GLOBE FEARON

WORLD
HISTORY

YOUR GUIDED
DISCOVERY
TOOL

GLOBE FEARON

WORLD
HISTORY

Color Transparencies

This comprehensive package of full-color transparencies supports Globe Fearon's World History program with political, physical geography, and special-purpose maps, as well as reproductions of fine art, artifacts, documents, and diagrams. These

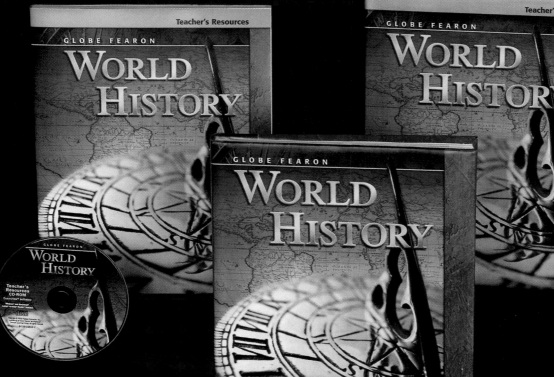

The following people have contributed to the development of this product:

Art & Design: Sharon Bozek, Eileen Brantner, Robert Dobaczewski, Kathleen Ellison, Salita Mehta, Jim O'Shea, Angel Weyant
Editorial: Linda Dorf, Elaine Fay, Mary Ellen Gilbert, Dena Kennedy, Alisa Loftus, Colleen Maguire, Jane Petlinski, Jennie Rakos, Maurice Sabean, Maury Solomon, Tara Walters
Manufacturing: Nathan Kinney
Marketing: Katie Erezuma
Production: Lorraine Allen, Irene Belinsky, Carlos Blas, Karen Edmonds, Cheryl Golding, Leslie Greenberg, Susan Levine, Cathy Pawlowski, Lisa Svoronos, Cindy Talocci, Susan Tamm, Meredith Tenety
Publishing Operations: Thomas Daning, Christine Guido, Richetta Lobban, Kate Matracia

Acknowledgments appear on pages 859–860, which constitutes an extension of this copyright page.

DK is a Pearson company specializing in the creation of high quality reference materials that combine educational value with strong visual style. This combination allows DK to deliver highly accessible and engaging educational content that is appealing to students, teachers, and parents worldwide.

Globe Fearon
Pearson Learning Group

1-800-321-3106
www.pearsonlearning.com

CONTENTS

GLOBE FEARON

WORLD HISTORY

Built on a Solid Foundation of Current Confirmed Research

What is considerate text?

Educational researchers Anderson and Armbruster have identified considerate text as text that provides readers with a well-organized, clear, coherent, and compelling body of information.

Globe Fearon World History *is a model of considerate text.*

This program contains the four key elements of considerate text: *structure, coherence, unity,* and *audience.*

✔ Each lesson in *Globe Fearon World History* is arranged in an outline *structure.*

✔ The clear and predictable outline format provides *coherence,* enabling students to see the relationships among ideas and to make logical connections from one idea to the next.

✔ Clean, uncluttered pages with an engaging narrative and large, attractive images provide *unity* of content and design. Topics are introduced through highly readable text and reinforced through visual elements such as photographs, maps, and charts.

✔ Your students are our *audience.* The appropriate concept load and the necessary vocabulary and reading support are built into the structure of each lesson to ensure comprehension.

SUPPORTS
No Child Left Behind

Why is text organization important to my students?

Literacy education researchers Dickson, Simmons, and Kame'enui have concluded that, "Well-presented physical text enables readers to identify the relevant information in text, including main ideas and relationships between ideas." The research makes it clear that students' ability to comprehend text is highly related to their awareness of the structure of text.

Globe Fearon World History *is organized in an accessible and readable outline format.*

- ✔ **Consistent and predictable outline format enables students to make connections among ideas and identify important topics.**

- ✔ **Clean, straightforward layout prevents distractions from core content.**

- ✔ **Upfront reading strategies, vocabulary terms, and learning objectives aid comprehension.**

- ✔ **Meaningful and relevant connections and high-interest features motivate students to read and learn.**

- ✔ **Graphic organizers structure students' reading and improve understanding.**

- ✔ **Comprehensive and coherent skill development enhances students' ability to acquire new content.**

Anderson, T. H., and B. B. Armbruster. 1984. "Content Area Textbooks." In *Learning to Read in American Schools*. R. C. Anderson, J. Osborne, and R. J. Tierney, eds. Hillsdale, NJ: Lawrence Erlbaum Associates, Inc. 193–226.

Anderson, T. H., and B. B. Armbruster; 1986. "Readable Textbooks, or Selecting a Textbook Is Not Like Buying a Pair of Shoes." In *Reading Comprehension: From Research to Practice*, J. Orasanu, ed. Hillsdale, NJ: Lawrence Erlbaum Associates, Inc. 151– 62.

Armbruster, B. B. and T. H. Anderson, 1988. "On Selecting 'Considerate' Content Area Textbooks." *Remedial and Special Education*, 9(1): 47–52.

Dickson, S. V., D. C. Simmons, and E. J. Kame'enui. 1998. "Text Organization: Research Bases." In *What Reading Research Tells Us About Children with Diverse Learning Needs: Bases and Basics*. D. C. Simmons and E. J. Kame'enui, eds. Mahwah, NJ: Lawrence Erlbaum Associates, Publishers

GLOBE FEARON

WORLD HISTORY

Accessibility
Without Compromise

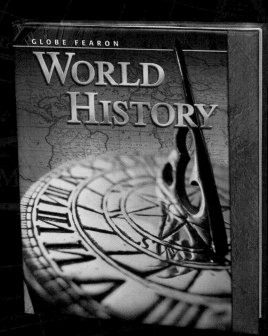

Student Edition

Written at a controlled reading level, this text provides accessibility without compromise. Your students will develop an appreciation of the world's history and diverse cultures without sacrificing content or rigor.

- Easy-to-follow outline format
- Comprehensive content and strong skills support
- Reading and vocabulary strategies
- Frequent opportunities to assess understanding
- Visual tools to enhance and support content

Teacher's Edition

The wraparound Teacher's Edition puts everything you need right at point of use. This resource reduces planning time and increases teaching time.

- Three-step lesson plans
- Extra vocabulary support
- Teaching options for mixed-level classrooms
- Motivating activities for different learning styles
- Easy-to-manage pacing and scheduling options
- Practical strategies that bring ancient cultures and civilizations to life

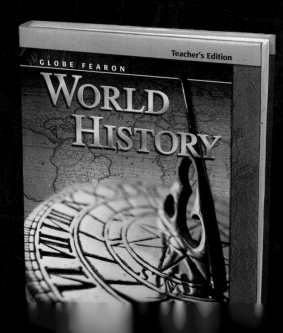

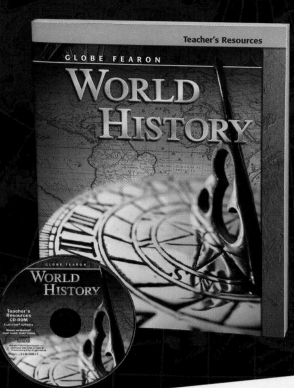

Teacher's Resources

Available in either book or CD-ROM format, the Teacher's Resources provides you with a comprehensive assessment program and support for every classroom.

- Reinforcement worksheets
- Graphic organizers
- Outline maps
- ESL/ELL worksheets
- Chapter tests, unit tests, and midterm and final exams
- Scoring rubrics
- CD-ROM test-generator software for customized tests

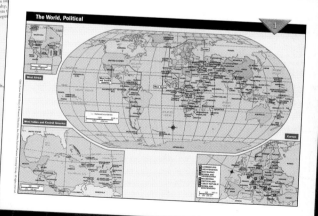

Transparencies

Transparencies support understanding by visually reinforcing and clarifying content.

- Full-color political, physical, and special-purpose maps
- Line and bar graphs containing current world statistics

Engaging chapter openers provide a snapshot of the upcoming material and improve student comprehension.

CHAPTER
14

The Renaissance and the Reformation
1300–1650

I. The Renaissance Begins
II. The Renaissance Spreads
III. The Reformation

The Renaissance was a time when people had new ideas and made new discoveries. Renaissance artists created works of art that were far more realistic than those of the Middle Ages. Ideas could be spread more rapidly because of the invention of the printing press. These and other developments caused life in Europe to change during the Renaissance. The most dramatic change, however, was a change in the way people thought. A new self-confidence was born. This self-confidence led to the exploration of unknown lands and challenges to the authority of the Roman Catholic Church.

One of the greatest figures of the early Renaissance was an architect and scholar named Leon Battista Alberti. Alberti expressed the Renaissance spirit in this way:

High-interest primary source quotes help students develop a perspective on world history.

66 *To you is given a body more graceful than other animals, to you power of apt and various movements, to you most sharp and delicate senses, to you wit, reason, memory like an immortal god.* 99

Timelines visually connect events covered in the chapter to world events.

1300s
Renaissance begins in Italian city-states.

1330s
Francesco Petrarca, a key figure in the early Renaissance, begins writing.

1450
Johann Gutenberg develops the printing press.

CHAPTER EVENTS

1300   1350   1400   1450

WORLD EVENTS

1325
Aztecs build Tenochtitlán.

1419
Prince Henry invites scholars to his court in Portugal.

314   UNIT 4   ◆   Europe Undergoes Change

Student Edition pages 314–315

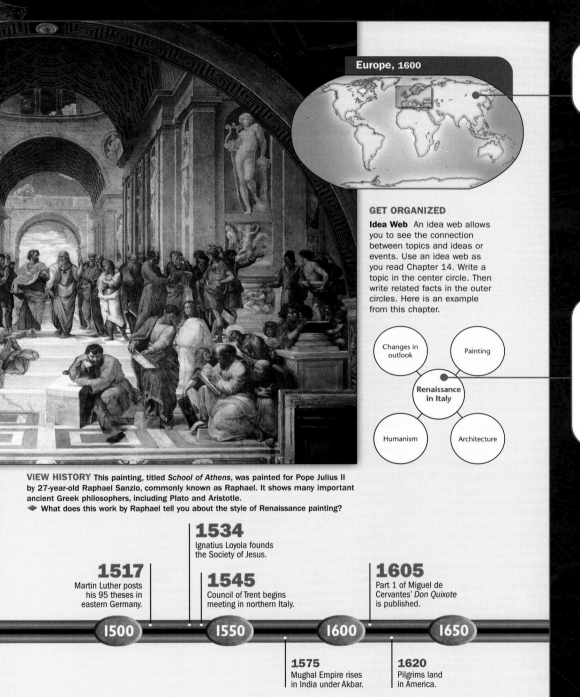

Europe, 1600

Locator maps set the geographical stage for the upcoming chapter.

GET ORGANIZED

Idea Web An idea web allows you to see the connection between topics and ideas or events. Use an idea web as you read Chapter 14. Write a topic in the center circle. Then write related facts in the outer circles. Here is an example from this chapter.

- Changes in outlook
- Painting
- Renaissance in Italy
- Humanism
- Architecture

Graphic organizers are introduced at the start of each chapter to structure students' reading and improve their comprehension.

VIEW HISTORY This painting, titled *School of Athens*, was painted for Pope Julius II by 27-year-old Raphael Sanzio, commonly known as Raphael. It shows many important ancient Greek philosophers, including Plato and Aristotle.
◆ What does this work by Raphael tell you about the style of Renaissance painting?

1534
Ignatius Loyola founds the Society of Jesus.

1517
Martin Luther posts his 95 theses in eastern Germany.

1545
Council of Trent begins meeting in northern Italy.

1605
Part 1 of Miguel de Cervantes' *Don Quixote* is published.

1500

1550

1600

1650

1575
Mughal Empire rises in India under Akbar.

1620
Pilgrims land in America.

Unique outline format and built-in reading support make world history accessible to all students.

Main ideas direct students' reading, introduce the outline format, and provide a purpose for reading the section.

Social studies terms are defined at the beginning of each section as well as shown in boldfaced type and defined in context.

The **outline format** organizes section content, helping students to maintain focus and successfully navigate the chapter.

Clear **maps** tied to the five themes of geography help students integrate geography skills into their study of history.

Section I

The Renaissance Begins

Terms to Know

Renaissance the great revival of art, literature, and learning in Europe

perspective an artistic technique used to give drawings a three-dimensional effect

humanism an intellectual movement that stemmed from the study of classical literature

patron a wealthy person who supports an artist

Main Ideas

A. Two major features of the Italian Renaissance were acceptance of nonreligious attitudes and the study of Greek and Roman cultures.

B. During this period, important contributions to science, art, politics, and manners were made by people such as Leonardo da Vinci, Niccolò Machiavelli, and Baldassare Castiglione.

C. The arts, including painting, sculpture, and architecture, flourished during the Renaissance.

Active Reading

COMPARE AND CONTRAST When you compare and contrast, you identify similarities and differences. As you read this section, compare and contrast Renaissance attitudes with the medieval outlook on human life and behavior.

A. The Renaissance in Europe

The **Renaissance** is the term now used by historians to refer to the rich flowering of European civilization from the fourteenth century into the sixteenth century. *Renaissance* means "rebirth" in the French language. The origins of the Renaissance lay in Italy. However, the spirit of the Renaissance soon spread to other places in Europe, including Germany, France, Spain, and England.

A Fresh Outlook

The Renaissance was a time of new attitudes about culture, life, and learning. During this time, people became more interested in the world around them. Individual achievement was valued as never before. The Renaissance marked a change from a spiritual emphasis to an emphasis on the human experience in the present. Human life was no longer seen as a preparation for eternal life. Renaissance thinking encouraged people to take control of their lives and to fulfill their potential.

The rebirth of ideas that took place during the Renaissance involved a renewed interest in learning for its own sake. Scholars became very interested in the writings of the ancient Greeks and Romans. Attitudes about a whole range of subjects changed dramatically. For example, people were no longer told to despise money or wealth. Instead, individuals were encouraged to use wealth to enhance themselves or their city. Renaissance leaders supported freedom of the individual. They encouraged positive attitudes about the human body. They praised curiosity and celebrated action.

The Renaissance Begins

Italy was a natural place for the Renaissance to begin. For one thing, Italy had been the center of the

Renaissance Italy, 1505

- Republic of Genoa
- Duchy of Milan
- Republic of Venice
- Republic of Florence
- Papal States
- Kingdoms under Spain
- Other city-states
- Cities

FRANCE
Avignon
Turin
Milan
Genoa
Pisa
Venice
Mantua
Florence
Rome
Corsica
Elba
Sardinia
Naples · Naples
Sicily
OTTOMAN EMPIRE
Adriatic Sea
Ionian Islands
Mediterranean Sea

0   100   200 mi
0   100   200 km

10°E   15°E   20°E
50°N
45°N
40°N

✔ Map Check

LOCATION Who controlled most of southern Italy?

ancient Roman Empire. The ruins of that empire surrounded the inhabitants of Italy and reminded them of how great it used to be.

Business and commerce also helped pave the way for the Italian Renaissance. As you learned in Chapter 13, northern Italy was one of the first regions in Europe to see the growth of towns and cities. Thriving commerce and trade brought Italian city-states such as Venice, Genoa, Milan, and Florence into contact with many other cultures. Trading ships sailed back and forth across the Mediterranean, from western Europe to the Middle East and from northern Africa to southern Europe. Its central location put Italy in a good position to profit from this trade. As trade grew, a new merchant class sprang up. Many merchants grew wealthy and used their money to support the arts.

Renaissance Figures in the Arts

An early Renaissance writer, Francesco Petrarca, known as Petrarch, began writing around 1337. His love sonnets, or poems, celebrated an imaginary woman named Laura. They are considered some of the greatest love poems in literature and served as models for later writers.

Other important figures of the early Renaissance included the painter Giotto and the architect Filippo Brunelleschi. Giotto painted lifelike, expressive figures. He was able to create the illusion of movement in his works. Brunelleschi is often credited with the discovery of **perspective**, which gave drawings a three-dimensional effect. One of his greatest achievements was the huge, eight-sided dome for the cathedral in Florence, Italy. Giotto and Brunelleschi were both from Florence. Although people from other cities, especially Venice and Rome, made important contributions, Florence was the single most important center of the Italian Renaissance.

Humanism

For Renaissance poets, historians, artists, and scholars, the classics—written works of Greek and Roman scholars—were an important source of inspiration. An intellectual movement developed that focused on classical ideals, styles, and forms. This movement was called **humanism**, and its members were called humanists. The humanists searched out manuscripts written in Greek and Latin with a wide range of topics, including history, literature, and grammar. The humanists studied, translated, and explained the manuscripts. Before the invention of the printing press, humanists copied manuscripts by hand. After the invention of the printing press, works such as those of Plato, Cicero, and Livy could be widely circulated. Printing helped spread the important texts of ancient Greece and Rome far and wide.

In his book *Oration on the Dignity of Man*, the humanist Giovanni Pico della Mirandola summed up the spirit of the age:

> 66 We have made thee neither of heaven nor of earth, neither mortal nor immortal, so that with freedom of choice and with honor, as though the maker and molder of thyself, thou mayest fashion thyself in whatever shape thou shalt prefer. 99

◆ How would you describe the fresh outlook of the Renaissance?

This dome is part of the great cathedral in Florence, Italy. It took more than 100 years to build, and many artists and sculptors worked on it.

> Relevant **visuals** reinforce and support students' content understanding.

ANALYZE PRIMARY SOURCES

DOCUMENT-BASED QUESTION
What does the quotation from Pico della Mirandola imply about the potential of human beings?

> **Comprehension questions** provide frequent opportunities for review.

Skill lessons and primary source documents prepare students for success.

Build Your Skills

◄ **Build Your Skills** lessons are included in every chapter. They provide opportunities for students to learn and practice critical thinking, social studies, and study skills, using content from the chapter.

Social Studies Skill

USE A TIMELINE

Timelines are important visual tools for students of history. They help put key events into chronological, or time, order. Timelines also help you understand how one event may have led to another.

Many people use a system of dividing time that was introduced by a Christian monk about 1,500 years ago. He classified events as *B.C.* and *A.D.* B.C. stands for "before Christ." A.D. stands for *anno Domini*, a Latin phrase meaning "year of the Lord." A.D. tells how many years have passed since the birth of Jesus Christ.

You may also see the abbreviations c. or ca. before a B.C. date. These abbreviations indicate that a date is approximate, or not exact. These abbreviations stand for the Latin word *circa*, which means "about."

Many historians today prefer to use the abbreviations B.C.E., which stands for "before the Common Era" and C.E., which stands for "the Common Era." The abbreviations B.C.E. and C.E. refer to the same years as B.C. and A.D.

Here's How

Use the steps below to read a timeline.

1. Look at the beginning and ending dates of the timeline to see what period it covers.

2. See if the timeline is divided into B.C. and A.D. To calculate the amount of time between an event that occurred in B.C. and one that occurred in A.D., add the two dates together. For example, around 3200 B.C., Stone Age people built the village of Skara Brae, which was discovered in A.D. 1850. The time between the building of the village and its discovery is 5,050 years (3,200 + 1,850).

3. Note the length of time between events. These intervals may be one year, 100 years, or some other spa[...]
shows wh[...]

Here's Why
Understand[...]
when event[...]
that Neande[...]
Cro-Magno[...]
the two may[...]

Practice the Skill
Study the timeline below. Then, answer the following questions.
1. Which is the earliest date on the timeline?
2. Which event has an approximate date listed?

Extend the[...]
Make a time[...]
first section[...]

Apply the S[...]
As you read[...]
construct a t[...]
events discu[...]

1.8 million B.C. *Homo habilis* inhabits Earth.	250,000 B.C. *Homo sapiens* inhabits Earth.	
2 million B.C.	1 million B.C.	100,000 B.C.
ca. 1.5 million B.C. Earth's earliest Ice Age occurs.		38,00[...] Cro-Magnon p[...] reach E[...]

tudent Edition page 9

Points of View pages use primary sources to highlight important topics in world history. Students develop basic writing skills while learning to analyze contrasting views of historical events. ▶

Points *of* View

Industrialization

Charles Dickens was a British writer who lived during the Industrial Revolution. He criticized the bad working conditions of mills in Great Britain. In 1842, Dickens traveled to the United States, where he toured the Massachusetts factories started by Francis Cabot Lowell. In his book *American Notes*, Dickens recorded a favorable impression of working conditions at the Lowell factories.

Other observers of the Lowell factories were much less impressed. Two years before Dickens's visit, the Unitarian minister Orestes A. Brownson wrote an article for the *Boston Quarterly Review* about the textile workers in Lowell. Brownson argued that factory conditions were so wretched that the workers were worse off than enslaved people.

During the 1800s, many young women worked at the Lowell factories operating machines that produced cloth.

"I happened to arrive at the first factory just as the dinner hour was over, and the girls were returning to their work. . . . They were all well dressed. . . . The rooms in which they worked, were as well ordered as themselves. In the windows of some, there were green plants, which were trained to shade the glass; in all, there was as much fresh air, cleanliness, and comfort, as the nature of the occupation would possibly admit of."

—Charles Dickens, *American Notes*, 1842

"We know of no sadder sight on earth than one of our factory villages presents, when the bell at break of day, or at the hour of breakfast, or dinner, calls out its hundreds or thousands of operatives [workers]. We stand and look at these hard working men and women hurrying in all directions, and ask ourselves, where go the proceeds of their labors? The man who employs them, and for whom they are toiling, is one of our city nabobs [big shots], reveling [enjoying] in luxury."

—Orestes A. Brownson, *Boston Quarterly Review*, 1840

ANALYZE PRIMARY SOURCES

DOCUMENT-BASED QUESTIONS

1. What details does Dickens mention to support his opinion?

2. What does Brownson see in his factory village?

3. **Critical Thinking** How do you think Brownson wants the reader to answer the question he asks about the "proceeds" of the workers' labors?

Frequent use of **primary source documents**, including **quotes** and **political cartoons**, prepares students for document-based test questions.

The images in this carving titled *The Loving Son* show the importance of filial piety.

ANALYZE PRIMARY SOURCES

DOCUMENT-BASED QUESTION Why do you think Confucius says you must follow your father's ways for three years after his death before considering yourself a filial child?

Primary Source Documents
You can read sections of the Analects on page 809.

The Five Relationships

Confucius taught that there were five relationships that governed society. First came the relationship between father and son. Next was the relationship between an older and younger brother. Then, came the relationships between husband and wife, between ruler and subject, and between friend and friend. As long as these relationships were in harmony, said Confucius, society would be in harmony. He taught that this harmony could be achieved by following an important rule: "What you do not wish for yourself, do not do to others."

The harmony of the family was central to the harmony of society. According to Confucius, children had to practice **filial piety**. Filial piety required a child to obey his or her parents during childhood, to care for them when they grew old, and to show respect for them after their death. Confucius explained filial piety in this way:

" When your father is alive observe his intentions. After he passes away, model yourself on the memory of his behavior. If in three years after his death you have not deviated from your father's ways, then you may be considered a filial child. "

The Analects and Confucian Influences

Confucius was a great and inspiring teacher. During his lifetime, many scholars learned from him. It is unclear whether Confucius ever wrote down his ideas. However, his followers did record his teachings. The collection of his sayings, called the Analects, contains his beliefs. In later centuries, the Analects was regarded as sacred. Students memorized the sayings, which soon became familiar to people in all levels of Chinese society.

The emperors of the Han Dynasty recognized the value of the Confucian scholar-gentleman. Men trained in Confucian learning became leaders of their communities. These men, in turn, sent bright young men to continue their Confucian education at schools in the capital. These Confucian officials formed an educated class that came from all parts of China. Members of this class were key ingredients in the development of Chinese civilization.

hat qualities did Confucius look for in a ruler?

oism

he third century B.C., a new system of beliefs began to challenge anism. Daoism, sometimes called Taoism, is very different from anism. Confucianists believed in order, ritual, and working hard to make rnment efficient. Daoists believed the opposite. They thought that rulers o as little as possible. They wanted their rulers to leave everybody alone.

ozi

Laozi, also known as *The Classic of the Way and Its Power*, contains the of Daoism. Lao Dan, who lived around 500 B.C., is thought by many been the original author, but most experts think the *Laozi* was

Primary Source Documents

From **Analects** (ca. 500 B.C.)

The main ideas of the teachings of Confucius were recorded by his followers in more than 450 verses. The exact number of Confucius's followers is uncertain. However, at least 22 are named throughout the Analects. In the following excerpts, Confucius stresses the importance of education, respect, and virtue in an individual's personal development. In addition, he discusses with some of his followers the characteristics of a superior person.

Confucius said: "A young man should serve his parents at home and be respectful to elders outside his home. He should be earnest and truthful, loving all . . . . After doing this, if he has energy to spare, he can study literature and the arts."

Meng I Tzu asked about the meaning of filial piety. Confucius said, "It means 'not diverging [from your parents].'" Later, when Fan Chih was driving him, Confucius told Fan Chih, "Meng Sun asked me about the meaning of filial piety, and I told him 'not diverging.'" Fan Chih said, "What did you mean by that?" Confucius said, "When your parents are alive, serve them with propriety; when they die, bury them with propriety, and then worship them with propriety."

Chi K'ang Tzu asked: "How can I make the people reverent and loyal, so they will work positively for me?" Confucius said, "Approach them with dignity, and they will be reverent. Be filial and compassionate and they will be loyal. Promote the able and teach the incompetent, and they will work positively for you."

Confucius said: "The Superior Man cares about virtue; the inferior man cares about material things. The Superior Man seeks discipline; the inferior man seeks favors."

Confucius said: "I don't worry about not having a good position; I worry about the means I use to gain position. I don't worry about being unknown; I seek to be known in the right way."

Confucius said that Tzu Chan had four characteristics of the Superior Man: In his private conduct he was courteous; in serving superiors he was respectful; in providing for the people he was kind; in dealing with the people he was just.

Confucius said: "Study as if you have not reached your goal—as if you were afraid of losing what you have."

Tzeng Tzu said: "The Superior Man doesn't worry about those things which are outside of his control."

Confucius said: "The Superior Man is humble in his speech but superb in his actions."

Confucius said: "Expect much from yourself and little from others and you will avoid incurring resentments."

Student Edition page 86

◀ **Primary Source Documents** library includes an array of our world's most important historical documents.

High-interest features make history come alive for students.

Student Edition pages 420–421

Past to...

INVENTIONS OF THE WESTERN WORLD

In the seventeenth and eighteenth centuries, there was an explosion of new scientific thinking. Ancient, outdated guesswork was replaced with ideas based on experiments and actual evidence. This Age of Enlightenment produced inventions, such as the "double-acting" steam engine, that would change people's day-to-day lives. Inventions to measure distance and view objects revolutionized ideas about Earth and the heavens.

MOVABLE METAL
Invented by Johann Gutenberg, individual metal letters could be rearranged after printing to make and print another page.

PRECISION MICROSCOPE
This precision microscope, invented by Anton von Leeuwenhoek around 1683, could magnify tiny objects 200 times. Through it, scientists could see human cells for the first time.

HOT STUFF
Although Thomas Savery patented the first crude steam engine in 1698, engineer James Watt improved the design. His "double-acting" steam engine of 1782 produced a circular motion, which could drive machinery. Soon it was being used in factories and in locomotives.

Piston rod

Lens

Cylinder

Fly wheel

Air pump   Cistern   Crankshaft

NEWTON'S TELESCOPE
Isaac Newton invented the world's first reflecting telescope in 1672. This telescope used a single curved mirror to gather light at its base. The more light a telescope gathers, the better it works for viewing details and faint objects, such as distant planets and st... Newton's reflector telescope was an improvement over earlier telescopes that used a lens to gather light.

STARING INTO SPACE
Although Galileo Galilei copied the design for his telescope from earlier ideas, he was the first to use it to study the planets. His telescopes magnified objects by up to 20 times—enough to identify the 4 moons of Jupiter.

ELECTRICAL EXPERIMENT
Benjamin Franklin was curious about electricity, so in 1752, he flew a kite in a thunderstorm. Small sparks appeared along the wet line of the kite, which proved that the lightning bolts were huge electrical charges—and that Franklin could have been electrocuted by his own experiment!

Mirror

Telescopic lens

Ivory scale

MOON AND STARS
The sextant was invented by John Campbell in 1757. It improved on an earlier design, known as an octant, which was used to calculate latitude and

...Present

Some of the greatest inventions of the present day are in the field of space exploration. Exploration has continued on the ground too, with improved tools and technology to measure distance. Optical research tools, especially in the field of medicine, have continued to become more sophisticated.

SATELLITE NAVIGATION
The Global Positioning System (GPS) means ships at sea can find their location to within several feet. Electronic equipment, such as this color GPS sensor (right), receives accurate information by satellite.

Viewers

DOUBLE VISION
By combining two single microscopes to make a double version, known as a binocular microscope, the viewer can use both eyes. This dual vision shows the image in depth and makes more detailed study possible.

External fuel tank

Rocket booster

Space shuttle, carrying the crew

GOING INTO ORBIT
A space shuttle is a rocket-launched vehicle that orbits Earth and can carry passengers to other orbiting spacecraft. To get off the ground, the shuttle needs a powerful boost from rocket engines, which detach once the

▲ **DK Past to Present** shows students how objects and events of the past connect to today.

Connect History provides ▶ interdisciplinary connections.

CONNECT
History&Archaeology

A Prehistoric Mystery

In 1991 two German hikers accidentally discovered the body of a man in melting ice on the slopes of the Italian Alps. At first it was feared that a fellow hiker had suffered a terrible accident. However, after digging the body out of the ice, it became clear that this man was not a hiker at all. What the German couple had stumbled upon was the body of a man who is now thought to be about 5,300 years old!

Being frozen in the ice had preserved the body of the "Iceman"—as he was now nicknamed. Both the frozen body and the tools archaeologists found with him provide clues about life thousands of years ago.

SCIENTISTS EXAMINED EVIDENCE of undigested food in the Iceman's stomach after moving the body to a laboratory in Austria. What they found was a kind of primitive wheat called einkorn that had been used to make bread. Finding this wheat suggested that the Iceman belonged to an agricultural community that made its home somewhere near where the body was found.

In addition to examining the body, scientists examined the contents of a tool kit the Iceman had been carrying with him. The tool kit contained a number of items, including mushrooms. Scientists believe that the mushrooms may have been used as food—but they also think that the mushrooms could have been used as a kind of medicine.

Other items found in the tool kit included a longbow with arrows in an animal-skin case, a small flint dagger, and a copper-headed ax. Before finding the Iceman, archaeologists believed that metal tools had not been used in that region until about 4,000 years ago. Yet here was a 5,300-year-old man with a copper-headed ax!

THE STORY CONTINUES as scientists research and examine evidence from the Iceman's body and his tool kit. Although hundreds of questions still surround the mystery of the Iceman, the most-often-asked question appears to be answered: Just how did the Iceman die? Many thought he had frozen to death in a sudden storm while

herding sheep. Instead, recent research now shows that the Iceman was killed, a victim of murder, warfare, or human sacrifice. X-rays have pointed to an arrowhead buried deep in the Iceman's left shoulder. The wound caused him to bleed to death over several hours and become buried in ice.

Critical Thinking

Answer the questions below. Then, complete the activity.

1. Without written records, how did archaeologists learn about the Iceman's history?

2. What objects were found in the Iceman's tool kit?

3. How do you think archaeology is similar to history? To science?

Write About It

Using the Internet and other sources, conduct your own research on the Iceman. Find at least two new interesting details about the Iceman and write a short essay on this topic.

The Iceman's body had been buried under snow and ice for about 5,300 years. The extreme cold preserved his body.

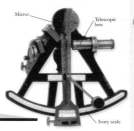

Margin features such as **Then & Now, Where in the World?** and **Global Connections** enhance students' understanding of world history.

Then & Now

MILITARY MIGHT
Similar to France's concern that Germany could pose a future military threat, nations today watch with alarm as more and more countries build military might.
In the twenty-first century, at least eight countries have nuclear weapons or the means to produce them.

The Treaty of Versailles required Germany to disarm many of its military operations.

The Bi...
threat to...
to be res...
force. T...
was redu...
airplane...
Rhine...
area th...

The L...
Th...
Nati...
to g...
Lea...
arm...

P...
fo...

V...
S...
t...

Angkor Wat in Cambodia was originally a Hindu temple. Its walls are covered with carvings of religious scenes.

would never again pose a...

Where in the World?

ANGKOR WAT
The Hindu temple of Angkor Wat is one of the greatest achievements of the ancient Khmer people. Five towers that represent the Mountain of the Gods rise from the center. Walls, courtyards, and moats surround the towers.
Angkor Wat was abandoned in the 1430s and mostly forgotten. It was not until the early 1900s that it was excavated and restoration was begun.

628 UNIT 7 ◆ Dec...
258 UNIT 3 ◆ Regional Civiliza...

Global Connections

BUILDING TOWNS
Pueblo is the Spanish word for town. Like the Southwest of the present-day United States, much of Spain has a hot, dry climate. The Spaniards built their towns of thick-walled, plain buildings around open squares, just as those built by the Anasazi.
To the Spanish invaders who arrived in the sixteenth century, the Anasazi pueblos looked just like their own towns. As a result, they referred to both towns and people as "pueblos." The name has stayed with these southwestern Native Americans ever since.

At Mesa Verde National Park in Mesa Verde, Colorado, multistory cliff dwellings that the Anasazi built still stand.

The Anasazi

The Anasazi peoples were Native Americans who settled in an area now known as the Four Corners—where the present-day U.S. states of Colorado, Arizona, New Mexico, and Utah meet. The Anasazi managed to grow crops in the dry, hot climate of the Southwest. They also produced items such as baskets, pottery, and cloth.

These early southwestern dwellers invented a new style of architecture that was well suited to the dry Southwest. Their houses, called **pueblos**, are made of adobe bricks, which are 3–5 inches thick. Thick walls kept the buildings cool in the summer and warm in the winter. The first pueblos were separate dwellings, but soon the Anasazi began building houses that resembled modern-day apartment houses. Each story of the building was narrower than the one below, so that the roof of the people on the lower floor provided a garden for the people above. The famous Cliff Palace at Mesa Verde, Colorado, was home to as many as 150 Anasazi.

The Anasazi began to move south toward the Rio Grande in about A.D. 1300. Historians believe they moved because drought had made their crops fail for several years. They built new, smaller pueblos where they settled. They are the ancestors of modern Pueblo Native Americans, who call the Anasazi ancestral Pueblos.

The Pueblos

Pueblo peoples, the descendants of the Anasazis, are not one nation, or group. *Pueblo* is a descriptive term referring to the culture, language, and lifestyle that groups such as the Hopi, the Zuñi, and the Acoma peoples have in common.

The Pueblo religion is largely based on prayers for a good harvest—important to survival in the harsh southwestern climate. In Pueblo religious practices, **kachinas**, or spirits of Pueblo ancestors, return to the earth in the forms of plants, animals, or people. The Pueblos hold kachina dances to honor these spirits. They believe that kachinas have power to heal the sick and to bring rain.

Farming was easier for the Pueblos than it had been for the Anasazis, because the Pueblos had the water of the Rio Grande for irrigation. They grew large fields of corn, beans, and squash.

Student Edition pages 628, 258, and 214

The Netherlands and the organization it created, the Dutch West India Company, expanded their trade to include the English and French colonies. Eventually, the Dutch took possession of all the Portuguese forts along the western coast of Africa, ending Portugal's trading activities.

France and England, which had colonies in the Americas, were resentful of the Dutch economic stronghold in Africa. Their governments encouraged merchants to form trading companies to compete with the Dutch. The French and English governments supported their newly formed trading companies with naval power. A series of wars between the three countries broke out, as the traders of each nation fought over control of the trading posts along the West African coast.

By 1713, Dutch power had weakened as a result of these wars. England and France continued to compete with each other for dominance. Throughout the 1700s, the Dutch continued to lose trade to the English, who were now the primary naval power in western Europe.

The Demand for Slaves Increases

The demand for African slaves led to more commercial activity along Africa's Gold Coast. By the late 1600s, a well-developed network for buying and selling slaves existed in Africa's inland regions as well as on its western Gold Coast. In the 1620s, about 10,000 slaves reached the Americas each year. By the end of the 1600s, it is estimated that about 1.5 million slaves had been brought to the Americas. Toward the end of the seventeenth century, that number had more than tripled.

Information about the slave trade comes from a variety of sources, including primary sources such as firsthand accounts and records. Olaudah Equiano, an African who was sold into slavery in the 1700s, later wrote about his experiences in Africa and the Americas.

➤ **Why did the Atlantic slave trade begin?**

They Made History highlights important people in history who influenced world events.

They Made History

Olaudah Equiano ca. 1750–1797

Olaudah Equiano, a West African, was sold into slavery when he was 12 and was taken to the West Indies. Equiano's life was luckier than many. He was given a little education and traveled with his master. Eventually, he became a free man.

Equiano moved to England where he worked to prohibit slavery. He traveled and lectured on the cruel treatment of Jamaican slaves at the hands of their English owners. In 1787, Equiano was an aide aboard the *Vernon*, a ship carrying about 600 freed slaves who would establish a settlement in Freetown, Sierra Leone, along the western coast of Africa.

Equiano is best known for his autobiography, written in 1789 and titled *The Interesting Narrative of the Life of Olaudah Equiano, or Gustavus Vassa, the African.* The book details Equiano's life in Africa before he was captured and presents arguments against slavery.

A former slave, Olaudah Equiano became a published writer and critic of slavery.

Critical Thinking Why do you think Olaudah Equiano was such an effective speaker against slavery?

CHAPTER 16 ◆ Europe Expands Overseas **379**

Student Edition page 379

Reference materials and handbooks put the world in the students' hands.

GEOGRAPHY HANDBOOK AND ATLAS

Why Study Geography?
A good place to begin your study of world history is with the study of geography. Geography is the study of the physical features of Earth and the people who live on it, including the relationship between people and their environment. Geography helps us to understand history by seeing how the characteristics of a place affect people and events.

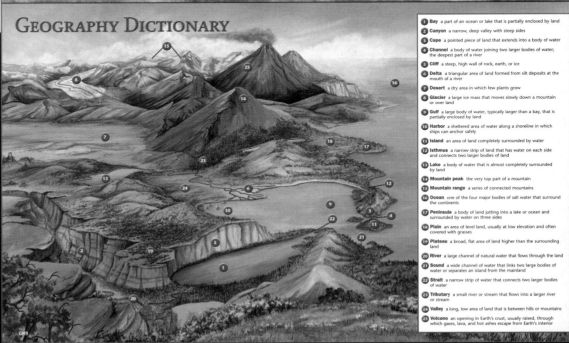

GEOGRAPHY DICTIONARY

1. **Bay** a part of an ocean or lake that is partially enclosed by land
2. **Canyon** a narrow, deep valley with steep sides
3. **Cape** a pointed piece of land that extends into a body of water
4. **Channel** a body of water joining two larger bodies of water; the deepest part of a river
5. **Cliff** a steep, high wall of rock, earth, or ice
6. **Delta** a triangular area of land formed from silt deposits at the mouth of a river
7. **Desert** a dry area in which few plants grow
8. **Glacier** a large ice mass that moves slowly down a mountain or over land
9. **Gulf** a large body of water, typically larger than a bay, that is partially enclosed by land
10. **Harbor** a sheltered area of water along a shoreline in which ships can anchor safely
11. **Island** an area of land completely surrounded by water
12. **Isthmus** a narrow strip of land that has water on each side and connects two larger bodies of land
13. **Lake** a body of water that is almost completely surrounded by land
14. **Mountain peak** the very top part of a mountain
15. **Mountain range** a series of connected mountains
16. **Ocean** one of the four major bodies of salt water that surround the continents
17. **Peninsula** a body of land jutting into a lake or ocean and surrounded by water on three sides
18. **Plain** an area of level land, usually at low elevation and often covered with grasses
19. **Plateau** a broad, flat area of land higher than the surrounding land
20. **River** a large channel of natural water that flows through the land
21. **Sound** a wide channel of water that links two large bodies of water or separates an island from the mainland
22. **Strait** a narrow strip of water that connects two larger bodies of water
23. **Tributary** a small river or stream that flows into a larger river or stream
24. **Valley** a long, low area of land that is between hills or mountains
25. **Volcano** an opening in Earth's crust, usually raised, through which gases, lava, and hot ashes escape from Earth's interior

▲ **Geography Handbook** teaches map skills, geographical terms, and the five themes of geography.

Student Edition pages GH1–GH2, GH9–GH10

S ◆ The World

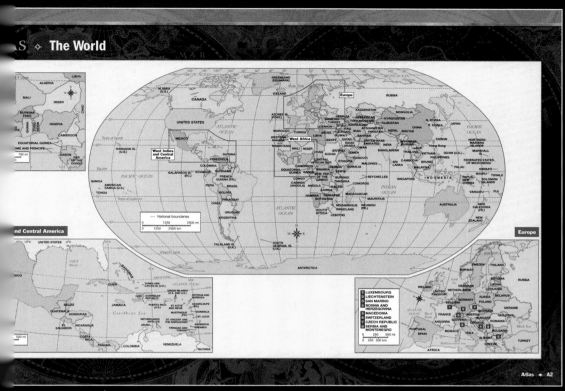

Atlas ◆ A2

dition pages A1–A2

▲ **Atlas** includes a variety of maps of the world.

The World at a Glance

Country	Official Name	Capital	Total Population	Principal Languages
AFRICA				
Algeria	People's Democratic Republic of Algeria	Algiers	32,277,942	Arabic, French, Berber
Angola	Republic of Angola	Luanda	10,553,547	Portuguese, Bantu, other African languages
Benin	Republic of Benin	Porto-Novo	6,834,795	French, Fon, Yoruba
Botswana	Republic of Botswana	Gaborone	1,579,436	English, Setswana
Burkina Faso	Burkina Faso	Ouagadougou	12,886,513	French, Sudanic languages
Burundi	Republic of Burundi	Bujumbura	5,965,127	Kirundi, French, Swahili
Cameroon	Republic of Cameroon	Yaoundé	15,428,030	African languages, English, French
Cape Verde	Republic of Cape Verde	Praia	408,760	Portuguese, Crioulo
Central African Republic	Central African Republic	Bangui	3,623,238	French, Sangho, Arabic, Hunsa, Swahili
Chad	Republic of Chad	N'Djamena	8,971,376	French, Arabic, Sara
Comoros	Federal Islamic Republic of the Comoros	Moroni	614,382	Arabic, French, Comorian, Shikomoro
Congo, Democratic Republic of the	Democratic Republic of the Congo	Kinshasa	55,041,752	French, Lingala, Kingwana, Kikongo, Tshiluba
Congo, Republic of the	Republic of the Congo	Brazzaville	2,908,048	French, Lingala, Monokutuba, Kikongo
Cote d'Ivoire	Republic of Cote d'Ivoire	Yamoussoukro	16,597,693	French, Dioula dialect
Djibouti	Republic of Djibouti	Djibouti	447,416	French, Arabic, Somali, Afar
Egypt	Arab Republic of Egypt	Cairo	73,312,559	Arabic, English, French
Equatorial Guinea	Republic of Equatorial Guinea	Malabo	498,144	Spanish, French, pidgin English, Fang, Bubi, Ibo
Eritrea	State of Eritrea	Asmara	4,305,577	Afar, Amharic, Arabic, Tigre and Kunama, Tigrinya
Ethiopia	Federal Democratic Republic of Ethiopia	Addis Ababa	65,253,938	Amharic, Tigrinya, Orominga, Guaragigna, Somali, Arabic
Gabon	Gabonese Republic	Libreville	1,288,229	French, Fang, Myene, Nzebi, Bapounou/Eschira, Bandjabi
Gambia, The	Republic of The Gambia	Banjul	1,455,842	English, Mandinka, Wolof, Fula, other African languages
Ghana	Republic of Ghana	Accra	20,163,149	English, African languages

Country	Official Name	Capital	Total Population	Principal Languages
Guinea	Republic of Guinea	Conakry	8,815,576	French
Guinea-Bissau	Republic of Guinea-Bissau	Bissau	1,333,453	Portuguese, Crioulo, African languages
Kenya	Republic of Kenya	Nairobi	31,223,158	English, Kiswahili
Lesotho	Kingdom of Lesotho	Maseru	1,857,866	Sesotho, English, Zulu, Xhosa
Liberia	Republic of Liberia	Monrovia	3,261,515	English, local languages
Libya	Socialist People's Libyan Arab Jamahiriya	Tripoli	5,368,585	Arabic, Italian, English
Madagascar	Republic of Madagascar	Antananarivo	16,473,477	French, Malagasy
Malawi	Republic of Malawi	Lilongwe	11,393,210	English, Chichewa
Mali	Republic of Mali	Bamako	11,300,445	French, Bambara
Mauritania	Islamic Republic of Mauritania	Nouakchott	2,828,863	Hasaniya Arabic, Pulaar, Soninke, Wolof, French
Mauritius	Republic of Mauritius	Port Louis	1,200,206	English, Creole, French, Hindi, Urdu, Hakka, Bhojpuri
Mayotte* (French Territory)	Territorial Collectivity of Mayotte	Mamoudzou	170,879	Mahorian, French
Morocco	Kingdom of Morocco	Rabat	31,167,783	Arabic, Berber dialects, French
Mozambique	Republic of Mozambique	Maputo	17,323,598	Portuguese, African dialects
Namibia	Republic of Namibia	Windhoek	1,896,845	Afrikaans, German, English
Niger	Republic of Niger	Niamey	10,760,206	French, Hausa, Djerma
Nigeria	Federal Republic of Nigeria	Abuja	130,499,978	English, Hausa, Yoruba, Igbo, Fulani
Réunion* (French Territory)	Department of Réunion	Saint-Denis	743,981	French, Creole
Rwanda	Republic of Rwanda	Kigali	7,668,223	Kinyarwanda, French, English, Kiswahili
Saint Helena* (British Territory)	Saint Helena	Jamestown	7,317	English
São Tomé and Principe	Democratic Republic of São Tomé and Principe	São Tomé	170,372	Portuguese
Senegal	Republic of Senegal	Dakar	10,311,497	French, Wolof, Pulaar, Jola, Mandinka
Seychelles	Republic of Seychelles	Victoria	80,098	English, French, Creole
Sierra Leone	Republic of Sierra Leone	Freetown	5,564,516	English, Mende, Temne, Krio

Easy-to-manage lesson plans allow you to spend less time planning and more time teaching.

Three-step lesson plans provide suggestions for introducing, teaching, and evaluating students' progress.

Terms to Know provide strategies for teaching social studies terms and other words or names that may be unfamiliar to students.

Active Reading presents opportunities to reinforce each section's reading strategy.

Teaching Options offer activities and strategies to address lesson planning and the learning styles of all students.

III. The War Expands
(pp. 672–675)

Section Summary

In this section, students will learn about Hitler's campaigns in the Soviet Union and North Africa. They will also learn how the United States entered the war in Asia and how it began to experience success on the Pacific front.

1 Introduce

Getting Started

Ask students to recall a time in recent history when the United States was attacked. (September 11, 2001—the destruction of the World Trade Center towers and the damage to the Pentagon) Ask students how Americans felt when this attack happened. (Possible answer: shocked, outraged, determined to fight back) Tell students that Americans had similar feelings when Pearl Harbor was attacked in 1941.

TERMS TO KNOW

Ask students to read the terms and definitions on page 672 and find each term in the section. After they have read the section, have them explain to a partner each term's relationship to World War II.

You may wish to preview the pronunciation of the following names with students.

Barbarossa (bahr buh RAW suh)
El Alamein (EHL a luh MAYN)
Guam (GWAHM)
Bataan (buh TAN)

ACTIVE READING

After students have read each subsection, pause and have them determine which events in the section show that the war is turning. Have students write two predictions—one for the war in Europe and one for the war in Asia. Have students save these predictions and review them for accuracy when they have finished reading the chapter.

Section III

The War Expands

Terms to Know

scorched-earth policy a wartime policy in which all goods useful to an invading army are burned or destroyed

infamy disgrace, or great evil

internment camp a place in which people are confined, especially in time of war

Main Ideas

A. Hitler's forces were overwhelmed by Allied attacks in the Soviet Union and Africa.

B. The United States was drawn into the war by a surprise attack on its military base in Hawaii by Japan.

Active Reading

PREDICT
When you predict, you analyze the information you know and make an educated guess about what events will occur. As you read this section, think about how the events of the war have occurred. Then, predict how the war will end for each nation.

A. Hitler Moves East

In 1941, Hitler turned his attention to the Soviet Union. Although he had signed a Nonaggression Pact with Stalin, Hitler's intent had always been to crush communism in Europe and defeat Stalin.

Hitler Invades the Soviet Union

On June 22, 1941, 3 million German soldiers moved into the Soviet Union and advanced toward three major targets—the Ukraine and the cities of Leningrad and Moscow. Hitler believed his troops could surround the Soviet armies and force them to surrender by autumn.

Within a few weeks, the Germans had advanced far into Soviet territory. However, as the Soviet army retreated, it followed a **scorched-earth policy**. Under this policy, the soldiers and civilians burned or destroyed everything that might be useful to the invaders. So, the German soldiers had to rely completely on their own supply lines for food, clothing, and weapons. The farther the German army advanced, the more difficult it was to keep them supplied.

Hitler believed that his Soviet invasion would be over in a matter of months. However, the campaign took much longer than planned, and cold weather arrived early. The German soldiers did not have winter clothing or adequate shelter from the below-freezing temperatures. Tanks and trucks had not been winterized, and the army was unable to move. In that winter of 1941, more than 500,000 German soldiers died from exposure or were captured.

The Siege of Leningrad

On September 8, 1941, German troops began an attack on Leningrad that would last two and a half years. This continuous assault would come to be known as the 900-day siege. The people of Leningrad had built fortifications around the city, which the Germans completely surrounded by November. Almost all supplies of food and military equipment were cut off. From time to time, a few supplies trickled in, keeping the city's 2 million people barely alive. In January 1944, Soviet troops arrived from the west and forced the Germans to retreat. The siege of Leningrad was over.

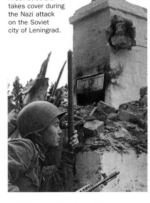
A Soviet soldier takes cover during the Nazi attack on the Soviet city of Leningrad.

672 UNIT 7 ◆ Decades of War

Teaching Options

Section 3 Resources

Teacher's Resources (TR)
Terms to Know, p. 41
Review History, p. 75
Build Your Skills, p. 109
Concept Builder, p. 244
Cause-and-Effect Chain, p. 325
Transparency 2

ESL/ELL STRATEGIES

Take Notes Help students to understand the information in this section by asking them to list the different strategies that are discussed. Help start them off with the three Terms to Know—*scorched-earth policy*, *infamy*, and *internment camp*. Have students work with partners to add to this list and then explain to each other the meaning of each term.

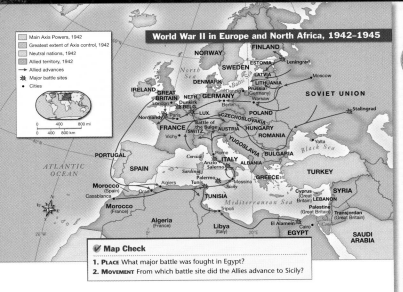

World War II in Europe and North Africa, 1942–1945

Main Axis Powers, 1942
Greatest extent of Axis control, 1942
Neutral nations, 1942
Allied territory, 1942
→ Allied advances
✹ Major battle sites
• Cities

✔ **Map Check**

1. **PLACE** What major battle was fought in Egypt?
2. **MOVEMENT** From which battle site did the Allies advance to Sicily?

The War in Africa

In the fall of 1940, the Italian dictator Mussolini sent his troops into Egypt, a British protectorate in northern Africa. However, the invasion was unsuccessful, and Hitler had to send one of his best commanders, Field Marshall Erwin Rommel, to help the Italians. By the summer of 1942, the combined forces of Germany and Italy had the British cornered in the city of El Alamein, near the Suez Canal. Both Great Britain and the United States, who had entered the war six months earlier, sent troops to defend the canal. The additional Allied troops turned the tide of battle, and by May 1943, they had gained control of all of North Africa.

◆ What factors slowed the German defeat of the Soviet Union?

B. The War in Asia

The United States had condemned Japan's attacks on China, and diplomats from the two nations were working to find a peaceful solution in Asia. Then, in 1941, Japan moved into the French colonies of Indochina, which included Vietnam, Cambodia, and Laos. The United States and Great Britain responded with economic sanctions, cutting off such goods as oil, iron, and steel. The Japanese leaders realized that they would have to deal with the United States if their expansion in the Pacific was to continue.

CHAPTER 28 ◆ World War II **673**

---

2 Teach

A. Hitler Moves East

Purpose-Setting Question What was the outcome of the siege of Leningrad? (After 2½ years, Soviet troops forced the Germans to retreat.)

TEACH PRIMARY SOURCES
Ask students to describe the photograph on page 672. (A Soviet soldier is taking cover by a bombed building in Leningrad.) Ask how soon the siege began after the beginning of the German invasion. (two months) Tell students that about one million of Leningrad's children, sick, and elderly were evacuated in 1942. At least 650,000 people died in the siege.

Using the Map

World War II in Europe and North Africa, 1942–1945

Ask students to describe the extent of Axis-controlled territory in 1942. (all of Europe except Great Britain and a few neutral nations; also, most of North Africa)

✔ **Map Check**
Answers
1. El Alamein
2. Tunis

Activity

Use a map Have students use the map on page 673 to trace the route of the Allies in the African campaign. (Great Britain to Algeria, then to Tunis, ending in Tripoli; another force from El Alamein to Tripoli)

◆ **ANSWER** The German army had to fight along a 2,000-mile front; the Soviet scorched-earth policy made supplying the army difficult; the Soviet winter brought the German assault to a standstill.

B. The War in Asia

Purpose-Setting Question Why did the United States and Great Britain impose economic sanctions on Japan in 1941? (to protest Japan's moving into Indochina)

CHAPTER 28 ◆ **T673**

Writing

AVERAGE
Have students write a letter from a Russian survivor of the siege of Leningrad, describing the horror of those 900 days. Encourage them to do further research and possibly include a quotation from a primary source in their letter.

CHALLENGE
Remind students that Napoleon also attacked Russia and was defeated there. Have students use the information in the textbook to compare and contrast Napoleon's and Hitler's Russian campaigns. Ask them to evaluate the kinds of mistakes both leaders made and to explain whether Hitler learned from Napoleon's errors.

Purpose-Setting Questions provide opportunities for discussion about core content.

Using the Map, Using the Graph, and **Using the Chart** provide additional information about each map, graph, and chart in the book.

Activities offer a variety of learning experiences to meet the needs of every classroom.

Answers are found at point-of-use.

Integrated assessments accurately monitor student performance.

Student Edition pages 266–267

CHAPTER 11 Review

Chapter Summary

Complete the following outline in your notebook. Then, use your outline to write a brief summary of the chapter.

Dynasties and Kingdoms of East Asia

I. Great Chinese Dynasties
  A. The Sui and Tang Dynasties
  B.
  C.
II. The Mongol Empire and the Ming Dynasty
  A.
  B.
III. Korea and Southeast Asia
  A.
  B.
IV. Japan: An Island Empire
  A.
  B.
  C.

Interpret the Timeline

Use the timeline on pages 242–243 to answer the following questions.

1. Which event happened first, the Japanese capital is transferred to Heian or the Chinese capital is moved to Beijing?

2. Which event happened later, the unification of Korea under the Silla Dynasty or the Mongol conquest of China?

3. **Critical Thinking** Which chapter event and world event involve the same group of people?

4. Select five events from the chapter that are not on the timeline. Create a timeline that shows these events.

266 UNIT 3 ◆ Regional Civilizations

Use Terms to Know

Select the term that best completes each sentence.

5. A landowner who lives elsewhere while earning money from landholdings is called
  a. a samurai.   c. a shogun.
  b. a daimyo.   d. an absentee landlord.

6. A person who flees to a foreign country is a
  a. daimyo.   c. tsunami.
  b. samurai.   d. refugee.

7. An alphabet using symbols to represent the sounds of the Korean language is
  a. hangul.   c. feudalism.
  b. tsunami.   d. daimyo.

8. A member of the Japanese warrior class was called a
  a. daimyo.   c. hangul.
  b. shogun.   d. samurai.

9. The order by which rulers follow one another in office is called
  a. tsunami.   c. feudalism.
  b. succession.   d. hangul.

Check Your Understanding

10. **Explain** why Tang emperors developed a program of land redistribution.

11. **Identify** how Wu Zhou was important to Chinese history.

12. **Identify** the improvements made to agriculture under the Song.

13. **Discuss** how China benefited under Mongol rule.

14. **Describe** the artistic advancements during the Ming Dynasty.

15. **Explain** how the Mongols affected Korea.

16. **Summarize** how China influenced Vietnam.

17. **Describe** the importance of Shinto to Japan.

18. **Identify** the importance of the daimyo in Japan.

19. **Describe** the effects of the Mongol invasion on Japan.

Critical Thinking

20. **Analyze Primary Sources** What does the quotation from Emperor Tai Zong on page 245 tell you about the values of the time?

21. **Analyze Primary Sources** How does the quotation from Marco Polo on page 253 describe the Mongol government of China?

22. **Analyze Primary Sources** What does the quotation from the Korean official on page 257 tell you about the relationship of Korea to China?

23. **Draw Conclusions** Why do you think Chinese influence decreased in Japan?

Put Your Skills to Work

24. **Compare and Contrast** You have learned that comparing and contrasting artifacts and ideas can help you understand what you read and see. Study the images below. Then, answer the following questions.

  a. What can you learn about the cultures that produced these statues?

  b. How are these statues alike and how are they different?

The statue to the right is a praying figure from Angkor Wat. The statue below is a Japanese Buddha.

Analyze Sources

25. Read more about Song reforms from this letter by Wang Anshi to one of his opponents. Then, answer the questions that follow.

  Now it is your opinion that I have overstepped my authority, caused trouble, pursued profit, and blocked criticism to the point where everyone in the world is enraged. In my view, I have received orders from my ruler, the policies were discussed in court, and executing them was delegated to the officials. . . . As for the abundance of resentment, this is something I expected. . . . Scholar-officials often prefer not to worry about the nation and merely content themselves with the status quo.

  a. How does Wang Anshi respond to criticism of his policies?

  b. What does Wang Anshi say about his opponents?

Essay Writing

26. China strongly influenced countries around it. They absorbed Chinese art, literature, and philosophy. Many of these countries adapted Chinese learning. They used it as it suited their needs. Choose one of the neighbors of China. Write an essay about how that neighboring country adopted and adapted Chinese ways.

In addition to the cultural developments of painting, architecture, garden art, and the tea ceremony, theater played an important role during the feudal age. Two forms of drama emerged.

The theater known as Kabuki was seen primarily by the common people. Several times a year, a group of traveling actors arrived in a town to perform. The theaters they used had no roofs, so the performers had to depend on good weather. They wore colorful costumes and heavy makeup. Their movements were exaggerated as they sang, danced, and acted out stories about love, war, and heroism. Sometimes members of the audience joined the actors on the stage, becoming part of the story. Performances often lasted up to 18 hours, so tea and food were sold during the plays.

The other form of drama was Noh drama. Unlike Kabuki theater, Noh drama was performed for the upper classes and had little action. Two actors wearing elaborate costumes and carved masks acted out simple stories on a wooden stage that was almost bare. The only scenery on the stage was a screen with a painting of a pine tree. The screen reminded the actors and audiences that Noh plays were first performed at Shinto shrines. Flutes and drums provided musical accompaniment for the actors. In addition, a chorus of men chanted. Their chants were about honor, unselfishness, and other ideals that were important in Japanese culture. Both Kabuki theater and Noh drama are still performed today in Japan.

This photograph shows masks used in Noh theater performances.

◆ **What beliefs and practices were part of Zen Buddhism?**

Review IV

Review History
A. How was Chinese culture transmitted to Japan?
B. What effect did the creation of kana have?
C. What was the role of the daimyo in Japan?

Define Terms to Know
Define the following terms: **tsunami, feudalism, shogun, daimyo, samurai**

Critical Thinking
Why do you think the worship of kami, or Shinto, is still practiced in Japan today?

Write About Culture
Write a paragraph about the impact of Zen on Japanese culture.

Get Organized
VENN DIAGRAM
Use a Venn diagram to organize information from this section. Choose a topic and then find supporting details. For example, what made the Heian and feudal periods similar and what made them different?

CHAPTER 11 ◆ Dynasties and Kingdoms of East Asia 265

▲ **Chapter Reviews** provide a multitude of opportunities for assessing students' mastery of chapter content.

Section Reviews assess students' understanding of section material. ▶

Unit 7

Portfolio Project

HISTORY QUIZ SHOW

Managing the Project
Plan for 3–4 class periods.

Set the Scene
Have students brainstorm names for their History Quiz Show. Write class suggestions on the board. Then, take a vote to determine the name of the show.

Your Assignment
Ask students to read the assignment on page 684. Point out that wars are events in which much history is made. A unit containing World Wars I and II will have plenty of available information for a quiz show. To make certain that students understand the proposed format of answer and question, you might provide one or two answers and ask volunteers to supply the questions.

PREPARE FOR THE SHOW
Make sure that students understand their varied assignments. The judges can prepare by becoming familiar with the contents of Unit 7. The quizmaster can prepare by watching several game shows at home and analyzing the hosts' behavior.

Participants should understand that they will end up with a total of 48 questions (16 from each team), based on the contents of Chapters 26–28.

Remind contestants and the audience that this is a game, and they are to conduct themselves in a courteous manner, even when they answer incorrectly or disagree with the quizmaster.

PUT ON THE SHOW
Use a podium and chairs at the front of the room to create a quiz-show setting. Encourage students to use music, sound effects, and other typical features of TV quiz shows.

Wrap Up
The final product from each team and the production crew will be a 30-minute quiz show. Afterwards, have the class evaluate what went well in the show, and also how the show could be made more exciting.

T684 ◆ **UNIT 7**

UNIT 7 PORTFOLIO PROJECT   COOPERATIVE LEARNING

History Quiz Show

YOUR ASSIGNMENT

Many people enjoy playing quiz-style games. Often the format of these quiz games involves being given an answer and then providing a question to match the answer. Here is an example:

Answer: This famous statesman was the prime minister of Great Britain during World War II.

Question: Who was Winston Churchill?

PREPARE FOR THE SHOW

Select Participants Ask for volunteers to take part in a history quiz show. First, select a quiz show host who will read the answers to the contestants. Next, select two student judges who will make decisions in case of any disputes over the interpretation or completeness of an answer. Finally, choose between 12 and 16 volunteers who are willing to serve as writers and contestants.

Write the Answers Form four teams of three to four students each. Each team will elect one member to serve as their contestant. The other members of each team will brainstorm to write 16 questions and answers based on material from the three chapters in Unit 7. The questions and answers will be divided equally into four categories: people, places, conflicts and treaties, and quotations. Remind students that, during the quiz, contestants will have to come up with questions that match the answers that are given to them.

After all the questions and answers have been written, a group consisting of one student from each team will review and edit the questions and answers for accuracy and to avoid repetition. This group will select the 40 best questions and answers to be used in the quiz.

Explain the Rules Each contestant will sit at a table or desk on which a small bell has been placed. Explain that the host will read an answer to a question. The first contestant to ring his or her bell will respond with the question. A correct response will be worth one point. An incorrect response will cost the contestant one point. If the first response is not correct, the next contestant to ring his or her bell will have a chance to respond.

There will be two rounds with 20 questions and answers in each round. After the first round, the two contestants with the best scores will take part in the final round to determine the winner.

PUT ON THE SHOW

Present Put on the quiz show in front of the entire class. Remind the students in the audience not to help the contestants in any way—except, of course, to encourage them with applause.

Multimedia Presentation

Turn your quiz show into a video to share with other classes in school. Teams should assign tasks such as videotaping and setting up props. Before actually taping, one or more rehearsals should be held to help people know where they should be and how they should act. Select a volunteer director to keep things running smoothly.

684 UNIT 7 ◆ Decades of War

Teaching Options

Multimedia Presentation

Adding music and sound effects will enhance the "reality" of the History Quiz Show. Students may want to add an introductory segment to the show as well as a closing. Students may also want contestants to introduce themselves. In between the two question segments, they may want to provide for station identification.

Alternative Assessment

Create a Bulletin Board Display Have three groups of students create a bulletin board display of Unit 7, Decades of War. Each group will focus on one chapter of the unit. Encourage students to use pictures of events, artifacts, portraits, maps, and charts in their display. Each visual should be accompanied by a caption explaining the historical significance of the visual and any other interesting information.

Teacher's Edition page T684

◀ **Portfolio Projects** provide ample opportunities for cooperative learning and research.

◀ **Alternative Assessment** offers additional methods for evaluating students' progress.

Assessment tools prepare students to succeed in a variety of test-taking situations.

Chapter tests, **unit tests**, and **midterm** and **final exams** use a variety of question formats to evaluate learning and provide practice for standardized tests.

Name _____ Date _____

Assessment

Chapter Test

Chapter 4

A. Answer each question on the lines provided

1. Which group developed the first Chinese

_____

2. What is produced during sericulture?

_____

3. According to the dynastic cycle, how d

_____

4. During which dynasty did education

_____

5. Give three reasons why Qin Shi H
   earlier kings.

_____

6. What were three major religio

_____

7. What type of economy did a

_____

8. Give two examples that sho
   astronomers and mathema

_____

Name _____

Date _____

Assessment

Unit Test, Chapters 22–25

Unit 6

A. Match each item with its description. Write the correct ___
on the line.

____ 1. sweeping series of changes in many areas of life beginning in the 1700s

____ 2. an area of land set aside for Native Americans

____ 3. served in field hospitals in the Crimean War

____ 4. invented the spinning jenny

____ 5. formed the American Federation of Labor

____ 6. one large business made up of a group of companies

____ 7. the result of a crop failure in Ireland

____ 8. basic principle of American foreign policy

____ 9. Chinese merchant

Name _____ Date _____

Midterm Exam *continued*

Assessment, Chapters 1–17

B. Analyze the graph, and answer the questions that follow on the lines provided.

The Atlantic Slave Trade 1450–1870

1601–1700	1701–1810	1811–1870

Years

d the number of slaves increase the most?

of slaves decrease between 1811 and 1870?

ted below. Use facts and specific
Write your essay on a separate

ars to capture the Holy Land from the Muslims.
usades highlight many of the central ideas about
es. Describe the impact of the Crusades during
should include the following:

ades

usades

Name _____ Date _____

Final Exam *continued*

Assessment, Chapters 18–33

22. Where did the first battle of the Spanish-American War take place?
    a. the United States
    b. the Philippine Islands
    c. Spain
    d. Cuba

23. The nations of the Triple Entente were
    a. Great Britain, France, and Russia.
    b. Germany, Great Britain, and France.
    c. Germany, Japan, and Italy.
    d. the United States, Great Britain, and France.

24. "The eleventh hour of the eleventh day of the eleventh month" was
    a. when Germany signed an armistice to end World War I.
    b. the beginning of the Russian Revolution.
    c. the end of World War II.
    d. when Archduke Franz Ferdinand was assassinated.

25. The Fourteen Points peace plan was developed by
    a. Winston Churchill.
    b. Theodore Roosevelt.
    c. Woodrow Wilson.
    d. Alfred von Schlieffen.

26. Which was Lenin's program for creating a more industrial nation in the Soviet Union?
    a. Great Leap Forward
    b. New Economic Policy
    c. Comintern
    d. Five Year Plan

27. Which was one important outcome of China's May Fourth Movement?
    a. Some Chinese Communists created a political party.
    b. Chinese leaders reinforced the ideas of Confucianism.
    c. China became a Japanese protectorate.
    d. Most Chinese leaders rejected western science.

28. Who demanded self-rule for the French colony of Indochina?
    a. Mao Zedong
    b. Ho Chi Minh
    c. Jiang Jieshi
    d. Sun Yat-sen

Assessment

A wide range of integrated ESL/ELL strategies help all students reach their maximum potential.

Student Edition page 533

◀ **Graphic organizers** provide visual aids to help students comprehend complex ideas.

Teacher's Edition page T672

Terms to Know ▶ point out words that may be difficult for ESL/ELL students.

ESL/ELL Strategies offer teaching ▲ tools that help students access information and achieve success with social studies content.

Globe Fearon World History helps students' test scores soar.

The national trend toward high-stakes testing affects all aspects of the school experience. The pressure for students to perform well on standardized tests impacts day-to-day learning in the classroom, teacher and school accountability, and parental concerns.

Research in test preparation shows that a three-stage approach is most effective in preparing students for tests: teach *subject-area content*, emphasize *critical thinking skills*, and provide students with useful *test-taking skills* as well as opportunities to practice these skills.

Globe Fearon World History *provides a complete, research-driven strategy for students to achieve success in high-stakes testing.*

- ✔ Full, *standards-based content coverage* is presented clearly and thoroughly so that every student in your classroom can master the material.

- ✔ Valuable *skill lessons* are included in every chapter to reinforce essential critical thinking skills, such as analyzing primary sources, decoding maps and visuals, and developing and supporting opinions.

- ✔ Frequent *opportunities to build and practice test-taking skills* are found throughout the Student Edition, Teacher's Edition, and Teacher's Resources. Students will become familiar with a variety of test formats and learn strategies to help them avoid common mistakes, gain confidence, and succeed on standardized tests.

Globe Fearon World History helps students gain confidence in their comprehension of content, learn how to think critically, and develop strong test-taking skills in order to perform better on standardized tests.

The Student Edition prepares students for success with test preparation questions that model standardized tests.

The **Test Preparation** feature in each Chapter Review reinforces the critical thinking skills required to succeed on social studies and other exams, such as generalizing, identifying problems and solutions, sequencing, distinguishing fact and opinion, and recognizing cause-and-effect relationships.

TEST PREPARATION

GENERALIZATIONS
Choose the correct answer to the question.

Which sentence best describes Henry the Navigator's goal for Portugal?

1. The Portuguese treasury would double in size.

2. Portugal would take the lead in European exploration in the 1400s.

3. Portuguese forts would be built around the world.

4. Portugal would be the first nation to establish a trade route to the Americas.

Clear **direction lines** help focus students on the task to be completed. Common words that appear in test directions are introduced to students to ensure comprehension.

Numbered multiple-choice items help students become familiar with this **standardized test format**. Two types of multiple-choice items are included: statements that answer a question (as shown) and phrases that complete a given statement. Some questions also include the option "all of the above" to give students practice with this type of answer.

TEST PREPARATION

SEQUENCING RELATED EVENTS
Read the question below and choose the correct answer.

Which event came after the Mongol conquest of China?

1. The Tang Dynasty began to decline.

2. Hong Wu established the Ming Dynasty.

3. Gunpowder was introduced as a weapon.

4. Wu Zhao became the first woman emperor in China.

The Teacher's Edition and Teacher's Resources offer test-taking strategies practice everyday.

Test Taking

To help students prepare for a multiple-choice test, write several sample questions on the board. Review the questions with students.

Point out that if students do not know the correct answer to a multiple-choice question, they can eliminate one or more incorrect choices and have a better chance of choosing the correct answer.

Teach your students useful test-taking strategies, such as eliminating incorrect items in a **multiple-choice question**. Practicing successful strategies gives students tools that allow them to earn high scores on standardized tests.

Test Taking

Give students a short quiz on subsection A that includes three short-answer questions. Remind students to read the directions carefully to determine if their answers should be a word, phrase, or sentence. Provide a sample question, such as the following: In a complete sentence, explain how Pericles got the money for his rebuilding program in Athens.

Reading the directions is a critical aspect of test taking. Students are taught to follow directions to ensure correct responses to **short-answer questions**.

Test Taking

Remind students that to get information from a map, they should start with the map title and key. In the map on this page, students will see that the map topic is early human migration. The map key tells which groups of early human migrations are shown. Ask students to write one question about the map. Then, have students exchange and answer the questions.

Social studies information is often presented through **maps**, **charts**, **graphs**, and **timelines**. Emphasize to students that the ability to examine titles, keys, and labels is essential to analyzing these informational visuals.

Test Taking

Tell students that essay questions sometimes ask them to compare and contrast two or more events, concepts, or historical figures. Making a list or chart can help students organize their thoughts about a topic. Have students make a two-column chart (TR, p. 328) to answer the essay question "How are the histories of Vietnam and Khmer alike and different?"

Prewriting strategies, such as outlining and listing, help students organize their ideas and write cohesive responses to **essay questions**. Additional essay writing strategies and practice can be found throughout the Student Edition and in the Essay Writing section of the Teacher's Resources.

Test-taking Strategies

Useful strategies such as preparing for a test, understanding direction lines and test questions, and managing available time help to build students' confidence in test-taking situations.

The **predictable format** ▶ of each lesson provides a formula for success. First, the test-taking skill is taught. Next, students are given the opportunity to practice the skill.

Test preparation worksheets ▶ include strategies for answering different types of standardized test questions about world history, including multiple-choice and short-answer formats.

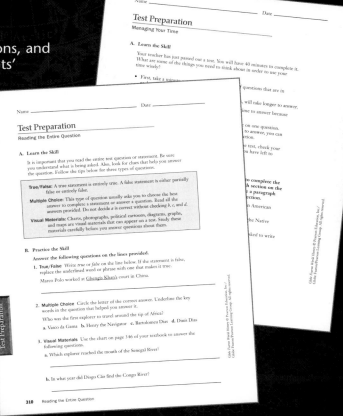

Teacher's Resources pages 310 and 308

Essay-writing Strategies

Most standardized tests contain an essay-writing component. Worksheets in the Teacher's Resources help prepare students to write effective essays about world history and other topics.

◀ By identifying components of a paragraph, students learn how the parts work together to create a cohesive whole.

Teacher's Resources page 295

Pacing Guide

The following pacing guide provides suggestions for teaching *Globe Fearon World History*. The guide is based on a 36-week school year. The model below provides suggestions for teaching both a one-year and a two-year world history course. The model for the two-year course is based on teaching world history from prehistory through the changes in Europe following the Renaissance and the Reformation in the first year and from the scientific revolution in Europe through the modern era in the second year.

	One-Year Course	Two-Year Course
Geography Handbook	Week 1	Year 1, Week 1
Chapter 1 **Early Peoples of the World**	Weeks 1 and 2	Weeks 1 and 2
Chapter 2 **Ancient Civilizations**	Week 3	Weeks 3 and 4
Chapter 3 **Ancient India**	Week 4	Weeks 5 and 6
Chapter 4 **Ancient China**	Week 5	Weeks 7 and 8
Chapter 5 **Ancient Greece**	Week 6	Weeks 9 and 10
Chapter 6 **Ancient Rome**	Week 7	Weeks 11 and 12
Chapter 7 **The Byzantine Empire, Russia, and Eastern Europe**	Week 8	Weeks 13 and 14
Chapter 8 **The Islamic World**	Week 9	Weeks 15 and 16
Chapter 9 **The Americas**	Week 10	Weeks 17 and 18
Chapter 10 **Kingdoms and City-States in Africa**	Week 11	Weeks 19 and 20
Chapter 11 **Dynasties and Kingdoms of East Asia**	Week 12	Weeks 21 and 22
Chapter 12 **The Early Middle Ages**	Weeks 13 and 14	Weeks 23, 24, and 25
Chapter 13 **The High Middle Ages**	Weeks 14 and 15	Weeks 26, 27, and 28
Chapter 14 **The Renaissance and the Reformation**	Week 16	Weeks 29 and 30

	One-Year Course	Two-Year Course
Chapter 15 **Exploration and Trade**	Week 17	Weeks 31 and 32
Chapter 16 **Europe Expands Overseas**	Week 18	Weeks 33 and 34
Chapter 17 **European Monarchies**	Week 19	Week 35 and 36
Chapter 18 **A Revolution in Science and Thought**	Week 20	Year 2, Weeks 1 and 2
Chapter 19 **The French Revolution and Napoleon**	Week 21	Weeks 3, 4, and 5
Chapter 20 **The Growth of Nationalism**	Week 22	Weeks 6 and 7
Chapter 21 **Asia, Africa, and Australia in Transition**	Week 23	Weeks 8 and 9
Chapter 22 **The Industrial Revolution and Social Change**	Week 24	Weeks 10, 11, and 12
Chapter 23 **Nationalism and Expansion**	Week 25	Weeks 13 and 14
Chapter 24 **Imperialism in Africa, India, and the Middle East**	Week 26	Weeks 15 and 16
Chapter 25 **Imperialism in Asia and Latin America**	Week 27	Weeks 17 and 18
Chapter 26 **World War I and the Russian Revolutions**	Week 28	Weeks 19, 20, and 21
Chapter 27 **Crises Around the World**	Week 29	Weeks 22 and 23
Chapter 28 **World War II**	Weeks 30 and 31	Weeks 24, 25, and 26
Chapter 29 **Europe**	Week 32	Weeks 27 and 28
Chapter 30 **North America and South America**	Week 33	Weeks 29 and 30
Chapter 31 **Asia**	Week 34	Weeks 31 and 32
Chapter 32 **Africa and the Middle East**	Week 35	Weeks 33 and 34
Chapter 33 **The World in a New Century**	Week 36	Weeks 35 and 36

Block Scheduling

Many schools have replaced traditional class periods with block scheduling. Block scheduling provides opportunities for flexible teaching.

Different Systems of Block Scheduling

Some block schedules allow teachers to meet with their classes every other day of an entire semester or year, depending on the length of the course. Other types of block schedules allow students to take only four classes each semester. In this second system, a year-long course is completed in one semester.

Benefits of Block Scheduling

Many schools that have implemented the block scheduling system have identified several benefits over traditional scheduling. These benefits are included in this system:
- More time for in-depth study
- Opportunities for a greater variety of in-class activities
- Fewer classes for students
- Fewer class changes and disruptions throughout the day
- Fewer class preparations for teachers

Challenges of Block Scheduling

Because classes are longer but meet less often, teachers must restructure their class formats. This situation leads to the following challenges:
- A greater need for varied activities to hold students' attention
- An increased demand for planning
- The need to rethink the pacing of instruction to ensure that all topics are covered

Tips for Teaching in a Block Schedule

Limit Lecture Time Do not expect students to listen to a longer lecture than they would in a traditional schedule. Most students are able to concentrate on teacher-led discussions for only a certain amount of time. Present the information you need to cover and then switch to a more student-centered activity.

Provide a Variety of Activities Change activities every 30 to 45 minutes. The longer class periods allow you to incorporate more hands-on and cooperative-learning activities into your classroom. Take advantage of the time students are in class to help them work together and share ideas. A greater variety of activities will keep students interested and learning throughout the duration of the class.

Allow Movement in the Classroom Use groupings to encourage students to work together and get up from their seats. Remember that 90 minutes is a long time for a student to sit in one place.

Using *Globe Fearon World History* With a Block Schedule

Globe Fearon World History includes many different activities and ideas that you can use in a block schedule. Technology-related activities are provided at the beginning of every unit as well as in every chapter review. The extended class periods in a block schedule provide the perfect setting for incorporating technology into your classroom. In addition, the numerous activities in the Teacher's Edition and Teacher's Resources offer an extensive array of student-centered activities from which you can choose. These activities can help you enrich students' learning experiences and keep them excited about studying world history.

Themes in *Globe Fearon World History*

Globe Fearon World History correlates to social studies themes developed by the National Council for Social Studies (NCSS).

Culture

All humans have some system of beliefs, knowledge, values, and traditions that make each culture unique.

Time, Continuity, and Change

The study of past events and patterns of change establishes a point of reference for students to understand their place in the world.

People, Places, and Environments

The understanding of geographic features and how people interact with their surroundings provides insights into the relationship between humans and nature.

Individual Development and Identity

Recognizing the effect of culture, surroundings, and institutions helps students define themselves in relation to others.

Individuals, Groups, and Institutions

Knowing how institutions that exist within a culture operate, what influence they have, and how they can be changed enables students to become actively involved in society.

Power, Authority, and Governance

By studying the development of power and authority in their country and other countries, students are better able to evaluate systems of government.

Production, Distribution, and Consumption

Studying the types of trading systems that have been used throughout history helps students recognize the growing interdependence of the world economy.

Science, Technology, and Society

The increasing complexity of today's science and technology and society's dependence on them creates an ever greater need for students to understand their influences.

Global Connections

Learning about past relationships among world cultures and the importance of future relationships helps students better evaluate the impact of world events on their lives.

Civic Ideals and Practices

One of the most important functions of social studies is the explanation of civic ideals and responsibilities. In order for students to participate fully in society, they must have a firm understanding of their rights and responsibilities.

Related Programs From Globe Fearon

These additional titles from Globe Fearon can help you to meet the diverse needs of your classroom. For more information about these and other Globe Fearon products please call 1-800-321-3106 or visit www.pearsonlearning.com.

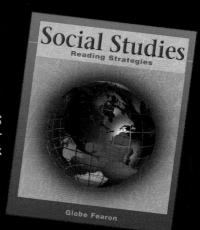

Social Studies Reading Strategies

This program helps students learn strategies for decoding text in social studies. The book includes unique strategies for reading maps, charts, and graphs.

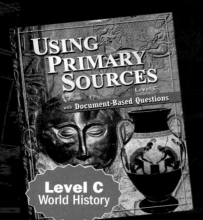

Using Primary Sources with Document-Based Questions

Using Primary Sources Level C provides in-depth instruction on a variety of world history primary-source documents. There are ample practice opportunities to reinforce and enhance skill development.

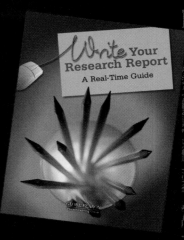

Write Your Research Report

This easy-to-use guide leads students through the ten steps of creating a research report for their language arts, social studies, and science classes.

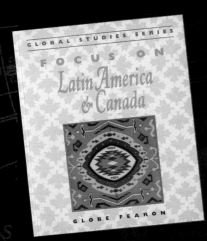

Global Studies

This program helps sudents learn about the geography, history, culture, economics, and politics of the major world regions.

Pearson Learning ◆ Core Knowledge History & Geography

This engaging program not only extends key world history themes but also provides rich nonfiction reading opportunities.

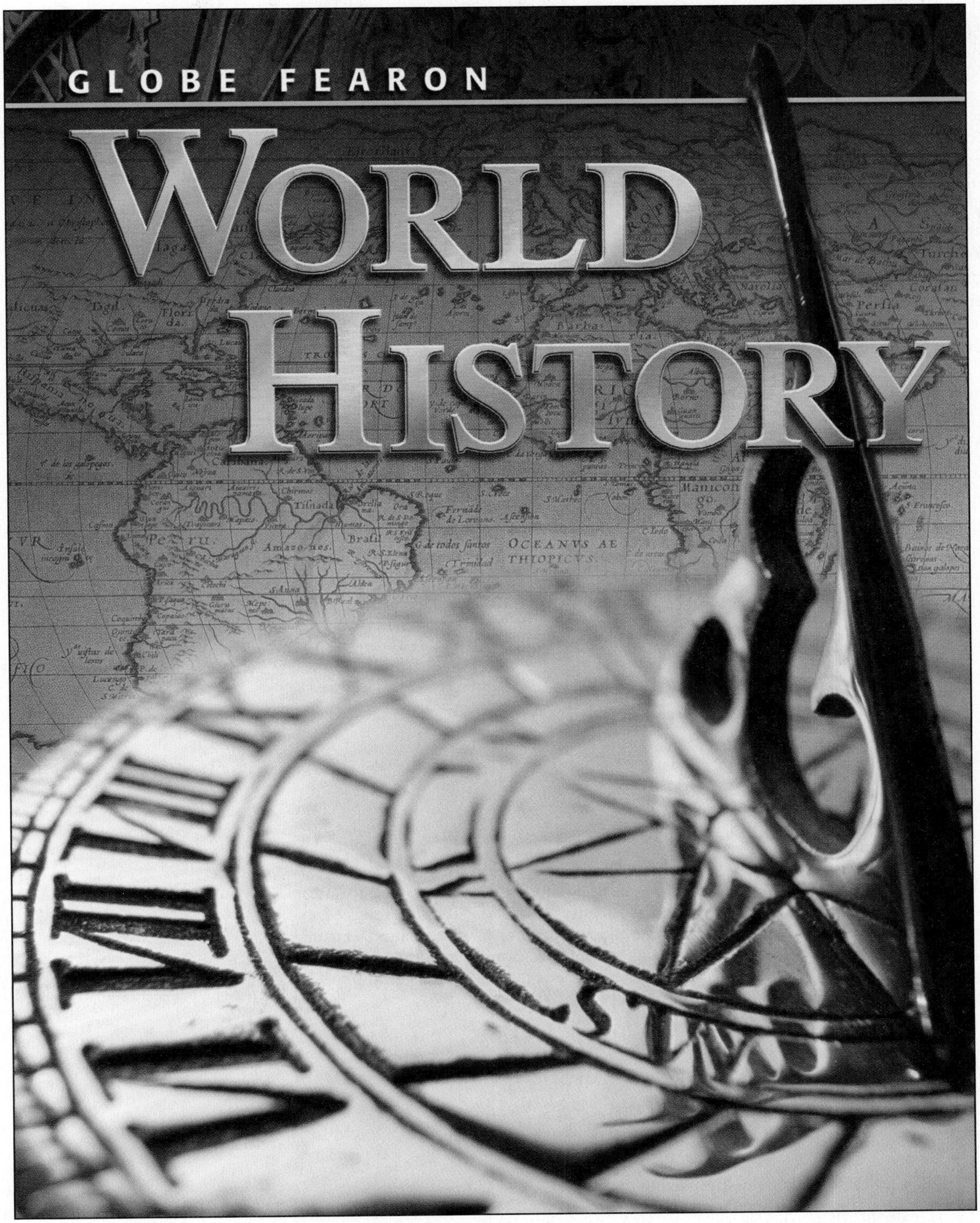

GLOBE FEARON

WORLD HISTORY

GLOBE FEARON

Pearson Learning Group

The following people have contributed to the development of this product:

Art & Design: Sharon Bozek, Eileen Brantner, Robert Dobaczewski, Kathleen Ellison, Salita Mehta, Jim O'Shea, Angel Weyant
Editorial: Linda Dorf, Elaine Fay, Mary Ellen Gilbert, Alisa Loftus, Colleen Maguire, Jane Petlinski, Jennie Rakos, Maurice Sabean, Tara Walters
Manufacturing: Nathan Kinney
Marketing: Katie Erezuma
Production: Lorraine Allen, Irene Belinsky, Carlos Blas, Karen Edmonds, Cheryl Golding, Leslie Greenberg, Susan Levine, Cathy Pawlowski, Lisa Svoronos, Cindy Talocci, Susan Tamm, Meredith Tenety
Publishing Operations: Thomas Daning, Christine Guido, Richetta Lobban, Kate Matracia

Acknowledgments appear on pages 859–860, which constitutes an extension of this copyright page.

ISBN 0-13-023992-5

Printed in the United States of America

1 2 3 4 5 6 7 8 9 10   07 06 05 04 03

 DK is a Pearson company specializing in the creation of high quality reference materials that combine educational value with strong visual style. This combination allows DK to deliver highly accessible and engaging educational content that is appealing to students, teachers, and parents worldwide.

1-800-321-3106
www.pearsonlearning.com

Globe Fearon gratefully acknowledges the contributions of the following consultants and reviewers.

Content Consultants

Carolyn A. Brown, Ph.D.
Associate Professor, Department of History
Rutgers University
New Brunswick, NJ
African studies

Manuel Chavez M., Ph.D.
Associate Director, Center for Latin American
    and Caribbean Studies
Professor, Latin American Studies and Journalism
Michigan State University
East Lansing, MI
Latin American studies

Linda L. Greenow, Ph.D.
Associate Professor and Chair,
Department of Geography
S.U.N.Y. New Paltz
New Paltz, NY
Geography

Richard E. Keady, Ph.D.
Comparative Religious Studies Program
San Jose State University
San Jose, CA
Religious studies

Akram Fouad Khater, Ph.D.
Associate Professor of Middle Eastern History
North Carolina State University
Raleigh, NC
Middle Eastern studies

Douglas R. Skopp
State University of New York
Distinguished Professor of History
Plattsburgh State University of New York
Plattsburgh, NY
European studies

Anand A. Yang
Director, Henry M. Jackson School of
    International Studies
University of Washington
Seattle, WA
Asian studies

Reviewers

John Boyd
Instructional Research and Evaluation Specialist
Office of Research, Evaluation, and Accountability
Osecola County School District
Kissimmee, FL

Carl Brownell
Social Studies Department Chairperson
Hinsdale Central High School
Hinsdale, IL

Robert Lemoine
Assistant Principal
Northeast High School
Philadelphia, PA

Maryanne Malecki
Instructional Supervisor
City School District of Albany
Albany, NY

Richard Thomas Mason
Social Studies Teacher and Curriculum Coordinator
Carter G. Woodson Public Charter School
Fresno, CA

Tamika S. Matheson
Assistant Principal, Social Studies
Paul Robeson High School
Brooklyn, NY

Elizabeth G. Salimbeni
Social Studies Teacher
Rio Rancho High School
Rio Rancho, NM

CONTENTS

Neanderthal Skull
(page 7)

| Unit 1 | From Prehistory to Early Civilizations |

Egyptian painting
(page 24)

Aryan god Indra
(page 60)

The British Museum

Ancient Greek vase
(page 123)

The Blue Mosque, Turkey
(page 171)

African mask
(page 226)

Marco Polo
(page 252)

Unit 4   Europe Undergoes Change 313

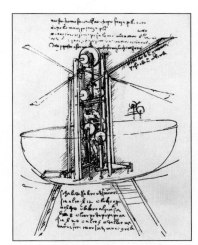

Drawing by Leonardo da Vinci
(page 318)

Elizabeth I
(page 389)

Napoleon Bonaparte
(page 457)

Qing Dynasty porcelain
(page 484)

Early phonograph
(page 518)

Simón Bolívar
(page 597)

Vladimir Lenin
(page 637)

Political cartoon
(page 666)

Dr. Martin Luther King Jr.
(page 714)

Nelson Mandela
(page 759)

MAPS

CHARTS AND GRAPHS

Timelines

Timelines Cont.

Build Your Skills

Past to Present

Connects topics in history to today

GEOGRAPHY HANDBOOK AND ATLAS

Introduce the Geography Handbook and Atlas

The Geography Handbook can be used to help students recognize the connection between geography and history. The Handbook includes a brief overview of basic geographical concepts and terms.

You may wish to use the Handbook as a complete unit of study or have students refer to specific pages as they encounter maps and map-related topics throughout the book.

Following the Geography Handbook is an Atlas. The Atlas contains a map of the world and maps of North America, South America, Europe, Africa, Asia and the Middle East, and Australia, New Zealand, and the Pacific Islands. Use these maps to help students locate countries around the world as they study the history of each region.

GEOGRAPHY HANDBOOK AND ATLAS

GH1

Teaching Options

ESL/ELL STRATEGIES

Organize Information As students read the first eight pages of the Handbook, have them maintain two lists of terms—geography terms (which would include the theme words) and map terms (which would include map parts). Students should write definitions of the terms in their own words and compare their lists with a partner.

Why Study Geography?

A good place to begin your study of world history is with the study of geography. Geography is the study of the physical features of Earth and the people who live on it, including the relationship between people and their environment. Geography helps us to understand history by seeing how the characteristics of a place affect people and events.

The Andes Mountains, shown here from Argentina, stretch across more than 5,000 miles of South America. Many of the peaks are more than 22,000 feet tall.

Using the Handbook
BUILDING VOCABULARY

Write the word *geography* on the board. Ask students to brainstorm terms that are related to geography or geographic features. Write students' terms on the board. Ask students to record these terms and keep a list of geography-related terms in their notebooks. Encourage them to add to their lists whenever they encounter a new term.

Why Study Geography?

Point out to students that geography and history are connected in many ways. Geography has often affected historical events in a place or an area. For example, ask students how geography might affect the outcome of a battle. (Sample answer: One side might have an advantage if its soldiers are positioned on higher ground than the other side's.) Explain that by studying geography, students may understand historical events better.

Closing
SUMMING UP

Have students create a SQR chart (TR, p. 322). Suggest that students review, or survey (S), the Geography Handbook (pp. GH3–GH10) to identify the topics being discussed. Have students write a survey topic in the top box. Then have students ask a question (Q) that they would like answered. Have them write the question in the center box. Finally, have students read (R) to find the answer and record their answer in the bottom box. Encourage students to share their SQR charts with the class and discuss what they have learned.

Test Taking

Point out that maps and globes usually contain a great deal of information and often, different types of data. In order to filter out unnecessary information when answering test questions, have students refer to the question to identify the information they will need from a map before they look at the map itself.

Introduce the Five Geography Themes

Tell students that a theme is a general idea or topic. Explain that in order to understand the connection between geography and history, geographers have developed five geography themes. Most events in history are connected to geography in one or more of these five ways. You may wish to refer to these themes as you discuss historical events presented in the text. Questions on maps throughout this book relate to these themes. After students have learned about a historical event, have them identify which one or more of the five themes relate to that event.

Using the Handbook

Location Point out that the words *location* and *place* are usually synonyms, except in geography. Have volunteers read the two descriptions on page GH3. Then, have students write their own definitions for the words and share their definitions with the class. Ask students to include examples of each word.

Place Ask students to describe a unique feature of their state, city, or community. Discuss how that feature has been important in the history or development of the community.

FIVE GEOGRAPHY THEMES

Geographers have developed five themes to show the connection between history and geography. These themes are location, place, region, movement, and human interaction.

Location Street signs in Charleston, South Carolina

Place

Geographers help us to find out what a place is like. The theme of place answers the question, "What do you find there?" Every place on Earth has its own features that make it different from every other place. Is the land flat? Is it hilly? What is the weather like? These are all questions about physical features of a place.

If you asked geographers to describe Hallstatt, Austria, they would point out physical features such as lakes, valleys, and mountains. They might also give its population and describe the kinds of buildings people have constructed there. So, a description of a place includes not only its geographical features, but also its human features. Questions such as "How many people live there? What languages do they speak? What customs do they follow?" are about the human features of a place.

Location

When you study events in history, you need to know exactly where in the world they take place. The theme of location answers the question, "Where is it?" To know precisely where a place is located, geographers have come up with a grid system of imaginary lines on maps and globes. These are called lines of latitude and lines of longitude. You will learn more about this grid system on page GH7.

Sometimes, it is useful to know where an area is in relation to another area. People often describe the location of a place by referring to another place. For example, Charleston, South Carolina, is in the southeast corner of the United States, close to North Carolina and Georgia. A specific location in Charleston could be the intersection of Queen Street and King Street.

Place The peaks of the Austrian Alps behind Hallstatt, Austria

GH3

Teaching Options

Cooperative Learning

Divide the class into five groups, and assign each group one of the geography themes on pages GH3–GH4. Have group members work together to write a brief description of their community that indicates its location, place, region, movement, or human interaction. Have groups share their descriptions with the class and develop a class description of their community.

Region

Because the world is so vast, it is sometimes convenient to think about it in terms of regions. A region is an area that has similar features and characteristics. These can include similar landforms, the type of climate the region has, or even its own particular culture. For example, the Outback in Australia is a region which covers about 75 to 80 percent of Australia. It is a low expanse of flat, dry, and sparsely populated land. Three deserts cover much of the Outback and few people live there.

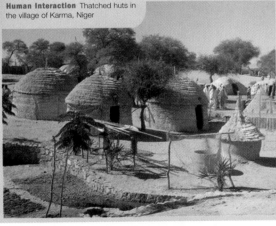

Region The Australian Outback with its reddish-brown soil

Movement Plane approaching an airport in Hong Kong, China

Movement

In early history, people moved around to hunt or gather food. Later, they traveled to explore, to conquer, and to gain riches. Some people left their homes to find good farmland, more space, or better jobs.

Today, movement has become a daily part of our lives. People use planes, trains, cars, buses, and subways to move from one place to another. Ships and planes crisscross the globe as goods and resources are exchanged among nations. When we study history, we look at the movement of people, ideas, and goods to understand the changes that have occurred.

Human Interaction Thatched huts in the village of Karma, Niger

Human Interaction

In the study of history, we look at the interaction between people and their surroundings. We might ask, "How does the environment of a place affect how people live?" The weather and resources of a place, for example, will determine how people use the land for business and recreation, as well as the types of houses people build. In the desert region of Niger, Africa, people build round huts called rondavels. These huts protect the people from the intense desert heat.

Geography Handbook ◆ **GH4**

Region Ask students to identify some regional features of their hometown. What common landforms are found in their region? What are some characteristics of the climate? How large an area, including nearby states, can also be included in this region?

Movement Have students speculate about what might have brought the first settlers to their area. What new trends in population movement can be seen in the area today?

Human Interaction Ask students how people have interacted with their surroundings in their area. In what ways do people use the land and other natural resources? How has the land been changed by people?

Closing

SUMMING UP

Have students create a main ideas/supporting details chart (TR, p. 319) to review each of the five themes. Have them list the geography theme in the center circle and include supporting details about each theme in the outer circles.

Connection to
SCIENCE

The interaction between people and their surroundings has had both positive and negative effects. Have students use a two-column chart (TR, p. 328) to list harmful and helpful effects of science and technology on the environment, such as chemical spills, destructive mining practices, new methods for cleaning streams, and increasing crop production.

Introduce Reading a Map

Ask students to think of the last time that they used a map. Have them explain what kind of map they used and why they used it. Explain to students that maps are useful not only in our everyday lives but also in learning about history and geography. They will see many maps as they learn about the historical events discussed in this book.

Point out to students that maps in this book may show both political and physical information.

Have students read and interpret the map on pages GH5–GH6. Then, have students apply their new skills at reading maps and map features to another map in this book.

Using the Handbook
BUILDING VOCABULARY

To help students learn the terms on these pages, have them write each of the following terms on separate index cards: *locator map, map title, compass rose, scale,* and *key.* Then, have students write an explanation of each term and draw a picture of it on the back of the card. Have students work in pairs to quiz each other, using their index cards.

READING A MAP

To understand geography, you need to know how to read a map and understand its parts.

Maps are drawings of places on Earth. To help you read maps, mapmakers—or cartographers—include certain elements on most maps they draw. These include the title, the key, the compass rose, the locator map, and the scale. Some maps also have an inset map. An inset map is a small map inside a larger one. It shows areas that are too large, too small, or too far away to show on the main map.

Maps that show general information about an area are called general-purpose maps. Two of the most common types of general-purpose maps are political maps and physical maps. A political map shows features determined by people, such as national boundaries, cities, and capitals. A physical map shows natural features, such as rivers and oceans. It also shows the differences in elevation, or height above sea level, of landforms in a particular area. Sometimes political and physical maps may be combined to make one map.

Maps that show specific kinds of information are called special-purpose maps. There are many types of special-purpose maps. Special-purpose maps include road maps, product maps, precipitation maps, climate maps, natural-resource maps, and time-zone maps. Special-purpose maps can also show human activities, such as exploration routes or battle sites. For example, a climate map is a special-purpose map that shows the temperature of a place or region. A product map is a map that shows where resources, such as coal, are found or where crops, such as cotton, are grown. A precipitation map can show the average yearly precipitation in a part of the world.

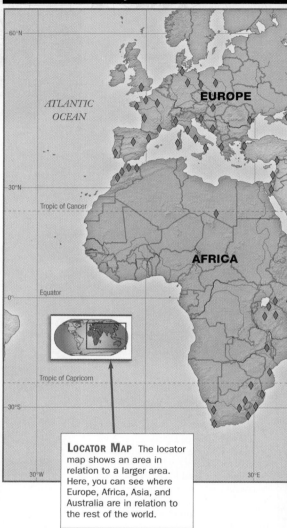

Evidence of Early Life

ATLANTIC OCEAN

EUROPE

AFRICA

Tropic of Cancer

Equator

Tropic of Capricorn

LOCATOR MAP The locator map shows an area in relation to a larger area. Here, you can see where Europe, Africa, Asia, and Australia are in relation to the rest of the world.

GH5

Teaching Options

MAP TITLE The title tells the subject of the map and what kind of information can be found on the map.

ASIA

PACIFIC OCEAN

INDIAN OCEAN

N
W ✦ E
S

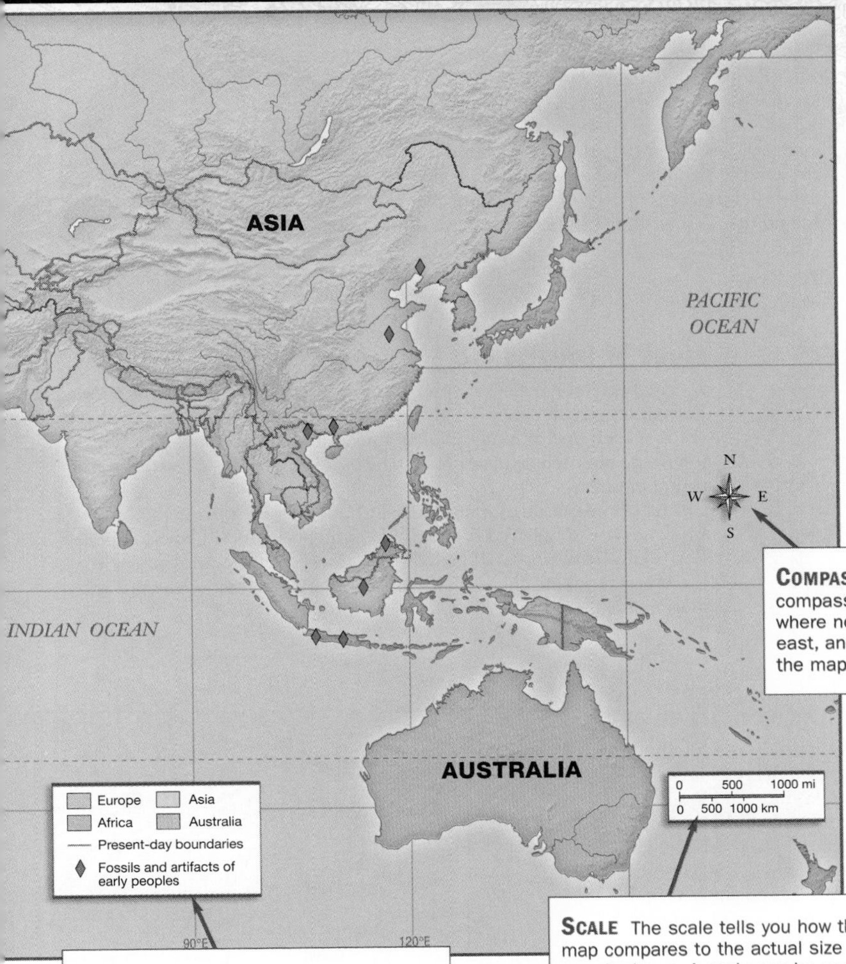

COMPASS ROSE The compass rose shows where north, south, east, and west are on the map.

AUSTRALIA

	Europe		Asia
	Africa		Australia

— Present-day boundaries

◆ Fossils and artifacts of early peoples

90°E   120°E

0   500   1000 mi
0 500 1000 km

KEY The key, or legend, explains what the symbols or colors on the map stand for.

SCALE The scale tells you how the map compares to the actual size of area it shows. A scale can be used to find distances on a map.

Ask students what each symbol in the key stands for. (Each of the four colored boxes stands for one continent, lines are present-day boundaries, and the diamond represents where fossils and artifacts have been found.) Ask students which continents are shown on the map (Europe, Africa, Asia, and Australia). Then challenge students to name the three continents that are not part of this map (North America, South America, and Antarctica). You may want to suggest that students use the locator map on page GH5 to help them answer this question.

Activity

Locate maps Have students skim through their textbooks to find an example of each of the following types of maps: political, historical, physical, special-purpose, and military. Have students share the maps they found with the class and explain what information each map conveys.

LINK TO TODAY

Tell students that maps have become much more sophisticated within the last decade due to the Global Positioning System (GPS). GPS is a system of 24 satellites that can identify the exact location on Earth of a person or object connected to a receiver. This system is being used as a navigational tool by the military, on commercial and private airplanes and ships, in automobiles, and even by hikers using handheld GPS receivers. Automobiles equipped with GPS receivers can provide a detailed map for the driver and give the driver specific directions to a destination.

Closing

SUMMING UP

Have individual students offer one piece of advice for reading maps more effectively. Have the class discuss the tips and decide which ones they will use most often.

Cooperative Learning

Have small groups create a detailed map of one part of their community, including several important landmarks. Tell students to use symbols on their maps and to include a key, map title, compass rose, and scale. Some possible roles for group members are: discussion leader, note taker, map designer and labeler, distance measurer, and presenter.

Introduce Latitude and Longitude

Have students arrange their desks in rows. Identify the lines of desks that go from the left side to the right side as rows and the lines of desks that go from the front to the back as columns. Tell students that you would like the person in row 2, column 1, to stand up. Then, ask another student to stand up referring only to the student's row and column numbers. Explain that you are using a type of grid system to identify students. Next, note that another type of grid system is used to identify places on maps and globes. This grid system is made up of lines of latitude and longitude.

Using the Handbook

Lines of Latitude

As a memory device, suggest that students think of latitude as the rungs of a ladder that go up or down a globe or map. These lines or rings start at the equator. The lines above the equator are marked with an **N**. The lines below the equator are marked with an **S**.

Lines of Longitude

Students may find that it helps to think of longitude as being the long lines that run from the North Pole to the South Pole.

Using Latitude and Longitude

Explain to students that when reading or writing a geographic coordinate the line of latitude is always given as the first number.

Closing

SUMMING UP

Have students locate five cities on the maps of Europe and Africa on Atlas pages A5 and A6 and write the approximate latitude and longitude coordinates for each city. Then, have students trade lists with a partner who has to identify the five cities.

LATITUDE AND LONGITUDE

Mapmakers have created a special kind of grid system to help people find the exact location of any place on Earth. You can locate any point on the surface of Earth if you know how to use lines of latitude and longitude.

Lines of Latitude

Latitude is the position of a place north and south of the equator. Lines of latitude run east to west around the globe. On the map, you can see that each line of latitude has a measurement in degrees (°).

The equator is the imaginary line of latitude that runs around the center of Earth. It is numbered 0° latitude. The equator also divides Earth into two halves, called hemispheres. The Northern Hemisphere lies north of the equator, and the Southern Hemisphere lies south of it.

Lines of Longitude

The lines on a map that run from the North Pole to the South Pole are lines of longitude. They are also called meridians. On the map, you can see that each line of longitude has a measure in degrees (°). Lines of longitude are used to measure distance in degrees east and west of the prime meridian.

The prime meridian is an imaginary line that runs through Greenwich, England. It is numbered 0° longitude. The prime meridian also divides Earth into hemispheres. The half that lies west of the prime meridian is the Western Hemisphere. The half that lies to the east of the prime meridian is the Eastern Hemisphere.

Using Latitude and Longitude

Once you know the latitude and longitude of a place, you can locate it quickly on a map. The point at which lines of latitude and longitude meet is the grid address, or coordinates, of an exact location. For example, in the United States the city of New Orleans, Louisiana, is located at 30°N/90°W. This means that New Orleans is 30° north of the equator and 90° west of the prime meridian. Use the map of the United States to find the approximate coordinates of Philadelphia, Pennsylvania.

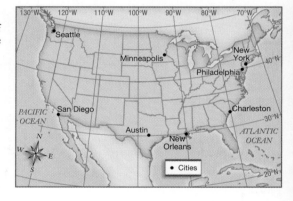

GH7

Teaching Options

MAP PROJECTIONS

A map projection is a way of showing the round Earth on a flat surface.

To locate places, geographers use maps and globes. Because a globe is the same shape as Earth, it shows the sizes and shapes of Earth's features accurately. Even though a globe has this advantage, flat maps are more convenient. A flat map allows you to see all of Earth's surface at the same time. The disadvantage of a flat map is that it distorts how the Earth really looks.

To solve this problem, mapmakers have developed different map projections. No map projection shows Earth correctly in every way. Some projections show the sizes of continents correctly but distort their shapes. Others show the correct shape of the landmasses but distort their sizes. On most maps, the regions near the center of the map are most accurate. Regions farther away from the center are distorted.

Mercator Projection

The Mercator projection shows the true shapes of landmasses, but distorts their sizes. On the Mercator projection, the actual curved lines of latitude and longitude are shown straight. Because the lines are straight, lands on either side of the equator must be stretched in size.

Robinson Projection

Today, many people use another kind of map projection called the Robinson projection. The lines of latitude and longitude are curved to show the curve of Earth's surface. The Robinson projection shows land and ocean sizes accurately, but the shapes of the land are slightly distorted.

MAP PROJECTIONS

Introduce Map Projections

Explain to students that map projections are different ways of showing what the round Earth looks like on a flat surface, like on a page in a book. Two such kinds of projections are the Mercator Projection and the Robinson Projection. Each projection is named after the mapmaker, or cartographer, who developed it.

Using the Handbook

Mercator Projection and Robinson Projection

On the board, create a large Venn diagram. Have the class compare and contrast the Mercator projection with the Robinson projection. (**Mercator:** shows lines of latitude and longitude as straight lines, shows true shape of landmasses, distorts the size of landmasses; **Robinson:** shows lines of latitude and longitude as curved lines, shows true sizes of land and water, distorts shapes of landmasses; **Overlap:** show a flat representation of Earth, include lines of latitude and longitude)

Closing

SUMMING UP

Have students use a two-column chart (TR, p. 328) to list the advantages and disadvantages of a flat world map. (**Advantages:** It is easier to handle, it lets you see all of Earth's surfaces at the same time; **Disadvantages:** it distorts the sizes and shapes of Earth and its features.)

F Y I

Mercator and Robinson

Gerardus Mercator, a Flemish cartographer, developed the Mercator projection in 1568. His map was one of the first to include lines of latitude and longitude. Arthur Robinson developed the Robinson projection during the 1960s. His map was one of the first to use computer-assisted cartography.

Introduce the Geography Dictionary

Explain to students that specific terms are used to refer to different geographic features. Knowing what each of these terms means can help students better understand geography. Point out that students should not only know the definitions of these terms but also be able to recognize the geographic features.

You may wish to refer back to these pages as students read about various geographical features throughout this book. Encourage them to use the visuals on these pages to refresh their memory of the geographical terms.

Using the Handbook

BUILDING VOCABULARY

Review the terms on page GH10 with students and discuss each definition. Have students locate the image of each term as you read the definition aloud.

Activity

Make a chart Have students use a two-column chart (TR, p. 328) to classify the terms as landforms or bodies of water. As a class, review students' charts, and discuss why each term was classified as it was.

GEOGRAPHY DICTIONARY

GH9

Teaching Options

Research

AVERAGE

Have students choose one of the geographical terms and use an atlas, encyclopedia, or almanac to research one famous example of that geographical feature. Ask students to gather information including the proper name of the feature, its location, and how it fits the term's definition. Have students report their findings to the class.

CHALLENGE

Have students choose one of the geographical terms and use an atlas, encyclopedia, or almanac to research famous examples of that geographical feature. Ask them to write a brief report explaining how the examples fit the term's definition and how they differ from each other. Suggest that students include pictures of their examples.

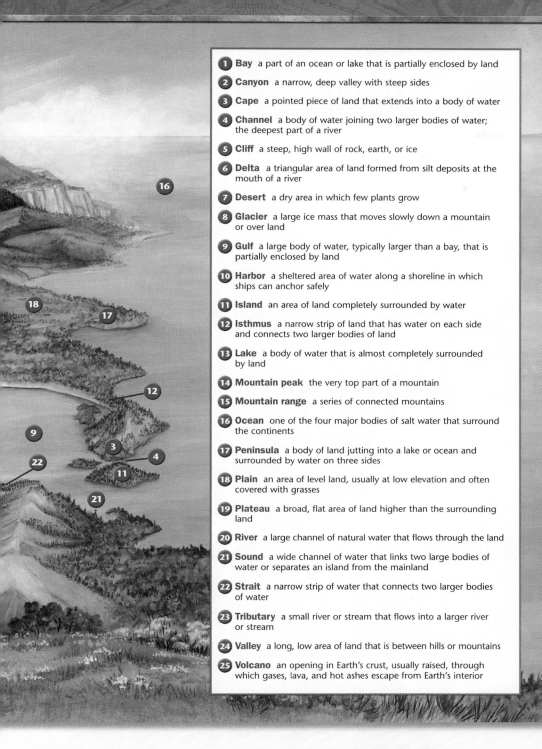

1. **Bay** a part of an ocean or lake that is partially enclosed by land

2. **Canyon** a narrow, deep valley with steep sides

3. **Cape** a pointed piece of land that extends into a body of water

4. **Channel** a body of water joining two larger bodies of water; the deepest part of a river

5. **Cliff** a steep, high wall of rock, earth, or ice

6. **Delta** a triangular area of land formed from silt deposits at the mouth of a river

7. **Desert** a dry area in which few plants grow

8. **Glacier** a large ice mass that moves slowly down a mountain or over land

9. **Gulf** a large body of water, typically larger than a bay, that is partially enclosed by land

10. **Harbor** a sheltered area of water along a shoreline in which ships can anchor safely

11. **Island** an area of land completely surrounded by water

12. **Isthmus** a narrow strip of land that has water on each side and connects two larger bodies of land

13. **Lake** a body of water that is almost completely surrounded by land

14. **Mountain peak** the very top part of a mountain

15. **Mountain range** a series of connected mountains

16. **Ocean** one of the four major bodies of salt water that surround the continents

17. **Peninsula** a body of land jutting into a lake or ocean and surrounded by water on three sides

18. **Plain** an area of level land, usually at low elevation and often covered with grasses

19. **Plateau** a broad, flat area of land higher than the surrounding land

20. **River** a large channel of natural water that flows through the land

21. **Sound** a wide channel of water that links two large bodies of water or separates an island from the mainland

22. **Strait** a narrow strip of water that connects two larger bodies of water

23. **Tributary** a small river or stream that flows into a larger river or stream

24. **Valley** a long, low area of land that is between hills or mountains

25. **Volcano** an opening in Earth's crust, usually raised, through which gases, lava, and hot ashes escape from Earth's interior

CHECK FOR COMPREHENSION

Have students work in pairs to quiz each other. One student identifies the name of each numbered feature in the visual while the other checks his or her partner's answers against the list of terms and definitions. Then, have students switch roles.

Closing

SUMMING UP

Have students play geography bingo. Ask them to draw a 4 × 4 grid. Have students write one geography term listed on this page in each square. Then, call out definitions one at a time as students mark off the appropriate term. Continue playing until one student has marked off four terms in a horizontal, vertical, or diagonal row.

Writing

AVERAGE

Ask students to write a short story set in one of the geographic places listed on this page. Encourage them to develop the story around the setting. After students have finished, have them read their stories to the class. As a class, discuss how the setting affected each story.

CHALLENGE

Have students write a short story in which the main character is a world traveler. Ask them to focus the story on experiences of the traveler in a variety of geographic places around the world. Encourage students to include various conflicts that stem from the diverse geography.

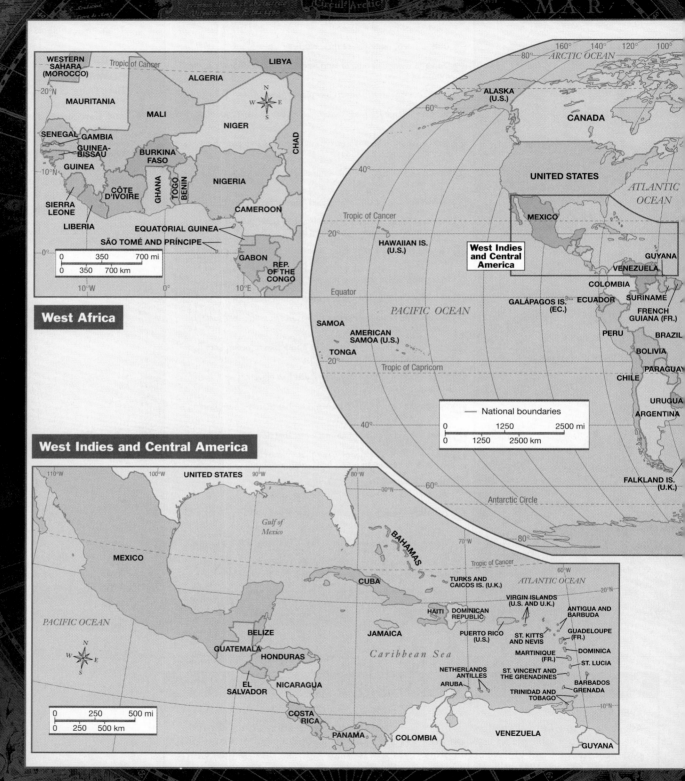

West Africa

West Indies and Central America

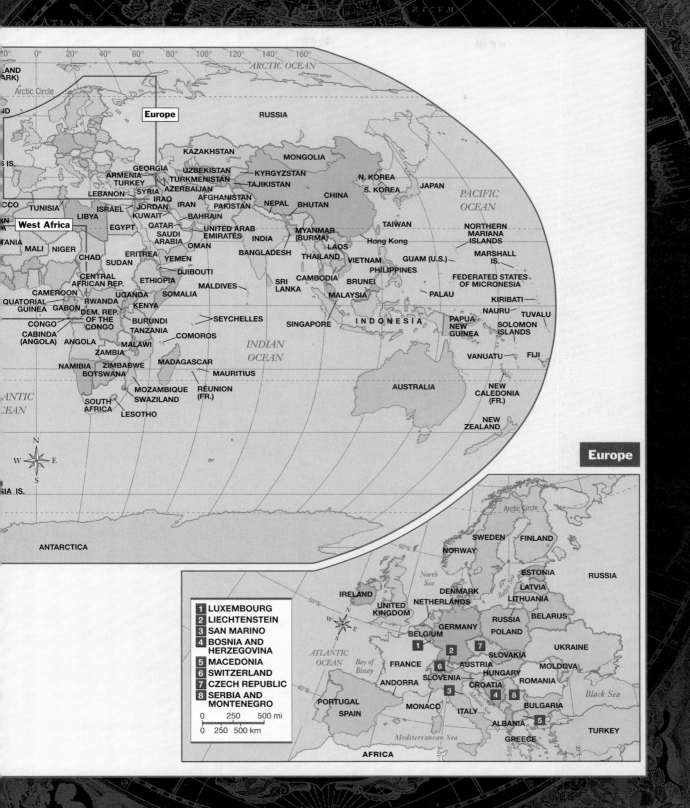

ARCTIC OCEAN

Arctic Circle

Europe

RUSSIA

KAZAKHSTAN

MONGOLIA

GEORGIA
ARMENIA
TURKEY
UZBEKISTAN
TURKMENISTAN
KYRGYZSTAN
TAJIKISTAN
N. KOREA
S. KOREA
JAPAN

PACIFIC OCEAN

LEBANON
SYRIA
AZERBAIJAN
IRAQ
AFGHANISTAN
CHINA
JORDAN
IRAN
PAKISTAN
NEPAL
BHUTAN

TUNISIA
ISRAEL
KUWAIT
BAHRAIN

West Africa

LIBYA
EGYPT
QATAR
SAUDI
ARABIA
UNITED ARAB
EMIRATES
OMAN
INDIA
MYANMAR
(BURMA)
TAIWAN

Hong Kong

NORTHERN
MARIANA
ISLANDS

MALI
NIGER
CHAD
SUDAN
ERITREA
YEMEN
BANGLADESH
LAOS
THAILAND
VIETNAM
GUAM (U.S.)
MARSHALL
IS.

CENTRAL
AFRICAN REP.
DJIBOUTI
ETHIOPIA
MALDIVES
SRI
LANKA
CAMBODIA
PHILIPPINES
FEDERATED STATES
OF MICRONESIA

CAMEROON
QUATORIAL
GUINEA
GABON
UGANDA
RWANDA
SOMALIA
KENYA
BRUNEI
MALAYSIA
PALAU
KIRIBATI

CONGO
DEM. REP.
OF THE
CONGO
BURUNDI
TANZANIA
SEYCHELLES
SINGAPORE
I N D O N E S I A
PAPUA
NEW
GUINEA
NAURU
SOLOMON
ISLANDS
TUVALU

CABINDA
(ANGOLA)
ANGOLA
MALAWI
COMOROS

INDIAN OCEAN

VANUATU
FIJI

ZAMBIA
ZIMBABWE
MADAGASCAR

NAMIBIA
BOTSWANA
MAURITIUS

AUSTRALIA

NEW
CALEDONIA
(FR.)

ANTIC
CEAN
MOZAMBIQUE
SWAZILAND
RÉUNION
(FR.)

SOUTH
AFRICA
LESOTHO

NEW
ZEALAND

N
W   E
S

GIA IS.

ANTARCTICA

Europe

Arctic Circle

SWEDEN
FINLAND

NORWAY

North
Sea

ESTONIA
RUSSIA

LATVIA
LITHUANIA

1 **LUXEMBOURG**
2 **LIECHTENSTEIN**
3 **SAN MARINO**
4 **BOSNIA AND
   HERZEGOVINA**
5 **MACEDONIA**
6 **SWITZERLAND**
7 **CZECH REPUBLIC**
8 **SERBIA AND
   MONTENEGRO**

IRELAND
UNITED
KINGDOM
DENMARK
NETHERLANDS

RUSSIA
BELARUS

BELGIUM
GERMANY
POLAND

1
2
7
UKRAINE

FRANCE
6
SLOVAKIA
AUSTRIA
HUNGARY
MOLDOVA

ATLANTIC
OCEAN
Bay of
Biscay
ANDORRA
SLOVENIA
3
CROATIA
4   8
ROMANIA

Black Sea

PORTUGAL
MONACO
ITALY
BULGARIA

0   250   500 mi
0   250 500 km

SPAIN
ALBANIA
5
TURKEY

Mediterranean Sea
GREECE

AFRICA

North America

ASIA

ARCTIC OCEAN

Bering Sea

Beaufort Sea

AK

Gulf of Alaska

Yukon Territory

Northwest Territory

Nunavut

GREENLAND

Arctic Circle

Baffin Bay

Labrador Sea

Hudson Bay

British Columbia

Alberta

Saskatchewan

Manitoba

Ontario

CANADA

Quebec

Labrador

Newfoundland and Labrador

Newfoundland

New Brunswick

Prince Edward Island

Nova Scotia

PACIFIC OCEAN

WA

OR

ID

MT

WY

ND

SD

NE

MN

WI

IA

MI

IL

IN

OH

Ottawa

NY

PA

VT

ME

NH

MA

RI

CT

NJ

DE

MD

Washington, D.C.

ATLANTIC OCEAN

NV

UT

CO

KS

MO

KY

WV

VA

CA

AZ

NM

OK

AR

TN

NC

SC

MS

AL

GA

TX

LA

FL

Gulf of Mexico

BAHAMAS

Nassau

Tropic of Cancer

PUERTO RICO (U.S.)

Havana

CUBA

Santo Domingo

HAITI

DOMINICAN REPUBLIC

MEXICO

Port-au-Prince

Kingston

JAMAICA

Caribbean Sea

Mexico City

BELIZE

Belmopan

GUATEMALA

HONDURAS

Guatemala City

Tegucigalpa

San Salvador

NICARAGUA

Managua

EL SALVADOR

San José

Panama City

SOUTH AMERICA

COSTA RICA

PANAMA

Legend

United States

National capitals

National boundaries

State/provincial boundaries

0   250   500 mi

0   250   500 km

N   E   S   W

160°   Kauai   156°

Nihau   Oahu   22°

Molokai

HI   Maui   20°

Hawaii

0   200 mi

0   200 km

120°W   110°W   100°W   90°W   80°W   70°W

80°N   70°N   60°N

50°N

40°N

30°N

20°N

10°N

South America

Caribbean Sea
Maracaibo
Caracas
VENEZUELA
Georgetown
Paramaribo
French Guiana (FR.)
Bogotá
GUYANA
Cayenne
Cali
COLOMBIA
SURINAME
Quito
ECUADOR
Guayaquil
Negro
Amazon
Equator 0°
Madeira
Tapajós
Xingu
Tocantins
PERU
BRAZIL
São Francisco
10°S
Lima
Lake Titicaca
Brasília
Arequipa
BOLIVIA
La Paz
Santa Cruz
Sucre
20°S
PARAGUAY
São Paulo
Tropic of Capricorn
Concepción
CHILE
Asunción
PACIFIC OCEAN
30°S
Valparaiso
Rosario
Salto
URUGUAY
Santiago
ARGENTINA
ATLANTIC OCEAN
Buenos Aires
Montevideo
40°S
N
W   E
S
National capitals
Cities
National boundaries
0   250   500 mi
0   250   500 km
Strait of Magellan
50°S
Falkland (Malvinas)
Islands (U.K.)
100°W   90°W   80°W   70°W   60°W   50°W   40°W   30°W   20°W
10°N

Europe

Reykjavik
ICELAND
Arctic Circle
60°N
Norwegian Sea
SWEDEN
FINLAND
NORWAY
Oslo
Helsinki
Stockholm
Tallinn
ESTONIA
RUSSIA
North Sea
Riga
LATVIA
Moscow
IRELAND
Copenhagen
Baltic Sea
LITHUANIA
Dublin
50°N
UNITED KINGDOM
DENMARK
Vilnius
Minsk
NETHERLANDS
Berlin
BELARUS
London
Amsterdam
RUSSIA
Warsaw
Brussels
GERMANY
POLAND
Kiev
BELGIUM
1
Luxembourg
Prague
7
UKRAINE
Paris
2
SLOVAKIA
Bratislava
ATLANTIC OCEAN
Vienna
Budapest
MOLDOVA
Bay of Biscay
FRANCE
6
Bern
AUSTRIA
HUNGARY
Chisinau
Ljubljana
SLOVENIA
Zagreb
ROMANIA
ANDORRA
Monte Carlo
3
CROATIA
Bucharest
Black Sea
40°N
Sarajevo
Belgrade
PORTUGAL
Madrid
MONACO
4
8
BULGARIA
Lisbon
SPAIN
Rome
Sofia
ITALY
Skopje
ASIA
Tiranë
5
ALBANIA
GREECE
Strait of Gibraltar
Aegean Sea
Athens
Valletta
MALTA
Mediterranean Sea
AFRICA

1	LUXEMBOURG
2	LIECHTENSTEIN
3	SAN MARINO
4	BOSNIA AND HERZEGOVINA
5	MACEDONIA
6	SWITZERLAND
7	CZECH REPUBLIC
8	SERBIA AND MONTENEGRO

⊛ National capitals
— National boundaries
0   200   400 mi
0   200   400 km

N W E S

0°   10°E   20°E   30°E

Africa

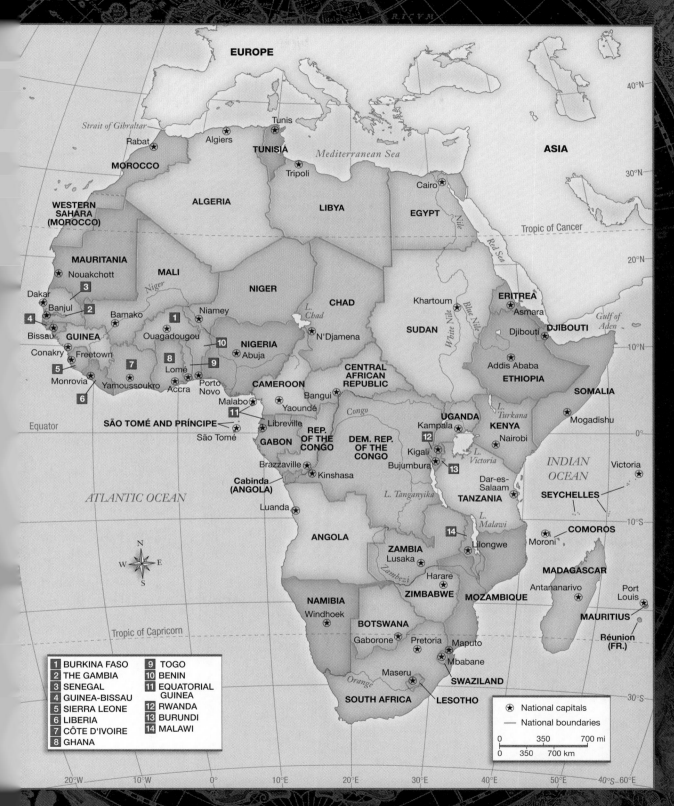

EUROPE

Strait of Gibraltar
Rabat ✪
Algiers ✪
Tunis ✪
TUNISIA
MOROCCO
Mediterranean Sea
ASIA
40°N

Tripoli ✪
30°N
Cairo ✪

WESTERN
SAHARA
(MOROCCO)
ALGERIA
LIBYA
EGYPT
Tropic of Cancer

MAURITANIA
Nouakchott ✪
MALI
NIGER
20°N

Dakar ✪
③
Banjul ✪
②
Bamako ✪
①
Niamey ✪
CHAD
Khartoum ✪
White Nile
Blue Nile
ERITREA
Asmara ✪
Gulf of
Aden
10°N

④
Bissau ✪
GUINEA
Ouagadougou ✪
⑩
NIGERIA
Abuja ✪
N'Djamena ✪
SUDAN
Djibouti ✪
DJIBOUTI

Conakry ✪
Freetown ✪
⑤
⑦
⑧
Lomé ✪
⑨
Addis Ababa ✪
ETHIOPIA
SOMALIA

Monrovia ✪
Yamoussoukro ✪
Accra ✪
Porto
Novo ✪
CAMEROON
CENTRAL
AFRICAN
REPUBLIC
Mogadishu ✪

⑥
Malabo ✪
Bangui ✪
Congo
L.
Turkana

⑪
Yaoundé ✪
UGANDA
KENYA
Equator
SÃO TOMÉ AND PRÍNCIPE
Libreville ✪
REP.
OF THE
CONGO
DEM. REP.
OF THE
CONGO
Kampala ✪
⑫
Nairobi ✪
0°

São Tomé ✪
GABON
Kigali ✪
L.
Victoria
Victoria ✪

Brazzaville ✪
Bujumbura ✪
⑬
INDIAN
OCEAN
SEYCHELLES

Cabinda
(ANGOLA)
Kinshasa ✪
Dar-es-
Salaam ✪
10°S

ATLANTIC OCEAN
L. Tanganyika
TANZANIA

Luanda ✪
L.
Malawi
COMOROS
Moroni ✪

N
W   E
S
ANGOLA
⑭
Lilongwe ✪
MADAGASCAR

ZAMBIA
Lusaka ✪
Zambezi
Antananarivo ✪
Port
Louis ✪

Harare ✪
MOZAMBIQUE
MAURITIUS

NAMIBIA
Windhoek ✪
ZIMBABWE
Maputo ✪
Réunion
(FR.)

Tropic of Capricorn
BOTSWANA
Mbabane ✪
30°S

Gaborone ✪
Pretoria ✪
SWAZILAND

Maseru ✪
Orange
SOUTH AFRICA
LESOTHO

20°W   10°W   0°   10°E   20°E   30°E   40°E   50°E   40°S 60°E

1	BURKINA FASO	9	TOGO
2	THE GAMBIA	10	BENIN
3	SENEGAL	11	EQUATORIAL GUINEA
4	GUINEA-BISSAU	12	RWANDA
5	SIERRA LEONE	13	BURUNDI
6	LIBERIA	14	MALAWI
7	CÔTE D'IVOIRE		
8	GHANA		

✪ National capitals
— National boundaries

0   350   700 mi
0   350   700 km

Asia and the Middle East

Australia, New Zealand, and the Pacific Islands

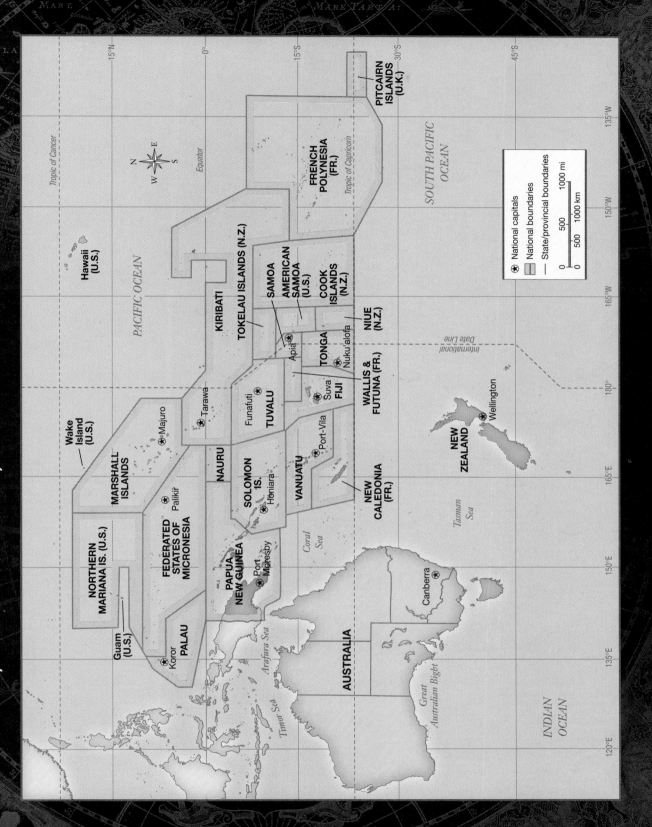

PITCAIRN ISLANDS (U.K.)

FRENCH POLYNESIA (FR.)

SOUTH PACIFIC OCEAN

Tropic of Capricorn

Tropic of Cancer

Equator

N
W E
S

Hawaii (U.S.)

PACIFIC OCEAN

KIRIBATI

TOKELAU ISLANDS (N.Z.)

SAMOA
AMERICAN SAMOA (U.S.)
COOK ISLANDS (N.Z.)

NIUE (N.Z.)

Apia

TONGA
Nuku'alofa

International Date Line

Wake Island (U.S.)

Majuro

Tarawa

MARSHALL ISLANDS

NAURU

Funafuti

TUVALU

WALLIS & FUTUNA (FR.)

Suva
FIJI

NEW ZEALAND

Wellington

NORTHERN MARIANA IS. (U.S.)

Palikir

FEDERATED STATES OF MICRONESIA

SOLOMON IS.
Honiara

Port-Vila

VANUATU

NEW CALEDONIA (FR.)

Tasman Sea

Guam (U.S.)

Koror
PALAU

PAPUA NEW GUINEA
Port Moresby

Coral Sea

AUSTRALIA

Canberra

Arafura Sea

Timor Sea

Great Australian Bight

INDIAN OCEAN

National capitals
National boundaries
State/provincial boundaries

0   500   1000 mi
0   500   1000 km

15°N
0°
15°S
30°S
45°S

120°E   135°E   150°E   165°E   180°   165°W   150°W   135°W

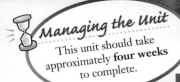

Managing the Unit
This unit should take approximately **four weeks** to complete.

PLANNING GUIDE

	Skills and Features	Projects and Activities	Program Resources	Meet Individual Needs

Chapter 1
 	
Early Peoples of the World,
pp. 1–21
 	
Plan for 4–5 class periods.
	Unit Technology, p. T1
	Use a Timeline, p. 9
	Connect History & Archaeology, p. 15
		Conflict Resolution, p. T5
		Test Taking, pp. T6, T7
		Cooperative Learning, p. T11
		Connection to Art, p. T12
		Research, p. T13
		Link to Today, T15
		Using Technology, p. T16
		Connection to Government, p. T17
		Writing, p. T18
			Teacher's Resources
			Terms to Know, p. 14
			Review History, p. 48
			Build Your Skills, p. 82
			Chapter Test, pp. 117–118
			Concept Builder, p. 217
			They Made History:
			  Louis and Mary Leakey,
			  p. 252
			Main Idea/Supporting
			  Details Chart, p. 319
			Transparencies 2, 10
				ESL/ELL Strategies,
				pp. T5, T10, T11
				Visual/Spatial, p. T4

Chapter 2
 	
Ancient Civilizations,
pp. 22–47
 	
Plan for 5–6 class periods.
	They Made History:
	Akhenaton, p. 26
	Read a Historical Map,
	p. 29
	📖 Past to Present:
	  Pyramids,
	  pp. 30–31
		Connection to Science, p. T26
		Connection to Literature, p. T30
		Connection to Economics, p. T32
		Using Technology, p. T33
		Teen Life, p. T35
		Writing, p. T39
		Cooperative Learning, p. T40
		Research, p. T43
		Test Taking, p. T44
			Teacher's Resources
			Terms to Know, p. 15
			Review History, p. 49
			Build Your Skills, p. 83
			Chapter Test, pp. 119–120
			Concept Builder, p. 218
			Idea Web, p. 321
			Transparencies 1, 6, 7,
			  10, 15
				ESL/ELL Strategies,
				pp. T24, T34, T38, T42
				Visual/Spatial, p. T25
				Verbal/Linguistic, p. T26
				Logical/Mathematical,
				p. T38

Chapter 3 **Ancient India,** pp. 48–71 Plan for 5–6 class periods.	Understand Cause and Effect, p. 55	Cooperative Learning, p. T51 Using Technology, p. T51 Connection to Economics, p. T53 Test Taking, p. T53 Writing, p. T57 Connection to World Languages, p. T58 Conflict Resolution, pp. T59, T65 World Religions, p. T62 Connection to Literature, p. T63 Research, p. T66 Connection to Art, p. T68	**Teacher's Resources** Terms to Know, p. 16 Review History, p. 50 Build Your Skills, p. 84 Chapter Test, pp. 121–122 Concept Builder, p. 219 Main Idea/Supporting Details Chart, p. 319 Transparencies 7, 10	ESL/ELL Strategies, pp. T50, T52, T58, T61, T67 Visual/Spatial, pp. T52, T68 Auditory, p. T59 Kinesthetic, p. T63
Chapter 4 **Ancient China,** pp. 72–96 Plan for 5–6 class periods.	Use Tables and Charts, p. 79 Points of View, p. 89	Using Technology, p. T75 Test Taking, p. T76 Connection to Art, p. T77 Connection to Culture, p. T77 Connection to Science, p. T81 Conflict Resolution, p. T82 Cooperative Learning, p. T83 Connection to Literature, p. T86 Research, p. T87 Take a Stand, p. T89 Link to Today, p. T89 Writing, p. T91	**Teacher's Resources** Terms to Know, p. 17 Review History, p. 51 Build Your Skills, p. 85 Chapter Test, pp. 123–124 Unit 1 Test, pp. 183–184 Concept Builder, p. 220 SQR Chart, p. 322 Transparencies 1, 7	ESL/ELL Strategies, pp. T74, T80, T90 Visual/Spatial, p. T83 Verbal/Linguistic, p. T92

Assessment Options

Chapter 1 Test, Teacher's Resources, pp. 117–118
Chapter 2 Test, Teacher's Resources, pp. 119–120
Chapter 3 Test, Teacher's Resources, pp. 121–122
Chapter 4 Test, Teacher's Resources, pp. 123–124
Unit 1 Test, Teacher's Resources, pp. 183–184

Alternative Assessment

Television Interview, p. 96
Write a Play, p. T96

Books for Students

AVERAGE

The Usborne Book of the Ancient World. Jane Chisholm and Anne Millard. Illustrated, detailed reference about the ancient civilizations in lands such as Egypt, India, and China. (EDC Publishing, 1996)

Ancient Medicine: From Sorcery to Surgery. Michael and Mary B. Woods. Overview of medical techniques used in ancient civilizations. (Lerner Publishing Group, 1999)

Mara, Daughter of the Nile. Eloise Jarvis McGraw. Historical fiction about a slave girl who becomes a spy in ancient Egypt. (Penguin Putnam, 1985)

Ancient Chinese Dynasties. Eleanor J. Hall. A review of the history and culture of six ancient Chinese dynasties. (Lucent Books, 2000)

CHALLENGING

The Classics of Mountains and Seas. Anne Birrell, translator. Reference with cultural information for ancient Chinese mythology. (Viking Press, 2000)

A Curse of Silence: A Mystery of Ancient Egypt. Lauren Haney. Fictional murder mystery set in ancient Egypt. (Avon Books, 2000)

Ajanta Caves: Artistic Wonder Of Ancient Buddhist India. Benoy K. Behl and Sangitika Nigam. Photographs and explanations of temple murals in the Ajanta Caves. (Harry N. Abrams, Inc. 1998)

The Search for Ancient China. Corinne Debaine-Francfort. Explains how archaeological discoveries help scientists understand ancient Chinese history and culture. (Abrams, 1999)

Books for Teachers

Historical Atlas of the Ancient World. John Haywood. Charles Freeman, Judith Toms, Paul Garwood. Reference with detailed maps and text of ancient civilizations. (Friedman, Michael Publishing Group, Incorporated, 2001)

Early Civilizations of the Old World: The Formative Histories of Egypt, the Levant, Mesopotamia, India, and China. Charles Keith Maisels. Reviews the development of ancient civilizations and their influences. (Routledge, 2001)

Ancient Egypt. David P. Silverman. Series of essays on the culture and daily life of ancient Egyptians, based on the latest archaeological evidence. (Oxford University Press, 1997)

Ancient Cities of the Indus Valley Civilization. Jonathan Mark Kenoyer. Overview of ancient Indus Valley civilizations, based on the latest archaeological evidence. (Oxford University Press, 1998)

Ancient China and its Enemies: The Rise of Nomadic Power in East Asian History. Nicola Di Cosmo. Reviews ancient China, using ancient writings among other sources. (Cambridge University Press, 2002)

You may wish to preview all referenced materials to ensure their appropriateness for your local community.

Audio/Visual Resources

Human Origins: 10,000,000 B.C.–8000 B.C. Traces the migration of early hominids from Africa across land bridges to other continents through archaeological evidence of rudimentary tools and weapons. Videocassette. (Social Studies School Service)

The Agricultural Revolution: 8000 B.C.–5000 B.C. Demonstrates how lifestyle changes accounted for growth in ancient civilizations and how differences in agricultural techniques can still be found today, from a series. Videocassette. (Social Studies School Service)

Ancient China: A Journey Back in Time. Explores five ancient Chinese dynasties from culture to architectural accomplishments. Videocassette. (Library Video Company)

Technology Resources

Egypt: Secrets of an Ancient World: www.nationalgeographic.com/pyramids/

Ancient India: www.wsu.edu:8080/~dee/ANCINDIA/ANCINDIA.HTM

History of China: www.travelchinaguide.com/intro/history/prehistoric/

Ancient Empires: Decisions, Decisions. The player must make decisions as ruler of an ancient city-state. Includes student books and teacher's guide. Software. (Social Studies School Service)

Globe Fearon Related Resources

History Resources

World History for a Global Age, Book 1: Ancient History to the Industrial Revolution. Reinforces understanding of early civilizations around the world and the factors that influence the development of civilization. ISBN 1-556-75683-6

Global Studies, Focus on East Asia, Volume 4. Activities and case studies explore the geography, history, cultures, economics, and politics of East Asia. ISBN 0-835-91939-0

Literature Resources

World Myths and Legends I: Ancient Middle Eastern. Anthology of cultural myths and legends from Egypt, Sumeria, and Babylonia. ISBN 0-822-44642-1

World Myths and Legends I: Far Eastern. Anthology of myths and legends from ancient China. ISBN 0-822-44643-X

World Myths and Legends II: India. Anthology of myths and legends from India. ISBN 0-822-44648-0

To order books, call **1-800-321-3106.**

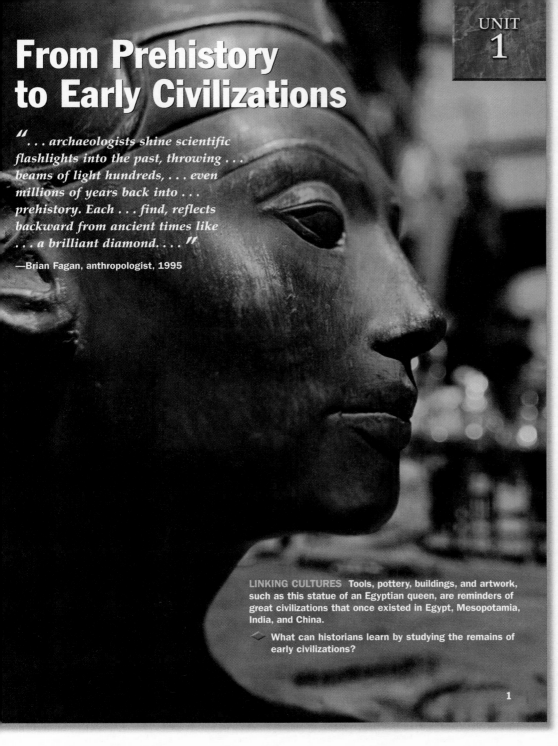

From Prehistory to Early Civilizations

"... archaeologists shine scientific flashlights into the past, throwing ... beams of light hundreds, ... even millions of years back into ... prehistory. Each ... find, reflects backward from ancient times like ... a brilliant diamond...."

—Brian Fagan, anthropologist, 1995

LINKING CULTURES Tools, pottery, buildings, and artwork, such as this statue of an Egyptian queen, are reminders of great civilizations that once existed in Egypt, Mesopotamia, India, and China.

◆ What can historians learn by studying the remains of early civilizations?

1

Teaching Options

UNIT TECHNOLOGY

Invite students to research art created by prehistoric humans and peoples of the earliest civilizations. Students will see some examples as they read Unit 1. To see other examples, have students use the Internet. Suggest that they use the following key words: cave art, ancient Egypt art, ancient India art, and ancient China art.

You may wish to identify possible Web sites for students and always monitor their activities on the Internet.

UNIT 1 — Portfolio Project

Television Interview

In the Portfolio Project for Unit 1 on page 96, students will conduct a television interview of a historical figure. Teams of students will select an individual and research the person and time he or she lived. The group will then conduct the interview for the class.

From Prehistory to Early Civilizations
(pp. 1–96)

Unit Summary

Unit 1 introduces the ages of prehistory, explains the rise of early settlements, and discusses ancient civilizations in Egypt, the Fertile Crescent, the Indus Valley, and ancient China.

CHAPTER 1
Early Peoples of the World

CHAPTER 2
Ancient Civilizations

CHAPTER 3
Ancient India

CHAPTER 4
Ancient China

Set the Stage
TEACH PRIMARY SOURCES

Photo This photo shows a reproduction based on the sculpted head of Nefertiti, who was queen of Egypt during the reign of Pharaoh Akhenaten, from 1353 to 1336 B.C. Nefertiti is an Egyptian phrase meaning "the beautiful one who has come." Ask students what they can infer about the ancient Egyptians from this portrayal. (that women were important in the civilization; that Egyptian artists were skilled)

Quote Brian Fagan's quote illustrates the importance of the findings of archaeologists. Ask students what they think the phrase "shine scientific flashlights into the past" means. Point out that those who study the earliest humans have no written records to rely on. Ask students what archaeologists in the future might think about today's culture if they found an item such as a spoon. (Encourage students to speculate what this item might suggest.)

◆ **ANSWER** They can learn about aspects of culture such as the kinds of tools people used, what they used the tools to create, and what the people looked like.

Early Peoples of the World
PREHISTORY–3300 B.C.

(pp. 2–21)

Chapter Objectives
• Describe how artifacts provide archaeological evidence of the existence of prehistoric peoples.
• Explain how permanent settlements lead to advances in agriculture, metalworking, and trade.
• Identify the key features that are characteristics of a civilization.

Chapter Summary
Section I focuses on the discovery of early humans and identifies characteristics of their cultures.
Section II describes the effects on prehistoric humans of permanent settlements and the advances in culture resulting from permanence.
Section III describes the geographic influences on the development of early civilizations and details characteristics of the early civilizations that developed in river valleys.

Set the Stage
TEACH PRIMARY SOURCES
Explain to students that art found in caves throughout Europe contained vivid paintings and sometimes sculpture. Point out to students that Annette Laming-Emperaire gives two possible reasons for the creation of the paintings, such as those in the Lascaux Cave. Ask students what the practical reason for cave paintings may have been (to represent animals that were hunted) and what the artistic reason may have been (to express a vision of the world).

CHAPTER
1

Early Peoples of the World
PREHISTORY–3300 B.C.

I. Prehistoric Times
II. Early Settlements
III. The Rise of Civilizations

On September 12, 1940, four teenagers were exploring a cave near Lascaux in southwestern France. There, they made a remarkable discovery. The cave was covered with about 600 paintings of animals and figures created more than 165,000 years ago.

Scientists have many ideas about the people who created these images. One scientist, Annette Laming-Emperaire, thought about what motivated early humans to decorate this cave:

66 *Paleolithic man was far more complex than is generally supposed and . . . the scope of his artistic inspiration extended far beyond . . . the hunt and its quarry [prey]. . . . these paintings . . . may represent man's first attempt to express his vision of the world and the relationship of one living creature with another.* 99

As more evidence of early humans is unearthed on all continents, more questions arise about the story of human life on Earth, which began millions of years ago.

7–6 million B.C.
Early human life appears in Africa.

1.8 million B.C.
Human ancestors begin walking upright.

CHAPTER EVENTS

6 million B.C.   **4 million** B.C.   **2 million** B.C.

WORLD EVENTS

ca. 3.4 million B.C.
Isthmus of Panama becomes a land bridge connecting the Americas.

2   UNIT 1   ◆   From Prehistory to Early Civilizations

Teaching Options

Chapter 1 Resources

REVIEW

Teacher's Resources (TR)
Terms to Know, p. 14
Review History, p. 48
Build Your Skills, p. 82
Concept Builder, p. 217
Chapter Test, pp. 117–118
Main Idea/Supporting Details Chart, p. 319
Transparencies 2, 10

ASSESSMENT
Section Review, pp. 8, 14, 19
Chapter Review, pp. 20–21
Chapter Test, TR, pp. 117–118

ALTERNATIVE ASSESSMENT
Portfolio Project, p. 96
Write a Play, p. T96

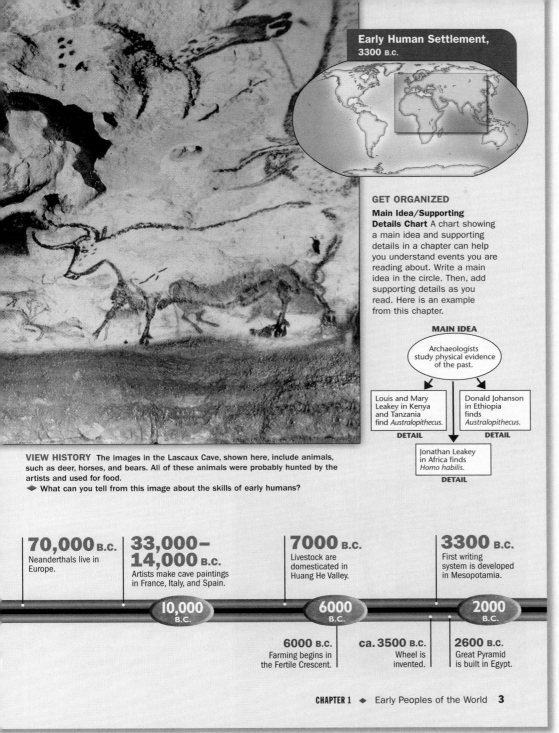

Early Human Settlement, 3300 B.C.

GET ORGANIZED

Main Idea/Supporting Details Chart A chart showing a main idea and supporting details in a chapter can help you understand events you are reading about. Write a main idea in the circle. Then, add supporting details as you read. Here is an example from this chapter.

MAIN IDEA

Archaeologists study physical evidence of the past.

Louis and Mary Leakey in Kenya and Tanzania find *Australopithecus*.

DETAIL

Donald Johanson in Ethiopia finds *Australopithecus*.

DETAIL

Jonathan Leakey in Africa finds *Homo habilis*.

DETAIL

VIEW HISTORY The images in the Lascaux Cave, shown here, include animals, such as deer, horses, and bears. All of these animals were probably hunted by the artists and used for food.
◆ What can you tell from this image about the skills of early humans?

70,000 B.C.	**33,000– 14,000** B.C.	**7000** B.C.	**3300** B.C.
Neanderthals live in Europe.	Artists make cave paintings in France, Italy, and Spain.	Livestock are domesticated in Huang He Valley.	First writing system is developed in Mesopotamia.

10,000 B.C.   **6000** B.C.   **2000** B.C.

6000 B.C. Farming begins in the Fertile Crescent.   **ca. 3500** B.C. Wheel is invented.   **2600** B.C. Great Pyramid is built in Egypt.

CHAPTER 1 ◆ Early Peoples of the World **3**

Chapter Themes
- Culture
- Time, Continuity, and Change
- Individuals, Groups, and Institutions
- Production, Distribution, and Consumption
- Global Connections
- People, Places, and Environment
- Science, Technology, and Society

F Y I

Cave Paintings of Lascaux

The Lascaux Cave, located in the Les Eyzies region of present-day France, is probably the most striking of the painted caves found in the region. The walls and ceilings of several areas of the cave have been painted in vivid red and black. One of the bulls is 18 feet long. Lascaux was closed to the public in 1963 to prevent damage from the outside air, moisture, and carbon dioxide.

Chapter Warm-Up

USING THE MAP
Have students find the locator map at the top of page 3. Ask what part of the world is highlighted. (Europe, Africa, and Asia) Explain that these areas are where fossil remains and artifacts from prehistoric times have been found. Ask students why all of this area, rather than North and South America, might have been inhabited by early humans. (The area is a single connected landmass.)

VIEW HISTORY
Explain to students that the majority of art caves found to date are located in present-day France and Spain. The art depicts animals in paint or in clay sculptures. Ask students what other things modern artists might depict that are not shown in the prehistoric art from the Lascaux Cave pictured on these pages. (human figures, landscape scenes)

◆ **ANSWER** Early humans observed the characteristics of animals they saw and were able to depict them realistically so that, even today, others could recognize most of the animals.

GET ORGANIZED
Main Idea/Supporting Details Chart
Discuss the graphic organizer shown on page 3. Explain that the main idea is the most important point the author is making about a topic. Details give more information about the main idea. Point out that identifying the main idea and details in each section of the chapter will help students remember the most important points and information about these main ideas. Also, explain that some main ideas may have more than three supporting details. Tell students to add detail boxes to their organizer as needed.

● **TEACH THE TIMELINE**
Explain that timelines are a way of explaining visually when events occur and how they relate to one another. The timeline on pages 2–3 shows events between 7–6 million years B.C. and 2600 B.C. Because the time span is so great, the timeline is broken to indicate a span of time that has been omitted. Explain that the parallel timeline at the beginning of each chapter shows events from the chapter and other events occurring at the same time around the world.

CHAPTER 1 ◆ T3

I. Prehistoric Times

(pp. 4–8)

Section Summary

In this section, students will learn how archaeological discoveries led scientists to believe that human prehistory began in Africa. They will also learn how some groups of prehistoric humans developed tools and how they adapted to changing conditions in their environment.

1 Introduce

Getting Started

Ask students what tools are common in modern households. (Answers will vary, but should include tools used for building, repair, kitchen implements, and so on.) Ask students why they think humans invented these tools.

TERMS TO KNOW

Ask students to read the words and definitions on page 4 and find each word in the section. Explain that this textbook underlines and uses boldface type for new terms and that near each term in the running text will be a *context clue*—a definition or explanation of the term so that students will see how it is used in the text.

Preview the names and pronunciations of the early hominid groups from the chart on page 6. You may want to point out that *Homo* means "man" and is part of the name scientists have given to several species of humans.

You may wish to preview the pronunciation of the following terms from this section with students.

Australopithecus
 (aw stray loh PIHTH uh kuhs)
Homo habilis (HOH moh HAB uh luhs)
Homo erectus
 (HOH moh ih REHK tuhs)
Homo sapiens
 (HOH moh SAY pee ehnz)

ACTIVE READING

As students complete the two-column chart (TR, p. 328) for subsection C of this section, explain that they should skim for words and phrases that signal cause-and-effect relationships.

Section I

Prehistoric Times

Terms to Know

archaeologist a person who studies the remains of the past

artifact any object made or changed by humans

hominid a primate of which only one species still exists today—humans

anthropologist a person who studies humans, especially their physical characteristics as well as their customs and social relationships

culture the way of life of a group of people that is handed down from one generation to the next

nomad a wanderer, usually in search of food

Archaeologists Louis and Mary Leakey searched for more than 20 years before finding the remains of an early hominid at Olduvai Gorge in Tanzania, Africa.

Main Ideas

A. Many exciting archaeological discoveries led scientists to believe that human life began in Africa.

B. Early humans developed skills necessary to survive and grow.

C. Early humans learned to adapt to changes that were taking place in nature.

 Active Reading

CAUSE AND EFFECT
When you focus on cause and effect, look for related events. As you read this section, "Prehistoric Times," use a two-column chart to show the relationship between causes and their effects.

A. The Earliest Humans

The time before events in history were recorded is called prehistory. Scientists, called **archaeologists**, study clues left behind by ancient people in order to learn more about prehistory. Often they find the remains of past human life and activities by digging and sifting through soil where ancient people probably lived. The items they find include bones, fossils, tools, and other objects. These clues help archaeologists to piece together the puzzle of prehistory and the earliest humans. For example, fossil evidence uncovered by archaeologists in Africa shows that early ancestors of humans lived in Africa as long as 6 to 7 million years ago.

Archaeologists at Work

Archaeologists also study **artifacts**, or objects such as pottery and tools, left by early groups of people. Until the 1800s, few people tried to study the past in an orderly way. At that time, archaeologists began developing methods to accurately study artifacts, including a three-era system for classifying their findings. They named the eras Stone Age, Bronze Age, and Iron Age, based on the materials humans knew how to use during each of these periods. Scientists further divided the ages into early, middle, and late periods.

The use of modern technology has made archaeology much more exact. An accurate way to determine the age of fossils is to measure the amount of a radioactive carbon, called carbon-14, left in them. Carbon-14 was discovered by Willard Libby, a chemist, and his assistants James Arnold and Ernie Anderson in the late 1940s. For his research, Libby won the Nobel Prize in Chemistry in 1960.

Finding a site, or a place where artifacts will be found, suitable to excavate, or uncover by digging, is almost as difficult as the excavation itself. Archaeologists use three main methods to locate sites. Perhaps the oldest is called fieldwalking. In fieldwalking, archaeologists identify and divide an area into sections of straight lines that they walk, looking for evidence of human activity.

Teaching Options

Section 1 Resources

Teacher's Resources (TR)
 Terms to Know, p. 14
 Review History, p. 48
 Build Your Skills, p. 82
 Concept Builder, p. 217
 Main Idea/Supporting Details Chart,
  p. 319
 Transparency 2

Meet Individual Needs:
VISUAL/SPATIAL LEARNERS

Invite students to create their own "cave art." Hang large sheets of paper along a wall in the classroom. Have students draw or paint pictures of the things they do in their life, such as school, music, videos, and so on. Ask students to view the paintings and explain how these paintings would help archaeologists of the future understand the present.

This early hominid skull was found in South Africa where lightning frequently strikes the plains. Lightning may have provided a source of fire that hominids used to roast meat.

Archaeologists also use sensors, or detectors, to find out what is beneath the ground. The sensors produce a computer printout to show the location of pits, ditches, and buried walls. Finally, photography from above may show light or dark patches on the land that may mark the presence of old paths, farms, and buildings.

Discoveries of Early Humans

The story of humankind begins more than 6 to 7 million years ago during the Stone Age. At that time, huge sheets of ice, called glaciers, covered parts of North America, Europe, and Asia. During these ice ages, Africa was free of ice. Great herds of animals lived there. When scientists began looking for evidence of early humans, they looked in Africa.

In 1924, archaeologist Louis Leakey had an idea, or theory, that early human remains could be found in East Africa. Louis and his archaeologist wife, Mary, searched for artifacts in Kenya and Tanzania. Finally, in 1959, at Olduvai Gorge in Tanzania, Mary discovered the remains of a **hominid**. Hominids are a biological family that includes humans and early humanlike creatures. Scientific studies showed that Mary Leakey's discovery was between 1.5 and 4.5 million years old! The Leakeys called this type of hominid *Australopithecus*. These hominids were bipedal, meaning they could walk upright on two legs, and they had thumbs that allowed them to pick up small objects.

One year later, in 1960, the Leakey's son, Jonathan, discovered the remains of another hominid called *Homo habilis*, a Latin term meaning "handyman." The remains of this hominid date to about 1.8 million years ago.

An **anthropologist** named Donald Johanson also spent many years searching for hominid fossils in Africa. Anthropologists are people who study humans, especially their physical characteristics. Johanson said he awoke feeling lucky one day in 1974 when he unearthed the bones of a three-and-a-half-foot-tall hominid in Ethiopia. As Johanson later recalled of that day:

> ❝ Right there in that 120° noonday sun, I had a sense that this was a terribly important momentous discovery . . . around 3 million-plus years old. ❞

Johanson and his team nicknamed their find Lucy. Lucy's remains also belong to the group of hominids called *Australopithecus*.

◆ **Why would archaeologists be interested in artifacts?**

BIRTHPLACE OF HUMANS
Because of the findings of the Leakeys, Johanson, and others, many scientists believe that the first humans lived in Africa and later traveled in groups to Europe, Asia, the Americas, and Australia.

ANALYZE PRIMARY SOURCES
DOCUMENT-BASED QUESTION
How did Johanson react to his archaeological find?

A. The Earliest Humans

Purpose-Setting Question
What do archaeologists do? (study clues such as fossils, bones, tools, and other objects of ancient people left before humans created written records)

Discuss How would the use of modern technology, such as carbon-14 dating, help archaeologists interpret their findings? (They can be much more precise in dating fossil finds or artifacts. This results in a more accurate understanding of when early humans lived.)

WHERE IN THE WORLD?

BIRTHPLACE OF HUMANS Many scientists believe that the first humans traveled in groups from Africa to Europe, Asia, the Americas, and Australia. Have students look at the map on page 7. Ask students which two continents would it have taken the first humans the longest to reach. (North America and South America)

Activity

Make a list Have students make a two-column chart (TR, p. 328) of the archaeologists and scientists named in subsection A. Next to each name, have them note what the person did or discovered.

ANALYZE PRIMARY SOURCES

DOCUMENT-BASED QUESTION
Donald Johanson was part of several expeditions to Ethiopia. In 1973, he discovered a small, humanlike knee. This was the first known hominid fossil recorded. The skeleton he found in 1974 is one of the most famous anthropological finds.

ANSWER He felt it was an extremely important, momentous discovery.

◆ **ANSWER** Artifacts give important clues to the culture of early humans. They help scientists understand what people and their surroundings were like in times before written records were kept.

Take Notes Ask students to take notes on the three primary methods archaeologists use when they search for a site to dig up, or excavate: fieldwalking, sensors, and aerial photography. Students may want to make a small sketch of each method to help them remember each term. Then, students should use their notes to discuss the pros and cons of each method.

Conflict Resolution

Historians often disagree about the conclusions drawn from the examination of fossils and artifacts. Help students understand that conclusions drawn from fossils and artifacts can sometimes be open to various interpretations. Ask students if they are ever involved in conflicts over people's opinions. Discuss how students would mediate such a conflict.

B. Humans Begin Making Tools

Purpose-Setting Question

What tools did early humans make? (Tools include stone cutting tools, choppers, axes, and spear points.)

Discuss Have the class make a list of animals and plants that were probably hunted or gathered by early humans. Ask students what these animals and plants tell them about the area where early humans lived. (what was available, what the environment was like)

TEACH PRIMARY SOURCES

Have students examine the photographs of early tools. Ask them what they might think if they saw just a picture of the tools. (Students may say they look like ordinary rocks.) Discuss how the caption adds information. Then, have them reexamine the photographs to identify places where there is evidence of deliberate chipping.

Using the Chart

Early Hominids

Remind students that hominids are primates—a group that includes early humans and humanlike creatures. Review the column and row headings. Ask questions about information on the chart to check that students are reading the chart. Ask students to identify the four groups of early hominids for which information is given on the chart. (*Australopithecus, Homo habilis, Homo erectus, Homo sapiens*)

✔ Chart Check

Answer *Homo erectus*

◆ **ANSWER** Humans are the only species that use tools to make other tools.

C. Adapting to Nature

Purpose-Setting Question What are some possible reasons why early humans migrated out of Africa? (changes in climate or shortage of game for food)

B. Humans Begin Making Tools

Early fossil remains indicate that around 2.6 million years ago, people had discovered how to shape tools from the stones around them. Scientists call these first toolmaking humans *Homo habilis*. Jonathan Leakey's 1960 hominid discovery is a member of this group.

The Earliest Tools

One of the first tools produced by *Homo habilis* was probably a stone cutting tool. To produce a cutting edge on a stone such as flint, early humans hit the flint against a harder stone. Pieces of the flint chipped off, leaving behind a sharp edge. Some of these cutting tools, known as choppers, date from 1.8 million years ago and have been found at Olduvai Gorge.

Humans are the only species on Earth to use tools to make other tools. For example, stone spear points were made by sharpening chips of stone that broke off of larger tools. Scientists believe that learning to make tools marked the beginning of human **culture**, or the way of life of a group of people that is handed down from one generation to the next.

While *Homo habilis* still existed, a new group of hominids appeared in East Africa. Known as *Homo erectus*, meaning "human who stands upright," this species showed greater intelligence and ability to adapt than *Homo habilis*. Archaeologists have evidence of this in the use of more complex tools. *Homo erectus* people created a variety of axes. Each form of ax took a bit more skill to produce. Around 4000 B.C., people had begun to grind the edges sharp and polish their axes.

Fire, Hunting, and Gathering

Archaeologists have found evidence that *Homo erectus* was the first hominid to use fire. *Homo erectus* most likely knew that fire kept people warm, frightened dangerous animals, and cooked food. The men probably hunted wild animals, and those who lived near rivers, oceans, or lakes also caught fish and other sea creatures. Women cared for children and gathered seeds, nuts, fruits, and berries.

Early tools were made by chipping pieces of stones until sharp edges formed.

Early Hominids				
	AUSTRALO-PITHECUS	**HOMO HABILIS**	**HOMO ERECTUS**	**HOMO SAPIENS**
PERIOD	4.5–1.5 million B.C.	ca. 1.8 million B.C.	1.8 million–250,000 B.C.	250,000 B.C. to present (includes Neanderthal and Cro-Magnon)
LOCATION	Africa	Africa	Africa, Asia, Europe	Every continent except Antarctica
TRAITS	Bipedal; primitive toolmaking	Bipedal; toolmaking; possible early speech	Advanced toolmaking; used fire; lived in caves	Large brain capacity; advanced writing and speech

✔ **Chart Check**

Which early hominid was first to travel outside of Africa?

◆ **How is human toolmaking different from toolmaking of other species?**

C. Adapting to Nature

Earth has had many major ice ages. The earliest Ice Age, probably about 1.5 million years ago, blanketed northern Europe and North America with ice and snow. Early humans survived because they could think and plan. Their skills in hunting and toolmaking continued to develop.

As *Homo erectus* developed more advanced hunting techniques, they began to migrate, or move, from

---

Teaching Options

Test Taking

Point out to students that tests often include visuals such as charts. To understand the information that is presented in a chart, tell students that they should look first at the title and then at the labels for the columns of information (generally given at the top of each column) and for the rows of information (generally given at the far left of the chart).

F Y I

The Impact of Fire

Fire served important functions besides being used for cooking. It scared away predators and kept people warm. It also was a likely force in drawing humans together. It would have been necessary to provide light in deep caves where cave art has been found. It may also have played a role in early religion.

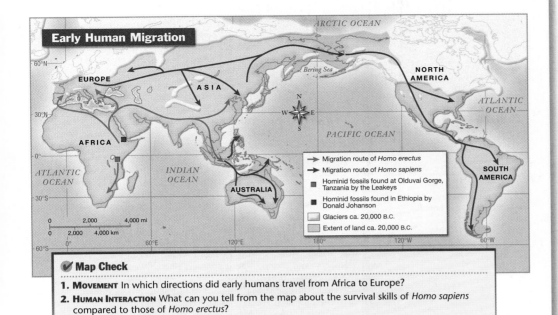

Early Human Migration

Migration route of *Homo erectus*
Migration route of *Homo sapiens*
Hominid fossils found at Olduvai Gorge, Tanzania by the Leakeys
Hominid fossils found in Ethiopia by Donald Johanson
Glaciers ca. 20,000 B.C.
Extent of land ca. 20,000 B.C.

✅ **Map Check**

1. **MOVEMENT** In which directions did early humans travel from Africa to Europe?
2. **HUMAN INTERACTION** What can you tell from the map about the survival skills of *Homo sapiens* compared to those of *Homo erectus*?

Africa into Asia and Europe. Because glaciers still covered much of Earth, sea levels were lower and more land was exposed. A land bridge connected Asia and North America across the Bering Sea. Many scholars believe that people from Asia walked across this land bridge to the Americas. They probably moved because of changes in climate or lack of food. These small groups of **nomads** moved from place to place, looking for good hunting grounds or areas in which plants grew. Nomads did not make permanent camps or build cities.

Neanderthal People

Evidence of the first modern humans, called *Homo sapiens*, which means "the wise man," has been found in Europe and Southwest Asia. Early *Homo sapiens* have some characteristics similar to *Homo erectus*, but their brains were much larger.

Neanderthals, so named because their remains were found in the Neander Valley in present-day Germany, are thought to be early *Homo sapiens*. However, some scientists disagree. What they do agree on is that Neanderthals lived in Europe during the last Ice Age, which began about 70,000 B.C. They knew how to hunt animals such as wild cattle and deer and used stone and wood to make tools. They lived mostly in caves.

Some scientists believe that the Neanderthals may have enjoyed music. A fossil with four holes that sound the notes *do, re, mi,* and *fa* seems to suggest that they made flutes. Other scientists, however, believe these holes are teeth marks from a large meat-eating animal.

No one knows why Neanderthals disappeared. Changes in climate may have been one reason. Some people believe that Neanderthals could not compete with a group of *Homo sapiens* living in Europe about 40,000 years ago.

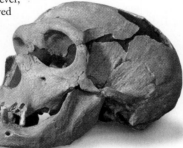

From this one skull, archaeologists learned a great deal about the Neanderthal people and how they differ from modern people.

CHAPTER 1 ◆ Early Peoples of the World **7**

Discuss What does the term *adapt* mean as it is used in the heading of subsection C? (to change or adjust to new conditions)

Using the Map
Early Human Migration

Have students use the map key to identify the two groups of early humans whose migration routes are shown. Ask them how the map indicates *Homo sapiens* may have reached North and South America. (A land bridge connected Asia and North America; from North America, the migration route continued into South America.)

✅ **Map Check**
Answers
1. Early humans traveled from Africa north into Europe. They entered Europe through present-day Spain or through the Middle East and Turkey.
2. *Homo sapiens* seem to have traveled more widely and may have been better able to adapt to a wide range of environments.

Explore Ask students to read the section titled "Neanderthal People." Ask students what are some things scientists agree on (*Homo sapiens* had bigger brains, Neanderthals lived in Europe, hunted animals, used stone and wood to make tools, and lived in caves.) and what are some things scientists disagree on. (Neanderthals were early *Homo sapiens*; enjoyed music, why they disappeared.) Discuss why scientists may disagree on how to interpret artifacts.

TEACH PRIMARY SOURCES

Have students study the photograph of the skull and read the caption. Remind students that the skull is an artifact. Ask them to identify the group of people mentioned in the caption. (Neanderthal) Discuss with students some similarities and differences between the skull in the photograph and the skulls of modern people.

Test Taking

Remind students that to get information from a map, they should start with the map title and key. In the map on this page, students will see that the map topic is early human migration. The map key tells which groups of early human migrations are shown. Ask students to write one question about the map. Then, have students exchange and answer the questions.

CHAPTER 1 ◆ T7

Make a chart Have students make a two-column chart (TR, p. 328) to compare the Neanderthal people and the Cro-Magnon people. The chart should include where they lived, what they hunted, tools they used, and other aspects of their culture. Have students share their charts with the class.

Extend Have students look back at the art from the Lascaux Cave shown on pages 2–3. Then, ask them to look at the detail of Cro-Magnon art shown on page 8. Ask students why they think Cro-Magnon people painted or carved animals.

◆ **ANSWER** The first people came to the Americas in search of food.

Section Close

Ask students to identify aspects of culture of the four groups of early hominids discussed in this section. Then show students Transparency 2 and have them identify the places where early peoples were found. Discuss with students the movement of people from one area to another.

3 Assess

Review Answers

Review History
A. The earliest human fossils have been found in Africa.

B. Learning to make tools is considered to be the beginning of human culture.

C. Changes in climate both forced and enabled early humans to move from place to place.

Define Terms to Know
archaeologist, 4; artifact, 4; hominid, 5; anthropologist, 5; culture, 6; nomad, 7

Critical Thinking
Artifacts can give information about the tools and technology people used to make objects, as well as information about the objects people used in their daily lives.

Cro-Magnons are known for their cave paintings, like this one in the Lascaux Cave in France.

Cro-Magnon People

Neanderthal's successors, the Cro-Magnon people, may have competed with Neanderthals for food, causing Neanderthals' numbers to decrease. Cro-Magnons reached Europe from Asia by about 38,000 B.C. They had advanced toolmaking skills that made them successful hunters. They created tools such as fishing tackle, harpoons, spears, and arrows. Cro-Magnons also had superior language skills compared with earlier hominids. Because of their intelligence and skills, Cro-Magnons flourished in many different environments. By about 8000 B.C., they were very much like modern-day humans.

Cro-Magnon Art

Cro-Magnons are perhaps most famous for their art. Their lifelike paintings decorate more than 300 caves and shelters in Europe, including the Lascaux Cave in France. The painters made pigments from soil and other natural substances to make the many images of animals on the walls of the caves.

Other artistic works of the Ice Age include carvings and engravings on ivory, antlers, and stone. These smaller, portable carvings were often of human figures or of birds and fish.

Stone circles in France and England continue to puzzle researchers. More than a thousand of these circles survive in England alone. One of the most famous circles is Stonehenge, which dates to around 2000 B.C. The huge stone blocks at Stonehenge weigh around 29 tons each and are over 13 feet high. Scientists are still not certain how such huge stones were moved to this location.

◆ **Why did the first people come to the Americas from Asia?**

Review I

Review History
A. Where have the earliest human fossils been found?
B. What was the importance of making tools to early humans?
C. What effect did changes in climate have on human life?

Define Terms to Know
Define the following terms:
archaeologist, artifact, hominid, anthropologist, culture, nomad

Critical Thinking
What kinds of information can artifacts provide about early forms of life?

Write About Geography
Write a brief paragraph discussing some of the challenges facing early humans as they migrated from Africa.

Get Organized
MAIN IDEA/SUPPORTING DETAILS CHART
Use a main idea/supporting details chart to show the artistic skills of the Cro-Magnons.

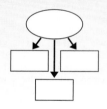

8 UNIT 1 ◆ From Prehistory to Early Civilizations

Write About Geography
Students' paragraphs should include the need to learn to hunt new animals and learn to eat new plants as early humans migrated from Africa. They would also have had to move by trial and error because the landforms and climate would have been unknown to them.

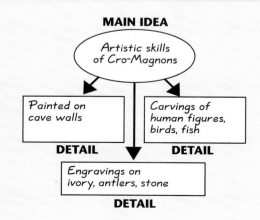

MAIN IDEA

Artistic skills of Cro-Magnons

Painted on cave walls
DETAIL

Carvings of human figures, birds, fish
DETAIL

Engravings on ivory, antlers, stone
DETAIL

Build Your Skills

USE A TIMELINE

Timelines are important visual tools for students of history. They help put key events into chronological, or time, order. Timelines also help you understand how one event may have led to another.

Many people use a system of dividing time that was introduced by a Christian monk about 1,500 years ago. He classified events as *B.C.* and *A.D.* B.C. stands for "before Christ." A.D. stands for *anno Domini*, a Latin phrase meaning "year of the Lord." A.D. tells how many years have passed since the birth of Jesus Christ.

You may also see the abbreviations c. or ca. before a B.C. date. These abbreviations indicate that a date is approximate, or not exact. These abbreviations stand for the Latin word *circa*, which means "about."

Many historians today prefer to use the abbreviations *B.C.E.*, which stands for "before the Common Era" and *C.E.*, which stands for "the Common Era." The abbreviations B.C.E. and C.E. refer to the same years as B.C. and A.D.

Here's How
Use the steps below to read a timeline.

1. Look at the beginning and ending dates of the timeline to see what period it covers.

2. See if the timeline is divided into B.C. and A.D. To calculate the amount of time between an event that occurred in B.C. and one that occurred in A.D., add the two dates together. For example, around 3200 B.C., Stone Age people built the village of Skara Brae, which was discovered in A.D. 1850. The time between the building of the village and its discovery is 5,050 years (3,200 + 1,850).

3. Note the length of time between events. These intervals may be one year, 100 years, or some other span of time. A break in the timeline shows when a period of time has been left out.

Here's Why
Understanding periods in history includes knowing when events occurred. Knowing, for example, that Neanderthals grew fewer in number after Cro-Magnons appeared tells you to look for ways the two may have influenced each another.

Practice the Skill
Study the timeline below. Then, answer the following questions.
1. Which is the earliest date on the timeline?
2. Which event has an approximate date listed?

Extend the Skill
Make a timeline using at least five dates from the first section of this chapter.

Apply the Skill
As you read the next two sections of this chapter, construct a timeline that includes at least ten events discussed in these sections.

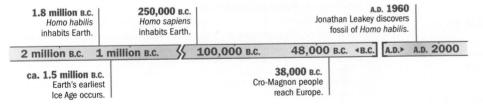

| 1.8 million B.C. *Homo habilis* inhabits Earth. | 250,000 B.C. *Homo sapiens* inhabits Earth. | A.D. 1960 Jonathan Leakey discovers fossil of *Homo habilis*. |

| 2 million B.C. | 1 million B.C. | 100,000 B.C. | 48,000 B.C. | ◄B.C. | A.D.► | A.D. 2000 |

| ca. 1.5 million B.C. Earth's earliest Ice Age occurs. | | 38,000 B.C. Cro-Magnon people reach Europe. |

Teaching Options

RETEACH
Have students use the list of events created in the opening activity and some personal dates to create a timeline of their own. Provide a blank timeline, divided into 13 or 14 equal units. Explain that since all events will be noted by dates A.D., it is not necessary to designate this information on the timeline.

CHALLENGE
Have students research recent archaeological discoveries and make a list of when each discovery occurred. Then, have students make a timeline that shows when the discovery was made. Have students include the dates of the discoveries mentioned in their textbook.

Build Your Skills

USE A TIMELINE

Teach the Skill
Ask the class to suggest ten events that have occurred in their lives. Ask them to identify the month and year of each event. Then, use the events to demonstrate how the same information can be shown on a timeline. Help students divide the model timeline into equal segments.

In order to help students practice the skill, refer them to the timeline at the bottom of the page. Explain that the first thing students should do in preparing to read a timeline is to identify the period of time it covers. They should look first at the far left to find the first date, then to the far right to find the last date.

Remind students that to find the number of years between an event that occurred B.C. (before the birth of Jesus) and one that occurred A.D., (*anno Domini*, or "in the year of the Lord") students must add the two dates. This is to account for a span of time between the date B.C. and the imaginary 0 on a timeline, and then to find the span between 0 and the date A.D.

Practice the Skill
ANSWERS
1. 1.8 million B.C.
2. Earth's earliest Ice Age occurs ca. 1.5 million B.C.

Extend the Skill
Students' timelines should reflect dates mentioned in Section 1 of the chapter. Check that the dates students use on the timeline are in order and that the intervals are even.

Apply the Skill
As students construct their timelines for the next two sections of Chapter 1, remind them to include at least ten events. Some students may find this easier to do if they first list each event on an index card and then put the cards in order.

II. Early Settlements
(pp. 10–14)

Section Summary
In this section, students will learn why nomadic life diminished and certain aspects of culture arose as early humans began to settle in villages and towns. They will also learn how trade began between early groups.

1 Introduce

Getting Started
Ask students what the word *revolution* brings to mind. (Some may say war or fighting.) Point out that the word can also refer to a large-scale change in thinking or in how things are done. Suggest that students keep this definition in mind as they read about the *agricultural* revolution.

TERMS TO KNOW
Ask students to read the words and definitions on page 10 and find each word in the section. Point out that the Latin root of the word *domesticate* is *domus*, meaning "home." Thus, domestic animals are those that have been tamed and live in or near someone's home. Ask students what they think a domestic worker would do and what a domesticated plant would be.

You may wish to preview the pronunciation of the following words from this section with students.

Çatalhüyük (chah tahl hyoo YOOK)
obsidian (uhb SIHD ee uhn)

ACTIVE READING
Tell students that to write a summary of subsection A, they may want to start by using the main idea statement at the top of page 10, the red heads, and the blue subheads within the section. As they summarize, remind them that headings and subheadings are placed in textbooks to help identify important ideas contained within the text. Have students share their summaries with a classmate.

Early Settlements

Terms to Know
domesticate to tame and breed wild animals

cultivate to prepare soil for growing crops

irrigate to artificially supply water to fields

metallurgy the science of making metals to create objects

ore a rock or mineral from which a metal can be separated

barter to trade by exchanging one item for another

Main Ideas
A. Humans began to plant crops and develop better tools.

B. Nomadic life decreased as people did more farming, pottery making, cloth making, and metalworking.

C. Early towns and villages began to appear.

D. Early people began to trade goods in exchange for resources they needed, as well as forming the first governments.

📖 Active Reading
SUMMARIZE
When you summarize, you include only the most important points of a text. As you read this section, concentrate on the main points about early settlements. Pause at the end to summarize what you have learned.

A. An Agricultural Revolution
When the last Ice Age ended, around 10,000 B.C., the glaciers that had covered much of Europe melted. The seas rose, covering land bridges that had been used by migrating groups of people. The climate improved in many regions, making more food resources available. However, more people began competing for these food resources. Instead of continuing to rely on hunting and gathering, people began to farm the land. Scientists know that women in most early cultures provided the majority of food, sometimes working together in food-hunting groups. They were most likely the ones who discovered that grains could be planted, tended, and grown into new crops. This shift from hunting and gathering to producing food is known as an agricultural revolution.

Farming in Asia and Europe
In addition to simple farming, early peoples also learned to **domesticate**, or tame, animals. By 7000 B.C., people in Asia had domesticated pigs, sheep, and goats. They grew lentils, wheat, peas, and barley. They also learned to fertilize their crops with manure from their animals.

A thousand years later, farming spread to Europe. There, people lived together in small villages. Living in communities allowed them to work together and to protect one another.

As people moved into central Europe, they had to adapt their farming practices to the cooler climate, richer soils, and forested lands. Pigs and cattle replaced sheep and goats because pigs were suited to life in forests. Crops were easier to **cultivate**, or prepare for growing, in Europe than in Asia. That is because the land was so fertile.

Advances in Farming Technology
Early settlements first developed along rivers, where floods provided water for crops. As people began moving inland, they learned to use hand tools to cut ditches and canals in the earth. They could then live farther from the river and **irrigate**, or provide water for, their fields.

Building irrigation canals required cooperation and teamwork. The bonds between people strengthened as they worked together. Canals also gave people a more efficient way to travel. Communication between settlements increased

Farming tools, such as this early sickle, were made from stone, bone, or wood.

Then & Now
EARLY FOODS
One of the earliest domesticated wheats, known as emmer, is still being grown along the eastern shores of the Mediterranean Sea.

Teaching Options

Section 2 Resources

Teacher's Resources (TR)
Terms to Know, p. 14
Review History, p. 48
Build Your Skills, p. 82
Concept Builder, p. 217
Main Idea/Supporting Details Chart, p. 319
Transparency 10

ESL/ELL STRATEGIES

Identify Essential Vocabulary Explain to students that writers often provide clues to unfamiliar words. For example, have a student read the definition of the word *cultivate* from the Terms to Know list. Then, read the sentence aloud from page 10 in which the word *cultivate* is used. Explain that the phrase within commas ("or prepare for growing") explains the term. Ask a volunteer to repeat this process with other Terms to Know.

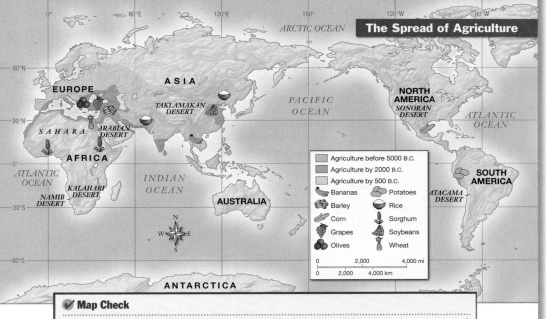

The Spread of Agriculture

Agriculture before 5000 B.C.
Agriculture by 2000 B.C.
Agriculture by 500 B.C.

Bananas	Potatoes
Barley	Rice
Corn	Sorghum
Grapes	Soybeans
Olives	Wheat

0   2,000   4,000 mi
0 2,000 4,000 km

✔ Map Check

1. **PLACE** Which geographic feature may explain why agriculture did not spread to some areas?
2. **LOCATION** On which continent, excluding Antarctica, was agriculture least established by 500 B.C.?

---

as ancient people used the rivers and canals in much the same way as modern people use roads.

As people learned to make tools for digging, such as hoes, axes, and sickles, planting also became easier. Harvesting cereal crops, such as wheat or barley, was easier using a sharp-edged sickle. Toolmakers also developed rakes and shovels.

◆ **How did climate changes encourage the spread of farming?**

B. Cloth, Pottery, and Metalworking

As early people turned to farming, rather than hunting, nomadic groups began to settle in one place. Evidence of advances in the skills of weaving, pottery making, and metalworking has been found by archaeologists in many early settlements.

Early Weavers and Potters

Early people probably wore clothing made from animal skins. By about 7000 B.C., however, people had learned to weave linen, a kind of cloth, from plant fibers. Later they began to weave fabric from wool. They gathered wool from sheep, twisted it on a spindle to make a single thread, and then stretched the thread vertically on a wooden loom. Next, a weaver passed additional threads horizontally through the threads on the loom. Weavers dyed their threads using colors from plants and soil.

Early people used a loom to weave plant fibers and animal hair into clothing and blankets.

CHAPTER 1 ◆ Early Peoples of the World   **11**

Extend Ask students what they think early pottery may have been used for. Why did humans begin making pottery? (Students may suggest it was used for storing food, for cooking, or for eating and drinking.)

Activity

Research Have students use library resources or the Internet to find out more about early metallurgy. Suggest that students find out how early people in different parts of the world used gold, copper, or ores. Then, ask them to find out how the metals are used today. Have students make a poster that shows how metal was used in the past and how it is used today.

◆ **ANSWER** Making pottery was an important skill because people then had containers to store food and water.

C. Two Early Settlements

Purpose-Setting Question How do you think permanent settlements changed the way people lived? (People could band together for protection and to accomplish tasks. Settlement led to the development of aspects of culture such as customs, law, and religion.)

Discuss Ask students what benefits there would be from having houses that were attached to each other and were entered from the roof. (safer from attack, people could easily support each other) Encourage students to describe what they think it might be like to live in a house in Çatalhüyük. Discuss why they think people might have painted the walls of their houses. You may wish to explain that Çatalhüyük is sometimes spelled Çatal hüyük.

Focus Display Transparency 10 and have students locate the area where Çatalhüyük was (south of Konya in present-day Turkey) and Jericho (in present-day Israel). Encourage students to discuss how they think the location of each settlement might have influenced its development.

Clay pots are common artifacts uncovered at archaeological excavations. The way in which pots were constructed and decorated provides historians with valuable information about the people who made them.

Potters made clay containers to store food and water. These containers are among the longest-lasting records of early societies. Because pottery is one of the most common artifacts recovered at archaeological excavations, a great deal is known about its history.

People made bowls by shaping the clay with their hands, so shapes and textures were irregular. The clay objects were then heated in a very hot fire to harden them. Bowls from as long as 12,000 years ago have been found in Japan.

More evenly shaped containers were made using a method that involves coils of clay. After removing the clay from the ground and mixing it with water, potters rolled it into sausagelike ropes. Then, they coiled a clay rope tightly to make a pot base and continued to coil the rope up the sides to finish the pot. Then, the potters smoothed the coils together. The coil method kept pots from cracking when they were fired. Once the pottery hardened, a piece of leather or cloth was used to polish the sides. Before firing the pots, potters often decorated the polished surfaces with glazes. Sometimes they cut or stamped a design into the surface. Some potters still use this method today.

The Beginnings of Metalworking

People also learned **metallurgy**, or the way to craft objects from metals found in the earth. Because copper and gold were soft enough metals to be hammered or cut into ornaments, these were the earliest metals used to form objects.

Gold and copper could sometimes be found in riverbeds. **Ores**, which are metals combined with rock, could be heated so that people could take out the metals. Around 4500 B.C., people in eastern Europe and western Asia began using this method to get metals.

Once separated from rock, a metal, such as copper, could be heated and poured into a mold carved from stone. The earliest artifact made by this method is a copper weapon from eastern Europe called a mace-head. Areas in eastern Europe and western Asia were early centers where people found and worked copper.

◆ **Why was making pottery an important skill?**

C. Two Early Settlements

Large permanent settlements changed the way people lived. People in these settlements were protected from other groups of people. They could work together to provide food for the entire settlement. In addition, people developed customs, laws were enforced, and organized religions grew.

A Town in Turkey

Between 1961 and 1965, a team of British archaeologists excavated Çatalhüyük, a 32-acre site located in modern Turkey. They discovered that the people of Çatalhüyük had lived there for more than 800 years, from 6300 B.C. to 5500 B.C. The residents of the site built flat-roofed houses that were attached to one another, like a honeycomb. There were no doors, so people entered their houses through a hole in the roof using a ladder. The houses were made of mud brick, plaster, and timber. Each had a large room for sleeping and cooking and one or two small storerooms. The walls were often decorated with elaborate paintings.

Teaching Options

Connection to
ART

Ask a volunteer to read aloud the information on the two methods of early pottery making on page 12. Point out that shaping clay by hand and using the coil method have been supplanted to a large extent by the use of a potter's wheel. Historians believe pottery was first produced in Japan in about 10,000 B.C. and that the potter's wheel was developed in Mesopotamia around 3500 B.C.

Archaeologists have learned a great deal about Çatalhüyük. At its largest, the town was home to between 5,000 and 6,000 people. Most citizens worked the land. They built irrigation canals to water the fields that surrounded the town. Lentils, barley, wheat, and peas were their major crops. However, residents also gathered nuts and fruits from the surrounding lands and kept domesticated goats, sheep, and pigs.

Potters made bowls and other vessels for storing grains and liquids. Local craftspeople and artists, called artisans, turned copper and other local metals into jewelry and tools, and they wove textiles.

Scientists are not certain about the religious beliefs of the people of Çatalhüyük. However, scientists believe they practiced ancestor worship because the dead were buried under the floors of their houses. In addition, they made clay figures of animals with stab wounds. This suggests that the people may have worshiped gods that could help them be successful in hunting. The people of Çatalhüyük might also have worshiped an earth goddess who was thought to control the growth of crops. Shrines, objects or buildings with religious significance, were found in the city honoring the goddess.

Stone Walls of Jericho

Jericho, located in present-day Israel, was another early settlement. British archaeologist Kathleen Kenyon found that the earliest village of Jericho had been settled nearly 12,000 years ago. This makes it one of the world's oldest continuously inhabited settlements. Jericho's earliest residents were hunter-gatherers who lived in round, single-roomed houses built partly in the ground.

Evidence shows that about 2,000 years later, the village had about 500 people. The residents of Jericho knew how to work with stone. Around the village, people built a wall made of at least 10,000 tons of stone. The wall was about 16 feet high and 10 feet thick. A ditch 27 feet wide ran in front of the wall. Just inside the wall was a stone tower 26 feet high and more than 30 feet wide at the base. The walls and ditch were most likely constructed for protection from outside groups. Parts of this wall and most of the tower still stand today.

Like the people of Çatalhüyük, the people of Jericho may have practiced ancestor worship. They buried family members who had died under the floors of their houses. The skulls of their ancestors were dug up and later covered with plaster and given shells for eyes and black paint for hair. The skulls were often placed in one room of the house as a shrine to those who had died.

◆ **What religious practice did the people of Çatalhüyük and Jericho most likely have in common?**

D. The Beginnings of Trade and Government

The growth of permanent settlements allowed some early people to become farmers, whereas others specialized in making pottery, weaving, or metalworking. A system developed that allowed people to trade the goods they made or the food they grew for other items.

Archaeologists uncovered a wall in what they believe to be one of the oldest cities discovered to date, Jericho.

Comparing cities Have students use a Venn diagram (TR, p. 323) to compare aspects of life in Çatalhüyük and Jericho. For example, students should consider houses, crops, number of inhabitants, and religious customs in their comparisons.

Discuss Ask students what scientists and historians have found that led them to infer that the peoples of Çatalhüyük and Jericho had some kind of religious beliefs. (They found skeletons buried under the floors of houses. The bodies were buried with objects. The skulls in Jericho were decorated. Also, shrines were found in both cities.)

◆ **ANSWER** Both groups of people probably practiced ancestor worship because archaeologists have found skeletons buried under the houses in both cities.

D. The Beginnings of Trade and Government

Purpose-Setting Question Why do you think government developed in early settlements? (Possible answers: to protect people, to regulate trade and other activities)

Extend Emphasize the relationship between specialization and the need for barter. If one person concentrates on producing a particular good (such as pottery), he or she will, over time, produce too many containers for his or her own use. At the same time, the pottery maker will need to obtain food or other goods produced by someone else. Thus, the need for trade or barter arises.

Explore The idea of "money" being something other than coins or paper may seem unusual to today's students. However, in economic terms, "money" used to barter or trade for goods can be almost anything that is relatively scarce and, that therefore, has value. For example, shells, animal pelts, grain, and even salt have been used as "money." Ask students to suggest valuable items that might be used today as money.

Research

AVERAGE

Have students use an atlas to locate the ancient city of Jericho. Then, have them use library resources or the Internet to find out three facts about Jericho not found in the text. Have each student list his or her findings and then share them with the class.

CHALLENGE

Have students use library resources or the Internet to find out more about the ancient city of Jericho. Then, have them explain to the class how their findings relate to aspects of culture that students have been studying, including agriculture, handicrafts, architecture, trade, and government.

Focus Show students how they can use the context surrounding the word *surplus* to determine its meaning. The phrase set off by commas immediately following the word ("or excess") shows the reader that the meaning of the word *surplus* is "excess." Make sure that students understand that societies barter when they have more of some items than they need. To barter successfully, other societies must need the excess items and have items to trade in return.

SPOTLIGHT ON ECONOMICS

EARLY COINS Before humans had coins, how do you think one person was able to get something that another person produced? (People would barter, or trade, to get items they wanted or needed.)

◆ **ANSWER** One opinion is that governments may have developed as warlords appointed by communities defended boundaries or water rights. Another opinion is that governments were connected to religion.

Section Close

Ask students how early settlements developed and what archaeologists have learned about the culture of these settlements.

3 Assess

Review Answers

Review History

A. Better tools made planting and harvesting easier.

B. the crafts of weaving, pottery making, and metalworking (metallurgy) developed and made life easier and better for people

C. The houses were built together and had no doors. People entered through the roof.

D. Permanent settlements brought specialization and the beginning of trade and government.

Define Terms to Know
domesticate, 10; cultivate, 10; irrigate, 10; metallurgy, 12; ore, 12; barter, 14

Critical Thinking
People would have had to learn to cooperate, to find suitable locations that would support a large number of people, and to develop some form of communication and some form of government or laws to prevent lawless behavior.

Spotlight on
Economics

EARLY COINS
The use of coins as money did not develop until about the seventh century B.C. The people of Lydia, a region north of the Mediterranean Sea, were the first to use a coin made from electrum, an alloy of gold and silver. The Lydians were wealthy because they had found gold in the Pactolus River, which flowed through their lands.

Bartering Brings New Goods

When people have a surplus, or excess, of goods, they can either store them or exchange, or **barter**, them for other goods. Because early settlements did not use money, people bartered goods. For example, people living in Çatalhüyük found obsidian, a glassy, black volcanic stone, nearby. Using obsidian, artisans made knives, axes, tools, and polished mirrors. Jericho, more than 500 miles away, was one of Çatalhüyük's trade partners. People from Jericho exchanged a stone called flint and shells for Çatalhüyük's obsidian.

In order for a system of bartering between settlements to be successful, people need to travel between the towns. Settlements, and later towns, were first built along rivers, which offered a way to move goods from place to place. In addition, residents of settlements traveled widely on foot, using well-worn paths and roads. Archaeological evidence has found bartered goods ranging from precious stones to timber to metal ores.

As trade expanded, a merchant class began to develop. Merchants are professional traders who buy and sell goods to make a living.

Early Governments

No one knows how the first governments developed. A government is an organized system that groups use in order to make laws and decisions. One opinion is that communities began to argue about boundaries or water rights. Each group appointed a warlord, or military leader, to defend its rights. These warlords eventually ruled over large armies.

Another opinion is that early governments were connected to religion. Temples served as government centers. Early writing shows that people brought goods and food supplies to the local temples. The priests then performed religious duties and distributed stored food in times of need.

◆ **What is one opinion about how governments developed?**

Review II

Review History
A. What advantages did humans gain from using better tools?

B. How would you describe the three crafts developed in early permanent settlements?

C. What is unusual about the way Çatalhüyük was constructed?

D. What were the benefits of living in a permanent settlement?

Define Terms to Know
Define the following terms: **domesticate, cultivate, irrigate, metallurgy, ore, barter**

Critical Thinking
What difficulties would people have to overcome in order to build settlements and towns?

Write About Government
Write a brief paragraph explaining anthropologists' opinions about the development of early governments.

Get Organized
MAIN IDEA/SUPPORTING DETAILS CHART
Create a main idea/supporting details chart based on this section entitled, Bartering Brings New Goods.

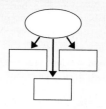

Write About Government
Students' paragraphs should include information about the opinion that governments probably developed for protection, to defend rights, and the opinion that early governments were connected to religion.

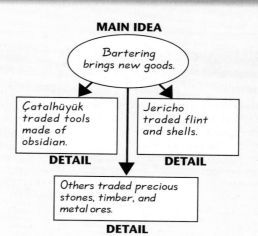

MAIN IDEA

Bartering brings new goods.

Çatalhüyük traded tools made of obsidian.
DETAIL

Jericho traded flint and shells.
DETAIL

Others traded precious stones, timber, and metal ores.
DETAIL

CONNECT
History & Archaeology

A Prehistoric Mystery

In 1991 two German hikers accidentally discovered the body of a man in melting ice on the slopes of the Italian Alps. At first it was feared that a fellow hiker had suffered a terrible accident. However, after digging the body out of the ice, it became clear that this man was not a hiker at all. What the German couple had stumbled upon was the body of a man who is now thought to be about 5,300 years old!

Being frozen in the ice had preserved the body of the "Iceman"—as he was now nicknamed. Both the frozen body and the tools archaeologists found with him provide clues about life thousands of years ago.

SCIENTISTS EXAMINED EVIDENCE of undigested food in the Iceman's stomach after moving the body to a laboratory in Austria. What they found was a kind of primitive wheat called einkorn that had been used to make bread. Finding this wheat suggested that the Iceman belonged to an agricultural community that made its home somewhere near where the body was found.

In addition to examining the body, scientists examined the contents of a tool kit the Iceman had been carrying with him. The tool kit contained a number of items, including mushrooms. Scientists believe that the mushrooms may have been used as food—but they also think that the mushrooms could have been used as a kind of medicine.

Other items found in the tool kit included a longbow with arrows in an animal-skin case, a small flint dagger, and a copper-headed ax. Before finding the Iceman, archaeologists believed that metal tools had not been used in that region until about 4,000 years ago. Yet here was a 5,300-year-old man with a copper-headed ax!

THE STORY CONTINUES as scientists research and examine evidence from the Iceman's body and his tool kit. Although hundreds of questions still surround the mystery of the Iceman, the most-often-asked question appears to be answered: Just how did the Iceman die? Many thought he had frozen to death in a sudden storm while herding sheep. Instead, recent research now shows that the Iceman was killed, a victim of murder, warfare, or human sacrifice. X-rays have pointed to an arrowhead buried deep in the Iceman's left shoulder. The wound caused him to bleed to death over several hours and become buried in ice.

Critical Thinking

Answer the questions below. Then, complete the activity.

1. Without written records, how did archaeologists learn about the Iceman's history?

2. What objects were found in the Iceman's tool kit?

3. How do you think archaeology is similar to history? To science?

Write About It

Using the Internet and other sources, conduct your own research on the Iceman. Find at least two new interesting details about the Iceman and write a short essay on this topic.

The Iceman's body had been buried under snow and ice for about 5,300 years. The extreme cold preserved his body.

Teaching Options

The study of medical evidence gave scientists a clue as to how the Iceman died. Today, forensic medicine continues to play a key role in determining how a person has died. Some students may wish to conduct a job investigation. Coroners and law enforcement experts today are often called upon to examine physical remains and from them to determine a cause of death.

F Y I
Mummies

A mummy is a body preserved from decay. Mummies can be intentionally preserved with chemicals, such as those found in tombs. The Iceman's body was mummified by chance, preserved because it was buried under ice and snow. Similarly, mummified bodies of prehistoric animals (such as a frozen baby mammoth, found in Siberia and about 40,000 years old) have been found buried in ice and snow.

CONNECT
History & Archaeology

A PREHISTORIC MYSTERY

Teach the Topic

Students will readily see the connection between history and archaeology since both disciplines involve the study of the past. Ask students to recall details from Sections 1 and 2 of the chapter. Ask what physical objects archaeologists study to learn about prehistoric humans. (artifacts such as pottery and tools, fossil remains, bones)

SCIENTISTS EXAMINED EVIDENCE Once students have read this section, ask what physical evidence archaeologists examined in the case of the Iceman. (his tool kit, his body, including the undigested remains of food)

THE STORY CONTINUES Ask students why scientists continued to examine evidence from the Iceman. (They wanted to know how he died.) Ask what traits this demonstrates about the scientists. (They were curious, persistent.)

Critical Thinking

1. They examined physical evidence, including his tool kit and the body itself.
2. Mushrooms, a longbow with arrows, an animal-skin case, a small flint dagger, and a copper-headed ax were all found in the Iceman's tool kit.
3. Students should indicate that both history and archaeology involve the study of past events and cultures. Both historians and archaeologists could be considered scientists because they observe, experiment, and organize their findings.

Write About It

Students' essays should include some of the information on page 15 and additional information that students have learned from their research. Have students share the sources they used.

Section Summary

In this section, students will learn about the characteristics of civilizations. They expand their knowledge through the introduction of early river valley civilizations. Students will learn more about these civilizations in later chapters.

1 Introduce

Getting Started

Ask students to speculate what type of geographic area they would pick to start a new community. Have students justify their answer by giving reasons why their choice is a good one. Some of their reasoning should reflect information they have learned so far in Chapter 1.

TERMS TO KNOW

Ask students to read the words and definitions on page 16 and then find each word in the section. Ask students which two terms have to do with government. (city-state, dynasty)

You may wish to preview the pronunciation of the following word from this section with students.

Menes (MEE neez)

ACTIVE READING

Explain to students that a generalization is a broad statement that applies to many facts or situations. A sound or logical generalization should be built from evidence. As students make generalizations from the information in this section, caution them that sometimes a generalization may not be valid because all the evidence is not available. Ask students to share their generalizations with the class. As they do, have the rest of the class tell whether they think there is enough evidence given to support each one.

Terms to Know

civilization the stage in human progress at which a complex and organized social order is developed

city-state a city and its surrounding territories having an independent government

cuneiform the wedge-shaped writing of early Mesopotamians

dynasty a powerful family or group that rules for a lengthy period of time

Main Ideas

A. The rise of cities was a major feature in the development of early civilizations.

B. Many of the first civilizations developed along river valleys.

 Active Reading

MAKE GENERALIZATIONS
When you generalize, you summarize many facts into a broad statement. For example: Early toolmakers designed tools that made their tasks easier. As you read this section, stop to generalize about what you read.

A. What Is a Civilization?

The progress that humans experienced from the time they moved from place to place to the time they began to settle in villages was a huge step in history. Yet another giant leap was about to take place—the birth of **civilization**, or the formation of a complex and highly organized society. One of the key features of the development of a civilization was the birth of cities. In fact, the word *civilization* comes from the Latin word *civilis*, which means "a community of citizens or a city." Historians have created a list of features, in addition to cities, that help to identify a civilization.

Cities and Government

Not all early people gathered in settlements that grew into large cities. Some continued to live as hunter-gatherers or nomads. Cities are, however, considered to be a basic feature of a civilization. In cities, large groups of people worked together to improve farming, develop artistic and technological skills, and to trade with other groups of people. As goods were traded, knowledge was passed from one city to another. Cities helped to promote the spread of knowledge among early peoples.

The large populations of cities created a need for laws to govern the people who lived there. Rulers established laws to maintain order. They also organized armies to enforce the laws and protect a city from outsiders. In addition, the first taxes began to be collected. Taxes are monies or goods that people pay to help support government. Separate officials slowly began to oversee different parts of government, such as tax collection, law enforcement, and military protection.

Job Specialization and Advanced Technology

As cities and food supplies grew, workers began to specialize in different areas. Farmers, pottery-makers, metalworkers, bricklayers, priests, soldiers, and rulers are just a few examples of the kinds of specialized workers found in early civilizations. Specialization allowed people to become experts in one area based on their abilities and the group's needs.

Experts in any field of work usually try to improve their tools and methods of working. These improvements made later humans better hunters, farmers, and artisans. As metalworkers learned new skills, for example, they created stronger weapons for armies to better protect cities. Improved metalworking skills also led to the creation of unique jewelry, which could be traded.

This sculpture is from the Sumerian civilization of Mesopotamia. It includes an early form of writing, found at the bottom of the statue.

16 UNIT 1 ◆ From Prehistory to Early Civilizations

Teaching Options

Section 3 Resources

Teacher's Resources (TR)
Terms to Know, p. 14
Review History, p. 48
Build Your Skills, p. 82
Concept Builder, p. 217
Chapter Test, pp. 117–118
Main Idea/Supporting Details Chart, p. 319
Transparency 10

Using Technology

Have students use the Internet, CD-ROM resources, and other media to find out about the early river valley civilizations from this section. Ask them to find at least one site for each early river valley civilization and take notes on what they learn. Suggest that students use the words *ancient* or *history* with each as key search terms.

This wall painting shows some activities of ancient peoples, such as writing, farming, and trading.

Social Classes and Religion

People in cities were divided into social classes, or groups with different levels of importance. Members of the highest class included rulers and priests. Below rulers and priests were farmers, merchants, and artisans. The lowest class was made up of slaves. They had either been captured in wars or sold into slavery.

Often, government and religious leaders were the same individuals, or they worked closely together to rule a city. Some rulers claimed that their power was based upon the approval of gods. Most ancient peoples believed in many gods who took care of every part of their life. This included weather, trade, war, the growth of crops, and many other events, such as birth, marriage, and death. Ancient peoples held a variety of activities ranging from dances to ceremonies to honor the gods. Religion played a major and growing role in their lives.

Writing and Record Keeping

As cities grew and became more complex, people needed a way to make and keep records. Merchants needed to keep records of their buying and selling. Rulers needed to record laws and taxes. As a result, many early civilizations developed forms of writing to keep records.

The earliest forms of writing, about 5,000 years ago, included pictographs, or simple drawings of the objects they represented. Later, symbols were added to represent ideas as well as objects. Writing, in any form, enabled people to record events and ideas in addition to communicating over great distances.

◆ **What are some reasons for the development of writing?**

B. Early Civilizations of the World

You now know that one of the key features of a civilization is the development of a city, but just how do cities begin? One of the most important factors for a city to develop is its location. Some of the earliest cities and civilizations first began along river valleys in Africa and Asia around 3500 B.C.

Connection to GOVERNMENT

The governments of early civilizations came into being to promote and regulate trade and to protect the community. Discuss with students the functions of government today. Ask students how they think the role of government is the same or different today. (Early functions have been maintained; the role of government expanded as civilizations became more complex.)

F Y I

Early Writing

The earliest writings are pictographs, or simplified pictures, found on clay tablets. The economic nature of these writings is clear: Writing was used to record lists of goods or receipts and was not meant to communicate a continuous "story," as much of today's writing is. Early humans probably had oral storytelling traditions before they used symbols to communicate their own history or beliefs.

---

2 Teach

A. What Is a Civilization?

Purpose-Setting Question How did job specialization help people in early civilizations? (Job specialization allowed people to become experts at certain skills.)

Focus Ask students to describe the social classes of early civilizations. Ask students why they think each group was given the status it had. Explain to students that they will learn about the social classes of many different societies. As they read about different societies, they should look for similarities and differences.

Extend Explain that early written records depended on pictographs or ideograms (representations of an idea). Alphabets or systems that represented sounds or syllables, rather than things, were probably a later invention. Ask students to invent a pictograph to represent the words *farm, tool, weather,* and *settlement.* Discuss the difficulties that arise in trying to depict abstract ideas and even in trying to interpret pictures in a standard way.

Activity

Explore other languages Ask students familiar with alphabetic symbols for languages other than English to show those to the class. For example, Arabic, Hebrew, Greek, Russian, and Chinese languages have different letter forms.

◆ **ANSWER** Writing developed as cities grew and became more complex. People needed a way to make and keep records. For example, rulers needed to record laws and taxes that were paid.

B. Early Civilizations of the World

Purpose-Setting Question Why was the river valley setting important to early civilizations? (Students should indicate that rivers provided fertile soil, and supplied water to support people, animals, and crops.)

Using the Map

Early River Valley Civilizations

Point out to students that the locator map in the map key shows the locations of river valley civilizations in relation to the rest of the world. Ask students to explain what each identifier in the map key means.

✔ Map Check

Answers
1. All four civilizations were located in river valleys.
2. Huang He Valley

Extend Much of the land called the Fertile Crescent, between the Tigris and Euphrates Rivers, looks very different today than it did thousands of years ago. Then, it was a lush land that could support farming and powerful settlements. Today, the climate has changed; much of the land is arid and the people who live there struggle to grow crops and raise animals. Have students use the Atlas map on page A7 or use Transparency 10 to locate the modern countries that are part of the Fertile Crescent. (parts of Iran, Iraq, Syria, and Turkey)

Discuss Have students locate Ur on the map. Ask what natural advantages the city-state had then that might have helped to make it the capital of the area. (near two rivers and the coast—it would have access to transportation and be able to trade with others)

Focus Ask students how many letters are in the English alphabet. (26) Remind students that the writing system cuneiform had about 500 images. Discuss how much harder cuneiform would be to learn and how it might limit communications.

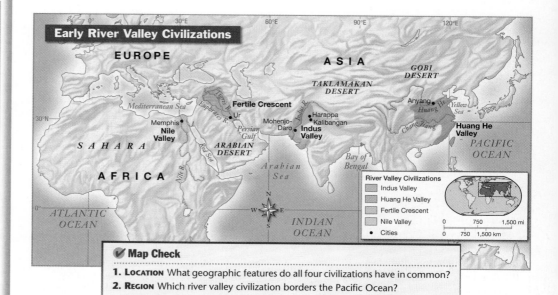

Early River Valley Civilizations

EUROPE

ASIA

GOBI DESERT

TAKLAMAKAN DESERT

Fertile Crescent

Anyang

Huang He

Yellow Sea

Mediterranean Sea

Ur

Memphis

Nile Valley

Mohenjo-Daro

Harappa

Kalibangan

Indus Valley

Huang He Valley

SAHARA

ARABIAN DESERT

Persian Gulf

Chang Jiang

PACIFIC OCEAN

AFRICA

Nile R.

Arabian Sea

Bay of Bengal

ATLANTIC OCEAN

INDIAN OCEAN

River Valley Civilizations
- Indus Valley
- Huang He Valley
- Fertile Crescent
- Nile Valley
- ● Cities

0   750   1,500 mi
0   750   1,500 km

✔ Map Check

1. **LOCATION** What geographic features do all four civilizations have in common?
2. **REGION** Which river valley civilization borders the Pacific Ocean?

The Fertile Crescent

One area of land that stretched from the Persian Gulf almost to the eastern end of the Mediterranean Sea had such rich soil that it came to be called the Fertile Crescent. Two rivers—the Tigris and the Euphrates—played a key role in the development of this area. The land between these two rivers, or the river valley, was home to one of the first civilizations of the Fertile Crescent—Mesopotamia, meaning "land between rivers" in the Greek language.

Because of the rich soils of the Fertile Crescent, the first farming settlements were established by around 6000 B.C., and the area attracted travelers and traders. Ideas were exchanged, goods moved freely to and from the area, and eventually, settlements grew to become cities. By around 3500 B.C., the first cities emerged in the southern part of Mesopotamia—a region called Sumer. Three hundred years later, in 3200 B.C., the cities had become powerful **city-states**. A city-state is an independent state that includes a city and its surrounding area. One of these city-states, Ur, had become the capital of southern Mesopotamia by about 2500 B.C.

In about 3300 B.C., the Mesopotamians developed the first primitive forms of writing. Before this time, tradespeople kept track of their goods by drawing symbols on clay tablets. These sketches later developed into **cuneiform**, a wedge-shaped script. About 500 of these wedges made up the Sumerian alphabet.

The Nile Valley

Another fertile river valley—the Nile Valley—was home to one of the greatest of all ancient civilizations—the Egyptian civilization. The Nile Valley was protected from invasion by rock and desert. Its rich soil was the result of the Nile's flooding its banks each year. This highly desirable location gave rise to the Egyptian civilization, which began around 3000 B.C. According to legend,

Teaching Options

Writing

AVERAGE

After students have read about the civilizations on pages 18–19, have them write a paragraph explaining which of the early civilizations they would have preferred to live in. Students should give reasons for their preference. Have students review their paragraphs with a classmate and then make suggested changes.

CHALLENGE

Ask students to create a two-column chart (TR, p. 328) that lists the pros and cons of living about 3300 B.C. Encourage students to consider information from the text and their own knowledge of current living conditions as they create the chart. Then, have students use their charts to create a two-paragraph summary of the advantages and disadvantages of life in 3300 B.C.

King Menes of Upper Egypt conquered Lower Egypt and united the two into one powerful kingdom. He also founded the first Egyptian **dynasty**, or family of rulers.

Around the same time, the Egyptians developed their own form of writing with pictographs. Their pictographs were shaped to resemble plants, animals, furnishings, tools, or human figures and body parts.

The Indus Valley

The Indus Valley in modern Pakistan was the site of another ancient river valley civilization. Cities along the Indus River served as seaports and trading centers, as well as farming areas. People in these cities lived in brick homes along streets set out in a gridlike pattern.

People living in settlements in the Indus Valley traded among themselves and with other cultures. Traders marked their merchandise with special seals to identify it.

Huang He Valley

Farmers in the valley of the Huang He, Yellow River in Chinese, began growing grains and raising pigs as early as 6000 B.C. People lived in walled towns or cities. While many inhabitants of the Huang He Valley were farmers, others were artisans. Around 1700 B.C., some artisans discovered that by combining copper and tin, they could produce an alloy, called bronze. This alloy, or mix of one metal with another, was much stronger than either metal alone. Better tools, weapons, and other goods were made from bronze.

The cities in the Huang He Valley were ruled by a king, who was assisted by members of the upper class. The king formed a large army to protect the area. His soldiers fought with bronze weapons and chariots pulled by horses.

◆ **Why did some towns in early civilizations specialize in certain goods?**

Seals, such as this one from the Indus Valley showing a bull, were used to identify goods being traded.

TEACH PRIMARY SOURCES

Have students study the seal on page 19. Ask students why merchants might want to identify goods that were being traded. Discuss with students what they think the writing on the seal might say.

Activity

Compare and contrast Have small groups choose two of the civilizations they have learned about and make a Venn diagram (TR, p. 323) to show similarities and differences between the civilizations. Have groups share their diagrams with the class. Conclude by asking students what they notice about all the different civilizations.

◆ **ANSWER** Towns specialized in certain goods because of their location. Some areas had more fertile soil, others had more metals and ores than they needed.

Section Close

Ask students to discuss whether a river valley is necessary for the development of a civilization. Then, ask students to give reasons to justify why the river valley is necessary or why it is not.

3 Assess

Review Answers

Review History

A. One major feature of a civilization is the existence of cities.

B. The growth of Mesopotamia was linked to the valley of the Tigris-Euphrates River system and the resulting fertile soil and ability of the people to farm and travel.

Define Terms to Know

civilization, 16; city-state, 18; cuneiform, 18; dynasty, 19

Critical Thinking

Factors that led to the growth of civilizations in the four river valleys are the rise of cities and governments with an established set of laws, spread of knowledge, job specialization, and advances in technology.

Review III

Review History
A. What is one major feature of a civilization?
B. In what ways is the growth of Mesopotamia tied to the geography of the area?

Define Terms to Know
Define the following terms: **civilization, city-state, cuneiform, dynasty**

Critical Thinking
Which factors do you think led to the growth of civilization in the four river valleys?

Write About Geography
You are a farmer living in one of the early cities located along a river. The spring floods have begun. Write a letter to a friend describing how the river affects your life.

Get Organized
MAIN IDEA/SUPPORTING DETAILS CHART
Use a main idea/supporting details chart to show three features of civilizations.

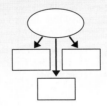

MAIN IDEA

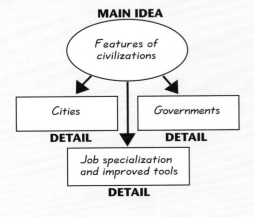

Features of civilizations

Cities — **DETAIL**

Governments — **DETAIL**

Job specialization and improved tools — **DETAIL**

Write About Geography
Students' letters should include information about the river's positive effects on their lives, using details they learned in this section.

Chapter Summary

A blank outline form is available in the Teacher's Resources (p. 318). Students should use the outline to complete their chapter summary. Chapter summaries should outline information about the earliest humans in prehistoric times, early human settlements, and the rise of civilizations along river valleys. Refer to the rubric in the Teacher's Resources (p. 340) to score students' chapter summaries.

⬤ Interpret the Timeline

1. 7–6 million B.C.
2. cave painting
3. The wheel would have helped workers transport the huge stone blocks that were used to build the pyramids, as well as transporting other supplies for building.
4. Check students' timelines to be sure the three events they use are from the chapter.

Use Terms to Know

5. hominid
6. irrigate
7. domesticate
8. civilization
9. artifact
10. nomad

Check Your Understanding

11. Early hominid findings included fossil evidence found in Africa, such as that found by Louis and Mary Leakey, and *Australopithecus* fossils found by Donald Johanson.
12. Archaeologists believe that the earliest tools were probably stone tools used for cutting or chopping.
13. Neanderthals lived in Europe during the last Ice Age.
14. Later stone tools were ground and polished. Later yet, tools were made more complex for improved hunting.
15. They made tools, weapons, and jewelry by separating metal from rock.
16. Cave paintings may have shown animals of prey as a simple record; they may also have been an expression of artistic vision.
17. Cities needed governments to create and enforce laws, to organize armies, and to collect taxes.

Chapter Summary

Complete the following outline in your notebook. Then, use your outline to write a brief summary of the chapter.

Early Peoples of the World

I. Prehistoric Times
   A. The Earliest Humans
   B. Humans Begin Making Tools
   C. Adapting to Nature

II. Early Settlements
   A. An Agricultural Revolution
   B. Cloth, Pottery, and Metalworking
   C. Two Early Settlements
   D. The Beginnings of Trade and Government

III. The Rise of Civilizations
   A. What Is a Civilization?
   B. Early Civilizations of the World

⬤ Interpret the Timeline

Use the timeline on pages 2–3 to answer the following questions.

1. About when did early human life appear in Africa?

2. Which occurred first, the development of writing or cave painting?

3. **Critical Thinking** How might the invention of the wheel have helped in the building of the Great Pyramid in Egypt?

4. Select three events from the chapter that are not on the timeline. Create a timeline that shows those events.

Use Terms to Know

Select the term that best completes each sentence in the paragraph below.

artifact	domesticate	irrigate
civilization	hominid	nomad

5. The remains of a _____ were found in 1959 in Tanzania.

6. Once early humans learned to _____ their fields, they could live farther away from rivers.

7. Early humans began to _____ animals, to have a steady supply of meat and work animals.

8. As settlements and towns grew into cities, _____ emerged.

9. An object that is made or changed by humans is called an _____.

10. A person who crossed the land bridge from Asia to the Americas was a _____.

Check Your Understanding

11. **Describe** some of the early hominid findings in Africa.

12. **Identify** what archaeologists believe were the earliest tools made.

13. **Identify** where Neanderthal people lived during the last Ice Age.

14. **Compare** how later tools improved over the first tools made.

15. **Describe** how early peoples used ores.

16. **Explain** why early peoples decorated caves with paintings.

17. **Explain** why government was needed in cities.

18. **Summarize** what some of the main characteristics of a civilization are.

19. **Compare and Contrast** how the river valley civilization of the Fertile Crescent was similar to the river valley civilization of ancient Egypt.

20. **Identify** an area of the world that was the first to see the growth of city-states.

---

18. Some of the main characteristics of a civilization are the existence of cities and a complex and organized social order; job specialization and advanced technology; social classes and religion; writing and record keeping.

19. Both were built in river valleys; both areas had rich soil; both had one or more forms of writing.

20. City-states first emerged in the Tigris-Euphrates valley, in the area called the Fertile Crescent, or Mesopotamia.

Critical Thinking

21. Draw Conclusions Based on the work of Louis and Mary Leakey at Olduvai Gorge in Tanzania, how have historians changed their ideas about how early peoples developed?

22. Compare and Contrast How did farming change as people moved inland?

23. Make Predictions Do you think civilizations would have developed in the Fertile Crescent if there had been no rivers there? Explain your answer.

24. Summarize What effect did advances in writing and technology have in the development and growth of civilizations?

Put Your Skills to Work

25. Use a Timeline You have learned how timelines help you understand events in the order in which they happened. Study the timeline below and answer the following questions.

a. How many years does the timeline cover?

b. Which event occurred before farming settlements were established in Mesopotamia?

c. When did Ur become the capital of Mesopotamia?

d. How many years came between the establishment of farming settlements and the development of the first writing in Mesopotamia?

10,000 B.C.
Last Ice Age ends.

3300 B.C.
First writing develops in Mesopotamia.

10,000 B.C.   7500 B.C.   5000 B.C.   2500 B.C.

5000 B.C.
People establish farming settlements in Mesopotamia.

2500 B.C.
Ur becomes capital of Mesopotamia.

Analyze Sources

26. In the early nineteenth century, Giovanni Belzoni explored the Nile River. Read the following quotation from his book about his adventures. Then, answer the questions that follow.

Thus I proceeded from one cave to another, all full of mummies piled up in various ways. . . . The purpose of my researches was to rob the Egyptians of their papyri [ancient writing material]; of which I found a few hidden . . . and covered by the numerous folds of cloth that envelop the mummy.

a. What were the caves full of?

b. What items was Belzoni specifically looking for?

c. According to Belzoni, what items had the ancient Egyptians hidden from intruders?

Essay Writing

27. Write a brief essay explaining the work of modern archaeology. Include work that is done at the site of the excavation and work that is done in the laboratories. Remember to include information about the recent inventions that have made archaeology a more exact science.

TEST PREPARATION

INCLUSION GROUPS
Choose the answer that correctly completes the sentence.

The Huang He, the Nile River, and the Indus River are all

1. polluted rivers that can no longer be used.

2. rivers located in Asia.

3. places where human life may have begun.

4. sites of early civilizations.

---

21. The Leakeys' discoveries in Africa showed that hominids could walk upright on two legs, and they had thumbs that allowed them to pick up small objects. This may have changed historians' ideas about where early peoples developed, how long ago, and what their characteristics were.

22. People adapted their farming to cooler climates, richer soil, and forested land. Different animals were raised; different crops were grown; and people began to irrigate their land.

23. Students' answers may vary. Some will believe that rivers provided the only resources for survival, whereas others may believe that humans would have found other ways to adapt and build civilizations.

24. They led to an increase in the trade of items such as jewelry and allowed people to communicate more easily.

Put Your Skills to Work

USE A TIMELINE
25a. time span of 7,500 years
25b. the last Ice Age ended
25c. in 2500 B.C.
25d. 1,700 years

Analyze Sources

26a. mummies
26b. papyri, or ancient writing material
26c. The papyri were hidden in the folds of cloth that covered the mummy.

Essay Writing

27. Students' essays should include explanations of techniques such as the use of sensors and aerial photography and methods used to date finds such as carbon-14 dating. You may also want to check for grammar, punctuation, and organization.

TEST PREPARATION

Answer 4. sites of early civilizations.

Ancient Civilizations
3500–500 B.C.
(pp. 22–47)

Chapter Objectives
• Discuss the role of the Nile River and its valley in the development of government and society in the kingdoms of ancient Egypt and explore the role of religion in ancient Egypt.
• Explain the role of the Tigris and the Euphrates Rivers in the development of early civilizations in Mesopotamia.
• Describe how the Akkadian, Babylonian, Assyrian, Persian, and Phoenician Empires of Mesopotamia contributed to the development of civilization.
• Discuss how the Hebrews developed a civilization and began a major world religion.

Chapter Summary
Section I focuses on the Old, Middle, and New Kingdoms that developed in Egypt.
Section II explores the early Mesopotamian communities and the Sumerian civilization that developed.
Section III explores the civilizations of the Akkadians, Babylonians, Assyrians, Persians, and Phoenicians.
Section IV focuses on the history of the ancient Hebrews and the development of Judaism.

Set the Stage
TEACH PRIMARY SOURCES
Explain that Hecataeus of Miletus (about 560–480 B.C.) was one of the first scientific geographers. He traveled from southern Russia to Egypt and wrote about the local customs and lifestyles of the people. He knew the geography of all the lands from the Caucasus Mountains to Gibraltar and from the Danube River to the Nile River. Discuss with students Hecataeus's thoughts about the Nile River and have them explain why he considered Egypt the Nile's gift. (Possible answer: Egypt could not have existed without the Nile. The Nile River made the entire civilization possible.)

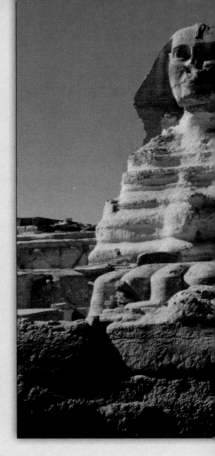

Ancient Civilizations
3500–500 B.C.

I. Ancient Egypt
II. Mesopotamia and Sumer
III. Empires of Ancient Mesopotamia
IV. The Beginnings of Judaism

Civilizations did not develop at the same time or even in the same parts of the world. However, the first civilizations formed in the fertile valleys of great rivers, which provided a sure supply of water. One of the greatest of these rivers, both in ancient times and today, is the Nile River. One of the greatest civilizations of all time, ancient Egypt had its beginning along the Nile. As Hecataeus of Miletus, an ancient Greek who traveled to the Nile River wrote:

❝ *Egypt is the gift of the Nile.* **❞**

Other ancient civilizations flourished as a result of great rivers, too. Unlocking the secrets of these civilizations has taken us more than 3,000 years. Even so, many mysteries still remain.

3100 B.C.
Egyptian civilization begins.
Wheel is invented in Mesopotamia.
Sumerians develop cuneiform writing.

3500 B.C.
First cities begin in Sumer.

2350 B.C.
Sargon I of Akkad conquers Sumer.

CHAPTER EVENTS

| **4000** B.C. | **3500** B.C. | **3000** B.C. | **2500** B.C. |

WORLD EVENTS

3372 B.C.
First date in Maya calendar is recorded.

2500 B.C.
Indian civilization begins.

Teaching Options

Chapter 2 Resources

REVIEW

Teacher's Resources (TR)
Terms to Know, p. 15
Review History, p. 49
Build Your Skills, p. 83
Concept Builder, p. 218
Chapter Test, pp. 119–120
Idea Web, p. 321
Transparencies 1, 6, 7, 10, 15

ASSESSMENT
Section Reviews, pp. 28, 36, 41, 45
Chapter Review, pp. 46–47
Chapter Test, TR pp. 119–120

ALTERNATIVE ASSESSMENT
Portfolio Project, p. 96
Write a Play, p. T96

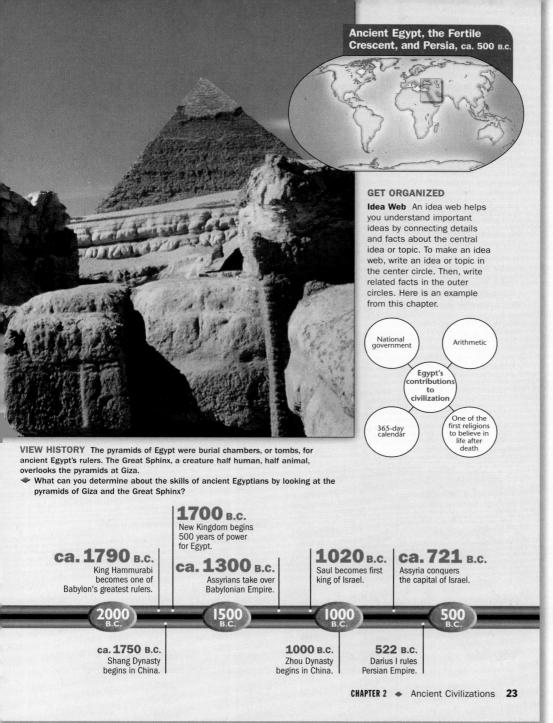

Ancient Egypt, the Fertile Crescent, and Persia, ca. 500 B.C.

GET ORGANIZED

Idea Web An idea web helps you understand important ideas by connecting details and facts about the central idea or topic. To make an idea web, write an idea or topic in the center circle. Then, write related facts in the outer circles. Here is an example from this chapter.

- National government
- Arithmetic
- **Egypt's contributions to civilization**
- 365-day calendar
- One of the first religions to believe in life after death

VIEW HISTORY The pyramids of Egypt were burial chambers, or tombs, for ancient Egypt's rulers. The Great Sphinx, a creature half human, half animal, overlooks the pyramids at Giza.
◆ What can you determine about the skills of ancient Egyptians by looking at the pyramids of Giza and the Great Sphinx?

ca. 1790 B.C.
King Hammurabi becomes one of Babylon's greatest rulers.

1700 B.C.
New Kingdom begins 500 years of power for Egypt.

ca. 1300 B.C.
Assyrians take over Babylonian Empire.

1020 B.C.
Saul becomes first king of Israel.

ca. 721 B.C.
Assyria conquers the capital of Israel.

2000 B.C. · · · **1500 B.C.** · · · **1000 B.C.** · · · **500 B.C.**

ca. 1750 B.C.
Shang Dynasty begins in China.

1000 B.C.
Zhou Dynasty begins in China.

522 B.C.
Darius I rules Persian Empire.

CHAPTER 2 ◆ Ancient Civilizations **23**

Chapter Themes
- Culture
- Time, Continuity, and Change
- People, Places, and Environments
- Individuals, Groups, and Institutions
- Power, Authority, and Governance
- Science, Technology, and Society

F Y I

The Great Sphinx
The Great Sphinx at Giza, Egypt, represents a mythological creature with the body of a lion and the head of a man. Constructed more than 4,500 years ago, its head and body are carved almost entirely from one limestone block. Its paws and legs are built of stone blocks. The sphinx is 240 feet long and about 66 feet high. It is one of the most famous monuments in the world.

Chapter Warm-Up

USING THE MAP
Point out the locator map on page 23. Explain that Egypt is located in the northeast corner of Africa. Challenge students to name the other continents near Africa and the bodies of water that border Egypt.

VIEW HISTORY
Discuss with students the materials used in Egyptian architecture as evidenced by the pyramids of Egypt (stone blocks) and the Great Sphinx (solid rock). Ask what impression the size of these monuments might have had on the ancient Egyptians. (huge size meant great importance)

◆ **ANSWER** The ancient Egyptians seem to have been great builders and stonecutters to build such large and well-designed pyramids and sculpt the Great Sphinx.

GET ORGANIZED
Idea Web
Discuss the idea web on page 23. Ask students where the main idea is listed (in the center) and how related ideas are connected to the main idea (put in surrounding circles). Point out that more details can be linked to the surrounding circles to expand the web. Encourage students to make an idea web for each section. (TR, p. 321)

TEACH THE TIMELINE
The timeline on pages 22–23 lists events from 3500 B.C. to 522 B.C. Remind students that the years identified as B.C. occurred before the birth of Jesus. The years count down to one. Point out that the timeline covers more than 2,700 years and that the intervals are every 500 years. Ask students to point out events on the timeline that deal with the development of Egypt. (Egyptian civilization begins, New Kingdom begins 500 years of power for Egypt.) Encourage students to refer to the timeline as they read the chapter.

Activity

Use a map Have students use the world map in the Atlas (pp. A1–A2) or Transparency 1 to locate the places referenced in the timeline. Point out that some place names have changed. Sumer, Babylon, and Assyria are in present-day Iraq. The Maya lived in present-day Mexico, Belize, and Guatemala.

CHAPTER 2 ◆ T23

I. Ancient Egypt
(pp. 24–28)

Section Summary
In this section, students will learn how the Nile River influenced the development of ancient Egypt. They will also learn about religion, government, and society in the three major periods in ancient Egypt and how hieroglyphics recorded aspects of Egyptian life.

1 Introduce

Getting Started
Ask students to describe the geography of the region where they live and its natural resources. Help them link these elements to the way people live in their community. Discuss with students how living close to a river can affect the kinds of jobs and houses that are available.

TERMS TO KNOW
Ask students to read the terms and definitions on page 24 and find each term in the section. Then have students start an "Ancient Civilizations" vocabulary file by writing each term on one side of an index card and its definition on the other side. As students begin each section, they can add more terms to their files.

You may wish to preview the pronunciation of the following words with students.

Hyksos (HIHK sohs)
Hatshepsut (hat SHEHP soot)
Amenhotep (ahm uhn HOH tehp)
Akhetaton (ahk uh TAHT ehn)
Akhenaton (ahk uh NAHT ehn)
Thutmose (thoot MOH suh)
Re (RAH)

ACTIVE READING
As students read each subsection, ask them to identify one problem the ancient Egyptians may have had as well as to suggest a solution. Have students record the problems and solutions in a two-column chart. You may wish to provide students with a blank two-column chart (TR, p. 328).

Ancient Egypt

Terms to Know
delta land formed from soil deposited at a river's mouth

cataract a large waterfall

papyrus a water plant used as a writing material like paper by ancient Egyptians

pharaoh a title given to the rulers of ancient Egypt

empire a group of countries, nations, territories, or peoples under the control of a single ruler

mummification a process that preserves dead bodies

hieroglyphics picture writing

Main Ideas
A. The Nile River was an important factor in the growth and development of ancient Egyptian civilization.

B. The three major periods of ancient Egypt—the Old Kingdom, the Middle Kingdom, and the New Kingdom—lasted 3,000 years.

C. Egyptian religion and government were closely tied together.

D. Egyptian writing recorded many aspects of life in ancient Egypt.

Active Reading
PROBLEMS AND SOLUTIONS
The first step in solving a problem is to identify what the problem is. As you read this section, think about the difficulties ancient Egyptians faced with their land and climate. Then, pay attention to the solutions they created.

A. The Nile River and Its Valley
The Nile River was key to the development of Egyptian civilization. Except for six miles of fertile soil deposited by flood waters on either side of the Nile, Egypt is a desert. The sources of the more than 4,000-mile-long river are in eastern Africa. From there, the Nile flows northward through Egypt and into the Mediterranean Sea. At the Nile's mouth, a **delta**, a triangular deposit of sand and soil, marks the end of the world's longest river. Along the southern part of the Nile there is a series of waterfalls, or **cataracts**.

Fertile Land Along the Nile
Every year between July and October, the Nile River swelled and overflowed it banks. The fertile soil left by the floods was ideal for growing grains, vegetables, and fruits. The fibers of flax plants were spun into linen thread, which was used to make clothing. Extra crops were traded to other countries for metals and hardwoods.

The ancient Egyptian people built irrigation systems to move water to where it was needed. Extra flood water was also stored for later use. Farmers could now water their crops during dry months. Egyptians had to work together to control their changing environment. They understood how important the Nile was to their survival.

This early painting shows the importance of the Nile River to early Egyptians.

Early Communities Along the Nile
Egyptian life revolved around the Nile. Most of Egypt's people farmed along the river's banks. They lived in mud-brick houses in villages along the Nile Valley, and transported goods by boat on the Nile's muddy waters. Thirsty livestock drank from the Nile's waters. **Papyrus**, a water plant that grew along the banks of the Nile, was used to make rope, sandals, and boats. Later, papyrus was used to make a writing material similar to our paper today.

◆ **Why was the yearly flooding of the Nile River important to the ancient Egyptians?**

Teaching Options

Section 1 Resources

Teacher's Resources (TR)
Terms to Know, p. 15
Review History, p. 49
Build Your Skills, p. 83
Concept Builder, p. 218
Idea Web, p. 321
Transparency 6

ESL/ELL STRATEGIES
Identify Essential Vocabulary Point out to students that some English words have more than one meaning. For example, the word *key* in the first line of the first paragraph means "important." The word *banks* in the second line of the second paragraph means "the land along the sides of a river."

B. The Kingdoms of Ancient Egypt

Early Egypt was divided into two parts. The southern part was called Upper Egypt. The northern part was called Lower Egypt. Here, the land was more fertile, and water more plentiful. Around 3100 B.C., a warrior king named Menes united Upper and Lower Egypt into one nation. He founded the world's first national government and named Memphis as its capital. This event marked the beginning of Egypt's spectacular 3,000-year history, which is generally divided into three main periods. They include the Old Kingdom, the Middle Kingdom, and the New Kingdom.

The Old Kingdom

The Old Kingdom lasted from about 2600 B.C. to 2150 B.C. During this period Egyptian civilization blossomed. The Egyptian rulers, called **pharaohs**, organized a strong nation. The pharaohs made laws and had absolute power, owning and ruling all the land. The pharaohs had huge pyramids built as burial places. The largest pyramid ever built was in Giza. It covers as much land as ten football fields! The pyramids are symbols of the strength of ancient Egyptian civilization. However, this strength began to decrease around 2100 B.C., when ancient Egypt underwent troubled times. The civilization was divided, as several rulers fought for power. Over time, new pharaohs took over to unite the land. This change marks the beginning of the Middle Kingdom.

The Middle Kingdom

During the period of the Middle Kingdom, from about 2100 B.C. to 1800 B.C., new pharaohs from Thebes in Upper Egypt gained control over the whole of Egypt. The capital was moved from Memphis to Thebes. The pharaohs began irrigation projects along the Nile, which made more farmland available. A canal was also dug to connect the Nile and the Red Sea.

It was also during this time that the Egyptians conquered part of Nubia, a gold-rich kingdom to the south. Nubia is also called Kush. Conquering Kush allowed the Egyptians to take over more trade routes, which led to the trading of gold, ebony, ivory, and leopard skins. In addition, a new middle class of workers who specialized in a variety of crafts helped increase trade.

The Middle Kingdom was brought to an end around 1800 B.C. by a powerful foreign enemy—the Hyksos. The Hyksos invaded Egypt and ruled it for about 100 years. They introduced the Egyptians to horse-drawn chariots and weapons made from iron. Around 1700 B.C. new Egyptian leaders came to power and drove out the Hyksos. They established the New Kingdom of Egypt, which would last for more than 500 years.

The New Kingdom

The pharaohs of the New Kingdom created a large and powerful **empire** in Egypt starting around 1700 B.C. An empire unifies people of many lands under the control of a single ruler. One of the most outstanding rulers of the

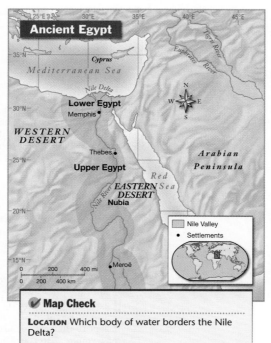

Ancient Egypt

Nile Valley

Settlements

✔ Map Check

LOCATION Which body of water borders the Nile Delta?

A. The Nile River and Its Valley

Purpose-Setting Question How did the Egyptians use papyrus? (Papyrus was used to make rope, sandals, boats, and a writing material similar to paper.)

◆ **ANSWER** The floods left fertile soil, which was important for growing crops. Also, the extra flood water was used to water crops during dry months.

B. The Kingdoms of Ancient Egypt

Purpose-Setting Question What were the major accomplishments of the Middle Kingdom? (A canal was built connecting the Nile River with the Red Sea. Irrigation projects increased farmland. A middle class of craftspeople emerged. Kush was conquered, which opened more trade routes.)

Using the Map
Ancient Egypt

Ask students to identify the compass rose and explain that the points between the main directions represent northeast, southeast, northwest, and southwest. Discuss what the dots on the map key indicate and what is common about the settlements on the map. (The dots indicate settlements. The settlements are located on the Nile River where water is available for farming.)

✔ Map Check

Answer Mediterranean Sea

Activity

Trace trade routes A canal, called the Egyptian Canal, linked the eastern part of the Nile Delta to the Red Sea. From there, traders could sail into the Indian Ocean and travel south around the Cape of Good Hope at the tip of Africa. Have students study the map of Africa on page A6 of the Atlas or Transparency 6 to trace this route.

Meet Individual Needs:
VISUAL/SPATIAL LEARNERS

Have students work in small groups to make posters that summarize the accomplishments of the three kingdoms of ancient Egypt. Students' posters for each kingdom should include its name, dates, a map of the area, and drawings that represent the accomplishments (i.e., for the Old Kingdom, a portrait of a pharaoh and a sketch of the Great Pyramid at Giza).

SPOTLIGHT ON ARCHAEOLOGY

KING TUT'S TOMB Howard Carter excavated King Tutankhamen's tomb for 10 years. Built in the New Kingdom, it is the only mostly intact tomb of an Egyptian king ever found. Thousands of Tutankhamen's objects were recovered, including a solid gold coffin and a gold mask of the king. Have students use library or Internet sources to discover other objects found in the tomb. Ask students to share their findings with the class.

Extend By 1150 B.C., the civilized world entered the Iron Age. Egypt had limited sources of iron and had difficulty importing it. Ask students how this lack of iron might have affected Egypt's decline. (Egypt could not compete against armies that had iron weapons.)

Focus Have students reread the information in their textbooks on page 26 and focus on the terms *Akhenaton* and *Akhetaton*. Discuss the differences between the two terms. (Akhenaton was the name of the pharaoh. Akhetaton was the place to which Akhenaton moved the government.)

◆ **ANSWER** The pyramids were built as burial places.

THEY MADE HISTORY
Akhenaton

Ask students how Egyptian daily life might have been affected by Akhenaton's revolutionary decision to worship one god, Aton, instead of several gods. (Possible answer: holy places and shrines that were once sacred were closed up; priests lost their power and wealth; tradesmen and craftsmen making a living from the old religion lost a means of support.)

Have students compare the statue of Akhenaton on page 26 with a full-length statue. (Use library sources or the Internet.) What is unusual about Akhenaton's body and head? (extremely tall stature, wide hips, overabundant belly, very long face, huge lower jaw, long slender neck) Explain that some scientists speculate that he suffered from a hereditary disease, possibly hyperpituitarism.

ANSWER Akhenaton believed that Aton was the one supreme god.

Spotlight on *Archaeology*

KING TUT'S TOMB

Archaeologists have increased their knowledge of ancient Egypt by studying the tombs of the kings and nobles. Howard Carter discovered King Tutankhamen's tomb in 1922. Three people connected with the tomb excavation died soon afterward, causing some to believe in the "curse of the mummy."

New Kingdom was Hatshepsut, an Egyptian queen who later declared herself pharaoh around 1500 B.C. Hatshepsut was the first-known female ruler.

Under the pharaoh Amenhotep IV, who ruled after Hatshepsut, the capital was moved from Thebes to Akhetaton. There, Amenhotep worshiped the god Aton, whose symbol is the sun's rays. The pharaoh even changed his own name to *Akhenaton*, meaning "servant of Aton."

After Akhenaton's death, Tutankhamen, a nine-year-old boy, became pharaoh of Egypt. Today, we call this pharaoh "King Tut." Although he ruled for only 9 years and died at the age of 18, Tutankhamen is perhaps the best-known of all Egyptian pharaohs. That is because he was buried in a solid-gold coffin in a tomb filled with gold and jewels.

Under other powerful pharaohs who ruled after Akhenaton and Tutankhamen, such as Thutmose III and Ramses II, Egypt led armies into Asia and conquered new lands. Under the military skills of Ramses II, the Egyptian Empire reached as far east as the Euphrates River.

During the New Kingdom, pharaohs resumed massive building projects—this time, of enormous temples and gigantic carved figures of gods and pharaohs. One of these is the statue of Ramses II found at the temple in Luxor, Egypt. After Ramses II's rule, which lasted from about 1290 B.C. to 1225 B.C., the Egyptian Empire slowly began to decline.

Egypt's Decline

Ancient Egypt began to lose power around 1085 B.C. Conflicts among the nobles and priests weakened the empire. More powerful nations arose around Egypt, including Assyria and Kush. The rich kingdom of Kush lay directly south of Egypt. As Egypt declined, people from Kush invaded and added Egypt to their own lands. For 100 years the kings of Kush ruled this large new empire. Later, around 650 B.C., the Assyrians attacked Egypt and pushed the Kushites back to their own lands.

◆ **For what purpose did the pharaohs have pyramids built?**

They Made History

A statue of Egyptian pharaoh Akhenaton

Akhenaton ca. 1380–1362 B.C.

Changes in Egypt's empire and traditions set the scene for the strange figure of Amenhotep IV. This pharaoh later changed his name to Akhenaton, or "servant of Aton." Akhenaton believed that Aton was the one supreme god. After moving his government to Akhetaton, Akhenaton worshiped Aton in a temple open to sunlight. His worship of Aton angered the priests who continued to worship Amon-Re, the Egyptians' most powerful god, and other gods. Some scholars think that the move to Akhetaton was meant to break the power of those priests. However, in poems that Akhenaton composed to Aton, it is evident that his devotion was sincere. Akhenaton's attention to his worship of Aton contributed to the decline of the Egyptian Empire. It weakened the power of the pharaoh and created conflict with the priests.

Critical Thinking What was Akhenaton's view of the god Aton?

Teaching Options

Connection to SCIENCE

The ancient Egyptians used astronomy and geography to develop a 365-day calendar. This calendar was based on the yearly flooding of the Nile River, which began soon after the star Sirius reappeared on the eastern horizon after being out of sight for months. This took place on or about June 20 each year. The calendar enabled the Egyptians to date much of their history.

Meet Individual Needs:
VERBAL/LINGUISTIC LEARNERS

Form three groups of students. Assign each group one of the three kingdoms. Have each group create a chant, song, or cheer to describe their kingdom and its accomplishments. Have groups share their work with the class.

C. Religion, Government, and Society

Religion was an important part of every Egyptian's life, beginning at a young age when they were told stories of gods and goddesses. In fact, religion formed the basis of Egyptian government and society.

Religion and Government

Egyptian people believed in one main god and many lesser gods. The sun god, Re, was the chief god among Egyptians. Only the pharaoh could take part in certain ceremonies for Re. The people of Thebes also worshiped a sun god named Amon. Re and Amon combined to become Amon-Re, the Egyptians' most powerful god.

Egyptian religion encouraged people to live good lives on Earth in order to have a happy afterlife, or life after death. Belief in the afterlife affected everyone—from the pharaoh to the lowest peasant. It was believed that in order to have an afterlife, each person's soul had to pass a test. The test had the god Anubis weighing a person's heart to see if it was good and truthful. If a heart passed the test, then the worthy soul entered a happy afterlife. Because Egyptians believed that the afterlife was similar to life on Earth, they buried people with all of the possessions they would need in their next life.

To give a soul use of its body in the afterlife, the Egyptians preserved the dead through __mummification__. During the mummification process, vital organs were taken out of a body. Then, the body was treated in order to preserve it. Afterward, it was wrapped in cloth to keep it from decaying. It was placed in a secure tomb or pyramid with all the things a person might need in the afterlife.

Religion played an especially important role in government. High priests not only performed religious duties, but also collected taxes that were paid in the form of agricultural products and other goods. In order to build pyramids, temples, statues, and tombs, the Egyptian priests used a system of forced labor involving slaves. Slaves were taken from among the peasants and criminals.

Social Organization and Daily Life

Egyptian people had many levels of society. At the very top of their society was the king, or pharaoh. The Egyptians believed that the pharaoh was half-divine, or godlike, and that everything they had belonged to him. High priests, landowners, government officials, army officers, and doctors formed the upper class. Merchants and craftspeople were in the middle class. Unskilled laborers, mostly farmers, made up the lower class. People could move to a higher class through marriage or hard work. Enslaved people, who were in the lowest class of all, could marry, inherit land, and be given their freedom.

Egyptian daily life centered on religion and family. Family members enjoyed leisure activities that included hunting, fishing, sailing, and watching sports such as wrestling. In addition, children played with toys and board games, such as the popular game called senet.

Most schools in Egypt were for children of the upper classes. Students studied reading, geography, math, and writing. Children of the lower classes learned skills from their parents such as farming and certain trades.

◆ Why did religion influence government in ancient Egypt?

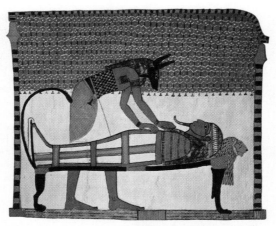

Anubis, the Egyptian god of preserving the dead, comes to weigh a dead man's heart.

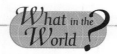

PLAYING SENET

Senet is a board game played in ancient Egypt that requires two players. The object of the game is to move the game pieces across 30 squares of the board. The first player to do so, wins the game. Players throw four dice sticks to find out how many spaces to move. Some squares force a player to start over. Game boards and pieces are made of wood and clay or of bone and ebony, a special black wood.

F Y I

Anubis

In Egyptian mythology, the god Anubis was responsible for overseeing the embalming of the dead and for protecting cemeteries. He guided the deceased through the underworld to the throne of Osiris, the chief god of the underworld. Anubis weighed the heart of the deceased to judge his or her worth. In the actual embalming process, the deceased's brain and all other internal organs were removed and placed in a jar.

C. Religion, Government, and Society

Purpose-Setting Question What was the role of religion in ancient Egyptian society? (Religion affected the actions of people in ancient Egyptian society and encouraged people to lead good lives in order to have a happy afterlife.)

TEACH PRIMARY SOURCES
Have students study the art on page 27 to identify the mummy, the funeral bed, Anubis's jackal head and tail, and his human body. Ask what Anubis is doing. (touching the area of the mummy near its heart) Explain that this scene is part of a mural painted on the walls of the tomb of King Sennedjem in Thebes.

Discuss Ask students in what ways the daily life of children in ancient Egypt was similar to that of children in the United States today. (Children played with toys and board games, and they were trained or educated.)

Activity

Role-play Ask pairs of students to role-play two middle-class city dwellers in ancient Egypt. They have not seen each other in a long time, and they meet by chance. They might discuss their families' daily activities, how they earn their living, how they entertain themselves, the sports they enjoy, and how the children in their households are educated.

WHAT IN THE WORLD?
PLAYING SENET We know about senet through archaeological discoveries of more than 40 senet boards and accompanying game pieces. Tomb paintings also show people playing senet. The game board has three rows of ten squares each. Most squares have symbols. Some symbols help a player advance, and others set a player back. Square 15 is the "square of rebirth." This square may have been the starting square. The original rules of senet are not known, although it is probably similar to the board game backgammon. Ask groups of students to draw their own senet boards, use modern die and markers, and create rules for playing the game.

◆ **ANSWER** High priests collected taxes and used a system of forced labor to build pyramids and temples.

D. Hieroglyphics and Writing

Purpose-Setting Question What kinds of information did the ancient Egyptians record in their writings? (mostly religious inscriptions, legal documents)

TEACH PRIMARY SOURCES
The picture on this page shows hieroglyphics on an Egyptian tomb. Ask students which pictures and symbols they recognize. (Possible answers: water, bird, staff, fish, tools, Egyptian worker)

Explore Point out that the Rosetta Stone gave the world a key to the language of ancient Egypt. Have students research its physical qualities (dimensions, shape, kind of stone, presentation of the languages) and the stone's message. (A summary by priests of how King Ptolemy V Epiphanes, 205–180 B.C., helped them.) Ask students to share what they have learned with the class.

◆ **ANSWER** Hieroglyphics could not convey abstract ideas, and creating them was difficult and slow.

Section Close

Ask students to summarize the advances made by the ancient Egyptians and discuss why it is valuable to study this civilization.

③ Assess

Review Answers
Review History
A. It provided fertile soil, water for crops and animals, and a means of transportation.

B. Conflict among the priests and nobles and invasions by other civilizations led to Egypt's decline.

C. The sun god Re was the chief god. He was eventually combined with Amon, another sun god, to become Amon-Re.

D. Hieroglyphics are pictures and symbols in a system of writing used by ancient Egyptians.

Define Terms to Know
delta, 24; cataract, 24; papyrus, 24; pharaoh, 25; empire, 25; mummification, 27; hieroglyphics, 28

D. Hieroglyphics and Writing

The Egyptians used a system of writing with pictures and symbols called **hieroglyphics**. Most examples of ancient Egypt's writing are from religious inscriptions and legal documents. Many examples of hieroglyphic writing can be found in stone carvings. About 700 hieroglyphs, or symbols, exist.

Two New Ways to Write

Hieroglyphics, however, had limitations. The symbols could not convey complex ideas, and making the symbols was difficult and slow. Two other kinds of writing did make writing easier and faster. Writing called hieratic was used with hieroglyphics in letters, wills, reports, and scientific texts until about 800 B.C. Hieratic script was written on sheets of papyrus. In about 700 B.C., scholars began using another simpler and faster form of writing called demotic. However, after about 1,000 years, Egyptians stopped using it, and its meaning and sound were lost.

The Rosetta Stone

When the New Kingdom declined, Egyptians stopped using hieroglyphics. The meaning of this system of writing was lost for many hundreds of years. Then, in 1799, French soldiers found a slab of black stone buried near the town of Rosetta in Egypt. This stone proved to be the key to the lost meaning of hieroglyphics.

The Rosetta Stone had writing in three scripts—Egyptian hieroglyphic, Egyptian demotic, and Greek. Scholars could only read the Greek, however. After studying the stone for more than 20 years, a French scholar named Jean-François Champollion figured out how to translate and read the Egyptian writing. Decoding the Rosetta Stone revealed the secrets of ancient Egypt—and unlocked the recorded history of the ancient Egyptians.

◆ **What were the limitations of using hieroglyphics?**

Early Egyptian writing was a system of pictures called hieroglyphics.

Review I

Review History
A. How did the Nile River influence the Egyptians?
B. What weakened ancient Egypt and led to its decline?
C. Before Aton, who was the Egyptians' chief god?
D. What are hieroglyphics?

Define Terms to Know
Define the following terms: **delta, cataract, papyrus, pharaoh, empire, mummification, hieroglyphics**

Critical Thinking
In what ways are the pyramids, temples, and huge carved figures statements about Egypt's power as an empire?

Write About History
Write a paragraph that compares the Old Kingdom of ancient Egypt with the New Kingdom.

Get Organized
IDEA WEB
Use an idea web to organize information from this section. Choose a topic and then find related facts. For example, what are some leisure activities that ancient Egyptians enjoyed?

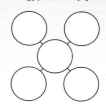

Critical Thinking
The large stone structures demonstrated Egypt's strength and abilities to construct and maintain an empire.

Write About History
Students' paragraphs should provide examples of how the Old Kingdom and the New Kingdom were similar (ruled by pharaohs, strong nations, built large projects) and different (rulers fought for power in the Old Kingdom, there was a queen pharaoh, and conquered new lands in the New Kingdom).

Hunting and fishing

Sailing

Leisure activities in ancient Egypt

Watching sports

Playing board games like senet

Build Your Skills

READ A HISTORICAL MAP

There are many different kinds of maps. Some give information about the physical features of a place, such as the location of mountains and rivers. Others show population growth, agricultural products, or road and highway information. Still other kinds of maps show information about the past. These maps are called historical maps.

By studying historical maps we learn where and how people once lived. Historical maps can show specific events, such as battles fought long ago. They might also show patterns from the past, such as the movement of people from place to place or the location of trade routes.

Here's How

Follow these steps to read a historical map.

1. Look at the title of the map to find the topic and the period of the map.
2. Look at the map key to learn the meanings of symbols on the map.
3. Read the labels to learn the names of the locations shown on the map.
4. Look for the scale to understand distances and to compare the sizes of places.

Here's Why

You have just read about the early trading kingdoms of ancient Egypt. Suppose you were asked to describe their trade routes. A historical map could help.

Practice the Skill

Use the map on this page to answer the following questions.

1. What does the title of the map tell you about the topic of the map and the period that it shows?
2. What information is given in the map key?
3. The Egyptian trade routes reach which eastern trade center?

Extend the Skill

Study the map to write three statements: one about the locations of the ancient Egyptian trade routes; another about the extent of trade in ancient Egypt; and a third about the location of cataracts as they relate to trade routes.

Apply the Skill

As you read the rest of this chapter, look for other historical maps. Compare the information that is given in those maps with the information that you read about in the section. Determine what new information you can learn as a result of reading historical maps.

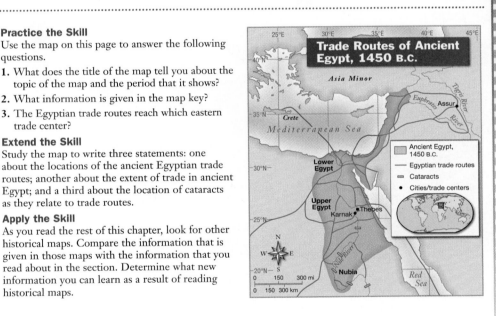

Trade Routes of Ancient Egypt, 1450 B.C.

CHAPTER 2 ◆ Ancient Civilizations **29**

Teaching Options

RETEACH

Review each item in the map key one at a time and ask students to locate each item on the map as you describe it. Then, have partners write five questions about the map, using information from the map key. Have partners exchange questions and answer them.

CHALLENGE

Provide students with a present-day map of Egypt. Have students compare the historical map on this page with the present-day map. Have students write a brief paragraph explaining the changes illustrated by the two maps.

Build Your Skills

READ A HISTORICAL MAP

Teach the Skill

Ask students to think of examples of maps that they may have used. They may mention road maps, geographical or political maps in textbooks, city maps, and so on. Point out that historical maps are different from other types of maps because they show information about the past. Discuss the challenges of reading a historical map. (The names of many places no longer exist; boundary lines have changed.)

You may wish to have students compare the historical map on page 29 with the Atlas maps of Africa (p. A6) and Asia and the Middle East (p. A7) or Transparencies 6 and 10. Ask where Asia Minor and ancient Egypt are today. (Asia Minor is in Turkey and ancient Egypt is in Egypt and Sudan.)

Ask students what it would be like to read a history textbook without any maps. Point out that historical maps help us to understand where ancient civilizations were located, how people saw the world in the past, and how to put key events and places into context.

Practice the Skill

ANSWERS

1. The title tells you that the map is about trade routes of ancient Egypt around 1450 B.C.
2. The map key identifies the symbol for the area of ancient Egypt, the Egyptian trade routes, the cataracts, and the cities and trade centers.
3. Assur

Extend the Skill

Student's answers will vary. Check that students' statements meet each requirement.

Apply the Skill

As a prereading activity, encourage students to study the historical map of each place studied in Sections 2 and 4 of this chapter. Ask students to write several statements about each map, using information from the map's title, key, labels, compass rose, and scale. Based on these statements, have students infer the topic of each section.

Past to...

PYRAMIDS

Teach the Topic

This feature focuses on the pyramids of ancient Egypt and the ways in which those pyramids have evolved and influenced architecture and building styles today. Ask students to picture a pyramid the size of their school. Explain that the pyramids are made of huge blocks of stone. Discuss with students how different it would be to move stone blocks without modern tools and equipment. Encourage students to suggest ways the ancient Egyptians might have moved the blocks.

STAIRWAY TO HEAVEN

The step pyramid was built during the time of Pharaoh Djoser. The original structure was an underground burial chamber. Once that was completed, additional layers were added in several stages to make a six-tiered pyramid. A statue of Djoser was found in the tomb chamber.

PLANNING A PYRAMID

After all these years, the pyramids at Egypt are still standing and show the careful planning that went into building them. Each side of one pyramid is the same length, usually within a few centimeters. Each side of a pyramid also points directly to one of the compass directions.

TOOLS FOR THE JOB

Ask students how each tool pictured might have been used. Encourage students to compare them to modern tools and discuss how these tools are used.

MAKING MUD BRICKS

Using straw and mud as a building material was common not only in ancient Egypt, but in other parts of the world as well. Explain that this is a good example of people using what they find in their environment to build structures.

Past to...

PYRAMIDS

Ancient Egyptians built pyramids as burial places for their pharaohs and members of the royal families. Chambers inside the pyramid protected the body of a royal person. Over time, these chambers were built with false doors and hidden passages to confuse intruders. Even though pyramids were used only in royal funerals, they had a shape that symbolized all life: The pointed peak represented the place on which the sun god, Amon-Re, stood when he created all the other gods.

STAIRWAY TO HEAVEN
The world's first large-scale stone pyramid is the "step pyramid" at Saqqara, Egypt, built around 2650 B.C. The pharaoh believed that, after death, he would climb the steps to reach heaven.

PLANNING A PYRAMID
The ancient Egyptians made sketches (left) and models to plan large building projects. They followed strict calculations when deciding on the dimensions of a pyramid.

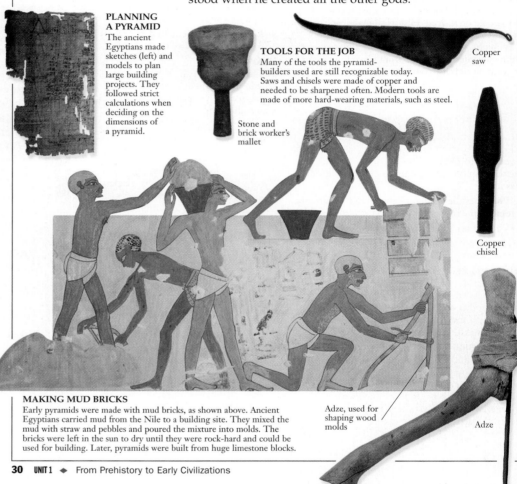

TOOLS FOR THE JOB
Many of the tools the pyramid-builders used are still recognizable today. Saws and chisels were made of copper and needed to be sharpened often. Modern tools are made of more hard-wearing materials, such as steel.

Copper saw

Stone and brick worker's mallet

Copper chisel

Adze, used for shaping wood molds

Adze

MAKING MUD BRICKS
Early pyramids were made with mud bricks, as shown above. Ancient Egyptians carried mud from the Nile to a building site. They mixed the mud with straw and pebbles and poured the mixture into molds. The bricks were left in the sun to dry until they were rock-hard and could be used for building. Later, pyramids were built from huge limestone blocks.

Teaching Options

F Y I

Pyramid Builders

Many of the laborers of the pyramids were farmers and craftsmen. The pyramids were *not* built only by slaves, as many people once thought. Scholars now believe that many workers were building the pyramids during the annual flooding on the Nile. People provided their labor in exchange for payment of their taxes. Workers were brought from all over the empire.

Connection to
LITERATURE

There are several very interesting books on the building of the pyramids. You may want to have students read one of the books and then have them explain to the class how the different pyramids were built. One book is *Pyramid* by David Macaulay (Houghton Mifflin, 1977).

KHUFU'S PYRAMID
The Great Pyramid (left) was built during ancient Egypt's Third Dynasty as the tomb of the pharaoh Khufu (right). For more than 20 years, builders cut and moved more than 2 million limestone blocks, each weighing 2 tons or more.

King's burial chamber

Queen's chamber

Ivory statue of Khufu

Entrance, 59 feet above ground level

Temple where offerings to the dead could be placed

...Present

Some of the most striking modern buildings today imitate the shape of ancient Egypt's pyramids. However, while the ancients built their pyramids by hauling large limestone blocks into place by hand, modern architects use sophisticated machinery and many different materials such as steel, concrete, and glass.

Glass and steel frame

Reinforced concrete sides

MODERN PYRAMIDS
The Transamerica Building (above), built in San Francisco, California, is earthquake-resistant partly because its pyramidal shape will not shake sideways. The Louvre pyramid (left) in Paris, France, uses glass instead of concrete on its four sides. The glass gives a fantastic view of the surrounding buildings.

CHAPTER 2 ◆ Ancient Civilizations **31**

Hands-On Activity

Have students work in small groups to research the history of some of the more famous pyramids in Egypt. Have students use library resources or the Internet to help them with their research. Ask students to make posters to show what they have learned about the pyramids they researched.

KHUFU'S PYRAMID
The Great Pyramid was built from about 2589 B.C. to 2566 B.C. and is located in Giza, which is the site of many pyramids. It contains more than 2,300,000 blocks of stone. The base of the pyramid covers about 13 acres.

...Present

MODERN PYRAMIDS
The Transamerica Building, located in downtown San Francisco, California, is the city's tallest building. It is 853 feet tall and is a 48-story building. The building is shaped in the style of a pyramid and is made of concrete, glass, and steel. At the very top of the building is a spire that rises above the uppermost floor.

From the top floors of the building, you can see the entire San Francisco Bay Area, including landmarks such as the Golden Gate Bridge, Alcatraz, Fisherman's Wharf, and Sausalito. There is an observation deck at the top of the building, but people are not allowed up because it is only 4 feet wide. The building has a camera that captures the view for people to see from the lobby.

Ieoh Ming Pei, or I. M. Pei as he is better known, designed the glass pyramid at the entrance to the Louvre in the 1980s. The pyramid is 71 feet high at the peak. The museum reception center is flooded with light because of the pyramid entrance. I. M. Pei is well known for his creative use of space and materials. He won the Pritzker Architecture Prize in 1983 for his design.

Many people did not like the design of the Louvre entrance when it was proposed because it was so different from the massive stone main building of the Louvre. However, it has now become a famous landmark.

Connect Past to Present
From the time of ancient Egypt to the present, people have been fascinated with pyramids. Ask students why they think people are still so interested in pyramids and why pyramids continue as an architectural form. You may wish to have students use the library or Internet to research other modern pyramids.

II. Mesopotamia and Sumer (pp. 32–36)

Section Summary

In this section, students will learn how the geography of Mesopotamia affected the development of farming settlements and the Sumerian civilization. They will also learn how a surplus food supply led to the growth of cities.

1 Introduce

Getting Started

Ask students to think about the town or city in which they live. Explain that Sumerian cities developed where there was rich soil for farming. Ask students why their town or city developed where it did and which features of their communities encourage growth.

TERMS TO KNOW

Ask students to read the words and definitions on page 32 and find each word in the section. Point out that one of the words contains the Greek combining form *theo-*. Have students use a dictionary to find its meaning (God or a god) and other words that contain *theo-*. (theology, theologian, monotheistic)

You may wish to preview the pronunciation of the following terms with students.

Mesopotamia
(meh suh puh TAY mee uh)
Euphrates (yoo FRAY teez) **River**

ACTIVE READING

Have students use a two-column chart (TR, p. 328) to compare and contrast Sumerian civilization and Egyptian civilization.

Terms to Know

theocracy a form of government in which a god is regarded as the supreme ruler, and power is in the hands of religious leaders

ziggurat a pyramid-shaped tower that stood several stories tall

scribe a person who copies information and keeps records

polytheism belief in many gods

Main Ideas

A. The hot, dry climate and the flooding of the Tigris and Euphrates Rivers influenced the growth of Mesopotamia.

B. Sumerian life was based on agriculture—with the first food surplus in history—and religion.

 Active Reading

COMPARE AND CONTRAST
When you compare and contrast, you look at the way an element in one area is the same as or different from that element in another area. As you read this section, think about the main points of Sumerian civilization. Then, compare and contrast them with what you have learned about Egypt.

A. The Land Between Two Rivers

As you learned in Chapter 1, the Fertile Crescent is an area of rich land reaching from the Mediterranean Sea to the Persian Gulf. It includes the Tigris and Euphrates Rivers and the valley between both rivers. This valley and the land around it came to be known as Mesopotamia.

Mesopotamia and Sumer

Legend:
▢ Mesopotamia
▢ Sumer
• Cities

0 150 300 mi
0 150 300 km

Black Sea
Asia Minor
ANTI-TAURUS MOUNTAINS
Nineveh
Euphrates River
Tigris River
ZAGROS MOUNTAINS
Mediterranean Sea
Tyre
SYRIAN DESERT
Ur
Nile Delta
Memphis
ARABIAN DESERT
EGYPT
Red Sea
Persian Gulf

✔ **Map Check**

LOCATION Which two major bodies of water border Mesopotamia?

Geography and Its Impact

The Fertile Crescent is bordered in the east by the Zagros Mountains and in the south by the Arabian Plateau. The Tigris and Euphrates Rivers played a huge role in the development of the region. Because both rivers deposited layers of rich soil in the valley each spring, a variety of crops could be grown. The plentiful crops supplied enough food to support a growing population. Although the area was rich in soil and water, there were few other natural resources, such as hard stone, metal, semiprecious stones, and trees.

People began settling in farming villages in this region by about 6000 B.C. In the north, hills and rainfall are more abundant than in the south. However, irrigation was more difficult in the north, which caused northern peoples to migrate south. The flat land in the southern region was ideal for growing crops. However, because the summers were hot and dry in the south, building irrigation ditches to carry water to planted fields was key to the area's success and growth. Once established, the farming communities produced an abundance of food. This extra quantity, or surplus, enabled large groups of people to live together and help establish one of the first civilizations.

Teaching Options

Section 2 Resources

Teacher's Resources (TR)
Terms to Know, p. 15
Review History, p. 49
Build Your Skills, p. 83
Concept Builder, p. 218
Idea Web, p. 321
Transparencies 7, 10

Connection to ECONOMICS

Tyre is one of the world's oldest cities and may have been founded around 2750 B.C. Located on the very eastern edge of the Mediterranean Sea, Tyre was controlled by Egypt until about 1100 B.C. It carried out trade with the peoples of Asia Minor and the Aegean Sea, and was a prosperous sea power. Tyre founded several colonies, including Carthage in North Africa, which added to its wealth.

The *Standard of Ur* is made from shells, gems, and colored stones. It shows daily life in ancient Mesopotamia, such as farming and raising livestock.

Early Mesopotamian Communities

Early Mesopotamia—a fertile valley between two rivers, the Tigris and the Euphrates—was an area of many natural riches. Wild wheat and barley grew abundantly in the fertile river valley, while wild sheep and goats roamed the green lowland. It was here, in this rich river valley, that people first began farming settlements about 8,000 years ago. They came because the land here was more fertile than in the surrounding region. However, little rain fell on the soil of the valley, so farmers had to dig irrigation canals from the rivers to bring water to the fields. Farming settlements grew larger as people banded and worked together to bring water to their land and grow crops.

The first farmers learned to grow, or cultivate, plants such as peas, lentils, carrots, and turnips. Then, farmers also began raising livestock. Livestock provided early Mesopotamians with another source of food as well as milk and animal skins.

Up to this time, the only tools that farmers used in order to prepare the soil for planting were sharp digging sticks. Then around 4000 B.C., Mesopotamians invented the plow. This invention was a huge breakthrough in the way soil was prepared for planting, making the work faster and less difficult. In addition to the plow, the people of Mesopotamia invented ovens for baking bread as well as pottery to use for storage. Some people were better at making pots and bread than at farming. As a result, people began specializing in the kind of work they did. While some remained farmers, others became traders or craftspeople. However, farming was still the central activity around which all the other tasks revolved.

The farming villages of Mesopotamia continued to grow and flourish over the next 500 years, from about 4000 B.C. to about 3500 B.C. The area was home to many people of different languages and cultures. While Mesopotamia had no set boundaries and no permanent capital, it was divided into three general areas. These areas included Assyria in the north and Akkad and Sumer in the south. Of these areas, Sumer was by far the largest. It was also there that the first Mesopotamian civilization began.

◆ **How did geography and climate affect farming in the northern and southern regions of the Fertile Crescent?**

B. Sumerian Civilization

The land known as Sumer was located in southern Mesopotamia between the Tigris and the Euphrates Rivers. Around 3500 B.C. some of the largest

CHAPTER 2 ◆ Ancient Civilizations **33**

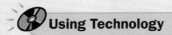
Using Technology

Have students do a search on the Internet using the phrase "Standard of Ur" as a search item. Have them check at least six sites, pick one that offers solid, interesting historical information, and take notes on what they learn. Suggest that students look for sites that have *.org* and *.edu* in their addresses, indicating nonprofit organizations or educational institutions.

A. The Land Between Two Rivers

Purpose-Setting Question What activity enabled people to plant more crops and grow an abundance of food? (building irrigation ditches)

Using the Map

Mesopotamia and Sumer

Ask students what the green color indicates on the map. (Mesopotamia) Then, discuss which map features are found within this green color (two rivers—Tigris and Euphrates; three cities—Nineveh, Tyre, Ur) and what impact they must have had on the area. (Rivers created fertile soil; cities provided centers of trade.)

✔ Map Check

Answer Mediterranean Sea and Persian Gulf

Review Have students review page 24 to determine which plants grew in ancient Egypt. (grains, vegetables, fruits, flax, papyrus) Then, have students compare those plants with plants that grew at the beginning of the Mesopotamian civilization. (wild wheat, barley, peas, lentils, carrots, turnips) Discuss reasons why there was a difference in the plants grown. (different climate, soil, or geographic conditions)

TEACH PRIMARY SOURCES Have students study the sections of the *Standard of Ur* shown on page 33. Discuss what these scenes show. (scenes of daily life, farming, and raising livestock)

◆ **ANSWER** The northern region had hills and rainfall, but irrigation was difficult. The southern region's flat land was good for growing crops, but the hot and dry climate made irrigation necessary for successful farming.

B. Sumerian Civilization

Purpose-Setting Question What were some functions of city-states in Sumer? (protect citizens from invaders; form armies; keep city walls strong and irrigation canals working; collect taxes and keep records; build temples and palaces)

CHAPTER 2 ◆ **T33**

Explore The Sumerians may have come to Mesopotamia from the highlands of Anatolia or western Asia. Explain that Anatolia is part of present-day Turkey. Have students use the map of Asia and the Middle East on page A7 of the Atlas or use Transparencies 7 and 10 to locate these places. Ask which modern-day countries located in western Asia the Sumerians might have come from. (Iran, Iraq, Syria, Israel, Lebanon, Jordan, Armenia, Azerbaijan; accept other reasonable answers)

Discuss Have students locate Ur on the map on page 32. Ask students how its location may have contributed to its growth as a city-state. (located at the mouth of the Euphrates River and edge of the Persian Gulf meant good access to trade, available water, and fertile soil) Ask what problems there might be with the location. (flooding, open to attack)

Focus Over time, the city-states switched from being headed by priests to being headed by war leaders. Ask students what this says about the priorities and experiences of the people and city-states. (Possible answer: defense became more important than religion) Discuss with students what would make priorities change.

Do You Remember?
Have students refer to "The Kingdoms of Ancient Egypt" on page 25 to recall other early governments that were based on the framework of city-states.

TEACH PRIMARY SOURCES
Have students study the photo of the ziggurat on page 34. Ask them what features they can identify. Suggest that students refer to the second paragraph under "Sumerian Government" for help. Remind students that a ziggurat was similar in construction and shape to the pyramids of Egypt. Ask what other civilizations had pyramids. (Egyptian and Maya)

Do You Remember?
In Chapter 1, you learned about the birth of cities. The word *civilization* comes from the word *city*.

and most active settlements in the area called Sumer grew into cities. Each city was the center of a farming region that became part of a larger city-state. The cities and city-states of Sumer varied in size. Ur, which began as a small farming village, grew to a population of 20,000 people by 2500 B.C. and covered more than 148 acres (about $\frac{1}{4}$ square mile) of land. In that same year, it also became the capital of Sumer.

Sumerian Government

To better protect themselves from invaders, Sumerian people organized themselves into city-states. Each city-state was a **theocracy**, a government ruled by a priest. The ruler could command an army, collect taxes, and put laborers to work building temples, palaces, and walls around the city.

At the center of each city was a building called a **ziggurat**. A ziggurat was a pyramid-shaped tower that was between three and seven stories high, with each story having its own terrace. At the very top was a temple in which priests honored their city's chief god or goddess. The people of Sumer saw the ziggurat as a link between Earth and the heavens.

By about 3300 B.C. Sumer had at least 12 city-states. The most powerful of these were Kish, Uruk, Lagash, and Ur, the capital of Sumer. As you have already learned, priests originally ruled the city-states. In time, however, war leaders came to rule as kings. Their courage and leadership in battle made them the natural choice for strong rulers. In each city-state, the king was responsible for keeping the city walls strong and the irrigation canals working correctly. Kings led armies into war and made sure that laws were obeyed. The rulers also performed religious duties and led ceremonies to serve each city-state's chief god or goddess. As government grew, these rulers had city-state officials collect taxes and keep records.

This ziggurat was built more than 4,000 years ago around 2100 B.C.

Teaching Options

ESL/ELL STRATEGIES

Take Notes Have partners work together in this oral activity that has them improve their study skills. Ask one partner to read aloud the text under *Sumerian Government* while the other partner listens and takes notes. Then, have both students check the notes against the text and evaluate accuracy. Have students switch roles and read the text under *Sumerian Writing and Literature*.

F Y I

Ziggurat—Chogha Zanbil
The ziggurat Chogha Zanbil was built around 1250 B.C. It served as a place of worship to the god Inshushinak. In 640 B.C., the Assyrians destroyed it. Clay inscriptions and sculptures of animals and men have been found at the site. At the bottom of the structure are mud-covered clay bricks. Archaeologists believe the ziggurat originally had luxurious entrances and stairways.

Sumerian Writing and Literature

The Sumerian people's first writing was in the form of pictographs, which represented objects, farm products, or other goods. Because clay was a main resource in the Fertile Crescent, Sumerians naturally used this material to make clay tablets on which they wrote. Later, around 3100 B.C., this writing became cuneiform, which you read about in Chapter 1. In cuneiform writing, a thin, pointed plant called a reed was used to make wedge-shaped marks on the soft clay tablets. The cuneiform system of writing remained in use for about 3,000 years.

While much of Sumerian writing is used to record surplus food or trade goods, other examples of their writing do exist. Such examples include myths, poems, and law codes. These examples show the highest cultural achievement of Mesopotamian civilization. In one piece of literature, a poem titled *The Epic of Gilgamesh*, 3,500 lines of cuneiform are written on 12 clay tablets. This poem, which is the Sumerians' favorite story, details the ruler of Uruk, an actual person whose name was Gilgamesh. Poems like *The Epic of Gilgamesh* were just one of many accomplishments that Sumerians created.

Although more than 3 million clay tablets exist today, scholars are still trying to decode some of the writing on them. These written records detail Sumerian government, trade, business, and other parts of life in Sumer. However, scholars are less certain about Sumerian civilization overall than they are about the civilization of ancient Egypt.

Inventions and Contributions

Mesopotamians had inventive minds that were put to good use in creating items that improved their daily lives. For example, you already have learned that the early Sumerian people invented the plow, pottery, and cuneiform writing. All of these were important inventions. Even more important, however, was the invention of the wheel—yet another idea that sprang from Sumer around 3100 B.C. Wheels changed forever how people and things moved from place to place.

Another invention that made travel easier and faster was the sail. Sumerian ships with sails could travel faster than ships powered by oars. This speed enabled them to send goods long distances for the purpose of trade. Some ships sailed to the Persian Gulf and even as far away as India.

The Sumerians were masters at recordkeeping—tracking the amount of land planted, products bought and sold, and the size of canals. All of these amounts had to be measured and calculated carefully, usually by a **scribe**. A scribe is a person who copies information and keeps records. As a result, the Sumerians invented a mathematical system, called the sexagesimal system, that was based on the number 60. We still use this system today on clocks and in geometry. Finally, the Sumerians also contributed to the growth of architecture with inventions that include the arch, the dome, the vault, and brick molds.

Development of Cuneiform Writing

MEANING	ORIGINAL PICTOGRAPH	EARLY CUNEIFORM	LATER CUNEIFORM
Sun			
Ox			
Fish			
Bird			
Grain			
Orchard			

✔ **Chart Check**

How did the original pictographs differ from later cuneiform?

Using The Chart
Development of Cuneiform Writing

Ask students what the information on the chart shows. (six pictographs and how they changed into wedge-shaped cuneiform writing) Discuss possible reasons for the change to cuneiform and why it took the form it did. Explain that cuneiform was easier to record information. The shape of the reed stylus determined the wedge-shaped writing. Ask students to create two more pictographs for the chart and then change them into cuneiform.

✔ **Chart Check**

Answer Over time, cuneiform depended more on abstract wedge shapes to depict objects.

Demonstrate Discuss how the sexagesimal system (based on 60 units) is used for clocks today. Have volunteers use an analog clock with a second hand to demonstrate how 60 seconds equal a minute and 60 minutes equal an hour.

Activity

Research Divide the class into five groups to research *The Epic of Gilgamesh*. Each group researches one of the following: the city-state of Uruk where the story takes place; Gilgamesh, king of Uruk; Enkidu the wild man; the adventures in the epic; and the epic's accomplishments as a work of literature. Then, have each group report its findings to the class.

Focus Ask students what they think life would be like without the wheel. Then, discuss how the wheel may have changed lives 5,000 years ago. Help them realize that the wheel would have made it easier to move objects and people.

Focus on
▶ TEEN LIFE ◀

Sumerian Education By around 2500 B.C., wealthy boys living in Sumerian cities studied at writing schools called tablet houses. These boys trained to become scribes. This would prepare them for a career as an administrator of the city-state, managing land, temples, and the palace.

Learning to inscribe cuneiform was the most important subject at school. Boys also studied mathematics, surveying, and music. During a typical day at school the boys would recite their tablets, prepare new tablets, and complete oral and written work. School rules were very strict; students could be struck with a wooden cane for talking, standing up, leaving the room, or having a poor copy of a tablet. Have students think about the daily activities of a Sumerian student and write a few paragraphs describing a day at school.

ANALYZING PRIMARY SOURCES

DOCUMENT-BASED QUESTION
To help students understand this quote, have them make a diagram that shows the relationship between each group.

ANSWER slave

Extend Point out that the Sumerians believed that floods, drought, disease, and other disasters were caused by a failure to care for the gods. Discuss how the Sumerians' lack of understanding of science may have encouraged these ideas. (Because they had little understanding of the natural causes of disasters, supernatural beings provided an answer.)

> ### Activity
>
> **Make a list** Have students reread the page to find three classes of Sumerian society. Have them list these classes, in order from highest to lowest. Students should also include the categories of workers who belonged to each class. (**upper class:** kings, priests and nobles; **middle class:** merchants and artists; **lower class:** farmers and laborers; **lowest class:** slaves)

◆ **ANSWER** a theocracy, which was ruled by a priest

Section Close

Discuss with students the advances the Sumerians made and why it is valuable to study this ancient civilization.

③ Assess

Review Answers

Review History

A. They deposited layers of rich soil in the valley each spring so that a variety of crops could be grown. They also provided water for irrigating the crops.

B. Answers should include three of the following: plow, pottery, cuneiform writing, epic poems, wheel, sail, sexagesimal system, arch, dome, vault, brick molds.

Define Terms to Know

theocracy, 34; ziggurat, 34; scribe, 35; polytheism, 36

Religion and Social Structure

Like the Egyptians, the Sumerian people practiced **polytheism**. This term means that they worshiped many gods and goddesses—about 3,000 in all. Because so many events in nature were unpredictable, Sumerians developed a system of beliefs that helped them feel in control of their world. In addition, each city had a chief god or goddess who protected that city from disasters in nature and in war. As you have also learned, each city maintained a temple for that god, and the city's ruler acted as the chief priest.

As to be expected, the ruler was at the very top of Sumerian society. He, along with priests and nobles, formed the upper class of Sumerian society. Merchants and artisans formed the middle class, whereas farmers and laborers made up the lower class. The following quote describes the social structure in Sumer:

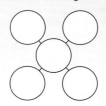
ANALYZE PRIMARY SOURCES
DOCUMENT-BASED QUESTION Who is the lowest member of Sumerian society, according to this quote?

> ❝ Man is the shadow of a god, and a slave is a shadow of a man; but the king is the mirror of a god. ❞

At the very bottom of the lowest class were slaves. While male slave labor was never a major part of the Sumerian economy, slavery did exist. A number of females were also slaves, mostly working in the temples. Under Sumerian law, slaves could own property and work during their personal time in order to earn money to buy their own freedom.

The backbone of Sumerian society was the family, and families tended to be close-knit. Men and women were married by family arrangements. The children they bore were highly valued and well treated. Only wealthy boys were educated formally in temple schools. There, they learned writing, grammar, science, astronomy, and math. Women and girls were not considered equal to boys. However, they had some rights, such as the right to own property, serve as witnesses in court, and carry out business negotiations.

◆ **What type of government did the Sumerians form?**

Review II

Review History
A. How did the Tigris and Euphrates Rivers contribute to Mesopotamia's growth?
B. What are three Sumerian inventions?

Define Terms to Know
Define the following terms:
theocracy, ziggurat, scribe, polytheism

Critical Thinking
Which Sumerian invention do you think changed their lives the most?

Write About Government
Write a letter to a friend describing what it would be like to live in a Sumerian city-state.

Get Organized
IDEA WEB
Use an idea web to organize information from this section. Choose a topic and then find related facts. For example, what are the elements found in cuneiform writing?

Critical Thinking

Answers will vary. Possible answers:
Writing: record events and literature; **wheel:** faster transportation and helped in the spread of ideas; **plow:** farming more efficient

Write About Government

Students' letters should describe various features of a city-state, including important structures, forms of government, and aspects of daily life and society.

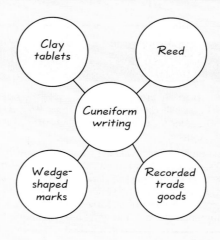

Empires of Ancient Mesopotamia

Terms to Know

patriarchal relating to a culture in which men are the most powerful members

satrap a governor of a region in ancient Persia

Main Ideas

A. The Akkadian Empire was the first empire in history.

B. Babylonia, a small Sumerian city-state, was destroyed by the Assyrians who were known for their military inventions and the fierceness of their soldiers.

C. The Persian Empire conquered Babylon in 539 B.C. and brought an end to the dominance of Mesopotamian empires.

D. The Phoenicians, mainly known for shipbuilding and far-reaching trade, created the basis for an alphabet used throughout the world today.

 Active Reading

PREDICT
When you predict, you build on your background knowledge to help you understand a subject or historical period. Before you read this section, review what you have learned about Mesopotamia's culture. Then, predict what the other cultures of the Fertile Crescent were like.

A. The First Empire

As you have learned, Sumer was not the only region of Mesopotamia. Other major regions included Akkad, Assyria, and Babylonia. As the Sumerian city-states weakened from constant fighting among themselves, outsiders from these other Mesopotamian regions looked to gain control of Sumer. Eventually, the high walls that protected Sumerian cities were not enough to keep out these foreigners. Although Sumer had been conquered, its civilization and achievements were not lost when their city-states became part of larger empires.

The Akkadian Empire

Around 2350 B.C., a military leader named Sargon waged battle against the city-states of Sumer and won. Sargon was from the region known as Akkad, a city-state located north of Sumer. By taking control of both the northern and southern regions of Mesopotamia, Sargon had created the world's first-known empire. He made the city of Akkad the capital of the new empire.

Because Sargon was a superb military leader, he continued to wage war and conquer new lands. Each victory expanded his territory even farther. The Akkadians had adopted many parts of the Sumerian civilization and culture. Sargon's conquests spread this culture to each new conquered land. At its peak, the Akkadian Empire and Sumerian culture stretched from the Mediterranean Sea in present-day Iran in the east, to present-day Turkey in the west.

Sumerian and Akkadian Civilization

Sargon lived to be very old. After his death, four kings succeeded him and continued his dynasty. In all, Sargon's dynasty ruled for almost 200 years. In that time, Sumerian and Akkadian cultures blended to become one. Both groups practiced the same religion and used the same social structure. In addition, both used the same systems of governing and writing and had similar economic and military practices.

The arts especially flourished at this time. Sculpture, carving, and seal making were particularly outstanding. Poetry was also important. In fact, one

In 2350 B.C., Sargon of the Akkadians conquered the Sumerian city-states and began a dynasty that continued for more than 200 years.

CHAPTER 2 ◆ Ancient Civilizations **37**

Teaching Options

Section 3 Resources

Teacher's Resources (TR)
Terms to Know, p. 15
Review History, p. 49
Build Your Skills, p. 83
Concept Builder, p. 218
Idea Web, p. 321
Transparencies 7, 10

 F Y I

Sargon of Akkadia

Sargon's fame gave rise to many legends about him. One legend describes the infant Sargon as being rescued from a basket floating in a river. The Bible tells a similar story about Moses, the great Israelite leader who lived about 1,000 years later.

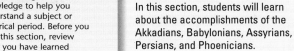

III. Empires of Ancient Mesopotamia
(pp. 37–41)

Section Summary

In this section, students will learn about the accomplishments of the Akkadians, Babylonians, Assyrians, Persians, and Phoenicians.

1 Introduce

Getting Started

Ask students to skim the section and notice how many different empires ruled varying regions in ancient Mesopotamia over 1,500 years. Discuss why so many civilizations wanted to conquer the region. (Invaders wanted more land to expand their territories, they wanted wealth from natural resources and slave labor, they sought freedom of religion. If they didn't try to conquer others, they were almost certain to be conquered by them.) As a class, decide if the world today suffers from the same types of problems.

TERMS TO KNOW

Ask students to read the words and definitions on page 37 and find each word in the section. Ask students to add these words to the vocabulary file they started in Section 1. Ask pairs of students to review the words.

You may wish to preview the pronunciation of the following words with students.

Babylonian (bab uh LOH nee uhn)
Hammurabi (ham uh RAH bee)
Phoenician (fuh NEE shuhn)

ACTIVE READING

Discuss the most important ideas that students have learned in Sections 1 and 2 about ancient Egypt and Sumer. (Students can reread the Main Ideas at the beginning of those sections to review the concepts.) Point out that since this is a chapter on ancient civilizations, they will probably be learning the same kinds of information about other empires of ancient Mesopotamia. Have students write several predictions and review them after they read the section to see if their predictions were correct.

A. The First Empire

Purpose-Setting Question What contributions did the Akkadian Empire make toward the development of civilization? (The arts flourished, especially sculpture, carving, seal making, and poetry. Akkadians also spread Sumerian culture.)

ANALYZE PRIMARY SOURCES

DOCUMENT-BASED QUESTION
Enheduana was the first known author in recorded history to write in the first person. She was in a very powerful position in Ur and had the clout and pride to include herself in her writings. Enheduana's hymns to Ishtar, the Akkadian goddess of love and war, are so intricate, that scholars call her the "Shakespeare of Sumerian literature."

ANSWER phrases such as "destroyer of the foreign lands," "foreign lands cower," and "their anguished outcry"

◆ **ANSWER** the Akkadians

B. The Babylonian and Assyrian Empires

Purpose-Setting Question How did the Babylonian Empire fall to the Hittites and eventually the Assyrians? (The Assyrians were skilled at war; had a well-organized army: used iron weapons, chariots, bows and arrows, and battering rams.)

Activity

Research Have students use library sources or the Internet to learn more about the Code of Hammurabi. Encourage students to list at least five facts, each one on a separate index card, and then create a logical, well-organized paragraph about the code. Some facts about the code follow: written in cuneiform Akkadian; intended to ensure that the strong did not oppress the weak; based on older collections of Sumerian and Akkadian laws; contained nearly 300 legal provisions; covered matters such as bearing false witness, witchcraft, and military service; stone column on which it was carved discovered in 1901 in Susa, Iran.

ANALYZE PRIMARY SOURCES
DOCUMENT-BASED QUESTION
Which words or phrases tell you that this poem is about war and conquest?

---

of Sargon's daughters, Enheduana, became the first female poet in history for whom we know a name. Here is one of her poems to Ishtar, the Akkadian goddess of love and war:

> ❝Destroyer of the foreign lands, you have given wings to the storm,
> Beloved of Enlil you made it blow over the land.
> My queen, the foreign lands cower [kneel] at your cry,
> In dread [and] fear of the South Wind, mankind
> Brought you their anguished outcry
> Brought before you the "great" lamentations [cries] in the city streets. ❞

Although Sargon's dynasty lasted for almost two centuries, the four kings who followed Sargon were weak. They could not hold the vast Akkadian Empire together. At this time, the city-states of Sumer regained their independence—but not for long.

◆ **Which group of people ruled in Mesopotamia after the Sumerians?**

B. The Babylonian and Assyrian Empires

Beginning around 2000 B.C. a wave of conquerors, called Amorites, invaded Mesopotamia from the west. They made the village of Babylon on the Euphrates River their capital and went on to make it a beautiful city with a grand ziggurat.

The Babylonian Empire

The Babylonian Empire of the Amorite peoples reached its peak around 1790 B.C. under the leadership of Hammurabi, the greatest of all Babylonian rulers. Hammurabi was an outstanding leader who became famous for building many fine palaces and temples such as the huge ziggurat located in the capital city. In time, Babylon became widely known for its wealth, entertainments, and beautiful gardens.

Hammurabi is best remembered for his code of laws. A code is similar to a list. While the Sumerians were the first to write laws, Hammurabi's code of laws was an attempt to write down all the laws of an empire in one document. In about 1780 B.C. he had the laws carved onto a huge stone column for everyone in the empire to see. He also made many copies of the laws that were distributed throughout his empire.

The Code of Hammurabi

The Code of Hammurabi helped the ruler do many things. First, it helped establish laws that everyone in his empire would know about and therefore, could obey. Second, and perhaps most important, the code helped to unify the many different peoples who made up the Babylonian Empire. Third, the code introduced the idea that government has some responsibility for how people act in society. The code set a pattern for later governments to follow.

The code lists 282 specific laws that deal with all aspects of Babylonian life, including marriage, land rights, business dealings, family relations, and crime and punishment. Some of the laws were complicated and often unfair. For example, even though the laws applied to everyone in the empire, it set different punishments for people of different classes and between men and women. Generally though, punishments for breaking laws or behaving criminally matched the bad deed. For example, one law stated: "If a man breaks the bone of another man, they (the people) shall break his bone."

The Code of Hammurabi was written on a stone monument about 8 feet tall. The top part, shown above, is a carving of Hammurabi standing next to the sun god.

Teaching Options

Meet Individual Needs:
LOGICAL/MATHEMATICAL LEARNERS

With students, create a two-column chart (TR, p. 328) to list the social structure of the Assyrian Empires. (**upper class:** king's advisors, military leaders, and nobles; **middle class:** merchants and artisans; **lower class:** farmers and slaves) Students may add additional columns to their charts to show the social structure of other peoples they have studied.

ESL/ELL STRATEGIES

Identify Essential Vocabulary Some students may be confused by phrases such as "a wave of conquerors," "The Babylonian Empire . . . reached its peak around," and "code of laws." Review each phrase with students and encourage them to identify the different meanings of some words. Suggest that students create a classroom file of phrases that use words in a way that they may not expect.

The Assyrian city of Nineveh contained many buildings, including a palace, library, and temple, as well as canals and gardens.

Babylonia Declines and the Assyrian Empire Rises

Later rulers of the Babylonian Empire were not able to hold onto all the lands that Hammurabi had conquered. The empire fell to outside warriors, called the Hittites, around 1590 B.C. Although Hittite rule was short, it marked the beginning of a time of turmoil for the Babylonian Empire. During the next 1,000 years, the empire was ruled by many people, including the Assyrians.

The Assyrian people came from the ancient city of Ashur, about 200 miles north of the city of Babylon. Around 1300 B.C. the Assyrians took over the Babylonian Empire and ruled it as their own. The Assyrians were greatly skilled at making war. They had a large, organized army that was well trained and could be ready to move at a moment's notice.

Assyrian soldiers used the latest tools to wage war, such as iron weapons, chariots, and bows and arrows. In addition, the Assyrians invented many new tools of war. This included the short sword, the shield and helmet, and the battering ram, a large, heavy wooden beam that could break down walls.

Through their military skill, the Assyrians built the greatest empire the world had seen up to that time. At the height of their power the Assyrians controlled not only Babylon and Mesopotamia, but also Syria, Phoenicia, the kingdom of Israel, and parts of Egypt.

Assyrian Social Order

There were many social classes in Assyrian society, with the king at the head of the social organization. The upper class was made up mostly of nobles, military leaders, and advisors to the king. The middle class consisted of merchants and artisans, whereas farmers and slaves made up the lower class. Assyria had a **patriarchal** society, one in which a man was the head of the family. Women's rank in society was below that of men.

The warlike Assyrians became so concerned with battle that they hardly had time for much else. Building projects, however, did occur, especially since they were a way for Assyrians to display their power. Over hundreds of years, the building projects of many kings included great palaces, especially in Nineveh, the capital of Assyria.

CHAPTER 2 ◆ Ancient Civilizations **39**

Activity

Create an idea web Point out that the scene on this page shows what one artist thought the city of ancient Nineveh looked like. Ask students to study the scene carefully to identify its parts: the multi-leveled palace, wooden boats, the towering ziggurat, shepherds with their flocks, and the tropical trees. Then, ask students to use the graphic organizer on TR page 321 to create an idea web. (**Central circle:** Nineveh; **Outer circles:** descriptive phrases about places and things in Nineveh as shown in the picture)

Explore Remind students that the Hittites conquered the Babylonian Empire around 1590 B.C. and ruled it for a short time. Have students use library sources or the Internet to research the Hittites. Students should look for information about where the Hittites came from; Hittite rulers and actions; Hittite government, society, economy, cultures, religion, and accomplishments; and what happened to the Hittite Empire. Ask students to share what they have learned with the class.

Discuss The Assyrians are described as warlike and great warriors. Ask students what part of Assyrian social order is consistent with a war-based society. Students may suggest patriarchal society and the lower rank of women.

Review To compare the place of women in Sumerian society with their low status in Assyrian society, have students reread "Religion and Social Structure" on page 36. Have students write one or two sentences that compare the rights of Sumerian women with the lack of status of Assyrian women. Then, encourage students to discuss why women might have a different status in the two different societies.

Writing

AVERAGE

Ask students to write one or two paragraphs that compare and contrast what they think Babylonian and Assyrian societies were like. Suggest that students discuss what each society considered important and how it dealt with other people and societies.

CHALLENGE

Have students write a short paper on the Code of Hammurabi. Students should discuss the importance of the code, the types of laws, the punishments, and how Hammurabi spread the laws. Encourage students to discuss how effective they think the code was.

ANSWER The Babylonians built palaces and temples and recorded one of the earliest written collections of laws, called the Code of Hammurabi. The Assyrians built the greatest empire the world had ever seen, controlling Babylon, Mesopotamia, Syria, Phoenicia, the kingdom of Israel, and parts of Egypt. The Assyrians invented the short sword, the shield and helmet, and the battering ram.

C. The Persian Empire

Purpose-Setting Question How was government organized during the Persian Empire? (The empire was ruled by an emperor; the empire was divided into small regions and ruled by governors.)

Demonstrate Have students use a classroom map, Transparencies 7 and 10, or the map of Asia and the Middle East on page A7 of the Atlas to locate central Asia, where the Persians came from. Then, point out that the Royal Road extended from Susa in the east to Sardis in the west. Have students research to discover where these places are today and locate them on the map.

Focus Remind students that the leader of the Persians, Cyrus the Great, used a very different approach with the people and areas he conquered. Explain that in other civilizations, soldiers conquering an area were often allowed, and even encouraged, to steal and destroy the property of people who were living there. Cyrus instructed his soldiers *not* to do this. Ask students how they think the conquered people felt about this approach. Help students realize that people would have been relieved, happy, felt better about the Persians. Explain that Cyrus's orders also meant that the people who were conquered would have food to eat, animals to help them, and enough goods to keep the economy running.

ANSWER The Persians built many roads, including the Royal Road, to make travel and communication easier. They encouraged a system of common weights and measures and the use of coins throughout the empire.

Darius I expanded the Persian Empire to make it one of the most powerful empires of ancient times.

The Assyrians eventually wore themselves out through constant fighting. When an outside group, the Chaldeans, attacked, the Assyrian Empire collapsed. In 612 B.C., the Assyrians disappeared from history altogether. The Chaldean people, however, rebuilt the city of Babylon under King Nebuchadnezzar, who ruled from 605 B.C. to 592 B.C. His spectacular buildings included his palace as well as a monumental gate called the Ishtar Gate. The Chaldean Empire lasted for less than 100 years. In 539 B.C., it was conquered by the Persians.

What were some of the Babylonian and Assyrian contributions to civilization?

C. The Persian Empire

The Persian people came from central Asia. Led by Cyrus the Great, Persians conquered the city of Babylon in 539 B.C., and Mesopotamia then became part of the Persian Empire.

Conquest and Contributions of the Persians

The Persians were the first people from outside the Fertile Crescent to conquer Mesopotamia. The Persians contributed much to the region culturally. For example, Cyrus the Great, the leader of the Persian army that defeated Babylon, was famous for building many roads to make travel and communication easier within the vast Persian Empire. This empire stretched from Egypt in the east all the way to India in the west. The most famous road that Cyrus had constructed was called the Royal Road. It carried advisors and messengers to and from all the major cities in the Persian Empire, including Susa and Sardis. Cyrus was also known for his method of governing, which was through kindness and cooperation. He gave strict orders to his army not to steal or destroy property of the areas they had conquered. In this way, he was able to control his huge empire through goodness and generosity rather than through cruelty and greed.

Other contributions of the Persian people included a system of common weights and measures and the use of coins throughout the empire. The coins were made of electrum, a natural mix of gold and silver. Because all the coins were of the same weight, they all had the same value. Using coins made trade more efficient and fairer in the exchange of one good for another.

Persian Government and Religion

The Persian king ruled his kingdom in much the same way as rulers from Sumer and Akkad had—with the help of nobles and as the spokesperson for the gods. Because the Persian Empire was so large, it was divided into small regions that were each ruled by a governor called a **satrap**. The satraps collected taxes that were paid in goods.

When Cyrus died in 530 B.C., his son extended the Persian Empire by conquering Egypt. Here, he publicly criticized the Egyptian gods and goddesses and had statues and other images of them destroyed. This action angered the Egyptians, who at the first opportunity, rebelled. Later, Darius I, who took the Persian throne in 522 B.C., spent the first three years of his rule putting down the revolts. He greatly extended the empire, adding parts of India and Afghanistan so that the entire empire covered more than 2,500 miles.

What were some contributions made by the Persians?

Teaching Options

Cooperative Learning

Have students work together in small groups to research the life of King Darius I of Persia. Each group can focus on a different aspect, such as his early achievements, military campaigns, the satrapies, trade with other countries, the Battle of Marathon, and his legacy. Then, the class may work together to prepare a visual report on his life and accomplishments.

D. The Phoenicians

At the same time that large empires were being formed in Mesopotamia, smaller city-states, such as Phoenicia, made their own contributions to civilization. The Phoenicians lived along the coast of the Mediterranean Sea in cities such as Tyre, Byblos, and Sidon.

Phoenicians and Trade

The Phoenician sailors were the greatest of the ancient world. They were also famed as traders. In small wooden boats, they boldly sailed the Mediterranean Sea to trade with peoples throughout the region. Some Phoenicians may even have sailed as far away as present-day Great Britain and southern Africa. To promote trade, the Phoenicians also set up colonies along the Mediterranean region in places such as Cyprus, Carthage, Sicily, and southern Spain. A colony is a place settled and ruled by people from a distant land.

Among the Phoenicians' most important trade products were lumber and purple dye that only they knew how to make from sea snails. The dye was so highly prized that it became the color of royalty.

A New Alphabet

The greatest of all Phoenician achievements was the development of a new alphabet, which eventually was spread throughout the regions in which the Phoenicians traded. The Phoenicians simplified cuneiform—the Sumerian writing system. This cuneiform system used more than 900 symbols. The Phoenician system used only 22, with each symbol, or letter, representing a single sound in speech. Later, the Greeks added more symbols, as vowels, to the Phoenicians' alphabet. This is what the English alphabet is based upon today.

◆ **How did the Phoenicians promote trade?**

Spotlight on
Economics

TRADE AT CARTHAGE
Carthage was a Phoenician city-state for about 400 years. One reason for its success in trade was its location on a peninsula and its two harbors. From Carthage, much trade in the western Mediterranean Sea was conducted. Trade for minerals in Spanish cities was especially important to Carthage.

Review III

Review History

A. Why were the Akkadians able to establish the first empire in history?

B. Why is Hammurabi remembered as a great ruler?

C. What was the Royal Road?

D. How did the Phoenician alphabet change the cuneiform system?

Define Terms to Know

Define the following terms:
patriarchal, satrap

Critical Thinking

Which of the empires in the Fertile Crescent do you think has had the most lasting effect on the world and why?

Write About Culture

Write an editorial about the Sumerian and Phoenician contributions to the development of writing.

Get Organized

IDEA WEB
Use an idea web to organize information from this section. Choose a topic and then find related facts. For example, what were the accomplishments of the Phoenicians?

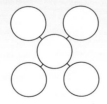

D. The Phoenicians

Purpose-Setting Question How did the geography of Phoenicia determine the way the people earned their livelihood? (They lived along the coast, so they became sailors and traders.)

Extend Point out that in the city-states of Tyre and Sidon, the Phoenicians produced the finest purple dye for clothing. Explain that this dye was extracted from a mollusk found on the Mediterranean shore and was extremely expensive to process. The high price made it accessible only to the extremely rich, mostly royalty. It later became known as "royal purple."

SPOTLIGHT ON ECONOMICS

TRADE AT CARTHAGE Explain that the Carthaginians had a monopoly on trade in the western Mediterranean Sea. Point out that *monopoly* is the exclusive control of a commodity, making it possible to regulate its price and supply, and to eliminate competition. Ask what the Carthaginians could probably do because of their monopoly on minerals from Spanish cities. (raise and lower the price of minerals at will; stop selling minerals to those they wanted to punish; destroy ships of competitors)

◆ **ANSWER** The Phoenicians promoted trade by setting up colonies along the Mediterranean region.

Section Close

Ask students what advances the Akkadians, Babylonians, Assyrians, Persians, and Phoenicians made and why it is valuable to study these ancient civilizations.

3 Assess

Review Answers

Review History

A. The Akkadians had a strong leader in Sargon and adopted many parts of the Sumerian civilization.

B. for building palaces and temples and recording his code of laws

C. It was an important route that made travel and communication easier in the Persian Empire.

D. The Phoenician alphabet, with 22 symbols, simplified the cuneiform system.

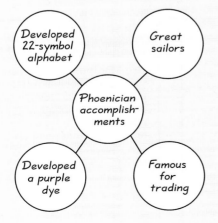

Define Terms to Know

patriarchal, 39; satrap, 40

Critical Thinking

Accept reasonable responses that are well supported.

Write About Culture

Students' editorials should address how both alphabets influenced the development of writing and how the alphabet is used today.

Section Summary

In this section, students will learn how the geography of Canaan influenced the development of the ancient civilization of the Hebrews. They will also learn how Judaism was founded, and later became a major world religion.

1 Introduce

Getting Started

Ask students how they know about their families' past. (photos, oral history, letters, precious objects) Have students discuss how archaeologists and historians know about the past of ancient peoples. (artifacts, sites, ancient writings, oral history) Point out that the beginnings of Judaism are known through the Hebrew Bible and other holy texts, as well as from artifacts and archaeological sites.

TERMS TO KNOW

Ask students to read the terms and definitions on page 42 and find each term in the section. Have students use the terms to prepare a quiz for a partner and exchange and answer quizzes.

You may wish to preview the pronunciation of the following words with students.

Canaan (KAY nuhn)
Torah (TAWR uh)
Leviticus (luh VIHT ih kuhs)
Deuteronomy (doot uhr AHN uh mee)

ACTIVE READING

Have students review what they already know about the way geography affects the development of civilizations. (Possible answer: It affects livelihood, trading, and the growth of cities.) Then, have students read subsection A to learn about the geography of Canaan and how it could affect people living there. Have students create an inference chart to record the information. (What I Already Know + What I Read = Inference)

Section IV — The Beginnings of Judaism

Terms to Know

covenant an agreement or contract

monotheism the belief that there is only one God

oral history the history of a people that is told by storytellers

Main Ideas

A. The civilization of the Hebrews, or Jewish people, began in the land of Canaan in the Fertile Crescent thousands of years ago.

B. The history of the Jewish people, as told in the Hebrew Bible, tells of their exile from Judah and how they scattered throughout the world.

Active Reading

MAKE INFERENCES
When you make inferences, you assume certain facts based on what you have read. As you read this section, think about how Hebrew society differed from other Fertile Crescent societies. Then, make inferences about how these differences have affected modern Western civilization.

A. The Land of the Hebrews

You have learned that many different groups of people, such as the Sumerians, Assyrians, Akkadians, and the Phoenicians, lived in the area of the Fertile Crescent. Yet another group who lived in the Fertile Crescent were the Hebrew people. Over time, the Hebrews came to develop their own ideas and traditions that set them apart from others living in the region.

Settling Canaan

Much is known about the early Hebrews because they recorded important events and religious instruction in a book called the Hebrew Bible. According to the first five books of the Hebrew Bible, the Hebrews were a small nomadic group of people who had once lived near the city of Ur in Mesopotamia.

✔ **Map Check**

LOCATION Between which two seas is Jerusalem located?

The Bible tells the story of a man named Abraham who brought the Hebrews from Mesopotamia to a land called Canaan. According to the Bible, God spoke to Abraham, and together they agreed to a contract, or **covenant**. This covenant was that Abraham and all those who followed him would worship only one god. The worship of one god is called **monotheism**. In return, God promised Abraham many descendants. Abraham's descendants would become the Twelve Tribes of Israel.

By worshiping only one God, the Hebrews were very different from the other peoples who lived in the region. They worshiped many gods and regarded the Hebrews as radical, or very different from traditional ideas and ways of doing things.

Moses and the Ten Commandments

The Twelve Tribes of Israel were mainly nomadic shepherds. When drought made life in Canaan difficult, many of the Hebrews traveled west to Egypt, where a pharaoh eventually enslaved them. After many generations, a great leader, Moses, arose and led the Hebrews out of Egypt.

Teaching Options

Section 4 Resources

Teacher's Resources (TR)

Terms to Know, p. 15
Review History, p. 49
Build Your Skills, p. 83
Concept Builder, p. 218
Chapter Test, pp. 119–120
Idea Web, p. 321
Transparency 15

ESL/ELL STRATEGIES

Use Manipulatives Review with students some of the geography terms used on pages 42–43, including *region, sea,* and *desert.* Have students write each term on one side of an index card and its definition on the other side. Suggest that students save their index cards to review with a partner throughout the year.

The Ten Commandments

1. I am the Lord thy God who brought you out of the land of Egypt, out of the house of bondage: Thou shalt have no other gods before Me.

2. Thou shalt not make unto thee a graven (carved) image, or any likeness of any thing that is in heaven above, or that is in the earth beneath, or that is in the water under the earth.

3. Thou shalt not take the name of the Lord thy God in vain.

4. Remember the Sabbath day, to keep it holy.

5. Honor thy father and thy mother, that you may long endure on the land that the Lord thy God is giving you.

6. Thou shalt not kill.

7. Thou shalt not commit adultery.

8. Thou shalt not steal.

9. Thou shalt not bear false witness against thy neighbor.

10. Thou shalt not covet thy neighbor's house... nor any thing that is thy neighbor's.

(Exodus 20:2–14)

The departure from Egypt is known as the Exodus. The Hebrews crossed the Red Sea and entered the Sinai Desert. They wandered in the desert for years. It was during this time that Moses received the Ten Commandments from God. The Commandments set the basic laws of Judaism, the religion of the Hebrews. God promised to make the Hebrews His own people if they followed His laws. In time, the Hebrews reached Canaan, which according to Moses was the land that God had promised Abraham and his descendants.

Kingdoms of the Israelites

Many peoples inhabited Canaan. The Hebrews, or the Israelites as they came to be known, had to battle to gain and keep land. It was necessary for the Twelve Tribes to unify under one leader. Around 1020 B.C., Saul became the first king. He was killed in battle. David was the next king. He strengthened his control over the tribes and created a strong kingdom—Israel. Jerusalem was its capital. David also made Jerusalem a religious center.

Solomon, David's son, made Israel a rich nation. The Israelites traded with Phoenicians and Egyptians. Solomon also created a large, powerful army and improved roads and ports. The most important thing that Solomon did was to build a great Temple in Jerusalem for the worship of God.

After Solomon's death, problems began to arise. People were upset about the taxes they had to pay to support all of Solomon's projects. The unity between the Twelve Tribes weakened. The tribes split into two separate kingdoms. The kingdom to the north continued to be called the kingdom of Israel. Its capital was Samaria. The kingdom of Judah, centered on Jerusalem, was to the south.

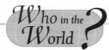

Who in the World?

DAVID
The second king of Israel and the one who ruled the longest was David. The Bible calls him a great warrior as well as a musician and poet. He established Israel as a major power in the area and expanded its territory.

David moved the Ark of the Covenant, the chest that contained the stone tablets with the Ten Commandments, to Jerusalem, making the city the spiritual center of Israel.

Ask students to study the relief sculpture at the bottom of page 44 from the Palace of Sennacherib at Nineveh. Ask what it tells historians about the exile of the Jewish people in Babylon. (The captives, entire families, traveled in oxen-driven carts or walked barefoot with their baggage.)

Discuss Tell students that some Jews chose to remain in Babylon. Ask students why they think some Jews decided not to return to Judah after the Persians conquered the Babylonian Empire. (They had established a life there—family, trade, personal relationships, wealth. It was easier to stay than to start a new life in a place only a few could remember.)

 ANSWER The stories, laws, and legends that were part of their oral history helped the Jewish people keep their traditions alive and their religious beliefs intact.

B. The Development of Judaism

Purpose-Setting Question
Why are the Dead Sea Scrolls so important? (They provide information about the Torah and the Hebrew Bible and are some of the oldest known copies of text from the Hebrew Bible.)

Activity

Make a timeline Have students research to find dates and events for a timeline of Jewish history. Possible events include the Babylonian captivity (586 B.C.), the rebuilding of the Temple in Jerusalem (538 B.C.), and the Jewish diaspora after the Persians were conquered (333 B.C.). Students can use the timeline (TR, page 320) to record the information.

Extend Judaism is considered to be the oldest monotheistic religion in the world today. Discuss with students other monotheistic religions that exist today. (Christianity and Islam) Use Transparency 15 to discover the areas where Judaism is practiced today.

The divided kingdoms remained independent for several hundred years until 721 B.C. when Assyria overwhelmed Israel. Most of the Israelites were forced to move to Assyria. After a few generations, these tribes became part of the Assyrian population and culture. Judah, the southern kingdom, survived for another 150 years until the king of Babylonia conquered it.

The Babylonian Captivity

The Babylonians captured Jerusalem and destroyed Solomon's great Temple. They also enslaved the people of Judah and sent them to Babylon. The people of Judah, who now became known as Jews, were held captive, or against their will, in Babylon for about 50 years. That is why this event has come to be called the Babylonian Captivity. During this time, the leaders and priests of Judah tried to keep the Jewish captives united and faithful to their religion. It is believed that during this time much of the **oral history**, or spoken history of the Jewish people, was written down.

When the Persians conquered the Babylonian Empire, the Jews were allowed to return to their kingdom. Upon their return to Jerusalem, they rebuilt the city and the Temple, and lived under Persian control.

◆ **What happened during the Babylonian Captivity that helped the Jews keep their identity?**

B. The Development of Judaism

The covenant that Abraham had made with God established Judaism as a monotheistic religion. The idea of a covenant between God and a people has lasted for centuries and is an idea that still influences religions today.

The Torah

To the Jewish people, the Torah is the most sacred text. The word *Torah* means "instruction" in the Hebrew language. The Torah was given by God to Moses, and then passed to the Jewish people.

The Torah most often refers to the Five Books—Genesis, Exodus, Leviticus, Numbers, and Deuteronomy. The first book of the Torah is Genesis, which

This relief sculpture shows the Jewish people leaving Jerusalem. About 30,000 Jews were forced into captivity in Babylon.

Teaching Options

F Y I

Babylonian Captivity
While in Babylon, the Jewish people built houses, businesses, and raised families. They gathered together on market days for a combination of worship and study. Some historians believe that these gatherings eventually became worship services. During this time, formal prayers were composed. When the exiled Jews returned to their kingdom, they took these prayers with them.

Test Taking
Remind students to read questions carefully. If they read too quickly, they may miss clues such as *some*, *all*, or *not* and choose the wrong answer. Ask students what clues are in these questions. (*not, some*)

• Which was not a factor in the formation of Jewish religious law?

• *T* or *F*: Some Jews decided to remain in Babylon.

tells the story of creation, Abraham and his covenant with God, and the story of Abraham's descendants. The second book is Exodus, which tells about the flight from Egypt. The next three books of the Torah are Leviticus, Numbers, and Deuteronomy. These books include Jewish laws and religious instruction.

In 1947, a collection of papers written in Hebrew and other languages was found in a cave near the Dead Sea. Many scholars consider the papers, called the Dead Sea Scrolls, to be the most important archaeological discovery of modern times. They provide much information about the Torah and the Hebrew Bible. The Hebrew Bible, or scriptures, is composed of 24 books, including the Five Books of the Torah. Before these scrolls were found, the oldest copies of text from the Hebrew Bible dated from around 800 A.D.

Laws and Justice

Another important part of the Hebrew Bible are the books that record the sayings of men who spoke in God's name, and reminded the Jewish people that they had responsibilities toward God and toward all people. They said to be fair, to share with neighbors, to care for those in need, and to show compassion for others. One of these men, Isaiah, spoke of God's desire that war between nations would end, and that all people would live in peace.

Judaism—a Major World Religion

The kingdom of Judah survived until about 63 B.C., when the Jews were forced to leave their homeland. After leaving their kingdom, Jews lived in many other parts of the world. Wherever they settled, however, Jews continued to follow the laws and traditions of their faith. Just as in ancient times, these traditions set Jews apart from other people, yet they also helped to bind Jewish people together. Throughout thousands of years, Jewish people have kept their ancient covenant that God made with Abraham, and as a result, have made Judaism one of the world's major religions.

◆ **Why is the Torah important to the Jewish religion?**

The Torah is the most sacred writing in the Jewish religion. The Hebrew word *Torah* means "instruction."

Review IV

Review History
A. Why was Solomon important to the kingdom of Israel?
B. Where did Jewish people live after they left the kingdom of Judah?

Define Terms to Know
Define the following terms:
covenant, monotheism, oral history

Critical Thinking
Why do you think the sacred writings of the Jews have lasted into the twenty-first century?

Write About Citizenship
Write an editorial supporting Jewish belief that God expects people to be fair and show compassion for others.

Get Organized
IDEA WEB
Use an idea web to organize information from this section. Choose a topic and then find related facts. For example, who are some of the important early figures in Jewish history?

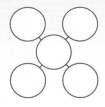

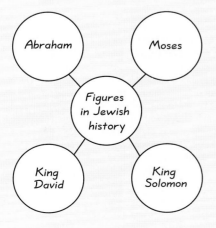

Critical Thinking
Answers will vary. Accept reasonable responses supported by accurate information.

Write About Citizenship
Answers will vary but should focus on the emphasis in the Hebrew Bible that God expects his followers to treat others well. Editorials should support the Jewish belief and explain why.

TEACH PRIMARY SOURCES
Ask students to view carefully the photo of the Torah and the case or covering that holds it. Explain that the Torah is in a very decorative covering. Many of these coverings are made of gold or silver. Others are made of fabric, such as velvet with gold or other colored trim. The purpose of this covering is to protect and beautify the Torah.

Have students discuss reasons why the Torah has been encased. (The Torah is very valuable; it needs to be kept clean, untouched, untorn.) Point out that when it is read, a pointer called a yad is used to follow along in the text.

Explore Have students learn more about the Dead Sea Scrolls and their significance to Jewish history by conducting research at the library or on the Internet. Have students make posters that explain how the Dead Sea Scrolls were found and why this archaeological discovery was so exciting.

◆ **ANSWER** The Torah tells about Jewish law and tradition. Throughout the centuries, it has provided, and continues to provide, instruction about the history and teachings of the Jewish people.

Section Close
Ask students what advances the Jewish people made and why it is valuable to study their history.

3 Assess

Review Answers

Review History
A. Solomon made Israel rich. He created a powerful army and improved ports and roads. Most importantly, he built the Temple in Jerusalem for the worship of God.

B. After leaving the kingdom of Judah, Jewish people spread throughout the world, keeping their faith and observing their traditions.

Define Terms to Know
covenant, 42; monotheism, 42; oral history, 44

CHAPTER
2
Review

Chapter Summary

A blank outline form is available in the Teacher's Resources (TR, p. 318). Chapter summaries should outline the civilizations of Egypt, Mesopotamia, Sumer, Babylon, Assyria, Persia, Phoenicia, and the kingdoms of ancient Israel. Refer to the rubric in the Teacher's Resources (p. 340) to score students' chapter summaries.

🌑 Interpret the Timeline

1. the invention of the wheel
2. 1700 B.C.
3. Answers will vary. Students may say the invention of the wheel or writing.
4. Check students' timelines to be sure that all events are in the chapter.

Use Terms to Know

5. oral history
6. satrap
7. patriarchal
8. hieroglyphics
9. monotheism
10. pharaoh
11. theocracy
12. delta
13. covenant

Check Your Understanding

14. Early Egypt was divided into two parts—the southern part was called Upper Egypt and the northern part was called Lower Egypt.
15. Egyptians believed in one main god over all the lesser gods. The king was half divine. People wanted to lead a good life because it meant that they would have a happy afterlife. For this purpose, bodies were preserved and buried with many possessions.
16. The king was at the top, and high priests, government people, landowners, army officers, and doctors were in the upper class. The merchants and craftspeople were in the middle class. The unskilled laborers—mostly farmers—were in the lower class. Enslaved people were in the lowest class.
17. Both societies depended on rivers to water their crops and to provide good soil; and in both places, people needed to work together to irrigate their crops. The Egyptians grew grains, vegetables, fruits, flax, and papyrus. The Mesopotamians grew wheat, barley,

peas, lentils, carrots, and turnips.
18. The Sumerians invented the wheel, a writing system, the plow, the arch, the dome, the sail, the vault, brick molds, ovens for baking bread, and pottery for storage.
19. The Code of Hammurabi was a collection of laws for an entire empire and tried to deal with all aspects of life. The code helped to unify many different peoples.

20. The Assyrians invented the battering ram, short sword, shields, and helmet.
21. The Persian Empire stretched from Egypt to India and needed a system of roads so that the king could keep in touch with all parts of it. The empire was divided into small regions. Each region was called a satrap.

22. The Phoenicians are remembered for trading and developing a new alphabet.
23. King David created a strong kingdom. He made Jerusalem the capital and religious center of ancient Israel.
24. Genesis, Exodus, Leviticus, Numbers, Deuteronomy

Chapter Summary

Complete the following outline in your notebook. Then, use your outline to write a brief summary of the chapter.

Ancient Civilizations

I. Ancient Egypt
   A. The Nile River and Its Valley
   B. The Kingdoms of Ancient Egypt
   C. Religion, Government, and Society
   D. Hieroglyphics and Writing

II. Mesopotamia and Sumer
   A. The Land Between Two Rivers
   B. Sumerian Civilization

III. Empires of Ancient Mesopotamia
   A. The First Empire
   B. The Babylonian and Assyrian Empires
   C. The Persian Empire
   D. The Phoenicians

IV. The Beginnings of Judaism
   A. The Land of the Hebrews
   B. The Development of Judaism

🌑 Interpret the Timeline

Use the timeline on pages 22–23 to answer the following questions.

1. Which occurred first, the invention of the wheel or the rule of Hammurabi?

2. In which year did the New Kingdom begin in Egypt?

3. **Critical Thinking** Describe an event on the timeline that marked an important turning point in history and technology.

4. Select four events from the chapter that are not on the timeline. Create a timeline that shows these events.

Use Terms to Know

Select the term that best completes each sentence.

covenant	monotheism	pharaoh
delta	oral history	satrap
hieroglyphics	patriarchal	theocracy

5. The history of a people that is told by storytellers is called _____.

6. A _____ was a Persian governor.

7. A culture in which men are the most powerful is called a _____ society.

8. _____ was the writing used in ancient Egypt.

9. _____ is a belief in one God.

10. _____ was a title given to the rulers of ancient Egypt.

11. _____ is a form of government in which a god is regarded as the supreme ruler and power is in the hands of religious leaders.

12. Soil deposited at the mouth of a river forms land called a _____.

13. A promise made between God and the Israelites is called a _____.

Check Your Understanding

14. **Explain** how Egypt was divided.

15. **Discuss** the religion of ancient Egypt.

16. **Describe** the organization of ancient Egyptian society.

17. **Compare** the agricultural conditions in ancient Egypt and Mesopotamia.

18. **Summarize** the achievements of the Sumerians.

19. **Describe** the Code of Hammurabi.

20. **Identify** the Assyrian military inventions.

21. **Describe** the Persian Empire during the reign of Cyrus the Great.

22. **Discuss** the two contributions the Phoenicians are remembered for.

23. **Discuss** the importance of King David to the kingdom of Israel.

24. **Identify** the Five Books of the Torah.

Critical Thinking

25. **Synthesize Information** Why do you think that so many empires of the Fertile Crescent were conquered?

26. **Compare and Contrast** How do you think the lives of Egyptian women differed from those of Assyrian women?

27. **Analyze Primary Sources** Which one of the Ten Commandments listed on page 43 emphasized how the Hebrews were set apart from other peoples at that time?

Put Your Skills to Work

28. **Read a Historical Map** You have learned how to read a historical map to help you understand events in a given time period. Study the map below. Then, answer the following questions.

    a. What information is shown in the key?

    b. What do the arrows on the map show?

    c. What other information does the map show?

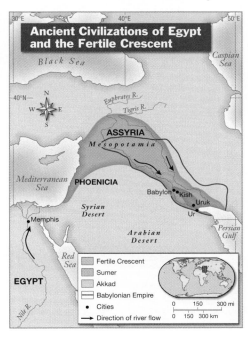

Analyze Sources

29. Read an Egyptian teacher's advice to his students. Then, answer the questions that follow.

    Do not give your heart to pleasures, or you shall be a failure. Write with your hand, read with your mouth, and take advice of those who know more than you. Be a scribe [person who writes]. It saves you from toil . . . and spares you torment, as you are not under many lords and numerous masters. He who works in writing is not taxed.

    Papyrus Anastasi III, Caminos 83;
    Papyrus Anastasi II, Caminos 51

    a. According to the author, from whom should you take advice?

    b. What were the advantages of being a scribe?

Essay Writing

30. Write a short essay in which you describe some of the reasons that the culture and technology of ancient civilizations might have developed in different ways.

Critical Thinking

25. There were always uprisings from within and without.
26. Egyptian women had more rights, so they were freer to move about in society. They could conduct business and earn a living. If they wanted to, they could divorce their husbands. They were probably happier because of their freedom.
27. The second of the Ten Commandments is about monotheism, which is the worship of one god. By worshiping one god, the Hebrews were very different from other peoples who lived in the same region.

Put Your Skills to Work

READ A HISTORICAL MAP

28a. The map key contains colored boxes for the Fertile Crescent, different empires, cities, a symbol for the direction the river flowed, and a scale.
28b. Each arrow shows the direction in which a river flows.
28c. The map shows rivers, some countries, bodies of water, and deserts.

Analyze Sources

29a. You should take advice from those who know more than you.
29b. It saves you from toil and spares you torment, because you are not under many lords and masters. People who are scribes are not taxed.

Essay Writing

30. Check that students' essays include a sufficient number of factors that may have contributed to differences among ancient civilizations such as geography, climate, natural resources, inventiveness, strength of rulers, religion, and roles of women. Also, check for correct use of grammar, punctuation, and spelling.

Ancient India
2500 B.C.–A.D. 500
(pp. 48–71)

Chapter Objectives
- Discuss how the geography of south Asia led to the development of civilization.
- Explain how the Aryan people affected society and religion.
- Contrast the religions of Hinduism and Buddhism.
- Contrast the civilizations of the Mauryan Empire and the Gupta Empire.

Chapter Summary
Section I focuses on the rise of and disappearance of the Indus Valley civilization that developed on the subcontinent of south Asia.

Section II identifies the Aryans as a nomadic people who were a major influence on society and religion in the region between 1500 B.C. and 1000 B.C.

Section III discusses the differences between the dominant religions on the subcontinent, Hinduism and Buddhism.

Section IV explores the differences between the Mauryan Empire and the Gupta Empire.

Set the Stage
TEACH PRIMARY SOURCES

Explain that Krishna is speaking to the warrior Arjuna as both an individual and the divine incarnation of one of the Hindu gods. Thus, he can tell Arjuna that to fight in the war is his religious and moral duty—he must accept the caste into which he was born. Discuss with students Arjuna's feeling about fighting. (grief) Then, discuss possible reasons for Arjuna's feelings.

CHAPTER 3

Ancient India
2500 B.C.—A.D. 500

I. Indus Valley Civilization
II. Aryan Civilization
III. Hinduism and Buddhism
IV. Ancient Indian Dynasties

Who am I? What am I to do? How should I see things? These are questions that Krishna answers for his friend Arjuna in the sacred Hindu text the *Mahabharata*. The conversation between the two begins when Arjuna sees his friends and relatives ready to fight in a battle and he is overcome by grief. He gives up his determination to fight when he thinks about all the people who might die in the battle. Krishna says to him,

> ❝ *But if you refuse to fight in this righteous war, you will be turning aside from your duty. You will be a sinner and will be disgraced. People will speak ill of you throughout the ages.* ❞

To the ancient peoples of India, religion played a major role in their lives. One of their religions, Hinduism, placed great emphasis on duty and personal sacrifice. The beliefs of the three main religions of ancient India—Hinduism, Buddhism, and Jainism—helped shape the Indian civilization. All three religions are still practiced today.

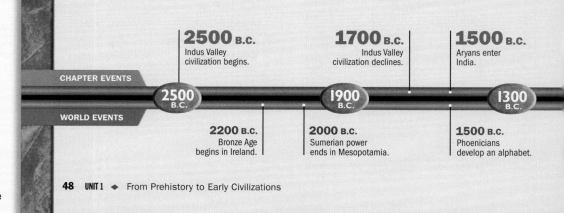

CHAPTER EVENTS

2500 B.C.
Indus Valley civilization begins.

1700 B.C.
Indus Valley civilization declines.

1500 B.C.
Aryans enter India.

2500 B.C. 1900 B.C. 1300 B.C.

WORLD EVENTS

2200 B.C.
Bronze Age begins in Ireland.

2000 B.C.
Sumerian power ends in Mesopotamia.

1500 B.C.
Phoenicians develop an alphabet.

48 UNIT 1 ◆ From Prehistory to Early Civilizations

Teaching Options

Chapter 3 Resources

REVIEW

Teacher's Resources (TR)
Terms to Know, p. 16
Review History, p. 50
Build Your Skills, p. 84
Concept Builder, p. 219
Chapter Test, pp. 121–122
Main Idea/Supporting Details Chart, p. 319
Transparencies 7, 10

ASSESSMENT
Section Reviews, pp. 54, 60, 64, 69
Chapter Review, pp. 70–71
Chapter Test, TR, pp. 121–122

ALTERNATIVE ASSESSMENT
Portfolio Project, p. 96
Write a Play, p. T96

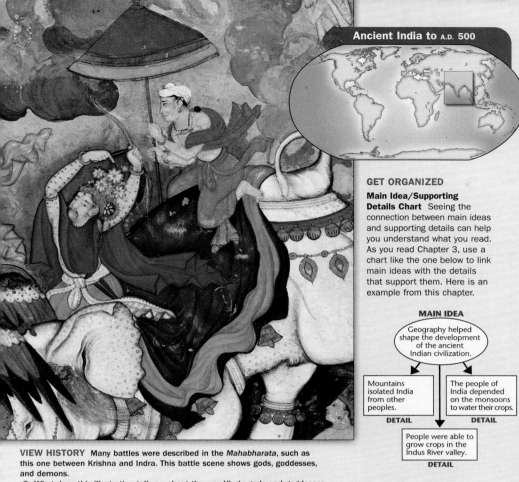

GET ORGANIZED

Main Idea/Supporting Details Chart Seeing the connection between main ideas and supporting details can help you understand what you read. As you read Chapter 3, use a chart like the one below to link main ideas with the details that support them. Here is an example from this chapter.

MAIN IDEA

Geography helped shape the development of the ancient Indian civilization.

Mountains isolated India from other peoples.
DETAIL

The people of India depended on the monsoons to water their crops.
DETAIL

People were able to grow crops in the Indus River valley.
DETAIL

VIEW HISTORY Many battles were described in the *Mahabharata*, such as this one between Krishna and Indra. This battle scene shows gods, goddesses, and demons.

➤ What does this illustration tell you about the way Hindu gods and goddesses were represented?

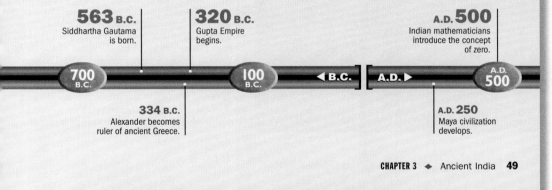

563 B.C.
Siddhartha Gautama is born.

320 B.C.
Gupta Empire begins.

A.D. 500
Indian mathematicians introduce the concept of zero.

700 B.C.

100 B.C.

◄ B.C.

A.D. ►

A.D. 500

334 B.C.
Alexander becomes ruler of ancient Greece.

A.D. 250
Maya civilization develops.

CHAPTER 3 ◆ Ancient India **49**

Chapter Themes
- Culture
- Time, Continuity, and Change
- People, Places, and Environments
- Individual Development and Identity
- Power, Authority, and Governance
- Production, Distribution, and Consumption
- Global Connections

F Y I
The Vedic Gods

There are more than 33 gods mentioned in the Veda. The Vedic gods exist on three planes—in the heavens, in the atmosphere, and on Earth. The gods can share power with one another. Indra is one of the chief gods. He is a warrior god and god of rain and thunder. He is known for killing the drought demon Vritra.

VIEW HISTORY
Discuss with students the use of color in this painting. Ask them if the colors blend together or seem to fight one another. (fight one another) Then, ask them how these colors help to convey the message of the painting. (The contrasting colors remind the viewer that there is a battle taking place.)

◆ **ANSWER** Possible answers: They were sometimes shown as animals; they were shown very strong and powerful; they were shown very colorful; they were shown with elements of nature.

GET ORGANIZED
Main Idea/Supporting Details Chart
Point out the main idea and supporting details in the chart. Suggest that students begin with a main idea, which they find by reading the headings and subheadings, and add details as they read the text.

⬤ TEACH THE TIMELINE
The timeline on pages 48–49 covers the period between 2500 B.C. and A.D. 500. Remind students that years labeled B.C. occurred before the birth of Jesus and count down to year one. Years labeled A.D. or *anno Domini*, Latin for "in the year of the Lord," count up from the year one to the present day.

Have students find the Chapter and World Events that discuss the ancient civilizations. (Indus Valley civilization begins, Sumerian power ends in Mesopotamia, Indus Valley civilization declines, Alexander becomes ruler of ancient Greece, Gupta Empire begins, Maya civilization develops.)

Activity

Make a timeline Have students look for some other interesting events that occurred between 2500 B.C. and A.D. 500. Make a classroom timeline with the additional events students find.

CHAPTER 3 ◆ **T49**

Section Summary

In this section, students will learn how the geography of the subcontinent affected the development and decline of the Indus Valley civilization. They will also learn about the archaeological evidence of the economic and cultural life of the people of Harappa and Mohenjo-Daro.

1 Introduce

Getting Started

Ask students to identify some geographic features of their city or town. Encourage them to suggest how these features have influenced the development of their city or town. Ask students how they think their city or town would change if it was isolated from other parts of the country.

TERMS TO KNOW

Ask students to read the terms and definitions on page 50 and then find each term in the section. After students have read the section, have them use the terms in sentences that clearly demonstrate their meanings.

You may wish to preview the pronunciation of the following terms from this section with students.

Khyber Pass (KY buhr PAS)
Deccan Plateau
  (DEHK uhn pla TOH)
Thar (TAHR)
Harappa (huh RA puh)
Mohenjo-Daro
  (moh HEHN joh DAHR oh)

ACTIVE READING

Have students use a cause-and-effect chain (TR, p. 325) to keep track of the cause-and-effect relationships in this section. Instruct them to write the event in the middle box, the cause in the top oval, and the effect in the bottom oval.

Indus Valley Civilization

Terms to Know

subcontinent a large part of a continent that is geographically separated from the rest of the continent

plateau a raised area of level land

monsoon a seasonal wind that creates a strong pattern of wet and dry seasons in parts of Asia

citadel a fort that commands a city

Fertile fields lay below the foothills of the Himalayas in Kulu Valley, India.

Main Ideas

A. Geography helped shape the development of the Indus Valley civilization.

B. The Indus Valley civilization was the first great civilization of ancient India.

C. Excavations at the sites of the ancient cities of Harappa and Mohenjo-Daro reveal many similarities in the way the cities were planned.

D. Many questions remain about the Indus Valley civilization and the reason it disappeared.

Active Reading

CAUSE AND EFFECT
Determining causes and effects helps you to understand what happened and why. As you read this section, ask yourself the following question: What factors caused the rise of the Indus Valley civilization as well as its decline and disappearance?

A. The Geography of South Asia

South Asia, which includes modern-day India, Pakistan, and Bangladesh, is a land of geographical contrasts. The region is located on a **subcontinent**. Geographically set off from the rest of Asia by mountains and water, the subcontinent forms a triangle. Its broadest part is in the north, and its narrowest part in the south. Wide expanses of ocean surround the lower part of the Indian subcontinent, making it a large, wide peninsula.

The Land, the Mountains, and the Rivers

The northern border of the Indian subcontinent is marked by the rough but beautiful Himalayas, the world's tallest mountains. These mountains made it difficult for people to enter India by land. The famous Khyber Pass, which is actually a narrow footpath cut into the Himalayas, was one of the only ways that people could cross the mountains into India.

South of the Himalayas is the Indo-Gangetic Plain, a plain that is watered by the Indus, the Ganges, and the Brahmaputra Rivers. It is a fertile area in which farming is possible. To the south of these two rivers is the Deccan Plateau. This **plateau**, or raised area of level land, makes up most of the interior of the Indian subcontinent. It has low hills and shallow valleys. The Western Ghats, a low-lying mountain range, lie along the western edge of the Deccan Plateau, while the Eastern Ghats stretch along the coast of the Bay of Bengal. In the western interior, the Thar, or Great Indian, Desert, bakes in India's heat.

The coastal plains lie on the eastern coast of India facing the Bay of Bengal. When people first lived in the area of the coastal plain thousands of years ago, they used the seas for fishing and trade.

Teaching Options

Section 1 Resources

Teacher's Resources (TR)
  Terms to Know, p. 16
  Review History, p. 50
  Build Your Skills, p. 84
  Concept Builder, p. 219
  Main Idea/Supporting Details Chart,
    p. 319
  Transparencies 7, 10

ESL/ELL STRATEGIES

Summarize Tell students that reading the headings in a textbook is a good way to preview the section content. Have students read the head of Section 1, subsection A. Then, ask them to write a sentence predicting the content. Finally, have them read that subsection and see whether the prediction was accurate.

The Climate

The climate of the Indian subcontinent varies quite a bit. India's climate is shaped by a weather pattern called a **monsoon**. Monsoons are characterized by seasonal winds from the Indian Ocean. The monsoon winds bring very heavy rainfall during part of the year. However, the winds reverse directions at certain times of the year, so dry seasons alternate with the wet ones.

The monsoons from the ocean last from about mid-June to early October. Moisture-bearing winds from the Indian Ocean drop heavy rainfall across the subcontinent, causing heavy flooding in some areas. The effects of the monsoon rains are felt most near the Bay of Bengal. Locations in that area receive some of the heaviest rainfall in the world, with an annual average of 450 inches. The people of India depend on monsoons to water their crops. However, if the rain is too heavy, floods can wash away entire villages. Between October and May, the monsoons blow from the land out to sea. During these months, the winds bring cooler, drier weather from central Asia.

Another feature of India's climate is the high temperatures. The Thar Desert and the Deccan Plateau are hot for much of the year. Temperatures in the desert region often rise as high as 123°F and as high as 100°F on the Deccan Plateau.

◆ **Which geographic features separate south Asia from the rest of Asia?**

B. The Indus Valley Civilization

Ancient India's first great civilization is called the Indus Valley civilization. The Indus Valley civilization was located in what is now Pakistan and northwestern India. The civilization existed for about 1,000 years and then vanished. Archaeologists have yet to uncover all the sites in the Indus Valley civilization. Our knowledge of this ancient culture comes almost completely from archaeological findings.

Farming and Trade

The geography of south Asia provided an attractive environment for humans. The Himalayas form a protective barrier from the harsh, northern winds blowing in from central Asia. Mountain passes to the northwest and the northeast of the Himalayas provided entries for people to enter the northern part of the subcontinent thousands of years ago. From there, people could have spread out to form settlements throughout the region. Around 3500 B.C., increasing numbers of human settlements began to appear in the Indus Valley region.

The Indus Valley people had many items to use for trade. Skilled craftspeople in the cities wove cotton and made jewelry and furniture. Potters made cooking utensils, as well as writing sticks, back scratchers, dice, and game pieces. Outside the cities, most of the people in the Indus Valley were farmers. They raised wheat, barley, cotton, and fruit on farmlands near the cities. Their technology was based on stone, copper, and bronze materials.

Indus Valley Civilization, 2500–1500 B.C.

Map Check

LOCATION Which geographical features made expansion of the Indus Valley civilization difficult?

Do You Remember?
In Chapter 1, you learned that around 4500 B.C. people in eastern Europe and western Asia began finding copper in riverbeds.

CHAPTER 3 ◆ Ancient India **51**

2 Teach

A. The Geography of South Asia

Purpose-Setting Question
What were the major industries of the subcontinent and where were they located? (farming on the Indo-Gangetic plain; when people lived on the coastal plains, they used the sea for fishing and trading)

Activity

Analyze the photograph Have students study the photograph on page 50. Then, ask students to describe what the weather there might have been like (warm) and what economic activities might take place there. (farming)

Using the Map

Indus Valley Civilization, 2500–1500 B.C.

Have students locate the cities of Mohenjo-Daro and Harappa on the map. Ask them to identify the river that runs near the two cities. (Indus River) Then, discuss how the river might have helped the growth of the civilization. (The river provided water for drinking and growing crops.)

Map Check
Answer mountains, Arabian Sea, and Thar Desert

◆ **ANSWER** Himalayas and Hindu Kush Mountains, Arabian Sea, Indian Ocean, and Bay of Bengal

B. The Indus Valley Civilization

Purpose-Setting Question
What are some occupations of the people of the Indus Valley civilization? (craftspeople, traders, and farmers)

Do You Remember?
Tell students that people discovered that mixing copper and tin made a stronger metal called bronze around 3000 B.C. Using the timeline on pages 48–49, find the year when the Bronze Age appeared on the continent of Europe. (2200 B.C., the Bronze Age begins in Ireland.)

Cooperative Learning

Have groups of students work together to pick an object that would best represent them as a group in the future. Each group should write a short speech about why it chose the object and present it to the class. Then have the class discuss all the objects and suggest what these objects would tell people in the future about them.

Using Technology

Have pairs of students use an Internet search engine to find out more information on how monsoons affect people on the subcontinent today. Have them choose key words for their search and write down the addresses of the Web sites they find. Finally, ask them to discuss how weather affects their lives.

Explore Ask students to discuss what we can learn from an artifact, such as a chessboard, about the culture of the people of Harappa. (A chessboard is part of a game, which may indicate that there was time for leisure activities in Harappa. Leisure pursuits are more common in wealthy societies where free time is an affordable luxury.)

◆ ANSWER People from other regions most likely came through mountain passes to the northwest and northeast of the Himalayas to enter south Asia.

C. The Cities of Harappa and Mohenjo-Daro

Purpose-Setting Question

What were some important elements of the cities of Harappa and Mohenjo-Daro? (There were houses with plumbing; cities were arranged according to grid patterns; citadels were constructed at the tops of hills with brick enclosures; bathhouses and granaries were located within the citadels.)

Discuss Ask students who they think might have lived at the residence in the citadel. (a ruler, a town manager) Then, ask students for reasons why food granaries were located inside the citadel. (to protect food from invaders; so the ruler could control distribution; to reserve grain in times of famine) Finally, have students discuss why a public bathhouse was located within the fortress. (The bathhouse may have been considered an important common meeting place.)

Artifacts such as this chessboard and terra cotta pot were discovered in the ruins of the ancient city of Harappa, pictured at the bottom of the page.

A Network of Settlements

The settlements of the Indus Valley had links with other villages located on or near the Indus River and beyond the Indus Valley itself. Over time, a gradual change occurred among some settlements that were located far from certain types of raw materials. For example, stone tools and beads began to appear in those villages even though the stones used were not found in the area. People in the villages must have imported, or brought in, the stones from other areas. This suggests they had a trade connection with other villages.

◆ **Where did people from other regions most likely enter south Asia?**

C. The Cities of Harappa and Mohenjo-Daro

The two largest Indus Valley archaeological locations are Harappa and Mohenjo-Daro. Modern-day excavations were first begun in these ancient cities in 1921. Each city probably covered about 1 square mile. Both locations have a similar layout and show careful planning.

The main streets of the cities formed a well-organized grid system, with streets running parallel to one another. Each settlement had a huge building that sat on top of a hill. This **citadel**, or fortress, was surrounded by a massive brick wall. Inside, the citadel had a public bathhouse, a residential building, and granaries, or buildings for storing grain. It seems clear that someone planned and directed the building of the cities. They could hardly have grown into such a regular pattern on their own.

Teaching Options

Meet Individual Needs:
VISUAL/SPATIAL LEARNERS

Have students plan and design their own city. Encourage them to follow the layout of Mohenjo-Daro and Harappa. Students should draw a street map of the city. The map should include a key, and all labeled items should be accompanied by short descriptive paragraphs. Students should also include a paragraph explaining the structure of the government of the city.

ESL/ELL STRATEGIES

Use Visuals Have students describe the artifacts and photograph on page 52. Create a list on the board of their descriptions. Encourage students to make connections between the descriptions listed on the board and the information in the text about the geography and culture of the Indus Valley.

Building Houses

The most common building material at Harappa and Mohenjo-Daro was brick. The sizes of houses varied from one-room barracks to large homes with central courtyards. Many of the larger homes had upper stories. Some had private wells for drinking and bath water. Excavated parts of Mohenjo-Daro show that families were housed in certain areas of the settlement, according to their specialized work.

The plumbing in these settlements was the most advanced in the world. Houses had bathrooms with drains. Water and sewage ran out through pipes into larger drains that ran under the streets.

Communication and Crafts

Many historians believe that frequent contact among the settlements of the Indus Valley must have occurred. One reason they believe this is because Indus Valley goods have been found in several neighboring areas, and goods from other areas have been found in the Indus Valley.

People of the Indus Valley may have been seafarers and traders who sailed along the coastline and on the region's many rivers. At sites throughout the valley, archaeologists have found gold from settlements in southern India, copper from settlements in present-day Afghanistan and India, and turquoise from settlements in present-day Iran.

Indus pottery found its way to Mesopotamia. Indus Valley seals, used to stamp labels on trade goods, have been found by archaeologists as far away as Sumer. This indicates that the people of these regions traded with one another.

Various objects found by archaeologists tell about games and toys of the Indus people. They had dice and stone marbles. The spots on the dice were arranged in exactly the same pattern that we use today. Among the toys were a clay monkey that could be made to slide down a string and a clay bull that wiggled its head.

◆ **What evidence suggests that there was communication among the different settlements?**

D. Culture, Religion, and Decline

Archaeological evidence from the Indus Valley civilization continues to be unearthed and analyzed. This newfound knowledge will eventually lead to a greater understanding of the Indus Valley civilization. At that time, historians may learn why it ultimately disappeared.

Writing and Language

One of the greatest unsolved mysteries about the Indus Valley civilization is the language of the Indus people. It appears that they had some sort of writing, but it is unclear what language they spoke. Archaeologists have found some seals with a type of script carved on them. However, no one knows how to read it. If we knew how to translate their language, we might learn more about the Indus people. We might discover where they came from and what happened to them.

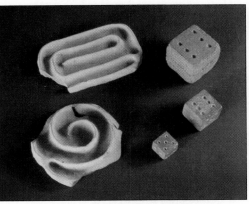

These dice and terra cotta maze games were among the artifacts found at Harappa.

Then & Now

V. GORDON CHILDE
V. Gordon Childe wrote about ancient India and noted several details of the Indus civilization that made it distinctly Indian. Some things such as *ikkas*, which are carts with a framed canopy, or top, have changed little and are still used in present-day India. Other items that have endured are uniquely Indian—seals with seated yogi gods and elaborate nose ornaments.

Activity

Use a map Have students use a map of Asia and the Middle East from the Atlas (p. A7 or Transparencies 7 and 10) to locate the places where evidence of trade has been found. Discuss how interactions with these areas may have influenced the people in the Indus Valley.

Discuss Have students discuss the role artifacts have in helping archaeologists uncover information about ancient civilizations. Then, have students decide which of their own belongings would help future archaeologists to learn about them. Have students share the item with the class and then let the class discuss its importance and meaning.

◆ **ANSWER** There was a great deal of uniformity among building materials and other aspects of the culture, such as the use of seals to stamp trade goods.

D. Culture, Religion, and Decline

Purpose-Setting Question How did historians obtain knowledge of the early people of the Indus Valley? (Archaeologists unearthed artifacts—such as seals, figurines, and buildings—and historians interpreted the artifacts.)

Then & Now

V. GORDON CHILDE Vere Gordon Childe (1892–1957) was referred to as one of "archaeology's few very great synthesizers." Childe was born in Australia and educated at Oxford University in England. He spent several years as private secretary to the premier of New South Wales. He published several books, including *Dawn of European Civilization* in 1925. He became professor of prehistoric archaeology at Edinburgh University in Scotland in 1927. Prior to his death, he held the directorship of the Institute of Archaeology of the University of London.

Connection to ECONOMICS

The craftspeople of the Indus Valley stamped seals on their goods. Have students discuss labels used on clothes, books, or other items. Ask students what these labels say about our economy. Do we trade with other nations? Are most products made by hand or by machine? What information about our economy cannot be revealed by reading labels?

Test Taking

Explain that tests sometimes ask students to identify the main idea and supporting details of a reading passage. Have students practice the skill by reading the paragraph under "Writing and Language." Then, have them choose the sentence that contains the main idea of the paragraph. (the first sentence)

SPOTLIGHT ON ARCHAEOLOGY

KALIBANGAN Kalibangan, Rupar, Lothal, Dholavira, and Banawali are all Indus Valley sites that have been discovered since the 1950s. Some scholars today contend that people who settled in Kalibangan and the other cities on the banks of the Sarasvati River provided the true support base of the civilization. To these scholars, Mohenjo-Daro and Harappa were just trading outposts.

Demonstrate Have students create a two-column chart (TR, p. 328) that summarizes the development and decline of the Indus Valley civilization. The column on the left should be labeled "Evidence of Existence." (planned city, indoor plumbing, seals, crafts, toys, religious artifacts) The column on the right should be labeled "Reasons for Collapse." (climactic change, agricultural disaster, natural disaster, invasion)

◆ **ANSWER** terra cotta figurines that appear to represent gods and goddesses and seals that may show religious scenes

Section Close

Discuss with students how the geography of the Indus Valley affected the growth and decline of civilization. (**growth:** fertile lands were good for farming; **decline:** Indus River may have changed course, possible flooding, earthquake, disease, or invasion)

③ Assess

Review Answers

Review History
A. The effects of the monsoon rains are felt the most near the Bay of Bengal.

B. They form a protective barrier from the harsh, northern winds blowing in from central Asia.

C. Objects from other areas have been found at the Indus Valley excavation sites, and Indus seals have been found as far away as Sumer.

D. Invasions by other tribes could have occurred; there may have been a sudden catastrophic event, such as an earthquake, flood, or disease.

Define Terms to Know
subcontinent, 50; plateau, 50; monsoon, 51; citadel, 52

Spotlight on *Archaeology*

KALIBANGAN

Kalibangan is another Indus Valley site, which lies on the bank of the dry bed of the Sarasvati River. It has been excavated by the Archaeological Survey of India. Most of the findings still remain unpublished. When the work is made public, it will add more to our knowledge of the Indus Valley civilization.

Indus Valley Religion

It is not clear what role religion played in the Indus Valley civilization. Archaeologists have identified some buildings as having a religious purpose, such as the Great Bath at Mohenjo-Daro, which is found in the citadel. This sunken bath with flights of stairs at either end measures 897 square feet, or 83 square meters.

Many terra cotta figurines, mostly of females, appear to represent gods or goddesses. Evidence also points to the beginning of an Indian religious belief system. Numerous seals have been unearthed. Many of them show animals standing in front of an object that may refer to scenes with religious or mythological meaning. In addition, the bodies of the dead were buried with their heads to the north. Historians do not know if this practice was related to religious belief.

The Decline and Disappearance of the Indus Valley Civilization

We still do not know why the Indus Valley civilization disappeared. Scientists have suggested several possible reasons. There may have been a gradual change in the climate that forced people to abandon the city. The Indus River could have changed its course, so that its water no longer fertilized the crops. As a result, there would not have been enough food to feed the people who lived there. There may have been a sudden, catastrophic event, such as an earthquake, flood, or disease. Invasions from other tribes living beyond the hills to the west of the Indus Valley could have occurred.

Archaeologists have found the remains of some bodies at Mohenjo-Daro that seem to never have been buried. This find may indicate that people abandoned the city quickly after a catastrophic event or an invasion. Perhaps a combination of these things led to the end of the Indus Valley civilization.

◆ **What are some artifacts that suggest the beginning of religion in the Indus Valley?**

Review 1

Review History
A. Where are the effects of the monsoon rains felt the most on the Indian subcontinent?
B. How do the Himalayas shelter the subcontinent?
C. Why was it likely that trade was a part of the Indus Valley civilization?
D. Which two events may have contributed to the decline and disappearance of the Indus Valley civilization?

Define Terms to Know
Define the following terms: **subcontinent, plateau, monsoon, citadel**

Critical Thinking
What evidence shows cooperation among the different settlements of the Indus Valley civilization?

Write About History
Write a short essay explaining why people of various settlements in the Indus Valley should cooperate with one another.

Get Organized
MAIN IDEA/SUPPORTING DETAILS CHART
Use a chart like the one below to show details that support each main idea in this section. For example, use this main idea: The geography of the Indian subcontinent provided an attractive environment for humans.

Critical Thinking
Possible answer: similar aspects of the culture, including building materials and city layout

Write About History
Students' essays should describe the ways that the people in the settlements could work together and how this would benefit everyone.

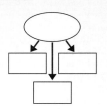

MAIN IDEA

The geography of the Indian subcontinent— good environment for humans

Himalayas— protected against harsh winds
DETAIL

The Indo-Gangetic Plain— a fertile area for farming
DETAIL

Coastal plains—access to fishing and trading
DETAIL

Build Your Skills

Critical Thinking

UNDERSTAND CAUSE AND EFFECT

When you read about history, you sometimes find yourself asking questions about events that happened long ago: "I wonder why the Indus Valley civilization was not more widespread?" "What really caused the decline of such a great civilization?" For many questions like these, answers cannot be proven because there were few, if any, written records. Instead, archaeologists unearth ancient settlements to try to find out what caused certain events to happen.

Understanding the cause means identifying the reason why certain actions or events happen. Understanding the effect means understanding the results of the cause or action. Sometimes causes and effects are easy to figure out. In science, many cause-and-effect relationships are explained every day, such as why grass turns brown in a drought or after a freeze, or why water puddles evaporate on a hot, sunny day.

However, as you read in Section I of this chapter, there are many times when cause-and-effect explanations are based purely on educated guesswork. The more facts that can be proven, the more likely an explanation will be accurate.

Here's How

Follow these steps to help you determine causes and effects.

1. Identify a cause by asking yourself why an action or event happened.

2. Identify an effect by asking yourself what was the result of the action or event.

3. Decide whether or not one action or event caused another action or event to happen. Look for key words such as *because*, *as a result*, *after*, *so that*, and *therefore*.

4. Make a cause-and-effect statement based on the evidence you have gathered.

Here's Why

Understanding cause and effect is a useful way to help us understand events, especially those that occurred in ancient times. By examining evidence yourself, you can come to your own conclusions about a particular time. This process will help you to become a more informed and independent thinker.

Practice the Skill

Copy the graphic organizer shown on the right on a separate sheet of paper. Read Section I again and look for cause-and-effect relationships. Fill in the missing parts of the graphic organizer.

Extend the Skill

Write a short paragraph in which you give your own ideas about the decline of the Indus Valley civilization. Include a topic sentence that states your position. Support your ideas with several details from the section.

Apply the Skill

As you read the rest of this chapter, think about the causes and effects of key events. Complete a cause-and-effect graphic organizer for other key events in the chapter.

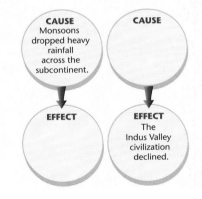

CAUSE
Monsoons dropped heavy rainfall across the subcontinent.

CAUSE

EFFECT

EFFECT
The Indus Valley civilization declined.

Teach the Skill

Have students think of examples of occurrences at school or home that are linked by cause and effect. Have students write sentences using the cause or effect words and phrases listed in step 3 in *Here's How*. Example: *I forgot my umbrella, so I got wet on my way home. I studied a lot for my history test, and as a result, I got an A.*

Ask students how thinking about cause and effect can help them explain events in history. (Knowing the cause and effect of an event could help them understand its impact and importance.)

Practice the Skill
ANSWER

Possible answers: **Effect:** The crops in the villages get watered; **Cause:** There may have been a gradual change in climate.

Extend the Skill

Students' theories should explain the causes and effects of the decline of the Indus Valley civilization using details from the section as support. Words that signal cause and effect should be used.

Apply the Skill

After reading Section 4, have students create a cause-and-effect graphic organizer like the one on page 55 for the Mauryan Empire.

Teaching Options

RETEACH

On an overhead projector, display the first paragraph under "The Land, the Mountains, and the Rivers" on page 50. Ask students to identify one cause and one effect in this paragraph. Then, allow a volunteer to underline the cause and draw an arrow to its effect on the transparency. (The cause and effect involves the Himalayas.)

CHALLENGE

Ask students to apply this skill to a current or recent event involving mass flooding or another natural disaster. Have them give a brief oral presentation on the causes and effects of the event. Students may want to use newspapers, news magazines, and Internet news sites to research a topic.

II. Aryan Civilization

(pp. 56–60)

Section Summary

In this section, students will learn who the Aryan people were and how knowledge about their culture was preserved through oral traditions and sacred writings called the Vedas. Students will also learn about the changes to Aryan society and religion that occurred during this period.

1 Introduce

Getting Started

The Aryan people settled in an area already inhabited by the people of the Indus Valley civilization. Ask students how new people moving into their community might affect their lives. Would students welcome the influx of new ideas and customs? Or, would they feel threatened that the new arrivals might compete for resources, such as jobs? Discuss how they would resolve these challenges.

TERMS TO KNOW

To help students become familiar with the terms on page 56, have them record the terms on index cards. Suggest that they write the terms on the front and the definitions on the back. Have pairs of students review the terms. Then, encourage students to refer to the cards as they read.

You may wish to preview the pronunciation of the following terms from this section with students.

Brahman (BRAH muhn)
Kshatriya (kuh SHAT ree yuh)
Vaisya (VIHS yuh)
Sudra (SOO druh)
Ramayana (rah MAH yuh nuh)
Mahabharata
  (muh hah BAH ruh tuh)
Bhagavad Gita
  (BUHG uh vuhd GEE tuh)

ACTIVE READING

Have students create a two-column chart (TR, p. 328) with the title "Did Aryans Strongly Affect India?" The columns should be labeled *Arguments* and *Facts*. Students should write notes in the chart as they read. After the chart is complete, students should use it to write a short statement about their position on the issue.

Aryan Civilization

Terms to Know

Vedas one of the earliest Hindu sacred texts
caste system the complex form of social organization that restricts its members to certain occupations
divinity a divine being; a god
epic a long, narrative poem about great heroes and their deeds

This sculpture shows warlike Aryans with weapons and horse-drawn chariots.

Main Ideas

A. The Aryans were nomads who entered the Indian subcontinent around 1500 B.C.
B. Knowledge about Aryan society comes from sacred writings first handed down orally by priests.
C. Two long poems based on stories from the Vedas spread throughout Southeast Asia.
D. The Aryan economy, society, and religion changed during the Vedic period.

📖 Active Reading

ARGUMENTS AND EVIDENCE
A strong argument uses good evidence to convince a reader or listener. As you read this section, look for evidence to support the argument that the Aryans had a strong effect on India. Then, decide if you agree or disagree with this view.

A. The Aryans

Archaeologists have little concrete information to help them understand what happened after the decline of the Indus Valley civilization. What is known is that groups of nomads invaded India around 1500 B.C. These nomads were skilled and brave fighters.

Aryan Migrations

For years, the common historical belief has been that invaders called the Aryans came through the Khyber Pass into northwestern India. The Aryans are thought to have made their way through the Indus River valley, then onto the Indo-Gangetic Plain. It is believed they were nomads from southern Russia and central Asia in search of pastureland for their sheep, goats, and cows.

Aryan People

Described as a fierce people, the Aryans were said to be skillful fighters who led horse-drawn chariots into battle. It has been thought that the Aryans conquered the Indus Valley peoples. Then, they gradually moved east toward the Ganges River, eventually conquering the entire northern plain. After entering the subcontinent, the Aryans settled on the lands they had conquered. The descendants of the Aryans became the rulers of many kingdoms in the subcontinent.

The nomadic lifestyle of the early Aryans meant they left few artifacts for modern archaeologists to uncover. Because they did not build cities, they left no ruins to tell their story. They had no written language, so they left no written sources for historians. Most of what we know about the early Aryans comes from hymns and chants.

◆ **Where might the Aryans have entered northwestern India?**

Teaching Options

Section 2 Resources

Teacher's Resources (TR)
Terms to Know, p. 16
Review History, p. 50
Build Your Skills, p. 84
Concept Builder, p. 219
Main Idea/Supporting Details Chart, p. 319

F Y I

Hitler's Aryans

Some students may recognize the word *Aryan* from Hitler's misappropriation of the word when the Nazis controlled Germany's government in the 1930s and 1940s. Hitler believed that Germans could supposedly trace their descent back to Aryan forebears. The Vedas—with glorified images of conquest—were incorporated into Nazi racist literature.

B. Aryan Society

The Aryans did not leave much in the way of physical evidence to examine, but they did leave the **Vedas**, a collection of hymns, prayers, and other religious teachings. Most of our knowledge about Aryan culture comes from the Vedas. They make up the earliest sacred writings of the Hindu religion.

The Vedas

The Vedas were memorized by priests and handed down orally for a thousand years before they were written. Experts disagree about when the Vedas were written. Western scholars believe Sanskrit, the language in which most of the Vedas are written, developed around 1500 B.C. The period from 1500 B.C. to 1000 B.C. is called the Vedic Age. Regardless of the exact time they were written, the Vedas have lasted through time. They have been recited daily by generations of people, like an unbroken chain. The message of the Vedas is one of peace and harmony:

> **❝**Let your aim be one and single,
> Let your hearts be joined in one,
> The mind at rest in unison
> At peace with all, so may you be. **❞**

In addition to the Vedas, other sacred writings included the Upanishads, which were complex explanations of the Vedas. The Upanishads were hard to understand, so most people listened to stories of the Vedas instead.

The Aryan Caste System

From the Vedas we know that Aryan society divided people into groups. This method of social division, called the **caste system,** may have been used to limit contact between Aryans and other peoples. The caste that an Aryan belonged to determined his or her place in society.

The castes were divided into varnas, or four main groups. These groups were the Brahmans, who were the priests and educated people; the Kshatriyas, who were rulers and warriors; the Vaisyas, who were merchants, farmers, traders, and artisans; and the Sudras, who were laborers and servants to upper castes.

A group ranked below the Sudra caste was called the untouchables. The untouchables were restricted to jobs such as cleaning baths and collecting trash. The untouchables lived a very difficult life. Their presence was considered harmful to members of the other castes.

In Aryan society, people were born into their caste for life. Their place in the caste determined what type of work they did, who they could marry, where they could worship, and who they could eat with. A person of a lower caste could not eat with people of a higher caste and could not marry outside their social level. In time, the castes themselves became divided into many smaller groups. The caste system shaped every aspect of people's lives in India.

Religious Beliefs

The Vedas showed that the Aryans worshiped many gods and goddesses. The Aryans held religious beliefs that would eventually influence all of Asia. Nature gods are some of the earliest **divinities**, or divine beings, mentioned in the Vedas. Like other early civilizations, the Aryans gave human characteristics to natural objects and forces, such as the Sun, sky, Earth, fire, wind, and rain. Indra was the god of war and the thunderbolt was his weapon.

ANALYZE PRIMARY SOURCES
DOCUMENT-BASED QUESTION What do you think the idea expressed in these lines reveals about Aryan religious beliefs?

Then & Now

THE CASTE SYSTEM
For centuries, the group known as the untouchables was ranked below the lowest caste. The caste system weakened over time. By 1950, the Indian constitution outlawed untouchability and gave the untouchables equal rights. However, this group still faces discrimination today.

A. The Aryans

Purpose-Setting Question How did descendants of Aryans come to be the rulers of many kingdoms in the subcontinent? (Aryans conquered the Indus Valley people, as well as others living on the northern plain at the time. They settled in the areas they conquered and eventually came to rule the land.)

TEACH PRIMARY SOURCES
Have students study the photograph on page 56 of the Aryan sculpture. Ask students to identify images in the sculpture that suggest the warlike image of the Aryan civilization.

◆ **ANSWER** The Aryans may have entered northwestern India through the Khyber Pass.

B. Aryan Society

Purpose-Setting Question
Without the use of artifacts, how did historians draw conclusions about the Aryan way of life? (from the Vedas, a collection of hymns, prayers, and religious teachings)

ANALYZE PRIMARY SOURCES

DOCUMENT-BASED QUESTION
The quotation cited is from *Rig Veda*, a collection of Vedic hymns. In Sanskrit, *rig* means "stanza of praise." The *Rig Veda* is the earliest of the four basic Vedas. It is a collection of 1,028 hymns, written in a style of literature known as the Samhita. Like each of the basic Vedas, the *Rig Veda* was taught in its own school, which produced literature that commented on the text.

ANSWER It may tell us that although the Aryans were warriors, their religion stressed peace as a way to bring people together.

Then & Now

THE CASTE SYSTEM Ask students if they think that laws can change the way people think about each other. Encourage them to provide examples that support their viewpoint.

Writing

AVERAGE

Have students write a journal entry about the daily activities of an Aryan from a specific caste. Journal entries should describe what the person did and how he or she felt about events or people. Remind students to indicate which caste the writer is part of.

CHALLENGE

Have students write a short comparative essay in which they compare a day in the life of a member of the Brahman caste with one of a member of the Sudra caste. Suggest that students have both people observe or participate in the same event.

◆ **ANSWER** Aryan society divided people into four main groups, or varnas. The caste an Aryan belonged to determined his or her place in Aryan society.

C. Poems About the Vedas

Purpose-Setting Question How do the epic poems the *Ramayana* and the *Mahabharata* reinforce the values of Aryan culture? (The *Ramayana's* main characters, Rama and Sita, symbolize the ideals of husband and wife because of their duty and devotion to one another even through hardships; the *Mahabharata's* Gita shows that the highest fulfillment in life is doing one's moral duty and that love and devotion to the god Vishnu is a way to salvation in the afterlife.)

TEACH PRIMARY SOURCES
Have students study the illustration on page 58 of a scene from the *Ramayana* in which Rama and his brothers marry their brides. What do they notice about the illustration? (There are many people present; there are musicians; the people look dressed up.) Then, discuss with students what a marriage ceremony might look like in the United States. Explore similarities and differences that they might expect to see.

Explore Point out to students that the *Ramayana* and the *Mahabharata* survived as oral traditions and are popular today. Ask students to share a tradition that has been passed down over time from their family or from that of someone they know or have read about. Students should hypothesize as to what values the tradition teaches and why that particular tradition continues to be practiced today.

He used the thunderbolt to destroy demons and to announce the arrival of the rain that was so important to Indian life. Other major gods included Varuna, the god of order and creation, and Agni, the god of fire. Agni was also a messenger who communicated between humans and gods.

Brahman priests had a great deal of influence in society because they interpreted the Vedas. They also performed complicated rituals and offered sacrifices of food and drink to the gods. The Aryans believed that they could call on the gods to bring them health and safety during war. The power of the Brahmans grew in Aryan society because they claimed they could lead the ceremonies needed to win the favor of the gods.

◆ **What do the Vedas tell us about the Aryan caste system?**

C. Poems About the Vedas

Some of the stories from the Vedas appeared in two long poems called **epics**. For thousands of years, these poems have survived as oral traditions. They are called the *Ramayana* and the *Mahabharata*. Both epic poems spread throughout Southeast Asia, especially in Cambodia, Indonesia, and Thailand. The stories continue to enjoy great popularity today in traditional theater and dance.

Ramayana

The *Ramayana* is a shorter epic that tells about the deeds of the hero Rama and his bride, Sita. Shortly after their wedding, Sita is kidnapped by Ravana, a demon-king. The epic tells about Rama's efforts to get his bride back.

This scene from the epic poem the *Ramayana* shows the marriage of Rama and his brothers to their brides. Many people were present for the celebration, which included food, music, and dance.

Teaching Options

ESL/ELL STRATEGIES

Role-play Divide the class into pairs or small groups. Ask each group to prepare and act out the scene from the *Ramayana* as described on pages 58–59 or the Gita from the *Mahabharata* as described on page 59. Have students explain the roles and message of the epics.

Connection to WORLD LANGUAGES

Sanskrit was, and still is, spoken and used by the learned pundits and the higher class in India. It may have been used as early as 1000 B.C. It is very similar to the language used in the *Rig Veda*, which was composed between 1500 and 1200 B.C. Sanskrit is an important language in recording and passing on Indic civilization.

The *Mahabharata* is an epic poem about the battles that take place between two groups of cousins as they struggle for power.

Rama is helped by a monkey-general named Hanuman. Ravana kills a duplicate of Sita before Rama's eyes to try to trick him, but Rama is not fooled. He continues to fight and eventually wins back his beloved Sita. Rama and Sita symbolize the ideals of husband and wife because of their duty and devotion to each other through many hardships.

Mahabharata

The *Mahabharata*, at almost 100,000 verses, is one of the longest poems in the world. It is India's greatest epic poem. It resembles the Old Testament of the Bible in that it is a collection of narratives.

Considered to have literary and religious value, the *Mahabharata* remains popular today because of its powerful images and timeless themes. One section of the *Mahabharata* is called the Bhagavad Gita, or Gita, for short. This section emphasizes that the highest fulfillment in life is doing one's moral duty. In addition, love and devotion to the god Vishnu is a way to salvation in the afterlife.

The *Mahabharata* describes a war between cousins in Aryan society for control of the kingdom. The conflict between the two groups of cousins, the Pandavas and the Kauravas, increases when the Pandavas lose their kingdom in a dice game to their cousins, and they must fight to regain it.

On the eve of battle, a dialogue takes place between Prince Arjuna, a Pandava, and his charioteer, Krishna. Arjuna confesses to Krishna that he does not want to fight his cousins, even though his cause is just. Krishna replies it is his duty as a warrior to fight:

> **❝** You ought not to hesitate; for, to a warrior, there is nothing nobler than a righteous war. **❞**

Arjuna resolves to fight. After 18 days of battle, he and his brothers are victorious.

◆ **Why is the *Mahabharata* still popular today?**

ANALYZE PRIMARY SOURCES

DOCUMENT-BASED QUESTION
Do you think Arjuna takes comfort in these words from Krishna? Why or why not?

Review Have students review the quotation and illustration from the Gita on pages 48–49 of the chapter opener. Then, have students review the quotation and illustration on page 59. How are the battle scenes in the illustrations different? (The battle illustrated on page 49 is between the gods, whereas, the one on page 59 is between two groups of mortals.) How are the quotations similar? (In both quotations, Krishna reminds Arjuna that it is his duty to fight.)

Activity

Write an epic verse Have students write one verse of epic poetry that might be found in the *Mahabharata*. Remind students that their verse does not have to rhyme and that epic poems traditionally are about a series of conflicts that a hero must overcome.

ANALYZE PRIMARY SOURCES

DOCUMENT-BASED QUESTION
Prince Arjuna is unwittingly in the complex position of being a mortal in conversation with a god. Chapter 11 of the Gita shows an awed and humbled Arjuna as it is revealed to him that he is, indeed, talking to a god and not to a friend and mortal.

ANSWER Possible answer: Arjuna takes comfort in these words because they support the idea of him doing his duty.

◆ **ANSWER** The *Mahabharata* is still popular today because of its powerful images and timeless themes.

Conflict Resolution

Have students discuss how jealousy and greed for power can sometimes lead to violent behavior. Invite students to conduct a dialogue between a Pandava cousin and a Kaurava cousin in which one cousin helps the other get over feelings of jealousy.

Meet Individual Needs:
AUDITORY LEARNERS

Have students read from an English translation of the Bhagavad Gita, such as *The Song of God: Bhagavad Gita*, translated by Swami Prabhavananda and Christopher Isherwood. Discuss how hearing the poetry read out loud enhances students' understanding of the context and adds to the mood and drama of the poem.

D. Changes in Aryan Society

Purpose-Setting Question What are some of the ways in which cultural change took place in Aryan society? (Aryans gave up their nomadic lifestyle and settled into villages and farmed. Trade began between villages.)

Review Remind students that the civilizations they read about in Chapters 1 and 2 followed a similar pattern. Nomadic lifestyles eventually became a more settled, village-based lifestyle, and then the villages began to trade with one another.

◆ **ANSWER** Possible answer: They learned to make iron; they used iron axes to clear land to establish more villages and make room for farming; leaders began fighting for land and power, causing little unity.

The Aryan god Indra, the god of war, is shown riding an elephant and holding symbols of power in his many hands.

③ Assess

Review Answers

Review History
A. Early Aryans were most likely nomads from present-day southern Russia and central Asia. It is thought that they came through the Khyber Pass into northwestern India. They conquered the people there and then settled in the area.

B. The Brahmans were the priests and educated people; the Kshatriyas were rulers and warriors; the Vaisyas were merchants, farmers, traders, and artisans; and the Sudras were laborers and servants to upper castes.

C. They teach about the ideals of husband and wife. They also teach that the highest fulfillment in life is doing one's moral duty.

D. The Aryans settled into villages tending cattle and growing crops. Villages began trading with one another.

Define Terms to Know
Vedas, 57; caste system, 57; divinity, 57; epic, 58

Critical Thinking
The writings tell about the values of the people in early Aryan society as well as early Aryan culture and religion.

D. Changes in Aryan Society

The early Vedic period may or may not have been a period of conquest, but it was certainly a time of a blending and transforming of different cultures.

Nomads to Farmers
The Vedic period was a time of change from a nomadic to a village economy. Aryans eventually gave up their nomadic lifestyle and settled into villages. In these villages they tended cattle and grew crops such as wheat, barley, beans, peas, and sugar cane. Villages began trading with one another, although poor transportation made it hard to trade with people from far away. Coins were not used until much later, so many villages bartered with one another. The Aryans learned farming and other skills from the people they traded and lived with.

Expanding Aryan Territory
In the later Vedic period, the Aryans began to expand their territory. They moved eastward into the plains of the Ganges River. They learned to make iron by about 1000 B.C. They used iron axes to clear some of the land in the plains to establish villages and make room for farming. Leaders among the Aryans began fighting for control of land and power. There was little unity because of these constant battles for control.

Aryan traditions and beliefs formed a framework for later Indian civilization. The Aryan civilization has shaped life in India to the present day. Aryan religious beliefs eventually evolved into two major world religions, Hinduism and Buddhism.

◆ **How did Aryan life change as a result of expansion in India?**

Review II

Review History
A. What do we know about early Aryan society?
B. What were the four varnas?
C. What kinds of lessons do the *Ramayana* and *Mahabharata* teach?
D. How did life change for the Aryans after they gave up their nomadic lifestyle?

Define Terms to Know
Define the following terms: **Vedas, caste system, divinity, epic**

Critical Thinking
What do the writings left by the Aryans tell about the beginning of Aryan culture and society?

Write About Economics
Write a want ad for a job opening aimed at a person belonging to the Sudra class. Describe expected duties and qualifications.

Get Organized
MAIN IDEA/SUPPORTING DETAILS CHART
Use a chart like the one below to link supporting details with a main idea in this section. Use this main idea: Aryan society changed during the Vedic period.

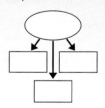

Write About Economics
Students' want ads should contain a brief description of an appropriate job for a person of the Sudra class and should include specific requirements for the position.

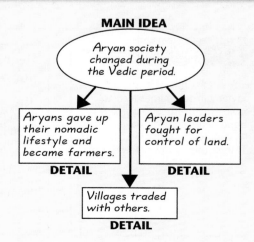

MAIN IDEA

Aryan society changed during the Vedic period.

Aryans gave up their nomadic lifestyle and became farmers.
DETAIL

Aryan leaders fought for control of land.
DETAIL

Villages traded with others.
DETAIL

Hinduism and Buddhism

Terms to Know

reincarnation the rebirth of a soul in another body

karma all the actions in a person's life that affect the next life

dharma an individual's duty in this life

Main Ideas

A. Hinduism became the dominant religion in ancient India.

B. Buddhism arose as an alternative to the formality of Hindu religious practices.

 Active Reading

COMPARE AND CONTRAST
When you compare and contrast two or more things, you look for similarities and differences. As you read this section, compare and contrast the beliefs of Hinduism, Jainism, and Buddhism.

A. Religious Traditions in Ancient India

Ancient India was home to several religious traditions. Hinduism, Jainism, and Buddhism arose out of a common culture and language. All three traditions have many similarities, although they differ from each other in some beliefs and practices.

Hinduism

Hinduism is one of the world's most complex religions. Unlike most major religions, Hinduism has no single founder and no single sacred text. It has no easily identifiable beginning and no central authority or organization. Different beliefs are emphasized by various groups, making it difficult to define the religion. It grew partly out of the religion of the early Aryans as described in the Vedas.

Hinduism grew out of a range of beliefs that came from the many peoples who settled in India over time. Hinduism embraces several aspects of Indian culture. It is at once a religion, a history, and a way of life. Although the religion is very diverse, all Hindus share certain basic beliefs.

Hindu Divinities—Many Out of One

Hinduism accepts the worship of all gods and goddesses, although some of them are considered more important than others. Early Hindu beliefs led some people to think that Hinduism is a polytheistic religion, with a belief in and worship of more than one god. However, Hindus believe that many divinities appear in several different forms, but that they are all part of one universal spirit called Brahman.

The most important Hindu gods are Brahma, creator of the universe; Vishnu, its preserver; and Shiva, its destroyer. Other gods worshiped by Hindus are represented in the spirits of trees, animals, and people.

All of these divinities are part of Brahman. The idea of one formless spirit is difficult for most people to understand. That is why the worship of many divinities in a concrete form arose. The many divinities, however, are simply part of the one Brahman.

Ganesh is an important god of Hinduism and is worshiped by people throughout India. Hindu gods are rarely shown with animal heads, but Ganesh is shown with an elephant head.

Teaching Options

Section 3 Resources

Teacher's Resources (TR)

Terms to Know, p. 16
Review History, p. 50
Build Your Skills, p. 84
Concept Builder, p. 219
Main Idea/Supporting Details Chart, p. 319

ESL/ELL STRATEGIES

Organize Information To help illustrate the concept of Brahman, have students create an idea web (TR, p. 321). Students should place Brahman in the center circle as the main idea. Then, have them create spokes from which the supporting deities are labeled. (Possible answers: Brahma, Vishnu, Shiva, trees, animals, people)

III. Hinduism and Buddhism

(pp. 61–64)

Section Summary

In this section, students will learn how Hinduism became the dominant religion in ancient India. Students will also learn about Jainism, a religion founded on the Hindu tradition of nonviolence, and Buddhism, a religion that arose as an alternative to the formality of Hindu religious practices.

 1 Introduce

Getting Started

Some religions that developed in India share in the belief that to be good in this life is a way to reach salvation in one's next life. Discuss with students how following this central belief affects every aspect of one's life—from what one chooses to eat to the way one greets one's neighbor. Have students think about a personal belief that guides them throughout their day.

TERMS TO KNOW

Ask several students to read aloud the terms and definitions on p. 61. As they read each term and its definition, expand on the definitions. Contrast *karma* and *dharma*.

You may wish to preview the pronunciation of the following terms from this section with students.

Jainism (JIHN ihz uhm)
ahimsa (uh HIHM sah)
Siddhartha Gautama
(sihd DAHR tuh GAOO tuh muh)

ACTIVE READING

Suggest that students use a Venn diagram with three circles to compare and contrast the beliefs of Hinduism, Jainism, and Buddhism.

A. Religious Traditions in Ancient India

Purpose-Setting Question Who are the most important Hindu gods? (Brahma, Vishnu, and Shiva)

Activity

Make a list Tell students that Hinduism is not just a religion; it is a way of life. Ask students to interpret this statement and list their answers on the board. As students read the section, have them adjust the list on the board.

Using the Map

Spread of Buddhism and Hinduism to A.D. 500

Have students preview the text on pages 63–64 to find the beliefs of Buddhism. (Possible answer: Any person could gain salvation by following the Eightfold Path.) Then, discuss with students how Buddhism differed from Hinduism and why Buddhism may have spread farther than Hinduism. (Possible answer: Buddhism's policy of enlightenment for all had greater appeal than the fixed caste system.)

✔ Map Check

Answers
1. about 1,100–1,300 miles
2. Japan

ANALYZE PRIMARY SOURCES

DOCUMENT-BASED QUESTION
Monotheism is the belief in one personal god. Scholars agree that monotheism is practiced in Judaism, Christianity, Islam, and Zoroastrianism, but not all agree it is practiced in Hinduism. Rather, some scholars say that Hindus practice monism. Monism is the union of the physical and the spiritual. It assumes unity but downplays personal monotheism.

ANSWER Possible answer: Brahman is part of everyone and everything; always has been and always will be.

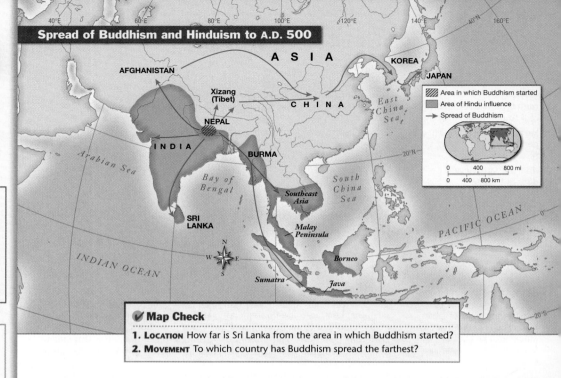

Spread of Buddhism and Hinduism to A.D. 500

ASIA · KOREA · JAPAN · AFGHANISTAN · Xizang (Tibet) · CHINA · East China Sea · NEPAL · INDIA · BURMA · Arabian Sea · Bay of Bengal · Southeast Asia · South China Sea · SRI LANKA · Malay Peninsula · PACIFIC OCEAN · INDIAN OCEAN · Borneo · Sumatra · Java

Area in which Buddhism started
Area of Hindu influence
Spread of Buddhism

0 400 800 mi
0 400 800 km

✔ Map Check

1. **LOCATION** How far is Sri Lanka from the area in which Buddhism started?
2. **MOVEMENT** To which country has Buddhism spread the farthest?

ANALYZE PRIMARY SOURCES
DOCUMENT-BASED QUESTION
What does the quote tell you about the qualities of Brahman?

Hindus believe that Brahman is everlasting and endless. Brahman is the cause, source, and reason for all existence. The Bhagavad Gita describes Brahman as being in all things:

❝ Innermost element, Everywhere, always, Being of beings, Changeless, eternal, For ever and ever. ❞

Hindu Beliefs

Hindus believe in **reincarnation**, or being reborn into another body, either human or animal. The law of **karma** states that every action in a person's life influences how the soul will be reborn in the next life. Those who live good lives will be reborn into a higher level of existence. Those who do evil will be reborn into a lower level of existence.

The importance of **dharma**, a person's religious and moral duties, is seen as a way for a person to escape the constant cycle of death and rebirth. If a person fulfills the duties of this life according to caste rules, then merit can be gained for the next life. Hindu beliefs strengthen the caste system because they teach that people must accept the caste into which they are born. They have a duty to accept it, because their caste is the result of all their good and bad actions in their past life. If people accept their caste in this life, they will be rewarded with a higher caste in the next life.

Another belief of Hinduism is the concept of ahimsa, or nonviolence to all living creatures. Ahimsa is the absence of the desire to harm oneself or others.

62 UNIT 1 ◆ From Prehistory to Early Civilizations

Teaching Options

Focus on WORLD RELIGIONS

Jainism A major tenet of Jainism is to accumulate merit in the afterlife through charity and good works. A charity that Jainism is well known for is the establishment of places to care for diseased animals. In fact, concern for animals is so important to the beliefs of Jains that many will not choose a job that might endanger animal life.

Have students learn more about the religion of Jainism, including where people practice the religion today, how many people practice the religion, and how the religion affects the everyday lives of the people who practice it. Then, have students focus on a specific topic and prepare reports to share with the class. (Possible topics: Mahavira, the founder of Jainism; ahimsa; vegetarianism; reasons for the decline of Jainism after A.D. 1000; or the practice of Jainism today)

Jainism

Jainism is a religion in India that was founded on the Hindu tradition of ahimsa. It is a religion of nonviolence. Jains believe in nonviolence to all living creatures, including the smallest insect. The rule against violence to animals kept many Jains from farming. They did not want to kill worms or other creatures in the earth. To make a living without farming, many Jains became merchants. Jainism began to decline after about A.D. 1000, but its ideas continued to influence many people in India.

◆ **Why is the Hindu religion difficult to define?**

B. The Rise of Buddhism

Buddhism began in northeastern India sometime around 500 B.C., in a period of great social change and religious activity. Many people were looking for less formality than that found in the Hindu rituals performed by Brahman priests.

The Enlightened One

Buddhism accepted some Hindu beliefs while rejecting others. The Hindu beliefs of karma and reincarnation were generally accepted by Buddhists. Buddhism rejected the caste system of Hinduism. Buddhists recognized the potential of all men and women, regardless of social class. The founder of Buddhism was Siddhartha Gautama, known as the Buddha.

Buddhist tradition claims the Buddha lived many lives before his birth as Siddhartha Gautama. The Buddha, which is not a proper name, but a title that means "awakened one" or "enlightened one," was born in northern India in 563 B.C. to a ruling class family. Before Siddhartha was born, his mother had a dream one night that a beautiful white elephant descended to her from heaven. Brahman priests who interpreted the dream foretold the birth of son who would become either a ruler or a wandering holy man.

Comparing Hinduism and Buddhism

HINDUISM
- One of the world's most complex religions
- No single human founder
- Many forms of divinities worshiped
- Belief in nonviolence to all living creatures
- Spread throughout India

- Karma
- Reincarnation

BUDDHISM
- Siddhartha Gautama founded Buddhism around 528 B.C.
- Any individual can gain enlightenment by following the Eightfold Path.
- Rejects elaborate rituals by Hindu priests
- Spread to other parts of Asia

✔ **Chart Check**

What are the similarities between Hinduism and Buddhism?

Connection to LITERATURE

Students may wish to read Herman Hesse's *Siddhartha*. It is a fictional story of a young man's search for enlightenment and is based on the life of Siddhartha Gautama, the founder of Buddhism. A major theme of the novel is that one must look to oneself to find true happiness rather than looking elsewhere.

Meet Individual Needs:
KINESTHETIC LEARNERS

Have students use index cards to help keep separate information about the three major religions of ancient India. On the front of an index card, students should list the name of the religion and a summary sentence. On the back of each card, they should list key details about that religion. These cards will be helpful study aids.

◆ **ANSWER** The Hindu religion is difficult to define because it has no single founder, no sacred text, no central authority or organization, and different beliefs are emphasized by various groups.

B. The Rise of Buddhism

Purpose-Setting Question Who is the Buddha and what does the title mean? (Siddhartha Gautama became the Buddha, which means "awakened one" or "enlightened one." He is the founder of Buddhism.)

Discuss Ask students how one religious tradition can develop into a new, separate religion. (Possible answer: A follower of the original religion will reinterpret that religion's beliefs and preach new teachings. If the teachings become popular, they will spread and be accepted by others, becoming their own religion.) Help students realize that Buddhism is its own religion. It does incorporate some of the beliefs of Hinduism.

Explore Have students think about a member of the Brahman varna in the caste system in ancient Hindu society. Ask them how this person might have felt about Buddha's message. (threatened, disapproving) Then, have students discuss how an untouchable might have felt about Buddhism. (hopeful)

Using the Chart
Comparing Hinduism and Buddhism

Review the Venn diagram with students. Encourage them to explain the differences between Hinduism and Buddhism in their own words. Ask how Hindus can practice monotheism and worship many gods at the same time. (All the divinities are part of the one Brahman.)

Point out to students that the concept of karma is a similarity of the two religions, but dharma is not. Ask students to explain this disparity. (The Hindu concept of dharma is the religious and moral duties of each caste. Buddhism rejects the caste system and, therefore, rejects the concept of dharma.)

✔ **Chart Check**
Answer They both believe in karma and reincarnation.

Explore Have students study the photograph of the Buddha statue on page 64. Ask students to name monuments that they may have visited. Then, discuss with the class the reasons why a culture builds monuments. (to honor a person or event)

Challenge students to think of the reasons why the creators of the Buddha in the photograph made the monument so massive. (Possible answer: Buddha was viewed by some as a god, larger than life.)

Activity

Make a poster Have students make a poster that illustrates the Four Noble Truths or the eight steps of the Eightfold Path. Allow students to use other references, if needed.

◆ **ANSWER** Buddha's followers helped him spread his teachings.

Section Close

Ask students to summarize the three major religions of ancient India by creating a three-column chart with the following labels: *Hinduism, Jainism,* and *Buddhism.* Have students complete the chart with information that describes what makes each religion unique.

3 Assess

Review Answers
Review History
A. belief in a universal spirit called Brahman; reincarnation; karma; dharma; ahimsa

B. All human existence is full of pain and suffering; the cause of suffering is selfish desire; the only freedom from suffering is to overcome desire; the only way to overcome desire is to follow the Eightfold Path.

Define Terms to Know
reincarnation, 62; karma, 62; dharma, 62

Critical Thinking
Possible answer: It may have given hope to members of the lower castes that if they fulfilled their duties in this life, they would be rewarded with a higher caste in the next life.

This massive carved rock statue in India shows Buddha meditating while sitting in the lotus position.

In Search of Truth

Siddhartha Gautama's father worried that Siddhartha would leave home and become a wandering holy man. He raised his son in luxury, hoping to keep him from seeing or hearing anything unpleasant.

Siddhartha did not follow his father's wishes. When he was 29, he left his father's palace to learn how other people lived. He saw an old man bent over with age, a sick man, and a dead man. He became so unhappy about people's suffering and pain that he decided to give up his life of ease and luxury and become a wandering holy man.

Siddhartha wandered for years, learning all he could about the way of truth. For six years, he gave up all comforts and pleasures. He ate so little that his skin hung from his bones, and his eyes sunk in their sockets. After he fainted from weakness, Siddhartha realized that he could not seek the truth if he did not remain healthy.

One day, Siddhartha decided to sit under a tree until he understood the mystery of life. He sat in meditation day and night. One day, he finally realized the meaning of life and became the Buddha, or Enlightened One. For the rest of his life, the Buddha taught others the Four Noble Truths:
- All human existence is full of pain and suffering.
- The cause of suffering is selfish desire.
- The only freedom from suffering is to overcome desire.
- The only way to overcome desire is to follow the Eightfold Path.

The Buddha explained that people should not worry about worldly cares. Instead, they should follow the Eightfold Path which consists of eight steps: "right view, right intention, right speech, right action, right way of making a living, right effort, right mindfulness, and right concentration."

The Buddha had followers to help him spread his teachings. Buddhism soon became a major religion in Asia. It is still one of the most important world religions today.

◆ **How did the Buddha spread his teachings?**

Review III

Review History
A. What are some of the basic teachings of Hinduism?
B. According to the Buddha, what were the Four Noble Truths that people should follow?

Define Terms to Know
Define the following terms:
reincarnation, karma, dharma

Critical Thinking
How might the belief in dharma have supported the Hindu social order?

Write About Culture
Write a short essay that supports Siddhartha Gautama's decision to become a wandering holy man.

Get Organized
MAIN IDEA/SUPPORTING DETAILS CHART
Use a chart like the one below to link details with main ideas in this section. For example, use this main idea: All Hindus share certain basic beliefs.

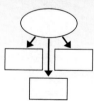

Write About Culture
Students' essays should describe Siddhartha Gautama's life and why he decided to become a wandering holy man. The essay should also provide support for the decision and the eventual outcome.

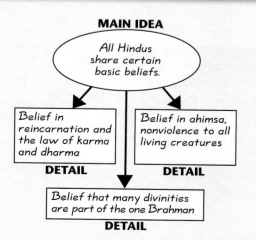

MAIN IDEA

All Hindus share certain basic beliefs.

Belief in reincarnation and the law of karma and dharma
DETAIL

Belief in ahimsa, nonviolence to all living creatures
DETAIL

Belief that many divinities are part of the one Brahman
DETAIL

Ancient Indian Dynasties

Terms to Know

bureaucracy a body of appointed or hired government officials who follow a set routine

edict an order or command given by an official and backed or supported by law

deity a supreme being or divinity

Main Ideas

A. The Mauryan Empire was successful because it united several different parts of the subcontinent into one political unit.

B. The Gupta Empire, which lasted for almost 300 years, marked a high point in Indian culture.

 Active Reading

CLASSIFY

When you classify, you put things into categories based on certain characteristics. As you read this section, look for cultural features of the Gupta Empire that show it to be a golden age.

A. The Mauryan Empire

By 400 B.C., some kingdoms in northern and eastern India, such as the kingdom of Magadha, had become especially large and powerful. The kings of Magadha built large armies. The people of Magadha traded products from their farms, forests, and mines with people in other lands, and increased their kingdom's wealth. Soon the Magadha kingdom took over neighboring lands.

The first great empire of India was formed around 321 B.C., by a man named Chandragupta Maurya. Chandragupta overthrew the Magadha kingdom in the Ganges River valley, swept west, and took control of the Indus River valley. He united the many kingdoms that existed in India and founded the Mauryan Empire. This empire would control most of the Indian subcontinent and parts of modern-day Afghanistan.

The Reign of Chandragupta

The Mauryan Empire was large but it worked well because it was a **bureaucracy**. A bureaucracy is a governmental system of departments run by appointed officials. High-level officials supervised the building of roads. Other officials ran the villages and collected taxes. Spies sent reports to the emperor about events in the villages and about plots against him. Chandragupta's huge army of 700,000 men, 9,000 elephants, and 10,000 chariots helped control his empire.

Chandragupta improved business and trade for his people. The emperor built canals that brought a steady supply of water to farms. The harvest of wheat, rice, and tea increased as a result. Chandragupta's bureaucracy created government jobs for some of its citizens. Chandragupta also built a road system that linked all parts of the empire. The roads made it easier to transport goods to ports. Ships from the Mauryan Empire traded goods along an area that stretched from Africa across the Arabian Peninsula into Asia.

The Mauryan Empire, 320–250 B.C.

HINDU KUSH MOUNTAINS
Gandhara
HIMALAYAS
Brahmaputra River
Indus River
Punjab
Indo-Gangetic Plain
THAR DESERT
Ganges River
INDIA
Magadha
Kalinga
Bay of Bengal
Arabian Sea
Deccan Plateau
Western Ghats
Eastern Ghats
INDIAN OCEAN

Mauryan Empire
Khyber Pass

0   250   500 mi
0   250   500 km

Map Check

LOCATION Which mountain range forms the northeastern boundary of the Mauryan Empire?

CHAPTER 3 ◆ Ancient India **65**

Teaching Options

Section 4 Resources

Teacher's Resources (TR)

Terms to Know, p. 16
Review History, p. 50
Build Your Skills, p. 84
Concept Builder, p. 219
Chapter Test, pp. 121–122
Main Idea/Supporting Details Chart,
   p. 319

Conflict Resolution

The strong central government of the Mauryan Empire united people from many different kingdoms. Ask students how they react when they are expected to interact with people they meet whose beliefs are different from their own. Discuss how people can find common ground.

IV. Ancient Indian Dynasties

(pp. 65–69)

Section Summary

In this section, students will learn about the reign of Chandragupta and the rise and fall of his political empire, known as the Mauryan Empire. Students will also learn about the Gupta Empire and the great advances in the arts and sciences during this period in ancient India.

1 Introduce

Getting Started

Tell students that throughout history there have been different types of leaders—strong, demanding, weak, kind, mean, and many have a mixture of these traits. Ask students what traits they think are best in a leader. Encourage them to discuss how they would feel with each type of leader. Explain that the people of ancient India had to deal with different types of leaders and this affected the civilizations that developed in ancient India.

TERMS TO KNOW

Ask students to read the terms and definitions on page 65. Then, ask volunteers to find the terms in this section and read the context sentences aloud. Have each student write a sentence using each term.

You may wish to preview the pronunciations of the following terms from this section with students.

Chandragupta Maurya
(chuhn druh GOOP tuh
MAH oor yuh)
Asoka (uh SOH kuh)
stupa (STOO puh)
Panchatantra
(puhn cheh TUHN treh)

ACTIVE READING

Suggest that students take notes about the Gupta Empire as they read the chapter. Students may want to classify different aspects of the culture, such as literature, art, and architecture. So, after the students write a note, they should classify, or label, it with one of the aspects of culture.

A. The Mauryan Empire

Purpose-Setting Question How did Asoka's conversion to Buddhism change the way he led his empire? (He led by good examples and stressed Buddhist virtues.)

Using the Map

The Mauryan Empire, 320–250 B.C.

After students correctly answer the Map Check question, ask them how the Himalayas might have affected Chandragupta's plans for expansion. (The Himalayas probably prevented a northeastern expansion because they were too difficult to pass.) Have students identify other geographic features that might have thwarted the spread of Chandragupta's power. (the Indian Ocean or the Hindu Kush Mountains)

✔ Map Check

Answer the Himalayas

ANALYZE PRIMARY SOURCES

DOCUMENT-BASED QUESTION

Asoka's inscribed edicts form the chief source of scholarly knowledge of his rule. Perhaps some of his most famous inscriptions were found in the archaeological site of Sarnath. These edicts proclaimed Asoka's belief in *ahimsa*. They also advocated tolerance of all faiths.

ANSWER Buddhists recognized the potential of all men and women, regardless of caste. So, Asoka wants everyone to achieve happiness in this world as well as the next.

Explore Asoka placed stone pillars along roads and carved laws and Buddhist teachings on them. Ask students in what ways travelers on U.S. roads can become familiar with U.S. laws and customs. (Travelers can learn the laws by reading road signs, and they can learn about the culture by reading shop signs, bulletins on telephone poles, or advertisements on signs.)

Asoka Rules the Mauryan Empire

It was Chandragupta's grandson, Asoka, who was the most admired of the Mauryan rulers. He became emperor around 274 B.C. Asoka ruled much like the kings who came before him, until an event happened during the eighth year of his reign that changed the way he ruled.

Asoka sent soldiers to conquer a kingdom called Kalinga on the eastern coast of India. The immense suffering and loss of more than 100,000 lives during the battles caused Asoka to think about the nature of violence. Filled with remorse, he became a follower of the Buddhist religion and declared he would never again go to war. He set out to win the support of India's people through kindness. Asoka saw himself as the protector of his people, saying:

ANALYZE PRIMARY SOURCES **DOCUMENT-BASED QUESTION** How does Asoka's statement reflect his Buddhist beliefs?

> ❝All men are my children, and just as I desire for my children that they may obtain every kind of welfare and happiness both in this world and the next, so do I desire for all men. ❞

Asoka devoted the rest of his life to practicing and spreading the teaching of the Buddha. He tried to lead his people by his good example, rather than by the use of force. To help spread his newfound beliefs, Asoka began placing **edicts**, or orders, on pillars and rocks throughout his empire in places people gathered. These edicts stressed the Buddhist qualities of goodness, compassion, truthfulness, purity, tolerance, and gentleness.

Mauryan Society

The Mauryan Empire was greatly improved by Asoka's conversion to Buddhism. He was the first Indian ruler who worked for the happiness and welfare of everyone in the empire. One of the improvements he made was having wells dug along major roadways to provide water for travelers and animals. Asoka also grew medicinal herbs and attempted to provide medical care for all living beings. In addition, he prohibited the slaughter of animals for food in accordance with his Buddhist beliefs.

Four lions guard the ancient edicts of Asoka, carved on this pillar in India more than 2,200 years ago.

Asoka appointed a special staff of ministers to help him achieve his aim of ruling over a more caring, tolerant society. The ministers encouraged better relations between members of different castes. They also promoted harmony among followers of different religious beliefs and encouraged charitable activities, such as giving assistance to the elderly.

In the spirit of helping others, Asoka personally donated great sums of money. These donations were used to carve out cave dwellings for holy men and to rebuild temples for Hindu priests. These actions helped unite the people of Asoka's empire. Asoka helped spread Buddhism to northwest India, south India, and Ceylon. In time, Buddhism was introduced to other parts of Asia.

The Decline of the Empire

The success of the Mauryan Empire lay in its ability to unite several different parts of the subcontinent into one political unit, which lasted for almost 100 years. Income to run the empire came from taxes on land and trade. Isolated regions were joined to the empire by means of road building, which improved communication and encouraged trade among regions.

Teaching Options

Research

AVERAGE

Have students write a summary about Chandragupta Maurya's empire. Ask them to find at least six additional facts about how he came to power and his main contributions to ancient Indian society. Remind students to use their own words in their summaries.

CHALLENGE

Ask students to put themselves in the role of a high official, a spy under Chandragupta's command, or a villager plotting against the king. Their task is to write an on-the-scene account of an attempt to overthrow Chandragupta Maurya. Encourage them to do additional research and to incorporate appropriate details and realistic quotations.

With the death of Asoka in 232 B.C., the Mauryan Empire began its decline. Fifty years after his death, the Mauryan Empire included only the Ganges Valley. There are several explanations for the decline of this first, great Indian empire. The economy may have weakened or agriculture may not have kept up with population growth.

Around 500 years passed between the breakup of the Mauryan Empire and the rise of a new empire called the Gupta Empire. A number of small kingdoms replaced the Mauryan Empire. Trade within the subcontinent and with distant regions led to wealth during this period.

◆ **What were some of the advances made in the empire during the reign of Chandragupta?**

B. The Gupta Empire

Around A.D. 320 the Gupta Empire arose in northeast India. Covering the northern and central parts of the subcontinent, the Gupta Empire was not as far reaching as the Mauryan Empire. Because the Gupta rulers were such strong military leaders, there were no threats of invasion for almost 300 years. During those peaceful years, the people of India could concentrate on developing art, music, and writing. During this period, artistic standards were established for Indian literature, art, and architecture. There was also widespread economic prosperity.

Gupta Rule and Rulers

Governmental power was more centralized in the cities and villages than it had been during the Mauryan period. The Gupta Empire was divided into separate territories, governed by imperial officers or by members of the royal family. Most of the power was left in the hands of individual villages. Leaders of the territories often existed side by side with groups of people that had a common set of interests, including associations of people in the same trade, or village. At the local level, merchants, artisans, and scribes governed together.

Chandragupta I, who was not related to the Mauryan Chandragupta, was the first of the great Gupta rulers. Chandragupta I strengthened the kingdom by marrying the daughter of a powerful family. This marriage brought him huge power, more resources, and fame. His son, Samudragupta, became king about A.D. 330. A great military general, Samudragupta also had an interest in promoting Indian culture. The reign of his son Chandragupta II, also called Vikramaditya, was important for its cultural and intellectual achievements. Chandragupta II extended the Gupta Empire from the Bay of Bengal to the Arabian Sea.

The decline of the Gupta Empire began during the reign of Chandragupta II's grandson, Skandagupta, with the invasion of the Huns. The Huns, a group from central Asia, invaded India about A.D. 650 and broke up the empire. Toward the end of the Gupta Empire, there were many kingdoms fighting for control in southern India.

The Gupta Empire, A.D. 400

HINDU KUSH MOUNTAINS
Gandhara
Punjab
Indo-Gangetic Plain
THAR DESERT
Indus River
HIMALAYAS
Brahmaputra River
Ganges River
INDIA
Magadha
Kalinga
Bay of Bengal
Deccan Plateau
Arabian Sea
Western Ghats
Eastern Ghats
INDIAN OCEAN

Gupta Empire
Khyber Pass

0   250   500 mi
0   250   500 km

✔ **Map Check**

LOCATION Which river marked the approximate location of the Gupta Empire's western boundary?

Who in the World?

CHANDRAGUPTA II
During the reign of Chandragupta II, there was great wealth and luxury throughout the empire. Chandragupta minted a large number of gold coins. The greatest number of Gupta coins found to date have come from his reign.

B. The Gupta Empire

Purpose-Setting Question Why was art, music, and writing able to develop during the Gupta Empire? (Gupta leaders were strong military leaders, so there was no threat of invasion. This peaceful time meant that people could concentrate on developing other things.)

Using the Map

The Gupta Empire, A.D. 400

Have students compare the map of the Gupta Empire with the map of the Mauryan Empire on page 65. Ask students which empire ruled a larger area. (Mauryan) Discuss with students how the size of an empire can affect its power. (The bigger an empire, the more powerful it is; however, a large empire can also be more difficult to unite, especially if geographic conditions are as diverse as they are on the subcontinent.)

✔ **Map Check**

Answer Indus River

WHO IN THE WORLD?

CHANDRAGUPTA II The gold, silver, and copper coins that Chandragupta II minted were issued to celebrate his reign. His coins featured many images, including one of him killing a lion and another of the god Vishnu. Ask students why a society embosses its currency with symbols and, in particular, images of its leaders. (Symbols represent a message; placing a leader's image on a coin honors that leader and sends the message that the society is united under one ruler.)

F Y I

Fa-hsien

Much information about the conditions of travel and the Buddhist sites of India during the reign of the Guptas comes to us from the travel writings of the Chinese Buddhist Fa-hsien. Fa-hsien was among the Chinese pilgrims who traveled to the holy sites of Buddhism to learn more about the religion and find Buddhist texts.

Tell students that the Ajanta caves are man-made and were decorated with wall paintings, or murals, of the gods. The caves also contain sculptures. A total of 29 caves have been discovered. The wall painting on page 68 is of the god Bodhisattva. Ask students why murals are an effective way to express an idea. (Possible answer: The size and location of most murals make them accessible to many people at one time.)

Activity

Compare empires Point out to students that a Venn diagram is a useful tool for classifying information. Suggest that students use a Venn diagram (TR, p. 323) with the labels *Mauryan Empire* and *Gupta Empire* for the outer portions of the ovals. Remind students to write the similarities in the overlapping portion of the ovals.

Discuss Ask students why they think so much of the art and architecture that survived from the Gupta Empire involved religion. (Religion must have been very important.)

Focus Have students use library sources or the Internet to find a photograph of the magnificent stone temples that were sponsored by the Gupta rulers or the stupas built by the Mauryan ruler Asoka. Students should also try to find the year the structure was built and its location. Have students share with the class. Encourage students to discuss what the temples or stupas say about Indian society.

Explore Ask groups of students to find other examples of the murals inside the cave temples at Ajanta. Have the groups discuss the elements in the mural and then see if these elements were also used in the murals found by another group in the class.

The murals of the cave temples of Ajanta contain detailed paintings of what life was like during the Gupta period.

Art and Architecture

The rulers of the Gupta Empire supported the arts, architecture, mathematics, and science. Art expressing both Hindu and Buddhist beliefs flourished. That is because the Gupta rulers, who were Hindu, allowed Buddhists to worship freely. Mural painting and sculpture prospered during this era. The wall paintings in the cave temples at Ajanta in western India are some of the best examples of murals. They are famous for their details of nature, architecture, and human activities.

Some of the scenes in the cave temples show the Buddha and his followers. Some show scenes of life in the Gupta Empire. These rock temples were developed by Asoka as places to hold religious ceremonies.

The Gupta rulers also sponsored the building of magnificent stone temples. Remains of these Hindu temples show that they had a very simple construction. They were usually square buildings with heavy walls that housed the image of a **deity**, or god. The Mauryan ruler Asoka also built thousands of stupas, or dome-shaped shrines. A shrine is a sacred place used for worship or devotion. The shrines that Asoka built were for housing artifacts and objects associated with the Buddha. The openings to these stupas had elaborate carvings that told stories of the life of the Buddha.

68 UNIT 1 ◆ From Prehistory to Early Civilizations

Teaching Options

Connection to -----------
ART ◁- - - - - - - - - - - - - - -

The Buddhist caves at Ajanta consist of 29 caves. Excavation on the caves began about 200 B.C. However, digging was abandoned in A.D. 650 in favor of the caves at Ellora. The Ajanta caves were "rediscovered" by a British tiger-hunting party in 1819. These caves, carved out of the side of a steep ravine, consist of five temples and 24 monasteries.

Meet Individual Needs:
VISUAL/SPATIAL LEARNERS

Ask students to make a five-column chart of the achievements of the Gupta Empire. The chart should have the following labels: *Art, Architecture, Literature, Mathematics,* and *Science.* Students should complete their charts with information from the text. You might want to have students illustrate their charts with pictures that represent each achievement. Encourage students to use their charts as a study aid.

Literature

The use of the Sanskrit language, which became the official language of the empire, became more widespread during the Gupta period. As a result, classical literature flowered. India's greatest Sanskrit poet and playwright during this era was Kalidasa. Kalidasa wrote a hundred-verse poem called *The Cloud Messenger*. It is the story of a man who misses his wife and decides to share his sadness with a passing cloud. It is one of the most famous poems of its time, especially for its beautiful descriptions of northern India's mountains, forests, and rivers.

Many other writers during this period collected fables and folk tales. A collection of animal fables called the *Panchatantra* was well known in India. The introduction to these fables says that they are meant to be used as a manual for the instruction of princes. Eventually, the tales spread to other parts of the world.

Advancement of Knowledge

Science, medicine, and education also flourished during the Gupta Empire. Gupta teachers formed the empire's great universities, or centers for learning, which were probably the first of their kind in the world. Students were taught medicine, physics, languages, mathematics, and literature.

Mathematics was more advanced in India during the Gupta Empire, probably more than anywhere else in the world. Indian culture was responsible for a number system with a decimal point and a zero. Aryabhata was a famous Hindu mathematician during the Gupta period. He is one of the first people to have used algebra, and he also devised a decimal system of counting in tens.

Some scientists during the Gupta Empire studied the stars. Indian astronomers—scientists who study the stars and planets—understood that Earth had a spherical, or round, shape and rotated on its axis. They also identified the seven planets that can be seen without the use of a telescope.

NALANDA

Nalanda, a famous Buddhist university, became the center of Indian learning during the Gupta Empire. It offered free education to thousands of students in its many buildings. Students studied the Vedas, grammar, and medicine.

◆ Why are the caves at Ajanta famous?

Review IV

Review History
A. Why did Asoka become a follower of Buddhism?
B. What advances were made in art, literature, and mathematics during the Gupta Empire?

Define Terms to Know
Define the following terms:
bureaucracy, edict, deity

Critical Thinking
How did the peaceful years of the Gupta Empire contribute to cultural achievements?

Write About Citizenship
Write an edict by Asoka that orders every person to strive to live according to Buddhist beliefs.

Get Organized
MAIN IDEA/SUPPORTING DETAILS CHART
Use a chart like the one below to link details with main ideas in this section. For example, use this main idea: The golden age in India was a period of cultural achievements.

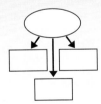

CHAPTER 3 ◆ Ancient India **69**

MAIN IDEA

The golden age in India—cultural achievements

Kalidasa writes **The Cloud Messenger**.
DETAIL

A collection of fables, **Panchatantra**, becomes popular.
DETAIL

Gupta teachers formed universities.
DETAIL

WHAT IN THE WORLD?

NALANDA Point out to students that the educational system of Nalanda was supported by the Gupta Empire in much the same way as federal and state governments support primary and secondary education in the United States. Discuss with students the advantages of a society providing free education for children.

◆ **ANSWER** The caves at Ajanta are famous for their wall paintings with details of nature, architecture, and human activities.

Section Close

Ask students what kind of leadership creates and maintains unity among diverse groups of people. Students should compare the methods used by Maurya and Gupta leaders to unify ancient India in order to answer the question.

3 Assess

Review Answers

Review History
A. He was filled with remorse for the suffering and loss of life in the campaign against Kalinga.
B. Mural painting and sculpture prospered, stone temples were built, classical literature flowered, mathematicians were responsible for a number system with a decimal point and a zero.

Define Terms to Know
bureaucracy, 65; edict, 66; deity, 68

Critical Thinking
Possible answer: Because the years during the Gupta Empire were peaceful, people were able to concentrate on things other than fighting and war. Art, music, and writing all developed during this period. There was also economic prosperity.

Write About Citizenship
Students should demonstrate an understanding of the qualities of Buddhism in their edicts, including goodness, compassion, truthfulness, purity, tolerance, and gentleness.

Chapter Summary

A blank outline form is available in the Teacher's Resources (TR, p. 318). Chapter summaries should outline the rise and decline of the Indus Valley civilization, the effect of the Aryan civilization on Indian society, the differences between Hinduism and Buddhism, and the differences between the Mauryan and Gupta Empires. Refer to the rubric in the Teacher's Resources (TR, p. 340) to score students' chapter summaries.

Interpret the Timeline

1. about 800 years
2. 1500 B.C.
3. Indian mathematicians introduce the concept of zero.
4. Check students' timelines to be sure all events are in the chapter.

Use Terms to Know

5. e. karma
6. f. monsoon
7. a. bureaucracy
8. b. caste system
9. h. reincarnation
10. d. edict
11. c. deity
12. g. plateau
13. i. Vedas

Check Your Understanding

14. The cities formed a well-organized grid system with parallel streets and a citadel on top of a hill surrounded by a brick wall; both cities had a similar layout that would not be possible without being planned and directed.
15. The house probably would be built of bricks and have a bathroom with drains connected to city pipes.
16. It grew partly from the religion of the early Aryans as described in the Vedas. Its beliefs also came from the many peoples who settled in India over time.
17. Jains believe in nonviolence to all living things. They did not want to kill worms or other creatures because of this belief.
18. Siddhartha saw an old man, a sick man, and a dead man. Siddhartha was so unhappy about people's suffering and pain, he decided to give up his life of ease and luxury.
19. Before his conversion, Asoka ruled like emperors before him. After his conversion, he tried to lead his people by his good example, not by

force. He decided he would never go to war again.
20. The Mauryan Empire declined when Asoka died. It may have declined because the economy declined or because agriculture did not keep up with population growth.
21. Magnificent stone temples were built; mural paintings with details of nature, architecture, and human character were done.

22. It gave beautiful descriptions of India's mountains, forests, and rivers.

Chapter Summary

Complete the following outline in your notebook. Then, use your outline to write a brief summary of the chapter.

Ancient India

I. Indus Valley Civilization
  A. The Geography of South Asia
  B. The Indus Valley Civilization
  C. The Cities of Harappa and Mohenjo-Daro
  D. Culture, Religion, and Decline
II. Aryan Civilization
  A. The Aryans
  B. Aryan Society
  C. Poems About the Vedas
  D. Changes in Aryan Society
III. Hinduism and Buddhism
  A. Religious Traditions in Ancient India
  B. The Rise of Buddhism
IV. Ancient Indian Dynasties
  A. The Mauryan Empire
  B. The Gupta Empire

Interpret the Timeline

Use the timeline on pages 48–49 to answer the following questions.

1. About how many years were there between the rise and fall of the Indus Valley civilization?
2. When did Aryans enter the Indian subcontinent?
3. **Critical Thinking** Which event on the timeline shows that knowledge was advanced during the Gupta period?
4. Select three events from the chapter that are not on the timeline. Create a timeline that shows these events.

Use Terms to Know

Match each term with its definition.

a. bureaucracy   d. edict   g. plateau
b. caste system   e. karma   h. reincarnation
c. deity   f. monsoon   i. Vedas

5. all the actions in a person's life that affect the next life
6. a seasonal wind that creates a strong pattern of wet and dry seasons in parts of Asia
7. a body of appointed or hired government officials who follow a set routine
8. the complex form of social organization that restricts its members to certain occupations
9. the rebirth of a soul in another body
10. an order or command given by an official and backed or supported by law
11. a supreme being or divinity
12. a raised area of level land
13. one of the earliest Hindu sacred texts

Check Your Understanding

14. **Explain** why archaeologists believe that the cities of Harappa and Mohenjo-Daro were planned.
15. **Describe** a family house in Mohenjo-Daro.
16. **Explain** how the Hindu religion came into being.
17. **Explain** why some Jains did not believe in farming.
18. **Summarize** the event that made Siddhartha decide to become a wandering holy man.
19. **Contrast** Asoka's life before and after his conversion to Buddhism.
20. **Describe** why the Mauryan Empire declined.
21. **Identify** some of the advances in art and architecture that were made during the Gupta Empire.
22. **Identify** why *The Cloud Messenger* was one of the most famous poems of its time.

Critical Thinking

23. Make Predictions How would being able to understand the written language found on seals add to our knowledge of the Indus Valley civilization?

24. Synthesize Information Why do you suppose some Hindu divinities take animal forms?

25. Analyze Primary Sources Do you think people thought Asoka's statement on page 66 was sincere? Why or why not?

26. Compare and Contrast In what ways were the Mauryan Empire and the Gupta Empire similar? In what ways were they different?

Put Your Skills to Work

27. Understand Cause and Effect In this chapter you learned about the relationship between cause and effect. One action or event is the cause of another action or event. You can understand more about the history of ancient India by identifying cause-and-effect relationships.

Copy the following chart. Identify two cause-and-effect relationships that you read about in this chapter. Write the causes in the circles at the top and the effects in the circles at the bottom.

Analyze Sources

28. Read more about Krishna in the Bhagavad Gita, as he discusses the nature of work. Then, answer the questions that follow.

You have the right to work, but for the work's sake only. Desire for the fruits of work must never be your motive in working. . . . Work done with anxiety about results is far inferior to work done without such anxiety, in the calm of self-surrender. Seek refuge in the knowledge of Brahman. They who work selfishly for results are miserable.

a. What does the "fruits of work" mean?

b. Why is work for work's sake better than work for some kind of reward?

Essay Writing

29. After Asoka's conversion to Buddhism, he expressed a desire to treat each of his subjects as he would his own children. Write an essay about how this desire led to a better society. Include details from the text as support.

TEST PREPARATION

CAUSE-AND-EFFECT RELATIONSHIPS
Choose the answer that correctly completes the sentence.

The exact cause of the decline of the Indus Valley civilization is a matter of making an educated guess based on what we know. Archaeologists believe that one of the most probable reasons for its disappearance was

1. a gradual change in the climate.

2. a natural event like a flood.

3. an invasion from other people.

4. a combination of factors.

Critical Thinking

23. Possible answer: It could give archaeologists a different view of the civilization.
24. Possible answer: Hindu divinities take animal forms to demonstrate the different aspects of the universal spirit call Brahman.
25. Possible answer: Yes, because Asoka devoted the rest of his life to improving the lives of others.
26. Similar: Both empires expanded and their rulers improved their empires; both empires were fairly large and powerful. **Different:** Governmental power was more centralized in the Gupta Empire; the Gupta Empire focused more on art, architecture, literature, and learning.

Put Your Skills to Work

UNDERSTAND CAUSE AND EFFECT
27. Possible answers: **Cause:** The rulers of the Gupta Empire supported the arts. **Effect:** Mural painting and sculpture prospered during this period. **Cause:** Brahman priests interpreted the Vedas. **Effect:** Brahman priests were very influential.

Analyze Sources

28a. Possible answers: getting paid, recognition, or thanks for a job well done
28b. Possible answer: A person working without concern for any kind of reward is more focused on the task itself.

Essay Writing

29. Check that students' essays meet all the requirements. In addition to correct grammar, spelling, and punctuation, and a logical organization, the essay must explain how Asoka's desire led to a better society.

TEST PREPARATION

Answer 4. a combination of factors.

Ancient China
1750 B.C.–A.D. 220
(pp. 72–96)

Chapter Objectives
• Discuss how the geography of ancient China led to the development of civilization, beginning with the Shang Dynasty.
• Compare the social, political, and cultural characteristics of the Zhou, Qin, and Han Dynasties.
• Identify the philosophies of Confucianism, Daoism, Legalism, and Buddhism, and understand their influences on Chinese society.
• Explain the importance of the family in ancient Chinese society and the advances in technology and culture during this period.

Chapter Summary
Section I focuses on the link between the geography of China's river valleys and the beginnings of civilization during the Shang Dynasty.

Section II discusses the rise and fall of the Zhou, Qin, and Han Dynasties and their political, social, and cultural influence on ancient China.

Section III explores the principles of Confucianism, Daoism, Legalism, and Buddhism, and explains how these beliefs and religions influenced Chinese civilization.

Section IV discusses the characteristics of ancient Chinese life and culture, including the role of the family, the importance of farming and trade, and the important advances in technology, science, and literature.

Set the Stage
TEACH PRIMARY SOURCES
Explain that this poem was written during a time when the king gave territory to his most loyal supporters in return for their military help. Discuss with students how the poet described the relationship between the Chinese king and his people. (The all-powerful king had complete control over everyone in the country.) Ask students to identify phrases that show the king's power extended beyond China. ("Everywhere under vast Heaven")

T72 ◆ **UNIT 1**

CHAPTER 4

Ancient China
1750 B.C.–A.D. 220

I. Early Civilization in China
II. The Zhou, Qin, and Han Dynasties
III. Religions and Beliefs in Ancient China
IV. Ancient Chinese Life and Culture

For centuries, the rulers of the various Chinese states battled each other for control of eastern Asia. As the kingdoms grew larger, so did the power of the kings. As a stanza from a poem in the ancient *Book of Songs* reported:

❝ *Everywhere under vast Heaven*
There is no land that is not the king's.
To the borders of these lands
There are none who are not the king's servants. ❞

Qin Shi Huangdi, powerful ruler of the Qin Dynasty, wanted to ensure his safety in the afterlife. His tomb was "guarded" by thousands of terra cotta soldiers and horses. Although no one has been hurt yet, people believe that the tomb is equipped with hidden traps designed to kill anyone attempting to rob it. Those who knew the secrets of the tomb's construction were buried alive inside it.

Today, the soldiers still stand guard over the tomb. The tomb and its soldiers serve as a reminder of China's ancient and powerful dynasties.

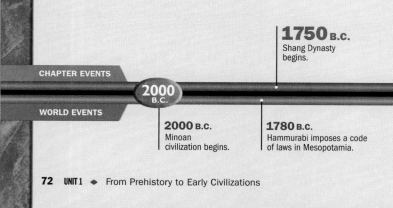

CHAPTER EVENTS

1750 B.C. Shang Dynasty begins.

1000 B.C. Zhou Dynasty begins.

2000 B.C.

1250 B.C.

WORLD EVENTS

2000 B.C. Minoan civilization begins.

1780 B.C. Hammurabi imposes a code of laws in Mesopotamia.

72 **UNIT 1** ◆ From Prehistory to Early Civilizations

Teaching Options

Chapter 4 Resources

REVIEW

Teacher's Resources (TR)
Terms to Know, p. 17
Review History, p. 51
Build Your Skills, p. 85
Concept Builder, p. 220
Chapter Test, pp. 123–124
SQR Chart, p. 322
Transparencies 1, 7

ASSESSMENT
Section Reviews, pp. 78, 84, 88, 93
Chapter Review, pp. 94–95
Chapter Test, TR pp. 123–124
Unit Test, TR pp. 183–184

ALTERNATIVE ASSESSMENT
Portfolio Project, p. 96
Write a Play, p. T96

Ancient China to A.D. 220

GET ORGANIZED

SQR Chart An SQR chart involves a three-step process that helps you better understand what you read. It organizes important ideas and facts. Use an SQR chart as you read Chapter 4. First, survey (S) a section to find a topic being discussed. Then, ask a question (Q). Finally, read (R) to find the answer. Here is an example from this chapter.

> **SURVEY**
> This section is about the geography of China.
>
> ↓
>
> **QUESTION**
> What role did geography play in China's cultural development?
>
> ↓
>
> **READ**
> Mountains and deserts prevented outside contact. People began farming in fertile river valleys.

VIEW HISTORY The "army" of Qin Shi Huangdi contains more than 7,000 terra cotta statues. Each one has a different face, indicating that the statues were individually molded.
◆ What does the number of statues suggest about Qin Shi Huangdi's concern for his own safety?

551 B.C.
Confucius is born.

221 B.C.
Qin Dynasty begins.

202 B.C.
Han Dynasty rises.

A.D. 220
Han Dynasty is overthrown.

500 B.C. ◄ B.C. ► A.D. ► **A.D. 250**

776 B.C.
First Olympic games are held in Greece.

44 B.C.
Julius Caesar is assassinated.

CHAPTER 4 ◆ Ancient China **73**

Chapter Themes
• Culture
• People, Places, and Environments
• Power, Authority, and Governance
• Individuals, Groups, and Institutions
• Time, Continuity, and Change
• Science, Technology, and Society
• Civic Ideals and Practices

F Y I

Terra Cotta Figures

The terra cotta figures are the earliest known life-size Chinese figures. Because the emperor who had them built died in 210 B.C., the figures show that making sculpture had a long history in China. The terra cotta army was found in three pits. Excavation of the pits revealed a huge army that included soldiers, cavalry, horses, infantry, and chariots. It was created to follow the emperor into the afterlife.

Chapter Warm-Up
USING THE MAP
Point out the highlighted area on the map at the top of page 73. To help students understand where China is, explain that China is part of Asia. Have them identify the Indian Ocean, Pacific Ocean, Africa, and Europe.

VIEW HISTORY
Point out that since the discovery of the terra cotta figures in 1974 by local farmers, the site has become a popular tourist attraction. Ask students to describe the impression made by this army of statues. (powerful, frightening, strong) Discuss the connection between the size and number of the statues and the king's power. (The statues reinforce the great power of the king.)

◆ **ANSWER** The king may have feared greatly for his safety.

GET ORGANIZED
SQR Chart
Discuss the SQR chart on page 73. Ask students to identify where the topic is located (top box), where the question is located (middle box), and where the answer is located (bottom box). Point out that an SQR chart can be used by students to organize information in sections of text as they read. Encourage students to make an SQR chart (TR, p. 322) for each section in the chapter.

 TEACH THE TIMELINE
The timeline on pages 72–73 covers the period between 2000 B.C. and A.D. 220. Point out that the timeline covers more than 2,000 years and covers dates identified as B.C. and A.D. Ask students what ideas are emphasized in the Chapter Events entries. (the rise and fall of early dynasties in China) Encourage students to identify other key events they can add to the timeline as they read the chapter.

Activity

Use a map Have students use a world map (Transparency 1) to identify where the civilizations referred to in the World Events section of the timeline are found. (**Minoan:** Crete; **Mesopotamian:** Iraq, Greece)

CHAPTER 4 ◆ **T73**

I. Early Civilization in China (pp. 74–78)

Section Summary

In this section, students will learn how ancient China's geography, particularly the mountain barriers and rivers, influenced the development of civilization while isolating the country from outside influences. Students will also learn about life in China during the Shang Dynasty and how distinct social classes developed.

Getting Started

Ask students about signs or pictures they may have seen as they move around their town. Discuss what the symbols on the signs or in the pictures mean. Students may suggest wheelchair (handicapped accessible), bed (hotel), or person reading a book (library). Ask how these symbols help people communicate with each other. (Some symbols have the same meaning regardless of the language a person speaks. These symbols represent a common language and help people who speak different languages to communicate.) Explain that the written language in ancient China used symbols.

TERMS TO KNOW

Ask students to read the terms and definitions on page 74 and then find each term in the section. Have students use each term in a sentence that includes context clues to explain the term's meaning.

You may wish to preview the pronunciation of the following terms from this section with students.

Huang He (HWAHNG HAY)
Shang (SHAHNG)

ACTIVE READING

Have students choose one of the subsections in Section 1 to preview. Use the headings and visuals to guide them. Suggest that they write a topic sentence based on the previewing strategy. As they read, you may want them to write the main idea and details related to the topic on a main idea/supporting details chart (TR, p. 319).

Terms to Know

elevation the height above sea level

loess a fine, yellowish-brown, rich soil

oracle a person, place, or thing that a god uses to reveal hidden knowledge

sericulture a process involved in silk production

Main Ideas

A. Eastern Asia's physical features isolated Chinese culture from outside influences and helped determine where Chinese people set up communities.

B. The Shang Dynasty developed the first Chinese civilization by uniting the agricultural communities that had developed in the river valleys of the North China Plain.

C. Shang society was divided into distinct social classes, with the king and royal family at the top and peasants at the bottom.

📖 Active Reading

PREVIEW

When you preview, you skim through a text to see what you can learn from headings and visuals before you actually read it. As you read this section, ask yourself this question: What topic is suggested by this heading? Then, read to learn the main idea and details.

Chinese civilization arose in fertile river valleys like the one shown here.

A. The Geography of China

Geography greatly affected how and where civilization developed in ancient China. China is a vast land that covers much of eastern Asia. Because of its size and location, China contains a variety of physical features. Rugged mountain ranges frame its western and northwestern borders. In its northeastern regions, plains run eastward to the coastline. Several rivers flow through these plains to seas that merge into the Pacific Ocean. Great deserts lie in parts of China's northern regions, whereas tropical rain forests grow on a strip of land along its southern coast.

The different climates of China are directly related to the varied landscapes. Snow-covered mountain peaks tower over regions with a highland climate. The temperature and precipitation of these regions depends on **elevation**, or distance above sea level. Deserts reflect their dry climate. The rain forests lie within the tropics, which generally has a hot and humid climate. China's southeast has a subtropical climate, which means that it is not quite as hot and humid as the tropical rain forests. In summer, winds called monsoons blow from the Pacific Ocean across China's coastline. Monsoons carry heavy rains into the plains regions.

Natural Barriers

China's natural barriers isolated it during prehistoric times, or the period before history was recorded. The high, rugged mountain ranges of the Himalayas and the Tian Shan were difficult to cross. People could not easily travel across the Gobi and Taklimakan Deserts.

In addition, groups of people within China's boundaries were isolated from one another. That is because the three major rivers in China run from west to east. Communication between the north and south was difficult.

Teaching Options

Section 1 Resources

Teacher's Resources (TR)
Terms to Know, p. 17
Review History, p. 51
Build Your Skills, p. 85
Concept Builder, p. 220
SQR Chart, p. 322

ESL/ELL STRATEGIES

Take Notes Tell students that in this section, they will read about the first group of rulers in ancient China, the Shang Dynasty. Have pairs of students work together to take notes on the characteristics of Shang society. Students' notes should include the different social classes and the roles of men and women. Students can identify unfamiliar words and define them for each other. Have students use their notes to quiz each other.

China's Agricultural Revolution

About 7000 B.C., agricultural communities began to spring up in China's river valleys. This was especially true where the earth was rich in **loess**. Loess is a fine-grained, yellow soil carried and deposited by wind and water. Loess is ideal for farming because it is very fertile and easy to work—even with prehistoric tools.

Between 4000 B.C. and 1000 B.C., an agricultural revolution took place in China. Soils rich in loess had been carried to the valleys of the major rivers by winds. Yearly flooding of the rivers during the monsoon season served to spread thick layers of this fertile soil on the valley floors. Farmers used water from the rivers to irrigate, or water, their crops. They built systems of canals to carry the water to fields that did not border the rivers. They also invented new and better tools for planting and harvesting crops.

A very important region for this agricultural revolution was the valley of the Huang He, or Yellow River. Farmers grew rice and other grains in the fertile soils of the valley. They also raised sheep and cattle. Like the Egyptians along the Nile River, the farmers in the Huang He valley learned how to build canals and walls to control the annual floods.

The building of canals and flood walls in the valley was a cooperative effort. That is, the farmers worked together to improve the entire valley region. This idea of working together for the good of all would lead to the development of one of the world's oldest systems of religious beliefs.

Local leaders governed the numerous small farming villages of the Huang He valley. Over hundreds of years, these villages grew into towns and small cities.

◆ What benefits did the Chinese gain in developing a civilization near a river?

Spotlight on
Geography

THE HIMALAYAS
The Himalayas are a series of mountain ranges that lie side by side. These ranges form the highest mountain system in the world. Nine of the world's tallest mountains are scattered throughout the Himalayas. Mount Everest, the world's highest, rises 29,028 feet (almost $5\frac{1}{2}$ miles) above sea level.

Sir Edmund Hillary and Tenzing Norgay were the first climbers to reach the top of Mount Everest. They did not accomplish this feat until 1953, more than 3,000 years after the rise of the first Chinese civilization.

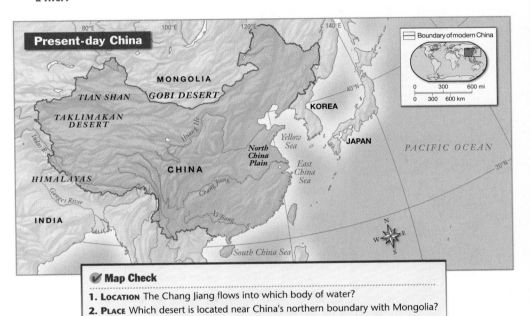

Present-day China

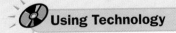

Map Check

1. **LOCATION** The Chang Jiang flows into which body of water?
2. **PLACE** Which desert is located near China's northern boundary with Mongolia?

---

2 Teach

A. The Geography of China

Purpose-Setting Question What geographic features isolated people living in ancient China from other countries and from one another? (Mountains and deserts prevented contact with other countries. Rivers ran from west to east, preventing people from reaching one another.)

Discuss Ask students what effect the farmers' new inventions had on China's agricultural revolution. (Without their invention of improved tools, an irrigation system, and dikes and canals to control floods, the agricultural revolution probably would not have taken place.)

SPOTLIGHT ON GEOGRAPHY
THE HIMALAYAS Ask students to predict how life in ancient China would have been different if people there had been able to cross the Himalayas. (Possible answer: The Chinese would have been able to make contact with people in other lands much earlier. This would probably have affected their cultural development as well as the cultures of neighboring regions.)

Using the Map
Present-day China

Ask students to identify the major geographical features on the map of China. (Gobi and Taklimakan Deserts, Himalayas in the west, Tian Shan Mountains in the north, North China Plain, Huang He, Chang Jiang, and Xi Jiang) Discuss in what geographic areas students would expect to find the earliest towns and cities and where there would probably be little or no settlement. (There would be cities and towns in the North China Plain and little or no settlement in the mountains and deserts.)

Map Check
Answers
1. East China Sea
2. Gobi Desert

◆ **ANSWER** They could grow enough crops for food and for trade. Also, they had a reliable source of transportation.

Using Technology

Ask students to use the Internet, CD-ROM resources, and other media to learn more about efforts to climb Mt. Everest. Have them identify the problems faced by mountain climbers and how they have attempted to overcome them. Encourage students to find out what a climbing expedition to Mt. Everest would involve today. They should note how many climbers have reached the top of Mt. Everest since Hillary's expedition.

B. The Shang Dynasty

Purpose-Setting Question In what geographic area did the Shang Dynasty start and develop? (The Shang Dynasty started in the Huang He valley and eventually developed southward to the Chang Jiang.)

Then & Now

ANYANG CITY, CHINA Ask students why it is important to maintain the archaeological site and treasures in Anyang for visitors and scholars. (These archaeological finds provide visitors with a window into the past, enabling them to understand what life was like during the first recorded dynasty in China.)

Focus Have students use a map of China in an atlas to locate the cities of Anyang and Zhengzhou. Why were the walled cities built in these locations? (They were both near the Huang He and would have sufficient food for their residents and access to water transportation.)

Discuss Ask students to evaluate the power that priests had during the Shang Dynasty. Have them support their answers with information from the text. (Possible answer: The priests were very powerful because they interpreted the oracle bones that supposedly answered the king's questions to his ancestors.)

Review Remind students that they learned in Chapter 2 that ancient Egyptians also believed in an afterlife. Their rulers were also buried with their jewelry, art objects, and other personal belongings in ornate tombs called pyramids.

Activity

Research Have students use library or Internet resources to find out more information about the ancient written Chinese language, which is based on individual symbols called characters. Each character represented an idea or object. Ask students to copy several of these Chinese characters on the left of a two-column chart (TR, p. 328). In the right column, students should provide a translation of the symbols.

◆ **ANSWER** because the different regions all had different dialects, so it was difficult for people to communicate

Then & Now

ANYANG CITY, CHINA

Anyang's history dates back more than 3,000 years. Once the major capital of the Shang Dynasty, Anyang remains a center of culture and archaeological treasures. Here, visitors can see ancient tombs, the first library of writings on animal bones, historic temples, and a canal more than 900 miles long.

Through the years, its scenic location near the Taihang Mountains made Anyang an attractive location. Today, a variety of modern industries contribute to Anyang's economy.

The Chinese used oracle bones to ask their ancestors about the future and to seek favors from the gods.

B. The Shang Dynasty

A Chinese people called the Shang built China's first recorded dynasty in the region of the Huang He valley. Artifacts led many historians to believe that the Shang Dynasty began about 1750 B.C. and flourished until around 1000 B.C. During this period, a number of clans, or extended families, united and formed a loose political union. The Shang Dynasty eventually grew southward to the banks of the Chang Jiang, or the Yangtze River.

Shang Rulers

At varying times, Shang rulers established walled capital cities. Anyang and Zhengzhou were among the most important. Archaeologists have found the remains of palaces and tombs at several sites in these locations.

The king probably oversaw lands near his capital city. Obedient princes and loyal nobles called lords helped control more distant areas. If nomads threatened their territories, the king took action. He led warrior-nobles from the walled capital to capture these invaders or to drive them out of the kingdom. Shang armies used wheeled chariots and bronze weapons to defeat their enemies. Slowly, the Shang kings gained more power over local leaders.

Ancestor Worship

Religious beliefs influenced Shang culture in many ways. Ancestor worship was at the heart of these beliefs. An ancestor is a person from whom a family or group is descended. The Shang believed that their ancestors could bring them good fortune. Shang families buried dead relatives with food and drink. Wealthier families sometimes included art objects. These gifts were meant to show respect to the ancestors in the next world.

The power of Shang kings was firmly rooted in religion. The Shang believed royal ancestors had a direct link to a powerful god. Kings sought their ancestors' advice in making decisions about life or politics. Priests developed rituals, or ceremonies, for contacting ancestors. They scratched symbols on a ceremonial object made of turtle shell or an animal bone. Today, these artifacts are known as **oracle** bones. An oracle is a person, place, or thing that a god uses to reveal hidden knowledge. The symbols on an oracle bone were arranged to form questions. When the oracle bone was touched with a hot metal poker, it cracked. The way the crack developed was read as an ancestor's answer.

Introduction of Writing

The Shang developed the first Chinese writing system. Many oracle bones have been found in Shang tombs. The writings on these artifacts are considered to be the first known examples of Chinese writing in complete sentences.

Shang writing used a symbol or simple picture to represent each object or Chinese word. Spoken Chinese varied widely among the groups of people living in different regions of China. These variations made it difficult for people from one area of China to talk with people in other parts of the land. One day, Chinese writing would solve this problem and help unify China. When people learned to read and write, they could communicate their thoughts to one another.

◆ **Why was the development of a Chinese writing system so important?**

Teaching Options

Test Taking

Tell students that short-answer questions ask them to provide a brief answer about a main idea in a section or chapter of a book. Making an SQR chart, such as the one on p. 73, will help them focus on the important ideas in each section of a chapter and help them prepare for a short-answer test.

F Y I

Chinese Written Language

Explain that the Chinese language does not have an alphabet like ours. The Wade-Giles system, developed by Sir Thomas Wade in 1879 and modified by Herbert A. Giles, used the Roman alphabet to help English-speaking people translate the sounds of the Chinese language. Another system, called Pinyin, was developed in the 1960s. Since then, the Pinyin system has been used to spell Chinese names and terms in English.

C. Shang Society

Shang society was divided into distinct social classes. The king was the most important warrior-leader. The royal family lived in a palace inside the capital city. Families of warrior-nobles held almost equal rank with the royal family. Although nobles followed the king's orders, many were former clan leaders who still controlled their own groups or territories.

Most Shang were peasants who lived in farming villages scattered throughout the kingdom. Peasants ranked lowest in the Shang social order. Their homes were huts with dirt floors. All members of a family worked many hours in the fields. Because no suitable metal for ordinary tools and farm equipment was available, peasants used simple stone and wood tools to plant and harvest crops. Peasants also dug canals and repaired flood walls. Sometimes nobles from different clans argued. If war broke out, nobles ordered peasant men to fight alongside them.

Ancient Chinese writings tell much about royal families and brave warriors. Many generations could only learn about ancient peasant life by memorizing and singing folk songs. One folk song expresses peasants' impressions of a war:

> **"** Long ago, when we started, the willows spread their shade.
> Now that we turn back the snowflakes fly.
> The march before us is long, we are thirsty and hungry, our hearts are stricken with sorrow but no one listens to our plaint. **"**

Artisans and Merchants

Artisans and merchants lived and worked outside the walls of early Chinese cities. However, they had no official rank in Shang society. Artisans crafted goods for nobles and merchants. Their creations included items made of silk, jade, or bronze. Merchants set up shops where they traded goods.

The beginning of the Shang Dynasty took place at the same time as the Bronze Age in China. Like many ancient world cultures, Chinese civilization developed as people learned how to make metal objects. Unfortunately, bronze was too soft to be used to make farm tools and equipment. However, the bronze objects produced by artisans tell us much about Shang culture. Many highly decorated bronze cups, bowls, vases, and artworks survive today. Most of these items were used during ceremonies. Warriors also fought with spears, axes, and daggers made from bronze.

Merchants traded farm products and objects produced by artisans for spices and goods found in other parts of China. In turn, they traded or sold unusual items such as cowrie shells to local people. Cowrie shells were popular among Shang nobility. These beautifully patterned seashells are not found in the coastal waters of northeastern China, but they have been discovered in royal Shang tombs. Some historians believe that the Shang valued these shells enough to use them as a form of money.

Women's Roles

At all levels of Shang society, men had more authority than women. Wives took direction from their husbands and cared for the children. However, some Shang women had rights and responsibilities usually associated with men in other cultures.

Women from royal families did not have political power equal to that of men because they could not become rulers. However, symbols arranged on several oracle bones tell much about Lady Hao, a wife of King Wu Ding, who lived about 1200 B.C. She was in charge of certain ceremonies and owned an

ANALYZE PRIMARY SOURCES **DOCUMENT-BASED QUESTION** What do the lyrics in this folk song suggest about the peasants' participation in war?

Artisans used bronze to make decorated containers that were used in ceremonies.

Connection to ART

Tell students that two of the great achievements of the Shang Dynasty were the development of horse-drawn war chariots and bronze vessels. Ask students to find pictures of these chariots or bronze vessels, using encyclopedia or Internet resources. Have them use these objects as the basis of original drawings, rendered in a realistic or impressionistic style.

Connection to CULTURE

Remind students that ancient cultures used a variety of objects and metals as money. Have students use Internet or classroom resources to research the different forms of money used in the ancient world in Egypt, the Fertile Crescent, and ancient India. They can present their findings in the form of brief, illustrated reports with examples of the different ancient currencies.

Purpose-Setting Question What were the main social classes in Shang society? (warrior-leaders, warrior-nobles, and peasants; artisans and merchants had no official rank)

ANALYZE PRIMARY SOURCES

DOCUMENT-BASED QUESTION
This folk song was written during a period when the warrior-leaders were engaged in fierce conflicts with each other and against neighboring enemies. While the ruling class rode into battle in elaborately decorated bronze chariots, the poor peasant soldiers followed them on foot. They had been forced to leave their families and farms to join the army. Their folk songs realistically describe the hardships they endured.

ANSWER The lyrics indicate that the peasants are very unhappy about the long military campaign, which has left them hungry, thirsty, and unable to voice their feelings.

Discuss Ask students what the status of artisans and merchants compared to that of warrior-nobles in Shang society shows about the culture. (The artisans and merchants had no official rank and lived and worked outside the walls of the cities. The warrior-nobles held almost equal rank with the royal family. This social division showed the low regard that artisans and merchants had in the culture.)

Activity

Make a chart Have students make a three-column chart to identify the two major social classes and the artisans and merchants group in Shang society. Have students list the characteristics of each.

TEACH PRIMARY SOURCES

Have students study the photograph of the bronze vessel. Explain that detailed molds with complicated designs based on animals found in China were created by artisans, who then poured metal in the molds. The vessel in the photograph is in the form of two owls. It was probably used in a ceremony for the dead.

LADY HAO'S TOMB

The discovery of Lady Hao's royal tomb at Anyang was an exciting event. This tomb is the only one never to have been robbed through the centuries.

Although there are no pictures of Lady Hao, oracle bones found elsewhere have told of her deeds. Within the tomb, many valuable objects were carefully arranged to honor her. These included nearly 500 bone hairpins, 750 jade objects, and 130 bronze weapons.

estate outside the capital. She even led armies as large as 13,000 troops to fight her husband's enemies in various parts of China. This information provides a glance at one woman's role in a royal family.

Silk Farming

Silk farming, or <u>**sericulture**</u>, was established in ancient China about 2600 B.C. In areas where silk was produced, women were responsible for all stages of sericulture. First, they took care of the silkworms that fed on the leaves of mulberry trees. Next, they gathered the cocoons created by these caterpillars. Each cocoon was made of a single strand of silk. Each strand could measure several thousand feet long. Then, the women carefully unraveled each strand from the cocoons to prepare for spinning. Several strands might be twisted together to form an even stronger thread. After spinning, they wove the threads to make a finished fabric.

By the time of the Shang Dynasty, Chinese women were already making fine, decorative silk fabrics and creating silk embroideries. Silk fabric is soft, lightweight, and strong. For centuries Chinese silk was the most prized and expensive fabric in the world. Only wealthy people could afford silk clothing and decorative silk tapestries.

Because silk was so valuable, its production was a great responsibility. An ancient Chinese saying, "Men plough and women weave," helps explain how work was divided in many farming villages.

◆ **What was life like for peasants in Shang society?**

Review I

Review History

A. What effect did mountains have on the development of Chinese culture?

B. What is an important feature of the writing found on oracle bones?

C. Describe the role of women in Shang society.

Define Terms to Know

Define the following terms: **elevation, loess, oracle, sericulture**

Critical Thinking

What likely caused the Chinese to name the Huang He, or Yellow River?

Write About Culture

Write a paragraph that describes the impact of the agricultural revolution in ancient China.

Get Organized

SQR CHART

Use an SQR chart to organize information from this section. Survey to find a topic from this section, such as China's agricultural revolution. Write a question and then read to find the answer.

SURVEY
This section is about the agricultural revolution in China.

QUESTION
How did the agricultural revolution affect villages?

READ
Villages formed in fertile valleys and grew into towns and cities.

Build Your Skills

USE TABLES AND CHARTS

Tables and charts are tools that organize information in categories. They are made up of columns and rows. The heading at the top of a column tells what kind of information can be found in that column. Labels can also appear before each row that help break down the information by person, place, year, or other categories.

You have learned that the Shang developed a system of writing that contributed to the development of the modern Chinese language. In 1859, language expert Thomas Wade developed a system for English-speaking people to translate the sounds of the Chinese language. Another expert, Herbert Giles, made some changes to the system in 1912. This system, known as Wade-Giles, is still widely used today.

In 1979, China adopted the Pinyin system of spelling and pronunciation. This system is used in schools throughout China today. Still, in the United States many maps and references are in use that were written before the conversion from Wade-Giles to Pinyin. A chart can help you to organize and understand Wade-Giles and Pinyin names.

Here's How
Follow these steps to read a table or chart.

1. Read the title, headings, and labels. Determine what type of information is being presented.
2. Read the information under each column. Determine how it relates to the heading.
3. Read the information in each row. Find relationships between the information in the headings, rows, and columns.

Here's Why
When you read tables or charts, they can help you understand and organize large amounts of information in a way that adds to what you have learned. They are useful reference tools when studying a variety of subjects, including history.

Practice the Skill
Read the chart on the right. It lists the names of some different dynasties in China. Use the chart to answer the following questions.

1. What do the title and headings tell you about the information being presented?
2. Which dynasty changes the most when it is converted from Wade-Giles to Pinyin?
3. Which dynasty has the same spelling in both systems?

Extend the Skill
Look up the names of three modern Chinese cities. Then, conduct research to discover the Wade-Giles pronunciation of these names.

Apply the Skill
As you read this chapter, create a chart that organizes information about Chinese dynasties and their rulers.

Some Chinese Dynasties	
WADE-GILES	**PINYIN**
Ch'in	Qin
T'ang	Tang
Sung	Song
Chou	Zhou
Shang	Shang

Build Your Skills

USE TABLES AND CHARTS

Teach the Skill
Bring in several examples of tables and charts that students use in their daily lives. (bus schedules, movie or television listings, school or sports schedules) Distribute the tables and charts to small groups of students. Ask the groups to identify the kind of information included in the table or chart. Explain how each one is read; and discuss why sometimes it is easier to use a chart or table instead of reading the same information in paragraph form.

Remind students to use the steps described in *Here's How* to read the table or chart. Discuss how making a table or chart would help students better organize their time when researching and writing a school paper.

Practice the Skill
ANSWERS
1. These are Chinese dynasties in both Wade-Giles and Pinyin systems of spelling.
2. Ch'in to Qin
3. Shang

Extend the Skill
Students' choices, if possible, should show names that are spelled differently in the two systems. Some cities, such as Shanghai, have the same spelling. One good example is Beijing (Pinyin)/Peking (Wade-Giles).

Apply the Skill
Ask small groups of students to make a chart for Section 2 that organizes information about the major accomplishments of the Zhou, Qin, and Han Dynasties. Remind students to review the chart to make sure the headings are correct and the information is accurate.

Teaching Options

RETEACH
Have students list the following information in a chart. Left column: *8:30, 9:15, 10:00, 10:45, 11:30*. Right column: *polar bears, penguins, seals, walruses, puffins*. Discuss with students what this information might mean. Then, title the chart *Zoo Feeding Schedule*. Add the column headings *Time* and *Animal*. Review the contents of the chart and have students answer questions using the chart.

CHALLENGE
Have students create their own charts to organize their time in 1-hour blocks during a 5-day school week. They should use different-colored inks to write labels for the days of the week and the hours of the day. They can create a system of stars or other marks to highlight projects or activities that are the highest priority to complete.

II. The Zhou, Qin, and Han Dynasties

(pp. 80–84)

Section Summary

In this section students will learn about the rise and fall of the Zhou, Qin, and Han Dynasties, the major contributions of each, and the social and cultural legacy of their rule.

 **Introduce**

Getting Started

Ask students how their school government is organized. Have them discuss the responsibilities of their elected student leaders, the election process, and the way in which school laws are amended or new laws are enacted. Explain that students will be learning about some different types of governments.

TERMS TO KNOW

Ask students to read the terms and definitions on page 80 and then find each term in this section. Have students review the terms with a partner. Encourage students to use the terms in their own sentences.

You may wish to preview the pronunciation of the following terms from this section with the students.

Zhou (JOH)
Qin Shi Huangdi
  (KIHN SHIH hoo ahng DEE)
Gaozu (GAOOD ZOO)

ACTIVE READING

Have students choose one of the three dynasties described in Section 2 and list the main events from its history on a flowchart (TR, p. 324).

 Section **II**

The Zhou, Qin, and Han Dynasties

Terms to Know

Mandate of Heaven a claim of the divine right to rule

dynastic cycle an explanation of the rise and fall of dynasties based on the Mandate of Heaven

civil war war between groups of people from the same country

authoritarian exerting complete power as a ruler

civil service people employed in government administration

Main Ideas

A. The Zhou believed they had the right to rule China with the Mandate of Heaven.

B. The Zhou Dynasty became a time of economic prosperity, but it ended with civil war.

C. Qin Shi Huangdi was successful in unifying China, but after his death the Qin Dynasty ended.

D. The Han Dynasty restored peace, strengthened government and education, and introduced a variety of technological advances.

Active Reading

SEQUENCE OF EVENTS
When you list a sequence of events, you place events in the order that they happened from first to last. As you read this section, ask yourself this question: How did events unfold from one dynasty to the next? Then, read to learn how a dynasty began, what happened during its rule, and what caused its end.

A. The Early Zhou

In the final centuries of the Shang Dynasty, a new union of clans developed, called Zhou. Around 1000 B.C., the Zhou became more powerful under their ruler, Wen Wang. At first, the Zhou conquered lands to the north and south of the Shang kingdom. Then, the Zhou challenged the Shang's authority. Wu Wang, Wen Wang's son, attacked the Shang and overthrew the cruel king who was then in power.

The Mandate of Heaven

The Zhou used religion to explain their overthrow of the Shang. They said that the king had earned the approval of a higher power, responsible for keeping order in the universe. This gave the king the authority to rule. This divine approval was called the **Mandate of Heaven**. As long as a king ruled well, it could be assumed that he had the mandate. The Zhou declared that heaven had become so unhappy with the cruelty of the last Shang king that the gods caused his ruin. The Zhou claimed that the Mandate of Heaven had passed to their leaders because they were kind and truthful.

The Dynastic Cycle

Chinese scholars carefully studied the idea of the Mandate of Heaven. They used what they learned to explain the concept of the **dynastic cycle**, or why dynasties rise and fall.

In the dynastic cycle, a dynasty gains control because it is kind and truthful. These characteristics win the approval of the gods. Over time, the dynasty neglects its duties and

The Dynastic Cycle

DYNASTY	AGING DYNASTY	NEW DYNASTY
Dynastic ruler has control.	Ruler loses control.	New ruler gains control.
Dynasty has kind and truthful officials.	Officials become dishonest.	Truthful officials lead to successful government.
Dynasty has Mandate of Heaven.	Loses Mandate of Heaven	Gains Mandate of Heaven
Building program for roads and canals	Roads and canals need repair.	Repair program begun for roads and canals

✔ **Chart Check**

What types of improvements were provided by a new dynasty?

Teaching Options

Section 2 Resources

Teacher's Resources (TR)

Terms to Know p. 17
Review History, p. 51
Build Your Skills, p. 85
Concept Builder, p. 220
SQR Chart, p. 322

ESL/ELL STRATEGIES

Use Resources Explain that the word *autocratic* comes from the Greek, as do many words in the English language. Have students use a dictionary to find the origins of four other vocabulary words from this or previous chapters. Have them write the origin of the word on one side of an index card and an original sentence that uses the word on the other side of the card. Have students share what they have learned about the words they chose with a classmate.

loses control. Violent events like earthquakes and severe floods signal heaven's displeasure. A new group arises to challenge the authority of the aging dynasty and overthrows its government. The leader of the group becomes the ruler of a new dynasty. The new dynasty provides a good, successful government. This achievement demonstrates to the people that the new dynasty has won the Mandate of Heaven.

◆ **How did the Zhou win the Mandate of Heaven?**

B. The Zhou Dynasty

The Zhou Dynasty was organized into a system based on social class and land ownership. Wu Wang, the first king of the Zhou Dynasty, began this system when he granted land to noble lords, relatives, and generals. Each lord appointed various officers to assist in running the daily affairs of his territory. Peasants lived on and farmed the lands.

Noble lords governed their lands in the king's name. In return for their rank and privileges, they were also expected to collect and pay taxes and provide services to the king. If war broke out, they organized armies to defend the king.

Times of Economic Prosperity

The Zhou period was a time of economic prosperity in China. The agricultural revolution had made farming profitable. During the Zhou period, better methods of irrigation increased the amount of land suitable for crops. The Zhou also developed blast furnaces, which allowed them to make cast iron. They used the iron to make weapons and farm tools. Because iron is harder and stronger than bronze, iron tools made farm work easier and more productive.

As farmers increased food production and artisans made more and varied goods, the Zhou expanded trade with groups outside their borders. During this period, the Zhou introduced money in the form of bronze coins. Some early coins were in the shapes of tools, such as knives and hoes. Later coins were round with holes in their centers, allowing merchants to string them on cords.

Early Books

At the start of the Zhou period, only people of the upper class could read and write. However, as the population increased and trade flourished, the need for court scribes and government officials grew. Education became more important, and tutors began to train young men for government service.

During this same period, educated people wrote books that would later be considered classics. For example, the *Book of Songs* contains a list of 305 of the earliest Chinese poems. These include love poems and songs that tell about the lives of ordinary people. The following stanza is from a love poem:

> **“**Please, Zhongzi,
> Do not leap over our wall,
> Do not break our mulberry trees,
> It's not that I begrudge the mulberries,
> But I fear my brothers.
> You I would embrace,
> But my brothers' words—those I dread. **”**

Chinese coins used during the Zhou period were created in various shapes.

ANALYZE PRIMARY SOURCES

DOCUMENT-BASED QUESTION
How does the speaker suggest that the relationship with Zhongzi might be a secret?

Connection to
SCIENCE ←

The first iron that was used for tools may have come from meteorites. By 1000 B.C., people were using iron ore, which is a mixture of iron and oxygen, to make tools and weapons. The iron ore, along with charcoal, was heated to very high temperatures in shallow hearths. Eventually the iron ore released the oxygen, leaving a shiny metal. The metal had to be reheated and hammered many times before it could be used.

Discuss Ask students to compare the power of the Zhou Dynasty with the power of the states during the warring states period. (As the warring states time continued, the Zhou rulers lost their authority and the lords of the states became even more powerful.)

➤ **ANSWER** Trade expanded because farmers increased food production and artisans made more and varied goods.

C. The Qin Dynasty

Purpose-Setting Question How was Qin Shi Huangdi, "the First Emperor," different from other earlier rulers of China? (He was an autocrat who concentrated all power in his hands. Unlike other rulers, he believed his government should meet the needs of the state rather than the people.)

Focus Have students look back at the chart on page 80. Ask them whether the rise of the Qin Dynasty follows the steps on the dynastic cycle. They should give reasons for their answer. (Yes. When the Zhou rulers lost power, the dynasty became the Aging Dynasty. After a period of civil war, the Qin Dynasty brought peace and became the New Dynasty.)

Discuss Ask students why they think the First Emperor divided the land of the noble families among the peasants. (It took away power from the noble families, who might be a threat to him, and made the peasants loyal to him.)

Extend Bring in a picture of the Great Wall of China and display it in class or have students look at the photograph on page 197. Point out that watchtowers were placed every 100 to 200 yards along the wall. Ask students how the watchtowers contributed to China's defense system. (Standing in the high towers, guards or soldiers could be on the lookout for enemies.)

The Decline of the Zhou Dynasty

From about 770–480 B.C., as the Zhou Dynasty aged, the lords of the outlying territory became more powerful. They challenged the authority of the Zhou kings and took over parts of the Zhou kingdom. This series of events began a period of war. In the end, Zhou kings only ruled the area around the capital city, Luoyang.

Constant war between groups of people from the same country, or **civil war**, marked this period. At first, the territories on the borders pushed outward to increase their land holdings. Rival territories in the center of the dynasty fought one another. Over time, the most powerful lords captured neighboring territories. By 300 B.C., only seven major territories survived. The wars would not end until one territory conquered all the lands.

➤ **What contributed to the expansion of trade during the Zhou period?**

C. The Qin Dynasty

Qin, the westernmost territory in the Zhou Dynasty, was one of the last to survive during this period of war. The Qin's leader, Zheng, drove his armies east, swallowing up other territories in his path. In 221 B.C., Zheng founded the Qin Dynasty.

The First Emperor

King Zheng concentrated more power in his own hands than earlier kings had. Declaring that he was now ruler of "all under heaven," Zheng named himself *Qin Shi Huangdi,* or the "First Qin Emperor."

Qin Shi Huangdi was determined to reunite China. He believed that the goal of government was to meet the needs of the nation, not the citizens. He ran an **authoritarian** government from his capital city, Xianyang. An authoritarian government is one in which a ruler has total control and power. One of Qin Shi Huangdi's first actions was to replace the territories with military districts. He ordered all noble families to move to the capital where they could be watched. Then, he divided their lands among the peasants.

The First Emperor did not favor the nobles. All Chinese people, regardless of their social class, paid high taxes to support the ruler's armies and projects. Qin Shi Huangdi made strict laws and enforced them. Anyone who broke a law was harshly punished. Those who disagreed with him could be tortured or killed.

Qin Shi Huangdi had no use for learning. He ordered that books be burned, including Zhou court records and copies of all literary books. Fortunately, scholars were able to hide many books.

Qin Shi Huangdi was successful in bringing unity to China. He introduced a set of coins and a system of weights and measures. He also repaired the damage that years of war had done to the roads and extended the canal system. In addition, Qin Shi Huangdi forced thousands to build projects, including his tomb. It would have taken the labor of many people to make terra cotta soldiers and construct the underground chambers where they were buried.

The Great Wall of China and the Final Days of the Qin Dynasty

Under the Zhou, many territories in northern China built high walls to protect their land against invaders. Qin Shi Huangdi ordered that the walls be joined to form a "Great Wall." Such a wall would protect the empire.

Teaching Options

Conflict Resolution

The First Emperor created strict rules and harshly enforced them. Ask students to come up with a list of classroom rules that they consider to be fair and a way to enforce these rules. Have them establish a democratic process that will enable students who are punished for breaking the rules to appeal their punishment.

F Y I

Great Wall of China

The Great Wall of China, including all its branches, extends about 4,500 miles east to west across China. Today, the Great Wall is an important tourist attraction. Historians study the structure to learn more about Chinese history, whereas scientists study the effects of earthquakes on the structure. In 1987, the Great Wall was added to UNESCO's World Heritage list.

During his reign, workers were forced to work under the harshest conditions. Many died. However, the task was not completed in the emperor's lifetime. It took centuries to join, rebuild, and extend the wall. When the Great Wall was finished, it was thousands of miles long.

The Qin Dynasty was short-lived. The First Emperor died in 210 B.C. One of his sons became the Second Emperor. His reign did not last long. Revolts broke out in all regions of the empire. Eventually, the Second Emperor was murdered. Liu Bang, a peasant leader, came to power. He would establish a new dynasty.

◆ **How did Qin Shi Huangdi control noble families?**

D. The Rise and Fall of the Han Dynasty

As emperor, Liu Bang took the name Gaozu. He reigned from 202 B.C. to 195 B.C. China found peace and prosperity under his leadership. He used scholars as advisors and established policies that became the foundation of a new dynasty, the Han. The peace brought stability to the country. A later Han ruler, Emperor Wudi strengthened the dynasty by building new roads and canals. He opened up an overland trade route, later called the Silk Road. China began to export, or send to another country for sale, its prized silk and other products. In turn, traders brought goods from as far away as Rome. This trade route eventually stretched more than 4,000 miles across central Asia to the Mediterranean Sea.

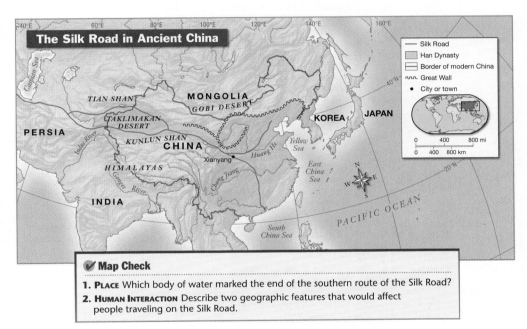

The Silk Road in Ancient China

Silk Road
Han Dynasty
Border of modern China
Great Wall
• City or town

✔ Map Check

1. **PLACE** Which body of water marked the end of the southern route of the Silk Road?
2. **HUMAN INTERACTION** Describe two geographic features that would affect people traveling on the Silk Road.

Focus Have students look back at the chart on page 80. Ask them whether the fall of the Qin Dynasty and the rise of Liu Bang follows the steps in the dynastic cycle. Have students provide reasons for their answer. (Yes. Civil wars took place and the peasants revolted. Then, a new dynasty came to power.)

◆ **ANSWER** He ordered all nobles to move to the capital and divided their land among the peasants.

D. The Rise and Fall of the Han Dynasty

Purpose-Setting Question How did Liu Bang's leadership affect China? (His leadership brought peace, prosperity, and stability to the country.)

Discuss Ask students how the Silk Road got its name. (This was the overland trade route that opened during the Han Dynasty so that China could export its silk goods and traders could bring in goods from other countries.)

Using the Map

The Silk Road in Ancient China

Ask students to use the map key to identify the Great Wall of China and the Silk Road. Discuss the connection between parts of the Great Wall and the Silk Road. (The Great Wall could protect trade along the easternmost part of the Silk Road.)

✔ Map Check

Answers
1. South China Sea
2. The Huang He, the Chang Jiang, the Kunlun Shan, the Tian Shan, the Taklimakan Desert

Cooperative Learning

Have groups of students work together to research and create a historical map of China during the Qin Dynasty. Students should create a map key with symbols for the Great Wall of China, the political boundaries of the Qin Dynasty, the capital, and major geographic features. They should title their maps. Ask students to compare the boundaries of the Qin Dynasty with those of the Han Dynasty, shown on the map on this page.

Meet Individual Needs:
VISUAL/SPATIAL LEARNERS

Have students create a Venn diagram (TR, p. 323) in order to compare the major characteristics of the Qin and Han Dynasties. They should list differences between the two dynasties in the outer parts of the two circles and common elements in the intersecting part of the circles. Have students compare their diagrams.

Spotlight on *Art*

CHINESE JADE AND IVORY
Since ancient times, Chinese artisans have carved many of the finest jade and ivory objects. Jade is a mineral used for jewelry and figurines because it is beautiful and long lasting. Chinese jade can be dark green, white, or a rare orange-yellow.

Ivory is white, but carvings become more brilliant and rich as they age. Elephant and other animal tusks are the source of ivory. Today, many countries have laws against harming animals to get this valuable material.

The Civil Service

As the business of government became more complex, Han rulers created a **civil service**. In this system, citizen employees helped to manage the government and keep its records. Education was an important qualification for civil servants because they had to be able to read and write.

In 124 B.C. an academy was established. Each year, 50 students studied for an examination. If they passed, they qualified for assignment to a government office. No candidate was excluded because of social status or wealth. However, women were not allowed to take civil service examinations.

From Golden Age to Decline

The Han period was a time of great advances in technology and the arts. Silk factories became more efficient. The Han invented the method for making paper from wood that is still used today. Bronze and iron stirrups and the horse collar made traveling more comfortable. Inventions like the wheelbarrow and a plow with movable parts made farming tasks easier.

The arts flourished. Pictures of daily life were woven into silk tapestries. The Han also built magnificent temples and palaces of wood. These buildings did not survive, but records from the period tell of their beauty.

Over the years, Han armies captured territories from modern-day Korea to northern Vietnam. When settlers arrived, they spread Chinese influences to nomads and other groups in these areas. At its peak, the Han Dynasty was approximately the size of the United States.

As the Han Dynasty aged, it faced problems similar to the dynasties before it. In A.D. 220, warlords attacked and overthrew the emperor. The Han Dynasty collapsed, and China broke into several kingdoms. The dynastic cycle had once again come full circle. This time, however, more than 350 years would pass before a new dynasty would arise.

◆ **What were some important advances in technology during the Han Dynasty?**

Review II

Review History
A. What did the Zhou believe gave them the right to rule?
B. What were three contributions made by the Zhou Dynasty?
C. Why was the Qin Dynasty so short-lived?
D. What role did the Silk Road play in the development of China's civilization?

Define Terms to Know
Define the following terms: **Mandate of Heaven, dynastic cycle, civil war, authoritarian, civil service**

Critical Thinking
Was Qin Shi Huangdi a good ruler? Why or why not?

Write About Government
Write an editorial stating your opinion about the exclusion of women from the Han civil service system.

Get Organized
SQR CHART
Use an SQR chart to organize information from this section. Survey to find a topic from this section, such as the Zhou Dynasty. Write a question and then read to find the answer.

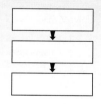

SURVEY
This section is about the Zhou Dynasty.

↓

QUESTION
How did the Zhou Dynasty's social system begin?

↓

READ
Wu Wang granted land to lords, relatives, and generals. Peasants farmed the land.

Religions and Beliefs in Ancient China

Terms to Know

philosopher a person who seeks wisdom or knowledge

filial piety the requirement that one must obey and respect one's parents

yin and yang the two basic forces of the universe according to the beliefs of Daoism

Legalism a belief in strong laws and the power of a ruler to reward and punish people in order to maintain control

Main Ideas

A. Confucius, China's great philosopher, taught that respect for one's parents is the foundation for a moral civilization.

B. Daoists believe that Dao is the energy of the universe and that nature is controlled by the interaction of negative and positive forces.

C. Both Legalism and Buddhism had followers in ancient China.

 Active Reading

COMPARE AND CONTRAST
When you compare and contrast, you use critical thinking skills to find similarities and differences. As you read this section, ask yourself the following questions: In which ways are the beliefs of Confucianists, Daoists, and Legalists the same? In which ways are they different?

Confucius's teachings on social behavior and government guided the development of Chinese civilization for centuries.

A. Confucianism

Out of the disorder in China during the Zhou period, a remarkable **philosopher**, or person who seeks wisdom or knowledge, appeared. His name was Kong Qiu, but he is known in the West as Confucius. He was born around 551 B.C. in the small state of Lu, which is in northeastern China. Even after the death of his parents when he was a child, Confucius worked hard and received a good education. As a young man, Confucius spent several years in the Lu court. However, he failed to gain recognition. He became increasingly worried about the conditions in China.

He left Lu in search of a king who would listen to his advice about good government. He never found the king he was looking for. Instead, he discovered that people in government were greedy and dishonest. They did not care about the needs of other people. Confucius decided to try to change the way people behaved. His teachings are called Confucianism.

Social Order

Confucius was an honest man of great learning. His study of the past left him convinced that the early Zhou period was a golden age. He felt that the early Zhou rulers had been good leaders who had run the land so that all things were in harmony. By harmony, he meant that people accepted their role in society and worked hard to fulfill their responsibility to others. Confucius believed that a ruler should lead by good example. He also believed that all people had an obligation to obey those who were superior to them. Those who were superior, in turn, had an obligation to treat their inferiors fairly.

Confucius taught that every man should try to be a *junzi*—a "princely man," or gentleman. A gentleman was a person who was educated, had good manners, and understood the importance of ritual and ceremony. Confucius said that the "gentleman understands what is moral. The small man understands what is profitable." A gentleman, according to Confucius, will take "as much trouble to discover what is right as lesser men take to discover what will pay."

Teaching Options

Section 3 Resources

Teacher's Resources (TR)
Terms to Know, p. 17
Review History, p. 51
Build Your Skills, p. 85
Concept Builder, p. 220
SQR Chart, p. 322
Transparency 7

III. Religions and Beliefs in Ancient China
(pp. 85–89)

Section Summary

In this section students will learn how the principles of Confucianism, Daoism, Legalism, and Buddhism influenced the culture, social order, government, and religion of ancient China.

1 Introduce

Getting Started

Ask students to identify rules in their classroom, school, or community that affect how people get along with each other. Students may suggest rules like no throwing items in class, no spitting, and no talking when others are talking. Discuss with students how these rules make it more pleasant to live with other people. Explain that some of the religions and beliefs in ancient China helped people get along peacefully.

TERMS TO KNOW

Ask students to read the terms and definitions on page 85 and then find each term in the section. Then, have them use each term in a sentence. Suggest that students look for additional terms that refer to the teachings of Confucians, Daoists, Legalists, and Buddhists, as they read the section.

You may wish to preview the pronunciation of the following words from the section with students.

Junzi (JOON dz)
Laozi (LOWD dz)

ACTIVE READING

Have students make a three-circle Venn diagram to help them identify the similarities and differences between Confucianism, Daoism, and Legalism. They should label the circles *Confucianism*, *Daoism*, and *Legalism*. Differences should be placed in the outer circles and similarities in the overlapping areas.

2 Teach

A. Confucianism

Purpose-Setting Question Why did Confucius consider the Zhou period a Golden Age? (He believed the Zhou leaders were moral and governed in a way that kept society in harmony.)

Discuss Ask students why they think the five relationships were so important. (They defined the relationships in life that are necessary to keep society in harmony.) Ask students to paraphrase the important Confucian rule in their own words. (Treat other people the way you want them to treat you.) Discuss how this is consistent with Confucius's goal of harmony.

ANALYZE PRIMARY SOURCES

DOCUMENT-BASED QUESTION

Explain that in ancient China, some men performed exaggerated acts of filial piety, such as never ending their period of mourning for their parents in order to show their respect.

ANSWER Because the relationship between father and son was the most important of the five relationships, Confucius wanted to ensure that the child was sincere in following his father's example.

TEACH PRIMARY SOURCES

Have students explain how the stone carving represents the philosophy of filial piety. (It visually reproduces the sense of responsibility that sons were supposed to show for their fathers and how that would keep society balanced.)

Focus To help students understand the teachings of Confucius, you may wish to have them read excerpts from the Analects on page 809.

◆ **ANSWER** He wanted a ruler to lead by good example and to run the land so that all things were in harmony.

B. Daoism

Purpose-Setting Question How did Daoism differ from Confucianism? (Unlike Confucianists, Daoists believed that the ruler should do as little as possible and leave the people alone.)

The images in this carving titled *The Loving Son* show the importance of filial piety.

ANALYZE PRIMARY SOURCES

DOCUMENT-BASED QUESTION Why do you think Confucius says you must follow your father's ways for three years after his death before considering yourself a filial child?

Primary Source Documents
You can read sections of the Analects on page 809.

The Five Relationships

Confucius taught that there were five relationships that governed society. First came the relationship between father and son. Next was the relationship between an older and younger brother. Then, came the relationships between husband and wife, between ruler and subject, and between friend and friend. As long as these relationships were in harmony, said Confucius, society would be in harmony. He taught that this harmony could be achieved by following an important rule: "What you do not wish for yourself, do not do to others."

The harmony of the family was central to the harmony of society. According to Confucius, children had to practice **filial piety**. Filial piety required a child to obey his or her parents during childhood, to care for them when they grew old, and to show respect for them after their death. Confucius explained filial piety in this way:

> ❝When your father is alive observe his intentions. After he passes away, model yourself on the memory of his behavior. If in three years after his death you have not deviated from your father's ways, then you may be considered a filial child.❞

The Analects and Confucian Influences

Confucius was a great and inspiring teacher. During his lifetime, many scholars learned from him. It is unclear whether Confucius ever wrote down his ideas. However, his followers did record his teachings. The collection of his sayings, called the Analects, contains his beliefs. In later centuries, the Analects was regarded as sacred. Students memorized the sayings, which soon became familiar to people in all levels of Chinese society.

The emperors of the Han Dynasty recognized the value of the Confucian scholar-gentleman. Men trained in Confucian learning became leaders of their communities. These men, in turn, sent bright young men to continue their Confucian education at schools in the capital. These Confucian officials formed an educated class that came from all parts of China. Members of this class were key ingredients in the development of Chinese civilization.

◆ **What qualities did Confucius look for in a ruler?**

B. Daoism

By the third century B.C., a new system of beliefs began to challenge Confucianism. Daoism, sometimes called Taoism, is very different from Confucianism. Confucianists believed in order, ritual, and working hard to make the government efficient. Daoists believed the opposite. They thought that rulers should do as little as possible. They wanted their rulers to leave everybody alone.

The *Laozi*

The *Laozi*, also known as *The Classic of the Way and Its Power*, contains the beliefs of Daoism. Lao Dan, who lived around 500 B.C., is thought by many to have been the original author, but most experts think the *Laozi* was

86   UNIT 1 ◆ From Prehistory to Early Civilizations

Teaching Options

F Y I

The Analects

To modern readers, the Analects may seem to be a collection of randomly organized and unrelated conversations, but this is not the case. This format reveals Confucius in thought and action, including his ambitions, fears, joys, and self-knowledge. The purpose of the Analects is not to present a philosophical argument or describe an event, but to involve the reader in taking part in an ongoing conversation with the great teacher.

Connection to
LITERATURE

In addition to the Analects, other works of Chinese literature reflected the spiritual and moral values that were revered in the culture. For example, *The Biographies of Heroic Women*, written by a scholar and biographer, Liu Xiang (79–8 B.C.), is a collection of the selfless actions of 125 women. Their virtues included loyalty to their ruler and wise counseling to their husbands and fathers.

compiled around 250 B.C. According to the *Laozi*, the Dao is the energy that controls all of the events in the universe. The natural order depends on the interaction of **yin** and **yang**. Yin is the negative force. It is dark and weak. Yang is positive, bright, and strong. Yin and yang work together to keep the forces of nature in balance.

The other major work on Daoism is the *Zhuangzi*, which was written by the philosopher Zhwang Zhou. The *Zhuangzi* urged Daoists not to worry about learning or working or fulfilling social obligations. They are to be free spirits. Daoists must not worry about worldly matters. They must spend their time meditating on nature.

Daoist Influences

Daoism was based both on Daoist beliefs and folk religion. The folk religions of China were based on popular myths, ancestor worship, and local gods. Along with a long Chinese tradition of seeking immortality, or a state of living forever, these religions combined easily with Daoist beliefs. Daoism influenced the cultures of all the countries that China touched. Japan and Korea were particularly affected by Daoism. In the twentieth century, a Western version of Daoism arose in Europe and North America.

Daoism influenced Chinese arts and sciences. Daoism's emphasis on nature has inspired many Chinese writers, artists, and architects throughout the centuries. The close relationship between Daoism and Chinese landscape painting was examined in *Introduction to Landscape Painting* by Zong Bing. Even amateur artists responded to Daoist influences. For example, the twelfth-century emperor Huizong was so moved by his love of nature that he painted a scene on silk and wrote a poem to accompany it.

Science also benefited from Daoist beliefs. The desire to learn more about nature led Daoists to study astronomy, medicine, and personal hygiene.

◆ **What did Daoists believe about government?**

C. Legalism and Buddhism

Xunzi was a student of Confucius. However, he had different beliefs about human nature and government. Confucius felt that rulers could inspire good behavior in the society they ruled. Xunzi disagreed. Xunzi's beliefs were called **Legalism** because they were based on a rule of law. Legalists called for strict laws and harsh punishments for wrongdoing.

Xunzi stated his beliefs in this famous passage from his writings: "Now the original nature of man is evil, so he must submit himself to teachers and laws before he can be just."

Han Feizi, a student of Xunzi, believed that people were like children. They could not be trusted to think for themselves. Therefore, a ruler must enforce the laws without exception. The wishes of a ruler were the highest law.

Legalism and the Qin

The Qin period was an example of how Legalist solutions created a strong government. The military replaced members of the upper class as government rulers. The land was divided into states. The head of each state was appointed by the government.

People could not travel without permits. They were heavily taxed and required to work on public projects without pay. To keep crime down, the government gathered families into small groups. Each group was responsible for any crimes committed by its members.

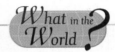

MUSIC
One of the ways that Xunzi believed a ruler could control his subjects was through the use of music. "Music is joy," he wrote, "an emotion which human beings cannot help but feel at times. Unable to resist feeling joy, they must find an outlet through voice and movement."

Xunzi believed that music affected everyone. By using music, a ruler could keep his subjects calm and under control.

Use a map Have students locate India on the map of Asia in the Atlas (p. A7) or Transparency 7. Ask students to identify the countries in Asia where Buddhism spread. (Sri Lanka, north and south China, Korea, Japan) Ask students to discuss the spread of Buddhism across Asia. Help them realize that Buddhism spread from country to country.

Do You Remember?
To review the Hindu beliefs, have students review pages 62–64 of Chapter 3.

Extend Have students use Internet resources or an almanac to find estimates on the number of people who practice each of the philosophies discussed in this section. Have students share what they have found out with the class.

Focus Have students refer to the map of the Silk Road on page 83. Ask them to speculate why Buddhism first spread to China as a result of trade along the Silk Road. (Possible answer: The Silk Road was close to the northern border of India, where Buddhism originated.)

◆ **ANSWER** The military replaced members of the upper class of government rulers. Heads of state were appointed by the government.

Section Close

Ask students to discuss which of the beliefs described in this section—Confucianism, Daoism, Legalism, and Buddhism—had the greatest impact on the civilization of ancient China and why.

3 Assess

Review Answers

Review History
A. The five relationships are father and son, older and younger brother, husband and wife, ruler and subject, and friend and friend

B. Yin and yang work together to keep the forces of nature in balance and maintain natural order.

C. Buddhism became popular because it promised freedom from suffering.

Define Terms to Know
philosopher, 85; filial piety, 86; yin and yang, 86; Legalism, 87

Do You Remember?
In Chapter 3, you learned that Buddhists generally accepted the Hindu beliefs of karma and reincarnation.

Buddhism Spreads to China

From its beginnings in India, Buddhism spread to Sri Lanka and then to north and south China. Eventually, it found believers in Korea, Japan, and throughout Southeast Asia.

Buddhism arrived in China as a result of trade along the Silk Road. Buddhism was not popular at first. It was, after all, a religion of foreigners. Eventually, the upper classes in China became interested in Buddhism. Then, the common people discovered it. Its appeal lay in its promise of freedom from suffering. Soon Buddhist temples rose in the towns and countryside. Wealthy people donated great sums of money to the temples. They believed that such generosity would earn them good karma, or good fortune in their next life.

Reactions to Buddhism

Confucianists and Daoists resented the Buddhists. They did not approve of certain Buddhist practices, such as the cremation, or burning, of the dead. In addition, they believed it was a violation of filial piety for monks, or religious men, not to marry or have children. The first obligation to one's ancestors was to have children. Critics also objected to the fact that the Buddhist monks paid no taxes.

On several occasions, the Chinese emperors listened to the critics and closed down the Buddhist temples. However, the temples were not closed permanently. They were reopened and Buddhism continued to be a major religion in China for many centuries.

◆ **How did Legalism create a strong government?**

Review III

Review History
A. According to Confucius, what are the five relationships that govern society?
B. What is the importance of the idea of yin and yang in Daoist philosophy?
C. Why did Buddhism become popular in China?

Define Terms to Know
Define the following terms: **philosopher, filial piety, yin and yang, Legalism**

Critical Thinking
In what ways did the beliefs of Xunzi and Han Feizi differ from those of Confucius?

Write About Citizenship
Write a brief essay explaining why you would or would not like to be the subject of a Legalist emperor.

Get Organized
SQR CHART
Use an SQR chart to organize information from this section. Survey to find a topic from this section, such as Confucianism. Write a question and then read to find the answer.

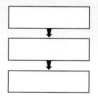

Critical Thinking
Confucius believed rulers could inspire good behavior in their citizens. Xunzi believed in a system of strict laws in order to govern people who were innately evil. His pupil Han Feizi believed that because people couldn't think for themselves, the ruler had to enforce the laws without exception.

Write About Citizenship
Students should support their opinions with facts about the practice of Legalism in ancient China.

SURVEY
This section is about Confucianism.

↓

QUESTION
How did Confucianism affect government in ancient China?

↓

READ
Confucianism teaches that leaders should set good examples.

Points of View

Confucianism Versus Legalism

Confucianism spread far and wide after Confucius died. Once his followers had gathered his wisdom into the Analects, the words of Confucius influenced rulers as far away as Korea, Japan, and Vietnam. At home in China, he was respected, and many emperors used at least part of his advice to help them rule their lands. His teachings became the Chinese model for official and personal behavior. The idea of a fair and honest ruler was central to the beliefs of Confucius.

The philosopher Xunzi disagreed with the teachings of Confucius. His student Han Feizi continued his teacher's argument, stating that there was no need for a ruler to be kind. Rather than be fair, Han Feizi said, a ruler must be strict. The people were like little children. It was better to keep them ignorant and let a ruler control them. These beliefs became the foundation of Legalism.

The dragon is the symbol of the Chinese emperor.

> " The Master said, 'Lead the people by means of government policies and regulate them through punishments, and they will be evasive and have no sense of shame. Lead them by means of virtue and regulate them through rituals [ceremonies] and they will have a sense of shame and moreover have standards.' "
>
> —Confucius, Analects

> " I know that only awe-inspiring power can suppress violence, while kindness cannot stop the rebellious. The sage [wise person], in governing a state, does not trust men to do good of themselves; he makes it impossible for them to do wrong. A ruler must concern himself with the majority, not with rare individuals. Thus he takes no account of virtue, but concerns himself rather with the law. "
>
> —Han Feizi, *Chinese Thought From Confucius to Mao*

ANALYZE PRIMARY SOURCES

DOCUMENT-BASED QUESTIONS

1. How does Confucius think a ruler should rule his subjects?

2. How does Han Feizi believe a ruler should control people?

3. **Critical Thinking** What might be the differences between a nation ruled by a Confucianist and one ruled by a Legalist?

Teaching Options

Take a Stand

Have students write a letter to the editor of a newspaper in which they support a government based on either Confucian principles or the political philosophy of Han Feizi. In their letter, they should clearly state their opinion, provide reasons to support it, and explain how the political position will benefit society.

LINK to TODAY

Although our country is a democracy, other nations are ruled by autocratic leaders who rely on the "awe-inspiring" power advocated by Han Feizi to control their citizens. Encourage small groups of students to use classroom or Internet resources to find information about recent political events in countries ruled by autocrats. Ask each group to briefly report on its findings in class.

Points of View

CONFUCIANISM VERSUS LEGALISM

Teach the Topic

These selections represent two points of view about how rulers should best govern in ancient China. The selection attributed to Confucius is from the Analects, the most sacred scripture in Confucian tradition. The second selection is from the writings of Han Feizi, who was a Legalist philosopher.

Have students list the advantages and disadvantages of each point of view on ancient Chinese society. (Confucius's belief in a benevolent ruler would probably result in less political dissent; however, political opponents would have greater freedom to express dissent. Han Feizi's position would result in a more authoritarian government that could also help the ruler implement his programs without opposition.)

Compare and Contrast Points of View

Ask students to analyze each selection, listing the reasons each writer gives for advocating his point of view. (Confucius believed his view of government would benefit the people; Han Feizi believed his view of government would benefit society by suppressing violence.) Have students identify how each writer views the role of virtue in his political system. (Confucius believes a leader will set an example for his people if his rule is based on virtue. Han Feizi believes a ruler should be concerned with the law rather than with virtue.)

ANALYZE PRIMARY SOURCES

DOCUMENT-BASED QUESTIONS

1. He thinks a ruler should lead by being virtuous himself and use rituals rather than fear of punishment to regulate their lives.

2. Han Feizi believes a ruler should control his subjects by being all-powerful and crushing dissent. The ruler should not trust people to rule themselves.

3. In a nation ruled by a Confucian, the people would have more control over their government and their own lives. In a society ruled by a Legalist, the government would be more authoritarian and the rights of the individual would be suppressed.

Section Summary

In this section, students will learn about the importance of the family in Chinese society and the preference for sons over daughters. They will also learn about the agrarian-based economy, including the difficult life of the peasant, and advances in technology and culture.

1 Introduce

Getting Started

Ask students to identify the technological advances in science, communication, or medicine that have had the greatest impact on their daily life. In these discussions, encourage students to identify the ways in which these breakthroughs have affected them. Tell students that technological advances made big changes in the lives of people in ancient China.

TERMS TO KNOW

Ask students to read the terms and definitions on page 90 and then find each term in the section. Ask students to explain the meaning of each term to the class.

You may wish to preview the pronunciation of the following terms from this section with students.

Ban Zhao (BAHN JOW)
lacquerware (LAK uhr wer)
Zhang Cang (JAHNG TSAHNG)
Zhu Chongzi (JOO KAHNG dz)

ACTIVE READING

Have students choose one of the subsections in Section 4 and write a summary in their own words of the most important points. Suggest that they use the headings, art, and captions to help them write their summaries.

Section IV
Ancient Chinese Life and Culture

Terms to Know

dowry a sum of money or goods paid to the family of the groom by the family of the bride

well-field system a division of land between individual farmers and the owner of the land

agrarian economy an economy that depends on farming

Then & Now

WOMEN IN CHINA
The role of women in China changed very little until the early twentieth century. Many leading Chinese intellectuals began in the 1900s to write about the unequal status of women. By the 1920s, more than 4.5 million girls and women were enrolled in schools. By 1935, more than 6,000 colleges and universities admitted women.
In China today, women hold a variety of jobs—an idea that would have horrified Ban Zhao.

Main Ideas

A. Chinese people wanted as many children as possible in order to have help in the fields, but they preferred sons over daughters.

B. China depended on an economy in which farmers were favored over merchants, while peasants had difficult lives.

C. Chinese scholars were skilled in many fields, including geography, mathematics, and medicine.

A. The Family

Families were the center of ancient Chinese society. Chinese religions and beliefs established rules that explained the proper way to behave among family members as well as among other people in society. In each family, children must obey their parents, wives must obey their husbands, and young people must obey and respect older people.

The Place of Children

In ancient China, children were the reason for the family. Even before Confucius, raising children was considered extremely important. The government needed farmers and soldiers. The more children a family had, the more would survive to adulthood.

Parents prayed that they would have sons. They believed that sons were stronger than daughters and could work longer hours in the field. In addition, only sons were allowed to perform the ceremonies that honored the family's ancestors. If a family had only daughters, there would be no one to care for the family tombs and show respect to the dead. In hard times, families would often leave infant daughters out in the open to die.

Female children were the least valued members of the family. They were also a financial burden. When daughters married, their families had to pay a **dowry**. A dowry is a sum of money, usually in the form of goods, that is paid by the parents of a bride to the family of the groom.

The Place of Women

Because women were considered to be inferior to men, little attention was paid to them by early writers. It was not until the Han period that even extraordinary women were noticed. Liu Xiang wrote the *Biographies of Heroic Women*. This book told of women who had performed acts of extreme self-sacrifice or had demonstrated wisdom.

Even when women spoke for themselves, they accepted a position lower than that of men. Ban Zhao, who was a teacher of girls at the royal palace, wrote a guide about the behavior of young women. Her *Admonitions for Girls* reflected the general opinion that women should keep their place:

Active Reading

SUMMARIZE
When you summarize, you include only the most important points of something that is written or said. As you read this section, stop after each part and think about what you have read. Then, summarize what you have learned about family life in ancient China.

Teaching Options

Section 4 Resources

Teacher's Resources (TR)
Terms to Know, p. 17
Review History, p. 51
Build Your Skills, p. 85
Concept Builder, p. 220
Chapter Test, p. 124
SQR Chart, p. 322
Transparency 1

ESL/ELL STRATEGIES

Organize Information Have pairs of students read aloud each paragraph in the subsection "The Place of Children." Suggest that students use a main idea/supporting details chart (TR, p. 319) to record the main idea and the supporting details. Have students and their partners compare and revise their charts as needed.

In China, the parents of the bride paid a dowry to the family of the groom. The bride's dowry is in the cart on the right.

ANALYZE PRIMARY SOURCES
DOCUMENT-BASED QUESTION How much opportunity did a woman have to develop interests of her own? How do you know?

❝ Humility means yielding and acting respectful, putting others first and oneself last . . . enduring insults and bearing mistreatment . . . Industriousness means going to bed late, getting up early, never shirking work morning or night . . . Continuing the sacrifice means serving one's master-husband with appropriate demeanor, keeping oneself clean and pure, never joking or laughing . . . There has never been a woman who had these three traits and yet ruined herself or fell into disgrace. ❞

◆ Why did Chinese parents prefer sons over daughters?

B. Farming and Trade

In the early Zhou period, most of China's farmland was divided according to the **well-field** **system**. Under this system, large areas of land were divided into nine plots. Eight of the plots were given to individual farmers. The ninth was farmed by all, and the crops were claimed by the noble landowner.

The Life of a Peasant

Peasants in China were very poor. They worked hard for their two meals a day. An ancient proverb states that "All a man needs in this life is a hat and a bowl of rice." Peasants expected little more than that, and even their bowl of rice was not guaranteed. Peasants faced many difficulties. They had to deal with floods and droughts. When taxes were due, they often had to sell their crops at half price to get cash. If they had no crops, they had to borrow money. Some were forced to sell all they had, including their children.

China had an **agrarian** **economy**. An agrarian economy depends on agriculture. During the Han period, the government did everything it could to help the farmers. It offered tax relief and free irrigation of crops. However, the government could not overcome the forces of nature.

China has experienced annual famines for thousands of years. Every year, in some part of China, peasants died of starvation. Because famines were so

---

Writing

AVERAGE

Have students write a short letter to the editor of a newspaper explaining why or why not the dowry system should be abolished in ancient China. Students' letters should be clearly written and contain as many supporting facts and details as possible.

CHALLENGE

Have students write a dialogue between Ban Zhao and a contemporary Chinese woman who has just graduated from a university with a degree in education. In the dialogue, the two women should discuss reasons for their different views about the roles of women in ancient and modern Chinese society.

---

2 Teach

A. The Family

Purpose-Setting Question In ancient China, why were children important? (The government needed farmers and soldiers.)

Activity

Make an idea web Have students create an idea web (TR, p. 321) to organize information about the family in ancient China. Suggest they use "importance of family" as the topic in the center circle. Have students list related ideas or events in the outer circles. (focus on children; value of sons; women in secondary roles; need farmers and soldiers)

Then & Now

WOMEN IN CHINA Beginning in the 1980s, all children in China were required by law to attend school for at least 9 years. Ask students how new educational opportunities would have changed the status of women. (They would have more opportunity to enter the workforce and more rights.)

ANALYZE PRIMARY SOURCES

DOCUMENT-BASED QUESTION
Ban Zhao, reflecting the culture of the period, believed that men and women had distinct social positions in their society. She encouraged women to concentrate on the virtues necessary for their social role. Ask students to identify these virtues in this selection. (hard work, subservience, humility, cleanliness, accepting mistreatment) What is the relationship between husband and wife? (They are not equals.)

ANSWER She had no opportunity to develop her own interests because she was subordinate to her husband.

◆ **ANSWER** Sons could work longer and harder, and sons could perform the ceremonies that honored the family's ancestors.

B. Farming and Trade

Purpose-Setting Question Why was the life of a peasant so difficult? (Peasants worked very hard for little food; they faced floods and drought; they often had to sell their crops at half price to raise money for taxes.)

Discuss Ask students to compare and contrast the lives of the wealthy and the peasants in ancient China. (While the rich had no trouble acquiring land, the peasants saw the size of their plots getting smaller and smaller as the land was divided and redivided among their sons, grandsons, and great-grandsons. As the plots of the peasants got smaller, the amount of food they could raise decreased. This increased the risk of famine among peasants.) Help students understand that wealthy people could easily acquire more land and therefore raise more crops and avoid famine.

Focus Explain that camel caravans carried silk and other products from China to the market at Damascus, the meeting place of East and West in the ancient world. Silk was then transported from Damascus to the Roman Empire and exchanged for other goods. Help students locate Damascus and Rome on a world map (pp. A1–A2 in the Atlas or Transparency 1). Discuss the distance that silk was transported.

◆ **ANSWER** Merchants were regarded as the lowest class—even below farmers and artisans—because they worked for profit, and Confucius had taught that working for profit was not a virtue.

C. Advances in Technology and Culture

Purpose-Setting Question What were some important technological advances made from the Shang Dynasty to the end of the Han Dynasty? (development of flood-control systems; processes for making bronze, silk, porcelain, and cast iron; invention of paper; a harness for farm animals that made plowing easier)

Discuss Ask students how the development of a calendar might have affected China's agrarian economy. (It would be important because it could help farmers plan their planting and harvesting.)

Merchants traveled along the Silk Road in ancient times, as shown below. The photo on the right shows the modern-day Silk Road.

common, it was not unusual for someone to be rich one year and ruined the next. Wealthy people had no trouble acquiring land. The peasants, however, left their plot of land to their sons when they died. Over time, the plots of land grew smaller and smaller as they were divided and redivided by sons, grandsons, and great-grandsons.

Merchants and Trade

Merchants were hardworking and clever at bargaining. In many cultures, these would be considered good qualities. Among the Chinese, however, these talents were looked down upon. Merchants were regarded as the lowest class of people—even below farmers and artisans. Confucius had taught that profit was the worst reason for labor. To merchants, it was the only reason. Even though they were widely disliked, the merchant class made China rich. They brought the products of China to many parts of the world.

For hundreds of years merchants traded silk and lacquerware along the Silk Road. Lacquerware was usually made from thin wood covered with as many as 30 coats of lacquer. Such luxury items made their way through Asia and to the West. Copper objects, including coins, made their way to India.

◆ **How were merchants regarded in ancient China?**

C. Advances in Technology and Culture

The period ranging from the time of the Shang Dynasty to the end of the Han Dynasty was one of impressive technological advances in China. Large-scale flood-control systems were invented. Processes for making bronze, silk, and fine porcelain were perfected. A process for producing cast iron was developed. A harness for farm animals made plowing land easier. Paper was invented in A.D 105.

Chinese scholars were excellent geographers and astronomers. Chinese astronomers during the Zhou Dynasty could calculate the times that eclipses

Teaching Options

Meet Individual Needs:
VERBAL/LINGUISTIC LEARNERS

To help students understand how merchants in ancient China traded goods, have pairs of students role-play a Chinese merchant bargaining with a prospective buyer in a Damascus market or along the Silk Road. The merchant would have silk, lacquerware, or copper objects to sell.

F Y I

Silk

According to legend, Xilingshi, the wife of Emperor Huangdi, discovered silk when she found white silkworms eating mulberry leaves and spinning cocoons. After accidentally dropping one in hot water, she saw a silk thread unraveling from the cocoon. She is also credited with the invention of the first silk loom.

would occur. The Chinese had a calendar with 12 months. From time to time, an extra month was added to make the calendar match the seasons of the year. One Chinese mathematician, Zhang Cang, wrote books on algebra and geometry in the second century. Another mathematician, Zhu Chongzi, calculated pi to six decimal places.

Medicine

Chinese medicine was practiced long before recorded history. Physicians relied on observation and careful study. During the Zhou period, physicians had to pass an examination in order to practice medicine. Books were written on surgery and the use of drugs. During the Han Dynasty, Chinese physicians also began to treat patients with acupuncture. This is a technique in which thin needles are inserted into a patient's body at certain points in order to relieve pain or treat an illness.

Literacy and Literature

Education in ancient China was available only to the upper classes. Many emperors saw the value of an educated class. Even under the First Emperor of the Qin, who did not approve of scholars, literacy, which is the ability to read, was considered important. As far back as 4500 B.C., there was evidence of a written language in China. However, the characters varied from time to time and place to place.

The earliest Chinese literature was written during the Zhou period. The *Book of Songs* is the earliest surviving work of the time. Known as the *Shijing*, it was one of the five classics of Confucian literature. The others were the *Book of Changes (Yijing)*, the *Book of Documents (Shujing)*, the *Book of Rites (Liji)*, and the *Spring and Autumn Annals*. The *Annals* was part of a written record from the early Zhou period. The five classics were considered the most important works one studied to become a scholar-gentleman.

 What were some advances in mathematics in ancient China?

 **Global Connections**

GEOMETRY

Shortly before Zhang Cang wrote his works on geometry and algebra, the Greek mathematician Euclid was organizing his great textbook, *Elements*. In it, he discussed axioms and postulates, which are the accepted truths of mathematics. He also proved more than 400 propositions in solid and plane geometry.

GLOBAL CONNECTIONS

GEOMETRY Contributions to mathematics were made throughout the ancient world. By 3000 B.C., Egyptians had developed basic geometry and surveying techniques. Ptolemy I invited Euclid to teach mathematics at an institute in Alexandria around 300 B.C. The Chinese developed a decimal system of numbers by the 100s B.C. and used counting rods to solve mathematical problems. A Chinese mathematician independently discovered the Pythagorean theorem, called the Gou-Gu theorem, in 263 A.D.

Extend Explain that today acupuncture is used in Asia, Europe, and the United States. It can be used alone or with Chinese herbs and western medicine. Researchers have found that acupuncture can cause the nervous system to change the pain signals sent to the brain as well as increase the production of the body's natural painkiller. In modern China, surgeons use acupuncture to relieve pain during major surgery while the patient remains awake.

ANSWER Advances in mathematics in ancient China included books on algebra and geometry and calculating pi to six decimal places.

Section Close

Ask students to identify what they consider the most important influence on the culture of ancient China. Have them give reasons for their answer. (Possible answer: the advances in technology and the emphasis on literacy, which created an educated class in China)

Review IV

Review History
A. Why did Chinese parents want large families?
B. In what way was the position of a wealthy merchant in China different from that of merchants in other parts of the world?
C. In your opinion, in what areas was Chinese science most advanced?

Define Terms to Know
Define the following terms:
dowry, well-field system, agrarian economy

Critical Thinking
What was family life like for children in ancient China?

Write About Economics
Write a speech from the point of view of a farmer in ancient China. Give reasons why the well-field system should be ended.

Get Organized
SQR CHART
Use an SQR chart to organize information from this section. Survey to find a topic from this section, such as family life in ancient China. Write a question and then read to find the answer.

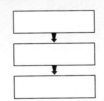

SURVEY
This section is about family life in ancient China.

↓

QUESTION
How did families treat their daughters?

↓

READ
Daughters were least valued and a financial burden.

Define Terms to Know
dowry, 90; well-field system, 91; agrarian economy, 91

Critical Thinking
Family life focused on respect for parents and elders; children, especially sons, were needed to help the family survive.

Write About Economics
Students' speeches should focus on the inequality of the well-field system and provide reasons for their opinions.

3 Assess

Review Answers

Review History
A. They wanted to ensure that more children would survive to adulthood and they wanted workers for the farm.

B. Unlike other countries where merchants had important positions in society, merchants in China were regarded as the lowest social class.

C. Answers will vary. Possible answers: medicine, mathematics, geography, astronomy

Chapter Summary

A blank outline form is available in the Teacher's Resources (p. 318). Chapter summaries should outline the beginnings of civilization in China; the Zhou, Qin, and Han Dynasties; religions and beliefs in ancient China; and ancient Chinese life and culture. Refer to the rubric in the Teacher's Resources (p. 340) to score students' chapter summaries.

⬤ Interpret the Timeline

1. 422 years
2. Hammurabi imposes a code of laws in Mesopotamia.
3. the Zhou Dynasty; It existed for the longest time.
4. Check that all events on students' timelines are in the chapter.

Use Terms to Know

5. filial piety
6. well-field system
7. Mandate of Heaven
8. sericulture
9. dynastic cycle
10. dowry

Check Your Understanding

11. Tian Shan and Himalayas
12. The Chinese made many bronze objects for use in their homes, as artwork, for trade, and as weapons.
13. Women would care for silkworms and feed them mulberry leaves, gather the cocoons, unwind the silk strands, spin silk into thread, and weave thread into cloth.
14. Dynasty flourishes and then begins to age; gods send earthquakes and floods to show their displeasure; new political union has good ideas for government and overthrows old dynasty; new group rules until it grows careless and corrupt; then, cycle begins again.
15. He regulated currency, standardized the system of weights and measures, built new roads, extended the canal system.
16. the employment of people to assist in the administration of government
17. Five Relationships: between father and son; older and younger brother; husband and wife; ruler and subject; friend and friend

Chapter Summary

Complete the following outline in your notebook. Then, use your outline to write a brief summary of the chapter.

Ancient China

I. *Early Civilization in China*
   A. *The Geography of China*
   B. *The Shang Dynasty*
   C. *Shang Society*

II. *The Zhou, Qin, and Han Dynasties*
   A. *The Early Zhou*
   B. *The Zhou Dynasty*
   C. *The Qin Dynasty*
   D. *The Rise and Fall of the Han Dynasty*

III. *Religions and Beliefs in Ancient China*
   A. *Confucianism*
   B. *Daoism*
   C. *Legalism and Buddhism*

IV. *Ancient Chinese Life and Culture*
   A. *The Family*
   B. *Farming and Trade*
   C. *Advances in Technology and Culture*

⬤ Interpret the Timeline

Use the timeline on pages 72–73 to answer the following questions.

1. How many years did the Han Dynasty last?

2. What event occurred elsewhere in the world at about the same time as the beginning of the Shang Dynasty?

3. **Critical Thinking** Which Chinese dynasty was the most successful? How does the timeline support your answer?

4. Select five events from the chapter that are not on the timeline. Create a timeline that shows these events.

Use Terms to Know

Select the term that best completes each sentence.

dowry   Mandate of Heaven
dynastic cycle   sericulture
filial piety   well-field system

5. _____ is the obligation to obey and respect one's parents.

6. _____ is the division of land among individual Chinese peasants and the owner of the land.

7. A claim of the divine right of a king to rule was called the _____.

8. Silk farming is called _____.

9. _____ is an explanation of the rise and fall of dynasties.

10. Money or goods paid to the family of a groom is called a _____.

Check Your Understanding

11. **Identify** two mountains that form China's western border.

12. **Explain** how the Bronze Age benefited China.

13. **Describe** sericulture.

14. **Explain** the dynastic cycle.

15. **Describe** some of the accomplishments of Qin Shi Huangdi.

16. **Describe** civil service.

17. **Identify** the five relationships of Confucianism.

18. **Compare** Confucianism and Daoism.

19. **Identify** the two forces that control the universe according to the Daoists.

20. **Discuss** two reasons why the Confucianists and the Daoists disapproved of the Buddhists.

21. **Explain** why raising children was so important in Chinese society.

22. **Describe** advances ancient Chinese scholars made in astronomy.

---

18. **Confucianism:** Study hard; demonstrate filial piety; work hard to help fellow humans. **Daoism:** Do not strive or study; do nothing but meditate; love nature; do not disturb pattern of yin and yang in nature and in life.
19. yin and yang

20. The Confucianists and Daoists objected to cremation and the fact that monks were childless and paid no taxes.
21. The government needed farmers and soldiers.
22. the ability to calculate eclipses and the development of a 12-month calendar

Critical Thinking

23. Recognize Relationships Describe the interaction among members of Shang social classes. In what ways did their actions affect each other?

24. Make Inferences Why was silk so expensive and highly prized throughout the world?

25. Draw Conclusions Why did the Zhou spread the idea that they had the Mandate of Heaven?

26. Make Inferences Why did Confucius consider filial piety so important to a harmonious society?

27. Analyze Primary Sources Do you think Ban Zhao's teaching, quoted on page 91, prepared a woman to be an equal partner in marriage? Why or why not?

Put Your Skills to Work

28. Use Tables and Charts You have learned that using tables and charts can help you organize and compare information. Look at the chart below, which organizes information about the religions and beliefs of ancient China. Copy the chart onto a separate sheet of paper and complete it by filling in the missing information. The first one has been done for you.

Chinese Religions and Beliefs

NAME	BELIEF	EFFECT ON CHINESE LIFE
Confucianism	Every man should try to be a gentleman.	
Daoism		
Legalism		
Buddhism		

Analyze Sources

29. Read this passage written by a Chinese philosopher. Then, answer the questions that follow.

A sage [wise person] governs this way:

He empties people's minds and fills their bellies.
He weakens their wills and strengthens their bones.
Keep the people always without knowledge and without desires.
For then the clever will not dare act.
Engage in no action and order will prevail.

a. Which Chinese belief does this passage reflect? Explain.

b. To whom is the writer giving advice?

c. What advantage might there be in keeping people's minds empty and their stomachs full?

Essay Writing

30. Write an essay discussing the rise of two dynasties discussed in this chapter and give reasons for their decline.

Critical Thinking

23. The warrior leaders controlled the peasants. When warrior nobles fought one another, peasants were forced to fight also. Women had almost no rights.

24. Sericulture was a long, labor-intensive process. Silk was only available in China, and it had to be transported a long distance.

25. They wanted to give the Shang reason to believe that their conquest was a good event that was approved of by the gods.

26. He believed that harmony in the family was the basis of harmony in the state.

27. No. The woman was considered to be little more than a willing slave; she could not be considered an equal partner to her husband.

Put Your Skills to Work

USE TABLES AND CHARTS

28. row 1, column 3: An educated class of people helped the development of Chinese civilization; **row 2, column 2:** Rulers should do as little as possible. People should meditate on nature; **row 2, column 3:** Daoism influenced the Chinese arts and sciences; **row 3, column 2:** There should be strict laws and harsh punishment for wrongdoing; **row 3, column 3:** A strong, harsh government was created; **row 4, column 2:** It promised freedom from suffering; **row 4, column 3:** Wealthy supporters donated money to temples because they thought their generosity would earn them good karma.

Analyze Sources

29a. Daoism
29b. a ruler
29c. They would be satisfied with their own lives and less likely to revolt.

Essay Writing

30. Students' essays should discuss two of the dynasties from the chapter. They should describe the dynasty and what led to its decline.

TEST PREPARATION

Answer 4. Zhou

Unit 1

Portfolio Project

TELEVISION INTERVIEW

Managing the Project
Plan for 3 class periods.

Set the Scene
Have students brainstorm the names of five contemporary political, entertainment, or sports figures that they would like to interview for a television program. Record their suggestions on the board. Then, ask students to explain why they would like to interview each person.

Your Assignment
Ask students to read the assignment on page 96. Then, divide the class into groups of 5 students and have the groups begin to work on the project.

RESEARCH A PERSON
After each group has chosen a historic figure from the list on page 96, have students decide what each member will do to research and present the interview, including playing the roles of the interviewer, the historic figure being interviewed, and other people who might contribute to the interview. Students may choose to elect a team leader who will be the director of the television show and ensure that the role-plays are presented convincingly.

REPORT TO YOUR CLASS
Once the research has been completed and the information assembled, the team should decide what questions to ask during the interview. The students playing the interviewees should prepare answers to the questions, and the researchers should make sure that the questions and answers are historically accurate. The director should oversee the rehearsals and make suggestions to improve the presentations.

Wrap Up
Groups should take turns presenting their interviews. They may want to use music, sets, and costumes to enhance their presentations. If video equipment is available, tape each interview and play it back in class.

Television Interview

YOUR ASSIGNMENT
Historians often regret that figures in the past cannot be interviewed about their feelings and reasoning at key points in their lives. Historic figures often have made choices in their lives that are important to explore and understand. Select one person from Unit 1 and prepare a television interview about the person's decisions and beliefs.

RESEARCH A PERSON

Choose a Topic As a group, choose one of the following people and topics to investigate.

Asoka, after the conquest of Kalinga

Hammurabi, on his code of laws

Cyrus the Great, on the expansion of the Persian Empire

Qin Shi Huangdi, on how to govern

Ban Zhao, on the education of females

Research Conduct research on the person and topic you have chosen. Use your textbook and other world history books, library periodicals, and the Internet as resources. After completing your research, organize the information to be used by different members of the group during the interview. In your interview, be sure to include individuals or groups whose lives were affected by the actions and beliefs of your historic figure. How were these people affected by this historic figure? Did the historic figure create or help to solve problems for the people around him or her?

REPORT TO YOUR CLASS

Plan Assemble your information on notecards in a logical order. As a team, decide how the interview will be conducted ahead of time. One member of the group can conduct the interview. Another member can be the historic figure being interviewed. Other members of the group can portray people who have been affected in some ways by the actions of the person being interviewed. You might have one or more rehearsals before conducting the interview in front of an audience.

Present Conduct your interview for your class. Be sure all members of your "cast" remain in character.

Work Individually Each member of the group should write a brief report about the importance of the historic figure's actions. Include a discussion of how important figures in modern times have made similar decisions, and how those decisions have affected the lives of people living today.

Multimedia Presentation
Turn your newscast into a newspaper feature story. Include pictures of the people being interviewed. You will need to create costumes and suitable backgrounds for the pictures. Put a newspaper headline on the story. Make copies of the article to distribute to your classmates.

Teaching Options

Multimedia Presentation
Help students brainstorm costumes and props for the photographs for their newspaper stories. Remind students to follow the Five *W*s of reporting: who, what, where, when, and why. These questions should be answered in the first few sentences.

Alternative Assessment
Write a Play Ask small groups of students to write a play about important events from Unit 1. Have them begin by brainstorming a list of the people, places, and events that could be included. Students should share responsibilities during the project. Have groups present their plays to the class. You may also refer to the rubric on page 341 of the Teacher's Resources.

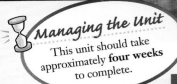

PLANNING GUIDE

	Skills and Features	Projects and Activities	Program Resources	Meet Individual Needs
Chapter 5 **Ancient Greece,** pp. 97–123 Plan for 5–6 class periods.	Unit Technology, p. T97 Analyze Artifacts, p. 105 They Made History: Pericles, p. 113 Points of View, p. 117	Using Technology, p. T101 Connection to Literature, p. T101 Writing, pp. T103, T120 Sports & Games, p. T107 Cooperative Learning, p. T109 Connection to Government, p. T109 Research, p. T110 Connection to Economics, p. T112 Test Taking, p. T113 Connection to Culture, p. T114 Conflict Resolution, p. T119	**Teacher's Resources** Terms to Know, p. 18 Review History, p. 52 Build Your Skills, p. 86 Chapter Test, pp. 125–126 Concept Builder, p. 221 They Made History: Demosthenes, p. 253 Idea Web, p. 321 Transparencies 1, 5, 7	ESL/ELL Strategies, pp. T100, T108, T114, T118 Visual/Spatial, p. T102 Kinesthetic, p. T106 Auditory, p. T119
Chapter 6 **Ancient Rome,** pp. 124–149 Plan for 5–6 class periods.	They Made History: Cicero, p. 128 Read a Special-Purpose Map, p. 131 Past to Present: The Legacy of the Roman Soldier, pp. 136–137	Teen Life, p. T128 Connection to Geography, p. T129 Connection to Literature, pp. T133, T136 Connection to Art, p. T134 Connection to Economics, p. T139 Conflict Resolution, p. T139 Using Technology, p. T140 Writing, p. T141 Cooperative Learning, p. T145 Test Taking, p. T145 Research, p. T146	**Teacher's Resources** Terms to Know, p. 19 Review History, p. 53 Build Your Skills, p. 87 Chapter Test, pp. 127–128 Concept Builder, p. 222 Cause-and-Effect Chain, p. 325 Transparencies 1, 15	ESL/ELL Strategies, pp. T127, T142, T144 Auditory, p. T129 Kinesthetic, p. T142
Chapter 7 **The Byzantine Empire, Russia, and Eastern Europe,** pp. 150–169 Plan for 4–5 class periods.	They Made History: Theodora, p. 153 Analyze Primary-Source Documents, p. 157	Using Technology, p. T153 Connection to Art, pp. T154, T159 Conflict Resolution, p. T155 Cooperative Learning, p. T159 Research, p. T160 Test Taking, p. T161 Writing, p. T162 Connection to Government, p. T165	**Teacher's Resources** Terms to Know, p. 20 Review History, p. 54 Build Your Skills, p. 88 Chapter Test, pp. 129–130 Concept Builder, p. 223 Main Idea/Supporting Details Chart, p. 319 Transparencies 1, 2, 5, 7	ESL/ELL Strategies, pp. T153, T158, T166 Visual/Spatial, p. T154 Logical/Mathematical, p. T165
Chapter 8 **The Islamic World,** pp. 170–196 Plan for 5–6 class periods.	Take Notes and Outline, p. 179 Connect History & Medicine, p. 185	Cooperative Learning, pp. T172, T190 Connection to Math, p. T173 Connection to World Languages, p. T174 Connection to Geography, p. T175 Test Taking, p. T176 World Religions, p. T177 Writing, p. T181 Connection to Literature, p. T182 Research, pp. T183, T191 Connection to Economics, p. T186 Conflict Resolution, p. T187 Using Technology, p. T188 Connection to Art, p. T188	**Teacher's Resources** Terms to Know, p. 21 Review History, p. 55 Build Your Skills, p. 89 Chapter Test, pp. 131–132 Unit 2 Test, pp 185–186 Concept Builder, p. 224 They Made History: Harun al-Rashid, p. 254 SQR Chart, p. 322 Transparencies 1, 10, 15	ESL/ELL Strategies, pp. T175, T180, T187, T192 Auditory, p. T182

Assessment Options

Chapter 5 Test, Teacher's Resources, pp. 125–126
Chapter 6 Test, Teacher's Resources, pp. 127–128
Chapter 7 Test, Teacher's Resources, pp. 129–130
Chapter 8 Test, Teacher's Resources, pp. 131–132
Unit 2 Test, Teacher's Resources, pp. 185–186

Alternative Assessment

Newscast: Turning Points in History, p. 196
Make a Poster, p. T196

Books for Students

AVERAGE

Technology in the Time of Ancient Rome. Robert Snedden. Illustrated reference highlighting innovations the ancient Romans used daily. (Raintree Publishers, 1998)

The Ides of April. Mary Ray. Fictional murder mystery set in ancient Rome. (Bethlehem Books, 1999)

Anna of Byzantium. Tracy Barrett. Almost-true autobiography told by the character, Anna Comnena. (Random House Children's Books, 2000)

Eyewitness: Islam. Philip Wilkinson. Illustrated reference discussing both the past and present Islamic world, from a series. (DK Publishing, Inc., 2002)

CHALLENGING

Pericles and His Circle. Anthony J. Podlecki. Political biography focusing on Pericles as he evolved into a statesman and on the people who influenced him. (Routledge, 1998)

Rome: Echoes of Imperial Glory. Dale M. Brown, editor. Illustrated reference discussing ancient Rome. (Time Life Custom Publishing, 1994)

Byzantium. Stephen R. Lawhead. Historical fiction about a young monk on an adventure to Byzantium. (HarperCollins Publishers, 1997)

Islam: Religion, History, and Civilization. Seyyed Hossein Nasr. Broad Islamic reference that reviews all aspects of the religion. (HarperCollins, 2002)

Books for Teachers

Ten Thousand: A Novel of Ancient Greece. Michael Curtis Ford. Historical novel based on the Greek book *Anabasis* by Xenophon. (St. Martin's Press, 2001)

As the Romans Did: A Sourcebook in Roman Social History. Jo-Ann Shelton. Collection of translations that reveals clues about ancient Roman life. (Oxford University Press, 1997)

Cicero: The Life and Times of Rome's Greatest Politician. Anthony Everitt. Historical biography of Cicero and life in Rome. (Random House, Incorporated, 2003)

Byzantium: The Bridge from Antiquity to the Middle Ages. Michael Angold. Explores the society and influence of the Byzantine Empire. (St. Martin's Press, 2001)

Classical Islam: A History 600–1258 G. E. Von Grunebaum. Translated by Katherine Watson. Review of the great classical period of Islamic history. (Barnes & Noble Books, 1996)

The Ottoman Empire: The Classical Age 1300–1600. Halil Inalcik. Accounts the history and growth of Turkey and the Ottoman Empire. (Sterling Publishing Company, Incorporated, 2001)

You may wish to preview all referenced materials to ensure their appropriateness for your local community.

Audio/Visual Resources

Greece and Rome: 1200 B.C.–A.D. ***200.*** Highlights influences of ancient Greece and Rome in modern society. Videocassette. (Social Studies School Service)

The Road to Ancient Rome. Reviews the history of ancient Rome, includes activities. CD-ROM. (Zenger Media)

Byzantium: The Lost Empire. Narration and footage from actual historical sites tell the history of the Byzantine Empire. Videocassettes. (Discovery Channel)

Islam: 600–1200. An overview of the Islamic world from its past to its present. Videocassette. (Social Studies School Services)

Technology Resources

The Ancient Greek World http://www.museum.upenn.edu

The Greeks: Crucible of Civilization http://www.pbs.org/empires/thegreeks/

The Roman Empire in the First Century http://www.pbs.org/empires/romans/

Byzantium http://www.fordham.edu/halsall/byzantium/

Islam: Empire of Faith http://www.pbs.org/empires/islam/

Globe Fearon Related Resources

History Resources

World History for a Global Age, Book 1: Ancient History to the Industrial Revolution. Reinforces an understanding of the histories of both eastern and western lands, includes activities. ISBN 1-556-75683-6

Core Knowledge History & Geography: Ancient Rome. Provides additional information on ancient Rome to extend students' knowledge. ISBN 0-7690-5098-0

Adapted Classics

Julius Caesar. A classic play by William Shakespeare about the life of Julius Caesar as a Roman leader. ISBN 0-835-91847-5

Odyssey. Epic poem by Homer that gives an account of Trojan War hero Odysseus's journey back to Greece. ISBN 0-835-90232-3

Literature Resources

World Myths and Legends I: Greek & Roman. Anthology of Greek and Roman myths and legends. ISBN 0-822-44636-7

World Myths and Legends II: Russia. Anthology of cultural myths and legends from Russia. ISBN 0-822-44647-2

To order books, call 1-800-321-3106.

The Growth of Empires and Governments

"As long as the Colosseum stands, Rome shall stand; when the Colosseum falls, Rome will fall; when Rome falls, the world will fall...."

—Bede, historian, 8th century

LINKING CULTURES As governments and empires developed, their rulers often built large structures as symbols of power and wealth. The Colosseum has stood in Rome, Italy, for nearly 2,000 years as a symbol of the dominance of the ancient Roman Empire.

What are some other recognizable structures around the world? How do these structures represent the power of a particular culture?

97

The Growth of Empires and Governments
(pp. 97–196)

Unit Summary
Unit 2 focuses on the rise and the cultural impact of new civilizations in the Mediterranean region and the growth of new empires throughout Europe and southern Asia.

CHAPTER 5
Ancient Greece

CHAPTER 6
Ancient Rome

CHAPTER 7
The Byzantine Empire, Russia, and Eastern Europe

CHAPTER 8
The Islamic World

Set the Stage
TEACH PRIMARY SOURCES
Photo The photo on this page shows the Colosseum in Rome at sunset. Explain that the Colosseum was used for celebrations and events such as races and fights. Have students describe the mixture of ancient and modern elements they see in the photo. (ruins, stone arches, a cross, and fences) Have students use the photo to compare life in Rome in ancient times to today.

Quote Bede, an English monk and historian in the early 700s, never visited Rome or saw the Colosseum, but he recognized the importance of the city and its famous landmark to the Christian world. Ask students why the Colosseum is still a major attraction today. (It shows the lasting nature of the ancient world and keeps alive interest in the Roman Empire.)

◆ **ANSWER** Possible answers: the pyramids in Egypt and Central America, the Great Wall of China, and Stonehenge in England. Check students' reasoning for why the structures represent the power of the particular culture.

Teaching Options

UNIT TECHNOLOGY

Have students use the Internet to research other well-known buildings from the civilizations discussed in this unit. Possible buildings include the Parthenon, the Roman Forum, Hagia Sophia, Cathedral of St. Basil, and the Great Mosque of Damascus.

You may wish to identify possible Web sites for students and monitor their activities on the Internet.

UNIT 2 Portfolio Project

Newscast: Turning Points in History

The Portfolio Project for Unit 2 (p. 196) is to create a newscast. Teams of students will plan and present a late-breaking news account of one of the significant events described in the unit. You may wish to encourage students to prepare music, sets, and visuals to enhance their presentation. As an additional activity, students may videotape their newscast.

Ancient Greece
2000–146 B.C.
(pp. 98–123)

Chapter Objectives
• Discuss how the geography of Greece led to the development of two early civilizations.
• Contrast the social and political characteristics of Sparta and Athens, and explain how Greek states united in the Persian Wars.
• Describe the development of political and religious ideas, art, drama, and architecture in Greece.
• Explain how Alexander conquered much of the known world and spread Greek culture throughout the Mediterranean region and Asia Minor.

Chapter Summary
Section I focuses on the Minoan and Mycenaean civilizations that developed in Crete and southern Greece.
Section II explores the Greek city-states such as Sparta and Athens, how they were similar and different, and how they united to defeat Persia in the Persian Wars.
Section III discusses new ideas in architecture, art, philosophy, history, drama, poetry, and science that developed in Athens. It also explores the Peloponnesian War.
Section IV focuses on the actions of Alexander, the king of Macedonia, as he conquered areas and built an empire. It also discusses the cultural and economic growth in the Hellenistic civilization.

Set the Stage
TEACH PRIMARY SOURCES
Explain that Pericles was a general and statesman who led Athens during the Persian Wars and oversaw the building of many of the city's most famous temples and palaces. Discuss with students Pericles' involvement with and his feelings for Athens. Ask the students if they are involved in their community and if they feel the same way about their community as Pericles did about Athens.

CHAPTER
5

Ancient Greece
2000–146 B.C.

I. Early Civilizations of Greece
II. Greek City-States Rise to Power
III. The Golden Age of Athens
IV. Alexander Builds a Great Empire

The people of ancient Greece created a civilization that had a lasting impact on many countries, including the culture and government of the United States. According to the historian Thucydides, the Athenian leader Pericles spoke these words about the city of Athens and its citizens in 431 B.C.:

" *Mighty indeed are the marks and monuments of our empire which we have left. Future ages will wonder at us, as the present age wonders at us now. . . . You should fix your eyes every day on the greatness of Athens as she really is, and should fall in love with her.* "

In Athens—one of the largest and most powerful of the Greek city-states in the fifth century B.C.—many citizens participated in government.

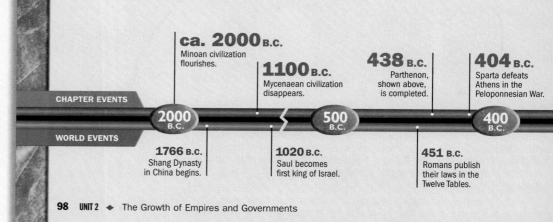

ca. 2000 B.C.
Minoan civilization flourishes.

1100 B.C.
Mycenaean civilization disappears.

438 B.C.
Parthenon, shown above, is completed.

404 B.C.
Sparta defeats Athens in the Peloponnesian War.

CHAPTER EVENTS

2000 B.C.

500 B.C.

400 B.C.

WORLD EVENTS

1766 B.C.
Shang Dynasty in China begins.

1020 B.C.
Saul becomes first king of Israel.

451 B.C.
Romans publish their laws in the Twelve Tables.

Teaching Options

Chapter 5 Resources

REVIEW

Teacher's Resources (TR)
Terms to Know, p. 18
Review History, p. 52
Build Your Skills, p. 86
Chapter Test, pp. 125–126
Concept Builder, p. 221
Idea Web, p. 321
Transparencies 1, 5, 7

ASSESSMENT
Section Reviews, pp. 104, 111, 116, 121
Chapter Review, pp. 122–123
Chapter Test, TR, pp. 125–126

ALTERNATE ASSESSMENT
Portfolio Project, p. 196
Make a Poster, p. T196

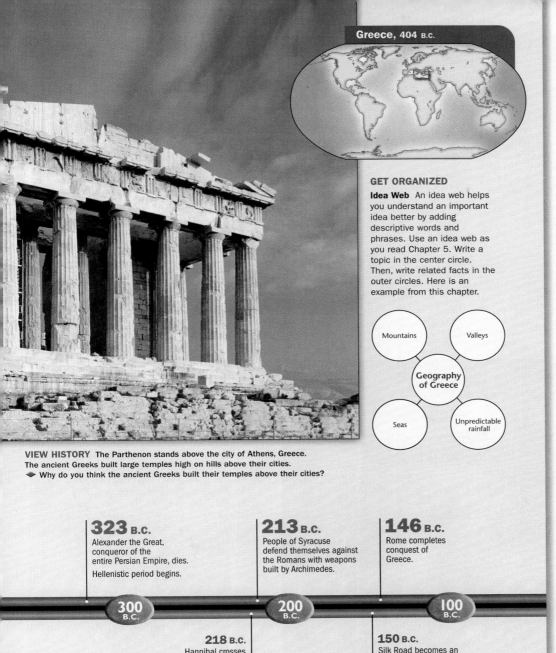

Greece, 404 B.C.

GET ORGANIZED

Idea Web An idea web helps you understand an important idea better by adding descriptive words and phrases. Use an idea web as you read Chapter 5. Write a topic in the center circle. Then, write related facts in the outer circles. Here is an example from this chapter.

Mountains — Valleys — **Geography of Greece** — Seas — Unpredictable rainfall

VIEW HISTORY The Parthenon stands above the city of Athens, Greece. The ancient Greeks built large temples high on hills above their cities.
◆ Why do you think the ancient Greeks built their temples above their cities?

323 B.C.
Alexander the Great, conqueror of the entire Persian Empire, dies. Hellenistic period begins.

213 B.C.
People of Syracuse defend themselves against the Romans with weapons built by Archimedes.

146 B.C.
Rome completes conquest of Greece.

300 B.C. — **200 B.C.** — **100 B.C.**

218 B.C.
Hannibal crosses the Alps and invades Italy.

150 B.C.
Silk Road becomes an important trade route between the Mediterranean region and China.

CHAPTER 5 ◆ Ancient Greece **99**

Chapter Themes
• Culture
• People, Places, and Environments
• Power, Authority, and Governance
• Individuals, Groups, and Institutions
• Time, Continuity, and Change
• Civic Ideals and Practices

F Y I

The Parthenon
The Parthenon, completed in 438 B.C., was built according to very strict standards for the number of columns and the length of the sides. It once housed a 40-foot gold and ivory statue of the goddess Athena, whom it was built to honor. It was used by different religions for centuries, starting as a Greek temple and later serving as a Byzantine church, a Latin church, and an Islamic mosque.

Chapter Warm-Up

USING THE MAP
Point out the locator map at the top of page 99. Help students understand where Greece is located in relation to North America (east), Africa (north), and Asia (west).

VIEW HISTORY
Discuss with students the features of Greek architecture evident in the Parthenon. (large pillars and carvings) Ask what impression is created by the angle from which the photograph was taken. (a sense of height, power, and majesty)

◆ **ANSWER** Possible answer: The ancient Greeks built their temples above their cities in order to protect their temples from destruction by enemies and to stress the importance of the gods in their lives.

GET ORGANIZED
Idea Web
Discuss the idea web on page 99. The first reference to the idea web can be found on page 25 of this book. Ask students to describe the geography of Greece using the idea web. Encourage students to organize information about each civilization using a different idea web (TR, p. 321).

TEACH THE TIMELINE
The timeline on pages 98–99 covers the period between 2000 B.C. and 100 B.C. Point out that the timeline covers nearly 2,000 years of time. Ask students what two ideas are emphasized in the Chapter Event entries. (civilization and war) Suggest that students look for those ideas as they read the chapter.

Activity

Use a map Use Transparencies 5 and 7, the outline maps for Asia and Europe (TR, p. 333 and p. 335), or have students trace the outline of a map of Europe and Asia from pages A5 and A7 of the Atlas. Have students locate Greece on the map and draw lines connecting it to places named in the world events part of the timeline. (China, Israel, Italy, the Alps)

I. Early Civilizations of Greece (pp. 100-104)

Section Summary

In this section, students will learn how the geography of Greece affected the development of two ancient civilizations of traders and palace builders. They will also learn about the economic and cultural life of the Minoans and Mycenaeans and how historical events have been preserved in legends and epics.

Introduce

Getting Started

Discuss with students all the ways they communicate events in their lives to family and friends. Then, have students discuss the role that verbal communication plays in recording the lives of their families and their culture.

TERMS TO KNOW

Ask students to read the terms and definitions on page 100 and find each term in the section. Point out that *civilization* and *monarchy* have Greek or Latin origins. Have students use a dictionary to find other words that begin with *civi-* or *mon-*. Then, ask students if the words have the same general meanings.

You may wish to preview the pronunciation of the following words from this section with students.

Peloponnesus
   (peh luh puh NEE suhs)
Phaistos (FYS tuhs)
Knossos (NAH suhs)
Mycenaean (my suh NEE uhn)
Tiryns (THIR ehnz)
archaeological
   (ahr kee uh LAHJ ih kuhl)
Odysseus (oh DIHS ee uhs)

ACTIVE READING

Have students choose one of the subsections in Section 1 and write a summary of its most important points. Suggest that they use the headings, the art, and the map to help them write their summaries.

Early Civilizations of Greece

Terms to Know

Western civilization the civilization that developed in Europe and spread to the Americas

monarchy a government that has a single ruler, such as a king, queen, or pharaoh

Greek civilization developed in the rocky coastal areas along the Mediterranean Sea.

Main Ideas

A. Mountains and seas influenced the growth and development of ancient Greek civilizations.

B. The Minoans developed a civilization on the island of Crete.

C. The Mycenaeans developed a civilization on the Greek mainland.

D. After the Mycenaean civilization declined, the memory of historical events was kept alive by storytellers and poets, including the poet Homer.

Active Reading

SUMMARIZE
When you summarize, you state only the important points of a passage. As you read this section, focus on the main points about early Greek civilizations. Then, pause to summarize what you have learned.

A. The Geography of Greece

Geography was a key factor in the development of ancient Greek civilization. Greece is located in a mountainous region in southeastern Europe. The mountains in Greece are called the Pindus Mountains. They isolated Greek people from one another and caused communities to develop in different ways. The rugged, mountainous land rises from the Aegean Sea, which is part of the larger Mediterranean Sea. The Greek mainland is in the southernmost part of the Balkan Peninsula, which extends into the Mediterranean Sea. A peninsula is land that is surrounded by water on three sides. The southern part of the Greek mainland is called the Peloponnesus. In addition, Greece has numerous islands.

The Land, the Climate, and the Sea

The land of Greece is difficult to farm. There are no great rivers to water the land. Rainfall is unpredictable, and most of it comes in winter. During the hot, dry summers, the small rivers and streams often dry up.

Still, farming in ancient Greece took root thousands of years ago. Farmers were able to grow barley, grapes, and olives in the rocky soil. They also raised pigs, sheep, goats, and chickens. However, no matter how hard Greek farmers worked, food was often scarce.

Fortunately, most Greek people lived within 40 miles of the sea. Although mountains often separated Greek communities, the seas linked the Greek people to the rest of the world. Many good harbors were located along the mainland and islands. The Greeks became good sailors, fishers, and traders. They traded goods all around the eastern Mediterranean Sea. Their ships carried olive oil, wine, wool, and marble to exchange for grain and metals.

Teaching Options

Section 1 Resources

Teacher's Resources (TR)
   Terms to Know, p. 18
   Review History, p. 52
   Build Your Skills, p. 86
   Concept Builder, p. 221
   Idea Web, p. 321

ESL/ELL STRATEGIES

Identify Essential Vocabulary Many English words with Greek origins have letter combinations that may cause students difficulty. Some examples in this section are the *eu* in *Europe*, the *ae* in *Mycenaeans*, the *ch* in *monarchy*, the *kn* in *Knossos*, or the *ph* in *geographic*. Have students work in pairs to look up the proper pronunciation of these words and then take turns sounding them out for each other.

Early Greek Communities

Many ancient Greek people lived on the mainland, while others lived on the numerous nearby islands. The early Greeks built their communities in the most fertile areas of their homeland, the mountain valleys. There, they were separated from neighboring communities by a fence of mountains. As a result of this separation, nearby communities often developed in very different ways. Sometimes even when there were no mountain barriers, nearby communities developed differently.

The Greeks believed that they lived in the most beautiful land on Earth. Their location by the sea would help them to produce a great civilization. The ancient Greeks laid the foundation for **Western civilization**, the civilization that developed in Europe and then spread to the Americas.

◆ How did the seas affect the lives of the ancient Greeks?

B. The Minoan Civilization

There is no written record of the beginnings of ancient Greek civilization that anyone is able to read. However, from ruins discovered on the large island of Crete, in the Aegean Sea, we know that the first great Aegean civilization developed there. This civilization is called Minoan, after Minos, a legendary king of Crete. It is believed that the Minoan people had a **monarchy**, a government with a single ruler. The Minoans produced fine crafts, built great palaces, and played sports. The symbol of the Minoan civilization is its palace centers on Crete—such as those in the cities of Mallia, Phaistos, and Kato Zakro. The most important palace of all was at Knossos, the economic and political center of Minoan civilization.

The Palace of Knossos

The Minoan civilization began to flourish with the building of palaces during the Bronze Age, around 2000 B.C. The Minoans used stone to build their palaces. Each palace was built around a central courtyard. Many palaces dotted the island of Crete, but the palace of Knossos was the largest.

The Minoan royal family, as well as its advisors, craftworkers, and servants, lived at Knossos. In addition to the courtyard, the palace included many rooms for the royal family, areas for worship, great storerooms, workshops, large bathrooms, and a complex plumbing system. Placed in the storerooms were large containers of oil, wine, and grain. These items were tax payments from the Minoan people to their king. In the palace workshops, craftspeople made decorative vases, ivory figurines, and jewelry.

Art was an important part of Minoan culture. In the many-storied palace of Knossos, the walls were covered with colorful frescoes, or watercolor paintings made on wet plaster. Images on the frescoes included animals such as bulls and leaping dolphins. People, sporting events, and nature scenes were also shown on frescoes.

Minoan and Mycenaean Civilizations

- ■ Major Minoan palace centers
- ■ Major Mycenaean palace centers
- ▣ Other settlements
- ▲ Mountain peak

✔ Map Check

MOVEMENT Why were sailors of ancient Greece usually able to stay close to land as they sailed the Aegean Sea?

Do You Remember?

In Chapter 1, you learned about the Bronze Age, when tools were made of bronze metal.

CHAPTER 5 ◆ Ancient Greece **101**

Connection to LITERATURE

Archaeological findings have supported some of the legends about the Minoans. For example, while excavating Knossos, archaeologists uncovered a maze of passages and storerooms for grain and honey. In the legend of Theseus and the Minotaur, Theseus, a Greek hero, goes through a labyrinth (maze) to hunt a bull-like creature guarding the palace of King Minos.

---

② Teach

A. The Geography of Greece

Purpose-Setting Question What conditions made farming difficult in ancient Greece? (The land was rocky and mountainous, there were no great rivers to water the land, and very hot and dry summers.)

Extend Ask students why Greeks traded so much of the food they grew and the livestock they raised even though food was often scarce. (They wanted to obtain foods they couldn't grow—such as grains— and metals they needed for tools and weapons.)

Using the Map

Minoan and Mycenaean Civilizations

Ask students what the different color squares indicate on the map. (the location of important palace centers or settlements of different cultures) Discuss what is common about the location of nearly all of these places. (They are near the coast and can be reached by boat.)

✔ Map Check

Answer There were many small islands in the Aegean Sea close to the mainland.

◆ **ANSWER** The seas linked Greeks to the rest of the world. They became good sailors, fishers, and traders. Most communities were by the sea.

B. The Minoan Civilization

Purpose-Setting Question What are some characteristics of the Minoan civilization? (peaceful, built large palaces for their monarchs, produced fine crafts, and played sports)

Do You Remember?

Remind students that the Bronze Age is the name historians gave to the period when people began to make and use the metal bronze.

THE MINOANS Evans worked for more than 30 years excavating and restoring the palace at Knossos. He and his team members uncovered 3,000 clay tablets containing writing in Linear A and Linear B (a Greek dialect they were able to read). Ask students how historians and archaeologists work together to help people understand old civilizations. (Archaeologists uncover artifacts of ancient peoples, and historians use these findings to write about how the people lived.)

Focus Have students look back at the map on page 101. Then ask them why Crete was an ideal location for the establishment of a new civilization. (It was located in the open waters of the Mediterranean, making trade possible with other civilizations throughout the region.)

Activity

Write an article Have students use library or Internet sources to find out more about the earthquake on Thera that weakened the Minoan civilization on Crete. Have them use their research to write an article for the front page of a newspaper about the event and its effects on the Minoan civilization.

Explore Have students study the photograph of the palace of Knossos. Encourage students to identify the architectural characteristics of Minoan civilization. (fresco on outside wall, decorative markings on top of columns, red columns, and decorative base on wall under columns at front)

◆ **ANSWER** The Minoans probably had a monarchy.

C. The Mycenaeans Grow Powerful

Purpose-Setting Question How do we know that the Trojan War actually occurred? (German businessman Heinrich Schliemann excavated the site of Troy in the 1870s and found evidence that a war occurred there around 1250 B.C.)

Spotlight on **Archaeology**

THE MINOANS

Knowledge about the Minoans is based on archaeological discoveries, not on written records. Although the Minoans had a system of writing, known as Linear A, no one has yet discovered how to read it!

Sir Arthur Evans, a British archaeologist, discovered the largest Minoan palace at Knossos in 1900. He restored some of the palace so that people could know what life was like in ancient Greece, but he used materials that the Minoans did not use themselves.

The palace of Knossos, on the island of Crete, was built of stone and decorated with frescoes.

Peaceful Sea Traders

The Minoan people seem to have lived in peace for a long time. Even though they used stone to build their palaces, the walls were not strong. They traded by sea but were not interested in warfare or conquest. The Minoans traded extensively with people on nearby islands, in Egypt, and in other areas of the eastern Mediterranean region. They also traded with people on the Greek mainland. Although the Minoans did not speak Greek, they influenced the Greek-speaking Mycenaeans—another palace civilization which was developing on the mainland.

Archaeologists do not know for certain what happened to the Minoans. One possibility is that a volcanic eruption on the nearby island of Thera may have destroyed the Minoan civilization in about 1600 B.C. Many archaeologists and historians think that after the eruption, the Minoans were greatly weakened and that another civilization developed.

◆ **What kind of government did the Minoans probably have?**

C. The Mycenaeans Grow Powerful

A short time after the development of the Minoan civilization, the Mycenaean civilization developed on the mainland of Greece. The origins of the Mycenaean people are not certain, but we know that they were the first Greek-speaking people to leave a written record. The Mycenaeans lived in Mycenae, Thebes, Athens, Pylos, Tiryns, and other cities on the mainland of Greece. The people were ruled by kings whose palaces were the centers of the kingdoms. The Mycenaeans dominated the mainland from about 1500 B.C. to 1200 B.C.

Teaching Options

Meet Individual Needs:
VISUAL/SPATIAL LEARNERS

To help students compare and contrast the Minoan and Mycenaean civilizations, have them create a Venn diagram (TR, p. 323). They should list differences between the two cultures in the outer parts of the two circles and common elements where the circles intersect. Post completed diagrams on a bulletin board for students to compare their findings.

F Y I
Sir Arthur Evans

Before Sir Arthur Evans began his excavations at Knossos, the idea of a Minoan civilization seemed more a legend than a reality. Evans worked very carefully and kept extensive notebooks of his daily activities. He later published books about his excavations and his attempts to translate tablets found at Knossos. As a mark of honor, a bust of Evans stands in the courtyard of the palace.

At first, the Mycenaeans traded peacefully with the Minoans. However, by the mid-1500s B.C., it appears that the Mycenaeans conquered Knossos and became the leading power in the Aegean. Instead of destroying the Minoan culture, the Mycenaeans borrowed from it. They adapted Minoan writing and made it their own. Mycenaean pottery and metalwork also show the influence of Minoan craftwork.

Mycenaean Palaces and Sea Traders

Like the Minoans, the Mycenaeans built great palaces. In fact, their name comes from their most important palace at Mycenae. However, unlike Minoan palaces, Mycenaean palaces were surrounded by thick walls. These walls provided a defense against possible invasions. Mycenaean palaces were centered around a great hall.

Inside the palace, a king lived in splendor. Frescoes that included scenes of men hunting, riding chariots, and battling were on the palace walls. Frescoes also showed animals such as lions and horses. In the village, farmers, traders, and craftworkers lived under the king's tight rule.

The Mycenaeans traded throughout the eastern Mediterranean. Their pottery has been found along the coast of present-day Asia Minor, in Syria and Palestine, and in Egypt, Mesopotamia, Sardinia, Sicily, and Malta. The Mycenaeans also set up colonies along the Mediterranean coast.

The Trojan War

The Mycenaeans are primarily known today for their role in the Trojan War. In this war, the Mycenaeans and other Greeks attacked the rich trading city of Troy, located near the western coast of present-day Turkey. According to legend, the war began after a Trojan prince named Paris kidnapped Helen, the wife of the brother of the Mycenaean king. In an effort to rescue her, the Greeks battled the Trojans and finally seized Troy, burning it to the ground.

For hundreds of years, people believed that the entire Trojan War may have been a legend. This belief changed in the 1870s when Heinrich Schliemann, a German businessman, found the site of Troy and excavated it. Schliemann found archaeological evidence that the legend was probably rooted in an actual war that took place about 1250 B.C.

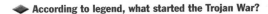

◆ According to legend, what started the Trojan War?

D. The Decline of Mycenae and the Age of Homer

By 1100 B.C., the Mycenaean people disappeared from history, and their palaces were either destroyed or abandoned. The causes of the destruction probably included internal warfare, natural disasters, and invaders, including a Greek-speaking people called Dorians.

At Home and Abroad

As Mycenaean cities were destroyed and abandoned, people settled in smaller villages. During this period, writing nearly disappeared and trade decreased. Storytelling, however, continued. Stories of the Bronze Age civilizations and the Trojan War were passed from one generation to the next.

Many Greeks left their homeland to settle elsewhere. They spread throughout the Mediterranean area from the coast of Asia Minor in the east to the coast of Sicily and southern Italy in the west. They took with them their culture and ideas. Gradually, Greeks at home began to rebuild their cities.

This gold mask, commonly known as the Mask of Agamemnon, is a striking artifact found by Heinrich Schliemann while excavating at Mycenae.

Where in the World?

ASIA MINOR

Asia Minor is the name for the peninsula that makes up the southwesternmost part of Asia. It lies to the east of Greece, just across the Aegean Sea. Asia Minor forms the greater part of present-day Turkey.

The southwestern coast of Asia Minor was settled by Greek peoples, including the Dorians, around 1000 B.C.

Discuss Ask students why the Mycenaeans would have surrounded their palaces with thick walls while the Minoans left their palaces more open. (The Minoans were a peaceful people, while the Mycenaeans were more warlike. Also, the Minoans lived on an island, so they may not have felt as threatened by attack.)

TEACH PRIMARY SOURCES

Ask students what the gold mask tells historians about the Mycenaean civilization. (Possible answers: It traded for gold; it was wealthy; King Agamemnon was important and respected; Mycenaean craftspeople were skilled at working with gold.)

Explore Point out that a number of idiomatic expressions are based on stories about the Trojan War and its heroes. Have students use dictionaries or library sources to find out the meaning and history behind the expressions *Achilles' heel, siren's song,* and *Trojan horse.*

WHERE IN THE WORLD?

ASIA MINOR Asia Minor and Greece came into conflict many times after the Trojan War. The Asia Minor peninsula was under Persian control during the Persian Wars in the fifth century B.C., and Alexander the Great later conquered most of Asia Minor. In more modern times, Greeks and Turks have long been enemies. Ask students what geographical and historical connections Greece and Asia Minor have. (They face each other on opposite shores of the Aegean Sea, the Dorians were their common ancestors, and they have fought many wars against each other.)

◆ **ANSWER** Paris, a Trojan prince, kidnapped Helen, the wife of the brother of the Mycenaean king. The Mycenaeans fought the Trojans to get her back.

D. The Decline of Mycenae and the Age of Homer

Purpose-Setting Question Why is Homer important? (His epic poems helped preserve events of the Trojan War and its heroes.)

Writing

AVERAGE

Sir Arthur Evans and Heinrich Schliemann both made important archaeological discoveries, but they used very different methods to do their work. Have students use library or Internet sources to discover more about the two men and their methods. Then have students write a paragraph explaining which one is a better role model for future archaeologists.

CHALLENGE

Heinrich Schliemann made many important discoveries. However, a number of his findings were later proven inaccurate. Have students research more about Schliemann's methods and findings. Then, they should use their research to write a brief essay discussing whether the value of Schliemann's findings outweighs the mistakes he made.

Agamemnon came to a tragic end, according to Homer. Upon his return from Troy, the Mycenaean king was killed in his bath by his wife Clytemnestra and her lover Aegisthus, who had ruled in Agamemnon's absence. Following the excavations at Troy, Schliemann began a search for Agamemnon's grave at Mycenae.

ANSWER The prediction is joyful because Agamemnon is predicting that Troy will be defeated, "Priam's self shall fall."

Extend The myths about the Greek gods and goddesses were explanations about things that happened in the world. Good or bad events were attributed to pleasing or displeasing a particular god or goddess. The gods competed with each other, so pleasing one could displease another. Ask students how this need to balance the desires of different gods might help to explain events in the lives of the ancient Greeks.

◆ **ANSWER** Greeks settled throughout the Mediterranean from the coast of Asia Minor to the coasts of Sicily and southern Italy.

Section Close

Ask students what advances the Minoans and Mycenaeans made and why it is valuable to study these ancient civilizations. Have them cite examples from the section.

3 Assess

Review Answers

Review History
A. The climate and soil of Greece made it difficult for the Greeks to grow food; they were able to fish and to trade goods for food and other resources.

B. Minoan palaces had courtyards, rooms for the royal family, religious areas, storerooms, large baths, plumbing, and frescoes.

C. The Mycenaeans borrowed writing, pottery, metalwork, and palaces.

D. *Iliad:* events that occurred toward the end of the Trojan War; *Odyssey:* the homecoming journey of Odysseus, a Greek hero of the war

---

The *Iliad* and the *Odyssey*

During this time, two epics or long narrative poems, the *Iliad* and the *Odyssey*, were created, probably by the poet Homer. They were later written down. The *Iliad* describes events during the last days of the Trojan War. The *Odyssey* tells the story of the long journey home of Odysseus, a Greek hero of the war.

In one section of the *Iliad*, the Greek king Agamemnon predicts what will happen to Troy and to Priam, the Trojan king.

> **ANALYZE PRIMARY SOURCES**
> **DOCUMENT-BASED QUESTION**
> Do you think Agamemnon is making a joyful prediction? Why or why not?

> 66 The day shall come, the great avenging day,
> Which Troy's proud glories in the dust shall lay,
> When Priam's powers and Priam's self shall fall,
> And one prodigious [enormous] ruin swallow all. 99

Greek Religion

Religion was important to the people of ancient Greece. They believed there were gods present in daily life. The gods were thought to have human feelings, such as love, hate, and jealousy, as well as human form. To have success in their lives, the ancient Greeks believed that they needed to please their gods. They built great temples of white marble to honor them. Many of these temples still stand today.

The Greeks believed that Zeus, the ruler of all the gods, lived on Mount Olympus, the highest mountain peak in Greece. He was the symbol of power, rule, and law. Athena, the goddess of wisdom, was Zeus's favorite child. The city of Athens was named in her honor. The Greek gods appear in Homer's epic poems as well as in myths. Myths are traditional stories about human beings' place in nature and their relationship to the gods.

◆ In what geographic areas did Greeks settle after 1100 B.C.?

Review I

Review History
A. Why did the ancient Greeks travel on the seas?
B. How would you describe the Minoan palaces?
C. What did the Mycenaeans borrow from the Minoans?
D. What events did the *Iliad* and the *Odyssey* tell about?

Define Terms to Know
Define the following terms:
Western civilization, monarchy

Critical Thinking
What are some reasons why civilizations might come to an end?

Write About Culture
Write a paragraph that compares and contrasts the Minoan and Mycenaean civilizations.

Get Organized
IDEA WEB
Use an idea web to organize information from this section. Choose a topic and then find related facts. For example, what were the main characteristics of the Mycenaean civilization?

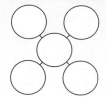

Define Terms to Know
Western civilization, 101; monarchy, 101

Critical Thinking
Possible answers: natural disasters, internal or external warfare, or invasions

Write About Culture
Students should describe parts of the Minoan culture that the Mycenaeans adopted and point out differences in the types of palaces the two cultures built.

Build Your Skills

Social Studies Skill

ANALYZE ARTIFACTS

When you want to find information, you go to a source. In history, one type of source is called a primary source. Primary sources are accounts of events created by people who were present at the events. They include letters, speeches, autobiographies, newspaper articles, political cartoons, advertisements, photographs, or artifacts. Artifacts are objects that are made or changed by people. Artifacts from a particular time can provide direct evidence about a person, a place, or an event in that time. They may include tools, paintings, drawings, pottery, utensils, and other objects.

In Chapter 1, you learned that archaeologists are scientists who dig for ruins and artifacts. Archaeologists study artifacts to learn what life was like in the past. The artifacts serve as clues in revealing how people lived.

Artifacts are particularly important when there is no readable written history. Much of the information about the Minoan and Mycenaean civilizations comes from the artifacts found at archaeological digs at those sites.

Here's How
Follow these steps to interpret an artifact.

1. Find out when, where, and how the artifact was discovered.

2. Identify the content, or main images, of the artifact. What do the images show about a person, a place, or an event?

3. Identify the purpose of the artifact. Is the content religious or does it show everyday life? Is the purpose to decorate, to teach, to inspire, or a combination of these purposes?

4. Learn more about the artifact and the period.

Here's Why
Analyzing artifacts can provide information about a particular time that you could not learn from reading about it. Many artifacts have images and scenes on them that help you see what people during a certain period looked like, what kinds of clothing they wore, what activities they were involved in, and what was important to them.

Practice the Skill
Study the Minoan fresco on this page. Then, answer the following questions.

1. What activity is shown in the fresco?

2. Based on the image in the fresco, how would you describe Minoan athletes?

Extend the Skill
Study the Minoan fresco carefully. Notice the different images, the colors, and the decorative borders. Then, write a description of the fresco. Include at least five details and what you think the purpose of the fresco is.

Apply the Skill
As you read the remaining sections of this chapter, study the paintings and photographs. Follow the steps in *Here's How* to learn more about them.

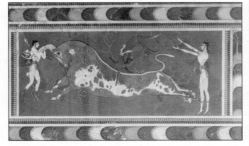

A Minoan fresco

Teaching Options

RETEACH
Provide students with several unusual kitchen or carpentry tools, if possible. Have students study the tools and speculate how they are used and what they say about the society they are used in.

Have students look through earlier chapters of this textbook to find photographs of artifacts. Ask them to explain when the artifact was created and when and where it was found. Ask students how the artifact helps them understand the past.

CHALLENGE
Have students use the Internet or library materials to locate photographs of additional artifacts discovered at Knossos, Mycenae, or Troy. Students can use these photographs to create a poster showing the artwork and explaining what it reveals about the civilization that created the original objects. Students should share their completed projects with the class.

ANALYZE ARTIFACTS

Teach the Skill
Ask students to describe a time they listened to a live speech by a politician, watched a televised broadcast of a news event, took a photograph of a live event, or wrote a letter describing something they saw or did. Point out that all of these activities involve primary sources. Discuss the difference between attending and observing an actual event compared to reading about it after it happens.

Explain that archaeologists use artifacts to tell how people lived, what they used, and what they thought was important. Tell students that the artifacts, as well as how they are decorated, help to tell the story of a people. Ask students what they think it might mean if archaeologists found many tools such as hoes or shovels. (The society farmed; farming was important.) What might it mean if the walls of a town had paintings of people fighting or dressed to fight? (War was a big part of the town's life; soldiers were honored.)

Finally, ask what the absence of artifacts might mean about a society. Help students realize that not all materials survive over time. The absence of hoes may not mean that the society didn't farm; it may mean that they used other tools to farm. Archaeologists need to look at many things to learn about a society.

Practice the Skill
ANSWERS
1. people leaping over a bull
2. strong, brave, and agile

Extend the Skill
Students' descriptions should include details about the appearance and activities of the athletes and the bull, the vivid colors used in the fresco, and its unusual border. Students may speculate that the fresco's purpose was probably to decorate.

Apply the Skill
Ask students to tell about the artifacts shown on pages 103, 107, and 120. Suggest that they look for additional artifacts illustrated in this chapter. Discuss why it is useful to include pictures of artifacts in a history book. Ask students to describe how the artifacts help bring ideas in the book to life.

II. Greek City-States Rise to Power

(pp. 106–111)

Section Summary

In this section, students will learn how Greek towns organized to form city-states with different forms of government. Sparta was governed by military leaders, and Spartan society emphasized military discipline. Athens developed a limited democracy in which only free adult men could participate. Sparta, Athens, and many other city-states united to defeat Persian invaders in the Persian Wars.

1 Introduce

Getting Started

Discuss with students some differences in the way students act and learn in a military school compared to other types of schools. Ask which type of school they prefer and why. Point out that, in ancient Greece, some communities followed very strict military discipline, and others had a more democratic government.

TERMS TO KNOW

Ask students to read the words and definitions on page 106 and then find each word in the section. Have students write each word on the front of an index card and write the definition and a sentence using the word in context on the back.

You may wish to preview the pronunciation of the following words from this section with students.

agora (AH goh rah)
ephors (EHF ers)
Cleisthenes (KLYS thuh neez)
Xerxes (ZERK seez)
Thermopylae (thuhr MAHP uh lee)
Herodotus (huh RAHD uh tuhs)

ACTIVE READING

Have students make a two-column chart (TR, p. 328), as they read sub-sections B and C. They should list facts about Sparta in one column and facts about Athens in the other column. Then, have them underline ways in which the two city-states were alike and circle ways in which they were different from each other.

Terms to Know

polis a Greek city-state

acropolis the highest part of a Greek city-state

aristocracy a government in which the upper class, or a privileged few, rule

oligarchy a government in which only a few powerful people rule

tyrant a leader who gains power by force; later, a leader who rules ruthlessly

legislature a lawmaking body in government

democracy a government that gives its citizens the ruling power

alliance an agreement between two or more people, groups, or nations to cooperate with one another

Do You Remember?

In Chapter 1, you learned about the city-states of ancient river valley civilizations, such as those on the Huang He and on the Nile, Tigris, Euphrates, and Indus Rivers.

Main Ideas

A. Greek people developed city-states with several types of governments.

B. Sparta became a powerful military city-state.

C. Athens developed a government in which many people participated, but other Athenians, including women and slaves, were not included.

D. Many Greek city-states, including Sparta and Athens, united to defeat the Persians in the Persian Wars.

A. City-States Develop

By about 800 B.C., the first Greek towns organized into larger political units. The Greeks called each political unit a **polis**, meaning "a city-state." Many city-states were small, with a population between a few hundred and a few thousand. City-states developed all over Greece and often competed against each other for control of land and trade.

Foundations of the City-State

The polis was made up of a city and the surrounding countryside. The size of a city-state was anywhere from a few square miles to a few hundred square miles. Part of the city was encircled by a fortress similar to those of Mycenaean towns. The fortress, usually built on a hilltop, was called an **acropolis**, or highest point. It offered protection from attacks and served as a center of government and religion. Often, great marble temples and monuments to gods and goddesses were built on the acropolis. Public buildings were also built on the acropolis.

Below the acropolis was the main section of the city-state. This section included housing as well as a public square and marketplace called the agora. Many ancient Greeks were farmers and shopkeepers who sold their crops and products in the agora.

In the agora, men also discussed political issues and gathered to conduct business. Government and politics were important to the polis. Greek people were proud of and loyal to their city-state. They were often willing to give up their lives for their polis.

Several city-states developed throughout Greece. While different in many ways, the Greeks of all city-states shared some common things. Citizenship was very important to the Greek city-state. The citizens of the polis—free adult men—took shared responsibility for the city's public affairs and for defense of the city. In return, each citizen benefited from the city's wealth and successes. The Greeks of all city-states also shared a common language. The Greeks adapted and expanded the Phoenician alphabet around 750 B.C. The alphabet and the reintroduction of writing transformed Greek culture. The expanded alphabet became the basis for their common language. The Greeks often regarded people who did not speak Greek as barbarians.

Active Reading

COMPARE AND CONTRAST
When you compare and contrast items, you learn to understand how they are the same and different. As you read this section, compare and contrast the different types of government that developed in ancient Greece.

Teaching Options

Section 2 Resources

Teacher's Resources (TR)

Terms to Know, p. 18
Review History, p. 52
Build Your Skills, p. 86
Concept Builder, p. 221
Idea Web, p. 321

Meet Individual Needs:
KINESTHETIC LEARNERS

Identify Essential Vocabulary To help contrast a monarchy, oligarchy, and democracy, write *Government Leaders* on the board. Below that, write *monarchy, oligarchy,* and *democracy.* Have one student stand under *monarchy;* have a small group of students stand under *oligarchy;* and have the class stand under *democracy.* Discuss how the process of making laws might be different in each government.

The Greek people also shared a common religion and culture. They believed in the same gods and honored them by building great temples. They also held festivals such as the Olympic games to recognize athletes. Greek festivals brought together people from different city-states.

Governments of the City-States

Although they shared some similarities, the city-states also prided themselves on their individuality and independence. Each polis tried to establish its own government. Many city-states began as monarchies. Such city-states were protected from enemies by citizen-soldiers called hoplites. The hoplites fought shoulder to shoulder in a formation known as a phalanx. They wore helmets and body armor. They also had round, heavy shields as well as spears and swords. Hoplites had to provide their own weapons, which were made of bronze. These weapons were not only required, but were expensive. As a result, only wealthy people, such as landowners, or their slaves could be soldiers. Some hoplites were paid for being soldiers.

In time, the wealthy landowners who served as soldiers demanded some form of power. Because of this, some city-states became **aristocracies**, or governments in which a group of noble landowners ruled. Nobles are people of high rank or birth. As trade expanded, wealthy businessmen wanted a share of the power, too. In some city-states, a group of nobles and businessmen formed an **oligarchy** of powerful men who controlled the government. The word *oligarchy* means "the rule of a few."

As people began to make iron tools and weapons around 800 B.C., power began to shift in the city-states. Because iron was more plentiful and cheaper than bronze, more people could afford to buy their own weapons and help defend their city. In time, they, too, demanded a voice in government.

In addition to having different forms of government, other differences existed among the city-states. These differences were never more apparent than in two of Greece's most powerful and most famous city-states—Athens and Sparta.

◆ **What were the physical characteristics of the polis?**

An ancient Greek festival chariot driver is assisted by Athena in this nineteenth-century painting based on an ancient Greek vase.

Then & Now

THE OLYMPICS
The first Olympic games were held in 776 B.C. at Olympia on the Greek mainland. The games were part of a religious festival in honor of the god Zeus. He and the other Greek gods were believed to live on Mount Olympus, above Olympia. The first games featured only one event— a footrace.

The first modern Olympic games were held in Athens, Greece, in 1896. In 2004, the games return to Athens.

A. City-States Develop

Purpose-Setting Question What are some characteristics that all Greek city-states had in common? (They had a common language, religion, and culture. Their citizens shared the responsibility for each city-state's public affairs and defense.)

Do You Remember?
Ask students how rivers or mountains in a region might lead to the development of city-states. (These geographical features separate communities from each other and encourage them to be independent of each other.)

Then & Now

THE OLYMPICS The first Olympics was a 1-day event. As more contests were added to the games— such as boxing, chariot and horse races, wrestling, jumping, discus, and javelin—the Olympics stretched to 5 days. The 2000 Summer Olympic Games in Australia lasted for more than 2 weeks, and athletes participated in 28 different individual and team sports.

Focus Ask students why there was such a close connection between serving in the military and participating in government in Greek city-states. (Citizens felt that if they served to protect the city-state, they deserved to help make its rules.)

Extend Many Greek city-states weren't content just to occupy their own small part of Greece. They needed more land and resources for their growing populations. These city-states established colonies all around the Mediterranean and Black Sea regions from Spain and Libya to what is now the Ukraine. Point out these areas on the maps of Europe and Africa in the Atlas. (p. A5 and p. A6)

◆ **ANSWER** The polis was made up of a city and the countryside around it. A fortress, called the acropolis, encircled part of the city and was usually built on a hilltop. Public buildings and temples were built on the acropolis. Housing, a public square, and a marketplace were built below it.

Focus on SPORTS & GAMES

Greek Athletic Competitions The Greeks believed that one way to please their gods was to develop strong and fit bodies. Therefore, they trained hard at different sports and held competitions as part of religious festivals. The Olympics was only one athletic competition. Others were held regularly at the city-states of Delphi, Corinth, and Nemea.

Athletes competed in such sports as boxing, wrestling, horse racing, running events (including one in full battle armor), and an unusual competition called the pankraton— a mixture of wrestling, boxing, and street fighting. Victorious athletes were often given cash prizes or other gifts when they returned home. Starting in the fifth century B.C., Athenian Olympics winners were given a free meal every day for the rest of their lives.

B. Sparta Becomes a Military State

B. Sparta Becomes a Military State

Purpose-Setting Question What is meant by the term "a Spartan life"? (a life that is very controlled and contains few luxuries)

Discuss According to legend, Spartan mothers sent their husbands and sons off to war with the words, "Come home with your shield or on it." This meant either come home as a victor or die. Ask students what they think of this statement and how it reflects the goals and culture of Sparta.

ANALYZE PRIMARY SOURCES

DOCUMENT-BASED QUESTION

Xenophon was an Athenian who had studied under Socrates before he became a mercenary soldier. He fought first with the Persian King Cyrus. Later, he joined the Spartan army and even fought against Athens. He was exiled from Athens and spent most of the rest of his life in Sparta. Since his children were educated in Sparta, he had firsthand knowledge of Spartan discipline.

ANSWER Spartan boys' lives were made more difficult because they went without shoes and had only one garment to wear throughout the year.

Activity

Prepare an exercise tape
Have students work in groups to prepare an exercise audiotape or videotape for Spartan boys or girls to use. The tape will include exercises to strengthen the bodies of Spartan children, and the "instructor" should emphasize Spartan values while directing the exercises. Have students present their tapes to the class and discuss how they would fit the Spartan way of life.

◆ **ANSWER** The main purpose was to produce strong, able soldiers and keep them in shape.

This bronze statue shows a Spartan warrior.

Located in southern Greece, the city-state of Sparta was probably founded in about 1000 B.C. by the Dorian people. In the 700s B.C., Sparta became wealthy and powerful by attacking and defeating its neighbors. Eventually, there were more conquered people in Sparta than there were Spartans. In order to control the conquered population, the Spartans created a way of life based on military ideas that was not shared by other Greek people. The Spartans sacrificed individual freedoms, family life, the arts, and most luxuries for the common interests of their city-state. Even today, *a Spartan life* means "one with few luxuries."

A Society of Soldiers

By the 600s B.C., Sparta had one of the earliest constitutions of the Greek city-states, called the Great Rhetra. Sparta was governed by two military leaders called kings and a 28-member council of elders, or men over 60 years of age. The council chose the issues to be presented to the assembly, or lawmaking group. The assembly voted on the issues. All free adult male Spartans over the age of 30 belonged to the assembly, which elected five ephors, or overseers. The Spartan kings were bound to consider the advice of the ephors. Also, the ephors were responsible for the education of Spartan youth and supervision of the kings.

The conquered people of Sparta had no role in the Spartan government. They were helots, or slaves of the state. Helots farmed the land, which was equally divided among all male citizens, worked as household servants, and sometimes assisted soldiers in war. Their labor enabled Spartan men to devote themselves to military training and warfare.

The entire Spartan society was organized for producing soldiers and keeping them in shape. Boys lived at home only until they were seven years old. Then, they moved to a barracks to begin their training to be soldiers. There, boys were underfed and only provided with light clothing year round in order to make them better soldiers. Xenophon, a Greek historian, described the rules for boys set by a Spartan lawmaker in *The Constitution of Sparta*:

DOCUMENT-BASED QUESTION According to Xenophon, in what two ways were Spartan boys' lives made more difficult?

> ❝Instead of softening the boys' feet with sandals he required them to harden their feet by going without shoes. . . . And instead of letting them be pampered in the matter of clothing, he introduced the custom of wearing one garment throughout the year.❞

Male Spartans lived in a barracks until they were 30 years old. At that time, they could live at home with their families, but they ate each day with their unit of soldiers. At age 30, they could also vote in the assembly. They remained available for military service until the age of 60.

Women of Sparta

Spartan women had more rights than other Greek women. For example, they could inherit land. Because many Spartan men were killed in warfare, women often gained control of property. Spartan women were encouraged to exercise and keep physically fit. The Spartans realized that healthy women would be more likely to bear strong babies.

Spartan girls were trained in physical fitness similar to the athletic training given to boys. Girls learned to run, wrestle, and throw a javelin, or spear. They also received some formal education.

◆ **What was the main purpose of Spartan society?**

Teaching Options

F Y I

Spartan Child

Spartan discipline began even before a child was seven. Newborn Spartan children were examined by public officials to determine if they were strong and healthy-looking. Healthy babies were allowed to live. Sickly babies were taken to nearby mountains and left to die.

ESL/ELL STRATEGIES

Take Notes Emphasize to students the value of using subheads as reading clues. Give students two large note cards. Have them write one of the two subheads found on this page at the top of each card. They should then write brief notes about that part of the text below the heading. Discuss how the notes present details that back up the main idea named in the subhead.

C. Athenians and Their Right to Govern

Athens was a city-state in Attica, northeast of Sparta. Athens developed in a far different way from Sparta. Unlike other important sites in Greece, Athens had not suffered widespread destruction at the end of the Bronze Age. Between 800 and 700 B.C., Athens grew quickly. As the city grew, merchants, soldiers, and free peasants wanted more power to govern. **Tyrants**, or rulers who gain power by force in the ancient Greek meaning of the word, sometimes won the support of these groups by promising reforms. After one such man tried to gain power, the Athenians appointed a man named Draco to establish new laws. However, Draco's laws were unpopular and considered harsh. Death was the penalty for most crimes, even minor ones.

Government Reforms and Limited Democracy

When civil war threatened to break out, Solon, a wise leader, was given authority to revise the laws. He tried to balance the power between rich and poor, outlawed making people slaves to repay debts, and freed the people already enslaved for debts. He also gave citizenship to some foreigners to attract tradespeople. Solon's reforms helped to stabilize the government of Athens and make it fairer, but wealthy landowners continued to hold the most power.

Later reformers included the tyrant Cleisthenes, who gave greater power to ordinary citizens. Cleisthenes created a council of 500 chosen citizens who proposed laws to the assembly. Under Cleisthenes, the assembly became a real lawmaking body, or **legislature**. This legislature was made up of free male citizens who were given the final authority to pass laws after free and open debate. This system created the foundations for Athenian **democracy**, or government by the people.

In Athens, although many people took part in government, many others, such as slaves and women, could not. Only free adult men were considered citizens in Athens. Athens had developed a limited democracy. There was no other place in the ancient world where so many people were involved in the political life of their state. However, many Athenian people were not given the right to govern themselves. They were left out of the democratic process and had few rights.

Education in Athens

In Athens, boys were tutored to prepare them to take part in the culture and politics of the city. They were expected to become well-rounded individuals. Education and literacy were very important. Boys not only learned how to read, write, and do arithmetic, but they also learned to play musical instruments, sing, and develop the body through exercise. In gymnasiums, boys trained in running, jumping, wrestling, discus and javelin throwing, and other athletic activities—events that are in the modern Olympic games. Some boys learned public speaking, debating, and other skills that would be useful in politics. They also recited from memory passages from poems, including Homer's *Iliad* and *Odyssey*.

Education was limited in ancient Athens. Tutors and schools were not paid for by the government. Therefore, wealthy citizens were usually the only people who received a full formal education. However, many Athenians did manage to pay for at least a few years of schooling for their sons. Girls received no formal education, although some girls probably learned to read and write at home. The Athenians were generally more literate than the rest of the ancient Greeks.

◆ What were the strengths and limitations of Athenian education?

SOLON

Solon was an Athenian statesman and reformer, but it was poetry that first made him famous. About 600 B.C., Solon read a poem aloud in public. In it, he called on discouraged Athenians to go back to war and win the island of Salamis from their neighbors. After hearing the poem, that is just what the Athenians did.

ORAL EPICS

Most scholars agree that Homer's *Iliad* and *Odyssey* are oral epics, or long poems created without the use of writing. Other great oral epics composed in the period 1000 B.C.–A.D. 200 include the Indian epics, the *Mahabharata* and the *Ramayana*. Like the Homeric epics, these poems served as a cultural foundation for the society that produced them.

C. Athenians and Their Right to Govern

Purpose-Setting Question What was education like for boys and girls in Athens? (Boys learned to read, write, do arithmetic, and received instruction in music and sports. Most girls received no formal education, although some learned to read and write at home.)

WHO IN THE WORLD?

SOLON Solon used poetry not only to convince Athenians to fight but also to lead better lives. Here is a verse from one of his poems written to convince Athenians not to be so money conscious:

> Some wicked men are rich,
> some good men poor,
> But I would rather trust in
> what's secure;
> Our virtue sticks with us and
> makes us strong,
> But money changes owners
> all day long.

Write the stanza on the board, and ask students if they agree with its message.

Focus Review with students the people who could participate in government in Athens. Tell students that they are all free adult citizens in Athens. Ask those who can participate in the government to stand up. (only the boys) Then tell the class that the people who can make the rules have passed a law that everyone must wear yellow shirts from now on. Have the girls explain how they feel about having to obey this law.

GLOBAL CONNECTIONS

ORAL EPICS Nearly every ancient society had an epic saga or epic heroes around whom legends were created. Have students use encyclopedias or the Internet to find descriptions of epic sagas such as the *Ramayana* (India), *Edda* (Viking), *Sundiata* (Mali), *Gilgamesh* (Babylonia), *Aeneid* (Rome), or *Beowulf* (Anglo-Saxon).

◆ **ANSWER Strengths**: Boys learned to read, write, do arithmetic, sing, play instruments, and develop a strong body through exercise. Some boys learned public speaking and debating. Some girls were educated at home. **Limitations**: Education was only for boys. It was not free, so only those from wealthy families received a full formal education, although many boys received some education.

Cooperative Learning

Have groups of students work together to prepare reports comparing growing up as boys and girls in Sparta and in Athens. Students should decide which group members will research each culture and gender. Then, each group should work together to write the reports and present their findings to the class.

Connection to GOVERNMENT

Both Sparta and Athens prepared a written constitution or a written body of laws to spell out the responsibilities of their citizens. Have students make a list of responsibilities or duties that citizens in their community have. Have students share their lists in class. Create a master list on the board, and ask students why each rule is necessary and useful.

D. Greek Unity in the Persian Wars

Purpose-Setting Question What events led to the start of the Persian Wars? (Greeks living in Persia rebelled against Persian rule, and Athens sent troops to support them. The troops burned the Persian city of Sardis. In response, Persian King Darius sent an army to invade Greece.)

Using the Map

The Persian Wars, 499–479 B.C.

Ask students about how far the Persian army traveled between Larissa and Athens. How can they tell? (They traveled more than 125 miles. Students can copy the length of the map scale to determine the measurement that represents 100 miles on the map, measure the length of the purple path with the 100-mile map scale, and then convert the measurement into miles.)

✔ Map Check

Answers
1. the Greeks
2. Larissa, Therma, and Abydus

Discuss Point out that even though the Battle of Thermopylae was a Persian victory, it ultimately helped lead to the Persians' defeat. Ask students why this was true. (The Persians were delayed long enough so that the Athenians could escape from harm and prepare for the Battle of Salamis.)

SPOTLIGHT ON CULTURE

RUNNING THE MARATHON The distance between Marathon and Athens is approximately 24.8 miles, and that was the distance that athletes ran in the first modern Olympics in 1896. The distance was changed to 26 miles, 385 yards during the London Olympics in 1908 so that the race could begin at Windsor Castle, where the Royal family lived. Since then, all marathon races have been 26 miles, 385 yards.

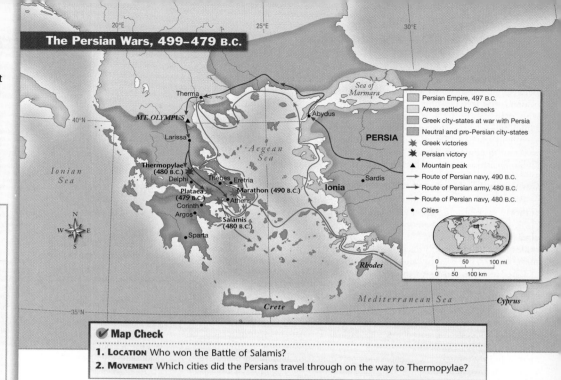

The Persian Wars, 499–479 B.C.

Map legend:
- Persian Empire, 497 B.C.
- Areas settled by Greeks
- Greek city-states at war with Persia
- Neutral and pro-Persian city-states
- ✴ Greek victories
- ✳ Persian victory
- ▲ Mountain peak
- → Route of Persian navy, 490 B.C.
- → Route of Persian army, 480 B.C.
- → Route of Persian navy, 480 B.C.
- • Cities

✔ Map Check

1. **LOCATION** Who won the Battle of Salamis?
2. **MOVEMENT** Which cities did the Persians travel through on the way to Thermopylae?

D. Greek Unity in the Persian Wars

In the late 400s B.C., many Greek city-states united against a common enemy, the Persian Empire. The battles that followed became known as the Persian Wars.

Events of the Persian Wars

The wars began as early as 499 B.C., when Greeks who had settled on the coast near Persia rebelled against Persian rule. Athens sent a small fleet to support the revolt. Its soldiers burned the Persian city of Sardis. Later, an angered King Darius of Persia sent a large army to invade Greece. On the plain of Marathon, in 490 B.C., the Athenians beat the Persians, even though the Greek forces were outnumbered three to one by the Persians.

Ten years later, however, the Persian king Xerxes continued the fighting. This time, many Greek city-states, including Sparta and Athens, fought against the Persians. A few hundred Spartans engaged several thousand Persian soldiers in battle at a narrow pass of land called Thermopylae. Although they were able to delay the advance of the Persian army, all the Spartans were killed. Xerxes then led his Persian troops on a march to Athens. The Persians burned the city-state to the ground, but most Athenians escaped harm.

At the great sea battle of Salamis, the Athenian navy beat the much larger Persian navy. In the waters off the island of Salamis, the Athenians sank about 300 Persian ships, while losing only about 40 of their own ships. The Battle of Salamis was the first large naval battle ever recorded.

Spotlight on
Culture

RUNNING THE MARATHON
There is a legend that an Athenian ran from Athens to Marathon, a distance of about 25 miles, to take part in the battle. After running back to Athens to announce the Greek victory, he died from exhaustion. His extraordinary effort gave the name "marathon" to the modern-day long-distance footrace.

110 UNIT 2 ◆ The Growth of Empires and Governments

Teaching Options

Research

AVERAGE

The Persians are an even older civilization than the Greeks. Today they live mostly in Iran. Have students use reference books or the Internet to find important dates in Persian history and prepare a Persian civilization timeline. Students can present their timelines to the class and discuss connections between ancient Persian and ancient Greek history.

CHALLENGE

Three ancient Persian leaders who interacted with the Greeks were Cyrus, Darius, and Xerxes. Have students use reference books or the Internet to find information about these three leaders and the extent of their empires. Then, students should prepare a report discussing the strengths and weaknesses of each leader.

Later, in 479 B.C., Athens and Sparta combined to beat the Persians in the Battle of Plataea, which took place northwest of Athens. This victory marked the end of the Persian Wars. The Persian army finally left Greece. We know about these events because of an important Greek historian named Herodotus. Herodotus wrote a history of the Persian Wars using storytelling, dialogue, and speeches.

The End of the Persian Wars

Athens, Sparta, and other city-states involved in the Persian Wars fought bravely against the Persians for many years. Afterward, however, the Spartans went home to their own concerns, including keeping the helots from rebelling. Athens, on the other hand, considered a larger issue: Would the Persians attack the Greeks again?

In response, Athens organized the Delian League in 478 B.C., an **alliance** that eventually included 140 Greek city-states that had fought in the Persian Wars. This alliance was a group of nations that promised to help defend each other. Each city-state contributed ships or money to the alliance. Athens led the League and decided how much money and how many ships each city-state contributed. The Delian League had its main headquarters on Delos, an island that was not partial to any particular city-state. Athens controlled the League through the use of its strong navy, which continued the attack against the Persian Empire. Sparta did not join the Delian League. It was already in control of another alliance called the Peloponnesian League.

By 454 B.C., the Delian League was moved to Athens. This move gave the city-state of Athens enormous power. With the end of the Persian Wars, the city-state of Athens entered what is often called its golden age, a time when Greek culture thrived.

◆ In what ways did the Delian League make Athens a more powerful city-state?

Review II

Review History
A. What were the three early types of government in Greek city-states?
B. Why was Sparta very concerned about its military strength?
C. How did Solon reform laws that governed public life in Athens?
D. How did the Persian Wars affect Greek unity?

Define Terms to Know
Define the following terms:
polis, acropolis, aristocracy, oligarchy, tyrant, legislature, democracy, alliance

Critical Thinking
What might cause problems in the Delian League?

Write About Citizenship
Both Sparta and Athens prepared boys for citizenship. Compare education in Sparta or Athens to education in the United States today.

Get Organized
IDEA WEB
Use an idea web to organize information from this section. Choose a topic and then find related facts. For example, what were the characteristics of life in Sparta?

Many slaves — Few luxuries — Life in Sparta — Women could own property — Focus on training soldiers

Critical Thinking
Some city-states might resent how much control Athens had over the alliance and over decisions about how much each member had to contribute.

Write About Citizenship
Comparisons should discuss Sparta's military training for young boys or Athens's emphasis on academic, athletic, and cultural education. Students should also discuss how education in Athens was private compared to modern-day public schools in the United States.

Focus Herodotus is known as the "father of history." He traveled around the entire Mediterranean area to study the places he wrote about and to learn stories about historical events that took place there. While he presented many facts in his writings, he also included many legends that were not true. Ask students if they think a historian is wrong to include in their works stories that may not be factual.

Activity

Write a newsletter Have students work in small groups to create a Delian League newsletter. The newsletter should mention when and why the League was created, which city-state organized it, and which city-state leads it. The newsletter should describe the League's move to Athens. If possible, allow students to use a computer to create the newsletter.

◆ **ANSWER** Athens led the League and decided how much money and how many ships each city-state contributed. The League was moved to Athens.

Section Close

Ask students to describe the impact the advances in government, athletics, and education made by the Greek city-states had on modern-day societies.

3 Assess

Review Answers
Review History
A. monarchy, aristocracy, and oligarchy
B. Sparta wanted to control the people it had conquered.
C. Solon outlawed enslaving people who were unable to repay debts and freed people who had already been enslaved because of debt. He gave citizenship to some foreigners in order to attract tradespeople.
D. Greek city-states, including Athens and Sparta, united to fight and ultimately defeat the Persians.

Define Terms to Know
polis, 106; acropolis, 106; aristocracy, 107; oligarchy, 107; tyrant, 109; legislature, 109; democracy, 109; alliance, 111

III. The Golden Age of Athens (pp. 112–116)

Section Summary

In this section, students will learn how Athens, under Pericles, expanded its democratic government, prospered economically, and experienced a golden age in which architecture, literature, and philosophy flourished. They will also learn how the Peloponnesian War brought an end to Greek unity.

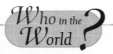

1 Introduce

Getting Started

Ask students what it means to be a good citizen of their community. List their ideas on the board. Discuss how they can participate as good citizens even if they are not old enough to vote or serve on a jury. Point out that in Athens citizens played a direct role in helping to make laws and seeing that laws were followed.

TERMS TO KNOW

Ask students to read the terms and definitions on page 112. Then, have them skim the section to locate each term, read the surrounding paragraph, and state a definition of the term in their own words.

You may wish to preview the pronunciation of the following words from this section with students.

Pericles (PER uh kleez)
orator (AWR uht uhr)
Sappho (SAF oh)
Aeschylus (EHS kih luhs)
Aristophanes (ar ih STAHF uh neez)
Socrates (SAK ruh teez)
Macedonia (mas uh DOH nee uh)
Lyceum (ly SEE uhm)
Euboea (yoo BEE uh)

ACTIVE READING

As students read the subsection "Three Great Thinkers" (pp. 114–115), ask them to write a timeline (TR, p. 320) showing the key events in the lives of Socrates, Plato, and Aristotle.

Section III — The Golden Age of Athens

Terms to Know

tribute a payment given by one nation to another more powerful nation; may be paid in exchange for protection

direct democracy a government in which citizens take part directly, rather than through their representatives

jury a group of people that considers the evidence in a trial and makes a judgment

Main Ideas

A. During the Age of Pericles, Athens became more democratic, prosperous, and powerful.

B. Athens experienced a golden age, in which art, architecture, literature, and the exploration of great ideas flourished.

C. The Peloponnesian War between the Delian League, led by Athens, and the Peloponnesian League, led by Sparta, destroyed hopes for Greek unity.

Active Reading

SEQUENCE OF EVENTS
When you put events in a sequence, you have placed them in the order in which they occurred. As you read this section, make a timeline of important events—for example, in the Peloponnesian War—to help you understand their sequence.

Who in the World?

SLAVES IN ATHENS
In ancient Athens, male citizens were busy in government, so most of the heavy work was done by slaves or by poor people. Most slaves were non-Greeks, and many worked in well-to-do households. Educated slaves might even tutor children.

Unlucky slaves, however, could be sent to do backbreaking work in the silver mines outside Athens. Some slaves were paid wages, which they could save to buy their freedom.

A. The Age of Pericles

When the Persian Wars ended, Athens was in ruins. The Persians had destroyed the Acropolis, buildings in the city, and farmhouses and crops in the countryside. However, within a short time Athens grew to become the richest, most powerful city-state in Greece.

One of the ways Athens became powerful was by demanding **tribute**, or payment in exchange for protection, from the members of the Delian League. You learned that the city-states in the Delian League eventually came under Athenian rule. This led to the birth of the Athenian Empire. It also led to the birth of the classical age, a period from about 480 B.C. to 323 B.C. During the classical age, Athenian politics, art, and literature flourished. The term *classical* refers to the Greek ideals of order, balance, and harmony. Part of this period, from 461 B.C. to 429 B.C., is also called the Age of Pericles, after the most important Athenian leader of that time.

Expanding Democracy

Pericles believed in **direct democracy**, a government in which large numbers of people take an active role. Thousands of Athenian citizens were eligible to serve in the assembly or on a **jury**. Members of a jury considered the evidence during a trial in order to make a judgment. However, Pericles saw that government service was difficult for poorer people because they lost their daily pay when they served in government. Using his skill as a great speaker, he convinced the assembly to approve a regular payment for jurors. Later, he also suggested payments for other government officers chosen by lot, or chance.

Juries in ancient Athens were much larger than juries in many countries today. In Athens, 6,000 jurors were chosen each year by lot. From this pool, juries were formed to serve as many as 200 days a year. On each day, a jury could range from about 200 to 2,500 members.

Not all government officials in Athens were chosen by lot. For example, citizens elected generals like Pericles from the educated, aristocratic class. People from the aristocratic class were thought to have the knowledge, experience, and time needed for high-level positions in government.

The Athenians developed another kind of election to get rid of unpopular leaders. The assembly could decide to call an unpopularity contest. The "winner" of the contest was exiled, or sent away, from Athens for ten years. This had the effect of ending his political career.

Teaching Options

Section 3 Resources

Teacher's Resources (TR)
Terms to Know, p. 18
Review History, p. 52
Build Your Skills, p. 86
Concept Builder, p. 221
Timeline, p. 320
Idea Web, p. 321

Connection to ECONOMICS

Under Pericles, the state became the major employer in Athens. The federal government is also the major employer in the United States. In the year 2000, more than 2,400,000 people were employed full time by the federal government in non-military jobs, and federal workers earned on average about $50,000 a year.

Rebuilding Athens

One of the reasons for the success of Pericles was his skill as an orator, or public speaker. Around 450 B.C., Pericles persuaded the Athenians to rebuild temples on the Acropolis and in other areas of the city. To rebuild, Pericles used money from member states of the Delian League as well as profits from the silver mines outside of Athens.

City-states in the League protested that their money should be spent for defense purposes like supporting the Athenian navy. Pericles used Athenian military power to make the other Greek city-states accept his plan. He argued that as long as Athens was protecting its allies, it could use the excess, or extra, money in any way it saw fit. The huge rebuilding program cost billions of dollars in today's money. However, it also helped the Athenian economy by giving jobs to artisans and other workers.

◆ **How were government officials chosen in Athens?**

B. Culture in the Golden Age

The Greeks often fought for their city-state. However, Greek citizens still found time to develop their own styles of architecture, art, and literature. During the fifth century B.C., Athens experienced a golden age. The city became a magnet for artists, writers, and thinkers who dared to ask, and answer, important questions in new ways. For example, they asked, "How can humans live a good life?" In earlier times, myths about the gods gave the answers to these questions. Now, thinkers were attempting to find other answers to these questions.

They Made History

Pericles ca. 495–429 B.C.

Pericles was not the only Athenian leader during the golden age of Athens. However, through his persuasive speaking skills, Pericles was able to get the Athenian assembly to support many of his ideas. Pericles wanted to make Athens the center of Greek culture and political life, and he largely succeeded. Today, he is most remembered for his rebuilding of the Acropolis, including the Parthenon. Completed in 438 B.C., the Parthenon was a temple built to house an immense statue of Athena as warrior goddess and protector of Athens. The Parthenon is one of the most famous buildings in the world.

Pericles was responsible for other building programs, too. For example, he built the Long Walls from Athens to the port of Piraeus. Within these parallel walls, goods could be moved safely, even when enemy forces were nearby. Pericles also built new temples and statues to show the greatness of Athens.

Pericles was a builder, a statesman, a supporter of culture and the arts, a great speaker, and a military leader. Proud of Athens and the cultural and political accomplishments of its citizens, Pericles declared, "Our city is the school of Greece."

Pericles helped shape the city of Athens into the ancient world's political and cultural capital.

Critical Thinking Do you think citizens, poor people, foreigners, and slaves had similar opinions about Pericles' building programs? Why or why not?

CHAPTER 5 ◆ Ancient Greece **113**

---

2 Teach

A. The Age of Pericles

Purpose-Setting Question How was Athens able to rebuild after the Persian Wars? (Athens used the tribute from the members of the Delian League and profits from the silver mines outside of Athens.)

Focus Athenian juries were intentionally large to make it harder for either side in a case to corrupt the jury and affect its decision. Juries consisted of a round hundred number plus one, such as 201, 501, 1,001, or 1,501. The extra one was to assure there would not be a tie vote on a decision.

WHO IN THE WORLD?

SLAVES IN ATHENS Slaves even served as police officers in Athens. It is thought that the Athenian police force contained about 1,000 archers from Scythia in northern Greece or other foreigners. The Scythians were slaves purchased directly by the state. They lived in barracks overlooking the agora and policed the entire city.

◆ **ANSWER** Some officials were elected; others were chosen by lot.

B. Culture in the Golden Age

Purpose-Setting Question Who were Aeschylus, Sophocles, and Euripides? (Three great Athenian playwrights who wrote tragedies.)

THEY MADE HISTORY
Pericles

Point out that Pericles' building programs put thousands of Athenians to work. Ask students to brainstorm the kinds of jobs that were created for both skilled and unskilled workers. (Craftsmen were needed to work with stone, bronze, wood, gold, and cloth; miners were needed to provide raw materials; boat builders and wagon makers were needed to help transport materials; unskilled laborers were needed to build roads and to lift, carry, and clean up.)

ANSWER Possible answer: Citizens and the poor who found work through the building programs were probably big supporters. Other poor Athenians might have resented spending so much money on buildings, while foreigners and slaves might have seen the programs as showing off.

Test Taking

Give students a short quiz on subsection A that includes three short-answer questions. Remind students to read the directions carefully to determine if their answers should be a word, phrase, or sentence. Provide a sample question, such as the following: In a complete sentence, explain how Pericles got the money for his rebuilding program in Athens.

CHAPTER 5 ◆ **T113**

Draw a floor plan Have students use library resources or the Internet to find more information about private homes in ancient Greece. Then have them draw a floor plan for a typical house. Ask volunteers to share their floor plans with the class and compare the Greek homes to their own houses or apartments.

Focus Point out that Greek plays were sometimes performed before audiences of 14,000–17,000 spectators at open-air theaters like the one shown in the photograph on page 114. Actors had no microphones, and there were no spotlights. Ask students how they think actors were able to make sure that audiences could understand their feelings and dialogue. (Possible answers: They wore masks to show if they were happy or sad; the chorus and actors spoke loudly; they made exaggerated movements on stage.)

Then & Now

WRITING MATERIALS The fact that merchants in Greece wrote their records on pieces of pottery has had some positive benefits for archaeologists. Thousands of inscribed fragments have been found in rubbish piles in ancient cities. These have provided insights into trade practices in ancient times.

Extend Much like public television or radio today, theatrical performances in ancient Athens were supported by contributions from private citizens. Each year, the government asked different wealthy citizens to pay for theatrical productions and other costs of the religious festivals at which the plays were performed. A play would typically cost between 300 and 5,000 drachmas to put on. This was a large sum, considering that 400 drachmas was enough to support an average small family in Athens for a year. Ask students if they think it was right for the government to require wealthy citizens to spend their money for public entertainment. Be sure students explain their thinking.

At open-air ancient Greek theaters, like this one in Delphi, Greece, people enjoyed plays.

Then & Now

WRITING MATERIALS
Today, people use the computer or paper to record their accounts, write letters, and produce creative writing.

In ancient Greece, however, writers did not have paper. Most ordinary people scratched or painted their names and messages on pieces of broken pottery. Others wrote on wax tablets. Writers like Sophocles and Plato wrote on papyrus, made from pressed strips of reeds and imported from Egypt.

Architecture and Art

The ancient Greeks built magnificent public buildings. These buildings were either temples for the gods or public structures in which political or commercial activities took place. Private homes, by contrast, were small and simply designed.

Great paintings and sculptures also were created for temples and other public buildings. Today, we think of the Greeks' painted pots and vases as art, but they were created for practical use. The Greeks did paint large pictures, but most of the painting that exists today is found on pottery. Subjects for painted pottery included the heroic acts of the gods, great historical events such as the Trojan War, and daily life.

Around 450 B.C., the Greeks developed a natural, fluid style of painting and sculpture. This style is in contrast to the geometric or rigid and blocklike styles of earlier Greek art. Humans were not shown as they actually appeared, but in an ideal, nearly perfect form.

Poetry, Drama, and History

The earliest Greek literature was written in the form of poetry. You have learned, for example, about the great epic poems of Homer. Famous poets who lived later included Sappho and Pindar. The great innovation of the Greeks, though, was drama. They held festivals to see who could write the best plays. Attending a play was a favorite activity. Plays could be tragedies or comedies. Tragedies explored deep conflicts and ideas. They dealt with suffering and misery. In Athens, there were three great writers of tragedies—Aeschylus, Sophocles, and Euripides. Their plays were presented in an open-air theater beside the Acropolis in Athens. Theaters were also built throughout other areas of the Mediterranean.

Comedies were also produced in ancient Greece. Aristophanes was a leading Athenian comic playwright. Greek comedies often poked fun at leaders and their policies. Although plays often were about what women should do for their families or the city-state, women could not perform in these plays. These roles were played by men.

Contests were held at drama festivals. The contests had rules to make them fair. For example, plays were limited to three actors, although each one could play several parts. Actors used masks to identify their characters, and they spoke in booming voices. There was little scenery, but costumes were elaborate, and dance routines could be very complicated.

Greek historians researched the past in a more balanced way than people had before. Herodotus, often called the Father of History, wrote about the Peloponnesian War, a war that involved many Greek city-states. Although he had experienced that war firsthand as an Athenian military commander, he tried to be fair and balanced in his account of it.

Three Great Thinkers

The first Greek philosophers lived in Ionia, a region of western Asia Minor, in the sixth century B.C. The term *philosopher* comes from a Greek word meaning "lover of wisdom." The earliest philosophers tried to answer the questions, "Where did the world come from?" and "What is the world made of?" Later, three great Greek philosophers—Socrates, Plato, and Aristotle—asked different questions, such as what it means to lead a good life.

Teaching Options

ESL/ELL STRATEGIES

Use Manipulatives Some students may have trouble keeping track of names and occupations of people discussed in this subsection. Suggest that students create separate index cards for poets, playwrights, historians, and philosophers. They should list each person's name on the front of the index card and a brief statement about him or her on the back. They might make additional cards for political or military leaders mentioned in the chapter.

Connection to CULTURE

Masks were an important part of Greek drama, but they were also used by actors and dancers in many other cultures. Have students use library or Internet sources to discover more about the use of masks in ancient Greek dramas, in Japanese Noh drama, in French comedies, in Indonesian dance theater, or in the arts of other cultures.

Socrates did not teach in a school. Instead, he often went to the Athenian agora, or marketplace, where he asked people questions. Socrates believed that goodness is knowledge and that doing evil is worse than suffering from evil. Young people flocked to hear him. However, Socrates' enemies said he was not respectful of the gods and that he corrupted the youth. In 399 B.C., a jury sentenced him to death. Socrates accepted the sentence and committed suicide by drinking hemlock, a powerful poison.

Most of our knowledge about Socrates comes from the writing of his student Plato. Plato wanted people to remember Socrates' talks, or dialogues, so he wrote some of them down. Plato also wrote about the ideal state, the ideal society, the nature of goodness and friendship, and the idea of truth. In 387 B.C., Plato founded a school called the Academy.

A few years after Plato's death in 347 B.C., his student Aristotle was invited to Macedonia, a kingdom in the northern part of the Balkan Peninsula. Here, he became the tutor of the young Alexander the Great, whom you will read about in Section IV. When Aristotle returned to Athens, he set up a school called the Lyceum. Aristotle taught his students to learn by observation. He considered what defines a good life and studied many forms of government to determine which were best. Eventually he, like Socrates, was accused of disrespect for the gods. He fled to the island of Euboea, where he later died.

Aristotle favored moderation, or avoiding extremes, in life and in politics. In his book *Politics*, for example, he praises the middle class:

> 66 The best political community is formed by citizens of the middle class. Those States are likely to be well administered in which the middle class is large, and larger if possible than both the other classes, or at any rate than either singly; for the addition of the middle class turns the scale and prevents either of the extremes from being dominant. 99

◆ **How did Socrates describe goodness and doing evil acts?**

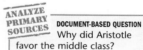

DOCUMENT-BASED QUESTION
Why did Aristotle favor the middle class?

This painting is titled *The Death of Socrates*. It was painted by Jacques-Louis David, a French artist, in 1787.

C. The Peloponnesian War

Purpose-Setting Question What advantage did each side have when the Peloponnesian War began? (Athens had the better navy, and Sparta had the better army.)

Activity

Label a map Give students an outline map of ancient Greece, or have them trace the map on page 110. Then, have them research which city-states were members of the Delian and Peloponnesian Leagues. They should then color-code their maps to show the sides in the Peloponnesian War.

◆ **ANSWER** two large alliances of city-states: the Delian League, led by Athens, and an alliance led by Sparta

Section Close

Ask students whether they would rather have lived in Sparta or Athens during the period of history described in this section. Have them explain their choice.

3 Assess

Review Answers

Review History

A. Pericles made it possible for poorer Athenian citizens to participate in government by convincing the assembly to approve regular payment for jurors.

B. It was a time when artists, writers, and thinkers flourished in Athens. There was an increase in art, architecture, poetry, drama, and the study and writing of history and philosophy.

C. Hopes for Greek unity ended, and corruption in the democracy of Athens grew. Philip II of Macedonia saw that the Greek city-states were weak, and he made plans to conquer them.

Define Terms to Know
tribute, 112; direct democracy, 112; jury, 112

Do You Remember?
In Section II, you learned that the Delian League included 140 Greek city-states.

C. The Peloponnesian War

Many of the great men of Athens, including Socrates, fought in a long and bitter struggle called the Peloponnesian War. This war involved most of the Greek city-states. Two large alliances dragged these states into conflict. Athens headed the Delian League. When the war began in 431 B.C., Athens had the superior navy, and Sparta had the better army.

War, Plague, and Starvation

The war began when the Spartans led an army into Attica, the countryside surrounding Athens. The Athenians, however, did not go out to meet the Spartans in battle. Instead, Pericles had his countrymen leave their farms and take shelter in the walled city of Athens. The plan backfired. Within months, a terrible plague broke out in the overcrowded city, killing many Athenians. Meanwhile, the Spartans destroyed crops and farmhouses throughout Attica. In 429 B.C., Pericles himself died from complications of the plague.

For eight more years, the fighting continued between Athens, Sparta, and their allies, but neither side was a clear winner. During the period 421 to 415 B.C., an uncertain peace existed until Athens invaded Sicily, a part of Italy, that had been settled by Greeks. In Sicily, the Athenian navy and army were both defeated. Inside Athens, there was turmoil as well, as an oligarchy overthrew the democracy. Finally, democratic rule was restored. Then, in 405 B.C., the Spartans surprised and destroyed the Athenian navy. Finally, in 404 B.C., Athens was starved into surrender by a Spartan blockade.

Aftermath

Although Sparta won the Peloponnesian War, conflict continued between city-states. Hopes for Greek unity ended. Within Athens, democracy had lost its energy, and corruption grew.

As the Greek city-states continued their quarrels, a great power was rising in the north—Macedonia. Its ruler, Philip II, had his eye on Greece. Philip was training his armies to conquer the Greek city-states one by one.

◆ **Who fought in the Peloponnesian War?**

Review III

Review History
A. How did Pericles make the Athenian government more democratic?
B. Why was the period following the Persian Wars called the golden age of Athens?
C. What were some results of the Peloponnesian War?

Define Terms to Know
Define the following terms: **tribute, direct democracy, jury**

Critical Thinking
If Athens had won the Peloponnesian War, what might have happened next?

Write About Citizenship
Write a dialogue in which Socrates asks you to explain what democracy means to you. Include at least three questions.

Get Organized
IDEA WEB
Use an idea web to organize information from this section. Choose a topic and then find related facts. For example, what were the characteristics of Greek drama?

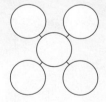

Critical Thinking
Possible answers: The Greek city-states might have united. War would have broken out again soon afterward because a defeated Sparta would never have accepted Athenian control.

Write About Citizenship
Students should provide three related questions Socrates might ask such as: What is democracy? What are the benefits of living in a democracy? What are the responsibilities of the citizens of a democracy?

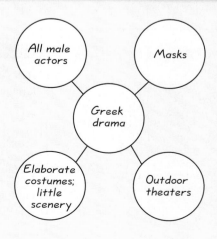

Points *of* View

Democracy in Athens

By 500 B.C., democracy was thriving in Athens. Thousands of male citizens were participating directly in Athenian government. Not all Greeks, however, supported democracy in Athens. Some critics expressed their opinions against this form of government.

One objector to democracy was known simply as the Old Oligarch. He opposed Athenian democracy in a pamphlet called the *Constitution of the Athenians*. This pamphlet was probably written between the 440s B.C. and the 420s B.C. Not much is known about this writer except that he strongly favored an oligarchy, or rule by a powerful few, over a democratic government.

The Athenian leader Pericles, on the other hand, supported democracy. In a speech to the Athenians in 431 B.C., Pericles stated his views on democracy. He also gave reasons for his belief that it was the best system of government. The historian Thucydides recorded this speech in his book, *History of the Peloponnesian War*.

A Greek orator

> 66 Our constitution is called a democracy because power is in the hands not of a minority but of the whole people. . . . When it is a question of putting one person before another in positions of public responsibility, what counts is not membership of a particular class, but the actual ability which the man possesses. No one, so long as he has it in him to be of service to the state, is kept in political obscurity because of poverty. 99
>
> —Speech by Pericles in Thucydides' *History of the Peloponnesian War*

> 66 Everywhere on earth the best element [group of people] is opposed to democracy. For among the best people there is . . . care for what is good, whereas among the [rest of the] people there is a maximum of ignorance, disorder, and wickedness; for poverty draws them rather to disgraceful actions, and because of a lack of money some men are uneducated and ignorant. 99
>
> —Old Oligarch, *Constitution of the Athenians*

ANALYZE PRIMARY SOURCES

DOCUMENT-BASED QUESTIONS

1. Why does Pericles think democracy is a good system of government?

2. What problems does the Old Oligarch see with democracy?

3. **Critical Thinking** Compare and contrast Pericles' views on democracy with those of the Old Oligarch.

Teaching Options

Take a Stand

Have students write an editorial for a newspaper in Athens that is either pro-democracy or opposed to democracy. Point out that describing the actions of those people in the editorial is a good way for students to demonstrate their opinion and will make their editorial more interesting. Have students read the editorials and decide which side each one takes.

LINK to TODAY

In most countries and communities, laws are usually passed by a small group of legislators or officials. However, in some small communities in New England, town meetings, like those in ancient Athens, are still held in which all citizens can vote to pass laws or make rules. While everyone has the right to vote in these meetings, most citizens don't attend. So, special-interest groups that do vote often get their way.

Points *of* View

DEMOCRACY IN ATHENS

Teach the Topic

These selections represent two differing opinions on the appropriateness of a democratic system of government in Athens. Point out that the statement from Pericles' speech was quoted by the historian Thucydides. The comments of the Old Oligarch were presented in a pamphlet handed out in Athens.

Ask students to whom each speaker is directing his message. Would the poor people in Athens be more likely to listen to a speech or read a pamphlet? (listen, because few could read) Ask students why rich and poor people might have different feelings about democracy.

Compare and Contrast Points of View

Ask students what word Pericles uses to describe the wealthy people of Athens in his speech (minority) and what phrase the Old Oligarch uses (best people). Also, how do the two speakers show differences in their feelings about the rest of the people in Athens? (Pericles says many are men who deserve positions of public responsibility, while the Old Oligarch thinks they are wicked, disgraceful, or ignorant.)

ANALYZE PRIMARY SOURCES

DOCUMENT-BASED QUESTIONS
1. Pericles thinks that everyone should have the chance to make a valuable contribution to the community based on ability, no matter what his class.
2. The Old Oligarch believes poor people, if put in positions of power, may do disgraceful things because they are uneducated and ignorant.
3. Pericles believes democracy is a good system because it encourages all citizens to take part in the government. The Old Oligarch feels that democracy is a bad system because it puts power into the hands of people who may not know how to use it properly.

Section Summary

In this section, students will learn how Philip II of Macedonia gained control over his own country and then over all of Greece, and how his son Alexander built a great empire that stretched from Egypt to India. They will also learn how Alexander's empire spread Greek culture throughout much of the ancient world.

1 Introduce

Getting Started

Ask students why they think a ruler of a country might be called "the Great." Can they think of any leaders in the world today that might be called "the Great"? If so, who? Tell students that they will learn about the military and cultural achievements of Alexander the Great in this section.

TERMS TO KNOW

Ask students to read the words and definitions on page 118 and then find each word in the section. Point out that even though the two words begin alike, they have very different origins. Have students look up the words in a dictionary to learn their origins.

You may wish to preview the pronunciation of the following words from this section with students.

Demosthenes (dih MAHS thuh neez)
Chaeronea (ker uh NEE uh)
Achilles (uh KIHL eez)
Hellenistic (hehl uhn IHS tihk)
Pharos (FER ahs)

ACTIVE READING

Have students read the "What in the World?" feature on page 118. Then, ask them what problem the sarissa helped solve. (how to attack an enemy in hand-to-hand combat with less risk of being injured)

Section IV — Alexander Builds a Great Empire

Terms to Know

assassination the murder of a leader, often for political reasons

assimilation the process of absorbing or taking on the cultural ideas and customs of another group and combining them into an existing culture

Main Ideas

A. King Philip II of Macedonia gathered and trained a great army and gained control of Greece in 338 B.C.

B. Philip's son Alexander, an admirer of Greek culture, conquered the Persian Empire.

C. Alexander's empire broke up after his death, but the spread of Greek culture throughout the area was a lasting achievement.

Active Reading

ANALYZE PROBLEMS AND SOLUTIONS
You can learn a lot about people by considering how they deal with different problems. As you read this section, pay attention to how Alexander the Great dealt with the problems he faced.

A. The Rise of Macedonia

After 404 B.C., the Greek city-states continued their squabbles. Sparta, and later Thebes, tried to control Greece. Neither of them succeeded. Meanwhile, north of the Greek mainland in the northern part of the Balkan Peninsula, the kingdom of Macedonia grew stronger.

Philip II Gains Control

In 359 B.C., Philip II gained the throne of Macedonia. He unified the two parts of the country, Lower and Upper Macedonia. Then, he turned his attention to the conquest of Greece. In time, Philip made friends with leaders in many city-states. He threatened, bribed, and charmed Greek leaders into allying themselves with him.

In Athens, the great political leader and orator Demosthenes warned his fellow citizens that Philip was a threat to Greek independence. By the time the Athenians listened, though, it was too late. At the Battle of Chaeronea in 338 B.C., Philip and his army defeated the southern Greek city-states, including Athens and Thebes. Philip's 18-year-old son, Alexander, led a successful attack on the Sacred Band of 300 Thebans, the best soldiers of Thebes.

Alexander Takes the Throne

Philip's goal was to form an alliance between Macedonia and Greece. Then, he planned to conquer the Persian Empire. However, two years after gaining control of Greece, Philip was murdered. He was the victim of an **assassination**. Alexander and his mother Olympias managed to eliminate other rivals to the throne. At the age of 20, Alexander became king of Macedonia and ruler of Greece. The young monarch would carry out his father's dream of conquering the Persian Empire.

◆ **What did Demosthenes try to tell the Athenians?**

B. Alexander Builds an Empire

Alexander had inherited the most powerful army in Europe. In 334 B.C., he led a Macedonian and Greek army into Asia Minor to attack Persia. While still in his twenties, Alexander conquered the entire Persian Empire. This amazing accomplishment earned him the title "the Great" in later times.

What in the World?

A GREEK WEAPON
Soldiers in Philip's army used a weapon called a sarissa. It was a 15-foot-long pike, or spear. Use of the long pike meant that Philip's army could engage enemy soldiers who were using hoplite spears at a safe distance because hoplite spears were shorter.

Teaching Options

Section 4 Resources

Teacher's Resources (TR)
Terms to Know, p. 18
Review History, p. 52
Build Your Skills, p. 86
Chapter Test, pp. 125–126
Concept Builder, p. 221
Idea Web, p. 321
Transparency 1

ESL/ELL STRATEGIES

Organize Information Suggest that pairs of students create a timeline (TR, p. 320) to keep track of events related to Alexander the Great's life before he took the throne, while he was building his empire, when he died, and following his death. Then, have the pairs use their timeline to prepare a newspaper obituary that might have been published after Alexander's death.

Alexander's March

Alexander inspired his troops to go places they had never been. When leading them into battle, he wore a hard helmet, a brightly colored cloak, and polished armor. His personal courage and his understanding of the nature of leadership made him an inspiring commander. He had a first-class education under Aristotle, and his parents had raised him to believe that he could accomplish anything he wanted.

Alexander believed that his glory equaled that of Achilles, the legendary hero of the Trojan War. To persuade his troops to do his will, Alexander sometimes sulked in his tent, as Achilles had done. However, Alexander also shared the hardships of his soldiers. Historians agree that he was one of the greatest military leaders of ancient times.

Throughout Asia Minor, Alexander and his forces never lost a battle. Starting in Macedonia, they moved south along the eastern side of the Mediterranean Sea and into Palestine. Then they moved southwest to Egypt, and eventually toward Babylon and other Persian cities. Alexander not only captured existing cities, he also established new ones. In 331 B.C., for example, he founded Alexandria on the northern coast of Egypt.

Alexander marched his troops toward India through 70 days of monsoon rains. Near a river, they defeated an army of soldiers who were mounted on elephants. Finally, in western India his soldiers refused to continue any farther—by then they had marched 11,000 miles! Alexander tried to shame the troops into continuing by talking about his father:

> 66 Philip found you a tribe of . . . vagabonds . . . he brought you down from the hills into the plains; he taught you to fight on equal terms with the enemy on your borders, till you knew that your safety lay not, as once, in your mountain strongholds, but in your own valor [courage]. He made you city-dwellers; he brought you law; he civilized you. 99

In spite of this speech, the army refused to go on, and Alexander was forced to set out for home.

Death and Division

Alexander and his men continued their homeward journey and finally reached Babylon. There, Alexander began to plan further actions. However, in 323 B.C., he died at age 33 from an infection or fever. According to legend, when he was asked who should inherit his empire, he replied that rulership should go "to the strongest."

Alexander's Empire, 336–323 B.C.

Extent of empire
→ Alexander's routes
✴ Major battles
0 250 500 mi
0 250 500 km

MACEDONIA · Granicus · Sardis · Miletus · Asia Minor · Issus · Black Sea · Caspian Sea · Aral Sea · Gaugamela · Tigris River · Euphrates River · Babylon · Susa · Persepolis · Mediterranean Sea · Alexandria · Tyre · Palestine · EGYPT · Nile River · Red Sea · Persian Gulf · Arabian Sea · Alexandria Eschate · Oxus River · INDIA

✔ Map Check

LOCATION Which battle took place along the Tigris River?

Here, Alexander the Great is shown as a young man.

ANALYZE PRIMARY SOURCES

DOCUMENT-BASED QUESTION What are some specific examples of Philip's support of the troops that Alexander describes in his speech to them?

A. The Rise of Macedonia

Purpose-Setting Question What role did Alexander play in helping his father gain control over Greece? (He led the successful attack against the best soldiers of Thebes, the Sacred Band of 300 Thebans.)

WHAT IN THE WORLD?

A GREEK WEAPON Some sarissas used by Philip's soldiers were 21 to 25 feet, though the shorter pikes proved easier to use and more effective. Ask students what disadvantages such a long weapon might pose. (Possible answer: It might be hard to hold up and control.)

◆ **ANSWER** Philip II of Macedonia was a threat to Greek independence.

B. Alexander Builds an Empire

Purpose-Setting Question What unusual problems did Alexander's army face in India? (They faced 70 days of rain, and an opposing army mounted on elephants.)

Using the Map

Alexander's Empire, 336–323 B.C.

Point out that Alexander's army crossed or approached many different bodies of water. Ask students to use the map to name as many of these as they can.

✔ Map Check

Answer Gaugamela

ANALYZE PRIMARY SOURCES

DOCUMENT-BASED QUESTION

Philip had made sure that Alexander learned not only how to read and write and how to fight but also how to be a public speaker. He believed that speaking well would help Alexander rouse his troops and be a good military leader.

ANSWER Philip improved their fighting abilities; taught them to trust in their courage, and turned them into city dwellers who lived by the law.

Meet Individual Needs:
AUDITORY LEARNERS

Have students take turns reading the paragraphs on this page aloud. Then, have them role-play a conversation between Alexander and some of the army leaders who don't want to go on fighting. You might have several students take turns playing Alexander and paraphrasing the quotation on the page.

Conflict Resolution

Point out that while Alexander nearly always got his way, he also knew when to compromise, as when he decided to stop fighting in India. Discuss how making compromises allows both sides to get something they want and helps to avoid problems that might result from a one-sided solution. Have students brainstorm qualities that leaders must have to resolve conflicts.

TEACH PRIMARY SOURCES

As in the mosaic pictured on this page, Alexander is often shown on horseback in paintings or statues. He rode the same horse, Bucephalus, in all of his battles, until it was killed in battle in India. Alexander held a state funeral for the horse and built a city in India that he named Bucephala to honor the horse. Discuss with students how Alexander's actions toward his horse reflect his character.

◆ **ANSWER** Alexander had personal courage, ambition, and the ability to inspire others. He was also willing to suffer the same hardships as his men.

C. Hellenistic Civilization

Purpose-Setting Question What different cultures' customs were blended into the Hellenistic civilization? (Greek, Egyptian, Persian, Indian, and other influences)

Discuss Ask students what made assimilation, which Alexander encouraged, different from the actions of other conquerors they have read about. (Assimilation involved a two-way sharing of ideas and cultures. Most conquerors forced the conquered civilizations to adopt their customs and laws and even made them slaves.)

Then & Now

ANCIENT LIGHTHOUSE The light of the Pharos lighthouse, as reflected by a mirror inside the structure, could be seen more than 35 miles offshore. It was finally destroyed by earthquakes in the early 1300s, but its memory lives on. The word for *lighthouse* in French is *phare*, and in Italian and Spanish, it is *faro*.

Activity

Plan a class trip Have students work in small groups. Each group should plan a class trip to the seven "wonders" of the ancient world listed on pages 120–121. Suggest that students use the outline map of the world (TR, p. 330) or Transparency 1 to help plan their trip. The groups should create an itinerary, a travel brochure, and a letter explaining the sites and the route the class will take. Suggest students use library sources or the Internet for information and pictures. Have each group share the plans for their trip with the class.

This mosaic, found in the ancient Roman city of Pompeii, shows Alexander, on the far left, fighting against the Persians.

Then & Now

ANCIENT LIGHTHOUSE
The Pharos lighthouse, built about 270 B.C., was destroyed by earthquakes. In recent years, underwater archaeologists in the Mediterranean Sea have found thousands of pieces of stone. Some of these pieces probably fell from the lighthouse when it was destroyed.

Today, the Egyptian government is planning an underwater park where divers can observe the lighthouse remains, statues, and sphinxes from ancient times.

Alexander's empire was too large for any other single leader to hold. After his death, three of his generals struggled for power. Finally, three kingdoms emerged. The richest and most powerful was Egypt. It was governed by the Macedonian general who became known as Ptolemy I.

◆ **What leadership qualities did Alexander display?**

C. Hellenistic Civilization

Although it did not last, Alexander's former empire continued to develop a culture heavily influenced by Greek ideas. Greeks settled in Alexander's new cities, bringing Greek language and culture with them. Through a process of **assimilation**, local peoples throughout the eastern Mediterranean region gradually took on many Greek customs. In addition, Greek settlers adopted local customs. Over time, a lively civilization developed that blended Greek, Egyptian, Persian, Indian, and other influences. This civilization was called Hellenistic. It lasted from about 323 B.C. to 146 B.C.

The Economy and the Growth of Cities

During the Hellenistic period, the use of money increased. For the first time there were real banks. The upper and middle classes lived well in beautiful homes. However, workers were poorly paid, and they competed with slaves and servants for work.

Some cities, such as Rhodes, became rich through trade. In Egypt, Alexandria was a busy port and the largest industrial center of the Hellenistic world. Planned by a Greek architect, Alexandria also became the greatest Hellenistic center of education and learning, replacing Athens. The city had the largest library and the second-highest structure in the world, the lighthouse on the island of Pharos. Rhodes also had a giant statue called the Colossus.

During the second century B.C., Hellenistic writers made lists of the great artistic achievements in the Mediterranean world. Seven "wonders" of the ancient world appeared on the majority of these lists: the Pyramids at Giza in Egypt, the Hanging Gardens at Babylon, the statue of Zeus at Olympia, the temple of Artemis at Ephesus in Asia Minor, the Mausoleum at Halicarnassus in Asia Minor, the Colossus of Rhodes, and the lighthouse of Pharos at Alexandria.

Teaching Options

Writing

AVERAGE
Point out that Alexander the Great built the world's largest empire, but it ultimately collapsed. Ask students to think about the question: Was Alexander the Great too ambitious? Have them use what they have read in this section or do additional research to help them answer the question. They should then write a brief persuasive essay stating their opinion.

CHALLENGE
Put the names of the following Greek leaders discussed in this chapter on the board: Solon, Cleisthenes, Pericles, Alexander. Ask students to rank them in order of the importance of their accomplishments to ancient Greece and to later civilizations. Then, have them write a short essay explaining their rankings and the ranking system they created and used.

Hellenistic Arts and Sciences

New philosophies, or beliefs, developed during the Hellenistic period. The Epicureans—followers of the philosopher Epicurus—believed that the ideal life was free from pain. The Cynics urged people to live simply, in tune with nature. Stoicism, founded by Zeno, taught that people should react with calm to life's events. Nevertheless, the Stoics believed that people should work with a sense of duty to protect human rights. Eventually, the Stoics had a major influence on the Christian religion.

During the Hellenistic period, mathematics and science bloomed, especially in Alexandria. Many of the discoveries and inventions of this period are still useful today. For example, the mathematician Pythagoras created a formula for expressing the relationship between the sides of a right triangle. This formula is still in use. The scientist and mathematician Eratosthenes accurately calculated the circumference of Earth and also invented a method for identifying prime numbers.

The Hellenistic period came to an end in 146 B.C., when the Romans conquered Greece. However, the culture of the ancient Greeks would continue as a strong and vital element for centuries to come.

◆ **What were the new philosophies of the Hellenistic civilization?**

Hellenistic Scientists and Mathematicians

NAME	CONTRIBUTION(S)
Archimedes	Helped develop geometry; invented the catapult, and the compound pulley; developed weapons to help when his city, Syracuse, was attacked in 213 B.C.
Eratosthenes	Calculated Earth's circumference; created a calendar with leap years; invented a method for identifying prime numbers
Euclid	Wrote *The Elements*, which became a standard geometry textbook used for more than 2,000 years
Hippocrates	Often considered the father of medicine; associated with the Hippocratic Oath
Pythagoras	Created a geometric formula for the relationship between the sides of a right triangle

✔ **Chart Check**

Which scientists studied geometry?

Review IV

Review History
A. How did Philip II gain control of the Greek city-states?
B. Why is Alexander called "the Great"?
C. What were the main characteristics of Hellenistic civilization?

Define Terms to Know
Define the following terms: **assassination, assimilation**

Critical Thinking
Why do you think mathematics and science flourished in the Hellenistic world?

Write About Culture
Hellenistic cities attracted people from many parts of the world. Write a paragraph in which you compare the appeal of Hellenistic cities with the appeal of present-day cities in the United States.

Get Organized
IDEA WEB
Use an idea web to organize information from this section. Choose a topic and then find related facts. For example, what advances in mathematics and science were made during the Hellenistic period?

CHAPTER 5 ◆ Ancient Greece **121**

Chapter Summary

A blank outline form is available in the Teacher's Resources (p. 318). Chapter summaries should outline the beginnings of early civilizations in Greece, the rise of city-states on the Greek mainland, Greek philosophy and art, and the empire-building of Alexander. Refer to the rubric in the Teacher's Resources (p. 340) to score students' chapter summaries.

⬤ Interpret the Timeline

1. the decline of the Mycenaean civilization
2. 292 years
3. the defeat of Athens by Sparta in 404 B.C.
4. Check students' timelines to be sure all events are in the chapter.

Use Terms to Know

5. monarchy
6. aristocracy
7. polis
8. legislature
9. jury
10. assimilation
11. tribute

Check Your Understanding

12. Ancient Greek culture laid the foundation for Western civilization in political, artistic, philosophical, and educational areas.
13. The Greeks believed that their gods were present in their daily lives and possessed human qualities such as love, hate, and jealousy. It was necessary to please the gods.
14. Different types of government included monarchy, or kingship; aristocracy, or rule by an upper class or a privileged group; oligarchy, or rule by a small and powerful elite; tyranny, or rule by a leader who seized power by force; and democracy, or rule by the people.
15. Sparta was a military state in which people lived by very strict standards of behavior designed to produce disciplined soldiers. The Spartan government consisted of two military leaders and an assembly that elected powerful overseers. Life in Athens was much freer. Boys' education in Athens included instruction in art, music, and exercise. All free male Athenian citizens could participate in the legislature that made laws, though wealthy landowners held the most power.

Chapter Summary

Complete the following outline in your notebook. Then, use your outline to write a brief summary of the chapter.

Ancient Greece

I. Early Civilizations of Greece
  A. The Geography of Greece
  B. The Minoan Civilization
  C. The Mycenaeans Grow Powerful
  D. The Decline of Mycenae and the Age of Homer
II. Greek City-States Rise to Power
  A. City-States Develop
  B. Sparta Becomes a Military State
  C. Athenians and Their Right to Govern
  D. Greek Unity in the Persian Wars
III. The Golden Age of Athens
  A. The Age of Pericles
  B. Culture in the Golden Age
  C. The Peloponnesian War
IV. Alexander Builds a Great Empire
  A. The Rise of Macedonia
  B. Alexander Builds an Empire
  C. Hellenistic Civilization

⬤ Interpret the Timeline

Use the timeline on pages 98–99 to answer the following questions.

1. Which occurred first, the decline of the Mycenaean civilization or the end of the Peloponnesian War?

2. How many years after the Parthenon was completed did Rome conquer Greece?

3. **Critical Thinking** What event shows the rivalry between two Greek city-states?

4. Select five events from the chapter that are not on the timeline. Make a timeline that shows these events.

Use Terms to Know

Select the term that best completes each sentence.

aristocracy   legislature   polis
assimilation   monarchy   tribute
jury

5. A _____ is a government with a king, queen, or pharaoh as ruler.

6. When wealthy landowners rule, the government is an _____.

7. A _____ was made up of a city and the surrounding countryside.

8. The lawmaking body, or _____, in Athens was made up of free male citizens.

9. In Athens, many citizens were chosen to serve on a _____.

10. During the Hellenistic period, there was a great deal of _____ of different cultures.

11. City-states that were members of the Delian League paid _____ to Athens.

Check Your Understanding

12. **Identify** the relationship between ancient Greek culture and Western civilization.

13. **Discuss** the religion of ancient Greece.

14. **Describe** the different types of government in ancient Greece.

15. **Contrast** the governments and ways of life in Sparta and Athens.

16. **Describe** the Persian Wars and their outcomes.

17. **Discuss** the significance of Pericles in the development of Athens.

18. **Summarize** the cultural accomplishments in Athens during its golden age.

19. **Identify** the two sides that fought in the Peloponnesian War.

20. **Describe** the achievements of Alexander the Great.

21. **Identify** two mathematical discoveries that were made during the Hellenistic period.

---

16. The Persian Wars included land and sea battles. Athenian armies were victorious on the plain of Marathon, but Spartan forces were defeated at Thermopylae. When the Persians then attacked and burned Athens, Athenians were able to escape from the city, and their navy met and defeated the larger Persian navy at Salamis. After one more Greek victory at Plataea, the Persians left Greece for good.

17. Pericles was both a military and political leader in Athens. Under his leadership, the city was fortified, and art and architecture flourished. He oversaw the rebuilding of the Acropolis, including the Parthenon.

18. Architecture, painting, and sculpture flourished during the golden age. Poetry and drama also reached a new level of excellence, with the tragedies of Aeschylus, Sophocles, and Euripides and the comedies of Aristophanes. Herodotus wrote historical accounts of the Peloponnesian Wars. The philosophers Socrates, Plato, and Aristotle opened people's minds to new ways of thinking.

19. In the Peloponnesian Wars, Athens and its allies in the Delian League were on one side, and Sparta and its allies were on the other side. The Spartan side was eventually victorious.

Critical Thinking

22. Draw Conclusions Why were the Minoan and Mycenaean palaces different?

23. Make Inferences Why were the city-states of Sparta and Athens rivals?

24. Analyze Primary Sources Do you agree with Aristotle's ideas in the quotation on page 115 about the importance of the middle class? Why or why not?

25. Analyze Primary Sources Do you think Alexander expected the speech quoted on page 119 to work? Why or why not?

Put Your Skills to Work

26. Analyze Artifacts You have learned how to interpret artifacts, which are a type of primary source. Interpreting an artifact can help you learn about the time when it was created as well as the people who lived during that time.

Study the ancient Greek vase below. It is called a red-figured vase because the background of the vase is painted black while the figures are left in the color of the reddish-orange clay. Write a paragraph that answers the following questions.

a. What can you learn from this artifact about the clothing of ancient Greek women?

b. Why would an artist have wanted to paint a scene such as this?

The British Museum.

An ancient Greek red-figured vase

Analyze Sources

27. Read more about a Spartan lawmaker's rules for boys as described by the historian Xenophon in *The Constitution of Sparta*. Then, answer the questions that follow.

Instead of softening the boys' feet with sandals he required them to harden their feet by going without shoes. He believed that if this habit were cultivated it would enable them to climb hills more easily and descend steep inclines with less danger. . . . And instead of letting them be pampered in the matter of clothing, he introduced the custom of wearing one garment throughout the year, believing that they would thus be better prepared to face changes of heat and cold.

a. What advantages could hardened feet give Spartan youth?

b. What was the purpose of having young Spartans wear only one garment year round?

Essay Writing

28. Ancient Greeks held festivals to see who could write the best plays. These plays were of two types: tragedies and comedies. Write an essay about a current topic that could be the subject of a play. Explain why the topic would be more appropriate as a tragedy or as a comedy.

TEST PREPARATION

CAUSE-AND-EFFECT RELATIONSHIPS
Choose the answer that correctly completes the sentence.

Although the exact cause of the destruction of the Minoan civilization has never been determined, archaeologists believe that its collapse was probably the result of

1. famine.
2. drought.
3. a volcanic eruption.
4. all of the above

CHAPTER 5 ◆ Ancient Greece **123**

---

20. Alexander conquered the Egyptians and Persians, built an empire that stretched from Egypt to India, and spread Greek culture throughout the ancient world.
21. During the Hellenistic period, Pythagoras created a formula for expressing the relationship between the sides of a right triangle, the circumference of Earth was calculated, and a method was invented for identifying prime numbers.

Critical Thinking

22. The Minoans were peaceful and lived on an island, while the Mycenaeans fought many wars and needed extra protection, because they lived on the mainland. Therefore, the Mycenaen palaces were well fortified.
23. Sparta and Athens were rivals because of their different approaches to life and government. Each thought its way was best and wanted other city-states to follow its ideas.
24. Possible answer: Aristotle was correct about the middle class, because if the middle class is large in a society, it has the power to make decisions benefiting the majority of the people.
25. Possible answers: No, because he was trying to get the men to feel guilty, a strategy that probably wouldn't work after such a long march. Yes, because the men owed their loyalty to Philip and Alexander. In addition, the men could be proud of their military accomplishments under both Philip and Alexander's leadership.

Put Your Skills to Work

ANALYZE ARTIFACTS
26a. Ancient Greek women dressed modestly in long, flowing robes.
26b. The artist may have wished to depict everyday life using an ornamental, decorative scene.

Analyze Sources

27a. Hardened feet could enable Spartan youth to climb hills and descend steep inclines more easily.
27b. Boys would be better prepared to endure changes of heat and cold.

Essay Writing

28. Possible essay topics: scandals in government or business; trends in fashion; changes in attitudes toward civility and neighborliness; the disgrace of a popular cultural figure

TEST PREPARATION

Answer 3. a volcanic eruption.

Ancient Rome
753 B.C.–A.D. 476
(pp. 124–149)

Chapter Objectives
• Explain how the geography of Italy helped Rome expand and gain control over its neighbors.
• Describe the end of the Roman republic and the rise of the Roman Empire.
• Identify reasons for Rome's decline and fall.
• Discuss how Christianity developed, from its origins until it became the official religion of the Roman Empire.

Chapter Summary
Section I focuses on the growth of Rome over a 600-year period, from a small village to a republic that controlled the lands around the Mediterranean Sea.
Section II explores factors leading to the republic's demise and the Roman Empire's birth, culminating in the Roman Empire's golden age.
Section III explains reasons for the empire's decline and its fall in A.D. 476.
Section IV discusses the rise of Christianity and how its relationship to the Roman Empire changed over time.

Set the Stage
TEACH PRIMARY SOURCES
Virgil is considered the greatest poet of ancient Rome. He died before finishing his epic *Aeneid*. The emperor Augustus appointed two of Virgil's friends to prepare the poem for publication. Ask students to contrast the achievements of Greece as described in the paragraph above the quotation with those of Rome in the quotation itself. (Greece excelled in literature, art and philosophy; Rome's strength lay in governing other peoples.)

CHAPTER 6

Ancient Rome
753 B.C.–A.D. 476

I. Early Rome and the Republic
II. From Republic to Empire
III. The Empire Declines
IV. The Development of Christianity

The Roman people developed one of the most powerful civilizations of the ancient world. With their army and their talents for law, engineering, and organization, they built a mighty empire. Rome also helped to pass on to later ages the Greek achievements in literature, art, and philosophy. In his epic *Aeneid*, the Roman poet Virgil summed up the ways in which Rome would excel:

❝ *[Y]ours will be the rulership of nations,*
remember, Roman, these will be your arts:
to teach the ways of peace to those you conquer,
to spare defeated peoples, tame the proud. ❞

The Romans left a permanent mark on the world as we know it. Even after the fall of the Roman Empire, many civilizations borrowed the ideas and ideals of the Romans.

The Metropolitan Museum of Art, Rogers Fund, 1903. (03.14.5) Photograph
The Metropolitan Museum of Art

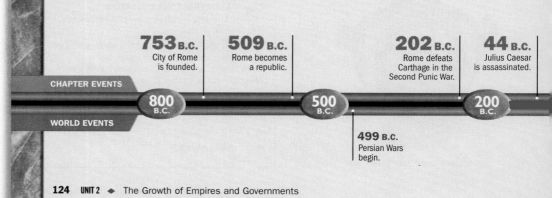

753 B.C. City of Rome is founded.

509 B.C. Rome becomes a republic.

202 B.C. Rome defeats Carthage in the Second Punic War.

44 B.C. Julius Caesar is assassinated.

CHAPTER EVENTS

800 B.C.

500 B.C.

200 B.C.

WORLD EVENTS

499 B.C. Persian Wars begin.

Teaching Options

Chapter 6 Resources

REVIEW

Teacher's Resources (TR)

ASSESSMENT

ALTERNATIVE ASSESSMENT

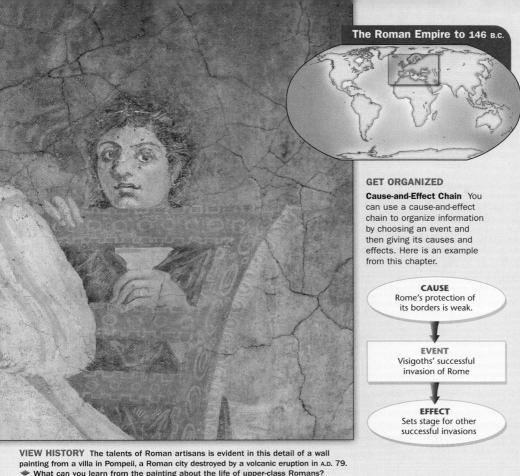

The Roman Empire to 146 B.C.

GET ORGANIZED

Cause-and-Effect Chain You can use a cause-and-effect chain to organize information by choosing an event and then giving its causes and effects. Here is an example from this chapter.

CAUSE
Rome's protection of its borders is weak.

↓

EVENT
Visigoths' successful invasion of Rome

↓

EFFECT
Sets stage for other successful invasions

VIEW HISTORY The talents of Roman artisans is evident in this detail of a wall painting from a villa in Pompeii, a Roman city destroyed by a volcanic eruption in A.D. 79.
◆ What can you learn from the painting about the life of upper-class Romans?

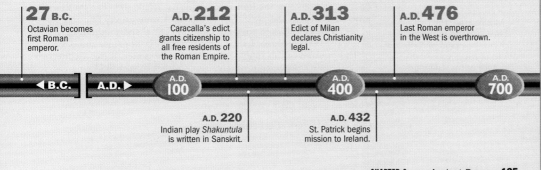

27 B.C.
Octavian becomes first Roman emperor.

A.D. 212
Caracalla's edict grants citizenship to all free residents of the Roman Empire.

A.D. 313
Edict of Milan declares Christianity legal.

A.D. 476
Last Roman emperor in the West is overthrown.

◀ B.C. | A.D. ▶ | A.D. 100 | A.D. 400 | A.D. 700

A.D. 220
Indian play *Shakuntula* is written in Sanskrit.

A.D. 432
St. Patrick begins mission to Ireland.

CHAPTER 6 ◆ Ancient Rome **125**

F Y I

The City of Pompeii

The wall painting on this page was found in the city of Pompeii. The city was buried in ashes in A.D. 79, when Mount Vesuvius erupted. People have been excavating Pompeii since the 1700s. Many artifacts from the time of the eruption have been found. Archaeologists have even found the remains of bodies that were preserved in the ashes. The world continues to learn much about ancient Rome from Pompeii's ruins.

Chapter Themes
- Culture
- Power, Authority, and Governance
- Individuals, Groups, and Institutions
- Production, Distribution, and Consumption
- Global Connections
- Civic Ideals and Practices
- Time, Continuity, and Change

Chapter Warm-Up

USING THE MAP
Point out the locator map at the top of page 125. Have students identify some of the landmasses that were part of the Roman Empire. (northern Africa, all of Europe, part of Asia)

VIEW HISTORY
One of the women in this first-century B.C. wall painting is playing a cithera, or zithara, which is a kind of lyre. From the names *cithera* or *zithara* come the instrument names *guitar* and *zither*. Discuss with students how a painting of life in a lower-class household might be different.

◆ **ANSWER** Possible answer: the upper-class women's clothing style, leisure-time activities, interest in the arts, and education

GET ORGANIZED
Cause-and-Effect Chain
Discuss the cause-and-effect chain on page 125. Ask students to begin by finding the event. (Visigoth's successful invasion of Rome) Then, have students find the cause and effect. Could there be other causes? Other effects?

TEACH THE TIMELINE
The timeline on pages 124–125 covers the period between 753 B.C. and A.D. 476. Point out the change from the term B.C. (before Christ) to A.D. (*anno Domini*, Latin for "in the year of the Lord"). Have students identify the common characteristic of almost all of the Chapter Events. (They deal with the growth and decline of Roman civilization.)

Activity

Review information Have students look back to the timeline for Chapter 5 on pages 98–99. Have them find the dates in the Chapter Events that pertain to Rome. (213 B.C. and 146 B.C.) Have them identify where Rome's conquest of Greece (146 B.C.) falls on the timeline on this page. (the defeat of Carthage (202 B.C.) and before Octavian becomes emperor (27 B.C.))

CHAPTER 6 ◆ **T125**

I. Early Rome and the Republic (pp. 126–130)

Section Summary

In this section, students will learn how the geography of Italy influenced Roman civilization. Students will also learn about the growth of the Roman republic and the reasons for its decline.

Introduce

Getting Started

Present this proverb: Rome was not built in a day. Ask students to explain what it suggests. (Roman civilization took centuries to develop.) Discuss the application of this proverb today. (Something of value takes time to develop.) Ask students to provide examples supporting the proverb. (getting an education, learning to drive, or learning a new sport or hobby)

TERMS TO KNOW

Ask students to read the terms and definitions on page 126 and find each term in the section. Ask students which topic most of these terms are related to. (government) Tell students that the language of ancient Rome was Latin. Point out that many English words have Latin roots. Have students use a dictionary to find other words that contain the root *pater* or *public*.

You may wish to preview the pronunciation of the following words with students.

Apennine (AP uh nyn)
Vesuvius (vuh SOO vee uhs)
Remus (REE muhs)
Etruscan (ih TRUHS kuhn)
paterfamilia
  (payt uhr fuh MIHL ee uh)
Scipio (SIHP ee oh)

ACTIVE READING

Have students make a prediction at the end of every subsection about the growth of Rome. Remind them that it is sometimes necessary to revise, or adjust, a prediction as they learn more about a subject. Have students use an organizer modeled on this equation: Prediction + Knowledge = Revised Prediction.

Early Rome and the Republic

Terms to Know

republic a government in which much of the power is held by elected representatives

veto to stop passage of a law

magistrate a government official

senate a council of representatives

patrician a descendant of a founding family of Rome

plebeian a commoner

tribune a plebeian official who could attend meetings of the assembly

Main Ideas

A. The long, mountainous Italian peninsula has a variety of climates and land uses.

B. Early Romans were a blend of people who were strongly influenced by the Etruscans and the Greeks.

C. Both the government and the society of the Roman Republic were divided into classes.

D. As Rome expanded, conflicts within the republic threatened its existence.

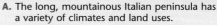 **Active Reading**

PREDICT
When you predict, you make an educated guess about what will happen next. As you read this section, think about the growth of Rome. Also consider the challenges that came along with that growth. Then, predict how you think Rome will change because of those challenges.

A. The Geography of Italy

When ancient Rome was at its most powerful, its land holdings were immense. Rome controlled most of Europe, northern Africa, parts of western Asia, and the Balkans. The origins and heart of Rome, however, were in Italy.

A Land of Geographic Differences

Italy is a boot-shaped peninsula extending southeast from a range of mountains called the Alps in the north, to the Mediterranean Sea in the south. The peninsula is about 700 miles long and only about 100 miles wide. The "toe" of the boot is located near the large island of Sicily. Italy's other major island is Sardinia.

The Apennine Mountain chain is the "backbone" of Italy. This chain runs for 857 miles from the Alps in the north, southward through the Italian peninsula and into Sicily. Between the Alps and the Apennines in northern Italy lies the basin of the Po River. Two other important rivers in Italy are the Arno and the Tiber Rivers.

Climate and Agriculture

Italy's climate ranges from cold in the north to semitropical in the south. The Apennines also influence Italy's weather patterns. The region on the western side is generally warmer and wetter than that on the eastern side.

As in Greece, the mountainous regions of Italy are poorly suited for agriculture. However, the Apennines are not as rugged as the mountains of Greece, and much of the Italian peninsula has fertile soil. The Po River basin provides northern Italy with rich farmland. A wide variety of crops is grown in the basin as well as in coastal regions of central and southern Italy. Today, as it was 2,000 years ago, Italy is a major producer of grapes and olives.

The location of this long peninsula near the center of the Mediterranean Sea has always provided profitable trade routes to surrounding areas. It did not take long for the Romans to recognize that Italy's location helped them in other ways as well. They came to realize that it was a perfect region from which to govern their growing empire.

◆ **What factors affect Italy's climate?**

Spotlight on *Geography*

VOLCANOES
People do not usually connect Europe with volcanoes. Italy, however, is home to Mount Vesuvius, the only active volcano on the European mainland.

Mount Etna, the highest active volcano in Europe, lies on the island of Sicily. Both of these volcanoes are part of the Apennine Mountain chain.

Teaching Options

Section 1 Resources

Teacher's Resources (TR)
Terms to Know, p. 19
Review History, p. 53
Build Your Skills, p. 87
Concept Builder, p. 222
Cause-and-Effect Chain, p. 325
Transparency 15

B. The Early Romans

According to legend, twin brothers named Romulus and Remus founded a city on the banks of the Tiber River. In a violent clash over who would rule the city, Romulus killed his brother. On April 21, 753 B.C., he named the city after himself and became its first king.

Historians believe that the earliest Romans were actually a mix of peoples called Latins, who were farmers and herders. The small town that would later become Rome developed as the Latins gathered to trade.

Influences on Early Rome

The Latins were not alone on the Italian peninsula. The Sabine people, for example, lived in the mountains to the northeast of Rome. The Etruscan people were a more powerful group located in central Italy. They had come to the Italian peninsula, possibly from Asia Minor, around 800 B.C. The Etruscans established city-states over much of central Italy. They had a written language and were skilled builders and artists. The early Romans learned about architecture and art from the Etruscans. They also adopted the Etruscan alphabet.

Around the time of the founding of Rome, the Greeks began to colonize Sicily and southern Italy. The Latins quickly saw that the Greeks had much to offer, such as a standard system of weights, measures, and money. Over time, the Romans would adopt many other elements of Greek culture.

The Roman Monarchy

Rome's first form of government was a monarchy. Tradition names seven kings of Rome. The early kings met with a council of advisors from the upper class. However, the seventh and last king, Lucius Tarquinius Superbus, or Tarquin the Proud, ruled alone—and harshly. He seized private property and had his opponents executed. In 509 B.C., a wealthy noble, Lucius Junius Brutus, led a successful revolt against the king.

◆ **How did the Etruscans and the Greeks influence the early Romans?**

C. Establishing a Republic

The Roman people did not replace Tarquinius Superbus with another monarch. Instead, they set up a new form of government—a **republic**. The root of this word is the Latin phrase *res publica*, or "property of the people." In a republic, voters choose people to represent them in the government.

The Government of Republican Rome

The government in republican Rome did not have a written constitution. Common ways of doing things became traditions that people followed as if they were laws. The government included the following characteristics:

- Each year, two people were elected to share the office of head of state. These men—for only men could hold office or vote—were the consuls. They proposed laws and led the army. One consul had the right to **veto**, or cancel, the actions of the other.

Early Romans were greatly influenced by Etruscan art, language, and religion. This Etruscan banquet scene and the figures on the Etruscan vase show similarities with later Roman ceremonies and styles of dress.

Romulus and Remus

Romulus and Remus were thought to be twin sons of Mars, the god of war, and Rhea Silvia, the daughter of the king of Alba Longa. Rhea's uncle forced her to abandon the twins in a basket on the Tiber River. According to legend, they were found by a wolf and a woodpecker, animals that were sacred to Mars. They cared for the twins until the king's herdsman, Faustulus, and his wife raised them.

ESL/ELL STRATEGIES

Take Notes Have students work with a partner in this oral activity that also targets study skills. Have one student read aloud a subsection of the text. Have the second student listen and take notes on the content. Then, have both students check the notes against the text and evaluate their accuracy. Finally, have students switch roles and complete the exercise for a different subsection of text.

---

2 Teach

A. The Geography of Italy

Purpose-Setting Question How were trade and agriculture in Rome affected by its geography? (Its location provided profitable trade routes to surrounding areas. The rich farmland of its river valleys allowed a variety of crops to be grown.)

SPOTLIGHT ON GEOGRAPHY

VOLCANOES People continue to live at the foot of Mount Vesuvius, even though it erupts on occasion. The fertile volcanic soil contributes to the fine vineyards in the region. Have students suggest other examples of people living in areas of natural danger. (Possible answers: earthquakes in California or Japan, avalanches in the Alps, hurricanes in Florida)

◆ **ANSWER** Answers should include the length of the peninsula from north to south, and the Apennine Mountains extending down its length.

B. The Early Romans

Purpose-Setting Question Who were some of the peoples who lived on the Italian peninsula with the early Romans? (Latins, Sabines, Etruscans, and Greeks)

Activity

Make a chart Have students create a two-column chart (TR, p. 328) that shows the contributions of the Etruscans and the Greeks to Roman culture.

◆ **ANSWER Etruscans:** architecture, art, alphabet; **Greeks:** system of weights, measures, and money; over time, other elements of Greek culture

C. Establishing a Republic

Purpose-Setting Question How did the establishment of a republic create stability in Rome? (Possible answer: Both patricians and plebeians were represented in government; power was distributed among several branches.)

SPOTLIGHT ON GOVERNMENT

CHECKS AND BALANCES Review the function of each branch of government. (**executive:** carries out laws; **legislative:** makes laws; **judicial:** interprets laws) Then, have students explain which Roman person or group correlated to each branch. (**executive:** consuls, most magistrates, dictator; **legislative:** senate and tribal assembly; **judicial:** praetors)

Activity

Make a chart Ask students to construct a cause-and-effect chain (TR, p. 325) explaining why the Romans created a republic. (**Cause:** king abused power; **Event:** Romans revolted; **Effect:** Romans set up a republic as their government.)

Focus Help students clarify the roles of government officials in the republic by asking them to write the name of each position on one side of an index card. On the other side, have them describe this position's function and responsibility. Group students into pairs and have them identify the roles by using these cards like flashcards.

Explore Ask students how women's positions differed in ancient Rome, ancient Greece, and modern times. (Women had more power and freedom in ancient Rome, though still less than they have today.)

THEY MADE HISTORY
Cicero

Point out to students the importance of oratory in ancient Rome. Ask students why speech-making was so important in government. (Possible answer: The Romans did not have all the other media available today; politicians could only make their views known through speeches.) Ask students what qualities make a good orator. (Possible answer: strong voice, organized, persuasive, command of facts, sense of humor)

ANSWER Possible answers: **Yes:** because Cicero was a highly educated scholar who witnessed many historic events. **No:** because Cicero was deeply immersed in politics and was biased toward the republican side.

Spotlight on
Government

CHECKS AND BALANCES

Why was Rome's republican government strong? Part of the reason was its system of checks and balances. No one person or group had all the power.

The United States is a strong republic, too. Like the Roman constitution, the U.S. Constitution contains checks and balances. As in the ancient Roman republic, the duties of the U.S. government are divided among the executive, legislative, and judicial branches.

- Consuls were the most important **magistrates**, or government officials. Other elected magistrates included the praetors, who headed the judiciary; the aediles, who supervised marketplaces; the questors, who were financial officers; and the censors, who counted the people every five years. Most magistrates held office for a one-year term.
- In many ways, the main governing power lay with the **senate**. A senate is a group of officials with the power to discuss matters important to the country and help make policy decisions. The first senators were **patricians**. Patricians, who were descendants of the founding families of Rome, formed the upper class.

Groups of Roman people also met to elect the magistrates and to approve laws recommended by the senate. One of these groups, the tribal assembly, was controlled by the **plebeians**, or common people. Around 450 B.C., this assembly won the right to elect their own officials, called **tribunes**. These tribunes could veto any government action.

The patricians ran the government, but the plebeians made up most of Rome's population and military. Before long, the plebeians forced the patricians to publish a written code of laws. In 451 B.C., work began on the Twelve Tables, the first Roman code of law.

Society in Republican Rome

Although they were divided into separate classes, patricians and plebeians had their freedom in common. A large group of people within Roman society, however, were slaves. Under Roman law, masters had the power of life and death over their slaves. Still, it was not unusual for a slave to earn or be granted freedom.

The situation of women in Rome changed during the republic. In the early years, women did not have the same rights as men. Over time, however, they gained more independence. By the end of the republic, some women took part in government decision making. Women could also own property.

They Made History

Cicero 106–43 B.C.

One official who rose through the ranks of the republic was Marcus Tullius Cicero. Cicero was educated in the law. He also studied literature, philosophy, and especially oratory, the art of effective speech-making. In 75 B.C., Cicero became a member of the senate. Twelve years later, he was elected consul.

Cicero watched Rome change from a republic to an empire. Still, he hoped to preserve the republic. Because of that view, he was labeled as a traitor, and he was later executed.

Cicero has been called the greatest orator of ancient Rome. Fortunately, many of his speeches, essays, and letters have survived. They provide valuable information about Rome during his lifetime.

Cicero was a Roman senator and orator.

Critical Thinking Do you think the writings of Cicero are reliable historical documents? Why?

Teaching Options

Focus on
❯ TEEN LIFE ❮

Education in Ancient Rome In early Roman society, education for boys was handled by the family. Boys learned to read and write, do simple math, and memorize the Twelve Tables. When a boy turned 16, he put on the toga, which adult males wore, and he was apprenticed in some career for a year to an older and honored friend of the family.

After the Romans came into contact with the Greeks, their idea of education expanded greatly. Upper-class Romans learned both Greek and Latin. Children attended schools, which were divided into primary, secondary, and higher education. In secondary schools, the focus was on poetry and rhetoric, the art of speaking and writing effectively. Giving an effective speech was an important accomplishment in secondary education.

Extent of Roman Lands
- End of the Punic Wars, 146 B.C.
- At Caesar's death, 44 B.C.
- At Augustus's death, A.D. 14
- Greatest extent of the empire, A.D. 130
- Hadrian's Wall
- Cities

Map Check

1. **REGION** By which date did Rome control the entire Mediterranean region?
2. **LOCATION** When was most of Spain added to the Roman Republic?

The heart of Roman society was the family. The head of each family was the paterfamilias, or the oldest male. He made all the important decisions and led the family's religious ceremonies. He also encouraged republican values in his family, such as discipline, industry, thrift, and self-sacrifice.

Religion in republican Rome borrowed much from the Greek and the Etruscan peoples. There were three main Roman gods. Jupiter was king of the gods. Jupiter's wife, Juno, was the protector of marriage. Minerva, the daughter of Jupiter, was the protector of wisdom. The Romans identified their gods with the Greek gods Zeus, Hera, and Athena.

◆ How did plebeians win a greater voice in the republic's government?

D. Expanding Roman Control

During the first 250 years of the republic, Rome waged a series of wars to conquer its neighbors in Italy. The Roman army defeated the Etruscan peoples and the Samnites, who were descendants of the Sabine peoples. Rome also seized Greek colonies in southern Italy. By 265 B.C., Rome ruled most of the Italian peninsula.

The Punic Wars

Control of southernmost Italy put Rome into conflict with Carthage, a city-state in northern Africa. At the time, Carthage controlled most of the western Mediterranean. Between 264 and 146 B.C., Rome and Carthage would fight three wars. These are called the Punic Wars.

Using the Map

The Roman Republic and Empire, 146 B.C.–A.D. 130

Have students describe the extent of the Roman Empire by A.D. 130. (The Roman Empire stretched from northern Africa, to southern and western Europe, to the eastern Mediterranean.)

✔ Map Check

Answers
1. A.D. 14
2. 146 B.C.

Focus Discuss with students what family life was like in ancient Rome. Ask how the role of the father differs from that of fathers in today's families. (In general, fathers had more authority in Rome.)

Extend Explain to students that the Greek and Roman gods had different names, but similar roles and personalities. In addition to the gods mentioned on page 129, other similar pairs are: Aphrodite—Venus; Ares—Mars; Eros—Cupid; Poseidon—Neptune. Ask students which of these gods they have heard about and what they know of their stories. You may want to have interested students read the stories of the gods and share them with the class.

◆ **ANSWER** Plebeians won the right to elect ten tribunes who could veto any government action. The plebeians forced the patricians to publish a written code of laws.

D. Expanding Roman Control

Purpose-Setting Question How did Rome expand its territory during the later years of the republic? (Rome conquered the Etruscans and Samnites in Italy, then fought the Punic Wars to defeat Carthage, adding Sicily and North Africa to its possessions. In 146 B.C. Rome completed the conquest of Greece.)

Connection to GEOGRAPHY

Have students examine the map on this page. Discuss the proximity of Carthage to both Rome and Sicily. Have students estimate the distances. (Carthage to Rome—about 375 miles; Carthage to Sicily—about 150 miles) Explore the discomfort of having an enemy so close to a country's shores.

Meet Individual Needs:
AUDITORY LEARNERS

Have students do library research or visit a Web site to find a collection of great speeches, including at least one of Cicero's. Have them examine one of Cicero's speeches and choose several paragraphs to read to the class. Ask them to explain why the speech is powerful. They may wish to tape and vary their presentation, then choose the most effective version.

GLOBAL CONNECTIONS
HANNIBAL AND QIN Shi Huangdi boasted many accomplishments, including the start of the Great Wall of China; however, he was a harsh ruler. Ask students to weigh the advantages and disadvantages of empires. (**advantages:** allowed for extension of culture and accomplishments; **disadvantages:** human rights often neglected)

ANALYZE PRIMARY SOURCES

DOCUMENT-BASED QUESTION
Polybius was a Greek historian, and therefore, had a heightened perspective on the growth of Rome. He was taken prisoner in 168 B.C., and when Rome conquered Greece, he helped negotiate a favorable treaty for the Greeks.

ANSWER According to Polybius, governing the conquered peoples is more difficult because those who know how to win do not necessarily know how to make the best use of their victory.

◆ **ANSWER** The First Punic War resulted in Rome's gaining control of Sicily. The Second Punic War ended with the defeat of Hannibal at Carthage. The Third Punic War saw the final destruction of Carthage.

Section Close
Discuss the six stages of human existence: birth, childhood, adolescence, maturity, old age, death. Then, ask students to compare the growth of Rome to that of a human being. At which stage of existence had Rome arrived by the second century B.C.? (adolescence)

3 Assess

Review Answers

Review History
A. Rome was centrally located, which eased trade with other areas and simplified the government of the empire. Also, it had rich farmland in the Po Valley.

B. the Etruscans and the Greeks

C. checks and balances and the separation of powers

D. Sicily

Define Terms to Know
republic, 127; veto, 127; magistrate, 128; senate, 128; patrician, 128; plebeian, 128; tribune, 128

Critical Thinking
Possible answer: It kept one person from accumulating too much power.

Write About Citizenship
Students' paragraphs should include information on senators' social class and the senate's function.

Global Connections

HANNIBAL AND QIN
Hannibal became a general in the Carthaginian army in 221 B.C. In that same year, the Chinese kingdom of Qin took over the last of its neighbors. The king of Qin proclaimed himself Qin Shi Huangdi, the first emperor of a unified China. The name *China*, in fact, is taken from *Qin*, or *Ch'in*.

ANALYZE PRIMARY SOURCES
DOCUMENT-BASED QUESTION According to Polybius, which is more difficult—winning a battle, or governing the conquered peoples?

The First Punic War lasted from 264 to 241 B.C. In this war, Rome and Carthage struggled for control of Sicily, the large island off the southern tip of Italy. The Romans won the First Punic War and gained control of Sicily.

A Carthaginian general named Hannibal was determined to gain control of Sicily. As a result, he and a large army marched through Spain and northward to a region called Gaul, now known as France. From here, Hannibal crossed the Alps into Italy. The Second Punic War, from 218 to 202 B.C., was an attempt by Hannibal to conquer Rome itself. After losing a major battle in Cannae, Italy, in 216 B.C., the Romans decided to invade Carthage. Hannibal was forced to return to northern Africa to defend his homeland. In 202 B.C., the Roman general Scipio defeated Hannibal's army at Zama, a town near Carthage.

In the Third Punic War, from 149 to 146 B.C., Roman forces destroyed Carthage and enslaved every survivor. What remained of Carthage became a Roman territory. Also in 146 B.C., Rome completed its conquest of Greece. Thus, the city of Rome, which had begun as a small village 600 years earlier, ruled the Mediterranean from Spain to Asia Minor.

Problems in the Late Republic
Expansion made Rome wealthy. However, it also widened the gap between rich and poor. Wealthy landowners built large houses, whereas many poor farmers lost their land. When Romans conquered new lands, they enslaved many captives and brought them to the city. Eventually, slaves outnumbered free people. Many Romans lost their jobs to slaves, who worked for no pay. These changes caused tension and unrest in Rome. The historian Polybius, writing about Rome in the second century B.C., said,

❝Those who know how to win are much more numerous than those who know how to make proper use of their victories.❞

◆ **What were the results of the three Punic Wars?**

Review I

Review History
A. How did Rome's location help the city to grow and prosper?
B. Which two neighbors had an important influence on early Rome?
C. What were two unwritten practices of the Roman republic?
D. What new territory did Rome gain as a result of the First Punic War?

Define Terms to Know
Define the following terms: **republic, veto, magistrate, senate, patrician, plebeian, tribune**

Critical Thinking
What advantages can you see in Rome's having two consuls, each of which had a term of only one year?

Write About Citizenship
Write a paragraph about the role of the senate in republican Rome.

Get Organized
CAUSE-AND-EFFECT CHAIN
Use a cause-and-effect chain to organize information from this section. Choose an event and then give its causes and effects. For example, what was the cause of the Second Punic War? What were the effects of that war?

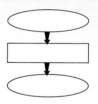

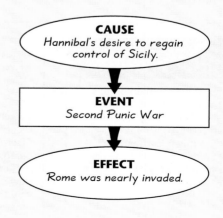

CAUSE
Hannibal's desire to regain control of Sicily.

EVENT
Second Punic War

EFFECT
Rome was nearly invaded.

Build Your Skills

READ A SPECIAL-PURPOSE MAP

As you study history, all types of maps are valuable tools to help you learn about the connections between history and geography. Maps come in many shapes and sizes. Most are political or physical maps.

A political map shows information such as national boundaries and the location of major cities. A physical map shows the natural features of an area or region such as mountains and rivers.

Other kinds of maps, called special-purpose maps, show specific kinds of information. A historical map, for example, might show battle sites, or the boundaries of an empire. An economic map might show trade goods and routes. A population map might show the population density of a region.

The map below is a special-purpose map that gives a variety of information about the Second Punic War between Carthage and Rome. Studying the information shown on this map will help you better understand Roman history.

Here's How

Follow these steps to read and interpret a special-purpose map.

1. Read the map's title, key, and scale. These tell you the subject and extent of the map.
2. Check the key to see what special-purpose symbols the map may contain. The map on this page uses a special symbol to mark the location of major battles during the Second Punic War.
3. Study the labels to identify each feature shown on the map.

Here's Why

Analyzing a special-purpose map can help you learn more about a place during a specific period. For example, reading about the Punic Wars gives you a sense of events that took place long ago. Studying a special-purpose map about these events allows you to understand the regions involved and the areas ruled by Rome and by Carthage.

Practice the Skill

Study the special-purpose map on this page. Then answer the following questions.

1. About how many miles did Hannibal's forces march to reach Cannae?
2. When was the battle of Zama fought?
3. From where did Scipio launch his invasion of Carthage?

Extend the Skill

Compare the map with a present-day political map of the Mediterranean region. Then, write a paragraph identifying some modern countries that correspond to the regions shown on the map at the right.

Apply the Skill

Study the maps in the rest of this chapter. Follow the steps in *Here's How* to interpret the maps.

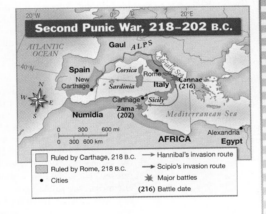

Second Punic War, 218–202 B.C.

Build Your Skills

READ A
SPECIAL-PURPOSE MAP

Teach the Skill

Have students offer instances in which they use maps in their everyday lives. (Possible answers: subway map, weather map, road map) Ask the purpose of each map. (to find routing on a subway, to find daily weather patterns, to determine directions to a location) Explain that all of these are special-purpose maps, which serve a particular function.

Have students examine the map on page 131. Have them determine what kind of special-purpose map it is. (historical) Explain that this map will expand their understanding of Roman history. Then, have students follow the three steps in *Here's How* to practice the skill of reading a special-purpose map. Encourage volunteers to share their answer to each step in *Here's How* with the class.

Practice the Skill
ANSWERS

1. about 1,400 miles
2. 202 B.C.
3. Scipio launched his attack from Sicily.

Extend the Skill

Responses will vary but should include some or all of the following: Turkey, Libya, Tunisia, Algeria, Morocco, France, Serbia, and Croatia.

Apply the Skill

Have students work in pairs to first apply the steps in *Here's How* to the maps on pages 142 and 146. Then, have each pair write a brief paragraph about the information provided on each map.

Teaching Options

RETEACH

Have students look through later chapters in the textbook to find additional examples of special-purpose maps. Have them list at least five maps, along with a notation describing what kind of special-purpose map each one is. They can also look for other chapters in which special-purpose maps might help explain historical battles and events, as well as using the special-purpose maps in Transparency 15.

CHALLENGE

Have students bring a special-purpose map into class. Possibilities include a weather map, a military map showing battle sites, a map showing topography or resources, or a road or subway map. Newspapers and newsmagazines are generally good sources for special-purpose maps. Have the students describe their map's purpose and explain any special symbols on the map.

Section Summary
In this section, students will learn how conflicts between military leaders and political parties led to civil war in Rome. Octavian's leadership ushered in the Roman Empire and many years of peace. For 200 years, Rome enjoyed peace, expansion, and prosperity.

1 Introduce

Getting Started
Ask students how they feel about change: Some people embrace it and some shun it. Discuss how some changes can be positive and other changes are negative. Ask students if their reaction to positive changes is different from their reaction to negative changes. Have students notice the changes in Rome as it moved from republic to empire, and how people responded to those changes.

TERMS TO KNOW
Ask students to read the terms and definitions on page 132 and find each term in the section. After they have read the section, have them explain each term's relationship to Roman government in the late republic.

You may wish to review the pronunciation of the following words with students.

Pompey (PAHM pay)
princeps (PRIHN cehps)
Flavian (FLAY vee uhn)
Caligula (kuh LIGH yoo luh)
Hadrian (HAY dree uhn)

ACTIVE READING
Have students choose one subsection of Section 2 and write a summary of its most important parts. Suggest that they use the heading, art, and chart in the subsection to aid their writing of the summary.

From Republic to Empire

Terms to Know
legion the chief fighting unit of the Roman army
triumvirate a group of three leaders

Main Ideas
A. Failed attempts at economic and social reform, as well as intense rivalries between military leaders, resulted in crisis and civil war in the late republic.
B. After Julius Caesar's assassination, his adopted son Octavian, later known as Augustus, succeeded in unifying Rome.
C. During the first two centuries of the empire, Rome continued to expand and to enjoy relative peace and prosperity.

Active Reading
SUMMARIZE
When you summarize, you state only the most important points, or highlights, of a passage. As you read this section, focus on the main points about the change in Rome from a republican to an imperial government. Then, pause to summarize what you have learned.

A. The End of the Republic
Beginning in the late second century B.C., conflicts within Rome became more intense. Two tribunes, Tiberious Sempronius Graccus and his brother, Gaius, tried to change some laws to help the poor. However, the Roman nobility would not agree to the changes. Both brothers died violently. Graccus was murdered in 133 B.C. His younger brother was killed in a riot 12 years later. Conflict in Rome eventually led to civil war.

Major Changes for Rome
One of the reasons for the conflict was the increasing power of the Roman army. By 107 B.C., a plebeian named Marius was elected consul. A gifted military leader, Marius had led his troops to many victories. Grateful Romans re-elected Marius over and over, even though the constitution stated that candidates had to wait 10 years before running for the same office.

Marius brought major changes to Rome. Many of these changes involved his **legions**. A legion was made up of about 5,000 foot soldiers and was the chief fighting unit of the Roman army. Marius rewarded his troops with money and newly conquered lands. As a result, soldiers were more loyal to their military leader than they were to the government overall.

Julius Caesar and Rome
In 60 B.C., two generals named Pompey and Crassus allied themselves with a general named Julius Caesar. This alliance is called the First **Triumvirate**. A triumvirate is a group of three leaders. The goal of Pompey, Crassus, and Caesar was to control the government. However, the alliance did not last long. Crassus was killed in 53 B.C., and Caesar and Pompey became rivals.

Caesar set out with his army to conquer Gaul—the region that is now France—and bring it under Roman control. While he was away, Pompey had the senate order Caesar to disband his army and return to Rome. Caesar refused. He knew that without an army, he would be defenseless against his enemies in the Roman government. In 49 B.C., Caesar and his victorious army returned to Italy and to civil war. Pompey and his supporters fled to Greece, where Caesar's army defeated them. Once back in Rome, the senate voted Caesar dictator for life.

This Roman coin has a likeness of Julius Caesar.

Teaching Options

Section 2 Resources

Teacher's Resources (TR)
Terms to Know, p. 19
Review History, p. 53
Build Your Skills, p. 87
Concept Builder, p. 222
Cause-and-Effect Chain, p. 325

During his reign, Caesar was responsible for a number of important reforms. Between 48 B.C. and 44 B.C., Caesar worked on reforms aimed at improving Romans' lives. He created new jobs and granted citizenship to more people. Caesar also gave public land to the poor and reorganized the government of Rome's territories. He also introduced a new calendar—called the Julian calendar—that is still used today. One month of the year was renamed *July*, the "month of Julius," in his honor.

Caesar's popularity was not well received by everyone. Many senators, fearing Caesar's ambition, conspired against him. On March 15, 44 B.C., Brutus and Cassius—two senators thought to be friends of Caesar—assassinated him on the floor of the senate. The date of this act on the new Julian calendar became known as the Ides of March. After Caesar's death, Rome entered another period of civil war.

◆ **What kind of ruler was Julius Caesar?**

B. Augustus and Rome's Golden Age

Julius Caesar's grandnephew Octavian was only 18 years old at the time of Caesar's assassination. Octavian and Mark Antony, a Roman general, joined forces to defeat Brutus and Cassius, Caesar's assassins, at the Battle of Philippi in Greece. However, the alliance between Octavian and Antony did not last long. The two were soon engaged in a struggle for power. In 31 B.C., Octavian defeated Antony and his ally, Queen Cleopatra of Egypt.

The Augustan Principate

Octavian knew that the Roman people had hated the idea of a monarchy for more than five centuries. For this reason, Octavian was careful not to call himself a king. However, in 27 B.C., he became the authority for all the power of the state. In other words, he became a king in fact, if not in name.

Octavian preferred to be called princeps, which means "first citizen." His rule is referred to as the principate, or the rule of the first among equals. He kept the senate, but he made sure that he controlled it. In 27 B.C., a grateful senate voted him the title of Augustus, which means "revered."

Augustus's main goal was to bring stability and order to Rome, and he largely succeeded. For the next 40 years, Rome prospered. The Roman world, weary of civil war, enjoyed a period of Pax Romana, or "Roman peace."

At home, Augustus worked hard to strengthen the government so it could successfully hold the empire together. To make the tax system more fair, he set up a census, or count of the number of people. He supported a huge building campaign in the capital, which was intended to give people jobs, beautify the city, and increase patriotism among Romans.

Culture in the Golden Age

Like the age of Pericles in Athens in the fifth century B.C., the Augustan era in Rome has been called a golden age. During this time, Augustus instructed the Roman army to maintain Rome's many roads and keep them safe from thieves. Augustus also had the army chase pirates from the sea trade routes. This resulted in more trade between Rome and distant lands such as China and India. Throughout the empire, building flourished. The military engineer Vitruvius wrote a manual on architecture and town planning. Temples and other religious buildings displayed impressive sculptures.

Statue of Augustus

CHAPTER 6 ◆ Ancient Rome **133**

A. The End of the Republic

Purpose-Setting Question
What brought about the end of the Roman republic? (Nobility would not agree to changes; soldiers became more loyal to leaders than to the state; military leaders conflicted; Caesar was elected dictator for life.)

Explore Review with students the qualities of a good leader. (Possible answers: cares about the state; cares about the people; honest; can make hard decisions; takes responsibility for actions) Tell students that Caesar was much beloved by his army, partly because he bore hardship with them. As a result, they fought hard for him and won many battles. Have students list the lasting achievements of Julius Caesar. (He created new jobs, granted citizenship to more people, gave land to the poor, reorganized the government of territories, and introduced a new calendar.)

◆ **ANSWER** Julius Caesar was a powerful leader, popular with the people, and responsible for many reforms.

B. Augustus and Rome's Golden Age

Purpose-Setting Question For what reasons did the Romans revere Augustus? (He brought them peace, stability, and prosperity.)

Discuss Ask students how years of civil war might have affected Romans' views of the republic. (Possible answer: They might have welcomed someone who established order and dictated to others.)

TEACH PRIMARY SOURCES
The statue of Augustus once stood in the home of Livia, Augustus's wife, but now it stands in the Vatican. Ask students what sense of Augustus's character it portrays. (Possible answer: a feeling of authority and control, conveyed by the outstretched arm; a feeling of peace and family, conveyed by the child)

F Y I

Julius Caesar
Julius Caesar was a brilliant military strategist, an accomplished writer, and a gifted statesman. He was also known for his memorable sayings. When he returned to Rome to battle, he said, "The die is cast." He crossed the Rubicon River to enter Roman territory, and today "crossing the Rubicon" describes an irrevocable decision. His message *veni, vidi, vici* ("I came, I saw, I conquered.") is often used today.

Connection to ---------
LITERATURE ◀- - - - -

In late sixteenth and early seventeenth-century England, William Shakespeare found worthy subjects for his plays in Roman history. Two of Shakespeare's most famous tragedies—*Julius Caesar* and *Antony and Cleopatra*—are based on the "players" in this section. Have interested students read these plays. Encourage groups of students to stage compelling scenes for the class.

CHAPTER 6 ◆ T133

◆ **ANSWER** Changes under Augustus included tax reform, a census, a building campaign, and support of the arts.

C. The Early Empire

Purpose-Setting Question After the first hundred years, why were the early years of the Roman Empire relatively stable? (Several of the emperors of that time ruled well.)

Focus Ask students to explain how rule was passed on in the Roman Empire. (Emperors declared successors in their own families. Occasionally civil war broke out, if and when there was a struggle to determine leadership.) Ask students to compare dynastic rule to the way a President comes to power in the United States. (A President is not chosen by another President, but is elected by the people and serves a maximum of eight years.)

ANALYZE PRIMARY SOURCES

DOCUMENT-BASED QUESTION

Edward Gibbon was born in Great Britain in 1737. The first volume of *The History of the Decline and Fall of the Roman Empire* was published in 1776. The sixth, and final, volume was published in 1788. The books are still used today to understand the Roman Empire and Western civilization.

ANSWER Gibbons considered Rome's earlier rulers to be more ruthless and selfish.

Roman artists and writers believed they were inspired by spirits, called muses. The Roman poet Virgil is shown seated in this mosaic with the muses Clio and Melpomene.

Augustus also supported poets, historians, and other artists. Roman literature began in the late 200s B.C. with the translation into Latin of classic Greek works, such as Homer's *Odyssey*. By the time of Augustus, Roman writers had developed their own styles. Augustus saw the value of such literature for promoting patriotic feelings among the Roman people. The poet Virgil, for example, told of the origins of Rome in his epic tale, the *Aeneid*. Horace wrote poems to celebrate the heroism of Augustus. The historian Livy wrote the history of Rome in 142 books.

◆ **What changes occurred in Rome under Augustus?**

C. The Early Empire

Despite his many successes, Augustus had trouble finding a successor. He eventually named his stepson Tiberius to succeed him. Augustus died in A.D. 14. For the rest of the first century A.D., Rome was governed by emperors of two dynasties, or series of rulers from the same family or group. These two dynasties were the Julio-Claudian and Flavian Dynasties.

The Julio-Claudian and Flavian Emperors

Few, if any, of the Julio-Claudian emperors were great rulers. While Tiberius was a good administrator, his harsh personality made him unpopular. His successor, Caligula, was assassinated after just four years. Both Tiberius and Caligula were cruel and brutal rulers. Claudius, Caligula's successor, completed the conquest of England. He was succeeded by Nero, an unstable ruler. Nero was blamed for a great fire that destroyed much of Rome. He committed suicide in A.D. 68.

After a year of turmoil, the Roman general Vespasian gained power, marking the start of the Vespasian dynasty in A.D. 69. His leadership made Rome stronger, and his reign was generally successful. Vespasian's son Titus was a fairly popular ruler. He completed the Colosseum, which was the largest arena in the Mediterranean world. This arena became the center of Rome's social life. Titus was succeeded by his brother, Domitian, who was a tyrant. His reign was cut short by assassination. His death marked the end of the Flavian dynasty.

Rome's Five "Good" Emperors

From about A.D. 100 to A.D. 200, a series of five rulers brought the Roman Empire to its height. Writing about these emperors, the English historian Edward Gibbon remarked in his classic work, *The History of the Decline and Fall of the Roman Empire*:

ANALYZE PRIMARY SOURCES **DOCUMENT-BASED QUESTION** Based on Gibbon's quote, what did the author think of Rome's earlier rulers?

❝ Their united reigns are quite likely the only period of history in which the happiness of a great people was the sole object of government. ❞

Teaching Options

Connection to
ART

The Romans were renowned for their architecture. In addition to houses, temples, and palaces, they built public baths, aqueducts, and outdoor arenas. They were masters of the arch and the vault, which allowed them to support roofs without columns. Have students find books about Roman architecture and use them to make a poster or bulletin board showing the beauty of Roman buildings.

After the brief reign of Nerva, a noble who was proclaimed emperor by the senate, Nerva's adopted son Trajan took power. Trajan was a skillful and popular military leader. He conquered the region of Dacia, in what is now modern Romania, built splendid new buildings in Rome, reduced taxes, and cooperated fully with the senate. Trajan's successor was his cousin Hadrian. Hadrian had his soldiers build a wall across England to hold back attackers. Hadrian's Wall still sits on the border between England and Scotland.

The fourth in this series of emperors was Antoninus Pius, chosen by Hadrian. He gradually centralized the government. Antoninus was succeeded by his nephew Marcus Aurelius who wrote a famous book called *Meditations*. Marcus had to spend much of his time putting down rebellions and fighting invasions. With the death of Marcus in A.D. 180, Rome's age of "good" rule came to an end. The empire entered an era of slow and often stormy decline.

◆ **What were the major accomplishments of Trajan?**

Rome's Five "Good" Emperors

NERVA A.D. 96–98	Reformed land laws in favor of poor; revised taxes
TRAJAN A.D. 98–117	Expanded the empire to its greatest extent; started a public building program
HADRIAN A.D. 117–138	Constructed Hadrian's Wall in England; codified Roman law; erected many buildings in Rome
ANTONINUS PIUS A.D. 138–161	Promoted art and science; started legal reform; constructed public works
MARCUS AURELIUS A.D. 161–180	Unified the Roman Empire economically; made legal reforms

✔ Chart Check

In what ways did the five "good" emperors strengthen Rome's empire at home?

Review II

Review History
A. Why was Marius a significant figure in the late Roman republic?
B. How would you describe Roman culture in the Augustan era?
C. Why were the five "good" emperors popular with the citizens of the empire?

Define Terms to Know
Define the following terms:
legion, triumvirate

Critical Thinking
Why do you think Augustus was able to unify Rome under his sole control?

Write About Culture
Write a paragraph evaluating the significance of either Julius Caesar or Augustus in Rome's history.

Get Organized
CAUSE-AND-EFFECT CHAIN
Use a cause-and-effect chain to organize information from this section. Choose an event, such as the death of Julius Caesar. Then, give the cause and an effect of this event.

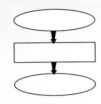

CAUSE
Caesar elected dictator for life; many fear his ambition.

↓

EVENT
Julius Caesar is assassinated.

↓

EFFECT
Rome enters period of civil war.

Define Terms to Know
legion, 132; triumvirate, 132

Critical Thinking
Possible answer: Augustus carefully avoided the appearance of wanting to be a monarch. He retained the magistracies of the republic, and he used propaganda skillfully.

Write About Culture
Students' paragraphs should describe Julius Caesar's or Augustus's accomplishments and explain why they were important in Rome's history.

Using the Chart
Rome's Five "Good" Emperors

Usually a chart consolidates textual information, but this chart actually adds information to what is already in the text. Have students choose one of the emperors in the chart and identify information that the chart adds to the text. (Possible answer: The chart tells that Nerva reformed land laws and revised taxes.)

✔ Chart Check
Answer reformed land laws, revised taxes, constructed public buildings, codified law, promoted art and science, unified empire economically, made legal reforms

Extend Marcus Aurelius was a rare combination—both an emperor and a philosopher. The Stoic philosophy that guided him originated in Greece around 300 B.C. The Stoics held that the good of society was more important than that of the individual, and that the world is ruled by a force of universal kindness. Ask students how this philosophy would influence a ruler.

◆ **ANSWER** Trajan conquered Dacia, built new buildings in Rome, reduced taxes, and cooperated with the senate.

Section Close

Ask students to write a paragraph describing the five most important events of the early Roman Empire. Rather than a list, have them think of the course of Roman history over those two centuries.

3 Assess

Review Answers
Review History
A. Under Marius, the army became stronger and more professional. The stage was set for such powerful generals as Pompey and Caesar.
B. Culture flourished in such areas as architecture, poetry, and history.
C. They expanded the empire, erected splendid new buildings, and reduced taxes. Also, happiness of the people was an important goal of the emperors.

CHAPTER 6 ◆ **T135**

Past to...

THE LEGACY OF THE ROMAN SOLDIER

Teach the Topic

This feature focuses on the armor and weapons of the Roman soldier, one of the linchpins of the Roman Empire. Discuss with students the importance of obedience in an army. (If soldiers do not follow orders, chaos ensues and their strength of number is lost.)

ROMAN SOLDIER'S UNIFORM

Point out to students that all of the materials for the Roman uniform were natural. Have students determine the sources of leather, linen, wool, and iron. (leather from cattle, wool from sheep, linen is a plant fiber, iron is a metal in Earth) Discuss the visibility of the Roman soldier. Ask in what way the soldiers' appearance might have been a strength of the army. (Seeing thousands of disciplined Roman soldiers on the attack would have been frightening to enemies; leaders in battle could be readily recognized.)

BEST FOOT FORWARD

Ask students to describe the advantage of the design of the caligae. (Possible answer: iron nails made soles of shoes long-lasting.) Tell students that Roman soldiers often marched as much as 25 miles a day. Remind students that Italy is about 700 miles in length. At 25 miles a day, about how long would it take soldiers to get from southern to northern Italy without stopping? (about 28 days)

BOLD AS BRASS

This was the Imperial Gallic helmet, designed about A.D. 30. The Romans continually improved the technology of their armor. Ask students what the effect of these improvements might have been. (Possible answers: easier to fight, greater protection, fit better on head)

BELTING UP

Ask students why the Romans might have used strips of weighted leather for the cingulum, instead of one large flap. (Possible answer: The strips were flexible, and they made it easier to march and sit.)

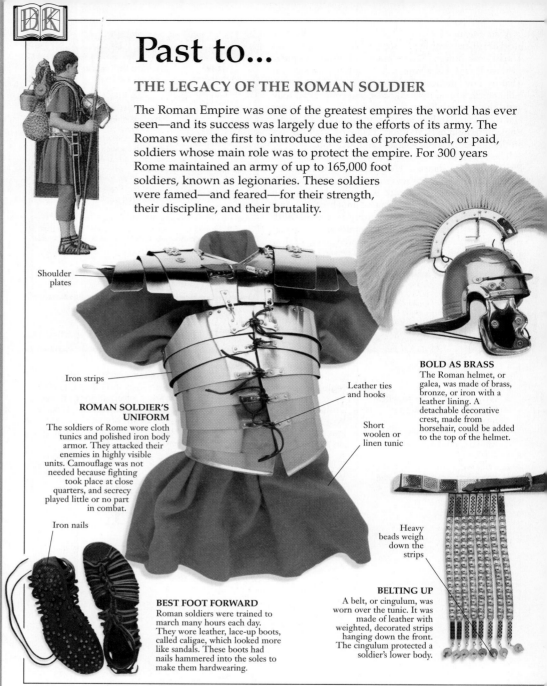

Past to...

THE LEGACY OF THE ROMAN SOLDIER

The Roman Empire was one of the greatest empires the world has ever seen—and its success was largely due to the efforts of its army. The Romans were the first to introduce the idea of professional, or paid, soldiers whose main role was to protect the empire. For 300 years Rome maintained an army of up to 165,000 foot soldiers, known as legionaries. These soldiers were famed—and feared—for their strength, their discipline, and their brutality.

Shoulder plates

Iron strips

ROMAN SOLDIER'S UNIFORM
The soldiers of Rome wore cloth tunics and polished iron body armor. They attacked their enemies in highly visible units. Camouflage was not needed because fighting took place at close quarters, and secrecy played little or no part in combat.

Iron nails

Leather ties and hooks

Short woolen or linen tunic

BOLD AS BRASS
The Roman helmet, or galea, was made of brass, bronze, or iron with a leather lining. A detachable decorative crest, made from horsehair, could be added to the top of the helmet.

Heavy beads weigh down the strips

BEST FOOT FORWARD
Roman soldiers were trained to march many hours each day. They wore leather, lace-up boots, called caligae, which looked more like sandals. These boots had nails hammered into the soles to make them hardwearing.

BELTING UP
A belt, or cingulum, was worn over the tunic. It was made of leather with weighted, decorated strips hanging down the front. The cingulum protected a soldier's lower body.

136 UNIT 2 ◆ The Growth of Empires and Governments

Teaching Options

Connection to LITERATURE

Students may be interested in reading Goscinny and Uderzo's *Asterix* books, a series of comic/cartoon novels about the conquest of Gaul. Written from the Gallic point of view, these novels poke fun mercilessly at the Roman army.

F Y I

The Life of a Roman Soldier

Roman soldiers enlisted for a period of 25 years, during which time they were not permitted to marry. Their life was hard, the food bad, the discipline harsh. So why did they sign up? Roman soldiers were paid very well and often received land at the end of their service. Those who were not already citizens also received citizenship as a reward for their service.

...Present

Today's foot soldiers, or infantry, travel in helicopters or personnel carriers and can be moved hundreds of miles in a day. Once on the ground, modern soldiers use long-range firearms instead of close-range stabbing weapons. This change has led to the use of camouflage in combat uniforms.

Water canteen

Mess tin

Turf cutter

Leather belt

ON THE MOVE
On reaching their destination, Roman soldiers pitched camp and often needed to build defenses. They carried backpacks containing essentials, such as food, tools, bedding, and cooking equipment. Each pack could weigh about 60 pounds.

Dagger, or pugio

Decorated scabbard

Short sword, or gladius

Heavy javelin, or pilum

WEAPONS OF WAR
Roman soldiers used mainly stabbing weapons, such as spears, swords, and arrows. A soldier's most important weapon was a short, sharp sword known as a gladius. In addition, soldiers used a pilum to pierce shields and body armor.

Helmet with cover

Flashlight

Hat

Desert boot

M16 Rifle

Rifle sling

Canteen

Personal equipment belt

Desert camouflage clothing

NOW YOU SEE US
Instead of hand-to-hand combat, today's soldiers face firearms from a distance of 200 feet or more. Camouflage clothing offers a degree of protection by making soldiers less visible to the enemy.

COMBAT CLOTHING
Bulletproof clothing, shown on the left, is made from many layers of artificial fabrics, such as Kevlar. A bullet flattens and slows as it hits the layers, causing bruising to the wearer rather than a wound.

CHAPTER 6 ◆ Ancient Rome 137

ON THE MOVE
The soldier's backpack contained personal items and a supply of rations for three days. Personal belongings included a clothes brush; shoe brush; soap; razor, shaving brush and shaving bowl; fork, knife, and spoon; and a cooking pot that doubled as a plate. Have students suggest why items that served dual purposes were welcome. (carrying fewer items made the backpack less heavy)

WEAPONS OF WAR
Unlike a regular spear, the long head of the pilum allowed the soldier to pierce the enemy's shield and armor. The iron shank of the pilum was made of softer iron, so that it bent on impact. The Romans did this to keep their enemies from reusing the weapons against the Romans themselves. The gladius is thought to have originated in Spain and was introduced in the First Punic War.

...Present

NOW YOU SEE US
Have students contrast the design of a modern soldier's uniform with that of the Romans. (The uniforms conform to the times. With the long-distance weapons of today, a camouflaged uniform is safer and more effective.)

COMBAT CLOTHING
Tell students that Kevlar® is up to five times stronger than steel. It is credited with saving hundreds of soldiers and law enforcement personnel from serious injury or death. There even is a Kevlar Survivors' Club, providing an opportunity for those individuals to share their stories. Have students explain why the chest is the most protected part of the body. (Soldiers who are hit in the chest are more likely to die than those who are hit in their arms, legs, or head.)

Connect Past to Present
Compare the illustration of the gladiator on page 136 with the photograph of the modern-day soldier on page 137. Ask students to list their similarities and differences. (**Similar:** headgear, supplies on belt or back, belt; **Different:** weapons, clothing—camouflaged today, colorful in Rome, shoes)

Hands-On Activity
As a class activity, have students write a letter to their local armed forces recruiting center and make arrangements to interview a representative. Have some students conduct the interview while others find out about further innovations in the technology of weapons and uniforms. Have both groups report to the class in a brief oral presentation.

III. The Empire Declines
(pp. 138–143)

Section Summary

In this section, students will learn about problems in Rome's government and social structure that weakened the empire. The Severan dynasty was followed by 50 years of turmoil. Diocletian and Constantine restored order for the next 50 years. Ultimately, the same problems surfaced, and Rome was overrun by invaders in the fifth century.

1 Introduce

Getting Started

Direct students' attention to the section title. Point out the slow downward trend implied by the word *decline*. Ask students what word would indicate a sharp decline. (Possible answers: fall, drop) Ask volunteers to use their hands to demonstrate the difference between these two meanings.

TERMS TO KNOW

Ask students to read the terms and definitions on page 138 and find each term in the section. Have students record the terms and their definitions on index cards. Then, have students work in pairs to write sentences on the back of the index card using each term in context.

You may wish to review the pronunciation of the following words with students.

Commodus (KAHM uh duhs)
Diocletian (dy uh KLEE shuhn)
Maximian (mak SIHM ee uhn)
Odoacer (oh doh AY suhr)

ACTIVE READING

Have students choose one subsection from Section 3 and list the reasons for the empire's decline that are described in that subsection. Have them evaluate the reasons and circle the one reason that they think is most responsible for the decline. Students should then write a paragraph explaining why they chose a specific reason.

Section III
The Empire Declines

Terms to Know

inflation a steep rise in prices, which has the effect of reducing people's purchasing power

province a territory

tetrarchy rule by four leaders

abdication voluntary resignation of a ruler

Main Ideas

A. From A.D. 180 to 235, economic problems in Rome increased and the military became more powerful.

B. Civil war and economic problems nearly caused the collapse of Rome during the mid-third century A.D.

C. In the late third and early fourth centuries, two leaders, Diocletian and Constantine the Great, reorganized the empire.

D. The division of the empire and foreign invasions finally toppled the western empire in A.D. 476.

📖 Active Reading

EVALUATE
When you evaluate, you weigh the importance of specific facts or evidence in order to make a judgment. As you read this section, evaluate the causes for Rome's decline and fall.

A. From Commodus to Severus Alexander

Starting with the reign of Marcus Aurelius's son Commodus, Rome suffered from a variety of economic, social, and political conflicts. These conflicts became worse during the next century, nearly causing the empire's collapse.

Leisure Time

Even during Rome's golden age, life was far from ideal for all the Roman citizens. There were sharp divisions between rich and poor. Unemployment was often high among the poor. Those without jobs depended on the emperor to provide free bread.

To make life a little easier for all the people of Rome, free entertainment was provided on a grand scale. Comedies and dramas were presented in theaters. Chariot races drew huge crowds to the Circus Maximus, a race track that could hold thousands of spectators. These crowds watched as teams of men, often slaves, raced chariots pulled by horses. The charioteer's tunic showed his team colors. Spectators cheered for their chosen team, calling out its color. The charioteer wore a helmet on his head, held a whip in his hand, and carried a dagger at his side to cut himself free if his chariot tipped over.

Perhaps the most popular form of entertainment was found at the Colosseum. The Colosseum's many tiers of marble seats could hold 45,000 people. Women could enjoy the spectacles from the top three tiers only, and slaves were only allowed to stand as they watched. In this huge arena, fierce battles were waged between wild animals and humans or between two gladiators. Gladiators were trained fighters, usually slaves or condemned criminals. These battles often ended in the death of one or both fighters.

Increasing Tensions

The reign of Emperor Commodus began a period of decline. First, Commodus was more interested in entertainment than in government. His special passion was fighting as a gladiator in the Colosseum. Identifying himself with the Greek hero Hercules, he ruled as a tyrant. When the government ran short of money, Commodus ordered the murder of rich citizens. The government then took over the wealth of these citizens.

Spotlight on *Culture*

GLADIATORS AND THE GAMES

The public shows held in arenas such as the Colosseum were among the most popular entertainments in ancient Rome.

Other games included bloody contests between men and animals and spectacular sea battles, for which the arena was flooded.

Teaching Options

Section 3 Resources

Teacher's Resources (TR)
Terms to Know, p. 19
Review History, p. 53
Build Your Skills, p. 87
Concept Builder, p. 222
Cause-and-Effect Chain, p. 325
Transparency 1

F Y I

Juvenal the Critic

The Roman satirist Juvenal (ca. 55–ca. 127) wrote a collection of poems, called *Satires*, about Roman life. The main theme of *Satires* is the corruption of life and human brutality. Juvenal used vivid description and strong rhythm to convey his points. In one poem he wrote about the Roman citizen: "Only two things does he anxiously wish for—bread and circuses."

In the Colosseum, gladiators fought bloody battles with animals and with each other. Some gladiators even developed a fan following, much like sports stars of today.

The Roman people saw hardships increase. The economy experienced severe **inflation**. Inflation is a steep rise in prices. When inflation occurs, people cannot buy as much with their money. In addition, Roman rulers became more and more brutal. The power of the army greatly increased, and the emperor relied more on the army as the senate grew weaker.

The Severan Dynasty

In A.D. 192, Commodus was assassinated, like so many Roman rulers before him. A period of civil war followed, and Septimius Severus, a strong general, seized power. During Septimius's reign, from A.D. 193–211, life in Rome was fairly stable.

Septimius's son, Caracalla, left his mark by building splendid baths. However, his most important political and economic decision was to give Roman citizenship to almost all free residents of the empire. Caracalla issued this edict, or official public decree, in A.D. 212.

In the final years of the Severan dynasty, Elagabalus and Severus Alexander served as rulers. Each became emperor at the age of 14, and each was weak.

◆ **What problems did the Romans face under Commodus?**

B. Fifty Years of Trouble

Starting in A.D. 235, the Roman Empire faced a number of problems. Over a period of 50 years, more than 20 emperors ruled, and ruled poorly. Only one or two of the rulers during this time died a natural death. The average length of time for a single ruler was about two years.

The Role of the Army

Severus Alexander was assassinated by his own troops because they thought his military policies were too weak. This murder set a pattern for the reigns of the emperors during the next 50 years. While the army took a leading role in making and breaking emperors, it also began to neglect one of its most important jobs. That job was to protect the empire's borders.

Connection to ECONOMICS

To help students understand the problem of inflation, use the following demonstration. Place ten coins on a table or draw them on the board. During Week 1, ten coins will buy five loaves of bread. In Week 2, ten coins will buy only four loaves of bread; in Week 3, three loaves, and so on. Have students explain what is happening to the value of the money.

Conflict Resolution

This period in Roman history could be considered a lesson in how *not* to resolve conflicts. Have students select an instance from page 138 or 139 in which violence settled a conflict. Then, have students "rewrite" history by writing a paragraph in which the people in conflict use an alternative method to solve the problem.

A. From Commodus to Severus Alexander

Purpose-Setting Question What evidence supports the statement that Rome was declining through the Severan dynasty? (Possible answers: high inflation, assassinations, and civil war)

SPOTLIGHT ON CULTURE
GLADIATORS AND THE GAMES
Discuss with students the unglamorous life of a gladiator. Then, have students discuss the characteristics of a culture that would stage this kind of entertainment.

Activity

Create an advertisement
Have students make a poster advertising the different forms of entertainment available to people in ancient Rome. Encourage them to use both words and images in their posters to convey their ideas.

TEACH PRIMARY SOURCES
Direct students' attention to the mosaic of the leopard and the gladiator. This detail is part of a scene in a circus. Ask students who will win this contest, and why. (Possible answer: the leopard, because of its greater strength)

◆ **ANSWER** Commodus was more interested in fighting as a gladiator than in governing the empire— inflation increased, the power of the army increased, and the senate grew weaker.

B. Fifty Years of Trouble

Purpose-Setting Question What led historians to label this period in Roman history as problematic? (economic misery, political chaos, more than 20 emperors in 50 years)

Explore Ask students to recall the predictions they made at the beginning of the chapter about what would happen to Rome. Discuss further evidence of Rome's decline. (invaders attacked Rome; Gaul split from Rome; population declined; trade, commerce, and industry declined) Ask students to now predict how long it would take for Rome to fall after the turmoil of these 50 years.

Discuss Review with students
Rome's various economic problems.
Help students understand that different parts of the economy are related
and problems in one area can cause
or intensify problems in other areas.

Activity

Write a letter Ask students to
write a letter from a Roman citizen
to a family member living far away,
describing the turmoil in Rome and
how it has affected family life.

◆ **ANSWER** The army made and
broke emperors.

C. Diocletian and Constantine

Purpose-Setting Question How
did Constantine try to stabilize the
Roman Empire? (He united the
eastern and western co-empires,
strengthened the armies, established new taxes, and founded
Constantinople, which became the
capital.)

Activity

Draw a diagram Have students
draw a diagram of a tetrarchy,
showing how this form of government worked. (Diagrams should
show an eastern and a western
emperor, with one chief assistant
below each.) Have students explain
the benefits of this type of organization. (Possible answer: With four
people, more could be accomplished and there was greater
oversight.)

Focus Discuss Diocletian's relin-
quishing power. Ask students why
this is remarkable. (Most Roman
leaders would not give up power
willingly.) Ask students what they
think this says about Diocletian's
personality. (He was confident; he
was concerned with the empire.)

Invaders from neighboring regions attacked Rome's borders. Gaul split from
the empire and formed a separate government in the third century A.D. The
Emperor Aurelian built a wall around the city of Rome—the first time that
such a defensive measure was needed since the days of Hannibal in the Second
Punic War. In the mid-200s A.D., Roman armies suffered damaging defeats at
the hands of the Goths in the lower Danube River region. In the east, Roman
armies had to defend against a newly powerful Persian Empire.

Economic Decline

The Roman economy during this period suffered from a number of severe
problems. As a result of war and disease, populations declined in cities.
Emperors took over many city treasuries to satisfy the army's demands for
higher pay. In addition, the emperors imposed high taxes to support the army
and government offices. This placed a heavy burden on Roman workers.

People in the countryside were at the mercy of invaders. Farm production
fell steeply. The value of money declined and the prices of goods and services
raced out of control. Inflation, or the sharp increase in prices, also caused a
significant drop in trade, commerce, and industry.

◆ **What was the role of the army during this period?**

C. Diocletian and Constantine

By the late third century, tensions and conflicts stretched the Roman Empire
to the breaking point. Many historians believe that Rome might have collapsed
altogether had it not been for the efforts of a strong reformer, Diocletian.

Diocletian

This coin shows Diocletian
wearing a laurel wreath
around his head.

Diocletian was a successful military leader from the **province**, or territory,
of Dalmatia. He seized power after another emperor was assassinated in
A.D. 284. He promptly set out to restore order to the empire.

Within a short time after becoming emperor, Diocletian made two key
decisions. These decisions would affect Roman history for the next 200
years. One of the decisions was to divide the leadership of the Roman
Empire. Diocletian shared his power with a co-emperor, Maximian. Several
years later, each co-emperor appointed a chief assistant, or deputy. In this
form of government, called a **tetrarchy**, responsibilities are divided among
four individuals.

Diocletian's second key decision was to split the empire in two—an
eastern half and a western half. Diocletian and his deputy took charge of the
more prosperous eastern empire. Maximian and his deputy ruled the
western empire.

Over the short term, the tetrarchy was a success. The men Diocletian had
chosen turned out to be capable officials and talented military commanders.
Under their leadership, Roman armies gained the provinces of England and
of Mauretania, in North Africa.

In addition to the formation of the tetrarchy and the division of the empire,
Diocletian made some other important changes. He doubled the size of the
army to about one-half million men. He organized provinces into smaller
units and improved the tax structure. Most importantly, he took steps to end
the economic decline of the empire. He tried to battle steadily rising prices
by fixing prices for goods and services.

Teaching Options

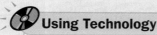

Using Technology

Have students use Internet sources, such
as an online encyclopedia, to obtain a
complete list of the Roman emperors and
their terms of office. If students have
trouble finding information, suggest they
type *Rome* and *emperor* into a search
engine. Then, have students use the
information to make a timeline of the
Roman emperors, beginning with
Octavian.

Diocletian also tried to improve his image. He used the title *dominus*, Latin for "lord" or "master." He surrounded himself with elaborate ceremonies. He wore purple robes decorated with gold and a crown adorned with jewels. Finally, in a remarkable act for a Roman leader, Diocletian and Maximian voluntary gave up their power in A.D. 305. They "retired."

Constantine the Great

Soon after the **abdication**, or voluntary resignation, of Diocletian and Maximian, the divided rule created by Diocletian broke down. Civil war broke out again. The new co-emperors of the empire, one of whom was Constantine, found themselves in a bitter battle for sole control of the empire. The final victor was Constantine. As sole emperor from A.D. 324–337, Constantine proved himself to be a capable ruler and brilliant military leader.

In the midst of a crucial battle during the civil war, Constantine had a vision. In this vision, a cross, the symbol of Christianity, appeared above the sun. On the cross was the motto "In this sign you will conquer." Constantine's victory in that battle led him to favor Christianity. The following year, A.D. 313, he issued the Edict of Milan, which granted the freedom to worship to all citizens of his empire. At the end of his life, Constantine converted to Christianity and became the first Christian emperor of the Roman Empire.

During his reign as emperor, Constantine reunited the eastern and western co-empires under his personal control. He strengthened the army and set up a new system of taxes. His most notable achievement was the founding of the city of Constantinople. Built on the site of the ancient city of Byzantium, Constantinople became the capital. This made the eastern part of the empire the seat of power. Today, Constantinople is the Turkish city of Istanbul, and is still located at the crossroads of Europe and Asia.

◆ **What sweeping changes did Diocletian make in the government of the Roman Empire?**

Constantine I founded the city of Constantinople and became the Roman Empire's first Christian emperor.

Ask students to identify the groups that invaded Italy. (Vandals, Visigoths, Ostrogoths, and Huns) Have students find Constantinople on the map. In contrast to Rome, how many groups invaded Constantinople? (none) Ask students to suggest a reason for this contrast. (Possible answer: Constantinople was easier to defend from a land attack.)

 Map Check

Answers

1. The Black Sea is north and the Mediterranean Sea is south.

2. south or southeast

D. The Fall of the Western Empire

Purpose-Setting Question Why did the western empire fall? (invasions on the frontiers; poor leadership; continuing economic problems)

ANALYZE PRIMARY SOURCES

DOCUMENT-BASED QUESTION

Review with students some of the problems the Roman Empire faced during the third century. These problems included poverty, inflation, bad leaders, and invasions.

ANSWER Possible answer: He felt that Rome had been good but was failing because of its problems.

Discuss Ask students why the Roman Empire was finding invaders more of a threat as the number of internal problems increased. Help students conclude that as the number of internal problems increased, leaders had less time and energy to deal with problems at the edges of the empire. Also, soldiers were needed closer to Rome to help maintain order. Explain to students that as attacks became more successful, the number of attacks increased.

Activity

Stage a debate Have students brainstorm about what might have saved Rome or about whether or not the fall of the Roman Empire was inevitable. Have groups of students support one or the other of these positions in a debate. Have them use evidence from the text to support their position.

T142 ◆ **UNIT 2**

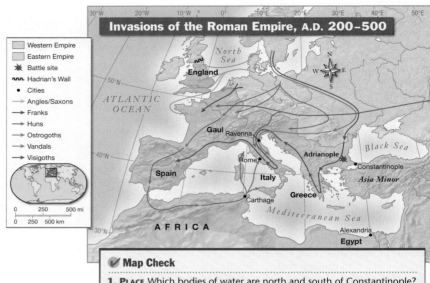

Invasions of the Roman Empire, A.D. 200–500

Legend:
- Western Empire
- Eastern Empire
- ✳ Battle site
- ⌁ Hadrian's Wall
- • Cities
- → Angles/Saxons
- → Franks
- → Huns
- → Ostrogoths
- → Vandals
- → Visigoths

0   250   500 mi
0   250   500 km

✔ Map Check

1. PLACE Which bodies of water are north and south of Constantinople?

2. MOVEMENT In which general direction did the Visigoths travel to reach Adrianople?

ANALYZE PRIMARY SOURCES

DOCUMENT-BASED QUESTION How would you describe the speaker's feelings about the decline of Rome?

D. The Fall of the Western Empire

After the death of Constantine, the empire gradually fell apart because of the same problems and conflicts that had nearly destroyed it in the third century. One Roman wondered,

❝ Who would believe . . . that Rome, built upon the conquest of the whole world, would itself fall to the ground? ❞

Living on Borrowed Time

Emperors who followed after Constantine generally continued the east-west division of the empire that Diocletian began in the late third century A.D. As the fourth century drew to a close, problems on the empire's borders became more severe. For centuries, the Romans had faced attacks from Germanic tribes that lived along their northern borders. Most of the battles were small and not well organized. Attacks of this type were not a real threat to the empire when it was strong. However, now the empire had problems within its own government, and it was weaker than it had been in the past. The Germanic tribes, such as the Visigoths and the Vandals, began to have success when they attacked Roman troops.

A successful general named Theodosius I became ruler of the eastern empire in A.D. 379. Shortly before his death in A.D. 395, he reunited the east and the west. Theodosius became the last Roman emperor to rule over the entire empire.

After the death of Theodosius, the empire was once again divided. However, cooperation between the two empires swiftly fell apart. The eastern empire was the stronger of the two, and its emperors used their

Teaching Options

Meet Individual Needs:
KINESTHETIC LEARNERS

Write the name of each group of foreign invaders on a piece of paper. Write the names of Rome, Constantinople, Gaul, Spain, and England on five more pieces of paper. Assign students to represent each of these groups and locations. Have the foreign invaders come out of the "north" and invade the Roman Empire, bypassing Constantinople.

ESL/ELL STRATEGIES

Identify Essential Vocabulary Write the following terms on the board: *plundered* (p. 142); *surrender* (p. 143). Ask students to work in pairs to explain each term, using a dictionary if necessary. (To *plunder* means to "ravage." To *surrender* means to "give up.")

political and economic strength to discourage foreign invasion of their region. The western empire, however, was not as fortunate.

Foreign Invasions and the Collapse of the West

In A.D. 410, the Visigoths, under their leader Alaric, attacked Rome, overcoming its defenses and plundering it. For the first time in eight centuries, Rome fell to a foreign invader.

From this time onward, more and more successful invasions of its borders marked the end of the Roman Empire in the west. In A.D. 429, the Vandals invaded North Africa. Within ten years, all of North Africa, including Carthage, had fallen. The Vandals then turned their attention to Italy. They crossed the Mediterranean and occupied Rome in A.D. 455. At about the same time, tribes of Angles and Saxons from the north attacked and conquered the Roman province of England.

The final collapse of the western empire occurred in A.D. 476, when the Ostrogoth leader Odoacer forced the emperor of Rome to surrender. At this point, Roman rule no longer existed in Europe and the western part of the Mediterranean Sea. Later historians would refer to this surrender of the Roman emperor as the "fall" of Rome.

◆ Who were the first people to successfully invade Rome?

Reasons for the Fall of Rome

POLITICAL CAUSES	• Harsh government • Corrupt officials • Divided empires in the east and west • Internal political struggles
ECONOMIC CAUSES	• Heavy taxes • Decline of population • Decline of empire's wealth
MILITARY CAUSES	• Foreign invasions • Weak border protection
SOCIAL CAUSES	• Self-interested upper class • Loss of traditional values • Lack of patriotism

✔ **Chart Check**

How was the fall of the Roman Empire linked to economic problems within the empire?

Review III

Review History
A. What were the most popular forms of entertainment during Rome's golden age?
B. What was the most common reason for a change in leadership during much of the third century A.D.?
C. What new city was founded by Constantine the Great?
D. What was Theodosius's major achievement during his reign as emperor?

Define Terms to Know
Define the following terms:
inflation, province, tetrarchy, abdication

Critical Thinking
What do you think was the most important cause for the decline and fall of the Roman Empire?

Write About Culture
Suppose you are a resident of Rome during Diocletian's early days as emperor. Write a journal entry describing the changes in government that took place.

Get Organized
CAUSE-AND-EFFECT CHAIN
Use a cause-and-effect chain to organize information from this section. Choose a topic or an event, such as the failure of the Roman army to protect its borders. Then, give a cause and an effect of this topic or event.

Reasons for the Fall of Rome

Ask students to identify the categories of causes listed in the chart. (political, economic, military, social) Have students examine the subsection "The Severan Dynasty" on page 139 and identify reasons in the chart that are discussed in the subsection. (political causes: corrupt officials, internal political struggle)

✔ **Chart Check**

Answer The fall of the Roman Empire was due, in part, to heavy taxes, a decline in the population and the number of people paying taxes, and a general decline of the empire's wealth.

Review Have students look back in Chapter 5 to the collapse of the Greek civilization. Discuss ways in which the falls of both civilizations were similar. (As Alexander had defeated the Greek city-states, the foreign invaders overran Rome.)

◆ **ANSWER** The first people to successfully invade Rome were the Visigoths.

Section Close

Review with students the different problems (political, economic, and military) that faced the Roman Empire after A.D. 180. Discuss how these problems contributed to the fall of the Roman Empire. Ask students to summarize the contributions of Roman civilization to the world today.

3 Assess

Review Answers

Review History
A. Chariot races and watching gladiators fight were the most popular forms of entertainment.
B. assassination of the emperor
C. Constantinople, located at the crossroads of Europe and Asia; present-day Istanbul in Turkey
D. Theodosius reunited the eastern and western empires; he was the last emperor to rule over the entire empire.

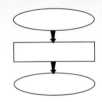

CAUSE
Roman army made and broke emperors.

EVENT
Roman army failed to protect its borders.

EFFECT
Invaders attacked frontiers.

Define Terms to Know
inflation, 138; province, 140; tetrarchy, 140; abdication, 140

Critical Thinking
Possible answers: economic hardship, poor leadership, foreign invasions, the disintegration of military discipline

Write About Culture
Students' journals should describe the dividing of the empire into east and west, having co-emperors, and the establishing of a tetrarchy.

IV. The Development of Christianity

(pp. 144–147)

Section Summary

In this section, students will learn about the political background of the Roman province of Judaea, against which the origins of Christianity are set. Students will learn about Jesus' teachings and crucifixion, and the subsequent rise of the Christian faith. They will read about the spread of Christianity throughout the Roman Empire and about early disputes in Christianity.

Getting Started

Ask students to discuss how different cultures can react when they are forced together. Encourage students to think about the different ways some cultures have interacted, including one culture absorbing another one, cultures merging, existing together, or clashing. Discuss with students the tensions that might arise and ways cultures can work together to ease the tension.

TERMS TO KNOW

Ask students to read the terms and definitions on page 144. Have them find each term in the section, skim the surrounding paragraph, and then record the meaning of the term in their own words. Ask students to explain the meaning of each term to a partner.

You may wish to review the pronunciation of the following terms with students.

Pontius Pilate (PUHN chuhs PY luht)
apostle (uh PAHS uhl)
Eucharist (YOO kuh rihst)

ACTIVE READING

When students come across a section that describes differing points of view, have them make a two-column chart (TR, p. 328), listing the parties involved and the differing points of view of each party.

The Development of Christianity

Terms to Know

persecution harsh treatment for following a set of religious beliefs

bishop a high-ranking Christian Church official

hierarchy a system or organization that is based on graded ranks

heresy a religious belief opposed to official teachings

missionary a person sent by religious authorities to spread a set of religious beliefs

Main Ideas

A. The Christian religion began with the teachings of Jesus, a Jew who lived during the early Roman Empire in the province of Judaea.

B. Despite persecutions by the state, Christianity grew rapidly from A.D. 100 to 300.

C. The conversion of Constantine and the edict of Theodosius I, as well as the efforts of clergy and of missionaries, laid the basis for Christianity as a world religion.

 Active Reading

POINTS OF VIEW
People often have different points of view. As you read this section, think about the viewpoints of the people and groups described. Ask yourself: What explains each point of view?

A. Jesus and the First Christians

By 100 B.C. Rome's empire stretched far beyond the city of Rome itself. A land known as Judaea, about 1,400 miles away at the eastern end of the Mediterranean Sea, came under Roman control in 63 B.C. Judaea became known as the birthplace of Jesus and the Christian religion—a religion that was to cause the empire's leaders great concern.

Judaea in Roman Times

As in many ancient cultures, the Roman people worshiped many gods and goddesses. The people believed that their gods could harm the empire if they were not respected. This belief was so strong that Roman law called for punishment of those who did not pay the gods proper respect.

However, Roman control over religion was not always strictly enforced. People living in distant regions of Rome's vast empire often had cultures and religious beliefs that were different from those of Romans. As long as people throughout the empire showed loyalty by honoring the Roman gods, they were allowed to worship as they pleased. Judaea, for example, was home to a large population of Jewish people who followed their own religious laws and leaders. Citizens of Judaea were allowed to worship as they pleased as long as there was no conflict with the policies of Rome.

Herod the Great ruled Judaea at the time that a child named Jesus was born in Bethlehem, a town in Judaea. Herod was skillful in balancing the interests of Rome and those of the Jewish population in Judaea. However, after Herod's death around 4 B.C., his successors had to deal with rebellions of Judaeans who had become angry about Roman interference in their daily lives.

In A.D. 6, the status of Judaea changed. It became a province of the Roman Empire. The Roman government sent new officials to govern the region. They were to make sure that Rome's laws were strictly obeyed.

The Life and Teachings of Jesus

While Judaea had become a Roman province, Judaeans still practiced their religion and listened to the preaching of religious teachers. One of these teachers was Jesus of Bethlehem, who had been born during Herod's rule. Like other Jewish teachers, Jesus taught belief in one God and in the Ten Commandments. Jesus was a popular teacher who attracted many disciples,

144 UNIT 2 ◆ The Growth of Empires and Governments

Teaching Options

Section 4 Resources

Teacher's Resources (TR)
Terms to Know, p. 19
Review History, p. 53
Build Your Skills, p. 87
Chapter Test, pp. 127–128
Concept Builder, p. 222
Cause-and-Effect Chain, p. 325

ESL/ELL STRATEGIES

Identify Essential Vocabulary Knowing word origins can help students who are unfamiliar with Christian theology. Tell students that *church* comes from the Greek *kyros*, meaning "power." *Messiah* comes from the Hebrew *meshiach* and means "anointed." *Priest* comes from the Greek *presbyteros* and means "elder." Have students find other words they do not know and look up the derivations in a dictionary.

or followers. However, he did not strictly follow Jewish law. According to his followers, Jesus called himself the Son of God and declared himself to be the messiah, or savior sent by God. As a result, Jesus had many enemies among Jewish leaders.

Around A.D. 30, the Roman governor, Pontius Pilate, found Jesus guilty of criminal actions. Pilate sentenced Jesus to be executed by crucifixion, the traditional Roman punishment for criminals. In a crucifixion, a person was nailed to a cross and left to die. The followers of Jesus believe that he rose from the dead three days after his crucifixion and commanded them to spread his teachings.

The First Christians

Before his death, Jesus had chosen 12 apostles, or main followers, to help him in his mission of teaching. Following Jesus' death, the apostles and other disciples spread Jesus' message. They spread the teachings of Jesus first throughout Judaea, then to other parts of the Roman Empire in which Greek was the common language.

Slowly, some people began to accept the idea that Jesus was the messiah, which in Greek is the word *christos*. Jesus came to be known as Jesus Christ. His growing number of followers became known as Christians, and their religion as Christianity.

Early Christians met in private houses scattered throughout Greek and Roman regions, where they shared their common faith. Christians believed in renouncing evil through baptism, a ritual in which their sins were forgiven by God. In addition, Christians assembled each Sunday to give thanks to God by celebrating the sacred meal of the Eucharist. This sacred meal symbolized Jesus and his last supper with the apostles before being crucified.

◆ What beliefs and practices did early Christians share?

B. The Christian Church and the Spread of Christianity

Gradually, the scattered communities of Christians who had worshiped in private houses began to organize themselves into a structured Christian Church. While the Church organization helped to expand the religion, Christians faced **persecution**, or harsh treatment for following their religious beliefs.

The Early Christian Church

Each Christian community was led by a priest. Since only men were allowed to become members of the clergy, all priests were male. The Christian religion was open to women as well as men—a factor that set it apart from many other religions. However, women played a different role in the religion, serving as teachers and officials.

In the early second century, it was recommended that each city have its own **bishop**, or Church official, who would be responsible for all Christians in an area. Cities of the Roman Empire such as Rome, Antioch, Alexandria, Jerusalem, and Constantinople, all had their own bishops. Over the course of time, the authority of the bishops grew. The bishops were given the title of patriarch, or highest Church official in a city. With the establishment of patriarchs, bishops, and priests, the Christian Church developed a **hierarchy**, a system of organization that is based on rank.

The anchor and fish images seen here in this stone engraving were common in early Christian art.

A. Jesus and the First Christians

Purpose-Setting Question How did Rome gain more control of Judaea when it became a province of the empire? (Rome sent new officials and could now govern the region and make sure that Rome's laws were strictly obeyed.)

Focus Ask students why the Roman government might allow people to worship as they pleased as long as they respected the Roman gods. Ask students to suggest a relationship between the size of the empire and the degree of control over its conquests. (The larger the empire, the harder it would be to exert control. So, to be less controlling made it possible for Rome to have a huge empire.)

Activity

Sequence events Ask students to place the following events in correct sequence: crucifixion; Christians celebrated the Eucharist; apostles helped Jesus teach; Jesus called himself the Messiah; and apostles spread Jesus' teachings. (Jesus called himself the Messiah; apostles helped Jesus teach; crucifixion; apostles spread Jesus' teachings; Christians celebrated the Eucharist)

◆ **ANSWER** Ten Commandments, belief in Jesus as son of God, baptism, and the Eucharist

B. The Christian Church and the Spread of Christianity

Purpose-Setting Question How did communities of Christians begin to organize themselves? (Scattered communities that had worshiped in private houses organized themselves into a Christian Church, which helped spread the religion but also brought about persecution.)

Extend Ask students to speculate on why the Christian faith gained popularity so quickly. (Possible answers: It dealt with a more spiritual side of human nature; people were tired of corruption.)

Cooperative Learning

Have students work in small groups to write a newspaper article about the life of Jesus. Have them assign a specific role to each member of the group. One member may devise interviews for the article, one may create a picture to accompany the article, one may be the writer, one, the proofreader, and so on. Have the groups "publish" their articles on a class bulletin board or class newspaper.

Test Taking

Give students a quiz on subsections A and B that has five short-answer questions. Remind students to read the directions carefully to see if their answer should be a word, phrase, or sentence. Provide a sample question, such as the following: In a complete sentence, explain why being a province of Rome did not benefit Judaea.

The Spread of Christianity to A.D. 476

Have students identify the areas where Christianity spread by A.D. 325. (areas around cities of Carthage, Rome, Thessalonica, Constantinople, Ephesus, Antioch, Jerusalem, and Alexandria, and other coastal and inland areas) Then, have them identify the general area in which Christianity had spread by A.D. 476. (most of the Roman Empire, such as Gaul, Spain, Italy, Syria, Egypt, and Greece; and sometimes beyond its borders)

✅ Map Check

Answers

1. west
2. Egypt—south of 30°N Latitude

Discuss Ask students why they think the Romans saw Christianity as a threat. (might cause civil disorder, went against official religion, it was growing and spreading) Remind students that many people view change as frightening, and that Christianity represented change for many people.

◆ **ANSWER** Possible answer: It was hurtful but also resulted in Christians becoming martyrs.

C. The Basis for a World Religion

Purpose-Setting Question
What allowed for the spread of Christianity? (The Edict of Milan allowed Theodosius I to make Christianity the religion of the Roman Empire.)

Do You Remember?
Review with students the event on page 141 that led to Constantine's conversion. Discuss with students what they think might have happened if Constantine had not won.

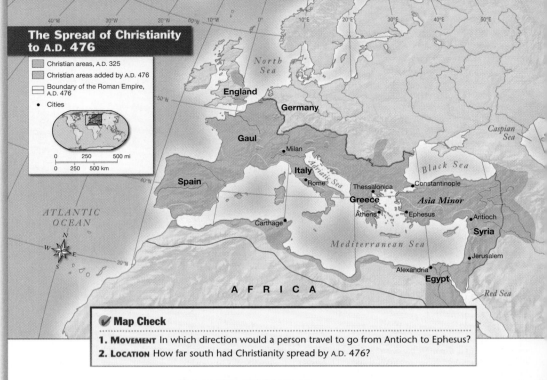

The Spread of Christianity to A.D. 476

- ☐ Christian areas, A.D. 325
- ☐ Christian areas added by A.D. 476
- ☐ Boundary of the Roman Empire, A.D. 476
- • Cities

✅ Map Check

1. **MOVEMENT** In which direction would a person travel to go from Antioch to Ephesus?
2. **LOCATION** How far south had Christianity spread by A.D. 476?

Persecution and Response

The spread of Christianity caused great concern for Roman leaders. In their view, the new religion seemed likely to spark civil disorder. Although Christians claimed there was no conflict between Christian faith and Roman citizenship, the Romans were not so sure. For one thing, the Christian belief in one God seemed to go against the official state religion of Rome, which supported belief in many different gods.

As a result of this uncertainty, more and more Christians were persecuted for following their religious beliefs. At first, Roman leaders thought that by persecuting Christians, they would ensure the loyalty of the rest of the empire's citizens. This loyalty would help unite the empire and make it stronger. However, persecution did not stop Christianity. In fact, many Christians showed the strength of their faith by becoming martyrs—people who are willing to suffer and die for their beliefs.

◆ **How did Roman persecution affect Christians?**

C. The Basis for a World Religion

When the Emperor Constantine the Great signed the Edict of Milan in A.D. 313, toleration was granted to all religions of the empire, including Christianity. In A.D. 380, the Emperor Theodosius I made Christianity the official religion of the Roman Empire.

Do You Remember?
In Section III, you learned that Constantine became the first Christian emperor of Rome.

Teaching Options

Research

AVERAGE

Have students conduct research to find out more about the four apostles who are credited with writing the Gospels—Matthew, Mark, Luke, and John. Have them write a short report about one of these men, including in their report the origin of the word *gospel*.

CHALLENGE

Have students conduct research on the Internet or in the library using a variety of reference materials and special-purpose maps to learn about the spread of Christianity after A.D. 476. Then, have students create two maps that show how Christianity spread by A.D. 1000 and again by A.D. 1500. Have them refer to Transparency 15 to view the extent of Christianity today.

Disputes and Divisions

Early Christians became involved in a number of disputes. One source of conflict was **heresies**, or beliefs that are contrary to the official teachings of a religion. To end such disputes, Church leaders met to decide what official Christian teachings should include.

Another source of conflict was the rivalry that arose among Church bishops. In the western part of the empire, the bishops of Rome claimed leadership of the Church as a whole. However, the bishops in the east believed that they should share in the leadership of the Church. In the end, the bishop of Rome became the pope, or leader of the Roman Catholic Church.

Spreading the Word

Christian writings played an important role in the growth of the religion. Letters by the apostles and disciples were saved and shared with later Christians. Other Christian writings include the Gospels, which describe Jesus' life and teachings. The Gospels of Matthew, Mark, Luke, and John make up part of the New Testament of the Christian Bible. The Old Testament contains the books of the Hebrew Scriptures.

With its growing organization and powerful writings, the Church continued to expand. One way to do this was to send out **missionaries**, or people who were sent out to spread the word of Christianity. Paul, an early Christian leader, traveled from city to city to spread the Christian religion. His missionary work set Christianity on the road to becoming a world religion.

How did the Roman Catholic Church expand?

Review IV

Review History
A. What important role did Pontius Pilate play in the history of Christianity?
B. What Christian belief was most difficult for Romans to accept?
C. How was the Edict of Milan beneficial to Christians?

Define Terms to Know
Define the following terms:
persecution, bishop, hierarchy, heresy, missionary

Critical Thinking
Why do you think Christianity survived despite persecution by the Roman authorities?

Write About Government
Conduct research about the rule of Herod the Great. Then, write a brief research paper explaining how Herod was able to balance the interests of Rome with those of Jewish people in Judaea.

Get Organized
CAUSE-AND-EFFECT CHAIN
Use a cause-and-effect chain to organize information from this section. Choose a topic or an event, such as Judaea's change to a province in the Roman Empire. Then, give a cause and effect of this topic.

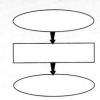

Explore Ask students to identify two ways that early Christian leaders resolved conflicts in the development of the Christian Church. (met to decide official teachings; bishop of Rome became leader of the Roman Catholic Church) Tell students that the Christian leaders of the eastern part of the region established a separate church—Eastern Orthodox Church—and that they will learn about this in the next chapter. Encourage students to discuss the different approaches that the early Christian leaders used to resolve conflicts.

Focus Point out to students that missionaries were very important to the spread of Christianity. These missionaries went to all areas of the Roman Empire telling people about Christianity. Contacting so many areas helped Christianity become a world religion.

ANSWER The Roman Catholic Church expanded by developing writings to describe Jesus' life and teachings and sending missionaries.

Section Close

Ask students to summarize in one sentence the development of Christianity through the sixth century. (Possible answer: Christianity grew from the teachings of one man, Jesus, into an influential world religion.)

3 Assess

Review Answers
Review History
A. Pontius Pilate sentenced Jesus to death by crucifixion; thus crucifixion became central to Christianity.
B. the belief in one god
C. The Edict of Milan allowed Christians to practice their religion and eventually led to Christianity becoming the official religion of the Roman Empire.

Define Terms to Know
persecution, 145; bishop, 145; hierarchy, 145; heresy, 147; missionary, 147

Critical Thinking
Answers will vary. Students may point out that Christianity offered believers a more satisfying creed than that of the Roman state religion.

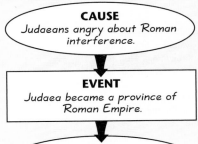

CAUSE
Judaeans angry about Roman interference.

EVENT
Judaea became a province of Roman Empire.

EFFECT
Roman laws had to be strictly obeyed.

Write About Government
Students' research papers should include information about the reign of Herod, including his policies, strengths, weaknesses, and skills at compromise and diplomacy.

Chapter Summary

A blank outline form is available in the Teacher's Resources (p. 318). Chapter summaries should outline early Rome and the republic, the movement from republic to empire, how the empire declined, and the development of Christianity. Refer to the rubric in the Teacher's Resources (p. 340) to score students' chapter summaries.

Interpret the Timeline

1. the founding of the Roman republic
2. 175 years (202 B.C.–27 B.C.)
3. the Edict of Milan (A.D. 313)
4. Check that all entries on students' timelines are from the chapter.

Use Terms to Know

5. inflation
6. triumvirate
7. republic
8. abdication
9. veto
10. heresy
11. magistrate

Check Your Understanding

12. It is cooler in the northern part of Italy; the southern tip of Italy is semitropical and well suited to agriculture.
13. The Etruscans and the Greeks influenced the early Romans.
14. Under the monarchy, the kings had the greatest role in government, and it was possible for a ruler such as Tarquin the Proud to become a despot. Under the republic, a system of checks and balances, as well as the separation of powers, prevented any one individual from gaining excessive power.
15. The paterfamilias, or oldest male, made all the important family decisions and led the family at religious ceremonies.
16. Marius's election as consul gave the army more power. His re-election eventually gave Marius more power. His support of the army resulted in the army being more loyal to the military leaders than the government.
17. By accepting his designation of dictator for life, Caesar gave supreme power to himself, thereby ending the republican system of government.

18. Nerva, Trajan, Hadrian, Antoninus Pius, and Marcus Aurelius
19. The army made and broke emperors, at the rate of one every two years or so.
20. Diocletian effected some important reforms. He split the Roman Empire into eastern and western halves, and he instituted the rule of a tetrarchy. He also doubled the size of the army, reformed the tax system, and attempted to fight inflation with a system of price controls.
21. Their attack in A.D. 410 resulted in Rome's first defeat in eight centuries.
22. Theodosius I proclaimed Christianity as the only official religion of Rome.

Chapter Summary

Complete the following outline in your notebook. Then, use your outline to write a brief summary of the chapter.

Ancient Rome

I. Early Rome and the Republic
   A. The Geography of Italy
   B. The Early Romans
   C. Establishing a Republic
   D. Expanding Roman Control
II. From Republic to Empire
   A. The End of the Republic
   B. Augustus and Rome's Golden Age
   C. The Early Empire
III. The Empire Declines
   A. From Commodus to Severus Alexander
   B. Fifty Years of Trouble
   C. Diocletian and Constantine
   D. The Fall of the Western Empire
IV. The Development of Christianity
   A. Jesus and the First Christians
   B. The Christian Church and the Spread of Christianity
   C. The Basis for a World Religion

Interpret the Timeline

Use the timeline on pages 124–125 to answer the following questions.

1. Which occurred first, the assassination of Julius Caesar or the founding of the Roman republic?

2. How many years after Rome defeated Carthage in the Second Punic War did Octavian become the first Roman emperor?

3. **Critical Thinking** Which event relates to the development of Christianity?

4. Select five events from the chapter that are not on the timeline. Create a timeline that shows these events.

Use Terms to Know

Select the term that best completes each sentence.

abdication   magistrate   triumvirate
heresy   republic   veto
inflation

5. A steep increase in prices that affects people's purchasing power is called _____.
6. A group of three leaders is a _____.
7. When voters elect people to represent them, the government is a _____.
8. Voluntary resignation of a ruler is called _____.
9. A _____ was used to stop the passage of a law.
10. Early Christians were sometimes divided because of _____.
11. A consul was the most important _____ of the Roman republic.

Check Your Understanding

12. **Compare** Italy's climate in the north with that in the south.
13. **Identify** two groups of people who had an important influence on the early Romans.
14. **Contrast** the systems of government under the Roman monarchy and the republic.
15. **Describe** the role of the paterfamilias in ancient Rome.
16. **Discuss** the significance of having Marius elected consul.
17. **Explain** how Julius Caesar changed the course of Roman history.
18. **Identify** the five "good" emperors.
19. **Summarize** the role of the army in the mid-third century A.D.
20. **Discuss** the achievements of Diocletian.
21. **Explain** why the successful invasion by the Visigoths was significant.
22. **Identify** the significance of Theodosius I in the development of Christianity.

Critical Thinking

23. Analyze Information What features of the Roman republican constitution were most important to the strength of the republic?

24. Make Inferences Why was Julius Caesar assassinated in 44 B.C.?

25. Analyze Primary Sources Do you agree with the poet Virgil's views on ways in which Rome would excel, as quoted on page 124? Why or why not?

26. Evaluate What qualities made Augustus a good statesman? Briefly explain your answer.

Put Your Skills to Work

27. Read a Special-Purpose Map You have learned how to read a special-purpose map. This type of map focuses on a specific topic or series of events.

Study the special-purpose map below, which details Roman trade routes around A.D. 200. Then, use the map to answer the following questions.

a. Which cities are located along trade routes?

b. What items did Spain trade with Rome?

c. From where did Rome receive wool?

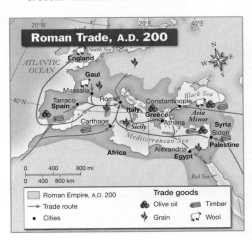

Roman Trade, A.D. 200

Analyze Sources

28. Read the passage below in which the historian Frank C. Bourne evaluates Julius Caesar in his book, *A History of the Romans*. Then, answer the questions that follow.

Julius Caesar was perhaps Rome's greatest mind; certainly he was its most versatile [adaptable]. He stood so far above his contemporaries [peers] in so many fields that it is hard to imagine how there could be a true partnership between him and them. He was a writer of clear, direct prose . . . ; he was greatly admired as an orator . . . ; and his talents were equally distinguished whether he took the role of a political thinker, organizer, administrator, [or] general. . . .

a. For what qualities does the writer praise Julius Caesar?

b. Do you agree with Bourne when he says, "it is hard to imagine how there could be a true partnership" between Caesar and his contemporaries? Why or why not?

Essay Writing

29. Write a brief essay in which you name the five "good" emperors and describe some accomplishments of each emperor.

TEST PREPARATION

RECOGNIZE FACT AND OPINION
Choose the correct answer to the question.

Which statement about the Roman Empire is a fact rather than an opinion?

1. Overall, Diocletian's division of the empire proved to be successful.

2. The Edict of Caracalla, issued in A.D. 212, gave almost all free residents of the empire Roman citizenship.

3. Economic problems were the major cause of the empire's decline and fall.

4. The invasion of the Visigoths eventually led to the end of 800 years of Roman rule.

CHAPTER 6 ◆ Ancient Rome **149**

Critical Thinking

23. Possible answer: checks and balances and the separation of powers
24. His enemies believed that Caesar was ambitious for supreme power, and other leaders feared his ambitions and power.
25. Possible answers: Yes, because the Romans proved themselves capable of gaining control of diverse regions and then governing them for a long time. No, because the Romans could not, in the end, resolve their own internal economic and political problems.
26. Students' answers should include that Augustus was concerned about Rome's citizens and their daily lives, and that he wanted to restore the values and traditions that had made Rome great.

Put Your Skills to Work

READ A SPECIAL-PURPOSE MAP
27a. Sidon, Alexandria, Constantinople, Athens, Rome, Carthage, Tarraco, and Massalia
27b. olive oil and timber
27c. England, Gaul, and Asia Minor

Analyze Sources

28a. versatility, his mind, his writing ability, his ability as an orator, and his ability as a political thinker, organizer, administrator, and general
28b. Possible answers: Yes, because Caesar's contemporaries inevitably envied his distinction and distrusted his ambitions. Caesar also felt superior. No, because other great leaders, such as Augustus, found ways to cooperate productively with their contemporaries.

Essay Writing

29. Students' essays should contain details about each of the five "good" emperors. **Nerva**: land law reform, tax revision; **Trajan**: conquered lands, building program, lowered taxes, worked with senate; **Hadrian**: built defensive wall, codified law, building program; **Antonius Pius**: centralized government, promoted art and science; **Marcus Aurelius**: wrote *Meditations*, economic unification of empire, fought invaders

TEST PREPARATION

Answer 2. The Edict of Caracalla, issued in A.D. 212, gave almost all free residents of the empire Roman citizenship.

CHAPTER 7
Overview

The Byzantine Empire, Russia, and Eastern Europe

330–1598
(pp. 150–169)

Chapter Objectives

• Identify the legacy of the Byzantine Empire and list the events that led to its decline.
• Describe the factors that contributed to the settlement and growth of Russia.
• Summarize the movement of the nomadic tribes that settled in Serbia, Bulgaria, Poland, and Hungary. Explain the influence they had on the region.

Chapter Summary

Section I relates the founding, the growth, and the decline of the Byzantine Empire, including some of its most important leaders.
Section II explores the influence of Byzantium on Russia as it was settled and grew.
Section III highlights the eastern European nations of Bulgaria, Serbia, Poland, and Hungary as they were settled, were governed, and grew in power.

Set the Stage

TEACH PRIMARY SOURCES
Point out to students that during the reign of Ivan the Great, many European travelers visited the city of Moscow in Russia. They left descriptions such as this one by Filofei. Explain that these descriptions help us understand the customs of the people, the power of the rulers, and the growth of both Moscow and of Russia. Ask students what Filofei means when he calls Moscow "the new Third Rome." (It is equal in greatness to Rome and Constantinople.) What evidence does he give for his opinion? (The Church shines brighter there than in any other place.)

The Byzantine Empire, Russia, and Eastern Europe
330–1598

I. The Byzantine Empire
II. The Rise of Russia
III. The Growth of Eastern European Culture

After the fall of the Roman Empire in the West, the Roman Empire in the East, founded by Constantine in 330, lasted another 1,000 years. This empire became known as the Byzantine Empire, and its capital, Constantinople, was called the "second Rome." However, just as Rome had fallen, Constantinople fell in 1453. Constantinople's fall was seen as an opportunity in Russia, where Byzantine culture had greatly influenced society. Some Russians believed that their city of Moscow was the "third Rome"— which would make it the successor to Rome and Constantinople. In the 1500s a Russian monk, Filofei, wrote:

“ *Heresy caused the downfall of old Rome. The Turks used their axes to shatter the doors of all churches of the Second Rome, the city of Constantinople. Now [in Moscow], the new Third Rome, the . . . Church . . . shines brighter than the sun. . . . Two Romes have fallen. The third stands [firm]. And there will not be a fourth.* ”

CHAPTER EVENTS			
330 Constantinople is founded on the site of Byzantium.	**537** Church of Hagia Sophia is completed.		**800** Charlemagne is crowned Roman emperor by the pope.

200	400	600	800

WORLD EVENTS

597 Church at Canterbury, England, is founded as the center of English Christianity.

622 Muhammad flees from Mecca to Medina.

150 UNIT 2 ◆ The Growth of Empires and Governments

Teaching Options

Chapter 7 Resources

REVIEW

Teacher's Resources (TR)
Terms to Know, p. 20
Review History, p. 54
Build Your Skills, p. 88
Chapter Test, pp. 129–130
Concept Builder, p. 223
Main Idea/Supporting Details Chart, p. 319
Transparencies 1, 2, 5, 7

ASSESSMENT
Section Reviews, pp. 156, 163, 167
Chapter Review, pp. 168–169
Chapter Test, TR, pp. 129–130

ALTERNATIVE ASSESSMENT
Portfolio Project, p. 196
Make a Poster, p. T196

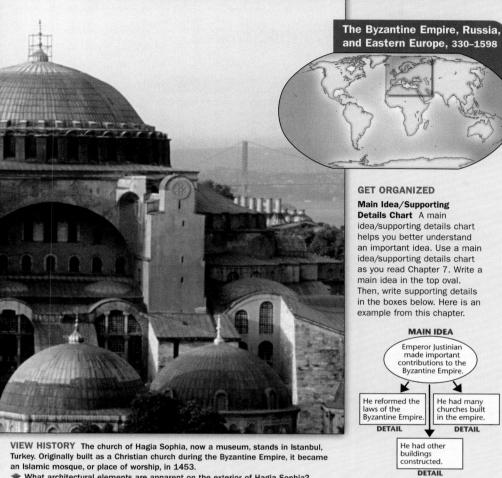

The Byzantine Empire, Russia, and Eastern Europe, 330–1598

GET ORGANIZED

Main Idea/Supporting Details Chart A main idea/supporting details chart helps you better understand an important idea. Use a main idea/supporting details chart as you read Chapter 7. Write a main idea in the top oval. Then, write supporting details in the boxes below. Here is an example from this chapter.

MAIN IDEA

Emperor Justinian made important contributions to the Byzantine Empire.

DETAIL — He reformed the laws of the Byzantine Empire.

DETAIL — He had many churches built in the empire.

DETAIL — He had other buildings constructed.

VIEW HISTORY The church of Hagia Sophia, now a museum, stands in Istanbul, Turkey. Originally built as a Christian church during the Byzantine Empire, it became an Islamic mosque, or place of worship, in 1453.
◆ What architectural elements are apparent on the exterior of Hagia Sophia?

1054 Permanent split occurs between Roman Catholic and Eastern Orthodox Churches.

1240 Mongols attack the Russian city of Kiev.

1386 Poland and Lithuania are linked under one monarchy.

1453 Ottoman Turks capture Constantinople. Byzantine Empire ends.

1000 **1200** **1400** **1600**

1099 Crusaders capture Jerusalem.

1492 Columbus sails from Spain to the Americas.

1517 Martin Luther nails a list of grievances to a church door, sparking the Protestant Revolution.

CHAPTER 7 ◆ The Byzantine Empire, Russia, and Eastern Europe **151**

Chapter Themes

- Culture
- People, Places, and Environments
- Power, Authority, and Governance
- Individuals, Groups, and Institutions
- Time, Continuity, and Change

F Y I

The Collapse of Hagia Sophia

When Emperor Justinian built the vast church of Hagia Sophia ("Holy Wisdom" in Greek) he meant it to show his power as ruler over all of Christendom. Its size and beauty surpassed any church built in the ancient or medieval world. Architecturally, the building was bold and daring. It was so daring, in fact, that its heavy dome was undersupported and collapsed not long after it was completed, helped along, perhaps, by earthquake tremors.

Chapter Warm-Up
USING THE MAP
Point out the locator map at the top of page 151. To help students recognize the large territory covered by the chapter, have them name the continents included in the box. (Europe, Asia, and Africa) Point out that Russia would eventually encompass almost all of northern Asia.

VIEW HISTORY
Tell students that the church shown on pages 150–151 is a basilica, a long, rectangular building with a curved apse, or altar area, and colonnaded aisles. The building is one of very few that still stands from the most opulent days of the Byzantine Empire. Ask students to describe the building. (solid, domed, detailed)

◆ **ANSWER** Domes, curved windows and walls, towers (or minarets), decoration such as relief carving on walls

GET ORGANIZED
Main Idea/Supporting Details Chart
Discuss the Main Idea/Supporting Details chart on page 151. Ask students to identify the main idea. (Emperor Justinian made important contributions to the Byzantine Empire.) Then ask them what the details all have in common. (They all give information about the main idea.) Have students make a Main Idea/Supporting Details chart (TR, p. 319) for each section.

● **TEACH THE TIMELINE**
The timeline on pages 150–151 covers events from 330 to 1517. Point out that some events on the timeline reveal that the regions covered in this chapter were influenced by western Europe. Have students point out such events. (Charlemagne is crowned; split between Roman Catholic and Eastern Orthodox Churches.)

Activity

Use the timeline Have students categorize the events on the timeline as religious or political. Suggest that students identify the relationship between events as they study the chapter.

CHAPTER 7 ◆ **T151**

I. The Byzantine Empire

(pp. 152–156)

Section Summary

In this section, students will learn how Byzantium was founded and how it grew to greatness under the Emperor Justinian. Also, students will trace the religious and political disagreements that led to conflict with the Roman Empire and ultimately to the defeat of the Byzantine Empire by the Ottoman Turks.

1 Introduce

Getting Started

Ask students how they think the civilization of the early twenty-first century will be remembered 1,000 years from now. Make the following suggestions: art, technology, and impact on the environment. Then, have students identify some of the positive and negative elements of our culture that might stand for centuries.

TERMS TO KNOW

Ask students to read the terms and definitions on page 152 and find each term in the section. Then, on one side of an index card, students should write the term. On the other side, students should put a historical example of the term and the page in the section on which it can be found. For example, for **autocrat,** students would write that Justinian ruled as an autocrat. (p. 152)

You may wish to preview the pronunciation of the following words with students.

Byzantine (BIHZ uhn teen)
Byzantium (bih ZAN tee uhm)
Agapetus (ag uh PEET uhs)
Cyrillic (suh RIHL ihk)
Mehmed (meh MEHT)

ACTIVE READING

The material in this section covers many centuries. Have students use a timeline (TR, p. 320) to track the events of the chapter. Then, have them identify a cause or an effect for each of the events on their timeline.

Section I

The Byzantine Empire

Terms to Know

autocrat a single ruler with absolute power

icon a religious image that is regarded as sacred

excommunicate to expel from the Church

Main Ideas

A. The emperor Justinian wanted to revive the glory of the Roman Empire.

B. The Byzantine Empire struggled against internal disputes and outside enemies.

C. Conflicts eventually destroyed the Byzantine Empire, but the empire had a lasting influence.

Active Reading

CAUSE AND EFFECT
Every event has a cause and an effect. As you read this section, think about the events that occurred during the time of the Byzantine Empire and their causes and effects.

A. Constantinople and the Age of Justinian

The Roman Empire was so immense that it was too much for one person to rule. In 395, rule of the Roman Empire was divided between two emperors. One emperor ruled in the east, and the other ruled in the west. When the last Roman emperor in the west was removed from power in 476, the richer and more populated eastern half of the empire continued.

Constantinople

Like other emperors, the emperor Constantine wanted to build a capital. After considering several sites in the east, he chose the Greek city of Byzantium. Byzantium's location had many advantages. Byzantium sat on a peninsula and could easily be defended. It could control trade routes between Europe and Asia. Also, it was located near the centers of Greek culture.

Constantine renamed the city Constantinople in 330. Constantinople was founded as the "New Rome." It became a center of trade, industry, and culture. There, Greek and Roman cultures blended and were influenced by Christianity. This blending created a new culture, called Byzantine. The eastern Roman Empire, therefore, became known as the Byzantine Empire.

Do You Remember?
In Chapter 6, you learned about the Emperor Constantine and the rise of Christianity in the Roman Empire.

The Age of Justinian

The emperor Justinian, who ruled from 527 to 565, was probably the last emperor to speak Latin as his native language. He was also determined to restore the Roman Empire to its full glory. In 534, Justinian began a series of wars to recover provinces in the west that had been conquered by Germanic invaders. Under the leadership of the general Belisarius, Byzantine armies reconquered North Africa, Italy, and southern Spain. These military victories caused the Byzantine Empire to reach its greatest territorial size. At the same time, the empire fought bitter wars with Persia in the east. The wars were expensive and drained Justinian's treasury.

Justinian ruled as an **autocrat**, or single ruler with absolute power. The emperor was considered the representative of God on Earth. He had complete authority over both the state and the Church.

A priest named Agapetus, who became a pope, wrote about the emperor:

> "In the authority attached to his dignity he is like God who rules over all."

ANALYZE PRIMARY SOURCES

DOCUMENT-BASED QUESTION How does Agapetus's statement describe the power of the emperor?

Teaching Options

Section 1 Resources

Teacher's Resources (TR)
Terms to Know, p. 20
Review History, p. 54
Build Your Skills, p. 88
Concept Builder, p. 223
Main Idea/Supporting Details Chart, p. 319

Justinian's wife, Empress Theodora, was also very powerful. She assisted and advised him. She challenged Justinian when she disagreed with his policies.

The Contributions of Justinian

Justinian is best known for reforming the laws of the empire. Early in his reign, he set up a commission, or group of people officially appointed for a specific purpose, to collect, organize, and revise all Roman laws. In the end, the commission produced the *Corpus Iuris Civilis*, or "Body of Civil Law." This collection of laws, known as the Justinian Code, became the foundation of law in the Byzantine Empire during and after Justinian's rule. In addition, the Justinian Code became the basis of some law codes in western Europe. The code even helped legal thinkers as they began to put together the international law that is used today. During Justinian's rule, he used the code of laws to unite the empire under his autocratic rule.

During Justinian's rule, a new silk industry started in the Byzantine Empire. Justinian encouraged the industry's beginnings and development. He also began an ambitious building program and ordered many public buildings constructed across the empire. Many churches, law courts, schools, hospitals, aqueducts, and fortresses resulted from his efforts. The most famous building is the church of Hagia Sophia, completed in 537 in Constantinople. *Hagia Sophia* means "Holy Wisdom" in Greek. The inside of the huge, domed church glittered with gold and colored marble as well as embroidered silk curtains and rich mosaics. Mosaics are pictures or designs made of small, colored materials, like stone, glass, or tile. Mosaics were an important Byzantine art form. Hagia Sophia inspired awe in all who saw it.

◆ **How did Justinian's wars affect the Byzantine Empire?**

Global Connections

A NEW SILK INDUSTRY

Emperor Justinian wanted a steady supply of silk, but his efforts to establish trade routes with China failed. Success came when smugglers stole silkworms and the technology to weave silk from China. Silkworms build cocoons made of silk that can be transformed into silk threads.

Soon a new silk industry was established. Many state-owned factories in Constantinople wove silk into cloth. Because the silk industry was very profitable, it added to the prosperity of the Byzantine Empire.

They Made History

Theodora ca. 497–548

Theodora came from simple beginnings as an actress in a family of entertainers. As a young woman, Theodora impressed the nephew of the emperor. That nephew was Justinian. They were married in 525, two years before he became emperor.

Theodora was Justinian's advisor and co-ruler—one of the first women known to have political power. She was a gifted politician. She was strong-willed, and she convinced Justinian to stay in Constantinople during a rebellion in 532. According to Procopius, who was the secretary of General Belisarius, Theodora said to Justinian, "Emperor, if you wish to flee, well and good . . . but I shall stay."

Theodora had great influence over policy in the empire. Divorce laws were changed to be fairer to women. Also, women were permitted to own property. Theodora often pursued her own interests, and she sometimes even challenged Justinian on policies if they conflicted with her interests. In 548, Theodora became ill and died.

This is a detail from a mosaic of Theodora (center).

Critical Thinking How did Theodora's personality help her to become a strong advisor and co-ruler?

A. Constantinople and the Age of Justinian

Purpose-Setting Question What is the Justinian Code? (collection of laws that became the foundation of law in the Byzantine Empire)

Do You Remember?
Suggest that students read page 141 to review the contributions of Constantine to Christianity.

ANALYZE PRIMARY SOURCES

DOCUMENT-BASED QUESTION
Make it clear to students that the people of Byzantium and the Byzantine Empire did not believe their king was a god.

ANSWER The emperor is all-powerful and whatever he says shall be considered true and final.

GLOBAL CONNECTIONS
A NEW SILK INDUSTRY Palace life in Byzantium involved elaborate rules of fashion, with different colors of cloth designating different ranks of people. The patterns on the silks were probably strictly regulated by the emperor.

◆ **ANSWER** The military victories caused the Byzantine Empire to reach its greatest territorial size. However, wars were expensive and drained the treasury.

THEY MADE HISTORY
Theodora
The rebellion of 532 was the Nika Revolt in which rioting crowds at a sporting event charged into the streets shouting, "Nika!" or "Conquer!" The people were actually angry at the harshness of the emperor's deputies in stopping a previous riot. The mob threatened to overthrow the emperor.

ANSWER She was strong-willed, brave, and willing to fight for what she believed in.

Organize Information Distribute a cause-and-effect chain (TR, p. 325) to students to help them complete the Active Reading suggestion on page 152. Have students work in pairs after each section to decide on the causes, events, and effects they have just learned about.

Using Technology

Have students use an Internet search engine to find an art museum exhibit of Byzantine art. Have them collect the details of the exhibit, including exhibit hours, highlights of the collection, and directions to get to the museum. If the museum is local, some students may wish to earn extra credit by going to the exhibit.

B. Difficult Times for the Byzantine Empire

Purpose-Setting Question Why was the pope's crowning of Charlemagne as Roman emperor a shock to the Byzantine people? (The Byzantine emperors believed that they were the only ones who could hold the title of Roman emperor. Charlemagne was not a Byzantine emperor. He was king of the Franks. This act widened the problems between the east and west.)

TEACH PRIMARY SOURCES

Empress Irene's husband, Leo, and his father, Constantine V, were both opposed to the use of icons and statues in worship. Leo was sickly and only ruled for five years. Upon his death, Irene assumed control of the empire along with her ten-year-old son. Irene reversed her husband's policies regarding icons. It is for her support of icons and statues that she received sainthood in the Eastern Orthodox Church.

Activity

Write an editorial People who worshiped images were once thought to be disobeying one of God's commandments. (Exodus 20:4) Tell students that the disagreement over the use of religious icons is usually referred to as the period of iconoclasm. Ask students to write an editorial explaining the issue and defending one side. The editorial should include reasons to substantiate the view, and a way to compromise on the disagreement over icons between the pope and the Eastern Orthodox Church.

Discuss Remind students that the Eastern Orthodox Church sent missionaries to other countries. Ask students how missionaries would be able to spread the culture of the country they come from and whether they think this might be an effective way to spread culture. Encourage students to explain their opinion.

Empress Irene, shown above, was married to Byzantine Emperor Leo, who ruled in 775. Also known as St. Irene in the Eastern Orthodox religion, she strongly supported the use of icons in the eastern church.

B. Difficult Times for the Byzantine Empire

After Justinian's rule ended in 565, the empire was attacked by outsiders. The Byzantine armies won the last war the empire fought against Persia. During the 600s and 700s, invaders burst forth from Arabia. Constantinople was attacked unsuccessfully several times.

In addition to the struggles against outside enemies, the Byzantine Empire dealt with religious conflict. At the time, there were growing divisions between the two branches of Christianity, which had some important differences. One branch was the western church, or Roman Catholic Church. The other branch was the eastern church. The eastern church was the Byzantine church, which was also called the Eastern Orthodox Church. The pope was the head of the Roman Catholic Church, and the Bible and services were written in Latin. A patriarch, nominated by the emperor, headed the Eastern Orthodox Church, and the Bible and services were written in Greek.

Divisions in the Empire and the Church

Religious disputes began from within the empire. Disagreements over the use of **icons**, or religious images that are regarded as sacred, turned violent in the 700s and 800s. Many people prayed to icons—images of Jesus, his mother Mary, and the saints. However, others believed that praying to icons violated God's commandments. The disagreement strained the relationship between the pope and the eastern church.

Then, in 800, the Byzantine people received a shock. A king named Charlemagne was crowned Roman emperor by the pope. Charlemagne was king of the Franks, a German-speaking people who had invaded the western Roman Empire. The Byzantine emperors believed they were the only ones who could possess the title of Roman emperor. The gap between the eastern and western churches grew wider.

The eastern, or Byzantine, church sent missionaries beyond the borders of the empire. The missionaries spread both Christianity and Byzantine culture. In 863, two brothers, Cyril and Methodius, adapted the Greek alphabet for the Slav language. They used the new alphabet, called Cyrillic, to translate the Bible. Byzantine missionaries converted many peoples, including the Bulgarian people, who lived in the Balkans, and the Russians.

In 1054, the eastern and western churches split over Church teachings and practices. The pope and the patriarch **excommunicated** each other. Excommunicate means to expel from the Church. The split between the Eastern Orthodox and Roman Catholic Churches was permanent.

Recovery and Disaster in the Byzantine Empire

After the attacks from outsiders during the 600s and 700s, the economy of the Byzantine Empire recovered. Constantinople was at the center of trade routes between Europe and Asia. The Byzantine gold coin, called the bezant, was circulated to so many countries that archaeologists have found it in places as far apart as Europe and China.

In the 900s and 1000s, the Byzantine Empire reconquered more lost land. Byzantine emperors, who were sometimes generals in the army, led soldiers against the Bulgarians and the Arabs. Byzantine territory expanded, stretching from southern Italy to Syria.

Then, in 1071, disaster struck the Byzantine Empire. Invaders from Normandy, a region in Gaul, which is present-day France, drove the Byzantines out of southern Italy. In the east, the Byzantine emperor led an army against a new enemy, the Seljuk Turks, a nomadic people from central

Teaching Options

Connection to ART

During the period of iconoclasm, destroyed icons were often replaced by crosses. For example, in 726, Leo III took down an image of Jesus at the palace gate and replaced it with a cross, which stood as a sign of salvation and pledge of faith. Because the cross did not depict a person (crucifixes appeared later), it was considered an object rather than an image or a likeness.

Meet Individual Needs:
VISUAL/SPATIAL LEARNERS

Explain to students that Byzantine art is some of the most widely studied art of all time. Have students find a catalog or book of Byzantine art in a library. Ask them to choose one image from the book and show it to the class. The students should give the name and date of the art as well as any details of content that give information about the Byzantine Empire. Ask the class to compare the pieces shown.

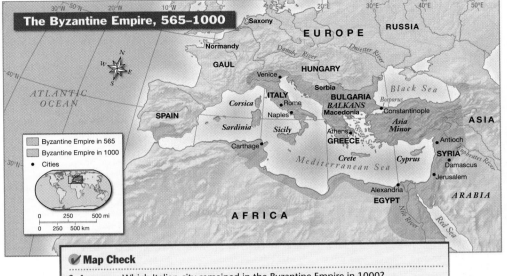

The Byzantine Empire, 565–1000

Map Check

1. LOCATION Which Italian city remained in the Byzantine Empire in 1000?

2. MOVEMENT About how far was Constantinople from the city of Rome?

Asia. The Byzantine army was destroyed, and the emperor was captured. The Byzantine Empire was defenseless.

◆ **What were the causes for the split between the Eastern Orthodox and the Roman Catholic Churches?**

C. The Byzantine Empire's Decline and Fall

Alexius I came to the throne in 1081. He wanted to reclaim the territory that the Seljuk Turks had taken, including the holy city of Jerusalem. Alexius turned to the pope for help because the Turks had closed the routes that pilgrims took to reach Jerusalem. These pilgrims were Christian people who made trips to see where Jesus had lived. The Seljuk Turks were Muslims, or followers of the Islamic religion. You will read about the Islamic religion in Chapter 8.

The pope sent Christian knights—or trained warriors—from western Europe to fight the Muslims and regain the holy city of Jerusalem. The knights did help Alexius reclaim some lands for the Byzantine Empire. Then, they continued on to Jerusalem. Later, in the 1200s, the Byzantine Empire would be attacked by other Christian knights, and the empire would continue to weaken.

Attacks on Constantinople

Trade disputes caused violence between the Byzantine Empire and Venice in Italy. In 1204, the Venetians persuaded the Christian knights to attack Constantinople. They captured the city, and after three days of looting, they sent much of its treasure to the West. These western Christians held the city for more than 50 years and went on to conquer other parts of the empire.

CHAPTER 7 ◆ The Byzantine Empire, Russia, and Eastern Europe **155**

WHO IN THE WORLD?

ANNA COMNENA was the author of a biography of her father, Emperor Alexis I. Her book offers some of the most reliable information about the Byzantine culture of her day. Ask students how a biography provides information about the culture of a time. (It shows how people lived, what they thought, as well as what was important to them.)

Review Remind students of the geographical advantages of Constantinople as discussed on page 152. Ask students why they think this would make the city particularly at risk for being attacked. (Other groups of people, such as the Ottoman Turks, recognized the advantages of the location and wanted to take control of it.)

◆ **ANSWER** The Ottoman Turks attacked Constantinople and captured the city, which they renamed Istanbul. It became the capital of the Ottoman Empire.

Section Close

Have students create a timeline (TR, p. 320) from the years 300 to 1500 for the Byzantine Empire. Be sure students include the emperors, the emperors' activities, the churches, and the wars waged or fought by the empire.

③ Assess

Review Answers

Review History

A. reforming the laws of the empire

B. The Churches permanently split over Church teachings and practices; the pope and the patriarch of Constantinople excommunicated each other.

C. Byzantine icons and mosaics made people feel connected with the sacred. Byzantine art and architecture influenced European art styles. Byzantine architecture was imitated by the Ottoman Turks.

Define Terms to Know

autocrat, 152; icon, 154; excommunicate, 154

ANNA COMNENA

Anna Comnena was the daughter of Emperor Alexius I. She was also one of the world's first female historians.

Anna wanted her husband instead of her brother John to follow her father as emperor. She tried, but failed, to convince Alexius to make her husband emperor. When John became emperor, she plotted with her mother to have him overthrown. Her plot failed, however.

A Byzantine emperor reclaimed Constantinople in 1261, but the empire never recovered its strength. Then, in 1453 Constantinople fell to its newest enemy—the Ottoman Turks. The Ottomans were another Turkish-speaking people who had migrated from Central Asia into southeastern Europe. Like the Seljuks, the Ottoman Turks had converted to Islam. To overrun Constantinople, the Ottomans used cannons. They renamed Constantinople Istanbul, and made this city the capital of the Ottoman Empire. Justinian's Christian church, the Hagia Sophia, now became an Islamic mosque, or house of worship, and the city itself became the centerpiece of Islamic culture.

Lasting Influence of the Byzantine Empire

The fall of the Byzantine Empire did not end its influence. The Byzantines had built upon Roman law and engineering. They kept alive Greek art, literature, philosophy, and science. Byzantine scholars produced their own works of history and literature. Historians such as Procopius and Anna Comnena wrote about their own times. The anonymous Byzantine poem *Digenis Akritas* describes a hero who defends the empire against bandits and invaders. Such poems helped shape popular Russian and western literature.

Byzantine art and architecture continued to be an influence in Europe. Icons and mosaics were popular religious art forms. In architecture, the Ottoman Turks imitated Byzantine designs. In the last years of the Byzantine Empire, scholars left Constantinople to go to Italy. There, they brought their knowledge and books to the universities in which they taught. They contributed to the beginning of the period in history known as the Renaissance, which you will read about in Chapter 14.

◆ **What happened to Constantinople in 1453?**

Review I

Review History

A. For what is Justinian best known?

B. What happened between the Eastern Orthodox and Roman Catholic Churches in 1054?

C. How did Byzantine art and architecture influence cultures in other parts of the world?

Define Terms to Know
Define the following terms: **autocrat, icon, excommunicate**

Critical Thinking
Why did relations between the Byzantine Empire and western Europe worsen?

Write About Culture
Write a short essay on how the Byzantine Empire contributed to western European culture.

Get Organized
MAIN IDEA/SUPPORTING DETAILS CHART
Use a main idea/supporting details chart to organize information from this section. Choose a topic and then find supporting details. For example, what were the reasons for the founding of Constantinople?

Critical Thinking

Possible answers: They had different beliefs; they had disputes over Charlemagne as Roman emperor; they distrusted each other.

Write About Culture

Students' essays may identify the following as influenced by the Byzantine Empire: art, architecture, literature, law, religion, and the Renaissance period.

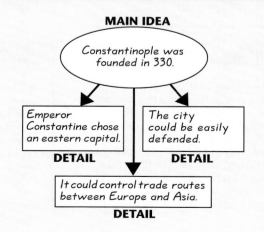

MAIN IDEA

Constantinople was founded in 330.

Emperor Constantine chose an eastern capital. **DETAIL**

The city could be easily defended. **DETAIL**

It could control trade routes between Europe and Asia. **DETAIL**

Build Your Skills

ANALYZE PRIMARY-SOURCE DOCUMENTS

Primary sources are produced by people who took part in events or were eyewitnesses to events. Primary sources include letters, speeches, autobiographies, newspaper articles, political cartoons, advertisements, photographs, and artifacts, or physical objects made by people. Documents from a particular time can provide direct information about a place, a person, or an event in that time. Documents can include novels, diaries, journals, poems, histories, speeches and quotations that are written, and many other kinds of writing.

Many writers have their own goals when they write. Some writers make judgments about their subjects. They can leave information out or distort it for their own goals. We say such writing is biased. When reading a primary-source document, it is important to keep in mind who the writer was, and the writer's purpose and audience.

Here's How
Follow these steps to interpret a document.

1. Find out who wrote the document and when it was written.
2. Identify the content of the document. What does the writer tell you about a person, a place, or an event?
3. Identify the purpose of the document. Is it about everyday life, or does it tell you about a person or event? Is the purpose to teach, to provide information, or to influence the reader?
4. Learn more about the document and the period.

Here's Why
Using primary sources can help you learn things about a particular time that you could not learn from other kinds of sources.

Practice the Skill
The passage on the right is from a book about Byzantine emperors written by Michael Psellus. This passage is about Romanus Diogenes. In the Byzantine Empire, there were two rival groups that sought power—the military and the non-military. Romanus Diogenes was a member of a military group which represented nobles from the countryside who led Byzantine armies. Diogenes became Emperor Romanus IV in 1068. Psellus, a scholar and teacher, was from the non-military group. This group included many scholars from Constantinople.

Read the passage in which Psellus writes about Romanus IV. Then, answer the following questions.

1. Who wrote the document, and what do you know about him?
2. About when was the document written?
3. What event is described in the quotation?
4. Based on the quotation, what is the author's opinion of the subject? Explain.

> "Romanus refused to believe anyone who detected the [Turkish ruler's] influence in [Turkish] successes. The truth is, he did not want peace. He thought he would capture the [Turkish] camp without a battle. Unfortunately for him, through his ignorance of military science, he had scattered his forces."

Extend the Skill
Write a paragraph that describes the author, his audience, and his purpose for writing. Be sure to include your reasoning.

Apply the Skill
Study the other primary source quotations in the rest of the chapter. Follow the steps in *Here's How* to learn more about the quotations.

Teaching Options

RETEACH
Write the following words or terms on the board: *speech, eyewitness account, newspaper story, history textbook, encyclopedia article, biography, autobiography, letter,* and *political cartoon*. Ask students to identify which are the primary sources. Have volunteers explain why the remaining items are not primary sources. Then, ask how the information from each source might be different.

CHALLENGE
Have students go to a library or use the Internet to find a primary source and a secondary source about an event in history. Have them write a paragraph explaining what the sources reveal about the event and how the information about the event differs from one source to the other.

Build Your Skills

ANALYZE PRIMARY-SOURCE DOCUMENTS

Teach the Skill
Ask students where they go to get official information about school events. (Possible answers: read the school newspaper, read bulletin-board displays put up by teachers or school staff, read the event flyers that are passed out by the student government) Explain that these documents are all primary sources.

Explain that historians use primary sources to find out firsthand information about conditions or events of the past. Primary sources are the most accurate version of events. For example, a student would get a more accurate description of a football game by interviewing one of the players (a primary source) than by interviewing a person who had heard about the game from a classmate.

Practice the Skill
ANSWERS
1. Michael Psellus was a scholar, a teacher, and a member of the nonmilitary group that sought power in the Byzantine Empire.
2. some time during or after 1068, when Romanus Diogenes became emperor
3. a battle to capture a Turkish camp
4. Possible answer: Psellus has a low opinion of Romanus IV; Psellus points out Romanus's ignorance of military science.

Extend the Skill
Paragraphs should focus on Michael Psellus, scholar and teacher. His purpose was to inform his audience about the actions of Byzantine emperors. His audience included people interested in Byzantine emperors.

Apply the Skill
Students should recognize that most textbooks are not primary sources since they were written by people who were not present at the events described. Encourage students to analyze speeches and quotations as they appear in their reading. For example, refer to the quotation on page 161, written by Grand Prince Vasilii to a community in 1460. Have students think about and discuss the conditions that the quotation reveals.

Section Summary

In this section, students will learn about the early formation of Russia, including the influences of Byzantium and the conquering Mongols. They will also learn about the early foundings of the cities of Kiev and Moscow.

1 Introduce

Getting Started

Tell students that geographically, Russia is larger than the United States. Ask students to identify some of the positive and negative aspects of living in an immense nation. (Possible answers: **Positive:** cultural diversity and land surplus; **negative:** communication and transportation barriers)

TERMS TO KNOW

Have students write the vocabulary terms on one side of index cards with the definition on the reverse. Assign partners and have students quiz one another on the terms and their definitions.

You may wish to preview the pronunciation of the following terms from this section with students.

Dnieper (NEE puhr) **River**
Kiev (KEE ihf)
Varangians (veh RAN yeh uhns)
Vladimir (vluh DYEEM yihr)
Yaroslav (yuh ruh SLAHF)
Novgorod (NAWV guh ruht)
Kulikovo (KOOL yih kah veh)

ACTIVE READING

As an alternate to the timeline, have students make a flowchart (TR, p. 324) of the events in the section. Encourage students to number the boxes of the flowchart to show the sequence of events.

Section II

The Rise of Russia

Terms to Know

tundra a plain without trees in an arctic region

steppe a great plain with few trees anywhere in southeastern Europe or Asia

boyar a Russian noble

czar the Russian word for *Caesar*, which means "emperor"

Main Ideas

A. Kiev was Russia's first capital and was heavily influenced by the Byzantine Empire.

B. The Mongol conquest had mixed results for Russia.

C. Czars Ivan the Great and Ivan the Terrible extended the power of Moscow over all of Russia.

Active Reading

SEQUENCE OF EVENTS
In order for history to make sense, you have to know the order in which events occurred. As you read this section, make a timeline and put events about the rise of Russia on it in the order they happened.

A. The Geography and People of Russia

Russia lies on the Eurasian plain. This plain stretches from Europe in the west to the edge of China in the east. Cartographers, or people who make maps, show the Ural Mountains in Russia as the boundary between Europe and Asia. However, since ancient times, the Urals have worn away from mountains to hills. Russia does not have many mountains, and there are few obstacles to movement.

Landforms and Climate

Russia is divided into three broad areas. The far north is the **tundra**, a frozen plain without trees, where almost no one lives. South of the tundra is a wide band of forest. Forests occupy more than half the land in Russia. Although it is bitterly cold in winter, this area of Russia offers fertile soil for farming. South of the forests is the **steppe**. The steppe is a great plain with few trees that extends from Russia east into Asia. Many nomadic groups used the steppe to travel from Asia to Europe.

Rivers have long been important to Russia. They serve as highways for travel and trade. The Dnieper, Don, and Volga Rivers are the most important. They flow south into the Black and Caspian Seas. These rivers once linked Russia with the Byzantine and the Arab peoples.

Varangians and Russians

During Roman times, the Slavs—any member of a group of Slavic-speaking peoples of east, southeast, and central Europe—moved into Russia and inhabited the area stretching from the Baltic Sea south to the Black Sea. Small groups of Slavs lived in Russian villages and earned their living by farming.

In the 700s, Vikings began migrating out of the northern European region of Scandinavia. In Russia, they were known as Varangians. The Varangians were expert sailors, merchants, and raiders. They sailed along the rivers of Russia, sometimes trading with the Slavs. Other times they demanded tribute—money paid for protection—because they were more powerful than the Slavs. The Varangian people also traveled along the rivers to trade with the Arabs and the Byzantines.

The Varangians settled at trade centers as well. The most important center of trade was the settlement of Kiev on the Dnieper River. Over the years, the Slavic and Viking peoples adopted each other's customs, blending into the first people we call Russians today.

Spotlight on *Economics*

VIKINGS IN THE 700s
The wealth of the Vikings, or Varangians, was based on their far-reaching trade routes. Rivers and seas connected Russia to Europe and Asia. Accounts of Russian traders come from Byzantine and Arab sources.
Artifacts from archaeological digs illustrate how far trade routes went: An Indian statue of Buddha was found at a Viking settlement in Sweden!

Teaching Options

Section 2 Resources

Teacher's Resources (TR)
Terms to Know, p. 20
Review History, p. 54
Build Your Skills, p. 88
Concept Builder, p. 223
Main Idea/Supporting Details
  Chart, p. 319
Transparencies 2, 5, 7

ESL/ELL STRATEGIES

Summarize The material in this chapter covers many years and large territories. Encourage students to get the big picture of each section by summarizing the text. You may wish to demonstrate how to summarize by reading one subsection aloud and writing a summary sentence on the board.

Kiev became the first capital of Russia in about 879. It remained as Russia's capital until 1169. From early times, Kiev was influenced by the Byzantine Empire. In times of peace, the people of Kiev traded with the Byzantines.

Byzantine Influence

The Byzantines sent missionaries to Kiev, and in 957, Princess Olga of Kiev converted to Eastern Orthodox Christianity. The religion only spread widely, however, in the time of her grandson, Prince Vladimir. Prince Vladimir sent ten trusted advisors to observe how people worshiped around the world. The advisors were impressed with the ornate, splendid Orthodox Christian churches in Byzantium. They reported their favorable impressions to Prince Vladimir when they returned. Prince Vladimir not only became an Eastern Orthodox Christian, he married the sister of the Byzantine emperor. Then, he ordered all the people in Kiev to become Eastern Orthodox Christians. In 990, Greek priests baptized all the Kiev citizens in the Dnieper River. A close connection between the Church and state occurred in Russia, just as it had in the Byzantine Empire.

The Byzantines had such a huge impact on culture in this region that later Russian rulers came to see themselves as the heirs to the Byzantine Empire. Russians used the Cyrillic alphabet. They adopted Byzantine religious art, architecture, and music. Their churches were built with the "onion domes" that even today show how much influence the Byzantines had in this region.

The Rise and Fall of Kiev

After Vladimir died, however, Kiev fell into decline when rivals battled for the throne. Yaroslav, Vladimir's son, eventually brought stability to Kiev in 1036. He came to be called Yaroslav the Wise for his many contributions to Kievan culture. He issued a written law code. He supported the arts. He translated Greek works into Russian. To strengthen his influence, he arranged marriages with other royal families in Europe. Under Yaroslav, Kievan lands stretched from the Baltic Sea almost to the Black Sea. His influence lasted until his death in 1054.

After Yaroslav's death, Kiev was divided between Yaroslav's sons, but they fought constantly. A nomadic group, the Cumans, threatened Russia from the steppe. In 1203, Kiev was destroyed. Then, after 1204, when Venetians destroyed Constantinople, Byzantine prosperity declined. Russian trading cities were hurt and trade with the Arabs declined. Problems continued for the Kievans. The territory of Novgorod in the north came under attack from a group of German knights, who were determined to conquer the non-Catholic lands along the Baltic Sea. Finally, the Mongol invaders from central Asia arrived.

◆ **How did trade affect the development of Russia?**

With its many onion-shaped domes, the Cathedral of St. Basil the Blessed stands in Moscow, Russia, as a symbol of Byzantine religious influence.

B. Mongol Conquest

Purpose-Setting Question Ask students to describe the Mongols. (nomadic, lived in small groups, herded animals, excellent horsemen, fierce warriors, and tolerant rulers)

Discuss Have students discuss the benefits gained by the Mongol rulers for tolerating religious differences among the Russians. Point out that the Mongols were interested in trade and land advantages rather than intellectual supremacy.

Activity

Describe a historical figure
Have one or more students read aloud a brief biography of Genghis Khan from an encyclopedia. Then as a class, brainstorm a list of personal qualities that Genghis Khan must have possessed to unite many different tribes, overcome tribal enemies, and conquer most of central Asia in his lifetime.

Explore Ask students to find out more about the biomes known as grasslands that the nomadic Mongol peoples lived on. Explain to them that a biome is a naturally occurring, large community of flora and fauna. A biome is often determined by its soil, the dominant, distinctive vegetation in the area, and a characteristic climate and animal life. Other types of biomes include deserts, tundra, and forests. Have students make guesses as to how living in grasslands might have influenced the actions of the Mongols.

Activity

Use a map Have students use a world map (Atlas pages A1–A2 or Transparency 2) to locate the extent of the Mongolian Empire and some of the places it included. Point out to students that this empire stretched from Hungary to Korea, included most of Asia and much of eastern Europe, and was the second largest land empire in human history. The Mongols' success in acquiring territory was partly due to their great skills as warriors. A Mongol warrior's main weapon was a compound bow. Made of yak horn, sinew, and bamboo, it was strung against the curve. This gave it great range.

B. Mongol Conquest

The Mongols were a nomadic people who lived in the grasslands north of China. They lived in small groups and herded animals. Although they were excellent horsemen and warriors, their skills in combat were usually directed at other tribes of nomads.

Then, a great leader united the Mongol tribes in 1206. He was given the title of Genghis Khan, which means "Universal Ruler." Under him, the Mongols quickly moved south into China and west across the steppe. When Genghis Khan died in 1227, his empire was divided among his four sons. Leadership and the title of Great Khan, who ruled the entire Mongol Empire, fell to his third son, Ogadai. Genghis Khan's successors continued his sweeping conquests.

Invasion of Russia

The Russian people first encountered the Mongols in 1223. An army of Mongols advanced on the Cumans. The Russians allied themselves with their former enemies, the Cumans, against the Mongols. Although the allied army was smashed, the Mongols left. They would, however, return.

In 1237, the Mongols, led by Batu, grandson of Genghis Khan and nephew of the Great Khan, once again attacked Russia. The quarreling Russian princes were not prepared. The Mongol invasion was rapid. Their horses carried them quickly over frozen rivers in winter. The Mongols burned 14 cities in a single month. In 1240, they attacked Kiev, destroying houses and other buildings. As in the other cities, the people were slaughtered. Russian resistance stopped after the fall of Kiev.

The invasion of Russia was only a part of the Mongol plan, however. Mongol armies swept into Europe. They destroyed towns and villages in Poland, Hungary, and the Balkans. Batu stopped the invasion in 1242, when his uncle, the Great Khan, died. The Mongols retreated east. However, all of Russia stayed under their rule. The Mongol khanate in Russia, called the Golden Horde because of the color of their tents, set up its headquarters on the Volga River and ruled Russia for about 200 years.

This Illustration from the 1200s shows a battle between rival Mongol tribes. Mongol warriors were such skilled horsemen that they could shoot arrows while riding at fast speeds.

Teaching Options

Research

AVERAGE

Have students look on the Internet to learn about modern Kiev or Moscow. Have them answer the following questions: What are the main attractions of the city? What problems does the city face today? What historical landmarks still stand in the city?

CHALLENGE

Have students find other early Russian cities that would have arisen around the same time as Kiev or Moscow. Have students identify the geographical features that made the cities important. Have them give the dates of each city's founding and details about its importance.

Impact of Mongol Rule

The Mongols were fierce warriors, but they were tolerant rulers. Although the Mongols selected the grand prince, or the leader of all the Russian princes, he and the other princes were allowed to continue ruling. The Mongols did, however, require the princes to pay them tribute. As long as the princes did this, they were left alone. In addition, the Mongols allowed the Russians to keep their own laws, customs, and religions.

The impact of the Mongols on Russia is still debated. Mongol rule brought peace to the lands between eastern Europe and China. Merchants benefited from the peace and new trade routes across this region. At the same time, the Mongols isolated Russia from the rest of Europe. Russia's close ties with Europe were broken. This prevented Russia from being part of the rapid European advances in arts and sciences that occurred at this time.

How much influence the Mongols had on the Russian style of rule is also still debated. The gap between rich and poor grew at this time. The **boyars**, or Russian nobles, gained more and more land, and became more wealthy and powerful. The peasants paid heavy taxes, however. Many peasants fell deeply into debt. Some fled to avoid this difficult situation, but many stayed. More and more peasants became workers bound to the land during this time. Although they farmed, the land they worked on belonged to the boyars and other landowners. The authorities brought back peasants who tried to leave their land. Grand Prince Vasilii wrote to a community in 1460, pledging to return peasants:

> "As for the peasants who live in their villages at the present time, I, the grand prince, order that these peasants not be allowed to go elsewhere; and if the . . . steward [person in charge] should need to have a constable [high-ranking official], he shall obtain one . . . to [return] those peasants who have left their villages."

During Mongol rule in Russia, the Russian Orthodox Church, which was part of the Eastern Orthodox Church, also became more powerful. The Russian Orthodox Church became increasingly independent of Constantinople when Russian bishops selected their own leader for their church in Moscow. Although the Mongols were not followers of the Eastern Orthodox religion, they were tolerant of its church in Moscow. Donations to the Church made it one of the greatest landowners in Russia.

The Mongols built roads and improved ways to communicate. Some Mongol words came to be part of the language that would be called Russian. Mongol customs and traditions influenced the Russians. Russian princes and boyars may have adopted from the Mongols the practice of isolating women. Many upper-class Russian women began living in separate quarters from men. Beginning in the 1200s, women of all classes were under male authority.

◆ **How did Mongol rule affect the peasants of Russia?**

The Growth of Russia, 1300–1584

Siberia
URAL MTS.
Ural River
Volga River
Don River
Dnieper River
Novgorod
Moscow
Vladimir
LITHUANIA
POLAND
Kiev
CARPATHIAN MTS.
HUNGARY
Eurasian Plain
Baltic Sea
Black Sea
Caspian Sea
Danube River
Constantinople
60°N
45°N
15°E
30°E
45°E
60°E
Moscow in 1300
Land added to Russia by 1462
Land added to Russia by 1584
Limit of Mongol expansion
Cities
0 300 600 mi
0 300 600 km

Map Check

MOVEMENT During which period did Russian territory expand the most?

ANALYZE PRIMARY SOURCES

DOCUMENT-BASED QUESTION What is the grand prince's solution for returning peasants who leave their villages?

Using the Map

The Growth of Russia, 1300–1584

Have students name the five rivers marked on the map. (Danube, Dnieper, Don, Volga, Ural) Identify the cities that they flow through and the seas they flow into. Discuss how merchants would have used them as trade routes.

Map Check

Answer 1462 to 1584

Focus It is not always easy for students to grasp the idea that fierce warriors could also be tolerant, even beneficent, leaders. Ask students to think about why this could be so. After they have thought about it for a while, explain to them that the invading warriors may have great respect for the culture they are invading and may often even come to adopt many of their ways. Ask students if they can name any other group that was known for great military success yet relatively gentle handling of conquered peoples. (the Romans)

ANALYZE PRIMARY SOURCES

DOCUMENT-BASED QUESTION

Under the system of feudalism, monasteries could own land and peasants just as boyars could. Wealthy people donated lands to monasteries in exchange for prayers for their souls. Monasteries also took over the lands inherited by their members.

ANSWER The land steward should ask for a constable to return the peasants to their villages.

◆ **ANSWER** The peasants had to pay a lot of taxes, and many of them went into debt. They became workers bound to land owned by others.

FYI

The English Link

In the 1500s, Russian rulers wanted to trade with Europe. German merchants who controlled the Baltic Sea, however, cut off most trade and travel to Russia.

In 1553, an English explorer reached the northern shore of Russia by way of the Arctic Sea and soon established direct relations between Moscow and England.

Test Taking

Remind students to read questions carefully. If they read too quickly, they may miss clues, such as *all, most*, or *not* and choose the wrong answer. Ask students what clues are in these questions. (*most, not*)

How did most Mongol princes rule the lands of Russia?

T or *F*: Mongol rulers were not tolerant.

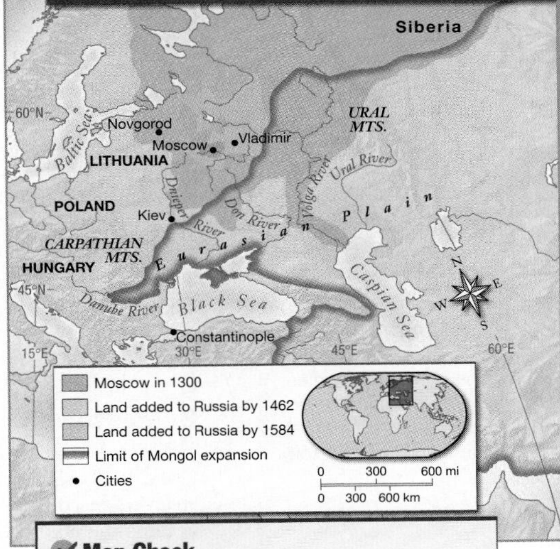

C. Moscow Dominates Russia

Purpose-Setting Question How did the princes of Moscow gain their power? (The princes collected taxes for the Mongols and for themselves. The Russian Orthodox Church was their powerful ally, siding with them when settling disputes. The decline of Mongol power strengthened the princes of Moscow as well.)

This is one of the earliest known paintings of Moscow. Moscow was located in the region known as Muscovy.

C. Moscow Dominates Russia

Moscow was a small town in the 1100s and remained so for almost 200 years. Its location next to a river meant that it was near important land and river trade routes. Moscow was the religious center of Russia, and later became the political center of Russia as well.

Moscow Benefits From Mongol Rule

During the Mongol period, the princes of Moscow increased their power by earning the Mongols' trust. The Mongols did not destroy Moscow, so people from other towns settled around this city. The princes collected taxes for the Mongols—and for themselves.

The Russian Orthodox Church was another powerful ally of the princes of Moscow. The head of the Russian Orthodox Church moved to Moscow. When he was asked to settle disputes, the head of the Church sided most often with the princes of Moscow.

The Rise of Moscow

Moscow replaced Kiev as the political center of Russia around 1300. As Mongol power declined, the princes of Moscow grew stronger and became champions of Russian independence. They united other Russian princes to fight against the Golden Horde. In 1380, they defeated the Mongols at Kulikovo. The Mongols were no longer thought of as unbeatable, yet they continued to control Russia for many years.

Then, Grand Prince Ivan III, known as Ivan the Great, propelled Moscow to greatness. He ruled Moscow from 1462 to 1505. In that time, he unified the remaining Russian settlements, conquering the last of them, Novgorod, in 1478. He enlarged the territory of Moscow so that it was the largest state at that time.

Ivan the Great, like others before him, looked to the Byzantine Empire for inspiration. In 1472, he married the niece of the last Byzantine emperor. He used a symbol of the Byzantine Empire, the two-headed eagle, and adopted Byzantine court rituals. He issued a code of laws. Ivan ruled Russia as an autocrat. Some members of his court developed the idea that Moscow was the "Third Rome," following Constantinople—the "Second Rome"—and therefore, the one true seat of the Eastern Orthodox faith and the Roman Empire.

Teaching Options

Writing

AVERAGE	CHALLENGE
Have students write a short dialogue between two peasants under Ivan the Terrible. The dialogue should include their ideas about the czar, their fears of his unstable leadership, and the impact of his leadership on their daily lives.	Have students write a flyer about Ivan the Terrible in which they give reasons why people should try to overthrow his rule. The flyer should include at least three details of Ivan's questionable leadership and disturbing actions.

Ivan the Terrible

Ivan IV, grandson of Ivan the Great, crowned himself **czar** at the age of 17. *Czar* is the Russian word for *Caesar*, which means "emperor." In the first half of his rule, he called a representative assembly. He began to replace centrally appointed governors with locally elected officials.

Besides supporting the development of an updated legal code, Ivan restarted trade with western Europe. He opened the large region of Siberia, in northern Russia, to Russian settlement.

After the death of his wife in 1560, Ivan became increasingly unstable. He sometimes flew into fits of rage. He distrusted everyone, and his fears gradually led him to introduce a reign of terror. He crushed all opposition, real or imagined. He created a group called the *oprichniki* to enforce his will. They dressed in black robes and rode black horses. The *oprichniki* killed many boyars and destroyed towns where people were thought to be disloyal. At the same time, Russia also was involved in wars that destroyed parts of the country. Ivan was so unstable that he even killed his oldest son in a fit of anger. His reign of terror earned him the name of Ivan the Terrible.

When Ivan the Terrible died in 1584, the reign of terror ended. His son, Feodor, became czar. Feodor was a weak ruler, and his advisor, Boris Godunov, became very powerful. After Feodor died in 1598, Boris claimed the throne. His action sparked a period that came to be known as the Time of Troubles.

◆ What were the *oprichniki* used for?

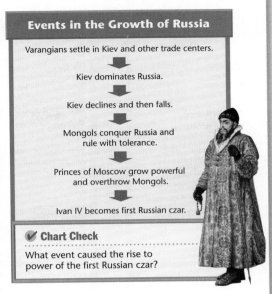

Events in the Growth of Russia

Varangians settle in Kiev and other trade centers.

⬇

Kiev dominates Russia.

⬇

Kiev declines and then falls.

⬇

Mongols conquer Russia and rule with tolerance.

⬇

Princes of Moscow grow powerful and overthrow Mongols.

⬇

Ivan IV becomes first Russian czar.

✔ **Chart Check**

What event caused the rise to power of the first Russian czar?

Review II

Review History
A. How did Kiev become the first Russian capital?
B. How did Mongol rule affect Russian merchants?
C. How did the princes of Moscow benefit from Mongol rule?

Define Terms to Know
Define the following terms: **tundra, steppe, boyar, czar**

Critical Thinking
How did contact with the Byzantine Empire affect Russia?

Write About Government
Write an editorial giving your opinion of the government of Russia under the princes of Moscow.

Get Organized
MAIN IDEA/SUPPORTING DETAILS CHART
Use a main idea/supporting details chart to organize information from this section. Choose a topic and then find supporting details. For example, how did the Mongol conquest affect Russia?

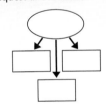

MAIN IDEA

Mongol conquest affected Russia.

↓ ↓

Russian princes had to pay tribute.
DETAIL

A time of peace benefited merchants.
DETAIL

Russia was isolated from Europe.
DETAIL

Discuss Explain to students that the father of Ivan the Terrible died when Ivan was only three years old, and his mother was murdered by boyars. Ivan and the nation were under the control of the boyars until Ivan turned 17, when he took over. Ask students to discuss how his childhood experiences could have negatively influenced Ivan.

Using the Chart

Events in the Growth of Russia

Ask students to estimate dates for the events listed on the chart. Point out that most of the events did not occur at an exact date but rather took place over decades or centuries.

✔ **Chart Check**

Answer The princes of Moscow grew powerful and overthrew the Mongols.

◆ **ANSWER** The *oprichniki* carried out Ivan IV's will. They killed many boyars and destroyed towns.

Section Close

Ask students to look at the chart "Events in the Growth of Russia." Have students write one paragraph, without reviewing the text, for each event, giving details that support the importance of the event in the growth of Russia. Then, once completed, allow students to go back into the book and add any forgotten details to their paragraphs.

③ Assess

Review Answers

Review History
A. It was the most important center of trade.
B. Merchants benefited from the peace and new trade routes across the region.
C. As long as the princes paid tribute regularly to the Mongols and recognized the Mongols' supremacy, the Mongols left the princes alone.

Define Terms to Know
tundra, 158; steppe, 158; boyar, 161; czar, 163

Critical Thinking
Possible answers: Russia adopted the religion, art, and architecture of the Byzantine Empire. An example of an architectural influence was the use of the onion domes on churches.

Write About Government
Possible answer: Even when the princes of Moscow were under the Mongols' control, they seemed powerful because the Mongols let the princes rule. They showed even more strength later, when they united to fight the Mongols and defeat them.

III. The Growth of Eastern European Culture

(pp. 164–167)

Section Summary

Students will read about the early settlement of the Balkans, including Bulgaria and Serbia. They will also learn about the settlement, governments, and societies of Poland and Hungary.

1 Introduce

Getting Started

Ask students to look at a world map (Atlas pages A1–A2 or Transparency 1). Have them locate the eastern European nations of Serbia, Bulgaria, Poland, and Hungary. Point out that these nations are located between the Slavic region of Russia to the east and the European nations to the west. Discuss how that location of the countries might impact culture and government.

TERMS TO KNOW

Ask students to think of synonyms for the vocabulary terms. For example, for *mercenary*, students may come up with *soldier, hired gun, maverick*. For *diet*, students may come up with *legislature, government, ruling body*. For *charter*, students might suggest *document, form*, or *code*. Allow students to use a thesaurus.

You may wish to preview the pronunciation of the following terms from this section with students.

Porphyrogenitus
   (poor fuh roh JEHN uh tuhs)
Queen Jadwiga (yahd VEE gah)
Wladyslaw Jagiello
   (vlah DIHS lahf hahg YEHL loh)
Magyar (MAG yahr)

ACTIVE READING

Have students go through the section and write one generalization based on the text under each heading. Then, have students share their generalizations with a partner. Partners may want to combine or revise their individual generalizations to more effectively summarize the text.

The Growth of Eastern European Culture

Terms to Know

mercenary a soldier paid to serve in a foreign army

diet a legislative assembly

ethnic group a large group of people who share the same language and cultural heritage

charter an official document in which rights are given by a government to a person or group

Do You Remember?

In Chapter 5, you learned that Greece is in the southernmost part of the Balkan Peninsula.

ANALYZE PRIMARY SOURCES

DOCUMENT-BASED QUESTION What was the military governor instructed to do in response to the revolt of the Slavs?

Main Ideas

A. The Balkans were settled by Slavs, Bulgarians, and Serbians who were influenced by Byzantine culture and religion.

B. Poland became one of the largest kingdoms in Europe.

C. The Magyars founded Hungary, which became a monarchy until the Ottomans took over most of the area.

A. The Balkans

The mountainous Balkan Peninsula is surrounded on three sides by seas. It stretches from Greece to the Danube River, one of the longest rivers in Europe and also one of the only passable rivers in the region.

The Romans conquered the Balkans in the first century A.D. The region remained under Roman and then Byzantine control until around 550. During the period of Roman rule, the Romans built many roads and fortresses throughout the region.

Slavic Settlement

Wars in the west and the east forced the Byzantines to leave the northern border of the Balkans undefended. Beginning around 550, Slavs poured into the Balkans, first as raiders and then as settlers. These southern Slavs settled the Balkans as far south as the Peloponnesus in Greece. The Byzantines eventually reconquered some of the lost territory and transmitted the Greek culture to the Slavs they conquered. Byzantine efforts were not all successful, however. Some Slavs did not accept the culture or the authority of the empire. Emperor Constantine Porphyrogenitus wrote in the mid-900s:

> ❝When the report of the . . . military governor of Peloponnesus arrived and was read in the presence of the emperor . . . and was found to contain news of the revolt of the . . . Slavs . . . this [military governor] was instructed to march against them and defeat and subdue and exterminate them. ❞

The Foundation of Bulgaria

In the late 600s, the Bulgars, a nomadic group, moved into the northern Balkans. They merged with the Slavic population and founded the state of Bulgaria. Although they fought many wars with the Byzantines, the Bulgarians were strongly influenced by Byzantine culture. They adopted Eastern Orthodox Christianity and the Cyrillic alphabet. In addition, they molded their art and literature after that of the Byzantines.

The greatest Bulgarian ruler was Simeon, who ruled from 893 until 927. Simeon had been a student in Constantinople. His daughter was promised in marriage to a Byzantine emperor. Simeon claimed that he should be the emperor and began a war. He also gave himself the title of emperor. The Byzantine emperor at the time, Romanus Lecapenus, only mocked Simeon.

Active Reading

GENERALIZE
When you generalize, you make broad statements from facts. As you read this section, concentrate on the main points of eastern European cultures. Then, pause to make general statements about what you have learned.

Teaching Options

Section 3 Resources

Teacher's Resources (TR)
   Terms to Know, p. 20
   Review History, p. 54
   Build Your Skills, p. 88
   Concept Builder, p. 223
   Chapter Test, pp. 129–130
   Main Idea/Supporting Details
      Chart, p. 319
   Transparencies 1, 5

Although Simeon's war was unsuccessful, he did conquer neighboring Balkan states. The Bulgarians stayed independent for another hundred years. In about 1000, the Byzantine Emperor Basil II, called "Slayer of the Bulgars," began a war against the Bulgarians. Town by town, he ground the Bulgarians down. After many years, his armies finally conquered them.

Serbia

Serbia was one of the early Slavic states in the Balkans. Like the Bulgarians, the Serbs were influenced by the Byzantine Empire. They adopted Eastern Orthodox Christianity. For a time, the Bulgarians and Byzantines dominated the Serbs. Then, in the late 1100s, Serbian prince Stefan Nemanja established an independent Serbia. Under his rule, Serbia became a strong state. His descendants ruled Serbia into the late 1300s.

In the 1200s, Serbia had begun to grow more powerful and wealthy at the same time that Serbia's neighbors were growing weaker. As a result, Serbia was able to conquer some neighboring lands. German immigrants came to work in new mines that had opened in Serbia. Wealth from these mines allowed Serbian rulers to hire **mercenaries**. A mercenary is a soldier serving in a foreign army for pay. Serbian rulers used their mercenaries to control independent nobles, who often had their own private armies.

Stefan Dusan ruled Serbia from 1331 to 1355. He was perhaps the greatest ruler of Serbia during the period, but his rule was not a peaceful one. He fought against groups such as the Byzantines and the Hungarians. He conquered lands in Macedonia and in Greece. His goal was to capture Constantinople. He took the title of emperor like the Bulgarian ruler Simeon had.

All of Stefan Dusan's efforts were not directed at warfare, however. He made many improvements at home and issued a code of laws. He made the Serbian Church independent of Constantinople. Serbia's days were numbered, however. The Ottoman Turks crossed into Europe from Asia in the 1350s. Within a few years, the Serbs were fighting the Ottomans. At the Battle of Kosovo in 1389, the Turks crushed Serbia's army and soon afterward gained control of Serbia.

In this illustration, Byzantine knights defeat Bulgar soldiers. Many wars and conflicts occurred between eastern Europe and the Byzantine Empire.

◆ What were Stefan Dusan's accomplishments for Serbia?

A. The Balkans

Purpose-Setting Question What groups settled in the Balkan region? (Slavs, Bulgarians, and Serbians)

ANALYZE PRIMARY SOURCES

DOCUMENT-BASED QUESTION
Constantine Porphyrogenitus was emperor of Byzantium from 913 to 959. His writings are some of the best sources for culture and learning of his day and region. Among his many books, Constantine wrote about the imperial administration of the Slavic and Turkish peoples. Little other evidence of these people exists outside of this writing.

ANSWER The military governor was instructed to defeat and kill the Slavs.

Extend Ask students to look at current news reports from Serbia and the Balkans. Have them identify the political, religious, and ethnic conflicts that still make it a region of turmoil.

Discuss Tell students that many countries and regions—including the region of the Balkans—are inhabited by people of different ethnic groups. Explain that an ethnic group is a large group of people who share a language and a cultural heritage. Discuss how ethnic diversity in a region could lead to tension, both culturally and politically.

Explore Ask students to look up *Cyrillic* in the dictionary and answer the following questions. Who first made the alphabet? (Saint Cyril) Where is it used? (Russia, Bulgaria, Slavic nations)

Activity

Use a map Have students study the map of Europe in the Atlas (p. A5) or Transparency 5 to identify each of the places mentioned in this section. Be sure that they locate the Balkan peninsula, the Danube River, present-day Bulgaria, present-day Serbia, Poland, the Black Sea, and Hungary.

◆ **ANSWER** Dusan conquered lands in Greece and Macedonia, made a code of laws, and made the Serbian church independent of Constantinople.

Meet Individual Needs:
LOGICAL/MATHEMATICAL

Have students make a four-column chart with the titles *Serbia, Bulgaria, Poland,* and *Hungary* at the top. Down the side, have students write *Geography, Settlers, Religion, Leaders.* Have students fill in the chart with the information from this section of the chapter. Suggest students use the chart to review the section.

Connection to
GOVERNMENT

Discuss the system within the Polish Sejm of *liberum veto,* in which a single voter could block legislation. Demonstrate the difficulties this veto would cause by setting up a class diet. Have the diet try to come to agreement about a school-related event, such as the theme for a dance or the destination for a class field trip. Allow diet members to discuss and argue the issues. Make sure to have one student always disagree.

B. Poland

Purpose-Setting Question What change took place in Polish society during the 1500s? (Poland became home to many different ethnic groups. Lords of large estates brought immigrants from Germany. Many Jewish people from western Europe came to settle in Kraków and other Polish cities. The settlers improved Poland's economy and brought with them technology and skills as farmers and craftspeople.)

WHERE IN THE WORLD?

KRAKÓW With a renowned university, Kraków was a cultural center and boasted architectural landmarks. Although the city fell into German hands during World War II, the Germans did not get the chance to destroy the historic buildings, which still stand as a testament to the proud history of the city and the nation.

Discuss Review the rule of the Polish diet that required all members to agree on legislation. As a class, discuss the advantages and disadvantages of this policy. Ask students to identify some of the ways that neighboring states could take advantage of this policy as included in the text. (Neighboring states could demand a certain action about trade or travel that limited the freedoms of the Polish people. The diet might have taken many sessions to come to agreement about how to address the conflict.)

◆ **ANSWER** to elect a king and pass laws

C. Hungary

Purpose-Setting Question What were the accomplishments of Stephen I? (He helped found Hungary, unified the Hungarians, and established the Roman Catholic Church in Hungary.)

Focus In the Balkans, peace was rare and life was harsh. Have students explain this statement by making a list of those groups that the Magyars in Hungary fought against during their occupation of the region.

In this painting titled *Oath of Queen Jadwiga*, Jadwiga swears loyalty to the Polish monarchy and to the Roman Catholic Church.

Where in the World?

KRAKÓW
Nestled in a valley in southern Poland, Kraków is one of the oldest cities in Poland. Many kings used Kraków as their capital.

The University of Kraków has been a center of culture and learning since the 1400s. One of its greatest students was Nicolaus Copernicus. Copernicus was an astronomer who devised the theory that Earth revolves around the Sun. His work was published in 1543, just before his death.

B. Poland

Geographically, the land of Poland is mostly a forested plain, though mountains lie to the south, and the Baltic Sea is to the north. West Slavs inhabited the region of Poland. They fought frequently with the Germans to the west.

Rulers of Poland

The rulers of Poland adopted Roman Catholicism in the 900s when missionaries from western and central Europe converted them to Christianity. The missionaries brought with them the Latin alphabet and western culture and ideas.

The first king of Poland was crowned in 1025. Poland expanded east, fighting other Slavs, Lithuanians, and Russians. A small force of Mongols attacked Poland in 1241. Most of the Mongol army was invading Hungary at the time, but the Polish defenders were defeated. However, Poland was not devastated like Russia or Hungary.

The reign of Queen Jadwiga brought a new age of greatness to Poland. Jadwiga married Grand Duke Wladyslaw Jagiello of Lithuania in 1386. The marriage linked Lithuania, a large state along Poland's eastern border, with Poland. Together, Poland and Lithuania controlled a vast territory, which stretched from the Baltic to the Black Sea. The Lithuanians, who before had their own religion, also converted to Roman Catholicism. Jadwiga and Jagiello also supported the University of Kraków, called the Jagiellonian University. It soon became the center of learning in Poland.

Changes in Government and Society

Royal power was decreased in Poland over time. The nobles of Poland met in a **diet**, or legislative assembly, called the Sejm. This group elected the king. In the 1500s and later, the king was often a foreigner. The diet also passed laws, and all members had to agree. If even one noble voted against a proposed law, the law was not passed. This situation made it difficult for the Polish government to be very effective.

Until the mid-1500s, Poland and Lithuania had separate governments. In 1569, the diets of Poland and Lithuania were joined into a single assembly. An agreement was made that officially united the two countries into one state. The state was now called Poland-Lithuania.

Over time, Poland became home to many different **ethnic groups**, or groups of people who shared the same language and heritage. Lords of large estates needed people to work the land. They brought immigrants from Germany to settle uninhabited lands. Many Jewish people from western Europe came to settle in Kraków and other Polish towns. They faced persecution in the west but were tolerated in Poland. The settlers improved the economy of Poland and brought with them technology and skills as farmers and craftspeople.

◆ **What was the purpose of the diet in Poland?**

C. Hungary

The Hungarian Plain is a wide region of grassland in central Europe. It is the westernmost part of the Eurasian—the combined European and Asian—steppe. Mountains surround it, but the Danube River cuts through its lands. The Magyars, a nomadic group from Russia, settled in Hungary.

Teaching Options

ESL/ELL STRATEGIES

Use Resources Have students look in an atlas to find a map of Poland. Have them locate the city of Kraków. Discuss its location in relation to other cities in Poland and Europe. Have students identify geographical and political factors that might have influenced the city.

F Y I

The Nazis in Kraków

At the beginning of World War II, the Germans took over Kraków, placing a German governor in the Wawel Castle, the traditional location for the crowning of Polish kings. Under the Nazi leadership, the German governor executed the teaching staff at the University. He also sent many of Kraków's Jewish population to the concentration camp at Auschwitz-Berkenau. Ultimately, nearly all of Kraków's 55,000 Jews were killed.

Magyar Invasion

For some time, the Magyars lived in the steppe of southern Russia. In the late 800s, they migrated into the Hungarian Plain. When they settled there, they became known as Hungarians.

In the first half of the 900s, as the Vikings raided by sea, the Hungarians attacked by land. They raided almost every corner of Europe, terrifying Europe's people as they destroyed towns. Many of the armies that stood against them were destroyed. The ruler of Germanic lands in western Europe rallied his forces against the Hungarians and defeated them at the Battle of Lechfeld in 955. The Hungarians were forced to accept peace. Hungarian raids into western Europe ended.

Saint Stephen

The first king of Hungary, Stephen I, ruled in the early 1000s. He unified the Hungarians. When he converted to Roman Catholicism, he established the Church in Hungary. As one of the founders of Hungary, Stephen was widely respected. Because of his deeds, the Church named Stephen a saint in the Roman Catholic Church.

The Hungarian king's authority was limited, however. King Andrew II of Hungary, for example, was forced to sign a **charter**—or official document—recognizing the rights of the nobles. Called the Golden Bull of 1222, it placed limits on royal power. The monarchy was weakened even more when some later kings came to power, not because they were in the royal family, but because they were elected by the nobles.

Hungary faced disaster in 1241 when the Mongol army destroyed the Hungarian army and massacred many Hungarians. Then, in 1526, the Ottoman Turks defeated the Hungarian army. The Ottomans took over most of Hungary, while Austria in the west took over the rest. Hungary was no longer independent.

◆ How did the Golden Bull of 1222 affect the government of Hungary?

Then & Now

CHARTERS OF RIGHTS
The Golden Bull of 1222 was just one charter of rights. The most famous one was the Magna Carta, which English nobles forced King John to sign in 1215.

The first modern charter of rights is the Bill of Rights in the U.S. Constitution. Like these earlier charters, it guarantees freedoms. Unlike them, rights are guaranteed for all citizens, and the Bill of Rights has remained in effect.

Review III

Review History
A. How did Serbia grow more powerful and wealthy in the 1200s?
B. How did Poland become one of the largest kingdoms in Europe?
C. What forced the Magyars to stop raiding western Europe?

Define Terms to Know
Define the following terms: **mercenary, diet, ethnic group, charter**

Critical Thinking
How were the governments of Poland and Hungary similar?

Write About History
Write a short essay comparing and contrasting Simeon and Stefan Dusan.

Get Organized
MAIN IDEA/SUPPORTING DETAILS CHART
Use a main idea/supporting details chart to organize information from this section. Choose a topic and then find supporting details. For example, what were some Byzantine cultural influences on the Bulgarians?

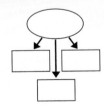

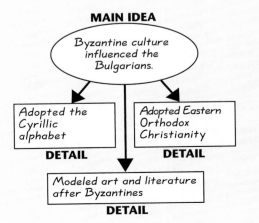

MAIN IDEA

Byzantine culture influenced the Bulgarians.

Adopted the Cyrillic alphabet
DETAIL

Adopted Eastern Orthodox Christianity
DETAIL

Modeled art and literature after Byzantines
DETAIL

Define Terms to Know
mercenary, 165; diet, 166; ethnic group, 166; charter, 167

Critical Thinking
Possible answer: Monarchs in both countries had their powers limited by the nobility.

Write About History
Possible answer: Simeon and Stephan Dusan were both strong leaders who took the title of emperor. Simeon claimed the Byzantine throne. Dusan wanted to capture Constantinople.

◆ **ANSWER** It limited the power of the king and recognized the rights of the nobles.

Section Close

Divide the class into three groups. Give each group a Main Idea/Supporting Details chart. (TR, p. 319) Have one group prepare a chart for each of the following: the Balkans, Poland, and Hungary. The main idea should be the establishment of the area named on the chart. Have students fill in as many details as they can remember. Then, have them exchange and add details to each other's charts.

3 Assess

Review Answers

Review History
A. Serbia conquered some lands. Its rulers used money from mining to hire mercenaries to control independent nobles.

B. The marriage of Jadwiga to Wladyslaw Jagiello linked Poland to Lithuania, and together Poland and Lithuania controlled a vast stretch of territory.

C. The Germans defeated the Hungarians at the Battle of Lechfeld in 955.

Chapter Summary

A blank outline form is available in the Teacher's Resources (p. 318). Chapter summaries should outline the founding, growth, and decline of the Byzantine Empire, the settlement and growth of Russia, and the early formation of the Eastern European countries of Serbia, Bulgaria, Poland, and Hungary. Refer to the rubric in the Teacher's Resources (p. 340) to score students' chapter summaries.

● Interpret the Timeline

1. The capture of Constantinople by the Ottoman Turks (1453)
2. 207 years
3. Answers will vary. They should include one of these events: Church of Hagia Sophia is completed; the Church at Canterbury, England, is founded as the center of English Christianity; a permanent split occurs between Roman Catholic and Eastern Orthodox Churches; crusaders capture Jerusalem; Martin Luther nails a list of grievances to a church door, sparking the Protestant Revolution.
4. Check that the events on students' timelines are from the chapter.

Use Terms to Know

5. boyar
6. autocrat
7. czar
8. steppe
9. diet
10. excommunicate
11. mercenary
12. icon
13. tundra

Check Your Understanding

14. Justinian reconquered part of the Roman Empire; he created a new law code; he started a building campaign.
15. There were disagreements over the use of icons, or religious images. Many people prayed to icons. However, others believed that this violated God's commandments.
16. Byzantine culture influenced Europe and the eastern Mediterranean area. The Byzantines kept Greek culture alive and built upon Roman law and engineering.

Chapter Summary

Complete the following outline in your notebook. Then, use your outline to write a brief summary of the chapter.

The Byzantine Empire, Russia, and Eastern Europe

I. The Byzantine Empire
  A. Constantinople and the Age of Justinian
  B. Difficult Times for the Byzantine Empire
  C. The Byzantine Empire's Decline and Fall

II. The Rise of Russia
  A. The Geography and the People of Russia
  B. Mongol Conquest
  C. Moscow Dominates Russia

III. The Growth of Eastern European Culture
  A. The Balkans
  B. Poland
  C. Hungary

● Interpret the Timeline

Use the timeline on pages 150–151 to answer the following questions.

1. Which happened later, the capture of Constantinople by the Ottoman Turks or the permanent split between the Roman Catholic and Eastern Orthodox Churches?

2. How many years after Constantinople was founded was the Church of Hagia Sophia completed?

3. **Critical Thinking** Which events on the timeline are about changes in Christianity and Protestantism?

4. Select five events from the chapter that are not on the timeline. Create a timeline that shows these events.

Use Terms to Know

Select the term that best completes each sentence.

autocrat	diet	mercenary
boyar	excommunicate	steppe
czar	icon	tundra

5. A Russian noble was called a _____.

6. An _____ is a ruler with complete power.

7. Ivan the Great's title was _____.

8. The _____ served as a way for many nomadic groups to travel from Asia to Europe.

9. Polish nobles attended the _____ to approve laws.

10. The pope could _____ an emperor from the Church.

11. A _____ serves in a foreign army for pay.

12. A religious image that is regarded as sacred is an _____.

13. The area of Russia that is a frozen plain without trees is the _____.

Check Your Understanding

14. **Summarize** the achievements of Justinian.

15. **Discuss** the religious dispute in the Byzantine Empire during the 700s and 800s.

16. **Describe** the lasting influence of the Byzantine civilization.

17. **Explain** how the Vikings encountered the Russians.

18. **Discuss** the effect the Mongol conquest had on Russia.

19. **Explain** how the Russian Orthodox Church became more powerful.

20. **Summarize** the achievements of Ivan the Great.

21. **Explain** how Bulgaria was founded.

22. **Describe** how the diets of Poland and Lithuania worked.

23. **Summarize** the events leading to the end of the Magyar raids.

Byzantine writers wrote history and literature. Europeans and the Ottoman Turks imitated Byzantine architecture.
17. In the 700s, the Vikings traveled on the rivers of Russia. They settled in trade centers such as Kiev.
18. Princes had to pay tribute to the Mongols; peasants were heavily taxed and many tried to leave the land; the Eastern Orthodox Church became more powerful; the princes of Moscow became more powerful.

19. The grand princes did not control the Russian Orthodox Church, and it became more independent. Russian bishops selected their own Church leader. Donations made the Church a large landowner.
20. unified Russian settlements, conquered Novgorod, freed Russians from Mongol rule, reconquered lands taken by Lithuania
21. The Bulgars moved into the northern Balkans and founded Bulgaria.

22. The diet was an assembly of nobles; the nobles elected a king; the nobles also passed laws; the laws needed the votes of all the nobles to pass.
23. The Magyars raided many places in Europe until the Germans defeated them at the Battle of Lechfeld in 955 and the raids stopped.

Critical Thinking

24. Draw Conclusions What were the successes and failures of the wars of Justinian?

25. Analyze Primary Sources What does the quotation from Grand Prince Vasilii's letter on page 161 say about relations between himself and the peasants?

26. Make Inferences How could the Polish adoption of Roman Catholic Christianity have affected relations with Russia?

Put Your Skills to Work

27. Analyze Primary-Source Documents You have learned how to interpret primary-source documents. Interpreting a document can help you learn more about the person, place, or event it describes.

Read the excerpt, or passage, below. It is a historical account arranged according to the order that events happened. The passage from the Russian chronicle describes the relations between Russian princes and the Mongols during the 1200s and 1300s. After you read the passage, answer the following questions.

a. Which people held the power in Russia at this time?

b. Who seems to have had the most power?

c. What were the orders of the khan?

d. How does this passage show that the Mongols were tolerant of the Russians?

"Prince Gleb Vasilikovich went to the [Mongol] land to Sartak [a Mongol lord]. Sartak honored him and dismissed him to his patrimony [estate inherited from his father]. That same winter, Aleksandr and Andrei returned from the khan [Mongol ruler], who ordered that Kiev and the entire Russian land be given to Aleksandr and that Andrei sit on the throne in Vladimir."

Analyze Sources

28. Read more about the relations between the Russians and the Pechenegs, as described by Byzantine Emperor Constantine Porphyrogenitus. The Pechenegs were part of the Mongols, and they controlled the lands between the Don and Danube Rivers. The emperor wrote about the Byzantine Empire and neighboring areas. After you read the passage, answer the questions that follow.

The Russians are much concerned to keep the peace with the Pechenegs. For they buy of them horned cattle and horses and sheep . . . since none of the aforesaid animals is found in Russia. Moreover, the Russians are quite unable to set out for wars . . . unless they are at peace with the Pechenegs. . . . Nor can the Russians come at this imperial city of the Romans [Constantinople] . . . unless they are at peace with the Pechenegs.

a. What do the Russians buy from the Pechenegs?

b. How do relations with the Pechenegs affect the Russians?

Essay Writing

29. Choose a topic about Russian or eastern European culture. Write an essay about how the Byzantine Empire affected that part of the culture of Russia or eastern Europe.

TEST PREPARATION

CAUSE-AND-EFFECT RELATIONSHIPS
Choose the answer that correctly completes the sentence.

A result of the wars of Justinian was

1. a decrease in the Byzantine Empire's territorial size.

2. an increased treasury.

3. that Byzantine armies reconquered North Africa, Italy, and southern Spain.

4. all of the above

Critical Thinking

24. Successes: recovered lands and reconquered North Africa, Italy, and southern Spain; Byzantine Empire reached its greatest size. **Failures:** Justinian's wars were expensive and drained the treasury.

25. Possible answer: Grand Prince Vasilii does not seem to care about the peasants' problems and just wants the peasants to be returned to their villages.

26. Possible answer: Relations could have worsened because of religious disputes, or relations would not be as close because of religious differences.

Put Your Skills to Work

ANALYZE PRIMARY-SOURCE DOCUMENTS
27a. the Mongols
27b. the khan, or Mongol ruler
27c. Kiev and all Russian land be given to Aleksandr and that Andrei be ruler of Vladimir
27d. Mongols honored Prince Gleb Vasilikovich, and they gave Russian princes land and ruling power.

Analyze Sources

28a. horses, cattle, and sheep
28b. Possible answer: If the Russians are not at peace with the Pechenegs, they cannot go to war with other countries or come to Constantinople.

Essay Writing

29. Students' essays should consider such topics as religion, language, literature, art, and architecture.

TEST PREPARATION

Answer 3. that Byzantine armies reconquered North Africa, Italy, and southern Spain.

The Islamic World
622–1629
(pp. 170–196)

Chapter Objectives
- Discuss how the religion of Islam began and then was spread to different parts of the world.
- Explore early Islamic society, family life, and achievements.
- Identify changes in India that were a result of Islamic invaders.
- Compare the Ottoman Empire to the Safavid Empire.

Chapter Summary
Section I focuses on the Islamic prophet known as Muhammad, the land in which Muhammad was born, his religious calling, and the subsequent spread of his teachings around the world.
Section II discusses how Islam affected all aspects of religious and secular society, which resulted in political, educational, and cultural improvements in many parts of the world.
Section III describes the succession of Islamic rulers who invaded India—including the Delhi sultanate, Tamerlane, and Babur—and how they affected the culture of the land.
Section IV demonstrates how the Ottomans sought to become the leaders of a united Islamic world and how the Safavid Empire affected Iran.

Set the Stage
TEACH PRIMARY SOURCES
The quotation on this page is from the holy book known as the Quran. Explore with students what the word *remits* in this quotation might mean. Encourage students to discuss why the idea of a savior—someone who absolves all sins and gives the reward of happiness to those who have faith—might find many supporters in a society.

The Islamic World
622–1629

I. The Rise and Spread of Islam
II. Islamic Achievements
III. Islamic Rulers in India
IV. The Ottoman and Safavid Empires

One of the major religions of the world, Islam began nearly 1,400 years ago in the Arabian city of Mecca. The teachings of Islam began with Muhammad. These teachings help shape the lives of Muslims—or people who belong to the Islamic faith—all over the world. There are more than 1.2 billion Muslims in the world today.

Muslims live in many countries throughout the world. As a result, they come from a variety of cultural backgrounds and speak many different languages. Yet Muslims all over the world share one very important thing—their religion. All Muslims regard the Quran as the holy book of their religion. Some Muslims memorize the entire Quran, even though the book contains more than 78,000 words. The Quran says the following about those who believe in what Muhammad taught:

> **❝** *Those who believe and work righteousness, and believe in what was sent down to Muhammad—which is the truth from their God—He remits their sins and blesses them with contentment.* **❞**

622
Muhammad flees from Mecca to Medina.

750
Abbasid Dynasty comes to power.

1099
Christian Crusaders from Europe capture Jerusalem.

CHAPTER EVENTS

600 · · · · · 800 · · · · · 1000

WORLD EVENTS

620
Production of porcelain begins in China.

800
Holy Roman Empire is established.

Teaching Options

Chapter 8 Resources

REVIEW

Teacher's Resources (TR)
Terms to Know, p. 21
Review History, p. 55
Build Your Skills, p. 89
Chapter Test, pp. 131–132
Concept Builder, p. 224
SQR Chart, p. 322
Transparencies 1, 10, 15

ASSESSMENT

Section Reviews, pp. 178, 184, 189, 193
Chapter Review, pp. 194–195
Chapter Test, TR, pp. 131–132
Unit Test, TR, pp. 185–186

ALTERNATIVE ASSESSMENT

Portfolio Project, p. 196
Make a Poster, p. T196

GET ORGANIZED

SQR CHART SQR stands for the words Survey, Question, and Read. An SQR chart helps you know what to look for when you read. First, survey the material. Look at the headings and visuals. Then, scan the text and write questions you hope to answer as you read. Finally, read and write the answers. Here is an example from this chapter.

SURVEY
This section is about the rise and spread of Islam.

↓

QUESTION
How did Islam begin?

↓

READ
Muhammad in Mecca and Medina

VIEW HISTORY Muslims worship in religious buildings called mosques, such as this one in Istanbul, Turkey. Called the Blue Mosque, it gets its name from the 20,000 blue tiles that line its interior. The center dome is 141 feet across and 77 feet high.
◆ What do you think is the purpose of the towers that surround the center dome?

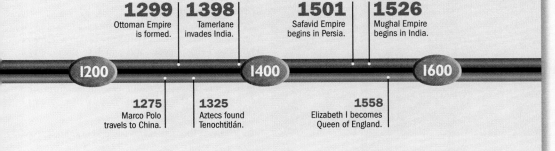

1299 Ottoman Empire is formed.

1398 Tamerlane invades India.

1501 Safavid Empire begins in Persia.

1526 Mughal Empire begins in India.

1200   1400   1600

1275 Marco Polo travels to China.

1325 Aztecs found Tenochtitlán.

1558 Elizabeth I becomes Queen of England.

CHAPTER 8 ◆ The Islamic World **171**

Chapter Themes
- Culture
- Time, Continuity, and Change
- Individual Development and Identity
- Individuals, Groups, and Institutions
- Power, Authority, and Governance
- Global Connections
- Science, Technology, and Society

F Y I

The Parts of a Mosque
A mosque is always orientated so that Muslims pray facing the *qibla* wall, or toward Mecca. A decorated alcove called a *mihrab* marks the *qibla*. Other parts of a mosque are a *mimbar*, or pulpit; a *maqsura*, or an enclosed space in which the caliph prays; a *minaret*, or tower from which the call to prayer is sounded; a *sahn*, or courtyard; and a *madrasa*, or space for a school.

Chapter Warm-Up

USING THE MAP
Point out the locator map at the top of page 171. To help students understand the far reach of Islam, have them identify Asia, Africa, Europe, and the Mediterranean Sea.

VIEW HISTORY
Discuss the mosque in the photograph with students. Ask them to describe its size, shape, color, and location. Then, ask them to describe a place of worship in their neighborhood, including its size and style of architecture. Discuss what the size and style of a building reveals about the people who built it. (The Blue Mosque, for example, is a very large and intricately built structure. It signifies the importance of religion to the community it serves.)

◆ **ANSWER** Possible answers: They may be used as decoration; they may be used as places from which to call people to prayer.

GET ORGANIZED
SQR Chart
Explain the steps of SQR to students. *Survey* includes scanning the titles and headings of a section to find out the main idea. *Question* includes writing down questions about the information in the text before reading. *Read* involves reading the text and locating the answers to questions identified in the *Question* section. Review the SQR chart on this page as an example for students.

⬤ TEACH THE TIMELINE
The timeline that is on pages 170–171 covers the period between 620 and 1558. Have students find events that involved the violent overthrow of the government of one nation or group by another nation or group. (1099, Christian crusaders from Europe capture Jerusalem; 1398, Tamerlane invades India.)

Activity
Use a map Several different countries are noted on the World Events part of the timeline. Have students locate these countries on the world map in the Atlas, pages A1–A2, or on Transparency 1.

Section Summary

In this section, students will learn about Muhammad, the founder of the monotheistic religion of Islam, and how he attracted followers all over the Arabian Peninsula. They will also learn the basic tenets of the religion and how it spread to Asia and the Mediterranean region. Lastly, students will learn how Turkish-speaking groups challenged Islamic rulers.

1 Introduce

Getting Started

Ask students to think of clubs or teams of which they are members. Then, ask them to describe some of the other members of that organization—their ideas, interests, where they live, and so on. Point out to students that without the shared experience of belonging to the organization, the members of the group are probably quite different. Tell students that Muhammad brought together independent nomadic groups by unifying them in their belief in one God, Allah.

TERMS TO KNOW

Ask students to read the terms and definitions on page 172 and then find each term in the section. Have them work with a partner and take turns using each term in a sentence.

You may wish to preview the pronunciation of the following terms with students.

Kaaba (KAH buh)
Quran (koo RAHN)
Abu Bakar (uh BOO BAK uhr)
Sunni (SOON ee)
Shiite (SHEE yt)
Abbasid (eh BA sehd)

ACTIVE READING

Have students write down the main points about the Arabian Peninsula on the left side of a sheet of paper as they read. Then, have them write a conclusion on the right side of the paper about how the geography of the region helped encourage the spread of Islam.

Section I

The Rise and Spread of Islam

Terms to Know

oasis a fertile place in a desert, due to the presence of water

prophet someone chosen by God to bring a message to people

hijra the flight of Muhammad and his followers from Mecca to Medina in 622

hajj a pilgrimage to Mecca; one of Five Pillars of Islam

jihad an effort carried out as a religious duty

caliph an Islamic ruler with the authority to rule from Muhammad

sultan the ruler of an Islamic state

Main Ideas

A. When Islam began, the Arabian Peninsula was a crossroad of trade.

B. Muhammad founded Islam based on revelations from God, which were collected in the Quran.

C. Islam spread quickly in Asia, North Africa, and Spain.

D. The empire of the caliphs did not remain united, and Turkish-speaking tribes moved into the Middle East.

Active Reading

DRAW CONCLUSIONS
When you draw conclusions, you make judgments about pieces of information. As you read this section, draw conclusions about the spread of Islam.

A. The Arabian Peninsula

The religion called Islam began on the Arabian Peninsula in southwestern Asia. The boundaries of the peninsula include the Red Sea to the west, the Persian Gulf to the east, the Indian Ocean to the south, and the Syrian Desert to the north. It is part of an area known as the Middle East. The Middle East stretches from Africa across the Arabian Peninsula into Asia.

The Arabian Peninsula has no permanent rivers or other bodies of water. The dry valleys, called wadis, fill with water when it rains, but the water disappears quickly. The peninsula consists of desert in the interior, with seacoast and mountains in the west. The central plateau, called Najd, has little vegetation, but there are some fertile **oases** where crops grow. An oasis is a fertile area in a desert.

Crossroads of Trade

Camels, which can survive for days without water, made travel across the desert easier. The people of Arabia carried on an active trade with peoples in Asia and Africa. Because of Arabia's location in the center of the Middle East, towns in Arabia became part of trade routes. Arabian products such as incense and animal hides were exchanged for spices, gold, ivory, and silk. These goods were sold in the fairs and markets around Mecca. Mecca, located on the west coast of the Arabian Peninsula, was Arabia's busiest trading center.

Bedouin Nomads

Many Arab clans lived in Arabia. One group of nomadic herders were known as the Bedouin nomads. They raised sheep, goats, and camels in the desert of the Arabian Peninsula. They traveled great distances on camels in search of pastures. In the town of Mecca and into this cultural environment, Muhammad, who was to become the most important figure in all of Islam, was born.

◆ **Why was there so much trade in Arabia?**

Camels are among the most useful animals in hot, dry lands, such as the Arabian Peninsula.

Teaching Options

Section 1 Resources

Teacher's Resources (TR)
Terms to Know, p. 21
Review History, p. 55
Build Your Skills, p. 89
Concept Builder, p. 224
SQR Chart, p. 322
Transparencies 10, 15

Cooperative Learning

Have students work in small groups to plan a journey to Mecca by caravan. Have them assign a specific role to each member of the group, such as caring for the camels, gathering food supplies, and packaging products to be sold at the market. Tell students to write a description of their plan. Finally, have them read their plan aloud to the other groups in the class.

B. Foundations of Islam

The desert and trade centers of the peninsula helped shape the early life of Muhammad—the founder of the Islamic religion. Muhammad was born in the city of Mecca more than 1,400 years ago, in about 570. Since both of Muhammad's parents died before he was seven years old, his uncle raised him. Muhammad is reported to have been thoughtful and honest.

Muhammad's Vision

Often Muhammad would go off by himself to think about life and how it should be lived. He sometimes went to a cave in the mountains near Mecca where he would pray for guidance. On one such occasion, around the year 610, Muhammad had a vision of the angel Gabriel—the first of many dreams that would change his life. During this vision, a voice told Muhammad to preach the word of God. At first, Muhammad was unsure how to begin. As more dreams and visions followed, Muhammad discussed his religious views with his family and friends. They told him he was meant to be a **prophet** who spoke on behalf of God. Muhammad's wife was the first to convert to, or join, the new faith he preached.

Soon Muhammad was preaching to large crowds at the market in Mecca. He taught the people of Mecca that Allah alone was God. *Allah* is the Arabic word for "God." To Allah alone, he insisted, the people must pray.

At first, only a few people in Mecca believed Muhammad's account of the angel's message. In time, Muhammad did win followers, and his opponents grew alarmed. They began to abuse and persecute those who believed Muhammad.

In 622, Muhammad and his followers decided to leave Mecca. This emigration, or leaving, is known as the **hijra**, which means "flight" in Arabic. Muhammad and his followers traveled to Medina, which became known as "the city of the Prophet." The escape of Muhammad and his followers is very important to Muslims. The Islamic calendar begins on the date of the hijra, July 16, 622.

The hijra marked the beginning of a new period in the history of Islam. Muhammad successfully converted all the citizens of Medina to Islam. He concentrated on building a community among the Arabs. He began to give Islam its own distinctive features.

Tensions grew between Mecca and Medina. Several years of war followed. Muhammad and the Muslims conquered Mecca in 630. Few Meccans fought against him. He destroyed the statues and other symbols of the many gods in the Kaaba—a shrine that houses a sacred black stone—and turned it into a holy place dedicated to Allah alone. Many of the people of Mecca began to convert to Islam after witnessing Muhammad's power. Mecca was now the center of the Islamic religion.

Teachings of Islam

Muhammad preached a religion in which all people were equal before God. He taught that there is but one Allah. Muhammad also said that in order for Muslims to gain Allah's grace, they must submit, or give in, to Allah's will. In fact, the word *Islam* means "submission to the will of Allah." The followers of the religion are called Muslims, those who have surrendered.

The black building in the center of this picture is the Kaaba. The Kaaba, located in Mecca, is Islam's most holy place.

Connection to MATH

The Islamic lunar calendar begins on the date of the hijra, July 16, 622. The calendar consists of 12 months. Some months have 29 days and others have 30 days. There are 354 days in a lunar year during a non-leap year. Ask students to compare and contrast the Islamic lunar calendar to the calendar they use (most likely the Gregorian calendar).

Connection to CULTURE

The Kaaba is a cubic stone structure, covered by a black cloth, that resides within the great mosque in Mecca, Saudi Arabia. Set in the outside of the Kaaba is a black stone, possibly a meteorite. This stone is revered and ritually kissed. Muslims believe that Abraham and his son Ishmael rebuilt the Kaaba, which is said to have been first built by Adam.

To be a good Muslim, a person must follow Islamic daily rules of living. A Muslim must also carry out the five major duties known as the Five Pillars of Islam. First, a Muslim must publicly declare that there is only one God, who is called Allah, and that Muhammad is Allah's prophet. Second, a Muslim must pray five times a day between dawn and dusk. Each time Muslims pray, they are to kneel and face the holy city of Mecca. Third, a Muslim must give alms, or donations to the poor. Alms include money, food, and clothing. Fourth, a Muslim must fast, or not eat, from dawn to sundown each day of the holy month of Ramadan. Ramadan is the ninth month of the Islamic calendar. Fifth, a Muslim must make a **hajj**, or pilgrimage, to Mecca. All Muslims who are able are expected to visit the Kaaba, Islam's most holy place, at least once in their lifetime.

The Quran

Muhammad's followers collected his teachings into one book of rules and laws called the Quran. Muslims believe that the Quran is the word of God revealed to Muhammad through the angel Gabriel. Muhammad spoke these words to his followers, who either memorized them or wrote them down. By 650, the entire collection of these revelations was complete. The Quran guides a believer through every aspect of life—moral, social, political, and legal.

The first chapters, or suras, of the Quran describe the goodness and power of Allah. They tell the people to worship Allah and to show their gratitude for what they have. The Quran states,

ANALYZE PRIMARY SOURCES
DOCUMENT-BASED QUESTION
What do you think it means to live a righteous life?

❝ Give good news to those who believe and lead a righteous life that they will always have gardens with flowing streams. ❞

There are many connections in the Quran to Jewish and Christian beliefs. Because Jewish people and Christians had Bibles, Muslims accepted these groups' right to continue practicing their religions if they paid a tax. The Quran called Jews and Christians "people of the book" because each religion had a holy book with teachings on how to conduct daily life. Jews and Christians were considered superior to others in society who worshiped more than one god. Islamic leaders were taught to extend religious tolerance to Christians and Jews.

Muhammad's Last Years

After conquering Mecca in 630, Muhammad lived only two more years. During that time, Islam spread throughout the regions surrounding Mecca and Medina, often through the efforts of Islamic warriors.

Muhammad taught that Muslims must spread Allah's rule. Doing so, he warned, might require **jihad**, that is, extraordinary effort and struggle. Sometimes, he said, that effort might take the form of fighting, even of war.

◆ **What are the Five Pillars of Islam?**

This page is from the Quran, the holy book of Islam.

Teaching Options

Connection to
WORLD LANGUAGES

The language of the Quran is considered classical Arabic and is used only as a written language or in formal settings. Modern, colloquial Arabic is used in general conversation. Today, colloquial Arabic is spoken throughout the Arabian Peninsula, the Middle East, Africa, and Asia. Colloquial Arabic is also one of the official languages of the United Nations.

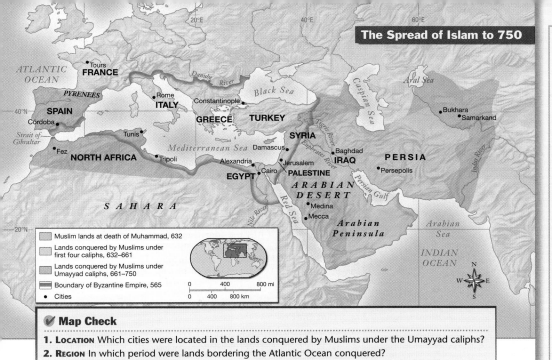

The Spread of Islam to 750

Muslim lands at death of Muhammad, 632

Lands conquered by Muslims under first four caliphs, 632–661

Lands conquered by Muslims under Umayyad caliphs, 661–750

Boundary of Byzantine Empire, 565

• Cities

0   400   800 mi
0   400   800 km

✔ Map Check

1. **LOCATION** Which cities were located in the lands conquered by Muslims under the Umayyad caliphs?
2. **REGION** In which period were lands bordering the Atlantic Ocean conquered?

C. Spread of Islam in Asia and the Mediterranean Region

When Muhammad died, he left no instructions for appointing a successor. His followers considered him the last of the prophets. However, Islam was spreading, and the Muslims knew they needed strong leadership to survive.

The Rightly Guided Caliphs

Although Muhammad did not name a successor, four men led the Muslims as religious and political leaders after his death. They were considered to be guided by Muhammad because they had known him personally. For this reason, they are called the rightly guided **caliphs**. The word *caliph* comes from the Arabic word *khalifat*, which means "successor." The four caliphs oversaw the spread of Islam throughout Syria, Palestine, Egypt, North Africa, and Persia. The caliphs acted as religious and political leaders. They used their powerful armed forces to control their growing empires.

Muhammad had told his followers to "spread the word." They did just that. Abu Bakr, the first caliph, was one of Muhammad's closest followers. He finished the job Muhammad had started of uniting the Arabian Peninsula under Islam. Under Umar, the second caliph, Islamic armies began to carry Islam to the lands outside Arabia. The third and fourth caliphs, Uthman and Ali, continued to expand Islamic territory eastward and westward.

Under the first four caliphs, Islamic armies marched from victory to victory. Their armies were tough to beat. Islamic soldiers were both good horseback riders and strong fighters. They depended on a combination of jihad, military strategy, and good fortune to accomplish their goals.

Point out to students that trade increased as the Muslims conquered new territory. Then, ask students how trade might have helped to further Muhammad's teachings. (Muslims would have had the opportunity to talk with people from many places and, possibly, convert them to Islam. Those converts would, in turn, return to their native lands, where they could convert more people. Thus, Islam could spread farther and quicker than a religion developing in a more isolated area.)

✔ Map Check
Answers
1. Córdoba, Fez, Tunis, Bukhara, Samarkand
2. under the Umayyad caliphs from 661–750.

C. Spread of Islam in Asia and the Mediterranean Region

Purpose-Setting Question How did new food crops from India improve life in the Middle East? (Tropical plants could be grown in the summer months, which meant a longer growing season and more types of crops.)

Extend Islam is the second largest religion in the world, with approximately 1 billion members. Review Transparency 15 with students to show how Islam has spread in the world today. The name of the religion comes from the word *salam*, which means peace. Have students do research to find out more about Muslim beliefs and how they relate to the meaning of the name of the religion.

Activity

Prepare and present an oral report Have students prepare and present an oral report on one of the following topics: (a) the history of Islam, (b) the teachings of Islam, or (c) the religious obligations of Islam. Students may wish to conduct additional research in the library using reference materials or search on the Internet to find information to complete their reports.

ESL/ELL STRATEGIES

Organize Information To help students chronicle the lives of the four caliphs who succeeded Muhammad, have them create a flowchart (TR, p. 324) and add an extra box at the end. Students should start with the death of Muhammad. Then, they should list each successor and summarize the major achievements of his reign. Encourage students to review their chart as needed as they read the rest of the chapter.

Connection to GEOGRAPHY

Point out to students that geography may have played a part in helping to spread Islam. Have students look at a map of the Middle East (Atlas p. A7 or Transparency 10). Point out that the lands east and west of Arabia are relatively flat and open. Thus, Muslim warriors could move swiftly from region to region as they conquered new territory.

Demonstrate Use maps of the Middle East and the Mediterranean region to help students locate the important battles fought by Muslim warriors. Point to various geographic features and ask students to speculate how these may have affected fighting strategies and outcomes. For example, the Balkan Mountains might have posed a challenge to Islamic expansion into eastern Europe.

Explore Ask students to discuss some of the differences that existed between the Sunni and the Shiites. (Each group had its own political and religious beliefs.) Encourage students to make a two-column chart (TR, p. 328) in which they can list these differences. Then, as a class, discuss how these differences might have affected the political and religious beliefs of both groups today.

Activity

Create a Venn diagram Have students use a Venn diagram (TR, p. 323) to compare and contrast the goals and accomplishments of the first two caliphs with those of the third and fourth caliphs. (Students should show that the first two caliphs continued to spread the word of Muhammad and to try to unite the Arabian Peninsula, whereas the third and fourth caliphs led armies to expand the territory of Islam; both groups were determined to spread the message of Islam throughout the region.)

Extend Like the schism between the Roman Catholic and Eastern Orthodox Christians, the divisions between Sunni and Shiite Muslims became permanent and have lasted to this day. Members of both branches believe in one God, Allah, refer to the Quran for guidance, and require the hajj. However, numerous differences have emerged, in such areas as religious practice, law, and daily life. Today, about 90 percent of Muslims are Sunni. Most Shiites live in Lebanon, Iraq, and Yemen. The Shiite movement itself has split into several different factions.

T176 ◆ **UNIT 2**

Sunni and Shiites

Even as the Muslims fought for the expansion of Islam, divisions developed among them. After Muhammad died, conflicts arose over who would succeed him. From these conflicts arose two distinct Islamic groups—the Sunni and the Shiites. These two groups exist among Muslims even today.

The differences between the Sunni and the Shiites were both political and religious. The Sunni, the larger group, supported the leadership of the early caliphs. They believed that the Quran was the only guide they needed between Allah and his followers. The Shiites disagreed. They believed that the only true successor had to be a direct descendant of Muhammad's daughter and son-in-law. They believed a person had to act as a guide between Allah and his followers. The division between Sunni and Shiite Muslims has survived to the present day. The division began as a political split, but the Shiites developed religious differences as well.

The Umayyads

After the death of Ali, the fourth caliph, the Umayyad family set up a dynasty that ruled the Islamic world until 750. The founder of the Umayyad Dynasty, Mu'awiyah, became caliph in 660. He moved his capital from Medina to Damascus in Syria. This location made controlling conquered territories easier. He and his successors conquered Rhodes, Sicily, North Africa, and Afghanistan.

Important Battles

By the year 636, Islamic armies had defeated the Byzantines at the Battle of Yarmak. One year later, Jerusalem was taken. The Muslims attacked Egypt and then attacked Persia. By 645, the Muslims controlled Persia, Syria, Iraq, Palestine, and Egypt.

The Islamic faith also spread south and west. All of North Africa fell to Islamic forces. North African Muslims, called Moors, crossed into territory that is now Spain and Portugal and conquered it by 719.

In 719 Islamic armies crossed the Pyrenees into what is now France. However, in 732 at a daylong battle near the city of Tours, they were defeated by an army led by Charles Martel. This was a very important battle. Martel's victory meant that most of Europe would remain Christian.

Far to the east, the Muslims defeated a Chinese army in 751 at the Battle of Tales, in central Asia. This too was a decisive battle. The Chinese Empire would never again reach that far west, and Islam replaced Buddhism as the major religion of central Asia.

The Abbasid Dynasty

Around 750, the Abbasid Dynasty came to power. Under the Abbasids, Islamic civilization became more splendid. The construction of mosques, schools, and hospitals throughout the empire came from a public works policy whose success depended on people's taxes. Economic prosperity was based primarily on agriculture and improved by commerce and manufacturing.

The second Abbasid caliph, Al-Mansur, built a new capital on the banks of the Tigris River.

Muslim warriors helped spread the Islamic faith.

Teaching Options

F Y I

Charles Martel

Charles Martel (ca. 688–741), grandfather of Charlemagne, eventually controlled the West Frankish kingdoms of Neustria, Burgundy, Aquitaine, and Provence. After he defeated the Spanish Muslims, he re-established the Franks as the rulers of Gaul. Although never officially given the title of king, Martel nevertheless divided the Frankish lands between his sons Pepin the Short and Carloman.

Test Taking

Essay questions often ask students to demonstrate the cause and effect of an event. To practice this skill, have students write an answer to the following essay question, using the text discussion on page 176: *What were the long-term consequences of the division of Muslims into Sunni and Shiites?*

Baghdad, the new capital, grew into a sprawling city of more than 1 million people.

The early years of the Abbasid Dynasty were very prosperous. New food crops were brought from India and planted in the Middle East. These new plants brought a great change in agriculture. Crops such as rice, sugar cane, lemons, limes, bananas, coconut palms, spinach, and eggplant allowed the growing season to be extended into the summer months, when other crops could not grow.

Trade also brought great wealth to the empire. Hundreds of ships came loaded with goods from every part of the empire and beyond—porcelain from China, ivory and gold from Africa, and furs from northern Europe. Shops in the empire sold spices, gems, linens and silk, ivory, and beautiful glassware.

The city of Baghdad reached its peak under Caliph Harun al-Rashid. Under his rule, the empire enjoyed a period of peace and prosperity. Because of his support of the arts and learning, a cultural awakening occurred. Literature, poetry, medicine, math, and astronomy flourished, as well as industry and commerce. For centuries, Harun al-Rashid was admired as a model ruler.

One order of Sufis is the Whirling Dervishes of Konya, Turkey. Dervishes try to achieve union with Allah through dancing.

Sufis

As the Muslims grew more powerful and Islam continued to spread throughout the world, many people longed for a more personal approach to religion. They found this approach in Sufism, a way to form a union with Allah in everyday life. Sufism arose during the Abbasid Dynasty. The Sufis believed in a union with Allah by continuous inner prayer, fasting, and other rituals. Some Sufis helped spread Islam to remote villages through missionary work.

◆ Who continued the spread of Islam after Muhammad died?

D. Caliph Rule Ends

The lands conquered by the Muslims contained a variety of peoples. Many of these conquered peoples adopted Islam. Many learned Arabic because this was the language of their conquerors. However, the empire of the caliphs did not remain united. Many disputes arose among different groups of Muslims. At one time there were three different caliphs, one in Baghdad, another in North Africa, and a third in Spain. Each of the caliphs claimed to be Muhammad's true successor. These divisions made it easier for Turkish-speaking tribes from central Asia to migrate to the Middle East.

Seljuk Turks

In the 900s, Turkish nomads, the Seljuks, began to settle in Islamic territories. Sometimes they served as soldiers of the caliph. Their advance marked the start of Turkish power in the Middle East. As the Abbasids grew weaker, the Seljuks grew stronger. They took over eastern areas of the empire and created a strong army to fight for them. They did not replace the caliph at the capital city of Baghdad, but the Seljuk leader—called the **sultan**—became the ruler of eastern Islamic lands.

The Seljuks also conquered the Anatolia peninsula, which was ruled by the Christian emperor at Constantinople. After the Seljuk conquest of Anatolia, the

These ancient gold dinar coins were used throughout the Islamic Empire as currency.

Discuss Ask students if they think some of the people whose land was conquered by Muslims may have resented being forced to adopt a new religion and culture. Have students explain their reasoning.

Explore There are many reports of Harun al-Rashid's wealth, generosity, and love of learning. Poets, physicians, philosophers, and artists all attended his court in Baghdad. Harun is said to have once rewarded his favorite poet with a robe of honor, a prize horse, and 5,000 dirhams. Harun also used gift giving to create closer ties with other rulers. For example, he sent the Frankish king Charlemagne a mechanical clock and an elephant. Harun hoped that the Franks would join him in an alliance against his rival caliph, Umayyad, in Spain. Harun amassed a great fortune in dirhams in his lifetime, in spite of lavish spending. In his treasuries were also huge amounts of jewels and gold.

Extend The name *Sufi* probably refers to the simple woolen cloak many Muslims wore called a *suf.* The original Sufis were mostly mystics, who believed that a direct, personal experience of God could be achieved through meditation and self-discipline. Because of their traditions, the Sufis were able to preserve the more spiritual and mystical aspects of early Islam. The path followed by mystics in Sufism was called a *tariqa.* The *tariqa* was a set of mental and physical exercises that were used to enhance communion with Allah. Eventually, the term *tariqa* came to refer to any group of people following a Sufi mystic.

TEACH PRIMARY SOURCES
Have students study the gold coins shown on page 177. Tell students that the Abbasid government issued the dinar. Tell students that the dinar was highly valued and used throughout the Islamic Empire.

◆ **ANSWER** The followers of Muhammad, beginning with the rightly guided caliphs, continued the spread of Islam.

D. Caliph Rule Ends

Purpose-Setting Question
Why did the Christian emperor of Constantinople ask the Roman pope for help? (The Seljuk Turks had conquered the Anatolia peninsula, which contained Constantinople.)

Focus on
WORLD RELIGIONS

Sufism The literature of Sufism is characterized by the prominence of Persian works, notably those of Jalal ad-Din Rumi. Rumi also is credited as the inspiration for one of the Sufi orders, the Whirling Dervishes of Konya, Turkey. During the dance of the Whirling Dervishes, the right hand is turned up toward heaven. One foot remains on the ground while the other propels the dancer. The dancer keeps rhythm by continuously reciting the name of Allah.

The poetry of Rumi and others helped Sufism to gain popularity in Asia and western nations, such as the United States. However, some conservative Muslims disagree with Sufi practices such as dancing. Ask students why Sufism's popularity is both its strength and weakness. (**Strength:** helps Sufism to spread; **Weakness:** some Muslims do not support it.)

Do You Remember?
Remind students that Christian pilgrims wanted to travel to Jerusalem and were prevented because of the Turks. You may wish to have students review pages 155–156.

◆ **ANSWER** Pope Urban wanted to send an army to conquer and rescue the Holy Land, including Jerusalem, from the Muslims.

Section Close
Discuss with students how the death of Muhammad affected Islam during the early years of the religion. (Without Muhammad to unite them, differences among the groups who practiced Islam ultimately divided and weakened the Islamic Empire.)

3 Assess

Review Answers

Review History
A. Camels were important because they made it possible for traders to cross the desert to carry goods between the Mediterranean Sea and the Indian Ocean.

B. There is only one God, Allah. Allah sent a prophet named Muhammad to teach people the true path, and Muhammad was the last prophet.

C. The early years of the Abbasid Dynasty were prosperous because new food crops were brought in and planted, and because of trade.

D. Caliph rule declined because disputes broke out among different groups of Muslims, causing disunity. Also, too many caliphs claimed to be Muhammad's true successors.

Define Terms to Know
oasis, 172; prophet, 173; hijra, 173; hajj, 174; jihad, 174; caliph, 175; sultan, 178

Do You Remember?
In Chapter 7, you learned that Turkish armies gained control over Jerusalem and blocked the route to the city.

Christian emperor sent a message to the pope in Rome asking for help. The emperor probably wanted trained fighting men to help his armies win back lost territory. However, Pope Urban II, who received the message, had a much more far-reaching plan. The pope wanted to send an army to conquer and rescue the Holy Land—the land where Jesus had lived— from the Muslims. Above all, he wanted the Christians to capture the city of Jerusalem.

In 1095, Pope Urban called on the knights of western Europe to join in a war against the Muslims. This was the first of a series of wars that were later called the Crusades—wars for the cross—between European Christians and Muslims in the Middle East.

The Crusaders
The Crusades further weakened the Islamic Empire. The army of the First Crusade, which was made up of knights and lords, reached Constantinople in 1097. Two years later, in 1099, the Crusaders captured Jerusalem. The fighting between Muslims and Christians was fierce, and neither side showed mercy. When the Crusaders took Jerusalem, they killed not only fighting men, but also many of the women and children. For 150 years, the city of Jerusalem passed back and forth between Muslims and Christians. You will learn in later chapters about the impact that the Crusades had on Europe.

The unity of the Islamic Empire was never recovered. Islam, however, continued to flourish, perhaps because of the diversity of the Islamic peoples.

◆ **What was Pope Urban's far-reaching plan?**

Review I

Review History
A. Why were camels so important to the people of the Arabian Peninsula?
B. What are some of the basic beliefs of Islam?
C. Why were the early years of the Abbasid Dynasty so prosperous?
D. What led to the decline of the caliph rule in Islamic lands?

Define Terms to Know
Define the following terms:
oasis, prophet, hijra, hajj, jihad, caliph, sultan

Critical Thinking
How was the religion of Islam able to grow and spread despite problems near Mecca?

Write About History
Write a short essay about how the geography of the Middle East might have helped Muslims spread the teachings of Islam.

Get Organized
SQR CHART
Use an SQR chart to organize information from this section. For example, this section is about the beginnings of Islam and its spread.

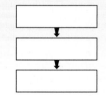

Critical Thinking
The religion of Islam was able to spread because of the faith of Muhammad and his followers.

Write About History
Students' essays should include: The geography helped Muslims spread the religion of Islam because of all the trade that took place there. Camels also made travel across the deserts easier.

SURVEY
This section is about the rise and spread of Islam.

⬇

QUESTION
How did Islam spread quickly?

⬇

READ
Muhammad received a revelation and converted many people to Islam. He and his followers conquered lands and converted others.

Build Your Skills

Build Your Skills

TAKE NOTES AND OUTLINE

Taking notes can help you to learn and to remember main ideas from your reading. It can also help you to prepare for tests and to write research papers. When you take notes, you write down important facts and ideas, adding supporting points and examples.

Leaving a line of space between notes makes them easier to read. You can also fill in additional notes between lines at a later time. Using index cards instead of paper is another way to take notes.

An outline helps you to group essential ideas and facts in an organized pattern. This will help you remember those pieces of information later. You can also record the logical sequence of whatever you are reading, such as this chapter. Use a pattern of letters and numbers to organize and write your outline. The goal of this type of outline is to write down important information to make it more understandable and useful at a later time.

Here's How

Follow these steps to take notes and to outline.

1. Write down main ideas and facts when taking notes. Look for titles, headings, lists, and charts in the material you are reading to find information. Look for words in boldface and italic type.

2. As you read, summarize key ideas and supporting details. Do not copy every word of a sentence.

3. Create an outline. Label main ideas with Roman numerals, subtopics with capital letters, and supporting details with numbers.

Here's Why

You have just read about the rise and spread of Islam. Suppose you needed to write an essay on the spread of Islam. Taking notes and outlining could help you write an informative essay about the topic. Your notes and outline could also be used later when you review this material.

Practice the Skill

Copy the outline on this page onto a sheet of paper. Complete the outline using the information in Section I of this chapter.

Extend the Skill

Answer the following questions.

1. How many main ideas are shown on the outline?

2. How many subtopics are listed under the first main idea?

Apply the Skill

As you read the remaining sections of this chapter, take notes and outline what you read. Then, use your notes to review information in this chapter.

> Topic: The Islamic Religion
> I. Origins of the Religion
>   A. Muhammad as God's prophet
>   1. Muhammad had a vision of the angel Gabriel.
>   2.
>   B. The Hijra
>   1. Muhammad and his followers traveled to Medina.
>   2.
> II. Beliefs of Islam
>   A. Five Pillars of Islam
>   1.
>   2.
>   B. The Quran
>   1.
>   2.

Build Your Skills

TAKE NOTES AND OUTLINE

Teach the Skill

Ask students to give examples of instances in which they take notes. They may mention they do so when listening to a lecture, when reading a textbook, or when researching a topic that they will need to write a paper on later.

Then, ask students what problems might result if a person writing a report did not make an outline first. They may say that the report could end up being disorganized, incomplete, or rambling. Point out that outlines can help them organize and explain information that otherwise might seem disjointed or disconnected.

Practice the Skill

Completed outlines may be similar to the following:

Topic: The Islamic Religion
I. Origins of the Religion
  A. Muhammad as God's prophet
    1. Muhammad had a vision of the angel Gabriel.
    2. Muhammad began to preach to large crowds.
  B. The Hijra
    1. Muhammad and his followers traveled to Medina.
    2. Medina was known as "city of the Prophet."
II. Beliefs of Islam
  A. Five Pillars of Islam
    1. Obligation of every Muslim
    2. Pilgrimage to Mecca
  B. The Quran
    1. The word of Allah revealed to Muhammad
    2. Guides a believer through life

Extend the Skill

ANSWERS
1. There are 2 main ideas.
2. two

Apply the Skill

For Sections 2, 3, and 4, encourage students to make an outline (TR, p. 318) before writing paragraphs for the *Write About Culture* activity on page 184, the *Write About Economics* activity on page 189, and the *Write About Citizenship* activity on page 193.

Teaching Options

RETEACH

Create a simple outline for one of the sections in Chapter 8. Then, on the board, write the items from the outline in random order, without the letters or numbers. Tell students to work with a partner to place the items in the proper order in an organized outline (TR, p. 318).

CHALLENGE

Ask students to apply this skill by taking notes, making an outline (TR, p. 318), and writing a report on a current event related to Islam. Students might use books, magazines, newspapers, and the Internet to research and write their reports.

II. Islamic Achievements
(pp. 180–184)

Section Summary

In this section, students will learn how the values of Islam affected both secular and religious activities. They will also learn how urban areas became centers of scientific and cultural achievements. Finally, students will learn about Persian and Spanish influences on Islam.

1 Introduce

Getting Started

Point out to students that one principle of the U.S. government is the separation of church and state. Nevertheless, there are instances in which religion and the U.S. government are linked. Have students brainstorm some of these instances. (For example, the U.S. one-dollar bill is printed with the motto, "In God We Trust.") Explain to students that in some other cultures, such as the Islamic culture, religion and government are fully integrated.

TERMS TO KNOW

Ask students to read the terms and definitions on page 180 and find each term in the section. Then, have pairs of students write a multiple-choice vocabulary quiz using the terms from the chapter. They need four possible definitions for each term, with only one being correct. Have pairs exchange and complete each other's quizzes.

You may wish to review the pronunciation of the following terms with students.

Rubáiyát (ru BAY yat)
Ibn Khaldun (ihb uhn kal DOON)
Ibn Sina (ihb uhn SEE nah)
Abd ar-Rahman
  (UHB door rach MAHN)

ACTIVE READING

Have students make a two-column chart (TR, p. 328) in which they list the characteristics of the two Islamic societies they are comparing. Have students label one side of their chart *Abbasids in Baghdad* and the other *Umayyads in Spain*. Suggest they add to their charts as they read.

Terms to Know

bureaucrat a government official

calligraphy an elegant style of handwriting

minaret a tall, slender tower with a balcony, on a mosque

mihrab an arched area in a mosque wall that is closest to Mecca

Main Ideas

A. Society and family life changed to reflect the values of Islam.

B. Cities became highly organized centers of government, education, and culture.

C. Islamic contributions to learning brought many improvements.

D. Persian cultural influences were strong during the Abbasid Dynasty, and culture flourished in Islamic Spain.

Active Reading

COMPARE AND CONTRAST
When you compare and contrast, you look for what is the same and what is different in two or more subjects. As you read this section, concentrate on the Abbasids in Baghdad and the Umayyads in Spain. Then, compare and contrast the two.

Section II Islamic Achievements

A. Society and Family Life

Islam brought new ideas and customs to the lands that the Islamic forces conquered. Although people of many cultural backgrounds made up the Islamic Empire, there were many unifying factors that made Muslims part of the same community. First, their religion gave them a common bond. Another factor in unifying Muslims throughout the world was the Arabic language. Many people still spoke their own languages, but Arabic was the sacred language of the Quran and of prayer.

Islamic Society

People throughout the Islamic Empire lived their lives according to the Quran. The Quran gave detailed instructions on how society should be organized and how the people should live. Kindness, generosity, honesty, and tolerance were valued.

All Muslims are supposed to be equal. However, this was not always the case. One group of people in the Islamic Empire were not considered equal. They were the slaves. Slavery was common in the cities of the Islamic Empire. Slaves who converted to Islam had to be freed, but slaves also might become soldiers, household servants, artisans, or **bureaucrats**, government officials. Muhammad urged people to free their slaves or to treat them fairly if they did not free them.

Roles of Women

Women in nomadic societies had fewer rights than men. Islam established the spiritual equality of men and women. The Quran says that women should be educated, should be allowed to earn a living, and should be able to inherit their father's property. Educated women in the Islamic Empire wrote poetry and played instruments. They had duties as teachers and prayer leaders for other women. Muslim women studied astronomy, medicine, law, philosophy, history, Arabic grammar, literature, theology, and chess. They also studied medicine in excellent medical schools. Parents arranged marriages in Islamic society. Muslim men were allowed to have more than one wife at a time, as long as the women were treated equally.

◆ **What was the role of women in the Islamic Empire?**

The Quran states that women should be educated and should be allowed to earn a living. This mural shows a woman writing poetry.

Teaching Options

Section 2 Resources

Teacher's Resources (TR)
Terms to Know, p. 21
Review History, p. 55
Build Your Skills, p. 89
Concept Builder, p. 224
SQR Chart, p. 322

ESL/ELL STRATEGIES

Use Resources To help students make use of the different sections of their textbook, demonstrate how they can use the index to locate information on the early Islamic Empire. Point out that the index is organized alphabetically. Have students find a term and turn to the page indicated. Then, they should skim the page to find information on the early Islamic Empire.

B. Urban Centers

Great cities arose in the Islamic Empire. Caliphs built luxurious palaces and gardens. Tax money financed mosques, schools, libraries, hospitals, and bazaars—from the Persian word for marketplace. The taxes paid by Muslims supported the army and public welfare. Many cities became centers of political power, of commerce, and of learning.

Islamic Cities

One of the most impressive buildings in an Islamic city was the mosque. Mecca had the Kaaba, the most sacred of all mosques. One of the holiest sites in the Islamic world is the Dome of the Rock, built in Jerusalem in 691. It was built on the spot where Muhammad is believed to have risen to heaven. Each Islamic city also had public buildings, public baths, and the bazaar.

The bazaar grouped merchants based on their products, such as food, spices, cloth, and rugs. Instead of delivery trucks, pack animals brought goods into the bazaar. Prices were fixed and the market inspector guaranteed fairness. Bazaars and shops crowded the streets of the city, making them more and more narrow.

House of Wisdom

Muslims rejoiced in learning. Muslims developed centers of learning throughout the empire where Arab, Asian, and Western scholars could share ideas. The caliph at Baghdad, the capital during the Abbasid Dynasty, established a center of learning, the House of Wisdom. Here, Islamic scholars preserved the learning of earlier civilizations by translating texts into Arabic. The translations made it possible for Muslims to study the works of Greek philosophers, such as Plato and Aristotle, as well as the Quran. The House of Wisdom had a large library and an astronomical observatory.

➤ **What kinds of buildings were found in Islamic cities?**

The Dome of the Rock was built in 691 on Temple Mount in Jerusalem. It is one of Islam's most holy places.

② Teach

A. Society and Family Life

Purpose-Setting Question How did the Quran affect people's rights? (Before Islam, slaves and women had few rights. After Islam, some slaves were granted or could buy their freedom. Islam enabled women to get an education, earn a living, and inherit property.)

➤ **ANSWER** Women received rights they had not previously had. There was opportunity to acquire an education, to earn a living, and to inherit property.

B. Urban Centers

Purpose-Setting Question How did the House of Wisdom help maintain what the world knows of Greek civilization? (The House of Wisdom was a center of learning. Scholars were able to translate Greek texts that were housed there into Arabic so others could learn.)

Activity

Hold a bazaar Have students plan and conduct a classroom bazaar by making crafts or auctioning services, such as raking leaves or making dinner. Students should design and run booths that advertise their wares. The students may barter goods or create their own currency.

Extend Astronomy was important to Muslims because it helped them to determine the beginning of the month of Ramadan, the hours of prayer, and the direction of Mecca. Muslims follow the lunar calendar, as required by the Quran. Months change according to the phases and sky positions of the moon. Each month begins with the first sighting of the crescent moon. This is especially important to know in the holy month of Ramadan, when fasting is required during the day.

➤ **ANSWER** Islamic cities had mosques, hospitals, libraries, schools, and bazaars.

Writing

AVERAGE

Have students write a paragraph about the ways slaves were thought of and treated in Islamic Empire territories. Students should keep in mind that slavery was a common institution at that time throughout many parts of the world.

CHALLENGE

Ask students to write a likely dialogue between a person whose parents arranged a marriage and a person who chose his or her own spouse. Point out to students that although a marriage may be arranged, it does not necessarily follow that there would be no love or friendship between those who are about to be betrothed.

C. Cultural Life

Purpose-Setting Question What were some of the benefits of living in the Islamic Empire during the time of the caliphs? (Doctors and pharmacists were highly skilled. A wide range of medicines was readily available. The caliphs supported philosophers and artists. Thus, it was a time of great artistic achievement and scientific discovery.)

Explore Have students conduct research in the library or on the Internet about the practice of medicine from about 700 to 1600. Students should split into different groups to research various parts of the world or different civilizations during this time. Students can summarize their findings in oral reports to the class.

Discuss Ask students what it says about Islamic society that women poets were well known and respected. (Women were educated and poets were respected for their work. Writing was open to anyone with talent, not just to men.) Encourage students to discuss whether or not they believe poets are respected in today's society.

Extend Ibn Khaldun set important standards for the study of history. He emphasized the importance of economic systems and social classes as causes of historical events. He also warned about common kinds of errors in historical writings, such as bias, exaggeration, and too much faith in the accuracy of one's sources. Khaldun urged historians to trust sources of information only after a thorough investigation had been conducted.

Activity

Write an interpretation Have students choose a poem, such as one from Omar Khayyám's *The Rubáiyát,* or some verses of a poem from one of the great Islamic poets of the period. Tell students to write two or three paragraphs on the poem's meaning or message, first as a literary work and then in relation to Islamic philosophy or society.

This illustration is from *A Thousand and One Nights*, a classical Arabic work. The scene shows an encounter between Sinbad the Sailor, a famous character from the story, and a creature he meets on one of his voyages.

C. Cultural Life

Wealthy people of the Islamic Empire helped to bring about an era of scientific discovery and artistic achievement. The caliphs were important supporters of learning and the arts. They invited poets, astronomers, mathematicians, and physicians to their courts.

The Practice of Medicine

Sickness and disease were a part of life in the ancient world. However, people who lived in the Islamic Empire were luckier than most who lived in other parts of the world. Serious illness was taken care of in clean hospitals that were free to the public. Islamic doctors were highly skilled. They were the first to describe measles and smallpox accurately, and they were the first to discover how some diseases spread. They had to pass examinations before they could practice medicine. The city of Baghdad had more than 800 doctors.

Some doctors became very famous. They studied Greek, Persian, and Hindu medical texts. Then, they wrote books that contained the best information from other cultures and added their own observations about diseases and their treatments.

The first pharmacies, or drugstores, opened in Baghdad during the ninth century. Pharmacists had to pass a test to obtain a license from the government. In the pharmacies, ordinary people as well as doctors could buy medicinal herbs, tonics, and ointments from all over the Islamic Empire.

Literature, History, and Philosophy

Islamic poets wrote poems of great beauty, and other Islamic writers told stories that are still read today. The greatest story collection in Islamic literature is *A Thousand and One Nights*, also known as *The Arabian Nights*. It includes such familiar tales as "Aladdin" and "Sinbad the Sailor."

Poetry had long been an important part of Islamic culture. Quite a number of poets were women. Some were Sufis who wrote deeply religious poems. Omar Khayyám is best known to westerners for *The Rubáiyát*, a collection of nature and love poetry. Caliphs in the Islamic Empire enjoyed listening to poetry that described the heroic deeds of the warriors who were conquering land for Islam.

Ibn Khaldun was an important historian of the time. He observed and studied countries and developed the idea that states and empires rise and fall in cycles. He was the chief historian of the time and the creator of a new science of history.

One philosopher and doctor in the Islamic Empire, Ibn Sina, became especially famous. It is said that by the time he was ten years old, he had memorized the entire Quran. The Quran has 114 chapters and more than 6,000 verses. As an adult, he wrote medical encyclopedias that were used to teach doctors. Ibn Sina described with great accuracy what was known about various diseases and their treatments. He also wrote books on philosophy, astronomy, and mathematics.

Teaching Options

Connection to
LITERATURE

Students may wish to read stories from *The Arabian Nights*. This collection of stories is made up mostly of the oral folklore of the time. Students may wish to take more than one translation of *The Arabian Nights* out of the library in order to compare and contrast how styles of different storytellers or translators vary.

Meet Individual Needs:
AUDITORY LEARNERS

Ask one student to read aloud one of the three subsections under *Cultural Life*. Have the second student listen and take notes on the content. Have both students compare the notes with the text and evaluate accuracy. Then, have students switch roles.

This arched area, called a mihrab, marks the direction of Mecca.

Discuss Point out to students that important phrases and messages can be found today on the walls of libraries, municipal buildings, federal and state courthouses, schools, and in other public places and spaces. Challenge students to identify important messages that they see often, maybe daily, in their school and community. Discuss where the message is placed and what it means. Ask students if they think this is an effective way to get a message across to many people.

Explore At the same time that Muslims were building monumental mosques, other types of buildings were being created in western Europe and in Central and South America. Have students conduct research on other forms of architecture built from 1000 to 1200. Students can present their findings in a short report that uses visuals.

Extend The earliest architectural monument of Islam that still retains most of its original form is the Dome of the Rock (Qubbat al-Sakhrah), constructed in Jerusalem around 691 on the site of the Second Jewish Temple. Muslims believe this to be the spot from which the prophet Muhammad ascended to heaven.

The Dome of the Rock is a shrine capped with a magnificent dome reminiscent of the domes and arches of Byzantine structures. Its mosaics depict scrolling vines and flowers, jewels, and crowns in greens, blues, and gold. Both the Dome of the Rock in Jerusalem and the later great Mosque of Damascus used the Syrian cut-stone technique of building and popularized the use of the dome.

◆ **ANSWER** Islamic doctors had to pass examinations before they could practice medicine.

Art and Architecture

During this time, some of the most beautiful buildings in the world were designed and built by Islamic architects and builders. Islamic art began as a way to glorify God. Muslims decorated mosques with wooden carvings, carpets, glass lamps, tiles, and mosaics. Islamic artists did not represent humans or animals in their religious art because they believed that only God could create life.

Islamic artists developed **calligraphy**, the art of elegant writing. Calligraphers had a high position in Islamic society. Writing the words of Allah from the Quran in calligraphy was considered to be the highest form of decorative art. The words of the Quran can be written anywhere—on metal, wood, stone, tiles, mosaics, stucco, fabrics, and pictures. Even today, calligraphy remains a living art.

Carpets from this region are also works of art that developed during this time. The most famous were Persian carpets that included geometric, rhythmic, and floral patterns. Nomads made their own carpets, which they used for saddlebags and tent furnishings.

Islamic architecture became a symbol of great artistic talent. The Muslims originally used many of the architectural styles of the Byzantine and Persian Empires. They combined these with other influences in a way that became their own.

As you have learned, mosques were among the most important buildings built by Muslims. Mosques did not have bell towers like those of many Christian churches. Instead, there were tall and slender towers with balconies, called **minarets**, where people would call others to pray every day. In addition, mosques had a courtyard for ritual washings, a gate, and a **mihrab**, a small arched area to mark the direction of Mecca.

◆ **What did Islamic doctors have to do before they could practice medicine?**

Research

AVERAGE

Ask students to conduct additional research on the Persian influence on regional carpet-making, gathering information from the library or on the Internet. Then, have students design a sketch of a carpet for a saddlebag or tent furnishing. Display finished sketches on a bulletin board in the classroom.

CHALLENGE

Have students conduct further research into the art of calligraphy. Ask them to gather information about other cultures (some already mentioned in this book) that use calligraphic writing as an artistic form of communication. Ask students to write a report explaining the use of calligraphy in past societies as well as how, where, and for what purposes it is used today.

D. Persian Influences and Islamic Spain

Purpose-Setting Question How did the Islamic Empire change the nature of cities in Persia and Spain? (It made Baghdad into the beautiful, busy capital city and Córdoba in Spain into a cultural center, with many scholarly opportunities.)

◆ **ANSWER** The Abbasids established their capital in a Persian village and were bound to be influenced by everything from Persian economics to architecture.

Section Close

Ask students if they think Islamic advancements in the arts and sciences during this time have had any effect on their lives today. (Yes, many Islamic achievements in art and science became the foundation of advancements today.)

③ Assess

Review Answers

Review History

A. Marriages were arranged; women had more rights, including the right to acquire an education, earn a living, and inherit their father's property; men could have more than one wife as long as each was treated equally.

B. Islamic cities were centered around the mosques. There were schools, hospitals, libraries, and covered bazaars, which received their goods by means of pack animals. There was a high level of intellectual life and beautiful architecture.

C. The Abbasids built the House of Wisdom in Baghdad to foster the translation of Greek texts. Islamic doctors studied Greek medical texts. Islamic scholars at the Library of Córdoba translated Greek and Roman texts.

D. Islamic Spain had many libraries and schools, which helped Muslims to reach high levels of achievement in science, literature, art, architecture, and medicine.

Define Terms to Know

bureaucrat, 180; calligraphy, 183; minaret, 183; mihrab, 183

Critical Thinking

Islamic art began as a way to glorify Allah. Mosques were highly decorated and had a mihrab to mark the direction of Mecca. Muslims also used calligraphy to write the words of the Quran.

Write About Culture

Students' essays may include the following: large number of doctors, first pharmacies, House of Wisdom where the work of translation was carried out, a library that was open to the public.

D. Persian Influences and Islamic Spain

Islamic rule spread from the Arabian Peninsula to the borders of India and China in the east, through North Africa, and into Spain in the west. Islam continued to link diverse people across an enormous area. In time, Islamic civilization blended many traditions from many different groups.

Persian Influences

As you have read, the Persians had a strong influence on the Islamic Empire. The Abbasids moved their capital to a Persian village, which became the elegant and busy city of Baghdad. Geographically, the Abbasids were in the center of Persian culture. The Persian influence was strongest in Arabic literature, court manners, and government. Persian social and economic traditions, architecture, and crafts all influenced the Islamic Empire.

Islamic Spain

The Islamic conquest of Spain began in 711 and was complete by 718. Until 1492, Spain flourished as a center of Islamic civilization. Caliph Abd ar-Rahman III brought Spain to a period of its strongest power and greatest cultural achievement. He recruited scholars, poets, philosophers, historians, and musicians. He paid them well and encouraged others to migrate to Spain.

Córdoba, the cultural center of Islamic Spain, had a library that was set up by Caliph al-Hakam II, also known as al-Mustansir. He hired book buyers to find books in Alexandria, Damascus, and Baghdad. His library housed 400,000 books. Many were translations of ancient Greek, Roman, and Middle Eastern writings, which Islamic scholars then passed on to Europe. Islamic scholars also wrote poetry, prose, and science books on mathematics, astronomy, and medicine. Many stars were named by Islamic astronomers from Spain.

By the late 1200s, however, the Spaniards had pushed the Muslims back. At this time, only the kingdom of Granada was under Islamic control.

◆ **Why was Persian influence so strong in Abbasid times?**

Spotlight on *Culture*

THE ALHAMBRA PALACE
The Islamic kings of Granada built a palace and fortress called the Alhambra between 1238 and 1358. The name Alhambra means "the red" in Arabic, from the color of the sun-dried bricks of the outer walls. It is famous for its courtyards, its arches, and its geometric tiles.

Review II

Review History
A. What effect did Islam have on family life?
B. What were some of the features of Islamic cities?
C. What was the Islamic role in preserving Greek and Roman culture?
D. In what ways did Spain flourish as a center of Islamic civilization?

Define Terms to Know
Define the following terms:
bureaucrat, calligraphy, minaret, mihrab

Critical Thinking
How did the religion of Islam affect Islamic art and architecture?

Write About Culture
Write a short essay about what it might have been like to live in Baghdad during the Islamic Empire.

Get Organized
SQR CHART
Use an SQR chart to help you organize information from this section. For example, this section focuses on Islamic cultural achievements.

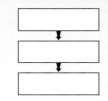

SURVEY
This section is about Islamic cultural achievements.

QUESTION
What were some major cultural achievements of the Islamic Empire?

READ
Books, poems, historical theory, medical information, calligraphy, carpets, mosques, libraries

CONNECT
History & Medicine

Islamic Advances in Medicine

Pay five pieces of gold to poor people when they get out of the hospital. That was the practice at many early Islamic hospitals where treatment was free to all. Giving money to former patients so they could take time to recover was based on the Islamic principle of giving alms to the poor and showing compassion to all.

The first hospitals as we know them and the first private pharmacies were built in the Islamic Empire. Trained, licensed, professional pharmacists dispensed medications. Many of these medications are still used today. Islamic pharmacists and chemists developed new treatments and methods that became the basis of important medical advances. Pharmacies used medicinal plants from many parts of the world to help the sick.

Islamic hospitals were clean, with fountains, musicians, and storytellers to entertain patients. Hospitals also had licensed doctors and outpatient clinics, and used anesthesia during surgery. Hospitals were government funded and most had medical schools and libraries. For the first time in history, doctors kept records of their patients and their treatments.

MUHAMMAD AL-RAZI was a famous doctor who had to select a site for a new hospital in Baghdad. He knew that dirty air was bad for sick people. So, to find the most healthful location for the hospital, he hung pieces of meat in different sections of the city. He built the hospital where the meat showed the least spoilage and contamination. Al-Razi is also known for writing a very important work describing the differences between smallpox and measles.

IBN SINA, a Persian physician known in Europe as Avicenna, wrote *The Canon of Medicine*. This huge book includes descriptions of many diseases and conditions, including rabies, cancer, and paralysis. It was used for hundreds of years in medical schools throughout the Islamic Empire and Europe.

Critical Thinking

Answer the questions below. Then, complete the activity.

1. How did physicians in the Islamic Empire add to medical knowledge?
2. Why do you think *The Canon of Medicine* was used in medical schools for such a long time?

Write About It

Use the Internet and reference books to learn more about medicine in the Islamic Empire during this time period. Then, write a paragraph that identifies and describes an Islamic contribution to medicine that is not described in your textbook.

An Islamic physician consults with a patient.

CONNECT
History & Medicine

ISLAMIC ADVANCES IN MEDICINE

Teach the Topic
Ask students what they know about medicine, hospitals, and pharmacies. Then, discuss the costs and procedures of healthcare in the community in which they live.

MUHAMMAD AL-RAZI Why do you think Al-Razi's practice of using healthful locations for hospitals was effective? (He probably found locations that were better protected from heat and insects, which could promote disease.) Ask students to suggest ways to determine where to locate a local hospital.

IBN SINA Why did Ibn Sina write such a large medical book? (in order to cover the vast amount of information he had gathered about disease from many different sources and cultures) Ask students why a long medical book might be valuable even if it is impossible to read from beginning to end. (Doctors and medical students could use it as a reference and read only the parts they need.)

Critical Thinking
1. Physicians in the Islamic Empire wrote about the differences between smallpox and measles, they wrote descriptions of many diseases, and they wrote many medical works based on their own observations and experiences.
2. *The Canon of Medicine* was used in medical schools for such a long time because it had descriptions of many common diseases and conditions and also because it was probably the first book of its kind to exist.

Write About It
Students' paragraphs should focus on important details of Islamic contributions to medicine and be accurate and well written. Suggest that students print out the first page of each Web site that they access as part of their research.

Teaching Options

LINK to TODAY

Islamic physicians were highly trained. Doctors were taught in hospitals, where they were tested regularly to ensure competency. In Baghdad, a medical student had to pass an exam in order to obtain a license to practice medicine. Ask students what steps a physician needs to take in order to practice medicine in the United States today. Then, have students compare these steps to medical training during the Islamic Empire.

FYI
Islamic Studies on Medicinal Plants

The word *alchemy* is derived from the Arabic word *al-kimiya*. Islamic chemists' exposure to many cultures brought them into contact with drugs unknown to earlier peoples, such as camphor, musk, sal ammoniac, and senna. Islamic pharmacists also used pleasant solvents, such as rose water and orange blossom water, to administer drugs.

Section Summary

In this section, students will learn about Muslims who invaded India. Some invaders, such as Tamerlane, pillaged the land and left. Other invaders, such as the Delhi sultanate and Babur, settled in India and improved conditions there. Students will also learn about the coexistence of Hinduism and Islam in India.

1 Introduce

Getting Started

Explain to students that to live in India between the thirteenth and seventeenth centuries was to live in a place of uncertainty: Who was in charge? More importantly, how would that person handle things? Ask students to describe how they would react if a totally unfamiliar person, such as a new teacher or coach, suddenly assumed the role of a school leader or principal. (Students might mention that they would be afraid, resentful, excited, or unsure of how they would react if a new person took over and changed how things were done.)

TERMS TO KNOW

Ask students to read the terms and definitions on page 186. Remind students that the sultan was the ruler of the Islamic state. Point out that the sultan was in charge of the sultanate the way a king or queen is in charge of a kingdom.

You may wish to review the pronunciation of the following terms with students.

Qutb ud-Aibak
 (KOOT bood eye BAHK)
Firuz Shah Tughlak
 (feh ROOZ SHAH took LOOG)
Tamerlane (tee moor LEHNG)
Babur (BAH boor)
Akbar (AK buhr)
Guru Nanak (GOO roo NAN uhk)

ACTIVE READING

Ask students to make a prediction at the end of each subsection about Islamic rulers in India. Remind students that it is sometimes necessary to adjust a prediction as they learn more about the subject.

Islamic Rulers in India

Terms to Know

sultanate a government headed by a sultan
militant ready and willing to fight in support of a cause

Main Ideas

A. In the thirteenth century, Islamic rulers in India established a government that lasted for 320 years.
B. Tamerlane, a Mongol nomad, invaded India in 1398.
C. The Mughal Empire, founded by Babur, brought about many accomplishments and reforms.

Active Reading

PREDICT
When you predict, you use your background knowledge to help you understand a subject or historical period. Before you read this section, review what you have learned about Islamic culture. What element of that culture might have been used in India?

A. Change Comes to India

After the collapse of the Gupta Empire in about 550, India entered a long period of political upheaval. The empire broke into small kingdoms, each under the control of a separate prince. For about 600 years, these princes fought for control of India. However, none was strong enough to unite India into one country. Tribes from central Asia added to the chaos. They crossed the mountains to raid and destroy Indian cities.

Muslims Gain Control

Islamic invaders who entered India carried off Hindu art, jewels, gold, silver, and slaves. One of the cruelest of these invaders was an Afghan ruler, or sultan, named Mahmud of Ghazni. He invaded India at least 17 times. In 1024, Mahmud led his forces into the town of Somnath. He robbed the Hindu temple of its treasures and carried off the gates of the town.

Until the twelfth century, few invaders settled in India. They took what they wanted and returned to their own kingdoms in central Asia. All this changed in 1186 when an Islamic Turk, Qutb ud-Aibak, started an Islamic state in northern India. After conquering the city of Delhi and the kingdoms around it, he took control of the whole area. The large kingdom was organized into a **sultanate**, or a government headed by a sultan. The Delhi sultanate was the beginning of Islamic rule in northern India.

Extending the Delhi Sultanate

The Delhi sultanate soon became famous as a center of Islam. One of Qutb ud-Aibak's first acts as sultan was to destroy the Hindu temples in northern India. Then, he set out to force the Hindus to convert to Islam. Hindus who would not accept Islam had to pay additional taxes. Others were imprisoned or sold as slaves.

With the wealth gained from trade and taxes, Qutb ud-Aibak and later sultans maintained lavish courts. They built beautiful mosques throughout the northern kingdom. One sultan, Firuz Shah Tughlak, built hospitals, schools, and irrigation systems. While he ruled, from 1351 to 1388, northern India was peaceful and prosperous.

This hand-carved tower with balconies rises above a mosque in Delhi, India. Towers such as these were built by the Delhi government.

Teaching Options

Section 3 Resources

Teacher's Resources (TR)
 Terms to Know, p. 21
 Review History, p. 55
 Build Your Skills, p. 89
 Concept Builder, p. 224
 SQR Chart, p. 322

Connection to ECONOMICS

Discuss with students how tax policies might affect the economic well-being of an empire or a nation. Point out that the relationship between taxes and economic health has always been a key issue in the United States. Ask students to compare the Delhi sultanate's tax policies to those of the U.S. government.

Hindu-Muslim Differences

Muslims and Hindus were uneasy neighbors in India. Conflicts developed when many of India's Hindus had to choose between converting to Islam and being killed or taken into slavery. The beliefs of the two groups were so different that their cultures did not blend easily. For example, music played an important part in Hindu religious ceremonies. Some strict Muslims, however, condemned the use of music and dance in religious ceremonies.

Even though Muslim and Hindu differences caused conflicts, the two groups did share some common ideas. For instance, a new language called Urdu developed. It combined the languages of the Hindus and the Muslims and was written with Arabic letters.

◆ **What was one of Qutb ud-Aibak's first acts as sultan?**

B. The Delhi Sultanate Is Destroyed

Delhi's success soon attracted the envy of rulers from other lands. A Mongol army led by Timur Lenk, or Tamerlane, invaded India in 1398. With a large force, Tamerlane swept into India, seizing everything in his path. Although the sultanate later regained the city, the rest of the area was split into smaller kingdoms. Tamerlane continued to destroy the region's countryside.

Tamerlane Captures Delhi

Stories of Tamerlane's cruelty spread terror throughout the region. Everywhere he went, he left death and destruction behind. He led a cavalry of almost 100,000 men into Delhi and nearly destroyed the city. It is said that "for two whole months not a bird moved a wing in the city." It took Delhi more than 100 years to recover from his army's attacks. However, after collecting his riches, Tamerlane left as quickly as he had come. He and his army were off to conquer other lands.

Other Attacks by Tamerlane

Tamerlane set out to establish control in the Middle East and central Asia. When cities rebelled against his rule, he destroyed them, killed all the people, and made towers of their skulls. In 1399, he advanced into Egypt. He destroyed Aleppo and Damascus in Syria. In 1401, he captured Baghdad, killed 20,000 people, and destroyed all its monuments. Then, in 1405, on his way to invade China, Tamerlane died.

◆ **What is Tamerlane remembered for?**

C. Mughal Empire

The Delhi sultanate never fully recovered from Tamerlane's attacks. The sultanate continued its decline and was finally destroyed by a new wave of Islamic invaders. In 1526, one of Tamerlane's descendants, Babur, marched into northern India. The area he controlled became known as the Mughal Empire.

Tamerlane was a Mongol ruler who hoped to establish control in the Middle East and central Asia.

Conflict Resolution

When cities rebelled against Tamerlane, he attacked them in retaliation, killing all the people who lived there. Ask students to discuss occasions in their own lives when trying to improve a situation created a larger problem. Ask them how the problem was eventually solved.

---

2 Teach

A. Change Comes to India

Purpose-Setting Question How did the organization of Indian kingdoms into a single sultanate change religious and secular life in India? (**Religious:** Hindus forced to convert to Islam; **Secular:** Courts, mosques, and infrastructure were built, and important health and educational services were offered.)

Activity

Create a chart Have students create a two-column chart (TR, p. 328) entitled *Hindu and Islamic Differences.* Label the column on the left *Hindu Beliefs and Customs.* Label the other column *Islamic Beliefs and Customs.* Students should fill in the chart with the following information: name(s) of God(s) worshiped; type of music allowed, if any; rules on equality; number of wives allowed; eating restrictions; and rules on consuming alcohol. Review the chart with students. Encourage them to explain the differences between Hinduism and Islam in their own words.

◆ **ANSWER** One of his first acts as sultan was to destroy the Hindu temples in northern India.

B. The Delhi Sultanate Is Destroyed

Purpose-Setting Question How did Tamerlane gain control of India? (He invaded India and destroyed anything that got in his way.)

◆ **ANSWER** He is remembered for his cruelty and for destroying many cities, including Delhi.

C. Mughal Empire

Purpose-Setting Question How did Akbar and his successors improve life in India? (Akbar tolerated all religions, reformed the economy and tax system, improved trade, and made advances in the arts. His successors also improved the economy and supported the arts.)

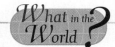

TIGER HUNT
  The Mughal armies expanded the empire by winning many battles. Akbar's soldiers kept in shape by hunting tigers and other animals. The soldiers formed a circle, closed in on the prey, and Akbar and the nobles killed the animals.

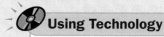
Akbar is shown praying on the bank of the Indus River.

Origins of the Mughal Empire

In 1526, an Islamic chief in northwestern India asked Babur to help him put down a Hindu rebellion. Babur conquered not only the rebels but also the chief who asked him for help. Babur, nicknamed the Tiger, founded what is considered to be the greatest of the Islamic empires of India—the Mughal Empire. *Mughal* is the Persian word for "mongol."

By the time Babur died in 1530, his empire had spread from Kabul, in Afghanistan, to the mouth of the Ganges River in the country now called Bangladesh. Because his conquests were based on weapons that used gunpowder, the Mughal Empire is sometimes called the first gunpowder empire.

The Rule of Akbar

Babur's grandson, Akbar, took over the empire in 1556, when he was only 13 years old. Many consider him the greatest Mughal ruler. His empire covered two-thirds of south Asia, most of present-day Afghanistan, Pakistan, and north and central India. During his reign, he created a strong central government and earned the title Akbar the Great.

Akbar felt that it would be impossible to keep his empire united if he tried to make all people live as Muslims. As a result, he allowed people of all religions to worship as they pleased. Besides Islam and Hinduism, religions practiced at this time were Buddhism, Christianity, and Sikhism, a new form of Islam. Akbar was fascinated by religion, inviting representatives of all faiths to his court. He also married a Hindu princess and gave important government jobs to Hindus.

Akbar also reformed the economy and the tax system, which enriched the empire. He did away with a special tax that people who were not Muslims had been forced to pay. He is remembered for military victories, improved trade, efficient government, advances in the arts, and religious tolerance. His policies helped the empire survive for 150 years.

Akbar's Successors

Akbar was succeeded by his son Jahangir, who ruled from 1605 to 1627. Political stability, excellent economic activity, and superb painting and architecture made him a popular ruler. His wife, Nur Jahan, ruled in his place for the last 16 years of his reign. Control of the empire then passed to Akbar's grandson Shah Jahan, who ruled from 1628 to 1658. Shah Jahan built the splendid Taj Mahal in northern India as a tomb for his wife. Both rulers continued Akbar's tolerant policies toward Hindus and expanded Mughal rule.

The Religion of the Sikhs

A new religion arose in India at this time. The Sikh religion began as a movement to combine the Hindu and Islam religions. The founder of the Sikh religion was Guru Nanak, born in 1469 into a Hindu family. He was a wandering holy man who believed that all people were brothers and sisters. He condemned all forms of inequality, including the caste system. Guru Nanak composed hymns that a Muslim friend put to music. He also organized groups to sing hymns in an eatery where both Muslims and Hindus of all castes would eat together. Guru Nanak asked his followers—known as Sikhs, or "disciples"—to find the truth within themselves.

188   UNIT 2   ◆   The Growth of Empires and Governments

Teaching Options

At first, the Sikh religion was a peaceful one. Later, however, Mughal rulers began to torture and kill Sikhs. To defend themselves, Sikhs became more **militant**, or willing to fight for a cause. They took the name Singh, which means "lion."

Decline of the Mughal Empire

There were a number of factors that led to the decline of the Mughal Empire. One reason was that Akbar's successors did not understand the importance of Hindu and Muslim harmony. They went back to the policy of persecution. For example, Aurangzeb, who ruled after Shah Jahan, required all citizens to practice Islam. No other religions were allowed.

Later Mughal rulers increased the size of their empire. At the height of Mughal power, the sultan controlled a very large area, which was costly even in times of peace. However, attacks against Hindus brought rebellions and cost an enormous amount of money. At the same time, European traders began arriving in India. They were anxious to profit from India's rich trade. As the Mughal Empire collapsed, the foreigners began to gain more and more power over troubled India's affairs.

◆ **Why was it important for the Mughals to be tolerant of many religions?**

The Golden Temple in northern India is a holy place for Sikhs.

Review III

Review History
A. What changes did the Delhi sultanate bring to India?
B. How was Tamerlane different from other rulers?
C. Why is Akbar remembered as a great ruler?

Define Terms to Know
Define the following terms:
sultanate, militant

Critical Thinking
Which elements of the Mughal Empire do you think have had the most lasting effect on the world?

Write About Economics
Write a speech to Babur, the Mughal leader, suggesting ways to improve business conditions in the empire.

Get Organized
SQR CHART
Use an SQR chart to organize information from this section. For example, this section is about the Mughal Empire.

SURVEY
This section is about the Mughal Empire.

↓

QUESTION
Who were the major figures of the Mughal Empire?

↓

READ
Babur founded it, Akbar created a prosperous state, Jahangir encouraged art and architecture, and Shah Jahan built the Taj Mahal.

Focus Ask students how religious factors contributed to the fall of the Mughal Empire. Then, ask students to list other contributing factors that led to the decline of the empire. (Religious tolerance was forgotten, and different religious groups fought and killed one another. Also, the size of the empire grew unwieldy and expensive, and foreign invaders seized on weaknesses and grew more powerful.)

◆ **ANSWER** Mughals had to be tolerant of many religions including Buddhism, Sikhism, and Christianity, in addition to Islam and Hinduism, in order to keep their empire united.

Section Close
Review with students some of the positive and negative changes Islamic invaders and rulers brought to India. Discuss which rulers had the most success and which had the least success in changing India for the better.

3 Assess

Review Answers
Review History
A. The Delhi sultanate marked the start of Islamic rule in northern India and soon became a center of Islam. It also built beautiful mosques, hospitals, schools, and irrigation systems.
B. Tamerlane was a very cruel ruler who left death and destruction in his wake.
C. Akbar is remembered as a great leader because he allowed people of all religions to worship as they pleased, he reformed the economy and tax system, and he improved trade.

Define Terms to Know
sultanate, 186; militant, 189

Critical Thinking
The establishment of an efficient government and the advancement of the arts by the Mughal Empire have had lasting and beneficial effects on the rest of the world.

Write About Economics
Students' speeches should implore Babur to develop new businesses, especially in the open market bazaars. They should also be well organized and factually accurate.

IV. The Ottoman and Safavid Empires

(pp. 190–193)

Section Summary

In this section, students will learn how the Ottoman Turks realized their dream to unite Muslims in the Middle East and parts of Europe under one vast empire. Students will also learn about the Safavids—Shiite Muslims who wrested power from the Sunni Muslims of the Ottoman Empire.

1 Introduce

Getting Started

Ask students how they might persuade someone to help them to realize an important personal goal. Then, have students speculate on the dreams of a leader of a nation: What if people are opposed to a leader's dream? Does the leader of that nation use force to achieve what he or she feels is right for the nation? Discuss what other methods might be used and why some methods might be better than others.

TERMS TO KNOW

Ask students to read the terms and their definitions on page 190 and then find each term in the section. After they have done this, have them rewrite each term and its definition in their own words.

You may want to review the pronunciation of the following terms with students.

Safavid (sah FAH vehd)
Suleiman (soo lay MAHN)
Isfahan (ehs fah HAHN)

ACTIVE READING

Suggest that students pause after reading each subsection to assess the point of view of a citizen of the empire on key issues, such as the fairness of the ruler. Students should list reasons for the citizen's stance or viewpoint.

The Ottoman and Safavid Empires

Terms to Know

millet a religious community of non-Muslims in the Ottoman Empire

janizary a soldier in an elite force of the Ottoman army

shah king

Main Ideas

A. The Ottoman Turks became the leaders of the Islamic world in the Middle East and Europe.

B. The Safavid Empire spanned a broad region of Persia and was controlled by Shiite Muslims.

Active Reading

POINTS OF VIEW
A point of view is how a person sees something. As you read this section, think about the viewpoints of the Ottoman Turks and the Shiite Muslims. Then, pause to consider what explains each point of view.

A. The Ottoman Empire

While the Mughals were ruling in India, two other empires dominated the Middle East and parts of Europe. These empires were the Ottoman Empire and the Safavid Empire. Dreaming of a single world united under the control of Islam, Ottoman Turks fought to conquer Constantinople in the 1400s and carry Islam deep into Europe.

Decline of the Seljuks

The Seljuk Turks were eventually weakened. In addition to fighting outside invaders, Seljuk leaders fought among themselves. Other problems were also brewing. When a ruler died, the Seljuks divided his province among his sons. This led to many power struggles. By the time Mughal warriors from Asia crossed Russia and invaded Persia in 1243, the Seljuks were in a state of disunity.

At the time of Mughal invasions, Asia Minor was overrun by several Turkic tribes from central Asia. As Seljuk power declined, one of these tribes, the Ottomans, formed an independent community in central Asia Minor. The tribe united under the rule of Osman to form the Ottoman Empire in 1299. Osman's troops captured Bursa, Turkey, in 1326 and made it their capital.

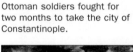
Ottoman soldiers fought for two months to take the city of Constantinople.

The Ottoman Turks

The Ottoman Empire replaced the remaining Seljuk Empire in Asia Minor. The Ottomans soon expanded beyond their Seljuk border and conquered Byzantine territories. By Osman's death in 1326, the western coast of Asia Minor was part of the Ottoman Empire. The Ottomans then pushed into Europe. In 1354, Ottoman troops seized the European part of modern-day Turkey. Over the next hundred years, the Ottomans conquered the Balkan kingdoms one by one, including Greece. By about 1450, all that remained under Byzantine control was Constantinople and the area surrounding it.

Teaching Options

Section 4 Resources

Teacher's Resources (TR)
Terms to Know, p. 21
Review History, p. 55
Build Your Skills, p. 89
Concept Builder, p. 224
Chapter Test, pp. 131–132
SQR Chart, p. 322

Cooperative Learning

Assign groups of students to develop interview questions for Constantine XI or Muhammad II after the fall of Constantinople. For example, students might ask the rulers about their reasons for fighting, the tactics they used, or the significance of the battle. Students should use prior knowledge and information from the text to answer the questions. Then, have a representative from each group read the interviews aloud to the class.

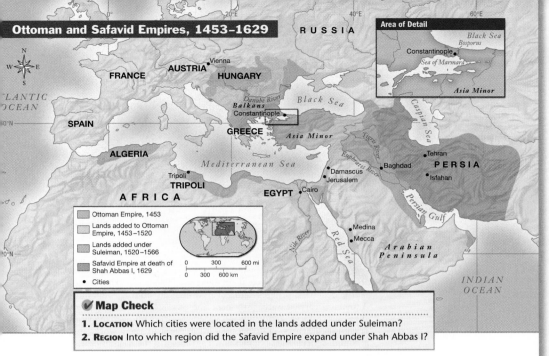

Ottoman and Safavid Empires, 1453–1629

Area of Detail

Legend:
- Ottoman Empire, 1453
- Lands added to Ottoman Empire, 1453–1520
- Lands added under Suleiman, 1520–1566
- Safavid Empire at death of Shah Abbas I, 1629
- • Cities

0   300   600 mi
0   300   600 km

✔ Map Check
1. **LOCATION** Which cities were located in the lands added under Suleiman?
2. **REGION** Into which region did the Safavid Empire expand under Shah Abbas I?

Fall of Constantinople

Finally in 1453, the Ottoman sultan Muhammad II, also known as Mehmet II, conquered Constantinople. People thought the city could not be attacked because of a great iron chain that kept ships from the harbor. However, Muhammad had 70 warships disassembled and moved over the land from the Bosporus—the waterway between Constantinople and Asia Minor—to the city's harbor. He then reassembled and launched the warships into the harbor outside the city. As Byzantine soldiers marched north to defend the city, troops of nearly 200,000 Ottoman soldiers marched to the city's landward side on the west. After two months, the city fell to the Ottoman Turks. The last Byzantine emperor, Constantine XI, was killed in the battle.

Ashikpashazade, a Turkic writer who was present at the fall of Constantinople, describes the scene:

> **❝** For fifty days the battle went on day and night. On the fifty-first day the [Ottoman] Sultan ordered free plunder. They attacked. On the fifty-first day, a Tuesday, the fortress was captured. . . . Gold and silver and jewels and fine stuffs were brought and stacked in the camp market. **❞**

ANALYZE PRIMARY SOURCES

DOCUMENT-BASED QUESTION Why do you think gold, silver, and jewels were brought to the camp market?

Suleiman the Magnificent

The greatest Ottoman sultan was Suleiman. He was an effective general who pushed even deeper into Europe. He extended Turkic rule west through much of Hungary to the borders of Austria. He was loved and respected by his people.

Research

AVERAGE

Have students find at least three additional facts about one of the major figures of the Ottoman Empire discussed in this chapter: Osman, Muhammad II, or Suleiman. Suggest that students find facts relating to the figure's youth, education, or background. Students should summarize their facts in a short paragraph.

CHALLENGE

Have students create a poster presenting a detailed timeline of major events in the Ottoman Empire. The timeline should be in the form of a list of short statements with a date preceding each statement. Suggest that the timeline include about 20 events.

---

❷ Teach

A. The Ottoman Empire

Purpose-Setting Question What was the main goal of the rulers of the Ottoman Empire? (to expand the world of Islam to the Middle East, Europe, and North Africa)

Using the Map

Ottoman and Safavid Empires, 1453–1629

As students study the map, point out the detail inset map in the upper right corner. Make sure that students realize that the inset is an enlargement of a section of the map.

Have students sketch a map of the Ottoman and Safavid Empires on a separate sheet of paper, using the map on page 191 as a guide. Then, ask students to reread the subsections *The Ottoman Turks* and *Fall of Constantinople*. As they read, have them plot battle sites and routes on their maps. Students should use completed maps as study aids.

✔ Map Check

Answers
1. Tripoli, Baghdad
2. Persia

ANALYZE PRIMARY SOURCES

DOCUMENT-BASED QUESTION

In the years following the fall of Constantinople, the city remained in ruins and was devastated by plague. The Turks were among the first and largest groups to resettle there. Ashikpashazade—who was a Turk himself—wrote that the sultan sent officers throughout the land to announce that whoever wished should come and freely take possessions from the city. When the people still did not come, Ashikpashazade reported that the sultan had to force people to move to his new capital. Thus, the city became repopulated.

ANSWER Gold, silver, and jewels were probably brought to the camp market so that the Ottoman Turks could take not only land but also riches from the people of Constantinople.

Activity

Prepare a brochure Have students work in groups to research, write, and illustrate a brochure that could be used to entice people to visit the cultural centers of the Ottoman Empire under Suleiman the Magnificent. Brochures should include information about the marketplaces, forms of architecture and new building projects, as well as cultural centers that visitors would want to investigate. Have student groups present their brochures to the class.

Explore Read aloud to students the following excerpt from a song about the practice of taking sons from a Christian family. Then, have them discuss the possible meaning(s) of the excerpt.

"You [the Emperor] catch and shackle the old and the arch priests

In order to take the children as Janissaries.

Their parents weep and their sisters and brothers too

And I cry until it pains me;

As long as I live I shall cry,

For last year it was my son and this year my brother."

Discuss Discuss with students why it might be a hardship to have a family member taken by the government. Then, ask students why some families might consider a chance to work in the Ottoman army as a great opportunity for their family or for personal success.

◆ **ANSWER** Suleiman had mosques, schools, hospitals, covered markets, and bridges built in his empire. He also rewrote laws to make them more fair.

During the reign of Suleiman the Magnificent, covered markets were built throughout the Ottoman Empire.

Suleiman led the Ottomans into a golden age. Under his leadership, Turkic laws were rewritten to make them more fair. Suleiman also had mosques, schools, baths, hospitals, bridges, and covered markets built throughout the empire. Aqueducts carried water into most homes. Turkic markets sold goods such as silks, ivory, spices, and fruits and vegetables from all over the world. Suleiman encouraged artists, craftspeople, and writers in their work. Because of his accomplishments, he became known as Suleiman the Magnificent.

Ottoman Culture

The Ottomans divided their people into four social classes. The sultan headed the government. At the top of the social classes were the "men of the pen." These were the scientists, lawyers, judges, and poets. Below them were the "men of the sword." These were the soldiers who protected the sultan. Below them were the "men of negotiation." This group of people collected taxes and were merchants and artisans. Below them were the "men of husbandry." This group included the herders and farmers who produced food.

The men of the sword and the men of the pen were mainly all Muslims. The men of negotiation and the men of husbandry included non-Muslims. In Ottoman society, non-Muslims were organized into **millets**, or religious communities. Although the communities of different religious groups reduced conflict, they did little to establish an Ottoman identity.

The Ottomans required Christians to give their sons to the sultan to train as soldiers or government officials. The boys almost always lost contact with their families. The best soldiers won a place in the **janizaries**, the highest-ranking group of the Ottoman army.

The Decline of the Ottoman Empire

The Ottoman Empire showed the first signs of weakness in the late 1700s. At that time, it lost the Crimea, a peninsula in the Black Sea, to Russia after a six-year war. In the 1800s, Greece won its independence. The empire also lost territories to France and Great Britain. As you will learn in Chapter 24, the Ottoman Empire had lost almost all of its European territory by 1914.

◆ **What achievements were made during the reign of Suleiman?**

Teaching Options

ESL/ELL STRATEGIES

Organize To best understand the social organization of Ottoman society, have students work in pairs to create a diagram. Students should have at the top of their diagram a box that reads *Sultan*. Underneath should be a box entitled *Men of the Pen*, followed by a box labeled *Men of the Sword*. The bottom two boxes should read *Men of Negotiation* and *Men of Husbandry*. Students should fill in each box with the type of people included in each group.

Connection to GOVERNMENT

Tell students that the sultan was at the head of the Ottoman government. An imperial council advised him. Military administrators and heads of millets answered to this council. Then, have students research and study the organization of the U.S. government. Finally, ask students to compare the two governments.

B. The Safavid Empire

The Safavid Empire existed in Persia between the time of Mughal India and the Ottoman Empire from 1501 to 1722. The Safavids were Shiite Muslims and enforced their beliefs throughout the empire. However, the Ottomans were Sunni Muslims who despised the Shiites. This led to constant warfare between the groups.

Shah Abbas I

The Safavid height of power came during the reign of the **shah**, or king, named Abbas I. He fought Portugal and Spain to keep them out of Islamic areas. European states sought his help against the Ottomans. Shah Abbas created a powerful military force, modeled after the Ottoman janizaries.

Persian culture experienced a rebirth during his reign. Miniature paintings, porcelains, clothes, and rugs were produced. In 1598, Abbas made Isfahan his capital, where he built religious monuments, mosques, palaces, gardens, and hospitals. Under Abbas, Isfahan flourished as a center of Persian culture.

Abbas strengthened the military, the economy, the government, and Islam. He modeled some policies on those of the Ottoman Empire. Because he trusted no one, he had his sons either blinded or put to death in order to avoid power struggles. It is said that Abbas liked to walk the streets of the capital city in disguise and talk with the people. He would always ask about their problems and see what he could do to help.

Decline of the Safavid Empire

The Safavid Empire declined after the death of Shah Abbas I in 1629. One possible cause of the decline was the pressure from Ottoman armies. Another possible cause was the continuing struggle that took place between the Sunni Muslims and the Shiite Muslims. Finally, a group of Afghan Sunni Muslims rebelled and captured Isfahan.

◆ **What policies did Shah Abbas I use to strengthen the Safavid Empire?**

Global Connections

SHAH-NAMEH
The *Shah-nameh* manuscript given to Shah Abbas in 1614 is now in the New York Public Library. Ferdowsi, the Persian epic poet, completed the 60,000-verse poem in 1010. It is the history of the kings of Persia from mythical times to the seventh century.

Review IV

Review History
A. What factors led to the fall of the Seljuks?
B. What were some of the achievements of Shah Abbas I?

Define Terms to Know
Define the following terms:
millet, janizary, shah

Critical Thinking
Why do you think the sultan in the Ottoman Empire wanted non-Muslims organized into millets?

Write About Citizenship
Write an editorial supporting or criticizing the system in the Ottoman Empire that required Christians to give their sons to the sultan to train as soldiers.

Get Organized
SQR CHART
Use an SQR chart to help you organize information from this section. For example, this section is about the Ottoman and Safavid Empires.

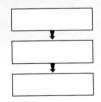

SURVEY
This section is about the Ottoman and Safavid Empires.

QUESTION
Who were the major figures of the Ottoman and Safavid Empires?

READ
Osman formed the Ottoman Empire, Muhammad II expanded it, and Suleiman helped it prosper. Shah Abbas I ruled the Safavid Empire.

B. The Safavid Empire

Purpose-Setting Question Why were the Ottomans and the Safavids opposed to one another? (The Ottomans were Sunni Muslims and the Safavids were Shiite Muslims.)

Review Ask students what the main ideological difference is between Shiite Muslims and Sunni Muslims. Students may refer to the first section of Chapter 8 for help in answering the question. (Both groups believe in Allah, but only the Sunni supported the leadership of the early caliphs.)

GLOBAL CONNECTIONS

SHAH-NAMEH Tell students that long sections of the *Shah-nameh* are memorized by heart and recited out loud at Iranian social gatherings. In many homes, the distinguished status of the *Shah-nameh* is demonstrated each year during the celebration of Nov-Ruz. At this time, a copy of the *Shah-nameh* is often put alongside the Quran in a place of honor. Discuss with students how the oral tradition of reciting the *Shah-nameh* helps to preserve Iranian culture.

◆ **ANSWER** He strengthened the military, the economy, the government, and religion. He reduced taxes on farmers and herders.

Section Close

Create a chart on the board or on an overhead transparency to review with students how the Ottomans and the Safavids gained control in the Middle East and Europe. Help students see both similarities and differences in each empire.

3 Assess

Review Answers

Review History
A. The centralized power of the Seljuks was broken by the system of inheritance, and there were many religious conflicts that caused splinter groups to form.

B. Shah Abbas, also known as Shah Abbas I, was known for strengthening the military, the economy, the government, and religion. He also made Isfahan his capital and built religious monuments and mosques there.

Define Terms to Know
millet, 192; janizary, 192; shah, 193

Critical Thinking
The sultan probably believed that he would have more control over the empire if non-Muslims were organized into millets.

Write About Citizenship
Students' editorials should express an opinion—either in favor of or against the system—and provide two or three reasons for their opinion.

Chapter Summary

A blank outline form is available in the Teacher's Resources (p. 318). Chapter summaries should outline how the religion of Islam began and spread, how it affected India, and how it flourished in the Ottoman and Safavid Empires. Refer to the rubric in the Teacher's Resources (p. 340) to score students' chapter summaries.

● Interpret the Timeline

1. the Abbasid Dynasty coming to power
2. 99 years (1299–1398)
3. Mughal Empire begins in India.
4. Check that students' events are all from the chapter.

Use Terms to Know

5. b. jihad
6. e. millet
7. g. oasis
8. h. prophet
9. i. sultan
10. c. mihrab
11. a. caliph
12. f. minaret
13. d. militant

Check Your Understanding

14. The Arabian Peninsula is an area that is mostly desert but has mountains and seacoast in the west. There is little rain and no permanent river. There are a few fertile oases to grow crops. The Arabian Peninsula is located in the center of the Middle East and is an area of trade; it is also the area where Islam began.
15. Islam began when a man named Muhammad saw a vision of the angel Gabriel and was instructed by him to preach the Word of God.
16. These men were called the rightly guided caliphs. They knew Muhammad personally and oversaw the spread of Islam throughout Syria, ancient Israel, Egypt, North Africa, and Persia.
17. Sunni Muslims supported the leadership of the early caliphs, and they believed that the Quran was the only guide they needed. The Shiites believed that the only true successor to Muhammad had to be a direct descendant of Muhammad's daughter and son-in-law. They also believed a person must act as a guide between Allah and his followers.

18. Islamic doctors discovered how some diseases spread, they wrote books, and they described many diseases. Islamic scholars translated many Greek books, and studied astronomy and mathematics.
19. Akbar allowed people of all religions to worship as they wanted; he gave important government jobs to Hindus; he reformed the economy and the tax system; he improved trade.

20. The Mughals brought efficient government, arts, and religious tolerance to India.
21. The Ottoman Empire declined because of lost territories and conflicts within its empire over religion.
22. The Ottomans had an efficient and stable government, fair laws, mosques, aqueducts, and covered markets. They also divided their people into social classes and organized non-Muslims into millets.

The Safavids experienced a rebirth in Persian culture; they had a strong military and economy. However, there was constant warfare among groups.

Chapter Summary

Complete the following outline in your notebook. Then, use your outline to write a brief summary of the chapter.

The Islamic World

I. The Rise and Spread of Islam
   A. The Arabian Peninsula
   B. Foundations of Islam
   C. Spread of Islam in Asia and the Mediterranean Region
   D. Caliph Rule Ends
II. Islamic Achievements
   A. Society and Family Life
   B. Urban Centers
   C. Cultural Life
   D. Persian Influences and Islamic Spain
III. Islamic Rulers in India
   A. Change Comes to India
   B. The Delhi Sultanate Is Destroyed
   C. Mughal Empire
IV. The Ottoman and Safavid Empires
   A. The Ottoman Empire
   B. The Safavid Empire

● Interpret the Timeline

Use the timeline on pages 170–171 to answer the following questions.

1. Which occurred first, the beginning of the Mughal Empire or the Abbasid Dynasty coming to power?
2. How many years after the Ottoman Empire was formed did Tamerlane invade India?
3. **Critical Thinking** Which event shows Islamic influence in India?
4. Select five events from the chapter that are not in the timeline. Create a timeline that shows these events.

Use Terms to Know

Match each term with its definition.

a. caliph	d. militant	g. oasis
b. jihad	e. millet	h. prophet
c. mihrab	f. minaret	i. sultan

5. an effort carried out as a religious duty
6. a religious community of non-Muslims in the Ottoman Empire
7. a fertile place in a desert, due to the presence of water
8. someone chosen by God to bring a message to people
9. the ruler of an Islamic state
10. an arched area in a mosque wall that is closest to Mecca
11. an Islamic ruler with the authority to rule from Muhammad
12. a tall, slender tower with a balcony, on a mosque
13. ready and willing to fight in support of a cause

Check Your Understanding

14. **Describe** the location and geographic significance of the Arabian Peninsula.
15. **Explain** how the Islamic religion began.
16. **Describe** the four men who led the Muslims after the death of Muhammad.
17. **Discuss** the differences between Sunni and Shiite Muslims.
18. **Identify** some of the scientific contributions that were made in the Islamic Empire.
19. **Describe** the rule of Akbar.
20. **Summarize** the achievements that were made during the Mughal Empire.
21. **Describe** the reasons why the Ottoman Empire declined.
22. **Compare and contrast** the strengths of the Ottoman and Safavid Empires.

Critical Thinking

23. **Make Inferences** Why were the Sunni Muslims and the Shiite Muslims rivals?

24. **Analyze Information** What are some of the reasons why Islam was able to spread as far as it did?

25. **Analyze Primary Sources** Based on the quotation on page 191, how do you think you would have felt if you had lived in Constantinople at this time?

26. **Draw Conclusions** Why do you think Suleiman was called the Magnificent?

Put Your Skills to Work

27. **Take Notes and Outline** You have learned how to take notes and to outline. Note taking and outlining can help you organize material so that it is easier to understand and remember.

    Take notes on the Ottoman and Safavid Empires using notecards or separate sheets of paper. Then, organize your notes, copy the outline below, and complete the outline by adding main ideas, subtopics, and important details.

    Topic: The Ottoman and Safavid Empires
    I.
      A.
      B.
      C.
      D.
      E.
      F.
    II.
      A.
      B.

Analyze Sources

28. Sufi Rabia spent long years praying, fasting, and studying. She became one of the most respected Sufis of all time. Read what her biographer said about her. Then, answer the questions that follow.

    Rabia of Basra [Iraq] was at the head of the women disciples and the chief of the women ascetics [one who leads a life of self-denial for religious purposes], of those who observed the sacred law, who were God-fearing and zealous . . . and she was . . . experienced in grace and goodness.

    a. What qualities would Rabia have to deserve such a description?

    b. What do you think the "sacred law" is?

Essay Writing

29. Throughout the centuries, Muslims made many contributions to learning and art. Choose a topic from the list below. Then, write a one-page essay describing how Islam affected this art form or area of study.

    - science
    - medicine
    - art
    - architecture

TEST PREPARATION

CAUSE-AND-EFFECT RELATIONSHIPS
Choose the correct answer.

Why did Akbar, the ruler of Mughal India, practice religious tolerance?

1. He was forced to by government policy.

2. Muslims were outnumbered, and it was wise to accept Hindus.

3. His mother was a Hindu.

4. He wanted to keep his empire united.

Critical Thinking

23. Sunni and Shiites had different religious beliefs, but they also both wanted political power.
24. Islam spread so far because of the conviction of the faithful followers of the religion; geography helped, as did, at times, force.
25. Answers will vary but may include that it was a frightening time because there was a lot of fighting and many people were being killed; there were soldiers everywhere, and goods and property were being destroyed.
26. Suleiman made the city of Istanbul beautiful, made and revised laws so that they were fair, supported the arts, conquered territory, and ran an orderly government.

Put Your Skills to Work

TAKE NOTES AND OUTLINE
27. Answers will vary but should be similar to the following outline.
Topic: The Ottoman and Safavid Empires
I. The Ottoman Empire
  A. Decline of the Seljuks
  B. The Ottoman Turks
  C. Fall of Constantinople
  D. Suleiman the Magnificent
  E. Ottoman Culture
  F. The Decline of the Ottoman Empire
II. The Safavid Empire
  A. Shah Abbas I
  B. Decline of the Safavid Empire

Analyze Sources

28a. She was holy, followed the religious rules, did not have any luxuries, and was liked by everyone.
28b. the law revealed in the Quran, the law of God

Essay Writing

29. Possible answers: **Science:** astronomy, aqueducts; **Medicine:** discovery of new diseases, clean hospitals, pharmacies, licensed doctors; **Art:** calligraphy, carpets, beautiful buildings, wooden carvings, tiles; **Architecture:** mosques, minarets, mihrabs, courtyards

---

TEST PREPARATION

Answer 4. He wanted to keep his empire united.

Unit 2

Portfolio Project

NEWCAST: TURNING
POINTS IN HISTORY

Managing the Project
Plan for 3–4 class periods.

Set the Scene
Have students list some newscasts that they have seen on television. Ask them to identify the different segments of a newscast and discuss the type of information that each provides. Then, ask them which news segments they tune into most when they watch a newscast.

Your Assignment
Ask students to read the assignment on page 196. Divide the class into groups and assign topics, or you may want to let students choose their own topic, based on which event they are most interested in.

RESEARCH YOUR STORY
After each group has chosen an event from the list on page 196, have it decide which role each member will play in the presentation, including who the guest interviewees will be. The group should also assign responsibilities for different parts of the research for the newscast.

REPORT TO YOUR CLASS
Once the research phase is completed, the reporters and anchor people should begin putting together their reports and interview questions, the directors should oversee technical tasks and rehearsals, the interviewees should prepare answers to the reporters' questions, and the researchers should make certain that the final reports are accurate.

Wrap Up
Have groups take turns presenting their newscasts. Suggest that groups may want to use costumes, props, and other realistic touches to add interest to their show.

Newscast: Turning Points in History

YOUR ASSIGNMENT

Much of world history is the story of extraordinary events and of the people who helped shape them. Often these "turning points in history" have a lasting impact, greatly influencing the course of future events. Select one event from Unit 2 and prepare a newscast from the perspective of a reporter from the time period.

RESEARCH YOUR STORY

Choose a Topic As a group, select one of the following turning points in history to investigate:

The Defeat of Greek City-States by Philip II of Macedonia, 338 B.C.

The Death of Alexander the Great, 323 B.C.

The Assassination of Julius Caesar, 44 B.C.

The Fall of the Western Roman Empire, A.D. 476

The Beginning of Mongol Rule of Russia, A.D. 1237

The Capture of Constantinople, A.D. 1453

The Founding of the Mughal Empire, A.D. 1526

Research Conduct research using your textbook, the Internet, and library sources. Prepare notecards to help you organize your information and create visuals, such as maps, charts, and posters, to illustrate your newscast. Be sure to answer these questions: What was happening before the event? What caused the event? How did the event unfold? Who was involved in the event? When and where did the event happen? What were some possible effects of this event?

REPORT TO YOUR CLASS

Plan Construct a plan that details the format of your newscast and the roles of all group members. Some members of the group can be news reporters, anchors, researchers, or directors. Include interviews of major historical personalities.

Rehearse Have a rehearsal before presenting your news report. Be sure that everyone knows what they are supposed to do during the presentation and the order in which the reports and interviews are presented.

Present Broadcast your news report to your class. Remember to stay in your assigned role and to refer to the visuals your group has created during your presentation.

Research and Write Individually Connect the significance of the topic your team selected to events today. In a report, draw broad conclusions about the impact that this "turning point in history" has on current social, economic, or political history.

Multimedia Presentation

Turn your newscast into a video presentation. Create a set for the show. Design costumes for the reporters and for the people they interview. Choose theme music. Present commercials for products of the time period. Use video equipment to tape your show. Then, screen the newscast for your class.

196 UNIT 2 ◆ The Growth of Empires and Governments

Teaching Options

Multimedia Presentation

Have students brainstorm commercials, theme music, sets, and other aspects of a newscast. Encourage students to be creative when preparing their commercials, sets, and costumes. If necessary, teach students how to use various features of video-recording equipment, such as fades, dissolves, and other effects.

Alternative Assessment

Make a Poster Have groups of students make a poster of turning points in history related to ancient civilizations in Greece, Rome, and the Islamic states. Have them draw an illustrated timeline on a large sheet of poster board. Encourage students to display information obtained from maps and other visuals in their textbooks as well as from the reading.

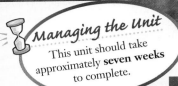
Managing the Unit
This unit should take approximately **seven weeks** to complete.

Unit 3 REGIONAL CIVILIZATIONS

PLANNING GUIDE

	Skills and Features	Projects and Activities	Program Resources	Meet Individual Needs
Chapter 9 **The Americas,** pp. 198–219 Plan for 4–5 class periods.	Unit Technology, p. T197 Understand Sequence, p. 205 They Made History: Pachacuti, p. 209	Cooperative Learning, p. T200 Sports & Games, p. T202 Research, pp. T207, T215 Connection to Math, p. T208 Writing, p. T209 Test Taking, p. T212 Connection to Literature, p. T213 Using Technology, p. T214 Conflict Resolution, p. T216	**Teacher's Resources** Terms to Know, p. 22 Review History, p. 56 Build Your Skills, p. 90 Chapter Test, pp. 133–134 Concept Builder, p. 225 Venn Diagram, p. 323 Transparencies 3, 4, 7	ESL/ELL Strategies, pp. T203, T210 Visual/Spatial, p. T208
Chapter 10 **Kingdoms and City-States in Africa,** pp. 220–241 Plan for 4–5 class periods.	Write a Persuasive Essay, p. 227 Past to Present: The Music of Africa, pp. 232–233	Cooperative Learning, p. T223 Connection to Science, p. T223 Connection to Culture, p. T225 Using Technology, p. T225 Connection to Economics, p. T228 Conflict Resolution, p. T229 Research, p. T230 Connection to Literature, p. T232, T236 Writing, p. T237 Connection to World Languages, p. T238	**Teacher's Resources** Terms to Know, p. 23 Review History, p. 57 Build Your Skills, p. 91 Chapter Test, pp. 135–136 Concept Builder, p. 226 They Made History: Sundiata, p. 255 Flowchart, p. 324 Transparencies 2, 6, 10	ESL/ELL Strategies, pp. T222, T234 Kinesthetic, p. T224 Visual/Spatial, p. T235
Chapter 11 **Dynasties and Kingdoms of East Asia,** pp. 242–267 Plan for 5–6 class periods.	Compare and Contrast, p. 249 They Made History: Toyotomi Hideyoshi, p. 264	Test Taking, pp. T246, T258 Conflict Resolution, pp. T246, T264 Connection to Art, pp. T247, T254 Research, p. T252 Connection to Literature, p. T253 Using Technology, pp. T254, T264 Writing, p. T261 Cooperative Learning, p. T262 Connection to Culture, p. T263	**Teacher's Resources** Terms to Know, p. 24 Review History, p. 58 Build Your Skills, p. 92 Chapter Test, pp. 137–138 Concept Builder, p. 227 Venn Diagram, p. 323 Transparencies 1, 7	ESL/ELL Strategies, pp. T245, T250, T256, T260 Visual/Spatial, p. T245 Verbal/Linguistic, p. T251
Chapter 12 **The Early Middle Ages,** pp. 268–287 Plan for 9–10 class periods.	Use Secondary Sources, p. 275 Points of View, p. 285	Test Taking, p. T270 Conflict Resolution, pp. T271, T276 Writing, p. T272 Connection to Economics, p. T273 Teen Life, p. T278 Using Technology, p. T280 Research, p. T283 Link to Today, p. T285	**Teacher's Resources** Terms to Know, p. 25 Review History, p. 59 Build Your Skills, p. 93 Chapter Test, pp. 139–140 Concept Builder, p. 228 Cause-and-Effect Chain, p. 325 Transparency 1	ESL/ELL Strategies, pp. T271, T277, T281 Visual/Spatial, pp. T277, T282
Chapter 13 **The High Middle Ages,** pp. 288–311 Plan for 9–10 class periods.	Distinguish Fact From Opinion, p. 295 Connect History & Economics, p. 301 They Made History: Joan of Arc, p. 304	World Religions, p. T291 Test Taking, p. T293 Research, p. T298 Using Technology, p. T299 Connection to Literature, p. T303 Conflict Resolution, p. T303 Writing, p. T304 Cooperative Learning, p. T305	**Teacher's Resources** Terms to Know, p. 26 Review History, p. 60 Build Your Skills, p. 94 Chapter Test, pp. 141–142 Unit 3 Test, pp. 187–188 Concept Builder, p. 229 Idea Web, p. 321	ESL/ELL Strategies, pp. T293, T296, T305, T308 Auditory, p. T292 Logical/Mathematical, p. T297

Assessment Options

Chapter 9 Test, Teacher's Resources, pp. 133–134
Chapter 10 Test, Teacher's Resources, pp. 135–136
Chapter 11 Test, Teacher's Resources, pp. 137–138
Chapter 12 Test, Teacher's Resources, pp. 139–140
Chapter 13 Test, Teacher's Resources, pp. 141–142
Unit 3 Test, Teacher's Resources, pp. 187–188

Alternative Assessment

Millennium Exhibition, p. 312
Create a Travel Brochure, p. T312

Books for Students

AVERAGE

The Mongol Empire. Mary E. Hull. A summary of the Mongol Empire, from its beginning to its lasting effects. (Gale Group, 1997)

Nelson Mandela's Favorite African Folktales. Nelson Mandela. A collection of 32 African tales. (Norton, W. W. & Company, Inc., 2002)

DK Discoveries: Aztecs. Richard Platt. An illustrated account of the conflict between the Aztecs and the Spanish expedition. (DK Publishing, Inc., 1999)

CHALLENGING

Along the Inca Road: A Woman's Journey into an Ancient Empire. Karin Muller. An account of the author's adventure along the Inca Road, including history of the Incas and present events. (National Geographic Society, 2001)

Hideyoshi. Mary Elizabeth Berry. A biography of Toyotomi Hideyoshi that explores the changes Japan underwent. (Harvard University Press, 1989)

The Year 1000: What Life Was Like at the Turn of the First Millennium: An Englishman's World. Robert Lacey and Danny Danziger. A month-by-month glance into the life of Europeans in the year 1000. (Little, Brown, & Company, 2000)

Joan of Arc: Her Story. Régine Pernoud and Marie-Véronique Clin. Translation. A biography based on primary sources. (Palgrave Global Publishing, 1999)

Books for Teachers

First Americans: American Indians. An illustrated overview, including Indian mythology, from a series. (Time-Life Custom Publishing, 1992)

Mexico: From the Olmecs to the Aztecs. Michael D. Coe and Rex Koontz. A history of ancient Mexico, including present-day discoveries. (Thames & Hudson, 2002)

Encyclopedia of African History and Culture, Vol. 1 and 2. Willie F. Page. Explores Africa from early beginnings through the sixteenth century with many resources. (Facts on File, Incorporated, 2001)

Daily Life in Traditional China: The Tang Dynasty. Charles D. Benn. A complete overview of the culture of the Tang Dynasty. (Greenwood Publishing Group, 2002)

The Early Middle Ages: Europe 400–1000. Rosamond McKitterick, editor. A detailed overview of all aspects of European society during this time. (Oxford University Press, 2001)

Europe in the High Middle Ages. William Chester Jordan. A thorough description of the events during this time. (Viking Press, 2003)

You may wish to preview all reference materials to ensure their appropriateness for your local community.

Audio/Visual Resources

The Americas Before the Europeans. Explores the Maya, Aztec, and Inca civilizations and the reasons they were conquered. Videocassette. (Social Studies School Service)

Africa Before the Europeans: 100–1500. Shows the lives and influences of the African civilizations from this time. Videocassette. (Social Studies School Service)

China and Japan: 1279–1600. Reviews the similarities and differences between China and Japan. Videocassette. (Social Studies School Service)

A Medieval Celebration. Review historical and cultural facts about this period with a story theme. CD-ROM. (Social Studies School Service)

Technology Resources

Native American History:
http://www.lib.washington.edu/subject/History/tm/native.html

Africa–Early History:
http://www.historyteacher.net/GlobalStudies/Africa_Early_History.htm

China:
http://emuseum.mankato.msus.edu/prehistory/china/

The Middle Ages:
http://www.learner.org/exhibits/middleages/

Globe Fearon Related Resources

History Resources

Global Studies: Focus on South and Southeast Asia, Volume 5. Primary source materials and activities explore all aspects of life in South and Southeast Asia. ISBN 0-835-91941-2

Core Knowledge History & Geography: Europe in the Middle Ages. Explores Europe in the Middle Ages to help students build a solid background. ISBN 0-7690-3081-5

Globe Adapted Classics

Beowulf. An epic poem about the adventures of a young, great prince. ISBN 0-835-95541-9

The Canterbury Tales. Geoffrey Chaucer's collection of short stories, told by English pilgrims on their way to Canterbury, England. ISBN 0-835-90869-0

Literature Resources

World Myths and Legends I: Native American. An anthology of Native American myths and legends. ISBN 0-822-44640-5

World Myths and Legends II: South America. An anthology of South American myths and legends. ISBN 0-822-44645-6

To order books, call 1-800-321-3106.

Regional Civilizations

"A general definition of civilization: a civilized society is exhibiting the five qualities of truth, beauty, adventure, art, and peace."
—Alfred North Whitehead,
  mathematician and philosopher, 1933

LINKING CULTURES Often separated by oceans and continents, most peoples of regional civilizations created powerful reminders of their way of life and thinking, such as ancient China's monumental structure called the Great Wall.

◆ What can a monument such as the Great Wall teach us about ancient civilizations?

197

Regional Civilizations
(pp. 197–312)

Unit Summary
Unit 3 discusses early civilizations that arose in the Americas, in Africa, and in Asia. It also introduces the development of European kingdoms in the Middle Ages.

CHAPTER 9
  The Americas

CHAPTER 10
  Kingdoms and City-States in Africa

CHAPTER 11
  Dynasties and Kingdoms of East Asia

CHAPTER 12
  The Early Middle Ages

CHAPTER 13
  The High Middle Ages

Set the Stage
TEACH PRIMARY SOURCES
Photo The unit photograph shows the Great Wall of China. Three Chinese dynasties actually had a part in the creation of the structure. The last of these, the Ming Dynasty, gave the wall its present form. Also, point out the watchtowers in the photograph. Fires were lit in the watchtowers, and the smoke was used to signal invasions and the number of invaders.

Quote Whitehead was a mathematician and philosopher. In this quote, he gives his definition of civilization as five qualities that represent the positive aspects of a civilized society. Ask students to recall some of the elements of civilization that were introduced in Chapter 1.

◆ **ANSWER** Structures created by ancient civilizations show us the organizational, mathematical, and engineering abilities of the people living at the time.

Teaching Options

UNIT TECHNOLOGY
Have students use the Internet, CD-ROM resources, and other media to research ancient art and architecture. Students can search by keywords and/or by the name of a specific civilization. Suggest students choose a culture on which to focus and to share their findings with the class. You may wish to identify possible Web sites for students before they begin.

UNIT 3 / Portfolio Project

Millennium Exhibition
The Portfolio Project for Unit 3 on page 312 is to create a millennium museum exhibition. Students will select visuals from a period in history. Then, they will plan and create the museum exhibit's layout, assign the role of tour guide for the exhibit, and plan a tour sequence.

The Americas
2500 B.C.–A.D. 1500
(pp. 198–219)

Chapter Objectives

• Describe the early civilizations of the Americas and explore how they developed.
• Identify characteristics and advances made by the Incan Empire.
• Discuss the early groups of the western and eastern regions in North America in relation to the variety of land and climate.

Chapter Summary

Section I focuses on a number of early civilizations that developed in the Americas, including the Olmec, the Maya, and the Aztec civilizations.
Section II describes the early peoples of Peru and explains the Incan civilization, the city of Cuzco, and the advances made by the Incas.
Section III discusses the groups who lived in North America and how the variety in geography and climate influenced these groups' development.

Set the Stage

TEACH PRIMARY SOURCES
Ask students to read the quotation on page 198. The structure and rhythm of the language of the quotation is that of a myth rather than that of a straightforward factual report. (The quotation is taken from *The Myth of Quetzalcoatl*.) Ask students how they might express the same message in a news bulletin, for example. (Possible answer: From the top of the mountain Tzatzitepetl, a public announcer shouted proclamations. People listened to learn about the laws and the commands of Quetzalcoatl.)

The Americas
2500 B.C.–A.D. 1500

I. Early Civilizations of the Americas
II. Peru and the Incan Empire
III. North American Groups

The Toltec people of ancient Mexico worshiped Quetzalcoatl, the god of both earth and sky. In the tenth century A.D., they believed that Quetzalcoatl had come to live among them in the form of a strong leader. Later, Spanish monks and native Mexican people translated what was written about his rule in the Toltec language, including the following words:

66 *There was a mountain called Tzatzitepetl (Mountain for Shouting), and that is its name today. From the top of it a public crier shouted announcements, and his messages spread over Anahuac [a great central plateau in Mexico]. He was heard and the laws were communicated. People came to learn and listen to what Quetzalcoatl had commanded.* 99

The Toltecs, and their god Quetzalcoatl, were part of one ancient society that developed in the Americas. Other peoples in different regions of North and South America created complex civilizations with great cities, as well. In what are present-day Canada and the United States, early Americans developed civilizations in different ways.

ca. 1000 B.C.
Adenas arrive in the Mississippi and Ohio River valleys.

ca. 2500 B.C.
People of ancient Mexico learn to grow corn.

ca. 1200 B.C.
Olmecs settle along the Gulf of Mexico.

CHAPTER EVENTS

2500 B.C.   1700 B.C.   900 B.C.

WORLD EVENTS

ca. 2500 B.C.
Egyptians build Great Pyramid of Cheops.
People of Mohenjo-Daro in the Indus Valley cultivate rice.

1100 B.C.
Zhou Dynasty begins in China.

198   UNIT 3   ◆   Regional Civilizations

Teaching Options

Chapter 9 Resources

REVIEW

Teacher's Resources (TR)
Terms to Know, p. 22
Review History, p. 56
Build Your Skills, p. 90
Chapter Test, pp. 133–134
Concept Builder, p. 225
Venn Diagram, p. 323
Transparencies 3, 4, 7

ASSESSMENT
Section Reviews, pp. 204, 211, 217
Chapter Review, pp. 218–219
Chapter Test, TR, pp. 133–134

ALTERNATIVE ASSESSMENT
Portfolio Project, p. 312
Travel Brochure, p. T312

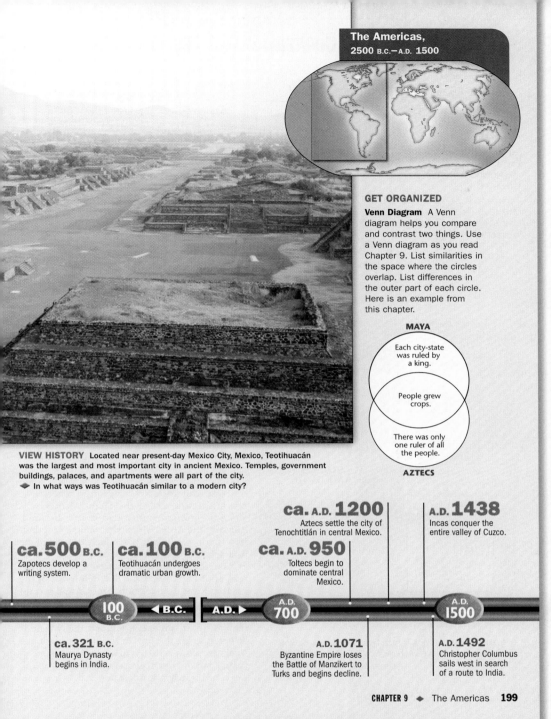

GET ORGANIZED

Venn Diagram A Venn diagram helps you compare and contrast two things. Use a Venn diagram as you read Chapter 9. List similarities in the space where the circles overlap. List differences in the outer part of each circle. Here is an example from this chapter.

MAYA

Each city-state was ruled by a king.

People grew crops.

There was only one ruler of all the people.

AZTECS

VIEW HISTORY Located near present-day Mexico City, Mexico, Teotihuacán was the largest and most important city in ancient Mexico. Temples, government buildings, palaces, and apartments were all part of the city.
◆ In what ways was Teotihuacán similar to a modern city?

ca. 500 B.C.
Zapotecs develop a writing system.

ca. 100 B.C.
Teotihuacán undergoes dramatic urban growth.

ca. A.D. 1200
Aztecs settle the city of Tenochtitlán in central Mexico.

A.D. 1438
Incas conquer the entire valley of Cuzco.

ca. A.D. 950
Toltecs begin to dominate central Mexico.

100 B.C. ◀ B.C. A.D. ▶ A.D. 700 A.D. 1500

ca. 321 B.C.
Maurya Dynasty begins in India.

A.D. 1071
Byzantine Empire loses the Battle of Manzikert to Turks and begins decline.

A.D. 1492
Christopher Columbus sails west in search of a route to India.

CHAPTER 9 ◆ The Americas **199**

Chapter Themes
- Culture
- Time, Continuity, and Change
- People, Places, and Environments
- Individuals, Groups, and Institutions
- Global Connections
- Power, Authority, and Governance

F Y I

The City of Teotihuacán
Teotihuacán was built by early civilizations in the Valley of Mexico. It was a major trading center for two or three centuries. It was probably also an important religious and ceremonial center because archaeologists have found it to be a large complex of pyramids and zpublic buildings. The city was mysteriously destroyed around the seventh century.

Chapter Warm-Up
USING THE MAP
Have students find the locator map at the top of page 199. The map shows the world and then highlights North, Central, and South America. Challenge students to name some of the present-day countries that are located in these areas.

VIEW HISTORY
The ruins of Teotihuacán represent many of the characteristics of early civilizations, a large city with temples and important public buildings. The Pyramid of the Sun, at the left of the photograph, rises above the ruins of the other buildings. Ask students how the Pyramid of the Sun compares to a polis. (The temples were above the public buildings.)

◆ **ANSWER** It had broad, straight streets and large buildings.

GET ORGANIZED
Venn Diagram
Discuss the graphic organizer, called a Venn diagram, on page 199. Remind students that the interlocking circles represent a way to visually show likenesses and differences. For example, when students use a Venn diagram to compare and contrast characteristics of the Maya and the Aztecs, the different characteristics of each civilization should be placed in the outer part of each circle. Students should place characteristics both civilizations shared in the area where the circles intersect.

● TEACH THE TIMELINE
The timeline on pages 198–199 shows events between 2500 B.C. and A.D. 1492. The intervals on the timeline are 800 years. Have students use the timeline to list all the different civilizations that settled at one time in present-day Mexico. (Olmecs, Toltecs, Aztecs) Tell students to watch for information on these civilizations as they read the chapter.

Activity

Interpret the timeline Have students note the early civilizations that had been developed in the Americas by the time the explorer Christopher Columbus sailed. (Olmecs, Adenas, Toltecs, Aztecs, Anasazis, Zapotecs, Incas)

I. Early Civilizations of the Americas
(pp. 200–204)

Section Summary
In this section, students will learn about the geography and climate of the area known today as Latin America and how these influenced the development of early civilizations there. Also, students will learn about several significant early civilizations of the region, including the Olmecs, Maya, and Aztecs.

1 Introduce

Getting Started
Ask students what characteristics of civilization in the present-day United States enable people to settle and live in towns and cities rather than live like nomads. (Possible answers: an adequate food and water supply, open jobs, or accessible transportation to jobs) Ask students if they think settlements brought improvements to the lives of early peoples, and why.

TERMS TO KNOW
Ask students to read the terms and definitions on page 200. Then, have students find each term in the section and write a sentence using each term in context.

You may wish to preview the pronunciation of the names of the early cities shown on the maps on pages 200 and 203 with students.

Tenochtitlán (tay nawch teet LAHN)
Tikal (tee KAHL)
Tula (TOO lah)
Teotihuacán (tay oh tee wah KAHN)

ACTIVE READING
Remind students that they learned about causes and effects in Chapter 3. Have them record causes and effects from Section 1. To help students get started, ask them to find the causes of these effects.
• The region that includes countries in North, South, and Central America is referred to as Latin America.
• Siberia and Alaska were once connected by a land bridge.

Terms to Know
annex to add to or take possession of
maize corn
glyph a picture or other symbol, often carved, that represents a word or an idea
chinampa a floating raft made of reeds and filled with earth on which the Aztecs grew crops

Main Ideas
A. Latin America is a diverse geographical region.
B. The earliest civilizations in the Americas began when people learned to grow corn and other crops.
C. The Aztecs developed a powerful civilization in Mexico.

Active Reading
CAUSE AND EFFECT
An effect is something that happens. The cause is what makes it happen. As you read this section, think about the major changes in early civilizations of the Americas and what caused these changes.

A. Geography and Its Impact
Early civilizations developed in North America, South America, and Central America. Central America is the area of land between North and South America, as shown on the map below. Central America is part of a region that is also called Latin America. Latin America also includes Mexico, South America, and some islands in the Caribbean Sea. Ancient civilizations developed differently in Latin America from other parts of the Americas, mostly due to geography.

Land and Climate of Latin America
The region known as Latin America stretches from Mexico in North America to the southernmost tip of South America at Cape Horn. The region is called Latin America because most of the people who live there today speak the Latin-based languages of Spanish, Portuguese, and French. At one time, parts of Latin America were **annexed**, or taken possession of, by European countries.

The geography of Latin America includes plains, mountains, and rain forests. Plains cover most of Mexico as well as parts of South America. Highland plateaus are good areas for farming or for grazing.

Mountains are located in both North and South America. In Mexico—in North America—a mountain chain called the Sierra Madres runs along the western and eastern coasts. In South America, the Andes Mountains run the length of its western coast. Many of the highest peaks of the Andes are in Peru.

Rain forests are an important geographical feature of Latin America. The rain forest of the Amazon River basin in South America and parts of Central America is the largest in the world.

Latin America has many different climate regions. In the mountain regions, the climate is colder than in the lowlands. The peaks of the Andes are always covered in snow. The climate in coastal and interior regions ranges from tropical, wet climates to hot, dry climates.

Early Civilizations of the Americas, A.D. 900–1500

NORTH AMERICA
Sierra Madres
Gulf of Mexico
MEXICO
Teotihuacán
Tenochtitlán
Tikal
Caribbean Sea
15°N
CENTRAL AMERICA
ATLANTIC OCEAN
Andes Mts.
0°
PACIFIC OCEAN
Amazon River
Amazon River Basin
PERU
Machu Picchu
Cuzco
SOUTH AMERICA
30°S
Andes Mts.
45°S
0   500   1,000 mi
0   500 1,000 km
Cape Horn
120°W 105°W 90°W 75°W 60°W 45°W 30°W 15°W

Maya civilization, A.D. 900
Aztec civilization, A.D. 1500
Incan civilization, A.D. 1500
• Cities

✔ Map Check
HUMAN INTERACTION Which two civilizations do you think would have been more alike geographically?

Teaching Options

Section 1 Resources

Teacher's Resources (TR)
Terms to Know, p. 22
Review History, p. 56
Build Your Skills, p. 90
Concept Builder, p. 225
Venn Diagram, p. 323
Transparencies 3, 4, 7

Cooperative Learning
Make groups with at most four students. Give each group three idea webs. (TR, p. 321) Each web should be labeled for one of the three major civilizations of the Americas: Aztecs, Maya, and Incas. Add two circles and label the circles Location, Religion, Recreation, Art, Government, and Architecture. Have the group work together to take notes about these major civilizations as they read this section.

The First Americans

During the Ice Age, most of Earth's water was frozen. The oceans were shallower than they are now. Therefore, less of the land was under water. It is believed that Siberia, in present-day northern Russia, and Alaska were once connected by a land bridge that was up to 1,000 miles wide. Some scholars believe that nomadic Asian peoples crossed this land bridge to the Americas about 13,000 years ago, probably in search of food. Some settled in what is now Alaska. Others continued traveling south and east, eventually scattering over North America and South America.

◆ **What are the three main geographical features of Latin America?**

B. Early Civilizations

The early peoples of the Americas slowly developed into social groups. Over time, people in some of these groups built cities and fought for control of their territories. They eventually created complex societies that continue to amaze us today.

Sometime between 3000 and 2500 B.C., the early Americans learned to cultivate **maize**, or corn. This crop became the basis of their diet. Maize is a highly nutritious cereal grain. It can be dried after harvest and stored to serve as a winter food supply. Then, it can be ground into flour for bread. It can also be cooked in a variety of ways.

The Olmecs and the Zapotecs

People known as the Olmecs developed the earliest known civilization in the Americas. They settled along the Gulf of Mexico in about 1200 B.C. The Olmecs lived by fishing and farming. Rubber is native to this part of Mexico, and the Olmecs harvested it and made it into rubber balls. The large stone courts on which they played ball games still survive today. Olmec art included gigantic carved stone heads. Other Olmec achievements included a calendar.

Global Connections

RICE

At the same time the early Americans were learning to cultivate maize, Asians were developing rice farming. Archaeologists have discovered that the inhabitants of Mohenjo-Daro in the Indus Valley cultivated rice in 2500 B.C.

Unlike maize, rice requires large amounts of water for growing and cannot survive in the environments in which maize thrives.

The Olmecs created giant stone heads like this one, which could weigh as much as several tons.

Connection to CULTURE

The calendar, writing system, and construction of large cities in the Olmec and Zapotec civilizations were adopted or adapted by later civilizations in the same area. For example, the Olmecs carved giant heads of stone. Ask students to speculate about what the heads depicted. (Possible answers: a powerful ruler, a priest, or a god) Have students read the chapter to find other cultures noted for carvings.

This Maya fresco shows a procession of musicians.

Explore The photograph of the procession of musicians at the top of page 202 is a fresco. Explain that a fresco is a painting originally done on a surface of moist plaster. The word comes directly from an Italian word meaning "fresh" because a fresco is made while the plaster is still moist, or fresh.

Activity

Role-play Ask students to identify the jobs held by the people who lived in the city of Teotihuacán. (farmers, craftworkers, artisans, builders, merchants, warriors, priests, and rulers) Ask students which of those jobs they would have liked to hold and why. Then, have students create the city of Teotihuacán in the classroom.

Assign a few students the role of customers who need some items built or pieces of art made. Assign the others the jobs they preferred. Have the customers discuss the job with the student with the correct job for the task and listen to the conversation. The customer should be asking for items that were made during this time and the worker should be able to explain how that item was made.

SPOTLIGHT ON CULTURE

MAYA BASKETBALL Ask students how the Maya ball game and the modern game of basketball are similar (Both used a ball and a hoop; both played in teams.) and how they are different (Maya players used a solid rubber ball and a stone ring hoop hung vertically from a wall; modern basketballs are not solid rubber and the hoops are string nets and are hung horizontally from a backboard.).

Review Ask students to recall the definition of a *city-state*. (A city-state is an independent government consisting of a city and its surrounding territories. Students can review the term on page 16.) The Maya civilization was unified by trade; however, many city-states existed, each having its own ruler.

The Zapotec people settled in southeastern Mexico, in the present-day state of Oaxaca. By 500 B.C., they had developed a writing system. Monte Alban, their capital city, was home to 40,000 to 50,000 people by 300 to 200 B.C. Monte Alban featured stone buildings, large plazas, and ceremonial pyramids.

Teotihuacán was an even larger city than Monte Alban. Located just northeast of modern Mexico City, Teotihuacán at its height was home to 125,000 people. From about 100 B.C. to A.D. 750, this city thrived as the most important political, religious, and economic power in Mexico.

The center of the city featured immense pyramids along a wide avenue called the Street of the Dead. The Pyramid of the Sun and the Pyramid of the Moon stood impressively in the city as did the Ciudadela, which was a courtyard surrounded by pyramids located at the city's geographic center. The central marketplace stood just across the street from it.

The people of Teotihuacán lived in stone apartments. Most of them were farmers who traveled outside of the city every day to farm the land. Others were craftworkers and artisans who worked in stone and clay, producing tools and other items that were traded with other groups. Some people worked as builders, merchants, and warriors. The priests and the rulers governed the city.

The Maya

Maya civilization reached its peak between A.D. 300 and 900. The Maya people occupied present-day Guatemala, Belize, and the Yucatán Peninsula. The Maya cleared forests and built raised fields on which they sowed their crops. They also played sports, including a game similar to basketball.

Maya civilization included a number of independent city-states linked by a common language and culture. Networks of roads linked Maya cities with one another, and all city-states benefited from trade among themselves.

A king ruled each city-state with the help and advice of priests and nobles. Artisans and merchants ranked below the nobles. The greatest number of Maya were peasants, laborers, and farmers. Wealthy Maya owned slaves, who were usually criminals or prisoners of war.

Spotlight on *Culture*

MAYA BASKETBALL
The Maya played the game that we know as basketball. Players used a solid rubber ball and a stone ring as a hoop. The ring was attached to a wall. Spectators watched their teams from the stands.

Teaching Options

Focus on ▷ SPORTS & GAMES ◁

Ball Games Many ancient civilizations developed a variety of sports and games, including different kinds of ball games. Men and women generally had different games and played separately. Children enjoyed the same games as the adults of a group.

Some of the early games seem to have been similar to games played today. For example, some women played *shinny* or *shinty*, a kind of field hockey. The Olmecs played ball games on large stone courts, which have been unearthed by archaeologists.

The Aztecs and Maya played a game in which teams of players tried to bounce a rubber ball through a vertical ring that was set high on a wall. Players could not use their hands, and scoring was difficult. The game was similar to today's soccer and basketball.

The city of Tikal became the Maya ceremonial center. Priests played an especially important role in Maya society. They performed daily rituals to please the gods, whom the Maya believed controlled the weather. Maya people built huge pyramid-shaped temples in honor of the gods, decorating them with murals that showed historic scenes or legends. The Maya also practiced human sacrifice to keep the gods happy.

The Maya had many achievements in the arts and sciences. They developed a $365\frac{1}{4}$-day calendar that was the most accurate in the world at that time. They studied astronomy and predicted solar eclipses. In mathematics, they were among the first people to understand and use the concept of zero. They also developed a system of writing that used **glyphs**, which are pictures or other symbols, often carved, that represent words or ideas.

◆ **What are some similarities between earlier civilizations and the Maya civilization?**

C. The Aztec Civilization

The Aztec people thrived later than the Maya. They were influenced by an earlier people called the Toltecs. Many elements of Aztec culture can be traced back to the Toltec people.

The Toltecs

An early Mexican history describes the Toltec people and their civilization:

> ❝ It is said that the Toltecs were very wealthy, and that they had all they needed for eating and drinking. The squash were huge, two meters [6 feet] in circumference. And the ears of maize were so big that a single pair of arms could not stretch around them. The amaranth plants were so thick that people could climb them like trees. ❞

The Toltecs dominated central Mexico from about A.D. 950 to 1200. The city of Tula was the capital of the Toltec Empire. It was located northwest of present-day Mexico City. Tula was the center of a powerful mining and trading empire. The Toltecs used copper and gold to make jewelry and weapons. Like the Maya, the Toltecs erected pyramid-shaped buildings.

The Toltecs worshiped a god called Quetzalcoatl. The name means "feathered serpent." The quetzal, a Central American bird, symbolized the sky. The Toltecs valued the bird's three-foot-long green tail feathers. The coatl, or snake, stood for Earth. Quetzalcoatl, therefore, symbolized a union of Earth and sky.

In the tenth century, a Toltec priest called Ce Acatl Topiltzín became identified with the god Quetzalcoatl. Topiltzín eventually disappeared. Around A.D 1200, Tula was destroyed and the Toltec civilization ended.

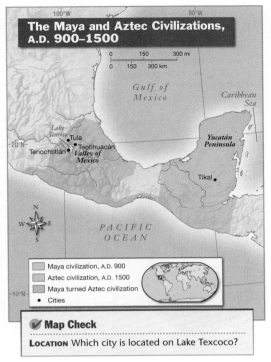

The Maya and Aztec Civilizations, A.D. 900–1500

100°W   90°W

0   150   300 mi
0   150   300 km

Gulf of Mexico

Caribbean Sea

Lake Texcoco • Tula
Tenochtitlán • • Teotihuacán
Valley of Mexico

Yucatán Peninsula

Tikal •

N
W E
S

PACIFIC OCEAN

20°N
10°N

☐ Maya civilization, A.D. 900
☐ Aztec civilization, A.D. 1500
☐ Maya turned Aztec civilization
• Cities

✔ **Map Check**
LOCATION Which city is located on Lake Texcoco?

ANALYZE PRIMARY SOURCES
DOCUMENT-BASED QUESTION
What are three products that show the wealth of the Toltecs?

Activity

Create your own language
Discuss with students the reasons why the Maya would create a writing system. Have groups of students create their own writing system, or language. Students should write out the symbols in the language, the rules of grammar, and the way to read the language. Then, have students write a message with an English translation to share with the class.

◆ **ANSWER** Earlier civilizations and the Maya civilization practiced farming, had monumental art and architecture, played sports, built cities, and developed a system of writing.

C. The Aztec Civilization

Purpose-Setting Question What did the Aztecs do that helped them establish a strong empire? (Possible answer: They were strong warriors; the conquered people had to pay them tribute; other conquered people were enslaved.)

Using the Map

The Maya and Aztec Civilizations, A.D. 900–1500

Ask students to use the map key to identify the area of land on the Pacific coast where both the Aztecs and the Maya controlled land.

✔ **Map Check**
Answer Tenochtitlán

ANALYZE PRIMARY SOURCES

DOCUMENT-BASED QUESTION
The source of the quotation on this page is *The Myth of Quetzalcoatl*. Ask students what clues suggest that this language is mythic rather than a literal description of Toltec wealth. (the exaggerated description of the size of the squash, ears of maize, and amaranth plants)

ANSWER huge squash, big ears of maize, and thick amaranth plants

WHAT IN THE WORLD?

THE AZTEC CALENDAR Discuss with students how the Aztec calendar differs from modern calendars. Note that for early peoples, calendars and aspects of astronomy were closely tied to religious beliefs. Thus, the main symbol on the Aztec calendar is the face of the sun god Tonatiuh.

◆ **ANSWER** The Aztec people developed a unified empire with one ruler chosen by nobles or priests to lead wars. They were harsh rulers; conquered people either paid tribute or became slaves or sacrifices.

Section Close

As a class, have students make a chart with five columns, one for each of the early civilizations: Olmec, Zapotec, Maya, Toltec, and Aztec. Have students list what they have learned, such as where each settled, the crops they grew, recreational activities, structures built, influences, government, achievements, and any other information that makes them stand out. Remind students that their charts will make good study aids.

3 Assess

Review Answers

Review History

A. The region is called Latin America because most people who live there speak a Latin-based language.

B. Characteristics of the earliest civilizations include the development of farming; the settlement of larger cities and the building of temples and government structures; the importance of religion; new inventions in the arts and sciences.

C. The Aztecs invaded and conquered lands held by other peoples; the conquered people paid tribute or became slaves or human sacrifices; children were educated.

Define Terms to Know

annex, 200; maize, 201; glyph, 203; chinampa, 204

THE AZTEC CALENDAR

In 1790, a round Aztec calendar stone was found in Mexico City. Mexicans call this Aztec calendar stone Piedra del Sol, or Stone of the Sun. A calendar is carved into the face of the 11-foot-wide stone. The central image is the face of the sun god, Tonatiuh. The outer carvings show time elements and religious symbols.

Aztec calendar stone

The Toltecs and later the Aztecs always believed Quetzalcoatl would return. As you will read in Chapter 16, this belief brought disaster to the Aztecs.

The Aztecs

Aztec peoples moved into the central plain of Mexico around A.D. 1200. Their capital city was Tenochtitlán on Lake Texcoco in central Mexico. The Aztecs developed a unified empire with one ruler, chosen by nobles and priests, to lead wars. Priests recorded Aztec laws and events. The Aztecs had an accurate calendar that was based on the Maya calendar.

During the fifteenth century, Aztec warriors began invading and conquering the city-states surrounding their capital. They forced the conquered people to give them tribute in the form of maize, tobacco, gold, and precious stones. They took many prisoners of war, some of whom became slaves to the Aztecs.

Most prisoners, however, became human sacrifices to the gods. Human sacrifice was an important part of the Aztec religion. The Aztecs believed that their gods demanded such sacrifices and that they were repaid by the gods with success in war and trade. They believed that to be sacrificed was an honor for the victim and his or her family.

The land around Lake Texcoco was swampy and difficult to farm. As a result, Aztec farmers planted their crops on **chinampas**, floating rafts made of reeds and filled with soil. They grew maize, squash, beans, and various vegetables.

Aztec boys attended schools, where priests taught them about astronomy and religion. They also taught them how to read and write hieroglyphics. Both boys and girls received training for their roles as adults. Boys learned the arts of war. Girls were educated by their mothers to enter certain professions. Girls became weavers and priestesses.

◆ **What kind of empire and rule did the Aztec people develop?**

Review I

Review History

A. How did Latin America get its name?

B. Describe the common characteristics of the earliest civilizations of the Americas.

C. How did the Aztec civilization become so powerful?

Define Terms to Know

Define the following terms: **annex, maize, glyph, chinampa**

Critical Thinking

What does the belief in Quetzalcoatl suggest about Toltec and Aztec society?

Write About Geography

Write a paragraph explaining how nomads migrated to the North American continent.

Get Organized

VENN DIAGRAM

Use a Venn diagram to compare and contrast early civilizations in the Americas. Choose two civilizations and note what they have in common and how they differ.

Critical Thinking

Possible answer: Quetzalcoatl symbolized a union of Earth and sky, so the Toltecs and the Aztecs felt that both were important in their lives.

Write About Geography

Students' paragraphs should include information about how Siberia and Alaska were once connected by a 1,000-mile-wide land bridge. Nomadic Asian people crossed this bridge about 13,000 years ago.

Maya

Priests and rulers governed cities; lived in stone apartments.

Developed writing system; most were farmers.

King ruled city-states; developed calendar.

Aztec

Build Your Skills

Build Your Skills

Critical Thinking

UNDERSTAND SEQUENCE

Have you ever made popcorn in a microwave oven? You need to follow the steps in a certain order. For example, you cannot open the bag and eat the popcorn before you pop it! Think about the steps you follow to make microwave popcorn.

The order in which events happen is their sequence. It is important to understand sequence so that you can study how events that happened in the past caused certain other events to happen.

One way to understand the sequence of specific events is to make a flowchart. A flowchart shows the order of events and can help you understand the order of the events you read about.

Most histories and biographies, or written histories about people's lives, are told in sequence. This chapter that you are reading, for example, describes history in the order in which civilizations in the Americas developed, or in chronological order.

Another visual tool to help you sequence events is a timeline. The timeline at the start of the chapter shows two sequences of events. The one shown on the top bar is the sequence of events happening in the chapter. The bottom bar shows the sequence of events happening elsewhere in the world.

Here's How
Follow these steps to make a flowchart of historical events.

1. Decide what the first and last events in your flowchart will be.

2. Identify the events you want to add to the chart. Look for dates and words such as *soon*, *before*, *later*, *after*, *then*, *while*, *first*, and *last* that can tell you when an event happened. Make a list of events in the order in which they happened.

3. Study the list. Try to find ways in which each event in your list caused the event that comes after it.

4. Use your list to make a flowchart like the one on this page.

Here's Why
You have just read about early civilizations in the Americas. You want to organize the events you read about to understand them better. Making a flowchart would help you to place the events in correct sequence.

Practice the Skill
Look at the flowchart on the right. It shows two important events about early American civilizations. Then, reread Section I. Copy the flowchart onto a sheet of paper and add events in the boxes to complete the chart.

Extend the Skill
Think about something you know how to do well. Make a flowchart to show the steps you take to do this activity. Make sure the flowchart shows the correct sequence of the steps.

Apply the Skill
As you read the next sections of the chapter, think about the sequence of events and ways you can use flowcharts to understand the order of important events you read about.

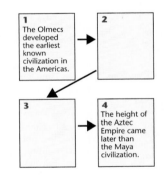

1. The Olmecs developed the earliest known civilization in the Americas.

2.

3.

4. The height of the Aztec Empire came later than the Maya civilization.

Teaching Options

RETEACH

Supply a blank flowchart (TR, p. 324) to students. Have students use events from Section 1 or from the Chapter Events section of the timeline on pages 198–199 to create a flowchart. Students may want to make a separate index card for each event, put the cards in order, and then fill in the events on the flowchart.

CHALLENGE

Ask students to find a current news article that presents events that happen in order. Have them place the events onto both a timeline and a flowchart. Ask them to display both formats together on posterboard. Discuss with students the similarities and differences shown by each format.

Build Your Skills

UNDERSTAND SEQUENCE

Teach the Skill
Recall for students the use of a timeline to represent events that happen in chronological order. Explain that when people write about events or steps of a process that happen in a certain order, they are using what is called sequence or sequential order. Point out that sequence is a typical writing style in a history textbook. Explain that a flowchart is another way to visually represent events that happen in chronological order, or in sequence.

In historical writing, the events that are presented in sequence often reflect a cause-and-effect relationship: one event happens first and causes another to happen.

To help students practice the skill, invite them to name some things they think are done, or happen, in order. (following a recipe or following instructions for how to put something together) Discuss how those steps could be represented as a list of steps or shown in a flowchart.

To make a flowchart, students need to identify what happens first and last, and events or steps that happen in between. A flowchart can have any number of boxes. Each event should be placed in a separate box. Arrows indicate the order or sequence of the events.

Practice the Skill
ANSWERS Possible answers: **Box 2:** The Zapotec people built the city of Monte Alban. **Box 3:** The Maya developed a system of writing using glyphs.

Extend the Skill
You may wish to distribute copies of the blank flowchart (TR, p. 324). Students' flowcharts should reflect a sequential process. Remind students that they may add additional boxes if necessary.

Apply the Skill
Have students construct flowcharts for either of the next two sections of Chapter 9. Students should skim the text for key dates. Caution students that in Section 3, some of the events are happening simultaneously.

Section Summary
In this section, students will learn about the early Peruvians as well as the rich and complex culture of the Incan Empire. They will identify elements of that culture, such as the strong system of government, the arts, and architecture.

1 Introduce

Getting Started
Have students describe the function and importance of various mail systems, such as the U.S. Postal Service, private companies that send mail and packages, and e-mail. Elicit that these systems help people of today communicate and send important messages quickly. Explain that in this section students will read about the Incan system of relaying messages.

TERMS TO KNOW
Ask students to read the terms and definitions on page 206 and find each term in the section.

You may wish to preview the pronunciations of the following terms.

Chavín (chah VEEN)
Moche (moh CHAY)
Machu Picchu
  (MAH choo PEEK choo)
Manco Capac
  (MAHNG koh KAH pahk)
Pachacuti (pah chah KOO tee)
Chimú (chee MOO)
Huayna Capac (WY nuh KAH pahk)

ACTIVE READING
Point out to students that to draw conclusions, they need to consider known information and evidence. As they read the section, they should use information they learn from the text and visuals to make some statements (conclusions) about ancient Peru and its people. Point out that a valid conclusion should be based on facts or evidence. So, students must be able to give reasons for their conclusions.

Terms to Know
adobe a sun-dried brick made from clay
quipu a long string with a knotted and colored group of smaller strings that was used to record numbers
ayllu a social unit made up of several families who owned land jointly

Main Ideas
A. The earliest people of Peru were accomplished artists, architects, and engineers.
B. Building projects, in the form of roads and bridges, helped unite the vast Incan Empire.
C. The Incas had a strict government, a rigid class structure, and a rich culture.

Active Reading
DRAW CONCLUSIONS
When you draw a conclusion, you must look at facts and evidence and think about what they suggest. As you read this section, look at the chart, photographs, and facts in the text and draw some conclusions about ancient Peru and its people.

A. Early Peoples of Peru
Peru is in central South America, on the Pacific coast between Chile and Ecuador. Much of the land is forested, and only a small percentage is suitable for farming. Ancient Peru was home to the Chavín and the Moche people, whose early cultures and societies were discovered by archaeologists.

The Chavín People
The Chavín culture flourished in northern Peru between 900 and 200 B.C. Architectural ruins and works of art of the Chavín culture remain for archaeologists and scholars to study.

People of the Chavín culture built stone temples in the mountains of Peru. They decorated their temples with carvings of Chavín gods and images of animals such as the jaguar, the serpent, and the caiman—an animal similar to an alligator. Along the coast, temples were more likely to be built of **adobe**, or sun-dried clay bricks, and painted with similar images. To build one temple, workers needed to produce about 50 million adobe bricks.

The Moche People
The Moche people of Peru emerged after the Chavín culture had faded, at about 200 to 100 B.C. They built no cities or urban centers. However, they controlled a vast area of land, and were an aggressive people. They were skilled engineers, building roads and irrigation systems of canals that brought water from the mountains to the valleys.

Like the people of the Chavín culture, the Moche people have left little behind except their art and their architectural ruins. Moche people had no written language. Unlike most ancient art in the Americas, Moche portraits are realistic representations of individuals. Their murals, figurines, and other works of art show people from every level of society involved in a wide variety of activities.

By A.D. 900, the Moche civilization had collapsed. The reasons for its collapse are not known for certain, although natural causes may have been involved. Some possible reasons for its collapse include earthquakes, a long period of drought, and severe flooding.

◆ **How was Moche art different from most ancient artwork?**

Courtesy of UCLA Fowler Museum of Cultural History

A Moche lord and his attendants are shown in this gold and turquoise earring (top). The figurine (bottom) is of a Moche musician.

Teaching Options

Section 2 Resources

Teacher's Resources (TR)
Terms to Know, p. 22
Review History, p. 56
Build Your Skills, p. 90
Concept Builder, p. 225
Venn Diagram, p. 323

B. Civilization of the Incas

The Incan people ruled a mighty empire on the western coast of South America by A.D. 1500. The ruins of the ancient Incan city of Machu Picchu were studied by an American history professor named Hiram Bingham in 1911. This city of Incan emperor Pachacuti, high in the Andes Mountains, provides a breathtaking record of Incan civilization. In his book, *Lost City of the Incas*, Bingham records his impressions of Machu Picchu:

> 66 Above all, there is the fascination of finding here and there under swaying vines . . . the rugged masonry [brickwork] . . . and of trying to understand the bewildering romance of the ancient builders who, ages ago, sought refuge . . . in a place where they might fearlessly and patiently give expression to their passion for walls of enduring beauty. 99

ANALYZE PRIMARY SOURCES
DOCUMENT-BASED QUESTION
What impressed Bingham about the builders of Machu Picchu?

History of the Incas

Little beyond legend is known of early Incan history. Most accounts state that around A.D. 1200, Manco Capac and his brothers and sisters traveled a few miles southwest of their home to settle in the valley of Cuzco. Manco Capac is considered the first ruler of the Incan people.

The Incas held the valley by attacking and conquering adjoining lands. By A.D. 1438, they had taken over the entire valley. Pachacuti, whose name means "Earth Shaker," became the first of the great Incan emperors. Under Pachacuti's rule, the Incas built their capital city of Cuzco and expanded their empire.

The ancient city of Machu Picchu is located high in the Andes Mountains, about 50 miles northwest of Cuzco.

An Incan noble receives a report from one of his officials who holds a long string called a quipu.

The City of Cuzco

The city plan of Cuzco was designed in the shape of a puma, or mountain lion—an animal sacred to the Incas. A fortress-temple was built at the head of the puma. The houses and palaces were laid out in a grid along the shape of its body. Houses were built in groups around rectangular or square enclosures. Four highways, one coming from each of the four quarters of the Incan Empire, came together in Cuzco's central plaza.

The Incas undertook many other building projects. They were highly skilled architects, able to build stone walls that needed no mortar to hold them together. They built roads and highways, which helped to unite the various parts of the empire. The Incas also built palaces, including Pachacuti's city, Machu Picchu. All Incas were responsible for serving on these projects.

A System for Messages

Because the empire had many roads, the Incas had an excellent postal system. Runners, called chasqui, carried messages along the roads. They were trained to run short distances at great speeds. Every three miles, they would come to a rest house. There, they would pass their messages on to the next runner. Messages could travel 150 miles in a day, which was very fast for the time.

The Incas did not have a writing system, so the runners had to remember the messages. If a message involved numbers or amounts of money, a runner might carry a **quipu**. This was a long string to which several smaller strings of different colors were tied. The quipu contained different groups of knots that represented numbers. The section closest to the main string stood for hundreds. The second section represented tens, and the third section represented ones. If there were no knots in a section, the section represented zero.

Government officials would tie knots on a quipu to record how many warriors were headed for a village or how much corn was in a storehouse. Maintaining a supply of food in the storehouses was important. If there were any crop failures, food from the storehouses was provided to the people.

Later Incan Emperors

Pachacuti's son Topa Inca succeeded him in A.D. 1471. Topa Inca greatly expanded the empire. His soldiers conquered the Chimú people, who were the only serious remaining threat to Incan rule in the region. Chimú artists influenced Incan styles and methods of painting, sculpting, and decorating. By the late 1400s A.D., the Incan Empire extended along most of South America's western coast. It also stretched far into the Andes, including much of the present-day countries of Peru, Ecuador, Bolivia, and Chile.

Huayna Capac succeeded his father, Topa Inca, in A.D. 1493. He left Cuzco to fight wars in the north. When Huayna Capac and his heir both died in A.D. 1527, others fought for the throne. Atahualpa won the conflict after a bloody war. He was the last of the independent Incan rulers before the Spanish conquest of the Americas.

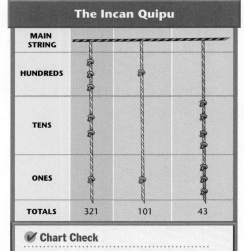

The Incan Quipu		
MAIN STRING		
HUNDREDS		
TENS		
ONES		
TOTALS	321	101	43

✔ Chart Check

According to the chart, which two groups of numbers are represented by no knots in a section?

Incan Government

The Incan government was a hereditary monarchy. This means that the emperor was the chief male member of the ruling family, and his direct descendants were his successors. The Incan Empire was divided into four quarters. Each quarter had its own governor. The governors and other important government officials were members of the emperor's extended family, all people of pure Incan blood. Other government jobs were filled by nobles from the outlying provinces, or territories, who were loyal to the emperor and his family.

◆ **What were some reasons for the success of the Incan civilization?**

C. Incan Society

Like the previous civilizations of the early Americas, the Incas had a highly developed religion and well-defined social classes. They were successful farmers as well.

Incan Religion

Incan religion, like many other ancient religions, was polytheistic: People believed not in one god, but in many. The chief god of the Incas was Viracocha, the creator of the Andean people. Other gods represented and controlled thunder, the Earth, the sea, and the moon. The sun god was worshiped as a special protector of the Incas. The emperor Pachacuti ordered temples built to all the major gods.

They Made History

Pachacuti ca. 1391–1473

When Pachacuti was growing up, his father, the king Viracocha Inca, looked upon Pachacuti unfavorably. The king made Pachacuti's brother, Inca Urcon, his heir. Then, a powerful northwestern group called the Chanca people began to march on Cuzco. Fearing for their lives, Viracocha Inca and Inca Urcon ran away. Pachacuti stayed in Cuzco. He and his army faced the more numerous Chanca with great courage. Just as the battle seemed lost, Pachacuti and his troops defeated the Chanca army.

Pachacuti took the throne and removed his brother's name from the list of kings. He fought a series of wars in which he expanded his empire. Then, he established a system of roads, set taxes to pay for improvements, and devised a means of communicating throughout the empire.

Pachacuti was a skilled politician. He used a policy of forced resettlement to maintain peace. He moved people from different cultural groups to various places in the Incan Empire. That made it difficult for them to get together and plot against him. Pachacuti's son succeeded him as the next Incan emperor.

Under Pachacuti's strong leadership, the Incan Empire grew and prospered.

Critical Thinking Why do you think Pachacuti removed his brother's name from the list of kings?

Explore Ask students to explain why they think the Incan Empire was divided into quarters. (The empire was too spread out for one ruler to control.) Discuss how the size of the empire made it difficult to govern it.

SPOTLIGHT ON GOVERNMENT

CONTROL OF THE CONQUERED

Have students identify the ways in which the Aztecs dealt with people they conquered. (enslaved them or sacrificed them to their gods) Discuss how the Incas differed in their treatment of conquered peoples and if the students feel this treatment by the Incas might have been more successful. (Possible answer: The Incan way led to assimilation, so the conquered people might have been more content to live under Incan rule.)

◆ **ANSWER** Possible answers: strong rulers, built good roads that connected regions, successful at farming and war

C. Incan Society

Purpose-Setting Question What were the Incas' religious beliefs? (They believed in many gods, the chief god was Viracocha. The Incas also believed that spirits lived in every aspect of nature.)

THEY MADE HISTORY
Pachacuti

King Viracocha chose one of his sons as his heir over another. Explain that a hereditary monarchy establishes a ruler whose direct descendants (generally male, in order of age, but in some cases also female) follow as rulers. Discuss with students how this plan of succession can be changed.

ANSWER Possible answer: Pachacuti did not think his brother deserved to be remembered as a king because he ran away instead of remaining to fight.

Writing

AVERAGE

Have students write a journal entry from the point of view of Pachacuti, explaining what his brother and father did as the Chanca approached and then the resulting actions he took. Remind students to include how Pachacuti felt about the events he described.

CHALLENGE

Have students write a journal entry from the point of view of Inca Urcon, Pachacuti's brother. The entry should explain what was going on, Urcon's actions as the Chanca approached, the reasons for his actions, and his feelings at the treatment he then received from his brother as Pachacuti took over the throne and made himself the king.

Artists in southern Peru influenced the Incas. These artists created the colorful cloak and gold and turquoise ceremonial knife, called a tumi, that are shown above.

Do You Remember?
In Chapter 5, you learned about ancient Greek social classes, including nobles, wealthy businessmen, and slaves.

The Incan people also believed that spirits lived in every aspect of nature. They believed that any unusual natural thing, such as an oddly shaped rock, indicated the presence of a spirit.

The Incas developed a calendar based on observations of the sun and moon. Festivals were tied to important seasons in the farming year, such as planting and harvesting. The chief reason for the festivals was to ask the gods for good health and a good harvest.

Priests served the gods by leading the festivals and tending to the people's needs. The sun god, called Inti, was especially important. His attendants were women selected from each region of the empire. This group was called the Chosen Women. For years they trained—studying the mysteries of the religion and learning to prepare food for the sun god. After the training ended, most of the Chosen Women remained attendants to the sun god. Some joined the emperor's court or married nobles.

Incan Social Classes

Incan people from the ruling family and other noble families considered themselves part of one extended family. They formed the first class of Incan society. There were fewer than 2 thousand of these "pure" Incas throughout the empire.

Below the pure Incas were the adopted Incas—the nobles from neighboring lands the Incas had conquered. The next lower class were the nobles from outlying provinces, whom the Incas allowed to rule large estates. Ordinary people, by far the largest group, made up the lowest class of society.

It was almost impossible for an Inca to change his or her social class. A soldier who displayed extraordinary courage in battle might improve his position. In addition, a servant in a noble's house who was extremely helpful to his master might be able to rise. For the most part, though, people remained in the social class into which they were born.

Incan Families

Incan families were organized into groups. One man served as an official administrator for each group. Instead of paying taxes in the form of money, the people were required to work in exchange for social services. Social services included being given food in times of drought or famine, and benefits for orphans and widows. The government also provided feasts for the people to enjoy on holidays.

The government was a strict ruler of most aspects of everyday life. People could not travel through the empire without permission. There were even laws about clothing. Unless the state gave an individual special permission, all citizens of the empire had to wear the clothing that was connected to the people and the place where they had been born.

Incan Farming

Each family belonged to a larger group of families called an **ayllu**. Members of an ayllu owned land jointly. They voted on any matters that related to the use of the land. The leaders of each ayllu made sure that government orders were followed. The leaders also decided who should do what job and organized the group to work the land. The Incas grew corn, squash, tomatoes, peanuts, cotton, and more than 200 kinds of potatoes. Growing potatoes was important because potatoes could be grown at high elevations, even on the slopes of the Andes Mountains.

Incan farmers also raised animals, including llamas and alpacas, which are South American animals with woolly coats. Incan women wove the wool into clothing. Families lived in one-room stone huts with thatched roofs. Boys did the same kind of work as their fathers did, whether it was farming or another type of trade. Girls learned skills such as weaving and cooking from their mothers. Part of the time, the Incas had to work for the empire and not just for their families and ayllu. However, they understood that doing so was to make the empire stronger and that this in turn would benefit them.

◆ How could Incas change their social class?

Review II

Review History
A. What were the major accomplishments of the earliest people of Peru?
B. How did the Incas develop a strong and powerful empire?
C. What were the purposes of an ayllu?

Define Terms to Know
Define the following terms:
adobe, quipu, ayllu

Critical Thinking
What connection do you see between the strength of the Incan Empire and the quality of the roads?

Write About Government
Write a brief essay discussing the advantages and disadvantages of the Incan system of government.

Get Organized
VENN DIAGRAM
Use a Venn diagram to compare and contrast the Chavín and the Moche people.

CHAPTER 9 ◆ The Americas **211**

Chavín people

Built stone temples; decorated with stone carvings.

Peru; left behind examples of art and architecture.

Built no cities; art very realistic.

Moche people

Discuss Have students list the types of crops grown by the Incas. (corn, squash, tomatoes, peanuts, cotton, and potatoes) Ask students why the Incas grew more than 200 kinds of potatoes. (Potatoes could be grown at high elevations, even in the Andes Mountains.)

◆ **ANSWER** Incas could change their social class by showing extraordinary courage in battle (a soldier) or by becoming extremely helpful to a noble master (a servant).

Section Close

Divide the class into three groups. Assign each group one of the civilizations: Chavín, Moche, and Inca. Then, have the group list what it knows about the civilization, such as where each settled, the crops each grew, recreational activities, structures built, influences, government, achievements, and any other information that makes them stand out. Have the group make a chart. Then, have the class compare this chart to the chart they completed for the Section Close in Section 1, page T204.

3 Assess

Review Answers

Review History
A. art, architecture, roads, and irrigation systems
B. Possible answers: They conquered peoples from neighboring lands and made them part of the empire. They established a strong central government with an emperor at its head. Well-built roads and a great system of communication unified the empire.
C. Members owned land jointly and voted on matters about land use. The leaders made sure members followed government orders, decided who did what job, and organized the group.

Define Terms to Know
adobe, 206; quipu, 208; ayllu, 211

Critical Thinking
Possible answer: Good roads and communication made travel between distant parts of the empire easier. So, the emperor was able to keep track of happenings all over the empire and respond faster.

Write About Government
Students' essays should include advantages such as unified empire, strong rulers, organized society, food provided by government when needed and disadvantages such as lack of personal freedom, inability to rise or change rank in society.

III. North American Groups (pp. 212-217)

Section Summary

In this section, students will learn how the varied climates and environments of North America influenced the development of distinct regional cultures in the western and eastern region.

1 Introduce

Getting Started

Ask students to describe what they know about the varied climate and topography of North America. (Possible answers: mountains, oceans, cold and warm climates) Show them a map of North America that illustrates geographical features (Transparency 3). Ask students how they think this variety influenced the early groups of people that developed in North America. (Possible answer: Some areas were easier to farm.)

TERMS TO KNOW

Ask students to read the terms and definitions on page 212 and then find each term in the section. Point out that the word *pueblo* has two meanings. With a lowercase *p*, the word *pueblo* refers to a style of architecture or type of building. With an uppercase *p*, the word becomes a proper noun or a proper adjective. The word *Pueblo* refers to a group of people, including Hopi, Zuni, and Acoma, and their culture.

You may wish to preview the pronunciation of the following terms with students.

Yupik (YOO pihk)
Anasazi (ah nuh SAH zee)
Adena (uh DEE nuh)
Dekanawidah
(duh kah nuh WEE duh)

ACTIVE READING

Recall for students that they have completed a main idea/supporting details chart in Chapter 1. Give students a main idea/supporting details Chart (TR, p. 319) as they read Section 3. Ask students to record the main ideas and the details that they identify in the section.

North American Groups

Terms to Know

potlatch a feast in which guests are given costly gifts
pueblo a dwelling made of adobe; also the name for some southwestern Native American groups
kachina the spirit of a Pueblo ancestor
longhouse a large one-story shelter made of logs
sachem a chief of the Iroquois nations

Main Ideas

A. The varied climates and environments of North America led to a variety of early American groups of people.

B. Early peoples in the western region survived in spite of settling in a harsh environment.

C. Early peoples in the eastern region created new forms of architecture and government.

Active Reading

MAIN IDEAS AND DETAILS
The main ideas of a text are the most important ideas the writer wants you to remember. The details provide more information about the main ideas. As you read this section, identify the main ideas and details.

A. The Geography of North America

The part of North America that is the United States and Canada developed differently from Mexico, Central America, and South America. The Asian peoples who crossed the land bridge into North America found themselves in a wide variety of land and climates, most of them fertile and welcoming.

Native Americans

North America had no unified empires, no cities, and no palaces. Instead, North America was home to a number of groups of people who survived by hunting, gathering, farming, and trading with one another. By the time the Europeans arrived, the early North Americans, who are called Native Americans today, had developed a wide variety of cultures, languages, styles of dress and architecture, and belief systems.

As they explored the continent and settled new areas, each group of Native Americans adjusted to the local climate. Instead of trying to control their environment, they adapted their lifestyle to it.

Land and Climates of North America

The continent of North America is a huge landmass with a number of different climates and countries. In the northeastern United States and Canada, the land is thickly forested, hilly, and sometimes rocky. There are four distinct seasons in a year—a cold winter, a warm spring, a hot summer, and a cool autumn. The southeastern United States has a warmer and more humid climate. The central section of the United States, called the Great Plains, is mainly flat and covered in grasses rather than trees. Winters in the Great Plains are quite cold and summers quite hot. The northwestern section is forested, with a long rainy season and a cool climate. The southwestern United States is arid, or dry, and hot. The southern Pacific Coast of the continent has a moderate climate all year round. Mountain ranges cover much of the western half of the continent.

Except for the deserts of the Southwest, North America has plenty of precipitation all year round. This rainfall fosters farming as well as supporting a variety of animals. Native American groups survived by hunting and by farming.

North America lies between the Atlantic and Pacific Oceans. It is crisscrossed with rivers such as the Mississippi, the Platte, and the Ohio. People often settled near these rivers, which served as highways as well as sources of water and food.

◆ **What function did North American rivers serve?**

Teaching Options

Section 3 Resources

Teacher's Resources (TR)
Terms to Know, p. 22
Review History, p. 56
Build Your Skills, p. 90
Chapter Test, pp. 133–134
Concept Builder, p. 225
Venn Diagram, p. 323
Transparency 3

Test Taking

To help students prepare for a multiple-choice test, write several sample questions on the board. Review the questions with students.

Point out that if students do not know the correct answer to a multiple-choice question, they can eliminate one or more incorrect choices and have a better chance of choosing the correct answer.

Native Americans in North America, A.D. 1450

Legend:
- Arctic/Subarctic
- Northwest Coast
- California/Great Basin/Plateau
- Southwest
- Great Plains
- Eastern Woodlands
- Southeast

0   500   1,000 mi
0   500 1,000 km

✔ Map Check

1. LOCATION Which three groups lived near 60° north latitude?

2. REGION Which groups lived in the Southwest region?

B. Western Groups

Most of the Asians who crossed the land bridge did not stay in the frozen, snowy area that is now called Alaska. A few of the most fearless and strong remained there. Others settled in the Northwest, Southwest, and Great Plains.

The Aleuts, Yupiks, and Inuits

The Aleuts, the Yupiks, and the Inuits (sometimes called Eskimos) lived in the Arctic region of present-day Canada and Alaska. The region was too cold for farming. The three groups had a hunting culture. They hunted seals, walruses, whales, and polar bears, as well as smaller game like caribou and foxes. The women turned the fur coats of polar bears and other game into warm clothing and blankets. They made tools and weapons from teeth and bones. Tents and boats were made from animal skins.

The northern peoples built kayaks, which are small boats that can hold one person. The umiak, a much larger boat, held several people.

Native Americans of the Northwest

The climate of the northwestern coast offered an easier life than that of Alaska. The rivers and the ocean were filled with fish. The forests were rich in game. The Native Americans of this region were able to accumulate, or gain, wealth through trade. A ceremony called the **potlatch** developed. At the potlatch, the host declared that he had certain rights. He might claim the title of someone who had died, for example. The guests would act as witnesses. The host would serve them a huge feast and give them costly gifts.

When hunting whales, Inuits put a harpoon bracket like this one on their large boat to hold a harpoon. An image of a whale is carved on the bracket.

Connection to
LITERATURE

Many groups of Native Americans developed mythology to explain happenings and forces of nature. Have students find and read from collections such as *From Sea to Shining Sea: A Treasury of American Folklore* and *Folk Songs* or *World Myths and Legends I: Native American.* Some students might enjoy reading aloud the stories they liked.

2 Teach

A. The Geography of North America

Purpose-Setting Question Why do you think many Native Americans thrived as hunters and gatherers? (The abundance of vegetation supported a great deal of wildlife.)

Activity

Using a map Refer students to the map of North America on page A3 of the Atlas or Transparency 3. Then, review which states are located in the five sections of North America discussed on page 212. Have small groups of students, using only the map for reference, describe the land features, and climate in summer and winter for each section. Have students read the subsection on page 212 called Land and Climates of North America to see if their descriptions are correct.

Discuss Ask students to compare the climate and geography of North America with those of Central and South America. Discuss how climate and geography influenced the lives of the civilizations that settled there.

◆ **ANSWER** Rivers served as highways and sources of food and water.

B. Western Groups

Purpose-Setting Question How did the first people use the resources of the northwestern coast? (They fished in the rivers and ocean, hunted game, and traded for wealth.)

Using the Map

Native Americans in North America, A.D. 1450

Have students locate where they live on the map. Then, ask students to locate the Native American group closest to their location.

✔ Map Check

Answers
1. Aleuts, Yupiks, and Inuits
2. Anasazis, Navajos, Pueblos, Apaches

BUILDING TOWNS

Pueblo is the Spanish word for *town*. Like the Southwest of the present-day United States, much of Spain has a hot, dry climate. The Spaniards built their towns of thick-walled, plain buildings around open squares, just as those built by the Anasazi.

To the Spanish invaders who arrived in the sixteenth century, the Anasazi pueblos looked just like their own towns. As a result, they referred to both towns and people as "pueblos." The name has stayed with these southwestern Native Americans ever since.

At Mesa Verde National Park in Mesa Verde, Colorado, multistory cliff dwellings that the Anasazi built still stand.

The Anasazi

The Anasazi peoples were Native Americans who settled in an area now known as the Four Corners—where the present-day U.S. states of Colorado, Arizona, New Mexico, and Utah meet. The Anasazi managed to grow crops in the dry, hot climate of the Southwest. They also produced items such as baskets, pottery, and cloth.

These early southwestern dwellers invented a new style of architecture that was well suited to the dry Southwest. Their houses, called **pueblos**, are made of adobe bricks, which are 3–5 inches thick. Thick walls kept the buildings cool in the summer and warm in the winter. The first pueblos were separate dwellings, but soon the Anasazi began building houses that resembled modern-day apartment houses. Each story of the building was narrower than the one below, so that the roof of the people on the lower floor provided a garden for the people above. The famous Cliff Palace at Mesa Verde, Colorado, was home to as many as 150 Anasazi.

The Anasazis began to move south toward the Rio Grande in about A.D. 1300. Historians believe they moved because drought had made their crops fail for several years. They built new, smaller pueblos where they settled. They are the ancestors of modern Pueblo Native Americans, who call the Anasazi ancestral Pueblos.

The Pueblos

Pueblo peoples, the descendants of the Anasazis, are not one nation, or group. *Pueblo* is a descriptive term referring to the culture, language, and lifestyle that groups such as the Hopi, the Zuñi, and the Acoma peoples have in common.

The Pueblo religion is largely based on prayers for a good harvest—important to survival in the harsh southwestern climate. In Pueblo religious practices, **kachinas**, or spirits of Pueblo ancestors, return to the earth in the forms of plants, animals, or people. The Pueblos hold kachina dances to honor these spirits. They believe that kachinas have power to heal the sick and to bring rain.

Farming was easier for the Pueblos than it had been for the Anasazis, because the Pueblos had the water of the Rio Grande for irrigation. They grew large fields of corn, beans, and squash.

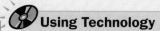

The Pueblos made clay from soil and water, shaped it into pots and other vessels, decorated it with patterns or with figures of birds and animals, and fired it. To this day, the Pueblos are famous for their pottery.

The Navajos and Apaches

Navajo means "large planted fields." The name refers to the area the Navajo people lived in and the work they were doing when the Spaniards first saw them. *Diné*, which means "human beings," is the Navajo's own name for their nation.

About 1,000 years ago, Athabascan people traveled south from Canada. They split into two groups as they crossed the Rocky Mountains. One group became the ancestors of the Apaches. The other group became the ancestors of the Navajos. The Apache and Navajo peoples probably settled in northern Mexico, Arizona, and New Mexico at about the same time the Anasazi people abandoned the Four Corners to move south.

The Apaches lived in the open plains of present-day Texas, northern Mexico, central Arizona, and eastern Colorado. Dry weather, extreme summer heat, fierce winds, and the lack of vegetation and water combined to make survival a challenge for the Apaches.

Except for farming on a small scale, the Apaches hunted for food. Most of their meat was from buffalo, deer, and rabbit that they chased and caught on the plains. Nothing was wasted. Apache women made clothing, blankets, and tipis—shelters of hides draped over a cone of sticks—from the animals' coats.

Unable to survive on hunting alone, the Apaches often raided other peoples' villages, stealing food, livestock, and other supplies. In Apache culture, the courage and skill it took to make a raid successful were highly valued.

◆ **Why did the Apaches become hunters?**

C. Eastern Groups

In the eastern region of North America as in the western region, Native Americans adapted their lifestyle to the climate and environment. Instead of deserts or snow and ice, they found a seasonal climate with distinct growing periods. They also found a great variety of vegetation and wildlife. Eastern Native American groups are responsible for some of the world's most unusual architecture and for a striking achievement in democratic government.

The Mound Builders

The mound builders of the Mississippi and Ohio River valleys are named for the structures they built. The Adenas, one group of mound builders, arrived in the Ohio River valley about 3,000 years ago. The Adenas built mounds of dirt over the graves of their leaders and chiefs. Bodies were buried near one another, and each time another person was buried, the Adenas would add another layer to the mound. The Adenas, and their descendants, the Hopewells, placed beautiful copper ornaments in these graves.

Not all mounds were built to honor the dead. The Great Serpent Mound, built 2,000 years ago and still standing in Ohio, is in the shape of a snake uncoiling itself.

The Great Serpent Mound in present-day Ohio is more than 440 yards long. The Adenas or the Hopewells probably built it.

Discuss Ask students which of the groups, Navajos or Apaches, they think were most like the Anasazi. Then, have students give reasons from the text on pages 214 and 215 or through extra research they complete. (Possible answer: the Navajos; they lived in settled villages.)

Review Ask students to recall the meaning of the word *nomad*. (a wanderer, usually in search of food) Ask them which group, the Navajos or the Apaches, they think were nomadic and why. (The Apaches; they followed and hunted game animals on the plains of the present-day United States.)

◆ **ANSWER** Dry weather, extreme summer heat, fierce winds, and the lack of vegetation and water allowed farming only on a small and limited scale; so, the Apaches hunted the animals that lived on the plains for food and other uses.

C. Eastern Groups

Purpose-Setting Question How did Native Americans in the eastern region resemble those in the western region in response to the climate and environment? (They adapted their lifestyle to them.)

Discuss Have students discuss why mounds were built by the Adenas and Hopewells and what archaeologists have found to give them the idea that the mounds were burial mounds. (The mounds were probably built to honor the dead. Archaeologists believe the mounds were burial mounds because copper ornaments were found in them.)

Focus Ask students to speculate why the Great Serpent Mound was built in the shape of a snake. (Possible answer: A snake may have been a symbol of power to the mound builders.)

TEACH PRIMARY SOURCES
As students look at the photograph on page 215, help them realize how long 440 yards is by telling them of an area in your school that would be about this long. Help students realize that the shape of the Great Serpent Mound is not as clear from the ground. Discuss how difficult it would be to build something on the ground when you could not see the final shape.

Research

AVERAGE
Native Americans in North America adapted to the climate and to their environment. Have students choose one group mentioned in this section and research additional details on how the group's culture reflected the environment.

CHALLENGE
Have students research the shape and location of the Great Serpent Mound. Then, have students research other mounds built by the Mississippians to see whether all the mounds were built in a particular shape. Ask students to draw the other shapes they find and to share their findings with the class.

Direct students' attention to the Iroquois wearing a mask and to the separate picture of the mask. Ask students what significance they think masks might have had in the Iroquois culture from these photographs. (Possible answer: Masks might have been used during ceremonies to keep the spirits happy or to tell one group from another during a celebration; masks might have been for decoration.)

Activity

Design an Iroquois mask Have groups of students use the Internet and other sources to research different Iroquois masks. Have the groups then decide on a common purpose for the masks they are going to design individually. Once decided, the members should draw and color their own masks on paper or posterboard. They can also mold papier-mâché to balloons, let them harden, remove the balloons, and then paint their masks. After the groups are finished, they can share their masks with the class. The students should also describe why they added certain features to their masks.

Explore Ask students to identify why Iroquois and Hurons built longhouses. (They needed shelter from the cold winters.) Have students describe the interior of a longhouse and explain why many families were able to live there. (Possible answer: Each family had its own platform.) Ask students what advantages or disadvantages longhouses had when compared to other types of shelter. (**advantages:** kept them warm, provided permanent shelter for many families; **disadvantages:** not portable, could get crowded)

An Iroquois wearing a mask stands in the doorway of an Iroquois longhouse. Deer skins cover part of the doorway. An Iroquois mask that was used in ceremonies is shown below.

Mississippian mound builders settled farther south than the Adena-Hopewells. Their name is taken from the Mississippi River, which was their chief source of water. The Mississippians farmed the fertile land along both the eastern and western banks of the river.

The Mississippian people built temple mounds as well as burial mounds. Some mounds are as high as 100 feet. They are in the shape of pyramids, with rectangular bases and sloping sides.

The mound builders had disappeared by the seventeenth century. Historians believe that crop failures or wars may have been responsible for the collapse of these Native American groups.

The Iroquois

The Iroquois and Hurons—some of the peoples who spoke the Iroquois language—occupied the area that is now New York State. Even though they spoke the same language, the two groups did not get along with each other. They spread out from the Great Lakes to the Finger Lakes.

The four seasonal climates of the northeastern region of North America enabled the Iroquois and Hurons to follow a seasonal calendar. They planted in the spring. Autumn was the time for hunting, harvesting, and holding councils to address any issues the community had.

The Iroquois and Hurons needed shelter that would keep them warm during the cold northeastern winters. They created a kind of shelter called a **longhouse**—a large, one-story shelter made from young trees called saplings. A longhouse contained two rows of platforms along its long walls, with an aisle down the building's center. Many families lived together in one longhouse. Each family had its own platform, which served as the living and sleeping area. Platforms had walls on both sides that separated different living areas. Each platform was open in the front—the area that faced the center aisle. Within this area were pits for indoor fires. Fires were used for cooking, heating water, and for warmth in cold weather. Smoke from the fire escaped in holes left in the roof of each longhouse.

All of the people worked to provide food. Fishing was an everyday task for the men. Women gathered food such as nuts and berries from the forests. Women also grew corn, beans, and squash in forest clearings. The people harvested sap from maple trees and used it as a sweetener. They made beadwork, called wampum, to give as gifts in honor of special events or to use in trade.

Although their culture was based on cooperation among families, Iroquois peoples often quarreled with one another. The search for solutions to disputes led to the establishment of the Iroquois League, also called the Iroquois Confederacy.

The Iroquois Confederacy

During the 1500s, Hiawatha, an Onondaga man from one of the Iroquois-speaking groups, met with a Huron man called Dekanawidah. Both men wanted to bring peace to their people. Dekanawidah hoped a council of elders and chiefs from each group would meet to discuss issues of importance and to settle all disputes.

Teaching Options

Conflict Resolution

Point out that many groups of Iroquois lived in an area where they regularly came in contact with one another. Ask students how this could lead to conflict. (People might have fought over land and hunting rights.) Have students discuss ways the groups could resolve such a conflict. Encourage students to suggest how they could use the methods of the Iroquois Confederacy to solve disputes with their friends and classmates.

Their plan became the basis for the Iroquois Confederacy. The Confederacy was made up of five Iroquois nations: the Mohawks, the Senecas, the Onondagas, the Oneidas, and the Cayugas. The Hurons were not part of the Iroquois Confederacy. However, Dekanawidah lived among the Senecas, who were part of the Confederacy. The five nations shared the same language and traditions. Each nation had its own council. The chiefs of each council were nominated by the women of the nation's families. The chiefs were called **sachems**.

In addition to each nation's council, a council of the nations met about larger issues. The Mohawk and Seneca chiefs, called the Elder Brothers, were the first to debate any question. They would reach an agreement, then explain their decision to the Oneida and Cayuga chiefs—the Younger Brothers. If they disagreed, the question would be taken to the Onondaga chief for a final decision. If the Brothers agreed, the Onondaga chief still had the power to adjust their decision.

The sachems' most important duty was to maintain peace within the Confederacy. All decisions were to be based on the welfare of the people:

> 66 In all of your . . . acts, self-interest shall be cast away. . . . Look and listen for the welfare of the whole people, and have always in view not only the present, but also the coming generations . . . the unborn of the future Nation. 99

◆ **What were the most important aspects of the Iroquois Confederacy?**

Then & Now

GOVERNMENT STRUCTURE

The structure of the Iroquois Confederacy resembled that of the U.S. government. Just as the Iroquois had its Elder and Younger Brothers, the United States has the two houses of Congress. In the same way that the Onondaga chief had the power to make a final decision in the council, the U.S. President can sign legislation into law.

ANALYZE PRIMARY SOURCES
DOCUMENT-BASED QUESTION According to the quotation, what is important to the sachems?

Review III

Review History
A. What effect did the climates and environments of North America have on early American groups?
B. How did early peoples of western regions survive the harsh climates?
C. Describe the achievements of the early peoples of the eastern regions of North America.

Define Terms to Know
Define the following terms:
potlatch, pueblo, kachina, longhouse, sachem

Critical Thinking
What made the Iroquois Confederacy successful?

Write About History
Write a paragraph that describes the different farming methods of the Pueblos and the Iroquois.

Get Organized
VENN DIAGRAM
Use a Venn diagram to compare and contrast early North American groups. Choose one eastern group and one western group. Note how they are alike and how they are different.

Then & Now

GOVERNMENT STRUCTURE Ask students how the Iroquois Confederacy was also like the United Nations organization. (Independent member nations are similar to the five independent Iroquois nations. Both the United Nations and the Iroquois Confederacy were formed so that representatives could come together to try to resolve disputes.)

ANALYZE PRIMARY SOURCES

DOCUMENT-BASED QUESTION
The values and laws suggested by the sachems were meant to accommodate the needs of their society peacefully. Each law was based on a moral structure, such as that of the quotation.

ANSWER the welfare of the whole people, in the present and the future

◆ **ANSWER** All five nations had the same language and traditions. Each had its own council. Council chiefs were nominated by women; the nations came together to debate questions.

Section Close

Ask students to discuss the accomplishments and lifestyle of each group in this section. Discuss how the environment influenced each of the groups.

③ Assess

Review Answers

Review History
A. The early North Americans adapted their lifestyles to the varied climates and environments.

B. Early peoples of the western region learned farming techniques and grew crops that could survive in a dry climate. Their shelters had thick walls built of adobe bricks to stay cool in summer and warm in winter.

C. Some groups built mounds while others formed the Iroquois Confederacy.

Define Terms to Know
potlatch, 213; pueblo, 214; kachina, 214; longhouse, 216; sachem, 217

Eastern/Iroquois

Built longhouses; farmers; organized Iroquois Confederacy.

Hunters

Made tipis from hides; raided villages; nomads.

Western/Apaches

Critical Thinking
Possible answer: It was a workable arrangement to which all members agreed. It was meant to protect the welfare of all the people.

Write About History
Students' paragraphs should state that both the Pueblos and the Iroquois grew corn, beans, and squash. The Pueblos irrigated their land. The Iroquois cleared forests for land, which they planted in the spring. Crops were harvested in the fall.

Chapter Summary

A blank outline form is available in the Teacher's Resources (p. 318). Students should outline information about the geography, the climate, and the rise of civilizations in both South and North America. They should then use the outline to complete their chapter summary. Refer to the rubric in the Teacher's Resources (p. 340) to score students' chapter summaries.

 Interpret the Timeline

1. Olmec
2. A.D. 1438
3. about 250 years
4. People of ancient Mexico learn to grow corn (ca. 2500 B.C.), and People of Mohenjo-Daro in India cultivate rice (ca. 2500 B.C.)
5. Check students' timelines to be sure all events are from the chapter.

Use Terms to Know

6. maize
7. adobe
8. glyph
9. ayllu
10. pueblo
11. sachem
12. chinampa

Check Your Understanding

13. Maize was the basis of their diet. It could be cooked in a variety of ways; it could be dried and stored for a winter food supply; it could be ground into flour.
14. Maya formed city-states, were the first to understand and use the mathematical concept of zero, and developed a calendar.
15. Aztec boys learned about astronomy, the Aztec religion, and the arts of war, and they were taught how to read and write. Girls were taught how to weave and be priestesses.
16. Pachacuti used a policy of forced resettlement. By moving different cultural groups, he made it difficult for them to get together and plot against him.
17. Their government was a hereditary monarchy with an emperor.
18. The Chosen Women studied the Incan religion and learned to prepare food for the sun god.

Chapter Summary

Complete the following outline in your notebook. Then, use your outline to write a brief summary of the chapter.

The Americas

I. Early Civilizations of the Americas
   A. Geography and Its Impact
   B. Early Civilizations
   C. The Aztec Civilization
II. Peru and the Incan Empire
   A. Early Peoples of Peru
   B. Civilization of the Incas
   C. Incan Society
III. North American Groups
   A. The Geography of North America
   B. Western Groups
   C. Eastern Groups

 Interpret the Timeline

Use the timeline on pages 198–199 to answer the following questions.

1. Which civilization—Aztec or Olmec—developed first?
2. Which date is significant in the development of the Incas?
3. About how many years after the Toltecs began to dominate central Mexico did the Aztecs settle the city of Tenochtitlán?
4. **Critical Thinking** Which chapter and world events are about farming?
5. Select four events from the chapter that are not on the timeline. Create a timeline that shows these events.

Use Terms to Know

Select the term that best completes each sentence.

adobe   glyph   pueblo
ayllu   maize   sachem
chinampa

6. The cereal grain also called corn is _____.
7. Chavín temples were built of sun-dried bricks, called _____.
8. A _____ is a picture or other symbol that represents a word or an idea.
9. An organization of several families that owned land jointly was called an _____.
10. The Spanish word for *town*, _____, is also applied to some southwestern Native American groups.
11. A _____ was a chief elected to represent his nation.
12. A floating raft filled with soil on which the Aztecs grew crops was called a _____.

Check Your Understanding

13. **Explain** why maize was so important to the early Americans.
14. **Identify** the achievements of the Maya civilization.
15. **Describe** what boys and girls learned in the Aztec civilization.
16. **Identify** Pachacuti's policy to improve control over his empire.
17. **Identify** the Incas' type of government.
18. **Describe** the role of the Chosen Women in Incan society.
19. **Discuss** how the peoples of the Arctic region survived in their environment.
20. **Explain** a potlatch.
21. **Describe** the mounds that the Mississippians built.
22. **Summarize** the structure of the Iroquois Confederacy.

19. They hunted water and land animals from the area. They built boats in which to travel and hunt. They dressed in furs from animals they hunted.
20. A potlatch was a gathering for a feast. The host proclaimed his rights and the guests would act as witnesses. The host would feed the guests a huge feast and give them costly gifts.

21. The Mississippians built temple mounds and burial mounds in the shape of pyramids.
22. The Iroquois Confederacy was made up of five groups or nations: the Mohawk, Seneca, Onondaga, Oneida, and Cayuga. They elected members to a council in order to discuss important issues and settle disputes.

Critical Thinking

23. Analyze Primary Sources What does the quotation on page 203 about the Toltecs tell you about their society?

24. Make Inferences What does the Aztec calendar stone tell you about Aztec religion?

25. Make Inferences How might the building of roads have helped the Moche people control a large area of land?

26. Cause and Effect What effects did Topa Inca and Huayna Capac have on the Incan civilization?

27. Draw Conclusions What does their willingness to adapt to the environment suggest about early North Americans?

28. Analyze Primary Sources Based on the quotation on page 217, what do you think the sachems of the Iroquois Confederacy would have thought about individual rights in their society?

Put Your Skills to Work

29. Understand Sequence You have learned that sequence, or the order in which things happen, is important to understanding history. A flowchart can help you understand a sequence of events. A flowchart can also help you to identify causes and effects and find relationships among events.

Copy the following chart. Fill in the boxes with events from this chapter that link the events described in the first and last boxes.

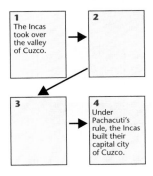

1 The Incas took over the valley of Cuzco.

2

3

4 Under Pachacuti's rule, the Incas built their capital city of Cuzco.

Analyze Sources

30. Read more about Hiram Bingham's impressions of Machu Picchu from his book *Lost City of the Incas*. Then, answer the questions that follow.

In the variety of its charms and the power of its spell, I know of no place in the world which can compare with it. Not only has it great snow peaks looming above the clouds more than two miles overhead, gigantic precipices [steep cliffs] of many colored granite [a very hard rock] rising sheer for thousands of feet above the foaming, glistening, roaring rapids; it has also, in striking contrast, orchids and tree ferns, the delectable beauty of luxurious vegetation, and the mysterious witchery of the jungle.

a. What are the geographic features and natural objects that Hiram Bingham describes?

b. What are some of the descriptive phrases that Bingham uses to help the reader picture Machu Picchu?

c. Why is Bingham unable to compare Machu Picchu with any place else in the world?

Essay Writing

31. Write an essay comparing and contrasting the development of civilizations in Central and South America with the development of Native American groups in North America. Explain why they developed so differently.

TEST PREPARATION

EXAMPLE/NONEXAMPLE
Choose the answer that correctly completes the sentence.

Each of these groups is an example of a group that created cities except the

1. Aztecs.
2. Inuits.
3. Incas.
4. Maya.

Critical Thinking

23. Possible answer: The quotation suggests that the Toltecs were very wealthy and had enough food and drink for everyone. Therefore, they probably lived comfortably.

24. Possible answer: The calendar stone shows that Aztec religion was connected to nature. The sun god's face is in the middle of the stone surrounded by religious symbols.

25. Possible answer: Roads would have made travel easier and improved communication, allowing the Moche people to control the vast area of land in the civilization.

26. Possible answer: Topa Inca had a positive effect. He expanded the Incan Empire. Huayna Capac abandoned Cuzco to fight wars in the north. This probably had a negative effect on the Incan civilization because Cuzco was the center of the empire.

27. Possible answer: Early North Americans respected nature and did not try to change it.

28. Possible answer: The sachems probably would not have supported individual rights. They were in favor of supporting "the welfare of the whole people" and were against self-interest.

Put Your Skills to Work

UNDERSTAND SEQUENCE

29. Box 2: The Incas won a decisive battle against invaders from the south. **Box 3:** Pachacuti became the first of the great Incan emperors.

Analyze Sources

30a. great snow peaks, precipices of steep cliffs, rapids, orchids, tree ferns, vegetation, jungle

30b. "great snow peaks," "gigantic precipices of many colored granite rising sheer for thousands of feet," "foaming, glistening, roaring rapids," "the delectable beauty of luxurious vegetation"

30c. Possible answer: Because it is so different that it can not be compared to other places.

Essay Writing

31. Students' essays should reflect the differences in geography and climate between North America and Central and South America. They should note how these influenced differences in architecture, cities, and government.

TEST PREPARATION

Answer 2. Inuits.

Kingdoms and City-States in Africa
1050 B.C.–A.D. 1500
(pp. 220–241)

Chapter Objectives

• Discuss how early civilizations, known for their trading and iron-making, developed in Africa, and explore how early African society was organized around family and religion.
• Describe the political and economic development of three major kingdoms and several smaller states in West Africa.
• Explain how trade played a major role in the development of East African kingdoms and led eventually to interaction with people from Asia and Portugal.

Chapter Summary

Section I discusses how early civilizations, characterized by defined social structure and traditional religion, developed in Africa.
Section II focuses on three important trading kingdoms—Ghana, Mali, and Songhai—which succeeded each other in West Africa.
Section III discusses how East African kingdoms in Aksum, Ethiopia, the Swahili region, and Zimbabwe developed unique cultures and established trade routes. They were later visited by Portuguese traders.

Set the Stage

TEACH PRIMARY SOURCES

Isaiah was a prophet, or a group of prophets, whose story is recorded in the Old Testament of the Bible in the book of Isaiah. This quotation is from the book of Isaiah. He is referring to the kingdom of Kush when he says "This land of whirring wings ... which is beyond the rivers of Ethiopia...." Isaiah is also describing the people of Egypt when he says "... to a nation, tall and smooth, to a people feared near and far...."

CHAPTER
10

Kingdoms and City-States in Africa
1050 B.C.—A.D. 1500

I. Early Civilizations in Africa
II. Major Kingdoms of West Africa
III. Major Kingdoms of East Africa

In 750 B.C., the people of Kush, a kingdom in eastern Africa, conquered the Egyptian Empire and established a powerful African civilization—one that lasted for nearly 100 years. Early biblical leaders, such as the prophet Isaiah, had warned the Egyptians of the strength and courage of these conquering peoples when he said,

> *This land of whirring wings which is beyond the rivers of Ethiopia; which sends ambassadors by the Nile, in vessels of papyrus upon the waters! Go you swift messengers, to a nation, tall and smooth, to a people feared near and far, a nation mighty and conquering, whose land the rivers divide.*

Early African kingdoms, such as Kush, later developed into major civilizations, especially in West Africa. Trade, religion, and education were often the foundation of these great kingdoms. In time, however, struggles over religious and economic control often led to war, eventually toppling even the most powerful African kingdoms.

CHAPTER EVENTS			
ca. 1050 B.C. Kush becomes a powerful civilization.	**750** B.C. Kushites conquer Egypt.	**500** B.C. Nok civilization is established.	

1500 B.C. ——————— **500** B.C.

WORLD EVENTS		
970 B.C. Solomon becomes king of Israel.	**612** B.C. Medes and Babylonians conquer Assyria.	**438** B.C. Building of the Parthenon in Greece is completed.

Teaching Options

Chapter 10 Resources

REVIEW

Teacher's Resources (TR)
Terms to Know, p. 23
Review History, p. 57
Build Your Skills, p. 91
Chapter Test, pp. 135–136
Concept Builder, p. 226
Flowchart, p. 324
Transparencies 2, 6, 10

ASSESSMENT
Section Reviews, pp. 226, 231, 239
Chapter Review, pp. 240–241
Chapter Test, TR, pp. 135–136

ALTERNATIVE ASSESSMENT
Portfolio Project, p. 312
Create a Travel Brochure, p. T312

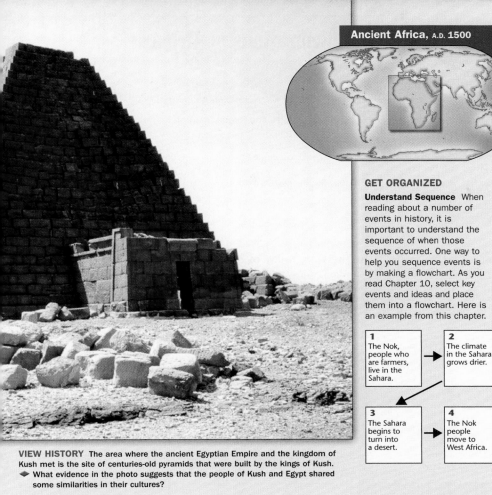

Ancient Africa, A.D. 1500

GET ORGANIZED

Understand Sequence When reading about a number of events in history, it is important to understand the sequence of when those events occurred. One way to help you sequence events is by making a flowchart. As you read Chapter 10, select key events and ideas and place them into a flowchart. Here is an example from this chapter.

```
1                    2
The Nok,     →       The climate
people who           in the Sahara
are farmers,         grows drier.
live in the
Sahara.
        ↓
3                    4
The Sahara    →      The Nok
begins to            people
turn into            move to
a desert.            West Africa.
```

VIEW HISTORY The area where the ancient Egyptian Empire and the kingdom of Kush met is the site of centuries-old pyramids that were built by the kings of Kush.
◆ What evidence in the photo suggests that the people of Kush and Egypt shared some similarities in their cultures?

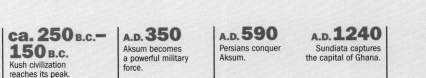

ca. 250 B.C.– 150 B.C.
Kush civilization reaches its peak.

A.D. 350
Aksum becomes a powerful military force.

A.D. 590
Persians conquer Aksum.

A.D. 1240
Sundiata captures the capital of Ghana.

A.D. 1498
Portuguese ships first reach West Africa.

◀ **B.C.** | **A.D.** ▶ | **A.D. 500** | **A.D. 1500**

A.D. 313
Christianity becomes the religion of the Roman Empire.

A.D. 750
Abbasid Dynasty comes to power in the Middle East.

A.D. 1096
First Crusade begins.

A.D. 1500
Maya Empire in Central America ends after 1,800 years.

CHAPTER 10 ◆ Kingdoms and City-States in Africa **221**

Chapter Themes

- Culture
- People, Places, and Environments
- Production, Distribution, and Consumption
- Power, Authority, and Governance
- Individuals, Groups, and Institutions
- Time, Continuity, and Change

F Y I

Kushite Kings

Kushite warriors conquered Egypt in 750 B.C. and borrowed many ideas from the Egyptians. One idea they borrowed was building a pyramid. However, unlike the Egyptians, the Kushite kings were buried under the pyramids. Kushite kings continued to build pyramids long after the Egyptians had stopped. Today, there are more pyramids in the Sudan than in Egypt.

I. Early Civilizations in Africa (pp. 222–226)

Section Summary

In this section, students will learn about the three diverse geographical regions of Africa and the development of early African civilizations, including the Kushites, the Nok people, and the Bantu-speaking people. They will also learn how early African society was organized.

1 Introduce

Getting Started

Discuss with students how living conditions in Africa around 600 B.C. might have been different from those in the Mediterranean or Asian regions they have already read about. What special problems might ancient African peoples have faced? (very hot temperatures, desert or jungle conditions) Then, discuss possible ways people adapted to their surroundings and established new civilizations.

TERMS TO KNOW

Ask students to read the terms and definitions on page 222 and then find each term in the section. Point out that the first term relates to geography and the other two relate to cultures and communities. Suggest that students look for other terms that relate to geography and culture as they read this section. (*desert, rain forest, hunter-gatherers, nomads*)

You may wish to preview the pronunciation of the following words from this section with students.

Serengeti (ser uhn GEHT ee)
desertification
  (dih zert uh fih KAY shuhn)
Kalahari (kah lah HAH ree)
Kush (KUSH)
Kushites (ku SHYTS)
Meroë (MER oh ee)

ACTIVE READING

Have students work with a partner to survey headings and visuals in the other two subsections of Section 1 and write a prediction of what information will be discussed. After they have read each subsection, they can compare predictions to see whose was more accurate.

Terms to Know

savanna a grassland with plants and scattered trees that can resist drought
lineage group several extended families combined into a larger community
matriarchal relating to a culture in which women are the most powerful members

Main Ideas

A. Africa has a varied landscape including grasslands, deserts, and forests.
B. Early African civilizations included the Kushites, the Nok people, and the Bantu-speaking people.
C. Early African society was organized around family and religion.

Active Reading

PREDICT
When you predict, you make an educated guess about what will happen. As you read this section, first skim the headings and visuals. Then, predict what information you will learn in the section titled "The Geography of Africa." Read the text to find out if your prediction is correct.

A. The Geography of Africa

Africa is the world's second largest continent in both population and area. About 825 million people live in villages, towns, and cities, most of them south of the Sahara, the world's largest desert. Africa's landmass of 11.7 million square miles fills about 20 percent of Earth's land surface. It can be divided into three major geographic regions: grasslands, called **savannas**, deserts, and forests. The land includes a large plateau, or high area toward the center of the continent. From there, rivers flow to the coastal regions, often forming waterfalls and rapids.

The Savanna Region

More than 40 percent of Africa is covered by a savanna. In this region, scattered trees, thorny bushes, and tall grasses grow. Temperatures rarely go below 50°F. As a result, the grasslands are very fertile. Animals and plants survive easily. During the rainy season on the Serengeti Plain, which is part of the African savanna, a square yard of grass can provide nearly 2 pounds of food each month. That amount is equal to 2,850 tons of food per square mile for

A herd of elephants crosses the African savanna.

Teaching Options

Section 1 Resources

Teacher's Resources (TR)
  Terms to Know, p. 23
  Review History, p. 57
  Build Your Skills, p. 91
  Concept Builder, p. 226
  Flowchart, p. 324
  Transparency 6

ESL/ELL STRATEGIES

Identify Essential Vocabulary Have students locate the compound words *landscape, landmass,* and *grasslands* on pages 222–223. Discuss how the meaning of each compound word combines the meanings of the words that make it up. Suggest that students look for other compound words as they read this chapter and use the word parts to help uncover their meaning.

people and animals during the rainy season. Because nearly half of all the plants in a savanna can be eaten, the Serengeti has many different animal species.

The Desert Region

Another 40 percent of the continent—the Sahara in the north and the Kalahari and Namib in the south—is desert. The Sahara is the world's largest desert, covering nearly 3.5 million square miles—an area about the size of the United States. The Sahara stretches from the Atlantic Ocean to the Red Sea. Both the Sahara and the Namib receive on average fewer than 6 inches of rainfall a year.

When the Sahara enjoyed a wetter climate, it had forests and grasslands. People hunted giraffes, elephants, and other animals. They also fished and farmed. Around 2500 B.C., the climate grew drier and the Sahara started turning to desert. In addition, people allowed their livestock to overgraze the land. Without plants, the soil can easily blow away, which causes vegetation to disappear. This process is known as desertification.

The Forest Region

Less than 20 percent of Africa is forest, and 8 percent of that is tropical rain forest. Many different evergreen trees grow in the rain forests of western Africa, Madagascar, and the Congo Basin. The northwestern mountains, the east African highlands, and parts of the south also have forests.

Tropical rain forests are the world's most varied ecosystems. An ecosystem is all the animals, plants, and bacteria that make up a particular community living in a certain environment. Although many of the trees in the forest look alike, every tree might be a different species. The temperature in the rain forest averages 77°F, hardly ever dropping below 68°F. Up to 155 inches of rain falls yearly in the rain forest.

◆ **What three geographic regions is Africa divided into?**

B. Early African Civilizations

Most of the early civilizations in ancient Africa were known for their extensive trading networks. Large deposits of iron ore helped some civilizations emerge as ironmaking centers. The Kush, Nok, and Bantu-speaking people are among the earliest known civilizations.

The Rise and Fall of Kush

The land of Nubia, also called Kush, was located in eastern Africa. Kush was a powerful civilization from about 1050 B.C. until A.D. 350. The people of Kush traded with Egypt. The Egyptians bought gold and copper from the Kush mines as well as cattle, ebony, ivory, and slaves. The Kushites, or people of Kush, adopted many of the Egyptians' ways.

STORIES ABOUT AFRICA
Twentieth-century American writer Ernest Hemingway traveled to Africa. His experiences there formed the background for one of his novels, *The Snows of Kilimanjaro*.

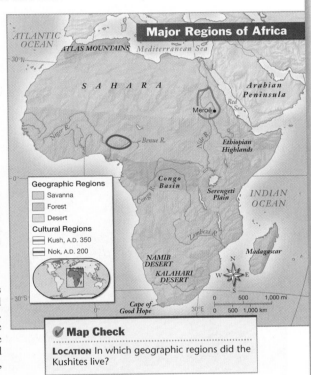

Major Regions of Africa

ATLANTIC OCEAN
ATLAS MOUNTAINS · Mediterranean Sea
30°N
S A H A R A
Arabian Peninsula
Meroë•
Red Sea
Niger R.
Benue R.
Nile R.
Ethiopian Highlands
0°
Congo Basin
Congo R.
Serengeti Plain
INDIAN OCEAN
Zambezi R.
Madagascar
NAMIB DESERT
KALAHARI DESERT
N
W E
S
30°S
Cape of Good Hope
30°E
0   500   1,000 mi
0   500 1,000 km

Geographic Regions
☐ Savanna
☐ Forest
☐ Desert
Cultural Regions
Kush, A.D. 350
Nok, A.D. 200

✔ **Map Check**

LOCATION In which geographic regions did the Kushites live?

CHAPTER 10 ◆ Kingdoms and City-States in Africa **223**

A. The Geography of Africa

Purpose-Setting Question What percentage of Africa is covered by savanna and what percentage is covered by desert? (about 40 percent each)

Extend Part of the Serengeti Plain has been designated a national park. It has been a protected area for plant and animal life since 1951. Students may want to find out more about the amazing plants and animals that live on the Serengeti and about the studies in ecology and animal behavior being conducted there.

Discuss Ask students how the actions of people can cause desert areas to expand. (People cut down shrubs and trees and overgraze grassland on the desert's edge.) Ask students to suggest ways to prevent desertification.

SPOTLIGHT ON CULTURE

STORIES ABOUT AFRICA In his writings about Africa, Ernest Hemingway introduced the word *safari* to readers in the United States and Europe. On safari in 1933, he hunted lions and other large game. Another Western writer, Danish author Isak Dinesen, spent many years in East Africa and wrote about her experiences in her book *Out of Africa*.

◆ **ANSWER** savanna, desert, and forest

B. Early African Civilizations

Purpose-Setting Question What important metals did the Kushites mine? (gold, copper, and iron)

Using the Map

Major Regions of Africa

Have students identify each cultural and geographic region on the map. Check that students understand how to read the map and key. Ask which geographic region is the largest. (savanna)

✔ **Map Check**

Answer desert and savanna

Cooperative Learning

Have students work in teams to create collages or photo essays of one of the regions of Africa—desert, savanna, or forest. Members of the team should share responsibilities, such as researching photographs in library resources or on the Internet, designing the display, and writing headings and captions. Have teams present their projects to the class.

Connection to
SCIENCE

Scientists from the United States and Gabon (on Africa's west coast) combined efforts to help preserve Gabon's rain forests. The scientists toured Gabon in 2002, and they convinced Gabon's government to open 13 new national parks to preserve the forests and protect the diverse plant and animal life found there.

Discuss Whereas Meroë never came under Roman control, there is some evidence that Roman soldiers did explore the area. Discuss with students possible reasons for Roman soldiers to explore Meroë. (Possible answer: to see if it was worth conquering for the Roman Empire)

Activity

Write an advertisement
Merchants from Meroë had many unusual and valuable items to sell in foreign markets. Have students prepare advertisements describing these goods and explaining what items the merchants might like to have in trade. Encourage students to make their ads as persuasive and attractive as possible.

Explore Have students compare the locations of Kush and Nok on the map on page 223. Ask why the Nok peoples would have been more involved in farming than the Kushites. You might also refer to Transparency 6, Africa's political and physical features, to locate geographic features. (The Nok had no easy access to waterways for trade; their location in the savanna meant they had more fertile soil.) Discuss the connection between location or environment and the ways in which people in a civilization make their living.

TEACH PRIMARY SOURCES
Have students study the photograph on page 224. Ask them what they think it would be like if they were standing in this photograph. (hot, dry, empty) Discuss the structures in the photograph.

Do You Remember?
In Chapter 2, you learned that priests used forced labor to build the pyramids in Egypt.

Over the next few centuries, Kush became an independent kingdom. The people of Kush conquered Egypt in 750 B.C. and ruled for nearly a century. In 663 B.C., the Assyrians invaded Kush. After the invasion, the Kushites moved their capital to Meroë on the Nile River. There, from 250 B.C. to 150 B.C., they enjoyed a new period of growth and achievement. The Kushites developed a writing system and built pyramids, a temple, and a royal palace. Unlike the pharaohs of Egypt who were buried inside their pyramids, the rulers of Meroë were placed in large burial chambers under the pyramids.

The knowledge of ironmaking became very important to the people of Kush. Under their new land were large deposits of iron ore. The Kushites made both weapons and farm tools from iron. Meroë became one of the earliest ironmaking centers of the ancient world.

One of Meroë's greatest advantages was its location. It was located across trade routes between the Nile River and the Red Sea. Meroë reached great power and wealth when the Greek and Roman civilizations prospered. Those nations imported luxury goods such as ostrich feathers, leopard skins, ivory, gold, and ebony from Meroë. Kush never came under Roman control. The Kushites were, however, defeated in A.D. 350 by the people from the rival city-state of Aksum, located southeast of Kush.

Nok Peoples

The Nok people were farmers who lived in villages in what is present-day Nigeria from about 500 B.C. to A.D. 200. When the Sahara dried up, they moved to West Africa. Their dwellings were huts made from reed frames covered with mud and straw. Archaeologists found many Nok artifacts between the Niger and Benue Rivers.

These ruins show the Kush pyramids in the Sudan.

Teaching Options

Meet Individual Needs:
KINESTHETIC LEARNERS

Have students role-play tours of ancient Meroë, including its pyramids and marketplaces. Some class members can serve as tour guides while others can be visitors from ancient Greece, Rome, India, or Egypt. The guides should emphasize the history, special characteristics, and products of Meroë, while the tourists might note differences to their own nations.

Like the Kushites, the Nok people learned to make iron. They were among the first civilizations south of the Sahara to use ironmaking. This technology changed the Nok culture. With stronger tools, they were able to cut down trees and settle nearby forests. Their crops included yams, palm nuts, peas, okra, and cereal grasses. The Nok people baked clay sculptures of human heads and animals. These sculptures may have influenced the beautiful art of later West African peoples.

Bantu Migrations

Modern linguists—scientists who study languages—have given the name *Bantu* to people who speak one group of African languages. With some 500 known languages and 85 million speakers, Bantu is the largest of the major language groups in Africa today. This group stretches across much of Africa south of the Sahara.

Originally, the Bantu-speaking peoples probably lived in the present-day Cameroon-Nigeria border area. Eventually, they probably moved south to the Namib Desert area and then east to the Great Lakes of East Africa. The Bantu people may have learned ironworking in this Great Lakes region. As they migrated, they took their language, their knowledge of agriculture, and their skills in pottery with them to a new area. Today, their language group spans a large area that extends from the region of the equator to the Cape of Good Hope.

◆ Why was the capital city of Meroë important in the kingdom of Kush?

C. Daily Life in Africa

Africa's earliest inhabitants were hunter-gatherers, nomads who moved around in constant search of food. Eventually, some nomads tamed some animals and raised other animals for food. Around 10,000 B.C., agriculture began to develop. When they grew their own food, early Africans were able to settle down and build communities. Yet, even today, some people who live in the deserts and rain forests of Africa are still hunter-gatherers.

African Society

Like the pharaohs of Egypt, the kings of various African civilizations had complete power over their people. Merchants were granted favors by the king. They, in turn, paid taxes to the king who upheld the laws and kept order so the merchants could conduct trade.

Most people lived in small villages in the countryside. They belonged to an extended family—usually composed of parents, children, grandparents, and other relatives—and a **lineage group**. A lineage group consisted of several extended families combined into a larger community. Members were expected to take care of one another.

In general, women were considered inferior to men in early African societies. Occasionally, they were prized for their work. The fact that they bore children was valued because this increased the size of the lineage group. When the village men hunted, women often worked in the fields. Some villages permitted women to be merchants. Many African societies were patriarchal, while some were **matriarchal**. In a matriarchal system, the mother, rather than the father, is the head of the family.

Baked clay sculptures, like this one, are common artifacts left by the Nok people.

Discuss Ask students how the Nok peoples used iron differently from the Kushites. How do the differences reflect the culture of each group? (The Nok, who were a farming people, made agricultural tools; the Kushites, who were often at war, made weapons, as well as farm tools.)

TEACH PRIMARY SOURCES
Have students describe distinctive features of the Nok sculpture on page 225. (triangular eyes, open pupils, distinct nose and lips, and elaborate hairstyle) Point out that almost all Nok sculptures unearthed so far have these common features.

Focus Nearly 500 different Bantu languages are spoken in Africa today. Ask students why they think so many different languages evolved from a common beginning. (Possible answer: As Bantu peoples migrated into different areas, they blended their language with that of the people already there.)

Discuss Ask students why they think iron ore and ironmaking would be important to a civilization. Help students realize that iron, because of its strength, meant better tools and weapons could be made.

◆ **ANSWER** Meroë was one of the earliest centers of ironmaking in the ancient world. It was located across trade routes between the Nile and the Red Sea.

C. Daily Life in Africa
Purpose-Setting Question How does a lineage group differ from an extended family? (An extended family is made up of the direct relatives within one family; a lineage group consists of several extended families combined into a larger community.)

Connection to
CULTURE ⟵

Even though the Nok culture died out long ago, modern-day Yoruban sculpture from western Nigeria shows some definite similarities to the Nok baked clay sculptures. Have students use library or Internet sources to find examples of modern and ancient sculptures that seem related, and share their findings with the class.
Using Technology

Have students use the Internet to locate examples of African masks and sculptures related to initiation ceremonies. If possible, have them print these examples in color and label which part of Africa each comes from. Then, have students place their examples on a bulletin board and have students organize these examples by location, if possible.

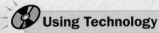

CHAPTER 10 ◆ **T225**

Discuss Ask students to review the information on ancient African religion discussed on page 226. Encourage students to discuss how the religions helped people understand their environment and the things that happened.

Extend Ancestor worship was not limited to Africa. Groups in China, Malaysia, and Polynesia also emphasized worshiping deceased relatives as part of their religions. Other groups, such as the Japanese, emphasized reverence for dead relatives as part of a living person's obligations. Ask students how connecting to ancestors could help strengthen a society. (Possible answer: It was a way to maintain traditions, pass along ethical standards, and provide hope that caring spirits among the dead would look out for the living.)

◆ **ANSWER** Women were usually considered inferior to men but were valued for their ability to bear children. Often they worked in the fields, and some became merchants. In some villages, women were the head of the family.

Section Close

Have students identify each of the three major groups discussed in this section. Then, ask them to describe each civilization and its accomplishments.

3 Assess

Review Answers

Review History
A. A savanna is a grassland that contains some trees, bushes, and lots of tall grasses.

B. The earliest known civilizations in ancient Africa are the Kush, the Nok, and the Bantu.

C. Some religions held the belief that ancestors had the power to influence the lives of their descendants.

Define Terms to Know
savanna, 222; lineage group, 225; matriarchal, 225

Critical Thinking
Possible answer: People might migrate to escape war or poor farming conditions caused by changing climate or overgrazing.

African priests sometimes wore elaborate masks during religious ceremonies.

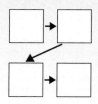

Religions of Ancient Africa

There were many different forms of religion in African cultures. Most religious groups believed in one supreme creator god. In addition to believing in a single supreme god, some groups believed that other lesser gods also existed. These lesser gods helped the supreme god and were closer to the people.

Some religious groups practiced ceremonies, or rituals, to communicate with the gods. The purpose of these rituals was to keep the gods satisfied so that they would protect the people from harm.

Rulers of some ancient African civilizations hired people known as diviners to contact the supreme god. Diviners felt they had the power to predict future events by communicating with the gods. In other groups, people believed their rulers were divine, or godlike. In Ghana and Benin, for example, the kings were too holy to speak to the people. The kings used a spokesperson rather than speak directly to their subjects. In other African religions, a priest told the people how they should live and behave. Priests were both religious leaders and healers. They often wore masks during special rituals.

Ancestors played an important role in some ancient African religions. An ancestor is an individual from whom a person has descended. Some religions held the belief that ancestors were close to the gods. As a result, the ancestors had the power to influence the lives of descendants. In an effort to please their ancestors, ancient African religious groups sometimes dedicated ritual ceremonies to them.

◆ **What was the role of women in most ancient African societies?**

Review I

Review History
A. What is a savanna?
B. Which civilizations were among the earliest known in ancient Africa?
C. Why were ancestors important in some ancient African religions?

Define Terms to Know
Define the following terms: **savanna, lineage group, matriarchal**

Critical Thinking
What might cause people to migrate from one area to another?

Write About Geography
Select one of the three geographic regions of Africa. Write a paragraph explaining how the region's climate would have affected Africa's early civilizations.

Get Organized
UNDERSTAND SEQUENCE
Copy this flowchart onto a sheet of paper and fill in the boxes with the major events in the history of Kush.

Write About Geography
Students' paragraphs will vary, but should include details such as the following: In the desert, people need to be near water sources. The heat could restrict activities. The savanna could be a good place to farm or raise cattle. The forest could be a source of farmland, and the tropical rain forests could be a good supply of food.

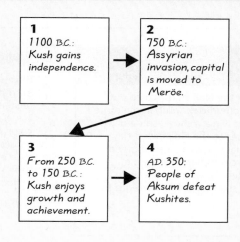

1
1100 B.C.:
Kush gains independence.

2
750 B.C.:
Assyrian invasion, capital is moved to Meröe.

3
From 250 B.C. to 150 B.C.:
Kush enjoys growth and achievement.

4
A.D. 350:
People of Aksum defeat Kushites.

Build Your Skills

Social Studies Skill

WRITE A PERSUASIVE ESSAY

Persuasion is one of the basic forms of writing and speaking. Persuasive writing uses facts and ideas to support a position, or a point of view. Facts can include statistics, while opinions from recognized experts can also be used to support a position. Persuasive writing that uses facts and opinions tries to convince others to agree with a position. However, persuasion may also appeal to the reader's emotions. For example, a writer might appeal to the reader's patriotism when the essay's purpose is to persuade the reader to support people in the military.

People write persuasive essays to support a number of ideas. For example, someone may write to support a candidate in an election or a law that should be passed. Knowing how to write a persuasive essay is a valuable tool.

Here's How

Follow these steps to write a persuasive essay.

1. Select an issue that you care about.
2. Write what your point of view, or position, is on the issue.
3. Develop reasons for your position and find evidence to support it.
4. Write a draft of your essay using a graphic organizer.

Here's Why

You have just read about Africa's varied geographical regions and ecosystems. Suppose you had to write a persuasive essay convincing scientists to help African countries conserve its geographical regions. The steps above would help you write your persuasive essay.

Practice the Skill

Consider the following position, or point of view:
I believe that scientists should find ways to help Africans conserve its varied geographical regions.

Read Section I again. Then, copy the graphic organizer onto a sheet of paper. Complete the organizer by writing two reasons for the position and two facts to support it.

Extend the Skill

Search your school or local library for books and magazines, and the Internet for information about what happens to a group of people or a place when its ecosystem is disrupted. Use this information to support the position.

Apply the Skill

As you read the rest of the chapter, look for issues about which you could form an opinion. Consider holding a class debate on one of these issues. Then, write a persuasive essay supporting your position.

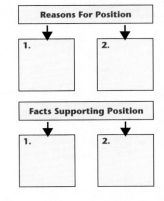

Reasons For Position

1. ☐   2. ☐

Facts Supporting Position

1. ☐   2. ☐

CHAPTER 10 ◆ Kingdoms and City-States in Africa **227**

Teaching Options

RETEACH

Have students bring in an editorial from a local newspaper on an issue that they think is important. Have students underline reasons and supporting facts in the editorial with different color pens or pencils. Ask them to analyze the editorial's argument using the graphic organizer on page 227. Then, have students use the editorial as a model and write their own persuasive essay on the issue. Suggest students take the opposing view.

CHALLENGE

Have students work in small groups to choose an issue and plan a persuasive essay in which they include statements of opinion by outside experts. They can interview the experts themselves or find quotations in library or Internet resources. Students can also work in groups to videotape their essay as television news editorials. The expert opinions can be included as breakaway segments of the editorials.

Build Your Skills

WRITE A PERSUASIVE ESSAY

Teach the Skill

Ask students to think of a time when they had read or heard something that made them take a position on an issue. Examples might have been a public service ad on television or radio, a political commercial, or a newspaper editorial. Have them share the issue and the action they decided to take. Then, ask what technique or combination of techniques the ad or editorial used to convince them, such as presenting a lot of factual details, appealing to their emotions, or citing the opinions of outside experts. Discuss why a persuasive essay that blends strong opinions with facts will usually be the most successful in persuading other people to agree with the writer's position.

Practice the Skill

Students can copy the graphic organizer on page 227. The first section of the graphic organizer can be labeled *Reasons for Position* and the other section *Facts Supporting Position*. Then, have students record two reasons and two facts that support facts based on their rereading of Section 1. Point out that, because they are trying to persuade scientists, their arguments should be strong and well supported. Have students share their graphic organizers with a partner to test whether the arguments are clear and strong; then, revise as needed.

Extend the Skill

Once students have completed their research, they should use a graphic organizer to help them organize their arguments in support of the new opinion statement.

Apply the Skill

As they read the rest of the chapter, have students point out issues that they feel strongly about and construct opinion statements clarifying their positions. Then, have them complete additional graphic organizers to back up their opinions. Finally, have students use their research to write a persuasive essay.

II. Major Kingdoms of West Africa

(pp. 228–233)

Section Summary

In this section, students will learn about the political and economic growth of three major empires in West Africa—Ghana, Mali, and Songhai. They will also learn how smaller states contributed to West Africa's development.

Introduce

Getting Started

Ask students what it takes to have a successful sales business. Discuss the importance of having products that others want, a good network to distribute the products, and assertive salespeople to bring in customer orders. Point out that in this section they will learn how several kingdoms noted for their successful trading practices rose in West Africa between A.D. 500 and 1500.

TERMS TO KNOW

Ask students to read the words and definitions on page 228 and then find each word in the section. Point out that their origins are from African languages.

You may wish to preview the pronunciation of the following words from this section with students.

Timbuktu (tihm buhk TOO)
Gao (gaw)
Songhai (SONG hy)
Ife (ee FAY)
Oyo (OH yoh)
Benin (beh NEEN)

ACTIVE READING

Review with students how to use a Venn diagram (TR, p. 323). Then, suggest that they use the diagram to compare and contrast two of the key leaders discussed in this section—Sundiata, Mansa Musa, Sonni Ali Ber, and Muhammad Askia.

Section II — Major Kingdoms of West Africa

Terms to Know

mansa a village head; later, the head of an empire

oba the king of a city-state in ancient Africa

Main Ideas

A. Ghana was the first major empire in West Africa.

B. The Islamic kingdom of Mali brought further wealth to West Africa.

C. The Songhai Empire replaced Mali as the most powerful empire in western Africa.

D. Smaller kingdoms also contributed to West Africa's development.

Active Reading

COMPARE AND CONTRAST
When you compare and contrast, you look for ways that two things are both alike and different. A Venn diagram is often the easiest way to see these likenesses and differences. As you read this section, look for ways to compare and contrast any of the two kingdoms in this section.

A. Ghana, the First Large Empire of West Africa

The kingdom of Ghana began developing around A.D. 500. It was ideally located along a trade route, about halfway between the salt mines of the Sahara and the forests of West Africa. The capital city was really two towns, the traders' town and the king's town. Archaeologists have found evidence of the traders' town, Koumbi Saleh. The artifacts found there include stones with verses from the Quran—the holy writings of the religion of Islam—and small glass weights that may have been used for weighing gold.

The Rise of Ghana

The earliest of the West African kingdoms, Ghana developed from a simple trading post. The kingdom grew prosperous from the profits and taxes gained through trade. The king built huge armies that were used to gain control over neighbors. In time, Ghana ruled a sprawling empire that covered a large part of western Africa. The lands that were conquered by Ghana sent tribute and soldiers to the king. In exchange, the king provided protection from invaders. The conquered lands usually continued to be ruled by their own leaders.

Ghana had large supplies of iron ore and gold. Gold was mined south of the kingdom and shipped north of the kingdom to trade for salt mined in the Sahara. In the ancient world, salt was used as a spice and also to prevent meat from spoiling in the heat. In addition, salt prevented people from becoming dehydrated. Salt was so valuable that it was traded for an almost equal amount of gold.

The peoples with whom Ghana traded gold for salt were called Berbers. They came from an area known as Arabia. The Berbers, and other traders from Arabia, brought their religion—Islam—to Ghana. The kings of Ghana did not convert to Islam, but they tolerated the new religion.

Kingdoms of West Africa, A.D. 500–1500

ATLANTIC OCEAN
SAHARA
AFRICA
Timbuktu
Gao
Niger River

- Songhai
- Ghana
- Mali
- Trade center

0   250   500 mi
0   250   500 km

Map Check

LOCATION Which West African kingdom extended the farthest east?

Teaching Options

Section 2 Resources

Teacher's Resources (TR)
Terms to Know, p. 23
Review History, p. 57
Build Your Skills, p. 91
Concept Builder, p. 226
Flowchart, p. 324

Connection to ECONOMICS

Salt was a very valuable commodity not only in Africa but also throughout the ancient world. The Latin word for *salt* is *sal*. Roman soldiers received part of their pay in salt. This portion was called a *salarium* and is the origin of our modern word *salary*. In Africa, small pieces of salt were used as money to buy goods, and people of Ghana would trade equal amounts of gold for salt.

At its height, the kingdom of Ghana had a population of about 15,000 to 20,000 people. Most of the common people lived as farmers and traders. Others mined gold, wove cloth, or made sculptures. They took these goods to the local market town to trade.

The Decline of Ghana

After the mid-1000s, Ghana experienced revolts from within and invasions from outside. The most serious invasion came in A.D. 1076 when an army of Muslims from North Africa attacked the kingdom.

Although the people of Ghana later regained some of their independence, they never regained their wealth. Then, the gold mines contained no more gold. Over the next several hundred years, two great empires rose up to replace Ghana. The first of these was Mali.

◆ What was the basis for the kingdom of Ghana's wealth?

B. The Kingdom of Mali

The kingdom of Mali came to power in the area that had been Ghana. It also expanded farther west. At its height, the kingdom covered 600 miles from north to south and 1,200 miles from east to west. Mali was larger than Ghana and far richer. The kingdom's wealth came from new gold mines located near the Niger River. Mali also won control of important trade routes across the Sahara. The cities of Timbuktu and Gao, both on the Niger River, became Mali's chief trading centers. Timbuktu became known for its wealth and learning. It later became one of the largest centers of Islamic learning on the African continent.

Mali Under Sundiata

In A.D. 1240, a man named Sundiata captured Ghana's capital, and the kingdom of Mali emerged. Sundiata became Mali's first great leader. He brought unity to the people and developed a strong government. Mali had new laws, a tax system, and a dedication to education.

Sundiata died in A.D. 1255, before he could see his empire become even more powerful. After his death, two of his sons took over the throne. The new leaders of Mali took the title of **mansa**, which means emperor. The mansa was the leader, both spiritually and legally, of the people.

Stories of Mali and other African peoples were passed down through oral tradition. Storytellers known as griots memorized the legends and recited or sang them. In Mali, the griots could be men or women.

Mali Converts to Islam

After Sundiata's death, Mali had a rich culture based on Islam. A fourteenth century visitor to Mali wrote,

> ❝ They are seldom unjust, and have a greater dislike of injustice than any other people. . . . There is complete security in their country. Neither traveler nor inhabitant in it has anything to fear from robbers or men of violence. ❞

In A.D. 1307, perhaps the greatest ruler in the history of Mali took the throne. His name was Mansa Musa. A devout Muslim, Mansa Musa made a pilgrimage across Africa to Mecca in A.D. 1324. He gave away so much gold on this trip that the price of gold in Egypt dropped for the next several years.

Trade in West Africa

EXPORTS	IMPORTS
salt	cloth
slaves	cowrie shells
cloth	animal harnesses
kola nuts	horses
sculptures	guns
carvings	salt
gold	

✔ **Chart Check**

Which items were both exported and imported?

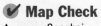
ANALYZE PRIMARY SOURCES

DOCUMENT-BASED QUESTION
In what ways was Mali secure?

CHAPTER 10 ◆ Kingdoms and City-States in Africa **229**

Conflict Resolution

The leaders of ancient Ghana helped to avoid revolts by sharing power with local leaders. Often, leaders of school organizations ask members to share in making rules and in leading activities. Discuss why having people participate in running an organization makes it run more smoothly.

A. Ghana, the First Large Empire of West Africa

Purpose-Setting Question What did Ghana do with the lands it conquered? (The lands sent tribute and soldiers to the Ghana king; the king provided protection; lands were usually ruled by their own leaders.)

Using the Map

Kingdoms of West Africa, A.D. 500–1500

Have students estimate how far the kingdom of Mali stretched from west to east. (about 1,200 to 1,300 miles) Discuss why such a large empire would be hard to control politically. (Transportation and communication would be difficult.)

✔ **Map Check**

Answer Songhai

Using the Chart

Trade in West Africa

Review the definition of the noun form of the words *import* and *export*.

✔ **Chart Check**

Answer salt, cloth

◆ **ANSWER** the profits and taxes gained through trade

B. The Kingdom of Mali

Purpose-Setting Question How were legends about ancient Mali preserved? (oral tradition; griots)

ANALYZE PRIMARY SOURCES

DOCUMENT-BASED QUESTION

Ibn Battuta spent many years traveling throughout Africa. His writings helped to spread knowledge about Mali to outsiders. This quote shows how impressed he was with the peacefulness he found in Mali.

ANSWER There was very little injustice, robbery, or violence.

Mansa Musa ruled Mali for 25 years.

Focus Mansa Musa was a generous and clever leader. Along with gold, he took about 60,000 people with him on his pilgrimage to Mecca. Ask students to suggest other adjectives they might use to describe Mansa Musa if they were writing about his travels.

TEACH PRIMARY SOURCES

Ask students how the painting of Mansa Musa reflects power and wealth. (He is holding a gold nugget in one hand and his royal scepter in the other.)

◆ **ANSWER** Sundiata brought unity to his people and developed a strong government that included new laws, a tax system, and a dedication to education.

C. The Songhai Empire

Purpose-Setting Question

How did Sonni Ali Ber control his kingdom? (He divided the empire into provinces and appointed a governor to rule each one.)

Explore Ask students how the presence of the Niger River affected the development of Songhai and the occupations of its people. (The river made it easier for traders to come and go. The fertile soil near the river made farming possible, and the river provided abundant fish for food and trade.)

◆ **ANSWER** Songhai descendants were part of the upper class; the next class was made up of traders, merchants, and soldiers; and the lowest class consisted of prisoners of war who were slaves.

D. Other West African Kingdoms

Purpose-Setting Question What was unusual about the villages and cities of the Hausa people? (They were surrounded by walls.)

When he returned to Mali, Mansa Musa wanted to continue developing Islamic culture in the kingdom. He brought architects to build new mosques and a magnificent palace. He also founded universities where people could study the writings of Islam.

Mansa Musa extended Mali's boundaries far and wide. He also increased trade. Mansa Musa died in A.D. 1332. After his death, the kingdom declined, and Songhai, the western part of the empire, grew in power.

◆ **What were Sundiata's accomplishments?**

C. The Songhai Empire

Around A.D. 750 the empire of Songhai was founded. Gao was its capital and chief trading center. It was located along the Niger River where the soil was fertile. The Songhai people were mainly fishers and farmers.

By the tenth century, the Songhai had converted to Islam. The next three centuries were spent resisting Mali rule. Around A.D. 1240, the Mali Empire absorbed Songhai. One hundred years later, however, the Songhai regained their freedom.

Songhai Under Two Rulers

Under the leadership of a warrior king, Sonni Ali Ber, the Songhai Empire replaced Mali as a dominant power around A.D. 1365. The Songhai recaptured Gao and Timbuktu, regaining control of the trading empire. Sonni Ali Ber kept his huge kingdom firmly under his control by dividing the empire into several provinces and appointing a governor to rule each one.

Late in the fifteenth century, the Songhai Empire reached the height of power during the reign of Muhammad Askia. He built Songhai into a strong kingdom. The empire grew, stretching about 1,000 miles along the Niger River. Its salt and gold trade made Songhai prosperous. The empire remained powerful until it was invaded by Morocco in the late sixteenth century.

Life in the Songhai Empire

Songhai had a strict social system. The upper class was made up of descendants of the original Songhai people. The next class included traders, merchants, and soldiers. The lowest social class included prisoners of war who were slaves. For hundreds of years, Africans had been taking prisoners of war and enslaving them. Slaves were often sold to other African kingdoms. Songhai, too, participated in this slave trade.

◆ **What were the different levels of the Songhai Empire's social system?**

D. Other West African Kingdoms

A number of smaller kingdoms emerged throughout West Africa between A.D. 1000 and A.D. 1500. Three of these kingdoms—Hausa, Yoruba, and Benin—greatly contributed to the development of West African civilization. The people of these kingdoms were organized into small villages or city-states.

Hausa

The Hausa people began developing their kingdom around A.D. 1000. Nomads from the southern part of the Sahara mixed with local farmers to form walled villages. The walls protected them from raiders. Eventually, the villages formed walled cities.

230   UNIT 3   ◆   Regional Civilizations

Teaching Options

Research

AVERAGE

Long after Sundiata and Mansa Musa died, griots told legends about their lives and deeds. Have students use library or Internet resources to find out more about the real-life and legendary activities of either leader. Then, have them present their findings to the class and discuss what made either man become a legendary figure.

CHALLENGE

Have students research more about the history of griots in Africa from ancient times to the present. Have students present their findings to the class and be prepared to discuss why, even with all of our modern communication techniques, the role of the griot is still important in some African communities today.

The Hausa people were also traders. One of the city-states sold prisoners for export to places such as Borneo in Malaysia and North Africa. In exchange for the slaves, the people of Hausa received guns, horses, and animal harnesses.

Because of the rivalry that existed between the various city-states in the Hausa civilization, no strong ruler emerged to form a united empire. As the rivalries continued, war ruined the countryside for farming.

The Kingdom of Yoruba

Yoruba covered the territory of the savanna woodlands from west of the lower Niger River to the forest near the coast. The people were mostly hunters, farmers, and traders who lived in small villages.

Farming was so successful that the villages could support artisans and court craftspeople. Ife, the capital of Yoruba, is best known for its artists. For them, art was a means of expressing religious ideas.

Between the twelfth and fifteenth centuries, artists produced beautiful brass and copper statues and pots, terra cotta—or red clay—sculptures, and wood and ivory carvings. Archaeologists believe that the people of Ife had a trade link to the Saharan copper mines. They probably traded ivory, food, and kola nuts for copper and salt.

Benin

The kingdom of Benin was located in present-day Nigeria. The **oba**, or ruler, Ewuare made Benin the most powerful kingdom in this part of Africa. He enlarged the army and expanded the empire in the mid-fifteenth century. Ewuare is said to have captured more than 200 towns. He appointed a council of district chiefs and had his son named as the next oba in order to avoid a war for power when he died.

Benin was a walled city with fine houses and wide streets. Like Yoruba, Benin is famous for its art. Artisans made figurines and heads out of bronze and brass to honor their rulers. In the late 1400s, the Portuguese arrived in Benin. The obas sold their war captives as slaves to the Portuguese, who in turn sold their slaves for gold.

◆ **What items did the people of Ife use for trading?**

Benin artisans crafted metal sculptures, such as this one, to honor their rulers.

▼ Review II

Review History
A. Why did Ghana prosper?
B. Who was Mali's greatest ruler?
C. Under which ruler did Songhai reach its height of power?
D. What three small kingdoms contributed to West African civilization?

Define Terms to Know
Define the following terms:
mansa, oba

Critical Thinking
What problems might be connected with having only one main item as the basis of trade?

Write About Culture
Write a brief essay explaining why it is important to preserve the art of a culture.

Get Organized
UNDERSTAND SEQUENCE
Copy this flowchart onto a sheet of paper and fill in the boxes with the major events in the rise and fall of the Mali Empire.

```
[  ] → [  ]
         ↓
[  ] → [  ]
```

Activity

Make a catalog Have students form groups to make catalogs of Benin bronze and brass art pieces from different periods. Each member of a group should make at least one catalog page that includes a reproduction and description of one or more art piece(s). Allow students to use library or Internet resources for their research. You may want to have groups use a computer software program to make the catalogs. Have each group share its catalog with the class.

TEACH PRIMARY SOURCES

Ask students what details they can identify in the sculpture on page 231. (hat, hair, neck wrap, eye shape, nose and nostril shape) Discuss with students if this is a realistic or more fanciful style of art.

◆ **ANSWER** ivory, food, kola nuts

Section Close

Discuss with students the ways the kingdoms of West Africa described in Section 2 were more advanced politically and economically than the earlier African civilizations they read about in Section 1.

③ Assess

Review Answers

Review History

A. Ghana prospered due to trade, huge armies, expanded lands, tribute, and soldiers.
B. Mansa Musa was Mali's greatest ruler.
C. Songhai reached its height of power under Muhammad Askia.
D. The kingdoms of Hausa, Yoruba, and Benin all contributed to West African civilization.

Define Terms to Know

mansa, 229; oba, 231

```
1
AD. 1240:
Kingdom of
Mali emerges.
```
→
```
2
Mali has new
laws, taxes,
and a
dedication
to education.
```
```
3
AD. 1307:
Mansa Musa
takes the
throne.
```
→
```
4
AD. 1332:
Mansa Musa
dies, Mali
begins to decline.
```

Critical Thinking

Answers should indicate that supplies of the one item, such as gold, might be depleted or that the market for that product might become flooded, which would cause prices to drop.

Write About Culture

Students' essays will vary but might include the idea that what a culture regarded as beautiful and what it kept reveal a lot about the values of the culture.

Past to...

THE MUSIC OF AFRICA

Teach the Topic

This feature focuses on the evolution of musical instruments from their African roots to modern electronic versions. Ask students to visualize a jazz band playing and to name as many instruments in the band as they can "see" or "hear" mentally. List their suggestions on the board in three categories: wind, string, and percussion. Point out that the roots of jazz music can be traced to African instruments and styles brought to the Western Hemisphere by slaves.

HANDY PIANO

Small thumb pianos called *mbiras* or *likembes* were usually played using the thumb and index fingers of both hands. They were often used by griots and other African storytellers to accompany their tales. Ask students why a griot might want to play music while he or she spoke. (easier to remember stories set to music, more entertaining for audience)

ANCIENT DRUMS

One distinctive feature of African music is that it is almost always accompanied by singing or dancing. The rhythm of the music is very important and is usually established by the drums. Drumming was also a way of echoing human speech. In colonial times, slave-owners feared the power of drums would build up the emotions of enslaved Africans and often outlawed the playing of drums on plantations.

SWEET STRINGS

Instruments created in different regions of Africa may have depended in part on environment. While drums were most popular in woodland areas, stringed instruments—made from gourds, skins, sticks, and string—were more prevalent in the savannas. Koras could have up to 21 strings. Ask students what modern five-string instrument the kora most resembles. (banjo) Note that the banjo was invented using the kora as a model.

Past to...

THE MUSIC OF AFRICA

Since ancient times, Africa has been enriched with musical traditions that featured a variety of percussion, stringed, and wind instruments. These traditions were brought to the Americas starting around 1520 when Africans were forcibly brought to these continents as slaves. African music—especially its rhythmical traditions—heavily influenced the music of both North and South America and has led to the creation of new musical forms.

HANDY PIANO
Narrow metal strips are arranged over a sounding board to make a "thumb-piano." This instrument is unique to Africa.

Goat or cowhide cover

Leather strips attach strings to neck

Animal skin

SWEET STRINGS
The kora, or harp lute, is from the Mali region of Africa. Strings are stretched over half a gourd and along a long, wooden neck.

ANCIENT DRUMS
Large African drums are either carved from a solid piece of wood or constructed from strips of wood bound together by iron hoops. A cover, made of animal skin, is stretched across the top of the drum and secured with wooden pegs. Wooden beaters are used to strike the animal skin covers.

Wooden beater

Leather straps

Teaching Options

Connection to LITERATURE

African American poet Langston Hughes was famous for his ability to capture the African American experience in his poetry. In his 1926 collection, *The Weary Blues*, Hughes blended musical rhythms with vivid words and images. Students may want to read some of the rhythm poems from this collection aloud in class.

LINK to TODAY

In the past, griots stayed close to their villages when telling old stories and legends. Some of today's griots have become international music stars. One such star, Amy Koita from Mali, says, "My grandmother sang songs about human nature that gave lessons about what to do and what not to do. My songs use the same themes, but I've also used violin and other western instruments, so the style has changed."

Cowrie shell decoration

JUST ADD WIND
Many African trumpets, such as the one shown above from Uganda, can be blown from the side. They are traditionally made from carved wood or animal horn, with a small mouthpiece made of gourd.

THAT'S JAZZ
In late nineteenth-century America, complex African rhythms joined with European-style harmonies and American spiritual songs to produce a new type of music known as jazz. By the early twentieth century, jazz had become a popular form of dance music.

...Present

Today's electronic machinery can analyze, record, and mimic a wide variety of sounds. Electrical sound signals are then transmitted to amplifiers and loudspeakers. Music is often composed using electronic instruments, or synthesizers, but may be performed live using standard instruments.

CRASH, BANG, WALLOP
Drummers may use each hand and each foot to play different drums and cymbals in different rhythms—all at the same time.

Crash cymbal

Hi-hat cymbals

Ride cymbal

Tom drums

Floor Tom

Snare drum

Hi-hat pedal

Bass drum pedal

Bass drum

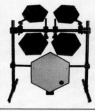

MODERN BEAT
Electronic drum pads produce a different type of sound than that of a standard drum kit.

Keyboard

Percussion controls

PLUGGED-IN MUSIC
A synthesizer can produce either a standard drum beat or an electronic drum beat—as well as other instrumental and non-instrumental sounds.

CHAPTER 10 ◆ Kingdoms and City-States in Africa **233**

Hands-On Activity

List these materials on the board: *two small wooden blocks; two sticks; dried gourds; beans; an empty tin can; string; leather strings; small pieces of metal; an animal horn; a hollowed log; a stretched piece of animal skin.* Ask students to write directions for using any of the materials to create a musical instrument. Have students describe their instruments.

JUST ADD WIND
Ask students how it might be possible for a musical instrument to "talk." Then, discuss with students why Africans may have created some flutes and trumpets. (Possible answers: to imitate the rhythm and pitch patterns of human voices; human-sounding calls could be sent over long distances)

THAT'S JAZZ
One common African musical technique was ring-shouting. A leader would shout or sing out words, and dancers would respond in chorus. This technique was brought to the Americas and it evolved into jazz. In jazz, one instrument would "shout" out a note pattern and others would respond.

...Present

CRASH, BANG, WALLOP
If any members of the class are percussionists, ask them to describe the different sounds and purposes of the percussion instruments in the pictured drum set. Discuss how modern drummers use both their hands and feet to produce sounds.

MODERN BEAT
Advantages of electronic drums include being able to produce almost any sound, being able to play with headphones so others are not disturbed no matter how loud the drums are played, and being able to record on a computer. Negatives include having a different sound to the ears from acoustic drums and needing a monitoring sound system in order to be heard.

PLUGGED-IN MUSIC
Musicians and engineers began experimenting with electronically produced music as early as 1867, but the first synthesizer was not made until 1955 in the United States.

Connect Past to Present
Have students create a three-column chart with the headings: *Drums Yesterday, Drums Today,* and *Drums Tomorrow.* Have students complete the first columns from the information on these pages and the third column with their own suggestions of future directions. Discuss how purposes of percussion instruments have or have not changed over time.

III. Major Kingdoms of East Africa

(pp. 234–239)

Section Summary

In this section, students will learn about the development of two contrasting kingdoms in the area southeast of Egypt: the powerful trading nation of Aksum and its successor, the Christian stronghold of Ethiopia. They will also learn how coastal towns in the region of Swahili were the first to be touched by civilizations outside of Africa, and how the kingdom of Zimbabwe built cities enclosed with stone walls to demonstrate its power.

1 Introduce

Getting Started

Ask students to describe what it is like to meet someone from a country or culture that is different from their own. Encourage students to share what they may have learned about the culture of the other person. Explain that they are going to learn about some African kingdoms and meetings between different cultures.

TERMS TO KNOW

Ask students to read the terms and definitions on page 234. Then, have them skim the section to locate each term, read the surrounding paragraph, and state a definition for the term in their own words.

You may wish to preview the pronunciation of the following terms from this section with students.

Ge'ez (gee EHZ)
Ibn Battuta (IHB uhn bat TOO tah)
Mogadishu (moh gah DEE shoo)
Limpopo (lihm POH poh)
Zimbabwe (zihm BAHB way)

ACTIVE READING

Students should also look for cause-and-effect relationships in other sections. For example, while reading subsection C on "The Region of Swahili," pages 236–238, students might focus on the effect of the region's coming into contact with Portuguese traders and explorers.

Section III — Major Kingdoms of East Africa

Terms to Know

stela a tall narrow column, usually carved; the plural form is stelae

dry stone a method of building without using mortar

This ancient stela from Aksum once stood about 13 stories tall and is the largest stela ever found.

Main Ideas

A. Aksum developed a powerful kingdom based on trade.

B. Ethiopia created a Christian kingdom in ancient Africa.

C. Swahili's coastal towns were the first to be touched by civilizations outside of Africa.

D. Zimbabwe builders formed impressive stone enclosures to show their power.

 Active Reading

CAUSE AND EFFECT
When you search for the reasons that an event occurred, you are investigating cause and effect. As you read this section, look for cause-and-effect relationships as they relate to the kingdom of Aksum.

A. The Ancient Kingdom of Aksum

Aksum was the name of both a kingdom and its capital city, located in Central Africa in what is now Ethiopia and Eritrea. The city of Aksum was built on a rugged plateau, about 20 miles from the northeastern seaport of Adulis on the Red Sea. In the first century A.D., the journey from Aksum to Adulis took 8 days.

The Aksum Peoples

Aksum may have been established around 1000 B.C. by Arabic peoples. It was a city divided by economic class. The wealthy people lived at the top of the plateau in stone houses. This location meant that their houses caught the sea breezes coming from the Red Sea 100 miles away. The artisans and people of lower economic classes lived at the base of the plateau. They built their houses from mud and reeds or branches and used straw for the roofs.

Aksum's climate was influenced by the monsoons that blew from the Indian Ocean to the Red Sea. Because the kingdom was built on high ground, the people were free of the diseases, such as malaria, more commonly found in the lowland.

Aksum became a powerful military force around A.D. 350. Around that time, King Ezana conquered Kush and built a kingdom. Thirty years later, he made Christianity Aksum's official religion. Christianity was a strong influence throughout the region.

The Stelae of Aksum

Aksum's most remarkable structures are the **stelae**, or carved pillars, which were believed to be grave markers for the tombs of rulers. More than 120 stelae have been found in the city. One of the largest was located in a park in Aksum. It is a single granite block carved to look like a 10-story building. A false door has been carved at the base.

The largest stela is as tall as a 13-story building. It is now broken into five pieces, but was probably the largest stone monument in the ancient world. The granite block was quarried 4 miles west of Aksum. Moving the granite was similar to moving the stones for the ancient Egyptian pyramids. Most likely, rollers and elephants were used to transport the granite.

Teaching Options

Section 3 Resources

Teacher's Resources (TR)

Terms to Know, p. 23
Review History, p. 57
Build Your Skills, p. 91
Chapter Test, pp. 135–136
Concept Builder, p. 226
Flowchart, p. 324
Transparencies 6, 10

ESL/ELL STRATEGIES

Organize Information Because this section is divided into four subsections, students might find it useful to complete an outline (TR, p. 318) of the text as they read. Suggest that they use the bold subheadings in the text as headings in their outline. Then, they should list key details from the text under the correct heading of the outline. The outline will help them review the section later.

Trade Brings Wealth

With Adulis, its famous port on the Red Sea, Aksum became a major trading power. From the interior of Africa came ivory, gold, and raw materials for trade. Aksum may have sold captives for the slave trade as well. Aksum itself added gum arabic, used in making medicine, glue, and candy to the trade.

Artisans made luxury goods from copper, brass, and glass beads to sell. Merchants in Aksum traded with Greece, Rome, Egypt, Persia, India, and Ceylon. They imported olive oil, silver, gold, and wine.

Trading with other nations created the need for a written language. In Aksum, this written language, Africa's oldest, is known as Ge'ez. Inscriptions from the seventh century B.C. indicate that Ge'ez was based on an Arabic script. Ge'ez was the forerunner of modern Ethiopian writing. It was also the language used for holy writings.

Aksumites used coins made of copper, silver, and gold. They were the first African civilization south of the Sahara to do so before the tenth century.

This Ethiopian Bible, written in Ge'ez script, illustrates a king on horseback above a dragon.

Persian and Islamic Conquests

Although Aksum had conquered many civilizations along the Nile River and the Red Sea, it was in turn conquered by Persians around A.D. 590. The Persians considered Aksum to be one of the four most important kingdoms in the world. However, as a result of the conquest, trade suffered.

A century later, Muslims conquered the Persians. The Muslims also captured Aksum's important port city, Adulis. Now, the people of Aksum felt isolated and cut off from trade. In addition, they were surrounded by non-Christian people. For the next 300 years, they fought both the Muslims and tribal peoples around them.

The kingdom eventually declined. Aksum gradually lost control over its trade routes and its territory. However, its culture survived in the East African kingdom of Ethiopia.

◆ What city was an important trade port in Aksum?

B. The Kingdom of Ethiopia

Like Aksum, the kingdom of Ethiopia was distinguished as being one of the oldest kingdoms in the world. The name *Ethiopia*—meaning "burnt face"—was given by the ancient Greeks to the kingdom of Ethiopia and the surrounding areas. Ethiopia's connection to the ancient peoples of Greece, Phoenicia, Egypt, and Rome was described in many trade records and historical writings. Ethiopia's connection to Aksum, however, was deeper—the two kingdoms were connected by a shared culture as well as by a shared religion.

Ethiopia's Christian Roots

When Aksum adopted the Christian religion, around A.D. 380, it slowly spread Christianity to neighboring regions, including Ethiopia. By around A.D. 500, Ethiopia, too, became a Christian kingdom.

When Muslims conquered Adulis in A.D. 700, the kingdom of Aksum began to decline, having lost control of its most important trade port. As a result of this conquest, Aksum culture and religious traditions moved to the south toward Ethiopia, which had resisted invasion and remained Christian.

A. The Ancient Kingdom of Aksum

Purpose-Setting Question What is significant about Ge'ez? (It is the oldest written language in Africa and was used for holy writings.)

Discuss Ask students how climate and geography influenced the development of Aksum. (Possible answers: monsoons provided rain for growing crops and mud for building houses; high elevations helped the people avoid lowland diseases such as malaria.)

Activity

Make a poster Explain that the Maya in Central America also erected stelae, many of which can still be viewed today. Have students use library or Internet resources to find information and photographs about both Aksumite and Maya stelae. Then, have students create posters that illustrate and compare the stelae of these civilizations.

TEACH PRIMARY SOURCES

Point out the Ethopian Bible on page 235. Explain that the Bible was translated into Ge'ez sometime between A.D. 400 and 600. Ge'ez continued to be used for Ethiopian literature through the sixteenth century although it had lost popularity as a spoken language long before that. Have students suggest similarities between Latin and Ge'ez. (Possible answers: used for religious purposes, still written but no longer spoken, connected to Christianity)

◆ ANSWER Adulis

B. The Kingdom of Ethiopia

Purpose-Setting Question Why did Ethiopia share culture and religion with the kingdom of Aksum? (They were neighboring regions and both were Christian. As Aksum declined, its culture and religious traditions moved south toward Ethiopia.)

Test Taking

Create analogy questions from material in this section. Remind students to look for a relationship in the given pair of words or phrases. Then, they should find the answer that makes the second pair have the same relationship. A sample might be:
stelae : Aksum :: pyramids :
(a) Mali; (b) Kush; (c) Ethiopia; (d) Ghana (Answer: b Kush)

Meet Individual Needs:
VISUAL/SPATIAL LEARNERS

Suggest that students create a product map using an outline map of Africa (TR, p. 334) to help them keep track of the goods exported by the African nations discussed in this chapter. Have students make a key with product symbols, such as gold, salt, ivory, copper, and iron. Then, have them write in the names of the nations and draw the product symbols for each nation's key exports.

Activity

Write a press release Have students assume the role of King Lalibela's public relations expert. Their job is to write a press release describing the building and purpose of the 11 stone churches and encourage Ethiopian Christians to make a pilgrimage to the churches. Suggest that students include quotations from the king and other church leaders in their press release.

ANALYZE PRIMARY SOURCES

DOCUMENT-BASED QUESTION

The churches served a double function as places of worship and as a kind of museum of Christian holy places in Jerusalem. From solid stone, the builders chiseled the outside walls, entry ways, courtyards, and elaborate interior decorations.

ANSWER Possible answer: the work was so intricate that people felt the churches were built with holy intentions.

◆ **ANSWER** Cyprus, Egypt, and the Holy Land

C. The Region of Swahili

Purpose-Setting Question What were the three levels of Swahili society? (**Top level:** Arabic Islamic leaders, court officials, wealthy merchants; **middle level:** Muslim African townspeople; **lowest level:** non-Muslim slaves)

Focus Point out that Swahili is a language that blends words from Bantu and Arabic languages. Ask students how this blending came about. (Arabs settled along the East African coast, intermarried with Bantu settlers, and converted the people to Islam. Over time, their languages blended.) You may wish to use Transparency 10 to help students understand locations in the Middle East.

This underground church was carved out of stone in the region of Ethiopia around A.D. 1200.

By the tenth century, new rulers gained control of the area once controlled by Aksum. These rulers, who were Christians, founded a new capital at Roha, about 150 miles south of the old capital city of Aksum. These rulers also preserved the ancient Ethiopian language, Ge'ez, and re-established a formal connection to the Christian Church.

King Lalibela

One of the most famous of these Christian rulers, King Lalibela, ruled in the early thirteenth century. He ordered 11 underground churches to be carved out of stone in Roha. Some people believed that the builders had divine help:

> **ANALYZE PRIMARY SOURCES**
> **DOCUMENT-BASED QUESTION**
> Why do you think some people believed that the builders had divine help?

❝ Angels joined the workers, the quarry men, the stone cutters, and the laborers. The angels worked with them by day and by themselves at night. The men . . . doubted whether the angels were doing this work because they could not see them, but Lalibela knew, because the angels, who understood his virtue, did not hide from him. **❞**

Lalibela was considered a saint for having built such marvelous structures. In fact, the city of Roha was renamed for him. Lalibela's churches still exist to this day, with names that represent Christian saints or holy places. Some historians believe that the churches may have been intended to take the place of a pilgrimage to Jerusalem.

During Lalibela's reign, Ethiopians also journeyed to many places, such as Cyprus and Egypt. They also went on pilgrimages to the Holy Land.

◆ **Under King Lalibela's rule, to which places did Ethiopians travel?**

C. The Region of Swahili

Around the tenth century, Arabs settled along the East African coast. They intermarried with local people and converted these people to Islam. A new language developed in East Africa. The new language, Swahili, was a mixture of Arabic and Bantu languages. The word *Swahili* is based on an Arabic word

Teaching Options

Connection to
LITERATURE ⟵

Until the 1990s, there were groups in Ethiopia that practiced a simple form of Judaism and claimed to be descendants of King Solomon's son. These Jews, called *falashas*, often suffered discrimination because of their religion. During civil wars in Ethiopia in the 1980s and 1990s, about 45,000 falashas felt they were "returning home" when they left Ethiopia for Israel.

that means "coast dwellers." Swahili is both a group of people and a language. Swahili speakers were not from a single ethnic group. They were bound together by both their language and their connection to trade.

Swahili Society

The Swahili people came out of the mix of people descended from Arabic and Bantu peoples. By the early A.D. 800s, a form of the Swahili language was being spoken in settlements along the East African coast. These settlements later grew to be towns. More than 40 coastal towns formed the basis of the Swahili city-states between the tenth and fourteenth centuries. Each city-state was independent, governed by a sultan, the Arabic word for ruler.

These Arabic Islamic rulers, with their court officials and wealthy merchants, were at the top of a three-level class society. At the next level were most of the Muslim African townspeople—the artisans, clerks, and ships' captains. The lowest class included the non-Muslim slaves who worked for the wealthy landowners.

Swahili City-States

People living in city-states along the coast of the Indian Ocean, such as Kilwa, Mombasa, and Mogadishu, were the first people to be touched by other civilizations. Traders from Arabia, India, and countries along the Red Sea came to these coastal towns.

Some of the Swahili people moved to islands, such as Zanzibar, off the eastern coast of Africa. For more than 1,000 years, Zanzibar was a center for the slave trade to Arabia and across the Indian Ocean.

Other places that prospered through trade included Malindi, a seaport town, and Lamu. In fact, the connection between Malindi and China was so close that in A.D. 1415, the people of Malindi sent a giraffe to the emperor of China. Giraffes were unknown in China at that time. The gift was so astonishing that poems were written about it, and it became the subject of paintings.

Kilwa was one of the most well-known African city-states. It was a walled city with wide streets and impressive palaces. Around A.D. 1200, Kilwa gained control of the gold trade. For the next 200 years, it was probably the wealthiest of Africa's city-states. Ibn Battuta, a world traveler, writer, and geographer, said that Kilwa was "one of the most beautiful and well-constructed towns in the world." Modern archaeologists have uncovered a huge trade center and a large mosque there.

The people of Kilwa lived in stone houses. Kilwa's merchants bought gold, ivory, copper, and iron from inland towns. They traded these goods for products from other lands, including porcelain from China and cotton from India. Kilwa's traders were extremely prosperous. Most of their houses were filled with many luxury items.

Ibn Battuta also visited Mogadishu. Battuta related that when merchants came into port, young men carrying food boarded their ships to welcome them. The merchants were then invited to a host's house to sell goods and to make purchases.

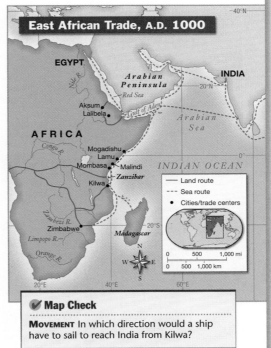

East African Trade, A.D. 1000

✔ Map Check

MOVEMENT In which direction would a ship have to sail to reach India from Kilwa?

Discuss Ask students why they think the city-states in Africa did not unite against the Portuguese. (Possible answer: They had been competing for trade and power for years, and were not used to cooperating.) Encourage students to discuss other city-states they have learned about (Greek city-states of Athens and Sparta) and how cooperating helped these city-states defeat their enemies.

GLOBAL CONNECTIONS
THE CRUSADES AND THE MUSLIMS
While the Crusaders did not win back the Holy Land from the Muslims, they did gain a greater appreciation for the many literary, mathematic, and scientific advances of the Islamic world. As students will learn in Chapter 13, contact with these advancements helped to fuel a cultural rebirth in Europe. Ask students what they think the Portuguese gained from their contact with Africa. (new markets for trade, areas to colonize)

◆ **ANSWER** Portugal was able to control East African trade by conquering the city-states or making agreements with them. The city-states did not work together to stop Portugal.

D. The Kingdom of Zimbabwe

Purpose-Setting Question
Which two rivers served as the borders of the ancient kingdom of Zimbabwe? (the Zambezi and Limpopo Rivers)

TEACH PRIMARY SOURCES
The Great Zimbabwe enclosure had a circumference of 820 feet and was the largest single ancient structure south of the Sahara. Scientists have estimated that the structure contains 120,000 tons of stone. Among objects unearthed in the ruins was Ming Dynasty pottery from China, showing that Zimbabwe carried on extensive trade.

Global Connections

THE CRUSADES AND THE MUSLIMS
Portugal thought that by capturing African Muslims, Christianity would remain strong. In the Middle Ages, European knights went on Crusades to the Middle East to capture the Holy Land from Muslims. The Europeans thought that they had a more advanced civilization than the Muslims. However, when they arrived, they saw that Islamic civilization was very advanced.

These are the stone ruins of the Great Zimbabwe.

Portugal Gains Control

For a long time, Portuguese explorers from the European country of Portugal had been seeking a route to India that did not require going all the way around the southern tip of Africa. Vasco da Gama, the famous explorer, first came to the Swahili coast in A.D. 1498. The Portuguese were impressed with the wealth of the region. Five years later, da Gama returned, prepared to do battle. He demanded that the towns declare loyalty to Portugal and pay tribute every year. If a town refused, it was attacked and looted. The first city-state to fall was Zanzibar around A.D. 1500.

The town of Malindi agreed to the terms. A few years later, Portugal attacked Mombasa and Kilwa. Both towns fell to the Portuguese forces. Portugal believed that by conquering these African Islamic towns, it was preventing the downfall of Christianity.

The city-states of Swahili had never formed an alliance. They were not accustomed to working together for a common goal. They were not prepared to fight an enemy attacking from the sea with cannons. The Portuguese forces won and built a fort. Portugal controlled the East African trade after this time. However, the empire Portugal was building was too large to control. The forts that had been built in Swahili towns were abandoned by the end of the seventeenth century.

◆ **Why was Portugal able to control East African trade?**

D. The Kingdom of Zimbabwe

In southern Africa, several great kingdoms developed and faded in the years between A.D. 1000 and 1500. The Shona were a Bantu-speaking people. By about A.D. 1000, they settled between the Zambezi and Limpopo Rivers in present-day Zimbabwe. Zimbabwe was in a rich region that contained large amounts of gold, copper, and iron.

Zimbabwe's Economy

The Shona farmed, raised cattle, and traded. People living near the Zimbabwe plateau in southern Africa had learned to mine gold around the ninth century. Within the next several hundred years, the people of Zimbabwe expanded their gold and ivory trade as far as Asia. Kilwa was the coastal city to which they sent their items for trade. In exchange for gold and copper, the people of Zimbabwe imported Chinese porcelain.

Rulers demanded gold and ivory as tribute from the people in the large area that they controlled. In the 1100s, the wealthy rulers in this kingdom began building large stone enclosures around their villages. About 200 zimbabwes, a word that means "stone buildings," have been found in this southeastern area of Africa. The enclosures were home to society's most important people: kings, priests, and court officials. Great Zimbabwe was probably the largest and most important of these enclosures. Ordinary people lived in mud huts in the area outside the walls.

Teaching Options

Great Zimbabwe

Over a period of 400 years, the settlement known as Great Zimbabwe was almost completely enclosed. The walls were more than 16 feet thick and 30 feet high. No mortar—a mixture of sand or crushed stone and water—was used to hold the stones together. This technique for building stone walls was called <u>dry</u> <u>stone</u>. The walls seem to slope because each level of stone was set back a bit from the one it sat on.

There were many rooms and mazelike passageways inside the Great Zimbabwe. The outer walls had decorative towers built along the top. The entrances were rounded. The walls were not built for defense but as a display of power.

When Europeans first explored Great Zimbabwe in the nineteenth century, they assumed that the queen of Sheba or King Solomon had built the city. They were mistaken. At the time, early explorers and archaeologists knew little about the advanced civilizations of Africa south of the Sahara.

During the thirteenth and fourteenth centuries, Great Zimbabwe reached the height of its power. Between 11,000 and 18,000 people lived at the site. Because of its location on the trade routes and by its control of cattle herds, the town grew wealthy.

A stronger kingdom to the north may have taken control of Great Zimbabwe in the late fifteenth century. Great Zimbabwe was later abandoned, perhaps because the land had been overfarmed or because the area suffered from droughts. Another explanation is that the population grew too fast. The supply of land and water may not have been sufficient to support the people. In addition, many trees were cut down for firewood. This action increased erosion of the soil. During the 100 years or so that the area prospered, a great deal of damage was done to the land.

◆ **What was unusual about the stone walls surrounding Great Zimbabwe?**

Review III

Review History
A. How did Aksum acquire its wealth?
B. What is King Lalibela best known for?
C. How did Ibn Battuta describe the city of Kilwa?
D. Why might the zimbabwes have been built?

Define Terms to Know
Define the following terms:
stela, dry stone

Critical Thinking
How did African trade increase the spread of cultural practices between Africa and the European continent?

Write About Geography
Write a persuasive essay about why farmers in ancient Zimbabwe should not damage their natural environment by overfarming and pollution.

Get Organized
UNDERSTAND SEQUENCE
Copy this flowchart onto a sheet of paper and fill in the boxes with the major events in the development of East African trade.

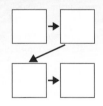

CHAPTER 10 ◆ Kingdoms and City-States in Africa **239**

Then & Now
ZIMBABWE'S NATIONAL SYMBOL
Within the Great Zimbabwe enclosure, large birds carved of soapstone sat on columns outside the palace. When the nation of Zimbabwe gained independence from Great Britain in 1980, one of these birds became the national symbol. The present nation of Zimbabwe is named in honor of this civilization.

Then & Now
ZIMBABWE'S NATIONAL SYMBOL
The Zimbabwe bird appears on the country's flag, seal, and airplanes. On the flag and seal, the bird is perched regally on a throne. On Zimbabwe airplanes, the bird is shown with wings back, as if in flight. While the bird is the country's national symbol, its official national bird is the fish eagle.

Focus Many of the Europeans who came to Zimbabwe in the 1800s believed that it was the legendary "Land of Ophir," the place in which King Solomon obtained the gold for his temple. There is evidence that ancient Great Zimbabwe did indeed have large deposits of gold and copper nearby, and it is possible that the area may have had a reputation as being a source of gold in biblical times.

◆ **ANSWER** The stone walls surrounding Great Zimbabwe were 16 feet thick and 30 feet high and were built with a technique called dry stone, which does not use mortar to hold the stones in place.

Section Close
Have students create a two-column chart (TR, p. 328) in which they list the four nations or regions from this section in the left column and the "most unusual or interesting feature" in the right column.

3 Assess

Review Answers

Review History
A. Aksum acquired its wealth through trade.
B. King Lalibela is best known for ordering that 11 underground churches be carved out of stone.
C. Ibn Battuta described Kilwa as "one of the most beautiful and well-constructed towns in the world."
D. Possible answer: to show power and provide protection from invaders

Define Terms to Know
stela, 234; dry stone, 239

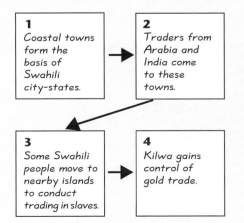

1	2
Coastal towns form the basis of Swahili city-states.	Traders from Arabia and India come to these towns.

3	4
Some Swahili people move to nearby islands to conduct trading in slaves.	Kilwa gains control of gold trade.

Critical Thinking
Possible answer: The merchants and traders exchanged ideas, languages, and customs, thereby spreading cultural practices between Africa and Europe.

Write About Geography
Students' paragraphs will vary, but should mention that by depleting the land of natural resources, it will make it too damaged to farm.

CHAPTER 10 Review

Chapter Summary

A blank outline form is available in the Teacher's Resources (p. 318). Chapter summaries should outline the early civilizations in Africa, the rise of major kingdoms in West Africa, and the development of trading nations in East Africa. Refer to the rubric in the Teacher's Resources (p. 340) to score students' chapter summaries.

Interpret the Timeline

1. Kush becomes a powerful civilization.
2. about 300 years
3. A.D. 350, Aksum becomes a powerful military force; A.D. 590, Persians conquered Aksum
4. Check students' work to ensure that all events are from the chapter.

Use Terms to Know

5. matriarchal
6. lineage group
7. oba
8. dry stone
9. mansa
10. savanna
11. stela

Check Your Understanding

12. Africa is ranked second in area and population among the continents.
13. The desert is hot, sandy, and dry. The savanna has tall grasses, bushes, and trees. The forest has many different types of evergreen trees. Less than 20 percent of Africa is forest and 8 percent of that is tropical rain forest.
14. 750 B.C. Kush conquered Egypt. After being conquered by the Assyrians in 663 B.C., Kush moved its capital to Meroë and reached its peak between 250 B.C. and 150 B.C.
15. The Bantu-speaking people probably originally lived in the present-day Cameroon-Nigeria border area; then, moved south to Namib Desert area and then east to the Great Lakes of Africa.
16. Possible answer: The people belonged to an extended family and a lineage group; members were expected to take care of one another.
17. Salt was used as a spice and also to keep meat from spoiling in the heat, and people from becoming dehydrated; it was traded for an almost equal amount of gold.

Chapter Summary

Complete the following outline in your notebook. Then, use your outline to write a brief summary of the chapter.

Kingdoms and City-States in Africa

I. Early Civilizations in Africa
  A. The Geography of Africa
  B. Early African Civilizations
  C. Daily Life in Africa
II. Major Kingdoms of West Africa
  A. Ghana, the First Large Empire of West Africa
  B. The Kingdom of Mali
  C. The Songhai Empire
  D. Other West African Kingdoms
III. Major Kingdoms of East Africa
  A. The Ancient Kingdom of Aksum
  B. The Kingdom of Ethiopia
  C. The Region of Swahili
  D. The Kingdom of Zimbabwe

Interpret the Timeline

Use the timeline on pages 220–221 to answer the following questions.

1. Which occurred first, Kush becomes a powerful civilization or Sundiata captures the capital of Ghana?

2. How many years after Kush established a powerful civilization did it conquer Egypt?

3. **Critical Thinking** Which events involve the rise and fall of the kingdom of Aksum?

4. Select four events from the chapter that are not on the timeline. Create a timeline that shows these events.

Use Terms to Know

Select the term that best completes each sentence.

dry stone   matriarchal   savanna
lineage group   oba   stela
mansa

5. A culture in which women are the most powerful members is called _____.

6. Several extended families combined into larger communities are called a _____.

7. A king of a city-state in ancient Africa is called an _____.

8. A method of building that requires no mortar is called _____.

9. A _____ is a village head who later becomes the head of the empire.

10. A grassland with plants and scattered trees that can resist drought is called a _____.

11. A tall narrow column that is usually carved is called a _____.

Check Your Understanding

12. **Identify** Africa's rank in area and population among the continents.
13. **Describe** briefly the three geographic regions of Africa.
14. **Summarize** the rise of the kingdom of Kush.
15. **Describe** where Bantu-speaking peoples originally lived.
16. **Describe** family life in an early African village.
17. **Discuss** the importance of salt in African trade.
18. **Describe** the development of Islamic culture in Mali.
19. **Identify** three West African kingdoms.
20. **Explain** why Aksum was a successful trade center.
21. **Summarize** how the culture of Aksum survived.
22. **Discuss** the effect of Portuguese explorers on Swahili city-states.
23. **Discuss** the expansion of Zimbabwe's trading.

18. Possible answer: Mali had a rich culture based on Islam; Mansa Musa continued to develop the Islamic culture by establishing universities so that people could study the writings of Islam.
19. Hausa, Yoruba, Benin
20. It had a port on the Red Sea, Adulis.
21. Aksum culture and religious traditions spread south to Ethiopia after the Muslims conquered Adulis in A.D. 700.

22. Portuguese explorers attacked the towns and took over the trade.
23. Zimbabwe expanded their gold and ivory trade as far as Asia. The people of Zimbabwe sent their items for trade to Kilwa. In exchange for gold and copper, they imported Chinese porcelain.

Critical Thinking

24. Draw Conclusions Why was the spread of ironmaking so important?

25. Make Inferences What effect did Islam have on African cities?

26. Compare and Contrast How did the rulers of Zimbabwe differ from the mansas in the kingdom of Mali?

27. Cause and Effect What effect did Mansa Musa have on the kingdom of Mali?

28. Make Predictions What do you think happened to the walls that completely enclosed the settlement of Great Zimbabwe?

Put Your Skills to Work

29. Write a Persuasive Essay Write a persuasive essay in which you convince modern African nations to construct a museum that highlights the significance of trade in African history.

Use the graphic organizer below to help you prepare your essay. Remember to use as many facts as possible to construct your argument.

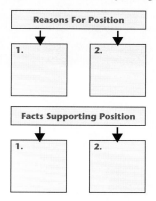

Analyze Sources

30. Read the following quotation about the discovery of ruins believed to be the lost palace of a famous ancient queen—Sheba—who traveled throughout Ethiopia. Then, answer the questions that follow.

[E]very find, however remote, was tied to the Mediterranean world, wherever possible. Such was the case with Great Zimbabwe in central Africa in 1871, where [a] German geologist became convinced that he had found the queen of Sheba's lost palace, on the grounds that a wooden lintel support beam smelled the same as his cedarwood pencil!

a. Who was looking for the queen of Sheba's lost palace?

b. For what reason did the geologist think he had found the queen of Sheba's lost palace?

Essay Writing

31. Use details from the chapter to write an essay that describes how trade expanded in ancient Africa, allowing people to exchange goods, services, and ideas throughout the world. Then, explain what impact this ancient trade network has on our lives today.

TEST PREPARATION

CHRONOLOGICAL
Read the question below and choose the correct answer.

Which sequence best shows the ruling kingdoms of West Africa?

1. Ghana, Songhai, Mali
2. Mali, Songhai, Ghana
3. Ghana, Mali, Songhai
4. Mali, Ghana, Songhai

Critical Thinking

24. Possible answer: Ironmaking allowed people to make stronger tools and weapons. They could farm more easily and defend themselves in war.
25. Possible answer: Muslims founded some African cities as centers of learning.
26. The rulers of Zimbabwe were concerned primarily with collecting tribute, while the mansa was the leader, both spiritually and legally, of the people.
27. Possible answer: Mansa Musa extended Mali's borders and increased trade, making the kingdom of Mali stronger and more powerful.
28. Possible answer: The walls are probably still standing because they were so thick.

Put Your Skills to Work

WRITE A PERSUASIVE ESSAY
29. Check students' graphic organizers to ensure that there are reasons and supporting facts for the positions of the entries. Students should use the information in their graphic organizers in their essays.

Analyze Sources

30a. a German geologist
30b. A wooden support beam smelled the same as the geologist's cedarwood pencil.

Essay Writing

31. Students' essays will vary but should explain how trade caused the exchange of ideas and explain how the ancient networks impact life today.

TEST PREPARATION

Answer 3. Ghana, Mali, Songhai

Dynasties and Kingdoms of East Asia
500–1600
(pp. 242–267)

Chapter Objectives
- Compare and contrast the political, social, and cultural achievements of the Tang and Song Dynasties.
- Discuss the effects of the Mongol conquest of China, and the subsequent rise of the Ming Dynasty.
- Understand the relationship between Korea and China and the cultural interaction between India, China, and other Southeast Asian countries.
- Describe Chinese and Korean influence on early Japanese culture and the development of a feudal society in Japan.

Chapter Summary
Section I focuses on the influence of the Tang and Song Dynasties in China.

Section II discusses the Mongol conquest of China, the expansion of the Mongol Empire, and the rise of the Ming Dynasty.

Section III explores the influence of Chinese culture on Korea and the Chinese and Indian influences on other countries in Southeast Asia.

Section IV focuses on the influence of China and Korea on early Japanese culture, the emergence of Japanese tradition during the Heian period, and life in feudal Japan.

Set the Stage
TEACH PRIMARY SOURCES

Explain that the scholar Cho'oe Malli strongly opposed using a new Korean writing system because it would make adapting Chinese culture impossible. How does he refer to the status of the Korean people if the Chinese writing system is discarded? (barbarians) How would developing a distinctly Korean script make Korea independent of China? (It would create a distinctly Korean culture and reinforce the Korean people's identity.)

CHAPTER
11

Dynasties and Kingdoms of East Asia
500–1600

I. Great Chinese Dynasties
II. The Mongol Empire and the Ming Dynasty
III. Korea and Southeast Asia
IV. Japan: An Island Empire

China dominated eastern Asia for more than 1,000 years. The art, literature, and philosophy of China influenced the cultures of its neighbors. Neighboring countries used the Chinese government as a model for their own governments. To do otherwise was often unthinkable to many people. When the Korean king created a new writing system for Korea, a scholar wrote,

> ❝ It has been said that the barbarians are transformed only by means of adopting Chinese ways; we have never heard of the Chinese ways being transformed by the barbarians. . . . Now, however, our country is devising a Korean script separately in order to discard the Chinese, and thus we are willingly being reduced to the status of barbarians. ❞

Despite the Korean king's actions, most states along the borders of the Chinese Empire continued to adapt Chinese culture to their own needs.

CHAPTER EVENTS

589 Sui Wendi reunifies China.

668 Korea is unified under the Silla Dynasty.

794 Japanese capital is transferred to Heian.

500 — **750** — **1000**

WORLD EVENTS

622 Muhammad flees from Mecca to Medina.

1054 Permanent split occurs between Roman Catholic and Eastern Orthodox Churches.

242 UNIT 3 ◆ Regional Civilizations

Teaching Options

Chapter 11 Resources

REVIEW

Teacher's Resources (TR)

Terms to Know, p. 24
Review History, p. 58
Build Your Skills, p. 92
Chapter Test, pp. 137–138
Concept Builder, p. 227
Venn Diagram, p. 323
Transparencies 1, 7

ASSESSMENT

Section Reviews, pp. 248, 255, 259, 265
Chapter Review, pp. 266–267
Chapter Test, pp. 137–138

ALTERNATIVE ASSESSMENT

Portfolio Project, p. 312
Travel Brochure, p. T312

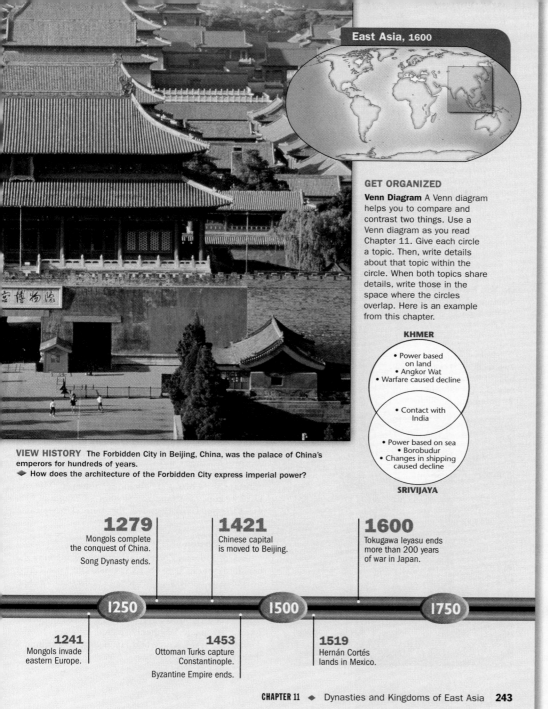

East Asia, 1600

GET ORGANIZED

Venn Diagram A Venn diagram helps you to compare and contrast two things. Use a Venn diagram as you read Chapter 11. Give each circle a topic. Then, write details about that topic within the circle. When both topics share details, write those in the space where the circles overlap. Here is an example from this chapter.

KHMER
- Power based on land
- Angkor Wat
- Warfare caused decline

- Contact with India

- Power based on sea
- Borobudur
- Changes in shipping caused decline

SRIVIJAYA

VIEW HISTORY The Forbidden City in Beijing, China, was the palace of China's emperors for hundreds of years.
◆ How does the architecture of the Forbidden City express imperial power?

1279
Mongols complete the conquest of China. Song Dynasty ends.

1421
Chinese capital is moved to Beijing.

1600
Tokugawa Ieyasu ends more than 200 years of war in Japan.

1250   1500   1750

1241
Mongols invade eastern Europe.

1453
Ottoman Turks capture Constantinople.
Byzantine Empire ends.

1519
Hernán Cortés lands in Mexico.

CHAPTER 11 ◆ Dynasties and Kingdoms of East Asia   **243**

Chapter Themes
- Culture
- Individuals, Groups, and Institutions
- Power, Authority, and Governance
- Global Connections
- People, Places, and Environments
- Time, Continuity, and Change

F Y I

The Forbidden City
The Forbidden City lies within the Inner City, which is one of two, large rectangular areas in the Old City of Beijing. The other area is called the Imperial City. Because only the emperor's household was permitted to enter the Forbidden City, this area was given its distinctive name. Today, the buildings are preserved as museums, which are visited by tourists from all over the world.

Chapter Warm-Up
USING THE MAP
Point out the locator map at the top of page 243. To help students understand where East Asia is, have them identify Europe, Africa, Australia, the Pacific Ocean, and the Indian Ocean. Ask them to identify the other oceans and continents.

VIEW HISTORY
Point out some of the features of Chinese architecture that are evident in this photograph of the Forbidden City, such as the massive tiled roofs supported by intricate wooden supports and terraces. Ask how the people in the photograph might have been feeling as they approached the Forbidden City. (They were probably in awe of the architectural and political achievements of ancient China.)

◆ **ANSWER** Possible answer: Students may refer to the size and number of the buildings.

GET ORGANIZED
Venn Diagram
Discuss the Venn diagram on page 243. Remind students that they used this diagram in Chapter 9 (p. 199). Ask students to identify where the shared idea is recorded. (in the overlapping part of the circles) Remind students that a Venn diagram is used to show similarities and differences between two topics. Encourage students to make a Venn diagram for each section. (TR, p. 323)

● TEACH THE TIMELINE
The timeline on pages 242–243 covers the period between 589 and 1600, which is about 1,000 years of history. Ask students to identify the type of events that are referred to in the Chapter Events entries. (political events, dynasties, war, and the transfer of capital cities) Which event in the World Events entries takes place in North America? (Hernán Cortés lands in Mexico.)

Activity
Writing Have students choose one of the World Events on the timeline to research. Then, have them write a summary of the causes that led to the event they selected.

I. Great Chinese Dynasties (pp. 244–248)

Section Summary

In this section students will learn how the Sui and Tang Dynasties reunified China and achieved a golden age of culture. They will also learn about China's tremendous economic growth during the reign of the Song rulers.

1 Introduce

Getting Started

Ask students if they have ever been in a school when a new principal arrived or when a new teacher started in the middle of the school year. Encourage students to describe how this person affected the way the school or class was run. Explain to students that China had many new rulers, all of whom changed the way the country was governed.

TERMS TO KNOW

Ask students to read the terms and definitions on page 244 and find each term in the section. Have students write each term on the front of an index card and a sentence using the term in context on the back of the card. Students may add terms for the other sections.

You may wish to preview the pronunciation of the following terms from this section with students.

Sui Wendi (SWAY WEHN dee)
Changan (chahng AHN)

ACTIVE READING

Have students consider the viewpoints of the Tang and Song emperors reflected in the reforms made under each of the dynasties. Ask them to summarize these viewpoints on a two-column chart (TR, p. 328). Based on their summaries, encourage students to explain the reasons for these different points of view.

Terms to Know

tributary state a conquered state that makes payments, called tributes, to the conquering state

absentee landlord a landowner who lives elsewhere while earning money from landholdings

Do You Remember?
In Chapter 4, you learned about the Han Dynasty, Confucianism, and Daoism.

This painting shows the large boat of Emperor Yangdi. The brief Sui Dynasty ended with Yangdi's assassination.

Main Ideas

A. The Sui and Tang Dynasties reunified China on the model of the Han Dynasty.

B. China experienced economic growth under the Song Dynasty.

C. China reached a golden age of culture under the Tang and Song Dynasties.

Active Reading

POINTS OF VIEW

People often have different points of view on history. As you read this section, think about the points of view of the people described. Then, ask what explains each viewpoint.

A. The Sui and Tang Dynasties

You have learned that one of China's greatest dynasties, the Han, came to an end in 220. The period following the collapse of the Han Dynasty was one of almost constant war for more than 300 years. Invaders poured into the empire and settled in the north, where they set up kingdoms. They all wanted China's resources.

In this time of disorder, Buddhism grew in popularity. This religion had been introduced into China about 100. By 500, it had spread throughout China. At times, Buddhism conflicted with Confucianism and Daoism. However, Buddhism adapted to Chinese culture, and eventually Buddhism, Confucianism, and Daoism all existed together.

The Sui Dynasty

The Sui Dynasty began when a Chinese general took over the throne of a northern kingdom. This general went on to conquer the south and to reunify China in 589. He took the name of Sui Wendi.

Wendi founded the Sui Dynasty. He and his son, Yangdi, began a program to restore the glory of the Chinese Empire. They increased the power of the central government, built a system of roads and canals to unite northern and southern China, and repaired the Great Wall. The high cost of the construction and constant wars brought rebellions, however. The Sui Dynasty ended with the assassination of Yangdi in 618. After the Sui Dynasty ended, the Tang Dynasty came to power.

Tang Expansion

In 626, Tang Tai Zong became emperor, marking the beginning of the Tang Dynasty. Under the Tang, China expanded its borders farther west than ever before. The dynasty included new territories in central Asia and Southeast Asia. China's influence also remained strong over certain **tributary states**. These were conquered states that made payments, called tributes, to the conquering state. Korea and Japan were two tributary states of the Tang Dynasty.

Teaching Options

Section 1 Resources

Teacher's Resources (TR)
Terms to Know, p. 24
Review History, p. 58
Build Your Skills, p. 92
Concept Builder, p. 227
Venn Diagram, p. 323

F Y I

Zen Buddhism

In China, Buddhism focused on moral standards, as well as on the concepts of rebirth and life after death. Chinese Buddhists looked to the many gods they worshiped for help in difficult times. One school of Buddhism, Zen Buddhism, originated in ancient China. There, it was called Chan. This form of Buddhism emphasizes a close relationship between pupil and master.

Tang emperors restored and improved the civil service system in which citizens helped to manage the government and keep its records. The emperors issued a new law code and demanded that an accurate population count, or census, be made. A Board of Censors was created to expose wrongdoing in government. Emperor Tai Zong wrote,

❝ The emperor, living in the palace, is blocked from direct access to information. For fear that faults might be left untold or defects unattended, he must . . . elicit loyal suggestions and listen attentively to sincere advice. ❞

Tang emperors began a program of land redistribution. Large estates were broken up, and land was given to peasants. The poor peasants could then support themselves and pay taxes.

One of the best-known Tang rulers was Wu Zhao, the only woman emperor of China. Wu Zhao had left home at the age of 13 to work at the Tang court. Her intelligence and ability paid off. Eventually, she married the emperor, Kao Tsung, and became empress. When her husband became ill, Wu Zhao ran the government. When Kao Tsung died, she took the title of emperor so that she could officially rule China. In China, only emperors ruled.

Wu Zhao was a skilled but cruel ruler. Anyone who threatened her power was executed, and in time the people came to hate her. At age 83, she was driven from office by a group of generals.

Prosperity of the Tang

In the time between the Han and Tang Dynasties, the population of China increased greatly. Much of the population increase was in the area of the Chang Jiang (Yangtze River) in the south. As the population of the south grew, the primary farming region moved to the area surrounding the Chang Jiang. The largest crop in China changed as well. The north produced mostly wheat, but rice was the south's main crop.

China prospered under the Tang. The system of roads and canals made trade and travel in China easier. The largest canal was the Grand Canal. It linked the Huang He (Yellow River) with the Chang Jiang. The Grand Canal made it possible for grain from the south to be transported to the capital in the north. The canals also made communication easier.

As the empire prospered, the large cities grew. The capital, Changan, was one of the largest cities in China. Changan lay at the end of the trade route through central Asia. The city was laid out like a checkerboard, with long straight avenues. The population of the city and nearby areas reached almost 2 million. Many foreigners visited the capital, and foreigners brought the religions of Christianity and Islam to China.

ANALYZE PRIMARY SOURCES
DOCUMENT-BASED QUESTION
Why does Emperor Tai Zong value direct access to information?

For 15 years, Wu Zhao ruled as emperor—the only time a woman would do so in Chinese history.

A. The Sui and Tang Dynasties

Purpose-Setting Question What were the most important achievements of the Sui Dynasty? (It increased the power of the central government, built roads and canals, and repaired the Great Wall.)

Do You Remember?
Remind students of the different beliefs and religions they have studied, along with ones they know personally. You may wish to suggest that students review pages 83–84 and 85–87 of Chapter 4.

Activity

Make an idea web Have students make an idea web (TR, p. 321) to connect information about the important ways in which the Tang Dynasty changed ancient China. (**Center circle:** Tang Dynasty changed ancient China. **Outer circles:** conquered new lands; improved civil service system; made new code of laws; distributed land to peasants)

ANALYZE PRIMARY SOURCES

DOCUMENT-BASED QUESTION
This quotation is from a text written in 648 in which Tai Zong, near the end of his life, expressed his views on how a monarch governs effectively. It was written as advice to his heir apparent. Ask students whether or not they think his successor should follow this advice. Have them support their opinions.

ANSWER He valued direct access because otherwise the emperor might overlook problems in the empire that he does not know about.

Meet Individual Needs:
VISUAL/SPATIAL LEARNERS

To help students understand the rise and fall of the Tang Dynasty, have them create a two-column chart (TR, p. 328) with the headings *China During the Tang Dynasty* and *Fall of Tang Dynasty*. They should list important details under each heading. Ask students to compare their completed charts.

ESL/ELL STRATEGIES

Summarize Have pairs of students work together to write summaries of the subsection, "Prosperity of the Tang." Remind them that their summaries should restate the main ideas of the section in their own words. Ask pairs of students to take turns reading their summaries to each other.

B. The Song Dynasty

Purpose-Setting Question How did the Song emperors change China? (They reunited the country and made the government more efficient. Because the army was poorly equipped and trained, China was defeated in wars on its northern border.)

Activity

Make a chart Have students create a main idea/supporting details chart (TR, p. 319) to identify the important economic reforms of Wang Anshi. (**Main Idea:** Wang Anshi improved the Chinese government income. **Supporting Details:** low-cost loans to peasants; regulated farm prices; reformed the military; improved the civil service)

Focus Discuss with students the benefits of improved strains of rice and the ability to raise two crops per year. Remind students that many peasant farmers were able to raise only enough food for themselves. Help students understand that having a surplus of crops resulted in a healthier population, and some people no longer had to grow crops to live, but could produce other products.

Using the Map
China, 618–1126

Ask students what red and green indicate on the map. (They show the boundaries of the Tang and Song Dynasties during different time periods in China's history.) Have them locate major waterways, along with the Grand Canal. Where are the major cities located? (Three of the cities are located on or near the Huang He and Chang Jiang. Hangzhou is located near the coast.)

✔ Map Check

Answer Nanjing

Tang Decline

The Tang Dynasty began to decline in the mid-700s. There were wars at the borders and a struggle for power. Revolts began to break out, and the last Tang emperor was forced to leave office in 907. China once more broke into smaller, warring states.

◆ What led to prosperity in Tang China?

B. The Song Dynasty

In 960, General Tai Zu took control of one of China's northern kingdoms. Over the next 18 years, he and his successor once again united China. The Song Dynasty, which Tai Zu founded, lasted until 1279.

Song emperors improved on the government policies of the Tang, making government more efficient. In Song China, the importance of the military was reduced. The army that remained was poorly equipped and trained. China was not able to stand against invaders. As China was repeatedly defeated in wars on its northern borders, the victorious armies demanded large tributes from China.

The Reforms of Wang Anshi

Frequent wars were costly, and government expenses continued to increase. By 1041, the military spent almost 80 percent of the annual budget.

In 1069, the government finally took action to solve the economic crisis. The emperor appointed Wang Anshi to make reforms, or changes, in the government. Wang looked for new ways to increase government income. First, the government gave low-cost loans to peasants. These loans helped poor peasants and the interest on the loans earned money for the government. In addition, the prices of farm products were regulated. Wang also reformed the military and reduced its size and improved the civil service. Civil service examinations—which tested candidates for government positions—were changed to test practical subjects, such as economics, law, and medicine.

The reforms of Wang Anshi did not last, however. Some government people opposed his reforms. Political opponents had him removed from office twice, the last time in 1085.

During 1125 and 1126, Song China suffered a great disaster. The Jurchen people of central Asia took over northern China. They forced the Song people to move their capital to Hangzhou in the south. The Jurchen established the Jin Dynasty in the north. Song China never recovered its lands in the north, but it did exist in the south until 1279.

Song Prosperity

The Song Dynasty was a golden age for the Chinese economy, technology, and arts. Farm production greatly improved under the Song. Farmers developed new strains of rice that allowed two crops of rice to be cultivated in a year. Better

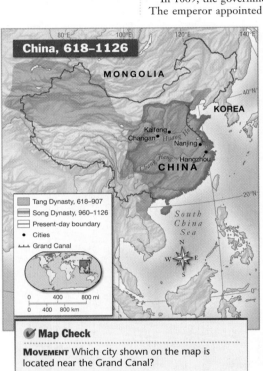

China, 618–1126

MONGOLIA

KOREA

Kaifeng
Changan • *Huang He*
Nanjing •
Chang Jiang Hangzhou
CHINA

South China Sea

Tang Dynasty, 618–907
Song Dynasty, 960–1126
Present-day boundary
• Cities
Grand Canal

0   400   800 mi
0   400   800 km

✔ Map Check

MOVEMENT Which city shown on the map is located near the Grand Canal?

Teaching Options

Test Taking

Explain that multiple-choice format questions sometimes ask students to identify the main idea and then choose a supporting detail of a reading passage. Have students practice this skill by reading the second paragraph under the "The Reforms of Wang Anshi" on this page. Have them choose the sentence that best expresses the paragraph's main idea. (first sentence)

Conflict Resolution

Discuss the ways in which conservative bureaucrats expressed their opposition to Wang Anshi's reforms. Ask students to explain how they can express their dissatisfaction with the way in which an elected class or school official is handling a problem. (Possible answer: They can attend class or student council meetings and express their opinions there. They can circulate a petition. They can vote for another candidate in the next election.)

tools and irrigation also helped with farm production. Fewer farmers needed to work the land to produce the same amount of food.

The biggest advances, however, were in technology. Gunpowder was first introduced as a weapon in the early 900s. New methods of casting iron included the use of water-powered machines. Ceramic production also improved and increased. Porcelain, a type of ceramic, was developed in the 1100s. A mathematical device called the abacus became the main calculating tool of east Asian merchants. The abacus makes use of beads on wires to add, subtract, multiply, and divide. Improvements in shipbuilding and development of the magnetic compass helped ocean travel.

The Chinese economy boomed. Roads and canals made transportation much cheaper. Trade increased dramatically, both within China and with other countries. This increased trade caused more goods to be produced. Cities that were centers of trade began to appear. Chinese goods were in high demand across Asia and Europe.

◆ **What advances in technology were made in Song China?**

C. Culture and Society Under the Tang and the Song

During the golden age of the Tang and Song Dynasties, the arts flourished. The prosperity of this time set the pattern of Chinese society for many centuries to come.

The Arts

The new wealth encouraged development of the arts in China. Much of the art of the period was an improvement to Chinese and other Asian traditions. Porcelains became finer. In architecture, multistoried buildings became more common. The Indian stupa, a large domed Buddhist structure, became the Chinese pagoda, a multistoried tower.

Landscape painting became a major art form in the Song Dynasty. Literature also reached new heights under the Tang and Song Dynasties. Better education and improved methods of printing led to the spread of literature and knowledge. Popular stories blended romance and adventure.

Chinese art flourished during the Song Dynasty. This piece shows women ironing silk. It was painted by the Song emperor Hui Zong, who loved art and taught himself to paint.

CHAPTER 11 ◆ Dynasties and Kingdoms of East Asia **247**

Connection to
MATH

Explain that the abacus is a simple device that can be used to add, subtract, multiply, divide, and calculate square roots and cube roots. Have pairs of students research the abacus and make a diagram of the device. Ask student pairs to make up a simple mathematical problem and explain to the group how to solve it.

Connection to
ART

Chinese porcelain, which was first made during the Tang Dynasty, and later produced in royal factories during the Song Dynasty, became world famous. The Chinese used a dark outline to separate each color in a design. Ask students to study examples of Chinese porcelain in classroom, library, or Internet resources. Then, have them create their own designs.

Discuss Ask students how different advances in technology during the Song Dynasty affected both Chinese economy and culture. (Possible answer: The development of porcelain created an important product that could be exported; the use of the abacus enabled merchants to make more precise calculations; the development of the magnetic compass resulted in improved trade and communications with other countries.)

SPOTLIGHT ON ECONOMICS
CASH AND PAPER NOTES Although the Chinese began using paper money during the 600s, it was not used in Europe until the 1600s. Ask students how the use of paper notes during the Song Dynasty might have solved some of the problems created by a coin-based currency. (The lightweight paper notes were easier to carry and to use than coins for conducting business. Also, merchants could more easily hide paper money while traveling.)

◆ **ANSWER** In Song China, advances were made in the use of gunpowder as a weapon, new methods of casting iron, ceramic production, development of porcelain, calculation on the abacus, improvements in shipbuilding, and development of the magnetic compass.

C. Culture and Society Under the Tang and the Song

Purpose-Setting Question How did the arts change during the Tang and Song Dynasties? (Arts were encouraged, porcelain became finer, more multistoried buildings were built, landscape paintings became a major art form, and literature reached new heights.)

Discuss Ask students to name some conditions that are necessary for the arts to flourish. (peace, good crops, educated people, leisure time) Then, discuss how these conditions were met during these dynasties.

Make an idea web Have students make an idea web (TR, p. 321) to show the connection between the Tang and Song Dynasties and the arts in China. (**Center Circle:** artistic change during the Tang and Song Dynasties; **Outer Circles:** finer porcelain; Chinese pagoda; impressionistic landscape paintings; spread of literature and knowledge)

Extend Footbinding, which began during the Tang Dynasty, was still practiced in China during the twentieth century. At the age of seven, a girl's feet were bound by wrapping them tightly in cloth and sewing the cloth together. Then, a cotton thread was used to connect the front and rear of the bound foot. Generally, girls' feet were rebound on a weekly basis. This process was extremely painful. After each rebinding, the girl was given slightly smaller shoes to wear. In one memoir, a Chinese woman noted that as a result of the binding, her feet were only 3 inches long. Many women were not able to stand or walk much if their feet were bound.

◆ **ANSWER** Merchants did not make and produce goods; they earned their money from the work of others.

Section Close

Ask students to evaluate the Sui, Tang, and Song Dynasties by listing the accomplishments and problems during each period on a three-column chart.

This photograph shows a Chinese woman with bound feet.

Social Order

China had a well-ordered society under the Tang and Song emperors. At the head of their society was the emperor, who ruled over a court of aristocrats. Beyond the court, most people were peasants, merchants, and wealthy landowners.

Peasants made up the bulk of the population. They often found employment in the army or in mines. Many of those jobs were in the cities. The cities, as a result, grew rapidly during this period.

The demand for education increased. Any male could take the civil service examinations. If a talented peasant boy was educated and passed the examinations, he could become a civil servant. As a civil servant, both he and his family would rise in status.

Merchants grew wealthier. However, merchants had a lower social status than peasants did, because they did not produce anything. They earned their money from the work of others.

The gentry was a class of wealthy landowners. Many of the gentry were **absentee landlords**, people who lived elsewhere while earning money from their land. They either rented their property or paid others to work their fields and harvest their crops.

In general, the status of women declined during this time. In Confucian tradition, women were considered inferior to men. This was especially true in wealthy families in the cities, where the custom of footbinding arose. Girls' feet were tightly bound with strips of cloth, preventing the feet from growing. In time, tiny feet were seen as a sign of feminine beauty.

Chinese society and culture built on and improved past traditions. The Sui, Tang, and Song Dynasties picked up where the Han had left off. Like Rome, the ideal of the Chinese Empire survived. Unlike the Roman Empire, which never revived in anything but name, the Chinese Empire was rebuilt.

◆ **Why was the status of merchants so low in the Tang and Song societies?**

Review I

Review History
A. What made trade and travel easier in the Tang Dynasty?
B. What affected the economic growth of Song China?
C. What was the importance of education in Tang and Song China?

Define Terms to Know
Define the following terms: **tributary state, absentee landlord**

Critical Thinking
Why do you think that Wang Anshi's reforms met with so much opposition?

Write About Economics
Write a short essay on the relationship between technology and the economy in Tang and Song China.

Get Organized
VENN DIAGRAM
Use a Venn diagram to organize information from this section. Choose a topic and then find supporting details. For example, what were the similarities and differences of the Tang and Song Dynasties?

Review Answers

Review History
A. a system of roads and canals, including the Grand Canal
B. Construction of roads and canals, development of technology, and foreign trade all affected the growth of the Song economy.
C. The education system trained people to serve in government. Education helped people rise in status because anyone who could pass the civil service exams could become a civil servant.

Define Terms to Know
tributary state, 244; absentee landlord, 248

Critical Thinking
Conservative bureaucrats opposed modification of ancient traditions.

Write About Economics
Students should discuss how agricultural techniques, new inventions, and improved transportation helped the economy.

Tang

Borders expanded; peasants taxed; new code of laws

Bureaucracy; civil service exams; economic prosperity; culture developed

Military reduced; north conquered by others; technology advanced

Song

Build Your Skills

COMPARE AND CONTRAST

When you compare and contrast two or more items, you look for both their similarities and their differences. Comparing and contrasting items can help you better understand the information you read and the visuals you see.

When you study history, you may compare and contrast such things as literature, artwork, events, cultures, and points of view. Comparing and contrasting two things can help you understand them more clearly. For example, it can be useful to compare and contrast cultures to better understand the different elements of those cultures.

Here's How
Follow these steps to compare and contrast.
1. Find out what is being compared and contrasted.
2. Identify the similarities between the two items.
3. Identify what is different about the two items.

Here's Why
Comparing and contrasting can help you understand how societies change over time, how cultures are different, and how to distinguish different points of view.

Practice the Skill
The two paintings below show Chinese women. The painting on the left shows women at work picking fresh tea leaves that will be dried later. The painting on the right shows women, probably from a wealthier class, flying kites. Study the paintings carefully. Then, follow the directions in *Here's How* to compare and contrast the two paintings.

Extend the Skill
Create a Venn diagram that compares and contrasts the two paintings. Include information about the location, clothing, activities, and subjects of the two paintings.

Apply the Skill
As you read the remaining sections of this chapter, continue to compare the different Chinese dynasties and kingdoms as well as different artifacts from them. Create Venn diagrams to help you distinguish similar and different characteristics.

This painting shows a group of women flying kites.

This painting shows two women picking tea leaves.

CHAPTER 11 ◆ Dynasties and Kingdoms of East Asia **249**

Teaching Options

RETEACH
Have students exchange the Venn diagrams they prepared in *Extend the Skill* with a partner and then review the diagrams. Tell students to underline the similarities with a red pencil and the differences with a blue pencil. Discuss what words help to tell the reader which is a similarity and which is a difference between the paintings.

CHALLENGE
Ask pairs of students to identify an issue that has been the subject of debate in their school or community. Have them use a Venn diagram (TR, p. 323) to illustrate the way supporters and opponents feel about the issue. On the diagram they should illustrate how the points of view are similar and different. Have student pairs display their diagrams in class.

Build Your Skills

COMPARE AND CONTRAST

Teach the Skill
Invite students to brainstorm how they make comparisons and contrasts when evaluating events, objects, and situations in their daily lives. For example, they may compare and contrast types of computers or other electronic equipment, clothes, television programs and movies, or the candidates in a school election.

Briefly discuss the three steps in *Here's How* with the group. Point out the importance of first identifying what is being compared and contrasted, next identifying similarities, and finally identifying what is different about the two items.

Then, have students work in small groups to discuss times when they've had to compare and contrast—for example, two recent movies they have seen, school plays, or books that they are reading for another class. Ask a volunteer from each group to explain how using the three steps in the *Here's How* helped them understand the topics.

Practice the Skill
Similarities: Both show Chinese women; both take place outside and show nature.
Differences: The pictures show differences in clothing styles. The picture on the left is a close-up, the colors are paler, more details are shown, and it seems more realistic; the picture on the right is a landscape, it has less detail and stronger colors.

Extend the Skill
Provide students with a Venn diagram. (TR, p. 323) Remind students that similarities are recorded in the overlap area and differences in the outer circles.

Apply the Skill
Students may also consider other comparisons for their Venn diagrams (TR, p. 323), such as the technology or culture of different dynasties.

CHAPTER 11 ◆ **T249**

Section Summary

In this section students will learn about the rise of the Mongol Empire, which brought economic stability to the area, and the subsequent decline of the empire. They will also learn about the effect of Mongol rule on Chinese culture, and how the Ming Dynasty restored Chinese rule.

1 Introduce

Getting Started

Ask students to think about a time in their lives, such as when they worked on a school committee, when a strong leader controlled a group and would not tolerate any opposition. How did students feel? What steps did they take to resolve the conflict?

TERMS TO KNOW

Ask students to read the terms and definitions on page 250 and then find each term in the section. Point out that one of the words ends with the suffix *-ion*. Have students use a dictionary to find the meaning of the suffix and look for other examples of words ending in *-ion* as they read this section.

You may wish to preview the pronunciation of the following terms from this section with students:

Kublai Khan (KOO bluh KAN)
Ibn Battuta (IHB uhn bat TOO tah)

ACTIVE READING

Suggest that students use a cause-and-effect chain (TR, p. 325) to identify the causes and effects of events described in one of the subsections in Section 2.

Section II

The Mongol Empire and the Ming Dynasty

Terms to Know

clan a group of families with a common ancestor
succession the order by which rulers follow one another in office

Main Ideas

A. The Mongol Empire fostered economic growth.
B. The Ming Dynasty restored the glory of the Chinese Empire.

Active Reading

CAUSE AND EFFECT
Almost all events have causes and effects. As you read this section, concentrate on what caused the events and what effects those events had later on. Then, pause to write down what you have learned.

A. Mongol Conquest and the Yuan Dynasty

North of China lie the vast grasslands of the Eurasian steppe. Chinese power had often extended into this region. Various nomadic tribes lived on the steppe. Among these were the Mongolian tribes. These nomads were expert horsemen and skilled warriors. The Great Wall, which had been built under Shi Huangdi in 221 B.C., was intended not only to keep these people out, but to impress them with the power of the empire. No attempt was made to permanently conquer this region.

Many times, however, these nomads raided or invaded the Chinese Empire. The wall failed to keep them out, but it did impress them with the wealth of the empire. In fact, many of these nomadic tribes wanted to share China's prosperity. As you have learned, one such tribe, the Jurchens, set up the Jin Dynasty in the north.

The Mongolian leader Genghis Khan raided and eventually defeated the Jin Dynasty in northern China.

The Mongols made up another group of nomads that successfully invaded China. Early on, the Mongols were divided into **clans** and tribes with no leader and no common goal. A clan is a group of families with a common ancestor. In 1206, Genghis Khan united the Mongols into a fierce fighting group.

The Mongol Invasions

Genghis Khan began a series of invasions of nearby states. He began with the kingdom of Xixia. The Mongols destroyed cities and killed the inhabitants. Soon their reputation as fierce, brutal invaders became widely known.

In 1211, Genghis Khan turned his attention to China and the Jin Dynasty. In his first invasion, he destroyed the capital city of the Jin Dynasty. He also gained the services of many people of the conquered region. One of these men, Yelu Chucai, convinced him not to completely destroy China. Instead, Yelu taught the Mongols how to collect taxes and encourage industry. The Mongols also learned how to use gunpowder.

During the 1200s, the Mongols continued to expand their empire. They conquered a Turkish empire in central Asia. This empire included rich cities along the Silk Road, a famous trade route.

Teaching Options

Section 2 Resources

Teacher's Resources (TR)
Terms to Know, p. 24
Review History, p. 58
Build Your Skills, p. 92
Concept Builder, p. 227
Venn Diagram, p. 323
Transparencies 1, 7

ESL/ELL STRATEGIES

Use Manipulatives Have students make a set of index cards with sequence words, such as *first, next, then, after, before, finally,* and *last.* Explain that these words help order events. Have students use the words to help them summarize the events that are in this section. Have pairs of students share the summaries and make necessary changes.

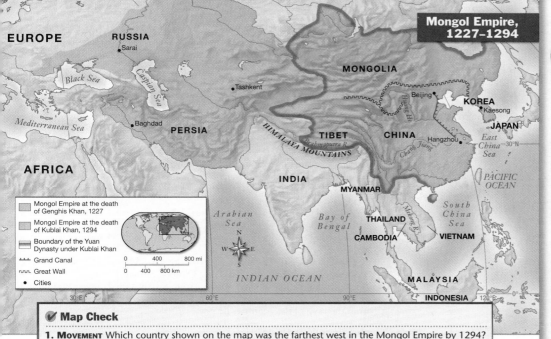

EUROPE
RUSSIA
• Sarai
Black Sea
Caspian Sea
MONGOLIA
• Tashkent
Beijing •
KOREA
• Kaesong
JAPAN
Mediterranean Sea
• Baghdad
PERSIA
TIBET
CHINA
Hangzhou •
East China Sea
30°N
AFRICA
HIMALAYA MOUNTAINS
Brahmaputra R.
Chang Jiang
PACIFIC OCEAN
INDIA
MYANMAR
South China Sea
Arabian Sea
Bay of Bengal
THAILAND
Mekong R.
N
W   E
S
CAMBODIA
VIETNAM
INDIAN OCEAN
MALAYSIA
INDONESIA
30°E   60°E   90°E   120°E

Mongol Empire at the death of Genghis Khan, 1227
Mongol Empire at the death of Kublai Khan, 1294
Boundary of the Yuan Dynasty under Kublai Khan
Grand Canal
Great Wall
• Cities

0   400   800 mi
0   400   800 km

✔ Map Check

1. **MOVEMENT** Which country shown on the map was the farthest west in the Mongol Empire by 1294?
2. **PLACE** Which Chinese city did the Yuan Dynasty rule that Genghis Khan did not?

Although Genghis Khan died in 1227, his sons and grandsons continued his conquests. The Jin Dynasty was finally conquered in 1234, and the takeover of Russia was completed by 1241. The expansion continued in the west and south. Song China, despite its weakness, held out for several decades before being defeated.

Genghis Khan's grandson Kublai Khan completed the conquest of China. He became the Great Khan in 1260 and ruled until 1294. He adopted the Chinese name of Yuan for his new dynasty in 1271 and continued the campaign against the remaining Song. The last resistance to the Mongols was crushed in 1279. Kublai Khan became the first foreigner to conquer all of China.

The Mongol Empire

The Mongol Empire spread across much of Asia. It stretched from China west to Russia and Persia. It was the largest empire the world had yet seen. Because the empire was too large for one person to rule directly, it was divided into four parts. Kublai Khan ruled over all four. The Mongol Empire lasted for just over 100 years.

The Mongols allowed people to live much as they had before in most of the empire. They allowed their subjects to continue with their own governments as long as they paid tribute. In conquered lands, they tolerated the religions of the conquered people. Religious establishments were free from taxation. The Mongol Empire included many Buddhists, Daoists, Muslims, and Christians. In many parts of the empire, Mongols adopted local religions.

Spotlight on
Geography

MONGOL CONQUEST
Geography helped determine just how far the Mongols were able to travel and conquer. On horseback, they were able to cross the flat, open areas of the steppe very easily.

Mountains, seas, and the dense northern forests proved difficult barriers for them. However, the Mongols did develop a type of navy, which was used in their successful invasion of south China.

CHAPTER 11 ◆ Dynasties and Kingdoms of East Asia **251**

---

2 Teach

A. Mongol Conquest and the Yuan Dynasty

Purpose-Setting Question How did China become part of the Mongol Empire? (Genghis Khan invaded China in 1211, destroying the capital city. His grandson, Kublai Khan, completed the conquest and adopted the dynastic name of Yuan.)

Using the Map

Mongol Empire, 1227–1294

Ask students what the different colored areas indicate on the map. (They show the boundaries of the Mongol Empire at the deaths of Genghis Khan and Kublai Khan.) Have students compare the relative sizes of the Mongol Empire in 1227 and 1294. (The empire was about twice as large in 1294.) Ask students to identify the regions and countries that were within the boundaries of the Yuan Dynasty. (Mongolia, Tibet, China, Korea)

✔ Map Check
Answers
1. Russia
2. Hangzhou

SPOTLIGHT ON GEOGRAPHY

MONGOL CONQUEST Show students Transparency 7 and ask them to consider the geography of China and to speculate why the Mongols used a navy to invade south China. (Ships could invade China from the South China Sea and the Pacific Ocean, which would be faster and easier than going overland from the north.)

Discuss Ask students to identify the advantage and the disadvantage of dividing the Mongol Empire into four parts. (**Advantage:** It was easier to govern. **Disadvantage:** Each kingdom would have a strong national identity and might revolt.)

Activity

Make a timeline Have students create a timeline (TR, p. 320) with the important events on pages 250–251 presented in chronological order.

F Y I

Gers

The nomadic Mongols lived in tentlike structures called gers. They were made of wooden poles covered with animal skins or handwoven cloth. Inside the tents were all the items the family required to live and travel. The tents were carried on large wooden wagons drawn by oxen. Modern nomadic Mongolian families still live in tents similar to those used by their ancestors.

Meet Individual Needs:
VERBAL/LINGUISTIC LEARNERS

Have students write a summary of the contributions of Genghis Khan and his grandson Kublai Khan in creating the Mongol Empire. Ask students to read their summaries aloud in small groups and discuss which Mongol leader contributed more to the establishment of the empire.

IBN BATTUTA World traveler Ibn Battuta wrote *Rihlah (Travels)*, one of the most famous travel books in history. His love of travel stemmed from his desire to learn about new places and peoples. Throughout his life he followed his own rule, "Never travel any road a second time." Because of his great fame, many rulers gave him money, which enabled him to continue his adventures. During his travels, he visited Egypt, Syria, Arabia, Africa's eastern coast, Crimea, India, Spain, and Constantinople. Have students identify some of the places he visited on the world map on pages A1–A2 of the Atlas or Transparency 1.

Discuss Ask students how the Silk Road affected the exchange of ideas between different cultures. (China exported its cultural, scientific, and technological advancements westward. Trade, which would have facilitated this cultural exchange, flourished between Southeast Asia and China.)

Extend Explain to students that some historians have questioned whether Marco Polo actually visited China at all. These historians point out some of the fictional events he describes, such as birds that could fly with elephants, and the fact that he is not mentioned in any accounts written in China. Other historians defend Marco Polo and are confident that he was in China. Discuss with students why there are different interpretations of historical information.

Review You may want to remind students that they read about the Silk Road in Chapter 4. Have them identify important cities along the trade route on the map on page 83.

Make a chart Have students create a two-column chart (TR, p. 328) to identify the advantages and disadvantages of Mongol rule in China. (**Advantages:** trade flourished; cultural exchange with west expanded; numerous building projects; **Disadvantages:** Chinese were discriminated against; heavy taxes; only Mongols and non-Chinese people could hold important government positions.)

Global Connections

IBN BATTUTA
The Arabs were the most traveled people in the world in the 1300s. Ibn Battuta was the ultimate traveler. He traveled from West Africa to China, India, and Indonesia. On his journeys, he met many Muslims and Arabs. He studied with great scholars. He was a guest of rulers. He even met one Arab traveler in China, and later met the man's brother in the Sahara!

Marco Polo lived in China during the reign of Kublai Khan. Stories of his travels informed Europeans about Asian culture.

Mongols and Trade

The Mongols brought peace and stability to their large empire. Although the north of China was devastated by the initial Mongol invasion, the south was left almost untouched. Peasants continued to farm the land. The large estates of the wealthy were left intact. The cities were left as centers of commerce. Trade flourished during this time, especially along the Silk Road. Chinese culture and ideas traveled west with traders along the Silk Road. Printing, paper money, gunpowder, porcelain, art, and medical advances all made their way west. The Mongols also established a postal system along the highways of their empire. The postal system was one of the Mongols' greatest achievements during Kublai Khan's rule. He created the postal system so that information could be sent and received more quickly. He ordered new roads and more than 1,400 postal stations to be built throughout China.

An Italian merchant, Marco Polo, traveled to China during the time of Mongol control. He spent 17 years in the court of Kublai Khan during the late 1200s. He wrote a book about his travels, *Description of the World*, in which he described the wonders of China. At the time, Europeans thought it was too fantastic to be believable. Many of the details of Polo's journey were later shown to be true.

Muslim merchants traded successfully along the Silk Road. By sea and land, trade between southwest Asia and China flourished. The Arab scholar Ibn Battuta traveled throughout Asia and North Africa between 1325 and 1355, along the Arab trade routes. His writings are the most detailed accounts from the time of the countries he saw.

Mongol Rule in China

The Mongols used the Chinese system of government to rule over China. They kept the system of the Tang and Song Dynasties. The Mongols were few in number, so they relied on the Chinese to fill the posts in the government. The civil service examinations were suspended for a while but then reinstated.

The Mongols taxed China heavily, using different systems in the north and the south. Peasants paid their taxes in goods and labor rather than in money. Using the vast wealth of China, the Mongols started huge building projects. They rebuilt the Grand Canal, which had fallen out of use in the late 1100s and early 1200s. The canal connected the south with the new capital of Beijing. Along the canal, the Mongols built a new paved highway.

Mongol Effects on Chinese Culture

Unlike many other foreign invaders, the Mongols made an effort to keep their own culture. The Mongols kept their native dress. They also kept their customs and language. They were the only fully nomadic people to conquer China. The Mongols were determined not to become absorbed into Chinese culture as many other conquerors had been.

The Mongols did not treat the Chinese people as equals. Only Mongols or other non-Chinese people could hold important positions in the government. Even punishments for crimes varied between the Mongols and the Chinese. For example, if a Mongol was found guilty of a crime, he might receive a fine, whereas a Chinese criminal might be executed for the same crime. Marriage between different groups of people was forbidden.

Under the Mongols, China came into direct contact with the West. Merchants, missionaries, and travelers came from Europe and southwest Asia into China. However, increased contact with the West had little lasting effect on Chinese culture.

Teaching Options

Research

AVERAGE
Have students research Marco Polo's life, particularly his travels with his father and uncle to Asia. Distribute copies of the outline map of the world (TR, p. 330). Ask small groups to show the route the Polos followed after they sailed from Venice in 1271 until Marco Polo arrived in the Chinese city of Yangzhou.

CHALLENGE
Have students read and summarize a chapter or section in a translation of Marco Polo's famous book, *Description of the World*, in which the adventurer told the world about Kublai Khan's empire. Ask small groups of students to use their summaries to discuss Marco Polo's impressions of thirteenth century China.

Decline of the Mongols

Chinese people hated the Mongol invaders for devastating China. Marco Polo described the hatred of the Chinese people for the Mongols:

> ❝You must understand that all the Cathayans [Chinese] hated the government of the Great Khan, because he set over them Tartar rulers, mostly Saracens [Arabs and Turks], and they could not endure it, since it made them feel that they were no more than slaves. ❞

After Kublai Khan's death, Mongol rule over China weakened. Disputes over **succession** to the throne caused chaos. Succession is the order by which rulers follow one another in office. A series of rulers took over the throne, but the Chinese people rebelled against these rulers. The country experienced other problems as well. The Chang Jiang flooded repeatedly, ruining farmlands. Fifteen years of famine devastated the north. China was falling into ruin.

◆ How were Chinese people treated under Mongol rule?

B. The Ming Dynasty

In the 1350s, several rebel leaders challenged the Yuan Dynasty—the dynasty that Kublai Khan had established in 1271. The rebel leaders struggled against each other and against the last of the Yuan rulers. The eventual victor was Zhu Yuanzhang.

ANALYZE PRIMARY SOURCES

DOCUMENT-BASED QUESTION
According to Marco Polo, why did Chinese people hate the Mongols?

This Ming Dynasty painting shows what the summer residence of the Ming emperors might have looked like.

< Connection to ------------
LITERATURE ◁- - - - -

Using the notes he kept during his years in China, Marco Polo dictated the story of his travels. In his book, Polo described many Chinese customs, including the postal system, the use of coal as fuel, and the use of paper currency, all of which were unknown in Europe at the time. The book was copied by hand and read throughout Europe.

F Y I
Chinese Paper

The ancient Chinese developed paper about 2,000 years ago. Originally they made paper from hemp or the inner bark of the mulberry tree. Later they obtained paper from a pulp made by pounding rags, rope, or old fishing nets. Early Chinese paper was too coarse to be used for writing, so it was used for wrapping and clothing instead.

Discuss Ask students what cultural and geographical factors made China less affected by the Mongol conquest. (Possible answer: The size of the country and the fact that the Mongols remained culturally distant from the Chinese probably left the country less affected by the conquest.)

ANALYZE PRIMARY SOURCES

DOCUMENT-BASED QUESTION
This quotation is from Marco Polo's account of his adventures in China, *Description of the World*. In the book, he describes the cultural, scientific, and technological achievements of Kublai Khan's empire.

ANSWER According to Polo, the Chinese hated the Mongols because the Mongols used members of other groups as rulers and the Chinese felt they were treated like no more than slaves.

Activity

Make an idea web Have students make an idea web (TR, p. 321) to identify the factors that contributed to the decline of the Mongol Empire. (**Center Circle:** decline of Mongol Empire; **Outer Circles:** disputes over succession; rebellions; famines; floods)

◆ **ANSWER** The Mongols allowed the Chinese people to live much as they had before they were conquered as long as they paid tribute. They tolerated the religions of the Chinese. However, Chinese people could not hold important government jobs, and they were severely punished for crimes.

B. The Ming Dynasty

Purpose-Setting Question How did the Chinese finally overturn Mongol rule? (After defeating other rebel leaders, Zhu Yuanzhang threw out the Mongols and founded the Ming Dynasty.)

Discuss Ask students how the government in China changed during Hong Wu's rule. (Hong Wu introduced new laws and organized the government so that many high officials reported directly to him.) Discuss with students how these changes might have made the government and country stronger.

Explore Ask students how the economic revival under the first Ming emperor affected agriculture and industry. (Building irrigation systems and restoring canals resulted in land being reclaimed. This in turn led to increased farm production. New technologies, increased demand, and reconstruction brought increased production.)

WHERE IN THE WORLD?

THE FORBIDDEN CITY The site of the Forbidden City was added to UNESCO's World Heritage List in 1987 because of its importance as the center of Chinese power for about 500 years and for its impressive architecture. In the late twentieth century, several of the palace buildings were restored. Ask students how restricting access to the Forbidden City affected the relationship between the Chinese people and their rulers. (Possible answer: It probably reinforced the sense of isolation of the ruling family and a lack of connection between commoners and rulers; however, it also added to the ruler's mystique.)

Activity

Write a dialogue Have small groups of students write a dialogue or script of a meeting between a person who lives in the Forbidden City and a high government official. Have the official explain conditions for most people in China. Then, have the person from the Forbidden City try to understand the explanation based on the life he or she knows.

Focus Ask students what the building complex in the Forbidden City illustrated about life in China during the Ming Dynasty. (Possible answer: The buildings illustrate the power and authority of the Ming rulers and their emphasis on Chinese achievements in art and architecture. They also illustrate the separateness of the Chinese rulers from the ordinary people and everyday life.)

THE FORBIDDEN CITY
The Ming palace in Beijing is known as the Forbidden City. It is actually a huge walled area with many buildings. The emperor's family lived there. Just outside was the Imperial City, where government officials worked.

Few people were allowed to enter the Forbidden City. Common people never could.

Chinese women weave silk into cloth in this detail from a Ming Dynasty vase.

Zhu was born a peasant, but he made himself into the leader who threw the Mongols out of China. In 1368, he defeated the last of his rivals. He gave himself the name of Hong Wu, and he founded a new dynasty, which he called the Ming, meaning "brilliant." As the first Ming emperor, he ruled China for 30 years.

Rebuilding China

Hong Wu took steps to make China a strong country again. He introduced new laws and organized the government so that many high officials reported directly to him. Hong Wu, who had grown up poor, was concerned about China's poor people. He established laws to protect poor farmers from rich and powerful nobles and made it a crime to take land from them.

After decades of war and natural disasters, the first Ming emperor began to rebuild China. He rebuilt irrigation systems and repaired canals. New forests were planted in some areas. Farm production rose.

The reconstruction increased trade and production of goods. Goods once again had a large market, and increased demand brought higher production. New technologies also increased production.

Overseas trade also increased. New crops were introduced from the Americas. The Chinese no longer relied on middlemen, like the Arabs, for trade. Chinese merchants sailed abroad with Chinese goods.

In 1421, the capital of the empire was transferred to Beijing. Beijing was located at the edge of the empire. The Ming emperors lived in the Forbidden City, a huge palace complex surrounded by walls. The emperors lived in splendor in the city's many palaces, courtyards, and gardens.

The emperor's family often moved from one palace to another. Other buildings in the Forbidden City contained large reception halls in which the emperor met with his officials and important foreign visitors.

Chinese Voyages

Hong Wu's successors wanted to impress others with Chinese power. They gathered and trained a large army and attacked neighboring countries. To show off the wealth and power of the empire, Ming emperors sent out expeditions of exploration by sea.

The most famous expeditions of the Ming Dynasty were commanded by Zheng He, a Muslim admiral. Zheng He's fleet included more than 300 ships and a crew of almost 28,000 men. His immense fleet went on seven expeditions around Southeast Asia and the Indian Ocean between 1405 and 1433. The expeditions demonstrated the power and technology of China.

After Zheng He died in 1433, there were no more expeditions past Southeast Asia. Historians have long debated why. Some historians suggest that such distant expeditions were too expensive at a time when money was needed to fight wars with Mongolia. Others have thought that those who had gained power after Zheng He's death opposed the expeditions.

Teaching Options

Using Technology

Have small groups of students use Internet resources to research the layout of the building complex in the Forbidden City in Beijing. Ask them to print a copy of the first page of each Web site they visit in order to keep a log of their research. Encourage the groups to discuss the results of their research. Focus discussion on how students decide if a Web site is a valid research tool.

Connection to ART

Calligraphy, the art of fine handwriting, originated during the Shang Dynasty and was used in many Chinese paintings. Ask students to research and study examples of Chinese calligraphy and its use in scroll paintings. Have them make their own scroll paintings on drawing paper, using very fine paintbrushes and black ink. Encourage students to share their work.

Cultural Flowering of the Ming

The Ming Dynasty saw a further development of literature and the arts. Ming artists created new styles of portrait and landscape painting and created beautiful blue and white porcelain. Chinese porcelain came to be called "chinaware" or just "china" in the West. Ming writers preferred the novel to other forms of fiction. New printing techniques allowed more books to be printed.

In the 1500s, the Ming period also saw the first influence from western Europe. Europeans and Chinese exchanged ideas and technology directly. Both cultures were exposed to new knowledge in mathematics, astronomy, medicine, and weapons.

Decline of the Ming

In the early 1600s, a group called the Manchu became a serious threat to the Ming Dynasty. A Ming general asked the Manchus to enter China to help him put down a rebellion. The Manchu then captured Beijing, and 15 years later put down the rebellion. In the meantime, the leader of the Manchu declared himself emperor. He set up a new dynasty called the Qing, meaning "pure."

◆ **What were Hong Wu's rebuilding and repairing efforts?**

The Ming Dynasty is probably best known for its beautiful porcelain craftsmanship.

CHAPTER 11 ◆ Dynasties and Kingdoms of East Asia **255**

Review II

Review History
A. How did Mongol rule encourage trade?
B. What was the purpose of Zheng He's expeditions?

Define Terms to Know
Define the following terms:
clan, succession

Critical Thinking
Why do you think the Mongols tolerated the religions of the Chinese people?

Write About Government
Write an editorial about Chinese opposition to Mongol rule. Explain the reasons for opposition and the results of the opposition.

Get Organized
VENN DIAGRAM
Use a Venn diagram to organize information from this section. Choose a topic and then find supporting details. For example, how were the Yuan and Ming Dynasties alike and different?

Focus During the Ming period, Chinese artists used a blue and white underglaze, which was applied to a piece of porcelain before the final glaze. This porcelain became world famous. In addition, artists frequently painted on the underglaze with enamel colors. Ask students to describe the techniques used on the vase from the Ming Dynasty shown on page 255. (It appears to have a blue-and-white underglaze with red or rust enamel added.)

Activity

Make a flowchart Have students make a flowchart of the events that led to the decline of the Ming Dynasty and related events. (**Box 1:** Ming general asked Manchus to help put down rebellion; **Box 2:** Manchu captured Beijing; **Box 3:** Manchu put down rebellion; **Box 4:** Manchu leader declared himself emperor.)

◆ **ANSWER** Hong Wu rebuilt irrigation systems, repaired canals, planted new forests, and improved farm production.

Section Close

Discuss with students the effects of the Mongol invasion and the Ming Dynasty on the area of present-day China. Encourage students to describe the changes that occurred as a result of these two empires.

3 Assess

Review Answers

Review History
A. Mongol rule brought peace and stability; the Mongols also built roads and canals.
B. Zheng He's expeditions were meant to demonstrate Chinese power and technology.

Define Terms to Know
clan, 250; succession, 253

Critical Thinking
Possible answers: The Mongols might not have felt that it was important for everyone to have the same religion, or they did not feel strongly about any particular religion.

Yuan

Foreign rulers; racial discrimination; conquered other areas

Heavy taxes; foreign trade expanded

Literature and arts grew; Chinese rulers; naval expeditions; new technology

Ming

Write About Government
Students' editorials might refer to the ways in which the Mongol rulers oppressed the Chinese people and how the Chinese felt about being considered inferior to the Mongols.

III. Korea and Southeast Asia (pp. 256–259)

Section Summary
In this section students will learn about the cultural interaction between Korea and China, as well as the blending of cultures of India and China with various countries in Southeast Asia.

1 Introduce

Getting Started
Ask students to discuss how people from different cultures live together in their community, enjoying each other's foods and traditions. Focus on the ways in which members of the community share their cultures at street fairs or other community events. Encourage students to talk about what they have learned about the traditions of their neighbors.

TERMS TO KNOW
Ask students to read the terms and definitions on page 256 and then find each term in the section. Have students write context sentences for each term. Ask student pairs to substitute the definitions for each term as they read their sentences aloud.

You may wish to preview the pronunciation of the following terms from the section with students.

Koguryo (koh goor YOH)
Paekche (PAK chuh)
Silla (SIH luh)
Srivijaya (sree WIH jaw yuh)
Khmer (kuh MER)
Angkor Wat (ANG kawr WAHT)
Anawrahta (an aoo RAHT uh)

ACTIVE READING
Have students choose one of the subsections in Section 3 and make a timeline (TR, p. 320) putting the major events in chronological order.

Section III — Korea and Southeast Asia

Terms to Know
refugee a person who flees to a foreign country

hangul an alphabet using symbols to represent the sounds of the Korean language

Main Ideas
A. Korea was strongly influenced by Chinese culture but maintained its own identity.

B. Countries of Southeast Asia mixed their own cultures with those of China and India.

Active Reading
SEQUENCE OF EVENTS
In order for history to make sense, you have to know the order in which events occurred. As you read this section, make a timeline and insert events on it in the order they happened.

A. Korea
Korea is a peninsula to the northeast of China. It is extremely mountainous with a few large, level plains. Only one-fifth of the land can be farmed. Korea does, however, have a long coastline, and especially along the western coast, Korea has many harbors and small islands. This long coast allowed many Korean people to earn a living by fishing. Located between China and Japan, Korea has often exchanged ideas and technology with both groups.

Early History
By the second century B.C., a kingdom had developed in northern Korea. In 194 B.C., a Chinese rebel seized the throne of this kingdom and ruled for many years. Then, in 108 B.C., the Han emperor invaded the Korean peninsula. He set up a military colony that survived for more than 400 years. The colony exposed the Korean people to Chinese culture.

Between A.D. 300 and 600, Korea formed three kingdoms that controlled the peninsula. These were Koguryo, Paekche, and Silla. The three kingdoms fought one another as well as with Chinese and Japanese forces.

Chinese influence in this period increased. The wars after the collapse of the Han Dynasty sent waves of **refugees** into Korea. A refugee is a person who flees to a foreign country. Missionaries introduced the Indian religion of Buddhism to Korea. Refugees and missionaries brought Chinese arts and learning with them. The northern kingdom of Koguryo fought off invasions from Sui China in the late 500s and early 600s.

Unified Korea
The kingdom of Silla united Korea in 668 with Chinese help. The rulers of Silla joined with the Tang emperor of China. Working together, the armies of Silla and China conquered Paekche and Koguryo. Then, Silla drove the Tang from Korea.

During the early 900s, a new kingdom challenged Silla rule. Koryo, from which the country of Korea is named, took control of the peninsula.

✔ Map Check

LOCATION Which kingdom borders two other kingdoms?

Teaching Options

Section 3 Resources

Teacher's Resources (TR)
Terms to Know, p. 24
Review History, p. 58
Build Your Skills, p. 92
Concept Builder, p. 227
Venn Diagram, p. 323
Transparency 7

ESL/ELL STRATEGIES

Use Resources Tell students that the word *geography*, like many of the words in our daily vocabulary, comes to us from the ancient Greek. It is made up of two Greek roots, *geo-*, which means "relating to Earth" and *-graphy*, which means "writing." Ask pairs of students to use a dictionary or book of word histories to find the origins of five other words from this section.

This Yi Dynasty Korean scroll shows images from nature.

Koreans adopted Chinese arts and learning during this time. Artists produced works of art to rival those of China. Scholars used the Chinese language to read and write. Poetry and histories were written in Chinese. Korean potters also learned the art of making porcelain from the Chinese. Then, they perfected the technique of making celadon, a kind of porcelain with a green glaze.

Beginning in 1231, the Mongols invaded Korea six times in 30 years. The struggle ended in the early 1270s, when Korea became part of the Mongol Empire. Koryo kings were allowed to rule, but they had to pay large tributes to the Mongols. In addition, they were forced to build ships for the failed Mongol invasions of Japan.

Yi Dynasty

In 1392, a general named Yi Songgye seized the throne and established the Yi, or Choson, Dynasty. The Yi Dynasty lasted until 1910. Yi Songgye gave a fresh start to the Chinese system of government in Korea. The civil service examinations became more difficult. The Ming criminal code was adopted in 1395. Yi adopted the ideas of Confucianism, and the influence of Buddhism shrank.

Korean culture, despite Chinese influence, remained different from that of China. Korean people still spoke their native language. In 1446, King Sejong introduced **hangul**, an alphabet using symbols to represent the sounds of the Korean language. Hangul was easier for Koreans to learn. Its use led to large numbers of Korea's people being able to read and write. Confucian scholars, however, did not like hangul. They claimed that it would isolate Korea and that it was against tradition. One official wrote,

> 66 Ever since the founding of the dynasty, our court has pursued the policy of respecting the senior state with the utmost sincerity and has tried to follow the Chinese system of government. . . . Although the letter shapes are similar to the old seal letters, the use of letters for phonetic value violates ancient practice and has no valid ground. 99

ANALYZE PRIMARY SOURCES

DOCUMENT-BASED QUESTION Why did Korean officials oppose the use of hangul?

The Yi Dynasty had frequent power struggles. In the 1590s, an ambitious Japanese warlord wanted to invade China through Korea. Korea was not prepared for the invasion. The Koreans used hit-and-run tactics of fighting against the Japanese invaders. They attacked Japanese ships using "turtle boats," which were ironclad warships. Still, the Japanese invaders devastated the countryside for six years before they were forced to leave.

 How did China affect Korean culture?

F Y I

Turtle Boats

The turtle boat was an ironclad warship that looked like a 100-foot long turtle. The boat had a long, rounded roof covered with spikes. In battle, the sails were lowered and the boat was powered by oars. Cannons, firearms, and arrows were housed in ports above the oars. In the front of the boat, smoke poured out from a dragon's head to terrify the enemy.

---

2 Teach

A. Korea

Purpose-Setting Question How was Korea exposed to Chinese culture? (A Han emperor set up a military colony in Korea.)

Using the Map

Korea, 300–668

Ask students what the names in capital letters on the map refer to? (They are the names of countries.) What country is southwest of Korea? (China)

✔ Map Check

Answer Silla

Discuss Ask students why Korea might have absorbed more from Chinese culture than from Mongol culture. (Possible answer: Mongols allowed Koryo kings to rule the country; they tended to mingle very little with the populations they conquered.)

Extend Tell students that originally celadon was plain, because the potters were more concerned with the beautiful color and the shapes of the vessels they produced than they were with ornamentation. However, from 1150 to 1250, inlaid celadon was produced. Korean artists invented the technique, which involves cutting designs out of the porcelain and then filling in the designs with white or black clay. Sometimes they scraped away the background and filled it in with the clay to make a reverse design.

ANALYZE PRIMARY SOURCES

DOCUMENT-BASED QUESTION

Some Confucian scholars opposed Korea's adoption of its own writing system. This quotation is from a document explaining the reasons for one official's opposition.

ANSWER The officials considered hangul to be a violation of tradition.

◆ **ANSWER** Koreans adopted Chinese arts and learning. The Chinese language was used by scholars, and poetry and histories were written in Chinese. Potters learned to make porcelain from the Chinese.

Angkor Wat in Cambodia was originally a Hindu temple. Its walls are covered with carvings of religious scenes.

B. Southeast Asia

Purpose-Setting Question How did India and China influence the region of Southeast Asia? (Southeast Asia lay along the trade routes between India and China and benefited when trade flourished. The cultures of India and China blended with the different cultures of Southeast Asia.)

WHERE IN THE WORLD?

ANGKOR WAT Angkor Wat was built as an administrative center for the Khmer Empire as well as a temple. A system of canals and moats represent the ocean that surrounds the Mountain of the Gods. After French archaeologists began restoring the site, many of the original sculptures were moved to museums. Restoration work on the complex was stopped in the 1960s because of political turmoil in Cambodia.

Discuss Ask students how the Han invasions affected the culture and government of Vietnam. (The invasion by the Chinese resulted in the establishment of the Nan Yue regime. Chinese immigrants brought their ideas of government, art, and Buddhism and Daoism when they settled in the region.)

Explore Have students use the map of Asia in the Atlas (p. A7) or Transparency 7 to locate the areas mentioned in this section, including Vietnam, Cambodia, Thailand, Sumatra, Malay Peninsula, Java, Borneo, Malaysia, and Myanmar (Burma). Discuss the location of these places and how they relate to each other.

Activity

Write an article Ask students to find out more information about the archaeological restoration of Angkor Wat using an encyclopedia or the Internet. Have them use their research to write a magazine article describing the scientific exploration of the site.

Where in the World?

ANGKOR WAT
The Hindu temple of Angkor Wat is one of the greatest achievements of the ancient Khmer people. Five towers that represent the Mountain of the Gods rise from the center. Walls, courtyards, and moats surround the towers.

Angkor Wat was abandoned in the 1430s and mostly forgotten. It was not until the early 1900s that it was excavated and restoration was begun.

B. Southeast Asia

The region of Southeast Asia is made up of a large peninsula and several large island chains. There are mountain ranges but also broad plains and river valleys. Southeast Asia's location along trade routes between India and China helped it prosper when trade flourished. Both Indian and Chinese cultures blended with the native cultures of Southeast Asia. These cultures stemmed from the early kingdoms of Nan Yue, Angkor, Srivijaya, and Pagan.

Vietnam

Some 2,000 years ago, the heart of what is now Vietnam lay in the Red River delta near the border with China. As a result of the Han invasion in 111 B.C., the region of Nan Yue was established. Many Chinese immigrants settled in the region, and Chinese ideas of government were introduced to the Vietnamese people. The immigrants brought with them the arts and learning of China and introduced Buddhism and Daoism.

At the end of the Tang Dynasty, Nan Yue broke free from Chinese rule. In the early tenth century A.D., Vietnamese leaders expanded their control of the country all the way to the Mekong Delta. Although Mongol invaders ravaged much of the country, they were not able to conquer it. Early Ming leaders tried to make Vietnam a province of China but were driven out by A.D. 1427.

Khmer

Angkor was the main city of the Khmer Empire, which included much of present-day Cambodia and Thailand. Unlike the Vietnamese, the Khmer people were never conquered by any foreign nations. Contact with outsiders came mostly through trade and missionaries from India. The Khmer adopted Indian writing, art, and architecture.

In the 500s and 600s, rulers began to unite the Khmer. The heart of the empire lay in the rice-growing area near the Tonle Sap, which means "great lake." It was in this area that rulers built the capital of Angkor. The greatest achievement of the Khmer Empire was the temple complex of Angkor Wat. King Suryavarman II built Angkor Wat in the early 1100s.

258 **UNIT 3** ◆ Regional Civilizations

Teaching Options

Test Taking

Tell students that essay questions sometimes ask them to compare and contrast two or more events, concepts, or historical figures. Making a list or chart can help students organize their thoughts about a topic. Have students make a two-column chart (TR, p. 328) to answer the essay question "How are the histories of Vietnam and Khmer alike and different?"

In the late 1100s and early 1200s, the Khmer Empire declined. Invaders captured Angkor Wat in the late 1180s. In 1431, Angkor was abandoned.

Srivijaya

Srivijaya began to grow in power around the year 600. It included the island of Sumatra and parts of the Malay Peninsula, Java, and Borneo in present-day Indonesia. Srivijaya controlled the Strait of Malacca, which grew in importance as trade routes shifted.

At the heart of trade routes, Srivijaya was exposed to many influences. Sumatra became a center of Buddhism. The Buddhist temple of Borobudur was built in Java around 778. Like Angkor Wat, it was covered in elaborate carvings. Then in the 1400s, the religion of Islam reached the kingdom.

Srivijaya faced attacks by southern Indian kings in the eleventh century and Mongols in the thirteenth century. Increased shipping from China reduced the importance of local Malay shipping. Weakened, Srivijaya would later face European attacks.

Pagan

Myanmar, which was once called Burma, is a region that borders India. For centuries, rival cities in the region competed with one another for control.

In 1044, King Anawrahta united the Burman people into the kingdom of Pagan. He brought Buddhism to the kingdom, making the city of Pagan a major Buddhist center.

The kingdom of Pagan flourished for 200 years after Anawrahta's death. In 1287, however, the Mongols invaded and conquered Pagan. Mongol rule was short-lived. When the Mongols left, Burma was again a divided region.

◆ **What was the greatest achievement of the ancient Khmer people?**

Then & Now

ISLANDS OF TRADE

Srivijaya was a huge country, stretching across a number of islands. The islands lay along thriving trade routes. A wide mix of peoples and cultures flourished in Srivijaya.

Today, the lands of Srivijaya are in Malaysia and Indonesia. Trade routes still pass through the islands. The modern city-state of Singapore is a major economic power because of this trade.

Review III

Review History
A. How did Chinese learning and arts influence Korea?
B. Why was Srivijaya able to prosper?

Define Terms to Know
Define the following terms:
refugee, hangul

Critical Thinking
What were the similarities and differences of the countries of Southeast Asia?

Write About Culture
Write a paragraph about the opposition to the adoption of hangul in Korea.

Get Organized
VENN DIAGRAM
Use a Venn diagram to organize information from this section. Choose a topic and then find supporting details. For example, how were Korea and Southeast Asia similar and how did they differ?

Korea

Influenced by China; used Chinese language; celadon; hangul

Mongol invasion; Buddhism; Chinese trade

Blend of Indian and Chinese cultures; influenced by other countries

Southeast Asia

Write About Culture
Answers should indicate that opponents of hangul feared that its adoption would make Korea an outsider in its own region of the world.

Discuss Ask students how the culture of the Khmer people was affected by making contact with outsiders through trade and missionary work, rather than as the result of invasion by foreign powers. (Possible answer: They were not forced to accept the culture of another country because of conquest. Instead, they had a freer cultural exchange with other countries.)

Then & Now

ISLANDS OF TRADE Due to its location, Singapore is a major center of trade today, just as it was in the 1200s and 1300s. Ask students to name cities in their state or region whose economy is linked to geography.

◆ **ANSWER** The greatest achievement of the Khmer people was the temple complex of Angkor Wat.

Section Close

Ask students to discuss whether China had a greater influence on Korea or on Southeast Asia and to give reasons for their opinions.

3 Assess

Review Answers
Review History
A. Koreans adopted Chinese arts and learnings. Scholars used the Chinese language to read and write. Poetry and history were written in Chinese. Korean potters learned the art of making porcelain from the Chinese and then perfected the technique of making celadon.

B. Srivijaya was able to prosper because it was located near the Strait of Malacca, which was crucial to trade routes.

Define Terms to Know
refugee, 256; hangul, 257

Critical Thinking
Similarities: All the countries were at least partly Buddhist; **Differences:** China influenced Vietnam, India influenced the rest of Southeast Asia; Khmer, Pagan, and Vietnam had agriculture-based economies; Srivijaya had an economy based on trade and maritime industries.

Section Summary

In this section students will learn how Japanese culture was affected by Korean and Chinese influences, and how Japanese traditions developed during the Heian period. They will also learn about the development of a feudal society in Japan.

1 Introduce

Getting Started

Ask students how peers sometimes influence their choice of clothes and their interests in music and popular entertainment. In the discussion, encourage students to talk about instances when they have rejected peer influence and made their own choices based on personal taste.

TERMS TO KNOW

Ask students to read the terms and definitions on page 260 and then find each term in the section. Have pairs of students create a crossword puzzle using the words and definitions in this section and the previous sections in this chapter. Ask student pairs to exchange papers and solve each other's puzzles.

You may wish to preview the pronunciation of the following terms from this section with students.

Yamato (yah mah toh)
Shotoku (shoh toh koo)
Heian (hayn ahn)
Fujiwara (fooj ee wah rah)
Kamakura (kah mah koor ah)
Toyotomi (toh yah toh mee)

ACTIVE READING

Have students write a general statement based on the main points of one of the subsections, such as *The Heian Period*. Suggest that they focus on identifying facts in the subsection to help them write their generalizations.

Section IV — Japan: An Island Empire

Terms to Know

tsunami a huge ocean wave that can sweep over land and destroy everything in its path

feudalism a system of government in which lesser lords owe service to greater lords

shogun the supreme military commander of Japan

daimyo a Japanese lord

samurai a Japanese warrior

Main Ideas

A. Ties with China and Korea strongly influenced early Japanese culture.

B. Chinese and Japanese cultures blended in the Heian period.

C. Changes in government produced a feudal society in Japan.

Active Reading

GENERALIZE
When you generalize, you make broad statements based on facts. As you read this section, concentrate on the main points of Japanese culture. Then, pause to make general statements about what you have learned.

A. The Geography and Early History of Japan

Japan, like Korea and Vietnam, has been strongly influenced by China. At the same time, Japan has also kept its own distinctive culture. Chinese influences merged with that culture.

Geographically, Japan is a chain of islands off the coast of east Asia. The four main islands are generally mountains. Four-fifths of Japan's land is too mountainous to farm, so people generally settled along the narrow coastal plains and in river valleys. Japan has suffered from volcanic eruptions and earthquakes. An off-shore, underwater earthquake can produce a **tsunami**. A tsunami is a huge, fast-moving wave that can sweep over land and destroy everything in its path.

The sea has dominated life in Japan. It provides the Japanese people with food and gives Japan a mild climate and plenty of rainfall. The sea has both isolated Japan and protected it from attack. The isolation has reduced the influence of other cultures on Japan.

Huge ocean waves, called tsunamis, can be more than 60 feet high and can cause terrible damage when they come on shore.

Teaching Options

Section 4 Resources

Teacher's Resources (TR)
Terms to Know, p. 24
Review History, p. 58
Build Your Skills, p. 92
Concept Builder, p. 227
Chapter Test, pp. 137–138
Venn Diagram, p. 323

ESL/ELL STRATEGIES

Organize Information Divide the class into three groups, and assign one of the subsections to each group. Have students read their subsection together to identify the main idea. Then, have them discuss the supporting details and work together to create an outline (TR, p. 318) of the subsection.

The people we know as Japanese migrated to Japan several thousand years ago. The Japanese migrants displaced an earlier group of settlers, the Ainu. The Ainu were pushed farther and farther north as more Japanese people colonized the islands.

Early Traditions

Early Japanese society was divided into two main groups, the uji and the be. Under each group there were several clans. Uji clans were aristocratic clans. Each clan had a hereditary chieftain and worshiped a clan god who was considered the ancestor of the clan. Clan leaders were also priests. Women often were leaders of their clans. Below the uji clans were the be clans. These clans were made up of people organized by occupation, such as farming and weaving. Most people belonged to a be clan.

The most powerful uji clan was the Yamato clan, which claimed to have descended from the sun god. By about 500, the Yamato clan dominated part of central Japan. This region became the heartland of the Japanese state. The Yamato organized the clans underneath it into ranks. Chief ministers to the early Yamato rulers came from the highest of these ranks. In 645, the ruler of the Yamato clan became emperor of Japan. He chose the rising sun as the symbol of his empire.

The early Japanese people worshiped kami, or nature spirits. They believed their spirits lived in natural wonders, such as waterfalls, mountains, great trees, and unusual rocks. Shrines were typically located in places of great natural beauty. A shrine is a place in which a saint or god is prayed to or honored. A shrine can be an altar, chapel, or any place that is sacred. The worship of kami came to be called Shinto, "The Way of the Gods." It is still practiced in Japan today. There are many Shinto shrines along the Japanese countryside. Shinto did not attract followers outside Japan.

Influences on Early Japan

Early Japan was open to influences from Korea and China. A steady flow of people moved from Korea to Japan until the early 800s. Immigrants brought their Korean and Chinese culture with them, including their knowledge of crafts, writing, literature, and art. They also brought Confucianism and Buddhism. Skilled immigrants were given a prominent place in Japanese society.

In the early 600s, a powerful Yamato prince became fascinated with China. Prince Shotoku was determined to have Japan adopt more of Chinese civilization. He encouraged Confucian values.

Shotoku also supported the growth of Buddhism. He and his successors sent students to acquire knowledge and skills in China. When they returned to Japan, they were given a great deal of respect.

The reforms of Prince Shotoku influenced Japanese society. Students who went to China brought back Chinese ideas, art, and technology. Japanese rulers created a government modeled after the Tang government. Japanese rulers called themselves emperors, but they had little power. Their code of law was similar to that of China. They divided the country into provinces, and people paid taxes on their land.

The Islands of Japan

CHINA

• Cities

0   150   300 mi
0   150   300 km

Sea of Japan

KOREA

Hokkaido

Honshu
Heian (Kyoto)
Edo (Tokyo)
• Nara

Shikoku

Kyushu

PACIFIC OCEAN

✔ **Map Check**

LOCATION On which island is Heian (Kyoto) located?

A. The Geography and Early History of Japan

Purpose-Setting Question Why was the sea so important in Japanese history? (Japan is a chain of islands surrounded by the sea, which provides the people with their food and a mild environment. The sea also isolated and protected Japan.)

TEACH PRIMARY SOURCES
Explain that the art on page 260 is an example of Japanese woodblock printing and presents a very stylized image of a tsunami wave. Ask students to discuss what the artist is showing the viewer about the tsunami wave. (Possible answer: The print illustrates the great force, size, and power of the wave.)

Using the Map
The Islands of Japan

Ask students to identify the four main islands of Japan and the bodies of water that surround the islands. (Kyushu, Shikoku, Honshu, Hokkaido; Sea of Japan, Pacific Ocean)

✔ **Map Check**
Answer Honshu

Discuss Ask students why the Yamato clan claimed descent from the sun god and how this claim affected the clan's power. (Claiming descent from the sun god, which was considered the greatest clan god, would have given the clan more power.)

Activity

Make an idea web Have students make an idea web (TR, p. 321) to show how Prince Shotoku's reforms affected the Japanese state. (**Center Circle:** effect of Shotoku's reforms; **Outer Circles:** government imitated Tang; leaders were called emperors; law code is similar to that of China; land was taxed; rulers had little power)

Writing

AVERAGE
Ask students to write a letter to a Japanese newspaper of the period in which they support or oppose Prince Shotoku's reforms. Remind them to clearly state their opinions in the first paragraph and support their points of view with facts. Have student volunteers share their letters in small groups.

CHALLENGE
Have students write a letter to the editor of a current newspaper supporting the idea of "selective borrowing," or the process of adapting some customs and rejecting others. Suggest that students support their argument with examples of selective borrowing in their lives or communities.

The Japanese emperor had the new capital city of Nara built in 710. The period from 710 to 784 is considered the highest point of Chinese influence on Japan. The emperor's palace had Chinese-style buildings. The court used Chinese ceremonies. Nobles studied Chinese literature and wore Chinese clothing. Scholars and officials wrote in Chinese. Confucianism and Buddhism spread, and pagodas, or multistoried towers, were built.

Japanese people did not completely adopt Chinese culture, however. In time, enthusiasm for Chinese culture declined. Japanese people kept some Chinese customs but not others. Sometimes they kept a custom only after changing it. This process is called selective borrowing. One example of selective borrowing is in government. The Japanese people adopted a Chinese-style government, but they did not adopt the civil service examinations. In the 800s, when the Tang Dynasty began to decline, the Japanese people lost interest in learning from China. They began to develop and change what they had already learned.

◆ **How did selective borrowing affect Japanese society?**

B. The Heian Period

Chinese influence did not disappear completely in Japan. In 794, the Emperor Kammu established a new capital city, Heian. Heian, like Nara, was built after the pattern of the Chinese city of Changan. Heian later became the modern city of Kyoto, which remained the capital of Japan until 1868.

The Heian period lasted from 794 until 1185. During that time, Chinese influence on Japan weakened. Chinese culture blended with Japanese culture. New, purely Japanese traditions emerged.

Heian Culture

During the Heian period, Chinese culture was adapted to Japanese tastes. Art and literature flourished. A new painting style developed.

Lady Murasaki wrote *The Tale of Genji*, the most famous literary work from the Heian period in Japan.

Japanese scholars developed a new writing system called kana, with characters that represent the sounds of the Japanese language. With the new kana, there was an explosion of literature in Japanese. Because only men were allowed to write in Chinese in the court, women wrote in Japanese. The most famous literary work of this period is *The Tale of Genji*, written by Murasaki Shikubu, a lady at the Heian court. It is a story about the romantic adventures of a fictional prince named Genji and his son.

The Heian Court

In the 800s, the Fujiwara, a wealthy court family, gained almost complete control of the Japanese government. The emperors had little political power. The Fujiwara held the real power. The Fujiwara were the greatest landholders in Japan and frequently married off their daughters to the heirs to the throne. Yet, they never tried to seize the throne itself.

During this time, Heian court nobles lived in luxury. The court was lavishly decorated and surrounded with gardens and ponds. The Heian court was known for elegance, good manners, and love of beauty.

◆ **What contribution did women in the Heian culture make?**

Teaching Options

C. Feudal Japan

As the central government during the Heian period declined, armed struggles between rival clans increased. Landowners began to keep armed guards. A system was emerging. This system was called **feudalism**, in which lesser lords owe service to greater lords.

The Japanese Feudal System

The emperor remained the social and religious leader of Japan. However, he had little power. The real power lay with the **shogun**, or supreme military commander of Japan. The shogun, however, only controlled a small part of Japan. He relied on the **daimyo** to help him control the rest. The daimyo, landowners during the Heian period, commanded great numbers of **samurai**. The samurai were mounted warriors, and their weapons were the bow and the curved sword. The samurai had a code of behavior that stressed courage, honor, and loyalty to one's lord.

Confucian ideas influenced how the samurai thought about the social order. Below them were peasants, artisans, and merchants. Peasants worked on the estates of the samurai and formed the majority of the population. Sometimes they fought as foot soldiers in the armies of the daimyo. Artisans were the craftspeople of society. They manufactured goods, including the weapons and armor of the samurai. Merchants were regarded as less important than peasants and artisans.

Developments of the Feudal Age

Minamoto Yoritomo was given the title of shogun in 1192. He set up the Kamakura shogunate, or military government, that kept order and peace for almost 150 years in Japan.

In the late 1200s, the Mongols conquered China and Korea. During that time, Kublai Khan sent a delegation to Kyoto in Japan to demand tribute, but the delegation was turned away. In 1274, the Mongols launched an invasion of Japan. The Mongol fleet was driven back by storms.

Several years later, the Mongols launched another invasion fleet, which landed in Japan. However, the Japanese army kept the invaders confined to the beach for two months. Then a typhoon struck, destroying as much as half of the Mongol fleet and forcing them to withdraw. The Japanese celebrated the kamikaze, or "divine wind," of the typhoon.

The Japanese army was kept together for several more years to defend against any further invasion. None came. The cost of defense, however, was high. Feudal ties of loyalty weakened. Finally, a struggle over succession led to a civil war that lasted 50 years.

As Kamakura power weakened, the rival Ashikaga clan emerged. Its members became shoguns beginning in 1338. The Ashikaga shoguns kept the title for more than 200 years, but the Ashikaga shoguns never fully controlled Japan.

In 1467, Japan fell into a state of constant warfare. The daimyo divided Japan among themselves. They issued their own legal codes for their lands. All resources were devoted to increasing military power.

Feudal Society in Japan

Emperor

Shogun

Daimyo

Samurai

Peasants, Artisans, Merchants

Armor for a samurai warrior

✔ Chart Check

Who is directly above the samurai in feudal society?

Then & Now

EMPEROR OF JAPAN

Japanese emperors were once the most powerful people in Japan. They were thought to have had divine ancestors. Kyoto was the center of culture and government.

As time went by, the emperors lost power to military leaders. Emperors still reign, but Japan is now a democracy. The emperor's role is ceremonial.

C. Feudal Japan

Purpose-Setting Question Why did the feudal system develop in Japan? (As the power of the central government declined, landowners used armed guards to protect them. The result was the development of feudalism.)

Using the Chart

Feudal Society in Japan

Point out that the chart illustrates the various classes in Japanese feudal society, in order of descending importance. Ask students why the peasants, artisans, and merchants are at the bottom of the chart. (They were lowest in the social order.)

✔ Chart Check

Answer The daimyo are above the samurai.

Then & Now

EMPEROR OF JAPAN Have students identify examples of figures or symbols that have largely ceremonial functions in their school, community, or city, and do not have authority to make changes. (Possible answer: school mascots; individuals who are honorary chairpersons of committees or special events because of their past service to the community; homecoming queens; prom kings and queens)

Activity

Make a chart Have students make a two-column chart (TR, p. 328) of the shoguns and ruling families in Japan. Students can list the shogun in the left column and important information about the shogun in the right column. Remind students that they can use their charts to review for tests.

Connection to CULTURE

Have pairs of students give an oral presentation about the rise and fall of the samurai warriors in Japan. Suggest that students identify the qualities epitomized by the samurai and how they compare to the heroic qualities of today. They might want to discuss the Edo Mura Village in Nikko, Japan, which recreates the Shogun period.

In the late 1500s, warlords began to reunite Japan. The most famous were Oda Nobunaga, Toyotomi Hideyoshi, and Tokugawa Ieyasu. Through years of war, they ground down opposition. By 1590, Hideyoshi had reunified Japan. Hideyoshi also attacked Korea in the 1590s, but he was forced to withdraw. Tokugawa Ieyasu crushed his opponents in 1600 and established the Tokugawa shogunate. The age of warfare had ended.

Culture in the Feudal Age

The feudal age was a time of record economic growth in Japan. A flowering of culture came with economic growth. The Zen sect of Buddhism strongly influenced Japanese culture. Imported from China, it stressed devotion to duty and meditation. During meditation, the seeker tries to achieve a state of "no-mind." Zen believers feel that through meditation the seeker can free his or her mind and arrive at enlightenment. The simple philosophy of Zen appealed to the samurai.

Zen dominated the arts of the period. Zen stressed simplicity and tranquility. Simple designs became popular. The Japanese love of nature combined with Zen ideas produced tranquil landscape paintings that were done only in black ink. Zen ideas influenced Japanese architects who designed buildings that promoted meditation. These buildings were set among Zen gardens. Garden artists carefully chose and placed rocks, moss, water, and well-raked sand in the gardens. Zen also influenced flower arranging, which was considered an art. Even samurai practiced the art of flower arranging to achieve tranquility.

Zen priests developed a tea ceremony. Tea helped the priests stay awake for long periods of meditation. During the tea ceremony a group met in a simple room to drink tea in a strict ritual. The tea ceremony became part of Japanese culture, and the ritual remains popular today.

They Made History

Toyotomi Hideyoshi 1536–1598

Toyotomi Hideyoshi was one of the greatest generals in Japanese history. Hideyoshi was born a peasant, without even a family name. As a young man, he joined the army of Oda Nobunaga and worked his way up through the ranks. When Nobunaga was assassinated in 1582, Hideyoshi was a general. Over the next eight years, he took control of Japan through diplomacy and, when needed, force. He launched an invasion of Korea and had dreams of conquering China.

He preferred being known for his generosity. The family name he adopted, Toyotomi, means "abundant provider." He lavished money on the court. He also supported the arts. He had a statue of Great Buddha built in Kyoto. His public tea ceremonies were huge art festivals. Thousands came to see the displays of art and performances of plays at the festivals. After Hideyoshi's death, the emperor gave him the Shinto title Hokoku, which means "Wealth of the Nation."

Toyotomi Hideyoshi reunified Japan.

Critical Thinking What is the significance of Hideyoshi's rise to power to the society of Japan?

In addition to the cultural developments of painting, architecture, garden art, and the tea ceremony, theater played an important role during the feudal age. Two forms of drama emerged.

The theater known as Kabuki was seen primarily by the common people. Several times a year, a group of traveling actors arrived in a town to perform. The theaters they used had no roofs, so the performers had to depend on good weather. They wore colorful costumes and heavy makeup. Their movements were exaggerated as they sang, danced, and acted out stories about love, war, and heroism. Sometimes members of the audience joined the actors on the stage, becoming part of the story. Performances often lasted up to 18 hours, so tea and food were sold during the plays.

The other form of drama was Noh drama. Unlike Kabuki theater, Noh drama was performed for the upper classes and had little action. Two actors wearing elaborate costumes and carved masks acted out simple stories on a wooden stage that was almost bare. The only scenery on the stage was a screen with a painting of a pine tree. The screen reminded the actors and audiences that Noh plays were first performed at Shinto shrines. Flutes and drums provided musical accompaniment for the actors. In addition, a chorus of men chanted. Their chants were about honor, unselfishness, and other ideals that were important in Japanese culture. Both Kabuki theater and Noh drama are still performed today in Japan.

This photograph shows masks used in Noh theater performances.

◆ What beliefs and practices were part of Zen Buddhism?

Review IV

Review History
A. How was Chinese culture transmitted to Japan?
B. What effect did the creation of kana have?
C. What was the role of the daimyo in Japan?

Define Terms to Know
Define the following terms:
tsunami, feudalism, shogun, daimyo, samurai

Critical Thinking
Why do you think the worship of kami, or Shinto, is still practiced in Japan today?

Write About Culture
Write a paragraph about the impact of Zen on Japanese culture.

Get Organized
VENN DIAGRAM
Use a Venn diagram to organize information from this section. Choose a topic and then find supporting details. For example, what made the Heian and feudal periods similar and what made them different?

Heian

Chinese influence; selective borrowing; kana; literature

Emperor; weak central government

Loyal to daimyo or shogun; Zen; constant warfare

Feudal

Critical Thinking
Possible answer: Japanese people today appreciate how Shinto values nature and might want to continue this tradition of worshiping nature spirits.

Write About Culture
Students' paragraphs should include specific examples of ways in which Zen influenced the arts and culture of Japan.

Chapter Summary

A blank outline form is available in the Teacher's Resources (p. 318). Chapter summaries should outline the development of great dynasties in China, the effects of invasions on China, the development of Korea and other areas of Southeast Asia, and the history of Japan. Refer to the rubric in the Teacher's Resources (p. 340) to score students' chapter summaries.

⬤ Interpret the Timeline

1. The Japanese capital is transferred to Heian.
2. the Mongol conquest of China
3. Mongols invade eastern Europe, and Mongols complete the conquest of China.
4. Check students' timelines to be sure all events are in the chapter.

Use Terms to Know

5. d. an absentee landlord
6. d. refugee
7. a. hangul
8. d. samurai
9. b. succession

Check Your Understanding

10. The land redistribution program was developed to ensure that peasants worked on their own land so they could support themselves and pay taxes.
11. Wu Zhou was the first female emperor of China.
12. New strains of rice were developed so that two crops could be cultivated in a year, new tools were introduced, and irrigation was improved.
13. The Mongols built new roads; rebuilt the Great Canal; encouraged peace and stability; opened up trade routes; and established a postal system.
14. Artists during the Ming period created new portrait and landscape styles. Ming artists also created beautiful blue-and-white porcelain.
15. The Mongols allowed Koryo kings to rule but forced them to pay tribute to the Mongols; Korea was forced to build ships for the Mongol invasion of Japan.
16. Chinese immigrants introduced Chinese ideas of government to Vietnam.

17. Shinto is a religion based on the worship of nature spirits and is still practiced today.
18. The daimyo were the great landowners in Japan; they controlled large numbers of samurai and were vassals of the shogun; the shogun relied on the daimyo to help them control Japan.
19. The Mongols' unsuccessful invasion attempt resulted in Japan's keeping its army together.

Chapter Summary

Complete the following outline in your notebook. Then, use your outline to write a brief summary of the chapter.

Dynasties and Kingdoms of East Asia

I. Great Chinese Dynasties
 A. The Sui and Tang Dynasties
 B. The Song Dynasty
 C. Culture and Society Under the Tang and the Song
II. The Mongol Empire and the Ming Dynasty
 A. Mongol Conquest and the Yuan Dynasty
 B. The Ming Dynasty
III. Korea and Southeast Asia
 A. Korea
 B. Southeast Asia
IV. Japan: An Island Empire
 A. The Geography and Early History of Japan
 B. The Heian Period
 C. Feudal Japan

⬤ Interpret the Timeline

Use the timeline on pages 242–243 to answer the following questions.

1. Which event happened first, the Japanese capital is transferred to Heian or the Chinese capital is moved to Beijing?

2. Which event happened later, the unification of Korea under the Silla Dynasty or the Mongol conquest of China?

3. **Critical Thinking** Which chapter event and world event involve the same group of people?

4. Select five events from the chapter that are not on the timeline. Create a timeline that shows these events.

Use Terms to Know

Select the term that best completes each sentence.

5. A landowner who lives elsewhere while earning money from landholdings is called
 a. a samurai.　　c. a shogun.
 b. a daimyo.　　d. an absentee landlord.

6. A person who flees to a foreign country is a
 a. daimyo.　　c. tsunami.
 b. samurai.　　d. refugee.

7. An alphabet using symbols to represent the sounds of the Korean language is
 a. hangul.　　c. feudalism.
 b. tsunami.　　d. daimyo.

8. A member of the Japanese warrior class was called a
 a. daimyo.　　c. hangul.
 b. shogun.　　d. samurai.

9. The order by which rulers follow one another in office is called
 a. tsunami.　　c. feudalism.
 b. succession.　　d. hangul.

Check Your Understanding

10. **Explain** why Tang emperors developed a program of land redistribution.

11. **Identify** how Wu Zhou was important to Chinese history.

12. **Identify** the improvements made to agriculture under the Song.

13. **Discuss** how China benefited under Mongol rule.

14. **Describe** the artistic advancements during the Ming Dynasty.

15. **Explain** how the Mongols affected Korea.

16. **Summarize** how China influenced Vietnam.

17. **Describe** the importance of Shinto to Japan.

18. **Identify** the importance of the daimyo in Japan.

19. **Describe** the effects of the Mongol invasion on Japan.

Critical Thinking

20. Analyze Primary Sources What does the quotation from Emperor Tai Zong on page 245 tell you about the values of the time?

21. Analyze Primary Sources How does the quotation from Marco Polo on page 253 describe the Mongol government of China?

22. Analyze Primary Sources What does the quotation from the Korean official on page 257 tell you about the relationship of Korea to China?

23. Draw Conclusions Why do you think Chinese influence decreased in Japan?

Put Your Skills to Work

24. Compare and Contrast You have learned that comparing and contrasting artifacts and ideas can help you understand what you read and see. Study the images below. Then, answer the following questions.

a. What can you learn about the cultures that produced these statues?

b. How are these statues alike and how are they different?

The statue to the right is a praying figure from Angkor Wat. The statue below is a Japanese Buddha.

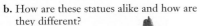

Analyze Sources

25. Read more about Song reforms from this letter by Wang Anshi to one of his opponents. Then, answer the questions that follow.

Now it is your opinion that I have overstepped my authority, caused trouble, pursued profit, and blocked criticism to the point where everyone in the world is enraged. In my view, I have received orders from my ruler, the policies were discussed in court, and executing them was delegated to the officials. . . . As for the abundance of resentment, this is something I expected. . . . Scholar-officials often prefer not to worry about the nation and merely content themselves with the status quo.

a. How does Wang Anshi respond to criticism of his policies?

b. What does Wang Anshi say about his opponents?

Essay Writing

26. China strongly influenced countries around it. They absorbed Chinese art, literature, and philosophy. Many of these countries adapted Chinese learning. They used it as it suited their needs. Choose one of the neighbors of China. Write an essay about how that neighboring country adopted and adapted Chinese ways.

TEST PREPARATION

SEQUENCING RELATED EVENTS
Read the question below and choose the correct answer.

Which event came after the Mongol conquest of China?

1. The Tang Dynasty began to decline.

2. Hong Wu established the Ming Dynasty.

3. Gunpowder was introduced as a weapon.

4. Wu Zhao became the first woman emperor in China.

Critical Thinking

20. Possible answer: The quotation suggests that the Chinese valued wisdom and that wisdom included knowing when to listen to others.
21. Possible answer: The quotation illustrates a system of discrimination in which the Mongols were at the top, followed by such peoples as Turks and Arabs, with the Chinese in the lowest position at the bottom.
22. Possible answer: The quotation suggests that China was seen as the source of culture and civilization, and that all worthwhile traditions came from China.
23. Possible answer: The Japanese might have wanted to develop more independently from Chinese influence.

Put Your Skills to Work

COMPARE AND CONTRAST
24a. You can learn what is important to the culture, such as praying and the Buddha, and that art and sculpture are important to both cultures.
24b. Similarities: Both are at rest, are images dealing with religion, and are wearing hats; **Differences:** Angkor Wat figure is praying, and we do not know who it is; Buddha is contemplating something and is a well-known figure.

Analyze Sources

25a. He states that he is following the orders of the emperor. The policies were discussed in court and executing the policies is delegated to the officials.
25b. He states that the scholar-officials would rather maintain the status quo than do anything constructive.

Essay Writing

26. Check that students' essays meet all the requirements. In addition to grammar, punctuation, and organization, the essay should clearly explain how the neighboring country adopted and adapted Chinese ways to its own culture.

TEST PREPARATION

Answer 2. Hong Wu established the Ming Dynasty.

The Early Middle Ages
481–1100
(pp. 268–287)

Chapter Objectives
• Summarize how European kingdoms developed in the early Middle Ages and realize the importance of a nation's close relationship with the pope.
• Identify the impact of the Viking invasions on Europe, and explain the social and economic structure of feudalism that existed throughout Europe.
• Describe the power of the Roman Catholic Church throughout society as well as its construction of grand Gothic-style cathedrals. Tell how Jewish people endured medieval anti-Semitism.

Chapter Summary
Section I begins with an overview of the geography of western Europe and details the rise of Charlemagne, his alliance with the pope, and the decline of his influence.
Section II explores the expansion of the Vikings, the Norman Conquest, and the political and economic structure of feudalism.
Section III describes the power of the Roman Catholic Church, the growth of religious communities, the emergence of the Gothic style of architecture, and the treatment of Jewish people in Europe.

Set the Stage
TEACH PRIMARY SOURCES
Explain that this type of pledge was typical between peasants and lords under the social structure of feudalism. A similar pledge would have been spoken at a homage ceremony in which one man declared that he had become the "man" of another. Homage ceremonies were some of the most important ceremonies of feudal Europe.

CHAPTER
12

The Early Middle Ages
481–1100

I. Early European Kingdoms
II. Feudalism and the Manor System
III. The Church in Medieval Times

The period after the fall of Rome has been called an age of darkness in which tribes of rude, lawless barbarians cared only about their own needs. In fact, the period was one of great interdependence among people of different social classes. Peasants depended on lords for food, shelter, and protection. Lords depended on peasants to farm their lands, service their castles, and fight their battles. All people depended on the Church to guide them toward the path to heaven. Such dependence can be seen in a typical pledge made by a peasant to his lord:

> 66 . . . [Because] it is known to all . . . that I . . . [am unable] to feed and clothe myself, I have asked of your pity, and your goodwill has granted to me permission to deliver and commend myself into your authority and protection . . . in return you have undertaken to aid and sustain me in food and clothing. . . . And for as long as I shall live, I am bound to serve you and respect you as a free man ought. 99

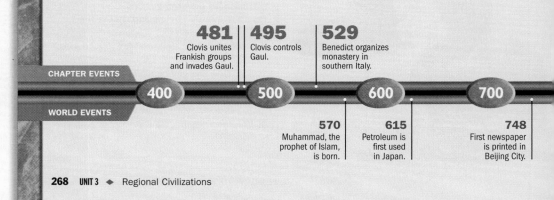

CHAPTER EVENTS

481
Clovis unites Frankish groups and invades Gaul.

495
Clovis controls Gaul.

529
Benedict organizes monastery in southern Italy.

400 — 500 — 600 — 700

WORLD EVENTS

570
Muhammad, the prophet of Islam, is born.

615
Petroleum is first used in Japan.

748
First newspaper is printed in Beijing City.

268 UNIT 3 ◆ Regional Civilizations

Teaching Options

Chapter 12 Resources

REVIEW

Teacher's Resources (TR)
Terms to Know, p. 25
Review History, p. 59
Build Your Skills, p. 93
Chapter Test, pp. 139–140
Concept Builder, p. 228
Cause-and-Effect Chain, p. 325
Transparency 1

ASSESSMENT
Section Reviews, pp. 274, 279, 284
Chapter Review, pp. 286–287
Chapter Test, TR, pp. 139–140

ALTERNATIVE ASSESSMENT
Portfolio Project, p. 312
Create a Travel Brochure, p. T312

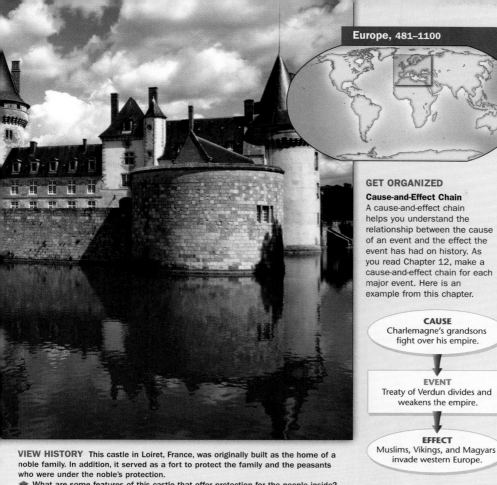

Europe, 481–1100

GET ORGANIZED

Cause-and-Effect Chain
A cause-and-effect chain helps you understand the relationship between the cause of an event and the effect the event has had on history. As you read Chapter 12, make a cause-and-effect chain for each major event. Here is an example from this chapter.

CAUSE
Charlemagne's grandsons fight over his empire.

↓

EVENT
Treaty of Verdun divides and weakens the empire.

↓

EFFECT
Muslims, Vikings, and Magyars invade western Europe.

VIEW HISTORY This castle in Loiret, France, was originally built as the home of a noble family. In addition, it served as a fort to protect the family and the peasants who were under the noble's protection.
◆ What are some features of this castle that offer protection for the people inside?

800
Charlemagne is crowned Roman emperor.

814
Charlemagne dies.

911
Vikings establish first settlement in Normandy.

1066
Normans conquer England.

800 — 900 — 1000 — 1100

800
Ancient kingdom of Ghana becomes a powerful trading state in Africa.

900
Arab physician Rhases describes smallpox.

1000
Maya civilization begins to collapse.

CHAPTER 12 ◆ The Early Middle Ages **269**

Chapter Themes
• Culture
• Time, Continuity, and Change
• People, Places, and Environments
• Individuals, Groups, and Institutions
• Power, Authority, and Governance
• Civic Ideals and Practices

F Y I

Why Castles Were Built
Castles were built for protection and for prestige. Great nobles tried to outdo one another with the beauty and grandeur of their castles. Within the castle were lodging places for servants and animals, as well as storehouses and the offices for governing the manor. Most castles were designed to support and protect a small village during a siege.

Section Summary

In this section, students will learn why its geographical features made western Europe ideal for settlement in the early Middle Ages. They will read about the leaders who united the Franks and fostered culture and learning. Students will evaluate the importance of Christianity to Charlemagne's leadership.

1 Introduce

Getting Started

Have students preview the section, looking at the pictures, reading the captions, and scanning the maps and chart. Discuss what these visuals reveal about the time period.

TERMS TO KNOW

Ask students to read the terms and definitions on page 270 and then find each term in the section. Have them write sentences using each term in context.

You may wish to preview the pronunciation of the following words from this section with students.

Clovis (KLOH vihs)
Gaul (GAWL)
Charlemagne (SHAR luh mayn)
Alcuin (AL kwihn)
Magyars (MAG yahrs)

ACTIVE READING

Have students make a timeline (TR, p. 320) for the section that spans the years 400–800, with 100-year intervals. Then, have them work in small groups to compare and improve their timelines. Suggest that these timelines be used as students review for a quiz or chapter test.

Early European Kingdoms

Terms to Know

medieval of the Middle Ages

revival a renewed interest in a part of the past

Main Ideas

A. The weakened defense of the old Roman borders cleared the path for Germanic-speaking groups to invade Europe.

B. Charlemagne was crowned Roman emperor, ruler of a large empire in western Europe.

C. Charlemagne's rule encouraged culture and learning to develop in western Europe.

Active Reading

SEQUENCE OF EVENTS
When you sequence events, you put them in the order in which they occurred. As you read this section, create your own timeline to keep track of the order of events in Europe during the medieval period.

A. The People and Land of the Middle Ages in Europe

The term *Middle Ages* covers the time between the fall of Rome and the beginning of what is known as modern history. In Latin, the term for Middle Ages is **medieval**. That is why this time period is also called the medieval period.

During the Middle Ages, western Europe lacked the strong, unified leadership and glorious culture of ancient Rome. However, Europe was not without its social and religious structures. It was a time of powerful Church leadership and tightly woven communities of farmers, traders, and lords.

The Geography of Western Europe

Much of the land of western Europe during the early Middle Ages was covered with thick forests. The soil was rich, and mineral resources lay beneath the forests and mountains. The large, swift rivers were easy for trading ships to navigate, and were full of fish.

Yet, at the dawn of the sixth century, there were few settlers in western Europe. People had left the cities, such as Paris and Rome, and moved to the countryside, where they could grow their own food. Western Europe was largely cut off from the troubled Romans and the cities of the Middle East, China, and India. The sturdy Roman roads, which had once been the pride of a powerful empire, were now badly in need of repair. Roman warriors were no longer assigned to defend the old borders, so the outlying regions of the empire were soon overcome by invading groups.

The People of the Middle Ages in Europe

The people of northern Europe did not share the culture or the Latin language of the Romans. These people, often organized into groups, spoke Germanic languages, with words from Latin, Greek, and Hebrew. As a result, they have been called Germanic peoples.

Germanic peoples lived in small groups of farmers and herders. As a nomadic people, they moved from place to place. Sometimes, they had to defend themselves from attack. Other times, they fought to gain new lands that had better soil for farming and better grazing for their animals. For this reason, groups were almost always led by the strongest warrior.

◆ **What event marks the beginning of the Middle Ages?**

Soldier from the Middle Ages

Teaching Options

Section 1 Resources

Teacher's Resources (TR)
Terms to Know, p. 25
Review History, p. 59
Build Your Skills, p. 93
Concept Builder, p. 228
Cause-and-Effect Chain, p. 325

Test Taking

Give students examples of true/false statements using the information in this section. Remind students that only one part of a statement needs to be false to make the entire statement false. Example: Carolus Magnus, who was called Charles the Terrible, lived to be 72 years old and ruled as king of the Franks for 46 years. (False)

B. The Empire of the Franks

One strong leader was a man named Clovis. He was the ruler of one of several Germanic-speaking groups called the Franks. Language and custom connected the Frankish groups to each other, but each group was ruled by a different leader. The groups lived on the east bank of the lower Rhine River. During the third and fourth centuries, the Franks tried to expand their territories into Roman-held territories. These attempts were largely unsuccessful.

Uniting the Franks

Around 481, Clovis was able to unite several of the Frankish groups. He led a combined force against the collapsing Roman army into Gaul. Gaul is an area that includes most of present-day France, Belgium, northern Italy, and western Germany. By 495, Clovis had brought most of Gaul under his control and established a unified Frankish kingdom.

After Clovis conquered Gaul in 496, he converted to Christianity. This proved to be a very wise move. As a Christian, he gained the support of the people of Gaul. He also made an ally of the remaining leaders of Rome and of the powerful Roman Catholic Church. In their eyes, his conversion set him above the leaders of other Germanic groups who had not adopted Christianity.

Clovis began a dynasty of rulers that would remain in power for a long time. Then, in the eighth century, the descendants of Clovis were displaced by the grandfather of the famous ruler Charlemagne.

Then & Now

FRENCH LANGUAGE
The Franks who invaded and settled the northern regions of Europe were strongly influenced by Roman customs. Their language, for example, took on many new Latin words and phrases. It changed from Germanic into a very old form of the language spoken in France today.

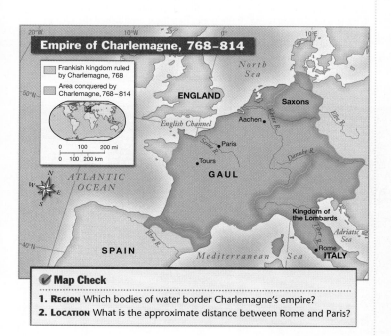

Empire of Charlemagne, 768–814

- Frankish kingdom ruled by Charlemagne, 768
- Area conquered by Charlemagne, 768–814

✔ Map Check

1. **REGION** Which bodies of water border Charlemagne's empire?
2. **LOCATION** What is the approximate distance between Rome and Paris?

Conflict Resolution

Explain to students that Clovis's conversion to Christianity was almost certainly a political move calculated to avoid possible conflict with the Roman people of the region. Have students discuss Clovis's conversion. Ask how Clovis's decision to assimilate allowed him to both appear strong and avoid conflict. (Christians saw that he was on solid moral ground and willing to adopt some of the customs of the new land.)

ESL/ELL Strategies

Summarize Have students work with proficient English readers and speakers to read the paragraphs under subsection B. Ask each ESL/ELL student to summarize the information in his or her own words. Then, have the pair of students work together to improve the summaries.

---

2 Teach

A. The People and Land of the Middle Ages in Europe

Purpose-Setting Question What geographical features made western Europe ideal for settlers? (The soil was rich, the rivers were navigable, and the forests were thick.)

◆ **ANSWER** The fall of the Roman Empire marked the beginning of the Middle Ages.

B. The Empire of the Franks

Purpose-Setting Question How did Clovis conquer Gaul? (Clovis united Frankish groups and then led the combined forces against the Roman army.)

Then & Now

FRENCH LANGUAGE Point out that English is also a melding of many languages for the same reasons. Ask students to identify English words that come from other languages. Start with an easy topic, such as food. (Possible words: *spaghetti, sushi, fajita*)

Using the Map

Empire of Charlemagne, 768–814

Point out that Charlemagne expanded on three fronts: southwest, southeast, and northeast. Discuss why winning and maintaining control of these three new areas would have taken enormous resources and efficient organization and leadership. (Possible answers: Part of the army probably stayed behind in the conquered areas to govern and protect, and the army would need replacements; also, food for the army's journeys would be expensive.)

✔ Map Check

Answers
1. Mediterranean Sea, Atlantic Ocean, English Channel, North Sea, and Adriatic Sea
2. about 650 miles

Activity

Write a letter Have each student write a letter to Charlemagne from Leo III. The letter should use stately, diplomatic language to invite Charlemagne to come to Rome on Christmas Day, in the year 800. Remind students that Pope Leo III was setting a precedent for a pope to approve an emperor because he believed he was the more powerful leader. Students may wish to decorate their letters.

TEACH PRIMARY SOURCES

Legend has it that Charlemagne claimed he would never have entered the Church that Christmas Day had he known the pope was going to crown him emperor. Have students study the illustration on page 272 showing Pope Leo III crowning Charlemagne. Ask them to describe what they see. Have them provide as many details as possible.

Who are the people standing around? How can they tell? What can they surmise about medieval coronation ceremonies from the art? (There are many nobles and religious figures in attendance. They are all richly dressed and probably have some political influence. The pope's robe is probably being held off the floor by an official of the Roman Catholic Church. Charlemagne is receiving a gold crown and has a thoughtful look on his face.)

◆ **ANSWER** The pope wanted to challenge the emperor of Constantinople's claim as ruler of all Roman territories, and he wanted to establish the idea that the pope had the power to crown the emperor.

The Rise of Charlemagne

Carolus Magnus was also called Charles the Great, or Charlemagne in French. Charlemagne lived to be 72 years old, nearly twice the average life span at the time. He ruled as king of the Franks for 46 years, from 768 to 814.

During the first ten years of Charlemagne's rule, he conquered the Lombard kingdom in present-day northern Italy, fought against the Saxons in northern Europe, and invaded Spain. By the end of this period, he had united under him the largest region since the fall of Rome. For the remaining 36 years of his reign, he focused on defending his vast territory from invasions. He also improved culture, education, and law within his kingdom.

A Christian King

As Charlemagne expanded his kingdom, he tried to force the conquered peoples to become Christian. He had his priests perform baptisms on the populations of entire cities. He also demanded strict punishment for anyone who practiced other religions. His promotion of Christianity sealed his friendship with the leader of the Church in Rome, Pope Leo III.

Leo hoped that an alliance with Charlemagne would solve his own problems. The pope's main rival was the emperor in Constantinople, who claimed to be sole ruler over all Roman territories. To challenge this claim, Pope Leo III crowned Charlemagne as the new Roman emperor on Christmas Day in the year 800.

The crowning of Charlemagne accomplished three things. First, it gave the Romans an emperor for the first time since 476. Second, it gave Charlemagne the blessing of the pope. Finally, it established the idea that the pope had the power to crown an emperor. In later years, this tradition would lead to bitter battles between popes and leaders who could be denied the crown if the pope did not approve of them.

This illustration shows the coronation, or crowning, of Charlemagne in 800.

◆ **Why did the pope crown Charlemagne emperor of Rome?**

272 UNIT 3 ◆ Regional Civilizations

Teaching Options

Writing

AVERAGE

Have students write a letter in the person of Charlemagne, or one of his agents, inviting a prominent scholar to come to Aachen, Charlemagne's home city, to become a teacher at the center of learning. Remind students that many scholars considered Charlemagne an ignorant nomad from the mountains. Letters should be persuasive and full of praise for the scholar, as well as dignified, as befits a king.

CHALLENGE

Have students write letters of reply to Charlemagne's invitation to teach at the center of learning. The letters are from two different European scholars. One scholar eagerly accepts the invitation and the other declines it. Students should explain the reason for each decision. Remind students that they are writing to a powerful emperor and the tone must show respect.

C. The Age of Charlemagne

Charlemagne was determined to make his kingdom a center of learning and culture. To do this, he brought great artisans to his court in Aachen, in what is now northwestern Germany. Trade flourished as wealthy people ordered luxury goods, such as fine clothing, foods, and household items that were only available in Rome or other cultural centers.

Schools and Learning

Charlemagne wanted to foster culture and learning. He could read, but he could not write. During the Middle Ages, most people could not read or write. However, the clergy were expected to be able to read and write in Latin. Unfortunately, many did not read and write well. To help change this situation, Charlemagne brought in scholars from England, Germany, Spain, and Italy, including one of the greatest scholars of the time, Alcuin of York.

Alcuin arrived in 782 and organized a school in the palace for the children of Charlemagne and other nobles. The courses at the palace school were based on advances in education in England and Ireland.

Under Alcuin's influence, Charlemagne issued the *Charter of Modern Thought*. This document was addressed to religious officials. In it, Charlemagne noted that the letters he had received from the clergy were filled with errors in grammar. He told them that, in the future, he expected that the clergy would work to make sure that their letters were better written. Charlemagne also wanted everyone in the clergy to learn to read and write to the best of his ability. To accomplish this, he encouraged the establishment of cathedral schools.

In addition, Alcuin set up schools throughout the kingdom. Priests were told to establish schools in every village. These village schools would be open to all children. Parents were charged no fee, or tuition, but they could contribute whatever they could afford.

Culture

Charlemagne's interest in learning led to a **revival**, or renewed interest, in the cultures of Rome and Greece. Most books were produced by monks and were handwritten copies of the Bible and other books on early Christianity. As interest in learning grew and expanded, the monks were also instructed to make copies of works by ancient Roman authors. Their efforts preserved many works that otherwise would have been lost to the world.

Although Charlemagne could not write, he understood the importance of keeping careful records and accurate accounting. One historian explained how careful Charlemagne expected his recordkeepers to be:

> " Not an egg, a nail, or a plank was to be omitted from the accounts which the king's managers had to render [present] every Christmas. "

Charlemagne's careful attention to detail extended to all parts of his kingdom. He assigned nobles to travel around the kingdom and report back on everything. He wanted news of the conditions of the roads, the state of the crops, and the loyalty of local administrators. The nobles were also instructed

---

| **School Subjects Taught in Charlemagne's Kingdom** | |
CATHEDRAL SCHOOLS	VILLAGE SCHOOLS
grammar (language and some poetry)	religion
rhetoric (the art of speaking)	plainsong (church music)
dialectic (reasoning with speech as a means of argument)	simple grammar (reading and writing)
geometry and arithmetic	manual training
music	
astronomy	

✔ **Chart Check**

What subjects were taught in both cathedral schools and village schools?

ANALYZE PRIMARY SOURCES

DOCUMENT-BASED QUESTION
What can you tell about Charlemagne from this historian's description of his recordkeeping?

F Y I

Dignified and Stately

The historian Einhard described Charlemagne: "He had a broad and strong body of unusual height. His skull was round, the eyes were lively and rather large, the nose of more than average length, . . . the face friendly . . . [he] made a dignified and stately impression even though he had a thick, short neck and a belly that protruded somewhat."

Connection to ECONOMICS

Ask students to keep a record of their expenses for one week. Have them record every penny they spend, as Charlemagne had his officers do. Set up some rules for the project. For example, students should include the cost of snacks but not family groceries. At the end of the week, have students evaluate their expenditures. Also, create a class total for the week.

C. The Age of Charlemagne

Purpose-Setting Question
What were some of the activities that took place during the Age of Charlemagne? (Possible answers: trade flourished, the *Charter of Modern Thought* was issued, and priests established schools in every village)

Using the Chart

School Subjects Taught in Charlemagne's Kingdom

Have students make a Venn diagram (TR, p. 323) to evaluate the similarities and differences between village schools and cathedral schools. Point out that the text and the chart on page 273 will help students complete the diagram.

✔ **Chart Check**
Answer grammar and music

ANALYZE PRIMARY SOURCES

DOCUMENT-BASED QUESTION
Government officials of today must keep careful records of revenue and expenditures. Keeping a log of expenses and income was not a commonplace practice for royalty, nobility, or large landowners during the Middle Ages. Explain to students that Charlemagne's insistence on accurate recordkeeping was one of the reasons for his political and military success.

ANSWER Possible answer: He was detail-oriented and wanted to know where every bit of money was spent.

Extend Tell students that Charlemagne was said to have had boundless energy and trouble sleeping. In his many wakeful hours, he planned campaigns and learned Latin. Point out that other famous leaders have been insomniacs, or people unable to sleep through the night, such as Winston Churchill, the leader of Great Britain during World War II. Have students research the effects of insomnia on the body and mind and modern treatments for it.

Using the Map

Invasions of Europe, 700–1000

Ask students to determine the most active invaders shown on the map. (the Vikings) As a class, make a list of the regions the Vikings invaded. (Russia, Germany, Byzantine Empire, France, England, Iceland, Ireland, Italy) Point out that the sheer number of invasions may have contributed to the Vikings' reputation for ferocity.

✔ Map Check

Answer west or southwest

◆ **ANSWER** Charlemagne wanted to make his kingdom a center of learning. He also wanted everyone in the clergy to learn how to read and write to the best of his ability.

Section Close

Review with students the accomplishments of Clovis and Charlemagne. Discuss how they united different groups and what they were able to do by bringing groups together. Explore with students the role Christianity played in the success of both men.

③ Assess

Review Answers

Review History

A. Land: mostly thick forest, rich soil with mineral resources, and rivers that were easy to navigate, full of fish, and excellent for trading; **People:** lived in small groups of farmers and herders, were nomadic, and spoke Germanic languages

B. Clovis gained the support of the people of Gaul, leaders in Rome, and the Roman Catholic Church.

C. He unified much of the former Roman Empire, christianized western Europe, and brought culture and education to Europe.

Define Terms to Know

medieval, 270; revival, 273

Critical Thinking

Possible answer: Charlemagne wanted the people of his kingdom to be able to read and write. He himself could read, but could not write.

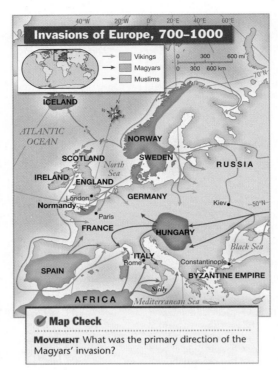

✔ Map Check

MOVEMENT What was the primary direction of the Magyars' invasion?

to settle court cases and see that justice was done. His leadership brought about so many reforms and improvements that the period of his reign has come to be called the Age of Charlemagne.

The Decline of Charlemagne's Empire

With Charlemagne's death in 814, the empire he had built went into slow decline. In 843, after almost 30 years of conflict, his three grandsons signed the Treaty of Verdun. This treaty divided Charlemagne's empire into three kingdoms. Eventually, the lack of strong leadership allowed invaders to conquer large parts of the kingdom.

Muslim forces attacked southern Italy and gained control of Sicily in the late 800s. A nomadic group called Magyars lived in the area that is now Hungary. Around 896, they began an invasion of Europe, looting parts of France, northern Italy, and eastern Europe. Finally, the Vikings invaded northern Europe.

The empire that Charlemagne had created did not last long after his death. However, his standards for learning and governing remained a model for many centuries.

◆ **Why did Charlemagne encourage learning in his kingdom?**

Review 1

Review History

A. How would you describe the land and people of medieval Europe after the fall of Rome?
B. How did converting to Christianity help Clovis?
C. What were some of Charlemagne's most important achievements?

Define Terms to Know

Define the following terms: **medieval, revival**

Critical Thinking

Why was education an important issue for Charlemagne?

Write About Government

Explain the advantages for Charlemagne's government in converting conquered lands to Christianity.

Get Organized

CAUSE-AND-EFFECT CHAIN
Use a cause-and-effect chain to analyze information from this section. For example, what were the causes and effects of the fall of Charlemagne's empire?

Write About Government

Students may state that when everyone is practicing the same religion, it is easier to govern the people. Also, everyone is then following the same rules and feels like they belong to the same group.

CAUSE
Death of Charlemagne

EVENT
Fall of Charlemagne's empire

EFFECT
Kingdom is divided; invaders conquer parts of the kingdom

Build Your Skills

USE SECONDARY SOURCES

Secondary sources are sources such as books, magazines, newspapers, research papers, and Web sites. They are sources that are written by people and are based on knowledge from primary sources. For example, a biography of Charlemagne written by a modern historian would be a secondary source.

Some secondary sources are more reliable than others. For example, an encyclopedia or other reference book is often more reliable than a Web site that contains information on a similar topic. Sometimes, a secondary source may provide information that supports a point of view. One historian of the Middle Ages may use primary sources to prove that Charlemagne was a kind and tolerant leader. Another historian might use other documents to show that he was cruel.

When using secondary sources in your research, it is important to read several secondary sources on the same subject to be sure that you get a full picture of an event in history.

Here's How
Follow these steps to evaluate a secondary source.
1. Select a book or chapter in a history book on your subject.
2. Evaluate the knowledge and background of the author.
3. Read the source thoroughly, watching carefully for biased, or one-sided, judgments or unusual points of view.
4. Look for an additional secondary source on the same topic to check the author's bias.

Here's Why
Using secondary sources will let you quickly learn general ideas about a subject. It will also point you toward useful primary sources in your search to gather reliable information on a topic.

Practice the Skill
Read the paragraph on the right from a secondary source called *The Age of Chivalry*. Then, answer the following questions.
1. What primary sources does the author cite to support her work?
2. What words or phrases does the author use that may indicate her bias about village social life?
3. What position does the author hold about village life?

Extend the Skill
Compare the details in this paragraph to the paragraphs on page 280 about religious life. How are they similar? How are they different?

Apply the Skill
After completing the last chapter in this unit, conduct research, using secondary sources, to complete the Portfolio Project. Compare several sources on the same topic.

"The Church and the manorial court were the most important centers of village social life. A court of elected jurors with the power to fine and punish wrongdoers helped to ensure everyone's best behavior. However, writers of the time complain about the loose morals of the villagers: dancing in the churchyard and holding beauty contests are cited as evidence. The parish priests, on the other hand, would have organized more wholesome entertainment such as pilgrimages to local shrines, celebrations on holy days, and religious plays."
—*The Age of Chivalry* by Silvia Wright

Teaching Options

RETEACH
Provide a passage from a secondary source that contains obviously biased material, such as a printout of an advertiser's Web page. Ask students to evaluate the reliability of the author, the bias of the material, and the suitability of the information for history research papers.

CHALLENGE
Have students choose a topic from the chapter on the Middle Ages, such as Clovis, Charlemagne, or knighthood. Then, have them find two secondary sources and compare them for their bias. Have students write a paragraph in which they evaluate the background for each source, the author, and how the information presented differs between the two sources.

Build Your Skills

USE SECONDARY SOURCES

Teach the Skill
Collect several secondary sources that students are familiar with, such as an encyclopedia, a printout from a Web site, a biography, and a student research paper. Explain that these are all considered secondary sources. Ask students to evaluate the expertise of the author for each source. Discuss which source would be the most reliable if all the topics were the same. (The encyclopedia would be more reliable than the student research paper. Depending on the person who produced it, the Web site and the biography may or may not be reliable sources.)

Practice the Skill
1. Wright cites writers of the time that tell about village social life.
2. The author says "ensure everyone's best behavior" and "loose morals," which show that she does not like the villagers' behavior. She says "wholesome entertainment" to show that she approves of or likes the activities planned by the priests.
3. The author believes that activities in village life planned by the villagers were not "wholesome" and that she likes the activities that the parish priests would have planned.

Extend the Skill
Both selections point out the importance of the parish priest to village life. In Section 3, the description deals with religious obligations in villages. The selection on this page deals with entertainment in villages.

Apply the Skill
Remind students that there are very few documents that have survived from the Middle Ages, and the existing ones are written in very old forms of Latin, French, English, German, or other languages. For most research on this period, students will rely on secondary sources. As a class, brainstorm various types of secondary sources that they might find to help complete the Portfolio Project. (biography of Charlemagne, general history about knighthood, tour guides of castles, etc.)

II. Feudalism and the Manor System

(pp. 276–279)

Section Summary

In this section students will read about the impact of the Viking invasions on Europe, which led to the Norman Conquest of England. They will also learn about the social and economic structure of feudalism in medieval society.

1 Introduce

Getting Started

As a class, complete an SQR Chart (TR, p. 322) on feudalism. Have students write *feudalism* in the Survey box on the chart. Then, ask students to write about what they wish to know about the topic in the form of a question in the Question box. After reading, have students come back to this chart and fill in the Read box with the information they learned about. Students can then share their completed charts with the class.

TERMS TO KNOW

Explain to students that many words take on prefixes or suffixes to become different parts of speech or to change the meaning. Ask students to look up the terms in a dictionary and list the other forms they find. For example, *chivalry* takes on an adjective form as *chivalrous*. *Manor* can become the adjective *manorial*. *Serf* can become another noun, *serfdom*, which means the state of being a serf, like slavery.

ACTIVE READING

Emphasize that an evaluation must be based on facts. Have small groups of students read the material under subsection B. As they read, have them write down statements of fact on posterboard. These facts should be labeled, *Facts About Feudalism*. Then, each group should evaluate the facts and write an opinion statement about them. The opinion statement should be written at the bottom of the posterboard and labeled *Evaluation of Feudalism*. Ask each group to share its poster.

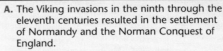

Terms to Know

manor the land and property under a lord's control

vassal a person who has taken a pledge of loyalty to a lord

liege lord the lord to whom a vassal owes first service

chivalry the code of conduct expected of knights

serf a peasant who is legally bound to the land belonging to a lord

Main Ideas

A. The Viking invasions in the ninth through the eleventh centuries resulted in the settlement of Normandy and the Norman Conquest of England.

B. Feudal societies brought safety to Europe and a new class of nobility.

C. Feudalism benefited both lords and peasants, while technology improved their lives.

📖 Active Reading

EVALUATE
When you evaluate events in history, you examine the facts and form an opinion. As you read this section, concentrate on the feudal structure of society. Then, evaluate what you have learned.

A. The Viking Invasions of Europe

The Vikings lived in Scandinavia. They were called Norseman, or Northmen, by Europeans because they sailed from the north. The Vikings were daring warriors as well as skilled craftspeople and experienced traders and travelers. Evidence of their settlements can be seen today in Greenland, Iceland, and even Newfoundland, Canada.

Historians disagree about why Vikings began raiding in the ninth century. Some believe that the population of Vikings in Scandinavia had grown too large for the land to support. Others point out that European kingdoms had grown weak, tempting the Vikings to raid Europe.

The Crisis of Power in England

In the tenth century, the Vikings took advantage of the fighting among Charlemagne's heirs. Raiding parties attacked and settled land along the Seine River in northern Europe. This was the first settlement in the region that would be called Normandy.

As the Norman rulers became stronger, they set out to expand their power. The most important campaign was by William of Normandy. By some reports, William had been chosen to inherit the throne of England from King Edward the Confessor, who had no children. During his reign, Edward had established close ties with the Normans. Grateful for the help he had received from William, Edward had reportedly promised him the crown. However, shortly before his death in 1066, Edward named Harold, Earl of Wessex, to be his successor.

The Norman Conquest

An unhappy William of Normandy invaded England in October 1066. The Normans defeated the English army at the Battle of Hastings, in which Harold was killed. William marched next to London, where the undefended nobles were ready to submit to his rule. William, now known as William the Conqueror, was crowned king of England on Christmas Day in 1066. The victory of William's army over the English is known as the Norman Conquest.

◆ **What led to William's invasion of England?**

Spotlight on *Geography*

VIKING TRAVELS

In good weather, it takes only seven days to sail from Norway to Iceland. Greenland is only two days beyond that.

As early as 870, the Vikings traveled in longboats to colonize these islands. They found abundant fish and game. The growing season was so short that livestock starved because the first settlers did not grow enough grain to feed them during the long winter.

Teaching Options

Section 2 Resources

Teacher's Resources (TR)
Terms to Know, p. 25
Review History, p. 59
Build Your Skills, p. 93
Concept Builder, p. 228
Cause-and-Effect Chain, p. 325
Transparency 1

Conflict Resolution

Give students the following scenario: You have two best friends and two tickets to a sporting event or concert. Ask students to think about how they would decide which friend to take to the event. Then, have students apply the decision-making process to the situation involving King Edward's choice of a successor.

B. Feudalism

Changes in England came quickly after the Norman Conquest. The English nobles who had supported Harold lost their lands to William. William granted his Norman warriors large parcels of English land as rewards for their loyalty. His policy of granting land to loyal subjects was not entirely new. The system was called feudalism.

Land Grants and Service

In a feudal society, a king might grant a large parcel of land, called a **manor**, to a lord or knight. In exchange for the land, the lord would promise the king his loyalty. The manor often included a small town and the peasants who worked the land. The lord could pass the manor on to his children, but he did not actually own the land. The lord could also divide his manor into smaller portions and give each portion to another person. The lord was a **vassal** of the king, which meant that he owed the king his loyalty and support. Each person who received a part of the manor was a vassal of the lord.

Both the lord and his vassal had an obligation to one another. The lord agreed to protect his vassal from attack. The vassal pledged his loyalty to the lord. He agreed to work the land, make a small payment to the lord, and spend 40 days in military service each year. In this way, the lord had an income from his land and a military force to defend the land.

The feudal system was often complicated. A person could be a lord to vassals below him and a vassal to a lord above him. Some vassals pledged loyalty to more than one lord. In this case, a vassal often had one **liege lord**, or primary lord, to whom he owed first service. These relationships became difficult when two lords went to war. Sometimes one man was vassal to both lords.

Knighthood

In the early Middle Ages, the lord of a manor was, by definition, a noble and a knight. He had earned his land as a reward for military service to the king. However, being a knight meant more than being a good warrior. Knights were supposed to behave according to a code of conduct called **chivalry**. This code required knights to be loyal, brave, and honest. Knights were supposed to defend the weak and less privileged.

A knight who was a good warrior might win land or receive it as a reward from his lord. More land meant more vassals, greater strength, and more wealth. A knight needed to be wealthy because his equipment was very expensive. He had to maintain his horse and his armor. He also had to feed, clothe, and provide horses for the servants who traveled with him to war.

Importance of Castles

Kings and lords built great castles with high, strong walls to protect themselves and their families from other lords. Many castles were surrounded

Structure of Feudalism

King

Nobles and Church Officials

Knights

Peasants

✔ Chart Check

Which group was at the lowest end of the social structure?

A. The Viking Invasions of Europe

Purpose-Setting Question What are some of the possible reasons the Vikings began raiding in the ninth century? (Possible answers: The Viking population had grown too large for the land to support; European kingdoms were growing weaker.)

Review Ask students to look back at the map on page 274 to see how widely the Vikings traveled during the eighth through the eleventh centuries. Have them find Normandy on the map.

SPOTLIGHT ON GEOGRAPHY

VIKING TRAVELS Show students a map of the world (Transparency 1). Trace the path the Vikings would have taken to get from Scandinavia to Iceland, Greenland, and Newfoundland. Make sure students realize how difficult this trip would have been.

◆ **ANSWER** William had been chosen to inherit the throne of England from King Edward. However, before his death, Edward named Harold, Earl of Wessex, to be his successor.

B. Feudalism

Purpose-Setting Question What were some of the responsibilities of a knight in the Middle Ages? (good warrior, behave according to a code of conduct, be loyal, brave, and honest, defend the weak and oppressed)

Using the Chart

Structure of Feudalism

Have pairs of students study the chart on page 277. Have pairs describe the role of each person or group. Have students take notes about this information. Have more sources available. When completed, the class should share their notes on the chart and each person should add any missing information to his or her notes.

✔ Chart Check

Answer peasants

Meet Individual Needs:
VISUAL/SPATIAL LEARNERS

Explain to students that one of the most remarkable achievements of the Viking culture was the invention of the longboat, often called a long ship. Tell students to locate a diagram of a Viking longboat and trace it. Students should then label the parts of the longboat, such as oars, rudder, mast, and sail.

ESL/ELL STRATEGIES

Identify Essential Vocabulary Have students look up the word *liege* in a dictionary. Ask a volunteer to read the definitions aloud. Emphasize that, as an adjective, the meaning is "loyal or faithful." Ask students to create a sentence that uses the word in a context not related to feudalism.

Discuss Explain that castles were mainly built to keep out enemies. Stone and wood were the most-used building materials. Slate and thatch (thick bundles of reeds or other plants) were used for roofs but not for walls. Wood was easy to use but did not last very long, and it could easily be set on fire by an enemy. Stone buildings needed little maintenance and could last a long time. However, stone castles were cold, damp, and dark.

Tell students that before cannons and gunpowder, one of the only ways to bring down a stone wall was to dig a hole under it. The hole would cause a portion of the wall to collapse into it. Some castles were built on solid rock, to prevent digging. Have students present some ideas of their own for building a strong castle that could withstand an attack.

> **Activity**
>
> **Write a journal entry** Have students write a journal entry that would come from a medieval woman's journal. Entries should include a description of daily life and an opinion about how she views her life.

◆ **ANSWER** The lord agreed to protect his vassals from attack. The vassals pledged loyalty to the lord. Vassals agreed to work the land, make small payments to the lord, and spend 40 days in military service each year. The lord had an income from his land and a military force to defend the land.

C. The Economics of Feudalism

Purpose-Setting Question How did landowners in medieval Europe use their land? (People who did not have enough money to buy land made an agreement to work on the landowner's land and to serve part-time in the military. The landowner provided food, shelter, clothing, and protection from invasion.)

by a moat of water. A moat kept enemies at a distance. Inside the castle were rooms where the lord and his family lived. There were also areas where horses and weapons were kept. Other areas held large supplies of food and water, so that when the castle was attacked, the people inside had everything they needed to survive for some time.

Castles were often located in key places that were important to trade or travel, such as at the mouth of a river or at the entrance to an important mountain pass. Eventually, castles became symbols of status and wealth.

Women in the Middle Ages

During the Middle Ages, the legal status for all women was below that of men. While a woman could own land, her land and her belongings became the property of her husband when she married. For daughters of nobles, marriages were arranged for political, financial, or territorial gain. The lord of a manor often arranged for the peasant women on the manor to marry at a young age. He hoped that the women would have many children, which meant more workers for the manor.

The daily life of women depended in large part on their social status. For peasant women, life was full of hard work. In addition to caring for her family, she also worked long hours in the fields and helped to care for the animals. Peasants generally lived in one- or two-room cottages and usually ate vegetables, brown bread, grain, cheese, and soup.

Ladies of the manor were usually responsible for running the household. They went to the fields to see how hard the peasants were working. They supervised the buying of food and its preparation, including the preserving of food for the winter. They were trained to spin, weave, and make the clothing for the family. These upper-class women were also expected to care for the sick and entertain guests in their homes. Often they learned to play a musical instrument, to sing, and to play games. They were also responsible for defending the manor when their lord was away.

◆ **How were the lord and his vassals dependent upon one another?**

C. The Economics of Feudalism

During the early Middle Ages, wealth was generally measured in land. Having land meant that a person could grow food to eat. Yet, most people did not have enough money to buy land. Instead, they made an agreement with a landowner to work on his land and to serve part-time in the military. In exchange, the landowner would provide food, shelter, clothing, and protection from invasion. This economic system was called manorialism, because it was based on the manor as an economic unit.

Peasants

During this time, most people living on the land were peasants. Some peasants were free to move from place to place as they wished, but most were **serfs**. Serfs were peasants who were legally bound to the land of the manor where they worked.

Upper-class women in medieval times were often responsible for entertaining guests. The two women here are playing chess.

278 UNIT 3 ◆ Regional Civilizations

Teaching Options

> **Focus on**
> **TEEN LIFE**
>
> **Teens in the Middles Ages** Life was harsh during the Middle Ages, and disease was common. The average life expectancy was about 30 years. Most people married in their teens. Men fought as knights and farmed during their teen years. Life expectancy was no different among the nobility and royalty, which explains why many rulers, including William the Conqueror, took on leadership roles at a very young age.
>
> Have student groups plan a manual for young people of the Middle Ages that identifies the information they will need as they take on adult responsibilities. The manual should cover all disciplines, including science (keeping animals healthy), mathematics (logging income and expenses), and music (playing an instrument).

One source described the role of a serf in this way:

> ❝It is seemly that men should plow and dig and work hard in order that the earth may yield the fruits from which the knight and his horse will live.❞

Serfs could be sold with the land they lived and worked on. Most owned very little—usually a few animals and some tools. Serfs were not allowed to leave the land without the lord's permission, and the lord could not force them to leave. Serfs paid rent, usually in the form of food produced, and agreed to work three days a week in the lord's fields. The lord, in turn, provided a house and protection for the serfs and their families.

Technology Brings Improvement in Farming

By the eleventh century, life in Europe had improved somewhat. People generally had plenty of food and were not being killed in battle. As a result, the population began to grow.

At the same time, new inventions made farming easier. The new iron plow could cut through hard, rocky soil. A system of harnessing animals one behind the other allowed teams of animals to pull heavier loads. A system of crop rotation kept the soil from wearing out.

As new lands opened up, conditions for free peasants and serfs improved. Lords realized that they might lose workers if they found more favorable conditions elsewhere. The lords had to extend new privileges or remove some of the heavier burdens from their peasant workers.

◆ **What were the advantages for serfs under feudalism?**

ANALYZE PRIMARY SOURCES

DOCUMENT-BASED QUESTION
Was this statement written from the point of view of the peasant or the knight? Explain your answer.

Review II

Review History
A. How did Viking culture spread to England?
B. In what ways did feudalism shape society in the early Middle Ages?
C. How did the system of feudalism benefit both lords and peasants?

Define Terms to Know
Define the following terms:
manor, vassal, liege lord, chivalry, serf

Critical Thinking
What changes did William of Normandy bring to England?

Write About Economics
Write a paragraph explaining why a person would agree to become the vassal of a lord.

Get Organized
CAUSE-AND-EFFECT CHAIN
Use a cause-and-effect chain to analyze information from this section. For example, what was the cause and effect of the Norman Conquest?

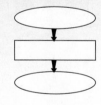

CHAPTER 12 ◆ The Early Middle Ages **279**

CAUSE
Death of English king

⬇

EVENT
Norman invasion and conquest of England

⬇

EFFECT
Norman warriors receive parcels of English land.

Critical Thinking
William granted his Norman warriors large parcels of English land. His policy of granting land was called feudalism.

Write About Economics
Students' paragraphs should include protection, land, and food as reasons to agree to become a vassal to a lord.

ANALYZE PRIMARY SOURCES

DOCUMENT-BASED QUESTION
Explain that the usual view of medieval people was that serfs existed for the sake of the higher orders, the knights and the lords. Society was strictly structured, and there was little opportunity to move between social classes.

ANSWER It was written from the point of view of the knight. It implies that it is only right that peasants farm, so that the knight and his horse can eat.

Focus Explain to students that crop rotation involved dividing fields into three sections. One section was left unplanted. Another was planted in the spring. The third was planted in the fall. Each year the sections would be rotated. Ask students how they think the peasants kept track of the complicated system if none of them knew how to read or write.

◆ **ANSWER** Under feudalism, a serf had a house to live in, land to farm, and protection from raiders and other enemies.

Section Close

Return to the SQR chart from the beginning of the section. Ask students to fill in the Read box with the information they learned about feudalism.

---

3 Assess

Review Answers

Review History
A. The Vikings conquered and settled in Normandy. Later, William of Normandy conquered England and brought the culture to England.

B. It created a class of landowners who were loyal to and supported the king and vassals who pledged their loyalty to the lord.

C. Lords had food grown for them. Peasants had land to farm and protection from enemies.

Define Terms to Know
manor, 277; vassal, 277; liege lord, 277; chivalry, 277; serf, 278

Section Summary

In this section, students will learn how the Roman Catholic Church was a major part of society, providing moral guidance as well as supporting religious communities of monks and nuns. Students will read about how the elaborate and costly Gothic-style cathedrals grew from the wealth and power of the Church. Finally, students will observe how European rulers treated Jewish people in medieval Europe.

1 Introduce

Getting Started

Have students look through the section. On the board, make an outline of the headings and subheadings in the section. Ask students to predict what they will learn under each heading.

TERMS TO KNOW

Explain to students that sometimes a vocabulary term is easier to remember if they think of an example of the term. Have students find or think of an example for each vocabulary term. Students should then write the term on one side of an index card and the example on the other. For example, have them find the name and location of a convent and a monastery.

ACTIVE READING

Give an example of how to make a generalization. Read the first paragraph of the section aloud. Ask students to identify its facts and details. Then, as a class, have them write a generalization. Tell students to use that exercise as a model for making their own generalizations as they read each subsection.

Terms to Know

tithe a tax equal to one-tenth of a person's income

monastery a religious community of men

convent a religious community of women

Gothic style a style of architecture used for churches in medieval Europe

anti-Semitism prejudice against Jewish people

Main Ideas

A. Men and women in the Middle Ages took part in the Roman Catholic Church as members or as monks and nuns.

B. During the early Middle Ages, the authority of the Church could be seen in the power of the pope and in lavish cathedrals, while Jewish people were free to worship their own religion.

Active Reading

GENERALIZE
When you generalize, you make an assessment from the facts and details you have read. As you read this section, think about the many ways the Church was part of medieval life. Then, make a generalization about its importance.

A. The Importance of the Church

It is almost impossible to imagine how important the Roman Catholic Church was during the early Middle Ages in western Europe. Nearly everyone in society worshiped according to the rules of the Church. The Church unified the people of a country by providing a common set of beliefs. It also provided a common meeting place for people in a village and a place to hold celebrations and other social activities, or functions. In terms of power, even a king was not equal to the head of the Roman Catholic Church, the pope.

Religion in Everyday Life

The parish, or village church, was the center of village life during the early Middle Ages. Everyone was expected to go to church on Sundays and on other holy days, such as the feast days of important saints. The Roman Catholic Church service, called Mass, was given in Latin.

This nineteenth-century painting shows a woman kneeling inside a highly decorated medieval church.

The parish priest was often the only educated person in the village or town. His job was to perform marriages, baptisms, and funerals as well as to teach the rules and values of the Roman Catholic Church.

In addition, the priest cared for the sick and poor of the community by supplying food and shelter. In some cases, a priest would run a school for the children of his parish. For most people, the parish priest was their only contact with the Church. The parish priest was a very important man in the village.

The services of the Church were paid for by the parishioners. They were obligated to pay to the Church a **tithe**, or a tax that equaled one-tenth of their income. Their money or goods went to care for the parish church and to provide food and shelter for the parish priest. In addition to the tithe, many wealthy families gave gifts or paid for improvements to their church.

Above the parish priest was a bishop. The bishop was in charge of the parishes in a certain

---

Teaching Options

Section 3 Resources

Teacher's Resources (TR)

Terms to Know, p. 25
Review History, p. 59
Build Your Skills, p. 93
Concept Builder, p. 228
Chapter Test, pp. 139–140
Cause-and-Effect Chain, p. 325

Using Technology

Provide the opportunity for students to search for information about Benedictine monks using a CD-ROM encyclopedia or the Internet. Ask students to record in a brief paragraph some of the details they find and then refer to these details as they read the section.

geographic region, called a diocese. It was the bishop's job to oversee the parish priests and to settle disputes that involved the Church. Above the bishop was the archbishop, who was in charge of many dioceses. Above the archbishop was a senior archbishop, and then the pope. There was no higher authority in the Roman Catholic Church than the pope.

Religious Communities

Some men and women chose to practice their religion by withdrawing from society and joining religious communities called **monasteries** and **convents**. Religious men who joined monasteries were called monks. Monks took vows of poverty, purity, and obedience to the abbot, who was the head of the monastery. Monks spent their time working for the monastery and praying. People in medieval times believed that prayer directly benefited those who had died.

The monastery contained a church or chapel where the monks worshiped, dormitories where they slept, and other buildings where the monks ate and worked. In addition to their life of prayer, monks were expected to perform some kind of work. In many cases, the monks of a particular monastery became experts at certain tasks, such as raising sheep for wool.

Religious women who joined convents were called nuns. Most early convents accepted only well-born women who brought with them an inheritance of land and money. Later, convents accepted women from all social classes. Convents were run by women called abbesses. The abbess was often a woman of noble background or even a member of a royal house.

Wealthy people often gave gifts of land to monasteries and convents in exchange for special prayers for salvation, or the saving of one's soul. As a result, these religious communities grew, and the abbots and abbesses became overlords to many vassals and peasants. The land and its workers provided an income for the religious community, allowing it to pay for food and shelter and to care for the buildings. Many monasteries and convents grew quite wealthy and powerful.

The Roles of Monasteries and Convents

In addition to being places of prayer, monasteries and convents filled other roles in society. They became places of learning. Some monasteries were known for the beautiful books they produced. The monks would hand copy each page, often decorating the pages. Other monasteries and convents served as hospitals. Travelers could stay at a convent or monastery at night, knowing that they would be safe and fed.

Some monks felt that they had to leave the monastery and spread their religious message. These monks, called missionaries, helped convince most of western Europe to become Roman Catholic by 1050.

Benedictine Rule

Around 530, a holy man named Benedict organized a monastery in southern Italy. During his time as abbot, he wrote a series of rules for his monks to follow. The rules urged the monks to lead simple, orderly lives of prayer, study, and work. The rules also had monks lead lives of poverty so that they could concentrate on their religious duties. These rules were called the Benedictine Rule and were followed by most monasteries of Europe and England for many centuries.

As monasteries grew wealthy, some of the abbots who ran them lived well and entertained lavishly. Many of the other abbots and monks called for reform. They felt that these monasteries were not following Benedict's rule of poverty.

Then & Now

CONVENTS AND MONASTERIES

During the Middle Ages, the majority of people who chose to live in a religious community were men. In 1066, for example, there were just 13 convents compared to 48 monasteries in England.

By the nineteenth and twentieth centuries, these numbers had reversed. About three-fourths of the people in Roman Catholic religious communities were now women.

This page of a manuscript copied by monks shows the first initial of the text on the page, as well as Benedictine monks in prayer.

A. The Importance of the Church

Purpose-Setting Question Why was the Roman Catholic Church important in the Middle Ages? (Nearly everyone worshiped according to its rules; it unified the people of a country; it provided a common set of beliefs; it was a common meeting place and a place to celebrate, even a king was not equal to the pope.)

Focus Students may not understand how important the Roman Catholic Church was in the everyday lives of European people during this time in history. To help students understand, ask them to suggest as many ways as they can think of that government controls or influences their lives. Remind them that the local, state, and federal governments have many laws regulating where we live, where we go to school, what we learn, how we travel, and so on. Help students understand that the Roman Catholic Church assumed many of the roles that government has today.

Then & Now

CONVENTS AND MONASTERIES Have students find a present-day monastery or convent by looking in a telephone book or on the Internet. Have students find out the name, location, and mission of the religious community, and the number and gender of its population.

Activity

Make an idea web Make an idea web (TR, p. 321) on the board. In the center, write *The Life of a Monk or Nun in the Middle Ages*. Have students suggest information from the text to include in each circle.

Extend Decorated, or illuminated, manuscripts took months or years to make. They were printed by hand on pages made from animal skins. Illuminations were often inlaid with gold leaf. Ask students how they think people treated books in the Middle Ages. (with great care and respect)

ESL/ELL STRATEGIES

Use Visuals Remind students that an adjective is a word that describes a noun. Ask students to look at the image of the medieval church that is shown on page 280. Ask them to write as many adjectives as they can think of to describe the church and the woman praying in the church. Ask a volunteer to make a class list of the adjectives on the board.

Make a chart Have groups of 3–4 students make a chart with one column for each religious order covered in the following sections on pages 281–282: Benedictine Rule and New Religious Orders. (4 columns: Benedictines, Carthusians, Dominicans, and Franciscans) Under each heading, have the groups write facts from the text about the lifestyle and mission of the order. Then, have the group decide which order they believe was truly wealthy.

TEACH PRIMARY SOURCES
Have students study the photograph of the monastery of Saint Michel. Ask students what images or feelings the monastery suggests. (strength, security, long lasting, success, awe inspiring, wealth) Discuss how these images helped reinforce the power and role of the Roman Catholic Church.

Discuss Review with students the ways the different orders operated. Then, ask them which orders they think would have had the most impact on the lives of the peasants in medieval Europe and why they think this way.

◆ **ANSWER** Many wealthy families gave gifts or paid for large improvements in monasteries and convents.

B. Church, Religion, and Power

Purpose-Setting Question Why was the Roman Catholic Church so powerful? (Almost all men and women were members of the Roman Catholic Church. The pope had the power to excommunicate Church members. Excommunication meant that a person's soul would not go to heaven, a person could not have a Christian marriage or burial, and others would avoid the excommunicated person. Great nobles, kings, and even the toughest warriors feared the authority of the pope.)

The monastery at Saint Michel shows the wealth of some religious communities in medieval Europe.

New Religious Orders

Some monks started their own religious orders. Their members focused on prayer and living simply. Some groups were so strict that they had very few members. For example, Carthusian monks lived as hermits, sheltered from the outside world. Each monk had his own hut and did not have any contact with people except during services. The Carthusian monks did not even see the servants who brought their meals. A small opening was built into each hut through which a dish was silently placed at mealtimes.

The ideas of the Roman Catholic Church were spread throughout parts of Europe by wandering priests. One order, or group, of such priests was the Dominicans. Founded by a Spanish priest named Dominic, the Dominican order considered studying to be very important. As a result, many priests in this order were scholars.

Some religious organizations had orders of nuns. The nuns did not travel from place to place, preaching the ideas of the Church. The main responsibility of these nuns was to care for the sick and the poor.

The Franciscan order was another important group. Founded in France by Francis of Assisi, members of this order chose to live as beggars. They lived in poverty and traveled about helping the poor and the sick. Members of this order called themselves friars, which means *brothers*. The Franciscan friars were deeply respected because of their simple lifestyle and good works. Women were also welcomed by the Franciscans. The Franciscan order for women, called the Poor Clares, also helped the poor and the sick.

◆ **How did monasteries and convents gain wealth?**

B. Church, Religion, and Power

The power of the pope came from hundreds of years of Church tradition. According to this tradition, the pope held supreme power on Earth and in heaven. Medieval people believed that the pope spoke with the voice of God and from Him, to his bishops and priests.

The Pope's Reach

The ultimate weapon of the pope was excommunication, the expelling of a person or group of people from the Church. To believers, this punishment was dreadful, because it meant that a person's soul would not go to heaven. Also, it meant that he or she could not receive a Christian marriage or burial. In addition, others would avoid an excommunicated person for fear of being punished in the same way. The pope could also issue an order to excommunicate an entire town or kingdom.

Almost all men and women at this time were members of the Roman Catholic Church. Most people were superstitious and afraid of evil forces loose in the world. Their religion served as a shield. Great nobles, kings, and even the toughest warriors feared the authority of the pope.

Teaching Options

The Cistercian Order

The Cistercian order of monks also rejected luxury. The following passage gives some evidence of the daily life of a Cistercian monk. "From the Ides of September till Easter . . . they do not take more than one meal a day, except on Sunday. They never leave the cloister but for purpose of labour, nor do they ever speak, either there or elsewhere, save only to the abbot or prior."

Meet Individual Needs:
VISUAL/SPATIAL LEARNERS

Have students draw a stained glass window on paper. The scene should tell a story about the Middle Ages. It does not need to be a biblical story. The window should be shaped as a long rectangle, perhaps with a rounded peak at the top, and it should be colorful. Students should then give the window to another student to see if the window communicates the intended story.

Cathedral Architecture

The outward expression of the power of the Church could be seen in the grand medieval cathedrals. A cathedral is a church that houses a bishop's throne, or *cathedra* in Latin.

The cathedral was usually the largest church in a parish, or diocese. It was also the most richly decorated. Cathedrals were designed to hold grand processions and religious celebrations involving many people. The cathedrals were enormously expensive and demanded the talents of thousands of workers over many years.

During the early Middle Ages, churches and cathedrals were built with round arches and heavy roofs. Their walls were thick, and the interior contained many pillars. There were usually small windows in the walls that let in very little light. This was known as the Romanesque style of architecture.

In the later part of the Middle Ages, the style of cathedrals changed. Due to improvements in building techniques—pointed, ribbed vaults to support the roofs and flying buttresses to support the walls—churches were more open and rose much higher. This architecture is called **Gothic style**, and it spread across medieval Europe. The arches and spires, or tall stone peaks, pointed toward the sky and were supposed to draw the attention of the faithful up toward God.

Gothic-style cathedrals also contained beautiful stained-glass windows. Most people at the time could not read, so the windows served to illustrate stories from the Bible. The light shining through the windows would change the appearance of the interior of the church during the course of a day.

Notre Dame Cathedral in Paris, France, is typical of the Gothic-style architecture of the Middle Ages.

Demonstrate Show students how the light coming through stained glass windows can change the appearance of a room. Place tinted panels of plastic on the classroom windows. Show students how the colors change positions and intensity as the sun moves in the sky. Remind students that this color movement would have been an extraordinary sight in the days before electricity.

Activity

Compare and contrast
Student groups should research pictures of churches and cathedrals that were constructed in the early Middle Ages and others that were constructed in the later Middle Ages. The pictures should be labeled and placed on posterboard. Then under the pictures, have students compare and contrast these buildings and their features. Students' findings should be written on the posterboard.

Focus Explain to students that it took many years and many workers to build the Gothic-style cathedrals. Ask students what types of tradespeople would be needed to build a cathedral. (manual laborers, stonemasons, artists, woodcarvers, carpenters, and others)

TEACH PRIMARY SOURCES

Ask students to look at the details in the photograph of Notre Dame in Paris, France. Ask students to describe the details they can see in the photograph. Tell students that construction of this famous cathedral was begun in 1163 and was finally completed almost 200 years later in 1345. The cathedral was built in the same spot as was used by the Celts, Romans, and earlier Christians for worship.

Research

AVERAGE
Have students find, photocopy, and display images of one or more Gothic-style cathedrals. With each image, have them identify the name, location, and date of construction. Also, have students label directly on the image some of the extraordinary features of the cathedral. Display the images together in the classroom.

ADVANCED
Have students research one Gothic-style cathedral. Have them collect images of its construction, façade, floor plan, sculpture, and interior artwork. Display the images on posterboard along with a paragraph that identifies the name, location, date of construction of the cathedral, as well as the importance of each image displayed.

Discuss Ask students what jobs Jewish people were allowed to hold. (merchants who traded spices, silks, and jewels; bankers who lent money) Discuss why they were allowed to hold these jobs.

SPOTLIGHT ON ECONOMICS

BANKS AND LOANS For Christians, charging interest on a loan was a sin. However, it was not sinful for a Christian to borrow money from a non-Christian or to pay interest to a non-Christian.

Because Jewish people existed largely outside of European society, a Christian borrower could be certain of almost no legal consequences for neglecting to pay back a loan. However, most people who needed large sums of money were very careful to treat their Jewish moneylenders fairly so that they would be willing to provide another loan in the future. Ask students to identify the consequences for neglecting to repay a loan today. Point out that some of these consequences are no different than they were in the Middle Ages.

◆ **ANSWER** The Jewish merchants kept the trade routes open between western Europe and the Middle East; they acquired goods otherwise not available to wealthy Europeans; and they made large loans to kings or nobles.

Section Close

Ask students to list the ways religion played a part in society in the Middle Ages. Then, ask them to explain this statement made by one medieval historian, "The Middle Ages was the Church."

Review Answers

Review History
A. All people gave tithes to the Roman Catholic Church. Wealthy people gave gifts to the Church. Some men and women joined religious orders.

B. People believed that the pope spoke with the voice of God; the pope could excommunicate those he felt were wrong.

Define Terms to Know
tithe, 280; monastery, 281; convent, 281; Gothic style, 283; anti-Semitism, 284

Do You Remember?
In Chapter 2, you learned about the beginnings of Judaism.

Spotlight on
Economics

BANKS AND LOANS
In medieval times, Christians were not allowed to charge interest on a loan. This was considered a sin. Charging interest was not forbidden by Judaism. Yet, because courts were not likely to rule in favor of a Jewish person, banking was risky business, and interest rates were high.

Jewish People and European Economics

The Middle Ages was a time of **anti-Semitism**, or attacks and prejudice against Jewish people. Jews were restricted from owning land and from working in most professions. However, during the early Middle Ages, most Jews lived quite peacefully in the Christian lands of northern Europe and were free to practice their own religion. Jews in Spain were also left alone when Muslims ruled the region. The Muslim leaders were more interested in collecting taxes than in converting Jews to their religion.

Jewish merchants were able to keep the lines of trade open between the Middle East and Europe during times that Muslims and Christians were at war. As traders, they acquired goods that were otherwise not available to wealthy Europeans. These goods included spices, silks, and jewels as well as furs, swords, and lumber.

Their skill as traders made many Jewish families quite wealthy. The Jewish banking families often made large loans to kings or nobles. As a result, powerful lords and political families protected the Jewish communities because they needed the trading and banking services. During this period, Jews typically could not own land. Their wealth was often in the form of gold, precious stones, and other goods.

The protection of Jews ended around the eleventh century for several reasons. First, Christian traders became more successful and more common. Foreign goods were no longer the sole property of Jewish traders. Second, Church policy started to allow Christians to charge interest on loans. Third, Christianity became more violent during the Crusades of the eleventh century, which you will read about in Chapter 13. The attacks against Jews and Muslims in the Middle East led to more violence against Jews in Europe. Certain bishops called for Jews to convert to Christianity or be expelled from their lands. As a result, many Jews left England and France and moved to the regions of present-day Germany and Poland. There, they could be farther away from the great Christian powers and could live in relative peace.

◆ **Why did powerful lords protect Jewish people from persecution?**

 Review III

Review History
A. What were some of the ways men and women participated in the activities of the Church in medieval times?
B. What was the authority of the pope, and how could it be used?

Define Terms to Know
Define the following terms: **tithe, monastery, convent, Gothic style, anti-Semitism**

Critical Thinking
Why was excommunication a feared punishment for Roman Catholics?

Write About Culture
Write a paragraph that describes the Gothic style of architecture.

Get Organized
CAUSE-AND-EFFECT CHAIN
Use a cause-and-effect chain to analyze events from this section. For example, what were some of the causes and effects of the wealth acquired by monasteries and convents?

Critical Thinking
Excommunication meant that a person's soul would not go to heaven, and that other people would avoid any person who had been excommunicated.

Write About Culture
Students' paragraphs may include that churches built in the Gothic style of architecture were large and impressive, showing God's power. The arches and spires pointed toward the sky and God.

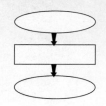

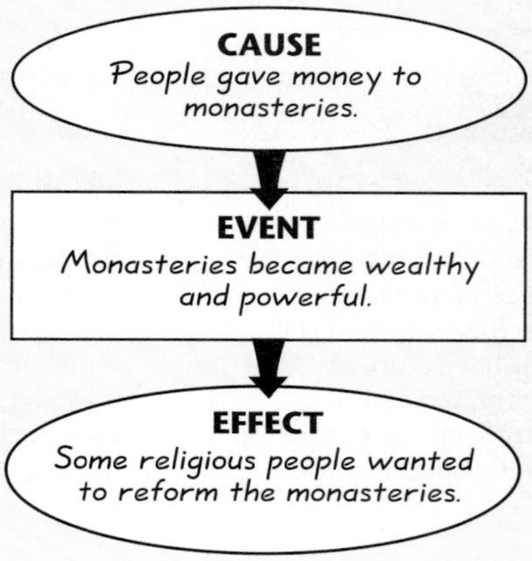

CAUSE
People gave money to monasteries.

EVENT
Monasteries became wealthy and powerful.

EFFECT
Some religious people wanted to reform the monasteries.

Points *of* View

Decoration in Monasteries

During the Middle Ages the Christian Church dominated many aspects of life and culture. Churches and monasteries could be found in almost every city and town.

Benedictine Rule required monks and nuns to put aside worldly possessions. Over time, however, it became more difficult to live simply. Monasteries grew wealthier because of donations of money and gifts by the aristocracy. Monastery churches became grander, often having lavish decorations. By the 1100s, a debate arose over how correct it was to have decoration in monasteries. Two powerful abbots, Abbot Suger and Abbot St. Bernard, expressed these differing views. Abbot Suger wrote a report about the rebuilding of his grand abbey church in 1135. Abbot St. Bernard, who ran a monastery that followed the Benedictine Rule, was an outspoken critic of decoration in monasteries.

Thirteenth-century gold chalice from a monastery in Belgium

❝[B]ecause of my delight in the beauty of the house of God, the splendor of the multicolored gems tears me away from external cares. To me . . . it always has seemed right that the most expensive things should be used above all for the administration of the holy Eucharist. To be sure . . . holy mind, pure heart, and faithful intention . . . are the things that matter most; yet . . . we should also serve God with the external ornaments of sacred vessels. . . . ❞

—Abbot Suger, St. Denis Monastery
The Book of Abbot Suger of St. Denis,
ca. 1144

❝[T]he immense height of the [abbey] churches . . . their . . . sumptuous [lavish] decoration and finely executed pictures . . . divert the attention of those who are praying . . . and impede devotion. . . . It may be that they are . . . to God's honor. I, however, [ask] 'what business has gold in the sanctuary?' We . . . who have renounced [given up] anything precious or attractive . . . what do we expect to arouse by these [worldly] means?❞

—Abbot St. Bernard, Clairvaux Monastery
Letter to Guillaume de St. Thierry, ca. 1124

ANALYZE PRIMARY SOURCES

DOCUMENT-BASED QUESTIONS

1. According to Abbot Suger, what purpose do gems and other church ornaments serve?

2. According to Abbot St. Bernard, what effect does lavish decoration have on a churchgoer?

3. **Critical Thinking** Which view presents the strongest argument for or against decoration in monastery churches? Explain your answer.

CHAPTER 12 ◆ The Early Middle Ages **285**

Points *of* View

DECORATION IN MONASTERIES

Teach the Topic

These selections present two different points of view concerning the medieval practice of decorating monasteries in an elaborate fashion. The authors of these two quotations were both respected leaders of their time.

Abbot Suger was a statesman and a historian. As a statesman he sought to strengthen royal power, improve agriculture, commerce, and trade, and reform the justice system. As an abbot he introduced major reforms. Abbot St. Bernard was high born, highly educated, especially in literature and poetry, and known for his piety and kindness.

Compare and Contrast Points of View

Ask students how the authors of these quotations felt about the issue of elaborate decorations in monasteries. What were some of the reasons each abbot might have felt the way he did? How do we know how they felt? What specific words or phrases were used in each case that indicated how they felt? Have students compare the arguments and decide whose viewpoint they would support.

ANALYZE PRIMARY SOURCES

DOCUMENT-BASED QUESTIONS
1. They serve to help churchgoers escape from external cares.
2. Churchgoers would find such decoration distracting.
3. Possible answers: Abbot Suger's argument is stronger, because it shows how the love and worship of God can be expressed through the beautiful objects found in his church. Abbot St. Bernard's argument is stronger, because it gives examples of ways in which decoration in monastery churches is distracting to the people who use the church.

Teaching Options

LINK to TODAY

Places of worship today are decorated in many different styles. Some are extremely decorative and others are very simple or plain. If possible, have students visit or study photographs of places of worship in their community. Have students discuss the different styles and then categorize the places of worship by style.

F Y I

Glastonbury and King Arthur

Glastonbury is one of England's oldest monasteries. Legend has it that in 1190, during the rebuilding of the monastery, the monks came upon a grave 7 feet below the surface containing a stone slab with words in Latin: *Here lies the renowned King Arthur in the isle of Avalon with his second wife Guinevere.* Today, a sign marks the grave from which the royal remains disappeared after King Henry VIII ordered the monastery closed in 1539.

Chapter Summary

A blank outline form is available in the Teacher's Resources (p. 318). Chapter summaries should outline the development of early European kingdoms, the rise of feudalism and its effects on society, as well as the importance of the Roman Catholic Church. Refer to the rubric in the Teacher's Resources (p. 340) to score students' chapter summaries.

⬤ Interpret the Timeline

1. 155 years
2. 14 years
3. Clovis unites the Frankish groups, Charlemagne is crowned Roman emperor, Vikings establish first settlement in Normandy, and Normans conquer England.
4. Check that students' events are from the chapter and are listed in order.

Use Terms to Know

5. vassal
6. convent
7. anti-Semitism
8. serf
9. medieval
10. manor
11. liege lord
12. chivalry

Check Your Understanding

13. The soil was rich, mineral resources were available, and the area had navigable rivers. People were nomadic or farmers and spoke Germanic languages.
14. Clovis united several Frankish groups, and formed an army that was powerful enough to defeat the Romans in Gaul. He then created a strong kingdom to rule the area.
15. He brought great artisans and scholars to his kingdom and established schools.
16. Charlemagne's kingdom was divided among his grandsons, who were weak leaders. Poor leadership allowed invaders to conquer large parts of the kingdom.
17. The Vikings conquered and then established settlements in Normandy. Later, William the Conqueror, a Norman, invaded and conquered England.

Chapter Summary

Complete the following outline in your notebook. Then, use your outline to write a brief summary of the chapter.

The Early Middle Ages

I. Early European Kingdoms
   A. The People and Land of the Middle Ages in Europe
   B. The Empire of the Franks
   C. The Age of Charlemagne
II. Feudalism and the Manor System
   A. The Viking Invasions of Europe
   B. Feudalism
   C. The Economics of Feudalism
III. The Church in Medieval Times
   A. The Importance of the Church
   B. Church, Religion, and Power

⬤ Interpret the Timeline

Use the timeline on pages 268–269 to answer the following questions.

1. How many years passed between the time that the Vikings founded Normandy and the Normans conquered England?
2. For how many years did Charlemagne rule the Roman Empire?
3. **Critical Thinking** Which events show the merging of different groups of people in Europe?
4. Select four events from the chapter that are not on the timeline. Create a timeline that shows these events.

Use Terms to Know

Select the term that best completes each sentence.

anti-Semitism   liege lord   serf
chivalry   manor   vassal
convent   medieval

5. A person who has taken a pledge of loyalty to a lord is a _____.
6. A _____ is a religious community for women.
7. Prejudice against Jewish people is _____.
8. A peasant legally bound to the land is a _____.
9. The word _____ means "Middle Ages."
10. A _____ is the land and property under a lord's control.
11. The person to whom a vassal owes first service is his _____.
12. _____ is the code of conduct for knights.

Check Your Understanding

13. **Describe** the land and people of western Europe in the early Middle Ages.
14. **Explain** how Clovis changed who held power in Europe.
15. **Describe** the way Charlemagne made his kingdom a place of learning and culture.
16. **Explain** why Charlemagne's empire declined after his death.
17. **Summarize** the successes of the Viking invasions of the early Middle Ages.
18. **Explain** why William of Normandy believed he had a claim to the English crown.
19. **Describe** a serf's obligations to his lord in a feudal system.
20. **Identify** three of the duties of an upper-class woman in the Middle Ages.
21. **Explain** why land was important during the Middle Ages.
22. **Identify** the major role of the parish priest in the Middle Ages.

18. William had helped Edward, who was king of England and childless. In exchange, Edward had promised William the crown.
19. Serfs worked land belonging to the lord, paid dues—usually food—and fought in military service for the lord.
20. Any three of the following: manage the household; run the estate when the lord is away; make clothing; care for the sick; supervise the buying, cooking, and preparation of food; check on peasants working in the fields, and entertain guests.
21. Land was a measure of wealth. It meant that a person could grow food to eat.
22. The parish priest performed marriages, baptisms, and funerals; taught the rules and values of the Church; cared for the sick and poor; and often ran the village school.

Critical Thinking

23. Draw Conclusions Why would the Roman Catholic pope want the authority to approve rulers in Europe?

24. Make Inferences What effects did the Norman Conquest have on the English?

25. Analyze Primary Sources How does the quote about the role of peasants on page 279 support the social system of feudalism?

26. Make Inferences How were Jewish people important to the economy of Europe during the Middle Ages?

27. Make Inferences How did early medieval Europeans treat Jewish people?

Put Your Skills to Work

28. Use Secondary Sources Read the selection below from a secondary source that tells about Vikings and their raids. Then, answer the following questions.

a. What assessments can you make about the reliability of the secondary source?

b. What biases do you detect?

c. Based on the author's description, what is a major characteristic of the Vikings?

> ". . . Vikings on the rampage were a terrible force to be reckoned with. They frequently turned on each other in raids just as grisly as those they would later unleash against the rest of Europe. 'I've been with sword and spear slippery with bright blood where kites wheeled,' runs one tenth century poem. 'And how well we violent Vikings clashed! Red flames ate up men's roofs, raging we killed and killed, and skewered bodies sprawled sleepy in town gateways.'"
> —*Vikings: Raiders from the North*

Analyze Sources

29. Read this selection from a book about the nature of knighthood by a medieval writer, Diaz De Gamez. Then, answer the questions that follow.

Of what profit is a good knight? I tell you that through good knights is the king and the kingdom honored, protected, feared, and defended. I tell you that the king, when He sends forth a good knight with an army and entrusts him with a great enterprise, on sea or on land, has in him a pledge of victory. I tell you that without good knights, a king is like a man who has neither feet nor hands.

a. What is the value of the knight to the kingdom, according to the author?

b. To what does the writer compare a king without good knights?

Essay Writing

30. Many present-day relationships are built on mutual obligations, just as they were in feudal society. Describe the mutual obligations you have to another person, such as your parent or teacher. Then, write a pledge to that person describing the obligation and write a similar pledge from that person to you.

TEST PREPARATION

CAUSE-AND-EFFECT RELATIONSHIPS
Choose the answer that correctly completes the sentence.

One cause of the Viking raids in western Europe was probably

1. overpopulation in the the Vikings' native lands.

2. a desire to live in a warmer climate.

3. a lack of skilled artisans.

4. a wish to become more cultured.

Critical Thinking

23. The pope wanted the authority because it made him more powerful in western Europe and helped protect him because the kings he supported would then support him.
24. The English who had supported William's opponent lost their lands. William granted his Norman warriors large parcels of English land. This would introduce Norman culture into England. This policy of granting land to loyal subjects was known as feudalism.
25. The quotation reinforces the position of peasants and knights and describes the role of the peasant.
26. Jewish people were the merchants, traders, and bankers in medieval Europe. In these roles, they were very important to the economy.
27. Early medieval Europeans were generally tolerant of Jewish people and did not attack them.

Put Your Skills to Work
USE SECONDARY SOURCES
28a. The source is probably reliable because it uses a primary source.
28b. The source is a poem that might embroider the truth. The poet may wish to depict Vikings as more fierce than they actually were.
28c. A major characteristic of the Vikings is their violent nature.

Analyze Sources

29a. A knight protects the kingdom.
29b. a man without feet or hands

Essay Writing

30. Students' pledges should reflect mutual obligations, such as doing required work, helping each other, loyalty, respect, etc.

TEST PREPARATION

Answer 1. overpopulation in the Vikings' native lands.

The High Middle Ages
962–1492
(pp. 288–311)

Chapter Objectives

• Identify the Crusades and how they affected medieval Europe.
• Describe social and economic consequences of the growth of towns and the Black Death.
• Discuss the development of nation-states in Europe.
• Explain the Great Schism and identify further troubles of the Roman Catholic Church.

Chapter Summary

Section I focuses on the Crusades, how they began, and how they impacted European life.
Section II explains how trade and towns grew, and how the Black Death affected Europe.
Section III describes how conflicts between France and England led to greater political unity within each country, how conflicts between popes and kings continued in the Holy Roman Empire, and how Spain was reclaimed from the Muslims.
Section IV explores reasons for the Great Schism and further challenges to the Church's authority.

Set the Stage

TEACH PRIMARY SOURCES

Explain to students that Geoffrey Chaucer (ca. 1342–1400) was the first court writer to write in the English language, and, over 600 years later, is still considered one of the greatest English poets.

Discuss the verses from *The Canterbury Tales* on this page. Tell students that the word *martyr* means "a person who chooses death rather than renounce his religion." Ask students why people might have liked to take pilgrimages in April in particular. (Possible answer: Winter was over, and travel was easier.) Tell students that the martyr referred to in the verse is Thomas Becket, who was killed in Canterbury Cathedral over 200 years before Chaucer wrote his account (see p. 302).

CHAPTER 13

The High Middle Ages
962–1492

I. The Crusades Begin
II. Trade and Towns Grow
III. Organized Kingdoms Develop
IV. The Roman Catholic Church Faces Crises

Beginning around the year 1000 in Europe, trade became more active, and the population increased steadily. More towns and cities grew, and unified countries began to develop. This later period of the Middle Ages from about 1000 to 1300 is known as the High Middle Ages.

During this time, the Church continued to be an important force in people's lives. Pilgrimages, or journeys to holy places, were common. These journeys combined travel, adventure, and entertainment with religious devotion. In the late 1300s, the English poet Geoffrey Chaucer introduced a fictional account of a pilgrimage to Canterbury, England, in his book *The Canterbury Tales*:

> ❝*When in April the sweet showers fall*
> *And pierce the drought of March to the root, and all . . .*
> *Then people long to go on pilgrimages . . .*
> *And specially, from every shire's [county's] end*
> *Of England, down to Canterbury they wend [go]*
> *To seek the holy blissful martyr, [who was] quick*
> *To give his help to them when they were sick.*❞

962
Otto I of Germany is crowned Holy Roman emperor by Pope John XII.

987
Hugh Capet is elected king of France.

1095
Council of Clermont calls for a crusade to recapture Jerusalem.

CHAPTER EVENTS

| 800 | 900 | 1000 | 1100 |

WORLD EVENTS

1117
Hoysala Dynasty builds the Temple of Belur in south India.

288 UNIT 3 ◆ Regional Civilizations

Teaching Options

Chapter 13 Resources

REVIEW

Teacher's Resources (TR)
Terms to Know, p. 26
Review History, p. 60
Build Your Skills, p. 94
Chapter Test, pp. 141–142
Concept Builder, p. 229
Idea Web, p. 321

ASSESSMENT

Section Reviews, pp. 294, 300, 306, 309
Chapter Review, pp. 310–311
Chapter Test, TR, pp. 141–142
Unit Test, TR, pp. 187–188

ALTERNATIVE ASSESSMENT

Portfolio Project, p. 312
Create a Travel Brochure, p. T312

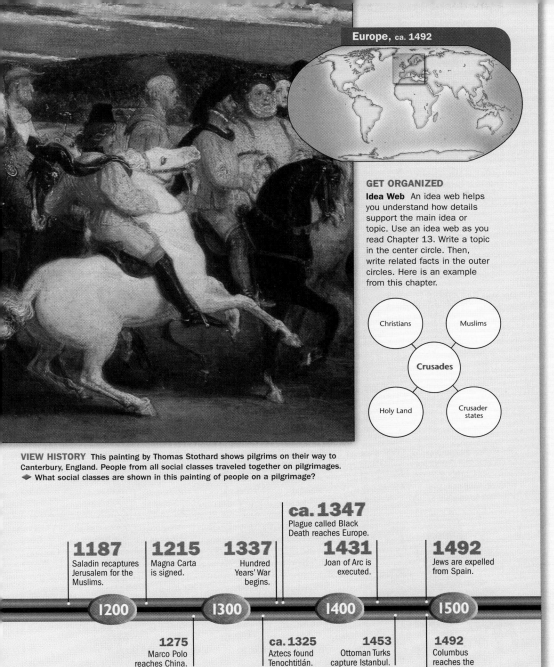

Europe, ca. 1492

GET ORGANIZED
Idea Web An idea web helps you understand how details support the main idea or topic. Use an idea web as you read Chapter 13. Write a topic in the center circle. Then, write related facts in the outer circles. Here is an example from this chapter.

Christians
Muslims
Crusades
Holy Land
Crusader states

VIEW HISTORY This painting by Thomas Stothard shows pilgrims on their way to Canterbury, England. People from all social classes traveled together on pilgrimages.
◆ What social classes are shown in this painting of people on a pilgrimage?

ca. 1347
Plague called Black Death reaches Europe.

1187
Saladin recaptures Jerusalem for the Muslims.

1215
Magna Carta is signed.

1337
Hundred Years' War begins.

1431
Joan of Arc is executed.

1492
Jews are expelled from Spain.

1200   **1300**   **1400**   **1500**

1275
Marco Polo reaches China.

ca. 1325
Aztecs found Tenochtitlán.

1453
Ottoman Turks capture Istanbul.

1492
Columbus reaches the West Indies.

CHAPTER 13 ◆ The High Middle Ages   **289**

Chapter Themes

• Culture
• Power, Authority, and Governance
• Production, Distribution, and Consumption
• Individuals, Groups, and Institutions
• Time, Continuity, and Change
• Civic Ideals and Practices

F Y I
Thomas Stothard

Thomas Stothard (1755–1834) painted *The Pilgrimage to Canterbury* in the early 1800s, long after the pilgrimages of the Middle Ages took place. When Stothard completed his painting, it was exhibited in a private home and then went on a tour of the British Isles. It was an extremely popular painting. Stothard is best known for his graceful, richly colored paintings.

Chapter Warm-Up
USING THE MAP
Point out the locator map at the top of page 289. Help students identify Europe in relation to Asia and Africa. Have them find the Atlantic Ocean and the Mediterranean Sea. Then, have them find England, where the pilgrimage in the painting took place.

VIEW HISTORY
Ask students how many people they can count in the painting of the pilgrimage. (about 15) Ask students to describe the pilgrims. (men and women in a variety of dress; some old, some young) Tell students that a pilgrimage to Canterbury in the Middle Ages was the equivalent of a vacation over spring break today.

◆ **ANSWER** wealthy people, the military, the clergy, common people

GET ORGANIZED
Idea Web
Discuss the idea web on page 289. Have students identify the main idea. (Crusades) Ask what details the chart focuses on. (Christians, Muslims, the Holy Land, crusader states) Tell students they may add circles as needed to develop the web; for example, there may be more circles for the detail "Muslims." Ask students to make an idea web for each section (TR, p. 321).

⬤ TEACH THE TIMELINE
The timeline on pages 288–289 covers the period 962–1492, or 530 years. Ask students which events deal with the Crusades. (1095 Council of Clermont and 1187 Saladin recaptures Jerusalem.) Have students find the two events that occurred in the same year. (1492 Jews are expelled from Spain and Columbus reaches the West Indies.) Encourage students to refer to the timeline as they read the chapter, to help place events in historical perspective.

Activity
Make a timeline Have students use an encyclopedia or almanac to find interesting events from the period 900–1500 in Europe. As a class, make a timeline for this period of European history. Then, compare the events on the class timeline to those events on the book's timeline, pages 288–289.

I. The Crusades Begin

(pp. 290–294)

Section Summary

In this section, students will learn about the religious and political reasons for the Crusades. They will also learn about the first four Crusades and how the Crusades impacted Europe and the Mediterranean region.

Getting Started

Ask students how they would go about reclaiming something that they believed had been taken from them. (Possible answers: ask politely, negotiate, just take it) Discuss the meaning of the word *crusader*. (It has evolved beyond a religious context to refer to someone who undertakes a cause with great enthusiasm.) Ask students to suggest examples of more recent crusaders. (Possible answers: Mohandas Gandhi, Martin Luther King Jr.)

TERMS TO KNOW

Ask students to read the terms and definitions on page 290 and find each term in the section. Ask students to write a brief paragraph using all three terms.

You may wish to preview the pronunciation of the following terms with students.

Nicaea (ny SEE uh)
Seljuk Turks
   (SEHL jook TERKS)
Saladin (SAL uh dihn)

ACTIVE READING

Draw a cause-and-effect chain on the board, with *The Crusades* written in the event rectangle. Then, as the class reads the section, have volunteers list causes and effects of the Crusades. Discuss how the Crusades led to sweeping changes in Europe. Students should keep a copy of this chart in their notebooks to refer to as well.

The Crusades Begin

Terms to Know

papacy the office and rule of the pope, or bishop of Rome

schism a separation or division

crusader state a state established by western European Christians

Main Ideas

A. A variety of causes led to religious wars called the Crusades, which spanned more than two centuries.

B. During the First Crusade, Jerusalem was recaptured and crusader states were established in the eastern Mediterranean.

C. The Crusades had lasting effects on medieval Europe.

Active Reading

CAUSE AND EFFECT
When you identify cause and effect, you determine the reasons for an event and the results, or consequences, of it. As you read this section, think about the background and the outcome of the Crusades, both in western Europe and in the eastern Mediterranean area. What were the causes of the Crusades? What were some effects of these wars?

Do You Remember?

In Chapter 12, you learned about the knightly code of chivalry. This code promoted standards of honor for knights.

Friars, like this one below from Chaucer's *The Canterbury Tales*, were among those who went on religious pilgrimages after the Crusades ended.

A. The Background of the Crusades

The Crusades were Christian wars to capture the Holy Land—the land where Jesus had lived—from the Muslims. The causes and effects of these wars highlight many of the central ideas about the later period of the Middle Ages. The later Middle Ages is the period in Europe from about 962 to 1492. Among these central ideas are the power of the **papacy**, or the office of the pope, the growth of trade in western Europe, and the military spirit encouraged by the Crusades, or holy wars.

The Growth of Papal Power

In early medieval Europe, lawlessness and violence were common. During the late 900s, bishops and Church councils in France promoted a social reform movement called the Peace of God. By the terms of its ruling, those who broke the peace—by robbing the poor or a church or attacking priests or other clergy—could be excommunicated, or excluded from the church. The clergy extended the Peace of God by declaring another reform called the Truce of God. The Truce banned warfare on certain days. For example, when the Truce was first established, knights and soldiers had to stop fighting from Saturday night until Monday morning.

Around this same time, the Byzantine, or Eastern Orthodox Church and the Roman Catholic Church began to disagree on the role of the pope. The Byzantine Church did not accept the pope's claim that he was the sole head of the Christian faith. In 1054, representatives of the Roman Catholic Church excommunicated Michael Cerularius, the patriarch, or leader, of the Byzantine Church. Cerularius, in turn, then excommunicated those Roman Catholic representatives. This disagreement led to a separation, or **schism**, that divided the two churches then and still continues today. The separation weakened the power and role of the papacy for a while.

Pope Gregory VII wanted to restore the power of the papacy. Gregory claimed that the pope was the head of the Church—leader of all society. As such, he was unable to be judged by anyone on Earth.

As a result of Pope Gregory's efforts to strengthen his power, he was often in conflict with emperors, kings, and nobles. For example, Pope Gregory

290 UNIT 3 ◆ Regional Civilizations

Teaching Options

Section 1 Resources

Teacher's Resources (TR)
   Terms to Know, p. 26
   Review History, p. 60
   Build Your Skills, p. 94
   Concept Builder, p. 229
   Idea Web, p. 321

F Y I

Gregory VII and Henry IV

In 1075, Pope Gregory VII declared the practice of appointing bishops and other Church officials by kings illegal. Henry IV then declared the pope deposed. Gregory retaliated by excommunicating Henry. Realizing he needed Gregory, Henry followed the pope to a castle in the Apennines. It is said that he stood barefoot in the snow for three days before the pope absolved him.

This painting shows the conquest of Antioch, one of the early battles of the Crusades.

and King Henry IV of Germany disagreed about who had the power to appoint bishops and other church leaders. Until this time, political leaders had been doing this. However, Pope Gregory insisted that only a pope could appoint clergy, especially to powerful positions. The conflict was finally resolved in 1122 during the reign of Henry's son, King Henry V. The two sides reached an agreement in which only Church officials could elect bishops.

The Pope Calls for a Crusade

As the eleventh century drew to a close, the city of Jerusalem had been in Muslim hands for more than 450 years. Sacred to Jews, Christians, and Muslims alike, the holy city was one of the most important destinations in the world for pilgrims. However, tension in the Islamic-held region was making Christian pilgrimages increasingly difficult. Conflict arose between the Seljuk Turks—followers of Islam—and the Byzantine Empire. The Seljuk Turks threatened to invade Constantinople, the Byzantine capital. To stop their invasions, the Byzantine emperor turned to the West for help, appealing to Pope Urban II in Rome.

Like Pope Gregory VII, Urban believed in the supreme power of the pope. In 1095, at the Council of Clermont in France, he called on western leaders to join in a war to win back the Holy Land. This cause was to be a crusade, from the Latin word for *cross*. Joining a crusade—or taking the cross, as this act was called—appealed to people for many reasons: Some people went on a crusade because of strong religious feelings. However, soldiers wanted military glory; merchants wanted new markets for their goods; and others hoped to gain new land and wealth.

◆ **What factors led to Pope Urban's call for a crusade?**

Focus on
▶ WORLD RELIGIONS ◀

Explore Judaism, Christianity, and Islam Judaism, Christianity, and Islam all arose in the same part of the world. Judaism is the oldest of the three religions and was the first to proclaim monotheism, a belief in one God. In Islam, God is called Allah. Both Christianity and Islam follow the teachings of a charismatic leader—Jesus and Muhammad, respectively. All three religions use a collection of sacred writings: in Islam, this is the Quran; in Judaism, the Torah; and in Christianity, the Bible. Finally, all three have strong beliefs about the correct way to live. Most of the time people of different faiths live together in peace. Problems arise when people of one faith mistrust other faiths. Ask how people of different religions can establish tolerance. (Possible answer: educate all people in different cultures and religions)

A. The Background of the Crusades

Purpose-Setting Question How did the struggle for power between popes and political leaders lead to the Crusades? (The Byzantine Empire asked Pope Urban II of the west to help stop Turkish invasions. Pope Urban II then called on western leaders to join in a war to win back the Holy Land. This act asserted papal supremacy over political leaders.)

Review Remind students of the origins of the power struggle between the Eastern Orthodox Church and the Roman Catholic Church. Have students look back to Chapter 6 to review how this struggle began.

Activity

Make a list Ask students to review the subsection and list at least three examples of conflict among groups or individuals. Have them explain how each conflict was resolved, or how the people involved tried to resolve the conflict.

TEACH PRIMARY SOURCES
Have students study the painting on page 291. Explain that this painting is from the fifteenth-century work *Le Miroir Historial* by Vincent de Beauvais.

Discuss Ask students how the pope enticed people to go on crusades. (He told them that by going on a crusade, a person could follow in the way of Jesus and make amends for his or her sins.) Discuss what this reveals about the power of the pope at that time.

◆ **ANSWER** the growth of papal power under Pope Gregory VII, disruptions of Christian pilgrimages to the Holy Land caused by tensions in the Islamic world between the Seljuk Turks and Byzantine Empire, and Turkish invasions of the Byzantine Empire by the Seljuk Turks

B. The First and Second Crusades

Purpose-Setting Question How did the First and Second Crusades differ? (The First Crusade aimed to regain Jerusalem and was successful; the Second Crusade aimed to protect the crusader states and was a failure.)

ANALYZE PRIMARY SOURCES

DOCUMENT-BASED QUESTION

This account of the reclamation of Jerusalem is by the Muslim historian Ibn al-Qalanisi. Another historian, Ibn al-Athir, reported that the crusaders pillaged for a week and killed more then 70,000 people when they took Jerusalem.

ANSWER Possible answer: The writer probably thought the crusaders were brutal and out of control.

SPOTLIGHT ON CULTURE

CRUSADING WOMEN The women who stayed behind in Europe also played a role in the Crusades. Noble women had to run their husband's estates while their husbands were away. Peasant women had to tend and harvest the crops during this time. Women also worked in inns and stores that the crusaders used on their trips.

◆ **ANSWER** The crusader states brought wealth and power to settlers; the need to protect these states was a direct cause of later Crusades.

C. Later Crusades

Purpose-Setting Question What was the cause of the Third Crusade? (The Muslim warrior Saladin defeated the Christians and recaptured Jerusalem. As a result, three European rulers joined together to fight for Jerusalem.)

ANALYZE PRIMARY SOURCES | **DOCUMENT-BASED QUESTION** How do you think the writer of this account felt about the actions of the crusaders?

Spotlight on *Culture*

CRUSADING WOMEN
During the Crusades, most European women were left at home because they were seen as fragile and in need of protection from war. However, some took an active part in the Crusades.
Eleanor of Aquitaine led 300 women and 1,000 knights in the Second Crusade. Other women were also at the Crusades. Some tended to the wounded, some helped to plan battle strategies, and some actually fought in the wars.

B. The First and Second Crusades

Pope Urban II asked crusaders to recapture Jerusalem, the holy city in which Jesus had died. By taking the cross, Pope Urban promised, people could follow in the way of Jesus and save their souls. This promise of forgiveness was a powerful part of the Crusades' appeal. Perhaps equally strong was the promise of military adventure and the chance of seizing land and goods from captured people.

The Quest for Jerusalem

The First Crusade, which began in 1096, was the first of a series of wars between European Christians and Muslims. In 1097, the crusaders took the city of Nicaea, near Constantinople, from the Turks. Then, a Christian army marched southeast across Anatolia—or present-day Turkey—and conquered Edessa, which lies northeast of the Mediterranean Sea. Here, the victors set up their first **crusader state**, or kingdom founded by European Christians.

In 1099, the crusaders succeeded in their main goal—they conquered Jerusalem and founded a crusader state there. It was not easy for the crusader states to survive because they were surrounded by Muslim territories.

The First Crusade may have been a success for the Christians, but it was a disaster for the Muslims and Jews in the area. As the crusaders captured Jerusalem they killed many Muslims, including women and children. In addition to Muslims, the crusaders also killed many Jews who lived in Jerusalem. One Middle Eastern historian described the events this way:

> 66 The Jews had gathered in their synagogue and the Franks [crusaders] burnt them alive. They also destroyed monuments of saints and the tomb of Abraham, may peace be upon him. 99

The Second Crusade

Crusader states in the eastern Mediterranean were important for two reasons. These states brought new wealth and power to their settlers. In addition, the need to protect the crusader states and settlers from attack led to further Crusades during the next two centuries.

In 1144, the Muslims captured the crusader state of Edessa. Pope Eugenius III called for another crusade to protect western interests in the eastern Mediterranean. This time, two of the most powerful monarchs in Europe, King Louis VII of France and Emperor Conrad III of Germany, led the crusaders. Eleanor of Aquitaine, married to Louis, also joined the Second Crusade, which lasted from 1147 to 1149.

The effort to defend the crusader states ended in failure. At the urging of Christian leaders in Jerusalem, the crusaders tried to take control of Damascus in Syria. Their attack on that city was overwhelmingly defeated by Muslim forces. Embarrassed by another failure, the crusaders returned to Europe.

◆ **What were two reasons that the crusader states were important?**

C. Later Crusades

A new crisis arose in the year 1187. At the battle of Hattan near Jerusalem, the brilliant Muslim warrior Saladin defeated the Christians. Saladin had succeeded in uniting the Muslims under his rule. When Saladin recaptured Jerusalem, the stage was set for further crusades.

Teaching Options

Meet Individual Needs:
AUDITORY LEARNERS

Have students use a tape recorder to record themselves reading Section 1 aloud. Encourage them to use the recording to make notes about the section, including examples of cause and effect. Students may use the notes and the recording as study aids.

FYI
Military Knights

The Knights Templar, or Templars, and Knights of the Hospital of St. John, or Hospitalers, were monastic military orders formed at the end of the First Crusade. The mission of these groups was to protect Christian pilgrims en route to the Holy Land. These groups stayed in the region for many years and often worked to develop better working relationships with the Muslim princes in the area.

The Crusades, 1096–1204

Legend:
→ First Crusade
→ Second Crusade
→ Third Crusade
→ Fourth Crusade
▨ Muslim lands
• Cities

0   200   400 mi
0   200   400 km

Map Check

1. **MOVEMENT** Which Crusade involved the longest sea voyages?
2. **LOCATION** Where did the Fourth Crusade begin?

Using the Map
The Crusades, 1096–1204

Ask students what the different-colored arrows on the map mean. (the different Crusades, First through Fourth) Ask if any of the Crusades bypassed Constantinople, and if so, which one(s). (yes, the Third)

✔ **Map Check**
Answers
1. the Third Crusade
2. Venice

Focus Ask students what was ironic about the Fourth Crusade. (The crusaders were supposed to attack Egypt and then go north to the Holy Land. Instead, they attacked Constantinople, which was a Christian city.) Discuss the reason or reasons for this action.

Review Remind students of the Code of Chivalry they learned about in Chapter 12. Ask students to compare the ideals from the Code of Chivalry to the realities of the Crusades. (In many instances, crusaders acted contrary to the knightly Code of Chivalry. They were not always loyal to their cause, nor did they always protect the weak.)

Activity

Write a letter Tell students that they live in the Middle Ages and have just spoken with a crusader who has returned home from one of the Crusades. (Let students choose which Crusade to use in the letter.) Explain to students that they are going to write a letter to a friend and explain all that they have just learned. Be sure student letters include the name of the Crusade, its dates, places, and events. Suggest students use the map on page 293 for additional information.

The Third and Fourth Crusades

The Third Crusade, which lasted from 1189 to 1192, was the direct result of Saladin's victory. Three European rulers joined together to fight for Jerusalem. King Richard I—also called the Lionhearted—of England and King Philip II Augustus of France traveled to the Holy Land by sea. Emperor Frederick I Barbarossa of Germany marched by land. In 1191, the crusaders recaptured the city of Acre, north of Jerusalem, from the Muslims. However, Frederick drowned between Acre and the Holy Land, and Philip returned to France. That left Richard I as the only Christian leader to face Saladin. After a series of battles, the two leaders signed a peace agreement in 1192. Under the terms of the truce, Jerusalem was to remain under Muslim control. However, Saladin guaranteed that Christian pilgrims would be allowed to visit the holy sites.

Then, in 1198, a new pope, Innocent III, was elected. Like Gregory VII a century before him, Innocent believed in the supreme power of the papacy. He soon called for a new crusade to return the Holy Land to Christian control.

The strategy of the Fourth Crusade, which lasted from 1202 to 1204, was to attack Egypt first and then march north to the Holy Land. Instead, the crusaders became involved in Italian and Byzantine conflicts. Merchants from Venice, Italy, convinced the crusaders to attack trade rivals and cities that had rebelled against Venetian rule. Then, the crusaders attacked the Christian city of Constantinople, the Byzantine capital. When the crusaders entered Constantinople, they took control of both the city and the Byzantine Empire. The Fourth Crusade then came to an end. However, none of the original goals were achieved.

CHAPTER 13 ◆ The High Middle Ages **293**

ESL/ELL STRATEGIES

Organize Information Help students to distinguish among the four Crusades by creating a chart with a column for each Crusade described in the text. Have them include the following information: Name of the Crusade, dates, goal, crusaders, outcome.

Test Taking

Many tests use multiple-choice items in the form of incomplete statements followed by a list of choices. Use information on this page to provide an example for students. Remind them to read the question and all the answer choices first. If they are not sure of the answer, have them rule out obviously incorrect choices, then select the best option.

Extend Perhaps the most tragic crusade event of this period was the Children's Crusade in 1212. Thousands of young people between the ages of 10 and 18 believed they could regain Jerusalem, because they were poor and had faith. Children from France and Germany began marching toward Jerusalem, expecting that God would part the Mediterranean Sea so that they could cross. None of them reached Jerusalem. Some froze to death or starved. Some drowned at sea or were sold into slavery. Only a fraction managed to reach home again.

◆ **ANSWER** A peace agreement between Richard I and Saladin left Jerusalem in Muslim hands, but allowed Christian pilgrims free access to the city.

Section Close

Direct students' attention to the idea web about the Crusades on page 289. Ask students how they would expand the web. Ask what other method of organization might be used. (Possible answer: One could organize the information crusade by crusade, so that one circle is the First Crusade, and so on.)

3 Assess

Review Answers

Review History

A. He claimed that the pope was the head of the Church, the leader of all society, and unable to be judged by anyone on Earth; he insisted that only the pope had the power to appoint clergy.

B. The crusaders regained control of Jerusalem and established several crusader states.

C. Saladin's role in the Crusades was to unite the Muslims under his rule and recapture Jerusalem. This led to the Third Crusade. He signed a peace agreement with Richard I. As a result, Jerusalem remained under Muslim control, but Christian pilgrims were allowed to visit.

Define Terms to Know

papacy, 290; schism, 290; crusader state, 292

When not fighting in the Crusades, knights often staged battles called tournaments.

The Results of the Crusades

Throughout the thirteenth century, crusades continued to be organized. For one reason or another—political schemes, poor preparation, and the deaths of key western leaders—most of these efforts failed. The Crusades ended in 1291 after almost 200 years of fighting. The goal of the Crusades was to take the Holy Land from the Muslims. Only the First Crusade reached that goal.

The Christian religious spirit, which motivated the Crusades, had a dark side. Serving in the Crusades in order to achieve religious goals was part of the knightly code of chivalry. However, the crusaders often turned into persecutors of Muslims and Jews. Many Muslims and Jews died during the Crusades, in both southwest Asia and in Europe. The tensions between the Roman Catholic Church and the Byzantine Church also increased as a result of the Crusades.

Despite the fact that the Crusades were not successful overall, they had a lasting impact on Europe and the Mediterranean region. First, the Crusades strengthened the power of the medieval Church. The popes, who organized the Crusades, became more powerful. Second, Europeans were introduced to new goods from southwest Asia and trade grew. Merchants returning from the wars introduced Europeans to foods such as sugar, lemons, rice, apricots, and melons. New spices, such as ginger, pepper, cloves, and cinnamon, now seasoned European foods as well. Third, the crusaders returned to their homes with new ideas and inventions. Plans for new military machinery and new methods of fortifying, or strengthening, castles would change the future of European warfare. Inventions, such as the windmill, the compass, and the clock, made life more comfortable for much of the population. Although the Crusades were sad and costly, they brought about a sharing of cultures and many changes to Europe.

◆ **What was the outcome of the Third Crusade?**

Review I

Review History
A. How did Pope Gregory VII strengthen the papacy?
B. What were the successes of the First Crusade?
C. What was Saladin's role during the Crusades?

Define Terms to Know
Define the following terms: **papacy, schism, crusader state**

Critical Thinking
How do you think the Muslims regarded the Christian crusaders? Briefly explain your answer.

Write About Culture
Suppose you are a crusading soldier. Write a letter to a family member telling about some of your experiences on a crusade.

Get Organized
IDEA WEB
Use an idea web to organize information from this section. Choose a topic and then find related facts. For example, what were some of the reasons people wanted to join a crusade?

Critical Thinking
Possible answer: as invaders and persecutors, because the Muslims also considered Jerusalem to be a holy place and were living there

Write About Culture
Students' letters might include information about the clothing, food, and language of the peoples; dramatic sights, such as the desert; and descriptions of pilgrimage sites in Jerusalem.

Build Your Skills

Critical Thinking

DISTINGUISH FACT FROM OPINION

In order to read and think critically, you need to be able to distinguish facts from opinions. A fact is a statement that can be proven to be true. Facts can be proven from records, such as primary-source documents or observations. For example, historical records show that Pope Urban II called for a crusade at the Council of Clermont in 1095.

An opinion is a personal belief, judgment, or claim. Unlike facts, opinions cannot be proven. Opinions, however, can be based on evidence. For example, it is the opinion of many historians that the Crusades were fought for economic reasons, rather than for religious reasons. Often, there is evidence to support both sides of an opinion.

As you read history, focus on trying to distinguish facts from opinions. Being able to separate one from the other will make you a more critical reader.

Here's How
Follow these steps to distinguish fact from opinion.

1. Ask yourself how a specific statement can be proven to be true. Dates, names, and places are usually facts that can be proven. For example, can the statement be checked in an encyclopedia, an atlas, or another source?

2. Decide which statements are opinions. Phrases such as *I think* and *I believe* signal that a writer is giving an opinion.

Here's Why
You have just read about the Crusades to recapture the Holy Land. Suppose you had to write a factual account about one of the Crusades. Separating the facts from the opinions would help you to write a more accurate account.

Practice the Skill
Read the passage on the right, which was written about some of the Crusades by a modern historian. Decide if each statement is a fact or an opinion. Then, answer the following questions.

1. What mixture of fact and opinion does the first sentence of the passage contain?

2. How does the word *appalling* in the eleventh line indicate the writer's opinion about the crusaders?

Extend the Skill
Write a paragraph commenting on the historian's use of facts and opinions in the passage.

Apply the Skill
Choose a brief passage or two from another section of this chapter, and analyze the passage(s) for facts and opinions. Discuss your findings with classmates.

"The Crusades, as they came to be called, went on for more than two centuries, and though they were to be unsuccessful in their claim of delivering the Holy Land from Islamic rule, they would leave profound marks . . . on European society and psychology. The first four were the most important. The earliest and most successful was launched in 1096. Within three years the crusaders recaptured Jerusalem, where they celebrated the triumph of the Gospel of Peace by an appalling massacre of their prisoners, women and children included. . . . Then in 1187 Saladin recaptured Jerusalem for Islam. The Third Crusade which followed (1189–1192) was socially the most spectacular. A German emperor . . . and the kings of England and France all took part. They quarreled and the crusaders failed to recover Jerusalem."

CHAPTER 13 ◆ The High Middle Ages **295**

Teaching Options

RETEACH
Collect a series of statements that are facts, opinions, or a combination of both. Provide each student with three index cards—one with *Fact* written on it, one with *Opinion,* and one with *Both.* Read each statement to the class. Have students hold up the index card that characterizes that statement. Have students who chose correctly explain how they made their choice.

CHALLENGE
Tell students that although most newspaper articles are supposed to relate facts, a newspaper editorial is a place where the editor can express opinions. Provide copies of a newspaper editorial to pairs of students. Ask students to underline or highlight facts in one color and opinions in another color. Then have student pairs compare their analysis with that of another pair of students.

Build Your Skills

DISTINGUISH FACT FROM OPINION

Teach the Skill
Ask volunteers to explain what a fact is, what an opinion is, and how facts and opinions differ. Then, ask students to name times in their lives when being able to distinguish facts from opinions is important. (Possible answers: reading advertisements, evaluating different sides of an argument or an issue) Explain to students that being able to distinguish facts from opinions will make them better students of history and better decision-makers. Have the class use the *Here's How* steps to develop the skill of distinguishing fact from opinion.

Discuss the steps in *Here's How.* Point out that opinions can often be of great value. You may wish to use the example of an illness and a doctor's diagnosis of that illness to illustrate the difference between facts and opinions: The symptoms are the facts, or what is seen on the surface. The opinion can be likened to the diagnosis, or what to *do* with the facts.

Practice the Skill
ANSWERS
1. **Fact:** The Crusades went on for more than two centuries; they were unsuccessful; **Opinion:** they left profound marks on the societies and psychology of Europeans.
2. The word *appalling* has a negative tone, so it shows that the author highly disapproves of the crusaders' actions.

Extend the Skill
Responses should include examples of both fact and opinion. Students' views on the balance between fact and opinion will vary.

Apply the Skill
Have students work in small groups and use a two-column chart (TR, p. 328) to list facts and opinions. Have students compare their results and justify their choices. Point out to students that as they read the rest of this chapter, they should focus on the facts.

II. Trade and Towns Grow
(pp. 296–300)

Section Summary

In this section, students will learn how trade revived as a result of agricultural improvements and the growth of trade fairs. They will also learn how trade contributed to the growth of towns, and how it was adversely affected by the Black Death. Students will also learn about the cultural achievements of the period.

1 Introduce

Getting Started

Ask students what they would do if they had made a product and had made more of it than they themselves needed. (Possible answers: Give away the extra; trade it; sell it) Discuss under what conditions they would not just give the product away. (perhaps if they needed money) Have students offer examples of product trades they have made.

TERMS TO KNOW

Ask students to read the terms and definitions on page 296 and find each term in the section. Have students give examples of the kinds of functions the burgher and guild served. Have them explain their examples.

You may wish to preview the pronunciation of the following words with students.

Bruges (BRUEZH)
Ypres (EE puhr)
Chola (COH luh)
Aquinas (uh KWY nuhs)
Dante (DAHN tay)

ACTIVE READING

Have students work in pairs. Ask partners to use a main idea/supporting details chart (TR, p. 319) to summarize important points in the section. As they continue to read the section, have students add detail rectangles to the chart as necessary. At the end of the section, have pairs write a brief summary based on the information in their charts.

Terms to Know

burgher a resident or an official of a city or town

guild an association of merchants or craftspeople

epidemic a widespread disease

Main Ideas

A. The development of trade fairs and trade centers created an interest in western European trade in the later Middle Ages.

B. The growth in trade was linked to the development of towns and cities, especially in northern Italy and its surrounding regions.

C. In the fourteenth century, western Europe suffered a series of disasters, in particular, the plague called the Black Death.

D. The later Middle Ages witnessed such cultural achievements as the beginnings of universities and the development of literature.

Active Reading

SUMMARIZE
When you summarize, you state only the most important points, or highlights, of a passage. As you read this section, focus on the main points about the development of trade, towns, universities, and literature. Then, pause to summarize what you have learned.

This illustration, taken from a French manuscript from the 1200s, shows several trades that existed at that time.

A. The Revival of Trade

By the year 1000, agricultural changes in western Europe had paved the way for a revival, or renewed growth, in trade. These changes included the invention of an iron plow and better methods for harnessing horses. Windmills were built in Europe, offering a new source of power. The three-field system of rotating crops led to a large increase in the food supply. Farmers soon began to look for markets in which they could sell their surplus, or extra, crops.

Trade at Home and Abroad

Fairs, where merchants could sell and exchange goods, offered one of the best means for local trade. Fairs grew up at key locations on trading routes, which were often near rivers. Held at regular intervals, fairs offered a safe setting for merchants to do business. In addition to purchasing goods, the people who attended the fairs could also socialize, share news, and enjoy entertainment.

In the Middle Ages, international fairs developed that drew people from great distances. These fairs expanded into cycles, with each city in a region acting as the host in turn. One center for such an event was Flanders, which is part of Belgium and the Netherlands today. Fairs in Flanders were held in cities such as Bruges and Ypres.

Regional Trade Routes

Trade routes in the later Middle Ages centered on two regions. The northern region was in the area of the Baltic and North Seas. The southern region was in the area of the Mediterranean. The city of Venice, in Italy, was a key center of trade in the southern region. Venetian merchants traded silks and spices from Asia, as well as woolen cloth from Flanders. By the 1200s, Venice had become rich, not only through trade, but also from the goods brought back by the crusaders in return for their use of the large Venetian navy.

Genoa, another Italian port city, played such a large role in the expanding European trade that it needed money-changers to deal

---

Teaching Options

Section 2 Resources

Teacher's Resources (TR)
Terms to Know, p. 26
Review History, p. 60
Build Your Skills, p. 94
Concept Builder, p. 229
Idea Web, p. 321

ESL/ELL STRATEGIES

Use Visuals Have students use the visuals in the section to stimulate a discussion of the content of each subsection. Then, have them write a sentence or two relating the visual to the section in which it appears. Encourage students to explain how the visuals help the reader understand and enhance the content of the section.

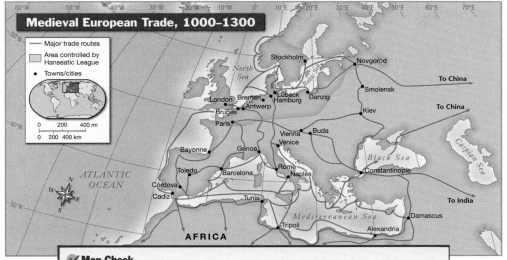

Medieval European Trade, 1000–1300

Major trade routes
Area controlled by Hanseatic League
Towns/cities

ATLANTIC OCEAN

North Sea

Baltic Sea

To China
To China
To India

Black Sea
Caspian Sea
Mediterranean Sea

AFRICA

Stockholm, Novgorod, Smolensk, Kiev, London, Bremen, Lübeck, Hamburg, Danzig, Bruges, Antwerp, Paris, Vienna, Venice, Buda, Bayonne, Genoa, Toledo, Barcelona, Rome, Naples, Constantinople, Cordova, Cadiz, Tunis, Tripoli, Damascus, Alexandria

✔ Map Check

1. **LOCATION** From Stockholm, which body of water had to be crossed to conduct trade?
2. **MOVEMENT** What is true about most of the towns along the trade routes?

with all of the different coins traded in that city. The money-changers went to the port and worked out what each country's money was worth compared to the money of countries it traded with. Then, they exchanged one for the other. Eventually, the money-changers became bankers—the first ever in medieval Europe.

In the northern region, German trading companies joined together in the 1160s to form what would become the Hanseatic League. The league's purpose was to protect its member companies from attacks by pirates and from foreign competition. By the 1200s, it had more than 70 members.

These Hanseatic League wax seals were used on trade documents.

➤ How did progress in agriculture lead to the growth of trade?

B. The Growth of Towns

Improved agricultural methods, a rising population, and the expansion of trade led to the rapid growth of medieval towns and cities. Before the year 1000, medieval life had centered on the manor, and society was organized by the feudal system. During the next 300 years, life became much more urbanized, or centered in cities. The number of serfs declined as peasants migrated from manors to the new towns.

Merchants and the New Middle Class

It has been estimated that 1,000 new towns developed in western Europe. The growth of towns was directly related to the expansion of trade. Merchants settled at important crossroads on trade routes. These commercial centers often developed into towns. Craftspeople from the manors followed the merchants' lead. Populations of early European towns ranged from a few hundred to two or three thousand.

Meet Individual Needs:
LOGICAL/MATHEMATICAL LEARNERS

Before the invention of the three-field system of crop rotation, the Roman two-field system was used. If necessary, explain that in the three-field system, the two planted fields had different crops. Ask students what the annual percentage of increase in planted fields was under the three-field system. (an increase from 50% [1 of 2 fields being used] to $66\frac{2}{3}$% [2 of 3 fields being used]— $66\frac{2}{3}$% – 50% = $16\frac{2}{3}$%)

Working Women in the Middle Ages

During the Middle Ages, both girls and boys were apprenticed in trades. Girls and women worked in a variety of occupations, but most often in the food and clothing trades. They belonged to guilds. Toward the end of the Middle Ages, some girls in towns attended school. However, women were not allowed to work in the fields of medicine, law, and scholarship.

2 Teach

A. The Revival of Trade

Purpose-Setting Question What factors led to the revival of trade in the later Middle Ages? (improvements in agriculture, development of trade fairs and trading centers)

Extend Explain to students that a newer kind of harness allowed horses to be hitched to a plow; before then, oxen did the work of pulling. Because a horse can pull a plow three to four times faster than an ox can, horses quickly became popular among those European farmers who could afford them.

Using the Map
Medieval European Trade, 1000–1300

Ask students to describe what the map shows. (trade routes in Europe from 1000–1300) Have students find Venice on the map and explain its advantageous position for trade. (good location in relation to central Europe and easy access to the Mediterranean Sea)

✔ Map Check
Answers
1. the Baltic Sea
2. They are near water.

TEACH PRIMARY SOURCES
Have students examine the photograph of the seals from the Hanseatic League. Made of wax, each seal represents a different city. Ask students to explain the purpose of the league. (to protect members from attacks by pirates and foreign competition)

➤ ANSWER Agricultural improvements resulted in a large increase in the food supply; farmers began to look for markets at which they could sell their surplus crops.

B. The Growth of Towns

Purpose-Setting Question What three causes contributed to the growth of towns in the Middle Ages? (improved agricultural methods, rising population, expansion of trade)

CHAPTER 13 ◆ **T297**

Merchants and craftspeople had no wish to remain within the feudal system. They wanted to govern themselves. The ancient concept of a city-state, with its own government and laws, was reborn in cities such as Pisa, Genoa, and Florence in Italy, as well as in towns such as Bruges and Ghent in Flanders. In France and England, towns asked their kings for charters, or written agreements. These agreements gave the towns the right to choose their own officials and to set up their own courts. In return for these rights, people had to pay taxes to the king in place of their feudal obligations. As time passed, merchants and craftspeople became **burghers**, or free town citizens, who enjoyed the right of personal liberty. Burghers formed a new middle class, the class that existed between the nobles and the peasants.

Establishing Guilds

Merchants and craftspeople living in cities formed groups or associations called **guilds**. Guilds linked people in the same specialty or craft together much like a trade union does today. Merchants, bakers, weavers, tailors, dyers, goldsmiths, and many other types of workers had guilds. The basic purpose of a guild was to promote the business and the personal well-being of its members. The guilds served a number of other important functions, both for their members and for the town as a whole.

First, guilds set quality standards for products and services. Guild members who did not obey the association's rules or who produced poorly made products were fined. Second, guilds regulated, or controlled, competition between members with rules about working conditions and hours.

Third, guilds provided education and career training for its male members. A boy would typically begin work in a trade or craft as an apprentice for a master craftsworker. An apprentice was not paid, but a master was expected to clothe, feed, and provide shelter for him. After several years of training, an apprentice, now a young man, would advance to the rank of journeyman. The name comes from the French word *jour,* meaning "day." A journeyman could earn wages by working for any master. Finally, a skillful journeyman might become a master himself by showing his own "master piece" to the guild leaders. As a master, he would employ journeymen and train apprentices.

In addition to their educational function, guilds played an important social role in medieval towns. The guild hall served as a club for its members. Guild members also helped other members and members' families in times of need.

◆ **What were four functions served by the medieval guild system?**

C. Plague and Social Upheaval

In the first half of the fourteenth century, European expansion and prosperity suffered a series of setbacks. Food shortages caused a rise in prices and hardship in cities. Then, the most serious crisis in European life—the plague, known as the Black Death—struck. It got its name because it caused spots of blood to turn black under the skin. Scholars have estimated that during the 1300s from 25 to 33 percent of the European population died as a result of famine and plague.

The Spread of the Plague

Between 1347 and 1352, the Black Death caused the deaths of about 25 million people. It spread from Asia to Sicily and then north through Italy into the rest of Europe, Scandinavia, and even as far away as Iceland and Greenland.

LONDON GUILDS
London trade guilds became known as livery companies because members wore livery, or special clothing. Edward III granted charters to the first London guilds in the 1300s. Guild members were recognized as leading members of society and had the authority to elect local government officials.

Members of livery companies still elect the lord mayor of London. There are nearly 100 livery companies today. Some, such as the Air Pilots and Navigators, were formed in the twentieth century.

Teaching Options

Research

AVERAGE
The people of the Middle Ages had no idea that insects or animals could spread a disease. Have students do research to find out what people of the time thought was the cause of the Black Death and how people tried to prevent the disease. Have them write a brief summary of their research.

CHALLENGE
Have students find and read a firsthand account of the plague. Have them note how the disease spread, what the symptoms were, and what its effects on survivors were. Have them write a report summarizing their research.

At the time, no one knew how the **epidemic**, or a disease that affects a large number of people, spread or how to protect against it. The best defense was to leave a town or city in which the plague was killing people and hope to go somewhere safe. Scholars today believe that fleabites caused the most commonly known form of the Black Death. The fleas bit infected rats that traveled on merchant ships and bit humans on the ships or in the ports. Because people in the 1300s did not know that keeping themselves and their homes very clean would help to eliminate the fleas, thousands of people were bitten and became infected.

Although the plague epidemic was named the Black Death, scientists now believe that it was really a combination of three or four diseases. Some people died very quickly, almost as though they were poisoned. Others fell into a coma, a sleep-like state, and lived for almost a week. Those who had the black spots under their skin probably had the bubonic plague. Another form of the disease, called the pneumonic plague, was spread through the air and caused people's lungs to fail. Still another form struck the nervous system and made people look like they were doing a strange dance. Whatever the disease, it was almost always deadly.

Some regions of Europe were harder hit than others. In Florence, Italy, more than half of the population died because of the Black Death. In England, about 1,000 villages disappeared completely. The few people who survived the epidemic in those villages could not bury all of the dead, so they moved to towns and villages that seemed safe. About 250 years would pass before Europe would again have the same population it had before the plague arrived.

Consequences of the Black Death

The Black Death may have been the most significant natural event during the Middle Ages. It had a huge effect on all the areas it touched—population, economics, and society. As a result of the plague, the population of entire villages died and many fields were not planted. However, the fields that were planted and harvested usually provided enough food for the now much smaller population. Trade also was affected. It became difficult to produce goods or obtain them because of a shortage of workers. Because there were fewer workers, they were able to demand more wages and better working conditions for their labor.

◆ **How was the Black Death spread?**

D. Life and Culture

Despite the setbacks to European life and culture from the plague, the High Middle Ages saw achievements in philosophy, education, and literature.

Philosophy, Education, and Literature

Possibly the most important philosopher during the High Middle Ages was St. Thomas Aquinas. A great admirer of the ancient Greek philosopher Aristotle, Aquinas wanted to unite classical, Christian, and worldly knowledge into a single system of belief.

The dark, gloomy scene shown in this painting illustrates the devastation that resulted from the spread of the plague throughout Europe.

Extend Tell students that the plague was called the Black Death because a victim's lymph glands swelled up and the spots of blood under the skin became blackened and discolored. The word *bubonic* comes from *bubo*, the technical term for the swollen glands.

Activity

Make a chart Ask students to use the information in this subsection to make a cause-and-effect chain (TR, p. 325) with this event in the rectangle: *Workers charge more for their labor.* (**Cause:** shortage of workers because of Black Death; **Effect:** weakening of feudal system)

TEACH PRIMARY SOURCES

Explain to students that the painting on page 299 about the Black Death was done by Ben Stahl (1910–1987) and exhibits a modern style and perspective. Ask students what details in the painting set the scene in the Middle Ages. (cobblestone street; wooden wagon; people's clothing; woman throwing liquid out of second-story window)

◆ **ANSWER** The Black Death was spread by fleas that had bitten infected rats, which then bit people.

D. Life and Culture

Purpose-Setting Question In what areas of culture did medieval society make great strides at this time? (philosophy, education, and literature)

Focus Some of Aristotle's thinking posed problems for Christian philosophers. For example, Aristotle believed that the world had always existed; this belief conflicted with the biblical story of creation. Ask students how Christian philosophers might have felt about St. Thomas Aquinas's publication of a unified system of beliefs. (Possible answer: relieved that he had solved a problem for Christians)

Using Technology

Ask students to browse the Internet for Web sites about either the Black Death or the first universities in western Europe. Have them list several Web sites, their addresses, and the kind of content on each site. Students may include printouts if they like. Ask them what these Web sites contribute to the field of knowledge about the event(s).

Discuss Explain the phenomenon before the Middle Ages of people speaking in one language and nearly all writing being in another language—Latin. Ask what might be the effects of producing literature in the vernacular. (Possible answer: make people proud of their culture; develop national pride; make common people feel that literature is for them; increase demand for books)

ANALYZE PRIMARY SOURCES

DOCUMENT-BASED QUESTION

Tell students that in *The Divine Comedy*, Dante is guided by the Roman poet Virgil on part of the journey. This use of Virgil marked a general movement of looking back to the ancients as guides to learning after centuries of defaming or ignoring them.

ANSWER Possible answer: Dante implies that human beings should use their free will to love and serve God.

◆ **ANSWER** by writing in the vernacular, or common spoken language of the day

Section Close

Have students identify each subhead in the section. Have them summarize the section by creating a brief outline of it, using the heads and subheads. Then, have them take turns with a partner, elaborating on each of the heads they have written down.

3 Assess

Review Answers

Review History

A. to protect its members from piracy and from foreign competition

B. They had no wish to remain in the feudal system, they wanted to govern themselves.

C. The Black Death spread from Asia to Sicily and then north through Italy into the rest of Europe, Scandinavia, Iceland, and Greenland.

D. They were two of the most important poets in the Middle Ages; Dante wrote an epic, *The Divine Comedy*, Chaucer wrote the poem, *The Canterbury Tales*.

Define Terms to Know

burgher, 298; guild, 298; epidemic, 299

Geoffrey Chaucer is the author of the poem, *The Canterbury Tales*.

ANALYZE PRIMARY SOURCES | **DOCUMENT-BASED QUESTION** What might Dante be implying about the importance of human beings using their free will?

At this time as well, the first universities were founded in western Europe. During the 1200s, universities began to flourish in a number of cities, including Paris, France; Bologna, Italy; and Oxford, England. The universities became legally recognized institutions of education. People could now study specialty areas such as theology, or the study of religious teachings, law, or medicine.

Before the Middle Ages, Latin had been the language used by educated people in western Europe. During the Middle Ages, however, people began speaking in vernacular, or everyday, language. Writers also started using vernacular language in their works.

Vernacular literature took on several forms, including poetry, romance fiction, comedy, and drama. Because this type of literature was written in everyday speech, it appealed to a larger audience. Common people who may not have had much education were able to enjoy these literary works.

Two Medieval Writers

Italian poet Dante Alighieri wrote in the vernacular, or the language spoken by the residents of Florence, his native city in Italy. Today Dante is regarded as the Father of Italian Literature, and his epic masterpiece, *The Divine Comedy*, is often considered the most important Christian poem. In it, Dante writes an imaginary tale of his soul's ten-day journey from hell to heaven:

❝ The greatest gift that God in His bounty made in creation, and the most conformable [suited] to His goodness, and that which He prizes the most, was the freedom of the will, with which the creatures with intelligence, they all and they alone, were and are endowed. ❞

Dante's example encouraged other poets to write in their own vernacular language. Geoffrey Chaucer, an English poet, wrote *The Canterbury Tales*. This poem is told from the point of view of a group of pilgrims, and was written in a form of English known as Middle English.

◆ **How did medieval writers expand their audience?**

Review II

Review History
A. What were the goals of the Hanseatic League?
B. Why did the merchants and craftspeople who settled new towns seek political rights?
C. Into which areas did the Black Death spread?
D. What were some of the achievements of Dante Alighieri and Geoffrey Chaucer?

Define Terms to Know
Define the following terms: **burgher, guild, epidemic**

Critical Thinking
What were some of the benefits of membership in a trade guild?

Write About Culture
Write a short essay in which you describe life in a medieval town during the Middle Ages.

Get Organized
IDEA WEB
Use an idea web to organize information from this section. Choose a topic and then find related facts. For example, how did the plague affect Europe and Europeans?

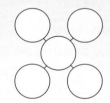

Critical Thinking
enforced quality standards and regulated competition; provided a means by which new workers were trained; provided a place to socialize; and dispensed charity

Write About Culture
Students' essays should include the growth of trade, function of guilds, the plague, and cultural developments.

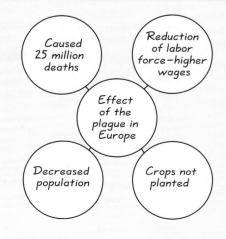

Caused 25 million deaths

Reduction of labor force—higher wages

Effect of the plague in Europe

Decreased population

Crops not planted

CONNECT
History&Economics

Trade Fairs

During the Middle Ages, trade fairs offered merchants and craftspeople an important opportunity to exchange goods. Fairs were a key element in trade, especially before the development of permanent commercial centers in western Europe.

EARLY FAIRS in Europe dated from the 700s. One of these was located at St. Denis, near Paris, France. The products exchanged at early fairs were mostly agricultural, including wool, grain, and vegetables. Fairs were held at special times of a year, such as the feast days of saints, religious festivals, or important holidays. Merchants from all over Europe traveled to towns and set up tents and stalls in which they displayed goods to trade. Visitors came from near and far to these events, which lasted from a single day to several weeks.

LATER FAIRS in the High Middle Ages were larger and featured manufactured and imported products from other areas of the world. By the 1100s, for example, metal objects from England and Spain, wine from France, and silk from China could be found at the great fairs.

Champagne, a region in northeastern France, held a series of fairs during the High Middle Ages called the great fairs. Six fairs, lasting about six weeks each, took place every year in one of the four towns within the region. These fairs provided a centralized location for merchants throughout Europe.

These fairs also played an important role in the development of economic practices still in use today. Because people came from so many different areas, a common system of assigning value to various goods became necessary. For example, a standard weight system was needed to determine the value of goods sold by weight. The troy weight—named after the city of Troyes in the Champagne region—was established to weigh silver and gold. In addition, money-changers had to estimate the value of currencies from the different regions. This estimate became known as the foreign exchange rate. Both the troy weight and the foreign exchange rate are still very important today in international trade.

Critical Thinking

Answer the questions below. Then, complete the activity.

1. Why did fairs develop in the early Middle Ages?
2. How were trade fairs different in the High Middle Ages from earlier fairs?
3. What new economic methods developed at the great fairs in Champagne?

Write About It

Use the Internet and reference books to learn about state fairs and trade fairs today. What similarities and differences can you identify between modern and medieval fairs? How do fairs today promote, or increase, economic growth? Write a paragraph to present your research.

In an illustration made in the early twelfth century, the Bishop of Paris is shown blessing a street fair at Notre Dame Cathedral in Paris, France.

CHAPTER 13 ◆ The High Middle Ages 301

CONNECT
History& Economics

TRADE FAIRS

Teach the Topic
Explain that trade is an essential element of economics. Before cities were well established in the Middle Ages, it made sense for people to gather and exchange goods from time to time. Remind students that they learned that as farming equipment and techniques improved, people began to have a surplus of goods. Ask students if they have ever traded items with friends. Discuss what makes a good trade. (when everyone is equally pleased with the trade)

EARLY FAIRS Discuss why most of the goods at early fairs were agricultural in nature. (In the early Middle Ages, people were mostly farmers.) Ask why trade fairs were often held on feast days of saints. (Possible answer: People were gathering for the feast day, so they could also attend the fair.)

LATER FAIRS Discuss what the goods available at later fairs showed about countries' economies. (People were traveling more and beginning to produce and import more sophisticated goods.) Have students identify reasons to attend a fair. (Possible answers: safe environment for entertainment, eating and buying different foods and other goods, seeing people and hearing news)

Critical Thinking
1. for the exchange of goods and for entertainment; as a key element in long distance trade, especially important before the development of commercial centers
2. Fairs in the High Middle Ages were larger and featured manufactured and imported goods in addition to agricultural products.
3. Establishment of a standard system of weights and a way to exchange currency—these made trade between different regions easier.

Write About It
Students can use a Venn diagram (TR, p. 323) to help organize their thoughts about similarities and differences between modern and medieval fairs.

Teaching Options

Ask students to find out about their region's modern-day economy. What goods are produced on a local level? Have the class as a whole use this information to stage a mock trade fair, complete with food, entertainment, and advertisements of goods for sale. Other classes and grades could be invited.

More Than Trade Fairs
Juggling, acrobats, and dancing bears were forms of entertainment at medieval fairs. People also played games and watched wrestling matches. One popular food was a chewet—a baked or fried meat pie.

CHAPTER 13 ◆ T301

III. Organized Kingdoms Develop

(pp. 302–306)

Section Summary

In this section, students will learn how both royal power and individual liberties grew steadily in England and France during the later part of the Middle Ages. They will also learn that nationalism developed more slowly in the Holy Roman Empire, and how the Spanish *reconquista* achieved success.

1 Introduce

Getting Started

Power struggles are a part of many people's daily lives. Ask students to think of relationships they have in which power can be an issue. (Possible answer: relationships with parents, siblings, friends, teachers, coaches) Ask how these power struggles are different from those a king or queen might have. (A political leader's power struggle is likely to affect an entire country and may even lead to war between nations.)

TERMS TO KNOW

Have students read the terms and definitions on page 302 and find each term in the section. Ask them to compare *Parliament* and *Estates General*.

You may wish to preview the pronunciation of the following words with students.

Aquitaine (A kwuh tayn)
Capet (KAY peht)
Capetian (kuh PEE shun)
Crécy (kreh SEE)
Poitiers (pwah TYA)
Orléans (or lay AHN)

ACTIVE READING

As students read, ask them to take notes that will help them to evaluate factors affecting the development of European nations. They may wish to have a different sheet of notes for each nation or political entity. Ask them to select what they think was the most important factor affecting each nation or empire.

Section III Organized Kingdoms Develop

Terms to Know

common law the traditional body of law in England that blends English and Norman elements

Parliament the assembly that advises the king or queen of England

Estates General the assembly that advised the king of France

nationalism the belief that people should be loyal to their country, not just to their leader

Inquisition the court of the Roman Catholic Church responsible for identifying and punishing heretics

King John signs the Magna Carta in 1215 under pressure from the English barons.

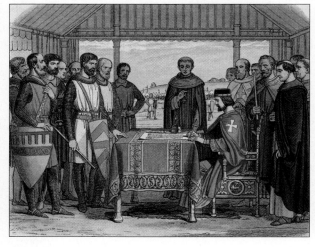

Main Ideas

A. Conflicts arose in England as a result of the growth of royal power.

B. The Capetian Dynasty in France succeeded in laying the foundations for a nation-state.

C. Alliances and conflicts united and divided Europe, and Christians succeeded in regaining control of Spain from the Muslims.

Active Reading

EVALUATE
When you evaluate, you weigh the importance of specific facts or pieces of evidence in order to make a judgment. As you read this section, evaluate the factors that affected the development of organized nations in Europe.

A. England

William the Conqueror's conquest of England in 1066 led to sweeping changes in government, law, and society as a whole. He brought the feudal system with him from Normandy, and claimed the English throne. Then, he tightened his control by requiring lords to swear their loyalty to him. His successors tried to maintain and increase the power of the king.

Henry II, Common Law, and Conflicts with the Church

King Henry II of England, who ruled from 1154 to 1189, became one of the most powerful European monarchs. He controlled England and half of what is present-day France. His wife, Eleanor of Aquitaine, who had been married to Louis VII of France, was an enthusiastic supporter of both music and literature. Partly because of their interests, culture and learning flourished in both regions.

Henry II's creation of jury systems, courts, and other legal reforms contributed to the growth of English **common law**. Common law is the body of law that developed out of English and Norman legal traditions. One important feature of common law was the system in which people gave sworn evidence in a legal trial. Another feature was a special jury set up to review the evidence for criminal charges. These features were the basis for the modern court system.

It was in legal matters, however, that Henry had one of his major setbacks. The king and Thomas Becket, the archbishop of Canterbury, disagreed over the right of the royal courts to place on trial clergy members who had already been tried in Church courts. After Becket refused to allow the clergy to be subject to the king's laws, he was murdered in his own cathedral by four of Henry's knights in 1170. Soon afterward, Thomas Becket was declared a saint by the Roman Catholic Church.

Teaching Options

Section 3 Resources

Teacher's Resources (TR)
Terms to Know, p. 26
Review History, p. 60
Build Your Skills, p. 94
Concept Builder, p. 229
Idea Web, p. 321

F Y I

Eleanor of Aquitaine
Eleanor of Aquitaine (1122–1204) was a wealthy, beautiful French noble. She married Louis VII and was queen of France for 15 years. In 1147, she accompanied Louis on the Second Crusade. Their marriage was annulled in 1152. Eleanor soon after married Henry Plantagenet, who became King Henry II of England. Two of her sons—Richard the Lionhearted and John—became kings of England.

King John, the Magna Carta, and Parliament

King John was the youngest son of Henry II and Eleanor of Aquitaine. He ruled from 1199 to 1216. Troubles with his nobles began because John insisted that as king, he had the power to do whatever he wished. In time, the nobles banded together and threatened to go to war against the king unless he accepted limits on his power.

In 1215, a group of English nobles forced John to sign a document guaranteeing them certain basic rights. This document is called the Magna Carta, which is Latin for "great charter." By signing the Magna Carta, King John admitted that a king was subject to the laws of the land, not above them. The rights given to the nobles in the Magna Carta included protection under the law. Perhaps the most important part of the Magna Carta that granted individuals certain rights was the following:

> 66 No free man shall be seized or imprisoned, or stripped of his rights or possessions, or outlawed or exiled, . . . except by the lawful judgment of his equals or by the law of the land. 99

King John and the pope later rejected the Magna Carta. However, the document inspired later legal and political reformers. During the late 1200s, another step was taken that further limited the power of an English king or queen. In 1295, the **Parliament**, or English legislative body, met for the first time—nobles together with commoners. Parliament began to represent the people of England. Gradually, over the next two centuries, the English Parliament became more and more important.

From 1455 to 1485, England was split internally by conflict and civil war. During the war, Parliament gained more authority as two noble families, Lancaster and York, fought for the throne. This conflict is called the Wars of the Roses because each side used a rose as its symbol. The Lancasters used a red rose and the Yorks used a white rose. Eventually, Henry Tudor, a Lancastrian, defeated Richard III, the York king, and was crowned as Henry VII. A strong new leader took the throne while a strong Parliament represented his people.

◆ **What features of English common law are used today?**

B. France

In France, a series of strong kings faced many problems. These problems included unifying their territory, securing the loyalty and cooperation of powerful nobles, and ensuring succession of their heirs to the throne.

The Capetians

The election of Hugh Capet as king in 987 ended a long struggle among the descendants of Charlemagne. Starting out with a small region around Paris, Hugh Capet laid the foundations of the French monarchy. His line, called the Capetian Dynasty, lasted for more than 300 years. Later, Capetian kings began to increase the territory and power of the French monarchy.

Hugh Capet ruled for only nine years, but he was able to establish an important principle of succession: The bishops agreed to make the monarchy hereditary. As a result, Hugh's eldest son was selected as the next king of France.

Two strong later Capetian monarchs were Philip II Augustus and Louis IX. Both monarchs enjoyed long reigns. Philip II ruled from 1179 to 1223. He centralized the kingdom around Paris and made Paris the capital of France.

Primary Source Documents

You can read sections of the Magna Carta on page 810.

ANALYZE PRIMARY SOURCES

DOCUMENT-BASED QUESTION
What important right does this part of the Magna Carta give freemen?

Hugh Capet began a dynasty in which French kings had great power.

---

2 Teach

A. England

Purpose-Setting Question How did Henry II extend royal power in England? (He made the clergy subject to the king's laws.)

Discuss Explain to students that common law is based on custom rather than rules made by a legislature or a king. Discuss the effects of establishing common law. (encouraged a belief in the justice system and nationalism) Ask students how trial by jury was an improvement over other forms of trial at the time, such as fighting between two opponents. (Trial by jury establishes peace and order and is grounded in logic.)

ANALYZE PRIMARY SOURCES

DOCUMENT-BASED QUESTION
Ask students to reflect on an agreement that has been in effect for almost 800 years. Tell students that much of the Magna Carta deals with the issues of the times, but two clauses deal more generally with English rights.

ANSWER The clause gives freemen the right to judgment by their equals.

Activity

Analyze documents Have students read sections of the Magna Carta on page 810. Direct their attention to Clause 40: "To none will we sell, to none deny or delay, right or justice." Discuss this clause's meaning. (Everyone deserves and will get justice; there is justice under the law.)

◆ **ANSWER** The two features are a system in which people give sworn evidence in a legal trial and a special jury set up to review the evidence for criminal charges.

B. France

Purpose-Setting Question How did France assume almost all of the territory that it occupies today as a nation? (In 1429, the French defeated the English at Orléans; then, after 20 years, Charles VII succeeded in driving his enemies out of most of France, ending the Hundred Years' War.)

Connection to LITERATURE

As a challenge activity, students may want to read T. S. Eliot's *Murder in the Cathedral*. A play in verse, it touches on the relationship between Thomas Becket and Henry II. Another play that deals with a conflict between English royalty and the Roman Catholic Church is Robert Bolt's *A Man for All Seasons*, about Sir Thomas More and Henry VIII in the sixteenth century.

Conflict Resolution

The conflict between King John and the nobles of England led to the Magna Carta, a document that promoted individual liberties. The establishment of Parliament was a further refinement in the way the English monarchy and the aristocracy chose to resolve conflicts. Ask students what effects these peaceful resolutions of conflicts had on English history. (Possible answer: promoted sense of cooperation between royalty and subjects)

He established a regular army and conquered Normandy, which had been under English control, in 1204. Philip used marriages and inheritances to triple the size of his territory.

Louis IX ruled from 1226 to 1270. He allowed the provinces of his kingdom to keep their own customs, as long as they were loyal to the French monarchy. Louis's reputation for wisdom and justice led to his being widely regarded as the ideal monarch. About 30 years after his death, the Roman Catholic Church formally declared him a saint.

During the 1300s, as Parliament was gaining more authority in England, assemblies were also developing in France. By the end of the 1400s, the national assembly in France included representatives of three groups: the clergy; the nobility; and the merchants, craftspeople, and peasants. These three social classes were called "estates." Later, reporters and newspapers became known as the "fourth estate." The assembly came to be known as the **Estates General**.

The Hundred Years' War

In 1337, England invaded Normandy in France, which caused the beginning of the Hundred Years' War. The war extended over the reigns of five English and five French kings and lasted from 1337 to 1453. The struggle was actually a series of wars—broken by truces and treaties—to determine who would rule western France. The first phase of the war was marked by English successes under King Edward III. On battlefields in France, English archers used their longbows to pierce the armor of the French knights. One of the most famous battles was fought in the French town of Agincourt.

Archer with longbow

They Made History

Joan of Arc ca. 1412–1431

Joan of Arc was an uneducated, deeply religious peasant girl from northern France. At about the age of 13 she began having visions of the Roman Catholic saints. The visions urged her to help Charles, the future king of France. She persuaded Charles that she had been called upon to drive the English forces out of France. Her great faith convinced others to follow her.

Charles sent Joan to free the city of Orléans, which had been under attack by an English army. Dressed in armor, Joan led the French forces to victory. For that reason, Joan is also known as the "Maid of Orléans."

Joan of Arc eventually became a prisoner of the English, who were embarrassed to have been defeated by a teenage girl. They charged her with witchcraft and heresy because she claimed to hear voices of God and the voices of saints. Joan was convicted and burned on a wooden cross known as the stake.

In 1920, the Roman Catholic Church made Joan of Arc a saint. In France, she is regarded as a national hero.

Joan of Arc helped France defeat the English in 1429.

Critical Thinking How did Joan of Arc help to strengthen the kingdom of France?

Teaching Options

Writing

AVERAGE
Have students find out more about the reasons for the Hundred Years' War. How did land ownership figure in the conflict? Ask students to write a paragraph explaining these reasons.

CHALLENGE
Have students research to find out about one of the events listed in the chart on page 305. Have them write a brief essay, describing the event and explaining why the victor won. Have them discuss the effect of the event's outcome on the war in general.

A large, powerful French army was defeated by a small English army. It seemed that England would take over all of France.

Then, a 17-year-old girl persuaded French leaders to let her lead an army. In 1429, a young peasant named Joan of Arc led the defeat of the English army in the French town of Orléans. Charles VII was crowned the new king of France. Inspired by Joan's courage, the French rallied around Charles and drove his enemies out of most of France. The only French territory still in English hands was the port of Calais. The Hundred Years' War was finally over.

Despite the economic damage caused by the war, the power of the monarchy, both in England and France, was strengthened. As a result of the war, France assumed much of the same territory that it occupies today as a nation.

➧ Despite the French victory over the English in Orléans, what French territory remained under English control?

Turning Points of the Hundred Years' War

YEAR	EVENT	NOTABLE LEADER
1337	Outbreak of war	Edward III
1346	French defeat at Crécy	Edward III
1347	English victory at Calais	Edward III
1356	French defeat at Poitiers	Edward III
1360	Truce	Edward III
1415	English victory at Agincourt	Henry V
1429	English defeat at Orléans	Joan of Arc
1453	English withdrawal from France, except for Calais	Charles VII

✔ Chart Check
During the first 20 years of the war, which side won more wars?

C. The Holy Roman Empire and Spain

Besides England and France, other areas of western and central Europe were starting to lay the foundation for **nationalism**, or the belief that people should be loyal to their country. These areas included the Holy Roman Empire and Spain.

The Holy Roman Empire

Charlemagne's empire continued in various forms for centuries after his death in 814. In Rome, which was part of his empire, there was a strong alliance between the pope and the rulers of the German-speaking areas of the empire. In 962, the German king Otto I was crowned emperor by Pope John XII. In addition to ruling Germany, Otto now had control of northern Italy.

In the 1200s, the Hapsburg family took over the empire. It was at this point, having been blessed by the pope, that it became known as the Holy Roman Empire. The Holy Roman Empire included the area of present-day Germany, Switzerland, and Austria, as well as parts of eastern France, northern Italy, and the Czech Republic.

Although the boundaries of the empire changed over the centuries, struggle for power continued. The kings of other emerging European nations, the Holy Roman emperors, and the popes of Rome often tried to gain or keep power. However, at times, they worked together to support the goals of the various crusades.

Nationalism was slower to develop in Germany and the Holy Roman Empire than in other parts of western Europe. Nevertheless, in the 1100s and early 1200s, German culture flourished with the building of magnificent cathedrals and the writing of epics and poems.

Do You Remember?
In Chapter 12, you learned that Charlemagne was crowned as the Roman emperor by Pope Leo III in 800.

CHAPTER 13 ◆ The High Middle Ages **305**

Review Remind students of the Muslim conquest of Spain in the 700s, which they read about in Chapter 8. Under Muslim rule, Christians, Jews, and Muslims lived together peacefully in Spain.

TEACH PRIMARY SOURCES

Have students find Granada on a map of this period. Then, direct students to the painting on page 306. Titled *The Fall of Granada in 1492,* this work was painted by Carlos Luis Ribera y Fieve in the nineteenth century. Ask students to identify the focal point of the painting. (the king and queen exulting over their victory) Then, have them locate the Christian presence in the painting. (priests with crosses on the left)

◆ **ANSWER** Christians captured the Muslim stronghold of Granada; Ferdinand and Isabella sponsored the first voyage of Christopher Columbus.

Section Close

Have students work in pairs and act as newscasters recapping this period of development in European nations. Have each pair write a brief summary of events in England, France, Spain, and Germany. Then, have them try to model their summaries on TV news broadcasting programs.

3 Assess

Review Answers

Review History

A. Parliament began as an advisory council to the king; later nobles, clergy, and representatives from the new towns and cities met to discuss government matters.

B. The power of the monarchy was strengthened in England and France; France assumed roughly the territory that it occupies as a nation today.

C. The Jews were expelled from Spain; a victory for the Inquisition; power of Spanish monarchs was strengthened.

Define Terms to Know

common law, 302; Parliament, 303; Estates General, 304; nationalism, 305; Inquisition, 306

King Ferdinand and Queen Isabella are shown at the fall of Granada in Spain in 1492.

Christians Reconquer Spain

As you have read, the Muslims conquered much of Spain in the early 700s. In the mid-1100s, Portugal succeeded in becoming an independent kingdom. Beginning in the early 1200s, the Christian states of Aragon and Castile in northern Spain began a determined effort to drive the Muslims out of that region. This effort is known as the *reconquista,* which is Spanish for "reconquest."

By the mid-1260s, many cities in southern Spain had been reclaimed by the Christians, including Córdoba, Cádiz, and the Muslim capital of Seville. It took the Christians until 1492, however, to capture the Muslim stronghold of Granada.

That year was a landmark year in the history of Spain for two other reasons. King Ferdinand of Aragon and his wife Isabella of Castile sponsored the first journey of the Italian explorer Christopher Columbus. In that same year, Ferdinand and Isabella expelled the Jewish people from Spain. The expulsion of the Jews, who had been responsible for major cultural achievements in Spain, followed a pattern of their persecution in Europe. From the late 1200s to the late 1400s, Jews were expelled from France, England, Spain, and Portugal. Many of them settled in eastern Europe and Russia.

The expulsion of the Jews from Spain marked a victory for the Spanish **Inquisition**. The Inquisition was a Roman Catholic Church court that enforced the Church's teachings. The Inquisition was known for its harshness and cruelty to people who were accused of having ideas against those of the Church. The fear caused by the Inquisition further strengthened the power of the Spanish monarchs.

◆ **Why was the year 1492 important in Spanish history?**

Review III

Review History

A. What were the origins of the Parliament in England?

B. What were the major effects of the Hundred Years' War on England and France?

C. What changes took place in Spain after the Christians regained control of it from the Muslims?

Define Terms to Know

Define the following terms: **common law, Parliament, Estates General, nationalism, Inquisition**

Critical Thinking

What were the most important factors affecting the development of organized kingdoms during the Middle Ages?

Write About Government

Write a paragraph explaining why more people became involved in the governments of England and France during the Middle Ages.

Get Organized

IDEA WEB

Use an idea web to organize information from this section. Choose a topic and then find related facts. For example, what were the accomplishments of the Capetian Dynasty?

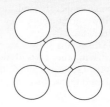

Critical Thinking

Possible answers: strong leadership; parliaments; rivalry between France and England; *reconquista* in Spain

Write About Government

Students should include some or all of the following: development of trial by jury; establishment of Parliament in England; establishment of the Estates General in France.

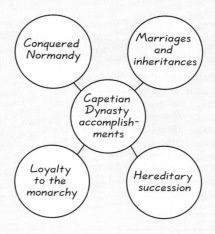

Conquered Normandy

Marriages and inheritances

Capetian Dynasty accomplishments

Loyalty to the monarchy

Hereditary succession

Section IV
The Roman Catholic Church Faces Crises

Terms to Know

Great Schism the split dividing the papacy in the High Middle Ages

antipope a pope not officially recognized by the entire Roman Catholic Church

indulgence a release by the Roman Catholic Church for some or all of a person's sins

Main Ideas

A. For more than a century, the papacy was troubled by its physical separation from Rome and by rival popes claiming authority.

B. By the fourteenth century, debates within the Roman Catholic Church had increased.

Active Reading

MAIN IDEAS AND DETAILS
When reading history, you will find it helpful to identify main ideas and supporting details. Main ideas often appear in the heads and subheads of each section and details follow in the text. As you read this section, look for the main ideas and details about problems developing in the Roman Catholic Church.

Then & Now

AVIGNON

Today, Avignon is a popular tourist destination in the southeastern region of France known as Provence. In addition to its other attractions, you can still see the magnificent palaces of the popes there. Another tourist attraction in Avignon is an international arts festival, which is held during the summer. This festival is especially known for its experimental theater.

A. The Papacy at Avignon and the Great Schism

During the Middle Ages, the papacy played an important role in politics and in the development of organized nations. The medieval popes were political leaders, who ruled over large territories in Italy, as well as religious leaders. The powerful influence of the Roman Catholic Church meant that the popes could help or hurt kings and emperors.

From Rome to Avignon

Since the days of the early Christian Church, Rome had been a symbol for Christians. Over time, the bishop of Rome became the most powerful bishop and worldwide leader of the Church.

In 1309, a French pope, Clement V, moved the seat of the papacy from Rome to Avignon, in France, to avoid civil wars in Italy. Two new palaces were built for the popes, who remained in Avignon until 1377. There were seven popes during this time and all of them were French.

The Great Schism

Pope Gregory XI returned the papacy to Rome in 1377. He died a year later. The cardinals—the high-ranking church officials—elected an Italian pope, Urban VI. Urban soon proved to be unruly and cruel. The cardinals declared his election invalid and elected a French candidate, Clement VII. Urban refused to resign, and Clement retreated to Avignon.

For the next 40 years, the Church was divided by the **Great Schism**, in which a succession of rival popes claimed authority. The popes at Avignon are sometimes called **antipopes** because they were not recognized as the real popes by many Roman Catholics. France, Sicily, and parts of Spain supported the popes at Avignon. However, most of the rest of Europe, including England and Ireland, supported the popes in Rome.

Starting in 1417, a group of Church leaders met in Constance, Switzerland, to discuss Church unity. They brought the separate papacies together at the meeting, called the Council of Constance. The leaders elected Martin V as the one pope to unify the papacy. The Council of Constance established that a general council of the whole Church had authority that even popes had to obey.

◆ **What caused the Great Schism?**

Teaching Options

Section 4 Resources

Teacher's Resources (TR)
Terms to Know, p. 26
Review History, p. 60
Build Your Skills, p. 94
Chapter Test, pp. 141–142
Concept Builder, p. 229
Idea Web, p. 321

F Y I

The Great Schism

The Great Schism damaged the dignity of the Church deeply. The popes excommunicated each other, as well as everyone who supported that pope. So, for a time everyone in Christendom was excommunicated. Before the Council of Constance met, there was a Council of Pisa, which tried to depose the two sitting popes by electing a third. The two popes refused to resign, and so for a few years there were *three* popes.

Section Summary

In this section, students will learn about the papacy being seated in Avignon for almost 70 years and about the Great Schism that followed when the Church moved the papacy back to Rome. They will also learn about outspoken critics of the Church at this time—John Wycliffe, the Lollards, and Jan Hus.

1 Introduce

Getting Started

Discuss with students how they respond when they witness something wrong happening. Ask what they would do if a respected member of their household or community committed a wrongful act. (Some students will confront the person, whereas others may overlook the act.) Discuss the courage needed to confront a person at such a time.

TERMS TO KNOW

Ask students to read the terms and definitions on page 307 and find each term in the section. Point out that the prefix *anti-* means "against."

You may wish to preview the pronunciation of the following words with students.

Avignon (a veen YOHN)
Rhône (ROHN)
Wycliffe (WY klihf)

ACTIVE READING

Have students use a main idea/supporting details chart (TR, p. 319) to list the main ideas of the section and the details that support these ideas. In this section, they will probably find four or five main ideas, and beneath those will be a variety of details. So, students should be given four or five charts or asked to draw charts as necessary, linking them together with arrows.

A. The Papacy at Avignon and the Great Schism

Purpose-Setting Question What papal problems was the Roman Catholic Church forced to deal with between 1309 and 1417? (The pope's residence moved to Avignon. Then the Church split between those who wanted a pope in Avignon and those who wanted a pope in Rome.)

Discuss Ask students why French kings would want the papacy at Avignon. (to have more control over the pope's actions) Ask students what the economic effect of two papacies might be. (more expensive to run two papacies)

Then & Now

AVIGNON In 1947, the actor and director Jean Vilar founded the festival of Dance, Music and Theatre in Avignon. Now the festival events occur all around Avignon, including at historical monuments and in the streets. People from all over the world attend the festival.

◆ **ANSWER** the refusal of Pope Urban VI to resign and the election by the cardinals of the antipope Clement VII, who relocated his office in Avignon

B. Internal Tensions Grow

Purpose-Setting Question How did John Wycliffe and Jan Hus alarm leaders of the Roman Catholic Church? (They questioned Roman Catholic Church doctrines and policies.)

Explain Ask students to name Wycliffe's three major objections to Church teachings and practices. (some clergy were too wealthy, including the pope; the Bible was the highest source of religious authority; people should be able to read and interpret the Bible for themselves) Discuss whether these objections were reasonable.

The pope's palaces in Avignon, France, overlook the Rhône River.

B. Internal Tensions Grow

The medieval Roman Catholic Church was the most powerful institution in Europe. During the twelfth and thirteenth centuries, the Church was at the height of its political, social, and philosophical influence. For most of the Middle Ages, believers were willing to accept whatever the Church taught. This began to change in the High Middle Ages. By the fourteenth century, critics began to question Church teachings and practices.

John Wycliffe Calls for Reforms

Before the Great Schism, the most serious internal conflict among Christians had been the split between Rome and Constantinople in 1054. The patriarch, or leading bishop, of Constantinople, had refused to acknowledge the authority of the pope in Rome. As a result, two branches of Christianity developed: the western European Roman Catholic Church and the Eastern Orthodox Churches.

At the same time that the Great Schism was dividing Roman Catholics, John Wycliffe, an English teacher and priest, criticized many Church teachings and practices. Wycliffe, like some earlier critics, objected to the wealth of many members of the clergy, including the pope. Wycliffe argued that the Bible, not the Church or its officials, was the highest source of religious authority. He felt that people should be able to read and interpret the Bible for themselves. Church officials accused Wycliffe of being a heretic, someone who publicly expresses beliefs that differ from the official teachings of the Roman Catholic Church. The English royal court protected him, so he was not executed like many others of that time.

Besides his arguments on faith, Wycliffe also helped launch the first translation of the Latin Bible into English. The result was that many more people could read the Bible and decide for themselves what it said.

In England, followers of John Wycliffe called themselves Lollards, and spread the belief that individuals ought to be able to interpret the Bible for themselves. The Lollards also criticized the wealth of the clergy.

308 UNIT 3 ◆ Regional Civilizations

Teaching Options

ESL/ELL STRATEGIES

Role-play Help students to understand the conflict within the Roman Catholic Church at this time. Have pairs of students role-play John Wycliffe or Jan Hus being accused of heresy by Roman Catholic Church leaders and defending himself. Before beginning their defense, the pair should list points that they wish to make in the trial. They may wish to write a short script as well.

Connection to CULTURE

Discuss the practice of labeling a person a heretic. Then, discuss with students how the Roman Catholic Church justified this act and the possible reasons for it. Ask students the following question: If there were heretics today in the United States, would they be protected like Wycliffe was in the Middle Ages? (Yes; in the United States, we have freedom of speech and religion.)

The Lollards posed such a threat to established interests that England denounced the reformers as heretics and introduced the death penalty for heresy in 1401. A Lollard uprising was harshly put down in 1414, and the Lollards were driven into hiding.

Challenges to the Church

Wycliffe's ideas also influenced the Czech religious reformer Jan Hus. At the University of Prague in present-day Czech Republic, where he studied and taught, Hus called for reform of Church practices. Hus objected particularly to the Church's sale of **indulgences**. For many years, the Church allowed people to buy an indulgence instead of doing penance to gain forgiveness for their sins. Penances could involve praying for many hours or days, giving all of one's possessions to poor people, or even going on a crusade. Many people were happy to buy an indulgence instead of doing a penance, and the Church was happy to take their money. Hus felt this practice was not in keeping with Church teachings.

When the archbishop of Prague burned John Wycliffe's writings, Hus strongly protested. Conflicts with the Church and the king forced him to leave Prague in 1412. Two years later, the Council of Constance condemned Hus as a heretic. He was burned to death at the stake in 1415.

John Wycliffe, the Lollards, and Jan Hus all raised important issues that challenged Roman Catholic teachings and authority. For a while, the Church was successful in resisting efforts at reform. However, calls for reform in the Church continued to spread in the early 1500s. Wycliffe, the Lollards, and Hus led the calls for Church reform. Their ideas survived, and other reformers took up the same demands.

◆ **Why did John Wycliffe and Jan Hus call for reforms in the Roman Catholic Church?**

INDULGENCES

According to Church teaching, people who confessed their sins could be forgiven. However, the Church required that such sinners make amends, either by doing penance in this life or by suffering for a time after death in Purgatory. In exchange for donations and prayers, the Roman Catholic Church believed it had the authority to cancel either part or all of this penance.

Review IV

Review History
A. What is Avignon's significance in Church history?
B. What did the Lollards believe in?

Define Terms to Know
Define the following terms:
Great Schism, antipope, indulgence

Critical Thinking
How did the challenges to Church authority at the end of the 1300s affect its power in Europe?

Write About History
Write a news article about the Council of Constance and its outcome. Describe what you think it would have been like to be at the meeting and how returning to a single pope would change life for most people.

Get Organized
IDEA WEB
Use an idea web to organize information from this section. Choose a topic and then find related facts. For example, what were the beliefs and achievements of John Wycliffe?

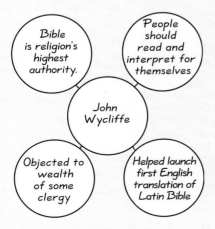

- Bible is religion's highest authority.
- People should read and interpret for themselves
- John Wycliffe
- Objected to wealth of some clergy
- Helped launch first English translation of Latin Bible

Critical Thinking
Challenges to the Church eventually weakened the control the Church had over the people in Europe.

Write About History
Students' news articles should describe the events at the Council and describe what the events would mean to most people.

Chapter Summary

A blank outline form is available in the Teacher's Resources (p. 318). Chapter summaries should outline the Crusades, the growth of trade and towns, how organized nations developed, and the crises faced by the Roman Catholic Church. Refer to the rubric in the Teacher's Resources (p. 340) to score students' chapter summaries.

 Interpret the Timeline

1. The capture of Jerusalem by Saladin occurred first.
2. 61 years (1431–1492)
3. One event is the outbreak of the Hundred Years' War.
4. Check that the events students choose are all in the chapter.

Use Terms to Know

5. Inquisition
6. epidemic
7. papacy
8. Parliament
9. indulgence
10. guild

Check Your Understanding

11. Possible answers: Gregory VII, Innocent III, Urban II
12. The First Crusade was a success in that the crusaders were able to recapture Jerusalem from the Muslims and to establish several crusader states in the East.
13. The Crusades expanded trade, strengthened the Roman Catholic Church, and served as a vehicle for the cross-cultural exchange of ideas and inventions. At the same time, the Crusades encouraged religious hatred that often resulted in persecution.
14. Agricultural improvements, the development of new markets for agricultural goods, the development of fairs, the establishment of the Hanseatic League, and the invention of new banking practices and institutions were all significant factors in the revival of trade.
15. The basic purpose of a guild was to promote the business and the personal well-being of its members.
16. The economic consequences of the Black Death were devastating, contributing to the decline of feudalism.

Chapter Summary

Complete the following outline in your notebook. Then, use your outline to write a brief summary of the chapter.

The High Middle Ages

I. The Crusades Begin
   A. The Background of the Crusades
   B. The First and Second Crusades
   C. Later Crusades

II. Trade and Towns Grow
   A. The Revival of Trade
   B. The Growth of Towns
   C. Plague and Social Upheaval
   D. Life and Culture

III. Organized Kingdoms Develop
   A. England
   B. France
   C. The Holy Roman Empire and Spain

IV. The Roman Catholic Church Faces Crises
   A. The Papacy at Avignon and the Great Schism
   B. Internal Tensions Grow

 Interpret the Timeline

Use the timeline on pages 288–289 to answer the following questions.

1. Which occurred first, the capture of Jerusalem by Saladin or the Hundred Years' War?

2. How many years after the death of Joan of Arc were the Jews expelled from Spain?

3. **Critical Thinking** Name an event on the timeline that is linked to the struggle for power between England and France during the High Middle Ages.

4. Select five events from the chapter that are not on the timeline. Create a timeline that shows these events.

Use Terms to Know

Select the term that best completes each sentence.

| epidemic | indulgence | papacy |
| guild | Inquisition | Parliament |

5. The Church court charged with finding and punishing heresies was the _____.

6. A widespread disease that attacks people is an _____.

7. The _____ refers to the office and rule of the pope.

8. The _____ is the assembly that advises the rulers of England.

9. By issuing an _____, the Roman Catholic Church could cancel the penance that sinners needed to perform to gain forgiveness.

10. During the Middle Ages, a merchant or craftsperson in a town was likely to be a member of a _____.

Check Your Understanding

11. **Identify** two strong popes during the later Middle Ages who believed in the supreme power of the papacy.

12. **Describe** the achievements of the First Crusade.

13. **Discuss** the lasting impact of the Crusades on medieval Europe.

14. **Explain** the revival of trade after the year 1000.

15. **Identify** the basic purpose of a guild in medieval towns and cities.

16. **Summarize** the consequences of the Black Death in Europe.

17. **Discuss** the significance of the Magna Carta.

18. **Describe** the role of Joan of Arc in the outcome of the Hundred Years' War.

19. **Explain** why the papacy moved to Avignon, France, in 1309.

20. **Discuss** the challenges posed to the Roman Catholic Church by John Wycliffe, the Lollards, and Jan Hus.

---

17. The Magna Carta established the principle that the king was not above the law. Furthermore, it assured freemen the basic right of trial.

18. Joan of Arc inspired the French army to defeat the English army at Orléans. After this defeat, Charles VII was crowned king of France. Eventually, Charles drove the English out of most of France.

19. The papacy was moved to Avignon to avoid political unrest in Italy.

20. John Wycliffe attacked clerical wealth and power, proclaimed the Bible as the supreme source of religious authority, wanted people to be able to read and interpret the Bible for themselves, and helped to get the Bible translated into English. The Lollards asserted that individuals should be able to interpret the Bible for themselves. They also criticized the wealth of the clergy. Jan Hus protested against the Church's sale of indulgences.

Critical Thinking

21. Make Inferences Why was Jerusalem such an important focal point for the crusaders?

22. Analyze Information What was the long-term importance of the decision by Dante and Chaucer to use the vernacular for their works?

23. Compare and Contrast How would you compare and contrast these two strong monarchs of the High Middle Ages: King Henry II of England and King Louis IX of France?

24. Draw Conclusions What conclusions do you draw from the internal conflicts of the Roman Catholic Church during the period from 1378 to 1417?

Put Your Skills to Work

25. Distinguish Fact From Opinion You have learned how to distinguish facts from opinions. Facts can be checked and proven with records or sources. Opinions, however, are statements of judgment, value, or belief.

Read the passage below about the poet Dante Alighieri. Then, answer the following questions.

a. What are one opinion and one fact about Dante in the first sentence?

b. What are two other facts in this passage about Dante?

c. What do you think the writer of this passage thought about Dante? What supports your opinion?

"Dante was the most accomplished poet of the Middle Ages. He grew up in the Italian city of Florence, where he was active in city politics. After political opponents exiled him from the city in 1302, Dante spent the last 20 years of his life in exile. During his exile, he wrote an epic poem—*Commedia*, or *Comedy* (later called *The Divine Comedy*)—a triumph of world literature that has placed Dante in the company of Homer and Shakespeare as among the greatest writers who ever lived."

Analyze Sources

26. Read the passage below about the achievements of later medieval Europe, written by the modern historians R. R. Palmer and Joel Colton. Then, answer the questions that follow.

The people of the High Middle Ages did not develop the conception of progress, because their minds were set upon timeless values and personal salvation in another world, but the period was nevertheless one of rapid progress in nonreligious or "secular" things. It was a period in which much was created that remained fundamental far into modern times.

a. According to Palmer and Colton, why did people not develop the concept of progress during this period?

b. Do you agree with the authors' evaluation of this period as a time of rapid and far-reaching progress? Why or why not?

Essay Writing

27. During the High Middle Ages, Europe expanded on many levels. For example, trade expanded greatly, kings and popes tried to increase their power, and towns and cities developed. Write an essay on the theme of expansion during this period. Was expansion always positive? Support your main ideas with facts, examples, and reasons.

TEST PREPARATION

COMPARING AND CONTRASTING IDEAS
Choose the correct answer.

Unlike Henry II of England, Louis IX of France strengthened his control of his kingdom by

1. imposing heavy new taxes.

2. introducing a system of common law.

3. holding frequent meetings of the Estates General.

4. allowing the provinces to keep their regional customs, as long as they were loyal to the French monarchy.

Critical Thinking

21. As the place where Jesus was put to death, Jerusalem was sacred to Christians and an important destination for Christian pilgrims.

22. Possible answer: Their decision to use the vernacular led to the rise of national literatures, which were read by more people.

23. Both monarchs were involved in laws and justice. Henry II created a legal system for the entire country. Louis IX allowed areas to keep their own customs as long as they were loyal to the king. Louis IX was later declared a saint.

24. The Roman Catholic Church, which had earlier been very powerful and influential, was weakened by internal conflict during this period.

Put Your Skills to Work

DISTINGUISH FACT FROM FICTION
25a. Fact: poet in the Middle Ages; **Opinion:** most accomplished poet in the Middle Ages

25b. He grew up in Florence and was active in city politics.

25c. The writer thinks that Dante is a wonderful poet. He calls Dante an "accomplished" poet and ranks him with Homer and Shakespeare.

Analyze Sources

26a. Their minds were set upon timeless values and personal salvation in another world.

26b. Possible answer: Yes, because of the revival of trade, the rise of towns and cities, the development of organized nations, and such achievements as Gothic-style architecture and literature in the vernacular.

Essay Writing

27. Students' essays may mention such positive factors as increased prosperity, the development of political rights for towns and individuals, the development of national literatures, the establishment of universities, and calls for Church reform. Essays may also mention negative aspects and tensions such as persecution and greed during the Crusades and the Inquisition's suppression of religious freedom.

TEST PREPARATION

Answer 4. allowing the provinces to keep their regional customs, as long as they were loyal to the French monarchy.

Unit 3
Portfolio Project
MILLENNIUM EXHIBITION

Managing the Project
Plan for 4–5 class periods.

Set the Scene
Ask students if their families keep family albums or videotapes. Discuss the value of these keepsakes. (to preserve the memories of the family's past) Explain that museum exhibits have a similar function, although their scope is broader.

Your Assignment
Have students read the assignment on page 312. Then, divide the class into groups of 5–6 to begin work on the project.

RESEARCH YOUR EXHIBIT
Have each group choose a topic from the list on page 312. Each group may be further divided into work areas, such as research, production, and presentation. Be sure that responsibilities are clearly defined. Groups may begin by obtaining information from the textbook. Then, have them turn to the Internet and library for additional resources. Remind them that a museum exhibit is predominantly visual, supported by short descriptive captions or paragraphs.

SET UP AND PRESENT YOUR EXHIBIT
Once the research phase has been completed, the group as a whole should decide on which items to focus on. Encourage students to organize their exhibits in an attractive and easily followed format. Written information should be brief. Have the whole group proofread the written materials. Be sure that the whole group supports the museum guide's presentation.

Wrap Up
The final product will be a museum exhibit, including attractive visuals with descriptive captions. The exhibits will provide a summary of world history and culture at this time.

Millennium Exhibition

YOUR ASSIGNMENT
In the late 1990s, many news stories reported that a thousand years earlier, people widely feared the destruction of the world in the year 1000. Your assignment is to put together a museum exhibit of photos, charts, posters, and other visuals that focus on world history and culture at the end of the first millennium and the beginning of the next.

RESEARCH YOUR EXHIBIT
Select a Topic Below are some topics you and your group may find useful for research.

> Maya art and architecture
> city-states and trading centers in Africa
> the kingdom of Venice in Italy
> the Song Dynasty in China
> the spread and effects of the Black Death
> the early Capetian monarchy in France
> medieval trade fairs
> knights in armor

Research Conduct research using your textbook, the Internet, and library sources. Use notecards to organize your information and create visuals such as maps, charts, and posters. Be sure to answer these questions: What does this information show about life in or around the year 1000? What comparisons and contrasts does the information reveal?

SET UP AND PRESENT YOUR EXHIBIT

Plan Make a plan that organizes the items in your exhibit in a logical way that is easy to follow. Some members of the group can discuss with your teacher where the exhibit should be set up. Other members can write informative captions for photos and other visuals. Still other members can create displays for the items, setting up creative backdrops if possible.

Present Choose one member of your group to take on the role of museum guide. This spokesperson will lead visitors around the exhibit. Other members can describe and comment on a specific item or group of items in the exhibit.

Work Individually In a report, compare and contrast culture in this period with the culture of the present.

Multimedia Presentation

Turn your exhibit into a slide show or video program. Write a script describing the items in your exhibit and choose theme music. Then, present or screen your program for a small audience of classmates or friends.

Teaching Options

Multimedia Presentation

Help students take pictures for the slide show, and teach them to run a slide projector. If students are videotaping, be sure they are familiar with the equipment. Have students practice their presentations in advance to be sure that they are coordinated.

Alternative Assessment

Create a Travel Brochure Have students work in five small groups to create pages for a Travel Back in Time brochure. Each page should focus on a period or culture found in Unit 3. Have groups include information about the location, geography, climate, activities, or historical events that took place, and at least one visual.

Managing the Unit
This unit should take approximately **four weeks** to complete.

Unit 4 EUROPE UNDERGOES CHANGE

PLANNING GUIDE

	Skills and Features	Projects and Activities	Program Resources	Meet Individual Needs

Chapter 14
 	
The Renaissance and the Reformation,
pp. 314–335
Plan for 4–5 class periods.
	Unit Technology, p. T313
	Analyze and Answer a Document-Based Question, p. 321
	Connect History & Literature, p. 327
		Connection to World Languages, p. T316
		Cooperative Learning, p. T317
		Writing, p. T318
		Using Technology, p. T319
		Connection to Geography, p. T323
		Research, p. T324
		Test Taking, p. T325
		Link to Today, p. T327
		Conflict Resolution, p. T329
		Teen Life, p. T330
			Teacher's Resources
			Terms to Know, p. 27
			Review History, p. 61
			Build Your Skills, p. 95
			Chapter Test, pp. 143–144
			Concept Builder, p. 230
			They Made History:
			  Johann Gutenberg,
			  p. 256
			Idea Web, p. 321
			Transparencies 5, 15
				ESL/ELL Strategies,
				  pp. T317, T322, T328
				Visual/Spatial, p. T323
				Verbal/Linguistic, p. T332

Chapter 15
 	
Exploration and Trade,
pp. 336–357
Plan for 4–5 class periods.
	Draw Conclusions, p. 343
	They Made History:
	  Vasco da Gama, p. 347
	[DK] Past to Present:
	  Asia and European
	  Trade Connections
	  pp. 354–355
		Test Taking, pp. T339, T346
		Connection to Geography, p. T340
		Research, p. T341
		Connection to Literature, pp. T345, T354
		Writing, p. T347
		Conflict Resolution, p. T348
		Using Technology, p. T351
		Cooperative Learning, p. T352
			Teacher's Resources
			Terms to Know, p. 28
			Review History, p. 62
			Build Your Skills, p. 96
			Chapter Test, pp. 145–146
			Concept Builder, p. 231
			SQR Chart, p. 322
			Transparencies 1, 6
				ESL/ELL Strategies,
				  pp. T338, T344, T350
				Verbal/Linguistic, p. T340
				Visual/Spatial, p. T345

Chapter 16
 	
Europe Expands Overseas,
pp. 358–383
Plan for 5–6 class periods.
	Formulate and Support Opinions, p. 365
	They Made History:
	  Olaudah Equiano, p. 379
		Using Technology, p. T361
		Cooperative Learning, p. T361
		Writing, p. T363
		Sports and Games, p. T367
		Connection to Science, p. T368
		Connection to Culture, pp. T370, T378
		Research, p. T373
		Conflict Resolution, p. T374
		Test Taking, p. T375
			Teacher's Resources
			Terms to Know, p. 29
			Review History, p. 63
			Build Your Skills, p. 97
			Chapter Test, pp. 147–148
			Concept Builder, p. 232
			Idea Web, p. 321
			Transparencies 1, 3, 4, 5
				ESL/ELL Strategies,
				  pp. T360, T369,
				  T375, T378
				Visual, p. T380

Chapter 17
 	
European Monarchies,
pp. 384–410
Plan for 5–6 class periods.
	Make Inferences, p. 391
	Points of View, p. 407
		Writing, p. T389
		Connection to Government, pp. T393, T398
		Connection to Art, p. T395
		Using Technology, p. T400
		Conflict Resolution, p. T403
		Cooperative Learning, p. T403
		Test Taking, p. T404
		Research, p. T405
		Take a Stand, p. T407
			Teacher's Resources
			Terms to Know, p. 30
			Review History, p. 64
			Build Your Skills, p. 98
			Chapter Test, pp. 149–150
			Unit 4 Test, pp 189–190
			Concept Builder, p. 233
			They Made History:
			  Oliver Cromwell, p. 257
			Cause-and-Effect Chain,
			  p. 325
			Transparencies 1, 5
				ESL/ELL Strategies,
				  pp. T388, T399, T402
				Auditory, p. T387
				Visual/Spatial, p. T392
				Verbal/Linguistic, p. T394

Assessment Options

Chapter 14 Test, Teacher's Resources, pp. 143–144
Chapter 15 Test, Teacher's Resources, pp. 145–146
Chapter 16 Test, Teacher's Resources, pp. 147–148
Chapter 17 Test, Teacher's Resources, pp. 149–150
Unit 4 Test, Teacher's Resources, pp. 189–190

Alternative Assessment

Drama: History in Action, p. 410
Write a Dramatic Monologue, p. T410

Books for Students

AVERAGE

The Riddle of the Compass: The Invention That Changed the World. Amir D. Aczel. Reviews the origination of the compass and the changes it made in trade and navigation. (Harvest Books, 2002)

You Are the Explorer. Nathan Aaseng. Novel in which the reader is part of the story and makes choices. (Oliver Press, Incorporated, 2000)

Kidnapped Prince: The Life of Olaudah Equiano. Olaudah Equiano and Ann Cameron. Adapted autobiography of Olaudah Equiano. (Alfred A. Knopf Publishing Group, 2000)

CHALLENGING

The Renaissance: A Short History. Paul Johnson. Highlights the famous figures and developments of the Renaissance. (Random House Adult Trade Publishing Group, 2002)

Who's Who in Shakespeare's England. Alan Warwick and Veronica Palmer, editors. Biographies of people who influenced, knew, or were famous during the time of Shakespeare. (Tom Doherty Associates, LLC, 2000)

Columbus in the Americas. William Least Heat-Moon and Lois Wallace. Primary sources describe the events and consequences of Columbus's voyages. (John Wiley & Sons, Inc., 2002)

Women All on Fire: The Women of the English Civil War. Alison Plowden. Examines the women who took part in the English war of the mid-1600s. (Sutton Publishing, 2000)

Books for Teachers

Voices of Morebath: Reformation and Rebellion in an English Village. Eamon Duffy. Using a primary source, the lives of citizens from sixteenth century Morebath are explored. (Yale University Press, 2001)

1587: A Year of No Significance: The Ming Dynasty in Decline. Ray Huang. Uses seven people to describe the politics of the Ming Dynasty. (Yale University Press, 1993)

Slavery, Atlantic Trade and the British Economy, 1660–1800. Kenneth Morgan. Reviews how slavery and the Atlantic trade were factors of the British economy from 1660–1800. (Cambridge University Press, 2001)

American Colonies: The Settling of North America. Alan Taylor. Explores the many cultural influences that shaped America. (Penguin Group (USA) Inc., 2001)

Peter the Great: The Struggle for Power, 1671–1725. Paul Bushkovitch. Reviews the change in the Russian government and its effects on the culture. (Cambridge University Press, 2001)

You may wish to preview all referenced materials to ensure their appropriateness for your local community.

Audio/Visual Resources

The Renaissance. Probe the changes in areas, such as art and philosophy that occurred in this period. CD-ROM. (Social Studies School Service)

The Silk Road. Different adventures, chosen by the player, review history, people, places, and culture. CD-ROM. (DNA Multimedia)

Expansion of Europe: 1250–1500. Reviews the changes and events in Europe during this time. Videocassette. (Social Studies School Service)

Technology Resources

History of China: The Imperial Era: III: www-chaos.umd.edu/history/imperial3.html

Creating French Culture: Treasures from *Bibliothèque Nationale de France*: www.loc.gov/exhibits/bnf/bnf0005.html

The Renaissance: http://renaissance.dm.net/

Renaissance, Reformation & Scientific Revolution. Explores Europe during the years 1400–1700. CD-ROM. (Entrex)

The Renaissance Explorers: John Cabot and the Merchant Venturers. Students become an explorer, use tools such as an astrolabe, and read biographies and maps. Activity sheets included. CD-ROM. (Social Studies School Service)

Globe Fearon Related Resources

History Resources

Core Knowledge History & Geography: The Age of Exploration. Provides additional information on the age of exploration. ISBN 0-7690-3086-6

Core Knowledge History & Geography: The Renaissance. Provides additional information on the Renaissance. ISBN 0-7690-3087-4

Global Studies, Focus on Europe and Eurasia, Volume 3. Primary source materials and activities are used to explore all aspects of life in these regions. ISBN 0-835-91937-4

Adapted Classics

Gulliver's Travels. Jonathan Swift's novel describes three voyages of Lemuel Gulliver. ISBN 0-835-90853-4

Hamlet. William Shakespeare's play about a prince who pretends to be mad for revenge. ISBN 0-835-91864-5

Othello. Play by William Shakespeare about a marriage destroyed by lies and jealousy. ISBN 0-835-95555-9

Romeo and Juliet. William Shakespeare's play about a boy and a girl from opposing families and their forbidden love. ISBN 0-835-91845-9

To order books, call 1-800-321-3106.

Europe Undergoes Change

> *"Dare to know."*
> —Immanuel Kant, philosopher, 1784

LINKING CULTURES Between the fourteenth through seventeenth centuries, people searched for new lands and examined fresh ideas about religion, education, and government. Such ideas challenged the establishment and labeled free thinkers as dangerous. This monument to Prince Henry of Portugal is a tribute to the courage of all those who "dared to know."

◆ What do the monument and the quotation suggest about the changes Europe might undergo as it entered into an age of discovery?

313

Teaching Options

UNIT TECHNOLOGY

Have students use the Internet (CD-ROM resources and other media) to research other well-known monuments and statues from the periods discussed in this unit. Possible suggestions include the *Pietà*, *David*, *Saint Theresa of Ávila*, *Christopher Columbus*, *Fontana di Trevi*, and the *Basilica of Saint Peter* in the Vatican.

You may wish to identify possible Web sites for students and always monitor their activities on the Internet.

UNIT 4 / Portfolio Project

Seeing History in Action

The Portfolio Project for Unit 4, on page 410, is to write a movie or television program about a person from this unit who had a dramatic impact on history. Teams of students will select an individual from history, and research the accomplishments of the person they chose and the time that person lived. The teams will then write and present the program they created to the class.

Europe Undergoes Change
(pp. 313–410)

Unit Summary
Unit 4 focuses on the impact of the Renaissance and the Reformation on European life, exploration, and overseas trade.

CHAPTER 14
The Renaissance and the Reformation

CHAPTER 15
Exploration and Trade

CHAPTER 16
Europe Expands Overseas

CHAPTER 17
European Monarchies

Set the Stage
TEACH PRIMARY SOURCES
Photo This photograph shows the monument to Prince Henry the Navigator. Explain that Prince Henry of Portugal was the leading promoter of exploration and the study of geography in the 1400s. Have students describe the monument and explain why they think Prince Henry is holding a sailing ship. (Henry, leading his navigators, looks out from Lisbon harbor to the sea. The sailing ship symbolizes exploration by sea.)

Quote Immanuel Kant, an eighteenth century German philosopher, was interested in the nature and limits of human knowledge. He believed people could know things that they had not experienced as well as those they had experienced. Based on his beliefs, ask students what they think this quotation means. (Possible answers: People should take it upon themselves to discover many new things. They should not be afraid to try or to learn something new.)

◆ **ANSWER** Possible answer: Filled with self-confidence that was based on new ideas, Europeans were ready and willing to explore unknown areas, thus expanding their own horizons.

The Renaissance and the Reformation
1300–1650
(pp. 314–335)

Chapter Objectives

• Discuss how the acceptance of nonreligious attitudes and the study of Greek and Roman culture led to the development of the Renaissance and influenced the arts.
• Explain how the Italian Renaissance spread to northern and western Europe and affected writers and artists in those areas.
• Describe how calls for reform of the Roman Catholic Church led to the Reformation and how the Church reformed in response.

Chapter Summary

Section I discusses the development of the European Renaissance and focuses on Italian Renaissance innovations in writing and the arts.
Section II explores the spread of the Renaissance to the nation-states of northern and western Europe and the innovations in writing and the arts that accompanied it.
Section III focuses on the causes of the Reformation, how it spread throughout Europe, and how the Roman Catholic Church changed in response to it.

Set the Stage
TEACH PRIMARY SOURCES
Ask students who the *you* refers to in Leon Battista Alberti's quotation. (humans) Discuss Alberti's feelings about humans and encourage students to point out terms in the quotation that express these feelings. (graceful, power, sharp and delicate senses, wit, reason, and memory) Explain that Alberti believed that a burst of civilization depended on "self-confidence." Ask students to discuss whether they believe self-confidence can make a difference in achieving things in their own lives.

CHAPTER
14

The Renaissance and the Reformation
1300–1650

I. The Renaissance Begins
II. The Renaissance Spreads
III. The Reformation

The Renaissance was a time when people had new ideas and made new discoveries. Renaissance artists created works of art that were far more realistic than those of the Middle Ages. Ideas could be spread more rapidly because of the invention of the printing press. These and other developments caused life in Europe to change during the Renaissance. The most dramatic change, however, was a change in the way people thought. A new self-confidence was born. This self-confidence led to the exploration of unknown lands and challenges to the authority of the Roman Catholic Church.

One of the greatest figures of the early Renaissance was an architect and scholar named Leon Battista Alberti. Alberti expressed the Renaissance spirit in this way:

❝ *To you is given a body more graceful than other animals, to you power of apt and various movements, to you most sharp and delicate senses, to you wit, reason, memory like an immortal god.* ❞

1300s
Renaissance begins in Italian city-states.

1330s
Francesco Petrarca, a key figure in the early Renaissance, begins writing.

1450
Johann Gutenberg develops the printing press.

CHAPTER EVENTS

| 1300 | 1350 | 1400 | 1450 |

WORLD EVENTS

1325
Aztecs build Tenochtitlán.

1419
Prince Henry invites scholars to his court in Portugal.

314 **UNIT 4** ◆ Europe Undergoes Change

Teaching Options

Chapter 14 Resources

REVIEW

Teacher's Resources (TR)
Terms to Know, p. 27
Review History, p. 61
Build Your Skills, p. 95
Chapter Test, pp. 143–144
Concept Builder, p. 230
Idea Web, p. 321
Transparencies 5, 15

ASSESSMENT
Section Reviews, pp. 320, 326, 333
Chapter Review, pp. 334–335
Chapter Test, TR, pp. 143–144

ALTERNATIVE ASSESSMENT
Portfolio Project, p. 410
Write a Dramatic Monologue, p. T410

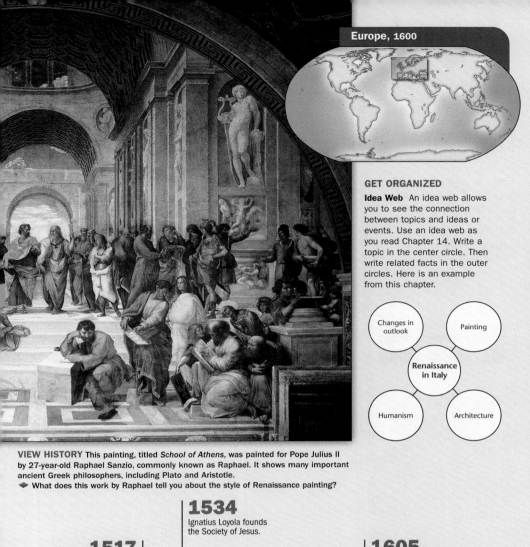

Europe, 1600

GET ORGANIZED

Idea Web An idea web allows you to see the connection between topics and ideas or events. Use an idea web as you read Chapter 14. Write a topic in the center circle. Then write related facts in the outer circles. Here is an example from this chapter.

Changes in outlook

Painting

Renaissance in Italy

Humanism

Architecture

VIEW HISTORY This painting, titled *School of Athens*, was painted for Pope Julius II by 27-year-old Raphael Sanzio, commonly known as Raphael. It shows many important ancient Greek philosophers, including Plato and Aristotle.
◆ What does this work by Raphael tell you about the style of Renaissance painting?

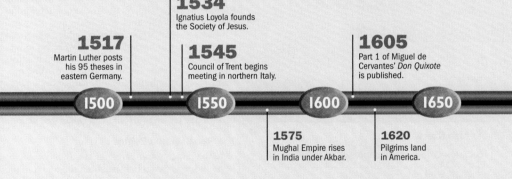

1517
Martin Luther posts his 95 theses in eastern Germany.

1534
Ignatius Loyola founds the Society of Jesus.

1545
Council of Trent begins meeting in northern Italy.

1605
Part 1 of Miguel de Cervantes' *Don Quixote* is published.

1500　1550　1600　1650

1575
Mughal Empire rises in India under Akbar.

1620
Pilgrims land in America.

CHAPTER 14 ◆ The Renaissance and the Reformation **315**

Chapter Themes
- Culture
- Time, Continuity, and Change
- People, Places, and Environments
- Individuals, Groups, and Institutions
- Power, Authority, and Governance
- Science, Technology, and Society
- Civic Ideals and Practices

F Y I

Raphael
Raphael Sanzio was an artist who mastered the use of perspective. In *School of Athens*, he created depth by placing Plato and Aristotle close to the center of the painting with high arches above them and the floor and a few steps below them leading back toward a distant step. Also, scholars in the foreground are drawn larger than those in the background.

I. The Renaissance Begins (pp. 316–320)

Section Summary

In this section, students will learn how an acceptance of nonreligious attitudes and the study of Greek and Roman cultures were major features of the Italian Renaissance. They will also learn that important contributions were made to science, art, politics, and manners, and that the arts flourished during this period.

Getting Started

Ask students to think of a time that they felt very sure of themselves, perhaps in sports, music, or schoolwork. Discuss how this self-confidence affected their ability to accomplish something. (Possible answer: Positive attitude helped me believe I could do it!) Point out that this new confidence at the beginning of the Renaissance had a huge effect on the people. They explored new lands, challenged the Church, invented new machines, and created new kinds of art.

TERMS TO KNOW

Ask students to read the terms and definitions on page 316 and find each term in the section. Have students write a short paragraph about the Renaissance in which they use all the terms.

You may wish to preview the pronunciation of the following names from this section with your students.

Niccolò Machiavelli
(nee koh LOH mahk yah VEHL ee)
Filippo Brunelleschi (fay LEE poh broo nayl LAYS kee)
Baldassare Castiglione
(bahl dahs SAHR ay kahs teel YOH nay)

ACTIVE READING

Ask students to use a Venn diagram (TR, p. 323) to record similarities and differences between the Renaissance attitudes and the medieval outlook on human life and behavior. Suggest that students scan subsection A of Section 1 to find the comparisons.

T316 ◆ UNIT 4

The Renaissance Begins

Terms to Know

Renaissance the great revival of art, literature, and learning in Europe

perspective an artistic technique used to give drawings a three-dimensional effect

humanism an intellectual movement that stemmed from the study of classical literature

patron a wealthy person who supports an artist

Main Ideas

A. Two major features of the Italian Renaissance were acceptance of nonreligious attitudes and the study of Greek and Roman cultures.

B. During this period, important contributions to science, art, politics, and manners were made by people such as Leonardo da Vinci, Niccolò Machiavelli, and Baldassare Castiglione.

C. The arts, including painting, sculpture, and architecture, flourished during the Renaissance.

Active Reading

COMPARE AND CONTRAST
When you compare and contrast, you identify similarities and differences. As you read this section, compare and contrast Renaissance attitudes with the medieval outlook on human life and behavior.

A. The Renaissance in Europe

The **Renaissance** is the term now used by historians to refer to the rich flowering of European civilization from the fourteenth century into the sixteenth century. *Renaissance* means "rebirth" in the French language. The origins of the Renaissance lay in Italy. However, the spirit of the Renaissance soon spread to other places in Europe, including Germany, France, Spain, and England.

A Fresh Outlook

The Renaissance was a time of new attitudes about culture, life, and learning. During this time, people became more interested in the world around them. Individual achievement was valued as never before. The Renaissance marked a change from a spiritual emphasis to an emphasis on the human experience in the present. Human life was no longer seen as a preparation for eternal life. Renaissance thinking encouraged people to take control of their lives and to fulfill their potential.

The rebirth of ideas that took place during the Renaissance involved a renewed interest in learning for its own sake. Scholars became very interested in the writings of the ancient Greeks and Romans. Attitudes about a whole range of subjects changed dramatically. For example, people were no longer told to despise money or wealth. Instead, individuals were encouraged to use wealth to enhance themselves or their city. Renaissance leaders supported freedom of the individual. They encouraged positive attitudes about the human body. They praised curiosity and celebrated action.

The Renaissance Begins

Italy was a natural place for the Renaissance to begin. For one thing, Italy had been the center of the

Renaissance Italy, 1505

- Republic of Genoa
- Duchy of Milan
- Republic of Venice
- Republic of Florence
- Papal States
- Kingdoms under Spain
- Other city-states
- • Cities

Milan · Turin · Venice · Mantua · Avignon · FRANCE · Genoa · Pisa · Florence · Corsica · Elba · Rome · Sardinia · Naples · Naples · Sicily · OTTOMAN EMPIRE · Adriatic Sea · Ionian Islands · Mediterranean Sea

0 100 200 mi
0 100 200 km

✔ Map Check

LOCATION Who controlled most of southern Italy?

316 UNIT 4 ◆ Europe Undergoes Change

Teaching Options

Section 1 Resources

Teacher's Resources (TR)
Terms to Know, p. 27
Review History, p. 61
Build Your Skills, p. 95
Concept Builder, p. 230
Idea Web, p. 321

Connection to
WORLD LANGUAGES

Point out to students that each language has its own rules of pronunciation. Explain that in Italian, if the letter *c* is followed by the vowels *a, o, u,* or the consonant *h,* it is pronounced /k/ as in *cat.* If *c* is followed by *e* or *i,* it is pronounced /ch/ as in *cherry.* Using these rules, help students pronounce Michelangelo and da Vinci.

ancient Roman Empire. The ruins of that empire surrounded the inhabitants of Italy and reminded them of how great it used to be.

Business and commerce also helped pave the way for the Italian Renaissance. As you learned in Chapter 13, northern Italy was one of the first regions in Europe to see the growth of towns and cities. Thriving commerce and trade brought Italian city-states such as Venice, Genoa, Milan, and Florence into contact with many other cultures. Trading ships sailed back and forth across the Mediterranean, from western Europe to the Middle East and from northern Africa to southern Europe. Its central location put Italy in a good position to profit from this trade. As trade grew, a new merchant class sprang up. Many merchants grew wealthy and used their money to support the arts.

Renaissance Figures in the Arts

An early Renaissance writer, Francesco Petrarca, known as Petrarch, began writing around 1337. His love sonnets, or poems, celebrated an imaginary woman named Laura. They are considered some of the greatest love poems in literature and served as models for later writers.

Other important figures of the early Renaissance included the painter Giotto and the architect Filippo Brunelleschi. Giotto painted lifelike, expressive figures. He was able to create the illusion of movement in his works. Brunelleschi is often credited with the discovery of **perspective**, which gave drawings a three-dimensional effect. One of his greatest achievements was the huge, eight-sided dome for the cathedral in Florence, Italy. Giotto and Brunelleschi were both from Florence. Although people from other cities, especially Venice and Rome, made important contributions, Florence was the single most important center of the Italian Renaissance.

Humanism

For Renaissance poets, historians, artists, and scholars, the classics—written works of Greek and Roman scholars—were an important source of inspiration. An intellectual movement developed that focused on classical ideals, styles, and forms. This movement was called **humanism**, and its members were called humanists. The humanists searched out manuscripts written in Greek and Latin with a wide range of topics, including history, literature, and grammar. The humanists studied, translated, and explained the manuscripts. Before the invention of the printing press, humanists copied manuscripts by hand. After the invention of the printing press, works such as those of Plato, Cicero, and Livy could be widely circulated. Printing helped spread the important texts of ancient Greece and Rome far and wide.

In his book *Oration on the Dignity of Man*, the humanist Giovanni Pico della Mirandola summed up the spirit of the age:

> 66 We have made thee neither of heaven nor of earth, neither mortal nor immortal, so that with freedom of choice and with honor, as though the maker and molder of thyself, thou mayest fashion thyself in whatever shape thou shalt prefer. 99

◆ How would you describe the fresh outlook of the Renaissance?

This dome is part of the great cathedral in Florence, Italy. It took more than 100 years to build, and many artists and sculptors worked on it.

ANALYZE PRIMARY SOURCES

DOCUMENT-BASED QUESTION
What does the quotation from Pico della Mirandola imply about the potential of human beings?

A. The Renaissance in Europe

Purpose-Setting Question
What new attitudes emerged in the Renaissance? (People were more interested in the world around them and individual achievement; emphasis was put on human experience in the present; individuals wanted to control their lives and fulfill their potential.)

Using the Map
Renaissance Italy, 1505

Ask students to use the map key to locate the different areas in Renaissance Italy. Have them name the city within each area. Point out that most of the cities are located near water. Discuss why these cities might have developed there. (easy access for trade)

✔ Map Check
Answer Spain

Activity

Write a poem Read some of Petrarch's sonnets with students. Then, have students work in pairs to write a sonnet that describes the ideal day or event. Have students share their sonnets and compare their descriptions.

ANALYZE PRIMARY SOURCES

DOCUMENT-BASED QUESTION
Oration on the Dignity of Man is a well-known work that some believe represents Renaissance thought. Count Giovanni Pico della Mirandola wrote *Oration on the Dignity of Man* for a gathering of European scholars. At this gathering, Pico planned to discuss 900 theses of different philosophers as well as his own thoughts. Thirteen of the theses were deemed heretical, and the gathering was not allowed to take place.

ANSWER Possible answer: Human beings have the potential to become whatever they would like, to make a good life for themselves.

◆ **ANSWER** Possible answers: new attitudes, rebirth, optimism

---

ESL/ELL STRATEGIES

Identify Essential Vocabulary Have students choose a paragraph from pages 316–317 and write words they do not understand. Then, have students work in pairs to try to use context clues to learn the words' meanings. Have students use a dictionary to check the meanings of the words. Monitor students' progress in the use of this strategy.

Cooperative Learning

Divide the class into four groups and explain that each group will be hosting a dinner for a famous Renaissance person. Assign Petrarch, Giotto, Filippo Brunelleschi, or Pico della Mirandola to a group. Have groups use library sources and the Internet to learn more about the person. One person from each group is the host, a second is the Renaissance person, and the others are guests at the dinner. Have each group discuss history, philosophy, literature, or art.

B. Italian Renaissance Writers

Purpose-Setting Question How did the books of Machiavelli and Castiglione affect the thinking of individuals during the Renaissance? (*The Prince* helped readers take a cold, hard look at how rulers had to act if they wanted to stay in power; *The Courtier* informed readers of the manners and qualities expected of a Renaissance gentleman.)

> **Activity**
>
> **Write headlines** Have students choose either Machiavelli's *The Prince* or Castiglione's *The Courtier* and write several newspaper headlines announcing its groundbreaking ideas. Then, have students complete a Five *W*s chart (TR, p. 326) that could be used to write a news article discussing the new ideas from the book.

Discuss Ask students to identify the qualities of a Renaissance gentleman as described by Castiglione. (noble birth, handsome, graceful, strong, courageous, accomplished in learning) Have students discuss possible reasons for the book's immense popularity. Then, allow groups to use library sources or the Internet to find books from today that might be similar to *The Courtier*. Groups should be able to discuss the similarities and differences between the books.

◆ **ANSWER** He held different government positions; so, he saw how the government worked.

C. Italian Renaissance Artists

Purpose-Setting Question What are some of the most famous works in painting and sculpture completed during the Italian Renaissance? (**Painting:** *La Gioconda, The Last Supper*, the ceiling of the Sistine Chapel, *School of Athens*; **Sculpture:** *David, Pietà*)

Focus Have students study the sketch of the helicopter from Leonardo's notebook and locate the man in the center. Then, discuss what they think the man is doing in order to make the machine fly. (powering the rotating wings) Point out that it was not for about another 450 years until the first practical helicopter was invented.

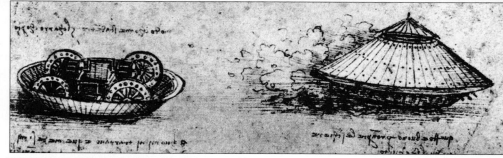

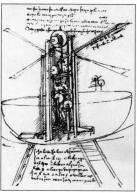

Leonardo da Vinci drew these sketches of a submarine (top) and a helicopter (above) in his notebooks.

B. Italian Renaissance Writers

During the Renaissance, there were many books that told how to live and act. They were available in print. Two of these most famous and influential books were *The Prince* and *The Courtier*.

Machiavelli and Government

Niccolò Machiavelli spent much of his time in Florence. From 1498 until 1512, he held a number of positions in government. Each position allowed him to observe how government worked or did not work. Machiavelli was most interested in how rulers gained and kept power.

Machiavelli's most famous book was *The Prince*. Many consider *The Prince* to be the first secular, or nonreligious, analysis of politics. The book was based on what Machiavelli had learned about politics in Italy. It tells how rulers really acted, not how they ought to act. The book helped readers take a cold, hard look at how rulers had to act if they wanted to stay in power.

The Writing of Castiglione

Another influential book of the Italian Renaissance was *The Courtier* by Baldassare Castiglione. In this manual of manners published in Venice in 1528, Castiglione discusses the qualities of the ideal courtier, or Renaissance gentleman. The perfect courtier should be of noble birth, handsome, graceful, strong, and courageous. The ideal courtier, according to Castiglione, should also be accomplished in learning. Castiglione's book was a best seller. It was read by both men and women and was soon translated into French, German, Spanish, Russian, and English.

◆ **How did Machiavelli learn about politics?**

C. Italian Renaissance Artists

The Renaissance witnessed an explosion of creativity in the fine arts. Three fields in which especially beautiful works were created include painting, sculpture, and architecture.

Leonardo da Vinci as Renaissance Man

When people speak of a Renaissance man, they mean someone who is highly skilled in many fields. If one figure of the Renaissance deserves such praise, it is Leonardo da Vinci.

Da Vinci is most widely known as a painter. His great masterpieces include *The Adoration of the Magi, The Last Supper*, and *La Gioconda*, more commonly called Mona Lisa. For more than 500 years, these works have been praised by painters and art historians alike for their unique expressive power.

318 UNIT 4 ◆ Europe Undergoes Change

Teaching Options

Writing

AVERAGE

Have students use library sources or the Internet to learn more about Machiavelli's life, including his early career, the intent and contents of *The Prince*, and his banishment from Florence. Have students make an outline (TR, p. 318) with the information they find. Then, have students use this outline to write a three-to-four-paragraph paper about Machiavelli.

CHALLENGE

Machiavelli believed that a strong state required a realistic, iron-willed ruler who was not afraid to use his power. Ask students if they agree or disagree with this statement, and have them write an essay based on their point of view. Essays should include an introductory paragraph, a body of several paragraphs that offers support for the point of view, and a closing paragraph to sum up the point of view.

Artists like Leonardo da Vinci were sought out by wealthy and powerful church and government leaders. These leaders gave money to support the artists and were called **patrons**. The artists, in turn, decorated the rooms, halls, and chapels owned by their patrons with wonderful paintings and statues. This system of support for the arts continued for many centuries. The Medici were a wealthy banking family in Florence who for generations spent lavishly on the arts. The Medici were patrons of da Vinci.

Da Vinci was also a sculptor, a mathematician, an architect, and a scientist. However, it was in the field of science that he was so ahead of his time. Leonardo da Vinci dissected corpses at a hospital in Florence to gain an accurate knowledge of human anatomy. His scientific sketches of the human body are works of art. Da Vinci also drew sketches of submarines and airplanes in his many notebooks. He even wrote about the use of parachutes and poison gases. Da Vinci was truly a Renaissance man.

Painting

Two other well-known painters of the Italian Renaissance were Michelangelo Buonarroti and Raphael Sanzio. Michelangelo moved to Rome at a young age. Like so many artists before him, he was fascinated by the ancient city's sculpture, architecture, and paintings. His first major work in Rome earned him the reputation of a master sculptor. Later, the pope gave Michelangelo the task of painting the ceiling of the Sistine Chapel, where many papal ceremonies were held. Michelangelo shut himself in the huge room and labored under extremely difficult situations. The finished work was a masterpiece. The Sistine Chapel is Michelangelo's most famous work.

The paintings on the ceiling of the Sistine Chapel took Michelangelo nearly four years to complete.

Extend Point out that Leonardo da Vinci could write backwards and that he wrote this way in his voluminous notebooks throughout his life. When he wanted to read his notes, he simply held them up to a mirror. Ask students why they think he wrote in this manner. (to keep other people from reading his ideas)

Explore Have students find a photograph of *The Last Supper* in an art book or on the Internet, and ask them to identify the person at the center (Jesus) and those around him (his disciples). Discuss with students what is shown in the painting. (It is the last supper of Jesus' life) Discuss why da Vinci might have been asked to create this scene. (Biblical themes were valued during the Renaissance.)

WHAT IN THE WORLD?

THE SISTINE CHAPEL Many Renaissance artists decorated the walls of the Sistine Chapel. These paintings tell the stories of Moses and Jesus. However, it was Michelangelo who painted the ceiling of the chapel with what experts believe are some of the world's greatest paintings. It took Michelangelo nearly 4 years of work, lying on his back, suspended from the ceiling, to complete. The ceiling shows biblical scenes. Most famous of all is *The Creation of Adam*, in the center of the ceiling.

Activity

Create an idea web Have students create an idea web (TR, p. 321) whose topic is Leonardo da Vinci. In the outer circles, have students record areas in which da Vinci was skilled. They should include at least one accomplishment in each area. Students can add extra circles and do research for more information. (Possible answers: **Engineering:** diversion of rivers; **Geology:** rock formations; **Architecture:** designs for fortifications; **Music:** invented instruments; **Painting:** *La Gioconda*)

Using Technology

Ask students to use Internet search engines to find and gather information about da Vinci's great works of art. Have them find out which sites now offer tours. They might be able to download photographs or other visuals from these sites to share with the class.

F Y I

Mona Lisa

La Gioconda, better known as Mona Lisa is the portrait of the wife of a Florentine merchant named Gioconda. It is one of the most famous portraits ever painted. Mona Lisa's smile is mysterious—no one knows for sure if she is happy or sad. Da Vinci created a mountain landscape behind her to provide perspective for the portrait and to portray a person in harmony with her surroundings in the natural world—a goal of Renaissance thinking.

Many people consider the *Pietà* as Michelangelo's greatest sculpture.

Raphael Sanzio also worked in Rome. Because he was a few years younger than Michelangelo and da Vinci, he was able to study their works. His best known painting is called *School of Athens*. In it, he sums up the Renaissance ideals of harmony, balance, and classical culture. The painting is an imaginary gathering of great scientists and thinkers. Sanzio even included the faces of Michelangelo, da Vinci, and himself in the painting.

Sculpture and Architecture

In the Middle Ages, most sculptures were created primarily for the great cathedrals. Sculptures of human figures represented saints and kings in typical poses. The figures were usually wearing robes or crowns. Most statues were part of a building to which they were attached.

During the Renaissance, however, sculptors began to create free-standing statues. The human body became a major subject of sculpture. For example, one of the most famous works of sculpture from this period is Michelangelo's *David*. This statue is of the young biblical hero David, who killed the giant Goliath. The statue almost seems alive—as if it is about to spring into action. Another important work is the *Pietà*, which is a sculpture of Mary cradling the dead body of Jesus in her lap.

The influence of Greece and Rome was also noticeable in Renaissance architecture. Architects used many of the classical forms: columns, domes, and arches, for example. Symmetry and harmony were popular themes of architectural style. Symmetry means that things on either side of a line drawn down the middle are the same size and are arranged the same way. Harmony means that objects are arranged in a pleasing way according to color, size, and shape. Many of the great Renaissance architects—Brunelleschi, Michelangelo, Raphael, and Bramante—were artists who also painted and sculpted as well.

◆ **What did sculptors begin to portray during the Renaissance?**

Review History

A. To what period of history did many Renaissance scholars turn for models and inspiration?

B. What were the contributions of Niccolò Machiavelli and Baldassare Castiglione?

C. What were some fields in which Leonardo da Vinci was active and achieved distinction?

Define Terms to Know

Define the following terms: **Renaissance, perspective, humanism, patron**

Critical Thinking

How would you contrast the Renaissance outlook on human life and behavior with medieval attitudes?

Write About Government

In a paragraph or two, state and support your opinion of Machiavelli's ideas on government and the need for a strong leader or "prince."

Get Organized

IDEA WEB

Look back over Section I. Use an idea web to connect the information in the section. For example, what were some of the major contributions made during the Renaissance?

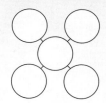

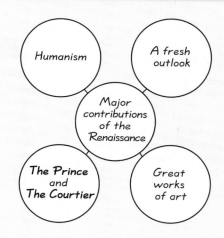

Build Your Skills

ANALYZE AND ANSWER A DOCUMENT-BASED QUESTION

You have learned that examining primary sources is an important part of the study of history. Primary sources are accounts of events created by people who took part in the events or by people who were eyewitnesses to the events. Primary sources include letters, speeches, autobiographies, newspaper articles, and photographs. They may also include visuals such as a political cartoon or a painting by an eyewitness to an event.

The content, style, and point of view in primary sources offer valuable evidence concerning people, places, and events of a particular time.

Documents are an important type of primary source. Sometimes you will be called upon to analyze and answer a document-based question. Usually, this assignment involves your analyzing a document or a series of related documents. You would then answer multiple-choice or short-answer questions about each primary source. Then, you may be asked to write an essay related to the primary source, or series of sources.

Here's How

Follow these steps to analyze and answer a document-based question.

1. Study each document or political cartoon to get an overall view of the subject matter and the writer's main ideas. Pay special attention to the opening and closing sentences. Underline any unfamiliar words. If you are looking at a visual, you will want to read the caption or introduction.

2. Carefully read the question or questions related to each document. Be sure you understand exactly which points your answer is expected to address.

3. Read each document a second time. Write down any evidence or ideas that relate to the document-based question. Try using context clues to determine the meaning of any unfamiliar words.

Here's Why

The ability to analyze and answer a document-based question will help you improve your test scores and will add to your knowledge of history.

Practice the Skill

Study the passage from Niccolò Machiavelli's *The Prince.* Then, analyze and answer the following questions.

1. What action does Machiavelli recommend to a ruler in this passage?

2. What are two advantages of this action?

Extend the Skill

Write a paragraph in which you elaborate on the role of a ruler according to Machiavelli.

Apply the Skill

As you read other chapters in this textbook, look for examples of primary sources and document-based questions. Use the steps in *Here's How* to answer these and other document-based questions.

> "But when one acquires states in a province where the language, the customs, and the laws are different, there are difficulties; here both fortune and great ability are needed to keep them. One of the best and most ready solutions is for the new ruler to reside there. This expedient would make the new possession safer and more lasting. . . . Being on the spot, one may observe disorders as they arise and quell them quickly; not being present, one will learn about them only when they have assumed such proportions that they cannot be quelled."

CHAPTER 14 ◆ The Renaissance and the Reformation **321**

Teaching Options

RETEACH

Have students look through earlier chapters of this textbook to find other passages from actual historical documents. For each document, ask them to identify the writer and explain the writer's message. Have students discuss why textbook authors include these sources.

CHALLENGE

Have students use library sources or the Internet to find additional primary source documents—letters, autobiographies, speeches—about Machiavelli or *The Prince.* Students can take the role of Renaissance writers and, based on their research, write a letter to a friend about Machiavelli and what his book reveals about the way rulers should govern.

Build Your Skills

ANALYZE AND ANSWER A DOCUMENT-BASED QUESTION

Teach the Skill

Collect copies of several different kinds of primary source documents, such as a famous letter (i.e., Abigail Adams to John Adams), a speech (i.e., Nelson Mandela's Inaugural Address), a newspaper article (i.e., Sinking of the *Titanic*), a passage from a political document (i.e., Magna Carta on page 810), and a quotation (i.e., Immanuel Kant's "Dare to know," on page 313). Divide the class into small groups to study each type of document collected. Ask groups to decide what their document tells about the time period and the point of view of the person who wrote it.

Explain that historians study and interpret primary sources in order to understand cultures of the past. Ask students to discuss some of the challenges to interpreting primary sources. (difficulties in getting accurate translations from foreign languages; lack of understanding of the background of the document; having different values or experiences from the primary source)

Practice the Skill
ANSWERS

1. Machiavelli recommends that a ruler personally reside in a new territory that has a different language, laws, and customs.

2. The ruler can observe disorders as they arise and quell, or put down, the disorders quickly.

Extend the Skill

Students' paragraphs should contain details on how a ruler observes disorders and quells them when he lives in a foreign state he acquires.

Apply the Skill

Encourage students to complete each step listed in *Here's How* when they answer document-based questions. Remind students that it is important to read the passage more than once.

Section Summary

In this section, students will learn how the spread of the Italian Renaissance to northern and western Europe contributed to the development of literature and the arts in those areas.

1 Introduce

Getting Started

Discuss with students how they would communicate something very important to as many people as possible in the shortest amount of time. Point out that during the Renaissance there were no telephones, computers, and other electronic devices. Discuss the impact of the printing press, an invention that was revolutionary then. Ask what role it probably played in the lives of the people and the way they communicated new ideas.

TERMS TO KNOW

Ask students to read the terms and definitions on page 322 and find each term in the section. Then, have them write context sentences for these terms. For example, "Newtown was such a problem-free, well-run village, it seemed like a *utopia*." Have students substitute their definitions for each term as they read their sentences out loud for the class.

You may wish to preview the pronunciation of the following names from this section with your students.

Johann Gutenberg
   (yoh HAHN GOOT uhn buhrg)
François Rabelais
   (fran SWAH rab uh LAY)
Pieter Brueghel
   (PEE tuhr BROI guhl)

ACTIVE READING

Have students choose one of the subsections in Section 2 and write a summary of its most important points. Suggest that they use the headings and illustrations to help them write their summaries.

T322 ◆ UNIT 4

Section II — The Renaissance Spreads

Terms to Know

satire the use of ridicule or scorn to expose the vices or misbehavior of others

engraving an art form in which an artist cuts a design on a metal plate and then uses the plate for printing

utopia an ideal or perfect society

Main Ideas

A. During the 1500s, the Renaissance spread across northern and western Europe.

B. Northern Renaissance writers made important contributions.

C. Achievements in art were made when the Renaissance spread to northern Europe.

D. English writers made great contributions to the Renaissance.

Active Reading

SUMMARIZE
When you summarize, you state only the most important points, or highlights, of a passage. As you read this section, focus on the main points about the spread of the Renaissance throughout Europe. At the end of each section, pause to summarize what you have learned.

A. The European Renaissance Spreads Outside Italy

The influence of the Renaissance spread from Italy to northern and western Europe in the 1500s. A wider area of Europe was now set for the spread of humanist values and Renaissance styles in the arts.

Johann Gutenberg and the Printing Press

Many factors helped spread the Renaissance into northern Europe. The invention of the printing press around 1450 by Germany's Johann Gutenberg was one of the most important. Gutenberg developed an efficient way of printing with movable type. This invention allowed numerous copies of the same publication to be produced quickly and cheaply. The printing press made it possible to share the knowledge the humanists had gathered by printing and distributing multiple copies. Classical works such as Castiglione's *The Courtier* began to appear in printed form. By 1600, *The Courtier*, had been translated into many European languages and printed in more than 100 editions.

This illustration is an artist's interpretation of what a print shop must have looked like. Shops like this could produce many works in a short time.

The Spread of Ideas

Translation of the printed word was just one of many ways in which the ideas and values of Renaissance Italy were spread throughout the rest of Europe. The ideas of the Renaissance also were carried outside Italy by Italian artists who traveled to other countries. Da Vinci, for example, spent his final years in France as painter, engineer, and architect to King Francis I. Other Italian artists of the Renaissance also worked outside Italy, sharing their skills.

Visitors to Renaissance Italy often carried home their respect for Italy's ancient civilization and its artistic discoveries. They found inspiration in Italy and gladly shared it with citizens of their home countries.

◆ **How were the ideas of the Renaissance carried outside Italy?**

Teaching Options

Section 2 Resources

Teacher's Resources (TR)
   Terms to Know, p. 27
   Review History, p. 61
   Build Your Skills, p. 95
   Concept Builder, p. 230
   Idea Web, p. 321
   Transparency 5

ESL/ELL STRATEGIES

Take Notes Tell students that reading the headings in a textbook is a good way to preview the section content. Have students read the head of Section 2, subsection A. Then, ask them to write a sentence or two predicting the content of the subsection. Finally, have them read that subsection and see whether their prediction was accurate.

B. Northern Renaissance Writers

The Renaissance humanists produced important scholarship and philosophy, but they also motivated others. Humanist ideas sparked important achievements in literature and the arts.

Erasmus Spreads Humanism

One of the most important figures of the Renaissance in northern Europe was Desiderius Erasmus. Erasmus was an ordained priest from Rotterdam, a city in the Netherlands. He spent many years in Italy where he studied Greek. After he left Italy, he headed to England.

When Erasmus reached England, he lived for a time in the house of his friend, Thomas More. It was in More's house that Erasmus wrote his most powerful work, *The Praise of Folly*. In it, Erasmus attacked wrongdoing, stupidity, and meaningless Church ceremony. Erasmus was a loyal Roman Catholic priest who was disturbed by corruption in the Church. He called for reform. Erasmus was also a humanist, a person who wants to deal with the problems people face in this life rather than in the next one.

In addition, Erasmus wanted people to know more about the teachings of Christianity. Since he wanted all people to be able to read the Bible, he called for a translation of the Bible into the vernacular, or everyday language of ordinary people.

François Rabelais

You have learned that Erasmus criticized social institutions that needed reform. Erasmus's tone in his work, however, was mild and restrained. A generation after Erasmus, the French humanist François Rabelais used a humorous tone in his work *Gargantua and Pantagruel*. This work is a collection of stories about the giant Gargantua and his son Pantagruel. Rabelais uses these characters to tell others his opinions on religion, education, and greed.

Rabelais, who had trained for both the priesthood and medicine, made fun of greed, clerical abuses, and the educational system. Rabelais instead believed in civilized education, intelligent government, and balanced living.

Montaigne's Personal Essays

Another important French humanist and author was Michel de Montaigne. Montaigne's father loved Renaissance values and ideals. He is said to have spoken only Latin to his son until the boy was six years old. He also made sure that young Michel would awaken every morning to the pleasing sound of music.

As an adult, after a term of service in government, Michel de Montaigne spent many years in private study. He wrote his thoughts and feelings in personal essays. Montaigne used his essays to gain and share self-knowledge. Among the topics he discussed were education, friendship, suffering, politics, death, freedom, and nature.

Cervantes and the First European Novel

Renaissance Spain also produced one of the greatest writers of that age. That writer was

This illustration is from Rabelais's humorous novel *Gargantua and Pantagruel*.

A. The European Renaissance Spreads Outside Italy

Purpose-Setting Question In the 1500s, where did the influence of the Renaissance from Italy spread? (northern and western Europe)

TEACH PRIMARY SOURCES
Have students study the illustration of the print shop on page 322 to identify what the men are doing. (Possible answer: preparing a page of type, printing a page by pressing the type onto a sheet of paper) Discuss how this new process affected the spread of ideas and works.

◆ **ANSWER** Possible answer: The ideas of the Renaissance were carried outside of Italy through translations, printing numerous copies with the printing press, by Italian artists who traveled to other countries, and by visitors to Italy.

B. Northern Renaissance Writers

Purpose-Setting Question Who were the most important writers of the northern Renaissance and Renaissance Spain? (Erasmus, Rabelais, Montaigne, and Cervantes)

Discuss Remind students that Rabelais used humor to get his message across to people. Discuss with students why a writer might use humor to get a serious message across to people. Have the class discuss other ways to get a message across and explain which way they like best.

Meet Individual Needs:
VISUAL/SPATIAL LEARNERS

To help students organize the information in this section, have them create a three-column chart titled *Contributions of the Northern Renaissance*. The columns should address the contributions made by writers and artists of northern Europe and the writers of England. These charts will be excellent study aids for students.

Connection to
GEOGRAPHY

Some of the great Renaissance writers came from the Netherlands (Erasmus), France (Rabelais, Montaigne), and Spain (Cervantes). Have students use the map of Europe on page A5 or Transparency 5 to locate these countries and to determine their direction and distance from Italy. Discuss land and sea routes that travelers could have taken from Italy to these parts of Europe.

C. Northern Renaissance Artists

Purpose-Setting Question Who were some of the most important artists of the northern Renaissance? (van Eyck, Brueghel, Rubens, Dürer)

Explore Explain that Flanders is a region or section of Belgium. Tell students that the size of Flanders has changed over time. The region known as Flanders is located in northwestern Europe, on the North Sea. Its land has included parts of Belgium, France, and the Netherlands. Have students use the map of Europe on page A5 or on Transparency 5 to find these countries. Encourage students to use the Internet to learn about Flanders' significance as an artistic center of today in northern Europe.

> **Activity**
>
> **Make a list** Point out that Pieter Brueghel painted paintings of everyday life. Have students study *Peasant Wedding* and make a list of details based on their observations. Students can compare their lists with the rest of the class. (Possible answers: wedding guests are eating and drinking; musicians play in the background; a child in a red feather cap is completely absorbed in his food; two waiters are carrying a large tray of food.) Then, have students explain what the details in the painting tell about life in this time.

Miguel de Cervantes, known simply as Cervantes. After an action-packed career as a soldier, Cervantes settled down to write poems, plays, and stories. His literary fame came from the publication of *Don Quixote*. This book is often called the first European novel. The hero, Don Quixote, has a good heart but does many foolish things as he tries to imitate the brave knights he has read about. In one scene from the book, Don Quixote insists that a simple peasant girl is really a noble princess. He fights against windmills, thinking they are evil giants. Today, we use the word *quixotic* to describe someone who is impractical or trying to reach for an impossible goal.

Cervantes wrote *Don Quixote* as <u>satire</u>, poking fun at Spanish nobility and the cruelty of his time. *Don Quixote* was an immediate success throughout Europe. Today, it remains one of the most widely read novels ever written.

◆ **What ideas did Erasmus promote as a humanist?**

C. Northern Renaissance Artists

You have learned that, beginning with the works of Giotto in the 1300s, the Italian Renaissance produced a stunning series of masterpieces in painting. The spread of the Renaissance to northern Europe was marked by major achievements in this art.

Flemish Painters

One important school of art was located in Flanders, a region of Belgium. Flanders became the artistic center of northern Europe. In Flanders, a group of painters developed their own style of painting by using oil on canvas.

Jan van Eyck was the first great Flemish Renaissance painter. He developed new standards for the realistic portrayal of the human figure and was among the

Peasant Wedding, by Pieter Brueghel the Elder, was completed in 1568. The bride is shown sitting in front of a piece of green cloth that is hanging on the wall.

324 UNIT 4 ◆ Europe Undergoes Change

Teaching Options

Research

AVERAGE

Point out that *Don Quixote* is considered to be the first novel ever written. Have students research its plot to find the names of the characters, the adventures they had, and their goals. Have small groups work together to write a dialogue between Don Quixote, who symbolizes the ideal in life, and Sancho Panza, who symbolizes reality. Students can perform their dialogues for the class.

CHALLENGE

Explain that Cervantes got ideas for *Don Quixote* from his early careers as a soldier and a grain collector. Have students use library sources or the Internet to research this part of his life and write magazine articles describing his adventures and the lessons he learned. (Possible answers: His captivity as a slave in Algiers provided plot ideas. Travels in southwest Spain gave him an understanding of human nature.)

first painters to use oil paint. Van Eyck paid great attention to detail and used striking colors in his works. His works included landscapes, pictures of townspeople, and religious scenes. His most popular piece of art is titled *Adoration of the Lamb*.

Pieter Brueghel the Elder was a famous Flemish painter who painted everyday scenes of peasants at work and at play, the countryside, and village festivals. In his lively paintings, he used rich colors and details.

Peter Paul Rubens was another outstanding artist of the northern Renaissance. He created monumental works on themes from the Bible and classical mythology.

Dürer Invents the Woodcut

One of the greatest German painters of this time was Albrecht Dürer. At a young age, Dürer's father discovered his son had a remarkable talent for drawing. He apprenticed him to a local artist, where young Dürer quickly mastered the technique of designing woodcuts. These are blocks of wood that are carved and inked and then used to make illustrations.

After he finished his apprenticeship, Dürer traveled to France. There he improved the engraving skills he had learned. **Engravings** are images carved onto metal plates with a sharp tool. The plates are then inked for printing. Dürer was to do some of his finest work as an engraver and woodcutter.

Dürer then traveled to Venice. There he discovered new artistic styles and new forms of expression that were quite different from anything he had experienced in his native country. While in Venice, he copied the paintings of well-known artists to improve his technique. He also studied mathematics, read poetry, and carefully observed the landscapes and life that surrounded him.

Dürer returned to Germany and established his own workshop. He soon became enormously popular, both as a painter and an engraver. Two of his most remarkable paintings were self-portraits. He also painted and drew many other portraits, including one of Erasmus. However, his main interest was in creating engravings and woodcuts.

◆ **What art form was developed by Albrecht Dürer?**

D. The English Renaissance

In England, the Renaissance reached its height in the late sixteenth and early seventeenth centuries. In many European countries, it was the sculptors, painters, and architects who made the greatest contributions to the Renaissance. In England, it was the writers.

Renaissance Models: Thomas More and Philip Sidney

Two men who lived almost a century apart, Thomas More and Philip Sidney, summed up the spirit of the English Renaissance. Thomas More became a brilliant lawyer. As a young man, he formed a close friendship with the Dutch humanist Desiderius Erasmus. In 1516, with Erasmus's encouragement and help, Thomas More published one of his greatest books, *Utopia*, which he wrote in Latin. A **utopia** is an ideal or perfect society. Thomas More's subject was the search for the best possible form of government. More's writing gifts did not only include political philosophy. He also wrote biography, history, theology, and poetry.

Albrecht Dürer created this engraving in 1514. It shows Saint Jerome in his study.

Extend Provide students with art books for them to review. Have small groups of students choose a Renaissance artist and study his work. Then, have groups teach the rest of the class about the artist. You may want to have students use the Internet to research their artist.

Focus Dürer completed many revealing self-portraits and wrote letters and a travel diary. Ask students what kinds of things his art works and writings may have revealed to historians about him. (Possible answers: his appearance as a teenager; how his appearance changed as he aged; where he traveled; what he learned in his travels; whom he met)

◆ **ANSWER** designing woodcuts

D. The English Renaissance

Purpose-Setting Question How did Italy influence the plays of William Shakespeare? (shared Renaissance interest in classical Greek and Roman texts; some plays took place in Italian city-states)

Activity

Role-play Ask students to work with partners to role-play a scene between Thomas More and his friend Desiderius Erasmus. The setting is London in 1516. The scene focuses on Erasmus' encouragement and help in the publishing of More's book *Utopia*. Students can use library or Internet sources for additional information on Erasmus, More, and *Utopia*. If they wish, partners can role-play the scene in costume.

F Y I

Peter Paul Rubens

Like many artists of the northern Renaissance, Peter Paul Rubens had traveled to Italy. There he studied Roman sculpture and the paintings of Renaissance artists: Michelangelo, Raphael, Tintoretto, Titian, and Veronese. Like the Italian Renaissance artists, he too painted themes from the Bible and ancient Greece and Rome. For large-scale works, Rubens formed a large workshop with assistants who painted a large part or all of the paintings.

Test Taking

Many standardized tests require students to read a passage and answer questions about the information they read. Sometimes these questions relate to cause and effect. Have students read a paragraph from page 324 or 325 and write a sample cause-and-effect question about the passage. Ask students to read their questions to the class and discuss the answers.

Then & Now

THE GLOBE THEATRE
Many of Shakespeare's plays were first staged at London's Globe Theatre. This playhouse was built on the south bank of the Thames River in 1598. The original building lasted only 15 years, however, before it burned down. In 1644, a second Globe Theatre was destroyed by the Puritans, who strongly objected to entertainments such as plays.

In 1996, a replica of the original Globe Theatre opened in London.

Sir Philip Sidney brought together the style and accomplishments of the Renaissance gentleman in England. Sidney was a brilliant diplomat and soldier, as well as a major poet and literary critic. One story from Sidney's military career gives a sense of his reputation for chivalry. At a battle in Holland, where Sidney was fatally wounded, he caught sight of a dying soldier. He gave the man his water bottle, saying "Thy necessity is yet greater than mine."

Sidney is remembered for his series of sonnets called *Astrophel and Stella*. The sonnet became one of the most popular poetic forms in the Renaissance. A sonnet is a 14-line lyric poem with a complicated rhyme scheme. Many of the greatest writers of the English Renaissance followed Sidney in his use of writing sequences, or cycles, of sonnets.

Shakespeare, Playwright and Poet

During this period, a number of poets and playwrights wrote books and plays that are still read and performed today. Among them was William Shakespeare, often called the greatest playwright of all time. Shakespeare was born in Stratford-upon-Avon, England, in 1564. Before he was 30, he moved to London where he established himself as both a playwright and a poet.

There is no record that Shakespeare ever visited Italy. However, the influence of Italy is apparent in many of his plays. For example, *The Merchant of Venice* is a drama based on a merchant in Renaissance Italy. *Othello* is a tragedy about a general in the same city. *Romeo and Juliet* takes place in Verona, Italy.

Shakespeare also shared the Renaissance interest in classical Greek and Roman texts. He wrote several plays about ancient Greece and four tragedies based on ancient Roman texts, including *Julius Caesar* and *Antony and Cleopatra*.

Shakespeare also wrote comedies, histories, romances, and poems of all sorts. Such Shakespearean plays as *Hamlet*, *King Lear*, and *Macbeth* are among the greatest works of English literature. A reason for their lasting fame is Shakespeare's understanding of human nature.

◆ **What themes did Thomas More explore in his writings?**

Review II

Review History
A. How did Gutenberg's invention of the printing press affect the spread of Renaissance ideas?

B. Why did Erasmus want to translate the Bible into the vernacular?

C. How did Jan van Eyck contribute to the development of European painting?

D. Why was Thomas More an important figure in the English Renaissance?

Define Terms to Know
Define the following terms:
satire, engraving, utopia

Critical Thinking
How would you describe the connections between humanist philosophy and some landmark achievements in literature and the arts during this period?

Write About Culture
Write a dialogue in which two Renaissance humanists—for example Thomas More and Desiderius Erasmus—exchange ideas.

Get Organized
IDEA WEB
Use an idea web to organize information from this section. Choose a topic and then find related facts. For example, who were some of the leading European artists and writers who expressed the spirit of the Renaissance?

CONNECT
History&Literature

Shakespeare

If you were to say that William Shakespeare was the best writer ever in the English language, someone might disagree with you. However, it is not likely. Shakespeare's plays capture every human emotion. For that reason, his works have remained popular for nearly 400 years.

There are many connections between history and the plays of William Shakespeare. Shakespearean drama is commonly divided into four types of plays: tragedies, comedies, histories, and romances.

THE HISTORY PLAYS written by Shakespeare usually focused on English monarchs during the time of the Hundred Years' War and the Wars of the Roses. These kings included Richard II, Henry IV, Henry V, Henry VI, and Richard III—all of whom "gave" their names to Shakespearean plays. Shakespeare's principal sources for the history plays were the chronicles written by Raphael Holinshed, which were published in 1577. To increase dramatic interest, however, Shakespeare did not hesitate to alter some of the historical facts.

THE ROMAN PLAYS also draw extensively on history. They are called the Roman plays because they focus on historical figures during Rome's ancient history. These three plays, *Julius Caesar*, *Antony and Cleopatra*, and *Coriolanus* are usually classified as tragedies, however.

Shakespeare's historical source for the Roman plays was the Greek historian Plutarch's collection of biographies of leading Greeks and Romans, simply called *Lives*. These biographies had been translated by Sir Thomas North in 1579. Here again, Shakespeare felt free to alter some of the historical facts. He also included anachronisms, or references that are chronologically out of place.

Finally, Shakespeare's plays reflect some of the notable events of the playwright's own time. For example, the play *The Tempest* was probably inspired by accounts of voyages of discovery to the Americas.

Critical Thinking

Answer the questions below. Then, complete the activity.

1. Which periods of English history did Shakespeare usually focus on in his history plays?

2. What was Shakespeare's historical source for his Roman plays?

Write About It

Use the Internet and library reference books to learn more about one of Shakespeare's history plays. Then, write a brief essay in which you summarize the play's plot and comment on Shakespeare's use of history for stage drama.

Ms. WILLIAM
SHAKESPEARES
COMEDIES,
HISTORIES, &
TRAGEDIES.
Published according to the True Originall Copies.

LONDON
Printed by Isaac Iaggard, and Ed. Blount. 1623.

The first collected edition of Shakespeare's plays was published in 1623.

CONNECT
History& Literature

SHAKESPEARE

Teach the Topic

Point out that William Shakespeare combined events from history with observations and experiences to create plots for his plays. Ask students what events from history, observations, and experiences they could use for story plots. Write a list of their ideas on the board so students can visualize the variety of possibilities. Help students organize the ideas into tragedies, comedies, histories, and romances.

THE HISTORY PLAYS Ask students why they think Shakespeare chose the particular monarchs he did for his plays. (Possible answers: Information was available in Raphael Holinshed's chronicles; Shakespeare was deeply involved in London life and knew people who were informed about these topics; playgoers were interested in this part of their more recent history.) Ask students how they feel about Shakespeare's changing or adding events to make the events depicted in his plays more interesting.

THE ROMAN PLAYS Ask students why they think Shakespeare chose to write plays about ancient Rome. (Possible answers: During the Renaissance, there was a return to an interest in biblical and Greco-Roman themes. Information was available to Shakespeare from Plutarch's biographies of leading Greeks and Romans.)

Critical Thinking

1. Hundred Years' War and the Wars of the Roses
2. Plutarch's collection of biographies of leading Greeks and Romans called *Lives*.

Write About It

Students' essays should provide a summary of the plot of one of Shakespeare's historical plays and support for a point of view about how Shakespeare used history for stage drama.

Teaching Options

LINK to TODAY

Some of Shakespeare's plays reflect notable events of the period he lived in, such as voyages to the Americas in *The Tempest*. Point out that today, plays and movies in the United States focus on notable events in our own time. Discuss recent plays, movies, and TV shows that students have seen about such events as the terrorist attacks on the United States and crises around the world.

F Y I

The Elizabethan Age

Shakespeare's plays reflect the culture and beliefs of the Elizabethan Age. During the reign of Elizabeth I, people believed in ghosts, witches, and magicians. Ghosts play an important part in *Hamlet, Julius Caesar, Macbeth,* and *Richard III.* Witches are major characters in *Macbeth.* The hero of *The Tempest,* Prospero, is a magician.

Section Summary

In this section, students will learn about the desires to change the Roman Catholic Church, how this led to the Reformation, and how the Reformation spread throughout Europe. They will also learn how the Roman Catholic Church responded to the Protestant Reformation.

1 Introduce

Getting Started

Ask students to consider some of the important issues and concerns that Americans face today. Discuss how leaders could go about making reforms, or changes. (Possible answers: rallies, strikes, petitions, e-mail messages, writing books and pamphlets, declaring war) Point out that in the 1500s, church leaders faced important issues. List on the board ways these leaders might have addressed such issues. After reading the section, have students compare their ideas with what actually happened.

TERMS TO KNOW

Ask students to read the terms and definitions on page 328 and find each term in the section. Point out that both terms end with the suffix *-tion* which means "state of being." Hence, the term *Reformation* means "the state of being reformed."

ACTIVE READING

As students read subsection A, have them find specific facts or evidence that will help them identify and evaluate the causes of the Reformation. Suggest that they use the headings to direct them in their search.

Terms to Know

Reformation the European movement calling for reform within the Roman Catholic Church

predestination a religious teaching that God determines who will gain salvation

Main Ideas

A. After previous calls for Church reform had failed, Martin Luther took up the challenge and began the Reformation.

B. The Reformation spread rapidly throughout Europe, resulting in a number of different forms of dissent.

C. The Roman Catholic Church responded to the Protestant Reformation.

Active Reading

EVALUATE
When you evaluate, you weigh the importance of specific facts or evidence in order to make a judgment. As you read this section, evaluate the causes and then the spread of the Reformation. Also evaluate the Roman Catholic response to the Reformation.

A. Causes of the Reformation

The **Reformation** was a movement in the 1500s that called for urgent reforms within the Roman Catholic Church. Like the Renaissance, this movement was local at first but soon spread throughout Europe. The Reformation resulted in the birth of a number of Protestant branches of Christianity in western Europe and in England.

Religious, Social, and Political Factors

The Roman Catholic Church was deeply in debt by the late 1400s. The Church owed money for its armies and for rebuilding Saint Peter's Basilica in Rome. The Church also owned huge amounts of land, and many Church officials had become used to a life of luxury. These wealthy clergy often forgot that they had promised to obey the laws of God and the laws of the Church. Many were willing to use dishonest methods to raise money. The Church often raised money through the sale of indulgences, or a release from all or part of the punishment for committing a sin. Many people believed this practice was doing great harm to the Church.

The Renaissance, with its emphasis on the individual and on human potential, increased people's desire for change within the Church. Humanistic values and ideals broadened people's horizons. The growth of trade and the middle class in European cities also increased enthusiasm for Church reform. People increasingly wanted to manage their own religious affairs. They saw the Roman Catholic Church as old-fashioned.

The Spread of Knowledge

One of the most important factors leading to the Reformation was the invention of the printing press by Johann Gutenberg, which you read about earlier. Gutenberg's invention changed the way in which knowledge and opinions were communicated.

The Gutenberg Bible was one of the most celebrated products of Gutenberg's press. Within several generations, the Bible had achieved wide circulation. The reformers called on all Christians to read and interpret the Bible for themselves. The invention of printing made this idea more possible than ever.

Gutenberg's Bible was probably printed in 1455. The decorations were added by hand.

Teaching Options

Section 3 Resources

Teacher's Resources (TR)
Terms to Know, p. 27
Review History, p. 61
Build Your Skills, p. 95
Chapter Test, pp.143–144
Concept Builder, p. 230
Idea Web, p. 321
Transparencies 5, 15

ESL/ELL STRATEGIES

Identify Essential Vocabulary Many English words have more than one meaning, which may cause students difficulty. Two examples in this subsection are *movement* on page 328, and *roots* on page 329. Have students discuss what they think these words mean and then have them work in pairs to determine the meanings as used in the sentences. Ask students to confirm their meanings by looking up the words in a dictionary.

Martin Luther nailed his 95 theses to the door of Wittenberg's Castle Church in 1517. These statements explained Luther's religious ideas.

The Challenge of Martin Luther

The Reformation began on October 31, 1517, when a young monk named Martin Luther posted 95 theses, or statements, on a church door in Wittenberg, Germany. In his theses, Luther attacked the sale of indulgences. He also argued that God saved sinners through faith alone, rather than through a person's own goodness—such as prayer, charitable gifts, and a religious lifestyle. In other words, salvation according to Luther had its roots in the grace of God rather than in human achievement.

Martin Luther had originally studied to become a lawyer but then entered a monastery to become a priest. In 1507, he was ordained, or installed, as a priest. On a visit to Rome a few years later, he was shocked by the wealth and power of the pope and the high-ranking clergy.

Less than four years after Luther's public call for reforms, the Church excommunicated him. Luther, however, remained defiant. During the 1520s, he began translating the Bible into German. This work, published in 1534, was the first complete translation of the Bible from the original Greek and Hebrew into a modern European language.

Luther urged his followers to read the Bible in order to find for themselves the truths of the Christian religion. He insisted that the Bible provided all the guidance people needed to live a Christian life.

Luther also criticized the luxury and abuses of the clergy. He argued that the clergy should be allowed to marry. Finally, he issued a call that Church authorities found especially threatening. He urged the German princes to enforce reform by, in effect, taking over the Church in Germany.

Within several decades, it was clear that Luther had set in motion a great religious upheaval in Europe. Those who agreed with Luther's protests against the Church became known as Protestants. The opening lines of one of Luther's hymns became a symbol of the Protestant Reformation:

> A mighty fortress is our God,
> A bulwark [defensive wall] never failing.
> Our helper He amid the flood
> Of mortal ills prevailing. "

◆ **What were three important factors leading to the Reformation?**

Do You Remember?

In Chapter 7, you learned that a person who is excommunicated is expelled from the Church.

ANALYZE PRIMARY SOURCES **DOCUMENT-BASED QUESTION** What image does Luther use for God in the hymn?

Conflict Resolution

Ask students how people today can resolve disagreements with each other. Point out that one way is to publicize grievances to gain support—distribute pamphlets or speak to large groups of people. Then, ask if they think one person posting a list of complaints on a church door in a small town in 1517, could bring about a resolution to a conflict. Discuss the advantages of posting statements in a well-trafficked area.

---

2 Teach

A. Causes of the Reformation

Purpose-Setting Question How did the invention of the printing press affect the spread of the Reformation? (It changed the way knowledge and opinions were communicated; the Bible achieved wide circulation; people could interpret the Bible for themselves.)

Review Remind students that they learned in Chapter 7 that excommunication was a terrible punishment. Suggest that students review page 154 of Chapter 7 to remind themselves about the power of excommunication.

Discuss Point out that when Martin Luther was excommunicated from the Roman Catholic Church, it meant he was excluded from its sacraments, rights, and privileges. Discuss why Luther's actions seemed so awful that the Roman Catholic Church sought to take this step. (Possible answers: His reformist ideas seemed blasphemous to the Roman Catholic Church; his public calls for reforms had spread throughout Europe; the Church felt he was responsible for its decline.)

ANALYZE PRIMARY SOURCES

DOCUMENT-BASED QUESTION

This quotation is a translation from the German. It comes from a hymn called *Ein' Feste Burg*, which Martin Luther wrote in 1529. The hymn was arranged by Johann Sebastian Bach. The following translation of the quotation, published in 1868, may be easier for students to understand:

A mighty Fortress is our God,
A trusty shield and weapon;
He helps us free from every need
That hath us now o'ertaken.

ANSWER mighty fortress, bulwark, helper

◆ **ANSWER** Possible answers: dissatisfaction with the Roman Catholic Church and Renaissance emphasis on individual and human potential; the growth of trade and the middle class; the invention of the printing press

B. The Spread of Protestantism

Purpose-Setting Question How were John Calvin's beliefs different from Martin Luther's? (Calvin placed more emphasis on predestination; his outlook toward society and the state; he wanted to build a Christian society with no separation between politics and religion.)

Then & Now

CHURCH NUMBERS EXPAND There are almost 2 billion Christians in the world. Most people in South America (92%), North America (86%), Australia (85%), and Europe (76%) identify themselves as Christians. Christianity is the most practiced religion in Africa. However, only 9% of the people in Asia identify themselves as Christians. Use Transparency 15, which identifies the location of the major religions, to help students understand the spread and strength of Christianity. Ask students why they think such a small number of Asians are Christians. (Other religions, such as Islam, Buddhism, Hinduism, Confucianism, and Shintoism are more powerful there; Christian missionaries were not as successful in Asia as in other places.)

Using the Map

Catholicism and Protestantism in the 1500s

Ask students what continent the map represents (Europe) and what the different colored squares indicate. (different religious affiliations in the 1500s) Have students compare the size of Roman Catholic areas with Protestant areas. (about two-thirds of Europe was Roman Catholic)

✔ Map Check

Answers
1. Norway, Sweden, Denmark, areas around the Baltic Sea
2. France, Scotland, the Netherlands, and England

Explore Ask students to compare this historical map of Europe in the 1500s with the map of Europe on page A5 or Transparency 5. Ask which place names are different. (Holy Roman Empire no longer exists; England, Wales, Scotland, and Northern Ireland are now called the United Kingdom; today many more European countries exist.)

Catholicism and Protestantism in the 1500s

Legend:
- Roman Catholic
- Lutheran
- Anglican
- Calvinist
- → Spread of Calvinism
- • Cities

✔ Map Check

1. **LOCATION** In which areas was Lutheranism dominant?
2. **MOVEMENT** To which countries did Calvinism spread from Geneva?

B. The Spread of Protestantism

Martin Luther's challenge to the Church spread rapidly. Soon the Protestants themselves split into various groups. These new groups included a religion modeled on the ideas of John Calvin, a French scholar, and the establishment of the Anglican Church in England.

Calvinism

Calvinism refers to the beliefs and practices of the followers of French theologian John Calvin. Like Martin Luther, who was a generation older, Calvin began his studies in law. His religious conversion brought him in contact with Reformation ideas. In 1536, he published *Institutes of the Christian Religion*. In this book, he explained his religious beliefs. It was read by Protestants throughout Europe. He would rewrite and expand this book several times during his life.

Calvin's beliefs had much in common with Luther's. However, Calvin put far more emphasis than Luther did on the idea of **predestination**—the teaching that only certain individuals have been chosen by God for eternal salvation. Calvinism also differed from Lutheranism in its outlook toward society and the state. The Calvinists wished to build a thoroughly Christian society in which there would be no separation between politics and religion. They therefore rejected the institution of bishops. Instead, Calvinist churches were governed by elected groups of elders, or presbyteries.

During the 1540s, Calvin set up a religious community in Geneva, Switzerland. He drew up a new set of rules for the community. These rules

Then & Now

CHURCH NUMBERS EXPAND
In 1500, there were only Roman Catholic Churches in western Europe. Within the next 50 years, many new churches came into existence.

Many of the churches you see in your community today—Baptist, Methodist, Presbyterian, and others—grew out of changes that started in the Reformation.

330 UNIT 4 ◆ Europe Undergoes Change

Teaching Options

Focus on TEEN LIFE

Teenagers in the Sixteenth Century Teenage life in the sixteenth century depended on social class and gender. Teenage boys from the upper class were taught subjects such as Latin, philosophy, and rhetoric, and even swordsmanship and riding. Boys were either tutored at home or attended a school in poor conditions for long hours. Teenage girls from the upper class were trained to be good marriage candidates. Teenage boys in the peasant class were generally not educated but went to work as young as possible. Some teenage sons of artisans were taught a trade at home or in an apprenticeship. Have students make a chart about teenage life in sixteenth century Europe. Allow students to use library sources or the Internet, as necessary, to complete the chart.

were based on the Bible. A group of elders and pastors, or ministers, would oversee the behavior of everyone in the community. Calvin placed restrictions on activities such as gambling, singing, dancing, and drinking alcohol. Worship was plain and strict. Images, candles, and incense were all banished. Lengthy sermons and hymns dominated the service.

Calvinism spread widely from Geneva. People from all over Europe visited Geneva and carried Calvin's ideas home with them. In France and England, Calvinism had only limited success. However, in the Netherlands and Scotland, Calvinism eventually became the dominant form of religion.

The English Reformation

The course of the Reformation in England was different from its spread on the European continent. England was a nation divided by religion. King Henry VIII rebelled against the Roman Catholic Church for personal reasons. He was determined to pass the monarchy to a male heir. His wife, Catherine of Aragon, did not give him the son he wanted, so he requested a divorce from her. The pope refused to grant Henry the divorce, so he divorced her anyway and married a young lady named Anne Boleyn. In response, the Roman Catholic Church excommunicated Henry. Henry proceeded to establish the Church of England, with himself as its head. In 1534, the Act of Supremacy declared Henry VIII as head of the Church of England.

Although he claimed to be independent, Henry VIII was not a drastic reformer in matters of belief. He rejected most Protestant beliefs and kept most Catholic forms of worship. Many people in England, however, favored some or all of the ideas of the European Protestant reformers.

When Henry died in 1547, his son Edward VI took over the throne. Under his rule, Protestantism grew in popularity. Edward died after ruling for only six years, and his older half-sister, Mary Tudor, came to the English throne. She tried to reinstate Roman Catholicism and burned several hundred Protestants at the stake for heresy. Many English citizens were horrified by these public executions. They also disapproved of Mary's marriage to King Philip II of Spain. The hostility of her subjects earned her the name "Bloody Mary."

It fell to Mary's successor, Queen Elizabeth I, to stabilize the religious situation in England. Elizabeth I was Protestant, though she liked many of the Roman Catholic rituals and practices. Under her leadership, a compromise was reached between Protestant and Roman Catholic practices. The Church of England was re-established. Priests wore robes, as they did in the Roman Catholic Church, but they were allowed to marry. Church services were held in English, as the Protestants wanted, but altars were decorated with crucifixes in the style of Roman Catholic cathedrals. Under Elizabeth I, neither Roman Catholics nor Protestants were persecuted for their religion.

 How did political concerns, rather than religious debate, cause the Reformation in England?

C. Catholics Respond to the Reformation

With the challenges of Luther, Calvin, and Henry VIII, the Roman Catholic Church faced the urgent task of responding to the Reformation. Many high-ranking church officials in Rome recognized that reform was long overdue. This movement was known as the Roman Catholic Reformation and its leader was Pope Paul III.

Henry VIII began the Protestant Reformation in England.

Global Connections

AKBAR THE GREAT
The reign of the Mughal emperor Akbar the Great in India (ruled 1556–1605) almost exactly overlapped with that of Elizabeth I in England. Like Elizabeth, Akbar was remarkably skillful at balancing religious tensions in his land. He himself was a Muslim, but he ordered toleration of Hindus and Christians. Also like Elizabeth, Akbar was an energetic patron of literature and the arts.

Focus Have students study the portrait of Henry VIII. Ask students what it reveals about the king. (Possible answers: His expression and stance show determination and pride; his clothes show great wealth; his dagger symbolizes great power.)

GLOBAL CONNECTIONS

AKBAR THE GREAT Akbar, a Muslim, took the throne at the age of 13 and ruled for 49 years. He controlled most of north and central India and Afghanistan. Under his rule, scholars, priests, and mystics of all religions debated at court. He also gave important government jobs to Hindus, making them more loyal to him. Have students review page 188 in Chapter 8 for additional information.

Activity

Make a timeline Have students use the timeline (TR, p. 320) to organize important events discussed in this section that occurred during the Reformation. (Possible events: 1517, Luther posts his 95 theses; 1534, Bible translated; 1536, Calvin publishes *Institutes of the Christian Religion*; 1545, Council of Trent)

◆ **ANSWER** Henry VIII broke with the Roman Catholic Church and established the Church of England, with himself as its head, after the pope refused to grant him a divorce.

C. Catholics Respond to the Reformation

Purpose-Setting Question What issues did the Council of Trent address over its 18 years of existence? (how to attain salvation, whether priests can marry, what the source of truth is, what the language of worship is)

Discuss Point out that the Roman Catholic Reformation is sometimes called the Counter-Reformation. Discuss why this term is used to describe the internal reform in the Roman Catholic Church. (The Counter-Reformation was meant to "counteract" the Protestant Reformation started by Martin Luther. It countered, or answered, charges against the Roman Catholic Church brought about by the Protestants.)

groups. Ask each group to review
what they know about the Council of
Trent, and then discuss what they
think the history of the Roman
Catholic Church would have been
like if the Council of Trent had not
occurred. Finally, have all the groups
come together and discuss their
conclusions.

Focus Point out that the Council of
Trent was held in the city of Trent in
northern Italy. Have students study
the painting of the Council and
determine how well attended the
session was according to the painting. (It was well attended.) Ask what
else they can learn about the
Council from the painting. (The
Council met in the cathedral in Trent;
the most important attendees were
seated at the center; the sessions
were formal occasions.)

Explore Place students into small
groups. Then, have each group
research minutes or information
about one of the 25 meetings held by
the Council of Trent. Suggest to students that they use an Internet
search with the words *Council of
Trent.* Have the groups summarize
the meeting they were responsible
for and share this information with
the class.

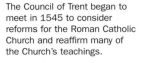

Create a journal entry Have
students assume the role of Martin
Luther during the time of the
Council of Trent. Have the students
write one journal entry discussing
his feelings toward the Council, if
he feels the meetings are worthwhile and productive. Allow students to use library sources or the
Internet for any information needed. Then, have students share their
entry with the class.

The Council of Trent

Pope Paul III called a meeting of Church leaders to define the official
Church position on matters of doctrine, or policy. Called the Council of
Trent, the group began meeting in northern Italy in 1545. It met on and off
for 18 years during the reigns of five popes. Sessions were often interrupted
and poorly attended. Nevertheless, the Council of Trent was able to address
many of the major issues that the Protestants had challenged.

The council restated supreme papal authority. It also declared that
salvation—one of Martin Luther's central issues—came from a combination of
faith and good works. The council also ruled that priests were a special group
set aside from the ranks of society as a whole. Priests were forbidden to marry.

The Council of Trent rejected the Protestant belief that the Bible was the
only source of authority. The Church as well as the Bible were declared to be
sources of truth. Individuals did not have the right to interpret the Bible. The
council also maintained devotion to the saints and the honoring of Mary,
mother of Jesus. Finally, Latin was declared the language of worship
throughout the universal Church. Native languages could not be used for the
celebration of the Roman Catholic Mass.

The Council of Trent also acted to end the abuses within the Church. For
example, the practice of indulgences was spelled out, but indulgences could no
longer be sold. The council also ordered that seminaries be set up for the
education and training of priests.

How effective was the Council of Trent? In the opinion of some historians,
the council occurred too late to reunify the Church. The restatement of
Roman Catholic beliefs still put the Church on a collision course with the
reformers. The Church's own efforts to reform itself would take time and

The Council of Trent began to
meet in 1545 to consider
reforms for the Roman Catholic
Church and reaffirm many of
the Church's teachings.

Teaching Options

Meet Individual Needs:
VERBAL/LINGUISTIC LEARNERS

Tell students that they live in Trent, Italy,
during the time the Council of Trent convened. They have just attended their first
session conducted by Roman Catholic
clergy. Based on this information and what
they already know about the Roman
Catholic Reformation, have students write a
journal entry describing what they have just
seen and heard and their ideas about it.

determination. However, if Pope Paul III had not succeeded in calling the council, the division within the Roman Catholic Church might have been even greater.

Spreading Catholicism

A few years before the first meetings of the Council of Trent, Pope Paul III took another significant step in the Catholic Reformation. He gave permission to Ignatius of Loyola, a Spanish soldier-turned-priest, to found a new order, or group of Catholic clergy. It was called the Society of Jesus and was founded in 1534. Its members were called Jesuits. Their goals were to be soldiers of the Church, missionaries for the Christian faith, and educators of the young. Loyola, who later became a saint, outlined strict disciplinary requirements for the Jesuits. All Jesuits were also required to take a special oath of obedience to the pope. Within the Church, the Jesuits played a major role in the Roman Catholic Reformation.

Along with Loyola's loyalty to the Church, another supporter of Catholic renewal was Saint Theresa of Ávila. Theresa was a Spanish nun who set up many convents throughout Spain. The nuns in her convents lived in isolation and devoted their lives to prayer and meditation. Through her writings and inspiring example, she became an important role model for the Church's new spirit.

◆ **What was the Council of Trent?**

In 1522, Ignatius of Loyola wrote *Spiritual Exercises*, a book that gave a plan for meditation.

◆ **What was the Council of Trent?**

Review III

Review History
A. What were three important issues in Martin Luther's challenge to the Church?
B. What were some of the beliefs of John Calvin and his followers?
C. How did the Jesuits contribute to the Roman Catholic Reformation?

Define Terms to Know
Define the following terms:
Reformation, predestination

Critical Thinking
Why do you think the Protestant Reformation spread so rapidly?

Write About History
Write a letter from Martin Luther to John Calvin in which you briefly discuss the similarities and differences in your views on what course the Reformation should take.

Get Organized
IDEA WEB
Use an idea web to organize information from this section. Choose a topic and then find related facts. For example, what were the main events in the development of the Reformation in England?

CHAPTER 14 ◆ The Renaissance and the Reformation **333**

Henry VIII divorced his wife.

Pope excommunicated Henry VIII.

Events in the English Reformation

Henry VIII established Church of England.

Henry VIII's Act of Supremacy

Write About History
Answers will vary but should include reference to the doctrine of predestination and to the different outlooks in Lutheranism and Calvinism on the relationship of the Church to the state and society as a whole.

CHAPTER 14 Review

Chapter Summary

A blank outline form is available in the Teacher's Resources (p. 318). Chapter summaries should outline the start of the Renaissance in Italy, how it moved north and west to the rest of Europe, and the Protestant Reformation that developed. Refer to the rubric in the Teacher's Resources (p. 340) to score students' chapter summaries.

 Interpret the Timeline

1. the beginning of the Renaissance in Italian city-states
2. 28 years
3. Martin Luther posts his 95 theses in eastern Germany, 1517.
4. Students' events will vary, but they must be taken from the chapter.

Use Terms to Know

5. predestination
6. patron
7. humanism
8. Renaissance
9. utopia
10. Reformation

Check Your Understanding

11. The word means "rebirth."
12. emphasis on human experience in the present; encouragement of human beings to take control of their lives and to fulfill their potential
13. Possible answer: He was highly skilled in many fields and far ahead of his time in science.
14. Machiavelli wrote the first secular analysis of politics, *The Prince.* In his book *The Courtier,* Castiglione identified and described the qualities of the ideal Renaissance gentleman.
15. During the Renaissance, sculpture focused on freestanding, individualized, heroic figures, and the human body became a major subject. Medieval sculptures were created mostly for great cathedrals, and the figures were mostly saints and kings wearing robes.
16. Erasmus wanted people to deal with the problems they face in this life rather than in the next one.
17. Rabelais used humor to criticize greed, clerical abuses, and the educational system of his day. Montaigne wrote essays in order to gain and

Chapter Summary

Complete the following outline in your notebook. Then, use your outline to write a brief summary of the chapter.

The Renaissance and the Reformation

I. The Renaissance Begins
   A. The Renaissance in Europe
   B. Italian Renaissance Writers
   C. Italian Renaissance Artists
II. The Renaissance Spreads
   A. The European Renaissance Spreads Outside Italy
   B. Northern Renaissance Writers
   C. Northern Renaissance Artists
   D. The English Renaissance
III. The Reformation
   A. Causes of the Reformation
   B. The Spread of Protestantism
   C. Catholics Respond to the Reformation

 Interpret the Timeline

Use the timeline on pages 314–315 to answer the following questions.

1. Which occurred first, the founding of the Society of Jesus or the beginning of the Renaissance in Italian city-states?

2. How many years after Martin Luther posted his 95 theses did the Council of Trent begin to meet?

3. **Critical Thinking** Which event on the timeline is linked to criticism of Church teachings and practices?

4. Select five events from the chapter that are not on the timeline. Create a timeline that shows these events.

Use Terms to Know

Select the term that best completes each sentence.

humanism   predestination   Renaissance
patron   Reformation   utopia

5. The idea that God chooses only certain people for salvation is called _____.

6. A wealthy person who supports an artist is a _____.

7. In the intellectual movement called _____, scholars focused on classical models and on human values and potential.

8. The _____ was a flowering of European culture between the Middle Ages and the modern period.

9. An ideal or perfect society is a _____.

10. The _____ was a European movement that called for reform within the Church and resulted in the establishment of Protestant branches of Christianity.

Check Your Understanding

11. **Identify** the meaning of the word *Renaissance.*

12. **Describe** two major features of the Italian Renaissance.

13. **Explain** why Leonardo da Vinci may be called the ultimate Renaissance man.

14. **Summarize** the contributions of Machiavelli and Castiglione to the Renaissance.

15. **Compare and contrast** Renaissance sculpture with medieval sculpture.

16. **Describe** the humanism of Desiderius Erasmus.

17. **Explain** the contributions to literature of François Rabelais, Michel de Montaigne, and Miguel de Cervantes.

18. **Identify** the title and subject of Thomas More's most famous work.

19. **Discuss** the effect of Gutenberg's invention on Bible reading.

20. **Describe** the principal differences between Lutheranism and Calvinism.

share self-knowledge. Cervantes wrote what many people consider the first European novel, *Don Quixote.*
18. *Utopia,* about the search for the best possible form of government
19. The printing press made it easier to make copies of the Bible; therefore, more people were able to read it and understand its messages for themselves.

20. The Calvinists put more emphasis on predestination and aspired to forging a totally Christian state in which there would be no separation between politics and religion.

Critical Thinking

21. Compare and Contrast How would you compare and contrast the medieval outlook on human life with the attitudes of the Renaissance?

22. Evaluate What was the significance of Gutenberg's invention of the printing press, both for the Renaissance and for the Reformation?

23. Make Inferences Why do you think Renaissance architects used many of the classical forms—such as columns, domes, and arches—in their buildings?

24. Draw Conclusions What conclusions can you draw about the achievements of the Council of Trent during the Roman Catholic Reformation?

Put Your Skills to Work

25. Analyze and Answer a Document-Based Question You have studied how to analyze and answer a document-based question. Read the brief passage below about Thomas More's *Utopia*. Then, write a few sentences to answer the following questions.

a. What is the main idea of this passage?

b. How does the writer support this idea?

"Utopia was a playful work, laced with puns, jokes, and satirical sketches. But this is not the same as saying that it was not a serious work. In grappling with the best-state exercise, tackling the problem of true nobility, exploring the social meaning of friendship, and founding a better society on a human motivation steered by the calculation and pursuit of individual interests, More's project went to the heart of the Erasmian humanist agenda. In that sense, it is one of the great achievements of the late Renaissance."

Analyze Sources

26. Read the passage below from William Shakespeare's tragedy *Hamlet*. Then, answer the questions that follow.

What a piece of work is a man, how noble in reason, how infinite in faculties, in form and moving how express [exact] and admirable, in action how like an angel, in apprehension how like a god.

a. For what qualities does the speaker praise humanity?

b. How might this passage be regarded as typical of Renaissance attitudes?

Essay Writing

27. The Renaissance and the Reformation both marked turning points in the history of western Europe. In an essay, discuss the significance of each of these movements. Develop a main idea for your essay, then support it with specific evidence, such as facts, examples, and reasons.

TEST PREPARATION

CHRONOLOGICAL
Choose the correct answer.

The printing press was developed

1. after the Reformation.
2. before the Renaissance began.
3. after the Pilgrims landed in America.
4. before the Council of Trent met.

Critical Thinking

21. Possible answer: In the medieval outlook, human life was brief and insignificant when compared to eternity. Things of this world were to be spurned or disregarded. By contrast, the Renaissance fostered the celebration of human life in the present and the potential of the individual.
22. Possible answer: Printing aided the dissemination of humanist values and Greco-Roman works during the Renaissance. Printed copies of the Bible also made possible individual study and interpretation of the Scriptures during the Reformation.
23. Possible answer: Renaissance architects were strongly influenced by Greco-Roman models.
24. Possible answer: The Council of Trent was only partially successful. The Council firmly reasserted the Church's teaching authority and the special status of the clergy. The Council did not reunify the Church or halt the Reformation.

Put Your Skills to Work

ANALYZE AND ANSWER A DOCUMENT-BASED QUESTION

25a. Possible answer: The main idea of the passage is that Thomas More's *Utopia* was in the mainstream of humanist thought, as represented by the goals and values of Erasmus.
25b. The writer refers to various aspects of More's work: for example, the problem of true nobility, the social meaning of friendship, and the quest for a better society.

Analyze Sources

26a. The writer praises humanity for its ability to reason, mental and emotional diversity, action, and apprehension (or sensitivity).
26b. Possible answer: The passage is representative of Renaissance attitudes because of its optimism and its celebration of human potential.

Essay Writing

27. Students' essays should include the contrast between the medieval and Renaissance outlooks on human life and behavior, the concerns and achievements of the humanists, the growth in literature and the arts during the Renaissance, the challenges to Roman Catholic Church authority and the response of the Roman Catholic Church.

TEST PREPARATION

Answer 4. before the Council of Trent met.

Exploration and Trade
1200–1700
(pp. 336–357)

Chapter Objectives

• Explain how the growing European interest in the East led to the search for direct trade routes and the desire to spread Christianity.
• Describe the discoveries of the explorers who Prince Henry the Navigator of Portugal sent out on expeditions and the rise of Dutch, English, French, Portuguese, and Spanish trading empires.
• Compare and contrast China's limited contact with other countries during the Ming and Qing Dynasties with Japan's isolation from the outside world.

Chapter Summary

Section I describes Europe's growing interest in the East, which resulted in a search for new trade routes and the spread of Christianity, and it explains the impact of new navigation technologies on exploration.
Section II discusses Prince Henry the Navigator, who sponsored the first expeditions seeking a sea route to the East; the later Portuguese explorers; and the rise and fall of Portugal's trading empire.
Section III focuses on China's relationship with the outside world during the Ming and Qing Dynasties and on Japan's years of isolation from Europe during the rule of the Tokugawa family.

Set the Stage

TEACH PRIMARY SOURCES
In this speech, Hernán Pérez de Oliva highlighted a striking development in western Europe. Ask students what he is saying about the place of Europe in the changing world order. (Possible answer: Earlier, Europe had considered itself geographically isolated. Now, it sees itself as part of a much larger world.) Encourage students to discuss what he means by a "change in our fortunes." (Possible answer: a positive economic shift as a result of trade and exploration)

Exploration and Trade
1200–1700

I. Europe Looks Outward
II. Portugal Leads the Way
III. China, Japan, and Foreign Trade

In the 1400s and 1500s, Europeans began to explore and trade in new areas of the world. As a result, their vision of the world and their place in it changed.

In a speech to city leaders in Córdoba, Spain, in 1542, Hernán Pérez de Oliva described this new European view of the world:

❝ *Formerly we were at the end of the world, and now we are in the middle of it, with an unprecedented change in our fortunes.* ❞

At about the same time that Europeans began looking outward to new corners of the world, people from China and Japan also experienced increased contact with others through travel and trade. They welcomed these contacts at first. However, over time, they pulled away from the outside world.

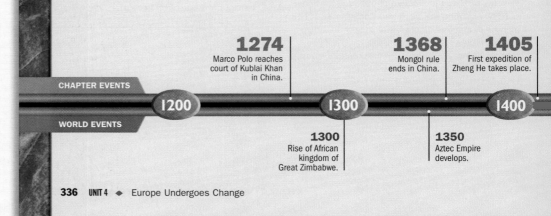

CHAPTER EVENTS

1274
Marco Polo reaches court of Kublai Khan in China.

1368
Mongol rule ends in China.

1405
First expedition of Zheng He takes place.

1200 **1300** **1400**

WORLD EVENTS

1300
Rise of African kingdom of Great Zimbabwe.

1350
Aztec Empire develops.

336   UNIT 4   ◆   Europe Undergoes Change

Teaching Options

Chapter 15 Resources

REVIEW

Teacher's Resources (TR)
Terms to Know, p. 28
Review History, p. 62
Build Your Skills, p. 96
Chapter Test, pp. 145–146
Concept Builder, p. 231
SQR Chart, p. 322
Transparencies 1, 6

ASSESSMENT

Section Reviews, pp. 342, 349, 353
Chapter Review, pp. 356–357
Chapter Test, TR, pp. 145–146

ALTERNATIVE ASSESSMENT

Portfolio Project, p. 410
Write a Dramatic Monologue, p. T410

Exploration and Trade, 1700

VIEW HISTORY Traders from Portugal arrived in Japan in the 1540s. They were the first Europeans the Japanese had ever seen.
◆ What impressions might the people from Portugal and Japan have had of each other?

GET ORGANIZED

SQR Chart An SQR chart helps you find purpose in what you are reading. Use an SQR chart as you read Chapter 15. Survey, or look at, the material to see what it is about. Write questions you want to answer as you read. Finally, read and write the answers. Here is an example from this chapter.

SURVEY
This section is about Europe beginning to look outward.

↓

QUESTION
Why did Europeans begin to explore the world?

↓

READ
Europeans were interested in direct trade routes and new technology. They wanted to spread Christianity.

1475
Fernão Gomes arrives at kingdom of Benin.

1497
Vasco da Gama sails around Africa to India.

1557
China allows Portuguese trading posts at Macao.

1571
Portugal sets up trading post at Nagasaki, Japan.

1641
Dutch control spice trade.

1500

1600

1700

1453
Ottoman Turks capture Constantinople.

1517
Martin Luther posts 95 theses.

1524
Giovanni da Verrazano explores the coast of North America.

1607
English set up colony at Jamestown.

1682
Peter the Great comes to power in Russia.

Chapter Themes
- Culture
- People, Places, and Environments
- Individuals, Groups, and Institutions
- Science, Technology, and Society
- Global Connections
- Time, Continuity, and Change
- Production, Distribution, and Consumption

Chapter Warm-Up

USING THE MAP
Point out the locator map at the top of page 337. To help students understand where Europe, Asia, Africa, and Australia are, have them identify the Atlantic, Pacific, and Indian Oceans; the Bay of Bengal; the Sea of Japan; and the Mediterranean Sea. Then, ask students to identify the other continents.

VIEW HISTORY
The art on pages 336–337 is a detail from a folding screen of the Edo Period in seventeenth-century Japan. The artist used ink, colors, and gold leaf. Ask students to identify the elements that characterize the Japanese setting of this picture. (architecture, costumes, foliage)

◆ **ANSWER** Possible answer: Each group probably thought that the other was unusual because of differences in dress, language, and behavior.

GET ORGANIZED
SQR Chart
Discuss the SQR chart on page 337. Point out that it was introduced in Chapter 4 on page 72. Review with students that "survey" involves scanning the titles and headings of a section to find the main or most important ideas. "Question" entails writing questions about the information before beginning to read. "Read" involves reading the text and locating the answers to the questions. Review the SQR chart on this page as an example. Have students make an SQR chart (TR, p. 322) for each section of the chapter.

● TEACH THE TIMELINE
The timeline on pages 336–337 covers the period between 1274 and 1682. Ask students what theme most of the Chapter Events emphasize. (exploration) Have students identify the areas of the world that were explored within the time frame of this timeline. (Asia, Africa, Western Hemisphere, North America)

Activity

Write a headline Have students work in small groups. Assign each group one Chapter Event. Have them skim the chapter to find out about their event and then write a newspaper headline for it.

Section Summary
In this section, students will learn how the Polo family's travels to China stimulated European interest in the East and led to the search for direct trade routes to the area as well as the arrival of Christian missionaries from Europe. Technological advancements facilitated exploration during this period.

1 Introduce

Getting Started
Ask students to describe a visit to a historical site or a museum in their community. Have students discuss whether their reactions to the place prompted their friends or classmates to visit the same site.

TERMS TO KNOW
Ask students to read the words and definitions on page 338 and then find each word in this section. Have students use a dictionary or book of word histories to find the origins of five other words in this section and write the information for each word on a separate index card.

You may wish to preview the pronunciation of the following terms from this section with students.

Crimea (kry MEE uh)
Cathay (ka THAY)
Giovanni da Montecorvino
  (joh VAHN nee DAH
  mohn tay kaw VEE noh)
Bernal Díaz (ber NAHL DEE ahs)
portolan (por tuh LAN)

ACTIVE READING
Have student pairs choose one of the subsections in Section 1 to preview. Then, ask each student to write a one- or two-sentence summary of what the subsection may be about. Have the pairs compare summaries. If they do not agree, they should review the main points in the subsection together. After reading the subsection, have students reread their predictions and see if they were correct.

Section I

Europe Looks Outward

Terms to Know
ambassador a person who acts as a messenger or representative
navigation the control of the direction of a boat or a ship

Main Ideas
A. European interest in the East increased after travelers reached China in the thirteenth century.
B. Europeans began searching for direct trade routes to the East.
C. An important goal of European explorers was to spread Christianity.
D. Advances in technology helped make exploration possible.

Active Reading
PREVIEW
When you preview an item you are reading, you look at headings, key terms, and illustrations to identify what the selection is about. Before you read this section, study these identifiers. Then, think about what they tell you about the section.

A. Growing Interest in the East
Since ancient times, people in Europe and Asia connected with each other by establishing land routes for trade. Caravans had carried all kinds of goods over these routes, from China in the East to the Mediterranean region in the West. Around the 1200s, European contact with other parts of the world began to increase. There was a great demand in Europe for silk and spices from the East. Merchants from Italian cities such as Venice traded for these goods in markets in the Middle East. As trade increased, ideas and travelers passed through markets and over the routes that joined the West with the East.

Italian Traders Reach China
In about 1260, Niccolo and Maffeo Polo, two brothers from a merchant family in Venice, Italy, set out on a trading trip to the Crimea, on the western edge of the Mongol Empire. In 1265, a group journeying farther to the East invited the Polos to join them. They were headed to the court of Kublai Khan in China, or Cathay as it was then known.

Marco Polo's journey to China along the Silk Road is shown on this ancient map.

No serious trader would have passed up the chance to visit Kublai Khan's court. Like other Europeans, the Polos had heard amazing stories about Cathay and its walls of silver and towers of gold. Kublai Khan's power stretched from the Yellow Sea in the east to the Black Sea in the west. Important trade routes crossed this territory.

The Polo brothers became friends with the Mongol leader. They traveled home to Italy as his **ambassadors**, or people who act as messengers. They carried letters from Kublai Khan to the pope. Two years later, the Polo brothers were on their way back to the Mongol court. This time they brought along Niccolo's son, Marco.

Teaching Options

Section 1 Resources

Teacher's Resources (TR)
  Terms to Know, p. 28
  Review History, p. 62
  Build Your Skills, p. 96
  Concept Builder, p. 231
  SQR Chart, p. 322

ESL/ELL STRATEGIES

Identify Essential Vocabulary Point out to students that each Term to Know can be heard in students' everyday lives. Have students write each term on one side of an index card and then its definition with relevant examples on the other. For *ambassador*, have students look up the names of people who hold this position in government or the United Nations. For *navigation*, have students find out what tools are currently used for navigation.

Tales of the East

The Polos stayed in China for 16 or 17 years. As you learned in Chapter 11, Marco Polo worked at Kublai Khan's court and traveled to many parts of the empire in that time. He took notes about what he saw and heard about distant lands. After his return to Venice, Marco Polo's notes became a book, *The Travels of Marco Polo.* This book was instantly popular. It opened new worlds to Europeans. Polo wrote that Cathay's capital had "everything that is most rare and valuable in all parts of the world." Japan, or Cipango as it was called by Polo, was a place with "gold in the greatest abundance." At least that is what Polo had heard from merchants and sailors who had been there.

◆ Why were Europeans interested in Marco Polo's book?

B. Looking for New Trade Routes

Marco Polo's description of the riches of the East inspired European merchants. Perhaps they could find a direct route to the East. Then, they could get eastern goods more cheaply.

High Prices for Eastern Goods

Trade in eastern goods was brisk during the 1300s. European demand for cinnamon, nutmeg, cloves, pepper, and other spices from India and China was especially great. Europeans used spices not only to season food but also to preserve it. Spices were also used in cosmetics and perfumes and as medicines.

Do You Remember?

In Chapter 11, you learned that Kublai Khan became the first foreigner to conquer all of China.

Trade Routes, 1000–1400

✔ Map Check

1. **REGION** Who controlled the trade routes in the Mediterranean Sea?
2. **MOVEMENT** What was the land route that crossed China called?

Test Taking

Some tests require students to find the meaning of a word by using context clues found in the same sentence or in surrounding sentences. Have students read the first two sentences in the subsection "High Prices for Eastern Goods" and then define the word *brisk* using context clues. (very active or lively)

F Y I

Marco Polo's Travels

Because Marco Polo worked for Kublai Khan, he traveled throughout China and wrote detailed reports about the cities, ports, and provinces that he visited. In his own book about China, he described the well-designed system of roads throughout the country. Under Kublai Khan, trees were planted to shade travelers in the summer and mark their path in the winter.

---

2 Teach

A. Growing Interest in the East

Purpose-Setting Question What factors contributed to the Europeans' increased interest in the East? (There was a great demand in Europe for silk and spices from the East. Because of trade, ideas from the East spread to the West.)

Focus Explain that the picture on page 338 is a detail of an antique map. Have students identify the elements in the detail and discuss possible meanings or reasons these elements were used. (use of symbols for landmarks or markers, lines representing a grid that could have been used to show distance)

Do You Remember?
Have students reread page 251 in Chapter 11 to review how Kublai Khan conquered China.

Discuss Ask students to discuss the effect on his audience of Marco Polo's vivid writing and his positive view of China. (Possible answer: He would have inspired readers to visit China; his reference to rare objects and an abundance of gold would have fascinated Europeans.)

◆ **ANSWER** It opened new worlds to them.

B. Looking for New Trade Routes

Purpose-Setting Question Why were the prices Europeans paid for Eastern goods, such as spices, so high? (Traders traveled a long way and through many lands; each time the goods changed hands, the prices became higher.)

Using the Map
Trade Routes, 1000–1400

Ask students to identify which of the three trade routes on the map covered the most distance. (Arab trade routes) Have students identify two cities along the Italian trade route. (Bruges, Lisbon)

✔ Map Check
Answers
1. the Italians
2. the Silk Road

Make a flowchart Have students make a flowchart (TR, p. 324) to show the route that spices and other goods traveled from the East to Europe. (1. Chinese and Indian merchants sold goods to Arab traders; 2. Arab traders traveled to the Middle East; 3. Arab traders sold goods in Middle Eastern markets to Italian traders; 4. Italian traders took goods back to Europe.)

Ask students why they think one merchant didn't take the goods from China to Europe. (Possible answers: Countries or areas might limit trade to their own citizens; merchants might not want to leave a country or an area; the trip was too long.) Discuss the effect of having so many merchants and traders involved. (Costs went up.)

Focus Have students locate Constantinople on the map on page 339. Ask them to show which overland routes were blocked by the Ottoman Empire, which controlled this important city. (Arab and Italian trade routes) Have students identify the sea route that Europeans would eventually follow to reach the East. (They would most likely sail around Africa.)

Then & Now

CONSTANTINOPLE Constantinople's geographic location between Europe and Asia made it an important commercial and political center. Ask students to identify cities in their state or region that are important centers of commerce because of their location.

◆ ANSWER They wanted to avoid dealing with Venetian and Arab traders so they could get Eastern goods more cheaply.

C. Spreading Christianity

Purpose-Setting Question Why did European missionaries travel to the East? (to urge Mongols to accept the Christian faith; to learn more about the Mongol Empire)

At a Turkish bazaar in Istanbul, merchants traded spices and other goods from Asia.

Then & Now

CONSTANTINOPLE
Constantinople was located on a triangle of land between Europe and Asia. The city of Byzantium was located there in ancient times. Emperor Constantine expanded the city and made Constantinople the eastern capital of the Roman Empire in 330. Today its name is Istanbul.

Traders who brought spices and other goods from the East traveled a long way and through many lands before they reached Europe. For example, Chinese and Indian merchants sold goods to Arab traders. These traders then traveled west to markets in the Middle East. There they sold goods from the East to merchants and traders from Venice, Italy. These Italian traders then took the goods across the Mediterranean Sea to Europe. By the time the eastern goods reached Europe, they were expensive. Each time the goods changed hands, the prices rose.

Europeans had no choice but to pay the prices Venetian merchants charged for eastern goods. Venice had complete control of trade in the Middle East. By the beginning of the fifteenth century, however, European countries were already considering how they could get around dealing with the Venetians and the Arabs. Their plan included sailing to Asia, where the goods were produced. All they needed was to find a safe, direct route.

Dangerous Land Routes

In the late 1300s, the huge Mongol Empire began to break apart. As a result, the East-West trade routes on land became more and more dangerous for western merchants. The days in which the Mongol ruler could promise westerners such as the Polos a safe trip home were over.

New Muslim powers were rising in Asia Minor, the part of Asia closest to Europe. Of these groups, the Ottoman Turks posed the greatest threat to the West. They looked upon Christians as nonbelievers. They felt that it was their sacred duty to wage a jihad, or holy war, against them. As the Mongol Empire crumbled, the Ottomans extended their control over a broad area. By 1402, they conquered the Balkans, on the edge of Europe. In 1453, they seized Constantinople, a busy port and trade center where West met East. With Constantinople under their control, the Ottomans could block the overland trade routes to the East.

◆ Why did Europeans want to find a sea route to Asia?

C. Spreading Christianity

Exploring new trade routes was important for economic reasons. In addition, religious leaders in the West looked outward for a completely different reason—to spread Christianity. They believed that people who converted, or changed, to Christianity from other religions would be allies, or supporters, of Europe. After the failure of the Crusades, Christians in Europe especially wanted allies against followers of Islam.

Missionaries Head East

Even before the Polos had begun their travels, missionaries were traveling eastward to urge the Mongols to accept the Christian faith. The pope sent monks to the East in order to learn more about the Mongol Empire and to

Teaching Options

**Connection to ----------
GEOGRAPHY**

In 1326, the Ottoman Empire was a small state in Anatolia (now Turkey). By the late 1400s, it had expanded into eastern Europe. Two centuries later, it was the world's largest empire. Have groups research the expansion of the Ottoman Empire and show two different stages in the growth of the empire on the outline map of the world. (TR, p. 330)

Meet Individual Needs:
VERBAL/LINGUISTIC LEARNERS

To help students understand the steps in the trading process, ask them to act out what happened along the trade route as spices and other goods from the East traveled to the Istanbul market. Have students include a description of the scene depicted in the sixteenth-century manuscript on this page.

spread Christian beliefs. The monks followed the caravan routes, trading ideas with people they met along the way.

Later, several monks reached China. Giovanni da Montecorvino, an active missionary, became archbishop of Beijing. Da Montecorvino stayed in China for more than 30 years. Another active missionary was Oderic of Pordenone who traveled throughout Asia. He traveled to China by way of India and Malaya. He was the first European to visit Tibet in China. Like Marco Polo, he wrote a fascinating account of his journey.

Voyages With Several Purposes

When European explorers and conquerors began their sailing expeditions in the fifteenth and sixteenth centuries, they had several purposes. The Portuguese explorer Vasco da Gama stated plainly that he was searching for both "Christians and spices." Bernal Díaz wrote that he sailed to the Indies

> **❝** . . . to serve God and his Majesty, to give light to those who were in darkness and to grow rich as all men desire to do. **❞**

Kings, queens, and others who sent forth these expeditions were also motivated by religion, the chance to find new trade routes, and hopes for finding gold and silver in faraway lands. Expeditions were also conducted in order to gather information about how far the power of non-Christians, especially Muslims, actually extended.

◆ **Why did European rulers want to spread Christianity?**

D. Sailing With New Technology

Europeans set out on their voyages of exploration during the Renaissance. It was a time of great curiosity and independent thinking and action. It was also a period that saw the development of new technology. Advances in technology that began in the Middle Ages helped Europeans explore the world. European explorers set sail on new kinds of ships with new means of defense. They also had new techniques and tools for navigation.

Tools for Navigation

By the mid-1400s, Europeans setting sail on the high seas carried two important tools, a magnetic compass and an astrolabe. In the 1100s, European sailors had discovered that they could magnetize an iron needle. By the 1300s, sailors created a magnetic compass to find direction. This compass had a magnetized needle that turned on a pin above a card marked with the points of direction. Sailors also used an astrolabe to help them figure out their ship's latitude, or distance north or south of the equator. With these tools, Europeans could sail far from land and explore unknown places.

More detailed charts and maps also gave sailors a better idea of where they were. Portolan charts helped a ship's pilot figure out the course from one harbor to another along known coastlines. When people sailed unknown and uncharted waters, they relied on stars to guide them in their **navigation**, or steering the ship in the correct direction. New maps of previously uncharted territory were made.

ANALYZE PRIMARY SOURCES **DOCUMENT-BASED QUESTION** What image does Díaz use to describe converting people to Christianity?

Global Connections

ASTROLABE
The astrolabe was developed by ancient Greek mathematicians and astronomers. The Arabs improved the astrolabe. They used it to determine when it was time to pray and which way to face when they prayed toward Mecca, their holiest city. The astrolabe came to the West sometime before 1000, after Europeans came into contact with Arabs in Spain.

Astrolabe

Fast, light, and easy to navigate into the wind, the caravel was an excellent ship for long voyages.

Ships for Long Trips

European sailors in the fifteenth century took to the seas on two types of ships: the long ship and the round ship. The long ship had both oars and sails. It was fast and easy to handle. However, it also needed a large crew and had little room for supplies or weapons. The round ship was powered by sail alone and was less costly to run. It had plenty of room for storage and weapons. It was also a stronger ship than the long ship. It could better face the stormy weather that whipped up on the open ocean.

For long voyages on the open sea, early European explorers preferred a type of round ship known as a caravel. The caravel was a small, light ship with sails the shape of triangles. It was easy to move the caravel about in waters with changing winds and currents.

The caravel's triangular sails also allowed it to sail into the wind. This made it easier to sail any route. A caravel could carry heavy weapons along its sides. The weapons could be used to attack enemy ports and ships as needed. Caravels and other round ships sat deep in the water. They required deep water ports and harbors, which meant that many European ports had to be expanded.

◆ **Why was the caravel a good ship for long-distance travel?**

Review I

Review History
A. Why did the Polos want to travel to Kublai Khan's court in China?
B. Why did the land routes to the East become dangerous?
C. What, besides trade, did Europeans hope to do on their voyages?
D. What new tools did sailors have for exploring?

Define Terms to Know
Define the following terms: **ambassador, navigation**

Critical Thinking
Do you think you would have believed Marco Polo's descriptions of his travels? Why or why not?

Write About Economics
Write a short paragraph explaining why Europeans wanted to find a sea route to the East.

Get Organized
SQR CHART
Use an SQR chart to organize information from this section. Choose one of the main parts and use the chart to find a purpose for reading it. Make an SQR chart for "Sailing With New Technology," for example.

Critical Thinking
Students will likely state that they would have believed Marco Polo's descriptions because they had already heard some of the amazing stories about Cathay and its walls of silver and towers of gold.

Write About Economics
In their paragraphs, students should explain that Europeans were no longer willing to pay high prices to Venetian merchants for Eastern goods that came overland.

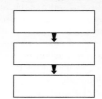

SURVEY
This section is about using new technology to explore.

QUESTION
What kind of technology did explorers use?

READ
Magnetic compass, astrolabe, maps, charts such as the portolan chart, caravel

Build Your Skills

Critical Thinking

DRAW CONCLUSIONS

A conclusion is a decision you reach or an idea you form about something after carefully considering the facts. To draw a conclusion, you put new information together with what you already know. What you already know may be other facts you have gathered or ideas from your own experiences.

Knowing how to draw conclusions is a useful skill in many everyday situations. You can draw a conclusion anytime you have enough factual information about something. For example, if you wake up in the morning and see that the sidewalk is wet, what conclusion can you draw? You would probably conclude that it rained during the night, based on previous experiences and your knowledge of weather.

Drawing conclusions is an important reading and study skill. When you read, you can use information or clues in the text to draw conclusions about what is not directly stated. In history, being able to draw conclusions helps you understand why events happen and how events are connected.

Here's How
Follow these steps to draw a conclusion.
1. Carefully examine the facts or clues about a topic.
2. Gather information or ideas from your own experiences. Ask yourself: "What do I already know about this? Do I have any experience that applies to this?"
3. Put the new facts and what you already know together to draw a conclusion.

Here's Why
You have just read about Europeans' search for new lands. Drawing conclusions can help you understand what influenced Europeans to explore other parts of the world.

Practice the Skill
Copy the graphic organizer onto a separate sheet of paper. The top box of the graphic organizer provides new information about the Polos. Fill in the box called "What I Already Know" with information you learned about the Polos' trip to China. Then, draw a conclusion based on the new facts and what you already know.

Extend the Skill
Read about a current event reported in the newspaper. Use this information and what you already know to draw a conclusion about the event.

Apply the Skill
In the next section, you will learn about Portugal's explorations. Set up a graphic organizer like the one on this page. Fill in the "New Information" box with facts you already learned about Portugal from Section I. Then, complete the organizer and draw a conclusion about Portuguese exploration.

The Polos' Trip to China

NEW INFORMATION
- The Polos had a very successful trading trip to the Crimea.
- They planned to return to Venice in 1262.
- War kept them from returning.

WHAT I ALREADY KNOW

CONCLUSION

CHAPTER 15 ◆ Exploration and Trade **343**

DRAW CONCLUSIONS

Teach the Skill
Have students discuss a conclusion they have drawn recently about a school or community event or situation. Ask small groups to identify the facts or clues, including information from their own experience, to draw a conclusion. Suggest that they refer to the three steps in the *Here's How* to help them explain the process they used.

Practice the Skill
ANSWERS
What I Already Know:
- The Polos set out on a trading trip to the western edge of the Mongol Empire around 1260.
- In 1265, a group journeying to the court of Kublai Khan invited the Polos to join them.

Conclusion:
- Possible answer: If war had not kept them from returning to Venice, they probably would not have traveled to Kublai Khan's court.

Extend the Skill
Students' conclusions should reflect the new facts they read in the newspaper and what they already knew about the event.

Apply the Skill
Have students use the same method to draw some conclusions about Portugal's explorations in Section 2. Discuss the importance of following the three steps listed in *Here's How*. Remind students to examine facts or clues, not opinions. You may wish to review the difference between fact and opinion with students. (Possible answer for "What I Already Know": Explorers set out to find a sea route to Asia, to spread Christianity, and to find gold and silver.)

Teaching Options

RETEACH

Have the class use the graphic organizer on this page to draw a conclusion about a class event or situation. Call on volunteers to write a title for the chart and to complete "New Information" and "What I Already Know." Then, invite different students to draw a conclusion based on the information.

CHALLENGE

Ask pairs of students to track for 1–2 weeks news coverage of a social, cultural, or political issue affecting their community, city, or state. Have students identify the facts about the issue. Based on these facts and their own prior knowledge, ask them to draw a conclusion about the issue. Have student pairs discuss the conclusions they drew. Encourage them to identify facts and conclusions that may have changed over time.

Section Summary

In this section, students will learn that Prince Henry the Navigator sent out explorers, including Vasco da Gama, to seek a sea route to the East around the African continent. Students will also learn about the trading empires established by the Portuguese, English, Dutch, Spanish, and French in the East.

1 Introduce

Getting Started

Ask students if they have ever helped their classmates achieve something that was important to their class, such as working on a school newspaper or winning an athletic or a music competition. Discuss how long the classmates worked together before achieving their goal and how they felt when they finally succeeded.

TERMS TO KNOW

Ask students to read the words and definitions on page 344 and then find each word in this section. Then, have them use each word in a sentence. Point out to students both of these words are economic terms.

You may wish to preview the pronunciation of the following words from the section with students.

Madeira (muh DIHR uh)
Gil Eanes (GIHL YA neesh)
Fernão Gomes
   (fuhr NAOO GOH mihs)
Bartolomeu Dias
   (bar toh loo MAYOO DEE ahs)
Malacca (muh LAH kuh)
Moluccas (moh LUH kuhz)
Macao (muh KAOO)

ACTIVE READING

Have students choose one of the subsections in Section 2, identify the most important events, and then list them in sequence. Ask pairs of students to compare their sequences of events. You may wish to have students use a flowchart (TR, p. 324) to help sequence events.

Terms to Know

commodity something that can be bought or sold

shareholder an investor who provides a company with money

Main Ideas

A. Prince Henry the Navigator sent expeditions to explore the West African coast.

B. After Bartolomeu Dias sailed round the southern tip of Africa, the Portuguese explorer Vasco da Gama sailed around Africa to India.

C. First the Portuguese and then the English, Dutch, and French set up trading empires in the East.

Active Reading

SEQUENCE OF EVENTS When you put events in the order in which they happened, you create a sequence. As you read this section, list events in sequence. Use dates and signal words such as *first*, *then*, and *next* to figure out the sequence of events.

Portugal's Prince Henry, holding the map, earned the title "Henry the Navigator" for his enthusiastic support of navigation, mapmaking, and shipbuilding.

A. Exploration Under Henry the Navigator

The Portuguese were the first Europeans to sail out in search of a sea route to the East. In 1419, Portuguese sailors landed on the island of Madeira, in the Atlantic Ocean southwest of Portugal. Their ships had been supplied by the king of Portugal's son, Henry. Over the next 40 years, Prince Henry sent out many other expeditions. He also supported research in navigation and ship design. These achievements earned him the name "Henry the Navigator."

A Sailing Study Center

Around 1419, Prince Henry set up a center for the study of navigation at Sagres, on the southwestern coast of Portugal. Prince Henry brought together the best sailors and geographers in Europe. The work at the school would help the search for a sea route to Asia around Africa.

Sailors, shipbuilders, mapmakers, astronomers, and makers of tools for navigation came to work at the school. The maps they made were more exact and had more detail than others of the time. People at the school also developed the caravel, which you read about in Section I, and improved tools for navigation.

Henry had many reasons for supporting exploration. He was curious about the world, and navigation and shipbuilding fascinated him. He also wanted to find direct routes to places that had valuable goods such as gold, ivory, and pepper. He had religious reasons for his interest, too. In addition to introducing others to Christianity, he wanted to use contact with other people to oppose the power of the Muslims.

Teaching Options

Section 2 Resources

Teacher's Resources (TR)
   Terms to Know, p. 28
   Review History, p. 62
   Build Your Skills, p. 96
   Concept Builder, p. 231
   SQR Chart, p. 322
   Transparencies 1, 6

ESL/ELL STRATEGIES

Summarize Explain to students that summarizing the main ideas in a section of text is a useful way to study the most important points in that section. Ask students to write a summary of one of the subsections. Remind them that their summaries should be shortened versions of the main ideas and must be written in their own words. Point out that summaries can be used to study for tests.

Portuguese traders built forts, such as this one, along the Gold Coast of Africa.

Down the African Coast

Beginning in 1415, Henry sent out one expedition after another. Portuguese sailors reached the Azores, a group of islands in the mid-Atlantic off the coast of Portugal. In 1434, Portuguese explorer Gil Eanes was sent to find a route to Africa. He sailed around Cape Bojador above Cape Verde in western Africa, looking for valuable goods such as gold. Dinís Dias arrived at the mouth of the Senegal River in 1445. In 1446, Nuño Tristão sighted the Gambia River located in Gambia, Africa. Each expedition explored a little farther south than the ship before. These expeditions explored every twist and turn of the coastline, naming bays, capes, and rivers as they went.

Until this time, the Portuguese found African trade fairly disappointing. They traded for fish, sealskins, and seal oil. Farther south, however, there were more valuable **commodities**, or trade goods. These included gold dust, ivory, pepper, and slaves. In 1441, Africans were shipped back to Portugal to work as slaves. As a result, the slave trade grew rapidly. To handle the slave trade, Henry had a fort built on Arguin Island, off the coast of West Africa. It was the first overseas trading post set up by Europeans.

Between 1450 and 1460, Henry focused mainly on trade with areas of Africa the Portuguese had reached. However, Henry also sent out several more expeditions for exploration. Between 1455 and 1456, Alvise Cá da Mosto and Diogo Gomes found several Cape Verde Islands, which are northwest of Gambia. By the year of Henry's death in 1460, the Portuguese had traveled as far south as Sierra Leone on the coast of West Africa. In 1471, Fernão Gomes reached Africa's Gold Coast. Gomes arrived at the kingdom of Benin in Africa around 1475. Then in 1482, Diogo Cão found the Congo River.

◆ **What new commodity did the Portuguese trade at their first overseas trading post?**

SAILING MARKERS
Stone markers were set up by Portuguese explorers at important places along their routes.
Portuguese captain Diogo Cão placed his first marker by the mouth of the Congo River. He placed his last at Cape Cross, where his expedition ended. Vasco da Gama set up a marker at Calicut to show he had reached India.

Connection to
LITERATURE ←------

Around the World In a Hundred Years: From Henry the Navigator to Magellan, by Jean Fritz (The Putnam and Grosset Group, New York, 1998), describes many of the fifteenth-century European voyages of exploration in an especially engaging, informative style that will appeal to students. Encourage students to read selected chapters or the entire book and share their impressions in small groups.

Meet Individual Needs:
VISUAL/SPATIAL LEARNERS

Suggest that pairs of students create a timeline (TR, p. 320) that shows the important events on pages 344–345. Have students make up three questions that can be answered by the information on their timelines. Have pairs of students exchange papers and answer each other's questions.

---

② **Teach**

A. Exploration Under Henry the Navigator

Purpose-Setting Question How did Prince Henry earn the name Henry the Navigator? (He supplied expeditions in search of a sea route to the East and supported research in navigation and ship design.)

Discuss Point out that although Prince Henry supported more than 50 voyages of exploration, he never went on a voyage himself. Ask students to speculate why he did not participate in any of the sailing expeditions he subsidized. (Possible answer: He probably thought it was more important to organize and support the voyages of exploration.)

Activity

Write an article Have students write a newspaper article about the center at Sagres that Prince Henry established. They can supplement the information in their texts by using encyclopedias and the Internet. Remind them to write headlines for their articles.

Explore Have pairs of students identify on a map of Africa (Transparency 6) the places reached by various explorers who sailed for Portugal. They can mark the sites with colored pieces of paper or flags. As a class, encourage students to discuss the significance of these discoveries for the explorers. (Possible answer: Explorers working for Portugal continued to expand their knowledge of Africa as a result of their discoveries.)

WHAT IN THE WORLD?
SAILING MARKERS On an enlarged copy of a world map (pp. A1–A2 or Transparency 1) have students identify the locations where Portuguese explorers placed their stone markers. Discuss with students the reasons why explorers left markers at important places along their route.

◆ **ANSWER** African slaves

B. Toward the Indian Ocean

Purpose-Setting Question How did exploration of the coast of West Africa change after Prince Henry's death? (It slowed because the coastline was more challenging to navigate where his expeditions left off. Also, sailors felt less certain of their courses.)

Explore Have students trace the route of Bartolomeu Dias's expedition in 1487, using the world map on pages A1–A2 or Transparency 6. Have them discuss the significance of Dias's discovery for future explorers. (By rounding the tip of Africa, he found that the coastline turned northeast and thereby proved that there was a sea route around Africa.)

Discuss Ask students why the Cape of Storms was renamed the Cape of Good Hope. (The original name would have frightened future explorers; "Cape of Good Hope" would have encouraged explorers to continue sailing up the east coast of Africa.)

SPOTLIGHT ON GEOGRAPHY

PTOLEMY'S WORLD Ask students how the map made in 1459 would have encouraged explorers to sail around Africa. (By showing that the Indian Ocean wasn't surrounded by land, a water route became possible.) Have students discuss the importance of revising maps during this period of exploration. (Maps could reflect new discoveries and knowledge about Earth's geography; the better the maps, the less fearful explorers would be.)

Portuguese Expeditions to Africa, 1434–1497

EXPLORER	DATE	ACHIEVEMENTS
Gil Eanes	1434	Rounded Cape Bojador
Dinís Dias	1445	Reached mouth of Senegal River
Nuño Tristão	1446	Sighted Gambia River
Alvise Cá da Mosto and Diogo Gomes	1455–1456	Found several of Cape Verde Islands
Fernão Gomes	1471; ca. 1475	Reached Gold Coast; arrived at kingdom of Benin
Diogo Cão	1482	Found Congo River
Bartolomeu Dias	1487	Rounded the tip of Africa
Vasco da Gama	1497	Crossed the Indian Ocean from East Africa to Calicut

✔ Chart Check

Which explorer reached the Gold Coast in 1471?

Spotlight on *Geography*

PTOLEMY'S WORLD
Europeans did not know much about world geography in the fifteenth century. They often referred to a world map made in the second century by Ptolemy, an astronomer and geographer. Ptolemy's map showed three continents: Europe, Africa, and Asia. It also showed the Indian Ocean locked in by land.

A map made in 1459 by a monk in Venice, however, suggested that Ptolemy was wrong about the Indian Ocean. Perhaps it was possible to sail around Africa.

B. Toward the Indian Ocean

After Henry the Navigator's death, exploration of the West African coast slowed. The coastline was more challenging to navigate where Henry's expeditions had left off. Sailors also felt less certain of their course. Near the equator they could no longer see the Pole Star, or North Star, which helped them find their way. Nevertheless, the Portuguese pushed on, reaching the Guinea coast in the 1470s. Trade there was excellent, supplying slaves, gold, and pepper. To protect the Guinea trade, King John II of Portugal ordered a fort built.

Bartolomeu Dias Rounds Africa

From the Guinea coast, the coastline of Africa seemed to stretch south endlessly. Some people, however, held out hope that the coastline would eventually turn northeast. If so, it would be possible to sail around Africa to the Indian Ocean and then on to the East. King John sent out several expeditions to test this idea.

In 1487, three Portuguese ships led by Bartolomeu Dias sailed down the west coast of Africa. As Dias went south, the weather turned bad, and visibility was reduced to almost nothing. In the wind and rain, Dias rounded the tip of Africa without knowing it. As he sailed on, however, he realized that the African coastline had taken a turn and now stretched northeast. Dias's crew persuaded him to turn back, perhaps because they feared what lay ahead in unknown territory. In addition, a lack of food and a need for ship repairs forced Dias to make the decision to return to Portugal. As he sailed west, he rounded the tip again, seeing it for the first time. Dias named the tip the Cape of Storms. On hearing of Dias's accomplishment, the ruler of Portugal renamed the Cape of Storms. He called it the Cape of Good Hope. Dias's journey proved that there was a sea route around Africa.

Vasco da Gama Sails to India

The Portuguese were still determined to reach Asia by sailing around Africa. However, it was 10 years before they set out again to accomplish that goal. In 1497, Vasco da Gama set sail with 170 sailors and 4 ships. His goal was to reach Calicut, on the west coast of India. This time, however, da Gama traveled with the newest maps. In the past, once ships crossed the equator, the navigational markers such as the North Star were no longer useful. Now, however, da Gama had the tools and tables he needed to find direction in places where the North Star was not in sight.

Da Gama sailed from Portugal, heading south down the west coast of Africa. He used the winds to guide him toward the Cape of Good Hope. In spite of better weather, rounding the cape was no easier for da Gama than it had been for Dias. Rough seas and storms are common near the Cape of Good Hope, but da Gama's crew was up to the task. Once on the east side of Africa, the ships stayed close to land until they reached Mozambique, along Africa's east coast.

Teaching Options

Test Taking

Point out that students should skim all the test questions before beginning the test. This previewing technique will enable them to identify those questions they will have more difficulty answering. After answering the questions they know, they can go back to the other, more difficult ones at the end of the test.

In the spring of 1498, da Gama crossed the Indian Ocean from East Africa to Calicut. In 1499, he returned with just 2 ships and 44 sailors. The ships were filled with Indian pepper, cinnamon, and other spices. Da Gama had sailed around Africa to India and back again. The Portuguese had found their long-sought sea route to India. The discovery would have great impact on the politics and business interests of the known world.

◆ **Why did Portuguese exploration slow for a while after 1460?**

C. Trading Empires

For the Portuguese, exploration was mainly a way to obtain wealth. As they sailed down the West African coast, the Portuguese quickly took control of the gold trade. They protected their interests by building trading posts that included forts. Trade in the region and the wealth it created was theirs. East Africa and India presented a different situation. Although unknown to the Portuguese until then, the rim of the Indian Ocean was already an active trading area. Trade there was largely controlled by the Arabs. The Portuguese would have to fight for their share of trade in that region.

The Portuguese Take Control

When the Portuguese returned to the Indian Ocean after Vasco da Gama's expedition, they were ready to use force to take control of trade. They brought a permanent fleet of ships to stand guard. Then they built bases for their ships and merchants.

The Arabs saw that the Portuguese were a threat and sent a large fleet out to attack them. In their long ships and with their old methods of attack, however, the Arabs were no threat to the Portuguese. The Portuguese had the latest technology for fighting on the sea.

They Made History

Vasco da Gama ca. 1460–1524

Vasco da Gama knew the sea. Before becoming a ship captain, he studied astronomy and navigation. Then, he served in the Portuguese navy, sailing up and down the coast of Portugal. He led an expedition around Africa to India.

Da Gama's expedition was well equipped when it sailed. He had several ships, including a caravel and a storage ship. Also on board were two people who spoke Arabic and another who knew some African languages. Bartolomeu Dias, the first captain to round South Africa, sailed beside da Gama part of the way down the West African coast.

Da Gama did not receive a warm welcome on the east coast of Africa or in India. Still, da Gama managed to return to Portugal with spices and other Indian goods. In 1502, he made a second voyage to India to increase trade there.

Vasco da Gama rounded Africa's Cape of Good Hope and established a trade route to India by sea.

Critical Thinking How was the Portuguese effort to sail around Africa similar to the effort to explore space in the twentieth century?

Discuss Ask students about the significance of da Gama's achievement for the Portuguese. (By crossing the Indian Ocean, he discovered a sea route to India. As a result, Portugal could establish a trading empire in the East.)

◆ **ANSWER** The coastline of Africa became more challenging to explorers.

C. Trading Empires

Purpose-Setting Question What problems did the Portuguese encounter in establishing a trading empire in the Indian Ocean region? (Trade there was largely controlled by the Arabs, and they would have to fight for their share of trade in that region.)

Review Remind students that they read about the Portuguese ships, the caravels, on page 342. Ask them how these ships would have given the Portuguese the advantage in their fight against the Arabs. (The caravel was a small, light ship with triangular sails that could easily move through water with changing winds and currents. Also, the caravel could carry heavy weapons along its sides.)

THEY MADE HISTORY
Vasco da Gama
In 1502, Admiral da Gama returned to Calicut with a fleet of 20 ships to establish Portuguese control of the Indian Ocean region. After bombarding Calicut, he gained control of it for Portugal. Ask students to use encyclopedias and the Internet to create a timeline (TR, p. 320) of the most important events relating to his explorations. Ask students to explain the significance of the globe in the portrait. (It emphasizes his achievements as an explorer.)

ANSWER Both show how people want to explore what is out there and expand their knowledge of the world.

Writing

AVERAGE
Ask students to write a newspaper article about da Gama's second voyage to India in 1502. If necessary, they can do additional research. Suggest that students complete a Five Ws chart (TR, p. 326) to organize their information before they write their article. Remind students to write a headline for their article. Students can share their writing in small groups.

CHALLENGE
Have students write two journal entries, one by Vasco da Gama, the other by someone living in Calicut, that describe the arrival of da Gama at Calicut. The journal entries should reflect different points of view about the arrival of the Portuguese in 1502.

Make a chart Have students create an idea web (TR, p. 321) reviewing Portuguese control of trade in the Indian Ocean. The center circle should say, "Portuguese control Indian Ocean trade." (Possible answers for the outer circles: controlled the spice trade; destroyed Arab control of trade; developed another trading area in China Sea; set up trading posts in region)

Discuss Ask students to identify causes for the breakup of Portugal's trading empire and to explain their choices. (Possible answer: Portugal had not sponsored any more explorations for a sea route around Africa to the East, but Spain sponsored some of its own.)

Explore Have groups of students use encyclopedias or the Internet to research the Treaty of Tordesillas. Work with students to identify the Spanish and Portuguese areas of influence that were created as a result of this treaty.

Using the Map
Trading Empires, 1700

Ask students to explain what the different-colored diamonds on the map legend represent. (trading posts controlled by different European countries) Where were most trading posts located? (India) What did all of these trading posts have in common? (They were located on the coasts of continents or were important islands.)

✔ Map Check
Answers
1. the Dutch
2. India

By 1513, only 15 years after da Gama reached Calicut, the Portuguese had destroyed the Arabs' hold on trade in the Indian Ocean. The spice trade was finally theirs. Portugal now controlled the ocean traffic from Hormuz, in the Persian Gulf, east to Malacca, in Malaya.

The Portuguese used Malacca as a springboard to another trading area centered in the China Sea. The Chinese and Japanese controlled trade here. The first stop of the Portuguese was the Moluccas, or Spice Islands. Then, they sailed to China and Japan. Over a period of about 40 years, they set up trading posts throughout the region, in places such as Java, Timor, Sumatra, and Macao in China and Nagasaki in Japan. Missionaries accompanied them whenever possible.

Power Shifts in the East

The Portuguese trading empire in the East began to break up about 1580. It had been 100 years since King John II of Portugal had brought new energy to the search for a sea route around Africa to the East. Meanwhile, the country of Spain sponsored its own expeditions. The Spaniards made conquests in the Americas and in Asia. Spain became very wealthy and powerful. In 1494, Spain and Portugal agreed to the Treaty of Tordesillas. Under the treaty, lands to the west of an imaginary vertical line drawn in the Atlantic Ocean, including most of the Americas, belonged to Spain. Land to the east of this line, including Brazil, belonged to Portugal. Now, under the treaty, Spain controlled the Philippines.

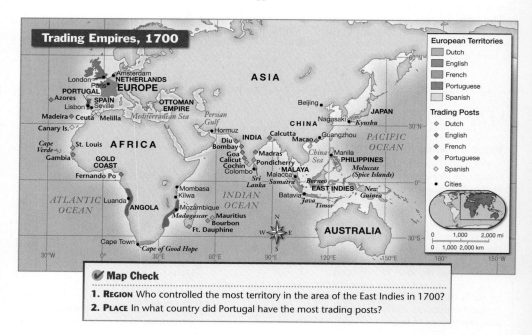

✔ Map Check
1. **REGION** Who controlled the most territory in the area of the East Indies in 1700?
2. **PLACE** In what country did Portugal have the most trading posts?

Teaching Options

F Y I

Treaty of Tordesillas

In 1493, Pope Alexander VI established an imaginary line, called the Line of Demarcation, to settle land claims between Spain and Portugal and prevent disputes. In 1494, under the Treaty of Tordesillas, the line was moved about 1,100 miles west of the Cape Verde Islands. Later, Portugal used the treaty to support its claim to territory in what eventually became eastern Brazil.

Conflict Resolution

Point out that the Portuguese destroyed Arab control of trade in the Indian Ocean by using military force. Explore with students some methods countries use today to resolve trade disputes. (negotiate, get other countries to help, make compromises or treaties) Discuss with students the methods they would use to share school resources, such as use of computer or video equipment, between two or more classes or grades.

Other European countries wanted a share in eastern trade. In the 1600s, they traded in the region through special companies. For example, the East India companies had the legal right, given by the government, to conduct trade between England and the East Indies. The East Indies included India, China, and Southeast Asia. The Dutch, people from the Netherlands, made similar arrangements through the Dutch East India Company. Shares, or parts of the company, were owned by investors called **shareholders**. These shareholders provided the trading company with money.

Over the next 60 years, the Dutch took control of one Portuguese territory or trading post after another. They gained control of the Moluccas. They also captured the important port of Malacca from the Portuguese, and they began trading with China. By 1641, the spice trade belonged to the Dutch.

In the same period, English traders were establishing themselves in India. They set up the British East India Company. The French traders became active in the region after the French East India Company was formed in 1664. For the Dutch, English, and French people, trade was the way they could gain more power.

◆ How did Portugal take control of trade in the Indian Ocean?

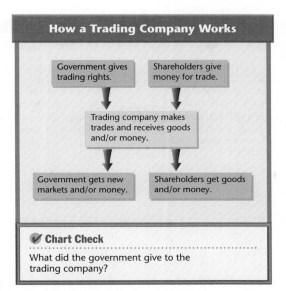

How a Trading Company Works

Government gives trading rights.

Shareholders give money for trade.

Trading company makes trades and receives goods and/or money.

Government gets new markets and/or money.

Shareholders get goods and/or money.

✔ **Chart Check**

What did the government give to the trading company?

Review II

Review History
A. What goods did the Portuguese trade for in Africa?
B. What route did Vasco da Gama find?
C. What other Europeans besides the Portuguese began to trade in the East?

Define Terms to Know
Define the following terms:
commodity, shareholder

Critical Thinking
Suppose a center for the study of navigation had not been set up. What effect would this have had on trade?

Write About Geography
Suppose you are a sailor with Vasco da Gama. Write a letter home about sailing around Africa to India.

Get Organized
SQR CHART
Use an SQR chart to organize information from this section. Choose one of the main parts and use the chart to find a purpose for reading it. Make an SQR chart for "Toward the Indian Ocean," for example.

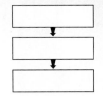

SURVEY
This section is about expeditions to the Indian Ocean.

QUESTION
Who reached the Indian Ocean?

READ
Dias went around Africa to the Indian Ocean but turned back. Da Gama crossed the Indian Ocean.

Critical Thinking
Possible answer: The lack of financial support and gathering of people would have slowed exploration; the lack of accurate maps and efficient boats would have made it difficult to find trading ports with valuable commodities.

Write About Geography
Students should describe the hard work and fear of the unknown associated with sailing around Africa and across the Indian Ocean.

Discuss Have students discuss how the creation of special companies to conduct trade affected the influence of European countries in the East. (These trading companies enabled the Dutch, English, and French to establish powerful trading empires in the East and provided an important source of revenue for the countries.)

Using the Chart
How a Trading Company Works

Point out that the chart shows how the trading company benefited both the government and the shareholders. Ask students what the shareholders give the trading company. (money for trade) Who had the actual responsibility for making the trades? (the trading company)

✔ **Chart Check**
Answer trading rights

◆ **ANSWER** They brought a permanent fleet there, built bases for their ships and merchants, and won a sea war against the Arabs.

Section Close
Ask students how European nations were able to establish trade centers in the East and what effect these centers had on the Europeans.

3 Assess

Review Answers
Review History
A. fish, sealskins, seal oil, gold dust, ivory, pepper, and slaves
B. Vasco da Gama found a sea route to India.
C. The Dutch, English, French, and Spanish all began to trade in the East.

Define Terms to Know
commodity, 345; shareholder, 349

China, Japan, and Foreign Trade

III. China, Japan, and Foreign Trade

(pp. 350–353)

Section Summary

In this section, students will learn about China's limited foreign contact during the Ming and Qing Dynasties, and the Tokugawa family's rule in Japan for more than 200 years.

1 Introduce

Getting Started

Have students discuss how much interaction their grade has with other grades in the school. For example, do they compete against each other in athletics or participate in any joint cultural programs? Encourage students to discuss the advantages of maintaining contact with other grades within a school. Then, expand the discussion to other schools. Explain that China and Japan had limited contact with other countries. This influenced the development of those countries.

TERMS TO KNOW

Ask students to read the words and definitions on page 350 and then find each word in the section. Have students write context sentences for each word. Then, have them substitute the definition for the word as they read the sentences to a partner.

You may wish to preview with students the pronunciation of the following terms from the section.

Hong Wu (HAWNG WOO)
Zheng He (JEHNG HAY)
Manchu (man CHOO)
Qing (CHIHNG)
Xinjiang (shihn JYAHNG)
daimyo (DYM yoh)
Tokugawa Ieyasu
(toh koog AH wah ee eh YAHS oo)

ACTIVE READING

Have students compare and contrast two of the dynasties or rulers they read about in this section. Ask them to create a Venn diagram (TR, p. 323) with the information they find.

Terms to Know

fleet a group of ships that is under one command

monopoly the control of goods or services by one person, group, or company

ANALYZE PRIMARY SOURCES
DOCUMENT-BASED QUESTION
Which of the king's questions shows an interest in Chinese culture?

A brilliant military leader, Hong Wu founded the Ming Dynasty and ruled as emperor.

Main Ideas

A. During the Ming and Qing Dynasties, China had limited contact with foreigners.

B. The Tokugawa rulers closed Japan to almost all foreigners for more than 200 years.

Active Reading

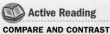

COMPARE AND CONTRAST
When you compare and contrast, you think about how two things are similar and how they differ. As you read this section, compare and contrast China and Japan. Then, list ways they were similar and different in their action toward foreigners.

A. China and the Outside World

In 1508, six Portuguese ships were sent to Malacca in Malaya to meet the Chinese in port. They also had special orders from the king of Portugal. They were to

> ask after the Chijns [Chinese], and from what part they come, and from how far, and what times they come to Malacca, . . . and the merchandise that they bring, and how many of their ships come each year, . . . and if they are wealthy merchants, . . . and if they have arms [weapons] . . . and what clothes they wear, . . . and if they are Christians or heathens, if their country is a great one, and if they have more than one king amongst them.

Nearly 200 years had passed since European people and Chinese people had direct contact with each other. Now, they would meet again in the ports of the China Sea.

The Ming Dynasty Rebuilds China

Mongol rule of China ended in 1368. In the final years of the Mongol Empire, civil war broke out among the Chinese people. As you learned in Chapter 4, a civil war is a war between people of the same country. After many years of fighting, a rebel leader known as Hong Wu, meaning "great military power," captured Beijing from the Mongols and made himself emperor of China. Hong Wu founded a new dynasty, the Ming. The Ming, or "brilliant," Dynasty would remain in power for almost 300 years.

The Ming emperors rebuilt Chinese society after many years of foreign rule under the Mongols. The Ming reconstructed the great cities of China, such as Nanjing and Beijing, making them more spectacular than before. They recreated the bureaucracy, or body of government workers. The bureaucracy was huge, extending from top officials in the capital to local administrators in the villages. As time passed, the emperor enjoyed greater power. He became an autocrat, or ruler with unlimited power.

China's own culture flourished under the Ming rulers. Artists and scholars became as important as army officers. Students studied China's past. Schools encouraged the study of classical Chinese writing and culture.

Teaching Options

Section 3 Resources

Teacher's Resources (TR)
Terms to Know, p. 28
Review History, p. 62
Build Your Skills, p. 96
Concept Builder, p. 231
Chapter Test, pp. 145–146
SQR Chart, p. 322
Transparency 1

ESL/ELL STRATEGIES

Organize Information Have students organize the information in one of the subsections in this section using a main idea/supporting details chart (TR, p. 319). Suggest that students review their charts with a partner and have students reread the subsection and make any necessary changes. Point out that organizing information in this way is useful when reviewing for a test.

Foreign Contacts Under the Ming

China also expanded its power during the Ming Dynasty. Mongolia, Korea, and Southeast Asia all became subject to the emperor's authority. They recognized the power of the Chinese emperor by sending tribute, or payments of goods. Foreign trade developed. The Ming expanded their interest.

The early Ming developed more contacts across the seas. Yongle, the third Ming emperor, took unusual steps to encourage foreign contact. In 1405, Yongle sent a **fleet** of ships to India and Southeast Asia. A fleet is a group of ships that is under one command. Zheng He, a member of the court and a Muslim, was commander. The expedition carried nearly 28,000 people, including officials and troops. Six more expeditions followed, all headed by Zheng He.

The purpose of the expeditions was to display China's power, encourage trade, and win new tribute-paying states. Zheng He sailed to more than 30 countries. He sailed from the Indian Ocean and its chain of islands to the east African coast to the Persian Gulf and the Red Sea port of Aden. The ships carried porcelain, silk, gold, and silver from China. They returned with valuable goods such as ivory, spices, and pearls. Zheng He used force as needed to make states agree to send tribute to the emperor.

Direct contact with other lands did not last, however. The Chinese expeditions ended suddenly in 1433. Their great cost was one likely reason. Later emperors were also more concerned about growing troubles within China than with becoming a power overseas. This left the seas open to others, such as Arabs and Europeans. In 1557, the Chinese gave the Portuguese permission to set up a trading post at Macao in southeast China.

Expansion and Trade During the Qing Dynasty

The Ming Dynasty slowly lost its control of outlying regions in the 1500s. Many states stopped paying tribute. There was unrest in China. By 1644, the Ming could no longer handle the troubles in China on their own. They turned to the people from Manchuria, called Manchus, for help. The Manchus took advantage of the uncertain situation in China. They invaded China, overthrew the Ming government, and set up their own dynasty. The Qing, or "pure," Dynasty remained in power until 1912.

The key to the Manchus' long rule was their respect for Chinese culture. Although they were foreigners, the Manchus were willing to adapt to Chinese ways of life. For example, they recognized and supported the role that Confucianism played in the public and personal lives of the Chinese. They made few changes in the structure of government in China. The Chinese people continued to live in much the same way as they had under the Ming rulers.

The Qing rulers increased China's territory. China stretched into Central Asia and included Mongolia, Tibet, and Xinjiang. Korea, Vietnam, Nepal, and Burma became tribute states. Local people served as administrators in the new territories. They were allowed to organize their local government in ways familiar to them.

Zheng He commanded a fleet of ships to impress China's neighbors and to demand tribute payments to the emperor.

Then & Now

TIBET

China took control of Tibet in the 1700s during the Qing Dynasty. When Qing rule ended in 1911, the Tibetans drove Chinese troops out. Chinese forces returned to Tibet under the Communists in the 1950s. The Tibetan leader, known as the Dalai Lama, left Tibet in 1959.

Since then, the Dalai Lama has worked hard to end Chinese control of Tibet. However, he refuses to use violence to win Tibet's independence. The Dalai Lama received the Nobel Peace Prize in 1989. China still claims Tibet today.

A. China and the Outside World

Purpose-Setting Question Why did the Portuguese king instruct the trading ships to find out so much information about the Chinese? (Nearly 200 years had passed since the Europeans and the Chinese had had direct contact with each other, and the Portuguese king wanted to know what these people were like.)

ANALYZING PRIMARY SOURCES

DOCUMENT-BASED QUESTION

Discuss with students the ways the sailors would approach the Chinese traders to ask these questions, and how the Chinese traders might feel about the questions. (Possible answer: Because the sailors and the Chinese did not speak the same language, the sailors might use polite, friendly gestures to communicate the king's questions. The Chinese traders would sense the sailors' friendliness and feel comfortable enough to communicate with gestures also.)

ANSWER the questions about their clothes, their religion, and if they have more than one king

Discuss Ask students to discuss whether the Ming Dynasty lived up to its name, the Brilliant Dynasty. (Possible answer: Yes, the Ming period was outstanding, or brilliant, especially in the arts. Also, during this period scholars became important, the bureaucracy was recreated, and great Chinese cities were reconstructed.)

Focus Using the world map on pages A1–A2 or Transparency 1, have students identify the countries that Zheng He's expeditions visited. Ask students what Portugal gained by getting China's permission to set up a trading post in Macao. (The Portuguese could establish an important trade center in China.)

Then & Now

TIBET Point out that the current Dalai Lama lives in India, where he maintains a government in exile. Ask students to discuss any times in history when people from different countries left their homelands because of political repression or because other countries gained control of their governments. Discuss how these people felt about their homeland.

Using Technology

Ask small groups of students to use the Internet, CD-ROM resources, and other media to prepare a report about some aspect of life in China under the Manchu Dynasty. Have students use word processing software and computer graphics to create a chart that presents their findings in an interesting way. Encourage students to display their completed charts in class.

F Y I

Manchu Rule

Although the Manchus adopted the Ming traditions and government, they also took steps to ensure their control. Half of the higher-level government officials were Manchu. They created the Army of the Green Standard, which included Chinese leaders who had surrendered. These troops were stationed throughout the country, whereas the Manchu troops stayed in the capital.

B. Japan Shuts a Door

Discuss Discuss with students how trade increased under the Qing rulers. Ask students if they feel that trade would have increased if Europeans had not been allowed into Canton. (Possible answer: No, trade could not have increased because no outsiders could have entered China.) Then, discuss the role of the missionaries in China. (Possible answer: They shared their knowledge and skills with the Chinese people.) Ask students how China's decision to allow trade only in Canton benefited China. (China got the benefits of trade but limited the influence from other countries.)

Extend Tell students that, in addition to his official post, Father Johann Adam Schall von Bell was also responsible for reforming the old Chinese calendar. Ask students to study the seventeenth-century color engraving of the missionary. Encourage them to analyze why he is pictured holding navigational tools and standing beside a globe. (The artist is highlighting his achievements as an astronomer and a scientist.) Have students discuss why the young emperor accepted Schall von Bell. (Because the Chinese respected European learning, the emperor was probably impressed with von Bell's scholarship.)

◆ **ANSWER** By paying tribute, states demonstrated that they recognized the authority of the Chinese emperor.

B. Japan Shuts a Door

Purpose-Setting Question How would you compare Japan's contact with the outside world with China's? (Japan was more isolated from Europe than China was; the first Europeans didn't arrive in Japan until the 1540s.)

Explore Have pairs of students do additional research about the daimyo Oda Nobunaga, who is mentioned in this section. Students should create a timeline (TR, p. 320) of events in the life of the daimyo. If possible, students should photocopy a picture of the daimyo, as well. Students can then share their timeline and picture with the rest of the class.

The Jesuit missionary, Johann Adam Schall von Bell became head of the bureau of astronomy under the Qing.

Trade also increased somewhat under the Qing rulers. At first the Qing were not sure whether to allow foreigners to trade in China. Then they decided to let Europeans trade in the city of Canton only. Some Chinese merchants formed a group to create a **monopoly**, or complete control of trade, in Canton. They were the only merchants the Europeans could deal with there. The Qing did not stop the group. They asked only that it make sure the Europeans acted properly and paid all the necessary fees.

China had other contacts with Europeans during the Qing Dynasty. Missionaries were welcomed in the Qing court. Many were experts in science and mapmaking. They shared their knowledge and skills with the Chinese people. Missionaries such as Johann Adam Schall von Bell even served in the bureau of astronomy in Beijing. In the early 1700s, missionaries carried out land surveys, or measurements, of the Qing Empire. The Chinese admired the learning of European visitors. However, they were selective about which foreign ways to accept. China developed on its own, more or less isolated from the rest of the world.

◆ **What was the purpose of the tribute certain states paid to China?**

B. Japan Shuts a Door

The Japanese people were more isolated from the outside world than the Chinese people. The first Europeans to reach Japan did not arrive until 1542 or 1543. Their arrival was something of an accident. They were Portuguese sailors and traders headed to the Chinese port of Macao. They landed on an island off the coast of Kyushu when their boat was driven ashore there. Kyushu is one of the four main islands of Japan.

Europeans Arrive in Japan

The 1500s were unsettled times in Japan. The daimyo, or warrior lords, were fighting a civil war. Their armies spread across the countryside to guard the lords' farmland. Armies of warrior-monks defended the land holdings of temples. People everywhere used weapons to protect themselves, their families, and their communities.

A Portuguese missionary and several priests arrived in the midst of this conflict. In the beginning, they were welcomed. They had come not only to convert the Japanese people to Christianity but to help Portuguese traders sell the Japanese goods from Europe, including weapons. Soon, the Japanese were making copies of the weapons they had bought. These weapons changed fighting in Japan.

As you read in Chapter 11, a powerful daimyo named Oda Nobunaga wanted to unite Japan and be its leader. Nobunaga was a fierce warrior, and soon half of Japan was under his control. After Nobunaga was killed, one of his generals, Toyotomi Hideyoshi, completed his work of uniting the country. During his rule, Hideyoshi was helped by another warrior lord, Tokugawa Ieyasu.

Teaching Options

Cooperative Learning

Have groups of students prepare a script for a 10-minute video about life in Japan during the 1500s. Students should include interviews with historical figures and Japanese warriors, peasants, and merchants who lived at different times during this period. Some students should do research, others should write the scripted interviews, and a third group should be responsible for production. If video equipment is available, have each group tape its part of the program.

The Tokugawas Send Foreigners Away

In 1603, the Tokugawa family came to power and ruled for more than 250 years. In the first years of rule, the Tokugawas worked to bring peace and set up a new government system. At the top was the shogun, or military ruler. Tokugawa Ieyasu was the first Tokugawa shogun. The Tokugawas made rule hereditary, so that it passed from one member of the ruling family to the next. Power under the shogun was shared by 250 lords. Each was the head of a region of Japan that was loyal to the shogun.

Next, the Tokugawas needed to deal with the many foreigners who were in Japan. Portugal had set up a trading post at Nagasaki in 1571. Spanish missionaries had crossed to Japan from the Philippines in 1592. Dutch and English traders had built trading posts in Hirado in the early 1600s. At first, the Japanese government welcomed the Europeans because it wanted European guns and gunpowder from trade.

In a short time, however, thousands of Japanese people had become Christians. The Tokugawas feared that the missionaries might bring armies to conquer Japan. They ordered the missionaries to stop converting people and they forced Japanese Christians to stop practicing the religion. When these orders failed, they expelled the missionaries and became strict with the Japanese Christians. By 1640, Christianity had nearly disappeared from Japan.

To keep order, the Tokugawas finally cut Japan's contacts with the outside world. The Japanese people were forbidden to leave the country. All European traders except for the Dutch were forced to leave Japan. Since the Dutch were not Catholics, the Japanese did not consider them to be Christian, although they were, of course, mistaken. The Dutch could trade only on one small island near Nagasaki. They were allowed to unload only one ship a year there.

Japan was not completely isolated. Japan traded actively with China and Korea. The Japanese people learned about what was going on in the rest of the world from their trading partners. By limiting Japan's outside contact, however, the Tokugawas thought they were keeping Japan safe.

◆ **How did Europeans change life in Japan?**

Global Connections

DUTCH LEARNING
Although foreigners were not allowed in Japan, European ideas began to spread among Japanese in high circles in the 1700s. The Japanese called these ideas "Dutch learning." Foreign books on science, medicine, and geography were translated into Japanese. Some Japanese people even learned the Dutch language. A Japanese-Dutch dictionary was published in 1745.

Review III

Review History

A. What was the purpose of the expeditions led by Zheng He?

B. Why did the Tokugawas make European missionaries leave Japan?

Define Terms to Know
Define the following terms:
fleet, monopoly

Critical Thinking
In your opinion, why was Japan more isolated from the rest of the world than China was?

Write About Culture
Write a brief essay about why the Manchus were able to stay in power in China for so long.

Get Organized
SQR CHART
Use an SQR chart to organize information from this section. Choose one of the main parts and use the chart to find a purpose for reading it. Make an SQR chart for "Japan Shuts a Door," for example.

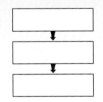

SURVEY
This section is about Japan's isolation from the outside world.

↓

QUESTION
Why did Japan decide to send foreigners away?

↓

READ
Japan's rulers were afraid that missionaries might bring armies.

Critical Thinking
Japan expelled foreigners and forbade the Japanese people to leave the country. The Tokugawas cut Japan's contact with European countries. China developed and encouraged foreign trade and developed contacts across the seas.

Write About Culture
Students' essays should focus on the Manchus' respect for Chinese culture.

Discuss Ask students how making the Tokugawa's rule hereditary affected government in Japan. (Making their rule hereditary would have ensured that their family would continue to rule Japan for generations to come, it should help eliminate wars when a ruler dies.)

GLOBAL CONNECTIONS

DUTCH LEARNING Have students identify the Netherlands on the map of Europe on page A5. Discuss with the class the reasons Japan did not shut out the Dutch. Also, ask students if they feel that unloading one ship a year in Japan was worth it for the Dutch. Then, ask students why the Japanese called European ideas "Dutch learning." (The Dutch were the only European traders Japan had contact with, so the ideas had to come from them.)

Activity

Make a cause-and-effect chain Ask students to organize information about Christianity in seventeenth-century Japan on a cause-and-effect chain (TR, p. 325). (**Cause:** Missionaries arrive in Japan; **Event:** Tokugawas order missionaries to stop converting Japanese and order citizens to stop practicing Christianity; **Effect:** Missionaries are expelled.)

◆ **ANSWER** They introduced weapons to the Japanese and spread Christianity.

Section Close

Ask students to compare and contrast Japan's and China's history of contact with foreigners.

3 Assess

Review Answers

Review History

A. to display China's power, encourage trade, and win new tribute-paying states

B. In a short time, thousands of Japanese had become Christians. The Tokugawas began to fear that the missionaries might bring armies to conquer Japan.

Define Terms to Know
fleet, 351; monopoly, 352

Past to...

ASIAN AND EUROPEAN TRADE CONNECTIONS

Teach the Topic
Before students begin to read, ask what they already know about Asian imports, such as cars, computers, and video equipment. Have students discuss how these goods play a part in their daily lives. Encourage them to talk about how the design and function of these imported goods may change in the future.

CURVED CARVING
The Eight Immortals were thought to be holy. Each of them had earned the right to become immortal. The figures are popular in Chinese art and are shown in a single group, standing alone, or in small groups. As a group they are often presented bearing gifts to the god of longevity.

SHIPS OF THE DESERT
Camels were used to transport goods and people in desert regions. Have small groups of students research the physical characteristics of camels that allow them to travel easily in the desert. Ask them to organize their findings in an idea web (TR, p. 321) or an illustrated poster.

THE SILK ROAD
Explain that from the 100s B.C. to the A.D. 1500s, the Silk Road extended about 5,000 miles across Asia. Today, however, the only part of the famous road that still exists is a paved highway connecting Pakistan and a region in China. The United Nations' plan for a modern trans-Asian highway was inspired by this historic road. Have students identify the major geographical features along the Silk Road. (Gobi Desert, Hindu Kush Mountains, Plateau of Tibet, Caspian Sea, Mediterranean Sea, Black Sea)

LOVELY LACQUER
Lacquerware can be coated with up to several hundred coats of either lacquer or shellac. In Asia, the sap of the lacquer or varnish tree is collected, strained, and dried by heat. The resulting dark brown liquid, which has the consistency of syrup, is used as lacquer.

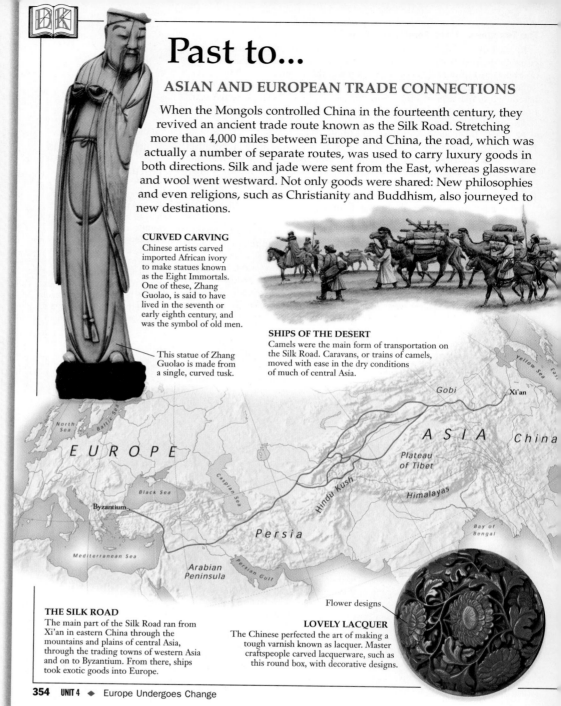

Past to...

ASIAN AND EUROPEAN TRADE CONNECTIONS

When the Mongols controlled China in the fourteenth century, they revived an ancient trade route known as the Silk Road. Stretching more than 4,000 miles between Europe and China, the road, which was actually a number of separate routes, was used to carry luxury goods in both directions. Silk and jade were sent from the East, whereas glassware and wool went westward. Not only goods were shared: New philosophies and even religions, such as Christianity and Buddhism, also journeyed to new destinations.

CURVED CARVING
Chinese artists carved imported African ivory to make statues known as the Eight Immortals. One of these, Zhang Guolao, is said to have lived in the seventh or early eighth century, and was the symbol of old men.

This statue of Zhang Guolao is made from a single, curved tusk.

SHIPS OF THE DESERT
Camels were the main form of transportation on the Silk Road. Caravans, or trains of camels, moved with ease in the dry conditions of much of central Asia.

THE SILK ROAD
The main part of the Silk Road ran from Xi'an in eastern China through the mountains and plains of central Asia, through the trading towns of western Asia and on to Byzantium. From there, ships took exotic goods into Europe.

LOVELY LACQUER
The Chinese perfected the art of making a tough varnish known as lacquer. Master craftspeople carved lacquerware, such as this round box, with decorative designs.

Flower designs

Teaching Options

Connection to LITERATURE

Students interested in reading a nonfiction book about the Silk Road can read *Cave Temples of Mogao: Art and History on the Silk Road* by Roderick Whitfield, Susan Whitfield, and Neville Agnew (Getty Publications, 2001). This book features photographs of the art and statues as well as describes the manuscripts that were created by Buddhist monks.

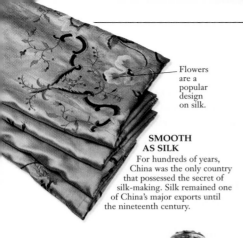

Flowers are a popular design on silk.

SMOOTH AS SILK
For hundreds of years, China was the only country that possessed the secret of silk-making. Silk remained one of China's major exports until the nineteenth century.

FRAGILE BEAUTY
China did not have a large-scale glassmaking industry until the seventeenth century. As a result, the Chinese imported fine and fragile European glassware that was transported along the Silk Road.

POPULAR POTS
Porcelain is often called china because of its country of origin. Blue-and-white porcelain, such as this Ming Dynasty vase, was particularly desired in Europe.

...Present

Goods still flow between Europe and Asia but primarily by sea rather than by land. The types of goods traded have also changed. Luxury items from the East might now include the latest model of Japanese car, while the West is a major exporter of petroleum.

20–40 foot containers

CARGO BY WATER
With the improvement of seafaring techniques and equipment, sea routes are now the most popular way of moving goods from one country to another. Container vessels store most of the cargo in the hull, or main body, of the ship, and the remainder on deck.

PRECIOUS OIL
Russia, the United States, and Saudi Arabia are the world's largest producers of petroleum. The Organization of Petroleum Exporting Countries (OPEC) decides the price of this valuable and limited resource.

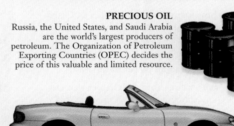

A FOUR-WHEELED SUCCESS STORY
In the mid-twentieth century, Japanese automobile companies became the biggest producer of cars in the world. However, many of these are now part-owned by non-Japanese companies.

F Y I

Silk
For about 3,000 years, only the Chinese knew the secret of silk making. Although countries in the West had heard about the silkworm, no one actually saw it until about 550. The Byzantine emperor, Justinian I, instructed two monks, sent to China as spies, to smuggle out silkworm eggs and mulberry seeds in a hollow bamboo cane. This ended the Chinese and Persian monopolies on silk production.

Hands-On Activity
The Eight Immortals
Place students into groups of at least four. Each group should collectively find information on the Eight Immortals. Groups should then create a presentation for the class, including pictures or art of the Immortals.

CHAPTER 15 Review

Chapter Summary

A blank outline form is available in the Teacher's Resources (p. 318). Chapter summaries should outline how the growing interest in the East led to explorations for direct trade routes, the desire to spread Christianity, and the establishment of trading empires. Also, summaries should outline the limited contact China and Japan had with the outside world and their reasons for this limited contact. Refer to the rubric in the Teacher's Resources (p. 340) to score students' chapter summaries.

 Interpret the Timeline

1. Zheng He's first expedition
2. 144 years
3. Dutch control spice trade
4. Students' answers will vary. Check that all entries are from the chapter.

Use Terms to Know

5. commodity
6. monopoly
7. fleet
8. shareholder
9. navigation
10. ambassador

Check Your Understanding

11. The goods passed through the hands of many merchants, and each time they changed hands, the prices rose.
12. magnetic compass, astrolabe
13. He set up a center for the study of navigation where the caravel was developed, more exact maps were made, and tools for navigation were improved. He also sent out expeditions that explored the West African coast.
14. They traded through special companies. For example, the East India companies had the legal right, given by the government, to conduct trade between England and the East Indies.
15. The Ming emperors rebuilt Chinese society, reconstructed great cities, and recreated bureaucracies.
16. He sailed to more than 30 countries all around the Indian Ocean. He sailed from the Indian Ocean to the East African coast to the Persian Gulf and the Red Sea port of Aden. He returned with valuable goods. He also used force to make states send tribute to the emperor.

Chapter Summary

Complete the following outline in your notebook. Then, use your outline to write a brief summary of the chapter.

Exploration and Trade

I. Europe Looks Outward
  A. Growing Interest in the East
  B. Looking for New Trade Routes
  C. Spreading Christianity
  D. Sailing With New Technology
II. Portugal Leads the Way
  A. Exploration Under Henry the Navigator
  B. Toward the Indian Ocean
  C. Trading Empires
III. China, Japan, and Foreign Trade
  A. China and the Outside World
  B. Japan Shuts a Door

 Interpret the Timeline

Use the timeline on pages 336–337 to answer the following questions.

1. Which occurred first, Vasco da Gama's voyage to India or Zheng He's first expedition?

2. About how many years after Vasco da Gama sailed around Africa to India did the Dutch control the spice trade?

3. **Critical Thinking** Which event shows the end of Portugal's trading power in the East?

4. Select four events from the chapter that are not on the timeline. Create a timeline that shows these events.

Use Terms to Know

Select the term that best completes each sentence.

ambassador   fleet   navigation
commodity   monopoly   shareholder

5. A _____ is something that can be bought or sold.

6. When one group controls goods or services, it has a _____.

7. A group of ships under one commander is called a _____.

8. An investor who provides a company with money is called a _____.

9. The control of the direction of a boat or a ship is called _____.

10. An _____ is a person who acts as a representative.

Check Your Understanding

11. **Explain** why goods that traveled over land from the East were expensive.

12. **Identify** two tools that European explorers used on their voyages.

13. **Summarize** what Henry the Navigator of Portugal did to help the search for a sea route around Africa to Asia.

14. **Describe** how European countries other than Portugal began to trade in the East.

15. **Describe** the accomplishments of the Ming emperors.

16. **Describe** the voyages of Zheng He.

17. **Explain** how the first contact between Japan and Portugal changed fighting in Japan.

18. **Discuss** the reasons Japan allowed the Dutch to trade on one of its islands.

19. **Describe** two steps that the Tokugawas took to keep Japan safe.

20. **Explain** the reasons that Christianity nearly disappeared in Japan by 1640.

17. The Portuguese traders sold weapons to the Japanese. The Japanese learned how to make these weapons. This changed the way they fought.
18. Because the Dutch were not Catholics, the Japanese did not consider them to be Christian, although they were mistaken.

19. The Tokugawas forced all European traders except for the Dutch to leave Japan. They also ordered the missionaries to stop converting people, and they forced Japanese Christians to stop practicing their religion. They eventually expelled the missionaries and became strict with the Japanese Christians.

20. The government threw out the missionaries and forced the Japanese Christians to stop practicing their religion.

Critical Thinking

21. Make Inferences Why did Europeans begin to explore the world after the Middle Ages?

22. Identify Cause and Effect Why do you think the Portuguese trading empire in the East broke up?

23. Analyze Primary Sources According to the passage on page 350, how do you know that the king of Portugal was concerned about the power of China when he gave orders to the traders sent to Malacca?

24. Synthesize Information How did life improve in China under early Ming emperors?

25. Synthesize Information Why did troubles within China develop during the Ming Dynasty?

Put Your Skills to Work

26. Draw Conclusions You have learned how to draw conclusions by putting new facts together with information you already know. Drawing conclusions can help you understand why events happened.

Study the new information in the graphic organizer below. Then, think about what you already know from this chapter. Put the two together to draw a conclusion. Next, copy the graphic organizer onto a separate sheet of paper. Add the information you learned from the chapter and your conclusion to your graphic organizer.

Improvements Under Tokugawa Rule

Analyze Sources

27. Alfonso de Albuquerque, a Portuguese officer, led his soldiers in the attack of Malacca. Read how de Albuquerque explained to his men some of the goals of their mission before the battle. Then, answer the questions that follow.

[This is a] great service we shall perform to our Lord in casting the Moors [members of a Muslim people] out of the country and quenching the fire of the sect [a small group of people having the same opinion] of Mahomet . . . and the service we shall render to the king Don Manoel in taking this city because it is the source of all the spiceries and [medicines] . . .

a. Why does de Albuquerque tell his men to attack Malacca?

b. Do you think the order in which de Albuquerque expresses his ideas reflects how important each reason is to him? Explain.

c. What goods was Malacca the source of?

Essay Writing

28. In an essay, explain how technology affected the exploration that took place during the fifteenth and sixteenth centuries. Give at least three specific examples to support your ideas.

Critical Thinking

21. With an increase in trade, Europeans wanted to be able to get Eastern goods more cheaply.
22. Other European countries began to trade in the region.
23. He asked the traders to find out whether the Chinese had weapons, how large their country was, and whether they had more than one ruler.
24. The Ming emperors rebuilt Chinese society. Culture flourished. Trade expanded.
25. China stopped sending out expeditions. Many states stopped paying tribute.

Put Your Skills to Work

DRAW CONCLUSIONS
26. Possible answers for **What I Already Know:** worked to bring peace; set up new government; power was shared. Possible answer for **Conclusion:** Tokugawas wanted to improve Japan, were skilled at restoring order and making plans, and wanted to improve life for all social classes.

Analyze Sources

27a. to render service to God, to serve the king, and to capture a source of spices and medicines
27b. Possible answers: Yes, because spreading Christianity was a sincere reason for exploring, and it is mentioned first; or No, because gaining wealth motivated most of the explorers.
27c. spices and medicines

Essay Writing

28. Students' essays may mention the many innovations that made exploration and conquest possible, such as the astrolabe, the compass, improved maps, gunpowder and cannons, improved ships, and improved techniques for warfare.

Europe Expands Overseas
1492–1780
(pp. 358–383)

Chapter Objectives

• Discuss how Columbus's voyages led to further exploration of the Americas and the first circumnavigation of the world.
• Describe how Spanish and Portuguese colonies were established in the Americas and how they affected native peoples.
• Contrast the Dutch, French, and English colonies in the Americas and the impact each had on Native Americans.
• Explain the causes of the Atlantic slave trade and their effects on Europeans, Africans, Native Americans, and American colonists.

Chapter Summary

Section I focuses on the voyages of Columbus and other early explorers and their impact on Europe and the Americas.
Section II explores the Spanish and Portuguese colonies in Mexico, Central America, and South America and their impact on the native peoples.
Section III compares the reasons for establishing Dutch, French, and English colonies in North America and their impact on Native American ways of life.
Section IV discusses the development of the Atlantic slave trade by Europeans and the effects of triangular trade.

Set the Stage

TEACH PRIMARY SOURCES
Explain that today Columbus is considered a controversial figure. He is viewed by some with disdain and by others with admiration. Point out that Zvi Dor-Ner, however, wants us to recognize Columbus's indisputable accomplishment. Based on the quotation, ask students what they think that accomplishment was. (his determined search to find a new way to do something) Ask students why that is so important to all of us, even today. (It addresses the human quest for knowledge, profit, power, and glory.)

Europe Expands Overseas
1492–1780

I. Conquests in the Americas
II. Spanish and Portuguese Colonies
III. Dutch, French, and English Colonies
IV. Africa and the Atlantic Slave Trade

On August 3, 1492, an Italian navigator, Christopher Columbus, set sail across the Atlantic Ocean in search of a new route to the riches of Asia. On October 12, more than two months into the journey, Columbus and his men caught their first sight of the land to be called the Americas. They had no way of knowing their voyage of discovery would forever change the world in ways both good and bad. Writer Zvi Dor-Ner had this to say about the success of Columbus:

❝ *If there is a core of nobility to Columbus, . . . it is the part of him that searched for a new route, a new way. . . . It is, after all, what moves us in our own search for new ways of knowledge.* ❞

CHAPTER EVENTS			
1492 Columbus makes his first voyage.	**1533** Pizarro conquers the Inca Empire in Peru.	**1588** England defeats the Spanish Armada.	**1620** Pilgrims sail to America.

1500 — **1560** — **1620**

WORLD EVENTS		
1514 Copernicus develops the theory of a Sun-centered universe.	**1568** Japanese unification begins.	**1609** Galileo constructs an astronomical telescope.

Teaching Options

Chapter 16 Resources

REVIEW

Teacher's Resources (TR)
Terms to Know, p. 29
Review History, p. 63
Build Your Skills, p. 97
Chapter Test, pp. 147–148
Concept Builder, p. 232
Idea Web, p. 321
Transparencies 1, 3, 4, 5

ASSESSMENT
Section Reviews, pp. 364, 371, 376, 381
Chapter Review, pp. 382–383
Chapter Test, TR, pp. 147–148

ALTERNATIVE ASSESSMENT
Portfolio Project, p. 410
Write a Dramatic Monologue, p. T410

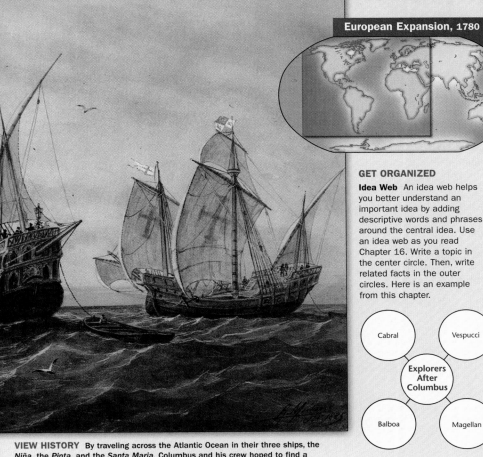

GET ORGANIZED

Idea Web An idea web helps you better understand an important idea by adding descriptive words and phrases around the central idea. Use an idea web as you read Chapter 16. Write a topic in the center circle. Then, write related facts in the outer circles. Here is an example from this chapter.

```
        Cabral          Vespucci

              Explorers
               After
              Columbus

        Balboa          Magellan
```

VIEW HISTORY By traveling across the Atlantic Ocean in their three ships, the *Niña*, the *Pinta*, and the *Santa Maria*, Columbus and his crew hoped to find a western sea route to Asia. Columbus landed in the Americas but believed he had arrived in the East Indies.
➤ How are the ships shown in this painting different from modern sailing vessels?

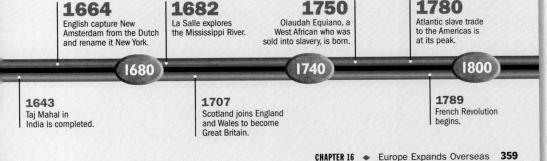

1664
English capture New Amsterdam from the Dutch and rename it New York.

1682
La Salle explores the Mississippi River.

1750
Olaudah Equiano, a West African who was sold into slavery, is born.

1780
Atlantic slave trade to the Americas is at its peak.

1680

1740

1800

1643
Taj Mahal in India is completed.

1707
Scotland joins England and Wales to become Great Britain.

1789
French Revolution begins.

Chapter Themes

- Culture
- Time, Continuity, and Change
- Individuals, Groups, and Institutions
- Power, Authority, and Governance
- Production, Distribution, and Consumption
- Global Connections
- Science, Technology, and Society

F Y I

Caravels

Some of Columbus's ships were caravels—small, fast, wooden sailing vessels developed by the Portuguese in the fifteenth century. Caravels had high sides, either three or four masts, and were broad and deep. Columbus's flagship, the *Santa Maria,* was larger than a caravel and was called a *nao,* which means "ship."

Chapter Warm-Up
USING THE MAP
Point out the locator map at the top of page 359. Ask students which continents and oceans are in the highlighted box. (Africa, Europe, part of Asia, North America, South America, Atlantic Ocean, and parts of the Pacific and Indian Oceans) Explain that they will be learning about people who sailed to all of these areas.

VIEW HISTORY
Discuss with students the features of Columbus's ships, as evident in the painting. (three-masted sailing vessels with square and triangular (lateen) sails; high structures at front and back were probably made of wood) Point out that Columbus sailed on the *Santa Maria.* Ask students which one they think is the *Santa Maria,* and why. (the largest one at the center; because Columbus sailed on it, it was the most important)

➤ **ANSWER** The sailing ships in the painting have hulls and masts built from wood, several natural fabric sails, lookout ledges on the masts, and they were made from all-natural materials.

GET ORGANIZED
Idea Web
Discuss the idea web on page 359. Ask students what the main idea is (Explorers After Columbus) and what the related names are (Cabral, Vespucci, Balboa, Magellan). Point out that more details can be linked to the surrounding circles to expand the web. Encourage students to make an idea web for each section. (TR, p. 321)

⬤ TEACH THE TIMELINE
The timeline on pages 358–359 lists events from 1492 to 1789. Have students identify dates that tell of European exploration or conquest of places in the Americas. (1492, 1533, 1620, 1664, and 1682) Suggest that students look for these events as they read the chapter. Encourage them to refer to the timeline to help place events in historic perspectives.

Activity

Create a timeline Have students create their own "Europe Expands Overseas" timeline. (TR, p. 320) They should include the explorations and conquests on pages 358–359 and add other explorations and conquests noted in the text.

I. Conquests in the Americas (pp. 360–364)

Section Summary

In this section, students will learn how the voyages of Columbus led to the colonization of the Americas. They will also learn about other explorers, including Magellan, whose expedition circumnavigated the world.

1 Introduce

Getting Started

Ask students to describe the longest journey they have ever taken. On the board, write their starting and ending points and their modes of transportation (land, sea, or air). Then, ask them to think about what it would have been like to take the same journey 500 years ago.

TERMS TO KNOW

Ask students to read the terms and definitions on page 360 and find each term in the section. Have students create a glossary for this chapter by writing the words and definitions on page 360. Encourage them to add new terms to their glossaries as they read the chapter.

You may wish to preview the pronunciation of the following terms with students.

Treaty of Tordesillas
(tawr day SEEL yahs)

Amerigo Vespucci
(ahm ay REE goh veh SPOO chee)

Vasco Núñez de Balboa
(vahs KOH NOON yehz day
bahl BOH uh)

ACTIVE READING

Have students choose one of the subsections in Section 1 and identify the main idea of each paragraph in the subsection. Then, have students work in pairs to write a short summary of the subsection.

Section I — Conquests in the Americas

Terms to Know

indigenous occurring naturally in a region

circumnavigate to sail completely around a landmass or Earth

mercantilism an economic system that stresses increasing national wealth by selling more to other nations than buying from them

balance of trade the difference in value between a country's imports and its exports over a period

Main Ideas

A. The four voyages of Christopher Columbus were the start of the colonization of the Americas.

B. Many explorers followed Columbus west across the Atlantic Ocean.

C. The expedition led by Ferdinand Magellan was the first to sail around the world.

 Active Reading

MAIN IDEA
A main idea includes only the most important point of a passage. As you read this section, ask yourself what the main idea is behind the theory of mercantilism.

A. The Voyages of Columbus

Europeans had long been looking for a better way to reach areas filled with riches in Asia. Improvements in navigation and shipbuilding encouraged explorers to continue to look for a better, faster sea route to Asia.

A Route West

Italian navigator Christopher Columbus was a skilled sailor and expedition organizer who wanted to discover a new route to the riches of Asia. Because he, as well as many other educated Europeans, knew that Earth was round, Columbus thought he would reach Asia if he sailed west across the Atlantic Ocean. Columbus convinced King Ferdinand and Queen Isabella of Spain to finance, or pay for, his voyage.

Columbus's plan had two flaws. First, he thought the distance around Earth was less than it actually is. Second, he thought Earth had more land than water. He expected to reach Asia after a short sea voyage.

The First Journey

Columbus's fleet set sail from Spain on August 3, 1492. The fleet stopped in the Canary Islands, off the northwest coast of Africa, for repairs and fresh supplies before setting sail again on September 6. Columbus captained the *Santa Maria*. Two slightly smaller vessels, the *Niña* and the *Pinta*, sailed with the *Santa Maria*. There were about 90 crew members altogether who sailed on the expedition. The crew included a translator, three doctors, a secretary, an accountant, and servants for the ship's captains. The ship's log that Columbus kept during the journey is a valuable and reliable source of information about the voyage. As Columbus himself wrote:

ANALYZE PRIMARY SOURCES **DOCUMENT-BASED QUESTION** Why do you think the log that Columbus kept is still valued by scholars today?

❝ I decided to write down everything that I might do and see and experience on this voyage from day to day, and very carefully. ❞

Columbus kept track of the distance the ships covered, the weather, compass headings, and his impressions of the lands and peoples the explorers encountered. Life on board ship was hard, and the work seemed endless. The sails and ropes needed constant maintenance and repairs. Water that washed into the ship had to be pumped out. Cooking was done on deck with portable wood-burning stoves. There was little variety to the sailors' diet—stews of salted meat or fish, hard biscuits, and watered wine were the main meal. A few officers had bunks, but everyone else slept on deck in good weather or below deck during storms.

Teaching Options

Section 1 Resources

Teacher's Resources (TR)
Terms to Know, p. 29
Review History, p. 63
Build Your Skills, p. 97
Chapter Test, pp. 147–148
Concept Builder, p. 232
Idea Web, p. 321
Transparencies 1, 3

ESL/ELL STRATEGIES

Use Resources Point out to students that the English language contains many synonyms, or words with similar meanings. Ask students to use a thesaurus to find synonyms for the following words that appear on pages 360–362: *encouraged, expedition, establish, voyage,* and *indigenous.*

Finding New Lands

On October 12, the crew spotted land in the group of islands in the Caribbean Sea presently called the West Indies. Columbus thought he had landed in the East Indies, a group of islands near the mainland of east Asia. This mistaken belief is why he called the people who lived on the island Indians. Columbus named the island on which they landed San Salvador. He described the islanders, called the Táino, as gentle and primitive. They were skilled cotton farmers who had a village society and well-developed government. Columbus's crew explored the area, including the northern coast of Hispaniola, home to present-day Haiti and the Dominican Republic.

Columbus took several captured islanders with him back to Spain. A grand reception given by King Ferdinand and Queen Isabella awaited Columbus when he arrived in Spain with some gold trinkets and the few Táino people who had survived the voyage.

Columbus made three more voyages during the next ten years, taking colonists with him to settle the islands. His hope was to establish colonies for Spain. However, Columbus's main goal was to find gold. Columbus forced all male Táinos over the age of 14 to pan for gold.

Impact of Columbus's Voyages

Columbus's search for a new sea route to Asia led to contact between Europe and the Americas. This contact triggered many changes in the cultures of both worlds. Explorers mapped parts of the coastlines of North and South America and claimed and colonized parts of the interiors of both continents. The Europeans were quick to use the abundant natural resources they found in the

VOYAGE RE-ENACTMENT
Spanish authorities constructed a replica fleet of the *Niña*, the *Pinta*, and the *Santa Maria* to mark the five hundredth anniversary of Columbus's first voyage. In 1992, the ships were sailed across the Atlantic in a voyage that traced the explorer's original route.

Columbus showed gold and some Táino people to King Ferdinand and Queen Isabella as proof of the success of his first voyage.

CHAPTER 16 ◆ Europe Expands Overseas **361**

A. The Voyages of Columbus

Purpose-Setting Question What was the purpose of Columbus's first voyage? (to discover a new route to the riches in Asia)

ANALYZE PRIMARY SOURCES

DOCUMENT-BASED QUESTION
The history of Columbus's log is curious. The original, presented to Ferdinand and Isabella when he returned from his first voyage, has disappeared. At the time, however, Columbus was presented with a copy, which was passed down to his heirs. Luckily, the copy survived long enough for Bartolomé de las Casas to use it in his *History of the Indies* before it too was lost.

ANSWER It contains information about navigation techniques, distances traveled, weather conditions, and people met, as well as insights into Columbus's thoughts.

Then & Now

VOYAGE RE-ENACTMENT For the sailors on Columbus's ships in 1492, the trip across the Atlantic Ocean was a dangerous adventure. In 1992, what factors helped make the trip easier? (Sample answer: better weather forecasts and mapping of trouble spots, more durable ships, and high technology navigation and communication tools)

Activity

Start an SQR Chart Work with students to start an SQR chart (TR, p. 322) for conquests in the Americas. Have them survey the section and record what they think the section is about in the first box. Then, in the second box, have them record a question to which they want an answer. Have students complete their charts during the Section Review. (p. 364)

Focus Point out that the illustration on this page offers information about the Royal Court of Barcelona, Spain. Have students identify Ferdinand and Isabella, the Native Americans, and the priests. Ask students how they would role-play this scene. What might the various people say?

Using Technology

Have students research one of Columbus's three other trips. Then, have them use presentation software to retell the story. Instruct students to use main ideas to create a brief summary of the trip. Ask students to prepare one slide for each main idea, with appropriate visuals and sound effects. Finally, have students present their illustrated stories to the class.

Cooperative Learning

Ask groups of students to find out more about the Táino, and report their findings to the class. Suggest that group members assign themselves different topics to research about this indigenous culture, such as political organization, social organization, daily life, language, sports, music, and art. Students then prepare the report together. You may want to suggest that students use *Táino* as a search word when looking for information on the Internet.

Some Land Claims in the Americas, 1502

✔ Map Check

LOCATION Portugal claimed land that bordered which body of water?

Global Connections

SAILING SHIPS
Chinese sailing vessels called junks were the world's most reliable ships during the Song Dynasty in China, which lasted from 960 to 1260.

Americas, creating vast fortunes for many. This wealth helped western European countries dominate much of the world for centuries to come.

The arrival of the Europeans was devastating to the **indigenous**, or native, populations of the Americas. When Columbus first arrived in the Caribbean, more than 40 million Native Americans lived in the Americas. About 80 years later, their numbers had decreased to about 3 to 4 million. While many died from overwork and abuse, illnesses, such as measles, smallpox, and tetanus, killed most of the native population. The illnesses had been brought over from Europe by the crews of the ships. The indigenous populations had no natural defenses against these illnesses.

◆ **What were two flaws of Columbus's plan to sail across the Atlantic Ocean?**

B. Other European Explorers

During the 1400s, the Portuguese and the Spanish were the world's major explorers. In 1494, Portugal and Spain signed the Treaty of Tordesillas. This treaty drew an imaginary line from north to south through the Atlantic Ocean and what is present-day Brazil. Portugal claimed all the lands east of the line and Spain claimed all the lands west of the line. The treaty set the course for future explorations and land claims on the part of both countries.

Cabral Sails for Portugal

In 1500, Pedro Alvarez Cabral, representing Portugal, sailed southwest across the Atlantic Ocean. On April 22, he sighted land, which he called Island of the True Cross. The land Cabral found is present-day Brazil. After claiming the land for Portugal, Cabral sent a ship back to inform the king. This newly claimed possession of Portugal became a stopping-off point for later long voyages from Europe to India. Ships would sail southwest to the Island of the True Cross, and then head southeast to Africa's Cape of Good Hope. From the cape, ships sailed to the Indian Ocean.

America's Namesake

Amerigo Vespucci, an Italian navigator, made at least two voyages to the Americas between 1499 and 1502. During the first Spanish-financed expedition, Vespucci reached the northern coast of South America near what is now Guyana. It is believed that he discovered the mouth of the Amazon River. He then sailed to the island of Trinidad off the coast of present-day Venezuela. Here, he sighted the mouth of the Orinoco River before heading to Haiti.

Vespucci's second expedition was financed by Portugal. Vespucci reached the coast of Brazil and continued southward, possibly as far as Patagonia in present-day Argentina. Vespucci's second voyage was important because he and others were convinced that the newly explored lands were not Asia, but some sort of a "new world." In 1507, a German mapmaker who had read of Vespucci's expeditions called this new land America in Vespucci's honor. Eventually, the name took hold.

Discovery of the Pacific

Vasco Nuñez de Balboa joined a Spanish expedition in 1501. He explored the northern coast of South America, settled on the island of Hispaniola for a time, and led expeditions into Panama. Native peoples told him that gold could be found across the mountains.

In 1513, Balboa followed trails across the Isthmus of Panama. After three weeks of walking, his native guides told him that a great sea could be seen if he climbed a nearby mountain. Instructing his men to stay behind, Balboa climbed the mountain. There, he became the first European to sight what is now called the Pacific Ocean. Soon after, Balboa waded into the ocean, which he called the South Sea, to claim it and all its coastline for Spain. The exploration party found pearls and gold along the coast. This discovery would fuel Spanish exploration and conquest of the western coast of South America.

◆ **How did the Americas come to be named after Amerigo Vespucci?**

C. Around the World

Ferdinand Magellan was a Portuguese navigator and explorer who first sailed for Portugal and later for Spain. When he offered his services to King Charles I of Spain, Magellan proposed to sail west across the Atlantic. He hoped to find a strait—a narrow waterway—through the landmass of the Americas to the Pacific Ocean.

Magellan had a practical reason for his proposal. He wanted to prove that the Spice Islands, or the Molucca Islands in present-day Indonesia, were located west of the line established by the Treaty of Tordesillas. The Spice Islands were then controlled by the Portuguese, and Portugal earned great wealth from the sale of spices. If Magellan's theory was correct, Spain could claim the riches of the Spice Islands that Portugal now claimed. Magellan would benefit by getting a share of the profits and the right to govern any lands he discovered.

Magellan's Journey

Magellan set off from Spain on September 20, 1519, with 5 ships and a crew of about 250 men. Magellan sailed south along the African coast. He crossed the Atlantic at the ocean's narrowest point, instead of taking the usual route west from the Canary Islands. When his fleet came within sight of South America, they headed south, landing at the site of the present-day city of Rio de Janeiro. They made their way down the coastline, exploring each inlet as a possible route to the Pacific Ocean.

On October 21, 1520, the fleet entered the eastern end of a dangerous 350-mile strait, located near the southern tip of South America. It took about a month to navigate a passage through the narrow, twisted strait. The strait, named the Strait of Magellan, was a major sailing route from the Atlantic Ocean to the Pacific Ocean until 1914.

When the fleet emerged on the western end of the strait, they found themselves in a new body of water. Magellan named this body of water the Pacific Ocean because of its relatively calm waters. This body of water is the same one that Balboa had called the South Sea. During the next four months, Magellan and his fleet sailed westward across the Pacific Ocean, hoping to find Asia.

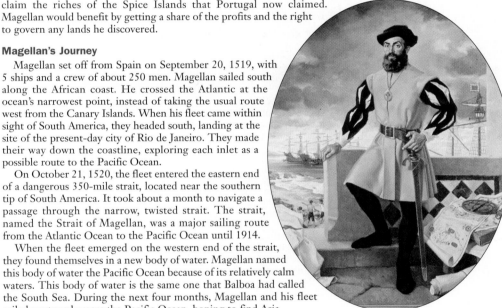

Ferdinand Magellan led the expedition that sailed around the world. Magellan was killed on the trip.

This 1492 globe helped people of that time visualize the placement of the continents they knew about.

After restocking supplies on what is now the island of Guam, the fleet continued toward the Spice Islands. While stopping off in the Philippine Islands, Magellan was killed in a battle with some village chieftains. Now down to two ships, the sailors continued their journey. Later, Portuguese sailors captured one ship. Finally, on September 6, 1522, the *Victoria*, the sole surviving ship, leaking, but filled with spices, returned to Spain, almost three years after starting the voyage.

The Growth of Mercantilism
As part of Magellan's voyage, sailors had for the first time **circumnavigated**, or sailed around, the world. This achievement, which started with the belief of Christopher Columbus that a ship could sail west across the Atlantic to reach Asia, was accomplished when the last ship of Magellan's fleet limped into port.

This new knowledge of the world would be used primarily for material gain. European nations practiced an economic theory called **mercantilism**. Under this system, governments tried to increase national wealth by selling more goods to other countries than they bought from those same countries. A **balance** of **trade**, the difference between a country's imports and exports, was considered favorable if exports were greater than imports. Government policies encouraged an increase of gold and silver, a favorable balance of trade, and establishment of foreign trading monopolies.

Europeans viewed the Americas as new markets for their exports. The colonies they established supplied raw materials for the home countries. Manufacturing, or the production of items, was forbidden in the colonies. All commerce between a colony and its home country was set up so that only the home country would profit. Europeans believed the only way a nation could grow rich was at the expense of another. This view was to have disastrous consequences for the indigenous peoples of the Americas.

◆ **What were the goals of Magellan's voyage?**

Review 1

Review History
A. Why were the indigenous peoples of the Caribbean called Indians?
B. What did Balboa discover when he crossed the Isthmus of Panama?
C. Why was manufacturing forbidden in European colonies?

Define Terms to Know
Define the following terms: **indigenous, circumnavigate, mercantilism, balance of trade**

Critical Thinking
What motives do you think explorers had to sail for countries other than their native country?

Write About Geography
Write a journal entry describing the hardships of being a sailor on Columbus's voyage.

Get Organized
IDEA WEB
Use an idea web to organize information from this section. Choose a topic and find related details. For example, what impact did the voyages of Columbus have on the Americas?

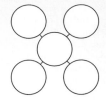

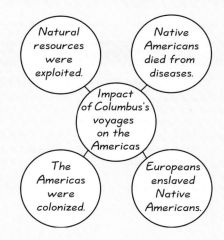

Natural resources were exploited.

Native Americans died from diseases.

Impact of Columbus's voyages on the Americas

The Americas were colonized.

Europeans enslaved Native Americans.

Build Your Skills

FORMULATE AND SUPPORT OPINIONS

As you read about European explorers, you probably found yourself forming opinions about them such as: "Magellan must have been as skillful as he was fearless to cross through the strait that bears his name."

When you study history, you find yourself reading factual passages or looking at historical illustrations that lead you to formulate opinions. Anyone can state an opinion, which is simply a person's viewpoint or position about a topic. The key to formulating an opinion that can be supported is to base it on factual evidence—pieces of information that can be proven to be correct.

For example, when you read about Cabral discovering Brazil, you learned that future expeditions would use Brazil as a stopping-off place for ships sailing around Africa to India. Based on geographical facts, you may have said to yourself, "Even though that route is a roundabout way to get to Asia, it was a workable route at the time."

Here's How
Follow these steps to help you formulate and support your opinions.
1. Read the text and look at any visuals.
2. Look for evidence that supports or disproves a particular opinion or point of view.
3. Look for other details that may not be obvious at first.
4. Formulate an opinion based on the evidence you have gathered.

Here's Why
Being able to formulate and support your own opinions is an important skill because it helps you make informed judgments about the people you read about in history. This skill also helps you to persuade others to support your opinion. Practice in this skill can help you gain an understanding about the time you are studying.

Practice the Skill
Read the passage to the right and look at the visual of a half-hour glass. Then, answer the following questions.
1. How do you think this half-hour glass was used to tell time?
2. How sturdy do you think this half-hour glass was during a storm?

Extend the Skill
Formulate an opinion about the accuracy of the half-hour glass. Support your opinions with at least one fact.

Apply the Skill
Carefully look at the illustrations, paintings, and other visuals in the rest of this chapter. Formulate an opinion for each remaining section. Share your opinions with the class.

"The half-hour glass was an object of vital importance on a ship of the sixteenth century. It recorded the length of a sailor's watch at sea and was a necessary tool to help navigate a ship."

Half-hour glass

Teaching Options

RETEACH
Give pairs of students an index card with one of the following opinions written on it: *Fruits and vegetables are healthy foods. Team sports help you learn to work together. Prices for clothes are high.* On separate slips of paper, have students write at least two facts that support the opinion and two facts that do not. Put the slips into an envelope, and have pairs exchange envelopes. Ask student pairs to find the slips that support the opinion.

CHALLENGE
Give pairs of students a copy of a newspaper editorial. Have them underline one opinion in black and facts that support it in another color. Then, discuss the rationale behind the markings as a class. Discuss any factual support that students may have missed.

Build Your Skills

FORMULATE AND SUPPORT OPINIONS

Teach the Skill
Make copies of a recent local, national, or world news article for students to read. When they finish reading, ask groups of students to formulate opinions based on the article. List these opinions on the board. For example, *The United States is well prepared to fight terrorism.* For each opinion, encourage students to find at least one factual passage or illustration to support the opinion. Explain that when they study history, students need to follow the same process to make informed judgments about people and events. Ask students what challenges they may face when formulating and supporting opinions. (distinguishing facts from opinions, too much information, extraneous information)

Practice the Skill
ANSWERS
1. The weight of the grains of sand caused them to fall through the narrow "waist" of the glass in a steady stream until they were all in the bottom part. It took a half-hour for the top part to empty. Then, the glass would be turned over to count the next half-hour.
2. Not very sturdy at all because a large part of it is made of glass, which breaks easily. It is also unreliable because sand grains clump together in humid or wet weather.

Extend the Skill
Possible answer: The half-hour glass was not very accurate. The glass could be turned over before a half-hour was up if a sailor wanted to end his watch a little early, or not turned when the sand had run out, if it was not watched carefully.

Apply the Skill
You may wish to have students make a two-column chart (TR, p. 328) for each section of this chapter. Students can record the description of each visual in the first column and an opinion based on it in the second column.

Section Summary

In this section, students will learn how the establishment of Spanish colonies in Mexico and Peru affected native peoples and how the government of the colonies affected settlers who lived in them. They will also learn about the establishment of the Portuguese sugar-producing colony in Brazil.

1 Introduce

Getting Started

Ask students how they behave when they go to a new place, such as a new school or a friend's house, for the first time. What strategies do they use to assimilate to or merge with their new environment? What are their goals? (Possible answers: to fit in, to figure out what is acceptable, to stand out) Write student responses on the board. Compare and contrast them to methods that European explorers and settlers used upon arriving in the Americas.

TERMS TO KNOW

Ask students to read the terms and definitions on page 366 and find each term in the section. Remind students to add these terms and other new terms to the glossaries they started in Section 1.

You may wish to preview the pronunciation of the following words with students.

conquistador
(kahn KEES tuh dawr)
Moctezuma (mawk tay SOO mah)
Quetzalcoatl (keht sahl koh AHT ihl)
Tenochtitlán (tay nawch teet LAHN)
Atahualpa (ah tah WAHL pah)

ACTIVE READING

Encourage students to look for facts and opinions as they read this section. Have them use a two-column chart (TR, p. 328) to record the facts and opinions they find. Then, have partners exchange charts and verify that the statements are classified correctly.

Section II — Spanish and Portuguese Colonies

Terms to Know

viceroy a governor of several countries or provinces who rules as the representative of a monarch

encomienda a system in which Spanish colonists were given land and Native Americans to care for, in return for the Native Americans' labor or tribute

cash crop a crop grown mainly to sell, not for personal use

Main Ideas

A. Spain established colonies in Mexico and in Peru.

B. A land grant system gave colonists the right to force labor or tribute from native peoples.

C. Colonial society reflected the blending of Spanish, Native American, and African cultures.

D. Brazil became a profitable sugar-producing colony for Portugal.

Active Reading

FACT AND OPINION Pieces of evidence based on things that can be observed or proven are facts. Views based on facts are formulated opinions. As you read this section, decide whether Spanish missionary Bartolomé de las Casas relied more on facts or opinions to persuade colonizers to stop enslaving Native Americans.

A. Spain's Vast Empire

During the 1500s, Spain acquired the world's largest overseas land holdings as Spanish explorers colonized the Americas. Conquistadors, the Spanish word for "conquerors," heard stories about the immense wealth of great empires that lay beyond the shores of the Caribbean islands. Expeditions made contact with the Maya civilization of present-day Mexico. It was there that the Spaniards learned of the riches of the Aztec Empire and others.

Cortés Invades Mexico

In February 1519, the Spanish conquistador Hernán Cortés set out for the Yucatán coast, in present-day Mexico, with 11 ships, 508 soldiers, 100 sailors, and 16 horses. When he arrived, Cortés formed alliances with local peoples, gathering information about a nearby civilization—the Aztecs.

Over the next several months, Cortés worked his way to the Mexican interior. Along the way, Cortés made connections with various indigenous groups. Cortés used to his advantage the bitter resentment felt by many groups that were forced to pay tribute to the Aztecs. More than 200,000 Native Americans became his allies.

Moctezuma's Fall

Many Aztec people, including their emperor Moctezuma, believed in a legend about a bearded god called Quetzalcoatl, whom they feared and expected would return to rule someday. Moctezuma, thinking Cortés might be the god Quetzalcoatl, tried unsuccessfully to keep Cortés away from the Aztec capital of Tenochtitlán. Cortés, however, entered the city on November 8, 1519, with his men and 1,000 Native American allies. Bernal Díaz, one of Cortés's soldiers, described the city:

> ❝ When we saw the level causeway leading to [Tenochtitlán], we were astounded. . . . Buildings rising from the water, all made of stone, seemed like an enchanted vision. . . . Indeed, some of our soldiers asked whether it was not all a dream. ❞

ANALYZE PRIMARY SOURCES
DOCUMENT-BASED QUESTION What does this quotation reveal about the Aztec Empire?

Teaching Options

Section 2 Resources

Teacher's Resources (TR)

Terms to Know, p. 29
Review History, p. 63
Build Your Skills, p. 97
Chapter Test, pp.147–148
Concept Builder, p. 232
Idea Web, p. 321
Transparencies 1, 4, 5

F Y I

Tenochtitlán

Tenochtitlán was built on an island in a lake where Mexico City lies today. It had palaces, plazas, and pyramids topped with temples. The Great Temple, standing about 130 feet tall, dominated the center of the city. Canals crisscrossed the city, and raised roads linked it to the mainland. Celebrations, religious sacrifices, and other rituals were held to honor the gods. Gold, silver, cocoa, bark paper, and other types of tribute arrived along streets and canals.

When the two leaders met, Moctezuma greeted Cortés with great honor. The two exchanged gifts. Moctezuma gave Cortés gold, jade, and feathers. Cortés pretended to be respectful of Moctezuma, but in fact, he was interested only in the riches of the city and the Aztec Empire. He took Moctezuma captive. The Aztecs fought back and drove the Spaniards out of the city, but Moctezuma was killed during the battle. Cortés attacked the city for almost three months and eventually won. By 1521, the Aztec Empire had fallen and Cortés had extended Spain's territory from the Caribbean Sea to the Pacific Ocean.

Pizarro and the Incas

In 1531, Francisco Pizarro set off with a small expedition of 180 men and 37 horses to the Inca Empire in present-day Peru. The Incan emperor, Atahualpa, agreed to meet with Pizarro.

A priest who was Pizarro's spokesperson urged the Incan people to accept Christianity and agree to be ruled by the king of Spain. When Atahualpa refused, Pizarro attacked and imprisoned the emperor. Atahualpa offered a huge ransom of pure gold for his release, which Pizarro accepted before having the emperor put to death. When Incan armies heard of their leader's death, they retreated. Pizarro took the royal capital of Cuzco without a struggle in 1533.

In a short period, two great civilizations, the Aztecs and the Incas, had fallen. The conquistadors succeeded for several reasons. The Spanish explorers had more effective weapons. They fought on horseback and used cannons, guns, and swords against the spears and bows and arrows of the Native Americans, who fought on foot. The resentment that divided the Aztec Empire worked to the advantage of Cortés, as did the belief that he might be the god Quetzalcoatl. Finally, European diseases killed many Aztecs and Incas during this period.

◆ **What was Cortés's intention when he met the Aztec leader Moctezuma?**

Then & Now

MESOAMERICA
Up to the sixteenth century, two great civilizations, the Maya and the Aztec, controlled a territory now called Mesoamerica. The region included central and southern Mexico, and much of present-day Central America.

The heart of the Aztec Empire was its capital city of Tenochtitlán. Today, Mexico City is built on the ruins of that great capital.

Spanish conquistador Hernán Cortés exchanged gifts with the Aztec ruler, Moctezuma. Cortés later attacked the Aztec city of Tenochtitlán for its gold.

Focus on
⊱ SPORTS & GAMES ⊰

The Ball Game In many pre-Columbian cultures, a ball game similar to soccer was played by teams of men and women. The ball could be hit with the head, arms, hips, and legs. Hands were used only to put the ball into play. Although there were different rules, sizes of teams, and types of courts, this game was important to all cultures.

The game had secular and religious meanings. To the Aztecs, the ball symbolized the cyclical journey of the Sun. Among the Maya, the game served as a re-enactment of war, in which captives were forced to lose the game and were then sacrificed. Have students conduct research and write a report on the rules of the ball game in one pre-Columbian culture.

② Teach

A. Spain's Vast Empire

Purpose-Setting Question Why were Spanish conquistadors able to conquer the great Aztec and the Inca civilizations? (superior weapons, they fought on horseback, a divided Aztec empire, European diseases killed many Aztecs and Incas, belief that Cortés was a god)

ANALYZE PRIMARY SOURCES

DOCUMENT-BASED QUESTION
Until recently, Bernal Díaz's *True History of the Conquest of Mexico* and Cortés's letters to King Charles V of Spain have been the two primary works historians used to judge the conquest of the Aztecs. However, today historians use indigenous accounts, some written as early as 1528. These writings make up a brief history of the conquest as told by the victims who survived the siege—native priests and wise men.

ANSWER The Aztec Empire was a strong civilization capable of building impressive buildings and cities.

Then & Now

MESOAMERICA Today, the ruins of the great Maya cities are tourist attractions. Sites in Mexico include Palenque, Chichén Itzá, and Bonampak. Tourists also visit Tikal in Guatemala and Copán in Honduras. Ask students to locate these sites on a map of Mexico and Central America. Have them brainstorm a list of items they might expect to see at these ruins. (plazas, stone buildings, pyramids with a temple on top, stone figures of gods, raised ceremonial platforms, ball courts)

Activity

Write a dialogue Discuss the action that is taking place in the painting on page 367. Then, assign groups of students the parts of Cortés, Moctezuma, Aztec warriors, Aztec women, and Spanish conquistadors. Have each group work together to write dialogue for a scene based on the painting and perform the scene for the class.

◆ **ANSWER** Cortés intended to make Moctezuma a captive and take the Aztec riches for Spain.

Purpose-Setting Question What was the Columbian Exchange? (It was the exchange of customs, food, and animals between Europe and the Americas that began with Columbus.)

TEACH PRIMARY SOURCES

Have students study the wooden cup and read the caption. Discuss with students what the warrior on the cup might indicate about the Incan society. (Possible answers: Warriors were important; people liked warrior images.)

Discuss Tell students that there was a chain of command in Spain's empire in the Americas. It started with the Spanish monarch and ended with the colonists and Native Americans. Ask students to reread the subsection "Government and the Economy" and describe this chain. (Spanish monarch, Council of the Indies, viceroys, lesser officials, colonists, Native Americans)

Activity

Write a job description Discuss the extensive powers that viceroys had in the Spanish colonies. Then have students write a job description for the position of viceroy. The job description should list the viceroy's powers (collect royal taxes, nominate colonial officials, enforce laws, protect the indigenous population, oversee conversions to Christianity, and grant encomiendas) and the type of skills that they think a viceroy might need.

ANALYZE PRIMARY SOURCES

DOCUMENT-BASED QUESTION

By 1510, Bartolomé de las Casas had become a Spanish missionary in Hispaniola. He was one of the first Europeans to defend the rights of Native Americans who were enslaved by Spaniards. He gained a reputation for being a great protector of indigenous people.

ANSWER The king and queen were probably amazed at the beauty and richness of the items.

The image of a warrior is shown on this wooden Incan cup.

ANALYZE PRIMARY SOURCES

DOCUMENT-BASED QUESTION What impression do you think the gifts Columbus brought made on the king and queen?

B. Governing Spain's Empire

Despite Spain's conquest of native peoples, there was ongoing resistance by Native Americans to the European invaders. In the Yucatán, Maya fought Spanish rule. Incan revolts erupted in Peru after the death of their emperor. Native Americans also fought to preserve their cultures and resisted conversion to Christianity.

Government and the Economy

In 1524, the Spanish monarchy created the Council of the Indies, a lawmaking body for their new possessions. **Viceroys**, representatives of the monarch, were the principal governors of the American colonies, which were divided into provinces. The viceroys were chosen from among Spanish noble families and were required to report to the Council of the Indies in Spain. Viceroys were aided by lesser officials and audiencias, a court that shared responsibilities with the viceroy.

Viceroys had many powers and duties. These allowed them to govern both the many Spanish colonists who came to the Americas as well as the conquered peoples. Viceroys collected royal taxes, nominated colonial officials, enforced laws, protected Native Americans and oversaw their conversion to Christianity, and granted **encomiendas**. An encomienda was a land grant system in which land and the Native Americans who lived on that land were given over to Spanish colonists. These colonists were, in turn, expected to care for the Native Americans and the land on which they worked. In exchange, the Native Americans were expected to serve the colonists through either labor or tribute in gold.

The encomienda system was both an economic and legal system that was intended to protect the native population and enrich the Spanish Empire. In many areas of the Americas, not as much gold was found as expected. As a result, the crops grown in the colonies were an even more important source of wealth. These crops included sugar, rice, tobacco, coffee, and cocoa beans.

In reality, the system became a form of slavery. The native peoples were often abused and overworked, and many died. However, even more devastating to the native population were diseases brought by the Europeans. The natives had no immunity to the diseases and many more died. To replace the lost workers, African slaves were imported.

The Columbian Exchange

As you read earlier in this chapter, Christopher Columbus described his first voyage to the Americas in 1492 to King Ferdinand and Queen Isabella when he returned to Spain. Bartolomé de las Casas described this meeting and the news Columbus brought of this new region:

> ❝[Columbus] set out in the finest clothing he possessed, taking the Indians with him. . . . He also brought green parrots, which were very beautiful and colorful, and also guaycas, which are jeweled masks made from fishbones, inlaid and decorated with pearls and gold. ❞

Ferdinand and Isabella hoped to use the wealth of this new land to their advantage. In addition, Columbus had brought back plants and animals from the Americas that were unknown in Europe. As he prepared for his second voyage, Columbus took European plants and animals to the Americas. This interchange of plants, animals, and cultures is sometimes called the Columbian Exchange.

Teaching Options

Connection to
SCIENCE

European diseases were devastating to Native Americans, who had no immunity to them. Today, few Americans get diseases such as measles or whooping cough because most people are immunized against them by vaccines or serums. Vaccines cause the body to make disease-fighting substances called antibodies. Serums provide immunity by adding antibodies directly to a person's blood.

The Impact of the Columbian Exchange

As part of the Columbian Exchange, new foods and beverages were introduced to Europe from the Americas. Tobacco and cocoa became popular in Europe, and the potato became a staple, or basic, food in northern and central Europe. People in the Americas were also exposed to European foods, animals, and ideas. Cotton was introduced in the Americas. Sugar cane, brought to the West Indies, became the main **cash crop** of that region. A cash crop is one that is grown for sale rather than for use by a farmer. From Europe also came the horse, a new mode of transportation, and cattle, a new protein source.

The exchange also affected the movement of peoples. As cash crops became a profitable source of income, many Europeans migrated to the Americas. They imported enslaved Africans to work their large plantations and mine their precious metals.

The Role of Missionaries

As Spain and the rest of Europe benefited from the new products and ideas obtained through the Columbian Exchange, Spain's Christian missionaries hoped to gain other things from the Americas. These missionaries wanted to convert Native Americans to Christianity as well as establishing Spanish colonies. As a result, the Roman Catholic Church sent missionaries to the Americas. Missionaries traveled widely, establishing churches in which Native Americans were instructed in the Catholic faith and taught a variety of trades.

Bartolomé de las Casas was a Spanish missionary who was granted an encomienda in 1513. Eventually, Las Casas decided that the encomienda system was wrong because it enslaved the Native Americans. In 1514, Las Casas announced he was returning his encomienda and the Native Americans to the governor. After several years, he felt he needed to speak out about the mistreatment of the indigenous people.

Las Casas returned to Spain to ask that the system be reformed. He wrote a book, entitled *The Devastation of the Indies: A Brief Account*, to help convince the king of Spain that the encomienda system needed to be changed.

Finally, in 1542, Las Casas was able to get laws passed that abolished, or put an end to, the encomienda system. Las Casas urged Spain to treat Native Americans justly. He observed that greed seemed to be a motivating factor in the colonists' treatment of Native Americans.

Efforts to enforce these laws were not successful at first. It was difficult for the king to make sure the Native Americans were treated fairly because the Americas were thousands of miles away from Spain. As a result, Native Americans continued to suffer. In addition, many colonists and Roman Catholic Church officials believed that Native Americans were destined to be enslaved and should be converted to Christianity. This attitude lasted for years before the encomienda system lost its effectiveness.

➤ **Who replaced the Native Americans who died from overwork, abuse, and disease?**

The Columbian Exchange

TO AFRICA, ASIA, AND EUROPE	TO THE AMERICAS
corn	olives
tomatoes	turnips
vanilla	bananas
potatoes	coffee beans
beans	peaches
peanuts	pears
cocoa	sugar cane
peppers	honeybees
pineapples	wheat
avocados	rice
sweet potatoes	cotton
turkeys	cattle
squash	sheep
pumpkins	pigs
tobacco	horses
	smallpox
	typhus
	influenza
	African slaves

✔ **Chart Check**

What diseases were introduced to the Americas?

Demonstrate To help students visualize the location and extent of the Columbian Exchange, have them look at Transparency 1 or the map of the world in the Atlas on pages A1–A2 and locate the areas covered. (Africa, Asia, Europe, North America, South America) Tell students that almost every continent on the globe was involved in the Columbian Exchange. Ask which continents were not involved in the exchange. (Australia and Antarctica)

Using the Chart
The Columbian Exchange

Ask students which column on the chart represents items in the Columbian Exchange that came from the Americas (left side) and which came from Africa, Asia, and Europe (right side). Discuss which items students believe were the best and worst items exchanged.

✔ **Chart Check**

Answer smallpox, typhus, and influenza

Discuss Point out that in 1557, the Spaniards founded a mission, or religious settlement, at San Pedro de Atacama, Chile. (See photo on page 370.) It became an administration center for the Spanish missionary movement. Ask students what an administration center was probably used for and why San Pedro was probably selected for this role. You may want students to first locate San Pedro on a map of South America. If you wish to show students the general location, use the map on page A4 of the Atlas or Transparency 4. San Pedro is located in northern Chile near the southern most point of Bolivia. (The church needed a place to coordinate its missionary efforts. San Pedro is located near the largest population center in the area.)

➤ **ANSWER** enslaved Africans

ESL/ELL STRATEGIES

Take notes To help students understand information that is related orally, have them take notes as you or a student volunteer reads aloud a subsection from this chapter. Then, have students work in pairs to compare their notes and help each other with any comprehension problems.

C. Spain's Influence on Colonial Society

Purpose-Setting Question What was the role of cities in the Spanish colonies? (center of government, religious life, culture, and trade)

Discuss Have students study the photograph and then discuss how it represents what a typical Spanish colonial mission looked like. (The mission had a church, other public buildings, and living quarters; all buildings were of a similar design and made of adobe; adobe walls surround the mission.)

Extend Tell students that the mix of cultures in the Spanish colonies created many innovations in music, art, architecture, government, sports, and cuisine. Ask students what the mix of cultures in the United States today has added to American life. (Accept specific innovations in music, art, architecture, government, sports, cuisine, and so on.)

WHERE IN THE WORLD?

IBERIAN PENINSULA Have students use the Atlas (p. A5) or Transparency 5 to locate the Iberian Peninsula. Explain that the Iberian Peninsula was once home to the Iberians, one of the oldest European peoples. They probably came from Africa during prehistoric times. Descendants of Iberians now live in Italy, Spain, and Portugal.

Ask students what geographical and historical connections Spain and Portugal have. (They share the Iberian Peninsula, with Portugal facing the Atlantic Ocean, and Spain, more than five times Portugal's size and to its east, bordering the Atlantic Ocean and the Mediterranean Sea. They share common ancestors. They have fought wars against each other.)

Extend One of the greatest poets on the American continent during the seventeenth century was Sor Juana, who was born in 1651 in a village south of Mexico City. She wrote about secular subjects, but in 1690, Sor Juana criticized a Jesuit priest in a private letter. The letter was published without her permission, and she was attacked by the Roman Catholic Church. Her books, musical instruments, scientific equipment, and personal possessions were confiscated, and she never wrote works for public consumption again. She had strongly advocated women's right to an education.

◆ **ANSWER** Native Americans and Africans

Catholic missions, such as this one in Chile, South America, were used to help convert Native Americans to Christianity. Conversion was an important goal of Spain.

C. Spain's Influence on Colonial Society

With so many conquests and land claims in the Americas, Spain now controlled a vast empire—one that spanned both sides of the Atlantic Ocean. Spain sought to impose its traditions and way of life on the peoples of the Americas by establishing towns and cities throughout its colonies. In addition, Spain sought to blend Spanish culture with the culture of the indigenous populations.

Colonial Cities

Most Spanish settlers in the Americas preferred to live in cities. As a result, cities were established throughout the colonies and grew quickly. To the Spaniards, colonial cities were centers of government, religious life, culture, and trade. Almost all of these Spanish cities had the same design—a central square bordered by a church, a government building, and a house for the viceroy, or governor. Rectangular blocks of houses surrounded the square. The higher a person's social status, the closer that person lived to the main square.

Colonial Culture

Colonial culture was a mixture of Spanish, Native American, and African traditions. Although Spanish culture was dominant in all of Spain's colonies, its mixture with different traditions led to the formation of a unique blended culture in Spanish America. This blended culture was reflected in styles for art and architecture, methods of farming, religion, and even cooking.

As in most societies, different classes provided a framework for colonial social structure. Peninsulares, people born in Spain, held the highest and most powerful positions in both colonial government and the Roman Catholic Church. Creoles, American-born descendants of Peninsulares, occupied the next highest level of society. Mestizos, a mix of Native American and Spanish peoples, and mulattoes, people of African and Spanish descent, were socially above those who had the least power—Native Americans and Africans.

◆ **Which two social groups had the least power in Spanish America?**

Where in the World?

IBERIAN PENINSULA
Spain and Portugal are located on the Iberian Peninsula, which is where the word *Peninsulares* comes from.

Teaching Options

Connection to CULTURE

Creoles in Cuba became landowners, cattle raisers, tobacco and sugar planters, teachers, lawyers, priests, and journalists. Their wealth, however, was appropriated by the Peninsulares. By the late eighteenth century, Creoles demanded an end to economic and political restrictions. They were influenced by the writings of Voltaire, Rousseau, and Paine, as well as by the U.S. Declaration of Independence.

D. The Portuguese Colony of Brazil

As you learned earlier in this chapter, the Treaty of Tordesillas effectively divided the areas of the Americas that Spain could claim as opposed to the areas that Portugal could claim. In South America, Portugal claimed Brazil and issued land grants to Portuguese nobles in the hopes of encouraging settlement in the region.

Portugal's Expansion In Brazil

As more and more Portuguese people were encouraged to move to Brazil to establish permanent cities and farms in the 1500s, the colony slowly but steadily grew. At first, the Portuguese settlers established themselves on Brazil's coastline. There, they traded with Native Americans for brazilwood, which the settlers then exported to Europe. As time passed, however, settlers moved into Brazil's interior to establish farms and plantations, especially plantations that produced sugar cane. Some regions of Brazil developed into major sugar producers, which turned the entire colony into one of Portugal's most profitable. By 1600, some farming regions had twice as many enslaved Africans and Native Americans—most of whom worked as field laborers—as colonists.

Competition from Caribbean sugar plantations forced some colonists to look for new sources of income. Cattlemen looking for new pastures and miners searching for gold ventured farther into Brazil's interior. When gold was discovered at the end of the 1600s, it replaced sugar as Brazil's main export.

Portuguese Society and Culture

As in Spanish America, Portuguese culture in Brazil was a mix of European, Native American, and African traditions. European culture dominated class and race divisions in Brazilian society as it did in Spain's colonies. Here too, the Roman Catholic Church played an important role in providing a shared tradition for all classes of society.

◆ What replaced sugar as Brazil's main export at the end of the 1600s?

Review II

Review History
A. How did Atahualpa's death help Pizarro?
B. Why were laws abolishing the encomienda system hard to enforce?
C. How did the Spaniards impose their culture quickly in their colonies?
D. Why did the new colonies in Brazil look for new sources of income?

Define Terms to Know
Define the following terms:
viceroy, encomienda, cash crop

Critical Thinking
How did the encomienda system contribute to the inequality between the Spanish and the Native American population in the Americas?

Write About Economics
Write a brief explanation of the benefits and problems of the Columbian Exchange.

Get Organized
IDEA WEB
Use an idea web to organize information from this section. Choose a topic and find related details. For example, what were the main parts of Spanish colonial life?

Encomienda system

Social class system

Spanish colonial life

Native peoples convert to Christianity.

Blend of European, African, and native cultures.

Critical Thinking
The system favored the Spanish by giving them legal title to lands in the Americas and by requiring Native Americans to work on these lands or pay tribute.

Write About Economics
Students' explanations should point out benefits, such as new foods, animals, ideas, and cultures. Problems should include the destruction of existing cultures, diseases, and African slavery in the Americas.

D. The Portuguese Colony of Brazil

Purpose-Setting Question How did Brazil become one of Portugal's most important colonies? (Some regions of Brazil developed into major sugar producers making Brazil very profitable for Portugal.)

Focus Review with students the progress of the settlers in Brazil. Ask students how settlers responded to the environment. (traded brazilwood, established farms and plantations, mined for gold)

Activity

Compare and contrast Have students work in pairs and use a two-column chart (TR, p. 328) to compare and contrast Portuguese and Spanish cultures and colonies. Some topics to include are use of land grants, exports, slavery, and culture blending. Have pairs share their findings with the class.

◆ **ANSWER** gold

Section Close
Discuss the Spanish and Portuguese colonies with students and ask students how the colonies changed over time.

3 Assess

Review Answers
Review History
A. Atahualpa's death caused the Incan armies to retreat, allowing Pizarro to take Cuzco without a struggle.
B. Spain was too far from the Americas to enforce laws in the colonies, and many people believed Native Americans were destined to be slaves and converted to Christianity.
C. They built towns and cities and converted Native Americans to Christianity.
D. Competition from sugar cane plantations in the Caribbean forced some colonists to look for new sources of income.

Define Terms to Know
viceroy, 368; encomienda, 368; cash crop, 369

CHAPTER 16 ◆ **T371**

Section Summary

In this section, students will learn how the development of Dutch, French, and English colonies impacted Native American ways of life. They will also learn how the commercial revolution in Europe affected global domination.

1 Introduce

Getting Started

Discuss the meaning of the word *risk*. (the chance of loss or injury) Ask students what experiences they have had that involved risk. (changing schools, competing in sports or academics, making new friends) With students, make a list of ways that people minimize risk. (share the risk with others, vary efforts, plan well) Explain that starting a colony in the Americas was a risk that was not always successful. Discuss the kinds of risks colonists probably faced. (illness, injury, famine, conflicts with Native Americans, and death)

TERMS TO KNOW

Ask students to read the terms and definitions on page 372 and find each term in the section. Remind students to add new terms to the glossaries they started in Section 1.

You may wish to review the pronunciation of the following names with students.

Giovanni da Verrazano
(joh VAHN nee duh
vayr rah SAHN oh)
Jacques Cartier (ZHAHK kahr TYAY)
Samuel de Champlain
(SAM yuhl DUH sham PLAYN)
Robert Cavelier, Sieur de la Salle
(raw BER kaw vuhl YAY
suhr duh luh sal)
Massasoit (mas uh SOYT)
Wampanoag (wahm puh NAWG)

ACTIVE READING

Have students use a three-column chart to list features of the Dutch, French, and English colonies as they read the section. Then, at the end of the section, have them make a three-part Venn diagram (TR, p. 323) to compare and contrast the different colonies.

Terms to Know

capitalism an economic system based on the investment of money in businesses for profit

investor a person who puts money in a company, hoping to make a profit

joint-stock company a group of investors who share both risk and profit

Main Ideas

A. Dutch colonies appeared in the Caribbean, South America, and North America.
B. New France, established by French explorers, attracted fur traders, merchants, and missionaries.
C. England established 13 colonies in North America during the 1600s and 1700s.
D. European colonizers had a huge impact on the Native American way of life.
E. Expanding markets changed the economy of Europe forever.

 Active Reading

COMPARE AND CONTRAST
When you compare and contrast two or more things, you look for similarities and differences. As you read this section, compare and contrast the Dutch, French, and English colonies. How did they differ from Spanish and Portuguese colonies?

A. The Dutch Colonies

Before the 1600s, Spain was the only European country that had established colonies in the Americas. The Netherlands, France, and England had been busy with wars. The situation changed in the early 1600s. These countries wanted land in the Americas as well.

Dutch Interests

In the early 1600s, the Dutch—people who lived in the Netherlands—became Europe's strongest naval power. They held this position until the late 1600s. The Dutch sailed the world's oceans, waging war against Spain and Portugal. What the Dutch especially wanted was to take over Portugal's hold on world commerce. They acquired much of Portugal's eastern trading empire and seized part of Brazil after an invasion beginning in 1624. They established colonies in the Caribbean and on the northern coast of South America.

The Dutch in North America

In 1609, Henry Hudson, an English explorer hired by the Dutch to find a water route through North America to Asia, sailed up a river in present-day New York State. Today this river is known as the Hudson River. Hudson claimed the land around the river for the Netherlands. The Dutch built trading posts in the area. By 1624, the Dutch had established a colony and had named the area New Netherland. The colony's largest settlement, New Amsterdam, was located on Manhattan Island. The Dutch colonists prospered by trading with the Native Americans for furs.

The colony was more interested in profits than in religion. This openness to different religions meant that the colony was tolerant of many religions and attracted people of different faiths and from other countries. The population of New Netherland included Catholics, Protestants, Muslims, and Jews. It was one of the more diverse areas in the Americas. The English captured the colony in 1664 and named it New York in honor of the Duke of York. The Dutch attempt to colonize North America was over.

◆ **Why was New Netherland able to attract a variety of colonists?**

Dutch colonists

Teaching Options

Section 3 Resources

Teacher's Resources (TR)
Terms to Know, p. 29
Review History, p. 63
Build Your Skills, p. 97
Chapter Test, pp.147–148
Concept Builder, p. 232
Idea Web, p. 321
Transparency 3

B. French Settlements in the Americas

France was slow to establish a presence in North America. Early in the sixteenth century, French ships fished for cod off the coast of Newfoundland, Canada. Giovanni da Verrazano explored part of North America's coastline for France in 1524. Ten years later, Jacques Cartier sailed up the St. Lawrence River. However, the French did not attempt to explore or colonize New France, as they called Canada, for the rest of the 1500s.

France's best-known explorer, Samuel de Champlain, went to Canada in 1603. He founded Quebec in 1608, the first permanent French settlement in North America. Champlain also fought the Native Americans of New York, encouraged the fur trade, explored west to Lake Huron in 1615, and brought in missionaries to convert the Native Americans.

Colonizing New France

New France became a province in 1663. French troops arrived two years later to protect settlers against the Iroquois—the Native Americans of that region. The Iroquois had no interest in sharing their lands with the settlers of New France. As a result, relations were openly unfriendly. Missionaries worked their way west, hoping to convert Native Americans to Christianity. However, most Native Americans rejected the missionaries' efforts.

Adventurers continued their travels across North America throughout the seventeenth century. Fur traders had already pushed westward to Lake Superior. Robert Cavelier, known as Sieur de la Salle, headed south. He sailed from the Great Lakes down the Mississippi River to the Gulf of Mexico. In 1682, La Salle claimed the entire river basin for France. La Salle called the territory Louisiana after King Louis XIV of France.

The French government had trouble attracting colonists to New France. The long winters and attacks by the Native Americans in the area discouraged many farmers. Many of the settlers were Roman Catholic priests who wanted to convert the Native Americans. Others were young, single men who constantly moved farther west to become fur trappers, a much more profitable occupation than farming.

French West Indies

French settlements in the Caribbean began in 1625. Four decades later, France possessed 14 Caribbean islands. Guadeloupe and Martinique were its main holdings. Haiti was added later. Slaves were imported from Africa as early as 1642 to work the large plantations, where sugar was the main crop.

The French society was similar to Spanish and Portuguese society. White people occupied top positions of power and owned the largest plantations as well. They were followed by merchants, buccaneers (pirates), and small farmers. Hired workers from France and enslaved Africans occupied the lowest positions in West Indian society.

◆ **Why did the French have trouble attracting colonists to New France?**

Robert Cavelier, known as Sieur de la Salle, sailed down the Mississippi River and claimed the entire river basin for France.

A. The Dutch Colonies

Purpose-Setting Question What was the Netherlands' main goal in colonizing in the Americas? (It wanted to take over Portugal's hold on world commerce.)

Extend Have students study the map of North America on Transparency 3 or in the Atlas on page A3, to find the body of water that Henry Hudson discovered, which was subsequently named for him. Ask students to describe its location. (Hudson Bay; above present-day Ontario, Canada.)

◆ **ANSWER** The colony was more interested in profits than religion, which meant that people of different faiths could live there and were tolerated.

B. French Settlements in the Americas

Purpose-Setting Question Where were the French land claims in the Americas located? (Newfoundland; St. Lawrence River; Quebec; Great Lakes region; Mississippi River valley; Caribbean islands)

Activity

Make a chart Have students use a two-column chart (TR, p. 328) to compare and contrast the social structure, from highest to lowest, of French settlements in the West Indies with Spanish settlements in Spanish America. (page 370) (**French:** white people, merchants, buccaneers, small farmers, French contract laborers, enslaved Africans; **Spanish:** Peninsulares, Creoles, mestizos, mulattoes, Native Americans, enslaved Africans)

Focus Point out that this painting shows La Salle claiming the Mississippi River valley for France. Historians tell us he erected a cross and a column bearing the French coat of arms. Ask them to identify La Salle (in the center) and the others in the painting. (Native Americans, French Jesuit priests, French explorers)

◆ **ANSWER** long winters, Native American attacks, more interest in fur trapping than farming

---

Research

AVERAGE

Have students find at least five additional facts about one of the explorers discussed in this chapter: Henry Hudson, Giovanni da Verrazano, Jacques Cartier, Samuel de Champlain, Robert Cavelier (Sieur de la Salle), and John Cabot. Suggest that students find facts relating to the explorer's youth, education, training, or major accomplishments.

CHALLENGE

Have students learn more about an explorer in this chapter. Ask them to find out how the explorer's background and experiences led him to become an explorer, what the risks were, how the explorer obtained patronage, and how the explorer led and organized the expedition. Have students explain this to the class.

C. The English in North America

Purpose-Setting Question What did all thirteen English colonies have in common? (agriculture and shipping)

Then & Now

JAMESTOWN
England's first permanent colony in North America was originally located on a peninsula. By the mid-nineteenth century, it had become an island. Archaeological excavations of Jamestown began in 1934. Many artifacts and traces of the original fort have been found.

The island is now part of the Colonial National Historical Park and features seventeenth-century colonial replicas. Artifacts continue to be unearthed to this day.

The signing of the Mayflower Compact proclaimed the right of the Pilgrims to make and enforce their own laws.

C. The English in North America

John Cabot claimed much of the North Atlantic coast for England in 1497. While the English were interested in finding a way to Asia, they were occupied with the Spaniards. In 1588, a large fleet of Spanish ships, called the Spanish Armada, tried to invade England. With help from a storm, the English fleet defeated the Spaniards. This defeat made it possible for the English to colonize North America.

The English had many reasons for colonizing North America. People came to get rich, to find a new trade route to Asia, to slow the spread of the Spanish colonies, and to have religious freedom and better economic opportunities.

Early English Colonies

Founded in 1607, Jamestown, Virginia, was the site of the first successful English colony in North America. England's King James I issued a charter, or official document, to the Virginia Company allowing it to send settlers to the Atlantic coast of North America.

Jamestown, which was named after King James, faced problems from the beginning. Many settlers died from disease because the settlement was in a swampy, mosquito-infested area. In addition, in the early years, many settlers were more interested in searching for gold than in farming. Eventually, the colony started growing tobacco, established a representative government, and brought the first enslaved Africans to the English colonies.

Plymouth Colony was the first English settlement in New England. Founded in 1620, the colony was home to a group of people, called Pilgrims, who sought economic opportunity and religious freedom. One of the organizers of the expedition was William Bradford. Bradford helped write the historic Mayflower Compact, an agreement of cooperation that was to become the foundation of Plymouth government.

Bradford kept a journal that detailed the experiences of the settlers. As a result, we know that many Pilgrims died in the first few years. Eventually, the colonists learned how to survive from local Native Americans.

Thirteen Colonies

Thirteen English colonies were established in North America during the 1600s and 1700s. All thirteen colonies were agricultural, but geographic conditions fostered different ways of life.

In the New England colonies, those farthest north, farming was difficult due to poor soil and harsh winters. In the Middle Atlantic colonies, those in the middle of the eastern coastal region, farms were larger and more diversified because of a milder climate and more fertile soil. In the Southern colonies, those farthest south, there were many large landowners who used the labor of enslaved Africans to grow tobacco, rice, and indigo on large plantations. Many of these crops were later exported to other colonies, or even to Europe.

Teaching Options

Conflict Resolution

Point out that William Bradford and the Pilgrims signed the Mayflower Compact to ensure cooperation in the new colony. This document spelled out the rules for living together in a community. Have students discuss the advantages and disadvantages of signing such a contract. Then, ask students what they would do to ensure cooperation within a new community.

F Y I

John Cabot

The Italian navigator John Cabot (Giovanni Caboto) made his first trip to the Americas only five years after Columbus had. After being refused ships by Portugal and Spain, he was given a ship to sail by England. Like Columbus, he believed he had reached Asia (or the East Indies). Cabot never returned to England after his second voyage. Most historians believe he was lost at sea.

Colonial shipping encouraged the growth of towns and cities along the Atlantic seaboard. By 1763, there were several cities, including Boston, New York City, Philadelphia, Baltimore, and Charleston, along the coast and inland waterways.

◆ **What event happened in 1588 that opened the way for English colonization in North America?**

D. Native Americans

Colonial expansion in North America by the Dutch, French, and English had a devastating effect on the indigenous population. Like Native Americans of the West Indies and South America, many died from European diseases, such as smallpox, even before the colonists arrived. Epidemics had swept through the area after the earliest explorers arrived.

Sharing Land

European nations followed different policies toward native North Americans, according to each country's aims. The main interest of the Dutch was to establish trade markets and networks. They were very tolerant of others, and they did not have a strong interest in converting Native Americans to their religion—Protestantism. After its defeat at New Netherland in 1664, the Dutch colony became English.

France was mostly interested in establishing a profitable fur trade with the Native Americans. The number of French settlers was fairly small, and many French colonists traveled either as fur traders or missionaries.

It was the English colonists who would have the biggest impact on Native Americans. English settlers who colonized Plymouth lived in peace with local Native Americans for many decades. Massasoit, chief of the Wampanoags, saw the value of trading with the newcomers. His people helped the early settlers survive by teaching them planting, fishing, and cooking techniques, which were essential to the Pilgrims' survival. Problems began as more English settlers arrived.

King Philip's War

As more colonists arrived, the demand for land grew. The colonies spread west, taking more and more land from Native Americans. As a result, more conflicts arose between the groups. Native Americans were concerned about losing their freedom and way of life.

When Massasoit died, his son Metacomet, known as King Philip, became chief of the Wampanoags. Metacomet wanted to stop the colonists from expanding into new areas. In 1675, Native Americans raided frontier settlements along the Connecticut River and in the Massachusetts Colony. The colonists fought back, attacking Native American villages. During the conflict, many colonial settlements were destroyed, and entire Native American groups were wiped out. By the spring of 1676, Native American resistance collapsed. This conflict is called King Philip's War.

◆ **Which European colonists had the biggest impact on Native Americans?**

CHAPTER 16 ◆ Europe Expands Overseas **375**

Land Claims in North America, ca. 1700

0 500 1,000 mi
0 500 1,000 km

Newfoundland
St. Lawrence River
New France
Nova Scotia
Boston
New York City
Baltimore
Philadelphia
Louisiana
Mississippi River
Charleston
30°N
PACIFIC OCEAN
ATLANTIC OCEAN
Florida
Gulf of Mexico
Bahamas
West Indies
Caribbean Sea
120°W
90°W

- English territory
- French territory
- Spanish territory
- Cities

✔ **Map Check**

LOCATION What geographical characteristic is shared by all of the cities located in English territory?

◆ **ANSWER** The English fleet defeated the Spanish Armada.

D. Native Americans

Purpose-Setting Question What factors determined the way different European nations treated Native Americans? (each country's aims: The Dutch and French had commercial aims that did not conflict with Native American aims, The English demand for land conflicted with Native American interests.)

Using the Map

Land Claims in North America, ca. 1700

Ask students to use the map key to identify English, French, and Spanish territories in North America. (**English:** parts of Canada, including Newfoundland and Nova Scotia; colonies along the Atlantic coast; **French:** Louisiana Territory extending into eastern Canada and north along the St. Lawrence River; **Spanish:** almost the entire western part of North America, Florida, and islands in the Caribbean Sea) Have students refer back to the map on page 362 to compare Spanish claims in North America in 1502 to those in 1700. (Spanish claims were greater in 1700 and farther north.)

✔ Map Check

Answer They border the Atlantic Ocean.

Extend The Wampanoag group saw the value of trading with the English settlers at Plymouth. Discuss what the Wampanoags hoped to gain. (trade) What did the colonists hope to gain? (survival techniques: planting, fishing, and cooking)

◆ **ANSWER** the English

ESL/ELL STRATEGIES

Identify Essential Vocabulary Point out that many words in English are compounds, made up of two words. By discovering the meaning of each word within a compound word, students can often figure out its meaning. Have students work with partners to discover the meanings of the following compound words found on this page: *inland, waterways, smallpox,* and *newcomers.*

E. The Commercial Revolution

Purpose-Setting Question Why did European investors take a chance on risky overseas investments? (They heard tales of great wealth.)

TEACH PRIMARY SOURCES

Explain that the coins shown on this page are Spanish silver coins from the year 1622. Have students describe the coins' shape (round but irregular), and how they probably were made. (hand hammered and stamped) Ask students to suggest how the coins were found. (They were salvaged from a shipwreck.)

◆ **ANSWER** Overseas trade and the expansion of European empires in the Americas led to the growth of capitalism, the investment of money in companies and business enterprises in the Americas. Expanding markets changed Europe's economy. Capitalism flourished.

Section Close

Ask students how Dutch, French, and English explorers contributed to the opening of trade between Europe and North America.

Review Answers

Review History

A. Hudson claimed the land around the Hudson River.

B. He founded Quebec, the first permanent French settlement; he fought the Iroquois; and he encouraged fur trading.

C. Geographic conditions affected the types of farms and crops the colonists could establish, from small farms in New England to larger, more varied farms in the milder climate of the Middle Atlantic, to the large plantations of the Southern colonies.

D. to establish trade markets and networks

E. Increased amounts of gold and silver from the Americas and Spain in Europe caused prices to rise.

Define Terms to Know

capitalism, 376; investor, 376; joint-stock company, 376

E. The Commercial Revolution

Even before the exploration of the Americas, European trade and industry as well as banking began to increase. These changes came to be known as the commercial revolution. European discoveries in the Americas helped to stimulate this revolution. Gold and silver from the new American colonies replaced the barter exchange and helped to form a money-based economy.

Rising Prices

As you read earlier in this chapter, gold and silver that came from the Americas to Spain caused prices of Spanish goods to increase. Higher prices led Spaniards to buy cheaper goods from other countries. The silver and gold left Spain when Spaniards purchased these cheaper foreign goods. Spanish wars caused even more money to leave Spain. As increased amounts of Spanish gold and silver arrived in other countries, prices for goods rose quickly in those countries as well. In England, for example, prices increased 250 percent during this period. As you learned in Chapter 6, this sharp increase in the price of goods is called inflation.

Overseas Investments

Overseas trade as well as the expansion of European empires in the Americas led to the growth of __capitalism__, the investment of money for profit. People who invest, or put money into a business in the hope that the business will earn a profit, are called __investors__. Many European investors heard tales of great wealth in the Americas. As a result, they eagerly invested their money in overseas companies and business enterprises.

Almost all overseas investments were considered risky and could not guarantee a profit to the investor. However, one type of investment that slightly reduced the risk of losing money was called a __joint-stock__ __company__. In a joint-stock company the costs and profits are shared by many investors, thus reducing the risks. As more Europeans invested in the Americas, capitalism flourished. Expanding markets changed the economy of Europe forever.

◆ **How did the American colonies change the European economy?**

These gold and silver coins are symbols of the economic growth stimulated by European exploration in the Americas.

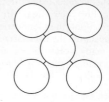

Review III

Review History

A. Which lands did Henry Hudson claim for the Dutch?

B. What were some accomplishments of French explorer Samuel de Champlain?

C. How did geographic conditions affect the way of life in the English colonies?

D. What was the main interest of the Dutch colonists in North America?

E. What caused prices to rise in Europe after colonies were started in the Americas?

Define Terms to Know

Define the following terms: **capitalism, investor, joint-stock company**

Critical Thinking

Why would English settlers have the biggest impact of all the European colonists on Native Americans?

Write About Culture

Describe the development of the 13 English colonies in North America.

Get Organized

IDEA WEB

Use an idea web to organize information from this section. Choose a topic and find related details. For example, what were the different goals of English settlers in North America?

Critical Thinking

Possible answer: Their large numbers and desire for land caused Native Americans to lose their lands and their way of life.

Write About Culture

Students' paragraphs should include the difficulty in initially establishing settlements in the Americas and the valuable assistance settlers received from Native Americans. They should also mention the regional agriculture and businesses, such as shipping, that developed.

Have religious freedom

Gain economic opportunities

Goals of English settlers

Find a trade route to Asia

Support a cash economy in Europe

Africa and the Atlantic Slave Trade

Terms to Know

triangular trade a trading system involving a three-way exchange of goods and people among Europe, Africa, and the Americas

Middle Passage the second leg of the triangular trade route in which slaves were shipped across the Atlantic

Main Ideas

A. Portuguese sailors traded with Africans for gold and eventually for slaves.

B. A labor shortage in the Spanish colonies led to an increased demand for African slaves.

C. Enslaved Africans were forced to endure horrible conditions on the journey to the Americas.

 Active Reading

CAUSE AND EFFECT
Cause and effect helps you to determine what happened and why. As you read this section, ask yourself what influenced the growth of the slave trade to the Americas and what effect the forced enslavement had on African society in the Americas.

A. European Exploration in Africa

While slavery had been practiced for centuries in many regions of the world, it reached new levels in Africa, especially along the western Gold Coast region, by the 1500s. This increase was due primarily to the European exploration of the African continent, which began in the 1400s.

Slavery in Africa

Do You Remember?
In Chapter 15, you learned that Africans were shipped to Portugal to work as slaves in 1441.

Slavery existed in Africa as early as 1000—during the development of the early West African kingdoms. Until the 1400s, many African societies considered slavery a form of punishment for criminals and prisoners of war. These prisoners of war were thought of as a part of the local communities. They were treated more like servants than property, and some slaves were able to regain their freedom after serving a specific term of service. In addition, slavery was not hereditary. The children of slaves were not automatically born into slavery, but were considered free. However, this form of slavery changed after Europeans began to arrive in West Africa in the early fifteenth century.

Elmina Castle, along the Gold Coast of Africa, was a place where enslaved people were commonly traded.

Teaching Options

Section 4 Resources

Teacher's Resources (TR)
Terms to Know, p. 29
Review History, p. 63
Build Your Skills, p. 97
Chapter Test, pp. 147–148
Concept Builder, p. 232
Idea Web, p. 321
Transparency 1

IV. Africa and the Atlantic Slave Trade
(pp. 377–381)

Section Summary

In this section, students will learn how European exploration of Africa encouraged the use of slave labor and eventually led to the Atlantic slave trade. They will also learn about triangular trade and its impact on enslaved Africans in the Americas as well as on West African culture and population.

① Introduce

Getting Started

Point out that slavery has existed among different civilizations for thousands of years. Refer students to Chapter 2, "Ancient Civilizations," and review which civilizations used slaves and how they were treated. Ask students to name some ways that slaves have been treated more as property than as people. (were bought and sold; used to accomplish hard work; kept locked up; replaced as needed)

TERMS TO KNOW
Ask students to read the terms and definitions on page 377 and find each term in the section. Point out that the term *triangular trade* begins with the prefix *tri-*, which means "three." Ask students to explain the meanings of these terms with *tri-*: *tricycle, triangle,* and *tricolor.* Remind students to add new terms to the glossaries they started in Section 1. Encourage pairs of students to test each other on all glossary terms.

You may wish to preview the pronunciation of the following name with students.

Olaudah Equiano
(oh LAU duh ehk wee AHN oh)

ACTIVE READING
As students read this section, have them list events that they encounter and their causes and effects. For example, the growth of the slave trade in the Americas was caused by labor shortages in the colonies. Students may wish to use a cause-and-effect chain (TR, page 325).

A. European Exploration in Africa

Purpose-Setting Question From whom did Europeans buy African slaves when the slave trade first began in the 1440s? (African rulers)

Discuss Talk with students about the difference between the African view of slavery, in which slavery was punishment for criminals and prisoners of war, and the European view of slavery, in which people were treated as property. Ask students to identify what happened to children of African slaves and European slaves. (Children of African slaves were born free, and children of European slaves were born slaves.)

◆ **ANSWER** They were looking for a sea route to India and Asia.

B. The Atlantic Slave Trade

Purpose-Setting Question Which European nations were involved in the Atlantic slave trade? (Portugal, the Netherlands, England, Spain, and France)

Activity

Make a chart Have students use the problem/solution chart (TR, p. 327) to record problems that Europeans faced in developing trade with the Americas. (Sample answers: **Problem:** There was a labor shortage in the Spanish colonies. **Solution:** The Atlantic slave trade began. **Problem:** European diseases devastated the native population in the Caribbean. **Solution:** The Portuguese supplied Spanish colonies and their own colony in Brazil with slaves. **Problem:** England and France established colonies in the Caribbean and needed cheap labor. **Solution:** The Dutch West India Company supplied slaves.)

Review Remind students that they already learned about the rise of the Dutch as a commercial and naval power. Have students reread page 372. Then, discuss how Dutch power was weakened by 1713. (wars with France and England) Ask how long the Dutch were powerful. (They rose to power in the early 1600s and declined by 1713; about 110 years)

Enslaved Africans worked as field laborers on Caribbean sugar plantations.

Unlike the Africans, Europeans considered slaves as possessions to buy and sell for profit or to work as field hands or other kinds of laborers.

The Portuguese in Africa

In the 1400s, Portuguese sailors began exploring the western coast of Africa looking for a route to India and the rest of Asia. The Portuguese were mainly interested in trading for gold. They built forts along the coast to use as trading posts and to repair and restock their ships. This area of western Africa became known as the Gold Coast.

It is believed that African slaves were sold to Portuguese sailors as early as the 1440s. These slaves were sold to the Portuguese by African rulers. After establishing colonies on the Cape Verde Islands off the coast of Africa, the Portuguese imported many more enslaved Africans to work on the sugar plantations. Slaves were sent to the Canary Islands, and later, Brazil. The enslaved Africans were not well treated by the Portuguese. The slaves were forced to work long hours under harsh conditions in the fields.

◆ **Why did the Portuguese sailors explore the western coast of Africa?**

B. The Atlantic Slave Trade

The Atlantic slave trade began as a way to address the labor shortage in the Spanish colonies. Slavery had almost died out in medieval Europe. However, the Portuguese revived it in the fifteenth century. By the end of the 1500s, about 275,000 African slaves had been shipped across the Atlantic Ocean. A profitable business developed involving millions of Africans who were sent across the Atlantic to work on tobacco and sugar plantations. From 1701 to 1810, it is estimated that more than 6 million Africans were sent to the Americas.

Plantation Laborers

African slave labor attracted the attention first of Spain and then of other European nations. These countries saw that the Portuguese used enslaved people to work their plantations off the African coast. By the 1520s, small numbers of slaves had been sent from Africa to the Caribbean.

Sugar was the most important crop grown on Caribbean plantations. Plantation agriculture required large supplies of cheap labor to be profitable. European diseases had a devastating impact on the native populations who had been working the fields to harvest the sugar crop. As a result, plantation owners needed a new source of labor. This source came from Africa.

Another reason why Spain turned to African slaves was due to the concerns of Bartolomé de las Casas. As a defender of Native Americans, he suggested that Africans replace indigenous laborers. He argued that Africans were more likely to fight European disease than the native Caribbean population. As a result, the use of Africans as slaves began to increase in the Caribbean.

Competing for Trade

In addition to using enslaved Africans in the Caribbean, the Portuguese supplied enslaved workers to Spanish colonists and to their own colony in Brazil. Then, in 1598, the Dutch established their first trading posts on the western coast of Africa. African coastal traders welcomed them, eager to break the Portuguese monopoly. By 1640, the Dutch were the main supplier of enslaved Africans to the Spanish plantations in the Caribbean.

England and France began to establish colonies on the smaller Caribbean islands. Like Spain, they wanted a cheap source of labor for their plantations.

Teaching Options

ESL/ELL STRATEGIES

Identify Essential Vocabulary Discuss with students the meaning of the word *profitable,* found under the "Plantation Laborers" heading. (capable of making a profit, gain, or benefit) Ask students to find or explain the meaning of the suffix *-able.* (capable of being) Have students identify five other words that use this suffix. Then, have students explain to other students the meanings of these terms.

Connection to CULTURE

West African Art Have students use the Internet or library resources to learn about Benin artists who were known for wood and ivory carving and bronze casting. Few people outside of Africa knew about this West African art until the early 1900s, when it became a major influence on Pablo Picasso, George Braque, and Henry Moore.

The Netherlands and the organization it created, the Dutch West India Company, expanded their trade to include the English and French colonies. Eventually, the Dutch took possession of all the Portuguese forts along the western coast of Africa, ending Portugal's trading activities.

France and England, which had colonies in the Americas, were resentful of the Dutch economic stronghold in Africa. Their governments encouraged merchants to form trading companies to compete with the Dutch. The French and English governments supported their newly formed trading companies with naval power. A series of wars between the three countries broke out, as the traders of each nation fought over control of the trading posts along the West African coast.

By 1713, Dutch power had weakened as a result of these wars. England and France continued to compete with each other for dominance. Throughout the 1700s, the Dutch continued to lose trade to the English, who were now the primary naval power in western Europe.

The Demand for Slaves Increases

The demand for African slaves led to more commercial activity along Africa's Gold Coast. By the late 1600s, a well-developed network for buying and selling slaves existed in Africa's inland regions as well as on its western Gold Coast. In the 1620s, about 10,000 slaves reached the Americas each year. By the end of the 1600s, it is estimated that about 1.5 million slaves had been brought to the Americas. Toward the end of the seventeenth century, that number had more than tripled.

Information about the slave trade comes from a variety of sources, including primary sources such as firsthand accounts and records. Olaudah Equiano, an African who was sold into slavery in the 1700s, later wrote about his experiences in Africa and the Americas.

◆ Why did the Atlantic slave trade begin?

They Made History

Olaudah Equiano ca. 1750–1797

Olaudah Equiano, a West African, was sold into slavery when he was 12 and was taken to the West Indies. Equiano's life was luckier than many. He was given a little education and traveled with his master. Eventually, he became a free man.

Equiano moved to England where he worked to prohibit slavery. He traveled and lectured on the cruel treatment of Jamaican slaves at the hands of their English owners. In 1787, Equiano was an aide aboard the *Vernon,* a ship carrying about 600 freed slaves who would establish a settlement in Freetown, Sierra Leone, along the western coast of Africa.

Equiano is best known for his autobiography, written in 1789 and titled *The Interesting Narrative of the Life of Olaudah Equiano, or Gustavus Vassa, the African.* The book details Equiano's life in Africa before he was captured and presents arguments against slavery.

The British Museum

A former slave, Olaudah Equiano became a published writer and critic of slavery.

Critical Thinking Why do you think Olaudah Equiano was such an effective speaker against slavery?

C. Triangular Trade Routes

Purpose-Setting Question What three continents were involved in triangular trade? (Europe, Africa, and North America)

Using the Map

Triangular Trade Routes, 1700s

Point out that the colored arrows on the map show the routes among the three continents involved in triangular trade. Ask students to identify each trade route. (**raspberry:** goods from Europe; **orange:** goods from the thirteen colonies; **green:** goods from Africa; **purple:** goods from the West Indies) and to identify products that were exported from each area. (**Europe:** manufactured goods went to Africa and the thirteen colonies; **Africa:** enslaved Africans and gold went to the West Indies; **West Indies:** molasses and cotton went to Europe; enslaved Africans, molasses, and sugar went to the thirteen colonies; **Thirteen Colonies:** rum, tobacco, cotton went to Europe; rum went to Africa.)

✔ Map Check

Answers
1. Goree and Elmina
2. rum, tobacco, and cotton

Explore Point out that the map on this page shows only a few of the triangular trade routes in the 1700s. Ask students to research other routes and report to the class.

Discuss The Middle Passage that carried enslaved Africans to America is documented as a journey so terrible that it seems incomprehensible to us today. If Africans tried to rebel, they were severely beaten and sometimes thrown overboard. Despite this possibility, there were more than 250 documented slave revolts at sea. Ask students what these revolts tell us about the enslaved Africans. (determined to be free at any cost; extremely brave, fearless)

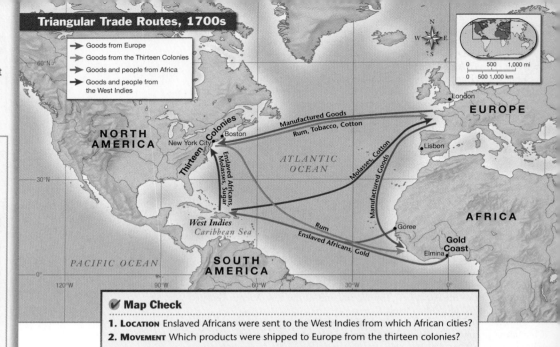

Triangular Trade Routes, 1700s

- Goods from Europe
- Goods from the Thirteen Colonies
- Goods and people from Africa
- Goods and people from the West Indies

✔ Map Check

1. **LOCATION** Enslaved Africans were sent to the West Indies from which African cities?
2. **MOVEMENT** Which products were shipped to Europe from the thirteen colonies?

C. Triangular Trade Routes

The slave trade from West Africa was one part of a system known as **triangular trade**. This system of transatlantic trade formed a three-way exchange of goods and people among Europe, Africa, and the Americas.

There were several different triangular trade routes connecting the Americas to Europe and Africa. One route started in England, went to Africa and then went on to the West Indies and other parts of North America. This route, shown on the map above, involved trading goods for enslaved Africans.

On the first leg of this triangle, European ships carried manufactured goods such as guns and cotton cloth to Africa's west coast in exchange for slaves and gold. The **Middle Passage** was the next part of the route. On it, slaves and gold were moved from Africa to the West Indies and later to the English colonies in North America. The last leg of this route included carrying rum, tobacco, and cotton from the plantations of the Americas to Europe. Other trade routes differed slightly; however, they all formed a triangular pattern in their routes.

The Middle Passage

The estimates for the number of slaves arriving in the Americas do not account for the number of slaves who left Africa. As many as 15 to 20 percent may have died from disease, harsh treatment, or disasters at sea on the voyage across the Atlantic Ocean.

The Middle Passage in which hundreds of enslaved men, women, and children were packed onto one ship in a single voyage, was devastating to the Africans who were forced to make the journey. Leg irons and handcuffs joined pairs of slaves together before they were sent below deck. The space below deck was so

Teaching Options

Meet Individual Needs:

VISUAL LEARNERS

To help students understand the desperate conditions under which enslaved Africans made the trip from West Africa to the Americas, have them view the film *Amistad*. This movie chronicles the trip and attempts by Africans to escape their fate. Discuss how the film enhanced students' understanding of the Atlantic crossing that was known as the Middle Passage.

cramped that people often could not sit up and were forced to lay on their sides. They were only allowed above deck to eat and exercise once or twice a day. One enslaved African, Olaudah Equiano described the conditions below deck:

> 66 The closeness of the place, and the heat of the climate, added to the number in the ship, which was so crowded that each had scarcely room to turn himself, almost suffocated us. 99

Great suffering was inflicted on those who endured the filthy conditions below deck. Many enslaved people tried to resist. Some tried to jump overboard. If they were caught, they were beaten for attempting to escape. After enduring the voyage, Africans faced a life of hard work and abuse. The slave trade continued for about 400 years.

Some African leaders resisted the slave trade, but in the end, their efforts were unsuccessful. Traders offered good prices for slaves, and many local people were tempted by quick profits and European goods.

Impact of the Slave Trade on Western Africa

Population statistics for western Africa can only be estimated during the period from the 1400s to the 1800s. The total population for this part of Africa may have been around 25 million. During peak years in the 1700s, about 78,000 Africans a year were shipped to the Americas. This loss of people slowed population growth in the region.

Plantation owners in the Americas were primarily interested in strong, healthy males as slaves because of the hard work required of them. This loss of so many men may have changed parts of African cultures forever. Some groups disappeared completely and parts of some cultures were lost. As great as the loss was, the population of Africa continued to grow. New African states appeared that were dependent on the slave trade and European products. Rulers waged war for more slaves and territory.

◆ What was the system known as triangular trade?

Review IV

Review History
A. How did West Africa come to be known as the Gold Coast?
B. Which two countries fought with the Netherlands for control of trade along the West African coast?
C. What were the conditions on the Middle Passage?

Define Terms to Know
Define the following terms:
triangular trade, Middle Passage

Critical Thinking
How might the loss of so many young people in West Africa affect the villages in which they lived?

Write About Culture
Write a brief essay that describes how the Atlantic slave trade benefited the Portuguese colonies in the Americas.

Get Organized
IDEA WEB
Use an idea web to organize information from this section. Choose a topic and find related details. For example, which geographic locations were part of the triangular trade route?

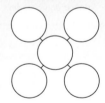

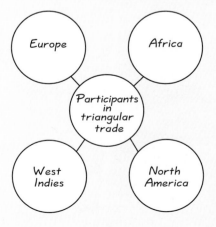

Critical Thinking
Possible answer: The loss of young people would mean that fewer children would be born to continue their way of life in the villages. Some villages could die out.

Write About Culture
Students' essays should explain that the African slave trade was profitable for the Portuguese and provided workers for the plantations in Brazil. The successful plantations helped to make Brazil Portugal's most important colony.

ANALYZE PRIMARY SOURCES

DOCUMENT-BASED QUESTION

This quotation was taken from Equiano's famous autobiography, *The Interesting Narrative of the Life of Olaudah Equiano,* published in 1780. Equiano wrote it as a free man in England, where he lived most of his life. The autobiography became a bestseller all over Europe and made Equiano a rich man. His book helped to advance the antislavery movement.

ANSWER The description suggests that many people did not survive the trip and those who did were not in good physical condition.

Discuss Some historians believe that the loss of so many Africans during the 1700s may have changed parts of African culture forever. Have students discuss whether they agree or disagree with this statement, and why. (Possible answers: West African cultures lost their strongest, most able-bodied people; the population was depleted; there were fewer able men to tend crops, govern, and defend the tribes.)

◆ **ANSWER** It formed a three-way exchange of goods and people among Europe, Africa, and the Americas, creating a triangular pattern.

Section Close

Review with students what the effects of slavery in the Americas were. Have students discuss why it is valuable to study the issue of slavery.

3 Assess

Review Answers

Review History
A. While looking for a sea route to India and Asia, the Portuguese established ports on the West African coast where they could trade for gold and spread Christianity.

B. England and France

C. The conditions were harsh. Ships were crowded and uncomfortable. Slaves were often handcuffed and forced to lie on their sides below deck. Many died from disease, starvation, or disasters at sea.

Define Terms to Know
triangular trade, 380; Middle Passage, 380

Chapter Summary

A blank outline form is available in the Teacher's Resources (p. 318). Chapter summaries should outline the events discussed in this chapter, including the voyages of early explorers, Spanish and Portuguese colonies, the establishment of Dutch, French, and English colonies, and the Atlantic slave trade. Refer to the rubric in the Teacher's Resources (p. 340) to score students' chapter summaries.

⬤ Interpret the Timeline

1. 160 years
2. 1533
3. England's defeat of the Spanish Armada in 1588
4. Check students' timelines to be sure all events are in the chapter.

Use Terms to Know

5. g. viceroy
6. e. mercantilism
7. f. triangular trade
8. a. cash crop
9. d. indigenous
10. c. encomienda
11. b. circumnavigate

Check Your Understanding

12. Possible answer: The voyages led to contact between the Americas and Europe, which brought about the interchange of plants, animals, and ideas and created huge fortunes for European countries. They also introduced European diseases to indigenous peoples in the Americas.
13. Magellan proposed that by sailing west across the Atlantic, he would find a strait through the landmass of the Americas to the Pacific Ocean.
14. Queztalcoatl was supposed to be bearded. The Spanish leader had this characteristic.
15. Bartolomé de las Casas
16. Missionaries served to convert native peoples to Christianity and establish churches in the colonies.
17. fur trader and farmer
18. religious freedom and economic opportunity
19. Jamestown, Virginia, was the first successful English settlement.
20. The Portuguese began exploring the west coast of Africa in their search for a route around Africa to India and Asia.

T382 ◆ **UNIT 4**

Chapter Summary

Complete the following outline in your notebook. Then, use your outline to write a brief summary of the chapter.

Europe Expands Overseas

I. Conquests in the Americas
  A. *The Voyages of Columbus*
  B. Other European Explorers
  C. Around the World

II. Spanish and Portuguese Colonies
  A. Spain's Vast Empire
  B. Governing Spain's Empire
  C. Spain's Influence on Colonial Society
  D. The Portuguese Colony of Brazil

III. Dutch, French, and English Colonies
  A. The Dutch Colonies
  B. French Settlements in the Americas
  C. The English in North America
  D. Native Americans
  E. The Commercial Revolution

IV. Africa and the Atlantic Slave Trade
  A. European Exploration in Africa
  B. The Atlantic Slave Trade
  C. Triangular Trade Route

⬤ Interpret the Timeline

Use the timeline on pages 358–359 to answer the following questions.

1. About how many years were there between the arrival of the Pilgrims in America and the peak of the Atlantic slave trade?

2. When did Pizarro conquer the Inca Empire?

3. **Critical Thinking** What event shows a turning point in the increasing naval power of England?

4. Select three events from the chapter that are not on the timeline. Create a timeline that shows these events.

Use Terms to Know

Match each term with its definition.

a. cash crop   e. mercantilism
b. circumnavigate   f. triangular trade
c. encomienda   g. viceroy
d. indigenous

5. the governor of several provinces who ruled as the representative of the king of Spain

6. an economic system that stresses increasing national wealth by selling more to other nations than buying from them

7. trading system involving a three-way exchange of goods and people

8. a crop grown mainly to sell, not for personal use

9. people, plants, or animals that are found naturally in a region

10. a system in which Spanish colonists were given land in return for Native Americans' labor or tribute

11. to sail completely around a landmass or Earth

Check Your Understanding

12. **Summarize** the impact Columbus's voyages had on the Eastern and Western Hemispheres.

13. **Describe** the route that Magellan proposed to King Charles I of Spain.

14. **Explain** why the Aztecs believed Cortés might be Quetzalcoatl.

15. **Identify** the person who worked to abolish the encomienda system.

16. **Discuss** the role of missionaries.

17. **Describe** two occupations of the people who went to New France.

18. **Describe** what the Pilgrims were seeking in the Americas.

19. **Identify** the first successful English settlement.

20. **Explain** why the Portuguese began exploring Africa's west coast.

21. **Explain** why some African leaders were unsuccessful in stopping the slave trade.

---

21. Traders offered good prices for slaves, and many local people were tempted by quick profits and European goods.

Critical Thinking

22. Draw Conclusions How did the decision Columbus made to enslave the Táino people affect the treatment of other peoples by conquistadors?

23. Make Inferences Why do you suppose Spain wanted to impose its society on the natives in the areas it conquered?

24. Synthesize Information Why do you suppose Columbus brought back people, animals, and other items from the Americas to show to the Spanish monarchs?

25. Analyze Primary Sources What details from Olaudah Equiano's quotation on page 381 reveal the slaves' suffering on the Middle Passage?

Put Your Skills to Work

26. Formulate and Support Opinions You have learned how to formulate and support an opinion by looking carefully at factual evidence, which may be written or visual. You also know that before forming an opinion, you should examine all facts and look for other details that support your opinion. Look at the illustration below. Then, answer the following questions.

a. How can you tell which group of fighters are the Spaniards?

b. Based on the drawing, who will win this battle? Support your answer.

Spaniards fighting the Aztecs

American Museum of Natural History Library; Image # 286838

Analyze Sources

27. Read about the reactions of the Pilgrims on the night before they landed on the coast of North America, after having crossed the Atlantic Ocean. Then, answer the questions that follow.

Being thus arrived in a good harbor, and brought safe to land, they fell upon their knees and blessed the God of Heaven who had brought them over the fast and furious ocean, and delivered them from all the perils and miseries therof, again to set their feet on the firm and stable earth, their proper element.

a. Why were the Pilgrims happy to have their journey over?

b. Do you think a sailor would agree with the opinion that Earth is the "proper element" for people? Why or why not?

Essay Writing

28. Because of the concern he felt about the way Native Americans were treated, Bartolomé de las Casas suggested instead that Africans be used for labor on plantations. Write an essay about why he might later regret this statement. Include details from this chapter as support.

TEST PREPARATION

RECOGNIZE FACT AND OPINION
Choose the correct answer to the question.

Which statement is a fact rather than an opinion about the colonization of North America?

1. The French colonists were less skilled at agriculture than at fur trading.

2. Local Native Americans lived peacefully with the English settlers for many years.

3. The English placed more emphasis on colonizing than the French did.

4. The Dutch were more skillful at trading than at colonizing.

Critical Thinking

22. Possible answer: His decision set a pattern for others to follow.

23. Possible answer: They wanted to ensure dominance, politically, economically, and culturally. Converting Native Americans to Christianity was one way to ensure cultural dominance. They believed that their society was superior.

24. Possible answer: He wanted to impress with a wide variety of products and people so that the Spanish monarchs would finance more trips.

25. the closeness, the heat, the number of people, scarcely room to turn, almost suffocated us

Put Your Skills to Work

FORMULATE AND SUPPORT OPINIONS

26a. The Spaniards are fighting with guns and cannons as well as with powerful bows and arrows.

26b. Possible answer: The Spaniards because they have powerful weapons such as guns and a cannon.

Analyze Sources

27a. Possible answer: Their journey was long and hard, so they were happy to be back on solid ground.

27b. A sailor would probably not agree that Earth is the proper element, because sailors make their living on the water.

Essay Writing

28. Check that students' essays meet all the requirements. In addition to using grammar, punctuation, and organization, students must explain why Bartolomé de las Casas might regret that Africans be used in place of Native Americans for labor on plantations and include details from the chapter to support the view.

TEST PREPARATION

Answer 2. Local Native Americans lived peacefully with the English settlers for many years.

European Monarchies
1526–1796
(pp. 384–410)

Chapter Objectives

• Explain the religious and political factors that led to the growth and decline of Spain's empire.
• Describe the leadership of France's Louis XIV, including his political and cultural influence on foreign nations.
• List the leaders and the political conditions that led Prussia and Russia into the western European political arena.
• Identify the protest, revolt, and eventual triumph of England's Parliament, which led to a limited monarchy.

Chapter Summary

Section I discusses how the powerful Hapsburg Empire enforced Roman Catholicism, encouraged cultural growth, and came into conflict with the Netherlands and England and also describes the growing power of Spain in Europe.
Section II discusses the long rule of Louis XIV in France, which brought culture, political power, and military strength to the country.
Section III explores the destruction in Germany after the Thirty Years' War and the growth of Prussia and Russia into major European powers under the leadership of Frederick the Great, Peter the Great, and Catherine the Great.
Section IV examines the conflict over religion and royal power that prompted a civil war in England, leading to the beheading of the king, the establishment of a commonwealth, the demand for a Bill of Rights, and limits on the monarchy.

Set the Stage

TEACH PRIMARY SOURCES
The remark by Louis XIV reflects the idea that the state would not exist without the king. Ask students to list the privileges and the responsibilities of having such absolute authority.

CHAPTER 17

European Monarchies
1526–1796

I. Spain's Power Grows in Europe
II. Louis XIV Rules France
III. The Rulers of the Holy Roman Empire, Prussia, and Russia
IV. A Limited Monarchy in England

Organized nations began to develop in Europe during the High Middle Ages. Most of these nations were monarchies, ruled by a king or queen. After about 1500, strong monarchs emerged at different times in Spain, France, England, Prussia, and Russia. Most of these rulers believed that they had complete authority. One monarch, Louis XIV of France, is credited with declaring:

❝ *L'état, c'est moi – I am the state.* **❞**

From 1500 to 1800, European nations faced several key issues. These issues included the successes and failures of monarchy as a system of government, the links between religion and the state, and the efforts to prevent any nation from gaining too much power in Europe.

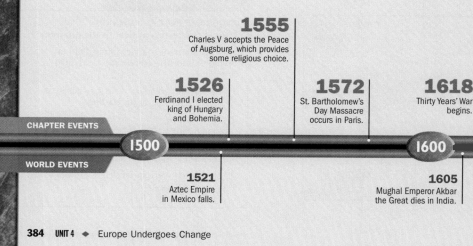

1555
Charles V accepts the Peace of Augsburg, which provides some religious choice.

1526
Ferdinand I elected king of Hungary and Bohemia.

1572
St. Bartholomew's Day Massacre occurs in Paris.

1618
Thirty Years' War begins.

CHAPTER EVENTS

1500

WORLD EVENTS

1600

1521
Aztec Empire in Mexico falls.

1605
Mughal Emperor Akbar the Great dies in India.

Teaching Options

Chapter 17 Resources

REVIEW

Teacher's Resources (TR)
  Terms to Know, p. 30
  Review History, p. 64
  Build Your Skills, p. 98
  Concept Builder, p. 233
  Chapter Test, pp. 149–150
  Cause-and-Effect Chain, p. 325
  Transparencies 1, 5

ASSESSMENT
  Section Reviews, pp. 390, 396, 401, 406
  Chapter Review, pp. 408–409
  Chapter Test, pp. 149–150
  Unit Test, TR, pp. 189–190

ALTERNATIVE ASSESSMENT
  Portfolio Project, p. 410
  Write a Dramatic Monologue, p. T410

The Rise of Monarchies, 1796

GET ORGANIZED
Cause-and-Effect Chain
Recognizing the cause and effect of an event can help you understand the relationship between the cause of an event and the effect the event has had on history. Use a cause-and-effect chain as you read about the events in Chapter 17. Here is an example from this chapter.

CAUSE
Many German princes became Protestants.

↓

EVENT
The Peace of Augsburg

↓

EFFECT
Holy Roman Empire states have some religious choice.

VIEW HISTORY During her reign in the 1500s, Queen Elizabeth I of England often traveled with her court on journeys called progresses. During these journeys, Elizabeth visited many castles and manors in different villages, where her subjects were able to see her.
◆ What do you think this painting suggests about the role of the monarch during this time?

1649
English Civil War ends, and Oliver Cromwell begins to rule England as a republic.

1689
Parliament approves the English Bill of Rights.

1703
Peter the Great founds Saint Petersburg.

1756
Seven Years' War begins.

1700

1800

1681
William Penn founds the English colony of Pennsylvania.

1775
American Revolution begins.

CHAPTER 17 ◆ European Monarchies **385**

Chapter Themes
- Culture
- Time, Continuity, and Change
- People, Places, and Environments
- Individuals, Groups, and Institutions
- Power, Authority, and Governance
- Civic Ideals and Practices
- Individual Development and Identity

F Y I

Queen Elizabeth I
Queen Elizabeth I was unmarried and was called the Virgin Queen. Her courtiers speculated intensely about a suitable husband, but Elizabeth declared that she did not wish to marry. She declared that she was wed to her kingdom, although she allowed many men to believe that she cared especially for them. At one public event, when one of her favorites demanded a favor, she said, "I will have here but one mistress [England] and no master."

Chapter Warm-Up
USING THE MAP
Ask students to look carefully at the boxed area of the locator map. Explain that this chapter will focus on events in Europe and in Russia. Ask students to name the two continents included in the boxed region of the map. (Asia and Europe)

VIEW HISTORY
Point out that Queen Elizabeth wore gowns that were adorned with many jewels and elaborate embroidery. Her extravagance helped project her image as a person of power and authority. Such extravagant styles also set the standard for fashion among women during her reign. Ask students how Elizabeth's elaborate gown helped her political image. (She is the most opulently dressed. She wanted to be revered and admired by her subjects.)

◆ **ANSWER** The monarch represented wealth, was the most important person, and was to be respected and admired by all.

GET ORGANIZED
Cause-and-Effect Chain
Review the use of a cause-and-effect chain and explain that it is a type of graphic organizer that helps find the reasons and results of particular events. Point out that some events may have several causes or several effects. These can be added to a cause-and-effect chain as needed. Suggest that students use a cause-and-effect chain (TR, p. 325) to evaluate events described in Section 3, such as the rise of Russia and Prussia.

⬤ **TEACH THE TIMELINE**
The timeline on pages 384–385 shows events from the years 1521 to 1775. Point out to students that the turmoil in England was partly responsible for the rise of the colonies in America. Ask students how many years elapsed between the approval of the English Bill of Rights and the American Revolution, when the colonists fought for their own rights. (86 years)

Activity
Use a map Have students use the world map (Transparency 1) to find the foreign countries referenced in the world events. (Mexico, India, America)

CHAPTER 17 ◆ **T385**

I. Spain's Power Grows in Europe

(pp. 386–390)

Section Summary

In this section, students will read about the dominance of the Hapsburg Empire during the height of Spain's political power. They will also learn how England emerged as a political power by defeating the Spanish Armada.

1 Introduce

Getting Started

Ask students what the term *absolute power* means to them. If they had absolute power over a country, what commands would they give to their subjects? How would they expect their subjects to treat them? Point out that in this chapter they will read about some monarchs with absolute power and some who chose to give up some of their power.

TERMS TO KNOW

Have students create a glossary for this chapter. Instruct students to write in their glossaries the terms and definitions found on page 386. Encourage students to add new terms to their glossaries as they read the chapter.

You may wish to preview the pronunciation of the following names with students.

Hapsburg (HAHPS buhrg)
Bohemia (boh HEE mee uh)
Valois (vahl WAH)
Calais (kah LAY)

ACTIVE READING

Encourage students to use a flowchart (TR, p. 324) to make a visual presentation of the sequence of events that led to Spain's growth as described in this section.

Spain's Power Grows in Europe

Terms to Know

inheritance the receiving of property or possessions, especially from a relative when that person dies

divine right a belief that a monarch's right to rule comes directly from God, not from the consent of the people

absolute monarchy a monarchy in which the ruler is not limited by a constitution or law

treason an act of betrayal against one's country

Charles V ruled the Holy Roman Empire in the 1500s.

Main Ideas

A. Several monarchies in Europe became linked with the Holy Roman Empire.

B. Although King Philip II believed he ruled Spain with complete authority, his power proved to be limited.

C. Fighting between the English and Spanish fleets marked a climax in the conflict between England and Spain.

 Active Reading

SEQUENCE OF EVENTS
You can better understand the information you read by noticing the order in which events take place. As you read this section, keep track of the sequence, or order, of events that led to the revolt in the Netherlands.

A. Charles V and the Hapsburg Empire

It rarely happens that a single family can dominate the affairs of an entire region for centuries. However, this claim can be made for the Hapsburg Dynasty. The Hapsburgs had their roots in what is now Austria, where they ruled for more than 600 years. Hapsburg influence, though, spread so far throughout Europe that it became its own empire.

The Holy Roman Empire

You have learned that the Holy Roman Empire was a geographical area in western and central Europe. The area included parts of modern Germany, Switzerland, Austria, eastern France, and northern Italy. The empire lasted, in one form or another, for about 1,000 years, beginning with the crowning of Charlemagne in 800. Holy Roman emperors, who were originally crowned by the pope, were later elected by princes in the Holy Roman Empire.

Germany formed the heart of the Holy Roman Empire. It is important to remember, though, that Germany was not a unified nation at this time. Instead, there were dozens of states of different types: states controlled by princes and other rulers, church states governed by bishops or abbots, and states free from those types of control.

The Hapsburgs, who gained power in Austria in the late 1200s, came to dominate the Holy Roman Empire. In fact, every emperor from 1452 until 1806, with one exception, was a Hapsburg. Although the status of the Holy Roman emperor carried great honor, the emperors often found themselves at odds with the papacy and with the rulers of the small princely states. Their actual power, as Charles V would discover in the 1500s, was limited.

Teaching Options

Section 1 Resources

Teacher's Resources (TR)
  Terms to Know, p. 30
  Review History, p. 64
  Build Your Skills, p. 98
  Concept Builder, p. 233
  Flowchart, p. 324
  Cause-and-Effect Chain, p. 325
  Transparency 5

The Growth of Hapsburg Influence

Dynasties such as that of the Hapsburgs could expand their influence in three ways: through marriage, military campaigns, and <u>inheritances</u>, or the receiving of something from a family member or someone else when that person dies. In the late 1400s, Emperor Maximilian I used all three methods to increase Hapsburg power. Through his marriage to Mary of Burgundy, Maximilian I claimed large areas of eastern France. The couple also inherited the kingdom of Castile in Spain. The Spanish connection was strengthened when their son Philip married Juana, the daughter of Spain's King Ferdinand II and Queen Isabella. Lastly, Maximilian's army waged military campaigns against France, the Netherlands, and the Ottoman Empire.

These alliances and territorial expansions meant that when it was time for Philip and Juana's son Charles to claim his inheritance, he was one of the most powerful rulers in the Western world. He actually had two titles. As Holy Roman emperor, he was known as Charles V. As king of Spain, he was Charles I.

Besides Spain and Austria, Charles's possessions included parts of the Netherlands and southern Italy as well as the entire Spanish Empire in the Americas. In 1526, Hungary and Bohemia, which is the present-day Czech Republic, feared the advance of the Ottoman Turks and elected Charles's brother Ferdinand as king. It seemed to some observers that the Hapsburgs might dominate all of Europe.

The Reign of Charles V

Throughout his long reign, Charles V discovered that he did not have complete authority. As Holy Roman emperor, he was expected to keep the Roman Catholic faith in Europe. However, he found that the Reformation had severely damaged the scope of the Roman Catholic Church. Many of the German princes became Protestant, and they were determined to preserve their religious freedom. At a meeting called the Peace of Augsburg in 1555, Charles V was forced to accept an arrangement by which each state in the empire could choose to be either Lutheran, a group within the Protestant religion, or Roman Catholic.

Charles V also found himself in disagreement on a number of other issues. Although a skilled leader in warfare, Charles preferred to settle conflicts by compromise. However, his peace negotiations with King Francis I of France and with Sultan Suleiman I of the Ottoman Empire, his main rivals, had few positive results. Perhaps exhausted by the burdens of monarchy, Charles V gave up his position as Holy Roman emperor in 1556. He left Spain, the Netherlands, southern Italy, and Spanish America to his son Philip II. Charles's brother Ferdinand I inherited Austria as well as Hungary and Bohemia. Thus, for the rest of its history, the Hapsburg Dynasty had two branches.

◆ **What were the two branches of the Hapsburg Dynasty?**

King Ferdinand II and Queen Isabella ruled Spain during the fifteenth and sixteenth centuries.

A. Charles V and the Hapsburg Empire

Purpose-Setting Question What happened as a result of the Peace of Augsburg? (Each state in the empire could choose to be Lutheran or Roman Catholic.)

Explore You may wish to explain to students that the *Hapsburg* name is sometimes spelled *Habsburg*. Both spellings are acceptable.

Extend The Hapsburg family came to power with the election of Count Rudolf as German king and Holy Roman Emperor in 1273. In 1278, Rudolf took over certain territories in Bohemia. These lands and others, later identified with Austria, soon became the center of the Hapsburg domains and were ruled by the family without interruption until 1918. The Hapsburgs also controlled Hungary and ruled Spain and the Spanish Empire for almost two centuries.

Discuss Ask students to discuss the decision of Charles V to abdicate and retire to a monastery. Do they think his decision was right? Why or why not? Would they have been willing to give up wealth and power as Charles did?

Focus Although Charles retired as emperor, he did not give up the good life. Living in a monastery in northern Spain, he had nearly 150 attendants and dined on excellent meals. Charles particularly enjoyed fish, eels, frogs, and oysters, which were brought to him at the monastery.

Activity

Make a family tree As students read the section, have them create a Hapsburg family tree. When the section is completed, have pairs of students compare their Hapsburg family trees and make any changes or corrections.

◆ **ANSWER** One branch included Spain, the Netherlands, southern Italy, and Spanish America; the other branch included Austria, Hungary, and Bohemia.

F Y I

Peace of Augsburg

The Peace of Augsburg was a compromise to settle religious disputes. However, Charles V did not want to recognize the divisions among Christians in western Europe. He did not want to make any compromises over religion. For this reason, he refused to go to the Augsburg negotiations. Instead, he sent his brother Ferdinand to settle all questions.

Meet Individual Needs:
AUDITORY LEARNERS

Have students work in pairs. Give each student several index cards. Have one student in each pair read the segment "The Growth of Hapsburg Influence" (p. 387) aloud while the other takes notes. Then, have the students switch roles to read aloud and take notes on the segment "The Reign of Charles V" (p. 387). Have students share their notes.

B. The Golden Age in Spain

Purpose-Setting Question

Where did Philip II believe his authority to rule came from? (Philip II believed his right to rule came directly from God.)

TEACH PRIMARY SOURCES

Identify the features of *Las Meninas* that make it an extraordinary masterpiece. Point out that the artist himself is depicted at the left. He is looking at the subjects of his canvas, the back of which shows on the left of the painting. The framed mirror on the back wall of the room reflects the subject of his painting, the king and queen of Spain. The child in the center is being urged to join her parents and pose for the artist. Encourage students to learn more about the painting by using the Internet, encyclopedias, or other reference sources.

GLOBAL CONNECTIONS

DIVINE RULERS Ask students to consider what ancient Egyptians, the people of imperial Japan, or the people ruled by Philip II would think about the way Americans feel about the President of the United States. Discuss differences between regarding a political leader as a divine ruler, with authority directly from God, or regarding him or her as simply a fellow citizen.

◆ **ANSWER** A dispute over religious freedom; a group of Protestant and Roman Catholic Dutch nobles petitioned King Philip II of Spain to ban the Inquisition from the Netherlands. When the king refused, rebellion broke out.

This famous painting by Velázquez is titled *Las Meninas* (*Maids of Honour*). Many people consider it to be one of the greatest paintings of all time.

Global Connections

DIVINE RULERS

In Europe, many monarchs believed that their right to rule came directly from God. However, they did not think that they were divine, or godlike. In ancient Egypt and Rome, rulers were actually regarded as divine or were declared to be gods after their death. For centuries, the emperors of Japan were considered to be divine.

B. The Golden Age in Spain

During the reign of Philip II of Spain in the second half of the 1500s, Spain reached its greatest power and influence. This period of Spanish history ushered in a golden age. Spanish literature and the arts experienced a renaissance, with achievements such as Miguel de Cervantes's *Don Quixote*, which has been called the first European novel, the plays of Lope de Vega and Pedro Calderón de la Barca, and the paintings of El Greco, Diego Velázquez, and Bartolomé Murillo.

Philip II and Rule by Divine Right

By nature Philip II, who also ruled Portugal as Philip I, was strict and severe. Like most other European monarchs of the time, he believed that the authority of his kingship rested on **divine right**, or the right to rule coming directly from God and not from the consent, or approval, of the people. He ruled in an **absolute monarchy**, or a monarchy in which the ruler is not limited by a constitution or law.

Philip II was also a strong supporter of the Roman Catholic faith. He was determined not only to root out heresy but to restore Roman Catholicism wherever he could. More than anything else, these goals set the tone of Philip's long reign and set the stage for later conflicts.

In 1554, after the death of his first wife, Philip married Mary Tudor, the queen of England and the daughter of Henry VIII. This alliance made Philip, in theory, the English king—much to the alarm of English Protestants. To their relief, Philip was content to remain in the palace he had built for himself outside Madrid in central Spain.

Meanwhile, Mary tried energetically to restore Roman Catholicism in England. She had several hundred Protestants burned at the stake as heretics. This act of burning at the stake horrified many of her subjects. By the time she died in 1558 and was succeeded by her sister, Elizabeth I, she had earned the nickname Bloody Mary.

The Revolt of the Netherlands

Besides England, Scandinavia, and many parts of Germany, another center of European Protestantism was the Netherlands. Like Germany, this area was not a unified state in the late 1500s. The Netherlands was ruled by Spain. The Dutch people of the Netherlands were unified in their hatred of Philip II's rule. Many Dutch were Calvinists, a Protestant group that followed the teachings of John Calvin, whom Philip considered heretics. The Dutch disliked that Philip was a Roman Catholic. They were especially concerned about Philip's use of the Inquisition.

In 1566, a group of Protestant and Roman Catholic Dutch nobles urged Philip to ban the Inquisition from the Netherlands. When the king refused, rebellion broke out. For more than two decades, Philip was at war with his own subjects. The Dutch had begun the revolt in order to preserve religious freedom. As the conflict unfolded, their goals focused on gaining independence.

◆ **What dispute brought the Netherlands into conflict with Philip II?**

Teaching Options

C. England Enters the World Stage

One of the most important challenges faced by Queen Elizabeth I was to prevent religious conflict from tearing England apart. Not only did she succeed in this aim, but she was also able to achieve a victory against Roman Catholic Spain. This accomplishment paved the way for England to emerge as a major power in Europe.

Roman Catholics and Protestants

As you have learned, the Reformation in England had political rather than religious roots. During the sixteenth century, England gradually rejected Roman Catholicism and Calvinism, or the religion of the Calvinists. The Church of England, also called the Anglican Church, became England's established denomination, or religious group, of Christianity.

In the 1550s, Mary Tudor's short marriage to Philip II of Spain increased religious tensions. In 1576, ten years after the beginning of the Dutch rebellion against Spain, Philip II sent his half-brother Don Juan to the Netherlands to put down the revolt. Then he planned to use the Netherlands as a base for the invasion of England.

Don Juan died in 1578 before he could achieve this plan. However, Elizabeth took steps to ensure England's security by forming an alliance with the Dutch rebels. In 1585, Elizabeth sent 6,000 English troops to the Netherlands to help in the struggle against Spain. The following year, the imprisoned Mary Queen of Scots, who was Roman Catholic and had been queen of Scotland, joined a plot against her cousin, Elizabeth, in an attempt to take over the English throne. Mary was charged with **treason**, which is an act of betrayal against one's country. Elizabeth signed an order for her execution in early 1587.

Do You Remember?
In Chapter 14, you learned about the English Reformation. During this period, the Act of Supremacy declared the king as head of the Church of England.

Elizabeth I ruled England for nearly 50 years. During her reign, England advanced to become a major European power in politics, trade, and the arts.

Writing

AVERAGE

Have students write a letter in the person of Mary Queen of Scots. The letter could be written to Queen Elizabeth or to one of Mary's allies who conspired against Queen Elizabeth. Students may choose to have Mary use the letter to beg for mercy or to try to justify her political actions.

CHALLENGE

Have students write a letter to Queen Elizabeth in the person of Mary Queen of Scots. Have them write a second letter that is a reply from Queen Elizabeth. Each letter should clearly state a position and support it with details from the text or from outside research.

C. England Enters the World Stage

Purpose-Setting Question How did England's defeat of the Spanish Armada affect the fortunes of both Spain and England? (England became a world power; Spain's power declined.)

Do You Remember?
Remind students that Parliament passed the Act of Supremacy in order to separate the Church of England from the Roman Catholic Church after the pope refused to permit Henry VIII to divorce his wife and marry another woman. Ask students how the conflict between Queen Elizabeth and her cousin Mary Queen of Scots reflected continued disagreements between the two churches. (Mary was a Roman Catholic and wanted to re-establish the Roman Catholic Church as the official English church. Elizabeth, who was Anglican, wanted to maintain the Church of England. Eventually, Elizabeth agreed to have Mary executed for treason.)

Review Have students look back at Chapter 14, which covers the Reformation. Have them scan the headings to recall the issues. Ask volunteers to describe key details about the Reformation.

Activity

Research Have students research the Tower of London and the imprisonment of Mary Queen of Scots within the Tower. Suggest that they start with Web sites on London tourism. Some students might like to use their research to create a travel brochure of the tower and its most famous occupant.

Extend Elizabeth came to the throne in 1558 highly educated and widely read. During the age that was named for her, she inspired many writers, such as Shakespeare and Christopher Marlowe. Queen Elizabeth was herself a writer of various works, including translations, speeches, and poetry. Her poem "On Monsieur's Departure" might have been written to the French duke of Anjou, a former suitor, or to the Earl of Essex, one of her favorite courtiers.

Demonstrate
On a map of Europe (Atlas, page A5, or Transparency 5) have students trace the course of the Spanish Armada from Spain, to Calais, around Scotland, and back to Spain. Have students describe the difficulties of this trip.

Focus
Up until the time of the Spanish Armada, Spain had been the strongest naval power in Europe and had controlled the seas. Point out to students that the defeat of the Spanish Armada changed the power structure in Europe forever. England became a major power and remained so for many centuries, while Spain's power declined.

◆ **ANSWER** Elizabeth's decision helped the Netherlands become independent from Spain. England was drawn into war with Spain. England won, which led to England's becoming a world power.

Section Close
Have students recap the growth and decline of Spain's power. They should describe the golden age of Spain, the Inquisition, and the sea battle involving the Spanish Armada and England's naval fleet.

3 Assess

Review Answers
Review History
A. The Hapsburg Dynasty began in Austria.

B. The goals of King Philip II were to root out heresy and restore Roman Catholicism wherever he could.

C. The defeat of the Spanish Armada helped England to become a world power and led to the decline of Spain as a world power. The Netherlands also became independent after the Armada's defeat.

Define Terms to Know
inheritance, 387; divine right, 388; absolute monarchy, 388; treason, 389

Critical Thinking
Possible answer: English aid to the Dutch rebels brought England into direct conflict with Spain.

Sir Francis Drake led the English navy to an unexpected victory against the mightier Spanish Armada in 1588.

The Defeat of the Spanish Armada
Now that England had openly challenged Spain, Philip II prepared for a massive invasion of England. His fleet, called the Armada, consisted of 130 ships, 30,000 men, and 2,400 weapons. The Armada set sail for England in May 1588.

The Spanish ships were first sighted off the southwestern coast of England in late July. The English fleet, under the command of Charles Howard and Sir Francis Drake, sailed from Plymouth, England, to do battle. The English had approximately the same number of ships as the Spaniards had, but their vessels were lighter and more heavily armed with weapons.

After several small battles in the English Channel, the Spanish Armada anchored at the French port of Calais. The commanders hoped to pick up additional troops from the medieval county of Flanders, which today is the Dutch-speaking part of Belgium. However, the English set fire to the anchored Spanish ships and caused heavy damage. The English then destroyed many of the fleeing vessels. Blocked by westerly winds and by part of the English fleet, the Spaniards had no choice but to sail eastward and north. They returned to Spain the long way—all around Scotland—and suffered more damage from heavy storms. The invasion had ended in utter failure, with only about half the fleet returning safely.

The defeat of the Armada in 1588 ensured independence for both England and the Netherlands. The English had great pride in their nation and were pleased with the leadership of Elizabeth I. Both the English and the Dutch began to explore the East Indies, a development that would have major economic consequences in the seventeenth century. England and the Netherlands also became active in establishing colonies in North America. Finally, as Spain declined, England rose as a world power.

◆ **What consequences did Elizabeth I's decision to ally England with the Netherlands have for both countries?**

Review I

Review History
A. Where did the Hapsburg Dynasty have its roots?

B. What were the goals of King Philip II of Spain?

C. What was the historical significance of England's defeat of the Spanish Armada in 1588?

Define Terms to Know
Define the following terms: **inheritance, divine right, absolute monarchy, treason**

Critical Thinking
Why did the revolt in the Netherlands lead to a critical conflict between Spain and England?

Write About Government
In a paragraph, explain how the idea of divine right conflicts with individual liberty.

Get Organized
CAUSE-AND-EFFECT CHAIN
Think about the main events in this section. Use a cause-and-effect chain to show the cause and effect of an event. For example, what was the cause and effect of the defeat of the Spanish Armada?

Write About Government
Possible answer: The theory of divine right doesn't allow for individual liberty, because monarchs have all the power to make decisions for everyone. In addition, the idea that a king's power comes from God and not from the consent of the people conflicts with the liberty of individuals to pick their rulers.

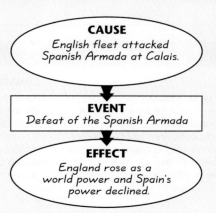

CAUSE
English fleet attacked Spanish Armada at Calais.

EVENT
Defeat of the Spanish Armada

EFFECT
England rose as a world power and Spain's power declined.

Build Your Skills

Critical Thinking

MAKE INFERENCES

A skill that helps you to think and read critically, or with careful analysis and judgment, is the ability to make inferences. An inference is a reasonable conclusion or judgment based on evidence. For example, from the evidence in Section I of this chapter, you can make the inference that religious conflict and national rivalry played major roles in European history during the 1500s.

The evidence supporting this inference includes the reign of Charles V as Holy Roman emperor during the early stages of the Protestant Reformation, the efforts of Philip II of Spain to preserve Roman Catholicism, and the actions of Mary Tudor and Mary Queen of Scots. The clash between England and Spain, in particular, the English defeat of the Spanish Armada in 1588, also supports this inference.

Here's How
Follow these steps to make inferences.
1. Study the evidence, noting relationships between facts and ideas.
2. Ask yourself about unstated or suggested meanings.
3. Test your inferences against additional evidence, and revise them if necessary. Keep in mind that valid inferences are supported by a wide range of facts or examples.

Here's Why
Making valid inferences allows you to join facts and ideas into a meaningful conclusion or judgment.

Practice the Skill
Read and study the passage on the right, which comes from a modern history book of the British monarchy. Then, answer the following questions.

1. What inference can you make about Philip's motives in supporting Mary Queen of Scots?
2. What inference can you make about Mary being held in English custody?
3. What inference can you make about the attitude of Parliament and Elizabeth's attitude on this issue?

Extend the Skill
Think about some precautions you should take about making inferences. Then, examine how you reached the inferences in the questions above.

Apply the Skill
Choose a brief section or two from this chapter and analyze the passage(s) for inferences that you can reasonably make. Test your inferences using additional evidence.

"The conflict between Philip and Elizabeth brought Mary Queen of Scots into play once more. Since 1567 she [Mary] had been a captive in English custody, the Scottish throne being occupied by her young son, James VI. Philip's obvious move was to effect her rescue and place her on the [English] throne by force of arms. In August 1586 . . . evidence made Mary's complicity in the plot abundantly clear. Mary was tried in October and found guilty. The following month Parliament begged Elizabeth to proceed to execution. In February 1587, after an agony of indecision, Elizabeth had her cousin beheaded."

Mary Queen of Scots

Teaching Options

RETEACH
Ask students to look at one of the images in the chapter, such as the chapter opener painting of Queen Elizabeth on pages 384–385 or the painting of Versailles on page 395. Have them evaluate the images and make inferences about monarchies in Europe during the period covered in the chapter. Encourage students to test their inferences by rereading the text or doing additional research.

CHALLENGE
Have students make inferences about the targeted audience of a television program. Students should choose one program and use clues such as the subject matter, commercial messages, and the time of the program broadcast to make their inferences. Have students summarize their inferences in a brief paragraph. Students should share their information and their inferences with the class.

Teach the Skill
Have students think of inferences they make every day. For example, students might infer that a class is almost over when a teacher begins to recap the lesson. Challenge students to think of other types of inferences they have made today.

Ask students to speculate what would happen if they were not able to make inferences. For example, what if the sound of a car horn did not give them the idea that they may be in danger? (Possible answer: Many car accidents would occur.) Point out to students that using common sense and prior knowledge helps people make inferences.

Practice the Skill
ANSWERS
1. Possible answer: Philip's motive was to use Mary Queen of Scots as a way of overthrowing the Protestant monarch, Elizabeth I, and putting a Roman Catholic monarch in Elizabeth's place.
2. Possible answer: The English did not trust Mary.
3. Possible answer: Parliament wanted to avoid the possibility of a Roman Catholic conspiracy. Elizabeth was reluctant to have her cousin Mary killed, but finally agreed.

Extend the Skill
Possible answer: One precaution is to make sure that inferences are clearly based on information presented. An inference is a guess based on evidence, not a wild guess.

Apply the Skill
Students' inferences may vary. The inferences should be reasonable and should be able to be tested using additional evidence.

Section Summary

In this section, students will read about the conflicts over religion during the sixteenth century as well as the negotiations that helped resolve the conflicts. They will read about the reign of Louis XIV, his influence on French culture, and his interactions with and influences on foreign nations.

1 Introduce

Getting Started

Tell students that Louis XIV ruled France for 54 years. Ask them to think about the influence on the United States if one person ruled for such a long period of time. Discuss the ways such a ruler would impact the nation.

TERMS TO KNOW

Ask students to read the terms and definitions on page 392 and find each term in the section. Then, have them write sentences using each term so that its definition is clear. If students started a glossary for the chapter in Section 1, remind them to add the new terms.

You may wish to preview the pronunciation of the following words with students.

Catherine de Médicis
(kah TREEN duh may dee SEES)
Henry of Navarre
(HEHN ree uhv nuh VAHR)
Gaspard de Coligny
(gah SPAHR duh kau lee NYEE)
Edict of Nantes
(EE dihkt uhv NAHNT)
Jacques Bossuet
(ZHAHK bah SWAH)
Versailles (ver SY)
René Descartes
(ruh NAY day KAHRT)

ACTIVE READING

Have students create an outline for this section. A blank outline form is available in the Teacher's Resources (p. 318). As students read, they should write down the headings and then list the main points under each heading. This will help students remember the text and focus on the main points, instead of on little details, when they write their summaries.

Section II — Louis XIV Rules France

Terms to Know

regent someone who rules in a monarch's place, usually because the monarch is too young to rule alone

balance of power a system in which no single state is strong enough to dominate all the others in its region

Main Ideas

A. Clashes between French Protestants and Roman Catholics in the late 1500s threatened to tear France apart.

B. The long reign of Louis XIV brought France to a peak of political and cultural influence throughout Europe.

C. Opposition to the foreign policy of Louis XIV, which called for almost constant war, prevented him from dominating all of Europe.

📖 Active Reading

SUMMARIZE
When you summarize, you state only the most important points of a passage. As you read this section, focus on the main points about the conflicts that divided France and then on the ways in which Louis XIV unified and strengthened that country. Then, pause to summarize what you have learned.

A. The French Wars of Religion

The Protestant Reformation in sixteenth-century Europe followed different paths. In France, the ideas of John Calvin, a French native, spread rapidly. French Calvinists were called Huguenots, a term that by the 1500s came to include all Protestant groups in France.

Religious Conflict

In the 1500s, French Protestants, or Huguenots, were especially numerous among the nobility. This situation threatened French monarchs such as King Francis I and King Henry II, who were Roman Catholics. They tried to prevent the Huguenots from gaining more power and influence in France. By the 1550s, French Protestants were being burned at the stake for heresy.

After the death of Henry II in 1559, his widow Catherine de Médicis ruled France as **regent** for the couple's sons, who were too young to rule. Despite persecution, more than one-third of French nobility was Protestant. Roman Catholic and Protestant groups each tried to seize the monarchy or, at the very least, control the state's policy on religious issues. During the period from 1560 to 1600, there were at least nine civil wars in France.

In 1572, many Huguenots assembled in Paris to celebrate the marriage of Henry of Navarre, one of their leaders. Catherine de Médicis feared the growing influence of Admiral Gaspard de Coligny, a Huguenot, on her son, Charles IX. She encouraged her son to order a massacre, which he did. Thousands of Huguenots, including Coligny, were killed. This event is known as the Saint Bartholomew's Day Massacre because it began on that saint's feast day, August 24. Henry, who had been raised as a Protestant, escaped death by renouncing, or giving up, his Protestant religion.

During the Saint Bartholomew's Day Massacre in Paris, thousands of Huguenots were killed.

Teaching Options

Section 2 Resources

Teacher's Resources (TR)
Terms to Know, p. 30
Review History, p. 64
Build Your Skills, p. 98
Concept Builder, p. 233
Cause-and-Effect Chain, p. 325
Transparency 5

Meet Individual Needs:

VISUAL/SPATIAL LEARNERS

Before they begin reading, ask students to look carefully at the image on page 392. Discuss the elements the artist uses to reveal facts about the Saint Bartholomew's Day Massacre. Then, ask students to write a summary of the event based on what they learned from the painting and the caption. Once completed, have students share their summaries with the class.

Henry IV and Cardinal Richelieu

Far from settling matters, the Saint Bartholomew's Day Massacre led to a period of even more violent civil war. Spanish troops entered France to support Roman Catholics. Some French towns with many Protestants, such as Rouen, called on England for help. Gradually, however, groups from both sides began to find common ground. Known as the "politicals," these people argued that religion could not justify the civil wars that were tearing the country apart. They chose Henry of Navarre, who returned to Protestantism, as their leader. In 1589, Henry III, was assassinated. Henry of Navarre, who had been appointed the heir to the French throne in 1584, then became king of France. He ruled as Henry IV from 1589 to 1610.

Henry IV was determined to reunify the country. As a realist, he knew that the Huguenots, however numerous, were still a minority in France. Henry thus put into effect a two-part compromise. In 1593, he rejected his Protestant faith again. He then returned to Roman Catholicism and begged the pope for forgiveness. In 1598, he issued the Edict of Nantes, which guaranteed basic civil rights and some religious freedoms for French Protestants. The Edict of Nantes effectively brought the bitter religious conflicts in France to an end. In effect, Henry ordered the country to adopt a policy of toleration.

In 1610, Henry IV was succeeded by his nine-year-old son, Louis XIII. For most of Louis XIII's reign, however, state affairs were managed by his chief minister, Cardinal Richelieu. As a high-ranking member of the Roman Catholic clergy, Richelieu was opposed to any Huguenot participation in state affairs. He amended, or changed, the Edict of Nantes, canceling the Huguenots' rights to maintain fortified cities and Protestant armies. Once again, the trend was to organize the power of the state in a single figure—the monarch.

◆ What was the significance of the Edict of Nantes?

B. Louis XIV: The Sun King

Louis XIII died in 1643. He left a young son and heir who was just five years old. Once again, a member of the Roman Catholic clergy, Cardinal Mazarin, held power as chief minister. After the cardinal's death in 1661, the young king, Louis XIV, took control of his reign.

The Great Monarch

In 1661, Louis XIV began to govern France personally. In the tradition of his grandfather, Henry IV, Louis believed in absolute monarchy. A Roman Catholic bishop, Jacques Bossuet, laid down the ideas for absolute monarchy in France. All power comes from God, Bossuet argued, and kings are God's representatives on Earth. Royal power is absolute, but it must be just and reasonable as well. In a sermon in Paris, Jacques Bossuet is said to have exclaimed, "Kings, you are gods."

Louis XIV's long reign lasted until his death in 1715. His policy might generally be described as peace at home and war abroad. Because royal control of the army was important to these goals, Louis XIV's government supervised military recruiting, training, supplies, and promotions. The king also greatly enlarged the army, raising it to a strength of 400,000 men, four times its size when Louis inherited the throne.

Louis XIV ruled France as an absolute monarch.

A. The French Wars of Religion

Purpose-Setting Question
What were some causes and effects of the Saint Bartholomew's Day Massacre? (**Possible causes:** Huguenots gathered for a wedding; Catherine de Médicis feared the influence of the Huguenots and had them killed. **Possible effects:** a civil war between the Roman Catholics and the Protestants)

Extend Ask students where in today's world religious conflicts or religious intolerance have led to periods of violence or unrest. (e.g., the Middle East, Northern Ireland, India and Pakistan) Ask students if they have any suggestions for building more tolerance.

Focus Ask if any students have read the novel *The Three Musketeers* or seen a movie version of the book. Point out that Cardinal Richelieu is a central character in the book, and he is often involved in spying and plotting. Note that the real Richelieu often needed to use both trickery and force to help assure the power of the French king in the early 1600s.

◆ **ANSWER** It brought the bitter religious conflicts in France to an end and encouraged the country to adopt a policy of religious tolerance.

B. Louis XIV: The Sun King

Purpose-Setting Question What were some of the changes made during the reign of Louis XIV? (Possible answers: absolute monarchy strengthened, army expanded to 400,000 men, economy strengthened, Edict of Nantes revoked, Versailles built, culture promoted)

Discuss Have students reflect on possible positive and negative effects of an absolute monarchy. Comments might include less unrest and political infighting but also less freedom and less voice in government for the average citizen.

Connection to GOVERNMENT

One of the most basic civil rights of Americans is the right to assemble. This includes the right to have religious, social, or political assemblies. Explain to students that the French under Catherine de Médicis did not have this right. For this reason, they could be murdered at the whim of the king, as occurred in the assembly that took place during the Saint Bartholomew's Day Massacre.

Rows of sparkling chandeliers adorn the interior of Versailles.

ANALYZE PRIMARY SOURCES **DOCUMENT-BASED QUESTION** What does the quotation tell about the royal image that Louis XIV tried to show?

Louis XIV's chief minister of finance, Jean Baptiste Colbert, worked hard to raise the revenues, or money, necessary to support the army and the king's other projects. Colbert's policy of mercantilism strengthened the French economy.

In matters of religion, Louis XIV felt that a unified state required a single state religion. As a result, he cancelled the Edict of Nantes in 1685, and many Protestants left France so they would not have to become Catholics.

A Grand Palace

Like many other monarchs, Louis XIV showed the grandeur of his reign by constructing a large new palace. This splendid residence was Versailles, some 10 miles outside Paris.

In the principal royal residence at Versailles, hundreds of rooms were stunningly furnished with tapestries, chandeliers, and dazzling mirrors. Formal parks and gardens had fountains, elaborate landscape patterns, and marble statues. The king's wealth and power became the envy of Europe. Versailles was more than a residence. It was a symbol of absolute monarchy. In a popular phrase, Louis XIV was described as the "Sun King," the source of all life and splendor.

At Versailles, as elsewhere, Louis XIV's needs were catered to with great ceremony. One of the house rules for the serving of meals gives a sense of the atmosphere:

     66 His Majesty's meals shall be brought in thus: two of the guards will walk in first, then the doorkeeper, the maître d'hôtel carrying his staff, the gentleman who serves bread, the controller-general [chief accounting officer], the controller's clerk, the squire of the kitchen, and the keeper of table settings. 99

Arts and Culture Under Louis XIV

Like other successful monarchs, the reign of Louis XIV brought about a cultural flowering. The arts during Louis XIV's reign are considered to represent the peak of the Baroque style. The main feature of the Baroque style is its ornate decoration. This style was especially evident in architecture, sculpture, and music. In music, Jean Baptiste Lully enjoyed the direct patronage, or support, of Louis XIV, creating chamber music, ballets, and operas.

The literature and painting of the period are often described as neoclassical, or a revival of classical style and form. This is due to the authors' interest in classical Greek and Roman subjects and the artists' stress on balanced, classical forms. Outstanding French painters during Louis's reign included Nicolas Poussin, who specialized in biblical and classical Greek and Roman subjects, and Claude Lorrain, whose greatest work was in landscapes.

Three of France's greatest writers dominated literature and drama during this period. These writers were Pierre Corneille and Jean Racine, whose works often focused on subjects from Greek and Roman history, and Jean Baptiste Poquelin, known as Molière. Corneille is regarded as the creator of

Teaching Options

FYI

Versailles

Versailles was a grandiose palace and became a symbol of royal extravagance. During the time of Louis XIV, the palace housed about 1,000 courtiers with 4,000 attendants. As many as 14,000 soldiers were quartered in annexes or in the nearby town. Today, the palace is a major tourist attraction and the lodging place for visiting heads of state.

Meet Individual Needs:

VERBAL/LINGUISTIC

Explain to students that the name "Sun King" is a metaphor. The name compares King Louis XIV to the Sun. Demonstrate why this comparison is appropriate by asking students to think of adjectives that can describe both the Sun and the king.

French classical tragedy, and Racine is considered one of the greatest French poets. Molière is thought to be the greatest of all French comedy playwrights.

In science and philosophy, René Descartes introduced ways to apply mathematics to all areas of knowledge, whereas Blaise Pascal explored the relationships of science and religion. Skepticism, or doubting knowledge by challenging its reliability, had a great deal of influence on seventeenth-century France.

◆ **What did Versailles symbolize?**

C. France and the Rest of Europe

During the reign of Louis XIV, as well as the reigns of other European monarchs of this period, power was of greatest significance. One important principle that monarchs such as Louis XIV came to understand was the principle of **balance of power**. Balance of power was a system in which each state tried, through its foreign policy, to increase its own influence and to prevent any other state from gaining too much power within the region.

Louis XIV's Foreign Policy

Louis XIV was strongly committed to the peaceful unification of France at home. In foreign affairs, however, Louis pursued a policy of almost constant war. He was particularly concerned about the power of the Hapsburgs, whose possessions came close to surrounding France.

The splendor of Versailles is illustrated in this French painting. Besides the palace, Versailles had 15,000 acres of gardens, lawns, and woods.

Use a map Have students use the map of Europe in the Atlas (p. A5) or Transparency 5 to locate the countries against which Louis XIV fought. Have students highlight the nations joined in the Grand Alliance of 1701. Then, have students highlight the nations ruled by Louis XIV and his grandson.

Discuss Ask students to reflect on changes and developments in France under Louis XIV. How was the country improved under his rule? (Possible answers: arts and culture expanded; French territory was expanded; Versailles had been built; and the monarchy was strengthened.)

Focus Point out that while Louis XV inherited a stronger France, it would weaken under his poor leadership, and, within 75 years, the monarchy would be overthrown.

◆ **ANSWER** to preserve the balance of power by keeping France and Spain from uniting

Section Close

Ask students to recall a definition for the following terms: *Huguenots, Baroque style, Versailles*, and the *War of the Spanish Succession*. Ask them to explain the significance of each to the time period of the section.

3 Assess

Review Answers

Review History
A. The St. Bartholomew's Day Massacre increased religious tensions between French Roman Catholics and Protestants.

B. The government of Louis XIV supervised military recruiting, training, supplies, and promotions. Louis XIV greatly increased the size of the army.

C. The possessions of the Hapsburgs came close to encircling France.

Define Terms to Know
regent, 392; balance of power, 395

Critical Thinking
Possible answer: Louis XIV supported writers, artists, and musicians. Other important people encouraged and served as patrons for artists.

Louis attempted to expand the borders of France by waging war against the Netherlands and the Holy Roman Empire. His most significant military campaign, though, was the War of the Spanish Succession, fought from 1702 to 1713. This war began when King Charles II of Spain died and left all Spanish territories to Louis XIV's grandson. To preserve the balance of power, King William III of England formed the Grand Alliance of 1701 with the Netherlands and the Holy Roman Empire. This alliance opposed the transfer of territories from Louis XIV to his family members.

For more than a decade, the war continued without a winner. Finally, the French were defeated. The Spanish territories were divided among the countries of the Grand Alliance by the Treaty of Utrecht in 1713. Louis XIV's grandson was allowed to rule Spain on the condition that the French and Spanish thrones would never be united.

The Legacy of Louis XIV

Louis XIV's absolute monarchy ensured his country's unification and made France one of Europe's leading powers. French culture had a strong influence throughout Europe and even beyond the continent. At the same time, Louis was less than successful in some of his economic and foreign policies. Projects such as Versailles and foreign wars required huge amounts of money. Royal taxes on the peasants caused extreme hardship. Peasants and serfs lived on the verge of starvation.

Louis XIV was king of France for 72 years. He lived longer than his son and grandson. When Louis XIV died in 1715, his great-grandson, who was five years old, inherited the throne. The child became Louis XV, ruler of one of the strongest European countries at the time.

◆ **Why was the War of the Spanish Succession fought?**

Review II

Review History
A. What was the importance of the Saint Bartholomew's Day Massacre?
B. How did Louis XIV control the army?
C. Why was Louis XIV concerned with the power of the Hapsburgs?

Define Terms to Know
Define the following terms: **regent, balance of power**

Critical Thinking
How did Louis XIV's reign benefit the arts in France?

Write About Government
Write a paragraph in which you discuss the achievements of Louis XIV during his long reign as king of France.

Get Organized
CAUSE-AND-EFFECT CHAIN
Think about the main events in this section. Use a cause-and-effect chain to show the cause and effect of an event. For example, what was the cause and the effect of the Saint Bartholomew's Day Massacre?

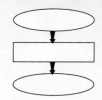

Write About Government
Students' paragraphs should include such achievements as France becoming a leading power in Europe, enlarging the army, building Versailles, strengthening the economy, and allowing culture to flower.

```
CAUSE
Catherine de Médicis
feared the growing influence
of Huguenots.
        ↓
EVENT
Saint Bartholomew's Day Massacre
        ↓
EFFECT
Civil war in France
between the Huguenots and
the Roman Catholics
```

The Rulers of the Holy Roman Empire, Prussia, and Russia

Terms to Know

militarism a policy in which a military's needs and values take priority

standing army a permanent army of paid soldiers

enlightened despotism an absolute monarchy in which the ruler uses his or her power to bring beneficial political and social changes to his or her subjects

A major battle during the Thirty Years' War occurred in 1622 in the town of Fleurus in present-day Belgium.

Main Ideas

A. The Thirty Years' War caused devastation in central Europe and brought the Holy Roman Empire to an end as a political force.

B. In northeastern Europe in the 1700s, Prussia rose to become an important military power.

C. In Russia, Peter the Great encouraged modernization and brought his country into closer contact with Europe.

Active Reading

EVALUATE
When you evaluate, you weigh the importance of specific facts or evidence in order to make a judgment. As you read this section, evaluate the factors that played a role in the development of Prussia and Russia as significant powers.

A. The Thirty Years' War

Absolute rulers in Europe used military and economic policy to increase their power. However, in the region that is now Germany, there was no organized nation in the seventeenth century. The leaders of dozens of small states jealously guarded their independence. Even Charles V, the powerful Holy Roman emperor of the 1500s, had not been able to force his will on the small German states.

Germany and Civil War

In 1612, Ferdinand II came to the throne of Bohemia, which is today the Czech Republic. As a Hapsburg, Ferdinand dreamed of succeeding where Charles V had failed. Allying himself with his cousins, the Spanish Hapsburgs, he attempted to stamp out Protestantism from the Holy Roman Empire. The Bohemian nobles resisted strongly and forced Ferdinand to step down from the throne, replacing him with a Protestant ruler. This began the Thirty Years' War in 1618, a long and bloody conflict that spread from Bohemia and Germany all across Europe.

After years of war, peace was declared in 1635. The agreement was broken, however, by Cardinal Richelieu, Louis XIII's chief minister of French affairs. He feared Hapsburg power and led France into war against Spain. Now the fighting spread to the Netherlands, Italy, Spain, and Scandinavia—Denmark, Norway, and Sweden.

The Thirty Years' War was largely fought by mercenaries, or hired soldiers who were paid for their services by the kings and princes. When money for salaries ran out, as it often did, these soldiers helped themselves to whatever loot they could find. Entire communities were attacked and robbed. At the end of the struggle, much of Germany lay in ruins. One-third of the population had died in battle or from plague or undernourishment.

Teaching Options

Section 3 Resources

Teacher's Resources (TR)
Terms to Know, p. 30
Review History, p. 64
Build Your Skills, p. 98
Concept Builder, p. 233
Cause-and-Effect Chain, p. 325
Transparency 5

III. The Rulers of the Holy Roman Empire, Prussia, and Russia
(pp. 397–401)

Section Summary

Students will read about the civil war in Germany that ended the reign of the Holy Roman Empire. They will also learn how politics and war helped to make both Prussia and Russia major European powers. Students will study such important historical figures as Frederick the Great, Peter the Great, and Catherine the Great.

1 Introduce

Getting Started

Have students examine the two maps in this section, including the map of Europe on page 398 and of Russia on page 400. Have students read the keys and draw conclusions about the political conditions of the period.

TERMS TO KNOW

Explain that sometimes it is possible to remember a word by inventing a mnemonic device or by associating an image with the word. For example, suggest that students can remember the vocabulary term *standing army* by imagining a group of soldiers standing up, waiting for something to happen.

You may wish to preview the pronunciation of the following words with students.

Voltaire (vawl TER)
czar (ZAHR)
Romanov (ROH mah nohf)
Diderot (dee DROH)

ACTIVE READING

As students read, have them complete an idea web (TR, p. 321) with the various factors that helped the country of Prussia to rise to power in Europe and a separate idea web for Russia's rise to power. Encourage students to use these idea webs as they write their evaluations at the end of the section.

A. The Thirty Years' War

Purpose-Setting Question What was the purpose of the Peace of Westphalia? (It ended the Thirty Years' War and gave religious freedom to Protestants in the Holy Roman Empire. It also marked the end of the Holy Roman Empire as a political force and allowed France to become a leading European power.)

Using the Map

Europe, 1648

Ask students to read the "Where in the World?" feature about Westphalia on page 398 and then find Westphalia's approximate location on the map. Ask students what other Prussian province lay between Westphalia and the rest of Prussia. (Brandenburg)

✔ Map Check

Answers
1. Sicily and Sardinia
2. the Austrian Hapsburgs

WHERE IN THE WORLD?

WESTPHALIA In 1945, Westphalia stopped being a province of Prussia. During World War II, the province was split between three German lands: Nordhein-Westfalen, Lower Saxony, and Hessen.

◆ **ANSWER** When money for their salaries ran out, the mercenaries would pillage and loot the land for whatever they could find.

B. The Rise of Prussia as a European Power

Purpose-Setting Question What were some of the significant achievements of Frederick the Great during his reign in Prussia? (He was a great patron of the arts, he supported religious liberty, and he led military campaigns that expanded Prussian territory.)

Europe, 1648

- Spanish Hapsburgs
- Austrian Hapsburgs
- Brandenburg-Prussia
- Dutch Netherlands
- Holy Roman Empire

✔ Map Check

1. **REGION** Which islands did the Spanish Hapsburgs control?
2. **LOCATION** Who controlled Silesia and Bohemia?

Where in the World?

WESTPHALIA
Westphalia is a region in present-day western Germany that is near the border of the Netherlands. It is located just east of the Rhine River. From 1816 to 1945, Westphalia was governed by Prussia, which was a northeastern region of Europe.

The Peace of Westphalia

Negotiations for peace were renewed in 1640 but—like the war itself—they dragged on and on. It was not until 1648 that the parties could agree on terms and stop the conflict. The Hapsburgs were forced to give up their dream of restoring Roman Catholicism to central Europe. The Peace of Westphalia in 1648 marked the end of the Thirty Years' War and secured the religious freedom of Protestants. It also weakened Germany's power, which allowed France to become the leading European nation. In addition, the Peace of Westphalia divided the Holy Roman Empire into more than 300 separate and mostly independent states. This marked the end of the Holy Roman Empire as a political force. It continued in name only.

◆ **Why did mercenaries cause destruction during the Thirty Years' War?**

B. The Rise of Prussia as a European Power

Prussia, a northeastern region in Europe of German-speaking peoples, occupied parts of what are now eastern Germany, Poland, and western Russia. During the 1700s, expert leadership and military might made Prussia one of the most important European powers.

A Military State

In the early 1600s, Prussia came under the control of the German state of Brandenburg. Under the leadership of Frederick William during the Thirty Years' War, a policy of **militarism** gradually took shape. Militarism stresses military needs and values. Seeing the horrors of the Thirty Years' War, Frederick William was determined to build a strong, capable army in Prussia that could defend his territory if the need arose.

Teaching Options

Connection to GOVERNMENT

For Frederick the Great, religious tolerance was more a political or an economic issue than a humane concern. He once wrote, "If the sovereign . . . declares himself for one religion or another, . . . persecutions will commence and, in the end, the religion persecuted will leave the fatherland, and millions of subjects will enrich our neighbors by their skill and industry."

In 1701, as the War of the Spanish Succession was about to begin, the Hapsburg emperor asked Frederick III, Frederick William's successor, to supply 8,000 troops. Frederick agreed, provided that the emperor would recognize him as king of Prussia. Thus, Frederick III became King Frederick I. Through skillful negotiation, he had achieved a unique position among the German princes.

Although the Prussians did not invent the idea of a **standing army**, they applied great energy to strengthening their military. A standing army is a permanent army of professional, or paid, soldiers. King Frederick William I, the son of Frederick I, was an especially strong supporter of the military. He doubled the size of the army, invented a system for recruiting new soldiers, and founded a group of younger people for military training. By the end of Frederick William's reign, out of a population of about 100,000 in Berlin, 20,000 were soldiers. Unusual for a European monarch at the time, Frederick William preferred saving money to spending it. When his son inherited the throne in 1740, Prussia had become strong, not only militarily but also financially.

Frederick the Great

From 1740 until his death in 1786, Frederick II, known as Frederick the Great, ruled Prussia. Unlike his father, who looked down on cultural pursuits, he loved literature and philosophy. He became a great patron of the arts, and he supported religious liberty. He was also one of the most brilliant military leaders of the time.

Soon after becoming king, Frederick boldly led the Prussian army southward and conquered the region of Silesia, most of which lay in present-day Poland. This act began the War of the Austrian Succession among European nations, which was fought from 1740 to 1748. When peace was finally made, Prussia emerged as the big winner. The other European powers recognized the Prussian annexation, or taking possession, of Silesia.

However, Frederick was forced on the defensive in the 1750s, when Austria, Russia, and France formed an alliance against Prussia. In the Seven Years' War, which was fought from 1756 to 1763, Frederick was able to save his kingdom, even though the population of his enemies outnumbered Prussia by about ten to one. The discipline and loyalty of the Prussian army saved Frederick and his state.

Frederick the Great's rule of Prussia is an example of a certain style of monarchy called **enlightened despotism**. Enlightened despotism is an absolute monarchy in which the ruler uses his or her power to bring about political and social changes that benefit his or her subjects. Enlightened despotism developed in the 1700s. Frederick described this style of monarchy in a letter to one of his close friends, the French philosopher Voltaire:

Frederick the Great ruled Prussia for nearly 50 years. Under his leadership, Prussia's influence in Europe developed.

> ❝ My chief occupation is to fight ignorance and prejudices in this country. . . . I must enlighten [free from ignorance and misinformation] my people, cultivate their manners and morals, and make them as happy as human beings can be, or as happy as the means at my disposal permit. ❞

Frederick's use of centralized authority to make important decisions while he ruled Prussia was clear. His most important fault, perhaps, was his failure to train a capable successor. Twenty years after Frederick's death, a French leader named Napoleon was able to defeat the Prussians.

 How did King Frederick William I strengthen the Prussian military?

ANALYZE PRIMARY SOURCES

DOCUMENT-BASED QUESTION
What goals does Frederick the Great stress in his letter to Voltaire?

C. The Russian Empire Emerges

Purpose-Setting Question What were some of the outside influences on Peter the Great? (He spent a year in western Europe learning about western culture; he wanted to create a strong army, just as the monarchs of France and Prussia were doing.)

SPOTLIGHT ON HISTORY

SAINT PETERSBURG Ask students to research and list places in the United States that were also named in honor of famous historical figures. (Possible answers: the states of Washington and Pennsylvania or the cities of Houston, Columbus, and Pittsburgh)

Using the Map

The Growth of Russia, 1689–1796

Point out the huge size of Russia. Ask students to estimate the number of degrees of longitude that Russia covers. (about 180 degrees)

✔ Map Check
Answers
1. Baltic Sea
2. Prussia

 **Activity**

Play a name game Adding a meaningful adjective or description to a person's name can be a good strategy for remembering something about a historical figure. Suggest that students make up names as they take notes or study. For example, they might call Peter I, Peter the Great Modernizer.

Explore Ask students to examine the ways that Saint Petersburg is like Versailles. Students may wish to work in groups to make a Venn diagram (TR, p. 323) comparing the city and the palace as symbols and as political capitals.

C. The Russian Empire Emerges

Until the late 1600s, Russia had not developed into an organized nation. Also, Russia had very little contact with the rest of Europe. The reasons included religion, foreign invasion, and geography. Russia followed the religion of the Eastern Orthodox Church and was influenced by Constantinople rather than by Rome. Also, from 1250 to about 1500, the Mongols controlled Russia. Finally, the lack of warm-water ports made Russian contact with Europe difficult.

In the 1500s, absolute monarchy took shape in Russia under the rule of Ivan IV, known as Ivan the Terrible. In 1613, after a period of civil war, the Russians chose a new czar, or leader, named Michael Romanov. He was the first of the Romanovs, a dynasty that lasted until the Russian Revolution of 1917.

Peter the Great

Russia's development into an organized nation took place most rapidly under Peter I, known as Peter the Great. At the age of 25, Peter spent a year in western Europe. He was determined to bring the ideas and influence of western Europe to his own country. He also wanted to create a strong army just as the monarchs in France and Prussia were doing.

Military campaigns dominated Peter the Great's reign. His principal enemies were the Swedes, whom he eventually defeated in 1709. Russian conquests in the Baltic region were especially important because they provided new access to the sea.

Peter the Great also built a new capital with a splendid royal residence. This city, named in his honor, was Saint Petersburg. Like the Versailles of

Spotlight on *History*

SAINT PETERSBURG
After the city's founding in 1703 by Peter the Great, Saint Petersburg replaced Moscow as the Russian capital. The city's name was changed in 1914 to Petrograd and in 1924 to Leningrad, in honor of V. I. Lenin, the leader of the Russian Revolution. In 1918, Moscow once again became the capital.
After the breakup of the Soviet Union in 1991, Saint Petersburg became known again by its original name.

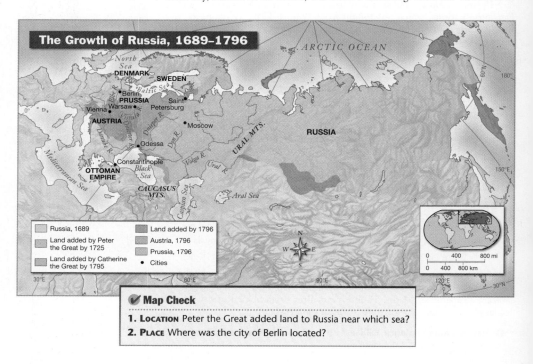

The Growth of Russia, 1689–1796

Legend:
- Russia, 1689
- Land added by Peter the Great by 1725
- Land added by Catherine the Great by 1795
- Land added by 1796
- Austria, 1796
- Prussia, 1796
- • Cities

✔ Map Check
1. **LOCATION** Peter the Great added land to Russia near which sea?
2. **PLACE** Where was the city of Berlin located?

400 UNIT 4 ◆ Europe Undergoes Change

Teaching Options

 Using Technology

Have students use the Internet to experience firsthand the splendor of Saint Petersburg. Have them make a list of the most important historical landmarks or cultural centers of the city. As a class, make a travel itinerary that includes these places. Students should also print as many pictures of these landmarks and cultural centers as possible to include in the itinerary.

Louis XIV, Saint Petersburg was symbolic as well as spectacular. The city represented the czar's opening of Russia to the technological and cultural achievements of the West.

In economics, Peter the Great adopted mercantilism, as Louis XIV's minister Colbert had done in France. He encouraged the development of mining and textile work, and he tried to increase exports. Peter also supported education, requiring all sons of Russian aristocrats to attend school.

Although many of these actions were progressive, Peter the Great ruled Russia as an absolute monarch. His continual financial needs put heavy burdens on peasants and serfs. He also refused to follow the custom by which most monarchs passed on their rule by inheritance. Peter had his own son tried for treason and tortured to death. He then decided that he would choose his successor. However, he died without naming one.

Catherine the Great

The absence of a policy for transferring power from one monarch to another had predictable results. For nearly 30 years, there was chaos in Russia. Finally, in 1762, Catherine II—who, like Peter, is known as the Great—proclaimed herself czarina.

Catherine's reign was an example of enlightened despotism. She liked and admired Voltaire and Diderot, the French philosophers of the 1700s. She also supported a certain degree of religious toleration. Like Peter the Great, however, Catherine enjoyed using her power. She severely crushed a peasant rebellion in 1773. Under her reign, serfs in Russia became powerless.

In addition, Catherine added significantly to Russian territory. Together with Frederick the Great and the Austrian empress Maria Theresa, she divided Poland. She also gave Russia another outlet to the sea by winning the northern coast of the Black Sea from the Turkish sultan in 1774. Soon afterwards in that region, the Russians founded the seaport of Odessa.

◆ Why did Russia have little contact with the rest of Europe until the late 1600s?

This Russian cartoon shows Peter the Great cutting off the beard of a Russian aristocrat. The cutting of beards was symbolic of becoming more like western Europeans.

Focus Catherine was actually German and not Russian. Her marriage to Peter, the heir to the Russian throne, was arranged by Peter's mother in 1743. Once Peter assumed the throne, he proved to be an ineffective ruler, and the royal couple grew to hate each other. The nobles and common people of Russia were happy when Catherine overthrew her husband, had him murdered in 1762, and assumed the throne herself.

◆ **ANSWER** Russia followed the religion of the Eastern Orthodox Church, not the Roman Catholic Church; the Mongols controlled Russia; and there were no warm-water ports to connect Russia to other European countries.

Section Close

Remind students that one of the reasons Russia emerged as a world power was because its leaders began to emulate western nations. Ask students to identify some of the political, economic, and cultural influences that changed Russia.

③ Assess

Review Answers

Review History

A. The Hapsburgs were forced to give up their dream of restoring Roman Catholicism to central Europe, and the Protestants—both Lutherans and Calvinists—in the German states were guaranteed religious freedom.

B. The other European powers recognized the Prussian annexation of Silesia.

C. Peter the Great defeated the Swedes, got new access to the Baltic Sea, built Saint Petersburg, adopted mercantilism, encouraged mining and textile work, and supported education for sons of Russian aristocrats.

Define Terms to Know

militarism, 398; standing army, 399; enlightened despotism, 399

Critical Thinking

Possible answer: Religion played a central role, with Roman Catholics and Protestants fighting each other over control of the Holy Roman Empire.

Review III

Review History
A. What were the main results of the Thirty Years' War?
B. What did Frederick the Great accomplish for Prussia in the War of the Austrian Succession?
C. What were some of Peter the Great's achievements during his reign in Russia?

Define Terms to Know
Define the following terms:
militarism, standing army, enlightened despotism

Critical Thinking
What role did religion play in the Thirty Years' War?

Write About Government
In a paragraph or two, compare and contrast absolute monarchy with enlightened despotism.

Get Organized
CAUSE-AND-EFFECT CHAIN
Think about the main events in this section. Use a cause-and-effect chain to show the cause and effect of an event. For example, what was the cause and effect of the Thirty Years' War?

CAUSE
Ferdinand II wanted to stamp out Protestantism. Bohemian nobles replaced him with a Protestant ruler.

EVENT
Thirty Years' War

EFFECT
The Peace of Westphalia in 1648 secured religious freedom for Protestants.

Write About Government
Students' comparisons should note that although an enlightened despot is an absolute ruler with total control, he or she uses power to bring about political or social change to benefit royal subjects. Many absolute rulers would not accept any social responsibility.

IV. A Limited Monarchy in England

(pp. 402–406)

Section Summary

Students will read about the conflicts between the kings of England and Parliament over religion and political power. They will learn how Parliament gradually took on more and more power and imposed significant limitations on the monarchy with the English Bill of Rights.

1 Introduce

Getting Started

Call on students' prior knowledge about the U.S. system of checks and balances. Ask students to tell why this system is important. Explain that power in many countries today is not balanced nor are there any checks on power. Point out that in this section, they will learn how the English government established the concept of checks and balances.

TERMS TO KNOW

Discuss the vocabulary terms with the class. For the first three terms, have students look for clues to the meaning within the term itself. For example, students know both parts of the compound word *Commonwealth.* Suggest that they use this strategy as they learn other new terms. Remind students to add the new terms to their glossaries.

You may wish to preview the pronunciations of the following terms with students.

Anglican Church
(AYN glih kan CHERCH)
Whig (HWIHG)
Tory (TAWR ee)
habeas corpus
(HAY bee uhs KAWR puhs)

ACTIVE READING

Students may find it useful to record the main ideas and details in a main idea/supporting details chart (TR, p. 319). Remind students that the headings usually present main ideas.

Section IV

A Limited Monarchy in England

Terms to Know

Commonwealth the English republic declared by Oliver Cromwell

martial law the law administered by military forces with the government's approval

English Bill of Rights a statement of subjects' rights and of the relationship of Parliament to the monarchy

habeas corpus a Latin term for a legal requirement that a person cannot be held in prison without being charged with a specific crime

Main Ideas

A. The policies of two kings of England, James I and Charles I, put these monarchs in opposition to Parliament.

B. The Glorious Revolution of 1688 limited the powers of the monarchy and resulted in the creation of the English Bill of Rights.

Active Reading

MAIN IDEAS AND DETAILS
While reading history, it is helpful to identify main ideas and supporting details. As you read this section, look for supporting details that explain how the powers of the monarchy were limited after the Glorious Revolution.

A. The Early Stuarts and the English Civil War

When Queen Elizabeth I died in 1603, her distant cousin James VI of Scotland came to the English throne. He ruled as King James I. James was the son of Mary Stuart, who is also known as Mary Queen of Scots. Under his rule, the thrones of England and Scotland were united for the first time. The four kings who ruled England for most of the seventeenth century are known as the Stuarts, from their family name.

James I and Rule by Divine Right

James I was far less skillful than Elizabeth had been at balancing conflicting interests. Many members of Parliament were Puritans, who believed that the Church of England, also called the Anglican Church, still resembled the Roman Catholic Church too much. In addition, Puritans did not strongly support Protestant ideas. Moreover, almost all members of Parliament were property owners. James I was strongly anti-Puritan, and his need for money alarmed landowners and merchants, who feared new taxes.

James I believed that he ruled by divine right.

The king showed an open disregard for Parliament. James I claimed that he ruled by divine right. He had written a book entitled *True Law of Free Monarchy* in which he argued that monarchs ought to be free from the interference of Parliament or control by the Church of England. Kings, according to James, possessed their authority directly from God, and they were responsible only to God.

Parliament disagreed. Many members were not ready to accept the king's claim that he could make any laws he wished. They denied that the king had the right to raise taxes or the power to decide cases in the courts on his own authority. Such absolute powers went against English tradition.

James I remained anti-Puritan and did not support the Puritans' call for reforms. During his reign, the Bible was translated into English. This translation of the Bible is called the King James Version. This Bible remains one of the most widely used English translations.

During King James's reign, Puritans began to leave England. One of the groups that left for Holland later sailed to North America aboard the *Mayflower.*

Teaching Options

Section 4 Resources

Teacher's Resources (TR)
Terms to Know, p. 30
Review History, p. 64
Build Your Skills, p. 98
Concept Builder, p. 233
Chapter Test, pp. 149–150
Cause-and-Effect Chain, p. 325

ESL/ELL STRATEGIES

Organize Information Have students make a chart listing each monarch discussed in this section. Each column should be titled with a monarch's name. Under each name, have students list the monarch's main strengths, weaknesses, and actions. Have students work in pairs to improve and complete their charts.

Charles I and Civil War

Charles I, James's son, succeeded him in 1625. Like his father, he believed that monarchs ruled by divine right. As a result, he created tension between himself and Parliament by trying to rule without the interference of Parliament. Once again, religious and economic issues put the king in opposition to Parliament. Charles's marriage to a French Roman Catholic princess was unpopular in England. His strong support of the Anglican Church angered many Puritans. Large numbers of them left England, and many traveled to the new colonies in North America. Charles also tried to raise money to improve the navy without the consent of Parliament.

Through inheritance, Charles I was also king of Scotland. Scotland was a heavily Calvinist country. In 1637, however, Charles attempted to force the Anglican system of bishops on the Scottish Church. When the Scots rebelled, Charles called on Parliament to help defeat the revolt. Far from sympathizing with the king, however, Parliament took the opportunity to focus on its own problems with the king.

The English Civil War broke out in 1642. Oliver Cromwell, a Puritan member of Parliament who had great military and organizational abilities, led the king's opponents. Cromwell gradually defeated the king's forces, and Charles I was imprisoned. In 1649, some members of Parliament tried the king for treason. Charles I was beheaded, which at the time was quite extraordinary.

Oliver Cromwell and the Commonwealth

After the execution of Charles I, Oliver Cromwell ruled England as a republic called the **Commonwealth**. Scotland rebelled again—this time out of shock that the king had been executed. Cromwell soon found that he was no more successful than the Stuart monarchs had been in resolving conflicts within England. During Cromwell's rule, harsh campaigns were carried out against Irish Roman Catholics. Imposing **martial law**, which is the law administered by military forces with the government's approval, Cromwell named himself the "Lord Protector" of England. When he died in 1658, however, his son was overwhelmed by the struggle for power between the army and Parliament.

Oliver Cromwell (center) led Parliamentary forces, called the Roundheads, into battle during the English Civil War.

2 Teach

A. The Early Stuarts and the English Civil War

Purpose-Setting Question What did Charles I do to alienate Parliament? (He tried to rule without the interference of Parliament, particularly on issues involving religion and economics.)

Focus Although today the argument for absolute control by a president or national leader is rarely heard, at one time it was a lively and legitimate debate. Have students make the case for absolute control by Charles I to Parliament. Write on the board the reasons and details that support the argument.

Explore Have students compare Cromwell's Commonwealth to a monarchy. In what ways was Cromwell like a king? (He led the military, imposed power on the people, controlled the government, attempted to work with Parliament.)

Discuss Ask students why they think the English quickly re-established the monarchy after Cromwell died. Discuss the symbolic and political needs a monarch seemed to provide for England.

Activity

Write a journal entry Have students write a journal entry for Charles II after his father, Charles I, was beheaded. Students should include his feelings regarding the seriousness of the struggle between the army and the Parliament. Suggest that students use the text or do more research to obtain more information.

Extend Cromwell was a fascinating figure. Biographies of Cromwell far outnumber those of any English or British monarch. Despite being a devout Puritan, Cromwell drank, danced, hunted, enjoyed music, and did not even object to horse racing or plays. Cromwell is said to have loved practical jokes. In spite of his achievements and successes, in January 1661, twelve years after the execution of Charles I and three years after his death, Cromwell's corpse was dug up and brought to Tyburn, the traditional site of public execution. There his body was hanged and then decapitated.

Conflict Resolution

Explain to students that the beheading of King Charles I was an unheard of act of defiance. Ask students to explain how the act created more problems for the country. Have students work together to brainstorm other solutions that might have been used to resolve the conflicts between the king and Parliament.

Cooperative Learning

Hold a mock trial of the case of Parliament versus Charles I. Assign groups of students to act as the major players in the trial, witnesses, jury members, the defense team, and the prosecution team. The defense and the prosecution should meet to formulate their arguments. After the case is presented, jury members should meet to decide the outcome of the trial based on the arguments given.

B. Restoration, Revolution, and the Triumph of Parliament

Purpose-Setting Question How did Parliament try to prevent a Roman Catholic king from coming to power? (Parliament issued the Test Act, which required all officials to take part in the communion service of the established Church of England.)

Focus One reason that Charles II was called the merry monarch was that it was thought that he was more interested in money and in living well than in power. He agreed to give Parliament control over taxation in England in exchange for a yearly personal income of 1 million pounds. Charles also signed a secret treaty with King Louis XIV of France, requiring him to restore the Roman Catholic Church to supremacy in England in exchange for a substantial yearly payment. Parliament's angry reaction to attempts by Charles II for greater tolerance of Roman Catholics in England led to the passage of the Test Act.

Then & Now

WHIGS AND TORIES Point out that the terms *Whigs* and *Tories* have also been part of U.S. history. American colonists loyal to England during the Revolutionary War were called Tories, and William Henry Harrison and Zachary Taylor were Presidents who were members of the Whig Party.

Discuss Have students discuss the reasons absolute monarchy succeeded in Spain, France, and Russia, whereas it became limited in England. (Possible answer: the strength of the English Parliament; even powerful rulers, such as Henry VIII and Elizabeth I, had been careful to give the appearance, at any rate, of sharing power with Parliament.)

The coronation procession of Charles II proceeded from the Tower of London to Westminster Abbey, the London church in which Charles was crowned king of England in 1660.

Then & Now

WHIGS AND TORIES
Whigs and Tories remained the standard name for the two major political parties in the British Parliament for about 150 years.

Now, the two major parties are called Labour and Conservative. Some people still use the term *Tories* for the Conservatives.

404 UNIT 4 ◆ Europe Undergoes Change

The great majority of people in England were now exhausted by civil war. By Parliamentary consent, England turned again to the monarchy. Charles I's son, who had spent 11 years in France, returned to England in 1660 as Charles II.

◆ **What conflicts divided the monarchy and Parliament?**

B. Restoration, Revolution, and the Triumph of Parliament

Charles II was a more capable politician than his father and grandfather had been. Nevertheless, there were tensions between the king and Parliament for the next quarter of a century. Charles II, however, was well aware of his father's fate, and he was cautious about angering members of Parliament.

Charles II and the Restoration

Charles II, who ruled from 1660 to 1685, is sometimes called the merry monarch. During the Restoration, the common name for this period, there was a departure from the strict, severe style of the Puritan Commonwealth. The new king admired French taste, and he enjoyed watching plays. The theaters in London, which had been closed by the Puritans in 1642, promptly reopened. A brilliant generation of playwrights delighted audiences, and women actors appeared onstage for the first time.

Charles II was generally tolerant on religious issues—too tolerant, in fact, for the majority of Parliament. The members feared that the king personally favored Roman Catholicism. Because Charles had no children of his own, the religious issue came to be linked with the issue of royal succession during the 1670s. Charles's brother James was next in line to the throne. James had publicly announced his conversion to Roman Catholicism. Parliament responded by passing the Test Act in 1673. This law, which Charles was forced to approve, required all officials to take part in the communion service of the established Church of England.

In 1681, Parliament tried again to prevent a Roman Catholic king from coming to the throne. They debated a bill that would specifically exclude James from the succession. The bill's supporters were known by the nickname Whigs, whereas the king's supporters were called Tories. For a long time afterward, these names continued to identify the two leading political parties in Parliament. To block the exclusion bill, as it came to be called, Charles II ended Parliament. After Charles's death in 1685, his brother became king and ruled as James II. His reign was not to last long.

Teaching Options

More on Charles II

Soon after Charles succeeded to the throne of Britain, there were two major catastrophes—the Plague of 1665, when 70,000 died in London alone, and the Great Fire of London in 1666. About 75,000 people died from the plague. The Great Fire, which lasted four days, damaged four-fifths of London. As a result of the fire, London was rebuilt with a more open design.

The Glorious Revolution and the English Bill of Rights

Soon after coming to power, James II appointed many Roman Catholic officials. In the eyes of Parliament, these appointments directly violated the Test Act. Furthermore, James and his Roman Catholic wife had a son, who was baptized as a Roman Catholic. Now, even the Tories refused to support the king any longer. In 1688, Parliament offered the English throne to William of Orange in the Netherlands, who was married to James's daughter Mary. Later that year, William and Mary arrived in England with their army and James II was forced to abdicate, or step off the throne. This event, which took place with almost no bloodshed, became known as the Glorious Revolution. James II then fled the country, first to France and then to Ireland, where his army was eventually defeated by William in 1690. James's fate was described this way by modern historian Gilbert Burnet:

> **"** A great king, with strong armies and mighty fleets, a vast treasure and powerful allies, fell all at once; and his whole strength, like a spider's web, was . . . broken with a touch. **"**

ANALYZE PRIMARY SOURCES **DOCUMENT-BASED QUESTION** How does this historian evaluate James's actions?

In 1689, when William III and Mary officially took the throne, Parliament approved a Bill of Rights. Like the Magna Carta nearly 500 years earlier, the **English Bill of Rights** was a statement of subjects' rights and of the relationship between Parliament and the monarchy. The terms of the English Bill of Rights gave most of the political power to Parliament. Parliamentary consent was required for passing laws, raising taxes, and maintaining an army. The English Bill of Rights also confirmed the legal requirement of **habeas corpus**, which was issued in 1679. Habeas corpus, a Latin term, is a legal requirement that no English subject could be arrested or imprisoned without

Major Terms of the English Bill of Rights

- The monarch does not have the power to execute or suspend laws without Parliament's consent.
- No taxes may be raised without the consent of Parliament.
- Maintaining an army in peacetime without Parliament's consent is illegal.
- There must be free elections of members of Parliament and free speech within Parliament.
- Courts must have juries. Church and royal courts are illegal.
- No one can be punished without a trial and conviction, and there should be no cruel or unusual punishments.
- There must be frequent meetings of Parliament.

This medal was created in honor of the marriage of Mary, daughter of James II, to William of Orange in 1640.

✔ Chart Check

Which three terms of the English Bill of Rights involve Parliament's consent?

Focus Have student volunteers explain why *Glorious Revolution* is a good name for the overthrow of James II. Have other members of the class give reasons why they agree or disagree with the volunteers' arguments.

Activity

Make a timeline To help trace the events of the civil war and the revolution in England, make a timeline (TR, p. 320) of the events described in this section. Have students copy this timeline in their notebooks and use it as they review the chapter.

ANALYZE PRIMARY SOURCES

DOCUMENT-BASED QUESTION
As perhaps the least popular of all the English monarchs, James II spent much of his life in exile. After William of Orange defeated his army, James fled to France, where he lived for 13 years.

ANSWER Gilbert Burnet thinks that James II had both great wealth and power but that it all was lost very quickly.

Using the Chart
Major Terms of the English Bill of Rights

Have students choose one of the items from the list of rights and write a brief paragraph that explains why it was included in the English Bill of Rights and why it is still an important rule for governments to follow.

✔ Chart Check

Answer the monarch's executing or suspending laws, the raising of taxes, and the maintenance of an army in peacetime

---

Research

AVERAGE
Have students look at the Bill of Rights in the U.S. Constitution. Have them evaluate the differences and similarities between the U.S. Bill of Rights and the English Bill of Rights. Ask them to summarize their findings in a brief report.

CHALLENGE
Point out that the United States and England are not the only governments to have a Bill of Rights as part of their political tradition. Challenge students to find another nation with a Bill of Rights. Have them write a summary of the document they find and compare it to the English Bill of Rights, shown in the chart on page 405.

Explore Discuss the words *treatise* and *contract* with students. Then, ask students to suggest what terms might be part of an ideal contract between citizens and their government. List their suggestions on the board. Ask students whether they think a contract can exist in an absolute monarchy or an enlightened despotism. Why or why not? Suggest that students read the excerpt of *Two Treatises of Government* on page 811.

 **ANSWER** He appointed many Roman Catholic officials, which Parliament viewed as violating the Test Act. James also baptized his son as a Roman Catholic, alarming Parliament at the prospect of a Roman Catholic successor.

Section Close

Have students recap the section by asking them to explain how limited monarchy came about in England and how the power of Parliament increased.

③ Assess

Review Answers

Review History

A. Both James I and Charles I believed in absolute monarchy, in which the king's authority is based on divine right.

B. The Glorious Revolution was the decision of Parliament in 1688 to force James II to abdicate. Parliament invited William III of Orange of the Netherlands to take the throne of England. The revolution took place with almost no bloodshed.

Define Terms to Know

Commonwealth, 403; martial law, 403; English Bill of Rights, 405; habeas corpus, 405

Critical Thinking

Possible answer: The struggles between the monarchy and Parliament had religious aspects because both Puritans and Roman Catholics were dissatisfied under the Church of England, also called the Anglican Church. These struggles were also political because Parliament refused to accept the absolutist rule of the Stuart monarchs.

---

being charged with a specific crime. A court would have to meet promptly to decide if there was cause for the person to be arrested or imprisoned.

Change in England

The result of the English Bill of Rights was that a person called the prime minister would be chosen by the leading party in Parliament. The prime minister became the real head of government. William and Mary had to limit their powers as England's rulers. These limits were spelled out in the English Bill of Rights. This type of rule is known as a limited monarchy. William and Mary agreed that Parliament would have the right to pass laws, to tax citizens, and to approve the existence of a permanent army.

At the time that Parliament approved the English Bill of Rights and William and Mary agreed to the terms, an English philosopher named John Locke wrote about the rights of English subjects. Locke contributed greatly to the study of politics and government. One of his most famous works was *Two Treatises of Government*. In this book, he argued against one person having absolute power in government. Locke believed that governments were formed because people allowed them to be formed. Locke's theory was called the contract theory of government. A government made a contract with the people to protect certain rights, such as life, liberty, and property. If government failed to protect these rights, the contract was broken. Then, a new government could be put in place.

In 1701, Parliament passed the Act of Settlement, declaring that no Roman Catholic could be king of England. Then, in 1694, Mary died. Six years later, William became ill. Since he had no children, Parliament amended the act to ensure that James II could not return as king of England. In 1707, the Act of Union merged the parliaments of England and Scotland. Scotland joined England and Wales, which all together became Great Britain, or Britain.

◆ **How did the actions of James II cause Parliament to react?**

Primary Source Documents
You can read sections of *Two Treatises of Government* on page 811.

Review IV

Review History
A. What theory of monarchy did James I and Charles I both hold?
B. What was the Glorious Revolution?

Define Terms to Know
Define the following terms: **Commonwealth, martial law, English Bill of Rights, habeas corpus**

Critical Thinking
How was religious conflict linked with political conflict in seventeenth-century England?

Write About Economics
In a paragraph, explain why Parliament was eager to secure its right to raise taxes.

Get Organized
CAUSE-AND-EFFECT CHAIN
Think about the main events in this section. Use a cause-and-effect chain to show the cause and effect of an event. For example, what was the cause and the effect of the English Civil War?

Write About Economics

Possible answer: Parliament did not want the monarchy to be able to control taxes and possibly raise them to enrich itself or wage an unpopular war. Parliament also recognized that by controlling taxation, it could have more power in making governmental decisions.

CAUSE
Charles I tried to impose the Anglican system of bishops on the Scottish Church, and the Scots rebelled.

↓

EVENT
The English Civil War

↓

EFFECT
Charles I was beheaded; Oliver Cromwell ruled England.

Points of View

King Versus Parliament

In several European nations from 1500 to 1800, rule by an absolute monarch was supported by the theory of the "divine right of kings." According to this theory, God was the ultimate source of all power. The monarch was God's chosen representative on Earth. Therefore, it was the obligation of all the monarch's subjects to obey him or her. Monarchs, such as Philip II in Spain, Louis XIV in France, and James I in England, used the theory of divine right to defend their supreme power.

Not all of these monarchs were equally successful, however. In England, Parliament had a long history, dating back to the thirteenth century. Individual rights were guaranteed by the Magna Carta, signed by King John in 1215. Members and supporters of Parliament viewed it as a way to ensure a balance of power between the monarch and Parliament. In this view, monarchs were bound to consult with Parliament and not to override its laws. In his *Two Treatises of Government*, the philosopher John Locke supported the idea that the people are the only source of power.

Members of Parliament met to discuss laws.

> **"**Kings exercise a manner of resemblance of divine power on earth . . . they have power of raising and casting down; of life and death; judges over all their subjects and in all causes, and yet accountable to none but God only.**"**
>
> —James I, *Speech to Parliament* (1610)

> **"**The people alone can appoint the form of the commonwealth, which is by constituting the legislative, and appointing in whose hands that shall be. And when the people have said, 'We will submit, and be governed by laws made by such men, and in such forms,' nobody else can say other men shall make laws for them.**"**
>
> —John Locke, *Two Treatises of Government* (1690)

ANALYZE PRIMARY SOURCES

DOCUMENT-BASED QUESTIONS

1. According to James I, what powers do kings have?

2. According to John Locke, who has the power to decide a state's form of government?

3. **Critical Thinking** By taking absolute power in the government and economy of a state or nation, how do monarchs limit the growth of those they rule?

Teaching Options

Take a Stand

Have students use the information in Section 4 and the quotations here to form an opinion about the amount of power a national leader should have. Students should summarize their opinions in several paragraphs. The summary should include a clear viewpoint that is supported by details, facts, and examples.

F Y I

John Locke's Influence

John Locke's ideas about freedom, authority, and government made him the first philosopher of the Enlightenment. They also inspired the shapers of the American Revolution and later the authors of the U.S. Constitution. His writings are considered the classic expression of liberalism and are still influential today.

Points of View

KING VERSUS PARLIAMENT

Teach the Topic

The selections represent two differing opinions about the basis of government power. Point out that one statement was made by an absolute monarch. The other was written by an influential thinker, John Locke. Locke's book on government was widely read and summarized the most important arguments for a limited monarchy.

Ask students to summarize the power and authority of the leader of the United States. Point out that the President proposes laws but does not pass them. Ask students how the American people can indicate their dissatisfaction with their leaders. (by electing others)

Compare and Contrast Points of View

Have student volunteers read the passages aloud, changing the third person point of view to the first person. For example, they would begin the first passage, "I exercise a manner of resemblance . . ." Ask students if they understand the dangers of placing such great authority in one person.

ANALYZE PRIMARY SOURCES

DOCUMENT-BASED QUESTIONS
1. Kings have the "power of raising and casting down; of life and death; judges over all their subjects and in all causes."
2. the people
3. Possible answer: Absolute monarchs have control over decisions that affect all people, so people do not have independence to make their own decisions that could make their lives better.

CHAPTER
17 Review

Chapter Summary

A blank outline form is available in the Teacher's Resources (p. 318). Chapter summaries should outline the growth of Spain, the events in the reign of Louis XIV, the decline of the Holy Roman Empire, the rise of Prussia and Russia, and the events that led to the limited monarchy in England. Refer to the rubric in the Teacher's Resources (p. 340) to score students' chapter summaries.

 Interpret the Timeline

1. the Thirty Years' War
2. 1555
3. Ferdinand I is elected king of Hungary and Bohemia, Oliver Cromwell begins the rule of England as a republic, and Parliament approves the English Bill of Rights.
4. Check students' timelines to ensure that all events are from the chapter.

Use Terms to Know

5. habeas corpus
6. enlightened despotism
7. militarism
8. divine right
9. balance of power

Check Your Understanding

10. Dynasties could expand their influence through marriage, military campaigns, and inheritances.
11. Charles V found that he could not re-establish Roman Catholicism in the German states. He was forced to accept the Peace of Augsburg in 1555, by which each state could choose to be either Lutheran or Roman Catholic.
12. The revolt of the Netherlands against Spain brought England into confrontation with Spain.
13. By granting religious freedoms to Huguenots, the Edict of Nantes helped end civil war in France and reunify the country.
14. Louis XIV put great emphasis on the army. His government supervised recruiting, training, supplies, and promotions.
15. The term *neoclassical* emphasized the authors' interest in Greek and Roman subjects and the artists' stress on balanced, classical forms.
16. The Thirty Years' War began in Bohemia in 1618. The Bohemian nobles removed Roman Catholic

---

Chapter Summary

Complete the following outline in your notebook. Then, use your outline to write a brief summary of the chapter.

European Monarchies

I. Spain's Power Grows in Europe
  A. Charles V and the Hapsburg Empire
  B. The Golden Age in Spain
  C. England Enters on the World Stage

II. Louis XIV Rules France
  A. The French Wars of Religion
  B. Louis XIV: The Sun King
  C. France and the Rest of Europe

III. The Rulers of the Holy Roman Empire, Prussia, and Russia
  A. The Thirty Years' War
  B. The Rise of Prussia as a European Power
  C. The Russian Empire Emerges

IV. A Limited Monarchy in England
  A. The Early Stuarts and the English Civil War
  B. Restoration, Revolution, and the Triumph of Parliament

 Interpret the Timeline

Use the timeline on pages 384–385 to answer the following questions.

1. Which occurred first, approval of the English Bill of Rights or the beginning of the Thirty Years' War?

2. In which year was a document issued that provided religious freedom?

3. **Critical Thinking** Which events on the timeline show changes that took place in government?

4. Select five events from the chapter that are not on the timeline. Create a timeline that shows these events.

Use Terms to Know

Select the term that best completes each sentence.

balance of power   habeas corpus
divine right   militarism
enlightened despotism

5. The legal requirement called _____ states that a person cannot be held in prison without being charged with a specific crime.

6. In _____, the ruler uses his or her power to bring about political and social change that benefits his or her subjects.

7. A policy of _____ existed in Prussia because the region felt it was important to defend itself.

8. King James I of England is an example of a monarch who believed that he ruled by _____.

9. _____ was important to many rulers in Europe so that no single state dominated the others in its region.

Check Your Understanding

10. **Identify** ways in which dynasties could expand their influence.

11. **Explain** how Holy Roman Emperor Charles V found that his power was limited.

12. **Summarize** the international importance of the revolt of the Netherlands in the mid-1500s.

13. **Discuss** the significance of the Edict of Nantes.

14. **Describe** Louis XIV's policy toward the army in France.

15. **Explain** why literature and painting in France during Louis XIV's reign are called neoclassical.

16. **Identify** how, when, and where the Thirty Years' War began.

17. **Identify** two European monarchs of this period who ruled as enlightened despots.

18. **Explain** the causes of the English Civil War.

19. **Discuss** the outcome of the Glorious Revolution in England.

King Ferdinand II and replaced him with a Protestant ruler. This action led to the outbreak of war.
17. Frederick the Great of Prussia, Catherine the Great of Russia
18. Charles I tried to rule without the interference of Parliament. Some of his actions were unpopular in England. He married a French Roman Catholic, and he supported the Anglican Church, which offended many Puritans. After

Charles tried to force the Anglican system of bishops on the Scottish Church and the Scots rebelled, Parliament gathered forces to fight Charles and his supporters.
19. The Glorious Revolution assured the triumph of Parliament, the reinforcement of individual subjects' rights, and a Protestant line of succession in England.

Critical Thinking

20. Make Inferences Why did the marriage of King Philip II of Spain to Mary Tudor alarm many people in England?

21. Draw Conclusions What was the symbolic significance of Versailles during the reign of Louis XIV?

22. Compare and Contrast How would you compare and contrast Frederick the Great in Prussia with Catherine the Great in Russia?

23. Analyze Information How do the terms of the English Bill of Rights show the strength of Parliament in its struggle with the monarchy?

Put Your Skills to Work

24. Make Inferences You have learned how to make inferences, or reasonable conclusions or judgments, by evaluating facts and ideas as evidence.

Read the passage below. Then, answer the following questions.

a. What inference can you make from the passage about William III's attitude toward England and his kingship there?

b. What inference can you make about the relationship between France and the Netherlands?

c. What inference can you make about the future of the Netherlands if France and the Netherlands went to war and England was not involved?

> "The year 1688 gave England a Dutch king, Queen Mary's husband, William III, to whom the major importance of the 'Glorious Revolution' of that year was that England could be mobilized against France, now threatening the independence of the [Netherlands]."

Analyze Sources

25. Read the passage below from John Locke's *The Second Treatise of Government*. Then, answer the questions that follow.

> *It is true governments cannot be supported without great charge, and it is fit every one who enjoys his share of the protection should pay out of his estate his proportion for the maintenance of it. But still it must be with his own consent—[namely], the consent of the majority, giving it either by themselves or their representatives chosen by them.*

a. What does Locke mean by "charge"?

b. Who does Locke think should pay the "charge"?

c. How does Locke think the "charge" should be paid?

d. What important principles of government does this passage support?

Essay Writing

26. Write an essay discussing the different types of rule you have learned about in this chapter: absolute monarchy, enlightened despotism, and limited monarchy. In your essay, include the major features of each type of rule, as well as specific examples of each type of rule in Europe from 1500 to 1800. Then, compare and contrast the different types of rule.

TEST PREPARATION

CAUSE-AND-EFFECT RELATIONSHIPS
Choose the answer that correctly completes the sentence.

The most important effect of the Glorious Revolution in England was to

1. increase the conflict between Roman Catholics and Protestants.

2. lead England into a lengthy war with Spain.

3. ensure the political power of Parliament.

4. support the belief in divine right.

Critical Thinking

20. Possible answer: The English feared that Philip II would aid Mary Tudor in her efforts to reinstate Roman Catholicism in England.

21. Versailles served as a symbol of the power and magnificence of King Louis XIV and of absolute monarchy in France.

22. Both rulers might be described as enlightened despots. They used their power to gain additional territory. Both rulers admired French culture. Frederick the Great supported religious liberty. Catherine the Great supported a degree of religious tolerance. Frederick the Great was a strong military leader and supported the policy of militarism. Catherine the Great crushed a peasant uprising, leaving serfs powerless.

23. Possible answer: The English Bill of Rights emphasized the powers of Parliament and limited the powers of the monarchy.

Put Your Skills to Work

MAKE INFERENCES

24a. William III did not have much use for England or his kingship there. He saw his kingship only as a way to protect the Netherlands from France.

24b. France threatened the Netherlands, so the relationship between the two countries would have been very tense.

24c. The Netherlands might lose to France if England were not involved.

Analyze Sources

25a. Locke means "cost" or "expense."

25b. everyone who receives a share of the government's protection

25c. Locke says the charge should be paid out of each person's estate.

25d. Possible answer: The passage supports the principles that the costs of government are paid by the people but only by the consent of the majority.

Essay Writing

26. Students' essays should include the major features of the different types of rule and examples of each type. Students' essays should also compare and contrast the different types of rule.

TEST PREPARATION

Answer 3. ensure the political power of Parliament.

Unit 4

Portfolio Project

DRAMA: HISTORY IN ACTION

Managing the Project

Plan for 3–4 class periods.

Set the Scene

Encourage students to narrow the scope of their play to one episode in the life of their historical figure. To get started, have them answer the following question: What scene was most important or most interesting about the historical figure you chose?

Your Assignment

Ask students to read the assignment on page 410. Then, divide the class into groups of 5–6 to begin work on the project. You may want to suggest that students research several events from their person's life before choosing one event for their play.

RESEARCH YOUR STORY

After each group has chosen a historical figure, encourage students to take a vote on the scene that will be the subject of their play. Students who do not wish to perform should be encouraged to write; coordinate sets, costumes, or props; or to act as stage manager for the play.

REPORT TO YOUR CLASS

Once the research phase is complete, allow class time for team meetings. Encourage groups to limit their plays to 7–10 minutes so that each group will have an opportunity to perform its play. Remind students that they need to explain the context of the play through dialogue or through narration.

Wrap Up

The finished play should have props, costumes, and a script. The play should have a clear beginning, middle, and end.

Multimedia Presentation

Use a video camera to videotape your play. Before you videotape, make signs to display the title of the play and the names of the cast and crew members. Once everyone is ready, begin the video recording. Then, show your videotape to other history classes in your school.

Drama: History in Action

YOUR ASSIGNMENT

A movie or a television program about a person who has had a dramatic impact on history usually leaves you with the feeling that you better understand why he or she was important and interesting. Often, knowing something about a great person in history makes you want to know more, not only about this individual but about the time period as well. Select one person from Unit 4 and write a short play about that person's life.

RESEARCH YOUR STORY

Choose a Topic Working with a small group of classmates, select one of the following people to investigate:

Leonardo da Vinci	Ferdinand Magellan
Johann Gutenberg	Elizabeth I
Marco Polo	Frederick the Great
Prince Henry	Peter the Great
Moctezuma	Catherine the Great

Research Conduct research using your textbook, the Internet, and library resources. Prepare notecards to help you organize your information and create visuals, such as maps and posters, to illustrate settings in your play. Be sure to find the answers to these questions:

- What was happening before the play?
- How did the person achieve or carry out his or her actions?
- What were the effects of the person's actions or life?

REPORT TO YOUR CLASS

Plan Make a plan that details the scenes, the props, the settings, and the costumes for your play and the roles of all group members. For example, you might use a map of the country the historical person is from as a backdrop or as an introduction. Different roles of group members might include actors, researchers, director, set and lighting designers, and prop and costume managers.

Present Act out your play for the class. If the lines are too long for you to memorize, you could have one group of students read the lines while another group does the acting.

Work Individually Write a brief report about the major achievements of the person who is the subject of your play. In your report, make inferences about who or what might have had the biggest influence on this person.

Teaching Options

Multimedia Presentation

Encourage students to add music and narration to their video presentation. You may wish to have students videotape their plays outside of class and then present only the videotape to the class.

Alternative Assessment

Write a Dramatic Monologue Have students write and present a dramatic monologue in the person of one of the historical figures listed on page 410 or elsewhere in the unit. Have students present their dramatic monologues to the class without identifying the speaker and have the class guess the speaker's identity.

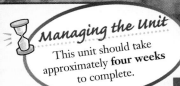

Managing the Unit
This unit should take approximately **four weeks** to complete.

PLANNING GUIDE

	Skills and Features	Projects and Activities	Program Resources	Meet Individual Needs
Chapter 18 **A Revolution in Science and Thought,** pp. 412–433 Plan for 4–5 class periods	Unit Technology, p. T411 Conduct a Debate, p. 419 Past to Present: Inventions of the Western World, pp. 420–421	Test Taking, pp. T416, T417 Connection to Literature, p. T420 Connection to Government, p. T423 Cooperative Learning, p. T424 Conflict Resolution, p. T425 Connection to Music, p. T427 Writing, p. T428 Sports & Games, p. T429 Research, p. T430	**Teacher's Resources** Terms to Know, p. 31 Review History, p. 65 Build Your Skills, p. 99 Chapter Test, pp. 151–152 Concept Builder, p. 234 They Made History: Mary Wollstonecraft, p. 258 Five *W*s Chart, p. 326	ESL/ELL Strategies, pp. T415, T422 Visual/Spatial, p. T414 Logical/Mathematical, p. T417
Chapter 19 **The French Revolution and Napoleon,** pp. 434–459 Plan for 5–6 class periods	Interpret Political Cartoons, p. 441 Points of View, p. 457	Using Technology, p. T437 Connection to Literature, p. T437 Writing, p. T439 Research, p. T443 Cooperative Learning, p. T444 Teen Life, p. T445 Connection to Geography, p. T448 Test Taking, p. T449 Connection to Math, p. T449 Connection to Art, pp. T451, T454 Conflict Resolution, p. T451 Connection to Government, p. T455 Take a Stand, p. T457 Link to Today, p. T457	**Teacher's Resources** Terms to Know, p. 32 Review History, p. 66 Build Your Skills, p. 100 Chapter Test, pp. 153–154 Concept Builder, p. 235 They Made History: Olympe de Gouges, p. 259 Cause-and-Effect Chain, p. 325 Transparency 5	ESL/ELL Strategies, pp. T436, T442, T450, T453 Verbal/Linguistic, p. T438 Auditory, p. T446 Visual/Spatial, p. T454
Chapter 20 **The Growth of Nationalism,** pp. 460–481 Plan for 4–5 class periods	Identify Ideologies, p. 467 They Made History: Florence Nightingale, p. 470 Connect History & Government, p. 479	Test Taking, p. T464 Using Technology, p. T465 Connection to Geography, p. T469 Connection to Literature, p. T470 Writing, pp. T471, T476 Cooperative Learning, p. T474 Conflict Resolution, p. T477 Connection to Math, p. T477 Link to Today, p. T479	**Teacher's Resources** Terms to Know, p. 33 Review History, p. 67 Build Your Skills, p. 101 Chapter Test, pp. 155–156 Concept Builder, p. 236 Cause-and-Effect Chain, p. 325 Transparencies 1, 5	ESL/ELL Strategies, pp. T463, T468, T475 Visual/Spatial, p. T464 Kinesthetic, p. T469
Chapter 21 **Asia, Africa, and Australia in Transition,** pp. 482–502 Plan for 4–5 class periods	Improve Your Test-Taking Skills, p. 489	Cooperative Learning, p. T485 Connection to Music, p. T485 Research, p. T486 Connection to Culture, p. T487 Connection to Art, p. T491 Using Technology, p. T491 Writing, p. T492 Connection to Government, p. T493 Conflict Resolution, p. T495 World Religions, p. T496 Connection to Music, p. T497 Test Taking, p. T498 Connection to Geography, p. T498	**Teacher's Resources** Terms to Know, p. 34 Review History, p. 68 Build Your Skills, p. 102 Chapter Test, pp. 157–158 Unit 5 Test, pp 191–192 Concept Builder, p. 237 Five *W*s Chart, p. 326 Transparencies 1, 5, 7, 8	ESL/ELL Strategies, pp. T484, T497 Visual-Spatial, p. T487 Verbal/Linguistic, p. T493

Assessment Options

Chapter 18 Test, Teacher's Resources, pp. 151–152
Chapter 19 Test, Teacher's Resources, pp. 153–154
Chapter 20 Test, Teacher's Resources, pp. 155–156
Chapter 21 Test, Teacher's Resources, pp. 157–158
Unit 5 Test, Teacher's Resources, pp. 191–192

Alternative Assessment

Debate: Conflicts and Disputes in History, p. 502
Write an Editorial, p. T502

Books for Students

AVERAGE

Call for Independence: The Story of the American Revolution and its Causes. Stephen Meyeroff. Describes events and people involved with the war. (Oak Tree Publishers, 1996)

The French Revolution. Don Nardo, ed. Series of essays discussing causes and events of the Revolution. (Greenhaven Press, Inc., 1999)

Simón Bolívar: South American Liberator. David Goodnough. Biography of this general who helped free South America from Spain. (Enslow Publishers, Incoparted, 1998)

Folk Tales and Fables of Asia and Australia. Barbara Hayes. Compilation of seventeen stories from Asia and Australia. (Chelsea House Publishers, 1994)

CHALLENGING

Ingenious Pursuits: Building the Scientific Revolution. Lisa Jardine. Explores the scientific developments in the sixteenth and seventeenth centuries and the interaction among the people involved. (Anchor Books, 2000)

Scaramouche. Rafael Sabatini. Fictional adventure that takes place during the French Revolution. (W. W. Norton & Company, Inc., 2002)

Florence Nightingale: Lady with the Lamp. Sam Wellman. Biography that discusses her career from the time when she was in Turkey. (Barbour Publishing, Inc., 1999)

The Crimean War. John Sweetman. Reviews the Crimean War and highlights developments in fields such as war correspondence and nursing. (Osprey Publishing Ltd., 2001)

Books for Teachers

The Scientific Revolution. Steven Shapin. Discusses how science developed and was influenced by philosophy, politics, and religion. (University of Chicago Press, 1998)

American Revolution. David F. Burg. Primary sources are used to explore how the war affected those living at that time. (Facts on File, Inc., 2001)

The Days of the French Revolution. Christopher Hibbert. Describes the events, places, culture, and people of the Revolution. (Perennial, 1999)

Crimea: The Great Crimean War, 1854–1856. Trevor Royle. Explores the events that led to and occurred during the war, as well as the effects of the war. (St. Martin's Press, 2000)

The Last Emperors: A Social History of Qing Imperial Institutions. Evelyn S. Rawski. Reviews this dynasty from the cultural and social perspective of two different cultures. (University of California Press, 2001)

Australia: Biography of a Nation. Phillip Knightley. Narrative history of Australia that starts with the founding of the British colony. (Jonathan Cape, Limited, 2002)

You may wish to preview all referenced materials to ensure their appropriateness for your local community.

Audio/Visual Resources

Galileo: The Challenge of Reason. Discusses Galileo's contributions and discoveries and their effects on the world. Videocassette. (Social Studies School Service)

History Through Art: The Enlightenment. Reviews accomplishments, art, people, and places of the eighteenth century. Videocassette/CD-ROM. (Clearvue/EAV)

The Age of Revolutions: 1776–1848. Explores the reasons for the French Revolution, roles of certain leaders, and the affect on other continents. Videocassette. (Social Studies School Service)

Technology Resources

The European Enlightenment: Scientific Revolution: www.wsu.edu:8000/~dee/ENLIGHT/SCIREV.HTM

Liberty, Equality, Fraternity: Exploring the French Revolution: http://chnm.gmu.edu/revolution/

Toussaint L'Ouverture: http://www.pbs.org/wgbh/aia/part3/3h326.html

Qing Dynasty: http://emuseum.mnsu.edu/prehistory/china/later_imperial_china/qing.html

American Revolution. Allows students to explore the camps, the people, and a battle during 1651–1789. CD-ROM. (Entrex)

Globe Fearon Related Resources

History Resources

Core Knowledge History & Geography: American Revolution. Extends knowledge of the American Revolution to help build a solid background. ISBN 0-7690-3079-3

Core Knowledge History & Geography: Independence for Latin America. Extends the topic to help build a solid background. ISBN 0-7690-3089-0

Pacemaker and Adapted Classics

The Time Machine. H. G. Wells's novel about a scientist who travels into the future. ISBN 0-822-49256-3

Frankenstein. Mary Shelley's story of a scientist and his creation. ISBN 0-835-91116-0

20,000 Leagues Under the Sea. Jules Verne's adventure of underwater exploration. ISBN 0-835-90217-X

A Tale of Two Cities. Charles Dickens' novel during the French Revolution. ISBN 0-835-90219-6

Les Misérables. Victor Hugo's novel of an imprisoned peasant takes students into the Parisian underworld and the uprising of 1832. ISBN 0-835-90473-3

To order books, call 1-800-321-3106.

Enlightenment and Revolution

" *Sacred love of country*
Restore us to our daring and our pride!
My country gave me life
And I shall give it liberty. "

—Daniel François Auber, composer, *La Muette de Portici*, 1828

LINKING CULTURES When Enlightenment ideas opened people's minds to new ways of looking at the world, they began to question things they had always taken for granted. In countries around the world, people started to believe that they had the right to govern themselves. Many revolutions in thought led to revolutions on battlefields.

What do the painting and the quotation suggest about the attitudes of those who participated in revolutions?

411

Teaching Options

UNIT TECHNOLOGY

Invite students to research additional information about the historical figures involved in revolutions in Europe and Latin America. Students will encounter examples of leaders of revolution as they read Unit 5.

You may wish to identify possible Web sites for students and monitor their activities on the Internet.

UNIT 5 Portfolio Project

Debate: Conflicts and Disputes in History

The Portfolio Project for Unit 5 asks students to prepare and conduct a debate on topics from this unit. Students will prepare both affirmative and negative sides of the argument. As an extension, students can prepare their debate as a panel discussion for radio or television.

Enlightenment and Revolution
(pp. 411–502)

Unit Summary

Unit 5 introduces the ideas and key figures of the Enlightenment. It discusses how new ideas led to political revolutions in the United States and France. Finally, it details the spread of nationalism in eastern Europe, Latin America, Asia, Africa, and Australia.

CHAPTER 18
A Revolution in Science and Thought

CHAPTER 19
The French Revolution and Napoleon

CHAPTER 20
The Growth of Nationalism

CHAPTER 21
Asia, Africa, and Australia in Transition

Set the Stage

TEACH PRIMARY SOURCES
Painting The painting on page 411 depicts Simón Bolívar presenting the flag of liberation (the Venezuelan flag) after the Battle of Carabobo in June 1821. Bolívar, the leader of independence in Latin America, is sometimes referred to as the Liberator. He organized an army to fight against Spanish rule and hoped to unite countries of South America in a way similar to the United States. Western Europe and Latin America were inspired by the Enlightenment thinking that first led to revolution in the United States and France.

Quote Daniel Auber's opera, *La Muette de Portici*, is set in Naples, Italy. In the second act, a young fisherman sings of his love for his land. The opera inspired Belgians to revolt against the Dutch who ruled them. This revolution was one of many that swept western Europe in the first half of the 1800s.

◆ **ANSWER** They believed that love of country was sacred and liberty was worth fighting for.

A Revolution in Science and Thought
1628–1789
(pp. 412–433)

Chapter Objectives

• Identify advances in science and the scientists that challenged the old view of the world.
• Describe the ideas of the Enlightenment and how they influenced society, government, economics, and the arts.
• Explain the influence of the ideas of the Enlightenment on the American Revolution and on the new government of the United States.

Chapter Summary

Section I focuses on the scientific revolution and the changes in thinking that came about as scientists tested new ideas and challenged old ones.
Section II describes the effects of the ideas of the Enlightenment and the *philosophes* on political, economic, and social thought.
Section III focuses on the American Revolution and how it grew out of ideas of the Enlightenment.

Set the Stage
TEACH PRIMARY SOURCES

Explain to students that scientific discoveries and the belief that ideas could be tested and confirmed led to new ways of thinking about society. If humans could—as Alexander Pope wrote—"measure earth, weigh air, and state the tides"— then scientific reasoning could also be applied to areas beyond science.

Ask students who they think the "wondrous creature" in Pope's quotation is. (Students should realize that Pope is addressing his words to humankind; the "creature" is a human being.) Pope's *Essay on Man* included the often-quoted line "Hope springs eternal in the human breast." This reflects the optimistic view of most of the Enlightenment thinkers.

CHAPTER 18

A Revolution in Science and Thought
1628–1789

I. The Scientific Revolution
II. The Enlightenment
III. The American Revolution

Scientific discoveries of the 1600s and 1700s began to change the way Europeans thought about the world. People began to put their faith in reason and progress and to believe that in time, science could solve all the mysteries of the universe. Science could bring about marvels of technology. In his *Essay on Man*, the poet Alexander Pope wrote:

> ❝ *Go, wondrous creature! mount where Science guides;*
> *Go, measure earth, weigh air, and state the tides;*
> *Instruct the planets in what orbs [spheres] to run,*
> *Correct old time, and regulate the sun.* ❞

Progress, however, was more than science. Many believed that progress included the ideas of reason, and that reason could solve all of society's problems.

CHAPTER EVENTS

1633
Galileo is ordered before the Inquisition.

1660
Royal Society of London is founded.

1687
Newton publishes his theory of gravity.

1689
Locke publishes his *Two Treatises of Government.*

1625 — 1650 — 1675 — 1700

WORLD EVENTS

1637
Foreigners are expelled from Japan.

1664
Ming Dynasty is overthrown.

1681
Academy of Sciences is founded in Moscow.

412 UNIT 5 ◆ Enlightenment and Revolution

Teaching Options

Chapter 18 Resources

REVIEW

Teacher's Resources (TR)
Terms to Know, p. 31
Review History, p. 65
Build Your Skills, p. 99
Chapter Test, pp. 151–152
Concept Builder, p. 234
Five *Ws* Chart, p. 326

ASSESSMENT
Section Review, pp. 418, 426, 431
Chapter Review, pp. 432–433
Chapter Test, TR, pp. 151–152

ALTERNATIVE ASSESSMENT
Portfolio Project, p. 502
Write an Editorial, p. T502

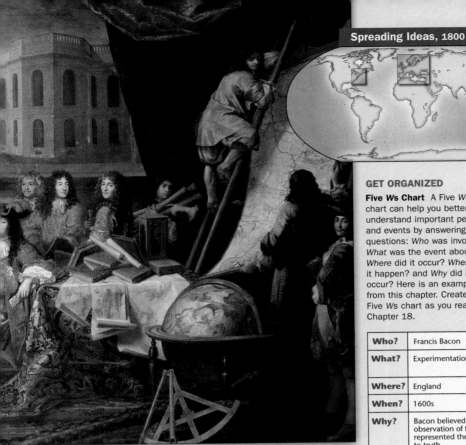

Spreading Ideas, 1800

GET ORGANIZED

Five Ws Chart A Five Ws chart can help you better understand important people and events by answering the questions: *Who* was involved? *What* was the event about? *Where* did it occur? *When* did it happen? and *Why* did it occur? Here is an example from this chapter. Create a Five Ws chart as you read Chapter 18.

Who?	Francis Bacon
What?	Experimentation
Where?	England
When?	1600s
Why?	Bacon believed direct observation of facts represented the road to truth.

VIEW HISTORY This painting shows the Royal Society of London, an organization founded in 1660 to allow intellectuals to gather and share scientific information. In the 1600s, scientific institutes were founded in many countries in Europe.
◆ How could institutes of science help scientists?

1770
Boston Massacre occurs.

1776
British colonies in North America declare independence.

1789
George Washington is elected President of the United States.

1725   1750   1775   1800

1734
War breaks out between Turkey and Persia.

1771
First edition of the *Encyclopedia Britannica* is completed.

1779
Spain declares war on Great Britain.

Chapter Themes

- Culture
- Time, Continuity, and Change
- Individual Development and Identity
- Individuals, Groups, and Institutions
- Power, Authority, and Governance
- Science, Technology, and Society
- Global Connections
- Civic Ideals and Practices

F Y I

The Royal Society

Starting in the middle of the seventeenth century, academies and learned societies, such as the Royal Society of London and the French Academie des Sciences, were founded. The Royal Society was founded in 1660. There, new scientific ideas were exposed through lectures given by members and subsequent discussion of these ideas. Wealthy and influential patrons often supported the ideas of Royal Society members.

Chapter Warm-Up

USING THE MAP

Have students find the locator map at the top of page 413, which shows the world and then highlights the areas of Europe and North America, where ideas of the Enlightenment and the Age of Reason led to political revolutions. Ask students why they think these areas were the first to be affected by these new ideas. (Possible answer: All these areas were connected by colonial relationships, so there was transportation of both people and ideas.)

VIEW HISTORY

Explain to students that the Royal Society of London and the French Academy of Science were two organizations that encouraged discussion and publication of the new ideas. The members included both scientists and amateurs who made discoveries and wanted their ideas spread to a wider audience.

◆ **ANSWER** Possible answer: They could support new ideas more effectively as a group than an individual scientist could. They could provide financial support for materials, expeditions, and publication of members' ideas.

GET ORGANIZED
Five Ws Chart

Discuss the graphic organizer shown on page 413. Explain that answering the five questions that begin with the letter *W—Who? What? Where? When? Why?—* is an excellent way to summarize the most important ideas of a section of text. Explain that in some cases students may not find an answer to every one of the five questions. Have students create a Five Ws chart (TR, p. 326) for each section.

● TEACH THE TIMELINE

The timeline on pages 412–413 shows events between 1633 and 1789. Ask students to find the names of people listed with Chapter Events. (Galileo, Newton, Locke, Washington) Suggest that students look for information about these people as they read Chapter 18.

Activity

Interpret the timeline Ask students to find events that support science and scientific thought. Suggest that students look for more information on these events as they read the chapter.

Section Summary

In this section, students will learn how scientific discoveries of the 1500s and 1600s challenged the teachings of established political and religious groups. They will also learn how the scientific method played a key role in encouraging people to rely on evidence and proof.

1 Introduce

Getting Started

Ask students what they know about the approach to gathering and explaining information known as the scientific method and why it is important. (Answer: Students will likely know from their science classes that an important feature of the scientific method is developing a hypothesis and then testing it. The original hypothesis is then either confirmed or changed.) Explain to students that they will learn how the scientific method came to be used.

TERMS TO KNOW

Ask students to read the terms and definitions on page 414 and find each term in the section. Explain that the prefix of the word *heliocentric* comes from the Greek word *helios*, meaning "sun." Have volunteers use a dictionary to find other words beginning with the prefix.

You may wish to preview the pronunciation of some of the names found in this section.

Ptolemy (TAHL uh mee)
Tycho Brahe (TOO koh BRAH huh)
Johannes Kepler
  (yoh HAHN uhs KEHP luhr)
Galileo Galilei
(gal uh LEE oh gal uh LAY)

ACTIVE READING

As students read Section 1, remind them to identify people or groups connected with the traditional view of the universe and those who promoted new ideas. Explain that in order to convince others of your point of view, it is important to have proof. Ask students what proof supported each group's perspectives.

Terms to Know

heliocentric Sun-centered
scientific method a way of carefully gathering and explaining information
hypothesis a possible explanation
gravity a force that pulls objects toward each other, with more massive objects having a greater pull

Do You Remember?
In Chapter 12, you learned that the Middle Ages covers the time from the fall of Rome to the start of the Renaissance.

This photograph shows a model of Ptolemy's earth-centered universe.

Main Ideas

A. Astronomers challenged the teachings of ancient philosophers and of Church leaders.
B. Francis Bacon and René Descartes helped develop the scientific method.
C. Scientists gained more support from monarchs and made new discoveries.

 Active Reading

POINTS OF VIEW
People have different points of view or perspectives. As you read this section, think about the perspectives of the people described. Then, ask what explains each point of view.

A. Revolutionary Thinking

While the Protestant Reformation was taking place, another revolution was taking place in Europe. This revolution was not a war, but a revolution of the mind. During this revolution, scientists began to approach their work in a new way. They began to test their ideas and conduct experiments to see if their ideas were correct. The result was a revolution in how people thought about the world. This dramatic change in the way of thinking became known as the Scientific Revolution.

The Old View

In the Middle Ages, most European thinkers accepted the traditional view of the universe, based on the ideas of Aristotle and other early writers. They explained natural events by observing them and by using logic to reason about their causes. When philosophers of the Middle Ages studied nature, they accepted things as they seemed. They observed the world around them and formed ideas about what they saw. They used logic in reaching their conclusions, but they did not test their ideas to see if their reasoning and conclusions were accurate.

During the Renaissance and early Reformation, people looked to the past for ideas. Humanists turned to the writings of ancient philosophers, and leaders of the Reformation looked to the Bible and writings of early Christians. The writings of Ptolemy, an early Greek astronomer, provide a classic example of an ancient idea that was accepted by thinkers of a later period in history.

Ptolemy had made an extensive study of the motions of the stars and planets. Based on his observations, he concluded that Earth was at the center of the universe. In other words, all heavenly bodies—stars, planets, and even the Sun—revolved around Earth. Thousands of years later, both the Roman Catholic Church and Protestant Churches accepted Ptolemy's ideas. Church leaders believed that God had created all things. Therefore, it seemed logical that Earth, believed to be one of God's greatest creations, would be at the center of the universe.

As the printing press made more books available and more people learned to read, people began to question many of the ideas of earlier thinkers. In the 1500s and 1600s, scientists began to question the methods that had been used by earlier philosophers in reaching their conclusions. They now began using accurate measurements and conducting experiments to support their observations and test their ideas. This new approach ultimately led to the Scientific Revolution.

Teaching Options

Section 1 Resources

Teacher's Resources (TR)
  Terms to Know, p. 31
  Review History, p. 65
  Build Your Skills, p. 99
  Concept Builder, p. 234
  Five *Ws* Chart, p. 326

Meet Individual Needs:
VISUAL/SPATIAL LEARNERS

Ask students to create drawings to show the geocentric solar system of Ptolemy (Earth at the center) and the heliocentric (Sun-centered) solar system of Copernicus. Have students explain how the two views are different and why Copernicus's view upset people.

Nicolaus Copernicus and Watchers of the Stars

Nicolaus Copernicus was a Polish scholar who had studied the writings of the ancients and spent much of his time observing the stars. His observations, however, did not agree with the writings of Ptolemy. At first, Copernicus may have hoped to use his observations to bring Ptolemy's ideas up to date. The more he observed, however, the more he realized that Ptolemy's ideas about a universe with Earth at its center were wrong. Just before his death in 1543, Copernicus published *On the Revolutions of the Heavenly Spheres*. Based on careful observations, he laid out a **heliocentric**, or Sun-centered, model of the universe. According to Copernicus, the Sun stood at the center of the universe. Earth was one of several planets that revolved around the Sun.

Most scholars rejected Copernicus's writings. Europe's scientific knowledge was based on classical writings, and scholars were not eager to give up on ideas that had guided their thought for centuries. In addition, his model of a heliocentric solar system shocked leaders of the Roman Catholic Church, who insisted that everything in the universe revolved around God's great creation, Earth.

Later astronomers continued to observe the heavens. Their evidence suggested that Copernicus was right. The Danish astronomer Tycho Brahe watched the stars for years. Every night, he tracked the positions of the stars and planets and recorded them. His student, Johannes Kepler, a brilliant mathematician, used Brahe's data to confirm that the planets move around the Sun. Kepler also found that planets move in oval paths, not in perfect circles as Copernicus had believed. This idea helped to explain some of the unusual observations of planetary motion.

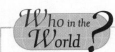

TYCHO BRAHE

Today's moviemakers might consider Tycho Brahe as a good model for a mad scientist. He built a huge castle on a Danish island. He filled the castle with observatories and laboratories. He and his team of assistants studied astronomy, astrology, and alchemy. His observations of the stars were the best in Europe at the time.

This seventeenth-century Dutch illustration is a drawing of the Copernican theory showing the Sun in the center of the revolving universe.

ESL/ELL STRATEGIES

Identify Essential Vocabulary Define the term *scholar* for students. (A scholar is a person who has learned a great deal about a topic through serious study.) The term comes from the Latin *scholar,* or *school.* Relate this to other words students may know, such as *school* and *scholarship.*

2 Teach

A. Revolutionary Thinking

Purpose-Setting Question What does the term *revolutionary thinking* imply? (a drastic change in a way of thinking)

Do You Remember?
Ask students to recall what European society was like during the Middle Ages. Suggest students skim Chapters 12 and 13 to find ideas. Remind students of the strength of the Roman Catholic Church and its teachings at the time.

Extend Ask students why they think scientists were the first people or group to promote new ideas in the 1500s and 1600s. (Possible answers: Scientists were encountering finds that were at odds with accepted beliefs of the past. They were among the first to approach their work in a new way. They made observations and tested ideas rather than simply accepting the ideas of the past.)

Focus Ask students why they think the heliocentric model of the solar system was so shocking to leaders of established religion. (Possible answer: The established view of the creation of human beings led people to believe that Earth was all-important, and thus it would be logical to them that Earth, not the Sun, was the center of the solar system.)

WHO IN THE WORLD?

TYCHO BRAHE Ask students what movies they know of that portray a "mad scientist." Suggest, if students do not, that Dr. Frankenstein and Dr. Jekyll are generally shown in laboratories surrounded by bubbling vats and conducting wild experiments. If possible, show a video of one of these movies. (Be sure students understand that the observations of Tycho Brahe were sound and advanced for his time and that Brahe was not "mad.")

TEACH PRIMARY SOURCES

The Dutch drawing of the universe as Copernicus accepted it, with the Sun at the center, was a new viewpoint. Ask students to compare this heliocentric view to that of Ptolemy. (Ptolemy believed that Earth, not the Sun, was the center of the universe.)

Discuss Ask students how Galileo was able to gather new information about the universe. (He invented a new, more powerful telescope than those that had been used before.) Encourage students to identify some of the discoveries Galileo made with his telescope. (Moon's surface was rough, the Sun had dark, changing spots, and four moons circling Jupiter)

◆ **ANSWER** Galileo was brought before the Inquisition because his ideas about the solar system and the universe challenged the accepted ideas of the Roman Catholic Church.

B. A New Scientific Method

Purpose-Setting Question How was the new scientific method different from science practice of the past? (It relied on observation, experimentation, and logical reasoning and not simply on what seemed to be true or on what the Roman Catholic Church taught was true.)

Activity

Make a chart Have students make a two-column chart (TR, p. 328) listing the names of all the scientists they read about in this section in the left column. Then, ask them to note the accomplishments of each person in the right column. The chart should be given a title, and each column should have a heading. Students may find the chart a helpful study tool.

ANALYZE PRIMARY SOURCES

DOCUMENT-BASED QUESTION

Descartes is known to many as the author of the often quoted, "I think, therefore I am." This may be the ultimate statement of ideas of the Enlightenment, representing a deep-seated belief in the power of thought to give validity to one's own existence.

ANSWER Descartes's rules begin with the assumption that one should doubt everything. The first rule is useful to scientists because it suggests that scientists should not accept anything as true without testing it for themselves.

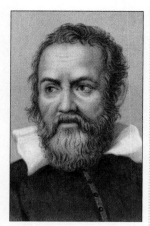

Galileo was interested in determining the laws that govern the movement of physical objects in space.

ANALYZE PRIMARY SOURCES

DOCUMENT-BASED QUESTION How can Descartes's first rule be useful to a scientist?

Galileo Galilei

The idea of a Sun-centered solar system was supported strongly by Galileo Galilei, who was born in 1564. As a young man, Galileo entered the University of Pisa in Italy to study medicine. While there, he became very interested in math and science. When Galileo learned of the invention of the telescope, he developed a new telescope more powerful than any other then in use.

Using this powerful telescope, Galileo studied planets and stars and gathered valuable new information about the universe. Since early times, people had believed that heavenly bodies never changed. However, the universe as seen through Galileo's telescope was different. He saw that the Moon's surface was rough. The Sun had dark, changing spots. Galileo also found that four moons circled Jupiter. This showed that not all heavenly bodies moved around Earth. Galileo now had evidence that Copernicus's ideas were correct.

When Galileo wrote about his findings in the early 1600s, he made many people angry. Authorities of the Catholic Church warned that such ideas were dangerous to religion. Galileo was told by Church leaders not to defend or teach his ideas.

Finally, in 1633, Galileo was ordered before the Inquisition. Under the threat of torture, he was forced to deny that the ideas of Copernicus were true. He was placed under house arrest for the rest of his life. However, Galileo never changed his views, and he continued to write until his death.

◆ **Why was Galileo brought before the Inquisition?**

B. A New Scientific Method

Despite resistance, new scientific thinking was gaining acceptance in the 1600s. This new science relied on observation, experimentation, and reason.

Champions of the New Science

Two philosophers who had a huge influence on the Scientific Revolution were Francis Bacon and René Descartes. Both men disagreed with the methods of the old science. Bacon was interested in solid facts. He urged scientists to experiment because he believed that direct observation of facts represented the road to truth. Scientists should, he said, gather facts first and then study and test them. Scientists could then use the tested facts to form a conclusion.

Descartes, on the other hand, believed that nature and philosophy should be studied by mathematical analysis. As a result of this approach, he believed that everything except God and the human soul could be viewed as mechanical. Complex ideas should be broken down into smaller, simpler parts to arrive at the truth. Descartes thought that a person should begin any study by doubting everything. He wrote several rules, starting with the following:

> ❝ The first rule was never to accept anything as true unless I recognized it to be certainly and evidently such: that is, carefully to avoid all precipitation [rush] and prejudgment [judgment without all the evidence], and to include nothing in my conclusions unless it presented itself so clearly and distinctly to my mind that there was no reason or occasion to doubt it. ❞

Descartes made known his ideas through his writings. His most famous work, *Discourse on Method*, was published in 1637.

Teaching Options

Test Taking

Point out to students that good notes are valuable study tools to use when they are about to take a test. Suggest that they use a Five *W*s chart, as well as other techniques they have learned—such as finding main ideas and details—to take notes as they read the chapter, in preparation for the Chapter Test.

F Y I

The Inquisition and Galileo

The Inquisition was established by the Roman Catholic Church to punish people who opposed the Church's teachings. Some members of the Inquisition tortured suspected heretics and condemned them to death if they did not change their views. Because of his age, Galileo was allowed to serve his imprisonment in a villa outside Florence.

The Methods of Science

The ideas of Bacon and Descartes helped create a new approach to science—an approach that is still used today. It is called the **scientific method**, a way of carefully gathering and explaining information.

Although there is no single scientific method, scientists do share a general approach. They make careful observations of the world around them and study the observations of others. Next, scientists try to explain their observations by developing a **hypothesis**, or a possible explanation. They then test the hypothesis to see if it explains their observations. A key part of an experiment is that someone else can repeat it with the same results. If an experiment does not show consistent results, the scientist rejects the hypothesis or modifies it until repeated experiments verify or confirm the results.

◆ **Why does a scientist repeat the steps of the scientific method?**

C. Science Continues to Advance

As scientists made more discoveries, European monarchs helped support scientific research. King Charles II of England founded the Royal Society of London. King Louis XV of France helped establish the new French Academy of Science. These societies brought together teams of scientists and paid for their research.

Isaac Newton

Isaac Newton, a brilliant mathematician, was the first person to explain the laws of force and motion that operate in the universe. Newton is also one of the people credited with inventing the branch of mathematics called calculus.

Newton's greatest discovery was the law of **gravity**. According to Newton, gravity is a force that pulls objects toward each other. The force of gravity

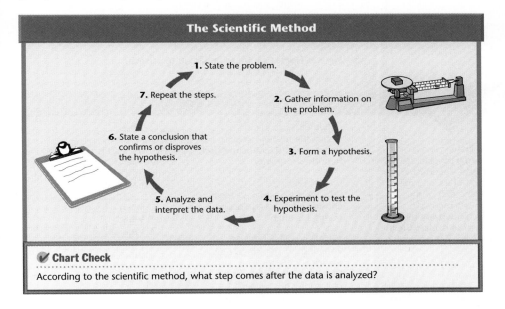

The Scientific Method

1. State the problem.
2. Gather information on the problem.
3. Form a hypothesis.
4. Experiment to test the hypothesis.
5. Analyze and interpret the data.
6. State a conclusion that confirms or disproves the hypothesis.
7. Repeat the steps.

✔ **Chart Check**

According to the scientific method, what step comes after the data is analyzed?

Advances in science were helped by improvements in scientific instruments, such as Galileo's telescope shown here.

between two objects depends on the mass, or amount of matter, in each object. This force also depends on the distance between the objects. The heavenly bodies, like all other objects, have gravity. The Sun's gravity is the strongest of all bodies in the solar system because it has the most mass. The Sun's gravity holds the planets in their orbits as they move around the Sun. In 1687, Newton published his theory of gravity in his famous book, *Mathematical Principles of Natural Philosophy*.

Newton continued his work in science all his life. He explained why planets travel in oval paths, as Kepler had found. He developed the world's first reflector telescope which used a mirror to gather light. Newton also investigated the nature of light and was the first to explain why objects appear to have color. He used science to show that the universe was orderly and worked by natural laws.

Other Discoveries

Once scientists began to use accurate observation and measurement as the basis for their work, they made great progress. Chemists began to study the gases that make up the air. During the 1700s, hydrogen, oxygen, and carbon dioxide were discovered. Antoine Lavoisier, a French scientist, discovered the true nature of fire. He demonstrated that fire is caused by material uniting with oxygen.

Life sciences and medicine also benefited from the new scientific methods of observation and measurement. Just as the telescope revealed the heavens, the microscope revealed living things too small for the naked eye to see. A Dutch scientist, Anton van Leeuwenhoek, used a microscope to examine red blood cells, bacteria, and some of the smallest forms of life.

Advances in technology also assisted advances in science. Improvements in the steam engine made by James Watt had a great effect on transportation and the manufacturing of precision parts. The invention and construction of precise instruments was a need recognized by scientists. Slowly, better methods of building instruments were devised. Improved telescopes and microscopes assisted astronomers and biologists in their work. Barometers, thermometers, and air pumps helped the study of chemistry.

◆ **Why was Newton's work so important to science?**

Review I

Review History
A. Why did scholars reject the ideas of Copernicus?
B. Which of Bacon's ideas became part of the scientific method?
C. Which discovery by Newton helped to explain the motions of the planets?

Define Terms to Know
Define the following terms:
heliocentric, scientific method, hypothesis, gravity

Critical Thinking
Why were Copernicus's ideas considered so revolutionary during his time?

Write About Philosophy
Write a short speech on how the ideas of Bacon and Descartes influenced the philosophy of science.

Get Organized
FIVE Ws CHART
A Five Ws chart is a good way to understand important events. Complete a Five Ws chart about Isaac Newton and his ideas.

Who?	
What?	
Where?	
When?	
Why?	

418   UNIT 5   ◆   Enlightenment and Revolution

Build Your Skills

CONDUCT A DEBATE

Debates can help you understand opposing sets of ideas. In a debate, two people or two teams present evidence that supports their viewpoints on an issue or on a topic in the arts, science, history, or politics, for example. They may offer opposing solutions to the same problem or different ways of handling an issue. Debaters must back up their opinions and statements with evidence. Events, statistics, or scientific data can support their statements.

In Section I, you learned that science advanced through a debate of ideas. Like other ideas, scientific ideas can be challenged when there is enough evidence.

Debaters must know their subject ahead of time and conduct thorough research on the topic. Debaters often take notes on the important points to cover during the debate. From their research, the debater identifies the evidence that supports both sides of the argument. That way, he or she can counter the arguments the other side will make and find good evidence to support their own position.

Here's How
Follow these steps to conduct a debate.

1. Choose an issue or topic to debate. Prepare a written statement about the issue or topic, such as: *Planets, including Earth, revolve around the Sun.*
2. Choose a side of the issue to debate.
3. Research the issue. Make sure you thoroughly know your side of the issue, as well as knowing information about your opponent's side.
4. Take notes on the important points to cover during the debate.
5. Debate the issue with your opponent.

Here's Why
Debating helps you understand both sides of an issue so you can take well-informed positions.

Practice the Skill
The dispute between the followers of Ptolemy and Aristotle and those of Copernicus and Galileo is an example of a debate. Choose one side to debate. Then, conduct research to find evidence to use in a mock debate. Look at the organizer on the right. Copy it onto a separate sheet of paper and use it to take notes.

Extend the Skill
Read the editorial section of your local newspaper. List the issues that would lend themselves to debate topics. Conduct research to support one of the views.

Apply the Skill
As you read the chapter, find other topics that would be appropriate for a debate. Choose one topic, and research information in preparation for a debate.

Issue: The Heliocentric Model of
the Universe
Facts:
•
•
•

In favor of:

Against:

Teaching Options

RETEACH
Have students create a list of topics of interest at your school or in the local community. Help them state each topic as an issue. Discuss what the argument would be if a person were in favor of the issue and what the argument would be if a person were against it.

CHALLENGE
Have students, working in small groups, select a local issue or topic to debate. Have the groups choose a side and then research the issue. Remind groups to research both sides of the issue so that they are better prepared. Then, have groups conduct the actual debate.

Build Your Skills

CONDUCT A DEBATE

Teach the Skill
Inform students that a debate is a discussion or argument in which people (an individual or a team) take opposite sides of a question and present their viewpoints. Debates are often governed by formal rules so that both sides of a question can be presented in an orderly way. Arguments are presented for (pro or affirmative) a topic or issue, or against (con or negative). Ask students why they think it is important to know both sides of an argument before beginning to give their own side.

In order to help students practice the skill, copy the outline card shown on page 419 on the board. Suggest an issue that students can discuss in class, such as *Should students be required to wear uniforms to school?* List any facts students know about wearing uniforms to school. Then, ask students to think of arguments for or against the issue. Record their viewpoints in favor of wearing uniforms and their arguments against the issue.

Practice the Skill
Have students do research for a debate on two views of the universe.

FACTS:
• Ptolemy and Aristotle—geocentric universe. They observed the movement of the Sun, which seemed to move around Earth.
• Ptolemy and Aristotle—common-sense observations
• Copernicus and Galileo—better instruments
• Copernicus—careful observation
• Other astronomers were able to support Copernicus.

Extend the Skill
Students should list any current news issues that would be likely topics for debate. After stating the issue, they should choose a side—for or against—and then conduct research to support their viewpoint.

Apply the Skill
Students' lists of topics should include ideas from the chapter. Then have students research one topic.

Past to...

INVENTIONS OF THE WESTERN WORLD

Teach the Topic

This visual feature explores some important inventions, both past and present. Ask students what other inventions of the past they are familiar with. (telephone, telegraph, camera, microscope, telescope, and so on) What other modern inventions do they know of? (Students may mention computer technology, including the Internet.)

MOVABLE METAL

Point out that with Gutenberg's method, a printer had to place individual letters to create words and sentences. Ask students to compare the letter on metal (a "slug") with the workings of a typewriter and computer. How does the labor involved compare?

PRECISION MICROSCOPE

Ask students to compare the microscope of 1683 with those they use in science classes and with the binocular microscope pictured on the page. How have microscopes been improved over time? (Possible answer: They use greater magnification and more precise lenses, and show more detailed images.)

HOT STUFF

Explain to students that the steam engine changed not only manufacturing, but also transportation. Ask them what forms of transportation used steam engines. (locomotives, steamboats, and cars such as the Stanley Steamer)

NEWTON'S TELESCOPE

Have students discuss the discoveries made by Newton with this telescope. (planetary travel, gravity of planets, nature of light)

Past to...

INVENTIONS OF THE WESTERN WORLD

In the seventeenth and eighteenth centuries, there was an explosion of new scientific thinking. Ancient, outdated guesswork was replaced with ideas based on experiments and actual evidence. This Age of Enlightenment produced inventions, such as the "double-acting" steam engine, that would change people's day-to-day lives. Inventions to measure distance and view objects revolutionized ideas about Earth and the heavens.

MOVABLE METAL
Invented by Johann Gutenberg, individual metal letters could be rearranged after printing to make and print another page.

Lens

PRECISION MICROSCOPE
This precision microscope, invented by Anton von Leeuwenhoek around 1683, could magnify tiny objects 200 times. Through it, scientists could see human cells for the first time.

HOT STUFF
Although Thomas Savery patented the first crude steam engine in 1698, engineer James Watt improved the design. His "double-acting" steam engine of 1782 produced a circular motion, which could drive machinery. Soon it was being used in factories and in locomotives.

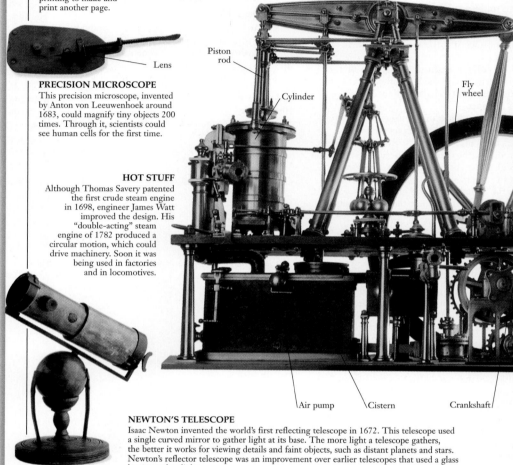

Piston rod

Cylinder

Fly wheel

Air pump   Cistern   Crankshaft

NEWTON'S TELESCOPE
Isaac Newton invented the world's first reflecting telescope in 1672. This telescope used a single curved mirror to gather light at its base. The more light a telescope gathers, the better it works for viewing details and faint objects, such as distant planets and stars. Newton's reflector telescope was an improvement over earlier telescopes that used a glass lens to gather light.

Teaching Options

Connection to
LITERATURE

Have students read a book about imaginary inventions, such as *The Time Machine* or *20,000 Leagues Under the Sea*. (See page T411B for references for these books.) These and other novels seem to foreshadow actual inventions. Encourage students to explain how more recent inventions are similar to the ones in these books.

F Y I

Steam Engines for Cars

Explain to students that in early cars of the late 1800s steam and electric engines were as popular, or more popular, than gasoline engines. One of the chief benefits of steam was its cleanliness. However, these cars needed a lot of water to run. Water troughs used for horses supplied water for motorists as well. The Stanley Steamer, made by the Stanley brothers, was the most famous steam-driven automobile.

STARING INTO SPACE

Although Galileo Galilei copied the design for his telescope from earlier ideas, he was the first to use it to study the planets. His telescopes magnified objects by up to 20 times—enough to identify the 4 moons of Jupiter.

ELECTRICAL EXPERIMENT

Benjamin Franklin was curious about electricity, so in 1752, he flew a kite in a thunderstorm. Small sparks appeared along the wet line of the kite, which proved that the lightning bolts were huge electrical charges—and that Franklin could have been electrocuted by his own experiment!

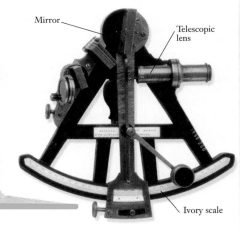

Mirror

Telescopic lens

Ivory scale

MOON AND STARS

The sextant was invented by John Campbell in 1757. It improved on an earlier design, known as an octant, which was used to calculate latitude and longitude at sea. Viewers could now work out their location by measuring the angle of the horizon in relation to a planet or star, and by knowing Greenwich Mean Time (GMT).

...Present

Some of the greatest inventions of the present day are in the field of space exploration. Exploration has continued on the ground too, with improved tools and technology to measure distance. Optical research tools, especially in the field of medicine, have continued to become more sophisticated.

SATELLITE NAVIGATION

The Global Positioning System (GPS) means ships at sea can find their location to within several feet. Electronic equipment, such as this color GPS sensor (right), receives accurate information by satellite.

Viewers

DOUBLE VISION

By combining two single microscopes to make a double version, known as a binocular microscope, the viewer can use both eyes. This dual vision shows the image in depth and makes more detailed study possible.

External fuel tank

Rocket booster

Space shuttle, carrying the crew

GOING INTO ORBIT

A space shuttle is a rocket-launched vehicle that orbits Earth and can carry passengers to other orbiting spacecraft. To get off the ground, the shuttle needs a powerful boost from rocket engines, which detach once the shuttle is underway. Modern shuttles are reusable and return to land on Earth.

Hands-On Activity

Have students research additional information on navigation tools, such as the compass, sextant, and astrolabe from the past and the more modern radar, satellites, or the Global Positioning System. Ask them to show photos or to draw pictures to show one past and one present navigation tool and to explain how it works.

STARING INTO SPACE

Have volunteers conduct research on modern reflector telescopes that use lenses and mirrors (Mt. Palomar), radio telescopes (the Parkes Observatory or Green Bank, WV), and electron telescopes (carried by the *Voyager*). Ask them to find out how these telescopes work, and to compare these with the telescope of Galileo's day. (A reflector telescope collects light; radio telescopes collect radio waves, and electron telescopes sample light and give "time histories" of the universe.)

ELECTRICAL EXPERIMENT

Many students will be familiar with the story of Benjamin Franklin's kite experiment with electricity. What does this say about scientific experiments and potential danger? (Possible answer: You can hypothesize about an experimental outcome, but you don't know the outcome until you actually try it—and this can be dangerous!)

MOON AND STARS

Challenge your confident readers to read the book *Latitude* to learn the difficulty of calculating position while at sea. Have them share what they learn with the class.

...Present

SATELLITE NAVIGATION

Have students read about the Global Positioning System (GPS), used to locate naval vessels today. Some students may know that GPS is also available on certain cars to provide locations and directions for the driver.

DOUBLE VISION

Ask students why using both eyes would make it easier to see more details. Discuss how this would be helpful.

GOING INTO ORBIT

Have students visit the NASA Web site for students. There they will be able to read about experiments conducted in space and what life is like for astronauts. Ask students to present what they learn to the class.

Connect Past to Present

Ask students which of the inventions shown on these pages is the most significant and why. Students can apply their debating skills to this issue.

II. The Enlightenment
(pp. 422–426)

Section Summary

In this section, students will learn how Enlightenment thinkers' influence grew beyond science. They will see how new ideas also influenced thinking about human behavior, government, economics, and the arts.

1 Introduce

Getting Started

Explain to students that the word *Enlightenment* refers to a period of time. The word *enlighten* is a verb that means "to give knowledge and understanding." Enlightenment thus suggests the gaining of knowledge and understanding. Ask students to keep this in mind as they read this section. Ask them what new knowledge and understandings were becoming part of society, beyond what they read about in Section 1.

TERMS TO KNOW

Ask students to read the terms and definitions on page 422 and find each term in the section. Point out that the terms all have to do with government and that they describe two views of government—positive and negative. Help students use a two-column chart (TR, p. 328) to categorize the Terms to Know, with positive connotations in one column (natural law, laissez faire, free market economy) and negative connotations in the second column (social contract, censorship).

You may wish to preview the pronunciation of some of the names found in this section.

Voltaire (vohl TER)
Montesquieu (MOHN tehs kyoo)
Rousseau (roo SOH)
Denis Diderot (duh NEE dee DROH)

ACTIVE READING

To help students make generalizations, suggest that they refer to the subheadings of the section and, after reading, make a general statement about each one. By asking a question, they can provide an answer that is a generalization. (For example: Why did people search for natural law? Generalization: People wanted to solve the problems of society through reasoning.)

T422 ◆ **UNIT 5**

Terms to Know

natural law the conditions that govern human behavior

social contract an agreement in which people give up the state of nature for an organized society

laissez faire letting businesses run without government intervention

free market economy an economy in which the buying and selling can be carried out without regulation

censorship the policy of prohibiting objectionable materials

Main Ideas

A. Philosophers used the reason of science to change the way people thought about such topics as human behavior, government, and economics.

B. In France, a group of Enlightenment thinkers called *philosophes* tried to improve society through science and reason.

C. Ideas of the Enlightenment influenced society, government, and the arts.

Active Reading

GENERALIZE
When you generalize, you make broad general statements based on facts. As you read this section, concentrate on the main points of Enlightenment thought. Then, pause to make general statements about what you have learned.

A. Political, Economic, and Social Thought

The late 1600s and 1700s in Europe include the period called the Enlightenment. During that period, ideas from the Scientific Revolution spread to other areas of thought. Scientists such as Isaac Newton had discovered the laws of the universe through mathematical reasoning. Might there also be laws of society and human behavior? Enlightenment thinkers were certain they could use the power of reason to solve all human problems and improve people's lives. Because of this growing belief in the power of reason, the Enlightenment is also called the Age of Reason.

The Search for Natural Law

The chaos of the Reformation and wars of religion had shaken a belief system that had been accepted by society throughout the Middle Ages. Then, the revolt against tradition shattered older ideas. This revolt inspired thinkers to question nearly every aspect of life, including human nature, rules governing society, and accepted forms of government.

People began looking for **natural law**, or the conditions that govern human behavior. Thinkers began to believe that the problems of society could be solved through reasoning. They wanted a just society and a good government, and they wanted to design a sensible economy.

Not everyone agreed with the emphasis on scientific reasoning, though. Many still supported the old order. Kings, for example, still claimed to rule by divine right, and the Roman Catholic Church continued to hold great power.

Enlightenment Thinkers

One of the first philosophers to search for the natural laws of government was England's Thomas Hobbes. Hobbes believed that people were by nature evil and needed strong government. The violence of England's civil wars left him with the belief that people were cruel, greedy, and selfish. Without strict government control, people rob, kill, enslave one another, and live a life filled with misery. He believed people could escape such a fate by entering into a **social contract**. A social contract is an agreement to give up individual freedom to live in an organized society that provides safety and security. Hobbes believed that a strong government could keep order, and therefore, that government should have absolute power.

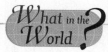

LEVIATHAN
Leviathan is a book written by Thomas Hobbes in 1651. In it, Hobbes described people as being naturally cruel and interested only in themselves. He believed that their desire to protect their own lives must always lead to conflict. Hobbes felt that the only way to stop this conflict was to establish a strong government.

Teaching Options

Section 2 Resources

Teacher's Resources (TR)
Terms to Know, p. 31
Review History, p. 65
Build Your Skills, p. 99
Concept Builder, p. 234
Five *W*s Chart, p. 326

ESL/ELL STRATEGIES

Identify Essential Vocabulary Explain to students that words or terms such as *laissez faire* often enter the English language in their original form from other languages. Give examples, and ask students if they are familiar with other words from a home language that are part of everyday English. Examples: *coffee* (Italian), *chocolate* (Aztec), *café* (French), and *raja* (Hindu).

Thomas Hobbes

John Locke

Thomas Hobbes and John Locke were two English writers who were central to the Enlightenment view of natural law.

As you learned in Chapter 17, another English philosopher, John Locke, proposed new theories on people and government. In 1689, Locke published his book *Two Treatises of Government*. His ideas did not agree with those of Hobbes. Locke argued that government was based on a cooperative agreement between the people and the government of their choice. Locke had a more hopeful view of human nature than Hobbes. Locke thought that people in a state of nature are guided by reason and good will. Individuals possess the natural rights of life, liberty, and property.

Locke believed that the power to govern was a trust given to a ruler by the people. This idea is known as consent of the governed. If a ruler does not work for the public good, Locke wrote, the people have the right to change that government. The duty of the government to protect the rights of the governed became important to democracy in Europe and North America.

New Views of the Economy

During this time, another group of thinkers developed new ideas about economics. They used scientific reasoning to try to discover natural laws that explained the economy. Most rejected government interference in the economy, especially the practices of heavily taxing people and regulating trade. These thinkers argued for a policy of **laissez faire**, the practice of letting businesses run without government intervention. They argued that wealth came from the land, and therefore farming, logging, and mining were the true sources of wealth.

Adam Smith, a Scottish philosopher, was influenced by the ideas of the new economic thinkers. He published his best-known work, *The Wealth of Nations*, in 1776. Smith believed that the buying and selling of goods should not be regulated, or controlled, by government. This is called a **free market economy**. He showed how supply and demand in the free market affected wages and prices. He disliked government interference in the economy. Smith's work has been the most influential book on economics ever written. It still influences economic policies today.

◆ According to John Locke, what was the duty of government?

B. The Ideas of the *Philosophes*

Purpose-Setting Question

Which English writers influenced Voltaire? (Newton and Locke)

Discuss Ask students to make generalizations about the beliefs of the *philosophes*. (Possible answer: The *philosophes* believed in progress through education.)

Using the Chart

Major Ideas of the Enlightenment

Have a volunteer state the purpose of the chart on this page. (to present some of the major ideas of the Enlightenment) Ask the volunteer how the information on this chart differs from the same information that was presented in running text. (Possible answer: Information in the chart is organized, making it easier to relate the major thinkers of the Enlightenment with their ideas.)

 Chart Check

Answer Adam Smith

Extend Ask students to think about some of the beliefs they have learned about in this chapter. Ask students whose beliefs, those of Hobbes or Locke, would the *philosophes* have been more comfortable with. (the beliefs of Locke)

Focus An important idea of the Enlightenment was that reason and knowledge could overcome ignorance. Diderot's *Encyclopedie* compiled information and ideas, and pointed out that intolerance should not interfere with debate and freedom to publish and speak about new ideas. Ask students how they think Diderot's work was like a modern encyclopedia. (Possible answer: Both are collections of writings on various subjects.) How were they different? (Possible answer: Articles in an encyclopedia today are not meant to voice opinions or arguments in favor or against particular ideas. Diderot's purpose was to voice his opinions.)

◆ **ANSWER** The *philosophes* influenced ideas about society by publishing their ideas, by speaking strongly for their beliefs, and by gathering in salons to share ideas.

Major Ideas of the Enlightenment

PHILOSOPHER	IDEA
Thomas Hobbes	People needed strict government control
John Locke	Natural rights—life, liberty, property
Adam Smith	Free market economy among the branches of government
Baron de Montesquieu	Separation of powers
Jean-Jacques Rousseau	Government based on an agreement made by the people
Mary Wollstonecraft	Equality of women and men through education

✔ Chart Check

Which philosopher's ideas dealt mainly with economics?

B. The Ideas of the *Philosophes*

In France, the thinkers of the Enlightenment were known as *philosophes*, meaning "lovers of wisdom." The *philosophes* believed that science and reason could work together to improve the lives of the people. These *philosophes* believed strongly in progress through education. For this reason, they were interested in preserving knowledge from the past as well as spreading their own ideas. The *philosophes* spoke out strongly for individual rights such as freedom of speech and freedom of worship.

Famous *Philosophes*

One of the leading *philosophes* was the great French writer Voltaire. Voltaire spent two years in England and met the great English writers of the time. He eagerly studied the ideas of Newton and Locke. Voltaire was delighted by the freedom of speech he found in England. When he returned to Paris, he began to write about the natural laws of government and the rights of all people as a model for the citizens of France. Until his death in 1788, Voltaire wrote many essays, letters, and plays in which he urged reform of French society. He became one of the most influential and famous of the French *philosophes*.

The Baron de Montesquieu further influenced political thought, especially through his harsh criticism of France's absolute monarchy. In *The Spirit of the Laws*, Montesquieu discussed different forms of government. He believed that power should be divided among different parts of the government, which he identified as the executive, legislative, and judicial branches. Montesquieu also believed that these different branches of government limited the power of the others. His ideas later influenced the formation of the government of the United States.

Jean-Jacques Rousseau was another French *philosophe* whose ideas had great influence. Rousseau believed that human beings were born good but were spoiled by society. Society set people against each other and made them unequal and unhappy. Rousseau urged people to return to simpler ways of living. In Rousseau's most famous book, *The Social Contract*, he spoke out strongly against the government and society of his day. Like Locke, Rousseau believed that government was based on an agreement made by the people.

The *Encyclopedie*

The *philosophe* Denis Diderot did a lot to spread the ideas of the Enlightenment. Through travel and letters, the *philosophes* of the Enlightenment exchanged ideas with rulers and thinkers in other countries. As these ideas became more widely known and accepted, Diderot decided to bring them all together in one collection. The subjects included science, religion, government, philosophy, and the arts. All the writings were put together in the *Encyclopedie*. The work filled 35 volumes. Articles contained in it encouraged freedom of expression, urged education for all, and criticized slavery and religion. The *Encylopedie* was one of the greatest achievements of the Enlightenment.

◆ **How did the *philosophes* influence ideas on society?**

Teaching Options

Cooperative Learning

Assign students to groups of four or five. Have them work together to add other philosophers and their ideas to the chart on page 424. For example, students might add Voltaire and Diderot as major Enlightenment thinkers. Have students decide within the group who will record the information and who will report the group's findings to the rest of the class.

F Y I

Rousseau and Education

Jean-Jacques Rousseau felt children should be taught with patience and understanding. Strict discipline and tiresome lessons were discouraged. These ideals were taken by others to promote child-centered schooling, in which teachers appealed to children's interests. Some people incorrectly felt he had intended that children's thoughts and behavior should not be controlled.

C. The Enlightenment and Society

Enlightenment ideas spread quickly. Educated people all over Europe read the works of the *philosophes*. Developments in printing had made information widely available. Pamphlets were printed on broad ranges of issues. Because the pamphlets were cheap enough for many to afford, people everywhere discussed these new ideas. *Philosophes* gave people a new vision of society—a vision that a just society should ensure justice and happiness for all people, regardless of their rank.

The Enlightenment Salons

Many of the *philosophes* knew each other personally. They frequently gathered in salons, rooms in the private homes of the rich. These salons provided a gathering place for authors and artists to mingle with wealthy patrons, or supporters of culture. Usually the groups that gathered held informal discussions, with topics ranging from morals to physics.

Salon gatherings began in the 1600s when noblewomen in Paris invited some friends over for poetry readings. By the 1700s, even people in the middle class were holding such gatherings. Soon, it became fashionable to have these gatherings not just in France but also all over Europe. The salon was one of the most important ways that ideas spread during the Enlightenment.

The *philosophes* believed in freedom and equality—but only for men. They believed women had natural rights, too, but not the same rights as men. By the mid-1700s, inspired by the new ideas of the Enlightenment, some women began protesting for rights equal to those of men. These women included Mary Wollstonecraft in Great Britain. Wollstonecraft believed that women should not be completely dependent on men. She argued for equal education of both girls and boys. Through education, she believed, women could join in public life as men's equals.

Literature, the arts, science, and philosophy were regular topics of discussion in salons.

CHAPTER 18 ◆ A Revolution in Science and Thought **425**

C. The Enlightenment and Society

Purpose-Setting Question Why did the ideas of the Enlightenment spread quickly? (Developments in printing made inexpensive pamphlets widely available.)

Extend Explain to students that the salon was an actual room in a home. The salon would compare most closely to the room called a parlor or living room in homes at a later time. Because of the meetings held there, it soon became a more expanded concept. When people spoke of a salon, they came to mean the meeting itself. Ask students what topics might be discussed at a salon today. (Possible answer: politics, religion, current events, science, movies, and shows)

Discuss Explain to students that in most places in Europe and North America in the 1700s, women had very few rights. Often they could not own property and any property they might have belonged to their husband when they married. Women were expected to care for their houses and children and help their husbands. Ask students which philosophers' ideas might have supported the idea of equal rights for women. (Locke, Rousseau, Voltaire)

Activity

Role-play Have students act out a modern salon gathering. Point out that their discussions should convey the optimistic outlook of the *philosophes* at the early salon gatherings.

TEACH PRIMARY SOURCES

The painting on page 425, *A Soiree with Mme. Geoffrin,* shows a salon gathering in Paris. It was painted in the eighteenth century by Gabriel Lemonnier. Male salon attendees were known as *philosophes* and their female counterparts were called *salonnieres.* Since most women did not receive extensive formal education at the time, the salons were the sole source of education for many of the *salonnieres.*

Conflict Resolution

Point out that the new ideas of the Enlightenment generally applied to men. Publications put forth ideas of freedom, equality, and natural rights, but women were excluded from sharing in most of these ideals. Ask students how they would convince people of the 1500s and 1600s that rights for all humans were important.

Discuss Ask students why some leaders believed that the Enlightenment threatened them. (fear of change, more power to people, loss of power to themselves) Encourage students to describe what type of leader they think would have welcomed the ideas behind the Enlightenment. (confident, open-minded, progressive)

◆ **ANSWER** Although government and church officials tried to stop the spread of Enlightenment ideas through censorship, they failed when books were published in other countries or secretly smuggled over borders to be made widely available.

Section Close

Ask students why the ideas of the Enlightenment are important to us today. Discuss which ideas are part of society today.

3 Assess

Review Answers

Review History

A. Hobbes thought that government should have absolute power. He felt people should enter into a social contract, giving up some freedoms for the safety and security provided by organized society and by a strong government.

B. The *philosophes* believed science and reason could improve lives. They believed in education, freedom of speech, and freedom of worship.

C. A few rulers changed their policies. They became known as enlightened despots because they used their power to foster social and political change.

Define Terms to Know

natural law, 422; social contract, 422; laissez faire, 423; free market economy, 423; censorship, 426

Critical Thinking

Locke and Hobbes had different views of the nature of people and so their views on government also differed. Hobbes believed that people were cruel and selfish and that government should have absolute power. Locke had a positive view of human nature and believed that power was given by the people and that people had the right to change their government.

Handel was one of the great composers of baroque music.

Although the Enlightenment had many supporters, not everyone approved of its ideas. Governments and the Roman Catholic Church considered the new ideas a threat. They believed their duty was to defend the order and stability of the old beliefs. As a result, some authors were prosecuted.

Government and Church officials tried to prevent the spread of new ideas. They regulated printing. They practiced **censorship**, or restricting access to ideas and information. They banned and burned many books. These policies failed, however. Books printed in countries that did not censor ideas were smuggled over borders. Other books were published secretly.

Enlightened Despots

Enlightenment thinkers thought that if they could influence rulers to change their policies to match Enlightenment ideas, then society would also change. In some cases, their strategy worked, and a few rulers did change their policies. These enlightened despots included Frederick II of Prussia, Catherine the Great of Russia, and Joseph II of Austria. Under Frederick II, Prussia practiced religious toleration and had policies aimed at improving the lives of peasants. Catherine the Great established some schools and made limited political reforms. Joseph II granted toleration to Protestants and Jews in his Roman Catholic empire and ended censorship.

Arts and Culture

Art forms continued to develop and change during the Age of Reason. The ideas of the Enlightenment transformed many of the arts. Patrons, people who hired artists to create works of art for them, often funded artists and writers.

The styles of the Renaissance gave way to the baroque, the ornate art style of the 1600s. Baroque art was grand, energetic, and theatrical. It influenced painting, sculpture, music, and theater. Baroque paintings were large, colorful, and full of excitement. Baroque buildings were huge and ornately decorated. Baroque music was deeply expressive, and its greatest composers were Johann Sebastian Bach and George Frideric Handel.

◆ **How did the policies of censorship fail during the Enlightenment?**

Review II

Review History

A. What kind of government did Thomas Hobbes believe was necessary?
B. What were some of the basic beliefs of the *philosophes*?
C. How did the ideas of the Enlightenment affect some rulers?

Define Terms to Know

Define the following terms:
natural law, social contract, laissez faire, free market economy, censorship

Critical Thinking

How were John Locke's ideas different from those of Thomas Hobbes?

Write About Culture

Write a short essay on how the ideas of the Enlightenment could have affected the arts of the 1600s and 1700s.

Get Organized

FIVE Ws CHART
A Five *Ws* chart is a good way to understand important people and events. Complete a Five *Ws* chart about Jean-Jacques Rousseau and his ideas.

Who?	
What?	
Where?	
When?	
Why?	

Write About Culture

Students' essays should reflect that reason and new freedoms of the Enlightenment also applied to the arts and culture. The baroque style of art, music, and architecture grew out of the Age of Reason. It was grand and expressive and conveyed a sense of excitement.

Who?	Jean-Jacques Rousseau
What?	The Social Contract
Where?	France
When?	1762
Why?	Believed that government was based on an agreement between rulers and people

Terms to Know

propaganda the promotion of certain ideas to influence people's opinions

guerrilla warfare fighting involving surprise raids

recession a decline in economic activity

federal republic a government in which power is shared between the central government and the states

amendment a change or an addition

This trading ship is shown in Salem, Massachusetts, in the 1780s. It shows how cargo was stored below the deck of the ship.

Main Ideas

A. Growing discontent with British rule in America eventually led to war.

B. American patriots declared independence from Great Britain and defeated British forces.

C. The new country adopted a Constitution based on Enlightenment ideas.

 Active Reading

CAUSE AND EFFECT
Nearly every event has causes and effects. As you read this section, concentrate on what caused events to happen, and what effects those events had later on. Then, pause to write down what you have learned.

A. Causes of the American Revolution

The ideas of the Enlightenment spread beyond Europe to the British colonies in North America. Here, they merged with a growing unhappiness with British rule. The mix proved to be explosive.

The American Colonies

By the 1770s, Great Britain had established a powerful empire in the Americas. Thirteen colonies had been settled along the eastern coast of North America. These colonies were important to Great Britain's economy. Many British trading ships were built in the colonies. Colonial cities such as Boston and New York were centers of trade that linked North America to trade with Africa, the West Indies, and Europe. Although Great Britain tried to control colonial trade, trade laws were not well enforced, and smuggling was common.

Colonial life was different from life in Europe. Although wealthy people still dominated government and society, class differences that were so important in Great Britain were blurred in the colonies. Because it was difficult to control government from thousands of miles away, colonial assemblies controlled local affairs.

War With France

In 1763, the French and Indian War, a long struggle with France for territory in North America, ended in a British victory. When this war ended, British leaders faced two problems. One was keeping order on the western edge of its colonies. The other was paying off the huge debt caused by the war. Great Britain looked to the colonies for help with both of these problems.

British troops guarded the American frontier, but it was expensive to keep an army so far from home. To cut down on conflicts with Native Americans, the British government issued a proclamation that prohibited settlement beyond the frontier. British officials also believed that the colonists should pay for part of their own defense. To recover expenses and increase revenue, British authorities began to enforce laws regulating trade more strictly. Parliament also passed laws to increase taxes paid by the colonists.

CHAPTER 18 ◆ A Revolution in Science and Thought **427**

Section Summary

In this section, students will learn how growing discontent with British policies led the American colonies to a war for independence. Students will also see how the ideas of Enlightenment thinkers influenced the colonial leaders as they founded a new government and wrote the U.S. Constitution.

1 Introduce

Getting Started

Ask students to suppose they are participating in a protest gathering in the 1770s. Have them tell what they are protesting and why. Then, ask what things people in the United States today might protest. (In the 1770s, people likely would have protested against British taxes, the prohibition on settlement beyond the frontier, the Sugar Act, and the Stamp Act. Modern protests might involve local or national issues.)

TERMS TO KNOW

Ask students to read the terms and definitions on page 427 and then find each term in the section. After reading the section, have them use each term in a sentence. Their sentences should reflect students' understanding of each term and should not simply restate a definition.

ACTIVE READING

The events that led to the American Revolution provide an excellent understanding of causes and effects. After they read the section, have students review the material and use a cause-and-effect chain (TR, p. 325) to show what caused events to happen and what effects those events had.

Teaching Options

Section 3 Resources

Teacher's Resources (TR)
Terms to Know, p. 31
Review History, p. 65
Build Your Skills, p. 99
Concept Builder, p. 234
Chapter Test, pp. 151–152
Five *W*s Chart, p. 326

Connection to MUSIC

Have students listen to the music and lyrics from a soundtrack of the musical *1776*. The characters of this musical include many of the leading figures of the colonial era and the American Revolutionary War. Discuss with students how the song lyrics express some of the same ideas stated in the text in Section 3.

2 Teach

A. Causes of the American Revolution

Purpose-Setting Question What made the people of the colonies in North America unhappy with British rule? (Possible answer: People of the colonies did not want to be taxed and controlled by others.)

Discuss Compare social distinctions and social rank in Europe with those of the colonies in the Americas. (Social rank was very important in Europe. The wealthy people dominated government and society there. In the colonies, wealth and social rank were less important. People tended to feel themselves more equal to one another.)

ANALYZE PRIMARY SOURCES

DOCUMENT-BASED QUESTION
Thomas Paine published a very popular pamphlet, *Common Sense.* It was published anonymously. It was one of many documents that colonists were reading, urging independence from British rule; however, it was more influential than most.

ANSWER Possible answer: Paine says that Britain was too far away and too "ignorant" of the matters of the new continent to be able to do justice to management of the colonies. He said that it would be too difficult for a distant power to understand the needs of the colonies. Paine also said if the British could not conquer the colonies, they could not govern.

◆ **ANSWER** The French and Indian War made the colonists more unhappy with the British. It led to British troops on the American frontier. It also led to stricter enforcement of British trade laws and to increased taxes on the colonies.

B. War for Independence

Purpose-Setting Question Did the delegates to the Continental Congress in 1774 at first intend to declare independence? (No; the original intent of the 1774 Continental Congress was to discuss ways to negotiate peace with Great Britain.)

Growing Discontent

In the years following the French and Indian War, new laws and taxes were passed that were irritating to the colonists. For example, in 1764, Parliament passed a Sugar Act that increased taxes on many goods. The Stamp Act of 1765 created a tax in the form of special stamps required for newspapers and other printed items.

Discontent led to violence. In 1770, when a crowd in Boston threw snowballs and rocks at British soldiers, the soldiers fired on the crowd. Five colonists were killed in the Boston Massacre. In 1773, a small group of colonists protested taxes on tea by breaking into a ship carrying fresh tea and throwing it overboard. Their protest became known as the Boston Tea Party. When the British punished Boston for the protest, colonists from other colonies came to their defense.

Colonists in favor of independence began using **propaganda** to gather support for their cause. Propaganda is the spreading of ideas favorable to a cause. Pamphlets urging independence were distributed in colonial cities. Thomas Paine, a colonial writer and editor, published a pamphlet, *Common Sense,* in early 1776. In lines such as the following, Paine urged colonists to break from Britain and form their own government:

> 'Tis not in the power of Britain to do this continent justice; the business of it will soon be too weighty and intricate [hard to understand] to be managed with any tolerable [reasonable] degree of convenience, by a power so distant from us, and so very ignorant of us; for if they cannot conquer us, they cannot govern us.

ANALYZE PRIMARY SOURCES DOCUMENT-BASED QUESTION Why does Paine say that Britain can no longer rule the colonies?

◆ **What effect did the French and Indian War have on the colonists?**

B. War for Independence

Eventually, the crisis grew worse. In September 1774, colonial leaders called for a meeting in Philadelphia, Pennsylvania, to discuss what to do next. This meeting, called the Continental Congress, included delegates from all the colonies except Georgia. At first, delegates discussed ways to negotiate peace with Great Britain.

Declaration of Independence

After fighting broke out between British forces and colonial forces in 1774 and 1775, the Continental Congress approved the creation of an army. George Washington was named as its commander. Washington had excellent qualifications to lead the Continental army. He was levelheaded and able to command respect and loyalty from his troops. These qualities became increasingly important as the war progressed because the odds were often heavily in favor of the British. His army fought the British near Boston and in Canada.

Then, in 1776, the Continental Congress voted to declare independence. A draft of the formal document, the Declaration of Independence, was written by Thomas Jefferson of Virginia. The ideas in the document, however, were not entirely original. Jefferson was influenced by the ideas of

This painting shows American soldiers fighting British redcoats at Penobscot, Massachusetts.

Teaching Options

Writing

AVERAGE
Review the reasons why the colonists were unhappy with British rule. Have students choose one reason. Then, ask them to assume the role of a colonist and write a one- or two-paragraph letter to a friend explaining why he or she is unhappy with British rule. Remind students to include examples from the textbook.

CHALLENGE
Have students take the part of an American colonist and write a propaganda piece urging their fellow colonists to support the cause of independence. Remind students to give reasons why others should join the cause and to use persuasive writing techniques. Students' propaganda pieces should cite the same reasons that are given in this section.

John Locke, and many ideas in the Declaration of Independence came from Locke's writings. Locke felt that all people had certain rights. These rights include the right to "life, liberty, and the pursuit of happiness." He felt that government should provide these three basic rights. If a government failed its citizens, the citizens should have the right to do away with the government.

The American Revolution

People were divided about revolution, both in America and in Great Britain. In America, some of the population still supported Britain. Many served in the British army. In Great Britain, people criticized Parliament. They still hoped for a peaceful resolution.

Both sides faced problems while fighting in the American Revolution. The American military was poorly equipped and trained, and they faced a well-organized British army. The Continental Congress had few resources and little money. The British controlled most major cities. Still, American soldiers knew the land and controlled the countryside. They were fighting for their lands and their homes.

Turning Point of War

In 1777, the war reached a turning point. American forces defeated the British at Saratoga, New York, and Great Britain's old enemy, the French, joined the war on the side of the Americans the next year. Entering the war, they could strike back at their old enemies, the British. The French gave the Americans needed supplies and trained soldiers. The French navy also gave the Americans much-needed help.

Even with European help, the fighting was bitter. When the fighting moved into the Southern colonies, the Americans suffered many defeats in open battle. American soldiers practiced **guerrilla** **warfare**, or fighting through hit-and-run attacks. They came at the British army from unlikely locations, attacked isolated units, and captured British supplies.

The British lost their last major battle against the Americans in 1781, when Washington had the British blocked at Yorktown, Virginia. Because the French fleet blocked any help or escape route for British troops, General Cornwallis, the British commander, surrendered to the Americans.

In 1783, the British and Americans signed a peace treaty in Paris, France, called the Treaty of Paris, which officially ended the war. The British recognized the independence of the Americans. The treaty also established the American western boundary at the Mississippi River.

◆ **Why did France join the Americans against Great Britain?**

Primary Source Documents
You can read sections of the Declaration of Independence on page 812.

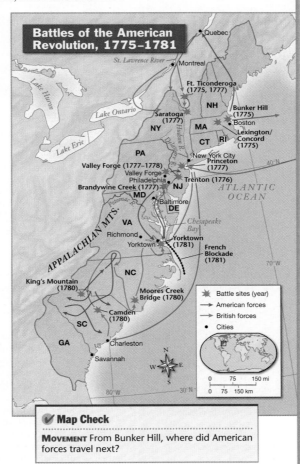

Battles of the American Revolution, 1775–1781

✔ Map Check

MOVEMENT From Bunker Hill, where did American forces travel next?

Activity

Hold a debate Have students use their debating skills to conduct a debate on the following topic, from the point of view of a colonist of 1776: *We should fight a war against the British to become independent.*

Have some students take the affirmative side and others take the negative side. Students should use facts given in the section to back up their arguments. Suggest that students review the debating skills on page 419.

Focus Have students read sections of the Declaration of Independence on page 812. Ask which ideas represent the ideas of the Enlightenment.

Using the Map

Battles of the American Revolution, 1775–1781

Have students use the map key to identify the significance of the red starbursts (battle sites) and black dots (cities), and then to identify what color arrow is used to show American troop movements (blue) and British troop movements (red). Ask them to identify the state in which each of the following battles occurred: Trenton (NJ); Yorktown (VA); Moores Creek Bridge (NC); Camden (SC).

✔ Map Check

Answer American forces moved north from Bunker Hill to Quebec.

Extend Explain that the Marquis de Lafayette brought assistance from France to the American colonies in their fight against the British. Discuss with students why French assistance was so helpful to the colonists. (Possible answer: France provided supplies, soldiers, ships, sailors, and knowledge of war.) You may wish to have students research Lafayette and share what they learn with the class.

◆ **ANSWER** The French joined the Americans because France and Great Britain had been enemies (in North America they fought the French and Indian War); by entering the war, France could strike back at Great Britain.

Focus on
SPORTS & GAMES

Recreation in North American Colonies Life in the North American colonies was often harsh, both before and after independence. People needed diversions and means of recreation. The need to "practice" for the work of daily life meant that many forms of recreation combined work and play. At social gatherings, for example, games and contests were held such as plowing contests, footraces, or horse races.

Children played games such as hopscotch, leapfrog, or London Bridge. Most toys were homemade, and included kites, balls, and dolls. Children of wealthy families had toys imported from Europe, such as fancy dolls, tea sets, and toy soldiers.

C. A New Nation

Activity

Make a chart Have students use a two-column chart (TR, p. 328) to identify some of the central ideas of the Enlightenment thinkers that became part of the new Constitution of the United States of America. Suggest that students use the column heads "Ideas" and "Enlightened Thinker." (Possible answers: three branches of government, Montesquieu; government is a contract between rulers and those governed, Locke, Rousseau; right to life, liberty, property, Locke)

SPOTLIGHT ON GOVERNMENT

CONSTITUTIONAL CONVENTION As president of the convention, it was George Washington's responsibility to enforce the secrecy rule. Ask students why they think the delegates to the Constitutional Convention felt it was important to meet in secret. (Possible answer: They may have wanted to be able to meet and talk without anyone overhearing the discussion before a final decision was made. This allowed them to change their minds without being criticized by people who were not involved in the convention.)

Focus Have students closely examine the painting on this page. Ask them if they can identify any of the famous men depicted. (Benjamin Franklin in chair at center; George Washington standing next to desk)

In this painting, George Washington watched as delegates signed the U.S. Constitution on September 17, 1787.

Spotlight on *Government*

CONSTITUTIONAL CONVENTION

The delegates to the Constitutional Convention suffered through miserable conditions for 17 weeks as they wrote the U.S. Constitution. They met during one of the hottest summers in years.

Temperatures soared in the meeting room because the windows had been shut for secrecy. In addition, the men wore heavy jackets and powdered wigs, as was the fashion in 1787.

C. A New Nation

Recovery from the war was slow for the Americans. Their new country had staggering debts from the war, and the economy fell into a severe downturn, called a **recession**. Worse, the new nation had no way to collect money to pay its debts except through voluntary contributions from the states.

Then, in 1777, a document titled the Articles of Confederation was adopted. The articles formally united the states into a single country. However, the new government was weak and ineffective. It could not raise money on its own nor successfully settle disputes between states. Individual states held most of the power. They were reluctant to give up any of it to a central government that might come to be as powerful as European monarchies.

A New Constitution

By 1787 it was clear that the Articles of Confederation did not work. Once again, delegates gathered in Philadelphia. They originally planned to improve the Articles of Confederation. In the end, they created the Constitution of the United States of America.

As they debated the shape that the new Constitution would take, the delegates were influenced by the ideas of the Enlightenment. They had absorbed ideas from John Locke, Jean-Jacques Rousseau, and Baron de Montesquieu, and had studied the histories of many countries, including ancient Rome. Following the ideas of Locke and Rousseau, they saw government as part of the social contract.

The government the delegates created was a **federal republic**, a form of government in which power is shared between the central government and the states. The idea of a republic was taken directly from the government structure of Rome. The delegates were aware, however, of Rome's shortcomings.

The delegates also borrowed ideas from Montesquieu. The new United States government would consist of three branches. Congress, the legislative branch, would make the laws. The chief executive, the President, would see

Teaching Options

Research

AVERAGE

Have students choose one of the major figures of the Constitutional Convention of 1787 and research that person to learn more about his life and to illustrate his contributions to the new government. Suggest students research George Washington, Gouverneur Morris, Alexander Hamilton, William Paterson, or James Madison.

CHALLENGE

Have students read the Bill of Rights to the U.S. Constitution and then research recent court cases that have been decided based on these amendments. Have students share what they have learned with the class.

that the laws were enforced. A system of courts, the judicial branch, was set up to interpret the laws. The delegates also devised a system to prevent any one of the branches of the government from taking complete power.

The Constitution was not perfect, however. The delegates knew that the United States would grow and change. They realized that the Constitution would have to change to meet new circumstances and challenges. That is why it is called a "living document." The delegates outlined a process by which **amendments**, or written changes, could be added to the Constitution. However, the amendment process was set up to be difficult in order to discourage minor or frequent changes.

Experience had taught some of the delegates to be very careful to preserve basic human rights. They pushed other members to spell out these rights in the Constitution itself. James Madison was one of the delegates who fought to include citizens' rights. Ten amendments were added to the Constitution in 1791. They are known as the Bill of Rights. They protect individual rights, such as the freedoms of religion, speech, and assembly. These rights were based on the ideas of natural rights expressed by many Enlightenment philosophers.

The U.S. Constitution was approved by most states in 1789. In that same year, George Washington was elected President of the United States, taking office in April. The U.S. Constitution became the supreme law of the land.

Effects of the American Revolution

America's Revolution and new democratic society changed the way people thought about governments. Never before had a group of colonies rebelled against a monarch with such success. In France, Spain, the German states, and Latin America, people were encouraged by the success of the new American government. They realized that they no longer had to accept the idea that only the nobility had a right to influence the government. People in parts of Europe and in South America eventually came to fight for that right.

◆ **What effect did the American Revolution have on other countries?**

Then & Now

THE U.S. CONSTITUTION

The first ten amendments, known as the Bill of Rights, showed that the Constitution could be changed when needed.

The Constitution has been amended only 27 times in more than 200 years. The last amendment was added in 1992. It addressed changes in the salaries of senators and representatives.

Review III

Review History
A. What were some of the causes of the American Revolution?
B. Which military tactic helped the Americans defeat the British in battle?
C. How are the ideas of Baron de Montesquieu reflected in the U.S. Constitution?

Define Terms to Know
Define the following terms: **propaganda, guerrilla warfare, recession, federal republic, amendment**

Critical Thinking
Why did many people in the American colonies support independence from Great Britain?

Write About Government
Write a short essay on how the ideas of the Enlightenment affected the delegates who helped create the U.S. Constitution.

Get Organized
FIVE Ws CHART
A Five Ws chart is a good way to understand important people and events. Complete a Five Ws chart about James Madison and his ideas.

Who?	
What?	
Where?	
When?	
Why?	

Who?	James Madison
What?	Bill of Rights to the U.S. Constitution
Where?	United States
When?	1791
Why?	To protect the rights of the people

Write About Government
Students' essays should incorporate ideas from this section and should trace those aspects of the U.S. Constitution that were founded on Enlightenment ideas. For example, students should mention the ideas of government structure and the mutual obligations of government and those governed.

Extend Tell students that Delaware was the first state to ratify the Constitution. New Jersey, Pennsylvania, Georgia, and other states soon followed. The new government was approved when the ninth state, New Hampshire, ratified the Constitution in June 1788.

Then & Now

THE U.S. CONSTITUTION Ask students why they think the Constitution has been amended only 27 times in more than 200 years. (Possible answers: It was a sound base and provided for most needs; the Founding Fathers made it difficult to pass amendments.)

◆ **ANSWER** It encouraged people in other countries to influence their governments and sometimes to fight for that right.

Section Close

Discuss with students why it is important to understand the thinking of the Enlightenment and the American Revolution in a world history class.

3 Assess

Review Answers

Review History
A. Some of the causes of the American Revolution were the laws enforced by Great Britain regulating trade and increased taxes, such as taxes created by the Sugar Act and the Stamp Act.
B. guerrilla warfare
C. Montesquieu's ideas about separation of branches of government were reflected in the U.S. Constitution, which set up three branches of government.

Define Terms to Know
propaganda, 428; guerrilla warfare, 429; recession, 430; federal republic, 430; amendment, 431

Critical Thinking
Reasons to support independence: taxes were being imposed on them unfairly because they had no voice in the government; land on the frontier had been closed to them; supporters felt it was their right to overthrow a government that was not providing for their interests.

Chapter Summary

A blank outline form is available in the Teacher's Resources (p. 318). Students should outline information about the scientific revolution, the Enlightenment, and the influence of those movements on the American Revolution. They should then use the outline to complete their chapter summary. Refer to the rubric in the Teacher's Resources (p. 340) to score students' chapter summaries.

⬤ Interpret the Timeline

1. 2 years
2. Galileo's trial
3. The founding of the Royal Society of London or founding of the Academy of Sciences in Moscow
4. Check students' timelines to be sure all events are in the chapter.

Use Terms to Know

5. guerrilla warfare
6. laissez faire
7. social contract
8. propaganda
9. gravity
10. heliocentric
11. scientific method
12. free market economy
13. natural law

Check Your Understanding

14. Nicolaus Copernicus set out to revise the ideas of Ptolemy.
15. According to Johannes Kepler, the planets moved in oval, or elliptical, orbits around the Sun.
16. Galileo Galilei discovered that the Moon's surface was rough; that the Sun had dark, changing spots; and that four moons circled Jupiter. These observations confirmed the ideas of Copernicus.
17. Locke believed government could be overthrown if the ruler did not work for the public good and if the rights of the people were not protected.
18. Adam Smith thought that government should not regulate the economy. He believed in a free market economy.
19. Propaganda affected the American colonists by encouraging them to participate in rebellion against the British.

Chapter Summary

Complete the following outline in your notebook. Then, use your outline to write a brief summary of the chapter.

A Revolution in Science and Thought

I. The Scientific Revolution
   A. Revolutionary Thinking
   B. A New Scientific Method
   C. Science Continues to Advance

II. The Enlightenment
   A. Political, Economic, and Social Thought
   B. The Ideas of the *Philosophes*
   C. The Enlightenment and Society

III. The American Revolution
   A. Causes of the American Revolution
   B. War for Independence
   C. A New Nation

⬤ Interpret the Timeline

Use the timeline on pages 412–413 to answer the following questions.

1. How many years passed between the publication of the ideas of Newton and Locke?

2. Which happened first, Galileo's trial or the Boston Massacre?

3. **Critical Thinking** Which event shows the increasing respect science was given in society?

4. Select five events from the chapter that are not on the timeline. Create a timeline that shows these events.

Use Terms to Know

Select the term that best completes each sentence.

free market economy   natural law
gravity   propaganda
guerrilla warfare   scientific method
heliocentric   social contract
laissez faire

5. Attacks involving surprise raids are used in _____.

6. _____ is the belief that governments should not interfere in business.

7. People make a _____ to form a society that provides them safety and security.

8. Writers can use _____ to get people to agree with them.

9. Newton's theory of _____ was published in one of his most famous books.

10. A universe in which the Sun is the center is called _____.

11. The _____ is a way of carefully gathering and explaining information.

12. A _____ is an economy in which the buying and selling can be carried out without regulation.

13. The rules that govern human behavior are known as _____.

Check Your Understanding

14. **Explain** what Nicolaus Copernicus set out to accomplish.

15. **Describe** how the planets moved according to Johannes Kepler.

16. **Describe** what Galileo Galilei discovered through his telescope.

17. **Identify** under what circumstances John Locke believed a government could be overthrown.

18. **Summarize** what Adam Smith thought about government.

19. **Discuss** how propaganda affected American colonists.

20. **Explain** why the U.S. Constitution is called a "living document."

20. The U.S. Constitution is called a "living document" because it can be changed, or amended, to meet new conditions or circumstances.

Critical Thinking

21. Recognize Relationships How did Newton improve on the ideas of Copernicus and Galileo?

22. Draw Conclusions Why did government and Church officials censor books?

23. Make Inferences How did the Bill of Rights reflect ideas from the Enlightenment?

Put Your Skills to Work

24. Conduct a Debate You have learned how to conduct debates. Debates can help you understand an issue by exploring it from every side. You can find out which points can be defended and which points cannot.

Study the arguments used by Thomas Hobbes and John Locke concerning the role government should play in people's lives. Then debate the issues as a class. Use the questions below and the notecard to help you prepare for the debate.

a. What did Hobbes believe about the basic nature of people?

b. What world events helped Hobbes to reach his conclusions?

c. How did Locke's ideas about the role of government differ from those of Hobbes?

Issue:

Facts:
-
-
-

In favor of:

Against:

Analyze Sources

25. Read about Voltaire's opinions of French society. Then, answer the questions that follow.

In France, the title of marquis is given gratis [free] to any one who will accept of it; and whosoever arrives at Paris from the midst of the most remote provinces with money in his purse . . . , may strut about, and cry, "Such a man as I! A man of rank and figure!" And may look down upon a trader with sovereign [superior] contempt. . . .

a. What sort of person does Voltaire say can become a marquis?

b. How does Voltaire think nobles treat merchants in France?

Essay Writing

26. The Enlightenment was an age of faith in reason and progress. Writers and thinkers embraced ideals of justice and equality. They wanted to build a society that made sense. Write an essay about how the ideals of the Enlightenment still affect society today.

CHAPTER 18 ◆ A Revolution in Science and Thought **433**

Critical Thinking

21. Newton provided a mathematical reason why the planets orbited the Sun by explaining the laws of force, motion, and gravity. Thus, his ideas were based on scientific proof and not observation alone.

22. Possible answer: They believed the ideas were dangerous because they went against the teachings of the Roman Catholic Church and the authority of government. Their power was threatened by the ideas contained in books.

23. The Bill of Rights reflects ideas from Locke and Montesquieu that people possess natural rights and that government should be the protector of those rights.

Put Your Skills to Work

CONDUCT A DEBATE

24a. Possible answer: Hobbes believed that people were evil by nature.

24b. the violence of England's civil wars

24c. Hobbes believed in a strong government with absolute powers. Locke believed in a government that served to meet the needs of the governed and could be changed if it failed in its responsibilities.

Analyze Sources

25a. Voltaire says anyone with money and the right name can become a marquis.

25b. Nobles look down on merchants.

Essay Writing

26. Students' essays should include explanations of how Enlightenment ideals about society and government still exist today. These are reflected in the use of the scientific method, the U.S. Constitution and Bill of Rights, the continued faith in a free market economy, and the separation of powers and federal structure of governments.

The French Revolution and Napoleon
1789–1815
(pp. 434–459)

Chapter Objectives

• Describe the factors that led up to the French Revolution.
• Discuss the violence that resulted in the overthrow of the French monarchy and the establishment of the Reign of Terror.
• Explain how Napoleon Bonaparte rose from the ranks of the military to become emperor of France.
• Explore events that led to Napoleon's fall from power.

Chapter Summary

Section I explores how the ideas of the Enlightenment and foreign revolutions combined with problems within France to prompt French common people to call for changes in their government.
Section II discusses mob violence within France that led to the overthrow of the monarchy and a wave of terrorism that swept the country.
Section III focuses on Napoleon Bonaparte's rise within the ranks of the French army to become emperor of France.
Section IV explores how military setbacks weakened Napoleon and led to his surrender and exile, followed by an unsuccessful attempt to retake power.

Set the Stage

TEACH PRIMARY SOURCES
Explain that Charles Dickens, an Englishman, was concerned that social problems in England in the 1850s might lead to revolution, just as they had in France 60 years earlier. Discuss which words in the quote seem to describe a storm (*sea raging and thundering*) and those that describe a war (*roar, attack*).

The French Revolution and Napoleon
1789–1815

I. Beginnings of the French Revolution
II. Revolution and Terror
III. Napoleon Bonaparte
IV. Napoleon's Power Ends

On July 14, 1789, the people of Paris marched on the Bastille, a state prison in which many writers and thinkers, including Voltaire, had once been held. The people who marched on the Bastille destroyed the building and seized its store of weapons and ammunition. In his novel *A Tale of Two Cities*, British novelist Charles Dickens brings the scene to vivid life:

> **"** *With a roar that sounded as if all the breath in France had been shaped into the detested word [Bastille], the living sea rose, wave on wave, depth on depth, and overflowed the city to that point. Alarm-bells ringing, drums beating, the sea raging and thundering on its new beach, the attack began.* **"**

The attack on, or storming of, the Bastille marked the beginning of the French Revolution. Through this long and violent process, France ended its absolute monarchy and became an empire under a military dictator.

1789
People of Paris storm the Bastille.

1793
French monarch Louis XVI and his wife Marie Antoinette are executed.

CHAPTER EVENTS

1780 — **1785** — **1790** — **1795**

WORLD EVENTS

1787
Group of freed slaves from Great Britain form a settlement in Sierra Leone.

1789
United States of America adopts its new constitution.

Teaching Options

Chapter 19 Resources

REVIEW

Teacher's Resources (TR)
Terms to Know, p. 32
Review History, p. 66
Build Your Skills, p. 100
Chapter Test, pp. 153–154
Concept Builder, p. 235
Cause-and-Effect Chain, p. 325
Transparency 5

ASSESSMENT
Section Reviews, pp. 440, 447, 452, 456
Chapter Review, pp. 458–459
Chapter Test, TR, pp. 153–154

ALTERNATIVE ASSESSMENT
Portfolio Project, p. 502
Write an Editorial, p. T502

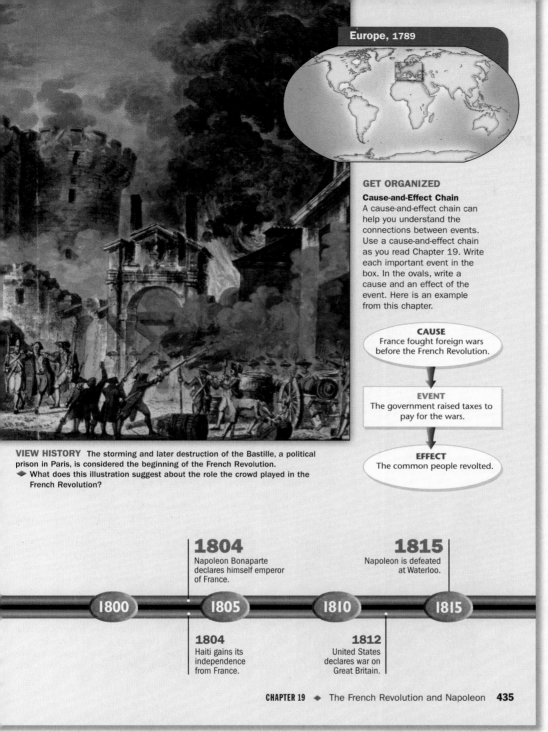

Europe, 1789

VIEW HISTORY The storming and later destruction of the Bastille, a political prison in Paris, is considered the beginning of the French Revolution.
◆ What does this illustration suggest about the role the crowd played in the French Revolution?

1804
Napoleon Bonaparte declares himself emperor of France.

1815
Napoleon is defeated at Waterloo.

1800 | 1805 | 1810 | 1815

1804
Haiti gains its independence from France.

1812
United States declares war on Great Britain.

Chapter Themes
- Culture
- People, Places, and Environment
- Power, Authority, and Governance
- Individuals, Groups, and Institutions
- Time, Continuity, and Change
- Civic Ideas and Practices
- Individual Development and Identity

F Y I

The Place de la Bastille
The Bastille no longer stands in Paris, but its location is marked by a crossroads known as the Place de la Bastille and a monument, the Colonne de Juillet (Column of July). The monument honors both the events of July 1789 and the death of French commoners who revolted in 1830. In the subway station beneath the square, stones from the Bastille's foundation can still be seen.

Chapter Warm-Up

USING THE MAP
The French Revolution affected France as well as much of the rest of Europe. Have students point out the area of France on the map and then name as many other European countries as they can that fall within the highlighted area on the map. Use Transparency 5 to point out the locations of England, Italy, and Russia, which will be discussed in relation to Napoleon in the chapter.

VIEW HISTORY
Discuss with students the prisonlike features of the Bastille. Ask how the painting reflects the toppling of old institutions by people intent on bringing about change.

◆ **ANSWER** The illustration shows that the attack on the Bastille was made by civilians rather than soldiers, suggesting that the common people played a central role in the French Revolution.

GET ORGANIZED
Cause-and-Effect Chain
Discuss the cause-and-effect chain on page 435. Ask students how the event connects to both the cause and to the effect. (The event is the result of the cause and leads to the effect.) Point out that there may be more than one cause leading up to the event and more than one effect linked to the event. Encourage students to organize information by making a cause-and-effect chain (TR, p. 325) for each section.

● **TEACH THE TIMELINE**
The timeline on pages 434–435 covers the period between 1787 and 1815. Ask students which two rulers are noted in the Chapter Events on the timeline and what happens to them (Louis XVI and Napoleon; Louis is executed, Napoleon is defeated). Ask students to look for reasons behind the overthrow of these rulers as they read the chapter.

Activity

Make a classroom timeline
Have groups of students look at timelines in other chapters in this textbook and other resources and identify five to seven events that happened during the years covered in this chapter. Then, have groups put their events together into a classroom timeline. Discuss the different events that were going on around the world.

Section Summary

In this section, students will learn how political ideas, foreign revolutions, and economic problems led to the French Revolution. They will also focus on the makeup of French society before the Revolution, the lifestyle and actions of the monarchy, the effects of those factors on the people, and the sweeping government changes proposed by the Estates-General when it met in 1789.

1 Introduce

Getting Started

Ask students to provide a definition for the word *revolution* that relates to politics (a government overthrow) and a definition that relates to science (a circular path). Point out that the French Revolution involved both a political upheaval and a complete turnaround in the government and society of France.

TERMS TO KNOW

Ask students to read the words and definitions on page 436 and then find each word in the section. Have them use a dictionary to find the etymology and the glossary at the back of the book for the correct pronunciation of *bourgeoisie*. Ask students to name other English words of French origin that still maintain their French spelling and pronunciation (e.g., *ballet, bureau, café, chauvinist, patois, fillet*).

You may wish to preview the pronunciation of the following names from this section with students.

Duc d'Orleans (dook dor LAY ahn)
Marie Antoinette
  (mah REE ahn twah NEHT)

ACTIVE READING

As students think of problems and solutions discussed in this section, suggest that they use a problem/solution chart (TR, p. 327) to record the information and help them visualize each situation.

Terms to Know

estate a French legal term that indicates a person's status in society based on property ownership and ancestral rights and customs

bourgeoisie the middle class

Main Ideas

A. The roots of the French Revolution lay in ideas of the Enlightenment, foreign revolutions, economic problems, and corruption.

B. Before the Revolution, France had three levels of society.

C. The absolute monarchs of France had the power to affect the lives of their subjects.

D. The 1789 meeting of the Estates-General led to sweeping changes in the government.

Active Reading

PROBLEMS AND SOLUTIONS
A problem is a difficulty. A solution is a way out of the difficulty. As you read this section, think about the problems faced by different levels of French society, including the monarchs. Read to see how they tried to solve their problems.

A. The Roots of the Revolution

Several factors led to the French Revolution. Included among these factors were the Enlightenment of the eighteenth century, successful revolutions in Great Britain and America, and government spending and corruption.

The Enlightenment

The ideas of the Enlightenment were based on reason and tolerance, or the acceptance and respect of beliefs different from one's own. You learned that the thinkers, or *philosophes*, behind the Enlightenment spoke out strongly for individual freedoms and equality, right of self-government, freedom of religion, and freedom of speech and thought without censorship.

The French government censored books and pamphlets and sent thinkers and writers to prison. Still, people found ways to get their work published and read. The discussion of new books and ideas was encouraged in places such as coffee houses and salons. Public opinion became a force and a power in society.

Revolutions in Great Britain and America

As you learned in Chapter 17, Great Britain's Glorious Revolution of 1688, also known as the "Bloodless Revolution," was not an armed conflict. It was basically a political revolution. The two main parties of Parliament opposed the policies of the reigning monarch, James II. When faced with this opposition, James fled the country and William and Mary were appointed joint rulers. Under their rule, the powers of the monarch were greatly limited.

Great Britain was now a constitutional monarchy. Under this system, certain men elected representatives to the lower house of Parliament. One of these members of the house would then be appointed prime minister by the monarch.

In America, the thinkers who wrote the Declaration of Independence, and later the Constitution, relied heavily on the ideals of the Enlightenment. After a victorious revolution, the United States became a republic in which some citizens had the right to vote for the President and the lawmakers.

The success of these two types of representative government brought out strong reactions in France.

This illustration shows a group of thinkers discussing ideas of the Enlightenment. Voltaire is shown with his hand raised.

Teaching Options

Section 1 Resources

Teacher's Resources (TR)
  Terms to Know, p. 32
  Review History, p. 66
  Build Your Skills, p. 100
  Concept Builder, p. 235
  Cause-and-Effect Chain, p. 325

ESL/ELL STRATEGIES

Use Visuals Discuss with students types of cartoons with which they are familiar. Then, explain that this chapter includes political cartoons. Discuss the purpose of a political cartoon. Suggest that students pay special attention to the political cartoons used in the chapter. As students encounter a cartoon in the chapter, they should write a brief paragraph about it.

The monarch, the government, and the aristocrats were alarmed. Such examples of representative government were a threat to the power of all monarchs. On the other hand, French intellectuals were pleased with the examples of representative government. The British example proved that a limited monarchy could result in a successful government and a peaceful society. The American example showed that citizens could elect a leader and others to represent them.

France's Economy

In the years leading up to the Revolution, France's economy began to fail. By 1789 it was in turmoil. The cost of foreign wars had forced the French ministers to raise taxes on the part of the population that could least afford it. The common people resented having to pay these taxes. Waste, corruption, and poor harvests also damaged the economy.

The French government tried to raise money by changing the tax system to force landowners to pay taxes. This attempt failed. Starting in 1783, the French government survived by borrowing money from European banks. However, wasteful and extravagant spending by the royal family hurt the economy and increased the people's resentment of the government.

Extreme weather conditions, including floods, drought, and storms, destroyed much of the grain crops of 1787 and 1788. Unemployment rose and prices soared. By the spring of 1789, bread had become scarce and very expensive. Riots broke out throughout the countryside and even in the cities. People broke into warehouses and stole whatever food they could find. The king and his ministers were unable to resolve the economic crisis. Their only remaining option was to call a meeting of the Estates-General, a body of representatives that the king could call at will for advice and counsel. Although this body was made up of representatives of all the people, it had not met for 175 years!

◆ **Why was France's economy in turmoil by 1789?**

B. French Society

The structure of French society had not changed much since the Middle Ages. Like most European societies at this time, it was a pyramid with the monarch at the top and the peasants at the bottom. Politically, everyone belonged to one of three **estates**, or ranks.

The First Estate

The First Estate was made up of the clergy—priests, bishops, and other men who held high-ranking positions in the Roman Catholic Church. The clergy did not have to pay taxes, in spite of the fact that the Church owned enormous amounts of land. Peasants were required to pay one-tenth of their incomes to the Church. This custom had helped the Church to grow rich.

Many parish priests were commoners and were nearly as poor as the peasants who came to their churches. The high-ranking members of the clergy, such as the bishops and cardinals, on the other hand, were usually aristocrats who lived well in luxurious surroundings.

This painting shows a woman making and selling bread on a street when bread was scarce in France in the late 1700s.

Using Technology

Have students use word processing or desktop publishing software to create a French Revolution newspaper that they will publish while working through this chapter. Have students work in groups to write articles or editorials about events of the Revolution as they read about them. Students might also locate pictures or political cartoons on the Internet or from library resources to include in their newspapers.

Connection to
LITERATURE ←------

A Tale of Two Cities is only one familiar novel set in the time of the French Revolution. Students might also enjoy other books, such as *The Scarlet Pimpernel* by Baroness Orczy, *Scaramouche* by Rafael Sabatini, *A Far Better Rest* by Susanne Alleyn, and *The Dark Tower* by Sharon Stewart. For stronger readers, *A Place of Greater Safety* by Hilary Mantel focuses on the leaders of the Reign of Terror.

---

2 Teach

A. The Roots of the Revolution

Purpose-Setting Question What political changes in Great Britain and the United States had an impact on France by the late 1700s? (the Glorious Revolution in Great Britain that led to establishment of a constitutional monarchy and the American Revolution that led to establishment of a republic)

Discuss Ask students why the French government might have wanted to censor books and pamphlets that stressed ideas of the Enlightenment. (France had an absolute monarchy. Enlightenment writers were trying to spread the ideas of self-government and individual freedom. This would mean an overthrow of the monarchy. So, the monarchs did not want these ideas to spread and would have tried to censor the material.)

TEACH PRIMARY SOURCES
Have students study the illustration on page 436 and discuss what is going on. (thinking, eating, talking, sharing ideas) Remind students that they learned about the Enlightenment in Chapter 18, pages 424–426.

Focus Students may have heard that Marie Antoinette, who was queen of France at the time of the French Revolution, made light of the bread shortages by saying that if the peasants do not have bread, "let them eat cake." The queen never actually said these words. In fact, she took an active role in trying to alleviate the famine in France.

◆ **ANSWER** foreign wars, waste of resources and money, corruption, and a series of poor harvests

B. French Society

Purpose-Setting Question What factors enabled the Roman Catholic Church in France to increase its wealth? (The clergy did not have to pay taxes, and the peasants were required to pay one-tenth of their incomes to the Church.)

Ask students why the pie graph is particularly useful for presenting this kind of information. (It shows very clearly that the Third Estate was home to the overwhelming majority of French citizens.) Have them match each of the colors on the pie graph to the illustrations, and describe how the statistics and pictures work together.

✔ **Graph Check**

Answer Third Estate or peasants

Activity

Draw graphs Write the following statistics relating to land ownership in France in 1789 on the board:
   First Estate—10%
   Second Estate—25%
   Third Estate—65%
Have students draw a pie graph to show this distribution. Then, have them compare their graphs to the one on page 438 that relates population by social class. Discuss the inequities and potential problems raised by these inequities.

◆ **ANSWER** Taxpayers were members of the Third Estate.

C. The French Monarchy

Purpose-Setting Question How did the French monarch see himself? (He ruled by divine right and was above the law.)

ANALYZE PRIMARY SOURCES

DOCUMENT-BASED QUESTION

France was run by the king, his council of ministers, and 13 regional courts, called *parlements*. Members of the *parlements* were nobles. By the 1780s, *parlements* located outside of Paris were trying to increase their power and weaken the control of the king and the central government. Louis delivered this speech in 1766 to the *parlement* of Paris to reassert his absolute power and authority.

ANSWER the rights and interests of the nation

Population by Social Class in France, 1789

■ First Estate
■ Second Estate
■ Third Estate

1.5%
0.5%
98%

Noble (Second Estate)   Member of the Clergy (First Estate)   Peasant (Third Estate)

✔ **Graph Check**

Based on the graph and the drawing, which Estate had the largest percentage of the French population but the least wealth, power, and privileges?

ANALYZE PRIMARY SOURCES **DOCUMENT-BASED QUESTIONS** What does Louis XV say rests entirely in his hands?

438   UNIT 5 ◆ Enlightenment and Revolution

The Second Estate

The Second Estate consisted of the aristocracy, or nobles who had inherited wealth and titles. Aristocrats, like the clergy, did not have to pay taxes. They held most of the land not owned by either the Church or the state. They were the only people who could hold high government office.

Louis XIV had begun the custom of requiring all members of the Second Estate to spend a certain amount of their time attending his court at Versailles. Aristocrats were taken away from their lands for several months a year. This system widened the gap between the nobles and the peasants. The feudal relationship in which a lord protected and cared for his people in exchange for their loyalty and hard work was now over.

The Third Estate

The Third Estate included all French subjects who did not belong to the First Estate or the Second Estate. It was by far the largest of the three estates. It included a mix of people—peasants, artisans, and successful business people. Unlike the clergy and the aristocracy, the common people paid taxes. They had less power and influence over the government than the other two estates, in spite of having the largest membership. The Third Estate included about 98 percent of the people.

During the eighteenth century, a middle class, or **bourgeoisie**, had begun to arise in France. It included people who were educated and who had made money in trade, manufacturing, or a profession such as law or banking. The *philosophes* of the Enlightenment found a ready audience in these people. They were ambitious and eager to play important roles in society and government.

◆ **In which estate were the people who paid taxes?**

C. The French Monarchy

In 1766, Louis XV made the following statement to the *parlement*, or court, of Paris:

❝ [I]n my person alone lies that sovereign power. . . . From me alone the courts receive their existence and authority. The fullness of this authority, which they exercise in my name only, remains permanently vested in me. . . . Legislative power is mine alone. . . . My people are one with me, and the rights and interests of the nation . . . are of necessity united with my own and rest entirely in my hands. ❞

The French monarch believed he ruled by divine right and was considered above the law. Louis XIV had been one of the most powerful monarchs in Europe. The two kings who followed Louis XIV tried to rule as he had. However, Louis XV and Louis XVI were weak and ineffective at a time when France needed strong leaders.

Teaching Options

Meet Individual Needs:

VERBAL/LINGUISTIC LEARNERS

Have students role-play, and possibly audiotape or videotape, a newscast of Louis's speech before the *parlement* of Paris. Have one student read Louis's words while others portray members of each of the three estates, serving as commentators and analyzing the remarks from their points of view.

F Y I

The Estates-General

The Estates-General was first convened by King Philip IV in 1302. Before that time, there had been provincial assemblies in France, but no national gathering of representatives of the clergy, nobility, and townspeople. One of the main responsibilities of the Estates-General was to approve changes in taxation. Because tax laws seldom changed, there was not much need to convene the body.

Louis XV

In 1715, Louis XV inherited the crown from his great-grandfather, Louis XIV. Because Louis XV was only five years old, a regent, or temporary ruler, was appointed to run the government. The Duc d'Orleans ruled until his death in 1723. For the next 21 years, different chief ministers appointed by Louis governed the country.

Louis XV finally took over the monarch's responsibility in 1744. However, he had little interest in governing. He relied on the advice of his ministers rather than setting policies based on his own convictions.

France fought costly wars during Louis XV's reign. The people might have accepted these expenses if the wars had been successful, but they were not. France won lands in the War of Austrian Succession but gave them up in 1748. In 1756, France allied itself with Austria in a war against Prussia and Great Britain. By the end of these wars, France was deeply in debt.

A king with a strong personality might have been able to reform the social system and save the monarchy. Louis XV, who was not very intelligent or interested in government, was not the one. He was apparently aware of his shortcomings and the damage he had done to the nation. On his deathbed, in 1774, he is said to have remarked, "After me comes the flood!" predicting the disaster his successor's reign would bring.

Louis XV was only five years old when he inherited the throne from his great-grandfather, Louis XIV.

Louis XVI and Marie Antoinette

In 1770, the heir to the throne of France married Austrian princess Marie Antoinette. Four years later, Louis XVI succeeded his grandfather, Louis XV. Crowned in 1774, Louis XVI would reign until 1793.

Louis XVI inherited an empty treasury and unhappy subjects. Unfortunately, his queen was as extravagant as she was lovely. Royal spending on personal luxuries was really only a small part of the national debt, but the public believed otherwise. The queen's spectacular gowns and the glittering balls and court life at Versailles all suggested that the royal family wasted far too much money when their people were starving. The people felt that their high taxes should be used to improve their living conditions, not to throw expensive parties for the aristocracy.

Like his grandfather, Louis XVI was weak. Early in his reign, and partly at the queen's urging, he dismissed many of Louis XV's experienced ministers. With their dismissal, the possibility of reform faded. In the end, Louis XVI and his ministers could not solve the kingdom's financial crisis. The king was forced to bring in the Estates-General. This decision set off the chain of events that would end by abolishing the monarchy.

◆ **How did the common people feel about the way Louis XVI and his wife lived?**

D. From Estates-General to National Assembly

On May 5, 1789, the members of the Estates-General met for the first time in more than 175 years. The outcome of this conference would provide the first stepping stone toward national revolution.

Extend While Louis XV was too young at age five to rule France, he was not the youngest person ever to be crowned king of France. In 1422, Henry VI became king of England when he was less than nine months old. A month later, he was also crowned king of France. Ask students what problems might arise from naming a king who was too young to rule. (Possible answers: Ineffective or greedy regents or relatives would fight for the throne; people would not know who to serve; enemies might think the country was vulnerable.)

Explore Louis XVI and Marie Antoinette met only 2 days before their wedding. He was 15 years old and she was 14 at the time. Their marriage had been arranged as a way to strengthen the alliance between France and the Holy Roman Empire, of which Marie's mother was empress. Despite her style and beauty, Marie was never fully accepted by many French people, who viewed her as an outsider. Have students research to find other royal marriages arranged for political purposes. Students should find out the country of origin of both the bride and the groom and the political purposes for which the marriage was arranged.

◆ **ANSWER** Possible answer: The people felt that Louis and his wife wasted money that should have been used to improve the living conditions of the common people.

D. From Estates-General to National Assembly

Purpose-Setting Question What was the Tennis Court Oath? (an agreement made by members of the Estates-General in 1789 not to separate and to continue meeting until a constitution was established for France)

Writing

AVERAGE

Louis XV and Louis XVI were both ineffective kings, but they had very different personalities and motives as rulers. Have students research both men to find out about their education, interests, and capabilities as king. Then, have them write a paragraph or brief essay comparing and contrasting the last two Bourbon kings. Give students a Venn diagram (TR, p. 323) to use as they research.

CHALLENGE

By the mid-1700s, the role of monarchs was changing throughout Europe. Have students research to find out more about changes in the status of European monarchies in the 1700s and have them use their research to write an essay to explain how and why monarchs were losing their positions as absolute rulers of their countries.

Make a petition Activists often create petitions calling for political change and ask others to sign the petitions to show their support. Have students create a petition from members of the Third Estate to persuade clergy and nobles to change the voting system. Have students share their petitions.

ANALYZE PRIMARY SOURCES

DOCUMENT-BASED QUESTION

On June 13, 1789, three parish priests from the First Estate declared support for voting changes. By June 17, the National Assembly was adopted by a vote of 491–89. On June 19, the members of the clergy voted by a narrow margin to join the National Assembly. Then came the lockout and Tennis Court Oath on June 20. By June 27, the king gave in and invited the members of the First and Second Estates to join the National Assembly.

ANSWER The members were determined to work together to gain all votes to establish a Constitution of the Kingdom.

◆ **ANSWER** Members of the Third Estate felt that the voting system was unfair.

Section Close

Ask students why some people living in France in 1789 supported the king and others supported the idea of revolution. Discuss the given reasons behind each position.

③ Assess

Review Answers

Review History

A. the Enlightenment, foreign revolutions, and the poor condition of the French economy

B. It was very much like it had been since the Middle Ages. The king was at the top; then the nobles and clergy; and finally the workers, artisans, and peasants.

C. All the kings' decisions and actions had an immediate effect on their people.

D. The first political battle of the Revolution had been fought.

Define Terms to Know

estate, 437; bourgeoisie, 438

Critical Thinking

Louis XVI was weak as a king and the state of the nation was in unrest and in a financial crisis.

Write About Citizenship

Students' essays may include the following: All citizens were required to obey the monarch. The First and Second Estates paid no taxes. The Third Estate paid all the taxes and did most of the work. Citizens could play no active role in the government.

Meeting at Versailles

On May 5, 1789, the deputies of the Estates-General were presented to the king at Versailles. Louis XVI was gracious to the deputies of the First and Second Estates but ignored those of the Third Estate. He refused to listen to their complaint that the voting system was unfair. Deputies within an estate voted as a block. So, on any question of reform, the Third Estate would be outvoted two to one. The wealthy members of the First and Second Estates were not likely to change a system that protected their privileges.

The National Assembly

The conference remained deadlocked for more than a month. Finally, deputies of the Third Estate asked the poorer deputies of the First Estate for their support. On June 17, many deputies of the First Estate voted with deputies of the Third Estate to set up a National Assembly. This vote was the first outward act of revolution.

On June 20, 1789, deputies of the National Assembly found themselves locked out of the conference rooms. Instead, they met at a nearby building that housed the royal indoor tennis courts and took the following oath:

ANALYZE PRIMARY SOURCES **DOCUMENT-BASED QUESTION** Why did the members of the National Assembly swear not to separate?

❝ We decree that all members of this Assembly shall immediately take a solemn oath not to separate, and to meet again wherever circumstances require, until the Constitution of the Kingdom is established upon firm foundations. ❞

This oath came to be called the Tennis Court Oath. Politically, the French Revolution had begun.

◆ **What complaint did members of the Third Estate express to the king?**

Review 1

Review History
A. What were some root causes of the French Revolution?
B. What was French society like before the Revolution?
C. What effect did the absolute monarchs of France have on the lives of their subjects?
D. What was the result of the 1789 meeting of the Estates-General?

Define Terms to Know
Define the following terms:
estate, bourgeoisie

Critical Thinking
What was the connection between the character and abilities of Louis XVI and the state of the nation?

Write About Citizenship
Explain what it meant to be a citizen of France at the dawn of the Revolution. Remember to discuss the different social classes and responsibilities.

Get Organized
CAUSE-AND-EFFECT CHAIN
Use a cause-and-effect chain to show a cause and an effect of the destruction of grain crops in 1787 and 1788.

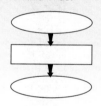

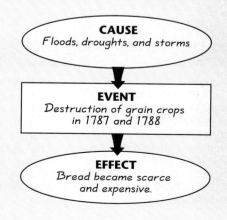

CAUSE
Floods, droughts, and storms

EVENT
Destruction of grain crops in 1787 and 1788

EFFECT
Bread became scarce and expensive.

Build Your Skills

Build Your Skills

INTERPRET POLITICAL CARTOONS

A political cartoon is the visual equivalent of a newspaper editorial. It is a drawing showing the cartoonist's view of a political issue. Like an editorial, a political cartoon uses facts to support a point of view.

Political cartoons often use symbols to represent nations or political parties. For example, a globe can represent the nations of the world, one soldier can stand for an entire army, and a dollar sign can stand for a nation's treasury or its banks.

Political cartoons are often humorous, poking fun at national issues and leaders. Cartoonists often exaggerate and distort visual elements to create this humor. For example, Marie Antoinette dressed extravagantly. A cartoonist might exaggerate her appearance to add to the humor of the cartoon. Such exaggeration often makes an image more memorable and allows cartoonists to express their feelings on an issue more clearly.

The main purpose of a political cartoon is to persuade. The cartoonist wants to convert viewers to his or her point of view on some political figure or issue.

Here's How

Follow these steps to interpret a political cartoon.

1. Look at the images and read the text. Cartoons often include dialogue balloons and other text within the drawing, as well as a caption underneath.

2. Identify the people and symbols in the cartoon. In modern U.S. cartoons, for instance, an elephant usually represents the Republican Party.

3. Note exaggerated elements, such as changes in a well-known person's appearance, alteration of the relative sizes of countries, and so on. Think about how these changes affect your view of the people or objects.

4. Formulate your opinion of what the cartoonist is trying to say. Make sure each detail in the cartoon supports your interpretation.

Here's Why

You have just read about some of the reasons why the French Revolution began. The cartoon below is about the relationship among members of the three social divisions, or estates, in France.

Practice the Skill

Look at the political cartoon on this page. Each person shown in the cartoon represents one of the Three Estates.

1. What does this cartoonist want you to think about the purpose of the estate that the peasant represents?

2. What do you think the cartoonist thinks about the other two estates?

Extend the Skill

Find a political cartoon in a newspaper or magazine. Use the steps above to interpret the cartoon.

Apply the Skill

As you read Section III, look at the political cartoon. Follow the steps in *Here's How* to understand the point the cartoonist is trying to make.

This political cartoon shows a peasant holding a cane (left), a member of the clergy (center), and a noble (right).

CHAPTER 19 ◆ The French Revolution and Napoleon **441**

Teach the Skill

Ask students to name two different kinds of cartoons they can find in most daily newspapers. (comic strips and political cartoons) Have several examples of both types of cartoons available for students to analyze. Ask students what the purpose is of each type of cartoon and how the purposes differ. (Comic strips usually seek to entertain viewers or to show a humorous side of real life; political cartoons are designed to make fun of something, point out a political or social problem, and push for change.)

Discuss with students ways that political cartoonists use exaggeration in their drawings and sarcastic captions to get their point across. Ask students in what ways humor or satire can be more effective than fiery speeches in getting people to see the need for change.

Practice the Skill

ANSWERS

1. Members of the Third Estate carry a heavy burden and must support the First and Second Estates.

2. Members of the First and Second Estates are lazy and take advantage of members of the Third Estate.

Extend the Skill

Ask students to analyze their cartoons by pointing out important elements and relating the cartoon to the political situation or event it addresses.

Apply the Skill

After studying the cartoon and reading the caption, students should identify the person (Napoleon) and symbols (French flag, eagle). Then, they should note the exaggerated element (large shadow cast by Napoleon) and formulate an opinion about what the cartoonist is conveying (Europe's wariness of the threat presented by Napoleon's army and his ambitions).

Teaching Options

RETEACH

Have students work together in pairs or small groups to analyze their cartoons for the *Extend the Skill* activity. For each cartoon, have students identify the subject and any symbols or personalities they recognize. Then, have groups present their cartoons to the class and lead a discussion on what they feel the cartoons mean and how effectively the cartoonists get their message across.

CHALLENGE

Have students draw a political cartoon about a current community or school issue or an issue they have read about in this textbook. Then, ask students to exchange cartoons with a partner. Have students critique each other's cartoons and captions for clarity, creativity, use of symbolism, humor, and effectiveness.

II. Revolution and Terror

(pp. 442-447)

Section Summary

In this section, students will learn how the French Revolution began with acts of violence and that a new government was built through painful steps. They will also learn how France's royal family was imprisoned and executed and how a violent Reign of Terror took over the government.

1 Introduce

Getting Started

Discuss the idea that the term *mob* is usually used to imply violence and lack of control. Point out that the French Revolution began with mobs of people marching through Paris. Have students predict what might happen as the Revolution begins.

TERMS TO KNOW

Ask students to read the terms and definitions on page 442 and then find each term in the section. Suggest they write each term and definition on a separate index card. Then, have students write a sentence using that term in context on the back of the index card.

You may wish to preview the pronunciation of the following terms from this section with students.

"La Marseillaise"
(lah mar seh LEHZ)
Claude-Joseph Rouget de Lisle
(KLOHD ZHOH zef roo ZHEH duh LEEL)
Tuileries (TWEEL reez)
Girondin (juh RAHN dihn)
Jacobin (JAK uh bihn)
sans-culottes (sanz koo LAHTS)
Robespierre (ROHBZ pyer)

ACTIVE READING

Have students make an idea web (TR, p. 321) as they read subsection B. In the center circle, have them write *March on Versailles*. Then, in each outer circle write the point of view of the king, the women, the soldiers, and the members of the Assembly toward the march. Be sure that students have reasons for each point of view also listed in the circle.

 Section II

Revolution and Terror

Terms to Know

tricolor the red, white, and blue flag of revolutionary France

guillotine a device with a blade, used to cut off the heads of convicted criminals

Main Ideas

A. The French Revolution began with acts of mob violence.

B. By painful steps, the new leaders of France moved toward a new government.

C. France's king and queen tried to escape the country, but they were captured and later executed.

D. The Reign of Terror threatened anyone identified as an enemy of the republic.

 Active Reading

POINTS OF VIEW
Points of view are ways of looking at issues, events, or people. As you read this section, think about the different views that the common French people, Louis XVI, and the aristocrats had of important events. Try to find reasons for their points of view.

A. The Revolution Begins

The National Assembly presented Louis XVI with a list of demands for reform. On June 23, 1789, the king made a speech accepting only those reforms that were most acceptable to the aristocracy. The king's list included taxes, individual liberty, and freedom of the press. He ignored other demands, such as equal employment opportunity for government offices and a reform of the social order. The National Assembly decided to put their reforms into action without the king's consent. On June 27, Louis XVI gave in. He invited all members of the First and Second Estates who had remained loyal to him to join the National Assembly.

The Storming of the Bastille

Fourteen miles away in Paris, mobs were gathering every day to listen to the news from Versailles. Bread prices were at an all-time high and thousands of people were out of work. Everyone was excited about the hints of coming reforms. However, the reforms did not come soon enough for the people.

On July 11, news reached Paris that Jacques Necker and several other ministers had been fired. Necker was popular with the common people because he had always favored reform. When the people heard this news, they took matters into their own hands.

There were large numbers of troops in Paris, but many of the soldiers were no longer loyal to the king. They had suffered as much as anyone from the shortages of food and the rising prices. The palace guards and many other soldiers sided with the Parisians. On the evening of July 12, mobs of people looted gunsmiths' shops. At dawn on July 14, the mobs broke into the military hospital and stole its supply of muskets. Now armed, the mobs marched on the Bastille.

The Bastille had been built in 1370 as a fortress. Under Louis XIV, it became a state prison. Anyone who, in the king's opinion, wrote or spoke against the government was likely to end up as a prisoner in the Bastille. It had become a hated symbol of the old government. There were few prisoners within its walls at the time of the attack, but there was a large store of weapons and ammunition.

The Bastille's guards could not hold back the attackers, who rushed in to take over the prison. By the afternoon, the Bastille belonged to the people. They freed the prisoners, stole the weapons inside, and dragged the prison warden and the

Spotlight on *Culture*

FRENCH NATIONAL ANTHEM "LA MARSEILLAISE"
Claude-Joseph Rouget de Lisle's "War Song for the Army of the Rhine" became the French national anthem in 1795. Its lyrics perfectly fit the revolutionary mood:
To arms, citizens!
Form your battalions!
March on, march on,
Let impure blood water
our furrows!

Teaching Options

Section 2 Resources

Teacher's Resources (TR)
Terms to Know, p. 32
Review History, p. 66
Build Your Skills, p. 100
Concept Builder, p. 235
Cause-and-Effect Chain, p. 325

ESL/ELL STRATEGIES

Identify Essential Vocabulary Explain that the machine used to behead King Louis and other enemies of the state during the revolution was called a *guillotine*, after a French doctor named Joseph Guillotin, who advocated its use during the French Revolution. Many other common words are based on the names of people. Have students find the history and meaning of words such as *braille, diesel, pasteurize, silhouette,* and *sideburns.*

governor out into the streets. These men died violent deaths at the hands of the mob. Their heads were then cut off, rammed onto long, sharpened sticks called pikes, and paraded through the streets of Paris.

The Peasants React

News of the violence in Paris quickly reached other towns, where people followed the Parisian example. They forced mayors and officials to step down from their offices, and mob rule governed.

In the countryside things happened somewhat differently. At the same time that the Parisians were attacking the Bastille, peasants were attacking the stately homes of their lords, looting, burning, and often killing. Like the Parisians, they had had high hopes of the meeting of the Estates-General. Like the Parisians, they were not content to wait for the slow process of establishing a new government and a new social order. False rumors spread that various aristocrats were coming with troops to attack and that peasants' crops would be seized. Peasants armed themselves and kept watch during this period of confusion and panic known as the Great Fear.

This painting shows the storming of the Bastille on July 14, 1789.

 Why did the people storm the Bastille?

B. Toward a New Government

On August 27, 1789, the National Assembly approved the Declaration of the Rights of Man and the Citizen. This document, published before the Assembly began work on a national constitution, set forth the rights and privileges of all French citizens.

Declaration of the Rights of Man and the Citizen

The deputies of the National Assembly argued through the night of August 4, trying to decide which reforms everyone could agree on and which were the most important. Some of the deputies from the old Second Estate showed that they were willing to give up certain privileges for the sake of a just government. After several days of debate, the Assembly published a report. They did away with the old feudal society. Personal privilege for aristocrats was ended. Employment was open to all people, regardless of class. Serfdom was abolished. Peasants would no longer have to tithe, or pay the Roman Catholic Church one-tenth of everything they earned.

The Assembly's next task was to write a constitution. Having done away with the old social order, the deputies knew that they would have to set up a new one. Days and weeks of debate ended with the decision to publish a document that would set out the rights, privileges, and responsibilities of all French citizens. This document would be the foundation for the new France.

On August 26, the Assembly voted on the Declaration of the Rights of Man and the Citizen. In a preamble, or introduction, and 17 articles, this document stressed equality under the law. It also provided for freedom of speech, of the press, and of religion. It stated that laws were the true rulers of France.

Primary Source Documents
You can read sections of the Declaration of the Rights of Man and the Citizen on page 813.

A. The Revolution Begins

Purpose-Setting Question Why did the troops in Paris not stop the people from rioting? (Many of the troops sided with the Parisian mobs against the king because they were also suffering from food shortages and rising prices.)

SPOTLIGHT ON CULTURE

FRENCH NATIONAL ANTHEM "LA MARSEILLAISE" "La Marseillaise" was more than just a marching song to French people in the 1790s. Even before being adopted as the French national anthem, it became one of the most popular songs in Paris. It was sung at weddings, funerals, and even between acts at plays. Ask students what adjectives they would use to describe the song, based on the lyrics presented here. (Possible answers: stirring, warlike, intense, patriotic)

Extend Today, July 14 is a national holiday in France. The French celebrate Bastille Day in much the same way Americans celebrate Independence Day on July 4, with parades, speeches, and the setting off of fireworks.

◆ **ANSWER** The people stormed the Bastille because it was a hated symbol of the old government, and they wanted the large store of weapons and ammunition that was inside.

B. Toward a New Government

Purpose-Setting Question What were some reforms agreed upon by the National Assembly? (abandoning the old feudal society, removing personal privilege for aristocrats, opening employment to all classes of people, abolishing serfdom, and ending the requirement that peasants tithe to the church)

Focus Have students read the sections of the Declaration of the Rights of Man and the Citizen on page 813. Discuss how these rights would make life better for people.

Research

AVERAGE

Point out that neither the constitution that was adopted by the National Assembly in France nor the U.S. Constitution granted full rights to all members of society. Have students research which parts of society were left out in the original constitution of each country and how those groups gained more rights over time.

CHALLENGE

Have students research what happened during the meetings in which the constitutions of France and the United States were developed. What issues were debated most intently? What ideas were eventually omitted from each document and why? What process was undertaken to adopt or ratify each constitution? Have students report their findings to the class.

However, in order to be valid these laws were to be applied equally to all and had to be just and reasonable. The slogan "Liberty, Equality, Fraternity," was the battle cry of the Revolution and expressed its main ideas.

The March on Versailles

In the meantime, rioting and mob unrest continued throughout Paris. Little had been done to ease the food shortages, and it was still too early in the year to harvest the crops. Amid this violence, Louis XVI still would not agree to adopt the Declaration of the Rights of Man and the Citizen. Instead, he summoned troops from the town of Flanders. He hoped that their arrival in Versailles would make the angry citizens back down from their demands.

The opposite happened. The troops arrived at the end of September. On October 5, the women of Paris tired of asking for bread and formed a mob. A ragged band of women marched along the road to Versailles, armed with sticks and kitchen knives. When they reached the palace, they forced their way into the hall where the National Assembly was meeting and demanded to see the king.

Thousands of National Guard soldiers followed the women. The National Guard was a citizen's army that had formed in Paris after the fall of the Bastille. Faced by both an angry mob and a small army, Louis XVI realized that he had no choice but to give in to their demands. He promised bread to the women and agreed to accompany the National Guard back to Paris. He also promised the Assembly that he would sign the Declaration of the Rights of Man and the Citizen and a constitution that would limit the king's powers.

On October 6, the royal family and its escort returned to the capital city. The soldiers waved the __tricolor__, the new French flag of red, white, and blue stripes. The king and queen, with a few courtiers, were imprisoned in the long-abandoned palace of the Tuileries.

◆ **What made Louis XVI accept the Declaration of the Rights of Man and the Citizen?**

C. The End of the Monarchy

In their long hours in the dusty prison of the Tuileries, the king and queen wondered what would happen to them. It was becoming clear to them that the French people no longer wanted a monarch but rather a representative government of elected officials. Convinced that there would be no place in this new France for them, the king and queen were afraid for their lives. Together, they determined to leave the country.

An Attempt to Escape

On a June night in 1791, Louis XVI dressed in old clothing belonging to a servant. He quietly left the palace, unnoticed by the guards, and made his way to a waiting coach. The driver set out on the road for Austria. Louis hoped to find protection, and perhaps, an army willing to fight for him, at his brother-in-law's court.

The coach made a brief stop in a small town along the road. The postmaster recognized the king in spite of his disguise. In the next town, Varennes, Louis was arrested and taken back to Paris under guard.

Meanwhile, the deputies of the National Assembly had originally intended to create a constitutional monarchy, with Louis XVI as its figurehead. The people would elect representatives who would make the laws. However, the royal family would play a ceremonial role, and the king would have limited

Teaching Options

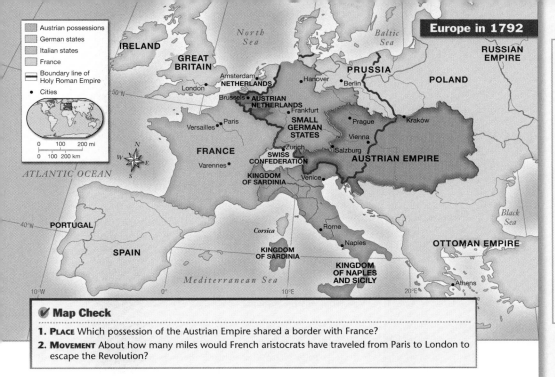

Europe in 1792

Austrian possessions
German states
Italian states
France
Boundary line of Holy Roman Empire
• Cities

North Sea
Baltic Sea
IRELAND
GREAT BRITAIN
RUSSIAN EMPIRE
PRUSSIA
POLAND
NETHERLANDS
Amsterdam
London
Hanover
Berlin
Brussels AUSTRIAN NETHERLANDS
Frankfurt
Prague
Kraków
Versailles Paris
SMALL GERMAN STATES
Vienna
FRANCE
Zurich
Salzburg
Varennes
SWISS CONFEDERATION
AUSTRIAN EMPIRE
KINGDOM OF SARDINIA
Venice
ATLANTIC OCEAN
Black Sea
PORTUGAL
Corsica
Rome
SPAIN
KINGDOM OF SARDINIA
Naples
OTTOMAN EMPIRE
KINGDOM OF NAPLES AND SICILY
Mediterranean Sea
Athens

✔ Map Check

1. **PLACE** Which possession of the Austrian Empire shared a border with France?
2. **MOVEMENT** About how many miles would French aristocrats have traveled from Paris to London to escape the Revolution?

legislative powers. After the king's attempted escape, however, the deputies reconsidered. Could they trust a king who had run away in disguise?

The Legislative Assembly

In October 1791, the National Assembly was replaced by a new Legislative Assembly. Members of this Legislative Assembly fell into two groups. One group believed that the National Assembly's model of constitutional monarchy was the best idea for the new government. The other group wanted to abolish the monarchy altogether. This group wanted to make France a republic. Louis XVI would have preferred a constitutional monarchy. However, his flight to Varennes had shaken the deputies' confidence in the monarchy. So, they were more willing to listen to ideas of the radicals.

Many people besides the king had thoughts of leaving France. The mob violence of 1789 had frightened the aristocrats. They realized that they might be forced to pay with their lives for their centuries of privilege. Thousands of members of the old Second Estate sailed to Great Britain or crossed the borders into Germany and Austria. Once settled in these foreign lands, the aristocrats began to plot to overthrow the Assembly and bring an end to the Revolution.

While all this was going on, France was also faced with the possibility of a foreign war. Leaders of other nations feared that the revolutionary ideas would spread from France to their countries. The aristocrats who had fled France urged the leaders of Austria and Prussia to invade France and restore Louis XVI to the throne. The Legislative Assembly responded to these threats by declaring war on Austria in April 1792.

Discuss Point out that following the Glorious Revolution, Great Britain established a constitutional monarchy, whereas after the American Revolution, the United States established a republic. Ask students why the French, like the British, might have wanted to retain a monarchy. (Possible answer: Many French people still felt loyalty to the king, who might provide more stability and better relations with surrounding kingdoms and empires.) Then, ask why the United States rejected the idea of a monarchy. (Possible answer: It had just fought a war to be free of Great Britain and its king.)

Focus Point out that the declaration of war passed by the Legislative Assembly in April 1792 marked a major turning point in the way wars were fought in Europe. Before that time, European wars had always been declared by monarchs, who were usually defending agreements or treaties. They were fought by royal troops or by mercenaries. Representatives of the French people made the decision to go to war this time, and many troops of the revolutionary army were volunteers and not professional soldiers.

Focus on
TEEN LIFE

Work and Teens Working-class teenagers during the time of the French Revolution had two choices—they could work on farms in the countryside or work in Paris where they could learn a trade. Many boys and girls as young as 13 years old went to Paris to become apprentices. All worked long hours and usually had little to eat. Most of their conversation outside of the workplace was about the Revolution. They also had to make sure to wear a tricolor cockade pinned to their hats whenever they went walking on the streets of Paris. The cockade proved that the young person was an ardent patriot. Revolutionaries were suspicious of anyone not wearing a cockade.

DOCUMENT-BASED QUESTION
In the initial vote at the trial of
Louis XVI, 361 deputies voted for
death whereas 360 voted for other
punishments. The Girondins continued to appeal for clemency, but the
final vote at the trial was 380–310
for death.

ANSWER Possible answer: He
seems to have died without complaint, hopeful for the future of
France, but maintaining his innocence.

◆ **ANSWER** The National
Convention was established to
decide the fate of the king and to
write a new constitution.

D. The Reign of Terror

Purpose-Setting Question How
did the Jacobins, including
Robespierre, support the Reign of
Terror during the French Revolution?
(The Jacobins, and one of its members, Robespierre, wanted immediate changes to the French government and revenge on members of
the aristocracy. They supported acts
of violence, such as beheading by
guillotine, during the Reign of Terror.)

Focus Ironically, beheading was
proposed by Dr. Joseph Guillotin, a
member of the National Assembly,
as a "humane" way of executing
capital offenders. Previously, convicted French nobles were executed
by sword and peasants by hanging.
Guillotin opposed this unequal punishment and felt that both ways
caused too much suffering. During
the Reign of Terror, many assembly
members died at the guillotine, and
Guillotin himself was arrested and
faced execution. He was spared
when the killing fever faded after
Robespierre's death.

Activity

Make a Venn diagram Have
students use a Venn diagram
(TR, p. 323) to compare and contrast the Jacobins and Girondins.
(**Overlap:** member of National
Convention, from bourgeoisie, democratic; **Jacobins:** wanted immediate change, supported fixing prices
and rationing food; **Girondins:** more
slow to act, not ready to fix prices
or ration food, wanted to change
carefully)

The National Convention

In the fall of 1792, the people voted for yet another new governing body,
the National Convention. The 750 members of this body would vote to decide
on the fate of the king and would write a new constitution. Most of the
deputies were from the bourgeoisie. Their political beliefs were democratic.
They quickly abolished the monarchy and declared France to be a republic.

As with other legislative bodies, the Convention soon was divided into two
groups with widely different views. Some deputies believed the king was a
traitor and should be executed. Other deputies argued unsuccessfully for
mercy. During his brief trial, Louis XVI refused to admit to any wrongdoing.
A large majority of the deputies found the king guilty. A much smaller
majority voted to execute the king.

On January 21, 1793, Louis XVI was taken to the scaffold and executed.
An eyewitness recalled the king's last words:

❝ I die perfectly innocent of the so-called crimes of which I was accused.
I pardon those who are the cause of my misfortunes. Indeed, I hope that
the shedding of my blood will contribute to the happiness of France. **❞**

Marie Antoinette lived for nine months after her husband was beheaded.
Then, on October 16, 1793, she was executed as well.

◆ **What was the National Convention established to do?**

D. The Reign of Terror

Perhaps the most familiar image of the French Revolution is the **guillotine**,
a device with a sharp, heavy blade that was used to cut off the heads of
convicted criminals. Prisoners found guilty of treason were carried to places of
public execution in clumsy, heavy farm carts called tumbrels. The victims were
executed by means of a guillotine, much to the pleasure of cheering crowds.

The Jacobins

During the hectic meetings of the National Convention, the legislative body
became divided into two major groups—the Girondins and the Jacobins.
Members of the Girondins preferred to move carefully when making changes.
The Jacobins wanted immediate changes. It was the Jacobins who led the effort
to have the king tried for treason, found guilty, and executed.

Outside the halls of the National Convention, the working people of Paris
also wanted change. These people were called sans-culottes, after the
comfortable, loose-fitting trousers that they wore. The sans-culottes
supported the Jacobins, who were willing to ease food shortages and inflation
by fixing prices and rationing food. The Girondins were not ready to make
such changes. On June 2, 1793, a mob of sans-culottes attacked the Tuileries,
where the Girondins held their meetings. Politically, this marked the end of
the Girondins. It also was another step forward in the brutal campaign known
as the Reign of Terror.

Robespierre and the Committee of Public Safety

In late June 1793, the National Convention's Committee of Public Safety
became the most powerful organization in the French government. It had
authority over all civil servants and all state bodies. At the center of the
committee was Maximilien Robespierre, an emblem of the Reign of Terror,
or Terror, as it came to be called.

The guillotine was a dreaded
symbol of the Reign of Terror.

DOCUMENT-BASED QUESTION
What impression
do you have of Louis XVI
based on his last words?

Teaching Options

F Y I
Leftists and Rightists

The labeling of political liberals or radicals
as "leftists" and conservatives as "right-
ists" originated in the French Legislative
Assembly. The more radical Jacobins sat
together on the upper left benches of the
Assembly, while the more conservative
Girondins sat on the right side.

Meet Individual Needs:
AUDITORY LEARNERS

Have different students read aloud individual paragraphs in subsection C while other
students act out the king's attempted
escape and capture, his trial, and his execution. Discuss reasons for the fall of the
king and help students understand the
political changes that led to his being
removed from power and eventually killed.

Robespierre was a lawyer who had been one of the deputies to the Estates-General in 1789. A Jacobin, he favored the king's execution. Robespierre did not invent the ideas of the Terror, but he supported them.

The Jacobins were from the old Third Estate, as were the sans-culottes who supported them. They wanted revenge on the members of the old First and Second Estates. With the king's execution and the fall of the Girondins, the Revolution was on shaky ground. People feared a rebellion by the old Second Estate, or an invasion by a foreign power.

During the Terror, anyone accused of plotting, speaking, or writing against the Republic was imprisoned, tried in a mock trial, and hauled to the guillotine for execution. It was also a crime to show sympathy for any "enemy of the state." Many of those aristocrats who stayed in France were beheaded.

Aristocrats were not the only people who were beheaded. Common citizens such as Olympe de Gouges were also victims of the Reign of Terror. De Gouges, like many women, had been disappointed that the Declaration of the Rights of Man and the Citizen did not give equal citizenship to women. In 1791, she wrote the Declaration of the Rights of Woman and the Female Citizen. She proclaimed that all men and women citizens were equal. She argued that women deserved to hold political positions as much as men did.

The government did improve some rights of women for a short time. For example, women could inherit property and divorces were made easier. However, two years after de Gouges wrote the Declaration of the Rights of Woman and the Female Citizen, a committee of the National Convention criticized women for being involved in politics. Women's political clubs were stopped. Women who continued to meet were arrested. Some were imprisoned and executed by guillotine. In 1793, de Gouges was guillotined, because she criticized the Jacobins, opposed the Reign of Terror, and spoke publicly and repeatedly in support of women's rights.

In 1794, the Terror ended. It sickened people who realized that executions were not necessary to preserve the state. As a sign of the change in public opinion, Robespierre was one of the last to be guillotined.

◆ **Who was Robespierre?**

Primary Source Documents
You can read sections of the Declaration of the Rights of Woman and the Female Citizen on page 813.

Review II

Review History
A. How did the French Revolution begin?
B. What kind of government did the new leaders of France design?
C. What became of King Louis XVI and Marie Antoinette?
D. What was the purpose of the Reign of Terror?

Define Terms to Know
Define the following terms:
tricolor, guillotine

Critical Thinking
Why did members of the old First and Second Estates take so little part in the new government?

Write About Government
Write a brief editorial describing what kind of government you think France should design after the Revolution. Support your argument.

Get Organized
CAUSE-AND-EFFECT CHAIN
Use a cause-and-effect chain to show a cause and an effect of the storming of the Bastille.

CHAPTER 19 ◆ The French Revolution and Napoleon **447**

Activity

Write a letter Have students write a letter to the editor of an underground French newspaper during the time of the Revolution in which they oppose the effect that the Reign of Terror has had on life in France. Students' letters might explain how the Terror has negated some of the important principles of the Revolution.

Discuss Ask students why they think some women might have felt that the Revolution was not equal. (Women did not gain more rights or representation.) Have students read the Declaration of the Rights of Woman and the Female Citizen on page 813 and discuss what rights women wanted.

◆ **ANSWER** Robespierre was a Jacobin who led the Committee of Public Safety, which led the Reign of Terror.

Section Close

Have students create a two-column chart (TR, p. 328) in which they list positive changes and negative effects of the French Revolution. Ask students to evaluate whether the Revolution improved the life of most French people or not. Then, have them explain their view.

3 Assess

Review Answers

Review History
A. with the storming of the Bastille
B. democratic government
C. They were executed by guillotine.
D. to destroy all enemies of the republic; to frighten people into loyalty; to prevent a royalist attack on the republic; to get revenge on the wealthy First and Second Estates

Define Terms to Know
tricolor, 444; guillotine, 446

Critical Thinking
Possible answer: Many were personally loyal to the king and many more supported the old traditions and system. Also, the new government was led by the Third Estate who did not want the First and Second Estates involved.

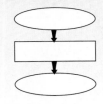

CAUSE
Jacques Necker and other ministers were fired.

EVENT
Storming of the Bastille

EFFECT
Mob stole weapons, freed prisoners, killed warden and guards.

Write About Government
Students' editorials might suggest a representative government in which all adult citizens could vote because this would be fair to everyone. Students may suggest a limited role for the monarch.

Section Summary

In this section, students will learn how Napoleon quickly rose within the ranks to become a general in the French revolutionary army; how he began to play a larger role within France's government until he was named emperor for life; and how he led successful attacks against other European powers and built a French empire.

1 Introduce

Getting Started

Ask students what qualities they feel a military leader must have to be successful (courage, willingness to take risks, forcefulness, charisma) and what qualities might lead to a military leader's downfall (excessive pride, recklessness, poor judgment). Point out that in the next two sections they will learn how Napoleon rose to become one of the world's most successful military leaders and how he ultimately fell.

TERMS TO KNOW

Ask students to read the terms and definitions on page 448. Then, have them skim the section to locate each term, read the surrounding paragraph, and write their own definition of the term.

You may wish to preview the pronunciation of the following terms from this section with students.

Napoleon Bonaparte
 (nah POH lay ohn BOH nuh pahrt)
Kutuzov (koo TOO zuhf)
Austerlitz (AOOS tuhr lihts)

ACTIVE READING

Present students with a list of Napoleon's actions that are discussed in this section: ordering the firing of grapeshot, invading Italy, attacking Great Britain in Egypt, devising the Code Napoléon, crowning himself emperor, fighting the Battle of Austerlitz. Have them use a two-column chart (TR, p. 328) to list the actions in one column and their judgment about each action in the second column.

Terms to Know

émigré a person who left France after the fall of Louis XVI and later returned

concordat an agreement between a pope and a monarch or head of a government

Main Ideas

A. Napoleon Bonaparte quickly rose to become a general in the French revolutionary army.

B. Napoleon became emperor of France and led many successful attacks on other European nations.

Active Reading

MAKE JUDGMENTS
When you make a judgment, you form an opinion of a person or an issue or of event-based facts. As you read this section, try to form a judgment about Napoleon Bonaparte.

A. Napoleon's Beginnings

As the Reign of Terror died down, the French began to realize that their revolution had not been successful so far. Many innocent people had been killed. The government was poorly organized, and its authority was shaky. What France needed was a confident leader who would step in and make order out of chaos. The most unlikely person possible—an army officer from Corsica by the name of Napoleon Bonaparte—took advantage of a chaotic situation.

Early Life and Achievements

Napoleon Bonaparte was born in 1769 on the Mediterranean island of Corsica. His parents were descended from minor Italian nobility. Because of the family's noble status, Napoleon won a place at an exclusive French preparatory school and went on to a military academy. There, he displayed extraordinary skills in mathematics and geography.

Napoleon quickly became an officer. He was among the army officers who tried to control the mobs during the first few months of the Revolution. After the attempted escape of Louis XVI, all soldiers were required to take an oath of loyalty to the constitution. Many refused out of loyalty to the monarch, but Napoleon was perfectly willing. He was made a captain in 1792.

Napoleon is shown at military school in 1784.

Early Victories

In 1793, France declared war on Britain, the Netherlands, and Spain. These nations had joined with Austria in hopes of defeating the revolutionary forces. Civil wars also broke out in France. The opponents were the royalists—or people who supported the old form of government—and those who supported a new form. The army sent Napoleon to fight against the royalists. His organizational abilities were soon recognized, and he was quickly promoted to general.

In September 1794, at Napoleon's urging, France launched a surprise attack on the Austrians and beat them. This victory brought Napoleon further recognition and praise. He returned to Paris, hoping to persuade the National Convention to send him to fight the Turks.

"A Whiff of Grapeshot"

Paris in October 1794 was restless. The National Convention was still in existence. However, many people were not satisfied with its actions. The Jacobins, the royalists, and the moderates wanted to force change. A group made up mostly of royalists banded together to form a mob.

Teaching Options

Section 3 Resources

Teacher's Resources (TR)
 Terms to Know, p. 32
 Review History, p. 66
 Build Your Skills, p. 100
 Concept Builder, p. 235
 Cause-and-Effect Chain, p. 325
 Transparency 5

Connection to GEOGRAPHY

Some of the most important national leaders in history were actually born outside the borders of the countries they rose to control. Napoleon came from Corsica, which, at the time, was not part of France. Alexander the Great was Macedonian, not Greek. William the Conqueror was from Normandy, not England. Adolf Hitler was from Austria, not Germany. Joseph Stalin was Georgian, not Russian.

The National Convention ordered Napoleon to maintain order, placing all soldiers in Paris at his disposal.

Napoleon decided to threaten the mob with grapeshot—clusters of small musketballs fired at close range from cannons. These balls would scatter over a wide area and might spill a great deal of blood, but they rarely killed. Napoleon intended to scare the mob, not massacre them. Napoleon's plan was a great success, even though the grapeshot killed and wounded many people. It ended the attempted takeover of the Convention and made Napoleon famous.

As his reward, Napoleon asked to be put in charge of the campaign against Italy. He intended to invade and conquer the Italian kingdoms and make them part of France. The Convention agreed to his detailed plans. This plan marked a change in the foreign policy of the Republic, because Napoleon was leading an attack rather than a defensive war.

By May 1796, Napoleon had successfully invaded and conquered much of Italy. In February 1797, he went on to defeat the Austrians, France's traditional enemy. Napoleon negotiated a treaty with Austria that extended France's lands to the east into what is now Belgium. By now he was universally recognized as France's most important military figure. He returned to Paris in triumph in 1797 to create a new government.

◆ How did Napoleon use the military to advance himself?

This cartoon shows that the threat of invasion by Napoleon cast a long shadow over much of Europe.

A NEW CALENDAR
The National Convention designed a new calendar to go with the new Republic. Each of the twelve 30-day months was divided into three 10-day weeks. A harvest festival would be held on the five (or six) days remaining at the end of the year.

Months were given new names to celebrate the seasons: *Messidor* means "harvest," *Brumaire* means "fog," and so on. Because no other nation had such a calendar, it was not practical and was abandoned in 1805.

2 Teach

A. Napoleon's Beginnings

Purpose-Setting Question What did Napoleon do to earn his first major promotion in the revolutionary army? (He signed an oath of loyalty to the National Assembly after the attempted escape of Louis XVI.)

Focus Napoleon's decision to sign the oath of loyalty was not so much political as practical. It fit with his philosophy of joining the side that seemed most likely to win. In a letter to his brother, he once noted, "Since one must take sides, one might as well choose the side that is victorious, the side which devastates, loots, and burns. Considering the alternative, it is better to eat than be eaten." Read this quotation aloud to students and ask what adjectives they would use to judge Napoleon based on his remark. (Possible answers: ruthless, unfeeling, selfish)

WHAT IN THE WORLD?
A NEW CALENDAR French mathematicians and poets joined together to help create the new calendar. The poets contributed the names of the months, which were arranged in groups of three rhyming names that fit with their seasons. The mathematicians contributed division of weeks and months into equal decimal measures. The French also established a new clock based on the decimal system, with each day divided into 10 hours, each of which consisted of 100 minutes divided into 100 seconds.

TEACH PRIMARY SOURCES
Have students use the steps in *Here's How* on page 441 to interpret the political cartoon. Then, ask students to share their interpretation with the class.

◆ **ANSWER** He used the army to put down civil wars by opponents of the new government, to end the mob attempt to take over the Convention, to conquer much of Italy, and to defeat the Austrians—all of which showed his qualities as a leader and promoter of change.

Test Taking

Standardized tests often require students to read passages and answer questions related to cause and effect. Have students work in pairs as they read subsection A. Each student should write two cause-and-effect questions, in the short-answer question format, based on the text. Have students exchange papers and answer the questions.

Connection to MATH

French scientists were determined to adopt a national measurement system based on decimals as well as the new calendar and clock. Starting in 1791, scientists proposed a system based on a unit called a meter that was one ten-millionth of the distance between the North Pole and the equator. The new metric system was adopted in France in 1795 and, by 1900, was used by most of the world.

Purpose-Setting Question What was the Directory? (The Directory was the legislative group that replaced the National Convention in 1795. It consisted of two councils made up of former Convention members and new members elected by local assemblies throughout France.)

Discuss Ask students to summarize the actions of the Directory and discuss the motivations of the members of the Directory. (passed laws against émigrés, arrested priests, suppressed the Roman Catholic Church; revenge against those who used to be in power and to protect their own authority) Discuss with students how this may have resulted in the loss of people who did have experience running a country and may have been sympathetic to the new government.

Extend Although Napoleon's incursion into Egypt was a failure from a military standpoint, it did have one positive outcome. In 1799, French soldiers found a slab of black rock buried near the town of Rosetta in the Nile Delta. This stone, called the Rosetta Stone, had the same message inscribed on its surface in three different forms of writing. These inscriptions were to provide the key to deciphering, or decoding, Egyptian hieroglyphics that no one had been able to translate.

Activity

Hold a debate Have two groups of students represent deputies in the Directory who are debating whether Napoleon should be named First Consul or not. One group should present arguments in favor of Napoleon's appointment based on his past service to France. The other group should present arguments opposing Napoleon based on past actions, as well.

This nineteenth-century painting is titled *Napoleon and His General Staff in Egypt* by Jean Léon Gérôme.

B. Rise to Power

The short time it took for Napoleon to rise through the military to the rank of general was impressive. However, the speed of his rise to the position of "emperor for life" was unbelievable.

The Directory

By 1795, the people had grown tired of the National Convention. Some believed that there were too many royalists among its members. Others hated and feared it because of its connection to the Reign of Terror. So, by November of that year, the Convention had been replaced by a legislative group called the Directory.

The Directory had two councils, with a total of 750 deputies. Two-thirds of the deputies were former members of the Convention. The other one-third were freely elected by the local assemblies throughout France. The Directory had been created to mark the true end of the Revolution and the beginning of the Republic. However, the leaders of the Directory were poorly organized and unsure of the best way to govern. They were mainly concerned with protecting their new positions of authority.

In 1797, the Directory passed laws against returning **émigrés**—members of the old Second Estate who had fled the nation after the fall of Louis XVI. They were suspected of having royalist sympathies and conspiring to restore the monarchy. Some deputies suggested banishing all former aristocrats from the country. In the end, the laws allowed them to remain but with no political rights. The Directory also took its share of revenge on the First Estate. More than a thousand priests were arrested. Many were deported, or sent off, to Africa and others were sent to prison in outlying areas of France. The Directory suppressed the Roman Catholic Church, which seemed to the revolutionaries a hated symbol of the old order.

Rise to First Consul

The Directory rewarded Napoleon for his military victories by making him a member of the Institute, the nation's chief association of men of arts and letters. Napoleon enjoyed the honor but soon found himself looking for something more active to do.

In 1798 he had found what seemed to be the perfect idea. He decided to attack Great Britain in Egypt, where Britain had become an important force. The members of the Directory were pleased with the idea of sending Napoleon far from Paris, where he had become more popular and important than the people who ran the government.

The Egyptian expedition was not a military success. Napoleon's army failed to drive out the British. He gave up the attempt in August 1799 and set out for France. He arrived in Paris in October and was warmly welcomed by the people.

While Napoleon was in Egypt, things had not gone well for the leaders of the Directory. France still did not have a clear, popular constitution that would have spelled out the Directory's authority. Many citizens did not trust or respect the Directory. Eventually, the leaders decided to dissolve the Directory, hoping to set up a more workable government. Because Napoleon

Teaching Options

ESL/ELL STRATEGIES

Organize Information As they read this section, have students create a graphic organizer in the form of a ladder to chart Napoleon's rise to power. Each rung of the ladder should note a new position for Napoleon and the year he reached that position. Students might extend their ladders downward in the next section to chart Napoleon's fall.

FYI

Rosetta Stone
Two forms of writing on the Rosetta Stone were types of hieroglyphics. The third form was Greek. Because scholars could translate Greek, they were eventually able to decode the hieroglyphics. This made it possible for archaeologists to begin translating the thousands of surviving Egyptian records written in hieroglyphics.

was the most powerful military leader, the members of the Directory knew that they would need Napoleon's help in keeping control over the people. On November 9 and 10, the Directory was dissolved, and a body made up of three powerful officials, called consuls, was created. Napoleon quickly became First Consul, the only one of the three that had any real power.

The Code Napoléon

Napoleon set about organizing the French government from the local to the national level. He set up a public school system and a national bank. He improved the organization of the nation. Napoleon felt that the Roman Catholic Church was too important a part of France's history to be suppressed as the Directory had done. In September 1801, Napoleon signed a **concordat**, or agreement, with the pope. By this agreement, the Church was slightly reorganized and placed more firmly under the ruler's control.

The Code Napoléon, the set of civil laws that still governs France today, is thought by many to be Napoleon's greatest achievement. The Convention had begun working to codify the laws in 1793, and by 1801 Napoleon had many rough drafts and ideas with which to work. He revised and finalized the Code, which went into effect in 1804.

The Code Napoléon set forth many of the basic rights of citizens—the right to own property, the right to make contracts, and the equal application of the laws to all citizens. This work was already done by the time Napoleon became First Consul. Napoleon's great contribution was to try to combine some traditions of the old form of government with the ideas of the new one.

In August 1802 Napoleon was chosen as permanent First Consul, with the right to name his successor. There had been several attempts to kill him, and he wanted to secure his position of power. Napoleon was now a military dictator, the sole ruler of the nation. In another proclamation, he was named Napoleon I, hereditary emperor of France for life.

Spotlight on
Citizenship

WOMEN'S RIGHTS

Admirable though it was, the Code Napoléon was a setback to the cause of women's rights in France. It reversed most of the gains women had made since 1789. In 1804, women became once again the property of their husbands, with no rights over their own households. In the divorce court, a husband now had greater rights than his wife.

At his coronation, Napoleon is shown about to place a crown on his wife, Josephine.

Connection to
ART

Artist Jacques-Louis David's fortunes rose and fell with the French Revolution. An ardent Republican, his paintings of revolution heroes earned him great fame. David was imprisoned after Robespierre's fall but rose to prominence again with his paintings glorifying Napoleon, such as the *Coronation of Napoleon*. After Napoleon's fall, David went into exile in Brussels and his career waned.

Conflict Resolution

The concordat that Napoleon signed with the pope was an agreement that helped to avoid a confrontation between two opposing sides. Discuss the value of working out agreements rather than fighting for control in difficult situations and explain how an agreement can help both sides. Relate the agreement to present-day attempts at mediation, such as those favored by the United Nations.

Discuss The motto of the French Revolution was "liberty, equality, fraternity." However, when the constitution that set up the three-consul system was adopted in 1799, it guaranteed property and personal security, but it did not include much about individual liberty and rights. Discuss with students how the events of the Revolution may have turned people from thinking about liberty to concentrating more on security for themselves and their property.

Extend The Code Napoléon became the legal system for areas that the French took over under Napoleon. It was also spread to French-controlled areas of North America. When Louisiana drew up its civil code in 1825, more than 20 years after the Louisiana Purchase, the Code Napoléon was its model. Students might research to find which parts of the French code are still reflected in Louisiana's laws.

SPOTLIGHT ON CITIZENSHIP

WOMEN'S RIGHTS Explain to students that not only women's rights were abridged under the Code Napoléon. The codes also favored employers over workers in any disputes, and tradespeople and laborers were forbidden to form unions. In addition, workers had to carry passbooks issued by local authorities, a practice that oppressive regimes have continued into present times.

TEACH PRIMARY SOURCES

Napoleon carefully staged the coronation ceremony portrayed in the painting on page 451. Point out to students that the laurel wreath he is wearing was similar to one worn by Roman emperors. Napoleon wanted people to know that he had taken over the leadership of the Holy Roman Empire. The pope sits solemnly in the center of the painting but is not involved in the coronation itself. The woman in a prominent spot at the top center of the painting is Napoleon's mother.

Ask students why they think the French people, who had overthrown their monarch just a few years before, now accepted Napoleon as emperor. (Possible answers: He promised stability and strength; he had come from the Third Estate; they feared his power; they still believed in the monarchy.)

Do You Remember?

Suggest that students review pages 271–274 in Chapter 12 to revisit Charlemagne and his accomplishments. Remind students that after Pope Leo III crowned Charlemagne, future popes had a great deal of power and authority over future kings.

Activity

Label a map Provide students with an outline map of Europe (TR, p. 333) or use Transparency 5. Then, have students use atlases or other references to find out where to label the Alps, Marengo, and Austerlitz on their maps. Students should then link the labels by drawing Napoleon's "path to victory" on the map.

◆ **ANSWER** He never allowed his army to be attacked. He always attacked first at the opponent's weakest points, defeated his enemy, and then made peace on terms that were favorable to France.

Section Close

Ask students to analyze Napoleon's strengths and weaknesses based on what they read in this section. Then, have them use what they know to predict what they think is going to happen to Napoleon in the next section and to explain their predictions.

3 Assess

Review Answers

Review History

A. Once Napoleon took the oath of loyalty to the National Assembly, he became a captain; his organizational abilities were soon recognized in the civil wars and he became a general.

B. Because Napoleon was the most powerful military leader, the Directory knew that they would need his help in keeping control over the people. So, once the Directory was dissolved, he became First Consul, the only one with real power; he was a military dictator, and a proclamation named him Napoleon I, hereditary emperor of France for life.

Do You Remember?

In Chapter 12, you learned that Pope Leo III crowned Charlemagne as the Roman emperor in 800. The crowning of Charlemagne established the idea that the pope had the power to crown an emperor.

In an elaborate ceremony in 1804, Napoleon chose to crown himself to avoid giving the impression that he owed his authority to a pope, or to anyone else. He had learned this lesson from Charlemagne!

Napoleon's Victories

Napoleon was first and foremost a military commander. Throughout his reign as First Consul and then emperor, he was constantly on horseback, leading his soldiers into battle. Napoleon never fought a war in which his army was attacked first. He always attacked the enemy army at its weakest point, defeated it, and made peace on terms favorable to France.

One of Napoleon's best-known victories in this period was the invasion of Italy in pursuit of the Austrians in May 1800. In a surprise move, Napoleon organized his soldiers into a march across the Alps. Napoleon got his army across and faced the Austrians at the Battle of Marengo in mid-June. He won decisively, and the Austrians surrendered numerous fortresses.

In 1805 Napoleon found himself on the march against both the Austrians and the Russians, who had formed an alliance. The Austrians planned to attack the French first. Russian reinforcements, or supporting troops, would march west and arrive at an agreed time. Napoleon attacked the weak point of the enemy's position. He anticipated every Austrian move and was able to counter the moves successfully. On October 20, the Austrians surrendered.

The Russian reinforcements had not yet arrived. When the Russian general, Kutuzov, heard of the Austrian defeat, he decided to retreat. On December 2, the French fought both the Austrians and Russians. The battle took place at Austerlitz, a town about 50 miles north of Vienna. When French reinforcements arrived, the tide of battle turned in Napoleon's favor. About 25,000 Austrian and Russian soldiers were killed. About 8,500 French soldiers lost their lives.

The Treaty of Pressburg ended the war and did away with the historic Holy Roman Empire. The Confederation of the Rhine, under French control, took its place. The Battle of Austerlitz is considered Napoleon's greatest victory. After this, France seemed unstoppable.

◆ **What was Napoleon's strategy for fighting wars?**

Review III

Review History
A. How did Napoleon become a general in the French army?
B. How did Napoleon become First Consul, then emperor of France?

Define Terms to Know
Define the following terms:
émigré, concordat

Critical Thinking
Why did Napoleon spend so much of his time fighting wars?

Write About Government
Write an editorial attacking or defending the Code Napoléon as the basis for French society.

Get Organized
CAUSE-AND-EFFECT CHAIN
Use a cause-and-effect chain to show a cause and an effect of the establishment of the Directory.

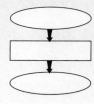

Define Terms to Know

émigré, 450; concordat, 451

Critical Thinking

Possible answer: He liked the excitement of battle better than he liked staying in Paris and governing the nation.

Write About Government

Students can defend the Code based on its insistence on the rule of law for all citizens. They may attack it for its revocation of women's rights.

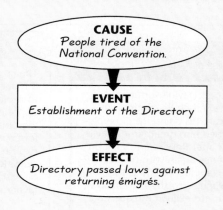

CAUSE
People tired of the National Convention.

EVENT
Establishment of the Directory

EFFECT
Directory passed laws against returning émigrés.

Napoleon's Power Ends

Terms to Know

conscript a person drafted into military service

satellite state a country that is dependent on another country for its economic and political well-being

veteran a person who has served in the military

Main Ideas

A. Invasions of Spain and Russia brought about Napoleon's fall from power.

B. Rather than accepting exile to Elba, Napoleon attempted to retake control of France and was defeated at Waterloo.

 Active Reading

MAIN IDEAS AND SUPPORTING DETAILS
The main idea of a text is the most important idea the writer wants you to remember. As you read this section, identify the most important ideas about Napoleon's decline and downfall and the details that support the main ideas.

A. Napoleon's Military Fall

By 1810, Napoleon seemed unstoppable. His armies had never been defeated in direct combat, and he had greatly expanded France's territory. However, after 1810 nothing went well for Napoleon.

Nationalism, Threat, and Unity

Thousands of French troops had died on the battlefields of various military campaigns. In most cases, Napoleon could replace fallen troops with **conscripts**. These conscripts were soldiers drafted from **satellite states**, countries that were dependent on France. However, these soldiers lacked both personal loyalty to the emperor and nationalism—loyalty to France as their native land. Such passionate loyalty had brought down the Bastille. Nationalism and ambition had carried the French army across the Alps. Soldiers fighting for a country that was not their own could not be expected to be so strongly motivated.

Napoleon had made many enemies. All foreign governments hated him and wanted to bring him down because he had succeeded so well in his wars against them. No other nation was pleased with France expanding its power base farther and farther into Europe. France had simply become too much of a threat. All these nations would find it necessary to put aside their quarrels with one another to unite against Napoleon.

The constant French threat began to arouse feelings of nationalism among the peoples of Europe. Germany and Italy were not unified nations when Napoleon became emperor. However, after Napoleon's exile, or forced removal from France, their governments began working toward unification.

France and Its Satellites, 1807

GREAT BRITAIN — *North Sea* — *Baltic Sea*
Amsterdam — Holland — Hanover — PRUSSIA
London — Westphalia — Berlin — Duchy of Warsaw — RUSSIAN EMPIRE
Saxony
Paris — Baden — Prague
FRANCE — Wurt — Bavaria — Munich — Vienna
Geneva — Switzerland — AUSTRIAN EMPIRE
Kingdom of Italy — Venice
SPAIN — Toulon — Kingdom of Etruria
Corsica — Papal States — Rome
KINGDOM OF SARDINIA — Naples — Kingdom of Naples
Mediterranean Sea

Legend:
- France
- French satellites
- Cities
- Boundaries

0 150 300 mi
0 150 300 km

✔ Map Check
REGION Which French satellite was located the farthest east from France?

Section Summary

In this section, students will learn how Napoleon's decisions to invade Spain and Russia led to defeats and his fall from power. They will also learn how Napoleon refused to accept his first exile from France and attempted to return to power, only to be defeated at Waterloo and be banished for life.

1 Introduce

Getting Started

Ask students how the expression "whatever goes up must come down" can apply both in science and in politics. Ask students to predict reasons that might lead to Napoleon's fall. As they read ahead, they can check on the accuracy of their predictions.

TERMS TO KNOW

Ask students to read the terms and definitions on page 453 and then find each term in the section. Have students use each term in a sentence that demonstrates the meaning of the term. Ask students to suggest a link between *conscripts* and *veterans*.

You may wish to preview the pronunciation of the following names from this section with students.

François Lejeune
(frahn SWAH luh ZHUHN)
Leipzig (LIHP sihk)
Charles-Maurice de Tallyrand
(shahrl maw REES duh tahl leh RAHN)

ACTIVE READING

Have students use a main ideas/supporting details chart (TR, p. 319) to arrange the main ideas and supporting details they identify as they read each subsection.

Teaching Options

Section 4 Resources

Teacher's Resources (TR)
Terms to Know, p. 32
Review History, p. 66
Build Your Skills, p. 100
Concept Builder, p. 235
Chapter Test, pp. 153–154
Cause-and-Effect Chain, p. 325

ESL/ELL STRATEGIES

Use Visuals Suggest that students refer often to the map on page 453 as they read this section to help them visualize where Napoleon's final major battles were fought (Spain and Russia). Discuss why Napoleon's forces would have been stretched thin by campaigns against both Spain and Russia. (They required fighting on two fronts far from each other.)

A. Napoleon's Military Fall

Purpose-Setting Question How did the threat posed by France affect other European nations? (The countries put aside their quarrels with each other and united against a common enemy, Napoleon. Germany and Italy also began unification of their separate states to form national governments.)

Using the Map

France and Its Satellites, 1807

Have students compare the map on page 445 with the map on page 453 to see how Europe had changed since 1792. Ask how Germany and Italy appear different in the two maps. (In 1792, both countries were made up of separate small republics or states; in 1807, they seem even more divided, but the states are linked under French control.)

✔ Map Check

Answer Duchy of Warsaw

Focus Even before being named by Napoleon to rule Spain following the Peninsular War, Napoleon's brother Joseph had been appointed as ruler of the Kingdom of Naples. Napoleon also separated the Kingdom of Westphalia from Prussia and put another of his brothers, Jerome, in charge there. Ask students how they think the conquered people felt about these appointments. (Possible answers: very angry, embarrassed) Discuss with students why Napoleon might have put his brothers on thrones in Europe. (reward his brothers, put people loyal to him in charge)

Extend In fighting against their French occupiers, the Spaniards used a type of warfare, which they called *guerrilla*, based on the Spanish word for "war." Bands of Spanish resistance fighters would ambush or snipe at French troops, raid supply trains, poison food supplies, or carry out other unexpected actions that eventually destroyed the morale of French troops. Have students research more information on the beginnings of this type of warfare.

This painting by Francisco Goya shows the fierce fighting during a battle of the Peninsular War.

The Peninsular War

Trade was the reason for the outbreak of the Peninsular War between Spain and France in 1808. France had refused to allow goods from Great Britain and its colonies to be imported into any European territory under French control. Portugal, which was not under French control, developed an economy that relied heavily on British trade. With Spanish cooperation, Napoleon soon invaded and controlled Portugal.

Because Spain would be a valuable ally, Napoleon wanted someone he trusted absolutely in charge. He therefore decided to overthrow the family that ruled Spain. He had them imprisoned and placed his brother Joseph on the throne.

The Spaniards were outraged and rose up in protest. Rioting, looting, and terrible acts of violence were committed. If Napoleon himself had been in Spain, he might have been able to bring matters under control, but he was in France.

The British were ready to fight on the side of any nation that opposed France. In 1809, the Duke of Wellington arrived with thousands of troops. He conserved his army's energy, attacked now and then, and soon began to win major battles, commanding English, Portuguese, and Spanish forces.

The French generals in Spain surrendered to Wellington in 1814 when they received the news that Napoleon had abdicated, or stepped down from his throne. He had long given up the war in Spain as lost and had turned his attention to an invasion of Russia. This decision would lead to the worst failure of his career and ended his rule over France and much of Europe.

Invasion of Russia

By the beginning of 1812, Napoleon had decided to invade Russia. Czar Alexander I had not responded well to Napoleon's interest in marrying his sister. In addition, the two rulers had disagreed over issues of trade and the future of Poland.

Because so many French **veterans**, men who had served in the military, were fighting in Spain, Napoleon conscripted men from all of France's satellite states. By the end of June, an army of 650,000 was at the Russian border. They trudged eastward toward Moscow through the barren plains in the intense summer heat. There were no forests to offer them shade, no crops to steal for food, and few sources of fresh water. Soldiers were dying by the hundreds. Horses were dying too, killed by their starving riders for meat.

In September, the French soldiers faced the Russian troops. Fighting lasted for several hours and ended in a victory for Napoleon. However, the victory came at the cost of 50,000 men and much ammunition—none of which could be replaced so far from home.

The Russians then began a strategic retreat toward Moscow. They knew that the coming winter would be their best defense against the French. When the Russians reached the city, they evacuated it and then set it on fire. Built mostly of wood, Moscow was quickly destroyed. The French moved into what was left of the capital and waited for the Russian surrender that never came.

In October, Napoleon acknowledged the need to retreat. His armies would starve if they stayed through the winter months. Several rivers lay between the French soldiers and the Russian border, and the Russians had burned the

454 UNIT 5 ◆ Enlightenment and Revolution

Teaching Options

Meet Individual Needs:

VISUAL/SPATIAL LEARNERS

Have students focus on the artwork on pages 454 and 455 as a starting point for discussion about the defeat of the French army and the fall of Napoleon. You might also ask students to compare the bleak or frightening mood of these pieces of art with the elegance of the painting of Napoleon's coronation on page 451. Discuss how much things seem to have changed during this short timeframe.

Connection to ART

Some of the most brutal and heroic fighting of the Peninsular War occurred in the small Spanish town of Zaragosa. Despite being heavily outnumbered by French troops, the town's men, women, and children drove back their initial attack. Goya later visited Zaragosa and created a series of etchings entitled *Los Desastres de la Guerra* ("Disasters of War") that portrayed the horror of the fighting.

bridges on the way to Moscow. French engineers and artillery fighters quickly built new bridges so that the retreat could continue. By now, however, the Russians had turned west in pursuit of the French. General Louis François Lejeune described the scene:

Troops are shown retreating from Russia after Napoleon's unsuccessful invasion.

> 66 [The Russian] artillery poured shells upon the struggling crowds, beneath whose weight the bridges were bending till they were under water. Those who could swim flung themselves into the river. . . . On either side the hapless fugitives pressed on, driving others into the water, many clutching at the ropes of the bridges in the hope of being able to climb on to them. In the awful struggle none who fell ever rose again. 99

The last of Napoleon's army crossed the Russian border on December 14. Napoleon himself had already left for Paris. No good news awaited him there. Allies were deserting him, Wellington was winning battles in Spain, and the future held little hope. In October 1813, he led his forces against Austrians, Russians, Prussians, and Swedes in the Battle of Leipzig, but it was a doomed effort. Napoleon's armies lost 38,000 men. In April 1814, Napoleon abdicated.

◆ **Why did Napoleon's armies fail in Spain and Russia?**

B. The Downfall of Napoleon

After Napoleon abdicated, his empire fell to pieces. France would again become a monarchy under Louis XVI's brother, who would rule as Louis XVIII with Charles-Maurice de Talleyrand as his chief minister. Napoleon was neither arrested nor executed. Instead, he was banished, or exiled, from France.

Exile and Return

Napoleon arrived on the small Mediterranean island of Elba in May 1814. Bitter and bored with his surroundings, Napoleon was always eager for news from France. Many soldiers wrote to him, pleading that he return and once

ANALYZE PRIMARY SOURCES **DOCUMENT-BASED QUESTION** Why did so many soldiers drown trying to cross the river?

Focus When Napoleon left Elba and landed in southern France, he declared, "I am the sovereign of the Island of Elba and have come with 700 men to attack the King of France and his 600,000 soldiers. I shall conquer this kingdom." Soon, thousands of Napoleon's former troops came over to his side. Ask students what they think about Napoleon's return to France and to back up their answer with reasons.

THE UNITED NATIONS The UN has been sending peacekeeping troops to different "hot spots" around the world ever since 1948, when soldiers went to Jerusalem to supervise the truce between the new State of Israel and the Arab nations after the first Arab-Israeli war. Students can get the latest information about UN peacekeeping efforts by selecting the United Nations Web site and then checking the News Center.

◆ **ANSWER** He was taken prisoner and was banished to the South Atlantic island of Saint Helena.

Section Close

Ask students what they most remember about Napoleon. Have a volunteer make a list on the board. Then, ask them whether they think most French people today would have the same items listed. Why or why not?

③ Assess

Review Answers

Review History

A. Napoleon lost the Peninsular War against Spain and led a disastrous campaign into Russia. His failures forced him into exile.

B. Napoleon escaped from Elba and returned to France, where he regained power.

Define Terms to Know

conscript, 453; satellite state, 453; veteran, 454

Critical Thinking

Possible answer: Napoleon had been tremendously popular. The army remained loyal to him. If he had been executed, the army might have turned against the government. Civil war might have broken out.

---

again take over the government. After less than a year on Elba, Napoleon made his plans to return.

Napoleon prepared well for his journey. He took with him a million francs in gold, 700 soldiers, and plenty of ammunition. The ship sailed for France in early 1815. Once Napoleon arrived at the coast, he marched north, coming face to face with a French infantry battalion. When he approached them, a cheer for the returning emperor went up.

Napoleon continued toward Paris. Louis XVIII fled the city when he heard the news of Napoleon's march. Upon his arrival in Paris, Napoleon took control of the government and raised an army. Meanwhile, the leaders of the European nations were gathering. As soon as they had received the news of Napoleon's march, they agreed that he must be stopped. For the second time, a united Europe acted swiftly to oppose Napoleon.

The European allies appointed the Duke of Wellington, victor in the Peninsular War, to head the allied troops. His army was stationed in Belgium. The Prussian army, his ally, was about nine miles away. Napoleon decided to attack from the center, thus separating the two armies and hoping to defeat each in turn.

The Battle of Waterloo

Wellington prepared for Napoleon's attack by moving his troops to a strategic position overlooking the field of Waterloo in 1815. Waterloo is near Brussels, Belgium. The fighting went on all day. The French were defeated when the Prussians broke through the French lines. Several thousand men on both sides lost their lives in the battle. Napoleon had suffered a crushing defeat. Nearly half of his troops were dead or wounded. The defeat caused the end of his rule in France. Napoleon surrendered to the British, who declared him a prisoner of war and banished him to the South Atlantic island of Saint Helena. He died there in May 1821.

◆ **What happened to Napoleon after the Battle of Waterloo?**

Review IV

Review History
A. How did Napoleon fall from power?
B. What did Napoleon do after he was exiled to Elba?

Define Terms to Know
Define the following terms: **conscript, satellite state, veteran**

Critical Thinking
Why did the French and British banish Napoleon, instead of executing him as they had Louis XVI and Charles I?

Write About Geography
Write an essay discussing the effect of Russia's geography on the outcome of Napoleon's invasion in 1812.

Get Organized
CAUSE-AND-EFFECT CHAIN
Use a cause-and-effect chain to show a cause and an effect of Napoleon's invasion of Russia.

Write About Geography
Answers should discuss Russia's vast size, the grasslands that did not provide crops the invading army could steal and eat, and the extreme summer heat and winter cold for which the French were unprepared.

CAUSE
France and Russia disagreed on trade and Poland.

EVENT
Napoleon invades Russia.

EFFECT
Russians destroyed Moscow.

Points *of* View

Napoleon Bonaparte

Napoleon Bonaparte, an officer in the French army, became emperor of France in 1804. Before and during his reign, he led his soldiers to victory in battle after battle. Only after 1810 did he begin to suffer defeats—in Spain, Russia, and finally on the field of Waterloo in Belgium.

Historians are sharply divided on whether Napoleon was a villain or a hero. People in his own day were equally divided. He was popular with some and hated by many others.

Below are two soldiers' opinions of Napoleon, both written during the 1812 military campaign against Russia. Nineteen-year old Nadezhda Durova disguised herself as a man, took the name "Alexander Sokolov," and joined the Russian cavalry in 1807. Jakob Walter was a German stonemason whose home state of Württemberg had become part of France. He was drafted into Napoleon's army in 1806.

Napoleon Bonaparte strikes a familiar pose.

❝Napoleon . . . watched his army pass by in the most wretched condition. What he may have felt in his heart is impossible to surmise. His outward appearance seemed indifferent and unconcerned over the wretchedness of his soldiers; only ambition and lost honor may have made themselves felt in his heart; and, although the French and Allies shouted into his ears many oaths and curses about his own guilty person, he was still able to listen to them unmoved.❞

—Jakob Walter, *The Diary of a Napoleonic Foot Soldier*

❝Despite Napoleon's countless admirers, I make so bold as to think that, for one considered such a great genius, he is much too confident both of his luck and his capabilities. . . . [To] believe that it [the Russian army] is retreating for fear of encountering the enemy? To believe in the timidity of the Russian army within the borders of its native land?❞

—Nadezhda Durova, *The Cavalry Maiden: Journals of a Female Russian Officer in the Napoleonic Wars*

ANALYZE PRIMARY SOURCES

DOCUMENT-BASED QUESTIONS

1. How does Walter describe Napoleon's outward appearance?

2. What does Durova think Napoleon is too confident about?

3. **Critical Thinking** How are these two views of Napoleon similar? How are they different?

Teaching Options

Take a Stand

Have students consider where they stand on Napoleon as a military leader. Tell students to create a political cartoon about Napoleon for either a pro-Napoleon French newspaper or an anti-Napoleon Russian newspaper. Remind students that their position should be clear in their cartoon. They might use some of either writer's words to help them develop their images or captions.

Modern-day psychologists have coined the term *Napoleon complex* to refer to a person who is small in stature or feels small or inferior in some other way and compensates by being overly aggressive. Suggest that students find out more about this syndrome using library or Internet resources and report their findings to the class.

Points *of* View

NAPOLEON BONAPARTE

Teach the Topic

The selections on page 457 represent two opinions that differ on whether Napoleon was someone to be admired or someone to be hated. Point out that both comments are taken from diaries kept by soldiers who fought either with Napoleon's forces or against them.

Ask students which writer probably had more personal knowledge of the French general (Walter) and which was responding to what he or she had heard from someone else. (Durova) Ask why each writer may have had negative feelings about Napoleon. (Walter was German, not French, and had been drafted into Napoleon's army, possibly against his will; Durova was a soldier in the Russian army, which fought bitterly against the French.)

Compare and Contrast Points of View

Ask students what aspect of Napoleon's personality each quote focuses on. (Walter focuses on Napoleon's ambition and lack of concern about what hardships he may cause others. Durova focuses on Napoleon's overconfidence and contempt for his enemies.) Discuss what each writer admires about Napoleon despite their negative thoughts. (Walter admires Napoleon's ability to keep focused on his ambition; Durova admires Napoleon's genius, even though she thinks it may be overrated.)

ANALYZE PRIMARY SOURCES

DOCUMENT-BASED QUESTIONS
1. He describes Napoleon's appearance as expressionless, showing no emotion.
2. He is overconfident about his luck and his capabilities.
3. Possible answers: **Similar:** Both are critical. Walter describes Napoleon as "guilty" and Durova thinks he is overconfident. **Different:** Walter feels some compassion for Napoleon's "lost honor" and respect for his ability to hide his feelings. Durova dismisses the idea that Napoleon is a "great genius" and scoffs at the leader's stupidity in thinking that the Russians would retreat in their own land out of fear of the French army.

Chapter Summary

A blank outline form is available in the Teacher's Resources (p. 318). Chapter summaries should outline the factors leading up to the French Revolution, the early events of the Revolution and the Reign of Terror, the rise of Napoleon Bonaparte and his empire-building efforts, and the eventual fall of Napoleon. Refer to the rubric in the Teacher's Resources (p. 340) to score students' chapter summaries.

 Interpret the Timeline

1. the storming of the Bastille
2. 1815
3. Haiti gains its independence.
4. Check students' timelines to be sure all the events are in the chapter.

Use Terms to Know

5. f. tricolor
6. c. émigré
7. d. estate
8. a. concordat
9. b. conscript
10. e. guillotine

Check Your Understanding

11. The First Estate was the clergy. The Second Estate was the aristocracy. The Third Estate included everyone else.
12. As a result of wars during the reign of Louis XV, France lost land, was deeply in debt, and the people were very discontented with the ruined economy.
13. Each Estate had one vote. This procedure was unfair because most French citizens were members of the Third Estate.
14. The Declaration of the Rights of Man and the Citizen guaranteed natural freedom and equality; freedom of speech, religion, and the press; and that all laws applied equally to all citizens and must be reasonable and just.
15. The women interrupted the Assembly meeting to demand an audience with the king, of whom they demanded bread. The king agreed to give it to them and to accompany the guard back to Paris.
16. He was afraid for his life and the lives of his family, and he hoped to get help from Austria.
17. Napoleon loaded cannons with grapeshot and fired them into the crowd to scare them off.

18. Napoleon won foreign wars and controlled mobs, leading the Directory to make him a member of the Institute. He later became First Consul, signed an agreement with the Church, established the Code Napoléon, and eventually was named emperor.
19. The conscripts were not loyal to France or to Napoleon, a factor that helped undermine Napoleon's campaign in Russia.

20. Other European nations hated Napoleon, mainly for his military successes and expansion into so many European states and kingdoms.
21. Many French troops died due to extreme weather conditions and great distances they had to travel, making victory over Russia impossible.

Chapter Summary

Complete the following outline in your notebook. Then, use your outline to write a brief summary of the chapter.

The French Revolution and Napoleon

I. Beginnings of the French Revolution
  A. The Roots of the Revolution
  B. French Society
  C. The French Monarchy
  D. From Estates-General to National Assembly

II. Revolution and Terror
  A. The Revolution Begins
  B. Toward a New Government
  C. The End of the Monarchy
  D. The Reign of Terror

III. Napoleon Bonaparte
  A. Napoleon's Beginnings
  B. Rise to Power

IV. Napoleon's Power Ends
  A. Napoleon's Military Fall
  B. The Downfall of Napoleon

 Interpret the Timeline

Use the timeline on pages 434–435 to answer the following questions.

1. Which happened first, the executions of Louis XVI and Marie Antoinette or the storming of the Bastille?
2. In which year was Napoleon defeated at Waterloo?
3. **Critical Thinking** Which world event directly involved France?
4. Select six events from the chapter that are not on the timeline. Create a timeline that shows these events.

Use Terms to Know

Match each term with its definition.

a. concordat   c. émigré   e. guillotine
b. conscript   d. estate   f. tricolor

5. the red, white, and blue flag of revolutionary France
6. a person who left France after the fall of Louis XVI and later returned
7. a French legal term that indicates a person's status in society based on property ownership and ancestral rights and customs
8. an agreement between a pope and a monarch or head of a government
9. a person drafted into military service
10. a device with a blade, used to cut off the heads of convicted criminals

Check Your Understanding

11. **Identify** the members of the three estates of French society.
12. **Summarize** the results of wars fought during the reign of Louis XV.
13. **Explain** why the traditional voting procedure was unfair to the Third Estate.
14. **Identify** what the Declaration of the Rights of Man and the Citizen guaranteed.
15. **Describe** what happened when the women of Paris and the National Guard marched to Versailles.
16. **Summarize** why Louis XVI tried to escape from Paris.
17. **Describe** how Napoleon halted the mob's attempt to overthrow the National Convention.
18. **Summarize** how Napoleon became emperor of France.
19. **Analyze** why the use of conscripts caused problems for Napoleon's army.
20. **Discuss** how other European nations reacted to Napoleon's success.
21. **Explain** why the invasion of Russia was a disaster for the French.

Critical Thinking

22. Draw Conclusions What was the chief cause of the French Revolution?

23. Cause and Effect What effect did the common people have on the Revolution?

24. Evaluate How would you evaluate the system of consuls?

25. Make Inferences What can you infer about Napoleon's popularity after his return from exile on Elba?

Put Your Skills to Work

26. Interpret Political Cartoons You have learned that a political cartoon uses exaggeration and humor to make a point. Study the political cartoon below and answer the following questions.

   a. What does Napoleon's pose suggest?

   b. Who is the small man on the right? Why is he so much smaller than Napoleon?

   c. What is the cartoonist trying to say about international politics?

A STOPPAGE to a STRIDE over the GLOBE

Napoleon is shown sitting on a globe.

Analyze Sources

27. In 1804, German composer Ludwig van Beethoven was writing his Symphony no. 3, which he had titled *Bonaparte* after the French general. Read the following account of Beethoven's reaction on learning that Napoleon had crowned himself emperor. Then, answer the questions that follow.

[H]e flew into a rage and cried out: "Now he too will trample on all the rights of men and indulge only his ambition. He will exalt himself above all the others and become a tyrant." Beethoven went to the table, took hold of the title page by the top, tore it in two and threw it on the floor.

   a. Why do you think Beethoven would have named his symphony after Napoleon?

   b. What were Beethoven's feelings about Napoleon based on his actions and words?

   c. Do you think Beethoven's prediction about Napoleon was reasonable?

Essay Writing

28. Write an essay discussing the causes of the French Revolution. Explain why you think the situation in France led to open rebellion and bloodshed instead of a peaceful solution.

Critical Thinking

22. Answers will vary. Possible answers include taxes, unemployment, rising food prices, and destruction of grain crops; the resentment among the three estates; the excesses of the monarch; and the examples of successful revolutions in Great Britain and America.

23. Their violent acts, such as the storming of the Bastille, alarmed the aristocrats and the royal family. The people's demands for revenge helped to fuel the Reign of Terror.

24. The system of consuls proved to be effective because, as First Consul, Napoleon held all the power.

25. The French people, especially the military, still loved Napoleon and were anxious to follow him.

Put Your Skills to Work

INTERPRET POLITICAL CARTOONS

26a. It suggests that he rules the world or at least the countries on which he is sitting.

26b. The small man stands for Great Britain. He is protecting his country from Napoleon's sword and the large nation of France. He is small to show he has less power.

26c. The cartoonist is trying to say that France has all the power but that Great Britain is determined not to give in.

Analyze Sources

27a. At one time, Beethoven must have admired Napoleon for his reorganization of France's government and for drawing up the Code Napoléon.

27b. Beethoven despises Napoleon for becoming a dictator.

27c. Beethoven was correct; Napoleon did become a tyrant.

Essay Writing

28. Answers should suggest that unlike Great Britain and the United States, France had no political or philosophical tradition of freedom and equality. The monarch's rule was absolute. Students should also refer to the hatred between the classes that the monarchs had both strengthened and helped to perpetuate.

TEST PREPARATION

Answer 3. Louis XVI deserved to be executed after he tried to escape.

The Growth of Nationalism

1800–1900

(pp. 460–481)

Chapter Objectives

• Explain how the ideas of nationalism and liberalism spread in the nineteenth century, and how they affected France, among other nations.
• Identify changes in eastern Europe throughout the 1800s, and explore the nature of Russia's involvement with the Ottoman Empire.
• Describe how Enlightenment thought developed in Europe and North America and led to independence in much of colonial Latin America.

Chapter Summary

Section I discusses the rise of liberalism and nationalism in the 1800s, how these ideologies affected political events in France, and the backlash of conservatism whose proponents fought against these ideologies.
Section II focuses on the effects of nationalism in eastern Europe, and how other European countries involved themselves in political affairs in eastern Europe.
Section III describes the social structure of colonial Latin America, how the Age of Enlightenment affected Latin Americans, and how most of Latin America gained independence in the early 1800s.

Set the Stage

TEACH PRIMARY SOURCES

Explain that Simón Bolívar was known as the George Washington of South America. Six countries—Venezuela, Colombia, Panama, Peru, Ecuador, and Bolivia—see him as their liberator from Spanish rule. In fact, Bolivia is named in Bolívar's honor. Discuss the quotation on page 460. Have students restate the last sentence in their own words. Ask what this statement shows about Bolívar's feelings for his homeland. (He loves it more than life itself.) Ask students if they can relate to this kind of patriotism and love of country. For example, how do they feel when they see the flag or sing the national anthem?

CHAPTER 20

The Growth of Nationalism

1800–1900

I. New Ideas, New Directions
II. Change in Eastern Europe
III. Wars of Independence in Latin America

In the early 1800s, a huge independence movement swept Latin America as it had in North America and Europe. Ordinary people expected, as well as desired, a voice in the way their governments were run. The greatest leader of this independence movement was Simón Bolívar, called The Liberator. With his help, several Latin American countries gained their independence from Spain.

Life after independence was not always easy. Conflicts arose. Bolívar reminded people of their common heritage and values. One week before he died in 1830, he wrote a letter to the people of Colombia. He told them:

> ❝ *As I depart from your midst, . . . My last wishes are for the happiness of our native land. If my death will help to end party strife and to promote national unity, I shall go to my grave in peace.* ❞

Indeed, loyalty to one's "native land" was an important ideal in many parts of the nineteenth-century world.

CHAPTER EVENTS

1810
Miguel Hidalgo y Costilla leads a peasant revolt in Mexico.

Simón Bolívar begins to organize revolts against Spanish rule in South America.

1821
Mexico proclaims independence.

| 1775 | 1800 | 1825 |

WORLD EVENTS

1803
United States purchases the Louisiana Territory from France.

1815
Napoleon is defeated at Waterloo.

Teaching Options

Chapter 20 Resources

REVIEW

Teacher's Resources (TR)
Terms to Know, p. 33
Review History, p. 67
Build Your Skills, p. 101
Chapter Test, pp. 155–156
Concept Builder, p. 236
Cause-and-Effect Chain, p. 325
Transparencies 1, 5

ASSESSMENT
Section Reviews, pp. 466, 472, 478
Chapter Review, pp. 480–481
Chapter Test, TR, pp. 155–156

ALTERNATIVE ASSESSMENT
Portfolio Project, p. 502
Write an Editorial, p. T502

Nationalism Expands, 1825

GET ORGANIZED

Cause-and-Effect Chain A cause-and-effect chain shows relationships among certain events. Use a cause-and-effect chain as you read Chapter 20. Fill in the center link first by naming a chapter event. Then, look for an event that helped cause it and an event that resulted from it. Here is an example from this chapter.

CAUSE
Charles X does away with the legislature.

↓

EVENT
Workers in Paris revolt and drive off the king's troops.

↓

EFFECT
Charles X abdicates and flees to Great Britain.

VIEW HISTORY Simón Bolívar and his soldiers journeyed throughout South America, often crossing plains, mountains, and rivers, to fight for independence from Spain.
◆ What hardships of war are evident in the painting?

1830
French rebellion replaces Charles X with Louis Philippe, the "Citizen King."

1835
In Africa, Boers in Cape Colony begin Great Trek to escape British control.

1848
Revolutions sweep much of Europe.

1853
Crimean War begins.

1850

1861
Czar Alexander II ends serfdom in Russia.

1868
Rule in Japan is restored to an emperor.

1875

1877
Russo-Turkish War begins.

1894
Dreyfus Affair begins.

Nicholas II becomes czar of Russia.

1893
New Zealand gives voting rights to women.

1900

Chapter Themes

- Power, Authority, and Governance
- Civic Ideals and Practices
- Time, Continuity, and Change
- Culture

F Y I

Bolivia

What is now Bolivia was once part of the ancient Inca Empire. Simón Bolívar did not actually lead the region's movement for independence from Spain—General Antonio José de Sucre did, in 1825. However, to honor Bolívar's achievements and his role in drafting the nation's constitution, the new country was named for him.

Chapter Warm-Up

USING THE MAP

Point out the locator map at the top of page 461. Ask students to identify the highlighted continents. (North America, South America, Europe, Asia) Ask students whether they would expect the United States to be discussed in this chapter based on the highlighting. (no)

VIEW HISTORY

While fighting for independence in New Granada, Simón Bolívar led a small detachment of troops. He used swift, aggressive troop movements to fight the enemy. Later, he rewarded his soldiers without regard for their social background.

◆ **ANSWER** The soldiers would have to survive in harsh environments and cross difficult terrain during times of war. There are some men who are not on horseback, which suggests there may be a lack of supplies.

GET ORGANIZED
Cause-and-Effect Chain

Discuss the cause-and-effect chain on page 461. Have students identify the event in the chain. (Workers in Paris revolt and drive off the king's troops.) Have them turn this statement into a "Why" question. (Why did workers revolt and drive off the king's troops?) Then, have them look at the cause in the chain for the answer to this question. Encourage students to make a cause-and-effect chain (TR, p. 325) for each section.

⬤ TEACH THE TIMELINE

The timeline on pages 460–461 covers the period between 1803 and 1894. Discuss the locations mentioned in the Chapter Events. Help students notice that even though the period in this chapter is brief, the areas affected are vast. Ask students to find one or two words that express the main idea in the Chapter Events on the timeline. (revolution, independence, war) Suggest that students look for these concepts as they read the chapter.

Activity

Writing Have students choose one of the World Events on the timeline. Have them find out more about the event and write a brief paragraph explaining it. Ask them to suggest why the event might have been used on the timeline for this chapter.

I. New Ideas, New Directions

(pp. 462–466)

Section Summary

In this section, students will learn about the rise of nationalism and liberalism in Europe and about the conservatives' struggle to prevent change. They will also learn about changes of governments in France after Napoleon and how the French secured political rights as the nineteenth century progressed.

Introduce

Getting Started

Ask students how it feels to them to be living in the United States. (Possible answers: proud of the country they live in and its freedoms, grateful to live here, may be willing to defend the country if attacked) Have students consider how the idea of the nation-state "the United States" came into existence. Remind students that the United States, like many other countries, had to fight a war to win its independence.

TERMS TO KNOW

Ask students to read the terms and definitions on page 462 and find each term in the section. Ask students which three terms belong together. (ideology, conservatism, liberalism) Ask students to write a brief paragraph using all of the terms.

You may wish to preview the pronunciation of the following words with students.

ultraroyalist (ul truh ROY uhl ihst)
banquet (BANG kwuht)
abdicate (AB dih kayt)
Dreyfus (DRY fuhs)

ACTIVE READING

Ask students to examine one of the subsections in this section and list the differing points of view found there. To determine which point of view was most influential in the outcome of an event, have students think in terms of which side "won," or prevailed.

Terms to Know

ideology a belief and plan for social and political change

nation-state a self-governing land whose people share the same cultural background, language, and history

conservatism the idea that generally supports existing ways of doing things and opposes quick, major changes

liberalism the idea that generally encourages individual freedom and social progress

Do You Remember?

In Chapter 19, you learned that Napoleon organized the French government and finalized a set of civil laws called the Code Napoléon.

Main Ideas

A. Largely in reaction to the decisions of the Congress of Vienna, new ideas spread throughout Europe.

B. The political and economic scene in France was troubled during the late 1800s.

 Active Reading

POINTS OF VIEW
When you understand points of view, you are able to identify and analyze opinions. As you read this section, create a list of the opinions that shaped events in France at this time. For each major event, decide which point of view had the most influence.

A. Changes in Political Thinking

Between 1789 and 1815, Europe changed dramatically. The French Revolution tore France apart. It created unrest in other parts of Europe, too. The Napoleonic Wars also caused destruction and disorder across the continent. New **ideologies**—beliefs and plans for social and political change—were forming. As a result, Europe would continue to change.

The Rise of Nationalism

Throughout Europe, people began to admire the idea of a **nation-state**. A nation-state is a self-governing land in which most people have the same cultural background, language, and history. As you read in Chapter 19, loyalty to one's country is called nationalism. Nationalism would shape much of Europe's history in the nineteenth century. Nationalism also grew in other parts of the world that Europeans had settled.

The Congress of Vienna

In September 1814, the chief ministers of the great European powers met in Vienna, Austria, to find a way to undo the changes brought about by the French Revolution and Napoleon. Nearly every European nation sent delegates. Prince Klemens von Metternich represented Austria. He took charge of the negotiations among the ministers. Charles Talleyrand represented France, speaking for Louis XVIII. The Duke of Wellington was among the British representatives, and Prince Karl August von Hardenberg represented Prussia. Alexander I, czar of Russia, represented the Russian Empire. Historians call this meeting the Congress of Vienna.

Metternich and the leaders of the Congress of Vienna believed in the ideals of **conservatism**. Conservatives believe that things should return to the way they were. Many of the choices made at the Congress of Vienna showed conservative ideas in action. Metternich felt that Europe should be restored, or returned, to the way it was before the French Revolution. To achieve this, he guided the decisions made at the Congress of Vienna based on three main ideas. The first was that all countries that had suffered the most while fighting Napoleon had to be paid back for what they had lost. The second was that the balance of power had to be restored in Europe, so no nation would be too powerful. Third, all royal families who had ruled before Napoleon became emperor had to be restored to power.

Teaching Options

Section 1 Resources

Teacher's Resources (TR)
Terms to Know, p. 33
Review History, p. 67
Build Your Skills, p. 101
Concept Builder, p. 236
Cause-and-Effect Chain, p. 325
Transparency 1

Ensuring Peace in Europe

The representatives at the Congress of Vienna worked out a plan to maintain peace in Europe and restore the balance of power. The plan redrew the map of Europe. To the north of France, they added Belgium and Luxembourg to Holland, creating the kingdom of the Netherlands. To prevent France from expanding to the east, they gave Prussia lands along the Rhine River, and Austria part of northern Italy. France would now be surrounded by strong countries, so it could not threaten the peace of Europe again.

In Germany, the Congress of Vienna organized the many German states into the German Confederation. A confederation is a group of states or countries. Austria would head this group.

To protect the new plan, a peacekeeping alliance called the Concert of Europe was formed. The leaders of all the major European nations in the alliance promised to maintain the balance of power set up by the Congress of Vienna.

Nationalism and Liberalism in Europe

To Metternich and most other leaders at the Congress of Vienna, the nationalism and **liberalism** spread by the French Revolution and Napoleon were dangerous forces. Nationalism made many of the peoples of Europe want to achieve independence and self-government. Liberalism is a set of political ideas, called ideology, that promotes social change and individual freedoms. Liberals supported such ideas as freedom of speech, freedom of the press, and religious freedom.

In 1830 and 1831, serious uprisings broke out in France, Belgium, Poland, and Italy. In France, the king fled the country, and a new, more liberal king came to the throne. In 1831, Belgium succeeded in gaining its independence

European delegates met in Vienna, Austria, during the Congress of Vienna to plan peace for Europe.

A. Changes in Political Thinking

Purpose-Setting Question What was the goal of the Congress of Vienna? (to restore Europe to the way it was before the French Revolution)

Do You Remember?
Remind students about the scope of the Code Napoléon, which they read about in Chapter 19. Discuss whether the code promoted the cause of nationalism or not. (It promoted it in France, less so in other countries.)

Activity

Make a chart Ask students to make a three-column chart listing characteristics of nationalism, conservatism, and liberalism. Ask students if nationalism can develop under both conservative and liberal ideologies. (It can, but in this chapter, it is most closely linked with liberalism.)

Focus Between 1815 and 1848 central Europe was dominated by Prince Metternich, the leader of Austria. Metternich believed that revolution was a kind of disease, requiring international cooperation to cure it. In practice, this meant that revolutions and uprisings must be suppressed everywhere, not only in one's own country.

TEACH PRIMARY SOURCES
Ask students to describe the scene in the engraving on page 463. Ask what evidence of wealth is in the picture. (large, beautiful room; expensive clothing) Discuss whether the engraving is suggestive of a liberal or conservative ideology. (Conservative; this display of wealth and high living is what people at the Congress of Vienna wanted to preserve.)

Extend Ask students to try to think of all the freedoms Americans have. (freedom of speech, the press, religion, etc.) Ask them where these freedoms are guaranteed. (in the U.S. Constitution and in state laws and state constitutions) Conversely, ask students to name some things Americans are not free to do, such as take another's life or steal from others. Have students discuss why Americans are not free to do these things.

ESL/ELL STRATEGIES

Identify Essential Vocabulary Tell students that the word *ideology* has the same origin as the word *idea*. Ask students how these words are related. (An ideology is an idea of how people should live.) Ask how a person becomes attracted to a particular ideology. (Possible answers: Parents or respected elders believe it; the person attended a political function that was inspiring; the person read about it in a book or on the Internet.)

Discuss Ask the students to identify the causes of the 1848 uprisings. (Nationalists wanted self-rule; liberals wanted human rights.) Then, ask students to distinguish between the immediate and the long-term effects of the uprisings. (**Immediate:** Uprisings were crushed, except in France. **Long-term:** Ideas of nationalism and liberalism would eventually return.)

◆ **ANSWER** Prince Klemens von Metternich

B. France After Napoleon

Purpose-Setting Question How did France's government change over much of the 1800s? (It went from monarchy to republic to empire to republic.)

Review Refer students to the cause-and-effect chain on page 461. Ask students if these events are an example of liberalism or nationalism. (liberalism)

SPOTLIGHT ON CITIZENSHIP
VOTING IN FRANCE The Charter of 1814 was the constitution of the French restoration. The tax qualification of 300 francs made it possible for very few Frenchmen to vote. Ask students how the French government might have justified this kind of restriction. (Possible answer: After the French Revolution, it was necessary to keep power out of the hands of poor, uneducated people.)

Activity

Make a family tree Louis Philippe of France was a member of the Bourbon family, a European ruling family, originally of France but with ties to the Spanish throne and other former European kingdoms. Have students conduct research to find out about this ruling family and its various branches in Europe. Then, have them create a tree of the line, leading to Louis Philippe and beyond.

---

from the Netherlands. However, in Poland and Italy, when nationalists tried to win freedom from foreign rule, Russian and Austrian troops put an end to the uprisings.

In 1848, a wave of uprisings spread across Europe. In France, the people overthrew the king and established a republic. Austrians in Vienna rose up and forced Metternich to leave the country. The Czechs and Hungarians also rebelled against Austrian control. Revolts broke out in several German and Italian states. However, except in France, these uprisings were quickly crushed.

The leaders at the Congress of Vienna were able to keep peace by redrawing national boundaries in Europe. However, they overlooked the national cultures of the people whose lands they were dividing. When the people tried to voice their views, their leaders responded with force. Most of the uprisings between 1830 and 1848 failed. Yet throughout Europe, the ideals of nationalism and liberalism grew stronger. Before long, these forces would lead to the creation of several new European nations.

◆ **Who took charge of the negotiations during the Congress of Vienna?**

Spotlight on
Citizenship

VOTING IN FRANCE
The Charter of 1814 gave the vote to French men who were at least 30 years old and who paid at least 300 francs in taxes each year. More people had a voice in the government—but, for the most part, it was the voice of the well-to-do.

B. France After Napoleon

Members of the Congress of Vienna believed that a monarchy was the best way to bring peace to France. Therefore, they agreed to the restoration, or return, of Louis XVIII to power. Louis accepted a constitution that limited his power.

From Charles X to Citizen King

Louis XVIII did face some opposition. One group of ultraroyalists, or Ultras, wanted to return France to the kind of government that it had had before 1789. These aristocrats wanted back the property and power they had lost in the Revolution. Led by the king's brother Charles, they often challenged Louis XVIII.

When Louis XVIII died in 1824, his brother took the throne as Charles X. Unlike Louis, Charles believed that the king should hold all the power of government in his own hands. He believed that the constitution of France had no authority over his actions and he did away with much of it. He favored his supporters and increased the power of the Roman Catholic Church in France. The crisis came in 1830 when Charles X dissolved the legislature and limited the right to vote. He also ended freedom of the press. Angry citizens in Paris revolted. About 2,000 people died in three days of street fighting. Charles X gave up the throne and fled to Great Britain.

Some legislators wanted France to be a republic again. Others still supported a monarchy. Together, the legislators chose a new king: Louis Philippe, the Duke of Orléans and brother of Charles X. Louis Philippe called himself the "Citizen King." He held many liberal views and agreed to accept the new constitution of France that was written in 1814. This constitution recognized the right of the people to elect a lawmaking body, and it included a bill of rights to protect the individual citizen.

Trouble at Home

The upper and middle classes generally liked Louis Philippe, but there were people who wanted change. Many working-class people felt that Louis Philippe was not working in their best interest. Most people were still not allowed to vote. In addition, working-class people resented their low wages and the high prices of essential goods. Between 1846 and 1848, workers grew angrier because of food shortages and rising unemployment.

464 UNIT 5 ◆ Enlightenment and Revolution

Teaching Options

Meet Individual Needs:
VISUAL/SPATIAL LEARNERS

Have students make a chart that shows the progression of leaders in France. Suggest students include one or two phrases for each leader that describes his actions and reasons for leaving the throne. Students can use their charts as a review later.

Test Taking

Tell students that essay questions often ask them to compare and contrast events or ideologies. Remind them that comparing is finding similarities, and contrasting is examining differences. Have students list the beliefs of liberals and conservatives and then write a short essay comparing and contrasting the two ideologies.

After Charles X of France dissolved the legislature in 1830, a revolution broke out in the streets of Paris, as shown in this painting. Louis Philippe, shown on horseback, was chosen as the new French king.

Beginning in 1847, people critical of the government held political gatherings called banquets to organize their forces. When Louis Philippe banned a huge banquet, riots broke out. He sent troops to end the riots. To his shock, the troops joined the protesters and the disturbance grew. At last, like his brother Charles X, Louis Philippe abdicated. He, too, fled to Great Britain.

The group of revolutionary leaders in Paris set up a new government, the Second Republic. They called for an election in which all Frenchmen could vote—a first for Europe. Most of the representatives who were elected, however, were moderates and conservatives. One of their first actions was to end a program of national workshops that provided jobs for the unemployed. The result was "June Days," a 4-day revolt in Paris. Government troops crushed the revolt, and its leaders were imprisoned, exiled, or executed.

That fall, the French elected Louis Napoleon, the nephew of Napoleon Bonaparte, as president. Louis Napoleon worked hard to gain the support of the people and the army. Voters authorized him to revise the French constitution. Louis Napoleon had been waiting for this moment. In 1852 he dropped the title of "president" and became Emperor Napoleon III. In what now was the Second Empire, all Frenchmen continued to vote. France still had a constitution. However, Napoleon crushed those who opposed him. The legislature was strictly controlled by Napoleon III. Newspapers that criticized him were censored.

Trouble Abroad

Napoleon III tried to quiet unhappy voices at home by seeking glory for France abroad. His first target was Russia. With England and the Ottoman Empire as allies, France went to war against Russia in 1854 in the Crimean War. You will read more about this war in Section II.

Napoleon III then built up the French presence elsewhere. He attempted to extend French influence in North Africa, mostly by supporting the construction of the Suez Canal in Egypt. In Asia, Napoleon III established French control over the region of Cambodia. He also tried to establish a foothold for France in Mexico but was unsuccessful.

Global Connections

REVOLTS IN SPAIN AND PORTUGAL

Like France, Spain and Portugal wrestled over the way in which they were to be governed. In 1820, a revolt in Spain forced Ferdinand VII to accept a constitution that he had set aside. A year later, John VI of Portugal also accepted a constitution.

Using Technology

Have students conduct research using an online encyclopedia and other Internet Web sites to find more information about the "June Days." Have students explain what caused the revolt. Have them list several Web sites devoted to this event and explain how the Web sites supplemented information from the encyclopedia.

Napoleon III, the nephew of Napoleon Bonaparte, was elected president of France in 1848. Like his uncle, he later declared himself emperor.

Prussia was the next target of Napoleon III. Prussia was trying to unite Germany. To the French, a united Germany was a threat. France declared war on Prussia in 1870, and it proved a disaster for France. Napoleon III was captured and later died in exile. Prussian forces took Paris, and France was forced to negotiate a peace in 1871.

The Third Republic

French rebels revolted over the terms of the peace treaty between Prussia and France. An uprising broke out in Paris in March 1871. Government troops, however, restored order in the city in May.

In 1871, France became a republic once more—the Third Republic. Legislators settled on a new constitution in 1875. The constitution restated that France was a republic. Tired, but still hopeful for social progress and national glory, France would not return to a monarchy again.

A serious crisis in the Third Republic began in 1894. Alfred Dreyfus, a Jewish captain in the French army, was charged with selling military secrets to Germany. He was convicted of treason and sentenced to life imprisonment on Devil's Island, a prison colony in South America. Soon afterward, evidence that Dreyfus was innocent appeared. The army, however, refused to review the case. Over the next few years, the case divided the French people. Liberals generally wanted the Dreyfus case reopened. Most conservatives continued to believe in his guilt. Finally, the real traitor was found. The government brought Dreyfus home and gave him a pardon. To the supporters of Dreyfus, a pardon was not enough. They wanted him declared innocent. Finally, in 1906, Alfred Dreyfus's name was cleared.

◆ **What were the policies of Napoleon III at home and abroad?**

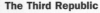

Review 1

Review History
A. Why did chief ministers of the European powers meet in Vienna, Austria, in 1814?
B. What events and forces led to the abdication of Louis Philippe?

Define Terms to Know
Define the following terms:
ideology, nation-state, conservatism, liberalism

Critical Thinking
Why do you think conservatives and liberals differed in their view of nationalism?

Write About Citizenship
Write a journal entry from the point of view of a factory worker in Paris in 1848. Explain why you think that your rights are being denied.

Get Organized
CAUSE-AND-EFFECT CHAIN
Use a cause-and-effect chain to organize information from this section. Choose a topic and then find related facts. For example, think about what led to the Congress of Vienna. Then, think of a result of the Congress.

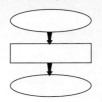

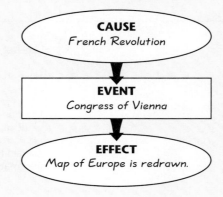

CAUSE
French Revolution

EVENT
Congress of Vienna

EFFECT
Map of Europe is redrawn.

Build Your Skills

Build Your Skills

IDENTIFY IDEOLOGIES

As you have learned, an ideology is a system of thought that includes ideas about how government should function. It may also include ideas about how people should behave and think in society. Both kinds of ideas are included in conservatism and liberalism, two examples of ideologies.

Here's How

Follow these steps to interpret an ideology in a written or visual piece, such as a political cartoon.

1. Describe the main idea of the ideology. For example, if the ideology is expressed in writing, find a sentence that states the main idea. If the ideology is expressed visually, then look to see which images make the most impact. Read any words on the visual that help you figure out the main idea.

2. Think about where and when the piece was created. Ask yourself what you know about the history of that time and place, such as important events and people.

3. Identify an ideology represented in a cartoon by reading any words in the cartoon and by carefully examining the visual. In a written piece, identify the writer's ideology by examining the major points of his or her statement.

Here's Why

Ideologies are more than just ideas that people think about. They are ideas that shape actions and political systems. Being able to identify ideologies will help you better understand why some historical events happened as they did.

Practice the Skill

Look at the poster on the right, which relates to the Alfred Dreyfus affair in France in 1894. Then, answer the following questions.

1. What does the image of the serpent represent?
2. What does the cartoonist think about Dreyfus?
3. Remember the history of this event. Which ideology—conservatism or liberalism—does this cartoon reflect?

Extend the Skill

Suppose that your ideology is the opposite of the one in this cartoon. Describe how you would show Dreyfus in a political cartoon.

Apply the Skill

Study other quotations and visuals in this chapter. Follow the steps in *Here's How* to figure out the ideologies that inspired them.

The case against Alfred Dreyfus produced strong emotions. This poster shows Dreyfus as a serpent. The French words *le Traitre* mean "the traitor" in English.

Build Your Skills

IDENTIFY IDEOLOGIES

Teach the Skill

Bring in several different daily newspapers to class, enough for several small groups to examine one paper each. Ask the groups to select two articles or editorials from each paper—one with a conservative point of view and one with a liberal point of view. Ask students why it is important to be able to recognize ideologies. (Possible answers: It helps to understand causes of some events; it helps to evaluate information that we read about or hear on a daily basis.)

Practice the Skill

ANSWERS

1. The serpent represents treachery and evil.
2. Possible answer: The cartoonist thinks that Dreyfus is a traitor who is evil.
3. It reflects conservatism. Conservatives generally believed that Dreyfus was guilty; in addition, the idea of being cautious about reversing a judicial decision would relate more to conservatism than to liberalism.

Extend the Skill

Students' cartoons would show Dreyfus in a sympathetic light, perhaps as a victim of persecution or as innocent.

Apply the Skill

You may want to select certain visuals in the textbook for students to examine, such as that of the Congress of Vienna on page 463. Ask students if an absolute monarch, such as Czar Alexander II, shown on page 472, is shown in a positive or negative light.

Teaching Options

RETEACH

Supply students with photographs or pictures of posters from World War I or World War II, or from another period in which ideologies were clearly defined. Even though the students may not be familiar with the era of these historical posters, they should be still able to apply the steps of *Here's How* to determine the ideologies the posters show.

CHALLENGE

Have students find other political cartoons, either from this period or from later periods. They may even use a contemporary cartoon from a current newspaper. Have students explain how the cartoon illustrates a point and how that point is suggestive of a particular ideology.

II. Change in Eastern Europe (pp. 468–472)

Section Summary

In this section, students will learn how nationalism influenced the Greek and Serbian peoples to fight for independence. They will also learn how Russia's involvement in eastern Europe caused the Crimean War and how Russia's czars in the 1800s ruled their country.

1 Introduce

Getting Started

Discuss with students their growing independence from their parents. Ask if they anticipate gaining greater freedom over the next several years. (Most will anticipate this.) Ask how they would feel if their parents refused to grant them the rights and responsibilities of a young adult. (Many would be angry or hurt.) Tell students that many countries in eastern Europe experienced similar feelings in the 1800s. Many of them were even willing to fight for the independence they felt they deserved.

TERMS TO KNOW

Write the terms on page 468 on the board. Ask students what they already know about these terms. Add their responses to the terms on the board. Have students find each term in the text and read it in context. Then, have them add new information to the list on the board. Finally, have students read the definitions on page 468.

You may wish to preview the pronunciation of the following words with students.

Croatia (kroh AY shuh)
Crimean (krih MEE uhn)
Ypsilantis (ihp suh LANT ehz)
Herzegovina
  (hert suh GOV vee nuh)

ACTIVE READING

Tell students that a Venn diagram (TR, p. 323) is a good aid to use when comparing and contrasting two things. Have students use a Venn diagram to compare and contrast the independence movements of two of the countries they read about in this section.

Section II — Change in Eastern Europe

Terms to Know

self-determination the belief that a people have the right to decide their own form of government

neutral not taking one side or the other

reactionary a person who opposes change

Main Ideas

A. A rising belief in nationalism inspired revolts in Greece and other parts of eastern Europe.

B. Russia's interest in the Ottoman Empire led to clashes with other major European powers.

C. Russia's nineteenth-century czars, with the exception of Alexander II, opposed liberal reforms.

Active Reading

COMPARE AND CONTRAST
When you compare two or more things, you are looking for ways in which they are alike. Contrasting means looking for ways in which things are different. As you read this section, compare and contrast independence movements in eastern Europe and the czars of nineteenth-century Russia.

A. Nationalism Leads to Revolt

As nationalism spread throughout Europe in the 1800s, so did peoples' thoughts about **self-determination**. Self-determination is a belief that people have the right to decide their own form of government.

The Ottoman Empire and the Balkans

At the beginning of the 1800s, the Ottoman Empire covered a huge area that stretched as far east as Persia. It included parts of Egypt, northern Africa, and land in southeastern Europe. This area of southeastern Europe on the Balkan Peninsula was known as the Balkans.

As the nineteenth century began, the Ottoman Empire was faced with two problems that threatened its unity and strength. The first problem was the sultan's decreasing influence over the empire's many provinces. The second problem was the rise of nationalism, especially among the peoples of the Balkans.

The Balkans consisted of many nation-states. Among them were Greece, Albania, Romania, Serbia, Croatia, and Bulgaria. Each nation-state had a different language, culture, and history that set it apart from its Ottoman rulers.

In addition, most of the people of the Balkans were Christians, whereas their Ottoman rulers were Muslims. As Christians, the people of the Balkans were denied rights that were granted to Muslims. They also paid heavy taxes to support an Ottoman army in which they could not serve. These differences and limited freedoms weakened Balkan loyalty to the Ottoman Empire.

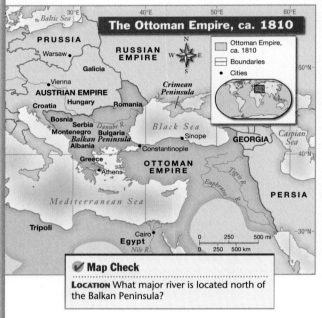

The Ottoman Empire, ca. 1810

Ottoman Empire, ca. 1810
Boundaries
• Cities

✔ Map Check

LOCATION What major river is located north of the Balkan Peninsula?

Teaching Options

Section 2 Resources

Teacher's Resources (TR)
  Terms to Know, p. 33
  Review History, p. 67
  Build Your Skill, p. 101
  Concept Builder, p. 236
  Cause-and-Effect Chain, p. 325
  Transparency 5

ESL/ELL STRATEGIES

Organize Information Have students develop a four-column chart to organize information about the Balkan states' independence. In the first column, they will write the state's name; in the second, whether it became independent; in the third, when it attained independence (if information is available); and in the fourth, any comments on how the independence was achieved.

Trouble in Serbia and the Balkans

In the early 1800s, several Balkan groups rebelled against the Ottomans who had ruled them since the late 1400s. The first Balkan people to revolt were the Serbs in 1804. In two different revolts between 1804 and 1817, the Serbs fought bitterly against the Ottomans, suffering massive defeats both times. Finally, in 1829 they were granted limited self-rule within the Ottoman Empire. Their long fight against the Ottomans helped shape a sense of national identity among Serbians.

Greek Independence

In 1821, the people of Greece also rebelled against Ottoman rule. Leaders of the rebellion, especially a man named Alexander Ypsilantis, encouraged Greeks to rally as a nation in order to win back their independence. They reminded

Over the course of several years, the Greeks battled the ruling Ottoman Turks in order to gain their independence.

Greeks that their ancient civilization had fostered democracy. The leaders of the Greek rebellion took this message to western Europeans, many of whom sided with the Greeks and sent money to support their fight for freedom. Some Europeans even journeyed to Greece to join the freedom fighters.

In 1825, France, Russia, and Great Britain agreed to support Greece in their rebellion by supplying a combined naval force to the Balkan region. By the late 1820s, these allies had forced the Ottomans to grant independence to some parts of Greece. By 1830, Greece was formally declared an independent kingdom. The independence gained by Greece, and the self-rule granted to Serbia gave other Balkan nations hope that they could gain independence for themselves.

As more Balkan states rebelled, pushing for freedom, the Ottoman Empire's power weakened. Europeans described the Ottoman Empire as "the sick man of Europe." By the 1850s, Russia and other countries in Europe rushed to divide up Ottoman lands. Russia, especially, was eager to control the region near the Black Sea and Istanbul, which the Russians still called Constantinople. The Austrian Empire seized Bosnia and Herzegovina. This action angered the Serbs because they had hoped to expand there. In addition, Great Britain and France also looked for Ottoman lands to control. All of this competition to grab Ottoman lands contributed to more fighting and more wars.

◆ **How did the Ottoman Empire lose its control over Greece?**

B. Russia's Involvement Grows

Beginning in the 1850s, Russia fought several wars against the Ottomans. Russia was not only the largest nation in Europe but was also a major world power. France and Great Britain, also world powers, feared that if Russia gained more lands it would grow even more powerful and threaten them. Over the next 30 years, as Russia battled the Ottomans for power and control, France and Great Britain sometimes sided with the Ottomans and sometimes sided with the Russians. This seesaw of power and control continued for many decades.

Meet Individual Needs:
KINESTHETIC LEARNERS

Help demonstrate a balance of power by bringing in a balance scale and several foods of approximately the same size. Label one Russia, one Great Britain, one France, and one Austria-Hungary. Have students experiment to find a balance. Explain that the political balance of power works similarly: Nations ally themselves according to beliefs and also to ensure that other nations do not grow too powerful.

Connection to
GEOGRAPHY ◁----

Help students find Istanbul on the map of Europe (Transparency 5 or p. A5 of the Atlas). Review the city's strategic importance as a window between Europe and Asia. Discuss with students why Russia wanted access to the Mediterranean Sea. Explain that whoever controlled this area controlled much of the trade between Europe and Asia.

A. Nationalism Leads to Revolt

Purpose-Setting Question How did countries in eastern Europe express growing nationalistic feelings? (Many countries in the Balkan Peninsula began to move purposefully toward independence, beginning with Serbia and Greece.)

Using the Map
The Ottoman Empire, ca. 1810

Have students name countries in Europe today that they recognize as being part of the Ottoman Empire at the time represented on the map. (Albania, Serbia, Bosnia, Hungary, Bulgaria, Greece, Romania)

✔ Map Check
Answer the Danube River

Review Remind students of the expansion of the Ottoman Empire into eastern Europe, as described in Chapter 8. Ask students to estimate the number of years the Ottoman Empire had been a strong presence in Europe. (since 1453; around 400 years)

◆ **ANSWER** The people of Greece began to rebel against Ottoman rule. Leaders of the rebellion tried to convince several western European nations to side with the Greeks. In 1825, France, Russia, and Great Britain agreed to support the rebels by supplying a combined naval force. This forced the Ottomans to grant independence to parts of Greece.

B. Russia's Involvement Grows

Purpose-Setting Question Why was Russia involved in the events that developed in nation-states in the Balkan Peninsula? (Russia wanted to control the lands along the Danube River, which would connect Russia to the Mediterranean Sea.)

Explore Discuss Russia's aggressive acts that led to the Ottoman Turks' declaring war in 1853. (Russia needed access to the Mediterranean Sea via Ottoman lands along the Danube.) Then, ask students why they think Great Britain and France entered the war. (Possible answer: They didn't want to see Russia win, because it would make Russia too powerful, and Russia could then be a threat to European nations.)

Activity

Use a map Have students locate the Crimean Peninsula on the map on page 468. Ask students to list the Ottoman states along the Danube River. (Serbia, Romania, Bulgaria)

Extend Although there were several causes for the Crimean War, the earliest hostilities involved a Franco-Russian dispute over the holy places in Palestine, particularly over who had the right to guard the key to Bethlehem's Church of the Nativity. Have students find out more about the religious dispute that led to the war and prepare a brief written report on it.

THEY MADE HISTORY
Florence Nightingale
Tell students that the Crimean War was the first war to be covered by newspaper photographers and correspondents. Ask how this might have affected the arrival of Florence Nightingale. (Possible answer: People in Britain would quickly know that British soldiers were suffering needlessly, and they would want something to be done about the soldiers' condition.)

Tell students that the American Civil War began just five years after the end of the Crimean War. American women—both northerners and southerners—were aware of Florence Nightingale's writings and activities. In the Civil War, thousands of American women modeled themselves after Florence Nightingale and became nurses for both the Union and the Confederate armies.

ANSWER Possible answers: Many people did not think highly of the nursing profession; many men did not think a woman should be in a dirty, disease-ridden hospital; they saw her as someone who went there to criticize the work of the male doctors and other officials who ran the hospital.

The Crimean War

One of Russia's major goals in fighting the Ottomans was to gain control of the Ottoman lands along the Danube River. This would give Russia important access to the Mediterranean Sea. The struggle to win these lands resulted in the Crimean War, which began in 1853. Great Britain, France, and the Italian kingdom of Sardinia sided with the Ottomans against the Russians. Most of the battles of the war took place in Crimea, a peninsula in southern Russia that juts into the Black Sea.

The fighting in the Crimean War was brutal, with many casualties on both sides. During the winter, thousands of soldiers died from the cold, illness, and malnutrition. To tend to the many wounded soldiers, temporary hospitals were set up near the actual fields of battle. Such hospitals became known as field hospitals. One of the army nurses who worked in a field hospital during the Crimean War was a British woman named Florence Nightingale. She insisted that field hospitals provide sanitary conditions for wounded soldiers. Nightingale is credited with saving many soldiers' lives during the Crimean War.

Finally, after years of fighting in the war, Russia turned away in defeat. The Crimean War ended with a treaty that was drawn up in 1856. The treaty blocked Russia's growth in the area—at least for a time.

The Russo-Turkish War of 1877

In 1876, the Bulgarians and other Balkan peoples revolted against Ottoman rule. Russia used the occasion to declare war—called the Russo-Turkish War—on the Ottoman Empire once more.

They Made History

Florence Nightingale 1820–1910

During the Crimean War, conditions at the military hospital in a district of the city of Istanbul, once known as Constantinople, were horrible. Wounded soldiers lay on dirty, bare floors. The hospital had no soap, no medicine, no nurses, and not enough bandages. Many soldiers died from infection and fever. An English nurse, Florence Nightingale, wanted to help.

When she was 25, Nightingale had become interested in nursing. She had gone to Egypt and Germany, where she had trained to become a nurse. Back in London, she had run a small private hospital.

When she heard about conditions at the military hospital in Istanbul, Nightingale volunteered to go there. She arrived with 38 nurses. She had the hospital cleaned and set up a program of patient care. She wrote reports and demands for supplies. Conditions and hygiene improved. Even the men who had opposed her work at first were impressed.

After the war, Nightingale began a nursing school in England. She continued to give advice about hospital planning and nursing. Almost single-handedly, Florence Nightingale shaped the nursing profession as we know it today.

Florence Nightingale improved hospital conditions during the Crimean War.

Critical Thinking Why do you think Nightingale was not accepted in the beginning?

Teaching Options

F Y I

The Crimean War: Cause and Effect

One of the causes of the Crimean War was that Russia demanded authority over Eastern Orthodox Christians in the Ottoman Empire. Another was that Russia and France were arguing over protection of Roman Catholic and Russian Orthodox Churches in the Holy Land. One effect of the war was that Alexander II became aware of the need to reform Russia.

Connection to
LITERATURE ◀------

During the Battle of Balaklava in 1854, a small British brigade attacked a strong Russian position. Of the 673 men in this "light brigade," about 250 were wounded or killed. Alfred, Lord Tennyson wrote a celebratory poem—"The Charge of the Light Brigade"—that is renowned for its glorification of war. Ask interested students to find the poem in an anthology of English literature and read it aloud to the class.

In the Russo-Turkish War, the European nations remained **neutral**. They did not take sides. In this war, without European aid, the Ottomans lost. Russia and many Balkan nationalists were victorious. Serbia, Romania, and Montenegro gained full independence. Russia took control of many of the smaller Balkan states.

France, Germany, and Austria-Hungary thought that Russia had too much power in the Balkans. They demanded that the major European nations organize a conference to discuss the matter. Great Britain and Austria-Hungary forced Russia to attend this conference, which was called the Congress of Berlin.

The Congress of Berlin met in 1878. It set up three independent Balkan nations: Serbia, Romania, and Montenegro. The Congress of Berlin also distributed parts of the Balkans to different European nations, such as Great Britain and Austria. In the end, Russia was left with little power. It had won the war but lost the peace.

◆ **Why was the Crimean War fought?**

C. Russia Faces Other Problems

Czar Alexander I ruled Russia from 1801 to 1825. Up until this time, Russian czars had, for centuries, ruled with absolute power. They did not share power with any other person or group, but rather held it all themselves. There was no parliament or congress to vote on new laws. The czars tried to control every part of Russian society, and they expected to be obeyed. They often did not seek to improve the lives of their subjects.

In the early part of Alexander's reign, he made some improvements to Russian life. He reorganized the government and expanded Russia's educational system. He also limited the use of secret police. In later years, though, Alexander I became more conservative and reversed some of these changes. In addition, at the Congress of Vienna, Alexander I joined the conservative powers in opposing nationalist movements in Europe.

Czar Nicholas I

Many Russians opposed the czar's changes. These Russians began meeting in secret to discuss revolt. When Alexander I died suddenly in 1825, his brothers Constantine and Nicholas each said that the other should be the new czar. In the confusion, a group of army officers tried to take over the government. These officers demanded a Russian constitution. They were called the "Decembrists." On December 14, 1825, they marched their troops into Senate Square in Saint Petersburg, Russia. By then, however, Russian officials had already pledged their loyalty to Czar Nicholas I. The Decembrists would not surrender and government troops opened fire, killing many of them. The survivors were dealt with harshly. Some of the leaders were executed and many more were sent into exile.

Czar Nicholas I was a **reactionary**, a person who is opposed to change. After the revolt in December, he started a special secret police to watch for groups that might work against the government. The police would arrest or take the property of any person who had liberal ideas about giving power to the people. Nicholas acted quickly against any who opposed him.

Wars and Revolts in the Ottoman Empire	
1804	Serbia revolts against Ottoman rule.
1825	Greece fights for independence from Ottoman rule.
1829	Serbia is granted limited self-rule.
1830	Ottoman Empire declares Greece an independent kingdom.
1853–1856	Russia fights against the Ottomans, Great Britain, France, and Sardinia to gain control of Ottoman lands in the Crimean War.
1876	Bulgaria revolts against Ottoman rule.
1877	Russia begins fighting the Russo-Turkish War with the Ottoman Empire.

✔ **Chart Check**

Which event took place in the Ottoman Empire in 1829?

Extend Tell students that Bosnia was part of a country called Yugoslavia for about 70 years until 1992. Yugoslavia was dominated by Serbs, but Muslims and Croats also lived there. When Bosnia became independent, Bosnian Serbs immediately attacked and seized about 70 percent of Bosnian territory. They terrorized Muslims and Croats and besieged the capital city of Sarajevo. About 250,000 Bosnians were killed. The warring factions reached an accord in 1995, but a lasting peace is far from certain, especially after the assassination of the Serbian Prime Minister in 2003. Ask students what ideology gripped the Serbs at the time the civil war began. (a conservative nationalism based on ethnicity)

◆ **ANSWER** Russia wanted control of land along the Danube River that would give it access to the Mediterranean Sea.

C. Russia Faces Other Problems

Purpose-Setting Question What problems did Russia face in the 1800s? (conflicts over who would be in power and over the extent of the czar's power; complaints of the serfs)

Focus Ask students to speculate on why change was so difficult to achieve in Russia. (Possible answer: The czar did not want things to change, and government officials dealt harshly with people who did.)

Using the Chart

Wars and Revolts in the Ottoman Empire

Ask what three Balkan countries are discussed in the chart. (Serbia, Greece, Bulgaria) Ask students to make a generalization about the Ottoman Empire in the 1800s. (Possible answer: The Ottoman Empire was falling apart, nation by nation.)

✔ **Chart Check**

Answer Serbia is granted limited self-rule.

Writing

AVERAGE

Ask students to consider the sentence on page 471 at the end of subsection B: "It [Russia] had won the war but lost the peace." Have students write a paragraph or two explaining the meaning of this statement. Students should also explain whether they agree with the statement and should be sure to support their opinion with specific details.

CHALLENGE

Ask students to research more about the Congress of Berlin. Have them find out what part Germany played in settling international problems and how the alliances in Europe shifted as a result. Ask them to include information on the Balkan nations' feelings about the treaty resulting from the Congress of Berlin. Have students write a brief essay discussing the importance of this event.

Use a diagram Refer students to the Active Reading paragraph at the top of page 468. Ask them to use a Venn diagram (TR, p. 323) to compare and contrast the reigns of Russian czars Nicholas I and Alexander II.

◆ **ANSWER** Unlike earlier Russian czars, Alexander I tried to improve the lives of the Russian people through reforms of the government, educational system, and secret police.

Section Close

Alphonse Karr, a French novelist and journalist, once said, "The more things change, the more they are the same." Have students consider this saying in relation to eastern Europe at this time. Have them list something that changed in one country and something that remained the same in another country. (Possible answer: Greece gained independence; Russia remained under the control of the czars.)

3 Assess

Review Answers

Review History
A. They sought independence because of religious differences with the Ottomans and the limited freedoms that Ottoman rule imposed on them.

B. Russia wanted access to the Mediterranean. The Ottomans had land along important waterways that Russia wanted, so the nations went to war.

C. After the death of Alexander I, each of his brothers claimed the other should be the new czar. This lack of leadership and confusion led to a revolt by the Decembrists.

Define Terms to Know
self-determination, 468; neutral, 471; reactionary, 471

Czar Alexander II introduced great reforms to Russia.

Within Russia, Nicholas I censored newspapers and textbooks. He banned any writing that disagreed with the government. He limited university attendance and class subjects. Finally, Nicholas I refused to listen to the complaints of the serfs.

Reforms of Alexander II

Nicholas I died in 1855, during the Crimean War. His son became Czar Alexander II. Unlike his father, Alexander II believed in reform. He introduced trial by jury to Russia and expanded Russia's railway system.

His most important reform, however, came in 1861. At that time, some 25 million serfs were still being forced to work for wealthy landowners. The serfs lived in extreme poverty, their work was exhausting, and they had few legal protections. Alexander II agreed to end serfdom. The Edict of Emancipation set the serfs free and took millions of acres of land from landowners. Former serfs could buy a piece of this land and pay for it over several years. The new system had its problems, however: To buy land, many serfs went into debt. They were worse off than before. Just the same, the end of serfdom would change Russia dramatically.

In 1881, a revolutionary group assassinated Alexander II. His son, Czar Alexander III, was a reactionary who put new restrictions upon the Russian people. He was succeeded in 1894 by Nicholas II, another autocrat who would be the last of Russia's czars.

◆ **How was Alexander I different from earlier Russian czars?**

Review II

Review History
A. Why did various peoples of the Balkans seek independence from Ottoman rule?
B. What factors led to the Crimean War?
C. How did the death of Czar Alexander I lead to the revolt of the Decembrists?

Define Terms to Know
Define the following terms: **self-determination, neutral, reactionary**

Critical Thinking
What advantage did nations in Europe hope to gain by having countries in the Balkan Peninsula become independent?

Write About Government
Prepare an outline in which you list the governmental reforms of both Czar Alexander I and Czar Alexander II. Then, write a paragraph about the changes in Russia's government between 1820 and 1860.

Get Organized
CAUSE-AND-EFFECT CHAIN
Use a cause-and-effect chain to organize information from this section. Choose a topic and then find related facts. For example, what was one cause and one effect of the Congress of Berlin?

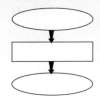

Critical Thinking
Possible answer: Because the Ottoman Empire was becoming unstable, the major powers of Europe were afraid that Russia would take over the countries ruled by the Ottomans. They preferred to have those countries become independent in the hopes of preserving the balance of power.

Write About Government
Students' paragraphs should discuss both governmental and educational changes in Russia.

CAUSE
Russo-Turkish War ends in treaty favorable to Russia.

↓

EVENT
Congress of Berlin is formed.

↓

EFFECT
Russia loses power in the Balkans.

Wars of Independence in Latin America

Terms to Know

constitutional monarchy
a government in which a ruler's powers are limited to those that the constitution and the laws of the country allow

Western Hemisphere
the half of Earth that includes North and South America

Main Ideas

A. The colonial society of Latin America had distinct classes based on birth and race.

B. The Age of Enlightenment influenced Latin Americans and resulted in independence for Haiti.

C. Most of colonial Latin America gained its independence between 1810 and 1825.

 Active Reading

SEQUENCE OF EVENTS
When you determine a sequence of events, you think of a logical order—for example, which event happened first, next, and so on. As you read this section, find the order of the events taking place in Latin America. Also, think about what was happening in Europe at the same time.

Section Summary

In this section, students will learn about the class structure of colonial Latin American society. They will learn how Enlightenment thinkers influenced Latin American leaders and how Haiti won its independence. They will also learn how other Latin American countries gained independence by 1825.

 **Introduce**

Getting Started

Ask students what a fad is. (Possible answers: a craze, the fashion) Discuss why people respond to fads. (Possible answer: They feel a need to; if others are doing it, it must be good.) Then, tell students that in the 1800s, the idea of independence spread through Latin America. In a way, it was like a fad but much more serious in that people dedicated their lives for it. The idea of independence also changed the way people lived.

A. Social Structure in Latin America

Latin America is a region that includes Mexico, Central America, South America, and the Caribbean islands. In the late 1700s, much of this region was under Spanish control. Portugal, however, governed the colony of Brazil in South America. The French, Dutch, and British also claimed small parts of Latin America.

Latin American society reflected two major influences. One was the culture of the governing countries. The other was a population with large numbers of native-born residents and enslaved workers.

Classes of Society

In the parts of Latin America controlled by Spain and Portugal, white people who were born in Europe were at the top of society. As you read in Chapter 16, the Spaniards called these people Peninsulares because they came from the Iberian Peninsula—where Spain and Portugal were located. Peninsulares held the best, most powerful jobs. They made the most money. More than any other class, they preserved the cultures of their homelands.

This painting shows a mother and child, both of whom are mestizos, setting up a fruit stand for market day.

Below them were Criollos, or Creoles. These white people were born in Latin America, but their parents and ancestors were born in Spain. Creoles owned the most land and the mines. However, even well-educated Creoles worked at less important jobs and made less money than the Peninsulares did. The Creoles were jealous of the Peninsulares and angry because they seldom were allowed to hold important jobs in government. As a result, relations between the two groups were usually tense.

Both the Peninsulares and Creoles were united on one issue, though. This issue concerned people of mixed race—mestizos and mulattoes. Mestizos were part Native American and part Spanish. Mulattoes were of European and African ancestry. The upper classes generally viewed both groups as inferior.

TERMS TO KNOW
Ask students to read the terms and definitions on page 473 and find the terms in the section.

You may wish to preview the pronunciation of the following words with students.

Peninsulare (puh NIHN soo ler)
Toussaint L'Ouverture
(TOO sahn loo ver TUHR)
Jean Jacques Dessalines
(ZHAN ZHAHK DAY sah leen)
João (ZHWAW)
Simón Bolívar
(see MOHN boh LEE vahr)
Agustín de Iturbide
(ah goos TEEN DAY ee toor BEE thay)

ACTIVE READING
Encourage students to use a timeline, modeled on the timeline on pages 460–461, to record events in Latin America and in Europe between 1800 and 1830. Students may review Sections 1 and 2 for details. Then, have students read Section 3, adding important dates as they read.

Teaching Options

Section 3 Resources

Teacher's Resources (TR)

Terms to Know, p. 33
Review History, p. 67
Build Your Skills, p. 101
Chapter Test, pp. 155–156
Concept Builder, p. 236
Cause-and-Effect Chain, p. 325

F Y I

Creole

The word *Creole* has taken on different meanings over time and place. In the West Indies, it means anyone who is part of the Caribbean culture. In Louisiana, it means a white descendant of Spanish or French settlers, but it also refers to people who speak a form of French and Spanish. In Peru, it refers to a way of living—including national pride and enjoyment of social occasions.

A. Social Structure in Latin America

Purpose-Setting Question What social groups were at the bottom of the class structure of colonial Latin America? (Native Americans, Africans, and people of mixed races)

Activity

Use a diagram Draw a triangle on the board, and create four classifications by drawing horizontal lines in the triangle. Have students use the diagram to describe the social structure in Latin America before independence. (Peninsulares at the top, then Creoles, then mestizos and mulattoes, and at the bottom Native Americans, Africans, and people of mixed Native American and African ancestry)

Discuss Ask students what was unfair about the social structure in colonial Latin America. (Possible answer: Poor people did not have equal opportunities; everyone was not equal.) Ask why people accepted this structure. (Possible answer: Force may have been used to maintain it; people may have thought it was the way life had to be.) Remind students of the social structures in Europe during the Middle Ages. Discuss how the structures of the societies were similar.

Explore Discuss how the Roman Catholic Church supported the social structure in colonial Latin America. (It upheld social differences based on race.) Ask how the Church helped society. (It established hospitals and orphanages and set up charitable works.)

◆ **ANSWER** from the Iberian peninsula, where Spain and Portugal are located today

B. Challenges to the System

Purpose-Setting Question How were people who were living in Latin America affected by the Age of Enlightenment? (It gave them hope that they, too, could achieve independence.)

Although mestizos and mulattoes had enough training to work at skilled jobs and could read and write, they were not allowed to own land.

The lowest classes in the social structure included Native Americans, Africans, and people with both Native American and African backgrounds. The rights of Native Americans varied from place to place. In general, though, they were viewed as peasants. They worked the lands owned by the upper classes or they lived in isolated villages. Most Africans living in Latin America were slaves. Most slaves could often buy or earn their freedom. Even though Spanish colonial laws promised enslaved people protection from harsh treatment, these laws were rarely enforced.

The Role of the Church

From the beginning, Roman Catholicism was an important part of life in Latin America. The monarch of Spain was also the head of the Church in Spain's colonies. He or she decided how the Church would collect and spend money, and also chose many of the Church's leaders. Settlers in Latin America quickly built churches in new communities. In addition, missionaries brought Christianity and Spanish culture to the Native Americans.

The Church in Latin America grew very wealthy. In Mexico, for example, the Church came to own about one third of the land. In some cases, that wealth helped expand missionary activity. It also paid for hospitals, orphanages, and other charitable works.

With few exceptions, the Church supported the government and society in Latin America. Some people within the Church protested the mistreatment of Native Americans, but little was said about the slave population. In fact, the Church itself owned thousands of enslaved workers.

◆ **From where did the Peninsulares originate?**

Some women from the upper classes of Latin American society, such as Sor Juana Inés de la Cruz, shown in this painting, became nuns in the Roman Catholic Church.

B. Challenges to the System

In Europe and the United States, great changes were underway. Latin Americans who were unhappy with their lives listened with interest to news about those changes.

The Age of Enlightenment Reaches Latin America

The Enlightenment dramatically influenced European thought during the 1700s. Latin Americans who visited or studied in Europe discovered the ideas of such writers as John Locke, Voltaire, and Rousseau. As Latin Americans—especially young Creoles—applied these ideas to their situations at home, their desire for change grew. They returned from Europe with Enlightenment ideas.

During the later 1700s, Latin Americans turned their attention to the American Revolution. Many Latin Americans admired leaders such as George Washington and Thomas Paine. They read translations of the Declaration of Independence and other U.S. documents. After the war, Latin Americans who had visited the United States voiced praise for the new nation. After all, the American Revolution gave the people of the United States independence. If such change was possible in a former English colony, they thought, perhaps it was possible at home.

474 UNIT 5 ◆ Enlightenment and Revolution

Teaching Options

Cooperative Learning

Have students work in groups of five or six to create tableaus of life in colonial Latin America. Have several students find out more about the roles of different social classes, including differences in dress. Other students may prepare brief statements to give to the class. Allow class time for each group to stage its tableau for the rest of the class.

François Dominique Toussaint, shown with the red hat, rose from slavery to become the lieutenant governor of Saint Domingue. Here, he is shown on his way to prison after surrendering to French troops.

Hopes rose higher with news of the French Revolution. Here was another case in which the people rose up against their rulers and demanded rights. The Declaration of the Rights of Man and the Citizen was read across Latin America. Other revolutionary literature, even when banned, found an audience. Latin Americans talked eagerly about liberty and equality. The Creoles—who felt that they would gain the most from independence—watched for a time when they might take control from the Peninsulares and the European colonial governments.

Independence for Haiti

The French Revolution gave people of the West Indies the motivation to rebel. The first successful uprising took place in the French colony of Haiti on the island of Hispaniola. Haiti was called Saint Domingue at that time.

Saint Domingue was France's wealthiest colony. Its sugar and coffee plantations depended upon the labor of half a million enslaved workers. Even though there were more slaves than white people, the French settlers quickly put down revolts. News about the French Revolution quickly led to an uprising by the colony's free mulattoes. In August 1791, enslaved African workers followed with a revolt. They wanted the same rights as French settlers.

In the troubled months that followed, a leader named François Dominique Toussaint emerged. Toussaint, a slave, grew up on a plantation. The plantation's owners treated slaves kindly. Toussaint learned to read and write and was allowed to read books in the owner's library. At the start of the revolt,

TEACH PRIMARY SOURCES

The painting on page 475 shows François Dominique Toussaint being taken to prison in France by officers on a French ship. Ask students if they think that justice was served in the case of François Dominique Toussaint. (Most will say no, they don't think he was dealt with fairly.)

Activity

Start an SQR chart Work with students to start an SQR chart (TR, p. 322) based on this statement: *This section is about Latin American countries gaining independence.* Have students turn the statement into a question and then read the textbook to gather information. As they read, have them complete the chart with additional information.

Discuss Ask students how the ideas of the Enlightenment spread. (Possible answers: through writings; through people traveling to other countries) Ask why the Creoles felt they would gain the most from independence. (They were hopeful of displacing the Peninsulares, who had long held the most power.)

Focus Turn students' attention to a discussion of Haiti's struggle for independence. Point out that, unlike much of South America, Haiti, which was originally called Saint Domingue, was a French colony. Ask why the French wanted to hold on to Saint Domingue. (It was France's wealthiest colony because of its sugar and coffee plantations.) Discuss the emergence of François Dominique Toussaint. Ask how he repaid the family to whom he had been enslaved. (He moved them to a safe place before the revolt began.)

ESL/ELL STRATEGIES

Role-play Ask pairs of students to role-play scenes in which Latin Americans hear about the Declaration of the Rights of Man and the Citizen. Have students discuss their views of independence and how they may be affected by the independence movement.

DOCUMENT-BASED QUESTION

Tell students that one of Toussaint's strengths was his shrewdness in dealing with the French on the matter of Saint Domingue. For example, he hired French deserters to instruct the slaves in troop discipline and military tactics.

ANSWER The terms came from the French Revolution, an event with which he was very familiar. Because he could read, he may have seen the terms in revolutionary literature as well.

◆ **ANSWER** The news inspired some Latin Americans to think of independence for their lands and others into open revolt against colonial governments.

C. Revolution Spreads

Purpose-Setting Question How did Napoleon's actions in Europe affect the political status of Latin American countries? (When Napoleon invaded Portugal, the Portuguese royal family fled to Brazil and re-established itself there. When Napoleon deposed the Spanish king, Spanish colonies in Latin America saw the turmoil in Spain as an opportunity to seize their independence.)

Using the Map

Latin America, 1828

Review the key with students, particularly the date of declaring independence. Ask which two countries gained independence in the same year. (Mexico and Venezuela, 1821) Ask what this same map would have looked like in 1803. (It would have been all the same color for colonies under European control, not the color of independent nation-states.)

✔ Map Check

Answer Haiti

DOCUMENT-BASED QUESTION
How do you think Toussaint became familiar with the terms *liberty* and *equality*?

Do You Remember?

In Chapter 19, you learned that Napoleon took the title of Emperor of France for life in 1804.

Latin America, 1828

✔ Map Check

HUMAN INTERACTION Which Latin American country was the first to gain independence?

---

he helped move the family to a safe place. Then, he took the name *L'Ouverture*—French for "the opening"—and devoted himself to the cause of freedom. He led a series of revolts against the French for freedom in Saint Domingue. In 1793, he published this statement:

> ❝ I desire the establishment of Liberty and Equality in St. Domingue. I strive to bring them into being. Unite with us, brothers, and fight with us in the common cause. ❞

Toussaint and his army were successful in the revolt. In 1794, France passed a law freeing all slaves. Toussaint was made lieutenant governor of Saint Domingue and instituted many reforms there. As time went on, the European governors were eased out, and Toussaint took control over the entire island by 1801.

Meanwhile, Napoleon had taken over the government in France. Napoleon was in favor of slavery, and was not pleased about a former slave governing a French colony. Napoleon sent a large fleet and more than 20,000 troops to retake the island. Yellow fever killed many French soldiers. Toussaint finally surrendered. He was sent to France, where he died in prison in 1803.

Toussaint's generals, Jean Jacques Dessalines and Henri Christophe, took over his cause and drove the French troops out of Saint Domingue. Jean Jacques Dessalines declared himself emperor of the independent republic in September 1804 and called it Haiti.

Haiti would continue to have problems in the years ahead. It remained a free country, however, ending Napoleon's hopes of establishing an empire in the Americas. Haiti also served as an inspiration to the rest of Latin America.

◆ **How did news of the French Revolution affect Latin Americans?**

C. Revolution Spreads

In South America, the push for independence followed news of trouble abroad. When Napoleon invaded Portugal in 1807, Prince John, or João as he was called, and his family fled to Brazil. Brazil was a Portuguese colony located in South America. It became the center of the Portuguese Empire. In 1808, Napoleon forced out King Charles IV of Spain and placed his own brother, Joseph Bonaparte, on the Spanish throne. With two governing countries in turmoil, Latin American revolutionaries made their move.

Simón Bolívar as Liberator

A great number of people took part in South America's march toward independence. From 1810 on, however, a few revolutionary leaders made such an impact that they were called "liberators."

One of those liberators was Simón Bolívar, a young Creole aristocrat. Bolívar had traveled to

---

Teaching Options

Writing

AVERAGE
Have students use an encyclopedia to find out more about the lives of one of Latin America's liberators—François Dominique (Toussaint) L'Ouverture, José de San Martín, or Bernardo O'Higgins. Have them note any interesting characteristics of their subject and also try to find out what motivated him to lead a revolt.

CHALLENGE
Ask students to read a biography of one of the great liberators of Latin America—Simón Bolívar, Miguel Hildalgo y Costilla, or Agustín de Iturbides. Have them consider whether or not their subject was a good leader, and instruct them to be prepared to explain their position.

Europe and read Enlightenment works by Voltaire and John Locke. He vowed to free Venezuela, his homeland, from Spain's control. Bolívar also encouraged an independence movement in New Grenada, the colony next to Venezuela. After winning back Caracas, Venezuela, from Spain, he was named dictator in 1814. However, Spanish troops drove him out of the country. He went to Haiti in the West Indies and gathered supplies and troops. Bolívar then returned to South America, where he and his troops defeated the Spaniards in New Grenada in 1819. Next, he moved to Venezuela, achieving victory there in 1821. He became president of the new Republic of Gran Colombia—a union of Venezuela, Colombia, and Panama. Its first constitution was written in 1821. However, this was just the beginning of Bolívar's plans. Next, with the help of Antonio José de Sucre, Bolívar ended colonial rule in Ecuador. It, too, became part of Gran Colombia.

Now, only Peru remained to be liberated. However, another liberator was already there. His name was José de San Martín.

The great Creole leaders, José de San Martín and Simón Bolívar meet to discuss the liberation of Peru.

José de San Martín

A skilled Creole military leader named José de San Martín had been fighting since 1813 to liberate southern South America. San Martín trained an army in the Andes Mountains. He then took the army into Chile. Chile was struggling to keep its independence, which had been declared in 1818. San Martín's forces were victorious. Bernardo O'Higgins, San Martín's aide, led the new Chilean government. San Martín's forces then moved north into Peru. They captured Lima in 1821 and liberated most of Peru. There were still Spanish forces remaining in some parts of Peru, however.

In 1822, José de San Martín and Simón Bolívar met to discuss how to achieve the total liberation of Peru. San Martín resigned and Bolívar went on to claim total victory in Peru in 1824, driving the Spaniards out for good. The next year, Upper Peru became independent and was named Bolivia in honor of Bolívar.

Brazil's story was somewhat different. When King John VI returned to Portugal from Brazil, he left his son, Pedro, to rule Brazil. Brazil's Creole people persuaded Pedro to declare Brazil's independence, which he did in 1822. Brazil became a **constitutional monarchy**, a government in which the ruler's powers are limited to those that the constitution and the laws of the country allow.

Mexico and Central America

In 1810—an important year in Mexico's history—a priest named Miguel Hidalgo y Costilla led a peasant army in revolt against the Spanish government. Hidalgo sought reform and independence. He issued a call for support for his rebellion from Native Americans, Africans, and mestizoes. Hidalgo ended slavery in central Mexico where his army gained control. Before long, though, Hidalgo was arrested and executed. The revolution was taken up by another priest, José Maria Morelos y Pavón. Pavón issued a declaration of independence but was captured and executed in 1815.

In 1821, Agustín de Iturbide, a Spanish Creole general, joined the rebels in Mexico. With Iturbide's help, Mexico declared its independence that same year. Iturbide continued briefly as emperor of the new country.

Primary Source Documents

You can read sections of Miguel Hildago's The Abolition of Slavery in Mexico on page 814.

Explore Have students work in pairs. One student will read the first paragraph on page 477 (it begins on p. 476), and the other student will list the countries Bolívar liberated and the dates they were liberated. (New Grenada—1819; Venezuela—1821; Republic of Gran Colombia—1821; and so on.)

TEACH PRIMARY SOURCES

Tell students that this picture of the meeting of San Martín and Bolívar is an engraving, made by cutting an image into a metal plate and then using the plate to print the image. Photography was not widely used until the mid-1800s, years after Bolívar had died. Ask students to speculate on the specific nature of the conversation in the engraving. (Possible answer: One of the leaders might be trying to persuade the other of something.)

Discuss Ask how José de San Martín helped liberate Latin America. (He trained an army in the Andes Mountains, and won independence for Chile and Peru.)

Focus Ask students how the beginning of Mexico's struggle for independence differed from that of other Latin American countries. (It was begun by priests—first Miguel Hidalgo y Costilla and then José Maria Morelos y Pavon.) Have students contrast these priests with the description of the Roman Catholic Church on page 474. (The Church supported the colonial system, but Hidalgo and Morelos supported change.) Have students read Miguel Hildago's The Abolition of Slavery in Mexico on page 814 and discuss his ideas.

Activity

Make a chart Have students make a chart comparing the different types of monarchies, including absolute monarchies, limited monarchies, and constitutional monarchies. Have them identify in their charts some of the countries that have had or still have these kinds of governments. Then, have them summarize the differences between the constitutional monarchies and democracies or republics such as the United States.

Conflict **Resolution**

No one knows what José de San Martín and Simón Bolívar discussed when they met in 1822, but San Martín was a disappointed man when he returned to Peru after the meeting. He resigned his protectorship and lived in Europe for the remainder of his life. Tell students that sometimes a conflict is resolved by one party simply bowing out of the situation.

Connection to
MATH

Ask students to follow the path of Simón Bolívar and the liberation of South American countries. Have them set up an equation and calculate how many years this journey of liberation took. (1814 to 1825—a period of 11 years)

Make a flowchart Ask students to make a flowchart (TR, p. 324) showing the events leading to independence in Mexico and Central American countries.

Explore Discuss the effect of the Monroe Doctrine in Latin America. (The United States would respect the independence of Latin American countries. The United States also warned European nations to stay away from Latin America, except for the colonies that were already there.)

◆ **ANSWER** Simón Bolívar, José de San Martín, and Agustín de Iturbide were all Creole military officers who were at the forefront of the independence movement. As Creoles, they were aware of the ways in which they were kept from power; as military officers, they had the training and experience to lead a rebellion.

Section Close

Ask students to make a general statement of how the ideas of nationalism and liberalism changed the world in the 1800s. (led to many people struggling for independence and to the establishment of new countries in the 1800s)

3 Assess

Review Answers
Review History
A. European Latin Americans had better opportunities than did native-born white Latin Americans; both had better opportunities than did mixed-race Latin Americans, Africans, and Native Americans.

B. Enlightenment ideas focused on liberty and individual rights and encouraged a change in the rigid Latin American social system.

C. The United States issued the Monroe Doctrine, which promised that it would not interfere with Europe's remaining colonies in the Western Hemisphere and warned European nations not to try to take back their former colonies there.

Define Terms to Know
constitutional monarchy, 477; Western Hemisphere, 478

Iturbide's empire included much of Central America, in the area where people had also sought independence from Spain. In 1823, Iturbide was forced out of office. Representatives from parts of Central America met and formed the United Provinces of Central America. This union continued until 1838. It then became the countries of Guatemala, El Salvador, Honduras, Nicaragua, and Costa Rica. By 1825, therefore, only parts of Latin America remained under European control. They included the British, French, and Dutch Guianas, British Honduras, Cuba, Puerto Rico, Jamaica, and a few small Caribbean islands.

Reaction in the United States

Years of fighting for independence had weakened the economies of Latin American countries. As a result, they were not prepared to govern themselves. Knowing this, Spain urged its European allies to help it regain control of its former colonies. Great Britain had strong economic reasons for not wanting Latin America to be controlled by Spain again. Britain approached the United States to make a joint declaration to protect the independence of the new Latin American nations. The United States considered Britain's request. However, the United States rejected it, preferring to issue its own policy statement.

In 1823, President James Monroe issued a statement that has become known as the Monroe Doctrine. In it, Monroe promised that the United States would not interfere in European affairs or with Europe's remaining colonies in the **Western Hemisphere**. The Western Hemisphere is the half of Earth that includes North and South America. At the same time, he warned Europeans not to try to take back their former colonies in the Western Hemisphere. European nations denounced the doctrine, but no one challenged it. For more than 100 years, the Monroe Doctrine remained the key to U.S. policy in the Americas.

◆ **What role did Creole military officers play in bringing independence to Latin America?**

Review III

Review History
A. How did race and place of birth limit the opportunities of many Latin Americans?
B. Why were many Latin Americans attracted to Enlightenment ideas?
C. How did the United States act to protect the newly independent Latin American countries?

Define Terms to Know
Define the following terms: **constitutional monarchy, Western Hemisphere**

Critical Thinking
Why do you think Simón Bolívar has often been called "the George Washington of South America"?

Write About Government
Write a brief conversation that might have taken place between Simón Bolívar and José de San Martín during the liberation of Peru.

Get Organized
CAUSE-AND-EFFECT CHAIN
Use a cause-and-effect chain to organize information from this section. Choose a topic and then find related facts. For example, think of an event, a cause, and an effect relating to the efforts of Touissant L'Ouverture in Haiti.

Critical Thinking
Possible answer: Bolívar was a leader in the independence movement; he brought about the independence of more South American countries than any other person.

Write About Government
Students' conversations should focus on how to achieve independence and what kind of government to establish.

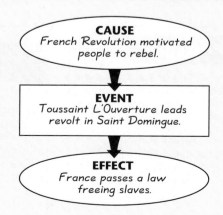

CAUSE
French Revolution motivated people to rebel.

EVENT
Toussaint L'Ouverture leads revolt in Saint Domingue.

EFFECT
France passes a law freeing slaves.

CONNECT
History&Government

Constitutional Monarchies

A constitutional monarchy is a system of government in which a nation's monarch is given limited power by that nation's lawmaking and governing body.

A constitutional monarchy has two main features. First, a monarch—king, queen, or emperor—is the hereditary head of state. Second, a constitution describes the way that the various parts of a government function.

Constitutional monarchies existed in Spain, Portugal, and Brazil, for example, and still exist today. In many of them, a constitution gives its legislature much of the governing power. In some cases, the monarch's advisors, or leaders such as a prime minister, make many of the executive decisions. The power given to the monarch varies from country to country.

Listed below are some countries that have constitutional monarchies as their form of government.

UNITED KINGDOM has a queen who has no official power. Most government decisions are made by the prime minister and his or her cabinet, and by the Parliament, which includes a House of Commons and a House of Lords.

SPAIN, in Europe, has a king as its ceremonial head of state. Spain's legislature consists of the Senate and the Congress of Deputies.

DENMARK, in Europe, has a queen as its head of state. She has the power to appoint the prime minister and the cabinet.

LESOTHO, in Africa, has a king with no official power. Most government decisions are made by the prime minister and cabinet. Its parliament consists of a National Assembly and a Senate.

BAHRAIN, in the Middle East, is led by a king who will help shape the new government. Its new government is currently being formed.

JAPAN, in Asia, has an emperor who has no official power. Most government decisions are made by an elected prime minister and a legislature.

Critical Thinking
Answer the questions below. Then, complete the activity.

1. What are the main characteristics of a constitutional monarchy?

2. Do you think that constitutional monarchies serve a purpose in the world today? Why or why not?

Write About It
Japan and the United Kingdom probably are today's two best-known constitutional monarchies. Use the Internet and reference books to learn more about their governments. Then, make a chart or Venn diagram that gives information about both governments and that shows their similarities and differences.

Japanese Emperor Akihito giving a speech in Tokyo in 2001.

Teaching Options

LINK to TODAY

Ask students to list the characteristics of a constitutional monarchy. Then, have them identify the kind of government we have in the United States. (republic) Have students make a Venn diagram (TR, p. 323) or another graphic organizer that shows the similarities and differences between a constitutional monarchy and the U.S. government.

FYI
Emperor Akihito
Tell students that in the photograph on page 479, Emperor Akihito is giving the opening oath for the National Diet (the Japanese legislature) in 2001. Emperor Akihito has ruled since the death of his father, Hirohito, in 1989. Japanese tradition says that he is the 125th direct descendant of Japan's first emperor, Jimmu.

CONSTITUTIONAL MONARCHIES

Teach the Topic
Ask students how French monarchs of the 1800s felt about a constitutional monarchy. (Louis XVIII accepted it; Charles X tried to get rid of it; Louis Philippe and Napoleon III accepted it, although Napoleon III restricted the legislature.)

UNITED KINGDOM Over time, the power of the House of Commons has increased. Ask students how that reflects social change in Great Britain. (It shows the growth of a middle class that wants representation in government.)

SPAIN After the death of dictator Francisco Franco in 1975, the Spanish monarchy was restored, and a constitution was established. Discuss the problems of a country transitioning from dictatorship to constitutional monarchy.

DENMARK Have students find the Danish constitution on the Internet. Have them look for the parts of the constitution having to do with a monarch's power.

LESOTHO According to Lesotho's constitution, a college of chiefs determines who will be king.

BAHRAIN The king of Bahrain promises to institute a prime minister and a cabinet of ministers, as well as a two-house National Assembly.

JAPAN Emperors have reigned in Japan for more than 1,500 years and have all descended from the same imperial family.

Critical Thinking
ANSWERS
1. A hereditary ruler is the head of state, but the functions of government are outlined in a constitution.
2. Possible answers: **No:** people need a voice in government, making the legislature more important. **Yes:** A monarch is important as a symbol of national unity.

Write About It
Students' charts should show the kind of monarchy and the name of the monarch in the United Kingdom and Japan.

CHAPTER
20 Review

Chapter Summary

A blank outline form is available in the Teacher Resources (p. 318). Chapter summaries should outline the new ideas and new directions in political thinking in the 1800s, the changes in France and eastern Europe as a result of these new ideas, and how these ideas led to wars of independence in Latin America. Refer to the rubric in the Teacher's Resources (p. 340) to score students' chapter summaries.

⬤ Interpret the Timeline

1. 1803
2. Serfdom was ended.
3. This was a time of great change in history, a time of hope for many.
4. Check that all events on students' timelines are in the chapter.

Use Terms to Know

5. c. liberalism
6. b. constitutional monarchy
7. e. reactionary
8. f. Western Hemisphere
9. d. nation-state
10. a. conservatism

Check Your Understanding

11. The ideology conservatism believes in supporting the existing way of doing things, and in opposing quick, major changes. Liberalism believes in individual freedom and social progress.
12. Where nationalism is strong, the people generally have a sense of unity that comes from a shared ethnic and cultural heritage, language, history, and experiences.
13. Working-class people rebelled and drove Louis Philippe out of France when he tried to shut down protests over food shortages and low employment.
14. In the first few years after the Congress of Vienna, Metternich remained very influential. He was committed to keeping peace and stability in Europe, so he pressured the major powers to stay out of the Greek war.
15. The Ottoman Empire was the "sick man of Europe," as its power declined and it lost its control over territories in the nineteenth century.

Chapter Summary

Complete the following outline in your notebook. Then, use your outline to write a brief summary of the chapter.

The Growth of Nationalism

I. New Ideas, New Directions
   A. Changes in Political Thinking
   B. France After Napoleon
II. Change in Eastern Europe
   A. Nationalism Leads to Revolt
   B. Russia's Involvement Grows
   C. Russia Faces Other Problems
III. Wars of Independence in Latin America
   A. Social Structure in Latin America
   B. Challenges to the System
   C. Revolution Spreads

⬤ Interpret the Timeline

Use the timeline on pages 460–461 to answer the following questions.

1. When did France sell the Louisiana Territory to the United States?
2. Why was the year 1861 a milestone for Russian serfs?
3. **Critical Thinking** What do all of the revolts in South America and Latin America tell you about this period of time in history?
4. Select five events from the chapter that are not on the timeline. Create a timeline of those events.

Use Terms to Know

Match each term with its definition.

a. conservatism   d. nation-state
b. constitutional   e. reactionary
   monarchy
c. liberalism   f. Western Hemisphere

5. the idea that generally encourages individual freedom and social progress
6. a government in which a ruler's powers are limited to those that the constitution and the laws of the country allow
7. a person who opposes change
8. the half of Earth that includes both North and South America
9. a self-governing land whose people share a common background, language, and history
10. the idea that generally supports existing ways of doing things and opposes quick, major changes

Check Your Understanding

11. **Summarize** the ideologies known as conservatism and liberalism.
12. **Identify** the conditions that are generally true in a place in which nationalism is strong.
13. **Explain** why Louis Philippe, the "Citizen King," left France for Great Britain.
14. **Explain** why the major powers of Europe were slow to become involved in the Greek war for independence.
15. **Summarize** the meaning of the expression "sick man of Europe."
16. **Identify** the two sides in the Crimean War and the main reason for their conflict.
17. **Contrast** the attitudes of Czar Nicholas I and Czar Alexander II toward the serfs of Russia.
18. **Explain** why France was not willing to grant independence to its colony on Hispaniola.
19. **Describe** the role of Simón Bolívar in South America's independence movement.

16. In the Crimean War, Russia faced an alliance of the Ottoman Turks, France, England, and Sardinia. The immediate cause of the war was Russia's move into Ottoman lands.
17. Nicholas I did nothing to help the serfs. Alexander II, on the other hand, set the serfs free in 1861 and established a program through which they could own land.

18. Saint Domingue, or Haiti, was the most productive French colony.
19. Simón Bolívar was perhaps the greatest leader of South America's independence movement. He helped bring about the liberation of Venezuela and was instrumental in securing the independence of other South American countries, including Colombia, Ecuador, and Peru.

Critical Thinking

20. **Evaluate** Was Charles X an effective leader of France? Why or why not?

21. **Hypothesize** Why do you think that Czar Alexander II was assassinated, despite his reforms?

22. **Analyze Primary Sources** Reread the words of Toussaint L'Ouverture on page 476. How does his statement illustrate the idea of nationalism?

Put Your Skills to Work

23. **Identify Ideologies** You have learned how to interpret an ideology, or a system of political thought, in political cartoons and written documents. Read the statement made by Prince Klemens von Metternich below. Then, answer the following questions.

   a. What is the main idea of Prince Metternich's statement?

   b. According to Prince Metternich, from where do kings get power?

   c. Which ideology does Prince Metternich support in this statement—conservatism or liberalism?

> "I am a true friend to order and public peace. As such . . . I am absolutely convinced that the governments ruled by kings must . . . stop the rioting and social unrest. By taking whatever steps are necessary, the kings will fulfill the duties which God . . . has given them power to do."
>
> —Adapted from Prince Metternich, *Secret Memorandum for Alexander I,* December 15, 1820

Analyze Sources

24. During the first half of the nineteenth century, Belgium, as well as many nation-states in the Balkans, gained their independence. Austrian chancellor Prince Klemens von Metternich is reported to have said at that time:

When Paris sneezes, Europe catches cold.

   a. What did Metternich probably mean when he referred to the "sneezing" of Paris?

   b. What did Metternich see as the relationship between events in Paris and events in the rest of Europe?

   c. Do you think that Metternich approved of the changes in Europe? On the basis of this quotation, how can you tell?

Essay Writing

25. Haiti sought independence earlier than any other Latin American country did. In addition, the independence movement swept Latin America more quickly than it swept Europe. In an essay, explain why you think the widespread push for independence happened in Latin America before it happened in Europe.

CHAPTER 20 ◆ The Growth of Nationalism **481**

Critical Thinking

20. Possible answer: Charles X was not an effective leader because he failed to understand and respond to the needs of most of his people. He took away many of their constitutional rights and tried to silence his critics.

21. Possible answer: His assassins may have felt that his reforms did not go far enough or that he was not dealing effectively with the problems of the new landowning system. Perhaps they wanted to get rid of the Russian monarchy altogether.

22. He calls for unity, urging his "brothers"—that is, enslaved black workers, people with a shared heritage and shared experiences—to join him in improving conditions in the land that they considered their home.

Put Your Skills to Work

IDENTIFY IDEOLOGIES

23a. He is against the ongoing struggles of people against their government and believes that kings should put an end to social unrest.
23b. from God
23c. conservatism

Analyze Sources

24a. Possible answer: It takes very little to cause big trouble.
24b. Very close; Europe relied on France for stability.
24c. No; he seemed to think the rest of Europe blew France's revolution out of proportion.

Essay Writing

25. Answers will vary. The fact that Latin Americans lived in colonies at a great distance from direct European control made an earlier, faster independence movement possible. Students may suggest that Latin America was in a more desperate economic situation than was Europe.

TEST PREPARATION

Answer 3. Napoleon Bonaparte abandoned the Americas.

Asia, Africa, and Australia in Transition
1550–1850
(pp. 482–502)

Chapter Objectives
• Discuss how the Qing Dynasty affected life in China and identify key characteristics of the Tokugawa Shogunate of Japan.
• Explore societies of Africa and how contact with Europeans changed the African societies.
• Describe the impact of colonization on Australia, New Zealand, Southeast Asia, and the Pacific Islands, and discuss the diverse cultures of those regions.

Chapter Summary
Section I focuses on the social orders, governments, philosophies, religions, economies, cultures, and the arts of the Qing Dynasty of China and the Tokugawa Shogunate of Japan.
Section II identifies various peoples of Africa and explains the history of their language, culture, and interaction with foreigners.
Section III describes the history, cultures, development, and colonization of Australia, Southeast Asia, and the Pacific Islands.

Set the Stage
TEACH PRIMARY SOURCES
The quotation on this page is the boast of a warrior chief about his military prowess. Discuss with students the importance of a strong military ruler both to the citizens of a nation and to other nations. (Students might point out that a military leader might be less tolerant of ideas from his citizens if their ideas contradict his rule. However, a strong military is an asset when protecting one's nation from invasion or attack by another nation.)

Asia, Africa, and Australia in Transition
1550–1850

I. Asian Empires
II. African Societies and States
III. Australia and Southeast Asia

The period between the sixteenth to nineteenth centuries was a time of transition, or change, in many parts of the world. On the continents of Asia, Africa, and Australia, power shifts and cultural changes affected progress. In Asia, the Qing Dynasty ruled China while the shoguns dominated Japan.

African societies continued to develop, but were under constant threat by Europeans. In response to this threat, one African group—the Zulus—established a strong military presence. Shaka, the most famous Zulu king, composed this song about his strength in the region:

66 *Who is it that opposes us?*
When we stab we proceed forward,
While there are some who retreat. 99

During this same period, Australia and New Zealand were just being colonized, while Pacific Island cultures were facing changes brought by Europeans.

CHAPTER EVENTS			
1596 First Dutch traders arrive in Southeast Asia.	**1600** Tokugawa Shogunate begins.	**1644** Manchus found Qing Dynasty.	

1550 ————————————————— 1650

WORLD EVENTS	
1588 English fleet defeats the Spanish Armada.	**1643** Louis XIV is crowned king of France.

482 UNIT 5 ◆ Enlightenment and Revolution

Teaching Options

Chapter 21 Resources

REVIEW

Teacher's Resources (TR)
Terms to Know, p. 34
Review History, p. 68
Build Your Skills, p. 102
Chapter Test, pp. 157–158
Concept Builder, p. 237
Five *W*s Chart, p. 326
Transparencies 1, 5, 7, 8

ASSESSMENT
Section Reviews, pp. 488, 494, 499
Chapter Review, pp. 500–501
Chapter Test, TR, pp. 157–158
Unit Test, TR, pp. 191–192

ALTERNATIVE ASSESSMENT
Portfolio Project, p. 502
Write an Editorial, p. T502

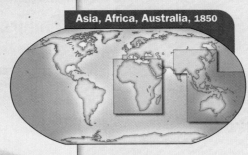

Asia, Africa, Australia, 1850

GET ORGANIZED

Five Ws Chart A Five Ws chart helps you to organize the most important details of an event, a place, or a person. Use Five Ws charts as you read Chapter 21. Make a chart with the Five Ws questions in one column. Then, fill in the other columns as you read. Here is an example from this chapter.

Who?	Tokugawa Shogunate
What?	Line of Tokugawa shoguns
Where?	Japan
When?	1600–1868
Why?	Tokugawa Ieyasu started a line of shoguns to control Japan.

VIEW HISTORY

Tell students that the illustration is of Zulu soldiers preparing for battle. Discuss with students what the illustration reveals about African warfare at this time. (Possible answer: People fought with spears and shields at close range.) Then, ask students how this compares to modern warfare. (Possible answer: Modern warfare is fought with bullets, bombs, planes, and other technological advances. Modern battles do not always involve hand-to-hand combat.)

ANSWER The painting shows that the Zulus fought with sharp spears and long shields.

GET ORGANIZED
Five Ws Chart
Review the five Ws chart with students. Point out that all five facts together give a complete picture of an event. Have students use the information in the chart to write a sentence that includes all five Ws. (Sample answer: In 1600, the Tokugawa period began, and the Tokugawa Shogunate controlled Japan until 1868.)

VIEW HISTORY The Zulu nation, in southern Africa, had strong military power. Zulu soldiers were taught to fight with sharp spears and were trained to move quickly. In this painting, a Zulu officer is inspecting his troops.
◆ What does the painting tell you about the types of weapons the Zulu troops used?

1770
Australia is claimed for Great Britain by James Cook.

1788
First convicts arrive in Australia from Great Britain.

1816
King Shaka of the Zulus begins rule.

1750

1850

1703
Peter the Great, czar of Russia, founds St. Petersburg.

1830
France invades Algeria.

CHAPTER 21 ◆ Asia, Africa, and Australia in Transition **483**

TEACH THE TIMELINE
The timeline on pages 482–483 covers the period between 1588 and 1830. Have students find events that involve the beginning of a new rule. (1600, Tokugawa Shogunate begins; 1643, Louis XIV is crowned king of France; 1644, Manchus found Qing Dynasty; 1816, King Shaka of the Zulus begins rule.)

Activity

Extend the timeline Without providing them with the relevant dates, have students research the following events and decide where they should be placed on the timeline: Akbar begins rule in India (1556); Shakespeare is born (1564); Roggeveen reaches Easter Island (1722).

Chapter Themes
• Culture
• Time, Continuity, and Change
• People, Places, and Environments
• Individual Development and Identity
• Individuals, Groups, and Institutions
• Power, Authority, and Governance
• Global Connections

F Y I

Shaka Zulu's Successors
A major challenge for Shaka's successors was the migration of Boer settlers. Shaka's immediate successor, Dingane, fought and killed many Boers. However, Boer intervention in Zulu domestic affairs led to his defeat. Mpande then became king of Zulu, and his son, Cetshwayo, came to power in 1872. Cetshwayo fought Great Britain for control over Zulu and the Boer republic of Natal but was defeated on July 4, 1879.

Section Summary

In this section, students will learn about the Manchus, the ruling family of the Qing Dynasty, and how this dynasty changed Chinese society. They will also learn about the third shogunate of Japan, begun by Tokugawa Ieyasu, and how Ieyasu's militaristic rule brought about a period of peace, prosperity, and culture.

1 Introduce

Getting Started

Tell students that sometimes rulers are from other areas or countries than those that they rule. These rulers are often more successful if they gain the respect of the people they rule. Ask students to suggest ways a leader can earn the respect of the people in the country. (Answers will vary.)

TERMS TO KNOW

Ask students to read the words and definitions on page 484 and find each word in the section. Then, have them look up the derivation of each word in the dictionary.

You may wish to preview the pronunciation of the following terms with students.

hui-kuan (hway gwan)
kung-so (koong saw)
Beijing (BAY jihng)
Tokugawa Ieyasu
  (toh koog ah wah ee eh yahs oo)
Shogunate (SHOH guh nayt)

ACTIVE READING

As students read this section, have them list events that they encounter and their causes and effects. For example, higher literacy during the Qing Dynasty caused the printing of more books. As a result, scholarship and creative writing flourished. You may want to distribute a cause-and-effect chain (TR, p. 325) to students.

Terms to Know

queue the pigtail worn by Chinese men to show submission to Manchus

Bushido the samurai code of loyalty and courage, and the preference of death to dishonor

Main Ideas

A. The Qing Dynasty in China had a peaceful and prosperous reign.

B. The Tokugawa Shogunate in Japan was a period of peace, prosperity, and culture.

Active Reading

CAUSE AND EFFECT
When you use cause and effect, you look for the reason that something happened. As you read this section, think about what caused the Qing Dynasty to be so successful. Then, think about the effects this dynasty had on Chinese society.

A. The Qing Dynasty in China

The Ming Dynasty managed to keep China secure until the Manchurian invasion in 1644. In that year, the Manchu people overthrew the Ming Dynasty and conquered China. They set up the Qing Dynasty, which remained in power until 1911. The Manchus, like the Ming before them, kept China isolated. This policy would cause serious problems for China when it had to deal with foreign countries in later years.

Rulers of the Qing Dynasty

The first emperor of the Qing Dynasty was six-year-old Fu-lin. Because of his young age, a regent ruled until Fu-lin was old enough to take over. As emperor, Fu-lin took the name Shunzi. He died of smallpox at age 23, and his six-year-old son, Kangxi, succeeded him. Kangxi reigned for 61 years and was considered one of the greatest emperors in Chinese history. During his reign, the empire increased its wealth and enjoyed relative peace and prosperity.

The Qing Dynasty lasted for more than 260 years. It ruled over an area unequaled in Chinese history. At its greatest, the dynasty controlled three times as much land as the Ming Dynasty had.

Social Order in the Qing Dynasty

Under the Qing Dynasty in China, the ruling class was at the top of the social order, followed by the farmers. Farmers were highly ranked because they produced food and paid taxes. Artisans produced goods but not food, so they were ranked just below farmers. Merchants moved goods, but they did not produce anything. Thus, they found themselves at the bottom of the social order.

There was some chance to move upward in rank. For example, a poor boy could move up by passing civil service exams. However, it was expensive to receive the education needed to pass the exams.

During the prosperity of the Qing Dynasty, people created new kinds of social ties. One of these was shared partnerships in which several people pooled their resources to start a business. A second type of organization was *hui-kuan*, a partnership in which people helped others who came from their same geographic area. There were special groups for officials and exam candidates, for immigrants, and for merchants. The *hui-kuan* gave people financial aid and a place to live.

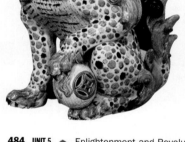

Artists of the Qing Dynasty were known for their fine porcelain figures, such as the dog shown here.

Teaching Options

Section 1 Resources

Teacher's Resources (TR)
Terms to Know, p. 34
Review History, p. 68
Build Your Skills, p. 102
Chapter Test, pp. 157–158
Concept Builder, p. 237
Five *W*s Chart, p. 326
Transparency 1

ESL/ELL STRATEGIES

Identify Essential Vocabulary Discuss the difference between a regent, a figurehead, and an emperor. A regent is a person appointed to rule when a monarch is absent, disabled, or too young. A figurehead is a person in a position of seeming power but who has no real authority. An emperor refers to the sovereign, or supreme, male monarch of an empire.

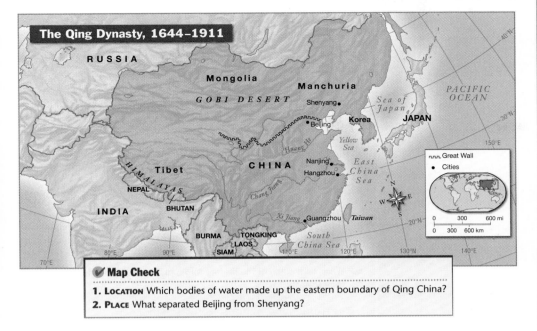

The Qing Dynasty, 1644–1911

RUSSIA

Mongolia

Manchuria

GOBI DESERT

Shenyang

Sea of Japan

PACIFIC OCEAN

Beijing

Korea

JAPAN

Yellow Sea

Tibet

CHINA

Nanjing

Hangzhou

East China Sea

HIMALAYAS

NEPAL

Chang Jiang

Huang He

Great Wall
Cities

INDIA

BHUTAN

Xi Jiang

Guangzhou

Taiwan

BURMA

TONGKING

LAOS

SIAM

South China Sea

0   300   600 mi
0   300   600 km

✔ **Map Check**
1. **LOCATION** Which bodies of water made up the eastern boundary of Qing China?
2. **PLACE** What separated Beijing from Shenyang?

A third type of organization was the *kung-so*, or guild. People in the same profession banded together to help one another.

Culture and the Arts

During the Qing Dynasty, art often attempted to recover customs and values of the past. Many people began to collect rubbings of inscribed stones from the Han period, about 1,800 years earlier. However, painting and porcelain were the most popular visual arts. Porcelain was in high demand in Europe. Europeans admired the beauty of porcelain and collected it. Other arts that developed and flourished at this time were furniture design and printmaking.

Literacy, or the ability to read and write, during the Qing Dynasty encouraged the printing of more books. Poetry was the highest art form. Other literary forms included collections of winning exam essays, route books for commercial travelers, and religious pamphlets and scriptures. In the 1730s, the emperor decided to publish all Chinese literature, which greatly benefited scholarship. However, censors burned all controversial books.

The Beijing opera began in 1790 as part of the emperor's birthday celebration. The actors and singers in a Chinese opera have painted faces. The colors of the face paint indicate a character's qualities, such as red for loyalty and black for boldness. The opera is sung in Mandarin Chinese dialect. A dialect is a form of spoken language peculiar to a place or group of people.

Government and Economics

The Manchu Qing rulers kept the same government organization as the Ming, the previous dynasty, had. The government's official philosophy was neo-Confucian, a way of controlling people by insisting on the values of the past. The Manchu were considered a foreign dynasty and were in the

Spotlight on
Culture

CHINESE PORCELAIN
The European demand for Chinese porcelain was high. The early Qing era, from 1680 to 1750, produced magnificent porcelain. Qing porcelain, made both for the court and for export, was known for its detailed decoration and variety of colors.

Cooperative Learning

Have students work in groups to prepare displays on some aspect of life during the Qing Dynasty, such as social order, government, economy, religion, philosophy, or the arts. Groups should assign roles for various tasks so that some students prepare commentary while others create the display. Have groups present their displays to the class.

Connection to
MUSIC ←

Chinese opera combines singing, acting, dancing, acrobatics, poetry, and music to create a total story. Play an example of Chinese opera to the class—such as *White Snake*, an opera based on a fairy tale about a snake that can metamorphose into a beautiful woman. Encourage students to comment on the instrumentation of the music. Share an English translation of opera with students if available.

---

2 Teach

A. The Qing Dynasty in China

Purpose-Setting Question What are three new types of social ties that were created during the Qing Dynasty? (shared partnerships, *hui-kuan* partnership, and *kung-so*, or guilds)

Discuss Ask students why new organizations might develop in a society when old bonds, such as kinship, lose their power. (They fill a need, people like to be part of groups, people need connections to others.)

Using the Map
The Qing Dynasty, 1644–1911

Remind students that under the Ming Dynasty, the area of the Chinese Empire was significantly smaller than the area controlled by the Qing Dynasty. (The western border of the Ming Dynasty extended just past the Huang He.) Ask students if the additional territory made the Qing Dynasty more powerful. (Answers should show an understanding that more land equals more resources and more people but also more responsibility and difficulty in keeping borders protected and different peoples united.)

✔ **Map Check**
Answers
1. Pacific Ocean, South China Sea, East China Sea, Yellow Sea, Sea of Japan
2. the Great Wall

SPOTLIGHT ON CULTURE

CHINESE PORCELAIN Ask students how the export of Chinese porcelain might affect the Europeans' view of Chinese society. (Students might say that Europeans considered the Chinese highly skilled in the technical aspect of porcelain making and in the craft of decorative arts. This might have led them to think that the Chinese were an intelligent and creative people.)

minority. Therefore, they had to balance their culture with the culture of the Chinese. The Qing rulers encouraged Manchu people to keep their language and culture, and all government documents were written in both Chinese and Manchu. The most hated policy of the Manchu was that they forced Chinese men to wear their hair in one long pigtail, called a **queue**, as a sign of loyalty and submission to Manchu rule.

Philosophical and Religious Ideas

China's main religions and philosophies remained Confucianism, Daoism, and Buddhism. At this time, Confucianism stressed moral standards, a well-ordered society, avoidance of extremes or excesses, and respect for ancestors and for the past. Daoism influenced the art of the time. It emphasized nature and harmony. Buddhism, while receiving no state support, still attracted followers.

Toward the end of the eighteenth century, a group called the White Lotus was dedicated to overthrowing the Manchu government. During this time, many people in China suffered from famine and poor living conditions. The leaders of the White Lotus society promised people that Buddha would return and end their suffering if the people rebelled. The rebellion against the Manchus lasted for nine years before it was stopped.

◆ **What were some of the literary forms that were printed during the Qing Dynasty?**

B. The Tokugawa Shogunate in Japan

In the last years of the Ming Dynasty, China's neighbor Japan was also undergoing changes. As you learned in Chapter 11, Japan's 66 provinces were brought together by warlords, such as Toyotomi Hideyoshi, under one government. Hideyoshi built a strong group of alliances. These alliances helped establish peace throughout the land.

After Hideyoshi's death in 1598, however, the alliances broke apart. Several generals fought for control of Japan. Finally, in 1600, Tokugawa Ieyasu became the new shogun, or supreme military governor. Ieyasu started a line of Tokugawa shoguns who ruled for more than 250 years. The emperor, who had little military power, continued his role as figurehead, or symbolic ruler.

Tokugawa Rule

As leader of Japan, Ieyasu built a strong government. He moved the center of government to Edo, which is now Tokyo. He also formed a secret police to keep watch for any plans against the government. The samurai, or warrior class, defended Ieyasu from his enemies. The daimyo, or Japanese lords, kept their lands in the countryside. However, Ieyasu restricted their power. Daimyo now needed permission from the shogun to sign a contract or arrange a daughter's marriage. Also, the daimyo had to live in Edo every other year. Their families had to live in Edo year-round as a way to prevent the daimyo from rebelling against the shogun.

Another method of control enforced by the shogun was to isolate, or limit contact, between Japan and the rest of the world. European traders and Christian missionaries began going to Japan in the 1540s. By 1639, almost all the foreigners had been expelled from Japan or killed. No Japanese people were allowed to leave the country, and

This painting on a silk scroll shows a shogun of the Tokugawa Shogunate.

486 UNIT 5 ◆ Enlightenment and Revolution

Teaching Options

Research

AVERAGE

Have students research information about the development of kabuki theater under the support of the Tokugawa shoguns. Then, ask students to prepare and present an oral report about kabuki drama that focuses on its origins, major characteristics, and audience. Students might want to add value to their reports by creating accompanying visuals.

CHALLENGE

Have students research and then compare and contrast the samurai and the medieval knight. Students may use material from Chapter 12, library sources, and the Internet. Students should write essays that focus on required skills, the allegiance pledged to the emperor or lord, and the daily life of a samurai or knight.

those already abroad were killed if they returned. Foreign trade was restricted to Chinese, Dutch, and Korean ships. Japan kept this isolation policy until 1853.

Social Order Under the Shoguns

Japanese social order was based on the Chinese system, which used Confucian principles of a well-ordered society. The emperor, although powerless, and the shogun were at the very top. The main classes of society were based on their usefulness. The most useful, and thus ranked highest, were the samurai. The farmers were ranked the second highest because they produced food.

Artisans were producers of goods, not food. Therefore, as in China, they were ranked lower than farmers. Merchants produced nothing, but moved goods from one person or group to another. They were regarded as less important than farmers or artisans. Most people had to remain in the class into which they were born, with few exceptions.

The samurai served their daimyo and, by extension, the shogun. The samurai protected both the daimyo and shoguns from attack and enforced laws. Even though the Tokugawa Shogunate was considered peaceful, there were more than 2,000 peasant rebellions. The samurai worked to put down these rebellions. Samurai were expected to exhibit loyalty, honor, courage, and self-discipline. Their code was called **Bushido**.

Art and Culture

During the Tokugawa Shogunate, art and culture flourished. The isolation of the country forced artists to concentrate on Japan and Japanese culture. Peacetime also gave the Japanese people more time to enjoy art and culture. Even the samurai turned their attention to other arts. The fifth Tokugawa shogun set up schools that taught Japanese philosophy along with samurai skills. These schools began to hold games that trained the body and the mind. Many samurai learned to write as well as to fight.

Under the Tokugawa shoguns, two kinds of theater appeared. One was kabuki theater, a popular musical drama with elaborate and colorful costumes, painted faces, and stories based on current society or history. Kabuki was the first theater for common people in Japan. The second type of theater was the bunraku puppet shows. Large, lifelike puppets would act out adventure or love stories.

Do You Remember?
In Chapter 11, you learned that the emperor was the social and religious leader in Japan. However, he had little power. The real power lay with the shogun.

The actors in this modern-day performance are continuing a tradition dating to the time of the Tokugawa Shogunate.

Do You Remember?
Discuss the reasons for having an emperor if he had no real power. (Students may say that he kept the country unified and preserved social and religious values rather than enforcing laws.)

Activity

Write a book review Have students write a review of a historical book on the Tokugawa Shogunate. The review should include information on one aspect of the government. Remind students that the object of a book review is to entice others to read the book. For help with writing style, students might want to read actual reviews in the newspaper or on the Internet.

Extend Have students conduct research in the library or on the Internet to learn more about the samurai code, Bushido. Students should look for information about Bushido's connections to Buddhism, Zen, Confucianism, and Shintoism. When they have completed their research, students should share what they have learned with the rest of the class.

TEACH PRIMARY SOURCES
Direct students' attention to the photograph of a modern-day kabuki performance on page 487. Have them describe the scene. (Students might mention the elaborate makeup and costumes and the outdoor setting.) Have students compare the photograph to a drama that they might have seen in the United States: What style of costumes and makeup was used? What kind of stage design was used? What was the purpose of the play? (Answers will vary.) Then, ask students how kabuki and theater in the United States continue cultural traditions. (Possible answer: Plays—and the style in which they are performed—are a living record of history and culture.)

Meet Individual Needs:
VISUAL/SPATIAL LEARNERS

Have students view the 1954 action film *The Seven Samurai* by Akira Kurosawa. The film is set in sixteenth-century Japan. It tells the story of a small village that hires seven unemployed samurai to defend it against bandit raids. After viewing the film, discuss how it enhanced students' understanding of samurai during the time of the shogun.

Connection to
CULTURE

The tea ceremony is a Japanese ritual conducted in simple teahouses or special rooms. It is based on Zen Buddhism and intended to promote purity, cleanliness, harmony, respect, and a tranquil mind. Ritual tea drinking was first performed in China. It began in Japan when Zen monks drank tea to stay awake for meditation.

ANALYZE PRIMARY SOURCES

DOCUMENT-BASED QUESTION

The haiku on page 488 can be found in Basho's travel journal, *The Narrow Road to the Deep North*. Basho (1644–1694) based this work on his five-month journey into the country northwest of Edo in 1689. Recent scholars claimed to have found the original manuscript of this work in the library of an Osaka bookseller. *The Narrow Road to the Deep North* is still read by most Japanese high school students.

ANSWER It means that warriors dream of things that they may not have.

◆ **ANSWER** The role of the samurai was to protect their daimyo and the shogun from attack and rebellion and to enforce laws.

Section Close

Have students create a two-column chart (TR, p. 328) that compares the Qing Dynasty of China to the Tokugawa Shogunate of Japan. Rows of the chart should include type of government, economy, social order, religions, and popular arts and entertainment.

3 Assess

Review Answers

Review History

A. Possible answers: It was peaceful and prosperous. Kinship bonds loosened, art and literature flourished. It was traditional, and government philosophy was Confucianism.

B. bonsai gardening, haiku and senryu poetry, kabuki theater, bunraku puppet shows, woodblock printing

Define Terms to Know

queue, 486; Bushido, 487

Poems were part of the popular literature during the Tokugawa period. Haiku, which is still popular, is a type of short poem. A haiku has only 17 syllables and is divided into three lines. It tries to capture a scene or mood in a few words. The theme is usually nature or the seasons. Matsuo Basho is the best-known haiku poet. He made haiku into a serious form of writing in the late 1600s. Another short poem style that became popular was the senryu. Its form was similar to the haiku, but it used humorous themes. Here is an English translation of a Japanese haiku by Basho:

ANALYZE PRIMARY SOURCES
DOCUMENT-BASED QUESTION
What do you think this haiku means?

> ❝ Summer grass
> All that remains
> Of warriors' dreams. ❞

Woodblock prints and paintings of everyday themes were also very popular in Japan during the Tokugawa Shogunate. Other forms of beauty developed at this time were bonsai, or landscape gardening, and a form of the tea ceremony. Weaving, pottery, ceramics, and lacquerware also were very advanced.

Isolation of Japan

For most of its history under the Tokugawa shoguns, Japan remained isolated from the West. For a brief time, Ieyasu allowed Christian missionaries from Portugal and Spain to teach their religion in Japan. In exchange, the Japanese traded with Portuguese and Spanish merchant ships. However, Iemitsu, Ieyasu's grandson, feared that the Europeans would change his people. In 1640, he ended the Portuguese and Spanish visits to Japan and kept the Japanese from sailing to Europe. He expelled the missionaries and treated the Japanese Christians harshly. He feared the Christians would grow strong enough to overthrow him. Following these actions by the shogun, Japan had little contact with the West for the next 200 years.

◆ **What was the role of the samurai?**

Review I

Review History
A. What were two important features of the Qing Dynasty?
B. What were some of the arts that developed during the Tokugawa period?

Define Terms to Know
Define the following terms:
queue, Bushido

Critical Thinking
Why do you think the shogun imposed restrictions on the daimyo?

Write About History
Write a letter to a daimyo stating your reasons for wanting to be a samurai and why you believe you are qualified.

Get Organized
FIVE Ws CHART
Use a Five *W*s chart to organize information from this section. Choose a topic and then find the answers to the five questions. For example, what are the important facts about the Qing Dynasty?

Who?	
What?	
Where?	
When?	
Why?	

Critical Thinking

Possible answer: The shogun probably imposed restrictions on the daimyo to keep them from gaining too much power and rebelling against the shogun.

Write About History

Students' letters should include at least two to three reasons for wanting to be a samurai, such as their qualifications: good physical condition, expertise with a sword, and a sense of commitment.

Who?	Manchu emperors
What?	A family of emperors who set up the Qing Dynasty
Where?	China
When?	1644-1911
Why?	Longest reigning in Chinese history

Build Your Skills

Build Your Skills

IMPROVE YOUR TEST-TAKING SKILLS

Study Skill

IMPROVE YOUR TEST-TAKING SKILLS

Standardized tests usually have four types of questions. They are multiple-choice, true-false, short-answer, and matching questions. There are many strategies to help you do well on a test. Learn as much as you can about the test format.

First, make a study checklist, using notes and the text to make an outline of the major topics you have studied and are expected to know for the test.

The next step is to make a detailed summary sheet for each major topic, using key words or phrases. It is helpful to write the key words in a question form. If you do so for all of the topics, you can use the summary sheet to review for the test, and you will not need to use the textbook.

Other important strategies include reading and following the directions carefully, budgeting your time, and checking your work carefully.

Here's How
Follow these steps to help you succeed on a standardized test.

1. Read the entire test item and all of the answer choices before answering.

2. Rephrase each question in your own words to make sure you understand it, especially in sentences that contain double negatives.

3. Answer the questions you know first.

4. Your first instinct is usually correct. Do not change your answer unless you are reasonably sure that you were wrong.

Here's Why
Improving your test-taking skills is a good way to improve your test scores.

Practice the Skill
Use what you have learned about good test-taking strategies to answer the Test Preparation questions on the right.

Extend the Skill
Use the information found in Section I of this chapter to write another test question and possible answers using a format of your choice. Exchange your questions with a classmate and answer the question.

Apply the Skill
As you read the rest of the chapter, create a detailed summary sheet for each main topic. Then, use your summary sheets to complete the Chapter Review.

TEST PREPARATION

Read the questions below and choose the correct answers.

A. Which of the following does not describe the Qing Dynasty in China?

1. It was first ruled by Fu-lin.

2. It was a dynasty that lasted for more than 260 years.

3. It was not a prosperous dynasty.

4. More books were printed during this dynasty.

B. Which of the following statements is true?

1. Japan's provinces split apart in the sixteenth century.

2. By 1639, Japan was isolated from the rest of the world.

3. Japan's shogun was allowed to be foreign-born.

4. Art and culture suffered during the Tokugawa Shogunate.

CHAPTER 21 ◆ Asia, Africa, and Australia in Transition **489**

IMPROVE YOUR TEST-TAKING SKILLS

Teach the Skill
Ask students to name some factors that make test taking difficult. (Sample responses: finding time to study, being sure of the material that the test will cover, getting "stuck" on difficult questions, choosing between similar answers, organizing answers to essay questions)

Explain that the steps in *Here's How* can help them improve their scores on both objective and subjective tests. Review the tips with students and invite them to suggest other techniques they have found to be helpful. If anyone describes a self-defeating practice, such as "cramming" the night before, help students recognize the potential negative effects of the practice.

Practice the Skill

TEST PREPARATION

Answers
A: 3. It was not a prosperous dynasty.
B: 2. By 1639, Japan was isolated from the rest of the world.

Extend the Skill
After pairs share their questions with each other, provide time for sharing with the class. Encourage feedback from the class as you listen closely to determine whether students have a clear understanding of this study technique.

Apply the Skill
After students complete their summary sheets, have partners review them for accuracy. If students have difficulty in completing their sheets, you may wish to create a sample summary. It can serve as a model when students prepare for future tests.

Teaching Options

RETEACH
After students read each section of Chapter 21, work as a class to write section summaries. Encourage students to write detailed summaries about the entire content of the section and avoid focusing on just one or two subheadings. Remind them to include information about features and visuals.

CHALLENGE
Encourage pairs of students to exchange their summary sheets and review each other's work. Have pairs give each other feedback on any important section concepts that are not included in their summary sheets.

II. African Societies and States (pp. 490–494)

Section Summary

In this section, students will learn about the peoples of West and Central Africa. They will also learn about the livelihoods of the Khoisan and Bantu-speaking peoples of southern Africa. Lastly, students will learn about European interactions with Africans and the impact those interactions had on African society.

1 Introduce

Getting Started

Ask students to describe what they would do if a resource they depended on was no longer available where they lived. (Possible answers: They would purchase it on the Internet or at a store that carried imports; they would move to a place where the resource was more readily available.) Tell students that between the sixteenth and eighteenth centuries, Africans traded or migrated to obtain essential resources.

TERMS TO KNOW

Ask students to read the words and definitions on page 490 and find each word in the section. Then, have students write a sentence using each of the words.

You may wish to preview the pronunciation of the following terms with students.

Ashanti (uh SHAN tee)
Osei Tutu (oh SAH too too)
Khoisan (KOY sahn)
Nguni (uhn GOO nee)
Xhosa (KOH sah)

ACTIVE READING

Ask students to write a summary statement at the end of each subsection. You may wish to have students use the main idea/supporting details chart (TR, p. 319) to record details that support each summary sentence.

Section II — African Societies and States

Terms to Know

chiefdom centralized African political system with hereditary offices

Boers Dutch settlers in South Africa

Main Ideas

A. Several large kingdoms developed in West and Central Africa in the sixteenth through the eighteenth centuries.

B. Southern Africa was home to many distinct culture groups, each having its own heritage.

C. Portuguese, Dutch, and British traders became settlers in southern Africa.

Active Reading

SUMMARIZE
When you summarize, you include only the main points. As you read this section, concentrate on the main points about the African states and societies. Then, pause to summarize what you have learned.

A. West and Central African States and Societies

The sixteenth through the eighteenth centuries in Africa was a time of many great empires, migrations of nomadic groups, and the beginnings of contact with Europeans. In the 1700s, Muslim religious reformers waged holy wars in western Africa to strengthen Islam.

West African Kingdoms and States

By 1700, the largest kingdoms in West Africa were the Ashanti, the Benin, and the Kanem-Bornu. A group of seven states, known as the Hausa States, was also powerful, but not united under a single government.

The Ashanti kingdom on Africa's Gold Coast was made up of many small states that had once been independent. These states were forced to unify under a single king in the 1600s. One of these kings was Osei Tutu. His reign, followed by that of his grandnephew, lasted for about 150 years.

This bronze plaque from Benin shows an armored chief accompanied by armed warriors.

During the late 1600s, the Ashanti kingdom expanded—both in population, which swelled to several million people, and in physical size. One important industry of the Ashanti kingdom at this time was the production of small weights made of brass, a mixture of the metals copper and zinc. These weights were used to weigh gold dust collected from the region's rivers.

Many Ashanti served the king as warriors. Their job included the defense of the kingdom as well as the expansion of its borders. Warfare, however, did not always benefit the kingdom. Several of the wars weakened the Ashanti kingdom and eventually helped bring it to its end.

Benin, one of Africa's largest and most successful kingdoms in the sixteenth and seventeenth centuries, was known for its bronze art, which is still highly prized today. Benin was also known for its architecture. Its *iya*, or earthen walls, have been compared to the Great Wall of China. The Benin people used these walls to protect themselves against outsiders. Benin men were also skilled warriors. Their armor included battle shields made from raffia, a fiber from a leaf that is used as a string and woven.

Another of Africa's largest kingdoms included Kanem-Bornu, which developed in the Sudan around Lake Chad. It was an important center in the trans-Saharan trade. Kanem-Bornu also

Teaching Options

Section 2 Resources

Teacher's Resources (TR)
Terms to Know, p. 34
Review History, p. 68
Build Your Skills, p. 102
Chapter Test, pp. 157–158
Concept Builder, p. 237
Five *W*s Chart, p. 326
Transparency 5

F Y I

Griots

Most West African societies had no universal system of reading and writing. Oral literature—including histories, myths, songs, and proverbs—was communicated by a *griot*. A griot, or praise singer, would combine a narrative with music and use call-response techniques. A griot's job was essential to his people, entertaining them and educating them about their ancestors and traditions.

traded with Egypt and Kush to the east. In 1086, the king of Kanem-Bornu converted to Islam. This strengthened the kingdom's ties to Muslims in the north and east. By the late sixteenth century Kanem-Bornu controlled a huge portion of the trans-Saharan trade, and gained fame for having an effective cavalry. This armored cavalry helped support and expand the kingdom. Kanem-Bornu lasted until the mid-1800s.

The Hausa States were loosely united by their first king in 999. The states thrived on agriculture and trade and competed with one another for control of the trade routes. The great wealth of the region led to invasions by outsiders, causing its eventual downfall.

Central African Kingdoms

In Central Africa, the Kongo kingdom began in the fourteenth century and lasted until the seventeenth century. In 1491, the Portuguese converted many of Kongo's people to Christianity. By 1578, a Portuguese writer referred to Kongo as a large kingdom of six provinces, each ruled by a governor. Although the king had political and religious power, he had no army.

Kongo artisans excelled in cloth production. They also raised grains, rice, citrus fruits, bananas, coconuts, cucumbers, pineapples, and several kinds of palm trees. From the different palm trees they obtained wine, vinegar, oil, fruit, and bread.

The Luba and the Lunda were Bantu-speaking groups in south-central Africa. The Luba kingdom, which thrived in the 1500s and 1600s, had a powerful army and traded in copper, iron tools, and salt. The Lunda kingdom became one of central Africa's largest empires around the 1740s.

◆ **What was the Benin kingdom known for?**

B. Southern African Peoples

Southern Africa was home to many different groups and kingdoms from the sixteenth through the eighteenth centuries. Mobility was a characteristic shared by many southern African peoples.

The Zimbabwe Region

The region around what is now Zimbabwe saw a number of groups rise to power. One group called the Torwas moved the capital of the region from the ancient walled city of Great Zimbabwe to Khami. The Torwas continued to use the techniques of stonebuilding and pottery making of the Zimbabwe people until the end of the seventeenth century.

The Khoisan

The Khoisan people formed from two groups, the Khoikhoi, or Khoi, and the San. These groups had very little in common except language. Both used clicking sounds as consonants.

The San were hunter-gatherers, and the only domestic animals they kept were dogs. Their hunting groups consisted of small bands of people. The San had few material possessions except for their bows and arrows. The San also

African Kingdoms, 1500–1800

Mediterranean Sea

SAHARA
HAUSA STATES
KANEM-BORNU
ASHANTI
BENIN
Lake Chad
IBO
ETHIOPIA
Lake Victoria
ATLANTIC OCEAN
LUBA
KONGO
Lake Tanganyika
LUNDA
Lake Nyasa
MWENE MATAPA
ROZWI
KALAHARI DESERT
Sotho-Tswana
KHOISAN
Nguni
INDIAN OCEAN
Red Sea

African kingdoms
Area of Ottoman control

0   500   1,000 mi
0 500 1,000 km

✔ Map Check

REGION In which area of Africa was the Luba kingdom located?

Do You Remember?
In Chapter 10, you learned that the settlement known as Great Zimbabwe began in the 1100s and reached its height during the thirteenth and fourteenth centuries.

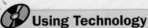

Connection to ART

African art has had a lasting effect on modern examples of various styles of creative media. For example, Western artists—such as Pablo Picasso, Henri Matisse, and Jacques Lipchitz—were influenced by African art. Many modern African American and Caribbean music genres—such as ragtime, jazz, and reggae—also use African syncopated rhythms as the foundation of their sounds.

Using Technology

Have students do a search on the Internet using the phrase "Hausa States" as a search term. Have them check at least four sites; pick one that offers solid, interesting historical information; and take notes on what they learn. Suggest that students look for sites that have .org and .edu in their addresses, indicating nonprofit organizations or educational institutions. Then, have students present an oral report of their findings.

② Teach

A. West and Central African States and Societies

Purpose-Setting Question In which western and central African kingdoms was trade important to the economy? (Kanem-Bornu kingdom, Hausa States, Luba kingdom)

Using the Map
African Kingdoms, 1500–1800

Remind students that many kingdoms in Africa developed because of trade with other lands. Discuss with students the different modes of travel that were available at that time. (camels, ships, caravans) Have students study the map on page 491. Ask students to plot out a trade route from a western African kingdom, such as Benin to the Mediterranean Sea. Then, have them plan a route from a southern African kingdom, such as Khoisan to the southern tip of the Red Sea. Lastly, have students suggest a trade route from the Ethiopian kingdom to the Ashanti kingdom. Students may plot their courses on an outline map (TR, p. 334) or they may describe their routes in a short paragraph.

✔ Map Check
Answer Central Africa near Lake Tanganyika

◆ **ANSWER** Benin is known for its bronze art and unique architecture.

B. Southern African Peoples

Purpose-Setting Question What were the major industries of the southern African peoples? (hunting and gathering, herding, agriculture)

Do You Remember?
Discuss with students how the stone wall enclosures of Great Zimbabwe offered protection for a capital city and why people of this region later moved the capital to a different location. (One reason for moving the location of a capital might be that people have migrated to a different region.)

Extend Ask students to speculate on problems that might have occurred in a Khoi chiefdom because an official's qualifications were based solely on heritage. (Possible answer: Tribal problems were not solved because the official did not have any problem-solving skills.)

Then & Now

WAR SHIELDS Shields—made of material strong enough to stop the piercing point of a spear—were considered an essential part of a warrior's uniform. Ask students how the concept of the shield is incorporated into modern-day uniforms of most police officers and soldiers. (They wear bulletproof vests or clothing.)

◆ **ANSWER** The San and Khoi had a common language, and both used clicking sounds as consonants.

C. Europeans in Southern Africa

Purpose-Setting Question What are some ways that Europeans changed the cultures of the peoples of southern Africa? (Possible answers: Europeans overtook the trading power of certain kingdoms; Europeans claimed African territory as their own; Europeans introduced Christianity to Africa.)

---

created beautiful rock paintings that have been useful to historians in studying the San way of life.

The Khoi people were cattle herders. Cattle provided them with a source of food as well as clothing. In addition to herding cattle, the Khoi also raised sheep, and they hunted and gathered. They did not, however, raise crops.

Over a number of years, the two groups blended their cultures and ways of life. The Khoi learned better hunting techniques from the San. The San adapted their ways to Khoi **chiefdoms**, centralized political systems with hereditary offices. A chiefdom typically had several hundred people. When a chiefdom became too large to herd all the cattle together, the groups would be split into two chiefdoms.

Bantu-Speaking People

Many Bantu-speaking groups also lived in southern Africa. As their population increased, they spread into ever-wider areas and developed many language and culture groups. The two major groups are the Nguni—which include the Zulus—and the Sotho-Tswanas.

The Nguni people were a settled group that hunted and grew crops. However, its main wealth was in cattle. The Sotho-Tswana people lived to the north of the Nguni and were more dependent on agriculture. Both Bantu-speaking groups were organized into chiefdoms. However, unlike the Khoisan, the leadership of the chiefdoms was not hereditary.

The Zulus and King Shaka

The Zulus were farming people in southern Africa. A serious drought caused them to seek new grazing lands. In addition, Europeans were beginning to push the Zulus from their lands. King Shaka was a Zulu military leader from 1816 to 1828. He invented a short-handled stabbing spear to replace the long-handled throwing spear. Shaka also designed a body-length cowhide shield for better protection in battle. As a field commander, Shaka devised battle formations that improved his army's chances for winning and gave his kingdom strong military power. Shaka conquered more than a hundred chiefdoms to expand his kingdom.

Shaka was often a cruel ruler. When his mother died, he had his army kill many people because they did not show enough sorrow. In 1828, Shaka was killed by his half-brothers, one of whom, Dingane, became king.

◆ **What did the San and Khoi peoples have in common?**

C. Europeans in Southern Africa

First the Portuguese, then the Dutch, and finally the British found reasons to set up trading posts, supply stations, or other settlements in southern Africa. These groups forever changed the cultures of the native peoples who had lived there for thousands of years.

The Portuguese

The Portuguese voyages to both the east and west coasts of southern Africa helped to bring the continent into the world economy. In addition, they placed Africa under the domination of Europe. Portuguese traders wanted ivory, gold, and other minerals from southern Africa. As a result, they began trading relations with the people living in the region. By the late 1600s, the Portuguese had succeeded in completely overtaking the trading power of the indigenous peoples.

Then & Now

WAR SHIELDS
Zulu war shields were made by stretching and drying cowhide in the sun, then burying the shields under manure for two days, and finally pounding them with stones. The hides were taken from cattle bred for their skin patterns and colors, so that all of the warriors in a regiment had the same color shield.

Today, riot police who need to control large crowds also carry shields. Made from clear polycarbonate, the shields protect police officers from bullets and flying objects.

Teaching Options

Writing

AVERAGE

Have students write a summary about the governments of the southern African peoples. Ask them to reread and take notes on pages 491 and 492 before they begin writing. Remind them to use their own words in their summaries and to include only key details from the text.

CHALLENGE

Ask students to write a poem or story about the blending of culture and ways of life between the Khoi and San peoples. Encourage students to include realistic details by using information in the text and outside resources. Have volunteers read their poems or stories aloud to the class.

In addition to establishing trade networks, Portugal was also interested in spreading Christianity in the region. Missionaries to southern Africa saw some success in their efforts to convert indigenous peoples to Christianity.

The Dutch

The British were the first Europeans to claim parts of present-day South Africa in 1615. However, they did not establish a permanent settlement. In 1652, Jan van Riebeeck and 125 men working for the Dutch East India Company set up a supply station and claimed the Cape of Good Hope for the Netherlands. Their goal was to establish a place for Dutch ships to stock up on supplies on their way to and from the East Indies. In 1657, some of the company's employees began to farm and raise cattle. The farmers were not allowed to enslave the local people, so slaves were brought from other parts of Africa and from Southeast Asia to work the farms.

The Dutch Cape settlers were called **Boers** from the Dutch word for farmer. Huguenots, or Protestants escaping persecution in Roman Catholic France, joined them in the 1680s. The group of Dutch, French, and other settlers living in the Cape of Good Hope colony eventually called themselves Afrikaners. They spoke a blended language they called Afrikaans.

The British

The British government took the Cape Colony from the Dutch in 1795. They established their own colony to protect their sea route to India and to expand their markets. Traders, settlers, and Christian missionaries made up the colony. Despite the resistance of Dutch farmers who depended on slave labor, the British abolished slavery in 1834.

Boer farmers were unhappy with British policies, especially the abolition—or elimination—of slavery. They began a journey, known as the Great Trek, which led them north and east. The Great Trek was a revolt against radical British policies. Most of the Trekkers believed that it was God's will that they

In 1652, Jan van Riebeeck founded a resupply station for the Dutch East India Company at Table Bay.

Do You Remember?
In Chapter 16, you learned that Europeans became involved in the slave trade and sold African slaves to the Americas.

Meet Individual Needs:
VERBAL/LINGUISTIC LEARNERS

Tell students that the Portuguese first arrived in an area known as the Gold Coast in West Africa. Gold had been found there and then traded across the Sahara and into North Africa. Ask students to speculate about how the first Portuguese gained knowledge about the rich resources of the area. Then, have them create a dialogue between a Portuguese explorer and an African leader about establishing a trading relationship.

Connection to
GOVERNMENT

Explain to students that the Dutch and the British continued to battle over control of South Africa throughout the nineteenth and twentieth centuries until the latter half of the twentieth century when Afrikaners took control of the government. They established apartheid, a legal system of strict racial segregation. It was not until 1990 and 1991 that South Africa repealed its apartheid laws.

Discuss Ask students why they think the early Dutch farmers were not allowed to enslave the local Africans. (Possible answers: This might have created bad relationships with the local people; local slaves might have found it easier to escape.)

Do You Remember?
Ask students to recall how the slave trade began and how it benefited the Europeans as well as some Africans. (The slave trade began in the 1400s when Europeans used African slaves to work as laborers on large plantations. The slave trade benefited some African rulers, European merchants, and European and American plantation owners.)

Activity

Write test questions Have students work individually to write possible test questions and the answers about the different groups of people in southern Africa. Then, have pairs of students exchange and answer the questions. Select different types of questions for the class to discuss together.

Focus Ask students to name the four European countries that most settlers in southern Africa came from. (Portugal, Great Britain, the Netherlands, and France) You may wish to use Transparency 5 to reinforce the location of these countries.

TEACH PRIMARY SOURCES
Have students examine the painting on page 493. Ask students to describe what is happening. (Jan van Riebeeck and his men are conversing with native Africans while holding a flag of the Netherlands.) Have students comment on how the painting depicts the relationship between the Dutch explorers and the Africans. For example, would they describe the two sides as equal? If not, which side seems more powerful? What details in the painting support their responses? (Possible answer: The Dutch are shown as more powerful because they are fully clothed and standing tall while the native Africans are scantily dressed and sitting or crouching.)

3 Assess

The Voortrekker Monument in South Africa commemorates the Great Trek.

establish their own society where they could maintain the separation of the races.

Southern African Conflicts

The resources of southern Africa were valuable to both the native peoples of southern Africa as well as to European colonizers. Both sides fought to control the land and trade networks. In the end, however, the superior arms of the Europeans overpowered the resistance of the Africans.

The Xhosa people were one group who tried to keep the Dutch out of southern Africa in the area of the Cape of Good Hope. The Xhosa had initially traded with the Dutch in the 1700s. Eventually, the two groups disagreed over a number of trade and territorial issues. As a result, the Xhosa and the Dutch fought three wars between 1779 and 1801.

At the same time that the wars between the Dutch and the Xhosa were being fought, other rebellions against the Dutch occurred. The Khoisan servants of the Dutch in southern Africa rose up against their employers. The Dutch referred to these rebellions as Kaffir Wars. Others called them Cape Frontier Wars.

Hostility toward the Dutch in southern Africa was not the only source of conflict in the region. The Zulu expansion under King Shaka forced many people off their native lands in southern and central Africa. These same people then competed with each other for water and grazing lands in other areas. Still other groups competed against one another for cattle and the trade of ivory goods.

The result of all of the conflicts in southern Africa was that the people in this region took part in about 20 years of warfare during the early nineteenth century. The results were disastrous, both economically as well as culturally.

◆ **How did the Xhosa people try to keep their land?**

Review II

Review History
A. For what did the Kanem-Bornu Empire gain fame?
B. Which two war tools did Shaka improve?
C. What was the Great Trek?

Define Terms to Know
Define the following terms:
chiefdom, Boers

Critical Thinking
For what reasons do you think the Xhosa people wanted to keep the Dutch out of the area of the Cape of Good Hope?

Write About Culture
Write a letter to a friend in which you describe a visit to a central or southern African kingdom.

Get Organized
FIVE Ws CHART
Use a Five Ws chart to organize information from this section. Choose a topic and then find the answers to the five questions. For example, what are the important facts about the Zulu King Shaka?

Who?	
What?	
Where?	
When?	
Why?	

Who?	King Shaka
What?	Zulu king, military leader
Where?	Southern Africa
When?	1816–1828
Why?	Good military techniques, improved weapons and shield for defense

Australia and Southeast Asia

Terms to Know

penal colony a colony to which convicted criminals are exiled

archipelago a group of islands

Main Ideas

A. The colonization of Australia and New Zealand occurred in the nineteenth century when Great Britain sent convicted criminals to Australia to serve their prison sentences.

B. The nations of Southeast Asia have many different cultures and traditions.

C. Pacific Island cultures experienced changes with the coming of the Europeans.

Active Reading

MAKE INFERENCES
When you make inferences, you assume certain facts based on what you read. As you read this section, think about being in an unfamiliar place. Then, make inferences about how the settlers in Australia and the explorers in the Pacific might have coped with the hardships they encountered.

Section Summary

In this section, students will learn about the history and colonization of the island cultures of Australia and New Zealand. Students will also learn about the complex geography and cultures of the island nations in Southeast Asia and the Pacific.

1 Introduce

Getting Started

Suppose that a guest in your home or school began to mistreat you and others. How would this make you feel? (hurt, angry, confused) Point out to students that the European explorers, traders, and settlers whom they had welcomed colonized the indigenous people of Australia, New Zealand, Southeast Asia, and the Pacific Islands.

A. Australia and New Zealand

For thousands of years, the island continent of Australia and its neighboring island, New Zealand, escaped intrusion from outsiders. By the time the fifteenth century arrived, more than 1 million people lived in Australia alone. Little did they know that their peaceful lives were about to change.

Unknown Southern Land

About 1,900 years ago, the Greek geographer Ptolemy had a theory that there had to be landmasses south of Asia and Europe. This area that no European had even seen before became known as the Unknown South Land, or *terra australis incognita*. Spanish, Portuguese, and Dutch explorers all sailed in the area of this unknown land before 1650. It was not until the next century, however, that the Australian coastline was explored and mapped by Europeans. On his first voyage in 1770, Captain James Cook claimed the eastern part of the Australian continent for Great Britain.

These Aboriginal boys are using a laptop computer in the desert.

Settlers in Australia

The first people to settle Australia came from the Asian mainland over 40,000 years ago. In time, Europeans called them Aborigines. The name comes from Latin and means "from the beginning."

The Aborigines did not live in permanent settlements. Instead, they roamed the land setting up temporary settlements. Men fished and hunted large animals. Women gathered seeds, fruits, and roots. The Aborigines believed that each piece of land was protected by spiritual beings, so they did not take another group's land. Although conflicts did arise from time to time, traditional society was mostly peaceful.

When the Aboriginal peoples first met the Europeans, they were shocked by the European way of thinking about the land. The British settlers did not recognize Aboriginal rights to their land.

CHAPTER 21 ◆ Asia, Africa, and Australia in Transition **495**

TERMS TO KNOW

Ask students to read the terms and definitions on page 495. Then, have them write a paragraph about Australia or New Zealand that uses both terms.

You may wish to preview the pronunciation of the following words with students.

Aborigine (ab uh RIHJ uh nee)
Maori (MAH oh ree)
Myanmar (MYAHN mahr)

ACTIVE READING

Tell students to write facts about the early hardships of settlers in Australia and the explorers in the Pacific Islands as they read this section. Then, ask them how these facts support their inferences.

Teaching Options

Section 3 Resources

Teacher's Resources (TR)

Terms to Know, p. 34
Review History, p. 68
Build Your Skills, p. 102
Chapter Test, pp. 157–158
Concept Builder, p. 237
Five *W*s Chart, p. 326
Transparencies 7, 8

Conflict Resolution

When the British declared that they owned land inhabited by Aborigines, the Aborigines initially did not resist. Ask students to think of a time when they gave in to someone in order to keep the peace. What happened as a result? Have students discuss situations in which this strategy is useful and situations in which it is not.

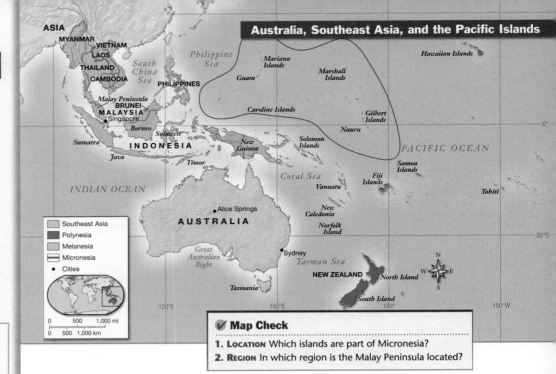

Australia, Southeast Asia, and the Pacific Islands

Map legend:
- Southeast Asia
- Polynesia
- Melanesia
- Micronesia
- Cities

✔ Map Check
1. **Location** Which islands are part of Micronesia?
2. **Region** In which region is the Malay Peninsula located?

2 Teach

A. Australia and New Zealand

Purpose-Setting Question
What groups of people inhabited the islands of Australia and New Zealand between the seventeenth and nineteenth centuries? (**Australia:** Aborigines, British soldiers and convicts; **New Zealand:** Maori, European traders)

Focus Review with students the beliefs of the Aborigines about land. Help students understand the different view of the British settlers toward land.

Using the Map

Australia, Southeast Asia, and the Pacific Islands

Have students locate Sydney, Australia, on the map on page 496. Tell students that the first group of colonists arrived in Sydney in 1788. Ask students to use an atlas to locate other major cities in Australia and New Zealand. What do most have in common? (Most major cities in Australia and New Zealand are coastal cities.) Discuss with students why many settlements developed along the coast. (Possible answers: The interior terrain is uninhabitable; the coast provides water and trade/travel routes; people tend to settle where they first arrive if there are enough immediate resources.)

✔ Map Check

Answers
1. Mariana Islands; Marshall Islands; Gilbert Islands; Guam; Caroline Islands; Nauru
2. Southeast Asia

Extend Tell students that convicts who were sent to Australia were given land if they were discharged for good behavior. They could also buy land and settle.

Because Aborigines did not farm the land, the British decided they did not own it. It has been only since the 1990s that Australian legal courts have recognized some of the land claims made by early descendants of Australia's first people.

European Arrivals

The first Europeans to inhabit Australia were convicted criminals, or convicts. Starting in 1788, the British began to use Australia as its **penal colony**, a colony to which convicted criminals are sent. Over the next 80 years, more than 160,000 convicts were exiled to Australia.

The first group, called the First Fleet, arrived in Sydney, Australia, with 568 male convicts, 191 female convicts, and 13 children of the convicts. A number of soldiers were sent along to serve as guards, some of whom brought their wives and children.

Survival was difficult at first. Food supplies were short, there were few tools, the soil was poor, and fertilizer was in short supply. However, as hard as life was for the convicts, the Aboriginal people fared worse. Many Aborigines died of smallpox spread by the Europeans.

Settlement Beginnings

Colonial traders and former convicts began to survive by shipbuilding and trading in whale oil and sealskins. In 1797, the first sheep were brought to Australia by Henry Waterhouse. In the early 1800s, sheep raising and the export of wool became the backbone of the economy. It is said that Australia

496 UNIT 5 ◆ Enlightenment and Revolution

Teaching Options

Focus on WORLD RELIGIONS

Aboriginal Spirituality Aboriginal spirituality assumes an equal relationship between humans and the land. Aborigines' creation story is called the Dreaming, or Dreamtime. In the Dreaming, Aboriginal ancestors arose from beneath the earth to form parts of nature, such as animals, water, and the sky. To Aborigines, their ancestors are still spiritually alive, metamorphosed into nature as rock formations or rivers, for example.

Today, there are approximately 400,000 Aborigines living in Australia. Outside interest in Aboriginal spirituality has been growing. In Australia in particular, there is a desire to understand the Dreaming and other aspects of Aboriginal culture. Ask students why the Aboriginal beliefs might be of interest to nonbelievers. (Possible answer: Land is important to everyone because of the many and varied resources it offers.)

"rode to prosperity on the back of a sheep." By the 1830s, the value of wool exports was greater than that of all other products.

The colonies in Australia grew slowly until 1851, when gold was discovered. Suddenly everyone wanted to go to Australia. Newcomers came not only from Great Britain, but from the rest of Europe and Asia as well.

In 1901, six former Australian colonies became states in the Commonwealth of Australia. Australians decided to build a new capital city. It was named Canberra—an Aboriginal word meaning "meeting place."

New Zealand

As you can see from the map on page 496, New Zealand consists of two main islands— North Island and South Island—and a number of smaller ones. The Maori arrived in New Zealand over many hundreds of years, beginning in about the year 700. It is believed that they came from islands in the Pacific Ocean.

On the same voyage in which he explored Australia, James Cook claimed New Zealand for Great Britain. In contrast with the Aborigines in Australia, the Maori accepted British firearms and traded eagerly with Europeans.

In 1840, British settlers and a group of Maori signed the Treaty of Waitangi. The Maori agreed to accept Queen Victoria as their ruler and sell their land only to the government. In return, the British government agreed to protect Maori land and rights. As with other treaties between European powers and native people, however, the British failed to live up to the agreement. Conflict over land and ownership arose between the government and the Maori.

◆ **How did Europeans first colonize Australia?**

B. Southeast Asia

As the map on page 496 shows, the geography of Southeast Asia includes part of mainland Asia, both large and small islands, and island groups called **archipelagos**. An archipelago is a chain of islands. In fact, two nations— Indonesia and the Philippines—include more than 20,000 islands between them.

Nations of Southeast Asia

Ten nations make up Southeast Asia. These nations are: Myanmar, which was formerly called Burma; Thailand; Vietnam; Cambodia; Laos; Malaysia; Indonesia; the Philippines; Brunei; and Singapore.

The cultures and traditions found in different parts of Southeast Asia are as varied as the geography. The islands of the region made it possible for small isolated communities to develop. This isolation allowed each community to establish a unique culture and lifestyle. However, many of these island civilizations shared certain characteristics. For example, their economies were based on fishing and growing rice.

People flocked to Australia to look for gold in the mid-1800s. Tents were set up as temporary shelters in areas where gold digging took place.

Early Powers in Southeast Asia

REGION	CONTROLLING POWER
Brunei	Great Britain
Cambodia, Laos, Vietnam	France
Indonesia	Holland
Malaysia	Great Britain
Myanmar	Great Britain
Philippines	Spain, United States
Singapore	Great Britain

✔ Chart Check

Which country held power in the most regions?

---

498 UNIT 5 ◆ Enlightenment and Revolution

Religion in Southeast Asia

Religious beliefs in Southeast Asia were primarily influenced by either India or China. As a result, Hinduism and Buddhism were two of the chief religions of the region. Indian influence had spread Hindu and Buddhist practices in Southeast Asia for centuries.

Another chief religion of Southeast Asia was, and still is, Islam. When Marco Polo arrived in Sumatra in the late thirteenth century, he found that some people had converted to Islam. This was accomplished mainly through merchants and sailors who spread the Islamic religion in Southeast Asia. Islam's simple rituals appealed to the people of this part of the world, and the religion adapted itself to the local cultures. Today, Indonesia has one of the largest Muslim populations in the world.

Europeans in Southeast Asia

For hundreds of years, traders from the Middle East, India, and China had the rich markets of Southeast Asia to themselves. After 1500, the Europeans made their way to the region. Portuguese traders were the first to arrive. They set up trading posts in several ports, including Borneo and Java. They were driven out of the region by the Dutch, who arrived in Java in 1596. The Dutch were closely followed by traders from Spain, Great Britain, and France.

From 1800 to the mid-twentieth century, five European powers controlled much of Southeast Asia and its rich markets. The British ruled in Burma; the Dutch in Indonesia; the French in Laos, Cambodia, and Vietnam; the Spaniards in the Philippines; and the Portuguese in Timor. By the late 1800s, Thailand was the only nation in Southeast Asia that remained free of colonial control.

Europeans were able to expand colonial rule because of their superior technology and the presence of a strong European merchant community in the region. Their motivation for expanding was the intense competition for control among the powers for territory.

◆ **What were the main reasons that Europeans went to Southeast Asia?**

C. Pacific Island Cultures

The Pacific Islands are divided into three geographic areas: Polynesia, Melanesia, and Micronesia. Polynesia includes present-day Hawaii, Easter Island, New Zealand, Samoa, and Tahiti. Melanesia includes New Caledonia, present-day New Guinea, the Solomon Islands, and Vanuatu. Micronesia has 2,000 tiny islands, the best known being Guam, the Caroline Islands, Fiji, the Mariana Islands, the Marshall Islands, the Gilbert Islands, and Nauru.

European Explorers

Several Europeans explored the South Pacific region from the sixteenth to the eighteenth centuries. In 1521, Ferdinand Magellan reached Guam. In 1567, the Spaniard Alvaro de Mendaña found the Solomon Islands. James Cook, an excellent navigator, made three trips to explore the Pacific region between 1768 and 1779. During these voyages, he sailed to Tahiti and charted New Zealand and the east coast of Australia. He reached most of the Pacific Islands.

Teaching Options

European Traders and Settlers

People began coming to the Pacific Islands for a variety of reasons. Traders were the first to arrive. They came for coconut oil and sandalwood, the fragrant wood of the sandalwood tree. Sandalwood is used to make furniture and incense. Whalers and sea hunters came from a variety of countries in search of new hunting grounds. Fur traders also came to the region.

Colonization of the Pacific Islands did not begin, however, until around 1850, when Great Britain, France, Germany, Spain, and the United States competed for control of the islands. Settlers who came from these countries started plantations in which pineapples, coconuts, sugar cane, and coffee beans were grown.

James Cook made several voyages to the Pacific Islands.

The Pacific Islands also served as a valuable source of supplies to the Australian settlement. During the late 1700s, European ships set out from Australia to trade for sandalwood, pearl shell, and sea cucumbers with the native peoples of the Pacific Islands. From 1793 to 1826, pigs from Tahiti were an important Australian import.

Missionaries came to convert the native peoples of the Pacific Islands to Christianity. They also convinced many islanders to give up their traditional beliefs and customs. Some islanders had no problems with adopting the new religion. This was especially true of leaders, who converted to Christianity for political reasons. However, becoming Christian posed a problem for others, such as the Polynesians. They were unwilling to give up their traditional beliefs. As a result, there were several revolts against the Christians by those who supported the old ways in Tahiti and in Tonga.

◆ **What are the three geographic divisions of the Pacific Islands?**

Review III

Review History

A. How did Australia first become settled by Europeans?
B. How did Islam reach to Southeast Asia?
C. Why did European traders go to the Pacific Islands?

Define Terms to Know

Define the following terms:
penal colony, archipelago

Critical Thinking

Why is the history of Australia, Southeast Asia, and the Pacific Islands often told in terms of contact with Europeans?

Write About Government

Write a letter to the British prime minister against sending convicts to Australia.

Get Organized

FIVE *Ws* CHART

Use a Five *Ws* chart to organize information from this section. Choose a topic and then find the answers to the five questions. For example, what are the important facts about the colonization of Australia?

Who?	
What?	
Where?	
When?	
Why?	

Activity

Make a resource chart

Distribute a copy of a two-column chart (TR, p. 328) to students. Title the left column *Nation* and the right column *Resources*. Then, list the following nations in the rows of the left column: Australia, New Zealand, Vietnam, Thailand, Tahiti, Guam, and Fiji. Work as a class to research the resources of each of these nations that European hunters, traders, and settlers exploited in the 1700s and 1800s. List the resources in the right column of the chart. Encourage students to use their charts as a study aid.

◆ **ANSWER** Polynesia, Melanesia, and Micronesia

Section Close

Imperialism and colonization were major forces in the lives of the peoples of Australia, New Zealand, Southeast Asia, and the Pacific Islands. Have students discuss the impact of these forces on the indigenous cultures of these areas.

3 Assess

Review Answers

Review History

A. British convicts were sent there to serve their terms and guards were sent to watch the convicts.
B. Islam was brought to Southeast Asia by merchants and sailors.
C. European traders went to the Pacific Islands for coconut oil and sandalwood.

Define Terms to Know

penal colony, 496; archipelago, 497

Critical Thinking

Possible answers: History is often told from the point of view of those who write it, in this case from European explorers and settlers. Contact with Europeans changed the cultures and countries and led to how many of the current countries exist.

Write About Government

Accept all logical and well-supported answers. Students' letters should include at least two to three reasons against sending convicts to Australia, such as the lack of food, tools, and other essentials to survive. Some students may say that going to Australia is a less harsh punishment than being sent to a prison in Great Britain.

Who?	*Convicts from Great Britain and soldier guards*
What?	*Penal colony*
Where?	*Near Sydney*
When?	*1788*
Why?	*Great Britain exiled criminals to Australia.*

Chapter Summary

A blank outline form is available in the Teacher's Resources (p. 318). Chapter summaries should outline the Qing Dynasty of China and the Tokugawa Shogunate of Japan, the various peoples of Africa, and the development of Australia, Southeast Asia, and the Pacific Island cultures. Refer to the rubric in the Teacher's Resources (p. 340) to score students' chapter summaries.

● Interpret the Timeline

1. the beginning of the Tokugawa Shogunate (1600)
2. 18 years
3. Dutch traders were active in Southeast Asia, and James Cook claimed Australia for Great Britain.
4. Check students' timelines to be sure all events are in the chapter.

Use Terms to Know

5. d. chiefdom
6. f. queue
7. c. Bushido
8. a. archipelago
9. e. penal colony
10. b. Boer

Check Your Understanding

11. Merchants were ranked low in the social order because they did not produce anything.
12. Painting, porcelain, furniture design, and printmaking were popular during the Qing Dynasty.
13. Chinese men were forced to wear their hair in queues as a sign of loyalty and submission to Manchu rule.
14. The samurai was loyal to his daimyo and would die for his honor. Samurai protected the daimyo and put down rebellions. Samurai had to pay land taxes to their daimyo.
15. The Kanem-Bornu were able to strengthen and expand their empire because they had an effective cavalry.
16. The Khoi people and the San people shared a language that used clicking sounds as consonants.
17. The Zulu became stronger during Shaka's reign because he invented a new spear, a longer body shield, and new and very effective military techniques. He conquered many kingdoms.
18. The Aborigines did not live in

Chapter Summary

Complete the following outline in your notebook. Then, use your outline to write a brief summary of the chapter.

Asia, Africa, and Australia in Transition

I. Asian Empires
  A. The Qing Dynasty
  B. The Tokugawa Shogunate in Japan

II. African Societies and States
  A. West and Central African States and Societies
  B. Southern African Peoples
  C. Europeans in Southern Africa

III. Australia and Southeast Asia
  A. Australia and New Zealand
  B. Southeast Asia
  C. Pacific Island Cultures

● Interpret the Timeline

Use the timeline on pages 482–483 to answer the following questions.

1. Which occurred first, the beginning of the Qing Dynasty or the beginning of the Tokugawa Shogunate?

2. How long after James Cook claimed Australia for Great Britain did convicts begin to arrive there?

3. **Critical Thinking** What can you learn about trade and exploration from the timeline?

4. Select five events from the chapter that are not on the timeline. Create a timeline that shows these events.

Use Terms to Know

Match each term with its correct definition.

a. archipelago d. chiefdom
b. Boer e. penal colony
c. Bushido f. queue

5. centralized African political system with hereditary offices
6. Chinese men in the Qing Dynasty had to wear their hair in this manner
7. the samurai code of loyalty and courage
8. a group of islands
9. a place where convicts are exiled
10. a Dutch settler in South Africa

Check Your Understanding

11. **Explain** why merchants were ranked so low in the social order during the Qing Dynasty.
12. **Discuss** types of art that were popular during the Qing Dynasty.
13. **Explain** why Chinese men were forced to wear their hair in a queue during the Qing Dynasty.
14. **Describe** the relationship between a daimyo and his samurai.
15. **Explain** why the Kanem-Bornu were able to strengthen and expand their empire.
16. **Identify** the one characteristic that the Khoi people and the San people had in common.
17. **Describe** how King Shaka helped to make the Zulu warriors such an effective fighting force.
18. **Explain** the lifestyle of the Aboriginal peoples.
19. **Describe** what life was like for the first Europeans who inhabited Australia.
20. **Explain** why the Europeans were able to expand colonial rule in Southeast Asia.
21. **Identify** some of the explorers who went to the Pacific Islands.
22. **Identify** the motivating forces that took people to the Pacific Islands.

---

permanent settlements. Instead, they roamed the lands fishing and hunting for large animals. Women gathered seeds, fruit, and roots.
19. Life was difficult for the first Europeans who inhabited Australia. Food supplies were short, the soil was poor, and fertilizer was in short supply.
20. The Europeans were able to expand colonial rule in Southeast Asia because of their technology

and because of the presence of a strong European merchant community in the region.
21. Ferdinand Magellan, Alvaro de Mendaña, and James Cook were all explorers who went to the Pacific Islands.
22. People began going to the Pacific Islands for trading reasons, to start plantations, and to get supplies for the new Australian settlement.

Critical Thinking

23. Compare and Contrast How was social order in the Qing Dynasty different from social order under the shoguns in Japan? How were they the same?

24. Make Inferences Why do you think the Zulu were so successful in their expansion?

25. Analyze Primary Sources Reread the haiku poem on page 488. What does the poem tell you about warriors in Japanese society?

Put Your Skills to Work

26. Improve Your Test-Taking Skills You have learned how to improve your scores on standardized tests. Doing well on a test shows that you have a solid grasp on the subject you are studying and have mastered strategies to help you succeed on future tests.

Study the chart below. Then, answer the following short-answer and multiple-choice questions.

a. Short-Answer From the chart, what can you learn about the Khoi people?

b. Multiple-Choice The San people are known for their

1. bronze art.
2. cloth production.
3. rock paintings.
4. stabbing spears.

African Kingdoms

PEOPLE	KNOWN FOR
Ashanti	Brass weights
Benin	Bronze art, earthen walls
Khoi	Cattle herding
Kongo	Cloth production
San	Rock paintings
Zulu	Stabbing spears

Analyze Sources

27. Read what Chinese Emperor Kangxi wrote after defeating a Mongol named Galdan. Then, answer the questions that follow.

Now Galdan is dead. . . . My great task is done. In two years I made three journeys, across deserts combed by wind and bathed with rain, eating every other day, in the barren and uninhabitable deserts—one could have called it a hardship . . . ; people all shun such things but I didn't shun them. The constant journeying and hardship has led to this great achievement.

a. After reading this passage, what qualities do you think Kangxi has?

b. Why would an emperor undertake such a task when he could avoid it?

Essay Writing

28. Write an essay about what life must have been like in Japan under the Tokugawa Shogunate. You may include some of the following points in your essay.

- the Japanese social order
- Tokugawa schools
- popular literature
- the arts

TEST PREPARATION

DEFINITION
Choose the answer that correctly completes the sentence.

The White Lotus is

1. a beautiful tree.
2. a famous Buddhist painting.
3. a seventeenth-century Chinese novel.
4. a secret religious group in China.

Critical Thinking

23. In the Qing Dynasty, the ruling class was ranked at the top, followed by the farmers, artisans, and merchants. During the Tokugawa Shogunate, the emperor and shogun were ranked at the top, followed by the samurai, the farmers, the artisans, and the merchants. Both had the ruling class ranked highest and artisans and merchants lowest. One difference is the ranking of the farmers; they were ranked higher in Chinese society.

24. The Zulu were a strong and unified people, had good military techniques, and developed new weapons.

25. The poem might tell you that Japanese warriors felt very strongly about their position in society and were frustrated if they were not able to meet their goals.

Put Your Skills to Work

IMPROVE YOUR TEST-TAKING SKILLS
26a. They were known for cattle herding.
26b. 3. rock paintings.

Analyze Sources

27a. Possible answer: He was probably very tough and well disciplined. He was also proud of himself for having made the journeys.
27b. Possible answer: He had all he needed, so he wanted to do something that staying home would not bring him.

Essay Writing

28. Students' essays should contain accurate and specific information about the Tokugawa Shogunate in Japan.

TEST PREPARATION

Answer 4. a secret religious group in China.

Unit 5
Portfolio Project

DEBATE: CONFLICTS AND DISPUTES IN HISTORY

Managing the Project
Plan for 2–3 class periods.

Set the Scene
Review with students the purpose and rules of a debate. Point out that for each debate topic, there will be two groups, one for each side. Each group will present evidence to support its side. Then, both groups will have a chance for rebuttal.

Your Assignment
Ask students to read the assignment on page 502. Then, divide the class into small groups and assign topics. You may want to let students vote on a choice of topic, based on which event they are most interested in and then divide the students into groups.

PREPARE FOR THE DEBATE
Have students meet as teams before the debate to research their position. Then, teammates should decide how to present their argument. Students also should be prepared to respond to their opponents' arguments. Provide time for teams to practice their debate points and rebuttals.

CONDUCT YOUR DEBATE
Encourage team members to help each other respond to rebuttals. Help each team keep its points organized on note cards so members may quickly and quietly pass information to the speaker.

Wrap Up
Discuss with students the evidence presented during the debate. Ask students which evidence they think made the strongest impression and why. Discuss with students the importance of how they talk as well as what they are saying.

Multimedia Presentation

Turn your debate into a panel discussion for radio or television. Have one student act as the moderator who questions members of the panel of experts. Other students should be prepared to represent differing or conflicting points of view on the topic selected.

Debate: Conflicts and Disputes in History

YOUR ASSIGNMENT
In this unit you have read about many conflicts and contrasts. For example, the dispute between the followers of Ptolemy and Aristotle versus those of Copernicus and Galileo; the approach to science of Francis Bacon versus that of René Descartes; the autonomy of Balkan Kingdoms versus the rule of the Ottoman Empire; and southern African native peoples versus European colonizers. Together with a small team of classmates, conduct a debate on one of the conflicts in this unit.

PREPARE FOR THE DEBATE
Agree on a Debate Topic Below are some statements you and your group may want to debate. These statements are called propositions.

- Scientists should base their thinking only on solid facts.
- The British had a right to tax the colonists because the colonists were British subjects.
- Louis XVI was responsible for his fate during the French Revolution.
- Napoleon caused more harm than good for France.
- People in Europe, South America, Asia, and Africa during the 1800s had the right to determine their own political futures.

One team will gather evidence and use it to argue in favor of the proposition. The other team will look for evidence to argue against it.

Choose Teams Select two debate teams, one for the affirmative (in favor of the statement) and one for the negative (against the statement). Agree on a time limit for each speaker and an order of speakers.

Research Conduct research to support your position using your textbook, the Internet, and library sources. Meet with your teammates to decide how you will present your argument. Be prepared to respond to your opponents' arguments. Use notecards to organize your information. Think about how visuals, such as charts or photographs, and quotations, might strengthen your presentation.

CONDUCT YOUR DEBATE
Present Conduct your debate based on the evidence you have researched. You may conduct the debate in front of an audience or judging panel.

Vote on a Winner Have audience members discuss and comment on the debate. A panel of students and teachers, or a majority vote by the audience may determine the winner.

Work Individually In a report, discuss and evaluate the points that were made during your debate. Explain which debate team had a stronger argument and why.

Teaching Options

Multimedia Presentation

You may wish to videotape the debates. Then, have the class watch the videotape and evaluate the effectiveness of particular arguments. You may want to let groups study their part of the debate and allow them to make changes to their arguments to make them better.

Alternative Assessment

Write an Editorial Have groups of students use the information they have collected for the debate to write a newspaper editorial. Students should state their opinions on their topic and support those opinions with evidence from the debate. Display editorials on a school Web site or bulletin board.

Managing the Unit
This unit should take approximately **four weeks** to complete.

PLANNING GUIDE

	Skills and Features	Projects and Activities	Program Resources	Meet Individual Needs

Chapter 22
 	
The Industrial Revolution and Social Change,
pp. 504–531
Plan for 5–6 class periods.
	Unit Technology, p. T503
	Conduct Research, p. 513
	Points of View, p. 519
		Using Technology, p. T507
		Connection to Science, p. T509
		Test Taking, p. T510
		Cooperative Learning, p. T510
		Connection to Culture, pp. T511, T520
		Connection to Literature, p. T511
		Research, p. T517
		Take a Stand, p. T519
		Link to Today, p. T519
		Connection to Language Arts, pp. T521, T526
		Writing, p. T522
		Conflict Resolution, p. T526
		Connection to Government, pp. T527, T528
			Teacher's Resources
			Terms to Know, p. 35
			Review History, p. 69
			Build Your Skills, p. 103
			Chapter Test, pp. 159–160
			Concept Builder, p. 238
			They Made History:
			  Elizabeth Blackwell,
			  p. 260
			SQR Chart, p. 322
			Transparencies 1, 5
				ESL/ELL Strategies,
				pp. T506, T514, T523, T525
				Verbal/Linguistic, p. T508
				Visual/Spatial, p. T515

Chapter 23
 	
Nationalism and Expansion,
pp. 532–557
Plan for 5–6 class periods.
	Interpret Bar Graphs, p. 539
	Past to Present: Native American Life on the Plains, pp. 546–547
		Connection to Math, pp. T535, T552
		Connection to Science, p. T536
		Cooperative Learning, p. T537
		Using Technology, p. T541
		Conflict Resolution, p. T543
		Connection to Literature, pp. T543, T546
		Connection to Government, p. T544
		Writing, p. T549
		Test Taking, p. T550
		Research, p. T553
			Teacher's Resources
			Terms to Know, p. 36
			Review History, p. 70
			Build Your Skills, p. 104
			Chapter Test, pp. 161–162
			Concept Builder, p. 239
			They Made History:
			  Giuseppe Mazzini, p. 261
			Cause-and-Effect Chain,
			  p. 325
			Transparencies 1, 3
				ESL/ELL Strategies,
				pp. T535, T542, T554
				Visual/Spatial, pp. T536, T550
				Kinesthetic, p. T541
				Verbal/Linguistic, p. T554

Chapter 24 **Imperialism in Africa, India, and the Middle East,** pp. 558–583 Plan for 5–6 class periods.	Write a Research Paper, p. 565 Connect History & Art, p. 571	Connection to Economics, p. T562 Test Taking, pp. T562, T574 World Religions, p. T563 Cooperative Learning, pp. T566, T573 Research, pp. T567, T579 Connection to Literature, pp. T568, T578 Conflict Resolution, p. T568 Writing, p. T569 Link to Today, p. T571 Connection to World Languages, p. T572	**Teacher's Resources** Terms to Know, p. 37 Review History, p. 71 Build Your Skills, p. 105 Chapter Test, pp. 163–164 Concept Builder, p. 240 They Made History: Kemal Atatürk, p. 262 Main Idea/Supporting Details Chart, p. 319 Transparency 1	ESL/ELL Strategies, pp. T560, T574, T580 Visual/Spatial, pp. T573, T577
Chapter 25 **Imperialism in Asia and Latin America,** pp. 584–608 Plan for 5–6 class periods.	Predict Consequences, p. 591 Points of View, p. 605	Writing, p. T589 Research, p. T594 Test Taking, p. T595 Cooperative Learning, p. T598 Conflict Resolution, p. T599 Using Technology, p. T599 Connection to Science, p. T602 Sports & Games, p. T603 Take a Stand, p. T605 Link to Today, p. T605	**Teacher's Resources** Terms to Know, p. 38 Review History, p. 72 Build Your Skills, p. 106 Chapter Test, pp. 165–166 Unit 6 Test, pp 193–194 Concept Builder, p. 241 They Made History: Carlotta, p. 263 SQR Chart, p. 322 Transparency 1	ESL/ELL Strategies, pp. T587, T593, T597 Logical/Mathematical, p. T600

Assessment Options

Chapter 22 Test, Teacher's Resources, pp. 159–160
Chapter 23 Test, Teacher's Resources, pp. 161–162
Chapter 24 Test, Teacher's Resources, pp. 163–164
Chapter 25 Test, Teacher's Resources, pp. 165–166
Unit 6 Test, Teacher's Resources, pp. 193–194

Alternative Assessment

Book of Letters and Journal Entries, p. 608
Make a Brochure, p. T608

Books for Students

AVERAGE

The Industrial Revolution. Anita Louise McCormick. Discusses the inventors and their creations, and how they changed America. (Enslow Publishers, Inc., 1998)

At Her Majesty's Request: An African Princess in Victorian England. Walter Dean Myers. The true story of a West African princess who became a member of Queen Victoria's royal court and her protégé. (Scholastic, Inc., 1999)

Remember the Maine: The Spanish-American War Begins. Tim McNeese. Reviews the incident using primary sources. (Morgan Reynolds, Inc., 2001)

Orphan Train Rider: One Boy's True Story. Andrea Warren. Tells one boy's story with the orphan train and explores the role of these trains. (Houghton Mifflin, Co., 1998)

Commodore Perry in the Land of the Shogun. Rhoda Blumberg. Describes Commodore Perry's goal, expedition, and achievements in 1850s Japan. (HarperTrophy, 2003)

CHALLENGING

Industry and Empire: The Birth of the Industrial Revolution. Eric Hobsbawm. Traces 250 years of the Industrial Revolution and how it affected society and the world. (The New Press, 1999)

Voices from the Trail of Tears. Vicki Rozema. Uses primary sources to give an account of what happened during this time. (John F. Blair, Publisher, 2003)

Four Sisters of Hofei: A History. Annping Chin. Chronicles the lives of the Chang sisters while telling the history of China. (Scribner, 2002)

Books for Teachers

Women's Rights Emerges within the Anti-Slavery Movement 1830–1870: A Short History with Documents. Kathryn Kish Sklar. Primary sources help explain the beginnings of the women's movement. (Palgrave Macmillan, 2000)

Seedtime for Fascism: The Disintegration of Austrian Political Culture, 1867–1918. George V. Strong. Explores the causes and effects of nationalism on Austria-Hungary. (M. E. Sharpe, Inc., 1998)

Zenith of Imperialism, Volumes I and II. Eugene M. Wait. Covers the events, people, and trends from 1899 to 1907, such as the Boxer Rebellions. (Nova Science Publishers, Inc., 2001)

Economics of the Industrial Revolution. Joel Mokyr, ed. A collection of writings covering the causes and effects of industrialization in Great Britain, focusing on the lives of the workers. (Rowman & Littlefield Publishers, Inc., 1989)

The Path Between the Seas: The Creation of the Panama Canal, 1870–1914. David G. McCullough. A description of the creation of the Panama Canal. (Simon & Schuster Trade Paperbacks, 1978)

You may wish to preview all referenced materials to ensure their appropriateness for your local community.

Audio/Visual Resources

The Industrial Revolution – Second Edition. Two-part review of all aspects of the Industrial Revolution. Videocassette. (CLEARVUE/eav)

Bismarck: Germany from Blood and Iron. Learning Corporation of America. Shows how Otto von Bismarck paved the way for the unification of Germany. Videocassette. (Social Studies School Services)

Imperialism. Explores imperialism using three different countries. CD-ROM. (CLEARVUE/eav)

Technology Resources

Age of Industrialization: http://history.evansville.net/industry.html

Make the Dirt Fly! www.sil.si.edu/Exhibitions/Make-the-Dirt-Fly/whybuild.html

The Boer War: http://ubh.tripod.com/afhist/saw/saw0.htm

American History Inspirer: The Civil War. Tom Snyder. Students search for specific information about America between 1820 to 1865 in a game format. Includes a teacher's guide. Software. (Social Studies School Services)

Globe Fearon Related Resources

History Resources

World History for a Global Age, Book 2: Age of Imperialism to the Present. Reviews the goals of imperial powers seeking colonies. ISBN 1-556-75684-4

Core Knowledge History & Geography: Industrialization and Urbanization in America. Helps students explore topics of industrialization and urbanization. ISBN 0-7690-3091-2

Core Knowledge History & Geography: Immigration. Provides additional information on immigration. ISBN 0-7690-3090-4

Adapted Classics

The Jungle. A 1906 novel by Upton Sinclair about the meat-packing industry in Chicago. ISBN 0-835-94982-6

Narrative of the Life of Frederick Douglass. An autobiography by Frederick Douglass. ISBN 0-835-91118-7

My Antonia. A novel by Willa Cather about an immigrant and pioneer in early America. ISBN 0-835-95543-5

The Red Badge of Courage. Stephen Crane's novel of a young Civil War soldier. ISBN 0-835-90032-0

Things Fall Apart. A novel by Chinua Achebe that describes the effect of European culture on one man's life and African society. ISBN 0-13-023501-6

Heart of Darkness. Joseph Conrad's novel of one man's search for another in Africa. ISBN 0-835-90877-1

To order books, call 1-800-321-3106.

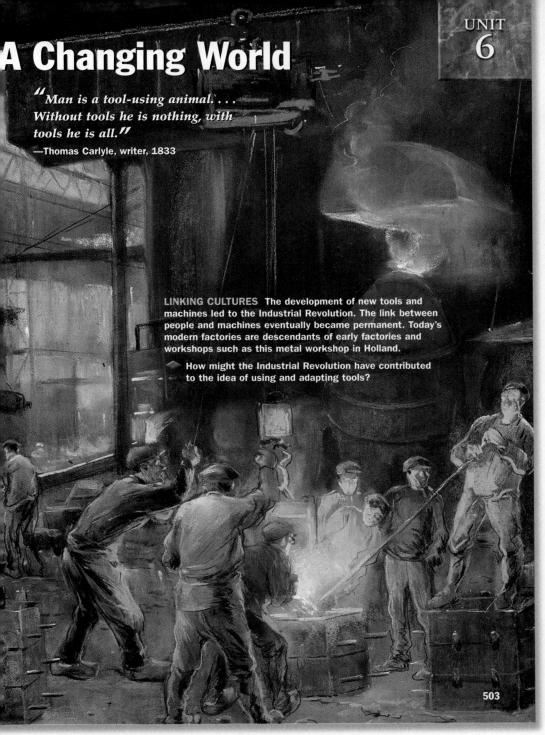

A Changing World

"Man is a tool-using animal. . . . Without tools he is nothing, with tools he is all."

—Thomas Carlyle, writer, 1833

LINKING CULTURES The development of new tools and machines led to the Industrial Revolution. The link between people and machines eventually became permanent. Today's modern factories are descendants of early factories and workshops such as this metal workshop in Holland.

How might the Industrial Revolution have contributed to the idea of using and adapting tools?

503

A Changing World
(pp. 503–608)

Unit Summary
Unit 6 focuses on the Industrial Revolution and its social, economic, technological, and political effects from the early eighteenth to the early twentieth centuries.

CHAPTER 22
The Industrial Revolution and Social Change

CHAPTER 23
Nationalism and Expansion

CHAPTER 24
Imperialism in Africa, India, and the Middle East

CHAPTER 25
Imperialism in Asia and Latin America

Set the Stage
TEACH PRIMARY SOURCES
Photo This twentieth-century gouache painting, by Haeyenbrock, shows workers in a nineteenth-century metal workshop in Rotterdam's naval depot. Have students identify items they see in the painting. (Possible answers: molten ore, the furnace pulley, the workers wearing caps, glasses, and aprons, and the assembly line process used in manufacturing the metal)

Quote Thomas Carlyle was a nineteenth-century British essayist, historian, and biographer. The quote is from his book *Sartor Resartus*, a philosophical satire. Ask students what the quote shows about attitudes toward the nineteenth-century worker. (Possible answer: Tools are what make people better than other animals.)

➥ ANSWER People could bring toolmaking and tool use to new heights due to new situations.

Teaching Options

UNIT TECHNOLOGY

Have students use the Internet to research labor laws during nineteenth-century England. Tell them that such laws affected conditions in factories and workshops during the Industrial Revolution. Students can use "labor laws during Victorian England" as a search phrase.

You may wish to identify possible Web sites for students and monitor their activities on the Internet.

UNIT 6 Portfolio Project
Book of Letters and Journal Entries

The Portfolio Project for Unit 6 is to create a book of letters and journal entries. First, teams of students research the life of any Unit 6 historical figure and then write journal entries or letters from that individual's point of view. You may suggest to students that they include visuals relating to the life of the historical person, to enhance their journals.

The Industrial Revolution and Social Change
1733–1928
(pp. 504–531)

Chapter Objectives

• Describe the beginnings of the Industrial Revolution and how it affected people's daily lives.
• Contrast the spread of the Industrial Revolution in parts of Europe and the United States with the relative lack of industrialization in Asian colonies.
• Understand how the Industrial Revolution affected immigration, cities, and the middle class.
• Discuss the social and political reforms and economic theories that developed during the nineteenth century.

Chapter Summary

Section I focuses on how the Industrial Revolution affected the textile, mining, and transportation industries as well as everyday life, and led to new economic theories.
Section II explores the spread of the Industrial Revolution and the development of the factory system, progress in transportation, communications, science, and technology.
Section III discusses the growth of cities and the rise of the middle class.
Section IV focuses on social, political, and labor reforms and the development of new economic theories during the nineteenth century.

Set the Stage

TEACH PRIMARY SOURCES
Explain that Hollingshead's quotation is from his book, which was based on ten letters published in the *London Morning Post* in January 1861, under the heading "London Horrors." Discuss with students the meaning of the metaphor, "the spreading limbs of a great city." (He is comparing the growth in capital and population in London to growing tree branches.) What is the writer contrasting in this quote? (the way the city looks in real life for those who live there)

CHAPTER 22

The Industrial Revolution and Social Change
1733–1928

I. The Industrial Revolution Begins
II. The Spread of Industry
III. Cities and the Middle Class
IV. An Age of Reforms

The Industrial Age began in the 1700s in Great Britain and soon spread to other parts of Europe and to the United States. Machines, factories, and cities were part of the Industrial Age. This revolution in progress caused conflict. Some people celebrated the changes. Others, such as John Hollingshead, a British journalist and author who grew up poor in London, wrote about the city's growth during the Industrial Revolution in 1861:

❝ [T]he spreading limbs of a great city may be healthy and vigorous, while its heart may gradually become more choked up and decayed. ❞

1733	1765	1769	1793	1807
John Kay invents the flying shuttle.	James Watt improves the design of the steam engine.	Richard Arkwright invents the water frame.	Eli Whitney invents the cotton gin.	Robert Fulton successfully sails the first steam riverboa...

CHAPTER EVENTS

1730 — 1770 — 1810

WORLD EVENTS

1743	1770	1789	1804
Maria Theresa, Hapsburg empress, is crowned.	New South Wales is annexed for Great Britain by James Cook.	United States adopts its new constitution.	Haiti becomes independent of France.

Teaching Options

Chapter 22 Resources

REVIEW

Teacher's Resources (TR)
Terms to Know, p. 35
Review History, p. 69
Build Your Skills, p. 103
Chapter Test, pp. 159–160
Concept Builder, p. 238
SQR Chart, p. 322
Transparencies 1, 5

ASSESSMENT

Section Reviews, pp. 512, 518, 524, 529
Chapter Review, pp. 530–531
Chapter Test, TR pp. 159–160

ALTERNATIVE ASSESSMENT

Portfolio Project, p. 608
Make a Brochure, p. T608

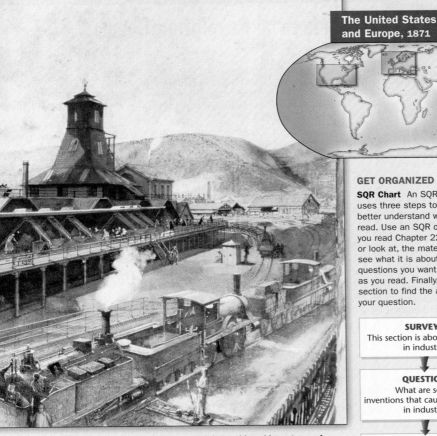

GET ORGANIZED

SQR Chart An SQR chart uses three steps to help you better understand what you read. Use an SQR chart as you read Chapter 22. Survey, or look at, the material to see what it is about. Write questions you want to answer as you read. Finally, read the section to find the answer to your question.

```
┌─────────────────────────────┐
│          SURVEY             │
│  This section is about changes │
│        in industry.         │
└─────────────────────────────┘
              ↓
┌─────────────────────────────┐
│         QUESTION            │
│       What are some         │
│  inventions that caused changes │
│        in industry?         │
└─────────────────────────────┘
              ↓
┌─────────────────────────────┐
│           READ              │
│   Water frame, cotton gin,   │
│    steam engine, locomotive  │
└─────────────────────────────┘
```

VIEW HISTORY Mechanical inventions increased the wealth and importance of many nations during the Industrial Revolution. However, mechanical inventions also brought new problems, such as smoky air filled with soot and steam.
◆ What in the painting shows the problems brought by the Industrial Revolution?

1825
George Stephenson builds the first railroad locomotive.

1848
Seneca Falls Convention meets to support women's rights.

1869
Transcontinental railroad is completed.

1893
British Labour Party is formed.

1920
Women in the United States get the right to vote.

1928
Women in Great Britain get the right to vote.

1850   1890   1930

1821
Mexico, Guatemala, and Peru win independence from Spain.

1847
Liberia is proclaimed an independent republic.

1911
Hiram Bingham finds the ancient Peruvian city of Machu Picchu.

CHAPTER 22 ◆ The Industrial Revolution and Social Change   **505**

Chapter Themes
- Culture
- Time, Continuity, and Change
- Individuals, Groups, and Institutions
- Individual Development and Identity
- Production, Distribution, and Consumption
- Science, Technology, and Society
- Global Connections

F Y I

Gouache Paintings

Gouache is a medium used by artists. It is an opaque watercolor paint, sometimes called poster paint or body color. It provides a stronger color than regular watercolor. The art on pages 503 and 504–505 are examples of the use of gouache. Artists such as Vincent van Gogh and Paul Klee have used gouache. It has been used in art as early as the mid-fifteenth century.

Chapter Warm-Up

USING THE MAP
Point out the locator map at the top of page 505. To help students understand where the United States and Europe are located, have them identify the Atlantic Ocean, North America, and Asia. Ask students to identify the other continents and oceans.

VIEW HISTORY
The 1866 ink and gouache painting, *The Pits of St. Pierre & St. Paul at Le Creusot,* shows the daily activity at a coal mine. The artist is Ignace Francois Bonhomme. Ask students to identify details in the drawing. (Possible answers: the railway and the locomotive used to transport the coal, people on the platform)

◆ **ANSWER** The smoky air and the steam rising from the railroad show the problems brought on by the Industrial Revolution.

GET ORGANIZED
SQR Chart
Remind students that they first learned how to use an SQR chart in Chapter 4. Then, discuss the SQR chart on page 505. Ask students to identify the topic of the section using the chart. (changes in industry) Then, have them identify the question about the topic and the answer. Point out that this type of chart helps people organize information found in text.

⬤ TEACH THE TIMELINE
The timeline on pages 504–505 covers the period between 1733 and 1928. Ask students to compare the topics of events emphasized in the Chapter Events and the World Events entries. (**Chapter Events:** inventions that advanced industry and women's rights; **World Events:** political and cultural) Encourage students to look for these topics as they read the chapter.

Activity

Extend the timeline Give students a copy of the timeline on pages 504–505. As students read the chapter, have them add other key events onto this timeline.

Section Summary

In this section, students will learn about the beginning of the Industrial Revolution in the 1700s, its effects on the textile industry, and the development of steam power. They will also learn how industrialization affected people's lives and resulted in new economic theories.

1 Introduce

Getting Started

Have students list different steps in the manufacturing of an object in the classroom, such as a window, book, pen, or computer. Ask students if it is likely that one worker performed all the steps. Explain that the word *manufacture* comes from Latin roots that mean "made by hand" but that in this section they will learn how manufacturing changed from a one-person job done by hand to a job involving many different people using machines.

TERMS TO KNOW

Ask students to read the terms and definitions on page 506 and then find each term in the section. Have pairs of students make a multiple-choice quiz using these terms and providing correct answers. Student pairs can exchange quizzes and answers.

You may wish to preview the pronunciation of the following terms from this section with students.

madras (MA dras)
chintz (CHINTS)
Arkwright (AHRK ryt)
Newcomen (NYOO kuh muhn)
Fernand Braudel
(fer nahn broh DEHL)

ACTIVE READING

Have students choose two of the inventions or important developments described in Section 1 and use a Venn diagram (TR, p. 323) to compare and contrast them.

Terms to Know

capital the money or property used by a businessperson to make a profit

crop rotation a system of growing different crops one after the other on the same land to help restore the soil

enclosure the fencing off of common land by private landowners in Great Britain

textile industry the manufacturing of cloth from wool, cotton, and other materials

factory system the mass production of goods in a central building or buildings

A family breaks flax fiber in order to make linen fabric. Before the Industrial Revolution, goods like clothing were made by hand at home.

Main Ideas

A. Economic and social factors set the stage for the beginnings of the Industrial Revolution in Great Britain in the 1700s.

B. Textiles were the most important focus in the first stage of the Industrial Revolution.

C. Progress in the mining industry led to the development of steam power and then to a revolution in transportation.

D. Industrialization affected people's everyday lives and led to new economic ideas.

📖 Active Reading

COMPARE AND CONTRAST
When you compare and contrast, you identify similarities and differences. As you read this section, compare and contrast everyday life before and after the Industrial Revolution.

A. Before Industrialization in Great Britain

The Industrial Revolution is the term used to describe the sweeping series of changes that took place in many areas of life beginning in the 1700s. At the root of these changes was the shift from the use of hand tools to power machinery. This era also marked the shift of people from working in their homes to working together in central places, called factories, to make goods.

Early Industry

Before the Industrial Revolution, people and animals, as well as moving water and wind, provided power. As a result of the Industrial Revolution, power was multiplied greatly by new sources, such as steam and electricity.

Before industrial times, people made goods, or products, by hand—usually in their homes. They made their own clothes and grew their own food. Local craftspeople dominated the economy in most regions. A few industries such as cloth making, or textiles, employed large numbers of workers.

By modern standards, though, manufacturing—the making of goods—was primitive. Sources of power, which included the water wheel and the windmill, had not changed much for 600 years. By most estimates, a typical water wheel output produced five horsepower—a unit of energy. A windmill's output might be double this, or perhaps more, but only in windy areas like the Netherlands. Moreover, wind did not provide power on a consistent basis.

Transport and travel were so slow that a merchant's investment in trade usually took years to pay off—if the merchant made a profit at all. **Capital**, or the money that merchants use in business to produce more wealth, was tied up for a long time. In addition, the dangers of trade—such as shipwreck, piracy, and war—often led to the failure and bankruptcy of merchants.

Teaching Options

Section 1 Resources

Teacher's Resources (TR)
Terms to Know, p. 35
Review History, p. 69
Build Your Skills, p. 103
Concept Builder, p. 238
SQR Chart, p. 322
Transparency 1

ESL/ELL STRATEGIES

Take Notes Have students take notes on one of the subsections in Section 1. Remind them to include only the most important ideas and supporting details in their notes. You can give students a main ideas/supporting details chart (TR, p. 319) to help them avoid including unimportant information. Then, ask them to use the notes to write a short newspaper article about the subject of the subsection.

Developments Toward Industrialization

The Industrial Revolution began in Great Britain during the 1700s. Several important developments set the stage. First, after the Glorious Revolution of 1688, Parliament and the monarchy settled their differences. The result was that Britain's politics became more stable.

Second, an agricultural revolution swept through Britain. Well-to-do landowners experimented with new methods and tools that made farms more efficient. New farming methods focused on **crop rotation**—a system of growing different crops one after the other on the same land. This practice helps to restore the soil. The new tools included the seed drill and the horse-hoe.

Third, landowners sought to increase the size of their holdings. Together with the merchants of London, well-to-do British "gentlemen" farmers controlled Parliament. They found it easy, therefore, to pass a series of laws that allowed them to fence off, or enclose, large areas of land. Before the **enclosures**, these areas had belonged to the residents of a village or a town. However, during the 1700s, a small group of wealthy landlords controlled most of the land. These owners usually leased their land in large blocks to a relatively small number of farmers who paid for the use of the land.

Advantages for Great Britain

This system led to more efficient management of larger tracts, or areas, of land. As a result, the food supply increased. Fewer people were needed to manage the land. More people—the labor supply—were available for other tasks. Great Britain's labor supply was plentiful because it had witnessed a greater than 50 percent population increase. Britain's rivers and ports allowed for easier transportation. All of these things combined to make Great Britain an especially suitable place for the start of the Industrial Revolution.

Finally, by the mid-1700s, Britain had a large overseas empire. Besides the colonies in the Americas, the country was working to establish its hold in India. Britain had won control of the high seas. Merchants had huge overseas markets available to them, if only more products could be created more rapidly. The possibility of profit was particularly great for the sale of cloth.

◆ **What was the significance of the enclosure laws in Great Britain?**

This illustration shows the enclosures, hedges, and fences that marked land holdings in Great Britain during the 1700s.

 **Using Technology**

Ask pairs of students to find three Web sites that provide information about the Industrial Revolution in Great Britain in the 1700s. Have them print the information and include a list of the Web sites they used. Encourage small groups of students to compare the sources they used and discuss which ones were most valuable in their research.

A. Before Industrialization in Great Britain

Purpose-Setting Question What were two of the most important changes in people's lives during the Industrial Revolution? (Possible answers: used power machinery instead of hand tools, worked in factories instead of in their homes)

Activity

Make an idea web Have students use an idea web (TR, p. 321) to organize information about life before the Industrial Revolution. (**Center circle:** life before the Industrial Revolution; **Outer circles:** goods produced at home by hand; primitive making of goods; slow transportation; used water wheel and windmill for power)

Explore Ask students why the term Industrial Revolution was used to describe the many changes in life in eighteenth-century Europe. (It was a complete change in the way goods were manufactured.)

Discuss Ask students why the Industrial Revolution began in Great Britain rather than in other European countries or the American colonies. (Important developments took place in Great Britain that contributed to the beginning of the Industrial Revolution, including new farming methods, political stability, the enclosure laws, and a large overseas empire.)

Extend Ask pairs of students to research *division of labor* in encyclopedias or on the Internet and explain how this manufacturing method, which developed during the Industrial Revolution, increased production. (Possible answer: By dividing the work on one big project so that smaller tasks were completed by many people, production was greatly increased.)

◆ **ANSWER** The enclosure laws led to more efficient management of the land, an increase in the food supply, and freed the labor supply for other tasks.

B. The Textile Industry

Purpose-Setting Question Why was the textile industry in Great Britain so important during the beginning of the Industrial Revolution? (Great Britain had an established textile industry. The earliest inventions mechanized the cloth-making industry.)

Explore Have students use library resources or the Internet to find examples of madras, calico, and chintz cloth.

GLOBAL CONNECTIONS

A GLOBAL TRADE Ask students to identify the coasts of Africa and Brazil on the world map in the Atlas (pp. A1–A2) or use Transparency 1. Have them trace possible routes that British vessels would have followed to reach these destinations.

Extend Ask small groups of students to discuss the ways developments in technology today affect their lives compared with the ways the Industrial Revolution affected the lives of people during the 1700s and 1800s. Have the groups share their answers with the class.

Make an illustrated timeline
Ask students to create an illustrated timeline (TR, p. 320) that shows the inventions that revolutionized the textile industry. Have them use library resources or the Internet to find pictures of the flying shuttle and the spinning jenny to include in their timelines.

Discuss Ask students why the invention of the water frame was a more significant achievement than that of the flying shuttle or the spinning jenny. (It was powered by water and produced strong, 100 percent cotton thread that resulted in cheaper cotton fabric. Also, the machinery, which required mechanical power, could not be used in workers' homes; thus the factory system began.)

Global Connections

A GLOBAL TRADE
Demand for cotton spread rapidly. On the coasts of Africa, traders exchanged cotton cloth for slaves. In 1808, the British started to make use of the cotton trade in Brazil.

Richard Arkwright's water frame used the power of water to spin strong cotton thread.

B. The Textile Industry

The **textile** **industry** manufactures cloth from such materials as wool and cotton. It was most important in the first stage of the Industrial Revolution. Cloth making from wool had been a traditional art for centuries in England. At the start of the Industrial Revolution, however, the demand for cotton was high.

The Demand for Cotton

In the early eighteenth century, cotton—along with spices, rugs, and china—was among the most important items in Europe's trade with Asia. The supply of cotton fabrics from India is evident from the names for different kinds of cloth. *Madras* and *calico* are from the names of the Indian cities Madras and Calicut, and *chintz* is from a Hindi word meaning "spotted." Cotton was popular largely because of its texture and the bright range of printed designs on the fabrics. Cotton could be washed without shrinking as much as wool, and cotton could absorb color dyes better.

The demand for cotton in Europe was so heavy, in fact, that it caused concern for cloth-makers of silk, wool, and linen. The French government banned cotton imports from India. Cotton continued to find its way into Great Britain, though.

Before the days of power machinery, India produced cotton fabrics that were cheaper than those made in Europe or the United States. This situation was about to change because of developments in technology. Technology became the basis of the Industrial Revolution.

Toward More Rapid Production

British merchants had organized a cotton cloth industry with people working in their homes. In this "putting-out" system, raw cotton was given to families who spun it into thread. Then, the thread was given to other families who wove the thread into cloth. After the cloth was made, artisans in nearby towns finished and dyed the cloth. This production system was slow.

The key challenge for the makers of cotton fabrics and other textiles was how to speed up the production process. This was a gradual process that took about 60 years. Four major figures: John Kay, James Hargreaves, Richard Arkwright, and Eli Whitney created inventions that improved the process. All except for Whitney were British. Whitney was an American.

In 1733, John Kay began the process of modernizing textile production. He invented a machine called the flying shuttle. This machine made it possible for one person, rather than two, to operate a loom. Then, in 1764, the engineer James Hargreaves further improved matters with his invention of the spinning jenny. This hand tool doubled production because many threads could be spun at the same time.

Although the flying shuttle and the spinning jenny were significant mechanical inventions, they fell short of being power machinery. In 1769, the inventor Richard Arkwright designed a water-powered spinning machine that truly deserved the name "industrial." The machine was called the water frame. It produced cotton thread that was much stronger than the thread made by a spinning jenny. Therefore, the need for the previously stronger linen fibers was eliminated. Because linen was more expensive than cotton, 100 percent cotton cloth meant that the price for cotton fabrics fell.

Arkwright's water frame was a far larger and heavier machine than the spinning jenny. It required mechanical power—first

508 UNIT 6 ◆ A Changing World

Teaching Options

F Y I

Cotton Producing Countries

Although the cotton plant originated in subtropical countries that had warm temperatures all year round, today more than half of all cotton grows in temperate climates with hot summers and cold winters. China, the leading producer, grows about one quarter of the world's cotton, whereas the United States, the second largest producer, grows about one-fifth of the world's cotton.

Meet Individual Needs:
VERBAL/LINGUISTIC LEARNERS

Write the terms *flying shuttle, spinning jenny,* and *water frame* on index cards. Have students choose a card, read the term aloud, and explain how the invention named on the card helped to modernize the eighteenth-century textile industry.

water, then steam—to operate. Now it was no longer practical for people to work at home.

In the 1770s, Arkwright began building the first factories, called mills, in Britain. Workers on the new machines spun thread and wove cloth. Thus, at first with the water frame and afterward with the power loom, the **factory** **system** began. The factory system is the mass production of goods in a central building or buildings.

One problem remained—how to efficiently process raw cotton. The challenge was to mechanically remove the seeds from the plant's fibers. Eli Whitney, an American, solved this challenge in 1793. Whitney's invention, the cotton gin, resembled a box with small slits down one side. It was cheap to make and easy to operate. It multiplied production of raw cotton by 5,000 percent. By 1830, more than half of all British exports consisted of cotton fabric. For the first time, British cotton goods started to compete directly with goods imported from India.

At a British textile mill, workers used machines to produce cloth.

◆ What were four achievements in the development of the textile industry?

C. The Development of Steam Power

Textiles dominated the first stage of the Industrial Revolution in Great Britain. Not long afterward, however, came important progress in the technology of steam power.

Building Better Steam Engines

Besides its political stability and large labor force, Britain also had a plentiful supply of natural resources like iron and coal. Beginning in the early 1700s, mining became an important activity. Wood had become scarce. Coal was needed, both as a source of fuel and as energy for the process of smelting iron. In this process, iron ore was melted to separate the iron metal from the ore.

To extract more coal from the ground, however, miners needed to drill deeper and deeper shafts. This problem made it necessary to have an efficient method for pumping out the water that flooded the mines. The search for better pumps was directly linked to the development of better steam engines.

As early as 1702, an English engineer named Thomas Newcomen had invented the first practical steam engine. By later standards, it was regarded as primitive because it used a huge amount of fuel. However, Newcomen's engine had the advantage of saving labor and making coal production less expensive.

The real breakthrough in steam power, however, came in 1765 when the Scottish inventor James Watt made his first improvement to Newcomen's steam engine. Watt went into partnership with Matthew Boulton. About 15 years later, steam engines were being used in textile mills. The replacement of water power by steam power gave mill owners new flexibility. Now mills did not need to be built near waterfalls or dams.

Steam engines were soon used in many parts of the world to power drills for coal mining and looms for textile production. The global spread of the machine age had begun.

HORSEPOWER

In addition to his other achievements, James Watt coined the word *horsepower*. As a unit of energy, horsepower is the power required to lift a weight of 550 pounds through a distance of 1 foot within 1 second.

Connection to
SCIENCE

Horsepower is not the only way to measure energy. The joule is a metric unit that measures all forms of energy, including mechanical energy, electrical energy, and heat. One joule is equal to about .239 calories, which is the amount of energy that can raise the temperature of 1 gram of water by 1 degree Celsius.

Activity

Write an article Have students write an article for an early nineteenth-century newspaper describing the first voyage of the *Clermont*. Remind them to write a dramatic headline and to answer the five *W*s in the opening paragraph. Allow students to use a five *W*s chart (TR, p. 326) to organize their articles. If students need additional information, allow them to use library resources or the Internet. Have students share their articles with the class.

Extend Have pairs of students create a poster advertising a trip on an early nineteenth-century American locomotive. Their posters should include text describing the advantages of this new method of transportation as well as illustrations.

SPOTLIGHT ON TECHNOLOGY

BRITISH LOCOMOTIVES Ask students to find pictures of George Stephenson's Rocket and Peter Cooper's Tom Thumb using library resources or the Internet. Have pairs of students compare the designs of these early locomotives.

◆ **ANSWER** A riverboat could be powered by a steam engine; the creation of the first railroad locomotive by British engineer George Stephenson.

D. Consequences of Industrialization

Purpose-Setting Question How did the French historian Fernand Braudel feel about the Industrial Revolution? (He believed it caused serious problems in Europe.)

Robert Fulton's steamboat, the *Clermont*, brought about a new era in steam-powered transportation. The principles of steam power eventually led to the development of the railroads.

Spotlight on *Technology*

BRITISH LOCOMOTIVES
In 1829, a competition for locomotives was held. George Stephenson's locomotive, the Rocket, which he and his son built, won the competition. When the railroad opened, it began with eight locomotives—all of them built by Stephenson. As the railroad industry grew, Stephenson stayed very involved. He built locomotives and solved problems of locomotive construction and design.

A Revolution in Transportation

Steam power soon led to a revolution in transportation. In 1807, Robert Fulton, an American inventor and engineer, successfully demonstrated that a steam engine could power a riverboat. The engine had been imported from the firm of Boulton and Watt. The riverboat was named the *Clermont*.

John Fitch had designed a steamboat about 20 years before Fulton. However, Fulton is generally given credit for the first usable or workable steamboat. In 1807, the *Clermont* made its first voyage on the Hudson River from New York City northward to Albany, New York, a distance of about 150 miles.

Within 5 years, another steamboat journeyed downstream from Pittsburgh to New Orleans. It cut the usual 4-week travel time in half. Even more dramatic time savings were achieved in upstream travel against the current. In the United States—and eventually in Europe—transport by steamboat increased profits through trade.

Another advance made possible by steam power was the railroad locomotive. In the late 1700s, the British mining industry began to use the locomotive. Horse-drawn wagons with wheels on wooden or iron tracks carried coal to canals or the sea. In the 1820s, steam engines began powering the wagons along the tracks. In 1825, British engineer George Stephenson created the first railroad locomotive. Then, he built a railroad locomotive called the Rocket in 1829. It traveled at a top speed of 16 miles per hour. In 1830, Peter Cooper built the first locomotive in the United States, the Tom Thumb.

People quickly realized that this new method of transportation had many advantages over canals and steamboats. Railroads could go almost anywhere, and transport was faster than by steamboat. For the first time in history, people who lived far away from one another could transact business within a relatively short amount of time.

◆ **What were two achievements of the revolution in transportation?**

D. Consequences of Industrialization

"Europe's example proves that, from its very beginnings, industrialization raises serious problems." Not everyone will agree with this statement by the leading French historian Fernand Braudel. Strong evidence does exist, though, that the shift from hand labor to machine labor had involved many hardships, tensions, and conflicts.

510 UNIT 6 ◆ A Changing World

Teaching Options

Test Taking

Explain that some tests include true/false statements. Point out that only one part of a statement has to be false in order to make the entire statement false. Make three true/false statements using information on this page and ask students to decide if each statement is true or false and then give reasons for their answer.

Cooperative Learning

Have students work together in small groups to plan an exhibit about the first railroad locomotives in the United States and Great Britain in the early nineteenth century. Members of each group should be responsible for different tasks, including research, planning, finding visuals, writing captions and brief reports, and making maps and posters. After each group has completed its exhibit, display the projects in class.

The Impact of Industrialization on Everyday Life

Over time, the Industrial Revolution had an impact on people's lives. The factory system was an economic reality that would grow. Work in the mills was demanding. Fourteen-hour days were common. The closed-in atmosphere and repetition in mill work made daily tasks a burden for many workers.

Mill workers had little say about their job conditions. Their wages were as low as the owner could make them. During the early stages of the Industrial Revolution, there were few attempts to regulate, or control by law, working conditions in the mills. Robert Peel, an owner of cotton mills, sponsored one such measure, the Factory Act of 1802. The law's goal was to regulate working conditions for children of the poor working in the textile industry. The law, however, failed to provide trained inspectors to enforce it.

In 1846, an American worker named Juliana wrote about conditions at the factory in which she worked in Lowell, Massachusetts.

> **“** Those who write . . . about the "Beauties of Factory Life," tell us that we are indeed happy creatures . . . [many] advantages are . . . enjoyed by the operatives [workers] . . . [but] when do they find time for all or any of these? When exhausted nature demands repose [rest]? **”**

ANALYZE PRIMARY SOURCES

DOCUMENT-BASED QUESTION What can you tell from Juliana's comments about real conditions in the factory?

Another factor affecting everyday life was the rapid growth of cities. For centuries, London had been the largest city in Britain and the country's capital and economic center. During the Industrial Revolution, though, new cities sprang up. They grew out of important clusters of mills that needed water power or steam power. New cities also developed near the sources of coal and iron, the resources that fueled steam power. These natural resources were concentrated in an area called Midlands and in the north.

Some Industrial Revolution Inventions, 1733–1825

INVENTOR	YEAR	INVENTION	EFFECT
John Kay	1733	Flying shuttle	Made possible one person's operation of a loom
James Hargreaves	1764	Spinning jenny	Made possible one person's spinning of two or more threads by hand
James Watt	1765	Improved steam engine	Replaced water power with steam power, at first in factories and later in transportation, with the steamboat and railroad locomotive
Richard Arkwright	1769	Water frame	Made possible the production of stronger thread by using water power in the spinning process
Eli Whitney	1793	Cotton gin	Made possible the rapid separation of seeds from cotton fibers
Robert Fulton	1807	Workable steam riverboat	Expanded water transportation
George Stephenson	1825	Railroad locomotive	Expanded rail transportation

Spinning jenny

✔ **Chart Check**

Which invention used water power to produce stronger thread?

Connection to
CULTURE

Mill owners in Lowell, Massachusetts, developed the Lowell system. It was designed to regulate the lives of the young girls recruited to work in the mills. Under this system, workers lived in clean boarding houses, received good wages, and were strictly supervised. However, as economic conditions began to decline, living conditions also deteriorated.

Connection to
LITERATURE

Sarah N. Cleghorn (1876–1959) was an American poet and novelist who wrote poems protesting social injustice. The theme of one of her most famous works is child labor in American factories:

The golf links lie so near the mill
That almost every day
The laboring children can look out
And see the men at play.

Discuss Ask students to identify the advantages and disadvantages of industrialization for the average worker. (Possible answers: **Advantages:** provided factory jobs for the workers; enabled people to learn new skills; **Disadvantages:** workdays were long, wages were low; the work was repetitive)

Activity

Write a letter Ask students to write a letter to the editor of a nineteenth-century British newspaper expressing their opinion about the Factory Act of 1802. Students should use facts in their letter to make their points persuasive. Students can use library resources or the Internet to find additional facts, if needed.

ANALYZE PRIMARY SOURCES

DOCUMENT-BASED QUESTION
Lowell, Massachusetts, was the first planned industrial town in the United States. By the middle of the nineteenth century, it had become one of the country's major industrial cities. Because of its tremendous reserve of water power, Lowell became an important center of textile manufacturing. The completion of the Boston and Lowell Railroad in 1835 and a canal system on the Merrimack River contributed to Lowell's economic growth.

ANSWER Possible answer: Factory workers found the conditions difficult.

Using the Chart
Some Industrial Revolution Inventions, 1733–1825

Ask students to identify the invention that made it possible for one person to spin two or more threads by hand. (spinning jenny) Ask students to identify two inventions that improved textile production. (flying shuttle; cotton gin)

✔ **Chart Check**
Answer water frame

Do You Remember?

Ask students whether laissez-faire and a free market economy would have benefited the mill owners or workers. Have them explain their answers. (Mill owners; they could run their businesses without government regulation for safety.)

Discuss Ask pairs of students to prepare five questions they would like to ask Adam Smith or Thomas Malthus about their economic theories. Have students present their questions in class and discuss how the economic theorists might have responded.

◆ **ANSWER** In his book *The Wealth of Nations*, Adam Smith supported capitalism.

Section Close

Ask small groups of students to list the advantages and disadvantages of the Industrial Revolution in eighteenth- and nineteenth-century Europe and the United States. Have groups compare their lists and combine them into a master list.

3 Assess

Review Answers

Review History

A. progress in farming methods, rivers and ports, and a good food supply and labor supply

B. Such inventions as the flying shuttle, the spinning jenny, the water frame, and the cotton gin made faster production of textiles possible.

C. James Watt improved the steam engine, which was used in the mills and in riverboats.

D. Mill workers worked 14-hour days, had repetitive routines, and low wages.

The British industrial cities of Manchester and Liverpool were prime examples of new towns with extraordinary population growth at this time. In 1772, for example, the population of Manchester was 25,000. By 1851, it was 455,000. The rapid growth overwhelmed the cities. Housing there was unplanned and overcrowded. Entire families lived in a single room. Water supplies were polluted. Fresh food was scarce. Police and fire protection and public health measures were almost nonexistent. Crime and disease were constant threats.

Capitalism and Laissez-Faire Economics

Along with the practical impact of the Industrial Revolution on people's everyday lives, there were also important developments in economic ideas. In fact, modern economics as a branch of knowledge dates from this period.

The most important figure was the Scottish economist Adam Smith, whom you read about in Chapter 18. As you have learned, Smith believed in the economic ideas of laissez faire and a free market economy. Smith's beliefs in these ideas called for government not to interfere with the supply and demand of goods and services. With his belief in these economic ideas, Smith favored the economic system of capitalism. Capitalism is based on the investment of money in businesses for profit. In capitalism, all or most of the means of production are privately owned. Wealth is created and increased by using the profits of business to stimulate further growth in business.

Smith's book *The Wealth of Nations* had a huge influence on economics. Among the most important of Smith's followers was Thomas Malthus. In 1798, Malthus published *An Essay on the Principle of Population*. In this work, Malthus argued that poverty could not be avoided because population growth would always be greater than society's ability to provide for everyone.

◆ **What economic system did Adam Smith support in** *The Wealth of Nations*?

Do You Remember?

In Chapter 18, you learned that laissez faire is the practice of letting business run without government intervention. A free market economy is the buying and selling of goods without the government's regulation.

Review I

Review History

A. Which factors allowed Great Britain to lead the Industrial Revolution?

B. How did technological innovations affect the textile industry?

C. How did James Watt contribute to the Industrial Revolution, both in Great Britain and in the United States?

D. What were job conditions like for mill workers?

Define Terms to Know

Define the following terms: **capital, crop rotation, enclosure, textile industry, factory system**

Critical Thinking

Write a letter as a British mill worker around 1820. Tell a friend how your working life has changed during the past 20 or so years.

Write About Economics

Do you think laissez-faire economics is a good idea? Write a paragraph stating and supporting your opinion.

Get Organized

SQR CHART

Use an SQR chart to organize information from this section. For example, one topic from this section might be the rise of factories.

Define Terms to Know

capital, 506; crop rotation, 507; enclosure, 507; textile industry, 508; factory system, 509

Critical Thinking

Letters should emphasize the contrast between industrial work in a mill and agricultural work on a farm or work done in the home.

Write About Economics

Students' opinions will vary, but they should support their views with examples and reasons.

Survey
This section is about the rise of factory systems.

Question
How did the factory system start?

Read
Larger and heavier machines that needed mechanical power to work made factories necessary.

Build Your Skills

CONDUCT RESEARCH

Assignments often require you to conduct research. Becoming familiar with research methods and tools can help you. Start your research by making a list of questions you have about a topic. Then, decide which of the following sources are appropriate for discovering answers to your questions: library resources, Internet resources, or interviews. Library resources include encyclopedias, atlases, almanacs, nonfiction books, biographical dictionaries, newspapers, periodicals, pamphlets, magazines, and bibliographies.

The Internet offers exciting potential for researching a topic. Much of the information is useful, but you need to examine it carefully to determine whether it is reliable, or based on facts.

Finally, consider using interviews when researching your topic. Experts and people who have lived through an event can furnish much valuable information.

Remember to use a variety of sources. Using more than one source allows you to cross-check the accuracy of information, and it exposes you to different opinions and points of view. Finally, make sure to document all the sources you use. You need to be able to identify these sources in your work.

Here's How
Follow these steps to conduct research.

1. Use an encyclopedia article to get an overview of your topic.
2. Use reference works, newspaper or periodical articles, books, and the Internet to gather information.
3. Be sure to use a variety of sources. Check to see that your sources contain accurate and up-to-date information.
4. Use notecards to record the author's ideas and words in quotation marks. Also, use them to record where you find each piece of information. Be sure to include all the source information that will tell others how to find it.
5. Consider using interviews to expand your research.

Here's Why
The ability to conduct research is a valuable skill. Not only will it help you with your schoolwork, but it will also be useful for general problem solving and career opportunities.

Practice the Skill
Copy the chart on the right onto a sheet of paper. Reread Section 1 to review the three topics listed on the chart. Then, visit your school or local library to find three sources you could use to prepare a report on each topic. List the sources in the second column.

Extend the Skill
Choose one of the topics on the chart and write a one-page report. Share your report with the class.

Apply the Skill
As you read the remaining sections of this chapter, take notes on the people, places, and events mentioned. Then, go to your school or local library to learn more about them.

TOPIC	SOURCES
Robert Fulton	• A biographical dictionary • *A History of the Modern World*, R. R. Palmer • www.historychannel.com
Factory Act of 1802	
Early railroad locomotives	

CHAPTER 22 ◆ The Industrial Revolution and Social Change **513**

Teaching Options

RETEACH
Ask pairs of students to choose a topic from an early chapter in their textbook to research. Have students work in pairs to identify five sources they would use to research the topic. Remind students to use a variety of sources. Student pairs should compare their lists and then, list the sources under appropriate headings on a chart.

CHALLENGE
Ask students to research a career that interests them by using a variety of sources: library reference material, the Internet, and interviews. You may need to help students formulate interview questions and identify appropriate people to interview. Have groups of students discuss what they learned about the career and what other careers they may want to research.

Build Your Skills

CONDUCT RESEARCH

Teach the Skill
Ask students to identify a place of interest in your community or state to visit on a class trip. You may wish to bring in a state or community map. Have students discuss how they would use the steps in *Here's How* to find more information about their destination in order to plan the trip.

Encourage students to discuss other sources of information they could use to research the site, such as community or state historical societies, the information centers at state parks or museums, or automobile associations. Have students discuss which research source would be the most valuable and efficient and explain the reason for their choice. Finally, have students draw a map to show where their site is, explain how they would get there, and describe what they expect to see.

Practice the Skill
Students should provide three sources for each topic and note all information needed to locate the source again. Students should demonstrate that they could find appropriate sources for their topics. Their results should show an understanding of the topic they have researched.

Extend the Skill
Reports should be one page in length. Students should present their reports to the class and be able to describe the sources they used and why they selected those sources.

Apply the Skill
Students should be able to select people, places, and events from the remaining three sections of the chapter that can be researched. Have students share what they have learned with the class.

II. The Spread of Industry (pp. 514–518)

Section Summary

In this section, students will learn about the spread of the Industrial Revolution to other countries and how industrialization affected the United States. They will also learn about the disparity between industrialization in western and Asian countries and their colonies.

1 Introduce

Getting Started

Ask students what advantages a country would have if it had automobiles and power engines and other countries did not. (move people and goods faster and cheaper) Explain to students that some countries did not want to share the technological advances that were made by their citizens with other countries.

TERMS TO KNOW

Ask students to read the terms and definitions on page 514 and then find each term in the section. Have students work with a partner, taking turns using each term in an original sentence.

You may wish to preview the pronunciation of the following terms from this section with students.

Le Creusot (LUH kroo ZOH)
Joseph Marie Jacquard
(ZHOH zehf mah REE zhah KAHR)
Wilhelm Roentgen
(vihl HEHLM ROONT guhn)

ACTIVE READING

Have students choose one of the subsections of Section 2 and write a summary of its most important ideas. Remind them that their summaries should be written in their own words. They can use section headings, captions, and key words to help them.

Terms to Know

interchangeable parts identical parts that can be used in place of one another

protective tariff a tax put on imported goods to encourage consumers to buy those same goods from their own country

transcontinental across a continent

colonialism the rule of a foreign territory for economic gain and military power

This tapestry, titled *Lady with the Unicorn*, was handwoven in the fifteenth century. After the invention of the power loom, tapestries could be produced cheaply in French and Belgian mills.

Main Ideas

A. The Industrial Revolution spread from Great Britain to other parts of Europe and to the United States.

B. The factory system, the arms industry, and rapid progress in transportation and communications were notable features of the Industrial Revolution in the United States.

C. In the 1800s, science and technology continued to be linked with industrialization, but colonies of foreign powers were generally not allowed to industrialize.

A. The Spread of Industry in Europe

Just as the Renaissance spread northward from Italy and the Reformation spread outward from Germany and Geneva, Switzerland, the Industrial Revolution in Great Britain soon affected European countries. The newly independent United States of America was affected as well.

Following Britain's Lead

The rapid advances in the textile industry, as well as the development of steam power, created a strong British economy. At the same time, the British were well aware that if other nations became industrialized, they would compete fiercely with Great Britain. Therefore, Britain passed laws forbidding people to take the designs of new machines abroad or overseas. The laws did not work very well, however, and industrialization spread. Although the British had a commanding head start in the Industrial Revolution, their attempt to control industry failed.

Except for the United States, the first nations to industrialize after the British were countries located nearby: Belgium, France, and Germany. A British mechanic named William Cockerill, together with his sons, took the plans for a mill to Belgium. There, they set up a textile machine industry. Belgium became the first European nation outside Britain to industrialize.

France was especially eager to follow in Britain's footsteps. The French offered large rewards to spies who could provide them with information about the new industrial technology. William Wilkinson, a British metalworker, set up a metalworking center at Le Creusot in France. Germany became a major industrial nation by the late 1800s. Its electrical and chemical industries were particularly strong.

Perhaps the most spectacular example of industrial spying involved the case of Samuel Slater. A skilled mechanic, Slater had worked for Richard Arkwright's partner, Jedediah Strutt. Arkwright's water frame had proved so successful that by the late 1700s, there were almost 100 cotton mills in Great Britain. In 1789, Slater left Britain for the United States. He had memorized the designs for cotton-spinning machinery. Within 2 years of landing in New York, he created a partnership with Moses Brown, a Rhode Island businessman. Together, they built a factory for spinning cotton thread.

Active Reading

SUMMARIZE
When you summarize, you state only the most important points, or highlights, of a passage. As you read this section, focus on the main points about the spread of the Industrial Revolution. At the end of each section, pause to summarize what you have learned.

Teaching Options

Section 2 Resources

Teacher's Resources (TR)
Terms to Know, p. 35
Review History, p. 69
Build Your Skills, p. 103
Concept Builder, p. 238
SQR Chart, p. 322
Transparency 5

ESL/ELL STRATEGIES

Organize Information Ask pairs of students to use a main idea/supporting details chart (TR, p. 319) to identify the most important idea and the supporting details in the subsection Following Britain's Lead. Have student pairs compare charts and add any details as necessary.

An Uneven Process

The Industrial Revolution involved a set of events rather than a single occurrence. Many of the important discoveries were made in Great Britain. However, Eli Whitney's cotton gin was an American contribution. In 1801, Joseph Marie Jacquard invented a power loom in France. French coal fields used steam-powered machines possibly as early as 1750.

The Industrial Revolution also grew at an uneven rate. Industrialization soon reached areas that enjoyed political stability, a large labor force, and plentiful natural resources. By the end of the nineteenth century, mechanized industry was far more common in western than in eastern Europe.

◆ How did Great Britain attempt to completely control industrialization?

B. Industrialization in the United States

After the United States gained independence, it was not at all clear that the new nation would become an industrial power. In 1790, more than 95 percent of the American population was rural, or living on farms.

Alexander Hamilton, an important statesman, argued that the United States needed to become a manufacturing country. In a report to the U.S. Congress in 1791, Hamilton listed the benefits of industrialization. Among these benefits was the "promoting of emigration [the movement away] from foreign countries." Industrialization soon enriched the U.S. economy, and it also added more opportunities for many people.

Here is how one promoter of manufacturing argued in a letter to the magazine *American Museum* in 1787:

   ❝Why all this opposition to our working up those materials that God and nature have given us? Surely . . . it was the only way to our real independence, and to render [make] the habitable [liveable] parts of our country truly valuable.—What countries are the most flourishing and most powerful in the world? Manufacturing countries.**❞**

The Early Phase of Manufacturing

After the American Revolution, the new government of the United States was still concerned about national defense, or protection of the country from outsiders. Eli Whitney, the inventor of the cotton gin, also played an important part in the development of the weapons, or arms, industry. At that time, all guns were handmade, and their parts were each slightly different. If a part broke, a new one had to be handcrafted for that particular weapon. Whitney realized that the production of arms could be made far more efficient if guns were made with standardized, or **interchangeable parts**. These identical parts could be used in place of one another.

A cotton mill co-owned by Samuel Slater in Pawtucket, Rhode Island, was a sign of the arrival of the industrial age in the United States.

ANALYZE PRIMARY SOURCES
DOCUMENT-BASED QUESTION
What benefits of manufacturing does the writer point out?

CHAPTER 22 ◆ The Industrial Revolution and Social Change **515**

---

2 Teach

A. The Spread of Industry in Europe

Purpose-Setting Question How did the Industrial Revolution spread to other countries? (Industrial spies gave other countries information about the new industrial technology.)

Discuss Ask students why they think that the Industrial Revolution spread more quickly in western than in eastern Europe. (Possible answer: Western European countries had the same advantages as Great Britain, such as political stability, a large labor force, and plentiful natural resources. Eastern European countries did not have these advantages.)

Extend Have pairs of students use the Internet to find more information about Samuel Slater's cotton mill. Have them share their findings with the class.

◆ **ANSWER** Great Britain passed laws forbidding people to take the designs of new machines abroad.

B. Industrialization in the United States

Purpose-Setting Question Why did Alexander Hamilton encourage industrialization in the United States? (He realized the benefits of industrialization, including encouraging people from other countries to move to the United States and providing more opportunities for many people.)

ANALYZE PRIMARY SOURCES

DOCUMENT-BASED QUESTION
This excerpt is from one of three letters published in the magazine *American Museum* in 1787. The letters were signed, "A Plain, but Real Friend to America," and supported the viewpoint that America should manufacture more of its own products, rather than import them from other countries.

ANSWER Possible answers: real independence, a flourishing economy, and making the habitable parts of the United States truly valuable

Focus Point out that the Erie Canal, the first important national waterway built in the United States, provided a link between east and west. While settlers and manufactured goods could be transported westward, agricultural products and timber could be transported eastward. The canal helped New York City to become the leading port in the United States during the nineteenth century. However, railroads lessened the importance of the Erie Canal after 1865 and eventually it became part of a larger waterway.

TEACH PRIMARY SOURCES
The location of the golden spike used to complete the transcontinental railroad is now a National Historic Site in Utah. Have students identify details of the ceremony that are visible in the photograph on page 516. (Possible answers: large crowd, the trains assembled for the ceremony) Ask students to discuss the significance of having a photograph of a historic event such as this one. (Possible answer: A photograph can preserve the event for future generations.)

Discuss Ask students how the telegraph and telephone would have affected life in nineteenth-century America. (Both advances enabled Americans to communicate with one another and with people in other countries of the world more quickly and more easily for the first time. These inventions were the first steps in a future communications revolution.)

◆ **ANSWER** Eli Whitney developed the idea of interchangeable parts for weapons.

The factory system soon caught on in the United States, but it took advantage of children. Children worked in unhealthy conditions and were paid less than adults. Not all factory owners, however, were cruel. Francis Cabot Lowell's highly successful spinning factory in Waltham, Massachusetts, was the first fully mechanized spinning and weaving operation in the United States. It opened in 1814. In 1850, Lowell's companies employed about 10,000 workers in Waltham and Lowell, Massachusetts. In the "Lowell system," as it was called, the company workers—many of them young, unmarried women—lived in dormitories. They were provided with educational resources, a church, and a minister. The system, however, had its defenders and critics.

In order to encourage American industry, Congress enacted taxes called **protective** **tariffs** in the early 1800s. These tariffs made goods imported from abroad more expensive than goods produced at home. Therefore, consumers were motivated to buy goods made in the United States.

Transportation and Communications

Fulton's demonstration of the *Clermont* brought about a new era for transportation in the United States. To take advantage of water transportation, many canals were dug. The Erie Canal was completed in 1825. This inland waterway connected the Great Lakes to the Hudson River and thus to the Atlantic Ocean. While canals and shipbuilding flourished, it was the railroads that truly revolutionized transportation. In 1869, a **transcontinental**, or across-the-continent, railroad was completed. It connected the East coast and the West coast, and played a major role in settling the western United States.

Two advances in the United States affected long-distance communications. The first was the telegraph, invented by Samuel F. B. Morse in 1844. In 1866, North America was linked to Europe by telegraph through a cable laid across the ocean floor. In 1876, Alexander Graham Bell invented the telephone.

◆ What was Eli Whitney's role in the development of the U.S. arms industry?

The ceremony celebrating the completion of the transcontinental railroad is shown in the photograph on the far right. The last spike hammered into the track is shown on the near right.

Teaching Options

F Y I

Transcontinental Railroad

When the transcontinental railroad was completed, North America had a rare distinction—it was the first continent linked by rail from coast to coast. The Union Pacific laid the rails westward, beginning near Omaha, Nebraska, while the Central Pacific laid the track eastward from Sacramento, California. This engineering feat involved crossing the Rocky Mountains and Sierra Nevadas.

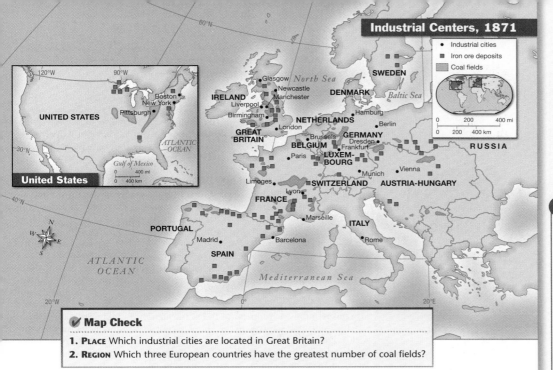

Industrial Centers, 1871

- Industrial cities
- Iron ore deposits
- Coal fields

United States

UNITED STATES

Boston
New York
Pittsburgh

ATLANTIC OCEAN

Gulf of Mexico

IRELAND
Glasgow *North Sea*
Newcastle
Manchester
Liverpool
Birmingham
London
GREAT BRITAIN
Brussels
BELGIUM
Paris
LUXEM-BOURG
Limoges
FRANCE
Lyon
PORTUGAL
Madrid
SPAIN
Barcelona
Marseille

SWEDEN
DENMARK *Baltic Sea*
Hamburg
NETHERLANDS
Berlin
GERMANY
Dresden
Frankfurt
RUSSIA
SWITZERLAND
Munich
Vienna
AUSTRIA-HUNGARY
ITALY
Rome

ATLANTIC OCEAN

Mediterranean Sea

✔ Map Check

1. **PLACE** Which industrial cities are located in Great Britain?
2. **REGION** Which three European countries have the greatest number of coal fields?

C. Advances and Setbacks

Competition within industries and among nations encouraged some countries to grow wealthy at the expense of others. Some countries often deliberately held other countries back.

Advances in Technology and Science

During the later 1800s, scientific discoveries quickened the pace of the Industrial Revolution. In the 1850s, a British inventor named Henry Bessemer and an American iron manufacturer named William Kelly, working independently, developed a process for making steel quickly and cheaply. It came to be known as the Bessemer process. The key was blasting air into a furnace as iron was melted and transformed into steel. The air helped eliminate impurities and produced stronger steel. The Bessemer process allowed for larger quantities of steel to be produced.

By 1880, most steel produced in the United States used this faster and less-expensive method. Steel output increased and helped other industries expand. The stronger steel was used to make taller buildings, longer bridges, and miles of railroad tracks. A wealth of natural resources also helped the steel industry to expand. The United States had plenty of coal for fuel and iron ore, the raw material of steel.

In the field of medicine, Horace Wells, an American dentist, first used an anesthetic—a drug that stops pain during surgery. Joseph Lister, an English surgeon, began to use antiseptics—chemicals which reduce infection—when he performed surgery.

CHAPTER 22 ◆ The Industrial Revolution and Social Change **517**

Activity

Role-play Ask pairs of students to role-play an interview between Thomas Edison and a newspaper reporter. The reporter should ask Edison about his inventions and his life. Encourage students to do additional research about Edison. Call on student pairs to present their interviews in class.

Extend Explain to students that Marie Curie shared the 1903 Nobel Prize for physics. She was also awarded the 1911 Nobel Prize for chemistry for the isolation of pure radium. She did extensive research about the chemistry of radioactive substances and how these substances could be used in medicine. Curie was the first woman to teach in the Sorbonne in Paris.

Discuss Have students draw conclusions about the reasons why industrialization was not encouraged in European colonies. (Possible answer: The colonies of European powers, such as Great Britain and the Netherlands, were seen as sources of raw materials. If the colonies became industrialized they could become independent.)

◆ **ANSWER** The Bessemer process resulted in stronger steel used to build taller buildings, longer bridges, and more railroad tracks.

Section Close

Have small groups of students identify the positive and negative effects of the Industrial Revolution in a two-column chart (TR, p. 328). Ask the groups to compare their lists and discuss any differences.

3 Assess

Review Answers

Review History
A. Belgium, France, and Germany
B. They encouraged people to buy more goods at home than from abroad.
C. microphone, phonograph, and electric light bulb

Define Terms to Know
interchangeable parts, 515; protective tariff, 516; transcontinental, 516; colonialism, 518

T518 ◆ UNIT 6

The American inventor Thomas Alva Edison transformed everyday life with his discoveries. In 3 years alone, from 1877 to 1879, Edison invented the microphone, the phonograph, or record player, and the electric light bulb. Edison also introduced the concept of a research laboratory in Menlo Park, New Jersey. There, teams of scientists worked together on projects and sets of problems.

Toward the end of the nineteenth century, the German physicist Wilhelm Roentgen discovered X rays. Three French physicists—Antoine Becquerel and Pierre and Marie Curie—discovered radioactivity. Like Roentgen, they won a Nobel Prize for their work. Finally, just after the turn of the twentieth century, a German physicist who would later become an American, Albert Einstein, revolutionized physics with his theory of relativity.

European Policies in India and Indonesia

The height of the Industrial Revolution happened at the same time as European **colonialism** in many parts of the world, especially in Africa and Asia. Colonialism is the rule of foreign territory for economic and military power. By the mid-nineteenth century, Great Britain's lead in the Industrial Revolution, its vast sea power, and its overseas possessions had made it the richest and most powerful country in the world.

In 1857, Britain put down a rebellion in India called the Mutiny and strengthened its rule there. The economic goal of British rule was to hold India back. What made Britain wealthy was the cheap supply of Indian raw materials, such as raw cotton, tea, jute, and wheat. While there, the British also misused the environment in India, cutting down millions of teak trees.

Much the same was true of the Dutch colonialists in Indonesia. In the early 1800s, Dutch power was confined to the island of Java. However, the colonial interests of Britain, Germany, and France in nearby areas motivated the Dutch to expand their own empire. Sugar, coffee, and spices were important products. Like the British who controlled India, the Dutch ruled Indonesia. India did not become independent until 1947. Indonesia gained independence in 1949.

◆ **What was the effect of the Bessemer process?**

An Edison standard phonograph with cylindrical records is shown here. Thomas Edison invented the phonograph in 1877.

Review II

Review History
A. After Great Britain, which were the next three European countries to begin to industrialize?
B. What was the purpose of protective tariffs?
C. What were three of Edison's inventions?

Define Terms to Know
Define the following terms:
interchangeable parts, protective tariff, transcontinental, colonialism

Critical Thinking
What do you think would have happened to the U.S. economy if industrialization had not spread there?

Write About Economics
Suppose you are an American newspaper editor in 1790. Write a brief editorial arguing either for or against the development of manufacturing in the United States.

Get Organized
SQR CHART
Use an SQR chart to organize information from this section. For example, one topic from this section might be advances in transportation and communications.

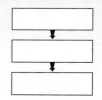

518 UNIT 6 ◆ A Changing World

Critical Thinking
Possible answer: The U.S. economy would have grown at a slower rate than it did.

Write About Economics
Students' editorials should include at least two or three reasons or examples that support their opinion, which should be explicitly stated in the first paragraph.

Survey
This section is about advances in transportation and communications.

Question
What were the transportation and communications advances?

Read
Canals and railroads were transportation advances. The telegraph and telephone were communications advances.

Points of View

Industrialization

Charles Dickens was a British writer who lived during the Industrial Revolution. He criticized the bad working conditions of mills in Great Britain. In 1842, Dickens traveled to the United States, where he toured the Massachusetts factories started by Francis Cabot Lowell. In his book *American Notes*, Dickens recorded a favorable impression of working conditions at the Lowell factories.

Other observers of the Lowell factories were much less impressed. Two years before Dickens's visit, the Unitarian minister Orestes A. Brownson wrote an article for the *Boston Quarterly Review* about the textile workers in Lowell. Brownson argued that factory conditions were so wretched that the workers were worse off than enslaved people.

During the 1800s, many young women worked at the Lowell factories operating machines that produced cloth.

> " I happened to arrive at the first factory just as the dinner hour was over, and the girls were returning to their work. . . . They were all well dressed. . . . The rooms in which they worked, were as well ordered as themselves. In the windows of some, there were green plants, which were trained to shade the glass; in all, there was as much fresh air, cleanliness, and comfort, as the nature of the occupation would possibly admit of. "
>
> —Charles Dickens, *American Notes*, 1842

> " We know of no sadder sight on earth than one of our factory villages presents, when the bell at break of day, or at the hour of breakfast, or dinner, calls out its hundreds or thousands of operatives [workers]. We stand and look at these hard working men and women hurrying in all directions, and ask ourselves, where go the proceeds of their labors? The man who employs them, and for whom they are toiling, is one of our city nabobs [big shots], reveling [enjoying] in luxury. "
>
> —Orestes A. Brownson,
> *Boston Quarterly Review*, 1840

ANALYZE PRIMARY SOURCES

DOCUMENT-BASED QUESTIONS

1. What details does Dickens mention to support his opinion?

2. What does Brownson see in his factory village?

3. **Critical Thinking** How do you think Brownson wants the reader to answer the question he asks about the "proceeds" of the workers' labors?

Teaching Options

Take a Stand

Have students write a letter to the editor of a nineteenth-century American newspaper that either praises the conditions in the Lowell factories or criticizes them. Their letters should clearly state their opinions and include factual details to support them. Encourage students to do more research about the Lowell system of factory management. Have students read their letters aloud and have others identify the opinion expressed.

Today, investigative journalists and authors write magazine or newspaper articles and books about various social issues. Provide an example of a recent investigative magazine or newspaper article about a social issue that would be of interest to students. Photocopy the article and ask students to identify the writer's opinion.

Points of View

INDUSTRIALIZATION

Teach the Topic

These selections present two different points of view about the effects of industrialization on the working conditions in factories in Lowell, Massachusetts. The quote by Charles Dickens, a famous British author, is from a book of travel sketches about American life. Brownson's impression was recorded in an American magazine article.

Ask students to identify reasons why the writers had such different opinions of the same experience. (Possible answers: To Dickens, who was visiting America, the working conditions in Lowell were probably better than those in industrialized cities in Great Britain; Brownson, an American, had a more personal view of the factory system in Lowell. Also, he probably compared the working conditions of the millworkers with those of American farmworkers.)

Compare and Contrast Points of View

Ask students to paraphrase Dickens's and Brownson's points of view about the effects of industrialization on the workers in the Lowell mills. (Charles Dickens found the working and living conditions of the workers to be satisfactory. Orestes Brownson believed the millworkers, whom he called "operatives," weren't being well treated by the mill owners, who reaped the benefits of the workers' labor.) Have students make up headlines for a magazine or newspaper article of the period in which these two writers express their points of view about industrialization in Lowell.)

ANALYZE PRIMARY SOURCES

DOCUMENT-BASED QUESTIONS

1. Possible answers: well-dressed workers, cleanliness of the workroom, and green plants
2. Brownson sees hardworking men and women hurrying in various directions around the factory village when the factory bell rings.
3. Possible answer: Brownson wants us to infer that the proceeds go to the factory owners while the workers are poorly paid.

III. Cities and the Middle Class (pp. 520–524)

Section Summary

In this section, students will learn how the Industrial Revolution and increased immigration resulted in rapid urban growth in Europe and the United States. They will also learn about the harsh conditions of urban life and the relationship between the growth of cities, which became cultural centers, and the growth of the middle class.

1 Introduce

Getting Started

Ask students to discuss some of the factors that have contributed to the growth of their community or city. These may include economic expansion, a good transportation system, location, the quality of the school system, universities, and job or cultural opportunities.

TERMS TO KNOW

Ask students to read the terms and definitions on page 520 and then find each term in the section. Have pairs of students write context sentences for each word. Student pairs should exchange papers and substitute the definitions for each word as they read the sentences out loud.

You may wish to preview the pronunciation of the following terms from this section with students.

Lazarus (LAZ uh rus)
cholera (kahl UHR uh)
Philharmonic (fil hahr MAHN ihk)
Carnegie Mellon
  (kahr NEH gee MEHL uhn)
Cornelius Vanderbilt
  (kawr NEEL yuhs VAN duhr bihlt)

ACTIVE READING

Have students work in groups to choose one of the subsections in Section 3, such as Conditions of Urban Life, and evaluate specific facts before making a judgment about the information. Ask students to discuss why certain facts were more important than others in helping them make their judgment.

Terms to Know

urbanization the movement of more and more of a country's population from rural to urban areas

immigration the act of coming to a new country to live there

tenement a run-down apartment building

Main Ideas

A. The Industrial Revolution caused the growth of cities in Europe and the United States.

B. The conditions of urban life in the 1800s were challenging and often quite harsh.

C. The growth of cities was accompanied by an increase in the population of the middle class and by the development of cities as centers of culture.

Active Reading

EVALUATE
When you evaluate, you weigh the importance of specific facts or evidence in order to make a judgment. As you read this section, evaluate the advantages and disadvantages of urban life during the 1800s.

A. The Growth of Cities

In the late Middle Ages and during the Renaissance, the development of towns and cities owed much to increases in trade. The Industrial Revolution rapidly created great possibilities for manufacturing and business. The growth in population and the need for fewer farm laborers also caused cities to grow. It is little wonder, then, that cities grew swiftly, both in number and size, during the nineteenth century.

Cities and the Industrial Revolution

In Great Britain and in the United States, the development of cities was linked to the factory system. Factories tended to be located near sources of energy, so cities grew up near rivers or dams. The most rapid growth in Great Britain was in the Midlands and the north, the center of the mining industry. The population in the Midlands city of Manchester exploded during the 1800s. Not far to the west of Manchester, the busy port of Liverpool also greatly increased in population.

In 1800, Europe had only a few cities, such as London and Paris, with populations of over 500,000. By 1900, London had more than 6 million people—more than 7 times the number of people it had 100 years before. Paris had more than 3 million people, and Berlin, Germany, had almost 3 million people. Glasgow in Great Britain, Moscow and Saint Petersburg in Russia, and Vienna, in Austria-Hungary, each had more than 1 million residents. Across Europe, new chances for wealth and the demand for industrial labor drew people to the cities in huge numbers.

The process of **urbanization**, or the movement of more and more people from rural areas to cities, was equally evident in the United States. The chart on page 521 shows the increases in population in some of the largest cities between 1850 and 1900.

People from all over Europe, such as this family, came to the United States in the 1800s.

Immigration to the United States

During the second half of the 1800s, cities in the midwestern and western regions of the United States grew enormously. This growth reflected the expansion of the American West. Along with the settlement of the West, however, there was another important factor in the nationwide growth of cities in all U.S. regions: **immigration**. Immigration is the act of coming to another country to live there.

520 UNIT 6 ◆ A Changing World

Teaching Options

Section 3 Resources

Teacher's Resources (TR)
Terms to Know, p. 35
Review History, p. 69
Build Your Skills, p. 103
Concept Builder, p. 238
SQR Chart, p. 322

Connection to CULTURE

In Great Britain and the United States, settlement houses helped improve conditions for the urban poor. When immigration to the United States skyrocketed in the late 1800s, settlement houses provided services to help newcomers adjust to life in America. The houses offered lectures, art exhibits, courses in English and industrial education, and kindergartens for the young.

Beginning in the 1830s, the pace of immigration grew rapidly. In that decade, about 600,000 immigrants entered the United States. In the 1850s, the figure was 2.6 million. Most of these immigrants were Irish, German, or British. Immigrants had a variety of reasons for leaving their homelands. Poor people looked forward to economic opportunities in a young and vigorous country. Some immigrants fled their native lands to avoid religious or political persecution. Others immigrated because land in northern Europe was crowded or unavailable, and land in the United States was plentiful and cheap.

For most immigrants, the cities seemed the logical place to settle. This was because the Industrial Revolution increased the demand for labor, especially in cities. In addition, steamships and railroads made mass movements of people possible for the first time in history.

Immigration and Cities

Many immigrants were too poor to buy land, so they lived in cities and worked at low-skilled jobs. Many people from Germany moved to escape political and economic problems in their homeland. Because many Germans were craftspeople, they settled in cities where there were markets for their goods.

Each group of immigrants brought some part of its culture. One city could contain many separate cultures, because people from different countries created their own neighborhoods. As a result, a diversity, or a variety, of people from different cultures began to grow in the United States.

After 1850, immigration to the United States increased even more. Over the next 90 years, about 32 million immigrants arrived in the United States. Many immigrants in the later 1800s were from southern and central Europe. Starting in 1892, the great majority of them passed through the reception center at Ellis Island in New York harbor. Ellis Island is now a national monument.

Close to Ellis Island stands the Statue of Liberty. A gift from France, the statue was completed in 1885 as a symbol of freedom, hope, and opportunity. Engraved on the pedestal of the statue is a poem by Emma Lazarus. The poet imagines that the statue speaks these words of welcome:

> ❝Give me your tired, your poor,
> Your huddled masses yearning to breathe free,
> The wretched refuse of your teeming shore.
> Send these, the homeless, tempest-tost [tossed about] to me,
> I lift my lamp beside the golden door! ❞

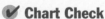 **What were some of the reasons for immigration to the United States?**

B. Conditions of Urban Life

During the 1800s, cities in Europe and the United States grew so rapidly that their development was largely unplanned. Most cities grew faster than the number of services that their residents needed. Daily life was often difficult, confusing, and even violent.

Growth of U.S. Cities, 1850–1900		
CITY	POPULATION IN 1850	POPULATION IN 1900
New York	696,000	3,437,000
Chicago	30,000	1,699,000
Philadelphia	121,000	1,294,000
St. Louis	78,000	575,000
Boston	137,000	561,000
San Francisco	35,000	343,000

Source: *The World Almanac and Book of Facts* (2002 edition)

✔ **Chart Check**

Which U.S. city had fewer than 100,000 people in 1850 and more than 1,000,000 people in 1900?

ANALYZE PRIMARY SOURCES

DOCUMENT-BASED QUESTION What do you think the "lamp" and the "golden door" may stand for, or symbolize?

Do You Remember?

In Chapter 13, you learned about the development of towns and cities during the later Middle Ages.

A. The Growth of Cities

Purpose-Setting Question
What was one factor that led to the growth of cities during the Industrial Revolution? (Possible answer: the development of the factory system near sources of energy)

Using the Chart

Growth of U.S. Cities, 1850–1900

Ask students to locate the cities listed in the chart on a map of the United States. Discuss with students the geographical factors that would have contributed to the growth of these cities. (Possible answer: The cities are all located near major ports or on major river systems.)

✔ **Chart Check**

Answer Chicago

ANALYZE PRIMARY SOURCES

DOCUMENT-BASED QUESTION

Ask students to discuss the impression the poem might have had on immigrants. (The poem gives immigrants promises of hope and safety in the United States.)

ANSWER The lamp, or flame, may symbolize hope that never goes out. The golden door may symbolize an opening to economic opportunity and freedom.

◆ **ANSWER** Possible answers: desire to own land, economic opportunity, and freedom from religious or political persecution

B. Conditions of Urban Life

Purpose-Setting Question What was a serious consequence of the rapid growth of cities in the 1800s? (Possible answer: There were not enough services, so daily life was difficult.)

Do You Remember?
Ask students to identify why cities grew so rapidly in the Middle Ages. Then, compare and contrast these reasons to the growth of cities during the Industrial Revolution.

F Y I

Ellis Island
Ellis Island is named after Samuel Ellis, who owned the land in the late 1700s. It was first used as an immigration station by the government in 1892. Its busiest period as a processing center was between 1918 and 1924. The main building on Ellis Island is now the Ellis Island Immigration Museum, which includes exhibits of clothing, toys, and passports of immigrants.

Connection to
LANGUAGE ARTS

Ask students to write letters from the point of view of a recent immigrant to the United States during the Industrial Revolution to family members who still live in the immigrant's country of origin. The letter should discuss the reasons for coming to the United States and hopes for the future. Have volunteers read the letters in class.

Write a letter to the editor
Have students write letters to the editor of nineteenth-century newspapers in which they express their feelings about the living conditions in their cities. Call on volunteers to read their letters aloud in class.

TEACH PRIMARY SOURCES
Have students study the photograph on page 522 that was taken in the early 1900s. Ask students to identify items in the photograph that might contribute to the problems faced by people in urban areas (crowded streets, food out in the open)

Discuss Ask students to contrast the realities of living conditions in nineteenth-century tenements with the hopes of the many immigrants who had left their homelands to come to the United States. (The immigrants came to the United States in search of a better life, but many found themselves living in poverty.)

Then & Now

URBANIZATION Ask pairs of students to research industrialization in one of the countries identified in this feature and discuss their findings in small groups.

◆ **ANSWER** Cities in the 1800s had few paved streets, no motorized vehicles, no sanitation or sewage systems, and no street lighting. Before the late 1800s, most cities and towns did not have police departments and had only volunteer fire departments.

C. The Impact of Cities on Society as a Whole

Purpose-Setting Question How did the Industrial Revolution contribute to the expansion of the middle class? (The factory owners, merchants, artisans, and professional people who worked hard, benefited from the economic prosperity of the period.)

The rapid population growth in American cities, such as New York City, pictured here, contributed to many social problems, including disease, crime, and poverty.

Then & Now

URBANIZATION
Urbanization during the 1800s in Europe and the United States has parallels today in cities located in nations where industrialization has occurred. These countries include Thailand, India, Malaysia, Nigeria, and Brazil.

Public Spaces

Many features of cities today did not exist during the Industrial Revolution. For example, most streets were unpaved. Transport of heavy goods by horse and wagon was difficult and it was almost impossible in rainy, muddy conditions.

There were almost no sanitation or sewage systems, no motorized vehicles, and—until the late 1800s—no street lighting. Only by the late 1800s did most cities and towns have public police departments. Until the late 1800s, fire departments were mostly run by volunteers. Garbage was often dumped into the streets. The result was that epidemics posed a frequent danger to public health. Cholera, which is caused by polluted water, was a particularly serious threat in cities. The lack of lighting and, in some cases, the lack of police meant that travel by night could be dangerous. Fire was another danger in cities because most buildings were made of wood and were built close together.

City Life

Despite unsanitary and difficult conditions, people moved to cities for job opportunities. Because many workers spoke little English, the jobs they were offered involved physical labor. Many men paved streets and built bridges. Women often sewed clothes, either at home or in garment factories. All these jobs paid very little.

Many workers who were poor lived in overcrowded conditions. Whole families often occupied a single room in rundown apartment buildings, called **tenements**. Tenements often had no plumbing, heating, electricity, or windows. Overcrowded tenements with poor living conditions and dangers of violence and disease were all factors of the lives of people who lived in cities. In Great Britain and the United States, critics of urban life began to demand reform.

◆ **What were some ways in which cities of the 1800s differed from modern cities?**

C. The Impact of Cities on Society as a Whole

You have seen that nineteenth-century cities had some major problems. However, the overall economic progress accompanying urbanization had some positive effects on society as a whole.

The Rise of the Middle Class

One important result of the Industrial Revolution was the expansion of the middle class in Europe and the United States. The middle class—factory owners, merchants, skilled artisans, and professionals such as doctors and engineers—was not wealthy. However, middle-class people profited from hard work. This hard work, together with ambition, and respect for family and society members contributed to the culture of this time period. The time between 1840 and 1900 is often called the Victorian Age. This period roughly corresponds to the reign of Queen Victoria in Great Britain.

Teaching Options

Writing

AVERAGE

Have students choose one of the nineteenth-century reformers, such as Jacob Riis or Jane Addams, to research. They can use library resources and the Internet for research. Ask them to prepare one-page reports in which they summarize the works of the reformer and how he or she contributed to the reform movement of the period.

CHALLENGE

Ask students to write a series of three to five journal entries written from the point of view of one of the nineteenth-century reformers, such as Jacob Riis or Jane Addams, who worked to improve conditions in American tenements and to help immigrants living in impoverished neighborhoods. Their journal entries should reflect the reformer's feelings about his or her work and the social problems of the time.

Middle-Class Way of Life

The middle class developed its own way of life, especially during the Victorian Age. Families often lived in single-family houses or attractive apartment buildings. Strict rules were followed regarding social behavior. For example, there were rules for how to dress for all kinds of occasions, how to entertain visitors, and how long to mourn dead relatives.

Children in middle-class families were supposed to "be seen but not heard." Parents were strict. A child who misbehaved was a bad reflection not only on himself or herself, but also on the entire family.

A notable gap between middle-class people and working-class people soon developed. Working-class people were people who earned wages that were less than the incomes earned by middle-class people. In the 1800s, working-class people often worked in factories and mines. They also worked in their own homes sewing clothes for others or in the home of a middle-class person as a cook. Unskilled laborers, such as people who dug canals, built railroads, or did other physical work, were in the working class as well in the 1800s. The gap between middle-class people and working-class people occurred because middle-class people in cities did not want to live near working-class tenements. Before the Industrial Revolution, well-off and poorer residents lived near each other.

The expansion of the middle class also had effects on the roles and organization of family members. More and more, husbands became the sole providers for middle-class families. Women were expected to stay home and settle into a domestic role. Before industrialization, many wives had worked alongside their husbands. Children had also worked, even when quite young. With the Industrial Revolution, as you have seen, children were employed in many factories. This practice, however, declined during the 1830s, when laws in several countries began to restrict child labor and encourage school attendance. Children began to be viewed as individuals requiring protection and education. However, many children whose families were poor still worked to support their families. At the same time that poor families were struggling, a new upper-middle class of wealthy industrialists, bankers, and merchants was growing.

Cities as Centers of Culture

The growth of the middle class and economic progress increased the amount of leisure time many people had. Family entertainment, especially reading and music, was popular. Outside the home, middle-class people also attended lectures and symphony performances. The New York Philharmonic Symphony Orchestra, for example, began performing in 1842.

In this photograph taken in the 1800s, a family is having afternoon tea in the parlor, or living room, of their middle-class home.

The painting on page 524 shows a group of Coney Island visitors watching a puppet show on the beach in 1880. Encourage students to identify details in the painting.

Discuss Ask students why cities became the sites of important cultural institutions in the nineteenth century. (Possible answers: There was more wealth concentrated in cities, or cities were more socially and economically diverse.)

Make a timeline Have small groups of students make a timeline (TR, p. 320) that shows when important cultural institutions were founded. Encourage students to do additional research and extend their timelines. (Possible answers: 1848: Boston Public Library; 1857: Central Park in New York City)

◆ **ANSWER** Possible advantages: Middle-class children did not have to work; they could be educated. **Possible disadvantages:** Parents were strict; middle-class children were supposed to "be seen but not heard."

Section Close

Have small groups of students prepare a two-column chart (TR, p. 328) that shows how the Industrial Revolution affected the middle class and working class of the period. Invite groups to display their charts in class. Discuss which social class they believe benefited the most from industrialization.

3 Assess

Review Answers

Review History
A. Possible answer: London's population in 1900 was 6 million—7 times its population in 1800.

B. Possible answers: epidemics, the lack of paved streets, no sanitation or sewage systems, no street lighting

C. Possible answer: the founding of museums, libraries, and concert halls

Define Terms to Know
urbanization, 520; immigration, 520; tenement, 522

Economic prosperity increased the desire for leisure time activities, like a day on the beach at Coney Island in New York.

In the second half of the nineteenth century, cities became the sites of important cultural institutions. Libraries and museums were founded. For example, the Boston Public Library was founded in 1848 and the Metropolitan Museum of Art in New York City was founded in 1870. An increase in leisure led to the planning of beautiful urban parks, such as Central Park in New York City in 1857 and Golden Gate Park in San Francisco in 1870. The parks provided fresh air and health benefits that helped to lessen the likelihood of diseases. Music halls and theaters gave people a chance to enjoy concerts and plays. Artists founded associations to show their artwork.

Some institutions, such as large urban libraries, were founded or sponsored by extremely wealthy people. Andrew Carnegie, owner of a steel company just outside Pittsburgh, Pennsylvania, donated nearly $60 million to open 2,500 libraries. He founded Carnegie Hall in New York, one of the country's leading concert halls, in 1891. Then, in 1900, he founded Carnegie Mellon University in Pittsburgh. He also created the Carnegie Foundation for the Advancement of Teaching to help improve education.

John D. Rockefeller, owner of a large oil company, helped found the University of Chicago. He also helped found the Rockefeller Institute for Medical Research, now called Rockefeller University, in New York. Leland Stanford and Cornelius Vanderbilt, who became rich from the railroad industry, helped establish Stanford and Vanderbilt universities in Stanford, California, and Nashville, Tennessee.

◆ **What were some advantages and disadvantages of being a child in a middle-class family in the 1800s?**

Review III

Review History
A. What is one specific example of the rapid growth of cities during the 1800s?
B. What are some of the problems that made urban life difficult and sometimes dangerous in the 1800s?
C. What are some of the ways in which cities became centers of culture in the second half of the nineteenth century?

Define Terms to Know
Define the following terms:
urbanization, immigration, tenement

Critical Thinking
Why do you think extremely wealthy people, such as Andrew Carnegie, donated money for libraries and other cultural institutions?

Write About History
In a short essay, evaluate the advantages and disadvantages of urban life in the 1800s.

Get Organized
SQR CHART
Use an SQR chart to organize information from this section. For example, one topic from this section might be urbanization.

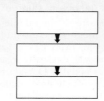

Critical Thinking
Students may state that wealthy people might donate money because they are generous or because they want recognition. Also, some come from poor backgrounds and want to give others advantages.

Write About History
Students' essays will vary but may include such advantages as economic and cultural opportunities and such disadvantages as overcrowding, crime, and disease.

Survey
This section is about urbanization in the 1800s.

Question
What were the causes of urbanization?

Read
Causes of urbanization included the growth of factories and economic opportunities in cities.

An Age of Reforms

Terms to Know

suffrage the right to vote

labor union an association of workers that protects and promotes the interests of its members

collective bargaining talks between a union and an employer about working conditions

Progressive movement the American movement that urged social and economic reforms in the early 1900s

socialism an economic system in which the means of production are collectively owned or owned by the government, and economic exchanges are regulated for the common good

communism an economic system in which the means of production are controlled by the government, and property is owned by everyone equally

Main Ideas

A. During the 1800s, women campaigned for their rights, and some also took leadership roles in society.

B. Reformers worked to improve conditions in factories in the late 1800s.

C. The economic ideas of capitalism, socialism, and communism took hold during the Industrial Revolution.

 Active Reading

CAUSE AND EFFECT
When you identify cause and effect, you determine the reason(s) for and the consequence(s) of an event. As you read this section, think about the ways in which the Industrial Revolution encouraged people to work for social reform. What were some results of these reforms?

A. Women's Rights

You have learned that the Industrial Revolution produced social changes. Along with changes in working conditions, there were shifts in family organization and in the roles of family members. When middle-class families were able to live on a husband's income, a wife was no longer expected to work outside the home. Some of these women began to devote their time to social reform, or the improvement of society.

The Seneca Falls Convention

Lucretia Mott and Elizabeth Cady Stanton were two women who were strongly opposed to slavery in the United States. In 1840, they attended an international antislavery convention in London. Mott had been chosen as a delegate, or representative, to the convention. However, she was forbidden to speak because she was a woman.

Both Mott and Stanton were also interested in women's rights. As a young teacher at a school in New York State, Mott had received only half the salary that male teachers were paid. Many working women in the 1800s were also paid only half as much as men were for the same work.

In July 1848, Mott and Stanton called a women's rights convention in Seneca Falls, New York. This meeting marked the beginning of the women's **suffrage** movement in the United States. Suffrage means the right to vote. The convention issued a declaration that strongly criticized the fact that women did not have equal rights. The convention members especially stressed the fact that women were not permitted to vote. Women also lacked property rights and the right to equal educational and job opportunities. Sixty-eight women and 32 men signed the document, called the Declaration of Sentiments. Here is one part of it:

ANALYZE PRIMARY SOURCES
DOCUMENT-BASED QUESTION What is mankind accused of in this quotation?

> 66 The history of mankind is a history of repeated injuries and usurpations [takeovers] on the part of man toward woman. 99

Women began to make important strides in the long process toward equality. Dr. Elizabeth Blackwell became the first female doctor in the United States. Lucy Stone, who kept her maiden name after marriage, lectured for the rights of women. Susan B. Anthony worked to obtain women's right to vote.

CHAPTER 22 ◆ The Industrial Revolution and Social Change **525**

IV. An Age of Reforms
(pp. 525–529)

Section Summary

In this section, students will learn about the women's rights movement and efforts to achieve labor reforms in the nineteenth century. They will also learn about the economic theories of capitalism, socialism, and communism that developed during the Industrial Revolution.

1 Introduce

Getting Started

Ask students how they would organize a campaign in support of a social or political issue that affects their school, community, or city. Possible issues include preserving neighborhood gardens or increasing their school's budget. Encourage students to provide specific examples of what they would do, such as writing letters to their city or state political leaders or sponsoring a phone or fax campaign in support of the issue.

TERMS TO KNOW

Ask students to read the terms and definitions on page 525 and then find each term in the section. Point out that several of the terms include suffixes, such as *-age*, *-ive*, or *-ism*. Have students use a dictionary to find the meanings of these suffixes and explain how each one changed the meaning of the root word. Encourage students to look for other terms that use these suffixes as they read the section.

You may wish to preview the pronunciation of the following names from this section with students.

suffragist (SUHF ruh jihst)
Dorothea Dix (dawr uh THEE uh DIHKS)
muckraker (MUK rayk er)
Jacob Riis (JAY kuhb REES)
François Noël Babeuf (frahn SWAH noh UHL bah BOOF)
Charles Fourier (CHAHR uhlz foor YAY)

ACTIVE READING

Have students identify the cause(s) and effect(s) of a particular event or idea that is discussed in a subsection of this section. They can organize this information on a cause-and-effect chain (TR, p. 325).

Teaching Options

Section 4 Resources

Teacher's Resources (TR)
Terms to Know, p. 35
Review History, p. 69
Build Your Skills, p. 103
Chapter Test, pp. 159–160
Concept Builder, p. 238
SQR Chart, p. 322

ESL/ELL STRATEGIES

Use Resources Have pairs of students brainstorm a list of four reformers who are referred to in this section. Ask them to use library resources to find more information about the accomplishments of these individuals. Students can summarize their findings in a two-column chart (TR, p. 328).

CHAPTER 22 ◆ **T525**

2 Teach

A. Women's Rights

Purpose-Setting Question What was the significance of the women's rights convention at Seneca Falls? (It marked the beginning of the movement that supported women's suffrage and equality of rights for women.)

Explore You may want to refer students to sections of the Declaration of the Rights of Woman and the Female Citizen on page 813.

ANALYZE PRIMARY SOURCES

DOCUMENT-BASED QUESTION
The model for this document was the U.S. Declaration of Independence. Give students a copy of the Declaration of Sentiments. Then, have students find phrases from the Declaration of Independence (p. 812) that are repeated in the Seneca Falls declaration and compare the way these phrases are used in each document.

ANSWER Mankind is accused of holding power over women.

WHO IN THE WORLD?

HELEN KELLER Keller became a well-known author. One of her best-known works, *The Story of My Life*, was published in 1902. The Broadway play, *The Miracle Worker*, which was later made into a movie, focuses on Anne Sullivan's experiences teaching Helen to communicate as a child.

◆ **ANSWER** Possible answers: women's rights, education for people with physical limitations, the temperance movement, the treatment of mentally ill people and prisoners, and the health field

B. The Rights of Workers

Purpose-Setting Question What were working conditions like for most workers during the Industrial Revolution? (harsh and unhealthy; worked long hours and received low wages)

Who in the World?

HELEN KELLER
Helen Keller successfully developed both reading and speaking skills that had never been developed before by someone with no sight and no hearing. With her teacher Anne Sullivan, Keller learned to read by feeling raised words in cardboard—a system called braille.

Keller learned to speak with the help of Sarah Fuller. Keller was admitted to Radcliffe College in Cambridge, Massachusetts, in 1900. She graduated in 1904.

Clara Barton was a nurse during the American Civil War and founded the American Red Cross.

526 UNIT 6 ◆ A Changing World

The Right to Vote

Mott, Stanton, and Anthony continued to support women's rights in the late 1800s. None of them lived long enough, though, to see passage of the Nineteenth Amendment to the U.S. Constitution. This amendment finally gave American women the vote in 1920.

Women over the age of 21 in Britain won the right to vote in 1928 after a long campaign. The first women's suffrage association was founded in Manchester in 1865. Around 1900, the struggle for the right to vote became more active. Some women activists, called suffragists, staged public demonstrations and even went to jail for their beliefs.

Changing Roles of Women

Besides being active in the causes of women's rights and ending slavery, a number of women took leadership roles in other areas of social reform. One of these efforts involved education for the blind. In Boston, Massachusetts, a special school for people with limited or no eyesight was started in the 1830s. One of the school's graduates, Anne Sullivan, later became the teacher of Helen Keller. Helen Keller had grown up without both sight and hearing. Keller became a noted lecturer and supporter of people with physical limitations.

Another area of social reform was the temperance movement, which worked to outlaw alcoholic beverages. One more drive for reform centered on the treatment of mentally ill patients. Dorothea Dix from Massachusetts played a leading role in improving conditions for mentally ill patients. As a result of her efforts, a number of U.S. states provided institutions in which mentally ill people received better care than in the prisons that had previously housed them.

Some reformers focused on conditions in prisons. They worked to eliminate brutal punishments such as whipping. These reformers also worked to make prisons cleaner and to separate first offenders from hardened criminals.

Some of the most dramatic reforms occurred in the health field. As you read in Chapter 20, Florence Nightingale became the founder of the modern profession of nursing in the 1850s. A British woman, Nightingale served in field hospitals in the Crimean War. She then founded a training school for nurses in London. In the United States, Clara Barton founded the American Red Cross in the 1880s. For her work during the American Civil War and the Franco-Prussian War in Europe, Barton earned the nickname of the "angel of the battlefield."

◆ What were some social reforms in the 1800s?

B. The Rights of Workers

Child labor, long hours, and low wages were common conditions in factories during the Industrial Revolution. People in factories were often injured and even killed because of accidents with machinery. Poor lighting, pollution, and loud noise added to the harsh conditions. Workdays usually stretched to 10 or 12 hours. The normal workweek was six days. If workers demanded higher pay or better conditions, they risked being fired. Gradually, reformers mounted strong campaigns to improve conditions for workers.

Teaching Options

Conflict Resolution

The passage of a constitutional amendment gave women in the United States the right to vote. Ask the class to brainstorm an important issue that affects their school. Have students discuss the steps they would have to take to make a change in their school constitution in order to address this issue.

Connection to LANGUAGE ARTS

Have students write newspaper articles for nineteenth-century periodicals about the Seneca Falls Conference. Remind them to answer the five *W*s in the first paragraph and to include an interesting headline. Students may find it easier to start filling in a five *W*s chart (TR, p. 326) before writing the article.

The Union Movement

One of the most important movements for workers' rights was the union movement. A **labor union** is an association of workers formed to protect and promote the welfare, interests, and rights of its members. One of the first unions was the Knights of Labor, formed in Philadelphia, Pennsylvania, in 1869.

One of the labor leaders was Samuel Gompers. Gompers upheld the workers' right to strike, or to refuse to work, if negotiations broke down. He supported **collective bargaining**, a system in which union officials, elected by the membership, negotiate with business owners. In 1886, he formed the American Federation of Labor (AFL). Gompers was president of the AFL for nearly 40 years.

During this period, labor unions were strongly opposed by many people, including wealthy, powerful people and businesses. They saw the unions as unwanted forces in the free market of capitalism. The labor movement itself had disagreements. Some leaders thought that only skilled workers should be members. Thus, for some years, the AFL did not reach out to unskilled workers. Nevertheless, Gompers's efforts won results for many workers in the form of higher wages, the passage of child labor laws, and workers' pay for injuries.

The union movement in Great Britain started around this time. Unions became legal through the Trade-Union Act of 1871. However, while Gompers tried whenever possible to keep the AFL in the United States out of politics, British labor leaders were politically involved. Their efforts led to the formation of a labor party in 1893.

An international labor movement, with the first association called the International Working Men's Association, created a unifying force for labor in Europe. As the labor union movement was developing in Europe and the United States, the People's Party, better known as the Populist Party, became an established political party in the United States in 1892. A populist is a person who supports the rights of the common people. The Populist Party specifically supported the interests of American farmers. They felt that farmers should get fair prices to ship their grain and other farm products to markets.

The Progressives in the United States

In the early 1900s, the growth of labor unions to protect workers' rights led to a more general reform movement in the United States. The **Progressive movement** focused on the need for reform on a wide range of issues.

Some of the most forceful Progressives were called "muckrakers." The muckrakers used newspapers, magazines, and novels to expose social concerns and problems. Ida Tarbell wrote a series of articles about corruption at the Standard Oil Company. Her magazine reports claimed that the company's owner, John D. Rockefeller, had acquired his tremendous wealth and power through corrupt methods.

ANALYZE PRIMARY SOURCES

DOCUMENT-BASED QUESTION According to the cartoon below, what did Rockefeller's company control?

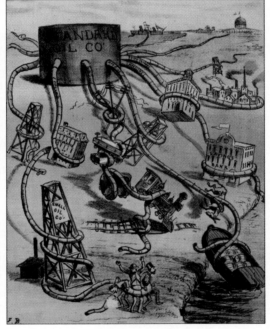

This cartoon shows John D. Rockefeller's Standard Oil Company as an octopus with far-reaching control.

Connection to GOVERNMENT

Great Britain's Labour Party has its roots in the country's labor union movement of the late 1800s. Have students work in small groups and use library and Internet resources to find out more about the past and present Labour Party. Remind them to use the British spelling, *labour*, when referring to the Labour Party.

Discuss Ask students why they think labor unions were able to gain some improvements for workers. (Possible answers: When people band together to support the same cause, they are stronger and more organized. A large group of workers could also be more effective if threatening to strike.) Explain that companies knew that unions could interfere with their businesses. They often fired anyone who joined a union.

Activity

Create slogans Ask pairs of students to research the strike organized by the Knights of Labor against the Union Pacific Railroad at the end of the nineteenth century. Have the students make slogans that the strikers might have used to make the public aware of the issues.

ANALYZE PRIMARY SOURCES

DOCUMENT-BASED QUESTION

In 1870, at age 31, Rockefeller established the Standard Oil Company, the business that would make him one of the wealthiest people of the era. Rockefeller increased his control over the oil business by secretly buying related companies and making secret deals. Despite giving large amounts of money to charity, his ruthless business tactics earned him a reputation for greed.

ANSWER oil wells, buildings, locomotives, towns, boats, and people

Extend Point out that the Populist Party was an outgrowth of local political action groups, known as Farmers' Alliances, which were active in the United States in the 1880s. These groups appealed to farmers in the Midwest and the South, who were concerned about crop failures. James B. Weaver, the presidential candidate of the Populist Party in 1892, won more than 1,000,000 popular votes.

Activity

Ask a journalist Ask pairs of students to make up a list of questions they would like to ask the muckraker journalists about the methods they used when investigating the subjects of their magazine articles and books. Call on students to discuss their questions in class.

Lewis Hine took this photograph of children working in a canning factory as an adult supervises them.

Lincoln Steffens attacked corrupt city government in his book *The Shame of the Cities*. In *The Jungle*, novelist Upton Sinclair focused on the threats to workers' health because of unsanitary conditions in the meat-packing industry. Some people applauded the muckrakers' efforts, whereas others objected to their work.

Not all Progressives were muckrakers. The Danish-American journalist and photographer Jacob Riis focused public attention on poor tenements in his 1890 book *How the Other Half Lives*. Lewis Hine, a photographer, raised awareness of the harsh reality of child labor across the United States in his photos of urban life.

Progressives and Politics

Progressives steadily worked to tie state and city governments more to the people. In 1913, the U.S. Constitution was amended to give voters the right to elect senators directly. Before passage of this amendment, senators had been elected by state legislatures—in other words, by other politicians.

Another target of the Progressive movement was large corporations. A corporation is a business that is usually made up of many investors. By the end of the 1800s, some large corporations had enormous power. Many corporations had a monopoly—or complete control over a supply, service, or market. Some companies formed a trust—one large business made up of a group of companies. In 1890, the U.S. Congress passed the Sherman Antitrust Act. This act put an end to monopolies that limited trade between states. However, this law proved hard to enforce. The trust problem remained serious. It received the special attention of U.S. President Theodore Roosevelt, who agreed with many ideas of the Progressive movement.

◆ Who were three leading muckrakers, and on what issues did they focus?

C. Economic Systems

In addition to reform, the Industrial Revolution sparked interest in economics and the ideas about how economies work.

Capitalism

As you have learned, capitalism is an economic system in which all or most of the means of production are privately owned. Owners invest capital, or money, to create or acquire the means of production—for example, a factory. Owners then hope to make a profit from selling goods and services. They pay wages to their workers. In return for their investment, they keep most of the profits. Profits are then invested in the business to encourage economic growth.

In his book *The Wealth of Nations*, Adam Smith argued in favor of capitalism. Smith believed in free enterprise and free markets. During the 1800s, many people agreed with Smith's ideas. Throughout the Industrial Revolution and today, many people believe that the ideas of capitalism mean independence, hard work, competition, inventiveness, and risk taking. Many Americans identify capitalism with the American character and way of life.

528 UNIT 6 ◆ A Changing World

Teaching Options

Other Economic Systems

During the Industrial Revolution, economic ideas opposed to capitalism arose. Two of the most important were socialism and communism. In **socialism**, the means of production are collectively owned or owned by the government. Economic exchanges are regulated for the common good. In the 1700s, socialists such as François Noël Babeuf and Charles Fourier in France and Robert Owen in Great Britain attacked the capitalist system as unfair. They criticized capitalists as selfish, and they disliked competition. The aims of the early socialists were social harmony and a more even distribution of income.

Fourier and Owen set up model communities to achieve these goals. Fourier's idea failed to take hold in France. Fourier's idea, however, influenced the experimental community of Brook Farm in West Roxbury, Massachusetts. Brook Farm was set up in the early 1840s. In Britain, Owen—wealthy owner of a cotton mill—completely changed conditions for his workers. He raised wages, built schools, cut working hours, and created company stores and housing. Owen also sponsored a model community in New Harmony, Indiana. However, this effort, like Brook Farm, lasted for only 2 years. The model communities in West Roxbury and New Harmony were examples of utopian thinking.

Many of the beliefs of socialism were also shared by **communism**. The basic beliefs of communism are that the production of goods and services are controlled by the government, and property is owned by everyone equally. Communism went beyond socialism, however, in claiming that violent revolution is necessary to overthrow capitalism. Karl Marx, a German social philosopher, economist, and revolutionary, was a key figure in the establishment of communism. In his books *The Communist Manifesto* and *Das Kapital*, Marx argued that the working classes would—and should—overthrow the capitalist system through violent revolution. Marx hoped that in the future, there would be no need for government and all people would be equal.

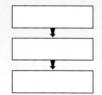

Robert Owen was an important utopian socialist. Owen believed that competition caused society's problems.

◆ How did communism differ from socialism?

Review IV

Review History
A. Which rights for women did the Seneca Falls Convention of 1848 emphasize?
B. What were some of the goals of the Progressive movement in the United States?
C. Charles Fourier and Robert Owen believed that the goals of socialism could be achieved in what way?

Define Terms to Know
Define the following terms:
suffrage, labor union, collective bargaining, Progressive movement, socialism, communism

Critical Thinking
Why do you think people such as the Progressives used photographs to express their opinions?

Write About Economics
Prepare an outline comparing and contrasting socialism and communism. Then, write a short essay based on your outline.

Get Organized
SQR CHART
Use an SQR chart to organize information from this section. For example, one topic from this section might be social reform.

```
┌──────────┐
│          │
└──────────┘
     │
     ▼
┌──────────┐
│          │
└──────────┘
     │
     ▼
┌──────────┐
│          │
└──────────┘
```

Survey
This section is about social reform.

↓

Question
What happened at the Seneca Falls Conference?

↓

Read
The women's suffrage movement began in the United States.

Critical Thinking
Possible answer: Photographs provide evidence that reveals the reality of a situation, such as poor living conditions in tenements; words are not as effective as one photo.

Write About Economics
Students' outlines should reflect the information in the text. Check students' essays for accuracy and grammar.

Discuss Ask students to compare two of the most important economic theories during the Industrial Revolution, socialism and communism. (**Socialism:** advocated that the means of production are collectively owned or owned by the government; **Communism:** stressed communal ownership of property and government control of the production of goods and services.)

Extend Brook Farm's well-known educational system, which included an infant school, primary school, and a 6-year college preparatory course, was intended to increase personal responsibility and a love of learning. The schools were part of the 175-acre farm, which included teachers, farmers, and craftspeople among its 70–80 members. Nathaniel Hawthorne fictionalized some aspects of Brook Farm in his novel, *The Blithdale Romance* (1852).

◆ **ANSWER** Communists claimed that a violent revolution was needed to overthrow capitalism.

Section Close
Ask students to evaluate the different reforms that were instituted during the Industrial Revolution and the economic theories that took hold during the period. Then, have them identify the reforms that had the greatest impact on the lives of the workers.

3 Assess

Review Answers
Review History
A. the right to vote, property rights, and equal opportunity in education and jobs
B. Possible answers: to end monopolies, corrupt government, unsanitary conditions in workplaces, poor living conditions in tenements, child labor, and to have people vote directly for U.S. senators
C. by creating model communities

Define Terms to Know
suffrage, 525; labor union, 527; collective bargaining, 527: Progressive movement, 527; socialism, 529, communism 529

Chapter Summary

A blank outline form is available in the Teacher's Resources (p. 318). Students should outline information about beginnings, growth, and effects of the Industrial Revolution on people and countries, as well as the reforms of the 1800s and the economic theories that took hold during this period. They should then use the outline to complete their chapter summary. Refer to the rubric in the Teacher's Resources (p. 340).

⬤ Interpret the Timeline

1. the invention of the water frame
2. to gain support for women's rights
3. Seneca Falls Convention (1848); women in the United States get the right to vote (1920); women in Great Britain get the right to vote (1928); Haiti becomes independent of France (1804); Mexico, Guatemala, and Peru win independence from Spain (1821); Liberia is proclaimed an independent republic (1847).
4. Check that all events selected by students are from the chapter.

Use Terms to Know

5. tenement
6. capital
7. colonialism
8. factory system
9. urbanization
10. textile industry
11. suffrage

Check Your Understanding

12. The Industrial Revolution refers to the shift from making articles by hand to manufacturing them through the use of machines or power tools and the shift from people working in their homes to working together in factories to make goods.
13. Cotton was popular because of its texture and bright range of designs. It could be washed without shrinking. There was a heavy demand for it in Europe.
14. Adam Smith argued in favor of laissez-faire, an economic policy in which government is strongly discouraged from interfering in the supply and demand of goods and services. Smith favored capitalism. Thomas Malthus argued that population growth would always be greater than society's ability to provide for everyone so poverty and distress are unavoidable.

Chapter Summary

Complete the following outline in your notebook. Then, use your outline to write a brief summary of the chapter.

The Industrial Revolution and Social Change

I. The Industrial Revolution Begins
   A. Before Industrialization in Great Britain
   B. The Textile Industry
   C. The Development of Steam Power
   D. Consequences of Industrialization

II. The Spread of Industry
   A. The Spread of Industry in Europe
   B. Industrialization in the United States
   C. Advances and Setbacks

III. Cities and the Middle Class
   A. The Growth of Cities
   B. Conditions of Urban Life
   C. The Impact of Cities on Society as a Whole

IV. An Age of Reforms
   A. Women's Rights
   B. The Rights of Workers
   C. Economic Systems

⬤ Interpret the Timeline

Use the timeline on pages 504–505 to answer the following questions.

1. Which occurred first, the invention of the water frame or the invention of the cotton gin?
2. What was the purpose of the Seneca Falls Convention?
3. **Critical Thinking** Which events on the timeline are about individual rights and independence?
4. Select five events from the chapter that are not on the timeline. Create a timeline that shows these events.

Use Terms to Know

Select the term that best completes each sentence.

capital   suffrage   textile industry
colonialism   tenement   urbanization
factory system

5. A _____ is a run down apartment building.
6. Money that is used in business is called _____.
7. The rule of a foreign territory for economic gain is _____.
8. In the _____, goods are mass produced at a central location.
9. The movement of people from rural to urban areas is _____.
10. In the _____, cloth is manufactured from wool or cotton.
11. Women in the 1800s began to fight for the right to vote, which is called _____.

Check Your Understanding

12. **Identify** the meaning of the phrase "Industrial Revolution."
13. **Discuss** the reasons why cotton was important to the textile industry.
14. **Summarize** the economic ideas of Adam Smith and Thomas Malthus.
15. **Identify** two important contributions by Eli Whitney.
16. **Explain** how Great Britain attempted to control industry.
17. **Describe** the Lowell system.
18. **Discuss** the conditions of urban life in Great Britain and the United States during the Industrial Revolution.
19. **Summarize** the ideas of family during the Victorian Age for the middle class.
20. **Identify** the areas of social reform in which women took leadership roles during the 1800s.
21. **Summarize** the goals and methods of the union movement.

---

15. Eli Whitney invented the cotton gin, which greatly speeded up the processing of raw cotton. He also produced standardized, or interchangeable parts for weapons.
16. Great Britain passed laws forbidding the export of designs for the new industrial machines. Despite these measures, however, industrialization spread abroad.
17. In the Lowell system, many employees were young, unmarried women. They lived in dormitories, were provided with educational resources, a church, and a minister.
18. Urban life could be difficult and even dangerous. Overcrowding was common in the cities, which lacked paved streets, public sanitation and sewage systems, and streetlighting. Epidemics, such as cholera, were caused by serious diseases. Until the late 1800s, most cities did not have public police departments. Fires also posed danger, because many buildings were made of wood.
19. The ideas of family during the Victorian Age for the middle class included strict rules for social behavior. Children were expected to always be well-behaved. Men were the sole providers, and women were expected to take care of the home and family. Children from middle-class families were educated and did not work.

Critical Thinking

22. **Analyze** What factors set the stage for the Industrial Revolution in Great Britain?

23. **Make Inferences** How did the rapid advances in transportation and communications during the 1800s affect people's lives?

24. **Draw Conclusions** Despite the drawbacks of urban life, why do you think cities grew so quickly in the 1800s?

25. **Compare and Contrast** What was the main difference between the American and British union movements?

Put Your Skills to Work

26. **Conduct Research** You have learned about a variety of sources that you can use when you are conducting research. You can find many of these sources at your school or local library. Before you start your research, you will need to decide which kinds of sources are appropriate for the topic you want to research. For most topics, an encyclopedia article about the topic is a good place to begin your research.

Copy the chart below onto a separate sheet of paper. In the first column, list some people, places, or events covered in this chapter about which you would like to know more. Then, in the second column, list three sources in which you could find more information.

TOPIC	SOURCES
Clara Barton	• A biographical dictionary • *Encyclopedia of American History* • www.redcross.org/museum

Analyze Sources

27. Read the comment below by historian Fernand Braudel. Then, answer the questions that follow.

Europe's example proves that, from its very beginnings, industrialization raises serious problems. Any country that undertakes to industrialize itself must envisage [expect] at the same time a change in its social structure. . . .

a. What does Braudel think countries that industrialize must expect?

b. What place that has industrialized is Braudel using for an example of his point?

c. What does Braudel think industrialization causes?

Essay Writing

28. In a brief essay, discuss some ways in which the Industrial Revolution is still very much a part of our daily lives. Think about the many inventions and technologies that you have read about in this chapter. Consider and write about how you use some of the inventions and technologies that occurred during the Industrial Revolution in your life today. Include in your essay how life would be different without these inventions and technologies.

TEST PREPARATION

COMPARING AND CONTRASTING IDEAS
Choose the answer that correctly completes the sentence.

Unlike socialism, communism holds that

1. revolution is necessary to overthrow capitalism.

2. capitalism should be encouraged on a limited basis.

3. utopian communities should be encouraged.

4. population growth will mean the end of cities.

Critical Thinking

22. Possible answer: Important factors included political stability, the enclosure acts, a plentiful labor supply, the urge to exploit economic markets, and British sea power.
23. Possible answer: These advances expanded economic opportunities by making more markets available at greater distances, made immigration easier, and contributed to the growth of cities.
24. Possible answer: Cities grew rapidly because of the availability of jobs, expanding opportunities for merchants and factory owners to exploit markets, and the greater cultural opportunities.
25. Possible answer: While the American union movement tried, when possible, to stay out of politics, the British union movement involved itself in politics.

Put Your Skills to Work

CONDUCT RESEARCH

26. Students should list some people, places, or events in the first column and list three sources for each in the second column. Possible sources include encyclopedias, periodicals, newspapers, magazines, nonfiction books, biographical dictionaries, almanacs, atlases, interviews, and Internet sources.

Analyze Sources

27a. a change in social structure
27b. Europe
27c. serious problems

Essay Writing

28. Students' essays should include inventions and technologies such as electricity, the telephone, machinery for the textile industry, the Bessemer process, the microphone, and X-rays. Essays should explain how these inventions and technologies have allowed for things in students' everyday lives. Students should include information about how their lives would be different without these inventions and technologies.

TEST PREPARATION

Answer 1. revolution is necessary to overthrow capitalism.

20. Women took leadership roles in women's rights issues, ending slavery, education for the blind, the temperance movement, and the treatment of mentally ill patients.
21. The goals of the union movement were to promote and protect the rights of working people. The union movement supported higher wages, child labor laws, and pay for workers who were injured. The methods of the union movement included collective bargaining in which union officials, representing workers, negotiated with business owners.

Nationalism and Expansion
1800–1900
(pp. 532–557)

Chapter Objectives

• Explain how political reforms in Great Britain led to a more democratic government for some groups but not for others.
• Describe the connection between westward expansion in the United States and the Civil War.
• Compare the way in which Italy and Germany each achieved unification.
• Discuss the changes that the Austro-Hungarian Empire endured in the nineteenth century.

Chapter Summary

Section I focuses on political reform in Great Britain during the Victorian Age and earlier and the changes in the relationships between Great Britain and both Ireland and Canada.
Section II explores the era of westward growth, the Civil War, and increased immigration to the United States.
Section III discusses the unification of Italy and of Germany and the leaders that led each country to its unification.
Section IV focuses on the fall of Metternich as leader of the Austro-Hungarian Empire and the effects of nationalism on the empire during the nineteenth century.

Set the Stage
TEACH PRIMARY SOURCES

Tell students that Ernest Renan (1823–1892) was a French historian who wrote about many topics. The quotation on this page is from his essay, "What Is a Nation?" Renan gave the essay as a lecture at the Sorbonne University, in Paris, France, in 1882. Ask students to identify the two things that make up the soul of a nation, according to Renan. (the past and the present) Ask whether students agree with Renan. Do they think that there are other things that make up the soul of a nation? Have students discuss what they think makes up the soul of the United States.

Nationalism and Expansion
1800–1900

I. Changes in Great Britain and Its Empire
II. Growth and Change in the United States
III. Italy and Germany Become Unified Nations
IV. The Austro-Hungarian Empire

Nationalism, or the ideas of having pride in being part of a nation, was on the rise in the 1800s. The question "What is a nation?" was on many people's minds. Books, newspapers, and even songs reminded people of their desire to belong to one nation. Gradually, people began to be loyal also to their language, history, and culture.

Ernest Renan, a French historian of the period, supplied his answer to what a nation was in an essay in 1882:

> 66 *A nation is a soul. . . . Two things . . . make up this soul. . . . One . . . lies in the past, the other in the present. The one is the possession in common of a rich heritage of memories; and the other is actual agreement, the desire to live together, and the will to continue to make the most of the joint inheritance.* 99

Nationalism became an important force throughout many parts of the world—from Italy and Germany to the United States and Great Britain—in the 1800s.

CHAPTER EVENTS				
1801 Ireland is made part of the United Kingdom.	**1803** United States buys the Louisiana Territory.	**1819** Peterloo Massacre occurs in Manchester, England.	**1832** Reform Act gives the British middle class the right to vote.	

| **1800** | | **1820** | | **1840** |

WORLD EVENTS			
	1807 Robert Fulton sails the *Clermont*.	**1816** Shaka begins rule of the Zulu Empire.	**1821** Mexico becomes independent.

Teaching Options

Chapter 23 Resources

REVIEW

Teacher's Resources (TR)
Terms to Know, p. 36
Review History, p. 70
Build Your Skills, p. 104
Chapter Test, pp. 161–162
Concept Builder, p. 239
Cause-and-Effect Chain, p. 325
Transparencies 1, 3

ASSESSMENT

Section Reviews, pp. 538, 545, 551, 555
Chapter Review, pp. 556–557
Chapter Test, TR, pp. 161–162

ALTERNATIVE ASSESSMENT

Portfolio Project, p. 608
Make a Brochure, p. T608

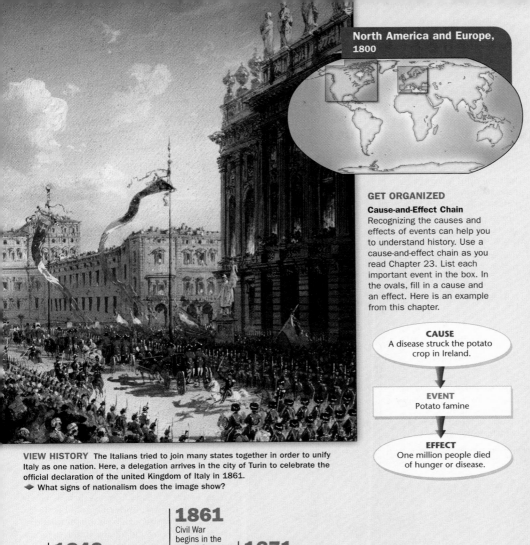

GET ORGANIZED

Cause-and-Effect Chain
Recognizing the causes and effects of events can help you to understand history. Use a cause-and-effect chain as you read Chapter 23. List each important event in the box. In the ovals, fill in a cause and an effect. Here is an example from this chapter.

CAUSE
A disease struck the potato crop in Ireland.

⬇

EVENT
Potato famine

⬇

EFFECT
One million people died of hunger or disease.

VIEW HISTORY The Italians tried to join many states together in order to unify Italy as one nation. Here, a delegation arrives in the city of Turin to celebrate the official declaration of the united Kingdom of Italy in 1861.
◆ What signs of nationalism does the image show?

1848
Revolutions occur in France, Austria, Prussia, and Italy.

1861
Civil War begins in the United States. Kingdom of Italy is officially proclaimed.

1871
Unified German nation becomes the German Empire.

1860

1880

1900

1844
First YMCA is founded in London, England.

1853
Commodore Matthew Perry lands in Japan.

1869
Suez Canal opens.

1894–1895
China and Japan come into conflict in the Sino-Japanese War.

CHAPTER 23 ◆ Nationalism and Expansion **533**

Chapter Themes
• Time, Continuity, and Change
• People, Places, and Environments
• Individuals, Groups, and Institutions
• Power, Authority, and Governance

Chapter Warm-Up

USING THE MAP
Point out the locator map on page 533. Ask students what continents are highlighted on the map and what large body of water is between them. (North America and Europe, Atlantic Ocean) Explain that this chapter will focus on these two areas of the world.

VIEW HISTORY
Following the proclamation of Italian unification in 1861, Turin became the capital of Italy. In 1865 the capital moved to Florence, and then to Rome five years later. Ask students what details in the painting show that Turin was an important city and that an exciting event was occurring. (large buildings, a grand square, flags, many people, a procession)

◆ **ANSWER** The grand and colorful presentation of flags and parading of the troops, plus the large gathering of citizens to watch the festivities, are all signs of nationalism.

GET ORGANIZED
Cause-and-Effect Chain
Discuss the cause-and-effect chain on page 533. Remind students that the event is always listed in the center, the cause is always listed above the event, and the effect is always listed below the event. Point out that some events may have more than one cause and more than one effect. Encourage students to make a cause-and-effect chain for each section. (TR, p. 325)

⬤ TEACH THE TIMELINE
The timeline on pages 532–533 covers the 100-year period between 1800 and 1900. Point out the intervals in between, which are every 20 years. Ask students what ideas are emphasized on the timeline. (revolution, unification, reform, civil war) Encourage students to refer to the timeline as they read the chapter to help them place events in historical perspective.

Activity

Use a map Have students use the world map in the Atlas (p. A1) or Transparency 1 to locate the places referenced in the timeline events. Point out that some places no longer exist and will not be on the map. For example, students will find Prussia and the Zulu Empire only on historical maps.

I. Changes in Great Britain and Its Empire

(pp. 534–538)

Section Summary

In this section, students will learn how Great Britain reformed its political system and gave the vote to more people. They will also find out how Ireland became part of the United Kingdom and how Canada gained some autonomy from Great Britain.

Getting Started

Ask students if they are familiar with voting procedures in the United States. Have them discuss the age at which people can vote (18), who is eligible to vote (U.S. citizens), and whether voting choices are confidential (they are). Then, tell students that they will be reading about political power and voting procedures in Great Britain during the 1800s. Explain to them that before political reform in Great Britain, most citizens were not eligible to vote.

TERMS TO KNOW

Ask students to read the terms and definitions on page 534 and find each term in the section. Ask students to scan the section to find the terms in context. In addition, point out that another word for *franchise*, as it is defined here, is *suffrage*. Ask students to look in the dictionary to find other definitions for *franchise*.

You may wish to preview the pronunciation of the following words from this section with students.

massacre (MAS uh ker)
borough (BER oh)
emancipation
   (ee man suh PAY shuhn)

ACTIVE READING

As students read each subsection, ask them to write a sentence describing the viewpoints expressed by each nation or group discussed. Suggest that they make a two-column chart (TR, p. 328) that lists the nations or groups in one column and the different viewpoints in another column.

T534 ◆ **UNIT 6**

Changes in Great Britain and Its Empire

Terms to Know

franchise a right or privilege, especially the right to vote

rotten borough a borough in Great Britain that had few voters but had the right to send a representative to Parliament

home rule self-government for a dependent country

dominion a self-governing nation

The Peterloo Massacre took place in 1819 when soldiers attacked a crowd of about 60,000 in the industrial city of Manchester, England.

Main Ideas

A. The middle classes gained political power in Great Britain in the nineteenth century.

B. People in Ireland wanted to be independent of Great Britain.

C. Canada became a self-governing nation within the British Empire and expanded westward.

Active Reading

POINTS OF VIEW
A point of view is what someone thinks and feels about an issue. As you read this section, try to identify the points of view of different groups in Great Britain, Ireland, and Canada. Then, for each group, write a brief sentence that describes its point of view.

A. Political Changes in Great Britain

After the wars against Napoleon, Great Britain entered a period of unrest at home. As the Industrial Revolution continued, members of both the new middle class and the working class wanted to improve conditions for the workers and the poor. Many people also began to want political reforms. By the 1830s, many British people were demanding the right to vote and a greater voice in government.

Demands for Reform

Middle-class and working-class people desired greater freedom and wanted to be represented in the government. They wanted the **franchise**, or right to vote. They also called for other reforms, or changes, that would give them more economic opportunities.

Desire for reform and bad economic times led to trouble for the British government. Workers in villages and towns were hungry because of poor harvests and high food prices. Workers in the cities put up with difficult conditions in factories. Some lost their jobs or could not find work. People, unhappy with their situation, demanded reform. In August 1819, workers gathered peacefully in St. Peter's Fields in Manchester, England, to press their demands for political reforms. Suddenly, soldiers began to attack the crowd of about 60,000 people. Eleven people were killed, and hundreds were hurt. This attack in Manchester became known as the Peterloo Massacre.

British Parliament

Since the 1600s, British monarchs had been required to share their power with Parliament, the British legislature. Monarchs were not above the law. They could not interfere in elections to Parliament, and they needed Parliament's approval to raise taxes. Parliament's duty was to check the monarchs and protect the rights of the people.

534 **UNIT 6** ◆ A Changing World

Teaching Options

Section 1 Resources

Teacher's Resources (TR)
   Terms to Know, p. 36
   Review History, p. 70
   Build Your Skills, p. 104
   Concept Builder, p. 239
   Cause-and-Effect Chain, p. 325
   Transparency 3

F Y I

The Peterloo Massacre

Richard Carlile, publisher of a radical newspaper, published the art print of the Peterloo Massacre shown on this page. Carlile wrote an account of the event in his paper that was critical of the government for its part in the incident. He was sent to jail for criticizing the government, an illegal act in Great Britain at this time. His arrest upset many people, and circulation of his newspaper increased.

The British Parliament has two parts: the House of Lords and the House of Commons. Members of the House of Lords either inherit their positions or are appointed. Members of the House of Commons are elected by the British people. Still, in the early nineteenth century, the British government was far from democratic. Many people felt it was in need of reform.

Representation and Voting

An important problem with the British government in the 1800s was that not all people were represented in Parliament. The number of representatives from each borough, or voting area, was supposed to be based on population. However, the number of representatives in each borough had not been changed as the population rose or fell. Large, underpopulated farming areas, owned mostly by aristocratic families, had the greatest representation. On the other hand, new factory cities, where the population was growing the fastest, had no one representing them in Parliament. In boroughs in which the population had fallen, local landowners still sent members to Parliament. Boroughs of this kind were called **rotten boroughs**.

The number of voters was another problem. In the early 1800s, there were only 245,000 eligible voters in Britain out of a population of 9 million. Only men who owned a certain amount of land had the right to vote. This left farm workers, business people, factory workers, and women without a vote.

The Reform Act of 1832

Parliament worried that there might be a revolution in Great Britain if changes were not made. The government became more willing to listen to people's demands for change. Many members of Parliament recognized that reform was necessary. After months of debate, the Reform Act of 1832 was passed. This act was the first important reform in nineteenth-century Great Britain. It helped business people and merchants by lowering the amount of property they needed in order to be allowed to vote. The Reform Act also got rid of many rotten boroughs, and made representation in Parliament more equal by including the new factory cities. Still, only about 5 percent of the total British population could vote.

Movements for Reform

For some, the Reform Act was not enough. Middle-class men could vote, but not working-class men. In 1838, a working-class group listed its hopes for political changes in a document called the People's Charter. This reform group was known as the Chartists. They called for voting rights for all adult men and a secret ballot for all voting. They also wanted equal electoral districts and yearly elections for the House of Commons.

The Chartists sent a petition to Parliament. A petition is a formal request to someone in authority. More than 1 million people had signed the petition, but Parliament rejected it. It also rejected a second petition with more than 3 million signatures. Finally, the Chartists dropped their demands.

Workers, however, kept on pressing for equal voting rights and democratic reform. They finally achieved their goals in the later half of the 1800s. In 1858, it was decided that a person no longer needed to own property to become a member of Parliament. In 1867, a new reform bill gave the right to vote to all men living in cities, whether they owned property or not. In 1872, the secret ballot, which would allow people to cast their votes without announcing them publicly, became law.

What in the World?

POCKET BOROUGHS
Even those who could vote in Great Britain in the early 1800s were not treated fairly. A rich property owner often told the people living in his borough how they should vote. These were called pocket boroughs because they were in the "pocket" of one man. He could be sure that people voted as he wished, because voting was not done in secret until 1872.

A. Political Changes in Great Britain

Purpose-Setting Question Who benefited most from political reforms passed during the 1800s in Great Britain? (Middle-class and working-class men benefited the most because they gained the right to vote and the right to become members of Parliament.)

Extend Tell students that in 1819, immediately after the Peterloo Massacre, Parliament reacted by passing harsh measures that became known as the Six Acts. These acts included provisions that allowed the government to search for and seize weapons from anyone, prohibited the organizing of meetings of more than 50 people without consent, and forbade criticism of the government.

Discuss Ask students to speculate about how the Industrial Revolution affected citizen representation in Great Britain's Parliament. (Because of the Industrial Revolution, many people left the farms and moved to cities to work in factories. Crowded cities had no representation in Parliament, whereas lightly populated rural boroughs had too much representation.)

Activity

Draw a political cartoon Ask students to look at examples of political cartoons on the Internet or in library resources, including newspapers. Then, have them work in groups to draw a political cartoon that expresses an opinion about one of the following topics in this section, including rotten boroughs, the Reform Act of 1832, or the Chartist movement.

ESL/ELL STRATEGIES

Role-play Have students act out a discussion about political reform in Great Britain from different points of view. Divide the class into three groups. Assign each group one of the following roles to play: working-class people, middle-class people, and upper-class people. Allow students time to prepare a summary of their group's viewpoint on political reform. Then, have them discuss the issue.

Connection to MATH

Have students review the figures that show how many people could vote in the early 1800s. (245,000 of a population of 9 million) Ask them to use these numbers to calculate what percentage of the total population could vote. (about 2.7 percent)

WHAT IN THE WORLD?

POCKET BOROUGHS Be sure that students understand what pocket boroughs are. Then, discuss how in Great Britain voting was not done in secret until 1872. Before then, people cast their votes by announcing them publicly. Ask students how having a secret ballot would have affected voting in pocket boroughs. (People would probably vote the way they really wanted to vote, knowing that their vote would be kept secret.)

ANSWER The Reform Act of 1832 reduced the amount of property business people and merchants were required to have in order to vote. It also reduced the number of rotten boroughs and gave some representation to factory cities.

B. The Irish Question

Purpose-Setting Question How did Ireland's relationship with Great Britain change during the 1800s? (Through the Act of Union, which took effect in 1801, Ireland became part of the United Kingdom. Ireland's parliament was disbanded, but Ireland was permitted 100 seats in the British House of Commons. A major issue was discrimination against Roman Catholics, which was partly resolved through the Emancipation Act.)

GLOBAL CONNECTIONS

DISEASE OVERSEAS Tell students that the potato is not native to Ireland. It originally came from South America and was introduced to Ireland in the late sixteenth century. Have students review Chapter 16, page 369, to identify other foods that were introduced to Europe from the Americas during the colonial era.

Focus Explain to students that for many poor Irish people, potatoes were the only food they ate at most of their meals. In many fields, the entire potato crop was destroyed. Discuss how dependence on one food made the situation so much worse for the Irish people.

Extend Daniel O'Connell, born in Ireland in 1775, was adopted by his wealthy, aristocratic Roman Catholic uncle, who sent him to top Roman Catholic colleges in Europe. Though dedicated to fair treatment for Ireland, O'Connell was appalled by the excesses of the French Revolution and hated violence. His thinking was also influenced by Thomas Paine and others.

Queen Victoria, who is shown here with Benjamin Disraeli, a prime minister of Great Britain, believed in the idea of government by the people.

Global Connections

DISEASE OVERSEAS

The disease that destroyed the potato crop in Ireland is known as "late blight." It is caused by the fungus *Phytophthora infestans*. The fungus was accidentally brought to Ireland from North America in 1845. Cool and wet conditions in Ireland that year allowed the disease to grow.

In the twentieth century, late blight destroyed most of the tomato crop in the eastern United States.

The Victorian Age

The person who ruled during this time of political change was Queen Victoria. She became queen of Great Britain in 1837 at the age of 18. Her reign of nearly 64 years was the longest in British history. The time period when Victoria reigned is called the Victorian Age.

During the reign of Queen Victoria, the idea of government by the people and not the monarch grew stronger. Victoria spoke often with government leaders, though she felt it was not her duty to take sides. However, the queen was a great help in settling fights between parties in Parliament. Queen Victoria was a popular monarch throughout her long reign. Her quiet, dignified way of life and her strong beliefs about proper behavior set the tone for the age.

What did the Reform Act of 1832 do?

B. The Irish Question

Developments in Ireland had been a concern for centuries. Most Irish people lived in poverty and suffered under harsh British rule. By 1800, Irish hatred of the British was strong. The British could no longer ignore what they called the Irish Question. Should the Irish be allowed to govern themselves?

Part of the United Kingdom

Hatred toward the British and the examples of the American and French Revolutions sparked a rebellion in Ireland in 1798. The Irish wanted their independence. Although the uprising failed, it got the attention of the British. To prevent an Irish revolution, Parliament passed the Act of Union, which took effect in 1801. It made Ireland part of the United Kingdom of Great Britain and Ireland. Ireland lost its own parliament, but it received 100 seats in the House of Commons. Roman Catholics, however, could not serve.

Without Roman Catholics as members, Parliament did not truly represent Ireland's people. Daniel O'Connell, a Roman Catholic leader in Ireland later known as the Liberator, demanded that Roman Catholics be allowed to run for the House of Commons. Hundreds of thousands in Ireland supported him when he ran for and won a seat in Parliament in 1828. In 1829, Parliament passed the Emancipation Act. It allowed Roman Catholics in Ireland and Britain to serve in public office.

The Great Potato Famine

Without true economic and political reform, the Irish still struggled. Ireland's population was growing, but the country had little industry. Most people farmed on rented land and gave part of their crop to the landowners as rent. Almost half of the people in Ireland depended on potatoes for food in the early 1840s. When the potato crop failed in 1845, famine struck. A famine is a great lack of food. Disease destroyed both the leaves and roots of the potato plant. More than 1 million Irish people died of hunger or disease.

The British government did little to ease the suffering caused by the potato famine. The government expected Ireland's landowners to help the starving people. However, the landowners ran out of money when the farmers could not pay rent. During the famine, larger Irish farms exported meat and grain to Great Britain, where people had money to buy them. The Irish poor, hardest hit by the famine, had no money.

Teaching Options

Years of Change

Ireland continued to suffer in the years following the great potato famine. Many Irish people looked for better lives in North America. Some moved to Great Britain to find work in factories and ports. New landowners took the place of old ones in Ireland.

After the British government's poor response to the famine, some Irish people began to demand **home rule**, or self-government. They wanted Ireland to have its own parliament so that it could control its own domestic affairs. Ireland would remain part of the United Kingdom. Others, however, did not support the idea of home rule. Protestants were afraid that the Roman Catholics would control an Irish parliament. The British government rejected bills for home rule in 1886 and 1893. Home rule was not approved until 1914. It did not take effect immediately, however, because of World War I.

◆ How did the British government respond to Ireland's potato famine?

C. Self-Government for Canada

Canada's relationship with Great Britain was different from that of Ireland. The British won control of Canada in 1763 by defeating France in the French and Indian War. For a time, Canada's population stayed mostly French. However, many immigrants from Great Britain began to settle in Ontario, where they often came into conflict with French Canadians. To keep the peace, the British divided Canada into two provinces, or parts, in 1791. Upper Canada, or Ontario, along the upper Saint Lawrence River, would be British. Lower Canada, or Quebec, would be French. It would have its own governor, legislative council, and elected assembly.

Lord Durham's Report

In 1837, rebellions against British rule broke out in both Lower Canada and Upper Canada. Although the rebellions did not last long, they made the British aware of serious problems in Canada. The British sent the Earl of Durham to Canada to study the situation. In an 1839 report, Lord Durham made two main recommendations. First, he called for the two Canadas to be united. Second, he believed that the area should be given control over its own affairs. Lord Durham's two main recommendations were accepted.

The British House of Commons was divided over the issue of granting Ireland self-government.

Ask students why they think the British government opposed Irish home rule. (Protestants in the government did not want Roman Catholics in control of an Irish parliament.) Then, ask what happened when home rule was finally approved in 1914. (It was delayed due to the outbreak of World War I.) Explain that after years of warfare, 26 southern counties of Ireland gained independence from Great Britain in 1921. Six northern counties are still part of the United Kingdom.

TEACH PRIMARY SOURCES

Ask students to note the clothing and wigs members of Parliament are wearing in the picture. Tell students that today members of the House of Lords wear robes and wigs, but members of the House of Commons do not. In spite of the fancy dress, the House of Lords has less power than the House of Commons. Ask students to find out how many members there are in the House of Commons and in the House of Lords. (House of Commons has 659 members; the House of Lords has about 670 members, called peers.)

◆ **ANSWER** During the potato famine the British government did very little to help the Irish. The British expected Irish landowners to help the people, but the landowners lacked the resources to do so.

C. Self-Government for Canada

Purpose-Setting Question How did Canada gain the status of a self-governing territory? (After rebellions in 1837, Great Britain followed Lord Durham's recommendation to give Canada control over its own domestic affairs. Great Britain maintained control over Canada's foreign affairs.)

Activity

Create a tourist guide The province of Quebec in Canada still shows a strong French heritage. For example, French is an official language of the area. Have students use the Internet or library resources to find out how the Quebec province reflects its French heritage and how Quebec is different from the rest of Canada. Then, have students make a tourist guide, complete with illustrations, that show the French influence.

Cooperative Learning

Have students work in small groups to research Ireland's potato famine with the aim of preparing an outline for a 30-minute documentary. Tell students to prepare a list of topics they would cover and images they would show during their documentary. Have groups share their outlines with the rest of the class.

CANADA'S LAND AREA Have students study the map of North America in the Atlas (p. A3) or Transparency 3. In addition, you may ask them to find a population density map and a climate map of Canada on a larger atlas or on the Internet. Based on the information they find on the maps, ask students why they think most Canadians live near the U.S.-Canadian border. (The climate is milder and the physical features less harsh in southern Canada.)

◆ **ANSWER** Lord Durham recommended that Upper and Lower Canada be united and that the area should be given control over its own affairs.

Section Close
Review with students the various events that led up to changes in the way Ireland and Canada are ruled today. Discuss which changes helped democracy grow and expand.

Assess

Review Answers

Review History
A. In 1858, the property qualification for members of Parliament was eliminated. In 1867, all men in cities received the vote.

B. It passed the Act of Union to prevent a revolution in Ireland.

C. The Dominion of Canada was able to expand because other provinces could be added as people moved west, and a rail line that linked east to west was built.

Define Terms to Know
franchise, 534;
rotten borough, 535;
home rule, 537;
dominion, 538

Critical Thinking
Possible answer: The British government recognized that O'Connell had a great deal of support, and it may have feared an uprising if it did not satisfy at least some of the demands of the Roman Catholics in Ireland.

Write About Citizenship
Students' editorials should address why the right to vote, when it is extended to the general population, could encourage positive changes and how it would most likely be more representative of all citizens.

Spotlight on
Geography

CANADA'S LAND AREA
Today, Canada is the second largest country in the world in land area. Only Russia covers more land. Although Canada has plenty of land, three-fourths of its population chooses to live in the south, near Canada's border with the United States. Living conditions are less severe there than in the far northern territories.

Upper Canada and Lower Canada became one unified Canada in 1841. It was given an elected legislature to determine domestic policies. However, Britain still kept control of foreign policy and trade.

The Dominion of Canada
People began talking about making Canada a confederation, or a group of joined independent states. They wanted Canada to become two provinces again. Each province would have control over local affairs. A central government would have authority over Canada as a whole.

In 1867, the British Parliament approved Canada's plan. It passed the British North America Act, which set up the Dominion of Canada. A **dominion** is a self-governing nation. The provinces of New Brunswick, Nova Scotia, Ontario, and Quebec made up the new Dominion. Under the act, the Dominion would have a government like Britain's, including a parliament with an elected House of Commons and an appointed Senate. Its prime minister would usually be the leader of the political party with the most seats in the House of Commons. This government would handle Canada's home affairs. Britain would handle foreign affairs for Canada. The British monarch would still be Canada's head of state.

Expansion of the Dominion
The British North America Act also said that the Dominion of Canada could include additional provinces. Other provinces were added as pioneers made their way to the Pacific Ocean. A rail line that linked east to west also helped the expansion of the Dominion. Hundreds of thousands of European immigrants helped settle the western prairies of the Dominion.

◆ **What were Lord Durham's two recommendations?**

Review I

Review History
A. What reforms made after 1850 increased the rights of middle-class British citizens?
B. Why did the British government pass the Act of Union?
C. How was the Dominion of Canada able to expand?

Define Terms to Know
Define the following terms:
franchise, rotten borough, home rule, dominion

Critical Thinking
Why do you think the British government passed the Emancipation Act after Daniel O'Connell was elected?

Write About Citizenship
Write a newspaper editorial supporting the right to vote in Great Britain in the early 1800s.

Get Organized
CAUSE-AND-EFFECT CHAIN
Think about the main events in this section. Use a cause-and-effect chain to show a cause and an effect of an event. For example, what was a cause and an effect of the Reform Act of 1832?

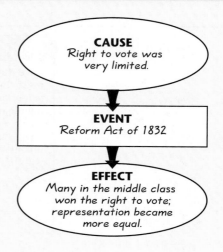

CAUSE
Right to vote was very limited.

EVENT
Reform Act of 1832

EFFECT
Many in the middle class won the right to vote; representation became more equal.

Build Your Skills

INTERPRET BAR GRAPHS

Graphs provide information in a visual format. They make it easy to compare statistics, or information that involves numbers. A bar graph is one type of graph. Bar graphs can help you compare changes over time or among categories of information.

To present statistics, bar graphs use vertical or horizontal bars. The bars show different quantities, or amounts, of things. On the axes, or vertical and horizontal sides of the graph, labels tell what the bars represent. The vertical axis of the graph usually provides a range of quantities. The horizontal axis identifies the years or places with the amounts shown.

As you study world history, you will examine bar graphs that provide information about many topics. Some of the topics include statistics about populations and population growth, industrial and agricultural production, and trade.

Here's How
Follow these steps to interpret a bar graph.
1. Read the title of the graph to find out what information is presented.
2. Examine the labels on the axes, or vertical and horizontal sides, of the graph to see what the bars show.
3. Study the lengths of the bars and compare the quantities they show.
4. Analyze the information in the graph by considering relationships among the statistics.

Here's Why
You have just read about changes in Great Britain and its empire during the 1800s. If you had to compare changes in population statistics in the British Empire during this time, a bar graph could help.

Practice the Skill
Study the bar graph on the right. Then, answer the following questions.
1. What is the subject of the bar graph?
2. On the basis of the information provided in the graph, how would you describe the change in Canada's population between 1851 and 1891?

Extend the Skill
Find a bar graph in a newspaper or news magazine. Study the statistics the graph presents. Then, write a brief summary of what you learned from the graph.

Apply the Skill
Carefully examine other bar graphs in this chapter. Follow the steps in *Here's How* to use the graphs to learn more about the United States and Europe in the nineteenth century.

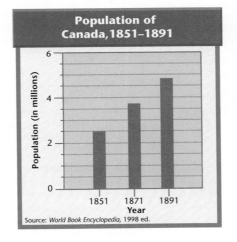

Population of Canada, 1851–1891

Source: *World Book Encyclopedia*, 1998 ed.

Teach the Skill
Bring to class examples of different kinds of graphs—bar graphs, pie or circle graphs, line graphs—from newspapers and magazines. Have students study the graphs and discuss with them the value of presenting information visually. Ask whether students can see the trends presented in the graphs. Tell them that in this lesson they will be learning how to interpret bar graphs.

Encourage students to think of information that would best be presented in a bar graph. (changes over time or information that compares data from different countries or groups) Take a class poll and present the data in a bar graph. Discuss the title for the graph and labels for the axes. Possible topics include students' favorite foods, most popular on-line services, or favorite types of music.

Ask volunteers to formulate questions about the information on the graph. Then, have them write a paragraph that summarizes the information.

Practice the Skill
ANSWERS
1. the population of Canada between 1851 and 1891
2. The population of Canada nearly doubled between 1851 and 1891.

Extend the Skill
Check students' summaries of their graphs for understanding and accuracy.

Apply the Skill
Students may interpret data about U.S. immigration or the nationalities of the Austro-Hungarian Empire.

Teaching Options

RETEACH

Review the steps in *Here's How*. Then, ask students the following questions to improve their ability to read the graph. What does the horizontal, or *x*-axis, show? (the years) What does the vertical, or *y*-axis, show? (population in millions) What was Canada's population in 1851? (2.5 million)

CHALLENGE

Have students use Internet or library resources to find the population changes in their state over a period of at least 50 years. Tell students to create a bar graph showing the population of their state. Ask them to explain the population trend. Is their state's population increasing or decreasing? Have them speculate why.

II. Growth and Change in the United States

(pp. 540–545)

Section Summary

In this section, students will learn about significant changes in the size of the United States during the 1800s. They will learn about U.S. territorial expansion, the causes and effects of the Civil War, and immigration to the United States during the 1800s. They will also find out how westward expansion affected Native Americans.

1 Introduce

Getting Started

Have students look at the map of the United States on page 541. Ask them to locate their state. Have them identify the region their state is in and note when their region became part of the United States. Have the class compile a list on the board that shows the acquisition of new territories in order of when they occurred. You may want to have students make a chart of this information, adding facts about each acquisition as they read about it.

TERMS TO KNOW

Ask students to read the terms and definitions on page 540 and find each term in the section. Have students use each term in a sentence that explains its definition.

You may wish to preview the pronunciation of the following words with students.

Sacagawea (sak uh jeh WEE uh)
abolitionist (ab uh LIHSH uhn ihst)

ACTIVE READING

Ask pairs of students to skim the section together and to predict what they think they will be learning. Have them record their predictions in one or two sentences. Save the predictions. After students have read the section, have them review their predictions and make necessary corrections. Discuss how they might make more accurate predictions in the future.

Terms to Know

Manifest Destiny the idea that the United States had the right to expand from the Atlantic Ocean to the Pacific Ocean

popular sovereignty control by the people

Union the United States of America

secede to withdraw from or leave

Main Ideas

A. By the late 1800s, the United States extended from the Atlantic Ocean to the Pacific Ocean.

B. The North fought the South in the U.S. Civil War, but the Union was saved.

C. At the same time that millions of immigrants were coming to the United States, Native Americans were being pushed off their lands.

 Active Reading

PREDICT
When you predict, you make a reasonable guess about what will happen. As you read this section, pay attention to each subhead. Before reading the text under each subhead, predict what the text will discuss. Then, check your prediction as you read.

A. The Nation Expands

Canada's move toward confederation was in part a response to the activities of its neighbor to the south. The United States of America had been expanding west since the early 1800s. Canadians feared that the United States might try to control all of North America.

The Louisiana Purchase

In 1803, the United States instantly doubled in size with the Louisiana Purchase. The Louisiana Territory extended from the Mississippi River west to the Rocky Mountains. It stretched north and south from Canada to the Gulf of Mexico. It covered more than 800,000 square miles. Spain had held this huge piece of land since the end of the French and Indian War in 1763. In 1800, the French emperor Napoleon bought the territory from Spain. However, Napoleon needed money to finance his wars in Europe more than he needed land. In 1803, he offered to sell the Louisiana Territory to the United States for $15 million.

The Louisiana Purchase was a positive development for the United States for many reasons. France was a great power, and the United States had viewed French control of Louisiana as a threat. The Louisiana Purchase also gave the United States the port city of New Orleans on the Gulf of Mexico. In time, 13 new states would be created from this territory.

Following the Louisiana Purchase, the United States, through various treaties and agreements, added more territory. The main gains were the Florida, Louisiana, and Oregon Territories. The United States shared control of the Oregon Territory with Great Britain. The other lands in what is now the United States belonged to Mexico. With these gains, the United States spanned the continent from coast to coast.

The Monroe Doctrine

While the United States was gaining these new lands, Spain was losing territory in both North and South America. Mexico, Argentina, Chile, and Colombia all won their independence from Spain in the early 1800s. Knowing that the governments of Latin America were unstable, Spain urged its European allies to help it regain control of its former colonies. The British suggested that the United States and Britain make a statement against such a plan. Britain had strong economic reasons for not wanting Latin America to

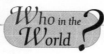

Who in the World?

SACAGAWEA
Sacagawea was a Native American woman who helped explore lands that were part of the Louisiana Purchase. In 1804, U.S. President Thomas Jefferson sent Meriwether Lewis and William Clark on an expedition to the Pacific Northwest. Sacagawea helped guide Lewis and Clark through the Rocky Mountains, where her band of the Shoshone Indians lived.

This stamp of Sacagawea was issued in 1993.

Teaching Options

Section 2 Resources

Teacher's Resources (TR)
Terms to Know, p. 36
Review History, p. 70
Build Your Skills, p. 104
Concept Builder, p. 239
Cause-and-Effect Chain, p. 325

F Y I

The Louisiana Purchase

In 1801, President Thomas Jefferson sent Robert Livingston and James Monroe to France to try to buy the city of New Orleans. They were to spend no more than $10 million. The French, in need of money, shocked the American negotiators by offering them all of the Louisiana Territory for $15 million, or just a few cents an acre.

return to Spanish control. Many British businesses had invested large sums in Latin America. If Spain regained control of Latin America, these British investments would be threatened. The United States rejected Britain's request, preferring to issue its own strong policy statement.

In December 1823, American President James Monroe called on European nations to stop establishing colonies in the Western Hemisphere. He warned that any action by a European power to interfere with a nation in the Americas would be taken as a threat to the United States. He also said that the United States would not interfere in European countries or the colonies they already had in the Western Hemisphere. This bold statement is known as the **Monroe Doctrine**. A doctrine is a statement of beliefs. The Monroe Doctrine became a basic principle of American foreign policy.

From Coast to Coast

By the time that the Monroe Doctrine was announced, people called pioneers had already crossed the Appalachian Mountains in the eastern part of the United States, and settled as far west as the Mississippi River. Soon these adventurous people were settling beyond the Mississippi. In the mid-1840s, pioneers pushed over the Rocky Mountains in the west into the Oregon Territory. They also reached lands in the west claimed by Mexico.

These pioneers saw no reason to stop their westward push. They believed in the **Manifest Destiny** of the United States. That is, they thought the United States had the right to expand from the Atlantic Ocean to the Pacific Ocean. Many people believed that the United States had a right to rule the entire continent. Its economy and political system were better than those of any other nation. Its population was also growing rapidly. Manifest Destiny expressed national pride and a sense of purpose.

Do You Remember?

In Chapter 20, you learned about the Latin American struggle for independence. Mexico won its independence from Spain in 1821.

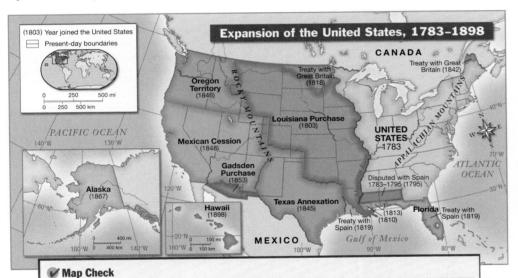

Expansion of the United States, 1783–1898

(1803) Year joined the United States
Present-day boundaries

0   250   500 mi
0   250   500 km

PACIFIC OCEAN
140°W   130°W

CANADA

Oregon Territory (1846)

Treaty with Great Britain (1818)

Treaty with Great Britain (1842)

ROCKY MOUNTAINS

Louisiana Purchase (1803)

UNITED STATES 1783

Mexican Cession (1848)

APPALACHIAN MOUNTAINS

ATLANTIC OCEAN

Alaska (1867)

Gadsden Purchase (1853)

Disputed with Spain 1783–1795 (1795)

Hawaii (1898)

Texas Annexation (1845)

Florida   Treaty with Spain (1819)

(1813)
(1810)

Treaty with Spain (1819)

MEXICO

Gulf of Mexico

70°W

60°W

40°N

30°N

20°N

120°W

400 mi
400 km

100 mi
100 km

100°W   90°W   80°W

✔ Map Check

1. PLACE Which two areas, added in the 1840s, extended the U.S. boundaries to the Pacific Ocean?

2. LOCATION What formed the eastern boundary of the Louisiana Purchase?

Meet Individual Needs:

KINESTHETIC LEARNERS

Have students work in groups to make a bulletin-board display with an illustrated map and a timeline featuring U.S. expansion from 1783 to 1898. Encourage groups to use Internet and library resources to add information and detail to the map and timeline.

💿 Using Technology

What has come to be called the Monroe Doctrine was part of President James Monroe's annual message to Congress delivered on December 2, 1823. Have students find the original speech or an excerpt containing the Monroe Doctrine on the Internet. Then, ask students to restate the speech in their own words and present it to the class.

A. The Nation Expands

Purpose-Setting Question Why were the French willing to sell the Louisiana Territory to the United States? (Napoleon needed the money for his war campaigns.)

WHO IN THE WORLD?

SACAGAWEA Historians believe that Sacagawea (ca.1788–ca.1825) was born in present-day Idaho. She acted as Lewis and Clark's inter-preter and negotiator with Native Americans in the region. She also suggested routes and passages through the mountains.

Do You Remember?

Have students refer to the subsec-tion "Mexico and Central America" on page 477.

Extend The term *Manifest Destiny* first appeared in 1845 in an article written by John L. O'Sullivan in the *United States Magazine and Democratic Review*. O'Sullivan wrote, "[It is] our manifest destiny to overspread the continent allotted by Providence for the free development of our yearly multiplying millions." Ask students how the opinions of Native Americans and Mexicans liv-ing in the west might have differed from O'Sullivan's. (Possible answer: They considered the land they lived on to be their homeland, not land open for "free development.")

Using the Map

Expansion of the United States, 1783–1898

Have students study the map. Then, ask them which territory the United States annexed in 1853. (the Gadsden Purchase) In which year did Florida become part of the United States? (1819) When did the United States annex Alaska and Hawaii? (in 1867 and 1898, respectively)

✔ Map Check

Answers
1. the Oregon Territory and the Mexican Cession
2. the Mississippi River

Create a map Have students use Internet or library resources to research the Texas War for Independence from Mexico (1835–1836) or the war with Mexico (1846–1848). Ask them to make a map for the war they choose. Their maps should show important battles and the routes of armies or navies. Remind students that their maps should have a key that shows which symbols they used to show battles, cities, routes, and other map features.

Extend The structure known as the Alamo was first built in 1718 as a mission. In 1836, the site became the "cradle of Texas Liberty." Rebelling against the policies of Mexico's self-proclaimed dictator, General Antonio López de Santa Anna, a band of 189 Texas volunteers at the Alamo defied the Mexican army for 13 days. All of the male defenders of the Alamo were killed. Soon after, the Texans defeated the Mexican army at the Battle of San Jacinto. "The Napoleon of the West," as Santa Anna called himself, was captured.

◆ **ANSWER** It doubled the size of the United States.

B. The Road to War

Purpose-Setting Question What issues divided the North and the South and led to the Civil War? (The North and the South held different views on slavery, had different ways of life, and both wanted to gain control of Congress.)

Discuss After students have read about life in the North and the South, ask them to compare the two regions. Suggest students describe the physical features, economic characteristics, and views on slavery.

Focus Have students study the picture of the plantation on this page. Ask students if they think this picture offers a pro-slavery or antislavery point of view and if it offers a realistic view of slavery. (Possible answer: The visual offers an idyllic and sentimental view of slavery, not a realistic one. Slaves are shown working in a beautiful field, are not shown as leading a miserable existence, and do not appear to be heavily supervised.)

This pride and purpose helped the United States expand farther. In 1835, American settlers in Texas rose up against Mexican rule and fought for Texas's independence. In 1845, Texas became a state. A year later, the United States went to war with Mexico over land they both claimed. In 1848, a treaty ended the war and gave the United States land from Texas west to the Pacific and north to the Oregon Territory. Great Britain also finally let go of its claim to the Oregon Territory. The United States completed its expansion in three more steps. It received a strip of land in southern Arizona and New Mexico through the Gadsden Purchase in 1853. It purchased Alaska from Russia in 1867, and it annexed Hawaii in 1898. The United States of America now stretched beyond its west coast border.

◆ **What was the main effect of the Louisiana Purchase?**

B. The Road to War

Westward expansion opened up new economic opportunities. It also added to troubles that had been developing in the United States. The northern and southern states had been pulling away from each other for some time. By the mid-1800s, many issues divided the North and the South. These differences would finally lead to war.

Two Ways of Life

The northern and southern parts of the United States had been different ever since colonial times. The South had a warm climate and fertile soils that supported agriculture. Enslaved people helped grow tobacco, cotton, and sugar cane on plantations. The southern way of life was generally rural. In the North, soils were poorer and the climate cooler. The North's economy focused on trade and manufacturing, not farming. Cities developed in the North. The northern way of life was more urban.

The two regions also differed greatly in their views of slavery. Northerners generally saw slavery as wrong. A movement to abolish, or end, slavery had developed in the North. Abolitionists gave speeches and wrote articles to put an end to slavery. The South saw slavery as necessary to its economy. Southern planters said that they would lose their farms without slaves to work them.

Many enslaved African Americans worked in the fields of large plantations.

542   UNIT 6   ◆   A Changing World

Teaching Options

ESL/ELL STRATEGIES

Take Notes Have students work together as pairs in this oral activity that also targets study skills. Ask one student to read aloud a subsection of the text while the other student listens and takes notes. Then, have both students check the notes against the text and evaluate accuracy. Finally, have students switch roles and repeat the process with the next subsection.

Slavery in the West

The debate about slavery raged in the U.S. Congress during the 1800s. One issue was whether slavery should be allowed in the new western lands. Most Southerners and other people who did not have a problem with slavery thought it should be allowed in new territories and states. Most Northerners and others against slavery wanted slavery to be against the law in the new territories and states. A third group supported the idea of **popular sovereignty**. These people thought the voters who lived in the new territories and states should decide whether to allow slavery.

In 1849, there were 15 slave states and 15 free states in the **Union**, giving southern and northern states a balance of power in Congress. The Union is another name for the United States of America. However, that year, California asked to be admitted to the Union as a free state. This presented a problem. The question that had to be answered was whether California was going to be allowed to enter the Union as a free state and upset the North-South balance of power. The Compromise of 1850 stated that California would be admitted as a free state. However, the compromise also included a strict law punishing runaway slaves and those who helped them. The Fugitive Slave Law angered abolitionists and increased the tension between North and South.

War Breaks Out

New political parties with new views on the problems of the nation emerged in the 1850s. A group of Americans against slavery formed the Republican Party. The party's main goal was to fight the extension of slavery into western lands. The party's choice for President of the United States was Abraham Lincoln. After Abraham Lincoln was elected President in 1860, it seemed that a war between the states could not be stopped.

To many Southerners, differences over slavery now seemed too great to resolve. In addition, many Southerners believed in states' rights. They thought that each state was independent and had the right to **secede**, or leave, the Union if it wanted to. In December 1860, South Carolina seceded from the Union. Before Lincoln was even inaugurated, six more states—Mississippi, Florida, Alabama, Georgia, Louisiana, and Texas—also voted to leave. These seven states formed the initial Confederacy, or the Confederate States of America, in 1861. Jefferson Davis became president of the Confederacy.

When Lincoln became President, he still considered the states that had seceded to be part of the United States. He hoped that the Union could be saved. However, war broke out in April 1861. This war was called the Civil War.

Europe's View of the War

Leaders of the South thought that France and Britain would help them in the war. After all, the European textile industry needed cotton from the South. The Confederate states, however, did not receive much help from Europe. The French and British also traded with the North and had begun to get cotton from India and China.

Many Europeans, however, had sympathy for the South. They saw the South's struggle to keep its way of life and be independent as a nationalist cause. In spite of this, no European government officially recognized the Confederate States of America as an independent nation.

American President Abraham Lincoln's main goal during the war was to restore the Union.

Spotlight on *Economics*

COTTON DIPLOMACY
Because the South supplied cotton to the European textile industry, southern leaders' attempts to win the support of powers such as France and Great Britain during the Civil War came to be known as "cotton diplomacy."

Although the South did not receive much aid from Europe, the Confederacy gained permission to build warships in European shipyards.

Discuss Ask students to discuss how they think relations between the North and the South were in the United States after the war. Ask students how they think Southerners and Northerners felt about each other at that time. (Students should recognize that resentment and anger were among the feelings most people were likely to have.)

◆ **ANSWER** Southerners believed that Lincoln's election would mean the end of slavery and the end of the southern way of life.

C. People on the Move

Purpose-Setting Question
Where did most immigrants to the United States come from before the year 1890? (northern and western Europe)

Using the Graph

Immigrants to the United States, 1831–1920

Have students review the Build Your Skills activity on page 539. Ask students to identify the title of the graph on this page (Immigrants to the United States, 1831–1920) and the information that appears on the axes. (year and number of immigrants in millions) Ask them how many immigrants arrived in the United States from 1831 through 1860. (about 5 million)

✔ **Graph Check**
Answer 1861–1890

The Union Saved

In 1865, after four years of bloody conflict, the North won the war. The unity of the United States had been saved. Now, the nation would have to rebuild. Bad feelings between North and South would have to heal. Former Confederate states would have to meet special terms to become part of the Union again. Southerners would need help getting back on their feet. This period of rebuilding after the Civil War is known as Reconstruction.

Former slaves also had new lives ahead of them after the war. In 1865, the Thirteenth Amendment to the U.S. Constitution ended slavery in the United States. The Fourteenth Amendment, passed in 1868, gave full rights of citizenship to African Americans. The Fifteenth Amendment was passed in 1870 and gave all male citizens over 21 the right to vote.

◆ **Why did states in the South secede after Lincoln was elected?**

C. People on the Move

The nineteenth century was a time of great change for people in the United States. Native Americans were pushed off their lands, and millions of immigrants came to the United States looking for a better way of life.

Newcomers

By the time of the Civil War, more than 31 million people lived in the United States. The country now had a larger population than Great Britain and almost as large a population as France. By the end of the century, the population of the United States would swell to more than 75 million.

Immigration was one of the main contributors to population growth in the 1800s. Nearly all of the immigrants came from Europe. Crop failures, famine, disease, and harsh governments drove some across the Atlantic. Others were farmers who had been pushed off their lands in Europe or craftspeople who had been put out of work by the Industrial Revolution. Some came looking for religious freedom. All looked to the United States as a land of opportunity where they could find work and make a better life.

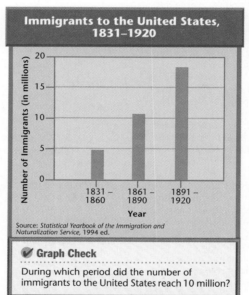

Immigrants to the United States, 1831–1920

Number of Immigrants (in millions)

Year
1831–1860
1861–1890
1891–1920

Source: *Statistical Yearbook of the Immigration and Naturalization Service, 1994 ed.*

✔ **Graph Check**

During which period did the number of immigrants to the United States reach 10 million?

Immigrants came to the United States in two waves. Before 1890, most came from northern and western Europe. They included large numbers from Ireland, Germany, and the Scandinavian countries of Sweden, Denmark, and Norway. Most immigrants in the first wave were Protestant, and many had some education and some experience living under a representative government. For these reasons, they adapted to life in the United States without much difficulty. While adapting, immigrants worshiped in their own churches, had their own social gatherings, and read newspapers in their own languages.

Around 1890, this population trend began to change. Immigrants from Hungary, Italy, Poland, Portugal, Russia, and Spain began to pour into the United States. This wave continued until around 1930. Many of these immigrants from southern and eastern Europe settled in the northeastern United States. Others traveled on to settle in cities across the country.

Teaching Options

First People

Native Americans—called Indians by the settlers—had lived in the land that became the United States long before any Europeans settled there. As European settlers and then American pioneers pushed west, the Native Americans were uprooted from the lands they had called home. Native Americans and settlers often came into conflict. In treaties that ended the fighting, Native Americans were usually forced to give up their lands.

From the point of view of the U.S. government, Native Americans stood in the way of westward expansion. The government's solution was to remove them from their lands, by force if necessary. In 1830, with the full support of U.S. President Andrew Jackson, Congress passed the Indian Removal Act. Under it, Native Americans in the East were forced to give up their lands east of the Mississippi River in exchange for land west of the river. The area they were given, now mostly in Oklahoma, was known as Indian Territory.

By 1860, almost all of the Native Americans in the East had been removed to Indian Territory. Over the rest of the nineteenth century, as white settlers pushed farther west, Native Americans would continue to be removed. They would be relocated to reservations, or areas of land set aside for them. The federal government broke treaties and sent soldiers to fight the Native Americans, until their way of life was eventually destroyed.

In 1838, more than 15,000 Cherokees were forced to set out on the Trail of Tears to a new home in the West.

◆ **Why were Native Americans removed to Indian Territory and reservations in the West?**

Review II

Review History

A. How did the United States gain so much land in the 1800s?

B. What events led to the start of the U.S. Civil War?

C. Why did so many immigrant groups come to the United States in large numbers in the 1800s?

Define Terms to Know

Define the following terms: **Manifest Destiny, popular sovereignty, Union, secede**

Critical Thinking

How did the South's and Lincoln's views of the Union differ?

Write About History

Write a brief essay describing the expansion of the United States in the 1800s and the concept of Manifest Destiny.

Get Organized
CAUSE-AND-EFFECT CHAIN

Think about the main events in this section. Use a cause-and-effect chain to show a cause and an effect of an event. For example, what was a cause and an effect of the U.S. Civil War?

Create a mural Have students use Internet and library resources to create a mural that illustrates immigration to the United States in the 1800s, the westward movement, and the removal of Native Americans. Divide the class into three groups and assign each group one of the topics to cover. Tell them to list the events they wish to illustrate. Then, provide them with large sheets of butcher paper on which to draw. Tell them to write captions explaining what their drawings depict.

◆ **ANSWER** They often came into conflict with white settlers over land, and the U.S. government thought Native Americans stood in the way of westward expansion.

Section Close

Have students create large, illustrated timelines that show the events discussed in this section. Remind them that their timelines must include events that show U.S. acquisition of territory, the Civil War, immigration, westward expansion, and removal of Native Americans.

3 Assess

Review Answers

Review History

A. through treaties, purchases, and victories in wars

B. expansion, division between the North and the South on the issue of slavery, the issue of states' rights, and the election of Abraham Lincoln to the presidency

C. Immigrants came for religious freedom, job opportunities, and to escape harsh governments, famine, failing crops, and disease.

Define Terms to Know

Manifest Destiny, 541; popular sovereignty, 543; Union, 543; secede, 543

Critical Thinking

The southern states saw themselves as independent states and believed they had the right to secede if they wanted to; Lincoln believed that the Union should be preserved.

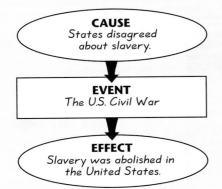

Write About History

Students' essays should discuss how the United States negotiated for and bought territory. They should include a brief explanation of Manifest Destiny.

Past to...

NATIVE AMERICAN LIFE
ON THE PLAINS

Teach the Topic

This feature highlights the life of Native Americans on the Great Plains in the past to their lives in the present. Help students locate the Great Plains on the Atlas map (p. A3) or use Transparency 3. Ask students if Native Americans are accurately portrayed in movies. (Students should recognize that most movies do not give an accurate picture of Native Americans.)

STANDING ON CEREMONY

Plains Native Americans wore headdresses during battles with other groups. Each group's headdress was distinctive so that those from the same group could identify one another in the heat of battle.

TRADITIONAL WEAPONS

Tell students that Native Americans would sometimes coat their arrows with deadly poison.

CATCHING YOUR DINNER

Make sure students understand that before Plains groups began using horses, hunting buffalo was a huge undertaking. As many as 300 people participated in annual buffalo hunts. Plains hunters surrounded a buffalo and attacked it as a group or forced it off a high cliff. Sometimes, they trapped the animal by setting fire to the prairies.

HOME, SWEET HOME

Point out the opening at the top of the tipi. Native Americans made fires for warmth and for cooking. This opening allowed smoke to escape from the tipi.

Have students work individually or in groups to research the variety of traditional Native American homes in different regions. Ask them to create models of some of these homes to display in class. Tell students to write a brief paragraph explaining why a particular home was appropriate for the climate or the physical features of the land on which the group lived.

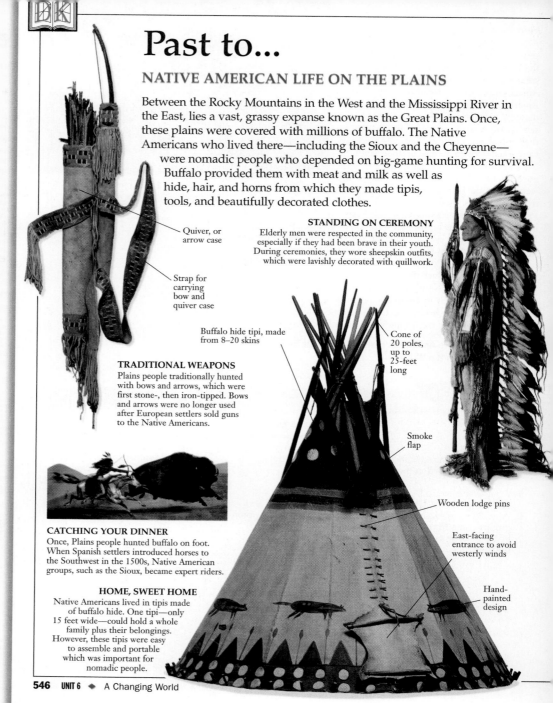

Past to...

NATIVE AMERICAN LIFE ON THE PLAINS

Between the Rocky Mountains in the West and the Mississippi River in the East, lies a vast, grassy expanse known as the Great Plains. Once, these plains were covered with millions of buffalo. The Native Americans who lived there—including the Sioux and the Cheyenne—were nomadic people who depended on big-game hunting for survival. Buffalo provided them with meat and milk as well as hide, hair, and horns from which they made tipis, tools, and beautifully decorated clothes.

Quiver, or arrow case

Strap for carrying bow and quiver case

STANDING ON CEREMONY
Elderly men were respected in the community, especially if they had been brave in their youth. During ceremonies, they wore sheepskin outfits, which were lavishly decorated with quillwork.

Buffalo hide tipi, made from 8–20 skins

Cone of 20 poles, up to 25-feet long

TRADITIONAL WEAPONS
Plains people traditionally hunted with bows and arrows, which were first stone-, then iron-tipped. Bows and arrows were no longer used after European settlers sold guns to the Native Americans.

Smoke flap

Wooden lodge pins

East-facing entrance to avoid westerly winds

Hand-painted design

CATCHING YOUR DINNER
Once, Plains people hunted buffalo on foot. When Spanish settlers introduced horses to the Southwest in the 1500s, Native American groups, such as the Sioux, became expert riders.

HOME, SWEET HOME
Native Americans lived in tipis made of buffalo hide. One tipi—only 15 feet wide—could hold a whole family plus their belongings. However, these tipis were easy to assemble and portable which was important for nomadic people.

Teaching Options

Connection to LITERATURE

You may wish to have some students read *Bury My Heart at Wounded Knee*, by Dee Alexander Brown. The book is a true account of the U.S. government's treatment of some groups of Native Americans. It tells of broken treaties, battles, and massacres from a Native American point of view.

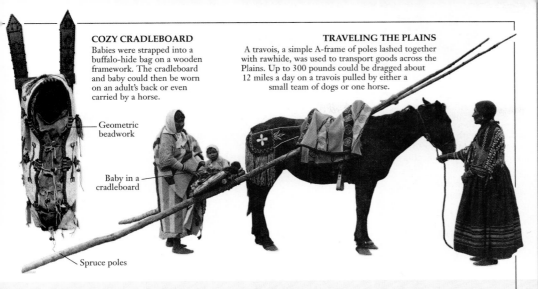

COZY CRADLEBOARD
Babies were strapped into a buffalo-hide bag on a wooden framework. The cradleboard and baby could then be worn on an adult's back or even carried by a horse.

Geometric beadwork

Baby in a cradleboard

Spruce poles

TRAVELING THE PLAINS
A travois, a simple A-frame of poles lashed together with rawhide, was used to transport goods across the Plains. Up to 300 pounds could be dragged about 12 miles a day on a travois pulled by either a small team of dogs or one horse.

...Present

With the immigration of white settlers, the arrival of the railroad, and the disappearance of the buffalo in the nineteenth century, the traditional life of the Plains people came to an end. While part of modern American culture today, Native Americans have kept many of their rich traditions alive throughout the Great Plains and other regions.

HEAD FOR HEIGHTS
Since the late nineteenth century, Mohawks have been known for their ability to work at great heights. Their superb sense of balance enables them to work on modern skyscrapers and bridges during construction.

ANCIENT CRAFT, MODERN PEOPLE
In the homeland of the Navajos in the southwestern United States, traditional weaving is still an important part of the local economy. Navajo blankets and rugs have beautiful geometric designs in natural colors.

COZY CRADLEBOARD
Cradleboards were made of oak and were about 2 feet long and 1½ feet wide. A wooden bow arched over the baby and supported a veil that protected the infant from the elements. Small objects were hung from the bow for the baby to swat at, much the same way as a mobile is hung over a baby's crib today. Babies were carried on their mother's backs in cradleboards or could ride on a travois, as shown at the top of page 547.

TRAVELING THE PLAINS
Ask students why they think a device such as a travois was important to a nomadic people. (Nomadic people would need a way to transport all their necessary items. A travois enabled them to carry 300 pounds of material.)

...Present

ANCIENT CRAFT, MODERN PEOPLE
According to Navajo legend, the Navajo people learned to weave from Spider Woman. Historians and archaeologists, however, believe that the Navajo people learned to weave from the neighboring Pueblo people. Before the Spanish conquest, Navajos used cotton to weave blankets and rugs. The Spaniards introduced sheep, and Navajos began weaving with wool.

HEAD FOR HEIGHTS
The Mohawks who work in construction are also called "skywalkers." Mohawk skywalkers helped build the Empire State Building in New York City in the 1930s. Then, in the 1950s, they put a 222-foot communications tower on it. Mohawks were originally from the Eastern Woodlands region.

Connect Past to Present
Have students study the two "Present" images. Ask whether they have ever seen such traditional Native American crafts as Navajo blankets, beadwork, or pottery. Discuss with students why it may be important to Native Americans to maintain tradition yet develop skills that allow them to make a living in the modern world.

Hands-On Activity
The Native American tradition of the powwow is as popular today as it was in the past. Powwows were traditionally held in spring, to celebrate the renewal of life. Participants came to sing, dance, meet friends, and trade goods. Today, powwows are held throughout the United States. Have students use the Internet to find out where powwows are being held near them.

Section Summary

In this section, students will read about the unification of Italy and Germany. They will find out about the revolutionary movements and the growth of feelings of nationalism in both countries.

1 Introduce

Getting Started

Explain to students that in the early 1800s, Italy and Germany were divided into small states and provinces. Ask them to think of reasons why countries that were more powerful may have wanted to keep Italy and Germany divided. (Possible answer: As many small states, these countries were weak.) Then, ask what challenges unification may have presented to Italy and Germany. (Local rulers may not have wanted to give up their power. People may have identified more with their local region than with the nation as a whole.)

TERMS TO KNOW

Ask students to read the words and definitions on page 548 and find each word in the section. Have them look in a dictionary to find the origin of the two words. (*Risorgimento* is the Italian word for *resurrection*; *kaiser* is from the Latin word for *Caesar*, the family name of the first Roman emperors.)

You may wish to preview the pronunciation of the following names with students.

Giuseppe Mazzini
(joo ZEHP pay mat TSEE nee)
Camillo Cavour
(kah MEEL loh kah VOOR)
Crimean (kry MEE uhn)
Metternich (MEHT uhr nihk)

ACTIVE READING

Tell students that creating a two-column chart (TR, p. 328) to compare and contrast will help them remember the main ideas and details about unification in this region. Ask them to look for similarities and differences between the unifications of Italy and Germany.

T548 ◆ UNIT 6

Terms to Know

Risorgimento a nationalist movement that worked for the unification of Italy

kaiser the emperor of unified Germany

Main Ideas

A. The Italian states were unified as the Kingdom of Italy.

B. A unified German nation came into being as the German Empire.

Active Reading

COMPARE AND CONTRAST
When you compare and contrast, you look for similarities and differences between things. As you read this section, compare and contrast the paths that Italian and German states took to reach unification. Then, list the similarities and differences in a simple chart.

A. Italy Becomes One

In the mid-1800s, as Americans debated issues that would affect the unity of their nation, nationalist ideas were spreading across Europe. As you read in Chapter 20, such ideas led to an uprising in France in February 1848. By March 1848 feelings of nationalism set off revolts in Italy.

Italian States and Provinces

Giuseppe Mazzini, an Italian patriot, founded Young Italy.

In 1815, the Congress of Vienna took control of Italy away from France and divided the country into small states and provinces. In the south, Naples and Sicily were joined into the Kingdom of the Two Sicilies. In central Italy, the Papal States were returned to the pope. The northern states of Lombardy and Venetia became parts of the Austrian Empire. The remaining northern states were independent. The most important independent state was the kingdom of Sardinia, which included the areas of Nice, Savoy, and Piedmont. In 1848, there were seven separate states in Italy.

The Road to Unification

People in the states of the Italian peninsula had been thinking about a united Italy since the early 1800s. A movement known as **Risorgimento** began to work for Italian unification. Many groups were part of the Risorgimento. A group called Young Italy was one of the most active. Young Italy was founded by the Italian patriot Giuseppe Mazzini in 1831. In just two years, its membership climbed from 40 to 50,000. Young Italy worked for a united, republican nation.

Other groups worked for unification too. In 1848, some groups led revolts in important Italian cities. New governments were set up in Milan, Venice, Rome, and Tuscany. None, however, could stand up to Austria. Austria crushed the revolutions and took over most of Italy again. Until Austria was driven out of Italy, it seemed, government reform and unification would not be possible.

Teaching Options

Section 3 Resources

Teacher's Resources (TR)
Terms to Know, p. 36
Review History, p. 70
Build Your Skills, p. 104
Concept Builder, p. 239
Cause-and-Effect Chain, p. 325

FYI

Giuseppe Garibaldi

In the 1830s, Giuseppe Garibaldi was forced to leave Italy to avoid a death sentence for taking part in a mutiny in 1834. He escaped to South America, where he participated in the fights for independence in Brazil and Uruguay. He returned to Italy in 1848, but he was forced to leave Italy again in 1849. Garibaldi returned to Italy again in 1854, this time staying for good and helping to achieve the unification of Italy.

The Kingdom of Sardinia

The Kingdom of Sardinia, under its prime minister Count Camillo Cavour, wanted to unite Italy under one government. He decided to make the Kingdom of Sardinia the leader of the rest of Italy. Cavour built railroads, encouraged the growth of new industries, introduced reforms in the law, and strengthened the military forces. The popularity of the king of Sardinia grew. Cavour's dream of an Italy united under the king of Sardinia was beginning to take shape.

Cavour realized that Italy could not free itself from Austrian control without the help of France. In 1855, Cavour sided with France in the Crimean War. Three years later, the French emperor Napoleon III promised to help drive Austria out of Italy. In return, France would get Savoy and Nice, the French-speaking parts of the Kingdom of Sardinia. Cavour hoped to gain control over the northern states of Lombardy and Venetia.

In 1859, Cavour cleverly provoked Austria into invading Sardinia. True to his word, Napoleon III sent his army to Sardinia's aid. With the help of the French, the Sardinians were able to push the Austrians almost as far east as Venice. By 1860, all of northern Italy, except Venetia, was a part of Sardinia.

Unifying Italy

Gaining the Kingdom of the Two Sicilies was the next step in bringing Italy together. Giuseppe Garibaldi, a popular Italian hero, led the fight for Sicily. Garibaldi sailed to the island of Sicily with a force of only 1,000 volunteers. This army, known as the "red shirts," quickly conquered the island. Then, Garibaldi's forces crossed to the mainland and seized the rest of the kingdom—the city of Naples and southern Italy. By the time Garibaldi had captured Naples, his forces numbered 40,000.

Garibaldi gave the land he had conquered to the Sardinian king, Victor Emmanuel II. When Garibaldi met the king on the border of the Papal States, he hailed him as the king of Italy. In 1861, Victor Emmanuel announced the formation of the Kingdom of Italy. It included all of the Italian peninsula except Venetia, Rome, and the country of San Marino.

Venetia became part of Italy in 1866. Rome followed in 1870 and was made the capital city of Italy. The unification of Italy was complete in 1870.

◆ **How did Garibaldi help create the Kingdom of Italy?**

B. Germany Comes Together

Germany's movement toward nationalism actually began in the minds of its philosophers. In the early 1800s, philosophers such as Georg Hegel pointed out that Germans shared the same language, customs, and history. Hegel thought that making the Germans aware of their heritage would help them unite.

Unification of Italy, 1858–1870

Kingdom of Sardinia, 1858
Added to Sardinia, 1859 and 1860
Added to Italy, 1866
Added to Italy, 1870
• Cities

✔ Map Check

PLACE Which cities shown on the map were part of the Kingdom of Sardinia in 1858?

A. Italy Becomes One

Purpose-Setting Question What actions did Count Camillo Cavour take to unite Italy? (Cavour built railroads, developed the economy, supported political reform, and strengthened the military in the Kingdom of Sardinia. He also sided with France in the Crimean War to ensure that France would be Sardinia's ally.)

Discuss Have students discuss the advantages and disadvantages of making alliances. This discussion will help prepare them for the study of World War I and one of its underlying causes: alliances. Ask students what alliance Count Cavour made to help Italy (Cavour made an alliance with France) and what were the advantages of making this alliance. (Cavour gained France's help in driving Austria out of Italy.) Finally, ask what might be the disadvantages of the alliance with France. (He had to sacrifice Italian lives to help France in the Crimean War, and he might owe France favors in the future.)

Using the Map
Unification of Italy, 1858–1870

Have students explain what the different colored areas on the map represent. Then, have them write a paragraph describing the unification of Italy. (Answers should reflect the information on the map and in the text.)

✔ Map Check
Answer Genoa and Turin

◆ **ANSWER** He conquered the Kingdom of the Two Sicilies and gave the land to King Victor Emmanuel II of Sardinia.

B. Germany Comes Together

Purpose-Setting Question Why did German unification fail in 1848? (The Frankfurt plan did not please all the German states. The assembly did not agree about whether Austria or Prussia should lead the new nation.)

Writing

AVERAGE

Have students work with a partner to "interview" either Giuseppe Mazzini or Count Camillo Cavour. Encourage students to use the text as well as Internet and library resources to write a list of questions and possible answers. Then, have students role-play their interviews, with one student as the interviewer and the other as the subject to be interviewed.

CHALLENGE

Have students use the text as well as Internet and library resources to write a newspaper article about Giuseppe Garibaldi's battle for Sicily and Naples. Remind students that a newspaper article must answer the five *W*s: *Who, What, Where, When,* and *Why.* Have students illustrate their articles with their own drawings or with pictures they find on the Internet.

German States

Germany in 1800 was divided into more than 250 independent states. Most of these states were loosely joined in the Holy Roman Empire, headed by Austria. In 1806 Napoleon I, having defeated Austria, dissolved the Holy Roman Empire. His armies took over many of the German states. Napoleon reduced the number of German states to about 100.

As you learned in Chapter 20, the Congress of Vienna met to restore the balance of power in Europe. The Congress reduced the number of German states to 38 to form the new German Confederation. Metternich's Austria was the strongest member of the confederation. Prussia was the second strongest member. The states in the confederation remained independent. Most were ruled by kings or princes, and each state kept its own laws and armies.

Germans Revolt

As in other parts of Europe, however, nationalist feelings had been developing in the German states for some time. By the 1840s, Germans throughout the confederation were eager for change. Some talked of getting rid of the confederation and creating a unified nation.

In March 1848, the Germans rose up against governments in Vienna, Berlin, and other German capitals. Rulers reacted by making some changes. German nationalist leaders saw that simply bringing together states would not make a nation. In May 1848, about 500 liberal leaders formed an assembly at Frankfurt to write a constitution for all the German states. The Frankfurt plan failed to please everyone however. The assembly could not agree, for instance, about whether Austria or Prussia should lead the new nation. In 1849, the assembly broke up, and the German Confederation was set up again.

Unification of Germany, 1865–1871

Prussia, 1865
Added to Prussia, 1866
Added to Prussia, 1867
Added to form German Empire, 1871
Boundary of German Empire, 1871
• Cities

0   75   150 mi
0   75   150 km

✔ Map Check
1. LOCATION How far west did the German Empire extend in 1871?
2. PLACE Which cities shown on the map were in the area added to Prussia in 1866?

Teaching Options

Meet Individual Needs:

VISUAL/SPATIAL LEARNERS

As students read subsection B, tell them to take notes with the objective of making an illustrated timeline containing events leading to the unification of Germany. Have students find or draw illustrations to accompany their timeline entries.

Test Taking

Remind students to read questions carefully on multiple-choice tests. Then, tell them to begin eliminating choices they know are wrong. Have students write a multiple-choice question about subsection B. Then, have students exchange questions and identify which choices they can eliminate and which answer is correct.

Germany's Unification

After the unification of Italy, nationalist movements became active again in central Europe. Various German groups gathered to discuss the possibility of a German nation. At the same time, Prussia took its own steps to increase its power and become the leader of such a nation. Its actions would lead finally to the unification of Germany. Prussia brought German states together under its leadership through a series of short wars. This course of action was the idea of Prussia's new prime minister, Otto von Bismarck.

In a war in 1864, Prussia and Austria took Schleswig and Holstein from Denmark and added them to the German Confederation. Two years later, Prussia defeated Austria itself in the Seven Weeks' War. With Austria out of the way, Prussia was all-powerful. Prussia ended the German Confederation, taking over some of its territory. Then, Prussia set up the North German Confederation. Four German states in the south, which stayed independent, became allies of Prussia.

Now, only France stood in the way of German unification. The French saw the rise of a strong, united Germany as a serious threat. France finally declared war on Prussia in July 1870.

During the Franco-Prussian War, the four southern German states joined the North German Confederation. They all fought as a united German nation led by Prussia. The Germans won the war in 1871. Under the peace treaty, France gave up part of Lorraine and nearly all of Alsace. The new German nation was a German Empire. Wilhelm I became its emperor, or **kaiser**. He named Bismarck as the chancellor and head of government.

Otto von Bismarck (wearing a white jacket) stands at the foot of the stairs as King Wilhelm I of Prussia (center, top of stairs) is crowned emperor of Germany.

 How did Bismarck bring the four independent German states in the south into the new German nation?

Review III

Review History
A. What was the outcome of the revolts of 1848 in Italy?
B. What events helped bring the German states together under Prussia?

Define Terms to Know
Define the following terms:
Risorgimento, kaiser

Critical Thinking
Why do you think Giuseppe Garibaldi gave the land he had conquered to the Sardinian king?

Write About Government
Write a paragraph explaining why Italians and Germans who revolted in 1848 wanted new governments.

Get Organized
CAUSE-AND-EFFECT CHAIN
Think about the main events in this section. Use a cause-and-effect chain to show a cause and an effect of an event. For example, what was a cause and an effect of German unification?

```
  ⬭
  ↓
 ▭
  ↓
  ⬭
```

CHAPTER 23 ◆ Nationalism and Expansion **551**

Section Summary

In this section, students will read about the rise of the Austro-Hungarian Empire and the ebb and flow of its power and prestige. They will also read about the rise of nationalism and its effects on this region.

1 Introduce

Getting Started

Discuss with students some of the different cultures that exist and languages that are spoken in their school or community. Help students understand that the United States has a great deal of diversity. Explain that the Austro-Hungarian Empire in the 1800s was also quite diverse and sometimes this diversity caused problems.

TERMS TO KNOW

Have students read the terms and definitions on page 552 and find each term in the section. Ask them whether they believe the United States is multinational and explain why it is. (Students should acknowledge that the United States is multinational. It is a country that contains people from many different nations.) Ask whether they know of other countries that are multinational. (Canada is one example, though many countries are multinational.)

You may wish to preview the pronunciation of the following names with students.

Magyar (MAG yahr)
Istvan Szechenyi
  (IHSHT vahn SAY chehn yih)
Lajos Kossuth
  (LAY yawsh KAW shoot)

ACTIVE READING

Ask students to take notes as they read. As they begin reading the section, remind them to identify the problems faced by Austria. If students are having trouble suggesting solutions, have the class brainstorm solutions. Then, have the class choose the most realistic solutions.

Section IV

The Austro-Hungarian Empire

Terms to Know

dual monarchy rule of two kingdoms by one person
multinational including many nationalities

Main Ideas

A. Revolutions shook the Austrian Empire in 1848 but were finally put down by the conservative government.

B. Austria and Hungary were joined under one ruler in 1867.

📖 Active Reading

PROBLEMS AND SOLUTIONS
Problems seldom have just one solution. As you read this section, try to identify problems faced by Austria, and later by Austria-Hungary. Think of at least two solutions for each problem. Then, read on to see how each problem was actually solved.

A. The Austrian Empire

In the 1800s, the Austrian Empire was made up of many different peoples living within the empire. Each group had its own territory and its own language. Yet until 1867, all power in the empire was held by only one of these groups, the Germans. After 1867, power was divided between two of the empire's groups, the Germans and the Hungarians.

The Austrian Empire

In 1815, Austria was a land of many peoples. The largest ethnic group was the Germans. Numbering about 12 million, they lived mostly in Austria and Bohemia. Magyars, or Hungarians, numbered about 10 million and lived in Hungary. About 8.5 million Czechs and Slovaks and 5 million Poles lived in the northern parts of the empire. In the east and south, Ukrainians, Romanians, Croats, Serbs, Slovenes, and a small Italian population accounted for an additional 15.5 million people. Each group had its own language and culture. Many wanted self-government within the empire.

The Hapsburgs and Metternich

During this time, Austria was ruled by a narrow-minded emperor, Francis I. Francis I was one in a long line of European rulers from the Hapsburg family. The Hapsburgs had ruled the Holy Roman Empire for almost 400 years. Through marriage and other arrangements, they also governed other kingdoms and states throughout Europe. Hapsburg ties with Austria dated back to the thirteenth century. Rudolph, the first Hapsburg to be Holy Roman emperor, conquered Austria soon after being crowned. Austria became the Hapsburg family's home and remained so through the nineteenth century.

Francis began his rule in 1806. His government was against reform and suspicious of any new ideas. His belief in government was, "Rule, and change nothing." Francis kept a close grip on affairs within his country. For example, he tried to limit freedom of speech by setting up a censorship bureau to make sure that antigovernment writings were not printed.

Although a Hapsburg ruled the Austrian Empire, Klemens von Metternich, the Austrian minister of foreign affairs, had even greater power. As you learned in Chapter 20, Metternich played a key role in reshaping Europe after Napoleon's defeat. He helped choose rulers and set boundaries in Europe. He also influenced the European powers to put down movements devoted to the

Klemens von Metternich was an Austrian prince and statesman.

Teaching Options

Section 4 Resources

Teacher's Resources (TR)
  Terms to Know, p. 36
  Review History, p. 70
  Build Your Skills, p. 104
  Chapter Test, pp.161–162
  Concept Builder, p. 239
  Cause-and-Effect Chain, p. 325

Connection to
MATH ◄

Have students review the population data under the subhead "The Austrian Empire." Ask them to compile the data given and calculate the total population of Austria in 1815. (51 million) Have them create a bar graph with the information. Suggest that students refer to the Build Your Skills feature on page 539.

causes of nationalism and liberalism. Metternich's impact on Europe in the early part of the nineteenth century was so great that the period is sometimes called the Age of Metternich.

Metternich was a conservative. He saw nationalism and liberalism as threats to keeping Europe as it had been in the past. He once remarked:

 Two words are enough to create evil; two which because they are empty of any practical meaning delight the visionaries. The words are liberty and equality. 🔟

ANALYZE PRIMARY SOURCES

DOCUMENT-BASED QUESTION
What does Metternich think of the meaning of liberty and equality?

Revolution in the Empire

Metternich tried to stop Europe from changing. However, talk of revolution began in the 1820s, and uprisings occurred in various cities in the 1830s. In 1848, the French revolted against their king. News of the revolution in France spread quickly, leading to revolts across Europe. Revolutions broke out in different parts of the Austrian Empire, including Vienna and Hungary.

The first revolt in the Austrian Empire began in Budapest, Hungary. Two leaders rose up among the Magyars. These were Count Istvan Szechenyi and Lajos Kossuth. When revolution broke out in France in 1848, Kossuth saw this as a time for Hungary to rise against the Austrians. In passionate speeches, Kossuth urged people to fight for their liberty.

In Vienna, people crowded the streets. They wanted basic freedoms, such as freedom of speech and the press. They wanted a more liberal government. They demanded that Metternich resign. The government called out troops

Revolts in Europe, 1848

Legend:
- Austrian Empire
- Prussia
- German states
- German Confederation
- Revolts

✔ Map Check

1. PLACE Which places in the Austrian Empire were centers of revolt?

2. REGION Where in the German Confederation did people revolt?

CHAPTER 23 ◆ Nationalism and Expansion **553**

Explore Tell students that Lajos Kossuth was the first foreign statesman officially invited to address the U.S. House of Representatives since the Marquis de Lafayette in 1824. A statue of Kossuth is located in the Capitol in Washington, D.C. Words on the statue proclaim him the Father of Hungarian Democracy. Have students find out more about the Hungarian nationalist Lajos Kossuth and his trip to the United States. Ask them to present their findings in an oral report.

◆ **ANSWER** His views and policies were too conservative and the people wanted change.

B. Austria-Hungary

Purpose-Setting Question How did Emperor Franz Joseph try to unify his empire? (He made German the language of government and schools. He tried to eliminate differences in laws and customs.)

Discuss Ask students why Franz Joseph's efforts to unify the Austrian Empire failed. Discuss with them whether the emperor's solution was a good one. (Franz Joseph's efforts failed because he tried to suppress ethnic differences. This suppression resulted in a surge of nationalistic feelings among the various ethnic groups. Students' opinions will vary regarding his decision to create a dual monarchy.)

Activity

Write a biography Have students write mini-biographies of Franz Joseph or Klemens von Metternich. They should supplement information in their textbook with material from the Internet and other sources. Encourage students to include information about the personalities of these two men, as well as their failures and accomplishments.

and even fired on the crowds. In the end, Metternich was forced out and escaped to Great Britain.

As a result of this revolt, Hungary won almost complete independence from Austria. However, the Magyars refused to share the rights they had won with other groups in Hungary. Groups such as the Croats staged revolts. The Austrians hoped to take advantage of attacks on Hungary and sent troops to support the rebels. Attempts were made by the Austrians to bring down the new government. Kossuth responded by declaring complete independence from Austria on April 14, 1849.

The Magyars put up a strong fight against the Austrians. The Hapsburgs turned to Russia for help and defeated the Hungarian army in August 1849. Austria again brought Hungary under its control, though not for long. Kossuth escaped to the United States, where his speeches about freedom and democracy won a large audience. He traveled to Italy and Britain as well, trying to gain support for Hungarian independence.

◆ **Why did people in Vienna during the revolt of 1848 want Metternich to resign?**

B. Austria-Hungary

By the early 1850s, Austria seemed to be powerful once more. It had put down revolts in Italian states it controlled and still had a powerful role in the German Confederation. However, as Italy and Germany moved toward unification in the 1850s and 1860s, Austria's power shrank.

Franz Joseph, Austrian Emperor

In 1848, 18-year-old Franz Joseph became Austrian emperor. Franz Joseph tried to put the empire back together by stamping out ethnic differences. He made German the language of government and schools. He wanted to get rid of differences in customs and laws. However, his changes only stirred more nationalistic feelings among Magyars and Slavs.

Sharing Power

Austria changed its policy after it was defeated by Prussia in the Seven Weeks' War of 1866. Having lost both land and power, Franz Joseph knew he must find a way to hold on to what was left of his empire. How could he strengthen an empire with so many different peoples? The answer was to come to terms with Hungary. Hungary wanted independence. It also wanted equal status, or standing, with Austria. In 1867, Austria and Hungary reached an agreement, or a compromise.

The compromise created a **dual monarchy**. The empire would be divided at the Leitha River. West of the river would be the empire of Austria. East of the river would be the kingdom of Hungary. The two would be equal. Each would have its own constitution and parliament. Each would manage its own affairs without the other interfering. Although Austria and Hungary would not have a common parliament, they would share ministries, or departments, of foreign affairs, defense, and finance. The empire was now called Austria-Hungary, or

Franz Joseph (center) is shown at a ball in Vienna in 1900 to celebrate the start of a new century.

Teaching Options

Meet Individual Needs:
VERBAL/LINGUISTIC LEARNERS

Ask students to suppose that they participated in the revolt in Vienna. Have them write a short speech expressing their desire for democracy, liberty, and equality. Remind students to state their feelings about Metternich and the monarchy.

ESL/ELL STRATEGIES

Use Visuals Ask students to study the picture on this page. Ask them to write at least five sentences using adjectives and adverbs to describe the people and surroundings. Encourage them to be as creative as possible in their descriptions. You may want to suggest that students work together in pairs to write their sentences.

the Austro-Hungarian Empire. The Hapsburg ruler would form a bridge between the two. He would be the emperor of Austria and the king of Hungary.

While Magyars and Germans were pleased by the new law, Slavic groups felt left out again. Slavic groups in Austria-Hungary included Croats, Czechs, Poles, Serbs, Slovaks, Slovenes, and Ukrainians. Only those who adopted German or Magyar languages and customs were able to prosper in the new Austro-Hungarian Empire. A bill to give Czechs in Bohemia their own government failed because of Magyar and German opposition. Then, some Slavic leaders wanted all Slavs to unite in an attempt to gain political and social power in Austria-Hungary. By 1900, the anger of the Slavic people was ready to explode.

The Reach of Empire

A large portion of eastern Europe belonged to the Austro-Hungarian Empire at its peak. The empire covered about 260,000 square miles. In 1878, Austria-Hungary won control of Bosnia and Herzegovina to its south. The province was added to the empire's area in 1908. Austria-Hungary's vast empire was **multinational**, including about 50 million people of many nationalities. Germans formed the majority in the Austrian part of the empire. Magyars controlled the Hungarian side. Other major groups in the empire included Slavs, Romanians, and Italians. These groups spoke their own languages and observed their own customs. Together, they made up more than half of the empire's population. Yet they had no voice in its government.

◆ **How did the Magyars benefit from the dual monarchy?**

Nationalities of the Austro-Hungarian Empire, 1908

[Bar chart showing Population (in millions) on the y-axis from 0 to 25, and Nationality on the x-axis: Slavs (about 23), Germans (about 12), Magyars (about 10), Other Groups (about 5)]

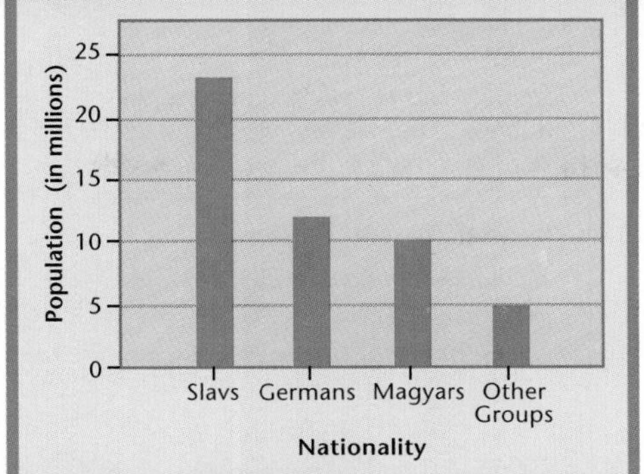

Source: *World Book Encyclopedia*, 1998 ed.

☑ **Graph Check**
Which was the largest national group in the Austro-Hungarian Empire?

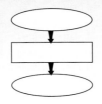

Review IV

Review History
A. Why is the early part of the nineteenth century sometimes called the Age of Metternich?
B. What were the main ethnic groups in the Austro-Hungarian Empire?

Define Terms to Know
Define the following terms:
dual monarchy, multinational

Critical Thinking
How did the revolt in Hungary in 1848 differ from that in Vienna?

Write About Geography
Write a short description of the location of the Austro-Hungarian Empire in relation to France, Germany, and Italy.

Get Organized
CAUSE-AND-EFFECT CHAIN
Think about the main events in this section. Use a cause-and-effect chain to show a cause and an effect of an event. For example, what was a cause and an effect of the dual monarchy?

[Diagram: oval → rectangle → oval]

CAUSE
Austria wanted control of Hungary; Hungary wanted equal status.

↓

EVENT
Creation of dual monarchy

↓

EFFECT
Empire of Austria and kingdom of Hungary were recognized as equals.

Write About Geography
Students should use the cardinal and intermediate directions and geographic features to describe Austria-Hungary's location in relation to France, Germany, and Italy.

Using the Graph

Nationalities of the Austro-Hungarian Empire, 1908

Have students review the feature Build Your Skills on page 539. Ask them how many Germans there were in the Austro-Hungarian Empire. (about 12 million) How many in the category of "other groups"? (about 5 million)

☑ **Graph Check**
Answer the Slavs

◆ **ANSWER** The Magyars kept their independence and had equal status with Austria.

Section Close

Ask students what they think was the most serious problem that the Austro-Hungarian Empire faced during the nineteenth century. (Possible answers: ethnic rivalry; rise of nationalism) What solutions did the empire find to this problem? (Answers will vary based on students' answers to the first question.)

③ Assess

Review Answers
Review History
A. Metternich had a great impact on Europe in the early part of the nineteenth century. He helped choose rulers, set boundaries, and influenced the European powers to put down movements devoted to the causes of nationalism and liberalism.

B. Germans, Magyars, Slavs, Romanians, and Italians

Define Terms to Know
dual monarchy, 554; multinational, 555

Critical Thinking
The revolt in Hungary was tied to nationalist feelings, whereas the revolt in Vienna emphasized liberal ideas.

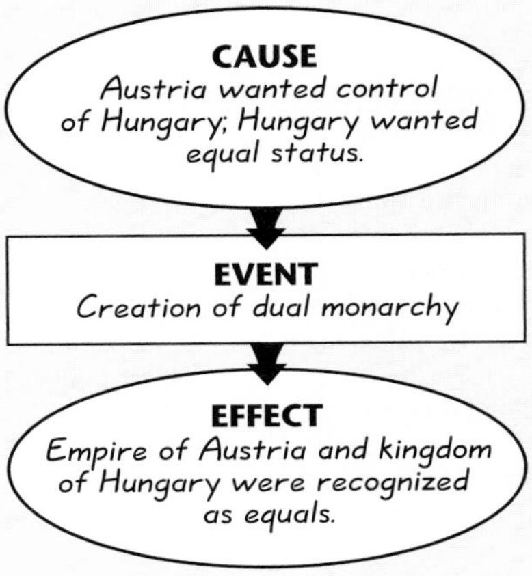

Chapter Summary

A blank outline form is available in the Teacher's Resources (p. 318). Chapter summaries should outline the events discussed in this chapter, including political changes in Great Britain and the United States, unification of both Italy and Germany, and the issues that divided the Austro-Hungarian Empire. Refer to the rubric in the Teacher's Resources (p. 340) to score students' chapter summaries.

 Interpret the Timeline

1. 42 years
2. the United States buying the Louisiana Territory
3. revolutions in France, Austria, Prussia, and Italy in 1848
4. Check students' timelines to be sure that all events are in the chapter.

Use Terms to Know

5. a. dominion
6. h. secede
7. b. dual monarchy
8. c. franchise
9. f. Manifest Destiny
10. e. kaiser
11. d. home rule
12. i. Union
13. g. popular sovereignty

Check Your Understanding

14. The Chartists wanted voting rights for all adult men, a secret ballot, equal electoral districts, and yearly elections for the House of Commons.
15. The Irish Question was whether the British should allow the Irish to govern themselves.
16. Ireland was directly ruled by Great Britain and became part of the United Kingdom; Canada had more independence. As a dominion, Canada had control over its own domestic affairs.
17. Its goal was to set up the Dominion of Canada. Canada would have a parliament and a prime minister.
18. The Monroe Doctrine was a statement made by U.S. President James Monroe that any European interference in the affairs of a nation in the Americas would be taken as a threat to the United States.
19. Conditions in the South supported agriculture. Enslaved people helped grow crops on plantations

T556 ◆ UNIT 6

Chapter Summary

Complete the following outline in your notebook. Then, use your outline to write a brief summary of the chapter.

Nationalism and Expansion

I. *Changes in Great Britain and Its Empire*
   A. *Political Changes in Great Britain*
   B. *The Irish Question*
   C. *Self-Government for Canada*

II. *Growth and Change in the United States*
   A. *The Nation Expands*
   B. *The Road to War*
   C. *People on the Move*

III. *Italy and Germany Become Unified Nations*
   A. *Italy Becomes One*
   B. *Germany Comes Together*

IV. *The Austro-Hungarian Empire*
   A. *The Austrian Empire*
   B. *Austria-Hungary*

Interpret the Timeline

Use the timeline on pages 532–533 to answer the following questions.

1. How many years after the Peterloo Massacre took place did the Civil War break out in the United States?

2. Which happened first, the Reform Act or the United States buying the Louisiana Territory?

3. **Critical Thinking** Which events on the timeline show the rise of nationalism that took place in the 1800s?

4. Select four events from the chapter that are not on the timeline. Create a timeline that shows these events.

556 UNIT 6 ◆ A Changing World

Use Terms to Know

Match each term with its definition.

a. dominion   f. Manifest Destiny
b. dual monarchy   g. popular sovereignty
c. franchise   h. secede
d. home rule   i. Union
e. kaiser

5. a self-governing nation
6. to withdraw from or leave
7. rule of two kingdoms by one person
8. a right or privilege, especially the right to vote
9. the idea that the United States had the right to expand from the Atlantic Ocean to the Pacific Ocean
10. the emperor of unified Germany
11. self-government for a dependent country
12. the United States of America
13. control by the people

Check Your Understanding

14. **Identify** some of the demands of the Chartists.
15. **Explain** what the Irish Question was.
16. **Compare** Canada and Ireland's relationship with Great Britain.
17. **Summarize** the goals of the British North America Act.
18. **Describe** the Monroe Doctrine.
19. **Contrast** ways of life in the northern and southern parts of the United States before 1860.
20. **Discuss** the second wave of immigration to the United States.
21. **Identify** the Italian state that was a leader in unifying Italy.
22. **Explain** what the German Confederation was and how it was formed.
23. **Discuss** the role of the Hapsburgs in the Austro-Hungarian Empire.
24. **Describe** the population of the Austro-Hungarian Empire.

---

there. The southern way of life was generally rural. The economy of the North focused on trade and manufacturing. The northern way of life was more urban. Most people in the North were against slavery. Most people in the South were for it.

20. The second wave included immigrants from Hungary, Italy, Poland, Portugal, Russia, and Spain. It began around 1890 and ended around 1930. Many of the immigrants from southern and eastern Europe settled in the northeastern United States and in cities across the country.

21. the Kingdom of Sardinia

22. The German Confederation was a loose union of German states. It was formed by the Congress of Vienna mostly out of states from the Holy Roman Empire.

23. A Hapsburg ruler would rule the Austro-Hungarian Empire. He would be the emperor of Austria and the king of Hungary.

24. The empire included about 50 million people of many nationalities, or national groups. Germans formed the majority in the Austrian part of the empire. Magyars controlled the Hungarian side. Other groups in the empire included Slavs (Croatians, Czechs, Poles, Serbs, Slovenes, Slovaks, and Ukrainians), Romanians, and Italians.

Critical Thinking

25. **Make Inferences** Why did the Irish want independence from Great Britain?

26. **Draw Conclusions** What groups would have been concerned about the idea of Manifest Destiny?

27. **Compare and Contrast** Why do you think France supported Italy's unification but opposed unification for Germany?

28. **Analyze Primary Sources** Why do you think Metternich felt threatened by the words *liberty* and *equality*?

Put Your Skills to Work

29. **Interpret Bar Graphs** You have learned how to interpret bar graphs by comparing the quantities shown by vertical or horizontal bars. Interpreting bar graphs can help you understand changes over time.

    Study the bar graph below. Then, answer the following questions.

    a. What is the subject of the bar graph?

    b. What was the approximate population of the United States in 1920?

    c. By how many millions of people did the U.S. population grow between 1800 and 1880?

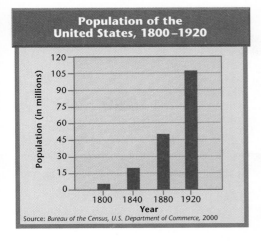

Population of the United States, 1800–1920

Population (in millions) / Year

Source: *Bureau of the Census, U.S. Department of Commerce, 2000*

Analyze Sources

30. In this speech by the French writer Victor Hugo, Hugo talks about Garibaldi's conquest of Sicily. Read the selection and answer the questions that follow.

    Italy a living entity [being], Italy now Italy! Where there was once a geographical term there is now a nation. . . . I tell you that there is but one reality: Right. If you would make comparisons between Right and Force, make trial by means of these figures. On 11 May eight hundred men landed at Marsala. Twenty seven days later, on 7 June, eighteen thousand scared men quit Palermo. The eight hundred represent Right, the eighteen thousand represent Force.

    a. Who had Right on their side?

    b. Who represented Force?

Essay Writing

31. A spirit of nationalism in Italy and Germany led each country to its unification in the second half of the nineteenth century. Nationalism also developed in Hungary. Write an essay about what the nationalist movement in Hungary gained in 1867. Compare and contrast Hungary's national status, or situation, with that of Italy and Germany.

TEST PREPARATION

SEQUENCING RELATED EVENTS
Read the question below and choose the correct answer.

Which of the following took place before Lord Durham's report on conditions in Canada?

1. Canada became a self-governing nation.

2. The Dominion of Canada was formed.

3. Canada was divided into Upper Canada and Lower Canada.

4. The British North America Act was passed.

Critical Thinking

25. Possible answer: Great Britain had controlled Ireland for hundreds of years. The British ruled harshly and discriminated against Roman Catholics.

26. Possible answer: British, Mexicans, and Native Americans

27. Possible answer: France saw a strong, unified Germany as a threat to itself.

28. Possible answer: People who want change will use such words in slogans to get others to revolt against the government. Metternich supported a monarchy and a return to a way of life that had existed before 1789.

Put Your Skills to Work

INTERPRET BAR GRAPHS
29a. population of the United States between 1800 and 1920
29b. about 105 million
29c. about 45 million

Analyze Sources

30a. Garibaldi and his troops, who wanted to unify Italy
30b. the troops of the ruler of Sicily

Essay Writing

31. In their essays students should comment on how nationalist ideas spread throughout Hungary and compare this movement to the nationalist movements in Italy and Germany. Students should highlight the similarities between the developing nations, from revolt and revolution to unified empires.

TEST PREPARATION

Answer 3. Canada was divided into Upper Canada and Lower Canada.

Imperialism in Africa, India, and the Middle East
1850–1923
(pp. 558–583)

Chapter Objectives

- Identify the economic, political, and social changes brought about by the Industrial Revolution that led to western imperialism.
- Explain how European imperialism affected the countries of Africa.
- Describe why British interest in India expanded and how British rule led to a desire for independence.
- Describe the collapse of the Ottoman Empire and how the imperialist practices of western Europe and Russia influenced the breakup of the empire.

Chapter Summary

Section I focuses on the Industrial Revolution and the factors that led to western imperialism.

Section II describes the growing interest of European nations in establishing colonies in Africa and how spheres of influence were established there.

Section III explores the growth of British interest in India and discusses the British influence on the politics, economics, infrastructure, and culture of India.

Section IV discusses the early expansion of the Ottoman Empire, the reasons for its decline, and how western Europe and Russia contributed to that decline.

Set the Stage

TEACH PRIMARY SOURCES

Explain to students that Edmund Burke was a British political philosopher. He reflected the thinking of many in the western world when he referred to the areas where Great Britain ruled as a "savage wilderness." Strategic and commercial reasons for imperialism were often accompanied by the romantic viewpoint that imperialism made a positive contribution to those who were ruled.

CHAPTER 24

Imperialism in Africa, India, and the Middle East
1850–1923

I. The Spread of Western Imperialism
II. Imperialism Divides Africa
III. British Imperialism in India
IV. Imperialism in the Islamic World

In 1877, Queen Victoria of Great Britain was proclaimed Empress of India. She was a symbol of the spread of European civilization and culture around the world. The expansion of western powers during the second half of the nineteenth century involved the whole world. The ideas behind the expansion included the spread of western ideals and civilization as well as financial gain. As Edmund Burke explained:

> ❝ *[O]ur ancestors have turned a savage wilderness into a glorious empire; and have made the most extensive and the only honorable conquests, not by destroying, but by promoting the wealth, the number, the happiness of the human race.* ❞

The countries of western Europe were determined to help "civilize" people in distant lands, whether or not their help was welcome.

CHAPTER EVENTS

1857 Indian soldiers mutiny against the British.

1869 Suez Canal opens.

1877 Queen Victoria proclaimed Empress of India.

1850 — **1865** — **1880**

WORLD EVENTS

1865 Civil War in the United States ends.

1877 Porfirio Díaz becomes president of Mexico.

Teaching Options

Chapter 24 Resources

REVIEW

Teacher's Resources (TR)

Terms to Know, p. 37
Review History, p. 71
Build Your Skills, p. 105
Chapter Test, pp. 163–164
Concept Builder, p. 240
Main Idea/Supporting Details Chart, p. 319
Transparency 1

ASSESSMENT

Section Reviews, pp. 564, 570, 575, 581
Chapter Review, pp. 582–583
Chapter Test, TR, pp. 163–164

ALTERNATIVE ASSESSMENT

Portfolio Project, p. 608
Make a Brochure, p. T608

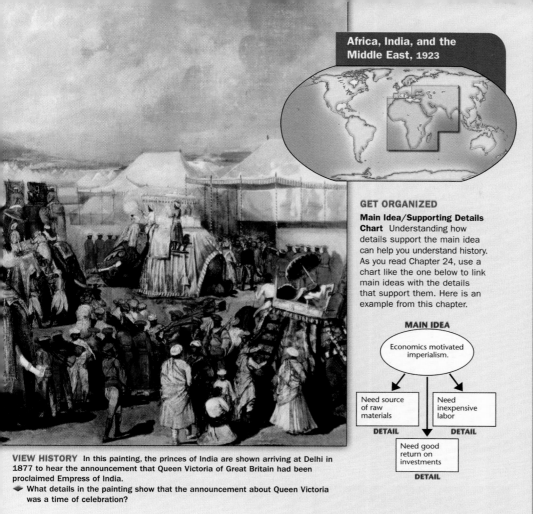

Africa, India, and the Middle East, 1923

GET ORGANIZED

Main Idea/Supporting Details Chart Understanding how details support the main idea can help you understand history. As you read Chapter 24, use a chart like the one below to link main ideas with the details that support them. Here is an example from this chapter.

MAIN IDEA

Economics motivated imperialism.

```
        ┌──────────┼──────────┐
        ▼          ▼          ▼
Need source    Need         Need good
of raw         inexpensive  return on
materials      labor        investments

DETAIL         DETAIL       DETAIL
```

VIEW HISTORY In this painting, the princes of India are shown arriving at Delhi in 1877 to hear the announcement that Queen Victoria of Great Britain had been proclaimed Empress of India.
◆ What details in the painting show that the announcement about Queen Victoria was a time of celebration?

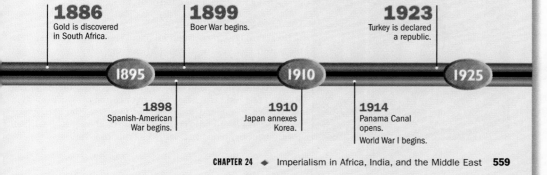

1886
Gold is discovered in South Africa.

1899
Boer War begins.

1923
Turkey is declared a republic.

1895 **1910** **1925**

1898
Spanish-American War begins.

1910
Japan annexes Korea.

1914
Panama Canal opens.
World War I begins.

CHAPTER 24 ◆ Imperialism in Africa, India, and the Middle East **559**

Chapter Themes
- Culture
- Time, Continuity, and Change
- Individuals, Groups, and Institutions
- Power, Authority, and Governance
- Production, Distribution, and Consumption
- Global Connections
- People, Places, and Environments

F Y I

Local Rule in India
Rajahs of imperial times in India were left in control of internal affairs of their local areas, which were like states. The British gave the title *maharajah* to princes who kept some authority under British rule.

The painting on pages 558–559 shows princes riding elephants. The "tent" on the back of the elephant is a *howdah*. The richly decorated *howdah* indicated the wealth of the prince who rode inside.

Chapter Warm-Up
USING THE MAP
Have students find the locator map on page 559. The map highlights the areas affected by European expansion in the late 1800s. Ask students why they think this area, rather than North and South America, was the target of European expansion. (Possible answer: Colonies in the Americas had already won their independence.)

VIEW HISTORY
Explain to students that the British in India are an example of imperial rule that was supported for a time by local rulers. The painting shows the respect shown to the British. Ask students to contrast the Indians in the painting who appear to be rulers with common people. (The common people are poorly dressed and subservient both to their fellow Indians and to the British.)

◆ **ANSWER** the fine clothing and decorations

GET ORGANIZED
Main Idea/Supporting Details Chart
Discuss the graphic organizer shown on page 559. Remind students that they have used this type of chart to record main ideas and details in earlier chapters. Tell students to use as many rectangular boxes as they need so that each detail is in its own box.

Point out that identifying the main idea and details in each subsection of text will help students remember the most important points and additional information about these points.

TEACH THE TIMELINE
The timeline on pages 558–559 shows events between 1857 and 1923. Ask students to figure out the interval between the ovals on the center part of the timeline. (15 years) Have them identify countries shown in the Chapter Events. (India, Great Britain, Egypt, South Africa, Turkey)

Activity
Interpret the timeline Explain that some of the World Events on the timeline also show the spread of imperialism. Ask students why some countries were seeking to expand and other countries became victims of this expansionism. (Possible answer: During the Industrial Revolution, industry spread and stronger countries took advantage of weaker ones.)

I. The Spread of Western Imperialism

(pp. 560–564)

Section Summary

In this section, students will learn how the changing economic conditions brought about by the Industrial Revolution motivated imperialism and the seeking of colonies by governments of western Europe. Students will also learn where imperialism spread and how western European nations justified establishing colonies in those areas.

1 Introduce

Getting Started

Ask students to suppose that they own a factory that makes ten cars a day. Ask what they would need if they suddenly could produce ten times as many cars. (raw materials, labor, storage)

Ask how they would go about selling the increased number of cars. Help students relate this issue to the conditions of manufacturing at the height of the Industrial Revolution. (Possible answer: Industrialization created the need for more raw materials and expanded markets.)

TERMS TO KNOW

Ask students to read the words and definitions on page 560 and find each word in the section. Challenge students to find the root in each word. (imperialism—imperium, empire; infrastructure—structure; protectorate—protect) Discuss how the government of a protectorate would differ from a colony's government.

ACTIVE READING

Students may wish to use a Venn diagram (TR, p. 323) to compare and contrast earlier forms of colonialism with western imperialism in the late 1800s. Remind students that they are being asked to find likenesses and differences. Students might compare such conditions as location and economic and political motivation.

The Spread of Western Imperialism

Terms to Know

imperialism the practice by which one nation gains and maintains political, social, and economic control over another nation

infrastructure a group of basic physical facilities, such as roads, railways, and factories, necessary for a community to operate efficiently

protectorate a state in which local government rules under the control of another government

Main Ideas

A. In the late 1800s, the Industrial Revolution in Europe and in the United States reached its peak.

B. Economic, political, and social factors served as important motives for western imperialism.

Active Reading

COMPARE AND CONTRAST
When you compare and contrast, you identify similarities and differences. As you read this section, compare and contrast earlier colonialism with western imperialism in the late 1800s.

A. Europe at the End of the Nineteenth Century

The Industrial Revolution—the shift from producing goods by hand to the use of power machines—resulted in sweeping economic and social changes. This revolution began in Great Britain in the late 1700s. By 1870, it had spread throughout much of the western world.

The Industrial Revolution in Full Stride

By 1850, Great Britain was the most industrialized nation in the world. Thanks to steamships, goods mass-produced in Britain could be transported worldwide. Britain's control of world markets continued for the rest of the nineteenth century.

The Great Exhibition of 1851, the first world's fair, was held in London, England. The goal of the exhibition was to celebrate British technology and industry. To emphasize British skills, the Great Exhibition was held in a building called the Crystal Palace, which had been built just for the exhibition. The stunning and unique Crystal Palace contained nearly 300,000 panes of glass and 5,000 iron beams and columns. People from all over the world traveled to London and were amazed.

France, Belgium, and the United States followed Britain's industrial lead in the early to mid-1800s. However, after 1871 a new industrial power emerged in Europe. This industrial power was Germany, which had united under the skillful, ambitious leadership of the German chancellor Otto von Bismarck. German finance, shipping, weapons, and manufacturing grew very rapidly over the next 30 years. By 1900, Germany was producing as much steel as France and Great Britain combined. In the early twentieth century, Germany also competed with Britain for control of the high seas.

This lifelike model of an iguanadon was a popular attraction in the gardens outside the Crystal Palace.

The Economic Picture

Breakthroughs in transportation and communications, such as the steam engine, the telegraph, and the telephone, brought nations and people closer together. Industrialization also affected countries economically. For example, during the U.S. Civil War, Britain could not depend on cotton imports from the American South. The need for a steady supply of cotton for their mills led the British to depend more on India, where raw cotton was readily available. To protect this new source of cotton, the British government tightened and unified its rule over India.

560 UNIT 6 ◆ A Changing World

Teaching Options

Section 1 Resources

Teacher's Resources (TR)
Terms to Know, p. 37
Review History, p. 71
Build Your Skills, p. 105
Concept Builder, p. 240
Main Idea/Supporting Details Chart, p. 319

ESL/ELL STRATEGIES

Identify Essential Vocabulary Point out the forms a word such as *colony* can take. For example, a colony (n.) is a group of people who live under the control of the country from which they came. To colonize (v.) is to establish a colony. A colonist (n.) is a person who lives in a colony. Colonialism (n.) is a governing policy based on control of people in a colony. Help students find examples of these words in this section and use each word form in a sentence.

The Crystal Palace was the site of the Great Exhibition of 1851. The structure was built of iron supports and glass.

The unification of India under British rule was made easier by the railroads. The British began an ambitious program of railway construction in India in the 1850s. In a short time, they had built an impressive network of railways. This network made it possible to quickly transport British soldiers to areas where they were needed.

The railway boom also had some unexpected effects on the economies of both Great Britain and India. Cotton goods cheaply produced in Great Britain were shipped by rail all over India. These goods could be sold for less than textiles turned out by local cloth-makers. Some parts of the Indian textile industry were almost put out of business because of competition from British goods.

As Europeans became a greater force in Asia and Africa, the industries of those places underwent a change. Instead of producing finished goods, they exported raw materials, such as raw cotton, jute, tin, gold, and rubber. These materials were then used by European industries to make finished products.

◆ **How did the industrialization of Europe change the industries of other nations?**

B. The Colonizers and the Colonized

Throughout most of recorded history, people have moved or migrated to seek out new opportunities. Sometimes their motives have been economic or political. Other times, people have migrated because of religious persecution or because of natural events that change an area.

European Defense of Imperialism

Colonialism and __imperialism__ are practices used to establish and maintain control over distant regions. Colonialism is generally concerned with expanding and protecting trade routes and markets. Imperialism is a practice by which one nation gains and maintains political, social, and economic control over another nation.

The industrialization of European nations gave them a great advantage over the nonindustrialized nations of Asia and Africa. The Europeans held a wide edge in manufacturing, transportation, and weapons. They developed strong

The Crystal Palace

The Crystal Palace covered nearly 20 acres of Hyde Park in London. Three huge elm trees stood inside the structure. Centrally placed was a fountain made of 4 tons of pure crystal glass. Eight miles of stands presented exhibits to extol human achievement in art and science. New products on display included the reaper and the Colt revolver.

Using the Chart

Causes and Consequences of Imperialism

Ask students what information the chart helps to summarize. (the causes of European imperialism and its consequences) Have students read across the chart and turn each cause and its corresponding consequence into a sentence that shows cause and effect. For example, the search for new economic markets led to the weakening of native industries.

✔ Chart Check

Answer search for new economic markets, weakening of native industries, need for raw materials, overuse of natural resources, competition of European nations

Hold a debate Have students debate whether European nations really helped the countries they colonized. Students might begin by listing advantages and disadvantages of imperialism, from the point of view of the colonies or protectorates. Have debate teams use specific examples from Section 1 to defend their viewpoint.

Extend Ask students to consider how industrialization affects relationships between countries today. (Possible answer: Highly industrialized countries continue to have an advantage and tend to be stronger economically.)

Causes and Consequences of Imperialism

CAUSES	CONSEQUENCES
Search for new economic markets	Weakening of native industries
Need for raw materials	Overuse of natural resources
Decline of aging, non-western empires	Mandates and protectorates
Competition of European nations	Rise of nationalist movements
Religious missions	• Prejudice • Advances in health and education • Scientific progress

✔ Chart Check
Which entries on the chart concern economic activities?

---

central governments that were able to impose their will on colonized regions.

As the Industrial Revolution spread throughout Europe, the need grew for steady supplies of raw materials, such as cotton and rubber. The powerful nations were more than willing to take over weaker countries that had the materials they needed. To this end, the British, the French, the Dutch, the Germans, and the Italians made large financial investments in Africa and Asia. These investments were used to create an industrial **infrastructure**, a number of basic physical facilities necessary for a community to operate efficiently. These facilities included roads, bridges, railroads, docks, factories, mines, banks, houses, and hotels. With such an infrastructure in place, the countries of Asia and Africa were able to function more like European countries.

Economics of Imperialism

Economics was always a major factor in imperialism. European nations needed many raw materials that only tropical regions could supply, such as tea, coffee, rubber, and jute. Most of these regions in Africa and Asia were poor and undeveloped, with plentiful raw materials and a huge resource of cheap labor.

Europeans also wanted to develop new markets for the products of their factories. The less-developed countries of Africa and Asia met these needs perfectly. Each European country's goal was to develop its own self-sufficient trading area.

Another important economic factor was the higher profits that could be made from investing money in Africa and Asia rather than in Europe. By 1914, the British had 25 percent of all their wealth invested outside Great Britain. Other Europeans were also investing their money in nations outside Europe. With so much of their money being invested in businesses outside Europe, it became necessary for the Europeans to place more control over the non-European nations.

Politics and Imperialism

As a driving force for imperialism, politics was probably second only to economics. The European nations were concerned with preserving the balance of power. In other words, no nation wanted any other nation to gain an advantage. In the 1600s, the concerns over balance of power had been confined to the European continent. By the 1800s, the field had expanded. Now, the lands of the colonial world beyond the boundaries of Europe were involved. The establishment of overseas territories was seen as proof of national greatness and power.

The European nations set up different types of governments in the areas they controlled. Some areas, such as Dutch-dominated Indonesia, were colonies. Other regions, such as Egypt under the British and Tunisia under the French, became **protectorates**. A protectorate is a system in which a local government continues to govern, but that government is under the control of another power.

Teaching Options

Connection to ECONOMICS

Ask students what aspects of a colony's economics are affected by imperialism and why. (The colony's local industries are often undersold, so the colony becomes a market for an imperialist nation and a provider of raw materials and cheap labor. The colonial power, with a more established industry, is able to satisfy its need for a greater and guaranteed source of raw materials.)

Test Taking

Tests that assess reading skills may require students to understand words with multiple meanings. Tell students to use the context to find clues to a word's meaning. Then, have students look on page 562 for a phrase that will help them understand *market* as it is used in the subsection Economics of Imperialism.

Religion, Culture, and Imperialism

Religious and social arguments were often used to support the idea of imperialism. Missionaries from Roman Catholic and Protestant groups were sent to convert the non-Christian peoples of Africa, Asia, and the Middle East. In addition to spreading the Christian word, missionaries promoted education. They built schools, taught in them, and trained local people to be teachers. Missionaries also built hospitals and provided medical care for local people. These were some of the ways that western culture was spread in these areas.

European writers and politicians spoke of the moral obligation of advanced countries to bring "culture," "reason," and "order" to developing regions. In 1899, British writer Rudyard Kipling wrote a poem that vividly expressed the imperialist viewpoint.

> " Take up the White Man's burden —
> Send forth the best ye breed —
> Go bind your sons in exile
> To serve your captives' need. . . . "

Other Factors Favoring Imperialism

Scientific curiosity and the urge for adventure also motivated imperialism. European settlement of remote areas allowed scientists and natural historians access to previously unexplored regions. Different kinds of plants and animals were collected and sent to western zoos and laboratories. Adventurers discovered the thrills of hunting exotic animals, such as lions, tigers, and elephants. For the wealthy Europeans, at least, the imperialist adventure provided new outlets for leisure and recreation.

Some people used sound scientific observations and altered them to fit ideas that supported imperialist beliefs. Social Darwinism is a perfect example of this practice. Charles Darwin was a natural scientist—a scientist

This is the interior of a school established by missionaries in the African Congo.

ANALYZE PRIMARY SOURCES — **DOCUMENT-BASED QUESTION** What do you think Kipling meant by "the White Man's burden"?

TEACH PRIMARY SOURCES Have students look at the photograph of the classroom of a mission school in the African Congo. Ask them what the photograph suggests about the relationship between the children and the missionaries. (Possible answer: The missionaries are teaching the children their European culture; the children are dressed in European clothing and the pictures on the walls are of Europeans.)

ANALYZE PRIMARY SOURCES

DOCUMENT-BASED QUESTION
Rudyard Kipling is the author of *The Jungle Books,* collections of stories describing the adventures of Mowgli, an Indian child. He is best known for his stories about India during the late 1800s. Kipling was born in India and was sent to boarding school in England. He returned to India as a young man and wrote for newspapers. In 1907, Kipling was awarded the Nobel Prize for literature.

ANSWER Possible answer: Kipling felt that it was the duty of western Europeans to travel to colonies in order to help educate and civilize "captive" non-European people.

Activity

Summarize Have students create an outline summarizing the religious, social, and cultural reasons people of western Europe were attracted to the idea of imperialism. If possible, have students provide an example for each reason in their outline.

Discuss Have students discuss the scientific motivations of imperialism. Then, ask students to suggest benefits to finding new plants and animals. (Possible answer: Scientists and natural historians who had access to unexplored regions might find new cures to existing diseases from the plants and animals found there.)

Focus on WORLD RELIGIONS

Missionaries and the Spread of Christianity As western imperialism spread, Westerners encountered strong, established religions. Many Europeans at that time viewed the religions practiced by people in Asia, Africa, and the Middle East as inferior or dangerous. In the nineteenth century, a new wave of missionary activity brought Christianity as one aspect of European culture to Asia, Africa, and the Middle East.

The attempt to establish Christianity in new regions often generated conflict. In India, there had been no separation of church and state; the rulers of society were teachers and religious leaders. In Africa, missionaries tried to spread monotheistic Christian beliefs to people who held polytheistic beliefs. Attempts to replace one system of religious beliefs with another helped fuel political strife that has often lasted to the present day.

AMERICAN IMPERIALISM The United States viewed the annexation of the entire North American continent as its "Manifest Destiny." The acquisition of overseas colonies, however, was a more hidden agenda. In addition to its acquisitions as a result of the Spanish-American War, the United States expanded its reach with its annexation of the Hawaiian Islands, the administration of Samoa, the acquisition of Puerto Rico as an overseas territory, and continued involvement in the affairs of Cuba. Ask why the United States was less open than European nations about such actions. (It had been a colony and professed to believe in freedom for all people.)

◆ **ANSWER economic:** desire to obtain raw materials, cheap labor, and expanded markets for manufactured goods; **political:** desire to maintain a balance of power drove nations to obtain new territory; **cultural:** Europeans often felt it was their duty to spread their religion and way of life to those who they believed were inferior or less fortunate.

Section Close

Ask students to identify both positive and negative aspects of imperialism. Have students also discuss how imperialism might be viewed as negative by the European powers as well as by the colonized nations.

3 Assess

Review Answers

Review History
A. The Industrial Revolution drove the need for more raw materials to feed European factories, and for expanded markets in which to sell manufactured goods. This led European nations to imperialism.

B. Economics was a major factor in imperialism, including the need for raw materials, new markets, and the higher profits that could be made from investing in Africa and Asia.

Define Terms to Know
imperialism, 561; infrastructure, 562; protectorate, 562

Global Connections

AMERICAN IMPERIALISM
American imperialism was less openly talked about in the United States than it was in Europe. The United States, after all, achieved independence through revolution against its colonizer, Great Britain. Nevertheless, in the late 1800s and early 1900s, imperialism was evident in the Spanish-American War, as well as in U.S. foreign policy toward the Panama Canal.

who studied living things in their natural environments. In his book *The Origin of the Species*, Darwin had written about how different species of animals changed, or evolved, over time in order to survive. Some of these changes eventually led to a new species that was stronger than the original species and was more likely to survive.

Social Darwinists adapted some of Darwin's ideas to explain human society. They applied Darwin's ideas to human ethnic groups, claiming that Europeans were more "advanced" than other groups and should be expected to rule over such groups.

Another misleading argument for imperialism was that Europeans needed living space to avoid "overcrowding" in their own countries. This argument was clearly false, because very few Europeans emigrated to new colonies after 1870. Most of the people who left Europe to live elsewhere settled in the United States.

In the end, imperialism had mixed results, some positive and some negative. On the negative side, people's homelands were taken over by foreign powers, and local people had to live under new sets of rules. Many of these people were forced to work under difficult conditions. In addition, local goods manufactured by hand could not compete with the mass-produced goods from Europe. As a result, many small, regional industries declined and even disappeared in some places.

On the positive side, Europeans built hospitals and schools. They provided medical care for the local people, helped educate the younger population, and trained adults to become teachers. The infrastructures built by the Europeans proved to be very useful to the people of the colonized nations when these nations gained their independence.

◆ **What were some of the important economic, political, and cultural factors that motivated European imperialism?**

Review 1

Review History
A. What were some connections between the Industrial Revolution and the rise of western imperialism?
B. What was the relationship between economics and imperialism?

Define Terms to Know
Define the following terms:
imperialism, infrastructure, protectorate

Critical Thinking
Do you think imperialism was basically caused by economic greed, or was it driven by a more complicated mixture of motives?

Write About Culture
Write an editorial for a British newspaper in which you condemn the policy of imperialism.

Get Organized
MAIN IDEA/SUPPORTING DETAILS CHART
Use a chart like the one below to show details that support each main idea in this section. For example, use this main idea: Factors leading to imperialism.

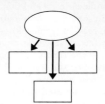

Critical Thinking
In their discussion, students should consider all the motives for imperialism discussed in this section, including economic, political, religious, and cultural factors, and support their decision.

Write About Culture
Students' editorials should reflect a personal reaction to imperialism through their tone, choice of words, and supporting evidence.

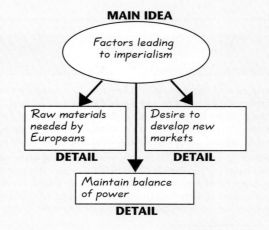

MAIN IDEA

Factors leading to imperialism

Raw materials needed by Europeans
DETAIL

Desire to develop new markets
DETAIL

Maintain balance of power
DETAIL

Build Your Skills

Build Your Skills

Study Skill

WRITE A RESEARCH PAPER

A research paper presents factual information about a specific topic. To begin your paper, first limit or focus the topic as much as possible. If your topic is too broad, you will not be able to include all the issues in a brief paper.

Next, begin the research part of your paper. Use a variety of current sources, such as reference books, periodicals, topical books, and Internet sources. Document each source you use, paying careful attention to quotations and footnotes. Take notes using the sources you have chosen.

Before you begin writing your paper, use your notes to make an outline of the information you will present. When you start writing your paper, state the main idea in a sentence or two. Then, write a first draft. Check your draft for errors and for missing information before writing the final copy of your paper.

Here's How
Follow these steps to write a research paper.
1. Choose a topic that is limited and focused.
2. Use a variety of sources to research the topic.
3. Take notes to record both the information you find and the sources.
4. Use your notes to prepare an outline to organize your information.
5. State your main idea in one or two sentences.
6. Prepare a first draft. Make corrections before writing the final copy.

Here's Why
Being able to present research findings in a paper or report is a valuable skill. It will not only help you with your work in school, but it will also help you learn how to research topics in a variety of subjects.

Practice the Skill
Read the chart on the right, which provides an example of narrowing a general topic. On a separate sheet of paper, state a main idea for the narrowed topic. Then, conduct research on the main idea. Write an opening paragraph of a research paper based on your main idea and research.

Extend the Skill
Choose a general topic from this chapter and then narrow this topic. Next, state a main idea for the narrowed topic.

Apply the Skill
Conduct research on your narrowed topic. Then, write a one-page research paper about this topic.

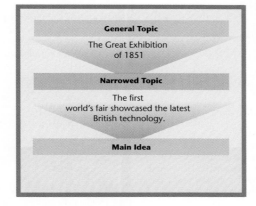

General Topic

The Great Exhibition of 1851

Narrowed Topic

The first world's fair showcased the latest British technology.

Main Idea

Teaching Options

RETEACH

Provide students with examples of broad topics from the chapter. Have them narrow each one to one or two more limited topics that would be suitable for a research report. Some broad topics you might suggest include Imperialism, the Industrial Revolution, and the World's Fair. From their narrowed topic, help students create a main idea statement.

CHALLENGE

Have students choose a topic for a research paper. Challenge them to research four or more different resources to find information about their topic. For example, students might use a newspaper, a magazine, a video, an Internet site, reference books, a CD-ROM, or a personal interview. Ask them to be prepared to share with the class the value of each type of reference source.

WRITE A RESEARCH PAPER

Teach the Skill
Ask students to recall instances in school when they have been asked to prepare a research report, perhaps for an English, a science, or a social studies class. Explain to students that often in school or at work people need to collect information to present in a report.

In order to help students practice the skill, refer them to the list of steps in *Here's How*. Explain that the first thing students should do in preparing to write a research paper is to identify a topic that is neither too large nor too limited.

Discuss reasonable sources for students' research papers, such as library books, periodicals, and the Internet. Stress to students that when they take notes they should document their sources. Unless they are taking an exact quotation, they should take notes in their own words, summarizing the information they find. Using notecards (an index card with one point, from a single source) is an excellent way to collect and organize information.

Practice the Skill
Students' opening paragraphs should incorporate the main idea statement and should entice the reader to want to read the rest of the report. You might suggest that students open with a quotation or interesting fact or statistic.

Extend the Skill
In choosing a topic, students should include a large general topic discussed in the chapter; a narrowed topic; and the main idea, which should state the viewpoint the student will take on the narrowed topic.

Apply the Skill
Explain to students how they should go about researching and writing the research paper. They might want to create a numbered list of steps to help them get through the process of developing a topic into a research paper.

II. Imperialism Divides Africa

(pp. 566–570)

Section Summary

In this section, students will learn about early European exploration and colonization of Africa. They will also learn how various European countries established spheres of influence in Africa.

1 Introduce

Getting Started

Write this twentieth-century proverb on the board: *Travel broadens the mind.* Ask students how travel can broaden a person's mind. (Possible answer: Travel lets people see that other cultures have created beautiful objects, such as buildings or statues.) Tell students that sometimes travelers can introduce new ideas to other cultures.

TERMS TO KNOW

Ask students to read the terms and definitions on page 566 and find each term in the section. Point out that both of these terms relate to governing and to power between nations.

Some students may be misled by the everyday meanings of the words *sphere* and *influence* as they read about spheres of influence. Discuss the concept of multiple meanings to eliminate misconceptions before students read the section.

You may wish to review the pronunciation of the following names with your students.

Angola (an GOH luh)
Mozambique (moh zahm BEEK)
Kalahari (kah luh HAHR ree)
Zambesi (zam BEE zee)
Otto von Bismarck
(AW toh FAWN BIHS mahrk)

ACTIVE READING

Remind students that to create a summary they should restate only the most important information in their own words. Have them use the main ideas at the top of page 566 as a starting point for their summary. Then, have them use the subheads to suggest supporting details for each heading.

Imperialism Divides Africa

Terms to Know

mandate a nation's assignment by an international body to govern or administer an area

sphere of influence a region in which one nation claims to have exclusive influence or control over other nations

Main Ideas

A. Until the late nineteenth century, most of Africa was unknown to Europeans.

B. Starting in the 1870s, European nations competed with each other to establish colonies in Africa.

📖 Active Reading

SUMMARIZE
When you summarize, you state only the most important points, or highlights, of a passage. As you read this section, focus on the main points about the partition of Africa. At the end of each section, pause to summarize what you have learned.

A. Africa in the Nineteenth Century

For hundreds of years after their first contact with Africans, Europeans concentrated on Africa's coastal regions. There were some exceptions. The Portuguese established colonies in Angola and Mozambique, and the Dutch settled parts of southern Africa in the 1650s. For the most part, however, Africa was thought of as a collection of ports. These ports served as sources of slaves for the colonizers of the Americas.

African Travels

In 1878, British explorer Henry Morton Stanley published a travel book telling of his adventures in Africa. The book's title was *Through the Dark Continent.* Stanley might have been referring to the skin color of Africans. The word *dark*, however, also summed up the ignorance of Europeans, who knew almost nothing about Africa until the late 1800s.

As a journalist, Stanley had accepted an assignment from the New York *Herald* in 1871. Stanley's project was to locate Dr. David Livingstone, a Scottish medical missionary who had traveled to Africa years earlier. Stanley located Livingstone in a village in central Africa. Stanley stayed and wrote about Livingstone's adventures in Africa.

This illustration shows Henry Stanley and Dr. Livingstone meeting at Ujiji, near Lake Tanganyika in Africa.

Teaching Options

Cooperative Learning

Review with students the goal of the partnership between Henry Morton Stanley and King Leopold II of Belgium. (development of the Congo River basin) Have students work in groups to explore current local development activity. Groups should identify what is being proposed, what the goal is, and how it is expected to affect the community. For example, students might note a proposal for a new school, hospital, store, transportation hub, or tract of homes.

Livingstone's story made for good travel reading. He had explored deep into the continent with a group of Africans in search of the source of the Nile River. In his travels, he had crossed the Kalahari Desert and was the first European to fully explore the Zambesi River. In 1855, he became the first white person to see Victoria Falls. After more than 30 years of self-sacrifice and service, Livingstone died in an African village in 1873.

Stanley was more interested in profit and development than in service. He made a second trip to explore the Congo River in Central Africa. Then, he went into partnership with King Leopold II of Belgium in order to develop the Congo River basin, which was a rich source of raw rubber. The two partners set up a company called the International Congo Association. Returning to Africa, Stanley set about making treaties with the local chiefs. This marked the beginning of the division of African lands for European profit.

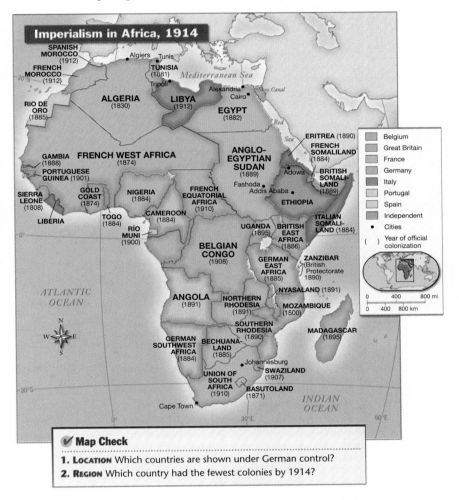

Imperialism in Africa, 1914

Legend:
- Belgium
- Great Britain
- France
- Germany
- Italy
- Portugal
- Spain
- Independent
- • Cities
- ( ) Year of official colonization

0   400   800 mi
0   400   800 km

✔ **Map Check**

1. **LOCATION** Which countries are shown under German control?
2. **REGION** Which country had the fewest colonies by 1914?

Research

AVERAGE

Have students research one of the countries of Africa shown on the map on page 567 during the time it was ruled by a western power. Have them write a summary of the imperialist relationship, including how the country was governed and what economic benefits were obtained by the ruling power.

CHALLENGE

Have students research one of the countries shown on the map on page 567 that was controlled by a western power and one of the countries that remained independent during this time. Have them write a research paper comparing and contrasting life in the two countries. Students might use a Venn diagram (TR, p. 323) to take notes for their reports.

A. Africa in the Nineteenth Century

Purpose-Setting Question What did Europeans know about Africa before the late 1800s? (Africa was thought of as a collection of ports for trading.)

Activity

Use television to view opinions Television shows such as the Tarzan series from the 1960s portray a stereotypical picture of the African continent that was likely similar to the view held by many Europeans. View one or more episodes of this series with your students. Discuss the characteristics of Africa that are portrayed and how people are characterized.

Extend Have students contrast the personalities and actions of David Livingstone and Henry Morton Stanley. Ask students to differentiate between each man's reason for being in Africa. (Livingstone explored Africa and worked with Africans; Stanley wrote about Livingstone but then went into business and exploited Africa's resources and people.)

Using the Map

Imperialism in Africa, 1914

Ask students to use the map key to identify the European countries that had established colonies in Africa by 1914. Then, have them compare the map on page 567 with the map of modern Africa on page A6 and note which country controlled the area where the Suez Canal would be built. (Great Britain)

✔ **Map Check**

Answers
1. Cameroon, Togo, German East Africa, and German Southwest Africa are shown under German control.
2. Belgium

Discuss Ask students to compare the amount of land in Africa controlled by European nations with the amount that was independent in 1914. (Far more was controlled by European nations or western powers than was independent.)

Discuss Ask students why the European countries believed that they could take the areas of Africa they wanted. (most Africans lived in villages or tribal groups; no kingdoms or large cities, no national boundaries)

Focus Remind students about the meaning of the term *protectorate* (page 562). Ask how a mandate differed from a protectorate. (With a mandate, the region is given to someone or to a group. With a protectorate, the local people control the day-to-day affairs of government.)

Explore Have students use an atlas to find an updated resource map of the continent of Africa. In addition to rubber, copper, and ivory, ask students to list at least five other resources from the continent. (Possible answers: diamonds, gold, iron ore, uranium, petroleum, tin, hardwood)

ANALYZE PRIMARY SOURCES

DOCUMENT-BASED QUESTION

Ask a volunteer to read aloud the quotation on this page. Ask others to identify words and phrases that establish the mood. (Possible answers: empty, impenetrable, sluggish, no joy, deserted, gloom)

ANSWER The atmosphere or mood Conrad establishes is one of mystery and lurking danger.

◆ **ANSWER** Possible answer: Stanley wrote about his adventures in Africa, thus spurring interest in the continent. He also went into partnership with King Leopold II of Belgium to develop and profit from the land. This would have led other Europeans to want a part of the potential profits.

B. European Influence in Africa

Purpose-Setting Question How did European countries claim land in Africa? (by establishing colonies and protectorates and by bringing in troops)

From the European point of view, the vast majority of African territory was available to anyone who wanted it. Most Africans lived in villages or tribal groups. Kingdoms and great cities were either in ruins or in decline. There were no national boundaries or frontiers. This situation set the stage for a new phase of European imperialism.

Europe Enters Africa

The International Congo Association was a private investment company, not a government undertaking. Nevertheless, around the time of its founding, other explorers were claiming, or about to claim, different parts of Africa. In November 1885, German chancellor Otto von Bismarck called a conference in Berlin to discuss how to deal with Africa on an international basis. Members of the conference, including the United States, agreed to the formation of the Congo Free State. The new state would have no official connection with any European nation, including Belgium. By international agreement, though, its government would be assigned to King Leopold of Belgium.

The arrangement with King Leopold was, in effect, a **mandate**. Sometimes called a trusteeship, a mandate is an assignment from an international body to govern a region. The conference agreed that all member nations had the right to conduct business in the Congo. Members also voted that the slave trade should be stopped and that the rights of local people should be protected.

The problem with these agreements was that no European nation had any way to make sure that they were upheld. King Leopold took advantage of this situation. To make the Congo profitable, Leopold used a harsh system of forced labor to collect the many natural resources of the region. These resources included rubber, copper, and ivory.

During the 15-year period after the Congress of Berlin, there was an explosion of colonizing activity in Africa. Products such as rubber and ivory brought huge rewards. In 1902, British writer Joseph Conrad published a short novel that captured the greed, the mystery, and even the horror of imperialism in Africa. The novel's title was *Heart of Darkness*. The central character was an evil, half-mad ivory trader named Kurtz, who abused native Africans. The story's narrator describes how he set out to find Kurtz deep in the jungle:

> **ANALYZE PRIMARY SOURCES**
> **DOCUMENT-BASED QUESTION**
> How would you describe the atmosphere or overall mood of this passage?

❝ Going up that river [the Congo] was like traveling back to the earliest beginnings of the world, when vegetation rioted on the earth and the big trees were kings. An empty stream, a great silence, an impenetrable forest. The air was warm, thick, heavy, sluggish. There was no joy in the brilliance of sunshine. The long stretches of the waterway ran on, deserted, into the gloom of over-shadowed distances. . . . You lost your way on that river as you would in a desert. . . . ❞

◆ **How did Henry Morton Stanley play a key role at the start of European imperialism in Africa?**

B. European Influence in Africa

Besides discussing the future of the Congo, the Berlin conference of 1885 tried to find a fair way for European countries to divide Africa. The members agreed that any country with territory on the coast had first "rights" to the interior of that region. Countries also had to keep each other informed about which regions they claimed, and they had to establish a government and settlements or troops in those regions.

Teaching Options

Connection to LITERATURE

Students may enjoy reading Joseph Conrad's *Heart of Darkness,* or you may wish to use the book as a read-aloud. Students might be interested in knowing that people compared the nightmarish quality of the war in Vietnam with Conrad's descriptions of Africa. In the film *Apocalypse Now,* Francis Ford Coppola explores the comparison: his portrayal mirrors Conrad's written descriptions.

Conflict Resolution

Ask students to debate as diplomats in the 1880s to determine how to settle the desire of seven or eight countries to split the continent of Africa. Have them discuss whether wealthier nations would get more or better territory. Ask students if the solution reached by the Berlin conference of 1885 seemed a reasonable way to come to an agreement.

This illustration shows shipping along the Suez Canal in 1869.

Egypt and North Africa

During the mid-1800s, Egypt was a semi-independent state within the Ottoman Empire. During the U.S. Civil War, Egyptian cotton exports became very important to Europe. Egypt's importance increased even further with the completion of the Suez Canal in 1869. The canal was one of the most important waterways in the world, linking the Mediterranean Sea with the Red Sea. This link greatly reduced the journey between Europe and southern and eastern Asia. Great Britain regarded the canal as a key link to its colonies in the East, such as India, Burma, and Malaya. In 1882, British troops bombarded the Egyptian city of Alexandria in a successful attempt to take over the region. As a result, Egypt became a British protectorate.

The French government's reaction to these events shows the European rivalry for colonies in the late 1800s. Deeply suspicious about British motives, the French government further developed Algeria, which it had declared a colony back in 1830. The French government increased its **sphere of influence** in North Africa by establishing protectorates in Tunisia in 1881 and Morocco in 1912. A sphere of influence is a region in which one nation claims to have exclusive control. France also established colonies in West Africa and parts of Central Africa. At one point, the French controlled an area of land in Africa that was as large as the continental United States.

Africa South of the Sahara

The area of Africa south of the Sahara is nearly as large as the continent of North America. Acting first in the form of a private company and later as a colonizer, Belgium took unfair advantage of the vast Congo River basin. Finally, protests in Great Britain and the United States forced King Leopold to turn over control of the Congo Free State to the Belgian parliament. In 1908, the region became known as the Belgian Congo. Today, it is the Democratic Republic of the Congo.

CHAPTER 24 ◆ Imperialism in Africa, India, and the Middle East **569**

Discuss Why was interest in Egypt so strong? (Exports such as cotton were important to Europe; the Suez Canal was a strategic waterway and whoever controlled it controlled the best access route between Europe and Asia.)

TEACH PRIMARY SOURCES
Have students examine the picture of shipping on the Suez Canal on page 569. Ask them to describe the kinds of boats that they see. (various types of sailboats) Then, ask them how the Suez Canal might appear 50 years after this picture was taken. (Possible answer: There would be steamships or ships powered by oil, and they would be much larger.)

Discuss Have students refer back to the map on page 567 as they read about European spheres of influence in Africa. Ask them which two European countries have control over the most land as of 1914 and why they think this is so. (Possible answer: Great Britain and France; because they were the strongest European powers or because they were so competitive)

Extend Have students locate the Suez Canal on a map of the Middle East or Africa in an atlas. Ask why they think the canal was and continues to be of great strategic and economic value. (Possible answer: It greatly cuts down the time and cost of shipping routes from Europe to Asia. This brings both political and economic advantage to the country that controls the canal.)

Activity

Use a map Have students use the information from the text on this page and the map on page 567 to list each European power and its African colonies or protectorates. Students should include France, Germany, Great Britain, Italy, Portugal, Belgium, and Spain as the imperialist powers.

Writing

AVERAGE
Have students write an advertisement for one of the European colonies or territories in Africa in 1914. The purpose of the advertisement is to encourage others from their country to live in that colony.

CHALLENGE
Have students research a European power that established a sphere of influence in Africa. Have them write a position paper stating what the European country hoped to accomplish by establishing its sphere of influence.

Boer fighters are shown in action in South Africa.

In East Africa, the major colonizers were Britain and Germany. They agreed to share this sphere of influence in order to preserve a balance of power, or equal power. Great Britain established British East Africa, now called Kenya, as a protectorate in 1886. Germany did the same in German East Africa, now called Tanzania, in 1891. Germany and Great Britain colonized other parts of Africa as well. Germany established a protectorate in southwest Africa, now called Namibia, as early as 1884. The British proclaimed Nigeria a protectorate in 1884, and their influence grew in the nearby Gold Coast.

Italy and Portugal also played important roles in imperialism. Italy occupied Somaliland and Eritrea in East Africa and then moved on to Ethiopia. The Italians were soundly defeated in 1896 by the Ethiopians at the Battle of Adowa. In 1912, the Turks yielded Libya to Italy. The Portuguese greatly expanded their hold on Angola in the southwest of Africa and on Mozambique in the southeast.

Ever since 1795, the British had maintained a political and military presence in South Africa at the Cape of Good Hope. The main purpose was to safeguard their shipping lanes to the East. The Cape had originally been settled in the 1650s by the Dutch. The descendants of these settlers, called Afrikaners or Boers, became more and more unhappy with British rule and moved inland. The discovery of diamonds and gold in the interior led to increasing conflict between the Boers and the British. In 1899, full-fledged warfare broke out. After three years of fighting with nearly 500,000 troops, the British finally won the Boer War and gained mining rights in the northern part of the region. In 1910, the unified country became the Union of South Africa.

◆ **Why did the British consider the Suez Canal so important?**

Review II

Review History
A. What did the Berlin conference of 1885 accomplish concerning European imperialism in Africa?
B. How did the French respond to the increasing British presence in Egypt?

Define Terms to Know
Define the following terms:
mandate, sphere of influence

Critical Thinking
Why did European nations scramble to claim regions in Africa between 1885 and 1900?

Write About Economics
In a paragraph, discuss how certain natural resources and precious metals in Africa affected the spread of European imperialism.

Get Organized
MAIN IDEA/SUPPORTING DETAILS CHART
Use a chart like the one below to show details that support each main idea in this section. For example, use this main idea: Countries created spheres of influence in Africa.

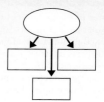

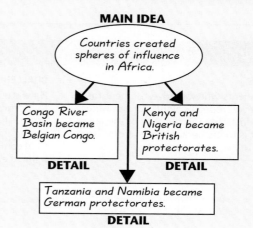

MAIN IDEA

Countries created spheres of influence in Africa.

Congo River Basin became Belgian Congo.

DETAIL

Kenya and Nigeria became British protectorates.

DETAIL

Tanzania and Namibia became German protectorates.

DETAIL

CONNECT
History & Art

African Weaving

The history of weaving in Africa goes back hundreds of years. In many parts of Africa, weaving textiles has played a major role in the culture of the region. Some of the best-known examples of weaving are from the Ashanti peoples of south-central Ghana in West Africa.

ASHANTI WEAVING includes highly prized textiles called kente cloth, or just kente. The word *kente* means basket. The outstanding features of kente are its bright colors and complex designs. Woven from imported silk, kente has been traditionally considered a royal textile. Beginning in the 1600s, Ashanti kings maintained control of kente production, and new patterns were offered first to the ruler. The Ashanti called this royal cloth *asasia*.

ASHANTI CULTURE AND RELIGION are closely associated with kente cloth. Ashanti myths link the origins of the cloth with the spider-hero, Anansi. In more recent times, kente designs have come to signify a wide range of associations. For example, some patterns honor specific people, such as kings and artists. Other designs refer to important cultural themes or lessons, such as the importance of peace, well-being, and wealth. Still other patterns relate to specific events or occasions, such as the actions of the Ashanti king in calling forth court members or acting as a judge to settle arguments.

MODERN KENTE FABRICS are worn by men and women. Men generally wear kente as a robe draped over their left shoulder. Women wear the fabric as a two-piece blouse and skirt. Today, there are more than 300 patterns of kente, and each has its own name. Some of these names are symbolic. For example, a pattern called liar's cloth has a notably zigzag design.

Critical Thinking
Answer the questions below. Then, complete the activity.

1. Why has kente been considered a royal textile?
2. What kinds of meanings for Ashanti culture are woven into kente?
3. How is kente used today?

Write About It
Use the Internet and library reference books to learn more about kente and about other African textiles, such as adinkra, which is also woven by the Ashanti peoples. Then write a brief report in which you summarize your findings.

A sample of a modern kente cloth is shown to the left. The photo above shows an Ashanti official wearing a kente robe.

Teaching Options

LINK to TODAY

Today, kente cloth is woven by hand and machine. It is worn by people all over the world. Colors often have symbolic meaning. For example, yellow symbolizes royalty, wealth, spirituality, and vitality. Red symbolizes blood, sacrifice, and struggle. Blue is associated with peacefulness, harmony, and good fortune. Purple and maroon are earth colors, associated with healing and Mother Earth.

FYI
Symbolism of Kente Cloths
Kente cloth originally was adopted as a royal cloth by the chief of the Ashanti people. Over its history, the type and quality of the yarn used for kente reflected the social status of the wearer. Various colors of yarns and their combination reflected the symbolic significance of kente cloth. The cloth itself symbolized social prestige, nobility, and cultural sophistication. Each kind of kente cloth has a name, and each pattern has a meaning, often given by the weaver.

CONNECT
History & Art

AFRICAN WEAVING

Teach the Topic
The weaving of kente cloth represents part of the African culture that was often scorned or ignored by Europeans during the period of imperialist domination. It also represents how local industry was threatened in many regions by competition from western industrialization.

ASHANTI WEAVING Cloth manufactured in Europe was exported to Asia, Africa, and the Middle East. Missionaries often insisted that local residents wear clothing that appeared western; thus, the cloth of local weavers was undervalued.

In more recent times, people have come to appreciate the complex patterns and tiny details woven in kente cloth by the Ashanti people.

ASHANTI CULTURE AND RELIGION Discuss that patterns of kente cloth are related to myths, specific people, or important events or occasions. Ask students to sketch or color their own pattern to symbolize a recent event or person.

MODERN KENTE FABRICS Ask students to speculate as to why a zigzag pattern might be used as the symbol of a liar. (A back-and-forth pattern might show a person trying to figure out how to tell a good lie.)

Critical Thinking
1. In the past, Ashanti kings controlled kente production, and new patterns were offered first to the ruler.
2. Kente designs signify Ashanti mythology, people, specific events, and cultural themes or lessons.
3. Today, kente fabrics are used in clothing. The fabric is usually worn by men as a robe and by women as a blouse or skirt.

Write About It
Students should include new information about kente cloth, adinkra, or other African textiles. Using the keywords *kente, cloth, Ashanti,* and *weaving,* students will find many Web sites with useful information.

Section Summary

In this section, students will learn how India became the most important overseas possession of the British Empire. They will also learn why feelings of nationalism grew in the opening years of the twentieth century.

1 Introduce

Getting Started

Ask students what they value above all else. Encourage them to explain why they value this item or idea. Explain that the British government considered India to be extremely important to the country. India was so important that it was often referred to as the "jewel in the crown." Ask students to explain this expression and how it shows the value Great Britain attributed to India.

TERMS TO KNOW

Ask students to read the words and definitions on page 572 and then find each word in the section. Explain that the term *Raj* can refer to a period of time and also to the rule of India by the British during that time.

You may wish to preview the pronunciation of the following names with your students.

Akbar (AK buhr)
Plassey (PLAH see)
Dalhousie (dal HAOO zee)
Meerut (MAY ruht)
Tata (TAH tah)
Mohandas K. Gandhi
(MOH huhn dahs GAHN dee)

ACTIVE READING

Tell students that in order to evaluate the section on British imperialism in India, they might ask questions such as:

• What were the conditions like in India before the British arrived? Did conditions improve?
• What was the Indian Civil Service? Did it provide any benefits for Indians?

Terms to Know

maharajah a king or prince who ruled an Indian state

Raj the British domination of India between 1757 and 1947

sepoy a native-born soldier in the Indian army controlled by the East India Company

Main Ideas

A. Beginning in the 1600s, British interest and influence in India grew steadily, and by the late 1850s, Great Britain had consolidated its rule in a large part of the country.

B. Even as India became the centerpiece of the British Empire, nationalism was growing and would eventually lead to Indian independence.

Active Reading

EVALUATE
When you evaluate, you weigh the importance of specific facts or evidence in order to make a judgment. As you read this section, evaluate the positive aspects, as well as the shortcomings, of the British Raj in India.

A. Controlling India

India is a vast land with a surface area about one-third the size of the United States. India has 16 major languages and hundreds of others. In addition, India is home to six major religions. For much of its history, India was not unified. Instead, it consisted of many regional states. Each state was ruled by a **maharajah**, a king or prince.

The East India Company

The Portuguese and the Dutch led European exploration of South Asia and the East Indies in the 1500s. In 1600, a group of British investors founded the East India Company for the purpose of conducting trade. During the seventeenth century, the British established factories and then permanent settlements at three strategic locations in present-day India: Madras in the southeast, Bombay in the west, and Calcutta in the east. Today, these are three of the four largest cities in India. The fourth is Delhi, in the north.

In the early 1600s, much of northern India had been under the control of the Mughals. The Mughal emperor Akbar, who ruled from 1556 to 1605, was very powerful. His annual income is said to have been 20 times that of the British monarch. With the death of the last great Mughal emperor in 1707, the empire went into a steep decline. This decline encouraged the British to strengthen their presence on the Indian subcontinent.

In 1757, an officer of the East India Company, Robert Clive, took advantage of the Mughal decline. He and his troops met Indian forces in the Battle of Plassey, in Bengal, a region that includes Calcutta. Clive also succeeded in driving the French trading company out of the region. After this, the East India Company controlled almost the entire eastern region of India.

British Control of India

Over time, the British Parliament became concerned about the activities of the East India Company and the power it held. As a result, Parliament unified the three main company posts at Bombay, Calcutta, and Madras. Parliament also required the company to get permission from British government officials before undertaking any political activities. As a final act of control, Parliament named a single chief administrator, or governor general, for all of British India.

During the first half of the nineteenth century, Great Britain steadily expanded its control over India. This domination by the British is referred to as **Raj**. Raj comes from an Indian word that means "king."

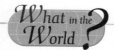
THE BLACK HOLE OF CALCUTTA

In 1756, the local ruler of Calcutta locked 146 Englishmen in a small, airless room and kept them there all night. Many died of suffocation. This event became known as the "black hole of Calcutta."

Teaching Options

Section 3 Resources

Teacher's Resources (TR)
Terms to Know, p. 37
Review History, p. 71
Build Your Skills, p. 105
Concept Builder, p. 240
Main Idea/Supporting Details Chart, p. 319

Connection to WORLD LANGUAGES

Explain that language can serve to promote the power of one group over another. Bengali, Hindi, Punjabi, Assamese, and Gujarati are some of the languages spoken in modern India. However, during the Raj, government and civil service affairs were conducted in English. As feelings of nationalism spread in India, Hindi was suggested as the national language.

One of the most dynamic administrators of India was Lord Dalhousie. He served as governor general from 1848 to 1856. At the end of his term, Dalhousie summed up his efforts to modernize India. According to his written account, he had worked to create "three great engines of social improvement . . . railways, uniform postage, and the electric telegraph." In India, these means of transportation and communication reinforced the links between the three leading British cities. In addition, the railway allowed the British to move troops swiftly to areas where they were needed.

During this time, the Indian Civil Service was created. As you learned, civil service is an organized group of trained officials who carry out government business. Entrance into Indian Civil Service, or ICS, as it was called, was gained by achieving a high score on an examination. At first, very few Indians qualified for the ICS. By the late 1800s, however, many native people of India became ICS officials.

◆ Why did the British Parliament become concerned about the East India Company?

B. The Jewel in the Crown

During the late 1800s, India under the British Raj was the largest colonial territory in the world. The British people considered it to be their most important possession. Some called India the "jewel in the crown" of the British Empire. Shortly after 1850, however, the British faced a serious challenge to their rule in India.

Indians Fight for Independence

By 1857, many Indians had become resentful of outsiders controlling their country. At this time, the army was still under control of the East India Company, and 80 percent of the troops were **sepoys**, or native-born soldiers.

An incident arose that led the Indians to rebel. This was the introduction of a new type of rifle that required soldiers to bite the ends off the bullet cartridges before loading them. These cartridges were rumored to be smeared with grease made from the fat of cows and pigs. This outraged the sepoys, many of whom were either Hindus or Muslims. To Hindus, cows are sacred, and Muslims do not eat pork.

This photograph shows a railroad station near Calcutta, India, in the 1860s.

Discuss Ask students why they think the British employed sepoys in their army. (Possible answer: They needed additional soldiers because there were not enough British troops to maintain control over such a large country. Also, they were a cheap source of labor.)

Explore Ask students to discuss the effect of the Sepoy Mutiny, or First War of Independence, on British rule in India. Ask why a rebellion led Great Britain to keep the existing maharajahs in power. (The British government took over direct control of India; however, because it needed the cooperation of the Indians, it left local rulers in power.)

Activity

Make a poster Have students work in small groups to create posters of life in India during the time Great Britain ruled. Have them make copies of photographs or illustrations and write captions for them on their posters. Tell them to write interesting titles for their posters at the top of the poster board.

TEACH PRIMARY SOURCES

Have students examine the illustration on page 574. Ask them to describe the picture. (Possible answer: It shows native troops fighting during the Sepoy Mutiny. Some soldiers are riding elephants, camels, or horses, and others are on foot. There are water buffalo and goats in the street and children are running. Some troops are carrying guns; others have swords or cudgels.) Ask students what they can learn from the picture. (A lot is happening. The fighting is taking place in the streets, not on a battlefield.)

When the sepoys refused to load their new rifles, they were punished by their British commanders. The troops mutinied, or rebelled. The resulting conflict is known as the Sepoy Mutiny, or the First War of Independence. It began in 1857 at Meerut, in northern India, and lasted for more than a year. After the British finally put down the rebellion, they transferred all rights of the East India Company to Great Britain. The British government then took over direct control of India. Realizing that it needed the cooperation of the Indians, Great Britain kept the existing maharajahs in power in their states. These states, in effect, became British protectorates.

Indians Under the Raj

Although the British government made allies of the native Indian rulers, it did not interfere with everyday life in India. Social contact between the British and the Indian people was limited, especially in public places. Many educated Indians believed that the British were holding India back from industrializing and were stripping the country of its natural resources.

In 1835, the British had decided to make English the language of education and government in India. This decision unified the country. English became a second "common language" for many upper-class Indians. The introduction of English also gave Indians a chance to gain a western education.

By the end of the nineteenth century, a new generation of Indian leaders of industry flourished. For example, the Indian industrialist Jamshed N. Tata made a fortune in cotton. His sons would go on to dominate iron, steel, and, eventually, motor vehicles.

This scene shows native troops fighting in India during the Sepoy Mutiny.

Teaching Options

ESL/ELL STRATEGIES

Organize Information Help students to use a cause-and-effect chain (TR, p. 325) to summarize causes and effects of western imperialism. Have students review the entire chapter as they do this activity. It might be helpful if they created a new chart for each world region discussed in the chapter—Africa, India, and the Middle East. Students can repeat the activity as they read Chapter 25 as well.

Test Taking

Explain to students that often on a test they will be asked to figure out the meaning of a word as it is used in a particular context. You might have students give the meaning of the word *mutinied* in the second sentence on page 574. Then, have them use the word in a sentence of their own.

The Indian National Congress

As education for Indians increased their opportunities, a growing movement for independence took shape. In 1885, the Indian National Congress was founded in Bombay. Most of the members of this organization were Hindus. Like the All-India Muslim League, founded in 1906, the National Congress would play a critical role in India's drive for independence during the early 1900s.

A few years after the Indian National Congress was founded, a young Indian named Mohandas K. Gandhi left India to study law in London. After completing his studies, Gandhi went to South Africa, remaining there for 20 years. There, Gandhi fought for the civil rights of Indian laborers working in South Africa. He felt that the laborers were being treated little better than slaves.

After returning to India in 1915, Gandhi became India's most eloquent spokesperson for independence from Great Britain. Gandhi spoke of achieving this goal through nonviolent measures.

> ❝ [The world of tomorrow] will be, must be, a society based on non-violence. It may seem a distant goal . . . but it is not in the least unobtainable, since it can be worked from here and now. An individual can adopt the way of life of the future—the nonviolent way—without having to wait for others to do so. And if an individual can do it, cannot whole groups of individuals? Whole nations? ❞

◆ **What part did the religious beliefs of the sepoys play in setting off the First War of Independence in India?**

ANALYZE PRIMARY SOURCES

DOCUMENT-BASED QUESTION According to Gandhi, what should be the first step in achieving a nonviolent society?

Review III

Review History
A. Where were the three major trading centers of the British East India Company located?
B. What was the significance of the British decision to make English the language of education and administration in India?

Define Terms to Know
Define the following terms:
maharajah, Raj, sepoy

Critical Thinking
In 1881, there were only about 100,000 British-born residents in India. The native population was several hundred million at that time. How do you think the British were able to rule such a vast country?

Write About History
In a short essay, evaluate the achievements of the British Raj in India.

Get Organized
MAIN IDEA/SUPPORTING DETAILS CHART
Use a chart like the one below to show details that support each main idea in this section. For example, use this main idea: Methods the British used to strengthen their power in India.

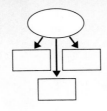

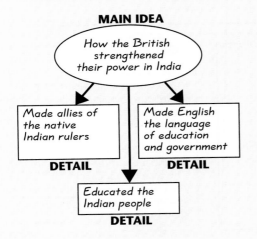

MAIN IDEA

How the British strengthened their power in India

Made allies of the native Indian rulers — **DETAIL**

Made English the language of education and government — **DETAIL**

Educated the Indian people — **DETAIL**

Critical Thinking
Possible answer: The British maintained a strong military force and used diplomacy to "divide and conquer" by making agreements with individual rulers of small Indian states.

Write About History
Remind students that when they are asked to evaluate, they should make judgments and express a viewpoint. Students' essays should exhibit an understanding of the major economic, political, and cultural achievements of the British Raj.

IV. Imperialism in the Islamic World

(pp. 576–581)

Section Summary

In this section, students will learn about the decline of the Ottoman Empire. They will also learn how the involvement of Russia and western Europe contributed to the empire's collapse.

Getting Started

Have groups of students brainstorm possible reasons for the Ottoman Empire's decline. Have students record their answers on the board. After the class has read the section, have them revisit this list and review it.

TERMS TO KNOW

Ask students to read the words and definitions on page 576 and then find each word in the section. Ask students to write a paragraph that incorporates each word in context.

You may wish to preview the pronunciation of the following names with your students before they read the section.

Abdülaziz (AHB dool ah ZEEZ)
Abdülhamid (AHB dool HAH meed)
Tunisia (too NEE zhuh)
Kemal Atatürk
  (kay MAHL AT uh tuhrk)

ACTIVE READING

Review with students the nature of cause-and-effect relationships. Historical events generally have one or more causes and lead in turn to one or more effects. As students read Section 4, have them consider the collapse of the Ottoman Empire. Have students list the multiple causes of this event. Then, ask them to list the effects.

Terms to Know

supremacy supreme power or authority

sector a district or region into which an area is divided

Main Ideas

A. The Ottoman Empire, which included vast territories on three continents, gradually declined in the 1800s.

B. Despite efforts at reform, the Ottoman Empire disintegrated and finally collapsed around 1920.

Active Reading

CAUSE AND EFFECT
When you identify cause and effect, you determine the reasons and the consequences of an event. As you read this section, think about the ways in which external pressures and internal conflicts caused the decline of the Ottoman Empire. Also, think about the effects of that decline.

A. The Ottoman Empire

The story of imperialism in the late nineteenth and early twentieth centuries usually involves the expansion of powerful nations. In the Islamic world, however, imperialism also involved the decline of the Ottoman Empire. Although this empire is sometimes referred to as Turkish, it extended far beyond the boundaries of present-day Turkey.

Origins and Geographic Extent of the Ottomans

As you learned in Chapter 8, the Ottoman Empire had its beginnings in the late 1200s. From a relatively small state in northwest Anatolia, the eastern part of modern Turkey, the Ottomans gradually expanded. They took their name from Osman I, the empire's first sultan, or king.

In the late 1300s, the Ottomans had conquered parts of the Balkans in eastern Europe. They had also added areas belonging to the Byzantine Empire. In 1453, under Sultan Muhammad II, the Ottomans captured the Byzantine capital, Constantinople. This event marked the end of the Byzantine Empire, which had lasted more than 1,000 years. Constantinople was later renamed Istanbul.

After 1453, western Europe became more and more involved in the policies and plans of the Ottoman Empire. The Ottoman rulers were Muslim, a fact that alarmed Christian Europe. However, the Ottomans proved to be relatively tolerant. Christians and Jews living in regions governed by the Ottomans, such as Greece, Serbia, and Bosnia, were free to practice their religions. In the cities, non-Muslims lived in their own communities, but they worked and traded alongside Muslims.

The Ottoman Empire reached its high point in the 1500s under Selim I and his son, Suleiman II, "the Magnificent." Selim became an absolute monarch in both religious and nonreligious affairs. Suleiman waged naval warfare against the Holy Roman Empire under Charles V. He also added most of Hungary to the Ottoman Empire, fought successfully against Persia, and conquered the Arabian coastal regions. A generous supporter of the arts, Suleiman made the city of Istanbul into one of the world's most beautiful capitals.

Do You Remember?
In Chapter 8, you learned about Ottoman Turks and their rise to power.

Suleiman II was sultan of Turkey in the late 1600s.

Teaching Options

Section 4 Resources

Teacher's Resources (TR)
Terms to Know, p. 37
Review History, p. 71
Build Your Skills, p. 105
Chapter Test, pp. 163–164
Concept Builder, p. 240
Main Idea/Supporting Details
  Chart, p. 319
Transparency 1

F Y I

The Turban

Draw students' attention to the head covering worn by Suleiman II in the photograph on page 576. Explain that this is called a turban. It is a head covering worn by some men in Muslim and Hindu countries and consists of a long scarf wound around the head or around a cap. The type of fabric, color, and decoration on a turban may indicate social rank. For example, princes of India wore silk and gold turbans.

A view of the city of Tophane, Karakoy, in the Ottoman Empire.

At its peak in the early 1600s, the Ottoman Empire stretched from Hungary in the west to the Caspian Sea and western Persia in the east. Much of northern Africa, as well as the coastal regions of Arabia, were also under Ottoman control. Starting in 1699, however, the Ottoman Empire began to decline. In this year, the Ottomans lost Hungary to the powerful Austrian nation.

Decline of the Ottoman Empire

There were many reasons why the Ottoman Empire began to decline. One problem was the lack of unity or identity among the many places under Ottoman rule. Another problem was the succession of Ottoman rulers. Succession is the way, or order, in which heirs rise to take their rightful place in office or on a throne. By tradition, any one of a sultan's sons could succeed him as an Ottoman ruler. Therefore, whenever a sultan died, or could no longer rule due to illness, power struggles often broke out within a royal family. Fratricide, or the murder of brother by brother, was common. Such struggles frequently expanded into civil war.

Another reason for the Ottoman decline was its loss of major territories. During the first half of the seventeenth century, for example, the empire lost Greece and Serbia, which became independent. In addition, Algeria became a colony of France.

Competition for the strategic location of the Ottoman Empire was another key reason why the empire went into decline. At its most powerful, the empire controlled access to the Mediterranean Sea, the Atlantic Ocean, and the Black Sea. Russia was particularly interested in using the trade routes offered by the Black Sea and the Mediterranean Sea. For years, the Russian government made several unsuccessful attempts to gain access to these routes. Finally, it resorted to war.

Do You Remember?
In Chapter 4, you learned that a civil war is fought by armies made up of people from the same country.

CHAPTER 24 ◆ Imperialism in Africa, India, and the Middle East **577**

Meet Individual Needs:

VISUAL/SPATIAL LEARNERS

Have pairs of students look at the view of Tophane, Karakoy, on page 577. Have them guess whether this picture was completed before or after the decline of the Ottoman Empire. Then, have them give reasons why. (Possible answer: It was completed before the decline because everyone seems busy and prosperous.)

A. The Ottoman Empire

Purpose-Setting Question What was the extent of the Ottoman Empire at its peak? (from Hungary in the west to the Caspian Sea and western Persia in the east, including much of northern Africa and the coastal regions of Arabia)

Do You Remember?
Remind students that the Ottomans were Turkish tribes that migrated west from central Asia.

TEACH PRIMARY SOURCES
Have students consider the view of the city of Tophane shown on page 577. Ask what this city tells about the Ottoman Empire. (Possible answer: It shows the grandeur of the architecture and the wealth of some of the citizens.)

Activity

Find supporting details Have students identify the topic sentence of the first paragraph under the head "Decline of the Ottoman Empire" on page 577. (There were many reasons why the Ottoman Empire began to decline.) Ask students what they expect to read about in the rest of the section. (reasons for the decline) Have them read to find these reasons. Explain that these are details that support the main idea. Have students make a list of the reasons for the empire's decline.

Extend Tell students that the tall, pencil-shaped structures in the view of Tophane are minarets, built as part of the dome-shaped mosques. The mosque is a place of worship for members of Islam. A member of the religious group called the crier, or *muezzin*, climbs the minaret and calls members to prayer five times a day.

Do You Remember?
Discuss why such a war is called a *civil* war. Tell students that the root of *civil* is the Latin *civis*, meaning "citizen." (A civil war takes place between citizens of the same country.)

British and French troops attack Russian troops during the Crimean War.

TEACH PRIMARY SOURCES

Have students examine the illustration of the soldiers attacking during the Crimean War. Have them explain how an attack today might differ from the one shown here. (Possible answer: Today, soldiers do not charge on horseback; they often attack via plane. Uniforms are camouflaged so that enemies will not see them easily.)

Discuss Ask students how the reporting of the Crimean War differed from the reporting of earlier wars. (It was the first war to be covered by newspaper correspondents at the front lines.) Have students speculate as to the results of close coverage of war. (Possible answer: Bringing the horrors of war closer to those who are not participating may make them understand the tragedy and feel more responsible for stopping it.)

Explore Explain that alliances in time of war are often made for political advantage. Have students review why France and Great Britain sided with the Ottoman Empire—not a natural alliance—during the Crimean War. (France and Great Britain sided with the Ottoman Empire against Russia because they did not want Russia to gain control of any more Ottoman territory.)

Focus Ask students what efforts the Ottomans made from 1856 to 1876 to save their empire from further decline. (They began to welcome western influences and their sultan, Abdülaziz, traveled to Europe.) Ask students to evaluate whether these actions would have produced positive effects. (Possible answer: Yes, because they would have acquired knowledge of some of the technological achievements accomplished by Europeans.)

Activity

Write a diary entry Have students write a diary entry of a British nurse who might have served with Florence Nightingale during the Crimean War. Have them discuss the accomplishments of Nightingale and the horrors of the war.

◆ **ANSWER** The Ottomans captured Constantinople, thus bringing the Byzantine Empire to an end. Western Europe became more involved in the affairs of the Ottoman Empire after 1453.

As you read in Chapter 20, the Crimean War, as it was called, involved Russia on one side and the Ottoman Empire, France, and Great Britain on the other side. France and Great Britain sided with the Ottoman Empire to prevent Russia from gaining control of any more of the Ottoman territory. The Russian army was eventually defeated.

The war was bloody and wasteful and resulted in many deaths. Alfred, Lord Tennyson wrote a poem, "The Charge of the Light Brigade," about one deadly battle. Around 600 English horsemen rode across an open valley, and almost half of them were killed by enemy fire.

The Crimean War was the first war to be covered by newspaper reporters at the front lines. This coverage allowed readers to learn more about the horrors of war. The Crimean War was also the first war to have professional nurses care for the wounded. As you read in Chapter 20, this nursing system was started by Florence Nightingale. After the war, she was involved in starting the Army Medical School and the Nightingale School for Nurses.

Attempts at Reform

After the Crimean War, the Ottoman government attempted a series of sweeping reforms. One reform created national citizenship for all people within the empire's borders. This reform also established equality before the law and the right of citizens to hold public office. For the first time, Christians could serve alongside Muslims in the army. Taxes and prison conditions were reformed, and torture was abolished. The government also guaranteed property rights for all citizens of the empire. The sultan promised to punish any public official who was found to be corrupt.

In the 20-year period from 1856 to 1876, a serious effort was made to save the empire from further decline. For a while it seemed as if this effort might succeed. The Ottomans began to welcome western influences, such as railways and newspapers, into their society. Abdülaziz became the first Ottoman sultan to travel to Europe, visiting Vienna, London, and Paris.

◆ **What event of 1453 proved to be a turning point in the history of the Ottoman Empire?**

Teaching Options

Connection to LITERATURE

Read aloud to students the poem "The Charge of the Light Brigade" or review the poem if they read it in Chapter 20. Discuss with students the literary devices Alfred, Lord Tennyson used to emphasize the horror of the battle. Tennyson uses metaphors such as "jaws of Death" and "mouth of hell." He also repeats the phrase "into the Valley of Death" to increase the feelings of suspense and horror.

F Y I

Florence Nightingale

Remind students that they read about Florence Nightingale in Chapter 20. When the British went to war with Russia in the Crimean War, Florence Nightingale traveled with 38 nurses and set up a hospital in Scutari in an old Turkish barracks. She became known as "The Lady with the Lamp" as she walked through the hospital at night caring for the wounded and wrote to British military officials demanding supplies.

B. The Ottomans Face Internal Conflicts

Any attempt to change a country or reform a society often leads to conflict. The struggle to modernize the Ottoman Empire in the late 1800s produced sharp differences among key figures within the empire.

In the mid-1870s, efforts underway to modernize the Ottoman Empire suddenly came to a halt. One reason was opposition by conservative officials. Another was the lack of qualified people with enough experience to carry out the reforms. The Ottoman government was deeply in debt, partly because of Sultan Abdülaziz's luxurious lifestyle.

A Harsh Ottoman Ruler

In 1876, a new Ottoman ruler came to power. His name was Abdülhamid II, and it was thought that he would continue the modernization of the empire. A year after Abdülhamid II became ruler, the first Turkish parliament met. Concealing his true intentions, Abdülhamid II issued a new constitution. It guaranteed personal liberty, freedom of education and the press, and a parliamentary government. A short time later, however, Abdülhamid II showed his true intentions. He dismissed the parliament and did away with the constitution. Abdülhamid II was determined to rule as an absolute monarch.

This sudden turn of events stunned those who were working to modernize and reform the empire. Such reform-minded people were nicknamed "Young Turks." Most of them were driven into exile by Abdülhamid II. The sultan's rule became increasingly harsh and violent. He responded savagely to nationalist feelings within the empire. As a result, Ottoman troops massacred thousands of peasants in Bulgaria in 1876 and thousands more in Armenia in 1894.

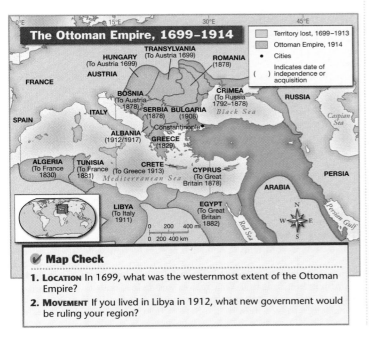

The Ottoman Empire, 1699–1914

Legend:
- Territory lost, 1699–1913
- Ottoman Empire, 1914
- • Cities
- ( ) Indicates date of independence or acquisition

HUNGARY (To Austria 1699)
TRANSYLVANIA (To Austria 1699)
ROMANIA (1878)
FRANCE
AUSTRIA
BOSNIA (To Austria 1878)
CRIMEA (To Russia 1792–1878)
RUSSIA
ITALY
SERBIA (1878)
BULGARIA (1908)
Black Sea
SPAIN
Constantinople
Caspian Sea
ALBANIA (1912/1917)
GREECE (1829)
ALGERIA (To France 1830)
TUNISIA (To Greece 1881)
CRETE (To Greece 1913)
CYPRUS (To Great Britain 1878)
PERSIA
Mediterranean Sea
ARABIA
LIBYA (To Italy 1911)
EGYPT (To Great Britain 1882)
Red Sea
Persian Gulf

0 200 400 mi
0 200 400 km

✔ Map Check
1. **LOCATION** In 1699, what was the westernmost extent of the Ottoman Empire?
2. **MOVEMENT** If you lived in Libya in 1912, what new government would be ruling your region?

B. The Ottomans Face Internal Conflicts

Purpose-Setting Question What effort resulted in internal conflict in the Ottoman Empire? (the struggle to modernize the Ottoman Empire in the late 1800s)

Focus Point out to students that Abdülhamid II started out as a reformer who seemed to want to modernize the Ottoman Empire. Ask students what actions he took that supported reform. (called the empire's first parliament; issued a new constitution that guaranteed personal liberty, freedom of education and the press) Discuss with students how these actions supported reform for the Ottoman Empire. Abdülhamid II then retracted all these changes. Ask students how they think reformers in the Ottoman Empire must have felt. (angry, frustrated, alarmed)

Using the Map
The Ottoman Empire, 1699–1914

Use the world map (pp. A1–A2 or Transparency 1) to show students the extent of the Ottoman Empire at its height. Review the territory that was lost from 1699 to 1913 and ask students to identify the nation that benefited in each case. For example, Bosnia was lost to Austria in 1878; Egypt was lost to Great Britain in 1882; Algeria was lost to France in 1830; Greece became independent in 1829.

✔ Map Check
Answers
1. Algeria
2. Italy

Research

AVERAGE

Have groups of students research the Crimean War and the role of the Light Brigade. Assign each group a different resource to use, such as different series of encyclopedias, the Internet, magazines, and even newspapers. Once the task is completed, have the groups summarize their findings and report on whether their source was useful.

CHALLENGE

Have students choose either Bulgaria or Armenia and research the history of its relationship to the Ottoman Empire. Students should find the way it came under Ottoman domination, describe some of the events during Ottoman rule, and explain how it eventually was removed from the empire.

Discuss How did the Russians contribute to the end of the Ottoman Empire? (They encouraged rebellion and nationalism in the Slavic regions, including Bosnia, Serbia, and Bulgaria. They fought a war against the Ottomans.)

Review Remind students that in the Crimean War, France and Great Britain fought on the side of the Ottoman Empire against Russia and Russia was defeated. France and Great Britain wanted to prevent Russia from gaining too much territory from the Ottoman Empire.

Activity

Analyze a name Discuss with students how nicknames often emphasize or play up a strong characteristic of a personality. Have students brainstorm a list of all the characteristics that come to mind from the nickname given to Otto von Bismarck, the Iron Chancellor.

Explore Ask students to evaluate the Treaty of Berlin. Ask how they view the fact that Russia and western European powers granted themselves permission to carve up much of the Ottoman Empire. (Possible answer: The treaty brought compromise between Russia and western Europe. Perhaps because they each got a piece of the Ottoman Empire, the countries were less suspicious of each other.)

ANALYZE PRIMARY SOURCES

DOCUMENT-BASED QUESTION
The statesman Otto von Bismarck was instrumental in unifying German principalities into a German national state. Germany became the strongest land power of western Europe. Bismarck's first quotation describes his pragmatic approach to getting things done; his second emphasizes his belief in using military might.

ANSWER Possible answer: Bismarck considered politics as a means to an end but that physical force would make the difference and win out in the end.

Focus Ask students to review the section "The Treaty of Berlin." Then, have them work with a partner and make a two-column chart (TR, p. 328), listing countries affected by the Treaty of Berlin and why each country was unhappy after the treaty.

Bismarck greets European leaders at the Congress of Berlin in 1878.

As you learned in Chapter 20, because of unrest in the Balkans and the gradual decline of the Ottoman Empire, Turkey and the rest of the empire came to be known as "the sick man of Europe." In this age of imperialism, Russia and the nations of western Europe waited like vultures for the "sick man" to die. Each nation was anxious to carve up the fading empire to its own best interests.

The End of the Ottoman Empire

Russia wanted the Ottoman Empire to completely break apart. Therefore, the Russians encouraged all efforts at rebellion in the Slavic regions of the Ottoman Empire. These regions included Bosnia, Serbia, and Bulgaria. Russia, being a Slavic country, hoped to unite all Slavic people against their common enemy—the Ottomans.

In 1877, Russia declared war on the Ottoman Empire. Unlike the Crimean War, when Ottomans had been allied with Great Britain and France against the Russians, the Ottoman army had to fight alone. After a series of victories in the Balkans, the Russians reached the Ottoman city of Istanbul. They forced the Ottomans to sign the Treaty of San Stefano in 1878. By this agreement, Serbia and Romania were granted outright independence. Semi-independent status was given to Bulgaria, and reforms were agreed to in Bosnia.

The terms of the treaty were so favorable to Russia that the western European states became alarmed. The British were especially concerned about the security of the Suez Canal. If the collapse of the Ottoman Empire was going to lead to Russian **supremacy**, or highest authority, in the eastern part of the empire, Great Britain was prepared for war again.

As you learned in Chapter 20, in 1878 the German chancellor, Otto von Bismarck, dominated the proceedings of an international conference called the Congress of Berlin. The task of this conference was to discuss the Eastern question: How would the fate of the declining Ottoman Empire be resolved?

Bismarck was a practical and skillful leader. During his long term in office, he was known as the "Iron Chancellor." Two of his quotes express his views on politics:

> Politics is the art of the possible.

> The questions of the time are not decided by speeches and majority decisions . . . but by iron and blood.

The Treaty of Berlin

The Congress of Berlin resulted in a new treaty that avoided war between countries in western Europe and Russia—at least for the moment. By the terms of this treaty, called the Treaty of Berlin, the Russians agreed to compromise on Bulgaria. That region was divided into three **sectors**, or districts, each with a varying degree of independence. Bulgaria and Bosnia officially remained within the borders of the Ottoman Empire. However,

ANALYZE PRIMARY SOURCES

DOCUMENT-BASED QUESTION
How would you describe Otto von Bismarck's philosophy?

Teaching Options

ESL/ELL STRATEGIES

Use Visuals Review with students the map on page 579 along with the text on pages 580–581 that discusses the Treaty of Berlin. Ask students to identify all the former Ottoman territories that were given over to Russian or European control by the treaty.

Austria-Hungary was permitted to administer Bosnia to balance Russian influence in the region. The British won an important new possession in Cyprus, a large island in the eastern Mediterranean Sea not far from the Suez Canal. France got permission to colonize Tunisia.

Germany gained no new lands from the treaty. However, over the next 30 years the Germans became extremely active in Turkey. Their special interest was the construction of a rail line running from Istanbul to Baghdad, the capital of Iraq. The British, the French, and the Russians all viewed this project with alarm. They assumed, quite correctly, that Germany was determined to expand its influence in the Middle East.

Although the Treaty of Berlin kept the peace in Europe for a time, it left many nations unhappy. Great Britain felt nervous about the long-term objectives of Russia and Germany. Nationalists in the Balkans and Slavs in Russia did not achieve their goals of unity. Most unhappy were the Turkish people. They rightly believed that peace had been achieved at their expense in carving up the Ottoman Empire. Even four years after the Congress of Berlin, Great Britain and France proclaimed protectorates in Egypt, Tunisia, and Morocco, all in North Africa. Thus, western imperialist efforts kept whittling away at the Ottoman Empire.

In the five-year period from 1908 to 1913, the Ottoman Empire suffered more losses. In 1908, the Young Turks seized control of the Turkish government. That same year, Bulgaria became fully independent, and two years later, Italy moved into Libya. Finally, as a result of two wars, the Ottoman Empire was forced to give up nearly all of its remaining European territory to the Balkan countries.

Events over the next nine years would finally bring an end to the Ottoman Empire. In 1922, a military leader named Kemal Atatürk seized power and abolished the sultanate in Turkey. One year later in 1923, Turkey was proclaimed a republic, with Atatürk as its first president.

◆ **What was the goal of the Congress of Berlin?**

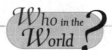 **in the World?**

THE FATHER OF MODERN TURKEY

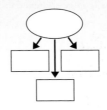

Kemal Atatürk is regarded as the father of modern Turkey. He established a new capital at Ankara in Anatolia. He introduced the use of the Roman alphabet to the Turkish language.

Although ruling as a dictator, Atatürk put in place many important governmental reforms. One of the most significant was to abolish the sultanate. This action cut the link between government and religion in Turkey.

THE FATHER OF MODERN TURKEY
Kemal Atatürk was a former Young Turk who established a new republic in Turkey. He ruled as an enlightened despot, amending the constitution to indicate that Turkey was no longer an Islamic state and giving new freedoms to women. The Grand National Assembly gave him the name Atatürk, meaning "Father of the Turks."

Tell students that today, the government of Turkey has usually remained friendly to the West. Turkey is now a member of NATO.

◆ **ANSWER** The goal of the Congress of Berlin was to decide the fate of the declining Ottoman Empire.

Section Close

Have students create an Ottoman Empire timeline (TR, p. 320). The dates should start with the late 1200s, when the Ottomans expanded from a small state in Anatolia, to 1923, when Turkey was proclaimed a republic, with Kemal Atatürk as the first president.

3 Assess

Review Answers

Review History
A. France and Great Britain wanted to prevent Russia from gaining any more of the Ottoman Empire's territory.

B. He pretended to be in favor of liberty for all, but in reality, he intended to become a dictator.

Define Terms to Know
supremacy, 580; sector, 580

Critical Thinking
The concept of the "balance of power" helps to explain the foreign policy of Russia, Germany, and Great Britain. None of the western powers wanted the Ottoman Empire to regain its vigor. At the same time, none of them wanted any of the others to gain an advantage in carving up the Ottoman Empire. So, they made agreements by which all of them shared in the territory that was formerly part of the Ottoman Empire, thus ensuring its disintegration.

Review IV

Review History
A. Why did France and Great Britain side with the Ottoman Empire during the Crimean War?
B. How did Abdülhamid II deceive the reform-minded members of the Ottoman government?

Define Terms to Know
Define the following terms:
supremacy, sector

Critical Thinking
Why is the concept of the "balance of power" useful in understanding the decline of the Ottoman Empire?

Write About History
In a paragraph, summarize the terms of the 1878 Treaty of Berlin.

Get Organized
MAIN IDEA/SUPPORTING DETAILS CHART
Use a chart like the one below to show details that support each main idea in this section. For example, use this main idea: Decay of the Ottoman Empire.

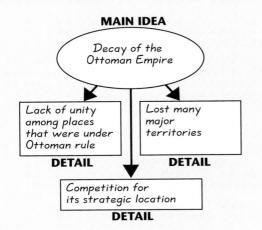

MAIN IDEA

Decay of the Ottoman Empire

Lack of unity among places that were under Ottoman rule
DETAIL

Lost many major territories
DETAIL

Competition for its strategic location
DETAIL

Write About History
Students' paragraphs should indicate that the 1878 Treaty of Berlin provided for a compromise on Bulgaria, administration of Bosnia by Austria-Hungary, ceding of Cyprus to Britain, and permission for France to colonize Tunisia.

Chapter Summary

A blank outline form is available in the Teacher's Resources (p. 318). Chapter summaries should outline the spread of western imperialism, how imperialism divided Africa, British imperialism in India, and imperialism in the Islamic world. Refer to the rubric in the Teacher's Resources (p. 340) to score students' chapter summaries.

⬤ Interpret the Timeline

1. the opening of the Suez Canal
2. 11 years (1899–1910)
3. the proclamation of Queen Victoria as Empress of India in 1877
4. Check students' events to ensure that all are from the chapter.

Use Terms to Know

5. sphere of influence
6. infrastructure
7. sepoy
8. imperialism
9. Raj
10. protectorate

Check Your Understanding

11. The Great Exhibition was the first world's fair. It was held in the Crystal Palace in London to highlight British supremacy in industry and technology.
12. Great Britain was unable to depend on the United States for a steady supply of cotton, so it had to look to other sources.
13. Possible answers: the search for new economic markets, the need for raw materials and natural resources, maintaining the balance of power, the decline of non-western empires, missionary zeal, and the urge for scientific knowledge and adventure.
14. Imperialism exploited countries for natural resources; it created infrastructure in less developed countries; it led to nationalist movements; it created conflicts and tensions among western European nations.
15. David Livingstone was a Scottish missionary who helped African villagers. Henry Morton Stanley was a British journalist and entrepreneur who developed the Congo River basin.
16. to safeguard the Suez Canal

Chapter Summary

Complete the following outline in your notebook. Then, use your outline to write a brief summary of the chapter.

Imperialism in Africa, India, and the Middle East

I. The Spread of Western Imperialism
  A. Europe at the End of the Nineteenth Century
  B. The Colonizers and the Colonized

II. Imperialism Divides Africa
  A. Africa in the Nineteenth Century
  B. European Influence in Africa

III. British Imperialism in India
  A. Controlling India
  B. The Jewel in the Crown

IV. Imperialism in the Islamic World
  A. The Ottoman Empire
  B. The Ottomans Face Internal Conflicts

⬤ Interpret the Timeline

Use the timeline on pages 558–559 to answer the following questions.

1. Which occurred first, the opening of the Suez Canal or the discovery of gold in South Africa?

2. How many years separate the beginning of the Boer War from the Japanese annexation of Korea?

3. **Critical Thinking** Which event on the timeline directly refers to imperialism?

4. Select five events from the chapter that are not on the timeline. Create a timeline that shows these events.

Use Terms to Know

Select the term that best completes each sentence.

imperialism   Raj
infrastructure   sepoy
protectorate   sphere of influence

5. In the late 1800s, European nations often sought to expand their _____ in Asia and Africa to have exclusive control over the area.

6. A community or nation's _____ consists of a group of basic physical facilities.

7. A _____ was a native-born soldier in the Indian army controlled by a British trading company.

8. _____ is the practice by which one nation gains complete control over other nations.

9. The British domination of India in the period 1757–1947 is called _____.

10. A _____ is a government run by local rulers but actually under the control of another government.

Check Your Understanding

11. **Identify** the Great Exhibition of 1851.

12. **Explain** how the Civil War in the United States affected the economy of Great Britain.

13. **Discuss** four important factors that contributed to European imperialism.

14. **Summarize** the major effects of imperialism.

15. **Identify** David Livingstone and Henry Morton Stanley.

16. **Explain** why Britain sent soldiers into Egypt in 1882.

17. **Describe** the ways in which the British strengthened their power in India after 1757.

18. **Identify** the immediate cause of the Sepoy Mutiny of 1857–1858.

19. **Discuss** the significance of the Indian National Congress.

20. **Explain** some of the reasons for the decline of the Ottoman Empire.

21. **Summarize** the results of the Congress of Berlin.

---

17. The British made English the language of education and administration; they constructed railways; they installed the electric telegraph and established uniform postage; after 1858 they ruled the country directly; they forged alliances with local rulers.
18. The British insisted that sepoys bite off the ends of cartridges, which were said to have been smeared with cow and pig grease, which offended Hindus and Muslims, respectively.
19. The Congress was an advocate of Indian independence.
20. lack of unity or identity, the succession of Ottoman rulers, loss of major territories, competition for the strategic location of the Ottoman Empire
21. The Congress of Berlin resulted in a new treaty that avoided war between Russia and countries in western Europe. Great Britain was given Cyprus, France got permission to colonize Tunisia, and Bulgaria was divided into three sectors with varying degrees of independence.

Critical Thinking

22. Analyze How did imperialism in the late 1800s differ from earlier practices of colonization?

23. Make Inferences What inference can you draw about the motives for King Leopold II's activities in the Congo?

24. Draw Conclusions What was the significance of the British decision to make English the language of education and administration in India?

25. Compare and Contrast How would you compare and contrast the Young Turks with Sultan Abdülhamid II?

Put Your Skills to Work

26. Write a Research Paper You have learned that you must think carefully before choosing a research topic. Narrowing the topic is important for producing a high-quality research paper.

Select a topic from this chapter for a research paper. Narrow your topic as much as possible. Then, state a main idea about the topic and the subject of your research paper. Copy the chart below to help you to narrow your topic and to state a main idea.

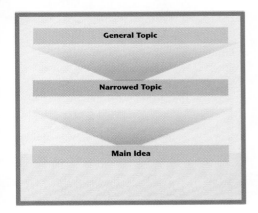

General Topic

Narrowed Topic

Main Idea

Analyze Sources

27. Read the comment below by historian Stanley Wolpert. Then, answer the questions that follow.

Dalhousie personally mapped the route of the first major Indian telegraph . . . He rightly predicted that the most critical use to which such a line would be put was political, and indeed it may have saved the empire for Britain in 1857, when word of the "mutiny" was flashed 824 miles from Agra to Calcutta.

a. Who mapped the route of the first Indian telegraph?

b. According to the passage, how may the telegraph line have saved the British Empire in 1857?

Essay Writing

28. In a brief essay, discuss some ways in which the balance of power played an important role in imperialist expansion in the late nineteenth century.

TEST PREPARATION

RECOGNIZING FACT AND OPINION
Choose the statement about the Ottoman Empire that is a fact rather than an opinion.

1. The Ottoman Empire's civil service was superior to the British civil service in India.

2. The Young Turks pushed reform too fast for the majority of people in the Ottoman Empire.

3. The Ottoman Empire sided with Britain and France against Russia during the Crimean War.

4. Sultan Abdülhamid II should have recognized that, in the absence of reforms, the empire was doomed.

Critical Thinking

22. Possible answer: It differed primarily in scale. Earlier colonialism was mainly concerned with trade. Imperialists in the late 1880s took over countries far more thoroughly as they established considerable infrastructure and systematically exploited natural resources and raw materials. They also governed more directly.

23. Possible answer: King Leopold's motives were primarily economic. He wanted the Congo venture to be profitable, so he resorted to a system of forced labor in order to exploit natural resources such as rubber.

24. Possible answer: The decision had the effect of developing national unity. It may also have helped the growth of feelings of nationalism by causing resentment among the people of India.

25. Possible answer: The Young Turks strongly advocated reform, whereas Sultan Abdülhamid, with equal determination, wanted to rule as an autocrat.

Put Your Skills to Work

WRITE A RESEARCH PAPER
26. Students' research papers should deal with a topic from the chapter, should reflect a suitably narrowed topic, and should include a main idea stating the topic of the paper.

Analyze Sources

27a. Dalhousie
27b. Possible answer: News of the mutiny was flashed promptly to Calcutta, which was a British stronghold. The British were thus able to respond quickly.

Essay Writing

28. Students' essays should mention the imperialist nations' concern that none of them gain an undue advantage over any other. This concern led to a scramble to create mandates, protectorates, and so on. It also led to many rounds of maneuvering, as in the western powers' deliberations over the fate of the Ottoman Empire.

TEST PREPARATION

Answer 3. The Ottoman Empire sided with Britain and France against Russia during the Crimean War.

Imperialism in Asia and Latin America

1821–1914

(pp. 584–608)

Chapter Objectives

• Examine the causes and effects of imperialism in China.
• Explain how Japan moved from a policy of isolationism to expansion and imperialism.
• List the reasons that the independent nations of Latin America could not break free from economic dependence on their former imperialist rulers.
• Identify the advantages and disadvantages of imperialism from a cultural, political, and economic standpoint.

Chapter Summary

Section I explains the Opium War and other rebellions that resulted from imperialism in China.
Section II discusses Commodore Perry's entry into Japan and the changes that resulted in the Sino-Japanese War and the Russo-Japanese War.
Section III introduces the legacy of imperialism on the economies of independent nations of Latin America.
Section IV focuses on the cultural, religious, economic, and political changes that imperialism brought as well as the scientific advances that helped control disease all over the world.

Set the Stage

TEACH PRIMARY SOURCES

Explain that when tea first arrived in Great Britain, it was advertised as a cure-all for problems such as gout or kidney infections. Some doctors recommended drinking many glasses of tea each day to maintain good health. Later, other doctors condemned tea drinking along with alcohol consumption. Nonetheless, tea became fashionable after Catherine of Braganza chose tea as the official court beverage in the 1660s. Ask students to respond to the quotation by telling whether people feel strongly today about tea or any other beverage.

Imperialism in Asia and Latin America

1821–1914

I. China Reacts to Western Influences
II. Japan Modernizes
III. Economic Imperialism in Latin America
IV. Worldwide Effects of Imperialism

Since the eighteenth century, when tea drinking first became popular in Great Britain, imports of tea from distant lands, such as China, rose. British woolen goods were exchanged for tea from China. By the nineteenth century, however, tea imports greatly increased as tea became the beverage of choice for many British people. François-Alexandre-Frédéric La Rochefoucauld-Liancourt, a French duke and writer who lived for a time in Great Britain, wrote in 1784 about the popularity of tea:

❝ *Throughout the whole of England the drinking of tea is general. You have it twice a day and though the expense is considerable, the humblest peasant has his tea just like the rich man.* ❞

When tea imports skyrocketed, the original exchange of woolen goods for tea was no longer equal. Great Britain was spending more on imported tea than it was earning from exported woolen goods. This situation led to one of the most shameful episodes in the age of imperialism: the sale of opium to China.

"Canton factories." Oil on glass, post 1780. Courtesy Peabody Essex Museum. Photo by Mark Sexton

CHAPTER EVENTS

1821
Mexico wins independence from Spain.

1839
Opium War begins between China and Great Britain.

1853
Commodore Matthew Perry lands in Japan.

1820 — **1840** — **1860**

WORLD EVENTS

1837
Victoria becomes queen in Great Britain.

1861
Czar Alexander II frees the serfs in Russia.

Teaching Options

Chapter 25 Resources

REVIEW

Teacher's Resources (TR)
Terms to Know, p. 38
Review History, p. 72
Build Your Skills, p. 106
Chapter Test, pp. 165–166
Concept Builder, p. 241
SQR Chart, p. 322
Transparency 1

ASSESSMENT
Section Reviews, pp. 590, 596, 601, 604
Chapter Review, pp. 606–607
Chapter Review, pp. 606–607
Unit 6 Test, TR, pp. 193–194

ALTERNATIVE ASSESSMENT
Portfolio Project, p. 608
Make a Brochure, p. T608

VIEW HISTORY This harbor in China was where foreign merchants docked while they conducted trade. It was here that the merchants arranged for the loading and unloading of their ships.
◆ What can you tell from the illustration about trade in this Chinese harbor?

GET ORGANIZED

SQR Chart An SQR chart helps you to better understand what you read by organizing ideas and facts. Use an SQR chart as you read Chapter 25. First, survey a section to discover a topic. Then, ask a question. Finally, read to find the answer. Here is an example from this chapter.

> **SURVEY**
> Western powers began to influence China and Latin America.

> **QUESTION**
> What events resulted from intervention by the United States and Great Britain in China and Latin America?

> **READ**
> Great Britain began selling opium to China and the Spanish-American War was fought.

Timeline

1863
Napoleon III of France installs Maximilian as emperor of Mexico.

1898
Spanish-American War is fought.

1904
Russo-Japanese War begins.

1914
Venustiano Carranza seizes power in Mexico.

1880   **1900**   **1920**

1869
Labor unions are legalized in Germany.

1896
First modern Olympics are held in Athens, Greece.

1914
World War I begins.

Chapter Themes

- Culture
- Time, Continuity, and Change
- Individuals, Groups, and Institutions
- Power, Authority, and Governance
- Production, Distribution, and Consumption
- Science, Technology, and Society
- Global Connections

F Y I

China's Trade

The art pictured on pages 584–585 is titled "Canton Factories." Canton was historically the major southern port in China, and it was the main trading outlet for exporting tea, silk, spices, and other goods. From the 17th century through 1842, all foreign imports were restricted to this port and were subject to strict regulations by the Chinese government.

Chapter Warm-Up

USING THE MAP
Explain that imperialism occurred all over the world, including Africa, Australia, and South America. However, the focus of this chapter is Asia and Latin America.

VIEW HISTORY
Have students look closely at the illustration and point out the ships that appear to be foreign to China. Ask students to identify the flags. What conclusions can they draw about the foreign nations that traded in the harbor? (Other countries, such as Great Britain and the United States, were allowed to trade in China.)

◆ **ANSWER** Since there are several boats and ships in the harbor, there was probably quite a bit of trade being conducted.

GET ORGANIZED
SQR Chart
Review the steps of SQR with students. *Survey* includes scanning the titles and headings of a section to find out the main idea. *Question* includes writing questions about the information before they begin reading. *Read* involves reading the text and locating the answers to their questions. Review the SQR chart on this page with students as an example.

⬤ TEACH THE TIMELINE
The timeline on pages 584–585 covers the period between 1821 and 1914, a span of about 100 years. Ask students to identify the events that involve Japan. (Perry lands in Japan, and Russo-Japanese War) Point out that Japan went from isolation to imperialist aggression in about 50 years.

Activity

Find the Presidents Have students find out which U.S. Presidents served during the period of this timeline. (Monroe, John Quincy Adams, Jackson, Van Buren, Harrison, Tyler, Polk, Taylor, Fillmore, Pierce, Buchanan, Lincoln, Andrew Johnson, Grant, Hayes, Garfield, Arthur, Cleveland, Harrison, McKinley, Theodore Roosevelt, Taft, Wilson)

I. China Reacts to Western Influences

(pp. 586–590)

Section Summary

In this section, students will learn how European imperialism reached China and created conflicts that forced the Chinese to sign several treaties. Students will read how the weakened imperial China faced rebellions that led to the downfall of the Manchu Dynasty.

1 Introduce

Getting Started

Have groups of students work together to list the ways Great Britain increased trade with China. Then, have the groups brainstorm other ways Great Britain could have increased trade. Once finished, have each group share their ideas with the class.

TERMS TO KNOW

Have students read the terms and definitions on page 586 and find each term in the section. Then have students write each term on the front of an index card. As students read, have them write important dates from China's history that relate to this term on the back of the card.

You may wish to preview the pronunciation of the following names from this section with students.

Guangzhou (GWANG joh)
Nanjing (nahn jihng)
Taiping (ty pihng)
Ci Xi (tsee shee)
Sun Yat-sen (soon yaht suhn)
Yuan Shikai (yoo AHN SHIUHR ky)

ACTIVE READING

Remind students that photographs, maps, charts, and captions will help them when they preview the section. When students are finished previewing the section, give each a main idea/supporting details chart (TR, p. 319) to use as he or she carefully reads the section.

China Reacts to Western Influences

Terms to Know

opium an addictive painkilling drug made from the dried juice of opium poppy pods

extraterritoriality an agreement that allows citizens of one country who live in another country to be governed by the laws of their own land

Main Ideas

A. When European imperialism reached China, it created conflicts and forced the Chinese to sign several treaties.

B. Imperialism led to rebellions in China and the overthrow of the Manchu Dynasty.

Active Reading

PREVIEW

When you preview, you skim through the text to see what you can learn from headings and visuals before you actually read the text. As you read this section, ask yourself this question: What is the topic suggested by this heading? Then, read to find the answer.

A. European Influence and Conflicts in China

For centuries, China did not need the outside world. Its standard of living was the highest in the world. Its civilization and technology were among the most advanced. By the end of the eighteenth century, however, the technology and weapons in some European nations were more advanced than China's.

Chinese leaders placed limits on foreign trade. By 1760, Europeans could trade only in one Chinese city, Canton, now Guangzhou. They were not allowed to live in China and could visit only to conduct business. The laws required Europeans to stay in one special section of the city. European traders could trade only through the city's merchant guild, the Co-hong. Co-hong members were the only merchants allowed to take part in foreign trading. In return, they had to guarantee the debt of foreign traders.

Instead of buying tea through the Co-hong in Guangzhou, British traders wanted to save money by buying black tea from the areas in which it was grown. They also wanted to sell more British goods in China.

The Chinese were happy to sell goods to British traders, but they did not want foreigners to live, trade, or move about freely in their country. They were not interested in the British trade proposals. Perfectly content with their own products and technology, they were not interested in buying British goods.

European nations wanted China's silk, tea, porcelain, and other products. The Chinese sold these products, and most of the money from trade flowed into China. However, Great Britain wanted to change its unfavorable balance of trade with China. In the 1700s, it found a way to make China start spending some of this money.

The Opium War

British traders sold **opium**, a painkilling yet highly addictive drug made from the poppy plant, to China. By the 1800s, many Chinese people were addicted to opium. Addicts included both rich people and poor people. Money from the sale of opium flowed out of China into British pockets. To protect their people, Chinese leaders passed laws against importing, growing, and smoking opium. However, the drug trade continued. The British sold opium through a network of smugglers, both foreign and Chinese. Gangs dealing in opium bribed police and officials. The job of stopping the trade in opium fell

Then & Now

DRUG WARS AND THE DRUG TRADE

Opium use for medicine is widespread today. Opium poppies can be legally used to make necessary medical drugs, such as the painkillers morphine and codeine. In the United States, growing, selling, and using opium is illegal. Unfortunately, many countries export opium in the form of heroin, an illegal and highly addictive drug.

Teaching Options

Section 1 Resources

Teacher's Resources (TR)

Terms to Know, p. 38
Review History, p. 72
Build Your Skills, p. 106
Concept Builder, p. 241
SQR Chart, p. 322

on the shoulders of an official named Lin Zexu. In a letter to Queen Victoria of Great Britain, he wrote,

> 66 Suppose there were people from another country who carried opium for sale to England and seduced [lured] your people into buying and smoking it; certainly your honorable ruler would deeply hate it and be bitterly [angrily] aroused. 99

Chinese leaders tried to pressure the British traders to stop smuggling opium into China. In 1839, Chinese officials seized and destroyed huge amounts of opium from British ships and warehouses. Battles broke out. In the battles, the Chinese were outmatched by superior British weapons, ships, and technology. In the end, China was badly beaten. This event became known as the Opium War.

The Treaty of Nanjing

In 1842, China was forced to sign the Treaty of Nanjing. Its terms forced China to pay Great Britain for the opium that was destroyed three years earlier. China had to give the city of Hong Kong to Great Britain. The possession of Hong Kong was a great bonus for Great Britain. It gave the British Empire a much needed port in Asia. The terms of the treaty granted some trade privileges that China had resisted for years. It also granted the right of **extraterritoriality**. Extraterritoriality meant that British subjects in China would be governed by the laws of Great Britain and not the laws of China. In effect, extraterritoriality left the Chinese government no authority over British foreigners within China's borders. The treaty also opened five ports to British traders and did away with the Co-hong. During the next two years, both France and the United States pressured China to sign similar treaties, which China did sign.

China resented these treaties. Sometimes China did not comply with, or follow, the treaties' terms. The British wanted to expand trade further. They looked for an excuse to use force. In 1856, a group of Chinese supplied the excuse when they boarded the British ship *Arrow*. They suspected that the

ANALYZE PRIMARY SOURCES

DOCUMENT-BASED QUESTION
What does Lin Zexu think would be Queen Victoria's reaction to the sale of opium to England?

Chinese war junks, or ships, were used in the fighting during the Opium War.

2 Teach

A. European Influence and Conflicts in China

Purpose-Setting Question What started the first Opium War? (China's people were addicted to opium that was first introduced and later smuggled into China by British traders. Chinese leaders tried to stop the smuggling, but nothing worked; so, Chinese officials seized and destroyed opium from British ships. This act caused battles to break out.)

Then & Now

DRUG WARS AND THE DRUG TRADE Like China in the 1800s, the U.S. government today works hard to outlaw the production, sale, and importation of illegal drugs. In reaction, huge networks of smugglers operate a dangerous black market much as they did in the nineteenth century. Ask students to look in a current newspaper for a story about drug traffic in the world today. Have students share their articles with the class.

ANALYZE PRIMARY SOURCES

DOCUMENT-BASED QUESTION
Lin Zexu's difficult task of stopping the opium trade was assigned after the emperor's son died as a result of opium addiction. Zexu carried out his task so aggressively that he led China into the Opium Wars. As a result, he was fired from his position and sent into exile.

ANSWER Lin Zexu thinks that Queen Victoria would hate the buying and selling of opium in England and would be very angry about it.

TEACH PRIMARY SOURCES

Explain to students that a junk, shown in the image, is a type of ship used in Japan and China. Have small groups of students work together to find as much information as possible about junks from the nineteenth century. Once completed, have the groups make a short presentation of the information they found. This presentation should include pictures.

ESL/ELL STRATEGIES

Organize Information To reinforce language learning through content, have each student draw a word web with the words *Treaty of Nanjing* in the middle. Have students add words and phrases to the web from the text or from prior knowledge that relate to the actions that caused China to sign the treaty and the stipulations of the treaty. Then, have pairs of students exchange webs and study them together, defining words as necessary.

Ask students which two nationalities had the largest spheres of influence in China. (British and Russian) Ask students to speculate about why this was the case. (Russia was a neighbor of China and may have had an interest in acquiring more land. Great Britain was interested in expanding its trade network throughout the world.)

✔ Map Check

Answer the Germans

Activity

Write a letter Have students write letters as Chinese citizens in the nineteenth century urging Queen Victoria to change the Unequal Treaties. Students should list what they feel is unfair about the treaties and possible suggestions that would make the treaties fairer to all. Be sure students keep the tone respectful, yet persuasive.

Explore Have students research the Open Door Policy. Allow students to use library resources and the Internet. Once students have found some information, ask them to share it with the class as a whole, comparing the information they found and the sources they used.

◆ **ANSWER** The British were selling opium to the Chinese people. Many Chinese people became addicted to the opium. The British did not listen to Chinese requests to stop selling the drug.

B. Toward Revolution in China

Purpose-Setting Question What was one possible cause of the Boxer Rebellion? (Possible answer: Many Chinese people were deeply angry at foreign nations for dividing their country into spheres of influence.)

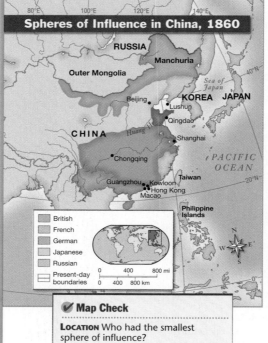

Spheres of Influence in China, 1860

RUSSIA

Manchuria

Outer Mongolia

Sea of Japan

Beijing
Lushup
KOREA   JAPAN
Qingdao

CHINA   Huang   Shanghai

Chongqing

PACIFIC OCEAN

Guangzhou Kowloon Taiwan
Hong Kong
Macao

Philippine Islands

- British
- French
- German
- Japanese
- Russian
- Present-day boundaries

0   400   800 mi
0   400   800 km

✔ Map Check

LOCATION Who had the smallest sphere of influence?

ship was involved in piracy, or robbery. The Chinese arrested the crew and lowered the ship's flag. The British regarded this action as a huge insult. Tensions between the two nations increased and war broke out. France joined Britain in attacking China. Between 1856 and 1860, Britain and France clashed with China in the Second Opium War. Once again, China was defeated and yet again it was forced to sign new treaties.

The Unequal Treaties

After the Second Opium War, several treaties were forced on China. All of the treaties were unfair to China. The treaties became known as the Unequal Treaties. In these treaties, trade in opium became legal in China. Ten more Chinese ports were opened to foreign trade and residents. The city of Kowloon was leased to Great Britain for 99 years. Duty, or tax, on goods imported into China could not be more than 5 percent.

The treaties gave foreign nations control over the entire Chinese economy. China could not even raise taxes on imports to cover the rising costs of some industries. Perhaps worst of all, opium use and addiction spread through China at an ever-increasing rate.

Spheres of Influence

China was weakened by the Taiping Rebellion, which occurred from 1850 to 1864. The leaders of the rebellion wanted more equal ownership of land and other reforms. Although the rebels gained control of part of China, the Chinese government finally defeated them. During the rebellion, 20 million people were killed.

After the Taiping Rebellion, China was an easy target of other countries. Japan joined the west in exploring China's resources. Japan drew China into war. The conflict was brief. However, China lost Taiwan, a large island off its coast. In 1860, Russia seized land on China's northern border to have a port on the Sea of Japan. By the end of the nineteenth century, France, Germany, Japan, and Great Britain had divided China into spheres of influence, or regions in which one nation has exclusive control.

The United States wanted to trade with China, but did not want to see China divided by imperialist powers. The United States proposed freedom of trade among the spheres of influence in China. This policy, called an Open Door Policy, was established to prevent nations from colonizing China. This policy gave the United States the same trading privileges that Great Britain, Russia, and the other nations enjoyed.

◆ **Why did Chinese leaders fight Europeans in the Opium Wars?**

B. Toward Revolution in China

By 1860, China's economy was almost completely dominated by foreign powers. These foreign nations put the profits they made from China into their own nations. This situation left too little money in the Chinese economy to allow Chinese business to prosper. It also left little money for the Manchu Dynasty to govern well.

Teaching Options

F Y I

The Taiping Rebellion

The Taiping Rebellion was a religious and political upheaval. Its leaders were influenced by Christian teachings from the West. The Taipings promised that they would impose shared property, so they appealed to many famine-stricken peasants. The rebellion attracted over a million soldiers who were fanatically loyal and rigorously disciplined.

China's people had lost confidence in the Manchu Dynasty for its failure to stand up to foreigners. In fact, even the Manchu rulers were resented as foreigners. As you learned in Chapter 21, the Manchu people invaded China in the 1600s and replaced the Ming Dynasty. As discontent spread in the late nineteenth century, some leaders began to focus their hatred on the Manchus. One such leader, Liang Qichao, announced, "If there were a way to save the nation and at the same time help us to take revenge against the Manchus, I would certainly be delighted to follow it."

The Boxer Rebellion

Many Chinese people were deeply angry at the foreign nations for dividing their country into spheres of influence. Some people blamed their troubles on missionaries and other foreigners. In 1899, they formed a secret society known as the Righteous Harmonious Fists. Europeans called this group Boxers because they were trained in Chinese fighting techniques.

Many Manchu leaders supported the Boxers. The Manchu empress Ci Xi thought that the Boxers would get rid of the foreigners. She said that the foreigners were aggressive with the common people.

Between 1898 and 1900, the Boxers attacked missionaries and other foreigners, killing many of them. They also surrounded the European section of Beijing, keeping the Europeans contained there for several months. Several foreign nations, including the United States, sent troops to free the foreign section of Beijing and defeat the Boxers. Approximately 20,000 foreign troops entered the city and looted Beijing.

After the failure of the Boxer Rebellion, the Manchu Dynasty decided to reform its government. Empress Ci Xi promised to reorganize the government's departments and modernize the army. Leaders made plans to form a limited constitutional government. However, reform was not the real issue. After years of discontent with the Manchu leaders, little could be done to satisfy the needs and growing discontent of the Chinese people.

Sun Yat-sen

When Empress Ci Xi died in 1908, China was ready for change. Some reformers wanted to replace the Manchu Dynasty with a republic. A republic is a government with an elected body of representatives. Sun Yat-sen became a passionate spokesperson for a Chinese republic. He was educated in western countries and western ways. As an adult, he became a Christian and later cut off his traditional pigtail.

Sun put together a group that included Chinese revolutionaries and foreign supporters to aid his cause. Sun traveled extensively, raising foreign funds to support the revolution. At home he reinforced the idea that the Manchus were not worthy of China's support:

> ❝Our ancestors refused to submit to the Manchus. Close your eyes and imagine the picture of the bitter battles, when rivers of blood flowed and the bodies of the fallen covered the fields, and you will realize that the conscience of our ancestors is clear.❞

The Boxers, members of a secret society, destroyed the property of foreigners and sometimes killed or tortured them.

ANALYZE PRIMARY SOURCES

DOCUMENT-BASED QUESTION What did Sun mean by "the conscience of our ancestors is clear"?

With the class, prepare a timeline on the board of the activities of Sun Yat-sen and General Yuan. Ask students to evaluate and discuss the actions of General Yuan as he came to power in the early 1900s. Challenge students to speculate about what life would be like for most people in China after Yuan died.

Create a constitution Have students research the constitution that was created in 1912 by the Chinese government. Then, ask groups of students to create their own constitution for China. Have students discuss the creation of parliament. Groups should discuss if they would allow for this in their constitution and then explain their thoughts and the role they would give parliament.

◆ **ANSWER** Revolutionaries fought against the Manchu Dynasty, provinces declared independence from the government, and the last Manchu emperor abdicated.

Section Close

Ask students to explain how strong foreign nations that pushed a thriving drug trade led to the conflicts and weakness in China. Remind students that opium use was rampant throughout all levels of society, and it was supported by powerful foreign nations.

Review Answers

Review History

A. China had to sign treaties that were known as the Unequal Treaties because they were unfair to China. In the treaties, China had to open ten more ports, trade in opium became legal, the city of Kowloon was leased to Great Britain for 99 years, duty, or tax on goods, could not be more than 5 percent, and foreign nations gained control over the entire Chinese economy.

B. a dictatorship, followed by parts of China being ruled by warlords

Define Terms to Know

opium, 586; extraterritoriality, 587

Yuan Shikai became president of the Republic of China in 1912 but soon ruled the country as a military dictator.

In 1911, uprisings spread through the provinces of China. Within 6 weeks, 15 provinces declared independence from the Qing, or Manchu, government. The Manchu armies were superior to the rebel forces. General Yuan Shikai, the top general of the Manchu Dynasty, had reorganized its armies and made them a strong force. Yuan defended the Manchu rulers vigorously, until the last Manchu emperor abdicated.

In January 1912, Sun Yat-sen formally declared China a republic. A constitution for the Chinese government was adopted, and a parliament was formed. Sun Yat-sen headed a political party called the Nationalist Party. Sun wanted to rebuild China so that the country would become strong again. He was elected temporary president of the new republic.

Sun tried to limit General Yuan's power. However, Yuan successfully used military force against Sun. Yuan forced Sun to resign the temporary presidency of the republic in 1912—the same year that Sun had been elected to that position. Yuan then established himself as temporary president of the republic.

In 1913, Sun Yat-sen organized a second uprising—this time against Yuan. When Sun failed to regain power, he fled to Japan. Yuan remained president of the republic until 1916. Although he was president, Yuan refused to let the constitution or parliament get in the way of his personal power. In 1914, Yuan dismissed the parliament. The ambitious general set himself up as a military dictator.

In 1916, Yuan declared himself emperor. However, he died suddenly in June. When he died, the central government became very weak. For the most part, local gangsters and former military leaders, called warlords, ruled different parts of China.

◆ **What happened in China that caused the end of the Manchu Dynasty?**

Review I

Review History
A. What was China forced to do after the Second Opium War?
B. What was the effect of revolution in China?

Define Terms to Know
Define the following terms:
opium, extraterritoriality

Critical Thinking
The Unequal Treaties created many changes for China. What do you think was the most significant change?

Write About History
Write a short speech a Boxer leader might use to encourage Chinese people to turn against missionaries and other foreigners.

Get Organized
SQR CHART
Use an SQR chart to organize information from this section. For example, you might survey this section to find the topic of the overthrow of the Manchu Dynasty.

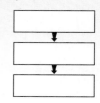

Critical Thinking
Possible answer: The opium trade was legalized; this led to increasing opium addiction.

Write About History
Speeches should cite the actions of foreigners and missionaries for China's problems, and should describe some specifics such as the Opium Wars and trade imbalance.

SURVEY
This section is about the overthrow of the Manchu Dynasty.

QUESTION
Why was the Manchu Dynasty overthrown?

READ
The Chinese people lost confidence in the Manchu Dynasty due to foreign domination and economic problems.

Build Your Skills

PREDICT CONSEQUENCES

Critical Thinking

PREDICT CONSEQUENCES

When you predict, you decide what you think will happen in the future. When you predict consequences, you make an educated guess about the effects of a given action or event. You do this by examining what you already know. Sometimes you might predict how the consequences of an event would have been different if someone had acted differently. Predicting the consequences of given actions or decisions helps you to better understand the events you read about.

In Section I, you learned that Yuan Shikai established himself as temporary president of the Republic of China. Then, he dismissed the parliament and made himself a military dictator and finally an emperor. After Yuan died, warlords took over China.

Here's How

Follow these steps to predict consequences.

1. Examine the event or action and the known facts.
2. Use your prior knowledge to examine what usually happens in such situations.
3. Form a prediction.
4. Think about ways in which consequences would be different under other circumstances.

Here's Why

Predicting consequences helps you to make better decisions. In studying printed material, predicting consequences also helps you to think critically about the information you have learned and encourages you to look and think ahead.

Practice the Skill

Predict the consequences of Yuan's actions 20 years after he declared himself emperor and died. Use the chart on the right to help organize your facts. Then, answer the following questions.

1. What facts did you use to make your prediction?
2. What is your prediction and why is it valid?

Extend the Skill

Predict what might have happened had Yuan not dismissed the parliament and become a military dictator and then an emperor. Explain your prediction.

Apply the Skill

Copy the chart on the right onto a sheet of paper. Then, think about a prediction and a consequence that relates to you and your schoolwork. Fill in the chart with facts. Share your prediction and consequence with a partner.

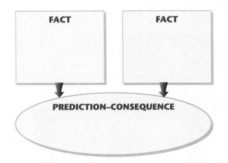

FACT   FACT

PREDICTION–CONSEQUENCE

PREDICT CONSEQUENCES

Teach the Skill

Have students make predictions about the consequences of an event in their own lives. These could range from the outcome of a sports event to the results of a recent test they have just completed.

Have students discuss their predictions with a partner and examine the process they used to come up with them. Have them identify the information they used to form their prediction. Then, ask students to compare the process they used to the one described in *Here's How*. Was the process similar? What steps in the process might have made a prediction more accurate?

Practice the Skill

ANSWERS

1. Possible answers: The central government was very weak; warlords ruled pieces of China; Sun had fled to Japan.
2. Possible answer: China was in chaos with many battles.

Extend the Skill

Possible answer: If Yuan had not dismissed the parliament and become a military dictator and emperor, China would probably have had a stronger national government more representative of the Chinese people. Then, the nation might not have been ruled by warlords.

Apply the Skill

Encourage students to discuss and refine their predictions. As an extension, ask students to use the graphic organizer to make predictions about the events in the rest of the chapter. For example, have students predict the consequences of Japan's isolationism of the nineteenth century in Section 2. In Section 3, ask students to predict the consequences of economic imperialism in Latin America.

Teaching Options

RETEACH

Demonstrate the basic principles of predicting consequences by asking a series of questions such as the following: What are the consequences of dropping an egg on the floor? What are the consequences of failing a test in class? Then, ask students to explain how they came up with their answers. Write their responses on the board. Use them as a guide for making predictions about the information in the chapter.

CHALLENGE

Ask students to use the chart on this page to make predictions about Sun Yat-sen and his rebel organization. Have them gather information from the text. Then, have students use a reference book or the Internet to find more information about Sun Yat-sen's revolutionary leadership. Have them compare their predictions to the actual events from their research.

II. Japan Modernizes

(pp. 592–596)

Section Summary

Students will learn how Japan was forced to open its ports to foreign trade. They will also learn about the advantages and disadvantages of the Meiji Restoration. Finally, they will evaluate the causes and effects of the conflicts that arose from Japan no longer being isolated from foreigners and becoming a world power.

1 Introduce

Getting Started

Explain to students that at one time, Japan was almost completely isolated from foreigners. Ask students to discuss the advantages and disadvantages of isolation for people and the rulers of an isolated nation. (**Possible advantage:** local business and trade is encouraged; **Possible disadvantage:** no exchange of ideas or technology)

TERMS TO KNOW

Have students use index cards to make vocabulary flashcards. On one side of the card, have them write the term and a sentence. On the other side, have them write the definition of the term. Have students work in pairs to make and use the cards.

You may wish to preview the pronunciation of the following terms with your students.

Calbraith (KAL brehth)
Edo (AY doh)
Kanagawa (kah NAH gaw wah)
Mutsuhito (moot soo hee toh)
Meiji (may jee)
Sino-Japanese
(SYN oh ja puhn NEEZ)

ACTIVE READING

Have students preview the section by reading the headings. Have them jot down some preliminary notes about Japan's transition from isolation to industrialization. Then, have them use the notes as they sequence the events of the chapter. A timeline (TR, p. 320) may help students keep their notes in order as they read.

Section II — Japan Modernizes

Terms to Know

consul a government official who lives and works in another country

peer a person of equal rank or social standing

imperial line emperors, their ancestors, and their descendants

mediator a person who settles differences between people and nations

Main Ideas

A. Challenges by western powers finally succeeded in opening Japan to foreigners and foreign traders.

B. The Japanese emperor Meiji was restored to power, and industrialization and social change followed.

C. Japan let go of its policy of isolation and became an industrial and military world power.

Active Reading

SEQUENCING EVENTS Sequencing events means placing events in the order in which they happened from first to last. As you read this section, ask yourself this question: How did events lead Japan to change from an independent, isolated country to an industrialized nation dependent on world markets?

This painting shows U.S. Commodore Matthew Perry's first meeting with Japanese officials in 1853.

Gessan Ogata/U.S. Naval Academy Museum

A. Challenges by Western Imperial Powers

In general, Japan tried to remain isolated from foreigners and foreign powers for years. Japanese people feared change and did not want their leaders to be overthrown. Trading ships were not allowed into Japanese ports. Foreign ships in need of supplies or help were turned away.

The Japanese, however, were not completely successful. In Nagasaki, for example, where the Dutch were allowed limited trade, there was information about western cultures. Some of the Japanese people were curious about the Westerners. Also, despite official bans, European traders and explorers had attempted to visit Japan. Others were interested in Japan as well. Russians had long been trying to sail to Japan and establish trade. In the early 1800s, Great Britain and the United States were interested in establishing trade relations. Many Japanese feared Russian expansion and the growing power of the West.

A Show of Force

In 1853, an event confirmed Japanese fears about foreigners. In that year, western power was used to force the Japanese into granting trade privileges.

It all began with the needs of the United States. Beyond trade advantages, the United States wanted its whaling ships in the Pacific to be allowed to restock their supplies when they crossed the vast Pacific. The American government sent a formal mission to the emperor of Japan. Headed by Commodore Matthew Calbraith Perry, four ships arrived in Edo Bay near Tokyo.

Tiny Japanese boats surrounded Perry's ships and tried to stop them. Ignoring the little boats, the ships sailed into the harbor. Perry landed and delivered a letter from U.S. President Millard Fillmore. The letter asked for better treatment of shipwrecked U.S. sailors, the sale of supplies to ships in need of them, and trade between Japan and the United States. Perry said firmly that he would return in a year for an answer from Japan. He informed the Japanese that he would bring a larger force with him when he returned.

Teaching Options

Section 2 Resources

Teacher's Resources (TR)
Terms to Know, p. 38
Review History, p. 72
Build Your Skills, p. 106
Chapter Test, pp. 165–166
Concept Builder, p. 241
SQR Chart, p. 322

The Japanese warlords were equipped only with medieval weapons. They were trained in small-scale battles. Alarmed by U.S. military equipment, they were afraid to resist. The discussion between the Japanese emperor, a shogun, and other officials continued for months. Should they agree to U.S. requests or should they stand firm and risk an attack?

The discussion ended when Perry returned with nine large ships in 1854. Japanese leaders agreed to Perry's demands. Japan was now opened to foreigners—although this had been accomplished by a show of superior force rather than because Japanese leaders wanted to open relations with foreign powers.

Treaty of Kanagawa

Perry and representatives of the emperor signed the Treaty of Kanagawa on March 31, 1854. It opened two ports to American trading ships and promised better treatment of American sailors. It also acknowledged that sometime in the future an American official would be useful to negotiate trade agreements. An American **consul** would live and work in Japan. A consul is a government official who is responsible for commercial interests and takes care of functions such as issuing passports. Great Britain, Russia, and the Netherlands were soon granted similar rights. Westerners living in Japan were governed only by the laws of their own countries or extraterritorially. They were not subject to Japan's laws.

◆ **What was Japan's policy toward foreign nations and foreigners in the early 1800s?**

B. Restoring Power to Japan

In the years that followed, Japan changed dramatically. A feudal system was replaced by a centralized imperial government. Over the years, Japan gained a constitution and elected representatives. A traditional, isolated society became a modern industrialized nation and joined a global community.

The Return of the Emperor

Internal conflicts and economic problems spread discontent among the Japanese people. Western interference, and seeing Japanese leaders bullied by foreign powers, destroyed confidence in the shogun and created unrest in Japan. In 1867, a reform group decided Japan would be better off if the emperor were restored to full power. They persuaded the last shogun to resign and give his power to Emperor Mutsuhito, a boy of 16. Emperor Mutsuhito took the name Meiji, which means "enlightened rule." This period is known as the Meiji restoration. Emperor Meiji signed the Charter Oath, five ground-breaking sentences that signaled a return to past traditions. One of the most dramatic signals of change was Article 5:

❝ Knowledge shall be sought throughout the world so as to strengthen the foundations of imperial rule. ❞

Emperor Meiji listens to the Charter Oath, which signaled a major break with Japanese traditions.

ANALYZE PRIMARY SOURCES

DOCUMENT-BASED QUESTION
How did Article 5 signal a change from the earlier policies of the Japanese government?

CHAPTER 25 ◆ Imperialism in Asia and Latin America **593**

Explore Have students research the Japanese constitution of 1889. Have them compare and contrast the two houses with the Senate and the House of Representatives in the government of the United States or Great Britain's parliament with two houses. Suggest students use a Venn diagram (TR, p. 323), if necessary, to organize their information.

Discuss The Meiji government brought western ideas to Japan, but these changes were not good for all people. Ask students to identify the ways that the changes both improved and damaged the nation. (Possible answer: Jobs were created and class distinctions were removed. Also, the government encouraged education. However, opposition to the government was discouraged and some workers were paid low wages.)

Focus Have students research the class system in Japan before the Meiji reform. Then, have students brainstorm the emperor's reasons for changing this system. Have students discuss the benefits to the people after these changes to Japanese society had occurred.

GLOBAL CONNECTIONS

CHEAP LABOR Have students use library resources or the Internet to find examples of how companies in the United States are trying to make working conditions better for all employees. (Possible answers: flexible schedules, healthy working environments, telecommuting bonuses) Then, have students discuss which of these benefits they would look forward to the most.

◆ **ANSWER** Emperor Meiji replaced feudal control with imperial control. A constitution and legislature were added, and voting rights were extended to a few.

The Tokyo-Yokohama Railway was built during the Meiji restoration with the assistance of foreign engineers.

Global Connections

CHEAP LABOR
Industrialization in Europe and the United States resulted in poor men and women working long hours under miserable conditions for low pay. Children also worked under these conditions. In both Japan and western countries, industries were built on cheap labor.

Government Changes Under Emperor Meiji

The new government set about centralizing power and breaking up feudalism. Feudal lords gave up their lands and became governors of their former kingdoms. Daimyo were retired and given government pensions. The samurai, or Japanese warriors, did not fare as well. Their government pay was reduced and later eliminated. This left many samurai in poverty. Because they were trained as warriors, many samurai did not fit into other professions or jobs. Eventually the samurai class was abolished altogether and an army was created.

The government also began moving in the direction of a constitutional government. In 1889, a constitution was announced. It provided for a legislature with two houses. Members of the upper house were made up of the ruling, or imperial, family as well as nobles appointed by the emperor. Such members were called **peers** because the upper house of the legislature was called the House of Peers. Peers are people of equal rank or standing. The representatives of the lower house were elected, not appointed. Because only men with a certain amount of money or property could vote, representatives were elected by a small percentage of Japanese citizens.

Under the constitution, the emperor did not give up much power. He could issue some laws and could decide to declare war or end a war. The emperor could also disband the lower and the upper houses.

Some discontented Japanese groups pressed for more reform. To keep unrest down, Japanese leaders encouraged citizens to be loyal to the nation and the emperor. In their school textbooks, students were told to worship the **imperial line**, which is the series of emperors within Japan.

Industrialization Under Emperor Meiji

Under government direction, rapid industrialization and modernization occurred during the Meiji restoration. The government began operating iron furnaces. It built ships, weapons, and railroads. To fuel industry, the government began mining for coal. The silk and cotton industries expanded. In 1880, silk accounted for 43 percent of Japanese exports. The silk and cotton industries depended on cheap labor.

Social Changes Under Emperor Meiji

Under Emperor Meiji, class distinctions were removed. People from differing classes could intermarry and dress as they chose. Also eliminated was the outcast class. Members of this class had been known as nonhumans. Outcasts had been allowed to marry only within their class and work only in jobs other people would not do. Outcasts lived in special areas and could be abused by members of other classes. Although such discrimination ended under the law, social discrimination of the outcasts continued.

The Meiji government also encouraged education for all Japanese. Besides loyalty to the nation and empire, Japanese education stressed science. Many students went abroad to study the science and technology of other countries.

◆ **What government changes were made under Emperor Meiji?**

Teaching Options

Research

AVERAGE
Have students choose one of the wars from the chapter, such as the Sino-Japanese War, the Russo-Japanese War, the Spanish-American War, or the Opium Wars. Have students research the conflict they choose and write a timeline and a brief summary of it. Summaries should identify the political and military leaders of each side as well as the major battles of the war.

CHALLENGE
Have students research one of the wars in the chapter and display their findings on a poster. The posters should include a timeline, a map, the name of the war, and photographs of relevant people, places, or battles. Display the posters in one area of the classroom. Encourage students to explain their posters to the class.

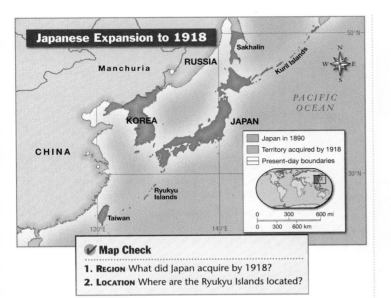

Japanese Expansion to 1918

- Japan in 1890
- Territory acquired by 1918
- Present-day boundaries

✔ **Map Check**

1. REGION What did Japan acquire by 1918?
2. LOCATION Where are the Ryukyu Islands located?

C. Japanese Foreign Policy

Once Japan became industrialized, its need for raw materials increased. A resource-poor nation, Japan was dependent on other countries for raw materials. It also needed markets for its products.

Japanese Imperialism

As Japan grew economically and politically, it looked for areas in which to expand. In 1879, Japan took over the Ryukyu Islands. The struggle for control of Korea was next. Korea had long been under Chinese control. In the past, Japanese efforts to trade with Korea and to take it from China had resulted in war. War was to happen again.

In 1894, the first Sino-Japanese War broke out between Japan and China. The modernized Japanese forces easily defeated the Chinese army and navy. The treaty that ended the war forced China to recognize the independence of Korea in 1895. The treaty also required China to give Japan the island of Taiwan.

The Russo-Japanese War

After the Sino-Japanese War, Japan gradually strengthened its army. Then, Japan came into conflict with Russia over Russian expansion. In 1900, after the Boxer Rebellion in China, Russia occupied Manchuria, which was part of China. From Manchurian bases, Russia began to push into northern Korea. This action worried Japan. The two countries tried to reach an agreement over who would control Korea, but negotiations failed. Russia refused to withdraw its troops from Manchuria. Nobody asked the Koreans or the Chinese how they felt about the conflict or what they wanted.

In 1904, the day after the talks broke off, a Russian naval force entered Korean waters. War broke out between Russia and Japan. This was called the Russo-Japanese War. After the Russians entered Korean waters, Japanese

Do You Remember?
In Chapter 24, you learned that during the 1800s industries in Asia and Africa began to export raw materials, such as cotton, gold, and rubber, instead of finished goods. These raw materials were used by industries in Europe to make finished products.

Extend Tell students that the Japanese took swift control of the seas in the Russo-Japanese War. Ask students what factors may have contributed to Japan's naval strength and Russia's naval weakness. (Possible answers: As an island nation, Japan depended on its seamanship for external contact. Also, Russia had few seaports on its east coast.)

◆ **ANSWER** Russia began to expand. Russia occupied Manchuria and, from there, began to push into northern Korea. This worried the Japanese. The two countries entered talks to see who would control Korea and whether or not Russia would leave Manchuria, but the talks failed.

Section Close

Ask students to recall the factors that helped Japan avoid colonization by strong foreign powers. (Possible answer: Japan allowed limited trade within its borders and then pursued its own imperialist interests in Korea and Taiwan.)

3 **Assess**

Review Answers

Review History
A. Commodore Perry sailed to Japan with several large, intimidating ships and advanced weapons. His show of force persuaded the Japanese to grant the requests he delivered.

B. Reformers persuaded the shogun to resign in favor of the emperor.

C. As Japan industrialized, it needed raw materials. It also needed markets for its products.

Define Terms to Know
consul, 593; peer, 594; imperial line, 594; mediator, 596

Critical Thinking
Possible answer: The influence of western technology and the ability to purchase western goods enabled Japan to use better weapons to defeat the Chinese and Russians.

U.S. President Theodore Roosevelt (center) acted as a mediator during the peace talks between Russia and Japan.

warships left Japan and headed for Korea. Japanese troops entered and occupied the Korean city of Seoul, and Japanese ships attacked and damaged Russian ships. Japan sent troops into Manchuria as well. A huge country with rugged terrain, Russia could not quickly move troops from Moscow to Manchuria.

After 18 months of battles on both land and sea, with many casualties, Japan won the war in 1905. Acting as a **mediator**, a person who settles differences between people and nations, U.S. President Theodore Roosevelt met with Russian and Japanese leaders. He helped them to reach an agreement on a peace treaty. Under the treaty, Russia withdrew from southern Manchuria and gave Japan a railroad for a set number of years. Russia also recognized Japan's control of Korea.

A New Imperialist Power

In little more than 50 years, a traditional, isolated Japan had become industrialized and emerged as a major international power. Once bullied by imperialist nations, it had now gained military power and became an imperialist nation itself.

Other industrialized imperialist nations, such as Great Britain and Russia, viewed the nation of Japan as a threat to the balance of power. Japan's achievements and victories sent ripples of concern through the western world.

◆ **How did Japan come into conflict with Russia?**

Review II

Review History
A. What opened Japan to western traders?
B. How was the Japanese emperor restored to full power?
C. Why did Japan become an imperialist nation?

Define Terms to Know
Define the following terms:
consul, peer, imperial line, mediator

Critical Thinking
How did opening Japan to trade with the West aid Japan in its own imperialist ambitions?

Write About Government
Write a letter of advice to Emperor Meiji stating your opinion about who should be allowed to vote and what qualifications should be required.

Get Organized
SQR CHART
Use an SQR chart to organize information from this section. For example, you might survey this section to find the topic of the Russo-Japanese War.

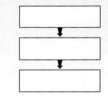

596 UNIT 6 ◆ A Changing World

Write About Government
Letters should present a well-supported case. For example, letters could recommend all Japanese-born residents over a certain age, excluding felons; or only property owners and taxpayers because they contribute more to funding the government.

SURVEY
This section is about the Russo-Japanese War.

↓

QUESTION
Why did Japan go to war with Russia?

↓

READ
Conflict with Russia over Korea and Russian expansion

Economic Imperialism in Latin America

Terms to Know

isthmus a narrow strip of land bordered on both sides by water between two larger masses of land

dictatorial rule a form of government in which the ruler has absolute power

Main Ideas

A. Even after Latin America gained independence, foreign nations continued to dominate.

B. During the late 1800s and early 1900s, the United States introduced its own brand of imperialism to Latin America.

C. After Mexico's independence from Spain, Mexico faced economic challenges and revolution.

 **Active Reading**

COMPARE AND CONTRAST
As you read this section, ask yourself the following questions: In which ways were the economic imperialism in China and in Latin America the same in the 1800s and early 1900s? In which ways were they different?

Section Summary

In this section, students will learn how many Latin American nations achieved independence only to fall victim to economic imperialism. They will learn how the United States took a role in keeping European imperialists out of Latin America.

A. Foreigners in Latin America

Imperialism in Latin America took the form of colonization by European countries. By 1825, however, most Latin American countries had declared independence from the European colonial powers. Even so, Latin Americans could not break free of the economic control by foreign nations.

Effects of Colonial Imperialism

Simón Bolívar led the independence movement in Latin America during the early 1800s.

Before Europeans arrived, Latin American economies were mostly self-sufficient. Families grew and produced most of what they needed, and traded with neighbors and local merchants for the rest. Native Americans survived and sometimes prospered without European help.

European interference permanently changed the economies of Latin America. The Spanish and Portuguese governments controlled industry and trade in their colonies. This left Latin America economically dependent on foreign nations.

Spanish and Portuguese governments and businesses did make important contributions to local economies. They invested money, contributed technology, and improved transportation and communications systems. Unfortunately, they also denied the Latin Americans any role in government. However, a wealthy Venezuelan Creole named Simón Bolívar, whom you learned about in Chapter 20, fought for the independence of several colonies.

Economic Imperialism in Latin America

Even after Latin Americans broke free of European political control, their economies still depended on trade with European countries. They needed markets for their export crops. They also needed sources for food crops and goods they did not produce. Europeans continued to invest money in Latin American businesses, railroads, and transportation networks. They made large loans to the new nations.

Some Latin American nations with many resources and good management built strong economies. Even so, most of the profits went only to a few wealthy people. Most Latin Americans were too poor to buy enough goods to support local industries.

Economic problems made it difficult or impossible for some new nations to pay off their loans. These unpaid loans soon provided an excuse for foreign interference in Latin America.

1 Introduce

Getting Started

Use Transparency 1 or the world map in the Atlas (pp. A1–A2) to point out the nations of Latin America that are the focus of the section. Demonstrate that the region is made up of many small nations by listing them on the board. List the nations from Mexico to Brazil.

TERMS TO KNOW

Have students read the terms and their definitions on page 597 and then find the terms in this section. Have students recall several examples of nations with dictatorial governments.

You may wish to preview the pronunciation of the following names from this section with students.

Guadalupe Hidalgo
(GWAD ihl loop hih DAHL goh)
Benito Pablo Juárez
(beh NEE toh PAHB loh KWAH rays)
Porfirio Díaz
(pawr FEER yoh DEE ahs)
Francisco Indalecio Madero
(frahn THEES koh een dah LAHTH yoh mah THAY roh)
Emiliano Zapata
(ay meel YAHN oh sah PAH tah)
Venustiano Carranza
(bay noos TYAHN oh kahr RAHN sah)

ACTIVE READING

To help students draw comparisons, have them scan Section 1 to remind themselves of the forms of imperialism in China. They may wish to refer to their notes from Section 1 as they compare and contrast. Have students use a Venn diagram (TR, p. 323) to organize their information.

Teaching Options

Section 3 Resources

Teacher's Resources (TR)
Terms to Know, p. 38
Review History, p. 72
Build Your Skills, p. 106
Chapter Test, pp. 165–166
Concept Builder, p. 241
SQR Chart, p. 322
Transparency 1

ESL/ELL STRATEGIES

Use Manipulatives Reinforce language learning by having students make a set of index cards with comparison words such as *unlike, in contrast, similar, likewise, although, on the other hand,* and *yet* on the front of the index cards and definitions on the back. They can use these cards for reference as they compare and contrast the text material for the Active Reading activity.

A. Foreigners in Latin America

Purpose-Setting Question How did European countries continue to influence Latin America after independence? (Europeans invested in Latin America businesses, railroads, and transportation networks and made loans to the new nations.)

Discuss Identify the weaknesses in Latin American nations after they obtained their independence. (Possible answers: These new nations needed to borrow large sums of money from the Europeans; they needed European markets to trade their crops and to get the crops and goods they did not produce.) Then, discuss with the class how these weaknesses led to economic imperialism.

◆ **ANSWER** Problems between social classes and troubled economies made it difficult for Latin American countries to unite.

B. United States Imperialism

Purpose-Setting Question What event sparked the Spanish-American War? (The battleship USS *Maine*, sent to protect Americans in Cuba, was destroyed. It was suspected that Spain was responsible, sparking outrage among many Americans.)

ANALYZE PRIMARY SOURCES

DOCUMENT-BASED QUESTION
The original caption for the political cartoon said "COASTING The old horse is too slow for Uncle Sam." The words on the horse's saddle say "Monroe Doctrine." Discuss with students the cartoonist's point of view and the elements in the cartoon that emphasize this view.

ANSWER No, the cartoonist is poking fun at the United States and the Monroe Doctrine.

Focus Have students recall the time frame of the American Revolution (1775–1783). Have them subtract to figure out how many years the United States had been governing itself when Monroe made his strong statement. (about 50 years)

Areas of Weakness

Problems between social classes and troubled economies made it difficult for Latin American countries to unite. These weaknesses invited foreign interference. Many Latin Americans felt no loyalty to the central governments of their nations. Powerful individuals took control of local areas and formed their own armies. Some individuals grew so powerful that they later became dictators. Former colonies did not have strong armies to defend themselves. They were at risk of further colonization because they could not defend their liberty.

The Monroe Doctrine

As revolutions ended Spanish and Portuguese rule in Latin America, U.S. citizens had watched eagerly. U.S. government leaders were aware that the newly independent Latin American governments were poorly prepared to defend themselves against further colonization.

As you learned in Chapters 20 and 23, U.S. President James Monroe had made a statement in 1823 that became known as the Monroe Doctrine. In it, he declared that the American continents were not open for further colonization by any European powers. He also declared that the United States would help American colonies maintain their independence.

The United States was not able to enforce the bold warnings. In fact, Europeans viewed the warnings of the young nation as comical. European countries made fun of the Monroe Doctrine. However, Great Britain feared that Spain would try to reconquer its former colonies in Latin America and stop Great Britain's trade with these new nations. Therefore, Great Britain opposed European colonization in Latin America and was willing to back up the United States if necessary.

◆ **What made it difficult for Latin American countries to unite?**

B. United States Imperialism

A growing spirit of imperialism convinced many Americans that the United States needed to take aggressive steps, both economically and militarily, to establish itself as a true world power. Both expansion and the extension of U.S. influence were supported by many citizens of the United States.

Through investment and trade, the United States gained economic control in Latin America. For example, when Cuba rebelled against Spanish rule, many sugar producers were ruined. Businesses in the United States then took over the sugar plantations and sugar mills.

The Spanish-American War

A Cuban revolution with the goal of gaining independence from Spain began in 1895. Most Americans were on the side of the Cubans. President McKinley sent the battleship USS *Maine* to Havana, the capital of Cuba, to help protect Americans there. Then on February 15, 1898, the *Maine* exploded

ANALYZE PRIMARY SOURCES

DOCUMENT-BASED QUESTION Do you think the cartoonist takes the United States seriously as a possible threat to a European nation?

European cartoonists made fun of the Monroe Doctrine.

Teaching Options

FYI

The Monroe Doctrine

The Monroe Doctrine had little meaning until the 1840s when U.S. Presidents began using it to justify the U.S. policy of expansion. They argued, for example, that the United States should have exclusive control over any canal connecting the Atlantic and the Pacific Oceans through Central America.

Cooperative Learning

Have students work in groups to prepare a debate on the issue of U.S. imperialism in Latin America. Assign members of the groups specific roles such as researching the pros and cons of imperialization and spokespeople for each side. Then have groups conduct their debates. Ask other groups to watch the debate and determine a winner based on the evidence presented.

in the Havana harbor. The explosion killed 260 American sailors. The cause of the blast was unknown. Today, many historians believe it may have been caused by an accident. In 1898, however, Americans blamed Spain for the disaster.

The headline "Remember the *Maine!*" echoed across the United States. In an effort to avoid war, President McKinley asked Spain to stop fighting and to grant Cuba its independence. Spanish officials refused. In April 1898, the United States went to war with Spain. The first battle of the Spanish-American War did not take place in Cuba, but in the distant Philippine Islands. In May 1898, the U.S. Navy defeated the Spanish navy at Manila Bay. The United States attacked Manila, the capital of the Philippine Islands. Soon after, President McKinley sent U.S. troops to fight beside the Filipino people. U.S. troops also fought beside the Cuban people in Cuba. Together, they defeated Spanish forces. In four months, Spain was totally defeated.

The United States and Spain negotiated and signed a peace treaty officially ending the war on December 10, 1898. Cuba was not asked about the terms of the treaty. In the treaty, Spain agreed to withdraw from Cuba, leaving it under temporary U.S. occupation. It also agreed to pay Cuban debts and give Puerto Rico, Guam, and the Philippines to the United States for $20 million. Cuba remained independent, but in 1901, the U.S. Congress added the Platt Amendment to Cuba's constitution. It gave the United States the right to step in on Cuban affairs. The Cuban constitution also gave the United States land in Cuba to be used for a U.S. naval base.

Big Stick Diplomacy

European imperialists had acquired territory and colonies all over the world. Instead of seeking colonies for the United States, President Roosevelt wanted treaties that would support U.S. businesses abroad. Many people accused him of being imperialistic. In foreign affairs, Roosevelt said it was

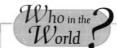
Who in the World?

THEODORE ROOSEVELT AND THE ROUGH RIDERS

Assistant Secretary of the U.S. Navy, Theodore Roosevelt, resigned his position to join the volunteer cavalry during the Spanish-American War. This cavalry, called the Rough Riders, built a reputation fighting in Cuba. The opportunity to distinguish himself in war may have helped Roosevelt in his political career. Years later, Roosevelt's presidency would expand U.S. imperialism in Latin America.

THEODORE ROOSEVELT AND THE ROUGH RIDERS The Rough Riders received more publicity for their flamboyant exploits than any other unit in the war. It came as no surprise that Roosevelt earned some fame from it. Ask students to name other military heroes who have become U.S. Presidents. (Possible answers: Dwight Eisenhower, George Washington, Andrew Jackson, John F. Kennedy)

Activity

Make a political cartoon Have students draw a political cartoon for or against the Spanish-American War. Cartoons should include details and a caption that reflect the circumstances of the war. The point of view should be obvious from the drawing, although the artistry may be simple.

Extend Tell students that one American politician called the Spanish-American War "a splendid little war." It was called this because the war was short and the United States forces won every conflict in the war but suffered few casualties.

The Spanish–American War, 1898

The Caribbean (From Spain)

UNITED STATES · ATLANTIC OCEAN · Florida · Tampa · Gulf of Mexico · Key West · Havana · Bahama Islands (Great Britain) · Cuba (Spain) · Daiquiri · Caribbean Sea · JAMAICA · HAITI · DOMINICAN REPUBLIC · San Juan · Puerto Rico (Spain)

→ U.S. Navy
→ U.S. Army
→ Spanish Fleet
✴ National capital
• Cities

The Philippines

CHINA · Taiwan · Hong Kong (Great Britain) · PACIFIC OCEAN · South China Sea · Manila Bay · Manila · Philippines (Spain)

0   200   400 mi
0   200   400 km

✔ Map Check

1. **LOCATION** Which Cuban city shown on the map is closest to the United States?
2. **MOVEMENT** From what city did the U.S. Navy ships sail for Manila in the Philippines?

CHAPTER 25 ◆ Imperialism in Asia and Latin America **599**

Using the Map

The Spanish-American War, 1898

Ask students where the Spanish fleet and the U.S. Navy ships met in Cuba. (Daiquiri) Have students identify the role that the U.S. Army played in the war. (The U.S. Army sailed from Tampa and met the navy and the Spanish fleet in Daiquiri.)

✔ Map Check
Answers
1. Havana
2. Hong Kong

Conflict Resolution

Point out to students that Latin American nations were weak because their people lacked loyalty to the central government of their nations. This led to a poor economy, and it left the nations vulnerable to imperialist powers. Ask students how they would advise their peers in a situation where a lack of loyalty, such as to a school or to the laws of a nation, creates weakness. Then, have students discuss ways to change the organization.

Using Technology

Have students do an Internet search to find out why the Panama Canal took just over ten years to complete. Have them report their findings by making a timeline covering 1904 to 1914. Timelines should include the major historical figures who took part in the project, the major technological breakthroughs, and details about construction challenges.

Ask students to use the map to figure out how many miles the Panama Canal shortens a cruise from San Francisco to New York City. (about 9,000 miles)

✔ Map Check

Answer Atlantic Ocean, Caribbean Sea, Panama Canal, and Pacific Ocean

Explore Ask students to make inferences about U.S. involvement in Panama's achieving independence. Have students discuss reasons for the United States recognizing the rebels who declared Panama independent and the ways the new Panamanian government repaid the United States for its support.

Activity

Use a map Have students locate the Panama Canal on a map of Panama. Ask them to trace the route of the Panama Canal, recognizing that the canal runs in a north-to-south direction because of the geographical formation of the isthmus of Panama.

◆ **ANSWER** It was a policy that was used at times to pressure Latin American countries to support U.S. interests and sometimes carried a threat of war.

C. Reform and Change in Mexico

Purpose-Setting Question What were the characteristics of Porfirio Díaz's rule in Mexico? (Díaz brought harsh dictatorial rule as well as order and modernization to Mexico.)

SPOTLIGHT ON GOVERNMENT
THE REPUBLIC OF TEXAS The period of independence for Texas was brief, but it fostered a pride in the history and heritage of Texas that still remains. The Republic of Texas adopted a national seal and flag. To this day the "Lone Star Flag" reminds Texans of the years in which Texas was its own nation. Ask students to name other nations that have declared independence. (the republics that used to make up the Soviet Union)

T600 ◆ **UNIT 6**

The Panama Canal and Water Routes

San Francisco • UNITED STATES • New York City

Water route around South America

Water route through the Panama Canal

6,100 miles (9,817 km)
15,100 miles (24,301 km)

ATLANTIC OCEAN

Caribbean Sea

Panama Canal

SOUTH AMERICA

PACIFIC OCEAN

Strait of Magellan

0   1,000   2,000 mi
0   1,000 2,000 km

✔ Map Check

MOVEMENT What bodies of water are crossed using the Panama Canal on a trip from New York City to San Francisco?

Spotlight on
Government

THE REPUBLIC OF TEXAS
During the period when Texas was an independent country, most Texans did not want it to remain independent. They wanted to join the United States.

Texas faced many problems. The government of Texas did not have money, and no other government recognized Texas as an independent republic. Texans knew that Mexico could send troops at any time to challenge their independence. They felt that Texas would prosper by being part of the United States.

600 UNIT 6 ◆ A Changing World

---

important to "speak softly and carry a big stick." This statement meant that a strong country could control others without making them colonies. The "big stick" sometimes carried a threat of war and was used at times to pressure Latin American countries.

The Panama Canal

The United States had long wanted to link its east and west coasts with a canal across Central America. Theodore Roosevelt negotiated a treaty with the government of Colombia in South America. Under the agreement, the United States would obtain the **isthmus** between North and South America located in the Colombian state of Panama. An isthmus is a narrow strip of land bordered on both sides by water between two larger masses of land. The Colombian senate, however, rejected the treaty. In 1903, a group of Panamanians who wanted a canal for themselves rebelled against Colombian rule and declared Panama independent. Three days later, the United States recognized the new Panamanian government. The new government used the U.S. Navy to prevent Colombia from stopping the rebellion.

Two weeks later, Panama signed a treaty giving the United States permission to build a canal. The United States agreed to guarantee Panama's independence and pay $10 million, plus an annual rental fee of $250,000. The Colombians were outraged. Work on the canal began in 1904 and was completed in 1914.

◆ **What was the "big stick" policy?**

C. Reform and Change in Mexico

Mexico was not ready to build a new republic after it won independence from Spain in 1821. Civil war had left the country unstable, and the economy was not able to produce enough tax money. From 1833 to 1855, a dictator named Antonio Lopez de Santa Anna ruled Mexico on and off. In 1835, the Americans who lived in Texas revolted against Mexican rule. In 1836, they created an independent republic. President James K. Polk annexed Texas to the United States in 1845. Mexico viewed this as a declaration of war.

After two years of fighting and several Mexican defeats, the two countries signed the Treaty of Guadalupe Hidalgo in 1848. Mexico withdrew its claim to Texas and gave up land to the United States. In return, the United States paid Mexico $15 million. The United States gained nearly half of Mexico's territory, including Texas. The states of California, Nevada, and Utah; most of Arizona; and parts of New Mexico, Colorado, and Wyoming were later created from this area.

Benito Pablo Juárez and Porfirio Díaz

Early in 1854, reformers launched a revolt against Santa Anna and took over the government in 1855. A great leader in the reform movement was Benito Pablo Juárez, a Native American who wanted to help poor people. In 1861, he became president of Mexico.

Teaching Options

Meet Individual Needs:

LOGICAL/MATHEMATICAL LEARNERS

Ask students to use an encyclopedia, almanac, or Internet search to find out how Panama has been impacted by the canal. Have them summarize the amount of money the canal generates for the nation as well as other details about the volume of traffic through the canal. Encourage students to show the information they find on a graph. Display graphs together on a bulletin board.

To help Mexico's economy recover, Juárez stopped payments on foreign loans. This action angered Napoleon III of France. In 1863, Napoleon III installed a European, Maximilian, as emperor of Mexico. In 1867, Juárez and his forces overthrew Maximilian.

In 1877, a Mexican general, Porfirio Díaz, led a series of revolts. He became president of Mexico. Under his harsh **dictatorial** **rule**, Díaz brought order and modernization to Mexico. Dictatorial rule is a form of government in which the ruler has absolute power. Díaz also strengthened the army and police. He encouraged the building of railroads and attracted foreign investors. Díaz favored the rich landowners and let them take lands that belonged to Native Americans. Many farmers became landless, and workers were underpaid and badly treated. Under Díaz, foreigners and a few Mexicans became rich, but the poor became poorer. In 1910, discontent exploded into revolt. Díaz resigned in 1911.

Emiliano Zapata and Pancho Villa

Francisco Indalecio Madero, a revolutionary leader, succeeded Díaz. Madero disappointed his revolutionary supporters, Native American Emiliano Zapata and former bandit Pancho Villa. In 1911, Zapata called for the immediate transfer of land to peasant farmers and the right of Mexican citizens to choose their own leaders. Zapata and Villa took up arms against Madero.

When Venustiano Carranza seized power in 1914, Zapata and Villa led rebellions against Carranza. Zapata was murdered in 1915. After Carranza was overthrown in 1920, Villa accepted the new government. Revolution continued to sweep through Mexico until 1920, when General Alvaro Obregón became president. The United States gave Obregón its support in 1923.

◆ **Why did Napoleon III install Maximilian as emperor of Mexico?**

Once an outlaw, Francisco "Pancho" Villa became a hero to the people of Mexico as a revolutionary leader.

Review III

Review History
A. Why did foreign domination continue in Latin America even after independence?
B. What form of imperialism did the United States pursue in Latin America?
C. Why were Emiliano Zapata and Pancho Villa important to the revolution in Mexico?

Define Terms to Know
Define the following terms: **isthmus, dictatorial rule**

Critical Thinking
How was U.S. imperialism different from the imperialism of European powers?

Write About Citizenship
Write a dialogue between two citizens of a country under a harsh dictator who has seized power. One citizen thinks citizens should obey laws and government leaders, and another explains why citizens should rebel.

Get Organized
SQR CHART
Use an SQR chart to organize information from this section. For example, you might survey this section to find the topic of the Spanish-American War.

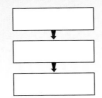

CHAPTER 25 ◆ Imperialism in Asia and Latin America **601**

SURVEY
This section is about the Spanish-American War.

↓

QUESTION
Why did the United States go to war with Spain?

↓

READ
In 1898, the U.S. battleship Maine exploded off the coast of Cuba, killing 260 American sailors.

Critical Thinking
Possible answer: The United States gained economic control in Latin America, while some European countries sought and established colonies.

Write About Citizenship
Students' dialogues should pit the obligation to uphold laws and government against the principle that citizens should reject governments that are not legitimate, democratic, and fair.

<Activity>

Make a flowchart Have students work in small groups to make a flowchart (TR, p. 320) of the change in leadership in Mexico that is discussed in this section. Tell students to add additional boxes to their flowcharts as needed. Ask students to use their flowcharts as a starting place to discuss the changes in leadership and how these changes might have affected the overall stability of the Mexican society and economy.

Discuss As in the rest of Latin America, a class system remained in Mexico after independence. Political and economic control passed to Spanish settlers and their descendants, called Creoles. Mestizos and Native Americans were poor and lacked power. Ask students to discuss the class system and identify several factors that could improve the disparity between the classes.

◆ **ANSWER** Napoleon III was angered by the fact that Juárez had stopped payments on foreign loans. He installed Maximilian, a European, as emperor of Mexico to regain control of Mexico.

Section Close

Have small groups of students discuss why the United States felt it should take a stand to defend the Latin American nations that had grown weak from internal conflicts and dependent on their colonial powers. They should find their evidence in the chapter. Once completed, have groups share with the class.

3 Assess

Review Answers

Review History
A. Economic dependence and foreign domination of trade left Latin Americans subject to foreign control.

B. investment, territorial expansion, and protection of U.S. businesses

C. Zapata and Villa were revolutionary leaders who fought for the rights of Mexican citizens and led rebellions against Mexican presidents.

Define Terms to Know
isthmus, 600; dictatorial rule, 601

CHAPTER 25 ◆ **T601**

IV. Worldwide Effects of Imperialism

(pp. 602–604)

Section Summary

Students will read about the scientific and technological advancements that occurred in the era of imperialism. They will also learn how imperialism affected nations economically, culturally, and politically.

1 Introduce

Getting Started

Ask students to consider how the United States would change if a foreign nation took over its government and social structures. How might everyday events such as school, television programming, or traffic laws change? Explain that such changes occurred in nations that were colonized during the age of imperialism.

TERMS TO KNOW

Ask students to read the terms and definitions on page 602 and then find each term in the section. Then, have them use each term in a sentence.

Explain to students that *pasteurization* comes from the last name of the man who invented the process, Louis Pasteur. Ask students to think of other words they know that come from people's names. (Possible answers: Columbus, Ohio, and Colombia; Phillips screwdriver)

You may wish to preview the pronunciation of the following name with your students.

Koch (KOOK)

ACTIVE READING

Remind students that the main idea of a paragraph is often contained in the first sentence. Finding the main ideas will help students structure their summaries. Allow students to use a main idea/supporting details chart (TR, p. 319) to organize the information for their summaries.

Terms to Know

pasteurization a process by which milk or other liquids are heated to kill germs

vaccine a substance that protects against a disease by using weakened or killed germs

Main Ideas

A. Both opposing and supporting views existed on the issue of imperialism.

B. Imperialism influenced worldwide changes including progress in medicine, public health, education, and science and technology.

Active Reading

SUMMARIZE
A summary contains the most important points. As you read this section, stop after each part and think about what you have read. Then, summarize what you have learned.

A. Views of Imperialism

Imperialism was considered a right and an obligation by many American and European leaders in the late 1800s. It was widely believed that countries in Asia, Latin America, and Africa were in need of what "civilized" nations could provide.

Some visitors from the West were shocked by the differences among themselves and the peoples they encountered. It seemed to most European and American observers that the native peoples of the rest of the world needed to be helped. However, while there were many people who supported imperialism, many other people strongly opposed it. Both supporters and opponents of imperialism had strong arguments for their positions.

Opposing Imperialism

In the United States, imperialism became a hotly debated issue. Many Americans thought that the United States should not have an overseas empire. They believed that the United States should stay out of the affairs of other countries. One U.S. Senator, George F. Hoar, stated his objection to imperialism in the debate over acquiring the Philippines:

> **ANALYZE PRIMARY SOURCES**
> **DOCUMENT-BASED QUESTION** What effect did Senator Hoar think a colony would have on its colonizing country?

> 66 If a strong people try to govern a weak one against its will, the home government will get despotic [dictatorial], too. You cannot maintain despotism in Asia and a republic in America. 99

Supporting Imperialism

Until the late 1800s, the United States had not been involved much in foreign affairs. Instead, Americans were mostly interested in expanding within North America. Thousands of settlers helped the United States to expand westward as far as the Pacific Ocean.

However, by the late 1800s, the United States began to consider the benefits of expanding overseas. Some European nations had built large empires. Many Americans wanted the United States to build a large overseas empire as well. They argued that expansion would greatly encourage economic growth. American industry and agriculture were producing more goods than the American people were buying. These surplus, or extra, products could be sold abroad. Such economic benefits caused many Americans to take a positive view of imperialism.

Some people also believed it was the responsibility of the United States to colonize and impose its culture upon the people with whom it traded. These

602 UNIT 6 ◆ A Changing World

Teaching Options

Section 4 Resources

Teacher's Resources (TR)
Terms to Know, p. 38
Review History, p. 72
Build Your Skills, p. 106
Chapter Test, pp. 165–166
Concept Builder, p. 241
SQR Chart, p. 322

Connection to SCIENCE

Explain that today almost all young children receive a standard series of vaccines. Have students find out about these common vaccines by speaking to their family members or doctor, asking the school nurse, or searching in a reference book. Have them present their findings as a list entitled "Diseases for Which Vaccines Are Available."

Americans believed that imperialism served the noble purpose of benefiting the native peoples who lived in the places that were being colonized.

◆ **How could the United States benefit economically by expanding overseas?**

B. Progress Under Imperialism

Imperialism had many effects around the world. Some of the positive effects came from improvements in technology introduced by western nations. The imperialists brought with them better healthcare, new means of communication, and new political ideas.

Medicine

Important scientific discoveries led to major breakthroughs in medicine. Once scientists understood that germs caused disease, they could control the spread of a disease. Cleanliness became necessary for good health. Towns and cities helped by maintaining clean drinking water and using healthy ways to dispose of garbage.

In the mid-1800s, Louis Pasteur, a French chemist and biologist, proved the germ theory of disease. Once he knew what caused disease, he was able to develop the process of **pasteurization** for milk and other products. Pasteurization involves heating milk or other liquids to kill germs. Pasteur also developed **vaccines** for several diseases. A vaccine is made from weakened or killed germs that are given to people or animals to protect them from getting a particular disease.

Robert Koch, a German scientist, made the study of germs into a systematic science. To this day, scientists apply his rules for linking a germ with a disease. Other scientists used what they learned from Pasteur and Koch to develop vaccines for diseases. One vaccine reduced the number of people who died of diphtheria, a major cause of death in Europe and the United States. Another vaccine dramatically reduced the number of deaths from typhoid, a disease that was widespread.

Public Health

The mingling of people from Europe and other continents resulted in more disease. Smallpox, for example, wiped out entire cities and native peoples in Latin America. Europeans took home other diseases. Eventually, discoveries by European scientists helped doctors control the spread of disease. Western doctors used this knowledge to help native peoples in Latin America, Asia, and Africa.

In addition to sending doctors, western nations established hospitals in other countries. Western medical knowledge and technology saved lives and helped people live longer. The numbers of babies dying in their first year fell. People who received medical care benefited greatly. Unfortunately, many poor people did not receive medical care. Also, economic conditions sometimes caused starvation, crowded cities, and dangerous or unhealthy working conditions.

Modern western medicine also had some negative effects. It caused people to abandon the sometimes valuable medical knowledge of traditional herbalists and healers.

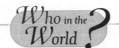

WHO in the World?

ROBERT KOCH
Robert Koch identified the germ that causes tuberculosis. He then traveled to other continents to find the causes of other deadly diseases. By 1883, cholera had become a widespread disease in India. Koch identified the germ that caused the disease. He further determined that the germ was spread to human beings through polluted water.

Later, Koch went to Africa. There he studied the causes of diseases carried by insects.

Louis Pasteur developed vaccines against anthrax and rabies.

A. Views of Imperialism

Purpose-Setting Question Why did some Europeans and Americans believe that colonizing other nations was a good thing? (They believed that expansion would encourage economic growth and that native peoples of the rest of the world needed to be helped.)

ANALYZE PRIMARY SOURCES

DOCUMENT-BASED QUESTION
Senator Hoar broke with his party to oppose maintaining troops in the Philippines. He felt that the U.S. presence in the Philippines would turn a friendly nation against the United States.

ANSWER He thought that controlling a colony would make the mother country unjust.

Discuss Reread Senator Hoar's opinion about imperialism and ask students if they believe Hoar is correct. Can one country be true to its founding principles while occupying another nation? Have students give their reasons.

◆ **ANSWER** The United States could expand its trade networks and sell more goods.

B. Progress Under Imperialism

Purpose-Setting Question What do you think life was like before vaccination and pasteurization? (Health suffered; people died at earlier ages.)

WHO IN THE WORLD?

ROBERT KOCH Point out to students that vaccines virtually wiped out many devastating diseases. However, today, other devastating diseases defy modern medicine. Have students identify modern diseases and discuss how scientists are working toward their eradication.

Activity

Write a speech Have students write speeches that might be given at a ceremony to honor either Louis Pasteur or Robert Koch. Speeches should explain how the scientist's work has had an impact on the world.

Focus on SPORTS & GAMES

Judo and Sumo During the age of imperialism, Europeans suppressed many traditional sports in the nations that they colonized. They also introduced sports of their own. However, in Japan, the two sports judo and sumo remained popular. The age of imperialism brought professionalism to athletics, making it possible for sumo wrestlers to make their living at the sport. Japanese judo took on its modern form in the late nineteenth century. It has become so popular that it is now included in the Olympic Games.

Have students choose one of these two sports to research. Ask them to work as a group to create a "sports page," including the rules of the game, a brief history of the sport, a profile of a successful player, and an account of a famous match. Have students copy and distribute their pages.

Discuss Have the class discuss the pros and cons of imperialism. Do students think that the areas colonized by western nations were better off or worse off than they had been before colonization? (Possible answers: They were better off because of education, technology, and public health. They were worse off because Europeans forced their ideas on them and caused them to lose their traditional ways.)

Explore Have students choose one country that was colonized by a European nation in the 1800s and research its history since colonization. Once students have gathered enough information, allow them to share with the class.

◆ **ANSWER** Contact with Europeans harmed the health of others by exposing them to new diseases such as smallpox. Also, the introduction of western medicine caused the knowledge of many traditional herbalists and healers to be forgotten. Contact with Europeans helped the health of others through new treatments for disease, the establishment of hospitals, and improved standard of living.

Section Close

Have the class summarize the changes in medicine, public health, science and technology, and education that occurred under imperialism.

Assess

Review Answers

Review History
A. Many Americans opposed imperialism because they thought the United States should not be involved in the affairs of other countries.

B. Possible answer: Imperialism brought improvements in health, medicine, and sanitation.

Define Terms to Know
pasteurization, 603; vaccine, 603

Critical Thinking
Possible answer: Many Americans strongly supported the independence of all people—not just in the United States but around the world. Other Americans strongly supported the economic opportunities of overseas expansion.

This illustration shows a Japanese silk factory in the 1800s.

Science and Technology

Western nations took their own technology to the countries they controlled or colonized. They built roads and established a network of railroads. Foreign investors poured money into the colonies to establish communications networks. Ports were modernized. Industries were developed that were as efficient and productive as those in the home countries.

Many people were eager for western technology. Sewers and water systems added to the quality of life. People in the right locations with enough money improved their standards of living with western technology and conveniences.

Education

European nations soon realized that they could not attract enough fellow Europeans to handle all the jobs that had to be done in their colonies. The new economies in the colonies required office workers, postal clerks, and other workers. These workers had to speak the language of their governing nation, and they had to have a basic western education. European schools taught promising students in the colonies. These students graduated to become part of the workforce. They were usually better paid than the rest of the population, but they did not receive pay equal to that of Europeans.

◆ **How did contact with Europeans both harm and help the health of people on other continents?**

Review IV

Review History
A. Why did many Americans oppose imperialism?
B. What benefits did imperialism bring to Latin American and Asian countries?

Define Terms to Know
Define the following terms:
pasteurization, vaccine

Critical Thinking
Why do you think that imperialism was such a hotly debated issue in the United States?

Write About Economics
Write an editorial from the early 1900s explaining why you think imperialism is economically beneficial to a country. Support your opinion with facts from this section or other sections.

Get Organized
SQR CHART
Use an SQR chart to organize information from this section. For example, you might survey this section to find a topic such as progress of medicine under imperialism.

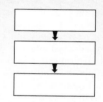

Write About Economics
Students' editorials should state the point of view and justify the position with facts from the chapter. Check that students maintain the same position throughout their editorial.

SURVEY
This section is about the progress of medicine under imperialism.

QUESTION
How did western medicine improve the health of people in colonies and former colonies?

READ
Pasteurization and vaccination eradicated diseases and led to improved health.

Points *of* View

United States and Imperialism

As a result of the Spanish-American War, the United States suddenly gained an overseas empire. This empire included Puerto Rico, Guam, and the Philippines—islands in the Caribbean Sea and the Pacific Ocean. Additionally, Cuba was partially controlled by the United States while Hawaii had been annexed in the same year that the war was fought.

Americans continued to debate whether the country should pursue a course of imperialism by expanding overseas or stay out of the affairs of other countries. Supporters of imperialism argued that the United States had a responsibility to bring law, good government, and American culture to the peoples in the Caribbean and the Pacific. Americans who opposed an overseas empire argued that imperialism was against the American ideals of liberty and democracy.

Below are two cartoons that illustrate the American debate about imperialism. Both cartoons use the image of Uncle Sam to represent the United States. The cartoon on the left focuses on the U.S. acquisition of a new overseas empire during the early 1900s. The cartoon on the right shows the intervention of U.S. forces in Veracruz, Mexico, in 1914.

This photograph of a globe shows the Western Hemisphere.

U.S. President William McKinley is shown as a tailor measuring a bloated Uncle Sam.

Uncle Sam intervenes in Veracruz, Mexico.

ANALYZE PRIMARY SOURCES

DOCUMENT-BASED QUESTIONS

1. In the cartoon on the left, why do you think William McKinley is portrayed as a tailor?

2. Do you think the cartoon on the right supports imperialism? Why or why not?

3. **Critical Thinking** How do you think each of the cartoonists views imperialism? Explain.

Points *of* View

UNITED STATES AND IMPERIALISM

Teach the Topic

The Spanish-American War forced Americans to debate the issue of imperialism. They did so in many forums, including newspapers, which reported on the war at length. The newspapers also offered political cartoons to illustrate their points of view.

Ask students whether they would be influenced if they saw the political cartoons shown on the page when they were first published. Would either one have changed their mind about imperialism? (Answers will vary, but most students, like most readers, might have made up their minds to some extent on an issue as controversial as imperialism.)

Compare and Contrast Points of View

Some reports on the Spanish-American War were considered biased and were termed "yellow journalism," for it was felt that the information they contained were purposely slanted in order to get readers to support imperialism. To this day, there is debate about political slants in the news media. How accurate is the news? Is there such a thing as an unbiased report? Students should look at the political cartoons and ask themselves if either political cartoon could have been entirely accurate.

ANALYZE PRIMARY SOURCES

DOCUMENT-BASED QUESTIONS

1. William McKinley supports imperialism, so he is helping Uncle Sam fit into new, larger clothes as the United States expands overseas.

2. It supports imperialism because it shows Uncle Sam bringing food, cleaning supplies, and law and order to Mexico.

3. The first cartoon shows a bloated, unhealthy Uncle Sam, whereas the second cartoon shows him as strong and lean. The first cartoonist opposes imperialism, presenting it as unhealthy. The second cartoonist supports imperialism, presenting it as helping other countries.

Teaching Options

Take a Stand

Have students draw a political cartoon for a newspaper around 1900 that either supports imperialism or criticizes it. Point out that the way in which the cartoon is illustrated—the technique, the vantage point, and so on—will make an impression on the "reader" as it does in the two cartoons on this page. Have students post their cartoons on either a "pro" imperialism or "anti" imperialism poster.

LINK to TODAY

Ask students to read newspapers or newsmagazines for political cartoons that they feel make a strong case for or against an issue. Have them bring them in and share the cartoons with the class. Ask students what they can learn from the cartoons about an issue. Have the class identify cartoons that they feel might sway readers either away from or toward a point of view.

Chapter Summary

A blank outline form is available in the Teacher's Resources (p. 318). Chapter summaries should outline the effects of imperialism in China; the end of isolationism in Japan; the economic imperialism in Latin America; and the cultural, political and scientific impact of imperialism throughout the world. Refer to the rubric in the Teacher's Resources (p. 340) to score the students' chapter summaries.

⬤ Interpret the Timeline

1. the Opium War
2. 16 years
3. Napoleon's installation of Maximilian as emperor of Mexico
4. Check students' timelines to be sure all events are in the chapter.

Use Terms to Know

5. vaccine
6. isthmus
7. pasteurization
8. extraterritoriality
9. consul
10. mediator

Check Your Understanding

11. Accept any two: Foreigners could only trade in one city, only through the city's merchant guild, were restricted to one section of the city, and could only be in China while actively conducting business.
12. Great Britain and China
13. Matthew Perry and the U.S. President wanted better treatment of shipwrecked crew members, for Japan to sell needed supplies to passing ships, and for Japan to trade with the United States.
14. In the early 1800s, Japan insisted on isolation and banned foreigners from its land. By the early 1900s, Japan had made use of western technology and knowledge and sought trade and new territory. It went from resisting imperialism to becoming imperialist itself.
15. As a result of the Spanish-American War Cuba was left under temporary U.S. occupation; Guam, Puerto Rico, and the Philippines became U.S. possessions.

Chapter Summary

Complete the following outline in your notebook. Then, use your outline to write a brief summary of the chapter.

Imperialism in Asia and Latin America

I. China Reacts to Western Influences
   A. European Influence and Conflicts in China
   B. Toward Revolution in China
II. Japan Modernizes
   A. Challenges by Western Imperial Powers
   B. Restoring Power to Japan
   C. Japanese Foreign Policy
III. Economic Imperialism in Latin America
   A. Foreigners in Latin America
   B. U.S. Imperialism in Latin America
   C. Reform and Change in Mexico
IV. Worldwide Effects of Imperialism
   A. Views of Imperialism
   B. Progress Under Imperialism

⬤ Interpret the Timeline

Use the timeline on pages 584–585 to answer the following questions.

1. Which event occurred first, the Russo-Japanese War or the Opium War?
2. How many years after the Spanish-American War was fought did Venustiano Carranza seize power in Mexico?
3. **Critical Thinking** What event shows a European power forcing a monarchy on a Latin American country?
4. Select five events from the chapter that are not on the timeline. Create a timeline that shows these events.

Use Terms to Know

Select the term that best completes each sentence.

consul   isthmus   pasteurization
extraterritoriality   mediator   vaccine

5. Doctors used a _____ to protect people from typhoid.
6. The _____ of Panama is a narrow strip of land bordered on both sides by water between two large masses of land.
7. Without _____, milk and other products would contain more germs.
8. An agreement that allows citizens of one country who live in another country to be governed by the laws of their own land is called _____.
9. A government official who lives and works in another country is called a _____.
10. A person who settles differences between people and nations is called a _____.

Check Your Understanding

11. **Describe** two ways China restricted foreign trade before the mid-1800s.
12. **Identify** the two countries involved in the first Opium War.
13. **Explain** what Matthew Perry and the U.S. President asked of Japan.
14. **Contrast** Japan's foreign policy in the early 1800s with its foreign policy during the late 1800s and early 1900s.
15. **Discuss** two outcomes of the Spanish-American War.
16. **Discuss** the reason the United States supported Panama's declaration of independence.
17. **Identify** two famous rebels in the Mexican Revolution.
18. **Explain** how European expansion overseas favorably affected many Americans' opinions about imperialism.
19. **Describe** two important scientific discoveries made in the mid-1800s.

16. Panamanians wanted the United States to build a canal, and Colombia would not permit it. If Panama was independent, the United States would be able to build a canal.
17. Pancho Villa and Emiliano Zapata
18. Many Americans wanted the United States to build large empires overseas like some European nations had built to encourage economic growth. These Americans favored imperialism because they saw the benefits imperialism brought to these European nations.
19. pasteurization and vaccines

Critical Thinking

20. **Make Inferences** How do you think Great Britain would have reacted if Chinese traders had sold large quantities of opium in Great Britain?

21. **Analyze Primary Sources** Do you think seeking knowledge throughout the world strengthened the foundations of imperial rule in Japan as stated in the quotation on page 593? Why or why not?

22. **Compare and Contrast** Compare and contrast the imperialism the United States displayed in the Spanish-American War and in supporting Panama's revolt.

23. **Analyze Primary Sources** According to the quotation on page 602, how do you think Senator Hoar would have voted on U.S. intervention in another country?

Put Your Skills to Work

24. **Predict Consequences** You have learned how to predict consequences and verify your predictions. Make the following prediction. Use the chart below to help organize data for your prediction. Then, review your prediction with classmates.

Predict what happened after Spain gave the Philippines to the United States. Explain your prediction. Verify your prediction using reference and Internet sources.

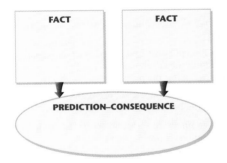

Analyze Sources

25. Japanese author Fukuzawa Yukichi, the son of a samurai, wrote about his father taking him to school. Read the passage. Then, answer the questions that follow.

The teacher lived in the compound of the lord's storage office, but, having some merchants' children among his pupils, he naturally began to train them in numerals. "Two times two is four, two times three is six etc." This today seems a very ordinary thing to teach, but when my father heard this, he took his children away in a fury [wild rage]. "It is abominable [very bad]," he exclaimed, "that innocent children should be taught to use numbers—the tool of merchants. There is no telling what the teacher may do next."

a. What does the author's father think about merchants? Explain.

b. What would you say to the father about how mathematics might help an ordinary person in daily life?

Essay Writing

26. Write an essay discussing Japan's relationship with the outside world during the Meiji period from 1868 to 1912.

TEST PREPARATION

COMPARING AND CONTRASTING IDEAS
Choose the answer that correctly completes the sentence.

The foreign trade policies of China and Japan were similar in that they both

1. looked for trade during the early 1900s.

2. restricted trade during the early 1800s.

3. enjoyed a favorable balance of trade after 1850.

4. suffered an unfavorable balance of trade after 1900.

Critical Thinking

20. Accept supported opinions. Most students would expect Great Britain to take violent offense.
21. Based on Japan's industrial, economic, and military successes, the answer would be yes.
22. In both, the United States supported a revolt for independence. In the Spanish-American War, the United States intervened on behalf of an American colony that wanted independence from a European power, to protect its established sugar interests, and in retaliation for an assumed attack on its boat. Panama's conflict was an internal revolt against a Latin American power, and the United States was after a canal treaty.
23. Possible answer: Senator Hoar's objections about being involved in another country seem to be a comment against intervention in general, so he would probably not support intervention in any country.

Put Your Skills to Work

PREDICT CONSEQUENCES
24. Predictions need not be historically accurate. The explanations should explain how they follow from known facts.

Analyze Sources

25a. The author's father thinks that merchants are lowly and beneath him and his children.
25b. Accept any useful life application of math, such as figuring out prices of purchases and change, making a budget, calculating time and distance, and so on.

Essay Writing

26. Essays should refer to seeking western knowledge and technology, industrialization, increasing economic interdependence, and aggressive imperialism.

TEST PREPARATION

Answer **2.** restricted trade during the early 1800s.

Unit 6

Portfolio Project

BOOK OF LETTERS AND JOURNAL ENTRIES

Managing the Project

Plan for 4–5 class periods.

Set the Scene

Ask students to identify the major contribution to society that each person on the list is known for. List the contributions on the board.

Your Assignment

Ask students to read the assignment on page 608. Then, divide the class into groups of three to four students to begin work. You may wish to have students form groups based on the historical person they want to research or have groups select an individual after the group is formed. Have each group focus on only one name from the list.

RESEARCH A PERSON'S LIFE

Explain that students should write an entry from the point of view of the historical figure. After some preliminary research, students may wish to focus their book of letters or journal entries on one particular period of the figure's life. Encourage groups to have every group member write one entry in the book. Students should review all the letters to revise, edit, and proofread one another's work.

COMPILE A COLLECTION

You may wish to provide a model of a collection of journal entries, an introduction, and a conclusion for students to refer to as they compile their own collections.

Wrap Up

Allow some class time for students to review the collections of other groups. Have students share the information that is new to them.

Book of Letters and Journal Entries

YOUR ASSIGNMENT

One of the most exciting things about studying history is learning about the people who have made a difference in the past. One way we learn about such personalities in history is through historical documents such as letters, speeches, diaries, and journal entries.

RESEARCH A PERSON'S LIFE

Choose a Historical Figure As a group, choose one person from this unit to learn about in depth. For example, you might choose one of the following people.

Otto von Bismarck	Commodore Matthew Perry
Thomas Edison	Theodore Roosevelt
Robert Fulton	Suleiman II
Mohandas K. Gandhi	Sun Yat-sen
Giuseppe Garibaldi	Ida Tarbell

Brainstorm As a group, brainstorm how the person you have chosen might have affected the history of the time period, a particular place in the world, and different people. For example, Thomas Edison changed the way people lived in North America and Europe in the 1800s with the invention of the incandescent electric light bulb.

Research Group members should research the person's life to learn more about the impact this person had on history. Use your textbook, library resources, and the Internet to conduct research. Record and organize the information from your research on notecards.

Write Have each group member use the research to write either a journal entry or letter from the point of view of the historical person. Remind members to write about how the person impacted history, including people and places.

COMPILE A COLLECTION

Plan Meet and read each other's journal entries and letters. Decide on a logical order. Publish them as a small book. One member of the group can bind the book. Another can design the cover. Another can write an introduction and conclusion, explaining the purpose of the collection.

Present Exchange books with another group. Read the books of all the groups in your class. Then, put the books in the classroom library.

Write Individually Write a brief summary of each book you read. Think about how different people in history affected world events.

Multimedia Presentation

Turn your journal entries into a documentary. Assume people from the past can be interviewed about their experiences. Present the journal entries orally as part of a television documentary about world events during the 1800s and early 1900s.

Teaching Options

Multimedia Presentation

Remind students that documentaries are made up of many aspects of a person's life. For example, a documentary might include a demonstration of a scientific experiment, a tour of a home, or the re-enactment of a battle. Encourage students to be creative about how they present their historical figure.

Alternative Assessment

Make a Brochure Tell students that they have been hired to prepare a brochure to be handed out to the people of a newly independent colonial nation. The brochure should include information about how the new nation should take control of its military, religious organizations, government, and trading policies. Students may want to use computer software to create their brochures.

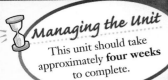

Managing the Unit
This unit should take approximately **four weeks** to complete.

Unit 7 DECADES OF WAR

PLANNING GUIDE

	Skills and Features	Projects and Activities	Program Resources	Meet Individual Needs
Chapter 26 **World War I and the Russian Revolutions,** pp. 610–635 **Plan for 5–6 class periods.**	Unit Technology, p. T609 Interpret Statistics, p. 617 Connect History & Technology, p. 623 They Made History: Czar Nicholas II, p. 631	Using Technology, pp. T613, T619 Conflict Resolution, p. T613 Writing, p. T615 Cooperative Learning, p. T619 Sports & Games, p. T620 Connection to Science, p. T621 Link to Today, p. T623 Test Taking, p. T625 Research, p. T626 Connection to Economics, p. T627 Connection to Geography, p. T631 Connection to Literature, p. T632	**Teacher's Resources** Terms to Know, p. 39 Review History, p. 73 Build Your Skills, p. 107 Chapter Test, pp. 167–168 Concept Builder, p. 242 They Made History: Woodrow Wilson, p. 264 SQR Chart, p. 322 Transparencies 1, 5	ESL/ELL Strategies, pp. T612, T621, T624, T630, T632 Visual/Spatial, pp. T614, T618 Kinesthetic, p. T628 Auditory, p. T631
Chapter 27 **Crises Around the World,** pp. 636–659 **Plan for 4–5 class periods.**	Interpret a Line Graph, p. 643 Points of View, p. 653	Conflict Resolution, pp. T638, T650 World Religions, p. T639 Connection to Science, p. T640 Connection to Economics, p. T645 Using Technology, p. T646 Test Taking, p. T649 Research, p. T651 Take a Stand, p. T653 Link to Today, p. T653 Writing, p. T656	**Teacher's Resources** Terms to Know, p. 40 Review History, p. 74 Build Your Skills, p. 108 Chapter Test, pp. 169–170 Concept Builder, p. 243 They Made History: Leon Trotsky, p. 265 Idea Web, p. 321 Transparencies 5, 7	ESL/ELL Strategies, pp. T640, T646, T650, T655 Visual/Spatial, p. T641 Auditory, p. T655
Chapter 28 **World War II,** pp. 660–684 **Plan for 9–10 class periods.**	Recognize Propaganda and Bias, p. 667 Past to Present: Wartime Spies to Modern Agents, pp. 676–677	Research, p. T664 Conflict Resolution, p. T665 Teen Life, p. T670 Writing, p. T673 Cooperative Learning, p. T674 Connection to Culture, p. T674 Connection to Literature, p. T676 Connection to Music, p. T678 Test Taking, p. T680	**Teacher's Resources** Terms to Know, p. 41 Review History, p. 75 Build Your Skills, p. 109 Chapter Test, pp. 171–172 Unit 7 Test, pp 195–196 Concept Builder, p. 244 Cause-and-Effect Chain, p. 325 Transparencies 2, 8	ESL/ELL Strategies, pp. T663, T668, T672, T679 Verbal/Linguistic, p. T680

Assessment Options

Chapter 26 Test, Teacher's Resources, pp. 167–168
Chapter 27 Test, Teacher's Resources, pp. 169–170
Chapter 28 Test, Teacher's Resources, pp. 171–172
Unit 7 Test, Teacher's Resources, pp. 195–196

Alternative Assessment

History Quiz Show, p. 684
Create a Bulletin Board Display, p. T684

Books for Students

AVERAGE

Eleanor's Story: An American Girl in Hitler's Germany.
Eleanor Ramrath Garner. Autobiography of an American teen who leaves the United States for Berlin, Germany, and ends up in World War II. (Peachtree Publishers, Ltd., 1999)

Navajo Code Talkers. Nathan Aaseng. Describes how Navajo Marines used their native language to create a secret code during World War II. (Walker & Co. 2002)

I Am Fifteen: And I Don't Want to Die. Christine Arnothy. Autobiography of a teenager living in Budapest during World War II and of her surviving the war. (Point, 1990)

The Girl With the White Flag. Tomiko Higa. Autobiographical account of a seven-year-old's survival on a World War II battlefield in Okinawa, Japan. (Kodansha International (JPN), 2003)

CHALLENGING

A People's Tragedy: The Russian Revolution, 1891–1924.
Orlando Figes. Looks at the events of the revolution from the perspective of the people involved. (Penguin Putnam Inc., 1998)

The Seamstress: A Memoir of Survival. Sara Tuvel Bernstein, Louise Toots Thornton, and Marlene Bernstein Samuels. Memoir about a Romanian Jew who survived the Holocaust. (Berkley Publishing Group, 1999)

Lusitania: An Epic Tragedy. Diana Preston. Describes the *Lusitania* incident and its effects on the world, with some new insights into the event. (Walker & Company, 2002)

Books for Teachers

Great Poets of World War I: Poetry from the Great War. Jon Stallworthy. Explores the lives and works of 12 poets who wrote during the war. (Carroll & Graf Publishers, 2002)

The Shadows of Total War: Europe, East Asia, and the United States, 1919–1939. Roger Chickering and Stig Forster, editors. Collection of essays that explores this period. (Cambridge University Press, 2003)

Gandhi: His Life and Message. Louis Fischer. A biography of the life of Gandhi. (New American Library, 1982)

Tuxedo Park: A Wall Street Tycoon and the Secret Palace of Science That Changed the Course of World War II. Jennet Conant. A biography of Alfred Loomis, who provided a laboratory and financing for research into radar systems and nuclear weapons. (Simon & Schuster, Inc., 2003)

The Nuremberg War Crimes Trial, 1945–1946: A Documentary History. Michael R. Marrus. Primary sources are used to review the trial. (Bedford/St. Martin's, 1999)

Liaison 1914. Edward Spears. A British officer recounts the beginning events of World War I. (Cassell, 2001)

You may wish to preview all referenced materials to ensure their appropriateness for your local community.

Audio/Visual Resources

The End of the Old Order: 1900–1929. Explores the end of World War I, the Russian Revolution, and the effects of Fascism. Videocassette. (Social Studies School Service)

The World in Conflict: 1929–1945. Discusses the Great Depression, Hitler, Mussolini, and three political philosophies. Videocassette. (Social Studies School Service)

Dear Home: Letters from the World Wars. History is told through letters from soldiers to their loved ones. Videocassette. (CLEARVUE/eav)

The Battle for Midway. Discusses this battle and shows the underwater search for a lost aircraft carrier. DVD. (National Geographic Society)

Technology Resources

First World War: www.firstworldwar.com

New Deal Network: The Great Depression of the 1930s: http://newdeal.feri.org

Anne Frank House: www.annefrank.nl/ned/default2.html

A More Perfect Union: Japanese Americans and the U. S. Constitution: http://americanhistory.si.edu/perfectunion

Globe Fearon Related Resources

History Resources

The Regional Studies: Japan and Korea. Overview of geography, history, culture, government, economy, and relations of Japan and Korea. ISBN 0-835-90430-X

Historical Case Studies: The Holocaust. Primary sources are used to study the cultural, economic, and political effects of the Holocaust. ISBN 0-835-91826-2

Multicultural Milestones in United States History, Volume 2, from 1900. Addresses the role of women in World War I. ISBN 0-835-91113-6

Globe Mosaic of American History: Women in the U.S. Work Force: 1876–1914. Primary sources give a multicultural perspective and information. ISBN 0-835-90621-3

Adapted Classics

All Quiet on the Western Front. Erich Maria Remarque's story about a young man's years in the German army during World War I. ISBN 0-835-91869-6

The Grapes of Wrath. John Steinbeck's novel about a family forced to move to California during a drought in the 1930s. ISBN 0-835-91885-8

Anne Frank: The Diary of a Young Girl. A Jewish teenager writes about her life during World War II. ISBN 0-835-90235-8

To order books, call 1-800-321-3106.

Decades of War

"Older men declare war. But it is youth who must fight and die. And it is youth who must inherit the tribulation, the sorrow, and the triumphs that are the aftermath of war."

—Herbert C. Hoover, former U.S. President, 1944

LINKING CULTURES Two world wars dominated the first half of the twentieth century. This photograph of American soldiers fighting in 1918 during World War I shows the devastation and human costs of war. Although wars represent the greatest failure in human relations, the sacrifices of those who fight and support such wars often mean freedom for others.

What ideas do the quotation and the photograph suggest to you about the ultimate sacrifices and benefits of war?

609

Teaching Options

UNIT TECHNOLOGY

Have students use the Internet, CD-ROM resources, and other media to find other positive and negative quotations about war during different periods of history. Students might also look online for additional photographs or paintings of war scenes to illustrate their quotations.

You may wish to identify possible Web sites for students and, as always, monitor their activities on the Internet.

UNIT 7 Portfolio Project

History Quiz Show

The Portfolio Project for Unit 7 on page 684 is to develop a quiz show based on Chapters 26–28. Teams of students will prepare and answer questions on people, places, conflicts, treaties, and quotations. The class will then participate in the show. As an additional activity, students can videotape their show to share with others.

Decades of War
(pp. 609–684)

Unit Summary
Unit 7 focuses on World War I and World War II and the feelings of unrest that settled over much of the world in the period between these two major wars, during which totalitarian governments and fascist dictatorships rose to power in several European and Asian countries.

CHAPTER 26
> World War I and the Russian Revolutions

CHAPTER 27
> Crises Around the World

CHAPTER 28
> World War II

Set the Stage
TEACH PRIMARY SOURCES
Photo The photograph on this page shows American soldiers fighting in the Argonne forest in France in September–November 1918. Explain that this fighting had both a positive and a negative side. **Positive:** The Allied powers finally broke through the German lines, leading to the end of the war; **Negative:** About 256,000 Americans were killed or injured in this battle and the second Battle of the Marne. Ask students to describe details they see in the photograph. (machine gun, burnt trees, soldiers with war gear)

Quote Herbert Hoover, the thirty-first U.S. President, served between the two world wars but delivered these remarks while U.S. troops were fighting in World War II. Ask students what words in the quotation reflect a positive side to war (*triumphs*) and a negative side (*sorrow*). Ask students who are the "older men" that Hoover mentions. (national leaders, diplomats, generals)

◆ **ANSWER** Sacrifices might include loss of life; destruction of the environment; and loss of comfort, security, and family. Benefits might include providing freedom for oppressed peoples, taking over corrupt governments, or assuring a better way of life.

World War I and the Russian Revolutions
1914–1920
(pp. 610–635)

Chapter Objectives
• Examine the national interests, alliances, and events that led to World War I.
• Describe the strategies and technology involved in fighting the war and the losses sustained by the countries on each side.
• Discuss the efforts to restore peace in Europe after the war while punishing the losing side.
• Explain how and why Russia endured two revolutions and a civil war during and following World War I.

Chapter Summary
Section I explores how European countries created alliances that maintained a shaky balance of power until a political assassination led to the outbreak of war.
Section II explains how new methods of fighting and modern technology resulted in a drawn-out conflict with heavy losses until the United States entered the war.
Section III focuses on the heavy toll of the war in lives lost and property damaged, and how world leaders went through a difficult process working out peace terms.
Section IV explores how long-time political unrest in Russia was increased by the war, leading to two revolutions and a civil war.

Set the Stage
TEACH PRIMARY SOURCES
Explain that W. B. Yeats was a poet, playwright, and political activist. His writing often reflected a pessimistic view of Ireland's struggle to become independent of Great Britain and of other European countries to emerge successfully from war. Ask students how a war might lead to a "blood-dimmed tide" that drowns innocence.

CHAPTER 26

World War I and the Russian Revolutions
1914–1920

I. Factors Leading to War
II. The War Is Fought
III. Peace in a New Europe
IV. The Russian Revolutions

World War I, the global conflict also known as the Great War, brought about dramatic shifts in power. The war shed the blood of a generation of youth, destroyed an enormous number of resources, and brought about the downfall of great empires. It allowed communism to grow in Russia and thrust the United States onto the world stage.

The Irish poet W. B. Yeats, who won the Nobel Prize in literature in 1923, wrote a poem called "The Second Coming." In it, he views the horrors unleashed by war.

> *Things fall apart; the centre cannot hold;*
> *Mere anarchy [political disorder] is loosed upon the world,*
> *The blood-dimmed tide is loosed, and everywhere*
> *The ceremony of innocence is drowned.*

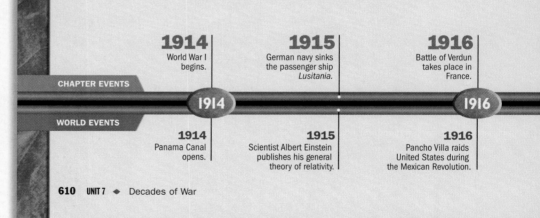

CHAPTER EVENTS

1914
World War I begins.

1915
German navy sinks the passenger ship *Lusitania.*

1916
Battle of Verdun takes place in France.

1914

1916

WORLD EVENTS

1914
Panama Canal opens.

1915
Scientist Albert Einstein publishes his general theory of relativity.

1916
Pancho Villa raids United States during the Mexican Revolution.

610   UNIT 7   ◆   Decades of War

Teaching Options

Chapter 26 Resources

REVIEW

Teacher's Resources (TR)
Terms to Know, p. 39
Review History, p. 73
Build Your Skills, p. 107
Chapter Test, pp. 167–168
Concept Builder, p. 242
SQR Chart, p. 322
Transparencies 1, 5

ASSESSMENT
Section Reviews, pp. 616, 622, 629, 633
Chapter Review, pp. 634–635
Chapter Test, TR, pp. 167–168

ALTERNATIVE ASSESSMENT
Portfolio Project, p. 684
Create a Bulletin Board Display, p. T684

The United States, Europe, and Russia, 1918

VIEW HISTORY During the fighting in the French town of Verdun in 1916, French soldiers stopped German troops from advancing.
◆ How does the painting show the drama of the fighting during World War I?

GET ORGANIZED

SQR Chart An SQR chart helps you better understand what you read by following three steps. First, survey the section to determine what it is about. Next, ask a question about the topic or topics in the section. Then, read the section to find the answer to your question. Use an SQR chart as you read Chapter 26. Here is an example from this chapter.

SURVEY
This section is about factors that led to World War I.

⬇

QUESTION
What were the factors that led to the war?

⬇

READ
Nationalism, imperialism, militarism, alliance system

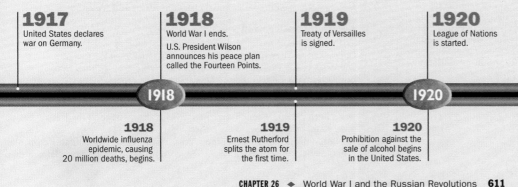

1917
United States declares war on Germany.

1918
World War I ends.
U.S. President Wilson announces his peace plan called the Fourteen Points.

1919
Treaty of Versailles is signed.

1920
League of Nations is started.

1918

1920

1918
Worldwide influenza epidemic, causing 20 million deaths, begins.

1919
Ernest Rutherford splits the atom for the first time.

1920
Prohibition against the sale of alcohol begins in the United States.

CHAPTER 26 ◆ World War I and the Russian Revolutions **611**

Chapter Themes
- Civic Ideals and Practices
- People, Places, and Environments
- Power, Authority, and Governance
- Individuals, Groups, and Institutions
- Time, Continuity, and Change
- Science, Technology, and Society
- Global Connections

F Y I

Verdun
The prolonged fighting between the French and Germans near Verdun was the bloodiest in the war up to that time. During the fighting, the Germans unveiled a new type of poison gas against which French gas masks could not provide protection. To inspire the troops, a French general issued a special order, "Ils ne passeront pas!" (They shall not pass!) that became a French rallying cry throughout World War I.

Chapter Warm-Up
USING THE MAP
Ask students which continents are included in the highlighted boxes on the locator map on page 611. (North America, Europe, Asia, and northern Africa) Explain that countries on four continents were involved in World War I.

VIEW HISTORY
Have students compare and contrast the painting on this page with the photograph on page 609. Discuss how both show a harsh view of war. (Both images focus on survival, death, and destruction.)

◆ **ANSWER** Possible answer: The painting reflects the intensity of soldiers' fighting and the damage being inflicted. Also, the snowy conditions shown in the image remind the viewer of soldiers' misery in war.

GET ORGANIZED
SQR Chart
Review the steps of an SQR Chart with students. *Survey* includes scanning the titles and headings of a section to find out the main idea. *Question* includes writing questions about the information before reading. *Read* involves reading the text and locating answers to questions. Review the SQR chart on this page as an example.

⬤ TEACH THE TIMELINE
The timeline on pages 610–611 covers the 6-year period from the beginning of World War I until the formation of the League of Nations that was supposed to prevent future wars. Ask students what World Events on the timeline reflect important technological advances. (opening of Panama Canal, publishing the theory of relativity, and splitting the atom) Explain that splitting the atom will have both positive and negative effects in the future. (nuclear power and nuclear weapons)

Activity

Research Have students use library resources or the Internet to find out more about the influenza epidemic noted on the timeline. Which countries of the world suffered the most losses? After students read the chapter, have them compare flu-related losses to war-related losses.

I. Factors Leading to War

(pp. 612–616)

Section Summary

In this section, students will learn how conflicting national interests led to a buildup of tensions in Europe, how countries formed alliances to achieve a fragile balance of power, and how the assassination of the Austrian archduke touched off the outbreak of war.

1 Introduce

Getting Started

Write the words *ally* and *alliance* on the board. Discuss how the words are related. (An *ally* is a friend or partner; *alliance* is a partnership or league in which members agree to support each other.) Point out that fulfilling obligations to alliance members was an important factor leading to World War I.

TERMS TO KNOW

Ask students to read the terms and definitions on page 612 and then find each term in the section. Suggest that students write each term and its meaning on a separate index card. They can later organize all of the new terms they encounter in this unit to form a personal dictionary of modern political terms.

You may wish to preview the pronunciation of the following terms from this section with students.

Alsace (ahl ZAS)
Pan-Slavism (PAN SLAHV ihz uhm)
Herzegovina (hert suh GOH vee nuh)
Sarajevo (sah rah YAY voh)
Gavrilo Princip
  (GAHV ree law PREENT seep)

ACTIVE READING

As students read this section, have them list all of the events they encounter and their causes and effects. For example, the Armenian revolt against the Ottoman Empire was caused by the sultan's raising taxes and Russia's support of Armenian revolutionaries. The effect was the killing of more than 50,000 Armenians. You may wish to distribute cause-and-effect chains (TR, p. 325) to students.

Section I

Factors Leading to War

Terms to Know

mobilize to assemble and be ready to move, as for war

entente an agreement between countries to follow common policies

ultimatum a final demand made with a threat to break off dealings or use force if not accepted

Global Connections

OLYMPIC GAMES
The first Olympic Games of modern times (the games began in 1896) reflected the nationalistic feelings of Europe. The games were planned as a peaceful competition between nations; but in reality, they encouraged national rivalry. They also promoted the military qualities of loyalty, strength, and fitness.

Main Ideas

A. Conflicting national interests led to a buildup of tensions in Europe.

B. European countries tried to find a balance of power by forming alliances with one another.

C. The assassination of Austrian Archduke Franz Ferdinand and his wife Sophie led to the outbreak of World War I.

Active Reading

CAUSE AND EFFECT
To understand why something happened, look for causes and their effects. As you read this section, ask yourself what caused countries to form alliances, and what effect the alliances had on contributing to tensions in Europe.

A. Europe on the Eve of War

One of the most influential military leaders in Europe at the start of the twentieth century was Alfred von Schlieffen, chief of the German great general staff between 1891 and 1905. As he lay dying, Schlieffen uttered the following words, "It must come to a fight." Schlieffen was predicting that the situation in Europe would end in war.

Conflicting National Interests

The second half of the nineteenth century had been a time of tremendous change in Europe. The last three decades were relatively peaceful. This period of peace allowed the European countries to focus on building their economies as the Industrial Revolution took hold. An increase in population followed better healthcare and nutrition. Social conditions improved.

National interests led countries to focus only on themselves without regard to neighboring countries. The conflicts caused by this new nationalism became increasingly tense in the early 1900s, and eventually led to war. Four factors contributed to the outbreak of war: imperialism, nationalism, militarism, and a tangled system of alliances.

Imperialism, as you recall, is the policy of extending a nation's power over another—politically, economically, or both. The Industrial Revolution spurred European nations to look for new markets and sources of raw materials. There was increased competition for overseas colonies, which led to high tensions between some countries. The British, French, and Germans, for example, fought over colonial claims in Africa and Asia.

A Push for Nationalism

The growth of nationalism in Europe was another cause of World War I. Politicians and newspaper editors reminded citizens of the dangers that other countries posed to their national security. Nationalist feelings were strong in both Germany and France. The French were especially upset about their 1871 defeat in the Franco-Prussian War. They were also angry about the German occupation of the French provinces of Alsace and Lorraine, which were both on the French-German border. Each country had unresolved, mistrustful feelings toward the other.

Nationalism had also become a powerful force in the Balkan Peninsula. A nationalist movement called Pan-Slavism began to form. It proclaimed that

---

Teaching Options

Section 1 Resources

Teacher's Resources (TR)

Terms to Know, p. 39
Review History, p. 73
Build Your Skills, p. 107
Concept Builder, p. 242
SQR Chart, p. 322
Transparency 5

ESL/ELL STRATEGIES

Identify Essential Vocabulary Point out that the suffix *-ism* is added to many English words related to politics—such as imperialism, nationalism, militarism, and Pan-Slavism. The suffix *-ism* means "a theory or practice." Show students how to break down each word to find its root (empire, nation, military, Slav). Suggest that students look for additional *-ism* words as they read this unit (e.g., communism, nazism).

all Slavic peoples, or people who spoke a form of a Slavic language, shared a common cultural background, regardless of where they lived. The goal of this movement was to unite all Slavic peoples. Because of Pan-Slavism, Russia, the largest Slavic country, stood ready to defend all Slavs, including the new nation of Serbia, against any threat.

Two empires that watched the rise of the Pan-Slavism movement with uneasiness were Austria-Hungary and the Ottoman Empire. Austria-Hungary had many Slavic peoples, including many Serbians in an area called Bosnia, who wanted to be free of the empire. The Serbian nation thought of Bosnia as part of its territory and promised to help free all the Slavs living there.

In 1912, several states in the Balkan Peninsula, where Serbia is located, attacked the Ottoman Empire. These Balkan states also fought among themselves over territory, which earned the peninsula the nickname, "the powder keg of Europe."

A nationalistic movement was also taking place within the borders of the Ottoman Empire. This movement contributed to tensions between that empire and Russia. In the late 1880s, almost 2 million Christian Armenians lived in the eastern provinces of the Ottoman Empire. Russia encouraged these Armenians to try to gain independence. When the Ottoman sultan raised their taxes in 1894, the Armenian people revolted. Thousands of them were brutally killed. The whole area was ready to explode.

Marching Toward War

France and other European countries remembered Germany's military might when Germany defeated France in 1871. Germany's continuing military buildup concerned them. The French worried about another German invasion. The Russians eyed Germany's growing ties with Austria-Hungary with distrust. The British were greatly concerned with the expansion of Germany's navy, which represented a threat to Great Britain's dominance of the seas.

Do You Remember?
In Chapter 20, you learned that the Balkan Peninsula consisted of many nation-states. In addition, most of the people on the Balkan Peninsula were Christians.

The growth of the German navy caused tension between Great Britain and Germany.

◆ **ANSWER** Nationalism caused tensions because countries became increasingly concerned about their own national security and did not care how other countries would be affected by their decisions. Independence movements by some groups threatened certain countries.

B. Forming Alliances

Purpose-Setting Question Why did German chancellor Bismarck want to prevent an alliance between France and Russia? (Such an alliance would isolate Germany and open it to attack from both the east and the west.)

ANALYZE PRIMARY SOURCES

DOCUMENT-BASED QUESTION

This cartoon, entitled "A Chain of Friendship," is believed to have appeared in an American newspaper in 1914. Have students describe how each country is portrayed in the cartoon. Discuss which figures look more militaristic. (Austria and Germany) Ask students how this chain might resemble a row of dominoes. (The countries are lined up in a row, and if one is pushed, the others may all topple, too.)

ANSWER The leaders are setting Europe up to be vulnerable to a chain reaction.

T614 ◆ **UNIT 7**

Another cause of World War I was the arms race that developed in Europe. An arms race is a rivalry among nations to gain the greatest military power. Many European leaders believed that force was the only way to settle disputes with other countries. Militarism, a policy in which the military's needs become most important to a country, arose out of fears that grew as European nations increased their military might. Armies continued to grow in size and strength, because generals believed that the strongest and largest army would be the winner if war broke out.

Most countries developed industries to produce guns, cannons, and other modern weapons. Many European nations also began to form reserve armies. In case of trouble, these reserves would be **mobilized**, or called to active duty, to serve in the army. Weapons and trained soldiers were supposed to give a country a sense of security. Instead, it appeared that Europeans were headed for war.

◆ **How did nationalism cause tensions in Europe?**

B. Forming Alliances

Under Prussian leadership, Germany united its confederation of states into a strong empire in 1871. This unity shifted the balance of power in Europe and caused other countries to form alliances for protection. The idea behind alliances is that peace can only be maintained if no one group or country becomes stronger than another.

The alliance system actually increased the likelihood of war rather than to prevent war. If one nation decided to attack another because it felt threatened, the member countries of the alliance could be drawn in, bound by their agreement with the country. A widespread conflict could happen, even if no one especially wanted that outcome.

The Triple Alliance

German chancellor Otto von Bismarck wanted to prevent an alliance between France and Russia, because it would isolate Germany. He feared being attacked on both Germany's western and eastern borders at the same time. In 1879, Bismarck formed the Dual Alliance with Austria-Hungary. Two years later, he set up an alliance called the Three Emperors' League with Austria-Hungary and Russia. In 1882, Bismarck made another alliance, called the Triple Alliance, with Austria-Hungary and Italy. According to this alliance, each nation promised to come to the aid of the others if they were attacked. The Triple Alliance upset the balance of power in Europe because it isolated France.

Eventually, Bismarck realized that Austria-Hungary and Russia might end up as enemies of each other over issues in the Balkans. Since Austria-Hungary had a more efficient army than Russia did, Bismarck allied with Austria-Hungary.

France and Russia

When Germany allied with Austria-Hungary, France took advantage of this situation by forming an alliance with Russia. Russia and France approved a treaty in 1893, a move that would lead to what Bismarck had feared.

ANALYZE PRIMARY SOURCES

DOCUMENT-BASED QUESTION What point is this cartoon making about the actions of Europe's leaders in forging alliances?

In this political cartoon, the effect of political alliances is illustrated as a chain of reactions among European nations.

614 UNIT 7 ◆ Decades of War

Teaching Options

Traditional enemies, Great Britain and France resolved colonial disputes over Morocco and Egypt by forming the Entente Cordiale in 1904. An **entente** is an agreement or understanding between countries to follow common policies. In 1907, Great Britain and Russia also formed an entente. They were able to form an alliance with France that same year, called the Triple Entente. The Triple Entente was an agreement between Great Britain, Russia, and France to cooperate with one another. This alliance provided a balance to the Triple Alliance of Germany, Austria-Hungary, and Italy.

◆ Why was the alliance system so dangerous?

C. War Breaks Out

Serbia, which became independent in 1878, hoped to become the leader of a Slavic state. Serbia wanted territories controlled by the Ottoman Empire and Austria-Hungary, especially Bosnia and Herzegovina, because of their location on the Adriatic Sea. When Austria-Hungary annexed Bosnia and Herzegovina in 1908, it added to the tension between Austria-Hungary and Serbian nationalists.

Great Britain did not trust Russia's influence in the Balkans, where Russia supported Serbia as a Slavic state. Russia, in turn, feared that Germany's relations with the Ottoman Empire would decrease Russia's chance of ever gaining access to the Mediterranean Sea.

An Assassination in Sarajevo

On June 28, 1914, the heir to Austria's throne was murdered in the Balkans. This action started a chain of events that led Europe into war. Archduke Franz Ferdinand of Austria visited Sarajevo, the capital of Bosnia. As the archduke and his wife Sophie rode in an open car, a Serbian nationalist named Gavrilo Princip fired two shots, killing both Ferdinand and his wife. Princip was a member of a nationalist society known as the Black Hand. This group wanted the Austro-Hungarians out of Bosnia. The Black Hand society believed that the assassination of Franz Ferdinand would help its cause.

Both the foreign minister and the chief of Austria-Hungary's general staff saw the murders as a chance for Austria-Hungary to get involved in the politics of the Balkans. Austria-Hungary delivered an **ultimatum** to Serbia. An ultimatum is a final set of demands. Serbia responded to the ultimatum, agreeing to some, but not all, of the demands. Austria-Hungary began to mobilize its troops. It declared war on Serbia on July 28, 1914.

Alliances Spread Conflict

The alliances between the European nations now caused the conflict to spread quickly. Because of the system of alliances, members of one alliance declared war on members of the other alliance. Great Britain, France, and Russia—members of the Triple Entente—became the leaders known as the Allied Powers, or the Allies. Italy, Japan, and other nations joined the Allies after the war broke out. The Triple Alliance became known as the Central Powers. It included Germany and

The assassination of Archduke Franz Ferdinand and his wife Sophie triggered the beginning of World War I.

Discuss Ask students how nationalist movements, such as Pan-Slavism, can be both good and bad for a country and its people. (**Good:** brings people together, creates a sense of pride; **Bad:** can lead a country to isolate itself from others, can lead to mistrust or hatred or fear)

Activity

Use a map Have students study the map of Europe in the Atlas (p. A5) or use Transparency 5 to locate some of the countries that would have been part of the huge Slavic state Serbia had hoped to lead. Encourage students to find out the history of some of these countries.

◆ **ANSWER** The alliance system increased the likelihood of war and the number of countries that would be involved in war.

C. War Breaks Out

Purpose-Setting Question Why did the Russians support an independent Slavic state in the Balkans? (The Russians were Slavs and supported their fellow Slavs; the Russians hoped to gain access to ports on the Mediterranean Sea.)

Extend Archduke Franz Ferdinand had been warned of a possible assassination plot on the day he was killed. He was a prime target because Serbians feared that if he ascended the throne, he would continue and even increase the persecution of Serbs living within the Austro-Hungarian Empire. The archduke chose to tour the capital on the anniversary of the 1389 battle of Kosovo. This battle was an embarrassment to Serbs because it marked a time when Serbia had lost its independence as a nation. The archduke ignored all warnings and proceeded with his tour.

Writing

AVERAGE

Have students write a letter to the editor of a French newspaper or a British newspaper discussing the military buildup of Germany in the 1910s and explaining why this buildup poses a problem for their own country. Have students read their letters aloud and compare the comments presented from the two different national viewpoints.

CHALLENGE

Have students prepare a formal written report from a French army general or British admiral describing Germany's military buildup, analyzing the threat it poses to their own country's military interest, and making specific proposals for dealing with the threat. Have students read their reports aloud and compare the two national points of view.

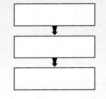

Austria-Hungary. Bulgaria and the Ottoman Empire joined the Central Powers soon after the war began. The United States was the last major nation to enter the war, joining the Allies in 1917. Before the war ended, 31 countries had entered the fighting, making it truly a worldwide war.

Many people believed that the war between the Central Powers and the Allies would be short, but this was not to happen. Both sides believed that they would win.

War and Society

As the war unfolded following the assassination of Archduke Franz Ferdinand, it required the total commitment of all of society, not just the military. People had to be willing to make sacrifices to gain victory. Posters, cartoons, marching songs, and editorials used propaganda, or the spreading of certain ideas, to boost support for the war. Much government propaganda was an appeal for financial support of the war. Great Britain especially tried to rally military support by using enlistment posters to encourage people to join its army, which was made up entirely of volunteers.

In addition, artists and writers who survived the war period expressed the brutality of war in new ways. German artists used bold lines and bright colors to illustrate highly emotional subjects. Their art shows the brutality and senselessness of war, such as the horrors of poison gas and new weapons that would be used against soldiers.

◆ Why did Serbia want the Slavic territories of Bosnia and Herzegovina that were controlled by Austria-Hungary?

Review I

Review History
A. What were four factors that contributed to the outbreak of war?
B. What was the Triple Entente?
C. What event happened on June 28, 1914?

Define Terms to Know
Define the following terms:
mobilize, entente, ultimatum

Critical Thinking
Do you think there would have been a war if the event on June 28, 1914, had not happened?

Write About Citizenship
Write an idea for a propaganda poster that urges citizens to support the war effort.

Get Organized
SQR CHART
Use an SQR chart to organize information from this section. For example, one topic from this section might be alliances.

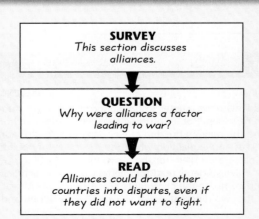

SURVEY
This section discusses alliances.

QUESTION
Why were alliances a factor leading to war?

READ
Alliances could draw other countries into disputes, even if they did not want to fight.

Build Your Skills

Social Studies Skill

INTERPRET STATISTICS

INTERPRET STATISTICS

Statistics is the science of collecting, analyzing, interpreting, and presenting data. As you read this chapter, you will find many statistics about World War I. These figures can be helpful in understanding the large amounts of resources countries committed to the war effort and the size of the losses each country suffered.

For example, the following numbers show the size of European armies during the early years of the war. Russia had an army of about 6 million soldiers in 1914. By the time Russia was fully involved in the war, it had an army of 12 million soldiers. France had an army of about 4 million soldiers in 1914. By the time France was fully involved in the war, it had an army of more than 8 million soldiers.

Being able to interpret statistics is an important skill, especially when numbers act as supporting details. Being able to interpret statistics can provide information about many historical events.

Here's How
Follow these steps to help you interpret statistics.

1. Study the statistical data carefully. If the data is presented in a chart or graph, identify the subject. If the data appears in a paragraph, as it does in the example just given, your job will be a little harder. In that case, you must pull out the data yourself from the text.
2. Look for patterns or relationships, such as an increase or decrease in numbers.
3. Interpret the data. What conclusions can you draw based on the data?

Here's Why
Being able to understand statistics is an important skill. In this chapter, it helps you to understand the huge resources it took to fight World War I. Practice in this skill can help you gain information about the time period you are studying so you can better understand historical events.

Practice the Skill
Study the information on the graph carefully. Then, answer the following questions.

1. Between which two countries is the difference in the number of soldiers the greatest?
2. Based on the information on the graph, did the Allies or the Central Powers have the greatest advantage in 1914?
3. Why do you think Germany was so worried about the alliance between France and Russia?

Extend the Skill
Write a brief paragraph based on the information on the graph. Be sure to use statistics to support your statements.

Apply the Skill
Carefully look at the statistics that appear in the rest of this chapter. Follow the steps in *Here's How* to help you learn how to better understand them.

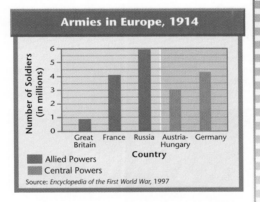

Armies in Europe, 1914

Number of Soldiers (in millions) — Country: Great Britain, France, Russia, Austria-Hungary, Germany

Allied Powers
Central Powers

Source: *Encyclopedia of the First World War, 1997*

INTERPRET STATISTICS

Teach the Skill
Ask students to list some jobs that require keeping or using statistics, such as salesperson, accountant, stockbroker, insurance actuary, sports scorekeeper, and office assistant. Record their suggestions on the board and discuss why knowing how to compile or read statistics is important for each job. Have sample spreadsheets, graphs, charts, or tables available for students to peruse. Ask what advantage these have over having to read the information in paragraph form.

Next, ask students why being able to interpret statistics is valuable in understanding history. Discuss the kinds of numbers historians need to keep track of (dates, population data, economic figures) and how that information is usually presented in history textbooks. Point out the graph on page 617 as one example. Discuss why a bar graph is a good way to present data you want to compare. (It clearly shows amount differences.)

Practice the Skill
ANSWERS
1. Great Britain and Russia
2. The Allies had the advantage because of the size of their armies.
3. because France and Russia both had very large armies compared to the other countries

Extend the Skill
Students' paragraphs should discuss the number of soldiers in each army. Students may also compare the size of each army. Paragraphs must include actual statistics from the graph.

Apply the Skill
Students should be able to point out statistics throughout the rest of the chapter and use the steps in *Here's How* to notice patterns or relationships and to interpret the statistics.

Teaching Options

RETEACH
Have students look through earlier chapters of this textbook to find three or four charts or graphs presenting statistics. Review with students how to read the charts or graphs. Have students, working in pairs, write a question based on the information in each chart or graph. Then, have them exchange papers with other pairs and answer the question.

CHALLENGE
Have students use the Internet or library materials to find statistics about World War I—such as the number of soldiers fighting for different sides, number of casualties suffered, or quantities of resources used up or destroyed. Have students create a graph or chart to present their statistics and then write three or four questions for classmates to answer as they interpret the data.

Section Summary

In this section, students will learn how new technology and fighting methods led to a long, drawn-out war with heavy losses sustained by the armies of many nations. They will also learn how the entrance into the war by fresh troops from the United States prompted Germany to seek an end to the fighting.

Introduce

Getting Started

Ask students to visualize a forest fire that starts in one location and keeps sending off sparks that cause new blazes to begin. Discuss why such a fire is so hard to put out. Point out that, in some ways, World War I was similar to the fire. New nations kept getting involved or being brought into the fray when they were attacked, and the fighting blazed at times, while smoldering and flaring up at other times.

TERMS TO KNOW

Ask students to read the terms and definitions on page 618 and then find each term in the section. Point out that the term *stalemate* represents a stoppage in the fighting. Suggest that students look for other terms in this section that relate to times of suspended fighting, such as *withdrawal*.

You may wish to preview the pronunciation of the following names from this section with students.

Schlieffen (SHLEE fuhn)
Ypres (EE pruh)
Verdun (vuhr DUHN)
Masurian Lakes
  (muh ZOOR ee uhn LAYKS)
Lusitania (loo suh TAY nee uh)
Château-Thierry (shah TOH ty REE)
Belleau Wood (BEH loh WOOD)

ACTIVE READING

Ask students to make an outline (TR, p. 318) to summarize each subsection. Suggest that students use the headings in each subsection to help them develop the main points of their outline and that they list several important details from the text below each main point.

Section II
The War Is Fought

Terms to Know

stalemate a situation in which neither side is able to defeat the other

trench warfare the act of waging war from the defense of trenches

Main Ideas

A. Many nations fought World War I using new technology.

B. The war dragged on with heavy losses and no end in sight.

C. The United States entered the war in 1917, which led Germany to eventually seek an end to the fighting.

Active Reading

SUMMARIZE

When you summarize, you include only the most important events. As you read this section, concentrate on the main events of World War I. Then, pause to summarize what you have read.

A. The War Unfolds

World War I, or the Great War as it was known, was the first war to involve nations from all areas of the world. Battles were fought in many countries, on every ocean, and in the skies. Newer and deadlier weapons changed the nature of warfare.

Military Resources and Strategy

Austria-Hungary began bombarding the Serbian city of Belgrade the day after it declared war on Serbia. Russia responded to this attack by mobilizing its troops. Austria-Hungary began gathering troops on its Russian border. Germany then sent a 12-hour ultimatum to Russia demanding a halt to its mobilization. In addition, it sent an 18-hour ultimatum to France demanding that it declare itself neutral, or not fighting on any side, if Russia and Germany went to war.

Russia and France ignored these German ultimatums. Germany declared war the next day against Russia, and France responded by mobilizing its troops. On August 1, 1914, Germany sent troops into Luxembourg and demanded that Belgium allow German troops to pass through its territory to get to France. At the time, Belgium was neutral. The next day, Germany declared war on France. When Germany marched into Belgium, Great Britain declared war on Germany, because Britain was committed to defending Belgium.

The Allies held the advantage against the Central Powers in terms of industrial resources and military forces. Allied armies grew larger as young men eagerly enlisted to fight in the war. In addition, the Allies had better naval access for trade with neutral countries, especially the United States, which was known as the Great Neutral.

Military resources include weapons, such as machine guns. This poster shows a Russian soldier preparing to use a machine gun during World War I.

The Allies had more troops, but the Russian armies were slow to mobilize and not well armed. Germany brought many advantages to the Central Powers with a superior railway network, a large, well-trained military, and its navy.

Germany's military strategy had been in place for years. Leaders had anticipated the possibility of having to fight a war on two fronts at the same time—against France to the west and Russia to the east. Alfred von Schlieffen, chief of the German great general staff from 1891 to 1905,

---

Teaching Options

Section 2 Resources

Teacher's Resources (TR)

Terms to Know, p. 39
Review History, p. 73
Build Your Skills, p. 107
Concept Builder, p. 242
SQR Chart, p. 322
Transparency 1

Meet Individual Needs:

VISUAL/SPATIAL LEARNERS

To help students visualize details in subsection A, have them draw a picture of a balance scale on their paper. One side of the scale will represent the Allies, and the other side will represent the Central Powers. On each side of the scale, have students list advantages each group had. Then, discuss whether they think the scale is balanced or one side outweighs the other.

had proposed a swift attack on northern France as the first move. This attack would be followed by an attack on Russia after France had been subdued. His proposal came to be known as the Schlieffen Plan.

A New Kind of War

Many new and deadly weapons were used for the first time in World War I. Machine guns and giant cannons forced both sides to seek protection. The British used the first armored tanks in 1916 to protect their soldiers from machine-gun fire. Germany, too, soon began using tanks. Both sides developed fighter planes. From planes, pilots could locate enemy lines and drop bombs. All of these weapons greatly increased the number of soldiers who were killed in the land battles of World War I.

Germany developed a new class of Unterseeboot (underseas boat), or U-boat. Armed with torpedoes, or self-propelled bombs, U-boats moved underwater and could sink ships on any ocean or sea.

◆ What was the Schlieffen Plan?

B. The War From 1914 to 1916

Fighting began on August 4, 1914, when Germany invaded neutral Belgium. Geography more than politics played a part in this decision. Belgium's flat coastal plain and its good railroad system were desirable to the German generals. They viewed Belgium as the most direct route to Paris, their final destination in France. The German army plundered the countryside as they advanced through Belgium. France and Britain came to Belgium's aid. Still, the Allies were quickly forced to retreat from German troops, who by August 25, had swept into northern France.

Europe During World War I

Legend:
- Allied Powers
- Central Powers
- Neutral nations
- ——— Eastern Front
- ——— Western Front
- ✹ Battle site

✔ Map Check
1. **PLACE** Which countries were not part of either alliance?
2. **HUMAN INTERACTION** Why might Germany face battles on both its eastern and western borders?

CHAPTER 26 ◆ World War I and the Russian Revolutions **619**

Using Technology

Have students use software programs or programs they download from the Internet to create a crossword puzzle or word search puzzle containing words and terms related to World War I. Suggest that students skim the chapter to select words before they begin to create their puzzles. Students can share their puzzles with classmates for them to solve.

Cooperative Learning

Have students work in groups to produce a World War I Yearly Highlights poster. Assign each group a different year during the war. Group members should divide the work, with some using computer software to create headlines for the year's top war events; others researching to find war-related photos or poems; and others creating drawings, maps, or charts that illustrate the war happenings for a particular year.

A. The War Unfolds

Purpose-Setting Question Why did Great Britain enter into the war? (Germany marched into Belgium and Great Britain had an agreement to defend Belgium.)

Focus Point out that Germany began the war by issuing ultimatums to Russia and France. The ultimatums demanded that Russia stop mobilizing its troops and that France stay neutral if Russia and Germany went to war. Ask students why they think Germany used this tactic. (to buy time to get its forces in place)

◆ **ANSWER** The Schlieffen Plan was Germany's military strategy of fighting a war on two fronts at the same time. There would be a quick attack on France, followed by an attack on Russia.

B. The War From 1914 to 1916

Purpose-Setting Question What happened at the first battle of the Marne? (The Allies stopped the German advance into France but were too weak to pursue the enemy and gain a quick victory.)

Using the Map
Europe During World War I

Ask students for one reason, from a geographic standpoint, why Great Britain was willing to defend Belgium. (Belgium is just across the English Channel from Great Britain. If Germany captured Belgium, its navy could easily attack England by sea.)

✔ Map Check
Answers
1. Norway, Sweden, Denmark, Belgium, the Netherlands, Luxembourg, Switzerland, Spain, and Morocco
2. Germany was at war with France to the west and Russia to the east.

Discuss In August 1914, Kaiser Wilhelm told German troops, "You'll be home before the leaves have fallen from the trees." What factors made his prediction wrong? (the stalemate at the Marne, trench warfare, a stronger response from the Allies)

The use of armored tanks and trench warfare became a common way of fighting on the Western Front.

ANALYZE PRIMARY SOURCES

DOCUMENT-BASED QUESTION What phrases does the general use to describe the horrors of war?

The Western Front

In early September, German troops came within 15 miles of Paris, the French capital. French and British troops stopped the German army at the Marne River. This important victory for the Allies meant that Germany's plan for a quick victory in France was now not possible.

After the German army was stopped, the fighting reached a **stalemate**, meaning that neither side was able to move ahead. Instead, both sides tried to hold their ground in France and Belgium. Both the French troops and the German troops dug trenches, or ditches, for protection. Fighting in trenches became known as **trench warfare**. Soldiers strung barbed wire in front of their defenses. The trenches stretched more than 400 miles from the border of Switzerland to the coast of the North Sea.

The area between the German and the French trenches became known as no man's land. This no man's land became a barren plain, where no trees stood and no grasses grew. One army would attack and gain ground one day only to have the opposing army take it back the next day.

Germans launched a second attack at Ypres in northwest Belgium, where Great Britain had suffered heavy losses five months earlier. The first day of the attack, April 22, 1915, Germans released poison gas along a four-mile-long stretch of trenches. French soldiers were distracted by the strange beauty of the grayish-green vapor as it came rolling in toward them and settled into the trenches. Soldiers had no experience with this poison gas, which caused terrible pain and death.

In 1916, the Germans attacked French forces in the French town of Verdun. More than 2 million bullets pounded French troops. Some contained explosives and others, poison gas. Along the six-mile-long front, Germans tried to kill as many soldiers as possible and create misery for those who survived. A French general wrote,

> ❝ Their expressions . . . seemed frozen by a vision of terror: their postures betrayed a total dejection; they sagged beneath the weight of horrifying memories. ❞

After ten months of fierce fighting, the French commander at Verdun and his troops stopped the German troops from advancing. His words, "They shall not pass," became a rallying cry as the French were determined to hold their land at all costs. The stalemate on the Western Front lasted until large numbers of American forces arrived in 1918.

The Eastern Front

At the same time that fighting was taking place on the Western Front, battles were also being fought on the Eastern Front, near Russia's border with Poland. The fighting between the German and Russian armies on the Eastern Front took a heavy toll on both sides. Fighting the Russian army weakened Germany, because the long front required so many German troops. Even so,

German and Austrian troops managed to win important battles along the Eastern Front. Russia's army was the largest in Europe, but it was poorly trained and lacked skilled military leaders. Russian soldiers were continually hungry because of scarce food supplies, and they became weary of fighting.

At the Battle of Tannenberg, in 1914, almost 100,000 Russians were captured, and much of their equipment was lost or destroyed. At the next battle, the Battle of Masurian Lakes, about 250,000 more Russians were captured.

◆ **Why did Germany invade Belgium?**

C. Global Involvement

Although the war was fought mostly in Europe, there were battlegrounds around the world. Soldiers from British colonies fought alongside European Allied soldiers. British and Japanese forces captured all of Germany's colonies in east Asia, while British and French troops seized most of Germany's African colonies. In Asia Minor, the Allies fought against the Ottoman Empire, and Russia invaded the empire's borders.

Fighting on the Sea

Great Britain and Germany set up blockades at sea, attempting to cut off each other's supply of food and raw materials. On May 7, 1915, a German submarine sank the British passenger ship *Lusitania*, which was also carrying weapons to Great Britain. More than 100 Americans were on board. This event angered Americans. Then, in 1916, a German submarine torpedoed the *Sussex*, a passenger ship. Some Americans were killed. U.S. President Woodrow Wilson threatened to break off diplomatic relations if Germany did not follow international law, which forbade the sinking of merchant and passenger vessels by submarines without warning.

Germany and Great Britain tried to blockade each other's ports, preventing supplies from getting through.

Connection to SCIENCE

At Ypres, the Germans released chlorine gas from cylinders into the air, where winds blew it toward the French lines. However, a change in wind conditions could result in the troops gassing themselves. This happened to the British in September 1915. After this mishap occurred, scientists on both sides began experimenting with ways to deliver their gas in artillery shells.

Extend The use of poison gas was considered "uncivilized" prior to World War I. However, by 1915 both sides decided that a new weapon was needed to overcome the stalemate created by trench warfare. Gas usage on both war fronts caused more than 1.2 million casualties and nearly 92,000 deaths. The use of gas in war was outlawed in 1925 by an international agreement, and it has been used very rarely since that time. Ask students if they agree that the use of gas or other biological or chemical weapons during a war is more "uncivilized" than the use of guns or bombs.

Focus Russia had one major advantage during the war—the huge number of soldiers available to fight—and one major disadvantage—poorly trained soldiers and leaders. As fighting began on the Eastern Front, Russian forces may have outnumbered Germans more than four to one (650,000 to 135,000). However, one of Russia's major strategic errors involved its officers giving commands over open radio lines that the enemy often intercepted. Because they knew Russia's plans at Tannenberg, the Germans were able to achieve a major victory.

◆ **ANSWER** Belgium was the most direct route to Paris, France, which was where the Germans wanted to go. Also, the Germans liked Belgium's flat terrain, and they wanted total access to Belgium's railroad system.

C. Global Involvement

Purpose-Setting Question What was the significance of the telegram intercepted by the British government? (It was a message sent from the German foreign secretary to the German ambassador in Mexico City urging Mexico to support the German effort. In return, Germany would help Mexico recover territories it had lost to the United States. Americans were outraged by the telegram.)

Discuss Ask students why the sinking of the *Lusitania* and *Sussex* influenced how people in the United States felt about the war. Help students realize that it brought the war closer to home and involved innocent Americans.

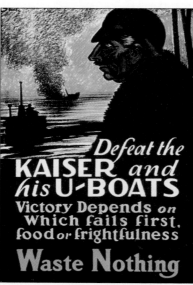

Propaganda posters, such as this one, encouraged Americans to support the war effort against Germany.

The United States Gets Involved

President Wilson had thus far kept the United States out of the war. However, two events happened in 1917 that supported U.S. entry into the war. First, the Central Powers announced they would resume unrestricted submarine warfare. German U-boats sank five American ships within one month. Second, the British government intercepted a telegram from Germany to its ambassador in Mexico City. The message urged Mexico to join the German effort. In return, Germany would help Mexico regain Texas, New Mexico, and Arizona, all former Mexican territories. This offer outraged Americans.

On April 2, 1917, President Wilson asked the U.S. Congress to declare war on Germany in order to make the world "safe for democracy." On April 6, the U.S. Congress declared war.

By 1918, U.S. soldiers had joined the Allies to stop the German advance in the town of Château-Thierry. Soon after, American soldiers fought in battles at Belleau Wood in France, in the Second Battle of the Marne, and at the Argonne Forest, where 1,200,000 American soldiers fought. Of those, 50,000 Americans were killed and 206,000 were wounded.

Clashes in Russia

The fighting in Russia on the Eastern Front made Russians weary of the war and desperate for peace. As a result, new leaders in the new Russian government signed a peace treaty with the Central Powers in March 1918 at the city of Brest-Litovsk. This treaty officially took Russia out of the war. However, the terms of the treaty were very harsh. It forced Russia to surrender 30 percent of its farmlands, 50 percent of its industry, and 90 percent of its coal mines. With Russia under the control of the Central Powers, Germany could withdraw its troops from the Eastern Front to concentrate their efforts on fighting elsewhere. As a result, U.S. troops were sent to Russia in August 1918 to guard Pacific and Arctic ports for the Allies and to strengthen Allied defenses on the Eastern Front.

◆ **What was the effect of the sinking of the *Lusitania* on the United States?**

Review II

Review History
A. What were three new weapons used in World War I?
B. How were trenches used in World War I?
C. Why was U.S. involvement in World War I so significant?

Define Terms to Know
Define the following terms:
stalemate, trench warfare

Critical Thinking
What might have happened in Europe if the United States had not entered the war?

Write About Geography
Write a paragraph describing the impact of geography on World War I.

Get Organized
SQR CHART
Use an SQR chart to organize information from this section. For example, one topic from this section might be new kinds of weapons that were used during World War I.

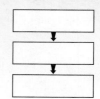

SURVEY
This section discusses new weapons used in World War I.

QUESTION
What new weapons were used in World War I?

READ
Heavy guns, armored tanks, hand grenades, poison gas, and smaller, lighter machine guns

CONNECT
History & Technology

Aviation

Great technological advances in the development of aircraft came rapidly during World War I. Before the war began, aircraft were not believed to be very important. Aerial reconnaissance, or observation, became more important once the Western Front was in a stalemate, with neither side victorious.

The main aircraft for surveying enemy artillery positions and troop movements were stationary, or nonmoving, gas-filled balloons, called zeppelins. These zeppelins were raised and lowered to the ground by cables. Military planners, who at first were not certain about how useful one- or two-seat propeller airplanes could be, soon realized that airplanes could cover more area because they were not stationary.

Soon airplanes were flown ahead of ground troops to gather information about the enemy. Pilots began shooting pistols at enemy aircraft. Nothing did much damage.

It was only when rifles were used instead of pistols that the fighting became serious. Still, the shooter had to overcome the difficulty of loading and aiming a rifle in the small space of the cockpit while flying a plane. Shooting at a moving target through the wires and spinning propeller blades was risky. A pilot could hit his own plane.

DOGFIGHTS were battles between planes. Pilots who shot down five or more planes were known as aces. Rapid development of more-powerful aircraft allowed pilots to take bombs and heavy machine guns into the air. Two challenges faced pilots: where to place the machine guns for easy access and how to keep from hitting one's own plane. In 1915, a technological breakthrough happened when Germany developed a mechanism that coordinated the firing of bullets with the spin of the propeller. In four months, the Allies developed a similar mechanism.

U.S. AIRCRAFT PRODUCTION in the United States got off to a slow start. In fact, the war was almost over before the United States sent planes to France. The newly formed United States Air Service used mostly French-built planes.

Critical Thinking

Answer the questions below. Then, complete the activity.

1. How did new developments in aviation affect the way in which World War I was fought?
2. Why do you think aircraft production got off to a slow start in the United States?

Write About It

Use the Internet and reference books to learn more about advances made in aviation during World War I. Then, write a paragraph that identifies and describes a particular aviation contribution that is not described in your textbook.

Airplanes were eventually equipped with guns, and aerial dogfights became a common type of battle.

Teaching Options

The Red Baron
The most famous World War I ace was Germany's Baron Manfred von Richthofen, whose red-painted plane earned him the nickname "The Red Baron." Richthofen shot down 80 Allied planes before he was shot down himself in April 1918. Mourning his death, one German general said, "He was worth as much to us as three divisions."

LINK to TODAY
Today's military aircraft crew has a range of weapons available that World War I aces could not even have imagined. Have students do research to identify the types of aircraft, missiles, and bombs used in modern wars, such as during the U.S. attacks on Afghanistan in 2002 and Iraq in 2003. Then, ask students to predict a new type of aircraft or aerial weapon that might be developed in the future.

CONNECT
History & Technology

AVIATION

Teach the Topic
Aircraft added a new dimension to fighting during World War I. Ask students to name the two major uses of aircraft during World War I. (reconnaissance and attack) Discuss the unique qualities that made aircraft appropriate to use for both types of missions.

Have students describe old aircraft they have seen in person or in photographs or movies. Discuss how the old airplanes were both more exciting and more dangerous to fly than today's warplanes.

DOGFIGHTS While much of the war news was either dull or sad, stories about aerial dogfights were exciting to read about and received a lot of attention in newspapers. Aerial aces often became celebrities.

U.S. AIRCRAFT PRODUCTION In 1917, the U.S. Congress voted to spend $640 million to build 22,000 airplanes based on French designs. It also authorized the building of more than 5,000 airplanes based on the British-designed Airco DH-4. In 1918, American-produced aircraft began arriving at the Western Front.

The first U.S. fighter patrols over German lines began in March 1918. The leading American flying aces at that time included Edward Rickenbacker, Frederick Gillet, and Wilfred Beaver.

Critical Thinking
1. Aircraft replaced air balloons for observation, and fights took place in the air.
2. Because the United States did not officially enter the war until 1917, the need to manufacture airplanes did not seem urgent.

Write About It
Students' paragraphs should show that they have researched and understood the aviation contribution that they cite.

III. Peace in a New Europe

(pp. 624–629)

Section Summary

In this section, students will learn about the armistice that ended World War I. They will analyze the economic and human costs of the war and learn how world leaders attempted to work out peace terms at the Paris Peace Conference in 1919.

1 Introduce

Getting Started

Ask students to suppose that they have just completed a long and stressful competition that they won. Have them describe how they feel. (relieved, exhausted, triumphant, etc.) Point out that the British, French, and Americans experienced all of these emotions and more following the end of World War I. Then, elicit from students another feeling that the victors must have had—anger at Germany for its aggressive role in the war.

TERMS TO KNOW

Ask students to read the terms and definitions on page 624. Then, have them skim the section to locate each term, read the surrounding paragraph, and state a definition of the term in their own words.

You may wish to preview the pronunciation of the following terms from this section with students.

Rhineland (RYN land)
Vladivostok (vla duh vuh STAHK)
Murmansk (moor MANSK)
pandemic (pan DEHM ink)
Georges Clemenceau (ZHAWZH kleh MAHN soh)
Schleswig (SHLAS vihk)
Versailles (ver SY)

ACTIVE READING

As students read about the armistice and how it brought about the end of the fighting, have them analyze how German soldiers might have viewed the fact that they had been defeated by the Allies.

Section III — Peace in a New Europe

Terms to Know

armistice an agreement to stop warfare

demobilization the disbanding or discharging of troops

reparation the payment for damages

demilitarized zone an area that military forces cannot enter

Main Ideas

A. Germany was the last of the Central Powers to sign an armistice that ended fighting.

B. The economic and human costs of World War I were enormous.

C. After the war, world leaders worked out strict treaties, and the United States did not join the League of Nations.

 Active Reading

POINTS OF VIEW
Governments of different countries often have different points of view. As you read this section, think about the viewpoints of the countries involved in peace treaties after the war. How valid is each point of view?

A. Signing an Armistice

Finding an end to war is a difficult political task. The task of ending World War I was extremely challenging, requiring the skill of all the Allied leaders.

The Eleventh Hour

As waves of fresh American troops continued to pour into Western Europe to relieve exhausted French and British troops in 1918, the German government finally lost hope of winning the war. Each of the other Central Powers had already signed an **armistice**, or an agreement to stop fighting. Finally, Germany agreed to sign as well. At 11:00 A.M. on November 11, 1918—the eleventh hour of the eleventh day of the eleventh month—Germany surrendered. After four years, the war was over.

The armistice set forth harsh terms for the Central Powers. According to these terms, the treaty with Russia at Brest-Litovsk was cancelled. Germany also had to surrender its submarines and a large part of its navy, release all war prisoners, and turn over all weapons. The final term of the armistice gave the Allies the right to occupy all German territory west of the Rhine River.

Disbanding Allied Troops

With the armistice signed, plans were started for the **demobilization**, or discharging from military service, of American and other troops who had fought in the war. Because there were so many troops, the process of demobilization was slow. French and British troops, who had fought the longest, were sent home first. The doughboys, the nickname for American soldiers during World War I, had to wait their turn. As a result, the last American troops did not leave Europe until 1923.

◆ **What were the terms of the armistice that ended World War I?**

B. Effects of the War

World War I, which lasted from 1914 to 1918, involved countries on four continents—Europe, Asia, North America, and Africa. The fighting took place on three continents—Europe, Africa, and Asia—and spanned three oceans—the Atlantic, the Pacific, and the Indian Oceans. As a global war on such a massive scale, it affected millions of people throughout the world.

Global Connections

FLU EPIDEMIC
As Allied troops waited to return home, more suffering came upon them in the form of a deadly influenza epidemic that had spread throughout the world. This worldwide epidemic—called a pandemic—occurred in 1918 and 1919. It was spread around the world by soldiers. About twenty million people worldwide died from the flu epidemic.

Teaching Options

Section 3 Resources

Teacher's Resources (TR)
Terms to Know, p. 39
Review History, p. 73
Build Your Skills, p. 107
Concept Builder, p. 242
SQR Chart, p. 322

ESL/ELL STRATEGIES

Identify Essential Vocabulary Explain to students that they can often create an antonym, or opposite, of a word by adding a negative prefix such as *un-, de-, in-, im-,* or *non-* to the original word. The vocabulary word *demobilization* in this section is an antonym of *mobilization.* Have students add negative prefixes to *necessary, possible, sane,* and *sense* to create their opposites. (unnecessary, impossible, insane, nonsense)

Total War

World War I has been called a total war. That is because it involved massive numbers of people as well as the movement of people and goods. World War I changed the face of the globe forever. It brought mass destruction to cities and towns throughout the war-torn countries of Italy, Serbia, Poland, Belgium, and France. It changed political boundaries of entire countries. It also changed the makeup of the workforce. Women, who had worked in factories and in hospitals during the war, now entered the workforce in other occupations. Women also gained the right to vote in Great Britain and in the United States soon after the war's end.

Costs of the War

The expenses of waging a total war, such as World War I, were staggering. Statisticians—people who work with statistics—added up the costs of the war in terms of lives and money. The numbers they came up with were record breaking. They calculated the direct financial cost to be about $186 billion dollars in 1918 dollars. In addition, there were indirect costs of the war. These included losses of production, shipping and property; the medical costs for the wounded; the future economic contributions of people killed; and the costs of supporting the families of the people who died.

Loss of Life

Wartime losses greatly exceeded those of previous wars. These losses marked a turning point in the history of warfare. World War I had been waged on a scale unequaled to that point. More than 65 million people were in the military service. Major battles often engaged a million people or more. The casualty rates, soldiers who were killed or wounded, were tremendous. Figures are not precise, because in many instances, data was not collected, especially for civilian casualties. It is known that Serbia, Russia, and Bulgaria, for instance, had more civilian than military losses.

In one of the war's most horrifying events, Christian Armenians living in what is now eastern Turkey, were killed by the Ottoman Turks. The Ottoman government, one of the Central Powers, had uncovered some cases of Armenians collaborating, or working with, Russian forces. They then concluded that all Armenians were disloyal. One-and-a-half-million Armenian men, women, and children were massacred.

Total estimates for the number of soldiers killed in battle during the war range from 7 to 11 million. About double that number were wounded, many disabled for life. Other soldiers died from disease. An entire generation of Europe's youth were killed. American total losses were relatively slight, by comparison—about 125,000 had died, half from disease. Many families in Great Britain, France, and Germany lost someone in the fighting.

◆ **Why was World War I called a total war?**

Spotlight on *History*

SHELL SHOCK

The new type of warfare introduced in World War I gave rise to a common disorder called shell shock. Shell shock was the term used to identify those who did not have physical wounds but were mentally disabled—including those who were terrorized by the noise and danger of explosives. It also included those affected by other frightening experiences, such as poison gas, liquid fire, and army tanks. This disorder is now called posttraumatic stress disorder.

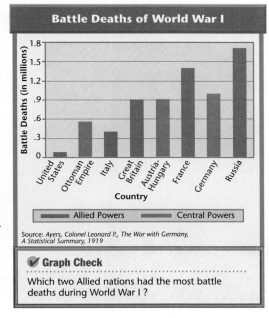

Battle Deaths of World War I

Battle Deaths (in millions) — Country: United States, Ottoman Empire, Italy, Great Britain, Austria-Hungary, France, Germany, Russia

Allied Powers / Central Powers

Source: Ayers, Colonel Leonard P., *The War with Germany, A Statistical Summary*, 1919

✔ **Graph Check**

Which two Allied nations had the most battle deaths during World War I ?

Test Taking

Point out that some test questions require students to interpret charts or graphs. Help students understand the information in the graph on page 625 by alerting them to carefully read the title, the labels, and the scale. Then, they should note the amount represented by the height of each bar and compare these amounts.

---

② Teach

A. Signing an Armistice

Purpose-Setting Question
When did the last American troops leave Europe and return home? (1923)

GLOBAL CONNECTIONS
FLU EPIDEMIC The flu epidemic might actually have begun at a U.S. army camp in Kansas in March 1918 and been carried to Europe by American soldiers heading to war. Returning soldiers brought the disease back with them. Ask students if they think more Americans died fighting in World War I or from the flu epidemic. (Approximate death totals are 116,516 for World War I and 650,000 for the flu.)

◆ **ANSWER** The terms of the armistice included canceling the treaty with Russia, the surrender of German submarines and navy, the release of all prisoners of war, and the right of the Allies to occupy part of Germany.

B. Effects of the War

Purpose-Setting Question What was the approximate total cost of World War I? ($186 billion in 1918 dollars)

SPOTLIGHT ON HISTORY
SHELL SHOCK While shell shock was a very real disorder, few soldiers received the medical care they needed. Many were sent back to the front. Ask students why doctors probably didn't send shell-shock patients home. (they knew that every soldier was needed; did not realize it was a real problem)

Using the Graph

Battle Deaths of World War I

Ask students to rank the Central Powers nations based on number of battle deaths suffered from greatest to fewest. (Answer: Germany, Austria-Hungary, Ottoman Empire)

✔ **Graph Check**
Answer Russia and France

◆ **ANSWER** because it involved massive numbers of people as well as the movement of people and goods

Purpose-Setting Question What were the first and last of President Wilson's Fourteen Points? (no secret treaties and the formation of an association of nations to guarantee independence for all nations)

Make a chart To help students remember President Wilson's Fourteen Points, have them make a three-column chart with the headings *Economic Points, Territory Points,* and *Independence Points.* Have students list each point under its appropriate heading. (**Economic:** 2, 3, 4; **Territory:** 1, 5, 6, 7, 8; **Independence:** 9, 10, 11, 12, 13, 14)

Review Ask students to recall the earlier Treaties of Paris. What war did those treaties conclude? What was similar about the two wars? (The earlier Treaties of Paris were signed in 1814 and 1815. They ended the Napoleonic Wars, which also involved armies of most major European powers.)

Discuss Have students read each of the Fourteen Points and then discuss which points a particular country might not like. Encourage students to support their choices.

Extend The Palace of Versailles was the official home of the kings of France from 1682 until 1790. It was originally built as a hunting lodge by Louis XIII and was greatly expanded by Louis XIV. The terrace that overlooked the original garden was removed to make way for the famed Hall of Mirrors.

TEACH PRIMARY SOURCES
Have students carefully examine the photograph on page 626. Ask them to describe how the image captures the mood and intensity of the negotiations of the forthcoming peace treaty.

C. The Terms of Peace

The war was not officially over until a plan for peace was established and a formal peace treaty was signed. U.S. President Woodrow Wilson had begun a first step toward world peace shortly after the armistice was signed. It was not until January 1919, however, that Allied delegates met in France to attend the formal Paris Peace Conference.

The Fourteen Points

In January 1918, about two months after the armistice had been signed by Germany, American President Woodrow Wilson made a speech in which he set forth his ideas about how countries of the world should exist after the war. Wilson's plan for world peace became known as the Fourteen Points. People everywhere, even in Germany, were impressed with Wilson's ideas. The Fourteen Points included:

1. No secret treaties
2. Freedom of the seas in war and peace
3. Free trade
4. Reduction of arms
5. A fair colonial settlement for the colonists as well as for the imperialists
6. Evacuation from Russian territory and the right of Russians to self-determination
7. The complete restoration of Belgium
8. Withdrawal of Germany from France and satisfaction for France concerning Alsace-Lorraine
9. A readjustment of the Italian border to accommodate ethnic groups
10. Self-determination for the peoples of Austria-Hungary
11. The restoration of Romania, Serbia, and Montenegro, with free access to the sea for Serbia and international guarantees of independence of the Balkan states
12. Self-rule for non-Turkish peoples in the Ottoman Empire
13. Independence for Poland with access to the sea
14. An association of nations to guarantee independence for all nations

The Paris Peace Conference

With Wilson's Fourteen Points as a basis for a peace plan, Allied leaders met in Paris to hammer out a formal peace treaty. Different committees worked on

Government representatives for each of the Allied nations gathered in Paris, France, to draft a treaty to end the war. None of the defeated nations was allowed to participate.

particular problems, such as determining who was responsible for the war, deciding who would make **reparations**, or payments for war damages, and settling territorial questions. Leaders of the Big Four, the four most powerful Allies—the United States, Great Britain, France, and Italy—drew up various treaties. One was known as the Treaty of Versailles, because the peace conference was held at the Palace of Versailles. Other Allied Powers outside of the Big Four only played a minor role. The Allied leaders at Versailles included President Wilson of the United States, David Lloyd George of Great Britain, Georges Clemenceau of France, and Vittorio Orlando of Italy.

During negotiations with other Allied Powers at the conference, each of the Big Four countries

---

Teaching Options

Research

AVERAGE

Have students do research on the Internet or in the library to find speeches President Wilson delivered to try to convince the American people and Congress to approve his peace plan and speeches delivered by politicians in opposition to Wilson's plan. Students should make a two-column chart listing the key arguments made on each side of the issue.

CHALLENGE

Have students find articles or editorials in old U.S. newspapers supporting or opposing establishment of the League of Nations after World War I and the United Nations near the end of World War II. Have students compare the arguments made in each situation and explain how the UN ultimately won U.S. approval whereas the League of Nations did not.

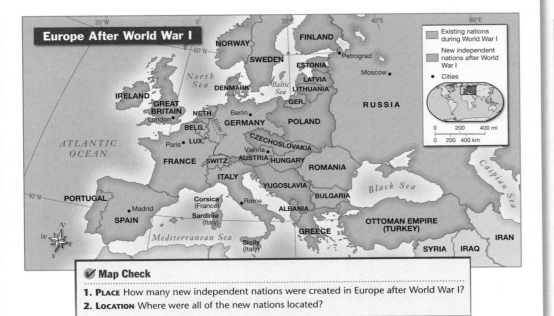

Europe After World War I

Existing nations during World War I

New independent nations after World War I

• Cities

Map Check

1. **PLACE** How many new independent nations were created in Europe after World War I?
2. **LOCATION** Where were all of the new nations located?

found items in the Fourteen Points they did not like. Great Britain, for example, opposed the point that called for freedom of the seas. Also, the Allies wanted to redraw the map of Europe on their own terms.

Treaty of Versailles

The defeated nations were not allowed to help draft the Treaty of Versailles. Delegates from these nations were shocked by the strict terms of the treaty and by the Allies' failure to honor promises made during negotiations before the treaty was written.

The treaty called for changes to Germany's population and territory, both of which were reduced by about 10 percent. The Alsace-Lorraine region in the west was returned to France. The Saarland, a coal-producing area on the French border, was placed under outside supervision until 1935. Three small areas in northern Germany were given to Belgium. Denmark received an area in northern Germany, Schleswig, after its people voted to leave Germany. To the east, Poland became a separate country again and was given access to the Baltic Sea. This move divided Germany's Prussian province in two. All of Germany's overseas colonies in China, in the Pacific, and in Africa were taken over by Allied nations. These colonies had been symbols of Germany's imperial power.

The hardest term of all for Germany to accept was the "war guilt" statement. It identified Germany as the aggressor in the war. Also humiliating were the terms of reparations that required Germany to pay the Allied nations for war damages and losses. A commission set the amount at $33 billion in reparations to be paid within 30 years. Economists pointed out that repayment of this huge debt could have an impact on international finances. If Germany fell behind on payments, the treaty allowed the Allies to take military action against Germany.

Connection to ----------
ECONOMICS ◁

The decision to require Germany to pay reparations backfired economically as well as politically. When Germany missed payments, France invaded the Ruhr area and took over German coal mines in 1923. The resulting flood of coal onto the market undercut prices of coal in Great Britain and was a main cause of a huge labor strike in Great Britain in 1926.

Using the Map

Europe After World War I

Have students compare this map to the one on page 619. Ask students which countries had territory reduced in order to create the independent nations formed after the war. (Germany, Russia, Austria-Hungary)

✔ **Map Check**

Answers
1. nine
2. In general, they were located east of Germany and west of Russia.

Discuss Ask students if they agree with the decision that prohibited defeated nations from helping to draft the peace treaty following World War I. Have students cite arguments on both sides of the issue. List their points on the board. Then, take a class vote on including or excluding the defeated nations in the peace process.

Focus The Treaty of Versailles punished Germany and rewarded the Allied nations. Review with students the conditions of the treaty and how it helped the Allies (money and territory) and punished Germany and the German people (loss of territory, large payments, loss of status).

Extend Germany was especially angered and humiliated by the peace process and final terms of the Treaty of Versailles. Ask students to predict how these feelings may have had an impact on later history. (Germany's displeasure led to the rise of Adolf Hitler and to Germany's decision to reassert its power, leading to World War II.)

Activity

Organize a protest Ask students to brainstorm ways to organize a peaceful protest against the Treaty of Versailles. Suggest that they use petitions or plans for rallies to be held in public places. They might also send letters to the editors of local newspapers. Ask students to determine the most effective means of peaceful protest.

Then & Now

MILITARY MIGHT

Similar to France's concern that Germany could pose a future military threat, nations today watch with alarm as more and more countries build military might.

In the twenty-first century, at least eight countries have nuclear weapons or the means to produce them.

The Treaty of Versailles required Germany to disarm many of its military operations.

The Big Four wanted to be certain that Germany would never again pose a threat to other countries in Europe. The treaty called for the German army to be restricted to 100,000 troops, reducing it to little more than a police force. The German high general staff was eliminated, and the German navy was reduced in the number of ships. The manufacture of armored cars, tanks, airplanes, submarines, and poison gas was prohibited. The area west of the Rhine River and 30 miles east of the river was made a **demilitarized zone**, an area that military forces cannot enter.

The League of Nations

The Treaty of Versailles also included the establishment of the League of Nations, which happened in 1920. This League called for member countries to guarantee one another's independence and territorial boundaries. The League would also manage certain territories and make plans to reduce armaments, or military forces and equipment.

For his efforts in making peace, Wilson received the 1919 Nobel Peace Prize. Of all the Fourteen Points, Wilson felt most strongly about the fourteenth point. He wanted the League of Nations to keep world peace.

However, in the United States, the League of Nations and the Treaty of Versailles were met with resistance. According to the U.S. Constitution, the Senate must approve all treaties made by the U.S. government. Wilson brought the Treaty of Versailles back to the Senate to be approved. However, Republicans, who made up the majority of the Senate, wanted to defeat Wilson's peace treaty. Many Republicans thought the League of Nations would limit American independent action in world affairs.

Wilson toured the United States by train to gain support for the treaty and the League of Nations. Without the League of Nations or some method to prevent conflict, he felt that there would surely be another world war.

During Wilson's tour of the country, he became seriously ill. He had to return to Washington, D.C., and could no longer work to gain more support for the peace treaty and the League. Wilson's illness eventually led to his death in 1924.

While the Treaty of Versailles was signed by other nations, it was not signed by the United States. The U.S. Senate rejected the treaty in 1919 and again in 1920. The Treaty of Versailles was signed in Paris, France, on June 28, 1919, exactly five years after Archduke Franz Ferdinand and his wife were assassinated. The United States made a separate treaty with Germany and never joined the League of Nations.

One of the main purposes of the League of Nations was to prevent aggression by enforcing the treaties made after World War I. However, the Treaty of Versailles and the League of Nations would not be enough to prevent another world war.

Other Treaties

In other treaties, the independence of Poland, Czechoslovakia, Hungary, and Yugoslavia—which

628   UNIT 7   ◆   Decades of War

Teaching Options

Meet Individual Needs:
KINESTHETIC LEARNERS

To help students understand the peace process that followed World War I, have them role-play a meeting of the Paris Peace Conference bringing out arguments made during the meetings and going over the final decisions for the Treaty of Versailles. Students can read sections of the text on pages 626–628 during their role-play or put the information into their own words.

F Y I

The Covenant

The basis of the League of Nations was the Covenant, which consisted of 26 articles from the Treaty of Versailles. Articles 1 through 7 outlined the structure of the league. It would have an assembly, composed of all member nations; a council composed of the great powers (originally Great Britain, France, Italy, and Japan) and four other, nonpermanent members; and a secretariat. In both the assembly and council, unanimous decisions were required.

included Serbia and Montenegro—were recognized when the political boundaries of Germany and Austria-Hungary were redrawn. Austria-Hungary's army was reduced and its navy was eliminated. Its ships were distributed among the Allies. Hungary lost two-thirds of its population to Czechoslovakia, Austria, Poland, Yugoslavia, Romania, and Italy. The Allies took away much of the Ottoman Empire's territory. Turkey lost territory to Greece and Italy, and Bulgaria was forced to give up territory to Greece and Yugoslavia. Mesopotamia, present-day Iraq, and Palestine, parts of which are now Israel, would be administered by the British.

Effects of the Peace Treaties

The harsh treaties resolved nothing permanently. The Allies ignored the dismay of their defeated enemies. This attitude allowed resentment to build. Germans were angered by the harshness of the settlement. The economic hardship of reparations encouraged the growth of military groups that would take control of the German government. American General Tasker H. Bliss, who had been at Versailles, predicted trouble ahead when he wrote in his diary,

ANALYZE PRIMARY SOURCES

> 66 We are in for a high period, followed by a low period. Then there will be the devil to pay all around the world. 99

DOCUMENT-BASED QUESTION Do you think the general foresaw an even bigger war on the horizon?

Less than 2 decades later, the unfinished business of the Great War of 1914–1918 would lead to another global conflict.

◆ **Why were the Treaty of Versailles and the League of Nations rejected in the United States?**

Review III

Review History
A. Why did Germany finally agree to sign an armistice?
B. What were some direct costs and some indirect costs of the war?
C. What was one of the main purposes of the League of Nations?

Define Terms to Know
Define the following terms: **armistice, demobilization, reparation, demilitarized zone**

Critical Thinking
How would being assigned to occupy Germany after the armistice was signed affect the spirits of American troops?

Write About Economics
Write a paragraph telling whether or not you think the amount of reparations Germany had to pay was fair. Be sure to give reasons for your opinion.

Get Organized
SQR CHART
Use an SQR chart to organize information from this section. For example, one topic from this section might be the Paris Peace Conference.

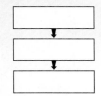

SURVEY
This section discusses the Paris Peace Conference.

↓

QUESTION
What was the result of the Paris Peace Conference?

↓

READ
The Treaty of Versailles was written. The terms of the treaty were harsh on Germany.

Critical Thinking
Possible answer: For many soldiers, it would have had a negative effect on their spirits not to be sent home when so many other soldiers were headed there.

Write About Economics
Students' essays should express their opinion and provide at least two or three reasons that support it.

ANALYZE PRIMARY SOURCES

DOCUMENT-BASED QUESTION
Earlier, General Bliss had commented unfavorably on the decision to send Japanese and American forces to guard areas of eastern Russia, feeling that either Japan or Russia might end up being part of a later war. "I have often thought," he wrote, "that this war, instead of being the last one, may be only the breeder of still more." Ask students to compare this statement with the one printed in the textbook.

ANSWER Yes. His comment is pessimistic, and he probably believed that Germany would eventually do something to destroy the peace that had been achieved.

◆ **ANSWER** Republicans in the Senate, who were the majority, rejected the peace treaty and the League of Nations because they thought the League of Nations would limit America's ability to act independently in world affairs.

Section Close

Note that this section ends on a pessimistic note, even though much of the section focuses on the peace process. Ask students to predict what might have happened in Europe after the Treaty of Versailles was signed.

3 Assess

Review Answers

Review History
A. because German commanders were convinced that Germany could not win the war

B. **Direct costs:** casualties and financial costs of fighting the war; **Indirect costs:** losses of production, shipping, property, medical costs for those injured, loss of economic contribution of those who were killed, and costs of supporting families of soldiers who had died

C. to guarantee the independence and territorial boundaries of member nations

Define Terms to Know
armistice, 624; demobilization, 624; reparation, 626; demilitarized zone, 628

Section Summary

In this section students will learn how Russia faced economic, social, and political problems for many years, leading to several revolutions; how Bolshevik leader V. I. Lenin led a revolution in 1917 and assumed power in the country; and how resistance to the Bolshevik revolution resulted in a civil war, after which the revolutionary party expanded its control over Russia.

1 Introduce

Getting Started

Direct students to one of the maps of Europe in this chapter (p. 619 or 627). Discuss the location and size of Russia compared to the other European countries. (larger, isolated, half in Europe and half in Asia, etc.) As students read this section, have them focus on Russia's differences from the rest of Europe politically as well as geographically.

TERMS TO KNOW

Ask students to read the words and definitions on page 630 and then find each word in the section. Point out that the words have a Latin, Russian, or Greek origin. Have students look up the words in a dictionary to learn their etymology and share their findings with the class.

You may wish to preview the pronunciation of the following names from this section with students.

Menshevik (MEHN shuh vihk)
Vladimir Ilich Ulyanov
(vluh DYEEM yihr ihl YEECH ool YAH nuhf)
Rasputin (ruh SPOOT yihn)

ACTIVE READING

Have students read the section on the Revolution of 1905 (p. 630) and make judgments about the czar's response to the march on the Winter Palace—firing on the marchers and later forming a Duma. Have students judge how effective those actions were and suggest better alternatives.

The Russian Revolutions

Terms to Know

proletariat the working people, especially industrial workers

soviet the elected governmental council set up by Russian revolutionaries

anarchy an absence of government; political disorder

Main Ideas

A. The Russian people were extremely discontented with their rulership in the years before the revolutions.

B. Resistance to the revolutions resulted in a civil war lasting three years and the spread of the revolutionary party in Russia.

 Active Reading

MAKE JUDGMENTS
When you make judgments, you piece together bits of information and come to a conclusion about what it all means. As you read this section, ask yourself how effective the temporary Russian government was after the first revolution of 1917.

A. Problems in Russia

Russia experienced many problems in the 1800s and early 1900s. Farm workers and peasants were starving because of a great population growth and the export of grain to strengthen the Russian economy. In the towns and cities, workers and a rising middle class wanted a chance to participate in government. Society underwent many changes as Russia became industrialized and urbanized.

Background to Discontent

During the reign of Russia's last czar, Nicholas II, there was a great deal of turmoil. As Czar Nicholas began ruling in 1894, dissatisfied people all over Russia formed organizations that they felt would better meet the needs of the people. One group, the Marxists, formed the Russian Social Democratic Labor Party in 1898 but split into two groups five years later. One group was called the Bolsheviks, and the other group was called the Mensheviks.

The Revolution of 1905, known as Bloody Sunday, was the first of three Russian revolutions during the early 1900s.

The Bolsheviks wanted party membership limited to a small group of professional revolutionaries. These revolutionaries would lead the **proletariat**, or working people. Vladimir Ilyich Ulyanov, better known as V. I. Lenin, led the Bolsheviks.

Beginning in 1899, Russian workers went on strike, and students protested against the rule of the czar. Revolts took place in the towns and countryside. A few years later, Russian expansion led to a war with Japan. The Russo-Japanese War ended with Russia's disastrous defeat in 1905.

The Revolution of 1905

On January 22, 1905, a Russian Orthodox priest named Father Gapon led thousands of people on a peaceful march to the czar's Winter Palace in the city of Saint Petersburg to ask for basic government reforms. They called for a democratically elected assembly. Hundreds of people were killed or wounded when the czar's soldiers fired on them. The Revolution of 1905, also known as Bloody Sunday, gave strength to the rebellion. However, Nicholas agreed to form a Duma, or parliament, to advise him after strikes disrupted the country.

Teaching Options

Section 4 Resources

Teacher's Resources (TR)
Terms to Know, p. 39
Review History, p. 73
Build Your Skills, p. 107
Chapter Test, pp. 167–168
Concept Builder, p. 242
SQR Chart, p. 322

ESL/ELL STRATEGIES

Organize Information Suggest that students create a flowchart (TR, p. 324) to keep track of events leading up to the Revolution of 1905, between the Revolution of 1905 and the March and November Revolutions, during the civil war, and after the civil war. Remind students to date their entries (month and year) and to include a short description of the event.

Later that year, revolutionaries set up a **soviet**, or elected governmental council, called the Saint Petersburg Soviet of Workers' Deputies. The czar gave the Duma more power in response to the revolutionaries, but strikes continued. In December 1905, the army was called in to put down another uprising. The Duma system was not perfect, because the czar and other wealthy, powerful men were not willing to give up much power. However, the Duma did provide a place for political discussion and debate.

◆ **What was the result of the Revolution of 1905?**

B. Two Revolutions and a Civil War

Nicholas took personal command of the military in the summer of 1915. His absence from Petrograd, which had previously been named Saint Petersburg, added to the general instability of the government. His wife, Alexandra, and Rasputin, a man who gained the royal family's trust, made important, but unwise decisions. Alexandra and Rasputin passed over qualified people to fill key positions. This action hurt the czar's chance of gaining popular support.

The March Revolution

During World War I, Russia experienced a heavy toll, with casualties in the millions. This ended the reign of Czar Nicholas. On March 8, 1917, people rioted in the streets of Petrograd over food and coal shortages. Soldiers, sent in to restore order, joined the revolt, which came to be known as the March Revolution. Czar Nicholas was forced to abdicate, thus ending a dynasty of more than 300 years of rule by the Romanov family.

The Duma set up a provisional, or temporary, government. The new government wanted to continue fighting on the Eastern Front against Germany. However, most Russians were fed up with the war. Soldiers were ill armed, poorly supplied, and had been defeated in a number of battles.

RASPUTIN
Grigory Yefimovich Rasputin was given the power to oversee appointments of church and state positions. In December 1916, supporters of the czar who feared that Rasputin's power would lead to the ruler's overthrow, plotted and carried out Rasputin's murder. It turned out to be quite difficult to kill him. Rasputin was poisoned, shot through the chest, beaten, shot again, and finally drowned in the icy Neva River.

They Made History

Czar Nicholas II 1868–1918

Nicholas II was the last czar, or emperor, of the Russian Empire. He ruled from 1894 until 1917, when he was forced to abdicate, or step down. Personally charming, Nicholas did not have the ability to be an effective ruler. His bad decisions led to military and political disasters. Nicholas's wife, the Empress Alexandra, and her adviser, Rasputin, made national policy decisions that were unsound.

As the March Revolution gained momentum, a small group of Nicholas's generals convinced him to give up his rule. He and his family were confined first to their Winter Palace in Petrograd and eventually to a city in the Ural Mountains. There, they were held as prisoners by the Bolsheviks. In July 1918, Nicholas, his wife, and their five children were placed in a room and shot to death by local Bolshevik authorities to prevent a possible rescue by the czar's supporters.

The last Russian czar, Nicholas II, poses with the Empress Alexandra and their children.

Critical Thinking Do you think Nicholas could have avoided his and his family's fate?

Meet Individual Needs:

AUDITORY LEARNERS

Have students take turns reading the paragraphs in subsection A aloud. Then, have pairs of students interview each other about the discussions between Father Gapon and Czar Nicholas at the Winter Palace on January 22, 1905. Each student should ask at least three questions concerning the problems Russia faced since 1898 and what led to the bloody confrontation on that day.

Connection to
GEOGRAPHY ⟨

Saint Petersburg has been renamed many times over the years. Peter the Great founded the city in 1703 and gave it his name. In 1914, Czar Nicholas changed the name to Petrograd. After Lenin died in 1924, the city was renamed Leningrad in his honor. In 1991, city residents voted to return to the name Saint Petersburg.

A. Problems in Russia

Purpose-Setting Question Who were the Bolsheviks and the Mensheviks? (two groups into which the Russian Social Democratic Labor Party split in 1903)

Discuss Ask students what the czar's response to the march on the Winter Palace showed about his relationship with his subjects. (distant, distrustful, out of touch) Discuss how events at the Winter Palace foreshadowed future events.

◆ **ANSWER** Hundreds of people were killed or wounded, but the event strengthened the revolutionary movement in Russia and forced Nicholas to form a Duma, or parliament, to advise him.

B. Two Revolutions and a Civil War

Purpose-Setting Question What was Russia's provisional government? (the government that served between the March and November 1917 Revolutions, a period of anarchy in Russia)

WHO IN THE WORLD?

RASPUTIN Rasputin came from a peasant family and was a troublemaker in his youth. He later assumed the role of a holy man though he never stopped his wild behavior. Despite his evil reputation, Rasputin was seen as a "man of the people" by many peasants, who were angry when he was killed.

THEY MADE HISTORY
Czar Nicholas II
Explain to students that Nicholas spent his entire life either guarded by secret police and soldiers or serving in the officer corps of the Russian army. This isolation added to his problems in understanding the demands made by the Russian revolutionaries and may have been a factor in his downfall.

ANSWER Possible answer: No. Nicholas's failure to govern wisely put him and his family at the mercy of the revolutionaries. They probably could not have escaped their fate.

Point out that the March Revolution had many parallels to the French Revolution. Present the following details to students and have them name the parallel events described in Chapter 19 of this book. Crowds of working-class people demanding peace marched in the capital city. (march of Parisian women on Versailles and storming of the Bastille) The czar ordered the Duma to disband, but most members simply moved to a new meeting place. (Tennis Court Oath) The czar was forced to abdicate (King Louis was overthrown); anarchy reigned in Russia for a time (the Reign of Terror). The czar was assassinated. (King Louis was guillotined.) A totalitarian regime eventually took power. (the rise of Napoleon)

ANALYZE PRIMARY SOURCES

DOCUMENT-BASED QUESTION

The sheer size of Russia added to the confusion and anarchy. It took weeks for representatives of the provisional government to arrive in some areas to explain what was happening. Meanwhile, unhappy workers and soldiers in areas far away from Petrograd had heard rumors of change and began making demands on their employers or deserting their posts, but they didn't have any real idea of who was in charge of the government.

ANSWER Petrograd, Moscow, and Kiev

Discuss Point out that the word *anarchy* literally means "without a ruler." Ask students if a leader is needed to be in charge of a government, an army, or a club. Discuss the role that leaders play and the problems that may occur without strong leadership. Ask students what problems arose in Russia's army and government when there was a "leadership gap."

Activity

Make a timeline Have students create a timeline (TR, p. 320) of the major events in the Communist takeover of Russia and the civil war between the White Army and the Red Army. Have them do research and include the birth and death dates of central figures during this period (such as Marx, Engels, Trotsky, Czar Nicholas II, Lenin).

The new provisional government's authority was challenged almost immediately by the Petrograd Soviet of Workers' and Soldiers' Deputies, who claimed to represent the people. On March 14, 1917, soldiers and sailors were told to ignore orders from their commanding officers. In addition, revolutionaries continued to set up soviets in other cities.

Between Revolutions

The provisional government was reorganized four times between March and October. None of the leaders could effectively address the problems facing the country. The government was unpopular with the people because it refused to end the war with Germany. In addition, independence movements of non-Russian peoples across the Russian Empire contributed to a state of **anarchy**, or political disorder. A French diplomat stationed in Petrograd commented on the anarchy that spread throughout Russia:

> ❝ The state of anarchy is confirmed and extends further and further every day. Petrograd is no longer the only centre [center]: it's the same everywhere, in Moscow, in Kiev, and confusion and disorder reign. ❞

By September, amid cries of "peace, land, and bread," the Bolsheviks and their allies won strong support among hungry urban workers and soldiers, who were deserting in large numbers.

The November Revolution

In November 1917, the Bolsheviks were ready to start uprisings and use force to seize power. V. I. Lenin saw that the time was ripe for a Bolshevik-led takeover and made plans with another Bolshevik leader, Leon Trotsky. On November 7, 1917, armed workers, soldiers, and sailors captured the Winter Palace in Petrograd. The Bolsheviks, under the leadership of Lenin, overthrew the provisional government in a nearly bloodless revolution.

The next day, Lenin ended private ownership of land and redistributed land taken from the upper classes. Workers were given control of the mines and factories. Soon, the Bolsheviks seized power in other cities as well. The Bolsheviks, renamed Communists, now controlled the Russian government under their leader V. I. Lenin.

The Russian Civil War

Weeks after the November revolution, two events occurred. The first was that Lenin signed the Treaty of Brest-Litovsk with Germany. The second was that counter-revolutionaries who still supported the czar, known as the White Army, began to resist the Communists, who were known as the Red Army. For nearly three years, both sides waged a civil war.

The White Army was supported by Allied forces. They did not want to see the Communists in power, because of their political beliefs. In 1920, when the Communists won the civil war, Russia became the first state controlled by a Communist Party.

DOCUMENT-BASED QUESTION
Which cities does this French diplomat specifically mention to support his observations about Russia?

Priests were sometimes attacked as the Bolshevik government tried to stop religious worship.

632 UNIT 7 ◆ Decades of War

Teaching Options

Connection to LITERATURE ←

John Reed, a left-wing American journalist, was in Petrograd during the November Revolution and wrote about it in *Ten Days That Shook the World.* Students might find the book interesting, though they should be aware that Reed had a strong pro-Communist bias that comes out in his description of revolutionary events. The movie *Reds* is a romanticized version of Reed's life and writing.

ESL/ELL STRATEGIES

Identify Essential Vocabulary Communism is an economic system characterized by collective ownership of property and the organization of labor for the common good of all members. In most forms of communism, the state controls the economy. The word *communism* comes from Old French and Latin words for "common." Suggest to students that they investigate the related terms of *commune* and *community*.

Lenin's Leadership

For a short time after the November revolution, Lenin had allowed peasant groups to keep farmland they had taken from the upper classes. He also allowed groups of workers to control factories. However, during the Russian Civil War, the Communist government took control of businesses and industries—the factories, railroads, mines, and banks. Also, many peasants were forced to provide food for the Red Army and for people living in the cities.

Views of Communism

The economic and political system practiced in Russia in 1917—known as communism—was a mix of the ideas of nineteenth-century German philosopher Karl Marx and the ideas of Lenin. Marx believed workers must be put in control to create a peaceful society. He believed capitalism, or private control of the economy, must be replaced with a government controlled by the proletariat. Workers should seize control by means of a violent revolution, because those in power would not willingly give up control. Eventually, a classless society would evolve, in which everyone would live in prosperous freedom. In this classless society, there would be no need for government.

Lenin agreed with Marx that only violence would bring about needed change. He differed from Marx in the belief that not all workers, but rather a small group, would lead the revolution. Instead of no government, the Communists believed in the need for an all-powerful government.

◆ **How did the Communists gain power in Russia?**

Ideas of Communism

- Society provides equality and economic security for everyone.
- Government owns the means of production—the land, factories, and other economic resources.
- Government plans most economic activities.
- Strict rules dominate the Communist Party and all of government.
- Government controls almost all aspects of people's lives.
- Collective, or group, needs are more valued than personal freedoms.

✔ Chart Check

Under communism, which are the three things that the government controls?

Review IV

Review History
A. What were some of the problems in Russia in the 1800s and early 1900s?
B. How did Lenin's view of communism differ from Marx's view?

Define Terms to Know
Define the following terms: **proletariat, soviet, anarchy**

Critical Thinking
Why do you think Marx and Lenin believed capitalism must be abolished?

Write About Government
Write an editorial for a Russian newspaper in 1917 in which you describe the March Revolution and its effects.

Get Organized
SQR CHART
Use an SQR chart to organize information from this section. For example, one topic from this section might be the revolutions and civil wars in Russia.

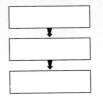

SURVEY
This section discusses revolutions and civil war in Russia.

QUESTION
When were the revolutions and civil war?

READ
There were revolutions in 1905 and two in 1917. A civil war occurred from 1917 to 1920.

Critical Thinking
Possible answer: Because owners, not workers, profited from capitalism; people did not benefit equally in capitalism.

Write About Government
Students' editorials may include the following: The March Revolution ended the reign of Czar Nicholas II and helped establish a new government that ultimately led to Communist rule.

Chapter Summary

A blank outline form is available in the Teacher's Resources (p. 318). Chapter summaries should outline the situation in Europe leading up to World War I, key developments during the war, the difficult peace process and its effects, and the revolutionary events going on in Russia during and after World War I. Refer to the rubric in the Teacher's Resources (p. 340) to score students' chapter summaries.

⬤ Interpret the Timeline

1. 4 years (1914–1918)
2. Panama Canal opens.
3. 1917
4. Approximately 25 million people around the world die from the influenza epidemic.
5. Check that students' events are all from the chapter.

Use Terms to Know

6. f. reparation
7. i. ultimatum
8. b. armistice
9. d. entente
10. e. mobilize
11. h. stalemate
12. a. anarchy
13. c. demobilization
14. g. soviet

Check Your Understanding

15. The Industrial Revolution spurred European nations to look for new markets and sources of raw materials, which meant increased competition for overseas colonies.
16. It would isolate Germany and he feared being attacked on both the eastern and western borders at the same time.
17. **Allies' advantages:** military troops and resources, industrial resources, better naval access. **Central Powers' advantages:** railway network, large and well-trained military, navy
18. Many Russian troops were killed, wounded, or captured and their equipment was lost or destroyed.
19. The United States, Great Britain, France, and Italy
20. Germany was forced to disarm and reduce much of its military operations so that it would not ever be a military threat again.

21. The Allies ignored the dismayed reaction of their defeated enemies, which caused resentment to build over the harshness of the treaties.
22. In the March Revolution, people rioted over food and coal shortages and were supported by the soldiers during the riot. After the uprising, Lenin let the peasants keep farmland they had taken from the nobles. In addition, he allowed workers to control factories and participate in government.
23. After the November Revolution, Lenin helped the Bolsheviks seize power with himself as their leader. The Communist government then reshaped the economic and political structure of Russia.

Chapter Summary

Complete the following outline in your notebook. Then, use your outline to write a brief summary of the chapter.

World War I and the Russian Revolutions

I. Factors Leading to War
   A. Europe on the Eve of War
   B. Forming Alliances
   C. War Breaks Out
II. The War Is Fought
   A. The War Unfolds
   B. The War From 1914 to 1916
   C. Global Involvement
III. Peace in a New Europe
   A. Signing an Armistice
   B. Effects of the War
   C. The Terms of Peace
IV. The Russian Revolutions
   A. Problems in Russia
   B. Two Revolutions and a Civil War

⬤ Interpret the Timeline

Use the timeline on pages 610–611 to answer the following questions.

1. How many years were there between the beginning and end of World War I?
2. Which world event happened the same year the war began?
3. When did the United States declare war on Germany?
4. **Critical Thinking** Which world event had the most immediate impact on the greatest number of people?
5. Select five events from the chapter that are not on the timeline. Create a timeline that shows these events.

Use Terms to Know

Match each term with its definition.

a. anarchy   d. entente   g. soviet
b. armistice   e. mobilize   h. stalemate
c. demobilization   f. reparation   i. ultimatum

6. the payment for damages
7. a final demand made with a threat to break off dealings or use force if not accepted
8. an agreement to stop warfare
9. an agreement between countries to follow common policies
10. to assemble and be ready to move, as for war
11. a situation in which neither side is able to defeat the other
12. an absence of government; political disorder
13. the disbanding or discharging of troops
14. the elected governmental council set up by Russian revolutionaries

Check Your Understanding

15. **Discuss** how the Industrial Revolution led to increased tensions among some European countries.
16. **Explain** why German chancellor Otto von Bismarck wanted to prevent an alliance between France and Russia.
17. **Discuss** the advantages of the Allies and of the Central Powers.
18. **Describe** what happened to Russian troops on the Eastern Front.
19. **Identify** the Big Four.
20. **Explain** why Germany was forced to disarm and reduce so much of its military operations.
21. **Explain** why there was no permanent resolution from the treaties signed after the armistice.
22. **Summarize** what happened during the March Revolution in Russia.
23. **Discuss** Lenin's leadership after the November Revolution.

Critical Thinking

24. **Analyze** Do you think there was any way World War I could have been avoided? Explain.

25. **Make Judgments** Explain what you think was the worst part of trench warfare.

26. **Make Inferences** Why do you think none of the defeated nations could participate in drafting the Treaty of Versailles?

27. **Analyze Primary Sources** Which words from the French diplomat's quotation on page 632 do you think best reveal his feelings about Russia in 1917?

Put Your Skills to Work

28. **Interpret Statistics** You have learned how to interpret statistics by looking carefully at factual evidence, which may be written or visual. Study the chart below, taking careful note of the statistics. Then, answer the following questions.

   a. Which resources did the Allied Powers have more of than the Central Powers?

   b. Why would having higher steel production be an advantage during the war?

   c. Based on the statistics in the chart, do you think the Allies had a significant advantage over the Central Powers? Explain.

Strength of the Warring Nations, 1914

RESOURCES	ALLIED POWERS	CENTRAL POWERS
Military forces	3,186,000	2,350,000
Steel production (in millions of metric tons)	15.3	17.0
Army divisions ready to mobilize	212	146
Modern battleships	39	20

Source: *Encyclopedia Britannica*

Analyze Sources

29. Read about one British woman's reaction after she learns of her family's first war casualty, the death of a cousin she barely knew. Then, answer the questions that follow.

   The original bullet wound behind the ear had not been serious, but he had lain untended for a week at Mudros, and was . . . operated on, too late, by an overworked surgeon. . . . [I]t was a shock to learn that lives were being thrown away through the inadequacy of the medical services.

   a. What shocks the woman?

   b. What does the woman say about her cousin's operation?

   c. What does the woman think was more serious than the bullet wound?

Essay Writing

30. Many ethnic groups controlled by large empires during the early 1900s wanted to govern themselves. Write an essay about why you think those in power resisted and who their supporters might have been. Include details from the chapter as support.

TEST PREPARATION

RECOGNIZING FACT AND OPINION
Choose the correct answer.

Which statement is an opinion rather than a fact about the Treaty of Versailles?

1. The terms of the treaty were harsh.

2. The Germans deserved the treaty's strict terms.

3. The treaty included the establishment of the League of Nations.

4. The Allies ignored the Germans' feelings about the treaty.

Critical Thinking

24. World War I probably could not have been avoided, because of the issues and tensions in Europe.

25. Possible answer: The worst part of trench warfare was that poison gas got trapped in the trenches, causing severe injuries to soldiers who breathed it.

26. Possible answer: The victorious nations did not believe that the defeated nations had a right to participate in drafting of the peace.

27. Possible answer: "Confusion and disorder reign."

Put Your Skills to Work

INTERPRET STATISTICS

28a. military forces, army divisions ready to mobilize, and modern battleships

28b. Possible answer: Steel could be used to make armored tanks and ships.

28c. Possible answer: Yes. The Allies led in three of the resource categories, and they had significantly more military personnel.

Analyze Sources

29a. She is shocked that lives were lost so easily due to a lack of medical services.

29b. He was operated on too late by a surgeon who was overworked.

29c. Her cousin had not been taken care of for a week, and the operation was too late.

Essay Writing

30. Students' essays should give reasons why nations with large ethnic populations, such as Austria-Hungary and the Ottoman Empire, would not want groups to become independent. Some possible reasons are loss of land, less money because less people would be taxed, and the loss of the labor force. Essays should include details from the chapter that support their conclusions, such as empires valued territory and did not want to lose it.

TEST PREPARATION

Answer 2. The Germans deserved the treaty's strict terms.

Crises Around the World
1919–1938
(pp. 636–659)

Chapter Objectives

- Explain how a new government developed in the Soviet Union under the leadership of Lenin and Stalin.
- Describe how western democracies began to recover from World War I and how that recovery was shattered by the Great Depression.
- Discuss how China was torn by civil war and how Southeast Asia and India began their push for independence.
- Identify how Mussolini in Italy and Hitler in Germany used their countries' troubles to rise to power.

Chapter Summary

Section I focuses on the establishment of the Soviet Union, including Lenin's changes in government and economics, and Stalin's reorganization of Russian agriculture and industry.

Section II explores the West's search for peace after the war, the brief prosperity followed by the Great Depression, and how Great Britain and France dealt with postwar crises.

Section III focuses on civil war in China between Communists and Nationalists, and on the beginnings of independence in Southeast Asia and India.

Section IV explores the causes and effects of Mussolini and Hitler's rise to power in Italy and Germany, respectively.

Set the Stage

TEACH PRIMARY SOURCES
Remind students of the devastation in Europe after World War I and the harsh peace terms of the Treaty of Versailles. Tell students that Vladimir Lenin became the leader of Russia after the revolution in 1917. His plan was to create a new Russia out of the ruins of the country's civil war. Ask students what Lenin's goal was, according to this excerpt. (to unite the Soviet republics to create a great, powerful nation) Joseph Stalin succeeded Lenin after his death in 1924.

Crises Around the World
1919–1938

I. Changing Government in the Soviet Union
II. Upheaval in the West
III. Unrest in China, Southeast Asia, and India
IV. The Rise of Dictatorships

The years after World War I were a time of both new hopes and great troubles. People had survived the horror of the war and now had high hopes for an era of peace, progress, and prosperity. Some of these dreams came true—at least for a time. Then, in 1929, a period of severe economic decline around the world shattered those dreams. People became desperate for jobs, housing, and even food. Many people began to look to strong leaders to restore order. One of these leaders, Vladimir Lenin, promised to lead the Soviet Union back to greatness. Joseph Stalin, a member of the policy-making group under Lenin's leadership, had this to say:

> ❝ *Comrades [friends], this day marks a turning point in the history of the Soviet power. . . . a landmark between the old period . . . when the Soviet republics, although they acted in common, yet each followed its own path and was concerned primarily with its own preservation, and the new period . . . when an end is being put to the isolated experience of the Soviet republics, . . .* ❞

CHAPTER EVENTS

1919
Adolf Hitler joins the Nazi Party.

1922
Benito Mussolini takes control in Italy.

1928
First Five Year Plan begins in Soviet Union.

| 1919 | 1923 | 1927 |

WORLD EVENTS

1923
Atatürk begins to modernize Turkey.

1928
Amelia Earhart is a passenger on a flight across the Atlantic Ocean.

Teaching Options

Chapter 27 Resources

Teacher's Resources (TR)
- Terms to Know, p. 40
- Review History, p. 74
- Build Your Skills, p. 108
- Chapter Test, pp. 169–170
- Concept Builder, p. 243
- Idea Web, p. 321
- Transparencies 5, 7

ASSESSMENT
- Section Reviews, pp. 642, 647, 652, 657
- Chapter Review, pp. 658–659
- Chapter Test, TR, pp. 169–170

ALTERNATIVE ASSESSMENT
- Portfolio Project, p. 684
- Create a Bulletin Board Display, p. T684

Crises After War, 1938

GET ORGANIZED

Idea Web An idea web allows you to see the connection between topics and ideas or events. Use an idea web as you read Chapter 27. Write a topic in the center circle. Then, list related ideas or events in the outer circles. Here is an example from this chapter.

- Started by Lenin in 1921
- State controlled large industries.
- New Economic Policy
- Created a more industrial nation
- Some profits were allowed.

VIEW HISTORY Vladimir Lenin was the leader of Russia from 1917 until 1924. Under his dictatorship, Russia became a one-party Communist nation, called the Soviet Union.
What does this poster tell you about the type of leader Lenin was?

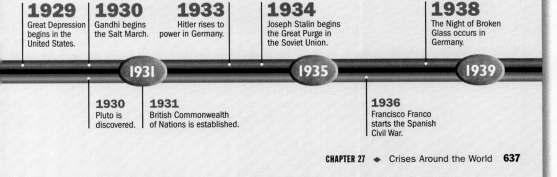

1929 Great Depression begins in the United States.

1930 Gandhi begins the Salt March.

1933 Hitler rises to power in Germany.

1934 Joseph Stalin begins the Great Purge in the Soviet Union.

1938 The Night of Broken Glass occurs in Germany.

1931   1935   1939

1930 Pluto is discovered.

1931 British Commonwealth of Nations is established.

1936 Francisco Franco starts the Spanish Civil War.

CHAPTER 27 ◆ Crises Around the World **637**

Chapter Themes
- Power, Authority, and Governance
- Culture
- Production, Distribution, and Consumption
- Individuals, Groups, and Institutions
- Civic Ideals and Practices

F Y I

Posters as Tools of Propaganda
The illustration on this page is a poster, a printed sheet of paper for public display. Posters usually use bright colors and simple illustrations to attract viewers. This poster was used in the early years of the Soviet Union. Lenin is pointing west, to Europe, from the Russian perspective. Ask students what Lenin might be saying. (Possible answer: Communism is the best form of government. It will help people all over the world.)

Chapter Warm-Up
USING THE MAP
Point out the locator map at the top of page 637. Have students identify the areas discussed in the chapter. (North America, Europe, Asia) Ask students to make a prediction regarding these areas of the world at this time. (Possible answer: The period after World War I was a time of crisis in many countries.)

VIEW HISTORY
Ask students to describe the poster. (Lenin is pointing to something, perhaps giving a speech.) Ask what is in the background. (tall chimneys of factories) Point out the drama of portraying Lenin in a diagonal pose across the poster, in contrast to the typical face-forward pose.

◆ **ANSWER** Lenin was a very strong and commanding leader.

GET ORGANIZED
Idea Web
Discuss the idea web on page 637. Ask students what the main idea is. (New Economic Policy) Explain that this was a plan devised by Lenin to help Russia gain economic stability. Remind students that the web can be expanded by adding more circles as links to the existing circles. Encourage students to make an idea web (TR, p. 321) for each section in the chapter.

⬤ TEACH THE TIMELINE
The timeline on pages 636–637 covers the period between 1919 and 1938, a period of 19 years. Remind students that these years fall between World War I and World War II. Ask students to identify the intervals on the timeline. (4 years) Have students identify the Chapter Events that involve Germany. (1919—Adolf Hitler joins the Nazi Party; 1933—Hitler rises to power in Germany; 1938—The Night of Broken Glass occurs in Germany.) Encourage students to refer to the timeline as they read the chapter to help place events in historical perspective.

Activity
Present an oral summary Tell students that the first commercial radio station began broadcasting in 1920. Have students work in pairs or groups to prepare and present a 1- to 2-minute oral summary of events between the years 1929 and 1933 for a radio station's news show.

CHAPTER 27 ◆ T637

I. Changing Government in the Soviet Union

(pp. 638–642)

Section Summary

In this section, students will learn how Lenin began to transform Russia into the Soviet Union, focusing on government and economics. They will also learn how Stalin took control after Lenin's death, implementing a dictatorship and a rule of terror in the Soviet Union.

1 Introduce

Getting Started

Use maps of Europe and Asia (pages A5 and A7 in the Atlas or Transparencies 5 and 7) to show students the extent of the former Soviet Union. Ask students to comment on its total size. Then, point out one of the smaller republics that are now independent nations (Georgia, Armenia, etc.), and have students discuss how this republic could do much more as part of the union than it could do on its own.

TERMS TO KNOW

Ask students to read the terms and definitions on page 638 and find each term in the section. Have them find smaller words that they recognize in *command economy*, and *collective. (command, collect)* Point out how these words are clues to the terms' meanings: *Command* tells that the economy was directed by orders; *collect* tells that people were gathered together.

You may wish to preview the pronunciation of the following word with students.

collectivization
(kuh lehk tih vih ZAY shuhn)

ACTIVE READING

After reading each subsection, suggest that students pause and attempt to answer the question, "What explains each viewpoint?" regarding Lenin and Stalin. Then, have students try to articulate a contrasting viewpoint as a possible response to each Soviet leader.

Changing Government in the Soviet Union

Terms to Know

command economy an economy in which a central government makes all economic decisions

collective a large farm that is worked by peasants but is owned by a government

quota a fixed amount

kulak a wealthy peasant in the Soviet Union

The sickle and hammer were symbols of the Soviet Union. The sickle stood for agricultural workers and the hammer for industrial workers.

Main Ideas

A. Vladimir Lenin laid the foundation of single-party Communist rule in the Soviet Union.

B. Stalin believed that harsh measures were needed to turn the Soviet Union into a strong industrial and military power.

 Active Reading

SUMMARIZE
When you summarize, you restate the main ideas in your own words. As you read this section, summarize the changes that took place in the Soviet Union under the leadership of Lenin and Stalin.

A. The Soviet Union Under Lenin

The Communists faced difficult times after they took control of the Russian government. Many of the nobles and large landowners hated them. The peasants, too, were angry because they were forced to give up their crops to this new government. Many people also feared the government's total control over their lives. As you learned in Chapter 26, the White Army, as the enemies of the Communists were called, fought to overthrow the Communist dictatorship in a civil war from 1917 to 1921. Great Britain, France, and the United States supported these groups and sent soldiers to help in the fight. However, the Communist armies had defeated the White Army by 1921.

The end of the civil war in 1921 left Russia in terrible shape. Hundreds of thousands of people had been killed. Many of Russia's farms and factories had closed, and many workers were out of jobs. Crop harvests were poor, and several million Russians died from hunger and disease. Vladimir Lenin, the country's new leader, knew that he must take strong steps to rebuild Russia.

Lenin ruled Russia, which was renamed the Soviet Union, until his death in 1924. For the first years of his rule, he was busy putting down another civil war. When the Communists were victorious, he turned to creating a new country out of the old one. He created a new system of government and a new economy.

Forming a New Government

Lenin moved to strengthen the country in many different ways. Because the nation included several major national groups, Lenin set up four republics in Russia. He changed the nation's name to the Union of Soviet Socialist Republics, or the Soviet Union. Lenin also organized the Communist Party into a strong, tightly run group.

In 1918, the Communists wrote a new constitution. Under this constitution, everyone had certain rights, and all citizens over 18 could vote. All political power, resources, and means of production would belong to the workers and peasants. The new constitution seemed to reflect the will of the people. In reality, however, the Communist Party controlled the government.

The people did not immediately accept Lenin's plans. Lenin believed that something was wrong with the people. He and other leaders believed that they needed to make the people accept communism, using force if necessary to convince the people about the benefits of the plan. Early on, Soviet

---

Teaching Options

Section 1 Resources

Teacher's Resources (TR)

Terms to Know, p. 40
Review History, p. 74
Build Your Skills, p. 108
Chapter Test, pp. 169–170
Concept Builder, p. 243
Idea Web, p. 321
Transparencies 5 and 7

Conflict Resolution

When Lenin saw the shambles of the Soviet economy in 1921, he adjusted his economic plan so that it could be more successful. The NEP combined communism and capitalism. Soon, the Soviet economy was on the upswing. Lenin perceived the conflict between communism and capitalism, but he could overlook this conflict for the good of the country. Ask students for instances when they have been able to reach such a compromise.

authorities established forced labor camps, places to which political prisoners were sent to do manual labor for the government. People who did not agree with communism often found themselves in such labor camps.

Lenin also set up Communist International, or Comintern. Comintern urged people around the world to revolt and overthrow capitalism and democratic governments. Comintern was in contact with Communist parties in other countries, and often directed their activities. For example, the British government found evidence that Soviets had tried to turn a labor strike into a revolution in Great Britain. As a result, Great Britain broke off relations with the Soviet Union.

A New Economic Plan

By 1921, the economy of the Soviet Union was in ruins. This happened because, as early as 1917, Lenin had given the state the right to control large industries and factories. The state also forced farmers to turn over products as needed. In addition, Lenin had made the following statement:

> 66 The right of private ownership of land is abolished forever. Land cannot be bought, sold, leased, mortgaged, or alienated [transferred to another] in any manner whatsoever. All lands . . . pass to the nation without any indemnification [damage or loss] and are turned over for the use of those who till them. 99

Because of harsh working conditions and government interference in the economy, no one wanted to produce anything for the government. Production was a fraction of what it was before the civil war. In the past, Russia had exported food. Now, the Soviet Union had to import it.

Lenin began the New Economic Policy, or NEP, in late 1921. His goal was to create a stronger, more industrial nation. Under the NEP, the government still owned all basic industries. However, it also allowed some private ownership of property. The government no longer took food from farmers. Peasants were allowed to sell their products again, and workers could start up small factories and workshops. These new factories were not controlled by the state. However, large industries, banks, and foreign trade stayed under state control.

Under the NEP, the Soviet economy began to recover. Production crawled back to prewar levels in a few years. Higher production brought renewed prosperity. People began to enjoy a higher standard of living. When Lenin died in 1924, the Soviet Union was once more becoming an important world power.

◆ **What were the main points of Lenin's New Economic Plan?**

B. Joseph Stalin Takes Control

After the death of Lenin, a power struggle began. Communist leaders struggled against each other to be the person who would take Lenin's place. The two main opponents were Leon Trotsky and Joseph Stalin. Trotsky was a brilliant Communist thinker.

ANALYZE PRIMARY SOURCES

DOCUMENT-BASED QUESTION
What happened to lands that were seized by the state under Lenin's order?

Peasants gather to trade goods in a square in Petrograd in the winter of 1922.

CHAPTER 27 ◆ Crises Around the World **639**

Focus on WORLD RELIGIONS

Communists and Religion Karl Marx, the founder of modern communism, once wrote, "Religion . . . is the opium of the people." The leaders of the new Soviet state took this saying to heart. They embarked on a campaign of repression and ridicule to discourage religious belief. Since the Russian Orthodox Church had links with the monarchy and was the dominant faith in Russia, the Communists concentrated their efforts toward its destruction. They nationalized all Church property. They classified priests as kulaks and had them killed or deported. They were equally ruthless with the followers of Roman Catholicism and Judaism, killing Catholic priests and desecrating Jewish synagogues. Today, the Communists are no longer in power, and the Russian people are returning to their faiths.

---

2 Teach

A. The Soviet Union Under Lenin

Purpose-Setting Question How did Lenin try to establish a stable Communist regime in Russia? (He created a new system of government and a new economy. He used force to maintain Communist Party control.)

Review Remind students of the outcome of the Russian Revolution in 1917, which they read about in Chapter 26.

Discuss Ask students in what ways the new constitution did not reflect the reality of life in Russia. (Possible answer: The Communist Party did not really reflect the will of many Russians; there was little or no personal freedom.)

ANALYZE PRIMARY SOURCES

DOCUMENT-BASED QUESTION
This statement is part of the Land Decree issued by Lenin. The Land Decree helped Lenin and the more radical Communists win support from the peasant masses, who thought they stood to gain land if this decree were upheld.

ANSWER The state owned the lands, but peasants were allowed to work the land.

Explore Have students identify aspects of the NEP that reflected Communist beliefs. (Government owned basic industries; banks and foreign trade stayed under state control.) Discuss why the NEP was successful. (Possible answer: It allowed some private ownership, which encouraged farmers and workers to work.)

◆ **ANSWER** The main points of the NEP were that government owned basic industries, some private ownership of property was allowed, government no longer took food from farmers, and peasants were allowed to sell their products.

B. Joseph Stalin Takes Control

Purpose-Setting Question What policies did Stalin enact in the Soviet Union? (His Five Year Plans created a command economy; he reorganized agriculture into giant collectives; he turned the Soviet Union into a repressive state.)

Spotlight on
Government

SOVIET BUREAUCRACY
The grand projects of the Soviet government gave rise to a huge bureaucracy. State control over the economy was very tight. Production on a mass scale needed many planners. The planners needed managers, and those managers needed supervisors. Whenever the economy was expanded, so was the government that controlled it.

He was one of the leaders of the revolution and was willing to use terror to reach Communist goals. Joseph Stalin was secretary-general of the Communist Party. Stalin, whose name meant "man of steel," believed that harsh measures were needed to turn the Soviet Union into a strong industrial and military power.

Trotsky and Stalin, however, had opposing views on how to rule. Trotsky backed worldwide revolution against capitalism. Stalin was more cautious. He urged "revolution in one country." He wanted to build up communism in the Soviet Union first.

Before his death, Lenin had doubts about both Trotsky and Stalin. He began expressing those doubts in 1922. He considered Trotsky too interested in violent action. He felt that Trotsky was not suited to actually running a country. He also thought that Stalin was too rude to rule a country. He tried to get other Communist Party leaders to replace Stalin.

Stalin outwitted Trotsky for control of the party. He placed his own supporters in positions of power. His supporters began to speak against Trotsky, and Trotsky became powerless. By 1927, Trotsky was expelled from the Communist Party. He was exiled from the Soviet Union in 1929. To Stalin, though, exile was not enough. In 1940, most likely as a result of Stalin's orders, Trotsky was assassinated in Mexico City. Stalin ruled as dictator of the Soviet Union until his death in 1953.

Command Economy

Stalin wanted to rapidly industrialize the Soviet Union. To reach this goal, he started to abandon the ideas of the NEP, and began a series of Five Year Plans. In 1928, Stalin began the first Five Year Plan.

The plan focused on expanding heavy industries such as steel, oil, and machinery production. Stalin believed that central planning would make the economy more efficient. He placed all economic activity under government control. The Soviet Union began to develop a **command economy**, or an economy in which the central government makes all economic decisions. This system replaced the market economy that had existed. As you learned in Chapter 18, a market economy is an economy in which the buying and selling of goods could take place without government regulation. Now, however, government officials decided what was produced, how much was produced, and where goods were to be delivered. Each Five Year Plan set goals for production.

The results of the Five Year Plans were mixed. Stalin's first Five Year Plan succeeded in expanding Soviet industries. Huge industrial projects were completed. Dams, canals, railways, steel mills, mines, and factories were all built under Five Year Plans. Steel, coal, and oil production increased greatly. More and more heavy equipment, such as farm machinery, was built.

Central planning was inefficient, however. With some goods, there were huge surpluses, while with others there were vast shortages. Managers were concerned only with meeting their goals. Factories often put out large quantities of low-quality goods. In addition, the Five Year Plans usually did not meet their own goals. When they did not, the government said they did anyway.

Market and Command Economies	
MARKET ECONOMY	**COMMAND ECONOMY**
Companies are privately owned.	Government controls all industry and companies.
Supply and demand govern manufacturing and trade.	Government decides what is needed, how much is needed, and where it is needed.
Industries and companies are run for profit.	Industries and companies are run for the benefit of the state.

✔ Chart Check

What is the difference between market and command economies in the making of goods?

Teaching Options

Most workers saw little improvement for themselves. Standards of living remained generally low. Factory workers in the cities lacked decent housing and clothing. Wages were low, and work was long and hard. Consumer goods were scarce.

Agriculture

Stalin also reorganized farming in the Soviet Union. Under the NEP, peasants had been allowed to have small plots of land. As with industry, the new goal was to make farming more efficient. Once again, land was seized and peasants were forced into **collectives**, or state-owned farms. The peasants worked on the collectives as a group. The state supplied the farms with modern equipment, such as tractors. The collectives now owned all tools and farm animals. The state set prices for farm goods. It also set a **quota**, or fixed amount, on crops each farm must produce and turn over to the state.

Many peasants resisted being forced into collectives, especially in the Ukraine, the country's richest farming area. They burned crops, slaughtered farm animals, and destroyed tools. Some began uprisings against the state. The state responded with brutality. Often, the army was called in to stop the uprisings.

Stalin wanted to destroy **kulaks**, or wealthy peasants. Stalin declared the kulaks enemies of communism and ordered millions of them killed or imprisoned. He seized their land and took their food from them. Soldiers shot many, and left others to starve. The state threw many more into forced labor camps. Stalin also forced the collective farmers in the Ukraine to give nearly all of their grain to the government for export. The result of this policy was a famine in which millions of peasants died across the Soviet Union. As many as 8 million died in the Ukraine alone.

Collectivization did not greatly increase farm production. It did, however, increase the Communist Party's control in the countryside. The remaining peasants were forbidden to travel. Once again, peasants were tied to the soil by the progressive Communist order.

Rule of Terror

Stalin's rule of the Soviet Union continued throughout the 1930s. Under Stalin, the oppressive Soviet state grew even worse. He extended state control beyond the economy. Stalin turned the Soviet Union into a state that attempted to control every aspect of its citizens' lives. The state used terror and propaganda, the spreading of ideas to influence how people think, to keep its citizens under control.

During the 1930s, Stalin gained absolute power within the Communist Party. He used force and terror to silence party members who criticized his actions or policies. Police monitored citizens' behavior. They followed people, read people's letters, and listened to people's private conversations using listening devices. They also hired spies to gather information about people.

In 1934, Stalin began the Great Purge. The purge, or removal of things that are considered harmful, was Stalin's campaign to get rid of any individuals he thought were disloyal to him. The police arrested many people. Included were people who had been involved in the Communist Party since the revolution. Soon, others were targeted as well, ranging from war heroes to ordinary citizens. Anyone who criticized the party could be arrested.

This Soviet poster shows collective farming in 1934. It reads, "Give first priority to gathering the Soviet harvest!"

GRAIN FARMS

Communist ideas were not Stalin's only source of ideas for collectives. He heard of the success of large grain farms in the United States. Because he considered small farms inefficient, he decided to set up large-scale "grain factories" in the Soviet Union. These farms would be models of modernization, with new equipment and efficient farming techniques.

TEACH PRIMARY SOURCES

Ask students why the poster on page 642 is considered propaganda. (Possible answer: It asks people to connect Stalin with patriotism; it portrays Stalin positively.) Tell students that this poster was created in 1937 in France, not Russia. Ask what this information suggests about communism. (Possible answer: It was a political force in western countries, too, at that time.)

◆ **ANSWER** Stalin used purges and secret police to maintain control.

Section Close

The Communists tried to change human nature, from being family-oriented to being state-oriented. Read to students this quotation by historian Ralph Raico about the changes in human nature required by communism: "The Communists soon discovered . . . that such an enterprise requires that terror be created into a system of government." Discuss whether this is an accurate portrayal of the first decades of the Soviet Union. Ask students to identify the change in human nature that is referred to. (Possible answer: change from private ownership to letting the state make all decisions)

3 Assess

Review Answers

Review History

A. Lenin set up the Soviet Union. He made the Communist Party the only political force. Lenin created the Comintern, and he started the NEP, which in turn led to a recovery in the economy.

B. Stalin began a series of Five Year Plans, eventually placing all economic activity under government control.

Define Terms to Know

command economy, 640; collective, 641; quota, 641; kulak, 641

This propaganda poster shows Stalin pointing upward at a Soviet flag.

Punishments were swift and severe. Police forced former Communist leaders to confess to crimes under torture. They convicted other party members without trials. Some, they simply executed. Others were sent to forced labor camps in isolated parts of Siberia, where many died. Millions suffered through the purges. When old opponents were removed, Stalin replaced them with new party members. These new members were young, enthusiastic, and very loyal to Stalin. Everyone knew the penalties for disloyalty.

The Communist Party controlled everything that was printed or broadcast. Censors, people who control free expression, eliminated anything that strayed from the party message. Communist victories and the evils of capitalism were announced everywhere. People were told how much better off they were in the Soviet Union than in capitalist countries. Industrial successes were glorified. People heard about how wise and wonderful Stalin was. Students were exposed to it in school. People heard it over loudspeakers and radios. They saw it on posters and they read it in the newspapers, including the Communist Party's newspaper *Pravda*, which means "truth."

 **How did Stalin try to keep control over people in the Soviet Union?**

Review I

Review History
A. What changes did Lenin bring to the Soviet Union?
B. What measures did Stalin take to control the economy?

Define Terms to Know
Define the following terms: **command economy, collective, quota, kulak**

Critical Thinking
Do you think Lenin or Stalin contributed more to the Communist Party's increase in power? Explain your answer.

Write About Economics
Write a short essay on how both Lenin and Stalin transformed the economy of the Soviet Union.

Get Organized
IDEA WEB
Use an idea web to organize information from this section. Choose an important idea or event and fill in details about it. For example, what were some details about Stalin's Five Year Plans in the Soviet Union?

Critical Thinking
Possible answer: Stalin contributed more to the increase in the Communist Party's power by establishing a command economy. Under Lenin, some private ownership existed. Under Stalin, however, everything was placed under government control.

Write About Economics
Students' essays should explain how Lenin's NEP used state control and how Stalin transformed the economy into a command economy.

Developed command economy.

Expanded Soviet industries.

Stalin's Five Year Plans

Completed industrial projects.

Surpluses and shortages of goods

Build Your Skills

Social Studies Skill

INTERPRET LINE GRAPHS

A graph is a drawing that presents information containing numbers. One type of graph is a line graph. Most often line graphs are used to show change over time. Numbers are usually shown along the left side of a line graph. Time is often shown across the bottom. A line shows the pattern of numbers going up or down over time.

Line graphs can show information about numbers of people employed, the value of goods produced, or changes in population. Sometimes, line graphs show several different sets of data over a particular period. This kind of graph can be useful in comparing the different sets of data.

When you read about history, you will often see information presented in line graphs. A line graph lets you see the trend, or the general direction, that something takes. For example, if the population of a city is growing, a line graph will very clearly show the increase. The trend, or general direction of the line, will go up.

Here's How

Follow these steps to interpret a line graph.

1. Read the title of the graph.
2. Identify the horizontal axis (the line across the bottom of the graph) and the vertical axis (the line along the left side). Read the labels of these axes.
3. Compare the information between periods.
4. Analyze the information on the graph and determine if there is a trend.

Here's Why

You have just read about how the Soviet Union set goals for the production of goods. Officials needed to be able to keep track of changes in production. Line graphs would help show those changes.

Practice the Skill

Look at the line graph on this page. Then, answer the following questions.

1. What does the graph show?
2. About what was the output of coal in 1933? In 1938?
3. What trend do you see reflected in the graph?

Extend the Skill

Write a paragraph explaining why production went up during Stalin's Five Year Plans.

Apply the Skill

As you read the next section of this chapter, interpret the line graph showing the changes in stock prices during the 1920s.

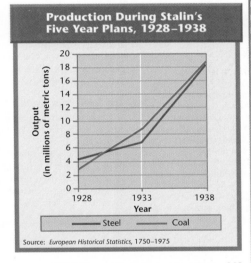

Production During Stalin's Five Year Plans, 1928–1938

Output (in millions of metric tons) vs. Year

Steel —— Coal ——

Source: *European Historical Statistics, 1750–1975*

CHAPTER 27 ◆ Crises Around the World **643**

Teaching Options

RETEACH

Have students clip or photocopy a line graph from a newspaper or news magazine. Ask students to write three questions about the graph and to write answers to the questions on another sheet of paper. Have students exchange questions with a partner and use the graph to answer the questions. Have them check their partners' answers and come to agreement on any discrepancies.

CHALLENGE

Have students apply this skill to current events by researching and creating a line graph on a subject of their choice. Students may also be interested in using computer software to create their graph. Ask students who use this software to share their knowledge about the software with the class.

Build Your Skills

INTERPRET LINE GRAPHS

Teach the Skill

Bring in several line graphs from newspapers or news magazines. Have students identify the title and horizontal and vertical axes of each graph. Then, ask students to identify what each graph shows. Suggest that students use each step in *Here's How* to interpret the graph. Be sure that students understand that line graphs generally show change over time.

Ask students to suggest information from their own lives that could be displayed on a line graph. (Possible answers: scores on tests, sports scores, after-school earnings) Have students explain how they would set up the line graph for these sets of information. (scores on the left side; time periods at the bottom) Have them identify the trend they would hope to find for quiz scores. (continually getting better scores)

Practice the Skill

ANSWERS

1. The line graph shows production of steel and coal during Stalin's Five Year Plans.
2. The output of coal in 1933 was about 9 million metric tons; in 1938 output was about 19 million metric tons.
3. The production of both steel and coal went up dramatically between 1928 and 1938.

Extend the Skill

Possible answer: Beginning in 1928, the Soviet government directed massive resources and labor to improve the economy.

Apply the Skill

Students should recognize the increase in stock prices in the 1920s until the stock market crash of 1929.

II. Upheaval in the West
(pp. 644–647)

Section Summary

In this section, students will learn how Europe tried to rebuild after World War I and how countries sought a permanent peace. They will also learn how the economic recovery in the 1920s was followed by the Great Depression. They will learn about the problems faced by France and Great Britain at this time and how these democracies tried to solve their crises.

1 Introduce

Getting Started

Ask students how people recover from natural catastrophes, such as earthquakes, floods, or tornadoes. Discuss what is involved in rebuilding economies, homes, and lives. Remind students that the federal government often steps in and helps with this rebuilding. Tell students that in the same way, the United States stepped in after World War I and helped European countries rebuild.

TERMS TO KNOW

Ask students to read the terms and definitions on page 644 and find each term in the section. After they read the section, have them explain to a partner each term's relationship to the upheaval in the West after World War I.

You may wish to preview the pronunciation of the following word with students.

Maginot (MAH zhee noh)

ACTIVE READING

As students read this section, have them list details they can use at the end of the section to make a generalization about Americans during the Great Depression.

Section II Upheaval in the West

Terms to Know

disarmament the reduction in number of a nation's military forces and equipment

debtor nation a nation that owes money

overproduction when the production of goods is greater than the demand for them

Great Depression the worldwide economic slowdown that caused massive unemployment

general strike a strike by workers in several different industries at the same time

Then & Now

THE UNITED NATIONS
Woodrow Wilson's idea of an organization that could prevent war did not die. Even though the United States did not join the League of Nations, other American leaders kept his dream alive.

In 1945, a new organization was born, the United Nations. Today, the Security Council of the United Nations organizes peacekeeping missions around the world.

Main Ideas

A. People in western Europe looked for ways to improve their economies after World War I.

B. The Great Depression shattered the prosperity of the 1920s.

C. Great Britain and France faced crises in the 1920s and 1930s but survived as democratic powers.

 Active Reading

GENERALIZE
When you generalize, you collect details, examine them, and make a general statement about them. As you read this section, make a generalization about the situation of Americans during the Great Depression.

A. Rebuilding After the War

In 1918, the Allied nations had, together, won World War I. Great Britain, France, and the United States were the forces behind the peace conference. Through the peace conference, new democratic countries were born. The development of these nations created new hopes for the spread of democracy.

However, World War I had taken a heavy toll on western Europe. In the war, millions had died. The war had torn up villages and towns throughout Europe and shattered countries' economies. The horrors of war behind them, the nations in western Europe looked to a brighter future.

Problems After the War

What developed after the war was often quite different from what people hoped and dreamed. The Treaty of Versailles, which ended the war, forced Germany to pay huge amounts of money and goods to the nations it invaded. The United States asked its allies to repay loans that it had made to them during the war. How could countries rebuild after the war if they had to pay large amounts of money to other countries?

The situation in Europe was desperate. Nations were suffering from inflation and unemployment. Another problem was war damage. Many factories in Germany, France, and Belgium had been destroyed by the fighting. European nations depended on Germany paying them money to rebuild. However, Germany was even worse off than these other nations. As a result, American loans were needed to help keep Germany and other European countries financially stable during the 1920s.

The Search for Lasting Peace

One hope after the war was for world peace. As you read in Chapter 26, American President Woodrow Wilson developed a peace plan called the Fourteen Points in 1918. The last point called for the establishment of an organization—what would become the League of Nations—to keep world peace. Member nations agreed to settle their disputes peacefully to prevent small conflicts from turning into another world war. These nations also tried to prevent war by cutting down on their supplies of weapons. The reduction in military power is called **disarmament**.

◆ **What country provided loans to help rebuild European countries?**

Teaching Options

Section 2 Resources

Teacher's Resources (TR)
Terms to Know, p. 40
Review History, p. 74
Build Your Skills, p. 108
Chapter Test, pp. 169–170
Concept Builder, p. 243
Idea Web, p. 321
Transparency 5

FYI

The League of Nations

The League of Nations came into being on January 10, 1920, when the Treaty of Versailles was ratified. Its headquarters was in Geneva, Switzerland, and its World Court was in The Hague, the Netherlands. U.S. opposition to the League stemmed from an isolationist thrust after World War I. Many Americans wanted to avoid obligations to warring European nations.

B. Boom and Bust

Prosperity began to return to western Europe in the 1920s. Peacetime trade and production resumed. Industrial workers won higher wages. They had a rising standard of living and could buy a variety of new goods, such as cars and radios.

The United States emerged from the war as the world's greatest economic power. Modern equipment helped the United States become the leading industrial power. The United States also went from being a **debtor** **nation** to a lender. American loans and investments helped Europe recover. As long as the U.S. economy was strong, the world economy remained fairly healthy.

Hidden Weaknesses

There were weaknesses to economic recovery after World War I, however. Better technology increased production of goods. Better farming techniques increased the supply of food. As supplies increased, prices began to drop. Industries began to suffer from **overproduction**, or when production of goods is greater than the demand for them. In spite of slowing demand, factories kept churning out products.

Many countries began raising tariffs on imported goods. Leaders wanted to protect their countries' industries from a flood of cheap imports. Eventually, products could neither be sold at home nor exported to other countries.

Financial problems also weakened the economy. Loans and credit became increasingly easy for people to get. Banks made loans to countries that had little ability to pay them back. In an attempt to find other ways to earn money, more and more people began to invest in the stock market.

Buying Into the U.S. Stock Market

Through most of the 1920s, the prices of U.S. stocks had risen higher and higher. Many Americans bought stocks in the hope of getting rich quickly. They expected the stock market to continue its upward climb. Investors took increasing risks, often buying stocks on margin, which meant that they paid a small percentage of the stock's price as a down payment and borrowed the rest from the seller of the stock. Then, if the value of the stocks rose, the buyer would sell the stocks and pay back what he or she owed. However, if the value of the stocks fell, the buyer then owed the seller what was borrowed.

In September 1929, some investors realized that prices could not rise forever. They began selling their shares, which caused prices to fall. Many stockbrokers asked margin buyers to make full payments. Those who could not pay were forced to sell their stocks. This selling caused prices to drop even more.

Worldwide Economic Crisis

Hopes for better times were shattered suddenly in October 1929—the start of the **Great Depression**. It began when the U.S. stock market in New York City crashed, causing a chain of events that plunged the world into

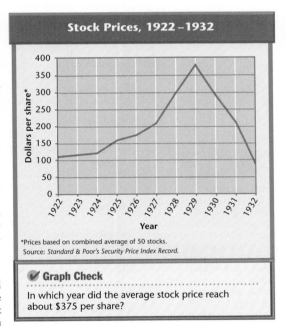

Stock Prices, 1922–1932

Dollars per share*

*Prices based on combined average of 50 stocks.
Source: Standard & Poor's Security Price Index Record.

✔ Graph Check

In which year did the average stock price reach about $375 per share?

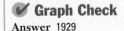

Connection to ECONOMICS ◄

Use play money to help students understand margin buying. A person who bought ten shares of stock at $10 per share would owe the broker $100. If the person bought on margin, however, he or she might pay only $10 for the ten shares; the broker would "loan" $90 to the buyer. If the stock price rose, the buyer could sell it, repay the broker, and still make a profit.

This photograph shows a common sight during the Great Depression, people eating at a charity soup kitchen. Ask students to describe the kinds of clothing worn by people in the photograph. (suits and ties, jackets and caps) Ask what the people's clothes tell about who was affected by the Great Depression. (Possible answer: It affected rich and poor alike.)

Extend Explain that the stock market "crash" of 1929 was not a physical event. The value of stocks fell quickly. This fall was so widespread that economists called it a crash. Unlike earlier depressions, which lasted for a year or two, the Great Depression lasted for about a decade.

Activity

Make a flowchart The Great Depression had a domino effect, first in the United States and then spreading to other countries. Have students create a flowchart (TR, p. 324) showing how the Great Depression widened.

◆ **ANSWER** Some investors realized that stock prices would not rise forever. They began to sell off their stocks, stock prices dropped, and people panicked and dumped all their stock.

C. Western European Democracies

Purpose-Setting Question What were the effects of World War I on France and Great Britain? (**France:** northern France was completely ruined; Germany's reparations helped France's economy recover; many political parties competed for power so coalition governments were formed; scandals brought down governments; France distrusted Germany. **Great Britain:** indebted government, economic crises, crumbling of empire)

WHAT IN THE WORLD?
POPULAR FRONT The Popular Front in France was a coalition of the Socialist, Radical, and Communist parties. Two years after the Popular Front was elected, a more centrist government took its place. Ask students why the French may have turned to the Popular Front. (Possible answer: They were frustrated with the continued depression.)

During the Great Depression in the United States, many people were forced to eat at charity soup kitchens.

economic ruin. People who had savings deposited in banks withdrew their money, and many banks were forced to close. As more banks failed, many Americans lost all of their savings. Then, American banks that were in danger of closing recalled money that had been loaned to European banks. This recall caused European banks to fail as well. Worse still, those who had money now stopped investing it in business and industry. As a result, industrial production and international trade fell sharply.

Countries tried to help themselves recover from the Great Depression in a number of ways. One approach was to put protective tariffs on all foreign goods. As you read in Chapter 22, the tariffs were supposed to encourage people to buy less costly domestic items, or those products made within a country. Even though these countries improved sales of goods at home, they lost many foreign markets. With fewer foreign markets available to them, people making the products lost their jobs.

◆ **What caused the U.S. stock market to crash in 1929?**

C. Western European Democracies

Great Britain and France were the great democratic powers of western Europe. They experienced the period following World War I differently, however. Each had its own political, social, and economic crises.

France

France was most directly affected by the war. Northern France had been completely ruined. More than a million French people had been killed, and many more were wounded in the war. The French government tried to make up for the devastation. In the Treaty of Versailles, France took back the industrial territories of Alsace and Lorraine from Germany.

In addition, Germany was forced to make huge reparations to France. These reparations helped France's economy recover quickly from the war. However, economic highs and lows made the country politically unstable. Many different political parties competed for power. Because no party had a majority in the legislature, coalition governments were formed. A coalition is

What in the World?

POPULAR FRONT
The Popular Front was formed in France by several political parties to solve problems brought on by the Great Depression. It won enough support to form a government in 1936. The Popular Front passed some social legislation and tried to solve labor problems.

646   UNIT 7 ◆ Decades of War

Teaching Options

Using Technology

Ask students to use the Internet to learn more about the Great Depression. Have students locate three to five general Web sites that deal with the Great Depression. Ask students to evaluate each site and prepare a summary of the information that is available on the site. Students can then collect the summaries into a book of useful sites. Have students print out the first page of each Web site to help them reference it in the future.

ESL/ELL STRATEGIES

Take notes Have students take notes on subsection A or B. Have them trade notes with a partner and take turns explaining the important points in the subsection. Encourage students to use their notes as a study aid.

a temporary alliance of various political parties. Frequent scandals brought down governments in France regularly.

Many people in France still distrusted Germany. Since its formation in 1871, Germany had invaded France twice. Determined to prevent future invasions, the government of France built a huge series of fortifications, or defensive walls, along its border with Germany. It was called the Maginot Line, and it gave the French people a greater sense of security.

Great Britain

Although victorious in the war, Britain faced many problems when the war ended. The government was deeply in debt. British manufacturing lagged behind its American competition. German U-boats had destroyed many British merchant ships and damaged overseas shipping. Unemployment was high, and wages stayed low. Angry workers often went on strike. In 1926, Britain was crippled for nine days by a **general strike**, or a strike by workers in different industries at the same time.

The Great Depression further deepened Britain's troubles. The three major political parties in Britain—the Liberal Party, the Labour Party, and the Conservative Party—formed a coalition government. The coalition eased hardships by giving benefits to the unemployed.

In addition, the British Empire began to lose territory. In 1914, Parliament passed a bill for Irish home rule. The government delayed implementing the law when war broke out later that year. After the war, however, the British government still failed to grant home rule. In 1919, a rebellion broke out in Ireland against Britain. The Irish Republican Army (IRA) waged war against the British. Britain made a treaty with Ireland in 1922, creating the Irish Free State.

In 1931, four former colonies were given full independence. These were Canada, Australia, New Zealand, and South Africa. They became part of the newly formed British Commonwealth of Nations and still had economic and cultural ties with each other and with Great Britain.

◆ **What led to rebellion in Ireland in 1919?**

Review II

Review History
A. What were some of the problems that developed after World War I?
B. What were two causes of the Great Depression?
C. What were some reasons why the British Empire lost territory after World War I?

Define Terms to Know
Define the following terms:
disarmament, debtor nation, overproduction, Great Depression, general strike

Critical Thinking
Compare and contrast the political and economic crises that took place in France and Great Britain after World War I.

Write About Economics
Write a short editorial about some of the weaknesses of the recovery in western Europe during the 1920s.

Get Organized
IDEA WEB
Use an idea web to organize information from this section. Choose an important idea or event and fill in details about it. For example, what were some details about the Great Depression?

(circles: Stock market crashed. / Bank closings / Great Depression / Loss of jobs / Industrial production fell.)

Write About Economics
Students' editorials may mention political instability in France and British unemployment, debts, and manufacturing woes.

Section Summary

In this section, students will learn how nationalism in China grew into a struggle between Communists and non-Communists. They also will learn about the beginnings of a struggle for independence in Southeast Asia and of the struggles and successes of the nationalist movement in India.

Getting Started

Display Transparency 7 or refer to page A7 in the Atlas and have students locate China, countries in Southeast Asia, and India. Review with students some of the reasons European countries wanted to control these areas. (access to raw materials, new markets, spread western culture and religions) Discuss with students why the people in these countries might want independence. Explain that they are going to learn about independence movements in these areas.

TERMS TO KNOW

Tell students that sometimes knowing the origins of terms makes them easier to remember. For example, *boycott* comes from the name "Charles C. Boycott," an English land agent in Ireland, who was ostracized for refusing to reduce land rents. *Satyagraha*, meaning "truth force," is a Sanskrit word. Sanskrit is a classical language in India.

You may wish to preview the pronunciation of the following terms with students.

Sun Yat-sen (soon yaht sun)
Guomindang (gwah meen dahng)
Jiang Jieshi (jee AHNG jee EHSH ee)
Mao Zedong (maood zee dawng)
Ho Chi Minh (hoh chee mihn)

ACTIVE READING

Have students use a main idea/supporting details chart (TR, p. 319) to list the main ideas from this section as well as two or three details that support each main idea.

Terms to Know

boycott a protest in which people refuse to buy certain goods

satyagraha a belief of Gandhi that emphasized passive resistance

civil disobedience the refusal to obey unjust laws

Main Ideas

A. China was torn by civil war between warlords, the Guomindang, and the Communists.

B. People in Southeast Asia began to resist French rule.

C. Indian nationalists began to push for independence from Great Britain.

Active Reading

SUPPORTING DETAILS
When you identify supporting details, you look for facts and examples that relate to the main idea. As you read this section, find supporting details that give you more information about India's struggle for independence from Great Britain.

A. China

Turmoil spread beyond Europe in the 1920s. Troubles tore at Asia as well. India had been made a colony by the British in the 1800s. Southeast Asia was mostly under French rule. China was still independent, but western countries had interests there.

The Chinese Republic

As you read in Chapter 25, nationalists overthrew the Qing, or Manchu, Dynasty and created a republic in 1911. Sun Yat-sen was the president of the Chinese republic. He hoped to rebuild China. Instead, the country fell into chaos. Western countries did not recognize the new government. Sun eventually stepped down in favor of an ambitious general, Yuan Shikai. Yuan wanted to set up a new dynasty, with himself as emperor. The military did not support his ambition. The country descended into further turmoil after his death in 1916.

The republic was a powerless government. The provinces fell into the hands of warlords, military leaders who battled each other for control of the country. They taxed the peasants to pay for their armies. The wars devastated the countryside. Peasants and businesses alike suffered terribly from the taxes and the wars. One Chinese newspaper published an article about a warlord in 1928:

ANALYZE PRIMARY SOURCES

DOCUMENT-BASED QUESTION
How does the newspaper describe the warlord?

❝ During the less than four years that Zhang Zongchang ruled, there was not one day that he failed to make money from the people. Besides the regular taxes, there were special taxes. . . . Whenever he needed a sum of money, he would issue an order to several counties to come up with the cash. ❞

Imperialism and the May Fourth Movement

Other countries took advantage of China's weakness. They had their "spheres of influence" in China. Merchants and soldiers kept control over these areas. In the turmoil, they extended their control deeper into the countryside. Japan was the most aggressive power. While the western countries were occupied with war, Japan put new pressure on China. Japan issued the Twenty-One Demands in 1915. The goal of the Twenty-One Demands was to make China a Japanese protectorate.

Teaching Options

Section 3 Resources

Teacher's Resources (TR)
Terms to Know, p. 40
Review History, p. 74
Build Your Skills, p. 108
Chapter Test, pp. 169–170
Concept Builder, p. 243
Idea Web, p. 321
Transparency 7

The Treaty of Versailles further outraged many Chinese nationalists. Japan was given former German colonies. It was also given the German "sphere of influence" in China.

On May 4, 1919, students began to protest in Beijing. They protested against the Japanese takeover of Chinese lands. They organized **boycotts** of Japanese goods. Protests spread to other cities, and local governments used police to put down the protests. These protests set off a reform movement called the May Fourth Movement.

Leaders of the May Fourth Movement wanted to strengthen China. Many of the leaders were educated in the West. They wanted China to learn from the West. With that new knowledge, they believed China could then throw off foreign control. They discarded Confucianism and many traditional practices. They believed western ideas could solve China's problems. They embraced western science and political ideas, such as democracy. Others, inspired by Marx and Lenin, turned to communism. By 1921, some Chinese Communists had created a political party. They won influence with factory workers in the cities.

Nationalists and Communists in China

Sun Yat-sen organized the Guomindang, or Nationalist Party, in southern China. He wanted to build an army to conquer the warlords and reunify China. Sun tried to get help from western countries. Only the Soviet Union agreed to help. The Soviets sent "experts" to arm and train the Chinese.

An army officer named Jiang Jieshi took over after Sun died in 1925. Jiang was determined to reunite China. He worked with the Chinese Communists, and for a time it looked like the Guomindang and the Communists might merge. In 1926, he began a campaign into northern China where he crushed local warlords and eventually captured Beijing.

Jiang decided to break with the Communists in 1927. The fierce fighting that followed between the Communists and the Guomindang claimed thousands of lives. The Guomindang beat the Communists and chased them into the countryside.

One of the Communists who emerged from the conflict was Mao Zedong. He was born in 1893 to a well-to-do peasant family. As a young man, he helped start the Chinese Communist Party. Mao believed that the Communists should look for support among the large peasant groups. He appealed to their hatred of the landlords. He began a peasant revolt in Hunan in 1927. The revolt failed, and he and his new army fled into the mountains. In the lands under Mao and other Communists, the peasants were treated better. Land was redistributed to them and they were offered schooling.

The Long March

Jiang wanted to destroy the Communists. Guomindang armies began a campaign to wipe them out. In 1934, the desperate Communists, under the leadership of Mao Zedong, fled to the north. Their retreat is known as the Long March. More than 100,000 people began the march, traveling over rugged terrain for more than 6,000 miles. They faced constant attacks from the Guomindang. Only a few thousand survived the march.

Do You Remember?
In Chapter 26, you learned that the Treaty of Versailles was the 1919 peace agreement between the Allies and Germany that ended World War I.

Jiang Jieshi led Guomindang armies in the fight against Communists in China.

Civil War in China, 1925–1935

Ask students to use the map key to note which areas were controlled by the Communists and which areas were controlled by the Guomindang. Ask which group controlled more area. (Guomindang) Have students describe the general directions of the Long March. (west, then north)

✔ Map Check

Answer the city of Yenan in Shaanxi province

Focus Point out to students that the Guomindang and Communists fought together against the Japanese. Explore with students why these two groups might cooperate. Ask students if they think this will be a long-term change.

Activity

Make a chart Have students construct a five *W*s chart (TR, p. 326), in which the *What* is civil war in China. Encourage students to use the chart as a study aid. (**Who**: Nationalists and Communists; **Where**: China; **When**: 1927; **Why**: Both groups wanted to control the country.)

◆ **ANSWER** The Long March gained support for the Communists because they treated the peasants well along their journey.

B. Southeast Asia

Purpose-Setting Question What western ideas influenced the educated class in Southeast Asia in the 1920s and 1930s? (civil rights, self-determination)

Discuss Remind students of the saying "Actions speak louder than words." Ask students how this saying applies to France's presence in Southeast Asia. (Possible answer: France fought for "liberty and equality" for its own citizens, but regarding a colony in Southeast Asia, it refused to recognize these ideals.)

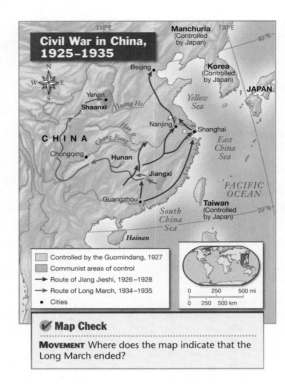

✔ Map Check

MOVEMENT Where does the map indicate that the Long March ended?

Mao Zedong became the supreme leader of the Communists during the Long March. He imposed discipline on his followers. He did not allow them to take anything from the peasants but instead required they pay for all goods. The soldiers were careful not to ruin the lands through which they passed. It was this behavior that made the peasants welcome the Communists. Many peasants had suffered at the hands of the warlords and the Guomindang. The Long March became a symbol of Communist heroism. Mao used it to inspire and persuade new people to join the Communist Party.

Civil war was not China's only problem. In 1931, Japanese forces conquered Manchuria, in northeastern China. By 1937, Japan struck Chinese cities once again. The Guomindang and the Communists agreed to fight together against Japan. Eventually, Japan launched a full-scale invasion of China.

◆ **How did the Long March affect support for the Communist Party?**

B. Southeast Asia

By the early 1900s, France ruled a large part of Southeast Asia. The French called their colony Indochina. It included Vietnam, Cambodia, and Laos. As elsewhere in Asia, a nationalist movement was growing. Many wanted to throw off French control.

French Rule in Southeast Asia

In ruling their colony in Southeast Asia, France had allowed the kings of Vietnam, Laos, and Cambodia to remain in place. However, the real authority lay with the French governor-general. He controlled a large, centralized administration.

The French government wanted to use the colony to make money. It became one of the world's largest exporters of rice and rubber. Workers were paid little, and the people were taxed heavily.

France did provide education for some in Southeast Asia. They trained officials for the lower ranks of the government. Education was also used to spread French culture.

Nationalist Movements

The educated class in Southeast Asia was influenced by western ideas. These ideas included civil rights and self-determination, the right of people to decide on their own form of government. In 1919, a Vietnamese leader named Nguyen Al Quoc, later known as Ho Chi Minh, demanded self-rule for the French colony. Western countries ignored his demand, which caused the Vietnamese nationalist movement to grow even stronger. By 1925, the Communists had formed a revolutionary party in Vietnam with Ho Chi Minh as one of the founding members.

Teaching Options

Conflict Resolution

Civil disobedience is usually a nonviolent way to confront a problem. It highlights an injustice, which is often formalized as a law. Ask students what the options for bringing attention to an unjust law are. (Possible answers: break the law; peaceful protest; change the law through legislation) Ask why civil disobedience is such a powerful tool of protest. (Because it is nonviolent, people respect and sympathize with the protesters.)

ESL/ELL STRATEGIES

Organize Information Have students create their own memory aids to make their learning more efficient. For example, they might use separate index cards to list important information about the many charismatic leaders in this section—Sun Yat-sen, Jiang Jieshi, Mao Zedong, Ho Chi Minh, and Mohandas Gandhi.

In the early 1930s, several major nationalist uprisings broke out against French rule. The French put them down savagely, executing hundreds. The nationalist movement was, for the moment, driven underground.

◆ **What did France use its colony in Southeast Asia for?**

C. India

India had been a British colony for more than half a century when World War I began. As part of the war effort, India contributed large sums of money and provided 1.5 million troops to military service. Indian soldiers fought bravely, and they returned home filled with ideas of liberty and self-determination.

The Struggle for Independence

Nationalists were outraged that Indians should fight in the British military when they did not have self-government. In 1919, violent protests broke out in Amritsar, a city in northern India. Nearly 400 Indians were killed and another 1,200 wounded when British soldiers opened fire on a crowd of unarmed demonstrators. The British government did not bring the soldiers to justice. Indians were outraged by the massacre. In the past, nationalists had wanted self-rule within the British Empire. Now, they began to call for full independence.

In 1920, Mohandas Gandhi became the leader of the Indian National Congress, India's most important political party. Gandhi was a lawyer who had studied in England. In 1893, he went to South Africa, where for more than 20 years he worked to end discrimination against Indians who lived there. After the massacre at Amritsar, he devoted his life to the struggle for independence. His integrity and personal courage earned him the title of Mahatma, or "great soul."

Then & Now

INDIAN NATIONAL CONGRESS
The Indian National Congress, which became known as the Congress Party, has had a long history. It was formed in 1885 and made increasing demands for Indian self-rule. By 1929, it was demanding full independence.

The Congress Party has dominated Indian politics since the country gained independence in 1947. In the 1950s, it adopted a policy of democratic socialism. Charges of corruption in the mid-1990s forced the Congress Party out of power.

These followers of Gandhi are deliberately breaking British law by evaporating salt from seawater.

◆ **ANSWER** France used the colony in Southeast Asia to make money because it was an exporter of rice and rubber.

C. India
Purpose-Setting Question Why were nationalists in India angry about India's role in World War I? (India contributed money and troops to the war effort, yet it did not have self-government.)

Then & Now

INDIAN NATIONAL CONGRESS Ask students to contrast Indian party politics to that of the United States. (Possible answer: Indian politics was dominated by one party. The United States has two major political parties.) Ask students what effect two main parties has on politics. (Possible answer: It gives people a choice. It makes both parties more aware of public opinion because there is competition.)

Activity

Cause-and-effect chain Have students develop a cause-and-effect chain (TR, p. 325), using the massacre at Amritsar as the central event. (**Cause:** Nationalists wanted self-government and protested. **Event:** Massacre at Amritsar; **Effect:** Nationalists called for full independence.)

Focus Have students read Gandhi's Quit India speech on page 814. Explain that the Congress Party wanted Great Britain to let India deal with Japan separately. Ask students to examine the speech with this in mind.

TEACH PRIMARY SOURCES
Ask students to identify who is in the picture, what they are doing, and why. (Indian women are evaporating salt from seawater as a protest of British law.) Tell students that the British had a monopoly on the production and sale of salt in India. Gandhi chose salt as the object of his protest because everyone—rich and poor—needed it. Discuss how this act is a form of civil disobedience. Have students contrast this protest with the protests that took place at the start of the French Revolution. (This is peaceful; those were violent.)

Research

AVERAGE
Have students use encyclopedia or library resources to find out more about the life of Mohandas Gandhi. Have them try to find out how he became convinced that civil disobedience was the answer to India's quest for independence. Ask them to explain if they, too, see Mohandas Gandhi as "the Great Soul."

CHALLENGE
Have students do research to find out about the Quit India campaign. Have them learn what Indian demands were in the campaign and how the British responded. Students should try to locate a copy of an original newspaper account of this event and bring it to class.

TEXTILES BOYCOTT Review the economics of the mother country and the colony. As the colony, India grew the raw material, cotton. India sent cotton to Great Britain, where it was made into cloth. Ask students how Gandhi was thwarting Great Britain's economic will by boycotting British cotton. (By not buying cotton cloth, Indians were refusing to be the market for Great Britain's cotton. India was trying to become more self-sufficient, too.)

Focus Use Transparency 7 or the map of Asia in the Atlas (p. A7) and have students locate Pakistan. Ask students where Pakistan is located in relationship to India. (north and west) Discuss with students why Muslims might have wanted their own country.

◆ **ANSWER** Gandhi worked to achieve independence through civil disobedience. He taught the Indian people to refuse to pay taxes, serve in the government, or obey British laws, because of injustice.

Section Close

Write the word *nationalism* on the board. Ask students to review the section and then write one sentence for each subsection, describing how that country was influenced by nationalism at the time.

3 Assess

Review Answers

Review History
A. Peasants in China welcomed the Communists because the Communists treated them better than either the warlords or the Guomindang.

B. The French established schools in order to educate officials for the lower levels of the colonial bureaucracy and to spread French culture.

C. Possible answer: He called for a boycott because Great Britain had destroyed native industries and because he believed India should be self-sufficient.

Define Terms to Know
boycott, 649; satyagraha, 652; civil disobedience, 652

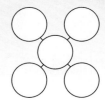

Spotlight on *Economics*

TEXTILES BOYCOTT
Gandhi called for a boycott of British goods in the 1920s. Textiles were the most important of these goods. The British bought cotton from India and used it to make cloth, which they sold back to India. In doing so, they could sell cloth more cheaply than local artisans could. Gandhi wanted India to become self-sufficient, and encouraged people to weave their own cloth. He made the spinning wheel the symbol of the nationalist movement.

Mohandas Gandhi and the Struggle for Independence

Gandhi believed that independence could be achieved through <u>satyagraha</u>, or "truth force." In practice, this term came to mean peaceful resistance to the British authorities. Gandhi's beliefs were based on <u>civil</u> <u>disobedience</u>. He urged the Indian people not to attack the British. Instead, they were encouraged to refuse to perform civil duties, such as paying taxes, serving in government, and obeying British laws. Laborers were urged not to work for foreign employers, and students were encouraged not to attend British schools.

Gandhi also set out to destroy the British salt monopoly. Natural salt was available at the seashore, but local people were forbidden to touch it. So, in 1930, Gandhi marched to the sea with some of his followers. As the marchers passed through villages, hundreds joined them. When Gandhi reached the sea, his followers numbered in the thousands. At the shore, he picked up a lump of salt. In doing so, he broke the law.

British authorities arrested and jailed Gandhi. Soon, Congress Party members were selling salt on the streets. They held up lumps of salt during rallies. They were all arrested for doing so. Jails were filled with tens of thousands of people who dared to sell salt.

In the 1930s, Britain began to grant more self-government to India. India's provinces gained greater freedom, and a national legislature was elected. However, Gandhi and the Congress Party insisted that India must be independent.

A Separate Muslim State

The nationalist movement in India was split between Hindus and Muslims. Muslims were a minority in India. Many did not want to belong to a country that was made up of mostly Hindus. Rioting broke out all over India. Muslims formed the Muslim League in 1906.

In the 1930s, the Muslim League had a new, able leader. His name was Muhammad Ali Jinnah. Like Gandhi, he was a lawyer from the middle class. Ali Jinnah supported the idea of a separate Muslim state. Eventually, the Congress Party allowed a new Islamic nation, called Pakistan, to be separated from India.

◆ **What role did Gandhi play in India's struggle for independence?**

Review III

Review History
A. Why did peasants in China welcome the Communists?
B. Why did the French establish schools in Southeast Asia?
C. What were some of the reasons why Gandhi called for a boycott of British goods?

Define Terms to Know
Define the following terms:
boycott, satyagraha, civil disobedience

Critical Thinking
Compare and contrast the beliefs of nationalists in China and India.

Write About Citizenship
Write a paragraph about Gandhi's views and how they reflect his ideas on the roles of citizens.

Get Organized
IDEA WEB
Use an idea web to organize information from this section. Choose an important idea or event and fill in details about it. For example, what were some details about the Long March?

Critical Thinking
Indian Nationalists struggled to expel a foreign power, whereas Chinese Nationalists wanted to reunify China. Indian Nationalists were divided between Hindus and Muslims; the Chinese, between the Guomindang and the Communists.

Write About Citizenship
Students' paragraphs should include an explanation of satyagraha and self-determination of nations.

Points *of* View

Mohandas Gandhi and Civil Disobedience

In the 1920s and 1930s, Mohandas Gandhi became one of the most active leaders of the Indian independence movement. He promoted the use of nonviolence and noncooperation to achieve his political goals. Many have called Gandhi's method of protest civil disobedience. He called nonviolence satyagraha, or "truth-force."

In a speech he gave in 1917, Gandhi outlined why he believed satyagraha works as a method to achieve political and other goals everywhere.

George Orwell was a British writer living at the same time as Gandhi. He is known for his criticism of governments that tried to control other nations and interfere in its own citizens' lives. Orwell was also much less optimistic about political movements and the use of civil disobedience. In the quotation below, he expresses doubts about how easily civil disobedience could be used in places other than India.

Hindu peacemaker Mohandas Gandhi in 1931

> **"** There are two methods for attaining the desired end: Truthfulness and Truthlessness. In our scriptures they have been described respectively as divine and devilish. In the path of satyagraha there is always unflinching adherence to Truth. . . . With truth for sword, he needs neither steel nor gunpowder. He conquers the enemy by the force of the soul, which is love. **"**
>
> —Mohandas Gandhi, address to the First Gujarat Political Conference, 1917

> **"** It is difficult to see how Gandhi's methods could be applied in a country where opponents of the regime [form of government] disappear in the middle of the night and are never heard from again. Without a free press and the right of assembly, it is impossible not merely to appeal to outside opinion but to bring a mass movement into being. . . . Is there a Gandhi in Russia at this moment? **"**
>
> —George Orwell, quoted in Paul Johnson's *A History of the Modern World*, 1983

ANALYZE PRIMARY SOURCES

DOCUMENT-BASED QUESTIONS

1. Why does Gandhi believe that civil disobedience works?

2. Why does Orwell question the effectiveness of civil disobedience?

3. **Critical Thinking** Compare and contrast Gandhi's and Orwell's views of government.

Teaching Options

Take a Stand

Ask students to clarify whether Orwell is opposed to civil disobedience. Then, ask them to tell whether they think Gandhi or Orwell is right and explain why they think this is the correct view of civil disobedience. Have them explain which point of view they would adhere to if they were taking a stand against an unjust law.

LINK to TODAY

Civil disobedience continues to exert a powerful draw on activist groups. Some recent examples include people protesting for animal rights, countries refusing to support apartheid in South Africa, and people against logging old-growth timber in the Pacific Northwest. Ask students to research one of these topics or another cause that has used civil disobedience.

Points *of* View

MOHANDAS GANDHI AND CIVIL DISOBEDIENCE

Teach the Topic

The issue of civil disobedience is often hotly debated when it is used as a technique to achieve an end. Some people believe it is appropriate to break or ignore unjust laws; other people feel that everyone must obey laws regardless of one's beliefs.

Gandhi's address and Orwell's essay express contrasting points of view about civil disobedience as a universal strategy to achieve political change. Explain to students that Gandhi's words come from a speech he made to the First Gujarat Political Conference in 1917. George Orwell's words are excerpted from his essay "Reflections on Gandhi."

Ask students whether people would be more likely to listen to a speech or read an essay. (probably listen to a speech) Ask students why people might have different points of view about civil disobedience.

Compare and Contrast Points of View

Ask students to express Gandhi's explanation in their own words. Then, have them do the same for Orwell's reply. Make sure that students understand that Orwell is not against the practice of civil disobedience—he is saying that there are places where it is inapplicable.

Vocabulary Builder

Demonstrate the meanings of *flinch* and *adhere* for students. Then, ask them to explain the meaning of *unflinching adherence*.

ANALYZE PRIMARY SOURCES

DOCUMENT-BASED QUESTIONS

1. He believes that the power of truth and love in one's soul will conquer one's enemies.
2. Orwell believes that civil disobedience would not work in countries without a free press or freedom of assembly.
3. Gandhi believes that civil disobedience will work under any circumstances, whereas Orwell believes that it will work only in countries that already have a degree of freedom.

IV. The Rise of Dictatorships
(pp. 654–657)

Section Summary

In this section, students will learn how Italy turned to a Fascist leader in the 1920s. They will also learn how Adolf Hitler rose to power in Germany in the 1930s.

1 Introduce

Getting Started

Show students a picture of a swastika. Ask them to identify the symbol and describe its meaning. Tell students that the swastika is an ancient symbol, found among peoples as diverse as the Native Americans of South America, the Greeks, and the Byzantines. It was adopted in 1920 by the Nazi Party and became one of the most hated symbols of all time. In this section, students will read about the dictatorship that the swastika symbolized.

TERMS TO KNOW

Ask students to read the terms and definitions on page 654 and find each term in the section. Have them use each term in a sentence.

You may wish to preview the pronunciation of the following words with students.

Mussolini (moos soh LEE nee)
Weimar (VY mahr)
Kristallnacht (krihs TUHL nahkt)

ACTIVE READING

Ask students to make a prediction at the beginning of each subsection about the rise of these dictatorships. As students read each subsection, remind them that it is sometimes necessary to adjust a prediction as they learn more about the subject. Have students use an organizer modeled on this equation:
Prediction + Knowledge = Adjusted Prediction

Section IV The Rise of Dictatorships

Terms to Know

fascism a political system that emphasizes nationalism and is ruled by a dictator

totalitarian state a government in which a one-party dictatorship regulates every aspect of citizens' lives

chancellor prime minister

concentration camp a place in which political prisoners and members of religious and ethnic groups were held

Benito Mussolini speaks on stage near Fascist soldiers.

Main Ideas

A. Benito Mussolini led the National Fascist Party in Italy.

B. Adolf Hitler used Germans' disappointment in the outcome of World War I and economic hard times to take control of Germany.

 Active Reading

PREDICT
When you predict, you use information in order to guess what will happen next. As you read this section, use information to predict how Adolf Hitler's formation of the Third Reich would change the world.

A. New Government in Italy

After World War I, Italy and Germany had their own crises. People lost faith in their governments. They felt their leaders had failed them. They turned to strong leaders who promised to restore their countries' lost glory.

Italy After the War

During the years following World War I, Italy's economy was very weak. Thousands of Italians were unemployed, many factories were closed, and food prices were high. The Italian government became less and less able to deal with the severe problems facing the country. At the urging of the Italian Socialist Party, which later became the Communist Party, labor unions went on strike and tried to force industries to raise workers' wages. Soon the strike became violent. Many feared a Communist revolution in Italy.

The Rise of Mussolini

In 1919, Benito Mussolini organized the National Fascist Party in Italy. The members of this political party supported **fascism**, a political system that emphasizes nationalism and is ruled by a dictator. Its members were determined to keep Italy from becoming a Communist country.

The Fascists believed the state—the nation—must be all-powerful. Rights of individuals or groups were less important than those of the state. The party took its name from the ancient Roman symbol of authority called a "fasces." Fasces were bundles of sticks wrapped around axes.

Mussolini, inspired by the revolution in Russia, rejected democracy in favor of direct action. He organized his Fascist followers into black-shirted gangs. These "Black Shirts" attacked Socialists.

In 1922, thousands of Fascists marched on Rome and demanded political power. Fearing a civil war, the king agreed to name Mussolini prime minister and allowed him to form a government.

Teaching Options

Section 4 Resources

Teacher's Resources (TR)
Terms to Know, p. 40
Review History, p. 74
Build Your Skills, p. 108
Chapter Test, pp. 169–170
Concept Builder, p. 243
Idea Web, p. 321

FYI

Benito Mussolini

Before World War I, Benito Mussolini (1883–1945) was a Socialist, with views that opposed his later Fascist policies. The Fascist Party originally appealed to war veterans, supporting government ownership of natural resources and the glorification of Italy. Mussolini promised to restore Italy to its former glory, but instead he led the country to bitter defeat in World War II.

Italy Under Mussolini

Italy was still a parliamentary monarchy. The real power lay with Mussolini, however. By 1925, Mussolini took on even more power. All political parties except the Fascist Party were outlawed. Civil liberties came to an end. The police arrested and often killed anyone who dared to criticize Mussolini or his policies. Labor unions and strikes were forbidden. All newspapers, books, and radio broadcasts were controlled by the Fascists. Mussolini turned Italy into a **totalitarian state**, or a state whose government attempts to control every aspect of its citizens' lives.

Many people welcomed fascism, even if it meant a loss of freedom, because Mussolini had brought new prosperity and order to Italy. Mussolini provided much-needed jobs through road-building and public works programs, as well as by expanding war industries. He ended riots and street fighting and improved Italy's economy.

Mussolini believed in the power of the state. Individuals were not important. Mussolini wrote,

> **"** The Fascist conception of the state is all-embracing; outside of it no human or spiritual values can exist, much less have value. Thus understood, Fascism is totalitarian [a complete dictatorship], and the Fascist state—a synthesis and unit inclusive of all values—interprets, develops, and potentiates the whole life of a people. **"**

Men were encouraged to sacrifice themselves for Italy. Women were called upon to stay at home and have as many children as possible. Fascist youth groups shaped children. They taught children strict military discipline. Constant propaganda reinforced these messages.

Under Mussolini, the economy was brought under state control. Workers and employers were organized into groups by industry, and the Fascist Party controlled them. Production increased, but most people received no personal benefits. Unions and the right to strike were abolished, and wages stayed low.

➤ **How did Mussolini's economic policies affect Italy?**

B. Nazi Germany

In 1919, the German nation had just been defeated in World War I. Some parts of Germany were still occupied by Allied armies. German soldiers were returning home, bitter and unhappy. Many of them were unable to find jobs. During this difficult time, the main hopes of the German people focused on the city of Weimar.

The Weimar Republic

In February 1919, the German national assembly met at Weimar to set up a new democratic government known as the Weimar Republic. They wrote a new constitution that provided a popularly

ANALYZE PRIMARY SOURCES
DOCUMENT-BASED QUESTION What is Mussolini's view of the state?

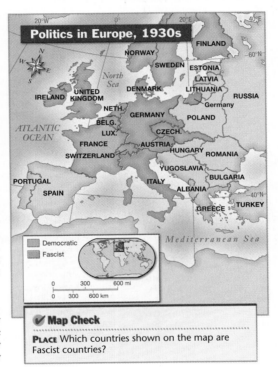

Politics in Europe, 1930s

Democratic
Fascist

✔ Map Check

PLACE Which countries shown on the map are Fascist countries?

---

2 Teach

A. New Government in Italy

Purpose-Setting Question Why did Italians turn to Benito Mussolini after World War I? (They had lost faith in their government. The economy was bad and people feared a Communist revolution in Italy.)

Discuss Ask students how Mussolini changed life in Italy. Have them categorize changes as positive or negative. (**Positive:** brought prosperity and order; provided jobs; ended riots; **Negative:** no other political party allowed; end to civil liberties; critics of Mussolini often killed; control of media)

ANALYZE PRIMARY SOURCES

DOCUMENT-BASED QUESTION
Tell students that this quotation comes from Mussolini's essay "Fundamental Ideas," which appeared in his book *Facism, Doctrine and Institutions* (1935).

ANSWER Mussolini saw the state as an all-powerful institution that should completely dominate peoples' lives.

Using the Map
Politics in Europe, 1930s

Ask students to use the map key to note which areas of Europe were democratic and which were Fascist. Ask whether more countries were democratic or Fascist. (democratic)

✔ Map Check
Answer Italy, Germany, Austria

➤ **ANSWER** The Fascists took control of industry, and production increased. However, workers could no longer strike and wages stayed low.

B. Nazi Germany

Purpose-Setting Question What economic climate in Germany led to the rise of Nazism? (Germany was burdened by war reparations and then by inflation. The Great Depression made the situation even worse.)

Nazi dictator Adolf Hitler poses with a young member of the Hitler Youth.

Global Connections

DICTATORSHIPS SPREAD

Italy and Germany were not alone as authoritarian countries. Eastern Europe, with many new countries after the war, faced similar turmoil. They all struggled with unstable democracies and economies. Some fell to authoritarian rulers. In 1926, Polish war hero Joseph Pilsudski founded a military dictatorship in Poland.

elected president who was given power over foreign policy and the armed forces.

From the start, the Weimar Republic was weakened by serious economic problems. Germany's economy was in ruins, but Germany was expected to make reparations to the victorious Allies. In 1923, Germany fell behind on payments to France. France occupied the Ruhr Valley, an industrial area, to take payment directly. The Germans attempted to defend themselves by refusing to work. To support the workers, the government decided to print more paper money than the treasury could cover. This action was one of the causes of runaway inflation in Germany in 1922 and 1923. The inflation shattered the public's confidence in its government. As more money came into use, it became less valuable. Wages could not keep up with prices. Many people's savings were wiped out.

Inflation was eventually brought under control. In 1924, the United States provided a plan for reducing German reparations. The French and British agreed. French troops withdrew from Ruhr. Loans from the United States helped the German economy recover. Then, the Great Depression began. At this time, a new leader promised to end the crisis and restore the glory of Germany.

Hitler Takes Control

Adolf Hitler was born in an Austrian town near the German border. When World War I started, Hitler joined the German army. After the war, Hitler became interested in politics. In 1919, he joined the National Socialist German Workers Party, which changed its name to the Nazi Party in 1920.

Like Lenin and Mussolini, Hitler hated democracy. Although he disliked the Communists, he admired some of their methods. Inspired by Mussolini, he formed the Nazis into gangs called "Brown Shirts." These gangs attacked Communists and other enemies. In 1923, he tried to overthrow communism in Munich. The attempt failed, and he was thrown into prison.

While in prison, Hitler wrote a book about his beliefs. The book, *Mein Kampf*, or *My Struggle*, expressed Nazi beliefs and goals. In it, he outlined his obsessions with nationalism and racism. He believed that the Germans were the "master race," destined to rule over all the other races. Germany must conquer "inferior" races such as the Slavs. He defined Jewish people as the enemy of all German people.

After leaving prison, Hitler gained a following. He made fiery speeches and published his book. The Great Depression helped him. As unemployment rose, so did Nazi Party membership. His beliefs appealed to people across all classes in Germany.

In the German national election of 1932, the Nazi Party received more votes than any other party. In 1933, President von Hindenburg appointed Hitler **chancellor**, or prime minister. Thus, Hitler came to power legally. Within two months, Hitler forced the German legislature to give up its authority and made himself absolute dictator of the country. Germany became a one-party state. All other parties were banned. The Nazi flag was substituted for the German flag. In 1934, Hitler took the title of Führer, or leader.

Teaching Options

The Third Reich

In 1933, Hitler announced the formation of what he called the Third Reich. The German word *reich* means "empire." While the Third Reich lasted for only 12 years, it changed the history of Germany and the world.

Hitler sought to give new life to the economy. New public works and military spending helped create new jobs. Business and labor were brought under government control. Many applauded his success with the economy and with reviving German pride.

Terror was Hitler's instrument of control. Hitler built up a secret police. He also began attacking Jewish people. They were deprived of civil rights and singled out for mistreatment. Some Jews fled Germany. On the night of November 9, 1938, Nazis launched a mass attack on Jews. The night was called *Kristallnacht*, or the Night of Broken Glass. Shops were looted, and synagogues were burned. Jews were beaten and murdered in the streets. Later, many Jews were sent to <u>concentration</u> <u>camps</u>, or places where prisoners were held.

Fascism, Communism, and Totalitarianism

Communists and Fascists claimed to be enemies. In reality, however, they were similar. In each, a small group claimed to represent the interests of the majority. Both thrived during hard times. Both established totalitarian states.

Mussolini had built a strong totalitarian state in Italy. It soon became a model for others, including Stalin and Hitler, who worked to increase state control over the population. All totalitarian states shared certain characteristics. All had single-party dictatorships and had state-controlled economies. All governments used propaganda and secret police to control the people and crush opposition. All used schools to instruct children. Finally, in all totalitarian states there was unquestioning obedience to a single leader.

◆ Why did Hitler deprive Jews of basic civil rights?

Businesses and properties owned by Jews were the target of Nazis during a night of vandalism known as *Kristallnacht*, or the Night of Broken Glass.

<table>
<tr><td colspan="3">

Review IV

</td></tr>
<tr>
<td>

Review History
A. How did Mussolini gain support in Italy?
B. Why did Hitler gain such a large following in the years after World War I?

</td>
<td>

Define Terms to Know
Define the following terms: **fascism, totalitarian state, chancellor, concentration camp**

Critical Thinking
Compare and contrast the conditions in Germany and Italy that brought dictators to power.

Write About Government
Write a newspaper article describing how governments can control people.

</td>
<td>

Get Organized
IDEA WEB
Use an idea web to organize information from this section. Choose an important idea or event and fill in details about it. For example, what are some details about the Third Reich?

</td>
</tr>
</table>

(Idea web: **Third Reich** center, connected to: Build up economy, Build up military, Use terror to control, Mistreat/kill Jewish people)

Chapter Summary

A blank outline form is available in the Teacher's Resources (p. 318). Chapter summaries should include changing government in the Soviet Union, upheaval in western countries, the unrest in China and India, and the rise of dictatorships. Refer to the rubric in the Teacher's Resources (p. 340) to score students' chapter summaries.

 Interpret the Timeline

1. the Great Purge
2. 14 years
3. the Great Purge in 1934; The Night of Broken Glass in 1938
4. Check students' timelines to be sure all events are in the chapter.

Use Terms to Know

5. collective
6. civil disobedience
7. totalitarian state
8. fascism
9. command economy
10. general strike
11. boycott

Check Your Understanding

12. Under the NEP, the Soviet economy began to recover. Production crawled back to prewar levels in a few years. Higher production brought renewed prosperity. People began to enjoy a higher standard of living.
13. Many farmers resisted collectivization, destroying their crops, equipment, and animals. They were punished by the government. Millions of peasants died, and farm production made few gains.
14. Many old Communist Party members were arrested and either executed or sent to forced-labor camps. People were terrorized and feared showing disloyalty to Stalin.
15. In Europe after World War I, there was inflation, unemployment, and damage from the war.
16. Loans and credit were easy to get. The price of stocks kept rising. People became margin buyers. When investors began to sell stocks, people panicked and the stock market crashed.
17. Jiang Jieshi used the army to conquer warlords. He also worked with the Communists for a while to gain popular support for the Guomindang.

Chapter Summary

Complete the following outline in your notebook. Then, use your outline to write a brief summary of the chapter.

Crises Around the World

I. Changing Government in the Soviet Union
  A. The Soviet Union Under Lenin
  B. Joseph Stalin Takes Control
II. Upheaval in the West
  A. Rebuilding After the War
  B. Boom and Bust
  C. Western European Democracies
III. Unrest in China, Southeast Asia, and India
  A. China
  B. Southeast Asia
  C. India
IV. The Rise of Dictatorships
  A. New Government in Italy
  B. Nazi Germany

 Interpret the Timeline

Use the timeline on pages 636–637 to answer the following questions.

1. Which happened last, the Great Purge or Gandhi's Salt March?

2. How many years passed between the time Adolf Hitler joined the Nazi Party and his rise to power in Germany?

3. **Critical Thinking** Which events on the timeline show totalitarian government in action?

4. Select five events from the chapter that are not on the timeline. Create a timeline that shows these events.

Use Terms to Know

Select the term that best completes each sentence.

boycott   fascism
civil disobedience   general strike
collective   totalitarian state
command economy

5. A farm owned and operated by the state is called a _____.

6. _____ is a way of opposing unlawful government action without resorting to arms.

7. A _____ tries to control every aspect of citizens' lives.

8. _____ is a political system that emphasizes nationalism and is ruled by a dictator.

9. In a _____, the government makes all economic decisions.

10. When workers of many different occupations stop work to protest, it is called a _____.

11. A protest in which people refuse to buy certain goods is called a _____.

Check Your Understanding

12. **Describe** the effects of the New Economic Policy.

13. **Discuss** the effects of Stalin's policy toward farmers.

14. **Describe** what happened during the Great Purge in the Soviet Union.

15. **Identify** some of the problems in Europe after World War I.

16. **Describe** some of the things that led to the Great Depression.

17. **Describe** how Jiang Jieshi worked to unify China.

18. **Summarize** the methods Mao Zedong used to gain popular support during the Long March.

19. **Describe** Gandhi's policy of civil disobedience.

20. **Identify** the beliefs of the National Fascist Party.

21. **Describe** some of the beliefs of Hitler.

---

18. Mao forbade his soldiers to take anything without paying for it, and he kept them from ruining the lands they passed through.
19. Civil disobedience was based on peaceful resistance to authorities. It meant not attacking the British, but refusing to obey unjust laws.
20. The National Fascist Party held that the state should be all-powerful and the rights of the individual were less important.

21. Hitler disliked democracy and admired some communist methods. He was obsessed with nationalism and racism. He believed that the Jews were Germany's enemies and that Germans were the "master race."

Critical Thinking

22. Compare and Contrast How were the NEP and Stalin's command economy different?

23. Draw Conclusions How did the stock market crash of 1929 contribute to the Great Depression?

24. Make Predictions What would have happened in China if the threat of conquest by Japan had been removed?

25. Recognize Relationships Why did the dictatorships of Mussolini, Stalin, and Hitler develop along similar lines?

Put Your Skills to Work

26. Interpret Line Graphs You have learned how to analyze line graphs, which are important for understanding information over a period. Study the line graph below. Then, answer the following questions.

a. What does the graph show?

b. How many people were unemployed in Great Britain in 1931?

c. In which country did a greater increase of unemployment occur?

Unemployment in Great Britain and Germany, 1929–1933

Source: *Twentieth Century Europe; A Documentary History*, 1967

Analyze Sources

27. Read about the general strike of the workers of Shanghai, China, in 1928. Then, answer the questions that follow.

> *The strike was a political, not an economic one; its purpose was to overthrow the rule of warlords . . . establish the political power of Shanghai's revolutionary masses . . . and expedite [speed up] the victory of the national revolutionary war. For these reasons, the workers of Shanghai rose to lead all oppressed people in their revolutionary struggle, and the general strike began.*

a. What kind of strike did the workers stage?

b. For whom are the workers of Shanghai striking?

Essay Writing

28. The 1920s and 1930s were a time of turmoil. World War I and the Great Depression had shaken the foundations of society. Some people began to look to strong leaders who promised a social revolution. Write an essay on how these leaders appealed to people in many countries.

TEST PREPARATION

CAUSE-AND-EFFECT RELATIONSHIPS
Choose the correct answer to the question.

Which of the following is a result of Stalin's drive to force peasants onto collectives?

1. Their standard of living increases.

2. Millions of peasants die of starvation.

3. The NEP is instituted.

4. Agricultural production skyrockets.

Critical Thinking

22. NEP allowed farmers and workers to sell their work for profit, although large industries were owned by the state; under Stalin's command economy, small enterprises were not allowed at all.

23. As stock prices fell, investors sold their stocks, causing a stock market crash. Business began a downward spiral as industrial production and international trade declined. With fewer foreign markets, people making the products lost their jobs.

24. Possible answer: If the threat of Japanese invasion was removed, the Guomindang and the Communists would resume their civil war.

25. All led small parties that claimed to represent the people of their countries and ruled in their name. All of them believed in autocratic, not democratic, government systems.

Put Your Skills to Work

INTERPRET LINE GRAPHS

26a. The graph shows the changes in unemployment in Great Britain and Germany from 1929 to 1933.

26b. about 2.7 million

26c. Germany

Analyze Sources

27a. Workers staged a general strike to overthrow the warlords.

27b. They are striking to lead all oppressed people in their revolutionary struggle.

Essay Writing

28. Students' essays should explain how strong leaders appealed to many people, and should identify the countries where these leaders assumed power.

TEST PREPARATION

Answer 2. Millions of peasants die of starvation.

World War II
1939–1945
(pp. 660–684)

Chapter Objectives
• Focus on the events in China, Ethiopia, and Spain as a prelude to global conflict, and explain why Germany began to annex neighboring territory.
• Identify the invasion of Poland as the beginning of World War II, and discuss the U.S. contributions to the Allied war effort.
• Discuss Hitler's fighting on two fronts, and explain how the United States entered the war.
• Describe the discovery of the Holocaust and the end of the war in Europe and in Asia.

Chapter Summary
Section I focuses on the Japanese invasion of China in the 1930s, Italy's invasion of Ethiopia, the Spanish civil war, and Hitler's annexation of Austria and Czechoslovakia.
Section II describes Hitler's invasion of Poland to start World War II, the progression of the war in Europe, and U.S. efforts to help the Allies.
Section III explores Hitler's invasion of Russia, the war in Africa, and the war in Asia after Japan attacks the United States.
Section IV explains how the war ended in Europe and how it finally ended in the Pacific with the explosion of two atomic bombs.

Set the Stage
TEACH PRIMARY SOURCES
In 1938, when Hitler took over Czechoslovakia he said he had no need to acquire further territory. Then, he invaded Poland. In the speech quoted on page 660, he stated that he had no desire for French territory. Ask students to suggest why other nations might have distrusted Hitler's words. (He had lied to them several times before.) Ask how Hitler used language to make himself sound trustworthy. (Possible answer: He said he offered friendship and cooperation to Great Britain, but he was really just trying to get the British to accept anything he did.)

CHAPTER
28

World War II
1939–1945

I. The Threat of War
II. Conflict in Europe
III. The War Expands
IV. The End of World War II

The Versailles Treaty that ended World War I left the German people angry and frustrated. The ambitions of Adolf Hitler and his Nazi Party renewed their spirit and set Germany on a path of expansion and destruction. On September 1, 1939, Germany invaded Poland. Hitler gave a speech in which he had these words for the nations of Europe:

❝ *I have declared that the frontier between France and Germany is a final one. I have repeatedly offered friendship and the closest co-operation to Britain, but this cannot be offered from one side only. . . .* ❞

Hitler had gone too far. The European nations, recognizing that Hitler's words did not match his actions, rejected his "offer of friendship." This set the stage for the deadliest war of all time.

CHAPTER EVENTS				
1939 Germany attacks Poland.	**1940** Germany invades western Europe.	**1941** Germany invades the Soviet Union. Japan attacks Pearl Harbor, Hawaii.	**1942** United States defeats Japan at the Battle of Midway.

1939 — **1940** — **1941** — **1942**

WORLD EVENTS			
1939 First baseball game is televised in the United States.		**1941** Manhattan Project to develop atomic bomb begins in the United States.	**1942** First U.S. jet airplane is built and tested.

660 UNIT 7 ◆ Decades of War

Teaching Options

Chapter 28 Resources

REVIEW

Teacher's Resources (TR)
Terms to Know, p. 41
Review History, p. 75
Build Your Skills, p. 109
Chapter Test, pp. 171–172
Concept Builder, p. 244
Cause-and-Effect Chain, p. 325
Transparencies 2, 8

ASSESSMENT
Section Reviews, pp. 666, 671, 675, 681
Chapter Review, pp. 682–683
Chapter Test, TR, pp. 171–172
Unit 7 Test, TR, pp. 195–196

ALTERNATIVE ASSESSMENT
Portfolio Project, p. 684
Create a Bulletin Board Display, p. T684

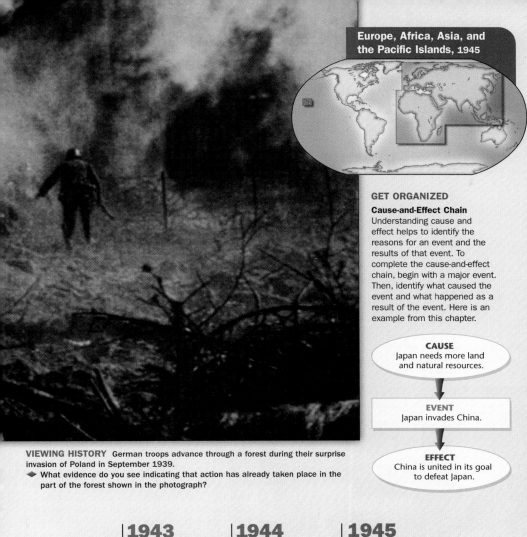

GET ORGANIZED

Cause-and-Effect Chain
Understanding cause and effect helps to identify the reasons for an event and the results of that event. To complete the cause-and-effect chain, begin with a major event. Then, identify what caused the event and what happened as a result of the event. Here is an example from this chapter.

CAUSE
Japan needs more land and natural resources.

EVENT
Japan invades China.

EFFECT
China is united in its goal to defeat Japan.

VIEWING HISTORY German troops advance through a forest during their surprise invasion of Poland in September 1939.
What evidence do you see indicating that action has already taken place in the part of the forest shown in the photograph?

1943
Allied forces invade Italy.

1944
D-day invasion in Europe begins.

1945
Germany surrenders.

United States drops atomic bombs on Japan.

World War II ends.

1943 **1944** **1945** **1946**

1943
Large-scale production of penicillin begins in the United States.

1944
Franklin D. Roosevelt re-elected U.S. President for a fourth term.

CHAPTER 28 ◆ World War II 661

Chapter Themes
- Power, Authority, and Governance
- Global Connections
- Culture
- Time, Continuity, and Change
- People, Places, and Environments
- Individuals, Groups, and Institutions
- Science, Technology, and Society

F Y I

German Technology and War Strategy
Hitler's blitzkrieg, or lightning war, involved powerful planes and speedy ground travel. Dive bombers would fire machine guns at the enemy as tanks rolled over plains and crashed through forests. Tank columns would penetrate far beyond enemy lines and then join up, so that the enemy found itself surrounded.

Chapter Warm-Up
USING THE MAP
Point out the locator map at the top of page 661. Have students identify the part of the world that is highlighted. (Europe, Africa, Asia, and islands in the Pacific Ocean) Ask why the conflict was called a world war. (It took place over much of the world, and nations on most continents were involved.)

VIEW HISTORY
Tell students that this photograph was taken in 1939, during the blitzkrieg, when German soldiers advanced during a surprise invasion of Poland.

◆ **ANSWER** Possible answer: Students may indicate the presence of smoke and damaged trees.

GET ORGANIZED
Cause-and-Effect Chain
Review the cause-and-effect chain with students. Point out that the content of the chain does not indicate whether Japan was right or wrong in what it did. The chain simply states the facts.

● **TEACH THE TIMELINE**
The timeline on pages 660–661 covers the period between 1939 and 1945. Help students notice the flow of the war by pointing out that the Chapter Events listed for the first three years are all attacks by the Axis powers. In contrast, have students classify the events in the last three years on the timeline. (The events are a mixture of both, with the Allies victorious.)

Activity

List related events Have students list events on the timeline that may be linked with one causing or contributing to another. As an example, point out that only four years after the Manhattan Project began, the United States dropped atomic bombs on Japan. (Other linked events: Germany invades western Europe and D-day invasion begins; the United States drops atomic bombs on Japan and World War II ends; Japan attacks Pearl Harbor and the United States fights Japan in the Battle of Midway.)

I. The Threat of War

(pp. 662–666)

Section Summary

In this section, students will learn about events in the 1930s that were prefaces to World War II, including Japan's invasion of China, Italy's invasion of Ethiopia, and the Spanish civil war. They will also learn how Hitler began appropriating territory for Germany in the late 1930s.

➊ Introduce

Getting Started

Ask students to think of music from a movie or television program that is suspenseful or full of dread. One possibility is the music from the movie *Jaws,* when the shark is about to attack. Have students discuss their feelings when they hear such music. Tell them that in the late 1930s, "political music" was playing, although not everyone in the world was listening. For those who were listening, the message was dreadful and terrifying.

TERMS TO KNOW

Ask students to read the words and definitions on page 662 and find each word in the section. The root of the word *appeasement* is the same as that of *peace*. The word *sanction* comes from the Latin *sanctus,* meaning "to make holy." Although a sanction used to refer to an ecclesiastical decree, it now means a penalty.

You may wish to preview the pronunciation of the following names with students.

Hideki Tojo (hee DEH kee TOH joh)
Haile Selassie (HY lee suh LAH see)
Guernica (guhr NEE kah)
Sudetenland (soo DAY tuhn land)
Edouard Daladier
(AY dwar dah LAHD yay)

ACTIVE READING

In order for students to draw conclusions about how the events in this section will be resolved, suggest that they use a main idea/supporting details chart (TR, p. 319) to make notes as they read about threats of war in the 1930s. Students should refer to their notes to draw their conclusions.

Terms to Know

sanction a penalty for breaking international laws or codes of conduct

appeasement giving in to demands in exchange for peace

Main Ideas

A. Military operations in China, Japan, Italy, and Spain were warning signs that war was brewing in Europe and Asia.

B. Germany's preparation for war included annexing Austria and Czechoslovakia and making a peace agreement with the Soviet Union.

Active Reading

DRAW CONCLUSIONS
When you draw conclusions, you evaluate information and decide its significance. As you read this section, concentrate on the conflicts developing in Europe and Asia. Then, draw your own conclusions about how these events will be resolved.

A. Rumblings of War in Asia and Europe

The aggression of Germany and the rising popularity of Adolf Hitler were not the only signs that serious trouble was developing. Conflicts in China, Japan, Italy, and Spain set the stage for worldwide war.

Japan Expands into Asia

As you read in Chapter 25, civil war was tearing China apart in the early part of the twentieth century. Communist rebel troops led by Mao Zedong were fighting government troops led by Jiang Jieshi. However, a much greater threat loomed over China's eastern horizon. That threat was the nation of Japan.

For some time, Japan had been looking for an excuse to invade the Asian mainland, particularly China. On September 18, 1931, an explosion rocked a Japanese-owned railroad in Manchuria, located in the northeast corner of China. The explosion, which had been staged by officers of the Japanese military, gave Japan the excuse it had been looking for. The Japanese quickly conquered Manchuria and established a government that was sympathetic to Japan.

The military leader of Japan was General Hideki Tojo, who later served as Japan's prime minister. Tojo and other military leaders believed that they had a right to rule all of Asia. Japan also had economic reasons for invading China—it needed land and raw materials. There was not enough farmland to support its many people. Japan also needed coal, iron, and oil for its growing industries.

After their successful invasion of Manchuria, the Japanese military continued to expand their control over surrounding regions. The League of Nations condemned the Japanese acts of aggression. However, member nations of the League were not willing to anger the powerful Japanese military forces. Japan soon withdrew from the League.

Members of the Japanese invasion force celebrate their victory in Manchuria.

Teaching Options

Section 1 Resources

Teacher's Resources (TR)
Terms to Know, p. 41
Review History, p. 75
Build Your Skills, p. 109
Concept Builder, p. 244
Cause-and-Effect Chain, p. 325

The Japanese military had many successes in China. Their powerful strikes on the coastal cities broke the Chinese forces there. The Chinese retreated up the Chang Jiang Valley toward the capital of Nanjing. This city was bombed for weeks by the Japanese and finally fell on December 13, 1937. Upon entering Nanjing, the victorious Japanese soldiers abandoned their discipline. For six weeks, they rampaged through the Chinese capital murdering and torturing more than 300,000 men, women, and children.

The effects of the massacre at Nanjing were far reaching. The Chinese people forgot the disagreements of the civil war. They became unified against a common Japanese enemy. Also, the media coverage of the event in the West portrayed Japan as a brutal aggressor.

Haile Selassie I was emperor of Ethiopia when it fell to the Italians under Benito Mussolini.

Italy Invades Ethiopia

In the 1930s, the dictator Benito Mussolini ruled Italy. Mussolini felt humiliated that other European nations had many rich colonies, while he had only what he called a "collection of deserts." He looked to Ethiopia in eastern Africa to fill his hopes for expansion.

In previous years, Mussolini had been a friend of Ethiopia, helping it to become a member of the League of Nations. However, he now began to look for an excuse to take over that nation. His excuse came in 1934 when troops serving under the Italian flag clashed with a small troop of Ethiopians. As a reaction, Mussolini invaded Ethiopia.

The League of Nations issued some economic **sanctions**, or penalties, against Italy for its actions against Ethiopia. However, most European nations were eager to remain on friendly terms with Mussolini and to keep Italy as an ally. Within a month, the British government asked that the sanctions be lifted. The conquered emperor of Ethiopia, Haile Selassie I, warned that European nations would live to regret their passive reaction. At a speech to the League of Nations he said, "It is us today. It will be you tomorrow."

Spain Fights a Civil War

The troubled decade of the 1930s saw more conflict in Spain. The Spanish civil war was a battle that would pit the forces of fascism against the forces of democracy. You read in Chapter 27 that fascism is a form of government that has a strong military dictator.

The ruling government of Spain angered some members of the military and some wealthy Spanish landowners. Fierce disagreements arose, and soon a civil war erupted. The two sides of the war in Spain were the Loyalists and the Nationalists. The Loyalists supported the existing government. The existing government had passed many reforms that helped poor people. Loyalists were mainly workers, trade unionists, and others who supported democracy. The Nationalists were the military leaders, landowners, and leaders of the Roman Catholic Church. Their leader was Francisco Franco. Franco was a Fascist, and the Nationalist rebels supported fascism.

War broke out in 1936, and promised to be a long one. Even Franco did not think his forces would accomplish a quick victory. He said:

> ❝ People are mistaken who think this business will be a brief affair. Far from it. It's going to be difficult, bloody and it'll last a long time. ❞

Franco was right. The Spanish civil war was long and bloody.

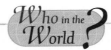

Who in the World?

SPANISH SAILORS
Not all Spanish troops supported their rebel military leaders. Just two days after the Spanish civil war began, most of the officers on board ships at sea had been killed by the enlisted crew members. These sailors refused to fight against the government.

ANALYZE PRIMARY SOURCES **DOCUMENT-BASED QUESTION**
Why do you think Franco gave this warning?

A. Rumblings of War in Asia and Europe

Purpose-Setting Question What events in Asia and Europe suggested that a global war was on the horizon? (Japan invaded China; Italy invaded Ethiopia; the Spanish civil war took place.)

Extend Tell students that Jiang Jieshi is also known as Chiang Kai-shek.

Discuss Ask students how Japan instigated a conflict with China. (staged an explosion, then conquered Manchuria) Ask why Japan invaded mainland Asia. (The Japanese believed they had a right to rule Asia; they wanted land and raw materials, too.)

Explore Have students turn their attentions to Italy and Ethiopia. Ask how this situation was similar to that of Japan and China. (Like Japan, Italy wanted more land. Like Tojo, Mussolini used a trumped-up excuse to invade.)

Focus Have students explain the cause of the Spanish civil war. (The military and wealthy landowners felt that the government was too liberal.)

WHO IN THE WORLD?

SPANISH SAILORS Many members of the Spanish navy were Loyalists, and their refusal to participate with the Nationalists was a problem for Franco, who was in Morocco when the conflict began. Italian and German planes were used to provide transport back to Spain for Franco and his men.

ANALYZE PRIMARY SOURCES

DOCUMENT-BASED QUESTION
A Popular Front coalition supported by leftist parties won in a general election in 1936. Five months later the military uprising began. Have students recall other wars that some people mistakenly thought would be over quickly. (Possible answer: World War I, U.S. Civil War)

ANSWER Possible answer: Franco may have wanted his followers to be ready for the worst.

F Y I

Abraham Lincoln Battalion

Most Americans who wanted to fight for the Loyalists in the Spanish civil war joined the Abraham Lincoln Battalion of the International Brigade. About 2,800 Americans joined during the war, and about 900 of these were killed in action. Ernest Hemingway was a correspondent in Spain during the war. Perhaps his greatest novel, _For Whom the Bell Tolls_ (1940), is about an American fighting in Spain for the Loyalists.

Ask students to explain how Picasso showed the horror of war in *Guernica*. (Possible answers: women screaming, dead child, fallen warrior) Tell students that in *Guernica*, the German bombers fired machine guns at the village for over three hours, systematically reducing it to rubble. One-third of the population was killed or wounded. *Guernica* had no strategic significance and was attacked simply to spread terror. In 1999, the German government apologized to the citizens of *Guernica* for Germany's role in the incident.

Discuss Ask students why the Spanish civil war has been called a rehearsal for World War II. (Possible answers: The forces of fascism fought the forces of democracy and communism/socialism. The Germans got fighting experience. The democracies saw that not getting involved was ultimately self-destructive.)

◆ **ANSWER** They were passive because they did not want to get involved, perhaps causing an escalation of the fighting.

B. Germany Plans for War

Purpose-Setting Question What events in Europe in the late 1930s led to World War II? (German troops in the Rhineland; German alliances with Italy and Japan; Anschluss; takeover of Czechoslovakia; Nazi-Soviet Nonaggression Pact)

Focus Ask students why sending German troops to the Rhineland was important to Hitler. (From there, Hitler could launch military action against France.)

Review Remind students that in Chapter 26, they learned that a demilitarized zone is an area that military forces may not enter. A demilitarized zone was set up after World War I by the Allied nations to make sure that Germany was contained in the future.

Spanish-born artist Pablo Picasso painted this mural, titled *Guernica*. It expressed his rage over the destruction of the ancient Spanish town of Guernica by Nazi bombers in 1937.

The Nationalist rebels looked to Italy and Germany for support for their cause. Mussolini sent planes, tanks, ships, cannons, weapons, and soldiers to support the attacks on the Spanish government. Germany sent planes and as many as 16,000 men. The Loyalists appealed to France, Great Britain, and the United States for help. France sent 200 planes, weapons, and 9,000 troops. Great Britain and the United States sent food, clothing, and medical supplies, but no weapons or troops. These nations did not want to anger Hitler or Mussolini.

As many as 60,000 volunteers from all around the world, including the United States and the Soviet Union, came to the aid of the Loyalists. About 40,000 of these people fought alongside the Loyalists. The rest provided medical aid. Even with the support they received, the Loyalists were weaker than the Nationalists. After three years of bitter fighting, Franco had crushed all resistance.

After Franco's Fascist government came to power, democratic nations such as France, Britain, and the United States began to regret their decision to stay out of the conflict. They realized that another strong military dictatorship increased their own danger.

Spain's civil war gave Germany and Italy some important advantages. It provided good fighting experience for Germany. In addition, Hitler had access to the iron resources of Spain. After his victory, Franco agreed that Spain would not take an active part in the battles of World War II.

◆ **How did members of the League of Nations react to the violence in Ethiopia?**

B. Germany Plans for War

In 1936, Adolf Hitler, the leader of Germany, moved his troops into the Rhineland, the demilitarized zone on either side of the Rhine River. In Chapter 26, you learned that the Treaty of Versailles had forbidden Germany to have troops in this area. However, Hitler ignored all objections to his actions. The placement of troops in the Rhineland had great strategic value. Now Hitler could safely launch military action against France and central Europe. That fall, Hitler also made alliances with Italy and Japan. These countries would be his allies in the great war that was to come.

Teaching Options

Research

AVERAGE

Have students choose one of the leaders mentioned in this section and find out more about him. Ask students to develop a biographical sketch of the person, including information on his background, political career, and five interesting facts about the person they chose.

CHALLENGE

Have students research in greater depth an event discussed in this section, such as the massacre at Nanjing or the selling out of Czechoslovakia in 1938. Have students list some of the interesting facts to come out of this research.

In 1937, Hitler announced that Germany needed more space. The German population was growing, and he wanted the farmlands of neighboring nations. Hitler was eager to take over the nearby nations of Austria and Czechoslovakia, and to stall the nations of France and Britain from taking any action against him. He also wanted to remain on friendly terms with the Soviet Union.

Germany Takes Over Austria and Czechoslovakia

Hitler's grand plan was to unite all German-speaking people under his power. This included the people in Austria. His goal was Anschluss, a union of Austria with Germany. In fact, many people in Austria had supported the Nazi ideals and were more than willing to follow Hitler's leadership. In early 1938, Hitler forced the leader of Austria to appoint Nazis to high-level government positions. Under great political pressure from Hitler, the Austrian government collapsed.

Although Austria did not have large mineral resources, it did have a great deal of foreign money. This money helped Hitler build steel factories and supply his military forces. By 1939, Austrian factories were producing fighter planes for the Nazis.

The takeover of Austria also meant that Czechoslovakia was surrounded on three sides by German-controlled lands. Conquering Czechoslovakia would be more difficult, because the nation had alliances with France and the Soviet Union. Hitler seized on the small strip of Czechoslovakian land near Germany called the Sudetenland, which was home to about 3 million people of German descent. He demanded that it should be annexed to Germany. Hitler's intentions alarmed Great Britain and France. However, neither nation was willing to go to war over problems in Czechoslovakia.

The Munich Conference

In September 1938, prime ministers Neville Chamberlain of Great Britain and Edouard Daladier of France met in Munich, Germany, with Hitler and Mussolini. Their purpose was to negotiate a settlement over the Sudetenland. Wanting to contain Hitler's aggression, the two prime ministers agreed to Hitler's demand that the Sudetenland be separated from Czechoslovakia and given to Germany. Hitler accepted this agreement immediately. In exchange, Hitler promised that he had no intentions for further aggressions.

At the Munich Conference, the four nations agreed that Czechoslovakia would remain independent. This agreement continued a policy of **appeasement** in which the democratic nations of Europe would give in to Hitler's demands in exchange for peace. Chamberlain returned to Great Britain in triumph, announcing that he had secured "peace in our time." Unfortunately, he was mistaken.

Germany then moved quickly into the rest of Czechoslovakia without European interference. As a result, the Czech factories and weapons were added to Germany's industrial power. They were used later against those very democracies that had negotiated for the independence of Czechoslovakia.

The swastika on this German flag became the symbol of the Nazi Party in Germany.

Neville Chamberlain of Great Britain believed that his negotiations with Hitler had prevented war with Germany.

CHAPTER 28 ◆ World War II **665**

CHAPTER 28 ◆ **T665**

Discuss Review with students the animosity between Fascists and Communists. Point out, however, the similarities between Hitler and Stalin. Tell students that the Nazi-Soviet Nonaggression Pact was like the final piece of a puzzle that Hitler needed to complete before World War II could begin. It assured Hitler that he would not have a war on two fronts.

TEACH PRIMARY SOURCES
Tell students that the cartoon on page 666 was created by Clifford K. Berryman, a political cartoonist for the *Washington Evening Star* from 1907 to 1949. Ask what is happening in the cartoon. (Hitler and Stalin are getting married.) Ask how the caption expresses a cynical attitude about this marriage. (Possible answer: The honeymoon is a time when the relationship is supposed to be at its best. The caption suggests that the honeymoon will be short.)

◆ **ANSWER** Germany gained all the industrial power of Czechoslovakia, which was used later against the Allies. Also, the Munich Conference reassured Hitler that the other European nations would not use force to resist him.

Section Close

Have students look back to their conclusions in the Active Reading activity on page 662. Ask if their conclusions were correct or need modifying. Discuss whether there was any way that war could be averted at this point. (Probably not, Hitler had grown too strong; other nations might have been able to prevent war if they had acted sooner regarding Hitler.)

3 Assess

Review Answers

Review History
A. In Spain, a Fascist government won the civil war. In Asia, Japan invaded China. Italy conquered Ethiopia.

B. He supported Franco in Spain, moved troops into the Rhineland, made alliances with Italy and Japan, and took over Austria and Czechoslovakia. He also signed a nonaggression pact with Stalin.

Define Terms to Know
sanction, 663; appeasement, 665

WONDER HOW LONG THE HONEYMOON WILL LAST?

As the cartoon indicates, many people believed that the "marriage" agreement between Adolf Hitler of Germany and Joseph Stalin of the Soviet Union would be short-lived.

Nonaggression Pact With the Soviets

Hitler knew that he must fight his enemies one region at a time. He had annexed Austria and Czechoslovakia, and he had put off attacks by France and Britain at the Munich Conference. Next, he had to be certain that the Soviet Union would not resist him as he carried out his plan to take over Europe.

In July 1939, Hitler and Joseph Stalin, the leader of the Soviet Union, came to an agreement. Their agreement, called the Nazi-Soviet Nonaggression Pact, was announced in August 1939. Publicly, the pact stated that the nations would not fight against one another. Secretly, the pact had divided up the regions that lay between the two nations.

The pact was good for both sides. Hitler did not want to fight a war on the eastern border of his country while he was busy in Europe on the western border. Even though Hitler despised the Soviets— he believed that Slavs were an inferior race—he needed to keep them on the sidelines while he invaded Poland. Stalin, in turn, detested the Nazis in Germany. However, he was eager for the territories that Hitler had promised him. He also knew the danger presented by Hitler's armies. The pact gave Stalin time to build up his military defenses.

The other nations of Europe resisted war at all costs. They were alarmed by Hitler's aggression, but they hoped he would be satisfied with the lands he had already occupied. However, it would not be long before they realized that Hitler would draw them all into a terrible war that would last for the next six years.

◆ **How did the results of the Munich Conference hurt European nations in the long run?**

Review I

Review History
A. What were signs that trouble was developing in Europe and Asia?
B. In what ways did Hitler prepare for large-scale war?

Define Terms to Know
Define the following terms: **sanction, appeasement**

Critical Thinking
Why do you think France and Great Britain did not oppose Hitler's plans for Czechoslovakia?

Write About Culture
Write a paragraph in which you explain why the conflicts in Ethiopia and Spain were good for Germany and Italy and bad for the United States and the democratic nations of Europe.

Get Organized
CAUSE-AND-EFFECT CHAIN
Use a cause-and-effect chain to organize information from this section. Choose an event and then identify the cause and effect. For example, what were the causes and effects of the Munich Conference?

Critical Thinking
France and Great Britain hoped that giving in to Hitler's demands would prevent a large-scale war.

Write About Culture
Students' paragraphs should discuss how the conflicts in Spain and Ethiopia helped Italy and Germany prepare for war, and how the United States and democratic nations of Europe were hurt by their lack of action and support for Spain and Ethiopia.

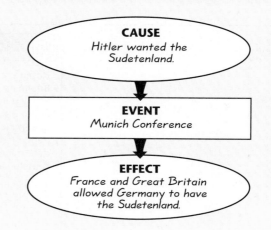

CAUSE
Hitler wanted the Sudetenland.

EVENT
Munich Conference

EFFECT
France and Great Britain allowed Germany to have the Sudetenland.

Build Your Skills

Social Studies Skill

RECOGNIZE PROPAGANDA AND BIAS

Propaganda is the promotion of certain ideas to advance, damage, or destroy a cause, especially a political cause. Usually, propaganda will contain some true statements. However, these statements are generally biased, and present only one side of an issue.

Bias is an idea that agrees more with one side of an argument than another side. Biased information does not present both sides of an argument equally.

Propaganda appears in materials written or created to persuade people. These materials include posters, political cartoons, speeches, films, and newspaper or magazine articles. During World War II, both sides used posters to spread propaganda. These posters were intended to appeal to people's emotions and influence their thoughts or actions.

Here's How
Follow these steps to interpret propaganda and bias.

1. Identify the type of material used for propaganda and tell why it is used.
2. Decide which techniques were used to support the biased ideas. Is there information missing? Is the idea made to appear glamorous?
3. Interpret the words and images and tell how they are used to persuade the reader or viewer.
4. Interpret the information in a piece of propaganda and decide who it is meant to influence.

Here's Why
Historians are interested in propaganda because it can help explain how historical events were viewed. Recognizing propaganda and interpreting it will help you form your own opinions.

Practice the Skill
Look at the poster on the right to answer these questions.

1. What is the subject of the poster?
2. Who is the poster meant to influence?
3. How does the poster try to influence the viewer?

Extend the Skill
Write a paragraph describing how you would have reacted to this poster if you lived in Germany in the 1940s. Explain the ways in which the poster appealed to German youths.

Apply the Skill
When a nation goes to war, its government uses propaganda to gain the support of the public. Study the primary sources and the visuals in the rest of the chapter. Identify how each side used propaganda to influence people during World War II.

The title of the propaganda poster announces "Young people serve the Führer" [Hitler].

CHAPTER 28 ◆ World War II **667**

Teaching Options

RETEACH

Provide students with several fliers, posters, or brochures about the local school district or the high school that they attend. Have students choose one of these pieces of literature. Ask students to follow the steps in *Here's How* to decide whether the publication is propaganda. If it is propaganda, have students note how it is biased.

CHALLENGE

Have students create a piece of propaganda relating to a local issue, a current event, or a school-related issue. Display students' work in the classroom. Using the steps in *Here's How,* have students analyze each piece of propaganda. Discuss which pieces are most effective, and have students explain why these pieces are the strongest.

Build Your Skills

RECOGNIZE PROPAGANDA AND BIAS

Teach the Skill
Ask students to think of political ads or strong persuasive appeals they have seen or heard on television or on the radio or in newspapers. Discuss how the appeals often stressed one side of an issue and avoided looking at both sides.

Ask students how propaganda differs from bias. (Possible answer: Propaganda is the showing of one side of an issue, and bias is the one-sided idea itself. You use bias when you create propaganda.)

Discuss with students why it is important to recognize propaganda. (to be able to look closely and see what has been left out of the presentation so that you are swayed by facts, not emotions) Explain to students that both sides of an issue use propaganda, so it is important to recognize what it is and view information accordingly.

Practice the Skill
ANSWERS

1. The subject is the service of young people to Hitler.
2. The poster is meant to influence all Germans and especially young Germans.
3. It shows that young people admire Hitler and want to serve him.

Extend the Skill
Students' paragraphs may state that students would have reacted positively to this poster. They may note that the poster makes it seem a noble thing to serve Hitler, and that such service would make you a better person.

Apply the Skill
Possible answer: All the speeches and visuals are designed to emphasize the views of the presenters and to sway the audience to accept those points of view.

Section Summary

In this section, students will learn how World War II began with the invasion of Poland and how Hitler soon conquered most of Europe, including France. They will also learn how the United States responded to the Nazi attacks, how resistance fighters helped fight the Nazis, and how women worked to help the Allies.

1 Introduce

Getting Started

Have students think of a time when they really needed someone's help. Ask how they felt when someone finally came to their aid. (Possible answer: relieved, grateful) Tell students that they will read about a time when some European countries desperately needed help.

TERMS TO KNOW

Ask students to read the words and definitions on page 668 and find each word in the section. Point out that one word—*blitzkrieg*—is German, and another—*sabotage*—is French. Ask students to write a brief paragraph using all of these words.

You may wish to preview the pronunciation of the following words with students.

Ardennes (ahr DEHN)
Luftwaffe (LOOFT vah fuh)
Pétain (pay TAN)

ACTIVE READING

Help students become more aware of sequence by asking them to write important events from the section and the dates on which they occurred on index cards. Then, have them create timelines by arranging the cards. Have students compare their timelines to see if they agree with the sequence of events.

Section II — Conflict in Europe

Terms to Know

blitzkrieg Hitler's method of fighting a "lightning war," involving powerful planes and speedy ground travel

arsenal a place for making or storing weapons

sabotage intentional damage or destruction by underground resistance groups

German troops are shown taking part in a blitzkrieg attack on Poland.

Main Ideas

A. The invasion of Poland forced the Allied Powers to take action.

B. President Franklin D. Roosevelt aligned the United States with the Allies by sending military supplies and other support for democratic nations.

Active Reading

SEQUENCE OF EVENTS
When you put events in a sequence, you put them in the order in which the events happened. As you read this section, concentrate on the events in the early years of World War II. Then, pause to put the events in sequence.

A. World War II Begins

The democratic nations of Europe had been turning their heads away and hoping for the best as Hitler took over first Austria, then Czechoslovakia. Because they had lived through World War I, most Europeans remembered the horrors of war vividly. They hoped that by appeasing Hitler, Europe would have peace. Finally, both France and Great Britain decided that they could no longer ignore the German advances. They agreed to intervene if Hitler attacked Poland, a move that seemed the next likely step after the Nazis took control of Czechoslovakia.

Invasion of Poland

As the French and British feared, on September 1, 1939, Hitler attacked Poland. Two days later, France and Great Britain declared war on Germany. In time, more than 40 other nations, including the United States and, eventually, the Soviet Union, would form an alliance called the Allied Powers, or Allies. These nations would wage a long, terrible war—known as World War II—against the Axis Powers, which included Germany, Italy, and Japan.

Hitler's invasion of Poland was the first real show of Nazi Germany's military power. During this invasion, the German armed forces demonstrated a new military strategy called **blitzkrieg**, which is German for "lightning war." Blitzkrieg was based on the use of bombs dropped by warplanes followed immediately by attacks using fast-moving tanks and trucks carrying troops and weapons.

The Polish army was overwhelmed by the quick-striking German forces. In a matter of days, the western regions of Poland were under German control. Then, on September 17, the Soviet Union invaded the eastern borders of Poland. By that time, the Polish military forces were in shambles, and the Soviets had an easy time defeating them. Within a month after the initial attack by the Germans, Poland

---

Teaching Options

Section 2 Resources

Teacher's Resources (TR)
Terms to Know, p. 41
Review History, p. 75
Build Your Skills, p. 109
Concept Builder, p. 244
Cause-and-Effect Chain, p. 325

ESL/ELL STRATEGIES

Organize Information Remind students that the Allies were Great Britain, France, and eventually the Soviet Union and the United States. Germany, Italy, and Japan made up the Axis Powers. Have students use a two-column chart (TR, p. 328) to classify the countries and their alliances. Encourage students to review the chart as they read the rest of the chapter.

no longer existed as a nation. The Germans and Soviets had rounded up the remaining Polish fighters and divided Poland according to the agreement in their Nonaggression Pact.

The Move West

Germany made no further advances during the winter of 1939–1940. However, the Soviet Union continued to advance and took Estonia, Latvia, Lithuania, and part of Finland. In April 1940, Hitler launched surprise attacks on Norway and Denmark. Denmark fell in less than one day. Norway held out for two months.

The Nazis' next move was to the west. In May 1940, Hitler's blitzkrieg overcame Luxembourg and the Netherlands. At the same time, the Germans began their invasion of France. The French had been expecting this attack. French and British troops had spent the winter in the trenches of the Maginot line, a series of heavily armed fortifications along France's border with Germany. However, Germany did not attack the Maginot line. Instead, their tanks and other armored vehicles raced around these defenses and through the Ardennes Forest to Belgium. Belgium surrendered to Germany on May 28, 1940.

The Miracle at Dunkirk and the Fall of France

Germany's swift defeat of Belgium left thousands of British and French soldiers stranded with little hope for escape. However, in a daring move, the British high command sent out a call for all available ships to cross the English Channel and rescue the soldiers. Stranded soldiers fought their way to the French coastal city of Dunkirk. In May 1940, boats of all sizes crossed the channel and rescued as many as 350,000 soldiers. The boats ranged from heavy British battle cruisers to tiny fishing boats. The rescue was called the "Miracle at Dunkirk," and it gave a huge boost to British spirits.

In early June, the German army began moving across France. The French leaders were stunned at the flying ability of the German Luftwaffe, or air force, and by the power and speed of the land attack. They had no plan of defense after the Germans had gone around the Maginot line. In addition, Italy invaded France from the south on June 10. By June 14, 1940, the Germans had taken Paris. A week later, the head of France, Marshal Phillipe Pétain, surrendered.

The Blitz in Britain

When Germany launched its western invasions, leaders in the British Parliament began to express unhappiness with Prime Minister Neville Chamberlain. They were annoyed at Chamberlain's inactivity and his foolish hope that Hitler would stop his military activity. On May 10, Chamberlain resigned and Parliament put Winston Churchill in his place. Churchill had been one of the few politicians to oppose the policy of appeasement in the 1930s.

British soldiers in the water are headed for a rescue ship during the "Miracle at Dunkirk."

A. World War II Begins

Purpose-Setting Question How did World War II begin? (Germany invaded Poland, then France, and Great Britain declared war on Germany.)

Review Remind students of the way Japan began its campaign to conquer neighboring lands by attacking Manchuria in 1931 (page 662). Tell students that Hitler began his attack on Poland in a similar way—by staging an attack on a German radio station that he said was committed by the Polish military but actually was committed by German soldiers in Polish uniforms.

Discuss Ask students to describe the Polish campaign. (Germany used its blitzkrieg to attack Poland, and the Polish succumbed. The Soviet Union surprised Poland by attacking several weeks later from the east.)

Activity

Use a map Have students use a map of western Europe from an atlas or other source to follow the German campaign in Belgium, north of the Maginot Line. Have them find Dunkirk on the map and estimate its distance to the English coast. (between 45 and 50 miles)

Focus Ask students what the "miracle" at Dunkirk was. (Using every boat available, the British sailed across the English Channel and rescued about 350,000 British and French soldiers. They would have become prisoners of war if this miracle had not happened.) Tell students that the success of the evacuation was due in part to the Royal Air Force, which provided air cover along the English coast.

F Y I

Winston Churchill

Sir Winston Churchill (1874–1965) led Great Britain when it stood alone against the Axis powers. Churchill was knighted in 1953, the same year he won the Nobel Prize for Literature. He denied being Great Britain's inspiration during the war. "It was the nation . . . that had the lion's heart," he said. "I had the luck to be called on to give the roar."

DOCUMENT-BASED QUESTION

This speech was made on May 13, 1940. Three days earlier, Germany had attacked Belgium, the Netherlands, and Luxembourg. Discuss Churchill's speech in light of these attacks.

ANSWER Listeners might have felt inspired to fight to any lengths against the Axis powers.

Explore Ask students why Hitler bombed England's air bases before bombing its cities. (He tried to eliminate its air force as a retaliatory threat.)

TEACH PRIMARY SOURCES

Tell students that this photograph of Winston Churchill was taken on November 8, 1939, after the war had begun but before Great Britain was attacked. Ask students to describe the expression on Churchill's face. (Possible answer: pensive, resolute, determined)

◆ **ANSWER** The speed of the blitzkrieg surprised them. They also did not expect the Germans to be able to go around the Maginot Line.

B. Responses to the Nazi Threat

Purpose-Setting Question What could the United States do as a result of the Lend-Lease Act? (It could lend or lease weapons to Allied nations for use in the war against Germany and Japan.)

Extend As a result of the Lend-Lease Act, American supplies worth tens of billions of dollars were sent to Great Britain, the Soviet Union, and China. President Roosevelt likened it to putting out a fire at your neighbor's house so that your own house would not catch fire as well.

Activity

Summarize Have students use a main idea/supporting details chart (TR, p. 319) to summarize the information in this subsection. (**Main idea:** People responded to the Nazi threat. **Supporting details:** Congress passed the Lend-Lease Act, and the Atlantic Charter strengthened the bond between the United States and Great Britain; resistance movements sprang up in conquered nations; women worked in factories and served in the armed forces.)

How might Churchill's listeners have responded to this speech?

When Churchill entered Parliament for the first time as Prime Minister, he made a memorable speech in which he said:

> ❝ I have nothing to offer but blood, toil, tears, and sweat. . . . You ask what is our policy? I will say: it is to wage war against a monstrous tyranny [cruel use of power]. . . . That is our policy. You ask, what is our aim? I can answer in one word: it is victory, victory at all costs . . . victory, however long and hard the road may be; for without victory, there is no survival. ❞

Churchill had been speaking out against appeasement of Hitler since 1935. He had read the warning signs of Hitler's military buildup as a dangerous threat to world peace. Churchill's leadership would prove to be an inspiration to all nations of the free world.

With France under the control of the Nazis, Hitler might have hoped that Great Britain would view the Soviet Union as a greater threat to world peace than Germany. In such a case, a British alliance against the Soviet Union might be possible. When this did not happen, Hitler attacked Great Britain. He began by bombing British air bases. Later, he concentrated on bombing the cities of England in what came to be called the Battle of Britain, or the "Blitz." In London, the Blitz lasted for 57 days in a row. Hitler believed that the constant air attacks would exhaust the British people and make them call for surrender. Instead, the attacks strengthened the will of the people and made them dig in stubbornly against the attackers.

During the Blitz in London, many British citizens camped out in bomb shelters and underground railway stations. Armed civilians watched the English Channel for signs of an invasion. Each day brought more destruction. In the city of London alone, about 14,000 people were killed in the bombings and the fires that followed.

◆ **Why was France surprised by the German invasion?**

B. Responses to the Nazi Threat

It took some time, but democratic nations around the world, the United States in particular, soon became involved in the growing conflicts abroad. When hostilities began in Europe and Asia, the United States had declared that it would remain neutral. The American people wanted to follow a policy of isolationism, which meant that they wished to keep out of any conflict that did not directly involve them. However, when France and Great Britain, the most important European allies of the United States, came under attack, U.S. public opinion began to shift.

Lend-Lease Act and the Atlantic Charter

The American President, Franklin D. Roosevelt, wanted to help the Allies without going against the nation's isolationist policies. In March 1941, he persuaded the U.S. Congress to pass the Lend-Lease Act. This act declared the United States to be the **arsenal**, or storehouse, of democracy. Under the Lend-Lease Act, the United States could provide weapons and equipment to Allied nations for use in the war against Hitler.

In August 1941, Roosevelt met with Winston Churchill for a secret conference. They agreed to support the right of all people to determine their own government. To achieve this, they agreed that Nazi Germany must be destroyed. This agreement, called the Atlantic Charter, strengthened the relationship between the United States and Great Britain.

Prime Minister Winston Churchill served as an inspiration to the British people during World War II.

Teaching Options

Focus on TEEN LIFE

Kindertransport After *Kristallnacht* (see page 657), many Jews tried to leave Germany. Tragically, few countries were willing to let them in. The British Jewish Refugee Committee appealed to the British Parliament, which agreed to admit children between the ages of 5 and 17. From December 1938 until September 1, 1939, approximately 10,000 Jewish children arrived in Great Britain. This influx is known as the Kindertransport. The children lived with foster families and in orphanages. Some worked on farms. When they came of age, many volunteered for service in the British armed forces to fight the Nazis. Most of them never saw their parents again. You may want to have students use the Internet to find out about the Kindertransport Association.

Resistance Movements

The people of Poland, France, Belgium and other European nations were under Hitler's control. Many were treated cruelly. Some fought fiercely against the invaders. Factories and farms in these countries were forced to supply the German military forces with manufactured goods and food.

Many people of the invaded countries in Europe resisted the takeover of their nations. In some cases, this resistance was well organized. Because of the secret nature of their activities, resistance groups were often referred to as the "underground."

French resistance fighters were among the best organized. French general Charles de Gaulle had escaped to Great Britain during the Nazi invasion. De Gaulle inspired the French underground movement by sending messages over British radio. In other occupied countries, and even in Nazi Germany, resistance took the form of work stoppages, spying, and **sabotage**. Sabotage is the intentional damaging or destruction of supplies or structures such as bridges and railroads.

Some resistance came in the form of helping Jewish people hide from the Nazis. At great risk to themselves, people hid individuals and even entire families for months or even years at a time.

Women in the War

During the war, millions of men left their jobs at factories and farms and entered the armed forces. Women took their places. Many women worked in factories, making airplanes, ships, tanks, and other military supplies. Other women worked in the fields, raising crops to feed the men in uniform and the people at home.

Many women also served in the armed forces. Women in Allied countries were not involved in direct combat. However, many did serve in occupations that placed them in danger. For example, one woman Marine was trained as an aerial photographer, flying in a plane at low altitudes over enemy territory.

During World War II, women, like these welders, showed that they could successfully carry on in jobs that had almost always been done by men.

◆ **What role could citizens at home fill to aid in the war efforts?**

Spotlight on *Economics*

WOMEN IN WORLD WAR II
At the peak of the war effort in the United States, women made up 37 percent of the total civilian workforce.

Review II

Review History
A. How did the Allies react when Hitler invaded Poland?
B. In what way did U.S. President Roosevelt help the Allied Powers?

Define Terms to Know
Define the following terms: **blitzkrieg, arsenal, sabotage**

Critical Thinking
What was miraculous about the Miracle at Dunkirk?

Write About Economics
Write a letter to President Roosevelt in which you explain why you do or do not support the Lend-Lease Act.

Get Organized
CAUSE-AND-EFFECT CHAIN
Use a cause-and-effect chain to organize information from this section. Choose an event and then write its cause and effect. For example, what were the causes and effects of Hitler's invasion of Poland?

CHAPTER 28 ◆ World War II **671**

CAUSE
Hitler controlled Austria and Czechoslovakia and wanted to expand into Poland.

↓

EVENT
Hitler invaded Poland.

↓

EFFECT
Germany quickly conquered Poland; France and Great Britain declared war on Germany.

Critical Thinking
It was miraculous that so many stranded soldiers could be saved by such a large number and wide variety of boats in such a short time.

Write About Economics
Students' letters should clearly explain their position on the Lend-Lease Act, and include a position on isolationism and the economic effects of producing weapons of war.

Section Summary

In this section, students will learn about Hitler's campaigns in the Soviet Union and North Africa. They will also learn how the United States entered the war in Asia and how it began to experience success on the Pacific front.

1 Introduce

Getting Started

Ask students to recall a time in recent history when the United States was attacked. (September 11, 2001—the destruction of the World Trade Center towers and the damage to the Pentagon) Ask students how Americans felt when this attack happened. (Possible answer: shocked, outraged, determined to fight back) Tell students that Americans had similar feelings when Pearl Harbor was attacked in 1941.

TERMS TO KNOW

Ask students to read the terms and definitions on page 672 and find each term in the section. After they have read the section, have them explain to a partner each term's relationship to World War II.

You may wish to preview the pronunciation of the following names with students.

Barbarossa (bahr buh RAW suh)
El Alamein (EHL a luh MAYN)
Guam (GWAHM)
Bataan (buh TAN)

ACTIVE READING

After students have read each subsection, pause and have them determine which events in the section show that the war is turning. Have students write two predictions—one for the war in Europe and one for the war in Asia. Have students save these predictions and review them for accuracy when they have finished reading the chapter.

Terms to Know

scorched-earth policy a wartime policy in which all goods useful to an invading army are burned or destroyed

infamy disgrace, or great evil

internment camp a place in which people are confined, especially in time of war

Main Ideas

A. Hitler's forces were overwhelmed by Allied attacks in the Soviet Union and Africa.

B. The United States was drawn into the war by a surprise attack on its military base in Hawaii by Japan.

 Active Reading

PREDICT
When you predict, you analyze the information you know and make an educated guess about what events will occur. As you read this section, think about how the events of the war have occurred. Then, predict how the war will end for each nation.

A. Hitler Moves East

In 1941, Hitler turned his attention to the Soviet Union. Although he had signed a Nonaggression Pact with Stalin, Hitler's intent had always been to crush communism in Europe and defeat Stalin.

Hitler Invades the Soviet Union

On June 22, 1941, 3 million German soldiers moved into the Soviet Union and advanced toward three major targets—the Ukraine and the cities of Leningrad and Moscow. Hitler believed his troops could surround the Soviet armies and force them to surrender by autumn.

Within a few weeks, the Germans had advanced far into Soviet territory. However, as the Soviet army retreated, it followed a **scorched-earth policy**. Under this policy, the soldiers and civilians burned or destroyed everything that might be useful to the invaders. So, the German soldiers had to rely completely on their own supply lines for food, clothing, and weapons. The farther the German army advanced, the more difficult it was to keep them supplied.

Hitler believed that his Soviet invasion would be over in a matter of months. However, the campaign took much longer than planned, and cold weather arrived early. The German soldiers did not have winter clothing or adequate shelter from the below-freezing temperatures. Tanks and trucks had not been winterized, and the army was unable to move. In that winter of 1941, more than 500,000 German soldiers died from exposure or were captured.

The Siege of Leningrad

On September 8, 1941, German troops began an attack on Leningrad that would last two and a half years. This continuous assault would come to be known as the 900-day siege. The people of Leningrad had built fortifications around the city, which the Germans completely surrounded by November. Almost all supplies of food and military equipment were cut off. From time to time, a few supplies trickled in, keeping the city's 2 million people barely alive. In January 1944, Soviet troops arrived from the west and forced the Germans to retreat. The siege of Leningrad was over.

A Soviet soldier takes cover during the Nazi attack on the Soviet city of Leningrad.

Teaching Options

Section 3 Resources

Teacher's Resources (TR)
Terms to Know, p. 41
Review History, p. 75
Build Your Skills, p. 109
Concept Builder, p. 244
Cause-and-Effect Chain, p. 325
Transparency 2

ESL/ELL STRATEGIES

Take Notes Help students to understand the information in this section by asking them to list the different strategies that are discussed. Help start them off with the three Terms to Know—*scorched-earth policy*, *infamy*, and *internment camp.* Have students work with partners to add to this list and then explain to each other the meaning of each term.

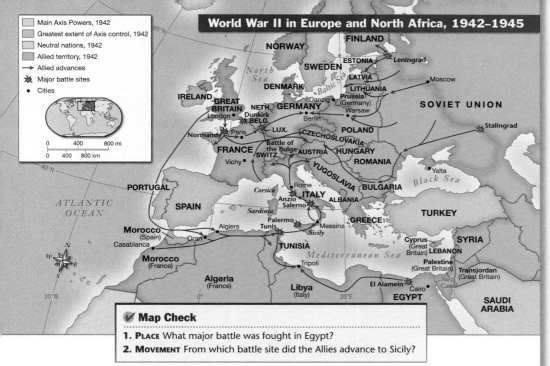

World War II in Europe and North Africa, 1942–1945

Legend:
- Main Axis Powers, 1942
- Greatest extent of Axis control, 1942
- Neutral nations, 1942
- Allied territory, 1942
- → Allied advances
- ✹ Major battle sites
- • Cities

✔ Map Check
1. **PLACE** What major battle was fought in Egypt?
2. **MOVEMENT** From which battle site did the Allies advance to Sicily?

The War in Africa

In the fall of 1940, the Italian dictator Mussolini sent his troops into Egypt, a British protectorate in northern Africa. However, the invasion was unsuccessful, and Hitler had to send one of his best commanders, Field Marshall Erwin Rommel, to help the Italians. By the summer of 1942, the combined forces of Germany and Italy had the British cornered in the city of El Alamein, near the Suez Canal. Both Great Britain and the United States, who had entered the war six months earlier, sent troops to defend the canal. The additional Allied troops turned the tide of battle, and by May 1943, they had gained control of all of North Africa.

◆ What factors slowed the German defeat of the Soviet Union?

B. The War in Asia

The United States had condemned Japan's attacks on China, and diplomats from the two nations were working to find a peaceful solution in Asia. Then, in 1941, Japan moved into the French colonies of Indochina, which included Vietnam, Cambodia, and Laos. The United States and Great Britain responded with economic sanctions, cutting off such goods as oil, iron, and steel. The Japanese leaders realized that they would have to deal with the United States if their expansion in the Pacific was to continue.

CHAPTER 28 ◆ World War II **673**

Writing

AVERAGE
Have students write a letter from a Russian survivor of the siege of Leningrad, describing the horror of those 900 days. Encourage them to do further research and possibly include a quotation from a primary source in their letter.

CHALLENGE
Remind students that Napoleon also attacked Russia and was defeated there. Have students use the information in the textbook to compare and contrast Napoleon's and Hitler's Russian campaigns. Ask them to evaluate the kinds of mistakes both leaders made and to explain whether Hitler learned from Napoleon's errors.

---

2 Teach

A. Hitler Moves East
Purpose-Setting Question What was the outcome of the siege of Leningrad? (After $2\frac{1}{2}$ years, Soviet troops forced the Germans to retreat.)

TEACH PRIMARY SOURCES
Ask students to describe the photograph on page 672. (A Soviet soldier is taking cover by a bombed building in Leningrad.) Ask how soon the siege began after the beginning of the German invasion. (two months) Tell students that about one million of Leningrad's children, sick, and elderly were evacuated in 1942. At least 650,000 people died in the siege.

Using the Map
World War II in Europe and North Africa, 1942–1945

Ask students to describe the extent of Axis-controlled territory in 1942. (all of Europe except Great Britain and a few neutral nations; also, most of North Africa)

✔ Map Check
Answers
1. El Alamein
2. Tunis

Activity
Use a map Have students use the map on page 673 to trace the route of the Allies in the African campaign. (Great Britain to Algeria, then to Tunis, ending in Tripoli; another force from El Alamein to Tripoli)

◆ **ANSWER** The German army had to fight along a 2,000-mile front; the Soviet scorched-earth policy made supplying the army difficult; the Soviet winter brought the German assault to a standstill.

B. The War in Asia
Purpose-Setting Question Why did the United States and Great Britain impose economic sanctions on Japan in 1941? (to protest Japan's moving into Indochina)

CHAPTER 28 ◆ **T673**

Direct students' attention to the map key. Ask why there are two ways of indicating areas under Japanese control. (One is for areas controlled in 1941, and the other is for the greatest extent of Japanese control, in 1942.)

✔ Map Check

Answers

1. Okinawa
2. The Allied troops moved west from the Hawaiian Islands.

Discuss Tell students that the attack on Pearl Harbor united Americans as never before. Ask why it might have been a mistake for Japan to attack as it did. (Possible answer: They won the battle but enraged a very powerful enemy.) Tell students that the United States had 20 times the productivity and 100 times the natural resources of Japan. It was only a matter of time before the United States would avenge the attack.

Then & Now

JAPAN Ask students to think of Japanese companies that have become household names. Tell students that Japan was in shambles at the end of World War II. However, with the help of the United States, it built itself up so that its economy was even stronger than before the war. Today Japan leads all industrial nations in eastern Asia. Only the United States and China have larger economies than Japan.

Extend After the Pearl Harbor attack, Canada also declared war on Japan. Then, like the United States, Canada interned more than 20,000 Japanese Canadians, most of whom were living in the province of British Columbia. Most of the Canadian internees lost all their property when they were seized.

World War II in the Pacific, 1941–1945

✔ Map Check

1. **LOCATION** Where was the last major battle of the war in the Pacific fought?
2. **MOVEMENT** In which direction did Allied troops move from the Hawaiian Islands?

Then & Now

JAPAN
During World War II, Japan was a major enemy of the United States. Today the nation is one of the most important economic and political allies of the United States.

Pearl Harbor

On the morning of December 7, 1941, Japan attacked the U.S. military base at Pearl Harbor, Hawaii, then a U.S. territory. The United States, which had engaged in peace talks with Japan over Japan's attacks on China, was caught totally by surprise. Japanese bombs destroyed or damaged more than 300 aircraft and several warships. Nearly 3,000 Americans were killed or wounded.

The following day, President Franklin D. Roosevelt asked the U.S. Congress to declare war on Japan. He described December 7, 1941, as "a day which will live in **infamy**," or disgrace. The vote in favor of declaring war on Japan took just 40 minutes. Three days later, Japan's allies, Italy and Germany, declared war on the United States.

Relocation of Japanese Americans

One unfortunate outcome of the attack on Pearl Harbor was a change in attitude toward Japanese people living in the United States. Many people feared that Japanese Americans, even those who were U.S. citizens by birth, might become spies for Japan. In response to this fear, the U.S. government relocated many Japanese Americans living on the west coast to **internment camps**, or places where people are forced to live in confinement. These Japanese Americans were crowded into temporary housing with little privacy and were not allowed to leave.

Not all Japanese Americans spent the war in internment camps. Many young men volunteered to serve in the U.S. military. They fought on the battlefields of Europe and received medals for their bravery.

674 UNIT 7 ◆ Decades of War

Teaching Options

Cooperative Learning

Divide the class into small groups. Explain that each group will present a talk show, hosting the leaders of the world's nations during World War II. Have students choose the role of one of the leaders, the show host, or a member of the audience. Provide each "leader" with one or two students to assist in research of that leader's position on various issues. Have group members assume the roles of their characters and discuss their feelings about the war.

Connection to CULTURE

After discussing the use of codes based on the Navajo language (Extend, p. T675), encourage students to learn more about the Navajo language and how the Navajo code was created. Suggest that they visit a Web site sponsored by the U.S. Department of the Navy for more information. To find the site, students should type *U.S. Navy, Navajo,* and *code* into a search engine.

Early Struggles in the Pacific

It would take time for the United States to build the military forces and weapons needed to be successful both in Europe and in Asia. So, for the first six months of 1942, Japan enjoyed a series of victories over several island nations in the Pacific Ocean.

U.S. General Douglas MacArthur was commander of the Philippines when Japan attacked that island nation. MacArthur was forced to leave the islands, vowing to return. The American and native Filipino troops left behind were forced to surrender on April 9, 1942. The Japanese forced 75,000 American and Filipino prisoners to march through a steaming jungle to the capital of Manila, a distance of 68 miles. During this ordeal, known as the Bataan Death March, an estimated 11,000 prisoners died. By the middle of 1942, Japan had conquered more than 1 million square miles of land and controlled more than 150 million people.

American Successes in the Pacific

America's earliest success in the Pacific came soon after the bombing of Pearl Harbor. Planes from American aircraft carriers bombed Tokyo, the capital of Japan. The bombing shocked the Japanese people. They had not expected any enemy to be able to invade their country.

In June 1942, American code experts learned of a planned Japanese attack on Midway Island. Midway Island was a U.S. territory in the Pacific and an important military base. When the attack came, U.S. planes based on aircraft carriers in the area were ready for it. They sank four Japanese aircraft carriers with hundreds of enemy planes on board. The Battle of Midway proved to be a turning point in the war in the Pacific. After its victory, the United States began a campaign in which they recaptured a number of islands from Japan. These islands gave the Allies bases from which to prepare an attack on Japan.

◆ **What was the immediate result of the attack on Pearl Harbor?**

Spotlight on Geography

THE ROLE OF GEOGRAPHY IN WORLD WAR II

Geography played an important role in the movement of troops during World War II. The English Channel helped to protect Great Britain from invasion by land. France's close location to Germany and the flat land of its coastal region helped Germany in its invasion of that country.

China and the Soviet Union were helped by the vastness of their land areas. The Pacific Ocean helped protect Japan from invasion, while the United States was protected by both the Atlantic and Pacific Oceans.

Review III

Review History
A. In what ways was Hitler weakened by the invasions of the Soviet Union and Africa?
B. Why was the United States so surprised by Japan's attack on Pearl Harbor?

Define Terms to Know
Define the following terms: **scorched-earth policy, infamy, internment camp**

Critical Thinking
Why did the attack on Pearl Harbor push Americans to change their isolationist policies?

Write About History
Research the topic of the use of aircraft carriers, and write a paragraph about the importance of aircraft carriers in the Pacific during World War II.

Get Organized
CAUSE-AND-EFFECT CHAIN
Use a cause-and-effect chain to organize information from this section. Choose a main event and then write the causes and effects. For example, what were the causes and effects of the U.S. entrance into World War II?

CAUSE
Japan attacked the military base at Pearl Harbor, Hawaii.

↓

EVENT
United States entered World War II.

↓

EFFECT
Japanese Americans were relocated to internment camps.

Critical Thinking
The attack made the war real to Americans. They were now defending their own lands.

Write About History
Students' paragraphs should include such advantages as increased mobility and nearness to targets, and such disadvantages as the difficulty of managing the planes and the vulnerability of the planes should a carrier be bombed.

Explore Ask students which battle is generally considered the turning point of the war in the Pacific. (Midway) Have students name important results of this battle. (Japanese control of the Pacific was halted; U.S. bases were established.)

Extend A contributing factor in the U.S. victory in the Pacific was the U.S. military's use of codes based on the Navajo language. In these codes, Navajo words were assigned military meanings, such as *turtle* for *tank*. These codes could not be broken by the enemy because there is no written Navajo language. Any message sent in this code could only be understood by another Navajo speaker.

SPOTLIGHT ON GEOGRAPHY
THE ROLE OF GEOGRAPHY IN WORLD WAR II Use Transparency 2 or the world map on pages A1–A2 of the Atlas to help students explore the role of geography. Help students locate each place mentioned.

◆ **ANSWER** The United States declared war on Japan; Germany and Italy declared war on the United States.

Section Close

Have students work together to create two flowcharts on the board, one for the important events in the war in Europe and North Africa, and one for important events in the war in Asia. Then, have students analyze the relationship among events in each flowchart.

3 Assess

Review Answers

Review History
A. Hitler's forces became spread too thin as he attacked the Soviet Union and sent troops to Africa. He also had difficulty keeping supply lines open to troops in the Soviet Union and Africa.

B. Possible answer: Diplomats from the United States and Japan were still engaged in peace talks.

Define Terms to Know
scorched-earth policy, 672; infamy, 674; internment camp, 674

Past to...

WARTIME SPIES TO MODERN AGENTS

Teach the Topic

This feature focuses on government spies, comparing the tools of espionage in World War II to those of today. Ask students what they would think of someone who spied on them. (Possible answer: would dislike it; would think less of the person) Ask if their feelings would change if a person spied for his or her country, especially in wartime. (Possible answer: That is different because it helps the war effort.) Then, tell students that some of the most interesting things about spies are the tools that they use to achieve their goals.

CLEVER CODES

Tell students that *enigma* is of Greek origin, meaning "something hard to understand" or "a mystery." Great Britain's ability to read the code of the Enigma machine was called the Ultra secret. It is credited with providing limited help during the Battle of Britain and in the North Africa campaign. Tell students that when a letter was typed on the machine, an internal system of gears yielded a letter that would not logically be repeated before 200 trillion further depressions. It took a machine called COLOSSUS to efficiently decode the codes created by the Enigma. The COLOSSUS was a first step toward the modern computer.

DANGEROUS MESSAGES

Remind students that radio waves move through the air and could be picked up by enemy receivers. Ask students what kind of messages a spy might send out via radio. (Possible answer: enemy troop movements, kinds and numbers of weapons, important people in the area) Ask students to write a message that a spy behind German lines might have sent.

FOOTPRINTS IN THE SAND

Ask students to provide an example of the kind of assignment that a spy who entered Nazi-controlled Europe using such footprints might have had. (Possible answer: He or she might have landed in northern France to check out the landing area and the towns in the event of an Allied invasion.)

Past to...

WARTIME SPIES TO MODERN AGENTS

Spies worked for both the Allied and Axis Powers during World War II. To keep their real identity secret, spies took on other identities and carried false papers. Many Allied spies were radio operators who sent important information to their country with details of enemy troop movements and weapons. If they were not able to send information home, they often took part in another form of active service by helping resistance movements attack the enemy.

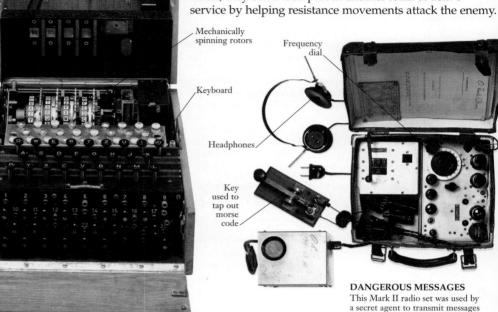

Mechanically spinning rotors

Keyboard

Frequency dial

Headphones

Key used to tap out morse code

DANGEROUS MESSAGES
This Mark II radio set was used by a secret agent to transmit messages to the Allies. This method of communication was very dangerous for the agent, because the enemy could trace the signal back to the radio and its operator.

CLEVER CODES
The Nazis invented Enigma, a machine that turned their messages into secret code. The Poles cracked this code and passed the information on to the British. Unknown to the Nazis, the Allies intercepted thousands of essential messages throughout World War II.

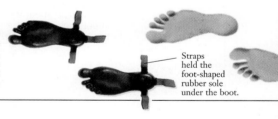

FOOTPRINTS IN THE SAND
Spies often entered occupied territory by parachute at night. If the spies landed on a beach, they taped footprint-makers onto the soles of their boots. The enemy's suspicions would not then be aroused by the sight of these footprints.

Straps held the foot-shaped rubber sole under the boot.

Teaching Options

FYI

Alan Turing

Alan Turing (1912–1954) was a brilliant British mathematician who worked to decipher Enigma codes during World War II. In the mid-1930s, he had developed one of the earliest computers, which was called a Turing machine. He is also considered one of the founders of artificial intelligence. Turing was made an officer of the Order of the British Empire toward the end of World War II for his work in code-breaking.

Connection to
LITERATURE

Suggest that students read *Under a War-Torn Sky* by Laura Elliott (Hyperion, 2001), a historical novel set in France during World War II. Henry Forester, a young American pilot, is shot down, survives the crash, and finds himself behind enemy lines. The story involves his journey across France to Portugal, where he finds help to go home. Forester meets spies and resistance fighters who assist him.

Bullet

Shoe heel

Ring with secret compartment

HIDDEN TRICKS
Secret tools were essential to wartime spies. Tricks included secret spaces in jewelry (above) or in the heels of shoes (left), or in patterned silk scarves that were actually maps (right). Weapons were disguised too: In an emergency, a single bullet could be fired from a pencil pistol (top left).

Code sheets

Map

SPY PURSE
Working from behind enemy lines, radio operator Yvonne Cormeau managed to send more than 400 coded messages to the Allies between 1943 and the end of the war. She used a secret compartment in her purse to hide her code sheets.

...Present

Today's spies, or intelligence agents as they are often known, still gather top-secret information, but they use very different technology. On the ground, they communicate using the smallest concealed radios. In the air, they use surveillance planes and satellites to monitor what is happening around the world.

Battery

Transmitter

Microphone

MINI COMMUNICATIONS
Since World War II, communications technology has become more sophisticated. The circuits of radio transmitters are now tiny enough to be concealed inside a working pen.

SURVEILLANCE FROM THE SKY
Today, drones, or spy planes flown without pilots, allow for safe surveillance of foreign lands and troop movements. The Predator (RQ-1A) can fly up to 40 hours without refueling. It uses ground controls and video technology to provide images to crews on the ground.

SPY SATELLITE
Satellites circle Earth taking pictures, which are then transmitted to a computer on the ground. The images can be used to determine the capability of an enemy.

CHAPTER 28 ◆ World War II **677**

Hands-On Activity
Have students work in small groups to role-play the meeting of a World War II spy with a contemporary spy. Have the dialogue include such topics as the kinds of tools used, the most difficult assignment, and an evaluation of the life of a spy.

SPY PURSE
Tell students that Yvonne Cormeau became a spy after her husband was killed during the Battle of Britain when a bomb destroyed their home. Cormeau helped the resistance in France by sending information that allowed other agents to cut power and telephone lines. Once, when the Germans seized her, she convinced them that she was a nurse and that her wireless equipment was an X-ray machine. Ask students what personality traits were essential for spies such as Yvonne Cormeau. (Possible answers: nerves of steel, love of danger, fearlessness, ability to lie convincingly)

HIDDEN TRICKS
Discuss the hidden tricks on page 677. Ask what might be hidden in a ring. (Possible answer: microfilm)

...Present

SPY SATELLITE
Ask students what satellites might take pictures of that would be of interest to a group such as the CIA. (Possible answers: concentration of troops, movement of troops, new construction of a missile site, chemical weapons laboratory)

MINI COMMUNICATIONS
Discuss the advantage of this kind of technology. (It is so small that it is almost impossible to detect.) Ask students what kinds of communication tools they have seen in recent spy movies. Tell them that these may become the tools of the future.

SURVEILLANCE FROM THE SKY
Ask what the advantages and disadvantages of this kind of surveillance are. (**Advantages:** can see over a wide area, soldiers do not get hurt; **disadvantage:** cannot get close-up pictures)

Connect Past to Present
Ask students what activities tie all the spy tools together. (seeking information or hiding information) Ask students if they think the information gathered in peacetime is different from what is needed in wartime. Help students realize that the specific types of information may change, but the need is still there. Discuss with students why information is so important to leaders during a war, and even in peacetime.

Section Summary

In this section, students will learn how the Allied troops gained strength from the entrance of American troops into the war. They will also learn about the end of the war in Europe and the discovery of the concentration camps. Finally, they will learn how the war in the Pacific ended when the United States dropped two atomic bombs.

1 Introduce

Getting Started

Ask students to consider what life would be like in a war-torn country. Does the mail get delivered when war is raging? Are schools open? Do favorite television shows still come on at the expected time? Lead students to understand how war disrupts a country. Then, ask students how the people of the world might have felt to learn that World War II was over. (Possible answer: ecstatic, unbelieving, looking forward to rebuilding)

TERMS TO KNOW

Ask students to read the terms and definitions on page 678 and find each term in the section. Ask students what the terms have in common. (They deal with the murder of civilian population.) Have students write a paragraph using the terms.

You may wish to preview the pronunciation of the following names with students.

Auschwitz (AOOSH vihts)
Buchenwald (BOO kuhn vahlt)
Iwo Jima (EE woh JEE mah)
Hiroshima (hir ROH SHEE muh)
Nagasaki (nah gah SAH kee)

ACTIVE READING

Encourage students to use a series of problem/solution charts (TR, p. 327) to record the problems they find in the section and the alternative solutions.

Section IV · The End of World War II

Terms to Know

genocide the planned killing of a racial or ethnic group
Holocaust Hitler's policy of killing European Jews and others considered "unfit to live"

Main Ideas

A. With the aid of American troops, the Allies were able to take control of Europe.
B. As Germany retreated, the Allies discovered Nazi concentration camps and freed the prisoners, while Allied leaders held peace discussions.
C. Americans fought the Japanese in the Pacific and ended the war with the atomic bomb.

Active Reading

PROBLEMS AND SOLUTIONS
When you analyze problems and solutions, you weigh the options and the possible consequences of each solution. As you read this section, concentrate on the problems that both sides of the war faced and consider the possible solutions to each problem.

A. Americans Shift the Balance in Europe

In December 1941, Hitler had control of Europe from the English Channel all the way to the outskirts of Moscow in the Soviet Union. However, when the United States declared war against Germany, the Allies finally had enough people and equipment to strike back against the Nazis.

The Tide Begins to Turn in Europe

In November 1942, American General Dwight D. Eisenhower led a combined force of British and American troops in an invasion of North Africa. Seven months later, the German and Italian troops under Field Marshal Rommel surrendered in Tunisia. From Africa, the combined British-American forces turned their attention to Italy. They invaded Sicily in July 1943, and Mussolini was forced out of power. The new government surrendered in September 1943. However, German troops in Italy continued to fight for another 18 months.

At about the same time as Rommel's surrender in North Africa, the Soviet Union struck a major blow against the Germans. In the Battle of Stalingrad, Soviet forces captured or killed some 300,000 German troops. Soviet troops then began to drive the German forces westward.

On D-day—June 6, 1944— these soldiers stormed the beaches of Normandy, France, as part of the greatest invasion force in history.

D-day

The Allies made secret plans to attack German-occupied Europe. Not even the military commanders in the field knew the location or the date for the attack. Allied leaders wanted to fool the Germans by attacking a small port city rather than a major port, where they might be expected. They hoped that the Germans would concentrate their strongest forces at the major ports and leave the smaller areas less guarded. The plan worked.

D-day came on June 6, 1944. General Dwight Eisenhower, Supreme Allied Commander, ordered more than 150,000 Allied troops to cross the English Channel and storm the beaches of Normandy, France. Many soldiers were killed by German machine guns positioned on cliffs above the beaches. However, the

Teaching Options

Section 4 Resources

Teacher's Resources (TR)
Terms to Know, p. 41
Review History, p. 75
Build Your Skills, p. 109
Chapter Test, pp. 171–172
Concept Builder, p. 244
Cause-and-Effect Chain, p. 325
Transparency 8

Connection to MUSIC

Popular songs during World War II covered the spectrum from patriotic to spiritual. Some of the great musicians and singers of the day included Benny Goodman, Glenn Miller, Duke Ellington, and Ella Fitzgerald. Ask students to find songs of the period, listen to them, and describe how the music of World War II differs from contemporary music.

stream of invading troops continued all day. Eventually, the Allied troops established a foothold on French soil. Within a month, more than 1 million Allied troops had joined their fellow soldiers in France.

◆ **How did the entry of the United States change the war?**

B. The War in Europe Ends

The Allied invasion of Normandy marked the beginning of the end for Hitler. Germany was now forced to fight the war on two long fronts—a western front in France and an eastern front in the Soviet Union. As a result, the German forces were spread too thin. Allied victory was in sight.

The Horrors of War

As Allied troops fought their way across Europe, the most horrifying part of Hitler's rule was exposed. The troops found and freed prisoners who were being held under inhumane conditions in concentration camps where political prisoners and members of certain racial and ethnic groups were sent from all over Europe.

More than 300 of these camps were discovered in such places as Auschwitz, Poland, and Buchenwald and Dachau in Germany. In these camps, Nazi leaders carried out Hitler's policy of **genocide**, a planned killing of an entire group of people. Hitler had sent millions of Jews and other groups, such as gypsies, to the concentration camps. In the larger death camps, prisoners were killed in gas chambers and their bodies reduced to ashes in special ovens. Those prisoners who were not killed were forced to work as slaves under brutal conditions, with little food or medical attention. Thousands died from starvation, disease, and physical abuse. This event is known as the **Holocaust**.

Victory in Europe

After D-day, the Allies advanced rapidly eastward, pushing the Germans back as they went. In December 1944, the Germans put up one final show of resistance. They launched a surprise attack, known as the Battle of the Bulge, against American troops in Belgium. At first, the Germans pushed the Allies back, creating a bulge in the Allied line. However, by January, Allied tanks led by U.S. General George S. Patton helped the Allies regain their earlier positions. By mid-September, most of France was under Allied control.

Soviet troops continued to push westward, and by April 1945, they had the city of Berlin surrounded. However, Hitler refused to surrender. On April 30, he killed himself, and one week later, Germany surrendered. Unfortunately, U.S. President Franklin Roosevelt did not live to enjoy the Allied victory. He died suddenly on April 12, 1945.

The day of the surrender was called V-E day, for Victory in Europe. On that day, General Eisenhower announced the surrender in the following short telegraph message:

❝ The mission of this Allied Force was fulfilled at 3:00 A.M., local time, 7 May 1945. Eisenhower. ❞

The world was horrified to discover what had happened in Nazi concentration camps.

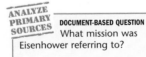

ANALYZE PRIMARY SOURCES

DOCUMENT-BASED QUESTION
What mission was Eisenhower referring to?

CHAPTER 28 ◆ World War II **679**

2 Teach

A. Americans Shift the Balance in Europe

Purpose-Setting Question What early victories did the American troops experience after entering World War II? (Early victories involving American troops include North Africa (November 1942–May 1943) and Italy (July–September 1943).

Extend Tell students that the D in D-day had no significance other than the fact that it was the "day" the invasion started. June 6, 1944, however, marked the largest amphibian operation ever undertaken, and it was the turning point of the war as well.

◆ **ANSWER** The entry of the United States gave the Allies a morale boost and greatly increased the supply of troops and equipment.

B. The War in Europe Ends

Purpose-Setting Question How did the Allies win the war in Europe? (The Allied forces advanced eastward, pushing the Germans back as the Soviet troops pushed westward.)

Discuss Ask students what they can tell about concentration camps based on the picture on page 679. (Possible answer: People were starving; they had very little clothing and poor shelter.) Tell students that an estimated 6 million Jews were killed in the Holocaust. Ask students what American troops must have thought or felt upon liberating concentration camps. (Possible answers: horrified, sickened, outraged)

ANALYZE PRIMARY SOURCES

DOCUMENT-BASED QUESTION
The actual surrender took place in a schoolhouse in Rheims, France. The Soviets insisted that the ceremony be repeated the following day in Berlin. Thus, May 8 is celebrated as V-E day.

ANSWER The mission was the defeat of the German forces.

ESL/ELL STRATEGIES

Summarize Have students work in pairs to summarize information in subsections A and B, with each student taking one of the subsections. Ask students to use the subheads as topics for their outlines, and have them write a sentence or two summarizing each topic. Have students explain their assigned subsections to their partners.

FYI

Auschwitz

Auschwitz, the largest German concentration camp, was located in Poland. Upon arrival, prisoners were separated into groups and were either killed immediately or put to work. Today, visitors to Auschwitz can tour the concentration camp where the bunkers, the gas chambers, and the ovens still stand. A museum on the site is dedicated to the victims of the Holocaust.

Explore Discuss the conferences at Yalta and Potsdam. Ask students to identify the main outcome of each conference. (**Yalta**: plans for ending the war, including the Soviet control of eastern Europe; **Potsdam**: terms for peace in Europe, including dividing Germany into four zones)

Focus Tell students that the "S" in President Truman's name does not stand for anything. The "S" was a compromise for his parents between the names of his two grandfathers: Anderson Shipp Truman and Solomon Young. Whether or not to use a period after the "S" has been a controversial subject for many years.

◆ **ANSWER** Hitler intended to kill all the Jews in Europe.

C. The War in the Pacific

Purpose-Setting Question What two strategies did the Americans use to win the war in the Pacific? (island hopping and dropping the atomic bomb)

Focus Use Transparency 8 to show students how island hopping worked. Point out that some of the islands were taken and some were skipped, or hopped over, until a later time. Be sure students grasp the concept of jumping forward over some islands, establishing a stronghold, and then claiming the islands in the middle.

TEACH PRIMARY SOURCES

Tell students that almost 7,000 American soldiers died during a 36-day battle to capture the island of Iwo Jima. Ask students to draw conclusions about the qualities of the soldiers in the picture. (Possible answers: brave, persistent, determined, exhausted) Tell students that this photograph by Joe Rosenthal won a Pulitzer Prize and later was transformed into a statue for the U.S. Marine Corps War Memorial, which stands next to Arlington National Cemetery in Virginia.

Activity

Hold a debate Have students stage a debate about whether or not President Truman's decision to drop two atomic bombs in August 1945 was a good one. Have two groups of students take pro and con positions, and have the groups present their arguments to the class.

T680 ◆ **UNIT 7**

During a long, fierce battle, a group of U.S. Marines raises the American flag on the Pacific Island of Iwo Jima.

The Conferences at Yalta and Potsdam

Several months before V-E day, it had become clear to the Allied nations that the defeat of Hitler was near. In February 1945, Churchill, Roosevelt, and Stalin met in the Soviet city of Yalta to discuss plans for ending the war. Because the United States was still fighting Japan, Roosevelt urged Stalin to join the war in Asia. Stalin agreed to do this in exchange for control of the eastern European nations after Hitler fell.

In July 1945, another conference was held at Potsdam, Germany, to discuss the terms for peace in Europe. U.S. President Harry S Truman, who took office after Roosevelt's death, agreed with Churchill and Stalin to divide Germany into four zones. The United States, the Soviet Union, Great Britain, and France would each administer one zone. Also at Potsdam, Truman told Stalin about the new weapon that he was considering against Japan—the atomic bomb.

◆ **What was Hitler's plan for the Jews in Europe?**

C. The War in the Pacific

After the success at the Battle of Midway, the United States followed a policy of "island hopping" in the Pacific. The Americans would recapture some Japanese-held islands, then "hop" over other islands that were strongly defended. Once a string of islands was occupied, the Americans cut off supply lines to other Japanese-held islands in the area.

The battles on these islands were bloody and costly. In battles on the islands of Guadalcanal, New Guinea, Saipan, Guam, and Iwo Jima, Americans found stiff resistance. The Japanese believed that surrender was shameful, so they fought fiercely and desperately. This refusal to surrender played an important part in the end of the war.

Truman Faces a Difficult Choice

When President Truman took office after Roosevelt's death, he was told for the first time about the Manhattan Project. This project was a secret effort to build a nuclear weapon. Roosevelt had been aware of the work on nuclear energy that was going on in Germany, and had directed American scientists to begin research on a nuclear weapon. Scientists worked under strict secrecy. Americans tested the bomb in New Mexico on July 16, 1945.

When scientists realized the devastating power of destruction contained in the bomb, some of them wrote a letter to President Truman. In this letter, the scientists expressed their deep concern that such a weapon should not be used against people.

Truman knew that the next step in the war was to attack the island of Japan. His advisors feared that invading Japan would result in massive loss of life for both sides. Truman's advisors believed that using the bomb in Japan would save at least 250,000 American lives and millions of Japanese lives. It would also end the war before Stalin could invade the Japanese islands and claim them for the Soviet Union.

Teaching Options

Meet Individual Needs:

VERBAL/LINGUISTIC LEARNERS

Some excellent literature emerged from events of World War II. Students may be interested in reading some of the books of author John Hersey: *A Bell for Adano* (1944), about the Allied occupation of a town in Sicily; *The Wall* (1950), a novel about Jewish resistance in the Warsaw ghetto; and *Hiroshima* (1946), a nonfiction account of the effects of the explosion on six survivors.

Test Taking

Tell students that some test questions require students to interpret charts. Help students understand the information contained in the chart on page 681 by explaining the features that will help them interpret the information. Students should first notice the title of the chart and the column headings. Then, they should compare the data in different rows of the chart.

Nuclear War

Truman sent the Japanese a message, "surrender or be destroyed." The Japanese ignored the message. On August 6, 1945, an atomic bomb was dropped on the Japanese city of Hiroshima. Three days later another bomb was dropped on Nagasaki. Both cities were destroyed. The Japanese and the world were astonished at the power of the bomb.

On August 15, the emperor of Japan, Hirohito, broke his traditional silence and spoke to the Japanese people for the first time over the radio. In his message he announced the surrender of Japan.

The Effects of the War

In the years after World War II, Europe and Asia reeled from the war's destruction and violence. Millions of people were homeless and diseased. Survivors from prison camps wandered hopelessly, trying to find something from their past lives. European nations had no resources to help them. The cost of the war in human lives was staggering. More than 50 million people around the world had died.

When the Allied leaders met before the end of the war, they agreed to hold trials of war leaders who had committed crimes against humanity. In Germany, these trials were held in Nuremberg. A total of 177 Germans and Austrians were tried, and 142 were found guilty. Some criminals were sentenced to prison. Others were given death sentences. Similar trials were held in Tokyo. Seven defendants, including former premier Hideki Tojo, were executed.

◆ **What was the policy of "island hopping"?**

Deaths in World War II

COUNTRY	MILITARY	CIVILIAN
Allied Powers		
China	1,310,224	Not known
France	213,324	350,000
Great Britain	264,443	92,673
Soviet Union	11,000,000	7,000,000
United States	292,131	6,000
Axis Powers		
Germany	3,500,000	780,000
Italy	242,232	152,941
Japan	1,300,000	672,000

Source: *Encyclopedia Britannica.* All figures are estimates.

✔ **Chart Check**

Which nation suffered the most deaths in World War II ?

Review History

A. In what way did the American presence influence the war against the Axis Powers?
B. What were some of the factors that led to the fall of Germany?
C. What were the major events in the war in the Pacific?

Define Terms to Know

Define the following terms:
genocide, Holocaust

Critical Thinking

Why was Truman's decision to use the atomic bomb a difficult one?

Write About Culture

Write a newspaper editorial in which you detail how the war in the Pacific has hurt both the United States and Japan.

Get Organized

CAUSE-AND-EFFECT CHAIN
Use a cause-and-effect chain to organize information from this section. Choose an event and then write the causes and effects of the event on the organizer. For example, what were the causes and effects of D-day?

CAUSE
The Allies wanted to invade France to attack German forces.

EVENT
On D-day, June 6, 1944, the Allies stormed the beaches of Normandy.

EFFECT
By mid-September, most of France was under Allied control.

Using the Chart
Deaths in World War II

Have students read the information in the chart. Ask how to determine the total number of people killed for a country. (Add numbers for military and civilian deaths.)

✔ **Chart Check**
Answer the Soviet Union

Focus Ask students if they think it is a good idea to try war leaders or soldiers for acts committed while a country is at war. (Some will say that it is important for people to be held accountable for their actions; others will think that soldiers have to follow orders in times of war.)

◆ **ANSWER** Americans would capture some Japanese-held islands and leave, or "hop over," ones that were strongly defended.

Section Close

Have the class discuss whether the Allies would have won the war if the United States had not entered on their side. (Students will probably say no. When the United States entered the war, the Axis Powers controlled most of Europe and much of North Africa. The United States added many more soldiers to the Allied forces. In addition, they brought industrial resources, equipment, and supplies.)

③ Assess

Review Answers

Review History

A. Americans brought fresh troops and equipment to the battle. They energized the Allies, making it possible to attack Europe and push Germany back.

B. Germany was fighting on two fronts. Germany also could not withstand the addition of American forces and supplies.

C. Major events included the attack on Pearl Harbor, the Battle of Midway, the struggle for the Philippines, and the bombings of Hiroshima and Nagasaki.

Define Terms to Know
genocide, 679; Holocaust, 679

Critical Thinking
Possible answer: The atomic bomb was a terrible weapon and would kill many people, but the invasion of Japan would also cost many lives.

Write About Culture
Students' editorials should include the enormous loss of life and the introduction of nuclear warfare.

CHAPTER
28 Review

Chapter Summary

A blank outline form is available in the Teacher's Resources (p. 318). Chapter summaries should outline the threat of war, the conflict in Europe, how the war expanded, and the end of World War II. Refer to the rubric in the Teacher's Resources (p. 340) to score students' chapter summaries.

 Interpret the Timeline

1. six years (1939–1945)
2. Japan attacked Pearl Harbor and the Manhattan Project started.
3. The Manhattan Project led to the development of the atomic bomb, which was dropped on Japan in 1945. The war ended shortly after this.
4. Students' responses should include events mentioned in the chapter.

Use Terms to Know

5. genocide
6. sanction
7. appeasement
8. Holocaust
9. blitzkrieg
10. scorched-earth policy

Check Your Understanding

11. As a result of Japan's victory at Nanjing, the Chinese became united against a common enemy—Japan—and media coverage in the West portrayed Japan as a brutal aggressor.
12. The Spanish civil war provided Germany with fighting experience and iron resources.
13. The democratic nations did not want to be drawn into a war with Germany.
14. Germany's invasion of Poland marked the beginning of World War II.
15. The U.S. Congress passed the Lend-Lease Act, which allowed the country to supply weapons and equipment to the Allies. The government also entered into the Atlantic Charter, which supported the right of all people to determine their own government.
16. Women took the places of men in factories and on farms, and many women served in the armed forces.
17. Possible answer: Hitler had to deal with the following problems: the Soviet policy of scorched earth forced Germans to rely on their own

supply lines; the vast size of the country; and the cold weather, for which Hitler was not prepared.
18. The bombing of their capital shocked the Japanese and made them realize that their country could come under attack.
19. The overall effect was to bring the United States into World War II.
20. The purpose of the Manhattan Project was to build a nuclear weapon.

Chapter Summary

Complete the following outline in your notebook. Then, use your outline to write a brief summary of the chapter.

World War II

I. The Threat of War
  A. Rumblings of War in Asia and Europe
  B. Germany Plans for War
II. Conflict in Europe
  A. World War II Begins
  B. Responses to the Nazi Threat
III. The War Expands
  A. Hitler Moves East
  B. The War in Asia
IV. The End of World War II
  A. Americans Shift the Balance in Europe
  B. The War in Europe Ends
  C. The War in the Pacific

 Interpret the Timeline

Use the timeline on pages 660–661 to answer the following questions.

1. How much time elapsed between Germany's attack on Poland and Germany's surrender?
2. What other event occurred in the year that Germany invaded the Soviet Union?
3. **Critical Thinking** How did the Manhattan Project affect the course of World War II?
4. Select five events from the chapter that are not on the timeline. Create a timeline that shows these events.

Use Terms to Know

Select the term that best completes each sentence.

appeasement   internment camp
blitzkrieg   sanction
genocide   scorched-earth policy
Holocaust

5. Following a policy of _____, Hitler tried to murder all Jews.
6. The set of economic limitations placed on Japan by the United States was a _____.
7. Although the policy of _____ kept the nations of Europe out of war for some years, it did not stop Hitler's ambitions.
8. The _____ was marked by the death of millions of Jews and other groups.
9. Hitler's use of _____ was not an effective means of attack on the Soviet Union because the nation was too big to take over quickly.
10. Stalin's use of a _____ helped defeat the Germans who invaded the Soviet Union.

Check Your Understanding

11. **Describe** the negative effects of the Japanese actions after their victory at Nanjing.
12. **Discuss** how the Spanish civil war helped the Axis Powers.
13. **Evaluate** the reasons that European nations did not come to the aid of Czechoslovakia.
14. **Identify** the event that marked the beginning of World War II.
15. **List** the ways that the United States supported the democratic nations of Europe before entering the war.
16. **Describe** the role of women in World War II.
17. **Identify** the problems that Hitler encountered when he invaded the Soviet Union.
18. **Describe** the effects of the bombing of Tokyo.
19. **Evaluate** the overall effect of Japan's bombing of Pearl Harbor.
20. **Identify** the purpose of the Manhattan Project.

Critical Thinking

21. **Analyze** What were the advantages of the Nazi-Soviet Nonaggression Pact for each side?

22. **Make Inferences** Do you think the policy of appeasement was a good one? Explain why or why not.

23. **Analyze Primary Sources** Reread the quotation by Hitler on page 660. Why do you think Hitler said he had offered friendship to the European nations?

24. **Make Generalizations** How did the Japanese shame of surrender affect the war?

Put Your Skills to Work

25. **Recognize Propaganda and Bias** You have learned how to recognize propaganda and bias on war posters. Study the poster below. Then, answer the following questions.

   a. What is the goal of the poster?

   b. What do the hands in the poster represent?

   c. What do the mother and baby represent?

A U.S. war poster

Analyze Sources

26. Winston Churchill, in a speech delivered in 1940, spoke about what was necessary for victory. Read the passage below. Then, answer the questions that follow.

   Very few wars have been won by mere numbers alone. Quality, willpower, geographical advantages, natural and financial resources, the command of the sea, and above all a cause which rouses the spontaneous surgings of the human spirit in millions of hearts—these have proved to be the decisive factors in the human story.

   a. What did Churchill consider most important for winning a war?

   b. Why did he consider "command of the sea" important?

Essay Writing

27. Write an essay commemorating the brave actions of the soldiers who fought in World War II and gave their lives for the cause of freedom.

Critical Thinking

21. For the Nazis, the pact kept them from fighting a war on two fronts. For the Soviets, the pact promised them territories to add to their own.

22. Answers should indicate that European democratic nations wanted to avoid war at all costs but that the policy allowed Hitler to take over many nations without any cost to himself—strengthening him and weakening the opposition to him. Thus, students should infer that appeasement was not a good policy.

23. Hitler did not want to appear to have made an unprovoked attack on Poland. If other nations did not accept his "friendship," it would make them appear to be aggressors.

24. Possible answer: The fact that the Japanese believed it was shameful to surrender meant that they fought to the death, which proved very costly in terms of human lives for the Americans. American leaders believed that they would not be able to win the war without killing millions of people, including Japanese civilians and American soldiers. For this reason, Truman decided to use atomic bombs on Japan.

Put Your Skills to Work

RECOGNIZE PROPAGANDA AND BIAS

25a. The goal is to encourage people to buy Victory Bonds.
25b. The hands represent the threat of the Nazis and the Japanese.
25c. They represent the United States and the American way of life.

Analyze Sources

26a. The most important factor was "a cause which rouses the spontaneous surgings of the human spirit in millions of hearts."
26b. Possible answer: Great Britain is an island nation and has always needed a strong navy to defend itself.

Essay Writing

27. Students' essays should name some of the battles in which Allied soldiers heroically sacrificed themselves for the cause of freedom.

TEST PREPARATION

Answer 1. America's use of the atomic bomb.

Unit 7

Portfolio Project

HISTORY QUIZ SHOW

Managing the Project
Plan for 3–4 class periods.

Set the Scene
Have students brainstorm names for their History Quiz Show. Write class suggestions on the board. Then, take a vote to determine the name of the show.

Your Assignment
Ask students to read the assignment on page 684. Point out that wars are events in which much history is made. A unit containing World Wars I and II will have plenty of available information for a quiz show. To make certain that students understand the proposed format of answer and question, you might provide one or two answers and ask volunteers to supply the questions.

PREPARE FOR THE SHOW
Make sure that students understand their varied assignments. The judges can prepare by becoming familiar with the contents of Unit 7. The quizmaster can prepare by watching several game shows at home and analyzing the hosts' behavior.

Participants should understand that they will end up with a total of 48 questions (16 from each team), based on the contents of Chapters 26–28.

Remind contestants and the audience that this is a game, and they are to conduct themselves in a courteous manner, even when they answer incorrectly or disagree with the quizmaster.

PUT ON THE SHOW
Use a podium and chairs at the front of the room to create a quiz-show setting. Encourage students to use music, sound effects, and other typical features of TV quiz shows.

Wrap Up
The final product from each team and the production crew will be a 30-minute quiz show. Afterwards, have the class evaluate what went well in the show, and also how the show could be made more exciting.

History Quiz Show

YOUR ASSIGNMENT
Many people enjoy playing quiz-style games. Often the format of these quiz games involves being given an answer and then providing a question to match the answer. Here is an example:

Answer: This famous statesman was the prime minister of Great Britain during World War II.

Question: Who was Winston Churchill?

PREPARE FOR THE SHOW

Select Participants Ask for volunteers to take part in a history quiz show. First, select a quiz show host who will read the answers to the contestants. Next, select two student judges who will make decisions in case of any disputes over the interpretation or completeness of an answer. Finally, choose between 12 and 16 volunteers who are willing to serve as writers and contestants.

Write the Answers Form four teams of three to four students each. Each team will elect one member to serve as their contestant. The other members of each team will brainstorm to write 16 questions and answers based on material from the three chapters in Unit 7. The questions and answers will be divided equally into four categories: people, places, conflicts and treaties, and quotations. Remind students that, during the quiz, contestants will have to come up with questions that match the answers that are given to them.

After all the questions and answers have been written, a group consisting of one student from each team will review and edit the questions and answers for accuracy and to avoid repetition. This group will select the 40 best questions and answers to be used in the quiz.

Explain the Rules Each contestant will sit at a table or desk on which a small bell has been placed. Explain that the host will read an answer to a question. The first contestant to ring his or her bell will respond with the question. A correct response will be worth one point. An incorrect response will cost the contestant one point. If the first response is not correct, the next contestant to ring his or her bell will have a chance to respond.

There will be two rounds with 20 questions and answers in each round. After the first round, the two contestants with the best scores will take part in the final round to determine the winner.

PUT ON THE SHOW

Present Put on the quiz show in front of the entire class. Remind the students in the audience not to help the contestants in any way—except, of course, to encourage them with applause.

684   UNIT 7 ◆ Decades of War

Multimedia Presentation

Turn your quiz show into a video to share with other classes in school. Teams should assign tasks such as videotaping and setting up props. Before actually taping, one or more rehearsals should be held to help people know where they should be and how they should act. Select a volunteer director to keep things running smoothly.

Teaching Options

Multimedia Presentation

Adding music and sound effects will enhance the "reality" of the History Quiz Show. Students may want to add an introductory segment to the show as well as a closing. Students may also want contestants to introduce themselves. In between the two question segments, they may want to provide for station identification.

Alternative Assessment

Create a Bulletin Board Display Have three groups of students create a bulletin board display of Unit 7, Decades of War. Each group will focus on one chapter of the unit. Encourage students to use pictures of events, artifacts, portraits, maps, and charts in their display. Each visual should be accompanied by a caption explaining the historical significance of the visual and any other interesting information.

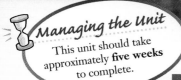

PLANNING GUIDE

	Skills and Features	Projects and Activities	Program Resources	Meet Individual Needs
Chapter 29 **Europe,** pp. 686–709 Plan for 5–6 class periods.	Unit Technology, p. T685 Read a Time-Zone Map, p. 693 They Made History: Margaret Hilda Thatcher, p. 697	Writing, p. T689 Conflict Resolution, p. T691 Connection to Economics, pp. T695, T705 Cooperative Learning, p. T696 Connection to Government, p. T696 Test Taking, p. T700 Connection to Science, p. T700 Research, p. T701 Using Technology, p. T702	**Teacher's Resources** Terms to Know, p. 42 Review History, p. 76 Build Your Skills, p. 110 Chapter Test, pp. 173–174 Concept Builder, p. 245 Main Idea/Supporting Details Chart, p. 319 Transparencies 1, 6	ESL/ELL Strategies, pp. T694, T699, T704 Visual/Spatial, pp. T688, T705 Auditory, p. T697
Chapter 30 **North America and South America,** pp. 710–733 Plan for 5–6 class periods.	Evaluate Information, p. 717 Points of View, p. 727	Conflict Resolution, p. T713 Connection to Geography, pp. T713, T719 Research, pp. T714, T725 Teen Life, p. T715 Connection to Languages, p. T720 Cooperative Learning, pp. T720, T722 Test Taking, p. T728 Writing, p. T729 Connection to Math, p. T730	**Teacher's Resources** Terms to Know, p. 43 Review History, p. 77 Build Your Skills, p. 111 Chapter Test, pp. 175–176 Concept Builder, p. 246 They Made History: César Chávez, p. 266 Flowchart, p. 324	ESL/ELL Strategies, pp. T712, T718, T724, T730 Logical/Mathematical, p. T724
Chapter 31 **Asia,** pp. 734–757 Plan for 5–6 class periods.	Develop a Multimedia Presentation, p. 741	Conflict Resolution, p. T737 Test Taking, p. T738 Connection to World Languages, p. T738 Connection to Culture, p. T739 Connection to Math, p. T744 Sports & Games, T745 Using Technology, p. T747 Writing, pp. T749, T752 Cooperative Learning, p. T751	**Teacher's Resources** Terms to Know, p. 44 Review History, p. 78 Build Your Skills, p. 112 Chapter Test, pp. 177–178 They Made History: Aung San Suu Kyi, p. 267 Cause-and-Effect Chain, p. 325	ESL/ELL Strategies, pp. T742, T748, T754 Verbal/Linguistic, p. T744 Visual/Spatial, p. T753
Chapter 32 **Africa and the Middle East,** pp. 758–783 Plan for 5–6 class periods.	Resolve Conflict Through Compromise, p. 765 Connect History & Geography, p. 771	Writing, p. T762 Conflict Resolution, pp. T763, T778 Cooperative Learning, pp. T763, T779 World Religions, p. T767 Using Technology, pp. T768, T780 Connection to Literature, p. T768 Connection to Science, p. T769 Research, p. T773 Connection to Geography, p. T774 Connection to Government, p. T777	**Teacher's Resources** Terms to Know, p. 45 Review History, p. 79 Build Your Skills, p. 113 Chapter Test, pp. 179–180 Concept Builder, p. 248 They Made History: Anwar el-Sadat, p. 268 SQR Chart, p. 322 Transparencies 2, 6, 10	ESL/ELL Strategies, pp. T766, T775, T779 Visual/Spatial, p. T761 Logical/Mathematical, p. T769 Verbal/Linguistic, p. T772 Kinesthetic, p. T775 Auditory, p. T780
Chapter 33 **The World in a New Century,** pp. 784–808 Plan for 5–6 class periods.	Develop a Historical Perspective, p. 789 Present to Future: Transportation Today—and Tomorrow, pp. 804–805	Connection to Culture, pp. T785, T797 Using Technology, pp. T787, T798 Conflict Resolution, p. T791 Connection to Science, p. T792 Cooperative Learning, p. T792 Research, p. T796 Test Taking, p. T798 Writing, p. T802 Connection to Literature, p. T804	**Teacher's Resources** Terms to Know, p. 46 Review History, p. 80 Build Your Skills, p. 114 Chapter Test, pp. 181–182 Unit 8 Test, pp. 197–198 Final Exam, pp. 207–214 Concept Builder, p. 249 Problem/Solution, p. 327	ESL/ELL Strategies, pp. T786, T790, T795, T800 Visual/Spatial, p. T795 Verbal/Linguistic, p. T801

Assessment Options

Chapter 29 Test, Teacher's Resources, pp. 173–174
Chapter 30 Test, Teacher's Resources, pp. 175–176
Chapter 31 Test, Teacher's Resources, pp. 177–178
Chapter 32 Test, Teacher's Resources, pp. 179–180
Chapter 33 Test, Teacher's Resources, pp. 181–182
Unit 8 Test, Teacher's Resources, pp. 197–198
Final Exam, Teacher's Resources, pp. 207–214

Alternative Assessment

Model UN, p. 808
Create Historical Maps, p. T808

Books for Students

AVERAGE

Of Beetles & Angles: A Boy's Remarkable Journey from a Refugee Camp to Harvard. Mawi Asgedom. An autobiography of an Ethiopian immigrant. (Little, Brown and Company, 2002)

Shabanu: Daughter of the Wind. Suzanne Fisher Staples. A twelve-year-old Pakistani girl must make a decision about her arranged marriage. (Laurel Leaf, 1991)

Red Scarf Girl: A Memoir of the Cultural Revolution. Ji-Li Jiang. A Chinese teenager describes her life during Mao Zedong's Cultural Revolution. (HarperTrophy, 1998)

One Thousand Paper Cranes: The Story of Sadako and the Children's Peace Statue. Takayuki Ishii. A story about Sadako Sasaki, who died of atomic bomb disease, and her quest to fold one thousand paper cranes. (Laurel Leaf, 2001)

Iqbal Masih and the Crusaders Against Child Slavery. Susan Kuklin. Describes the life of an enslaved Pakistani boy and the movement against children's exploitation. (Henry Holt and Company, Inc., 1998)

CHALLENGING

The Last Battle: The Mayaguez Incident and the End of the Vietnam War. Ralph Wetterhahn. Discusses the seizure of the SS *Mayaguez*, the raid, and the fate of three U.S. Marines left behind. (Plume, 2002)

Broken Glass Floats: Growing Up Under the Khmer Rouge. Chanrithy Him. A biography of the life of a child and her family in Cambodia. (W. W. Norton & Company, 2001)

Kaffir Boy: The True Story of a Black Youth's Coming of Age in Apartheid South Africa. Mark Mathabane. An autobiography by a South African boy who lived through apartheid. (Touchstone Books, 1998)

Books for Teachers

Looking for History: Dispatches from Latin America. Alma Guillermoprieto. Essays on Colombia, Cuba, and Mexico in the 1990s. (Vintage, 2002)

The Other Side of Silence: Voices from the Partition of India. Urvashi Butalia. Primary sources illustrate the effect the 1947 partition had on the people of India. (Duke University Press, 2000)

Understanding China: A Guide to China's Economy, History, and Political Culture. John Bryan Starr. Provides current information about China. (Hill and Wang, 2001)

Six Days of War: June 1967 and the Making of the Modern Middle East. Michael B. Oren. Explores this war and its effects on the current conflict in this region. (Oxford University Press, 2002)

Balkan Ghosts: A Journey Through History. Robert D. Kaplan. Discusses the Balkan region and its history. (Vintage, 1994)

You may wish to preview all referenced materials to ensure their appropriateness for your local community.

Audio/Visual Resources

Witness to History: Europe After World War II. Uses personal stories and primary sources to present events and people in Europe after World War II. Videocassette. (Guidance Associates Educational & Training Videos)

Liberation and Change: The Late 20th century (1945 to Present). Discusses the connection between literature and history in the late twentieth century. CD-ROM. (CLEARVUE/eav)

Populations on Earth. Videocassette. Explores the global concern of population growth and resource depletion in five countries. (Hawkhill)

Technology Resources

CNN—Cold War Experience: www.cnn.com/SPECIALS/cold.war/kbank/maps/global.html

Tiananmen: The Gate of Heavenly Peace: www.tsquare.tv/

Vietnam: Echoes from the Wall: www.teachvietnam.org/

African Voices: www.mnh.si.edu/africanvoices/

The Mideast: A Century of Conflict: www.npr.org/news/specials/mideast/history/index.html

Space Race: www.nasm.si.edu/galleries/gal114/gal114.htm

Globe Fearon Related Resources

History Resources

Historical Case Studies: Somos Mexicanos: Mexican Americans in the United States. Primary sources are used to study the cultural, economic, and political challenges faced by Mexican Americans. ISBN 0-835-91826-2

The United States: Its Past, Purpose, and Promise. Structured supplement for topics such as the Vietnam War. ISBN 0-835-94854-4

Global Studies, Focus on Latin America and Canada, Volume 1. Primary source materials and activities are used to explore life in Latin America and Canada. ISBN 0-835-91151-9

Global Studies, Focus on The Middle East and North Africa, Volume 2. Primary source materials and activities explore aspects of life in the Middle East and North Africa. ISBN 0-835-91153-5

Pacemaker and Adapted Classics

A Raisin in the Sun. Play by Lorraine Hansberry about an African American family in Chicago as they struggle with poverty and racism. ISBN 0-835-95542-7

The War of the Worlds. Science fiction by H. G. Wells about Martians invading Earth. ISBN 0-822-49345-4

To order books, call 1-800-321-3106.

The World Today

"The only credential the city asked was the boldness to dream. For those who did, it unlocked its gates and its treasures, not caring who they were or where they came from."
—Moss Hart, playwright, 1959

LINKING CULTURES Cities have long been magnets for people searching for new opportunities. Despite challenges facing the world's cities today, they continue to be places in which people can express their dreams for the future. The Manhattan skyline reflects the energy of the people and their hopes for a bright future.

◆ What ideas do the quotation and the photograph suggest to you about life in cities today?

The World Today
(pp. 685–808)

Unit Summary
Unit 8 focuses on political and economic developments in different parts of the world from the end of World War II to the present.

CHAPTER 29
Europe

CHAPTER 30
North America and South America

CHAPTER 31
Asia

CHAPTER 32
Africa and the Middle East

CHAPTER 33
The World in a New Century

Set the Stage
TEACH PRIMARY SOURCES
Photo The photograph on this page shows the New York City skyline at night. Ask students what aspects of modern life the photograph reflects. (tall commercial buildings, automobile traffic, bright lights) Ask students why many young people from all over the world move to big cities. What special opportunities do they think they will find? (jobs, culture, excitement)

Quote For Broadway playwright Moss Hart—whose family was so poor that he had to drop out of school and go to work—New York's theaters promised great opportunities and a magical future that came true for him. Ask students how a city can unlock its gates and treasures. (by providing opportunities for people of all backgrounds)

◆ **ANSWER** Possible answer: City life—as captured in the photograph and the quotation—promises equality of opportunity and a bright future filled with excitement, glamour, and wealth.

Teaching Options

UNIT TECHNOLOGY
A number of software programs are available that students can use to plan and create their own cities. Have students work in groups to use one of these software programs. Then, have them describe the types of buildings, businesses, and cultural institutions they included in their cities. Discuss the aspects of modern life that any large city—including the one they planned—reflects.

UNIT 8 Portfolio Project
Model UN

The Portfolio Project for Unit 8 is to stage a model United Nations meeting. Groups of students will select an issue from Unit 8, research and discuss the issue, and formulate a plan to resolve the issue. As a follow-up activity, students will turn their model UN meeting into a video presentation to show to the class.

Europe
1945–PRESENT
(pp. 686–709)

Chapter Objectives
• Describe the rivalry that existed between the Soviet Union and the United States after World War II.
• Discuss economic and political developments in Western Europe from the end of World War II to the present.
• Explain how oil crises in the 1970s led to a worldwide recession and how economic problems eventually led to the collapse of the Soviet system.
• Explore changes in Europe since the collapse of the Soviet Union.

Chapter Summary
Section I focuses on the emerging superpowers and the Cold War. Following World War II, the United States and the Soviet Union developed as economic and military leaders.

Section II explains the recovery in Western Europe. Western European countries cooperated economically as they rebuilt after the war. West Germany, France, and Great Britain developed political as well as economic stability.

Section III tracks political and economic changes during the 1970s. Cold War tensions began to ease, but economic and political problems in the Soviet Union eventually led to its collapse.

Section IV focuses on Russia and Europe after 1989. Europe underwent dramatic changes as new nations were created and ethnic tensions led to internal strife.

Set the Stage
TEACH PRIMARY SOURCES
Have students read the text on page 686 and the quotation from John F. Kennedy's speech. In the same speech, Kennedy spoke out harshly against the Berlin Wall, calling it "a vivid demonstration of the failures of the Communist system." Ask students what they think Kennedy meant by this description. (A wall was needed to keep people in East Germany against their will.)

CHAPTER
29

Europe
1945–PRESENT

I. Emerging Superpowers and the Cold War
II. Recovery in Western Europe
III. Political and Economic Changes
IV. Russia and Europe After 1989

After World War II, a division began between the Communist and democratic countries of the world. This division marked the beginning of a new type of war that would be waged in the world.

World War II left Germany a broken country. The winners of the war divided Germany into two countries. West Germany joined the Western world as a democratic country. East Germany came under the control of the Soviet Union as a Communist country. The city of Berlin was also divided by the Soviet Union into East and West Berlin. A wall was built in Berlin as a physical divide between Communist East Berlin and democratic West Berlin. On a visit to West Berlin in 1963, U.S. President John F. Kennedy said:

❝ *What is true of this city is true of Germany. Real lasting peace in Europe can never be assured as long as one German in four is denied the elementary right of free men, and that is to make a free choice.* ❞

In 1989, the Berlin Wall fell. East and West Germany joined as one country again. Once divided, Europe was now faced with the challenge of becoming a united continent.

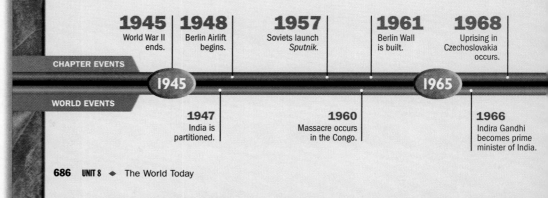

CHAPTER EVENTS

1945	1948	1957	1961	1968
World War II ends.	Berlin Airlift begins.	Soviets launch *Sputnik.*	Berlin Wall is built.	Uprising in Czechoslovakia occurs.

1945 1965

WORLD EVENTS

1947	1960	1966
India is partitioned.	Massacre occurs in the Congo.	Indira Gandhi becomes prime minister of India.

686 **UNIT 8** ◆ The World Today

Teaching Options

Chapter 29 Resources

REVIEW

Teacher's Resources (TR)
Terms to Know, p. 42
Review History, p. 76
Build Your Skills, p. 110
Chapter Test, pp. 173–174
Concept Builder, p. 245
Main Idea/Supporting Details Chart, p. 319
Transparencies 1, 6

ASSESSMENT
Section Reviews, pp. 692, 698, 703, 707
Chapter Review, pp. 708–709
Chapter Test, TR, pp. 173–174

ALTERNATIVE ASSESSMENT
Portfolio Project, p. 808
Create Historical Maps, p. T808

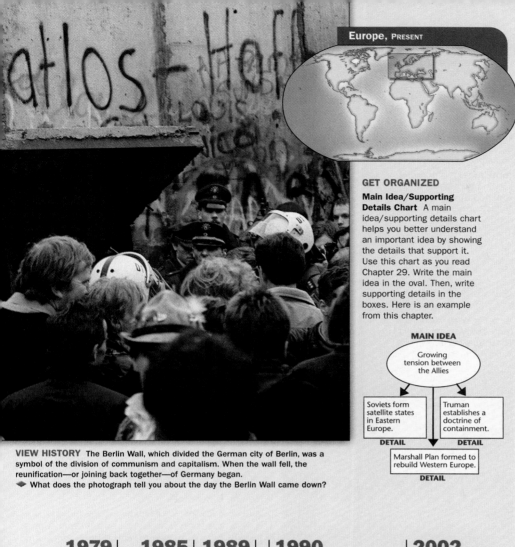

VIEW HISTORY The Berlin Wall, which divided the German city of Berlin, was a symbol of the division of communism and capitalism. When the wall fell, the reunification—or joining back together—of Germany began.
◆ What does the photograph tell you about the day the Berlin Wall came down?

Europe, PRESENT

GET ORGANIZED

Main Idea/Supporting Details Chart A main idea/supporting details chart helps you better understand an important idea by showing the details that support it. Use this chart as you read Chapter 29. Write the main idea in the oval. Then, write supporting details in the boxes. Here is an example from this chapter.

MAIN IDEA

Growing tension between the Allies

Soviets form satellite states in Eastern Europe.
DETAIL

Truman establishes a doctrine of containment.
DETAIL

Marshall Plan formed to rebuild Western Europe.
DETAIL

Timeline

1979 Margaret Thatcher is elected prime minister of Great Britain.

1985 Mikhail Gorbachev comes to power in Soviet Union.

1989 Berlin Wall falls.

1990 Soviet Union collapses.

2002 Euro becomes the currency of the European Union.

1985

2005

1969 U.S. astronauts walk on the moon.

1989 Tiananmen Square massacre occurs in China.

1994 Nelson Mandela is elected president of South Africa.

2003 United States and Great Britain join with other nations in war against Iraq.

Chapter Themes
• Culture
• People, Places, and Environments
• Power, Authority, and Governance
• Individuals, Groups, and Institutions
• Time, Continuity, and Change
• Science, Technology, and Society
• Global Connections

F Y I
Berlin Wall
The Berlin Wall separated East Berlin from West Berlin for almost 30 years. For East Germany, the Berlin Wall served a very practical purpose. It stopped the exodus of young, educated East Germans to the West. Erected on August 13, 1961, the wall was 103 miles long, 12 feet tall, and divided the city. The wall was a symbol of the division of ideas between East and West.

Chapter Warm-Up
USING THE MAP
Point out the locator map at the top of the page. Note that this chapter will focus on the political separation between Western and Eastern Europe after World War II. Discuss which part of Europe students think would most likely align with the United States and which part would most likely align with the Soviet Union.

VIEW HISTORY
Ask students to describe the expressions of East German soldiers as the Berlin Wall came down. Note that in the few days after the wall fell, millions of East Germans flocked across the border to ride free on subways and eat hamburgers at fast-food restaurants. Ask students why they think so many East Germans crossed the border. (They wanted to experience free movement and share in Western advances they had only heard about.)

◆ **ANSWER** Possible answer: The photograph might tell you that the event was very serious. People were not sure what to expect.

GET ORGANIZED
Main Idea/Supporting Details Chart
Discuss the main idea/supporting details chart on page 687. Ask students how each detail supports the main idea in the oval. Point out that the arrows could also be pointing in the other direction, to show the series of details leading to a main idea.

⬤ TEACH THE TIMELINE
The timeline on pages 686–687 covers the period between 1945 and the present. Ask students which Chapter and World Events demonstrate a positive change. (Possible answer: Berlin Wall falls, euro becomes the currency of the European Union, U.S. astronauts walk on the moon.)

Activity
Write a biographical sketch
Suggest that students research the life and career of one of the world leaders noted on the timeline. Then, have them write a brief biographical sketch that explains why the person deserves a place in the Twentieth Century History Hall of Fame.

I. Emerging Superpowers and the Cold War

(pp. 688–692)

Section Summary

In this section, students will learn how the United States and the Soviet Union developed as superpowers after World War II. They will also learn about the beginning of the Cold War.

1 Introduce

Getting Started

Ask students to name some words that start with the prefix *super-*, such as *superstar* and *superhuman,* and to explain what *super-* means in each word. (over and above) Discuss what qualities a country would probably have if it was called a superpower. (Possible answers: large size, strong economy, powerful military) Point out that two superpowers emerged after World War II and began to challenge each other in a different kind of war.

TERMS TO KNOW

Have students read the terms and definitions on page 688 and then find each term in the section. Ask them which terms seem to convey a positive feeling (*superpower*) and which convey a negative feeling. (*Cold War*)

You may wish to preview the pronunciation of the following names from this section with students.

Nikita Khrushchev
  (nyik YEE tuh kroos CHOF)
Czechoslovakia
  (chehk uh SLOH vahk ee uh)
Dubcek (DOOB chehk)

ACTIVE READING

Suggest that students focus on different events and ideas from the point of view of each side of the Cold War. For example, ask students how they think leaders of the Soviet Union may have felt about Churchill's iron curtain image. (Possible answers: angry, vengeful)

Emerging Superpowers and the Cold War

Terms to Know

superpower a country with overwhelming power
Cold War a conflict between countries with no actual fighting
containment a policy of keeping communism confined to the areas already under Communist control

Many European cities were badly damaged after World War II. This street is in Berlin, Germany.

Main Ideas

A. After World War II, tensions grew between American, British, and Soviet leaders.
B. Tensions following World War II led to the division of Europe and the beginning of the Cold War.

 Active Reading

POINTS OF VIEW
When you compare points of view, you look at an issue from the viewpoint of two or more groups of people. As you read this section, compare points of view toward the Cold War.

A. The Clash of Superpowers

World War II destroyed Europe. Whole cities lay in ruins, and tens of millions of people were dead. The victorious Allies occupied a defeated Germany. The Soviets had gained a large part of Eastern Europe, taking three small countries on the Baltic Sea, as well as a large part of Poland. In return, Poland received parts of eastern Germany.

Tensions Among the Allies

Tensions had begun to develop among the Allies even before the war ended. American, British, and Soviet leaders had different goals. The Americans and British distrusted the Soviet Union. Joseph Stalin, who ruled the Soviet Union from 1928 to 1953, feared losing power.

After the war, the United States and the Soviet Union surpassed all other countries in power. They did so because they had the strongest armies and economies. The United States and the Soviet Union became known as **superpowers**, or countries with overwhelming power. However, their ideals and goals were different. These differences put them in a new kind of conflict—a **Cold War**. A Cold War is a war that uses politics and economics instead of weapons. This period of increased tension lasted for nearly 50 years.

Widening Differences

American leaders defended democracy and capitalism. U.S. President Harry Truman and British Prime Minister Winston Churchill wanted to return European countries to democracy. They believed in private ownership of property and did not believe the government should control the nation's economy. They tried, but failed, to get Stalin to agree to hold free elections in Eastern Europe.

Stalin wanted to protect the Soviet Union, a totalitarian nation that practiced communism and was against capitalism. Stalin believed that the Soviet government should seize complete control of the nation's economy. The wishes of the individual were not important.

More tensions between the superpowers developed after the war over the issue of atomic weaponry. The arms

---

Teaching Options

Section 1 Resources

Teacher's Resources (TR)
  Terms to Know, p. 42
  Review History, p. 76
  Build Your Skills, p. 110
  Concept Builder, p. 245
  Main Idea/Supporting Details Chart,
    p. 319

Meet Individual Needs:

VISUAL/SPATIAL LEARNERS

To help students contrast the Cold War with a "hot war," have them make a Venn diagram (TR, p. 323). In the overlapping section, they should list some common goals or characteristics (high financial costs, desire to gain control). In the outer circles, have students list key differences (using spies instead of armies, providing economic help instead of military aid, etc.). Have students share their diagrams with the class.

race—a term used to describe the accumulation of huge stocks of weapons—began between the United States and the Soviet Union. During World War II, the United States tested the atomic bomb and then used it against Japan. The fact that the United States was the only nation with nuclear weapons worried the Soviet Union and many other nations. The Soviet Union decided to develop nuclear weapons of its own in order to restore the balance of power. Once it had developed similar weapons, the Soviet Union and the United States started a more intense race to make still more destructive weapons. Each wanted to have the superior defense. In this way, the rivalry between the two superpowers continued to grow.

The exploration of outer space was another area in which the United States and the Soviet Union soon became rivals. The two superpowers saw that space exploration would greatly increase their influence in the world and would serve a military purpose, as well. In the late 1950s, the Soviets began an impressive series of achievements in space. In 1957, the Soviet Union successfully launched *Sputnik*, the first artificial satellite, into space. Two years later, the Soviets landed the first rocket on the moon. In 1961, the first Soviet space capsule with a person on board orbited Earth. The Soviet space program was admired throughout the world.

The United States reacted to these events with alarm. In 1961, President John F. Kennedy ordered a large increase in government spending on research and exploration in space. The U.S. efforts were soon rewarded when American astronauts orbited Earth. In 1969, a U.S. team of astronauts were the first to land on the moon and explore its surface.

The Developing Conflict

Western leaders had long distrusted the Soviets in general, and Stalin in particular. Winston Churchill saw communism as an evil force, creeping across Europe. Leaders in Western nations referred to the iron curtain that separated the Soviet nations from the rest of Europe. The iron curtain was an invisible border between the Communist nations and the democratic nations of Europe. This iron curtain image became a symbol of the Cold War. The United States led the West's democratic countries. The Soviet Union dominated the countries in the East.

Like Churchill, the new American President, Harry S Truman, saw communism as an evil force that threatened capitalist countries. Truman and other Western leaders feared that more nations would become Soviet satellites, or controlled nations. He was determined that the United States would deal with the Soviet threat.

The Truman Doctrine

Conditions between the United States and the Soviet Union worsened. By 1947, U.S. President Truman supported the idea of **containment**, or keeping Soviet and Communist influence confined to the areas already under their control. In March 1947, President Truman asked the U.S. Congress to help Turkey and Greece defend themselves against Communists who were trying to take

British Prime Minister Winston Churchill was alarmed at the growth of Soviet influence in Eastern Europe.

Germany Divided, 1945

American zone
British zone
French zone
Soviet zone

0   75   150 mi
0   75   150 km

North Sea

NETHERLANDS

Baltic Sea

55°N

West Germany

POLAND

Berlin

Berlin

West Berlin   East Berlin

GERMANY

West Germany

50°N

FRANCE

CZECHOSLOVAKIA

AUSTRIA

SWITZERLAND

✔ Map Check

LOCATION Where was the American zone located in Berlin?

690   **UNIT 8** ◆ The World Today

over their countries. Congress agreed, and a new policy, called the Truman Doctrine, was established.

The new policy stated that the United States would help any country threatened by communism. Military and economic aid was given to Greece and Turkey to stop the Soviet-sponsored threat. To Stalin, the United States was now the enemy. Stalin thought that the capitalist world was trying to isolate the Soviet Union and destroy its authority and economic system.

The Marshall Plan

Another important part of Truman's foreign policy was the Marshall Plan. President Truman asked his Secretary of State, George C. Marshall, to create a plan to bring economic recovery to the battered countries of Europe.

In 1948, Truman offered Europeans money to rebuild their economies, and food to ease hunger. This program helped several Western European countries—including Britain, France, and West Germany—recover from the war's destruction. The basis of the Marshall Plan was the belief that as prosperity increased, the threat of communism in Western Europe would decrease.

◆ **What was the Truman Doctrine?**

B. The Cold War

As tensions increased and competition grew, the United States and the Soviet Union sank deeper into the Cold War. Americans and Soviets saw each other as threats. Each feared the other wanted to dominate the world.

A Divided Germany

After World War II, the Allies divided control of Germany and its capital, Berlin. It was divided into American, British, French, and Soviet zones, or areas. The Soviets used their zone's resources to rebuild their war-torn country. They installed a Communist government in East Germany. At the same time, Great Britain, France, and the United States rebuilt a democratic western Germany. It became West Germany.

In 1948, Stalin tried to force the western Allies out of Berlin. Railroads and highways into West Berlin were blocked. In response, the United States sent planeloads of food, fuel, and medical supplies to West Berlin. This response was called the Berlin Airlift. It was successful and eventually Stalin lifted the blockade.

West Berlin became a place of hope for the oppressed people of East Germany. Thousands of refugees, or people who leave a place to seek safety elsewhere, fled to West Berlin. To stop the flow of people from east to west, the Soviets built a huge concrete wall in 1961 that divided the city into two parts. The wall was topped with barbed wire and armed guard towers. Called the Berlin Wall, it remained a symbol of the Cold War and Communist oppression for almost 30 years.

The Cold War in Europe, 1955

Legend:
- NATO countries by 1955
- Warsaw Pact countries by 1955
- Nonmember nations

✅ **Map Check**

1. **PLACE** Which NATO countries share a border with West Germany?
2. **REGION** Which countries are nonmember nations?

New Organizations

Some leaders believed that the best way to contain communism was to stand together with other nations. In 1945, delegates from countries around the world met in San Francisco, California, to set up the United Nations, or UN. Like the League of Nations, the UN's purpose was to promote international cooperation. The member nations wanted to prevent wars and to bring a quick end to wars that did erupt.

To carry on its work effectively, the UN is made up of two major bodies—the General Assembly and the Security Council. The General Assembly has representatives from every nation. It debates problems that are brought before it and then suggests how they might be solved. The Security Council can respond to security threats and restore peace.

In 1949, the United States, Canada, and Western European countries formed the North Atlantic Treaty Organization, or NATO. The organization promised that if one nation was attacked, the others would come to its aid. The Soviet government saw NATO as a threat.

In response to the creation of NATO, Communist European nations formed a military defense agreement against a possible attack from the United States or other NATO members. This agreement was called the Warsaw Pact. With the formation of NATO and the Warsaw Pact, the division of power in Europe was made clear. Eastern Europe formed the Communist group of nations. Western Europe, the United States, and Canada formed the democratic group of nations.

Life Behind the Iron Curtain

From 1945 through the 1950s, the Soviet Union tightened its control of Eastern Europe. Soviet-controlled governments gave troops and money to

Do You Remember?

In Chapter 26, you learned that the League of Nations was established in 1920 as an organization to promote world peace. The League had the power to use force against any country that threatened peace.

CHAPTER 29 ◆ Europe **691**

Using the Map

The Cold War in Europe, 1955

Ask students to study the map and then explain why the Soviet Union wanted to include Turkey and Greece as part of the Warsaw Pact. (Both countries bordered on other Warsaw Pact countries and aligning with them would provide trading outlets to the Mediterranean Sea.)

✅ **Map Check**

Answers
1. Denmark, the Netherlands, Belgium, Luxembourg, France
2. Finland, Sweden, Ireland, Spain, Switzerland, Austria, Yugoslavia

Do You Remember?

In 1918, U.S. President Woodrow Wilson developed a peace plan called the Fourteen Points. The fourteenth point of his plan proposed an organization—what would become the League of Nations—to keep world peace. Wilson received the 1919 Nobel Peace Prize for his efforts at peacemaking.

Focus When NATO was formed, it was designed to protect Western Europe from Soviet attacks. After the fall of communism in 1989, three former members of the Warsaw Pact joined their old enemies. Hungary, Poland, and the Czech Republic became members of NATO.

Activity

Prepare a timeline Have small groups of students research instances since 1945 in which the UN Security Council has been asked to respond to security threats around the world. Ask students to make a chronological list of these instances and use their list to prepare a "UN timeline" (TR, p. 320). Students might use a color-coding system to differentiate between continents. Suggest that students start their research at the UN's Peace Keeping Web site.

Conflict Resolution

While a Cold War may seem less dangerous than a "hot" one, there is always one key fear: that feelings under the surface may flare up and lead to a full-blown conflict. To avoid such problems, both sides must communicate with each other openly. Use the Berlin Wall as an example. Discuss with students how building a wall may seem like protection, but it simply hides problems and does not resolve them.

F Y I

The Security Council

The UN Security Council consists of 15 member countries—five permanent members and ten member countries that serve two-year terms. The five permanent members are China, France, Russian Federation, United Kingdom, and United States. The purpose of the Security Council is to maintain international peace and security. All members of the UN, under the Charter, agree to follow all decisions of the Security Council.

Write captions Have students study the "Prague Spring" photograph on page 692 and write two new captions for the picture, one from the point of view of a Czech newspaper reporter in the crowd and one from the point of view of a Soviet reporter covering the event. Have students share their captions and discuss the differences in points of view.

◆ **ANSWER** The purpose of the UN is to promote international cooperation and to prevent wars.

Section Close

Ask students if they think there were any positive outcomes to the Cold War, and, if so, what were they. (Possible answers: Communism ultimately failed in Europe; the space race accelerated space exploration; the United States helped form organizations to maintain future peace and security; Europe may have been rebuilt more quickly following World War II because of U.S.-Soviet competition.)

3 Assess

Review Answers

Review History

A. The purpose of the Marshall Plan was to help to rebuild democratic countries in Western Europe after the war and to protect those countries against Communist takeovers.

B. NATO and the Warsaw Pact divided Europe into military alliances with the United States or with the Soviet Union. Europe was clearly divided between the two sides.

Define Terms to Know

superpower, 688; Cold War, 688; containment, 689

Critical Thinking

Possible answer: The Soviets controlled industries and depleted Eastern European resources. By 1953, people were trying to escape Soviet domination.

Prague, Czechoslovakia, residents surround Soviet tanks during the period known as "Prague Spring."

the Warsaw Pact. Secret police helped control the people. Governments controlled industries. Eastern European resources fed Soviet industries and left environmental disasters in their place. Under the Soviet system, however, Eastern Europe became more industrialized. Healthcare and education were available to everyone. More people gained specialized skills.

When Stalin died in 1953, Nikita Khrushchev became ruler of the Soviet Union. He publicly denounced Stalin's abuse of power and sought an end to the Cold War. In fact, the Cold War thawed briefly in 1960 when U.S. President Dwight D. Eisenhower and Khrushchev agreed to meet. A summit meeting, a meeting between important leaders of nations, was scheduled for late in the year. However, in May 1960, the Soviet Union announced it had shot down an American spy plane over Soviet territory. Eisenhower admitted that a spy plane had been sent to take pictures of Soviet military bases and agreed to stop all such flights over the Soviet Union. Yet, Khrushchev refused to attend the summit meeting. Relations between the two superpowers again grew cold.

In the 1950s and 1960s, two nationalists tried to escape Soviet domination. Imre Nagy, who gained power in Hungary in 1956, tried to pull Hungary from the Warsaw Pact. Khrushchev responded with force. The Soviets invaded Hungary, killed thousands, and executed Nagy. In Czechoslovakia, Alexander Dubcek introduced liberal reforms. This period of liberal reforms was known as "Prague Spring." Again, Khrushchev responded with force. Troops were sent in and a Communist dictatorship was restored. Because Khrushchev was so tough on those who opposed Soviet domination, it appeared that a return to Stalin's ways could take place at any time.

◆ **What is the purpose of the United Nations?**

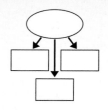

Review 1

Review History
A. What was the purpose of the Marshall Plan?
B. How did NATO and the Warsaw Pact divide Europe?

Define Terms to Know
Define the following terms: **superpower, Cold War, containment**

Critical Thinking
How did Soviet policies contribute to unrest in Eastern Europe after 1953?

Write About Government
Write a speech on the effects of the Cold War on the political stability of Europe after World War II.

Get Organized
MAIN IDEA/SUPPORTING DETAILS CHART
Use a main idea/supporting details chart to organize information from this section. Choose a topic and then find supporting details. For example, why did Western Europe fear the Soviet Union?

Write About Government

Students' speeches may state that communism divided Europe in half during the Cold War. Trade and relations between neighboring states were cut off. Europe was divided into two camps, separated by the iron curtain. This division caused instability in Europe after World War II.

MAIN IDEA

Western Europe feared the Soviet Union.

NATO and the Warsaw Pact were formed.
DETAIL

The Soviet Union kept large armies ready to fight.
DETAIL

The Soviet Union developed nuclear weapons.
DETAIL

Build Your Skills

READ A TIME-ZONE MAP

The world is divided into 24 time zones. Within each zone, it is a different time of day or night. When it is noon in one city, it can be a different time or day in another. Time zones are measured according to the distance from the prime meridian, or 0° longitude. To determine time in different parts of the world, you can use a time-zone map.

Here's How

Follow these steps in order to read a time-zone map.

1. Locate two places on the map.
2. Count the number of time zones between places.
3. As you move east, add an hour for each time zone you counted. As you move west, subtract an hour for each.

Here's Why

Reading a time-zone map can help you find out the time in a place that you are telephoning or traveling to.

Practice the Skill

Use the time-zone map below to answer the following questions.

1. How many time zones are between Moscow and Buenos Aires?
2. If it is midnight in Cairo, what time is it in Tokyo?

Extend the Skill

Name two cities on the map that are in the same time zone.

Apply the Skill

As you read this chapter, determine the time in different places discussed in the text.

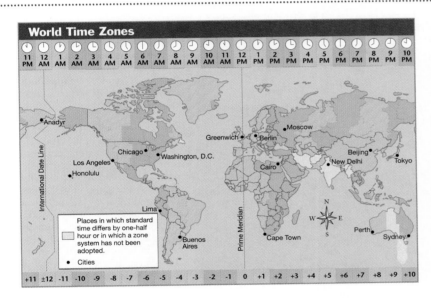

World Time Zones

CHAPTER 29 ◆ Europe **693**

Build Your Skills

READ A TIME-ZONE MAP

Teach the Skill

Describe a situation in which someone gets on an airplane at 10:00 A.M., travels five hours, and lands at 10:00 A.M. Ask students how that situation could be possible. (This situation would be possible if an airplane was flying west across different time zones.)

Ask students to describe instances in which they have been affected by time-zone changes, such as when they wanted to call someone in a different time zone and had to wait or when they have watched a live sports event on television at an unusual time. Discuss how communications, business transactions, and travel can be affected by time-zone changes.

Practice the Skill
ANSWERS

1. Moscow is six time zones away from Buenos Aires; there are five time zones *between* Moscow and Buenos Aires.
2. It is 7:00 A.M. in Tokyo.

Extend the Skill

Possible answers: Perth and Beijing; Washington, D.C., and Lima; Cairo and Cape Town

Apply the Skill

In Section 2, suggest that students find the difference in time between London and New Delhi, the capital of Great Britain's former colony of India. ($5\frac{1}{2}$ hours) In Section 3, have them indicate what time it would be in Moscow if Mikhail Gorbachev wanted to call Ronald Reagan at noon in Washington, D.C. (8:00 P.M.)

Teaching Options

RETEACH

After students have answered the questions in *Practice the Skill* and *Extend the Skill*, have them name foreign cities, which they can find on maps in the Atlas (pp. A1–A8) or Transparency 1. Work with the class to determine actual local time in these cities. Discuss what students may be doing in each city at the same moment in time.

CHALLENGE

Ask students to write an explanation for younger students of why time zones exist. Remind them that children may ask why it cannot be the same time everywhere, so their explanations should present clear reasons and examples. Have volunteers present their explanations to the class.

Recovery in Western Europe

II. Recovery in Western Europe (pp. 694–698)

Section Summary

In this section, students will learn how Western European countries rebuilt after the war and increased cooperation with each other. They will also focus on political developments in Germany, France, and Great Britain.

1 Introduce

Getting Started

Ask students why independent stores sometimes join together to buy or sell goods. What advantages does such joining provide? (Possible answers: can save by buying wholesale products in bulk, can reach more consumers, can offer lower prices) Point out that as Western European countries rebuilt after World War II, they benefited from international cooperation.

TERMS TO KNOW

Ask students to read the terms and definitions on page 694 and then find each term in the section. Suggest that they write each term and definition on the front of an index card and write a sentence using the term on the back.

You may wish to preview the pronunciation of the following terms from this section with students.

Konrad Adenauer
(KAHN rad AD ihn our)
Helmut Schmidt (HEHL moot SHMIHT)
Charles de Gaulle
(CHAHR ulz DUH GAWL)
Suez Canal (soo EHZ kuh NAL)
Rhodesia (roh DEE zhuh)

ACTIVE READING

Have students choose one of the countries discussed in this section—West Germany, France, or Great Britain—and write one or two generalizations about that country's political or economic development after World War II.

Terms to Know

Common Market the economic association of European nations that promotes trade and productivity

nationalize to convert from private to public control

partition divide

welfare state a government that takes responsibility for people's social and economic needs

British soldiers helped rebuild houses in 1945 as part of the recovery efforts that took place throughout Western Europe.

Main Ideas

A. When Western European countries rebuilt after the war, they benefited from international cooperation.

B. West Germany became the economic powerhouse of Western Europe and looked to reunify with East Germany.

C. Charles de Gaulle ended the political instability of France after World War II.

D. Great Britain lost its colonial empire after World War II.

Active Reading

GENERALIZE
When you generalize, you make broad statements based on facts you have heard or read. As you read this section, generalize by making a broad statement about economic recovery in Western Europe after World War II.

A. Western Europe Rebounds

Western Europe made a fairly quick recovery after World War II. When the war ended, the nations of Western Europe realized that they must work together in order to rebuild. With help from the United States, rapid economic growth helped create changes in Great Britain, France, and West Germany.

Political and Economic Trends

Growing unrest in their African and Asian colonies forced European countries to recognize that these colonies wanted independence. Some colonies, such as India, gained freedom after negotiation. Others, such as Algeria, fought long bloody wars for freedom. With fewer overseas colonies to govern, European countries were able to focus on issues at home.

The Marshall Plan helped Western Europe recover. It gave or lent about $13 billion to 17 countries. The money was used to rebuild bridges, factories, railroads, hospitals, and schools. It helped restore the economies of several Western European countries. It also helped democracy grow in Western Europe, while preventing future Communist takeovers.

Toward a United Europe

The rebuilding of the steel industry in Western Europe is one example of the benefits of international cooperation. Iron ore and coal are needed to make steel. France was rich in iron ore. Belgium and West Germany were rich in coal. Yet each country had high tariffs, or taxes, that limited trade of these materials. For example, a French steel mill had to pay tariffs in France on coal from Belgium. Therefore, in 1950, French foreign minister Robert Schuman proposed a plan

Teaching Options

Section 2 Resources

Teacher's Resources (TR)
Terms to Know, p. 42
Review History, p. 76
Build Your Skills, p. 110
Concept Builder, p. 245
Main Idea/Supporting Details Chart, p. 319
Transparency 6

ESL/ELL STRATEGIES

Identify Essential Vocabulary/ Summarize Note that this section, which deals with building Europe back up, contains many words that begin with the prefix *re-*, which means "back" or "again." Have students locate the words *recovery*, *rebuild*, and *restore* on page 694 and suggest several more *re-* words that they know. Then, have them write a summary of subsection A in which they use at least four *re-* words.

to help Western Europe produce steel cooperatively. His plan called for an end to tariffs on coal, ore, and steel in Western Europe. France, Italy, Belgium, West Germany, the Netherlands, and Luxembourg agreed to Schuman's plan. In 1951, they joined together to create the European Coal and Steel Community, or ECSC.

The success and cooperation of six ECSC nations led in 1957 to the formation of the European Economic Community, also called the **Common Market**. The goal of the Common Market was to reduce and then end tariffs on all products traded among the nations of Western Europe. In this way, the Common Market nations hoped to make Western Europe a large and important economic group of nations whose economies worked together. A treaty defined the Common Market's goals:

> ❝ It shall be the aim of the Community, by establishing a Common Market . . . to promote . . . a harmonious development of economic activities, a continuous and balanced expansion, an increased stability, an accelerated raising of the standard of living and closer relations between its Member States. ❞

The European Common Market was proof that Western Europe had recovered from World War II. Factories and mines greatly increased their output. Employment was high because the growth in industry and farming created new jobs. Trade among members of the Common Market was thriving.

In 1959, Great Britain, Austria, Denmark, Switzerland, Sweden, Portugal, and Norway organized the European Free Trade Association, or EFTA. EFTA, too, reduced tariffs and expanded trade among its member nations. Later, Great Britain, Ireland, Spain, Portugal, Denmark, and Greece joined the Common Market. In 1967, the Common Market became the European Community, or EC.

◆ **What was the goal of the Common Market?**

B. West Germany Gains Strength

West Germany became the leading economic power in Western Europe in the years after it became an independent nation. The German people were determined to forget the war years and to work hard to rebuild their part of the now-divided German nation.

German Prosperity

The West German government was headed by Konrad Adenauer, West Germany's chancellor, or chief minister, from 1949 to 1961. Under Adenauer, West German industries grew rapidly, producing steel and machinery that were sold to many other countries. West Germany's trade grew as rapidly as its industries. By the end of the 1960s, it was one of the world's leading industrial nations. West Germany's rapid and amazing change from a defeated nation to a great industrial country was known as the German "economic miracle."

West Germany became a close ally of the United States and the West during the Cold War. In 1955, West Germany joined NATO. Adenauer was opposed to communism and disliked the policies of the Soviet Union. Adenauer dreamed of someday uniting the two parts of Germany. However, the leaders of West Germany who came to power after Adenauer's death tried to improve West Germany's relations with the Soviet Union.

ANALYZE PRIMARY SOURCES **DOCUMENT-BASED QUESTION** According to the quotation, what was the purpose of the European Economic Community?

Connection to
ECONOMICS

The European Economic Community was one of the first multinational free trade regions in the world. Within it, goods and workers were permitted to travel across boundaries without paying duties. With fewer barriers to trade, goods became less expensive. Forming a united community also provided a huge internal market of up to 3 hundred million consumers for European goods.

A. Western Europe Rebounds

Purpose-Setting Question What was the purpose of the European Coal and Steel Community? (to end tariffs on coal, ore, and steel between France, Italy, Belgium, West Germany, the Netherlands, and Luxembourg)

Discuss Ask students why most historians consider the Marshall Plan to have been a success. (Possible answer: It helped Europe recover and built good will between the United States and Europe that would be important during the Cold War.)

ANALYZE PRIMARY SOURCES

DOCUMENT-BASED QUESTION
The European Economic Community is the official name of the Common Market. One of the first important accomplishments of the EEC was the establishment of common price levels for agricultural products. In 1968, tariffs on trade between member nations were eliminated. Ask students what value a "United States of Europe" might have. (Possible answers: freer trade within Europe, a more competitive position in world markets, regulation of certain industries or resources)

ANSWER The purpose of the EEC was to promote balanced economic development, to improve people's quality of life, and to improve the member states' relations with each other.

◆ **ANSWER** Its goal was to end tariffs on products traded among the nations of Western Europe.

B. West Germany Gains Strength

Purpose-Setting Question How did West Germany earn the name "economic miracle" in the years following World War II? (West German industries and trade grew, and it became one of the world's leading industrial nations.)

Focus Konrad Adenauer was already 73 years old when he became West German chancellor in 1949. Point out to students that Adenauer's skill as a diplomat was shown by his ability to connect Germany with its former enemies among the Western European powers.

Discuss Ask students why Germany was more interested in improving relations with the Soviet Union than were other Western European countries. (Germany was located closer to Eastern Europe than other Western European countries were. German leaders also hoped to reunite Germany in the future and knew they would need the support of the Soviet Union.)

◆ **ANSWER** Under Adenauer, West Germany's trade and industries grew rapidly. It earned the name the German "economic miracle." Adenauer also helped West Germany become a close ally of the United States.

C. Charles de Gaulle Stabilizes France

Purpose-Setting Question What changes took place in France under the leadership of Charles de Gaulle? (He improved France's relations with the Soviet Union, the standard of living in France improved, and he made France a nuclear power.)

Discuss Make sure that students understand the difference between nationalized and privatized industries. Ask which one involves more government spending (nationalized) and which relies more on competition (privatized). Ask students why a country might nationalize certain industries. (to maintain employment and ensure even distribution of goods) Also, ask students which industries they think are better run privately and why.

Role-play Have pairs of students role-play a conversation between Adenauer and de Gaulle when the two meet in 1958, as shown in the photograph on page 696. Before students present their role-playing, discuss the deep-seated distrust that the Germans and French had for each other coming out of World War II. Review the goals of each government as discussed in the text.

An Eastern Policy

In the mid-1960s, a coalition government was formed in West Germany. A coalition is a temporary alliance of persons, or countries, for joint action. Willy Brandt, became the foreign minister and later, chancellor of the new coalition government.

Brandt tried to improve relations between West Germany and the Soviets. His government officially recognized East Germany as an independent nation. Because of his actions, the division of Germany into two separate nations now seemed permanent.

Brandt was forced to resign from office in 1974, following charges that his close aide was an East German spy. During the 1970s and 1980s, West Germany's government was headed by two able leaders. Helmut Schmidt served as chancellor from 1974 to 1983. Helmut Kohl became chancellor in 1983. Under both leaders, the government played an active role in managing the nation's economic growth.

◆ **How did West Germany change under Konrad Adenauer?**

C. Charles de Gaulle Stabilizes France

The people of France, too, faced challenges at the end of World War II. France's economy had been badly damaged as a result of the fighting. However, the Marshall Plan aid helped French farmers and factory owners to recover. The French government also **nationalized**, or converted from private to public control, industries such as coal and gas. By the mid-1950s, France was beginning to build a stronger economy. The most difficult problem France faced after the war was its government.

The French National Assembly

The French National Assembly elected by the people had many political parties, including a strong Communist Party. However, no single party had enough votes to rule. In addition, French governments were made up of coalitions, or members of several political parties. These governments were often voted out of office. France's weak government led to a demand for change. In 1958, the French turned to Charles de Gaulle.

French President Charles de Gaulle and West German Chancellor Konrad Adenauer meet in Bad Kreuznach, West Germany, in 1958.

De Gaulle's France

In 1958, Charles de Gaulle, a World War II hero, was given power by the National Assembly to draft a new constitution for France. De Gaulle created a strong presidency with power to pass laws and a new National Assembly with fewer powers. The French people voted in favor of de Gaulle's plan.

De Gaulle was elected the first president of the new French Republic. He strongly believed that France was still a great nation. In fact, he wanted to make France the leader of Western Europe. De Gaulle feared that the United States might not be able to defend Europe. He also decided to improve France's relations with the Soviet Union, because he believed that Germany might someday again be France's chief enemy. For this reason, de Gaulle withdrew France from an active role in the NATO alliance.

Under de Gaulle, France prospered, and the standard of living improved. De Gaulle also made France a nuclear power by building nuclear weapons and making France one of

Teaching Options

Have students work in small groups to make a poster or brochure describing the history, members, and activities of one of the European organizations discussed in this section: the ECSC, Common Market, European Union, or NATO. Some group members can be responsible for designing and printing, others for drawing maps or charts, and others for presenting the finished project to the class.

In a two-party system, as in the United States, it is not difficult to get a majority vote on an issue if all legislators follow party lines. In most European countries, however, more than two parties are often represented in the national legislature. In order to develop a working majority to get bills passed, the party in power needs to form a *coalition,* or alliance, with members of several smaller parties.

Europe's largest producers of nuclear power. By the late 1960s, though, the French people became unhappy with de Gaulle's use of power. People objected to de Gaulle's handling of foreign affairs. When university graduates could not find jobs because of rising inflation, their discontent led to a student revolt and a general strike in 1968. The strike paralyzed the economy and threatened de Gaulle's power. De Gaulle finally resigned from office in 1969.

◆ **What were some of the problems France faced at the end of World War II?**

D. A New Course in Great Britain

Great Britain emerged from World War II as a weaker nation. It had lost its overseas empire of colonies that had provided much of its wealth. Its economy had been seriously hurt during the war. The British people voted into power a new government in 1945 ruled by the British Labour Party. The Labour Party ruled until 1979, when British voters turned to the Conservative Party led by Margaret Thatcher.

Loss of Empire

After the war, Great Britain was deeply in debt. When its colonies wanted independence, the British had little money and less desire for conflict. From 1956 to 1957, Egypt seized the Suez Canal. Britain and France invaded Egypt, expecting help from the United States. None came, and the invasion failed.

One by one, Britain lost its colonies. First, the British withdrew from India in 1947. India was **partitioned**, or divided, into a mainly Hindu India and a mostly Muslim Pakistan. However, tension about the boundary lines continues to this day. Then, African colonies gained independence in the 1950s and 1960s. The last African colony, Rhodesia, became an independent Zimbabwe in 1980.

They Made History

Margaret Hilda Thatcher 1925–

From a young age, Margaret Thatcher was politically active in Great Britain. By the age of ten, she was running errands for the local Conservative Party. Although she earned degrees in the field of chemistry, she changed careers and became a lawyer. She joined the Conservative Party and was elected to the British House of Commons in 1959.

Thatcher became secretary of state for education and science in the early 1970s. After the Conservative Party was defeated in an election, she challenged its leader and won control over the party in 1975.

Thatcher led the Conservatives to victory in 1979, and became the first woman prime minister in Great Britain. She won re-election in 1983 and 1987, when the Conservative Party won majorities in Parliament. When she left office in 1990, she had served as prime minister longer than any other British leader in the past 160 years.

Margaret Thatcher served as British prime minister for more than 10 years.

Critical Thinking What helped Thatcher win control over the Conservative Party?

Meet Individual Needs:

AUDITORY LEARNERS

Have students use a tape recorder to record themselves as they read part of this section aloud. Encourage them to use the recording to make notes and summarize the section. Suggest that students use the recording or their notes as study aids.

◆ **ANSWER** France's economy was badly damaged as a result of the fighting, and the government was in need of reform.

D. A New Course in Great Britain

Purpose-Setting Question What changes did Great Britain's Labour Party initiate when it came into power after World War II? (It set up a welfare state that provided free medical and health services, low-cost public housing, and increased pensions and jobless benefits. The government also nationalized the nation's coal mines, iron, and steel industries.)

Explore Have students find out when different British colonies received their independence following World War II and what name changes the newly formed countries underwent. Students might want to use an outline map of Africa (TR, p. 334) to make maps of pre-war and present-day Africa (page A6 of the Atlas or Transparency 6) showing the locations and names of the colonies.

THEY MADE HISTORY
Margaret Hilda Thatcher
Thatcher was the first female leader of a Western democracy and became the first British prime minister in the twentieth century to win three general elections in a row. She was sometimes called "the Iron Lady" because of her strong stance against communism and her leadership in crushing Argentine invaders who attacked Great Britain's colony in the Falkland Islands in the south Atlantic in 1982.

ANSWER The Conservative Party was defeated in an election, so Thatcher challenged the leader and won.

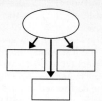

John Major and his wife at 10 Downing Street, which has been the official residence of Britain's prime minister since 1732.

The British Economy After World War II

The Labour government was in power from 1945 to 1951 and used its power to set up a **welfare state** in Great Britain. In a welfare state, the government provides for the basic needs of the people. The British Labour Party government provided free medical and health services, low-cost public housing, and increased pensions and jobless benefits. However, these programs drove up taxes. The government also nationalized, or took over the ownership of, the nation's coal mines, iron and steel industries, railroads, and telephone and electric services.

When the Conservative Party regained power in 1951, it accepted the welfare state reforms. In foreign policy, both parties supported the West in the Cold War. British armed forces also played a key role in NATO.

Fall of the Welfare State

During the 1960s and 1970s, rising costs forced the British government to cut some welfare state programs. In 1979, the Conservative Party came to power. Its leader, Margaret Thatcher, became prime minister.

Thatcher believed strongly that people should work hard, save money, and be responsible for improving their own lives. She also felt that the British government had gained too much power over its citizens' lives. Thatcher believed that industries would run better and make larger profits if private companies took them over. Therefore, she asked the government to sell many industries to private groups.

Thatcher's policies to cut expenses and reshape Great Britain's economy enjoyed considerable success. However, Thatcher's opposition to many elements of European unity and her support of an unpopular tax led to her resignation in 1990. John Major, the new Conservative Party leader, became prime minister.

◆ **What were some of Margaret Thatcher's beliefs about government?**

Review II

Review History
A. Why did Western Europe make a fairly quick recovery after World War II?
B. What happened to the West German economy under Konrad Adenauer?
C. Why did Charles de Gaulle withdraw France from an active role in NATO?
D. What does a welfare state provide for its people?

Define Terms to Know
Define the following terms:
Common Market, nationalize, partition, welfare state

Critical Thinking
What were the similarities and differences among West Germany, France, and Great Britain after the war?

Write About Economics
Write a brief essay on how European countries benefited from the European Community.

Get Organized
MAIN IDEA/SUPPORTING DETAILS CHART
Use a main idea/supporting details chart to organize information from this section. Choose a topic and then find supporting details. For example, how did the European Community affect Europe?

698 UNIT 8 ◆ The World Today

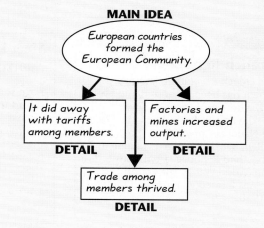

MAIN IDEA

European countries formed the European Community.

It did away with tariffs among members.
DETAIL

Factories and mines increased output.
DETAIL

Trade among members thrived.
DETAIL

Political and Economic Changes

Terms to Know

cartel a group formed by producers to control production and prices

embargo a stoppage of trade by political or military means

détente easing of tensions

standard of living level of comfort that a person or group wants or needs

perestroika the Soviet restructuring of its economy

glasnost the Soviet policy of openness in ideas and information

In response to the oil embargo of 1973, the Netherlands proclaimed "Sundays without cars."

Main Ideas

A. Oil crises led to a worldwide recession, and the European economy shifted from manufacturing to service industries.

B. Cold War tensions both eased and grew in the 1970s and 1980s.

C. Attempts to reform could not prevent the collapse of the Soviet Union.

 Active Reading

SEQUENCE OF EVENTS
When you try to make sense of history, you need to know the order in which events occurred. As you read this section, make a timeline of events leading to the collapse of Soviet-controlled Eastern Europe, and put events on it in the order in which they happened.

A. Oil and Recession

Economics and politics continued to change and shape the face of Europe in the 1970s and 1980s. During the same period, changes in the Cold War relationships affected not only Europe but also the world.

Economic Crisis and Renewal

The economies of industrial countries depended on oil. In the 1960s, oil-producing countries formed a **cartel**—a group that set the price of their oil as well as the amount produced. Called OPEC—Organization of Petroleum Exporting Countries—this cartel was dominated by Middle Eastern countries. In 1973, OPEC punished western countries for supporting Israel when several Arab countries attacked it. The cartel declared an oil **embargo**, or stoppage of trade, on the United States and the Netherlands. It also raised its oil prices many times over the next few years. A barrel of oil that cost $3.00 in 1973 cost ten times that by 1980.

The oil crisis hit European economies hard. Production slowed to a crawl. Many people lost their jobs. Workers went on strike. It was the worst slowdown, or recession, since the 1930s.

Welfare state programs helped people's suffering to some extent. Yet the countries of Western Europe also tried to lessen their dependency on OPEC oil. They began to conserve energy. Great Britain began to produce its own oil from deposits in the North Sea.

As a result of the economic recession, many Western European countries changed governments in 1974. France's Conservative Party president Georges Pompidou was replaced by Valéry Giscard d'Estaing, who led a business party. Great Britain's Conservative Party prime minister Edward Heath was replaced by the Labour Party's Harold Wilson. West German Social Democrat Willy Brandt resigned and Helmut Schmidt replaced him as chancellor.

CHAPTER 29 ◆ Europe **699**

1 Introduce

Section Summary
In this section, students will learn how policies of oil-producing countries in the Middle East led to a worldwide recession. They will also learn about Cold War tensions in the 1970s, and the collapse of the Soviet Union.

Getting Started
Introduce the economic concept of supply and demand to students. Ask them why, if the supply of a product goes down and the demand remains steady, the price will go up. (People will compete for the limited supply and be willing to pay more.) Similarly, if there is an overabundance of a product and demand remains constant or goes down, will the price fall? (Suppliers will need to cut prices to reduce their supply.) Point out that problems of supply and demand for oil in the 1970s led to a worldwide crisis.

TERMS TO KNOW
Ask students to read the terms and definitions on page 699. Then, have them skim the section to locate each term, read the surrounding paragraph, and state a definition of the term in their own words.

You may wish to preview the pronunciation of the following terms from this section with students.

Mikhail Gorbachev
(mee khah EEL GAWR buh chawf)
Chernobyl (chuhr NOH buhl)
Vaclav Havel (VAHT slahf HAH fuhl)

ACTIVE READING
Suggest that students create quizzes to test each other's understanding of the sequence of events in this section. Have them make a list of five events from the text in random order and then ask a partner to rearrange the events in their proper sequence.

Teaching Options

Section 3 Resources

Teacher's Resources (TR)
Terms to Know, p. 42
Review History, p. 76
Build Your Skills, p. 110
Concept Builder, p. 245
Main Idea/Supporting Details Chart, p. 319

ESL/ELL STRATEGIES

Identifying Essential Vocabulary Many Terms to Know in Sections 3 and 4 are political or economic concepts that students may not know. The text contains related terms, such as *recession, inflation, market economy,* and *reunification.* Have students keep a list of new economic and political terms as they read and define them in their own words. Then, have them work with a partner to test their knowledge of the terms.

CHAPTER 29 ◆ **T699**

A. Oil and Recession

Purpose-Setting Question What is OPEC? (the Organization of Petroleum Exporting Countries, which was formed in the 1960s to regulate supplies and prices of oil)

Explore The OPEC embargo encouraged scientists to test alternative energy sources to reduce dependency on Middle Eastern oil. Have students determine the advantages and disadvantages of such energy sources as wind, solar heating, nuclear energy, coal, and fuel cells.

Using the Map

The European Union, 1957–1995

Remind students that the EU started out as the EEC, or Common Market, in 1957. Ask how they can tell which countries were original members and which joined at different times. (Use the color code from the key.) Why is Germany shown with two colors? (It was two countries before reunification in 1990.)

✔ Map Check

Answer France, Germany, Luxembourg, Italy, Belgium, the Netherlands

---

◆ **ANSWER** Many countries changed governments as a result of the economic recession.

B. Tensions of the Cold War

Purpose-Setting Question What event caused Cold War tensions to rise again? (the movement of Soviet troops in Afghanistan in 1979)

SPOTLIGHT ON ECONOMICS
CHOICES OF A COMMAND ECONOMY A speeding up of the arms race between the United States and the Soviet Union in the 1980s put a huge strain on the Soviet economy. The Soviet Union could not afford to keep up with U.S. military spending without causing severe shortages in basic consumer goods, such as food, shoes, and paper products.

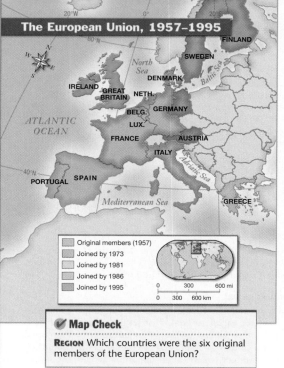

The European Union, 1957–1995

Key:
- Original members (1957)
- Joined by 1973
- Joined by 1981
- Joined by 1986
- Joined by 1995

0   300   600 mi
0   300   600 km

✔ Map Check

REGION Which countries were the six original members of the European Union?

Spotlight on *Economics*

CHOICES OF A COMMAND ECONOMY

The Soviet government wanted to be first among nations in the arms race. To achieve this goal, the government leaders had to deny their people many comforts that were taken for granted in Western European nations.

Eventually, the Soviet people would choose a different form of government when the opportunity arose.

Recovery in the 1980s

Conservative leaders came back into power in Great Britain and West Germany in the 1980s. In Britain, Margaret Thatcher attacked the welfare state as costly and inefficient. Conservative governments cut spending on social programs. They also offered businesses tax cuts to spur the economy. Slowly, prosperity returned.

France, on the other hand, elected a Socialist, François Mitterand, as president in 1981. The Socialist Party in France favored government ownership of the country's most important businesses and industries. These industries included the nation's railroads and airlines, coal mines, electricity, and gas. In the early 1980s, Mitterand's government took over other important industries, as well. The French government also spent large sums of money helping French businesses plan new products and modernize their factories. As a result of these government policies, the French people enjoyed a new prosperity in the 1980s.

In addition, the European Community (EC) continued to grow and work to make their economies better. Greece joined in 1981, and Spain and Portugal in 1986. When Germany was reunified, the former East Germany was also absorbed into the Community. In 1993, the European Community was reformed as the European Union, or EU.

◆ **Why did many Western European countries change governments in 1974?**

B. Tensions of the Cold War

In the 1970s and 1980s, changes in the Cold War were dramatic. In the 1970s, American and Soviet leaders tried to ease tensions between the superpowers. However, in the late 1970s and early 1980s, tensions heightened once again.

Easing of Tensions

U.S. President Richard Nixon and his national security advisor, Henry Kissinger, tried to decrease the tensions between the United States and the Communist superpowers of the world. This policy was known as **détente**, or easing of tensions.

In May 1972, Nixon and Kissinger traveled to the Soviet Union. They continued negotiations called Strategic Arms Limitation Talks (SALT), which had started in 1969. These talks were aimed at limiting certain kinds of nuclear weapons. During this visit, Nixon and Soviet leader Leonid Brezhnev signed an agreement known as SALT I. The treaty did not stop the arms race, but it did ease fears.

In 1975, U.S. President Gerald Ford met with delegates from Canada, the Soviet Union, and 35 European countries in Helsinki, Finland. Their goal

---

Teaching Options

Test Taking

Standardized tests often require students to recognize a correct sequence of events. For practice, name pairs of events discussed in this section and have students indicate which event came first. For example, ask students which came first: the OPEC oil embargo or the start of a war between Arab nations and Israel. (start of a war)

Connection to SCIENCE

The OPEC oil embargo led President Nixon to propose policies to reduce Americans' use of foreign oil. One suggestion was to lower speed limits on federal highways to 55 miles per hour to save gas. Scientists later determined that many engines were less efficient at 55 mph than at 60 or 65 mph. However, the reduced speed limits did reduce the number of highway accidents.

In 1989, Soviet troops rode out of Afghanistan on tanks.

was to reduce arms and control and ease tensions between the Soviet Union and other countries in Europe. These talks resulted in the signing of the Helsinki Accords. These agreements encouraged cooperation between Eastern and Western European countries, accepted national boundaries set after World War II, and established standards for human rights.

Tensions Rise

In 1979, Soviet troops moved into Afghanistan, a nation on the Soviet Union's southern border, and Cold War tensions soared again. The United States sent weapons to rebels in Afghanistan to help them fight against the Communists in this civil war. The Soviets could not defeat the rebel forces, however, and they withdrew in 1989. The Soviet pullout from Afghanistan was one of a number of steps that brought the Soviet Union and the rest of the world closer to an end of the Cold War.

◆ **What was the goal of the Helsinki Accords?**

C. Crisis in the Soviet Union

After Khrushchev was removed from power in 1964, Leonid Brezhnev assumed control of the Soviet Union. The economy was failing and harvests fell behind population growth. Shortages in food and other products were common. As military spending skyrocketed, the **standard of living**—the level of comfort that a person or group wants or needs—remained low. Then, in 1982, Brezhnev died. Two leaders succeeded him, but each died after little more than a year in office. In 1985, a new Soviet leader, Mikhail Gorbachev, introduced reforms that finally ended the Cold War.

Then & Now

WARS IN AFGHANISTAN
The United States supported the Afghan rebels in their struggle against communism. In 1992, the Communist government fell in Afghanistan. The country fell into chaos until 1996, when some Afghan rebels formed a group called the Taliban, and took control of the country.

In 2001, terrorists based in Afghanistan and backed by the Taliban launched an attack on the United States. The United States responded by attacking the Taliban in Afghanistan.

Then & Now

WARS IN AFGHANISTAN During the Soviet-Afghan war, the United States supported the Afghan rebels and the Soviets were forced to withdraw. Then, in 2001, U.S. forces helped to depose Taliban leaders, who had provided assistance to Arab terrorists planning attacks on the United States. Ask students to discuss the U.S. government's reactions to the terrorist events of 2001.

Focus The Cold War renewal also affected U.S. and Russian athletes. President Carter had U.S. athletes boycott the 1980 Summer Olympics, held in Moscow, in protest against Russian involvement in Afghanistan. Similarly, Russian athletes and those from many of its satellite states boycotted the 1984 Olympics held in Los Angeles.

◆ **ANSWER** The goal was to reduce arms and ease tensions between the Soviet Union and other countries.

C. Crisis in the Soviet Union

Purpose-Setting Question What economic reforms did Mikhail Gorbachev try to put into effect? (Gorbachev tried to reform the economy through a process he called perestroika. He proposed that industries and farms remain under state control. In addition, he limited military spending and offered incentives for productivity.)

Research

AVERAGE
Point out that historians have drawn comparisons between U.S. involvement in Vietnam and Soviet involvement in Afghanistan. Have students research to find comparative information about the two wars, such as number of troops involved, casualties, costs, and support or criticism at home. Have students report their findings to the class.

CHALLENGE
Have students research in American and foreign periodicals to find out how the Soviet Union's war in Afghanistan was reported and regarded during the 1980s. Students should write a brief summary of the responses and then use facts and opinions from their research to prepare an editorial supporting or opposing the war.

Do You Remember?
In Chapter 27, you learned about Lenin's New Economic Policy (NEP), in which the government allowed some private ownership of property.

ANALYZE PRIMARY SOURCES — **DOCUMENT-BASED QUESTION**
What relationship did Gorbachev see between democracy and restructuring?

U.S. President Ronald Reagan and Soviet leader Mikhail Gorbachev met several times.

Gorbachev's Reforms

When Mikhail Gorbachev took power in 1985, the Soviet Union had fallen far behind the West in technology, food production, and quality of life. While Gorbachev believed in Lenin's original Communist plan, he also saw the need for reform. To the older leaders of the Soviet Union, Gorbachev's plans for reforms were revolutionary. They were based on the belief that important changes had to be made if the Soviet Union was to survive and its people were to have better lives.

Gorbachev first tried to reform the economy through a process he called **perestroika**, or the restructuring of the economy. He proposed that industries and farms remain under state control. He offered rewards for productivity. He also began to limit military spending. In April 1986, the worst nuclear accident in history took place at the Chernobyl nuclear power station. It killed dozens of people and released a huge radioactive cloud, which drifted across Europe. Gorbachev's reforms tried to prevent the kind of mismanagement that led to the accident at Chernobyl.

Gorbachev also allowed public discussion of Soviet history and Communist Party policy. This development was called **glasnost**, or openness. In a speech to the United Nations in 1988, Gorbachev said,

> In order to involve society in implementing [accomplishing] the plans for restructuring [providing a new organization] it had to be made more truly democratic. . . . The . . . democratic reform of the entire system of power and government is the guarantee that the overall process of restructuring will move steadily forward and gather strength.

Glasnost helped the people of the Soviet Union. The government allowed the press more freedom, and new books were now allowed to be published. People were less fearful of the government. Gorbachev spoke openly about the harshness of Stalin's rule, and the government released information on bad harvests and poverty.

Gorbachev's ideas also transformed Soviet foreign policy. To Gorbachev, détente and making fewer weapons went together. He and U.S. President Ronald Reagan signed several nuclear weapons reduction agreements. He withdrew troops and weapons from Eastern Europe and ended the war in Afghanistan in 1989. His policies fostered cooperation and lessened tensions with the West.

The Collapse of the Soviet System

Gorbachev's reforms increased economic problems in the Soviet Union. Output of goods plummeted. Shortages grew worse, and prices shot up. Many state-owned factories closed, and workers lost their jobs. Ethnic tensions also grew. Many of the 15 republics of the Soviet Union demanded independence.

Reform also swept through Eastern European countries. They began economic and political reforms like those in the Soviet Union. People criticized harsh governments and their bad economies. Then, Gorbachev announced that the Soviet Union would no longer interfere in the affairs of Eastern Europe.

Once the Eastern European nations understood that the Soviet Union would no longer interfere in their affairs, they began to disassemble their Communist governments. In almost every instance, this amazing revolution was achieved without violence.

In Poland, the labor union called Solidarity was legalized because the Communist Party could not control the workers. For the first time in many decades, free elections were held. Solidarity candidates scored a stunning victory over the Communist Party candidates.

In November 1989, the East German government ordered the Berlin Wall to be opened. This hated symbol of the Cold War was destroyed. People began to talk about the reunification, or joining back together, of Germany.

In Czechoslovakia, the popular playwright Vaclav Havel led the reform. His group forced the country's Communist president to resign, and Havel was elected president.

The only violence occurred in Romania. There, President Nicolae Ceausescu's forces killed protesters. The revolt continued, however, and Ceausescu was tried in court and executed. Eastern European nations were finally in control of their own destinies.

Lech Walesa, the first democratically elected president of Poland, holds hands with members of a Polish youth group in 1993.

◆ Why did Gorbachev's policies lead to the collapse of the Soviet system?

Review III

Review History
A. How did the oil crises in the 1970s affect European economies?
B. What caused tensions to rise between the United States and the Soviet Union in the late 1970s?
C. How did glasnost affect the people of the Soviet Union?

Define Terms to Know
Define the following terms: **cartel, embargo, détente, standard of living, perestroika, glasnost**

Critical Thinking
How did détente help bridge the gap between the Soviet Union and Western Europe?

Write About Economics
Write a paragraph about the ways in which Western European governments tried to improve their economies in the 1980s.

Get Organized
MAIN IDEA/SUPPORTING DETAILS CHART
Use a main idea/supporting details chart to organize information from this section. Choose a topic and then find supporting details. For example, what effects did reform have on the Soviet Union?

Explore Assign teams of students to focus on one of the new leaders of Eastern Europe, such as Lech Walesa or Vaclav Havel. Have them prepare a class presentation that focuses on the person's background, key accomplishments, and influence on his country's political or economic direction in the 1990s.

Activity

Create a headline Have students research to find the date that each Eastern European Communist government fell. Then, have them write and date headlines that announce each government's change and arrange their headlines in proper time order.

◆ **ANSWER** Gorbachev's reforms increased economic problems in the Soviet Union and caused people to want reform.

Section Close

Ask students to suppose that they lived in one of the republics of the Soviet Union in the early 1990s. Discuss how they would feel about the collapse of the Soviet system. As a class, have students list some feelings they might have. Encourage students to use facts from the text to support their choices. Have students record these feelings and then share them with a partner.

3 Assess

Review Answers

Review History
A. Inflation rose and there was an economic recession.
B. The Soviet Union invaded Afghanistan to help the Communist government there.
C. It allowed the press more freedom; new books were allowed to be published; Gorbachev spoke openly about Stalin's rule and the people of the Soviet Union became less fearful of the government.

Define Terms to Know
cartel, 699; embargo, 699; détente, 700; standard of living, 701; perestroika, 702; glasnost, 702

MAIN IDEA

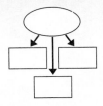

Effects of Gorbachev's reforms on the Soviet Union

The press was given more freedom. **DETAIL**

Gorbachev's policies decreased tensions with the West. **DETAIL**

People were less fearful of the government. **DETAIL**

Critical Thinking
Détente eased the fears of many Western European countries because arms reduction agreements and the Helsinki Accords were signed.

Write About Economics
Students' answers should mention that conservative governments came to power in the 1980s in Western Europe. They tried to stimulate the economy by cutting taxes and regulations and also by cutting spending on social programs. These policies helped their economies recover from the recession of the 1970s.

IV. Russia and Europe After 1989

(pp. 704–707)

Section Summary

In this section, students will learn how Europe underwent dramatic changes following the collapse of the Soviet Union. They will also learn about ethnic conflicts that broke out within the former Soviet Union and within Yugoslavia.

① Introduce

Getting Started

Ask students to think about a group of people who come from different families and backgrounds living together in the same house. Discuss what common interests might hold the group together and what potential problems might exist within the household. Point out that the Soviet Union, Czechoslovakia, and Yugoslavia were composed of different ethnic communities. These communities stayed together for a while, but could not survive after their central governments collapsed in the 1990s.

TERMS TO KNOW

Ask students to read the terms and definitions on page 704 and then find each term in the section. Discuss why *clean* is usually a positive word but an *ethnic cleansing* is a negative action. Ask students to name some other words they have learned that relate to destroying whole groups of people. (*massacre, genocide, holocaust*)

You may wish to preview the pronunciation of the following names from this section with students.

Chechnya (chech NYAH)
Slobodan Milosevic
(slo BOH dahn muh LOH suh vihk)

ACTIVE READING

Point out that cause-and-effect situations often form a chain, with the effect of one cause becoming the cause of another effect. For example, economic troubles in Eastern Europe caused these countries to move toward a market economy. The market economy led to closing of inefficient industries. The closing caused higher unemployment.

Russia and Europe After 1989

Terms to Know

default to fail to make payments
ethnic cleansing the act of eliminating one or more ethnic groups from a region or society

Main Ideas

A. Europe underwent dramatic changes after the fall of the Soviet Union.

B. Ethnic conflicts broke out in the former Soviet Union and in Yugoslavia.

C. European leaders looked for new ways to cooperate and solve problems.

Active Reading

CAUSE AND EFFECT
Every event has a cause and an effect. As you read this section, concentrate on what caused conflicts between ethnic groups, and what effects those conflicts had later on. Then, write down the relationship between the cause and the effect and these conflicts.

School children from East and West Germany formally celebrated the unification of Germany by raising the German flag in 1990.

A. The Changing Face of Europe

The rapid fall of the Soviet Union shocked the world. By 1989, the Eastern European countries controlled by the Soviets had abandoned state-controlled economies in favor of democratic governments and the free market system. Some political boundaries within these countries changed as well.

Shifting Boundaries

After the Berlin Wall was torn down, pressure mounted in both East and West Germany for reunification of the two areas. The two German states joined their economies and used the same currency. Formal reunification took place in 1990. West German Chancellor Helmut Kohl became chancellor of a united Germany. Within a few years, the capital of the new Germany was moved from Bonn to Berlin.

The collapse of the Soviet Union also created new, independent countries. In Czechoslovakia, the collapse of the central government revealed tensions between the Czechs and the Slovaks. Some leaders began to press for an independent nation of Slovakia. In 1993, two independent countries emerged—the Czech Republic and Slovakia.

Collapse of the Soviet Union

The borders of the Soviet Union also changed drastically. In 1990, Estonia, Latvia, and Lithuania declared their independence. In 1991, Boris Yeltsin, president of the Russian Republic, declared Russia's independence. A politically weakened Gorbachev resigned. Late in 1991, eleven of the twelve remaining republics formed the Commonwealth of Independent States (CIS). The Soviet Union simply ceased to exist.

The sudden shift from a command economy—where the government makes decisions about

---

Teaching Options

Section 4 Resources

Teacher's Resources (TR)
Terms to Know, p. 42
Review History, p. 76
Build Your Skills, p. 110
Chapter Test, pp. 173–174
Concept Builder, p. 245
Main Idea/Supporting Details Chart, p. 319
Transparency 6

ESL/ELL STRATEGIES

Use Visuals Suggest that students refer to the map on page 705 as they read this section. Have them compare it to the map on page 690 to help them visualize the "changing face" of Europe in the 1990s. Ask students to find the definition of the term "ethnic group" in the glossary. Then, discuss how differences in ethnic makeup led to the formation of many of the new nations in Europe.

production—to a market economy—where supply and demand control production—brought economic turmoil at first to both Eastern European countries and the CIS. Many inefficient industries shut down, and people lost their jobs. They suffered hardships and began to doubt their new freedoms.

Economic turmoil led to political chaos. Boris Yeltsin stayed in power but clashed frequently with Russia's parliament. Many former Communist members wanted to bring back the Soviet Union. Others who were extreme nationalists wanted to revive the glory of the Russian empire.

In 1998, Russia **defaulted**, or failed to make payments, on its foreign loans. In the face of economic and political unrest, Boris Yeltsin resigned in 1999. Vladimir Putin became the acting president of Russia and was voted into office in 2000.

In Western Europe, Germany paid a high price for reunification. East Germany's economy was in poor shape. The new German government poured huge sums of money into rebuilding projects. By the mid-1990s, Europe's economies began to grow.

◆ **What is a market economy?**

B. Conflicts Between Cultural Groups

The collapse of the Soviet Union led to many conflicts in that country as well as in other countries. Violent religious and ethnic conflicts broke out in a number of regions. Without the strict state to keep order, such conflicts were often violent.

Spotlight on
Government

FROM A SINGLE-PARTY TO A MULTIPARTY SYSTEM

There were actually many elected offices in the Soviet Union. However, because it was a one-party state, only members of the one party—Communist—could run for office. They did not often have opponents!

In the new Russian Federation, elections continued, but now there were many different parties and politicians who competed for power.

New Nations in Eastern Europe, 1993

Former Czechoslovakia
Former East Germany
Former Soviet Union
Former Yugoslavia
New country boundaries

0   150   300 mi
0   150   300 km

✔ **Map Check**

1. **LOCATION** Belarus formerly belonged to which country?
2. **PLACE** Which nations share a border with Latvia?

Meet Individual Needs:

VISUAL/SPATIAL LEARNERS

Point out that while many of the nations shown on the map on page 705 were newly formed, they had long histories as ethnic communities. Have students pick one of the new nations and find out more about its history, ethnic composition, and customs. Then, have them use their findings to create a poster about the "new" nation and share it with the class.

Connection to ----------
ECONOMICS ◁----

Under Gorbachev, the Soviet Union began moving from a command economy to a market economy. In a command economy, the government owns the industries and decides what to produce, how much to produce, and how much to charge for goods. In a market economy, most industry is privately owned and prices are determined by competition and profit motives. The United States is a market economy.

---

2 Teach

A. The Changing Face of Europe

Purpose-Setting Question What happened in Europe after the fall of the Soviet Union? (New, independent countries emerged and the borders of the Soviet Union changed.)

Explore Have students find out more about command and market economies. Encourage students to identify the advantages and disadvantages of each system. Ask students why it might be difficult to move from a command to a market economy. (Possible answers: need to build private ownership, factories may be outmoded, former key industries may not be competitive)

SPOTLIGHT ON GOVERNMENT
FROM A SINGLE-PARTY TO A MULTI-PARTY SYSTEM Remind students of the difficulties that political leaders sometimes have in developing a working coalition in a multiparty government. Then, discuss some of the advantages and disadvantages of a single-party, two-party, and multiparty system.

◆ **ANSWER** A market economy is an economy in which supply and demand control production.

B. Conflicts Between Cultural Groups

Purpose-Setting Question What causes ethnic conflicts to take place? (differences in cultures, languages, religions, or nationalities)

Using the Map

New Nations in Eastern Europe, 1993

Ask students which former countries became smaller as a result of political changes in the early 1990s (Soviet Union, Czechoslovakia, Yugoslavia) and which became larger (Germany).

✔ **Map Check**
Answers
1. the Soviet Union
2. Lithuania, Estonia, Belarus, and Russia

Extend Point out that Russia's problems with Chechnya were not resolved when the Russian armies withdrew in 1996. In 2002, Chechnyan rebels held more than 600 Russians hostage in a Moscow theater for several days. Most of the rebels and many of the hostages were killed when Russian troops used gas to try to resolve the situation. Have students find newspaper or magazine articles describing the incident and report details to the class.

Activity

Create a flag collage Have students research images of the flags of the former Soviet Union and former Yugoslavia and of the different nations formed from them. Suggest that they photocopy or print out the images of the flags and combine them in a collage. Have students present their collages to the class and explain the symbolism of the new flags.

GLOBAL CONNECTIONS

RWANDAN GENOCIDE Use a map of Africa (Transparency 6) to point out the location of Rwanda. Tell students that the Tutsi represent about 15 percent of the country's population, and the Hutu about 84 percent. There have been many power struggles between the groups over time. Discuss some of the problems that an ethnic group faces when it is a relatively small minority in a country. Ask students if they think anything can be done to avoid future incidents of ethnic cleansing in the world.

◆ **ANSWER** Peace continued in Yugoslavia because of the domination of communism.

C. Europe Today

Purpose-Setting Question What is the euro and when did it go into effect? (The euro is a new currency used by members of the European Union that went into effect in 2002.)

Activity

Track currency values Suggest that students use newspaper listings or the Internet to track the value of different currencies, including the euro, against the U.S. dollar for a two-week period. Discuss which currencies change the most and which seem the most constant during the period.

Wars in the Former Soviet Union

Russia is a huge area that includes a diverse mix of ethnic groups. When the Soviet Union broke apart, areas became republics or territorial units. Some ethnic groups in some areas demanded greater freedoms.

In 1991, one republic in the Caucasus region of Russia, Chechnya, declared itself an independent Islamic state. Russia invaded Chechnya in 1994. However, Russia withdrew in 1996, leaving destroyed cities and tens of thousands of dead behind. Russian troops returned to Chechnya in 1999. Human rights violations have been charged on both sides of the conflict.

Ethnic conflict also tore at other former Soviet republics. Many Russians who lived in those republics when they were part of the Soviet Union suddenly found themselves in newly formed foreign countries. In some of the republics, Russians faced hostility. In Georgia, small ethnic groups tried to break away from the larger nation in the 1990s, but the revolts were put down. Conflict continues between Armenia and Azerbaijan over disputed territory in Azerbaijan, where a majority of Armenians live.

Global Connections

RWANDAN GENOCIDE
Ethnic cleansing was not limited to the Balkans in the 1990s. In 1994, the small African country of Rwanda was also torn by ethnic tensions between Tutsi and Hutu groups. In a few weeks, more than 500,000 Tutsi were massacred by the Hutu. Order was soon restored, but the events left the world shocked.

Yugoslavia No More

Many of Yugoslavia's ethnic groups had strong nationalistic feelings. However, Communist leader Marshal Tito did not allow expression of these feelings. When Tito died in 1980, peace continued because of the domination of communism. After the Soviet Union fell in 1989, however, only Serbia and Montenegro wanted to keep Communist governments. Macedonia, Slovenia, and Croatia declared independence in 1991. Bosnia and Herzegovina declared independence in 1992.

Serbs, Croats, and Muslims lived in Bosnia. Civil war broke out when Serbia tried to keep areas of Bosnian Serbs under its control. Serbs and Croats began driving out and killing Muslims. They called this **ethnic cleansing**, which is another name for genocide. Human rights abuses on both sides horrified the world. In 1995, NATO peacekeepers came into the region, and an uneasy peace was restored by 1996.

In 1998, conflict broke out again when ethnic Albanians in the Serbian province of Kosovo tried to break away from Serbia. Serbian leader Slobodan Milosevic was accused of ordering the deaths of ethnic Albanians. NATO and the UN forced Milosevic to end the ethnic cleansing.

In 2000, Vojislav Kostunica was elected president of Serbia. Milosevic was sent to the World Court to face war-crime charges. In 2002, Serbia and Montenegro dropped the name *Yugoslavia* altogether and became the nation of Serbia-Montenegro.

◆ **Why did peace continue in Yugoslavia after the death of Tito in 1980?**

C. Europe Today

The major powers of Europe continued to seek political balance as they turned to a variety of forms of government in the 1990s.

The European Union

By the early 2000s, the European Union (EU) was an economic superpower. The addition of Austria, Finland, and Sweden in 1995 increased EU membership to 15 countries. Many more countries have asked to join the union, including many in Eastern Europe. In 1991, members of the EU agreed to have only one currency. The new currency, called the euro, went

Euro bank notes became the currency of the European Union in 2002.

Teaching Options

Slobodan Milosevic

In 1987, Slobodan Milosevic was a little-known Serbian Communist Party leader who helped calm a large crowd of Serbs being beaten by Muslim police in Kosovo. Two years later, he inspired a new wave of violence that helped him win an election to become president of Serbia. The many bloody incidents that occurred during his 13-year reign earned Milosevic the nickname Butcher of the Balkans.

into effect in 2002. The EU also established a new European central bank in Frankfurt, Germany.

Finding Political Solutions to Economic Problems

In the early 1990s, a recession in Europe caused widespread job losses. Britain's prime minister Tony Blair was willing to reduce the benefits of the welfare state to help the economy grow.

Similar programs were used in Germany and France. Unemployment dropped, and production and trade rose. A recession in the early 2000s weakened some gains, however. This recession was comparable to the economic problems in North America and Asia. It demonstrated how connected the economies of the world are.

Europe Into the Twenty-First Century

France's 14-year Socialist leadership ended in 1995, when François Mitterrand lost the presidency to Jacques Chirac, a conservative. Chirac promised to cut taxes, maintain law and order, and make state enterprises privately owned.

In contrast, Germans removed the Christian Democrat Helmut Kohl in 1998, in favor of the Social Democrat Gerhard Schröder. Great Britain also changed from Conservative to Labour leadership. Conservative John Major served as prime minister from 1990 to 1997, and Tony Blair, a moderate Labour leader, has served since 1997.

◆ **What did EU leaders agree to in 1991?**

Some European Leaders, 1981–2003

COUNTRY	LEADER	DATE OF SERVICE
Great Britain	John Major	1990–1997
	Tony Blair	1997–
Russia	Boris Yeltsin	1991–1999
	Vladimir Putin	2000–
France	François Mitterrand	1981–1995
	Jacques Chirac	1995–
Germany	Helmut Kohl	1990–1998
	Gerhard Schröder	1998–

✔ **Chart Check**
Which leaders came to power in 1990?

Using the Chart
Some European Leaders, 1981–2003

Which leader took power after Boris Yeltsin? (Vladimir Putin) Which leader came to power in 1998? (Gerhard Schröder) How many leaders came to power in 2000? (one)

✔ **Chart Check**
Answer Helmut Kohl and John Major

◆ **ANSWER** EU leaders agreed to have only one currency, called the euro, and to establish a new European central bank.

Section Close

Ask students to describe ways that Europe today is stronger politically and economically than it was in 1945. Discuss why a strong Europe is important to the United States as well. (as a trading partner, as a partner to prevent future wars, as a partner in scientific ventures)

3 Assess

Review Answers

Review History

A. East Germany and West Germany were reunited.

B. The country broke up into several independent countries, but ethnic and religious tensions led to brutal civil war.

C. The EU introduced a single currency and also created a central bank in Frankfurt, Germany.

Define Terms to Know
default 705; ethnic cleansing, 706

Critical Thinking
Communist governments suppressed ethnic conflicts while they tried to instill loyalty to the Communist government and ideals. When communism collapsed in the Soviet Union, so did the controls on ethnic conflicts. Ethnic loyalties grew into nationalist sentiments.

Review IV

Review History
A. What effects did the collapse of the Berlin Wall have on Germany?
B. What happened to Yugoslavia in 1991?
C. How did the European Union create greater economic cooperation?

Define Terms to Know
Define the following terms:
default, ethnic cleansing

Critical Thinking
How did the collapse of the Soviet Union set the stage for ethnic and nationalist conflicts in the region in the 1990s?

Write About Citizenship
Write a brief essay on how the breakup of the Soviet Union and Yugoslavia affected people in those countries.

Get Organized
MAIN IDEA/SUPPORTING DETAILS CHART
Use a main idea/supporting details chart to organize information from this section. Choose a topic and then find supporting details. For example, what were the effects of the fall of the Soviet government on Russia?

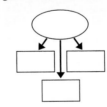

MAIN IDEA

Effects of the fall of the Soviet government on Russia

Russia faced severe economic problems.
DETAIL

Economic turmoil brought about political chaos.
DETAIL

Industries shut down and many people lost their jobs.
DETAIL

Write About Citizenship
Students' essays should note that with the breakup of the Soviet Union, many Russians discovered they were ethnic foreigners in various parts of the country, and were sometimes treated with hostility. Similarly, the former Yugoslavia broke up along ethnic lines, sometimes violently.

CHAPTER 29
Review

Chapter Summary

A blank outline form is available in the Teacher's Resources (p. 318). Chapter summaries should outline the rise of the United States and the Soviet Union as superpowers, developments in the Cold War, the economic and political rebuilding of Europe after World War II, the oil crisis of the 1970s, the collapse of the Soviet Union and its impact on European geography and economics since 1990, and the current status of Europe. Refer to the rubric in the Teacher's Resources (p. 340) to score students' chapter summaries.

 Interpret the Timeline

1. election of Margaret Thatcher
2. 42 years
3. the fall of the Berlin Wall in 1989
4. Check students' timelines to be sure all events are in the chapter.

Use Terms to Know

5. welfare state
6. default
7. nationalize
8. containment
9. glasnost
10. cartel
11. Common Market
12. Cold War

Check Your Understanding

13. The Marshall Plan rebuilt Western Europe's economy, and prevented Communist takeover of these countries.
14. He built the concrete wall to stop people from leaving East Germany.
15. The United Nations was important because its purpose was to promote international cooperation. This, in turn, would help prevent wars and promote peace.
16. Secret police helped control the people, governments controlled industries, Eastern Europe's industries caused environmental disasters, and healthcare and education were available to everyone.
17. People were less satisfied with de Gaulle's policies and were against his use of power; inflation was growing; and there were too few jobs for university graduates.
18. OPEC set the prices of oil and the amount of oil produced. It used this control of oil to achieve political goals by declaring an oil embargo

---

Chapter Summary

Complete the following outline in your notebook. Then, use your outline to write a brief summary of the chapter.

Europe

I. Emerging Superpowers and the Cold War
   A. The Clash of Superpowers
   B. The Cold War
II. Recovery in Western Europe
   A. Western Europe Rebounds
   B. West Germany Gains Strength
   C. Charles de Gaulle Stabilizes France
   D. A New Course in Great Britain
III. Political and Economic Changes
   A. Oil and Recession
   B. Tensions of the Cold War
   C. Crisis in the Soviet Union
IV. Russia and Europe After 1989
   A. The Changing Face of Europe
   B. Conflicts Between Cultural Groups
   C. Europe Today

⬤ **Interpret the Timeline**

Use the timeline on pages 686–687 to answer the following questions.

1. Which event happened first, the election of Margaret Thatcher or the fall of the Berlin Wall?
2. How many years passed between the Berlin Airlift and the collapse of the Soviet Union?
3. **Critical Thinking** Which symbolic event preceded the collapse of the Soviet Union in Europe?
4. Select five events from the chapter that are not on the timeline. Create a timeline that shows these events.

Use Terms to Know

Select the term that best completes each sentence.

cartel   containment   nationalize
Cold War   default   welfare state
Common Market   glasnost

5. A government that takes responsibility for people's social and economic needs is called a _____.
6. To _____ is to fail to make payments.
7. To convert a company from private to public control is to _____ it.
8. _____ is a policy of keeping communism confined to the areas already under Communist control.
9. _____ was the Soviet policy of openness in ideas and information.
10. A group of companies that sets production and prices for goods is a _____.
11. _____ is an economic association of European nations that promotes trade and productivity.
12. A conflict between countries with no actual fighting is called a _____.

Check Your Understanding

13. **Describe** the effects of the Marshall Plan.
14. **Summarize** why Stalin attempted to seal off Berlin.
15. **Discuss** the importance of the United Nations.
16. **Describe** what life was like in the Soviet Union from 1945 through the 1950s.
17. **Summarize** conditions that led up to the student protests in France in 1968.
18. **Identify** the causes of the oil crises in the 1970s.
19. **Describe** the effects of détente in the 1970s.
20. **Describe** how Mikhail Gorbachev tried to reform the Soviet economy.
21. **Identify** what took place in Chechnya from 1991 to 1996.

---

against the United States and other allies of Israel. Israel was engaged in a war against Arab countries. OPEC raised its oil prices many times over the next few years.

19. As a result of détente, the Soviet countries and the West signed arms control agreements that eased fears of nuclear war; they also signed the Helsinki Accords, which encouraged cooperation between Eastern and

Western countries, accepted the borders set up after World War II, and established standards for human rights.

20. Gorbachev tried to reform the economy by proposing that industries and farms remain under state control, offering incentives for production, and limiting military spending.

21. In 1991, Chechnya declared itself an independent Islamic state. In 1994, Russia went to war with Chechnya. In 1996, Russia withdrew from Chechnya, leaving destroyed cities and tens of thousands of people dead.

Critical Thinking

22. Analyze In what ways did the formation of NATO both unite and divide the nations of Europe?

23. Analyze Primary Sources According to the quotation on page 695, what were some of the reasons for the creation of the Common Market?

24. Analyze Primary Sources According to the quotation on page 702, why did Mikhail Gorbachev want to make democratic reforms in the Soviet Union?

25. Compare and Contrast How were the breakups of Czechoslovakia and Yugoslavia different?

Put Your Skills to Work

26. Read a Time-Zone Map You have learned how to read time-zone maps, which you can use to find out time in different places around the world. Interpreting a time-zone map can help you when you travel or when you communicate with people in different regions of the world.

Study the map on page 693. Then, answer the following questions.

a. How many time zones away from Berlin is Chicago?

b. If it is 2:00 P.M. in Berlin, what time is it in Beijing?

c. If it is 6:00 A.M. Monday in Los Angeles, what time and day is it in Perth?

d. You live in Washington, D.C. At 3:00 P.M. you call your friend in Tokyo. What might your friend be doing?

e. The prime meridian runs through which city?

f. If it is 5:00 P.M. in Washington, D.C., what time is it in Moscow?

Analyze Sources

27. During Hungary's attempted escape from Soviet domination, many Hungarians were injured and killed. Read a section of the Declaration by the Central Committee of the Hungarian Workers Party to the Soviets in 1956. Then, answer the questions that follow.

The new Government shall start negotiations with the Soviet Government in order to settle relations between our countries on the basis of independence. As a first step toward this end, Soviet troops will, after the restoration of order, return to their bases. Complete equality between Hungary and the Soviet Union corresponds to the interests of both countries, because on that basis alone can a truly fraternal, unbreakable Hungarian-Soviet relationship be built.

a. What does this declaration set out to do?

b. According to the declaration, what is the first step toward this end?

Essay Writing

28. The Cold War was a time of tension. At the same time, Western Europeans cooperated more closely than ever. Write an essay on the reasons why Western Europeans cooperated during this time.

TEST PREPARATION

CAUSE-AND-EFFECT RELATIONSHIPS
Choose the correct answer to the question.

Which of the following is a result of the breakup of the Soviet Union?

1. Russia immediately became prosperous.

2. Government in Russia was immediately more efficient and civil.

3. Russians faced increasing economic hardships.

4. Russia kept control over Eastern Europe.

Critical Thinking

22. NATO united many of the countries of Western Europe in a pact to support each other against Communist enemies. However, the formation of NATO was viewed as a threat by the Soviet Union and led many Eastern European countries to join the Soviet Union in the Warsaw Pact in opposition to NATO.

23. The Common Market was created to promote a harmonious development of economic activities, a continuous and balanced expansion, an increased stability, an accelerated raising of the standard of living, and closer relations between its member states.

24. Possible answer: He wanted to reform the government and economy of the Soviet Union, and he believed that democratic reforms would give strength to the restructuring.

25. Possible answer: Czechoslovakia had a long tradition of democracy already, and there were only two groups in distinct areas; Yugoslavia had only an authoritarian tradition, and the ethnic groups were more mixed, so the breakup was more violent.

Put Your Skills to Work

READ A TIME-ZONE MAP
26a. seven time zones
26b. 9:00 P.M.
26c. Tuesday, 10:00 A.M.
26d. sleeping
26e. Greenwich
26f. 1:00 A.M. the next day

Analyze Sources

27a. This statement aims to set the basis for equal relations between the Soviet Union and an independent Hungary.
27b. The first step is the withdrawal of Soviet troops.

Essay Writing

28. Answers should suggest that the Cold War brought Western Europeans together, partly because of the fear of nuclear annihilation that prompted them to seek collective security. It also promoted cooperation, because the Marshall Plan helped them work with the United States and with each other to help rebuild Europe.

TEST PREPARATION

Answer 3. Russians faced increasing economic hardships.

North America and South America
1945–PRESENT
(pp. 710–733)

Chapter Objectives

• Describe the United States after World War II, including its relationships with other nations and the internal struggles of various groups for equal rights.
• Compare the colonial histories of Canada and the United States and describe current relations between the two countries.
• Explain how U.S. policies have influenced the politics and the economies of Mexico, Central America, and the Caribbean islands in the modern era.
• Describe the economies and political climate of South America in the modern era.

Chapter Summary

Section I focuses on the United States after World War II including the Cold War conflicts, internal struggles, and describes the efforts of various groups for equal rights.
Section II describes the early settlement of Canada and the close relationship between Canada and the United States.
Section III describes the economies and political climate of Mexico, the nations of Central America and the island nations of the Caribbean, and the involvement of the United States with these nations.
Section IV describes the political, economic, and religious influences at work in nations of South America.

Set the Stage

TEACH PRIMARY SOURCES

U.S. Presidents from both the Republican and Democratic parties have supported NAFTA. The quote from U.S. President George Bush highlights benefits that proponents from both parties felt would come to the trading partners. Ask students to identify what George Bush expected those future benefits to be when he spoke in 1992. (increased prosperity, trade, and new jobs for each country)

CHAPTER 30

North America and South America
1945–PRESENT

I. The United States After World War II
II. Canada and the United States in a New Era
III. Mexico, Central America, and the Caribbean Islands
IV. South America

The last half of the twentieth century was filled with excitement and turmoil for people living in the Americas. Change and growth made the world a very different place from what it had been before World War II.

Free trade—trade without tariffs on goods and services bought and sold between countries—became a major issue in the Western Hemisphere. Countries developed trade agreements, such as the North American Free Trade Agreement (NAFTA) among the United States, Canada, and Mexico. After the agreement was signed in 1992, the three governments passed the agreement in 1993. NAFTA went into effect on January 1, 1994. U.S. President George Bush said in 1992,

❝ By building together the largest free trading region in the world, Mexico, the United States, and Canada are working to ensure that the future will bring increased prosperity, trade, and new jobs for the citizens of each of our countries. ❞

CHAPTER EVENTS

1946 General Juan Perón is elected president of Argentina.

1954 U.S. Supreme Court gives landmark ruling in *Brown* v. *Board of Education of Topeka.*

1959 Fidel Castro controls Cuba after a Communist revolution.

1962 Cuban Missile Crisis occurs between the United States and Cuba.

1945 — **1965**

WORLD EVENTS

1953 Queen Elizabeth II is crowned queen of the British Empire.

1961 Construction of the Berlin Wall in Germany begins.

1966 Cultural Revolution under Mao Zedong begins in China.

Teaching Options

Chapter 30 Resources

REVIEW

Teacher's Resources (TR)
Terms to Know, p. 43
Review History, p. 77
Build Your Skills, p. 111
Chapter Test, pp. 175–176
Concept Builder, p. 246
Flowchart, p. 324
Transparencies 3, 4

ASSESSMENT

Section Reviews, pp. 716, 721, 726, 731
Chapter Review, pp. 732–733
Chapter Test, TR, p. 175–176

ALTERNATIVE ASSESSMENT

Portfolio Project, p. 808
Create Historical Maps, p. T808

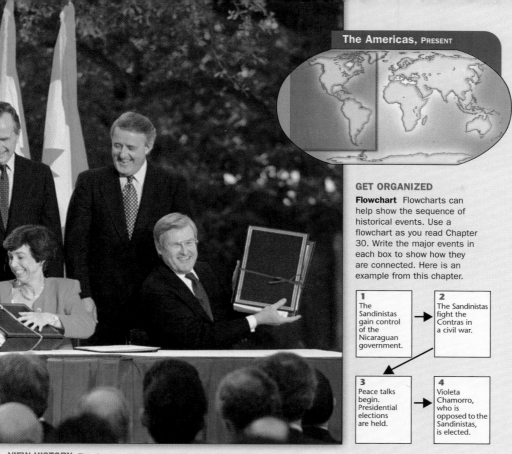

The Americas, PRESENT

GET ORGANIZED

Flowchart Flowcharts can help show the sequence of historical events. Use a flowchart as you read Chapter 30. Write the major events in each box to show how they are connected. Here is an example from this chapter.

1 The Sandinistas gain control of the Nicaraguan government.

→

2 The Sandinistas fight the Contras in a civil war.

3 Peace talks begin. Presidential elections are held.

→

4 Violeta Chamorro, who is opposed to the Sandinistas, is elected.

VIEW HISTORY The three people standing, Mexican President Carlos Salinas de Gortari (left), U.S. President George Bush (center), and Canadian Prime Minister Brian Mulroney (right), and their chief trade representatives (seated) celebrate the signing of the North American Free Trade Agreement (NAFTA) in 1992. The agreement eliminated tariffs among Mexico, the United States, and Canada.
◆ What do the leaders' expressions reveal about their opinions of NAFTA?

1973 Caribbean Community and Common Market (CARICOM) is formed.

1982 Canadians are freed from British Parliament's control.

1992 North American Free Trade Agreement (NAFTA) is signed.

2000 Panama gains control of the Panama Canal.

2001 World Trade Center and the Pentagon are attacked by terrorists.

1985

2005

1971 Aswan High Dam opens in Egypt.

1985 Mikhail Gorbachev becomes leader of the Soviet Union.

1990 Nelson Mandela is freed from prison in South Africa.

1993 European Union (EU) is created.

2003 Operation Iraqi Freedom ends the government of Saddam Hussein.

Chapter Themes

- People, Places, and Environments
- Time, Continuity, and Change
- Individuals, Groups, and Institutions
- Power, Authority, and Governance
- Production, Distribution, and Consumption
- Global Connections
- Civic Ideals and Practices

F Y I

The Passage of NAFTA

The photograph on this page was taken in San Antonio, Texas. The chief trade representatives, Jaime Serra Puche of Mexico, Carla Hills of the United States, and Michael Wilson of Canada are seated in front of the leaders of their respective countries. The NAFTA treaties were signed in San Antonio in 1992 but not ratified by the legislature of each country until a later date.

Chapter Warm-Up

USING THE MAP

Have students find the locator map at the top of page 711, which highlights the Western Hemisphere. The nations of North, Central, and South America and the Caribbean islands are the focus of Chapter 30. Have students use the maps in the Atlas (pp. A3–A4) or Transparencies 3 and 4 to identify and list individual nations in these areas.

VIEW HISTORY

Explain to students that the photograph on pages 710–711 shows a typical pose for an international group, with political figures and their nations' flags. Ask students to identify the flag of each nation. (The flags, from left to right, are those of Mexico, the United States, and Canada.)

◆ **ANSWER** Everyone appears to be smiling, laughing, or clapping. This shows that they all approve of NAFTA.

GET ORGANIZED
Flowchart

Discuss the graphic organizer shown on page 711. Remind students that historical events are often discussed in chronological, or time, order. Have students create flowcharts for major historical events discussed in Chapter 30. Explain to students that some flowcharts may have only three boxes, whereas others may have more than four. Each box on a flowchart represents one of the key steps, or related events.

● TEACH THE TIMELINE

The timeline on pages 710–711 shows events between 1946 and 2003. Ask students to identify the time interval represented by the ovals in the center of the timeline. (intervals of 20 years) Point out that the timeline shows major political and economic events of the modern era.

Activity

Interpret the timeline As students read about the Chapter Events, ask them to discuss each one shown on the timeline as a cause, an effect, or both. For example, the Cuban Missile Crisis was an effect of the U.S. fear of Soviet missiles in Cuba. It was a cause of the Bay of Pigs invasion and of continuing ill will between the United States and Cuba.

Section Summary

In this section, students will learn how society changed in the United States following World War II as the nation faced the Cold War and civil unrest. They will also learn about postwar administrations and about how a terrorist attack in modern times affected the nation.

1 Introduce

Getting Started

Explain to students that although the United States and the Soviet Union were allies during World War II, the countries soon came to distrust each other and were on opposite sides during the Cold War. The clashes resulted from a basic difference in political philosophy between democracy and communism.

TERMS TO KNOW

Ask students to read the terms and definitions on page 712 and find each term in the section. Discuss with students whether they live in a city, suburb, or rural area. Relate these terms to the term *migrant workers*. Ask students in which type of community migrant workers would most likely live. Relate the type of community also to the term *commute*.

You may wish to preview the pronunciations of the following names.

César Chávez (SAY sahr CHAHV es)
al Qaeda (AL KY dah)

ACTIVE READING

Remind students that when they preview material, the goal is to get a "big picture" of what the material is about. Ask students what features they should look for when they preview. (Headings, bold or highlighted words, visuals, and captions are some.) Have students preview Section 1 to find out what topics they expect to be reading about. Make a class list on the board. Ask students to copy the list and to take notes on each topic as they work through the chapter.

Section I

The United States After World War II

Terms to Know

suburb a community at the edge of a city

commute to travel back and forth regularly

migrant worker a person who moves from place to place to find work, usually harvesting crops

domino theory the belief that if one country falls to communism, others nearby will fall, one after the other

impeach to charge a high public official, such as the U.S. President, with a crime

Automobiles contributed to the growth of suburbs in the United States. People could live farther from their jobs and drive back and forth to work.

Chevy puts the purr in performance!

Main Ideas

A. In the 1950s, many Americans moved to communities outside of cities.

B. Cold War fears caused conflicts at home and abroad.

C. Many groups fought for equal rights before the law.

D. Wars, scandals, and terrorism greatly affected the United States in the last part of the twentieth century and the beginning of the twenty-first century.

A. Prosperity After World War II

The United States emerged from World War II economically stronger than ever before. The nations of Europe and Asia suffered great destruction to their cities and major loss of life. Although the United States lost many lives in the war, its cities and the people living in them had been spared.

New Communities

The idea of building houses quickly using mass production made sense to William Levitt, especially because soldiers returning from World War II and their families needed housing quickly. Levitt proceeded to build Levittown, the nation's first planned community. Levittown was located in a **suburb**, or a community at the edge of a city. It had thousands of small, almost identical houses on Long Island, near New York City. Many people began to move out of New York City into this and other suburbs. The trend continued throughout the country. City tax revenues began to decrease as upper- and middle-class people moved from cities to suburbs. Those who remained in the cities tended to be poorer and could not pay as much in taxes to support the city governments. Some city areas began to decline.

Changing Lifestyles

The growth of the suburbs that happened during the administrations of U.S. Presidents Truman and Eisenhower led to a number of changes in American life. As people moved farther from their jobs in the cities, they needed to **commute**, or travel back and forth from home to work. Many people bought cars as well as houses. Most middle-class women living in the suburbs stayed at home, caring for their children and homes. However, many other women worked at jobs outside their homes. The sales of houses and products and services for them and cars and gasoline strengthened the American economy after World War II.

◆ **What were some changes in the United States after World War II?**

Active Reading

PREVIEW

When you preview a section, you get an idea of what is to come. You can skim the section, noting headings in bold type, photos and captions, and special features. As you read this section, find out more about the important topics that you discovered in your preview.

Teaching Options

Section 1 Resources

Teacher's Resources (TR)
Terms to Know, p. 43
Review History, p. 77
Build Your Skills, p. 111
Concept Builder, p. 246
Flowchart, p. 324
Transparency 3

ESL/ELL STRATEGIES

Use Realia In order to help students understand the concept of a suburb such as Levittown, show photographs and maps of the area. Explain that, to answer the need for quick and inexpensive housing, builder William Levitt used a mass production model. He built a complete community and several models of nearly identical houses. He also planned carefully for schools and community centers.

B. Conflicts at Home and Abroad

Despite its prosperity, the United States faced continuing conflicts both at home and abroad. One of its most important concerns during most of the second half of the twentieth century was fear of the spread of communism.

Senator McCarthy

In 1950, U.S. Senator Joseph McCarthy of Wisconsin accused some government workers of being Communist supporters. People who were investigated often had difficulty getting or keeping jobs. For a time, government officials were afraid to criticize McCarthy, because they might also be suspected. In 1954, members of the armed forces who were accused of being Communists were questioned on television by McCarthy. Viewers could see that McCarthy had no real evidence to support his accusations. The U.S. Senate voted to censure, or condemn, McCarthy. The term *McCarthyism* refers to the practice of publicly accusing people of political disloyalty without real evidence.

The Korean Conflict

North Korea, which was under a Communist government, invaded democratic South Korea in 1950. President Truman sent U.S. troops to South Korea's defense. China, which was also under a Communist government, came to North Korea's aid. Negotiations to end the conflict dragged on for two years before an agreement was signed in 1953. The Southeast Asia Treaty Organization (SEATO) was formed the following year to protect nations in that region from conflicts. You will read more about the Korean conflict in Chapter 31.

Crises in Cuba

U.S. President John F. Kennedy, who was elected in 1960, had to face many problems abroad and at home. In 1959, for example, Fidel Castro took control of Cuba after a Communist revolution. At first Castro sought U.S. friendship. However, when he seized foreign property—most of which belonged to the U.S. government and U.S. businesses—the United States stopped trade with Cuba. Castro then turned to the Soviet government for military and economic aid.

Located only 90 miles off the Florida coast, Cuba seemed a big threat to Americans. The U.S. Central Intelligence Agency (CIA) trained about 1,500 Cuban exiles who attempted an invasion at the Bay of Pigs in Cuba in 1961. Exiles are people who are forced to live away from their home country. The invasion failed, and the exiles were captured. The United States had been unsuccessful against a much smaller country.

In 1962, a U.S. spy plane took aerial photographs of Cuba that showed Soviet nuclear missiles aimed at key targets in the United States. President Kennedy demanded that the missiles be removed and announced a blockade against ships going to Cuba.

Many people believed the United States should bomb Cuba. For several days, the world seemed on the verge of a nuclear war. Then, Kennedy negotiated an agreement that included a promise to remove U.S. missiles from Turkey, near the Soviet Union. The Soviet missiles were removed from Cuba. This event became known as the Cuban Missile Crisis.

◆ **How was the Cuban Missile Crisis resolved?**

In 1962, in Miami, Florida, U.S. President Kennedy (left) greeted a leader of the Cuban exiles after they were released from prison in Cuba. The exiles had attempted the invasion at the Bay of Pigs in 1961.

Conflict Resolution

Ask students to define McCarthyism and then to describe how this practice could turn people against each other. Ask them to suggest another possible course of action to take if they suspected someone of disloyalty.

Connection to GEOGRAPHY

The location of Cuba, approximately 90 miles off the coast of Florida, continues to cause problems between Cuba and the United States. Some Cubans have tried to enter the United States illegally. To reach the coast of Florida, many have used unsafe boats, rafts, and inner tubes. Some people have drowned in the attempt.

---

2 Teach

A. Prosperity After World War II

Purpose-Setting Question Why did the United States recover economically after World War II more quickly than nations in Europe and Asia? (It had not suffered the destruction of cities and major loss of life as had nations of Europe and Asia.)

Activity

Create a slogan Advertising is a strong force in a market economy. Ask students to discuss times they or people they know have been influenced by advertising. Have them read the slogan for the car on page 712 and then have students create a slogan for a car that is currently on the market.

◆ **ANSWER** Changes included the growth of suburbs and the need to commute, which resulted in the need for more cars. Also, more women worked at jobs outside of the home.

B. Conflicts at Home and Abroad

Purpose-Setting Question What was the greatest political fear during most of the second half of the twentieth century? (the spread of communism)

Discuss How do you think people would react to Senator Joseph McCarthy's message today? (Possible answer: Less concerned. The collapse of the former Soviet Union has reduced the fear of communism. A new concern, international terrorism, has led to more cooperation between the United States and some of its former Cold War enemies.)

◆ **ANSWER** The Cuban Missile Crisis was resolved when President John Kennedy negotiated with the Soviet Union: the United States would remove missiles from Turkey and the Soviet Union would remove missiles from Cuba. Thus, the threat of nearby missiles was reduced for both the United States and the Soviet Union.

C. The Struggle for Justice

Purpose-Setting Question Ask students to identify groups of people in the United States that felt they were being unfairly treated under the law. (African Americans, women, and migrant workers)

ANALYZE PRIMARY SOURCES

DOCUMENT-BASED QUESTION

Diane Nash grew up in Chicago, Illinois, and, as she admits, did not really notice segregation as it was practiced in the North. In the South, as a student at Fisk University in Nashville, Tennessee, she encountered institutional segregation: African American people were barred from most stores and restaurants and could not attend school with white people. Ask students how they would react to such acts of segregation.

ANSWER She resented African Americans not being allowed to eat in restaurants.

Extend Thurgood Marshall, appointed by President Lyndon Johnson, was the first African American to serve on the Supreme Court. He joined a Supreme Court that issued several far-reaching decisions during the 1960s. As a Justice, Marshall advocated free speech, school desegregation, and the rights of welfare recipients. He also fought against capital punishment. Probably the most famous case he presented to the Court as a lawyer was *Brown* v. *Board of Education of Topeka*. This case, which he won, legally ended the concept of "separate but equal" schools.

Discuss Ask students to evaluate the effectiveness of the tactics of 1960s civil rights leaders, such as Dr. Martin Luther King Jr. and Rosa Parks.

Focus Have students recall what they know about Rosa Parks. Discuss her role as a catalyst—a person who precipitates events. Her refusal to give up a seat on a segregated bus inspired others and led to a long boycott of the Montgomery buses by African American people and white supporters of the cause. Because Rosa Parks had broken the law, she was arrested. When her case went to the Supreme Court, the Court ruled that segregation on the Alabama buses was unconstitutional. This meant Rosa Parks had been unjustly convicted.

C. The Struggle for Justice

In the United States, several groups of people believed that they were being treated unfairly. They began to demand their equal rights before the law.

A Battle for Equal Education

In 1896, the U.S. Supreme Court had established a separate but equal doctrine, or policy, that became widely practiced in the South. African Americans could not enter some stores and restaurants, drink from certain water fountains, or go to schools with white people. Writing about her experiences in the 1950s, Diane Nash, an African American student supporter of basic civil rights, recalled,

> **ANALYZE PRIMARY SOURCES** **DOCUMENT-BASED QUESTION** How did Diane Nash feel about the exclusion of African Americans from restaurants?

❝ I resented not being able to go downtown . . . and have lunch with a friend. Also, when I was downtown, I saw lots of blacks sitting out on the curb or on the ground eating their lunches because they weren't allowed to sit in the restaurants and eat. ❞

In 1954, the U.S. Supreme Court gave a significant ruling in *Brown* v. *Board of Education of Topeka*. Supreme Court Chief Justice Earl Warren stated "that in the field of public education . . . 'separate but equal' has no place." The lawyer who argued the case against segregation, or separation of races, on behalf of the National Association for the Advancement of Colored People (NAACP) was Thurgood Marshall. Marshall became the first African American Supreme Court Justice in 1967.

Civil Rights Protests

In 1955, a woman named Rosa Parks refused to give up her seat on a bus for a white man, as required by law in Montgomery, Alabama, where buses were segregated. Parks was removed from the bus and arrested. On the day of her trial, the African American community took a stand against segregation by refusing to ride the Montgomery buses. The boycott lasted for more than one year. The trial went to the Supreme Court, which ruled that segregated seating on public transportation was unconstitutional and, therefore, not legal.

A man named Dr. Martin Luther King Jr. learned of Mohandas Gandhi of India and his principles of nonviolent protest. King used these principles when he started a civil rights movement in the South, where he was a minister. In 1963, protesters in Birmingham, Alabama, demonstrated for the right of African Americans to use public places. When Dr. King arrived, he was jailed for his role. After he was freed, he organized a march on Washington, D.C., in August 1963. There he spoke powerfully to a crowd of 250,000 people of his dream for true freedom and liberty for all Americans. In 1964, Congress passed the Civil Rights Act, which outlawed segregation in public places. U.S. President Lyndon Johnson supported the civil rights bill.

The next year, Dr. King organized a march in Alabama to encourage African Americans to register to vote. Twenty-five thousand people participated in the march. The Voting Rights Act, which outlawed discrimination—or unfair treatment—in voter registration, was passed in 1965. In 1968, King was asked to lead a protest in Tennessee. A few days before the protest, he was assassinated. King's followers continued to fight for equality, but the U.S. civil rights movement had lost its greatest leader.

Other Groups Seek Equal Rights

Women who supported the cause of African American equality began considering their own lives. Many jobs were closed to women. Often, they

Dr. Martin Luther King Jr. was jailed in Birmingham, Alabama, for leading civil rights demonstrations. His leadership in the civil rights movement encouraged others, including women, to demand equality.

Teaching Options

Research

AVERAGE

Have students investigate information about Dr. Martin Luther King Jr. Ask them to find at least five interesting facts about his life that are not mentioned in the textbook and write a brief report to present to the rest of the class. Remind students to cite their sources for each fact.

CHALLENGE

Have students compare and contrast tactics of nonviolence used by Dr. Martin Luther King Jr. and Mohandas Gandhi. Students should prepare a visual to present to the rest of the class that shows how the men's tactics were similar, how they were different, and how successful they were. You may want to suggest that students use a Venn diagram (TR, p. 323).

were paid less than men for doing the same jobs. Women demonstrated and marched in protest. As a result, more women were elected to political positions, and many others made progress toward higher salaries.

César Chávez led the fight for the rights of **migrant workers** through the Farm Workers Association. Migrant workers move from place to place to find work, usually harvesting crops. In 1965, Chávez joined a strike and persuaded many people to support a grape boycott.

In 1968, the U.S. Congress passed the Indian Civil Rights Act to protect the rights of Native Americans. Some Native Americans organized the American Indian Movement (AIM) that year and protested government regulations and policies. Eventually, Native Americans got back some lands that their ancestors had lived on and that the U.S. government had taken away.

◆ **How did Gandhi's principles shape protests in the United States?**

D. Wars, Scandals, and Terrorism

President Eisenhower sent military support to South Vietnam in Asia, which was fighting Communist North Vietnam. He did so because he believed in the **domino theory**—if one country of a region fell to the Communists, the others would follow as if they were a row of dominoes.

A Nation Divided Over War

The domino theory led four U.S. Presidents—Dwight Eisenhower, John Kennedy, Lyndon Johnson, and Richard Nixon—to send U.S. aid and troops to South Vietnam. The goal was to help South Vietnam fight against a Communist North Vietnamese takeover. In 1964, President Johnson asked the U.S. Congress to grant him the power to send more troops to Vietnam, which Congress granted. Public opinion in the United States was sharply divided.

As the war became more and more unpopular, it became clear that the United States could not continue its involvement. An agreement to stop the fighting was signed in 1973. In 1975, North Vietnam conquered South Vietnam, making the entire country a nation led by a Communist government. You will read more about the Vietnam War in Chapter 31.

A Time of Scandals

Scandal broke in 1972, when five men were caught breaking into the Watergate building in Washington, D.C. The purpose of the break-in was to steal records from the opposing political party. President Richard Nixon was accused of covering up the break-in. He denied any knowledge of the event. He resigned in 1974 to avoid being **impeached**. To impeach means to charge a high public official, such as the U.S. President, with a crime.

Later administrations also faced crisis and controversy. In 1979, during President Jimmy Carter's administration, Americans were taken hostage in Iran, in the Middle East. The crisis lasted for more than one year. The hostages were released the day Ronald Reagan became President in 1981.

In the 1980s, some members of President Reagan's administration secretly arranged the illegal sale of weapons to Iran. They used the money to support a group called the Contras in a revolution against the Sandinistas, a Communist group in power in Nicaragua, in Central America. Congress had already banned U.S. aid to the Contras. When news of these secret deals came out, the deals became known as the Iran-Contra scandal.

In the 1990s, President William Clinton was impeached. Accused of lying under oath, he was later acquitted, or found not guilty.

In addition to leading a grape boycott, César Chávez (shown holding a sign) led a boycott of lettuce.

Discuss Ask students to think about the way changes have been made in other countries they have read about. Help students understand that sometimes change has been very violent. Point out that while violence has sometimes been part of the process for change in the United States, it has been less common.

◆ **ANSWER** Gandhi's principles of nonviolent protest were used by Dr. Martin Luther King Jr. in the civil rights protests and by other groups that wanted change.

D. Wars, Scandals, and Terrorism

Purpose-Setting Question Ask students how many U.S. Presidents found themselves escalating the war in Vietnam? (four Presidents: Eisenhower, Kennedy, Johnson, and Nixon)

Discuss Ask students to evaluate the results of the war in Vietnam. (Students may say the war was a failure because the entire country of Vietnam was eventually taken over by the Communist regime in the north.)

Extend One of the most tragic events associated with student protests over the Vietnam War occurred on May 4, 1960, in Ohio. Four students were killed and nine were wounded by National Guardsmen brought in to keep an antiwar rally under control. Have students investigate the incident, known as the Kent State Massacre, and speculate on how it may have affected continued U.S. participation in the conflict.

Explore Ask students to infer how the Iran hostage crisis during President Jimmy Carter's administration influenced the election of 1980 between Carter and Ronald Reagan. (Possible answer: It encouraged people to elect Reagan because Carter had not been able to resolve the crisis or win the release of the hostages.)

TEACH PRIMARY SOURCES

Discuss with students the result of the terrorist attacks of September 11, 2001, on New York City and Washington, D.C. Point out to students that the two towers of the World Trade Center, each more than 1,350 feet tall, collapsed in the aftermath of the attack and the Pentagon was severely damaged. What does the photograph convey? (Possible answers: the extent of the destruction, the amount of rubble that had to be removed; the intensive efforts of local fire and police units to clear the area and rescue victims)

Focus Ask students how the threat of terrorism since September 11, 2001, has affected life in the United States. What changes have been made in response to the threat of future terrorism? (Possible answer: Travel and access to public places have been more restricted or more closely scrutinized.)

◆ **ANSWER** Operation Enduring Freedom resulted in a change of government in Afghanistan. The ruling Taliban was driven from power and a new government was established.

Section Close

Ask students to discuss how other nations were likely affected by the terrorist attack on the United States. You might point out that some alliances again shifted.

3 Assess

Review Answers

Review History
A. Possible answers: As people began moving to the suburbs, they bought cars and used more gasoline. Also, more women began to work outside of the home.

B. the Bay of Pigs invasion and the Cuban Missile Crisis

C. *Brown* v. *Board of Education of Topeka*

D. President Eisenhower and his administration believed in the domino theory: if one country fell to communism, others would follow. Because of this concern, he began sending military aid to South Vietnam.

Define Terms to Know
suburb, 712; commute, 712; migrant worker, 715; domino theory, 715; impeach, 715

New York City rescue workers and firefighters worked tirelessly at the site of the World Trade Center to rescue victims and clear the area following the terrorist attacks on September 11, 2001.

The Cold War ended with the collapse of the Soviet Union in 1991. By the mid-1990s, wars in the Persian Gulf and Bosnia had ended. In 2001, George W. Bush, son of George Bush, became President.

Troubles in a New Century

The nation's dreams of peace were shattered on September 11, 2001, when terrorists flew jets into New York City's World Trade Center and the Pentagon, near Washington, D.C. Several thousand people died as a result of those crashes and another crash in Pennsylvania.

The prime suspect behind the attacks was Osama bin Laden, the leader of a worldwide group of terrorists called al Qaeda. Bin Laden had hiding places in Afghanistan, a country in central Asia, where the Taliban government protected him. The United States wanted the Taliban to turn bin Laden over to it, but the Taliban refused. On October 7, 2001, the United States began Operation Enduring Freedom, bombing targets in Afghanistan. The Taliban and al Qaeda were driven from power by late 2001. The next year, a new Afghan government began restoring peace to its country. Americans carried on with their lives, but they would never forget the events of September 11, 2001.

In early 2003, Great Britain and the United States formed a coalition military force to fight a war in Iraq. This war, called Operation Iraqi Freedom, began after UN officials searched for weapons of mass destruction—biological, chemical, and nuclear—in Iraq. The United States and Great Britain believed that Iraq's president, Saddam Hussein, and his government had been stockpiling such weapons in violation of UN agreements. When Hussein did not fully cooperate with the UN weapons inspectors, U.S. President George Bush gave Hussein and his two sons 48 hours to leave Iraq. When Hussein refused to leave, the war in Iraq began. The war ended the government of Saddam Hussein. In May 2003, President Bush announced the end of major combat operations in Iraq.

◆ **What was the result of Operation Enduring Freedom?**

Review I

Review History
A. What contributed to the strength of the U.S. economy after World War II?
B. Which two conflicts occurred between Cuba and the United States?
C. What landmark U.S. Supreme Court case ruled against segregation of schools?
D. How did the domino theory relate to U.S. involvement in the Vietnam War?

Define Terms to Know
Define the following terms:
suburb, commute, migrant worker, domino theory, impeach

Critical Thinking
How might Dr. Martin Luther King Jr.'s commitment to civil rights have affected other movements?

Write About Economics
Write a paragraph explaining how equal wages could strengthen the American economy.

Get Organized
FLOWCHART
Think about some of the events in this section. Use a flowchart to show the sequence of what happened during one of the events. For example, show the sequence of U.S. involvement in the Vietnam War.

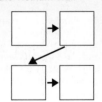

Critical Thinking
Dr. Martin Luther King Jr.'s commitment to civil rights and the tactics he used could have served as an example to others of how to win rights peacefully, without violence.

Write About Economics
Students' paragraphs should make the point that equal wages would raise the wages of the lowest paid workers. The government would have more tax revenue, and wage-earners would have more spending power.

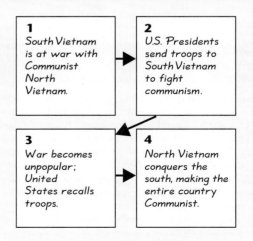

1	2
South Vietnam is at war with Communist North Vietnam.	U.S. Presidents send troops to South Vietnam to fight communism.

3	4
War becomes unpopular; United States recalls troops.	North Vietnam conquers the south, making the entire country Communist.

Build Your Skills

Critical Thinking

EVALUATE INFORMATION

EVALUATE INFORMATION

You have been assigned to write a report or a research paper. How can you find reliable information, or information that is based on facts? You can ask a librarian for help, but you will also want to find information on your own. Your school or local library is a good resource for reliable information. Sources for research include books, encyclopedias, magazines, academic journals, and the Internet.

Here's How

Use the steps below to evaluate information.

1. When using a book, look at it to see if the book has won any awards. Then, check the copyright publication date on the reverse side of the book's title page. Generally, more recent publications are based on the most up-to-date research. Also, check the book's back cover to read about the author and reviews of the book. What credentials does the author bring to the research?

2. When using a magazine, look for academic journals, sometimes called periodicals. They are often published with titles such as *The Journal of Your Subject* or *Your Subject's Quarterly Review.*

Such periodicals usually do not contain advertising. Each article usually offers a brief biography of the person who wrote it. As you do when evaluating books, determine if the author is qualified to write the article.

3. Online Internet sources vary in quality. Look for Web sites with addresses that include the endings for educational institutions (.edu), government agencies (.gov), or organizations (.org). Sources with a .com after their name may not be as reliable. Valid Web sites also give some information about the author and may include details about where the material was published.

Here's Why

Thousands of books and magazines are published every year. Large quantities of data are available online. As you write papers and prepare reports, you will need to wade through a huge quantity of information. Some published material contains bias, or a particular slant on a topic. Other material contains factual errors. When you are working on research, you want objective, accurate sources.

Practice the Skill

At your school or local library, log onto the Internet. Using a search engine, type in a few key words about a topic from Section I. Skim through the list of sites that result. Look for at least three reliable sources. Then, copy the chart on the right onto a sheet of paper. Take notes of the Web addresses, the contents of the Web sites, and why you think the Web sites are or are not reliable. Then, look for books and magazines about the topic and continue adding information to the chart.

Extend the Skill

Use the information in the sources you found to write a brief report about your topic. List your sources at the end of your report.

Apply the Skill

As you read the rest of the chapter, write ideas for other research topics. Select a topic and look for sources on that topic. Then, decide whether or not the sources are reliable.

TOPIC: U.S. CIVIL RIGHTS PROTESTS	
Source (book, magazine, or Web address)	The National Park Service www.cr.nps.gov Click on the search button and type in *civil rights.* Then, click on *Historic Places of the Civil Rights Movement.*
Content	history, photographs, bibliography
Reliability	good, government source intended for education

Teaching Options

RETEACH

Have students use the list of Web site domains from the Teach the Skill section and rank them on a scale of one to five in terms of reliability. Ask students to assign number one to the most reliable source and number five to the least reliable. Then, discuss students' evaluations to see if they all ranked the sites in the same way and why they ranked the sites as they did.

CHALLENGE

Have students find five Web sites from the commercial (.com) domain. Ask them to evaluate each one in terms of its reliability. Then, have students write an explanation of what they discovered as they looked at the sites. Ask them to discuss what makes a commercial site less reliable than others and to indicate which sites would be most useful for preparing a research paper.

EVALUATE INFORMATION

Teach the Skill

Have students recall five or more types of sources that they might consult to find information for a report. Mention Internet Web sites, if students do not. Then, explain that an important task after finding sources is to evaluate the source and the information. To help evaluate information, students might ask themselves these questions:

About the author: Does the author have qualifications that make him or her an expert on the topic? Does the author make biased statements or give opinions presented as facts? Has the author written other material on the topic? Does the author have any firsthand experience with the topic he or she is writing about?

About the timeliness: Is the information current, or is it too old to be relied on? Timeliness is especially important if the topic has to do with a field in which new discoveries are common or in which day-to-day events may make a statement inaccurate.

Inform students that they can use the domain, the last letters of a Web site address, to help evaluate a site. You may wish to list these on a chart and post them in the classroom:

.com—a business or commercial site
.edu—a site connected to education, such as a college or university
.gov—a government site
.mil—a military site
.org—a site connected to a professional or nonprofit organization

Practice the Skill

Students' charts should list at least three reliable Internet sources about a topic from Section 1, as well as several books and magazines. Their evaluations should comment on the reliability of each Web site and print source used.

Extend the Skill

Students' reports should explore the topic and list sources at the end.

Apply the Skill

As students read the rest of Chapter 30, have them list topics that would be interesting and appropriate for research. Later, students should choose a topic and find reliable sources for it.

Section Summary

In this section, students will learn that the United States and Canada have common interests as neighbors and as trading partners, most recently through the North American Free Trade Agreement (NAFTA). They will also learn about Canadian history and some areas of tension between the two countries.

1 Introduce

Getting Started

Have students talk briefly about how neighbors act toward each other, including how both friendly acts and sometimes minor arguments can be part of the relationship. Explain to students that in this section they will learn about relations between the United States and Canada, nations that are neighbors and trading partners on the North American continent.

TERMS TO KNOW

Ask students to read the terms and definitions on page 718 and then find each term in the section. Have them identify which term relates most closely to politics and which most closely to economics. (to politics: *asylum*; to economics: *gross domestic product*)

You may wish to preview the pronunciation of the following names.

Jean Chrétien (ZHAHN KRAY tyan)
Inuit (IHN oo iht)
Quebec (kay BEHK)

ACTIVE READING

Remind students that the terms *compare* and *contrast* refer to finding likenesses and differences between things. As students read Section 2, they should be alert to commonalities between Canada and the United States. They should also identify ways in which the two countries differ. Students can use a Venn diagram (TR, p. 323) or a two-column chart (TR, p. 328) to take notes on how Canada and the United States are alike and different.

Section II
Canada and the United States in a New Era

Terms to Know

asylum a place that gives protection, such as political protection

gross domestic product the value of all goods and services that a country produces during a year

acid rain rain, snow, or hail that contains toxic, or poisonous, chemicals

Main Ideas

A. Canada and the United States share both a border and common goals.

B. The people of Canada have achieved greater self-rule in recent decades.

C. Canada and the United States are strong trade partners but face some economic challenges.

 Active Reading

COMPARE AND CONTRAST
When you compare two things, you show how they are alike. When you contrast things, you show how they differ. As you read this section, look for ways to compare and contrast Canada and the United States.

A. Long-Standing Good Neighbors

Canada and the United States, which share a 4,000 mile border, have a history of being good neighbors and having common goals. For example, the construction of the Saint Lawrence Seaway, which links the Great Lakes and the Atlantic Ocean, was a joint project.

Population Movements Between Countries

Throughout history, four major waves of immigration to Canada from the United States have occurred. The first wave took place at the time of the American Revolution in the 1700s, when people loyal to Great Britain fled the colonies. A second large-scale movement happened in the 1800s, when enslaved Africans escaped from the southern region of the United States for freedom in Canada. The third wave happened in the early 1900s. Many farmers moved north to Canada, where land was being given away to encourage settlement. The fourth movement occurred during the Vietnam War. Many young men who opposed the war went to Canada to live, to escape being forced to fight in the war.

Today, most Canadians live within 200 miles of the border. Approximately 10,000 Canadians a year decide to move to the United States, where average incomes are higher and taxes are lower. This movement concerns the Canadian government. When skilled workers leave Canada for better opportunities elsewhere, Canada loses valuable human resources.

However, more than 200,000 immigrants, on average, move to Canada from other countries every year. As a peaceful nation, Canada often is a place where people seek political **asylum**. Asylum means giving protection, such as protection from unjust governments. More than 30,000 people sought asylum in Canada in 2000.

Do You Remember?
In Chapter 29, you learned about the founding of the United Nations in 1945, after World War II.

Fighting Terrorism

Canada has been a good neighbor to the world, as well as to the United States. Canada was among the first to join the United Nations in 1945 and actively supports UN programs. After the terrorist attacks on the World Trade Center and the Pentagon in 2001, Canada and the United States agreed to cooperate even more on matters of security and information about possible terrorist threats.

Teaching Options

Section 2 Resources

Teacher's Resources (TR)
Terms to Know, p. 43
Review History, p. 77
Build Your Skills, p. 111
Concept Builder, p. 246
Flowchart, p. 324
Transparency 3

ESL/ELL STRATEGIES

Identify Essential Vocabulary Point out the term *gross domestic product* and review its definition. Students may be familiar with the word *gross* in a different context. Explain that in financial terms, *gross* refers to complete or total. So, gross income is a person's total income, before any deductions such as taxes are taken out. Similarly, the gross domestic product is the total value of all goods and services produced during a set period, usually during one year.

Canadian Prime Minister Jean Chrétien (left) and U.S. President George W. Bush agreed to cooperate in the battle against terrorism.

The Smart Border Declaration, signed in December 2001, provided for U.S. National Guard troops to be stationed along the border. Canadian Prime Minister Jean Chrétien said to U.S. President George W. Bush,

❝ This problem of terrorism is a problem that concerns all the nations of the world . . . because it will disrupt the societies around the world. And I think that you know you have the support of Canadians. When you will need us, we will be there. **❞**

◆ **Why do some Canadians move to the United States?**

B. Freedom for Canada

Canada, located in the northern part of North America, has ten provinces and three territories. As part of the British Empire, Canada's symbolic ruler is the British monarch. However, Canada has achieved greater self-rule over time.

British Control Decreases

Canada's self-rule did not result from a dramatic revolution and break with Great Britain as it did for the United States. Instead, over the years, Canadians have pushed for greater freedom by working with the government of Britain. In 1982, Queen Elizabeth II of Great Britain signed the Constitution Act. Until that time, if Canada wanted to make a change in its constitution, approval from the British Parliament was required. Signing this act removed the final control that Britain's Parliament had over Canada. This act also gave rights to Canada's native peoples.

A New Territory

In 1999, the Nanavut Territory was created from the Northwest Territories of Canada. The Nanavut Territory is nearly as large as Alaska and California combined. The land in the new territory is thought to be rich in metal ores and oil. Snow covers the land for most of the year. The Nanavut Territory has 26 major communities, all of them separated by great distances. When the territory was formed, the unemployment rate was more than 30 percent.

ANALYZE PRIMARY SOURCES | **DOCUMENT-BASED QUESTION** Why does the prime minister believe it is necessary to deal with terrorism?

🌐 **Global Connections**

NATIVE PEOPLES
Native peoples around the world have been fighting for their rights over the past 30 years. Inuits have laid claim to 20 percent of the land of Canada. Australian Aborigines have gained the right to vote.

Connection to
GEOGRAPHY ◄- - - - - -

Ask students to locate the lands inhabited by Native Americans within the United States and the Nunavut Territory inhabited primarily by Inuits in Canada. Have students identify a common characteristic of the lands each of these peoples occupies today. (Possible answer: Both inhabit harsh lands within their respective nations.)

F Y I

The Constitution Act of Canada

The Constitution Act of 1982 was preceded by the original Constitution Act of 1867, also known as the British North America Act. This document, which became the backbone of the Canadian Constitution, united the areas of Ontario, Quebec, Nova Scotia, and New Brunswick under the Dominion of Canada and provided for a British-style parliament, house of commons, and senate.

Teach

A. Long-Standing Good Neighbors

Purpose-Setting Question In what ways have Canada and the United States been good neighbors? (They peacefully share a border, there have been few serious disagreements between the two countries, and Canada and the United States have been allies during wartime.)

Do You Remember?
Remind students that they learned that one of the goals of the United Nations was to prevent wars. You may wish to have students read about the United Nations on pages 690–691 of Chapter 29.

ANALYZE PRIMARY SOURCES

DOCUMENT-BASED QUESTION
Prime Minister Jean Chrétien made his remarks at a meeting with President George W. Bush. He cited the fact that the countries are neighbors, and he agreed to cooperate with the United States in fighting terrorism.

ANSWER Terrorism concerns all nations and disrupts societies around the world.

◆ **ANSWER** Some people move from Canada to the United States for economic reasons. They may find jobs with higher pay or they may pay lower taxes.

B. Freedom for Canada

Purpose-Setting Question How did Canada break away from Great Britain? (Its breaking away was gradual and peaceful. Over time, Canadians worked with the British government for greater freedom. There was no dramatic revolution.)

GLOBAL CONNECTIONS

NATIVE PEOPLES Have students identify the Nunavut Territory on the Atlas map (p. A3) or Transparency 3. This huge area is sparsely inhabited by Inuits. The struggles of this group of native peoples compares with the struggles of Native American groups in the United States and with those of the Aborigines in Australia.

Focus Talk with students about the issue of separatism in Canada and the province of Quebec. Explain that cultural factors such as language, religion, and the French influence on the province's history all combine to convince some people that Quebec should be separate from the rest of Canada. Compare Canada's separatist movements with the southern states in the United States that actually did secede at the time of the Civil War. So far, none of the current-day movements in Quebec have had enough voter support to bring about independence.

TEACH PRIMARY SOURCES
Draw students' attention to the photograph of the stop sign on page 720 and have them read the caption. Ask students why signs in Quebec would be written in both the French and English languages. (Many people in Quebec speak French. English is the language spoken by most other Canadians and the language used by government and public education in other provinces.)

◆ **ANSWER** The Constitution Act removed the British Parliament's control over Canada, particularly over Canada's ability to change its own constitution without approval of the British Parliament. It also gave rights to Canada's native peoples.

C. Trade Partners and Economic Challenges

Purpose-Setting Question What are two areas of concern between the United States and Canada? (Economic concerns stem from the effects of NAFTA and the Helms-Burton Act; environmental concerns are over fishing rights and pollution.)

Discuss Ask students why they think the United States and Canada made a free-trade agreement in 1988. (Possible answer: Both countries were expected to benefit from expanded trade.)

In Quebec, Canada, signs are written in both the French and English languages.

Most of Nanavut's citizens are Inuits, a group of native people who have lived in Canada since long before the English and French came. The lives of the Inuits have changed in many ways over the years. Today, for example, most Inuits live in houses made of wood instead of snow, and they tend to use snowmobiles, not dog sleds. However, the Inuits still hunt fish and seals, as their ancestors did.

Quebec Province

Unlike the other provinces in Canada, Quebec is heavily influenced by its French connections, which date back to 1608. That year the explorer Samuel de Champlain started the first permanent French settlement in Quebec. French is Quebec's official language. The dominant religion of Quebec is Roman Catholicism. Most of the rest of Canada is Protestant. Many of Quebec's citizens view themselves as a different society from the rest of Canada. They support a movement that calls for Quebec's separating from Canada and becoming an independent country. Quebec has demanded more independence within Canada. Government leaders have attempted to meet these demands. However, other provinces have protested any efforts that give Quebec different or favored treatment.

Quebec has attempted to secede, or break away, from Canada and form a new nation. In 1995, the province came close to voting for independence, but it did not have enough votes to win.

◆ **What is the significance of the Constitution Act?**

C. Trade Partners and Economic Challenges

Despite an economic recession during most of the 1990s, Canada had one of the highest **gross domestic product** rankings in the world. The gross domestic product is the value of all goods and services that a country produces during a year.

Although the United States and Canada are friendly neighbors, from time to time disagreements do arise. At the end of the twentieth century, two areas of conflict created tensions between Canada and the United States.

Canadian–U.S. Trade

In 2001, Canada exported to foreign countries goods and services worth nearly $275 billion and imported almost $240 billion worth of goods. This gave Canada a favorable trade balance, because it exported more goods than it imported.

Canada and the United States are each other's strongest trade partners. In 2001, for example, 86 percent of Canada's exports went to the United States, and 74 percent of Canada's imported goods came from the United States. The only other country with more than 3 percent of Canada's world trade in both imports and exports is Japan.

North American Free Trade Agreement

In 1988, Canada and the United States made a free-trade agreement that eliminated most tariffs on imports and exports between those two countries. The agreement was modeled after the European free-trade agreement. Mexico joined the agreement in 1992, which was then named the North American Free Trade Agreement (NAFTA). Citizens in all three countries are divided on the benefits of this agreement. You will read more about NAFTA in Section III.

Teaching Options

Connection to LANGUAGES

The French language belongs to the Indo-European family of languages. It is one of the Romance languages, which all developed from Latin roots. French is considered an international language and has been used as the language of diplomacy. Many English words have been adopted from French, for example *cafe* and *prison*.

Cooperative Learning

Have students work together in small groups to brainstorm reasons why Quebec should or should not separate from the rest of Canada. Have each group share their thoughts with the rest of the class. Ask each group to evaluate its own findings as to which side of the issue has more compelling arguments.

The Helms-Burton Act

In 1996, the United States passed an act that limited trade with Cuba. This act was called the Helms-Burton Act. Passage of the Helms-Burton Act upset many nations, including Canada. The Helms-Burton Act placed economic sanctions on countries that trade with Cuba. These sanctions prevent Cuban goods and services from being bought or sold in the United States. European nations, Canada, and Mexico saw the act as a way for the United States to control their foreign policy. Most countries disagree with the U.S. trade sanctions on Cuba. Canada was unhappy with the act because Cuba is one of Canada's important trading partners. Some Canadians blamed the act for high Canadian and Cuban unemployment rates in 1998.

Canadian factory workers prepare salmon to be sold. Fishing is one of Canada's most important industries.

Fishing and Other Environmental Concerns

A second area of disagreement between Canada and the United States has been over fishing, especially of salmon, in both the Atlantic and Pacific Oceans. Canadian fishers charge that the United States is overfishing the waters. Overfishing reduces the number of salmon that return to Canada to reproduce. Because fishing is a major Canadian industry, Canadians take the economic consequences of the loss of salmon and other fish very seriously.

Other issues between Canada and the United States concern the environment. American factory smokestacks cause chemical pollution that contributes to the **acid rain** that falls in northeastern Canada. Acid rain is rain, snow, or hail that contains toxic, or poisonous, chemicals. The United States and Canada have decided to work together to find solutions to these problems.

◆ Why do Canadians disagree with the Helms-Burton Act?

Review II

Review History
A. What is the Smart Border Declaration?
B. How has life changed for the Inuits in the Nanavut Territory?
C. What is a favorable trade balance?

Define Terms to Know
Define the following terms: **asylum, gross domestic product, acid rain**

Critical Thinking
What might happen to Canada if Quebec seceded?

Write About Economics
Write an editorial in favor of or opposed to the Helms-Burton Act. Support your opinion with specific evidence.

Get Organized
FLOWCHART
Think about some of the events in this section. Use a flowchart to show the sequence of what happened during one of the events. For example, use a flowchart to show the sequence of the decrease of British control in Canada.

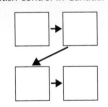

1
Canadians seek greater freedom.

2
Queen Elizabeth signs the Constitution Act of 1982.

3
Great Britain's Parliament can no longer approve or reject changes to Canada's constitution.

4
Great Britain's Parliament no longer controls the government of Canada.

Write About Economics
Student editorials that support the Helms-Burton Act should explain why the United States has the right to impose sanctions on Cuba's trading partners. Editorials that oppose the act should explain why the United States does not have this right.

Activity

Hold a debate Have students prepare to debate this issue: The United States should be able to stop other nations' trade with Cuba. Students can review debate skills on page 419 of the Student Edition.

Discuss Ask students if Canada has the right to be upset with the United States over environmental issues such as fishing and chemical pollution. (Possible answer: Yes, because U.S. actions threaten the Canadian fishing industry and the health of Canadian citizens.)

◆ **ANSWER** The Helms-Burton Act limits Canadian trade with Cuba, one of its major trade partners. The act places economic sanctions on any countries that trade with Cuba.

Section Close
Ask students to evaluate the overall state of the relationship between the United States and Canada, based on what they have read in this section.

3 Assess

Review Answers

Review History
A. The Smart Border Declaration is an agreement between the United States and Canada that allows hundreds of U.S. National Guard troops to be stationed at border crossings.
B. Inuits in the Nunavut Territory live in houses made of wood and use snowmobiles, but they still fish and hunt seals.
C. A favorable trade balance exists when a country exports more goods and services than it imports.

Define Terms to Know
asylum, 718;
gross domestic product, 720;
acid rain, 721

Critical Thinking
Possible answer: If Quebec was to secede, other provinces of Canada might be tempted to do the same. The country would no longer exist as a unified whole, with a common government, currency, and so on. Smaller, independent states might fight among themselves over trade and border issues.

III. Mexico, Central America, and the Caribbean Islands

(pp. 722–726)

Section Summary

In this section, students will learn about the relationship between the United States and Mexico. They will also learn about the governments and economies of nations of Central America, including Nicaragua, Guatemala, El Salvador, Panama, and the smaller island nations in the Caribbean.

1 Introduce

Getting Started

Ask students if they think the relationships between the United States and its neighbors to the south have been as positive as its relationship with Canada, which they have just read about in Section 2. Tell them that they should see if their prediction is correct as they read Section 3.

TERMS TO KNOW

Ask students to read the terms and definitions on page 722 and then find each term in the section. Point out that the prefix *counter-* means "against," or "opposite." Thus, a counterrevolutionary fights against a government set up by a previous revolution. Ask students what they think the word *counterterrorist* refers to. (a person who fights against terrorism) Have them list other words they may be familiar with that begin with the prefix *counter-*.

You may wish to preview the pronunciations of the following names.

Vicente Fox (vee SAYN tay FAHKS)
Nicaragua (nih kuh RAH gwuh)
Manuel Noriega
(mahn WEHL nor ee EHG ah)

ACTIVE READING

Remind students that when they read actively, they are reading with a purpose in mind. Looking for problems and solutions is a good way to be actively involved in reading. Have students identify problems that the nations mentioned in this section have and what has been done to solve the problems. Students might record the information on a problem/solution chart (TR, p. 327).

Mexico, Central America, and the Caribbean Islands

Terms to Know

amnesty a government pardon

counterrevolutionary a person who fights against a government set up by a previous revolution

Main Ideas

A. Mexico and the United States formed a new alliance in the 1990s.

B. Central American nations moved toward democracy.

C. The Caribbean islands made strides toward freedom.

Active Reading

PROBLEMS AND SOLUTIONS
As you read this section, look for the problems that nations in Mexico, Central America, and the Caribbean islands have faced and the ways that they have tried to solve these problems.

Mexican president Vicente Fox

ANALYZE PRIMARY SOURCES

DOCUMENT-BASED QUESTION What might Vicente Fox mean when he says that he had more opportunities than his childhood friends?

A. Mexico and the United States

Like Canada, Mexico shares a border with the United States. This border stretches for more than 2,000 miles along the southern states of Texas, New Mexico, Arizona, and California. About 24 million people from Mexico live in the United States—about two-thirds of the total Latino U.S. population. The overall relationship between the United States and Mexico as good neighbors is similar to the relationship between the United States and Canada.

NAFTA—A New Trade Agreement

The administrations of U.S. President George Bush, Canadian Prime Minister Brian Mulroney, and Mexican President Carlos Salinas de Gortari negotiated the North American Free Trade Agreement (NAFTA). Signed by the three nations' leaders in 1992, NAFTA went into effect on January 1, 1994. The treaty was not the first time the nations had cooperated, but the treaty made the cooperation formal and long lasting.

Vicente Fox was elected president of Mexico for a six-year term in 2000. Fox graduated from a Mexican university. Before becoming president of Mexico, he was president of an American company in Mexico. Fox understands the hopes of Mexican voters. He said,

> **❝**I fully understand the value of opportunities. I grew up on an ejido [ranch] with peasant children and the only difference between myself and my childhood friends lies in the opportunities I received. **❞**

Mexican Workers

During World War II, the United States started a program in which Mexicans came north to help harvest crops. The program was extended until 1964. The work of harvesting crops in the United States benefited both Mexican workers and American farmers. However, the practice set a pattern of both legal and illegal migrant workers. In 1965, a new U.S. program, the Border Industrialization Program, began. Some U.S. factories were established on the Mexican side of the U.S.-Mexican border. Many Mexicans who had been living in the United States went to work at these factories. The Border Industrialization Program continued until NAFTA went into effect in 1994.

Teaching Options

Section 3 Resources

Teacher's Resources (TR)
Terms to Know, p. 43
Review History, p. 77
Build Your Skills, p. 111
Chapter Test, pp. 175–176
Concept Builder, p. 246
Flowchart, p. 324
Transparency 3

Cooperative Learning

Have students work in small groups to create a promotional piece such as a flier advising Mexican workers of the new program for crop harvesting. Students should inform potential workers of the purpose of the program and explain who will benefit and why they will benefit. Then, have groups share their promotional pieces with the rest of the class.

Today, as in the past, Mexican workers are paid much less than American workers. As a result, many Mexicans are willing to work in the United States, where they can earn better wages. Some come legally to the United States. Others willingly take risks to enter the United States illegally. In 1986, U.S. President Ronald Reagan granted **amnesty**—a government pardon—to illegal workers who had been in the country since January 1, 1982. Many Mexicans received amnesty at that time.

Mexican President Vicente Fox visited the United States in September 2001 to speak with U.S. President George W. Bush about easing immigration. The next week, outside terrorists attacked the United States. The issue of immigration was put aside as the United States tightened its border security.

Factories and the Mexican Economy

A second, legal use of Mexico's workforce occurs in factories built along the U.S.-Mexican border. Many U.S. companies build factories in Mexico because of Mexico's lower labor costs. By the mid-1990s, more than 500,000 Mexicans worked in about 2,000 of these factories, assembling television sets and computers and manufacturing auto parts. Critics think that such factories take away jobs from U.S. workers. Supporters see the benefits to both the U.S. and Mexican economies.

Since World War II, Mexico has worked to strengthen its economy. The growth changed Mexico from an agricultural society into an industrial one. The 1970s were particularly strong for Mexico's oil industry. Then in the 1980s, a worldwide recession and other economic factors caused Mexico to fall into debt. In the 1990s, Mexico again headed toward economic recovery.

Concerns Over Illegal Drugs

Mexico is a major pipeline for illegal drugs coming from South American countries, such as Colombia, and entering the United States. Both marijuana and heroin are grown commercially in Mexico. Some experts believe that as much as two-thirds of the illegal drugs sold in the United States come from or through Mexico. Efforts to reduce Mexico's role in the drug trade and drug use in the United States continue on both sides of the border.

◆ How do U.S. factories in Mexico benefit both countries?

A man walks near a factory located along the Rio Grande. The Rio Grande is a natural border between the United States and Mexico.

F Y I

Maquiladoras

Maquiladoras are foreign-owned factories in Mexico. They have existed since the 1960s, and more than half are owned by U.S. firms that were invited into Mexico to provide jobs. However, some of these factories also brought pollution and the exploitation of women and child laborers. NAFTA has led to an increase in employment, better safeguards to protect the environment, and improved working conditions.

Connection to
CIVICS ←

Encourage students to read more about the positive and negative interactions between Mexico and the United States over time. Students can find excellent information in *Somos Mexicanos: Mexican Americans in the United States*, a book that is part of the Historical Case Studies series published by Globe Fearon (see p. T685B).

(see p. T685B).

2 Teach

A. Mexico and the United States

Purpose-Setting Question What official policies have brought workers from Mexico to the United States? (the U.S. program that encouraged workers between World War II and 1964 to harvest crops in the United States; the factories established on both sides of the border under NAFTA; and the Border Industrialization Program)

ANALYZE PRIMARY SOURCES

DOCUMENT-BASED QUESTION
The election of Vicente Fox in 2000 was unusual because he was not a member of the PRI (Partido Revolucionario Institucional). The PRI dominated politics in Mexico for most of the 1900s. Fox was the first Mexican president in 71 years to be elected from another party.

ANSWER Fox may have been able to travel or to receive more schooling. His parents may have had enough money to feed him well and provide quality healthcare.

Explore Ask students to evaluate the strength of the Mexican economy in relation to the pattern of legal and illegal border crossings. Help students understand that some workers are willing to take risks and even face death in crossing from Mexico into the United States illegally for a chance to earn more money. People have died in the hot deserts of the southwestern United States or drowned trying to cross the Rio Grande.

Extend Americans were first introduced to drugs such as morphine, heroine, codeine, and cocaine in the 1800s. Soon after these drugs were introduced for medicinal use, however, it became clear that using them could lead to serious problems such as drug addiction. Many American cities and states (starting with San Francisco in 1875) began passing antidrug laws. In 1906, the Pure Food & Drug Act forced the patent medicine industry to list on the label the presence of certain dangerous drugs. Have students do research on the creation of the U.S. Drug Enforcement Administration (DEA) in 1973.

◆ **ANSWER** They provide jobs for Mexicans and products with lower labor costs.

B. Central America Moves Toward Democracy

Purpose-Setting Question What forms of government were common in Central America before democracy? (Communist governments and dictatorships were common.)

Using the Map
Central America and the Caribbean, 1980–1992

Draw attention to the number of nations in Central America and the Caribbean. Ask students to infer how the relatively large number of countries in a relatively small area of the world may have affected internal and external relationships there. (Possible answer: It may have caused arguments and both internal and external political unrest.)

✔ Map Check
Answers
1. Guatemala, El Salvador, Nicaragua, Panama, and Grenada
2. Guantanamo Bay is located in Cuba.

WHAT IN THE WORLD?
ORGANIZATION OF AMERICAN STATES The OAS is an organization of 35 American countries. The United States has been a member since 1951. The organization was formed to provide self-defense. Aggression against any one member is regarded as aggression against all members. Cuba is officially a member of the OAS, although the other members voted to ban the current Communist government from the organization.

Activity

Hold a debate The United States has continually attempted to support stabilization and democratic governments in Central America. Ask students to debate whether the United States has been helpful or harmful to the region. Students should support their opinions with facts from the section and from additional outside sources.

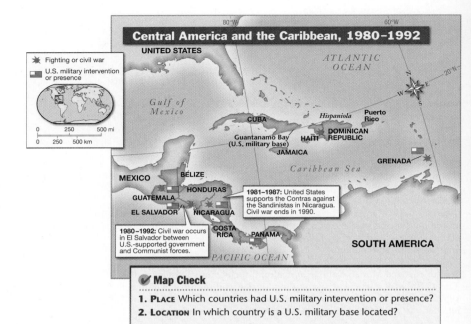

Central America and the Caribbean, 1980–1992

* Fighting or civil war
□ U.S. military intervention or presence

UNITED STATES
ATLANTIC OCEAN
Gulf of Mexico
CUBA
Hispaniola — Puerto Rico
Guantanamo Bay (U.S. military base)
HAITI — DOMINICAN REPUBLIC
JAMAICA
GRENADA
Caribbean Sea
MEXICO
BELIZE
HONDURAS
GUATEMALA
1981–1987: United States supports the Contras against the Sandinistas in Nicaragua. Civil war ends in 1990.
EL SALVADOR — NICARAGUA
1980–1992: Civil war occurs in El Salvador between U.S.-supported government and Communist forces.
COSTA RICA — PANAMA
SOUTH AMERICA
PACIFIC OCEAN

0   250   500 mi
0   250   500 km

✔ Map Check
1. **PLACE** Which countries had U.S. military intervention or presence?
2. **LOCATION** In which country is a U.S. military base located?

B. Central America Moves Toward Democracy

During the late twentieth century, many people in Central American nations fought to rid themselves of harsh dictators and unfair social systems. In some countries, a few powerful families controlled the resources, while most of the people lived in poverty. Revolutions and civil wars increased the problems. In 1987, though, leaders of Nicaragua, Costa Rica, Guatemala, El Salvador, and Honduras signed a regional peace agreement. The Central American Common Market (CACM), developed in 1960, was inactive during the mid-1980s. By the 1990s, the CACM was successfully re-established. The Organization of American States (OAS) also supports the development of Central American countries.

Nicaragua and Guatemala

From 1937 to 1979, Nicaragua was ruled by the Somoza family. In 1979, the corrupt Somoza dictatorship was overthrown by nationalists called Sandinistas. The Sandinistas were led by Daniel Ortega. They began land reform, giving away more than 20 percent of the land that the former dictator had owned. They also began to improve areas such as education, healthcare, and business. The U.S. government, however, worried about Sandinista ties to Cuba and the Soviet Union, both with Communist governments. In 1981, U.S. President Ronald Reagan supported the training of **counterrevolutionaries** called Contras. A counterrevolutionary is someone who fights against a government established by a previous revolution. The United States supported the Contras against the Sandinistas during a deadly civil war in Nicaragua.

Peace talks began in 1987. In the 1990 elections, Violeta Chamorro, who opposed the Sandinistas, was elected president. She was the first woman

What in the World?

ORGANIZATION OF AMERICAN STATES
The Organization of American States (OAS) was founded in 1948. Its purpose is to encourage democracy, understanding, and cooperation among Western Hemisphere nations. The OAS General Assembly meets every year to discuss issues.

Teaching Options

ESL/ELL STRATEGIES

Use Resources Explain to students that treaties, agreements, and groups are often best known by their acronyms. Help students compile a list of acronyms from this section, including NAFTA, OAS, CACM, and CARICOM. Have them use the text to find out what each acronym stands for and then to use other resources to find one fact not mentioned in the text about each. Encourage students to add other examples to the list of acronyms as they read.

Meet Individual Needs:
LOGICAL/MATHEMATICAL

Have students use the scale of miles on the map on page 724 to find the approximate distance of each nation shown from the southern tip of Florida. If students get different answers, have them explain how they found each answer. Help students understand that there may be more than one correct answer, depending on the end points of the distance being measured.

president of a Central American nation. During the 1990s, Nicaragua's economy grew as a result of increased exports. However, the unemployment rate remained high, and many people were still poor. Nicaragua is working toward a stronger economy for its future.

Like Nicaragua, Guatemala wanted a stable government. In 1954, rebels, with the support of the U.S. government, overthrew the Communist-supported government in Guatemala. During 36 years of civil war, more than 140,000 people were killed or disappeared. Many people went to Mexico to escape the violence. Guatemala has continued to be a nation of political unrest. In 1998, a Guatemalan bishop and human rights activist was murdered. Later that year, a busload of U.S. college students was attacked.

To support a stronger economy, the Guatemalan government has encouraged the nation to export a variety of products. However, Guatemala's economy is weakened. That is a result of debt it owes foreign nations, such as the United States, and because Guatemala imports more than it exports.

El Salvador and Panama

U.S. President Ronald Reagan focused attention on the nation of El Salvador during the early 1980s. A military force had overthrown the government there. The United States sent both military and financial assistance to the anti-Communist forces in El Salvador. After many years of civil war, peace came to the country in 1992 and reforms followed.

The civil war caused a very weak economy in El Salvador. The country also depended largely on one export, coffee. El Salvador receives foreign economic aid, but the country's economy continues to struggle.

The United States has had an interest in Panama since the building of the Panama Canal. A treaty signed in 1977 allowed the Panamanians to assume control of the canal over time. The canal remained under U.S. control until the end of 1999.

In 1989, U.S. troops invaded Panama to overthrow the president of the country, Manuel Noriega. They took him to the United States to stand trial for drug trafficking. In 1999, Panama elected its first woman president, Mireya Moscoso.

Spotlight on Geography

NATURAL DISASTERS
One of the most uncontrollable forces that Central America struggles against is the climate. The region has been hit by many hurricanes and earthquakes. In 1998, Hurricane Mitch destroyed more than $5 billion worth of property and took many lives.

Do You Remember?
In Chapter 25, you learned about the building of the Panama Canal in the early years of the twentieth century.

On January 1, 2000, control of the Panama Canal was officially transferred to Panama. The transfer ceremony, which occurred on December 14, 1999, is shown in this photograph.

Research

AVERAGE
Have students conduct research on the issues around President Reagan's support of the Contras in Nicaragua. Then have them write a short essay explaining whether they think President Ronald Reagan should have supported the Contras in Nicaragua against the wishes of the U.S. Congress. Students should state their opinion and then defend it with facts from research.

CHALLENGE
Have students take the role of President Reagan and write a persuasive speech to convince people in the United States that he was right in sending aid to the Contras in Nicaragua, in spite of the wishes of Congress. Students should use research to find out what aid was sent and what the results were, in order to make the case for this involvement.

SPOTLIGHT ON GEOGRAPHY

NATURAL DISASTERS Hurricanes and earthquakes have caused much death and destruction in Central America and the Caribbean over the years. For example, Hurricane Mitch in 1998 killed more than 11,000 people in Central America. Natural disasters in these areas tend to cause more destruction and loss of life than similar occurrences in the United States because buildings are not as stable and because of a lack of economic and political preparedness. Also, land-use restrictions may be ignored by local builders.

Discuss Remind students of the U.S. government's response to communism during the administrations of Eisenhower, Kennedy, and Johnson. Then, discuss why President Ronald Reagan's involvement with the Contras in Nicaragua seemed to many in the United States to be a logical next step.

Extend When the people of Panama declared themselves independent from Colombia, then-U.S. President Theodore Roosevelt quickly recognized Panama's independence and negotiated for a piece of land on which to build a canal. After much difficulty, the United States did succeed in building the Panama Canal, which was leased from Panama until the end of 1999. In 1989, then-President George Bush sent troops to Panama to capture the ruler of the country, Manuel Noriega. Noriega had ruled as a dictator and was involved in the drug trade.

Ask students why they think many people in the United States were reluctant to turn over the Panama Canal to Panama in 1999. (Possible answers: The United States had overcome many difficulties to build the canal. Political instability in Panama caused fear that the canal would be more susceptible to attack under Panama's control.)

Do You Remember?
Have students review the information about the building of the Panama Canal in Chapter 25. Ask them what hardships were overcome to build it. Point out that the U.S. feeling of entitlement for controlling this canal, which they had built, was similar to Great Britain's long involvement with, and feelings about, the Suez Canal.

C. The Caribbean Islands

Purpose-Setting Question What do many Caribbean islands' economies depend on? (tourism)

Explore Have students list at least ten island nations of the Caribbean. Then, assign pairs of students one nation and have them find out at least two facts about their assigned nation. Be sure students include Puerto Rico, although it is not a totally independent political entity.

Then & Now

PUERTO RICO Puerto Rico is a commonwealth of the United States, with international policy governed by the U.S. Congress. Most federal laws apply to Puerto Rico as if it were a state, but people there cannot vote in federal elections and do not pay federal taxes. Many Puerto Ricans want complete independence from the United States. Others want Puerto Rico to become a state. Still others want to maintain the current status. This last group carried the vote in referendums held in 1967, 1993, and 1998.

◆ **ANSWER** European nations

Section Close

Have students complete the problem/solution chart (TR, p. 327) and discuss what they think are the main problems facing Mexico, Central America, and the Caribbean islands today.

3 Assess

Review Answers

Review History

A. Mexicans work in companies in the United States and also in U.S. companies located in Mexico.

B. Nicaragua, Costa Rica, Guatemala, El Salvador, and Honduras

C. U.S. troops went to Haiti to restore the elected president to his office.

Define Terms to Know
amnesty, 723; counterrevolutionary, 724

T726 ◆ UNIT 8

Then & Now

PUERTO RICO
Puerto Rico became a U.S. possession following the Spanish-American War in 1898.

Today, there are almost 4 million people living in Puerto Rico and nearly 3 million Puerto Ricans living on the U.S. mainland. Some people believe this island could become the fifty-first state.

Panama's economy differs from those of other Latin American countries. Most of its gross domestic product is created by services, not agricultural and industrial products. The government encourages services, including tourism, that promote an awareness and support of the environment. The government also invests in improved rail and road systems.

◆ **Why was the election of Violeta Chamorro significant?**

C. The Caribbean Islands

The West Indies curve in an arc from Venezuela in South America to Florida. The largest islands are Cuba, Hispaniola, Jamaica, and Puerto Rico. Europeans colonized many of the islands soon after they reached the Americas. Until the late 1970s, many islands were controlled by nations in Europe.

Young Nations

Between 1962 and 1983, nine island nations became independent. Many island economies depend on tourism. The area wants to develop economically and politically. In the past, the United States has intervened many times. In 1983, U.S. troops went to Grenada to put down a Communist-led overthrow attempt. At times, U.S. military governments have ruled Haiti and the Dominican Republic, which share the island of Hispaniola. The United States intervened in Haiti to restore the elected president to his office in 1994.

Economic Challenges

In 1973, the Caribbean Community and Common Market (CARICOM) was formed. Members seek cooperation in areas of education, health, science, and economics. They hope to expand the area's economy, which has historically been based on crops such as sugar cane and bananas. This made the agricultural industry dependent on only a few cash crops.

◆ **Who controlled many Caribbean islands before their independence?**

Review III

Review History
A. In what two ways does the Mexican workforce interact with U.S. companies?
B. Which Central American countries have signed a regional peace agreement?
C. Why did U.S. troops go to Haiti in 1994?

Define Terms
Define the following terms: **amnesty, counterrevolutionary**

Critical Thinking
In what ways might a revolution or civil war affect a country's economy?

Write About Economics
Write a paragraph about the advantages of free trade. Then, write another paragraph about the disadvantages of free trade.

Get Organized
FLOWCHART
Think about some of the events in this section. Use a flowchart to show the sequence of what happened during one of the events. For example, use a flowchart to show the sequence of Mexico's economy since World War II.

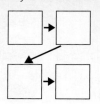

726   UNIT 8   ◆   The World Today

Critical Thinking
A revolution or civil war may affect shipping and transportation of goods around the country. The war may keep people from working and may cripple industries. Other countries may refuse to trade with a new government because of political differences.

Write About Economics
Students' paragraphs should use specific examples to show the advantages and disadvantages of free trade.

1 Since World War II, Mexico has worked to strengthen its economy.

2 Mexico has become a more industrialized society.

3 1980s worldwide recession and other factors caused Mexico to fall into debt.

4 Beginning in the 1990s, Mexico has moved toward economic recovery.

Points *of* View

Debate Over NAFTA

The North American Free Trade Agreement (NAFTA) has been in effect since 1994. Even so, politicians from each of the three North American countries have continued to debate whether the agreement benefits their nation.

The NAFTA agreement removes most tariffs and other trade barriers among Canada, Mexico, and the United States. NAFTA also gives Canadian and U.S. companies greater access to Mexican markets in banking, advertising, insurance, communications, and trucking.

Some of the greatest debate over NAFTA occurred before the agreement went into effect in 1994. U.S. President Bill Clinton wanted people in the United States to support NAFTA. He stressed the benefits that free trade could bring to the nation. Other political leaders disagreed. Representative Richard Gephardt, a leader in the U.S. House of Representatives, was and continues to be a strong critic of NAFTA.

Trucks carrying goods are regularly inspected at the border of the United States and Mexico.

> "The truth of our age is this–and must be this: Open and competitive commerce will enrich us as a nation.... And so I say to you in the face of all the pressures to do the reverse, we must compete, not retreat."
>
> —U.S. President Bill Clinton, February 26, 1993

> "If we just push trade at any cost, ... and we don't pay attention to people's ... real concerns about trade [such as] labor rights ... the environment ... human rights ... displaced workers from trade treaties, we're not going to deal with the human equation in trade–then trade is going to get a bad name, and a very important process in the furtherance of human rights [for] the whole world will go by the wayside."
>
> —U.S. Representative Richard Gephardt, April 26, 2001

ANALYZE PRIMARY SOURCES

DOCUMENT-BASED QUESTIONS

1. What does U.S. President Bill Clinton see as the benefit of NAFTA for the United States?

2. What does U.S. Representative Richard Gephardt think are people's real concerns about trade?

3. **Critical Thinking** What do you think is President Clinton's or Representative Gephardt's strongest argument for his point of view?

Teaching Options

Take a Stand

Divide the class into two groups. Have each group review the material about NAFTA on page 727 and in Sections 2 and 3 to draw conclusions about the benefits and drawbacks of NAFTA. Then, have one group prepare to debate the affirmative side and one to debate the negative side of the NAFTA issue. Suggest students review debating techniques on page 419.

LINK to TODAY

Have students work in small groups to brainstorm a list of benefits and drawbacks to the live interview as a medium for expressing opinions. (Possible answers: **Beneficial:** They are timely and likely to produce sincere, emotional responses. **Detrimental:** The interviewee may not have had time to think through her or his response.)

Points *of* View

DEBATE OVER NAFTA

Teach the Topic

Both before its passage in late 1993 and since then, people have debated the benefits of NAFTA. The goals, from the viewpoint of those in the United States who fought for it, were to open the borders of Western Hemisphere countries in order to increase trade and to make wages and industry practices more standard. A major concern of those who opposed NAFTA in the United States was that it would become easier for industry to set up jobs in Canada or Mexico, thus decreasing job opportunities for U.S. citizens.

In this feature, then-President Bill Clinton's quotation is taken from a more lengthy presidential statement on NAFTA; Representative Richard Gephardt's quotation is taken from an interview. Presidential statements are typically handed in print to the press, and may then be reported on television and in newspapers. Interviews, unless the entire interview is made available in print, have the potential for people to be misheard and later misquoted.

Compare and Contrast Points of View

The debate over NAFTA has been primarily economic. Neither the major disasters nor the full benefits have occurred as proponents and opponents predicted.

Have students state in their own words both President Clinton's and Representative Gephardt's points of view about the economic benefits and drawbacks. Besides economics, what other areas does Gephardt say that people are concerned about?

ANALYZE PRIMARY SOURCES

DOCUMENT-BASED QUESTION

1. He feels that NAFTA will result in competitive trade and enrich the United States as a nation.
2. Representative Gephardt believes people are concerned more about labor rights, the environment, and human rights, rather than economic issues.
3. Possible answers: **Clinton:** Competing in this way will "enrich us as a nation." **Gephardt:** Trade will get a bad name, and trade at any cost will lead to abuse of workers' rights.

IV. South America

(pp. 728–731)

Section Summary

In this section, students will learn about the economic and political climates of South America. They will also learn about the influence of the Roman Catholic Church there.

Getting Started

Ask students what they think it would be like to wake up one morning to a country that had an entirely different government. People who had power and authority would have lost everything, and entirely different people would now be in charge. Discuss the challenges that people would face in this situation. Explain to students that many countries in South America experienced these kinds of government changes.

TERMS TO KNOW

Ask students to read the terms and definitions on page 728 and then find each term in the section. You might wish to draw attention to the suffix *-ize* and point out that it can be added to adjectives to make new words, usually verbs, which denote action or activity. For example, the adjective *private* has been changed to the verb *privatize* with the suffix *-ize*. Ask students to list other words they know ending with the suffix *-ize* and discuss each one. (other words include *capitalize, finalize, specialize*)

You may wish to preview the pronunciations of the following names.

Salvadore Allende
(sahl vah TOR ahl YEHN day)

ACTIVE READING

Remind students that when they look for a main idea, they should look for a very important point that a writer wants them to understand. Details support, or tell more about, a main idea. To identify main ideas in this textbook, students can look at the listing at the beginning of each section and at the major headings in the section. Details can be found within the section.

Terms to Know

privatize to change from public to private control

El Niño a warm current in the Pacific Ocean, along the west coast of South America

Main Ideas

A. The countries of South America have experienced political and economic turmoil.

B. Economies of some nations in South America have demonstrated progress.

C. The Roman Catholic Church influences society in South America.

Active Reading

MAIN IDEAS AND SUPPORTING DETAILS
As you read this section, look for the main ideas and the details that support them. For example, find at least two supporting details for the main idea "Climate of Unrest."

A. Climate of Unrest

South America, like the rest of Latin America, has endured periods of turmoil and unrest. Revolutions and reforms against repressive governments have occurred across the region, often with violent results. Rapid population growth and huge increases in urban population have strained many countries' abilities to care for their people. By the end of the 1990s, many of these countries were also burdened by enormous debt and inflation.

Argentina

In 1946, General Juan Perón was elected president of Argentina. He and his wife Eva brought about reforms that were popular with working-class people, such as higher wages and stronger labor unions. However, they also denied people the freedom of speech and of the press. In addition, they drove the country into debt. Perón went into exile in Spain in 1955 after the military took control of the government. Military governments then controlled Argentina for years.

Eva Perón was the unofficial minister of health and labor for Argentina during her husband's first presidency. She helped women in Argentina win the right to vote.

Perón was elected president again on his return to Argentina in 1973, but died ten months later in 1974. The vice president, his second wife Isabel, became president. She was the world's first woman president. Isabel Perón stayed in power for two years. The country remained in political turmoil. In 1976, a group of military officers overthrew Perón. During the military rule, in the late 1970s, thousands of people were imprisoned without trial, tortured, or killed. To this day in the capital city, Buenos Aires, the Mothers of the Plaza de Mayo gather. These women march every Thursday in the plaza, demanding to know what happened to their children who were taken away.

In 1982, Argentina seized the Falkland Islands in the Atlantic Ocean. Both Great Britain and Argentina claimed the islands, which Argentina called the Malvinas. Britain had occupied the islands since 1833. The brief, undeclared war ended with a British victory. This defeat weakened Argentina's military power.

In 1983, after democratic elections, democracy returned. Argentina's economic problems continued to grow. The economy nearly collapsed in 1989, but the country's economy grew again in the 1990s. President Carlos Menem **privatized** businesses that had been state-owned for five decades by placing them in private control. However, at the beginning of the twenty-first century, Argentina was again in economic turmoil, partly due to its huge foreign debt and high unemployment rate.

Teaching Options

Section 4 Resources

Teacher's Resources (TR)
Terms to Know, p. 43
Review History, p. 77
Build Your Skills, p. 111
Chapter Test, pp. 175–176
Concept Builder, p. 246
Flowchart, p. 324
Transparency 4

Test Taking

Point out that essay questions on tests often require students to explain or describe main ideas. To fully explain or describe, they must provide details. Thus, identifying main ideas and details as they read is an important skill that will help them on tests. Have them practice the skill by finding the main ideas and details in this section.

Chile

The 1970s were a difficult time for Chile. In 1970, the Socialist Salvador Allende Gossens was elected president. Allende forced the breakup of many estates and raised workers' wages. His reforms were popular with workers but upset wealthier people who feared losing their property. The economy suffered because of declining productivity, food shortages, and inflation. The government printed more money for its needs.

In 1973, with the assistance of the U.S. State Department and the CIA, General Augusto Pinochet and his troops seized power. President Allende was killed during the attack. General Pinochet became president. Under his harsh government, many civil rights were suspended. He disbanded the country's legislature and outlawed political parties. Many people were killed or declared missing. They are still known as The Disappeared.

Allende's niece, Isabel, is a writer who now lives in North America. When asked in an interview about the events of 1973, she said,

> **❝** I think the events of 1973 marked my generation and divided the country in Chile. For 25 years, people have tried to silence the truth and to be cautious not to provoke any upheaval. . . . My life was shaped by that event because we had to leave my country. **❞**

By the late 1970s and during most of the 1980s, inflation had dropped, but unemployment increased dramatically. By the late 1980s, however, economic growth caused Chile to be one of South America's most prosperous nations.

In the 1988 national election, Pinochet was the only name on the ballot. Many people simply wrote "no" on the ballots. More than 50 percent of the voters opposed Pinochet. The next year free elections were held and Patricio Aylwin was elected president. During Aylwin's administration, the economy grew. Eduardo Frei Ruiz-Tagle followed Aylwin as Chile's president in 1994, and Chile continued its economic growth throughout the 1990s. Even when Chile faced issues of poverty and pollution during the 1990s, the nation's economy remained one of the strongest in South America.

◆ **Why were some Chileans upset over President Allende's reforms?**

B. Economic and Political Struggles

Most South American nations are struggling to gain the financial security enjoyed by many people in North America and Europe. You have just learned about Chile's political and economic instability followed by its political and economic success. These kinds of struggles have happened in other South American countries as well. Individual countries such as Brazil, Colombia, and Peru illustrate some economic successes.

ANALYZE PRIMARY SOURCES

DOCUMENT-BASED QUESTION What does Isabel Allende see as the results of the government overthrow in Chile?

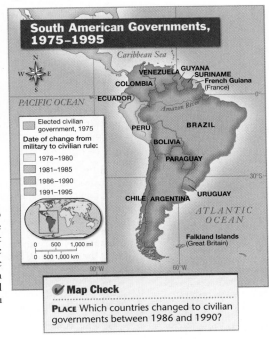

South American Governments, 1975–1995

Caribbean Sea
VENEZUELA
GUYANA
SURINAME
French Guiana (France)
COLOMBIA
PACIFIC OCEAN
ECUADOR
Amazon River
PERU
BRAZIL
BOLIVIA
PARAGUAY
CHILE
ARGENTINA
URUGUAY
ATLANTIC OCEAN
Falkland Islands (Great Britain)

Elected civilian government, 1975
Date of change from military to civilian rule:
1976–1980
1981–1985
1986–1990
1991–1995

0   500   1,000 mi
0   500 1,000 km

✔ **Map Check**

PLACE Which countries changed to civilian governments between 1986 and 1990?

A. Climate of Unrest

Purpose-Setting Question Why was General Juan Perón popular with the working-class people in Argentina? (He brought about reforms such as higher wages and stronger labor unions.)

Explore Explain to students that Eva Perón was also called Evita. She was her husband's contact with labor unions when he was president of Argentina. Perón tried to run for vice president herself in 1951 but was blocked by the military because she was a woman. Students may view the film *Evita* to learn more about her.

ANALYZE PRIMARY SOURCES

DOCUMENT-BASED QUESTION

Isabel Allende was born in Peru and raised in Chile. She worked as a journalist in Chile until the military takeover in 1973. Many of her books have been translated into English.

ANSWER She thinks it led people to be overly cautious.

Using the Map

South American Governments, 1975–1995

Ask students to identify the two areas of South America that were still controlled by European powers in 1995 and have them explain how this is shown on the map. (French Guiana and the Falkland Islands are shown in upper and lowercase letters; parentheses show the controlling nation.)

✔ **Map Check**

Answer Chile and Suriname

◆ **ANSWER** because his reforms favored workers

B. Economic and Political Struggles

Purpose-Setting Question What kinds of struggles were common to many South American nations? (struggles to gain economic and political stability)

Writing

AVERAGE

Remind students that Isabel Allende was forced to leave her country when Augusto Pinochet and his troops seized power. Have students use the information from the text and from Allende's quotation to write a newspaper article that answers the Five *W*s questions. Students might use a Five *W*s chart (TR, p. 326) to take notes on the information they find.

CHALLENGE

Have students use information from the text and from her quotation to write a speech Isabel Allende might have made about her own life if she were to return to Chile. Remind students that a speech is often used to motivate or inform individuals. You may want to have students read speeches by some well-known individuals before they write their own speeches.

Review with students the meaning of the words *import* and *export*. (Something that is imported is brought into a country, having been purchased from another country; exports are goods or services sold outside of the country.)

 Chart Check

Answer Brazil exports iron ore.

Discuss Have students use information in the chart and from the text to identify some of Brazil's important industries and export products. (**Industries:** automobile, shipbuilding, steel, machinery; **Exports:** iron ore, soybean bran, orange juice, footwear)

Activity

Research Have students investigate illegal drug trafficking that affects your state or community. How do drugs enter the United States? How do they come into your community? If possible, invite a local law enforcement officer to visit the class and have him or her explain the causes and effects of this illegal trade. Before the visit, have students prepare a list of questions they would like to discuss.

Then & Now

AMAZON RAIN FORESTS Ask students what a rain forest is and what the effect of cutting down rain forests is. (Rain forests are heavily wooded areas of tall trees that grow in warm tropical climates near the equator. Cutting down rain forests destroys plants and animals and disrupts the balance in the ecosystem. Rain forests have economic value in natural resources, including fibers, nuts, fruits, and chicle—an ingredient once used in chewing gum).

◆ **ANSWER** Peru and Brazil have both tried to develop industries that would provide them with products to export.

Brazil's Imports and Exports, 2000

	Imports	Exports
Amount	$55.8 billion	$55.1 billion
Products	Chemical products, oil, electricity	Iron ore, soybean bran, orange juice, footwear
Trading Partners	United States, Argentina, Germany	United States, Argentina, Germany

✔ Chart Check

Which resource that is mined does Brazil export?

Then & Now

AMAZON RAIN FORESTS
In the 1970s and 1980s, many of the rain forests in Brazil and Peru were cut down to provide people with wood, farmland, and pastures for cattle. However, by the 1990s, the number of rain forests being cut down decreased.

Today, the Amazon region in Brazil and Peru includes national parks and forests.

Brazil

Brazil is the largest country in South America. It is the world's fifth most populated country. In fact, more than half of South America's people live in Brazil. Eighty percent of Brazilians live within 200 miles of the Atlantic Ocean. In contrast, only 7 percent live in the Amazon region, which includes the rain forests. Most Brazilians live in the cities.

Brazil began a period of freedom after a dictatorship ended in 1945. Foreign companies moved in to build factories. Brazil's presidents encouraged automobile production, shipbuilding, and steel and machinery industries, so that Brazil would be less dependent on imports. Roads and power plants were built.

The 1960s and 1970s were very prosperous times for Brazil, although many people who moved to the cities looking for work were poor. The military took over the government from 1964 until 1985. In 1985, civilian government resumed. During the 1990s, government-run industries were privatized, and the economy improved. Brazil has been able to keep its economy strong.

Colombia

Although Colombia has often been close to civil war, it remains economically successful. The nation had a high economic growth rate during the last two decades of the twentieth century.

Colombia has experienced difficulties, however, with both drug dealers and guerrillas. The guerrillas are usually volunteer soldiers, not members of the army, who are skillful at making surprise raids. Drug trafficking is run in Colombia by organizations called drug cartels. Drug cartels supply many of the illegal drugs that are imported to countries in which there is a demand for illegal drugs.

Colombia produces more than 90 percent of the world's supply of emeralds. In addition, it is the largest gold producer in South America and has large reserves of oil and coal deposits. Colombia is second only to Brazil in coffee production. In addition to crops such as sugar cane and bananas, Colombia is a leading exporter of cut flowers.

Peru

In 1994, Peru had one of the highest economic growth rates in the world. Many businesses had been privatized. Unfortunately, as Peru continued to face political upheavals, the rapid growth rate of the early 1990s did not continue.

Although the largest gold mine in South America is in Peru, copper and zinc are the exports that earn the most money. Major crops for export include cotton, sugar, coffee, and rice. In the 1960s, Peru was the world's largest fishing nation. This industry declined because of the effects of **El Niño**, a warm ocean current along the west coast of South America. The warm waters that the weather system causes made the fish leave the area. In the 1990s, the industry recovered. Like Brazil, Peru has rain forests in the Amazon region. Brazil and Peru are trying to find a balance between using the rain forest land for agricultural and industrial purposes and maintaining the rain forests as they are naturally.

◆ **What strategy did both Peru and Brazil use to help their economies?**

Teaching Options

Connection to MATH ◁- - - - -

Have students use the information from the chart on page 730 to calculate the difference between the value of Brazil's imports and the value of its exports in 2000. Then, ask students to state whether Brazil had a favorable or unfavorable balance of trade in that year. (Imports were about $7 million greater so Brazil had an unfavorable balance of trade in 2000.)

ESL/ELL STRATEGIES

Identify Key Phrases Everyday expressions and figures of speech may be unfamiliar to students whose first language is not English. Draw attention to the following and discuss their meanings:

- "at the brink"
- "second only to"
- "face political upheaval"

C. Latin Americans and Religion

The Roman Catholic Church has long been the dominant religion in both Central and South America. In many Latin American countries, more than 90 percent of the people are Roman Catholics. During the early days of European colonization, Spain and Portugal sent missionaries, as well as armies, to their colonies. Today, the Roman Catholic Church is still a powerful force in this part of the world.

The Pope Visits

Never before had a pope come to South America. Crowds swarmed to see Pope Paul VI when he visited South America in 1968. His trip marked the beginning of a new excitement within the Roman Catholic Church. From 1979 until 1999, Pope John Paul II made 13 trips to Mexico and Central and South America. He visited nearly every predominately Roman Catholic nation and was well received almost everywhere.

During a visit to Peru in 1985, Pope John Paul II wore a Peruvian shawl as he greeted people.

Liberation Theology

The Church in Latin America is known for liberation theology. *Liberation* means "to set something free." Theology is the study of religion. Liberation theology stresses the need to help the poor by reforming politics and governments that hold people back. Roman Catholic leaders wanted to look at Christianity as the religion of the poor. Groups of Christians help others get basic needs such as food, water, and electricity. While many people have opposed the idea of liberation theology, many Roman Catholic leaders still preach this theology.

◆ **When did a pope first visit South America?**

Review IV

Review History
A. What were the effects of the war in the Falkland Islands?
B. What are some of Colombia's natural resources and products?
C. Why is the Roman Catholic Church so important in South America?

Define Terms to Know
Define the following terms:
privatize, El Niño

Critical Thinking
Why do you think countries with a variety of products might have stronger economies?

Write About Economics
Write a paragraph about some effects of privatizing businesses in South American countries.

Get Organized
FLOWCHART
Think about some of the events in this section. Use a flowchart to show the sequence of what happened during one of the events. For example, use a flowchart to show the sequence of Brazil's economic progress.

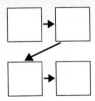

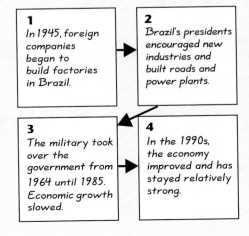

1
In 1945, foreign companies began to build factories in Brazil.

2
Brazil's presidents encouraged new industries and built roads and power plants.

3
The military took over the government from 1964 until 1985. Economic growth slowed.

4
In the 1990s, the economy improved and has stayed relatively strong.

Critical Thinking
Possible answer: If one product does poorly, there are still others that the country can depend on.

Write About Economics
Students' paragraphs should include both political and economic effects of privatization. In some cases, such as in Argentina after President Menem privatized businesses, the economy grew. Brazil and Peru have privatized businesses, too, and their economies have improved.

C. Latin Americans and Religion

Purpose-Setting Question
What is the dominant religion in South America and how was it spread? (Roman Catholicism; it was spread by missionaries from Spain and Portugal during the period of European colonization.)

Explore Help students understand the far-reaching effects of the separation of religion and politics in the United States. Explain that, to some people, this separation has had some controversial effects, such as banning prayer in public schools. In general, however, the policy has safeguarded the public in the United States from any one religion becoming too powerful in politics.

Discuss Ask students to explain liberation theology. (Liberation theology is an unofficial religious movement that stresses the need to reform politics and support the poor and powerless. Some leaders of the Roman Catholic Church practice liberation theology in countries in which people have been poor or politically oppressed for a long time, including many countries in Central and South America.)

◆ **ANSWER** Pope John Paul II was the first to visit South America, in 1968.

Section Close

Ask students to evaluate the major difficulties experienced by the countries of South America. Ask them to discuss whether they feel the Roman Catholic Church has been a favorable or an unfavorable factor.

3 Assess

Review Answers

Review History
A. Argentina lost the war, which weakened its military leaders.
B. emeralds, gold, oil, coal, coffee, sugar cane, bananas, and cut flowers
C. It is important because more than 90 percent of the people belong to it. Church leaders have taken an active role in civic affairs through the policy known as liberation theology.

Define Terms to Know
privatize, 728; El Niño, 730

Chapter Summary

A blank outline form is available in the Teacher's Resources (p. 318). Students should outline information about North America and South America in the modern era. They should then use the outline to complete their chapter summary. Refer to the rubric in the Teacher's Resources (p. 340) to score students' chapter summaries.

⬤ Interpret the Timeline

1. Communist revolution in Cuba
2. Canadians are freed from British Parliament's control, in 1982.
3. Accept any two of the following: the Caribbean Community and Common Market (CARICOM) is formed; the European Union (EU) is created; and North American Free Trade Agreement (NAFTA) is signed.
4. Check that all six events in students' timelines are in the chapter.

Use Terms to Know

5. i. suburb
6. f. domino theory
7. e. counterrevolutionary
8. a. acid rain
9. c. asylum
10. h. privatize
11. b. amnesty
12. d. commute
13. g. impeach

Check Your Understanding

14. It decreased the population of cities; populations of cities tended to be poorer; some city areas declined; more people commuting to work led to more cars and increased use of gasoline.
15. McCarthy's fear of communism led him to accuse many people in the United States of being Communists or Communist supporters. He questioned people on television.
16. U.S. involvement in both Korea and Vietnam began in response to the fear of communism. People in the United States generally supported aid to Korea. Aid to Vietnam divided public opinion, and the war eventually became unpopular. Agreements were signed in both cases that ended the fighting.
17. Four groups who moved to Canada were British Loyalists,

Chapter Summary

Complete the following outline in your notebook. Then, use your outline to write a brief summary of the chapter.

North America and South America

I. The United States After World War II
   A. Prosperity After World War II
   B. Conflicts at Home and Abroad
   C. The Struggle for Justice
   D. Wars, Scandals, and Terrorism

II. Canada and the United States in a New Era
   A. Long-Standing Good Neighbors
   B. Freedom for Canada
   C. Trade Partners and Economic Challenges

III. Mexico, Central America, and the Caribbean Islands
   A. Mexico and the United States
   B. Central America Moves Toward Democracy
   C. The Caribbean Islands

IV. South America
   A. Climate of Unrest
   B. Economic and Political Struggles
   C. Latin Americans and Religion

⬤ Interpret the Timeline

Use the timeline on pages 710–711 to answer the following questions.

1. Which event occurred first, the Cuban Missile Crisis or a Communist revolution in Cuba?
2. Which event involved Canada and Great Britain?
3. **Critical Thinking** Name two events that show collaboration between neighboring nations.
4. Select six events from the chapter that are not on the timeline. Create a timeline that shows these events.

Use Terms to Know

Match each term with its definition.

a. acid rain	f. domino theory
b. amnesty	g. impeach
c. asylum	h. privatize
d. commute	i. suburb
e. counterrevolutionary	

5. a community at the edge of a city
6. the belief that if one country falls to communism, others nearby will fall, one after the other
7. a person who fights against a government set up by a previous revolution
8. rain, snow, or hail that contains toxic, or poisonous, chemicals
9. a place that gives protection, such as political protection
10. to change from public to private control
11. a government pardon
12. to travel back and forth regularly
13. to charge a high public official, such as the U.S. President, with a crime

Check Your Understanding

14. **Explain** how moving to the suburbs changed the way people in the United States lived.
15. **Discuss** the actions of Senator Joseph McCarthy.
16. **Compare and Contrast** U.S. involvement in Korea and Vietnam.
17. **Identify** four groups of people who moved to Canada from the United States in the past.
18. **Identify** the reasons that many citizens in Quebec would like to secede from Canada.
19. **Describe** the Border Industrialization Program.
20. **Explain** the involvement of the United States in Panama.
21. **Summarize** the rule of the Perón family in Argentina.
22. **Identify** the ways in which Brazil improved its economy after 1945.

---

enslaved Africans, farmers, and some who opposed the draft during the Vietnam War.

18. Many citizens of Quebec would like to secede from Canada because they have a different background and religion from most of the rest of Canada. Quebec is heavily influenced by its past French connection. The dominant religion in Quebec is Roman Catholicism. Most of the rest of Canada feels closer to its English roots, and the Protestant religion is predominant.

19. The Border Industrialization Program began in 1965. U.S.-owned factories were established in Mexico, and many Mexicans who had been living in the United States returned to Mexico and went to work in these factories.

20. The United States became involved in Panama with the building of the Panama Canal and remained in control of the canal until the end of 1999, when it was turned back to Panama. While the United States was in control, the Panamanians had little say over the canal. In 1989, the United States invaded Panama to overthrow the president, Manuel Noriega. Noriega was captured, taken to the United States, and tried for drug trafficking.

Critical Thinking

23. Make Inferences Based on your study of U.S. military actions in the Americas during the last half of the twentieth century, what inferences can you make about how the threat of communism in the region influenced U.S. actions?

24. Make Judgments What do you think should be the policies that Canada and the United States follow when making laws that affect both nations?

25. Make Predictions What do you think will happen to the economic relationship between Mexico and the United States in the future?

26. Recognize Relationships What might the effects be of living in a nation in which the majority of the people are the same religion?

Put Your Skills to Work

27. Evaluate Information You have studied ways to evaluate sources. Practice evaluating sources by filling in a chart like the one below.

First, copy the chart onto a sheet of paper. Then, choose one nation you have studied in this chapter. Use sources, including books, encyclopedias, magazines, academic journals, and the Internet to locate information related to your topic. Determine whether those sources are reliable.

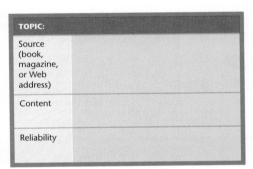

TOPIC:	
Source (book, magazine, or Web address)	
Content	
Reliability	

Analyze Sources

28. Read more about the U.S. Supreme Court's 1954 decision in *Brown* v. *Board of Education of Topeka*, in which the justices agreed that the segregation of children in public schools caused inequality. Supreme Court Chief Justice Earl Warren wrote the unanimous opinion. After reading the opinion, answer the questions that follow.

It is doubtful that any child may reasonably be expected to succeed in life if he is denied the opportunity of an education. Such an opportunity . . . is a right which must be available to all on equal terms. . . . Does segregation of children in public schools solely on the basis of race . . . deprive children of the minority group of equal educational opportunities? We believe that it does. . . . We conclude, unanimously, that in the field of public education . . . "separate but equal" has no place. Separate educational facilities are . . . unequal.

a. What does Chief Justice Warren write is important in order for a child to succeed?

b. What does Chief Justice Warren write about separate educational facilities?

Essay Writing

29. Write a brief essay that compares and contrasts revolutions toward democracy in any two countries in Central or South America. Consider the causes and effects of the revolutions.

TEST PREPARATION

CAUSE-AND-EFFECT RELATIONSHIPS
Read the question below and choose the correct answer.

Which development caused the other three?

1. Some city areas began to decline.

2. People bought more cars and gasoline.

3. City tax revenues began to decrease.

4. People moved to the suburbs.

Critical Thinking

23. Within the United States, it led to Senator McCarthy's hunt for Communists. Externally, the threat led the United States to be involved in conflicts in Korea and Vietnam. It led to the Bay of Pigs invasion of Cuba in 1961, to economic sanctions on countries that traded with Cuba, to the Cuban Missile Crisis, and to support for the Contras in Nicaragua.

24. Possible answer: The United States and Canada should work and plan together. Laws that affect both nations should be approved by both governments.

25. Possible answers: Some students may cite NAFTA and say that the economic relationship will grow stronger and improve. Some may say it will deteriorate due to unequal benefits from NAFTA and because of continuing illegal border crossings.

26. Possible answers: It might lead to involvement of religion in politics, greater harmony within the population, or discrimination against people of minority religions.

Put Your Skills to Work

EVALUATE INFORMATION

27. Students should copy the chart accurately and use it to record information about a nation they have studied in the chapter. Sources students can evaluate include encyclopedias, academic journals, and the Internet. Be sure students list a variety of sources and indicate whether or not they believe each source is reliable.

Analyze Sources

28a. Chief Justice Warren writes that it is important to have an opportunity for an education in order to succeed in life.

28b. He writes that separate educational facilities deprive children of equal educational opportunities and that separate facilities are unequal.

Essay Writing

29. Students' essays should focus on two countries in Central or South America with respect to their revolutions to introduce democratic governments.

TEST PREPARATION

Answer 4. People moved to the suburbs.

---

21. President Juan Perón and his wife Eva introduced reforms such as higher wages and stronger labor unions. They were popular with working-class people. However, they denied citizens basic freedoms such as freedom of speech and freedom of the press. Their economic policies also drove Argentina into debt. Perón went into exile in 1955, after the military had taken control of the

government. He returned in 1973 and was elected president again. After his death, his second wife, Isabel, became president. She served for two years.

22. After 1945, Brazil improved its economy by encouraging foreign companies to build factories there and by increasing production in automobile, shipbuilding, steel, and machinery industries so that the country would be less dependent

on imports. Roads and power plants were also built.

Asia
1945–PRESENT
(pp. 734–757)

Chapter Objectives
• Explain how the people of India achieved independence and have since struggled with religious tensions and social challenges.
• Identify the people and events that led to Communist control of China, and describe the events that led to the Korean War.
• Describe the factors that helped Japan recover from its defeat in World War II to become a powerful industrialized nation.
• Compare and contrast the struggles for independence and self-determination in the nations of Southeast Asia.

Chapter Summary
Section I focuses on the independence movement in India and the conflicts resulting from division of the Indian subcontinent.
Section II explains how China became a Communist state and describes the tensions that led to the Korean War.
Section III discusses the American occupation of post war Japan, and the factors that helped the Japanese nation become one of the world's industrial leaders.
Section IV draws comparisons between the conflicts over self-determination in the nations of Southeast Asia, including Cambodia, Myanmar, the Philippines, and Indonesia.

Set the Stage
TEACH PRIMARY SOURCES
Joseph Fewsmith is Professor of International Relations at Boston University. His book, *China since Tiananmen: The Politics of Transition*, discusses the struggle that led to the demonstrations in Tiananmen Square and how Chinese leaders have responded since then. Have students discuss why the demonstrators were primarily students. (Possible answer: Students were better educated and had more freedom than the average citizen. Also, they had learned about different types of governments.)

Asia
1945–PRESENT

I. Changes on the Indian Subcontinent
II. China and Korea
III. Japan Rebuilds
IV. Conflict in Southeast Asia

After World War II, most Asian nations moved from colonialism to independence. Some nations followed socialism or communism, whereas others tried to establish capitalist democracies. As in Europe in the 1800s, industrialization in Asia led to widespread social change. In addition, armed conflict broke out in many parts of Asia.

In 1989, students in China called for greater political freedom. They demonstrated in Tiananmen Square in Beijing and in other Chinese cities. Joseph Fewsmith, writer of the book, *China Since Tiananmen*, said,

> **❝** *The student demonstrators in Tiananmen Square and elsewhere, many believed, represented the wave of the future; few doubted that Chinese society, in contrast to the government, favored liberalism and democracy.* **❞**

The events in Tiananmen Square are a symbol not only of the great desire for freedom but also of the hardships that resulted from the attempts to achieve this goal.

1947
India gains independence from Great Britain.

1949
Communists come to power in China.

1945
U.S. military occupies Japan.

1950
Korean War begins.

1954
Cambodia gains independence from France.

1968
North Vietnam launches Tet Offensive against South Vietnam.

CHAPTER EVENTS

1945

1965

WORLD EVENTS

1945
World War II ends.

1955
Warsaw Pact is formed.

1960
Nigeria becomes independent from Great Britain.

1967
Six-Day War is fought between Israel and Arab countries.

734 UNIT 8 ◆ The World Today

Teaching Options

Chapter 31 Resources

REVIEW

Teacher's Resources (TR)
Terms to Know, p. 44
Review History, p. 78
Build Your Skills, p. 112
Chapter Test, pp. 177–178
Concept Builder, p. 247
Cause-and-Effect Chain, p. 325
Transparencies 1, 7

ASSESSMENT
Section Reviews, pp. 740, 746, 750, 755
Chapter Review, p. 756–757
Chapter Test, TR, pp. 177–178

ALTERNATIVE ASSESSMENT
Portfolio Project, p. 808
Create Historical Maps, p. T808

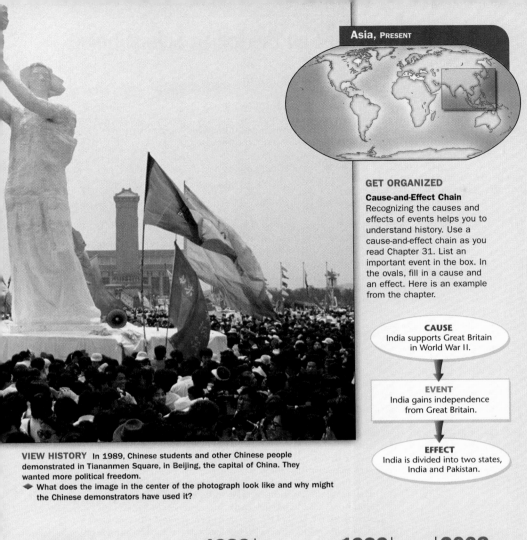

VIEW HISTORY In 1989, Chinese students and other Chinese people demonstrated in Tiananmen Square, in Beijing, the capital of China. They wanted more political freedom.

◆ What does the image in the center of the photograph look like and why might the Chinese demonstrators have used it?

GET ORGANIZED

Cause-and-Effect Chain
Recognizing the causes and effects of events helps you to understand history. Use a cause-and-effect chain as you read Chapter 31. List an important event in the box. In the ovals, fill in a cause and an effect. Here is an example from the chapter.

CAUSE
India supports Great Britain in World War II.

↓

EVENT
India gains independence from Great Britain.

↓

EFFECT
India is divided into two states, India and Pakistan.

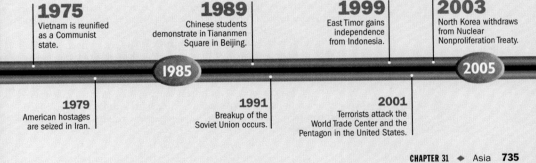

1975
Vietnam is reunified as a Communist state.

1979
American hostages are seized in Iran.

1985

1989
Chinese students demonstrate in Tiananmen Square in Beijing.

1991
Breakup of the Soviet Union occurs.

1999
East Timor gains independence from Indonesia.

2001
Terrorists attack the World Trade Center and the Pentagon in the United States.

2003
North Korea withdraws from Nuclear Nonproliferation Treaty.

2005

CHAPTER 31 ◆ Asia **735**

USING THE MAP
Point out the locator map at the top of page 735. To help students understand the location of the region, have them locate the Pacific Ocean and the Indian Ocean. Point out that much of the region is made up of islands.

VIEW HISTORY
Point out to students that the demonstrators in the photograph appear peaceful and orderly, yet this protest ended with a violent reaction by the Chinese government. Ask students why a government might object to this kind of protest.

◆ **ANSWER** Possible answer: It resembles the Statue of Liberty, which symbolizes liberty, freedom, and democracy.

GET ORGANIZED
Cause-and-Effect Chain
Discuss the cause-and-effect chain on page 735. Point out that the topic of the organizer is in the Event box. The boxes above and below relate directly to that event. Explain that some events can have more than one cause or effect, in which case, additional boxes could be drawn. Encourage students to make a cause-and-effect chain for each section (TR, p. 325).

● **TEACH THE TIMELINE**
The timeline on pages 734–735 covers the period from 1945 to the present. Point out that this period follows the end of World War II. Ask students which of the events on the timeline give information about war. (World War II ends, Korean War begins, Six-Day War is fought, North Vietnamese launch Tet offensive.) Explain that in addition to the wars, many of the timeline entries mark violent independence movements.

Chapter Themes
• Culture
• Time, Continuity, and Change
• Power, Authority, and Governance
• Production, Distribution, and Consumption
• Individual Development and Identity
• Individuals, Groups, and Institutions

FYI

Prodemocracy Protests in China

In early May 1989, about 100,000 prodemocracy protesters filled Tiananmen Square in Beijing. That number swelled to about 1 million by late May. On May 29, the statue "Goddess of Democracy" was lifted into place. On June 3, soldiers were ordered to clear the square. The soldiers fired on the demonstrators, killing and injuring thousands.

CHAPTER 31 ◆ **T735**

I. Changes on the Indian Subcontinent

(pp. 736–740)

Section Summary

In this section, students will learn that in 1947, the Indian subcontinent gained independence from Great Britain and was divided into two states: India and Pakistan. Since independence, India has been confronted with religious tension and social and economic challenges.

Getting Started

Ask students to draw on prior knowledge and identify various methods of nonviolent protest, such as boycotts, strikes, or protest rallies. Ask them to identify the advantages and disadvantages of nonviolent protest.

TERMS TO KNOW

Have students read the terms and definitions on page 736 and then find each term in the section. Students should write a sentence that defines each term.

Explain that prefixes such as *non-, pre-,* and *pro-,* are usually affixed to root words without a hyphen, as in *nonaligned.* Have students look for examples on page 736 of words with the *non-* prefix. (nonviolent, noncooperation)

You may wish to preview the pronunciation of the following names from this section with students.

Nehru (NEH roo)
Rajiv Gandhi (rah JEHV GAHN dee)
Ganges (GAN jeez)
Tamil Nadu (TA muhl NAH doo)

ACTIVE READING

As students read the section, have them use an idea web (TR, p. 321) to take notes. Then, have them refer to the idea web as they write a summary of the section.

Terms to Know

lobby to attempt to influence those in power to accept a particular point of view

separatist a citizen who wishes to break away from his or her country to form a new nation

Primary Source Documents

You can read sections of the "Quit India" speeches on page 814.

Main Ideas

A. After a long struggle, India achieved independence from Great Britain in 1947, and the subcontinent was divided into two separate nations: India and Pakistan.

B. Religious tensions, social challenges, and poverty have confronted India since independence.

Active Reading

SUMMARIZE
When you summarize, you state only the most important points, or highlights, of a passage. As you read this section, focus on the main points about the development of present-day India and then summarize what you have learned.

A. Independence and Partition

You learned in Chapter 27 that in the late 1800s, an Indian student named Mohandas K. Gandhi became a lawyer and then went to South Africa, where he lived for 20 years. It was there that he witnessed the painful discrimination suffered by Indians. When Gandhi returned to India, he led the Indian people in a struggle for independence from Great Britain. That struggle for independence ended when Great Britain kept a promise to India.

Gandhi's Leadership

Two organizations had been formed to lead the Indian struggle for independence from Great Britain. These organizations were the Indian National Congress, with a strong Hindu membership, and the All-India Muslim League, which was supported by Muslims. The All-India Muslim League believed that an independent Hindu-dominated India would discriminate against Muslims. Members of the Muslim League called for a separate Islamic state.

The main goal of the Indian National Congress, led by Gandhi, was independence from Great Britain. Beginning in 1942, their slogan sent a strong message to the British: "Quit India!" In moving speeches, Gandhi called on the British to leave India. He urged Indians to protest British control using such nonviolent means as boycotts and peaceful public demonstrations.

Gandhi firmly believed in using nonviolent methods of civil disobedience. His ideas of noncooperation and peaceful resistance influenced others worldwide. Gandhi's beliefs had a strong impact on Dr. Martin Luther King Jr., a leader of the U.S. civil rights movement in the 1950s and 1960s.

One of Gandhi's most effective methods was the boycott. He urged his fellow Indians to boycott cotton imported from Great Britain and to rely instead on native homespun fabric. The image of Gandhi seated in front of a spinning wheel making his own cloth became a powerful symbol.

Indian nationalists had called for independence from Great Britain since the late 1800s. In London, the British government had resisted the Indian independence movement until World War II. The British promised the Indians independence after the war in return for Indian support during the war.

When World War II ended, Great Britain kept its promise to India. However, as independence neared, a long-standing concern grew in importance. What would happen to Indian Muslims in an independent country with a mostly Hindu population?

Teaching Options

Section 1 Resources

Teacher's Resources (TR)
Terms to Know, p. 44
Review History, p. 78
Build Your Skills, p. 112
Concept Builder, p. 247
Cause-and-Effect Chain, p. 325

Two Separate Nations

Indian Muslims objected strongly to living in an independent state with a huge Hindu majority. Under the leadership of Muhammad Ali Jinnah, the All-India Muslim League **lobbied** for the establishment of a separate Islamic state. To lobby is to try to influence those in power to accept a particular point of view. Reluctantly, the Indian National Congress and the British agreed to a separate Islamic state.

Drawing borders would be a difficult task. In many parts of India, Hindus and Muslims lived side by side. Nevertheless, when the subcontinent achieved independence in August 1947, it was quickly partitioned, or divided, into two states: a Hindu state, India, and an Islamic state, Pakistan. Pakistan was divided into West Pakistan and East Pakistan. West Pakistan was located in the northwestern region of the subcontinent, where many Muslims lived. East Pakistan, located east of India on the Bay of Bengal, was separated from West Pakistan by hundreds of miles.

After the partition of India, about 10 million Hindus and Muslims crossed the borders of both countries. The two groups distrusted each other. Northern India erupted in violence. Hindus and Muslims massacred each other. One million or more people may have been killed. Independence was accompanied by chaos on the subcontinent.

India's dispute with Pakistan over the northern state of Kashmir was another conflict. The majority of the population of Kashmir was Muslim. However, it was included within India at the time of partition. The dispute over Kashmir persists to this day.

Gandhi refused to hold public office in India because of the violence that accompanied the partition. He had not been in favor of the partition. He felt that too many people had betrayed the ideals of nonviolence and truth. Then, on January 30, 1948, Gandhi was assassinated. Jawaharlal Nehru, India's first prime minister, told the nation,

> ❝ The light has gone out of our lives and there is darkness everywhere. ❞

Nehru was a highly educated lawyer. He led India for 17 years, until his death in 1964. Nehru's ideas for the nation's direction differed somewhat from those of Gandhi. Gandhi wanted India to cling to its traditional village roots. In contrast, Nehru was determined to transform the country into a modern, industrial power.

Indian Democracy

India's constitution of 1950 established a democratic government. This made India the largest democracy in the world. It is also one of the world's most diverse nations. India's constitution recognized more than a dozen official languages and 35 major regional languages.

Partition of India, 1947

AFGHANISTAN Kashmir CHINA Tibet WEST PKISTAN Sikkim BHUTAN NEPAL Ganges River INDIA EAST PAKISTAN Burma (Great Britain) Arabian Sea Bay of Bengal Ceylon (Great Britain)

India
Pakistan
Disputed area

0   300   600 mi
0   300   600 km

✔ Map Check

LOCATION Where were the two regions of Pakistan located in 1947?

ANALYZE PRIMARY SOURCES

DOCUMENT-BASED QUESTION Which key words does Nehru use to refer to Gandhi and his assassination?

Conflict Resolution

Point out to students that Gandhi is known for his philosophy that people who are struggling for their rights must not betray their obligation to respect life. Have students identify some forms of nonviolent protest, and ask them how nonviolence could play a part in conflicts they may encounter with their peers.

2 Teach

A. Independence and Partition

Purpose-Setting Question Why did Mohandas K. Gandhi refuse to hold public office in India? (Gandhi refused to hold office because of the violence that accompanied the partition of India; he had not favored partition.)

Focus Have students read the "Quit India" speeches on page 814. Encourage students to summarize the points in the speeches.

Review Have students recall how Gandhi protested the British tax on salt. (led a peaceful protest march to the sea) Then, review how he urged a boycott on British cotton. (spun his own cloth) Finally, discuss the effects of these protests.

Using the Map

Partition of India, 1947

Have students study the map showing the partition of India in 1947. Ask students what problems they think there might be in governing the countries, based on the map. (large territory, areas broken up) Ask students to identify the regions that remain colonies of Great Britain. (Ceylon and Burma)

✔ Map Check

Answer The two regions of Pakistan are located northwest and east of India.

ANALYZE PRIMARY SOURCES

DOCUMENT-BASED QUESTION

Gandhi was hugely popular. Yet, because his work to heal the nation after Indian independence was controversial, he earned some enemies. Gandhi was assassinated by a Hindu fanatic who disagreed with his efforts to heal the nation.

ANSWER Possible answer: *light* (Gandhi), *darkness everywhere* (his assassination)

Explore Draw a two-column chart on the board. Label the left column, *National Government*, and the right column, *State Government*. Then, have students work together to list the tasks that each government controls within our country. (Possible answers: **National:** foreign policy; **State:** road repair) Then, emphasize that India's federal system of shared powers is similar to that of the United States.

Focus Have groups of students research at least two of the different political parties in India today. Allow students to use library or Internet resources. Also, have students find one news article on either of their assigned political parties and share the information with the class. The class should try to find some similarities and differences between the parties.

◆ **ANSWER** Nehru was determined to turn India into a modern, industrial power; Gandhi wanted India to cling to its traditional village roots.

B. Challenge and Response

Purpose-Setting Question What are some of the reasons for the religious and ethnic tensions in India? (Possible answers: **Ethnic:** 1600s, Mughal Empire moved south, where Hindu kingdoms were established; Some Mughal rulers persecuted the Hindus; Not all Muslims left India since independence in 1947; Tamils waged war to form their own nation; **Religious:** tensions between Hindus and Sikhs; Sikhs in Punjab demanded independence from India and the Indian government refused.)

Activity

Research Have groups of students research information about modern India, such as the spoken languages, the practiced religions, or the current population count. Have a volunteer make a list from the shared information on the board.

In 1982, U.S. President Ronald Reagan and Indian Prime Minister Indira Gandhi met to discuss U.S.-Indian relations.

India set up a parliament modeled on Great Britain's government. India also had a federal system similar to that of the United States. A federal system divides power between the national government and the state governments.

As you read in Chapter 27, the Indian National Congress, or the Congress Party, had led India to independence. For more than 40 years, the party controlled the country's politics. During the same period, the Nehru family led India's government.

After Nehru's death, his daughter, Indira Gandhi, served as prime minister. She was succeeded by her son, Rajiv Gandhi. Except for a brief period of "emergency rule" during the 1970s, India maintained a parliamentary democracy. However, in the 1990s the country entered into a period of political instability. New political parties competed for control. As a result, power within the federal system frequently shifted from one party to another. The power of the Congress Party, which had ruled for decades, declined under charges of corruption. A Hindu nationalist party gained power in Parliament. In 1999, the Congress Party regained power, but in a weakened state.

Indian Foreign Policy

In foreign policy, Nehru did not want India to be allied with any side in a conflict. He called for an official neutrality between the great powers of the Cold War: the United States, the Soviet Union, and China—one of India's neighbors. Despite this policy, however, India accepted aid from both the United States and the Soviet Union.

India became involved in conflicts with some neighboring nations. It objected to China's occupation of Tibet in 1950. More armed conflict later developed between India and China over other border disputes in the 1960s.

In 1970, civil war developed between East Pakistan and West Pakistan. Political leaders in East Pakistan wanted independence. Riots broke out. When troops from West Pakistan arrived in East Pakistan to control the violence, India abandoned their policy of neutrality and strongly supported the **separatists**, those who wished to break away from their country to form a new country. It provided weapons and troops to East Pakistan. In 1971, East Pakistan split from West Pakistan to form the new nation of Bangladesh.

◆ **How did Prime Minister Nehru's aims for India after independence contrast with those of Mohandas Gandhi?**

B. Challenge and Response

India is a vast land of 25 states with a highly diverse population. With more than 1 billion people, India is home to six major religions and more than a dozen major languages. Even under the British, India was far from a unified country. It is remarkable that India has drawn together and maintained parliamentary democracy for more than half a century.

Teaching Options

Test Taking

To help students prepare for taking a test on this chapter, review how to answer multiple-choice questions. Write a multiple-choice question about the chapter on the board. Point out that even if students do not know the correct answer, they should try to eliminate as many choices as they can. Doing so will give them a better chance of selecting the correct answer.

Connection to
WORLD LANGUAGES

The official language of India is Hindi. However, India has many languages. There is a minority of people in India who do not speak Hindi, particularly those in the southern part of the country. Ask students to draw on their own experiences to suggest ways that India could help ease the relations among these different language speakers.

Religious and Ethnic Tensions

For many centuries, Hindus have lived alongside Muslims in India. Many Hindus have lived near the Ganges River and other rivers. Muslims first arrived in the subcontinent in the 700s. Then, in the early 1500s, the Mughals established an empire that ruled over much of the Indian subcontinent. In the late 1600s, the Mughal Empire moved south, where Hindu kingdoms had flourished since medieval times.

Some Mughal rulers had a policy of religious toleration. Others, however, persecuted Hindus. Their actions left long-lasting resentment. The British soon learned that in order to govern India successfully, they had to be aware of Hindu-Muslim relations and rivalries. Not all Muslims left India since independence and partition in 1947. As a result, the Hindu-Muslim conflict has continued to break out from time to time in India.

Religious tensions have also existed between Hindus and Sikhs. Sikhism is a religion that began in the 1500s as a reform movement within Hinduism. Sikhs, who are centered in the northwestern Indian state of Punjab, have developed their own set of beliefs and way of life. In the early 1980s, some Sikhs demanded independence from India. The Indian government, however, flatly refused these demands. This conflict led to an armed confrontation at a sacred Sikh shrine in 1984. A few months later, Prime Minister Indira Gandhi was assassinated by Sikhs.

The Tamils are a large ethnic group living in southeastern India in Tamil Nadu. Some Tamils also live in Sri Lanka, which was formerly called Ceylon. In this island nation off the southern coast of India, Tamils comprise a minority of the population. Beginning in the 1970s, the Tamils waged war in an effort to form their own nation. About 10 years later, Prime Minister Rajiv Gandhi sent troops to Sri Lanka to stop the rebellion. In response, a Tamil suicide bomber assassinated Gandhi in 1991.

Economic Concerns

Since independence, India has made significant progress economically. By the late 1970s, the nation was growing enough food to feed its people and could stop relying on imports. Certain industries made especially rapid advances, notably movie production and aerospace and computer technology.

Although 80 percent of Indians still live in villages, India has become a more urbanized nation since its independence. People have flocked to the cities for job opportunities and the chance for a better life. However, Indians are faced with a number of problems as a result of urbanization. As people continue moving to cities, it becomes difficult to provide adequate housing and basic

The making of Indian movies and television shows is an important industry for India's economy.

WHERE IN THE WORLD?

THE GANGES RIVER Have students use a map of India (Atlas p. A7 or Transparency 7) to locate the Ganges River and Varanasi. Have them locate the origin and the mouth of the river. Ask students why the location of the mouth of the Ganges River could be a problem for Indian Hindus. (It is in Bangladesh.)

Extend Tell students that the Indian constitution of 1950 called for religion and government to be kept separate. Recently, however, many Indians who support the Bharata Jaraytav Party (BJP) have argued that the Indian government should be guided by Hinduism. Hindus make up about 82 percent of the population. Discuss with students some of the advantages and disadvantages of running a country based on one religious belief system.

Discuss Ask students how they think minority groups in India, such as the Sikhs and Tamils, feel toward the Indian government. (Possible answers: angry, frustrated, unconnected to the government) Discuss how the actions of these groups may show their feelings. (armed confrontation at a Sikh shrine, assassinations of the leaders)

Activity

Create a list Have groups of students find different items that India exports. Allow students to use library or Internet resources. Once completed, have students create a list of all the exports. Ask students if they have seen any of India's exports for sale. If so, discuss where these items are for sale.

Review Ask students to recall the discussion in Chapter 22 describing the problems that rapid industrialization can cause. (greatly increased population; problems in cities, such as overcrowding, disease, and crime) Discuss how India is facing many of these problems.

Connection to CULTURE

Have students conduct research about the Hindu and Muslim faiths. Suggest that students review Chapter 3 and use an encyclopedia or the Internet to learn more about the primary beliefs and practices of each religion. Then, have students work in groups to create a chart that lists the major beliefs of each religion.

Mother Theresa devoted her life to the poor in India. She received the 1979 Nobel Peace Prize, an award for her work in helping to make the world better.

services to address their needs. Cities like Mumbai, formerly called Bombay, Delhi, and Chennai, once known as Madras, have become affected by poverty, disease, and pollution. The poorest of the Indian poor received international attention thanks to the efforts of Mother Theresa. Mother Theresa was an Albanian-born nun who for much of her life helped the poorest people living in Kolkata, also known as Calcutta.

India continues to struggle with the huge problems posed by a population boom. By the year 2000, India's population had passed the 1 billion mark. Experts predict that if current trends continue, India will replace China as the world's most populated country within the next 30 years. Efforts at population control have not been nearly as successful in India as they have been in China.

Social Strains

Despite the economic progress that India has made since its independence, India has had to deal with ongoing social challenges. Among the most important social challenges are those posed by the caste system. According to strict interpretations of this system, there can be no contact between members of the upper caste and those of the lower caste. Certain people called untouchables have been ranked below the lowest caste. Gandhi fought strongly for the rights of the untouchables, calling them *harijans*, or "children of God." Prime Minister Nehru spoke out strongly against the caste system. He believed in social justice and equality. The Indian constitution of 1950 outlawed the caste system and the discrimination that it caused. However, traditions that are thousands of years old are slow to change.

◆ **Since independence, what challenges has India faced from religious and ethnic divisions?**

Review I

Review History
A. How did India gain its independence?
B. What problems face Indians as a result of urbanization?

Define Terms to Know
Define the following terms:
lobby, separatist

Critical Thinking
Do you think Nehru acted in India's best interest by pursuing a policy of neutrality during the Cold War? Explain why or why not.

Write About Culture
In a paragraph, write about the caste system in India.

Get Organized
CAUSE-AND-EFFECT CHAIN
Think about the main events in this section. Use a cause-and-effect chain to show the cause and effect of an event. For example, what was a cause and an effect of urbanization in India?

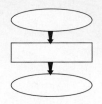

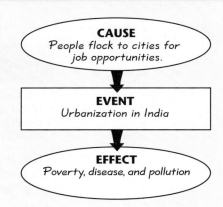

CAUSE
People flock to cities for job opportunities.

EVENT
Urbanization in India

EFFECT
Poverty, disease, and pollution

Build Your Skills

DEVELOP A MULTIMEDIA PRESENTATION

In a multimedia presentation, you use materials such as videotapes, audiotapes, and computer graphics to present a report and share information. The effective use of different media can make your report interesting and memorable.

Begin planning your multimedia presentation by asking yourself which features of your subject best lend themselves to different media. Statistical information, for example, will be clearer for your audience if you use a chart. If you are discussing geography, consider presenting maps in slide form. Using an excerpt, or section, from the speech of a political leader on audiotape may bring that person's qualities alive. Keep in mind that many multimedia resources may now be downloaded from the Internet.

Here's How
Follow these steps to develop a multimedia presentation.

1. Choose visual and audio cues that are clearly related to your material and convey key ideas.

2. Mark the text of your report to remind yourself where and how you will use multimedia elements.

3. Keep the needs of your audience in mind. For example, if you are using a poster or other visual display, be sure that it is large enough so that audience members can see it clearly.

4. Test your equipment thoroughly before your presentation. Be sure that slide projectors, VCRs, audiocassette players, overhead projectors, and other equipment are in good working order.

5. Rehearse your presentation so that you can coordinate the text of your report with multimedia elements smoothly.

6. Use gestures and verbal references to direct the audience's attention to each multimedia element.

Here's Why
You have just read about the 1947 partition of India. Presenting maps of the Indian subcontinent before and after the partition would clearly show the distance between West Pakistan and East Pakistan.

Practice the Skill
Copy the graphic organizer on the right onto a sheet of paper. Choose a presentation topic from Section I that interests you, such as Mohandas Gandhi. Write the topic in the top box. Then, list four types of media you could use to develop the presentation and explain how you would use each type.

Extend the Skill
Choose at least one type of media listed in your organizer. Develop a short presentation using that media. Share your presentation with the class.

Apply the Skill
As you read the remaining sections of this chapter, choose a topic and think about how you would present the information if you were asked to develop a multimedia presentation. Organize your ideas in a chart like the one on this page.

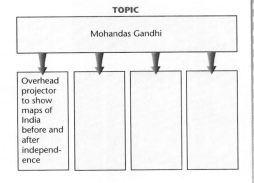

TOPIC

Mohandas Gandhi

Overhead projector to show maps of India before and after independence

---

Teaching Options

RETEACH

Ask students to identify different forms of media that could best illustrate the topics in Section 1. To do this, review the headings in the section and point out how video, audio, graphic images, or written material could help convey information effectively.

CHALLENGE

Have students conduct an Internet search on the topics covered in Section 1. Have them make a list of the various forms of media that Web page designers have chosen to convey information. Then, have students decide if the media chosen by the Web page designer was useful and engaging. If not, have students list suggestions to better convey the information on the Web page.

Build Your Skills

DEVELOP A MULTIMEDIA PRESENTATION

Teach the Skill

Ask students why presenters sometimes make and use a multimedia presentation. (more interesting, more exciting, can show information in different ways) Have students list various places that multimedia presentations might be useful. (workplaces, conferences, public speeches, classrooms) Discuss with students the different forms of media and the information these media would best convey. For example, a video is more effective than slides to show an action, whereas slides are more effective for a large group presentation than pictures from a book.

Discuss with students the steps they would take to make a multimedia presentation on industrialized India. Remind students to use the steps in *Here's How* as a reference.

Practice the Skill

Possible answers: a videotape of an interview with Gandhi, a slide or poster board presentation of photographs of Gandhi in action; computer graphics showing a timeline of his life.

Extend the Skill

Students' presentations should focus on the topic of Mohandas Gandhi. The medium they use should clearly help to explain the information, enrich the presentation, and engage the audience. Encourage students to practice their presentation before they make it to the class. You may wish to have the class provide useful feedback after each presentation.

Apply the Skill

As students read this chapter, ask them how they would incorporate topics they are reading about into a multimedia presentation. Invite students to give short presentations on these topics.

II. China and Korea

(pp. 742–746)

Section Summary

Students will learn how the Communist government under Mao Zedong and Deng Xiaoping implemented economic and social reforms. They will also read about the tensions between North and South Korea that led to the Korean War.

1 Introduce

Getting Started

Ask students how they would respond if the government told them that beginning today, no one was permitted to own any property individually. Instead, all property was to be owned by groups of people. Lead the discussion toward how students would feel about working if there were no personal rewards.

TERMS TO KNOW

Have students read the terms and definitions on page 742 and then find the terms in the section. Once students read the terms in context, have them write a definition in their own words.

You may wish to preview the pronunciation of the following names from this section with students.

Jiang Jieshi (je AHNG jee EHSH ee)
Deng Xiaoping (DUNG SHOU PING)

ACTIVE READING

You may want to suggest to students that they create two idea webs (TR, p. 321), one for each of the two leaders of China. As they read, students may add notes to each idea web. Students may use their notes to create a Venn diagram (TR, p. 323) that compares the Chinese leaders.

Terms to Know

commune a community in which there is no private ownership and people live and work together in large groups

socialist market economy an economic system that blends features of socialism with features of capitalism

Main Ideas

A. After nearly 40 years of conflict, China became a Communist state in 1949.

B. After the death of Mao Zedong in 1976, China pursued economic reforms and became an industrial power.

C. Tensions between Communist North Korea and democratic South Korea erupted into the Korean War.

📖 Active Reading

COMPARE AND CONTRAST
When you compare and contrast, you identify similarities and differences. As you read this section, compare and contrast two of China's leaders, Mao Zedong and Deng Xiaoping.

A. The People's Republic of China

In 1911, a revolution in China overthrew the Qing, or Manchu, Dynasty. The following year a republic was proclaimed. For many years, however, the Chinese found it hard to establish political stability. Local rulers controlled the country from 1916 to 1927. Then, Nationalist forces under Jiang Jieshi regained control of the government.

A Struggle Between Nationalists and Communists

As you read in Chapter 27, Jiang Jieshi led the Guomindang, the Chinese political party that had spearheaded the revolution in 1911. In 1924, this party formed an alliance with the Communists to achieve its goals. In 1927, however, Jiang turned against his Communist allies. Nationalist troops attacked the city of Shanghai. Jiang expelled the Communists from the government and ordered the murders of Communist Party members and workers who supported them. This action resulted in a lengthy civil war between the Nationalists and the Communists. The Communists were led by Mao Zedong.

The Communists, led by Mao Zedong, fought the Nationalists for power in China during the first half of the twentieth century.

The struggle between Nationalists and Communists was further complicated by Japan's invasion of Manchuria, located in northeastern China. The Nationalists and the Communists joined together again, this time to oppose the Japanese. On December 7, 1941, Japan bombed Pearl Harbor in Hawaii. On that day, approximately 18 ships were sunk or damaged. About 2,400 Americans were killed and many more Americans were wounded. The United States declared war on Japan. China and the United States became allies.

After Japan's defeat in World War II, the United States supported Jiang Jieshi and the Nationalists. The United States did not want civil war to break out again in China. However, civil war did break out again between the Nationalists and the Communists. The renewed struggle from 1945 to 1949 focused on control of China. Finally, the Communists defeated Jiang Jieshi. He and the Nationalists withdrew to the island of Taiwan, off China's southeastern coast. There he set up a government-in-exile and established the Republic of China. Mao Zedong and his followers proclaimed the Chinese mainland the People's Republic of China.

Teaching Options

Section 2 Resources

Teacher's Resources (TR)
Terms to Know, p. 44
Review History, p. 78
Build Your Skills, p. 112
Concept Builder, p. 247
Cause-and-Effect Chain, p. 325

ESL/ELL STRATEGIES

Identify Essential Vocabulary Have students create a list of words and phrases that are used for comparing and contrasting subjects, such as *similar, unlike, in contrast to,* and *on the other hand,* to help them make the comparison between China's leaders in the Active Reading activity. Have students work in pairs to compare and contrast the leaders.

China Under Mao

From 1949 to 1976, China was governed by Mao Zedong. Mao's power was nearly absolute, and the government functioned as a totalitarian state.

Mao's first goal, like Jawaharlal Nehru's in India, was to turn China into an industrial power. Building on the Soviet economic model, Mao nationalized the economy and abolished the system of rural landlords. In 1953, the first Five-Year Economic Plan focused on the development of heavy industry. In this period, China benefited a great deal from Soviet economic and technical aid.

In 1957, wishing for more rapid progress, Mao launched an even more ambitious economic effort. This program was called the Great Leap Forward. With this plan, the government greatly expanded the scale of collectives in agriculture. As you learned in Chapter 27, collectives are large farms that are worked by peasants but owned by the government. Collective farms were merged into larger units called people's **communes**. In the communes, private ownership did not exist. Peasants lived together in dormitories or buildings with beds for many people. They ate their meals in mess halls. The peasants' children were cared for in nurseries. Labor, production, and distribution were all carried out in common.

However, the Great Leap Forward turned out to be mostly a failure, due to the peasants' opposition and also to severe crop failures. In addition, the small-scale industries that the communes were ordered to develop produced poor-quality goods. The efforts to create these industries reduced the production of food. A famine swept the land, and some estimate that up to 30 million people died of hunger. China did make some progress with advances in transportation and healthcare.

The goals of the Communist government, however, were not only to expand in industry and agriculture. For Mao, revolution was extremely important. Here are some of Mao's beliefs on revolution and political power:

> ❝A revolution is not the same as inviting people to dinner, or writing an essay, or painting a picture. . . . A revolution is an insurrection [revolt against established government], an act of violence by which one class overthrows another. ❞

In 1966, Mao was eager to convince the Chinese people that constant revolution was necessary for China to achieve its Communist goals. His attempts to influence the people led to the Cultural Revolution. In this revolution, the government organized millions of young people into units called Red Guards. Mao called upon these troops to punish and attack anyone suspected of being counterrevolutionary. Cultural and educational leaders were publicly insulted and were often taken to the countryside to work on farms. Over a three year period, the Cultural Revolution affected 3 million people. Victims were sent to forced labor camps and tortured. Many were killed. The costs of the Cultural Revolution were enormous.

◆ **What were the aims of the Cultural Revolution?**

Mao's Attempts to Change China

PROGRAMS	RESULTS
First Five-Year Economic Plan (1953): focus on heavy industry	Successfully introduced heavy industry; less successful in agriculture
Great Leap Forward (1957): focus on expanding collectives and speeding up change	Mostly unsuccessful, due to peasant opposition, crop failures, poor-quality goods, and famine
Cultural Revolution (1966): focus on punishing and attacking suspected counterrevolutionaries	Resulted in chaos; Chinese people, including cultural and educational leaders, harshly treated or killed

✔ **Chart Check**

Which program had the most positive results?

ANALYZE PRIMARY SOURCES

DOCUMENT-BASED QUESTION
What does Mao think is the result of a revolution?

A. The People's Republic of China

Purpose-Setting Question
What led to the alliance between China and the United States? (China and the United States became allies during World War II in order to defeat Japan.)

Review Remind students that the dictator of Russia, Joseph Stalin, had implemented the idea of using Five-Year Plans to improve the economy and industry in his nation. Stalin's idea achieved many of its goals, but at great cost to Russian laborers. Discuss with students the advantages of economic and industrial strength versus the health and well-being of the people of a country.

Using the Chart

Mao's Attempts to Change China

Ask students to explain the purpose of the Great Leap Forward. (focus on collectivization and speeding up change)

✔ **Chart Check**
Answer First Five-Year Economic Plan (1953)

ANALYZE PRIMARY SOURCES

DOCUMENT-BASED QUESTION
Mao Zedong formed many of his revolutionary ideas when he was a student. He was part of a group of Chinese men and women who reformed the nation according to Communist principles.

ANSWER Possible answers: violence; one class overthrows another class

◆ **ANSWER** The aims of the Cultural Revolution were to punish and attack all people suspected to be counterrevolutionaries.

Great Leap Forward

The Great Leap Forward began with a plan to organize people into cooperatives. Then, they were organized into people's communes. People did not have the administrative experience or resources to establish and implement productive farm practices, so production fell and the economy suffered.

B. China After Mao

Purpose-Setting Question How did the Chinese government react to the call for political reform in the 1980s? (It quickly and harshly ended the protests by sending in the army with tanks to shoot protesters and by arresting, torturing, or executing demonstrators.)

Explore Ask one student to look up *socialism* in a dictionary and read its definition aloud. (the ownership and operation of the means of production and distribution by society rather than by private individuals) Ask another student to define from prior knowledge or to look up in the glossary or a dictionary *market economy*. (a system of exchange in which a buyer tries to achieve the lowest price and the seller, the highest) From these definitions, have students explain why these ideas are opposites.

Discuss Ask students to think about the ways a leader's visit can improve relations between two nations. Have them discuss the significance of President Nixon's visit to China in 1972.

Activity

Develop a Tiananmen Square multimedia presentation Have groups of students use the Internet to find information about the demonstration at Tiananmen Square in the spring of 1989. Be sure the groups record the sources they used. Tell students that they can choose the direction of the presentation. It can focus on any aspect or opinion they have of the demonstration. Students' presentations must include some visuals, including photographs, maps, charts, and graphs, and some written information. Once groups make their presentations, the class should discuss the effectiveness of the media used.

Focus Discuss with students some of the different political and economic changes that happened after the death of Deng. Help students determine if each change is political or economic. Ask students what types of changes the Chinese government was more apt to allow. (economic) Discuss with students why they think the Chinese leaders were more open to economic changes.

B. China After Mao

After the death of Mao in 1976, the Communist Party's iron grip on the Chinese people relaxed somewhat. However, Chinese leaders since Mao have been quick to put down any show of support toward democracy.

The Policies of Deng Xiaoping

After a struggle for power, Deng Xiaoping became the new leader of China in 1977. Deng set himself and the Communist Party on a new path of modernization. In economics, this program sharply departed from the Socialist methods of the past. Deng encouraged capitalist ideas. These ideas included free competition and production for profit. He called his blend of capitalism and socialism a **socialist market economy**.

For decades under Mao, China had been against the United States and other Western nations as supporters of imperialism. The United States remained deeply suspicious of Chinese communism and of the expansion of Chinese influence in Asia. Relations between the two countries improved somewhat with U.S. President Richard Nixon's visit to China in 1972.

Under Deng's leadership, Chinese contacts with the West increased. Deng encouraged foreign investment in China. He showed great interest in Western science and technology. Chinese consumer goods, agricultural production, and living standards improved. Under Deng in the 1980s, China's gross domestic product greatly increased. However, the rate of inflation in China grew as well.

Political Repression

In the 1980s, there were calls for political reform in China. Many young people wanted more freedom and an end to corruption. This democracy movement in China gained great support when large numbers of students began to demonstrate in the spring of 1989 at places such as Tiananmen Square, a historic public place in Beijing. In response, the government sent in the army with tanks to Tiananmen Square in June.

Chinese troops opened fire, killing many and injuring thousands of demonstrators. Other demonstrators were arrested and tortured. Some were even executed. The Communist Party was determined not to surrender its power.

After Deng's death in 1997, Jiang Zemin became China's new leader. He cautiously continued Deng's policies. Relations with the West have been unstable, with Western countries criticizing China for human rights violations against its government's opponents. In 1997, Great Britain turned over one of its last remaining colonies, Hong Kong, to China. The Communist government seems to want to continue many of Hong Kong's capitalist institutions. In late 1999, China and the United States signed an important treaty. This treaty normalized trade relations between the two countries. In 2003, the leader of the Chinese Communist Party, Hu Jintao, was elected as China's president.

Today, there are more than 1 billion people living in China. This large population is a strain on the nation's economy. To control population growth, the government started the one-child-per-family policy in the 1980s. Parents who followed this policy were rewarded with

U.S. President George W. Bush (right) met with Hu Jintao of China after President Bush gave a speech in Beijing in 2002.

744   UNIT 8 ◆ The World Today

Teaching Options

Connection to
MATH

Have students use the Internet to find China's Gross Domestic Product during the 1980s. Have students make a graph of the data. Remind students to include the names of their sources. Then, have students find the GDP data for the United States during the 1980s and show the data on the same graph. Have students present their graphs and data to the class. Then, the class should compare and contrast the graphs.

Meet Individual Needs:
VERBAL/LINGUISTIC LEARNERS

Have students write a song about the Chinese students at Tiananmen Square. Songs should include details from the text and should make a call for change.

better medical benefits or housing. Parents who did not follow the law were fined or given other penalties.

◆ **What were the policies of Deng Xiaoping?**

C. Korea Divided

Korea occupies a peninsula extending southward from northeast China. Korea is bound by the Yellow Sea to the west and the Sea of Japan to the east. Japan annexed Korea in 1910. For 35 years, Korea was a Japanese colony.

In 1945, after the Japanese defeat in World War II, Korea was divided into two zones. Soviet troops occupied the zone north of the 38th parallel of latitude (38°N). American troops occupied the south. In 1948, two separate governments were established: a Communist state in North Korea, and a republic in South Korea. Soviet and U.S. troops withdrew in 1949.

The Korean War

In June 1950, North Korean forces invaded South Korea. U.S. President Harry Truman ordered American troops to South Korea under the command of General Douglas MacArthur, who had commanded troops during World War I and World War II. Backed by UN troops, the American forces supported South Korea. The Soviet Union, which regarded North Korea as a satellite state, quickly provided it with military aid. As you learned in Chapter 19, a satellite state depends on another country for its economic and political well-being.

The Chinese government became concerned because American troops were advancing toward the Chinese border. China then entered the war on the side of North Korea. The Chinese army drove the UN forces back to the 38th parallel. General MacArthur wanted to attack China. President Truman believed that such a policy might draw the Soviet Union into the war. This possibility might lead to a larger war and the use of atomic weapons. When MacArthur publicly refused Truman's orders, the President relieved him of his command.

Between 1951 and 1953, a long series of negotiations took place. Then, under U.S. President Eisenhower, an armistice, or treaty, was signed. Korea remained divided, with a demilitarized zone, or DMZ, at the 38th parallel between the countries of North Korea and South Korea. There were more than 1 million casualties in North Korea and about the same number in South Korea. About 34,000 Americans were killed, and another 100,000, wounded.

After the Korean War, Cold War tensions remained. North Korea became a Soviet satellite, and South Korea signed a defense treaty and received aid from the United States. North Korea became a closed society with few contacts with other nations. U.S. forces are still in South Korea to help guarantee peace.

Global Connections

CHINA'S POPULATION
China's population in 2002 was 1.3 billion. This figure meant that about one out of five people in the world was Chinese in 2002.

The Korean War, 1950–1953

Legend:
- Farthest North Korean advance, September 1950
- Farthest UN advance, November 1950
- Farthest North Korean and Chinese advance, January 1951
- Armistice line, July 1953
- • Cities

Map labels: SOVIET UNION, CHINA, 125°E, 130°E, 42°N, 40°N, 38°N, 36°N, 34°N, Yalu River, Chosan, NORTH KOREA, Pyongyang, Panmunjom, 38th Parallel, Inchon Landing, U.S. troops land on September 15, 1950, Seoul, Inchon, SOUTH KOREA, Yellow Sea, Pusan, Sea of Japan, JAPAN, 0 50 100 mi, 0 50 100 km

✔ **Map Check**

MOVEMENT When did UN troops come closest to China?

GLOBAL CONNECTIONS
CHINA'S POPULATION During the period from 1950 to 1975, the population in China nearly doubled, rising from 554 million to 933 million. People were living longer, and infant mortality dropped dramatically with the improvement of medicine.

◆ **ANSWER** Deng Xiaoping introduced a socialist market economy in China, which blended socialism and capitalism; Deng increased contacts with the West and encouraged foreign investment in China. He did not support political freedom.

C. Korea Divided

Purpose-Setting Question In 1948, what kinds of governments were established in Korea? (a Communist government in North Korea and a republic in South Korea)

Activity

Invite a guest speaker Ask a community member to come to the class and relate his or her memories of the Korean War. Have students prepare questions for the guest beforehand.

Using the Map

The Korean War, 1950–1953

Ask students to use the map to find when troops landed at Inchon. (September 15, 1950)

✔ **Map Check**
Answer November 1950

Review Ask students to name the aggressors of the Cold War and tell what each nation feared from the other. (The United States and Soviet Union both feared the loss of military advantage and the possibility of nuclear attack.)

Explain Tell students that when North Korea and South Korea were formed, some families were split up. Due to the hostility that existed for the next 45 years, family members were not allowed to see each other or have any contact. Discuss with students how difficult it would be to have their own family split this way. In recent years, the North Korean and South Korean governments have let some family members visit each other.

 **ANSWER** North Korean forces invaded South Korea.

Section Close

Ask students to respond to the following statement, "China's people spent the twentieth century in peace and political stability." (no) Then, have students use information from the text to explain their answer.

Seoul, South Korea, hosted the 1988 summer Olympic Games.

From the American point of view, the Korean War had succeeded as an effort to stop the spread of communism in Asia. However, the Communists felt that the United States had been prevented from imposing its will on the East.

New Conflicts After the War

Since the Korean War, North Korea and South Korea have regarded each other with suspicion or hostility. In 1968, for example, North Korean troops slipped into Seoul, the South Korean capital, and tried to assassinate the South Korean president.

In 1988, South Korea hosted the summer Olympic Games. The International Olympic Committee refused to allow North Korea to co-host the games. North Korea boycotted the event.

In 1991, both Koreas joined the United Nations as separate states and agreed to recognize each other's existence. As relations between North Korea and South Korea seemed to be improving, conflicts developed between North Korea and other countries. In January 2003, North Korea withdrew from the Nuclear Nonproliferation Treaty, an international agreement that requires countries to reduce the number of its nuclear weapons. This action led to increased tensions between North Korea and nations that have signed this agreement. With leaders from these nations, including the United States, Japan, and South Korea, working together to discuss the issue with North Korea, a peaceful resolution remains a possibility.

◆ **In 1950, what triggered the Korean War?**

---

③ Assess

Review Answers

Review History

A. The Communists defeated the Nationalists and gained control of mainland China. The Nationalists withdrew to the island of Taiwan, where they set up a republican government-in-exile and established the Republic of China.

B. Many students began to demonstrate for more freedom and an end to political corruption. The government sent in the army to stop the protest. Demonstrators were killed, injured, arrested, tortured, or executed.

C. The United States, China, the Soviet Union, South Korea, and North Korea were all involved in the Korean War.

Define Terms to Know
commune, 743;
socialist market economy, 744

Critical Thinking
Possible answer: The government may have been reluctant to allow any reform that might lead to disorder or might call the government's authority into question.

Review II

Review History
A. What was the outcome of the struggle for power in China between Nationalists and Communists?
B. In 1989, what happened at Tiananmen Square in Beijing?
C. Which countries became involved in the Korean War?

Define Terms to Know
Define the following terms: **commune, socialist market economy**

Critical Thinking
Why do you think the Chinese government cracked down so harshly on the democratic movement in China?

Write About Government
In a paragraph, explain how Mao Zedong tried to achieve the goals of a Communist government in China.

Get Organized
CAUSE-AND-EFFECT CHAIN
Think about the main events in this section. Use a cause-and-effect chain to show the cause and effect of an event. For example, what was a cause and an effect of the Korean War?

Write About Government
Answers will vary. Students' paragraphs should explain how Mao Zedong tried to achieve the goals of a Communist government, and what the results were.

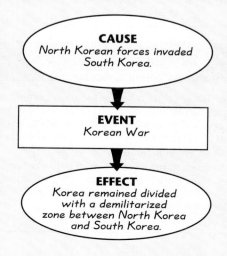

CAUSE
North Korean forces invaded South Korea.

EVENT
Korean War

EFFECT
Korea remained divided with a demilitarized zone between North Korea and South Korea.

Japan Rebuilds

Terms to Know

occupation the control of an area by the military force of a foreign state

business cycle the alternation of periods of economic prosperity and decline

Main Ideas

A. After its defeat in World War II, Japan rose to the challenge of rebuilding.

B. The Japanese economy, which had been strong for several decades, slipped into recession during the 1990s, and social tensions increased.

 Active Reading

PROBLEMS AND SOLUTIONS
When you examine problems and solutions, you consider ways in which challenges are met or problems are resolved. As you read this section, focus on the problems that confronted Japan after 1945 and the solutions. Also, focus on current problems in Japan.

Section Summary

In this section, students will read about Japan's recovery after its defeat in World War II. Students will learn about how Japan's economy, after several strong decades, slipped into recession, and social tensions increased.

1 Introduce

Getting Started

Ask students what they think would be most important for a country to do to recover after a war. Work with students to list some of the tasks (housing, food production, medical care, and rebuilding the economy) on the board. Explain to students that Japan faced all these problems after World War II. Japan needed help to rebuild.

A. Japan After World War II

The defeat of Japan by the United States and its allies brought World War II to a close in 1945. Japanese surrender was accomplished at a terrible cost, however. As you read in Chapter 28, the United States, wishing to end the war as quickly as possible, used atomic weapons to destroy the cities of Hiroshima and Nagasaki. The terms of the surrender forced Japan to give up all its Asian territories as well as the islands it had governed in the Pacific.

A Shattered Nation

In the autumn of 1945, Japan was a shattered nation. According to one estimate, the country had lost one-third of its total wealth. One-fourth of the country's housing had been destroyed by wartime bombing. Industrial and agricultural output had shrunk to 50 percent of prewar levels.

Urban life was especially difficult. After the war, the Japanese people called their cities scorched fields. Tens of thousands of people crowded together in shacks and huts. Even in 1948, three years after surrender in World War II, nearly 4 million Japanese families lacked housing.

It was not only housing that was scarce. Food, medicine, and jobs were all in short supply. Crop failures in 1945 and 1947 increased the hardships of middle- and working-class families. The United States helped to avoid mass starvation by shipping emergency supplies of wheat, corned beef, and powdered milk. Even with this aid, however, the average Japanese family spent about 70 percent of its income on food in 1947. This left little for other necessities.

With the public sanitation and health systems in chaos, disease reached epidemic levels. Cholera, typhoid, dysentery, and tuberculosis were especially severe. One historian estimated that between 1945 and 1947, a quarter of a million people died

TERMS TO KNOW

Have students read the terms and definitions on page 747 and then find each term in the text and use it in a sentence. As a class, have students brainstorm other events in history that involved an occupation.

You may wish to preview the pronunciation of the following names from this section with students.

Emperor Hirohito (hihr oh HEE toh)
Ainu (EYE noo)
Osaka (oh SAH kah)

ACTIVE READING

Ask students to identify a problem and its solution as they read each subsection. Suggest that they record each problem with its solution in a chart. You may wish to provide students with a blank problem/solution chart (TR, p. 327).

A man looks at the ruins of Hiroshima, Japan, after the atomic bomb destroyed the city on August 6, 1945.

Teaching Options

Section 3 Resources

Teacher's Resources (TR)
Terms to Know, p. 44
Review History, p. 78
Build Your Skills, p. 112
Concept Builder, p. 247
Cause-and-Effect Chain, p. 325

 Using Technology

Ask students to use the Internet to find three legitimate sources that record the conditions of postwar Japan. Ask them to keep a log of their search by printing a copy of the first page of each Web site they visit. Conclude the activity by discussing how to decide if a source will be valuable or not.

A. Japan After World War II

Purpose-Setting Question What were some reforms the U.S. occupation force introduced to Japan? (redistribution of land, legalization of labor unions, and reorganization of the education system)

Discuss Review with students the problems that Japan faced after World War II. Ask them how the actual problems compared with the list the class had made as part of the Getting Started activity on page T747.

ANALYZE PRIMARY SOURCES

DOCUMENT-BASED QUESTION

Some feel returning soldiers were harshly judged and that they were often treated as if they had failed their country.

ANSWER "Not a single person gave me a kind word. Rather, they cast hostile glances my way."

Activity

Make a list List MacArthur's three goals for rebuilding Japan on a three-column chart. Ask students to list the ways each goal was achieved. For each goal on the chart, have students include the advantages and disadvantages to the Japanese people.

Focus Review the new Japanese government created by Japan's new constitution. Discuss who was running the country after the war (diet and prime minister) and other changes. (women could vote, more local self-government) Ask students how they think some of these changes would have been received by the Japanese people.

ANSWER housing, food, jobs, and medicine were all in short supply; public sanitation and health systems in chaos; disease at epidemic levels

B. The Japanese Economy

Purpose-Setting Question How did the lack of a large standing military help Japan's recovery? (All the money that had supported the large military could now be used in business investments.)

from these diseases. Infant deaths rose to 77 deaths per 1,000 births—as compared to 5 per 1,000 in the mid-1980s.

Added to these hardships was the shock of defeat and widespread feelings of despair. Returning Japanese veterans suffered especially sharp conflicts. One veteran summed up these strains as follows:

> **66** My house was burned, my wife and children missing. What little money I had quickly was consumed by high prices, and I was a pitiful figure. Not a single person gave me a kind word. Rather, they cast hostile glances my way. **99**

ANALYZE PRIMARY SOURCES **DOCUMENT-BASED QUESTION** Which sentences tell how people treated this army veteran?

The American Occupation of Japan

From 1945 to 1952, the United States administered an Allied military **occupation** of Japan. An occupation is the control of a country by the armed forces of a foreign state. The American occupation of Japan was led by General Douglas MacArthur, who had played an important role in the Pacific during World War II. Japanese government officials carried out the orders of the occupation force.

MacArthur's three most important goals were demilitarizing Japanese society, encouraging political democracy, and rebuilding the Japanese economy. Demilitarization involved doing away with the Japanese army and navy as well as dealing with millions of demobilized, or discharged, troops. A small number of high-ranking politicians and military leaders were tried for war crimes. However, the emperor of Japan was permitted to retain his position and was not punished.

In 1946, MacArthur and his advisors drafted a new constitution for Japan. This document greatly changed the Japanese system of government. The emperor gave up his claim to divinity, or godlike status. Sovereignty, or the source of political power, was given to the people. In recognition of Japanese

General Douglas MacArthur (left), who led the American occupation of Japan, posed with Emperor Hirohito (right) of Japan in Tokyo in September 1945.

tradition, however, the emperor remained as the symbolic head of state.

Political power became centered in the diet, or two-part legislature. A civilian prime minister, elected by majority vote of the diet, became the head of government. The constitution also gave women the right to vote and encouraged local self-government. Finally, the constitution condemned war or the use of force in international disputes. Japan was permitted to maintain a small army, but only for defensive purposes.

In addition, the reforms of the occupation force included redistributing land, legalizing labor unions, and reorganizing the education system to increase opportunity for everyone.

◆ **What were some of the extreme hardships the Japanese people faced after World War II?**

B. The Japanese Economy

After defeat in 1945, the Japanese economy was badly damaged. Bombs had destroyed most factories, and unemployment was high. Many Japanese trading ships had been destroyed during the war. The value of the yen, or Japanese currency, had sunk so low that the country could not afford many foreign imports.

748 UNIT 8 ◆ The World Today

Teaching Options

ESL/ELL STRATEGIES

Summarize Help students simplify the paragraph beginning "MacArthur's three most." Show students how to shorten a sentence into a subject/verb/object format. Then, demonstrate the effect of modifiers. For example, the core of the first sentence is "Goals were demilitarizing, encouraging, and rebuilding." The remaining words modify this core sentence.

F Y I

Bullet Trains

Japan's bullet trains run at extraordinarily fast speeds. They also run very frequently, as often as every 7.5 minutes at rush hours. Such high speeds require each train to be equipped with elaborate safety measures. For example, the brake systems include cast-iron disks that allow the brakes to absorb extreme pressure and enormous friction.

The train pictured here, called a bullet train for its speed, is an example of Japanese modernization. A bullet train can reach speeds of almost 200 miles an hour.

Rising From the Ashes

The rapid recovery of Japan after World War II has often been called an economic miracle. The American occupation force, as well as the Japanese government, steered the rebuilding of Japanese industry. The United States provided financial and technical assistance. Two Japanese government departments were especially important: the Ministry of International Trade and Industry and the Ministry of Finance. By the mid-1950s, Japan's gross domestic product had regained prewar levels. For nearly two decades afterward, growth increased at an impressive yearly rate of nearly 10 percent. Japan had a favorable balance of trade. The country exported more goods than it imported.

Certain patterns in Japanese society aided economic growth. These patterns included dedication to work, company loyalty, self-discipline in saving money, and conservatism in investments. Another factor aiding economic recovery was the lack of a large military force. Money that had, in the past, gone to support the military could now be used in business investment. The Korean War also boosted Japan's economy. Japan produced and sold supplies to U.S. forces.

Along with strong economic expansion, social changes occurred rapidly in Japan. Many people moved to the cities, as in other industrialized countries. By the end of the twentieth century, 80 percent of Japanese people lived in urban areas. Family income greatly increased within a single generation. Some people whose families had been desperately poor became wealthy.

The economic boom in Japan after World War II was also steered by a labor shortage. This situation greatly encouraged the development of automation, or the use of machines or other equipment to perform manual labor. Japan became a leader in high-technology products, such as cameras, televisions, and automobiles. These high-tech industries made consumer products that were considered to be the best in the world. By the mid-1980s, Japan had become the world's second-strongest industrial economy, after the United States.

Global Connections

JAPANESE AUTOMOBILES
Automobile production and export figures give some idea of the Japanese economic miracle. In 1960, Japan produced about 481,000 autos and exported 8.1 percent of them. In 1970, the figure was 5.3 million, with 20.5 percent exported. In 1980, Japan made 11 million autos and exported 54 percent. Of the top four auto companies worldwide in 1983, two were American, and two were Japanese.

Demonstrate Ask students to look around the classroom and in their backpacks for items made in Japan. Have them discuss the reasons why Japan became a leader in technology and manufacturing.

TEACH PRIMARY SOURCES
Have students study the photograph of the bullet train. Remind students that the bullet train is an example of Japan's advanced technology. Then, ask students what else they see in the photograph. (three people harvesting wheat by hand) Explain that this photograph shows the complexity of the Japanese economy.

GLOBAL CONNECTIONS
JAPANESE AUTOMOBILES Ask students to make a list of words or phrases to describe the quality, reputation, or value of Japanese automobiles.

Allow students to use the Internet to find information, such as safety ratings, customer satisfaction, prices, and current marketing materials, to help them make the list of words and phrases. Once completed, have students share their information and list with the class.

Activity

Make a graph Use the information in the Global Connections feature to make two graphs on the board—one that shows auto production and the other percentage exported. Ask students to make suggestions about how the graphs ought to be constructed. After completing the graphs, ask students questions about the graphs.

Discuss Review with students some of the factors that contributed to Japan's economic growth. Explain to students that many people in Japan went to work for a company at the start of their career and never changed companies. Employees typically worked long hours. In exchange, companies took care of their employees and did not eliminate jobs when the company experienced problems. This relationship was successful as long as the economy was strong.

Writing

AVERAGE
Have students conduct research to write a profile of an actual Japanese person who lived in the postwar era. Students may focus on a returning soldier, a prosperous city dweller, or a farmer. Profiles should take the form of a letter, a narrative, or a description of the person, all based on the student's research.

CHALLENGE
Have students conduct research to write a profile of the different generations of one real-life Japanese family starting with the parents who lived during the postwar era and their children who lived during the rise of Japan. Students may write journal entries, letters, narratives, or descriptions in order to profile these people from two different generations.

A group of women motorcycle police officers patrol a neighborhood in Osaka, Japan.

Recovery Turns to Recession

A basic principle of economic theory is the concept of **business cycles**. A business cycle is the alternation of periods of prosperity and periods of decline. Perhaps, then, it was to be expected that Japanese prosperity would give way, sooner or later, to less favorable conditions. In the late 1980s, Japanese exports began to decrease. The country's strong currency and high labor costs made goods expensive. Japan also faced competition from low-cost manufacturing carried out in other countries, such as the Philippines and Indonesia.

In the early 1990s, serious problems also surfaced in the banking system. Banks had overextended themselves by making large loans to real estate investors. When property values fell, many borrowers could not repay these loans. This failure to repay bank loans made credit much harder to find. By raising taxes, the government deepened Japan's economic problems.

Along with economic decline, social unrest increased during the 1990s in Japan. Women pressed for changes in the workplace, which has traditionally favored men. Women demanded equal pay and treatment. Ethnic minorities, particularly the Ainu of the north, called for an end to discrimination. Charges of corruption in government were made. In a country that has traditionally prized respect for elders, a growing number of Japanese youth were involved in illegal actions. In 1997, for example, juvenile crime increased by 20 percent over the year before. Still, Japan remains one of the most wealthy, productive nations in the world, and it provides much foreign aid to countries in which industrialization is still taking place.

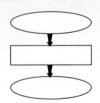 **What were some of Japan's problems during the 1990s?**

Review III

Review History
A. What were General Douglas MacArthur's three most important goals during the occupation of Japan after World War II?
B. What caused problems for the Japanese economy in the late 1980s?

Define Terms to Know
Define the following terms:
occupation, business cycle

Critical Thinking
Why might Japan provide much foreign aid even during difficult economic times?

Write About History
In one or two paragraphs evaluate the ways in which Japan and the United States, working together, succeeded in rebuilding Japan after World War II.

Get Organized
CAUSE-AND-EFFECT CHAIN
Think about the main events in this section. Use a cause-and-effect chain to show the cause and effect of an event. For example, what was a cause and an effect of the Japanese economic recovery after World War II.

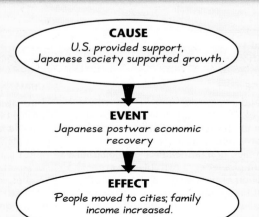

CAUSE
U.S. provided support, Japanese society supported growth.

EVENT
Japanese postwar economic recovery

EFFECT
People moved to cities; family income increased.

Conflict in Southeast Asia

Terms to Know

referendum a direct vote of the people on a law or policy

cease-fire agreement an agreement to end fighting

Main Ideas

A. In the 1960s and early 1970s, the United States became involved in a long and costly war in Vietnam in an effort to prevent the spread of communism in Asia.

B. Cambodia and Myanmar, formerly called Burma, have experienced dictatorship and bloodshed.

C. Since the late 1940s, Indonesia and the Philippines have struggled to establish self-determination and democracy.

 Active Reading

CAUSE AND EFFECT
When you identify cause and effect, you determine the reason(s) and the consequence(s) of an event. As you read this section, think about the causes and the effects of the Vietnam War.

Section Summary

In this section, students will learn about the causes of the Vietnam War. They will read about the bloodshed in Cambodia, as well as in Myanmar (Burma). Finally, they will read about the struggle for independence and democracy in Indonesia and the Philippines.

1 Introduce

Getting Started

Use a world map or Transparency 7 to point out Vietnam and the rest of Southeast Asia. Discuss the geographical factors that influence the region, such as climate, proximity to water, and topographic features, such as mountains and rain forests.

A. The Vietnam War

The Korean War of the early 1950s had convinced many American policy-makers that prompt, determined resistance could stop the spread of communism. Therefore, when conflicts arose in Vietnam, the way was paved for U.S. involvement.

Background and Causes

Vietnam, along with neighboring Cambodia and Laos, had been part of French Indochina since the nineteenth century. During and after World War II, a Vietnamese Communist, Ho Chi Minh, led the Vietnamese resistance, first against Japan and then against France. Communists fought side by side with non-Communists, and the French were forced to withdraw from Vietnam in 1954. An international conference proclaimed the independence of Vietnam, Cambodia, and Laos. Like Korea, Vietnam was partitioned into a northern and southern zone. It was divided at the 17th parallel of latitude (17°N). Elections were to be held for the entire country.

These arrangements left Ho Chi Minh in the Communist north dissatisfied. Likewise, anti-Communists in the south had no intention of living under a Communist government. In 1955, a **referendum**, or direct vote of the people on a law or policy, in the south proclaimed a separate, independent republic. Ngo Dinh Diem became president of the South Vietnam government. Ho Chi Minh then sent the Viet Cong—guerrilla troops loyal to the Communist cause—southward. Ho Chi Minh was determined to overthrow Diem and the South Vietnamese government. Both the Soviet Union and the People's Republic of China provided aid to North Vietnam. Meanwhile, South Vietnam turned to the United States for support.

The United States in Vietnam

During the late 1950s, Cold War tensions increased. American foreign policy supported resisting the spread of communism anywhere in the world. U.S. President Dwight Eisenhower sent military advisors as well as military and economic aid to South Vietnam. Eisenhower believed in the domino theory—that a Communist takeover of Vietnam would soon lead to Communist victories in the other nations of Southeast Asia. He used the image of a row of dominoes for a series of nations toppling over to the Communist cause.

Ho Chi Minh wanted Vietnam to have a Communist government.

Do You Remember?

In Chapter 30, you learned that the domino theory is the belief that if one country falls to communism, others nearby will also fall.

TERMS TO KNOW

Ask students to read the terms and definitions on page 751 and then find each term in the section. Write sentences on the board using the terms. For example, "The referendum on increasing the tax for schools passed by an overwhelming margin." Have students read the sentences aloud substituting the definition for the term.

You may wish to preview the pronunciation of the following names with students.

Ngo Dihn Diem
(NGOH DIHN dee EHM)
Tonkin (tahn KIHN)
Norodom Sihanouk
(NOOR uh duhm SEE uh nook)
Aung San Suu Kyi
(AWNG SAYN SOO CHEE)
Suharto (SOO HAHR too)
Megawati Sukarnoputri
(mehg eh WAH tee
soo kahr noh POO treh)
Corazón Aquino
(kaw ruh SAHN ah KEE noh)

ACTIVE READING

Suggest that students list each event individually on index cards. Have them note the causes and the effects on the card as they read. Then, provide students with a cause-and-effect chain (TR, p. 325) to complete, using the information from their index cards. Have partners compare their work.

Teaching Options

Section 4 Resources

Teacher's Resources (TR)

Terms to Know, p. 44
Review History, p. 78
Build Your Skills, p. 112
Chapter Test, pp. 177–178
Concept Builder, p. 247
Cause-and-Effect Chain, p. 325
Transparencies 1, 7

Cooperative Learning

Have students work in groups to make the front page for a newspaper covering the Vietnam War. The page should contain several articles on topics of students' choice, such as a report on a major battle, leadership conflicts, or fighting techniques. The page may also contain a map, a timeline, or other visual. Post the newspapers together in the classroom.

A. The Vietnam War

Purpose-Setting Question What role did France play in Vietnam? (Until 1954 when France was forced out, Vietnam had been part of French Indochina.)

Do You Remember?
Review the domino theory with students. Ask what other conflicts the United States was involved in to stop the expansion of communism. (Korean War)

Using the Map
The Vietnam War, 1968–1975

Ask students to name the countries in which the Ho Chi Minh Trail was located. (North Vietnam, South Vietnam, Cambodia, and Laos) Where did it begin and end? (It began in North Vietnam and ended in South Vietnam.)

✔ Map Check
Answer It began in Laos and Cambodia and continued into South Vietnam.

Extend Explain that the American and South Vietnamese military strategists were eager to destroy the Ho Chi Minh Trail, which was used to supply the North Vietnamese guerrillas. Discuss with students the risks Cambodia took by allowing the trail to operate.

Activity
Invite a guest Invite a fellow teacher or community member to talk about his or her experiences during the Vietnam War era. Have students prepare questions for the guest before the visit.

Then & Now
VIETNAM-U.S. RELATIONS Bring in a tourist promotion or travel guide for Vietnam, such as an Internet travel agency's promotion. Ask students to describe how Vietnam is portrayed in the promotion. What images support that portrayal?

The Vietnam War, 1968–1975

→ Tet Offensive, 1968
■ American bases
→ North Vietnam's final offensive, 1975
● Cities

0 100 200 mi
0 100 200 km

✔ Map Check
MOVEMENT In which countries did the Tet Offensive of 1968 start and into which country did it continue?

Then & Now
VIETNAM–U.S. RELATIONS
For some years after the Vietnam War, Vietnam was closed to American visitors. In 1989, however, Vietnam and the United States resumed relations and Vietnam has become a popular tourist destination.

752 UNIT 8 ◆ The World Today

American Involvement Increases

As Ho Chi Minh and Viet Cong troops continued their attempts to overthrow Diem, South Vietnamese people were unhappy with the corruption, inefficiency, and repression of Diem's government. Under U.S. President John F. Kennedy in the early 1960s, several thousand U.S. military advisors and support troops arrived in South Vietnam. However, sometime later, Diem was overthrown and assassinated by South Vietnamese military leaders.

In 1964, off the North Vietnamese coast in the Gulf of Tonkin, several torpedo boats attacked American destroyers. The U.S. Congress authorized President Lyndon B. Johnson to take "all necessary measures" to defend the United States and South Vietnam. Johnson's administration used this Gulf of Tonkin Resolution as a basis for swiftly escalating, or increasing, American involvement. By 1966, there were nearly 200,000 American troops in Vietnam. Three years later, in 1969, there were close to 550,000.

Despite massive bombing by the United States, the North Vietnamese refused to surrender. Their use of guerrilla warfare in the jungle terrain proved highly successful. In 1968, they mounted the Tet, or New Year's, Offensive.

Meanwhile, in the United States, opposition to the war was growing. Prospects for victory seemed very remote. Many students and other young people staged large demonstrations against the war. The reports of American casualties angered many observers. Some critics felt that the conflict in Vietnam was a civil war in which the United States should not be involved. Many politicians and journalists became convinced that a negotiated settlement would be necessary. Historians argued that Vietnam had a long history of independence. Even a unified Communist government there would not be likely to take orders from China or the Soviet Union.

The Vietnam War Ends

Under President Richard Nixon, the United States pursued a policy of Vietnamization—or turning over more and more of the responsibility to South Vietnam for its own defense. American troops began to slowly withdraw. However, in 1970, Nixon ordered air attacks in neighboring Cambodia against North Vietnamese supply lines.

Finally, a **cease-fire agreement**, or an agreement to end fighting, was concluded in Paris in January 1973. American forces withdrew from South Vietnam. A little more than two years later, the North Vietnamese captured Saigon, the South Vietnamese capital. It was renamed Ho Chi Minh City. The country was reunited as a Communist state.

The costs of the Vietnam War were enormous, not only in Vietnam, but in the United States as well. About 1.3 million Vietnamese died, and there were more than 58,000 American deaths. The faith of Americans in their political leadership and foreign policy was shaken. The war left scars that would take a long time to heal.

Teaching Options

Writing

AVERAGE
Have students research the events that led the United States to become involved in the Vietnam War. Have them use the information to make a timeline (TR, p. 320). Explain to students that the U.S. involvement had several causes. They should find at least three events to write on their timelines. Have students use timelines to write two or three summary paragraphs on the causes of the U.S. involvement in Vietnam.

CHALLENGE
Have students research the opposing viewpoints about U.S. involvement in Vietnam. Have them choose one side of the issue and write a speech to persuade Americans that they should or should not get involved in the war. Students should base their argument on historical facts.

In Vietnam, the people and the economy were devastated. For years, many people lived in extreme poverty. The United States and some other countries placed an embargo on Vietnam to decrease its trade. When Vietnam began some free-market policies in the 1990s, the country attracted foreign investment. The United States lifted the embargo and renewed their relations with the government of Vietnam.

◆ **What were the principal causes of the Vietnam War?**

B. Government by Extremes

The Vietnam War was a critical event for all of Southeast Asia. Communism and anti-communism flared to extremes in different parts of the region. During the 1960s and 1970s, two countries that served as examples of extreme government were Cambodia and Myanmar, formerly Burma.

Genocide in Cambodia

During World War II, Cambodia was occupied by Japan and Thailand. In 1954, France recognized Cambodia's independence. During the 1950s and 1960s, the country was ruled by Norodom Sihanouk.

During the Vietnam War, Viet Cong troops often went to Cambodia to avoid being captured. In addition, the Ho Chi Minh Trail—used by North Vietnam to transport supplies to the Viet Cong—ran through eastern Cambodia.

In 1970, the Cambodian general Lon Nol overthrew Sihanouk. He ruled the country as a dictator. As the Vietnam War continued, a group of Cambodian rebels, called the Khmer Rouge, were trained by Vietnamese Communists who had escaped to Cambodia for safety. In 1975, the Khmer Rouge captured the Cambodian capital of Phnom Penh and set up a new government under the leadership of Pol Pot.

Over the next four years, the new government inflicted a campaign of terror. Most city dwellers were driven into the countryside, where they were forced to work in labor camps. The government abolished religion, the use of money, and private property. The Khmer Rouge executed so many people that the government has been held responsible for genocide in Cambodia. Between 1975 and 1979, an estimated 2 to 3 million Cambodians died from execution, starvation, forced labor, or disease.

In 1978, Vietnam invaded and occupied Cambodia. By early 1979, Pol Pot's brutal government was defeated. Gradually, during the 1980s and 1990s, civil war ended and Cambodia began to build a democracy.

Military Dictatorship in Myanmar

Burma won independence from Great Britain in 1948. However, political and ethnic rivalries prevented the establishment of a stable parliamentary democracy. Beginning in 1960, civilian governments alternated with periods of military rule.

In 1962, General Ne Win suspended the Burmese constitution. He decided that the country should become a Socialist state. For the next quarter of a century, Ne Win's political party—the Burma Socialist Programme Party—was the only legal political party in the country.

A guerrilla soldier for the Khmer Rouge looks out from a hiding place in the Cambodian jungle.

F Y I

Khmer Rouge

The objective of Pol Pot and his Khmer Rouge was to obliterate all signs of western influence. The following quote, from *A Cambodian Odyssey* by Haing Ngor, explains the conditions in Cambodia. "There were no more cities. . . . No schools. No books or magazines. . . . Just the sun that rose and set, the stars at night and the rain that fell from the sky. And work. Everything was work."

Meet Individual Needs:

VISUAL/SPATIAL LEARNERS

Have students work in groups to make timelines (TR, p. 320) for Cambodia and Myanmar (Burma) using the information given in the text. Ask some groups to make a timeline for Cambodia and the other groups for Myanmar. Then, have the groups share their timelines with the class for comparison.

C. Struggles for Democracy and Self-Determination

Purpose-Setting Question How did the government of Indonesia deal with the self-determination movement in East Timor? (The government dealt harshly with such movements, although the violent conflict in East Timor resulted in the UN's assigning a peacekeeping force there. Eventually, Indonesia gave up its claim to East Timor.)

WHERE IN THE WORLD?
THE INDONESIAN ARCHIPELAGO
Ask students to locate Indonesia on a world map (Atlas pp. A1–A2) or Transparency 1. As a class, identify the major islands and cities of the nation.

Activity

Write a biography Ask students to find a profile on the Internet or in a reference book of one of the women leaders in Southeast Asia, Aung San Suu Kyi, Megawati Sukarnoputri, or Corazón Aquino. Have them summarize the leader's achievements in a brief biography. Ask student volunteers to read their biographies aloud.

Discuss Ask students what they have noticed about many of the governments in Southeast Asia. (They were authoritarian or dictatorships.) Discuss with students how the geography of Indonesia and the Philippines might have made it difficult to unite or govern these countries.

At the end of the 1980s, Burmese people began to demonstrate against the government, calling for the end of one-party rule. Thousands of protesters were killed. Once again, the army overthrew the government. A new set of military leaders took over. In 1989, this group changed the country's name to Myanmar.

Military dictatorship in Myanmar was courageously opposed by Aung San Suu Kyi. She was the daughter of a prominent fighter for Burmese independence. For six years, between 1989 and 1995, the military government kept Suu Kyi under arrest and guarded in her home. For her outspoken support of democracy and human rights, she won the Nobel Peace Prize in 1991.

◆ **How would you describe life in Cambodia during the campaign of terror?**

C. Struggles for Democracy and Self-Determination

Not all conflict in Southeast Asia was as violent as those in Cambodia and Myanmar. In Indonesia and the Philippines, political leadership took a less extreme course. However, these countries still experienced difficulties on the road to democracy and self-determination.

Indonesia After Independence

Indonesia had been dominated by the Dutch for several centuries, beginning around 1700. The Dutch East India Company obtained important trading rights in the vast Indonesian archipelago, or group of many islands. Nationalist feeling in Indonesia began to strengthen in the early 1800s. The Dutch had to confront numerous rebellions. In 1927, a freedom fighter named Sukarno founded the Indonesian National Party. During World War II, Japan occupied some parts of Indonesia. After the war, the Dutch tried but failed to regain control of the country. By 1949, the Dutch formally recognized Indonesia's independence.

Indonesia existed officially as a republic with parliamentary democracy. In actual fact, the country was ruled by a succession of authoritarian leaders. Sukarno ruled until 1965. Then, Suharto, a general, seized power from Sukarno. Suharto held power for more than 30 years. His government was able to promote economic growth, but not democracy. Then, Indonesia's economy declined in the 1990s. Suharto stepped down in 1998. Sukarno's daughter, Megawati Sukarnoputri, became president of Indonesia in 2001.

Indonesia's government dealt harshly with movements for self-determination. One of the most important movements occurred in East Timor, a Portuguese island colony that Indonesia had invaded in 1975. Much of the population of East Timor was Christian. They objected to rule by predominantly Muslim Indonesia. In August 1999, the East Timorese voted for independence from Indonesia. Violent conflict on the island resulted in the assignment there of a UN peacekeeping force. In late 1999, the Indonesian central government agreed to give up its claim to East Timor.

The Philippines

The United States ruled the island nation of the Philippines for nearly 50 years. In 1946, the United States gave the Philippines full independence. As in other regions of Southeast Asia, political and economic problems threatened Philippine stability. Communist groups fought over the redistribution of

THE INDONESIAN ARCHIPELAGO

The island nation of Indonesia has the fourth-largest population in the world. Indonesia is made up of more than 13,500 islands, 6,000 of them inhabited, which stretch along the equator.

General Suharto was the leader of Indonesia from 1967 to 1998.

Teaching Options

ESL/ELL STRATEGIES

Organize Information Have students make a chart for the national leaders mentioned in the section. After each name, have them identify the leader's nationality and the actions each leader is known for. Have students share their charts with each other and make necessary corrections.

land. Muslims demanded independence on islands where the majority of the population was Muslim rather than Christian. Despite aid from the United States, the economy remained weak.

In 1965, Ferdinand Marcos was elected president of the Philippines. He promised reform but made himself a dictator instead. In 1983, after nearly 20 years of rule by Marcos, his main political opponent, Benigno Aquino, was assassinated. Marcos was accused of being involved with Aquino's assassination. In response, this event touched off a series of trials, protest marches, and disputed elections. Finally, in 1986, Marcos was forced to leave the country. Aquino's widow, Corazón, was elected president.

Since 1986, the Philippines has faced continuing troubles in establishing a stable, democratic government. Islamic groups have continued to demand independence. Filipino politicians have faced charges of corruption. The future of democracy in the Philippines remains uncertain.

Corazón Aquino restored democracy to the Philippines in 1986. She served as the nation's president until 1992.

The Pacific Rim

In 1967, countries in Southeast Asia united for economic growth with the establishment of the Association of Southeast Asian Nations (ASEAN). ASEAN supports prosperity and promotes economic and cultural cooperation. Membership has grown to include most Southeast Asian nations.

Southeast Asia and East Asia are part of a large region called the Pacific Rim. The Pacific Rim includes countries in Asia and the Americas that border the Pacific Ocean. The countries of the Pacific Rim attract investors worldwide. Investment analysts think the area has great growth potential in the twenty-first century.

◆ **Why did East Timor want independence from Indonesia?**

Review IV

Review History
A. Why did the United States become involved in the Vietnam War?
B. What role has the military played in the government of Myanmar?
C. What problems threatened Philippine stability after it gained its independence in 1946?

Define Terms to Know
Define the following terms: **referendum, cease-fire agreement**

Critical Thinking
Explain why American participation in the Korean War may have led to U.S. involvement in the Vietnam War?

Write About History
In two paragraphs, compare and contrast government by extremes in Cambodia and Myanmar during the 1960s and 1970s.

Get Organized
CAUSE-AND-EFFECT CHAIN
Think about the main events in this section. Use a cause-and-effect chain to show the cause and effect of an event. For example, what was a cause and an effect of the Vietnam War?

CAUSE
Ho Chi Minh sent the Viet Cong to South Vietnam.

↓

EVENT
Vietnam War

↓

EFFECT
Vietnam was reunited under a Communist government.

◆ **ANSWER** East Timor wanted independence from Indonesia because much of the population of East Timor was Christian and it did not want to be ruled by the predominantly Muslim Indonesia.

Section Close

Ask students to recall the challenges to democracy that the nations of Southeast Asia have experienced in the late twentieth century. Discuss how each country has tried to establish itself as a self-governing country.

3 Assess

Review Answers

Review History
A. The United States became involved in Vietnam to prevent the spread of communism in Southeast Asia.

B. From 1960 to the present, Myanmar has been ruled mainly by a military dictatorship.

C. The region suffered economic difficulties, political conflicts among Communist groups, and religious conflicts between Muslims and Christians.

Define Terms to Know
referendum, 751; cease-fire agreement, 752

Critical Thinking
Possible answer: Both wars were fought to prevent the spread of communism. For many Americans, the Korean War had accomplished this objective successfully. They believed that the same goal might be achieved in Vietnam.

Write About History
Possible answer: In both Cambodia and Myanmar, people were denied their freedom. However, the totalitarian government in Cambodia was Communist and was responsible for the deaths of millions of people. A military dictatorship with Socialist goals ruled in Myanmar.

Chapter Summary

A blank outline form is available in the Teacher's Resources (p. 318). Chapter summaries should outline the causes and effects of independence in India, the move to communism in China, and the Korean War. It should also include the rebuilding of postwar Japan; causes and effects of the Vietnam War; and the conflicts in Cambodia, Myanmar, Indonesia, and the Philippines. Refer to the rubric in the Teacher's Resources (p. 340) to score the students' chapter summaries.

Interpret the Timeline

1. independence of India
2. 1949
3. 7 years (1968 to 1975)
4. 1947—India gains independence; 1954—Cambodia gains independence; 1960—Nigeria becomes independent; 1999—East Timor gains independence.
5. Check students' timelines to be sure that all events are from the chapter.

Use Terms to Know

6. e. referendum
7. f. socialist market economy
8. b. commune
9. d. occupation
10. a. business cycle
11. c. lobby

Check Your Understanding

12. The slogan means that Great Britain should leave India and give India its independence.
13. **Domestic:** transform India into a modern, industrial power; **Foreign:** did not want to ally with any side in a conflict; called for official neutrality with powers in Cold War
14. Possible answer: continuing existence of the caste system
15. Mao's first Five-Year Plan focused on the development of heavy industry.
16. A large number of students demonstrated in 1989. The Chinese government sent in the army, and many demonstrators were killed, injured, arrested, tortured, or executed.
17. In 1945, Korea was divided into two zones at the 38th parallel—a Communist state in North Korea and

Chapter Summary

Complete the following outline in your notebook. Then, use your outline to write a brief summary of the chapter.

Asia

I. Changes on the Indian Subcontinent
   A. Independence and Partition
   B. Challenge and Response
II. China and Korea
   A. Republic of China
   B. China After Mao
   C. Korea Divided
III. Japan Rebuilds
   A. Japan after World War II
   B. The Japanese Economy
IV. Conflict in Southeast Asia
   A. The Vietnam War
   B. Government by Extremes
   C. Struggles for Democracy and Self-Determination

Interpret the Timeline

Use the timeline on pages 734–735 to answer the following questions.

1. Which occurred first, the Korean War or the independence of India?
2. In which year did Communists come to power in China?
3. How many years passed between the launch of the Tet Offensive against South Vietnam and the reunification of Vietnam?
4. **Critical Thinking** Which events on the timeline involve the independence of countries?
5. Select five events from the chapter that are not on the timeline. Create a timeline that shows these events.

Use Terms to Know

Match each term with its definition.

a. business cycle   d. occupation
b. commune   e. referendum
c. lobby   f. socialist market economy

6. a direct vote of the people on a law or policy
7. an economic system that blends features of socialism with features of capitalism
8. a community in which people live and work together in large groups
9. the control of an area by the military force of a foreign state
10. the alternation of periods of economic prosperity and decline
11. to attempt to influence those in power to accept a particular point of view

Check Your Understanding

12. **Explain** the meaning of the slogan "Quit India!"
13. **Discuss** the domestic and foreign policies of Jawaharlal Nehru.
14. **Summarize** the social strains existing in present-day India.
15. **Explain** Mao's first Five-Year Economic Plan.
16. **Describe** the events of Tiananmen Square.
17. **Identify** the events leading up to the Korean War in 1950.
18. **Describe** the living conditions in Japan in the late 1940s.
19. **Discuss** the major features of the new Japanese constitution drafted by General MacArthur and his advisors.
20. **Identify** the Gulf of Tonkin Resolution.
21. **Describe** the conflict between the Indonesian government and East Timor.

---

a republic in South Korea. In June 1950, North Korean forces invaded South Korea.

18. Living conditions were harsh. Food, housing, jobs, and medicine were scarce. Public health and sanitation were in chaos. Disease reached epidemic levels.

19. The new Japanese constitution ended the emperor's claim of divinity; sovereignty was given to the people; political power was

centered in the diet; women's suffrage increased; local self-government was encouraged; there was a reduction of the military to a small defensive force.

20. The Gulf of Tonkin Resolution, passed by the U.S. Congress in 1964, gave President Lyndon B. Johnson the authority to take "all necessary measures" to defend the United States and South Vietnam.

21. East Timor was invaded by Indonesia in 1975. Many East Timorese are Christian and do not want to live under a primarily Muslim government. In 1999, they voted for independence, and a violent conflict resulted. UN peacekeeping forces intervened, and the Indonesian central government then agreed to give up its claim.

Critical Thinking

22. Analyze Causes and Effects What caused the Indian Muslims to object to living in an independent state?

23. Make Inferences Why do you think the Nehru family was able to lead India for more than 40 years?

24. Evaluate How would you evaluate the economic effort of the Great Leap Forward program?

25. Predict Consequences How might North and South Korea's relationship change during the twenty-first century? Explain.

26. Analyze What factors contributed to Japan's economic miracle after World War II?

27. Compare and Contrast How would you compare and contrast U.S. involvement in the Korean War and the Vietnam War?

Put Your Skills to Work

28. Develop a Multimedia Presentation You have learned that in a multimedia presentation, you use materials such as computer graphics, videotapes, slides, and audiotapes.

Copy the graphic organizer below. In the top box, write a topic for a presentation you could create using the information in this chapter. Then, list four types of media you would use to develop your presentation.

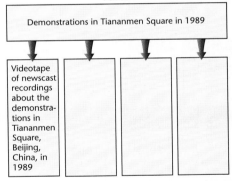

TOPIC

Demonstrations in Tiananmen Square in 1989

Videotape of newscast recordings about the demonstrations in Tiananmen Square, Beijing, China, in 1989

Analyze Sources

29. Read the comment below on Japan after World War II by historian W. G. Beasley. Then, answer the questions that follow.

Industry's success took on a different character from that of the early twentieth century, resting now on the production of high-tech goods for sale to the world's most advanced economies. It also spread affluence [wealth] more widely through the population at home. In a wider context, external influences on Japan, political, economic and cultural, came much more from America than Europe. . . .

a. How did Japanese industry after World War II differ from Japanese industry in the early twentieth century?

b. According to this passage, which country influenced Japan the most after World War II?

Essay Writing

30. Think about the Asian countries that have been discussed in this chapter and the events in those countries after World War II. Choose one Asian country and in an essay discuss the experiences for the people of that country after World War II.

TEST PREPARATION

RECOGNIZING FACT AND OPINION
Choose the correct answer to the question.

Which statement is a fact rather than an opinion?

1. In the history of India, Nehru was a more realistic leader than Gandhi.

2. Deng Xiaoping guided China's adoption of a socialist market economy.

3. The United States should have adopted a more hard-line policy during the Vietnam War.

4. Indonesia should not have invaded East Timor in 1975.

Critical Thinking

22. Indian Muslims objected to an independent state because they did not want to be a minority in a state that would have a huge Hindu majority. The Indian Muslims wanted a separate Islamic state so that they would not be discriminated against.

23. Possible answers: Nehru's political party led India to independence and then controlled politics in India. Most people must have been reasonably happy with the way Nehru and his family were running the country.

24. The Great Leap Forward was generally an economic failure due to opposition by the peasants, crop failures, and poor-quality manufactured goods.

25. Possible answer: North Korea and South Korea may have friendlier relations this century. Their leaders have met and there is even some hope of reunification.

26. Possible answers: Japanese dedication and hard work; U.S. economic assistance; focus on automation and high-tech products.

27. Possible answer: The United States became involved with both countries to stop the spread of communism. The United States had been involved in Korea since it was divided and supported South Korea against North Korea. North Vietnam invaded South Vietnam, and the United States aided the South Vietnamese government.

Put Your Skills to Work

DEVELOP A MULTIMEDIA PRESENTATION

28. Students' choices of media should reflect what they have learned about media presentations in Build Your Skills.

Analyze Sources

29a. In contrast to low-tech products for a domestic market early in the 1900s, after World War II, Japanese industry focused on high-tech goods for export to the world's most advanced markets.
29b. the United States

Essay Writing

30. Students' essays may focus on one of the following countries: India, China, Korea, Japan, Vietnam, Cambodia, Myanmar, Indonesia, or the Philippines. Essays should demonstrate familiarity with the textbook's discussion of the country selected.

TEST PREPARATION

Answer 2. Deng Xiaoping guided China's adoption of a socialist market economy.

Africa and the Middle East
1945–PRESENT
(pp. 758–783)

Chapter Objectives
- Identify the first African nations to gain independence after World War II.
- Describe how African nations dealt with the new challenges of self-government.
- Discuss the cessation of colonial rule in the Middle East.
- Identify conflicts in the Middle East between Arabs and Israelis, Iranians and Iraqis, and the international community and Iraq.

Chapter Summary
Section I focuses on the nations of Africa and their efforts to gain independence from colonial rule after 1945.

Section II describes the challenges that African nations faced after obtaining self-government, such as problems with leadership, the economy, and social issues.

Section III deals with nationalism and imperialism in the Middle East.

Section IV explores the reasons for conflict in the Middle East between Arabs and Israelis and Iranians and Iraqis; describes the international community's response to Iraq's invasion of Kuwait; and discusses Operation Iraqi Freedom.

Set the Stage
TEACH PRIMARY SOURCES
Have students analyze the quotation. Then, ask them what major issue divided South Africa before 1994. (racial equality) Have students list the key words or phrases that helped them to reach their conclusion. (all South Africans, both black and white; a rainbow nation)

Africa and the Middle East
1945–PRESENT

I. Independence in Africa
II. New Challenges for Africa
III. Struggles in the Middle East
IV. The Middle East and the Modern World

In Africa and the Middle East, movements to gain independence strengthened in the first half of the twentieth century. Some nations won independence through peaceful means, while others had to fight for freedom. The experiences of these nations shows that independence does not necessarily bring prosperity. It often brings responsibilities that some countries are not prepared for, and does not ease the hunger and poverty that still threaten millions of lives every year.

Nations within Africa and the Middle East face the responsibilities of independence in a modern world. In 1994, Nelson Mandela became South Africa's first black president. In his inaugural address, he expressed his hopes for South Africa:

❝ *We shall build a society in which all South Africans, both black and white, will be able to walk tall, without any fear in their hearts, assured of their inalienable right to human dignity—a rainbow nation at peace with itself and the world.* **❞**

CHAPTER EVENTS

1948 — State of Israel is established in Palestine.

1956 — Egypt takes control of the Suez Canal.

1960 — Nigeria wins independence from Great Britain.

1967 — Israel attacks Egypt in response to Egypt's military build-up.

1945 ———— **1965**

WORLD EVENTS

1949 — NATO is formed.

1950 — North Korea invades South Korea, beginning the Korean War.

1957 — Soviet Union launches *Sputnik*.

1962 — Cuban Missile Crisis heightens Cold War tensions.

758 UNIT 8 ◆ The World Today

Teaching Options

Chapter 32 Resources

REVIEW

Teacher's Resources (TR)
- Terms to Know, p. 45
- Review History, p. 79
- Build Your Skills, p. 113
- Chapter Test, pp. 179–180
- Concept Builder, p. 248
- SQR Chart, p. 322
- Transparencies 2, 6, 10

ASSESSMENT
- Section Reviews, pp. 764, 770, 776, 781
- Chapter Review, pp. 782–783
- Chapter Test, TR, pp. 179–180

ALTERNATIVE ASSESSMENT
- Portfolio Project, p. 808
- Create Historical Maps, p. T808

VIEW HISTORY Nelson Mandela became president of South Africa in 1994 when black South Africans voted for the first time in a national election.
◆ What does this photo reveal about the reaction of young, black South Africans to Nelson Mandela?

GET ORGANIZED

SQR Chart An SQR chart helps you know what to look for as you read. Use an SQR chart as you read each section in Chapter 32. Survey the text to see what it is about. Look at the headings and visuals. Then, write a question you want to answer as you read. Finally, read and find an answer to your question. Here is an example from this chapter.

> **SURVEY**
> The first moves African nations took toward freedom
>
> ↓
>
> **QUESTION**
> Which African nations were among the first to become independent?
>
> ↓
>
> **READ**
> Liberia, South Africa, Ethiopia, Libya, Egypt, Tunisia, Morocco, Ghana, Nigeria, Algeria

1979
Islamic revolution forces the shah to flee Iran.

1994
Nelson Mandela is elected president of South Africa.

2003
Iraq's government, led by Saddam Hussein, is overthrown in Operation Iraqi Freedom.

1985

2005

1975
Saigon falls and the Vietnam War ends.

1990
East Germany and West Germany are reunified.

2001
Terrorists attack the World Trade Center and the U.S. Pentagon.

CHAPTER 32 ◆ Africa and the Middle East **759**

Chapter Themes
- Culture
- Time, Continuity, and Change
- People, Places, and Environments
- Individuals, Groups, and Institutions
- Power, Authority, and Governance
- Production, Distribution, and Consumption
- Global Connections

F Y I

Nelson Mandela

While imprisoned, Nelson Mandela still was able to make positive changes. He started a system of prison education. During the workday, prisoners received instruction in a learning discipline. During rest hours, prisoners took part in cultural activities. Also from prison, Mandela successfully negotiated for his own release and for the country's transition to a democratic system of government.

Chapter Warm-Up
USING THE MAP
Point out the locator map at the top of page 759. To help students identify the many nations of Africa and the Middle East to be discussed in this chapter, have them compare the locator map to the maps of Africa and the Middle East in the Atlas (p. A6) or Transparencies 6 and 10.

VIEW HISTORY
Explain that Nelson Mandela was a leader in the African National Congress and was imprisoned under the apartheid system for more than 28 years. Mandela's election to the South African presidency was a monumental event.

◆ **ANSWER** It shows that young, black South Africans are very enthusiastic about Nelson Mandela's message. Their raised fists indicate that they identify with him.

GET ORGANIZED
SQR Chart
Explain the steps of SQR to students. *Survey* includes scanning the titles and headings of a section to find out the main idea. *Question* includes writing questions about the information before they begin actual reading. *Read* involves reading the text and locating the answers to their questions. Review the SQR chart on this page with students as an example.

TEACH THE TIMELINE
The timeline on pages 758–759 covers the period between 1948 and 2003. Remind students that after World War II, the map of the world was altered greatly as nations gained their independence. Have students find events that marked new national governments. (1948, the State of Israel is established in Palestine; 1960, Nigeria wins independence from Great Britain; 1990, East Germany and West Germany are reunified; 1994, Nelson Mandela is elected president of South Africa.)

Activity

Create a timeline Have students create their own timeline (TR, p. 320) of the dates of independence for African and Middle Eastern nations. They should include the information on Nigeria on page 758 and add other independence dates noted in the text.

I. Independence in Africa
(pp. 760–764)

Section Summary

In this section, students will learn about the gradual decline of European imperialism after World War II. They will also learn about the growing nationalist movement in Africa and its result—independent statehood for many nations.

Introduce

Getting Started

Ask students how they would feel if someone had come to their home unannounced and declared that it no longer belonged to them. (surprised, indignant, outraged) Tell students that many Africans found that, under colonialism, land that had been theirs for generations was taken over by foreigners. Years of this injustice led Africans to seek their independence.

TERMS TO KNOW

Ask students to read the terms and definitions on page 760 and then find each term in the section. Have them work with a partner and take turns using each term in a sentence.

You may wish to preview the pronunciation of the following names with students.

Kwame Nkrumah
(KWAH meh n KROO muh)
Nnamdi Azikiwe
(NAHM deh ah ZEHK wah)
Jomo Kenyatta
(JOH moh kehn YAHT uh)
Mau Mau (MOW mow)

ACTIVE READING

Point out to students that a chart is a useful tool for categorizing information. To classify the information in this section, suggest that students use a three-column chart with the following headings:

Independence from Great Britain
Independence from France
Independence from Belgium

Independence in Africa

Terms to Know

Pan-Africanism the unity of all black Africans, regardless of national boundaries

autonomy self-government

Main Ideas

A. Algeria, Ghana, and Nigeria were among the African nations to become independent following World War II.

B. Except for Rhodesia, the rest of Great Britain's African colonies won independence in the 1960s.

C. French and Belgian colonies gained independence in the 1950s and 1960s.

Active Reading

CLASSIFY

When you classify things, you organize them in groups based on characteristics they share. As you read this section, consider similarities and differences among the African nations mentioned. Then, classify them using characteristics you identify.

A. First Moves Toward Freedom

"Uhuru!," meaning freedom, was the cry of thousands of Africans as World War II ended. Many Africans felt that independence should be their reward for helping the Allies defeat the Axis Powers in North Africa. France, Great Britain, Germany, Italy, Portugal, Spain, and Belgium all claimed colonies in Africa before World War II. Over the next 35 years, however, Africa changed. As African nationalism, or the movement toward independence, grew, European imperialism in Africa declined.

Early Independent States

Nationalism was not a twentieth-century idea. The seeds of the struggle for independence in Africa had been planted almost 100 years earlier. In 1847, Liberia was founded as an independent African state governed by black people. The idea of **Pan-Africanism**—that black Africans have common interests and should unite—also began to form around this time. Nationalism and Pan-Africanism would stir Africans to action in the coming century.

The nation of South Africa became independent of Great Britain in 1931. Other African nations, however, did not gain independence until World War II. Ethiopia won its independence from Italy in 1941, while the world was still at war. Libya was also a colony of Italy before the war. After the war, Libya came under UN control but finally won its independence in 1951.

The situation in Egypt was more complicated. In 1922, Egypt had gained its independence from Great Britain. The British, however, continued to keep troops there. Egypt did not become truly independent until 1954 when the British finally pulled out. Two years later, in 1956, Tunisia and Morocco also became independent. Both had been protectorates of France. A protectorate is a country that is protected and controlled in some ways by another country.

This structure is a monument to Tunisian independence.

Teaching Options

Section 1 Resources

Teacher's Resources (TR)

Terms to Know, p. 45
Review History, p. 79
Build Your Skills, p. 113
Concept Builder, p. 248
SQR Chart, p. 322
Transparency 6

Connection to ------
HISTORY ◄------

Liberia was founded as a settlement for freed American slaves in 1821. Local chiefs gave the land, formerly known as Cape Mesurado, to officials of the American Colonization Society. Jehudi Ashmun was very important to the survival of the colony during its early years. In 1847, the colony was declared an independent republic.

Ghana

Nationalist movements were slower to develop in Africa south of the Sahara. With the end of World War II, however, nationalist groups sprang up throughout the continent. Africans, like people elsewhere, saw the Allies' triumph of World War II as a victory over tyranny and oppression. Africans too wanted to be free.

In the south, Ghana led the way toward independence. As a British colony, Ghana was known as the Gold Coast. In 1948, Africans revolted against British control. Kwame Nkrumah led the fight for Ghana's independence. The British put Nkrumah in prison for his activities, but they released him in 1951. In 1957, the Gold Coast became independent. Nkrumah became the nation's first prime minister. Three years later, he was elected president of the Gold Coast, by then known as Ghana.

Nigeria

The West African nation of Nigeria won its independence in 1960. Nigeria was the largest British colony in Africa. It included more than 200 cultural groups. Britain used local rulers to govern Nigeria indirectly. The people of Nigeria could take part in the government only up to a certain level.

In the 1920s, Nigerians demanded representation in the colonial government. The British responded by granting only limited representation. After World War II, however, Nigerians again demanded representation. In 1947, in a speech at Great Britain's Oxford University, the nationalist leader Nnamdi Azikiwe was direct about what Nigerians wanted:

> **❝**We demand the right to assume responsibility for the government of our country. We demand the right to be free and to make mistakes and profit from our experience. **❞**

The British created three political regions in Nigeria. Each had its own assembly with both African and British members. The assemblies advised the central government in Nagos. In 1954, Nigeria adopted a constitution that established a stronger union of the three political regions. These regions were further divided in the 1960s so that Nigeria's many cultural groups could share political power more fairly.

When it became independent in 1960, Nigeria had many of the important pieces of a democratic society in place. Whether the new government would work in a country as large as Nigeria and with as many people and cultural groups was not clear, however.

Algeria Moves Toward Independence

Algeria took a more violent path to independence. Algeria had been a French colony since the mid-1800s. European settlers quickly took over the best jobs in Algeria and held the most important positions in Algeria's government. The Arabs and Berbers who made up most of Algeria's population wanted equal status with the Europeans. The Europeans feared that the French government might give Algeria its independence. If that happened, the European settlers would lose their economic and political power.

When the French government did not answer the demands of the Arabs and Berbers, they revolted. French troops were able to crush these uprisings. In 1954, however, a nationalist movement known as the National Liberation Front (FLN) started a guerrilla war against France.

Kwame Nkrumah was elected president of Ghana in 1960.

ANALYZE PRIMARY SOURCES

DOCUMENT-BASED QUESTION
What does Azikiwe think is the value of making mistakes?

A. First Moves Toward Freedom

Purpose-Setting Question
Which African nations were among the first to gain independence from foreign colonists after World War II? (Libya, Egypt, Tunisia, Morocco, Ghana, Nigeria, Algeria)

Focus Ask students why they think Great Britain kept troops in Egypt even after Egypt had won its independence. (Egypt was a strategic military location for Great Britain.)

TEACH PRIMARY SOURCES
Have students analyze the photograph on page 760. Discuss with them how the monument symbolizes Tunisian independence. Ask students which symbols of nationalism surround the structure. (flags) Discuss the style of the monument (modern) and what message they think it conveys. (Possible answer: Its tall, modern stance symbolizes Tunisian pride in being progressive and independent.)

ANALYZE PRIMARY SOURCES

DOCUMENT-BASED QUESTION
Benjamin Nnamdi Azikiwe (1904–96) was a Nigerian statesman. As a young man, he studied in the United States. When he returned to Nigeria, he became involved in publishing and nationalist politics. He held several honorary government positions, such as the office of governor-general in 1960 and first president of the Republic of Nigeria in 1963. However, he ran unsuccessfully for the presidency of Nigeria twice.

ANSWER Nigerians would make mistakes because they did not have experience governing themselves, but they would learn from their mistakes.

Meet Individual Needs:

VISUAL/SPATIAL LEARNERS

Have students create a poster that illustrates Nigeria's opposition to colonial rule. Posters should show an understanding of change through passive resistance to government policies. Display posters in the classroom. Then, discuss with students other times in history when passive resistance affected gradual change (for example, the U.S. civil rights movement).

Focus The meaning of Pan-Africanism has varied historically. The First Pan-African Congress, held in 1919, favored gradual self-government. Later African organizations formed to demand African autonomy and independence. As independence was achieved by more African states, other interpretations of Pan-Africanism emerged. For example, the Organization of African Unity (OAU) was founded in 1963 to promote unity among all African states and to bring an end to colonialism.

◆ **ANSWER** Nationalism increased after World War II because the war had been fought to rid the world of tyranny and oppression. Africans, who had helped the Allies fight the war, wanted the same freedoms for themselves as other countries had.

B. British Rule Ends

Purpose-Setting Question
What pattern did many British-ruled African nations follow to gain independence? (An African nation made demands on the British government for independence. The British government responded by giving Africans greater representation in colonial assemblies. Then, the colonies were given independence as self-governing dominions. Finally, they became independent republics.)

Discuss Ask students why Europeans decided to settle in Kenya in the early 1900s. (to build coffee and tea plantations) Discuss the way the European settlers treated the Kikuyu. Encourage students to suggest other ways the settlers and Kikuyu could interact.

Extend The spectacular Serengeti National Park in Tanzania is one of the world's last great wildlife refuges. This vast region supports the largest remaining populations of plains animals in Africa. The name of the park comes from the Masai word *siringet*, meaning "endless plains." The park contains about 3 million large animals, including wildebeests and hundreds of thousands of zebras and gazelles. One valley in the Serengeti is famous for its abundance of lions and leopards.

These Algerian soldiers fought to gain independence for Algeria.

The conflict lasted more than seven years. The FLN turned to Egypt and other Arab states for help in pushing the French and other Europeans out. In 1959, French President Charles de Gaulle indicated that France was willing to work toward Algeria's independence. Some members of the French military in Algeria revolted, blocking streets and taking over government buildings. They said they would invade France and plotted to kill de Gaulle.

De Gaulle dealt quickly and firmly with the crisis in Algeria so that the French revolt stopped. The FLN, however, kept up its attacks for another year. When the French government promised that Algeria could begin to govern itself immediately, the FLN stopped fighting. In 1962, Algeria became fully independent, and the FLN took control of the government. It governed Algeria for the next 30 years.

◆ **Why did nationalism increase in Africa after World War II?**

B. British Rule Ends

As Great Britain's other colonies in Africa sought independence, a pattern of events similar to those in Nigeria and Ghana unfolded. First, nationalist movements made demands. The British government responded by giving Africans greater representation. Then, the colonies were given independence as self-governing dominions. Soon after, these dominions often became independent republics with a nationalist leader as president. Kenya and Uganda followed this general pattern.

Kenya Becomes Independent

European settlers came to Kenya in the early 1900s. They took charge of the government and the most important economic activities. They also took over the best land to build coffee and tea plantations. To do this, they drove the native peoples, the Kikuyu, off the land. As their population grew, the Kikuyu demanded the right to move into the area set aside for white people. Instead of working with the Kikuyu to solve this problem, the British passed strict laws to keep the Kikuyu from acting on their demands.

In the 1920s, a young nationalist named Jomo Kenyatta began to demand economic and political change in Kenya. Kenyatta campaigned for land reform and for African political rights. By 1952, Kikuyu terrorists, called Mau Mau, began killing both British landowners and Kenyans who worked for the landowners. In 1953, Kenyatta was jailed on suspicion of being the Mau Mau's leader. As the violence continued, the British saw that major changes had to be made in Kenya. In 1963, Kenya became independent. Jomo Kenyatta became prime minister and later president of Kenya.

Uganda Is Freed

Uganda won its independence from Great Britain in 1962. It was formed as a British protectorate in 1894. By 1896, it included the kingdom of Buganda and territories around it. There were many cultural groups in Uganda, as in Nigeria.

When Britain moved to unite Uganda with Kenya and Tanganyika, which is present-day Tanzania, the kingdom of Buganda tried to break away as a separate state, but it was unsuccessful. When Uganda became a republic in 1963, a year

Teaching Options

Writing

AVERAGE
Have students research the conflict between France and Algeria in 1954 over Algerian independence. Then, have them write a short essay on the conflict and how it failed to immediately achieve its goal for Algeria's independence.

CHALLENGE
Have students research guerrilla warfare tactics. Then, have them write a newspaper article that describes a battle between the National Liberation Front and the French government. Remind students that a newspaper journalist strives to be objective and to present the facts of the event as accurately as possible.

after its independence, the king of Buganda was elected ceremonial president. This helped unite the new nation, although only for a short time.

Colonies in Southern Africa Become States

The road to independence for the British colonies that became Zambia, Malawi, and Botswana was fairly smooth. Once known as Bechuanaland, Botswana became independent in 1966.

As colonies, Zambia and Malawi had been called Northern Rhodesia and Nyasaland. In the 1950s, the British combined the two colonies to form the Federation of Rhodesia and Nyasaland. The federation also included Southern Rhodesia. Zambia and Malawi did not want to be part of a federation that included Southern Rhodesia because Europeans controlled the government of that colony. Britain finally agreed to end the federation.

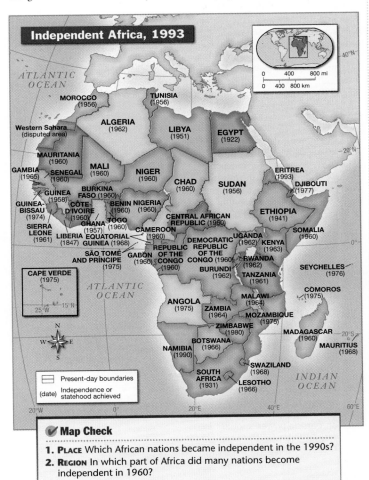

Independent Africa, 1993

Present-day boundaries
(date) Independence or statehood achieved

✔ Map Check

1. **PLACE** Which African nations became independent in the 1990s?
2. **REGION** In which part of Africa did many nations become independent in 1960?

Write a poem Have students write a poem expressing some aspect of the struggle for independence from an African point of view. Students' themes might include exploitation, resistance, or the growing spirit of nationalism. Have volunteers read their poems out loud to the class.

Explore Ask students why a ceremonial president—as opposed to an elected official—might have contributed to the short time span in which Uganda remained unified in 1963. (Possible answer: A ceremonial president has no real power to fix problems or make necessary changes.)

Review Discuss with students why the colonies of Zambia and Malawi did not want to become part of a federation that included Southern Rhodesia. (Possible answer: Because Europeans still controlled the government of Southern Rhodesia, Zambia's and Malawi's status as independent states might be challenged.)

Using the Map

Independent Africa, 1993

Have students use an outline map of Africa (TR, p. 334) to label each nation and the country from which it gained its independence, if applicable. Students can research this information from the chapter, an almanac, or other reference book. Then, have students tally the countries that formerly controlled Africa to determine which nation had the largest holdings on the continent.

✔ Map Check

Answers
1. Eritrea and Namibia became independent in the 1990s.
2. Many nations in the western and central regions of Africa became independent in 1960.

Conflict Resolution

Ask students to examine other ways to settle a disagreement besides leading a violent revolt the way the Mau Mau of Kenya did. Which techniques have students learned to find a solution that everyone involved can accept? (patient and careful listening, compromising, considering the other person's point of view, expressing your needs)

Cooperative Learning

Assign students the roles of various leaders they have read about in this section: Kwame Nkrumah, Nnamdi Azikiwe, Charles de Gaulle, or Jomo Kenyatta. Have them discuss their views of European colonialism, nationalist movements, independence, and other issues. Have the rest of the class ask questions of the leaders.

ANSWER In both countries, Europeans exercised control over the government and held onto the best jobs. The struggle for independence took a violent turn in both countries.

C. France and Belgium Bow Out

Purpose-Setting Question How did France and Belgium differ in their attitudes toward Africa after their colonies chose independence? (France continued to help its colonies, and they were able to develop their economies and armies; but Belgium left quickly without any aid, and the country quickly erupted into civil war and chaos.)

ANSWER France supported its colonies after they achieved independence by helping them economically and training their armies.

Section Close

Have students write on the board the various methods that African nations used to gain independence. Then, have students list underneath each method a nation that followed that route and to what end. If space allows, students might also want to list date of independence, former colonial ruler, and the first elected leader of the new republic.

Assess

Review Answers

Review History

A. The National Liberation Front fought for independence from France.

B. Zambia and Malawi did not want to be part of the federation because Southern Rhodesia was a member, and Europeans controlled the government of Southern Rhodesia.

C. France gave its colonies representation in the National Assembly in Paris; developed programs of economic, social, and legal reform in the colonies; and let colonies choose whether to keep ties or become independent.

Define Terms to Know

Pan-Africanism, 760; autonomy, 764

Cultural groups in different regions clashed when the Belgians left Congo. In this photograph, a soldier is chasing a group that was attacking the U.S. Consulate.

Shortly afterward, in 1964, both Zambia and Malawi won their independence. Southern Rhodesia became Rhodesia. It would be some time before Rhodesia would become independent.

How were the struggles for independence similar in Kenya and Algeria?

C. France and Belgium Bow Out

European powers gave up many African colonies during the 1950s and 1960s. Chief among these powers were France and Belgium.

French Colonies Make a Choice

While nationalism was rising in Algeria, France gave its African colonies representation in the National Assembly in Paris. It also developed a program of economic, social, and legal reform in the colonies. In the end, the French government decided to let the colonies choose to keep ties to France or become independent. While all of France's African colonies eventually chose independence, France continued to play a supportive role in the region. It helped the new nations develop their economies and train their armies.

A New Congo

Belgium had allowed its huge colony in central Africa little **autonomy**, or self-government, over the years. When neighboring French Congo became the independent Republic of the Congo in 1960, however, Belgian Congo could wait no longer for independence. The Belgian government pulled out of the Belgian colony in only six months. Civil war broke out as cultural groups and regions clashed in the new independent nation, which today is called the Democratic Republic of the Congo. The new nation's future did not look promising.

How did France stay involved after its colonies became independent?

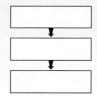

Review 1

Review History
A. What did the National Liberation Front fight for in Algeria?
B. Why did Zambia and Malawi not want to be part of the Federation of Rhodesia and Nyasaland?
C. What did France do for its African colonies to avoid the kind of conflict that developed in Algeria?

Define Terms to Know
Define the following terms:
Pan-Africanism, autonomy

Critical Thinking
Why do you think the French military in Algeria revolted?

Write About Government
Write a brief essay about why the citizens of a country, not an outside power, should have responsibility for the country's government.

Get Organized
SQR CHART
Use an SQR chart to organize information from this section. For example, this section is about the independence of African nations.

Critical Thinking
Possible answer: They did not want to give up their power in Algeria.

Write About Government
Students should use what they have learned and logical reasoning to support the suggested thesis. They may refer to the importance of freedom and self-determination and the idea that the people of a nation have a common heritage and similar values that may greatly differ from the heritage and values of an outside power.

SURVEY
This section is about the independence of African nations.

QUESTION
Which British colonies became independent after Nigeria and Ghana?

READ
Kenya, Uganda, Zambia, Malawi, and Botswana

Build Your Skills

Social Studies Skill

RESOLVE CONFLICT THROUGH COMPROMISE

Conflicts, or disagreements, are everyday occurrences. Members of a family or community may disagree. World leaders or countries may come into conflict. Conflicts arise between individuals and groups for various reasons. People may have different needs or wants. They may have different points of view on a particular issue.

People resolve conflict in different ways. Sometimes they choose to ignore the conflict. By doing this, they can let strong feelings die down and also have time to rethink the reasons for the conflict. Then, they can try to resolve, or end, the conflict at another time.

People also try to resolve conflict by winning the other side over to their point of view. They do this by showing why their way of thinking is best. Another way of resolving conflict is to make a compromise. A compromise gives each side something they want. To get what they want, each side must also give up something. To help two sides in a conflict reach a compromise, someone must look at each side objectively. A person such

as this is called a mediator. Mediators help people settle their differences by suggesting new ways of looking at issues.

Here's How
Follow these steps to resolve a conflict through compromise.

1. State clearly what you want. Then, listen to what the other side wants.
2. Make a plan for compromise by deciding what you are willing to give up.
3. Compare plans with the other side.
4. Talk about changes you are each willing to make to reach a compromise.

Here's Why
Knowing how to resolve conflict is a valuable skill that you can use in situations throughout your life. Being able to recognize conflict and the different methods people use to resolve it will increase your understanding of history and current events.

Practice the Skill
Study the information provided in the graphic organizer to the right about the conflict between Algeria's National Liberation Front (FLN) and France. Then, answer the following questions.

1. What did each side hope to gain?
2. What did each side give up to resolve the conflict?

Extend the Skill
Think of a conflict within your school or community. Make a graphic organizer that shows how it was, or could have been, resolved through compromise.

Apply the Skill
Identify conflicts in Africa and the Middle East described in this chapter. Follow the steps in *Here's How* to understand how these conflicts were, or could have been, resolved.

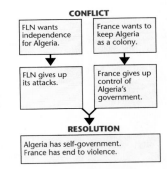

CONFLICT

FLN wants independence for Algeria.	France wants to keep Algeria as a colony.
FLN gives up its attacks.	France gives up control of Algeria's government.

RESOLUTION

Algeria has self-government. France has end to violence.

Teach the Skill
Ask students to give examples of conflicts in their own lives that needed to be resolved. Were they successful in resolving those conflicts? What methods did they use to achieve the results they did? Was a mediator involved? Students may want to refer to the steps in *Here's How* to explain the method they used. Then, have them tell what, if anything, changed in their lives as a result of the resolution of their issue.

Discuss whether or not students feel that resolving conflicts through compromise is easier or more difficult than through other methods. Ask students which methods of resolving conflicts have the most lasting and most positive results.

Practice the Skill
ANSWERS
1. The FLN wanted independence for Algeria; France wanted to keep Algeria as a colony.
2. The FLN stopped its attacks; France gave up control of the Algerian government.

Extend the Skill
Students' graphic organizers should demonstrate that compromise is an important method of resolving conflicts.

Apply the Skill
For Sections 2, 3, and 4, encourage students to make graphic organizers like the one on page 765 to identify conflicts and how they were resolved. Some other examples of graphic organizers that would be good to use include an SQR chart (TR, p. 322), a flowchart (TR, p. 324), and a problem/solution chart (TR, p. 327).

Teaching Options

RETEACH
Have students work in groups to research a current conflict in Africa or the Middle East. Have half of the groups research one point of view and have the other half represent the opposition. Pair the groups in sets that represent both sides of the issue. Have the pairs use the *Here's How* steps to attempt to find a solution to the conflict.

CHALLENGE
Have groups of students find, read, and perform scenes from a story, play, or film in which there is a conflict. Students may want to ask their English teacher for suggestions. After each performance, have students analyze and debate the way in which the conflict was handled. Encourage students to suggest alternative solutions if the conflict enacted was not resolved.

Section Summary

In this section, students will learn about the common problems of the new independent African nations, such as unstable governments, struggling economies, and social unrest. Students will also learn about apartheid in South Africa.

1 Introduce

Getting Started

Ask students to describe what occurred when they were given complete freedom to make an important decision. Have them explain both the positive and the negative consequences of their decision. Then, ask students to speculate on what decisions newly independent nations in Africa might have faced.

TERMS TO KNOW

Ask students to read the terms and definitions on page 766 and find each term in the section. Then, have them write a paragraph about Africa that uses both terms.

You may wish to preview the pronunciation of the following names with students.

Ibo (EE boh)
Hutu (HOO too)
Tutsi (TOOT see)

ACTIVE READING

Point out to students that generalizations often include the words *most, many, some,* or *frequently* or their opposites, such as *few* or *seldom.* Have students keep a running log of the sentences in the section that include generalizations. Ask them what is the point of making generalizations. (Possible answers: to introduce or conclude a discussion, to make a point of how common or universal a situation is)

Terms to Know

coup d'état the violent overthrow of a government by a small group

apartheid the policy of racial separation and discrimination in South Africa

The Hausa are one of the cultural groups in Nigeria.

Main Ideas

A. Unstable governments, all-powerful leaders, and conflict were common in the newly independent African nations.

B. White rule finally ended in Africa when Nelson Mandela was elected president of South Africa.

C. African nations face many economic and social problems, but some developments offer hope for the future.

Active Reading

GENERALIZE
When you generalize, you make a general statement based on specific facts. As you read this section, look for patterns in the information. Then, pause to generalize about developments in Africa.

A. Political Troubles

African nations faced many challenges after winning independence. The colonial powers had not given the new nations good models for leadership or democratic government. The new governments had trouble building unity among the different groups within their borders. Conflicts of various kinds divided the peoples of the new nations.

Leaders and Governments

It was natural for many of the newly independent nations to turn to nationalist leaders or groups for leadership. In many cases, however, this did not turn out to be the best decision. In Algeria, for example, the National Liberation Front (FLN) took power immediately after independence and stayed in power for the next 30 years. It was able to hold onto power because it was a one-party government. That means that there were no other parties to oppose it.

Other countries had been led to independence by a powerful leader. This person often seemed the obvious choice as leader of the new nation. The nationalist leader Kwame Nkrumah, for example, became president of Ghana when it won its independence. Nkrumah, however, took as much power as he could for himself. He banned all political parties but his own. Then, in 1964, he made himself president for life. He became a dictator.

Only two years later, Nkrumah was thrown out of office by the military. Over the next decade, Ghana experienced one military **coup d'état**, or overthrow of the government, after another. Attempts to set up a civilian, or nonmilitary, government continued to fail. The military kept its hold on Ghana through the 1990s.

Governments across Africa followed these same patterns. Military rule and the one-party system were common, as were autocratic leaders, who had unlimited power. African nations were not familiar with civilian government, a multiparty system, or leaders who shared power with others.

Teaching Options

Section 2 Resources

Teacher's Resources (TR)
Terms to Know, p. 45
Review History, p. 79
Build Your Skills, p. 113
Concept Builder, p. 248
SQR Chart, p. 322
Transparency 6

ESL/ELL STRATEGIES

Organize Information Have students work in pairs to create a chart of African nations listed in the section. As students read the section, have them fill in the chart with information from the text about the main problems and solutions of each nation. Students may then use their completed charts as study tools.

People in Conflict

In many countries, independence was followed by civil war and conflict. A terrible civil war broke out in Nigeria soon after independence. Cultural groups battled for political power within the different regions of Nigeria. Two of the largest groups, the Ibo in the southeast and the Hausa in the north, fought for control of the central government. The Ibo staged a military coup d'état, which the Hausa overturned several months later. When the Hausa started killing the Ibo, many Ibo fled to the east. They left Nigeria and founded a new, independent state called Biafra.

Civil war broke out between Nigeria and Biafra in 1967. It lasted almost three years. More than 1 million people died. Some were killed in the fighting. Others died of hunger as a result of Nigeria's blockade of Biafra. A blockade shuts off an area so people and supplies cannot go in or out. The Ibos finally joined Nigeria again, and the government worked to bring Nigeria's regions and cultural groups together. Military takeovers and other violence, however, made this difficult.

Civil Wars

Civil war divided other African nations. In Chad, Muslims from the north clashed with the government. In Ethiopia, the central government fought with Muslim and Christian groups from Eritrea. A terrible civil war raged in what is now the Democratic Republic of the Congo between the central government and rebels. The superpowers—the Soviet Union and the United States—became involved in some of the conflicts in Africa. For example, the United States led a UN force that intervened in a civil war in Somalia, and the Soviet Union sent aid to one group involved in a civil war in Angola.

Internal warfare between the Hutu and the Tutsi in Rwanda and Burundi was one of the worst examples of conflict in Africa. There had been tension between the two groups since colonial days. In the early 1990s, the tension led to violence, leaving thousands of people dead. In 1993, about 50,000 people, most of them Hutu, were killed in Burundi. The following year, Hutu killed about 500,000 Tutsi in Rwanda. Vast numbers of people also fled Rwanda and Burundi and became refugees. Hutu who did not support the action were also killed. The killing in Rwanda did not stop until Tutsi exiles who had been living in Uganda poured into Rwanda and set up a new government. Hutu fighters fled to the Democratic Republic of the Congo, called Zaire at the time, which was caught up in a civil war of its own. Violence expanded into warfare that involved three African nations.

These Hutu refugees fled the conflict with the Tutsi in Burundi.

◆ **Why did civil war break out in Nigeria after independence?**

B. Majority Rule Spreads

Other wars were fought in Africa. The Portuguese colonies of Guinea, Angola, and Mozambique were the scene of fierce fighting from the early 1960s to the mid-1970s. By the early 1970s, half of Portugal's budget paid for military operations in Africa. A revolt and change in the government in Portugal finally led to independence for its African colonies.

Focus on
WORLD RELIGIONS

Religions of Africa The people of Africa practice many different religions. Many Africans adhere to one or more of the following religions: indigenous African religions, Islam, or Christianity.

It is estimated that almost half of Africa's population is Muslim. Islam is successful in Africa because of its ability to absorb other traditions. Similarly, many Africans have established their own Christian churches—independent from the missions that introduced the religion. By the mid-twenty-first century, more than one-third of the world's Christians will live in Africa.

A. Political Troubles

Purpose-Setting Question What divided the African people after they gained their independence? (autocratic leadership, weak governments, cultural disputes, civil war)

Discuss What skills does a nationalist leader need? (power to inspire, willingness to try again after failure, passion for the cause) What skills does a president of a country need? (organizational skills, leadership skills, willingness to compromise, foresight, and openness to other ideas) Why might a nationalist leader not make a good president? (Possible answer: A nationalist leader might not be able to delegate power once the main goal is achieved.)

Activity

Create a newspaper Have students work together to create a front page for a newspaper about an African country covered in this section. The front page should include historic information about the country's leadership struggles and/or successes. Information may be presented as articles, illustrations, or political cartoons.

Explore Ask students to hypothesize about why so many African governments were made up of people in the military. (Possible answer: Many nationalist groups had a military component. Leaders who had military support were more likely to stay in power.)

Review Have students name other countries and societies they have already studied that also endured coup d'états. (Possible answers: ancient Rome, France)

◆ **ANSWER** Two different cultural groups, the Ibo and the Hausa, battled for power after independence.

B. Majority Rule Spreads

Purpose-Setting Question How did race affect politics in South Africa in the 1960s and 1970s? (The white minority controlled the government and passed discriminatory laws against the nonwhite majority. Eventually, political pressure from within the country and economic pressure from the international community led to reform and elections open to voters of all races.)

After Portugal's withdrawal from Africa, only a few countries in Africa remained under European colonial rule. In Rhodesia, the European minority refused to give up control of the government to the majority. In 1965, the white minority declared Rhodesia's independence from Great Britain. This action sparked a war between the white minority and nationalist groups hoping to achieve majority rule. One of these nationalist groups was led by Robert Mugabe. After 15 years of fighting, the white minority finally gave in, and Mugabe took power. In 1980, Rhodesia became the independent nation of Zimbabwe.

Separation of the Races

In the 1980s, South Africa had a population of more than 40 million. Black people numbered 30 million, and white people about 6 million. Another 4 million were nonwhite people. About half the white people were Afrikaners, descendants of Dutch immigrants who started coming to southern Africa as early as the 1650s. Most of the rest of the white people were descendants of immigrants who came from Great Britain in the 1820s.

After World War II, the Nationalist Party gained control of a whites-only parliament in South Africa. The Nationalists had the support of the Afrikaners. They wanted **apartheid**, or the policy of racial separation and discrimination. They believed that white people should dominate, or have the most powerful position in, society.

Over the next 10 years, the Nationalists passed law after law supporting apartheid. The separation of the races extended to all areas of life. It affected housing, jobs, land ownership, and transportation. Some 1 million nonwhite people were forced to move when the government set up self-governing homelands for different black cultural groups.

The South African government faced opposition around the world as it took steps to enforce apartheid. In 1961, it dropped out of the Commonwealth of Nations, completely cutting its ties with Great Britain.

Opposition to apartheid was also strong within South Africa. Both black people and white people protested the laws that separated the races. In addition to peaceful protests such as strikes and demonstrations, there were riots and other acts of violence. The police also used force. Hundreds of black protesters were hurt or killed at Sharpeville in 1960 and Soweto in 1976. Following the demonstration at Sharpeville, Nelson Mandela, the leader of the African National Congress (ANC), a major anti-apartheid organization, was put in prison.

Road to Democracy

After Soweto, the world took an even firmer stand against South Africa's policy of apartheid. Many nations, including the United States, took part in economic sanctions that limited trade and investment in South Africa. In the 1980s, many American and British companies and banks left South Africa. These developments greatly damaged the South African economy, which had been weakening since the mid-1970s. Anti-apartheid

Population of South Africa, Late 1980s

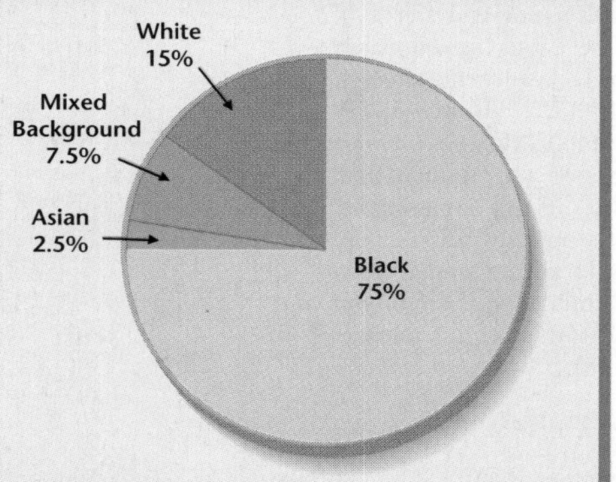

White 15%
Mixed Background 7.5%
Asian 2.5%
Black 75%

Source: *R. R. Palmer, A History of the Modern World, 2002*

✔ Graph Check

What percentage of the people living in South Africa were Asians?

Teaching Options

groups in Europe and the United States demanded reform. One of their demands was the release of Nelson Mandela from prison.

In the early 1980s, the South African government made some progress toward economic and social reforms that would benefit black people. However, when P. W. Botha became president in 1984, the government stepped up its crackdown on all opposition to apartheid. In 1985, Botha declared a state of emergency that allowed police, the military, and other forces to take whatever action they felt necessary to control opposition. Thousands of people were arrested, and many of them died in custody.

Meanwhile, a concerned group of black and white leaders began to plan for South Africa's future. They saw a future in which people of different races would live side by side and the country's black population would have political representation. Reforms would be needed to achieve this. Among those who supported reform was F. W. de Klerk, education minister under Botha. When Botha became ill in 1989, de Klerk took power.

An extraordinary chain of events followed, beginning with Nelson Mandela's release after 28 years in prison. Finally, in 1994, African majority rule became a reality. In the spring of that year, South Africa held its first elections open to voters of all races, and Mandela was elected president.

How did apartheid affect the lives of nonwhite people in South Africa?

C. Problems and Solutions

Positive political change had finally come to South Africa. Yet there were many other problems to solve. South Africa faced various economic and social problems familiar to other African nations. Among the most pressing were poverty, unemployment, food shortages, and disease.

Primary Source Documents

You can read sections of Nelson Mandela's Inaugural Address on page 815.

In the spring of 1994, South Africa held its first elections open to voters of all races. Twenty-two million people showed up to vote.

WHO IN THE WORLD?
DESMOND TUTU Have students write an introductory speech to present Desmond Tutu to an audience in Oslo, Sweden, as he accepts his 1984 Nobel Peace Prize. Students' speeches should focus on what apartheid was and how economic sanctions—such as the ones advocated by Tutu—affected the policy. Students' speeches may also focus on Desmond Tutu as a person if students conduct additional research on his life and work.

Extend As Minister of National Education, Frederik Willem de Klerk supported segregated universities and did not appear to be an advocate for social reform. Then, in February 1989, de Klerk became leader of the National Party. In his first speech as party leader, he called for a nonracist South Africa and for negotiations to decide the country's future. He soon lifted the ban on the ANC and set Nelson Mandela free, calling for a new constitution based on the principle of one person, one vote. In 1993, de Klerk shared the Nobel Peace Prize with Nelson Mandela.

ANSWER Apartheid affected housing, jobs, land ownership, and transportation. It also affected where people could live because the government set up self-governing homelands for different black cultural groups.

C. Problems and Solutions

Purpose-Setting Question What are some major economic and social issues that many African nations had to face after they gained political independence? (poverty, unemployment, food shortages, disease, foreign debt)

Meet Individual Needs:
LOGICAL/MATHEMATICAL LEARNERS

Ask students to construct a flowchart (TR, p. 324) that illustrates the sequence of events concerning the end of apartheid. Have students begin with the migration of white settlers into South Africa and end with South Africa's first election open to voters of all colors in 1994, when Nelson Mandela became the first black president of South Africa.

Connection to
SCIENCE

According to the United Nations, AIDS is now the leading cause of death in Africa—more than wars, famines, or floods. More than two-thirds of all people in the world who die from AIDS live in sub-Saharan Africa. Each day in Africa, approximately 6,000 people die from AIDS. Many African countries are now beginning to educate their people about the disease to help prevent it from spreading.

OIL PRICES IN THE EARLY 1970s
During the energy crisis of the 1970s, the price of a barrel of crude oil in the United States rose from $1.80 in 1971 to $11.65 in 1974. As a result of the rising price of oil, gasoline prices increased, and many Americans endured long lines at gas stations.

Focus Have students identify Jubilee 2000 and the purpose it is serving for African nations in debt. (Jubilee 2000 is an organized movement to speed up the process of removing debt from African nations.)

◆ **ANSWER** They turned to socialism, which meant they encouraged government control of agriculture and industry. They also ordered foreign companies to leave.

Section Close

Create an idea web with students that demonstrates how European colonists left a legacy of problems for the newly independent African nations. The main idea should read *Problems inherited from colonization.* Supporting details should include challenges for leaders and governments, border disputes, struggling economies, and social injustices.

③ Assess

Review Answers

Review History

A. New African nations had autocratic leaders because they were not familiar with civilian government, a multiparty political system, or leaders who shared power.

B. To show their opposition to apartheid, other nations took part in economic sanctions against South Africa.

C. They could not grow enough food or make needed goods, so African countries borrowed money to import food and goods.

Define Terms to Know

coup d'état, 766; apartheid, 768

Spotlight on
Economics

OIL PRICES IN THE EARLY 1970s
The economies of African nations were negatively affected in the early 1970s by a worldwide increase in oil prices. This situation occurred as many African nations had only recently gained independence. Increasing oil prices caused a dramatic rise in the prices that Africans paid for imported goods. As a result, many African nations went deeply into debt.

Economic Decline

Upon gaining independence, some leaders of new African nations turned to socialism for their economies. They rejected capitalism because they associated it with the colonial powers. They ordered foreign companies to leave. They encouraged government control of agriculture and industry. African governments, however, lacked the money, materials, and experience to support state-owned farms and factories. Production dropped. African nations could not grow much of their own food or make many of the goods they needed. They had to import food and goods. To pay for these items, they borrowed money from other countries.

African economies declined. Crop failures and falling prices on the world market for African goods added to the downturn. Africa's cities swelled with people looking for jobs. Natural disasters such as drought caused famine and the spread of disease. Many people became refugees.

Hope for the Future

Africa's political, economic, and social problems remain enormous. Certain developments, however, offer hope for the future. Among the most significant is debt relief.

Many African nations owe huge amounts of money to more developed countries, such as the United States. African nations spend more money paying off debt than they spend on health, education, or other social services. In the late 1990s, the World Bank developed a plan to help poor countries by removing debt. The movement Jubilee 2000 was organized to speed up the process. By the end of 2000, some African nations were approved for debt relief.

Countries chosen for debt relief must show that they are serious about reducing poverty. They must make plans for development. Debt relief and the development it requires are positive steps that will benefit poor African nations in the twenty-first century.

◆ **How did African leaders try to improve the economies of their nations?**

Review II

Review History
A. Why did many new African nations have autocratic leaders after they gained their independence?
B. How did other nations show their opposition to apartheid?
C. Why did African nations have to borrow money from other countries?

Define Terms to Know
Define the following terms:
coup d'état, apartheid

Critical Thinking
What are some of the challenges that Africa faces in the future?

Write About Economics
Write an editorial describing the economic decline in Africa and explaining how other nations around the world can help.

Get Organized
SQR CHART
Use an SQR chart to organize information from this section. For example, this section is about political troubles in Africa.

Critical Thinking

Answers will vary. Students may include disease, wars, poverty, famine, and overpopulation.

Write About Economics

In their editorials, students should synthesize what they have read about the decline of African economies and possible remedies.

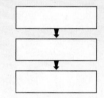

SURVEY
This section is about political troubles in Africa.

QUESTION
What are some of the political problems African nations face?

READ
One-party systems of government, autocratic leaders, military coup d'états, civil war, and cultural and regional conflicts

CONNECT
History & Geography

Preserving African Wildlife

Preserving wildlife is an important cause in Africa, as in the rest of the world. Hundreds of species, or kinds, of wildlife have disappeared from the face of the Earth over the past 2,000 years. Most of these species have become extinct, or died off, since the beginning of the twentieth century. Today, some African animals, including elephants, rhinos, hippos, lions, and antelopes, are in grave danger of becoming extinct.

THE IMPACT OF HUMANS is the main reason wildlife in Africa is at risk. Human populations are growing faster than ever before. Human activities such as farming and logging have destroyed animal habitats, or the places where they live. Poaching, or illegal hunting, has severely reduced animal numbers. Wars, government corruption, and building-development programs have also had an indirect effect on wildlife in Africa.

WILDLIFE PRESERVATION EFFORTS began about 1900 in Africa. Colonial governments set up the first game reserves, or special areas for the protection of animals, in South Africa. In 1933, a gathering in London discussed how to preserve African plants and animals. Ideas raised at this meeting led to the development of national parks in Africa. As African nations gained their independence, they continued the work started by colonial governments. By the end of the twentieth century, there were hundreds of protected areas.

Conservationists in Africa today believe that the survival of wildlife depends on the African people. Since colonial times, people living in rural areas in Africa have lost their rights to land and wildlife. At the same time, they have not received any benefit from the tourism and sport hunting that protected areas support. For this reason, wildlife is no longer valuable to many Africans. Many argue that to build local interest in preserving wildlife, local peoples must be given responsibility for Africa's wildlife resources again. They must manage and preserve wildlife in ways that agree with their traditions.

Critical Thinking

Answer the questions below. Then, complete the activity.

1. How did people in Africa lose their rights to local land and wildlife?
2. Do you think preserving wildlife is an important issue for people in the United States? Why or why not?

Write About It

Use the Internet and reference books to learn more about African wildlife and efforts to preserve it. Then, write an essay expressing your views about the methods of preservation being used today.

This photograph shows an African elephant calf.

Teaching Options

LINK to TODAY

Today, to help raise money for and an awareness of wildlife conservation, many African nations encourage ecotourism, a type of tourism that seeks to protect and respect natural resources while profiting from them. However, ecotourism is controversial because many ecotourist adventures disregard important environmental considerations. Have students research the debate on ecotourism.

F Y I
Biosphere Reserves in Africa

The definition of a biosphere reserve is an area of terrestrial and coastal ecosystems that promotes the conservation of biodiversity while developing, using, and sustaining the area's resources. The first idea for a biosphere reserve was created at a UNESCO conference in 1968. Now, there are 60 biosphere reserves in 28 African nations alone.

CONNECT
History & Geography

PRESERVING AFRICAN WILDLIFE

Teach the Topic

Ask students what they know about endangered animals. Then, have them name and describe efforts that they might have heard about to preserve wildlife. (Answers will vary, but students should remark on preservation game parks; international organizations that raise funds and awareness, such as the World Wildlife Federation; and other grass-roots efforts, such as raising funds within their own community.)

THE IMPACT OF HUMANS Ask students why governments in Africa might have a hard time convincing local people to protect wildlife. (Possible answers: Farmers want to protect their crops from wildlife, poachers can make money from wildlife, and African governments are reluctant to spend money on conservation when they need money for defense.)

WILDLIFE PRESERVATION EFFORTS Brainstorm with students about more policies, programs, or incentives that African governments could present to their communities to encourage preservation of wildlife. Write all answers on the board. Remind students that there are no "right" or "wrong" ideas when brainstorming—all contributions are valid. (Possible answer: The government could offer farmers a rebate program—for example, they could receive money from the government to supplement the percentage of their crop destroyed by animals.)

Critical Thinking

1. Africans lost their rights to local land and wildlife when large areas of land were taken over by Europeans for farms and game preserves.
2. Students should support their point of view with logical reasoning.

Write About It

In their essays, students should discuss African wildlife and efforts to preserve it. They should also express a point of view about preservation methods used throughout the world today.

III. Struggles in the Middle East

(pp. 772–776)

Section Summary

In this section, students will learn about the emergence of the Arab nations of Iraq, Jordan, Syria, Lebanon, and Saudi Arabia and the Jewish State of Israel. Students also will learn about Gamal Abdel Nasser and his desire to control a united Arab world.

1 Introduce

Getting Started

Have students think of an occasion when change happened so quickly that they did not have time to adjust to it—for example, when a younger sibling was born or when they moved to a new community or started in a new school. How did it make them feel? (confused, resistant, hostile) Tell students that many nations in the Middle East had difficulty adapting to their newfound independence after World War II, even though this was something they had fought for.

TERMS TO KNOW

Ask students to read the terms and definitions on page 772. Then, have students construct fill-in-the-blank quizzes, using these terms and the ones from the previous sections. Ask students to exchange quizzes and answer each other's questions.

You may want to preview the pronunciation of the following names with students.

Faisal (FY suhl)
Farouk (FAH rook)
Nasser (NAS uhr)

ACTIVE READING

As students read through this section, have them analyze the reasons for the rise of the Arab nations and the Jewish State of Israel. For example, why did the Iraqis not want the British to be involved in governing their country?

Terms to Know

kibbutz a farm cooperative in Israel in which settlers share the work and the produce

diaspora the scattered population of a cultural group throughout the world

Main Ideas

A. The Arab nations of Iraq, Jordan, Syria, Lebanon, and Saudi Arabia emerged in the first half of the twentieth century.

B. The Jewish State of Israel was created in Palestine in 1948.

C. Egyptian President Gamal Abdel Nasser wanted to unite the Arab world under his leadership.

Active Reading

ANALYZE

When you analyze, you look closely at information to figure out what it is about. As you read this section, try to identify the struggles in the Middle East being discussed. Then, write about the struggles in your own words.

A. The Rise of Arab States

Nationalist feelings were strong in many Arab nations after World War II. Since the end of World War I, Great Britain and France had governed Arab lands that had once been part of the Ottoman Empire. The League of Nations had given these lands to the British and French as mandates, or areas to prepare for self-government. Iraq and Palestine were British mandates. Syria was a French mandate.

Iraq and Jordan

Great Britain set up the state of Iraq in 1921. The new state was formed from three provinces in Mesopotamia: Basra, Baghdad, and Mosul. The provinces had little in common. They included a huge variety of cultural and religious groups, including Arabs, Kurds, Sunni and Shi'a Muslims, Christians, and Jews. Iraq won its independence in 1932. Its ruler was King Faisal I, an Arab prince chosen by the British and approved by the Iraqi people. Later, in 1939, his grandson Faisal II became ruler. Britain did not want to give up all ties to Iraq, however. It was interested in Iraq's oil fields. By an earlier treaty, Britain kept some control over Iraqi foreign policy. It also had the right to use air bases there.

Iraq's king, Faisal II, salutes the Moroccan flag upon his visit to Rabat, Morocco.

The Iraqis did not want the British to be involved in their country any longer. In World War II, they tried to become allies of the Axis Powers. At the same time, Great Britain tried to use its bases in Iraq. Iraq and Great Britain came into conflict. The British defeated the Iraqi army and remained in Iraq through the rest of the war. Britain continued to have a strong influence in Iraq until the late 1950s. In 1958, the military took over the government and declared Iraq a republic.

Besides the Mesopotamian provinces that became Iraq, Britain had also received Palestine as a mandate. Palestine was made up of lands west and east of the Jordan River. In 1921, Britain created a separate self-governing area from the lands east of the river. The area was called Transjordan because it was "across

---

Teaching Options

Section 3 Resources

Teacher's Resources (TR)

Terms to Know, p. 45
Review History, p. 79
Build Your Skills, p. 113
Concept Builder, p. 248
SQR Chart, p. 322
Transparencies 2, 10

Meet Individual Needs:

VERBAL/LINGUISTIC LEARNERS

Have students work with a partner to discuss imperialism in Arab lands and why the people of those lands desired independence. Then, have each pair of students make a list of actions that were taken to achieve independence for each Arab country.

the Jordan" from the rest of Palestine. In setting up Transjordan, the British hoped to make the region more stable. The area was desert and home to various nomadic tribes. These tribes did not observe borders and made frequent raids into Syria.

In 1922, Transjordan became an independent state. It was ruled by an emir, or prince, named Abdullah. The British, however, still controlled foreign policy, the military, and money matters in Transjordan. In 1946, Transjordan won complete independence, although the British still had a great deal of influence in its economy and army. In 1949, Transjordan became the Hashemite Kingdom of Jordan, and Abdullah became king.

Syria and Lebanon

France became even more involved in the affairs of its mandates than Britain. France had many reasons to hold onto Syria. It saw itself as the protector of Christians in the region. It wanted to protect the rail lines, ports, and trade it had established during Ottoman rule. It also thought that French control of Syria would balance British activity in the Middle East.

In 1920, France split Syria into Lebanon and Syria. Lebanon included a Christian area in Mount Lebanon and Muslim areas along the coast. France divided Syria into many parts based on the different groups living there. Instead of building national unity, these divisions encouraged religious and cultural differences.

To manage its mandates, France created a huge bureaucracy. France helped Lebanon write a constitution in preparation for self-government. Lebanon became independent in 1943 but was subject to French control until 1946. Syria also gained complete independence from France in 1946.

Saudi Arabia

Unlike the British and French mandates, Saudi Arabia became fully independent in the years between the two world wars. The Saud family had been increasing its power and land holdings in the Arabian peninsula since the 1700s. By the twentieth century, the Saud family controlled a large kingdom in Arabia, known as the Nejd. In 1925, the Nejd king, Abd al-Aziz ibn-Saud, defeated Sharif Hussein, ruler of the Hejaz, a kingdom to the west. Ibn-Saud united the kingdoms of Hejaz and Nejd to form the state of Saudi Arabia in 1926.

This vast desert state came into great riches soon after its formation. Some of the world's largest reserves of oil were discovered in eastern Saudi Arabia in the 1930s. The Saudi Arabian government gave the Arabian-American Oil Company (ARAMCO) the right to explore for oil and produce it. In exchange, ARAMCO helped create Saudi Arabia's infrastructure, which was largely undeveloped. ARAMCO also helped develop schools and health services for the people of Saudi Arabia. Saudi Arabia's oil industry grew rapidly after World War II.

◆ How was Saudi Arabia formed?

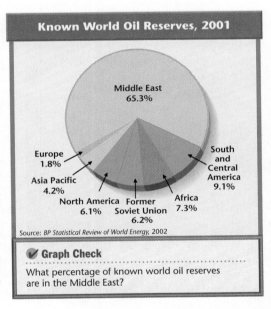

Known World Oil Reserves, 2001

Middle East 65.3%

Europe 1.8%

Asia Pacific 4.2%

North America 6.1%

Former Soviet Union 6.2%

Africa 7.3%

South and Central America 9.1%

Source: BP Statistical Review of World Energy, 2002

✔ **Graph Check**

What percentage of known world oil reserves are in the Middle East?

A. The Rise of Arab States

Purpose-Setting Question How did feelings of Arab nationalism conflict with the League of Nations mandate policy in the Middle East? (Arabs wanted foreigners out of their countries, but foreigners stayed involved because of their own self-interests.)

Discuss Review with students what a mandate is. (an area to be prepared for self-government) Have students discuss how the leaders of Syria, Lebanon, and Iraq must have felt as they were "prepared for self-government." (Possible answers: impatient, resentful) Have them identify how Iraq acted during World War II. (It tried to work against the British by attempting to join the Axis Powers.)

Focus Have students use map A7 in the Atlas or Transparency 10 to locate each nation mentioned in this section.

Using the Graph
Known World Oil Reserves, 2001

Ask students what advantages the Middle East has as the region with the most oil reserves. (Oil is a much sought-after commodity, which gives the Middle East power.) Then, ask students what disadvantages there may be to relying on one resource, such as oil, as the chief industry for a region's economy. (If the price of oil is low or if supplies run out, then the area is in economic trouble.)

✔ **Graph Check**
Answer 65.3 percent of the world's known oil reserves are in the Middle East.

◆ **ANSWER** Abd al-Aziz ibn-Saud, king of the Nejd in the Arabian Peninsula, defeated the ruler of the kingdom of Hejaz and united the kingdoms to form the state of Saudi Arabia in 1926.

Research

AVERAGE

Have students create fact sheets about the independence movement in Iraq, Jordan, Syria, Lebanon, or Saudi Arabia. Sheets should include information from the section. Based on research from other reference sources, fact sheets should also include important events, dates, and information concerning the leaders of the nation's independence movement.

CHALLENGE

Tell students that Africa's Pan-Africanism movement had a Middle Eastern equivalent: Pan-Arabism. Have students research and compare the two nationalist movements, drawing similarities and differences in a graphic organizer, such as a Venn diagram (TR, p. 323). Students should present their findings to the class along with a brief history of each movement.

B. The Creation of Israel

Purpose-Setting Question Why did the Jewish people feel that they needed a homeland? (Anti-Semitic feelings from the late 1800s on convinced Jews that other Europeans would never accept them. Thus, the Zionist movement began.)

Do You Remember?
Remind students that some people did not learn about the anti-Semitism in Europe and Nazi concentration camps until after the war. Ask students how such atrocities could go unnoticed. (Possible answers: The people who were discriminated against did not speak up for fear of more persecution, or they died in the concentration camps. Those who were perpetrating the crimes did not own up to them. Also, those who heard rumors could not believe anything so terrible could be true.)

Discuss Talk with students about the UN's suggestion regarding Palestine. Ask students why they think the Arab states rejected the plan. (Possible answer: They did not feel they should have to give up anything.)

Explore Ask students to describe how Jews and the Arab population living in Palestine might have interpreted the Balfour Declaration differently. (Possible answer: Jews probably were happy about the declaration because it offered them a homeland. Arabs probably felt threatened because the land they were living on suddenly belonged to someone else.)

Activity

Create a poster Have students learn more about the birth of the State of Israel and then create a poster that might have been displayed during the event. The poster could invite Jewish people from all over the world to come to Israel to celebrate and share in the building of the new state. It might promise citizens true religious freedom and a rich heritage to share in. Perhaps it would ask Arab neighbors to work with Israel to build a peaceful, prosperous Middle East.

Do You Remember?
In Chapter 27, you learned about anti-Semitism in Germany in the years before World War II.

A group of young people dance as the flag of the new State of Israel is raised on May 14, 1948.

B. The Creation of Israel

The first stirrings of Jewish nationalism began to surface in the late 1800s. At that time, anti-Semitism, or hostility toward Jews, seemed to be increasing in parts of Europe. Many Jews became convinced that they would never be accepted by other Europeans. These Jews began a movement called Zionism, which aimed at establishing a Jewish homeland in Palestine. Palestine was the ancient homeland of the Jews. Zionism spread rapidly throughout Europe.

The Beginning of Conflict

The first groups of Jewish immigrants arrived in Palestine in the 1880s. On November 2, 1917, the Zionist movement received the backing of the British government when Foreign Secretary Arthur Balfour issued the Balfour Declaration. This declaration stated Great Britain's official approval of the establishment of a national home for the Jewish people in Palestine.

The Balfour Declaration encouraged many Jews to move to Palestine after World War I. By 1936, they numbered about 400,000. The growing Jewish population was not welcomed by the native Arab population. Difficulties developed as more Jewish settlers arrived in Palestine. As they watched the Jewish population of Palestine increase, the Arabs became concerned. Jewish settlements were attacked in 1929 and during the 1930s.

The British sent in thousands of troops, but they were not able to keep the order. By the 1940s, Arabs and Jews were involved in an all-out war. In 1947, Britain turned the problem of Palestine over to the United Nations. The next year Great Britain pulled out its troops.

Independence and War

The United Nations suggested dividing Palestine into two states, one Jewish and one Arab. Jerusalem would be under international control. While Jewish leaders welcomed the plan, the Arabs rejected it. On May 14, 1948, the new State of Israel was born. The next day, Lebanon, Syria, Iraq, Jordan, and Egypt attacked Israel. They hoped to drive the Israelis, as the citizens of the new State of Israel called themselves, out of Palestine. However, they learned that the Israelis were determined to remain.

The Arabs and Israelis were at war until the middle of 1949. Israel increased its size by capturing territory that had been given to the Arabs. It held tightly to West Jerusalem. Jordan took over East Jerusalem and the West Bank, across the Jordan River. Egypt claimed the Gaza Strip. Peace agreements between Israel and the Arab countries ended the fighting. Violence between Arabs and Israelis continued to break out, however. The Arabs refused to recognize the existence of the State of Israel. The fighting forced thousands of Palestinian Arabs to flee their homeland into Syria, Jordan, and Lebanon. The problem of what to do with the Palestinian refugees became a source of conflict between Israel and Arab nations.

Building a Jewish Nation

After the 1948 War of Independence, Israel focused on building a modern state from its ancient homeland in

Teaching Options

Test Taking

Essay tests often ask students to identify and explain the significance of a person, place, or event in world history. To practice this skill, have students use information on this page to answer the following essay question: What was the Balfour Declaration, and how did it affect Arab and Israeli relations?

Connection to GEOGRAPHY

Water conservation is a critical issue in the Middle East. Often, keeping the peace is contingent on water rights issues. Some Middle Eastern nations have built dams and desalination plants. Desalination plants use different processes for taking salt out of water. In a common process called distillation, water is boiled and the steam is collected and condensed into drinkable water.

Palestine. Jewish settlers had already begun developing agriculture and industry in Palestine in the decades before the creation of Israel. They had built factories. They had also used irrigation to be able to farm in the desert. Israel's economy grew rapidly in the 1950s and 1960s. American economic aid and taxes in Israel provided money to invest in industry and agriculture. New industries produced goods such as electronics and military hardware, which were in demand elsewhere in the world.

By the early 1970s, Israel could grow all the food it needed. It began to export crops such as olives and citrus fruits. Many Israelis lived on a **kibbutz**, or a farm cooperative. Yet, Israel was quickly becoming an urban and industrialized society like those in the West. Israel's standard of living was higher than anywhere else in the Middle East.

During this time of expansion, Israel's population also grew. Jewish immigrants streamed into the new state, doubling its population between 1948 and 1951. Israel welcomed Jews from all over the world under the Law of Return. Israel's first prime minister, David Ben-Gurion, underlined this policy when he remarked,

> 66 Ours is a country built more on people than on territory. The Jews will come from everywhere: from France, from Russia, from America, from Yemen. . . . Their faith is their passport. 99

The Nationality Law, passed in 1952, gave automatic citizenship to Jewish immigrants from anywhere in the **diaspora**, or the scattered population of Jews throughout the world. It also gave Israeli citizenship to Arabs who had lived in Palestine prior to 1948. During the 1948 war, more than 700,000 Palestinian Arabs fled to Jordan and to other Arab states. Most remained there, living in poor conditions in refugee camps. Some 160,000 Palestinian Arabs, however, stayed in the new State of Israel after 1949.

◆ **Who could be a citizen of Israel?**

C. Arab Reaction to Defeat

From the Arab point of view, the Israeli victory in the 1948 war was a disaster. The Arab defeat created a huge refugee population. It also made Arabs question the strength of their own states and governments.

Nasser and the Suez Crisis

Egyptians blamed their ruler, King Farouk, for the Arab defeat. King Farouk had been ruler of Egypt since 1936. Many Egyptians who were unhappy with their government became followers of the Muslim Brotherhood, which believed that all of the former British mandate of Palestine should be given back to Arabs. It also wanted a strict Islamic government in Egypt. The military was also critical of King Farouk. In 1952, a group of army officers revolted and overthrew the king. The leader of the military coup was Gamal Abdel Nasser. Egypt became a republic. Nasser was elected president in 1956.

Many Israeli farmers work in a kibbutz—a community in which property, labor, and living quarters are shared.

ANALYZE PRIMARY SOURCES

DOCUMENT-BASED QUESTION
What did David Ben-Gurion mean when he said that faith was a passport for Jews going to Israel?

THE SUEZ CANAL Have students compare U.S. motives for building the Panama Canal in Central America with British, French, and Egyptian interests in building the Suez Canal. You may wish to point out to students that Nasser became a hero to the Arab peoples largely because of the way be handled the Suez crisis.

Extend Have students tell why Nasser became an Arab leader after the Suez Canal incident. (Possible answer: He stood up to world leaders to get the money to build the Aswan High Dam.) Ask students to speculate why the Arab unions founded after this incident did not last. (Possible answer: The Arab unions were not based on a long-term desire to be united.)

◆ **ANSWER** Egypt needed money to build the Aswan High Dam. After the United States and Great Britain withdrew their offer to help pay for the dam's construction, Nasser decided to use the canal tolls to pay for the dam.

Section Close

Have students review the section by turning heads and subheads into questions. For example, the head "The Rise of Arab States" might become the question, *Why and how did the Arab states rise?* Then, have them exchange their questions with a partner and answer them. Partners should check answers together to ensure accuracy.

3 Assess

Review Answers

Review History

A. They were mandates of Great Britain and France after World War I and eventually gained their independence.

B. War broke out between Israel and its Arab neighbors—Syria, Lebanon, Jordan, Egypt, and Iraq.

C. Nasser's dream was to unite the Arab world under his leadership.

Define Terms to Know

kibbutz, 775; diaspora, 775

THE SUEZ CANAL

After the 1948 war, the Suez Canal was closed to Israeli ships and ships trading with Israel. It was closed to all ships during the Suez crisis in 1956–1957 and later during the 1967 war between Arabs and Israelis. It was not officially reopened until 1975.

Today, the canal remains open to all oceangoing traffic, including Israeli ships.

Nasser had great plans for Egypt. He was especially interested in improving its economy. Nasser wanted to expand industry. He also wanted to reclaim desert land for agricultural use. To achieve his economic goals, Nasser organized various projects, including the building of the Aswan High Dam. Once constructed, the dam would hold back the waters of the Upper Nile. The reservoir behind the dam would provide irrigation for 2 million acres of land. The water could also be used to generate electric power. The United States and Great Britain promised funds to build the dam. Then, they withdrew their offer. Nasser reacted by taking over the Suez Canal in 1956. He said he planned to use the tolls from the canal to build the dam.

Nasser's action set off an international crisis. Britain and France owned the canal. When they could not come to an agreement with Nasser, Britain, France, and Israel planned to invade Egypt. Israel was ready. Palestinian Arabs had been making raids into Israel from the Gaza Strip for some time. Israel invaded and quickly took over the Sinai Peninsula. France and Britain sent in forces to take the canal back. The United States and the Soviet Union strongly opposed the actions of Great Britain, France, and Israel. The United Nations finally arranged a cease-fire. Israel gave up the land in the Sinai. UN troops were stationed on the Egypt-Israel border. The Egyptian government took control of the canal. It was again open to traffic, except from Israel.

Common Causes

The Suez crisis made Nasser a leader in the Arab world. It was Nasser's dream to unite the Arab world under his leadership. In 1958, Egypt, Syria, and part of what is now the country of Yemen formed unions with one another. These unions did not last long, however. In the end, these and other Arab states did not want to be under Nasser's control.

Other Arab states underwent changes in government and outlook similar to Egypt's after the 1948 war. The military took control in Syria and Iraq. Many Arabs throughout the Middle East began to support the Pan-Arab movement. Pan-Arabism called for Arab political unity. It also rejected western influence. Arabs were also united in opposing the existence of Israel.

◆ **Why did Nasser take over the Suez Canal?**

Review III

Review History

A. How did the Arab states of Iraq, Jordan, Syria, and Lebanon come into being?

B. What happened as soon as the State of Israel was established?

C. What was Egyptian President Nasser's dream?

Define Terms to Know
Define the following terms:
kibbutz, diaspora

Critical Thinking
Why do you think Israel required Arabs who wanted Israeli citizenship to prove that they had lived in Palestine prior to 1948?

Write About Geography
Write a paragraph explaining what happened to the British mandate of Palestine by 1948.

Get Organized
SQR CHART
Use an SQR chart to organize information from this section. For example, this section is about the rise of Arab states.

Critical Thinking

Possible answer: They probably thought this was a way to make sure that Arabs did not obtain Israeli citizenship; without citizenship, they would be unable to work against Israel and try to take back Palestine.

Write About Geography

Students should describe the creation of Transjordan and Israel.

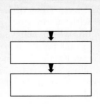

SURVEY
This section is about the rise of Arab states.

↓

QUESTION
Which Arab states in the Middle East came into being after World War II?

↓

READ
Jordan, Syria, and Lebanon

The Middle East and the Modern World

Terms to Know

intifada the uprising by Palestinians in territory held by Israel

secularize to change from religious to nonreligious use or control

fundamentalist someone who believes that religious beliefs and laws should be strictly followed

Main Ideas

A. The Arab-Israeli conflict continued as Israel occupied more territory in Palestine and Palestinians fought to establish their own state.

B. In 1979, a revolution overthrew the government of the shah of Iran and enforced traditional ways and strict Islamic law.

C. The United States led a mutlinational coalition to defeat Iraq's attempted takeover of Kuwait in 1991, and 12 years later began Operation Iraqi Freedom, a war to remove Iraq's president.

 Active Reading

MAIN IDEA AND SUPPORTING DETAILS
Writers use details to support their main idea. As you read this section about conflicts in various places in the Middle East, identify the main idea of each paragraph. Then, locate details that support the idea.

A. The Arab-Israeli Conflict

After the 1948 war, the Arab-Israeli conflict continued as Israel and its Arab neighbors fought again in 1956, 1967, and 1973. Palestinian guerrilla fighters made raids into Israel from Jordan, and the Israelis crossed the border into Jordan on raids of their own. Tensions were high. The Israelis feared that the Arabs might launch a joint military effort against them. The Arabs could not forget that the Israelis defeated them in 1948 and invaded Egypt in 1956.

Two More Wars

In 1967, several developments led to a war that became known as the "Six-Day War." When UN troops withdrew from the Egypt-Israel border, Gamal Nasser sent troops into the Sinai Peninsula. Then, he closed the Red Sea port of Aqaba to Israeli ships. Syria and Jordan entered into military agreements with Egypt.

Israel needed access to the Red Sea. Early in the morning on June 5, 1967, Israel attacked Egypt. Israeli warplanes quickly destroyed Egyptian air bases and most of its air force. Israeli troops took control of the Sinai Peninsula, the Gaza Strip, the West Bank, and East Jerusalem. Along its border with Syria, Israel seized the Golan Heights.

In just six days, Israel had defeated three Arab states: Egypt, Jordan, and Syria. It also greatly increased its territory. After the war, the Israelis decided that they would not return the territory they had won unless the Arab states recognized Israel's right to exist.

Just six years later, in 1973, Egypt and Syria launched an attack on Israel to take back the territory lost in 1967. The surprise attack took place on Yom Kippur, a Jewish holy day. After early Egyptian and Syrian gains, fighting shifted in Israel's favor. Israeli troops crossed the Suez Canal and marched toward Cairo, Egypt. They also defeated the Syrian army in the Golan Heights.

This photograph shows fighting during the Yom Kippur War, which took place in 1973 when Egypt and Syria launched an attack on Israel.

CHAPTER 32 ◆ Africa and the Middle East **777**

Section Summary

In this section, students will learn about continuing conflicts between Arabs and Israelis and international efforts to keep the peace. They will also learn about Iran and an Islamic revolution that called for a return to traditional ways. Lastly, they will learn about Iraq and its conflicts with Iran, Kuwait, the United Nations, and the international effort to remove Iraq's president.

1 Introduce

Getting Started

Have students volunteer information about themselves that they feel is different from other people they know. Then, ask students to explain how different people can live together peacefully within one community. Tell students that learning to tolerate differences is a daily issue for some nations in the Middle East.

TERMS TO KNOW

Ask students to read the terms and definitions on page 777 and then find each term in the section. Then, have them rewrite each definition in their own words.

You may wish to preview with students the pronunciation of the following names.

Sinai (SY ny)
Menachem Begin (muh NAH kuhm BAY gihn)
Yasir Arafat (yaw SER ar UH fat)
Ariel Sharon (AR ee ehl shah ROHN)
Ayatollah Ruhollah Khomeini (eye yuh TOH luh roo HAWL lah koh MAY nee)

ACTIVE READING

Have students use the main idea/supporting details chart (TR, p. 319) as they read each subsection. Encourage students to add more details if they feel they are needed.

Teaching Options

Section 4 Resources

Teacher's Resources (TR)
Terms to Know, p. 45
Review History, p. 79
Build Your Skills, p. 113
Chapter Test, pp. 179–180
Concept Builder, p. 248
SQR Chart, p. 322
Transparency 10

Connection to GOVERNMENT

In Israel, most men and women at age 18 are drafted into the Israeli Defense Forces. One Israeli woman believes that becoming a soldier bonds her with other Israelis: "Every soldier calls another one brother or sister." An increase in immigration and the birth rate, however, may eliminate Israel's need to draft 18-year-olds in the future.

2 Teach

A. The Arab-Israeli Conflict

Purpose-Setting Question
When and why were Israel and its Arab neighbors in conflict? (Arabs and Israelis fought over disputed territory in 1948, 1956, 1967, 1973, 1982, 1987, and from 2000 to the present.)

Discuss Have students volunteer what they know about the Jewish holiday of Yom Kippur. Then, ask them why Yom Kippur was a strategic day for Egypt to attack Israel. (Possible answer: Yom Kippur is the holiest day of the Jewish calendar; people would have been participating in daylong fasting and prayer and therefore not prepared for the attack.)

Explore Ask students why they think the United States became involved in the Arab-Israeli peace negotiations. (Possible answer: As long as the United States supported Israel and the Soviet Union supported Egypt, there would be tension between the superpowers. If a third party could succeed in initiating a plan for peace, this tension could be lessened.) Have students discuss whether the Camp David Accords helped or hurt the peace process.

Extend Have students research the cause-and-effect relationship between OPEC and the 1973 oil crisis. Students should report their findings in a short essay, which also should include a cause-and-effect graphic organizer (TR, p. 325) to represent their data visually.

GLOBAL CONNECTIONS
OLYMPIC TRAGEDY Ironically, many German people had hoped that the 1972 Olympics would show that their country had changed since the last time the Olympics had been held there—in 1936 during Hitler's regime. German president Gustav Heinemann welcomed the Olympics as "a milestone on the road to a new way of life with the aim of realizing peaceful coexistence among peoples."

President Anwar el-Sadat of Egypt, U.S. President Jimmy Carter, and Prime Minister Menachem Begin of Israel shake hands after signing the peace treaty between Israel and Egypt.

 Global Connections

OLYMPIC TRAGEDY
On September 5, 1972, during the Olympics in Munich, West Germany, a group of Palestinian terrorists, disguised as athletes, entered the Olympic village. Here, they held a group of Israeli athletes and coaches hostage. Twenty hours later, after an attempted rescue of the hostages, the terrorists had killed all 11 hostages. Five of the eight terrorists were also killed.

Peace Efforts

Following the war in 1973, the United States became actively involved in bringing peace to the Middle East. The United States and the Soviet Union supported different sides in the war. The United States sent supplies to Israel. The Soviet Union supplied Egypt and Syria. The possibility of open conflict between the superpowers existed as long as the Arab-Israeli conflict continued.

The need for oil was another factor in the U.S. decision to play peacemaker in the Arab-Israeli conflict. During the 1973 war, Arab states in the Organization of Petroleum Exporting Countries (OPEC) announced that they would reduce their oil production by 5 percent each month until Israel returned the territory it had taken. Saudi Arabia stopped all oil shipments to the United States. These actions caused an oil crisis—oil shortages and skyrocketing prices that caused major economic problems in the United States and Europe.

In 1970, Anwar el-Sadat became president of Egypt. After the war in 1967, Sadat decided to take a more moderate, or less extreme, stance toward Israel. Sadat believed that Egyptians and Israelis could work out their differences. In 1978, Sadat met with Israeli Prime Minister Menachem Begin and U.S. President Jimmy Carter. Sadat and Begin signed the Camp David Accords. Egypt agreed to recognize Israel's right to exist. Israel agreed to give up the part of the Sinai Peninsula that it still held. Both leaders also agreed that the Palestinians had a right to self-determination. The Camp David Accords set the stage for a peace treaty Egypt and Israel signed in 1979.

Many Arabs were upset about the Camp David Accords because they believed that Sadat had abandoned the Palestinian cause. In 1981, Sadat was killed by Muslims who claimed that he was a traitor to Arabs and to Islam.

The Palestinian Cause

Despite the Camp David agreement, Palestinians continued to fight for their cause. They were supported by the Palestinian Liberation Organization (PLO). Led by Yasir Arafat, the PLO dedicated itself to an armed struggle against Israel. In the 1960s and 1970s, Palestinian guerrilla groups attacked Israel. Israel responded by attacking Palestinian refugee camps in Jordan and Lebanon, where guerrillas were based. After being driven out of Jordan in 1971, the PLO began to launch attacks on Israel from Palestinian camps in southern Lebanon. In 1982, Israel drove the PLO out of southern Lebanon.

The PLO had two demands. It insisted that Israel leave all the territories it had occupied since 1967. It also called for the establishment of an independent Palestinian state in the West Bank and Gaza Strip. In 1987, the Palestinians mounted an **intifada**, or uprising. Young Palestinians used violent methods against Israeli soldiers, such as stone throwing and fire bombing. The Israeli military put the intifada down. They fired on protesters and leveled homes and villages. An international outcry arose from Israel's response to the intifada.

The Oslo Accord

Hope of establishing peace revived in 1992. After a new Israeli government came to power, new Israeli settlements in the West Bank were put on hold. Peace talks restarted in Oslo, Norway. The result was a historic agreement between Israel and the PLO. Israel recognized the PLO as the voice of the Palestinian people. Israel also agreed to withdraw from all or part of the occupied territories

Teaching Options

Conflict Resolution

Divide students into three groups. Then, present the class with a debate topic, such as "Should ninth graders be allowed to leave school grounds for lunch?" Have two groups debate the issue and the third group mediate. After the conflict is resolved, discuss with students how a third party helped or hindered the problem-solving process.

F Y I

Palestinian Refugee Camps
It is estimated that more than 3 million Palestinians live in or near the 59 refugee camps run by the United Nations. The United Nations Relief and Works Agency operates the camps' schools and health-care facilities. Conditions in the camps are often reported as being poor because of overcrowding and infrastructure damage from incidents with Israeli troops.

and to allow Palestinian control of these territories. The PLO recognized Israel's right to exist and said it would no longer use violence against Israel.

By the mid-1990s, Israel had begun to give up land, and the Palestinians were moving toward self-rule. In 2000, however, further peace talks stalled. A new intifada broke out, and Arafat could not control the violence. Israelis elected a new government in 2001, headed by Ariel Sharon. Chances for peace faded as Palestinians carried out suicide bombings on Israeli targets, and Israel responded by attacking Palestinians and reclaiming the lands they had promised for peace.

◆ **Why did Israel invade Lebanon in 1982?**

B. Iran and the Islamic Revolution

The 1960s and 1970s were also a time of change in Iran. Since World War II, Iran had been ruled by Shah Mohammad Reza Pahlavi. The shah was a friend to the West, especially the United States, but faced many opponents at home. As time went on, the shah clamped down on Iranians' civil rights and crushed opposition to his rule through the use of a secret police force.

The Shah in Iran

In the 1960s, the shah launched a development program to modernize Iran's economy and **secularize** Iranian society. *Secularize* means "to change from religious to nonreligious control." The program included land reforms reorganizing the military, improving education, and giving women the right to vote. These changes were criticized by people who lived in the countryside and by Muslim **fundamentalists**. Fundamentalists believe that religious beliefs and laws should be strictly followed. Muslim fundamentalists in Iran thought the changes the shah had introduced went against the teachings of Islam.

Return to Traditional Ways

After several years of protests, strikes, and riots, the shah was forced to flee Iran in 1979. Revolutionaries took control under the leadership of Ayatollah Ruhollah Khomeini. Khomeini was a Shiite Muslim religious leader and fierce critic of the shah's government. He proclaimed Iran an Islamic republic.

Khomeini and a revolutionary council began to enforce strict policies based on the teachings of Islam. One of the new government's first actions was to execute hundreds of officials with ties to the shah. It put down all opposition by banning political parties, shutting down universities, and getting rid of newspapers and magazines. Then, the government focused on bringing traditional Islamic ways of life back. Women had to wear loose-fitting garments and a head scarf. Men were encouraged to grow beards. Western influences were forbidden.

After hearing that the shah had entered the United States for medical treatment in the fall of 1979, a group of revolutionaries took over the U.S. embassy in Teheran, the capital of Iran. They held 52 Americans hostage and demanded the shah be returned to Iran for trial. The United States refused to meet their demands. The shah died in 1980. The hostages were finally released in January 1981.

To show their support of the Islamic revolution in 1979, Iranian women march and hold a poster of the Ayatollah Khomeini.

◆ **ANSWER** Israel invaded Lebanon in 1982 to stop guerrilla attacks on Israel from southern Lebanon.

B. Iran and the Islamic Revolution

Purpose-Setting Question Why were people unhappy about the society in Iran in the 1960s and 1970s? (People in the countryside and Muslim fundamentalists protested the shah's modernization program and secularization of the government.)

Discuss Have students discuss why the shah's policies were not well received by some of the Iranian people. (Possible answer: The shah's secularization of Iranian society went against traditional Muslim beliefs.) Ask them if the shah's relationship with the West hurt or helped his efforts. (The relationship hurt his efforts in Iran.)

You may want students to create a two-column chart comparing the shah's reforms mentioned in the text with traditional Muslim beliefs. This chart could be used as a basis for an essay.

Explore Have interested students research the various religious factions within Iran. Ask if Khomeini had any serious challenges to his rule. Have students present their findings to the class.

Extend Tell students that some people believe that if a third world war were to happen, it would start in the Middle East. Have students speculate on reasons why this is a common belief. (Student answers will vary but should show an understanding of volatile issues surrounding oil, terrorism, ideology, and the development of nuclear weapons technology.)

Activity

Create a propaganda poster Divide the class in half. Have one group of students create a propaganda poster for the shah of Iran to convince people to adopt western customs. Have the other group of students create a propaganda poster for Ayatollah Khomeini to convince people to reject secularization. Hang posters in the classroom and use them to launch a discussion about both points of view.

ESL/ELL STRATEGIES

Organize Have students create a main idea/supporting details chart (TR, p. 319) to help identify the various forces that shaped the modern Middle East. For example, supporting details might include nationalism, religious differences, territory disputes, and Islamic influences.

Cooperative Learning

Have groups of students research arguments about Israeli settlements on the West Bank to present in a debate. Tell students that the key issue is how these settlements affect the Palestinian population and peace in the region. Assign groups to different tasks—such as researcher, writer, or debater—according to their learning strengths and interests.

◆ **ANSWER** To enforce its policies, the government of Iran executed hundreds of officials with ties to the shah's government, banned political parties, shut down universities, and eliminated newspapers and magazines.

C. Wars in Iraq and Afghanistan

Purpose-Setting Question Why did Iraq invade Kuwait in 1990? (Iraq wanted Kuwait's oil and its access to the Persian Gulf.)

Using the Map

Persian Gulf War, 1991

Have students study the map on page 780. Ask students to describe the geography of Iraq, specifically whether or not there is access to major waterways. (Iraq has limited access to the Persian Gulf.) Then, ask students what geographic advantage Iraq would gain by taking control of Kuwait. (Iraq would gain full access to the Persian Gulf, which would give Iraq better control of oil shipments.)

✔ **Map Check**

Answer Israel, Kuwait, and Saudi Arabia

Explore Discuss with students Iraq's economic situation after its war with Iran. (It was deeply in debt.) Ask students if they think invading Kuwait was the answer to Iraq's financial problems. (Possible answer: The Iraqi government may have thought invading Kuwait would solve Iraq's financial problems, but the plan backfired because it upset other countries around the world as well as in the region.)

Focus Have students list the Arab countries involved in the UN coalition against Iraq. (Egypt, Saudi Arabia, Syria) Ask students how the Iraqi government may have felt toward these nations. (betrayed, angry)

Iran and Iraq Go to War

Saddam Hussein, the leader of Iraq, was afraid that the Islamic revolution in Iran might spread. In 1980, Iraq attacked Iran. The war did not end until 1988. The fighting cost tens of thousands of lives.

After the war, Iran softened its Islamic message somewhat. Khomeini died in 1989, and more moderate leaders led the Iranian government into the twenty-first century.

◆ **How did the fundamentalist government of Iran enforce its policies?**

C. Wars in Iraq and Afghanistan

After the war with Iran, Iraq had serious economic problems, including debts to other Arab countries. Saddam Hussein wanted the debts to be canceled. He also wanted the other countries in OPEC, especially Saudi Arabia and Kuwait, to help Iraq raise world oil prices. Raising oil prices would help bring more money into Iraq.

Operation Desert Storm

In August 1990, Saddam Hussein invaded Kuwait. Iraq wanted Kuwait's oil and its access to the Persian Gulf. More oil would make Iraq a more powerful member of OPEC and help Iraq's economy. The UN immediately passed a resolution against Iraq's invasion of Kuwait and set up a trade embargo. U.S. President George Bush worked to build an international coalition against Iraq. Countries in Europe, Asia, Africa, South America, and North America joined the coalition. Arab members of the coalition included Egypt, Saudi Arabia, and Syria, among other nations. The allies shared an interest in ensuring the availability of oil by protecting oil reserves and keeping open the Straits of Hormuz. This is a vital waterway that connects the Persian Gulf and the Gulf of Oman.

Iraq was given until January 15, 1991, to withdraw from Kuwait. When it refused, the international allies attacked first from the air and then on the ground. The air war, called Operation Desert Storm, was effective and fast. By the end of February, the Iraqi forces were surrounded. Saddam Hussein agreed to a cease-fire in early April, ending the Persian Gulf War.

Under the terms of the cease-fire, Iraq was to destroy all biological and chemical weapons and the plants where they were produced. It was also supposed to destroy any materials and plants it could use to make nuclear weapons. To try to make Iraq keep its promises, the UN imposed sanctions that kept Iraq from selling oil on the world market and from importing most goods. These sanctions hurt the Iraqi people.

War in Afghanistan

The Middle East became the center of another crisis in 2001 when terrorists hijacked four passenger airplanes. Three of

Persian Gulf War, 1991

Iraqi forces
Allied ground attacks
Allied naval forces
◉ Allied air and missile strikes
◉ Iraqi missile strikes
★ Capital cities

SYRIA
LEBANON
Mediterranean Sea
JORDAN
Jerusalem
ISRAEL
EGYPT
IRAQ
Baghdad
IRAN
Kuwait City
KUWAIT
Straits of Hormuz
BAHRAIN
Persian Gulf
Riyadh
QATAR
Gulf of Oman
SAUDI ARABIA
UNITED ARAB EMIRATES
Red Sea

0   150   300 mi
0 150 300 km

40°E   50°E   20°N   30°N

✔ **Map Check**

PLACE Which countries were the target of Iraqi missile strikes?

Teaching Options

Meet Individual Needs:

AUDITORY LEARNERS

Ask students to work in pairs for this activity. Have students take turns reading the text of one part of subsection B and taking notes on the reading. Then, have both students review the notes and compare them with the written text, making any needed corrections.

 **Using Technology**

Have students use the Internet, CD-ROM sources, or other media to find out more about Operation Desert Storm. Students can investigate major battles, weapons used, or the complete terms of the cease-fire agreement. Encourage students to share what they learn with the class.

the planes attacked the World Trade Center, in New York City, and the Pentagon building, near Washington, D.C. Thousands of people died in the attacks. The prime suspect behind the attacks was Osama bin Laden, a Saudi Arabian suspected of many terrorist acts. As you learned in Chapter 30, bin Laden ran a worldwide network of terrorists called al Qaeda.

Following the attacks, the United States declared war on terrorism. It launched an attack on Afghanistan. The purpose of the attack was to drive the government from power because it was controlled by the Taliban, Muslim fundamentalists who supported bin Laden. Frequent outbreaks of violence continue to occur in Afghanistan.

Operation Iraqi Freedom

In the decade following the Gulf War, Iraq challenged the terms of the cease-fire time and again. It also stood in the way of UN weapons inspectors.

Beginning in 2002, Iraq decided to allow UN inspectors into the country to determine if Iraq was producing and stockpiling biological and chemical weapons of mass destruction. Inspectors were also looking for evidence of nuclear arms production.

After many months, during which Iraq refused to fully cooperate with the UN inspectors, the United States, along with Great Britain and other nations, formed a coalition against Iraq. This coalition was convinced that Iraq, under the leadership of Saddam Hussein, had been hiding weapons of mass destruction. In 2003, Operation Iraqi Freedom—a war waged by coalition forces against the harsh government of Saddam Hussein—was fought. The goals of the war were to destroy weapons of mass destruction as well as to remove Hussein from power. The end of the war was declared in May 2003.

Saddam Hussein's statue was toppled in Baghdad, Iraq, after coalition forces gained control of that city.

◆ **How did other Arab states react to Iraq's invasion of Kuwait?**

Review IV

Review History
A. Besides defeating several Arab nations, what did Israel achieve in the 1967 war?
B. Why did Iraqi leader Saddam Hussein look upon Iran as a threat?
C. Why did the United Nations impose economic sanctions against Iraq after the Persian Gulf War?

Define Terms to Know
Define the following terms: **intifada, secularize, fundamentalist**

Critical Thinking
Why was Iraqi leader Saddam Hussein considered a threat to world peace and cooperation?

Write About Economics
Write a short paragraph explaining how oil from the Middle East has affected the U.S. role in the Arab-Israeli conflict.

Get Organized
SQR CHART
Use an SQR chart to organize information from this section. For example, this section is about conflict in the Middle East.

SURVEY
This section is about conflict in the Middle East.

↓

QUESTION
Which countries in the Middle East have been involved in conflict?

↓

READ
Israel, Egypt, Syria, Jordan, Lebanon, Iran, Iraq, Kuwait, Saudi Arabia, and Afghanistan

Critical Thinking
He has not obeyed the terms of the cease-fire agreement drawn up to end the Persian Gulf War, has interfered with UN weapons inspectors, and appears to have been hiding weapons of mass destruction.

Write About Economics
Students should briefly discuss the U.S. dependence on oil from the Middle East, the oil embargo of 1973, and the role of the United States as peacemaker.

Chapter Summary

A blank outline form is available in the Teacher's Resources (p. 318). Chapter summaries should outline Africa's first moves toward independence, the challenges that independence brought to the African and Middle Eastern nations, and the current issues that Middle Eastern nations face. Refer to the rubric in the Teacher's Resources (p. 340) to score students' chapter summaries.

⬤ Interpret the Timeline

1. Egypt's taking control of the Suez Canal
2. 1 year
3. Students should identify one event on the timeline and support their choice with logical reasoning.
4. Check to be sure the events and dates selected by students are in the chapter.

Use Terms to Know

5. a. apartheid
6. c. diaspora
7. b. autonomy
8. d. intifada
9. f. secularize
10. e. kibbutz

Check Your Understanding

11. The French held most of the political and economic power in Algeria; the Arabs and Berbers wanted equal status.
12. Jomo Kenyatta
13. The Belgian government pulled out very quickly. Civil war broke out as cultural groups and regions clashed for power and control of the country.
14. The country is very large and has a large population with many different cultural groups. There were civil wars, military takeovers, and other violence.
15. Military rule, the one-party system, and autocratic leaders were common forms of government in the African nations.
16. Both the civil war in Nigeria and the one in Rwanda resulted from tension between rival groups. Both resulted in many deaths and terrible hardship.
17. the Nationalist party, which was supported by Afrikaners

Chapter Summary

Complete the following outline in your notebook. Then, use your outline to write a brief summary of the chapter.

Africa and the Middle East

I. Independence in Africa
   A. First Moves Toward Freedom
   B. British Rule Ends
   C. France and Belgium Bow Out
II. New Challenges for Africa
   A. Political Troubles
   B. Majority Rule Spreads
   C. Problems and Solutions
III. Struggles in the Middle East
   A. The Rise of Arab States
   B. The Creation of Israel
   C. Arab Reaction to Defeat
IV. The Middle East and the Modern World
   A. The Arab-Israeli Conflict
   B. Iran and the Islamic Revolution
   C. Wars in Iraq and Afghanistan

⬤ Interpret the Timeline

Use the timeline on pages 758–759 to answer the following questions.

1. Which came first, Nelson Mandela's election as president of South Africa or Egypt's taking control of the Suez Canal?
2. How soon after the establishment of the State of Israel was NATO formed?
3. **Critical Thinking** Which event shown on the timeline, do you think, has had the greatest impact on relations among the nations of the world? Explain your answer.
4. Select five events from the chapter that are not on the timeline. Create a timeline that shows these events.

Use Terms to Know

Match each term with its definition.

a. apartheid   c. diaspora   e. kibbutz
b. autonomy   d. intifada   f. secularize

5. the policy of racial separation and discrimination in South Africa
6. the scattered population of a cultural group throughout the world
7. self-government
8. the uprising by Palestinians in territory held by Israel
9. to change from religious to nonreligious use or control
10. a farm cooperative in Israel in which settlers share the work and the produce

Check Your Understanding

11. **Explain** why Africans in Algeria revolted against the French government after World War II.
12. **Identify** the nationalist leader who became Kenya's first prime minister and later president.
13. **Describe** the situation in Belgian Congo when it became independent.
14. **Discuss** the challenges facing the independent nation of Nigeria.
15. **Summarize** government patterns in Africa after independence.
16. **Compare** the civil wars in Rwanda and Nigeria.
17. **Identify** the group that started the policy of apartheid in South Africa.
18. **Discuss** how Saudi Arabia came into great riches after it was formed.
19. **Explain** why Israel's economy grew so rapidly in the 1950s and 1960s.
20. **Describe** the terms of the Camp David Accords.
21. **Discuss** the reasons behind Operation Iraqi Freedom.

18. Saudi Arabia became rich because some of the world's largest reserves of oil were discovered there in the 1930s.
19. Israel developed new industries and goods, including electronics and military hardware, all of which could be exported.
20. In the terms of the Camp David Accords, Egypt agreed to recognize Israel's right to exist. Israel agreed to give up the part of the Sinai Peninsula that it still held. Both agreed that the Palestinians had a right to self-determination.
21. Iraq challenged the terms of the Gulf War cease-fire agreement and interfered with the work of UN weapons inspectors. A coalition, including the United States and Great Britain, was convinced that Iraq had been producing biological and chemical weapons. The war was fought to remove Iraq's harsh leader, Saddam Hussein, from power and to help establish a new government for the people of Iraq.

Critical Thinking

22. Draw Conclusions Why do you think the European powers resisted immediately meeting the demands of nationalist movements for independence in Africa?

23. Make Inferences Why is debt relief needed in Africa?

24. Analyze Primary Sources What developments following the establishment of the State of Israel contradict, or speak against, Ben-Gurion's statement on page 775?

25. Draw Conclusions How would getting rid of newspapers and magazines have assisted the aims of Khomeini and the revolutionary council?

Put Your Skills to Work

26. Resolve Conflict Through Compromise You have learned about different ways to resolve conflict. Understanding conflict and how it can be resolved helps you understand interactions between individuals and groups in history.

Copy the graphic organizer below onto a sheet of paper and fill in the missing boxes. Then, answer the following questions.

a. What does each side in the conflict want?

b. What compromise did each side make?

c. What resolution does each side end up with?

CONFLICT

Israel wants to keep occupied territory as part of Israel.	PLO wants to set up Palestinian state in what was Palestine.

RESOLUTION

Israel gets recognition that it exists. PLO gets some self-rule.

Analyze Sources

27. Read more about South Africa under apartheid in this passage from the speech given by South African Albert Luthuli on receiving the Nobel Peace Prize in 1961. Then, answer the questions that follow.

It is not necessary for me to speak at length about South Africa; its social system, its politics, its economics, and its laws have forced themselves on the attention of the world. It is a museum piece in our time, a hangover from the dark past of mankind, a relic of an age which everywhere else is dead or dying.

a. What do you think Luthuli means when he says that South Africa has forced itself on the attention of the world?

b. Why does Luthuli call South Africa a museum piece, a hangover from the dark past, and a relic from a dead age?

Essay Writing

28. Consider a conflict or situation in the Middle East that has not yet been resolved, such as the Israeli-Palestinian conflict. Write an essay that predicts what will happen in the conflict or situation you have chosen. Use what you have learned and your own experience or knowledge of world events to develop your prediction.

TEST PREPARATION

CAUSE-AND-EFFECT RELATIONSHIPS
Read the question below and choose the correct answer.

Which of the following is not an effect of the South African policy of apartheid?

1. nonviolent demonstrations

2. equality among the races

3. self-governing homelands

4. economic sanctions

Critical Thinking

22. Possible answer: European powers wanted to keep control over their African colonies for as long as possible so that they could use whatever resources their colonies might have.

23. Possible answer: Debt relief is needed because African nations with debt spend so much money paying off their debt that they do not have enough money for health, education, and other services for their people.

24. Possible answer: Israel's recapture of its territory in the 1967 war and afterward contradicts his statement that Israel is built more on people than on territory.

25. Possible answer: By getting rid of newspapers and magazines, the revolutionary council could control the information available to people and present their views without contradiction.

Put Your Skills to Work

RESOLVE CONFLICT THROUGH COMPROMISE

26a. Israel wants to keep the disputed territory as part of Israel; the PLO wants to set up a Palestinian state in what was Palestine.

26b. Israel gave up part of the Sinai Peninsula. Egypt had to recognize Israel's right to exist.

26c. Israel is recognized as a nation. The Palestinians gain some self-determination.

Analyze Sources

27a. Possible answer: The injustices of apartheid and its harmful effects have made the world pay attention to South Africa.

27b. Possible answer: He means that racial separation and discrimination ended in other places in the world some time ago.

Essay Writing

28. In their essays, students should use what they have learned and draw from their own experience or knowledge of world events to make and support a prediction about the resolution of a conflict or other situation in the Middle East.

TEST PREPARATION

Answer 2. equality among the races

The World in a New Century

1990–PRESENT

(pp. 784–808)

Chapter Objectives
• Understand how different elements of the global economy interact and how the economy has an effect on workers throughout the world.
• Discuss the environmental problems caused by pollution, population growth, and changing atmospheric and climatic conditions on Earth.
• Identify problems, such as poverty, disease, overpopulation, human rights violations, and regional conflicts, that threaten people around the world.
• Discuss ways in which scientific research, space exploration, and technological advancements in communications are improving the human condition.

Chapter Summary
Section I focuses on international economics, the ties between developed and developing countries, and the impact of these kinds of economic relationships on workers.
Section II explores the ways in which pollution, population growth, global warming, and damage to the ozone layer are causing worldwide environmental problems.
Section III explores the global challenges presented by poverty and disease, overpopulation, human rights abuses, and regional and international conflicts.
Section IV discusses how technology is being used to improve the human condition, explore outer space, and improve communications.

Set the Stage
TEACH PRIMARY SOURCES
Explain that Craig Kielburger began his own human rights group to end child slave labor. This quotation is from a book about his experiences. Ask students how Kielburger views the "dreamers" of the world. (He believes they were responsible for ending injustice and making important scientific breakthroughs.)

CHAPTER 33

The World in a New Century

1990–PRESENT

I. A Global Economy
II. Earth and the Environment
III. Facing Global Challenges
IV. Looking to the Future

What lies ahead for the future of our world? Craig Kielburger, a student from Toronto, Canada, thought about this question when he said:

"It was the dreamers of the world who thought that one day the Berlin Wall would fall, that apartheid in South Africa would end, and that a human would walk on the moon. Because we are young, full of ideals, and full of dreams, we are not afraid of taking an idea that seems impossible and making it a reality."

A lot has changed in the world today. There have been advances in communications, transportation, medicine, space exploration, and entertainment. The future will bring new challenges. By examining the past and adapting to new conditions, people all over the world can help shape the world of tomorrow.

CHAPTER EVENTS

1990
Hubble Space Telescope is launched.

1991
The World Wide Web is made available on the Internet.

1995
The World Trade Organization is established.

1990 — **1995**

WORLD EVENTS

1991
Boris Yeltsin is elected President of Russia.

1994
Nelson Mandela is elected president of South Africa.

784 UNIT 8 ◆ The World Today

Teaching Options

Chapter 33 Resources

REVIEW

Teacher's Resources (TR)
Terms to Know, p. 46
Review History, p. 80
Build Your Skills, p. 114
Chapter Test, pp. 181–182
Concept Builder, p. 249
Problem/Solution Chart, p. 327
Transparencies 1, 11

ASSESSMENT
Section Reviews, pp. 788, 793, 799, 803
Chapter Review, pp. 806–807
Chapter Test, TR, pp. 181–182
Unit 8 Test, TR, pp. 197–198
Final Exam, TR, pp. 207–214

ALTERNATIVE ASSESSMENT
Portfolio Project, p. 808
Create Historical Maps, p. T808

The World, PRESENT

VIEW HISTORY These flags are from countries all over the world. They display the colors, shapes, and symbols that each county stands for.
◆ Why is a collection of national flags an appropriate image for this chapter?

GET ORGANIZED

Problem/Solution Chart
Throughout history, people have faced problems and searched for solutions. Use a problem/solution chart as you read Chapter 33. In the top oval, write a problem faced by the people you read about. In the bottom oval, write the solution that has been found. Here is an example from this chapter.

PROBLEM
The ozone layer shows damage.

SOLUTION
World leaders are working on agreements to minimize emission of harmful gases.

1996
The first mammal is successfully cloned.

1997
Kyoto environmental conference is held in Japan.

1999
The world's population reaches 6 billion for the first time.

2001
The *Mars Odyssey* begins to orbit Mars.

2002
Iraq allows the return of UN weapons inspectors.

2003
Space shuttle *Columbia* breaks apart before landing.

Major combat of Operation Iraqi Freedom ends.

2000

2005

2000
USS *Cole* is attacked in Yemen by terrorists.

2002
Euro becomes official currency of many Western European nations.

CHAPTER 33 ◆ The World in a New Century **785**

Chapter Themes
• Culture
• Time, Continuity, and Change
• People, Places, and Environments
• Science, Technology, and Society
• Global Connections
• Civic Ideals and Practices

Connection to
CULTURE

Ask students if they can identify any of the flags shown on pages 784–785. Which flags, if any, represent countries to which students' families have connections? Ask students to find the symbolism of some of the flags shown.

Chapter Warm-Up
USING THE MAP
Direct students to look at the locator map at the top of page 785. Ask which regions of the world are highlighted. (all regions) Explain that all of the continents are highlighted because this chapter deals with the entire world. Have students identify each continent and ocean.

VIEW HISTORY
Discuss why flags are such important national symbols. (They represent the country's beliefs, national identity, struggles, and hopes for the future. Flags inspire patriotism and respect for a country's history.)

◆ **ANSWER** Possible answer: It represents many of the nations of the world as well as symbolizing the world's diversity.

GET ORGANIZED
Problem/Solution Chart
Discuss the problem/solution chart on page 785. Ask students to identify the problem (the ozone layer shows damage) and the solution (world leaders are working on agreements to minimize emission of harmful gases). Encourage students to make a problem/solution chart for each section (TR, p. 327).

TEACH THE TIMELINE
The timeline on pages 784–785 covers the period between 1990 and 2003. Point out that the timeline covers 13 years. Ask students to compare the kinds of Chapter Events emphasized with those events identified as World Events. (Most of the Chapter Events emphasize scientific and technological achievements and global problems. The World Events emphasize political action and world conflict.) Suggest that students look for these ideas as they read the chapter and add any other entries that they feel are appropriate to the timeline.

Activity

Research Have students conduct research on one of the events on the timeline and report on their research to the class.

CHAPTER 33 ◆ **T785**

I. A Global Economy

(pp. 786–788)

Section Summary

In this section, students will learn about the interdependence of developed and developing countries in the global economy. They will also learn how the world's workers are affected by the global economy.

1 Introduce

Getting Started

Ask students how their community's economy is affected by economic conditions in other countries of the world. For example, does their community trade with other nations? Do people in their community have personal and economic ties with people in other countries? Do people in their community use food or goods from other countries?

TERMS TO KNOW

Ask students to read the terms and definitions on page 786 and then find each term in the section. Link the first two terms by pointing out the difference between the suffixes *-ed* and *-ing.* Explain that *developed* refers to "completed action," whereas *developing* refers to "an ongoing process." Ask students to use each term in an original sentence.

ACTIVE READING

Have students use a Venn diagram (TR, p. 323) to compare and contrast how workers are treated in the United States and in India. Suggest that they discuss their findings in small groups.

Terms to Know

developed nation a country that is economically, socially, and politically advanced

developing nation a country in which industrialization is still taking place

interdependence the dependence of countries on resources, goods, and knowledge from other countries of the world

Main Ideas

A. Today, many nations of the world are linked economically.

B. The world's lowest-paid workers struggle to survive in today's growing and changing economy.

Active Reading

COMPARE AND CONTRAST When you compare and contrast, you can understand how items are the same and different. As you read this section, compare and contrast developed nations and developing nations.

A. Economic Systems

A global economy is one in which the production, distribution, and sale of goods take place on a worldwide scale. A global economy includes the economies of many, if not all, nations of the world. One feature of the current global economy is the wide gap between rich and poor nations.

Rich and Poor Nations

Industrialized nations are mainly located in the Northern Hemisphere. They are sometimes called **developed** **nations**. Developed nations usually have prosperous economies and high rates of literacy, or the ability to read and write. The labor force mostly works in professions requiring advanced training or education, such as teaching and medicine, or in service industries such as banking. Wages are usually high. Children in developed nations attend school and are prevented by law from working full-time until they reach a certain age. Although areas of poverty do exist, the standard of living is generally high. The United States, Japan, and Western European countries are examples of developed nations.

Nations in the process of becoming industrialized, sometimes called **developing** **nations**, are located mainly in the Southern Hemisphere. Developing nations may be in debt to other nations. In many developing nations, population growth is a serious problem. By the year 2050, the world's population is projected to reach 9 billion. Most of this growth is expected to be in developing nations. Because developing nations are often poor, wages for workers are usually low. Money is spent mostly on necessities such as groceries and housing. Most people work on farms, in mines, or in factories. Often, children work full-time at a very young age because their families need the added income.

Some developing nations have enjoyed strong growth, especially the oil-exporting nations of the Middle East. However, overall these nations remain poor. For most people in these countries, life is a daily struggle for survival. Examples of developing nations include India, most countries in Central America, and some African nations south of the Sahara.

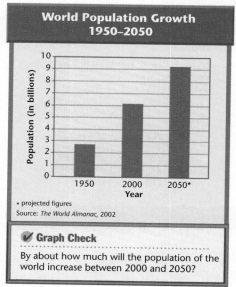

World Population Growth 1950–2050

Population (in billions)

* projected figures
Source: *The World Almanac,* 2002

✔ Graph Check

By about how much will the population of the world increase between 2000 and 2050?

786 UNIT 8 ◆ The World Today

Teaching Options

Section 1 Resources

Teacher's Resources (TR)
Terms to Know, p. 46
Review History, p. 80
Build Your Skills, p. 114
Concept Builder, p. 249
Problem/Solution Chart, p. 327
Transparency 11

ESL/ELL STRATEGIES

Organize Information Ask students to use a main idea/supporting details chart (TR, p. 319) to organize the information in one of the subsections in Section 1. Remind them that the main idea is the most important idea. The supporting details are smaller pieces of factual information that relate to the main idea. Have students make up questions and answers about the material in their charts.

Economic Interdependence

Interdependence is the dependence of countries on goods, resources, and knowledge from other parts of the world. Both developed and developing countries are linked by many economic ties. You have learned that countries export and import many goods. No country can manufacture or produce everything its people need. Many countries grow or produce more of certain crops or goods than their people need. Therefore, a country can trade its surplus crops or goods in exchange for items it cannot produce for itself. For example, Japan must import much of its food, but it exports more vehicles than any other nation in the world.

In an interdependent world, events in one country can affect people in another country. Countries are always willing to trade with their allies but not with their enemies. If two countries are at war, they will sometimes cut off trade relations.

Since communications have made the world one interconnected global economy, leaders have recognized that all nations depend on one another and must try to work together. The World Trade Organization, or WTO, was established in 1995. It is the first permanent institution with real power to regulate trade and to settle disputes among nations. As of 2002, the WTO had 144 member nations with some 30 more applicants for membership. It is the only global international organization that deals with rules of trade between nations.

 What are some of the characteristics of a developed nation?

B. Workers of the World

Developed nations control much of the world's capital—or wealth, trade, and technology. However, they depend on low-paid workers in developing countries to produce manufactured goods as inexpensively as possible. Much of the clothing imported by the United States and European countries is made in developing nations. When people in the United States and Europe shop for clothes, they are often surprised to see the variety of places that export clothing. Clothing made in the United States and Europe usually costs more

Garment factory employees work at long tables in a crowded workplace in Cambodia.

F Y I

The World Trade Organization

A member nation of the WTO must follow the WTO guidelines on international trade. After the organization makes a ruling in a trade dispute between member nations, the country found to be at fault must offer compensation or change its practices. If that country fails to comply, trade sanctions may be imposed. The WTO also regulates trade in intellectual properties such as books, computer software, and recordings.

Using Technology

Have pairs of students use the Internet to research the minimum wage of workers in two developed countries and two developing countries. Ask them to use graphing software to create a bar graph to organize their information. Call on student pairs to display their graphs in class and discuss the results of their research.

2 Teach

A. Economic Systems

Purpose-Setting Question How do the economies of the industrialized nations differ from those of nations that do not have well-developed industries? (The industrialized nations have prosperous economies, while nonindustrialized nations may be in debt to other nations.)

Using the Graph

World Population Growth, 1950–2050

Encourage students to discuss how the increase in the world population will affect the economic interdependence of countries. You may wish to show students the World Population Density map on Transparency 11. (As the world population increases, countries may have to use their surplus goods for their own needs rather than exporting them to other nations.)

✔ Graph Check

Answer The population of the world will increase by more than 3 billion.

Discuss Ask students how the economic differences between the developed nations and the developing nations affect the educational opportunities in these nations. (The developed countries can afford to spend more money on education. In the developing nations, much less money is available for educational needs.)

Focus Have pairs of students use a world almanac or the Internet to identify at least three products that the United States exports to other countries.

◆ **ANSWER** A developed nation has a prosperous economy, a high rate of literacy, high wages, and a generally high standard of living. The labor force mostly works in professions requiring advanced training.

B. Workers of the World

Purpose-Setting Question How does the building of factories help developing countries? (Factories help countries grow economically by providing jobs.)

Using the Graph

Workers Earning Less Than $2 per Day

Ask students to compare the number of East Asian workers earning less than $2 per day in 2002 with the projected number for 2015. (The number of workers earning less than $2 per day will drop from approximately 700 million to 300 million.) Then, ask which regions have the lowest number of low-paid workers. (Europe and Central Asia)

✔ Graph Check

Answer Africa Sub-Saharan

Extend Tell students that in 1912 Massachusetts became the first state to pass a minimum wage law. The Fair Labor Standards Act, passed in 1938, established the first federal minimum wage of 25 cents per hour. Amendments to this act have increased the minimum wage numerous times since its inception.

Discuss Ask students to evaluate the recommendations of the World Bank concerning child labor and give reasons for their opinions.

◆ **ANSWER** Many companies set up plants in developing nations because manufactured goods can be produced inexpensively there.

Section Close

Have students discuss how the interdependence of developed and developing nations affects the lives of workers.

3 Assess

Review Answers

Review History

A. Answers should include population growth, illiteracy, low wages, and child labor.

B. Children might work because there is no school for them to attend or because the family needs the child's wages in order to survive.

Define Terms to Know

developed nation, 786; developing nation, 786; interdependence, 787

Workers Earning Less Than $2 per Day

Number of Workers (in millions) vs Region

Legend: ■ in 2002 ■ in 2015*

* projected figures
Source: *The Economist: The World in 2002*

✔ Graph Check

In which region will the number of low-paid workers reach about 600 million in 2015?

---

than some imported clothing because European and American textile workers earn higher wages.

Worldwide Wages

In the United States, workers earned a minimum wage of $5.15 per hour in 2003. By federal law, no employer was permitted to pay less than this wage. Not all countries have such a law.

Many companies in developed nations are eager to build factories in developing countries because the workers are willing to accept lower wages. This type of investment in developing countries helps them to grow economically. However, when a company moves its factories to another country, jobs are lost at home. This loss sometimes causes political problems in the developed country.

Child Labor

Child labor—work performed by a child younger than the defined legal age—is common in some parts of the world. Children might work because there is no school for them to attend or because the family needs the child's wages in order to survive. Asia and Africa account for about 90 percent of the world's child labor. India alone has 44 million working children.

The World Bank has done a study of child labor. One of its recommendations is that developing nations, with the help of the international community, should help to improve the quality of education. Another suggestion is to subsidize, or provide money to, poor families so that their children can go to school rather than go to work. Efforts are also being made to stop the unfair treatment of children in the workplace.

◆ **Why do many companies set up plants in developing nations?**

Review I

Review History
A. What problems do developing nations face?
B. Why is child labor common in some parts of the world?

Define Terms to Know
Define the following terms:
developed nation, developing nation, interdependence

Critical Thinking
What connection can you find between prosperity and world peace?

Write About Economics
Write a brief essay describing the economic interdependence of the world's nations.

Get Organized
PROBLEM/SOLUTION CHART
Use a problem/solution chart to examine the problems you read about in Section I. For example, what major problem has the World Bank studied?

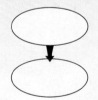

Critical Thinking
Possible answer: During times of prosperity, people have jobs and money and they are relatively content. Such conditions generally promote world peace and trade among nations.

Write About Economics
Students should explain that no country can produce all the goods it needs for its people. Therefore, most countries export surplus goods and import goods they cannot produce. So, nations trade with each other.

PROBLEM
Child labor is common in some parts of the world.

SOLUTION
Pay families to send children to school; pass laws banning child labor.

Build Your Skills

DEVELOP A HISTORICAL PERSPECTIVE

The word *perspective* means "having a point of view or outlook on an event, a person, an issue, or an idea." Developing a historical perspective means understanding events and historical figures from the past in the context, or setting, of their times. You do not judge the event or person from the past by current ideas and values, but take into account the beliefs of the time when the events actually happened.

For example, if an important historical event occurred last year, it would be difficult to develop a historical perspective on that event. One reason would be because you would be judging the event by today's values and beliefs. This would cloud your ideas about the event and its importance.

In order to develop a historical perspective, you must thoroughly understand an event, including its date and where it took place. Then, look for clues about the attitudes and values of the people who lived during that period. You might find these clues in reference texts, or on the Internet.

Here's How

Follow these steps to develop a historical perspective.

1. Identify the event and find out as much as possible about it, including the date of the event and its location.

2. Look for clues about attitudes and values during that time period in history. Use reference texts, periodicals, and the Internet to help you search for clues. List key words and phrases about the event and the time period.

3. Explain how peoples' actions or words reflected their attitudes, values, and emotions from that period in time.

Here's Why

Learning how to develop a historical perspective is useful in helping you to look objectively at people and events and understand them in the context of their own time. As a result, the history you study will be more relevant.

Practice the Skill

You have learned to develop a historical perspective. Read the passage on the right, written in 1989, about the ideas of socialism. Then, use what you have learned to answer the following questions.

1. What is the subject of this passage and the time period to which it refers?

2. What phrases does the author use to express his views on the failure of socialism?

3. Do you think that the author has developed a historical perspective of socialism? Explain.

Extend the Skill

Look on the Internet or in the library for a newspaper or magazine article about an issue or event from 5 to 10 years ago. Compare the article's perspective on the issue to your own perspective. How does historical perspective change your ideas about the issue?

> "Socialism is dead, finished. It was never anything more than an illusion. . . . . As a philosophy it is far superior to capitalism, but as an economic system it does not work. . . . Forty years of experimentation with a planned economy have ended in failure. Socialism is dead."
>
> —Professor D., University of Halle, East Germany, 1989

Apply the Skill

As you continue reading, think about the perspective present-day leaders have developed about events in the past. How can leaders use historical perspective to make the right decisions?

Teaching Options

RETEACH

Have students choose an event described in an earlier chapter in the textbook. Ask them to use the steps in *Here's How* to explain how they would develop a historical perspective on the event.

CHALLENGE

Have students choose an issue or event they have read about in previous chapters and research it in reference books and on the Internet. Ask students to write a newspaper editorial that reflects their historical perspective on the event.

Build Your Skills

DEVELOP A HISTORICAL PERSPECTIVE

Teach the Skill

Encourage students to select recent stories from their local newspaper that they think are important enough to be included in a time capsule to be opened in 100 years. Ask them to guess what people in the future might think about the event described in the article. Point out that people in the future will have to evaluate the event based on their historical perspective of the period.

Encourage students to use the steps in *Here's How* to determine how a future society would find out as much as possible about the subject of the article. What clues about current attitudes, customs, and values would people find in the news article? Have students explain how the events described in the article and the words quoted there reflect current attitudes, values, and emotions.

Practice the Skill

ANSWERS

1. The passage is about the death of socialism and the time period it refers to is around 1949, or 40 years before 1989.

2. "It was never anything more than an illusion"; "as an economic system it does not work."

3. Yes, he speaks of an issue that has been decided over the past 40 years; he knows the outcome.

Extend the Skill

Answers will vary depending on the issue chosen. Make sure that students can explain the difference between their feelings on the issue and the opinions expressed in the articles they choose.

Apply the Skill

Have students think about the conference on the world environment in Kyoto, Japan, in 1997. Ask them to consider what historical events or situations might have influenced those attending in making decisions concerning Earth's environment. (Possible answers: the destruction of the rain forests and the increase in ocean pollution)

II. Earth and the Environment

(pp. 790–793)

Section Summary

In this section, students will learn how Earth's environment has been damaged in a variety of ways, including pollution, population growth, global warming, and destruction of the ozone layer.

1 Introduce

Getting Started

Ask students to identify sources of pollution in their own communities and classify the sources as industrial, agricultural, or residential. What are local and state governments doing to correct the problem? Encourage students to identify ways they can help.

TERMS TO KNOW

Ask students to read the terms and definitions on page 790 and then find each term in the section. Have students use each term in a sentence that could be the lead sentence in a newspaper article.

You may wish to preview the pronunciation of the following words from this section with students.

Valdez (vahl DEHZ)
ozone (OH zohn)
chlorofluorocarbon
  (klohr oh FLOOR uh kahr buhn)

ACTIVE READING

Have students choose one of the subsections in Section 2, such as Earth's Changing Environment, and write a summary of its most important points. Remind students to use their own words to summarize the information. They can use the subheadings, art, and captions to help them write their summaries.

Terms to Know

pesticide any chemical used for killing insects or weeds

metropolitan area a large city and its surrounding towns and smaller cities

biodiversity variety of plant and animal species in an ecosystem

global warming the rise in the average temperature of Earth over time

greenhouse effect the process by which Earth is kept warm at all times

These women are throwing fertilizer on crops in Bolivia. Fertilizer is added to the soil to help improve the quality of plant growth.

Main Ideas

A. Pollution is causing many environmental problems around the world.

B. Population growth has also led to many environmental problems.

C. People have both caused and tried to stop damage to the environment.

Active Reading

SUMMARIZE
When you summarize information, you identify important facts from what you learn. As you read this section, summarize the most important ideas about pollution.

A. Pollution

Over the past century, economic development has taken a heavy toll on Earth's environment. Much of the world's water, air, and soil have been polluted and many natural resources have been used up.

The Use of Pesticides

Scientists pay close attention to the environmental effects of **pesticides**. Pesticides are chemicals that are used to kill insects and weeds that destroy crops. Pesticides that have been used to protect crops have sometimes caused illness in birds, animals, and humans. Because pesticides are carried by the wind and can linger up to 12 years in an area where they are sprayed, they can do tremendous damage to the environment. Today, farmers use fewer harmful pesticides and fertilizers in order to protect the environment.

Chemical Disasters

A dramatic example of modern technology threatening Earth occurred in the coastal waters off Alaska on March 24, 1989. On that day, the supertanker *Exxon Valdez* ran aground on a reef in Alaska's Prince William Sound. Prince William Sound is an important fishing ground for salmon, halibut, and shrimp. It is also home to wildlife such as seals, sea otters, birds, and whales. The broken hull of the tanker released more than 10 million gallons of oil into the sound. The oil slick quickly spread over approximately 1,300 miles of shoreline, killing wildlife and polluting waters. Similar oil spills have caused damage in other parts of the world.

Acid Rain

Acid rain has become a major concern throughout the world. As you learned in Chapter 30, acid rain is rain, snow, or hail that contains toxic chemicals.

Acid rain is especially dangerous because it can travel hundreds of miles from the source of the pollution. Acid rain can make a lake so acidic that living things in the lake die. Countries all over the world are working on ways to reduce acid rain.

◆ **Why has acid rain become a major concern throughout the world?**

Teaching Options

Section 2 Resources

Teacher's Resources (TR)
Terms to Know, p. 46
Review History, p. 80
Build Your Skills, p. 114
Concept Builder, p. 249
Problem/Solution Chart, p. 327

ESL/ELL STRATEGIES

Take Notes Ask pairs of students to take notes on one of the subsections. Remind them to write down only the most important information about the subsection topic. Then, have students exchange papers, read each other's notes, and use the notes to write the first paragraph of a newspaper article about the topic.

B. Impact of Population Growth

Urbanization is the movement from rural areas to cities. It is taking place all over the world. By the year 2000, a total of nearly 3 billion people, 47 percent of the world's population, lived in cities.

Overcrowding in these cities and in some **metropolitan areas** has led to many environmental problems, including pollution. A metropolitan area is a large city and its surrounding towns and smaller cities. Some metropolitan areas include New York City and the cities and towns around it as well as the Los Angeles metropolitan area. In England, London's metropolitan area covers about 620 square miles and includes the City of London, the City of Westminster, and districts in the West End. As population growth increases in the world's cities and metropolitan areas, the need for land and other resources increases as well. As a result, forests and other wild areas are sometimes destroyed, causing loss of plant and animal life.

Endangered Animals and Plants

In recent years, hundreds of different plants and animal populations all over the world have shrunk alarmingly, mostly due to human causes. These causes include overhunting, overfishing, urbanization that destroys habitats, climate changes, and pollution. Throughout the world, **biodiversity**—the number and variety of plants and animals that make up an ecosystem—is threatened. Scientists warn that the threat to biodiversity could have damaging effects on humans and the environment.

In 2001, the United Nations summed up the need to address the problem of endangered species, both animals and plants:

> ❝ The world's biodiversity is being lost at an alarming rate. For example, of the 1.75 million species that have been identified it is estimated that 3,400 plants and 5,200 animal species . . . face extinction. ❞

Because urbanization has destroyed their habitats, many wild elephants wander into villages. These cutouts of human figures are intended to scare wild elephants away from the villages in Sri Lanka.

ANALYZE PRIMARY SOURCES

DOCUMENT-BASED QUESTION Why is the United Nations concerned about biodiversity?

Conflict Resolution

Ask students to identify the method in place in their class or school government for correcting a problem that the students consider to be a threat to the school community. Have students explain whether they think the current method is working or if it should be improved or changed.

---

2 Teach

A. Pollution

Purpose-Setting Question What are the major causes of pollution in our environment? (the use of pesticides, chemical spills, and acid rain)

Activity

Make a chart Have students use a cause-and-effect chain (TR, p. 325) to organize information about the oil spill in Prince William Sound. (**Cause:** The supertanker *Exxon Valdez* ran aground. **Event:** More than 10 million gallons of oil were released into the water. **Effect:** Oil killed wildlife and polluted the water.)

Discuss Ask students to draw conclusions about the ways society can reduce the amount of acid rain produced each year. (reduce dependence on fossil fuels; develop other energy sources)

◆ **ANSWER** Acid rain can travel hundreds of miles from the source of the pollution.

B. Impact of Population Growth

Purpose-Setting Question How has overcrowding in cities affected the world environment? (It has led to many problems, including pollution. As population growth increases in the cities, the need for land increases. As a result, forests and other wild areas are sometimes destroyed.)

Explore Ask students to explain the environmental interdependence between countries around the world. (Possible answer: Change, such as pollution, in one country's environment often affects other countries.)

ANALYZE PRIMARY SOURCES

DOCUMENT-BASED QUESTION Have students use classroom resources or the Internet to identify examples of endangered animals and plants in their state or geographic region. Ask groups to compare their findings in class.

ANSWER The United Nations is concerned about biodiversity because it does not want to see animals or plants face extinction.

Focus Review the two main types of waste disposal with students. (consumer and industrial) Discuss with students which type of waste disposal they can help reduce the most. (consumer) Encourage students to suggest ways that they can reduce consumer waste.

◆ **ANSWER** Human causes, such as overhunting, overfishing, climate changes, and pollution are causing the number of some animals and plants to shrink.

C. Earth's Changing Environment

Purpose-Setting Question What is the relationship between the greenhouse effect and global warming? (The greenhouse effect, which results from the release of carbon dioxide and other gases into the atmosphere, is believed to be a major of cause of global warming.)

Using the Map
Condition of Earth's Ozone Layer, 2003

Ask students what problem faces areas with low ozone levels. (These areas receive less protection from the Sun's ultraviolet rays.) Discuss with students the meaning of the blue areas. (areas with low Dobson units)

✔ Map Check
Answers
1. The Arctic, parts of northern Canada and northern Russia
2. less than 280 Dobson units

Discuss Ask students how people in both developed and developing countries can work to slow or stop the destruction of the ozone layer. (Possible answer: They can greatly reduce practices that produce CFCs. Developed countries must conduct research to find compounds to replace CFCs; developing countries must stop using products that contain CFCs.)

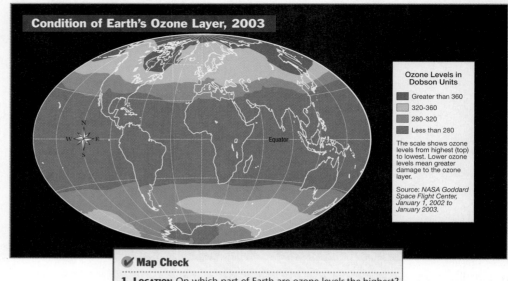

Condition of Earth's Ozone Layer, 2003

Ozone Levels in Dobson Units
- Greater than 360
- 320-360
- 280-320
- Less than 280

The scale shows ozone levels from highest (top) to lowest. Lower ozone levels mean greater damage to the ozone layer.

Source: NASA Goddard Space Flight Center, January 1, 2002 to January 2003.

✔ Map Check
1. **LOCATION** On which part of Earth are ozone levels the highest?
2. **REGION** What is the level of the ozone layer in most of Africa?

Waste Disposal

Industrialization and population also increase the amount of waste humans create. Contamination of water sources has led to research into effective waste disposal. Waste disposal is divided between consumer waste, which is ordinary garbage, and industrial waste, which can be hazardous and must be discarded according to industry and government regulations.

Recycling has been introduced in many cities. When glass, paper, metals, and plastics are recycled, they are broken down and reused. Some people also compost biodegradable waste, such as kitchen scraps and plant cuttings, by mixing it with soil. Soil, air, and water break down the potato peelings, apple cores, and other vegetable matter, and they return essential nutrients to the soil.

◆ **What has caused the numbers of some plants and animals to shrink?**

C. Earth's Changing Environment

Over the past century, people have made great advances in technology. However, these advances have had some negative effects on the planet as a whole.

The Ozone Layer

In recent years, many scientists who study global climate have become concerned about Earth's ozone layer. Earth is surrounded by a layer of ozone, a natural gas, that protects it from the Sun's ultraviolet rays. Chemical compounds called chlorofluorocarbons—or CFCs—found in air conditioners, refrigerators, insulation, and packaging, drift into Earth's atmosphere and react with the ozone, destroying it. Since scientists became aware of the problem, the ozone layer has been closely monitored. In response to the situation, some countries have agreed to eliminate all CFC production.

Teaching Options

Connection to SCIENCE

To study the greenhouse effect, scientists use computers that manipulate mathematical models. Another way to research this phenomenon is by drilling cores of ice in Greenland and Antarctica that provide environmental evidence of climate warming and cooling over the past 160,000 years.

Cooperative Learning

Have groups of students prepare presentations for a proposed school or community-wide environmental conference. Each presentation should include information about one of the environmental problems discussed in this section: global warming, ozone depletion, pollution, population growth, endangered animals and plants, and waste disposal—and proposed solutions. These reports should include visuals, such as graphs, maps, photographs, and posters.

Global Warming

In the 1980s, scientists documented that temperatures on Earth were slowly rising. Most scientists believe that this will cause worldwide climate changes. This increase is known as **global warming**.

Rising temperatures pose several dangers. If ice in the region of the North and South Poles were to melt, sea levels might rise. Many islands and low-lying coastal areas around the world could experience flooding. If Earth continues to grow hotter, some scientists believe weather patterns will change, affecting vegetation. If plants and crops die off in areas where they have always grown, food production is likely to be affected worldwide.

Scientists believe that the release of large amounts of carbon dioxide and other gases into the atmosphere causes global warming. These gases stay in the upper atmosphere, trapping Earth's heat. This condition is known as the **greenhouse effect**.

Carbon dioxide occurs naturally in the air, but human activities add large amounts of this gas to the environment. One source of carbon dioxide is the burning of fossil fuels, such as oil, gas, and coal. In developed countries, carbon dioxide and other gases come from cars, homes, and factories. In developing countries, these gases are produced by activities such as burning rain forests to clear land.

Efforts to Protect Earth's Atmosphere

People all over the world believe it is time to take action on global warming. In 1997, representatives of more than 150 countries met in Kyoto, Japan, for a conference on the environment. One of the goals of the conference was to find ways to reduce the amount of greenhouse gases being produced worldwide. The conference members agreed to reduce worldwide emission of greenhouse gases by a little more than 5 percent by 2010. Some people believe the treaty does not take strong enough action.

◆ What are some ways that global warming might affect people?

Review II

Review History
A. What have people done to damage their environments?
B. Why are so many species of plants and animals endangered?
C. What human activities add carbon dioxide to the environment?

Define Terms to Know
Define the following terms: **pesticide, metropolitan area, biodiversity, global warming, greenhouse effect**

Critical Thinking
What do you think is the greatest hazard to the environment?

Write About Geography
Write a paragraph identifying ways in which environmental problems are changing the planet's geography.

Get Organized
PROBLEM/SOLUTION CHART
Use a problem/solution chart to examine the problems you read about in Section II. For example, what are some of the problems world leaders face to repair the damage people have done to the environment?

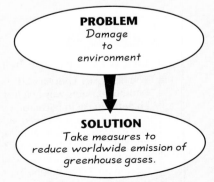

PROBLEM
Damage to environment

SOLUTION
Take measures to reduce worldwide emission of greenhouse gases.

Discuss Ask students how the Kyoto conference was intended to solve some of the problems affecting Earth's atmosphere. (The goal of the conference was to reduce the amount of greenhouse gases being produced around the world by 5 percent by the year 2010.)

Extend Although the United States signed the Kyoto treaty, President Clinton did not send it to the U.S. Senate for ratification because the chances of approval were slight. In 2001, another meeting was held in Bonn, Germany. Ask students to research the results of this meeting and present their findings in class.

◆ **ANSWER** Global warming may cause ice in the region of the North and South Poles to melt and sea levels to rise. Many islands and low-lying coastal areas could experience flooding. Weather patterns may change, affecting vegetation and food supplies.

Section Close

Ask students to discuss the environmental problems facing Earth and identify ways that, as world citizens, they can help protect the atmosphere. Have them prepare an advertising campaign to make other students in the school aware of these problems and join the efforts to solve them. Their campaign should include ads, slogans, and the scripts for a series of radio or television commercials.

3 Assess

Review Answers

Review History
A. They have added harmful materials to the environment, leading to pollution of air, land, and water.
B. Possible answer: Urbanization, clearing of forests, and pollution have destroyed habitats. People have fished and hunted beyond species' ability to reproduce.
C. Human activities, such as burning fossil fuels and burning rain forests have added carbon dioxide to the environment.

Define Terms to Know
pesticide, 790;
metropolitan area, 791;
biodiversity, 791;
global warming, 793;
greenhouse effect, 793

Critical Thinking
Possible answer: Students may say that the release of excess amounts of carbon dioxide and other gases into the atmosphere is the greatest hazard to the environment. One source is the burning of fossil fuels, such as oil, gas, and coal.

Write About Geography
Students may include such environmental problems as deforestation, creating deserts where there was water and vegetation, and increased air pollution.

III. Facing Global Challenges

(pp. 794–799)

Section Summary

In this section, students will learn how nations attempt to deal with a variety of global challenges, such as poverty and disease, overpopulation and human rights abuses, and political conflicts.

1 Introduce

Getting Started

Ask students to identify some social and economic problems in their own communities and discuss how the local and state governments are attempting to solve them. Encourage students to explain how these problems have an impact on their lives, and what they can do to help correct the situations.

TERMS TO KNOW

Ask students to read the terms and definitions on page 794 and then find each term in the section. Point out that the word *malnutrition* contains the prefix, *mal-* and the suffix *-tion*. The term *birth rate* is an example of an open compound term, which is a word or word group with two or more parts that act as a single unit.

You may wish to preview the pronunciation of the following names from this section with students.

James Orbinski (ohr BIHN skee)
Chechnya (CHEHCH nee yah)
Taliban (TAHL ih bahn)
Osama bin Laden
 (oh SAM eh bin LAH dehn)

ACTIVE READING

Have students form an opinion about a particular global challenge that is presented in this section. Using a two-column chart (TR, p. 328), ask students to list one argument about a global challenge in the first column and the evidence used to support the argument in the second column. After each statement of evidence, students should write *F,* for fact, or *O,* for opinion.

Facing Global Challenges

Section
III
Facing Global Challenges

Terms to Know

malnutrition undernourishment or the lack of a properly balanced diet

birth rate the measure of how many people are born each year in a country

Main Ideas

A. Many of the world's people suffer from poverty and disease.

B. Overpopulation and human rights are two of the challenges faced by today's leaders.

C. The world faces many challenges, including regional conflicts and the rise of terrorism.

 Active Reading

ARGUMENTS AND EVIDENCE
The facts and opinions a person uses to support his or her statements, or arguments, are called evidence. As you read this section, identify the arguments world leaders make about global challenges and the evidence they use to support those arguments.

A. Poverty and Disease

In 1971, a group of French doctors founded Doctors Without Borders, a nonprofit organization that provides medical aid to more than 80 countries worldwide. Doctors Without Borders helps people in areas devastated by war and people in developing nations. Volunteers and staff members commonly fight disease and **malnutrition**. Malnutrition is a condition resulting from poor nutrition or the lack of a properly balanced diet. War and poverty greatly contribute to malnutrition.

In 1999, Doctors Without Borders received the Nobel Peace Prize for its efforts around the world. In December of that year, James Orbinski of Doctors Without Borders accepted the prize. His speech described the challenges the organization faced:

ANALYZE PRIMARY SOURCES **DOCUMENT-BASED QUESTION** What does James Orbinski consider a major problem in treating diseases in poor countries?

❝ More than 90 percent of all death and suffering from infectious diseases occurs in the developing world. Some of the reasons people die from diseases like AIDS, TB [tuberculosis], sleeping sickness and other tropical diseases are that life saving essential medicines are too expensive. ❞

Poverty and the United Nations

As the chart on page 788 of this chapter shows, millions of the world's workers live on less than $2 per day. Many people work for a living at jobs that do not allow them to have such necessities as healthcare or adequate housing, especially in developing nations. In its Millennium Report, the United Nations pledged to take steps to see that children throughout the world remained in school. It is the hope of the UN that education will help to end poverty for future generations. The UN intends to see that schools provide children with at least one nourishing meal per day. The UN and other organizations also send relief workers to desperately poor areas, and wealthy nations have generously contributed food and medicines to them.

Fighting Malnutrition

Closely linked to poverty is malnutrition. All human beings need certain nutrients, or vitamins and minerals, in order to enjoy good health. Without these nutrients, people will eventually die. Many children around the world under the age of five die of malnutrition every year.

Teaching Options

Section 3 Resources

Teacher's Resources (TR)
 Terms to Know, p. 46
 Review History, p. 80
 Build Your Skills, p. 114
 Concept Builder, p. 249
 Problem/Solution Chart, p. 327
 Transparencies 1, 11

F Y I

Doctors Without Borders

The first relief effort organized by Doctors Without Borders was helping victims of an earthquake in Nicaragua in 1972. The group has also sponsored aid to victims of war in Afghanistan in 2001 and Iraq in 2003. Representatives from 45 nations serve in the organization, which sends more than 2,000 volunteers to 80 countries each year.

Malnutrition is widespread throughout developing nations. It is often a side effect of wars that lay waste to a land, destroying harvests and making it impossible for farmers and their families to find food.

Wealthy nations are trying to combat malnutrition by donating food and sending relief workers to countries in Africa south of the Sahara, eastern Europe, and other areas that have been devastated by war.

Battling the AIDS Virus

In 1983, Africa declared that it was suffering an AIDS (Acquired Immune Deficiency Syndrome) epidemic. By 2001, the United Nations reported that an estimated 36.1 million people were infected with some form of the AIDS virus. More than two-thirds of them live in Africa south of the Sahara. In some southern African countries, more than 15 percent of all adults have the virus. Throughout the region, there are 4 million new cases of AIDS each year.

AIDS has no cure, but a patient under treatment can live a long and productive life. Unfortunately, the cost of drugs used to treat AIDS is far beyond the ability of the developing nations to pay for them. Organizations such as Doctors Without Borders have persuaded drug companies to offer medicine to developing countries at huge discounts.

Global Connections

AIDS WORLDWIDE
Some countries have established strong AIDS prevention programs. As a result, the percentage of their population that tests positive for the AIDS virus has dropped significantly. Zambia and Uganda are two such nations.

◆ **What are some health threats to countries in Africa south of the Sahara?**

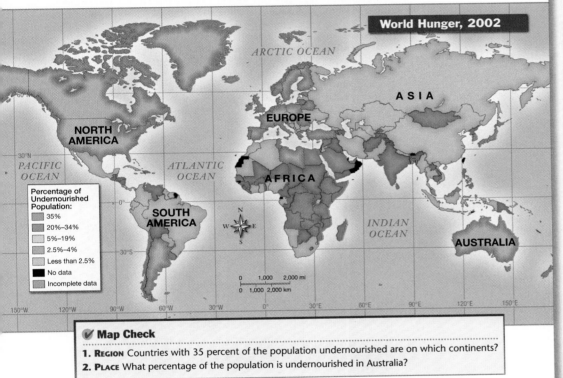

World Hunger, 2002

Percentage of Undernourished Population:
- 35%
- 20%–34%
- 5%–19%
- 2.5%–4%
- Less than 2.5%
- No data
- Incomplete data

✔ Map Check

1. **REGION** Countries with 35 percent of the population undernourished are on which continents?
2. **PLACE** What percentage of the population is undernourished in Australia?

B. The World's Population

Purpose-Setting Question How are the causes of overpopulation in developed nations different from those in developing nations? (Although death rates exceed birth rates in developed nations, immigration often results in increased population. In developing nations, people are living longer due to improved diet and healthcare.)

Explore Have students review Transparency 11 and identify the areas with the highest and lowest population densities. Discuss with students how the population density level affects people in developed and developing nations.

Activity

Write a news report Ask students to research programs, sponsored by world organizations, that are designed to end malnutrition. Have them write a brief news report about one of these programs. Remind them to answer the Five *W*s in the first paragraph and to include an interesting headline for their article. Ask students to read their articles in class.

SPOTLIGHT ON GEOGRAPHY

WATER IN INDIA Ask students to compare population distribution and rainfall maps of India from a classroom encyclopedia or an atlas. Have students identify the overpopulated areas with too little fresh water available.

Activity

Make a chart Ask students to make an idea web (TR, p. 321) that summarizes the Millennium Report's conclusions regarding women and girls. (**Center Circle:** Conclusions of the Millennium Report; **Outer Circles:** Women and girls need equal education; Women and girls need equal opportunities; the contributions of women and girls need to be valued; educating girls makes an economy stronger.)

TEACH PRIMARY SOURCES

Explain that the photograph on this page was taken in a shantytown in Lima called Marques. A shantytown is a section of a city where many poor people live in crudely built huts or houses. Ask students to express their reaction to the scene depicted in the photograph.

Spotlight on *Geography*

WATER IN INDIA
India is a nation in which water is a growing issue. By 2025, the population is expected to increase by another 400 million people. At that point, 75 percent of Indians will live in areas with too little water.

Much of the problem lies with how to get water to where it is needed. The debate over who should pay for modernizing a water system continues.

Children in Lima, Peru, wait for trucks to bring clean drinking water. In some countries, population growth has grown faster than the availability of fresh water.

B. The World's Population

In 2003, the world's population was more than 6 billion. Population continues to grow even though the **birth** **rate** in most nations has fallen. The birth rate is a measure of how many people are born each year in a country. The United Nations projects that by 2012, the world's population will reach 7 billion.

The Problems of Overpopulation

Improved diet and healthcare throughout the developed world and in developing countries means that people are living longer. In most developed nations, the death rate is higher than the birth rate—in other words, more people die each year than are born. However, the population of these nations continues to grow, swelled by immigration.

Overpopulation is a problem for many reasons. Water, food, housing, and jobs are all basic things that people need in order to survive. In some countries, population growth has already grown faster than the availability of fresh water. The United Nations is working with governments to develop ways of providing safe drinking water to these countries.

Human Rights

Human rights are the basic freedoms that all people should have. Western nations frequently accuse countries, such as China, of "human rights violations." This means that a country's citizens are denied basic freedoms. In China, citizens have not enjoyed freedom of speech. They cannot vote in free elections or participate in peaceful demonstrations. The government may take citizens' passports at any time.

The United Nations is especially concerned about the rights of women and girls in the developing world. In its Millennium Report, it stressed the necessity of equal education and opportunities for girls and the need to value their contributions to society. The report points out that when the girls of a society are educated, its economy is stronger. In addition, the people are more literate, the harvests are larger, and children become stronger and healthier.

Teaching Options

Research

AVERAGE

Have students use almanacs, encyclopedias, and the Internet to find at least four additional facts about the current world population and its growth. Ask them to list the facts and the sources for the information. Invite students to share their information with the class. Have students discuss which reference sources were most valuable.

CHALLENGE

Have groups of students use almanacs and the Internet to research the most current information about the population of each continent. Ask them to record the information on the outline map of the world. (TR, p. 330) Remind them to include a title and a map legend. Invite the students to draw conclusions about world population growth based on information in the map.

Achieving Literacy

In today's world, literacy means more than being able to read and write. Literacy also includes being able to do simple arithmetic and to apply one's knowledge to solving problems. A literate person has the ability to function in society.

The United Nations reports that about 113 million school-age children today do not go to school. These children are mostly poor, and their lack of literacy may force them to live in poverty. Approximately 880 million adults throughout the world cannot read or write. About two-thirds of these adults are women. In some societies, women are prevented from learning to read and write because of tradition or religious beliefs. Conditions are improving, however. In 2002, the United Nations reported that literacy rates worldwide were growing. Nearly 80 percent of people over the age of 15 are now literate. Literacy is also beginning to improve among women.

This woman is attending a literacy class in Senegal in Africa.

Modernization Versus Tradition

You have learned that throughout history, modernization has challenged traditional methods and values. Today, the pressure on traditional societies is greater than at any other time in history. Modern communications and speed of travel have made the world seem very small.

Western styles seem to be everywhere in the world. Modern products invite consumers to purchase them. Yet, traditionalists in many cultures fear that products and ideas from foreign countries will destroy their cultures.

In some countries, wealth is concentrated in the hands of a small privileged class. The majority of the people are relatively poor. They cannot afford modern appliances or automobiles because they do not have an adequate share of their country's wealth.

◆ Why is overpopulation such a big problem in the world?

C. Conflicts Throughout the World

The history of the world is a history of challenges faced by various groups of people. Often the challenges were about war. Sometimes they were about religion or politics. People and nations have their own set of challenges as they look forward to the future.

Participation in the Political Process

With the end of the Cold War, nearly all the world's nations have some form of representative government. Although there are still some hereditary monarchies, a few Communist governments, and some military dictatorships, a great deal of progress toward democracy has been made. There are far fewer such governments today than there were in the past.

As education and communications have improved, more and more people have demanded the right to choose their own leaders. The Internet has become a tool for democracy. Even the most repressive, or controlling, societies are not able to completely monitor people's access to the Internet. Throughout the world, people are able for the first time to learn about other cultures and ideas.

Discuss Ask students to draw conclusions about the impact of a high illiteracy rate on a nation. (Possible answer: In countries with high illiteracy rates, there is probably less economic growth, more poverty and disease, and greater social and economic inequality.)

Activity

Make a speech Divide students into pairs. Have each pair write a speech on the adoption of western styles in developing countries. Ask one student in the pair to write the speech as someone who is against it and the other as someone who supports it. Ask pairs of students to present their speeches to the class.

◆ **ANSWER** Overpopulation is a big problem in the world because, in some places, it has outpaced the availability of housing, food, and fresh water.

C. Conflicts Throughout the World

Purpose-Setting Question How would you categorize the different kinds of conflicts that societies have faced throughout history? (They have faced religious, political, and military conflicts.)

Explore Ask students to provide current examples of the problems they identified in the purpose-setting question.

Discuss Ask students to draw conclusions about the effect of improved education and communications on the development of representative government throughout the world. (Improved education and communications, especially the widespread use of the Internet, has resulted in a growth of representative government throughout the world, most likely because people are better informed and can apply knowledge to their immediate circumstances.)

Connection to
CULTURE

Before the 1400s, most people in medieval Europe were illiterate. Literacy spread unevenly throughout Europe from the 1400s to the 1900s. Factors determining literacy included gender, ethnic group, geography, social class, and economics. Ask students to research the current literacy rate by region in the United States and record the rates in a graph.

Activity

Write an interview Ask pairs of students to research recent developments in one of the regional conflicts identified in the subsection Regional Conflicts. Have students use current periodicals or the Internet to help them write an interview between an American journalist and one of the participants in the conflict. Call on student pairs to present their interviews in class.

Extend Have students use the World Map in the Atlas (pp. A2–A3), Transparency 1, or a classroom map or globe to find Northern Ireland, Israel, and Palestine. Invite students to identify other places in the world in which terrorism is currently a problem and find these countries on the map or globe as well.

Explore Have students review this chapter and identify all the countries that are mentioned. Challenge students to label each country on the outline map of the world (TR, p. 330). Work with the class to develop a map key that includes symbols for all of the global challenges mentioned in this chapter, such as AIDS, terrorism, and illiteracy. Students should add the symbols from the map key to their outline maps. After students complete the map, ask them what the map shows them. (There are problems and challenges all over the world.)

Discuss Ask students to express their opinions about current security measures in office and government buildings and airports in their community or city.

Regional Conflicts

At the beginning of the twenty-first century, many countries were torn by violence within their own boundaries. In 2003, for example, Russia and Chechnya struggled over a peace plan to stop a war over Chechnya's desire for independence. At the same time, nations in Africa were in the middle of their own wars. Rebel groups in the Ivory Coast nations of Liberia, Sierra Leone, and Guinea, were fighting wars over government and leadership.

In the Middle East, Israel and the Palestinian Authority continue their long struggle over boundaries. In Turkey, the Kurdish people have revolted over the right to establish their own identity and nation. Other parts of the world, including Indonesia and Latin America, were also torn by conflict in the twenty-first century.

For all the violence, however, there is still hope for peace. In some cases, talks are already underway to resolve the conflicts. Intervention by the United Nations or by other groups resolved many of the wars of the twentieth century. There is reason to believe that this will occur again in the twenty-first century.

The Rise of Terrorism

Terrorism has been a worldwide problem for many years. As you have read, Middle Eastern and other terrorists have demonstrated their hatred of the United States through various attacks, including the destruction of the World Trade Center in New York City and an attack on the Pentagon, near Washington, D.C. in 2001.

As a result of these attacks, people throughout the world have become more aware of the need for security. Airlines now rigorously screen passengers. New technology is being used to make certain that no weapons can be brought on board planes, trains, or buses.

The War on Terrorism

After the terrorist attacks on the United States, President George W. Bush and other leaders worked hard to make Americans secure. On September 11, 2001, the U.S. government grounded commercial airplanes and closed landmarks and government offices. Soon, military aircraft and ships were sent to port cities, and National Guard troops were stationed at airports. In addition, President George W. Bush promised that the United States would punish terrorists and the governments that protected them. Great Britain and other countries quickly promised to support U.S. efforts.

As you read in Chapter 32, the United States began the war on terrorism abroad in the country of Afghanistan. There, the Taliban government protected the terrorist Osama bin Laden and his al Qaeda followers. The United States wanted the Taliban to stop protecting bin Laden, but the Taliban refused. As a result, the United States began Operation Enduring Freedom by bombing targets in Afghanistan on October 7, 2001. U.S. soldiers on the ground helped Afghan opponents of the Taliban search for and defeat terrorists.

By 2002, the Taliban and al Qaeda had been driven from power in Afghanistan. A number of

With security at high levels, armed National Guard soldiers patrol a terminal at Baltimore/Washington International Airport in Maryland.

Teaching Options

Test Taking

Some tests ask students to identify a selection's main idea and supporting details. Ask students to identify the main idea and supporting detail in the subsection Regional Conflicts. (At the beginning of this century, many countries were torn by violence within their own boundaries, such as Russian troops in Chechnya and civil war in Liberia.)

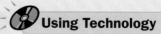

Using Technology

Have students use Internet resources, including periodical databases and search engines, to research for 2 weeks a current events story that relates to one of the global challenges in this section. Have students create a timeline (TR, p. 320) about the event. Collect the timelines and make a current events class newspaper.

terrorist training camps had been destroyed. As the Taliban left Afghan cities, many residents rejoiced. The Taliban government had enforced an extreme form of Islam in which movies and music were banned. Women were not allowed to work, and girls were forbidden to go to school.

Responding to Nuclear Threats

As you learned in Chapter 31, the Nuclear Nonproliferation Treaty is an international agreement requiring countries to reduce the number of nuclear weapons. As the Cold War ended, many nations began the slow process of reducing their number of nuclear weapons. However, Pakistan and India, two countries that did not agree to the Nuclear Nonproliferation Treaty, have tested nuclear weapons. In addition, North Korea withdrew from this treaty in early 2003, causing alarm in the United States and other countries.

The United States and its allies have been concerned about the possibility that Iraq was stockpiling chemical, biological, and nuclear weapons and could launch an attack. In 2002, United Nations weapons inspectors were sent to Iraq to search for weapons that violate UN policies.

At first, Iraq agreed to cooperate with the UN inspectors. However, Iraq's leader, Saddam Hussein, did not completely comply. As a result, the United States formed an international coalition to overthrow Hussein and his government and to destroy their weapons of mass destruction. This war, known as Operation Iraqi Freedom, was fought in 2003.

Despite setbacks in reducing nuclear weapons around the world, the ideas behind the Nuclear Nonproliferation Treaty are still viewed as valid. In the coming decades, the UN, as well as international leaders, will continue to work toward banning all nuclear weapons.

◆ **Why did many people rejoice when the Taliban left Afghan cities?**

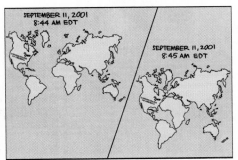

This cartoon, which appeared after the September 11, 2001, terrorist attacks in the United States, shows that the United States is close to some of the dangers facing the rest of the world.

Review III

Review History
A. What steps are being taken to end poverty and malnutrition throughout the world?
B. What did the United Nations report about human rights in its Millennium Report?
C. How has the United States changed since the events of September 11, 2001?

Define Terms to Know
Define the following terms: **malnutrition, birth rate**

Critical Thinking
How can countries of the world monitor each other to reduce the number of nuclear weapons?

Write About History
Write an essay discussing the significance of worldwide terrorism.

Get Organized
PROBLEM/SOLUTION CHART
Use a problem/solution chart to examine the problems you read about in Section III. For example, what are some of the international issues that world leaders face?

PROBLEM
The AIDS epidemic is a worldwide problem.

SOLUTION
Effective drugs are being developed and made available to many countries.

Critical Thinking
Possible answer: Countries can ask world organizations, such as the United Nations, to monitor the movement of nuclear fuels and, as necessary, send inspection teams into any member nation suspected of producing nuclear weapons.

Write About History
Students' answers should include that terrorism takes place all over the world and that terrorist acts can kill or injure many people.

Section Summary

In this section, students will learn how scientific research, space exploration, and technological advances will affect all nations of the world.

1 Introduce

Getting Started

Have students suggest ways in which technology is changing their lives. Ask them to consider technological advancements in communications, medicine, and travel. Help students make a list of advancements that they have seen in their lifetimes. Encourage them to predict what some of the next generation of technological advances will be.

TERMS TO KNOW

Ask students to read the terms and definitions on page 800 and then find each term in the section. Point out that these terms all relate to scientific breakthroughs that have affected our world and expanded our knowledge. Ask pairs of students to use each term in original sentences that include context clues. Have one student read the sentences aloud without the term. The second student should supply the missing term, based on the context clues.

You may wish to preview the pronunciation of the following name from this section with students.

Borlaug (BAWR lawg)

ACTIVE READING

Have students choose one of the subsections in Section 4 and identify the cause and effect of a particular event. Suggest that they use the cause-and-effect chain (TR, p. 325) to organize their information.

Section IV · Looking to the Future

Terms to Know

human genome the complete genetic makeup of human beings

genetic engineering the act of working on genes to change or copy them

clone to make an exact copy of an organism by duplicating genetic material

Main Ideas

A. Scientific research is being used to fight world hunger and identify genes that may lead to new medicines and cures.

B. Space exploration, both manned and unmanned, has allowed the world to see places that have not been explored before.

C. The Internet and other technological advances have increased communication among people all over the world.

Active Reading

CAUSE AND EFFECT
An effect is a result. A cause is what brings that result about. As you read this section, think about the causes and effects of developments in technology.

A. Technology Improves the Human Condition

Although a farming village in a developing country might appear very much as it did hundreds of years ago, much has actually changed. New crops, improved agricultural methods, and medical advances are being introduced. New methods, such as planting crops twice a year to double a harvest and new or improved grains, have increased crop yields. One major issue of the 2000s will be genetically modified, or changed, crops. A genetically modified crop contains genes from another type of plant. These plants have caused debate throughout the world. Many see these crops as a way to solve some serious problems. Others see them as a terrible threat.

The Green Revolution

The Green Revolution could be called a battle to provide the world's growing population with enough food for all. Scientists were certain that they could develop new varieties of plants that were hardier and easier to grow than existing ones. They also studied new agricultural methods.

In 1944, Norman Borlaug, an American scientist working in Mexico, developed a high-yielding wheat plant. At that time, Mexico imported half its wheat. Within 12 years, Mexico was growing enough wheat to feed its people. In 20 years, it was exporting its surplus wheat to other countries. This same wheat plant now also grows in Asia and Africa.

The Genetics Revolution

Every cell in the human body contains genes that are passed on from parents to child. These genes determine how a person's cells will function. Scientists have not yet identified all the genes in the human body, nor do they fully understand all that genes do. They have, however, identified many genes, including some connected to deafness, diabetes, kidney disease, certain cancers, and other diseases.

In 1990, scientists began the Human Genome Project to identify every human gene. The **human genome** is the complex genetic makeup of all humans. During their research, scientists discovered that up to 30,000 genes exist in the human body.

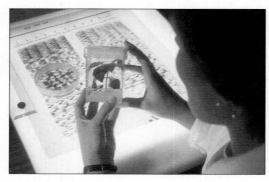

This woman is researching genetically modified tomato plants.

800 UNIT 8 ◆ The World Today

Teaching Options

Section 4 Resources

Teacher's Resources (TR)
Terms to Know, p. 46
Review History, p. 80
Build Your Skills, p. 114
Concept Builder, p. 249
Problem/Solution Chart, p. 327
Chapter Test, pp. 181–182
Unit Test, pp. 197–198
Final Exam, pp. 207–214

ESL/ELL STRATEGIES

Summarize Ask pairs of students to summarize two different subsections in Section 4. Remind students that summaries include the most important ideas in a section of text. Summaries should be written in the students' own words. Summarizing is one way to prepare for a test. Ask students to read each other's summaries and make up two questions about the section.

Scientists are now able to remove genes, take them apart, put them back together, and copy them—a process known as **genetic engineering**. Research into this area of genetics may lead to treatments for a wide range of disorders.

By working with genes, scientists can now **clone**, or copy, cells and entire organisms. In 1996, a sheep named Dolly was born in Scotland. Dolly was the first successful clone of an adult animal. She was cloned from a body cell of another adult sheep, and was an exact genetic copy of that sheep.

There are concerns about the safety of cloning and the possibility of passing diseases and defects to cloned animals. The latest research in genetic engineering involves the cloning of human beings. Some governments, however, have banned such research until solid guidelines are established.

◆ **What has the Green Revolution accomplished?**

B. Into Outer Space

Technology has allowed people to see places that have never been explored before. Scientists can search many kinds of places, from the tiniest inner spaces of the human body to the vast reaches of outer space.

Challenges to Space Exploration

During the 1970s, researchers at the National Aeronautics and Space Administration (NASA) created the technology of the space shuttle. The space shuttle served as a reusable rocket and spacecraft, allowing astronauts to use the same craft to enter orbit repeatedly. The first successful space shuttle, *Columbia*, was launched in April 1981.

In the more than 20 years of its operation, the space shuttle program has suffered two major setbacks. On January 28, 1986, the space shuttle *Challenger* exploded after liftoff. Seven astronauts, including a schoolteacher who was chosen to travel with them, were killed in the accident. Then, on February 1, 2003, the space shuttle *Columbia* broke apart several minutes before its scheduled landing, killing all seven astronauts on board.

Space Missions in the New Century

In 1998, the United States began working with 14 other countries to build an International Space Station. Today, the station is visited by crews of astronauts. These crews conduct scientific experiments and take space walks.

Another advance in the use of space technology is the use of high-powered telescopes that operate in space. The Hubble Space Telescope, launched in 1990, sends pictures of events and objects in space back to Earth.

Recent space missions have involved spacecraft with no crews on board. These spacecraft carry scientific instruments that are controlled by scientists on the ground. In 1997, the *Mars Pathfinder* set a machine called a rover on the surface of Mars. The rover sent back images from the planet's surface. In 2001, the *Mars Odyssey* began orbiting Mars. It was designed to search for water and certain minerals, and to study radiation levels on the planet.

◆ **What is the purpose of the International Space Station?**

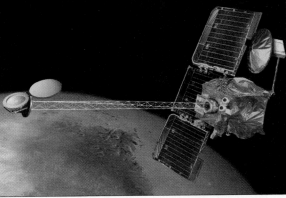

This drawing shows what the *Mars Odyssey* may have looked like as it was orbiting Mars.

A. Technology Improves the Human Condition

Purpose-Setting Question What are some ways that technological advances have improved our lives? (Medical advances, improved agricultural techniques, and new crops are some of the ways technology has improved our lives.)

Discuss Ask students why the term "green revolution" is a good name for the ongoing effort to increase the amount of food available to the world's growing population. (Possible answer: It is a good name because it implies a replacement of the existing system of food production with a new, improved system.)

Explore Ask students what scientists hope to accomplish with genetic engineering. (research treatments into diseases and disorders)

◆ **ANSWER** The Green Revolution has made it possible for many places in the world to increase their crop productions. For example, Mexico used to import half its wheat. Within 12 years it could feed its people and within 20 years it was exporting surplus wheat.

B. Into Outer Space

Purpose-Setting Question During the 1970s, what did researchers at NASA create and what did it allow astronauts to do? (Researchers created the technology of the space shuttle that allowed astronauts to use the same craft to enter orbit repeatedly.)

Focus Ask pairs of students to find examples of some of the photographs sent back by the *Mars Pathfinder* using encyclopedias or the Internet.

◆ **ANSWER** The International Space Station provides a place in which astronauts can conduct scientific experiments and undertake space walks.

The Moon Landing

On July 16, 1969, three American astronauts lifted off into space. On July 20, astronauts Neil Armstrong and Edwin (Buzz) Aldrin stepped onto the moon's surface. The astronauts' moonwalk, which lasted for $2\frac{1}{2}$ hours, enabled them to collect samples of moon rock and dust. They planted an American flag on the moon before leaving. Because there is no wind on the moon to blow the flag, they had to stiffen it with a metal rod.

Meet Individual Needs:

VERBAL/LINGUISTIC LEARNERS

Bring in a photograph of Earth as seen from outer space. Tell students they are astronauts orbiting Earth on a space mission. Have them write journal entries from an astronaut's point of view in which they express their feelings about what they see from outer space.

C. Technology in Communications

Purpose-Setting Question How can different technological advances promote cultural awareness? (Technologies, such as television, telephones, cell phones, and the Internet, enable people from all over the world to communicate with one another and learn more about each other's cultures.)

Discuss Ask students to predict what the impact of advances in communications technology will be on people in developing nations and how these advances will affect the relationship between developing and developed nations in the future. (Possible answer: Technological advances in communications, such as cellular phones, television, and the Internet, will help bring about closer cultural and economic ties between developed and developing countries. These advances will also have a positive impact on educational and social opportunities in developing countries.)

TEACH PRIMARY SOURCES

Ask students what the photograph on page 802 demonstrates about technological advances. (Possible answer: By showing a cell phone user at a historic Egyptian site using an ancient form of transportation, the photograph illustrates an interesting combination of modern communications technology and ancient modes of transportation and building technologies.)

Activity

Make a poster Have small groups of students research the history of one of the types of technological products discussed on page 802. Then, have the group make a picture-history poster of their product. Encourage each group to make a prediction of what its product will look like in 5 years.

A camel driver talks on his cell phone at the Great Pyramid in Egypt.

C. Technology in Communications

As the twentieth century ended, a revolution in communications began. This revolution made it possible for people to send and receive spoken and written messages by new means, more quickly, and in more places than ever. Technologies allow people from all over the world to have increasing contact with one another. These contacts promote widespread sharing of cultures.

Televisions and Telephones

Today, 98 percent of American households have televisions. The percentage in developing nations is lower. Television provides information about the world through news programs and documentaries. Cable and digital television have improved access and reception and made hundreds of channels available.

Beginning in the 1980s, people could rent videocassettes of films and watch them on their television screens, unedited and without commercial breaks. With the new century, DVDs—compact discs containing movies and extra footage—became a popular way to view films on televisions or computer monitors.

Cellular phones, also called mobile phones, are yet another revolution in technology. These hand-held phones without wires are considered mobile because they can pick up telephone signals over great distances using digital technology. As a result, people can use cell phones just about anywhere—in a desert, while riding a train, or hiking across mountains.

Cell phones are used today by hundreds of millions of people around the world—in developed countries as well as in developing countries. By the beginning of 2003, data companies estimated that there were about 600 million digital wireless subscribers, or customers, worldwide. That means that about 11 percent of the world's population subscribed to cellular phone use. In the United States alone, cellular phone users climbed from 5 million people in 1990 to 110 million in the year 2000.

802 UNIT 8 ◆ The World Today

Teaching Options

Writing

AVERAGE

Ask students to write a newspaper article about a recent team of astronauts to work at the International Space Station. Their articles should include summaries of the astronauts' experiments and their findings. Suggest that students use library resources or the Internet to research the articles. Remind them to answer the Five *W*s in the first paragraph and to include an interesting headline.

CHALLENGE

Have students use current research to extrapolate how an international space station might be used 50 years from now. Students should present their ideas in the form of a short paper, with visuals, such as charts, graphs, or pictures, to supplement their written report.

The Internet

Computers around the world can be connected to one another. This network of computers is called the Internet, and it is truly an "information superhighway." In September 2001, it was estimated that about 516 million people were using the Internet worldwide. One year later, this estimate climbed to about 606 million people. The Internet has become the world's largest communications network. By the year 2005, it is estimated that 1 billion people may be connected to the Internet.

The World Wide Web, introduced in 1991, has made it easier for people to use the Internet. The Web contains all the documents on the Internet. It enables people to send pictures and sound over the Internet as well as to create links from one site to another. Through the World Wide Web, people can now read a foreign newspaper, purchase airline tickets, find the text of a political speech, check the day's weather forecast, and send written or photographic messages to friends—all while sitting at a computer.

Challenges and Hopes

In the twenty-first century, people around the world wonder what new challenges await them. The world is always changing. We cannot know what the future will bring. We do know, however, that in order to grow and prosper, countries around the world must unite to defend the common goals of global peace and security. When faced with new challenges, people must come together. Economic, political, and environmental issues can bring nations closer together. Nations have begun to realize that they are all dependent on other nations. In the future, people all over the world will draw strength from their diversity and their commitment to freedom and equality.

◆ **What are some ways that computers have changed daily life?**

Review IV

Review History
A. In what way might genetic engineering benefit people?
B. What recent developments have changed space exploration?
C. How has the Internet changed life for many people?

Define Terms to Know
Define the following terms:
human genome, genetic engineering, clone

Critical Thinking
How might the knowledge of the structure and purpose of genes help scientists find cures for diseases?

Write About Government
Write a brief editorial urging the U.S. government to increase funding for an issue from this section. Defend your argument with evidence from the section.

Get Organized
PROBLEM/SOLUTION CHART
Use a problem/solution chart to examine the problems you read about in Section IV. For example, what are some of the problems technology and science have helped bring closer to a solution?

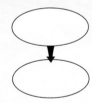

PROBLEM
A country cannot grow enough wheat to feed its people.

SOLUTION
A high-yielding wheat plant is developed and made available worldwide.

Present to...

TRANSPORTATION TODAY—AND TOMORROW

Teach the Topic

This feature describes various modes of transportation in use today and what we can expect in the future. Before students read and study the feature, ask them to identify the kinds of transportation they use every day and discuss the advantages and disadvantages of each. Invite them to offer solutions to transportation problems that affect their communities and cities.

FREIGHT HAULER

Ask students to discuss how the use of diesel-electric trains has affected rail transportation. (Because they are more fuel efficient, they are probably cheaper to operate than other types of trains.)

MODERN CLASSIC

A nickname for the Volkswagen New Beetle is the Bug. Ferdinand Porsche, an Austrian engineer, designed the original version of the car in the mid-1930s. He wanted to make a car that was compact, durable, and readily affordable. In fact, the word *Volkswagen* means "people's car."

MAGNET MARVEL

Maglev trains use powerful magnets to make them float above their tracks. Electrodynamic Maglev trains use magnetic repulsion to raise a train a few inches above the tracks. Although still in the early stages of development, it is expected that Maglev trains will be faster, quieter, and cleaner than trains powered by conventional engines.

BIG IS BEAUTIFUL

Ask small groups of students to use the Internet to research the most recent designs for the Boeing 747-400 jumbo jet. Have students make up a list of questions they would like to ask Boeing designers about the new planes.

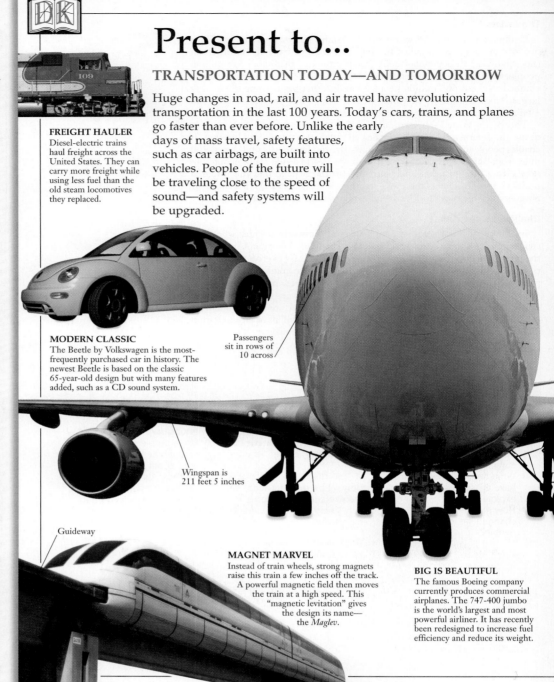

Present to...

TRANSPORTATION TODAY—AND TOMORROW

Huge changes in road, rail, and air travel have revolutionized transportation in the last 100 years. Today's cars, trains, and planes go faster than ever before. Unlike the early days of mass travel, safety features, such as car airbags, are built into vehicles. People of the future will be traveling close to the speed of sound—and safety systems will be upgraded.

FREIGHT HAULER
Diesel-electric trains haul freight across the United States. They can carry more freight while using less fuel than the old steam locomotives they replaced.

MODERN CLASSIC
The Beetle by Volkswagen is the most-frequently purchased car in history. The newest Beetle is based on the classic 65-year-old design but with many features added, such as a CD sound system.

Passengers sit in rows of 10 across

Wingspan is 211 feet 5 inches

Guideway

MAGNET MARVEL
Instead of train wheels, strong magnets raise this train a few inches off the track. A powerful magnetic field then moves the train at a high speed. This "magnetic levitation" gives the design its name— the *Maglev*.

BIG IS BEAUTIFUL
The famous Boeing company currently produces commercial airplanes. The 747-400 jumbo is the world's largest and most powerful airliner. It has recently been redesigned to increase fuel efficiency and reduce its weight.

Teaching Options

Connection to LITERATURE

Students will enjoy reading *Car*, by Richard Sutton. (DK Publishing, 2000) This nonfiction book, that is part of the *Eyewitness* series, is a history of the automobile, from the horseless carriage to the modern car. Chapters include information about the mechanics of designing cars and racing them.

F Y I

Electric Trains

Electric trains, which include subways, some freight trains, and high-speed passenger trains, are powered by an external electric source instead of an engine or a generator on the train itself. The "bullet train" used in Japan and the high-speed TGV train, used in France, are two examples of high-speed electric trains.

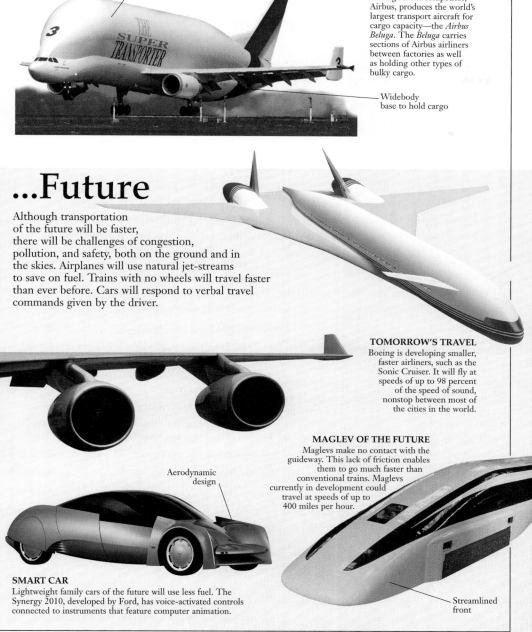

Cargo hold

SKY WHALE
Boeing's main competitor, Airbus, produces the world's largest transport aircraft for cargo capacity—the *Airbus Beluga*. The *Beluga* carries sections of Airbus airliners between factories as well as holding other types of bulky cargo.

Widebody base to hold cargo

...Future

Although transportation of the future will be faster, there will be challenges of congestion, pollution, and safety, both on the ground and in the skies. Airplanes will use natural jet-streams to save on fuel. Trains with no wheels will travel faster than ever before. Cars will respond to verbal travel commands given by the driver.

TOMORROW'S TRAVEL
Boeing is developing smaller, faster airliners, such as the Sonic Cruiser. It will fly at speeds of up to 98 percent of the speed of sound, nonstop between most of the cities in the world.

Aerodynamic design

MAGLEV OF THE FUTURE
Maglevs make no contact with the guideway. This lack of friction enables them to go much faster than conventional trains. Maglevs currently in development could travel at speeds of up to 400 miles per hour.

SMART CAR
Lightweight family cars of the future will use less fuel. The Synergy 2010, developed by Ford, has voice-activated controls connected to instruments that feature computer animation.

Streamlined front

CHAPTER 33 ◆ The World in a New Century **805**

...Future

TOMORROW'S TRAVEL
Ask students how the development of smaller, faster airliners, such as the Sonic Cruiser, will probably affect air travel in their community or state. (The use of the new, faster airliners will probably create better transportation links between students' geographical areas and cities all over the world.)

MAGLEV OF THE FUTURE
Ask students to find the distances between major cities in their state or geographical region. Then, have them make a train schedule for Maglevs that would travel between these cities at speeds of 400 mph. Call on students to compare their timetables.

SMART CAR
Ask students to discuss the advantages of lightweight family cars of the future, such as Synergy 2010. Then, have students design a car that will serve the needs of families in the year 2025. Ask students to display their designs in class and explain the features they have added.

Connect Present to Future
Ask small groups of students to identify the transportation needs of the future. Have them take into account environmental considerations, such as pollution, the world oil supply, security concerns, and the needs of an expanding world population. The groups can record their information on charts or posters. Ask the groups to share the results of their discussions with the rest of the class.

Hands-On Activity
Have pairs of students research one of the modes of transportation described on pages 804–805 to find out more information about future developments in this area. Have students role-play an interview that takes place 25 years in the future between a reporter and a designer of a new car, airplane, or train of that period. Have student pairs present their interview to the class.

CHAPTER
33
Review

Chapter Summary

A blank outline form is available in the Teacher's Resources (p. 318). Chapter summaries should outline the global economy, the environment, challenges facing the world, and ideas about the future. Refer to the rubric in the Teacher's Resources (p. 340) to score students' chapter summaries.

Interpret the Timeline

1. Nelson Mandela's election
2. 1999
3. Hubble Space Telescope is launched; *Mars Odyssey* orbits Mars.
4. Check students' timelines to be sure events are in chronological order and that all events are from the chapter.

Use Terms to Know

5. human genome
6. malnutrition
7. pesticide
8. biodiversity
9. global warming
10. birth rate
11. developing nation

Check Your Understanding

12. Possible answer: A developed nation has a prosperous economy, a high rate of literacy, and high wages. Most of these factors are just the opposite in developing nations.
13. Possible answer: Economic interdependence allows countries to exchange goods, resources, and knowledge.
14. Farmers use pesticides to protect crops from destruction by insects.
15. Possible answer: Overpopulation leads to overcrowding, environmental pollution, habitat destruction, and a loss of plant and animal populations.
16. CFCs damage the ozone layer that provides protection from harmful ultraviolet radiation from the Sun.
17. More than two-thirds of the estimated 36.1 million people infected with some form of the AIDS virus live in Africa south of the Sahara. In some southern African countries, more than 15 percent of all adults have the virus. Most of the people who have the AIDS virus die from the disease.

Chapter Summary

Complete the following outline in your notebook. Then, use your outline to write a brief summary of the chapter.

The World in a New Century

I. *A Global Economy*
  A. *Economic Systems*
  B. Workers of the World
II. *Earth and the Environment*
  A. Pollution
  B. Impact of Population Growth
  C. Earth's Changing Environment
III. *Facing Global Challenges*
  A. Poverty and Disease
  B. The World's Population
  C. Conflicts Throughout the World
IV. *Looking to the Future*
  A. Technology Improves the Human Condition
  B. Into Outer Space
  C. Technology in Communications

Interpret the Timeline

Use the timeline on pages 784–785 to answer the following questions.

1. Which event occurred first, the Kyoto environmental conference or Nelson Mandela's election as president of South Africa?
2. In what year did the population of the world reach 6 billion?
3. **Critical Thinking** What examples of advances in space exploration can be found on the timeline?
4. Select four events from the chapter that are not on the timeline. Create a timeline that shows these events.

Use Terms to Know

Select the term that best completes each sentence.

biodiversity
birth rate
developing nation
global warming
human genome
malnutrition
pesticide

5. The _____ is the complete genetic makeup of human beings.
6. _____ is the lack of a properly balanced diet.
7. A _____ is any chemical used for killing insects or weeds.
8. _____ is the variety in species of animals and plants in a given area.
9. _____ is the rise in the average temperature of Earth over time.
10. The measure of how many people are born each year in a country is called the _____.
11. A country in which industrialization is still taking place is called a _____.

Check Your Understanding

12. **Identify** the difference between a developed nation and a developing nation.
13. **Summarize** the benefits of economic interdependence.
14. **Explain** why many farmers use pesticides.
15. **Summarize** the environmental problems that come with overpopulation.
16. **Describe** the impact CFCs have on Earth's atmosphere.
17. **Discuss** the effect that AIDS has had on the population of Africa.
18. **Describe** the potential benefits of educating women in developing countries.
19. **Explain** how the United States is fighting a war on terrorism at home and abroad.
20. **Describe** two important space projects and their purposes.
21. **Summarize** some of the advances that have been made in televisions and telephones.

18. Possible answer: Educating women leads to a higher rate of literacy, a stronger economy, and healthier children.
19. Possible answer: At home, planes and ships are used to protect cities and ports, and troops are used to provide greater security. American troops were sent abroad to oust the Taliban government and to destroy terrorist strongholds in Afghanistan.

20. The International Space Station provides a platform for scientists to perform experiments, and the *Mars Odyssey* orbits Mars, allowing scientists to study that planet.
21. Advances in television include the development of cable and digital receivers that improve access and reception and make hundreds of channels available. Cellular telephones have made it possible to make and receive calls from just about any location.

Critical Thinking

22. Draw Conclusions How can a developing nation modernize its economy?

23. Cause and Effect Why did scientists work so hard to develop communications to such a sophisticated level?

24. Analyze Primary Sources What does the quote by James Orbinski on page 794 tell you about combating diseases in the future?

25. Make Inferences What is the greatest problem posed by waste disposal?

26. Generalize In what ways will this country's future challenges be different from those of the past?

Put Your Skills to Work

27. Develop a Historical Perspective You have learned that developing a historical perspective means distancing yourself from events so that you can evaluate them objectively. Read the quotation below and answer the following questions.

a. Which words in the passage suggest that this is not a historical perspective?

b. Do you think that this quotation describes space exploration today? Explain your answer.

> "If I could get one message to you it would be this: the future of this country and the welfare of the free world depends upon our success in space. There is no room in this country for any but a fully cooperative, . . . effort toward space leadership. No one person, no one company, no one government agency [office], has a monopoly on the . . . missions, or the requirements for the space program."
>
> —*U.S. Vice President Lyndon B. Johnson, speaking from the American Rocket Society on October 13, 1961*

Analyze Sources

28. Read part of the Nobel Lecture delivered by UN Secretary-General Kofi Annan, on December 11, 2001. Then, answer the questions that follow.

We have entered the third millennium through a gate of fire. If today, after the horror of 11 September, we see better, and we see further—we will realize that humanity is indivisible. New threats make no distinction between races, nations or religions. A new insecurity has entered every mind, regardless of wealth or status. A deeper awareness of the bonds that bind us all—in pain as in prosperity—has gripped young and old.

a. Why does Annan feel that the September 11, 2001, attacks brought the world's people closer together?

b. Do you think Annan is correct in his view? Explain.

Essay Writing

29. Write an essay discussing the changes in technology and science that you think you will see in your lifetime. In your essay, discuss new inventions you think you will see in the future. Also, discuss where you think space exploration may take us in the future.

TEST PREPARATION

GENERALIZATIONS

Read the question below and choose the correct answer.

Which of the following is a characteristic of a developing nation?

1. generally high standard of living
2. low rate of population growth
3. generally low wages
4. high rate of literacy

Critical Thinking

22. Possible answer: It can borrow money from developed countries and use it to expand industries. It can offer developed countries incentives to locate their businesses within its borders. It can expand its education systems so that its literacy rate will rise, allowing its people to become skilled and trained.

23. Possible answer: Scientists felt the need to make it easier to communicate over long distances.

24. Essential medicines must be made more affordable.

25. Consumer and industrial waste pollutes the environment. Disposal of certain types of industrial waste can be hazardous, so it must be monitored by the government.

26. Possible answer: Terrorism is now a large problem, so a major new challenge involves security. There are also challenges related to health-care, poverty, and the environment.

Put Your Skills to Work

DEVELOP A HISTORICAL PERSPECTIVE

27a. "The future of this country and the welfare of the free world depends upon our success in space."

27b. Possible answer: No. In modern times the United States and other countries work together to explore space. Today, most people do not believe that the future of any country or the welfare of the free world depends on space exploration.

Analyze Sources

28a. Possible answer: He is aware that people of all races, all classes, and all nationalities were killed in the attack. He knows that a similar attack could be made at any time anywhere on Earth.

28b. Answers will vary. Make sure students give reasons to support their opinions.

Essay Writing

29. Essays will vary but should include the changes and inventions in technology, science, and space exploration. Encourage students to explain how these changes will affect their lives.

TEST PREPARATION

Answer **3.** generally low wages

Unit 8
Portfolio Project

MODEL UN

Managing the Project
Plan for 3–4 class periods.

Set the Scene
Have students brainstorm a list of conflicts involving world powers that have been the subject of major news stories recently. Write their ideas on the board. Then, identify which of the issues has been dealt with by the United Nations and how UN involvement affected the outcome.

Your Assignment
Ask students to read the assignment on page 808. Then, divide the class into groups of six to begin work on the project.

RESEARCH YOUR ISSUE
After the groups have selected their issue from the list on page 808, have each group decide which role each member will play in the presentation. These roles include a representative of each nation involved in the UN debate. The group should also assign responsibilities for researching both sides of the issue and how a UN General Assembly debate is organized.

REPORT TO YOUR CLASS
After researching the issue or conflict, the group should begin constructing a plan for the UN discussion. This plan includes a list of speakers, representing different members of the world body, and what each speaker will contribute to the discussion. Next, the group should rehearse the presentation and make any necessary changes in the format or content.

After rehearsing, groups should hold their UN General Assembly debate for the class. Remind the audience that they are at a live broadcast of the model UN General Assembly discussion.

Wrap Up
Groups should take turns presenting in class. They may want to use visuals, such as maps and photographs, to enhance their presentations.

Multimedia Presentation
Turn your model UN meeting into a video presentation. Create a set for the model General Assembly. Use video equipment to tape your show. Then, screen the model General Assembly meeting for the class.

Model UN

YOUR ASSIGNMENT
Since it was first founded after World War II, the United Nations has taken on an increasingly active role in world affairs. The UN has sent troops into battle to resolve conflicts, addressed questions of world poverty and hunger, and fought for human rights and freedoms for all the world's population. Select one issue from Unit 8. Stage a model UN General Assembly meeting in which you discuss the issue and formulate a plan to resolve it.

RESEARCH YOUR ISSUE

Choose a Topic As a group, select one of the following issues as the basis for your model UN General Assembly.

Reducing the number of nuclear weapons

War around the world

Earth's environment/pollution

World health

Genetics and cloning

Global warming

Child labor around the world

World poverty

Malnutrition

World terrorism

Research Use your textbook as a starting point for your research. Do further research in the library and on the Internet. As a group, decide which nation your group will represent. Then, take notes on the issue, remembering to represent your chosen nation's point of view accurately. Decide which person in your group will represent the group (nation) in the model UN General Assembly meeting.

REPORT TO YOUR CLASS

Plan Construct a plan for presenting your nation's information to the rest of the UN members.

Present Hold your model UN General Assembly meeting in front of the class. Remember to have your representative stay in his or her assigned role and to listen with attention to the presentations of other group members.

Work Individually Connect the significance of the issue your group chooses to events today. Write a report summing up your thoughts on the issue discussed and how you think the United Nations could work to resolve it.

Teaching Options

Multimedia Presentation
Help students make up a list of sets, costumes, music, and commercials that might be used in their video presentations. Also, help students decide when to use different camera angles, such as close-ups and medium shots.

Alternative Assessment

Create Historical Maps Ask groups of students to make a historical map relating to one of the issues or conflicts that was discussed in Unit 8. These maps should reflect geographical and political changes in the history of the conflict or issue over time. Remind students to include map titles and legends, or key boxes.

Primary Source Documents

From Analects (ca. 500 B.C.)

The main ideas of the teachings of Confucius were recorded by his followers in more than 450 verses. The exact number of Confucius's followers is uncertain. However, at least 22 are named throughout the Analects. In the following excerpts, Confucius stresses the importance of education, respect, and virtue in an individual's personal development. In addition, he discusses with some of his followers the characteristics of a superior person.

Confucius said: "A young man should serve his parents at home and be respectful to elders outside his home. He should be earnest and truthful, loving all . . . . After doing this, if he has energy to spare, he can study literature and the arts."

Meng I Tzu asked about the meaning of filial piety. Confucius said, "It means 'not diverging [from your parents].'" Later, when Fan Chih was driving him, Confucius told Fan Chih, "Meng Sun asked me about the meaning of filial piety, and I told him 'not diverging.'" Fan Chih said, "What did you mean by that?" Confucius said, "When your parents are alive, serve them with propriety; when they die, bury them with propriety, and then worship them with propriety."

Chi K'ang Tzu asked: "How can I make the people reverent and loyal, so they will work positively for me?" Confucius said, "Approach them with dignity, and they will be reverent. Be filial and compassionate and they will be loyal. Promote the able and teach the incompetent, and they will work positively for you."

Confucius said: "The Superior Man cares about virtue; the inferior man cares about material things. The Superior Man seeks discipline; the inferior man seeks favors."

Confucius said: "I don't worry about not having a good position; I worry about the means I use to gain position. I don't worry about being unknown; I seek to be known in the right way."

Confucius said that Tzu Chan had four characteristics of the Superior Man: In his private conduct he was courteous; in serving superiors he was respectful; in providing for the people he was kind; in dealing with the people he was just.

Confucius said: "Study as if you have not reached your goal—as if you were afraid of losing what you have."

Tzeng Tzu said: "The Superior Man doesn't worry about those things which are outside of his control."

Confucius said: "The Superior Man is humble in his speech but superb in his actions."

Confucius said: "Expect much from yourself and little from others and you will avoid incurring resentments."

From **Magna Carta** (1215)

This charter, which English nobles forced King John to approve, limited the powers of the king of England and protected the basic rights of some English individuals. More than 500 years later, American colonists fought against the British for the same rights listed in the Magna Carta.

1. We have granted . . . that the English Church shall be free, and shall have its rights undiminished, and its liberties unimpaired. . . . This freedom we shall observe ourselves, and desire to be observed in good faith by our heirs in perpetuity.

   To all free men of our kingdom, we have also granted, for us and our heirs forever, all the liberties written out below, to have and to keep for them and their heirs, of us and our heirs.

9. Neither we nor our officials will seize any land or rent in payment of a debt, so long as the debtor has movable goods sufficient to discharge the debt.

20. For a trivial offense, a free man shall be fined only in proportion to the degree of his offense, and for a serious offense correspondingly, but not so heavily as to deprive him of his livelihood.

38. In future no official shall place a man on trial upon his own unsupported statement, without producing credible witnesses to the truth of it.

39. No free man shall be seized or imprisoned, or stripped of his rights or possessions, or outlawed or exiled, . . . except by the lawful judgment of his equals or by the law of the land.

40. To no one will we sell, to no one deny or delay, right or justice.

41. All merchants may enter or leave England, unharmed and without fear, and may stay or travel within it, by land or water, for purposes of trade.

42. In future it shall be lawful for any man to leave and return to our kingdom unharmed and without fear, by land or water.

45. We will appoint as justices, constables, sheriffs, or other officials, only men that know the law . . . and are minded to keep it well.

52. To any man whom we have deprived or dispossessed of lands, castles, liberties, or rights, without the lawful judgment of his equals, we will at once restore these.

60. All these customs and liberties that we have granted shall be observed in our kingdom in so far as concerns our own relations with our subjects.

63. It is accordingly our wish and command that the English Church shall be free, and that men in our kingdom shall have and keep all these liberties, rights, and concessions, well and peaceably, in their fullness and entirety for them and their heirs, of us and our heirs, in all things and all places forever.

From John Locke, Two Treatises of Government (1690)

John Locke, an English philosopher, believed that all people had natural rights of life, liberty, and property. In addition, Locke suggested that government is an agreement between the ruler and those being ruled. Above all, the ruler must protect people's rights. If the ruler violates people's rights, the people have a right to rebel. Locke's ideas influenced revolutions in Europe and North America.

But though men, when they enter into society, give up the equality, liberty, and executive power they had in the state of nature, into the hands of society, to be so far disposed of by the legislative, as the good of society shall require; yet it being only with an intention in every one the better to preserve himself, his liberty and property (for no rational creature can be supposed to change his condition with an intention to be worse); the power of the society, or legislative constituted by them, can never be supposed to extend farther than the common good; but is obliged to secure every one's property, by providing against those three defects above mentioned, that made the state of nature so unsafe and uneasy. And so whoever has the legislative or supreme power of any commonwealth, is bound to govern by established standing laws, promulgated and known to the people, and not by extemporary decrees; by indifferent and upright judges, who are to decide controversies by those laws; and to employ the force of the community at home, only in the execution of such laws, or abroad to prevent or redress foreign injuries, and secure the community from inroads and invasion. And all this to be directed to no other end, but the peace, safety, and public good of the people.

The reason why men enter into society, is the preservation of their property; and the end why they choose and authorize a legislative, is, that there may be laws made, and rules set, as guards and fences to the properties of all the members of the society, . . . Whensoever therefore the legislative shall transgress this fundamental rule of society; and either by ambition, fear, folly or corruption, endeavor to grasp themselves, or put into the hands of any other, an absolute power over the lives, liberties, and estates of the people; by this breach of trust they forfeit the power the people had put into their hands for quite contrary ends, and it devolves to the people, who, have a right to resume their original liberty, and, by the establishment of a new legislative, (such as they shall think fit) provide for their own safety and security, which is the end for which they are in society. . . .

From Declaration of Independence (1776)

By the late 1700s, many American colonists wanted to be free from Great Britain's rule. With the help of others, Thomas Jefferson wrote the Declaration of Independence to announce that the 13 colonies were forming a separate nation—the United States of America. The document describes the basic rights of American citizens and the government's responsibility to protect the rights of the people.

Preamble

When in the course of human events, it becomes necessary for one people to dissolve the political bands which have connected them with another, and to assume among the powers of the earth, the separate and equal station to which the laws of nature and of nature's God entitle them, a decent respect to the opinions of mankind requires that they should declare the causes which impel them to the separation.

We hold these truths to be self-evident, that all men are created equal, that they are endowed by their Creator with certain unalienable rights, that among these are life, liberty, and the pursuit of happiness. That to secure these rights, governments are instituted among men, deriving their just powers from the consent of the governed, that whenever any form of government becomes destructive of these ends, it is the right of the people to alter or to abolish it, and to institute new government, laying its foundation on such principles, and organizing its powers in such form, as to them shall seem most likely to effect their safety and happiness. . . .

We, therefore, the representatives of the United States of America, in General Congress, assembled, appealing to the Supreme Judge of the world for the rectitude of our intentions, do, in the name, and by the authority of the good people of these colonies, solemnly publish and declare, that these united colonies are, and of right ought to be, free and independent states; that they are absolved from all allegiance to the British Crown, and that all political connection between them and the state of Great Britain, is and ought to be totally dissolved; and that as free and independent states, they have full power to levy war, conclude peace, contract alliances, establish commerce, and to do all other acts and things which independent states may of right do. And for the support of this declaration, with a firm reliance on the protection of Divine Providence, we mutually pledge to each other our lives, our fortunes, and our sacred honor.

From Declaration of the Rights of Man and the Citizen (1789)

The French National Assembly issued the Declaration of the Rights of Man and the Citizen to help define a person's rights in society. The document included some ideas that had been set forth in the American Declaration of Independence. It proclaimed that all men were equal under the law. In addition, the document asserted that governments exist to protect the natural rights of citizens.

1. Men are born and remain free and equal in rights. Social distinctions may be founded only upon the general good.
2. The aim of all political association is the preservation of the natural and imprescriptible rights of man. These rights are liberty, property, security, and resistance to oppression. . . .
6. Law is the expression of the general will. Every citizen has a right to participate personally, or through his representative, in its foundation. It must be the same for all, whether it protects or punishes. All citizens . . . are equally eligible to all dignities and to all public positions and occupations, according to their abilities, and without distinction except that of their virtues and talents.
7. No person shall be accused, arrested, or imprisoned except in the cases and according to the forms prescribed by law. . . .
9. As all persons are held innocent until they shall have been declared guilty, if arrest shall be deemed indispensable, all harshness not essential to the securing of the prisoner's person shall be severely repressed by law. . . .
11. The free communication of ideas and opinions is one of the most precious of the rights of man. Every citizen may, accordingly, speak, write, and print with freedom, but shall be responsible for such abuses of this freedom as shall be defined by law. . . .

From Declaration of the Rights of Woman and the Female Citizen (1791)

Olympe De Gouges was a French writer who was devoted to the cause of women's rights. She believed that the Declaration of the Rights of Man and the Citizen did not grant equal citizenship to women. In response, she wrote this document to demand equality for women.

1. Woman is born free and lives equal to man in her rights. Social distinctions can be based only on the common utility.
2. The purpose of any political association is the conservation of the natural and imprescriptible rights of woman and man; these rights are liberty, property, security, and especially resistance to oppression. . . .
6. The law must be the expression of the general will; all female and male citizens must contribute either personally or through their representatives to its formation; . . . male and female citizens . . . must be equally admitted to all honors, positions, and public employment according to their capacity and without other distinctions besides those of their virtues and talents.
7. No woman is an exception; she is accused, arrested, and detained in cases determined by law. Women, like men, obey this rigorous law. . . .
13. For the support of the public force and the expenses of administration, the contributions of woman and man are equal; . . . therefore, we must have the same share in the distribution of positions, employment, offices, honors, and jobs. . . .

From Miguel Hidalgo, The Abolition of Slavery in Mexico (1810)

Father Miguel Hidalgo led a peasant army in a revolt against the Mexican government to gain more rights for the lower classes. During the rebellion, Hidalgo issued this declaration, which called for an end to slavery and improved conditions for Native Americans in Central America. He was later captured and executed before he could see the results of his efforts.

From the happy moment when the valiant American nation took up arms to shake off the heavy yoke that for three centuries had pressed upon it, one of the main objects was to end the many taxes which eroded all chances of raising oneself; but as in the critical circumstances Providence has not permitted us to complete that goal because of the heavy costs of war, nonetheless we shall address the most urgent situations by the following declarations:

1. That all the owners of slaves will have to free them, within the term of ten days, failure to do so merits capital punishment.
2. The tribute demanded of the Indians is to cease.
3. That in the courts, documents, writings and trials, all will be open and published rather than secret.

From Mohandas Gandhi, The Quit India Speeches (1942)

In the mid-1800s, Great Britain expanded its huge empire and gained control of the government in India. More than 50 years later, Mohandas Gandhi called for independence from British rule. In the following speech, he urged Indians to use nonviolent methods to gain freedom.

Ours is not a drive for power, but purely a non-violent fight for India's independence. In a violent struggle, a successful general has been often known to effect a military coup and to set up a dictatorship. But under the Congress scheme of things, essentially non-violent as it is, there can be no room for dictatorship. A non-violent soldier of freedom will covet nothing for himself, he fights only for the freedom of his country. The Congress is unconcerned as to who will rule, when freedom is attained. The power . . . will belong to the people of India, and it will be for them to decide to whom it placed in the entrusted. . . .

Our quarrel is not with the British people, we fight their imperialism. The proposal for the withdrawal of British power did not come out of anger. It came to enable India to play its due part at the present critical juncture. It is not a happy position for a big country like India to be merely helping with money and material obtained willy-nilly from her while the United Nations are conducting the war. We cannot evoke the true spirit of sacrifice and valor, so long as we are not free. I know the British Government will not be able to withhold freedom from us, when we have made enough self-sacrifice. We must, therefore, purge ourselves of hatred. . . . I have never felt any hatred. As a matter of fact, I feel myself to be a greater friend of the British now than ever before. One reason is that they are today in distress. My very friendship, therefore, demands that I should try to save them from their mistakes . . . they are on the brink of an abyss. It, therefore, becomes my duty to warn them of their danger even though it may . . . anger them to the point of cutting off the friendly hand that is stretched out to help them. People may laugh, nevertheless that is my claim. . . .

From Nelson Mandela, Inaugural Address (1994)

Nelson Mandela joined the African National Congress (ANC) in its effort to end the policy of apartheid, or racial separation, in South Africa. Despite being arrested and imprisoned in the early 1960s, Mandela remained a leader and a powerful symbol of the struggle against apartheid. After Mandela's release from prison in 1990, South Africa began changing apartheid laws. Nelson Mandela was later elected the first black president of South Africa.

Today, all of us do, by our presence here, and by our celebrations in other parts of our country and the world, confer glory and hope to newborn liberty.

Out of the experience of an extraordinary human disaster that lasted too long, must be born a society of which all humanity will be proud.

Our daily deeds as ordinary South Africans must produce an actual South African reality that will reinforce humanity's belief in justice, strengthen its confidence in the nobility of the human soul, and sustain all our hopes for a glorious life for all. . . .

The time for the healing of the wounds has come. . . .

The time to build is upon us.

We have, at last, achieved our political emancipation. We pledge ourselves to liberate all our people from the continuing bondage of poverty, deprivation, suffering, gender and other discrimination.

We succeeded to take our last steps to freedom in conditions of relative peace. We commit ourselves to the construction of a complete, just and lasting peace. . . .

We enter into a covenant that we shall build the society in which all South Africans, both black and white, will be able to walk tall, without any fear in their hearts, assured of their inalienable right to human dignity—a rainbow nation at peace with itself and the world. . . .

We dedicate this day to all the heroes and heroines in this country and the rest of the world who sacrificed in many ways and surrendered their lives so that we could be free.

Their dreams have become reality. Freedom is their reward. . . .

We understand it still that there is no easy road to freedom.

We know it well that none of us acting alone can achieve success.

We must therefore act together as a united people, for national reconciliation, for nation building, for the birth of a new world.

Let there be justice for all.

Let there be peace for all.

Let there be work, bread, water and salt for all. . . .

Let freedom reign.

The sun shall never set on so glorious a human achievement!

The World at a Glance

Country	Official Name	Capital	Total Population	Principal Languages
AFRICA				
Algeria	People's Democratic Republic of Algeria	Algiers	32,277,942	Arabic, French, Berber
Angola	Republic of Angola	Luanda	10,553,547	Portuguese, Bantu, other African languages
Benin	Republic of Benin	Porto-Novo	6,834,795	French, Fon, Yoruba
Botswana	Republic of Botswana	Gaborone	1,579,436	English, Setswana
Burkina Faso	Burkina Faso	Ouagadougou	12,886,513	French, Sudanic languages
Burundi	Republic of Burundi	Bujumbura	5,965,127	Kirundi, French, Swahili
Cameroon	Republic of Cameroon	Yaoundé	15,428,030	African languages, English, French
Cape Verde	Republic of Cape Verde	Praia	408,760	Portuguese, Crioulo
Central African Republic	Central African Republic	Bangui	3,623,238	French, Sangho, Arabic, Hunsa, Swahili
Chad	Republic of Chad	N'Djamena	8,971,376	French, Arabic, Sara
Comoros	Federal Islamic Republic of the Comoros	Moroni	614,382	Arabic, French, Comorian, Shikomoro
Congo, Democratic Republic of the	Democratic Republic of the Congo	Kinshasa	55,041,752	French, Lingala, Kingwana, Kikongo, Tshiluba
Congo, Republic of the	Republic of the Congo	Brazzaville	2,908,048	French, Lingala, Monokutuba, Kikongo
Cote d'Ivoire	Republic of Cote d'Ivoire	Yamoussoukro	16,597,693	French, Dioula dialect
Djibouti	Republic of Djibouti	Djibouti	447,416	French, Arabic, Somali, Afar
Egypt	Arab Republic of Egypt	Cairo	73,312,559	Arabic, English, French
Equatorial Guinea	Republic of Equatorial Guinea	Malabo	498,144	Spanish, French, pidgin English, Fang, Bubi, Ibo
Eritrea	State of Eritrea	Asmara	4,305,577	Afar, Amharic, Arabic, Tigre and Kunama, Tigrinya
Ethiopia	Federal Democratic Republic of Ethiopia	Addis Ababa	65,253,938	Amharic, Tigrinya, Oromigna, Guaragigna, Somali, Arabic
Gabon	Gabonese Republic	Libreville	1,288,229	French, Fang, Myene, Nzebi, Bapounou/Eschira, Bandjabi
Gambia, The	Republic of The Gambia	Banjul	1,455,842	English, Mandinka, Wolof, Fula, other African languages
Ghana	Republic of Ghana	Accra	20,163,149	English, African languages

Country	Official Name	Capital	Total Population	Principal Languages
Guinea	Republic of Guinea	Conakry	8,815,576	French
Guinea-Bissau	Republic of Guinea-Bissau	Bissau	1,333,453	Portuguese, Crioulo, African languages
Kenya	Republic of Kenya	Nairobi	31,223,158	English, Kiswahili
Lesotho	Kingdom of Lesotho	Maseru	1,857,866	Sesotho, English, Zulu, Xhosa
Liberia	Republic of Liberia	Monrovia	3,261,515	English, local languages
Libya	Socialist People's Libyan Arab Jamahiriya	Tripoli	5,368,585	Arabic, Italian, English
Madagascar	Republic of Madagascar	Antananarivo	16,473,477	French, Malagasy
Malawi	Republic of Malawi	Lilongwe	11,393,210	English, Chichewa
Mali	Republic of Mali	Bamako	11,300,445	French, Bambara
Mauritania	Islamic Republic of Mauritania	Nouakchott	2,828,858	Hasaniya Arabic, Pulaar, Soninke, Wolof, French
Mauritius	Republic of Mauritius	Port Louis	1,200,206	English, Creole, French, Hindi, Urdu, Hakka, Bhojpuri
Mayotte* (French Territory)	Territorial Collectivity of Mayotte	Mamoudzou	170,879	Mahorian, French
Morocco	Kingdom of Morocco	Rabat	31,167,783	Arabic, Berber dialects, French
Mozambique	Republic of Mozambique	Maputo	17,323,598	Portuguese, African dialects
Namibia	Republic of Namibia	Windhoek	1,896,845	Afrikaans, German, English
Niger	Republic of Niger	Niamey	10,760,206	French, Hausa, Djerma
Nigeria	Federal Republic of Nigeria	Abuja	130,499,978	English, Hausa, Yoruba, Igbo, Fulani
Réunion* (French Territory)	Department of Réunion	Saint-Denis	743,981	French, Creole
Rwanda	Republic of Rwanda	Kigali	7,668,223	Kinyarwanda, French, English, Kiswahili
Saint Helena* (British Territory)	Saint Helena	Jamestown	7,317	English
São Tomé and Príncipe	Democratic Republic of São Tomé and Príncipe	São Tomé	170,372	Portuguese
Senegal	Republic of Senegal	Dakar	10,311,497	French, Wolof, Pulaar, Jola, Mandinka
Seychelles	Republic of Seychelles	Victoria	80,098	English, French, Creole
Sierra Leone	Republic of Sierra Leone	Freetown	5,564,516	English, Mende, Temne, Krio

Country	Official Name	Capital	Total Population	Principal Languages
Somalia	Somalia	Mogadishu	7,753,310	Somali, Arabic, Italian, English
South Africa	Republic of South Africa	Pretoria	42,715,936	Afrikaans, English, Ndebele, Pedi, Sotho, Swazi, Tsonga, Tswana, Venda, Xhosa, Zulu
Sudan	Republic of the Sudan	Khartoum	37,090,298	Arabic, Nubian, Ta Bedawie, Nilotic, Nilo-Hamitic, Sudanic languages, English
Swaziland	Kingdom of Swaziland	Mbabane	1,150,161	English, siSwati
Tanzania	United Republic of Tanzania	Dar es Salaam	35,301,718	Kiswahili, Kiunguju, English, Arabic
Togo	Togolese Republic	Lomé	5,299,424	French, Ewe, Mina, Kabye, Dagomba
Tunisia	Republic of Tunisia	Tunis	9,815,644	Arabic, French
Uganda	Republic of Uganda	Kampala	24,888,694	Ganda or Luganda, English, other local languages
Zambia	Republic of Zambia	Lusaka	10,148,674	English, African languages
Zimbabwe	Republic of Zimbabwe	Harare	12,463,115	English, Shona, Sindebele

ASIA

Country	Official Name	Capital	Total Population	Principal Languages
Afghanistan	Islamic State of Afghanistan	Kabul	27,755,775	Afghan Persian, Pashtu, Uzbek, Turkmen
Armenia	Republic of Armenia	Yerevan	3,330,099	Armenian
Azerbaijan	Republic of Azerbaijan	Baku	7,798,497	Azerbaijani
Bahrain	Kingdom of Bahrain	Manama	656,397	Arabic, English, Farsi, Urdu
Bangladesh	People's Republic of Bangladesh	Dhaka	135,656,790	Bengali, English
Bhutan	Kingdom of Bhutan	Thimphu	2,094,176	Dzongkha, Tibetan dialects, Nepalese dialects
Brunei	Negara Brunei Darussalam	Bandar Seri Begawan	350,898	Malay, English, Chinese
Burma	Union of Burma	Rangoon	42,281,860	Burmese
Cambodia	Kingdom of Cambodia	Phnom Penh	12,890,312	Khmer, French, English
China	People's Republic of China	Beijing	1,279,160,885	Standard Chinese or Mandarin, Yue, Wu, Minbei, Minnan, Xiang, Gan, Hakka dialects
Cyprus	Republic of Cyprus	Nicosia	767,314	Greek, Turkish, English

Country	Official Name	Capital	Total Population	Principal Languages
East Timor	Democratic Republic of East Timor	Dili	952,618	Tetum, Portuguese, Indonesian, English, local languages
Georgia	Georgia	T'Bilisi	4,960,951	Georgian, Russian, Armenian, Azeri
India	Republic of India	New Delhi	1,034,172,547	Hindi, English, Bengali, Telugu, Marathi, Tamil, Urdu, Gujarati, Malayalam, Kannada, Oriya, Punjabi, Assamese, Kashmiri, Sindhi, Sanskrit
Indonesia	Republic of Indonesia	Jakarta	231,326,092	Bahasa Indonesian, English, Dutch, Javanese, Indonesian dialects
Iran	Islamic Republic of Iran	Tehran	67,538,065	Persian and Persian dialects, Turkic and Turkic dialects, Kurdish
Iraq	Republic of Iraq	Baghdad	24,001,816	Arabic, Kurdish, Assyrian, Armenian
Israel	State of Israel	Jerusalem	6,029,529	Hebrew, English, Arabic
Japan	Japan	Tokyo	127,065,841	Japanese
Jordan	Hashemite Kingdom of Jordan	Amman	5,307,470	Arabic, English
Kazakhstan	Republic of Kazakhstan	Astana	16,741,519	Kazakh, Russian
Kuwait	State of Kuwait	Kuwait	2,111,561	Arabic, English
Kyrgyzstan	Kyrgyz Republic	Bishkek	4,822,166	Kyrgyz, Russian
Laos	Lao People's Democratic Republic	Vientiane	5,777,564	Lao, French, English
Lebanon	Lebanese Republic	Beirut	3,677,780	Arabic, French, English, Armenian
Macau* (Administrative Region of China)	Macau Special Administrative Region	Macau	461,833	Portuguese, Chinese
Malaysia	Malaysia	Kuala Lumpur	22,662,365	Bahasa Melayu, English, Chinese dialects, Tamil, Telugu, Malayalam, Panjabi, Thai, local languages
Maldives	Republic of Maldives	Male	320,165	Maldivian Dhivehi, English
Mongolia	Mongolia	Ulaanbaatar	2,674,234	Khalkha Mongol, Turkic, Russian
Nepal	Kingdom of Nepal	Kathmandu	25,873,917	Nepali
North Korea	Democratic People's Republic of Korea	P'yongyang	22,215,365	Korean

Country	Official Name	Capital	Total Population	Principal Languages
Oman	Sultanate of Oman	Muscat	2,713,462	Arabic, English, Baluchi, Urdu, Indian dialects
Pakistan	Islamic Republic of Pakistan	Islamabad	147,663,429	Punjabi, Sindhi, Siraiki, Pashtu, Urdu, Balochi, Hindko, Brahui, English, Burushaski
Philippines	Republic of the Philippines	Manila	82,995,088	Filipino, English, Filipino dialects
Qatar	State of Qatar	Doha	793,341	Arabic, English
Saudi Arabia	Kingdom of Saudi Arabia	Riyadh	23,513,330	Arabic
Singapore	Republic of Singapore	Singapore	4,452,732	Chinese, Malay, Tamil, English
South Korea	Republic of Korea	Seoul	47,962,703	Korean
Sri Lanka	Democratic Socialist Republic of Sri Lanka	Colombo	19,576,783	Sinhala, Tamil
Syria	Syrian Arab Republic	Damascus	17,155,814	Arabic, Kurdish, Armenian, Aramaic, Circassian
Taiwan	Taiwan	Taipei	22,454,239	Mandarin Chinese, Taiwanese, Hakka dialects
Tajikistan	Republic of Tajikistan	Dushanbe	6,719,567	Tajik, Russian
Thailand	Kingdom of Thailand	Bangkok	63,645,250	Thai, English
Turkey	Republic of Turkey	Ankara	67,308,928	Turkish, Kurdish, Arabic, Armenian, Greek
Turkmenistan	Turkmenistan	Ashgabat	4,688,963	Turkmen, Russian, Uzbek
United Arab Emirates	United Arab Emirates	Abu Dhabi	2,445,989	Arabic, Persian, English, Hindi, Urdu
Uzbekistan	Republic of Uzbekistan	Tashkent	25,563,441	Uzbek, Russian, Tajik
Vietnam	Socialist Republic of Vietnam	Hanoi	80,577,466	Vietnamese, English, French, Chinese, Khmer; Mon-Khmer, Malayo-Polynesian
Yemen	Republic of Yemen	Sanaa	18,701,257	Arabic

AUSTRALIA, NEW ZEALAND, AND THE PACIFIC ISLANDS

Country	Official Name	Capital	Total Population	Principal Languages
American Samoa* (U.S. Territory)	Territory of American Samoa	Pago Pago	68,688	Samoan, English
Australia	Commonwealth of Australia	Canberra	19,546,792	English

Country	Official Name	Capital	Total Population	Principal Languages
Christmas Island* (Australian Territory)	Territory of Christmas Island	The Settlement	474	English, Chinese, Malay
Cocos (Keeling) Islands* (Australian Territory)	Territory of Cocos (Keeling) Islands	West Island	632	English, Malay
Cook Islands* (Self-governing Division of New Zealand)	Cook Islands	Avarua	20,811	English, Maori
Fiji	Republic of the Fiji Islands	Suva	856,346	English, Fijian, Hindustani
French Polynesia* (French Territory)	Territory of French Polynesia	Papeete	257,847	French, Tahitian
Guam* (U.S. Territory)	Territory of Guam	Hagatna	160,796	English, Chamorro, Japanese
Kiribati	Republic of Kiribati	Tarawa	96,335	English, I-Kiribati
Marshall Islands	Republic of the Marshall Islands	Majuro	55,147	English, Marshallese, Japanese
Micronesia	Federated States of Micronesia	Palikir	135,869	English, Trukese, Pohnpeian, Yapese, Kosrean
Nauru	Republic of Nauru	Yaren District- official government offices	12,329	Nauruan, English
New Caledonia* (French Territory)	Territory of New Caledonia and Dependencies	Nouméa	207,858	French, Melanesian-Polynesian dialects
New Zealand	New Zealand	Wellington	3,908,037	English, Maori
Niue* (Self-governing Division of New Zealand)	Niue	Alofi	2,134	Niuean, English
Norfolk Island* (Australian Territory)	Territory of Norfolk Island	Kingston	1,866	English, Norfolk
Northern Mariana Islands* (commonwealth in political union with the United States)	Commonwealth of Northern Mariana Islands	Saipan	77,311	English, Chamorro, Carolinian
Palau	Republic of Palau	Koror	19,409	English, Palauan, Sonsorolese, Tobi, Angaur, Japanese
Papua New Guinea	Independent State of Papua New Guinea	Port Moresby	5,172,033	English, pidgin English, Motu, local languages
Pitcairn Islands* (British Territory)	Pitcairn, Henderson, Ducie, and Oeno Islands	Adamstown	47	English, Pitcairnese
Samoa	Independent State of Samoa	Apia	178,631	Samoan, English

Country	Official Name	Capital	Total Population	Principal Languages
Solomon Islands	Solomon Islands	Honiara	494,786	Melanesian pidgin, English
Tokelau* (New Zealand Territory)	Tokelau	None	1,431	Tokelauan, English
Tonga	Kingdom of Tonga	Nuku'alofa	106,137	Tongan, English
Tuvalu	Tuvalu	Funafuti	11,146	Tuvaluan, English, Samoan, Kirabati
Vanuatu	Republic of Vanuatu	Port-Vila	196,178	English, French, Bislama
Wallis and Futuna* (French Territory)	Territory of the Wallis and Futuna Islands	Matâ'Utu	15,585	French, Wallisian

EUROPE

Country	Official Name	Capital	Total Population	Principal Languages
Albania	Republic of Albania	Tirana	3,544,841	Albanian, Tosk dialect, Greek
Andorra	Principality of Andorra	Andorra la Vella	68,403	Catalan, French, Castilian
Austria	Republic of Austria	Vienna	8,169,929	German
Belarus	Republic of Belarus	Minsk	10,335,382	Belarusian, Russian
Belgium	Kingdom of Belgium	Brussels	10,274,595	Dutch, French
Bosnia and Herzegovina	Bosnia and Herzegovina	Sarajevo	3,964,388	Croatian, Serbian, Bosnian
Bulgaria	Republic of Bulgaria	Sofia	7,621,337	Bulgarian
Croatia	Republic of Croatia	Zagreb	4,390,751	Croatian
Czech Republic	Czech Republic	Prague	10,256,760	Czech
Denmark	Kingdom of Denmark	Copenhagen	5,368,854	Danish, English, Faroese, Greenlandic
Estonia	Republic of Estonia	Tallinn	1,415,681	Estonian, Russian, Ukrainian, Finnish
Faroe Islands* (Self-governing Division of Denmark)	Faroe Islands	Tórshavn	46,011	Faroese, Danish
Finland	Republic of Finland	Helsinki	5,183,545	Finnish, Swedish
France	French Republic	Paris	59,925,035	French
Germany	Federal Republic of Germany	Berlin	82,350,671	German
Gibraltar* (British Territory)	Gibraltar	Gibraltar	27,714	English, Spanish, Italian, Portuguese, Russian
Greece	Hellenic Republic	Athens	10,645,343	Greek

Country	Official Name	Capital	Total Population	Principal Languages
Guernsey* (British Dependency)	Bailiwick of Guernsey	St. Peter Port	64,587	English, French, Norman-French dialect
Hungary	Republic of Hungary	Budapest	10,075,034	Hungarian
Iceland	Republic of Iceland	Reykjavík	279,384	Icelandic
Isle of Man* (British Dependency)	Isle of Man	Douglas	73,873	English, Manx Gaelic
Ireland	Ireland	Dublin	3,883,159	English, Gaelic
Italy	Italian Republic	Rome	57,926,999	Italian, German, French, Slovene
Jersey* (British Dependency)	Bailiwick of Jersey	Saint Helier	89,775	English, French, Norman-French dialect
Latvia	Republic of Latvia	Riga	2,366,515	Latvian, Lithuanian, Russian
Liechtenstein	Principality of Liechtenstein	Vaduz	32,842	German, Alemannic dialect
Lithuania	Republic of Lithuania	Vilnius	3,601,138	Lithuanian, Polish, Russian
Luxembourg	Grand Duchy of Luxembourg	Luxembourg	448,569	Luxembourgish, German, French
Macedonia	The Former Yugoslav Republic of Macedonia	Skopje	2,054,800	Macedonian, Albanian, Turkish, Serbo-Croatian
Malta	Republic of Malta	Valletta	397,499	Maltese, English
Moldova	Republic of Moldova	Chisinau	4,434,547	Moldovan, Russian, Gagauz
Monaco	Principality of Monaco	Monaco	31,987	French, English, Italian, Monegasque
Netherlands	Kingdom of the Netherlands	Amsterdam; (The Hague is the seat of government)	16,067,754	Dutch
Norway	Kingdom of Norway	Oslo	4,525,116	Norwegian
Poland	Republic of Poland	Warsaw	38,625,478	Polish
Portugal	Portuguese Republic	Lisbon	10,084,245	Portuguese
Romania	Romania	Bucharest	22,317,730	Romanian, Hungarian, German
Russia	Russian Federation	Moscow	144,978,573	Russian
San Marino	Republic of San Marino	San Marino	27,730	Italian
Serbia and Montenegro	Serbia and Montenegro	Belgrade	10,658,010	Serbian, Serbo-Croatian, Albanian

Country	Official Name	Capital	Total Population	Principal Languages
Slovakia	Slovak Republic	Bratislava	5,422,366	Slovak, Hungarian
Slovenia	Republic of Slovenia	Ljubljana	1,932,917	Slovenian, Serbo-Croatian
Spain	Kingdom of Spain	Madrid	40,077,100	Castilian Spanish, Catalan, Galician, Basque
Svalbard* (Norwegian Territory)	Svalbard	Longyearbyen	2,868	Russian, Norwegian
Sweden	Kingdom of Sweden	Stockholm	8,876,744	Swedish
Switzerland	Swiss Confederation	Bern	7,301,994	German, French, Italian
Ukraine	Ukraine	Kiev	48,396,470	Ukrainian, Russian, Romanian, Polish, Hungarian
United Kingdom	United Kingdom of Great Britain and Northern Ireland	London	59,912,431	English, Welsh, Scottish form of Gaelic
Vatican City	The Holy See (State of the Vatican City)	Vatican City	900	Italian, Latin, French

NORTH AMERICA

Country	Official Name	Capital	Total Population	Principal Languages
Anguilla* (British Dependency)	Anguilla	The Valley	12,446	English
Antigua and Barbuda	Antigua and Barbuda	Saint John's	67,448	English, local dialects
Aruba* (Dutch Territory)	Aruba	Oranjestad	70,441	Dutch, Papiamento, English, Spanish
Bahamas, The	Commonwealth of The Bahamas	Nassau	295,131	English, Creole
Barbados	Barbados	Bridgetown	276,182	English
Belize	Belize	Belmopan	259,946	English, Spanish, Mayan, Garifuna, Creole
Bermuda* (British Territory)	Bermuda	Hamilton	64,004	English, Portuguese
British Virgin Islands* (British Territory)	British Virgin Islands	Road Town	21,272	English
Canada	Canada	Ottawa	31,592,805	English, French
Cayman Islands* (British Territory)	Cayman Islands	George Town	40,762	English
Costa Rica	Republic of Costa Rica	San José	3,834,934	Spanish
Cuba	Republic of Cuba	Havana	11,224,321	Spanish
Dominica	Commonwealth of Dominica	Roseau	70,158	English, French patois

Country	Official Name	Capital	Total Population	Principal Languages
Dominican Republic	Dominican Republic	Santo Domingo	8,596,132	Spanish
El Salvador	Republic of El Salvador	San Salvador	6,353,681	Spanish, Nahua
Greenland* (Danish Territory)	Greenland	Nuuk (Godthåb)	56,376	Greenlandic, Danish, English
Grenada	State of Grenada	St. George's	89,211	English, French patois
Guadeloupe* (French Territory)	Department of Guadeloupe	Basse-Terre	435,739	French
Guatemala	Republic of Guatemala	Guatemala City	13,541,978	Spanish, Amerindian languages
Haiti	Republic of Haiti	Port-au-Prince	7,405,259	French, Creole
Honduras	Republic of Honduras	Tegucigalpa	6,514,412	Spanish, Amerindian languages
Jamaica	Jamaica	Kingston	2,680,029	English, English patois, Jamaican Creole
Martinique* (French Territory)	Department of Martinique	Fort-de-France	422,277	French, Creole patois
Mexico	United Mexican States	Mexico City	103,400,165	Spanish, Mayan dialects, Nuatl, Mexican languages
Montserrat* (British Territory)	Montserrat	Plymouth	8,437	English
Netherlands Antilles* (Dutch Territory)	Netherlands Antilles	Willemstad	214,258	Dutch, Papiamento, English, Spanish
Nicaragua	Republic of Nicaragua	Managua	5,023,818	Spanish
Panama	Republic of Panama	Panama City	2,920,150	Spanish, English
Puerto Rico* (U.S. Territory)	Commonwealth of Puerto Rico	San Juan	3,863,140	Spanish, English
Saint Kitts and Nevis	Federation of Saint Kitts and Nevis	Basseterre	38,736	English
Saint Lucia	Saint Lucia	Castries	160,145	English, French patois
Saint Pierre and Miquelon* (French Territory)	Territorial Collectivity of Saint Pierre and Miquelon	Saint-Pierre	6,954	French
Saint Vincent and the Grenadines	Saint Vincent and the Grenadines	Kingstown	116,394	English, French patois
Trinidad and Tobago	Republic of Trinidad and Tobago	Port-of-Spain	1,163,174	English, Hindi, French, Spanish, Chinese
Turks and Caicos Islands* (British Territory)	Turks and Caicos Islands	Grand Turk	18,738	English
United States	The United States of America	Washington D.C.	287,675,526	English, Spanish

Country	Official Name	Capital	Total Population	Principal Languages
Virgin Islands* (U.S. Territory)	United States Virgin Islands	Charlotte Amalie	123,498	English, Spanish, Creole

SOUTH AMERICA

Country	Official Name	Capital	Total Population	Principal Languages
Argentina	Argentine Republic	Buenos Aires	38,331,121	Spanish, English, Italian, German, French
Bolivia	Republic of Bolivia	La Paz (seat of government); Sucre (legal capital and seat of judiciary)	8,445,334	Spanish, Quechua, Aymara
Brazil	Federative Republic of Brazil	Brasília	179,914,212	Portuguese, Spanish, English, French
Chile	Republic of Chile	Santiago	15,498,930	Spanish
Colombia	Republic of Colombia	Bogotá	41,008,227	Spanish
Ecuador	Republic of Ecuador	Quito	13,447,494	Spanish, Quechua
Falkland Islands* (British Territory)	Falkland Islands	Stanley	2,967	English
French Guiana* (French Territory)	Department of Guiana	Cayenne	182,333	French, Creole, Taki-Taki, Amerindian languages
Guyana	Cooperative Republic of Guyana	Georgetown	699,572	English, Amerindian dialects, Creole, Hindi, Urdu
Paraguay	Republic of Paraguay	Asunción	5,884,491	Spanish, Guaraní
Peru	Republic of Peru	Lima	27,949,639	Spanish, Quechua, Aymara
Suriname	Republic of Suriname	Paramaribo	433,682	Dutch, English, Sranang Tongo, Surinamese, Hindustani, Javanese
Uruguay	Oriental Republic of Uruguay	Montevideo	3,386,575	Spanish, Portunol
Venezuela	Republic of Venezuela	Caracas	24,287,670	Spanish, local languages

*Dependency, Territory, Self-governing Division, Administrative Region

Sources: Population data from United States Census Bureau, Department of Commerce, 2002; *CIA World Factbook 2002*: **www.odci.gov/cia/publications/factbook**; *The World Almanac and Book of Facts,* 2002

Glossary

abdication (AB dih kay shuhn) voluntary resignation of a ruler (p. 141)

absentee landlord (ab suhn TEE LAND lawrd) a landowner who lives elsewhere while earning money from landholdings (p. 248)

absolute monarchy (AB suh loot MAHN uhr kee) a monarchy in which the ruler is not limited by a constitution or law (p. 388)

acid rain (AS ihd RAYN) rain, snow, or hail that contains toxic, or poisonous, chemicals (p. 721)

acropolis (uh KRAHP uh lihs) the highest part of a Greek city-state (p. 106)

adobe (uh DOH bee) a sun-dried brick made from clay (p. 206)

agrarian economy (uh GRER ee uhn ih KAHN uh mee) an economy that depends on farming (p. 91)

alliance (uh LY uhns) an agreement between two or more people, groups, or nations to cooperate with one another (p. 111)

ambassador (am BAS uh duhr) a person who acts as a messenger or representative (p. 338)

amendment (uh MEHND muhnt) a change or an addition (p. 431)

amnesty (AM nuhs tee) a government pardon (p. 723)

anarchy (AN uhr kee) an absence of government; political disorder (p. 632)

annex (AN nehks) to add to or take possession of (p. 200)

anthropologist (an throh PAHL uh jihst) a person who studies humans, especially their physical characteristics as well as their customs and social relationships (p. 5)

antipope (AN ty pohp) a pope not officially recognized by the entire Roman Catholic Church (p. 307)

anti-Semitism (AN ty SEHM uh tihz uhm) prejudice against Jewish people (p. 284)

apartheid (uh PAHR tyd) the policy of racial separation and discrimination in South Africa (p. 768)

appeasement (uh PEEZ muhnt) giving in to demands in exchange for peace (p. 665)

archaeologist (ahr KEE ahl uh jihst) a person who studies the remains of the past (p. 4)

archipelago (ahr kuh PEHL uh goh) a group of islands (p. 497)

aristocracy (ar ih STAH kruh see) a government in which the upper class, or a privileged few, rule (p. 107)

armistice (AHR muh stihs) an agreement to stop warfare (p. 624)

arsenal (AHR suh nuhl) a place for making or storing weapons (p. 670)

artifact (AHRT uh fakt) any object made or changed by humans (p. 4)

assassination (uh SAS uhn ay shehn) the murder of a leader, often for political reasons (p. 118)

assimilation (uh SIHM uh lay shuhn) the process of absorbing or taking on the cultural ideas and customs of another group and combining them into an existing culture (p. 120)

asylum (uh SY luhm) a place that gives protection, such as political protection (p. 718)

authoritarian (uh thawr uh TER ee uhn) exerting complete power as a ruler (p. 82)

autocrat (AWT uh krat) a single ruler with absolute power (p. 152)

autonomy (aw TAHN uh mee) self-government (p. 764)

ayllu (eye LOO) a social unit made up of several families who owned land jointly (p. 211)

balance of power (BAL uhns UHV POW uhr) a system in which no single state is strong enough to dominate all the others in its region (p. 395)

balance of trade (BAL uhns UHV TRAYD) the difference in value between a country's imports and its exports over a period (p. 364)

barter (BAHRT uhr) to trade by exchanging one item for another (p. 14)

biodiversity (BY oh duh ver suh tee) variety of plant and animal species in an ecosystem (p. 791)

birth rate (BIRTH RAYT) the measure of how many people are born each year in a country (p. 796)

bishop (BIHSH uhp) a high-ranking Christian Church official (p. 145)

blitzkrieg (BLIHTZ kreeg) Hitler's method of fighting a "lightning war," involving powerful planes and speedy ground travel (p. 668)

Boers (BAWRZ) Dutch settlers in South Africa (p. 493)

bourgeoisie (boor zhwah ZEE) the middle class (p. 438)

boyar (boh YAHR) a Russian noble (p. 161)

boycott (BOY kaht) a protest in which people refuse to buy certain goods (p. 649)

bureaucracy (byoo RAH kruh see) a body of appointed or hired government officials who follow a set routine (p. 65)

bureaucrat (BYOOR uh krat) a government official (p. 180)

burgher (BER guhr) a resident or an official of a city or town (p. 298)

Bushido (BOO shee doh) the samurai code of loyalty and courage, and the preference of death to dishonor (p. 487)

business cycle (BIHZ nihs SY kuhl) the alternation of periods of economic prosperity and decline (p. 750)

caliph (KAY lihf) an Islamic ruler with the authority to rule from Muhammad (p. 175)

calligraphy (kuh LIHG ruh fee) an elegant style of handwriting (p. 183)

capital (KAP uht ihl) the money or property used by a businessperson to make a profit (p. 506)

capitalism (KAP uht ihl ihz uhm) an economic system based on the investment of money in businesses for profit (p. 376)

cartel (kahr TEHL) a group formed by producers to control production and prices (p. 699)

cash crop (KASH KRAHP) a crop grown mainly to sell, not for personal use (p. 369)

caste system (KAST SIHS tuhm) the complex form of social organization that restricts its members to certain occupations (p. 57)

cataract (KAT uh rakt) a large waterfall (p. 24)

cease-fire agreement (SEES FYR a GREE muhnt) an agreement to end fighting (p. 752)

censorship (SEHN suhr shihp) the policy of prohibiting objectionable materials (p. 426)

chancellor (CHAN suh luhr) prime minister (p. 656)

charter (CHAHRT uhr) an official document in which rights are given by a government to a person or group (p. 167)

chiefdom (CHEEF duhm) centralized African political system with hereditary offices (p. 492)

chinampa (chihn NAM puh) a floating raft made of reeds and filled with earth on which the Aztecs grew crops (p. 204)

chivalry (SHIHV uhl ree) the code of conduct expected of knights (p. 277)

circumnavigate (ser kuhm NAV uh gayt) to sail completely around a landmass or Earth (p. 364)

citadel (SIHT uh dehl) a fort that commands a city (p. 52)

city-state (SIHT ee stayt) a city and its surrounding territories having an independent government (p. 18)

civil disobedience (SIHV uhl dis oh BEE dee uhns) the refusal to obey unjust laws (p. 652)

civilization (siv uh luh ZAY shuhn) the stage in human progress at which a complex and organized social order is developed (p. 16)

civil service (SIHV uhl SER vihs) people employed in government administration (p. 84)

civil war (SIHV uhl WAWR) war between groups of people from the same country (p. 82)

clan (KLAN) a group of families with a common ancestor (p. 250)

clone (KLOHN) to make an exact copy of an organism by duplicating genetic material (p. 801)

Cold War (KOHLD WAWR) a conflict between countries with no actual fighting (p. 688)

collective (kuh LEHK tihv) a large farm that is worked by peasants but is owned by a government (p. 641)

collective bargaining (kuh LEHK tihv BAHR guhn ihng) talks between a union and an employer about working conditions (p. 527)

colonialism (kuh LOH nee uhl ihz uhm) the rule of a foreign territory for economic gain and military power (p. 518)

command economy (kuh MAND ih KAHN uh mee) an economy in which a central government makes all economic decisions (p. 640)

commodity (kuh MAHD uh tee) something that can be bought or sold (p. 345)

common law (KAHM uhn LAW) the traditional body of law in England that blends English and Norman elements (p. 302)

Common Market (KAHM uhn MAHR kiht) the economic association of European nations that promotes trade and productivity (p. 695)

Commonwealth (KAHM uhn wehlth) the English republic declared by Oliver Cromwell (p. 403)

commune (KAH myoon) a community in which there is no private ownership and people live and work together in large groups (p. 743)

communism (KAHM myoo nihz uhm) an economic system in which the means of production are controlled by the government, and property is owned by everyone equally (p. 529)

commute (kuh MYOOT) to travel back and forth regularly (p. 712)

concentration camp (kahn suhn TRAY shun KAMP) a place in which political prisoners and members of religious and ethnic groups were held (p. 657)

concordat (kuhn KAWR dat) an agreement between a pope and a monarch or head of a government (p. 451)

conscript (kuhn SKRIHPT) a person drafted into military service (p. 453)

conservatism (kuhn SER vuh tihz uhm) the idea that generally supports existing ways of doing things and opposes quick, major change (p. 462)

constitutional monarchy (kahn stuh TOO shuh nuhl MAHN uhr kee) a government in which a ruler's powers are limited to those that the constitution and the laws of the country allow (p. 477)

consul (KAHN suhl) a government official who lives and works in another country (p. 593)

containment (kuhn TAYN muhnt) a policy of keeping communism confined to the areas already under Communist control (p. 689)

convent (KAHN vehnt) a religious community of women (p. 281)

counterrevolutionary (kownt uhr rehv uh LOO shuh ner ee) a person who fights against a government set up by a previous revolution (p. 724)

coup d'état (KOO day TAH) the violent overthrow of a government by a small group (p. 766)

covenant (KUHV uh nuhnt) an agreement or contract (p. 42)

crop rotation (KRAHP roh TAY shuhn) a system of growing different crops one after the other on the same land to help restore the soil (p. 507)

crusader state (kroo SAYD uhr STAYT) a state established by western European Christians (p. 292)

cultivate (KUHL tuh vayt) to prepare soil for growing crops (p. 10)

culture (KUHL chuhr) the way of life of a group of people that is handed down from one generation to the next (p. 6)

cuneiform (kyoo NEE fawrm) the wedge-shaped writing of early Mesopotamians (p. 18)

czar (ZAHR) the Russian word for *Caesar*, which means "emperor" (p. 163)

daimyo (DY myoh) a Japanese lord (p. 263)

debtor nation (DEHT uhr NAY shuhn) a nation that owes money (p. 645)

default (dee FAWLT) to fail to make payments (p. 705)

deity (DEE uh tee) a supreme being or divinity (p. 68)

delta (DEHL tuh) land formed from soil deposited at a river's mouth (p. 24)

demilitarized zone (dee MIHL uh tuh ryzd ZOHN) an area that military forces cannot enter (p. 628)

demobilization (dee moh buh lih ZAY shuhn) the disbanding or discharging of troops (p. 624)

democracy (dih MAHK ruh see) a government that gives its citizens the ruling power (p. 109)

détente (day TAHNT) easing of tensions (p. 700)

developed nation (dih VEHL uhpt NAY shuhn) a country that is economically, socially, and politically advanced (p. 786)

developing nation (dih VEHL uh pihng NAY shuhn) a country in which industrialization is still taking place (p. 786)

dharma (DAHR muh) an individual's duty in this life (p. 62)

diaspora (dy AS puh ruh) the scattered population of a cultural group throughout the world (p. 775)

dictatorial rule (dihk tuh TAWR ee uhl ROOL) a form of government in which the ruler has absolute power (p. 601)

diet (DY uht) a legislative assembly (p. 166)

direct democracy (duh REHKT dih MAHK ruh see) a government in which citizens take part directly, rather than through their representatives (p. 112)

disarmament (DIHS ahr muh muhnt) the reduction in number of a nation's military forces and equipment (p. 644)

divine right (deh VYN RYT) a belief that a monarch's right to rule comes directly from God, not from the consent of the people (p. 388)

divinity (duh VIHN uh tee) a divine being; a god (p. 57)

domesticate (doh MEHS tih kayt) to tame and breed wild animals (p. 10)

dominion (duh MIHN yuhn) a self-governing nation (p. 538)

domino theory (DAHM uh noh THEE uh ree) the belief that if one country falls to communism, others nearby will fall, one after the other (p. 715)

dowry (DOW ree) a sum of money or goods paid to the family of the groom by the family of the bride (p. 90)

dry stone (DRY STOHN) a method of building without using mortar (p. 239)

dual monarchy (DOO uhl MAHN uhr kee) rule of two kingdoms by one person (p. 554)

dynastic cycle (dy NAS tihk SY kuhl) an explanation of the rise and fall of dynasties based on the Mandate of Heaven (p. 80)

dynasty (DY nuhs tee) a powerful family or group that rules for a lengthy period of time (p. 19)

E

edict (EE dihkt) an order or command given by an official and backed or supported by law (p. 66)

elevation (ehl uh VAY shuhn) the height above sea level (p. 74)

El Niño (EHL NEEN yoh) a warm current in the Pacific Ocean, along the west coast of South America (p. 730)

embargo (ehm BAHR goh) a stoppage of trade by political or military means (p. 699)

émigré (EHM ih gray) a person who left France after the fall of Louis XVI and later returned (p. 450)

empire (EHM pyer) a group of countries, nations, territories, or peoples under the control of a single ruler (p. 25)

enclosure (ehn KLOH zhehr) the fencing off of common land by private landowners in Great Britain (p. 507)

encomienda (ehn kah MYEHN duh) a system in which Spanish colonists were given land and Native Americans to care for, in return for the Native Americans' labor or tribute (p. 368)

English Bill of Rights (IHN glihsh BIHL UHV RYTS) a statement of subjects' rights and of the relationship of Parliament to the monarchy (p. 405)

engraving (ehn GRAYV ihng) an art form in which an artist cuts a design on a metal plate and then uses the plate for printing (p. 325)

enlightened despotism (en LYT ihnd DEHS puh tihz uhm) an absolute monarchy in which the ruler uses his or her power to bring beneficial political and social changes to his or her subjects (p. 399)

entente (ahn TAHNT) an agreement between countries to follow common policies (p. 615)

epic (EHP ihk) a long, narrative poem about great heroes and their deeds (p. 58)

epidemic (ehp uh DEHM ihk) a widespread disease (p. 299)

estate (uh STAYT) a French legal term that indicates a person's status in society based on property ownership and ancestral rights and customs (p. 437)

Estates General (uh STAYTS JEHN uhr uhl) the assembly that advised the king of France (p. 304)

ethnic cleansing (EHTH nihk KLEHN zing) the act of eliminating one or more ethnic groups from a region or society (p. 706)

ethnic group (EHTH nihk GROOP) a large group of people who share the same language and cultural heritage (p. 166)

excommunicate (ehks kuh MYOO nih kayt) to expel from the Church (p. 154)

extraterritoriality (ehks truh ter uh tawr AL uh tee) an agreement that allows citizens of one country who live in another country to be governed by the laws of their own land (p. 587)

F

factory system (FAK tuh ree SYHS tuhm) the mass production of goods in a central building or buildings (p. 509)

fascism (FASH ihz uhm) a political system that emphasizes nationalism and is ruled by a dictator (p. 654)

federal republic (FED uhr uhl rih PUHB lihk) a government in which power is shared between the central government and the states (p. 430)

feudalism (FYOOD ihl ihz uhm) a system of government in which lesser lords owe service to greater lords (p. 263)

filial piety (FIHL ee uhl PY uh tee) the requirement that one must obey and respect one's parents (p. 86)

fleet (FLEET) a group of ships that are under one command (p. 351)

franchise (fran CHYZ) a right or privilege, especially the right to vote (p. 534)

free market economy (FREE MAHR kiht ih KAHN uh mee) an economy in which the buying and selling can be carried out without regulation (p. 423)

fundamentalist (fun duh MEHNT ihl ihst) someone who believes that religious beliefs and laws should be strictly followed (p. 779)

G

general strike (JEHN uhr uhl STRYK) a strike by workers in several different industries at the same time (p. 647)

genetic engineering (juh NEHT ihk ehn juh NIHR ihng) the act of working on genes to change or copy them (p. 801)

genocide (JEN uh syd) the planned killing of a racial or ethnic group (p. 679)

glasnost (GLAHS nohst) the Soviet policy of openness in ideas and information (p. 702)

global warming (GLOH buhl WAHRM ihng) the rise in the average temperature of Earth over time (p. 793)

glyph (GLIHF) a picture or other symbol, often carved, that represents a word or an idea (p. 203)

Gothic style (GAHTH ihk STYEL) a style of architecture used for churches in medieval Europe (p. 283)

gravity (GRAV ih tee) a force that pulls objects toward each other, with more massive objects having a greater pull (p. 417)

Great Depression (GRAYT deh PRESH uhn) the worldwide economic slowdown that caused massive unemployment (p. 645)

Great Schism (GRAYT SIHZ uhm) the split dividing the papacy in the High Middle Ages (p. 307)

greenhouse effect (GREEN hows eh FEHKT) the process by which Earth is kept warm at all times (p. 793)

gross domestic product (GROHS do MEHS tihk PRAHD uhkt) the value of all goods and services that a country produces during a year (p. 720)

guerrilla warfare (guh RIHL uh WAWR fer) fighting involving surprise raids (p. 429)

guild (GIHLD) an association of merchants or craftspeople (p. 298)

guillotine (GIHL uh teen) a device with a blade, used to cut off the heads of convicted criminals (p. 446)

habeas corpus (HAY bee uhs KAWR puhs) a Latin term for a legal requirement that a person cannot be held in prison without being charged with a specific crime (p. 405)

hajj (HAJ) a pilgrimage to Mecca; one of Five Pillars of Islam (p. 174)

hangul (hahn GOOL) an alphabet using symbols to represent the sounds of the Korean language (p. 257)

heliocentric (hee lee uh SEHN trihk) Sun-centered (p. 415)

heresy (HER uh see) a religious belief opposed to official teachings (p. 147)

hierarchy (HY urh ar kee) a system or organization that is based on graded ranks (p. 145)

hieroglyphics (hy uhr oh GLIHF ihks) picture writing (p. 28)

hijra (HIHJ ruh) the flight of Muhammad and his followers from Mecca to Medina in 622 (p. 173)

Holocaust (HAH luh kahst) Hitler's policy of killing European Jews and others considered "unfit to live" (p. 679)

home rule (HOHM ROOL) self-government for a dependent country (p. 537)

hominid (HAHM uh nihd) a primate of which only one species still exists today—humans (p. 5)

human genome (HYOO muhn JEE nohm) the complete genetic makeup of human beings (p. 800)

humanism (HYOO muh nihz uhm) an intellectual movement that stemmed from the study of classical literature (p. 317)

hypothesis (hy PAHTH uh sihs) a possible explanation (p. 417)

icon (EYE kahn) a religious image that is regarded as sacred (p. 154)

ideology (eye dee AHL uh jee) a belief and plan for social and political change (p. 462)

immigration (ihm uh GRAY shuhn) the act of coming to a new country to live there (p. 520)

impeach (ihm PEECH) to charge a high public official, such as the U.S. President, with a crime (p. 715)

imperial line (ihm PIHR ee uhl LYN) emperors, their ancestors, and their descendants (p. 594)

imperialism (ihm PIHR ee uhl ihz uhm) the practice by which one nation gains and maintains political, social, and economic control over another nation (p. 561)

indigenous (ihn DIHJ uh nuhs) occurring naturally in a region (p. 362)

indulgence (ihn DUHL jehns) a release by the Roman Catholic Church for some or all of a person's sins (p. 309)

infamy (IHN fuh mee) disgrace, or great evil (p. 674)

inflation (ihn FLAY shuhn) a steep rise in prices, which has the effect of reducing people's purchasing power (p. 139)

infrastructure (IHN fruh struhk chuhr) a group of basic physical facilities, such as roads, railways, and factories, necessary for a community to operate efficiently (p. 562)

inheritance (ihn HER ih tuhns) the receiving of property or possessions, especially from a relative when that person dies (p. 387)

Inquisition (ihn kwuh ZIHSH uhn) the court of the Roman Catholic Church responsible for identifying and punishing heretics (p. 306)

interchangeable parts (ihn tuhr CHAYN juh buhl PAHRTS) identical parts that can be used in place of one another (p 515)

interdependence (ihn tuhr dee PEHN duhns) the dependence of countries on resources, goods, and knowledge from other countries of the world (p. 787)

internment camp (ihn TERN muhnt KAMP) a place in which people are confined, especially in time of war (p. 674)

intifada (ihn tuh FAH duh) the uprising by Palestinians in territory held by Israel (p. 778)

investor (ihn VEHST er) a person who puts money in a company, hoping to make a profit (p. 376)

irrigate (IHR uh gayt) to artificially supply water to fields (p. 10)

isthmus (IHS muhs) a narrow strip of land bordered on both sides by water between two larger masses of land (p. 600)

janizary (JAN ih zer ee) a soldier in an elite force of the Ottoman army (p. 192)

jihad (jee HAHD) an effort carried out as a religious duty (p. 174)

joint-stock company (JOINT STAHK KUHM puh nee) a group of investors who share both risk and profit (p. 376)

jury (JER ee) a group of people that considers the evidence in a trial and makes a judgment (p. 112)

kachina (kuh CHEE nuh) the spirit of a Pueblo ancestor (p. 214)

kaiser (KY suhr) the emperor of unified Germany (p. 551)

karma (KAHR muh) all the actions in a person's life that affect the next life (p. 62)

kibbutz (kih BOOTS) a farm cooperative in Israel in which settlers share the work and the produce (p. 775)

kulak (koo LAHK) a wealthy peasant in the Soviet Union (p. 641)

labor union (LAY buhr YOON yuhn) an association of workers that protects and promotes the interests of its members (p. 527)

laissez faire (LEHS ay FER) letting businesses run without government intervention (p. 423)

Legalism (LEE guhl ihz uhm) a belief in strong laws and the power of a ruler to reward and punish people in order to maintain control (p. 87)

legion (LEE juhn) the chief fighting unit of the Roman army (p. 132)

legislature (LEHJ ihs lay cher) a lawmaking body in government (p. 109)

liberalism (LIB ruhl ihz uhm) the idea that generally encourages individual freedom and social progress (p. 463)

liege lord (LEEJ LAWRD) the lord to whom a vassal owes first service (p. 277)

lineage group (LIHN ee ihj GROOP) several extended families combined into a larger community (p. 225)

lobby (LAHB ee) to attempt to influence those in power to accept a particular point of view (p. 737)

loess (LOH ehs) a fine, yellowish-brown, rich soil (p. 75)

longhouse (LAWNG hows) a large one-story shelter made of logs (p. 216)

magistrate (MAJ ihs trayt) a government official (p. 128)

maharajah (mah huh RAH juh) a king or prince who ruled an Indian state (p. 572)

maize (MAYZ) corn (p. 201)

malnutrition (mal noo TRIHSH uhn) undernourishment or the lack of a properly balanced diet (p. 794)

mandate (MAN dayt) a nation's assignment by an international body to govern or administer an area (p. 568)

Mandate of Heaven (MAN dayt UHV HEHV uhn) a claim of the divine right to rule (p. 80)

Manifest Destiny (MAN uh fehst DEHS tuh nee) the idea that the United States had the right to expand from the Atlantic Ocean to the Pacific Ocean (p. 541)

manor (MAN uhr) the land and property under a lord's control (p. 277)

mansa (MAN suh) a village head; later, the head of an empire (p. 229)

martial law (MAHR shuhl LAW) the law administered by military forces with the government's approval (p. 403)

matriarchal (may tree AR chal) relating to a culture in which women are the most powerful members (p. 225)

mediator (MEE dee ay tawr) a person who settles differences between people and nations (p. 596)

medieval (mee dee EE vuhl) of the Middle Ages (p. 270)

mercantilism (MER kuhn tihl ihz uhm) an economic system that stresses increasing national wealth by selling more to other nations than buying from them (p. 364)

mercenary (MER suh ner ee) a soldier paid to serve in a foreign army (p. 165)

metallurgy (MEHT uh ler jee) the science of making metals to create objects (p. 12)

metropolitan area (meh troh PAHL ih tuhn ER ee uh) a large city and its surrounding towns and smaller cities (p. 791)

Middle Passage (MIHD ihl PAS ihj) the second leg of the triangular trade route in which slaves were shipped across the Atlantic (p. 380)

migrant worker (MY gruhnt WERK uhr) a person who moves from place to place to find work, usually harvesting crops (p. 715)

mihrab (MEE rahb) an arched area in a mosque wall that is closest to Mecca (p. 183)

militant (MIHL ih tuhnt) ready and willing to fight in support of a cause (p. 189)

militarism (MIHL uh tuh rihz uhm) a policy in which a military's needs and values take priority (p. 398)

millet (MIHL eht) a religious community of non-Muslims in the Ottoman Empire (p. 192)

minaret (mihn uh REHT) a tall, slender tower with a balcony, on a mosque (p. 183)

missionary (MIHSH uhn er ee) a person sent by religious authorities to spread a set of religious beliefs (p. 147)

mobilize (MOH buh lyz) to assemble and be ready to move, as for war (p. 614)

monarchy (MAHN uhr kee) a government that has a single ruler, such as a king, queen, or pharaoh (p. 101)

monastery (MAHN uh ster ee) a religious community of men (p. 281)

monopoly (muh NAHP uh lee) the control of goods or services by one person, group, or company (p. 352)

monotheism (MAHN oh thee ihz uhm) the belief that there is only one God (p. 42)

monsoon (mahn SOON) a seasonal wind that creates a strong pattern of wet and dry seasons in parts of Asia (p. 51)

multinational (mul tih NASH uh nuhl) including many nationalities (p. 555)

mummification (mum uh fih KAY shuhn) a process that preserves dead bodies (p. 27)

nationalism (NASH uh nuhl ihz uhm) the belief that people should be loyal to their country, not just to their leader (p. 305)

nationalize (NASH uh nuh lyz) to convert from private to public control (p. 696)

nation-state (NAY shehn STAYT) a self-governing land whose people share the same cultural background, language, and history (p. 462)

natural law (NACH uhr uhl LAW) the conditions that govern human behavior (p. 422)

navigation (nav uh GAY shuhn) the control of the direction of a boat or ship (p. 341)

neutral (NOO truhl) not taking one side or the other (p. 471)

nomad (NOH mad) a wanderer, usually in search of food (p. 7)

oasis (oh AY sihs) a fertile place in a desert, due to the presence of water (p. 172)

oba (OH buh) the king of a city-state in ancient Africa (p. 231)

occupation (ahk yoo PAY shuhn) the control of an area by the military force of a foreign state (p. 748)

oligarchy (AHL ih gahr kee) a government in which only a few powerful people rule (p. 107)

opium (OH pee uhm) an addictive painkilling drug made from the dried juice of opium poppy pods (p. 586)

oracle (AWR uh kuhl) a person, place, or thing that a god uses to reveal hidden knowledge (p. 76)

oral history (OR uhl HIS tuh ree) the history of a people that is told by storytellers (p. 44)

ore (AWR) a rock or mineral from which a metal can be separated (p. 12)

overproduction (oh vuhr proh DUHK shuhn) when the production of goods is greater than the demand for them (p. 645)

Pan-Africanism (PAN AF rih kuhn ihzm) the unity of all black Africans, regardless of national boundaries (p. 760)

papacy (PAY puh see) the office and rule of the pope, or bishop of Rome (p. 290)

papyrus (puh PY ruhs) a water plant used as a writing material like paper by ancient Egyptians (p. 24)

Parliament (PAHR luh muhnt) the assembly that advises the king or queen of England (p. 303)

partition (pahr TIHSH ehn) divide (p. 697)

pasteurization (pas chuhr ih ZAY shuhn) a process by which milk or other liquids are heated to kill germs (p. 603)

patriarchal (pay tree AHR kehl) relating to a culture in which men are the most powerful members (p. 39)

patrician (puh TRIHSH uhn) a descendant of a founding family of Rome (p. 128)

patron (PAY truhn) a wealthy person who supports an artist (p. 319)

peer (PIHR) a person of equal rank or social standing (p. 594)

penal colony (PEE nuhl KAHL uh nee) a colony to which convicted criminals are exiled (p. 496)

perestroika (per uh STROI kuh) the Soviet restructuring of its economy (p. 702)

persecution (per suh KYOO shuhn) harsh treatment for following a set of religious beliefs (p. 145)

perspective (per SPEHK tihv) an artistic technique used to give drawings a three-dimensional effect (p. 317)

pesticide (PEHS tuh syd) any chemical used for killing insects or weeds (p. 790)

pharaoh (FAR oh) a title given to the rulers of ancient Egypt (p. 25)

philosopher (fih LAHS uh fuhr) a person who seeks wisdom or knowledge (p. 85)

plateau (pla TOH) a raised area of level land (p. 50)

plebeian (plih BEE uhn) a commoner (p. 128)

polis (POH lis) a Greek city-state (p. 106)

polytheism (PAHL ih thee ihz uhm) belief in many gods (p. 36)

popular sovereignty (PAHP yuh luhr SAHV ruhn tee) control by the people (p. 543)

potlatch (PAHT lach) a feast in which guests are given costly gifts (p. 213)

predestination (pree dehs tuh NAY shuhn) a religious teaching that God determines who will gain salvation (p. 330)

privatize (PRY vuh tyz) to change from public to private control (p. 728)

Progressive movement (proh GREHS ihv MOOV muhnt) the American movement that urged social and economic reforms in the early 1900s (p. 527)

proletariat (proh luh TER ee uht) the working people, especially industrial workers (p. 630)

propaganda (prahp uh GAHN duh) the promotion of certain ideas to influence people's opinions (p. 428)

prophet (PRAHF iht) someone chosen by God to bring a message to people (p. 173)

protective tariff (pruh TEHK tihv TAR ihf) a tax put on imported goods to encourage consumers to buy those same goods from their own country (p. 516)

protectorate (pruh TEHK tuhr iht) a state in which local government rules under the control of another government (p. 562)

province (PRAHV ihns) a territory (p. 140)

pueblo (PWEHB loh) a dwelling made of adobe; also the name for some southwestern Native American groups (p. 214)

queue (KYOO) the pigtail worn by Chinese men to show submission to Manchus (p. 486)

quipu (KEE poo) a long string with a knotted and colored group of smaller strings that was used to record numbers (p. 208)

quota (KWOHT uh) a fixed amount (p. 641)

Raj (RAHJ) the British domination of India between 1757 and 1947 (p. 572)

reactionary (ree AK shuh ner ee) a person who opposes change (p. 471)

recession (rih SEH shuhn) a decline in economic activity (p. 430)

referendum (rehf uh REHN duhm) a direct vote of the people on a law or policy (p. 751)

Reformation (rehf uhr MAY shuhn) the European movement calling for reform within the Roman Catholic Church (p. 328)

refugee (rehf yoo JEE) a person who flees to a foreign country (p. 256)

regent (REE juhnt) someone who rules in a monarch's place, usually because the monarch is too young to rule alone (p. 392)

reincarnation (ree ihn kahr NAY shun) the rebirth of a soul in another body (p. 62)

Renaissance (REHN uh sahns) the great revival of art, literature, and learning in Europe (p. 316)

reparation (rehp uh RAY shun) the payment for damages (p. 626)

republic (rih PUHB lihk) a government in which much of the power is held by elected representatives (p. 127)

revival (rih VY vuhl) a renewed interest in a part of the past (p. 273)

Risorgimento (ree sawr jee MEHN toh) a nationalist movement that worked for the unification of Italy (p. 548)

rotten borough (RAHT ihn BER oh) a borough in Great Britain that had few voters but had the right to send a representative to Parliament (p. 535)

sabotage (SAB uh tahzh) intentional damage or destruction by underground resistance groups (p. 671)

sachem (SAY chuhm) a chief of the Iroquois nations (p. 217)

samurai (SAM uh ry) a Japanese warrior (p. 263)

sanction (SANK shuhn) a penalty for breaking international laws or codes of conduct (p. 663)

satellite state (SAT ihl yt STAYT) a country that is dependent on another country for its economic and political well-being (p. 453)

satire (SA tyr) the use of ridicule or scorn to expose the vices or misbehavior of others (p. 324)

satrap (SA trap) a governor of a region in ancient Persia (p. 40)

satyagraha (SUHT yuh gruh huh) a belief of Gandhi that emphasized passive resistance (p. 652)

savanna (suh VAN uh) a grassland with plants and scattered trees that can resist drought (p. 222)

schism (SIHZ uhm) a separation or division (p. 290)

scientific method (sy uhn TIHF ihk MEHTH uhd) a way of carefully gathering and explaining information (p. 417)

scorched-earth policy (SKAWRCHT ERTH PAHL uh see) a wartime policy in which all goods useful to an invading army are burned or destroyed (p. 672)

scribe (SKRYB) a person who copies information and keeps records (p. 35)

secede (sih SEED) to withdraw from or leave (p. 543)

sector (SEHK tuhr) a district or region into which an area is divided (p. 580)

secularize (SEHK yuh luh ryz) to change from religious to nonreligious use or control (p. 779)

self-determination (SEHLF dih ter muh NAY shuhn) the belief that a people have the right to decide their own form of government (p. 468)

senate (SEHN iht) a council of representatives (p. 128)

separatist (SEHP uh ruh tihst) a citizen who wishes to break away from his or her country to form a new nation (p. 738)

sepoy (SEE poi) a native-born soldier in the Indian army controlled by the East India Company (p. 573)

serf (SERF) a peasant who is legally bound to the land belonging to a lord (p. 278)

sericulture (SER uh kul cher) a process involved in silk production (p. 78)

shah (SHAH) king (p. 193)

shareholder (SHER hohl duhr) an investor who provides a company with money (p. 349)

shogun (SHOH gun) the supreme military commander of Japan (p. 263)

social contract (SOH shuhl KAHN trakt) an agreement in which people give up the state of nature for an organized society (p. 422)

socialism (SOH shuhl ihz uhm) an economic system in which the means of production are collectively owned or owned by the government, and economic exchanges are regulated for the common good (p. 529)

socialist market economy (SOH shuhl ihst MAHR kiht ih KAHN uh mee) an economic system that blends features of socialism with features of capitalism (p. 744)

soviet (SOH vee eht) the elected governmental council set up by Russian revolutionaries (p. 631)

sphere of influence (SFER UHV IHN floo uhns) a region in which one nation claims to have exclusive influence or control over other nations (p. 569)

stalemate (STAYL mayt) a situation in which neither side is able to defeat the other (p. 620)

standard of living (STAN duhrd UHV LIHV ihng) level of comfort that a person or group wants or needs (p. 701)

standing army (STAND ihng AHR mee) a permanent army of paid soldiers (p. 399)

stela (STEE luh) a tall narrow column, usually carved; the plural form is stelae (p. 234)

steppe (STEHP) a great plain with few trees anywhere in southeastern Europe or Asia (p. 158)

subcontinent (SUB kahnt uhn uhnt) a large part of a continent that is geographically separated from the rest of the continent (p. 50)

suburb (SUHB uhrb) a community at the edge of a city (p. 712)

succession (suhk SEHSH uhn) the order by which rulers follow one another in office (p. 253)

suffrage (SUF rihj) the right to vote (p. 525)

sultan (SULT ihn) the ruler of an Islamic state (p. 177)

sultanate (SULT ihn iht) a government headed by a sultan (p. 186)

superpower (SOO puhr POW uhr) a country with overwhelming power (p. 688)

supremacy (suh PREHM uh see) supreme power or authority (p. 580)

tenement (TEHN uh muhnt) a run-down apartment building (p. 522)

tetrarchy (teh TRAHR kee) rule by four leaders (p. 140)

textile industry (TEHKS tyl IHN duhs tree) the manufacturing of cloth from wool, cotton, and other materials (p. 508)

theocracy (thee AHK ruh see) a form of government in which a god is regarded as the supreme ruler, and power is in the hands of religious leaders (p. 34)

tithe (TYTH) a tax equal to one-tenth of a person's income (p. 280)

totalitarian state (toh tuhl uh TER ee uhn STAYT) a government in which a one-party dictatorship regulates every aspect of citizens' lives (p. 655)

transcontinental (trans kahn tuh NEHNT ihl) across a continent (p. 516)

treason (TREE zuhn) an act of betrayal against one's country (p. 389)

trench warfare (TREHNCH WAWR fer) the act of waging war from the defense of trenches (p. 620)

triangular trade (tri AYNG gyuh luhr TRAYD) a trading system involving a three-way exchange of goods and people among Europe, Africa, and the Americas (p. 380)

tribune (TRIHB yoon) a plebeian official who could attend meetings of the assembly (p. 128)

tributary state (TRIHB yoo tehr ee STAYT) a conquered state that makes payments, called tributes, to the conquering state (p. 244)

tribute (TRIHB yoot) a payment given by one nation to another more powerful nation; may be paid in exchange for protection (p. 112)

tricolor (TRY kul uhr) the red, white, and blue flag of revolutionary France (p. 444)

triumvirate (try UM vuh riht) a group of three leaders (p.132)

tsunami (tsoo NAH mee) a huge ocean wave that can sweep over land and destroy everything in its path (p. 260)

tundra (TUN druh) a plain without trees in an artic region (p. 158)

tyrant (TY ruhnt) a leader who gains power by force; later, a leader who rules ruthlessly (p. 109)

ultimatum (ul tuh MAYT uhm) a final demand made with a threat to break off dealings or use force if not accepted (p. 615)

Union (YOON yuhn) the United States of America (p. 543)

urbanization (ER buh nih zay shuhn) the movement of more and more of a country's population from rural to urban areas (p. 520)

utopia (yoo TOH pee uh) an ideal or perfect society (p. 325)

vaccine (vak SEEN) a substance that protects against a disease by using weakened or killed germs (p. 603)

vassal (VAS uhl) a person who has taken a pledge of loyalty to a lord (p. 277)

Vedas (VAY duhz) one of the earliest Hindu sacred texts (p. 57)

veteran (VEHT uhr uhn) a person who has served in the military (p. 454)

veto (VEE toh) to stop passage of a law (p. 127)

viceroy (VYS roi) a governor of several countries or provinces who rules as the representative of a monarch (p. 368)

welfare state (WEHL fer STAYT) a government that takes responsibility for people's social and economic needs (p. 698)

well-field system (WEL FEELD SIHS tuhm) a division of land between individual farmers and the owner of the land (p. 91)

Western civilization (WEHS tern sihv uh luh ZAY shuhn) the civilization that developed in Europe and spread to the Americas (p. 101)

Western Hemisphere (WEHS tern HEHM ih sfihr) the half of Earth that includes North and South America (p. 478)

yin and yang (YIHN UHND YAHNG) the two basic forces of the universe according to the beliefs of Daoism (p. 87)

ziggurat (ZIHG oo rat) a pyramid-shaped tower that stood several stories tall (p. 34)

Index

The following italicized abbreviations are used in the index to denote the following: *m* indicates a map; *c* indicates a chart; *crt* indicates a political cartoon; *g* indicates a graph; *p* indicates a photograph or painting; and *q* indicates a quote.

Aachen, 273
Abacus, 247
Abbas I, 193
Abbasids, 176–177, 184
Abd ar-Rahman III, 184
Abdülhamid II, 579–580
Abdullah, 773
Abolitionists, 542
The Abolition of Slavery in Mexico (Hidalgo), 814
Aborigines, 495–496, 495p, 719
Abraham, 42, 44, 45
Absolute monarchy, 388, 393, 393p, 394, 396, 397, 400, 407
Abu Bakr, 175
Acid rain, 721, 790
Acropolis, 106, 112, 113, 114
Act of Settlement (Great Britain, 1701), 406
Act of Supremacy (Great Britain, 1534), 331
Act of Union (Great Britain, 1707), 406
Act of Union (Great Britain, 1801), 536
Acupuncture, 93
Adbülaziz, 578, 579
Aden, 351
Adenas, 215, 216
Adenauer, Konrad, 695, 696p
Admonitions for Girls (Ban Zhao), 90–91, 91q
Adoration of the Lamb (Van Eyck), 325
The Adoration of the Magi (Da Vinci), 318
Adowa, Battle of (1896), 570
Adulis, 234, 235
Aegean Sea, 101, 103
Aeneid (Virgil), 124q, 134
Aeschylus, 114
Afghanistan
    Operation Enduring Freedom in, 716, 781, 799
    Persian rule of, 40
    Soviet invasion and withdrawal from, 701, 701p
    Taliban in, 701, 716, 781, 799
    Umayyad conquest of, 176
Africa, A6m. *See also specific countries in*
    AIDS in, 795
    Aksum peoples in, 234–236
    apartheid in, 768–769
    central kingdoms in, 491, 491m
    civil wars in, 767
    countries in, 816, 816c
    early civilizations in, 223–226

eastern kingdoms in, 234–239, 234p, 235p, 236p, 237m, 238p
economy in, 770
European exploration and colonization in, 238, 345, 345p, 346c, 377–378, 492–494, 566–570, 566p, 567m, 569p, 612
geography of, 222–223, 223m
independence in, 760–764, 763m
Kushites in, 223–224
missionaries in, 563, 563p
music of, 232–233, 232p, 233p
new challenges for, 766–770
Nok peoples in, 224–225, 225p
Northern, 176, 465
regional conflicts in, 798
religion in, 226, 235–236, 235p, 238, 563, 563p, 571
slavery in, 230, 231, 377–381, 378p
southern, 491–494
trade in, 345
weaving in, 571, 571p
western kingdoms in, 228–231, 228m, 229c, 230p, 231p, 381, 490–491, 490p, 491m
wildlife in, 771, 771p
World War II in, 673, 673m
Zulus in, 482, 482q, 482–483p
African Americans
    civil rights movement and, 714–715, 714p, 717c, 736
    slavery, 378, 379, 380–381, 380m, 525, 542, 542p, 544
    voting rights for, 544
African National Congress (ANC), 768
Afrikaners, 493, 570
Agincourt, 305
Agni, 58
Agora, 106
Agrarian economy, 91
Agricultural revolution, 10–11, 10p, 75, 507
Agriculture. *See also* Farming
    cash crops in, 369
    Columbian exchange, 368–369, 369c
    crop rotation in, 296, 507
    enclosure system in, 507, 507p
    encomienda system in, 368, 369
    genetically-modified crops in, 800, 800p
    Green Revolution in, 800, 800p
    kibbutz, 775, 775p
    Mexican migrant workers in, 715, 715p, 722–723
    three-field system of, 296
    well-field system in, 91
Ahimsa, 62–63
AIDS (Acquired Immune Deficiency Syndrome) epidemic, 795
Ainu, 750
Ajanta murals, 68, 68p
Akbar, 188, 188p, 331, 572
Akhenaton, 26, 26p
Akhetaton, 26
Akihito, Emperor of Japan, 479p

Akkad, 33, 37–38, 40
Aksum, Kingdom of, 224, 234–235, 234p, 236
Alaska, purchase of, from Russia, 542
Albania, nationalism and, 468
Alberti, Leon Battista, 314q
Albuquerque, Alfonso de, 357q
Alcuin of York, 273
Aldrin, Buzz, 715
Aleppo, 187
Aleuts, 213
Alexander I, Czar of Russia, 454, 462, 471
Alexander II, Czar of Russia, 472, 472p
Alexander the Great, 115, 118–120, 119, 119p, 119m, 120p
Alexandra, Empress of Russia, 631p
Alexandria, 119, 119m, 120
Alexius I, 156
Algeria, 569, 694, 761–762, 762p, 764, 766
Al-Hakam II, 184
Alhambra Palace, 184
Ali, 176
Alighieri, Dante, 300, 300q, 311
Allah, 173–174, 175, 176, 177, 177p, 183
Allende, Isabel, 729, 729q
Allied Powers
    in World War I, 615–616, 618, 619
    in World War II, 668, 678
All-India Muslim League, 575, 736, 737
Al-Mansur, 177
Al-Mustansir, 184
Alpacas, 211
Alphabet. *See also* Writing
    Cyrillic, 154, 159, 164
    hangul, 257
    Phoenician, 41, 106
Al Qaeda, 716, 781, 799
Al-Rashid, Harun, 177
Al-Razi, Muhammad, 185
Alsace, 551, 612, 646
Alsace-Lorraine, 627
Amazon rain forests, 730
Amazon River basin, 200
Amenhotep IV, 26
American Federation of Labor (AFL), 527
American Indian Movement (AIM), 715
American Red Cross, 526
American Revolution, 427–431, 428p, 429m
Americas. *See also* Central America; Latin America; North America; South America; *specific countries*
    colonies in, 366–371, 372–376
    early civilizations in, 200m, 201–204
    exploration of, 348, 366–370, 597
    farming in, 211, 215, 378
    geography of, 200–201
    independence in, 597–598, 597p, 598–600, 600–601, 601p, 724–726, 728–729, 729m, 750
    land claims in, 362m, 373p, 375m
    Panama Canal, 600, 600m, 725

Militarism, 398, 614
Milosevic, Slobodan, 706
Minarets, 183
Ming Dynasty, 253–255, 253p, 350–351, 484
Mining industry, 509
Minoan civilization, 101–102, 101m, 105, 105p
Minos, 101
Missionaries
    of Eastern Orthodox Church, 154
    Spanish, 369
    in spread of Christianity, 333, 340–341, 352–353, 352p, 369, 486, 488, 499, 563, 563p, 740, 740p
Mitterand, François, 700, 707c
Moche people, 206, 206p
Moctezuma, 366–367, 367p
Mogadishu, 237, 237m
Mohawks, 217
Mohenjo-Daro, 52–53, 201
Molière, Jean-Baptiste Poquelin, 394–395
Molucca Islands, 349, 363
Mombasa, 237, 237m, 238
Monasteries, 281, 281p, 285
Mongolia, 351
Mongols, 251–253, 251p, 340
    invasions by, 160–161, 160p, 250–251, 251p, 400
    missionaries to, 340–341
    rule of China by, 350
Monopolies, 528
Monotheism, 42
Monroe, James, 478, 541, 598
Monroe Doctrine, 478, 540, 598, 598crt
Monsoons, 51, 74, 75, 234
Montaigne, Michel de, 323
Montecorvino, Giovanni da, 341
Montenegro, 471, 629, 706
Montesquieu, Baron de, 424, 424c, 430
Montgomery bus boycott, 714
More, Thomas, 323, 325, 335q
Morelos y Pavon, Josée Maria, 477
Morocco, 569, 581, 614, 760
Morse, Samuel F. B., 516
Mosaics, 134p, 153, 153p
Moscoso, Mireya, 725
Moscow, 162, 162p, 454–455, 520, 672
Moses, 42–43
Mosques, 170–171p, 183, 186p
Mosto, Alvise Cá da, 345, 346c
Mothers of the Plaza de Mayo, 728
Mott, Lucretia, 525, 526
Mound builders, 215–216, 215p
Mount Etna, 126
Mount Everest, 75
Mount Olympus, 104, 107
Mount Vesuvius, 126
Mozambique, 346, 566, 570, 767
Mu'awiyah, 176
Muckrakers, 527–528, 527p
Mugabe, Robert, 768
Mughal Empire, 187–189, 739
Muhammad, 170, 171c, 172–175, 181
Muhammad II, 191, 576

Mulattoes, 473–474
Mulroney, Brian, 710–711p, 722
Munich Conference (1938), 665, 666
Music
    African, 232–233, 232p, 233p
    Baroque, 426
    Chinese, 87
Muslim League, 652, 736
Muslims, 170. See also Islam; Quran
    in Bosnia, 706
    in Byzantine Empire, 155
    conflict between Hindus and, in India, 187, 652, 736, 737, 739
    Crusades and, 178, 238, 289c, 290–294, 291p, 293m
    in East Timor, 754
    in India, 186–189, 186p, 187p, 188p, 189p, 573, 736, 737, 739
    nationalism and, 468
    in Pakistan, 697
    in Persia, 184, 235
    Shi'a, 772
    Shiite, 176, 193
    in Spain, 184
    Sunni, 176, 193, 772
    view of Christians by, 340
Mussolini, Benito, 654–655, 654p, 655q, 657, 673, 678
Mutsuhito, emperor of Japan, 593–594
Myanmar, 259, 753
Mycenaean civilization, 101m, 102–104, 103p, 105

NAFTA. See North American Free Trade Agreement (NAFTA)
Nagasaki, 348, 353, 592, 681, 747
Nagy, Imre, 692
Namib Desert, 223, 223m
Namibia, European interests in, 570
Nanavut Territory, 719–720
Nanjing, 350, 663
Nanjing, Treaty of (1842), 587–588
Naples, 549
Napoleon. See Bonaparte, Napoleon
Napoleon III, 465–466, 466p, 549, 601
Nara, 262
Nasser, Gamal Abdel, 775–776
National Association for the Advancement of Colored People (NAACP), 714
Nationalism, 305, 532, 760
    in Austrian Empire, 552–554, 553m
    as cause of World War I, 612–613
    Congress of Vienna and, 462–464
    in Germany, 305, 549–551, 550m
    in India, 651–652
    in Italy, 532–533p, 548, 548p, 549, 549m
    in Latin America, 460
    in Middle East, 772
    Napoleon and, 453

    in the Ottoman Empire and the Balkans, 468–469, 468m
Nationalists in Spanish civil war, 663–664
Nationality Law (Israel, 1952), 775
National Liberation Front (FLN), 761–762, 766
Native Americans, 212–217, 213m, 213p, 214p, 215p, 216p, 217q, 545, 545p. See also specific listings
    civil rights for, 715
    colonial expansion and, 375
    eastern groups, 215–217
    French and Indian War and, 427
    in Latin America, 473–474
    missions for, 369, 370p
    on the Plains, 546–547, 546p, 547p
    western groups, 213–215
NATO. See North Atlantic Treaty Organization (NATO)
Natural disasters, 725
Natural law, 422
Nauru, 498
Navajos, 215, 547, 547p
Navigation, tools for, 341, 341p
Nazi Party, 660, 665, 666
Neanderthal people, 7
Nebuchadnezzar, 40
Necker, Jacques, 442
Nehru, Jawaharlal, 737, 737q, 739, 743
Nejd, 773
Neo-Confucian philosophy, 485
Nepal, 351
Nero, 134
Nerva, 135, 135c
Netherlands. See also Dutch
    colonies of, 372, 372p, 378–379
    Congress of Vienna and, 463
    French Revolution and, 448
    as member of European Union, 695
    revolt of, against Spain, 388
    in World War II, 669
New Amsterdam, 372
New Caledonia, 498
Newcomen, Thomas, 509
New Economic Policy (NEP), 639
New England colonies, 374
Newfoundland, 276
New France, settlement of, 373, 373p
New Grenada, independence movement in, 477
New Guinea, 498, 680
Ne Win, 753
New Mexico, 600
New Netherland, 372
Newton, Isaac, 417–418, 422, 424
New York City, 427, 521c, 524, 685p, 791
New Zealand, 496m, 497, 647, 821c, A8m
Nguyen Al Quoc, 650
Nicaragua, 716, 724–725
Nicholas I, czar of Russia, 471–472
Nicholas II, czar of Russia, 472, 630, 631, 631p
Nigeria, 761, 767

S

Saarland, in Versailles Treaty, 627
Sabine people, 127, 129
Sacagawea, 540, 540*p*
Sadat, Anwar el-, 778, 778*p*
Safavid Empire, 191*m*, 193
Sahara, 223
Sails, 35, 342, 342*p*
Saint Bartholomew's Day Massacre, 392, 392*p*, 393
St. Bernard, Abbot, 285, 285*q*
Saint Domingue, 475–476, 475*p*
Saint Helena, 456
Saint Peter's Basilica, 328
Saint Petersburg, 400–401, 520
St. Peter's Fields, 534, 534*p*
Saipan, in World War II, 680
Saladin, 292, 293
Salamis, 109, 110
Salinas de Gortari, Carlos, 710*p*, 722
Salt March, 651*p*, 652
Samaria, 43
Samnites, 129
Samoa, 498
Samudragupta, 67
Samurai, 263, 263*c*
San, 491–492
Sandalwood, 499
Sandinistas, 716, 724–725
San Francisco Conference (1945), 690–691
San Martín, José de, 477, 477*p*
Sanskrit language, 69
San Stefano, Treaty of (1878), 580
Santa Anna, Antonio Lopez de, 600
Santa Maria, 358–359*p*, 360
Sappho, 114
Sardinia, 126, 470, 549
Sardis, 40, 110
Sargon, 37, 37*p*
Satellite navigation, 421, 421*p*
Satire, 324
Saudi Arabia, 773
Saul, 43
Savanna, African, 222–223, 222*p*
Savery, Thomas, 420
Saxons, 143
Schleswig, in Versailles Treaty, 627
Schlieffen, Alfred von, 612, 618–619
Schlieffen Plan, 619
Schliemann, Heinrich, 103
Schmidt, Helmut, 696, 699
School of Athens (Raphael), 314–315*p*, 320
Schröder, Gerhard, 707
Schuman, Robert, 695
Science. *See also* Astronomy; Mathematics
   advances in, 517–518, 518*p*, 604
   Chinese, 87
   Guptan, 69
   Hellenistic, 121, 121*c*
   Islamic, 184
   modern, 800–801, 800*p*

Scientific method, 416–417, 417*c*
Scientific revolution, 414–418, 422
Scipio, 130
Scorched-earth policy, 672
Scotland, under Charles I, 403
Sculpture. *See also* Art
   Aryan, 61*p*
   Egyptian, 31*p*
   Nok, 225, 225*p*
   Renaissance, 320*p*
   Sumerian, 16*p*
Sejong, King, 257
Selassie, Haile, 663, 663*p*
Selim I, 576
Seljuk Turks, 155, 177–178, 190, 291
Seneca Falls Convention (1848), 525–526
Seneca people, 217
Senegal River, 345
Senet, 27
Sepoy Mutiny, 574, 574*p*
Septimius Severus, 139
Serbia, 706
   early period of, 165
   independence of, 471, 580, 628–629
   nationalism and, 468, 469
Serbs, 706
Serengeti Plain, 222
Serfs
   in feudal Europe, 278–279, 279*q*
   in Russia, 401, 472
Sericulture, 78
Seven Weeks' War (1866), 551, 554
Seven Years' War (1756–1763), 399
Severus Alexander, 139
Seville, 306
Sexagesimal system, 35
Shah Jahan, 188, 189
Shah-nameh manuscript, 193
Shaka, Zulu king, 482, 482*q*, 492, 494
Shakespeare, William, 326, 327, 327*p*, 335*q*
The Shame of the Cities (Steffens), 527
Shang Dynasty, 76–78, 77*p*, 92
Sharpeville, 768
Shell shock, 625
Sherman Antitrust Act (1890), 528
Shiite Muslims, 176, 193, 772
Shikubu, Morasaki, 262, 262*p*
Shinto, 261
Shiva, 61
Shogun, 263, 482, 486–488
Shona, 238
Shotoku, Prince of Japan, 261–262
Shunzi, 484
Siberia, 163, 201
Sicily, 41, 116, 126
   Garibaldi's conquest of, 557*q*
   Muslim invasion of, 274, 274*m*
   Punic Wars and, 130
   Umayyad conquest of, 176
   in World War II, 678
Sidney, Sir Philip, 326
Sidon, 41
Sierra Leone, 345, 798
Sierra Madres, 200

Sikhism, 188–189, 189*p*, 739
Silesia, Prussian annexation of, 399
Silk farming, 78
Silk industry, in Byzantine Empire, 153
Silk making, 355
Silk Road, 83, 83*m*, 88, 92, 92*p*, 250, 252, 338*p*, 354
Simeon, 164–165
Sinai Desert, 43
Sinclair, Upton, 528
Singapore, 497
Sioux people, 546
Sistine Chapel, 319, 319*p*
Sita, 58–59, 58*p*
Sixtus IV, 319
Skandagupta, 67
Skepticism, 395
Slater, Samuel, 514
Slave revolt on Haiti, 475–476, 475*p*
Slaves
   in Africa, 230, 231, 377–379, 377*p*, 381
   in Athens, 109, 112
   Egyptian, 27
   Islamic, 180
   Roman, 128
   in Sparta, 108
   Sumerian, 36
   in the United States, 542, 542*p*, 543
Slave trade, 378–381, 380*m*
Slavs, 158–159, 555, 656
Slovakia, 704
Smart Border Declaration (2001), 719
Smith, Adam, 423, 424*c*, 512, 528
Social contract, 422
The Social Contract (Rousseau), 424
Social Darwinism, 563–564
Socialism, 529, 744
Social Studies Skills
   analyze and answer a document-based question, 321
   analyze artifacts, 105
   analyze primary-source documents, 157
   compare and contrast, 249
   conduct a debate, 419
   develop historical perspective, 789
   identify ideologies, 467
   interpret bar graphs, 539
   interpret a line graph, 643
   interpret political cartoons, 441
   interpret statistics, 617
   read a historical map, 29, 29*m*
   read a special-purpose map, 131, 131*m*
   read a time-zone map, 693, 693*m*
   recognize propaganda and bias, 667
   resolve conflict through compromise, 765
   use secondary sources, 275
   use tables and charts, 79
   use a timeline, 9
   write a persuasive essay, 227
Society of Jesus, 333
Socrates, 114–115, 115*p*